WEST'S BUSINESS LAW

Text and Cases

❖|Tenth Edition

. . . and all the study and review tools in the *Study Guide*

The student *Study Guide*, prepared by the text author Roger LeRoy Miller and William Eric Hollowell, is a valuable study and review tool. It contains the following helpful chapter-by-chapter features:

- A brief chapter introduction and chapter outline

- True-false, fill-in-the-blank, and multiple-choice questions as well as short essay problems to help you test yourself and prepare for exams

- Issue spotters

- A separate appendix at the end of the study guide containing answers to all questions and issue spotters

Visit our Bookstore
<u>Shop online</u> for textbook and digital solutions.

If your bookstore does not carry this study guide (ISBN 0-324-40196-5), you can order it directly online by visiting the "bookstore" at this text's Companion Website http://wbl.westbuslaw.com

Study Guide

Tenth Edition

WEST'S BUSINESS LAW

Text and Cases

Clarkson Miller Jentz Cross

Legal, Ethical, International, and E–Commerce Environment

Prepared by WILLIAM ERIC HOLLOWELL and ROGER LEROY MILLER

WEST'S BUSINESS LAW
Text and Cases ❖ Tenth Edition
Legal, Ethical, International, and E-Commerce Environment

Kenneth W. Clarkson
University of Miami

Roger LeRoy Miller
Institute for University Studies
Arlington, Texas

Gaylord A. Jentz
Herbert D. Kelleher
Emeritus Professor in Business Law
University of Texas at Austin

Frank B. Cross
Herbert D. Kelleher
Centennial Professor in Business Law
University of Texas at Austin

THOMSON
✴
WEST

Australia · Canada · Mexico
Singapore · Spain
United Kingdom · United States

West's Business Law

TEXT AND CASES

Legal, Ethical, International, and E-Commerce Environment

TENTH EDITION

Kenneth W. Clarkson **Roger LeRoy Miller** **Gaylord A. Jentz** **Frank B. Cross**

Vice President and Editorial Director:
Jack Calhoun

Publisher, Business Law and Accounting:
Rob Dewey

Acquisition Editor:
Steve Silverstein

Senior Developmental Editor:
Jan Lamar

Editorial Assistant:
Todd McKenzie

Executive Marketing Manager:
Lisa L. Lysne

Production Manager:
Bill Stryker

Technology Project Editor:
Christine A. Wittmer

Manufacturing Coordinator:
Charlene Taylor

Marketing Coordinator:
Jenny Stevens

Compositor:
Parkwood Composition

Printer:
RR Donnelley, Willard

Art Director:
Michelle Kunkler

Internal Designer:
Bill Stryker

Cover Designer:
Jennifer Lambert

Web Coordinator:
Scott Cook

INTERNATIONAL LOCATIONS

ASIA (including India)
Thomson Learning
5 Shenton Way
#01-01 UIC Building
Singapore 068808

AUSTRALIA/NEW ZEALAND
Thomson Learning Australia
102 Dodds Street
Southbank, Victoria 3006
Australia

LATIN AMERICA
Thomson Learning
Seneca, 53
Colonia Polanco
11560 Mexico
D.F.Mexico

CANADA
Thomson Nelson
1120 Birchmount Road
Toronto, Ontario
Canada M1K 5G4

UK/EUROPE/MIDDLE EAST/AFRICA
Thomson Learning
High Holborn House
50-51 Bedford Road
London WC1R 4LR
United Kingdom

SPAIN (includes Portugal)
Thomson Paraninfo
Calle Magallanes, 25
28015 Madrid, Spain

Contents in Brief

Contents

❖ Unit Nine
Government Regulation   869

❖ Unit Ten
Property   939

❖ Appendices

CONCEPT SUMMARIES LIST

EXHIBITS LIST

EMERGING TRENDS

CONTEMPORARY LEGAL DEBATES

Welcome to the world of business law and the legal environment. You are about to embark on the study of one of the most important topics you should master in today's changing world. A solid understanding of business law can, of course, help you if you are going into the world of business. If you decide on a career in accounting, economics, finance, political science, or history, understanding how the legal environment works is crucial. Moreover, in your role as a consumer, you will be faced with some legal issues throughout your lifetime—renting an apartment, buying a house, obtaining a mortgage, leasing a car, and so on. In your role as an employee (if you don't go into business for yourself), you will need to know what rights you have and what rights you don't have. Even when you contemplate marriage, you will be faced with legal issues.

What You Will Find in This Text

As you will see as you thumb through the pages in this text, we have tried to make your study of business law and the legal environment as efficient and enjoyable as possible. To this end, you will find the following aids:

1. **Mastering Terminology**—through *key terms* that are boldfaced, listed at the end of each chapter, and explained fully in a *glossary* at the end of the book.
2. **Understanding Concepts**—through numerous *Concept Summaries* and *Exhibits.*
3. **Observing the Law in the Context of the Real World**—through a *Reviewing Feature* at the end of every chapter.

4. **Seeing How Legal Issues Can Arise**—through *Video Questions* based on Web-available short videos, many from actual Hollywood movies.
5. **Figuring Out How the Law Is Evolving**—through a feature called *Emerging Trends*.
6. **Determining the Current Controversies in Today's Law**—through a feature called *Contemporary Legal Debates.*

The above list, of course, is representative only. You will understand much more of what the law is about as you read through the *court cases* presented in this book, including *longer case excerpts,* which will give you a feel for how the courts really decide cases, in the courts' language.

Improving Your Ability to Perform Legal Reasoning and Analysis

While business law may seem to be a mass of facts, your goal in taking this course should also be an increased ability to figure out how legal situations will be resolved, by using legal reasoning and analysis. To this end, you will find the following key learning features to assist you in mastering legal reasoning and analysis:

- **Finding and Analyzing Case Law**—In Chapter 1, there is a section with this title which explains
  1. Legal citations
  2. Standard elements of a case
  3. The different types of opinions a court can issue
  4. How to read and understand cases

- *Briefing a Case*—You will see in Appendix A how to brief and analyze case problems. This explanation teaches you how to break down the elements of a case and will improve your ability to answer the *case problems* in each chapter.
- *Questions with Sample Answers*—At the end of each chapter, there are several hypothetical factual scenarios that present legal issues. One such question has a *sample answer* presented in Appendix I. This allows you to practice and to see if you are answering such hypothetical problems correctly.
- *Case Problems with Sample Answers*—Each chapter has a series of chapter-ending *case problems.* You can find an answer to one problem in each chapter on this book's companion student Web site at: **http://wbl.westbuslaw.com**. You can easily compare your answer to the court's opinion in each real case.
- *Impact of This Case on Today's Law*—Each landmark and classic case concludes with a short section that explains the relevance of older case law to the way courts reason today.
- *What If the Facts Were Different?*—This section, found at the end of selected cases, encourages you to think about how the outcome of a case might be different if the facts were altered.

The Companion Student Web Site

As already mentioned, the companion student Web site at **http://wbl.westbuslaw.com** provides you with short videos on various legal topics and with sample answers to one case problem per chapter. In addition, you will find the following:

- *Online quizzes* for every chapter.
- A *glossary* of terms (as well as the Spanish-English glossary).

- *Interactive exercises* that introduce you to how to research the law online.
- *Relevant Web sites* for additional research for *Emerging Trends* features as well as links to the URLs listed in the *Law on the Web* section at the end of each chapter.
- *Court case updates* for follow-up on decisions presented in the text.

Interactive Assignments on the Web

Some of you may have instructors who provide assignments using our world-class interactive Web-based system, called **West's Business Law NOW: Online Assignments.**

West's Business Law NOW: Online Assignments allows you to improve your mastery of legal concepts and terminology, legal reasoning and analysis, and much more. Your instructor will give you further information if she or he decides to use this Web-based system.

Of course, whether or not you are using the NOW system, you will wish to consider purchasing the *Study Guide,* which can help you get a better grade in your course (see the inside cover for details).

The law is all around you, and will be for the rest of your life. We hope that you begin your first course in business law and the legal environment with the same high degree of excitement that we, the authors, always have when we work on improving this text, now in its Tenth Anniversary Edition. *West's Business Law* has withstood the test of time—several million students before you have already used and benefited by it.

Dedication

To Bob Disbrow—
Your advice on all
matters small and large
continues to make me wiser
and better off, but I'm still
not quite strong enough
to catch you, no matter
what the sport.
Perhaps some day . . .
(although I doubt it).
Thanks for everything,

R.L.M.

To my wife, JoAnn; my children, Kathy,
Gary, Lori, and Rory; and my grandchildren,
Erin, Megan, Eric, Emily, Michelle, Javier,
Carmen, and Steve.

G.A.J.

To my parents and sisters.

F.B.C.

UNIT ONE
The Legal Environment of Business

CONTENTS

CHAPTER 1

Introduction to Law and Legal Reasoning

One of the important functions of law in any society is to provide stability, predictability, and continuity so that people can be sure of how to order their affairs. If any society is to survive, its citizens must be able to determine what is legally right and legally wrong. They must know what sanctions will be imposed on them if they commit wrongful acts. If they suffer harm as a result of others' wrongful acts, they must know how they can seek redress. By setting forth the rights, obligations, and privileges of citizens, the law enables individuals to go about their business with confidence and a certain degree of predictability. The stability and predictability created by the law provide an essential framework for all civilized activities, including business activities.

What do we mean when we speak of "the law"? Although this term has had, and will continue to have, different definitions, they are all based on a general observation: at a minimum, **law consists of** *enforceable rules governing relationships among individuals and between individuals and their society.* These "enforceable rules" may consist of unwritten principles of behavior established by a nomadic tribe. They may be set forth in a law code, such as the Code of Hammurabi in ancient Babylon (c. 1780 B.C.E.) or the law code of one of today's European nations. They may consist of written laws and court decisions created by modern legislative and judicial bodies, as in the United States. Regardless of how such rules are created, they all have one thing in common: they establish rights, duties, and privileges that are consistent with the values and beliefs of their society or its ruling group.

Those who embark on a study of law will find that these broad statements leave unanswered some important questions concerning the nature of law. Part of the study of law, often referred to as **jurisprudence,** involves learning about different schools of jurisprudential thought and discovering how the approaches to law characteristic of each school can affect judicial decision making. We open this introductory chapter with an examination of that topic. We then look at an important question for any student reading this text: How does the legal environment affect business decision making? We next describe the basic sources of American law, the common law tradition, and some general classifications of law. We conclude the chapter with sections offering practical guidance on several topics, including how to find the sources of law discussed in this chapter (and referred to throughout the text) and how to read and understand court opinions.

SECTION 1 | Schools of Jurisprudential Thought

You may think that legal philosophy is far removed from the practical study of business law and the legal environment. In fact, it is not. As you will learn in the chapters of this text, how judges apply the law to specific disputes, including disputes relating to the business world, depends in part on their philosophical approaches to law.

Clearly, judges are not free to decide cases solely on the basis of their personal philosophical views or on their opinions about the issues before the court. A judge's function is not to *make* the laws—that is the function of the legislative branch of government—but to interpret and apply them. From a practical point of view, however, the courts play a significant role in defining what the law is. This is because laws enacted by legislative bodies tend to be expressed in general terms. Judges thus have some flexibility in interpreting and applying the law. It is because of this flexibility that different courts can, and often do, arrive at different conclusions in cases that involve nearly identical issues, facts, and applicable laws. This flexibility also means that each judge's unique personality, legal philosophy, set of values, and intellectual attributes necessarily frame the judicial decision-making process to some extent.

We look now at some of the significant schools of legal, or jurisprudential, thought that have evolved over time.

THE NATURAL LAW SCHOOL

An age-old question about the nature of law has to do with the finality of a nation's laws, such as the laws of the United States at the present time. For example, what if a particular law is deemed to be a "bad" law by a substantial number of that nation's citizens? Must a citizen obey the law if it goes against his or her conscience to do so? Is there a higher or universal law to which individuals can appeal? One who adheres to the natural law tradition would answer these questions in the affirmative. **Natural law** denotes a system of moral and ethical principles that are inherent in human nature and that people can discover through the use of their natural intelligence, or reason.

The natural law tradition is one of the oldest and most significant schools of jurisprudence. It dates back to the days of the Greek philosopher Aristotle (384–322 B.C.E.), who distinguished between natural law and the laws governing a particular nation. According to Aristotle, natural law applies universally to all humankind.

The notion that people have "natural rights" stems from the natural law tradition. Those who claim that a specific foreign government is depriving certain citizens of their human rights implicitly are appealing to a higher law that has universal applicability. The question of the universality of basic human rights also comes into play in the context of international business operations. Should rights extended to workers in the United States, such as the right to be free of discrimination in the workplace, be extended to workers employed by a U.S. firm doing business in another country that does not provide for such rights? This question is rooted implicitly in a concept of universal rights that has its origins in the natural law tradition.

THE POSITIVIST SCHOOL

In contrast, **positive law,** or national law (the written law of a given society at a particular point in time), applies only to the citizens of that nation or society. Those who adhere to the **positivist school** believe that there can be no higher law than a nation's positive law. According to the positivist school, there is no such thing as "natural rights." Rather, human rights exist solely because of laws. If the laws are not enforced, anarchy will result. Thus, whether a law is "bad" or "good" is irrelevant. The law is the law and must be obeyed until it is changed—in an orderly manner through a legitimate lawmaking process. A judge with positivist leanings probably would be more inclined to defer to an existing law than would a judge who adheres to the natural law tradition.

THE HISTORICAL SCHOOL

The **historical school** of legal thought emphasizes the evolutionary process of law by concentrating on the origin and history of the legal system. Thus, this school looks to the past to discover what the principles of contemporary law should be. The legal doctrines that have withstood the passage of time—those that have worked in the past—are deemed best suited for shaping present laws. Hence, law derives its legitimacy and authority from adhering to the standards that historical development has shown to be workable. Adherents of the historical school are more likely than those of other schools to strictly follow decisions made in past cases.

LEGAL REALISM

In the 1920s and 1930s, a number of jurists and scholars, known as legal realists, rebelled against the historical approach to law. **Legal realism** is based on the idea that law is just one of many institutions in society and that it is shaped by social forces and needs. The law is a human enterprise, and judges should take social and economic realities into account when deciding cases. Legal realists also believe that the law can never be applied with total uniformity. Given that judges are human beings with unique personalities, value systems, and intellects, obviously different judges will bring different reasoning processes to the same case.

Legal realism strongly influenced the growth of what is sometimes called the **sociological school** of jurisprudence. This school views law as a tool for promoting justice in society. In the 1960s, for example, the justices of the United States Supreme Court played a leading role in the civil rights movement by upholding long-neglected laws calling for equal treatment for all Americans, including African Americans and other minorities. Generally, jurists who adhere to this philosophy of law are more likely to depart from past decisions than are those jurists who adhere to the other schools of legal thought.

CONCEPT SUMMARY 1.1 | Schools of Jurisprudential Thought

SCHOOL OF THOUGHT	DESCRIPTION
THE NATURAL LAW SCHOOL	One of the oldest and most significant schools of legal thought. Those who believe in natural law hold that there is a universal law applicable to all human beings. This law is discoverable through reason and is of a higher order than positive (national) law.
THE POSITIVIST SCHOOL	A school of legal thought centered on the assumption that there is no law higher than the laws created by the government. Laws must be obeyed, even if they are unjust, to prevent anarchy.
THE HISTORICAL SCHOOL	A school of legal thought that stresses the evolutionary nature of law and that looks to doctrines that have withstood the passage of time for guidance in shaping present laws.
LEGAL REALISM	A school of legal thought, popular during the 1920s and 1930s, that left a lasting imprint on American jurisprudence. Legal realists generally advocated a less abstract and more realistic and pragmatic approach to the law, an approach that would take into account customary practices and the circumstances in which transactions take place. Legal realism strongly influenced the growth of the *sociological school* of jurisprudence, which views law as a tool for promoting social justice.

SECTION 2 | Business Activities and the Legal Environment

As those entering the world of business will learn, laws and government regulations affect virtually all business activities—from hiring and firing decisions to workplace safety, to the manufacturing and marketing of products, to business financing, and so on. To make good business decisions, a basic knowledge of the laws and regulations governing these activities is beneficial—if not essential. Realize also that in today's world a knowledge of "black-letter" law is not enough. Businesspersons are also pressured to make ethical decisions. Thus, the study of business law necessarily involves an ethical dimension.

MANY DIFFERENT LAWS MAY AFFECT A SINGLE BUSINESS TRANSACTION

As you will note, each chapter in this text covers a specific area of the law and shows how the legal rules in that area affect business activities. Though compartmentalizing the law in this fashion promotes conceptual clarity, it does not indicate the extent to which a number of different laws may apply to just one transaction.

Consider an example. Suppose that you are the president of NetSys, Inc., a company that creates and maintains computer network systems for its clients, including business firms. NetSys also markets software for customers who require an internal computer network. One day, Hernandez, an operations officer for Southwest Distribution Corporation (SDC), contacts you by e-mail about a possible contract concerning SDC's computer network. In deciding whether to enter into a contract with SDC, you should consider, among other things, the legal requirements for an enforceable contract. Are there different requirements for a contract for services and a contract for products? What are your options if SDC **breaches** (breaks, or fails to perform) the contract? The answers to these questions are part of contract law and sales law.

Other questions might concern payment under the contract. How can you guarantee that NetSys will be paid? For example, if payment is made with a check that is returned for insufficient funds, what are your options? Answers to these questions can be found in the laws that relate to negotiable instruments (such as checks) and creditors' rights. Also, a dispute may occur over the rights to NetSys's software, or there may be a question of liability if the software is defective. There may be an issue as to whether you and Hernandez have the authority to make the deal in the first place. A disagreement may arise from such circumstances as an accountant's evaluation of the contract. Resolutions of these questions may be found in areas of the law that relate to intellectual property, e-commerce, torts, product liability, agency, business organizations, or professional liability.

Finally, if any dispute cannot be resolved amicably, then the laws and the rules concerning courts and court procedures spell out the steps of a lawsuit. Exhibit 1–1 illustrates the various areas of law that may influence business decision making.

ETHICS AND BUSINESS DECISION MAKING

Merely knowing the areas of law that may affect a business decision is not sufficient in today's business world. Businesspersons must also take ethics into account. As you will learn in Chapter 5, *ethics* is generally defined as the study of what constitutes right or wrong behavior. In today's business world, business decision makers must consider not just whether a decision is profitable and legal but also whether it is ethical.

Throughout this text, you will learn about the relationship between the law and ethics, as well as about some of the types of ethical questions that often arise in the business context. For example, the unit-ending *Focus on Ethics* features in this text are devoted solely to the exploration of ethical dimensions of selected topics treated within the unit. Additionally, Chapter 5 offers a detailed look at the importance of ethical

EXHIBIT 1-1 **Areas of the Law That May Affect Business Decision Making**

considerations in business decision making. Finally, various other elements in this text, such as the ethical questions that conclude selected chapters, are designed to introduce you to ethical aspects of specific cases involving real-life situations.

SECTION 3 | Sources of American Law

There are numerous sources of American law. *Primary sources of law, or sources that establish the law*, include the following:

1. The U.S. Constitution and the constitutions of the various states.
2. Statutory law—including laws passed by Congress, state legislatures, or local governing bodies.
3. Regulations created by administrative agencies, such as the Food and Drug Administration.
4. Case law and common law doctrines.

We describe each of these important sources of law in the following pages.

Secondary sources of law are books and articles that summarize and clarify the primary sources of law. Examples include legal encyclopedias, treatises, articles in law reviews, and compilations of law, such as the *Restatements of the Law* (which will be discussed shortly). Courts often refer to secondary sources of law for guidance in interpreting and applying the primary sources of law discussed here.

CONSTITUTIONAL LAW

The federal government and the states have separate written constitutions that set forth the general organization, powers, and limits of their respective governments. **Constitutional law** is the law as expressed in these constitutions.

According to Article VI of the U.S. Constitution, the Constitution is the supreme law of the land. As such, it is the basis of all law in the United States. A law in violation of the Constitution, if challenged, will be declared unconstitutional and will not be enforced, no matter what its source. Because of its importance in the American legal system, we present the complete text of the U.S. Constitution in Appendix B.

The Tenth Amendment to the U.S. Constitution reserves to the states all powers not granted to the federal government. Each state in the union has its own constitution. Unless it conflicts with the U.S. Constitution or a federal law, a state constitution is supreme within the state's borders.

STATUTORY LAW

Laws enacted by legislative bodies at any level of government, such as the statutes passed by Congress or by state legislatures, make up the body of law generally referred to as **statutory law.** When a legislature passes a statute, that statute ultimately is included in the federal code of laws or the relevant state code of laws (these codes are discussed later in this chapter).

Statutory law also includes local **ordinances**—statutes (laws, rules, or orders) passed by municipal or county governing units to govern matters not covered by federal or state law. Ordinances commonly have to do with city or county land use (zoning ordinances), building and safety codes, and other matters affecting the local unit.

A federal statute, of course, applies to all states. A state statute, in contrast, applies only within the state's borders. State laws thus may vary from state to state. No federal statute may violate the U.S. Constitution, and no state statute or local ordinance may violate the U.S. Constitution or the relevant state constitution.

UNIFORM LAWS The differences among state laws were particularly notable in the 1800s, when conflicting state statutes frequently made trade and commerce among the states very difficult. To counter these problems, in 1892 a group of legal scholars and lawyers formed the National Conference of Commissioners on Uniform State Laws (NCCUSL) to draft **uniform laws,** or model laws, for the states to consider adopting. The NCCUSL still exists today and continues to issue uniform laws.

Each state has the option of adopting or rejecting a uniform law. *Only if a state legislature adopts a uniform law does that law become part of the statutory law of that state.* Note that a state legislature may adopt all or part of a uniform law as it is written, or the legislature may rewrite the law however the legislature wishes. Hence, even when a uniform law is said to have been adopted in many states, those states' laws may not be entirely "uniform."

The earliest uniform law, the Uniform Negotiable Instruments Law, was completed by 1896 and adopted in every state by the early 1920s (although not all states used exactly the same wording). Over the following decades, other acts were drawn up in a similar manner. In all, over two hundred uniform acts have been issued by the NCCUSL since its inception. The most ambitious uniform act of all, however, was the Uniform Commercial Code.

THE UNIFORM COMMERCIAL CODE The Uniform Commercial Code (UCC), which was created through the joint efforts of the NCCUSL and the American Law Institute,[1] was first issued in 1952. All fifty states,[2] the District of Columbia, and the Virgin Islands have adopted the UCC. It facilitates commerce among the states by providing a uniform, yet flexible, set of rules governing commercial transactions. The UCC assures businesspersons that their contracts, if validly entered into, normally will be enforced.

As you will read in later chapters, from time to time the NCCUSL revises the articles contained in the UCC and submits the revised versions to the states for adoption. During the 1990s, for example, four articles (Articles 3, 4, 5, and 9) were revised, and two new articles (Articles 2A and 4A) were added. In 2003, amendments to Articles 2 and 2A were approved. Because of its importance in the area of commercial law, we cite the UCC frequently in this text. We also present the UCC in Appendix C.

ADMINISTRATIVE LAW

An important source of American law is **administrative law,** which consists of the rules, orders, and decisions of administrative agencies. An **administrative agency** is a federal, state, or local government agency established to perform a specific function. Administrative law and procedures, which will be examined in detail in Chapter 43, constitute a dominant element in the regulatory environment of business. Rules issued by various administrative agencies now affect virtually every aspect of a business's operations, including its capital structure and financing, its hiring and firing procedures, its relations with employees and unions, and the way it manufactures and markets its products.

FEDERAL AGENCIES At the national level, numerous **executive agencies** exist within the cabinet departments of the executive branch. The Food and Drug Administration, for example, is an agency within the Department of Health and Human Services. Executive agencies are subject to the authority of the president, who has the power to appoint and remove officers of federal agencies. There are also major **independent regulatory agencies** at the federal level, such as the Federal Trade Commission, the Securities and Exchange Commission, and the Federal Communications Commission. The president's power is less pronounced in regard to independent agencies, whose officers serve for fixed terms and cannot be removed without just cause.

STATE AND LOCAL AGENCIES There are administrative agencies at the state and local levels as well. Commonly, a state agency (such as a state pollution-control agency) is created as a parallel to a federal agency (such as the Environmental Protection Agency). Just as federal statutes take precedence over conflicting state statutes, so federal agency regulations take precedence over conflicting state regulations.

CASE LAW AND COMMON LAW DOCTRINES

The rules of law announced in court decisions constitute another basic source of American law. These rules of law include interpretations of constitutional provisions, of statutes enacted by legislatures, and of regulations created by administrative agencies. Today, this body of judge-made law is referred to as **case law,** or the *common law*. Because of the importance of the common law in our legal system, we look at the origins and characteristics of the common law tradition in some detail in the pages that follow.

SECTION 4 | The Common Law Tradition

Because of our colonial heritage, much of American law is based on the English legal system, which originated in medieval England and continued to evolve in the following centuries. A knowledge of this system is necessary to an understanding of the American legal system today.

EARLY ENGLISH COURTS

The origins of the English legal system—and thus the U.S. legal system as well—date back to 1066, when the Normans conquered England. William the Conqueror and his successors began the process of unifying the country under their rule. One of the means they used to do this was the establishment of the king's

---

1. This institute was formed in the 1920s and consists of practicing attorneys, legal scholars, and judges.
2. Louisiana has not adopted Articles 2 and 2A (covering contracts for the sale and lease of goods), however.

CONCEPT SUMMARY 1.2 | Sources of American Law

SOURCE	DESCRIPTION
CONSTITUTIONAL LAW	The law as expressed in the U.S. Constitution and the state constitutions. The U.S. Constitution is the supreme law of the land. State constitutions are supreme within state borders to the extent that they do not violate a clause of the U.S. Constitution or a federal law.
STATUTORY LAW	Laws (statutes and ordinances) created by federal, state, and local legislatures and governing bodies. None of these laws may violate the U.S. Constitution or the relevant state constitution. Uniform statutes, when adopted by a state, become statutory law in that state.
ADMINISTRATIVE LAW	The rules, orders, and decisions of federal, state, or local government administrative agencies.
CASE LAW AND COMMON LAW DOCTRINES	Judge-made law, including interpretations of constitutional provisions, of statutes enacted by legislatures, and of regulations created by administrative agencies.

courts, or *curiae regis*. Before the Norman Conquest, disputes had been settled according to the local legal customs and traditions in various regions of the country. The king's courts sought to establish a uniform set of customs for the country as a whole. What evolved in these courts was the beginning of the **common law**—a body of general rules that applied throughout the entire English realm. Eventually, the common law tradition became part of the heritage of all nations that were once British colonies, including the United States.

COURTS OF LAW AND REMEDIES AT LAW The early English king's courts could grant only very limited kinds of **remedies** (the legal means to enforce a right or redress a wrong). If one person wronged another in some way, the king's courts could award as compensation one or more of the following: (1) land, (2) items of value, or (3) money. The courts that awarded this compensation became known as **courts of law,** and the three remedies were called **remedies at law.** (Today, the remedy at law normally takes the form of money **damages**—money given to a party whose legal interests have been injured.) Even though the system introduced uniformity in the settling of disputes, when a complaining party wanted a remedy other than economic compensation, the courts of law could do nothing, so "no remedy, no right."

COURTS OF EQUITY AND REMEDIES IN EQUITY
Equity is a branch of law, founded on what might be described as notions of justice and fair dealing, that

seeks to supply a remedy when no adequate remedy at law is available. When individuals could not obtain an adequate remedy in a court of law because of strict technicalities, they petitioned the king for relief. Most of these petitions were decided by an adviser to the king, called a **chancellor,** who was said to be the "keeper of the king's conscience." When the chancellor thought that the claims were fair, new and unique remedies were granted. Eventually, formal chancery courts, or **courts of equity,** were established.

The remedies granted by the equity courts became known as **remedies in equity,** or equitable remedies. These remedies include *specific performance* (ordering a party to perform an agreement as promised), an *injunction* (ordering a party to cease engaging in a specific activity or to undo some wrong or injury), and *rescission* (the cancellation of a contractual obligation). We discuss these and other equitable remedies in more detail at appropriate points in the chapters that follow, particularly in Chapter 18.

As a general rule, today's courts, like the early English courts, will not grant equitable remedies unless the remedy at law—money damages—is inadequate. For example, suppose that you form a contract (a legally binding agreement—see Chapter 10) to purchase a parcel of land that you think will be just perfect for your future country home. Further suppose that the seller breaches this agreement. You could sue the seller for the return of any deposits or down payment you might have made on the land, but this is not the remedy you really seek. What you want is to have the court order the seller to go through with the contract. In other words, you want the court to grant the equitable remedy of specific performance because money damages are inadequate in this situation.

EQUITABLE MAXIMS In fashioning appropriate remedies, judges often were (and continue to be) guided by so-called **equitable maxims**—propositions or general statements of equitable rules. Exhibit 1–2 lists some important equitable maxims. The last maxim listed in that exhibit—"Equity aids the vigilant, not those who rest on their rights"—merits special attention. It has become known as the equitable doctrine of **laches** (a term derived from the Latin *laxus*, meaning "lax" or "negligent"), and it can be used as a defense. A **defense** is an argument raised by the **defendant** (the party being sued) indicating why the **plaintiff** (the suing party) should not obtain the remedy sought. (Note that in equity proceedings, the party bringing a lawsuit is called the **petitioner,** and the party being sued is referred to as the **respondent.**)

The doctrine of laches arose to encourage people to bring lawsuits while the evidence was fresh. What constitutes a reasonable time, of course, varies according to the circumstances of the case. Time periods for different types of cases are now usually fixed by **statutes of limitations.** After the time allowed under a statute of limitations has expired, no action can be brought, no matter how strong the case was originally.

EXHIBIT 1–2 Equitable Maxims

1. *Whoever seeks equity must do equity.* (Anyone who wishes to be treated fairly must treat others fairly.)

2. *Where there is equal equity, the law must prevail.* (The law will determine the outcome of a controversy in which the merits of both sides are equal.)

3. *One seeking the aid of an equity court must come to the court with clean hands.* (Plaintiffs must have acted fairly and honestly.)

4. *Equity will not suffer a wrong to be without a remedy.* (Equitable relief will be awarded when there is a right to relief and there is no adequate remedy at law.)

5. *Equity regards substance rather than form.* (Equity is more concerned with fairness and justice than with legal technicalities.)

6. *Equity aids the vigilant, not those who rest on their rights.* (Equity will not help those who neglect their rights for an unreasonable period of time.)

LEGAL AND EQUITABLE REMEDIES TODAY

The establishment of courts of equity in medieval England resulted in two distinct court systems: courts of law and courts of equity. The systems had different sets of judges and granted different types of remedies. Parties who sought legal remedies, or remedies at law, would bring their claims before courts of law. Parties seeking equitable relief, or remedies in equity, would bring their claims before courts of equity. During the nineteenth century, however, most states in the United States adopted rules of procedure that resulted in combined courts of law and equity—although some states, such as Arkansas, still retain the distinction. A party now may request both legal and equitable remedies in the same action, and the trial court judge may grant either or both forms of relief.

The distinction between legal and equitable remedies remains relevant to students of business law, however, because these remedies differ. To seek the proper remedy for a wrong, one must know what remedies are available. Additionally, certain vestiges of the procedures used when there were separate courts of law and equity still exist. For example, a party has the right to demand a jury trial in an action at law, but not in an action in equity. In the old courts of equity, the chancellor heard both sides of an issue and decided what should be done. Juries were considered inappropriate. In actions at law, however, juries participated in determining the outcome of cases, including the amount of damages to be awarded. Exhibit 1–3 on the next page summarizes the procedural differences between an action at law and an action in equity.

THE DOCTRINE OF STARE DECISIS

One of the unique features of the common law is that it is *judge-made* law. The body of principles and doctrines that form the common law emerged over time as judges decided actual legal controversies.

CASE PRECEDENTS AND CASE REPORTERS When possible, judges attempted to be consistent and to base their decisions on the principles suggested by earlier cases. They sought to decide similar cases in a similar way and considered new cases with care because they knew that their decisions would make new law. Each interpretation became part of the law on the subject and served as a legal **precedent**—that is, a decision that furnished an example or authority for deciding

EXHIBIT 1-3 Procedural Differences between an Action at Law and an Action in Equity

PROCEDURE	ACTION AT LAW	ACTION IN EQUITY
Initiation of lawsuit	By filing a complaint	By filing a petition
Parties	Plaintiff and defendant	Petitioner and respondent
Decision	By jury or judge	By judge (no jury)
Result	Judgment	Decree
Remedy	Monetary damages	Injunction, specific performance, or rescission

subsequent cases involving similar legal principles or facts.

By the early fourteenth century, portions of the most important decisions of each year were being gathered together and recorded in *Year Books,* which became useful references for lawyers and judges. In the sixteenth century, the *Year Books* were discontinued, and other forms of case publication became available. Today, cases are published, or "reported," in volumes called **reporters,** or *reports*. We describe today's case reporting system in detail later in this chapter.

STARE DECISIS AND THE COMMON LAW TRADITION   The practice of deciding new cases with reference to former decisions, or precedents, became a cornerstone of the English and American judicial systems. The practice formed a doctrine known as ***stare decisis***[3] (a Latin phrase meaning "to stand on decided cases"). Under this doctrine, judges are obligated to follow the precedents established within their jurisdictions. The term *jurisdiction* refers to an area in which a court or courts have the power to apply the law—see Chapter 2.

The doctrine of *stare decisis* helps the courts to be more efficient, because if other courts have carefully analyzed a similar case, their legal reasoning and opinions can serve as guides. *Stare decisis* also makes the law more stable and predictable. If the law on a given subject is well settled, someone bringing a case to court can usually rely on the court to make a decision based on what the law has been in the past.

A TYPICAL SCENARIO   To illustrate how the doctrine of *stare decisis* works, consider an example. Suppose that the lower state courts in California have reached conflicting conclusions on whether drivers are liable for accidents they cause while merging into freeway traffic. Some courts have held drivers liable even though the drivers looked and did not see any oncoming traffic and even though witnesses (passengers in their cars) testified to that effect. To settle the law on this issue, the California Supreme Court decides to review a case involving this fact pattern. The court rules that in such a situation, the driver who is merging into traffic is liable for any accidents caused by the driver's failure to yield to freeway traffic—even if the driver looked carefully and did not see an approaching vehicle.

The California Supreme Court's decision on this matter is a **binding authority**—a case precedent or statute that must be followed. (Nonbinding legal authorities on which judges may rely for guidance, such as precedents established in other jurisdictions, are referred to as *persuasive authorities*.) In other words, the California Supreme Court's decision will influence the outcome of all future cases on this issue brought before the California state courts. Similarly, a decision on a given question by the United States Supreme Court (the nation's highest court) is binding on all courts.

DEPARTURES FROM PRECEDENT   Although courts are obligated to follow precedents, sometimes a court will depart from the rule of precedent if it decides that the precedent should no longer be followed. If a court decides that a ruling precedent is simply incorrect or that technological or social changes have rendered the precedent inapplicable, the court might rule contrary to the precedent. Cases that overturn precedent often receive a great deal of publicity.[4]

---

3. Pronounced *ster*-ay dih-*si*-ses.

4. For example, when the United States Supreme Court held in the 1950s that racial segregation in the public schools was unconstitutional, it expressly overturned a Supreme Court precedent upholding the constitutionality of "separate-but-equal" segregation. The Supreme Court's departure from precedent received a tremendous amount of publicity as people began to realize the ramifications of this change in the law. See *Brown v. Board of Education of Topeka,* 347 U.S. 483, 74 S.Ct. 686, 98 L.Ed. 873 (1954). (Legal citations are explained later in this chapter.)

Note that judges have some flexibility in applying precedents. For example, a trial court may avoid applying a Supreme Court precedent by arguing that the facts of the case before the court are distinguishable from the facts in the Supreme Court case and that, therefore, the Supreme Court's ruling on the issue does not apply to the case before the court.

WHEN THERE IS NO PRECEDENT Occasionally, the courts must decide cases for which no precedents exist, called *cases of first impression*. For example, as you will read throughout this text, disputes involving transactions conducted via the Internet have presented new problems for the courts. When existing laws governing free speech, pornography, fraud, jurisdiction, and other areas were drafted, cyberspace did not exist. Although new laws are being created to govern such disputes, in the meantime the courts have to decide, on a case-by-case basis, what rules should be applied.

Generally, in deciding cases of first impression, courts may consider a number of factors, including persuasive authorities (such as cases from other jurisdictions, if there are any), legal principles and policies underlying previous court decisions or existing statutes, fairness, social values and customs, **public policy** (governmental policy based on widely held societal values), and data and concepts drawn from the social sciences. Which of these sources is chosen or receives the greatest emphasis depends on the nature of the case being considered and the particular judge or judges hearing the case. In cases of first impression, as in all cases, judges must have legal reasons for ruling as they do on particular issues. When a court issues a written opinion on a case (we discuss court opinions later in this chapter), the opinion normally contains a carefully reasoned argument justifying the decision.

STARE DECISIS AND LEGAL REASONING

Legal reasoning is the reasoning process used by judges in deciding what law applies to a given dispute and then applying that law to the specific facts or circumstances of the case. Through the use of legal reasoning, judges harmonize their decisions with those that have been made before, as the doctrine of *stare decisis* requires.

Students of business law and the legal environment also engage in legal reasoning. For example, you may be asked to provide answers for some of the case problems that appear at the end of every chapter in this text. Each problem describes the facts of a particular dispute and the legal question at issue. If you are assigned a case problem, you will be asked to determine how a court would answer that question, and why. In other words, you will need to give legal reasons for whatever conclusion you reach.[5] We look here at the basic steps involved in legal reasoning and then describe some forms of reasoning commonly used by the courts in making their decisions.

BASIC STEPS IN LEGAL REASONING At times, the legal arguments set forth in court opinions are relatively simple and brief. At other times, the arguments are complex and lengthy. Regardless of the length of a legal argument, however, the basic steps of the legal reasoning process remain the same. These steps, which you also can follow when analyzing cases and case problems, form what is commonly referred to as the *IRAC method* of legal reasoning. IRAC is an acronym formed from the first letters of the following words: Issue, Rule, Application, and Conclusion. To apply the IRAC method, you would ask the following questions:

1. *What are the key facts and issues?* For example, suppose that a plaintiff comes before the court claiming *assault* (a wrongful and intentional action in which one person makes another fearful of immediate physical harm—part of a class of actions called *torts*). The plaintiff claims that the defendant threatened her while she was sleeping. Although the plaintiff was unaware that she was being threatened, her roommate heard the defendant make the threat. The legal issue, or question, raised by these facts is whether the defendant's actions constitute the tort of assault, given that the plaintiff was not aware of those actions at the time they occurred.

2. *What rules of law apply to the case?* A rule of law may be a rule stated by the courts in previous decisions, a state or federal statute, or a state or federal administrative agency regulation. In our hypothetical case, the plaintiff **alleges** (claims) that the defendant committed a tort. Therefore, the applicable law is the common law of torts—specifically, tort law governing assault (see Chapter 6 for more detail on intentional torts). Case precedents involving similar facts and

---

5. See Appendix A for further instructions on how to analyze case problems.

issues thus would be relevant. Often, more than one rule of law will be applicable to a case.

3. *How do the rules of law apply to the particular facts and circumstances of this case?* This step is often the most difficult one because each case presents a unique set of facts, circumstances, and parties. Although cases may be similar, no two cases are ever identical in all respects. Normally, judges (and lawyers and law students) try to find **cases on point**—previously decided cases that are as similar as possible to the one under consideration. (Because of the difficulty—and importance—of this step in the legal reasoning process, we discuss it in more detail in the next subsection.)

4. *What conclusion should be drawn?* This step normally presents few problems. Usually, the conclusion is evident if the previous three steps have been followed carefully.

FORMS OF LEGAL REASONING Judges use many types of reasoning when following the third step of the legal reasoning process—applying the law to the facts of a particular case. Three common forms of reasoning are deductive reasoning, linear reasoning, and reasoning by analogy.

—Deductive Reasoning. Deductive reasoning is sometimes called *syllogistic reasoning* because it employs a **syllogism**—a logical relationship involving a major premise, a minor premise, and a conclusion. For example, consider the hypothetical case presented earlier, in which the plaintiff alleged that the defendant committed assault by threatening her while she was sleeping. The judge might point out that "under the common law of torts, an individual must be *aware* of a threat of danger for the threat to constitute assault" (major premise); "the plaintiff in this case was unaware of the threat at the time it occurred" (minor premise); and "therefore, the circumstances do not amount to an assault" (conclusion).

—Linear Reasoning. A second important form of legal reasoning that is commonly employed might be thought of as "linear" reasoning because it proceeds from one point to another, with the final point being the conclusion. An analogy will help make this form of reasoning clear. Imagine a knotted rope, with each knot tying together separate pieces of rope to form a tight length. As a whole, the rope represents a linear progression of thought logically connecting various points, with the last point, or knot, representing the conclusion. For example, suppose that a tenant in an apartment building sues the landlord for damages for an injury resulting from an allegedly inadequately lit stairway. The court may engage in a reasoning process involving the following "pieces of rope":

1. The landlord, who was on the premises the evening the injury occurred, testifies that none of the other nine tenants who used the stairway that night complained about the lights.

2. The fact that none of the tenants complained is the same as if they had said the lighting was sufficient.

3. That there were no complaints does not prove that the lighting was sufficient but does prove that the landlord had no reason to believe that it was not.

4. The landlord's belief was reasonable because no one complained.

5. Therefore, the landlord acted reasonably and was not negligent with respect to the lighting in the stairway.

On the basis of this reasoning, the court concludes that the tenant is not entitled to compensation on the basis of the stairway's allegedly insufficient lighting.

—Reasoning by Analogy. Another important type of reasoning that judges use in deciding cases is reasoning by *analogy*. To reason by **analogy** is to compare the facts in the case at hand to the facts in other cases and, to the extent that the patterns are similar, to apply the same rule of law to the present case. To the extent that the facts are unique, or "distinguishable," different rules may apply. For example, in case A, the court held that a driver who crossed a highway's center line was negligent. Case B involves a driver who crosses the line to avoid hitting a child. In determining whether case A's rule applies in case B, a judge would consider what the reasons were for the decision in A and whether B is sufficiently similar for those reasons to apply. If the judge holds that B's driver is not liable, that judge must indicate why case A's rule is not relevant to the facts presented in case B.

THERE IS NO ONE "RIGHT" ANSWER

Many persons believe that there is one "right" answer to every legal question. In most situations involving a legal controversy, however, there is no single correct result. Good arguments can often be made to support either side of a legal controversy. Quite often, a case does not present the situation of a "good" person suing a "bad" person. In many cases, both parties have acted in good faith in some measure or have acted in bad faith to some degree.

Additionally, as already mentioned, each judge has her or his own personal beliefs and philosophy, which shape, at least to some extent, the process of legal reasoning. This means that the outcome of a particular lawsuit before a court can never be predicted with absolute certainty. In fact, in some cases, even though the weight of the law would seem to favor one party's position, judges, through creative legal reasoning, have found ways to rule in favor of the other party in the interests of preventing injustice.

SECTION 5 | The Common Law Today

Today, the common law continues to be applied throughout the United States. Common law doctrines and principles govern all areas *not* covered by statutory or administrative law. In a dispute concerning a particular employment practice, for example, if a statute regulates that practice, the statute will apply rather than the common law doctrine that applied prior to the enactment of the statute.

THE CONTINUING IMPORTANCE OF THE COMMON LAW

Because the body of statutory law has expanded greatly since the beginning of this nation, thus narrowing the applicability of common law doctrines, it might seem that the common law has dwindled in importance. This is not true, however. For one thing, even in areas governed by statutory law, there is a significant interplay between statutory law and the common law. For example, many statutes essentially codify existing common law rules, and regulations issued by various administrative agencies usually are based, at least in part, on common law principles. Additionally, the courts, in interpreting statutory law, often rely on the common law as a guide to what the legislators intended.

Furthermore, how the courts interpret a particular statute determines how that statute will be applied. If you wanted to learn about the coverage and applicability of a particular statute, for example, you would necessarily have to locate the statute and study it. You would also need to see how the courts in your jurisdiction have interpreted and applied the statute. In other words, you would have to learn what precedents have been established in your jurisdiction with respect to

CONCEPT SUMMARY 1.3	The Common Law Tradition	
ASPECT	**DESCRIPTION**
ORIGINS OF THE COMMON LAW	The American legal system is based on the common law tradition, which originated in medieval England. Following the conquest of England in 1066 by William the Conqueror, king's courts were established throughout England, and the common law was developed in these courts.
LEGAL AND EQUITABLE REMEDIES	The distinction between remedies at law (money or items of value, such as land) and remedies in equity (including specific performance, injunction, and rescission of a contractual obligation) originated in the early English courts of law and courts of equity, respectively.
CASE PRECEDENTS AND THE DOCTRINE OF STARE DECISIS	In the king's courts, judges attempted to make their decisions consistent with previous decisions, called precedents. This practice gave rise to the doctrine of *stare decisis*. This doctrine, which became a cornerstone of the common law tradition, obligates judges to abide by precedents established in their jurisdictions.
STARE DECISIS AND LEGAL REASONING	Legal reasoning refers to the reasoning process used by judges in applying the law to the facts and issues of specific cases. Legal reasoning involves becoming familiar with the key facts of a case, identifying the relevant legal rules, linking those rules to the facts, and drawing a conclusion. In linking the legal rules to the facts of a case, judges may use deductive reasoning, linear reasoning, or reasoning by analogy.

that statute. Often, the applicability of a newly enacted statute does not become clear until a body of case law develops to clarify how, when, and to whom the statute applies.

RESTATEMENTS OF THE LAW

The American Law Institute (ALI) has drafted and published compilations of the common law called *Restatements of the Law,* which generally summarize the common law rules followed by most states. There are *Restatements of the Law* in the areas of contracts, torts, agency, trusts, property, restitution, security, judgments, and conflict of laws. The *Restatements,* like other secondary sources of law, do not in themselves have the force of law but are an important source of legal analysis and opinion on which judges often rely in making their decisions.

Many of the *Restatements* are now in their second or third editions. We refer to the *Restatements* frequently in subsequent chapters of this text, indicating in parentheses the edition to which we are referring. For example, we refer to the second edition of the *Restatement of the Law of Contracts* simply as the *Restatement (Second) of Contracts*.

SECTION 6 | Classifications of Law

Because the body of law is so large, one must break it down by some means of classification. A number of classification systems have been devised. For example, one classification system divides law into substantive law and procedural law. **Substantive law** consists of all laws that define, describe, regulate, and create legal rights and obligations. **Procedural law** consists of all laws that delineate the methods of enforcing the rights established by substantive law. Other classification systems divide law into federal law and state law, private law (dealing with relationships between private entities) and public law (addressing the relationship between persons and their governments), national law and international law, and so on. Here we look at still another classification system, which divides law into civil law and criminal law, as well as at what is meant by the term *cyberlaw*.

CIVIL LAW AND CRIMINAL LAW

Civil law spells out the rights and duties that exist between persons and between persons and their governments, and the relief available when a person's rights are violated. Typically, in a civil case, a private party sues another private party (although the government can also sue a party for a civil law violation) to make that other party comply with a duty or pay for the damage caused by failure to comply with a duty. Much of the law that we discuss in this text is civil law. Contract law, for example, covered in Chapters 10 through 19, is civil law. The whole body of tort law (see Chapters 6 and 7) is civil law.

Criminal law, in contrast, is concerned with wrongs committed *against the public as a whole*. Criminal acts are defined and prohibited by local, state, or federal government statutes. Criminal defendants are thus prosecuted by public officials, such as a district attorney (D.A.), on behalf of the state, not by their victims or other private parties. (See Chapter 9 for a further discussion of the distinction between civil law and criminal law.)

CYBERLAW

Over the last ten years, the use of the Internet to conduct business transactions has led to new types of legal issues. In response, courts have had to adapt traditional laws to situations that are unique to our age. (For a discussion of one such situation, see this chapter's *Contemporary Legal Debates* feature on pages 16 and 17.) Additionally, legislatures have created laws to deal specifically with such issues. The growing body of law that deals specifically with issues raised by cyberspace transactions is often referred to as **cyberlaw.** Cyberlaw is not really a classification of law; rather, it is an informal term used to describe how traditional classifications of law, such as civil law and criminal law, are being applied to online activities.

Realize, too, that cyberlaw is not a new *type* of law. For the most part, it consists of traditional legal principles that have been modified and adapted to fit situations that are unique to the online world. Of course, in some areas new statutes have been enacted, at both the federal and state levels, to cover specific types of problems stemming from online communications.

Anyone preparing to enter today's business world will find it useful to know how old and new laws are being applied to activities conducted online, such as advertising, contracting, banking, filing documents with the courts or government agencies, employment relations, and a variety of other transactions. For that reason, many sections in this text are devoted to cyberlaw issues.

SECTION 7 | How to Find Primary Sources of Law

This text includes numerous citations to primary sources of law—federal and state statutes, the U.S. Constitution and state constitutions, regulations issued by administrative agencies, and court cases. (A **citation** is a reference to a publication in which a legal authority—such as a statute or a court decision or other source—can be found.) In this section, we explain how you can use citations to find primary sources of law.

FINDING STATUTORY AND ADMINISTRATIVE LAW

When Congress passes laws, they are collected in a publication titled *United States Statutes at Large*. When state legislatures pass laws, they are collected in similar state publications. Most frequently, however, laws are referred to in their codified form—that is, the form in which they appear in the federal and state codes. In these codes, laws are compiled by subject.

UNITED STATES CODE The *United States Code* (U.S.C.) arranges all existing federal laws of a public and permanent nature by subject. Each of the fifty subjects into which the U.S.C. arranges the laws is given a title and a title number. For example, laws relating to commerce and trade are collected in Title 15, "Commerce and Trade." Titles are subdivided by sections. A citation to the U.S.C. includes title and section numbers. Thus, a reference to "15 U.S.C. Section 1" means that the statute can be found in Section 1 of Title 15. ("Section" may also be designated by the symbol §, and "Sections," by §§.) Sometimes a citation includes the abbreviation *et seq.*, as in "15 U.S.C. Sections 1 *et seq.*" The term is an abbreviated form of *et sequitur*, which in Latin means "and the following"; when used in a citation, it refers to sections that concern the same subject as the numbered section and follow it in sequence.

Commercial publications of these laws and regulations are available and are widely used. For example, West Group publishes the *United States Code Annotated* (U.S.C.A.). The U.S.C.A. contains the complete text of laws included in the U.S.C., plus notes on court decisions that interpret and apply specific sections of the statutes, as well as the text of presidential proclamations and executive orders. The U.S.C.A. also includes research aids, such as cross-references to related statutes, historical notes, and library references. A citation to the U.S.C.A. is similar to a citation to the U.S.C.: "15 U.S.C.A. Section 1."

STATE CODES State codes follow the U.S.C. pattern of arranging law by subject. They may be called codes, revisions, compilations, consolidations, general statutes, or statutes, depending on the preferences of the states. In some codes, subjects are designated by number. In others, they are designated by name. For example, "13 Pennsylvania Consolidated Statutes Section 1101" means that the statute can be found in Title 13, Section 1101, of the Pennsylvania code. "California Commercial Code Section 1101" means that the statute can be found under the subject heading "Commercial Code" of the California code in Section 1101. Abbreviations may be used. For example, "13 Pennsylvania Consolidated Statutes Section 1101" may often be abbreviated "13 Pa. C.S. §1101," and "California Commercial Code Section 1101" may be abbreviated "Cal. Com. Code §1101."

ADMINISTRATIVE RULES Rules and regulations adopted by federal administrative agencies are initially published in the *Federal Register*, a daily publication of the U.S. government. Later, they are incorporated into the *Code of Federal Regulations* (C.F.R.). Like the U.S.C., the C.F.R. is divided into fifty titles. Rules within each title are assigned section numbers. A full citation to the C.F.R. includes title and section numbers. For example, a reference to "17 C.F.R. Section 230.504" means that the rule can be found in Section 230.504 of Title 17.

FINDING CASE LAW

Before discussing the case reporting system, we need to look briefly at the court system (which will be discussed in detail in Chapter 2). There are two types of courts in the United States, federal courts and state courts. Both the federal and state court systems consist of several levels, or tiers, of courts. *Trial courts*, in which evidence is presented and testimony given, are on the bottom tier (which also includes lower courts handling specialized issues). Decisions from a trial court can be appealed to a higher court, which commonly would be an intermediate *court of appeals*, or an *appellate court*. Decisions from these intermediate courts of appeals may be appealed to an even higher

International Jurisdiction and the Internet

As you will learn in Chapter 2, *jurisdiction* is an important legal concept that relates to the authority of a court to hear and decide a case. Within the United States, there is a federal court system, which has jurisdiction over specific types of cases. There are also fifty state court systems, each having jurisdiction over certain types of cases. In today's interconnected world, the issue of jurisdiction has become critical. Specifically, businesses using the Internet can reach individuals in any part of the world. Does that mean that every court everywhere has jurisdiction over, say, an Internet-based company in Chicago? This is one of today's legal debates.

THE MINIMUM-CONTACTS REQUIREMENT

Domestically, jurisdiction over individuals and businesses is based on the requirement of minimum contacts as outlined in *International Shoe Co. v. State of Washington.*[a] Essentially, this requirement means that a business must have a minimum level of contacts with residents of a particular state for that state's courts to exercise jurisdiction over the firm—see Chapter 2. In the context of the Internet, most courts have *not* viewed the mere existence of a *passive* Web site as sufficient minimum contacts to exercise jurisdiction over a person or entity located out of state. Rather, a site must offer some

---

a. 326 U.S. 310, 66 S.Ct. 154, 90 L.Ed. 95 (1945).

degree of interactivity (such as allowing a person to order goods from the site) to meet the minimum-contacts requirement. Internationally, other countries' courts are applying the requirement of minimum contacts as developed by the U.S. courts. As a result, a business in the United States offering products for sale via its Web site must comply with the laws of any jurisdiction in which it targets customers for its products.

THE FRENCH CASE AGAINST YAHOO

To understand some of the problems created by Internet commerce, consider a French court's judgment against the U.S.-based Internet company Yahoo!, Inc. Yahoo operates an online auction site on which Nazi memorabilia have been offered for sale. In France, the display of any objects representing symbols of Nazi ideology subjects the person or entity displaying such objects to both criminal and civil liability. The International League against Racism and Anti-Semitism filed suit in Paris against Yahoo for displaying Nazi memorabilia and offering them for sale via its Web site. The French court in which the suit was filed asserted jurisdiction over the U.S.-based company on the ground that the materials on the company's U.S.-based servers could be viewed on a Web site accessible in France. The French court ordered Yahoo to eliminate all Internet access in France to the Nazi memorabilia offered for sale through its online auctions.

---

court, such as a state supreme court or the United States Supreme Court.

STATE COURT DECISIONS Most state trial court decisions are not published. Except in New York and a few other states that publish selected opinions of their trial courts, decisions from state trial courts are merely filed in the office of the clerk of the court, where the decisions are available for public inspection. Written decisions of the appellate, or reviewing, courts, however, are published and distributed. As you will note, most of the state court cases presented in this book are from state appellate courts. The reported appellate decisions are published in volumes called *reports* or *reporters*, which are numbered consecutively. State appellate court decisions are found in the state reporters of that particular state. Official

reports are volumes that are published by the state, whereas unofficial reports are privately published.

—*Regional Reporters.* State court opinions appear in regional units of the National Reporter System, published by West Group. Most lawyers and libraries have the West reporters because they report cases more quickly, and are distributed more widely, than the state-published reporters. In fact, many states have eliminated their own reporters in favor of West's National Reporter System. The National Reporter System divides the states into the following geographic areas: *Atlantic* (A. or A.2d), *South Eastern* (S.E. or S.E.2d), *South Western* (S.W., S.W.2d, or S.W.3d), *North Western* (N.W. or N.W.2d), *North Eastern* (N.E. or N.E.2d), *Southern* (So. or So.2d), and *Pacific* (P., P.2d, or P.3d). (The *2d* and *3d* in the preceding abbre-

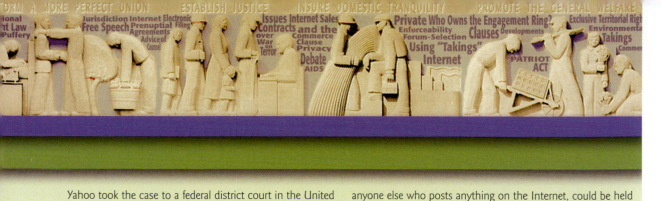

Yahoo took the case to a federal district court in the United States to resolve a much larger issue: Can a foreign court dictate what will or will not appear on a U.S. company's Web site? Or does such an order violate the U.S. constitutional right to free speech and expression under the First Amendment? The federal district court agreed with Yahoo's argument that the French court's order violated the First Amendment and was thus not enforceable in the United States.[b] In 2004, however, the U.S. Court of Appeals for the Ninth Circuit reversed the district court's decision on the ground that U.S. courts lacked personal jurisdiction over the French groups involved. According to the majority opinion, "If Yahoo violates the speech laws of another nation, it must wait for the foreign litigants to come to the United States to enforce the judgment before its First Amendment claim may be heard by a U.S. court."[c]

In the world of business, the *Yahoo* case represents the first time a U.S. court was asked to decide whether to honor a foreign judgment in the context of the Internet. The Ninth Circuit's ruling leaves open the possibility that Yahoo, and

anyone else who posts anything on the Internet, could be held answerable to the laws of any country in which the message might be received. Several other countries—including North Korea, Syria, the People's Republic of China, Cuba, Iran, Iraq, Belarus, and Saudi Arabia—have even stricter restrictions on free speech than France. What will happen if those countries start suing Internet companies for posting what they view as "politically undesirable" speech is still a matter of debate.

---

b. *Yahoo!, Inc. v. La Ligue Contre le Racisme et l'Antisemitisme,* 169 F.Supp.2d 1181 (N.D.Cal. 2001).

c. *Yahoo!, Inc. v. La Ligue Contre le Racisme et l'Antisemitisme,* 379 F.3d 1120 (9th Cir. 2004).

---

viations refer to *Second Series* and *Third Series,* respectively.) The states included in each of these regional divisions are indicated in Exhibit 1–4 on the next page, which illustrates West's National Reporter System.

—*Case Citations.*   After an appellate decision has been published, it is normally referred to (cited) by the name of the case (sometimes called the *style* of the case); the volume, name, and page number of the state's official reporter (if different from West's National Reporter System); the volume, unit, and page number of the National Reporter; and the volume, name, and page number of any other selected reporter. (Citing a reporter by volume number, name, and page number, in that order, is common to all citations; often, as in this book, the year the decision was made will be included in parentheses, just after the citations to reporters.)

When more than one reporter is cited for the same case, each reference is called a *parallel citation.*[6]

For example, consider the following case citation: *Yale Diagnostic Radiology v. Estate of Harun Fountain,* 267 Conn. 351, 838 A.2d 179 (2004). We see that the opinion in this case may be found in Volume 267 of the official *Connecticut Reports,* on page 351. The parallel citation is to Volume 838 of the *Atlantic*

---

6. Note that Wisconsin has adopted a "public domain citation system" in which the format is somewhat different. For example, a Wisconsin Supreme Court decision might be designated "2003 WI 40," meaning that the case was decided in the year 2003 by the Wisconsin Supreme Court and was the fortieth decision issued by that court during that year. (Parallel citations to the *Wisconsin Reports* and *West's North Western Reporter* are still required when citing Wisconsin cases, but they must follow the public domain citation.)

EXHIBIT 1-4   **National Reporter System—Regional/Federal**

Regional Reporters	Coverage Beginning	Coverage
Atlantic Reporter (A. or A.2d)	1885	Connecticut, Delaware, Maine, Maryland, New Hampshire, New Jersey, Pennsylvania, Rhode Island, Vermont, and District of Columbia.
North Eastern Reporter (N.E. or N.E.2d)	1885	Illinois, Indiana, Massachusetts, New York, and Ohio.
North Western Reporter (N.W. or N.W.2d)	1879	Iowa, Michigan, Minnesota, Nebraska, North Dakota, South Dakota, and Wisconsin.
Pacific Reporter (P., P.2d, or P.3d)	1883	Alaska, Arizona, California, Colorado, Hawaii, Idaho, Kansas, Montana, Nevada, New Mexico, Oklahoma, Oregon, Utah, Washington, and Wyoming.
South Eastern Reporter (S.E. or S.E.2d)	1887	Georgia, North Carolina, South Carolina, Virginia, and West Virginia.
South Western Reporter (S.W., S.W.2d, or S.W.3d)	1886	Arkansas, Kentucky, Missouri, Tennessee, and Texas.
Southern Reporter (So. or So.2d)	1887	Alabama, Florida, Louisiana, and Mississippi.

Federal Reporters		
Federal Reporter (F., F.2d, or F.3d)	1880	U.S. Circuit Courts from 1880 to 1912; U.S. Commerce Court from 1911 to 1913; U.S. District Courts from 1880 to 1932; U.S. Court of Claims (now called U.S. Court of Federal Claims) from 1929 to 1932 and since 1960; U.S. Courts of Appeals since 1891; U.S. Court of Customs and Patent Appeals since 1929; U.S. Emergency Court of Appeals since 1943.
Federal Supplement (F.Supp. or F.Supp.2d)	1932	U.S. Court of Claims from 1932 to 1960; U.S. District Courts since 1932; and U.S. Customs Court since 1956.
Federal Rules Decisions (F.R.D.)	1939	U.S. District Courts involving the Federal Rules of Civil Procedure since 1939 and Federal Rules of Criminal Procedure since 1946.
Supreme Court Reporter (S.Ct.)	1882	U.S. Supreme Court since the October term of 1882.
Bankruptcy Reporter (Bankr. or B.R.)	1980	Bankruptcy decisions of U.S. Bankruptcy Courts, U.S. District Courts, U.S. Courts of Appeals, and U.S. Supreme Court.
Military Justice Reporter (M.J.)	1978	U.S. Court of Military Appeals and Courts of Military Review for the Army, Navy, Air Force, and Coast Guard.

NATIONAL REPORTER SYSTEM MAP

Legend:
- Pacific
- North Western
- South Western
- North Eastern
- Atlantic
- South Eastern
- Southern

Reporter, Second Series, page 179. In presenting appellate opinions in this text, in addition to the reporter, we give the name of the court hearing the case and the year of the court's decision. Sample citations to state court decisions are explained in Exhibit 1–5, beginning on page 20.

FEDERAL COURT DECISIONS Federal district (trial) court decisions are published unofficially in West's *Federal Supplement* (F.Supp. or F.Supp.2d), and opinions from the circuit courts of appeals are reported unofficially in West's *Federal Reporter* (F., F.2d, or F.3d). Cases concerning federal bankruptcy law are published unofficially in West's *Bankruptcy Reporter* (Bankr. or B.R.).

The official edition of all decisions of the United States Supreme Court for which there are written opinions is the *United States Reports* (U.S.), which is published by the federal government. The series includes reports of Supreme Court cases dating from the August term of 1791, although many of the Supreme Court's decisions were not reported in the early volumes. Unofficial editions of Supreme Court cases include West's *Supreme Court Reporter* (S.Ct.), which includes cases dating from the Court's term in October 1882; and the *Lawyers' Edition of the Supreme Court Reports* (L.Ed. or L.Ed.2d), published by the Lawyers Cooperative Publishing Company (now a part of West Group). The latter contains many of the decisions not reported in the early volumes of the *United States Reports.* Sample citations for federal court decisions are also listed and explained in Exhibit 1–5.

UNPUBLISHED OPINIONS Many court opinions that are not yet published or that are not intended for publication can be accessed through Westlaw® (abbreviated in citations as "WL"), an online legal database maintained by West Group. When no citation to a published reporter is available for cases cited in this text, we give the WL citation (see Exhibit 1–5 for an example).

OLD CASE LAW On a few occasions, this text cites opinions from old, classic cases dating to the nineteenth century or earlier; some of these are from the English courts. The citations to these cases may not conform to the descriptions given above because the reporters in which they were published were often known by the names of the persons who compiled the reporters, which have since been replaced.

SECTION 8 | How to Read and Understand Case Law

The decisions made by the courts establish the boundaries of the law as it applies to virtually all business relationships. It thus is essential that businesspersons know how to read and understand case law. The cases that we present in this text have been condensed from the full text of the courts' opinions and are presented in a special format. In each case, we have summarized the background and facts, as well as the court's decision and remedy, in our own words and have included only selected portions of the court's opinion ("in the language of the court"). For those who wish to review court cases to perform research projects or to gain additional legal information, however, the following sections will provide useful insights into how to read and understand case law.

CASE TITLES

The title of a case, such as *Adams v. Jones,* indicates the names of the parties to the lawsuit. The *v.* in the case title stands for *versus,* which means "against." In the trial court, Adams was the plaintiff—the person who filed the suit. Jones was the defendant. If the case is appealed, however, the appellate court will sometimes place the name of the party appealing the decision first, so the case may be called *Jones v. Adams* if Jones is appealing. Because some appellate courts retain the trial court order of names, it is often impossible to distinguish the plaintiff from the defendant in the title of a reported appellate court decision. You must carefully read the facts of each case to identify the parties. Otherwise, the discussion by the appellate court may be difficult to understand.

TERMINOLOGY

The following terms, phrases, and abbreviations are frequently encountered in court opinions and legal publications. Because it is important to understand what is meant by these terms, phrases, and abbreviations, we define and discuss them here.

PARTIES TO LAWSUITS As mentioned previously, the party initiating a lawsuit is referred to as the *plaintiff* or *petitioner,* depending on the nature of the action, and the party against whom a lawsuit is brought is the *defendant* or *respondent.* Lawsuits frequently involve

EXHIBIT 1-5   **How to Read Citations**

State Courts

269 Neb. 82, 690 N.W.2d 778 (2005)[a]

N.W. is the abbreviation for West's publication of state court decisions rendered in the *North Western Reporter* of the National Reporter System. *2d* indicates that this case was included in the *Second Series* of that reporter. The number 690 refers to the volume number of the reporter; the number 778 refers to the first page in that volume on which this case can be found.

Neb. is an abbreviation for *Nebraska Reports,* Nebraska's official reports of the decisions of its highest court, the Nebraska Supreme Court.

125 Cal.App.4th 949, 23 Cal.Rptr.3d 233 (2005)

Cal.Rptr. is the abbreviation for West's unofficial reports—titled *California Reporter*—of the decisions of the California Supreme Court and California appellate courts.

1 N.Y.3d 280, 803 N.E.2d 757, 771 N.Y.S.2d 484 (2003)

N.Y.S. is the abbreviation for West's unofficial reports—titled *New York Supplement*—of the decisions of New York courts.

N.Y. is the abbreviation for *New York Reports,* New York's official reports of the decisions of its court of appeals. The New York Court of Appeals is the state's highest court, analogous to other states' supreme courts. (In New York, a supreme court is a trial court.)

267 Ga.App. 832, 600 S.E.2d 800 (2004)

Ga.App. is the abbreviation for *Georgia Appeals Reports,* Georgia's official reports of the decisions of its court of appeals.

Federal Courts

___ U.S. ___ , 125 S.Ct. 847, ___ L.Ed.2d ___ (2005)

L.Ed. is an abbreviation for *Lawyers' Edition of the Supreme Court Reports,* an unofficial edition of decisions of the United States Supreme Court.

S.Ct. is the abbreviation for West's unofficial reports—titled *Supreme Court Reporter*—of decisions of the United States Supreme Court.

U.S. is the abbreviation for *United States Reports,* the official edition of the decisions of the United States Supreme Court.

a. The case names have been deleted from these citations to emphasize the publications. It should be kept in mind, however, that the name of a case is as important as the specific numbers of the volumes in which it is found. If a citation is incorrect, the correct citation may be found in a publication's index of case names. The date of a case is also important because, in addition to providing a check on error in citations, the value of a recent case as an authority is likely to be greater than that of an earlier case.

EXHIBIT 1-5 **How to Read Citations (Continued)**

Federal Courts (continued)

394 F.3d 520 (7th Cir. 2005)

7th Cir. is an abbreviation denoting that this case was decided in the United States Court of Appeals for the Seventh Circuit.

340 F.Supp.2d 1051 (D.S.D. 2004)

D.S.D. is an abbreviation indicating that the United States District Court for the District of South Dakota decided this case.

English Courts

9 Exch. 341, 156 Eng.Rep. 145 (1854)

Eng.Rep. is an abbreviation for *English Reports, Full Reprint,* a series of reports containing selected decisions made in English courts between 1378 and 1865.

Exch. is an abbreviation for *English Exchequer Reports,* which included the original reports of cases decided in England's Court of Exchequer.

Statutory and Other Citations

18 U.S.C. Section 1961(1)(A)

U.S.C. denotes *United States Code,* the codification of *United States Statutes at Large.* The number 18 refers to the statute's U.S.C. title number and 1961 to its section number within that title. The number 1 refers to a subsection within the section and the letter A to a subdivision within the subsection.

UCC 2–206(1)(b)

UCC is an abbreviation for *Uniform Commercial Code.* The first number 2 is a reference to an article of the UCC and 206 to a section within that article. The number 1 refers to a subsection within the section and the letter b to a subdivision within the subsection.

Restatement (Second) of Contracts, Section 162

Restatement (Second) of Contracts refers to the second edition of the American Law Institute's *Restatement of the Law of Contracts.* The number 162 refers to a specific section.

17 C.F.R. Section 230.505

C.F.R. is an abbreviation for *Code of Federal Regulations,* a compilation of federal administrative regulations. The number 17 designates the regulation's title number, and 230.505 designates a specific section within that title.

EXHIBIT 1-5 **How to Read Citations (Continued)**

Westlaw® Citations[b]

2005 WL 27554

WL is an abbreviation for Westlaw®. The number 2005 is the year of the document that can be found with this citation in the Westlaw® database. The number 27554 is a number assigned to a specific document. A higher number indicates that a document was added to the Westlaw® database later in the year.

Uniform Resource Locators (URLs)[c]

http://www.westlaw.com[d]

The suffix *com* is the top level domain (TLD) for this Web site. The TLD *com* is an abbreviation for "commercial," which normally means that a for-profit entity hosts (maintains or supports) this Web site.

westlaw is the host name—the part of the domain name selected by the organization that registered the name. In this case, West Group registered the name. This Internet site is the Westlaw database on the Web.

www is an abbreviation for "World Wide Web." The Web is a system of Internet servers that support documents formatted in *HTML* (hypertext markup language). HTML supports links to text, graphics, and audio and video files.

http://www.uscourts.gov

This is "The Federal Judiciary Home Page." The host is the Administrative Office of the U.S. Courts. The TLD *gov* is an abbreviation for "government." This Web site includes information and links from, and about, the federal courts.

http://www.law.cornell.edu/index.html

This part of a URL points to a Web page or file at a specific location within the host's domain. This page is a menu with links to documents within the domain and to other Internet resources.

This is the host name for a Web site that contains the Internet publications of the Legal Information Institute (LII), which is a part of Cornell Law School. The LII site includes a variety of legal materials and links to other legal resources on the Internet. The TLD *edu* is an abbreviation for "educational institution" (a school or a university).

http://www.ipl.org/ref

ref is an abbreviation for "Internet Public Library Reference Center," which is a map of the topics into which the links at this Web site have been categorized.

ipl is an abbreviation for "Internet Public Library," which is an online service that provides reference resources and links to other information services on the Web. The IPL is supported chiefly by the School of Information at the University of Michigan. The TLD *org* is an abbreviation for "organization" (normally nonprofit).

b. Many court decisions that are not yet published or that are not intended for publication can be accessed through Westlaw®, an online legal database.

c. URLs are frequently changed as sites are redesigned and may not be working for other reasons, such as when a Web site has been deleted. If you are unable to find sites in this text with the specified URLs, go to the text's Web site at **http://wbl. westbuslaw.com**, where you may find an updated URL for the site or a URL for a similar site.

d. The basic form for a URL is "service://hostname/path." The Internet service for all of the URLs in this text is *http* (hypertext transfer protocol). Most Web browsers will add this prefix automatically when a user enters a host name or a hostname/path.

more than one plaintiff and/or defendant. When a case is appealed from the original court or jurisdiction to another court or jurisdiction, the party appealing the case is called the **appellant.** The **appellee** is the party against whom the appeal is taken. (In some appellate courts, the party appealing a case is referred to as the petitioner, and the party against whom the suit is brought or appealed is called the respondent.)

JUDGES AND JUSTICES The terms *judge* and *justice* are usually synonymous and represent two designations given to judges in various courts. All members of the United States Supreme Court, for example, are referred to as justices, and justice is the formal title usually given to judges of appellate courts, although this is not always the case. In New York, a *justice* is a judge of the trial court (which is called the Supreme Court), and a member of the Court of Appeals (the state's highest court) is called a *judge*. The term *justice* is commonly abbreviated to J., and *justices*, to JJ. A Supreme Court case might refer to Justice Kennedy as Kennedy, J., or to Chief Justice Rehnquist as Rehnquist, C.J.

DECISIONS AND OPINIONS Most decisions reached by reviewing, or appellate, courts are explained in written **opinions.** The opinion contains the court's reasons for its decision, the rules of law that apply, and the judgment.

—Unanimous, Concurring, and Dissenting Opinions. When all judges or justices unanimously agree on an opinion, the opinion is written for the entire court and can be deemed a *unanimous opinion.* When there is not a unanimous opinion, a *majority opinion* is written; the majority opinion outlines the view supported by the majority of the judges or justices deciding the case. If a judge agrees, or concurs, with the majority's decision, but for different reasons, that judge may write a *concurring opinion.* A *dissenting opinion* presents the views of one or more judges who disagree with the majority's decision. The dissenting opinion is important because it may form the basis of the arguments used years later in overruling the precedential majority opinion.

—Other Types of Opinions. Occasionally, a court issues a *per curiam* opinion. *Per curiam* is a Latin phrase meaning "of the court." In *per curiam* opinions, there is no indication of which judge or justice authored the opinion. This term may also be used for an announcement of a court's disposition of a case that is not accompanied by a written opinion. Some of the cases

presented in this text are *en banc* decisions. When an appellate court reviews a case *en banc*, which is a French term (derived from a Latin term) for "in the bench," generally all of the judges "sitting on the bench" of that court review the case.

A SAMPLE COURT CASE

To illustrate the elements in a court opinion, we present an annotated opinion in Exhibit 1–6 beginning on the next page. The opinion is from an actual case that the U.S. Court of Appeals for the Sixth Circuit decided in 2005.

BACKGROUND OF THE CASE A group of restaurant, bar, and bowling alley owners and an association of restaurant owners—collectively comprising an organization called D.A.B.E., Inc.—filed a suit in a federal district court against the city of Toledo, Ohio. The plaintiffs alleged that a city ordinance establishing tight restrictions on smoking in public places constituted a "taking" of the plaintiffs' right to their property. They also argued that the ordinance conflicted with a state law on the same subject and that therefore the ordinance was void. The court issued a judgment in favor of the city. The plaintiffs appealed to the U.S. Court of Appeals for the Sixth Circuit.

EDITORIAL PRACTICE You will note that triple asterisks (* * *) and quadruple asterisks (* * * *) frequently appear in the opinion. The triple asterisks indicate that we have deleted a few words or sentences from the opinion for the sake of readability or brevity. Quadruple asterisks mean that an entire paragraph (or more) has been omitted. Additionally, when the opinion cites another case or legal source, the citation to the case or other source has been omitted to save space and to improve the flow of the text. These editorial practices are continued in the other court opinions presented in this book. In addition, whenever we present a court opinion that includes a term or phrase that may not be readily understandable, a bracketed definition or paraphrase has been added.

BRIEFING CASES Knowing how to read and understand court opinions and the legal reasoning used by the courts is an essential step in undertaking accurate legal research. Yet a further step is "briefing," or summarizing, the case. Legal researchers routinely brief cases by reducing the texts of the opinions to their essential elements. Generally, when you brief a case, you first summarize the background and facts of the case, as the authors have done for the cases presented within this text. You then indicate the issue (or issues) before the court. An important element in the case brief is, of course, the court's decision on the issue and the legal reasoning used by the court in reaching that decision. Detailed instructions on how to brief a case are given in Appendix A, which also includes a briefed version of the sample court case presented in Exhibit 1–6.

EXHIBIT 1-6 **A Sample Court Case**

This section contains the case citation— the name of the case, the name of the court that heard the case, the year of the court's decision, and reporters in which the court's opinion can be found.	**D.A.B.E., INC. v. CITY OF TOLEDO** United States Court of Appeals, Sixth Circuit, 2005. 393 F.3d 692.
This line gives the name of the judge who authored the opinion of the court.	BOYCE F. MARTIN, JR., Circuit Judge. * * * *
The court divides the opinion into three parts, headed by roman numerals. The first part of the opinion summarizes the factual background of the case.	I. The City of Toledo has regulated smoking in public places since 1987 * * * . In early 2003, the City Council * * *
A law passed by a local government unit, such as a city or a county.	enacted a new Clean Indoor Air **Ordinance**, No. 509-03. Ordinance No. 509-03 regulates the ability to smoke in public
Present or current.	places, such as retail stores, theaters, courtrooms, libraries, museums, health-care facilities, and—most relevant to the **instant** case—restaurants and bars. In enclosed public places, smoking is generally prohibited except in a "separate smoking lounge" that is designated for the exclusive purpose of smoking * * * . * * * * * * * Appellants * * * [challenge] the ordinance on two grounds: first, that it constitutes a * * * taking of their property in violation of the Fifth [Amendment to the U.S.
Prevented from taking effect.	Constitution] * * * ; and second, that it is **preempted** by Section 3791.031 of the Ohio Revised Code, a state law that regulates smoking in places of public assembly but that does not apply to restaurants, bowling alleys and bars. * * * *
The second major section of the opinion sets out and applies the law to the plaintiffs' arguments.	II. * * * *
The first part of this section addresses the claim that the ordinance is a taking of the plaintiffs' property.	A. * * * **Taking Claim** The * * * Fifth Amendment * * * provides that private property shall not "be taken for public use, without just compen-

EXHIBIT 1-6 **A Sample Court Case (Continued)**

> Financially sustainable; capable of working, functioning, or developing adequately.

> The words of a writing in their apparent or obvious meaning.

> Absolutely, unqualifiedly.

> The second part of this section addresses the assertion that the city ordinance is void because a state statute already covers the subject and thus takes precedence.

sation." * * * [A] statute regulating the uses that can be made of property effects a taking if it denies an owner **economically viable** use of his land. * * *

The evidence presented in this case fails to establish that, **on its face**, the Clean Indoor Air Ordinance denies appellants economically viable use of their respective properties. Appellants have submitted affidavits alleging that they have lost—or fear they will lose—customers as a result of the ordinance, because smoking is an activity in which many customers wish to engage while patronizing their establishments. * * *

* * * First, there is nothing on the face of the Clean Indoor Air Ordinance that prevents the beneficial use of appellants' property. To the contrary, the ordinance has absolutely no effect on any aspect of appellants' businesses other than to restrict the areas in which appellants' patrons may smoke. Second, the ordinance does not **categorically** prohibit smoking inside appellants' establishments; it merely regulates the conditions under which smoking is permitted. We recognize that the construction of separate smoking lounges in most cases will require some financial investment, but an ordinance does not effect a taking merely because compliance with it requires the expenditure of money. Finally, for obvious reasons, the ordinance does not purport to regulate alternative uses of appellants' respective properties. Therefore, * * * it is clear that appellants have failed to establish that the Clean Indoor Air Ordinance, on its face, effects a * * * taking of their property.

B. Preemption Claim

Appellants' second argument is that the Clean Indoor Air Ordinance conflicts with—and, therefore, is preempted by—Section 3791.031(A) of the Ohio Revised Code.

A state statute takes precedence over a local ordinance when * * * the ordinance is in conflict with the statute * * * .

* * * [T]he test is whether the ordinance permits or licenses that which the statute forbids or prohibits, and vice versa. To the extent that the statute does not address or apply to an item or issue, however, an ordinance regulating the excluded item or issue does not conflict with the statute, even if it deals with the same general subject matter. * * *

EXHIBIT 1-6   **A Sample Court Case (Continued)**

In this case, Section 3791.031 of the Ohio Revised Code regulates indoor smoking throughout the State of Ohio within "places of public assembly." It explicitly provides, however, that "[r]estaurants, food service establishments, dining rooms, cafes, cafeterias, or other rooms used primarily for the service of food, as well as bowling alleys and places licensed by the division of liquor control to sell intoxicating beverages for consumption on the premises, are not places of public assembly." * * *

Appellants argue that because smoking is allowed in their establishments under state law but not under the ordinance, there is a conflict that renders the ordinance preempted by state law. The City argues, by contrast, that the statute "simply does not regulate the establishments" that are subject to the ordinance and, therefore, municipalities within the State of Ohio are free to regulate smoking within these establishments * * * .

* * * [B]y stating that certain types of establishments—such as restaurants, bars, bowling alleys, etc.—"are not places of public assembly," the legislature indicated not that these establishments were immune to smoking-related regulation, but that they simply did not fall within the * * * statute.

Our independent research reveals that other courts that have considered whether smoking-related ordinances are preempted by state law have reached similar conclusions. * * * The [statute] prohibits smoking in certain locations; it does not contain the slightest hint that the legislature intended to create a positive right to smoke in all public places where it did not expressly forbid smoking. Nothing in the [statute] is inconsistent with a local **jurisdiction's** decision to impose greater limits on public smoking. * * *

* * * *

III.

For these reasons, the district court's judgment is AFFIRMED.

> A government body with the authority to act within a certain geographic area.

> In the third major section of this opinion, the court states its decision and gives its order.

TERMS AND CONCEPTS TO REVIEW

administrative agency 7	cyberlaw 14	plaintiff 9
administrative law 7	damages 8	positive law 3
allege 11	defendant 9	positivist school 3
analogy 12	defense 9	precedent 9
appellant 23	equitable maxims 9	procedural law 14
appellee 23	executive agency 7	public policy 11
binding authority 10	historical school 3	remedy 8
breach 4	independent regulatory	remedy at law 8
case law 7	agency 7	remedy in equity 8
case on point 12	jurisprudence 2	reporter 10
chancellor 8	laches 9	respondent 9
citation 15	law 2	sociological school 4
civil law 14	legal realism 3	*stare decisis* 10
common law 8	legal reasoning 11	statute of limitations 9
constitutional law 6	natural law 3	statutory law 6
court of equity 8	opinion 23	substantive law 14
court of law 8	ordinance 6	syllogism 12
criminal law 14	petitioner 9	uniform law 6

 QUESTIONS AND CASE PROBLEMS

1–1. How does statutory law come into existence? How does it differ from the common law? If statutory law conflicts with the common law, which law will govern?

1–2. ⚖ **QUESTION WITH SAMPLE ANSWER**

After World War II, which ended in 1945, an international tribunal of judges convened at Nuremberg, Germany. The judges convicted several Nazis of "crimes against humanity." Assuming that the Nazi war criminals who were convicted had not disobeyed any law of their country and had merely been following their government's (Hitler's) orders, what law had they violated? Explain.

For a sample answer to this question, go to Appendix I at the end of this text.

1–3. Assume that you want to read the entire court opinion in the case of *Kelly v. Arriba Soft Corp.*, 280 F.3d 934 (9th Cir. 2002). The case considers whether a photographer's images could be legally displayed on another person's Web site without the photographer's permission. Explain specifically where you would find the court's opinion.

1–4. This chapter discussed a number of sources of American law. Which source of law takes priority in the following situations, and why?

(a) A federal statute conflicts with the U.S. Constitution.
(b) A federal statute conflicts with a state constitutional provision.
(c) A state statute conflicts with the common law of that state.
(d) A state constitutional amendment conflicts with the U.S. Constitution.

1–5. In the text of this chapter, we stated that the doctrine of *stare decisis* "became a cornerstone of the English and American judicial systems." What does *stare decisis* mean, and why has this doctrine been so fundamental to the development of our legal tradition?

1–6. What is the difference between a concurring opinion and a majority opinion? Between a concurring opinion and a dissenting opinion? Why do judges and justices write concurring and dissenting opinions, given that these opinions will not affect the outcome of the case at hand, which has already been decided by majority vote?

1–7. Courts can overturn precedents and thus change the common law. Should judges have the same authority to overrule statutory law? Explain.

1–8. "The judge's role is not to make the law but to uphold and apply the law." Do you agree or disagree with this statement? Discuss fully the reasons for your answer.

1–9. Assume that Arthur Rabe is suing Xavier Sanchez for breaching a contract in which Sanchez promised to sell Rabe a Van Gogh painting for $3 million.

(a) In this lawsuit, who is the plaintiff and who is the defendant?

(b) Suppose that Rabe wants Sanchez to perform the contract as promised. What remedy would Rabe seek from the court?

(c) Now suppose that Rabe wants to cancel the contract because Sanchez fraudulently misrepresented the painting as an original Van Gogh when in fact it is a copy. What remedy would Rabe seek?

(d) Will the remedy Rabe seeks in either situation be a remedy at law or a remedy in equity? What is the difference between legal and equitable remedies?

(e) Suppose that the trial court finds in Rabe's favor and grants one of these remedies. Sanchez then appeals the decision to a higher court. On appeal, which party will be the appellant (or petitioner), and which party will be the appellee (or respondent)?

LAW | on the Web

Today, business law and legal environment professors and students can go online to access information on virtually every topic covered in this text. A good point of departure for online legal research is the Web site for *West's Business Law*, Tenth Edition, which can be found at http://wbl.westbuslaw.com. There you will find numerous materials relevant to this text and to business law generally, including links to various legal resources on the Web. Additionally, every chapter in this text ends with a *Law on the Web* feature that contains selected Web addresses.

You can access many of the sources of law discussed in Chapter 1 at the FindLaw Web site, which is probably the most comprehensive source of free legal information on the Internet. Go to

> http://www.findlaw.com

The Legal Information Institute (LII) at Cornell Law School, which offers extensive information about U.S. law, is also a good starting point for legal research. The URL for this site is

> http://www.law.cornell.edu

The Library of Congress offers extensive links to state and federal government resources at

> http://www.loc.gov

Villanova University's Center for Information Law and Policy provides access to numerous legal resources, including opinions from the federal appellate courts. Go to

> http://www.law.vill.edu

The Virtual Law Library Index, created and maintained by the Indiana University School of Law, provides an index of legal sources categorized by subject at

> http://www.law.indiana.edu/v-lib/index.html#libdoc

LEGAL RESEARCH EXERCISES ON THE WEB

Go to **http://wbl.westbuslaw.com**, the Web site that accompanies this text. Select "Chapter 1" and click on "Internet Exercises." There you will find the following Internet research exercises that you can perform to learn more about some important sources of law discussed in Chapter 1 and other useful legal sites on the Web.

Activity 1–1: LEGAL PERSPECTIVE
Internet Sources of Law

Activity 1–2: MANAGEMENT PERSPECTIVE
Online Assistance from Government Agencies

Activity 1–3: SOCIAL PERSPECTIVE
The Case of the Speluncean Explorers

CHAPTER 2

Courts and Alternative Dispute Resolution

Today in the United States there are fifty-two court systems—one for each of the fifty states, one for the District of Columbia, and a federal system. Keep in mind that the federal courts are not superior to the state courts; they are simply an independent system of courts, which derives its authority from Article III, Section 2, of the U.S. Constitution. By the power given to it under Article I of the U.S. Constitution, Congress has extended the federal court system beyond the boundaries of the United States to U.S. territories such as Guam, Puerto Rico, and the Virgin Islands.[1] As we shall see, the United States Supreme Court is the final controlling voice over all of these fifty-two systems, at least when questions of federal law are involved.

Every businessperson will likely face a lawsuit at some time in his or her career. It is thus important for anyone involved in business to have an understanding of the American court systems, as well as the various methods of dispute resolution that can be pursued outside the courts. In this chapter, after examining the judiciary's role in the American governmental system, we discuss some basic requirements that must be met before a party may bring a lawsuit before a particular court. We then look at the court systems of the United States in some detail. We conclude the chapter with an overview of some alternative methods of settling disputes, including online dispute resolution.

SECTION 1 | The Judiciary's Role in American Government

As you learned in Chapter 1, the body of American law includes the federal and state constitutions, statutes passed by legislative bodies, administrative law, and the case decisions and legal principles that form the common law. These laws would be meaningless, however, without the courts to interpret and apply them. This is the essential role of the judiciary—the courts—in the American governmental system: to interpret the laws and apply them to specific situations.

As the branch of government entrusted with interpreting the laws, the judiciary can decide, among other things, whether the laws or actions of the other two branches are constitutional. The process for making such a determination is known as **judicial review.** The power of judicial review enables the judicial branch to act as a check on the other two branches of government, in line with the system of checks and balances established by the U.S. Constitution.[2]

The power of judicial review is not mentioned in the Constitution (although many constitutional scholars conclude that the founders intended the judiciary to have this power). Rather, this power was explicitly established by the United States Supreme Court in 1803 by its decision in *Marbury v. Madison,*[3] in which the Supreme Court stated, "It is emphatically the province and duty of the Judicial Department to say what the law is. . . . If two laws conflict with each other, the courts must decide on the operation of each. . . . So if the law be in opposition to the Constitution . . . [t]he Court must determine which of these conflicting rules governs the case. This is the very essence of judicial duty." Since the *Marbury v. Madison* deci-

---

1. In Guam and the Virgin Islands, territorial courts serve as both federal courts and state courts; in Puerto Rico, they serve only as federal courts.

2. In a broad sense, judicial review occurs whenever a court "reviews" a case or legal proceeding—as when an appellate court reviews a lower court's decision. When referring to the judiciary's role in American government, however, the term *judicial review* is used to indicate the power of the judiciary to decide whether the actions of the other two branches of government do or do not violate the Constitution.

3. 5 U.S. (1 Cranch) 137, 2 L.Ed. 60 (1803).

sion, the power of judicial review has remained unchallenged. Today, this power is exercised by both federal and state courts.

SECTION 2 | Basic Judicial Requirements

Before a lawsuit can be brought before a court, certain requirements must be met. These requirements relate to jurisdiction, venue, and standing to sue. We examine each of these important concepts here.

JURISDICTION

In Latin, *juris* means "law," and *diction* means "to speak." Thus, "the power to speak the law" is the literal meaning of the term **jurisdiction.** Before any court can hear a case, it must have two types of jurisdiction: jurisdiction over the person (defendant) or property involved and jurisdiction over the subject matter of the dispute.

JURISDICTION OVER PERSONS OR PROPERTY
Generally, a particular court can exercise **in personam jurisdiction** (personal jurisdiction) over any person or business that resides in a certain geographic area. A state trial court, for example, normally has jurisdictional authority over residents (including businesses) of a particular area of the state, such as a county or district. A state's highest court (often called the state supreme court)[4] has jurisdictional authority over all residents within the state.

A court can also exercise jurisdiction over property that is located within its boundaries. This kind of jurisdiction is known as **in rem jurisdiction,** or "jurisdiction over the thing." For example, suppose a dispute arises over the ownership of a boat in dry dock in Fort Lauderdale, Florida. The boat is owned by an Ohio resident, over whom a Florida court normally cannot exercise personal jurisdiction. The other party to the dispute is a resident of Nebraska. In this situation, a lawsuit concerning the boat could be brought in a Florida state court on the basis of the court's *in rem* jurisdiction.

—Long Arm Statutes.
Under the authority of a state **long arm statute,** a court can exercise personal jurisdiction over certain out-of-state defendants based on activities that took place within the state. Before a court can exercise jurisdiction over an out-of-state defendant under a long arm statute, though, it must be demonstrated that the defendant had sufficient contacts, or *minimum contacts,* with the state to justify the jurisdiction.[5] Generally, this means that the defendant must have enough of a connection to the state for the judge to conclude that it is fair for the state to exercise power over the defendant. For example, if the defendant caused an automobile accident or sold defective goods within the state, a court will usually find that minimum contacts exist to exercise jurisdiction over an out-of-state defendant. Similarly, a state may exercise personal jurisdiction over a nonresident defendant who is sued for breaching a contract that was formed within the state.

—Corporate Contacts.
In regard to corporations,[6] the minimum-contacts requirement is usually met if the corporation does business within the state, advertises or sells its products within the state, or places its goods into the "stream of commerce" with the intent that the goods be sold in the state. Suppose that a business incorporated under the laws of Maine and headquartered in that state has a branch office or manufacturing plant in Georgia. Does this facility constitute sufficient contacts with the state of Georgia to allow a Georgia court to exercise jurisdiction over the corporation? Yes, it does. If the Maine corporation advertises and sells its products in Georgia, or places goods within the stream of commerce with the expectation that the goods will be purchased by Georgia residents, those activities will likely suffice to meet the minimum-contacts requirement.

Some corporations, however, do not sell or advertise products or place any goods in the stream of commerce. Determining what constitutes minimum contacts in these situations can be more difficult, as the following case—involving an out-of-state creditor that refused to fix an alleged error in a resident's credit report—illustrates.

---

4. As will be discussed shortly, a state's highest court is often referred to as the state supreme court, but there are exceptions. For example, in New York the supreme court is a trial court.

5. The minimum-contacts standard was established in *International Shoe Co. v. State of Washington,* 326 U.S. 310, 66 S.Ct. 154, 90 L.Ed. 95 (1945).

6. In the eyes of the law, corporations are "legal persons"—entities that can sue and be sued. See Chapter 38.

| CASE 2.1 | Bickford v. Onslow Memorial Hospital Foundation, Inc. |

Supreme Judicial Court
of Maine, 2004.
2004 ME 111.
855 A.2d 1150.
http://www.courts.state.me.us/
opinions/supreme[a]

BACKGROUND AND FACTS *Roy Bickford was married in July 1997 and moved to Maine with his wife in June 1998. In September, his wife left him. She moved to North Carolina that December. The couple agreed that each would pay his or her own debts as of August 18, 1998. They divorced in 1999. Bickford's wife obtained medical care for her daughter at Onslow Memorial Hospital in North Carolina. Bickford was not legally related to his wife's daughter and never agreed to pay for the services. Without telling him, however, the hospital held him financially responsible and notified credit reporting agencies that he had been "placed in collection" for failing to pay. He asked the hospital to correct this statement, but it refused. Meanwhile, his bank would not qualify him for a mortgage because of the apparent outstanding debt. Bickford filed a suit in a Maine state court against Onslow Memorial Hospital Foundation, Inc., asserting various torts.[b] The defendant asked the court to dismiss the complaint on the ground that Maine did not have personal jurisdiction over the hospital. The hospital treats patients in North Carolina and does not own any property, have any contractual relationships, or solicit any business or funding in Maine or from Maine residents. The court dismissed the complaint. Bickford appealed to the Maine Supreme Judicial Court, the state's highest court.*

IN THE LANGUAGE OF THE COURT

SAUFLEY, C.J. [Chief Justice]
* * * *
* * * For Maine to exercise jurisdiction over a nonresident defendant, three conditions must exist * * * : (1) Maine must have a legitimate interest in the subject matter of this litigation; (2) the defendant, by its conduct, reasonably could have anticipated litigation in Maine; and (3) the exercise of jurisdiction by Maine's courts comports [is consistent] with traditional notions of fair play and substantial justice. * * * We address each condition in turn.
* * * *
Maine has a legitimate interest in allowing its residents a forum [court] in which to seek redress when out-of-state creditors refuse to correct erroneous credit reports. Credit reports substantially influence the ability of individuals to obtain financing for purchases that are vital to their lives and livelihoods. If a creditor actively refuses to correct the false credit report of a Maine resident, Maine has a legitimate interest in protecting the resident, *whether or not the creditor is located outside of Maine's boundaries.* * * * [Emphasis added.]
* * * *
In addressing [the] second [condition] Bickford relies on two United States Supreme Court cases in which the defendants were authors, editors, or publishers of periodicals that enjoyed circulation and readership in the states where suit was commenced. In each case, the Court emphasized that the effect of the allegedly [false] material was felt in the state where the suit was filed. Nonetheless, the commission outside the forum state of an act that has consequences in the forum state is *by itself* an insufficient contact where all the events necessary to give rise to a tort claim occurred outside the forum state. Rather, *the effect of the out-of-state conduct in Maine is merely a factor to be considered in light of the relevant facts that apply to the minimum contacts analysis.* [Emphasis added.]

We need not decide whether simply filing a report with a national credit agency that might share its information with lenders in Maine could establish a connection between the hospital and Maine that would justify Maine's exercise of control. In the present case, Bickford alleges that the hospital went beyond the mere act of reporting a credit incident. He alleges that the hospital realized the impact its report was having on a Maine resident after it engaged in an exchange with Bickford about the status of the credit report. Because the hospital was thereafter on notice that it was injuring a Maine resident by failing to take steps to eliminate the use of the allegedly [false] statement, it could reasonably have anticipated being required to respond to litigation in Maine courts. The hospital's conduct affected a Maine resident, and after Bickford contested the report, the hospital can be understood to have intentionally

---

a. In the "August 2004" section, click on the name of the case to access the opinion. The Judicial Branch of the State of Maine maintains this Web site.
b. A *tort* is wrongful conduct that causes injury to another. See Chapters 6 and 7.

CASE 2.1 Continued

directed its conduct toward a Maine resident. We conclude that the hospital could reasonably anticipate being haled into court in Maine.

      *   *   *   *

We must next address the third [condition's] requirement that the exercise of jurisdiction comport with traditional notions of fair play and substantial justice. The determination of fairness for purposes of personal jurisdiction depends upon the facts of each case. In making this determination, we consider the number, nature, and purpose of the defendant's contacts with Maine, the connection between those contacts and the cause of action, the interest of Maine in the controversy, and the convenience to both parties.

Maine has a strong interest in protecting its residents from abuses in credit reporting, and the hospital's alleged contact with Maine forms the basis for Bickford's tort claims against the hospital. Although the hospital's contact with Maine has not been voluminous, its action as a creditor failing to correct an erroneous report has allegedly resulted in a substantial impact on a Maine resident. Although it is inconvenient for the hospital to defend a suit in Maine and potential witnesses are out-of-state, it would also be burdensome for Bickford, whose credit has allegedly been compromised, to prosecute an action in North Carolina. *   *   * [Thus] it [does not offend] traditional notions of fair play and substantial justice to hale the hospital into court in Maine.

DECISION AND REMEDY *Maine's Supreme Judicial Court vacated the lower court's dismissal of Bickford's complaint and remanded the case to the lower court for "further proceedings consistent with this opinion." Maine's exercise of personal jurisdiction over the hospital met the three required conditions: Maine had a legitimate interest in the subject of the suit, the defendant reasonably could have anticipated litigation in Maine, and Maine's exercise of jurisdiction was in line with "traditional notions of fair play and substantial justice."*

WHAT IF THE FACTS WERE DIFFERENT? *Suppose that the hospital had only reported the incident to a credit agency but had not been in contact with Bickford and thus had no notice of Bickford's claims. How might this have affected the court's ruling in this case?*

JURISDICTION OVER SUBJECT MATTER Subject-matter jurisdiction refers to the limitations on the types of cases a court can hear. Certain courts are empowered to hear certain kinds of disputes.

—General and Limited Jurisdiction. In both the federal and state court systems, there are courts of *general* (unlimited) *jurisdiction* and courts of *limited jurisdiction*. A court of general jurisdiction can decide cases involving a broad array of issues. An example of a court of general jurisdiction is a state trial court or a federal district court. An example of a state court of limited jurisdiction is a probate court. **Probate courts** are state courts that handle only matters relating to the transfer of a person's assets and obligations after that person's death, including issues relating to the custody and guardianship of children. An example of a federal court of limited subject-matter jurisdiction is a bankruptcy court. **Bankruptcy courts** handle only bankruptcy proceedings, which are governed by federal bankruptcy law (discussed in Chapter 30).

A court's jurisdiction over subject matter is usually defined in the statute or constitution creating the court. In both the federal and state court systems, a court's subject-matter jurisdiction can be limited not only by the subject of the lawsuit but also by the sum in controversy, whether the case is a felony (a more serious type of crime) or a misdemeanor (a less serious type of crime), or whether the proceeding is a trial or an appeal.

—Original and Appellate Jurisdiction. A court's subject-matter jurisdiction is also frequently limited to hearing cases at a particular stage of the dispute. Courts in which lawsuits begin, trials take place, and evidence is presented are referred to as courts of original jurisdiction. Courts having original jurisdiction are courts of the first instance, or trial courts. In the federal court system, the *district courts* are trial courts. In the various state court systems, the trial courts are known by different names, as will be discussed shortly.

Courts having appellate jurisdiction act as reviewing courts, or appellate courts. In general, cases can be brought before appellate courts only on appeal from an order or a judgment of a trial court or other lower court. In other words, the distinction between courts of original jurisdiction and courts of appellate jurisdiction normally lies in whether the case is being heard for the first time.

JURISDICTION OF THE FEDERAL COURTS

Because the federal government is a government of limited powers, the jurisdiction of the federal courts is limited. Federal courts have subject-matter jurisdiction in two situations.

—*Federal Questions.* Article III of the U.S. Constitution establishes the boundaries of federal judicial power. Section 2 of Article III states that "[t]he judicial Power shall extend to all Cases, in Law and Equity, arising under this Constitution, the Laws of the United States, and Treaties made, or which shall be made, under their Authority." In effect, this clause means that whenever a plaintiff's cause of action is based, at least in part, on the U.S. Constitution, a treaty, or a federal law, a **federal question** arises. Any lawsuit involving a federal question comes under the judicial authority of the federal courts and can originate in a federal court. People who claim that their constitutional rights have been violated, for example, can begin their suits in a federal court. Note that in a case based on a federal question, a federal court will apply federal law.

—*Diversity of Citizenship.* Federal district courts can also exercise original jurisdiction over cases involving **diversity of citizenship.** This term applies whenever a federal court has jurisdiction over a case that does not involve a question of federal law. The most common type of diversity jurisdiction has two requirements:[7] (1) the plaintiff and defendant must be residents of different states, and (2) the dollar amount in controversy must exceed $75,000. For purposes of diversity jurisdiction, a corporation is a citizen of both the state in which it is incorporated and the state in which its principal place of business is located. A case involving diversity of citizenship can be filed in the appropriate federal district court. If the case starts in a state court, it can sometimes be transferred, or "removed," to a federal court. A large percentage of the cases filed in federal courts each year are based on diversity of citizenship.

As noted, a federal court will apply federal law in cases involving federal questions. In a case based on diversity of citizenship, in contrast, a federal court will apply the relevant state law (which is often the law of the state in which the court sits).

EXCLUSIVE VERSUS CONCURRENT JURISDICTION

When both federal and state courts have the power to hear a case, as is true in suits involving diversity of citizenship, **concurrent jurisdiction** exists. When cases can be tried only in federal courts or only in state courts, **exclusive jurisdiction** exists. Federal courts have exclusive jurisdiction in cases involving federal crimes, bankruptcy, and most patent and copyright claims; in suits against the United States; and in some areas of admiralty law (law governing transportation on the seas and ocean waters). State courts also have exclusive jurisdiction over certain subjects—for example, divorce and adoption.

When concurrent jurisdiction exists, a party may choose to bring a suit in either a federal court or a state court. The party's lawyer will consider several factors in counseling the litigant as to which choice is preferable. The lawyer may prefer to litigate the case in a state court because she or he is more familiar with the state court's procedures, or perhaps the attorney believes that the state's judge or jury would be more sympathetic to the client's case. Alternatively, the lawyer may advise the client to sue in federal court. Perhaps the state court's **docket** (the court's schedule listing the cases to be heard) is crowded, and the case could be brought to trial sooner in a federal court. Perhaps some feature of federal practice or procedure could offer an advantage in the client's case. Other important considerations include the law in the particular jurisdiction, how that law has been applied in the jurisdiction's courts, and what the results in similar cases have been in that jurisdiction.

JURISDICTION IN CYBERSPACE

The Internet's capacity to bypass political and geographic boundaries undercuts the traditional basis for a court to assert personal jurisdiction. This basis includes a party's contacts with a court's geographic jurisdiction. As already discussed, for a court to compel a defendant to come before it, there must be at least minimum contacts—the presence of a salesperson within the state, for example. Are there sufficient minimum contacts if the only connection to a jurisdiction is an ad on a Web site originating from a remote location?

---

7. Diversity jurisdiction also exists in cases between (1) a foreign country and citizens of a state or of different states and (2) citizens of a state and citizens or subjects of a foreign country. These bases for diversity jurisdiction are less commonly used.

THE "SLIDING-SCALE" STANDARD Gradually, the courts are developing a standard—called a "sliding-scale" standard—for determining when the exercise of personal jurisdiction over an out-of-state defendant is proper. In developing this standard, the courts have identified three types of Internet business contacts: (1) substantial business conducted over the Internet (with contracts and sales, for example); (2) some interactivity through a Web site; and (3) passive advertising. Jurisdiction is proper for the first category, improper for the third, and may or may not be appropriate for the second.[8] An Internet communication is typically considered passive if people have to voluntarily access it to read the message and active if it is sent to specific individuals.

In certain situations, even a single contact can satisfy the minimum-contacts requirement. In one case, for example, a Texas resident, Connie Davis, sent an unsolicited e-mail message to numerous Mississippi residents advertising a pornographic Web site. Davis falsified the "from" header in the e-mail so that it looked as if Internet Doorway had sent the e-mail. Internet Doorway filed a lawsuit against Davis in Mississippi, claiming that its reputation and goodwill in the community had been harmed. The federal court in Mississippi held that Davis's single e-mail to Mississippi residents satisfied the minimum-contacts requirement for jurisdiction. The court concluded that Davis, by sending the e-mail solicitation, should reasonably have expected that she could be "haled into court in a distant jurisdiction to answer for the ramifications."[9]

In the following case, the court considered whether jurisdiction could be exercised over defendants whose only contacts with the jurisdiction were through their Web site.

---

8. For a leading case on this issue, see *Zippo Manufacturing Co. v. Zippo Dot Com, Inc.*, 952 F.Supp. 1119 (W.D.Pa. 1997).

9. *Internet Doorway, Inc. v. Parks*, 138 F.Supp.2d 773 (S.D.Miss. 2001).

CASE 2.2 — Bird v. Parsons

United States
Court of Appeals,
Sixth Circuit, 2002.
289 F.3d 865.
http://pacer.ca6.uscourts.gov/
opinions/main.php [a]

HISTORICAL AND TECHNOLOGICAL SETTING *The creation of a Web site requires the reservation of a cyberlocation, called an Internet Protocol (IP) address, and a computer to host the contents of the site. To make using the Internet easier, a domain name is assigned to correspond to an IP address. A person who wants a specific domain name must apply for the name with a domain name registrar. To access a Web site, a user enters in a browser a domain name corresponding to an IP address and then is routed electronically to the computer that hosts the site at that address. Because not every person who establishes a site hosts it on his or her own Internet server, surrogate hosts license space on their servers to site owners.*

BACKGROUND AND FACTS *Darrell Bird, a citizen of Ohio, has operated Financia, Inc., a national computer software business, since 1983. Financia, Inc., owns the domain name financia.com. Dotster, Inc., a domain name registrar incorporated in Washington, operates its registry at* http://www.dotster.com.[b] *Dotster allows registrants who lack an Internet server to which a name can be assigned to park their names on Dotster's "Futurehome" page. Marshall Parsons registered the name efinancia.com on Dotster's site in 2000 and parked the name on the Futurehome page with the address* http://www.efinancia.com. *George DeCarlo and Steven Vincent, on behalf of Dotster, activated Parsons's site. The name efinancia.com was soon offered for sale at* http://www.afternic.com, *an auction site for the sale of domain names. Bird filed a suit against Dotster and others in a federal district court, alleging, in part, trademark infringement, copyright infringement, and cybersquatting.[c] Dotster, DeCarlo, and Vincent (the "Dotster defendants") asked the court to dismiss the complaint against them for, among other reasons, lack of personal jurisdiction. The court dismissed the suit. Alleging that Dotster sold 4,666 registrations to Ohio residents, Bird appealed to the U.S. Court of Appeals for the Sixth Circuit.*

---

a. This is a page within the Web site of the U.S. Court of Appeals for the Sixth Circuit. In the left-hand column, click on "Opinions Search." In the "Short Title contains" box, type "Parsons" and click on "Submit Query." In the "Opinion" box corresponding to the name of the case, click on the number to access the opinion.

b. Dotster's registration process is in conjunction with the Domain Registration of Internet Assigned Names and Numbers, which is maintained by Network Solutions, Inc. (owned by VeriSign), and regulated by the Internet Corporation for Assigned Names and Numbers (ICANN)(see Chapter 8). Dotster is an ICANN–accredited registrar.

c. *Cybersquatting* is registering another person's trademark as a domain name and offering it for sale. This is a violation of the Anticybersquatting Consumer Protection Act of 1999. Cybersquatting and trademark and copyright infringement are discussed in more detail in Chapter 8.

CONTINUED ▶

CASE 2.2 Continued

IN THE LANGUAGE OF THE COURT

RONALD LEE GILMAN, Circuit Judge.

* * * *

* * * [J]urisdiction over the Dotster defendants is permissible only if their contacts with Ohio satisfy [a] three-part test * * * :

> First, the defendant must purposefully avail himself of the privilege of acting in the forum state [the state in which the lawsuit is initiated] or causing a consequence in the forum state. Second, the cause of action must arise from the defendant's activities there. Finally, the acts of the defendant or consequences caused by the defendant must have a substantial enough connection with the forum state to make the exercise of jurisdiction over the defendant reasonable.

* * * We conclude that by maintaining a website on which Ohio residents can register domain names and by allegedly accepting the business of 4,666 Ohio residents, the Dotster defendants have satisfied the *purposeful-availment* [use] *requirement*. * * * [Emphasis added.]

The second requirement * * * involves an analysis of whether Bird's claims arise from the Dotster defendants' contacts with Ohio. * * *

The operative facts in the present case include Bird's allegation that the Dotster defendants committed copyright and trademark law violations by registering Parsons's domain name efinancia.com. Both the Dotster defendants' contacts with Ohio and Bird's claim of copyright and trademark violations stem from these defendants' operation of the Dotster website. As a result, the operative facts are at least marginally related to the alleged contacts between the Dotster defendants and Ohio. * * *

The final requirement * * * is that the exercise of jurisdiction be reasonable in light of the connection that allegedly exists between the Dotster defendants and Ohio. * * *

Although the Dotster defendants might face a burden in having to defend a lawsuit in Ohio, they cannot reasonably object to this burden given that Dotster has allegedly transacted business with 4,666 Ohio residents. Ohio has a legitimate interest in protecting the business interests of its citizens, *even though all of Bird's claims involve federal law.* Bird has an obvious interest in obtaining relief, and *Ohio might be the only forum where jurisdiction would exist over all of the defendants.* Although the state of Washington also has an interest in this dispute, because the claim involves its citizens, this interest does not override the other factors suggesting that personal jurisdiction in Ohio is reasonable. [Emphasis added.]

DECISION AND REMEDY *The U.S. Court of Appeals for the Sixth Circuit concluded that the lower court erred in granting the Dotster defendants' motion to dismiss for lack of personal jurisdiction. Bird had established that the court's exercise of jurisdiction over the Dotster defendants was proper.*

INTERNATIONAL JURISDICTIONAL ISSUES Because the Internet is international in scope, international jurisdictional issues have understandably come to the fore. We have already discussed some of these issues in the *Contemporary Legal Debates* feature in Chapter 1. The world's courts seem to be developing a standard that echoes the requirement of "minimum contacts" applied by the U.S. courts. Most courts are indicating that minimum contacts—doing business within the jurisdiction, for example—are enough to exercise jurisdiction over a defendant. The effect of this standard is that a business firm may have to comply with the laws in any jurisdiction in which it actively targets customers for its products.

VENUE

Jurisdiction has to do with whether a court has authority to hear a case involving specific persons, property, or subject matter. **Venue**[10] is concerned with the most appropriate location for a trial. For example, two state courts (or two federal courts) may have the authority

---

10. Pronounced *ven-yoo.*

CONCEPT SUMMARY 2.1 | Jurisdiction

TYPE OF JURISDICTION	DESCRIPTION
PERSONAL	Exists when a defendant is located within the territorial boundaries within which a court has the right and power to decide cases. Jurisdiction may be exercised over out-of-state defendants under state long arm statutes. Courts have jurisdiction over corporate defendants that do business within the state, as well as corporations that advertise, sell, or place goods into the stream of commerce in the state.
PROPERTY	Exists when the property that is subject to a lawsuit is located within the territorial boundaries within which a court has the right and power to decide cases.
SUBJECT MATTER	Limits the court's jurisdictional authority to particular types of cases. 1. *Limited jurisdiction*—Exists when a court is limited to a specific subject matter, such as probate or divorce. 2. *General jurisdiction*—Exists when a court can hear cases involving a broad array of issues.
ORIGINAL	Exists with courts that have the authority to hear a case for the first time (trial courts).
APPELLATE	Exists with courts of appeal and review; generally, appellate courts do not have original jurisdiction.
FEDERAL	1. *Federal questions*—When the plaintiff's cause of action is based at least in part on the U.S. Constitution, a treaty, or a federal law, a federal court can exercise jurisdiction. 2. *Diversity of citizenship*—In cases between citizens of different states when the amount in controversy exceeds $75,000 (or in cases between a foreign country and citizens of a state or of different states and in cases between citizens of a state and citizens or subjects of a foreign country), a federal court can exercise jurisdiction.
CONCURRENT	Exists when both federal and state courts have authority to hear the same case.
EXCLUSIVE	Exists when only state courts or only federal courts have authority to hear a case.
JURISDICTION IN CYBERSPACE	Because the Internet does not have physical boundaries, traditional jurisdictional concepts have been difficult to apply in cases involving activities conducted via the Web. Gradually, the courts are developing standards to use in determining when jurisdiction over a Web site owner or operator in another state is proper.

to exercise jurisdiction over a case, but it may be more appropriate or convenient to hear the case in one court than in the other.

Basically, the concept of venue reflects the policy that a court trying a suit should be in the geographic neighborhood (usually the county) where the incident leading to the lawsuit occurred or where the parties involved in the lawsuit reside. Venue in a civil case typically is where the defendant resides, whereas venue in a criminal case is normally where the crime occurred. Pretrial publicity or other factors, though, may require a change of venue to another community,

especially in criminal cases in which the defendant's right to a fair and impartial jury has been impaired.

STANDING TO SUE

In order to bring a lawsuit before a court, a party must have **standing to sue,** or a sufficient "stake" in a matter to justify seeking relief through the court system. In other words, to have standing, a party must have a legally protected and tangible interest at stake in the litigation. The party bringing the lawsuit must have suffered a harm or been threatened with a harm by the action about which he or she has complained. At times, a person can have standing to sue on behalf of another person. For example, suppose that a child suffers serious injuries as a result of a defectively manufactured toy. Because the child is a minor, another person, such as a parent or legal guardian, can bring a lawsuit on the child's behalf.

Standing to sue also requires that the controversy at issue be a **justiciable**[11] controversy—a controversy that is real and substantial, as opposed to hypothetical or academic. For instance, in the above example, the child's parent could not sue the toy manufacturer merely on the ground that the toy was defective. The issue would become justiciable only if the child had actually been injured due to the defect in the toy as marketed. In other words, the parent normally could not ask the court to determine what damages might be obtained if the child had been injured, because this would be merely a hypothetical question.

SECTION 3 | The State and Federal Court Systems

As mentioned earlier in this chapter, each state has its own court system. Additionally, there is a system of federal courts. Although no two state court systems are exactly the same, the right-hand side of Exhibit 2–1 illustrates the basic organizational framework characteristic of the court systems in many states. The exhibit also shows how the federal court system is structured. We turn now to an examination of these court systems, beginning with the state courts.

STATE COURT SYSTEMS

Typically, a state court system includes several levels, or tiers, of courts. As indicated in Exhibit 2–1, state courts may include (1) local trial courts of limited jurisdiction, (2) state trial courts of general jurisdiction, (3) state courts of appeals (intermediate appellate courts), and (4) the state's highest court (often called the state supreme court). Judges in the state court system are usually elected by the voters for specified terms. In some states, however, judges are appointed by an elected official and then confirmed by a public vote.

Generally, any person who is a party to a lawsuit has the opportunity to plead the case before a trial court and then, if he or she loses, before at least one level of appellate court. Finally, if a federal statute or federal constitutional issue is involved in the decision of a state supreme court, that decision may be further appealed to the United States Supreme Court.

TRIAL COURTS Trial courts are exactly what their name implies—courts in which trials are held and testimony taken. State trial courts have either general or limited jurisdiction. Trial courts that have general jurisdiction as to subject matter may be called county, district, superior, or circuit courts.[12] State trial courts of general jurisdiction have jurisdiction over a wide

---

11. Pronounced jus-*tish*-a-bul.

12. The name in Ohio and Pennsylvania is Court of Common Pleas; the name in New York is Supreme Court, Trial Division.

EXHIBIT 2-1 **The State and Federal Court Systems**

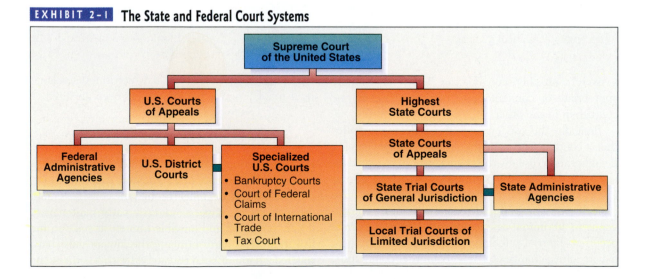

variety of subjects, including both civil disputes and criminal prosecutions. In some states, trial courts of general jurisdiction may hear appeals from courts of limited jurisdiction.

Courts of limited jurisdiction as to subject matter are often called special inferior trial courts or minor judiciary courts. **Small claims courts are inferior trial courts that hear only civil cases involving claims of less than a certain amount**, such as $5,000 (the amount varies from state to state). Suits brought in small claims courts are generally conducted informally, and lawyers are not required. In a small number of states, lawyers are not even allowed to represent people in small claims courts for most purposes. Decisions of small claims courts may sometimes be appealed to a state trial court of general jurisdiction.

Other courts of limited jurisdiction include domestic relations courts, which handle primarily divorce actions and child-custody disputes; local municipal courts, which mainly deal with traffic cases; and probate courts, as mentioned earlier.

APPELLATE, OR REVIEWING, COURTS Every state has at least one court of appeals (appellate court, or reviewing court), which may be an intermediate appellate court or the state's highest court. About three-fourths of the states have intermediate appellate courts. Generally, courts of appeals do not conduct new trials, in which evidence is submitted to the court and witnesses are examined. Rather, an appellate court panel of three or more judges reviews the record of the case on appeal, which includes a transcript of the trial proceedings, and then determines whether the trial court committed an error.

Usually, appellate courts focus on questions of law, not questions of fact. A **question of fact** deals with what really happened in regard to the dispute being tried—such as whether a party actually burned a flag. A **question of law** concerns the application or interpretation of the law—such as whether flag-burning is a form of speech protected by the First Amendment to the Constitution. Only a judge, not a jury, can rule on questions of law. Appellate courts normally defer to the trial court's findings on questions of fact because the trial court judge and jury were in a better position to evaluate testimony—by directly observing witnesses' gestures, demeanor, and other nonverbal behavior during the trial. At the appellate level, the judges review the written transcript of the trial, which does not include these nonverbal elements. Thus, an appellate court will tamper with a trial court's finding of fact only

when the finding is clearly erroneous (that is, when it is contrary to the evidence presented at trial) or when there is no evidence to support the finding.

HIGHEST STATE COURTS The highest appellate court in a state is usually called the supreme court but may be designated by some other name. For example, in both New York and Maryland, the highest state court is called the Court of Appeals. In Maine and Massachusetts, the highest court is labeled the Supreme Judicial Court. In West Virginia, the highest state court is the Supreme Court of Appeals.

The decisions of each state's highest court on all questions of state law are final. Only when issues of federal law are involved can the United States Supreme Court overrule a decision made by a state's highest court. For example, suppose that a city ordinance prohibits citizens from engaging in door-to-door advocacy without first registering with the mayor's office and receiving a permit. Further suppose that a religious group sues the city, arguing that the law violates the freedoms of speech and religion guaranteed by the First Amendment. If the state supreme court upholds the law, the group could appeal the decision to the United States Supreme Court—because a constitutional (federal) issue is involved.

THE FEDERAL COURT SYSTEM

The federal court system is basically a three-tiered model consisting of (1) U.S. district courts (trial courts of general jurisdiction) and various courts of limited jurisdiction, (2) U.S. courts of appeals (intermediate courts of appeals), and (3) the United States Supreme Court.

Unlike state court judges, who are usually elected, federal court judges—including the justices of the Supreme Court—are appointed by the president of the United States, subject to confirmation by the U.S. Senate. Article III of the Constitution states that federal judges "hold their offices during good Behaviour." In effect, this means that federal judges have lifetime appointments. Although they can be impeached (removed from office) for misconduct, this is rarely done. In the entire history of the United States, only seven federal judges have been removed from office through impeachment proceedings.

U.S. DISTRICT COURTS At the federal level, the equivalent of a state trial court of general jurisdiction is the district court. U.S. district courts have original jurisdiction in federal matters, and federal cases typically originate in district courts. There are other federal courts with original, but special (or limited), jurisdiction, such as the federal bankruptcy courts and others shown earlier in Exhibit 2–1 on page 38.

There is at least one federal district court in every state. The number of judicial districts can vary over time, primarily owing to population changes and corresponding changes in caseloads. Currently, there are ninety-four federal judicial districts. Exhibit 2–2 shows the boundaries of the U.S. district courts, as well as the U.S. courts of appeals (discussed next).

U.S. COURTS OF APPEALS In the federal court system, there are thirteen U.S. courts of appeals—referred to as U.S. circuit courts of appeals. Twelve of the federal courts of appeals (including the Court of Appeals for the D.C. Circuit) hear appeals from the federal district courts located within their respective judicial circuits, or geographic boundaries (shown in Exhibit 2–2).[13] The Court of Appeals for the Thirteenth Circuit, called the Federal Circuit, has national appellate jurisdiction over certain types of cases, such as those involving patent law and those in which the U.S. government is a defendant. The decisions of a circuit court of appeals are binding on all courts within the circuit court's jurisdiction and are final in most cases, but appeal to the United States Supreme Court is possible.

UNITED STATES SUPREME COURT At the highest level in the three-tiered federal court system is the United States Supreme Court. According to the language of Article III of the U.S. Constitution, there is only one national Supreme Court. All other courts in the federal system are considered "inferior." Congress is empowered to create other inferior courts as it deems necessary. The inferior courts that Congress has created include the second tier in our model—the U.S. circuit courts of appeals—as well as the district courts and the various federal courts of limited, or specialized, jurisdiction.

The United States Supreme Court consists of nine justices. Although the Supreme Court has original, or trial, jurisdiction in rare instances (set forth in Article III, Sections 1 and 2), most of its work is as an appeals court. The Supreme Court can review any case decided by any of the federal courts of appeals, and it also has appellate authority over cases involving federal questions that have been decided in the state courts. The Supreme Court is the final arbiter of the Constitution and federal law.

—Appeals to the Supreme Court. To bring a case before the Supreme Court, a party requests the Court to issue a writ of *certiorari.*[14] A **writ of *certiorari*** is an order issued by the Supreme Court to a lower court requiring the latter to send it the record of the case for review. The Court will not issue a writ unless at least four of the nine justices approve of it. This is called the **rule of four.** Whether the Court will issue a writ of *certiorari* is entirely within its discretion, and most petitions for writs are denied. (Thousands of cases are filed with the Supreme Court each year, yet it hears, on average, less than one hundred of these cases.[15]) A denial is not a decision on the merits of a case, nor does it indicate agreement with the lower court's opinion. Also, denial of the writ has no value as a precedent. Denial simply means that the lower court's decision remains the law in that jurisdiction.

—Petitions Granted by the Court. Typically, the Court grants petitions in cases that raise important constitutional questions or cases that conflict with other state or federal court decisions. Similarly, if federal appellate courts are rendering inconsistent opinions on an important issue, the Supreme Court may review the case and issue a decision to define the law on the matter. The justices, however, never explain their reasons for hearing certain cases and not others, so it is difficult to predict which type of case the Court might select.

SECTION 4 ｜ Alternative Dispute Resolution

Alternative dispute resolution (ADR) refers to the various methods by which disputes are settled outside the court system. **Litigation**—the process of resolving a dispute through the court system—is expensive and time consuming. Litigating even the simplest complaint is costly, and because of the backlog of cases pending in many courts, several years may pass before

---

13. Historically, judges were required to "ride the circuit" and hear appeals in different courts around the country, which is how the name "circuit court" came about.

14. Pronounced sur-shee-uh-*rah*-ree.
15. From the mid-1950s through the early 1990s, the Supreme Court reviewed more cases per year than it has since then. In the Court's 1982–1983 term, for example, the Court issued written opinions in 151 cases. In contrast, during the Court's 2003–2004 term, the Court issued written opinions in only 80 cases.

EXHIBIT 2-2 Geographic Boundaries of the U.S. District Courts and Courts of Appeals

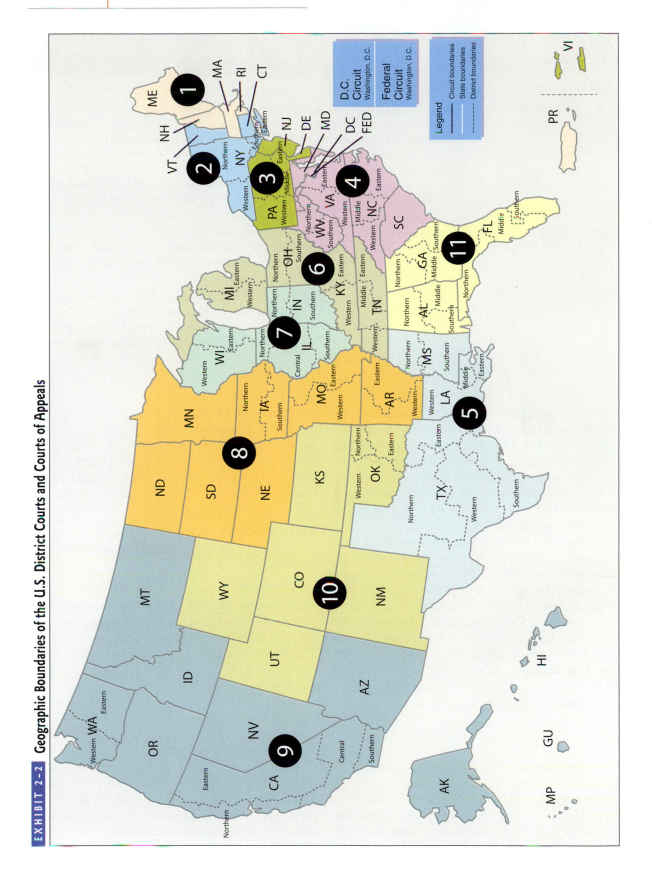

CONCEPT SUMMARY 2.2 | Types of Courts

COURT	DESCRIPTION
TRIAL COURTS	Trial courts are courts of original jurisdiction in which actions are initiated. 1. *State courts*—Courts of general jurisdiction can hear any case that has not been specifically designated for another court; courts of limited jurisdiction include domestic relations courts, probate courts, municipal courts, small claims courts, and others. 2. *Federal courts*—The federal district court is the equivalent of the state trial court. Federal courts of limited jurisdiction include the bankruptcy court and others shown in Exhibit 2–1 on page 38.
INTERMEDIATE APPELLATE COURTS	Courts of appeals are reviewing courts; generally, appellate courts do not have original jurisdiction. About three-fourths of the states have intermediate appellate courts; in the federal court system, the U.S. circuit courts of appeals are the intermediate appellate courts.
SUPREME COURT	The highest state court is that state's supreme court, although it may be called by some other name. Appeal from state supreme courts to the United States Supreme Court is possible only if a federal question is involved. The United States Supreme Court is the highest court in the federal court system and the final arbiter of the Constitution and federal law.

a case is actually tried. ADR, in contrast, usually entails fewer costs and allows disputes to be resolved relatively quickly. ADR also offers more privacy and flexibility than court proceedings. Disputes can be settled without the publicity of a trial using rules by which both parties have agreed to abide. Today, more than 95 percent of civil lawsuits are settled before trial using some form of ADR.

Methods of ADR range from neighbors sitting down over a cup of coffee in an attempt to work out their differences to huge multinational corporations agreeing to resolve a dispute through a formal hearing before a panel of experts. Traditionally, there were basically three forms of ADR—negotiation, mediation, and (normally binding) arbitration. Hence, we use that framework when discussing ADR in the pages that follow. Keep in mind, though, that new methods of ADR—and new combinations of existing methods—are continuously being devised and employed.

NEGOTIATION

One of the simplest forms of ADR is **negotiation,** a process in which the parties attempt to settle their dispute informally, with or without attorneys to represent them. Typically, during the pretrial stages of litigation, the parties and/or their attorneys may meet informally one or more times to see if a mutually satisfactory

agreement can be reached. In some courts, pretrial negotiation is mandatory before parties may proceed to trial. Only if the parties cannot reach an agreement will the court decide the issue. In other courts, negotiation is one of a menu of ADR options that the parties may (or must, in some situations) pursue prior to trial.

MEDIATION

In the **mediation** process, the parties themselves attempt to negotiate an agreement, but with the assistance of a neutral third party, called a mediator. The mediator talks with the parties separately as well as jointly, emphasizes points of agreement, helps the parties to evaluate their positions, and proposes solutions. The mediator, however, does not make a decision on the matter being disputed. The mediator, who need not be a lawyer, usually charges a fee for his or her services (which can be split between the parties). States that require parties to undergo ADR before trial often offer mediation as one of the ADR options or (as in Florida) the only option.

Mediation is not adversarial in nature, as lawsuits are. In litigation, the parties "do battle" with each other in the courtroom, while the judge is the neutral party. The mediation process, in contrast, tends to reduce the antagonism between the disputants and to allow them to resume their former relationship. For this reason mediation is often the preferred form of ADR for disputes involving business partners, employers and employees, or other parties involved in long-term relationships.

Today, characteristics of mediation are being combined with those of arbitration (to be discussed next). In *binding mediation,* for example, the parties agree that if they cannot resolve the dispute, the mediator can make a legally binding decision on the issue. In *mediation-arbitration,* or "med-arb," the parties agree to first attempt to settle their dispute through mediation. If no settlement is reached, the dispute will be arbitrated.

ARBITRATION

A more formal method of ADR is **arbitration,** in which an arbitrator (a neutral third party or a panel of experts) hears a dispute and renders a decision. The key difference between arbitration and the forms of ADR just discussed is that in arbitration, the third party hearing the dispute makes the decision for the parties. Usually, the parties in arbitration agree that the third party's decision will be *legally binding,* although the parties can also agree to *nonbinding* arbitration.

In both the federal and state court systems, many courts require the pretrial arbitration of disputes. Often, arbitration is required only in cases in which the dollar amount in controversy is under a specified threshold amount, such as $100,000 or $150,000. When a court mandates pretrial arbitration, normally the arbitrator's decision is not legally binding. If either of the parties is not satisfied with the decision, the court will try the case.

THE ARBITRATION PROCESS In some respects, formal arbitration resembles a trial, although usually the procedural rules are much less restrictive than those governing litigation. In the typical hearing format, the parties present opening arguments to the arbitrator and state what remedies should or should not be granted. Next, the parties present evidence supporting their respective positions, and witnesses may be called and examined by both sides. The arbitrator then renders a decision, called an **award.**

An arbitrator's award is usually the final word on the matter. Although the parties may appeal an arbitrator's decision, a court's review of the decision will be much more restricted in scope than an appellate court's review of a trial court's decision. The general view is that because the parties were free to frame the issues and set the powers of the arbitrator at the outset, they cannot complain about the results. The award will be set aside only if the arbitrator's conduct or "bad faith" substantially prejudiced the rights of one of the parties, if the award violates an established public policy, or if the arbitrator exceeded her or his powers (by arbitrating issues that the parties did not agree to submit to arbitration).

ARBITRATION CLAUSES AND STATUTES Virtually any commercial matter can be submitted to arbitration. Frequently, parties include an **arbitration clause** in a contract specifying that any dispute arising under the contract will be resolved through arbitration rather than through the court system. Parties can also agree to arbitrate a dispute after it arises.

Most states have statutes (often based in part on the Uniform Arbitration Act of 1955) under which arbitration clauses will be enforced, and some state statutes compel arbitration of certain types of disputes, such as those involving public employees. At the federal level, the Federal Arbitration Act (FAA), enacted in 1925, enforces arbitration clauses in contracts involving maritime activity and interstate commerce. Because of the breadth of the commerce clause (see Chapter 4), arbitration agreements involving transactions only slightly connected to the flow of interstate commerce may fall under the FAA.

ARBITRABILITY When a dispute arises as to whether the parties to a contract with an arbitration clause have agreed to submit a particular matter to arbitration, one party may file suit to compel arbitration. The court before which the suit is brought will not decide the basic controversy but must decide the issue of *arbitrability*—that is, whether the matter is one that must be resolved through arbitration. If the court finds that the subject matter in controversy is covered by the agreement to arbitrate, then a party may be compelled to arbitrate the dispute. Even when a claim involves a violation of a statute passed to protect a certain class of people, a court may determine that the parties must nonetheless abide by their agreement to arbitrate the dispute. Usually, a court will allow the claim to be arbitrated if the court, in interpreting the statute, can find no legislative intent to the contrary.

No party, however, will be ordered to submit a particular dispute to arbitration unless the court is convinced that the party has consented to do so.[16]

16. See, for example, *Wright v. Universal Maritime Service Corp.,* 525 U.S. 70, 119 S.Ct. 391, 142 L.Ed.2d 361 (1998).

Additionally, the courts will not compel arbitration if it is clear that the prescribed arbitration rules and procedures are inherently unfair to one of the parties.[17]

MANDATORY ARBITRATION IN THE EMPLOYMENT CONTEXT A significant question in the last several years has concerned mandatory arbitration clauses in employment contracts. Many claim that employees' rights are not sufficiently protected when they are forced, as a condition of being hired, to agree to arbitrate all disputes and thus waive their rights under statutes specifically designed to protect employees. The United States Supreme Court, however, has held that mandatory arbitration clauses in employment contracts are generally enforceable.[18]

Compulsory arbitration agreements often spell out the rules for a mandatory proceeding. For example, an agreement may address in detail the amount and payment of filing fees and other expenses. Some courts have overturned provisions in employment-related agreements that require the parties to split the costs when an individual worker lacks the ability to pay. The court in the following case took this reasoning a step further.

17. *Hooters of America, Inc. v. Phillips*, 173 F.3d 933 (4th Cir. 1999).

18. For a landmark decision on this issue, see *Gilmer v. Interstate/Johnson Lane Corp.*, 500 U.S. 20, 111 S.Ct. 1647, 114 L.Ed.2d 26 (1991).

CASE 2.3   **Morrison v. Circuit City Stores, Inc.**

United States Court of Appeals, Sixth Circuit. 2003. 317 F.3d 646. http://pacer.ca6.uscourts.gov/opinions/main.php [a]

KAREN NELSON MOORE, Circuit Judge.
* * * *

* * * Plaintiff-Appellant Morrison, an African-American female with a bachelor's degree in engineering from the U.S. Air Force Academy and a master's degree in administration from Central Michigan University, submitted an application for a managerial position at a Circuit City store in Cincinnati, Ohio. As part of the application process, Morrison was required to sign a * * * "Dispute Resolution Agreement." This document contained an arbitration clause that required resolution of all disputes or controversies arising out of employment with Circuit City in an arbitral forum. * * * Circuit City would not consider any application for employment unless the arbitration agreement was signed * * * .
* * * *

Pursuant to [the agreement] each party is required to pay one-half of the costs of arbitration following the issuance of an arbitration award * * * . In addition, * * * if an employee is able to pay her share of the arbitration costs within [ninety days], her costs (not including attorney fees) are then limited to the greater of either five hundred dollars or three percent of her most recent annual compensation.
* * * *

* * * Morrison began her employment at Circuit City on or about December 1, 1995. Two years later, on December 12, 1997, she was terminated. Morrison alleges that her termination was the result of race and sex discrimination.[b] She filed this lawsuit * * * in Ohio state court, alleging federal and state claims of race and sex discrimination * * * . Circuit City removed the case to federal court and then moved to compel arbitration and to dismiss Morrison's claims. The district court granted Circuit City's motion * * * .
* * * Morrison's appeal followed.
* * * *

We hold that *potential litigants must be given an opportunity, prior to arbitration on the merits, to demonstrate that the potential costs of arbitration are great enough to deter them and similarly situated individuals from seeking to vindicate [assert] their federal statutory rights in the arbitral forum.* * * * Thus, in order to protect the statutory rights at issue, the reviewing court must look to more than just the interests and conduct of a particular plaintiff. * * * [A] court considering whether a cost-splitting provision is enforceable should consider similarly situated potential

---

a. This a page within the Web site of the U.S. Court of Appeals for the Sixth Circuit. In the left-hand column, click on "Opinions Search." In the "Short Title contains" box, type "Morrison" and click "Submit Query." In the "Opinion" box corresponding to the name of the case, click on the number to access the opinion.
b. Employment discrimination is discussed in detail in Chapter 34.

CASE 2.3 Continued

litigants, for whom costs will loom as a larger concern, because it is, in large part, their presence in the system that will deter discriminatory practices. [Emphasis added.]

For this reason, *if the reviewing court finds that the cost-splitting provision would deter a substantial number of similarly situated potential litigants, it should refuse to enforce the cost-splitting provision in order to serve the underlying functions of the federal statute.* * * * [Emphasis added.]

* * * *

This analysis will yield different results in different cases. It will find, in many cases, that high-level managerial employees and others with substantial means can afford the costs of arbitration, thus making cost-splitting provisions in such cases enforceable. In the case of other employees, however, this standard will render cost-splitting provisions unenforceable in many, if not most, cases.

* * * Circuit City argues that Morrison could have avoided having to pay half of the cost of the arbitration * * * if she could have arranged to pay the greater of $500 or 3 percent of her annual salary (in this case, 3 percent of $54,060, or $1,622) within ninety days of the arbitrator's award. * * *

In the abstract, this sum may not appear prohibitive, but it must be considered from the vantage point of the potential litigant in a case such as this. Recently terminated, the potential litigant must continue to pay for housing, utilities, transportation, food, and the other necessities of life in contemporary society despite losing her primary, and most likely only, source of income. * * *

The provision reducing the (former) employee's exposure to the greater of $500 or three percent of her annual compensation presents a closer issue. However, a potential litigant considering arbitration would still have to arrange to pay three percent of her most recent salary, in this case, $1,622, within a three-month period, or risk incurring her full half of the costs * * * . Faced with this choice—which really boils down to risking one's scarce resources in the hopes of an uncertain benefit—it appears to us that a substantial number of similarly situated persons would be deterred from seeking to vindicate their statutory rights under these circumstances.[c]

Based on this reasoning, we hold that Morrison has satisfied her burden in the present case in demonstrating that * * * the cost-splitting provision in the agreement was unenforceable with respect to her claims.

---

c. The court also concluded that the provision could be severed from the agreement, which meant that the rest of the agreement could be enforced. Because the arbitration in this case had already occurred, and Morrison had not been required to pay any share of the costs, the court affirmed the lower court's order compelling arbitration, "on these different grounds."

QUESTIONS

1. On what argument did Morrison base her appeal of the court's order to arbitrate her employment-discrimination claims?
2. Why did the U.S. Court of Appeals for the Sixth Circuit hold in Morrison's case that the arbitration agreement's cost-splitting provision was unenforceable?

OTHER TYPES OF ADR

The three forms of ADR just discussed are the oldest and traditionally the most commonly used forms. As mentioned earlier, a variety of new types of ADR have emerged in recent years, including those described here.

1. In **early neutral case evaluation,** the parties select a neutral third party (generally an expert in the subject matter of the dispute) to evaluate their respective positions. The parties explain their positions to the case evaluator in any manner they choose. The case evaluator then assesses the strengths and weaknesses of the parties' positions, and this evaluation forms the basis for negotiating a settlement.

2. In a **mini-trial,** each party's attorney briefly argues the party's case before representatives of each firm who have the authority to settle the dispute. Typically, a neutral third party (usually an expert in the area being disputed) acts as an adviser. If the parties fail to reach

an agreement, the adviser renders an opinion as to how a court would likely decide the issue.

3. Numerous federal courts now hold **summary jury trials (SJTs),** in which the parties present their arguments and evidence and the jury renders a verdict. The jury's verdict is not binding, but it does act as a guide to both sides in reaching an agreement during the mandatory negotiations that immediately follow the trial.

4. Other alternatives being employed by the courts include summary procedures for commercial litigation and the appointment of special masters to assist judges in deciding complex issues.

PROVIDERS OF ADR SERVICES

ADR services are provided by both government agencies and private organizations. A major provider of ADR services is the **American Arbitration Association (AAA),** which was founded in 1926 and now handles over 200,000 claims a year in its numerous offices around the country. Cases brought before the AAA are heard by an expert or a panel of experts in the area relating to the dispute and are usually settled quickly. Generally, about half of the panel members are lawyers. To cover its costs, the AAA charges a fee, paid by the party filing the claim. In addition, each party to the dispute pays a specified amount for each hearing day, as well as a special additional fee in cases involving personal injuries or property loss.

Hundreds of for-profit firms around the country also provide dispute-resolution services. Typically, these firms hire retired judges to conduct arbitration hearings or otherwise assist parties in settling their disputes. The judges follow procedures similar to those of the federal courts and use similar rules. Usually, each party to the dispute pays a filing fee and a designated fee for a hearing session or conference.

CONCEPT SUMMARY 2.3 | Alternative Dispute Resolution (ADR)

TYPE OF ADR	DESCRIPTION
NEGOTIATION	The parties come together, with or without attorneys to represent them, and try to reach a settlement.
MEDIATION	The parties themselves reach an agreement with the help of a third party, called a mediator, who plays an active role in the dispute settlement. The mediator has discussions with the parties individually and jointly, assists the parties in evaluating their positions, and proposes possible solutions. Mediation is usually the preferred method of ADR in cases involving ongoing or long-term relationships.
ARBITRATION	In this more formal method of ADR, the parties submit their dispute to a neutral third party, the arbitrator, who renders a decision. The decision is binding unless the parties (or a court, in court-related arbitration) specify otherwise. Arbitration awards may be appealed to a court, but only in special circumstances (such as if the award is contrary to public policy) will a court set aside an arbitrator's award. If there is a question concerning the arbitrability of a certain type of claim, a court must decide the issue.

SECTION 5 | Online Dispute Resolution

An increasing number of companies and organizations are offering dispute-resolution services using the Internet. The settlement of disputes in these online forums is known as **online dispute resolution (ODR).** To date, the disputes resolved in these forums have most commonly involved disagreements over the rights to domain names (Web site addresses—see Chapter 8) and disagreements over the quality of goods sold via the Internet, including goods sold through Internet auction sites.

Currently, ODR may be best for resolving small- to medium-sized business liability claims, which may not be worth the expense of litigation or traditional methods of alternative dispute resolution. Rules being developed in online forums, however, may ultimately become a code of conduct for everyone who does business in cyberspace. Most online forums do not automatically apply the law of any specific jurisdiction. Instead, results are often based on general, more universal legal principles. As with offline methods of dispute resolution, any party may appeal to a court at any time.

NEGOTIATION AND MEDIATION SERVICES

The online negotiation of a dispute is generally simpler and more practical than litigation. Typically, one party files a complaint, and the other party is notified by e-mail. Password-protected access to the dispute-resolution service is possible twenty-four hours a day, seven days a week. Fees are generally low (often 2 to 4 percent, or less, of the disputed amount).

CyberSettle.com, Inc., clickNsettle.com, U.S. Settlement Corporation (ussettle.com), and other Web-based firms offer online forums for negotiating monetary settlements. The parties to a dispute may agree to submit offers; if the offers fall within a previously agreed-on range, they will end the dispute, and the parties will split the difference. Special software keeps secret any offers that are not within the range. If there is no agreed-on range, typically an offer includes a deadline within which the other party must respond before the offer expires. The parties can drop the negotiations at any time.

Mediation providers are also resolving disputes online. SquareTrade, for example, has provided mediation services for the online auction site eBay and also resolves disputes among other parties. SquareTrade uses Web-based software that walks participants through a five-step e-resolution process. Negotiation between the parties occurs on a secure page within SquareTrade's Web site. The parties may consult a mediator. The entire process takes as little as ten to fourteen days, and there is at present no fee unless the parties use a mediator.

ARBITRATION PROGRAMS

A number of organizations, including the American Arbitration Association, offer online arbitration programs. The Internet Corporation for Assigned Names and Numbers (ICANN), a nonprofit corporation that the federal government set up to oversee the distribution of domain names, has issued special rules for the resolution of domain name disputes.[19] ICANN has also authorized several organizations to arbitrate domain name disputes in accordance with ICANN's rules.

Resolution Forum, Inc. (RFI), a nonprofit organization associated with the Center for Legal Responsibility at South Texas College of Law, offers arbitration services through its CAN-WIN conferencing system. Using standard browser software and an RFI password, the parties to a dispute access an online conference room. When multiple parties are involved, private communications and breakout sessions with only some participants are possible via private messaging facilities. RFI also offers mediation services.

The Virtual Magistrate Project (VMAG) is affiliated with the American Arbitration Association, Chicago-Kent College of Law, Cyberspace Law Institute, National Center for Automated Information Research, and other organizations. VMAG offers arbitration for disputes involving users of online systems; victims of wrongful messages, postings, and files; and system operators subject to complaints or similar demands. VMAG also arbitrates intellectual property, personal property, real property, and tort disputes related to online contracts. The proceedings occur in a password-protected online newsgroup setting, and private e-mail among the participants is possible. A VMAG arbitrator's decision is issued in a written opinion. A party may appeal the outcome to a court.

SECTION 6 | International Dispute Resolution

Businesspersons who engage in international business transactions normally take special precautions to protect themselves in the event that a party with whom they are dealing in another country breaches an agreement. Often, parties to international contracts include special clauses in their contracts providing for how any disputes arising under the contracts will be resolved.

FORUM-SELECTION AND CHOICE-OF-LAW CLAUSES

As you will read in Chapter 20, parties to international contracts often include forum-selection and choice-of-law clauses. These clauses designate the jurisdiction (court or country) where any dispute arising under the contract will be litigated and the nation's law that will be applied. If no forum-selection and choice-of-law clauses have been included in an international contract, however, legal proceedings will be more complex

---

19. ICANN's Rules for Uniform Domain Name Dispute Resolution Policy are online at **http://www.icann.org/udrp/udrp-rules-24oct99.htm**. Domain names will be discussed in more detail in Chapter 8, in the context of trademark law.

and attended by much more uncertainty. For example, litigation may take place in two or more countries, with each country applying its own national law to the particular transactions.

Furthermore, even if a plaintiff wins a favorable judgment in a lawsuit litigated in the plaintiff's country, the defendant's country could refuse to enforce the court's judgment. As will be discussed in Chapter 52, for reasons of courtesy, the judgment may be enforced in the defendant's country, particularly if the defendant's country is the United States and the foreign court's decision is consistent with U.S. national law and policy. Other nations, however, may not be as accommodating as the United States, and the plaintiff may be left empty-handed.

ARBITRATION CLAUSES

Parties to international contracts often include arbitration clauses in their contracts that require a neutral third party to decide any contract disputes. In international arbitration proceedings, the third party may be a neutral entity (such as the International Chamber of Commerce), a panel of individuals representing both parties' interests, or some other group or organization. The United Nations Convention on the Recognition and Enforcement of Foreign Arbitral Awards[20]—which has been implemented in more than fifty countries, including the United States—assists in the enforcement of arbitration clauses, as do provisions in specific treaties among nations. The American Arbitration Association provides arbitration services for international as well as domestic disputes.

---

20. June 10, 1958, 21 U.S.T. 2517, T.I.A.S. No. 6997 (the "New York Convention").

REVIEWING COURTS AND ALTERNATIVE DISPUTE RESOLUTION

Stan Garner resides in Illinois and promotes boxing matches for SuperSports, Inc., an Illinois corporation. Garner created the concept of "Ages" promotion—a three-fight series of boxing matches pitting an older fighter (George Foreman) against a younger fighter, such as John Ruiz or Riddick Bowe. The concept included titles for each of the three fights ("Challenge of the Ages," "Battle of the Ages," and "Fight of the Ages"), as well as promotional epithets to characterize the two fighters ("the Foreman Factor"). Garner contacted George Foreman and his manager, who both reside in Texas, to sell the idea, and they arranged a meeting at Caesar's Palace in Las Vegas, Nevada. At some point in the negotiations, Foreman's manager signed a nondisclosure agreement prohibiting him from disclosing Garner's promotional concepts unless the parties signed a contract. Nevertheless, after negotiations between Garner and Foreman fell through, Foreman used Garner's "Battle of the Ages" concept to promote a subsequent fight. Garner filed a suit against Foreman and his manager in a federal district court located in Illinois, alleging breach of contract. Using the information presented in the chapter, answer the following questions.

1. | On what basis might the federal district court in Illinois exercise jurisdiction in this case?

2. | Does the federal district court have original or appellate jurisdiction?

3. | Suppose that Garner had filed his action in an Illinois state court. Could an Illinois state court exercise personal jurisdiction over Foreman or his manager? Why or why not?

4. | Assume that Garner had filed his action in a Nevada state court. Would that court have personal jurisdiction over Foreman or his manager? Why or why not?

5. | Now suppose that the federal district court in Illinois requires this dispute to be arbitrated prior to any trial on the matter. Explain whether this arbitration is likely to be legally binding on the parties.

TERMS AND CONCEPTS TO REVIEW

alternative dispute resolution (ADR) 40

American Arbitration Association (AAA) 46

arbitration 43

arbitration clause 43

award 43

bankruptcy court 33

concurrent jurisdiction 34

diversity of citizenship 34

docket 34

early neutral case evaluation 45

exclusive jurisdiction 34

federal question 34

in personam jurisdiction 31

in rem jurisdiction 31

judicial review 30

jurisdiction 31

justiciable controversy 38

litigation 40

long arm statute 31

mediation 42

mini-trial 45

negotiation 42

online dispute resolution (ODR) 46

probate court 33

question of fact 39

question of law 39

rule of four 40

small claims court 39

standing to sue 37

summary jury trial (SJT) 46

venue 36

writ of *certiorari* 40

 ## QUESTIONS AND CASE PROBLEMS

2–1. In an arbitration proceeding, the arbitrator need not be a judge or even a lawyer. How, then, can the arbitrator's decision have the force of law and be binding on the parties involved?

2–2. QUESTION WITH SAMPLE ANSWER

The defendant in a lawsuit is appealing the trial court's decision in favor of the plaintiff. On appeal, the defendant claims that the evidence presented at trial to support the plaintiff's claim was so scanty that no reasonable jury could have found for the plaintiff. Therefore, argues the defendant, the appellate court should reverse the trial court's decision. May an appellate court ever reverse a trial court's findings with respect to questions of fact? Discuss fully.

For a sample answer to this question, go to Appendix I at the end of this text.

2–3. Appellate courts normally see only written transcripts of trial proceedings when they are reviewing cases. Today, in some states, videotapes are being used as the official trial reports. If the use of videotapes as official reports continues, will this alter the appellate process? Should it? Discuss fully.

2–4. Marya Callais, a citizen of Florida, was walking one day near a busy street in Tallahassee, Florida, when a large crate flew off a passing truck and hit her, resulting in numerous injuries. She incurred a great deal of pain and suffering, plus significant medical expenses, and she could not work for six months. She wants to sue the trucking firm for $300,000 in damages. The firm's headquarters are in Georgia, although the company does business in Florida. In what court might Callais bring suit—a Florida state court, a Georgia state court, or a federal court? What factors might influence her decision?

2–5. STANDING. Blue Cross and Blue Shield insurance companies (the Blues) provide 68 million Americans with health-care financing. The Blues have paid billions of dollars for care attributable to illnesses related to tobacco use. In an attempt to recover some of this amount, the Blues filed a suit in a federal district court against tobacco companies and others, alleging fraud, among other things. The Blues claimed that beginning in 1953, the defendants conspired to addict millions of Americans, including members of Blue Cross plans, to cigarettes and other tobacco products. The conspiracy involved misrepresentation about the safety of nicotine and its addictive properties, marketing efforts targeting children, and agreements not to produce or market safer cigarettes. The defendants' success caused lung, throat, and other cancers, as well as heart disease, stroke, emphysema, and other illnesses. The defendants asked the court to dismiss the case on the ground that the plaintiffs did not have standing to sue. Do the Blues have standing in this case? Why or why not? [*Blue Cross and Blue Shield of New Jersey, Inc. v. Philip Morris, Inc.*, 36 F.Supp.2d 560 (E.D.N.Y. 1999)]

2-6. ARBITRATION. Alexander Little worked for Auto Stiegler, Inc., an automobile dealership in Los Angeles County, California, eventually becoming the service manager. While employed, Little signed an arbitration agreement that required the submission of all employment-related disputes to arbitration. The agreement also provided that any award over $50,000 could be appealed to a second arbitrator. Little was later demoted and terminated. Alleging that these actions were in retaliation for investigating and reporting warranty fraud and thus were in violation of public policy, Little filed a suit in a California state court against Auto Stiegler. The defendant filed a motion with the court to compel arbitration. Little responded that the arbitration agreement should not be enforced in part because the appeal provision was unfairly one sided. Is this provision enforceable? Should the court grant Auto Stiegler's motion? Why or why not? [*Little v. Auto Stiegler, Inc.*, 29 Cal.4th 1064, 63 P.3d 979, 130 Cal.Rptr.2d 892 (2003)]

2-7. **CASE PROBLEM WITH SAMPLE ANSWER**

Michael and Karla Covington live in Jefferson County, Idaho. When they bought their home, a gravel pit was across the street. In 1995, the county converted the pit to a landfill. Under the county's operation, the landfill accepted major appliances, household garbage, spilled grain, grass clippings, straw, manure, animal carcasses, containers with hazardous content warnings, leaking car batteries, and waste oil, among other things. The deposits were often left uncovered, attracting insects and other scavengers and contaminating the groundwater. Fires broke out, including at least one started by an intruder who entered the property through an unlocked gate. The Covingtons complained to the state, which inspected the landfill, but no changes were made to address their concerns. Finally, the Covingtons filed a suit in a federal district court against the county and the state, charging violations of federal environmental laws. Those laws were designed to minimize the risks of injuries from fires, scavengers, groundwater contamination, and other pollution dangers. Did the Covingtons have standing to sue? What principles apply? Explain. [*Covington v. Jefferson County*, 358 F.3d 626 (9th Cir. 2004)]

To view a sample answer for this case problem, go to this book's Web site at http://wbl.westbuslaw.com, select "Chapter 2," and click on "Case Problem with Sample Answer."

2-8. JURISDICTION. KaZaA BV was a company formed under the laws of the Netherlands. KaZaA distributed KaZaA Media Desktop (KMD) software, which enabled users to exchange, via a peer-to-peer transfer network, digital media, including movies and music. KaZaA also operated the KaZaA.com Web site, through which it distributed the KMD software to millions of

California residents and other users. Metro-Goldwyn-Mayer Studios, Inc., and other parties in the entertainment industries based in California filed a suit in a federal district court against KaZaA and others, alleging copyright infringement. KaZaA filed a counterclaim, but while legal action was pending, the firm passed its assets and its Web site to Sharman Networks, Ltd., a company organized under the laws of Vanuatu (an island republic east of Australia) and doing business principally in Australia. Sharman explicitly disclaimed the assumption of any of KaZaA's liabilities. When the plaintiffs added Sharman as a defendant, Sharman filed a motion to dismiss on the ground that the court did not have jurisdiction. Would it be fair to subject Sharman to suit in this case? Explain. [*Metro-Goldwyn-Mayer Studios, Inc. v. Grokster, Ltd.*, 243 F.Supp.2d.1073 (C.D.Cal. 2003)]

2-9. E-JURISDICTION. American Business Financial Services, Inc. (ABFI), a Pennsylvania firm, sells and services loans to businesses and consumers. First Union National Bank, with its principal place of business in North Carolina, provides banking services. Alan Boyer, an employee of First Union, lives in North Carolina and has never been to Pennsylvania. In the course of his employment, Boyer learned that the bank was going to extend a $150 million line of credit to ABFI. Boyer then attempted to manipulate the stock price of ABFI for personal gain by sending disparaging e-mails to ABFI's independent auditors in Pennsylvania. Boyer also posted negative statements about ABFI and its management on a Yahoo bulletin board. ABFI filed a suit in a Pennsylvania state court against Boyer, First Union, and others, alleging wrongful interference with a contractual relationship, among other things. Boyer filed a motion to dismiss the complaint for lack of personal jurisdiction. Could the court exercise jurisdiction over Boyer? Explain. [*American Business Financial Services, Inc. v. First Union National Bank*, __ A.2d __ (Pa.Comm.Pl. 2002)]

2-10. VIDEO QUESTION

Go to this text's Web site at http://wbl.westbuslaw.com and select "Chapter 2." Click on "Video Questions" and view the video titled *Jurisdiction in Cyberspace*. Then answer the following questions.

(a) What standard would a court apply to determine whether it has jurisdiction over the out-of-state computer firm in the video?

(b) What factors is a court likely to consider in assessing whether sufficient contacts existed when the only connection to the jurisdiction is through a Web site?

(c) How do you think the court would resolve the issue in this case?

LAW | on the Web

For updated links to resources available on the Web, as well as a variety of other materials, visit this text's Web site at http://wbl.westbuslaw.com.

For the decisions of the United States Supreme Court, as well as information about the Supreme Court, go to

http://supremecourtus.gov

Another Web site offering information about the United States Supreme Court, including information on the justices and links to opinions they have authored, can be accessed at

http://oyez.nwu.edu

The Web site for the federal courts offers information on the federal court system and links to all federal courts at

http://www.uscourts.gov

The National Center for State Courts (NCSC) offers links to the Web pages of all state courts. Go to

http://www.ncsconline.org

For information on alternative dispute resolution, go to the American Arbitration Association's Web site at

http://www.adr.org

To learn more about online dispute resolution, go to the following Web sites:

http://www.clicknsettle.com

http://www.cybersettle.com

http://www.SquareTrade.com

LEGAL RESEARCH EXERCISES ON THE WEB

Go to http://wbl.westbuslaw.com, the Web site that accompanies this text. Select "Chapter 2" and click on "Internet Exercises." There you will find the following Internet research exercises that you can perform to learn more about topics covered in this chapter.

Activity 2–1: **LEGAL PERSPECTIVE**
Alternative Dispute Resolution

Activity 2–2: **MANAGEMENT PERSPECTIVE**
Resolve a Dispute Online

Activity 2–3: **HISTORICAL PERSPECTIVE**
The Judiciary's Role in American Government

CHAPTER 3

Court Procedures

American and English courts follow the *adversarial system of justice*. Although clients are allowed to represent themselves in court (called *pro se* representation),[1] most parties to lawsuits hire attorneys to represent them. Each lawyer acts as his or her client's advocate, presenting the client's version of the facts in such a way as to convince the judge (or the judge and jury, in a jury trial) that this version is correct.

Most of the judicial procedures that you will read about in the following pages are rooted in the adversarial framework of the American legal system. In this chapter, after a brief overview of judicial procedures, we illustrate the steps involved in a lawsuit with a hypothetical civil case (criminal procedures will be discussed in Chapter 9).

SECTION 1 | Procedural Rules

The parties to a lawsuit must comply with the procedural rules of the court in which the lawsuit is filed. These rules specify what must be done at each stage of the litigation process. All civil trials held in federal district courts are governed by the **Federal Rules of Civil Procedure (FRCP).**[2] Each state also has rules of civil procedure that apply to all courts within that state. In addition, each court has its own local rules of procedure that supplement the federal or state rules.

Broadly speaking, the litigation process has three phases: pretrial, trial, and posttrial. Each phase involves specific procedures. Although civil lawsuits may vary greatly in terms of complexity, cost, and detail, they typically progress through the specific stages charted in Exhibit 3–1.

We now turn to our hypothetical civil case. The case arose from an automobile accident, which occurred when a car driven by Antonio Carvello, a resident of New Jersey, collided with a car driven by Jill Kirby, a resident of New York. The accident took place at an intersection in New York City. Kirby suffered personal injuries, which caused her to incur medical and hospital expenses as well as lost wages for four months. In all, she calculated that the cost to her of the accident was $100,000.[3] Carvello and Kirby have been unable to agree on a settlement, and Kirby now must decide whether to sue Carvello for the $100,000 compensation she feels she deserves.

SECTION 2 | Consulting with an Attorney

The first step taken by virtually anyone contemplating a lawsuit is to obtain the advice of a qualified attorney.[4] In the hypothetical Kirby-Carvello case, Kirby may consult with an attorney, who will advise her regarding what she can expect to gain from a lawsuit,

---

1. This right was definitively established in *Faretta v. California,* 422 U.S. 806, 95 S.Ct. 2525, 45 L.Ed.2d 562 (1975).

2. The United States Supreme Court has authority to set forth these rules as spelled out in 28 U.S.C. Sections 2071–2077. Generally, though, the federal judiciary appoints committees that make recommendations to the Supreme Court. The Court then publishes any proposed changes in the rules and allows for public comment before finalizing federal rules of civil procedure.

3. In this example, we are ignoring damages for pain and suffering or for permanent disabilities. Often, plaintiffs in personal-injury cases seek such damages.

4. See Chapter 42 for a discussion of the importance of obtaining legal counsel and for guidelines on how to locate attorneys and evaluate their services.

EXHIBIT 3-1 **Stages in a Typical Lawsuit**

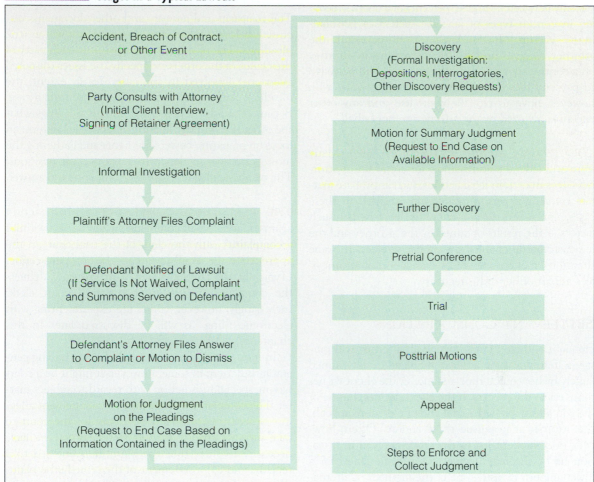

Accident, Breach of Contract, or Other Event

→

Party Consults with Attorney (Initial Client Interview, Signing of Retainer Agreement)

→

Informal Investigation

→

Plaintiff's Attorney Files Complaint

→

Defendant Notified of Lawsuit (If Service Is Not Waived, Complaint and Summons Served on Defendant)

→

Defendant's Attorney Files Answer to Complaint or Motion to Dismiss

→

Motion for Judgment on the Pleadings (Request to End Case Based on Information Contained in the Pleadings)

Discovery (Formal Investigation: Depositions, Interrogatories, Other Discovery Requests)

→

Motion for Summary Judgment (Request to End Case on Available Information)

→

Further Discovery

→

Pretrial Conference

→

Trial

→

Posttrial Motions

→

Appeal

→

Steps to Enforce and Collect Judgment

her probability of success if she sues, what procedures will be involved, and how long it may take to resolve the issue through the judicial process. Depending on the court hearing the case, the time costs of the litigation may be significant. Personal-injury cases may take two to three years to resolve, so this is an important factor for Kirby to consider.

LEGAL FEES

Another crucial factor that Kirby must consider is, of course, the cost of the attorney's time—the legal fees that she will have to pay in an attempt to collect damages from the defendant, Carvello. Attorneys base their fees on such factors as the difficulty of a matter, the amount of time involved, the experience and skill of the attorney in the particular area of the law, and

the cost of doing business. In the United States, legal fees range from $75 to $500 per hour or even higher (the average fee per hour is between $150 and $275). In addition, the client is also responsible for paying various expenses relating to the case (called "out-of-pocket" costs), including court filing fees, travel expenses, and the cost of expert witnesses and investigators, for example.

TYPES OF FEE ARRANGEMENTS For a particular legal matter, an attorney may charge one type of fee or a combination of several types. *Fixed fees* may be charged for the performance of such services as drafting a simple will. *Hourly fees* may be computed for matters that will involve an indeterminate period of time. Any case brought to trial, for example, may involve an expenditure of time that cannot be precisely estimated in advance. *Contingency fees* are fixed as a percentage (usually between 25 and 40 percent) of a client's recovery in certain types of lawsuits, such as a personal-injury lawsuit.[5] If the lawsuit is unsuccessful, the attorney receives no fee. If Kirby retains an attorney on a contingency-fee basis, she normally will not have to pay any fees unless she wins the case. (She will, however, have to pay the court fees and any other expenses incurred by the attorney on her behalf.)

COURTS CAN AWARD ATTORNEYS' FEES Many state and federal statutes allow for an award of attorneys' fees in certain legal actions, such as probate matters (settling a person's estate after death). In these cases, a judge sets the amount of the fee, based on such factors as the results obtained by the attorney and the fee customarily charged for similar services. In some situations, a client may receive an award of attorneys' fees as part of her or his recovery.

SETTLEMENT CONSIDERATIONS

Frequently, the extent to which an attorney will pursue a resolution of a legal problem is determined largely by how much time and money the client wishes to invest in the process. If the client decides that he or she can afford a lengthy trial and one or more appeals, the attorney may pursue those actions. Often, however, once a client learns the costs involved in litigation he or she may decide to settle the claim for a lower amount by using one of the methods of alternative dispute resolution discussed in Chapter 2, such as negotiation or mediation.

Another important factor in deciding whether to pursue litigation is the defendant's ability to pay the damages sought. Even if Kirby is awarded damages, it may be difficult to enforce the court's judgment. (We will discuss the problems involved in enforcing a judgment later in this chapter.)

SECTION 3 | Pretrial Procedures

The pretrial litigation process involves the filing of the *pleadings*, the gathering of evidence (called *discovery*), and possibly other procedures, such as a pretrial conference and jury selection.

THE PLEADINGS

The *complaint* and *answer* (and other documents discussed below), taken together, are known as the **pleadings.** The pleadings formally notify each party of the claims of the other and specify the issues (disputed questions) involved in the case. To an extent, the pleadings remove the element of surprise from a case. Because the attorneys learn from the pleadings what the other side will be claiming at trial, the lawyers can focus on preparing better arguments and gathering the most persuasive evidence to support their positions. The two basic pleadings are the complaint and answer.

THE PLAINTIFF'S COMPLAINT Kirby's action against Carvello will commence when her lawyer files a **complaint**[6] with the clerk of the trial court in the appropriate geographic area—the proper venue. (Typically, the lawyer or her or his assistant delivers the complaint in person to the trial court clerk. Increasingly, however, courts are experimenting with electronic filing, as will be discussed later in this chapter.)

In most states, the court would be one having general jurisdiction; in some, however, it might be a court having special jurisdiction with regard to subject matter. The complaint will contain (1) a statement alleging, or asserting, the facts necessary for the court to take jurisdiction; (2) a short statement of the facts necessary to show that the plaintiff is entitled to a remedy; and (3) a statement of the remedy the plaintiff is seeking. A typical complaint is shown in Exhibit 3–2.

The complaint will state that Kirby was driving her car through a green light at the specified intersection, exercising good driving habits and reasonable care, when Carvello negligently drove his vehicle through a red light and into the intersection from a cross street, striking Kirby's car and causing serious personal injury and property damage. The complaint will go on to state that Kirby is seeking $100,000 in damages. (Note that in some state civil actions, the amount of damages sought is not specified.)

—Service of Process. Before the court can exercise jurisdiction over the defendant (Carvello)—in effect, before the lawsuit can begin—the court must have proof that the defendant was notified of the

---

5. Note that attorneys may charge a contingency fee in only certain types of cases and are typically prohibited from entering this type of fee arrangement in criminal cases, divorce cases, and cases involving distribution of assets after death.

---

6. Sometimes, the document filed with the court is called a *petition* or a *declaration* instead of a complaint.

EXHIBIT 3-2 A Typical Complaint

IN THE UNITED STATES DISTRICT COURT
FOR THE SOUTHERN DISTRICT OF NEW YORK

CIVIL NO. 7-1047

JILL KIRBY

               Plaintiff,

v.

ANTONIO CARVELLO

               Defendant.

COMPLAINT

The plaintiff brings this cause of action against the defendant, alleging as follows:

1. This action is between the plaintiff, who is a resident of the State of New York, and the defendant, who is a resident of the State of New Jersey. There is diversity of citizenship between the parties.
2. The amount in controversy, exclusive of interest and costs, exceeds the sum of $75,000.
3. On September 10th, 2006, the plaintiff, Jill Kirby, was exercising good driving habits and reasonable care in driving her car through the intersection of Boardwalk and Pennsylvania Avenue, New York City, New York, when the defendant, Antonio Carvello, negligently drove his vehicle through a red light at the intersection and collided with the plaintiff's vehicle.
4. As a result of the collision, the plaintiff suffered severe physical injury, which prevented her from working, and property damage to her car.

WHEREFORE, the plaintiff demands judgment against the defendant for the sum of $100,000 plus interest at the maximum legal rate and the costs of this action.

By   *Joseph Roe*
      Joseph Roe
      Attorney for Plaintiff
      100 Main Street
      New York, New York

1/2/07

lawsuit. The process of notifying the defendant of a lawsuit is called **service of process.** Service of process involves serving the defendant with a summons and a copy of the complaint—that is, delivering these items to the defendant. The **summons** notifies defendant Carvello that he must answer the complaint within a specified time period (twenty days in the federal courts) or suffer a default judgment against him. A **default judgment** in Kirby's favor would mean that she would be awarded the damages alleged in her complaint because Carvello failed to respond to the allegations. A typical summons is shown in Exhibit 3–3.

—Method of Service. How service of process occurs depends on the rules of the court or jurisdiction in which the lawsuit is brought. Under the Federal Rules of Civil Procedure (FRCP), service of process in federal court cases may be effected by anyone who is not a party to the lawsuit and who is at least eighteen years of age. In state courts, the process server is often a county sheriff or an employee of an independent company that provides process service in the local area. Usually, the server effects the service by handing the summons to the defendant personally or by leaving it at the defendant's residence or place of business. In some states, a summons can be served by mail if the defendant so agrees. When the defendant cannot be reached, special rules provide alternative means of service; for example, leaving the summons with a designated person, such as the state's secretary of state, or publishing a notice in the local newspaper.

In the case discussed next, the issue was whether service of process could be accomplished via e-mail.

EXHIBIT 3–3   **A Typical Summons**

**UNITED STATES DISTRICT COURT
FOR THE SOUTHERN DISTRICT OF NEW YORK**

Jill Kirby	)	**Civil Action, File Number 7-1047**
Plaintiff,	)	
v.	)	*Summons*
Antonio Carvello	)	
Defendant.	)	

To the above-named Defendant:

You are hereby summoned and required to serve upon <u>Joseph Roe</u>, plaintiff's attorney, whose address is <u>100 Main Street, New York, New York</u>, an answer to the complaint which is herewith served upon you, within 20 days after service of this summons upon you, exclusive of the day of service. If you fail to do so, judgment by default will be taken against you for the relief demanded in the complaint.

<u>Samuel Raeburn</u>
CLERK

Mary Doakes

BY DEPUTY CLERK

<u>February 10, 2007</u>
DATE

CASE 3.1

Rio Properties, Inc. v. Rio International Interlink

United States
Court of Appeals,
Ninth Circuit. 2002.
284 F.3d 1007.

COMPANY PROFILE *Rio Properties, Inc., owns the Rio All Suite Casino Resort in Las Vegas, Nevada, the "Best Hotel Value in the World," according to* Travel and Leisure Magazine, *and the "Best Overall Hotel in Las Vegas," according to the* Zagat Survey of Resorts, Hotels, and Spas. *In addition to its hotel, Rio allows customers to wager on professional sports through the Rio Race & Sports Book. To protect its rights in the "Rio" name, Rio has registered numerous trademarks with the U.S. Patent and Trademark Office. When Rio sought to expand its presence onto the Internet, it registered the domain name playrio.com. At* http://www.playrio.com, *Rio operates a Web site that informs prospective customers about its hotel and accepts reservations.*

BACKGROUND AND FACTS *Rio International Interlink (RII) is a Costa Rican entity that participates in an Internet sports gambling operation, doing business as Rio International Sportsbook, Rio Online Sportsbook, or Rio International Sports, at* http://www.riosports.com, *RII grosses an estimated $3 million annually. When Rio became aware of RII's operation, Rio demanded that RII stop infringing Rio's trademark. RII disabled the "riosports" site but soon activated* http://www.betrio.com *to host an identical operation. Rio filed a suit in a federal district court against RII, alleging trademark infringement. To effect service of process, Rio attempted to locate RII, but its U.S. address housed only its international mail-forwarding service, which was not authorized to accept service on RII's behalf, and RII did not have an address in Costa Rica. RII advertised that it preferred communication through its e-mail address,* email@betrio.com, *Unable to serve RII by traditional means, Rio filed a motion for alternative service of process, asking the court for permission to serve RII via its e-mail address. The court granted the motion. When RII later failed to comply with the court's orders for discovery (discovery is discussed later in this chapter), the court entered a default judgment against RII. RII appealed to the U.S. Court of Appeals for the Ninth Circuit, alleging in part that the service of process was insufficient.*

IN THE LANGUAGE OF THE COURT

TROTT, Circuit Judge.

* * * *

* * * [W]e turn to the district court's order authorizing service of process on RII by e-mail at *email@betrio.com*. We acknowledge that we tread upon untrodden ground. The parties cite no authority condoning service of process over the Internet or via e-mail, and our own investigation has unearthed no decisions by the United States Courts of Appeals dealing with service of process by e-mail * * * . Despite this dearth of authority, however, we do not labor long in reaching our decision. Considering the facts presented by this case, we conclude not only that service of process by e-mail was proper—that is, reasonably calculated to apprise [inform] RII of the * * * action and afford it an opportunity to respond— but in this case, it was the method of service most likely to reach RII.

To be sure, *the Constitution does not require any particular means of service of process, only that the method selected be reasonably calculated to provide notice and an opportunity to respond.* In proper circumstances, this broad constitutional principle unshackles the federal courts from anachronistic [outdated] methods of service and permits them entry into the technological renaissance. * * * Electronic communication via satellite can and does provide instantaneous transmission of notice and information. No longer must process be mailed to a defendant's door when he can receive complete notice at an electronic terminal inside his very office, even when the door is steel and bolted shut. * * * [Emphasis added.]

Although communication via e-mail and over the Internet is comparatively new, such communication has been zealously embraced within the business community. RII particularly has embraced the modern e-business model and profited immensely from it. In fact, RII structured its business such that it could be contacted *only* via its e-mail address. RII listed no easily discoverable street address in the United States or in Costa Rica. Rather, on its website and print media, RII designated its e-mail address as its preferred contact information.

CONTINUED ▶

CASE 3.1 | Continued

* * * In addition, e-mail was the only court-ordered method of service aimed directly and instantly at RII * * * . Indeed, when faced with an international e-business scofflaw [habitual violator], playing hide-and-seek with the federal court, e-mail may be the only means of effecting service of process. Certainly in this case, it was a means reasonably calculated to apprise RII of * * * the lawsuit, and the Constitution requires nothing more.

DECISION AND REMEDY *The U.S. Court of Appeals for the Ninth Circuit upheld the lower court's order for service of process via e-mail. Because RII did not have an address in the United States or Costa Rica where service could be accomplished through traditional means, and RII advertised that it preferred contact through its e-mail address, service by e-mail was proper.*

—*Serving Corporate Defendants.* In cases involving corporate defendants, the summons and complaint may be served on an officer or on a *registered agent* (representative) of the corporation. The name of a corporation's registered agent can usually be obtained from the secretary of state's office in the state where the company incorporated its business (and, frequently, from the secretary of state's office in any state where the corporation does business).

—*Waiver of Formal Service of Process.* In many instances, the defendant is already aware that a lawsuit is being filed and is willing to waive (give up) her or his right to be served personally. The FRCP and many states' rules allow defendants to waive formal service of process, provided that certain procedures are followed. Kirby's attorney, for example, could mail to defendant Carvello a copy of the complaint, along with "Waiver of Service of Summons" forms for Carvello to sign. If Carvello signs and returns the forms within thirty days, formal service of process is waived. Moreover, under the FRCP, defendants who agree to waive formal service of process receive additional time to respond to the complaint (sixty days, instead of twenty days). Some states provide similar incentives to encourage defendants to waive formal service of process and thereby reduce associated costs and foster cooperation between the parties.

THE DEFENDANT'S RESPONSE Typically, the defendant's response to the complaint takes the form of an **answer.** In an answer, the defendant either admits or denies each of the allegations in the plaintiff's complaint and may also set forth any defenses to those allegations. Under the federal rules, any allegations that are not denied by the defendant will be deemed by the court to have been admitted. If Carvello admits to all of Kirby's allegations in his answer, a judgment will be entered for Kirby. If

Carvello denies Kirby's allegations, the matter will proceed further.

—*Affirmative Defenses.* Carvello can also admit the truth of Kirby's complaint but raise new facts to show that he should not be held liable for Kirby's damages. This is called raising an **affirmative defense.** As will be discussed in subsequent chapters, defendants in both civil and criminal cases can raise affirmative defenses. For example, a defendant accused of physically harming another might claim that he or she acted in self-defense. A defendant charged with breach of contract might defend on the ground (legal basis) of mistake or the fact that the contract was oral when it was required by law to be in writing. In the Kirby-Carvello case, assume that Carvello has obtained evidence that Kirby was not exercising good driving habits at the time the accident occurred (she was looking at a child in the backseat of her car instead of watching the road). Carvello could assert Kirby's own negligence as a defense. In some states, a plaintiff's contributory negligence operates as a complete defense. In most states, however, the plaintiff's own negligence constitutes only a partial defense (see Chapter 7).

—*Counterclaims.* Carvello could also deny Kirby's allegations and set forth his own claim that the accident occurred as a result of Kirby's negligence and that therefore Kirby owes Carvello money for damages to his car. This is appropriately called a **counterclaim.** If Carvello files a counterclaim, Kirby will have to submit an answer to the counterclaim.

DISMISSALS AND JUDGMENTS BEFORE TRIAL

Many actions for which pleadings have been filed never come to trial. The parties may, for example, negotiate a settlement of the dispute at any stage of the litigation process. There are also numerous procedural avenues for disposing of a case without a trial. Many of them involve one or the other party's attempts to get the case dismissed through the use of various motions.

A **motion** is a procedural request submitted to the court by an attorney on behalf of her or his client. When one party files a motion with the court, that party must also send to, or serve on, the opposing party a *notice of motion*. The notice of motion informs the opposing party that the motion has been filed. **Pretrial motions** include the motion to dismiss, the motion for judgment on the pleadings, and the motion for summary judgment, as well as the other motions listed in Exhibit 3–4.

MOTION TO DISMISS   Either party can file a **motion to dismiss** requesting the court to dismiss the case for the reasons provided in the motion. A defendant could file a motion to dismiss if the plaintiff's complaint fails to state a claim for which relief (a remedy)

EXHIBIT 3-4 Pretrial Motions

MOTION TO DISMISS

A motion normally filed by the defendant in which the defendant asks the court to dismiss the case for a specified reason, such as improper service, lack of personal jurisdiction, or the plaintiff's failure to state a claim for which relief can be granted.

MOTION TO STRIKE

A motion filed by the defendant in which the defendant asks the court to strike (delete) from the complaint certain paragraphs contained in the complaint. Motions to strike help to clarify the underlying issues that form the basis for the complaint by removing paragraphs that are redundant or irrelevant to the action.

MOTION TO MAKE MORE DEFINITE AND CERTAIN

A motion filed by the defendant to compel the plaintiff to clarify the basis of the plaintiff's cause of action. The motion is filed when the defendant believes that the complaint is too vague or ambiguous for the defendant to respond to it in a meaningful way.

MOTION FOR JUDGMENT ON THE PLEADINGS

A motion that may be filed by either party in which the party asks the court to enter a judgment in his or her favor based on information contained in the pleadings. A judgment on the pleadings will only be made if there are no facts in dispute and the only question is how the law applies to a set of undisputed facts.

MOTION TO COMPEL DISCOVERY

A motion that may be filed by either party in which the party asks the court to compel the other party to comply with a discovery request. If a party refuses to allow the opponent to inspect and copy certain documents, for example, the party requesting the documents may make a motion to compel production of those documents.

MOTION FOR SUMMARY JUDGMENT

A motion that may be filed by either party in which the party asks the court to enter judgment in his or her favor without a trial. Unlike a motion for judgment on the pleadings, a motion for summary judgment can be supported by evidence outside the pleadings, such as witnesses' affidavits, answers to interrogatories, and other evidence obtained prior to or during discovery.

can be granted. Such a motion asserts that even if the facts alleged in the complaint are true, they do not give rise to any legal claim against the defendant. If, for example, the allegations in Kirby's complaint do not amount to negligence on Carvello's part, Carvello could move to dismiss the case for failure to state a claim. Defendant Carvello could also file a motion to dismiss if he believed that he had not been properly served, that the complaint had been filed in the wrong court (for example, that the court lacked personal or subject-matter jurisdiction or that the venue was improper), or for other specific reasons.

Often, instead of filing an answer with the court, a defendant files a motion to dismiss. If the court denies the motion, the defendant generally is given an extension of time to file an answer. If the defendant fails to file the appropriate pleading, a judgment will normally be entered for the plaintiff. If the court grants the motion to dismiss, the defendant is not required to answer the complaint, and the plaintiff generally is given time to file an amended complaint. If the plaintiff does not file this amended complaint, a judgment will be entered against the plaintiff, and the plaintiff will not be allowed to bring suit on the matter again. The court can also dismiss a case on its own motion.

MOTION FOR JUDGMENT ON THE PLEADINGS

After the pleadings are closed—after the complaint, answer, and any other pleadings have been filed—either of the parties can file a **motion for judgment on the pleadings.** This motion may be filed when it appears from the pleadings that the plaintiff has failed to state a cause of action for which relief may be granted. The motion will only be granted when the pleadings indicate that no facts are in dispute and the only question is how the law applies to a set of agreed-on facts. For example, assume for a moment that in the Kirby-Carvello case, defendant Carvello admitted to all of Kirby's allegations in his answer and raised no affirmative defenses. In this situation, Kirby would file a motion for judgment on the pleadings in her favor.

The difference between this motion and a motion for summary judgment, discussed next, is that with a motion for a judgment on the pleadings, a court may consider only what is contained in the pleadings. In a motion for summary judgment, in contrast, the court may also consider sworn statements and other materials that would be admissible as evidence at trial.

MOTION FOR SUMMARY JUDGMENT A **motion for summary judgment** is similar to a motion for

judgment on the pleadings in that the party filing the motion is asking the court to grant a judgment in that party's favor without a trial. As with a motion for judgment on the pleadings, a court will grant a motion for summary judgment only if it determines that no facts are in dispute and the only question is how the law applies to the facts. A motion for summary judgment can be made before or during a trial, but it will be granted only if, when the evidence is viewed in the light most favorable to the other party, there clearly are no factual disputes in contention.

To support a motion for summary judgment, one party can submit evidence obtained at any point prior to trial (including during the discovery stage of litigation—to be discussed next) that refutes the other party's factual claim. The evidence may consist of **affidavits** (sworn statements by parties or witnesses), as well as documents, such as a contract. Of course, the evidence must be *admissible* evidence—that is, evidence that the court would allow to be presented during the trial. If Carvello, for example, had an affidavit from a city official that the stoplight was not working when he drove through the intersection, he could submit that as evidence with a motion for summary judgment. As mentioned, the use of additional evidence is one feature that distinguishes the motion for summary judgment from the motion to dismiss and the motion for judgment on the pleadings.

DISCOVERY

Before a trial begins, the parties can use a number of procedural devices to obtain information and gather evidence about the case. Kirby, for example, will want to know how fast Carvello was driving, whether he had been drinking or was under the influence of any medication, and whether he was wearing corrective lenses if he was required by law to do so while driving. The process of obtaining information from the opposing party or from witnesses prior to trial is known as **discovery.** Discovery includes gaining access to witnesses, documents, records, and other types of evidence.

The Federal Rules of Civil Procedure and similar state rules set forth the guidelines for discovery activity. The rules governing discovery are designed to make sure that a witness or a party is not unduly harassed, that privileged material is safeguarded, and that only information relevant to the case at hand—or likely to lead to the discovery of relevant information—is discoverable.

Discovery prevents surprises at trial by giving both parties access to evidence that might otherwise be hidden. This allows the litigants to learn as much as they can about what to expect at a trial before they reach the courtroom. Discovery also serves to narrow the issues so that trial time is spent on the main questions in the case.

DEPOSITIONS AND INTERROGATORIES   At a minimum, discovery involves the use of depositions, interrogatories, or both. A **deposition** is sworn testimony by a party to the lawsuit or by any witness, recorded by an authorized court official. The person deposed gives testimony and answers questions asked by the attorneys from both sides. The questions and answers are recorded, sworn to, and signed. These answers, of course, will help the attorneys prepare their cases. Depositions also give attorneys the opportunity to evaluate how their witnesses will conduct themselves at trial. In addition, depositions can be employed in court to impeach (challenge the credibility of) a party

or a witness who changes testimony at the trial. A deposition can also be used as testimony if the witness is not available at trial.

Interrogatories are written questions for which written answers are prepared and then signed under oath. The main difference between interrogatories and written depositions is that interrogatories are directed to a party to the lawsuit (the plaintiff or the defendant), not to a witness, and the party can prepare answers with the aid of an attorney. Whereas depositions are useful for eliciting candid responses from a party and answers not prepared in advance, interrogatories are designed to obtain accurate information about specific topics, such as, for example, how many contracts were signed, and when. The scope of interrogatories is also broader because parties are obligated to answer questions, even if it means disclosing information from their records and files.

What can a court do when a party refuses to respond to a discovery request? The following case illustrates the options.

| CASE 3.2 | Computer Task Group, Inc. v. Brotby |

United States
Court of Appeals,
Ninth Circuit, 2004.
364 F.3d 1112.

BACKGROUND AND FACTS *Computer Task Group, Inc. (CTG), hired William Brotby as an information technologies consultant in 1995. As a condition of the job, Brotby signed an agreement that restricted his ability to work for CTG's customers if he left CTG. Less than two years later, Brotby left CTG to work for Alyeska Pipeline Service Company, a CTG client for whom Brotby had contributed on a project. CTG filed a suit in a federal district court against Brotby, alleging a breach of the agreement that Brotby had signed when he joined the firm. During discovery, Brotby refused to fully respond to CTG's interrogatories. He gave contradictory answers, made frivolous objections, filed baseless motions with the court, and never disclosed all of the information that CTG sought. He made excuses and changed his story repeatedly, making it impossible for CTG to establish basic facts with any certainty. Brotby also refused to produce key documents. The court issued five separate orders compelling Brotby's cooperation and fined him twice. Finally, in 1999, CTG filed a motion to enter a default judgment against Brotby, based on his failure to cooperate. The court granted the motion. Brotby appealed to the U.S. Court of Appeals for the Ninth Circuit.*

IN THE LANGUAGE OF THE COURT

PER CURIAM [By the whole court].
* * * *

Federal Rule of Civil Procedure 37 permits the district court, in its discretion, to enter a default judgment against a party who fails to comply with an order compelling discovery. * * *

In deciding whether a sanction of dismissal or default for noncompliance with discovery is appropriate, the district court must weigh five factors: (1) the public's interest in expeditious [speedy] resolution of litigation; (2) the court's need to manage its docket [calendar]; (3) the risk of prejudice to the opposing party; (4) the public policy favoring disposition of cases on their merits; and (5) the availability of less drastic sanctions. Where a court order is violated, the first and second factors will favor sanctions and the fourth will cut against them. Therefore, whether terminating sanctions were appropriate in Brotby's case turns on the third and fifth factors.

CONTINUED ▶

CASE 3.2 | Continued

* * * Brotby engaged in a consistent, intentional, and prejudicial practice of obstructing discovery by not complying * * * with repeated court orders and not heeding multiple court warnings. Brotby violated court orders * * * by failing to provide clear answers to interrogatories, giving contradictory responses, making frivolous objections, filing frivolous motions and failing to provide the information CTG sought. He also failed to pay one of the [fines]. * * * Brotby violated orders * * * by failing to produce important financial documents and throwing up a series of baseless smoke screens that took the form of repeated groundless objections and contradictory excuses, which were absurd and completely unbelievable. The excuses included blaming the loss of documents on an earthquake, on a dropped computer and on a residential move. * * *

* * * [W]hatever Brotby actually produced was mostly incomplete or fabricated—and dribbled in only after a court order. In addition, Brotby changed his story numerous times with regard to his income from work done for Alyeska and the length of his contract with them, as well as the date of his resignation from CTG. These tactics unnecessarily delayed the litigation, burdened the court and prejudiced CTG. In the end, most of the documents CTG sought regarding the nature and extent of Brotby's work for Alyeska were never produced, despite court orders to do so * * * .

* * * *

* * * Brotby's baseless two-year fight against each and every discovery request and court order has been conducted willfully and with the intent of preventing meaningful discovery from occurring. It has clogged the Court's docket, protracted this litigation by years, and made it impossible for CTG to proceed to any imaginably fair trial.

We have held that failure to produce documents as ordered * * * is * * * sufficient prejudice. * * *

In deciding whether the district court adequately considered lesser sanctions, we consider whether the court (1) explicitly discussed the alternative of lesser sanctions and explained why it would be inappropriate; (2) implemented lesser sanctions before ordering the case dismissed; and (3) warned the offending party of the possibility of dismissal.

The [district court] judge appropriately considered the alternative of lesser sanctions. He ordered Brotby to comply with CTG's discovery requests five times * * * . The [judge] also imposed two lesser (monetary) sanctions against Brotby, but to no avail. * * * [I]t is appropriate to reject lesser sanctions where the court anticipates continued deceptive misconduct. *Brotby had sufficient notice that continued refusal to cooperate would lead to [the entry of a default judgment against him].* The * * * judge warned him that he should "stop playing games" if he wanted to stay in the game. The two monetary sanctions, five orders compelling him to cooperate and repeated oral warnings were enough to put Brotby on notice that continued failure to cooperate in discovery would result in * * * default. [Emphasis added.]

DECISION AND REMEDY *The U.S. Court of Appeals for the Ninth Circuit affirmed the judgment of the lower court. The appellate court held that "[i]n light of Brotby's egregious [horribly bad] record of discovery abuses" and his "abiding contempt and continuing disregard for [the court's] orders," the lower court properly exercised its discretion in entering a default judgment against him.*

WHAT IF THE FACTS WERE DIFFERENT? *Suppose that Brotby had not made frivolous objections and baseless motions but still had failed to comply with discovery requests. How might the court's ruling in this case have been different?*

REQUESTS FOR ADMISSIONS One party can serve the other party with a written request for an admission of the truth of matters relating to the trial. Any fact admitted under such a request is conclusively established as true for the trial. For example, Kirby can ask Carvello to admit that his driver's license was suspended at the time of the accident. A request for admission shortens the trial because the parties will not have to spend time proving facts on which they already agree.

REQUESTS FOR DOCUMENTS, OBJECTS, AND ENTRY UPON LAND A party can gain access to documents and other items not in her or his possession in order to inspect and examine them. Likewise, a party can gain "entry upon land" to inspect the premises. Carvello, for example, can gain permission to inspect and copy Kirby's car repair bills.

REQUEST FOR EXAMINATIONS When the physical or mental condition of one party is in question, the opposing party can ask the court to order a physical or mental examination by an independent examiner. If the court agrees to make the order, the opposing party can obtain the results of the examination. Note that the court will make such an order only when the need for the information outweighs the right to privacy of the person to be examined.

ELECTRONIC DISCOVERY Any relevant material, including information stored electronically, can be the object of a discovery request. Electronic evidence, or **e-evidence,** consists of all computer-generated or electronically recorded information, such as e-mail, voice mail, spreadsheets, word-processing documents, and other data. E-evidence can reveal significant facts that are not discoverable by other means. For example, whenever a person is working on a computer, information is being recorded on the hard disk without ever being saved by the user. This information includes the file's location, path, creator, date created, date last accessed, concealed notes, earlier versions, passwords, and formatting. It reveals information about how, when, and by whom a document was created, accessed, modified, and transmitted. This information can only be obtained from the file in its electronic format—not from printed-out versions.

The federal rules and most state rules (as well as court decisions) now specifically allow individuals to obtain discovery of electronic "data compilations" (or e-evidence). Although traditional means, such as interrogatories and depositions, may still be employed to find out whether e-evidence exists, the parties must usually hire an expert to retrieve the evidence in its electronic format. Using special software, the expert can reconstruct e-mail exchanges to establish who knew what and when they knew it. The expert can even recover files that the user thought had been deleted from the computer. Reviewing back-up copies of documents and e-mail provides useful—and often quite damaging—information about how a particular matter progressed over several weeks or months.

Electronic discovery has significant advantages, but it is also time consuming and expensive. Who should pay the costs associated with electronic discovery? For a discussion of this issue, see the *Contemporary Legal Debates* feature on pages 64 and 65.

PRETRIAL CONFERENCE

After discovery has taken place and before the trial begins, the attorneys may meet with the trial judge in a **pretrial conference.** The purpose of this conference is to clarify the issues that remain in dispute after discovery has taken place and to explore the possibility of settling the conflict without a trial. If a settlement is not possible at this time, the parties and the judge discuss the manner in which the trial will be conducted. In particular, the parties may attempt to establish ground rules to restrict the number of expert witnesses or the admissibility of certain types of evidence, for example. Once the pretrial conference concludes, both parties must turn their attention to the trial itself and, if the trial is to be a jury trial, to the selection of jurors who will hear the case.

THE RIGHT TO A JURY TRIAL

The Seventh Amendment to the U.S. Constitution guarantees the right to a jury trial for cases at law in federal courts when the amount in controversy exceeds $20. Most states have similar guarantees in their own constitutions, although many states set a higher minimum. For example, Iowa requires the dollar amount of damages to be at least $1,000 before there is a right to a jury trial. The right to a trial by jury need not be exercised, and many cases are tried without a jury. If there is no jury, the judge determines the truth of the facts alleged in the case. In most states and in federal courts, one of the parties must request a jury, or the judge presumes the parties waive this right.

JURY SELECTION

Prior to the commencement of any jury trial, a panel of jurors must be assembled. The clerk of the court will usually notify local residents by mail that they have been selected for jury duty. These prospective jurors are chosen in various ways, but often the court clerk selects names at random from lists of registered voters or lists of persons to whom the state has issued driver's licenses. These individuals then report to the courthouse on the date specified in the notice. There they are gathered into a single pool of jurors, and the process of selecting those jurors who will actually hear the case begins. Although some types of trials require twelve-person juries, most civil matters can be heard by six-person juries.

CONTEMPORARY LEGAL DEBATES

Who Bears the Costs of Electronic Discovery?

Generally, the party responding to a discovery request must pay the expenses involved in obtaining the requested materials. A court can limit the scope of the request or shift some of the cost to the requesting party, however, if compliance would be too burdensome or the cost would be too great. One matter that has become the subject of much debate today is how these traditional rules governing discovery will apply to requests for electronic evidence.

WHY COURTS MIGHT SHIFT THE COSTS OF ELECTRONIC DISCOVERY

Electronic discovery (e-discovery) has dramatically increased the costs associated with complying with discovery requests. It is no longer simply a matter of photocopying paper documents. Now the responding party may need to hire computer forensics experts to make "image" copies of desktop, laptop, and server hard drives, as well as removable storage media (including CD-ROMs, DVDs, and Zip drives), back-up tapes, voice mail, cell phones, and any other device that digitally stores data.

In cases that involve multiple parties or large corporations with many offices and employees, the e-discovery process can easily run into hundreds of thousands of dollars, if not more. For example, in one case concert promoters alleged that thirty separate defendant companies had engaged in discriminatory practices. The federal district court hearing the case found that the complete restoration of the back-up tapes of just one of

those defendants would cost $9.75 million. Acquiring 200,000 e-mail messages from another defendant would cost between $43,000 and $84,000, with an additional $247,000 to have an attorney review the retrieved documents. Restoring the 523 back-up tapes of a third defendant would cost $395,000, and $120,000 for the attorney to review them. The judge hearing the case decided that both plaintiffs and defendants would share in these discovery costs.[a]

WHAT FACTORS DO COURTS CONSIDER IN DECIDING WHETHER TO SHIFT COSTS?

Increasingly, courts are shifting part of the costs of obtaining e-discovery to the party requesting it (which is usually the plaintiff). At what point, however, should this cost-shifting occur? In *Zubulake v. UBS Warburg LLC,*[b] the court set forth a three-step analysis for deciding disputes over discovery costs.

1. If the data are kept in an accessible format, the usual rules of discovery apply: the responding party should pay the costs of producing responsive data. A court should consider cost-shifting *only* when electronic data are relatively inaccessible, such as in back-up tapes or deleted files.

2. The court should determine what data may be found on the inaccessible media. Requiring the responding party to

a. *Rowe Entertainment, Inc. v. William Morris Agency,* 2002 WL 975713 (S.D.N.Y. 2002).
b. 2003 WL 21087884 (S.D.N.Y. 2003).

VOIR DIRE The process by which the jury is selected is known as ***voir dire.***[7] In most jurisdictions, *voir dire* consists of oral questions that attorneys for the plaintiff and the defendant ask a group of prospective jurors to determine whether a potential juror is biased or has any connection with a party to the action or with a prospective witness. Usually, jurors are questioned one at a time, although when large numbers of jurors are involved, the attorneys may direct their questions to groups of jurors instead to minimize the amount of time spent in jury selection. Sometimes, jurors are

asked to fill out written questionnaires. Some trial attorneys use psychologists and other professionals to help them select jurors.

CHALLENGES DURING VOIR DIRE During *voir dire,* a party may challenge a certain number of prospective jurors *peremptorily*—that is, ask that these individuals not be sworn in as jurors without providing any reason for excluding them. The total number of peremptory challenges allowed each side is determined by statute or by the court. Furthermore, a party may challenge any juror *for cause*—that is, provide a reason why an individual should not be sworn in as a juror. If the judge grants the challenge, the individual is asked to step down. A prospective juror, however, may not be

7. Pronounced *vwahr deehr.* These old French verbs mean "to speak the truth." In legal language, the phrase refers to the process of questioning jurors to learn about their backgrounds, attitudes, and similar attributes.

RM A MORE PERFECT UNION   ESTABLISH JUSTICE   INSURE DOMESTIC TRANQUILITY   PROMOTE THE GENERAL WELFARE

onal
t Law
uffery

Jurisdiction Internet Electronic
Free Speech Prenuptial Filing
Agreements
Advice of
Counsel

Issues Internet Sales
Contracts and the
over Commerce
War Clause
on Privacy
Terror
Debate
AIDS

Private Who Owns the Engagement Ring?
Enforceability
Forum-Selection Clauses Developments
Using "Takings"
Internet

PATRIOT
ACT

Exclusive Territorial Righ
Environmenta
Takings
Commer

restore and produce responsive documents from a small sample of the requested medium is a sensible approach in most cases.

3. The court should consider a series of other factors, including, for example, the availability of the information from other sources, the total cost of production compared to the amount in controversy, and each party's ability to pay these costs.

Other courts, however, have declined to follow the *Zubulake* court's approach.[c]

PROPOSED CHANGES TO THE FEDERAL RULES OF CIVIL PROCEDURE

After five years of study, an advisory committee working for the federal judiciary has proposed changing the Federal Rules of Civil Procedure (FRCP) to better accommodate e-discovery. According to the committee, the enormous volume of electronic data, coupled with increasingly frequent requests for electronic evidence, or e-evidence, make this form of discovery more burdensome, costly, and time consuming than traditional discovery. The committee has therefore proposed that the parties only be required to provide electronic data that are "reasonably accessible." In addition, the committee recommends a "safe harbor" that would shield parties from

---

c. See, for example, *Toshiba America Electronic Components, Inc. v. Superior Court*, 124 Cal.App.4th 762, 21 Cal.Rptr.3d 532 (2004).

sanctions for failing to provide e-evidence as long as they have taken "reasonable steps to preserve the information" that they knew was discoverable.

Critics claim that the proposed new rules will allow more leeway to parties responding to e-discovery requests because they will only be penalized if they *willfully* fail to preserve e-evidence. (The current rules, in contrast, penalize even inadvertent destruction of evidence.) Many argue that the new rules simply are not necessary and that courts can do a better job of controlling the costs of e-discovery on a case-by-case basis.

WHERE DO YOU STAND?

As just discussed, the courts are still debating who should bear the costs of e-discovery. The federal judiciary has proposed changes to the FRCP that may decrease the burden on the responding party—the party who is asked to produce the e-evidence—by allowing it to produce only data that are "reasonably accessible." Should discovery of e-evidence be treated differently than other types of discovery just because it is more expensive? Should there be one rule establishing who pays the costs of e-discovery in all cases, or should the court determine who should bear the expense of providing e-evidence on a case-by-case basis? At what point, if ever, should the costs of producing e-discovery be shifted to the requesting party?

---

excluded by the use of discriminatory challenges, such as those based on racial criteria[8] or gender.[9] Of course, *proving* that a particular challenge is discriminatory can be difficult because an attorney may give another reason for the challenge even though the underlying basis may be discriminatory.

After both sides have completed their challenges, those jurors who have been excused will be permitted

to leave. The remaining jurors—those who have been found acceptable by the attorneys for both sides—will be seated in the jury box.

ALTERNATE JURORS Because unforeseeable circumstances or illness may necessitate that one or more of the sitting jurors be dismissed, the court, depending on the rules of the particular jurisdiction and the expected length of the trial, may choose to have up to three alternate jurors present throughout the trial. If a juror has to be excused in the middle of the trial, then an alternate may take his or her place without disrupting the proceedings. Once the jury members are seated, the judge will swear in the jury members, and the trial itself can begin.

---

8. *Batson v. Kentucky*, 476 U.S. 79, 106 S.Ct. 1712, 90 L.Ed.2d 69 (1986).

9. *J.E.B. v. Alabama ex rel. T.B.*, 511 U.S. 127, 114 S.Ct. 1419, 128 L.Ed.2d 89 (1994). (*Ex rel.* is an abbreviation of the Latin *ex relatione*. The phrase refers to an action brought on behalf of the state, by the attorney general, at the instigation of an individual who has a private interest in the matter.)

CONCEPT SUMMARY 3.1 | Pretrial Procedures

PROCEDURE	DESCRIPTION
PLEADINGS	1. *The plaintiff's complaint*—The plaintiff's statement of the cause of action and the parties involved, filed with the court by the plaintiff's attorney. After the filing, the defendant is notified of the suit through service of process. 2. *The defendant's response*—The defendant's response to the plaintiff's complaint may take the form of an answer, in which the defendant may admit to or deny the plaintiff's allegations. The defendant may raise an affirmative defense and/or assert a counterclaim.
PRETRIAL MOTIONS	1. *Motion to dismiss*—A motion requesting the judge to dismiss the case for reasons that are provided in the motion (such as failure to state a claim for which relief can be granted). 2. *Motion for judgment on the pleadings*—May be made by either party; will be granted only if no facts are in dispute and only questions of law are at issue. 3. *Motion for summary judgment*—May be made by either party; will be granted only if no facts are in dispute and only questions of law are at issue. Unlike the motion for judgment on the pleadings, the motion for summary judgment may be supported by evidence outside the pleadings, such as testimony and other evidence obtained during the discovery phase of litigation.
DISCOVERY	The process of gathering evidence concerning the case; involves (1) *depositions* (sworn testimony by either party or any witness); (2) *interrogatories* (in which parties to the action write answers to questions with the aid of their attorneys); and (3) requests for admissions, documents, examinations, or other information relating to the case.
PRETRIAL CONFERENCE	A pretrial hearing, at the request of either party or the court, to identify the matters in dispute after discovery has taken place and to explore the possibility of settling the dispute without a trial. If no settlement is possible, the parties plan the course of the trial.
JURY SELECTION	In a jury trial, the selection of members of the jury from a pool of prospective jurors. During a process known as *voir dire*, the attorneys for both sides may challenge prospective jurors either for cause or peremptorily (for no cause).

SECTION 4 | The Trial

Various rules and procedures govern the trial phase of the litigation process. There are rules governing what kind of evidence will or will not be admitted during the trial, as well as specific procedures that the participants in the lawsuit must follow.

RULES OF EVIDENCE

Whether evidence will be admitted in court is determined by the **rules of evidence**—a series of rules that have been created by the courts to ensure that any evidence presented during a trial is fair and reliable. The Federal Rules of Evidence govern the admissibility of evidence in federal courts.

EVIDENCE MUST BE RELEVANT TO THE ISSUES

Evidence will not be admitted in court unless it is relevant to the matter in question. **Relevant evidence** is evidence that tends to prove or disprove a fact in question or to establish the degree of probability of a fact or action. For example, evidence that a suspect's gun was in the home of another person when a victim was shot would be relevant—because it would tend to prove that the suspect did not shoot the victim.

Even relevant evidence may not be admitted in court if its reliability is questionable or if its probative (proving) value is substantially outweighed by other important considerations of the court. For example, a video or a photograph that shows in detail the severity of a victim's injuries would be relevant evidence, but the court might exclude this evidence on the ground that it would emotionally inflame the jurors.

HEARSAY EVIDENCE NOT ADMISSIBLE Generally, hearsay is not admissible as evidence. **Hearsay** is defined as any testimony given in court about a statement made by someone else who was not under oath at the time of the statement. Literally, it is what someone heard someone else say. For example, if a witness in the Kirby-Carvello case testified in court concerning what he or she heard another observer say about the accident, that testimony would be hearsay, or secondhand knowledge. Admitting hearsay into evidence carries many risks because, even though it may be relevant, there is no way to test its reliability.

Opening Statements

At the commencement of the trial, both attorneys are allowed to make **opening statements** concerning the facts that they expect to prove during the trial. The opening statement provides an opportunity for each lawyer to give a brief version of the facts and the supporting evidence that will be used during the trial.

Examination of Witnesses

Because Kirby is the plaintiff, she has the burden of proving that her allegations are true.

PLAINTIFF PRESENTS EVIDENCE Kirby's attorney begins the presentation of Kirby's case by calling the first witness for the plaintiff and examining, or questioning, the witness. (For both attorneys, the types of questions and the manner of asking them are governed by the rules of evidence.) This questioning is called **direct examination.** After Kirby's attorney is finished, the witness is subject to **cross-examination** by Carvello's attorney. Then Kirby's attorney has another

opportunity to question the witness in *redirect examination*, and Carvello's attorney may follow the redirect examination with a *recross-examination*. When both attorneys have finished with the first witness, Kirby's attorney calls the succeeding witnesses in the plaintiff's case, each of whom is subject to examination by the attorneys in the manner just described.

POTENTIAL MOTION AND JUDGMENT At the conclusion of the plaintiff's case, the defendant's attorney has the opportunity to ask the judge to direct a verdict for the defendant on the ground that the plaintiff has presented no evidence to support the plaintiff's claim. This is called a **motion for a directed verdict** (federal courts use the term *judgment as a matter of law* instead of *directed verdict*). In considering the motion, the judge looks at the evidence in the light most favorable to the plaintiff and grants the motion only if there is insufficient evidence to raise an issue of fact. (Motions for directed verdicts at this stage of a trial are seldom granted.)

DEFENDANT'S EVIDENCE The defendant's attorney then presents the evidence and witnesses for the defendant's case. Witnesses are called and examined by the defendant's attorney. The plaintiff's attorney has the right to cross-examine them, and there may be a redirect examination and possibly a recross-examination. At the end of the defendant's case, either attorney can move for a directed verdict, and the test again is whether the jury can, through any reasonable interpretation of the evidence, find for the party against whom the motion has been made. After the defendant's attorney has finished introducing evidence, the plaintiff's attorney can present a **rebuttal,** which includes additional evidence to refute the defendant's case. The defendant's attorney can, in turn, refute that evidence in a **rejoinder.**

Closing Arguments

After both sides have rested their cases, each attorney presents a closing argument. In the **closing argument,** each attorney summarizes the facts and evidence presented during the trial, indicates why the facts and evidence support his or her client's claim, reveals the shortcomings of the points made by the opposing party during the trial, and generally urges a verdict in favor of the client. Each attorney's comments must be relevant to the issues in dispute.

JURY INSTRUCTIONS

After the closing arguments, the judge instructs the jury (assuming it is a jury trial) in the law that applies to the case. The instructions to the jury are often called *charges*. A charge includes statements of the applicable laws, as well as a review of the facts as they were presented during the case. Because the jury's role is to serve as the fact finder, the factual account contained in the charge is not binding on the jurors. Indeed, they may completely disregard the facts as noted in the charge. They are not free to ignore the statements of law, however. The charge will help to channel the jurors' deliberations.

THE JURY'S VERDICT

After receiving the instructions, the jury retires to the jury room to deliberate the case. In a civil case, the standard of proof is a *preponderance of the evidence*. In other words, the plaintiff (Kirby in our hypothetical case) need not provide indisputable proof that she is entitled to a judgment. She need only show that her factual claim is more likely to be true than the defendant's. (As you will read in Chapter 9, in a criminal trial the prosecution has a higher standard of proof to meet—it must prove its case *beyond a reasonable doubt*.)

Note that some civil claims must be proved by "clear and convincing evidence," meaning that the evidence must show that the truth of the party's claim is highly probable. This standard applies in suits involving charges of fraud, suits to establish the terms of a lost will, some suits relating to oral contracts, and other suits in which the circumstances are thought to present a particular danger of deception.

Once the jury has reached a decision, it may issue a **verdict** in favor of one party; the verdict specifies the jury's factual findings and the amount of damages to be paid by the losing party. After the announcement of the verdict, which marks the end of the trial itself, the jurors will be dismissed.

CONCEPT SUMMARY 3.2 | Trial Procedures

PROCEDURE	DESCRIPTION
OPENING STATEMENTS	Each party's attorney is allowed to present an opening statement indicating what the attorney will attempt to prove during the course of the trial.
EXAMINATION OF WITNESSES	1. Plaintiff's introduction and direct examination of witnesses, cross-examination by defendant's attorney, possible redirect examination by plaintiff's attorney, and possible recross-examination by defendant's attorney. 2. At the close of the plaintiff's case, the defendant may make a motion for a directed verdict (or judgment as a matter of law), which, if granted by the court, will end the trial before the defendant presents witnesses. 3. Defendant's introduction and direct examination of witnesses, cross-examination by plaintiff's attorney, possible redirect examination by defendant's attorney, and possible recross-examination by plaintiff's attorney. 4. Possible rebuttal of defendant's argument by plaintiff's attorney, who presents more evidence. 5. Possible rejoinder by defendant's attorney to meet that evidence.
CLOSING ARGUMENTS	Each party's attorney argues in favor of a verdict for his or her client.
JURY INSTRUCTIONS	The judge instructs (or charges) the jury as to how the law applies to the issue.
JURY VERDICT	The jury renders its verdict, thus bringing the trial to an end.

SECTION 5 | Posttrial Motions

After the jury has rendered its verdict, either party may make a posttrial motion. The prevailing party usually files a motion for a judgment in accordance with the verdict. The nonprevailing party frequently files one of the motions discussed next.

MOTION FOR A NEW TRIAL

At the end of the trial, a motion can be made to set aside an adverse verdict and any judgment and to hold a new trial. The **motion for a new trial** will be granted only if the judge (1) is convinced, after looking at all the evidence, that the jury was in error but (2) does not feel it is appropriate to grant judgment for the other side. This will usually occur when the jury verdict is obviously the result of a misapplication of the law or a misunderstanding of the evidence presented at trial.

A new trial can also be granted on the grounds of newly discovered evidence, misconduct by the participants (such as the attorneys, the judge, or the jury) during the trial, or error by the judge. For example, in one personal-injury case, the plaintiff brought suit against Honda, a Japanese corporation. The plaintiff's attorney, during closing arguments, remarked that the case was about Honda's "corporate greed." When the jury returned a verdict in favor of the plaintiff, the court granted the defendant's motion for a new trial, based on the attorney's "improper and inflammatory" remarks to the jury.[10]

MOTION FOR JUDGMENT N.O.V.

If Kirby wins, and if Carvello's attorney has previously moved for a directed verdict, Carvello's attorney can now make a **motion for judgment n.o.v.**—from the Latin *non obstante veredicto*, meaning "notwithstanding the verdict." (Federal courts use the term *judgment as a matter of law* instead of judgment n.o.v.) The standards for granting a judgment n.o.v. often are the same as those for granting a motion to dismiss or a motion for a directed verdict. Carvello can state that even if the evidence is viewed in the light most favorable to Kirby, a reasonable jury should not have found in Kirby's favor. If the judge finds this contention to be correct or decides that the law requires the opposite result, the

---

10. *LeBlanc v. American Honda Motor Co.*, 141 N.H. 579, 688 A.2d 556 (1997).

motion will be granted. If the motion is denied, Carvello may then appeal the case. (Kirby may also appeal the case, even though she won at trial. She might appeal, for example, if she received a smaller money award than she had sought.)

SECTION 6 | The Appeal

Either party may appeal not only the jury's verdict but also any pretrial or posttrial motion. Many of the appellate court cases that appear in this text involve appeals of motions to dismiss, motions for summary judgment, or other motions that were denied by trial court judges. Note that few trial court decisions are reversed on appeal. In most appealed cases (approximately 90 percent), the trial court's decision is affirmed and thus becomes final.

FILING THE APPEAL

If Carvello decides to appeal the verdict in Kirby's favor, then his attorney must file a *notice of appeal* with the clerk of the trial court within a prescribed period of time. Carvello then becomes the *appellant*. The clerk of the trial court sends to the reviewing court (usually an intermediate court of appeals) the *record on appeal*. The record contains all the pleadings, motions, and other documents filed with the court and a complete written transcript of the proceedings, including testimony, arguments, jury instructions, and judicial rulings.

Carvello's attorney will file an appellate **brief** with the reviewing court. The brief contains (1) a short statement of the facts; (2) a statement of the issues; (3) the rulings by the trial court that Carvello contends are erroneous and prejudicial (biased in favor of one of the parties); (4) the grounds for reversal of the judgment; (5) a statement of the applicable law; and (6) arguments on Carvello's behalf, citing applicable statutes and relevant cases as precedents. The attorney for the *appellee* (Kirby, in our hypothetical case) usually files an answering brief. Carvello's attorney can file a reply, although it is not required. The reviewing court then considers the case.

The expenses associated with an appeal can be considerable, and sometimes the party who wins the appeal is awarded some of the associated costs. In the following case, the appellants argued that they should be reimbursed for the $16,065 they spent to prepare and file their briefs electronically.

CASE 3.3

United States
Court of Appeals,
Second Circuit, 2004.
356 F.3d 188.

Phansalkar v. Andersen Weinroth & Co.

PER CURIAM [By the whole court]:

* * * *

[Andersen Weinroth & Company (AW)] is a small * * * partnership that finds and creates investment opportunities for itself, its partners, and outside investors. * * *

* * * *

AW * * * paid [its] partners' * * * expenses, and provided them with opportunities to make certain investments * * * . These "Investment Opportunities" * * * were part of each partner's compensation * * * .

* * * *

[Rohit] Phansalkar joined AW in or about February 1998 as a nominal partner. * * * Throughout his tenure at AW, Phansalkar * * * was offered opportunities to invest in certain transactions.

Phansalkar remained at AW until June 2000, at which time he left to become the Chairman and [Chief Executive Officer] of Osicom Technologies, Inc. * * * AW * * * took the position that, after Phansalkar left AW, he was no longer entitled to the returns on certain Investment Opportunities that he had been given and had acted upon while at AW.

* * * *

* * * On October 16, 2000, Phansalkar filed this action against AW * * * . Phansalkar asserted claims for * * * breach of contract [among other things].

* * * *

* * * The court calculated damages on Phansalkar's * * * claim in the amount of $4,417,655.40 plus * * * interest.[a]

* * * *

On September 16, 2003, this Court [the U.S. Court of Appeals for the Second Circuit] reversed a judgment of approximately $4.4 million entered by the U.S. District Court for the Southern District of New York in favor of Phansalkar. On September 29, 2003, the AW parties submitted an itemized bill of costs. As appellants who have won a reversal, they are clearly entitled to costs for the docketing [scheduling] of the appeal and for printing the "necessary" copies of the regular and special appendices of appellants' main brief and reply brief, an amount totaling $16,112. That entitlement is supported by Rule 39 [of the Federal Rules of Appellate Procedure and] by this Court's Local Instructions for Bill of Costs * * * . In addition, the AW parties seek $16,065 in costs associated with preparing and submitting companion appendices and briefs in hyperlinked CD-ROM format.

The AW parties and Phansalkar vigorously dispute whether an agreement was ever reached over how these CD-ROM costs would be allocated between them following this appeal. There is no dispute, however, that if such an agreement was reached, it was never committed to writing * * * . The issue raised by the parties, which this Court has not yet decided, is whether Rule 39 and the rules of this Court contemplate [an award] of the costs of preparing such electronic submissions.

* * * *

Under Rule 25(a)(2)(D) of the Federal Rules of Appellate Procedure,

[a] court of appeals may by local rule permit papers to be filed, signed, or verified by electronic means that are consistent with technical standards, if any, that the Judicial Conference of the United States establishes.

This Court was among the first [federal courts of appeals] to promulgate such a local rule, by * * * order on October 17, 1997. That order was supplemented on January 30, 1998 with * * * Order 98-2 * * * , which states that *the submission of electronic format briefs is "allowed and encouraged" as long as "[a]ll parties have consented * * * or a motion to file has been granted."* Several other [federal courts of appeals] have adopted local rules that permit or even

---

a. This statement of the facts is taken from the court's previous opinion in this case, which can be found at *Phansalkar v. Andersen Weinroth & Co.*, 344 F.3d 184 (2d Cir. 2003).

CASE 3.3 | Continued

require the filing of electronic briefs, usually on companion disks. The submission of an electronic version of a paper brief very likely entails small incremental costs. [Emphasis added.]

CD-ROM submissions that hyperlink briefs to relevant sections of the appellate record are more versatile, more useful, and considerably more expensive. Our January 30, 1998 order allows and encourages the use of such "interactive CD-ROM" formats. The [U.S. Court of Appeals for the] Federal Circuit also allows CD-ROM briefs to be filed with the prior consent of both the court and the opposing party. To date, only the [U.S. Court of Appeals for the] First Circuit appears to have adopted formally a local rule that applies to submission of hyperlinked CD-ROM briefs. *Such submissions can assist judicial review and are welcomed, but they are not necessarily [part of an award] as costs.* [Emphasis added.]

We have found no local rule or holding from another circuit that allocates CD-ROM costs. No guidance can be found in the relevant text of Rule 39, which authorizes [an award] of costs incurred to produce "necessary" copies of briefs, appendices, and portions of the record relevant to an appeal and a variety of other costs of appeal, such as filing fees. * * * [I]n the absence of a specific textual reference in Rule 39, *an expense can be an allowable cost of appeal when it is analogous to one of the costs specifically authorized by Rule 39(e).* Citing this test, and our administrative orders encouraging the use of CD-ROM's, the AW parties argue that CD-ROM expenses are allowable costs under Rule 39. [Emphasis added.]

However, * * * several other factors * * * are also important in determining if a cost is authorized by Rule 39: whether the party seeking disallowance has clearly consented to the expense; whether a court has previously approved the expense; and whether the alternative arrangement costs less than the expense specifically authorized by the Rule. None of these factors assists the AW parties. In particular, it appears that a substantial portion of the costs were duplicative. Since the AW parties incurred costs both to produce hard copies of their appellate materials *and* to produce hyperlinked CD-ROM copies, Rule 25(a)(2)(D) suggests that the CD-ROM costs in this case were duplicative rather than an analog of hard copy production costs. [Awarding] the CD-ROM costs under such circumstances is inconsistent with our past applications of Rule 39.

Finally, it is decisive that there is no written stipulation or understanding between the parties concerning the allocation of the incremental costs of this useful technology.

* * * * *

For the reasons set forth above, the motion to disallow costs of $16,065 for CD-ROM preparation is hereby GRANTED.

QUESTIONS

1. Under the Federal Rules of Appellate Procedure, was it appropriate for the court to refuse the appellants' request for the cost of producing appellate documents in hyperlinked CD-ROM format? Why or why not?
2. Would the result in this case have been different if the court had required, rather than merely encouraged, the submission of electronic copies of the appeal documents? Explain.

APPELLATE REVIEW

As mentioned in Chapter 2, a court of appeals does not hear any evidence. Its decision concerning a case is based on the record on appeal and the briefs. The attorneys can present oral arguments, after which the case is taken under advisement. The court then issues a written opinion. In general, appellate courts do not reverse findings of fact unless the findings are unsupported or contradicted by the evidence.

An appellate court has the following options after reviewing a case:

1. The court can *affirm* the trial court's decision.
2. The court can *reverse* the trial court's judgment if it concludes that the trial court erred or that the jury did not receive proper instructions.
3. The appellate court can *remand* (send back) the case to the trial court for further proceedings consistent with its opinion on the matter.

4. The court might also affirm or reverse a decision *in part*. For example, the court might affirm the jury's finding that Carvello was negligent but remand the case for further proceedings on another issue (such as the extent of Kirby's damages).

5. An appellate court can also *modify a lower court's decision*. If the appellate court decides that the jury awarded an excessive amount in damages, for example, the court might reduce the award to a more appropriate, or fairer, amount.

HIGHER APPELLATE COURTS

If the reviewing court is an intermediate appellate court, the court may allow the losing party to appeal the decision to the state's highest court, usually called its supreme court. Such a petition corresponds to a petition for a writ of *certiorari* in the United States Supreme Court. If the petition is granted, new briefs must be filed before the state supreme court, and the attorneys may be allowed or requested to present oral arguments. Like the intermediate appellate courts, the supreme court may reverse or affirm the appellate court's decision or remand the case.

At this point, the case has reached its end unless a federal question is at issue—a question concerning a constitutional right, for example, or a question as to how a federal statute should be interpreted. If a federal question is involved, the losing party (or the winning party, if that party is dissatisfied with the relief obtained) may appeal the decision to the United States Supreme Court by petitioning the Court for a writ of *certiorari*. As discussed in Chapter 2, the United States Supreme Court may or may not grant the writ, depending on the significance of the issue in dispute.

CONCEPT SUMMARY 3.3 | Posttrial Options

PROCEDURE	DESCRIPTION
POSTTRIAL MOTIONS	1. *Motion for a new trial*—If the judge is convinced that the jury was in error, the motion normally will be granted. 2. *Motion for judgment n.o.v. ("notwithstanding the verdict")*—The party making the motion must have filed a motion for a directed verdict at the close of all the evidence during the trial; the motion will be granted if the judge is convinced that the jury was in error.
APPEAL	Either party can appeal the trial court's judgment to an appropriate court of appeals. 1. *Filing the appeal*—The appealing party must file a notice of appeal with the clerk of the trial court, who forwards the record on appeal to the appellate court. Attorneys file appellate briefs. 2. *Appellate review*—The appellate court does not hear evidence but bases its opinion, which it issues in writing, on the record on appeal and the attorneys' briefs and oral arguments. The court may affirm or reverse all (or part) of the trial court's judgment and/or remand the case for further proceedings consistent with its opinion. Most decisions are affirmed on appeal. 3. In some cases, further review may be sought from a higher appellate court, such as a state supreme court. If a federal question is involved, the case may ultimately be appealed to the United States Supreme Court.

SECTION 7 | Enforcing the Judgment

The uncertainties of the litigation process are compounded by the lack of guarantees that any judgment will be enforceable. Even if the jury awards Kirby the full amount of damages requested ($100,000), for example, Carvello's auto insurance coverage might have lapsed, in which event the company would not pay any of the damages. Alternatively, Carvello's insurance policy might be limited to $50,000, meaning that Carvello personally would have to pay the remaining $50,000.

REQUESTING COURT ASSISTANCE IN COLLECTING THE JUDGMENT

If the defendant does not have the funds available to pay the judgment, the plaintiff can go back to the court and request the court to issue a *writ of execution*—an order directing the sheriff to seize and sell the defendant's nonexempt assets (certain assets are exempted by law from creditors' actions). The proceeds of the sale would then be used to pay the damages owed and any excess proceeds of the sale would be returned to the defendant. Alternatively, the nonexempt property itself could be transferred to the plaintiff in lieu of an outright payment. (Creditors' remedies, including those of judgment creditors, as well as exempt and nonexempt property, will be discussed in more detail in Chapter 28.)

AVAILABILITY OF ASSETS

The problem of collecting a judgment is less pronounced, of course, when a party is seeking to satisfy a judgment against a defendant, such as a major corporation, that has substantial assets that can be easily located. Usually, one of the factors considered before a lawsuit is initiated is whether the defendant has sufficient assets to cover the amount of damages sought, should the plaintiff win the case. In addition, during the discovery process, attorneys should seek information to locate the defendant's assets that might potentially be used to satisfy a judgment.

REVIEWING COURT PROCEDURES

Ronald Metzgar placed his fifteen-month-old son, Matthew, awake and healthy, in his playpen. Ronald left the room for five minutes and on his return found Matthew lifeless. A toy block had lodged in the boy's throat, causing him to choke to death. Ronald called 911, but efforts to revive Matthew were to no avail. There was no warning of a choking hazard on the box containing the block. Matthew's parents hired an attorney and sued Playskool, Inc., the manufacturer of the block, alleging that the manufacturer had been negligent in failing to warn of the block's hazard. Playskool filed a motion for summary judgment, arguing that the danger of a young child choking on a small block was obvious. Using the information presented in the chapter, answer the following questions.

1. Suppose that the attorney the Metzgars hired agreed to represent them on a contingency-fee basis. What does that mean?

2. How would the Metzgars' attorney likely have served process (the summons and complaint) on Playskool, Inc.?

3. Is the question of whether a child could choke on one of the small blocks a question of fact or a question of law?

4. Should Playskool's request for summary judgment be granted? Why or why not?

5. Suppose that the judge denied Playskool's motion and the case proceeded to trial. After hearing all the evidence, the jury found in favor of the defendants. What options do the plaintiffs have at this point if they are unsatisfied with the verdict?

TERMS AND CONCEPTS TO REVIEW

affidavit 60

affirmative defense 58

answer 58

brief 69

closing argument 67

complaint 54

counterclaim 58

cross-examination 67

default judgment 56

deposition 61

direct examination 67

discovery 60

e-evidence 63

Federal Rules of Civil
    Procedure (FRCP) 52

QUESTIONS AND CASE PROBLEMS

3–1. If a judge enters a judgment on the pleadings, the losing party can usually appeal but cannot present evidence to the appellate court. Does this seem fair? Explain.

3–2. Attorneys in personal-injury and other tort lawsuits (see Chapters 6 and 7) frequently charge clients on a contingency-fee basis; that is, a lawyer will agree to take on a client's case in return for, say, 30 percent of whatever damages are recovered. What are some of the social benefits and costs of the contingency-fee system? In your opinion, do the benefits of this system outweigh the costs?

3–3. **QUESTION WITH SAMPLE ANSWER**

When and for what purpose is each of the following motions made? Which of them would be appropriate if a defendant claimed that the only issue between the parties was a question of law and that the law was favorable to the defendant's position?

(a) A motion for judgment on the pleadings.
(b) A motion for a directed verdict.
(c) A motion for summary judgment.
(d) A motion for judgment *n.o.v.*

For a sample answer to this question, go to Appendix I at the end of this text.

3–4. In the past, the rules of discovery were very restrictive, and trials often turned on elements of surprise. For example, a plaintiff would not necessarily know until the trial what the defendant's defense was going to be. In the last several decades, however, new rules of discovery have substantially changed this situation. Now each attorney can access practically all the evidence that the other side intends to present at trial, with the exception of certain information—namely, the opposing attorney's work product. Work product is not a clear concept. Basically, it includes all the attorney's thoughts on the case. Can you see any reason why such information should not be made available to the opposing attorney? Discuss fully.

3–5. During *voir dire*, the parties, through their attorneys, select those persons who will serve as jurors during the trial. The parties are prohibited, however, from excluding potential jurors on the basis of race or other discriminatory criteria. One issue concerns whether the prohibition against discrimination extends to potential jurors who have physical or mental disabilities. Federal law prohibits discrimination against an otherwise qualified person with a disability when that person could be accommodated without too much difficulty. Should this law also apply to the jury selection process? For example, should parties be prohibited from excluding blind persons, through either challenges for cause or peremptory challenges, from serving on juries if a reasonable accommodation can be made to allow them to serve? Discuss fully.

3–6. MOTION FOR A NEW TRIAL. Washoe Medical Center, Inc., admitted Shirley Swisher for the treatment of a fractured pelvis. During her stay, Swisher suffered a fatal fall from her hospital bed. Gerald Parodi, the administrator of her estate, and others filed an action against Washoe seeking damages for the alleged lack of care in treating Swisher. During *voir dire*, when the plaintiffs' attorney returned a few minutes late from a break, the trial judge led the prospective jurors in a standing ovation. The judge joked with one of the prospective jurors, whom he had known in college, about his fitness to serve as a judge, and personally endorsed another prospective juror's business. After the trial, the jury returned a verdict in favor of Washoe. The plaintiffs moved for a new trial, but the judge denied the motion. The plaintiffs then appealed, arguing that the tone set by the judge during *voir dire* prejudiced their right to a fair trial. Should the appellate court agree? Why or why not? [*Parodi v. Washoe Medical Center, Inc.*, 111 Nev. 365, 892 P.2d 588 (1995)]

3–7. **CASE PROBLEM WITH SAMPLE ANSWER**

To establish a Web site, a person must have an Internet service provider or hosting company, register a domain name, and acquire domain name servicing. Pfizer, Inc., Pfizer Ireland Pharmaceuticals, and Warner-Lambert Co. (collectively, Pfizer) filed a suit in a federal district court against Domains By Proxy, Inc., and other persons alleged to be behind two Web sites—genericlipitors.com and econopetcare.com. Among the defendants were an individual and a company that, according to Pfizer, were located in a foreign country. Without investigating other means of serving these two defendants, Pfizer asked the court for permission to accomplish service of process via e-mail. Under what circumstances is service via e-mail proper? Would it be appropriate in this case? Explain. [*Pfizer, Inc. v. Domains By Proxy*, __ F.Supp.2d __ (D.Conn. 2004)]

To view a sample answer for this case problem, go to this book's Web site at http://wbl.westbuslaw.com, select "Chapter 3," and click on "Case Problem with Sample Answer."

3–8. DISCOVERY. Advance Technology Consultants, Inc. (ATC), contracted with RoadTrac, L.L.C., to provide software and client software systems for the products of global positioning satellite (GPS) technology being developed by RoadTrac. RoadTrac agreed to provide ATC with hardware with which ATC's software would interface. Problems soon arose, however. ATC claimed that RoadTrac's hardware was defective, making it difficult to develop the software. RoadTrac contended that its hardware was fully functional and that ATC had simply failed to provide supporting software. ATC told RoadTrac that it considered their contract terminated. RoadTrac filed a suit in a Georgia state court against ATC, charging, among other things, breach of contract. During discovery, RoadTrac requested ATC's customer lists and marketing procedures. Before producing this material, ATC asked the court to limit RoadTrac's use of the information. Meanwhile, RoadTrac and ATC had become competitors in the GPS industry. How should the court rule regarding RoadTrac's discovery request? [*Advance Technology Consultants, Inc. v. RoadTrac, L.L.C.*, 236 Ga.App. 582, 512 S.E.2d 27 (1999)]

3–9. JURY SELECTION. Ms. Thompson filed a suit in a federal district court against her employer, Altheimer & Gray, seeking damages for alleged racial discrimination in violation of federal law. During *voir dire*, the judge asked the prospective jurors whether "there is something about

this kind of lawsuit for money damages that would start any of you leaning for or against a particular party?" Ms. Leiter, one of the prospective jurors, raised her hand and explained that she had "been an owner of a couple of businesses and am currently an owner of a business, and I feel that as an employer and owner of a business that will definitely sway my judgment in this case." She explained, "I am constantly faced with people that want various benefits or different positions in the company or better contacts or, you know, a myriad of issues that employers face on a regular basis, and I have to decide whether or not that person should get them." Asked by Thompson's lawyer whether "you believe that people file lawsuits just because they don't get something they want," Leiter answered, "I believe there are some people that do." In answer to another question, she said, "I think I bring a lot of background to this case, and I can't say that it's not going to cloud my judgment. I can try to be as fair as I can, as I do every day." Explain the purpose of *voir dire* and how Leiter's response should be treated in light of that purpose. [*Thompson v. Altheimer & Gray*, 248 F.3d 621 (7th Cir. 2001]

3–10. MOTION FOR JUDGMENT N.O.V. Gerald Adams worked as a cook for Uno Restaurants, Inc., at Warwick Pizzeria Uno Restaurant & Bar in Warwick, Rhode Island. One night, shortly after Adams's shift began, he noticed that the kitchen floor was saturated with a foul-smelling liquid coming from the drains and backing up water onto the floor. He complained of illness and went home, where he contacted the state health department. A department representative visited the restaurant and closed it for the night, leaving instructions to sanitize the kitchen and clear the drains. Two days later, in the restaurant, David Badot, the manager, shouted at Adams in the presence of other employees. When Adams shouted back, Badot fired Adams and had him arrested. Adams filed a suit in a Rhode Island state court against Uno, alleging that he had been unlawfully terminated for contacting the health department. A jury found in favor of Adams. Arguing that Adams had been fired for threatening Badot, Uno filed a motion for judgment as a matter of law (also known as a motion for judgment n.o.v.). What does a court weigh in considering whether to grant such a motion? Should the court grant the motion in this case? Why or why not? [*Adams v. Uno Restaurants, Inc.*, 794 A.2d 489 (R.I. 2002)]

LAW | on the Web

For updated links to resources available on the Web, as well as a variety of other materials, visit this text's Web site at **http://wbl.westbuslaw.com**.

If you are interested in learning more about the Federal Rules of Civil Procedure (FRCP) and the Federal Rules of Evidence (FRE), you can access them via the Internet at the following Web site:

http://www.cornell.edu

Procedural rules for several of the state courts are also online and can be accessed via the courts' Web pages. You can find links to the Web pages for state courts at the Web site of the National Center for State Courts. Go to

http://www.ncsc.dni.us/court/sites/courts.htm

The American Bar Association maintains a gateway to information on legal topics, including the court systems and court procedures, at

http://www.ABALawinfo.org

On January 9, 2002, the state of Michigan launched the nation's first "cybercourt." For information about this virtual court and how it is designed to operate, go to

http://michigancybercourt.net

LEGAL RESEARCH EXERCISES ON THE WEB

Go to http://wbl.westbuslaw.com, the Web site that accompanies this text. Select "Chapter 3" and click on "Internet Exercises." There you will find the following Internet research exercises that you can perform to learn more about topics covered in this chapter.

Activity 3–1: **LEGAL PERSPECTIVE**
Civil Procedure

Activity 3–2: **MANAGEMENT PERSPECTIVE**
Small Claims Courts

Activity 3–3: **TECHNOLOGICAL PERSPECTIVE**
Virtual Courtrooms

CHAPTER 4

Constitutional Authority to Regulate Business

The U.S. Constitution is the supreme law in this country.[1] As mentioned in Chapter 1, neither Congress nor any state may pass a law that conflicts with the Constitution. Laws that govern business have their origin in the lawmaking authority granted by this document.

In this chapter, we examine some basic constitutional concepts and clauses and their significance for businesspersons. We then look at certain freedoms guaranteed by the first ten amendments to the Constitution—the Bill of Rights—and discuss how these freedoms affect business activities.

SECTION 1 | The Constitutional Powers of Government

Following the Revolutionary War, the states created a *confederal form of government*. The Articles of Confederation, which went into effect in 1781, established a confederation of independent states and a central government of very limited powers. The central government could handle only those matters of common concern expressly delegated to it by the member states, and the national congress had no authority to make laws directly applicable to individuals unless the member states explicitly supported such laws. In short, the *sovereign power*[2] to govern rested essentially with the states. The Articles of Confederation clearly reflected the central tenet of the American Revolution—that a national government should not have unlimited power.

PROBLEMS WITH THE CONFEDERATION

The confederation, however, faced serious problems. For one thing, laws passed by the various states hampered national commerce and foreign trade by preventing the free movement of goods and services across state borders. By 1784, the nation faced a serious economic depression. Many who could not pay their debts were thrown into "debtors' prisons." By 1786, a series of uprisings by farmer debtors were proving difficult to control because the national government did not have the authority to raise revenues (by levying taxes, for example) to support a militia.

Because of these problems, a national convention was called to **amend** (change, alter) the Articles of Confederation. Instead of amending the Articles, however, the delegates to the convention, now called the Constitutional Convention, created the Constitution and a completely new type of government. Many of the provisions of the Constitution, including those discussed in the following pages, were shaped by the delegates' experiences during the confederal era (1781–1789).

A FEDERAL FORM OF GOVERNMENT

The new government created by the Constitution reflected a series of compromises made by the convention delegates on various issues. Some delegates wanted sovereign power to remain with the states; others wanted the national government alone to exercise sovereign power. The end result was a compromise—a **federal form of government** in which the national government and the states *share* sovereign power.

The Constitution sets forth specific powers that can be exercised by the national government and provides that the national government has the implied power to undertake actions necessary to carry out its

---

1. See Appendix B for the full text of the U.S. Constitution.
2. *Sovereign power* refers to that supreme power to which no other authority is superior or equal.

expressly designated powers. All other powers are retained by the states. According to the language of the Tenth Amendment to the Constitution, "The powers not delegated to the United States by the Constitution, nor prohibited by it to the States, are reserved to the States respectively, or to the people."

NATIONAL POWERS VERSUS STATE POWERS—AN ONGOING DEBATE The broad language of the Constitution has left much room for debate over the specific nature and scope of the respective powers of the states and the national government. Generally, it has been the task of the courts to determine where the boundary line between state and national powers should lie—and that line changes over time. For most of the twentieth century, for example, the national government met little resistance from the courts when extending its regulatory authority over broad areas of social and economic life. Today, in contrast, the courts, and particularly the United States Supreme Court, are more willing to interpret the Constitution in such a way as to curb the national government's regulatory powers and bolster the rights of state governments.

RELATIONS AMONG THE STATES The Constitution also includes provisions concerning relations among the states in our federal system. Particularly important are the privileges and immunities clause and the full faith and credit clause.

—The Privileges and Immunities Clause. Article IV, Section 2, of the Constitution provides that the "Citizens of each State shall be entitled to all Privileges and Immunities of Citizens in the several States." This clause is often referred to as the interstate **privileges and immunities clause.**[3] When a citizen of one state engages in basic and essential activities in another state (the "foreign state"), the foreign state must have a *substantial reason* for treating the nonresident differently from its own residents. Basic activities include transferring property, seeking employment, or accessing the court system. The foreign state must also establish that its reason for the discrimination is substantially related to the state's ultimate purpose in adopting the legislation or activity.[4] The idea is to

generally prevent any state from discriminating against citizens of other states in favor of its own.

Charging nonresidents $2,500 for a shrimp-fishing license, for example, when residents are charged only $25 for the same license, may be considered unconstitutional discrimination against nonresidents who are pursuing the essential activity of making a living.[5] Similarly, attempting to limit the practice of law to residents only (on the premise that it would help reduce the state's unemployment rate) may unconstitutionally restrict a nonresident's professional pursuit without substantial justification.[6]

—The Full Faith and Credit Clause. Article IV, Section 1, of the Constitution provides that "Full Faith and Credit shall be given in each State to the public Acts, Records, and judicial Proceedings of every other State." This clause, which is referred to as the **full faith and credit clause,** applies only to civil matters. It ensures that rights established under deeds, wills, contracts, and the like in one state will be honored by other states. It also ensures that any judicial decision with respect to such property rights will be honored and enforced in all states.

The full faith and credit clause originally was included in the Articles of Confederation to promote mutual friendship among the people of the various states. In fact, it has contributed to the unity of American citizens because it protects their legal rights as they move about from state to state. It also protects the rights of those to whom they owe obligations, such as a person who is awarded money damages by a court. This is extremely important for the conduct of business in a country with a very mobile citizenry.

THE SEPARATION OF NATIONAL GOVERNMENT POWERS

To prevent the possibility that the national government might use its power arbitrarily, the Constitution provided for three branches of government. The legislative branch makes the laws, the executive branch enforces the laws, and the judicial branch interprets the laws. Each branch performs a separate function, and no branch may exercise the authority of another branch.

---

3. Interpretations of this clause commonly use the terms *privilege* and *immunity* synonymously. Generally, the terms refer to certain rights, benefits, or advantages enjoyed by individuals.
4. *Supreme Court of New Hampshire v. Piper,* 470 U.S. 274, 105 S.Ct. 1272, 84 L.Ed.2d 205 (1985).

5. *Toomer v. Witsell,* 334 U.S. 385, 68 S.Ct. 1156, 92 L.Ed. 1460 (1948).
6. *Hicklin v. Orbeck,* 437 U.S. 518, 98 S.Ct. 2482, 57 L.Ed.2d 397 (1978).

Each branch, however, has some power to limit the actions of the other two branches. Congress, for example, can enact legislation relating to spending and commerce, but the president can veto that legislation. The executive branch is responsible for foreign affairs, but treaties with foreign governments require the advice and consent of members of the Senate. Although Congress determines the jurisdiction of the federal courts, the federal courts have the power to hold acts of the other branches of the federal government unconstitutional.[7] Thus, with this system of **checks and balances,** no one branch of government can accumulate too much power.

THE COMMERCE CLAUSE

To prevent states from establishing laws and regulations that would interfere with trade and commerce among the states, the Constitution expressly delegated to the national government the power to regulate interstate commerce. Article I, Section 8, of the U.S. Constitution expressly permits Congress "[t]o regulate Commerce with foreign Nations, and among the several States, and with the Indian Tribes." This clause, referred to as the **commerce clause,** has had a greater impact on business than any other provision in the Constitution. The commerce clause provides the basis for the national government's extensive regulation of state and even local affairs.

One of the early questions raised by the commerce clause was whether the word *among* in the phrase "among the several States" meant *between* the states or *between and within* the states. For some time, the courts interpreted the commerce clause to apply only to commerce between the states (*interstate* commerce) and not commerce within the states (*intrastate* commerce). In 1824, however, in *Gibbons v. Ogden,*[8] the United States Supreme Court held that commerce within the states could also be regulated by the national government as long as the commerce *substantially affected* commerce involving more than one state.

THE EXPANSION OF NATIONAL POWERS UNDER THE COMMERCE CLAUSE   In *Gibbons v. Ogden,* the commerce clause was expanded to cover activities that "substantially affect interstate commerce." As the nation grew and faced new kinds of problems, the commerce clause became a vehicle for the additional expansion of the national government's regulatory powers. Even activities that seemed purely local in nature came under the regulatory reach of the national government if those activities were deemed to substantially affect interstate commerce.

In a 1942 case,[9] for example, the Supreme Court held that wheat production by an individual farmer intended wholly for consumption on his own farm was subject to federal regulation. In *Heart of Atlanta Motel v. United States,*[10] a landmark case decided in 1964, the Supreme Court upheld the federal government's authority to prohibit racial discrimination nationwide in public facilities, including local motels, based on its powers under the commerce clause. The Court noted that "if it is interstate commerce that feels the pinch, it does not matter how local the operation that applies the squeeze." In *McLain v. Real Estate Board of New Orleans, Inc.,*[11] a 1980 case, the Supreme Court acknowledged that the commerce clause had "long been interpreted to extend beyond activities actually in interstate commerce to reach other activities, while wholly local in nature, which nevertheless substantially affect interstate commerce."

THE COMMERCE POWER TODAY   Today, at least theoretically, the power over commerce authorizes the national government to regulate all commercial enterprises in the United States. The breadth of the commerce clause permits the national government to legislate in areas in which Congress has not explicitly been granted power. In the last decade, however, the Supreme Court has begun to curb somewhat the national government's regulatory authority under the commerce clause. In 1995, the Court held—for the first time in sixty years—that Congress had exceeded its regulatory authority under the commerce clause. The Court struck down an act that banned the possession of guns within one thousand feet of any school because the act attempted to regulate an area that had "nothing to do with commerce."[12] Subsequently, the Court invalidated key portions of

7. As discussed in Chapter 2, the power of judicial review was established by the United States Supreme Court in *Marbury v. Madison,* 5 U.S. (1 Cranch) 137, 2 L.Ed. 60 (1803).
8. 22 U.S. (9 Wheat.) 1, 6 L.Ed. 23 (1824).
9. *Wickard v. Filburn,* 317 U.S. 111, 63 S.Ct. 82, 87 L.Ed. 122 (1942).
10. 379 U.S. 241, 85 S.Ct. 348, 13 L.Ed.2d 258 (1964).
11. 444 U.S. 232, 100 S.Ct. 502, 62 L.Ed.2d 441 (1980).
12. The United States Supreme Court held the Gun-Free School Zones Act of 1990 to be unconstitutional in *United States v. Lopez,* 514 U.S. 549, 115 S.Ct. 1624, 131 L.Ed.2d 626 (1995).

two other federal acts—the Brady Handgun Violence Prevention Act of 1993 and the Violence Against Women Act of 1994—on the ground that they exceeded Congress's commerce clause authority.[13]

MEDICAL MARIJUANA AND THE COMMERCE CLAUSE

The current trend of not allowing the federal government to regulate noncommercial activities that take place wholly within a state's borders has led to some controversial decisions in the lower courts. In 2003, for example, a federal appellate court decided a case involving marijuana use on commerce clause grounds. Eight states, including California, have adopted "medical marijuana" laws—legalizing marijuana for medical purposes. Marijuana possession, however, is illegal under the federal Controlled Substances Act (CSA).[14] Two seriously ill California women filed a suit in a federal district court after the federal government seized the marijuana that they were using on the advice of their physicians. The women argued that it is unconstitutional for the federal act to prohibit them from using marijuana for medical purposes that are legal within the state. The federal appellate court agreed, reasoning that the marijuana in this situation would never enter the stream of commerce, but the Supreme Court overturned that decision in 2005.[15]

THE REGULATORY POWERS OF THE STATES

As part of their inherent sovereignty, state governments have the authority to regulate affairs within their borders. This authority stems in part from the Tenth Amendment to the Constitution, which reserves all powers not delegated to the national government to the states or to the people. State regulatory powers are often referred to as **police powers.** The term does not relate solely to criminal law enforcement but rather refers to the broad right of state governments to regulate private activities to protect or promote the public order, health, safety, morals, and general welfare. Fire and building codes, antidiscrimination laws, parking regulations, zoning restrictions, licensing requirements, and thousands of other state statutes covering virtually every aspect of life have been enacted pursuant to states' police powers. Local governments, including cities, also exercise police powers.[16] Generally, state laws enacted pursuant to a state's police powers carry a strong presumption of validity.

STATE ACTIONS AND THE "DORMANT" COMMERCE CLAUSE

The United States Supreme Court has interpreted the commerce clause to mean that the national government has the *exclusive* authority to regulate commerce that substantially affects trade and commerce among the states. This express grant of authority to the national government, which is often referred to as the "positive" aspect of the commerce clause, implies a negative aspect—that the states do *not* have the authority to regulate interstate commerce. This negative aspect of the commerce clause is often referred to as the "dormant" (implied) commerce clause.

The dormant commerce clause comes into play when state regulations impinge on interstate commerce. In this situation, the courts normally weigh the state's interest in regulating a certain matter against the burden that the state's regulation places on interstate commerce. For example, in one case, the United States Supreme Court invalidated state regulations that, in the interest of promoting traffic safety, limited the length of trucks traveling on the state's highways. The Court concluded that the regulations imposed a "substantial burden on interstate commerce" yet failed to "make more than the most speculative contribution to highway safety."[17] Because courts balance the interests involved, it is extremely difficult to predict the outcome in a particular case.

THE SUPREMACY CLAUSE AND FEDERAL PREEMPTION

Article VI of the U.S. Constitution, commonly referred to as the **supremacy clause,** provides that the Constitution, laws, and treaties of the United States

---

13. See, for example, *Printz v. United States*, 521 U.S. 898, 117 S.Ct. 2365, 138 L.Ed.2d 914 (1997), involving the Brady Handgun Violence Prevention Act of 1993; and *United States v. Morrison*, 529 U.S. 598, 120 S.Ct. 1740, 146 L.Ed.2d 658 (2000), concerning the federal Violence Against Women Act of 1994.

14. 21 U.S.C. Sections 801 *et seq.*

15. *Gonzales v. Raich*, __ U.S. __, __ S.Ct. __, __ L.Ed.2d __ (2005).

16. Local governments derive their authority to regulate their communities from the state, because they are creatures of the state. In other words, they cannot come into existence unless authorized by the state to do so.

17. *Raymond Motor Transportation, Inc. v. Rice*, 434 U.S. 429, 98 S.Ct. 787, 54 L.Ed.2d 664 (1978).

are "the supreme Law of the Land." When there is a direct conflict between a federal law and a state law, the state law is rendered invalid. Because some powers are *concurrent* (shared by the federal government and the states), however, it is necessary to determine which law governs in a particular circumstance.

Preemption occurs when Congress chooses to act exclusively in an area in which the federal government and the states have concurrent powers. In this circumstance, a valid federal statute or regulation will take precedence over a conflicting state or local law or regulation on the same general subject. Often, it is not clear whether Congress, in passing a law, intended to preempt an entire subject area against state regulation. In these situations, it is left to the courts to determine whether Congress intended to exercise exclusive power over a given area. No single factor is decisive as to whether a court will find preemption. Generally, congressional intent to preempt will be found if a federal law regulating an activity is so pervasive, comprehensive, or detailed that the states have no room to regulate in that area. Also, when a federal statute creates an agency—such as the National Labor Relations Board—to enforce the law, matters that may come within the agency's jurisdiction will likely preempt state laws.

THE TAXING AND SPENDING POWERS

Article I, Section 8, provides that Congress has the "Power to lay and collect Taxes, Duties, Imposts, and Excises." Section 8 further provides that "all Duties, Imposts and Excises shall be uniform throughout the United States." The requirement of uniformity refers to uniformity among the states, and thus Congress may not tax some states while exempting others.

Traditionally, if Congress attempted to regulate indirectly, by taxation, an area over which it had no authority, the courts would invalidate the tax. Today, however, if a tax measure is reasonable, it is generally held to be within the national taxing power. Moreover, the expansive interpretation of the commerce clause almost always provides a basis for sustaining a federal tax.

Under Article I, Section 8, Congress has the power "to pay the Debts and provide for the common Defence and general Welfare of the United States." Through the spending power, Congress disposes of the revenues accumulated from the taxing power. Congress can spend revenues not only to carry out its expressed powers but also to promote any objective it deems worthwhile, so long as it does not violate the Bill of Rights. For example, Congress could not condition welfare payments on the recipients' agreement to refrain from criticizing government policies. The spending power necessarily involves policy choices, with which taxpayers may disagree.

SECTION 2 | Business and the Bill of Rights

The importance of a written declaration of the rights of individuals eventually caused the first Congress of the United States to submit twelve amendments to the Constitution to the states for approval. The first ten of these amendments, commonly known as the **Bill of Rights,** were adopted in 1791 and embody a series of protections for the individual against various types of interference by the federal government.[18] The protections guaranteed by these ten amendments are summarized in Exhibit 4–1 on the next page.[19] Some of these constitutional protections apply to business entities as well. For example, corporations exist as separate legal entities, or *legal persons,* and enjoy many of the same rights and privileges as *natural persons* do.

LIMITS ON BOTH FEDERAL AND STATE GOVERNMENTAL ACTIONS

As originally intended, the Bill of Rights limited only the powers of the national government. Over time, however, the United States Supreme Court "incorporated" most of these rights into the protections against state actions afforded by the Fourteenth Amendment to the Constitution. That amendment, passed in 1868 after the Civil War, provides in part that "[n]o State shall . . . deprive any person of life, liberty, or property, without due process of law." Starting in 1925, the Supreme Court began to define various rights and liberties guaranteed in the U.S. Constitution as constituting "due process of law," which was required of state governments under the Fourteenth Amendment. Today, most of the rights and liberties set forth in the

---

18. Another of these proposed amendments was ratified 203 years later (in 1992) and became the Twenty-seventh Amendment to the Constitution. See Appendix B.
19. See the Constitution in Appendix B for the complete text of each amendment.

EXHIBIT 4-1 Protections Guaranteed by the Bill of Rights

First Amendment: Guarantees the freedoms of religion, speech, and the press and the rights to assemble peaceably and to petition the government.

Second Amendment: States that the right of the people to keep and bear arms shall not be infringed.

Third Amendment: Prohibits, in peacetime, the lodging of soldiers in any house without the owner's consent.

Fourth Amendment: Prohibits unreasonable searches and seizures of persons or property.

Fifth Amendment: Guarantees the rights to indictment by grand jury, to due process of law, and to fair payment when private property is taken for public use; prohibits compulsory self-incrimination and double jeopardy (being tried again for an alleged crime for which one has already stood trial).

Sixth Amendment: Guarantees the accused in a criminal case the right to a speedy and public trial by an impartial jury and with counsel. The accused has the right to cross-examine witnesses against him or her and to solicit testimony from witnesses in his or her favor.

Seventh Amendment: Guarantees the right to a trial by jury in a civil case involving at least twenty dollars.[a]

Eighth Amendment: Prohibits excessive bail and fines, as well as cruel and unusual punishment.

Ninth Amendment: Establishes that the people have rights in addition to those specified in the Constitution.

Tenth Amendment: Establishes that those powers neither delegated to the federal government nor denied to the states are reserved to the states and to the people.

a. Twenty dollars was forty days' pay for the average person when the Bill of Rights was written.

Bill of Rights apply to state governments as well as the national government. In other words, neither the federal government nor state governments can deprive persons of those rights and liberties.

The rights secured by the Bill of Rights are not absolute. As you can see in Exhibit 4–1, many of the rights guaranteed by the first ten amendments are described in very general terms. For example, the Fourth Amendment prohibits *unreasonable* searches and seizures, but it does not define what constitutes an unreasonable search or seizure. Similarly, the Eighth Amendment prohibits excessive bail or fines, but no definition of *excessive* is contained in that amendment. Ultimately, it is the United States Supreme Court, as the final interpreter of the Constitution, that defines our rights and determines their boundaries.

FREEDOM OF SPEECH

A democratic form of government cannot survive unless people can freely voice their political opinions and criticize government actions or policies. Freedom of speech, particularly political speech, is thus a prized right, and traditionally the courts have protected this right to the fullest extent possible.

Symbolic speech—gestures, movements, articles of clothing, and other forms of expressive conduct—is also given substantial protection by the courts. For example, in a 1989 case, *Texas v. Johnson,*[20] the United States Supreme Court ruled that state laws that prohibited the burning of the American flag as part of a peaceful protest violated the freedom of expression protected by the First Amendment. Congress responded by passing the Flag Protection Act of 1989, which was ruled unconstitutional by the Supreme Court in 1990.[21] Similarly, participating in a hunger strike or wearing a black armband would be protected as symbolic speech.

Expression—oral, written, or symbolized by conduct—is subject to reasonable restrictions. For example, on the campus of a public high school, certain rights may be circumscribed or denied, in part to protect minors from predatory adults and to protect adults and others from predatory minors. A balance must be struck, however, between a government's obligation to protect its citizens and those citizens' exercise of their rights. These competing interests were at issue in the following case.

---

20. 491 U.S. 397, 109 S.Ct. 2533, 105 L.Ed.2d 342 (1989).
21. *United States v. Eichman,* 496 U.S. 310, 110 S.Ct. 2804, 110 L.Ed.2d 287 (1990).

CASE 4.1

United States
Court of Appeals,
Seventh Circuit, 2004.
355 F.3d 1048.

Hodgkins v. Peterson

ROVNER, Circuit Judge.

* * * *

Shortly after 11:00 P.M. on August 26, 1999, Colin Hodgkins and his three friends [all of whom were minors] left a Steak 'n Shake restaurant in Marion County, Indiana, where they had stopped to eat after attending a school soccer game. As they left the restaurant, police arrested and handcuffed them for violating Indiana's curfew regulation. The police took Colin and his friends to a curfew sweep processing site where he was given a breathalyser test and * * * tested for drugs. * * *

* * * At the time of Colin's arrest, the Indiana statute set a curfew of 11 P.M. on weekday nights [with a few exceptions].

* * * *

* * * Nancy Hodgkins is * * * the mother of * * * Colin * * *. Ms. Hodgkins would like to allow her children to participate in * * * activities protected by the * * * First Amendment * * *, however, she is concerned that if they do so, they will be subject to arrest. * * *

* * * She seeks [an] * * * injunction against defendants Bart Peterson, in his official capacity as Mayor of the City of Indianapolis and [other local government officials], barring them from enforcing the * * * curfew law. * * *

* * * *

* * * [T]he court found * * * only an incidental burden on minors' First Amendment rights. * * * The plaintiffs filed a timely appeal [to the U.S. Court of Appeals for the Seventh Circuit].

* * * *

The strength of our democracy depends on a citizenry that knows and understands its freedoms, exercises them responsibly, and guards them vigilantly. Young adults are not suddenly granted the full panoply [array] of constitutional rights on the day they attain the age of majority. We not only permit but expect youths to exercise those liberties—to learn to think for themselves, to give voice to their opinions, to hear and evaluate competing points of view—so that they might attain the right to vote at age eighteen with the tools to exercise that right. A juvenile's ability to worship, associate, and speak freely is therefore not simply a privilege that benefits her as an individual, but a necessary means of allowing her to become a fully enfranchised [endowed with the privileges of citizenship, especially voting rights] member of democratic society. * * *

[The Hodgkinses] assert that the consequences of violating the curfew law are so burdensome and intrusive that, rather than risk arrest, they will be discouraged from participating in expressive activity during curfew hours. In other words, the plaintiffs claim that the curfew regulation creates a "chill" that imposes on their First Amendment rights. * * *

* * * *

* * * The government claims that plaintiffs cannot mount a * * * challenge to the curfew law * * * because they have not demonstrated either that the curfew law imposes a disproportionate burden on those engaged in First Amendment activities or that it regulates conduct with an expressive element.

We agree that the Indiana curfew ordinance does not disproportionately impact First Amendment rights. As Colin Hodgkins can attest, it burdens minors who want to attend soccer games as much as it burdens those who wish to speak at a political rally. On the other hand, the curfew ordinance regulates minors' abilities to engage in some of the purest and most protected forms of speech and expression. [A] wide range of First Amendment activities occur during curfew hours, including political events, death penalty protests, late night sessions of the Indiana General Assembly, and neighborhood association meetings or nighttime events. A number of religions mark particular days or events with late-night services, prayers, or other activities: many Christians, for example, commemorate the birth of Christ with a

CONTINUED

CASE 4.1 | Continued

midnight service on Christmas Eve and the Last Supper with an all-night vigil on Holy Thursday; Jews observe the first night of Shavuot by studying Torah all through the night; and throughout the month of Ramadan, Muslims engage in late-evening prayer. Late-night or all-night marches, rallies, and sleep-ins are often held to protest government action or inaction. And it is not unusual for political campaigns, particularly in the whirlwind final hours before an election, to hold rallies in the middle of the night. Thus, during the last weeks of the 1960 presidential campaign, then-Senator John F. Kennedy addressed a group of University of Michigan students at 2:00 A.M. on the steps of the Michigan Union. In unprepared remarks, he asked the students whether they would be willing to devote a few years of their lives working in underdeveloped countries in order to foster better relations between the people of those nations and the United States. The students responded with a petition calling for the creation of the Peace Corps, which came into being the following year. These are but a few examples. *The curfew ordinance regulates access to almost every form of public expression during the late night hours. The effect on the speech of the plaintiffs is significant.* [Emphasis added.]

* * * *

* * * Any juvenile who chooses to participate in a late-night religious or political activity thus runs the risk that he will be arrested if a police officer stops him en route to or from that activity and he cannot prove to the officer's satisfaction that he is out after hours in order to exercise his First Amendment rights.

* * * *

* * * The prospect of an arrest is intimidating in and of itself; but one should also have in mind what else might follow from the arrest. * * * We have no doubt that the authorities are well meaning in administering the drug and alcohol testing and in questioning the minor and his parents about his friends and family life. But these are also rather serious intrusions upon one's personal and familial privacy, and they represent a substantial price for a minor to have to pay in order to take part in a late-night political or religious event. *The chill that the prospect of arrest imposes on a minor's exercise of his or her First Amendment rights is patent [evident].* [Emphasis added.]

* * * *

In sum, we hold that the curfew law * * * is not narrowly tailored to serve a significant governmental interest and fails to allow for ample alternative channels for expression. The statute restricts a minor's access to any public forum during curfew hours * * * . The concrete possibility of arrest * * * makes clear that the statute unduly chills the exercise of a minor's First Amendment rights. * * * Consequently, we reverse the judgment and remand with directions to enjoin [prevent] the enforcement of Indiana's curfew until such time as the State's legislature removes the chill that the statute places on the exercise of First Amendment rights by minors.

QUESTIONS

1. Why is it unfair to require minors to engage in protected activity only during noncurfew hours, during curfew hours accompanied by an authorized adult, or from the minors' homes by phone or over the Internet?

2. How might a curfew law be written to protect both the fundamental constitutional rights of minors and the safety of all citizens?

CORPORATE POLITICAL SPEECH Political speech by corporations also falls within the protection of the First Amendment. For example, in *First National Bank of Boston v. Bellotti*,[22] national banking associations and business corporations asked the United States Supreme Court to review a Massachusetts statute that prohibited corporations from making political contributions or expenditures that individuals were permitted to make. The Court ruled that the statute was unconstitutional because it violated the right of corporations to freedom of speech. Similarly, the Supreme Court has held that a law forbidding a corporation

22. 435 U.S. 765, 98 S.Ct. 1407, 55 L.Ed.2d 707 (1978).

from placing inserts in its billing to express its views on controversial issues violates the First Amendment.[23] Although in 1990 the Supreme Court reversed this trend somewhat,[24] corporate political speech continues to be given significant protection under the First Amendment.

COMMERCIAL SPEECH The courts also give substantial protection to *commercial speech*, which consists of communications—primarily advertising and marketing—made by business firms that only involve their commercial interests. The protection given to commercial speech under the First Amendment is not as extensive as that afforded to noncommercial speech, however. A state may restrict certain kinds of advertising, for example, in the interest of preventing consumers from being misled by the advertising practices. States also have a legitimate interest in the beautification of roadsides, and this interest allows states to place restraints on billboard advertising. For example, in one Florida case, the court found that a law preventing a nude dancing establishment from billboard advertising was constitutionally permissible because it directly advanced a substantial government interest in highway beautification and safety.[25]

Generally, a restriction on commercial speech will be considered valid as long as it meets the following three criteria: (1) it must seek to implement a substantial government interest, (2) it must directly advance that interest, and (3) it must go no further than necessary to accomplish its objective. The court in the following case applied these principles to determine the constitutionality of a county ordinance that regulated video games based on their content—the ordinance applied only to "graphically violent" video games.

---

23. *Consolidated Edison Co. v. Public Service Commission,* 447 U.S. 530, 100 S.Ct. 2326, 65 L.Ed.2d 319 (1980).

24. See *Austin v. Michigan Chamber of Commerce,* 494 U.S. 652, 110 S.Ct. 1391, 108 L.Ed.2d 652 (1990), in which the Supreme Court upheld a state law prohibiting corporations from using general corporate funds for independent expenditures in state political campaigns.

25. *Café Erotica v. Florida Department of Transportation,* 830 So.2d 181 (Fla.App. 1 Dist. 2002); review denied by *Café Erotica/We Dare to Bare v. Florida Department of Transportation,* 845 So.2d 888 (Fla. 2003).

CASE 4.2   Interactive Digital Software Association v. St. Louis County, Missouri

United States
Court of Appeals,
Eighth Circuit, 2003.
329 F.3d 954.

BACKGROUND AND FACTS *St. Louis County, Missouri, passed an ordinance that made it unlawful for any person knowingly to sell, rent, or make available "graphically violent" video games to minors, or to "permit the free play of" such games by minors, without a parent or guardian's consent.*[a] *Interactive Digital Software Association, and others that create or provide the public with video games and related software, filed a suit against the county in a federal district court. The plaintiffs asserted that the ordinance violated the First Amendment and filed a motion for summary judgment. The county argued that the ordinance forwarded the compelling state interest of protecting the "psychological well-being of minors" by reducing the harm suffered by children who play violent video games. A psychologist, a high school principal, and others offered their conclusions that playing violent video games leads to aggressive behavior, but the county did not provide proof of a link between the games and psychological harm. The court denied the plaintiffs' motion and dismissed the case. The plaintiffs appealed to the U.S. Court of Appeals for the Eighth Circuit.*

IN THE LANGUAGE OF THE COURT

MORRIS SHEPPARD ARNOLD, Circuit Judge.
* * * *
* * * If the first amendment is versatile enough to shield the painting of Jackson Pollock, music of Arnold Schoenberg, or Jabberwocky verse of Lewis Carroll, we see no reason why the pictures, graphic design, concept art, sounds, music, stories, and narrative present in video games are not entitled to a similar protection. The mere fact that they appear in a novel medium is of no legal consequence. Our review of the record convinces us that these violent video games contain stories, imagery, age-old themes of literature, and messages, even an ideology, just as books and movies do. * * *

---

a. St. Louis County Revised Ordinances Sections 602.425 through 602.460.

CASE 4.2 Continued

We recognize that while children have in the past experienced age-old elemental violent themes by reading a fairy tale or an epic poem, or attending a Saturday matinee, the interactive play of a video game might present different difficulties. The County suggests in fact that with video games, the story lines are incidental and players may skip the expressive parts of the game and proceed straight to the player-controlled action. But the same could be said of action-packed movies like "The Matrix" or "Charlie's Angels"; any viewer with a videocassette or DVD player could simply skip to and isolate the action sequences. *   *   *

We note, moreover, that *there is no justification for disqualifying video games as speech simply because they are constructed to be interactive;* indeed, literature is most successful when it draws the reader into the story, makes him identify with the characters, invites him to judge them and quarrel with them, to experience their joys and sufferings as the reader's own. In fact, some books, such as the pre-teen oriented "Choose Your Own Nightmare" series (in which the reader makes choices that determine the plot of the story, and which lead the reader to one of several endings, by following the instructions at the bottom of the page) can be every bit as interactive *   *   * . [Emphasis added.]

Whether we believe the advent of violent video games adds anything of value to society is irrelevant; *guided by the First Amendment, we are obliged to recognize that they are as much entitled to the protection of free speech as the best of literature.* *   *   * [Emphasis added.]

*   *   *   *

*   *   * [To] constitutionally restrict the speech at issue here, the County must come forward with empirical support for its belief that violent video games cause psychological harm to minors. In this case, *   *   * the County has failed to present the substantial supporting evidence of harm that is required before an ordinance that threatens protected speech can be upheld. *   *   * [T]he County may not simply surmise that it is serving a compelling state interest because "[s]ociety in general believes that continued exposure to violence can be harmful to children." Where First Amendment rights are at stake, the Government must present more than anecdote and supposition.

DECISION AND REMEDY *The U.S. Court of Appeals for the Eighth Circuit reversed the judgment of the lower court and remanded the case for the entry of an injunction preventing the county's enforcement of its ordinance. Video games are entitled to the same First Amendment protection as other types of speech, and the defendants failed to present the required evidence of harm to uphold a law threatening protected speech.*

UNPROTECTED SPEECH   The United States Supreme Court has made it clear that certain types of speech will not be protected under the First Amendment. Speech that harms the good reputation of another, or defamatory speech (see Chapter 6), is not protected under the First Amendment. Speech that violates criminal laws (threatening speech and pornography, for example) is not constitutionally protected. Other unprotected speech includes "fighting words" (speech that is likely to incite others to respond violently).

—*Obscene Speech.*   The Supreme Court has also held that the First Amendment does not protect obscene speech. The Court has grappled from time to time with the problem of establishing an objective definition of obscene speech. In a 1973 case, *Miller v.*

California,[26] the Supreme Court created a test for legal obscenity, including a set of requirements that must be met for material to be legally obscene. Under this test, material is obscene if (1) the average person finds that it violates contemporary community standards; (2) the work taken as a whole appeals to a prurient (arousing or obsessive) interest in sex; (3) the work shows patently offensive sexual conduct; and (4) the work lacks serious redeeming literary, artistic, political, or scientific merit.

Because community standards vary widely, the *Miller* test has had inconsistent applications, and obscenity remains a constitutionally unsettled issue. Numerous state and federal statutes make it a crime to

---

26. 413 U.S. 15, 93 S.Ct. 2607, 37 L.Ed.2d 419 (1973).

disseminate obscene materials, however, and the Supreme Court has often upheld such laws, including laws prohibiting the sale and possession of child pornography.[27]

—*Online Obscenity.* A significant problem facing the courts and lawmakers today is how to control the dissemination of obscenity and child pornography via the Internet. Congress first attempted to protect minors from pornographic materials on the Internet by passing the Communications Decency Act (CDA) of 1996. The CDA made it a crime to make available to minors online any "obscene or indecent" message that "depicts or describes, in terms patently offensive as measured by contemporary community standards, sexual or excretory activities or organs."[28] Civil rights groups immediately challenged the act as an unconstitutional restraint on speech, and ultimately the United States Supreme Court ruled that portions of the act were unconstitutional. The Court held that the terms *indecent* and *patently offensive* covered large amounts of nonpornographic material with serious educational or other value.

—*Subsequent Attempts to Regulate Online Obscenity.* Some of Congress's later attempts to curb pornography on the Internet have also encountered constitutional stumbling blocks. For example, the Child Online Protection Act (COPA)[29] of 1998 banned material "harmful to minors" distributed without some kind of age-verification system to separate adult and minor users. In 2002, the Supreme Court upheld a lower court's injunction suspending the COPA.[30] In 2000, Congress enacted the Children's Internet Protection Act (CIPA),[31] which requires public schools and libraries to block adult content from access by children by installing **filtering software.** Such software is designed to prevent persons from viewing certain Web sites by responding to a site's Internet address or its **meta tags,** or key words. The CIPA was also challenged on constitutional grounds, but in 2003 the Supreme Court held that the

act does not violate the First Amendment. The Court concluded that because libraries can disable the filters for any patrons who ask, the system is reasonably flexible and does not burden free speech to an unconstitutional extent.[32]

FREEDOM OF RELIGION

The First Amendment states that the government may neither establish any religion nor prohibit the free exercise of religious practices. The first part of this constitutional provision is referred to as the **establishment clause,** which has to do with the separation of church and state. The second part of the provision is known as the **free exercise clause.**

THE ESTABLISHMENT CLAUSE The establishment clause prohibits the government from establishing a state-sponsored religion, as well as from passing laws that promote (aid or endorse) religion or that show a preference for one religion over another. Establishment clause issues often involve such matters as the legality of allowing or requiring school prayers, using state-issued school vouchers to pay for tuition at religious schools, teaching evolutionary versus creationist theory, and giving state and local government aid to religious organizations and schools.

—*Sunday Closing Laws.* Federal or state laws that do not promote or place a significant burden on religion are constitutional even if they have some impact on religion. "Sunday closing laws," for example, make the performance of some commercial activities on Sunday illegal. These statutes, also known as "blue laws" (from the color of the paper on which an early Sunday law was written), have been upheld on the ground that it is a legitimate function of government to provide a day of rest to promote the health and welfare of workers. Even though closing laws admittedly make it easier for Christians to attend religious services, the courts have viewed this effect as an incidental, not a primary, purpose of Sunday closing laws.

—*Religious Displays on Public Property.* The First Amendment does not require a complete separation of church and state. On the contrary, it affirmatively mandates accommodation of all religions and

---

27. For example, see *Osborne v. Ohio,* 495 U.S. 103, 110 S.Ct. 1691, 109 L.Ed.2d 98 (1990).
28. 47 U.S.C. Section 223(a)(1)(B)(ii).
29. 47 U.S.C. Section 231.
30. *Ashcroft v. American Civil Liberties Union,* 535 U.S. 564, 122 S.Ct. 1700, 152 L.Ed.2d 771 (2002). Also see *American Civil Liberties Union v. Ashcroft,* 322 F.3d 240 (3d Cir. 2003).
31. 17 U.S.C. Sections 1701–1741.

---

32. *United States v. American Library Association,* 539 U.S. 194, 123 S.Ct. 2297, 156 L.Ed.2d 221 (2003).

forbids hostility toward any.[33] An ongoing challenge for the courts is determining the extent to which governments can accommodate a religion without appearing to promote that religion, which would violate the establishment clause. For example, in *Lynch v. Donnelly*,[34] the United States Supreme Court held that a municipality could include religious symbols, such as a Nativity scene, or crèche, in its annual holiday display as long as the religious symbols constituted just one part of a display in which other, nonreligious symbols (such as reindeer and candy-striped poles) were also featured. The Supreme Court applied this same reasoning in subsequent cases involving similar issues.[35] Nevertheless, disputes continue to arise involving religious monuments—particularly those depicting the Ten Commandments—on city or county property.[36]

THE FREE EXERCISE CLAUSE The free exercise clause guarantees that no person can be compelled to do something that is contrary to his or her religious

beliefs. For this reason, if a law or policy is contrary to a person's religious beliefs, exemptions are often made to accommodate those beliefs. When, however, religious practices work against public policy and the public welfare, the government can act. For example, regardless of a child's or parent's religious beliefs, the government can require certain types of vaccinations. Additionally, public school students can be required to study from textbooks chosen by school authorities.

For business firms, an important issue involves the accommodation that businesses must make for the religious beliefs of their employees. For example, if an employee's religion prohibits her or him from working on a certain day of the week or at a certain type of job, the employer must make a *reasonable* attempt to accommodate these religious requirements. Employers must reasonably accommodate an employee's religious belief even if the belief is not based on the tenets or dogma of a particular church, sect, or denomination. The only requirement is that the belief be religious in nature and sincerely held by the employee.[37] (See Chapter 34 for a further discussion of religious freedom in the employment context.)

The following case focused on a state scholarship program for college and university students. The case involved this question: Is the free exercise clause violated when the state bans students from using the scholarships to pursue degrees in theology?

---

33. *Zorach v. Clauson*, 343 U.S. 306, 72 S.Ct. 679, 96 L.Ed. 954 (1952).
34. 465 U.S. 668, 104 S.Ct. 1355, 79 L.Ed.2d 604 (1984).
35. See, for example, *County of Allegheny v. American Civil Liberties Union*, 492 U.S. 573, 109 S.Ct. 3086, 106 L.Ed.2d 472 (1989); and *Capitol Square Review and Advisory Board v. Pinette*, 515 U.S. 753, 115 S.Ct. 2440, 132 L.Ed.2d 650 (1995).
36. See, for example, *Van Orden v. Perry*, 351 F.3d 265 (4th Cir. 2001); *Summum, a Corporate Sole and Church v. Duchesne City*, 340 F.Supp.2d 1223 (D. Utah 2004); and *Modrovich v. Allegheny County, Pennsylvania*, 385 F.3d 397 (3d Cir. 2004).

37. *Frazee v. Illinois Department of Employment Security*, 489 U.S. 829, 109 S.Ct. 1514, 103 L.Ed.2d 914 (1989).

CASE 4.3   Locke v. Davey

Supreme Court of the
United States, 2004.
540 U.S. 712,
124 S.Ct. 1307,
158 L.Ed.2d 1.
*http://www.findlaw.com/
casecode/supreme.html*[a]

BACKGROUND AND FACTS *In 1999, the state of Washington created the "Promise Scholarship Program" to assist students with postsecondary education expenses. Those who meet the academic, income, and enrollment requirements can spend the funds on any education-related expense. Under the state constitution, however, students cannot use the scholarships to seek degrees in "devotional theology." A state statute refers to degrees that are "devotional in nature or designed to induce religious faith," but the schools, not the state, determine whether students' majors are "devotional." Joshua Davey was awarded a Promise Scholarship and chose to attend Northwest College, a private Christian college affiliated with the Assemblies of God denomination. When Davey decided to pursue a double major in pastoral ministries and business management/administration, he was denied the scholarship. Davey filed a suit in a federal district court against state officials, arguing in part that this denial violated the free exercise clause. The court issued a judgment in favor of the state. Davey appealed to the U.S. Court of Appeals for the Ninth Circuit, which ruled that the scholarship program was unconstitutional. The state appealed to the United States Supreme Court.*

---

a. In the "Browsing" section, click on "2004 Decisions." When that page opens, click on the name of the case to access the opinion.

CASE 4.3 | Continued

IN THE LANGUAGE OF THE COURT

Chief Justice *REHNQUIST* delivered the opinion of the Court.

* * * *

* * * [T]he Establishment Clause and the Free Exercise Clause are frequently in tension. Yet we have long said that there is room for play in the joints between them. In other words, *there are some state actions permitted by the Establishment Clause but not required by the Free Exercise Clause.* [Emphasis added.]

This case involves that play in the joints as described above. * * * [T]here is no doubt that the State could, consistent with the Federal Constitution, permit Promise Scholars to pursue a degree in devotional theology, and the State does not contend otherwise. The question before us, however, is whether Washington, pursuant to its own constitution, * * * can deny them such funding without violating the Free Exercise Clause.

Davey urges us to answer that question in the negative. He contends that * * * the program is * * * unconstitutional because it is not * * * neutral with respect to religion. We reject his claim * * * . [T]he State's disfavor of religion (if it can be called that) is of a far milder kind [than in other cases]. It imposes neither criminal nor civil sanctions on any type of religious service or rite. It does not deny to ministers the right to participate in the political affairs of the community. And it does not require students to choose between their religious beliefs and receiving a government benefit. The State has merely chosen not to fund a distinct category of instruction.

* * * *

* * * Because the Promise Scholarship Program funds training for all secular [lay, or nonreligious] professions, [it is contended that] the State must also fund training for religious professions. But training for religious professions and training for secular professions are not fungible [interchangeable]. Training someone to lead a congregation is an essentially religious endeavor. Indeed, majoring in devotional theology is akin to a religious calling as well as an academic pursuit. And *the subject of religion is one in which both the United States and state constitutions embody distinct views—in favor of free exercise, but opposed to establishment—that find no counterpart with respect to other callings or professions. That a State would deal differently with religious education for the ministry than with education for other callings is a product of these views, not evidence of hostility toward religion.* [Emphasis added.]

* * * *

Far from evincing [demonstrating] * * * hostility toward religion * * * , we believe that the entirety of the Promise Scholarship Program goes a long way toward including religion in its benefits. The program permits students to attend pervasively religious schools, so long as they are accredited. As Northwest advertises, its "concept of education is distinctly Christian in the evangelical sense." It prepares *all* of its students, "through instruction, through modeling, [and] through [its] classes, to use * * * the Bible as their guide, as the truth," no matter their chosen profession. And under the Promise Scholarship Program's current guidelines, students are still eligible to take devotional theology courses. * * *

In short, we find neither in the history or text of * * * the Washington Constitution, nor in the operation of the Promise Scholarship Program, anything that suggests *animus* [hostility] towards religion. Given the historic and substantial state interest at issue, we therefore cannot conclude that the denial of funding for vocational religious instruction alone is inherently constitutionally suspect.

* * * The State's interest in not funding the pursuit of devotional degrees is substantial and the exclusion of such funding places a relatively minor burden on Promise Scholars. If any room exists between the two Religion Clauses, it must be here. We need not venture further into this difficult area in order to uphold the Promise Scholarship Program as currently operated by the State of Washington.

DECISION AND REMEDY *The United States Supreme Court reversed the decision of the lower court. The Supreme Court held that Washington's "exclusion from an otherwise inclusive aid program" of students pursuing degrees in devotional theology "does not violate the Free Exercise Clause of the First Amendment." This exclusion furthers the state's interest in prohibiting the use of tax funds to support the ministry without suggesting hostility toward religion or imposing more than a minor burden on the program's participants.*

CONTINUED ▶

CASE 4.3 | Continued **WHAT IF THE FACTS WERE DIFFERENT?** *Suppose that the state constitution had allowed the scholarship to be given to students seeking degrees in Christian theology but not to students studying other religious theories. How might this have affected the Supreme Court's decision?*

SEARCHES AND SEIZURES

The Fourth Amendment protects the "right of the people to be secure in their persons, houses, papers, and effects." Before searching or seizing private property, law enforcement officers must obtain a **search warrant**—an order from a judge or other public official authorizing the search or seizure.

SEARCH WARRANTS AND PROBABLE CAUSE To obtain a search warrant, law enforcement officers must convince a judge that they have reasonable grounds, or probable cause, to believe a search will reveal a specific illegality. To establish **probable cause,** the officers must have trustworthy evidence that would convince a reasonable person that the proposed search or seizure is more likely justified than not. Furthermore, the Fourth Amendment prohibits *general* warrants. It requires a particular description of whatever is to be searched or seized. General searches through a person's belongings are impermissible. The search cannot extend beyond what is described in the warrant.

The requirement for a search warrant has several exceptions. One exception applies when it is likely that the items sought will be removed before a warrant can be obtained. For example, if a police officer has probable cause to believe that an automobile contains evidence of a crime and that the vehicle will likely be unavailable by the time a warrant is obtained, the officer can search the vehicle without a warrant.

SEARCHES AND SEIZURES IN THE BUSINESS CONTEXT Constitutional protection against unreasonable searches and seizures is important to businesses and professionals. As federal and state regulation of commercial activities increased, frequent and unannounced government inspections were conducted to ensure compliance with the regulations. Such inspections were at times extremely disruptive. In *Marshall v. Barlow's, Inc.*,[38] the United States

Supreme Court held that government inspectors do not have the right to enter business premises without a warrant, although the standard of probable cause is not the same as that required in nonbusiness contexts. The existence of a general and neutral enforcement plan will justify issuance of the warrant.

—Business Records. Lawyers and accountants frequently possess the business records of their clients, and inspecting these documents while they are out of the hands of their true owners also requires a warrant. A warrant is not required, however, for the seizure of spoiled or contaminated food. In addition, warrants are not required for searches of businesses in such highly regulated industries as liquor, guns, and strip mining. General manufacturing is not considered to be one of these highly regulated industries, however.

—Employee Safety. Of increasing concern to many government employers is how to maintain a safe and efficient workplace without jeopardizing the Fourth Amendment rights of employees "to be secure in their persons." Requiring government employees to undergo random drug tests, for example, may be held to violate the Fourth Amendment. In Chapter 33, we will discuss Fourth Amendment issues in the employment context, as well as employee privacy rights in general, in greater detail.

SELF-INCRIMINATION

The Fifth Amendment guarantees that no person "shall be compelled in any criminal case to be a witness against himself." Thus, in any federal proceeding, an accused person cannot be compelled to give testimony that might subject him or her to any criminal prosecution. Nor can an accused person be forced to testify against himself or herself in state courts because the due process clause of the Fourteenth Amendment (discussed in the next section) incorporates the Fifth Amendment provision against self-incrimination.

---

38. 436 U.S. 307, 98 S.Ct. 1816, 56 L.Ed.2d 305 (1978).

The Fifth Amendment's guarantee against self-incrimination extends only to natural persons. Because a corporation is a legal entity and not a natural person, the privilege against self-incrimination does not apply to it. Similarly, the business records of a partnership do not receive Fifth Amendment protection.[39] When a partnership is required to produce these records, it must do so even if the information provided incriminates the persons who constitute the business entity. In contrast, sole proprietors and sole practitioners (those who fully own their businesses) who have not incorporated cannot be compelled to produce their business records. These individuals have full protection against self-incrimination because they function in only one capacity; there is no separate business entity.

SECTION 3 | Due Process and Equal Protection

Other constitutional guarantees of great significance to Americans are mandated by the *due process clauses* of the Fifth and Fourteenth Amendments and the *equal protection clause* of the Fourteenth Amendment.

DUE PROCESS

Both the Fifth and Fourteenth Amendments provide that no person shall be deprived "of life, liberty, or property, without due process of law." The **due process clause** of these constitutional amendments has two aspects—procedural and substantive. Note that the due process clause applies to "legal persons" (that is, corporations), as well as to individuals.

PROCEDURAL DUE PROCESS *Procedural* due process requires that any government decision to take life, liberty, or property must be made equitably. For example, fair procedures must be used in determining whether a person will be subjected to punishment or have some burden imposed on her or him. Fair procedure has been interpreted as requiring that the person have at least an opportunity to object to a proposed action before an impartial, neutral decision maker (which need not be a judge). Thus, for example, if a

driver's license is construed as a property interest, some sort of opportunity to object to its suspension or termination by the state must be provided.

SUBSTANTIVE DUE PROCESS *Substantive* due process focuses on the content, or substance, of legislation. It generally requires that the government have an appropriate justification or goal in enacting the law and that the law, as applied, sufficiently furthers that goal.

—*When Fundamental Rights Are Involved.* If a law or other governmental action limits a *fundamental right*, it will be held to violate substantive due process unless it promotes a *compelling* or *overriding state interest*. Fundamental rights include interstate travel, privacy, voting, and all First Amendment rights. Compelling state interests could include, for example, the public's safety. Thus, even though laws designating speed limits affect interstate travel, they may be upheld if they are shown to reduce highway fatalities, because the state has a compelling interest in protecting the lives of its citizens.

Suppose that a state legislature enacted a law imposing a fifteen-year term of imprisonment without a trial on all businesspersons who appeared in their own television commercials. This law would be unconstitutional on both substantive and procedural grounds. Substantive review would invalidate the legislation because it abridges freedom of speech, a fundamental right. Procedurally, the law is constitutionally invalid because it imposes a penalty without giving the accused a chance to defend his or her actions.

—*When No Fundamental Rights Are Involved.* In situations not involving fundamental rights, a law or action does not violate substantive due process if it *rationally relates* to any *legitimate government purpose*. It is almost impossible for a law or action to fail this "rational basis" test. Under this test, virtually any business regulation will be upheld as reasonable—the United States Supreme Court has upheld insurance regulations, price and wage controls, banking controls, and controls of unfair competition and trade practices against substantive due process challenges.

EQUAL PROTECTION

Under the Fourteenth Amendment, a state may not "deny to any person within its jurisdiction the equal protection of the laws." The United States Supreme

---

39. The privilege has been applied to some small family partnerships. See *United States v. Slutsky*, 352 F.Supp. 1105 (S.D.N.Y. 1972).

Court has used the due process clause of the Fifth Amendment to make the **equal protection clause** applicable to the federal government. Equal protection means that the government must treat similarly situated individuals in a similar manner.

Both substantive due process and equal protection require review of the substance of the law or other governmental action rather than review of the procedures used. When a law or action limits the liberty of all persons to do something, it may violate substantive due process; when a law or action limits the liberty of some persons but not others, it may violate the equal protection clause. Thus, for example, if a law prohibits all advertising on the sides of trucks, it raises a substantive due process question; if it makes an exception to allow truck owners to advertise their businesses, it raises an equal protection issue.

In an equal protection inquiry, when a law or action distinguishes between or among individuals, the basis for the distinction—that is, the classification—is examined by the courts. The courts may use one of three standards: strict scrutiny, intermediate scrutiny, or the "rational basis" test.

STRICT SCRUTINY If a law or action prohibits or inhibits some persons from exercising a fundamental right, the law or action will be subject to "strict scrutiny" by the courts. Under this standard, the classification must be necessary to promote a *compelling state interest*. Also, if the classification is based on a *suspect trait*—such as race, national origin, or citizenship status—the classification must be necessary to promote a compelling state interest. Compelling state interests include remedying past unconstitutional or illegal discrimination but do not include correcting the general effects of "society's" discrimination. Thus, for example, if a city gives preference to minority applicants in awarding construction contracts, the city normally must identify the past unconstitutional or illegal discrimination against minority construction firms that it is attempting to correct. Generally, few laws or actions survive strict-scrutiny analysis by the courts.

INTERMEDIATE SCRUTINY Another standard, that of "intermediate scrutiny," is applied in cases involving discrimination based on gender or legitimacy. Laws using these classifications must be *substantially related to important government objectives*.

For example, an important government objective is preventing illegitimate teenage pregnancies.

Therefore, because males and females are not similarly situated in this regard—only females can become pregnant—a law that punishes men but not women for statutory rape will be upheld, even though it treats men and women unequally.

The state also has an important objective in establishing time limits (called *statutes of limitation*) for how long after an event a particular type of action can be brought. Such limits prevent persons from bringing fraudulent and stale (outdated) claims. Nevertheless, the limitation period must be substantially related to the important objective. For example, suppose that a state law requires illegitimate children to file a paternity action within six years of their birth in order to seek support from their biological fathers. This law will fail if legitimate children can seek support from their fathers at any time because distinguishing between support claims on the basis of legitimacy has no relation to the objective of preventing fraudulent or stale claims.

THE "RATIONAL BASIS" TEST In matters of economic or social welfare, the classification will be considered valid if there is any conceivable *rational basis* on which the classification might relate to a legitimate government interest. It is almost impossible for a law or action to fail the rational basis test. Thus, for example, a city ordinance that in effect prohibits all push-cart vendors, except a specific few, from operating in a particular area of the city will be upheld if the city provides a rational basis—such as reducing the traffic in the particular area—for the ordinance. In contrast, a law that provides unemployment benefits only to people over six feet tall would clearly fail the rational basis test because it could not further any legitimate government objective.

SECTION 4 | Privacy Rights

The U.S. Constitution does not explicitly mention a general right to privacy, and only relatively recently have the courts regarded the right to privacy as a constitutional right. In a 1928 Supreme Court case, *Olmstead v. United States*,[40] Justice Louis Brandeis stated in his dissent that the right to privacy is "the most comprehensive of rights and the right most val-

---

40. 277 U.S. 438, 48 S.Ct. 564, 72 L.Ed. 944 (1928).

ued by civilized men." The majority of the justices at that time did not agree, and it was not until the 1960s that a majority on the Supreme Court endorsed the view that the Constitution protects individual privacy rights. In a landmark 1965 case, *Griswold v. Connecticut*,[41] the Supreme Court held that a constitutional right to privacy was implied by the First, Third, Fourth, Fifth, and Ninth Amendments.

FEDERAL STATUTES AFFECTING PRIVACY RIGHTS

In the last several decades, Congress has enacted a number of statutes that protect the privacy of individuals in various areas of concern. In the 1960s, Americans were sufficiently alarmed by the accumulation of personal information in government files that they pressured Congress to pass laws permitting individuals to access their files. Congress responded in 1966 with the Freedom of Information Act, which allows any person to request copies of any information on her or him contained in federal government files. In 1974, Congress passed the Privacy Act, which also gives persons the right to access such information. Since then, Congress has passed numerous other laws protecting individuals' privacy rights with respect to financial transactions, electronic communications, and other activities in which personal information may be gathered and stored by organizations.

MEDICAL INFORMATION Responding to the growing need to protect the privacy of individuals' health records—particularly computerized records—Congress passed the Health Insurance Portability and Accountability Act (HIPAA) of 1996.[42] The HIPAA requires health-care providers and health-care plans, including certain employers who sponsor health plans, to inform patients of their privacy rights and of how their personal medical information may be used. The act also generally states that a person's medical records may not be used for purposes unrelated to health care—such as marketing, for example—or disclosed to others without the individual's permission. Covered entities must formulate written privacy policies, desig-

nate privacy officials, limit access to computerized health data, physically secure medical records with lock and key, train employees and volunteers on their privacy policies, and sanction those who violate the policies. These protections are intended to assure individuals that their health information, including genetic information, will be properly protected and not used for purposes that the patient did not know about or authorize.

THE PATRIOT ACT In the wake of the terrorist attacks of September 11, 2001, Congress passed legislation, commonly referred to as the USA Patriot Act, which gives increased authority to government officials to monitor Internet activities (such as e-mail and Web site visits) and to gain access to personal financial information and student information.[43] Using technology, law enforcement officials can track the telephone and e-mail conversations of one party to find out the identity of the other party or parties. The government must certify that the information likely to be obtained is relevant to an ongoing criminal investigation but does not need proof of any wrongdoing to gain access to this information. Privacy advocates argue that this law adversely affects the constitutional rights of all Americans, and it has been widely criticized in the media, fueling the public debate over how to secure privacy rights in an electronic age.

OTHER LAWS AFFECTING PRIVACY

State constitutions and statutes also protect individuals' privacy rights, often to a significant degree. Privacy rights are also protected under tort law (see Chapter 6). Additionally, the Federal Trade Commission has played an active role in protecting the privacy rights of online consumers (see Chapter 44). The protection of employees' privacy rights, particularly with respect to electronic monitoring practices, is an area of growing concern (see Chapter 33).

41. 381 U.S. 479, 85 S.Ct. 1678, 14 L.Ed.2d 510 (1965).
42. The HIPAA was enacted as Pub. L. No. 104-191 (1996) and is codified in 29 U.S.C.A. Sections 1181 *et seq.*

43. Uniting and Strengthening America by Providing Appropriate Tools Required to Intercept and Obstruct Terrorism Act of 2001, also known as the USA Patriot Act, was enacted as Pub. L. No. 107-56 (2001).

REVIEWING CONSTITUTIONAL AUTHORITY TO REGULATE BUSINESS

A state legislature enacted a statute that required any motorcycle operator or passenger on the state's highways to wear a protective helmet. Jim Alderman, a licensed motorcycle operator, sued the state to block enforcement of the law. Alderman asserted that the statute violated the equal protection clause because it placed requirements on motorcyclists that were not imposed on other motorists. Using the information presented in the chapter, answer the following questions.

1. | Why does this statute raise equal protection issues instead of substantive due process concerns?

2. | What are the three levels of scrutiny that the courts use in determining whether a law violates the equal protection clause?

3. | What type of government interest must be served to justify discriminatory classifications under each of these three standards of scrutiny?

4. | Which standard, or test, would apply to this situation? Why?

5. | Applying this standard, or test, is the helmet statute constitutional? Why or why not?

TERMS AND CONCEPTS TO REVIEW

amend 77	federal form of government 77	privileges and immunities clause 78
Bill of Rights 81	filtering software 87	probable cause 90
checks and balances 79	free exercise clause 87	search warrant 90
commerce clause 79	full faith and credit clause 78	supremacy clause 80
due process clause 91	meta tags 87	symbolic speech 82
equal protection clause 92	police powers 80	
establishment clause 87	preemption 81	

QUESTIONS AND CASE PROBLEMS

4–1. A Georgia state law requires the use of contoured rear-fender mudguards on trucks and trailers operating within Georgia state lines. The statute further makes it illegal for trucks and trailers to use straight mudguards. In approximately thirty-five other states, straight mudguards are legal. Moreover, in Florida, straight mudguards are explicitly required by law. There is some evidence suggesting that contoured mudguards might be a little safer than straight mudguards. Discuss whether this Georgia statute violates any constitutional provisions.

4–2. ⚖ **QUESTION WITH SAMPLE ANSWER**
Thomas worked in the nonmilitary operations of a large firm that produced both military and nonmilitary goods. When the company discontinued the production of nonmilitary goods, Thomas was transferred to a plant producing military equipment. Thomas left his job, claiming that it violated his religious principles to participate in the

manufacture of goods to be used in destroying life. In effect, he argued, the transfer to the war-materials plant forced him to quit his job. He was denied unemployment compensation by the state because he had not been effectively "discharged" by the employer but had voluntarily terminated his employment. Did the state's denial of unemployment benefits to Thomas violate the free exercise clause of the First Amendment? Explain.
For a sample answer to this question, go to Appendix I at the end of this text.

4–3. A business has a backlog of orders, and to meet its deadlines, management decides to run the firm seven days a week, eight hours a day. One of the employees, Abe Placer, refuses to work on Saturday on religious grounds. His refusal to work means that the firm may not meet its production deadlines and may therefore suffer a loss of future business. The firm fires Placer and replaces him with an employee who is willing to work seven days a week. Placer claims that by terminating his employment, his employer has violated his constitutional right to the free exercise of his religion. Do you agree? Why or why not?

4-4. The framers of the Constitution feared the twin evils of tyranny and anarchy. Discuss how specific provisions of the Constitution and the Bill of Rights reflect these fears and protect against both of these extremes.

4-5. EQUAL PROTECTION. With the objectives of preventing crime, maintaining property values, and preserving the quality of urban life, New York City enacted an ordinance to regulate the locations of commercial establishments that featured adult entertainment. The ordinance expressly applied to female, but not male, topless entertainment. Adele Buzzetti owned the Cozy Cabin, a New York City cabaret that featured female topless dancers. Buzzetti and an anonymous dancer filed a suit in a federal district court against the city, asking the court to block the enforcement of the ordinance. The plaintiffs argued in part that the ordinance violated the equal protection clause. Under the equal protection clause, what standard applies to the court's consideration of this ordinance? Under this test, how should the court rule? Why? [*Buzzetti v. City of New York*, 140 F.3d 134 (2d Cir. 1998)]

4-6. FREEDOM OF SPEECH. The city of Tacoma, Washington, enacted an ordinance that prohibited the playing of car sound systems at a volume that would be "audible" at a distance greater than fifty feet. Dwight Holland was arrested and convicted for violating the ordinance. The conviction was later dismissed, but Holland filed a civil suit in a Washington state court against the city. He claimed in part that the ordinance violated his freedom of speech under the First Amendment. On what basis might the court conclude that this ordinance is constitutional? (Hint: In playing a sound system, was Holland actually expressing himself?) [*Holland v. City of Tacoma*, 90 Wash.App. 533, 954 P.2d 290 (1998)]

4-7. 🏛 CASE PROBLEM WITH SAMPLE ANSWER

To protect the privacy of individuals identified in information systems maintained by federal agencies, the Privacy Act of 1974 regulates the use of the information. The statute provides for a minimum award of $1,000 for "actual damages sustained" caused by "intentional or willful actions" to the "person entitled to recovery." Buck Doe filed for certain disability benefits with an office of the U.S. Department of Labor (DOL). The application form asked for Doe's Social Security number, which the DOL used to identify his claim on documents sent to groups of claimants, their employers, and the lawyers involved in their cases. This disclosed Doe's Social Security number beyond the limits set by the Privacy Act. Doe filed a suit in a federal district court against the DOL, alleging that he was "torn * * * all to pieces" and "greatly concerned and worried" because of the disclosure of his Social Security number and its

potentially "devastating" consequences. He did not offer any proof of actual injury, however. Should damages be awarded in such circumstances solely on the basis of the agency's conduct, or should proof of some actual injury be required? Why? [*Doe v. Chao*, 540 U.S. 614, 124 S.Ct. 1204, 157 L.Ed.2d 1122 (2004)]

To view a sample answer for this case problem, go to this book's Web site at http://wbl.westbuslaw.com, select "Chapter 4," and click on "Case Problem with Sample Answer."

4-8. FREEDOM OF SPEECH. Henry Mishkoff is a Web designer whose firm does business as "Webfeats." When Taubman Co. began building a mall called "The Shops at Willow Bend" near Mishkoff's home, Mishkoff registered the domain name "shopsatwillowbend.com" and created a Web site with that address. The site featured information about the mall, a disclaimer indicating that Mishkoff's site was unofficial, and a link to the mall's official site. Taubman discovered Mishkoff's site and filed a suit in a federal district court against him. Mishkoff then registered various other names, including "taubmansucks.com," with links to a site documenting his battle with Taubman. (A Web name with a "sucks.com" moniker attached to it is known as a "complaint name," and the process of registering and using such names is known as "cybergriping.") Taubman asked the court to order Mishkoff to stop using all of these names. Should the court grant Taubman's request? On what basis might the court protect Mishkoff's use of the names? [*Taubman Co. v. Webfeats*, 319 F.3d 770 (6th Cir. 2003)]

4-9. DUE PROCESS. In 1994, the Board of County Commissioners of Yellowstone County, Montana, created Zoning District 17 in a rural area of the county and a planning and zoning commission for the district. The commission adopted zoning regulations, which provided, among other things, that "dwelling units" could be built only through "on-site construction." Later, county officials were unable to identify any health or safety concerns that were addressed by requiring on-site construction. There was no evidence that homes built off-site would negatively affect property values or cause harm to any other general welfare interest of the community. In December 1999, Francis and Anita Yurczyk bought two forty-acre tracts in District 17. The Yurczyks also bought a modular home and moved it onto the property the following spring. Within days, the county advised the Yurczyks that the home violated the on-site construction regulation and would have to be removed. The Yurczyks filed a suit in a Montana state court against the county, alleging in part that the zoning regulation violated their due process rights. Does the Yurczyks' claim relate to procedural or substantive due process rights? What standard would the court apply to determine whether the regulation is constitutional? How should the court rule? Explain. [*Yurczyk v. Yellowstone County*, 2004 MT 3, 319 Mont. 169, 83 P.3d 266 (2004)]

4–10. ⚖ A QUESTION OF ETHICS

In 1999, in an effort to reduce smoking by children, the attorney general of Massachusetts issued comprehensive regulations governing the advertising and sale of tobacco products. Among other things, the regulations banned cigarette advertisements within one thousand feet of any elementary school, secondary school, or public playground and required retailers to post any advertising in their stores at least five feet off the floor, out of the immediate sight of young children. A group of tobacco manufacturers and retailers filed suit against the state, claiming that the regulations were preempted by the federal Cigarette Labeling and Advertising Act (FCLAA) of 1965, as amended. That act sets uniform labeling requirements and bans broadcast advertising for cigarettes. Ultimately, the case reached the United States Supreme Court, which held that the federal law on cigarette ads preempted the cigarette advertising restrictions adopted by Massachusetts. The only portion of the Massachusetts regulatory package to survive was the requirement that retailers had to place tobacco products in an area accessible only by the sales staff. In view of these facts, consider the following questions. [*Lorillard Tobacco Co. v. Reilly,* 533 U.S. 525, 121 S.Ct. 2404, 69 L.Ed.2d 532 (2001)]

(a) Some argue that having a national standard for tobacco regulation is more important than allowing states to set their own standards for tobacco regulation. Do you agree? Why or why not?

(b) According to the Court in this case, the federal law does not restrict the ability of state and local governments to adopt general zoning restrictions that apply to cigarettes, as long as those restrictions are "on equal terms with other products." How would you argue in support of this reasoning? How would you argue against it?

LAW | on the Web

For updated links to resources available on the Web, as well as a variety of other materials, visit this text's Web site at http://wbl.westbuslaw.com.

For an online version of the Constitution that provides hypertext links to amendments and other changes, as well as the history of the document, go to

http://www.constitutioncenter.org

An ongoing debate in the United States is whether the national government exercises too much regulatory control over intrastate affairs. To find current articles on this topic, go to

http://www.vote-smart.org/issues/FEDERALISM_STATES_RIGHTS

For discussions of current issues involving the rights and liberties contained in the Bill of Rights, go to the Web site of the American Civil Liberties Union at

http://www.aclu.org

For a menu of selected constitutional law decisions by the United States Supreme Court, go to the Web site of Cornell Law School's Legal Information Institute at

http://supct.law.cornell.edu/supct/cases/conlaw.htm

LEGAL RESEARCH EXERCISES ON THE WEB

Go to http://wbl.westbuslaw.com, the Web site that accompanies this text. Select "Chapter 4" and click on "Internet Exercises." There you will find the following Internet research exercises that you can perform to learn more about topics covered in this chapter.

Activity 4–1: LEGAL PERSPECTIVE
Commercial Speech

Activity 4–2: MANAGEMENT PERSPECTIVE
Privacy Rights in Cyberspace

CHAPTER 5

Ethics and Business Decision Making

During the early part of the 2000s, the American public was shocked as one business ethics scandal after another became headline news. Each scandal involved serious consequences. Certainly, those responsible for grossly inflating the reported profits at WorldCom, Inc., ended up not only destroying shareholder value in the company but also facing possible prison terms. Those officers and directors at Enron Corporation who utilized a system of complicated off-the-books transactions to inflate current earnings saw their company go bankrupt—the largest bankruptcy in U.S. history at that time. They harmed not only their employees and shareholders but also the communities in which they worked—and themselves (some of them were sentenced to prison). The misdeeds of officers and directors at Tyco International landed that company and its shareholders in similar trouble.

In response to the public's outrage over these scandals, Congress passed the Sarbanes-Oxley Act of 2002, which will be explained in detail in Chapters 41 and 51. This act generally imposed various requirements on corporations in an effort to deter unethical behavior and encourage corporate accountability in the future. Nevertheless, new allegations of unethical business conduct continue to surface. For example, after the popular painkiller Vioxx was recalled in 2004 because of increased risk of heart attack and stroke, evidence surfaced that its maker, Merck & Company, knew about these dangers and allowed the drug to remain on the market. If these allegations are true, Merck's failure to recall the drug could potentially have adversely affected the health of thousands of patients—as well as exposing the company to years of litigation, investigations by the Justice Department and Congress, and a significant loss in market value.

Business ethics, the focus of this chapter, is not just theory. It is practical, useful, and essential. While a good understanding of business law and the legal environment is critical, it is not enough. Understanding how one should act in her or his business dealings is equally—if not more—important in today's business arena.

SECTION 1 | Business Ethics

Before we look at business ethics, we need to discuss what is meant by ethics generally. **Ethics can be defined as the study of what constitutes right or wrong behavior.** It is the branch of philosophy that focuses on morality and the way in which moral principles are derived or the way in which a given set of moral principles applies to one's conduct in daily life. Ethics has to do with questions relating to the fairness, justness, rightness, or wrongness of an action. What is fair? What is just? What is the right thing to do in this situation? These are essentially ethical questions.

WHAT IS BUSINESS ETHICS?

Business ethics focuses on what constitutes right or wrong behavior in the business world and on how moral and ethical principles are applied by businesspersons to situations that arise in their daily activities in the workplace. Note that business ethics is not a separate kind of ethics. The ethical standards that guide our behavior as, say, mothers, fathers, or students apply equally well to our activities as businesspersons. Business decision makers, though, must often address more complex ethical issues and conflicts in the workplace than they face in their personal lives.

WHY IS BUSINESS ETHICS IMPORTANT?

Why is business ethics important? The answer to this question is clear from this chapter's introduction. An in-depth understanding of business ethics is important to the long-run viability of a corporation. A thorough knowledge of business ethics is also important to the well-being of the individual officers and directors of the corporation, as well as to the welfare of the firm's employees. Certainly, corporate decisions and activities can significantly affect not only those who own, operate, or work for the company but also such groups as suppliers, the community, and society as a whole.

Throughout this text you will be exposed to a series of ethical issues at the end of every unit. These special *Focus on Ethics* features allow you to examine and apply the various concepts of business ethics that we present in this chapter.

Note that questions concerning ethical and responsible behavior are not confined to the corporate context. Business ethics applies to *all* businesses, regardless of their organizational forms. In a business partnership, for example, partners owe a *fiduciary duty* (a duty of trust and loyalty) to each other and to their firm. This duty can sometimes conflict with what a partner sees as his or her own best interest. Partners who act solely in their own interests may violate their duties to the other partners and the firm, however. By violating this duty, they may end up paying steep penalties—as the following case illustrates.

CASE 5.1   Time Warner Entertainment Co. v. Six Flags Over Georgia, L.L.C.

Georgia Court
of Appeals. 2002.
254 Ga.App. 598.
563 S.E.2d 178.

BACKGROUND AND FACTS *The Six Flags Over Georgia theme park in Atlanta, Georgia, was developed in 1967 as a limited partnership known as Six Flags Over Georgia, L.L.C. (Flags). The sole limited partner was Six Flags Fund, Limited (Fund). The general partner was Six Flags Over Georgia, Inc. (SFOG). In 1991, Time Warner Entertainment Company (TWE) became the majority shareholder of SFOG. The next year, TWE secretly bought 13.7 acres of land next to the park, limiting the park's expansion opportunities. Over the next couple of years, using confidential business information from the park, TWE began plans to develop a competing park. Meanwhile, TWE installed no major new attractions at the park, deferred basic maintenance, withheld financial information from Fund (the limited partner), and began signing future employment contracts with SFOG officers. TWE also charged Flags for unrelated expenses, including over $4 million for lunches in New York City and luxury automobiles for TWE officers. Flags and Fund filed a suit in a Georgia state court against TWE and SFOG, alleging, among other things, breach of fiduciary duty. A jury awarded the plaintiffs $197,296,000 in compensatory damages and $257,000,000 in punitive damages. TWE appealed to a state intermediate appellate court, alleging in part that the amount of the punitive damages was excessive.*

IN THE LANGUAGE OF THE COURT

ELLINGTON, Judge.
* * * *

We begin our analysis by examining the degree of reprehensibility [wrongfulness] of appellants' conduct in this case. *In examining the degree of reprehensibility of a defendant's conduct, [there are] a number of aggravating factors [to consider], including whether the harm was more than purely economic in nature, and whether the defendant's behavior evinced indifference to or reckless disregard for the health and safety of others.* Here, although the harm to Flags and Fund was primarily economic, it was caused by conduct we find especially reprehensible. Appellants' intentional breach of its fiduciary duty revealed a callous indifference to the financial well-being of its limited partners and their individual investors. [Emphasis added.]

* * * [T]he evidence [presented] supported the jury's conclusion that appellants acted in concert to breach SFOG's fiduciary duty to its business partners. * * * [T]his evidence clearly and convincingly supported an award of punitive damages * * * because the evidence showed that the appellants withheld vital business information from Fund and Flags, undertook to compete with them, took money belonging to them, and carried out a plan to depress the value of their investment, the Six Flags Over Georgia Park. Moreover, the jury found a specific intent to cause harm * * * .

Appellants' conduct toward its partners and those who invested in the limited partnership was part of a premeditated plan surreptitiously [secretly] executed over a period of years. Appellants' conduct was deceitful, self-serving, and financially damaging. More importantly, however, appellants' conduct was a breach of fiduciary duty, a violation of a confidential relationship of trust requiring the utmost in good faith. * * * Appellants' conduct was, in short, the kind of behavior we find deserving of reproof [disapproval], rebuke, or censure; blameworthy—the very definition of reprehensible. * * * *Trickery and deceit are reprehensible wrongs, especially when done intentionally through affirmative acts of misconduct.* * * * [Emphasis added.]

* * * *

In this case, the ratio of compensatory to punitive damages is 1 to 1.3. We see no shocking disparity inherent in this figure. Nor does it appear to approach that fuzzy line suggesting the bounds of constitutional impropriety. More importantly, however, given the amount of intentional economic damage inflicted by the appellants, corporate entities with collective assets measured in billions of dollars, we believe the award of punitive damages was reasonably calculated to punish them and to deter such conduct in the future.

DECISION AND REMEDY *The state intermediate appellate court affirmed the judgment of the lower court, finding that the award of punitive damages was not excessive, considering the defendants' financial status and "reprehensible" conduct toward the plaintiffs.*

WHAT IF THE FACTS WERE DIFFERENT? *If TWE had proceeded with its plans to build a competing park but had not otherwise acted "reprehensibly" with regard to Flags and Fund, how might the decision in this case have been different?*

SECTION 2 | Setting the Right Ethical Tone

Many unethical business decisions are made simply because they *can* be made. In other words, the decision makers not only have the opportunity to make such decisions but also are not too concerned about being seriously sanctioned for their unethical actions. Perhaps one of the most difficult challenges for business leaders today is to create the right "ethical tone" in their workplaces so as to deter unethical conduct.

THE IMPORTANCE OF ETHICAL LEADERSHIP

Talking about ethical business decision making means nothing if management does not set standards. Moreover, managers must apply those standards to themselves and to the employees in the company.

ATTITUDE OF TOP MANAGEMENT One of the most important factors in creating and maintaining an ethical workplace is the attitude of top management. Managers who are not totally committed to maintaining an ethical workplace will rarely succeed in creating one. Surveys of business executives indicate that management's behavior, more than anything else, sets the ethical tone of a firm. In other words, employees take their cues from management. If a firm's managers adhere to obvious ethical norms in their business dealings, employees will likely follow their lead. In contrast, if managers act unethically, employees will see no reason to behave any differently. For example, an employee who observes a manager cheating on her expense account quickly learns that such behavior is acceptable.

Managers can also reduce the probability that employees will act unethically by setting realistic production or sales goals. If a sales quota, for example, can be met only through high-pressure, unethical sales tactics, employees trying to act "in the best interests of the firm" may think that management is implicitly asking them to behave unethically.

LOOKING THE OTHER WAY A manager who looks the other way when she or he knows about an employee's unethical behavior also sets an example—one indicating that ethical transgressions will be accepted. Managers must show that they will not tolerate unethical business behavior. Although this may seem harsh, managers have found that discharging even one employee for ethical reasons has a tremendous impact as a deterrent to unethical behavior in the workplace. The following case illustrates what can happen when managers look the other way.

CASE 5.2

United States
District Court,
District of Alaska, 2004.
296 F.Supp.2d 1071.

In re the *Exxon Valdez*

HOLLAND, District Judge.

*   *   *   *

*   *   * On Good Friday, March 24, 1989, the oil tanker *Exxon Valdez* was run aground on Bligh Reef in Prince William Sound, Alaska.

On March 24, 1989, *   *   * Joseph Hazelwood was in command of the *Exxon Valdez*. *   *   *

*   *   *   *

Defendant Exxon Shipping [Company] owned the *Exxon Valdez*. Exxon employed Captain Hazelwood, and kept him employed knowing that he had an alcohol problem. The captain had supposedly been rehabilitated, but Exxon knew better before March 24, 1989. Hazelwood had sought treatment for alcohol abuse in 1985 but had "fallen off the wagon" by the spring of 1986. *   *   * Yet, Exxon continued to allow Hazelwood to command a supertanker carrying a hazardous cargo. Because Exxon did nothing despite its knowledge that Hazelwood was once again drinking, Captain Hazelwood was *the* person in charge of a vessel as long as three football fields and carrying 53 million gallons of crude oil. *   *   *

*   *   *   *

The best available estimate of the crude oil lost from the *Exxon Valdez* into Prince William Sound is about 11 million gallons. *   *   *

*   *   * Commercial fisheries throughout this area were totally disrupted, with entire fisheries being closed for the 1989 season. *   *   * Subsistence fishing by residents of Prince William Sound and Lower Cook Inlet villages was also disrupted. *   *   * Shore-based businesses dependent upon the fishing industry were also disrupted as were the resources of cities such as Cordova.

*   *   * Exxon undertook a massive cleanup effort. Approximately $2.1 billion was ultimately spent in efforts to remove the spilled crude oil from the waters and beaches of Prince William Sound, Lower Cook Inlet, and Kodiak Island. Also *   *   *, Exxon undertook a voluntary claims program, ultimately paying out $303 million, principally to fishermen whose livelihood was disrupted *   *   *.

*   *   *   *

[Lawsuits] (involving thousands of plaintiffs) were ultimately *   *   * consolidated into this case. *   *   *

*   *   *   *

*   *   * The jury awarded a breathtaking $5 billion in punitive damages against *   *   * Exxon *   *   *.

*   *   *   *

Exxon appealed *   *   * the amount of punitive damages [to the U.S. Court of Appeals for the Ninth Circuit]. *   *   *

*   *   *   *

*   *   * [T]he Ninth Circuit Court of Appeals in this case reiterated the *   *   * guideposts *   *   * for use in determining whether punitive damages are *   *   * grossly excessive [including] *   *   * the reprehensibility of the defendant's conduct *   *   *. The court of appeals remanded the case [and] *   *   * unequivocally told this court that "[t]he $5 billion punitive damages award is too high *   *   * " and "[i]t must be reduced."

CASE 5.2 Continued

*   *   *   *

*   *   * [T]he question before us is whether, under the circumstances of this case, an award of $5 billion in punitive damages is grossly excessive *   *   * .

*   *   *   *

*   *   * [T]he reprehensibility of the defendant's conduct is the most important *indicium* [indication] of the reasonableness of a punitive damages award *   *   * . In determining whether a defendant's conduct is reprehensible, the court considers whether:

> the harm caused was physical as opposed to economic; the tortious conduct evinced an indifference to or a reckless disregard of the health or safety of others; the target of the conduct had financial vulnerability; the conduct involved repeated actions or was an isolated incident; and the harm was the result of intentional malice, trickery, or deceit, or mere accident. *   *   *

*   *   *   *

The reprehensibility of a party's conduct, like truth and beauty, is subjective. One's view of the quality of an actor's conduct is the result of complex value judgments. The evaluation of a victim will vary considerably from that of a person not affected by an incident. Courts employ disinterested, unaffected lay jurors in the first instance to appraise the reprehensibility of a defendant's conduct. Here, the jury heard about what Exxon knew, and what its officers did and what they failed to do. Knowing what Exxon knew and did through its officers, the jury concluded that Exxon's conduct was highly reprehensible.

*   *   *   *

*   *   * *Punitive damages should reflect the enormity of the defendant's offense.* *   *   * Exxon's conduct did not simply cause economic harm to the plaintiffs. Exxon's decision to leave Captain Hazelwood in command of the *Exxon Valdez* demonstrated reckless disregard for a broad range of legitimate Alaska concerns: the livelihood, health, and safety of the residents of Prince William Sound, the crew of the *Exxon Valdez*, and others. Exxon's conduct targeted some financially vulnerable individuals, namely subsistence fishermen. Plaintiffs' harm was not the result of an isolated incident but was the result of Exxon's repeated decisions, over a period of approximately three years, to allow Captain Hazelwood to remain in command despite Exxon's knowledge that he was drinking and driving again. Exxon's bad conduct as to Captain Hazelwood and his operation of the *Exxon Valdez* was intentionally malicious. [Emphasis added.]

*   *   * Exxon's conduct was many degrees of magnitude more egregious [flagrant] [than defendants' conduct in other cases]. For approximately three years, Exxon management, with knowledge that Captain Hazelwood had fallen off the wagon, willfully permitted him to operate a fully loaded crude oil tanker in and out of Prince William Sound—a body of water which Exxon knew to be highly valuable for its fisheries resources. Exxon's argument that its conduct in permitting a relapsed alcoholic to operate an oil tanker should be characterized as less reprehensible than [in other cases] suggests that Exxon, even today, has not come to grips with the opprobrium [disgracefulness] which society rightly attaches to drunk driving. *   *   * Based on the foregoing, the court finds Exxon's conduct highly reprehensible.

*   *   *   *

*   *   * [T]he court reduces the punitive damages award to $4.5 billion as the means of resolving the conflict between its conclusion and the directions of the court of appeals.

*   *   *   *

*   *   * [T]here is no just reason to delay entry of a final judgment in this case. The court's judgment as to the $4.5 billion punitive damages award is deemed final *   *   * .

QUESTIONS

1. What might Exxon have done to avoid the tragic consequences in this case?
2. Are there situations in which a business's conduct would be more reprehensible than Exxon's behavior in this case? Explain.

PERIODIC EVALUATION Some companies require their managers to meet individually with employees and to grade them on their ethical (or unethical) behavior. One company, for example, asks its employees to fill out ethical checklists each week and return them to their supervisors. This practice serves two purposes: First, it demonstrates to employees that ethics matters. Second, employees have an opportunity to reflect on how well they have measured up in terms of ethical performance.

CREATING ETHICAL CODES OF CONDUCT

One of the most effective ways to set a tone of ethical behavior within an organization is to create an ethical code of conduct. A well-written code of ethics explicitly states a company's ethical priorities and demonstrates the company's commitment to ethical behavior. The code should set forth guidelines for ethical conduct, establish procedures that employees can follow if they have questions or complaints, and inform employees why these ethics policies are important to the company. A well-written code also might provide appropriate examples to clarify what the company considers to be acceptable and unacceptable conduct.

PROVIDING ETHICS TRAINING TO EMPLOYEES For an ethical code to be effective, its provisions must be clearly communicated to employees. Most large companies have implemented ethics training programs, in which management discusses with employees on a face-to-face basis the firm's policies and the importance of ethical conduct. Some firms hold periodic ethics seminars during which employees can openly discuss any ethical problems that they may be experiencing and learn how the firm's ethical policies apply to those specific problems. Smaller firms should also offer some form of ethics training to employees, because this is one factor that courts will consider if the firm is later accused of an ethics violation.

JOHNSON & JOHNSON—AN EXAMPLE OF WEB-BASED ETHICS TRAINING Creating a code of conduct and implementing it are two different activities. In many companies, codes of conduct are simply documents that have very little relevance to day-to-day operations. When Johnson & Johnson wanted to "do better" than other companies with respect to ethical business decision making, it created a Center for Legal and Credo Awareness. (Its code of ethical conduct is called its credo.)

The center created a Web-based set of instructions designed to enhance the corporation's efforts to train employees in the importance of its code of conduct. Given that Johnson & Johnson has over 110,000 employees in fifty-seven countries around the world, reinforcing its code of conduct and its values has not been easy, but Web-based training has helped. The company established a Web-based legal and compliance center, which consists of a set of interactive modules to train employees in areas of law and ethics. The curriculum is tailored to the individual employee based on his or her activities and job responsibilities. Moreover, employees can participate in the training right from their desks whenever they have the time, and the company can track the employees' progress. The Web-based courses are then integrated into an ethical training program that also involves face-to-face classes. This comprehensive program has contributed to Johnson & Johnson's receiving an award from the *Wall Street Journal* for having the best corporate reputation in America.

CORPORATE COMPLIANCE PROGRAMS

In large corporations, ethical codes of conduct are usually just one part of a comprehensive corporate compliance program. Other components of such a program, some of which were already mentioned, include a corporation's ethics committee, ethical training programs, and internal audits to monitor compliance with applicable laws and the company's standards of ethical conduct.

THE SARBANES-OXLEY ACT AND WEB-BASED REPORTING SYSTEMS The Sarbanes-Oxley Act of 2002[1] requires that companies set up confidential systems so that employees and others may "raise red flags" about suspected illegal or unethical auditing and accounting practices. The act required publicly traded companies to have such systems in place by April 2003.

Some companies have created online reporting systems to accomplish this goal. In one such system, employees can click on an icon on their computers that anonymously links them with Ethicspoint, an organization based in Vancouver, Washington. Through Ethicspoint, employees may report suspicious accounting practices, sexual harassment, and other possibly unethical behavior. Ethicspoint, in turn,

---

1. H.R. 3762. This act, which became effective on August 29, 2002, will be discussed in Chapters 41 and 51.

alerts management personnel or the audit committee at the designated company to the potential problem. Those who have used the system say that it is less inhibiting than calling a company's toll-free number.

CORPORATE GOVERNANCE PRINCIPLES Implementation of the Sarbanes-Oxley Act has prompted many companies to create new rules of *corporate governance*. As you will read in Chapter 41, corporate governance refers to the internal principles establishing the rights and responsibilities of a corporation's management, board of directors, shareholders, and *stakeholders* (those affected by corporate decisions, including employees, customers, suppliers, and creditors, for example). Corporate governance principles usually go beyond what is required to comply with existing laws. The goal is to set up a system of fair procedures and accurate disclosures that keeps all parties well informed and accountable to each other and provides a mechanism for the corporation to resolve any

problems that arise. Ultimately, good corporate governance should attract investors and stimulate growth while discouraging unethical behavior and fraud.

COMPLIANCE PROGRAMS MUST BE INTEGRATED
To be effective, a corporate compliance program must be integrated throughout the firm. For large corporations, ethical policies and programs need to be coordinated and monitored by a committee that is separate from the various corporate departments. Otherwise, unethical behavior in one department can easily escape the attention of those in control of the corporation or the corporate officials responsible for implementing and monitoring the company's compliance program.

The following case illustrates what happens when ethical behavior is not practiced in a corporate setting and how such occurrences might be avoided through the widespread implementation of ethics policies and programs.

CASE 5.3 **Securities and Exchange Commission v. WorldCom, Inc.**

United States District Court, Southern District of New York, 2003. 273 F.Supp.2d 431.

BACKGROUND AND FACTS *Corporate officers and others supposedly acting on behalf of WorldCom, Inc., committed perhaps the largest accounting fraud in history. The loss to WorldCom's shareholders alone is estimated to be as much as $100 billion. At the time of this writing, the individuals who allegedly perpetrated the fraud have been charged with crimes or are being investigated by the U.S. Department of Justice. WorldCom's creditors are seeking repayment in a federal bankruptcy court. Shareholders and employees have filed suits in federal district courts to recover what they can. Meanwhile, in another suit, the Securities and Exchange Commission (the Commission), which enforces federal securities laws (see Chapter 41), sought something different:*

—not just to clean house but to put the company on a new and positive footing;
—not just to enjoin future violations but to create models of corporate governance and internal compliance for this and other companies to follow;
*—not just to impose penalties but to help stabilize and reorganize the company and thereby help preserve more than 50,000 jobs * * * .*

With these goals in mind, the Commission and the company's new management submitted to the court for its approval an agreement for the payment of a penalty of $750 million—seventy-five times greater than any previous such penalty.

IN THE LANGUAGE OF THE COURT

RAKOFF, District Judge.

This case raises fundamental questions about how market regulators, and the courts, should respond when criminals use the vehicle of a public company to commit a massive fraud. While the persons who perpetrated the fraud can be criminally prosecuted, the exposure of the fraud often creates * * * pressures that can drive the company into bankruptcy, leaving * * * creditors with little and shareholders with nothing. Innocent employees may find their jobs in jeopardy, and, if the company is very large, entire segments of the market may be disrupted. In a situation where immense financial suffering is therefore likely, is there nothing government regulators can do to restore equilibrium?
* * * *

CONTINUED ▶

CASE 5.3 | Continued

The first step in this journey, taken at the very outset of the litigation, was the joint decision of the parties to have the Court appoint a Corporate Monitor to oversee the proposed transformation. * * *

Under the Corporate Monitor's watchful eye, the company has replaced its entire board of directors, hired a new and dynamic chief executive officer and begun recruiting other senior managers from without, fired or accepted the resignation of every employee accused * * * of having participated in the fraud, and terminated even those employees who, while not accused of personal misconduct, are alleged to have been insufficiently attentive in preventing the fraud. In this connection, the company has already spent more than $50 million of its own money to fund unrestricted investigations * * * , and their detailed reports have been given wide publicity.

The company has also consented to a permanent injunction authorizing the Corporate Monitor to undertake a complete overhaul of the company's corporate governance and authorizing a group of highly-qualified independent consultants to ascertain that the company has fully eliminated the many defects in the company's internal controls detected after a comprehensive review by the company's new outside auditors. The new corporate governance strictures will, among much else, mandate an active, informed, and highly independent board, prohibit related-party transactions and conflicts of interest, require a unique shareholder role in the nomination of directors, and impose significant restrictions on executive compensation packages. Moreover, even though not all of the specific changes in corporate governance and internal controls have yet been formulated, the company has committed in advance to adopt and adhere to all corporate governance and internal control recommendations made by the Corporate Monitor and the independent consultants, subject only to appeal to this Court. * * *

The permanent injunction also requires the company to provide a large segment of its employees with specialized training in accounting principles, public reporting obligations, and business ethics, in accordance with programs being specially developed for the company by New York University and the University of Virginia. At the behest of the Corporate Monitor, the Court also obtained from the new Chief Executive Officer a sworn "Ethics Pledge," requiring, on pain of dismissal, a degree of transparency well beyond [the Commission's] requirements. The company has since required its senior management to sign a similar pledge, and has plans to obtain similar pledges from virtually all employees.

The Court is aware of no large company accused of fraud that has so rapidly and so completely divorced itself from the misdeeds of the immediate past and undertaken such extraordinary steps to prevent such misdeeds in the future. While the Court, at the parties' express request, will continue to retain jurisdiction for however long it takes to make certain that these new controls and procedures are fully implemented and secured, the Court is satisfied that the steps already taken have gone a very long way toward making the company a good corporate citizen.
* * * *

[With respect to the agreement] *the Court is satisfied that the Commission has carefully reviewed all relevant considerations and has arrived at a penalty that, while taking adequate account of the magnitude of the fraud and the need for punishment and deterrence, fairly and reasonably reflects the realities of this complex situation.* Undoubtedly the settlement will be criticized by, among others, those shareholders unfamiliar with the severe limits imposed on their recovery by the bankruptcy laws, those competitors whose own self-interest blinds them to the broader range of public policies that such a settlement implicates, and those professed pundits [commentators] and ideologues for whom anything less than a corporate death penalty constitutes an "outrage." But the Court is convinced, for the reasons already outlined above, that the proposed settlement is not only fair and reasonable but as good an outcome as anyone could reasonably expect in these difficult circumstances. [Emphasis added.]

DECISION AND REMEDY *The court approved the agreement between the company's new management and the Securities and Exchange Commission to settle the "monetary penalty phase of this litigation" and issued a judgment to that effect. The parties agreed to pay $500 million in cash and $250 million in the company's new stock to be distributed to "qualifying claimants" (creditors).*

CONFLICTS AND TRADE-OFFS

Management constantly faces ethical trade-offs, some of which may lead to legal problems. As mentioned earlier, firms have implied ethical (and legal) duties to a number of groups, including shareholders and employees.

When a company decides to reduce costs by downsizing and restructuring, the decision may benefit shareholders, but it will harm those employees who are laid off or fired. When downsizing occurs, which employees should be laid off first? Cost-cutting considerations might dictate firing the most senior employees, who generally have higher salaries, and retaining less senior employees, whose salaries are much lower. A company does not necessarily act illegally when it does so. Yet the decision to be made by management clearly involves an important ethical question: Which group's interests—those of the shareholders or those of employees who have been loyal to the firm for a long period of time—should take priority in this situation?

In one case, for example, an employer facing a dwindling market and decreasing sales decided to reduce its costs by eliminating some of its obligations to its employees. The company established a subsidiary corporation that it expected to fail and transferred a number of its employees, and the administration of their retirement benefits, to that entity. When the subsidiary failed, several individuals who were left without retirement benefits sued the company for breaching its fiduciary duty under a federal law governing employer-provided pensions. Ultimately, the United States Supreme Court agreed with the plaintiffs, reasoning that "[l]ying is inconsistent with the duty of loyalty owed by all fiduciaries."[2]

SECTION 3 | Companies That Defy the Rules

One of the best ways to learn the ethical responsibilities inherent in operating a business is to look at the mistakes made by other companies. In the following subsections, we describe some of the ethical failures of companies that have raised public awareness of corporate misconduct and highlighted the need for ethical leadership in business.

ENRON'S GROWTH AND DEMISE IN A NUTSHELL

The Enron Corporation was one of the first companies to benefit from the deregulated electricity market. By 1998, Enron was the largest energy trader in the market. When competition in energy trading increased, Enron diversified into water, power plants, and eventually high-speed Internet and fiber optics (the value of which soon became negligible). Because Enron's managers received bonuses based on whether they met earnings goals, they had an incentive to inflate the anticipated earnings on energy contracts, which they did. Enron included these anticipated earnings in its current earnings profits reports, which vastly overstated the company's actual profit. Then, to artificially maintain and even increase its reported earnings, Enron created a complex network of subsidiaries that enabled it to move losses to its subsidiaries and hide its debts.

The overall effect of these actions was to increase Enron's apparent net worth. These "off-the-books" transactions were also frequently carried out in the Cayman Islands to avoid paying federal income taxes. In addition, Enron's chief executive officer engaged in a pattern of self-dealing by doing business with companies owned by his son and daughter. Enron's management was informed about these incidents of misconduct on numerous occasions, yet the company concealed the financial improprieties for several years—until Enron was bankrupt.

THE ENRON LEGACY

Deceptive accounting practices were at the heart of the Enron debacle, which led to one of the largest bankruptcies in the history of U.S. business. For years to come, the Enron scandal will remain a symbol of the cost of unethical behavior to management, employees, suppliers, shareholders, the community, society, and indeed the world. Enron's shareholders lost $62 billion of value in a very short period of time in the early 2000s as a result of management's deceptive accounting practices, conflicts of interest, and deviation from accepted ethical standards of business.

MERCK & COMPANY— A BRIEF HISTORY OF VIOXX

In 1999, Merck & Company, Inc., the maker of Vioxx, received approval from the U.S. Food and Drug Administration (FDA) to market Vioxx for the

---

2. *Varity Corp. v. Howe,* 516 U.S. 489, 116 S.Ct. 1065, 134 L.Ed.2d 130 (1996).

treatment of acute pain in adults. The FDA gave Vioxx a six-month priority review because it was thought that Vioxx caused fewer gastrointestinal side effects, such as bleeding, than other painkillers (including ibuprofen and aspirin). Merck spent millions of dollars persuading physicians and consumers to use Vioxx for pain, especially arthritis pain, instead of less expensive alternatives, which could cause stomach bleeding. Many people who used Vioxx found that it provided more effective short-term relief for pain, particularly from athletic injuries, than any other painkiller on the market at the time. At its peak, Vioxx had more than 20 million users.

Shortly after the drug's debut, however, troubling signs began to appear. In March 2000, Merck reported the results of a study of eight thousand people who had used Vioxx. The study compared the gastrointestinal effects of Vioxx to naproxen, another popular painkiller. Although the study ultimately found that patients taking Vioxx had less stomach bleeding than those taking naproxen, the study also indicated that patients taking Vioxx for eight months or longer had up to four times as many heart attacks and strokes as patients using naproxen. These results occurred even though the study had excluded patients with heart disease risks.

Independent studies of the drug—conducted in 2001, 2002, and 2004—all suggested correlations between Vioxx and increased risk of heart attack. Finally, Merck's own study revealed that Vioxx increased cardiovascular risks after eighteen months of daily use. Shortly after that, in September 2004, Merck voluntarily removed Vioxx from the worldwide market in the largest drug recall in history.

MERCK'S AWARENESS OF THE RISKS OF VIOXX

As mentioned, the initial 2000 study on Vioxx and naproxen showed that patients taking Vioxx for an extended period had up to four times as many heart attacks and strokes as those who took naproxen. Since the drug was often prescribed on a long-term basis for arthritis patients, this was a significant finding. Merck attributed the result to naproxen's strong protective effect on the heart. Merck never tested this theory, however, and scientists outside the company who found this explanation unlikely began to conduct independent studies of the drug.

In 2001, a cardiologist proposed to Merck a study of Vioxx in patients with severe chest pain, but Merck

declined. When a 2002 study found that patients who took high doses of Vioxx had significantly more heart attacks and strokes than similar patients, Merck stated that it still had confidence in the drug's safety. Merck maintained this stance even after receiving a warning letter from the FDA in 2001 reprimanding the company for minimizing the drug's potentially serious cardiovascular effects. The FDA required Merck to send letters to physicians across the country to correct false or misleading impressions and information.

MERCK'S CHOICE

In May 2000, Merck's top research and marketing executives met to consider ways to defend Vioxx against allegations that it posed cardiovascular risks. One suggestion was to develop a study that would directly test whether Vioxx posed these risks. That idea was rejected. Merck's marketing executives were apparently afraid that conducting a study would send the wrong signal about the company's faith in Vioxx. The company's position over the following years stayed the same: Vioxx was safe unless proved otherwise. At the time this book went to press, the company continued to maintain that stance, at least with respect to the hundreds of lawsuits filed blaming Vioxx as the cause of patients' injuries or deaths. Merck argued that every plaintiff in those suits must prove that the drug, not something else, caused the alleged injury or death. In August 2005, Merck lost its first Vioxx lawsuit, in which the jury awarded $253 million (reduced to $25 million due to Texas's cap on punitive damages) to Carol Ernst, widow of Robert Ernst.

THE DEBATE CONTINUES

The debate over the safety of Vioxx and whether Merck's conduct was ethical poses an interesting question—at what point does a corporation have an ethical duty to act when presented with evidence that its product may be harmful? Various studies estimate that as many as 139,000 people who used Vioxx suffered injury or death. This figure may seem large, but it accounts for less than 1 percent of Vioxx's total users. Some would argue that even one death is too many and that Merck should be responsible for compensating all those who were injured. Others would counter that there are risks involved in the use of any drug and that Merck did nothing wrong by waiting for conclusive evidence of harm before recalling Vioxx. It is likely that the outcome of the hundreds of lawsuits that have already been filed—which could ultimately cost Merck up to $18 billion in damages—and the litigation still to come will decide whether Merck's conduct was ethical. What is clear is that Merck's shareholders lost billions of dollars in value after the company recalled Vioxx and suspicions arose about Merck's conduct.

Shortly after Vioxx was recalled in 2004, questions were posed about the safety of two other drugs—Celebrex and Bextra—in the same class, called COX-2 inhibitors, which were made by different companies and competed with Vioxx. Concerns over drug safety, unethical practices by pharmaceutical companies, and mass consumer advertising of new medications have prompted many to criticize the FDA and recommend an overhaul of its drug-approval system. Even if the FDA eventually adopts revised procedures, however, questions remain over what exactly a corporation must do to fulfill its ethical duties with regard to notifying the public about the potential risks of using a product.

SECTION 4 | Business Ethics and the Law

Today, legal compliance is normally regarded as a **moral minimum**—the minimum acceptable standard for ethical business behavior. Had Enron Corporation strictly complied with existing laws and generally accepted accounting practices, very likely the Enron scandal, which came to light in the early 2000s, would never have happened. Simply obeying the law does not fulfill all business ethics obligations, however, as illustrated by the controversy surrounding the safety of the drug Vioxx. In the interest of preserving personal freedom, as well as for practical reasons, the law does not—and cannot—codify all ethical requirements. No law says, for example, that it is illegal to lie to one's family, but it may be unethical to do so.

It may seem that determining the legality of a given action should be simple. Either something is legal or it is not. In fact, one of the major challenges businesspersons face is that the legality of a particular action is not always clear. In part, this is because there are so many laws regulating business that it is possible to violate one of them without realizing it. The law also contains numerous "gray areas," making it difficult to predict with certainty how a court will apply a given law to a particular action.

LAWS REGULATING BUSINESS

Today's business firms are subject to extensive government regulation. As mentioned in Chapter 1, virtually every action a firm undertakes—from the initial act of going into business, to hiring and firing personnel, to selling products in the marketplace—is subject to statutory law and to numerous rules and regulations issued by administrative agencies. Furthermore, these rules and regulations are changed or supplemented frequently.

Determining whether a planned action is legal thus requires that decision makers keep abreast of the law. Normally, large business firms have attorneys on their staffs to assist them in making key decisions. Small firms must also seek legal advice before making important business decisions because the consequences of just one violation of a regulatory rule may be costly.

Ignorance of the law will not excuse a business owner or manager from liability for violating a statute or regulation. In one case, for example, the court imposed criminal fines, as well as imprisonment, on a company's supervisory employee for violating a federal environmental act—even though the employee was completely unaware of what was required under the provisions of that act.[3]

"GRAY AREAS" IN THE LAW

In many situations, business firms can predict with a fair amount of certainty whether a given action would be legal. For example, firing an employee solely because of that person's race or gender would clearly violate federal laws prohibiting employment discrimination. In some situations, though, the legality of a particular action may be less clear.

For example, suppose that a firm decides to launch a new advertising campaign. How far can the firm go in making claims for its products or services? Federal and state laws prohibit firms from engaging in "deceptive advertising." At the federal level, the test for deceptive advertising normally used by the Federal Trade Commission is whether an advertising claim would deceive a "reasonable consumer."[4] At what point, though, would a reasonable consumer be deceived by a particular ad?

---

3. *United States v. Hanousek*, 176 F.3d 1116 (9th Cir. 1999).
4. See Chapter 44 for a discussion of the Federal Trade Commission's role in regulating deceptive trade practices, including misleading advertising.

In addition, many rules of law require a court to determine what is "foreseeable" or "reasonable" in a particular situation. Because a business has no way of predicting how a specific court will decide these issues, decision makers need to proceed with caution and evaluate an action and its consequences from an ethical perspective. The same problem often occurs in cases involving the Internet when it is often unclear how a court will apply existing laws in the context of cyberspace. Generally, if a company can demonstrate that it acted in good faith and responsibly in the circumstances, it has a better chance of successfully defending its action in court or before an administrative law judge.

SECTION 5 | Approaches to Ethical Reasoning

Each individual, when faced with a particular ethical dilemma, engages in ethical reasoning—that is, a reasoning process in which the individual examines the situation at hand in light of her or his moral convictions or ethical standards. Businesspersons do likewise when making decisions with ethical implications.

How do business decision makers decide whether a given action is the "right" one for their firms? What ethical standards should be applied? Broadly speaking, ethical reasoning relating to business traditionally has been characterized by two fundamental approaches. One approach defines ethical behavior in terms of duty, which also implies certain rights. The other approach determines what is ethical in terms of the consequences, or outcome, of any given action. We examine each of these approaches here.

DUTY-BASED ETHICS

Duty-based ethical standards often are derived from revealed truths, such as religious precepts. They can also be derived through philosophical reasoning.

RELIGIOUS ETHICAL STANDARDS   In the Judeo-Christian tradition, which is the dominant religious tradition in the United States, the Ten Commandments of the Old Testament establish fundamental rules for moral action. Other religions have their own sources of revealed truth. Religious rules generally are absolute with respect to the behavior of their adherents. For example, the commandment "Thou shalt not steal" is

an absolute mandate for a person who believes that the Ten Commandments reflect revealed truth. Even a benevolent motive for stealing (such as Robin Hood's) cannot justify the act because the act itself is inherently immoral and thus wrong.

Ethical standards based on religious teachings also involve an element of *compassion*. Therefore, for example, even though it might be profitable for a firm to lay off a less productive employee, if that employee's family would suffer as a result, a religious person might give this potential suffering substantial weight. Compassionate treatment of others is also mandated to some extent by the "Golden Rule" ("Do unto others as you would have them do unto you"), which most religions follow.

KANTIAN ETHICS   Duty-based ethical standards may also be derived solely from philosophical reasoning. The German philosopher Immanuel Kant (1724–1804), for example, identified some general guiding principles for moral behavior based on what he believed to be the fundamental nature of human beings. Kant believed that human beings are qualitatively different from other physical objects and are endowed with moral integrity and the capacity to reason and conduct their affairs rationally. Therefore, a person's thoughts and actions should be respected. When human beings are treated merely as a means to an end, they are being treated as the equivalent of objects and are being denied their basic humanity.

A central theme in Kantian ethics is that individuals should evaluate their actions in light of the consequences that would follow if *everyone* in society acted in the same way. This **categorical imperative** can be applied to any action. For example, suppose that you are deciding whether to cheat on an examination. If you have adopted Kant's categorical imperative, you will decide *not* to cheat because if everyone cheated, the examination (and the entire education system) would be meaningless.

THE PRINCIPLE OF RIGHTS   Because a duty cannot exist without a corresponding right, duty-based ethical standards imply that human beings have basic rights. For example, the commandment "Thou shalt not kill" implies that individuals have a right to live. Additionally, religious ethics may involve a rights component because of the belief—characteristic of many religions—that an individual is "made in the image of God." This belief confers on the individual great dignity as a person. For one who holds this belief, not to respect that dignity—and the rights and status that flow from it—would be morally wrong.

The principle that human beings have certain fundamental rights (to life, freedom, and the pursuit of happiness, for example) is deeply embedded in Western culture. As discussed in Chapter 1, the natural law tradition embraces the concept that certain actions (such as killing another person) are morally wrong because they are contrary to nature (the natural desire to continue living). Those who adhere to this **principle of rights,** or "rights theory," believe that a key factor in determining whether a business decision is ethical is how that decision affects the rights of others. These others include the firm's owners, its employees, the consumers of its products or services, its suppliers, the community in which it does business, and society as a whole.

WHICH RIGHTS ARE MOST IMPORTANT? A potential dilemma for those who support rights theory, however, is that they may disagree on which rights are most important. When considering all those affected by a business decision, for example, how much weight should be given to employees relative to shareholders, customers relative to the community, or employees relative to society as a whole?

In general, rights theorists believe that whichever right is stronger in a particular circumstance takes precedence. For example, suppose that a firm can either shut down a plant to avoid dumping pollutants in a river, which would affect the health of thousands of people, or save the jobs of the twelve workers in the plant. In this situation, a rights theorist can easily choose which group to favor. (Not all choices are so clear-cut, however.)

OUTCOME-BASED ETHICS: UTILITARIANISM

"The greatest good for the greatest number" is a paraphrase of the major premise of the utilitarian approach to ethics. **Utilitarianism** is a philosophical theory developed by Jeremy Bentham (1748–1832) and modified by John Stuart Mill (1806–1873)—both British philosophers. In contrast to duty-based ethics, utilitarianism is outcome oriented. It focuses on the consequences of an action, not on the nature of the action itself or on any set of preestablished moral values or religious beliefs.

Under a utilitarian model of ethics, an action is morally correct, or "right," when, among the people it affects, it produces the greatest amount of good for the greatest number. When an action affects the majority adversely, it is morally wrong. Applying the utilitarian theory thus requires (1) a determination of which individuals will be affected by the action in question; (2) a **cost-benefit analysis,** which involves an assessment of the negative and positive effects of alternative actions on these individuals; and (3) a choice among alternative actions that will produce maximum societal utility (the greatest positive net benefits for the greatest number of individuals).

The utilitarian approach to decision making commonly is employed by businesses, as well as by individuals. Weighing the consequences of a decision in terms of its costs and benefits for everyone affected by it is a useful analytical tool in the decision-making process. Utilitarianism is often criticized, however, because it tends to reduce the welfare of human beings to plus and minus signs on a cost-benefit worksheet and to "justify" human costs that many find totally unacceptable.

SECTION 6 | Business Ethics on a Global Level

Given the various cultures and religions throughout the world, conflicts in ethics frequently arise between foreign and U.S. businesspersons. For example, in certain countries the consumption of alcohol and specific foods is forbidden for religious reasons. Under such circumstances, it would be thoughtless and imprudent for a U.S. businessperson to invite a local business contact out for a drink.

The role played by women in other countries may also present some difficult ethical problems for firms doing business internationally. Equal employment opportunity is a fundamental public policy in the United States, and Title VII of the Civil Rights Act of 1964 prohibits discrimination against women in the employment context (see Chapter 34). Some other countries, however, offer little protection for women against gender discrimination in the workplace, including sexual harassment.

We look here at how laws governing workers in other countries, particularly developing countries, have created some especially difficult ethical problems for U.S. sellers of goods manufactured in foreign nations. We also examine some of the ethical ramifications of laws prohibiting bribery and the expansion of ethics programs in the global community.

MONITORING THE EMPLOYMENT PRACTICES OF FOREIGN SUPPLIERS

Many U.S. businesses now contract with companies in developing nations to produce goods, such as shoes and clothing, because the wage rates in those nations are significantly lower than in the United States. Yet what if a foreign company hires women and children at below-minimum-wage rates, for example, or requires its employees to work long hours in a workplace full of health hazards? What if the company's supervisors routinely engage in workplace conduct that is offensive to women?

Given today's global communications network, few companies can assume that their actions in other nations will go unnoticed by "corporate watch" groups that discover and publicize unethical corporate behavior. As a result, U.S. businesses today usually take steps to avoid such adverse publicity—either by refusing to deal with certain suppliers or by arranging to monitor their suppliers' workplaces to make sure that the employees are not being mistreated.

THE FOREIGN CORRUPT PRACTICES ACT

Another ethical problem in international business dealings has to do with the legitimacy of certain side payments to government officials. In the United States, the majority of contracts are formed within the private sector. In many foreign countries, however, government officials make the decisions on most major construction and manufacturing contracts because of extensive government regulation and control over trade and industry. Side payments to government officials in exchange for favorable business contracts are not unusual in such countries, nor are they considered to be unethical. In the past, U.S. corporations doing business in these nations largely followed the dictum, "When in Rome, do as the Romans do."

In the 1970s, however, the U.S. press, and government officials as well, uncovered a number of business scandals involving large side payments by U.S. corporations to foreign representatives for the purpose of securing advantageous international trade contracts. In response to this unethical behavior, in 1977 Congress passed the Foreign Corrupt Practices Act (FCPA), which prohibits U.S. businesspersons from bribing foreign officials to secure beneficial contracts.

PROHIBITION AGAINST THE BRIBERY OF FOREIGN OFFICIALS The first part of the FCPA applies to all U.S. companies and their directors, officers, shareholders, employees, and agents. This part prohibits the bribery of most officials of foreign governments if the purpose of the payment is to get the official to act in his or her official capacity to provide business opportunities.

The FCPA does not prohibit payment of substantial sums to minor officials whose duties are ministerial. These payments are often referred to as "grease," or facilitating payments. They are meant to accelerate the performance of administrative services that might otherwise be carried out at a slow pace. Thus, for example, if a firm makes a payment to a minor official to speed up an import licensing process, the firm has not violated the FCPA. Generally, the act, as amended, permits payments to foreign officials if such payments are lawful within the foreign country. The act also does not prohibit payments to private foreign companies or other third parties unless the U.S. firm knows that the payments will be passed on to a foreign government in violation of the FCPA.

ACCOUNTING REQUIREMENTS In the past, bribes were often concealed in corporate financial records. Thus, the second part of the FCPA is directed toward accountants. All companies must keep detailed records that "accurately and fairly" reflect their financial activities. In addition, all companies must have accounting systems that provide "reasonable assurance" that all transactions entered into by the companies are accounted for and legal. These requirements assist in detecting illegal bribes. The FCPA further prohibits any person from making false statements to accountants or false entries in any record or account.

PENALTIES FOR VIOLATIONS In 1988, the FCPA was amended to provide that business firms that violate the act may be fined up to $2 million. Individual officers or directors who violate the FCPA may be fined up to $100,000 (the fine cannot be paid by the company) and may be imprisoned for up to five years.

OTHER NATIONS DENOUNCE BRIBERY

For twenty years, the FCPA was the only law of its kind in the world, despite attempts by U.S. political leaders to convince other nations to pass similar legislation. That situation is now changing. In 1997, the Organization for Economic Cooperation and Development created a convention (treaty) that made the bribery of foreign public officials a serious crime. By 2004, at least thirty-five countries had adopted the convention, which obligates them to enact legislation within their nations in accordance with the treaty. In addition, other international institutions, including the European Union, the Organization of American States, and the United Nations, have either passed or are in the process of negotiating rules against bribery in business transactions.

FOREIGN ETHICS CENTERS

The Ethics Resource Center, a nonprofit organization devoted to promoting ethics since 1922, has been instrumental in providing ethics-related training programs to business organizations in other nations. Since 1995, the center, which is located in Washington, D.C., has worked with ethics groups in different parts of the world to establish institutes for ethics training, including centers in Korea, Russia, South Africa, and Turkey. In 2004, the Ethics Resource Center worked with the United Arab Emirates to establish the Gulf Center for Excellence in Ethics (GCEE). The goal of the GCEE is to bring organizational ethics and corporate governance programs to business and government organizations throughout the Gulf and Arab world.

REVIEWING ETHICS AND BUSINESS DECISION MAKING

Isabel Arnett was promoted to chief executive officer (CEO) of Naturelles, Inc., a company that manufactures and sells herbal supplements. Before the board of directors appointed Arnett CEO, she had managed the company's production department, where she earned a reputation as a "slave driver" who routinely refused raises, benefits, and time off for long-term employees. As CEO, she continued her aggressive management style.

In April 2006, company researchers distilled a natural substance that radically increased the body's metabolism, causing significant weight loss without any change in diet or exercise habits. Although the researchers were reluctant to market the product, called Naturolean, without further study, Arnett initiated a massive marketing campaign and began distributing the supplement. Sales soared, shareholders profited, and the company gained value. Two years later, it was discovered that Naturolean caused irreparable brain damage to fetuses in women who had taken it just before or during pregnancy. Using the information presented in the chapter, answer the following questions.

1. Do employers have an ethical responsibility to give their employees raises, benefits, or time off under duty-based ethical standards? What about under a utilitarian model of ethics? Explain.

2. If the board of directors knew how Arnett treated company employees, was it unethical of them to promote her to CEO? Why or why not?

3. Suppose that Naturelles did have an ethical code of conduct and that Arnett's conduct in promoting Naturolean did not violate that code. Would that affect the determination of whether her conduct was ethical? Why or why not?

4. How might the presence of an ethics code affect a court's determination of whether the company's conduct was ethical?

 ## TERMS AND CONCEPTS TO REVIEW

business ethics 97

categorical imperative 108

cost-benefit analysis 109

ethical reasoning 108

ethics 97

moral minimum 107

principle of rights 109

utilitarianism 109

QUESTIONS AND CASE PROBLEMS

5-1. Some business ethicists maintain that whereas personal ethics has to do with "right" or "wrong" behavior, business ethics is concerned with "appropriate" behavior. In other words, ethical behavior in business has less to do with moral principles than with what society deems to be appropriate behavior in the business context. Do you agree with this distinction? Do personal and business ethics ever overlap? Should personal ethics play any role in business ethical decision making?

5-2. ⚖ QUESTION WITH SAMPLE ANSWER

If a firm engages in "ethical" behavior solely for the purpose of gaining profits from the goodwill it generates, the "ethical" behavior is essentially a means toward a self-serving end (profits and the accumulation of wealth). In this situation, is the firm acting unethically in any way? Should motive or conduct carry greater weight on the ethical scales in this situation?

For a sample answer to this question, go to Appendix I at the end of this text.

5-3. Susan Whitehead serves on the city planning commission. The city is planning to build a new subway system, and Susan's brother-in-law, Jerry, who owns the Custom Transportation Co., has submitted the lowest bid for the system. Susan knows that Jerry could complete the job for the estimated amount, but she also knows that once Jerry finishes this job, he will probably sell his company and retire. Susan is concerned that Custom Transportation's subsequent management might not be as easy to work with if revisions need to be made on the subway system after its completion. She is torn as to whether she should tell the city about the potential changes in Custom Transportation's management. If the city knew about the instability of Custom Transportation, it might prefer to give the contract to one of Jerry's competitors, whose bid was only slightly higher than Jerry's. Does Susan have an ethical obligation to disclose the information about Jerry to the city planning commission? How would you apply duty-based ethical standards to this question? What might be the outcome of a utilitarian analysis? Discuss fully.

5-4. Assume that you are a high-level manager for a shoe manufacturer. You know that your firm could increase its profit margin by producing shoes in Indonesia, where you could hire women for $40 a month to assemble them. You also know, however, that human rights advocates recently accused a competing shoe manufacturer of engaging in exploitative labor practices because the manufacturer sold shoes made by Indonesian women working for similarly low wages. You personally do not believe that paying $40 a month to

Indonesian women is unethical because you know that in their impoverished country, $40 a month is a better-than-average wage rate. Assuming that the decision is yours to make, should you have the shoes manufactured in Indonesia and make higher profits for your company? Or should you avoid the risk of negative publicity and the consequences of that publicity for the firm's reputation and subsequent profits? Are there other alternatives? Discuss fully.

5-5. Shokun Steel Co. owns many steel plants. One of its plants is much older than the others. Equipment at the old plant is outdated and inefficient, and the costs of production at that plant are now twice as high as at any of Shokun's other plants. Shokun cannot increase the price of its steel because of competition, both domestic and international. The plant is located in Twin Firs, Pennsylvania, which has a population of about forty-five thousand, and currently employs over a thousand workers. Shokun is contemplating whether to close the plant. What factors should the firm consider in making its decision? Will the firm violate any ethical duties if it closes the plant? Analyze these questions from the two basic perspectives on ethical reasoning discussed in this chapter.

5-6. ETHICAL CONDUCT. Richard and Suzanne Weinstein owned Elm City Cheese Co. Elm City sold its products to three major customers that used the cheese as a "filler" to blend into their cheeses. In 1982, Mark Federico, a certified public accountant, became Elm City's accountant and the Weinsteins' personal accountant. The Weinsteins had known Federico since he was seven years old, and even before he became their accountant, he knew the details of Elm City's business. Federico's duties went beyond typical accounting work, and when the Weinsteins were absent, he was put in charge of operations. In 1992, Federico was made a vice president of the company, and a year later he was placed in charge of day-to-day operations. He also continued to serve as Elm City's accountant. The relationship between Federico and the Weinsteins deteriorated, and in 1995, he resigned as Elm City's employee and as its accountant. Less than two years later, Federico opened Lomar Foods, Inc., to make the same products as Elm City by the same process and to sell the products to the same customers. Federico located Lomar close to Elm City's suppliers. Elm City filed a suit in a Connecticut state court against Federico and Lomar, alleging, among other things, misappropriation of trade secrets. Elm City argued that it was entitled to punitive damages because Federico's conduct was "willful and malicious." Federico responded in part that he did not act willfully and maliciously because he did not know that Elm City's business details were trade secrets. Were Federico's actions "willful and malicious"? Were they ethical? Explain. [*Elm City Cheese Co. v. Federico*, 251 Conn. 59, 752 A.2d 1037 (1999)]

5-7. CASE PROBLEM WITH SAMPLE ANSWER

Eden Electrical, Ltd., owned twenty-five appliance stores throughout Israel, at least some of which sold refrigerators made by Amana Co. Eden bought the appliances from Amana's Israeli distributor, Pan El A/Yesh Shem, which approached Eden about taking over the distributorship. Eden representatives met with Amana executives. The executives made assurances about Amana's good faith, its hope of having a long-term business relationship with Eden, and its willingness to have Eden become its exclusive distributor in Israel. Eden signed a distributorship agreement and paid Amana $2.4 million. Amana failed to deliver this amount in inventory to Eden, continued selling refrigerators to other entities for the Israeli market, and represented to others that it was still looking for a long-term distributor. Less than three months after signing the agreement with Eden, Amana terminated it, without explanation. Eden filed a suit in a federal district court against Amana, alleging fraud. The court awarded Eden $12.1 million in damages. Is this amount warranted? Why or why not? How does this case illustrate why business ethics is important? [*Eden Electrical, Ltd. v. Amana Co.*, 370 F.3d 824 (8th Cir. 2004)]

To view a sample answer for this case problem, go to this book's Web site at http://wbl.westbuslaw.com, select "Chapter 5," and click on "Case Problem with Sample Answer."

5-8. ETHICAL CONDUCT.

Richard Fraser was an "exclusive career insurance agent" under a contract with Nationwide Mutual Insurance Co. Fraser leased computer hardware and software from Nationwide for his business. During a dispute between Nationwide and the Nationwide Insurance Independent Contractors Association, an organization representing Fraser and other exclusive career agents, Fraser prepared a letter to Nationwide's competitors asking whether they were interested in acquiring the represented agents' policyholders. Nationwide obtained a copy of the letter and searched its electronic file server for e-mail indicating that the letter had been sent. It found a stored e-mail that Fraser had sent to a co-worker indicating that the letter had been sent to at least one competitor. The e-mail was retrieved from the co-worker's file of already received and discarded messages stored on the server. When Nationwide canceled its contract with Fraser, he filed a suit in a federal district court against the firm, alleging, among other things, violations of various federal laws that prohibit the interception of electronic communications during transmission. In whose favor should the court rule, and why? Did Nationwide act ethically in retrieving the e-mail? Explain. [*Fraser v. Nationwide Mutual Insurance Co.*, 352 F.3d 107 (3d Cir. 2004)]

5-9. ETHICAL CONDUCT.

Unable to pay more than $1.2 billion in debt, Big Rivers Electric Corp. filed a petition to declare bankruptcy in a federal bankruptcy court in September 1996. Big Rivers' creditors included Bank of New York (BONY), Chase Manhattan Bank, Mapco Equities, and others. The court appointed J. Baxter Schilling to work as a "disinterested" (neutral) party with Big Rivers and the creditors to resolve their disputes and set an hourly fee as Schilling's compensation. Schilling told Chase, BONY, and Mapco that he wanted them to pay him an additional percentage fee based on the "success" he attained in finding "new value" to pay Big Rivers' debts. Without such a deal, he told them, he would not perform his mediation duties. Chase agreed; the others disputed the deal, but no one told the court. In October 1998, Schilling asked the court for nearly $4.5 million in compensation, including the hourly fees, which totaled about $531,000, and the percentage fees. Big Rivers and others asked the court to deny Schilling any fees on the basis that he had improperly negotiated "secret side agreements." How did Schilling violate his duties as a "disinterested" party? Should he be denied compensation? Why or why not? [*In re Big Rivers Electric Corp.*, 355 F.3d 415 (6th Cir. 2004)]

5-10. VIDEO QUESTION

Go to this text's Web site at http://wbl.westbuslaw.com and select "Chapter 5." Click on "Video Questions" and view the video titled *Ethics: Business Ethics an Oxymoron?* Then answer the following questions.

(a) According to the instructor in the video, what is the primary reason why businesses act ethically?

(b) Which of the two approaches to ethical reasoning that were discussed in the chapter seems to have had more influence on the instructor in the discussion of how business activities are related to societies? Explain your answer.

(c) The instructor asserts that "[i]n the end, it is the unethical behavior that becomes costly, and conversely ethical behavior creates its own competitive advantage." Do you agree with this statement? Why or why not?

LAW | on the Web

For updated links to resources available on the Web, as well as a variety of other materials, visit this text's Web site at http://wbl.westbuslaw.com.

West's Legal Studies in Business offers an in-depth "Inside Look" at the Enron debacle at

http://insidelook.westbuslaw.com

You can find articles on issues relating to shareholders and corporate accountability at the Corporate Governance Web site. Go to

http://www.corpgov.net

For an example of an online group that focuses on corporate activities from the perspective of corporate social responsibility, go to

http://www.corpwatch.org

Global Exchange offers information on global business activities, including some of the ethical issues stemming from those activities, at

http://www.globalexchange.org

LEGAL RESEARCH EXERCISES ON THE WEB

Go to http://wbl.westbuslaw.com, the Web site that accompanies this text. Select "Chapter 5" and click on "Internet Exercises." There you will find the following Internet research exercises that you can perform to learn more about topics covered in this chapter.

Activity 5–1: LEGAL PERSPECTIVE
              Ethics in Business

Activity 5–2: MANAGEMENT PERSPECTIVE
              Environmental Self-Audits

Ethics and the Legal Environment of Business

In Chapter 5, we examined the importance of ethical standards in the business context. We also offered suggestions on how business decision makers can create an ethical workplace. Certainly, it is not wrong for a businessperson to try to increase his or her firm's profits. But there are limits, both ethical and legal, to how far businesspersons can go. In preparing for a career in business, you will find that a background in business ethics and a commitment to ethical behavior are just as important as a knowledge of the specific laws that are covered in this text. Of course, no textbook can give an answer to each and every ethical question that arises in the business environment. Nor can it anticipate the types of ethical questions that will arise in the future, as technology continues to transform the workplace and business relationships.

The most we can do is examine the types of ethical issues that businesspersons have faced in the past and that they are facing today. In the *Focus on Ethics* sections in this book, we provide examples of specific ethical issues that have arisen in various areas of business activity.

In this initial *Focus on Ethics* feature, we look first at the relationship between business ethics and business law. We then discuss various obstacles to ethical behavior in the business context. We conclude the feature with an examination of corporate social responsibility, which is a significant element of today's legal environment of business.

Business Ethics and Business Law

Business ethics and business law are closely intertwined because ultimately the law rests on social beliefs about right and wrong behavior in the business world. Thus, businesspersons, by complying with the law, are acting ethically. Mere legal compliance (the "moral minimum" in terms of business ethics), however, is often not enough. This is because the law does not—and cannot—provide the answers for all ethical questions.

In the business world, numerous actions may be unethical but not necessarily illegal. Consider an example. Suppose that a pharmaceutical company is banned from marketing a particular drug in the United States because of the drug's possible adverse side effects. Yet no law prohibits the company from selling the drug in foreign markets—even though some consumers in those markets may suffer serious health problems as a result of using the drug. At issue here is not whether it would be legal to market the drug in other countries but whether it would be *ethical* to do so. In other words, the law has its limits—it cannot make all ethical decisions for us. Rather, the law assumes that those in business will behave ethically in their day-to-day dealings. If they do not, the courts will not come to their assistance.

Obstacles to Ethical Business Behavior

People sometimes behave unethically in the business context, just as they do in their private lives. Some businesspersons knowingly engage in unethical behavior because they think that they can "get away with it"—that no one will ever learn of their unethical actions.

Examples of this kind of unethical behavior include padding expense accounts, casting doubts on the integrity of a rival co-worker to gain a job promotion, stealing company supplies or equipment, and so on. Obviously, these acts are unethical, and many of them are illegal as well. In some situations, however, businesspersons who would choose to act ethically may be deterred from doing so because of situational circumstances or external pressures.

Ethics and the Corporate Environment Individuals in their personal lives normally are free to decide ethical issues as they wish and to follow through on those decisions. In the business world, and particularly in the corporate environment, rarely is such a decision made by *one* person. If you are an officer or a manager of a large company, for example, you will find that the decision as to what is right or wrong for the company is not totally yours to make. Your input may weigh in the decision, but ultimately a corporate decision is a collective undertaking.

Additionally, collective decision making, because it places emphasis on consensus and unity of opinion, tends to hinder individual ethical assertiveness. For example, suppose that a director has ethical misgivings about a planned corporate venture that promises to be highly profitable. If the other directors have no such misgivings, the director who does may be swayed by the others' enthusiasm for the project and downplay her or his own criticisms.

Furthermore, just as no one person makes a collective decision, so no one person (normally) is held accountable for the decision. The corporate enterprise thus tends to shield corporate personnel from both individual exposure to the consequences of their decisions (such as direct experience with someone who suffers harm from a corporate product) and personal accountability for those decisions.

Ethics and Management Much unethical business behavior occurs simply because management does not always make clear what ethical standards and behaviors are expected of the firm's employees. Although most firms now issue ethical policies or codes of conduct, these policies and codes are not always effective in creating an ethical workplace. At times, this is because the firm's ethical policies are not communicated clearly to employees or do not bear on the real ethical issues confronting decision makers. Additionally, particularly in a large corporation, unethical behavior in one corporate department may simply escape the attention of those in control of the corporation or the corporate officials responsible for implementing and monitoring the company's ethics program.

Unethical behavior may also occur when corporate management, by its own conduct, indicates that ethical considerations take a second seat. If management makes no attempt to deter unethical behavior—through reprimands or employment terminations, for example—it will be obvious to employees that management is not all that serious about ethics. Likewise, if a company gives promotions or salary increases to those who consistently use unethical tactics to increase the firm's profits, then employees who do not resort to such tactics will be at a disadvantage. An employee in this situation may decide that because "everyone else does it," he or she might as well do it too.

Of course, an even stronger encouragement to unethical behavior occurs when employers engage in blatantly unethical or illegal conduct and expect their employees to do so as well. An employee in this situation faces two options, neither of which is satisfactory: participate in the conduct or "blow the whistle" on (inform authorities of) the employer's actions—and, of course, risk being fired. (See Chapter 33 for a more detailed discussion of this ethical dilemma and its consequences for employees.)

Corporate Social Responsibility

At one time, businesses faced few ethical requirements other than complying with the law. Generally, if an action was legal, it was regarded as ethical. By the 1960s, however, this attitude had begun to change significantly. Groups concerned with civil rights, employee safety and welfare, consumer protection, environmental preservation, and other causes began to pressure corporate America to behave in a more responsible manner with respect to these causes. Thus was born the concept of *corporate social responsibility*—the idea that corporations can and should act ethically and be accountable to society for their actions.

Just what constitutes corporate social responsibility has been debated for some time. Clearly, though, corporations that go too far in an attempt to increase their profits at the expense of individuals and groups affected by their decisions ultimately may face public outrage and government remedial action—as Enron, WorldCom, and other companies learned in the early 2000s.

Generally, the debate over corporate social responsibility has to do less with whether corporations *should* be responsible than with *how* and *to whom* they should be responsible. Today, there are a number of views on this issue, including those discussed next.

Profit Maximization Corporate directors and officers have a duty to act in the shareholders' interest. Because of the nature of the relationship between corporate directors and officers and the shareholder-owners, the law holds directors and officers to a high standard of care in business decision making (see Chapter 39). Traditionally, it was perceived that this duty to shareholders took precedence over all other corporate duties and that the primary goal of corporations should be profit maximization. Milton Friedman, the Nobel Prize–winning economist and a proponent of the profit-maximization view, saw "one and only one" social responsibility of a corporation: "to use its resources and engage in activities designed to increase its profits, so long as it stays within the rules of the game, which is to say, engages in open and free competition without deception and fraud."[1]

Those who accept this position argue that a firm can best contribute to society by generating profits. Society benefits because a firm realizes profits only when it markets products or services that are desired by society. These products and services enhance the standard of living, and the profits accumulated by successful businesses generate national wealth. Our laws and court decisions promoting trade and commerce reflect the public policy that the fruits of commerce (income and wealth) are desirable and good. Because our society regards income and wealth as ethical goals, corporations, by contributing to income and wealth, automatically are acting ethically.

The Stakeholder Approach Another view of corporate social responsibility stresses that a corporation's duty to its shareholders should be weighed against its duties to other groups affected by corporate decisions. Corporate decision makers should consider not only the welfare of shareholders but also that of *stakeholders*—employees, customers, suppliers, communities, and any group that has a stake in the corporation. The reasoning behind this "stakeholder view" of corporate social responsibility is that in some circumstances, one or more of these groups may have a greater stake in company decisions than do the shareholders.

Consider an example. A heavily indebted corporation is facing imminent bankruptcy. The shareholder-investors have little to lose in this situation because their stock is already next to worthless. The corporation's creditors will be first in line for any corporate assets remaining. Because in this situation it is the creditors who have the greatest "stake" in the corporation, under the stakeholder view, corporate

---

1. Milton Friedman, "Does Business Have Social Responsibility?" *Bank Administration*, April 1971, pp. 13–14.

directors and officers should give greater weight to the creditors' interests than to those of the shareholders.

Corporate Citizenship Another theory of social responsibility argues that corporations should actively promote goals that society deems worthwhile and take positive steps toward solving social problems. Because so much of the wealth and power of this country is controlled by business, business in turn has a responsibility to society to use that wealth and power in socially beneficial ways. To be sure, since the nineteenth century and the emergence of large business enterprises in America, corporations have generally contributed some of their shareholders' wealth to meet social needs. Indeed, virtually all large corporations today have established nonprofit foundations for this purpose. Yet corporate citizenship requires more than just making donations to worthwhile causes. Under a corporate citizenship view of social responsibility, companies are also judged on how they conduct their affairs with respect to employment discrimination, human rights, environmental concerns, and so on.

Critics of this view believe that it is inappropriate to use the power of the corporate business world to fashion society's goals by promoting social causes. Determinations as to what exactly is in society's best interest involve questions that are essentially political; therefore, the public, through the political process, should have a say in making those determinations. The legislature—not the corporate boardroom—is thus the appropriate forum for such decisions.

It Pays to Be Ethical

Most corporations today have learned that it pays to be ethically responsible—even if this means less profit in the short run (and it often does). Today's corporations are subject to more intensive scrutiny—by both government agencies and the public—than corporations of the past. "Corporate watch" groups monitor the activities of U.S. corporations, including activities conducted in foreign countries. With the availability of the Internet, complaints about a corporation's practices can easily be disseminated to a worldwide audience. Similarly, dissatisfied customers and employees can voice their complaints about corporate policies, products, or services in Internet chat rooms and other online forums. Thus, if a corporation fails to conduct its operations ethically or to respond quickly to an ethical crisis, its goodwill and reputation (and future profits) will likely suffer as a result.

There are other reasons as well for a corporation to behave ethically. For example, companies that demonstrate a commitment to ethical behavior—by implementing ethical programs, complying with environmental regulations, and promptly investigating product complaints, for example—often receive more lenient treatment from government agencies and the courts. Additionally, investors may shy away from a corporation's stock if the corporation is perceived to be socially irresponsible. Finally, unethical (and/or illegal) corporate behavior may result in government action, such as new laws imposing further requirements on corporate entities.

DISCUSSION QUESTIONS

1. | What might be some other deterrents to ethical behavior in the business context, besides those discussed in this *Focus on Ethics* feature?

2. | Can you think of a situation in which a business firm may be acting ethically but not in a socially responsible manner? Explain.

3. | Why are consumers and the public generally more concerned with ethical and socially responsible business behavior today than they were, say, fifty years ago?

4. | Perceptions of social responsibility differ among countries. Discuss some of the ethical implications of these differences for American firms that do business abroad.

5. | Suppose that an automobile manufacturing company has to choose between two alternatives: contributing $1 million annually to the United Way or reinvesting the $1 million in the company. In terms of ethics and social responsibility, which is the better choice?

Intentional Torts

Part of doing business today—and, indeed, part of everyday life—is the risk of being involved in a lawsuit. The list of circumstances in which businesspersons can be sued is long and varied. A customer who is injured by a security guard at a business establishment, for example, may attempt to sue the business owner, claiming that the security guard's conduct was wrongful. Any time that one party's allegedly wrongful conduct causes injury to another, an action may arise under the law of **torts** (the word *tort* is French for "wrong"). Through tort law, society compensates those who have suffered injuries as a result of the wrongful conduct of others.

Many of the lawsuits brought by or against business firms are based on the tort theories discussed in this chapter, which covers intentional torts, and the next chapter, which discusses unintentional torts. Intentional torts arise from intentional acts, whereas unintentional torts often result from carelessness (such as an employee at a store who knocks over a display case and causes injury to a customer). Most torts can occur in any context, but there are a few torts, referred to as **business torts,** that apply only to wrongful interferences with the business rights of others. Included in business torts are such vaguely worded concepts as *unfair competition* and *wrongfully interfering with the business relations of others*. In the concluding pages of this chapter, we look at how the courts have applied traditional tort theories to wrongful actions in the online environment. Tort theories also come into play in the context of product liability (liability for defective products), which will be discussed in detail in Chapter 23.

SECTION 1 | The Basis of Tort Law

Two notions serve as the basis of all torts: wrongs and compensation. Tort law is designed to compensate those who have suffered a loss or injury due to another person's wrongful act. In a tort action, one person or group brings a lawsuit against another person or group to obtain compensation (money damages) or other relief for the harm suffered.

THE PURPOSE OF TORT LAW

The basic purpose of tort law is to provide remedies for the invasion of various *protected interests*. Society recognizes an interest in personal physical safety, and tort law provides remedies for acts that cause physical injury or that interfere with physical security and freedom of movement. Society recognizes an interest in protecting property, and tort law provides remedies for acts that cause destruction or damage to property.

Society also recognizes an interest in protecting certain intangible interests, such as personal privacy, family relations, reputation, and dignity, and tort law provides remedies for invasion of these interests.

Of course, criminal law also involves wrongful conduct and societal interests. A crime, however, is an act so reprehensible that it is considered a wrong against the state or against society as a whole, as well as against the individual victim. Therefore, the *state* prosecutes and punishes (through fines and/or imprisonment—and possibly death) persons who commit criminal acts. A tort action, in contrast, is a civil suit because it involves only private parties and not the government. Nevertheless, some acts do provide a basis for both a criminal prosecution and a tort action—see Chapter 9.

CLASSIFICATIONS OF TORTS

There are two broad classifications of torts: *intentional torts* and *unintentional torts*. The classification of a tort depends largely on how the tort occurs (intentionally or negligently) and the surrounding circumstances. (Under the doctrine of strict liability, discussed in the following chapter, liability may be imposed regardless of fault.)

SECTION 2 | Intentional Torts against Persons

An **intentional tort,** as the term implies, requires intent. The **tortfeasor** (the one committing the tort) must intend to commit an act, the consequences of which interfere with the personal or business interests of another in a way not permitted by law. An evil or harmful motive is not required—in fact, the actor may even have a beneficial motive for committing what turns out to be a tortious act. In tort law, *intent* means only that the actor intended the consequences of his or her act or knew with substantial certainty that specific consequences would result from the act. The law generally assumes that individuals intend the *normal* consequences of their actions. Thus, forcefully pushing another—even if done in jest and without any evil motive—is an intentional tort (if injury results), because the object of a strong push can ordinarily be expected to go flying.

Intentional torts against persons include assault and battery, false imprisonment, infliction of emotional distress, defamation, invasion of the right to privacy, appropriation, and misrepresentation. We discuss these torts in the following subsections.

ASSAULT AND BATTERY

Any intentional, unexcused act that creates in another person a reasonable apprehension or fear of immediate harmful or offensive contact is an **assault.** Note that apprehension is not the same as fear. If a contact is such that a reasonable person would want to avoid it, and if there is a reasonable basis for believing that the contact will occur, then the plaintiff suffers apprehension whether or not she or he is afraid. The interest protected by tort law concerning assault is the freedom from having to expect harmful or offensive contact. The arousal of apprehension is enough to justify compensation.

The *completion* of the act that caused the apprehension, if it results in harm to the plaintiff, is a **battery,** which is defined as an unexcused and harmful or offen-

sive physical contact *intentionally* performed. For example, Ivan threatens Jean with a gun, then shoots her. The pointing of the gun at Jean is an assault; the firing of the gun (if the bullet hits Jean) is a battery. The interest protected by tort law concerning battery is the right to personal security and safety. The contact can be harmful, or it can be merely offensive (such as an unwelcome kiss). Physical injury need not occur. The contact can involve any part of the body or anything attached to it—for example, a hat or other item of clothing, a purse, or a chair or an automobile in which one is sitting. Whether the contact is offensive is determined by the *reasonable person standard*.[1] The contact can be made by the defendant or by some force the defendant sets in motion—for example, a rock thrown, food poisoned, or a stick swung.

COMPENSATION If the plaintiff shows that there was contact, and the jury agrees that the contact was offensive, the plaintiff has a right to compensation. There is no need to establish that the defendant acted out of malice. The underlying motive does not matter, only the intent to bring about the harmful or offensive contact to the plaintiff. In fact, proving a motive is never necessary. A plaintiff may be compensated for the emotional harm or loss of reputation resulting from a battery, as well as for physical harm.

DEFENSES TO ASSAULT AND BATTERY A defendant who is sued for assault, battery, or both can raise any of the following legally recognized defenses:

1. *Consent.* When a person consents to the act that damages her or him, there is generally no liability for the damage done.
2. *Self-defense.* An individual who is defending his or her life or physical well-being can claim self-defense. In a situation of either *real* or *apparent* danger, a person may normally use whatever force is *reasonably* necessary to prevent harmful contact (see Chapter 9 for a more detailed discussion of self-defense).
3. *Defense of others.* An individual can act in a reasonable manner to protect others who are in real or apparent danger.
4. *Defense of property.* Reasonable force may be used in attempting to remove intruders from one's home,

---

1. The *reasonable person standard* is an objective test of how a reasonable person would have acted under the same circumstances. See the subsection entitled "The Duty of Care and Its Breach" in Chapter 7.

although force that is likely to cause death or great bodily injury normally cannot be used just to protect property.

FALSE IMPRISONMENT

False imprisonment is defined as the intentional confinement or restraint of another person's activities without justification. It involves interference with the freedom to move without restriction. The confinement can be accomplished through the use of physical barriers, physical restraint, or threats of physical force. Moral pressure does not constitute false imprisonment. Furthermore, it is essential that the person being restrained not comply with the restraint willingly. In other words, the person being restrained must not agree to the restraint.

Businesspersons are often confronted with suits for false imprisonment after they have attempted to confine a suspected shoplifter for questioning. Under the privilege to detain granted to merchants in some states, a merchant can normally use the defense of *probable cause* to justify delaying a suspected shoplifter. Probable cause exists when there is sufficient evidence to support the belief that a person is guilty. Although the laws governing false imprisonment vary from state to state, generally they require that any detention be conducted in a *reasonable* manner and that the detention be for only a *reasonable* length of time.

INTENTIONAL INFLICTION OF EMOTIONAL DISTRESS

The tort of *intentional infliction of emotional distress* can be defined as an intentional act that amounts to extreme and outrageous conduct resulting in severe emotional distress to another. For example, a prankster telephones an individual and says that the individual's spouse has just been in a horrible accident. As a result, the individual suffers intense mental pain or anxiety. The caller's behavior is deemed to be extreme and outrageous conduct that exceeds the bounds of decency accepted by society and is therefore **actionable** (capable of serving as the ground for a lawsuit).

Emotional distress claims pose several problems. One major problem is that such claims must be subject to some limitation, or the courts could be flooded with lawsuits alleging emotional distress. A society in which individuals are rewarded if they are unable to endure the normal emotional stresses of day-to-day living is obviously undesirable. Therefore, the law usu-

ally focuses on the nature of the acts that fall under this tort. Indignity or annoyance alone is usually not sufficient to support a lawsuit based on intentional infliction of emotional distress.

Many times, however, repeated annoyances (such as those experienced by a person who is being stalked), coupled with threats, are enough. In a business context, for example, the repeated use of extreme methods to collect an overdue debt may be actionable. Also, an event causing an unusually severe emotional reaction, such as the severe distress of a woman incorrectly informed that her husband and two sons have been killed, may be actionable. Because it is difficult to prove the existence of emotional suffering, a court may require that the emotional distress be evidenced by some physical symptom or illness or by a specific emotional disturbance that can be documented by a psychiatric consultant or other medical professional.

DEFAMATION

As discussed in Chapter 4, the freedom of speech guaranteed by the First Amendment is not absolute. In interpreting the First Amendment, the courts must balance the vital guarantee of free speech against other pervasive and strong social interests, including society's interest in preventing and redressing attacks on reputation.

Defamation of character involves wrongfully hurting a person's good reputation. The law imposes a general duty on all persons to refrain from making false, defamatory *statements of fact* about others. Breaching this duty orally involves the tort of **slander;** breaching it in writing or other permanent form (such as a digital recording) involves the tort of **libel.** The tort of defamation also arises when a false statement of fact is made about a person's product, business, or title to property.

Often at issue in lawsuits alleging defamation (including online defamation, discussed later in this chapter) is whether the defendant's statement was one of fact or a *statement of opinion*. Statements of opinion normally are not actionable in tort because they fall under the protection of the First Amendment.

THE PUBLICATION REQUIREMENT The basis of the tort of defamation is the publication of a statement or statements that hold an individual up to contempt, ridicule, or hatred. *Publication* here means that the defamatory statements are communicated to persons other than the defamed party. If Thompson writes

Andrews a private letter falsely accusing him of embezzling funds, the action does not constitute libel. If Peters falsely states that Gordon is dishonest and incompetent when no one else is around, the action does not constitute slander. In neither case was the message communicated to a third party.

The courts have generally held that even dictating a letter to a secretary constitutes publication, although the publication may be privileged (a concept that will be explained shortly). Moreover, if a third party overhears defamatory statements by chance, the courts usually hold that this also constitutes publication. Defamatory statements made via the Internet are actionable as well. Note also that any individual who repeats, or republishes, defamatory statements normally is liable even if that person reveals the source of the statements.

DAMAGES FOR LIBEL Once a defendant's liability for libel is established, *general damages* are presumed as a matter of law. General damages are designed to compensate the plaintiff for nonspecific harms—such as disgrace or dishonor in the eyes of the community, humiliation, injured reputation, and emotional distress, for example—that are difficult to measure. In other words, to recover damages in a libel case, the plaintiff need not prove that he or she was actually injured in any way as a result of the libelous statement.

DAMAGES FOR SLANDER In contrast to cases alleging libel, in a case alleging slander, the plaintiff must prove *special damages* to establish the defendant's liability. The plaintiff must show that the slanderous statement caused the plaintiff to suffer actual economic or monetary losses. Unless this initial hurdle of proving special damages is overcome, a plaintiff alleging slander normally cannot go forward with the suit and recover any damages. This requirement is imposed in cases involving slander because slanderous statements have a temporary quality. In contrast, a libelous (written) statement has the quality of permanence, can be circulated widely, and usually results from some degree of deliberation on the part of the author.

Exceptions to the burden of proving special damages in cases alleging slander are made for certain types of slanderous statements. If a false statement constitutes "slander *per se,*" no proof of special damages is required for it to be actionable. The following four types of utterances are considered to be slander *per se:*

1. A statement that another has a loathsome communicable disease.

2. A statement that another has committed improprieties while engaging in a profession or trade.
3. A statement that another has committed or has been imprisoned for a serious crime.
4. A statement that a woman is unchaste or has engaged in serious sexual misconduct.

DEFENSES TO DEFAMATION Truth is almost always a defense against a defamation charge. In other words, if a defendant in a defamation case can prove that the allegedly defamatory statement of fact was actually true, normally no tort has been committed. Other defenses to defamation may exist if the speech is privileged or concerns a public figure.

—Privileged Speech. In some circumstances, a person will not be liable for defamatory statements because she or he enjoys a **privilege,** or immunity. With respect to defamation, privileged communications are of two types: absolute and qualified.[2] Only in judicial proceedings and certain government proceedings is *absolute* privilege granted. For example, statements made by attorneys and judges in the courtroom during a trial are absolutely privileged. So are statements made by government officials during legislative debate, even if the legislators make such statements maliciously—that is, knowing them to be untrue. An absolute privilege is granted in these situations because judicial and government personnel deal with matters that are so much in the public interest that the parties involved should be able to speak out fully and freely and without restriction.

In other situations, a person will not be liable for defamatory statements because he or she has a *qualified,* or conditional, privilege. For example, statements made in written evaluations of employees are qualifiedly privileged. Generally, if the communicated statements are made in good faith and the publication is limited to those who have a legitimate interest in the communication, the statements fall within the area of qualified privilege. The concept of conditional privilege rests on the common law assumption that in some situations, the right to know or speak is equal in importance to the right not to be defamed. If a communication is conditionally privileged, to recover damages, the plaintiff must show that the privilege was abused.

---

2. Note that the term *privileged communication* in this context is not the same as privileged communication between a professional, such as an attorney, and his or her client. The latter type of privilege will be discussed in Chapter 51, in the context of the liability of professionals.

—Public Figures. In general, false and defamatory statements that are made about **public figures** (public officials who exercise substantial governmental power and any persons in the public limelight) and published in the press are privileged if they are made without "actual malice." To be made with **actual malice,** a statement must be made *with either knowledge of falsity or a reckless disregard of the truth.*[3]

Statements made about public figures, especially when they are communicated via a public medium, are usually related to matters of general public interest; they refer to people who substantially affect all of us. Furthermore, public figures generally have some access to a public medium for answering disparaging falsehoods about themselves; private individuals do not. For these reasons, public figures have a greater burden of proof in defamation cases (they must prove actual malice) than do private individuals.

INVASION OF PRIVACY

A person has a right to solitude and freedom from prying public eyes—in other words, to privacy. As mentioned in Chapter 4, the courts have held that certain amendments to the U.S. Constitution imply a right to privacy. Some state constitutions explicitly provide for privacy rights. Additionally, a number of federal and state statutes have been enacted to protect individual privacy rights in specific areas. Tort law also safeguards these rights through the tort of *invasion of privacy.* Four acts qualify as invasions of privacy:

1. *The use of a person's name, picture, or other likeness for commercial purposes without permission.* For example, using without permission someone's picture to advertise a product or someone's name to enhance a company's reputation invades the person's privacy. (This tort, which is usually referred to as the tort of *appropriation,* will be examined shortly.)

2. *Intrusion on an individual's affairs or seclusion.* For example, invading someone's home or illegally searching someone's briefcase is an invasion of privacy. This tort has been held to extend to eavesdropping by wiretap, unauthorized scanning of a bank account, compulsory blood testing, and window peeping.

3. *Publication of information that places a person in a false light.* This could be a story attributing to someone ideas not held or actions not taken by that person.

(The publication of such a story could involve the tort of defamation as well.)

4. *Public disclosure of private facts about an individual that an ordinary person would find objectionable.* A newspaper account of a private citizen's sex life or financial affairs could be an actionable invasion of privacy.

APPROPRIATION

The use of another person's name, likeness, or other identifying characteristic, without permission and for the benefit of the user, constitutes the tort of **appropriation.** Under the law, normally an individual's right to privacy includes the right to the exclusive use of his or her identity. For example, in a case involving a Ford Motor Company television commercial in which a Bette Midler "sound-alike" sang a song that Midler had made famous, the court held that Ford "for their own profit in selling their product did appropriate part of her identity."[4]

A court ruled similarly in a case brought by Vanna White, the hostess of the popular television game show *Wheel of Fortune,* against Samsung Electronics America, Inc. Without White's permission, Samsung included in an advertisement for Samsung videocassette recorders a depiction of a robot dressed in a wig, gown, and jewelry, posed in a setting that resembled the *Wheel of Fortune* set, in a stance for which White is famous. The court ruled in White's favor, holding that the tort of appropriation does not require the use of a celebrity's name or likeness. The court stated that Samsung's robot ad left "little doubt" as to the identity of the celebrity that the ad was meant to depict.[5]

Cases of wrongful appropriation, or misappropriation, may also involve the rights of those who invest time and money in the creation of a special system, such as a method of broadcasting sports events. Commercial misappropriation may also occur when a person takes and uses the property of another for the sole purpose of capitalizing unfairly on the goodwill or reputation of the property owner.

FRAUDULENT MISREPRESENTATION

A misrepresentation leads another to believe in a condition that is different from the condition that actually exists. This is often accomplished through a false or an

---

3. *New York Times Co. v. Sullivan,* 376 U.S. 254, 84 S.Ct. 710, 11 L.Ed.2d 686 (1964).

4. *Midler v. Ford Motor Co.,* 849 F.2d 460 (9th Cir. 1988).
5. *White v. Samsung Electronics America, Inc.,* 971 F.2d 1395 (9th Cir. 1992).

incorrect statement. Misrepresentations may be innocently made by someone who is unaware of the facts. The tort of **fraudulent misrepresentation,** or *fraud*, however, involves intentional deceit for personal gain.

ELEMENTS OF FRAUD   The tort of fraudulent misrepresentation includes several elements:

1. A misrepresentation of material facts or conditions with knowledge that they are false or with reckless disregard for the truth.
2. An intent to induce another party to rely on the misrepresentation.
3. A justifiable reliance on the misrepresentation by the deceived party.
4. Damages suffered as a result of that reliance.
5. A causal connection between the misrepresentation and the injury suffered.

FACT VERSUS OPINION   For fraud to occur, more than mere **puffery,** or *seller's talk,* must be involved. Fraud exists only when a person represents as a fact something he or she knows is untrue. For example, it

is fraud to claim that the roof of a building does not leak when one knows that it does. Facts are objectively ascertainable, whereas seller's talk is not. "I am the best architect in town" is seller's talk. The speaker is not trying to represent something as fact because the term *best* is a subjective, not an objective, term.

Normally, the tort of fraudulent misrepresentation occurs only when there is reliance on a *statement of fact*. Sometimes, however, reliance on a *statement of opinion* may involve the tort of fraudulent misrepresentation if the individual making the statement of opinion has a superior knowledge of the subject matter. For example, when a lawyer, in a state in which she or he is licensed to practice, makes a statement of opinion about the law, a court would construe reliance on such a statement to be equivalent to reliance on a statement of fact.

Fraudulent and nonfraudulent misrepresentation will be examined further in Chapter 14 in the context of contract law. A growing problem in the online era is fraudulent misrepresentation in Internet transactions, a topic we examine in Chapter 44.

CONCEPT SUMMARY 6.1 | Intentional Torts against Persons

NAME OF TORT	DESCRIPTION
ASSAULT AND BATTERY	Any unexcused and intentional act that causes another person to be apprehensive of immediate harm is an assault. An assault resulting in physical contact is battery.
FALSE IMPRISONMENT	An intentional confinement or restraint of another person's movement without justification.
INTENTIONAL INFLICTION OF EMOTIONAL DISTRESS	An intentional act that amounts to extreme and outrageous conduct resulting in severe emotional distress to another.
DEFAMATION (LIBEL OR SLANDER)	A false statement of fact, not made under privilege, that is communicated to a third person and that causes damage to a person's reputation. For public figures, the plaintiff must also prove that the statement was made with actual malice.
INVASION OF PRIVACY	Publishing or otherwise making known or using information relating to a person's private life and affairs, with which the public has no legitimate concern, without that person's permission or approval.
APPROPRIATION	The use of another person's name, likeness, or other identifying characteristic, without permission and for the benefit of the user.
FRAUDULENT MISREPRESENTATION (FRAUD)	A false representation made by one party, through misstatement of facts or through conduct, with the intention of deceiving another and on which the other reasonably relies to his or her detriment.

SECTION **3** | Business Torts

Torts involving wrongful interference with another's business rights generally fall into two categories—interference with a contractual relationship and interference with a business relationship.

WRONGFUL INTERFERENCE WITH A CONTRACTUAL RELATIONSHIP

The body of tort law relating to *wrongful interference with a contractual relationship* has increased greatly in recent years. A landmark case in this area involved an opera singer, Joanna Wagner, who was under contract to sing for a man named Lumley for a specified period of years. A man named Gye, who knew of this contract, nonetheless "enticed" Wagner to refuse to carry out the agreement, and Wagner began to sing for Gye. Gye's action constituted a tort because it interfered with the contractual relationship between Wagner and Lumley. (Of course, Wagner's refusal to carry out the agreement also entitled Lumley to sue Wagner for breach of contract.)[6]

THE INTENT FACTOR In principle, any lawful contract can be the basis for an action of this type. The plaintiff must prove that the defendant actually knew of the contract's existence and *intentionally induced* the breach of the contractual relationship, not merely that the defendant reaped the benefits of a broken contract.

For example, suppose that Carlin has a contract with Sutter that calls for Sutter to do gardening work on Carlin's large estate every week for fifty-two weeks at a specified price per week. Mellon, who needs gar-

dening services, contacts Sutter and offers to pay Sutter a wage that is substantially higher than that offered by Carlin—although Mellon knows nothing about the Sutter-Carlin contract. Sutter breaches his contract with Carlin so that he can work for Mellon. Carlin cannot sue Mellon because Mellon knew nothing of the Sutter-Carlin contract and was totally unaware that the higher wage he offered induced Sutter to breach that contract.

REQUIRED ELEMENTS The elements necessary for wrongful interference with a contractual relationship to occur can be summarized as follows:

1. A valid, enforceable contract must exist between two parties.
2. A third party must know that this contract exists.
3. This third party must *intentionally* cause one of the two parties to the contract to breach the contract, and the interference must be for the purpose of advancing the economic interest of the third party.

The interference may involve a contract between a firm and its employees or a firm and its customers, suppliers, competitors, or other parties. Sometimes, a competitor of a firm draws away a key employee. If the original employer can show that the competitor induced the breach of the employment contract—that is, that the employee normally would not have broken the contract—damages can be recovered.

The following case illustrates the elements of the tort of wrongful interference with a contractual relationship in the context of a contract between an independent sales representative and his agent (agency relationships are discussed in Chapters 31 and 32). The case was complicated by the existence of a second contract between the sales representative and the third party.

---

6. *Lumley v. Gye*, 118 Eng.Rep. 749 (1853).

CASE 6.1

United States
Court of Appeals,
Eighth Circuit. 2002.
276 F.3d 1027.

Mathis v. Liu

BACKGROUND AND FACTS *Ching and Alex Liu own Pacific Cornetta, Inc. In 1997, Pacific Cornetta entered into a contract with Lawrence Mathis, under which Mathis agreed to solicit orders for Pacific Cornetta's products from Kmart Corporation for a commission of 5 percent on net sales. Under the terms, either party could terminate the contract at any time. The next year, Mathis entered into a one-year contract with John Evans, under which Evans agreed to serve as Mathis's agent to solicit orders from Kmart for the product lines that Mathis represented, including Pacific Cornetta, for a commission of 1 percent on net sales. Under the terms of this contract, either party could terminate it only on written notice of six months. A few months later, Pacific Cornetta persuaded Evans to break his contract with Mathis and enter into a contract with Pacific Cornetta to be its sales representative*

CASE 6.1 | Continued to Kmart. Evans terminated his contract with Mathis without notice. Two days later, Pacific Cornetta terminated its contract with Mathis. Mathis filed a suit in a federal district court against Ching and Alex Liu and Pacific Cornetta, alleging in part wrongful interference with a contractual relationship. The court issued a judgment that included a ruling in Mathis's favor on this claim, but Mathis appealed the amount of damages to the U.S. Court of Appeals for the Eighth Circuit.

IN THE LANGUAGE OF THE COURT

MORRIS SHEPHARD ARNOLD, Circuit Judge.

* * * *

* * * [A] defendant is liable for tortious interference only if the defendant's interference with some relevant advantage was improper. [The] courts [look at several considerations] to determine whether a defendant's interference is improper. These considerations include the nature of the actor's conduct[,] * * * the actor's motive[,] * * * the interests of the other with which the actor's conduct interferes[,] * * * the interests sought to be advanced by the actor[,] * * * the social interests in protecting the freedom of action of the actor and the contractual interests of the other[,] * * * the proximity or remoteness of the actor's conduct to the interference[,] and * * * the relations between the parties. [Emphasis added.]

We conclude that Mr. Mathis made out a * * * case on this element of his claim. If Mr. Evans's agency arrangement with Mr. Mathis had been purely at-will [a legal doctrine under which a contractual relationship can be terminated at any time by either party for any or no reason], we do not believe that Pacific Cornetta's successful effort to hire Mr. Evans * * * would have risen to the level of impropriety necessary to make out a case for tortious interference. That is because a party's interference with an at-will contract is primarily an interference with the future relation between the parties, and *when an at-will contract is terminated there is no breach of it*. In such circumstances, the interfering party is free for its own competitive advantage, to obtain the future benefits for itself by causing the termination, provided it uses suitable means. [Emphasis added.]

Mr. Evans's contract with Mr. Mathis, however, did not create a simple at-will arrangement because Mr. Evans could terminate it only after giving Mr. Mathis six months' notice of his intention to do so. In these circumstances, we think that the jury was entitled to conclude that Pacific Cornetta's blandishments [flattering statements] were improper, especially since *inducing a breach of contract absent compelling justification is, in and of itself, improper*. [Emphasis added.]

* * * *

Mr. Mathis asked for damages for the loss of anticipatory profits on his tortious interference claim. He argues that the damages that the jury awarded were supported by Mr. Evans's sales of * * * Pacific Cornetta products to Kmart [after Pacific Cornetta terminated its contract with Mathis].

* * * *

We reject this theory * * * . Mr. Mathis's losses on these sales were a result of Pacific Cornetta exercising its right to terminate its contract with him at will, not Pacific Cornetta's tortious interference, and the losses were therefore not recoverable under a theory of tortious interference.

DECISION AND REMEDY The U.S. Court of Appeals for the Eighth Circuit affirmed the judgment of the lower court. The appellate court concluded that the defendants had committed wrongful interference with Mathis's contract with Evans. Evans's sales of Pacific Cornetta products after Pacific Cornetta terminated its contract with Mathis could not furnish a basis for an award of damages on this claim, however, because the firm's contract with Mathis was terminable at will.

WHAT IF THE FACTS WERE DIFFERENT? Suppose that Mathis's contract with Pacific Cornetta had stated that Mathis could only be terminated for misconduct or with six months' notice. How might that have affected the court's ruling in this case?

WRONGFUL INTERFERENCE WITH A BUSINESS RELATIONSHIP

Individuals devise countless schemes to attract business, but they are forbidden by the courts to interfere unreasonably with another's business in their attempts to gain a share of the market. There is a difference between *competitive practices* and *predatory behavior*. The distinction usually depends on whether a business is attempting to attract customers in general or to solicit only those customers who have already shown an interest in the similar product or service of a specific competitor.

For example, if a shopping center contains two shoe stores, an employee of Store A cannot be positioned at the entrance of Store B for the purpose of diverting customers to Store A. This type of activity constitutes the tort of wrongful interference with a business relationship, often referred to as interference with a prospective (economic) advantage, and it is commonly considered to be an unfair trade practice. If this type of activity were permitted, Store A would reap the benefits of Store B's advertising.

REQUIRED ELEMENTS   Generally, a plaintiff must prove the following elements to recover damages for the tort of wrongful interference with a business relationship:

1. There was an established business relationship.
2. The tortfeasor, by use of predatory methods, intentionally caused this business relationship to end.
3. The plaintiff suffered damages as a result of the tortfeasor's actions.

DEFENSES TO WRONGFUL INTERFERENCE   A person will not be liable for the tort of wrongful interference with a contractual or business relationship if it can be shown that the interference was justified, or permissible. Bona fide competitive behavior is a permissible interference even if it results in the breaking of a contract.

For example, if Jerrod's Meats advertises so effectively that it induces Sam's Restaurant to break its contract with Burke's Meat Company, Burke's Meat Company will be unable to recover against Jerrod's Meats on a wrongful interference theory. After all, the public policy that favors free competition in advertising definitely outweighs any possible instability that such competitive activity might cause in contractual relations. Therefore, although luring customers away from a competitor through aggressive marketing and advertising strategies obviously interferes with the competitor's relationship with its customers, such activity is permitted by the courts.

SECTION 4 | Intentional Torts against Property

Intentional torts against property include trespass to land, trespass to personal property, and conversion. These torts are wrongful actions that interfere with individuals' legally recognized rights with regard to their land or personal property. The law distinguishes real property from personal property (see Chapter 47). *Real property* is land and things permanently attached to the land. *Personal property* consists of all other items, which are basically movable. Thus, a house and lot are real property, whereas the furniture inside a house is personal property. Money and securities are also personal property.

TRESPASS TO LAND

The tort of **trespass to land** occurs anytime a person, without permission, enters onto, above, or below the surface of land that is owned by another; causes anything to enter onto the land; or remains on the land or permits anything to remain on it. Note that actual harm to the land is not an essential element of this tort because the tort is designed to protect the right of an owner to exclusive possession. Common types of trespass to land include walking or driving on another's land; shooting a gun over another's land; throwing rocks at or spraying water on a building that belongs to someone else; building a dam across a river, thus causing water to back up on someone else's land; and constructing one's building so that it extends onto an adjoining landowner's property.

In the past, the right to land gave exclusive possession of a space that extended from "the center of the earth to the heavens," but this rule has been relaxed. Today, reasonable intrusions are permitted. Thus, aircraft can normally fly over privately owned land. Society's interest in air transportation preempts the individual's interest in the airspace.

TRESPASS CRITERIA, RIGHTS, AND DUTIES
Before a person can be a trespasser, the real property

owner (or other person in actual and exclusive possession of the property, such as a person who is leasing the property) must establish that person as a trespasser. For example, "posted" trespass signs expressly establish as a trespasser a person who ignores these signs and enters onto the property. Any person who enters onto another's property to commit an illegal act (such as a thief entering a lumberyard at night to steal lumber) is established impliedly as a trespasser, without posted signs.

At common law, a trespasser is liable for damages caused to the property and generally cannot hold the owner liable for injuries that the trespasser sustains on the premises. This common law rule is being abandoned in many jurisdictions, however, in favor of a "reasonable duty" rule that varies depending on the status of the parties. For example, a landowner may have a duty to post a notice that the property is patrolled by guard dogs. Also, under the "attractive nuisance" doctrine, a landowner may be held liable for injuries sustained by young children on the landowner's property if the children were attracted to the premises by some object, such as a swimming pool or an abandoned building. Finally, an owner can remove a trespasser from the premises—or detain a trespasser on the premises for a reasonable time—through the use of reasonable force without being liable for assault and battery or false imprisonment.

DEFENSES AGAINST TRESPASS TO LAND Trespass to land involves wrongful interference with another person's real property rights. If it can be shown that the trespass was warranted, however, as when a trespasser enters to assist someone in danger, a defense exists. Another defense exists when the trespasser can show that he or she had a license to come onto the land. A *licensee* is one who is invited (or allowed to enter) onto the property of another for the licensee's benefit. A person who enters another's property to read an electric meter, for example, is a licensee. When you purchase a ticket to attend a movie or sporting event, you are licensed to go onto the property of another to view that movie or event. Note that licenses to enter onto another's property are *revocable* by the property owner. If a property owner asks a meter reader to leave and the meter reader refuses to do so, the meter reader at that point becomes a trespasser.

TRESPASS TO PERSONAL PROPERTY

Whenever any individual, without consent, harms the personal property of another or otherwise interferes with the personal property owner's right to exclusive possession and enjoyment of that property, **trespass to personal property**—also called *trespass to personalty*—occurs. Trespass to personal property involves intentional meddling. If Kelly takes Ryan's business law book as a practical joke and hides it so that Ryan is unable to find it for several days prior to the final examination, Kelly has engaged in a trespass to personal property.

If it can be shown that trespass to personal property was warranted, then a complete defense exists. Most states, for example, allow automobile repair shops to hold a customer's car (under what is called an *artisan's lien,* discussed in Chapter 28) when the customer refuses to pay for repairs already completed. Trespass to personal property was one of the allegations in the following case. (For a discussion of whether spamming constitutes trespass to personal property, see the discussion of cyber torts later in this chapter.)

CASE 6.2 ## Register.com, Inc. v. Verio, Inc.

United States
Court of Appeals,
Second Circuit, 2004.
356 F.3d 393.

LEVAL, Circuit Judge.
 * * * *
 * * * [Register.com, Inc.] is one of over fifty companies serving as registrars for the issuance of domain names on the World Wide Web. As a registrar, Register issues domain names to persons and entities preparing to establish web sites on the Internet. Web sites are identified and accessed by reference to their domain names.
 Register was appointed a registrar of domain names by the Internet Corporation for Assigned Names and Numbers, known by the acronym "ICANN." ICANN * * *

CONTINUED ➡

CASE 6.2 | Continued

administer[s] the Internet domain name system. To become a registrar of domain names, Register was required to enter into a standard form agreement with ICANN * * * .

Applicants to register a domain name submit to the registrar contact information, including at a minimum, the applicant's name, postal address, telephone number, and electronic mail address. The ICANN Agreement, referring to this registrant contact information under the rubric "WHOIS information," requires the registrar * * * to preserve it, update it daily, and provide for free public access to it through the Internet * * * .

* * * [T]he ICANN Agreement requires the registrar to permit use of its WHOIS data "for any lawful purposes except to * * * support the transmission of mass unsolicited, commercial advertising or solicitations via e-mail (spam) * * * ."

* * * *

* * * An entity making a WHOIS query through Register's Internet site * * * would receive a reply furnishing the requested WHOIS information, captioned by a legend devised by Register, which stated,

> By submitting a WHOIS query, you agree that you will use this data only for lawful purposes and that under no circumstances will you use this data to * * * support the transmission of mass unsolicited, commercial advertising or solicitation via e-mail. * * *

* * * *

The defendant [Verio, Inc.] * * * is engaged in the business of selling a variety of web site design, development and operation services. * * * To facilitate its pursuit of customers, Verio undertook to obtain daily updates of the WHOIS information relating to newly registered domain names. To achieve this, Verio devised an automated software program, or robot, which each day would submit multiple successive WHOIS queries * * * . Upon acquiring the WHOIS information of new registrants, Verio would send them marketing solicitations by e-mail, telemarketing and direct mail. * * *

* * * *

Register wrote to Verio demanding that it cease * * * . Verio * * * refused * * * .

Register brought this suit [in a federal district court] on August 3, 2000 * * * . Register asserted, among other claims, that Verio was * * * trespassing on Register's chattels [personal property] in a manner likely to harm Register's computer systems by the use of Verio's automated robot software programs. On December 8, 2000, the district court entered a preliminary injunction. The injunction barred Verio from * * * [a]ccessing Register.com's computers and computer networks * * * by software programs performing multiple, automated, successive queries * * * .

* * * *

Verio * * * attacks the grant of the preliminary injunction against its accessing Register's computers by automated software programs performing multiple successive queries. This prong of the injunction was premised on Register's claim of trespass to chattels. Verio contends the ruling was in error because Register failed to establish that Verio's conduct resulted in harm to Register's servers and because Verio's robot access to the WHOIS database through Register was "not unauthorized." We believe the district court's findings were within the range of its permissible discretion.

*A trespass to a chattel may be committed by intentionally * * * using or intermeddling with a chattel in the possession of another, where the chattel is impaired as to its condition, quality, or value.* [Emphasis added.]

The district court found that Verio's use of search robots, consisting of software programs performing multiple automated successive queries, consumed a significant portion of the capacity of Register's computer systems. While Verio's robots alone would not incapacitate Register's systems, the court found that if Verio were permitted to continue to access Register's computers through such robots, it was "highly probable" that other Internet service providers would devise similar programs to access Register's data, and that the system would be overtaxed and would crash. We cannot say these findings were unreasonable.

Nor is there merit to Verio's contention that it cannot be engaged in trespass when Register had never instructed it not to use its robot programs. As the district court noted,

CASE 6.2 Continued Register's complaint sufficiently advised Verio that its use of robots was not authorized and, according to Register's contentions, would cause harm to Register's systems.

* * * *

The ruling of the district court is hereby AFFIRMED * * * .

QUESTIONS

1. Why should the use of a robot, or "bot," to initiate "multiple successive queries" have a different legal effect than typing and submitting queries manually?
2. Are there any circumstances under which the use of a bot to initiate "multiple successive queries" could be justified against claims of trespass to personal property?

CONVERSION

Conversion is defined as any act that deprives an owner of personal property without that owner's permission and without just cause. Conversion is the civil side of crimes related to theft. A store clerk who steals merchandise from the store commits a crime and engages in the tort of conversion at the same time. When conversion occurs, the lesser offense of trespass to personal property usually occurs as well. If the initial taking of the property was a trespass, retention of that property is conversion. If the initial taking of the property was permitted by the owner or for some other reason is not a trespass, failure to return it may still be conversion.

Even if a person mistakenly believed that she or he was entitled to the goods, a tort of conversion may still have occurred. In other words, good intentions are not a defense against conversion; in fact, conversion can be an entirely innocent act. Someone who buys stolen goods, for example, has committed the tort of conversion even if he or she did not know the goods were stolen.

A successful defense against the charge of conversion is that the purported owner does not in fact own the property or does not have a right to possess it that is superior to the right of the person in possession of the property. Necessity is another possible defense against conversion. If Abrams takes Mendoza's cat, Abrams is guilty of conversion. If Mendoza sues Abrams, Abrams must return the cat or pay damages. If, however, the cat had rabies and Abrams took the cat to protect the public, Abrams has a valid defense—necessity.

DISPARAGEMENT OF PROPERTY

Disparagement of property occurs when economically injurious falsehoods are made not about another's reputation but about another's product or property. *Disparagement of property* is a general term for torts that can be more specifically referred to as *slander of quality* or *slander of title*.

SLANDER OF QUALITY Publishing false information about another's product, alleging it is not what its seller claims, constitutes the tort of **slander of quality.** This tort has also been given the name **trade libel.** The plaintiff must prove that actual damages proximately resulted from the slander of quality. In other words, the plaintiff must show not only that a third person refrained from dealing with the plaintiff because of the improper publication but also that the plaintiff suffered damages because the third person refrained from dealing with him or her. The economic calculation of such damages—they are, after all, conjectural—is often extremely difficult.

It is possible for an improper publication to be both a slander of quality and a defamation. For example, a statement that disparages the quality of a product may also, by implication, disparage the character of a person who would sell such a product.

SLANDER OF TITLE When a publication falsely denies or casts doubt on another's legal ownership of property, and when this results in financial loss to the property's owner, the tort of **slander of title** may exist. Usually, this is an intentional tort in which someone knowingly publishes an untrue statement about another's ownership of certain property with the intent of discouraging a third person from dealing with the person slandered. For example, it would be difficult for a car dealer to attract customers after competitors published a notice that the dealer's stock consisted of stolen autos.

CONCEPT SUMMARY 6.2 | Intentional Torts against Property

NAME OF TORT	DESCRIPTION
TRESPASS TO LAND	The invasion of another's real property without consent or privilege. Specific rights and duties apply once a person is expressly or impliedly established as a trespasser.
TRESPASS TO PERSONAL PROPERTY	The intentional interference with an owner's right to use, possess, or enjoy his or her personal property without the owner's consent.
CONVERSION	The wrongful taking and use of another person's personal property for the benefit of the tortfeasor or another.
DISPARAGEMENT OF PROPERTY	Any economically injurious falsehood that is made about another's product or property; an inclusive term for the torts of *slander of quality* and *slander of title*.

SECTION 5 | Cyber Torts

Torts can also be committed in the online environment. Torts committed via the Internet are often called **cyber torts.** One of the tasks of the courts over the last ten years has been deciding how to apply traditional tort law to torts committed in cyberspace. Consider, for example, issues of proof. How can it be proved that an online defamatory remark was "published" (which requires that a third party see or hear it)? How can the identity of the person who made the remark be discovered? Can an Internet service provider (ISP) be forced to reveal the source of an anonymous comment? We explore some of these questions in this section, as well as some legal issues that have arisen with respect to bulk e-mail advertising.

DEFAMATION ONLINE

Recall from the discussion of defamation earlier in this chapter that one who repeats or otherwise republishes a defamatory statement is subject to liability as if he or she had originally published it. Thus, publishers generally can be held liable for defamatory contents in the books and periodicals that they publish. Now consider online message forums. These forums allow anyone—customers, employees, or crackpots—to complain about a business firm's personnel, policies, practices, or products. Regardless of whether the complaint is justified and whether it is true, it might have an impact on the firm's business. One of the early questions in the online legal arena was whether the providers of such forums could be held liable, as publishers, for defamatory statements made in those forums.

LIABILITY OF INTERNET SERVICE PROVIDERS

Newspapers, magazines, and television and radio stations may be held liable for defamatory remarks that they disseminate, even if those remarks are prepared or created by others. Prior to the passage of the Communications Decency Act (CDA) of 1996, the courts grappled on several occasions with the question of whether ISPs should be regarded as publishers and thus held liable for defamatory messages made by users of their services. The CDA resolved the issue by stating that "[n]o provider or user of an interactive computer service shall be treated as the publisher or speaker of any information provided by another information content provider."[7]

In a leading case on this issue, decided the year after the CDA was enacted, America Online, Inc. (AOL, now part of Time Warner, Inc.), was not held liable even though it failed to promptly remove defamatory messages of which it had been made aware. In upholding a district court's ruling in AOL's favor, a federal appellate court stated that the CDA "plainly immunizes computer service providers like AOL from liability for information that originates with third parties." The court explained that the purpose of the statute is "to maintain the robust nature of Internet communication and, accordingly, to keep government interference in the medium to a minimum."[8] The courts have reached similar conclusions in subsequent cases.[9]

---

7. 47 U.S.C. Section 230.
8. *Zeran v. America Online, Inc.*, 129 F.3d 327 (4th Cir. 1997); *cert.* denied, 524 U.S. 937, 118 S.Ct. 2341, 141 L.Ed.2d 712 (1998).
9. See, for example, *Noah v. AOL Time Warner, Inc.*, 261 F.Supp.2d 532 (E.D.Va. 2003).

Is an Internet dating service liable for a false profile of an actual person—in this case, an actress who has appeared in *Star Trek: Deep Space Nine* and other television shows and movies—posted by an identity thief who provided the content? That was the question in the following case.

CASE 6.3 Carafano v. Metrosplash.com, Inc.

United States
Court of Appeals,
Ninth Circuit, 2003.
339 F.3d 1119.

BACKGROUND AND FACTS *Matchmaker.com is a commercial Internet dating service. For a fee, members post anonymous profiles and view profiles of other members, contacting them via e-mail sent through Matchmaker. In October 1999, someone posted a profile of Christianne Carafano without her knowledge or consent. Under the stage name Chase Masterson, Carafano has appeared in films and television shows, including* Star Trek: Deep Space Nine *and* General Hospital. *Contacting the profile's e-mail address produced an automatic reply that included Carafano's home address and phone number. She began to receive messages responding to the profile, some of which were threatening. Alarmed, she contacted the police. She felt unsafe in her home and stayed away for several months. Meanwhile, Siouxzan Perry, who handled Carafano's e-mail, learned of the false profile and demanded that Matchmaker remove it immediately. Carafano filed a suit in a California state court against Matchmaker and its owner, Metrosplash.com, Inc, alleging invasion of privacy, appropriation, defamation, and other torts. The case was moved to a federal district court, which issued a summary judgment in the defendants' favor. Carafano appealed to the U.S. Court of Appeals for the Ninth Circuit.*

IN THE LANGUAGE OF THE COURT

THOMAS, Circuit Judge.

This is a case involving a cruel and sadistic identity theft. In this appeal, we consider to what extent a computer matchmaking service may be legally responsible for false content in a dating profile provided by someone posing as another person. * * *
* * * *

The dispositive [deciding] question in this appeal is whether Carafano's claims are barred by 47 U.S.C. Section 230(c)(1), which states that "[n]o provider or user of an interactive computer service shall be treated as the publisher or speaker of any information provided by another information content provider." Through this provision, Congress granted most Internet services immunity from liability for publishing false or defamatory material so long as the information was provided by another party. *As a result, Internet publishers are treated differently from corresponding publishers in print, television and radio.* [Emphasis added.]

Congress enacted this provision as part of the Communications Decency Act of 1996 for two basic policy reasons: to promote the free exchange of information and ideas over the Internet and to encourage voluntary monitoring for offensive or obscene material. Congress incorporated these ideas into the text of Section 230 itself, expressly noting that "interactive computer services have flourished, to the benefit of all Americans, with a minimum of government regulation," and that "[i]ncreasingly Americans are relying on interactive media for a variety of political, educational, cultural, and entertainment services." Congress declared it the "policy of the United States" to "promote the continued development of the Internet and other interactive computer services," "to preserve the vibrant and competitive free market that presently exists for the Internet and other interactive computer services," and to "remove disincentives for the development and utilization of blocking and filtering technologies."

In light of these concerns, reviewing courts have treated Section 230(c) immunity as quite robust, adopting a relatively expansive definition of "interactive computer service" and a relatively restrictive definition of "information content provider." *Under the statutory scheme, an "interactive computer service" qualifies for immunity so long as it does not also function as an "information content provider" for the portion of the statement or publication at issue.* [Emphasis added.]

* * * [T]he consensus developing across other [U.S.] courts of appeals [is] that Section 230(c) provides broad immunity for publishing content provided primarily by third parties.

CONTINUED ▶

CASE 6.3 Continued

* * * Congress made a policy choice * * * not to deter harmful online speech through the separate route of imposing tort liability on companies that serve as intermediaries for other parties' potentially injurious messages. Congress's purpose in providing the Section 230 immunity was thus evident. Interactive computer services have millions of users. The amount of information communicated via interactive computer services is therefore staggering. The specter of tort liability in an area of such prolific speech would have an obvious chilling effect. It would be impossible for service providers to screen each of their millions of postings for possible problems. Faced with potential liability for each message republished by their services, interactive computer service providers might choose to severely restrict the number and type of messages posted. Congress considered the weight of the speech interests implicated and chose to immunize service providers to avoid any such restrictive effect. Under Section 230(c), therefore, so long as a third party willingly provides the essential published content, the interactive service provider receives full immunity regardless of the specific editing or selection process.

* * * *

Thus, despite the serious and utterly deplorable consequences that occurred in this case, we conclude that Congress intended that service providers such as Matchmaker be afforded immunity from suit.

DECISION AND REMEDY *The U.S. Court of Appeals for the Ninth Circuit affirmed the lower court's decision. The appellate court held that under the Communications Decency Act, Matchmaker was not responsible for the "underlying misinformation" that characterized the false profile of Carafano.*

PIERCING THE VEIL OF ANONYMITY A threshold barrier to anyone who seeks to bring an action for online defamation is discovering the identity of the person who posted the defamatory message online. ISPs can disclose personal information about their customers only when ordered to do so by a court. Consequently, businesses and individuals are increasingly resorting to lawsuits against "John Does" (John Doe is a fictitious name that is used when the name of the particular person is not known). Then, using the authority of the courts, they can obtain from the ISPs the identities of the persons responsible for the messages.

In one case, for example, Eric Hvide, a former chief executive of a company called Hvide Marine, sued a number of John Does who had posted allegedly defamatory statements about his company on various online message boards. Hvide, who eventually lost his job, sued the John Does for libel in a Florida court. The court ruled that the ISPs, Yahoo and AOL, had to reveal the identities of the defendant Does.[10]

In some other cases, however, the rights of plaintiffs in such situations have been balanced against the defendants' rights to free speech. For example, a New Jersey court refused to compel Yahoo to disclose the identity of a person who had posted an allegedly defamatory message on Yahoo's message board. The court refused to compel disclosure because, in its view, more than a bare allegation of defamation is required to outweigh an individual's "competing right of anonymity in the exercise of [the] right of free speech."[11]

SPAM

Bulk, unsolicited e-mail ("junk" e-mail) sent to all of the users on a particular e-mailing list is often called **spam.**[12] Typical spam consists of a product ad sent to all of the users on an e-mailing list or all of the members of a newsgroup.

SPAM AS A FORM OF TRESPASS TO PERSONAL PROPERTY Spam can waste user time and network bandwidth (the amount of data that can be transmitted within a certain time). It also imposes a burden on an ISP's equipment as well as on an e-mail recipient's computer system. As a result, some courts have held that spam is a trespass to personal property.

---

10. *Does v. Hvide,* 770 So.2d 1237 (Fla.App.3d 2000).

11. *Dendrite International, Inc. v. Doe No. 3,* 342 N.J.Super. 134, 775 A.2d 756 (2001).

12. The term *spam* is said to come from a Monty Python song with the lyrics, "Spam spam spam spam, spam spam spam spam, lovely spam, wonderful spam." Like these lyrics, spam online is often considered to be a repetition of worthless text.

In one case, for example, Cyber Promotions, Inc., sent bulk e-mail to subscribers of CompuServe, Inc., an ISP at that time. CompuServe subscribers complained to the service about the ads, and many canceled their subscriptions. Handling the ads also placed a tremendous burden on CompuServe's equipment. CompuServe told Cyber Promotions to stop using CompuServe's equipment to process and store the ads—in effect, to stop sending the ads to CompuServe subscribers. Ignoring the demand, Cyber Promotions stepped up the volume of its ads. After CompuServe attempted unsuccessfully to block the flow with screening software, it filed a suit against Cyber Promotions in a federal district court, seeking an injunction on the ground that the ads constituted trespass to personal property. The court agreed and ordered Cyber Promotions to stop sending its ads to e-mail addresses maintained by CompuServe.[13]

STATUTORY REGULATION OF SPAM Because of the problems associated with spam, thirty-six states have enacted laws that prohibit or regulate its use. A few states, such as Washington, prohibit unsolicited e-mail that is promoting goods, services, or real estate for sale or lease. In some other states, including Minnesota, an unsolicited e-mail ad must state in its subject line that it is an ad ("ADV"). Many state laws regulating spam require the senders of e-mail ads to instruct the recipients on how they can "opt out" of further e-mail ads from the same source.

The most stringent state law is California's antispam law, which went into effect on January 1, 2004. That law follows the "opt-in" model favored by consumer groups and antispam advocates. In other words, the law prohibits any person or business from sending e-mail ads to or from any e-mail address in California unless the recipient has expressly agreed to receive e-mails from the sender. An exemption is made for e-mail sent to consumers with whom the advertiser has a "preexisting or current business relationship."

THE FEDERAL CAN-SPAM ACT In 2003, Congress enacted the Controlling the Assault of Non-Solicited Pornography and Marketing (CAN-SPAM) Act, which took effect on January 1, 2004. The legislation applies to any "commercial electronic mail messages" that are sent to promote a commercial product or service. Significantly, the statute preempts state antispam laws except for those provisions in state laws that prohibit false and deceptive e-mailing practices.

—Requirements. Generally, the act permits the use of unsolicited commercial e-mail but prohibits certain types of spamming activities, including the use of a false return address and the use of false, misleading, or deceptive information when sending e-mail. The statute also prohibits the use of "dictionary attacks"—sending messages to randomly generated e-mail addresses—and the "harvesting" of e-mail addresses from Web sites through the use of specialized software. Additionally, the law requires senders of commercial e-mail to do the following:

1. Include a return address on the e-mail.
2. Include a clear notification that the message is an ad and provide a valid physical postal address.
3. Provide a mechanism that allows recipients to "opt out" of further e-mail ads from the same source.
4. Take action on a recipient's "opt-out" request within ten days.
5. Label any sexually oriented materials as such.

—Effect of the CAN-SPAM Act. Because the federal CAN-SPAM Act preempts state laws, except for certain provisions relating to deceptive e-mailing practices, stricter provisions in state laws are no longer effective. Thus, it is apparent that the federal act reflects Congress's intent to protect the e-mail marketing industry against state laws, such as California's, that would make e-mail advertising extremely difficult. The federal government also sought to eliminate advertising by peddlers of financial scams and pornography.

Yet critics point out that the new law has done little to reduce the amount of unsolicited e-mail flowing through cyberspace. For one thing, many of the Internet ads being sent today already meet the requirements of the CAN-SPAM Act. For another, because the federal act uses an "opt-out" approach, the burden is placed on e-mail recipients to prevent the delivery of further ads from the same source. Additionally, the act cannot regulate spam sent from foreign servers. A survey conducted shortly after the act went into effect showed almost no noticeable reduction in the amount of spam received through e-mail.[14] Indeed, the volume of spam has actually increased since the CAN-SPAM Act was enacted.

---

13. *CompuServe, Inc. v. Cyber Promotions, Inc.*, 962 F.Supp. 1015 (S.D.Ohio 1997).

14. Pew Internet and American Life Project survey conducted from February 3 to March 1, 2004.

REVIEWING INTENTIONAL TORTS

Two sisters, Darla and Irene, are partners in an import business located in a small town in Rhode Island. Irene is married to a well-known real estate developer and is campaigning to be the mayor of their town. Darla is in her mid-thirties and has never been married. Both sisters travel to other countries to purchase the goods they sell at their retail store. Irene buys Indonesian goods, and Darla buys goods from Africa. After a tsunami (tidal wave) destroys many of the cities in Indonesia to which Irene usually travels, she phones one of her contacts there and asks him to procure some items and ship them to her. He informs her that it will be impossible to buy these items now because the townspeople are being evacuated due to a water shortage. Irene is angry and tells the man that if he cannot purchase the goods, he should just take them without paying for them after the town has been evacuated. Darla overhears her sister's instructions and is outraged. They have a falling-out, and Darla decides that she no longer wishes to be in business with her sister. Using the information presented in the chapter, answer the following questions.

1. | Suppose that Darla tells several of her friends about Irene's instructing the man to take goods without paying for them after the tsunami disaster. Under which intentional tort theory discussed in this chapter might Irene attempt to sue Darla? Would Irene's suit be successful? Why or why not?

2. | Now suppose that Irene wins the election and becomes the city's mayor. Darla then writes a letter to the editor of the local newspaper disclosing Irene's misconduct. What intentional tort might Irene accuse Darla of committing? What defenses could Darla assert?

3. | If Irene accepts goods shipped from Indonesia that were wrongfully obtained, has she committed an intentional tort against property? Explain.

4. | Suppose now that Irene, who is angry with her sister for disclosing her business improprieties, writes a letter to the editor falsely accusing Darla of having sexual relations with her neighbor's thirteen-year-old son. For what intentional tort or torts could Darla sue Irene in this situation?

5. | Would it change your analysis in any of the above questions if the statements that Darla and Irene made were posted on the Internet rather than published in a newspaper? Why or why not?

TERMS AND CONCEPTS TO REVIEW

QUESTIONS AND CASE PROBLEMS

6-1. Richard is an employee of the Dun Construction Corp. While delivering materials to a construction site, he carelessly backs Dun's truck into a passenger vehicle driven by Green. This is Richard's second accident in six months. When the company owner, Dun, learns of this latest accident, a heated discussion ensues, and Dun fires Richard. Dun is so angry that he immediately writes a letter to the union of which Richard is a member and to all other construction companies in the community, stating that Richard is the "worst driver in the city" and that "anyone who hires him is asking for legal liability." Richard files a suit against Dun, alleging libel on the basis of the statements made in the letters. Discuss the results.

6-2. QUESTION WITH SAMPLE ANSWER

Lothar owns a bakery. He has been trying to obtain a long-term contract with the owner of Martha's Tea Salons for some time. Lothar starts a local advertising campaign on radio and television and in the newspaper. This advertising campaign is so persuasive that Martha decides to break the contract she has had with Harley's Bakery so that she can patronize Lothar's bakery. Is Lothar liable to Harley's Bakery for the tort of wrongful interference with a contractual relationship? Is Martha liable for this tort?

For a sample answer to this question, go to Appendix I at the end of this text.

6-3. Gerrit is a former employee of ABC Auto Repair Co. He enters ABC's repair shop, claiming that the company owes him $800 in back wages. Gerrit argues with ABC's general manager, Steward, and Steward orders him off the property. Gerrit refuses to leave, and Steward tells two mechanics to throw him off the property. Gerrit runs to his truck, but on the way, he grabs some tools valued at $800; then he drives away. Gerrit refuses to return the tools.

(a) Discuss whether Gerrit has committed any torts.
(b) If the mechanics had thrown Gerrit off the property, would ABC be guilty of assault and battery? Explain.

6-4. Bombardier Capital, Inc., provides financing to boat and recreational vehicle dealers. Bombardier's credit policy requires dealers to forward immediately to Bombardier the proceeds of boat sales. When Howard Mulcahey, Bombardier's vice president of sales and marketing, learned that some dealers were not complying with this policy, he told Frank Chandler, Bombardier's credit director, of his concern. Before Chandler could obtain the proceeds, Mulcahey falsely told Jacques Gingras, Bombardier's president, that Chandler was, among other things, trying to hide the problem. On the basis of

Mulcahey's statements, Gingras fired Chandler and put Mulcahey in charge of the credit department. Under what business tort theory discussed in this chapter might Chandler recover damages from Mulcahey? Explain.

6-5. MISAPPROPRIATION. The United States Golf Association (USGA) was founded in 1894. In 1911, the USGA developed the Handicap System, which was designed to enable individual golfers of different abilities to compete fairly with one another. Between 1987 and 1993, the USGA revised the system and implemented new handicap formulas. The USGA permits any entity to use the system free of charge as long as it complies with the USGA's procedure for peer review through authorized golf associations of the handicaps issued to individual golfers. In 1991, Arroyo Software Corp. began marketing software, known as EagleTrak, that incorporated the USGA's system but did not incorporate any means for obtaining peer review of handicap computations. Arroyo's ads also used the USGA's logo without its permission. The USGA filed a suit in a California state court against Arroyo, alleging, among other things, misappropriation. The USGA asked the court to stop Arroyo's use of its system. Should the court grant the injunction? Why or why not? [*United States Golf Association v. Arroyo Software Corp.*, 69 Cal.App.4th 607, 81 Cal.Rptr.2d 708 (1999)]

6-6. TRESPASS TO PROPERTY. America Online, Inc. (AOL), provides services to its customers, or members, including the transmission of e-mail to and from other members and across the Internet. To become a member, a person must agree not to use AOL's computers to send bulk, unsolicited, commercial e-mail (spam). AOL uses filters to block spam, but bulk e-mailers sometimes use other software to thwart the filters. National Health Care Discount, Inc. (NHCD), sells discount optical and dental service plans. To generate leads for NHCD's products, sales representatives, who included AOL members, sent more than 300 million pieces of spam through AOL's computer system. Each item cost AOL an estimated $0.00078 in equipment expenses. Some of the spam used false headers and other methods to hide the source. After receiving more than 150,000 complaints from its members, AOL asked NHCD to stop. When the spam continued, AOL filed a suit in a federal district court against NHCD, alleging in part trespass to chattels—an unlawful interference with another's rights to possess personal property. AOL asked the court for a summary judgment on this claim. Did the spamming constitute trespass to chattels? Explain. [*America Online, Inc. v. National Health Care Discount, Inc.*, 121 F.Supp.2d 1255 (N.D.Iowa 2000)]

6-7. ⚖ CASE PROBLEM WITH SAMPLE ANSWER

In 1994, Gary Kremen registered the domain name "sex.com" with Network Solutions, Inc., to the name of Kremen's business, Online Classifieds. Later, Stephen Cohen sent Network Solutions a letter that he claimed to have received from Online Classifieds. It stated that "we have no objections to your use of the domain name sex.com and this letter shall serve as our authorization to the Internet registrar to transfer sex.com to your corporation." Without contacting Kremen, Network Solutions transferred the name to Cohen, who subsequently turned sex.com into a lucrative business. Kremen filed a suit in a federal district court against Cohen and others, seeking the name and Cohen's profits. The court ordered Cohen to return the name to Kremen and pay $65 million in damages. Cohen ignored the order and disappeared. Against whom else might Kremen attempt to obtain relief? Under which theory of intentional torts against property might Kremen be able to file an action? What is the likely result, and why? [*Kremen v. Cohen,* 337 F.3d 1024 (9th Cir. 2003)]

To view a sample answer for this case problem, go to this book's Web site at http://wbl.westbuslaw.com, select "Chapter 6," and click on "Case Problem with Sample Answer."

6-8. INVASION OF PRIVACY.

During the spring and summer of 1999, Edward and Geneva Irvine received numerous "hang-up" phone calls, including three calls in the middle of the night. With the help of their local phone company, the Irvines learned that many of the calls were from the telemarketing department of the *Akron Beacon Journal* in Akron, Ohio. The *Beacon's* sales force was equipped with an automatic dialing machine. During business hours, the dialer was used to maximize productivity by calling multiple phone numbers at once and connecting a call to a sales representative only after it was answered. After business hours, the *Beacon* programmed its dialer to dial a list of disconnected numbers to determine whether they had been reconnected. If the dialer detected a ring, it recorded the information and dropped the call. If the automated dialing system crashed, which it did frequently, it redialed the entire list. The Irvines filed a suit in an Ohio state court against the *Beacon* and others, alleging in part an invasion of privacy. In whose favor should the court rule, and why? [*Irvine v. Akron Beacon Journal,* 147 Ohio App.3d 428, 770 N.E.2d 1105 (9 Dist. 2002)]

6-9. DEFAMATION.

Lydia Hagberg went to her bank, California Federal Bank, FSB, to cash a check made out to her by Smith Barney (SB), an investment services firm. Nolene Showalter, a bank employee, suspected that the check was counterfeit. Showalter called SB and was told that the check was not valid. As she phoned the police, Gary Wood, a bank security officer, contacted SB again, and was informed that its earlier statement was "erroneous" and that the check was valid. Meanwhile, a police officer arrived, drew Hagberg away from the teller's window, spread her legs, patted her down, and handcuffed her. The officer searched her purse, asked her whether she had any weapons or stolen property and whether she was driving a stolen vehicle, and arrested her. Hagberg filed a suit in a California state court against the bank and others, alleging, among other things, slander. Should the absolute privilege for communications made in judicial or other official proceedings apply to statements made when a citizen contacts the police to report suspected criminal activity? Why or why not? [*Hagberg v. California Federal Bank, FSB,* 32 Cal.4th 350, 81 P.3d 244, 7 Cal.Rptr.3d 803 (2004)]

6-10. ⚖ A QUESTION OF ETHICS

Intel Corporation has an e-mail system for its employees. Ken Hamidi, a former Intel employee, sent a series of six e-mail messages to 35,000 Intel employees over a twenty-one-month period. In the messages, Hamidi criticized the company's labor practices and urged employees to leave the company. Intel sought a court order to stop the e-mail campaign, arguing that Hamidi's actions constituted a trespass to chattels (personal property) because the e-mail significantly interfered with productivity, thus causing economic damage. The state trial court granted Intel's motion for summary judgment and ordered Hamidi to stop sending messages. When the case reached the California Supreme Court, however, the court held that under California law, the tort of trespass to chattels required some evidence of injury to the plaintiff's personal property. Because Hamidi's e-mail had neither damaged Intel's computer system nor impaired its functioning, the court ruled that Hamidi's actions did not amount to a trespass to chattels. The court did not reject the idea that trespass theory could apply to cyberspace. Rather, the court simply held that to succeed in a lawsuit for trespass to chattels, a plaintiff must demonstrate that some concrete harm resulted from the unwanted e-mail. [*Intel Corp. v. Hamidi,* 30 Cal.4th 1342, 71 P.3d 296, 1 Cal.Rptr.3d 32 (2003)]

(a) Should a court require that spam cause actual physical damage or impairment of the computer system (by overburdening it, for example) to establish that a spammer has committed trespass? Why or why not?

(b) The content of Hamidi's messages caused much discussion among employees and managers, diverting workers' time and attention and thus interfering with productivity. Why did the court not consider this disruption to be sufficient evidence of harm? Do you agree with the court?

LAW | on the Web

For updated links to resources available on the Web, as well as a variety of other materials, visit this text's Web site at http://wbl.westbuslaw.com.

You can find cases and articles on torts, including business torts, in the tort law library at the Internet Law Library's Web site. Go to

http://www.lawguru.com/ilawlib

LEGAL RESEARCH EXERCISES ON THE WEB

Go to http://wbl.westbuslaw.com, the Web site that accompanies this text. Select "Chapter 6" and click on "Internet Exercises." There you will find the following Internet research exercises that you can perform to learn more about topics covered in this chapter.

Activity 6–1: **LEGAL PERSPECTIVE**
Online Defamation

Activity 6–2: **MANAGEMENT PERSPECTIVE**
Legal and Illegal Uses of Spam

CHAPTER 7

Negligence and Strict Liability

The intentional torts discussed in Chapter 6 all involve acts that the tortfeasor (the one committing the tort) intended to commit. In this chapter, we examine the tort of negligence, which involves acts that depart from a reasonable standard of care and therefore create an unreasonable risk of harm to others. Negligence suits are probably the most prevalent type of lawsuits brought against businesses today. It is therefore essential that businesspersons understand their potential liability for negligent acts. In the concluding pages of this chapter, we also look at another basis for liability in tort—*strict liability*. Under this tort doctrine, liability does not depend on the actor's negligence or intent to harm, but on the breach of an absolute duty to make something safe.

SECTION 1 | Negligence

In contrast to intentional torts, in torts involving negligence, the tortfeasor neither wishes to bring about the consequences of the act nor believes that they will occur. The actor's conduct merely creates a risk of such consequences. If no risk is created, there is no negligence. Moreover, the risk must be foreseeable; that is, it must be such that a reasonable person engaging in the same activity would anticipate the risk and guard against it. In determining what is reasonable conduct, courts consider the nature of the possible harm. Creating a very slight risk of a dangerous explosion might be unreasonable, whereas creating a distinct possibility of someone's burning his or her fingers on a stove might be reasonable.

To succeed in a negligence action, the plaintiff must prove each of the following:

1. That the defendant owed a duty of care to the plaintiff.
2. That the defendant breached that duty.
3. That the plaintiff suffered a legally recognizable injury.
4. That the defendant's breach caused the plaintiff's injury.

We discuss here each of these four elements of negligence.

THE DUTY OF CARE AND ITS BREACH

Central to the tort of negligence is the concept of a **duty of care.** This concept arises from the notion that if we are to live in society with other people, some actions can be tolerated and some cannot; some actions are right and some are wrong; and some actions are reasonable and some are not. The basic principle underlying the duty of care is that people are free to act as they please so long as their actions do not infringe on the interests of others.

THE REASONABLE PERSON STANDARD Tort law measures duty by the **reasonable person standard.** In determining whether a duty of care has been breached, for example, the courts ask how a reasonable person would have acted in the same circumstances. The reasonable person standard is said to be (though in an absolute sense it cannot be) objective. It is not necessarily how a particular person *would* act. It is society's judgment of how an ordinarily prudent person *should* act. If the so-called reasonable person existed, he or she would be careful, conscientious, prudent, even tempered, and honest. That individuals are required to exercise a reasonable standard of care in their activities is a pervasive concept in business law, and many of the issues dealt with in subsequent chapters of this text have to do with this duty.

In negligence cases, the degree of care to be exercised varies, depending on the defendant's occupation or profession, her or his relationship with the plaintiff, and other factors. Generally, whether an action constitutes a breach of the duty of care is determined on a case-by-case basis. The outcome depends on how the judge (or jury, if it is a jury trial) decides a reasonable person in the position of the defendant would act in the particular circumstances of the case. In the following subsections, we examine the degree of care typically expected of landowners and professionals.

DUTY OF LANDOWNERS Landowners are expected to exercise reasonable care to protect individuals coming onto their property from harm. In some jurisdictions, landowners may even have a duty to protect trespassers against certain risks. Landowners who rent or lease premises to tenants are expected to exercise reasonable care to ensure that the tenants and their guests are not harmed in common areas, such as stairways, entryways, and laundry rooms (see Chapter 48).

Retailers and other firms that explicitly or implicitly invite persons to come onto their premises are usually charged with a duty to exercise reasonable care to protect these **business invitees.** For example, if you entered a supermarket, slipped on a wet floor, and sustained injuries as a result, the owner of the supermarket would be liable for damages if, when you slipped, there was no sign warning that the floor was wet. A court would hold that the business owner was negligent because the owner failed to exercise a reasonable degree of care in protecting the store's customers against foreseeable risks about which the owner knew or *should have known*. That a patron might slip on the wet floor and be injured as a result was a foreseeable risk, and the owner should have taken care to avoid this risk or warn the customer of it.[1]

Some risks, of course, are so obvious that an owner need not warn of them. For example, a business owner does not need to warn customers to open a door before attempting to walk through it. Other risks, however, even though they may seem obvious to a business owner, may not be so in the eyes of another, such as a child. For example, a hardware store owner may not think it is necessary to warn customers that, if climbed, a stepladder leaning against the back wall of the store could fall down and harm them. It is possible, though, that a child could tip the ladder over while climbing it and be hurt as a result.

In the following case, the court had to decide whether a store owner should be held liable for a customer's injury on the premises. The question was whether the owner had notice of the condition that led to the customer's injury.

---

1. A business owner can warn of a risk in a number of ways—for example, by placing a sign, traffic cone, sawhorse, board, or the like near a hole in the business's parking lot. See *Hartman v. Walkertown Shopping Center, Inc.*, 113 N.C.App. 632, 439 S.E.2d 787 (1994).

CASE 7.1   Martin v. Wal-Mart Stores, Inc.

United States
Court of Appeals,
Eighth Circuit, 1999.
183 F.3d 770.
*http://www.findlaw.com/
casecode/courts/8th.html*[a]

BACKGROUND AND FACTS *Harold Martin was shopping in the sporting goods department of a Wal-Mart store. There was one employee in the department at that time. In front of the sporting goods section, in the store's main aisle (which the employees referred to as "action alley"), there was a large display of stacked cases of shotgun shells. On top of the cases were individual boxes of shells. Shortly after the sporting goods employee walked past the display, Martin did so, but Martin slipped on some loose shotgun shell pellets and fell to the floor. He immediately lost feeling in, and control of, his legs. Sensation and control returned, but during the next week, he lost the use of his legs several times for periods of ten to fifteen minutes. Eventually, sensation and control did not return to the front half of his left foot. Doctors diagnosed the condition as permanent. Martin filed a suit against Wal-Mart in a federal district court, seeking damages for his injury. The jury found in his favor, and the court denied Wal-Mart's motion for a directed verdict. Wal-Mart appealed to the U.S. Court of Appeals for the Eighth Circuit.*

---

a. This URL will take you to a Web site maintained by FindLaw, which is now a part of West Group. When you access the site, enter "Wal-Mart" in the "Party Name Search" box and then click on "Search." Scroll down the list on the page that opens and select the link to "Harold Martin v. Wal-Mart Stores."

CONTINUED ▶

CASE 7.1 Continued

IN THE LANGUAGE OF THE COURT

BEAM, Circuit J. [Judge]

* * * *

* * * [T]he traditional rule * * * required a plaintiff in a slip and fall case to establish that the defendant store had either actual or constructive notice of the dangerous condition. The defendant store [was] deemed to have actual notice if it [was] shown that an employee created or was aware of the hazard. Constructive notice could be established by showing that the dangerous condition had existed for a sufficient length of time that the defendant should reasonably have known about it.

* * * *

* * * [R]etail store operations have evolved since the traditional liability rules were established. In modern self-service stores, customers are invited to traverse the same aisles used by the clerks to replenish stock, they are invited to retrieve merchandise from displays for inspection, and to place it back in the display if the item is not selected for purchase. Further, a customer is enticed to look at the displays, thus reducing the chance that the customer will be watchful of hazards on the floor. * * * [C]ustomers may take merchandise into their hands and may then lay articles that no longer interest them down in the aisle. * * * The risk of items creating dangerous conditions on the floor, previously created by employees, is now created by other customers as a result of the store's decision to employ the self-service mode of operation. * * * *Thus, in slip and fall cases in self-service stores, the inquiry of whether the danger existed long enough that the store should have reasonably known of it (constructive notice) is made in light of the fact that the store has notice that certain dangers arising through customer involvement are likely to occur, and the store has a duty to anticipate them.* [Emphasis added.]

* * * *

Wal-Mart * * * claims that Martin * * * failed to establish that Wal-Mart had actual or constructive notice of the pellets in the action aisle. We disagree. We find there is substantial evidence of constructive notice in the record. Martin slipped on shotgun shell pellets on the floor which were next to a large display of shotgun shells immediately abutting the sporting goods department. The chance that merchandise will wind up on the floor (or merchandise will be spilled on the floor) in the department in which that merchandise is sold or displayed is exactly the type of foreseeable risk [that is part of the self-service exception to the traditional rule]. Under [this exception], Wal-Mart has notice that merchandise is likely to find its way to the floor and create a dangerous condition, and *it must exercise due care to discover this hazard and warn customers or protect them from the danger.* * * * Even assuming that the hazard was created by a customer, a jury could easily find, given that it had notice that merchandise is often mishandled or mislaid by customers in a manner that can create dangerous conditions, that, had Wal-Mart exercised due care under the circumstances, it would have discovered the shotgun pellets on the floor. [Emphasis added.]

DECISION AND REMEDY *The U.S. Court of Appeals for the Eighth Circuit affirmed the judgment of the lower court. There was sufficient evidence for a jury to find that Wal-Mart had constructive notice of the pellets on the floor in the main aisle.*

WHAT IF THE FACTS WERE DIFFERENT? *Suppose that Harold Martin had been in the store not to shop but only to use the restroom. In this situation, is it likely that Wal-Mart would have been liable for his injury?*

DUTY OF PROFESSIONALS If an individual has knowledge, skill, or intelligence superior to that of an ordinary person, the individual's conduct must be consistent with that status. Professionals—including physicians, dentists, architects, engineers, accoun- tants, and lawyers, among others—are required to have a standard minimum level of special knowledge and ability. Therefore, in determining what constitutes reasonable care in the case of professionals, the court takes their training and expertise into account.

In other words, an accountant cannot defend against a lawsuit for negligence by stating, "But I was not familiar with that general principle of accounting."

If a professional violates his or her duty of care toward a client, the client may bring a **malpractice** suit against the professional. For example, a patient might sue a physician for *medical malpractice*. A client might sue an attorney for *legal malpractice*. The liability of professionals will be examined in further detail in Chapter 51.

NO DUTY TO RESCUE Although the law requires individuals to act reasonably and responsibly in their relations with one another, if a person fails to come to the aid of a stranger in peril, that person will not be considered negligent under tort law. For example, assume that you are walking down a city street and see a pedestrian about to step directly in front of an oncoming bus. You realize that the person has not seen the bus and is unaware of the danger. Do you have a legal duty to warn that individual? No. Although most people would probably concede that in this situation, the observer has an *ethical* duty to warn the other, tort law does not impose a general duty to rescue others in peril. Duties may be imposed in regard to certain types of peril, however. For example, most states require a motorist involved in an automobile accident to stop and render aid. Failure to do so is both a tort and a crime.

THE INJURY REQUIREMENT AND DAMAGES

To recover damages (receive compensation), the plaintiff in a tort lawsuit must prove that she or he suffered a *legally recognizable* injury. In other words, the plaintiff must have suffered some loss, harm, wrong, or invasion of a protected interest. This is true in lawsuits for intentional torts as well as lawsuits for negligence. Essentially, the purpose of tort law is to compensate for legally recognized harms and injuries resulting from wrongful acts. If no harm or injury results from a given negligent action, there is nothing to compensate—and no tort exists.

For example, if you carelessly bump into a passerby, who stumbles and falls as a result, you may be liable in tort if the passerby is injured in the fall. If the person is unharmed, however, there normally can be no suit for damages because no injury was suffered. Although the passerby might be angry and suffer emotional distress, few courts recognize negligently inflicted emotional distress as a tort unless it results in some physical disturbance or dysfunction.

COMPENSATORY DAMAGES ARE THE NORM As already mentioned, the purpose of tort law is not to punish people for tortious acts but to compensate the injured parties for damages suffered. **Compensatory damages** are intended to compensate, or reimburse, a plaintiff for actual losses—to make the plaintiff whole. Compensatory damages compensate the plaintiff for property damage and physical injury, which may include medical expenses, lost wages and benefits, pain and suffering, and sometimes even emotional distress.

PUNITIVE DAMAGES ARE RARE Occasionally, however, punitive damages are also awarded in tort lawsuits. **Punitive damages,** or *exemplary damages*, are intended to punish the wrongdoer and deter others from similar wrongdoing. Punitive damages are rarely awarded in lawsuits for ordinary negligence and usually are given only in cases involving intentional torts. They may be awarded, however, in suits involving *gross negligence*, which can be defined as an intentional failure to perform a manifest duty in reckless disregard of the consequences of such a failure for the life or property of another. The amount of punitive damages awarded must be reasonable, however. The United States Supreme Court has held that punitive damages that exceed reasonable bounds may violate due process requirements (discussed in Chapter 4).[2]

CAUSATION

Another element necessary to a tort is *causation*. If a person breaches a duty of care and someone suffers injury, the wrongful activity must have caused the harm for a tort to have been committed.

CAUSATION IN FACT AND PROXIMATE CAUSE In deciding whether the requirement of causation is met, the court must address two questions:

1. *Is there causation in fact?* Did the injury occur because of the defendant's act, or would it have occurred anyway? If an injury would not have occurred without the defendant's act, then there is causation in fact. **Causation in fact** can usually be

---

2. See *State Farm Mutual Automobile Insurance Co. v. Campbell*, 538 U.S. 408, 123 S.Ct. 1513, 155 L.Ed.2d 585 (2003).

determined by use of the *but for* test: "but for" the wrongful act, the injury would not have occurred.

2. Was the act the proximate cause of the injury? In theory, causation in fact is limitless. One could claim, for example, that "but for" the creation of the world, a particular injury would not have occurred. Thus, as a practical matter, the law has to establish limits, and it does so through the concept of proximate cause. **Proximate cause,** or *legal cause,* exists when the connection between an act and an injury is strong enough to justify imposing liability. Consider an example. Ackerman carelessly leaves a campfire burning. The fire not only burns down the forest but also sets off an explosion in a nearby chemical plant that spills chemicals into a river, killing all the fish for a hundred miles downstream and ruining the economy of a tourist resort. Should Ackerman be liable to the resort owners? To the tourists whose vacations were ruined? These are questions of proximate cause that a court must decide.

Both questions must be answered in the affirmative for liability in tort to arise. If a defendant's action constitutes causation in fact but a court decides that the action is not the proximate cause of the plaintiff's injury, the causation requirement has not been met—and the defendant normally will not be liable to the plaintiff.

FORESEEABILITY   Questions of proximate cause are linked to the concept of foreseeability because it would be unfair to impose liability on a defendant unless the defendant's actions created a foreseeable risk of injury. Probably the most cited case on the concept of foreseeability as a requirement for proximate cause—and as a measure of the extent of the duty of care generally—is the *Palsgraf* case. The question before the court was as follows: Does the defendant's duty of care extend only to those who may be injured as a result of a foreseeable risk, or does it extend also to persons whose injuries could not reasonably be foreseen?

CASE 7.2   Palsgraf v. Long Island Railroad Co.

Court of Appeals
of New York, 1928.
248 N.Y. 339,
162 N.E. 99.

BACKGROUND AND FACTS   *The plaintiff, Helen Palsgraf, was waiting for a train on a station platform. A man carrying a package was rushing to catch a train that was moving away from a platform across the tracks from Palsgraf. As the man attempted to jump aboard the moving train, he seemed unsteady and about to fall. A railroad guard on the car reached forward to grab him, and another guard on the platform pushed him from behind to help him board the train. In the process, the man's package, which (unknown to the railroad guards) contained fireworks, fell on the railroad tracks and exploded. There was nothing about the package to indicate its contents. The repercussions of the explosion caused scales at the other end of the train platform to fall on Palsgraf, causing injuries for which she sued the railroad company. At the trial, the jury found that the railroad guards had been negligent in their conduct. The railroad company appealed. The appellate court affirmed the trial court's judgment, and the railroad company appealed to New York's highest state court.*

IN THE LANGUAGE OF THE COURT

CARDOZO, C.J. [Chief Justice]
* * * *

The conduct of the defendant's guard, if a wrong in its relation to the holder of the package, was not a wrong in its relation to the plaintiff, standing far away. Relatively to her it was not negligence at all. * * *

* * * *

* * * What the plaintiff must show is "a wrong" to herself; i.e., a violation of her own right, and not merely a wrong to someone else[.] * * * *The risk reasonably to be perceived defines the duty to be obeyed[.]* * * * Here, by concession, there was nothing in the situation to suggest to the most cautious mind that the parcel wrapped in newspaper would spread wreckage through the station. If the guard had thrown it down knowingly and willfully, he would not have threatened the plaintiff's safety, so far as appearances could warn him. His conduct would not have involved, even then, an unreasonable probability of invasion of her bodily security. Liability can be no greater where the act is inadvertent. [Emphasis added.]

CASE 7.2 **Continued**

* * * One who seeks redress at law does not make out a cause of action by showing without more that there has been damage to his person. If the harm was not willful, he must show that the act as to him had possibilities of danger so many and apparent as to entitle him to be protected against the doing of it though the harm was unintended. * * * The victim does not sue * * * to vindicate an interest invaded in the person of another. * * * He sues for breach of a duty owing to himself.

* * * [To rule otherwise] would entail liability for any and all consequences, however novel or extraordinary.

DECISION AND REMEDY *Palsgraf's complaint was dismissed. The railroad had not been negligent toward her because injury to her was not foreseeable. Had the owner of the fireworks been harmed, and had he filed suit, there could well have been a different result.*

INTERNATIONAL CONSIDERATIONS **Differing Standards of Proximate Cause** *The concept of proximate cause is common among nations around the globe, but its application differs from country to country. French law uses the phrase "adequate cause." An event breaks the chain of adequate cause if the event is both unforeseeable and irresistible. England has a "nearest cause" rule that attributes liability based on which event was nearest in time and space. Mexico bases proximate cause on the foreseeability of the harm but does not require that an event be reasonably foreseeable.*

IMPACT OF THIS CASE ON TODAY'S LAW

The *Palsgraf* case established foreseeability as the test for proximate cause. Today, the courts continue to apply this test in determining proximate cause—and thus tort liability for injuries. Generally, if the victim of a harm or the consequences of a harm done are unforeseeable, there is no proximate cause.

SECTION 2 | Defenses to Negligence

The basic defenses to liability in negligence cases are (1) assumption of risk, (2) superseding cause, and (3) contributory and comparative negligence.

ASSUMPTION OF RISK

A plaintiff who voluntarily enters into a risky situation, knowing the risk involved, will not be allowed to recover. This is the defense of **assumption of risk.** For example, a driver entering an automobile race knows there is a risk of being injured or killed in a crash. The driver has assumed the risk of injury. The requirements of this defense are (1) knowledge of the risk and (2) voluntary assumption of the risk.

The risk can be assumed by express agreement, or the assumption of risk can be implied by the plaintiff's knowledge of the risk and subsequent conduct. Of course, the plaintiff does not assume a risk different from or greater than the risk normally carried by the activity. In our example, the race driver assumes the risk of being injured in the race but not the risk that the banking in the curves of the racetrack will give way during the race because of a construction defect.

Risks are not deemed to be assumed in situations involving emergencies. Neither are they assumed when a statute protects a class of people from harm and a member of the class is injured by the harm. For example, courts have generally held that an employee cannot assume the risk of an employer's violation of safety statutes passed for the benefit of employees.

In the following case, a ball kicked by a player practicing on a nearby field injured a man who was attending his son's soccer tournament. The question before the court was whether a bystander who was not watching a soccer match at the time of injury had nevertheless assumed the risk of being struck by a wayward ball.

CASE 7.3

New York Supreme Court,
Appellate Division,
Third Department. 2004.
8 A.D.3d 855,
779 N.Y.S.2d 149.

Sutton v. Eastern New York Youth Soccer Association, Inc.

SPAIN, J. [Justice]
  * * * *

While attending a soccer tournament in which his son was a participant, plaintiff D. James Sutton (hereinafter plaintiff) was struck by a soccer ball kicked by a 16-year-old boy practicing on one of the soccer fields between games. Thereafter, plaintiff and his wife * * * commenced this personal injury action [in a New York state court] against organizations and teams sponsoring and/or participating in the tournament, as well as the boy who kicked the ball, seeking to recover damages for injuries he sustained to his knee as a result of the accident. [The] Court granted summary judgment to all defendants, finding that plaintiff had assumed the risk of being struck by a soccer ball, and dismissed the complaint. * * *

According to plaintiff, May 30, 1999 was a sunny, exceedingly hot day and his son, a member of defendant Latham Circle Soccer Club, was participating in a Highland Soccer Club Tournament at Maalyck Park in the Town of Glenville, Schenectady County [in New York]. Plaintiff attended as a spectator and had just finished watching his son's second game of the day from one of the sidelines when he walked to the end of the field to a tent which had been erected by his son's team some 30 to 40 yards behind the goal line in order to provide shade for the players while they were not engaged on the field. While walking past the field, plaintiff noticed six or seven players from defendant Guilderland Soccer Club on the field "hacking around" and warming up for the next game. Once under the tent, plaintiff was in the process of removing a sandwich from his son's cooler when he was struck in the chest and knocked off his feet by a soccer ball kicked from the field by a Guilderland player, defendant Ian Goss.

The first argument raised on appeal is that plaintiff was not a voluntary spectator of the soccer match at the point in time when he was injured; accordingly, plaintiffs argue, he cannot be found to have assumed the risk of injury. In support of this contention, plaintiffs point to the fact that a game was not in progress on the field and that, when injured, he was standing some 30 to 40 yards away from the field of play. We are unpersuaded. *The doctrine of assumption of risk can apply not only to participants of sporting events, but to spectators and bystanders who are not actively engaged in watching the event at the time of their injury.* Indeed, the spectator at a sporting event, no less than the participant, accepts the dangers that [are inherent] in it so far as they are obvious and necessary, just as a fencer accepts the risk of a thrust by his antagonist or a spectator at a ball game the * * * chance of contact with the ball * * * . The timorous [nervous] may stay at home. Here, plaintiff admitted that he was at the tournament as a spectator and was aware that players were practicing on the field when he walked past them. Furthermore, although plaintiff's son's team had just finished a game, the tournament involved hundreds of players with teams playing at various times on at least five fields and plaintiff had been at the tournament all morning, surrounded by this activity. Under these circumstances, we find that plaintiff's presence at the tournament rendered him a voluntary spectator to the soccer play in progress throughout the day. [Emphasis added.]

Next, plaintiffs contend that the placement of the tent behind the goal line of one of the soccer fields enhanced the risk to spectators at the game, thereby undermining the argument that plaintiff assumed the risk of getting struck by a ball. Plaintiffs rely on evidence * * * that spectators at soccer games should, for their safety, observe the game from the sidelines and that standing behind the goal line increases the chance of being struck by a kicked ball. This Court has not previously had occasion to address directly the duty of care owed to spectators at a soccer match. Existing jurisprudence surrounding the duty owed to spectators at a baseball game, though not controlling given the differences in the games of baseball and soccer, is nonetheless helpful to our analysis.

* * * Taking into consideration the independence of spectators who might want to watch a [baseball] game from an unprotected vantage point, and recognizing that even after the exercise of reasonable care, some risk of being struck by a ball will continue to exist, * * * the proprietor of a ball park need only provide screening for the area of the field behind home plate where the danger of being struck by a ball is the greatest. * * * [T]he municipal

CASE 7.3 | Continued

owner of a baseball park which has provided adequate space for spectators to view the game from behind the backstop [does] not owe a duty to install screens or netting above a fence running along the first baseline to protect spectators walking in the area between the fence and bathrooms against the risk of being struck by foul balls. * * *

Unlike baseball parks, outdoor soccer fields typically have no protective screening or fencing for spectators, presumably because the ball is larger and moves [more slowly], enabling the spectator who observes a ball coming his or her way to avoid being struck. Indeed, plaintiffs do not suggest that, in the exercise of reasonable care, defendants had a duty to provide any protective measures along the sidelines. Instead, plaintiffs assert that defendants unreasonably enhanced the risk of injury to plaintiff by essentially inviting him to stand at the end of the field through their placement of the team tent. Although we agree that a factual question has been presented as to whether the risk of being struck by a soccer ball is enhanced when a spectator is standing behind the goal line, we find that question immaterial to the disposition of this action. There is no suggestion that there was not adequate room for the spectators to remain along the sidelines; in fact, plaintiff was seated along the sidelines prior to moving to the tent to get a sandwich. Accordingly, just as the owner of a baseball park is not responsible for the spectator who leaves his or her seat and walks through a potentially more hazardous zone to reach a bathroom or concession stand, thereby assuming the open and obvious risk of being hit by a ball, *defendants here cannot be held responsible for the risk assumed by plaintiff when he, aware that players were active on the field, left the sidelines and stood in the tent positioned in the arguably more dangerous zone behind the goal line.* [Emphasis added.]

We also reject plaintiffs' contention that the risk of being struck while some 40 yards away from a field upon which no formal game was in progress was not open and obvious. *In the context of a sporting event, where the risks are fully comprehended or perfectly obvious, a participant will be deemed to have consented to such risk.* As discussed, plaintiff had been in attendance for hours at a tournament where soccer games were almost continuously in progress and had actual knowledge that players were kicking the ball around on the field when he opted to move to the tent behind the goal line. Further, he was familiar with the game of soccer having admittedly been a frequent spectator of the game for over 14 years. Under these circumstances, we hold that plaintiff should have appreciated the risk of being hit by an errant [stray] soccer ball when he opted to enter the tent in the area behind the goal. [Emphasis added.]

* * * *

ORDERED that the order is affirmed * * * .

QUESTIONS

1. What is the basis underlying the defense of assumption of risk, and how does that basis support the court's decision in the *Sutton* case?
2. Had the plaintiffs prevailed, how might the venues for soccer matches be different today?

SUPERSEDING CAUSE

An unforeseeable intervening event may break the causal connection between a wrongful act and an injury to another. If so, the intervening event acts as a *superseding cause*—that is, it relieves a defendant of liability for injuries caused by the intervening event. For example, suppose that Derrick, while riding his bicycle, negligently hits Julie, who is walking on the sidewalk. As a result of the impact, Julie falls and fractures her hip. While she is waiting for help to arrive, a small aircraft crashes nearby and explodes, and some of the fiery debris hits her, causing her to sustain severe burns. Derrick will be liable for the damages caused by Julie's fractured hip, but normally he will not be liable for the wounds caused by the plane crash—because the risk of a plane crashing nearby and injuring Julie was not foreseeable.

CONTRIBUTORY AND COMPARATIVE NEGLIGENCE

All individuals are expected to exercise a reasonable degree of care in looking out for themselves. Under the common law doctrine of **contributory negligence,** a plaintiff who was also negligent (failed to exercise a reasonable degree of care) could not recover anything from the defendant. Under this rule, no matter how insignificant the plaintiff's negligence was relative to the defendant's negligence, the plaintiff would be precluded from recovering any damages. Today, only a few jurisdictions still hold to this doctrine. In the majority of states, the doctrine of contributory negligence has been replaced by a **comparative negligence** standard.

The comparative negligence standard enables both the plaintiff's and the defendant's negligence to be computed and the liability for damages distributed accordingly. Some jurisdictions have adopted a "pure" form of comparative negligence that allows the plaintiff to recover damages even if her or his fault is greater than that of the defendant. Many states' comparative negligence statutes, however, contain a "50 percent" rule, under which the plaintiff recovers nothing if she or he was more than 50 percent at fault. Under this rule, a plaintiff who is 35 percent at fault could recover 65 percent of his or her damages, but a plaintiff who is 65 percent (over 50 percent) at fault could recover nothing.

SECTION 3 | Special Negligence Doctrines and Statutes

A number of special doctrines and statutes relating to negligence are also important. We examine a few of them here.

RES IPSA LOQUITUR

Generally, in lawsuits involving negligence, the plaintiff has the burden of proving that the defendant was negligent. In certain situations, however, the courts may presume that negligence has occurred, in which case the burden of proof rests on the defendant—that is, the defendant must prove that he or she was *not* negligent. The presumption of the defendant's negligence is known as the doctrine of *res ipsa loquitur,*[3] which translates as "the facts speak for themselves."

This doctrine is applied only when the event creating the damage or injury is one that ordinarily does not occur in the absence of negligence. For example, if a person undergoes knee surgery and following the surgery has a severed nerve in the knee area, that person

can sue the surgeon under a theory of *res ipsa loquitur*. In this case, the injury would not have occurred but for the surgeon's negligence.[4] For the doctrine of *res ipsa loquitur* to apply, the event must have been within the defendant's power to control, and it must not have been due to any voluntary action or contribution on the part of the plaintiff.

NEGLIGENCE PER SE

Certain conduct, whether it consists of an action or a failure to act, may be treated as **negligence** *per se* ("in or of itself"). Negligence *per se* may occur if an individual violates a statute or an ordinance providing for a criminal penalty and that violation causes another to be injured. The injured person must prove (1) that the statute clearly sets out what standard of conduct is expected, when and where it is expected, and of whom it is expected; (2) that he or she is in the class intended to be protected by the statute; and (3) that the statute was designed to prevent the type of injury that he or she suffered. The standard of conduct required by the statute is the duty that the defendant owes to the plaintiff, and a violation of the statute is the breach of that duty.

For example, a statute may require a landowner to keep a building in safe condition and may also subject the landowner to a criminal penalty, such as a fine, if the building is not kept safe. The statute is meant to protect those who are rightfully in the building. Thus, if the owner, without a sufficient excuse, violates the statute and a tenant is thereby injured, a majority of courts will hold that the owner's unexcused violation of the statute conclusively establishes a breach of a duty of care—that is, that the owner's violation is negligence *per se*.

"DANGER INVITES RESCUE" DOCTRINE

Under the "danger invites rescue" doctrine, if a person commits an act that endangers another, the person committing the act will be liable not only for any injuries the other party suffers but also for any injuries suffered by a third person in an attempt to rescue the endangered party. For example, suppose that Ludlam, while driving down a street, fails to see a stop sign because he is trying to end a squabble between his two young children in the car's backseat. Salter, on the

---

3. Pronounced *rihz ihp*-suh *low*-kwuh-duhr.

4. See *Edwards v. Boland,* 41 Mass.App.Ct. 375, 670 N.E.2d 404 (1996).

curb near the stop sign, realizes that Ludlam is about to hit a pedestrian walking across the street at the intersection. Salter runs into the street to push the pedestrian out of the way, and Ludlam's vehicle hits Salter instead. In this situation, Ludlam will be liable for Salter's injury, as well as for any injuries the other pedestrian sustained. Rescuers can injure themselves, or the persons rescued, or even bystanders, but the original wrongdoers will still be liable.

SPECIAL NEGLIGENCE STATUTES

A number of states have enacted statutes prescribing duties and responsibilities in certain circumstances. For example, most states now have what are called **Good Samaritan statutes.**[5] Under these statutes, persons whom others aid voluntarily cannot turn around and sue the "Good Samaritans" for negligence. These laws were passed largely to protect physicians and medical personnel who voluntarily render their services in emergency situations to those in need, such as individuals hurt in car accidents.

Many states have also passed **dram shop acts,** under which a tavern owner or bartender may be held liable for injuries caused by a person who became intoxicated while drinking at the bar or who was already intoxicated when served by the bartender. Some states have statutes that impose liability on *social hosts* (persons hosting parties) for injuries caused by guests who became intoxicated at the hosts' homes. Under these statutes, it is unnecessary to prove that the tavern owner, bartender, or social host was negligent. Sometimes, the definition of a "social host" is broadly fashioned. For example, in a New York case, the court held that the father of a minor who hosted a "bring-your-own-keg" party could be held liable for injuries caused by an intoxicated guest.[6]

SECTION 4 | Strict Liability

Another category of torts is called **strict liability,** or *liability without fault*. The modern concept of strict liability traces its origins, in part, to the 1868 English case of *Rylands v. Fletcher*.[7] In the coal-mining area of Lancashire, England, the Rylands, who were mill owners, had constructed a reservoir on their land. Water from the reservoir broke through a filled-in shaft of an abandoned coal mine nearby and flooded the connecting passageways in an active coal mine owned by Fletcher. Fletcher sued the Rylands, and the court held that the defendants (the Rylands) were liable, even though the circumstances did not fit within existing tort liability theories.

In justifying its decision, the court compared the situation to the trespass of dangerous animals: "the true rule of law is, that the person who for his own purposes brings on his land and collects and keeps there anything likely to do mischief if it escapes, must keep it at his peril, and, if he does not do so, is *prima facie* [at first sight; on the face of it] answerable for all the damage which is the natural consequence of its escape."

The doctrine that emerged from *Rylands v. Fletcher* was liberally applied by British courts. Initially, few U.S. courts accepted this doctrine, presumably because the courts were worried about its effect on the expansion of American business. Today, however, the doctrine of strict liability is the norm rather than the exception.

ABNORMALLY DANGEROUS ACTIVITIES

The influence of *Rylands v. Fletcher* can be seen in the strict liability rule for abnormally dangerous activities, which is one application of the strict liability doctrine. Abnormally dangerous activities have three characteristics:

1. The activity involves potential harm, of a serious nature, to persons or property.
2. The activity involves a high degree of risk that cannot be completely guarded against by the exercise of reasonable care.
3. The activity is not commonly performed in the community or area.

Clearly, the primary basis of liability is the creation of an extraordinary risk. For example, even if blasting with dynamite is performed with all reasonable care, there is still a risk of injury. Balancing that risk against the potential for harm, it seems reasonable to ask the person engaged in the activity to pay for any injury it causes. Although there is no fault, there is still

---

5. These laws derive their name from the Good Samaritan story in the Bible. In the story, a traveler who had been robbed and beaten lay along the roadside, ignored by those passing by. Eventually, a man from the region of Samaria (the "Good Samaritan") stopped to render assistance to the injured person.

6. *Rust v. Reyer,* 91 N.Y.2d 355, 693 N.E.2d 1074, 670 N.Y.S.2d 822 (1998).

7. 3 L.R.–E & I App. [Law Reports, English & Irish Appeal Cases] (H.L. [House of Lords] 1868).

responsibility because of the dangerous nature of the undertaking.

OTHER APPLICATIONS OF STRICT LIABILITY

Persons who keep wild animals are strictly liable for any harm inflicted by the animals. The basis for applying strict liability is that wild animals, should they escape from confinement, pose a serious risk of harm to persons in the vicinity. An owner of domestic animals (such as dogs, cats, cows, or sheep) may be strictly liable for harm caused by those animals if the owner knew, or should have known, that the animals were dangerous or had a propensity to harm others.

A significant application of strict liability is in the area of product liability—liability of manufacturers and sellers for harmful or defective products. Liability here is a matter of social policy and is based on two factors: (1) the manufacturing company can better bear the cost of injury because it can spread the cost throughout society by increasing prices of goods and services, and (2) the manufacturing company is making a profit from its activities and therefore should bear the cost of injury as an operating expense. We will discuss product liability in greater detail in Chapter 23. Strict liability is also applied in certain types of *bailments* (a bailment exists when goods are transferred temporarily into the care of another—see Chapter 47).

REVIEWING NEGLIGENCE AND STRICT LIABILITY

Alaina Sweeney went to Ragged Mountain Ski Resort in New Hampshire with her friend Derrick. Alaina was snow-tubing down a snow-tube run designed exclusively for snow tubers. There were no Ragged Mountain employees present in the snow-tube area to instruct Alaina on the proper use of a snow tube. On her fourth run down the trail, Alaina crossed over the center line between snow-tube lanes, collided with another snow tuber, and was injured. Alaina filed an action against Ragged Mountain seeking compensation for the injuries that she sustained. Two years earlier, the New Hampshire state legislature had enacted a statute that prohibited a person who participates in the sport of skiing from suing a ski-area operator for injuries caused by the risks inherent in skiing. Using the information presented in the chapter, answer the following questions.

1. What tort theory discussed in the chapter might provide the basis of Alaina's lawsuit?

2. What defense will Ragged Mountain probably assert?

3. The central question in this case is whether the state statute establishing that skiers assume the risks inherent in the sport bars Alaina's suit. What would your decision be on this issue? Why?

4. Suppose that the court concludes that the statute applies only to skiing and does not apply to snow tubing. Will Alaina's lawsuit be successful? Explain.

5. Now suppose that the jury concludes that Alaina was partly at fault for the accident. Under what theory might her damages be reduced in proportion to the degree to which her actions contributed to the accident and her resulting injuries?

TERMS AND CONCEPTS TO REVIEW

assumption of risk 145	dram shop act 149	proximate cause 144
business invitee 141	duty of care 140	punitive damages 143
causation in fact 143	Good Samaritan statute 149	reasonable person standard 140
comparative negligence 148	malpractice 143	*res ipsa loquitur* 148
compensatory damages 143	negligence 140	strict liability 149
contributory negligence 147	negligence *per se* 148	

QUESTIONS AND CASE PROBLEMS

7-1. In which of the following situations will the acting party be liable for the tort of negligence? Explain fully.

(a) Shannon goes to the golf course on Sunday morning, eager to try out a new set of golf clubs she has just purchased. As she tees off on the first hole, the head of her club flies off and injures a nearby golfer.

(b) Shannon goes to the golf course on Sunday morning. While she is teeing off at the eleventh hole, her golf ball veers toward a roadway next to the golf course and shatters a car's windshield.

(c) Shannon's physician gives her some pain medication and tells her not to drive after she takes it, as the medication induces drowsiness. In spite of the doctor's warning, Shannon decides to drive to the store while on the medication. Owing to her lack of alertness, she fails to stop at a traffic light and crashes into another vehicle, causing a passenger in that vehicle to be injured.

7-2. QUESTION WITH SAMPLE ANSWER

Ruth carelessly parks her car on a steep hill, leaving the car in neutral and failing to engage the parking brake. The car rolls down the hill and knocks down an electric line. The sparks from the broken line ignite a grass fire. The fire spreads until it reaches a barn one mile away. The barn houses dynamite, and the burning barn explodes, causing part of the roof to fall on and injure Jim, a passing motorist. Which element of negligence is of the greatest concern here? What legal doctrine resolves this issue? Will Jim be able to recover damages from Ruth?

For a sample answer to this question, go to Appendix I at the end of this text.

7-3. Kim went to Ling's Market to pick up a few items for dinner. It was a rainy, windy day, and the wind had blown water through the entrance to Ling's Market each time the door was opened. As Kim entered through the door, she slipped and fell in the approximately one-half inch of rainwater that had accumulated on the floor. The manager knew of the weather conditions but had not posted any sign to warn customers of the water hazard. Kim injured her back as a result of the fall and sued Ling's for damages. Can Ling's be held liable for negligence in this situation? Discuss.

7-4. Danny and Marion Klein were injured when part of a fireworks display went astray and exploded near them. They sued Pyrodyne Corp., the pyrotechnic company that was hired to set up and discharge the fireworks, alleging, among other things, that the company should be strictly liable for damages caused by the fireworks display. Will the court agree with the Kleins? What factors will the court consider in making its decision? Discuss fully.

7-5. NEGLIGENCE PER SE. A North Carolina Department of Transportation regulation prohibits the placement of telephone booths within public rights-of-way. Despite this regulation, GTE South, Inc., placed a booth in the right-of-way near the intersection of Hillsborough and Sparger Roads in Durham County. A pedestrian, Laura Baldwin, was using the booth when an accident at the intersection caused a dump truck to cross the right-of-way and smash into the booth. To recover for her injuries, Baldwin filed a suit in a North Carolina state court against GTE and others. Was Baldwin within the class of persons protected by the regulation? If so, did GTE's placement of the booth constitute negligence *per se*? Explain. [*Baldwin v. GTE South, Inc.,* 335 N.C. 544, 439 S.E.2d 108 (1994)]

7-6. DUTY OF CARE. As pedestrians exited at the close of an arts and crafts show, Jason Davis, an employee of the show's producer, stood near the exit. Suddenly and without warning, Davis turned around and collided with Yvonne Esposito, an eighty-year-old woman. Esposito was knocked to the ground, fracturing her hip. After hip-replacement surgery, she was left with a permanent physical impairment. Esposito filed a suit in a federal district court against Davis and others, alleging negligence. What are the factors that indicate whether Davis owed Esposito a duty of care? What do those factors indicate in these circumstances? [*Esposito v. Davis,* 47 F.3d 164 (5th Cir. 1995)]

7-7. CASE PROBLEM WITH SAMPLE ANSWER

New Hampshire International Speedway, Inc., owned the New Hampshire International Speedway, a racetrack next to Route 106 in Loudon, New Hampshire. In August 1998, on the weekend before the Winston Cup race, Speedway opened part of its parking facility to recreational vehicles (RVs). Speedway voluntarily positioned its employee Frederick Neergaard at the entrance to the parking area as a security guard and to direct traffic. Leslie Wheeler, who was planning to attend the race, drove an RV south on Route 106 toward Speedway. Meanwhile, Dennis Carignan was also driving south on Route 106 on a motorcycle, on which Mary Carignan was a passenger. As Wheeler approached the parking area, he saw Neergaard signaling him to turn left, which he began to do. At the same time, Carignan attempted to pass the RV on its left side, and the two vehicles collided. Mary sustained an injury to her right knee, lacerations on her ankle, and a broken hip. She sued Speedway and others for negligence. Which element of negligence is at the center of this dispute? How is a court likely to rule in this case, and why? [*Carignan v. New Hampshire International Speedway, Inc.,* 858 A.2d 536 (N.H. 2004)]

To view a sample answer for this case problem, go to this book's Web site at http://wbl.westbuslaw.com, select "Chapter 7," and click on "Case Problem with Sample Answer."

7–8. DUTY TO BUSINESS INVITEES. Flora Gonzalez visited a Wal-Mart store. While walking in a busy aisle from the store's cafeteria toward a refrigerator, Gonzalez stepped on some macaroni that came from the cafeteria. She slipped and fell, sustaining injuries to her back, shoulder, and knee. She filed a suit in a Texas state court against Wal-Mart, alleging that the store was negligent. She presented evidence that the macaroni had "a lot of dirt" and tracks through it and testified that the macaroni "seemed like it had been there awhile." What duty does a business have to protect its patrons from dangerous conditions? In Gonzalez's case, should Wal-Mart be held liable for a breach of that duty? Why or why not? [*Wal-Mart Stores, Inc. v. Gonzalez*, 968 S.W.2d 934 (Tex.Sup. 1998)]

7–9. DUTY OF LANDOWNERS. The Oklahoma State Board of Cosmetology inspected the equipment of the Poteau Beauty College and found it to be in satisfactory condition. A month later, Marilyn Sue Weldon, a student at Poteau, was injured when a salon chair failed to work properly. Weldon had washed the hair of a woman with the chair in a reclining position. The chair did not spring back, and due to a previous injury, the client had to be helped into an upright position. The chair was close to a manicure table, and in maneuvering around the table, Weldon twisted her back. Weldon filed a suit in an Oklahoma state court against Poteau and others, claiming in part that the college was negligent. Assuming that Weldon was an invitee, what duty did Poteau, as the owner of the premises, owe to her? On what basis might the court rule that Poteau was not liable? [*Weldon v. Dunn*, 962 P.2d 1273 (Okla.Sup. 1998)]

7–10. VIDEO QUESTION

Go to this text's Web site at http://wbl.westbuslaw.com and select "Chapter 7." Click on "Video Questions" and view the video titled *Jaws*. Then answer the following questions.

(a) In the video, the mayor (Murray Hamilton) and a few other men try to persuade Chief Brody (Roy Scheider) not to close the town's beaches. If Brody keeps the beaches open and a swimmer is injured or killed because he failed to warn swimmers about the potential shark danger, has Brody committed the tort of negligence? Explain.

(b) Can Chief Brody be held liable for any injuries or deaths to swimmers under the doctrine of strict liability? Why or why not?

(c) Suppose that Chief Brody goes against the mayor's instructions and warns townspeople to stay off the beach. Nevertheless, several swimmers do not heed his warning and are injured as a result. What defense or defenses could Brody raise under these circumstances if he is sued for negligence?

LAW | on the Web

For updated links to resources available on the Web, as well as a variety of other materials, visit this text's Web site at http://wbl.westbuslaw.com.

You can find cases and articles on torts, including business torts, in the tort law library at the Internet Law Library's Web site. Go to

http://www.lawguru.com/ilawlib

LEGAL RESEARCH EXERCISES ON THE WEB

Go to http://wbl.westbuslaw.com, the Web site that accompanies this text. Select "Chapter 7" and click on "Internet Exercises." There you will find the following Internet research exercises that you can perform to learn more about topics covered in this chapter.

Activity 7–1: LEGAL PERSPECTIVE
Negligence and the *Titanic*

Activity 7–2: MANAGEMENT PERSPECTIVE
The Duty to Warn

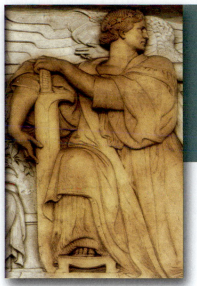

CHAPTER 8
Intellectual Property

Most people think of wealth in terms of houses, land, cars, stocks, and bonds. Wealth, however, also includes **intellectual property, which consists of the products that result from intellectual, creative processes.** Although it is an abstract term for an abstract concept, intellectual property is nonetheless wholly familiar to virtually everyone. *Trademarks, service marks, copyrights,* and *patents* are all forms of intellectual property. The book you are reading is copyrighted. The software you use, the movies you see, and the music you listen to are all forms of intellectual property. Exhibit 8–1 on page 155 offers a comprehensive summary of these forms of intellectual property, as well as intellectual property that consists of *trade secrets.* In this chapter, we examine each of these forms in some detail.

Intellectual property has taken on increasing significance in the United States as well as globally. Today, the value of the world's intellectual property probably exceeds the value of physical property, such as machines and houses. For many U.S. companies, ownership rights in intangible intellectual property are more important to their prosperity than are their tangible assets. As you will read in this chapter, a pressing issue for businesspersons today is how to protect these valuable rights in the online world.

The need to protect creative works was voiced by the framers of the U.S. Constitution over two hundred years ago: Article I, Section 8, of the U.S. Constitution authorized Congress "[t]o promote the Progress of Science and useful Arts, by securing for limited Times to Authors and Inventors the exclusive Right to their respective Writings and Discoveries." Laws protecting patents, trademarks, and copyrights are explicitly designed to protect and reward inventive and artistic creativity. Although intellectual property law limits the economic freedom of some individuals, it does so to protect the freedom of others to enjoy the fruits of their labors—in the form of profits.

SECTION 1 | Trademarks and Related Property

A **trademark** is a distinctive mark, motto, device, or implement that a manufacturer stamps, prints, or otherwise affixes to the goods it produces so that they can be identified on the market and their origin made known. In other words, a trademark is a source indicator. At common law, the person who used a symbol or mark to identify a business or product was protected in the use of that trademark. Clearly, by using another's trademark, a business could lead consumers to believe that its goods were made by the other business. The law seeks to avoid this kind of confusion. We examine in this section various aspects of the law governing trademarks.

In the following famous case concerning Coca-Cola, the defendants argued that the Coca-Cola trademark was entitled to no protection under the law because the term did not accurately represent the product.

CASE 8.1

Supreme Court of the
United States, 1920.
254 U.S. 143,
41 S.Ct. 113,
65 L.Ed. 189.
http://www.findlaw.com/
casecode/supreme.html[a]

The Coca-Cola Co. v. The Koke Co. of America

COMPANY PROFILE *John Pemberton, an Atlanta pharmacist, invented a caramel-colored, carbonated soft drink in 1886. His bookkeeper, Frank Robinson, named the beverage "Coca-Cola" after two of the ingredients, coca leaves and kola nuts. Asa Candler bought the Coca-Cola Company (http://www.cocacolacompany.com) in 1891, and within seven years, he made the soft drink available in all of the United States, as well as in parts of Canada and Mexico. Candler continued to sell Coke aggressively and to open up new markets, reaching Europe before 1910. In doing so, however, he attracted numerous competitors, some of which tried to capitalize directly on the Coke name.*

BACKGROUND AND FACTS *The Coca-Cola Company sought to enjoin (prevent) the Koke Company of America and other beverage companies from, among other things, using the word Koke for their products. The Koke Company of America and other beverage companies contended that the Coca-Cola trademark was a fraudulent representation and that Coca-Cola was therefore not entitled to any help from the courts. The Koke Company and the other defendants alleged that the Coca-Cola Company, by its use of the Coca-Cola name, represented that the beverage contained cocaine (from coca leaves), which it no longer did. The trial court granted the injunction against the Koke Company, but the appellate court reversed the lower court's ruling. Coca-Cola then appealed to the United States Supreme Court.*

IN THE LANGUAGE OF THE COURT

Mr. Justice *HOLMES* delivered the opinion of the Court.
* * * *
* * * Before 1900 the beginning of [Coca-Cola's] goodwill was more or less helped by the presence of cocaine, a drug that, like alcohol or caffeine or opium, may be described as a deadly poison or as a valuable [pharmaceutical item, depending on the speaker's purposes]. The amount seems to have been very small,[b] but it may have been enough to begin a bad habit and after the Food and Drug Act of June 30, 1906, if not earlier, long before this suit was brought, it was eliminated from the plaintiff's compound. * * *
* * * Since 1900, the sales have increased at a very great rate corresponding to a like increase in advertising. The name now characterizes a beverage to be had at almost any soda fountain. It means a single thing coming from a single source, and well known to the community. It hardly would be too much to say that the drink characterizes the name as much as the name, the drink. In other words *Coca-Cola probably means to most persons the plaintiff's familiar product to be had everywhere rather than a compound of particular substances.* * * * [B]efore this suit was brought the plaintiff had advertised to the public that it must not expect and would not find cocaine, and had eliminated everything tending to suggest cocaine effects except the name and the picture of [coca] leaves and nuts, which probably conveyed little or nothing to most who saw it. It appears to us that it would be going too far to deny the plaintiff relief against a palpable [readily evident] fraud because possibly here and there an ignorant person might call for the drink with the hope for incipient cocaine intoxication. The plaintiff's position must be judged by the facts as they were when the suit was begun, not by the facts of a different condition and an earlier time. [Emphasis added.]

DECISION AND REMEDY *The district court's injunction was allowed to stand. The competing beverage companies were enjoined (prevented) from calling their products "Koke."*

WHAT IF THE FACTS WERE DIFFERENT? *Suppose that Coca-Cola had been trying to make the public believe that its product contained cocaine. Would the result in this case likely have been different? Why?*

a. This URL will take you to a Web site maintained by FindLaw, which is now part of West Group. In the "Citation Search" section, enter "254" in the left box and "143" in the right box, and click on "Get It" to access the opinion.
b. In reality, until 1903 the amount of active cocaine in each bottle of Coke was equivalent to one "line" of cocaine.

 **Continued**

IMPACT OF THIS CASE ON TODAY'S LAW

In this early case, the United States Supreme Court made it clear that trademarks and trade names (and nicknames for those marks and names, such as the nickname "Coke" for "Coca-Cola") that are in common use receive protection under the common law. This holding is significant historically because it is the predecessor to the federal statute later passed to protect trademark rights—the Lanham Act of 1946, to be discussed next. In many ways, this act represented a codification of common law principles governing trademarks.

EXHIBIT 8-1 **Forms of Intellectual Property**

	DEFINITION	HOW ACQUIRED	DURATION	REMEDY FOR INFRINGEMENT
Patent	A grant from the government that gives an inventor the right to exclude others from making, using, and selling an invention.	By filing a patent application with the U.S. Patent and Trademark Office and receiving its approval.	Twenty years from the date of the application; for design patents, fourteen years.	Actual damages, including reasonable royalties or lost profits, *plus* attorneys' fees. Damages may be tripled for willful infringements.
Copyright	The right of an author or originator of a literary or artistic work, or other production that falls within a specified category, to have the exclusive use of that work for a given period of time.	Automatic (once the work or creation is put in tangible form). Only the *expression* of an idea (and not the idea itself) can be protected by copyright.	For authors: the life of the author, plus 70 years. For publishers: 95 years after the date of publication or 120 years after creation.	Actual damages plus profits received by the party who infringed *or* statutory damages under the Copyright Act, *plus* costs and attorneys' fees in either situation.
Trademark (Service Mark and Trade Dress)	Any distinctive word, name, symbol, or device (image or appearance), or combination thereof, that an entity uses to distinguish its goods or services from those of others. The owner has the exclusive right to use that mark or trade dress.	1. At common law, ownership created by use of the mark. 2. Registration with the appropriate federal or state office gives notice and is permitted if the mark is currently in use or will be within the next six months.	Unlimited, as long as it is in use. To continue notice by registration, the owner must renew by filing between the fifth and sixth years and, thereafter, every ten years.	1. Injunction prohibiting the future use of the mark. 2. Actual damages plus profits received by the party who infringed (can be increased under the Lanham Act). 3. Destruction of articles that infringed. 4. *Plus* costs and attorneys' fees.
Trade Secret	Any information that a business possesses and that gives the business an advantage over competitors (including formulas, lists, patterns, plans, processes, and programs).	Through the originality and development of the information and processes that constitute the business secret and are unknown to others.	Unlimited, so long as not revealed to others. Once revealed to others, they are no longer trade secrets.	Money damages for misappropriation (the Uniform Trade Secrets Act also permits punitive damages if willful), *plus* costs and attorneys' fees.

STATUTORY PROTECTION OF TRADEMARKS

Statutory protection of trademarks and related property is provided at the federal level by the Lanham Act of 1946.[1] The Lanham Act was enacted in part to protect manufacturers from losing business to rival companies that used confusingly similar trademarks. The Lanham Act incorporates the common law of trademarks and provides remedies for owners of trademarks who wish to enforce their claims in federal court. Many states also have trademark statutes.

TRADEMARK DILUTION   In 1995, Congress amended the Lanham Act by passing the Federal Trademark Dilution Act,[2] which extended the protection available to trademark owners by creating a federal cause of action for trademark **dilution.** Until the passage of this amendment, federal trademark law prohibited the unauthorized use of the same mark on competing—or on noncompeting but "related"—goods or services only when such use would likely confuse consumers as to the origin of those goods and services. Trademark dilution laws protect "distinctive" or "famous" trademarks (such as Jergens, McDonald's, RCA, and Macintosh) from certain unauthorized uses of the marks *regardless* of a showing of competition or a likelihood of confusion. More than half of the states have also enacted trademark dilution laws.

Although Congress passed the 1995 Federal Trademark Dilution Act in an effort to create uniformity and consistency in dilution cases, until recently, the federal courts were split in the level of proof required to show dilution. Some courts required proof that the defendant's use would cause "actual lessening" of selling power, whereas other courts required only a showing of "likelihood of dilution."

In 2003, the United States Supreme Court resolved this issue in favor of the higher standard (actual lessening of selling power) in the case of *Moseley v. V Secret Catalogue, Inc.*[3] In that case, famous lingerie maker Victoria's Secret brought a trademark dilution action against "Victor's Little Secret," a small retail store that sold adult videos, lingerie, and other items. The lower courts had granted Victoria's Secret an injunction prohibiting the adult store from diluting the trademark. The Supreme Court, however, concluded that likelihood of confusion is not enough and reversed the decision. To establish dilution under the federal act, the Court held that some evidence must establish that the junior user's mark actually reduces the value of the famous mark or lessens its capacity to identify goods and services.

USE OF A SIMILAR MARK MAY CONSTITUTE TRADEMARK DILUTION   In one of the first cases to be decided under the 1995 act's provisions, a federal court held that a famous mark may be diluted not only by the use of an *identical* mark but also by the use of a *similar* mark. The lawsuit was brought by Ringling Bros.—Barnum & Bailey, Combined Shows, Inc., against the state of Utah. Ringling Bros. claimed that Utah's use of the slogan "The Greatest Snow on Earth"—to attract visitors to the state's recreational and scenic resorts—diluted the distinctiveness of the circus's famous trademark "The Greatest Show on Earth." Utah moved to dismiss the suit, arguing that the 1995 provisions protect owners of famous trademarks only against the unauthorized use of identical marks. The court disagreed and refused to grant Utah's motion to dismiss the case.[4]

TRADEMARK REGISTRATION

Trademarks may be registered with the state or with the federal government. To register for protection under federal trademark law, a person must file an application with the U.S. Patent and Trademark Office in Washington, D.C. Under current law, a mark can be registered (1) if it is currently in commerce or (2) if the applicant intends to put it into commerce within six months.

In special circumstances, the six-month period can be extended by thirty months, giving the applicant a total of three years from the date of notice of trademark approval to make use of the mark and file the required use statement. Registration is postponed until the mark is actually used. Nonetheless, during this waiting period, any applicant can legally protect his or her trademark against a third party who previously has neither used the mark nor filed an application for it. Registration is renewable between the fifth and sixth years after the initial registration and every ten years thereafter (every twenty years for those trademarks registered before 1990).

---

1. 15 U.S.C. Sections 1051–1128.
2. 15 U.S.C. Section 1125.
3. 537 U.S. 418, 123 S.Ct. 1115, 155 L.Ed.2d 1 (2003).

4. *Ringling Bros.—Barnum & Bailey, Combined Shows, Inc. v. Utah Division of Travel Development,* 935 F.Supp. 763 (E.D.Va. 1996).

TRADEMARK INFRINGEMENT

Registration of a trademark with the U.S. Patent and Trademark Office gives notice on a nationwide basis that the trademark belongs exclusively to the registrant. The registrant is also allowed to use the symbol ® to indicate that the mark has been registered. Whenever that trademark is copied to a substantial degree or used in its entirety by another, intentionally or unintentionally, the trademark has been *infringed* (used without authorization). When a trademark has been infringed, the owner of the mark has a cause of action against the infringer. A person need not have registered a trademark in order to sue for trademark infringement, but registration does furnish proof of the date of inception of the trademark's use.

A central objective of the Lanham Act is to reduce the likelihood that consumers will be confused by similar marks. For that reason, only those trademarks that are deemed sufficiently distinctive from all competing trademarks will be protected.

DISTINCTIVENESS OF MARK

A trademark must be sufficiently distinct to enable consumers to identify the manufacturer of the goods easily and to distinguish between those goods and competing products.

STRONG MARKS Fanciful, arbitrary, or suggestive trademarks are generally considered to be the most distinctive (strongest) trademarks. This is because these types of marks are normally taken from outside the context of the particular product and thus provide the best means of distinguishing one product from another.

Fanciful trademarks include invented words, such as "Xerox" for one manufacturer's copiers and "Kodak" for another company's photographic products. Arbitrary trademarks include actual words used with products that have no literal connection to the words, such as "English Leather" used as a name for an aftershave lotion (and not for leather processed in England). Suggestive trademarks are those that suggest something about a product without describing the product directly. For example, the trademark "Dairy Queen" suggests an association between the products and milk, but it does not directly describe ice cream.

SECONDARY MEANING Descriptive terms, geographic terms, and personal names are not inherently

distinctive and do not receive protection under the law until they acquire a secondary meaning. A secondary meaning may arise when customers begin to associate a specific term or phrase (such as London Fog) with specific trademarked items (coats with "London Fog" labels). Whether a secondary meaning becomes attached to a term or name usually depends on how extensively the product is advertised, the market for the product, the number of sales, and other factors. Once a secondary meaning is attached to a term or name, a trademark is considered distinctive and is protected. The United States Supreme Court has held that even a shade of color can qualify for trademark protection, once customers associate the color with the product.[5]

GENERIC TERMS Generic terms that refer to an entire class of products, such as *bicycle* and *computer*, receive no protection, even if they acquire secondary meanings. A particularly thorny problem arises when a trademark acquires generic use. For example, *aspirin* and *thermos* were originally the names of trademarked products, but today the words are used generically. Other examples are *escalator*, *trampoline*, *raisin bran*, *dry ice*, *lanolin*, *linoleum*, *nylon*, and *corn flakes*.

Note that a generic term will not be protected under trademark law even if the term has acquired a secondary meaning. In one case, for example, America Online, Inc. (AOL), sued AT&T Corporation, claiming that AT&T's use of "You Have Mail" on its WorldNet Service infringed AOL's trademark rights in the same phrase. The court ruled, however, that because each of the three words in the phrase was a generic term, the phrase as a whole was generic. Although the phrase had become widely associated with AOL's e-mail notification service, and thus might have acquired a secondary meaning, this issue was of no significance in the case. The court stated that it would not consider whether the mark had acquired any secondary meaning because "generic marks with secondary meaning are still not entitled to protection."[6]

TRADE DRESS

The term **trade dress** refers to the image and overall appearance of a product—for example, the distinctive

---

5. *Qualitex Co. v. Jacobson Products Co.*, 514 U.S. 159, 115 S.Ct. 1300, 131 L.Ed.2d 248 (1995).
6. *America Online, Inc. v. AT&T Corp.*, 243 F.3d 812 (4th Cir. 2001).

decor, menu, layout, and style of service of a particular restaurant. Trade dress is a broad concept and can include either all or part of the total image or overall impression created by a product or its packaging. It can include such things as the cover of a book or magazine, the layout and appearance of a mail-order catalogue, the use of a lighthouse as part of the design of a golf hole, the fish shape of a cracker, or the G-shaped design of a Gucci watch.

Basically, trade dress is subject to the same protection as trademarks. In cases involving trade dress infringement, as in trademark infringement cases, a major consideration is whether consumers are likely to be confused by the allegedly infringing use.

SERVICE, CERTIFICATION, AND COLLECTIVE MARKS

A **service mark** is essentially a trademark that is used to distinguish the services of one person or company from those of another rather than its products. For example, each airline has a particular mark or symbol associated with its name. United Air Lines uses its slogan "Fly the Friendly Skies" as a service mark. Titles and character names used in radio and television are frequently registered as service marks.

Other marks protected by law include certification marks and collective marks. A **certification mark** is used by one or more persons other than the owner to certify the region, materials, mode of manufacture, quality, or accuracy of the owner's goods or services. When used by members of a cooperative, association, or other organization, it is referred to as a **collective mark.** Examples of certification marks are the phrases "Good Housekeeping Seal of Approval" and "UL Tested." Collective marks appear at the end of motion picture credits to indicate the various associations and organizations that participated in the making of the films.

TRADE NAMES

Trademarks apply to *products*. The term **trade name** is used to indicate part or all of a business's name, whether the business is a sole proprietorship, a partnership, or a corporation. Generally, a trade name is directly related to a business and its goodwill. A trade name may be protected as a trademark if the trade name is also the name of the company's trademarked product—for example, Pepsi-Cola. Unless also used as a trademark or service mark, a trade name cannot be registered with the federal government. Trade names are protected under the common law, however. As

with trademarks, words must be unusual or fancifully used if they are to be protected as trade names. The word *Safeway*, for example, was held by the courts to be sufficiently fanciful to obtain protection as a trade name for a food-store chain.[7]

SECTION **2** | Cyber Marks

In cyberspace, trademarks are sometimes referred to as **cyber marks.** We turn now to a discussion of issues in cyberspace relating to trademarks and how new laws and the courts are addressing these issues. One concern relates to the rights of a trademark's owner to use the mark as part of a domain name (Internet address). Other issues have to do with domain names and cybersquatting, meta tags, and trademark dilution on the Web. The use of licensing as a way to avoid liability for infringing on another's intellectual property rights in cyberspace will also be discussed.

DOMAIN NAMES

In the real world, one business can often use the same name as another without causing any conflict, particularly if the businesses are small, their goods or services are different, and the geographic areas in which they do business are distinctly separate. In the online world, however, there is only one geographic area of business—cyberspace. Thus, disputes between parties over which one has the right to use a particular domain name have become common.

A **domain name** is the core part of an Internet address—for example, "westlaw.com." It includes at least two parts. The top level domain (TLD) is the part of the name to the right of the period, such as *com* or *gov*. The second level domain (the part of the name to the left of the period) is chosen by the business entity or individual registering the domain name.

CONFLICTS OVER DOMAIN NAMES Conflicts over rights to domain names emerged during the 1990s as e-commerce expanded on a worldwide scale. The *.com* TLD came to be widely used by businesses on the Web. Competition among firms with identical or similar names and products for the second level domains preceding the *.com* TLD led, understandably, to numerous disputes over domain name rights. By using the same, or a similar, domain name, parties have attempted to profit from the goodwill of a competitor, to sell pornog-

---

7. *Safeway Stores v. Suburban Foods*, 130 F.Supp. 249 (E.D.Va. 1955).

raphy, to offer for sale another party's domain name, and to otherwise infringe on others' trademarks.

DISPUTE RESOLUTION THROUGH ONLINE ARBITRATION As noted in Chapter 2, the federal government set up the Internet Corporation for Assigned Names and Numbers (ICANN), a nonprofit corporation, to oversee the distribution of domain names. ICANN has also played a leading role in facilitating the settlement of domain name disputes worldwide. Since January 2000, ICANN has been operating an online arbitration system to resolve domain name disputes. Now, if trademark infringement involves a domain name, a party may submit a complaint to an ICANN-approved dispute-resolution provider instead of (or in addition to) filing a lawsuit. By 2005, ICANN-approved online arbitration providers were handling well over one thousand disputes annually.

ANTICYBERSQUATTING LEGISLATION

Cybersquatting occurs when a person registers a domain name that is the same as, or confusingly similar to, the trademark of another and then offers to sell the domain name back to the trademark owner. During the 1990s, cybersquatting became a contentious issue and led to much litigation. Often at issue in these cases was whether cybersquatting constituted a commercial use of the mark so as to violate federal trademark law. In 1999, Congress addressed this problem by passing the Anticybersquatting Consumer Protection Act (ACPA),[8] which amended the Lanham Act—the federal law protecting trademarks, discussed earlier in this chapter.

PROVISIONS OF THE ACPA The ACPA makes it illegal for a person to "register, traffic in, or use" a

---

8. 15 U.S.C.A. Section 1129.

domain name (1) if the name is identical or confusingly similar to the trademark of another and (2) if the one registering, trafficking in, or using the domain name has a "bad faith intent" to profit from that trademark. The act lists several factors that courts can consider in deciding whether bad faith exists. These factors include the trademark rights of the other person, whether there is an intent to divert consumers in a way that could harm the goodwill represented by the trademark, whether there is an offer to transfer or sell the domain name to the trademark owner, and whether there is an intent to use the domain name to offer goods and services.

APPLICABILITY OF THE ACPA AND SANCTIONS UNDER THE ACT The ACPA applies to all domain name registrations, even domain names registered before the passage of the act. Successful plaintiffs in suits brought under the act can collect actual damages and profits, or they can elect to receive statutory damages ranging from $1,000 to $100,000.

META TAGS

Search engines compile their results by looking through a Web site's key-word field. **Meta tags,** or key words, may be inserted into this field to increase the site's inclusion in search engine results, even though the site may have nothing to do with the inserted words. Using this same technique, one site may appropriate the key words of other sites with more frequent hits so that the appropriating site will appear in the same search engine results as the more popular sites. Using another's trademark in a meta tag without the owner's permission, however, normally constitutes trademark infringement.

In some situations, using another's trademark as a meta tag may be practically unavoidable. In those situations, the court must determine whether the particular use is permissible or impermissible. One such use of meta tags was at issue in the following case.

| CASE 8.2 | **Playboy Enterprises, Inc. v. Welles** |

United States Court of Appeals, Ninth Circuit, 2002. 279 F.3d 796.

T.G. NELSON, Circuit Judge.

* * * *

Terri Welles was on the cover of *Playboy* in 1981 and was chosen to be the Playboy Playmate of the Year for 1981. Her use of the title "Playboy Playmate of the Year 1981," and her use of other trademarked terms on her website are at issue in this suit. During the relevant time period, Welles' website offered information about and free photos of Welles, advertised photos for sale, advertised memberships in her photo club, and promoted her services as a spokesperson. A biographical section described Welles' selection as Playmate of the Year in 1981 and her years modeling for [Playboy Enterprises, Inc. (PEI)]. After the lawsuit began,

CONTINUED

CASE 8.2 | Continued

Welles included discussions of the suit and criticism of PEI on her website and included a note disclaiming any association with PEI.

PEI complains of * * * [Welles's use of] the terms "Playboy" and "Playmate" in the meta tags of the website * * * . PEI claimed [in part] that these uses of its marks constituted trademark infringement [and] dilution * * * . The [federal] district court [that heard the suit] granted defendants' [Welles and her "webmasters," Steven Huntington and Michael Mihalko] motion for summary judgment. PEI appeals the grant of summary judgment on its infringement and dilution claims * * *

* * * *

* * * [W]e conclude that Welles' uses of PEI's trademarks are permissible, nominative uses.[a] They imply no current sponsorship or endorsement by PEI. Instead, they serve to identify Welles as a past PEI "Playmate of the Year."

* * * *

* * * [The] test for nominative use [of a trademark is]:

First, the product or service in question must be one not readily identifiable without use of the trademark; second, only so much of the mark or marks may be used as is reasonably necessary to identify the product or service; and third, the user must do nothing that would, in conjunction with the mark, suggest sponsorship or endorsement by the trademark holder. * * *

* * * *

Welles includes the terms "playboy" and "playmate" in her meta tags. Meta tags describe the contents of a website using keywords. Some search engines search meta tags to identify websites relevant to a search. Thus, when an Internet searcher enters "playboy" or "playmate" into a search engine that uses meta tags, the results will include Welles' site. Because Welles' meta tags do not repeat the terms extensively, her site will not be at the top of the list of search results. Applying the three-factor test for nominative use, we conclude that the use of the trademarked terms in Welles' meta tags is nominative.

* * * Welles has no practical way of describing herself without using trademarked terms. In the context of meta tags, we conclude that she has no practical way of identifying the content of her website without referring to PEI's trademarks.

A large portion of Welles' website discusses her association with Playboy over the years. Thus, the trademarked terms accurately describe the contents of Welles' website, in addition to describing Welles. Forcing Welles and others to use absurd turns of phrase in their meta tags, such as those necessary to identify Welles, would be particularly damaging in the Internet search context. *Searchers would have a much more difficult time locating relevant websites if they could do so only by correctly guessing the long phrases necessary to substitute for trademarks.* We can hardly expect someone searching for Welles' site to imagine the same phrase proposed by the district court to describe Welles without referring to Playboy—"the nude model selected by Mr. Hefner's organization * * * ." Yet if someone could not remember her name, that is what they would have to do. Similarly, someone searching for critiques of Playboy on the Internet would have a difficult time if Internet sites could not list the object of their critique in their meta tags. [Emphasis added.]

There is simply no descriptive substitute for the trademarks used in Welles' meta tags. *Precluding their use would have the unwanted effect of hindering the free flow of information on the Internet, something which is certainly not a goal of trademark law.* Accordingly, the use of trademarked terms in the meta tags meets the first part of the test for nominative use. [Emphasis added.]

We conclude that the meta tags satisfy the second and third elements of the test as well. The meta tags use only so much of the marks as reasonably necessary and nothing is done in conjunction with them to suggest sponsorship or endorsement by the trademark holder. We note that our decision might differ if the meta tags listed the trademarked term so repeatedly that Welles' site would regularly appear above PEI's in searches for one of the trademarked terms.

* * * *

---

a. A *nominative use* of a trademark is one that does not imply sponsorship or endorsement of a product because the product's mark is used only to describe the thing, rather than to identify its source. See *New Kids on the Block v. News America Publishing, Inc.*, 971 F.2d 302 (9th Cir. 1992).

CASE 8.2 | Continued

Dilution works its harm not by causing confusion in consumers' minds regarding the source of a good or service, but by creating an association in consumers' minds between a mark and a different good or service. * * *

Uses that do not create an improper association between a mark and a new product but merely identify the trademark holder's products should be excepted from the reach of the [Federal Trademark Dilution Act]. Such uses cause no harm. The anti-dilution statute recognizes this principle and specifically excepts users of a trademark who compare their product in "commercial advertising or promotion to identify the competing goods or services of the owner of the famous mark."

For the same reason uses in comparative advertising are excepted from anti-dilution law, we conclude that nominative uses are also excepted. A nominative use, by definition, refers to the trademark holder's product. It does not create an improper association in consumers' minds between a new product and the trademark holder's mark.

When Welles refers to her title, she is in effect referring to a product of PEI's. She does not dilute the title by truthfully identifying herself as its one-time recipient any more than Michael Jordan would dilute the name "Chicago Bulls" by referring to himself as a former member of that team, or the two-time winner of an Academy Award would dilute the award by referring to him or herself as a "two-time Academy Award winner." Awards are not diminished or diluted by the fact that they have been awarded in the past. Similarly, they are not diminished or diluted when past recipients truthfully identify themselves as such. It is in the nature of honors and awards to be identified with the people who receive them. * * *
* * * *

For the foregoing reasons, we affirm the district court's grant of summary judgment as to PEI's claims for trademark infringement and trademark dilution * * * .

QUESTIONS

1. Welles also used the PEI marks in the headlines on her Web site and in the banner advertisements that could be transferred to other sites and linked to hers. Should these uses be permitted as nominative? Why or why not?
2. Why would PEI encourage its models to use its marks outside cyberspace but attempt to block such uses within cyberspace?

DILUTION IN THE ONLINE WORLD

As discussed earlier, trademark *dilution* occurs when a trademark is used, without authorization, in a way that diminishes the distinctive quality of the mark. Unlike trademark infringement, a dilution cause of action does not require proof that consumers are likely to be confused by a connection between the unauthorized use and the mark. For this reason, the products involved need not be similar.

In the first case alleging dilution on the Web, a court precluded the use of "candyland.com" as the URL for an adult site. The suit was brought by the maker of the "Candyland" children's game and owner of the "Candyland" mark.[9] In another case, a court issued an injunction on the ground that spamming under another's logo is trademark dilution. In that

case, Hotmail Corporation provided e-mail services and worked to dissociate itself from spam. Van$ Money Pie, Inc., and others spammed thousands of e-mail customers, using the free e-mail Hotmail as a return address. The court ordered the defendants to stop.[10]

LICENSING

One way to make use of another's trademark or other form of intellectual property, while avoiding litigation, is to obtain a license to do so. A license in this context is essentially an agreement permitting the use of a trademark, copyright, patent, or trade secret for certain purposes. For example, a licensee (the party obtaining the license) might be allowed to use the trademark of

---

9. *Hasbro, Inc. v. Internet Entertainment Group, Ltd.*, 1996 WL 84853 (W.D.Wash. 1996).

10. *Hotmail Corp. v. Van$ Money Pie, Inc.*, 1998 WL 388389 (N.D.Cal. 1998).

the licensor (the party issuing the license) as part of the name of its company, or as part of its domain name, without otherwise using the mark on any products or services. Often, selling a license to an infringer is an inexpensive solution to the problem, at least when compared with the costs associated with litigation.

SECTION 3 | Patents

A **patent** is a grant from the government that gives an inventor the right to exclude others from making, using, and selling an invention for a period of twenty years from the date of filing the application for a patent. Patents for designs, as opposed to inventions, are given for a fourteen-year period. The applicant must demonstrate to the satisfaction of the U.S. Patent and Trademark Office that the invention, discovery, process, or design is genuine, novel, useful, and not obvious in light of current technology. A patent holder gives notice to all that an article or design is patented by placing on it the word *Patent* or *Pat.*, plus the patent number. In contrast to patent law in other countries, in the United States patent protection is given to the first person to invent a product or process, even though someone else may have been the first to file for a patent on that product or process.

A significant development relating to patents is the availability online of the world's patent databases. The Web site of the U.S. Patent and Trademark Office (see the *Law on the Web* section at the end of this chapter for its URL) provides searchable databases covering U.S. patents granted since 1976. The Web site of the European Patent Office maintains databases covering all patent documents in sixty-five nations and the legal status of patents in twenty-two of those countries.

PATENT INFRINGEMENT

If a firm makes, uses, or sells another's patented design, product, or process without the patent owner's permission, the tort of patent infringement occurs. Patent infringement may arise even though the patent owner has not put the patented product in commerce. Patent infringement may also occur even though not all features or parts of an invention are identical, provided that the features are equivalent to those used in the patented invention.

Patent infringement litigation can be very costly. Often, rather than pursue litigation, the patent holder will offer to sell to the infringer a license to use the patented design, product, or process. Indeed, in many situations, licensing is the best option because the costs of detection, prosecution, and monitoring infringement are prohibitively high.

PATENTS FOR SOFTWARE

At one time, it was difficult for developers and manufacturers of software to obtain patent protection because many software products simply automate procedures that can be performed manually. In other words, the computer programs do not meet the "novel" and "not obvious" requirements previously mentioned. Also, the basis for software is often a mathematical equation or formula, which is not patentable. In 1981, however, the United States Supreme Court held that it is possible to obtain a patent for a process that incorporates a computer program—providing, of course, that the process itself is patentable.[11] Subsequently, many patents have been issued for software-related inventions.

PATENTS FOR BUSINESS PROCESSES

In a landmark 1998 case, *State Street Bank & Trust Co. v. Signature Financial Group, Inc.*,[12] the U.S. Court of Appeals for the Federal Circuit ruled that only three categories of subject matter will always remain unpatentable: (1) the laws of nature, (2) natural phenomena, and (3) abstract ideas.

After this decision, numerous technology firms applied for business process patents. Walker Digital applied for a business process patent for its "Dutch auction" system, which allowed consumers to make offers for airline tickets on the Internet and led to the creation of Priceline.com. About.com obtained a patent for its "Elaborative Internet Data Mining System," which extracts and pulls together the Web content of a large range of topics onto a single Web site. Amazon.com obtained a business process patent for its "one-click" ordering system, a method of processing credit-card orders securely without asking for the customer's card number or other personal information, such as the customer's name and address, more than once. Indeed, since the *State Street* decision, the number of Internet-related patents issued by the U.S. Patent and Trademark Office has increased by more than 800 percent.

---

11. *Diamond v. Diehr,* 450 U.S. 175, 101 S.Ct. 1048, 67 L.Ed.2d 155 (1981).

12. 149 F.3d 1368 (Fed. Cir. 1998).

SECTION 4 | Copyrights *expression of an idea*

A **copyright** is an intangible property right granted by federal statute to the author or originator of a literary or artistic production of a specified type. Today, copyrights are governed by the Copyright Act of 1976,[13] as amended. Works created after January 1, 1978, are automatically given statutory copyright protection for the life of the author, plus 70 years. For copyrights owned by publishing houses, the copyright expires 95 years from the date of publication or 120 years from the date of creation, whichever is first. For works by more than one author, the copyright expires 70 years after the death of the last surviving author.

These time periods reflect the extensions of the length of copyright protection enacted by Congress in the Copyright Term Extension Act of 1998.[14] Critics challenged this act as overstepping the bounds of Congress's power and violating the constitutional requirement that copyrights endure for only a limited time. In 2003, however, the United States Supreme Court upheld the act in *Eldred v. Ashcroft*.[15] This holding obviously favored copyright holders by preventing copyrighted works from the 1920s and 1930s from losing protection and falling into the public domain for an additional two decades.

Copyrights can be registered with the U.S. Copyright Office in Washington, D.C. A copyright owner no longer needs to place the symbol © or the term *Copr.* or *Copyright* on the work, however, to have the work protected against infringement. Chances are that if somebody created it, somebody owns it.

WHAT IS PROTECTED EXPRESSION?

Works that are copyrightable include books, records, films, artworks, architectural plans, menus, music videos, product packaging, and computer software. To obtain protection under the Copyright Act, a work must be original and fall into one of the following categories: (1) literary works (including newspaper and magazine articles, computer and training manuals, catalogues, brochures, and print advertisements); (2) musical works and accompanying words (including advertising jingles); (3) dramatic works and accompanying music; (4) pantomimes and choreographic works (including ballets and other forms of dance); (5) pictorial, graphic, and sculptural works (including cartoons, maps, posters, statues, and even stuffed animals); (6) motion pictures and other audiovisual works (including multimedia works); (7) sound recordings; and (8) architectural works. To be protected, a work must be "fixed in a durable medium" from which it can be perceived, reproduced, or communicated. Protection is automatic. Registration is not required.

SECTION 102 EXCLUSIONS Section 102 of the Copyright Act specifically excludes copyright protection for any "idea, procedure, process, system, method of operation, concept, principle, or discovery, regardless of the form in which it is described, explained, illustrated, or embodied." Note that it is not possible to copyright an *idea*. The underlying ideas embodied in a work may be freely used by others. What is copyrightable is the particular way in which an idea is expressed. Whenever an idea and an expression are inseparable, the expression cannot be copyrighted. Generally, anything that is not an original expression will not qualify for copyright protection. Facts widely known to the public are not copyrightable. Page numbers are not copyrightable because they follow a sequence known to everyone. Mathematical calculations are not copyrightable.

COMPILATIONS OF FACTS *Compilations* of facts are copyrightable. Section 103 of the Copyright Act defines a compilation as "a work formed by the collection and assembling of preexisting materials or data that are selected, coordinated, or arranged in such a way that the resulting work as a whole constitutes an original work of authorship." The key requirement in the copyrightability of a compilation is originality. Therefore, the white pages of a telephone directory do not qualify for copyright protection when the information that makes up the directory (names, addresses, and telephone numbers) is not selected, coordinated, or arranged in an original way.[16] In one case, even the Yellow Pages of a telephone directory did not qualify for copyright protection.[17]

---

13. 17 U.S.C. Sections 101 *et seq.*
14. 17 U.S.C.A. Section 302.
15. 537 U.S. 186, 123 S.Ct. 769, 154 L.Ed.2d 683 (2003).

16. *Feist Publications, Inc. v. Rural Telephone Service Co.*, 499 U.S. 340, 111 S.Ct. 1282, 113 L.Ed.2d 358 (1991).
17. *Bellsouth Advertising & Publishing Corp. v. Donnelley Information Publishing, Inc.*, 999 F.2d 1436 (11th Cir. 1993).

COPYRIGHT INFRINGEMENT

Whenever the form or expression of an idea is copied, an infringement of copyright has occurred. The reproduction does not have to be exactly the same as the original, nor does it have to reproduce the original in its entirety. If a substantial part of the original is reproduced, there is copyright infringement.

DAMAGES FOR COPYRIGHT INFRINGEMENT

Those who infringe copyrights may be liable for damages or criminal penalties. These range from actual damages or statutory damages, imposed at the court's discretion, to criminal proceedings for willful violations. Actual damages are based on the harm caused to the copyright holder by the infringement, while statutory damages, not to exceed $150,000, are provided for under the Copyright Act. Criminal proceedings may result in fines and/or imprisonment.

THE "FAIR USE" EXCEPTION

An exception to liability for copyright infringement is made under the "fair use" doctrine. In certain circumstances, a person or organization can reproduce copyrighted material without paying royalties (fees paid to the copyright holder for the privilege of reproducing the copyrighted material). Section 107 of the Copyright Act provides as follows:

> [T]he fair use of a copyrighted work, including such use by reproduction in copies or phonorecords or by any other means specified by [Section 106 of the Copyright Act], for purposes such as criticism, comment, news reporting, teaching (including multiple copies for classroom use), scholarship, or research, is not an infringement of copyright. In determining whether the use made of a work in any particular case is a fair use the factors to be considered shall include—
>
> (1) the purpose and character of the use, including whether such use is of a commercial nature or is for nonprofit educational purposes;
> (2) the nature of the copyrighted work;
> (3) the amount and substantiality of the portion used in relation to the copyrighted work as a whole; and
> (4) the effect of the use upon the potential market for or value of the copyrighted work.

Because these guidelines are very broad, the courts determine whether a particular use is fair on a case-by-case basis. Thus, anyone who reproduces copyrighted material may still be committing a violation. In determining whether a use is fair, courts have often considered the fourth factor to be the most important.

COPYRIGHT PROTECTION FOR SOFTWARE

In 1980, Congress passed the Computer Software Copyright Act, which amended the Copyright Act of 1976 to include computer programs in the list of creative works protected by federal copyright law.[18] The 1980 statute, which classifies computer programs as "literary works," defines a computer program as a "set of statements or instructions to be used directly or indirectly in a computer in order to bring about a certain result."

The unique nature of computer programs, however, has created many problems for the courts in applying and interpreting the 1980 act. Generally, the courts have held that copyright protection extends not only to those parts of a computer program that can be read by humans, such as the "high-level" language of a source code, but also to the binary-language object code, which is readable only by the computer.[19] Additionally, such elements as the overall structure, sequence, and organization of a program were deemed copyrightable.[20] The courts have disagreed on the issue of whether the "look and feel"—the general appearance, command structure, video images, menus, windows, and other screen displays—of computer programs should also be protected by copyright. The courts have tended, however, not to extend copyright protection to look-and-feel aspects of computer programs.

SECTION 5 | Copyrights in Digital Information

Copyright law is probably the most important form of intellectual property protection on the Internet. This is because much of the material on the Internet consists of works of authorship (including multimedia presentations, software, and database information), which are the traditional focus of copyright law. Copyright law is also important because the nature of the Internet requires that data be "copied" to be transferred online. Copies are a significant part of the traditional controversies arising in this area of the law.

---

18. Pub. L. No. 96-517 (1980), amending 17 U.S.C.A. Sections 101, 117.

19. See *Stern Electronics, Inc. v. Kaufman*, 669 F.2d 852 (2d Cir. 1982); and *Apple Computer, Inc. v. Franklin Computer Corp.*, 714 F.2d 1240 (3d Cir. 1983).

20. *Whelan Associates, Inc. v. Jaslow Dental Laboratory, Inc.*, 797 F.2d 1222 (3d Cir. 1986).

THE COPYRIGHT ACT OF 1976

When Congress drafted the principal U.S. law governing copyrights, the Copyright Act of 1976, cyberspace did not exist for most of us. At that time, the rights of copyright owners were threatened not by computer technology but by unauthorized *tangible* copies of works and the sale of rights to movies, television, and other media.

Some issues that were unimagined when the Copyright Act was drafted have posed thorny questions for the courts. For example, to sell a copy of a work, permission of the copyright holder is necessary. Because of the nature of cyberspace, however, one of the early controversies involved determining at what point an intangible, electronic "copy" of a work has been made. The courts have held that loading a file or program into a computer's random access memory, or RAM, constitutes the making of a "copy" for purposes of copyright law.[21] RAM is a portion of a computer's memory into which a file, for example, is loaded so that it can be accessed (read or written over). Thus, a copyright is infringed when a party downloads software into RAM without owning the software or otherwise having a right to download it.[22]

Today, technology has vastly increased the potential for copyright infringement. The question in the following case is whether a musician commits copyright infringement when he or she copies any part—even as little as two seconds—of a copyrighted sound recording without the permission of the copyright's owner.

---

21. *MAI Systems Corp. v. Peak Computer, Inc.*, 991 F.2d 511 (9th Cir. 1993).
22. *DSC Communications Corp. v. Pulse Communications, Inc.*, 170 F.3d 1354 (Fed. Cir. 1999).

CASE 8.3

United States
Court of Appeals,
Sixth Circuit, 2003.
383 F.3d 390.
http://www.findlaw.com/ casecode/courts/6th.html **b**

Bridgeport Music, Inc. v. Dimension Films[a]

BACKGROUND AND FACTS *Bridgeport Music, Inc., is in the business of music publishing and using musical composition copyrights. Westbound Records, Inc., is in the business of recording and distributing sound recordings. Bridgeport and Westbound own the composition and recording copyrights to "Get Off Your Ass and Jam" by George Clinton, Jr., and the Funkadelics. The recording "Get Off" opens with a three-note solo guitar riff that lasts four seconds. The rap song "100 Miles and Runnin" contains a two-second sample from the guitar solo, at a lower pitch, looped and extended to sixteen beats, in five places in the song, with each looped segment lasting about seven seconds. "100 Miles" was included in the sound track of the movie I Got the Hook Up, which was distributed by No Limit Films. Bridgeport, Westbound, and others filed a suit in a federal district court against No Limit and others, alleging copyright infringement. No Limit did not dispute that it had digitally sampled a copyrighted sound recording. The court found, however, that no reasonable juror, even one familiar with the works of George Clinton, would recognize the source of the sample and issued a summary judgment in the defendants' favor. Plaintiffs appealed the judgment to the U.S. Court of Appeals for the Sixth Circuit.*

IN THE LANGUAGE OF THE COURT

RALPH B. GUY, JR., Circuit Judge.

* * * *

* * * The copyright laws attempt to strike a balance between protecting original works and stifling further creativity. The provisions, for example, for compulsory licensing make it possible for "creators" to enjoy the fruits of their creations, but not to fence them off from the world at large. Although musical compositions have always enjoyed copyright

---

a. Initially, Dimension Films was also a defendant in this case. The claims against this company were dismissed pursuant to a settlement prior to trial.
b. This URL will take you to a Web site maintained by FindLaw, which is now a part of West Group. In the "Docket Number Search" box, type "02-6521" and click on "Get It" to access the opinion.

CONTINUED ▶

CASE 8.3 | **Continued**

protection, it was not until 1971 that sound recordings were subject to a separate copyright. If one were to analogize to a book, it is not the book, *i.e.*, the paper and binding, that is copyrightable, but its contents. There are probably any number of reasons why the decision was made by Congress to treat a sound recording differently from a book even though both are the media in which an original work is fixed rather than the creation itself. Not the least of [these reasons] certainly were advances in technology which made the "pirating" of sound recordings an easy task. The balance that was struck was to give sound recording copyright holders the exclusive right to duplicate the sound recording in the form of phonorecords or copies that directly or indirectly recapture the actual sounds fixed in the recording. This means that *the world at large is free to imitate or simulate the creative work fixed in the recording so long as an actual copy of the sound recording itself is not made.* That leads us directly to the issue in this case. If you cannot pirate the whole sound recording, can you "lift" or "sample" something less than the whole? Our answer to that question is in the negative. [Emphasis added.]

Section 114(b) [of the Copyright Act] provides that "[t]he exclusive right of the owner of copyright in a sound recording under clause (2) of Section 106 is limited to the right to prepare a derivative work in which the actual sounds fixed in the sound recording are rearranged, remixed, or otherwise altered in sequence or quality." In other words, *a sound recording owner has the exclusive right to "sample" his own recording.* We find much to recommend this interpretation. [Emphasis added.]

To begin with, there is ease of enforcement. Get a license or do not sample. We do not see this as stifling creativity in any significant way. It must be remembered that if an artist wants to incorporate a "riff" from another work in his or her recording, he is free to duplicate the sound of that "riff" in the studio. Second, the market will control the license price and keep it within bounds. The sound recording copyright holder cannot exact a license fee greater than what it would cost the person seeking the license to just duplicate the sample in the course of making the new recording. Third, sampling is never accidental. It is not like the case of a composer who has a melody in his head, perhaps not even realizing that the reason he hears this melody is that it is the work of another which he had heard before. When you sample a sound recording you know you are taking another's work product.

This analysis admittedly raises the question of why one should, without infringing, be able to take three notes from a musical composition, for example, but not three notes by way of sampling from a sound recording. * * * Our first answer to this question is what we have earlier indicated. We think this result is dictated by the applicable statute. Second, *even when a small part of a sound recording is sampled, the part taken is something of value.* No further proof of that is necessary than the fact that the producer of the record or the artist on the record intentionally sampled because it would (1) save costs, or (2) add something to the new recording, or (3) both. For the sound recording copyright holder, it is not the "song" but the sounds that are fixed in the medium of his choice. When those sounds are sampled, they are taken directly from that fixed medium. It is a physical taking rather than an intellectual one. [Emphasis added.]

DECISION AND REMEDY *The U.S. Court of Appeals for the Sixth Circuit reversed the lower court's summary judgment on the plaintiff's claims against No Limit and remanded the case. The appellate court held that digitally sampling a copyrighted sound recording of any length is copyright infringement.*

WHAT IF THE FACTS WERE DIFFERENT? *Suppose that instead of a sound recording, this case had involved three seconds of a copyrighted movie, which the defendants pirated off the Internet and incorporated as background in a music video production. Would this court's holding be different? Why or why not?*

FURTHER DEVELOPMENTS IN COPYRIGHT LAW

In the last several years, Congress has enacted legislation designed specifically to protect copyright holders in a digital age. Particularly significant are the No Electronic Theft Act of 1997[23] and the Digital Millennium Copyright Act of 1998.[24]

THE NO ELECTRONIC THEFT ACT   Prior to 1997, criminal penalties could be imposed under copyright law only if unauthorized copies were exchanged for financial gain. Yet much piracy of copyrighted materials was "altruistic" in nature; that is, unauthorized copies were made and distributed not for financial gain but simply for reasons of generosity—to share the copies with others. To combat altruistic piracy and for other reasons, Congress passed the No Electronic Theft (NET) Act of 1997.

NET extends criminal liability for the piracy of copyrighted materials to persons who exchange unauthorized copies of copyrighted works, such as software, even though they realize no profit from the exchange. The act also imposes penalties on those who make unauthorized electronic copies of books, magazines, movies, or music for *personal* use, thus altering the traditional "fair use" doctrine. The criminal penalties for violating the act are relatively severe; they include fines as high as $250,000 and incarceration for up to five years.

THE DIGITAL MILLENNIUM COPYRIGHT ACT OF 1998   The passage of the Digital Millennium Copyright Act (DMCA) of 1998 gave significant protection to owners of copyrights in digital information.[25] Among other things, the act established civil and criminal penalties for anyone who circumvents (bypasses, or gets around—by using a special decryption program, for example) encryption software or other technological antipiracy protection. Also prohibited are the manufacture, import, sale, and distribution of devices or services for circumvention.

The DMCA provides for exceptions to fit the needs of libraries, scientists, universities, and others. In general, the law does not restrict the "fair use" of circumvention methods for educational and other noncommercial purposes. For example, circumvention is allowed to test computer security, to conduct encryption research, to protect personal privacy, and to enable parents to monitor their children's use of the Internet. The exceptions are to be reconsidered every three years.

The DMCA also limits the liability of Internet service providers (ISPs). Under the act, an ISP is not liable for any copyright infringement by its customer *unless* the ISP is aware of the subscriber's violation. An ISP may be held liable only if it fails to take action to shut the subscriber down after learning of the violation. A copyright holder must act promptly, however, by pursuing a claim in court, or the subscriber has the right to be restored to online access.

MP3 AND FILE-SHARING TECHNOLOGY

Soon after the Internet became popular, a few enterprising programmers created software to compress large data files, particularly those associated with music. The reduced file sizes make transmitting music over the Internet feasible. The most widely known compression and decompression system is MP3, which enables music fans to download songs or entire compact discs (CDs) onto their computers or onto portable listening devices, such as Rio or iPod. The MP3 system also made it possible for music fans to access other music fans' files by engaging in file-sharing via the Internet.

PEER-TO-PEER (P2P) NETWORKING   File-sharing via the Internet is accomplished through what is called **peer-to-peer (P2P) networking.** The concept is simple. Rather than going through a central Web server, P2P networking uses numerous personal computers (PCs) that are connected to the Internet. Files stored on one PC can be accessed by others who are members of the same network. Sometimes this is called a **distributed network** because parts of the network are distributed all over the country or the world. File-sharing offers an unlimited number of uses for distributed networks. Currently, for example, many researchers allow their home computers' computing power to be accessed through file-sharing software so

---

23. Pub. L. No. 105-147 (1997). Codified at 17 U.S.C.A. Sections 101, 506; 18 U.S.C.A. Sections 2311, 2319, 2319A, 2320; and 28 U.S.C.A. Sections 994 and 1498.

24. 17 U.S.C. Sections 512, 1201–1205, 1301–1332; and 28 U.S.C. Section 4001.

25. This act implemented the World Intellectual Property Organization (WIPO) Copyright Treaty of 1996, which will be discussed later in this chapter.

that very large mathematical problems can be solved quickly. Additionally, persons scattered throughout the country or the world can work together on the same project by using file-sharing programs.

SHARING STORED MUSIC FILES File-sharing clearly offers many advantages. When file-sharing is used to download others' stored music files, however, copyright issues arise. Recording artists and their labels stand to lose large amounts of royalties and revenues if relatively few CDs are purchased and then made available on distributed networks, from which everyone can get them for free. In the following

widely publicized case, several firms in the recording industry sued Napster, Inc., the owner of the then-popular Napster Web site. The firms alleged that Napster was contributing to copyright infringement by those who downloaded CDs from other computers in the Napster file-sharing system. At issue was whether Napster could be held vicariously liable for the infringement.[26]

---

26. *Vicarious* (substitute) *liability* exists when one person is subject to liability for another's actions. A common example occurs in the employment context, when an employer is held vicariously liable by third parties for torts committed by employees in the course of their employment.

CASE 8.4   A&M Records, Inc. v. Napster, Inc.

United States
Court of Appeals,
Ninth Circuit, 2001.
239 F.3d 1004.
http://guide.lp.findlaw.com/
casecode/courts/9th.html [a]

HISTORICAL AND TECHNOLOGICAL SETTING *In 1987, the Moving Picture Experts Group set a standard file format for the storage of audio recordings in a digital format called MPEG-3, abbreviated as "MP3." Digital MP3 files are created through a process called "ripping." Ripping software allows a computer owner to copy an audio compact disc (CD) directly onto a computer's hard drive by compressing the audio information on the CD into the MP3 format. The MP3's compressed format allows for rapid transmission of digital audio files from one computer to another by e-mail or any other file-transfer protocol.*

BACKGROUND AND FACTS *Napster, Inc. (http://www.napster.com), facilitated the transmission of MP3 files among the users of its Web site through a process called "peer-to-peer" file-sharing. Napster allowed users to transfer exact copies of the contents of MP3 files from one computer to another via the Internet. This was made possible by Napster's MusicShare software, available free of charge from Napster's site, and Napster's network servers and server-side software. Napster also provided technical support. A&M Records, Inc., and others engaged in the commercial recording, distribution, and sale of copyrighted musical compositions and sound recordings, filed a suit in a federal district court against Napster, alleging copyright infringement. The court issued a preliminary injunction ordering Napster to stop "facilitating others in copying, downloading, uploading, transmitting, or distributing plaintiffs' copyrighted musical compositions and sound recordings, * * * without express permission of the rights owner." Napster appealed to the U.S. Court of Appeals for the Ninth Circuit.*

IN THE LANGUAGE OF THE COURT

BEEZER, Circuit Judge.
     *   *   *   *
     *   *   * In the context of copyright law, vicarious liability extends *   *   * to cases in which a defendant has the right and ability to supervise the infringing activity and also has a direct financial interest in such activities.
     *   *   *   *
     The ability to block infringers' access to a particular environment for any reason whatsoever is evidence of the right and ability to supervise. Here, plaintiffs have demonstrated that Napster retains the right to control access to its system. Napster has an express reservation of rights policy, stating on its website that it expressly reserves the "right to refuse service and terminate accounts in [its] discretion, including, but not limited to, if Napster believes that

---

a. This URL will take you to a Web site maintained by FindLaw, which is now a part of West Group. When you access the site, enter "Napster" in the "Party Name Search" box and then click on "Search." Select the *Napster* case dated "02/12/2001" from the list on the page that opens.

CASE 8.4 | Continued

user conduct violates applicable law * * * or for any reason in Napster's sole discretion, with or without cause."

To escape imposition of vicarious liability, the reserved right to police must be exercised to its fullest extent. *Turning a blind eye to detectable acts of infringement for the sake of profit gives rise to liability.* [Emphasis added.]

The district court correctly determined that Napster had the right and ability to police its system and failed to exercise that right to prevent the exchange of copyrighted material. * * *

Napster * * * has the ability to locate infringing material listed on its search indices, and the right to terminate users' access to the system. The file name indices, therefore, are within the "premises" that Napster has the ability to police. We recognize that the files are user-named and may not match copyrighted material exactly (for example, the artist or song could be spelled wrong). For Napster to function effectively, however, file names must reasonably or roughly correspond to the material contained in the files, otherwise no user could ever locate any desired music. As a practical matter, Napster, its users and the record company plaintiffs have equal access to infringing material by employing Napster's "search function."

Our review of the record requires us to accept the district court's conclusion that plaintiffs have demonstrated a likelihood of success on the merits of the vicarious copyright infringement claim. Napster's failure to police the system's "premises," combined with a showing that Napster financially benefits from the continuing availability of infringing files on its system, leads to the imposition of vicarious liability.

DECISION AND REMEDY *The U.S. Court of Appeals for the Ninth Circuit affirmed the lower court's decision that Napster was obligated to police its own system and had likely infringed the plaintiffs' copyrights. Holding that the injunction was "overbroad," however, the appellate court remanded the case for a clarification of Napster's responsibility to determine whether music on its Web site was copyrighted.*[b]

---

b. Napster later filed for bankruptcy but today offers a for-fee music downloading service. The case against *Napster* has not yet been fully resolved, however, the district court in 2005 did rule in the defendants' favor on one of the plaintiff's claims. ___ F.Supp.2d ___ (N.D.Cal. 2005).

NEW FILE-SHARING TECHNOLOGIES In the wake of the *Napster* decision, other companies developed new technologies that allow P2P network users to share stored music files, without paying a fee, more quickly and efficiently than ever. Today's file-sharing software is decentralized and does not use search indices. Thus, the companies have no knowledge or control over which music (or other media files) their users are exchanging. Unlike the Napster system, in which the company played a role in connecting people who were downloading and uploading songs, the new systems are designed to work without the company's input.

Software such as Morpheus and KaZaA, for example, provides users with an interface that is similar to a Web browser. This technology is very different from that used by Napster. Instead of the company locating songs for users on other members' computers, the software automatically annotates files with descriptive information so that the music can easily be categorized and cross-referenced (by artist and title, for instance). When a user performs a search, the software is able to locate a list of peers that have the file available for downloading. Also, to expedite the P2P transfer and ensure that the complete file is received, the software distributes the download task over the entire list of peers simultaneously. By downloading even one file, the user becomes a point of distribution for that file, which is then automatically shared with others on the network.

How will the courts decide the legality of these new digital technologies? The *Contemporary Legal Debates* feature on the next two pages discusses this issue.

SECTION **6** | Trade Secrets

Some business processes and information that are not, or cannot be, patented, copyrighted, or trademarked are nevertheless protected against appropriation by competitors as trade secrets. **Trade secrets** consist of customer lists, plans, research and development, pricing information, marketing methods, production techniques, and generally anything that makes an

New Technology and Copyright Infringement

Nearly 20 million Americans downloaded music from the Internet in 2004. Worldwide, it is estimated that 85 million songs and roughly half a million movies are downloaded from the Internet every day—90 percent of which constitute copyright infringement.[a] Clearly, any person who downloads copyrighted music or movies without permission from the copyright holder is liable for copyright infringement. But what about the companies that provide the software that enables users to exchange copyrighted materials? In what circumstances should these companies be held liable? Courts have had difficulty applying the traditional doctrines of contributory and vicarious copyright liability to new technologies.

THE GROKSTER CASE

Consider, for example, the situation faced by the court in *Metro-Goldwyn-Mayer Studios, Inc. v. Grokster, Ltd.*[b] In that case, organizations in the music and film industry (the plaintiffs) sued several companies that distribute file-sharing software used in P2P networks. The defendants included Grokster, Ltd., and StreamCast Networks, Inc. The plaintiffs claimed that the companies were contributorily and vicariously liable for the infringement of their end users.

The federal district court examined the technology involved and concluded that the defendants were not liable for contributory infringement because they lacked the requisite level of knowledge. According to the court, it was not enough

that the defendants *generally* knew that the software they provided might be used to infringe on copyrights; they also had to have *specific knowledge* of the infringement "at a time when they can use that knowledge to stop the particular infringement." Here, the companies had distributed free software. They had no specific knowledge of whether users were exchanging copyrighted files and had no ability to stop users from infringing activities. The court also held that the defendants could not be held vicariously liable for the infringement because they did not monitor, control, or supervise the software's use and had no duty to police infringements.

The district court's decision was affirmed on appeal.[c] The appellate court, relying on an earlier Supreme Court precedent, reasoned that the level of knowledge required depends on whether the product was "capable of substantial" or "commercially significant noninfringing uses."[d] Because file-sharing software is capable of commercially significant noninfringing uses, the appellate court held that the defendants must have reasonable knowledge of specific instances of infringement to be held liable.

THE UNITED STATES SUPREME COURT TAKES UP THE ISSUE

In June 2005, the United States Supreme Court unanimously overturned the appellate court's decision in the *Grokster* case and remanded the case for further proceedings. The Court held

---

a. Gregory G. Garre, "Copyright Bandits at Large," *Internet Law & Strategy*, Vol. 3, No. 1, January 2005.

b. 243 F.Supp.2d 1073 (C.D.Cal. 2003).

c. *Metro-Goldwyn-Mayer Studios, Inc. v. Grokster, Ltd.*, 380 F.3d 1154 (9th Cir. 2004).

d. See *Sony Corp. of America v. Universal City Studios, Inc.*, 464 U.S. 417, 104 S.Ct. 774, 78 L.Ed.2d 574 (1984).

---

individual company unique and that would have value to a competitor.

Unlike copyright and trademark protection, protection of trade secrets extends both to ideas and to their expression. (For this reason, and because a trade secret involves no registration or filing requirements, trade secret protection may be well suited for software.) Of course, the secret formula, method, or other information must be disclosed to some persons, particularly to key employees. Businesses generally attempt to protect their trade secrets by having all

employees who use the process or information agree in their contracts, or in confidentiality agreements, never to divulge it.

STATE AND FEDERAL LAW ON TRADE SECRETS

Under Section 757 of the *Restatement of Torts,* "One who discloses or uses another's trade secret, without a privilege to do so, is liable to the other if (1) he [or she] discovered the secret by improper means, or (2) his [or

that "one who distributes a device [software] with the object of promoting its use to infringe copyright, as shown by clear expression or other affirmative steps taken to foster infringement, is liable for the resulting acts of infringement by third parties."[e] The Court did not, however, specify what kind of "affirmative steps" are necessary to establish liability.

According to Justice Souter, who delivered the Court's opinion, there was ample evidence in the record that the defendants acted with the intent to cause copyright violations by use of their software. What was lacking, according to the Court, was evidence that the defendants "communicated an inducing message to their software users." The decision therefore left it up to the lower court on remand to determine if the defendants had actually induced their users to commit infringement.

The Supreme Court's decision in the *Grokster* case shifts the focus in secondary copyright infringement cases away from specific knowledge of acts of infringement to inducing or promoting infringement. Essentially, this means that file-sharing companies that have taken affirmative steps to promote copyright infringement can be held secondarily liable for the millions of infringing acts that their users commit daily. Nevertheless, because the Court did not define exactly what is necessary to impose liability, there is significant room for debate.

THE DEBATE CONTINUES

Many were hoping that the Supreme Court would spell out in the *Grokster* case exactly what is and is not legal in P2P and

file-sharing networks, but the decision failed to clarify that point. Thus, the future of P2P networks and file-sharing services remains unclear.

Critics claim that the Supreme Court's decision in the *Grokster* case creates a great deal of legal uncertainty and will stifle American innovation. Because the decision establishes a new theory of copyright liability that is based on whether the manufacturer created the technology with the intent of inducing infringement, critics claim it will unleash a barrage of litigation against technological innovators. Technology firms will have a harder time convincing banks, investors, and courts that their products are legal. The threat of legal costs and potential damage awards may ultimately lead many technological companies to modify their software and products to please the entertainment industry (copyright holders) rather than consumers.

WHERE DO YOU STAND?

The entertainment industry maintains that providers of the file-sharing services used to swap copyrighted files should be held liable because they know about and encourage their users' acts of infringement. Other groups, however, including the defendants in the *Grokster* case, compare the providers of file-sharing services to companies that sell copy machines. The courts do not hold Xerox Corporation liable when people use its copy machines to make infringing copies of copyrighted materials. Which side of this debate do you support? Is it possible for the courts to determine whether a company has promoted or induced copyright infringement? What is the best way to address the problem of music and movie piracy?

---

e. *Metro-Goldwyn-Mayer Studios, Inc. v. Grokster, Ltd.,* ___ U.S. ___, ___ S.Ct. ___, ___ L.Ed.2d ___ (2005). [2005 WL 1499402]

her] disclosure or use constitutes a breach of confidence reposed in him [or her] by the other in disclosing the secret to him [or her]." The theft of confidential business data by industrial espionage, as when a business taps into a competitor's computer, is a theft of trade secrets without any contractual violation and is actionable in itself.

Until about twenty-five years ago, virtually all law with respect to trade secrets was common law. In an effort to reduce the unpredictability of the common law in this area, a model act, the Uniform Trade

Secrets Act, was presented to the states for adoption in 1979. Parts of the act have been adopted in more than thirty states. Typically, a state that has adopted parts of the act has adopted only those parts that encompass its own existing common law. Additionally, in 1996 Congress passed the Economic Espionage Act,[27] which made the theft of trade secrets a federal crime. We will examine the provisions and significance of this act in Chapter 9, in the context of crimes related to business.

---

27. 18 U.S.C. Sections 1831–1839.

TRADE SECRETS IN CYBERSPACE

New computer technology is undercutting a business firm's ability to protect its confidential information, including trade secrets.[28] For example, a dishonest employee could e-mail trade secrets in a company's computer to a competitor or a future employer. If e-mail is not an option, the employee might simply walk out with the information on a computer disk.

SECTION 7 | International Protection for Intellectual Property

For many years, the United States has been a party to various international agreements relating to intellectual property rights. For example, the Paris Convention of 1883, to which about ninety countries are signatory, allows parties in one country to file for patent and trademark protection in any of the other member countries. We look next at the Berne Convention and another international agreement relating to intellectual property.

THE BERNE CONVENTION

Under the Berne Convention (an international copyright agreement) of 1886, as amended, if an American writes a book, every country that has signed the convention must recognize the American author's copyright in the book. Also, if a citizen of a country that has not signed the convention first publishes a book in a country that has signed, all other countries that have signed the convention must recognize that author's copyright. Copyright notice is not needed to gain protection under the Berne Convention for works published after March 1, 1989.

Currently, the laws of many countries, as well as international laws, are being updated to reflect changes in technology and the expansion of the Internet. Copyright holders and other owners of intellectual property generally agree that changes in the law are needed to stop the increasing international piracy of their property. The World Intellectual Property Organization (WIPO) Copyright Treaty of 1996, a special agreement under the Berne Convention, attempts to update international law governing copyright protection to include more safeguards against copyright infringement via the Internet. The United States signed the WIPO treaty in 1996 and implemented its terms in the Digital Millennium Copyright Act of 1998, which was discussed earlier in this chapter.

The Berne Convention and other international agreements have given some protection to intellectual property on a global level. Another significant worldwide agreement to increase such protection is the Trade-Related Aspects of Intellectual Property Rights agreement—or, more simply, the TRIPS agreement.

THE TRIPS AGREEMENT

Representatives from more than one hundred nations signed the TRIPS agreement in 1994. It was one of several documents that were annexed to the agreement that created the World Trade Organization, or WTO, in 1995. The TRIPS agreement established, for the first time, standards for the international protection of intellectual property rights, including patents, trademarks, and copyrights for movies, computer programs, books, and music.

IMPORTANT PROVISIONS OF THE AGREEMENT
Prior to the TRIPS agreement, one of the difficulties faced by U.S. sellers of intellectual property in the international market was that another country might either lack laws to protect intellectual property rights or fail to enforce what laws it had. To address this problem, the TRIPS agreement provides that each member country must include in its domestic laws broad intellectual property rights and effective remedies (including civil and criminal penalties) for violations of those rights.

Generally, the TRIPS agreement provides that member nations must not discriminate (in terms of the administration, regulation, or adjudication of intellectual property rights) against foreign owners of such rights. In other words, a member nation cannot give its own nationals (citizens) favorable treatment without offering the same treatment to nationals of all member countries. For example, if a U.S. software manufacturer brings a suit for the infringement of intellectual property rights under Japan's national laws, the U.S. manufacturer is entitled to receive the same treatment as a Japanese domestic manufacturer. Each member nation must also ensure that legal procedures are available for

---

28. Note that in at least one case, a court has held that customers' e-mail addresses may constitute trade secrets. See *T-N-T Motorsports, Inc. v. Hennessey Motorsports, Inc.*, 965 S.W.2d 18 (Tex.App.—Hous. [1 Dist.] 1998); rehearing overruled (1998); petition dismissed (1998).

parties who wish to bring actions for infringement of intellectual property rights. Additionally, as part of the agreement creating the WTO, a mechanism for settling disputes among member nations was established.

TYPES OF INTELLECTUAL PROPERTY COVERED BY THE AGREEMENT Particular provisions of the TRIPS agreement refer to patent, trademark, and copyright protection for intellectual property. The agreement specifically provides copyright protection for computer programs by stating that compilations of data, databases, and other materials are "intellectual creations" and are to be protected as copyrightable works. Other provisions relate to trade secrets and the rental of computer programs and cinematographic works.

THE MADRID PROTOCOL

In the past, one of the difficulties in protecting U.S. trademarks internationally was the time and expense involved in applying for trademark registration in foreign countries. The filing fees and procedures for trademark registration vary significantly from country to country. The Madrid Protocol, which President George W. Bush signed into law in 2003, may help to resolve these problems. The Madrid Protocol is an international treaty that has been signed by sixty-one countries. Under its provisions, a U.S. company wishing to register its trademark abroad can submit a single application and designate other member countries in which the U.S. company would like to register its mark. The treaty is designed to reduce the costs of international trademark protection by more than 60 percent, according to proponents.

Although the Madrid Protocol may simplify and reduce the cost of trademark registration in foreign countries, it remains to be seen whether it will provide significant benefits to trademark owners. Even assuming that the registration process will be easier, there is still the issue of whether member countries will enforce the law and protect the mark.

REVIEWING INTELLECTUAL PROPERTY

Two computer science majors, Trent and Xavier, have an idea for a new video game, which they propose to call "Hallowed." They form a business and begin developing their idea. Several months later, Trent and Xavier run into a problem with their design and consult with a friend, Brad, who is an expert in designing computer source codes. Before Hallowed is marketed, however, the video game Halo 2 is released for both the Xbox and Game Cube systems. Halo 2 uses the same source codes as Hallowed and imitates its overall look and feel. Using the information presented in the chapter, answer the following questions.

1. Is an idea for a video game patentable? Why or why not?

2. Suppose that Trent and Xavier did not file an application for a patent. Does that mean that they do not have a right to exclude others from making the game? Explain.

3. If Trent and Xavier did hold the patent on Hallowed, would the release of Halo 2 infringe on their patent? Why or why not?

4. Is an idea for a video game copyrightable? Is a video game copyrightable? At what point does copyright protection apply?

5. Based only the facts described above, could Trent and Xavier sue the makers of Halo 2 for copyright infringement? Why or why not?

6. Would the name "Hallowed" receive protection as a trademark or as trade dress?

7. Suppose that Trent and Xavier discover that Brad took the idea of Hallowed and sold it to the company that produced Halo 2. Which type of intellectual property issue does this raise?

TERMS AND CONCEPTS TO REVIEW

certification mark 158

collective mark 158

copyright 163

cyber mark 158

cybersquatting 159

dilution 156

distributed network 167

domain name 158

intellectual property 153

meta tag 159

patent 162

peer-to-peer (P2P)
networking 167

service mark 158

trade dress 157

trade name 158

trade secret 169

trademark 153

QUESTIONS AND CASE PROBLEMS

8–1. Professor Wise is teaching a summer seminar in business torts at State University. Several times during the course, he makes copies of relevant sections from business law texts and distributes them to his students. Wise does not realize that the daughter of one of the textbook authors is a member of his seminar. She tells her father about Wise's copying activities, which have taken place without her father's or his publisher's permission. Her father sues Wise for copyright infringement. Wise claims protection under the fair use doctrine. Who will prevail? Explain.

8–2. **QUESTION WITH SAMPLE ANSWER**

In which of the following situations would a court likely hold Ursula liable for copyright infringement?

(a) From a scholarly journal at the library, Ursula photocopies ten pages relating to a topic on which she is writing a term paper.

(b) Ursula makes blouses, dresses, and other clothes and sells them in her small shop. She advertises some of the outfits as Guest items, hoping that customers might mistakenly assume that they were made by Guess, the well-known clothing manufacturer.

(c) Ursula teaches Latin American history at a small university. She has a VCR and frequently tapes television programs relating to Latin America. She then takes the videos to her classroom so that her students can watch them.

For a sample answer to this question, go to Appendix I at the end of this text.

8–3. One day during algebra class, Diedra, an enterprising fourteen-year-old student, began drawing designs on her shoelaces. By the end of the class, Diedra had decorated her shoelaces with the name of the school, Broadson Junior High, written in blue and red (the school colors), and with pictures of bears, the school's mascot. After class, she showed the designs to her teacher, Mrs. Laxton.

When Diedra got home that night, she wrote about her idea in her diary, in which she also drew her shoelace design. Mrs. Laxton had been trying to think of a way to build school spirit. She thought about Diedra's shoelaces and decided to go into business for herself. She called her business Spirited Shoelaces and designed shoelaces for each of the local schools, decorating the shoelaces in each case with the school's name, mascot, and colors. The business became tremendously profitable. Even though Diedra never registered her idea with the U.S. Patent and Trademark Office or the U.S. Copyright Office, does she nonetheless have intellectual property rights in the shoelace design? Will her diary account be sufficient proof that she created the idea? Discuss.

8–4. TRADEMARK INFRINGEMENT. Elvis Presley Enterprises, Inc. (EPE), owned all of the trademarks of the Elvis Presley estate. None of these marks was registered for use in the restaurant business. Barry Capece registered "The Velvet Elvis" as a service mark for a restaurant and tavern with the U.S. Patent and Trademark Office. Capece opened a nightclub called "The Velvet Elvis" with a menu, decor, advertising, and promotional events that evoked Elvis Presley and his music. EPE filed a suit in a federal district court against Capece and others, claiming, among other things, that "The Velvet Elvis" service mark infringed on EPE's trademarks. During the trial, witnesses testified that they thought the bar was associated with Elvis Presley. Should Capece be ordered to stop using "The Velvet Elvis" mark? Why or why not? [*Elvis Presley Enterprises, Inc. v. Capece,* 141 F.3d 188 (5th Cir. 1998)]

8–5. TRADEMARK INFRINGEMENT. A&H Sportswear Co., a swimsuit maker, obtained a trademark for its MIRACLESUIT in 1992. The MIRACLESUIT design makes the wearer appear slimmer. The MIRACLESUIT, which was widely advertised and discussed in the media, was also sold for a brief time in the Victoria's Secret (VS) catalogue, which is published by Victoria's Secret

Catalogue, Inc. In 1993, Victoria's Secret Stores, Inc., began selling a cleavage-enhancing bra, which was named THE MIRACLE BRA and for which a trademark was obtained. The next year, THE MIRACLE BRA swimwear debuted in the VS catalogue and stores. A&H filed a suit in a federal district court against VS Stores and VS Catalogue, alleging in part that THE MIRACLE BRA mark, when applied to swimwear, infringed on the MIRACLESUIT mark. A&H argued that there was a "possibility of confusion" between the marks. The VS entities contended that the appropriate standard was "likelihood of confusion" and that, in this case, there was no likelihood of confusion. In whose favor will the court rule, and why? [*A&H Sportswear, Inc. v. Victoria's Secret Stores, Inc.*, 166 F.3d 197 (3d Cir. 1999)]

8-6. DOMAIN NAME DISPUTES. In 1999, Steve and Pierce Thumann and their father, Fred, created Spider Webs, Ltd., a partnership, to, according to Steve, "develop Internet address names." Spider Webs registered nearly two thousand Internet domain names at an average cost of $70 each, including the names of cities, the names of buildings, names related to a business or trade (such as air conditioning or plumbing), and the names of famous companies. It offered many of the names for sale on its Web site and through eBay.com. Spider Webs registered the domain name "ERNEST ANDJULIOGALLO.COM" in Spider Webs' name. E. & J. Gallo Winery filed a suit against Spider Webs, alleging, in part, violations of the Anticybersquatting Consumer Protection Act. Gallo asked the court for, among other things, statutory damages. Gallo also sought to have the domain name at issue transferred to Gallo. During the suit, Spider Webs published anticorporate articles and negative opinions about Gallo, as well as discussions of the suit and of the risks associated with alcohol use, at the URL ERNESTANDJULIO GALLO.COM. Should the court rule in Gallo's favor? Why or why not? [*E. & J. Gallo Winery v. Spider Webs, Ltd.*, 129 F.Supp.2d 1033 (S.D.Tex. 2001)]

8-7. ⚖ CASE PROBLEM WITH SAMPLE ANSWER

Gateway, Inc., sells computers, computer products, computer peripherals, and computer accessories throughout the world. By 1988, Gateway had begun its first national advertising campaign using black-and-white cows and black-and-white cow spots. By 1991, black-and-white cows and spots had become Gateway's symbol. The next year, Gateway registered a black-and-white cow-spot design in association with computers and computer peripherals as its trademark. Companion Products, Inc. (CPI), sells stuffed animals trademarked as "Stretch Pets." Stretch Pets have an animal's head and an elastic body that can wrap around the edges of computer monitors, computer cases, or televisions. CPI produces sixteen Stretch Pets, including a polar bear, a moose, several

dogs, and a penguin. One of CPI's top-selling products is a black-and-white cow that CPI identifies as "Cody Cow," which was first sold in 1999. Gateway filed a suit in a federal district court against CPI, alleging trade dress infringement and related claims. What is trade dress? What is the major factor in cases involving trade dress infringement? Does that factor exist in this case? Explain. [*Gateway, Inc. v. Companion Products, Inc.*, 384 F.3d 503 (8th Cir. 2004)]

To view a sample answer for this case problem, go to this book's Web site at http://wbl.westbuslaw.com, select "Chapter 8," and click on "Case Problem with Sample Answer."

8-8. FAIR USE DOCTRINE. Leslie Kelly is a professional photographer who has copyrighted many of his images of the American West. Some of the images can be seen on Kelly's Web site or other sites with which Kelly has a contract. Arriba Soft Corp. operates an Internet search engine that displays its results in the form of small pictures (thumbnails) rather than text. The thumbnails consist of images copied from other sites and reduced in size. By clicking on one of the thumbnails, a user can view a large version of the picture within the context of an Arriba Web page. Arriba displays the large picture by inline linking (importing the image from the other site without copying it onto Arriba's site). When Kelly discovered that his photos were displayed through Arriba's site without his permission, he filed a suit in a federal district court against Arriba, alleging copyright infringement. Arriba claimed that its use of Kelly's images was a "fair use." Considering the factors courts use to determine whether a use is fair, do Arriba's thumbnails qualify? Does Arriba's use of the larger images infringe on Kelly's copyright? Explain. [*Kelly v. Arriba Soft Corp.*, 280 F.3d 934 (9th Cir. 2002)]

8-9. PATENT INFRINGEMENT. As a cattle rancher in Nebraska, Gerald Gohl used handheld searchlights to find and help calving animals (animals giving birth) in harsh blizzard conditions. Gohl thought that it would be more helpful to have a portable searchlight mounted on the outside of a vehicle and remotely controlled. He and Al Gebhardt developed and patented practical applications of this idea—the Golight and the wireless, remote-controlled Radio Ray, which could rotate 360 degrees—and formed Golight, Inc., to make and market these products. In 1997, Wal-Mart Stores, Inc., began selling a portable, wireless, remote-controlled searchlight that was identical to the Radio Ray except for a stop piece that prevented the light from rotating more than 351 degrees. Golight sent Wal-Mart a letter claiming that its device infringed Golight's patent. Wal-Mart sold its remaining inventory of the devices and stopped carrying the product. Golight filed a suit in a federal district court against Wal-Mart, alleging patent infringement. How should the court rule? Explain. [*Golight, Inc. v. Wal-Mart Stores, Inc.*, 355 F.3d 1327 (Fed. Cir. 2004)]

8-10. VIDEO QUESTION

Go to this text's Web site at **http://blt.westbuslaw.com** and select "Chapter 8." Click on "Video Questions" and view the video titled *The Jerk*. Then answer the following questions.

(a) In the video, Navin (Steve Martin) creates a special handle for Mr. Fox's (Bill Macy's) glasses. Can Navin obtain a patent or a copyright protecting his invention? Explain your answer.

(b) Suppose that after Navin legally protects his idea, Fox steals it and decides to develop it for himself, without Navin's permission. Has Fox committed infringement? If so, what kind: trademark, patent, or copyright?

(c) Suppose that after Navin legally protects his idea, he realizes he doesn't have the funds to mass-produce the special handle. Navin therefore agrees to allow Fox to manufacture the product. Has Navin granted Fox a license? Explain.

(d) Assume that Navin is able to manufacture his invention. What might Navin do to ensure that his product is identifiable and can be distinguished from other products on the market?

LAW | on the Web

For updated links to resources available on the Web, as well as a variety of other materials, visit this text's Web site at **http://wbl.westbuslaw.com**.

An excellent overview of the laws governing various forms of intellectual property is available at FindLaw's Web site. Go to

http://profs.lp.findlaw.com

You can find answers to frequently asked questions (FAQs) about trademark and patent law—and links to registration forms, statutes, international patent and trademark offices, and numerous other related materials—at the Web site of the U.S. Patent and Trademark Office. Go to

http://www.uspto.gov

To perform patent searches and to access information on the patenting process, go to

http://www.bustpatents.com

You can also access information on patent law at the following Internet site:

http://www.patents.com

For information on copyrights, go to the U.S. Copyright Office at

http://www.loc.gov/copyright

You can find extensive information on copyright law—including United States Supreme Court decisions in this area and the texts of the Berne Convention and other international treaties on copyright issues—at the Web site of the Legal Information Institute at Cornell University's School of Law. Go to

http://www.law.cornell.edu/topics/copyright.html

Law.com's Web site offers articles, case decisions, and other information concerning intellectual property at

http://www.law.com/jsp/pc/iplaw.jsp

LEGAL RESEARCH EXERCISES ON THE WEB

Go to **http://wbl.westbuslaw.com**, the Web site that accompanies this text. Select "Chapter 8" and click on "Internet Exercises." There you will find the following Internet research exercises that you can perform to learn more about topics covered in this chapter.

Activity 8–1: **LEGAL PERSPECTIVE**
Unwarranted Legal Threats

Activity 8–2: **MANAGEMENT PERSPECTIVE**
Protecting Intellectual Property across Borders

Activity 8–3: **TECHNOLOGICAL PERSPECTIVE**
File-Sharing

CHAPTER 9

Criminal Law and Cyber Crimes

The law imposes various sanctions in attempting to ensure that individuals engaging in business in our society can compete and flourish. These sanctions include those imposed by civil law, such as damages for various types of tortious conduct (discussed in Chapters 6 and 7); damages for breach of contract (to be discussed in Chapter 18); and the equitable remedies discussed in Chapters 1 and 18. Additional sanctions are imposed under criminal law. Indeed, many statutes regulating business provide for criminal as well as civil penalties. Therefore, criminal law joins civil law as an important element in the legal environment of business.

In this chapter, after examining some essential differences between criminal law and civil law, we look at how crimes are classified, the basic requirements that must be met for criminal liability to be established, the various types of crimes that exist, and the defenses that can be raised to avoid criminal liability. We conclude the chapter with a discussion of crimes that occur in cyberspace, which are often referred to as *cyber crime*. Generally, cyber crime refers more to the way in which particular crimes are committed than to a new category of crimes.

SECTION 1 | Civil Law and Criminal Law

Recall from Chapter 1 that *civil law* pertains to the duties that exist between persons or between persons and their governments. Criminal law, in contrast, has to do with crime. A **crime** can be defined as a wrong against society proclaimed in a statute and punishable by a fine and/or imprisonment—or, in some cases, death. As mentioned in Chapter 1, because crimes are *offenses against society as a whole*, they are prosecuted by a public official, such as a district attorney (D.A.) or an attorney general (A.G.), not by victims.

MAJOR DIFFERENCES BETWEEN CIVIL LAW AND CRIMINAL LAW

Because the state has extensive resources at its disposal when prosecuting criminal cases, there are numerous procedural safeguards to protect the rights of defendants. We look here at one of these safeguards—the higher burden of proof that applies in a criminal case—as well as the harsher sanctions for criminal acts compared with civil wrongs. Exhibit 9–1 summarizes these and other key differences between civil law and criminal law.

BURDEN OF PROOF In a civil case, the plaintiff usually must prove his or her case by a *preponderance of the evidence*. Under this standard, the plaintiff must convince the court that based on the evidence presented by both parties, it is more likely than not that the plaintiff's allegation is true.

In a criminal case, in contrast, the state must prove its case **beyond a reasonable doubt.** If the jury views the evidence in the case as reasonably permitting either a guilty or a not guilty verdict, then the jury's verdict must be not guilty. In other words, the government (prosecutor) must prove that the defendant has committed every essential element of the offense with which she or he is charged beyond a reasonable doubt. If the jury is not convinced of the defendant's guilt beyond a reasonable doubt, the defendant is not guilty. Note also that in a criminal case, the jury's verdict normally must be unanimous—agreed to by all members of the jury—to convict the defendant. (In a civil trial by jury, in contrast, typically only three-fourths of the jurors need to agree.)

The higher burden of proof in criminal cases reflects a fundamental social value—the belief that it

EXHIBIT 9-1 Key Differences between Civil and Criminal Law

ISSUE	CIVIL LAW	CRIMINAL LAW
Party who brings suit	Person who suffered harm	The state
Wrongful act	Causing harm to a person or to a person's property	Violating a statute that prohibits some type of activity
Burden of proof	Preponderance of the evidence	Beyond a reasonable doubt
Verdict	Three-fourths majority (typically)	Unanimous
Remedy	Damages to compensate for the harm or a decree to achieve an equitable result	Punishment (fine, imprisonment, or death)

is worse to convict an innocent individual than to let a guilty person go free. We will look at other safeguards later in the chapter, in the context of criminal procedure.

CRIMINAL SANCTIONS The sanctions imposed on criminal wrongdoers are also harsher than those that are applied in civil cases. Remember from Chapters 6 and 7 that the purpose of tort law is to allow persons harmed by the wrongful acts of others to obtain compensation, or money damages, from the wrongdoer or to enjoin (prevent) a wrongdoer from undertaking or continuing a wrongful action. Tortfeasors are rarely subject to punitive damages—damages awarded simply to *punish* the wrongdoer. In contrast, criminal sanctions are designed to punish those who commit crimes in order to deter others from committing similar acts in the future. Criminal sanctions include fines as well as the much harsher penalty of the loss of one's liberty by incarceration in a jail or prison. The harshest criminal sanction is, of course, the death penalty.

CIVIL LIABILITY FOR CRIMINAL ACTS

Some torts, such as assault and battery, provide a basis for a criminal prosecution as well as a civil action in tort. For example, Jonas is walking down the street, minding his own business, when a person attacks him. In the ensuing struggle, the attacker stabs Jonas several times, seriously injuring him. A police officer restrains and arrests the wrongdoer. In this situation, the attacker may be subject both to criminal prosecution by the state and to a tort lawsuit brought by Jonas to obtain compensation for his injuries. Exhibit 9–2 on the following page illustrates how the same wrongful act can result in both a civil (tort) action and a criminal action against the wrongdoer.

SECTION 2 | Classification of Crimes

Depending on their degree of seriousness, crimes are classified as felonies or misdemeanors.

FELONIES

Felonies are serious crimes punishable by death or by imprisonment in a federal or state penitentiary for one year or longer.[1] The Model Penal Code[2] provides for four degrees of felony:

1. Capital offenses, for which the maximum penalty is death.
2. First degree felonies, punishable by a maximum penalty of life imprisonment.
3. Second degree felonies, punishable by a maximum of ten years' imprisonment.
4. Third degree felonies, punishable by up to five years' imprisonment.

Although criminal laws vary from state to state, some general rules apply when grading crimes by degree. For example, most jurisdictions punish a burglary that involves a forced entry into a home at night more harshly than a burglary that takes place during the day and involves a nonresidential building or

---

1. Some states, such as North Carolina, consider felonies to be punishable by incarceration for at least two years.
2. The American Law Institute issued the Official Draft of the Model Penal Code in 1962. The Model Penal Code contains four parts: (1) general provisions, (2) definitions of special crimes, (3) provisions concerning treatment and corrections, and (4) provisions on the organization of correction. The Model Penal Code is not a uniform code, however. Because of our federal structure of government, each state has developed its own set of laws governing criminal acts. Thus, types of crime and prescribed punishments may differ from one jurisdiction to another.

EXHIBIT 9-2 Civil (Tort) Lawsuit and Criminal Prosecution for the Same Act

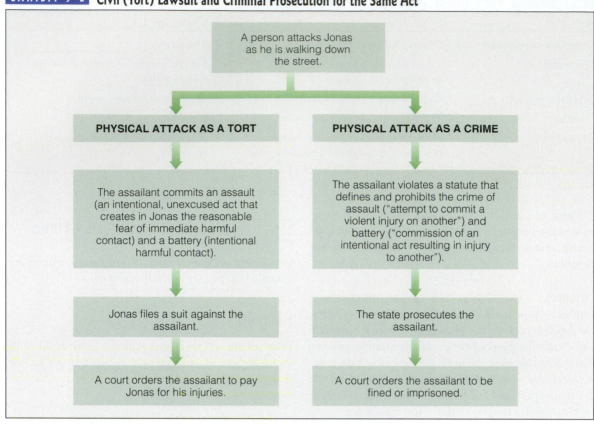

structure. A homicide—the taking of another's life—is classified according to the degree of intent involved.

For example, first degree murder requires that the homicide be premeditated and deliberate, as opposed to a spontaneous act of violence. When no premeditation or deliberation is present but the offender acts with *malice aforethought* (that is, with wanton disregard of the consequences of his or her actions for the victim), the homicide is classified as second degree murder. A homicide that is committed without malice toward the victim is known as *manslaughter. Voluntary manslaughter* occurs when the intent to kill may be present, as in a crime committed in the heat of passion, but malice is lacking. A homicide is classified as *involuntary manslaughter* when it results from an act of negligence (such as when a drunk driver causes the death of another person) and there is no intent to kill.

MISDEMEANORS AND PETTY OFFENSES

Under federal law and in most states, any crime that is not a felony is considered a **misdemeanor.** Misde-

meanors are crimes punishable by a fine or by incarceration for up to one year. If confined, the guilty party goes to a local jail instead of a penitentiary. Disorderly conduct and trespass are common misdemeanors. Some states have several classes of misdemeanors. For example, in Illinois, misdemeanors are either Class A (confinement for up to a year), Class B (not more than six months), or Class C (not more than thirty days). Whether a crime is a felony or a misdemeanor can also determine whether the case is tried in a magistrate's court (for example, by a justice of the peace) or a general trial court.

In most jurisdictions, **petty offenses** are considered to be a subset of misdemeanors. Petty offenses are minor violations, such as disturbing the peace and violations of building codes. Even for petty offenses, however, a guilty party can be put in jail for a few days, fined, or both, depending on state law.

Probation and community service are often imposed on those who commit misdemeanors, especially juveniles. Also, most states have decriminalized all but the most serious traffic offenses. These infractions are treated as civil proceedings, and civil fines are imposed. In many states, "points" are assessed against the violator's driving record (and the state will suspend a person's driver's license if too many points are accumulated).

SECTION 3 | The Essentials of Criminal Liability

Two elements must exist for a person to be convicted of a crime: (1) the performance of a prohibited act and (2) a specified state of mind, or intent, on the part of the actor. Additionally, to establish criminal liability, there must be a *concurrence* between the act and the intent. In other words, these two elements must occur together.

For example, suppose that a woman plans to kill her husband by poisoning him. On the day she plans to do so, she is driving her husband home from work and swerves to avoid hitting a cat crossing the road. The car crashes into a tree as a result, killing her husband. Even though she had planned to murder her husband, the woman would not be guilty of murder in this situation because she had not planned to kill him by driving her car into a tree.

THE CRIMINAL ACT

Every criminal statute prohibits certain behavior. Most crimes require an act of *commission*—that is, a person must *do* something in order to be accused of a crime. In criminal law, a prohibited act is referred to as the ***actus reus***,[3] or guilty act. In some cases, an act of omission can be a crime, but only when a person has a legal duty to perform the omitted act, such as filing a tax return. For example, in 2005 the federal government filed a criminal action against a former winner of the reality TV show *Survivor* for failing to report more than $1 million in winnings.

The *guilty act* requirement is based on one of the premises of criminal law—that a person should be punished for harm done to society. Thus, for a crime to exist the guilty act must cause some harm to a person or to property. Thinking about killing someone or about stealing a car may be morally wrong, but the thoughts do no harm until they are translated into action. Of course, a person can be punished for *attempting* murder or robbery, but only if substantial steps toward the criminal objective have been taken. Additionally, the punishment for an attempt to commit a crime is normally less severe than it would be if the act had been completed.

STATE OF MIND

A wrongful mental state (***mens rea***)[4] is also typically required to establish criminal liability. The required mental state, or intent, is indicated in the applicable statute or law. Murder, for example, involves the guilty act of killing another human being, and the guilty mental state is the desire, or intent, to take another's life. For theft, the guilty act is the taking of another person's property, and the mental state involves both the awareness that the property belongs to another and the desire to deprive the owner of it.

A guilty mental state can be attributed to acts of negligence or recklessness as well. *Criminal negligence* involves the mental state in which the defendant deviates from the standard of care that a reasonable person would use under the same circumstances. The defendant is accused of taking an unjustified, substantial, and foreseeable risk that resulted in harm. Under the Model Penal Code, a defendant is negligent even if she or he was not actually aware of the risk but *should have been aware* of it.[5] The Model Penal Code defines *criminal recklessness* as "consciously disregard[ing] a substantial and unjustifiable risk."[6] In other words, a defendant is reckless if he or she is *actually aware* of the risk. A defendant who commits an act *recklessly* is more blameworthy than one who is criminally negligent.

SECTION 4 | Corporate Criminal Liability

As will be discussed in Chapter 38, a corporation is a legal entity created under the laws of a state. Both the corporation as an entity and the individual directors and officers of the corporation are potentially subject to liability for criminal acts.

---

3. Pronounced *ak*-tuhs *ray*-uhs.

4. Pronounced *mehns ray*-uh.
5. Model Penal Code Section 2.02(2)(d).
6. Model Penal Code Section 2.02(2)(c).

LIABILITY OF THE CORPORATE ENTITY

At one time, it was thought that a corporation could not incur criminal liability because, although a corporation is a legal person, it can act only through its agents (corporate directors, officers, and employees). Therefore, the corporate entity itself could not "intend" to commit a crime. Under modern criminal law, however, a corporation may be held liable for crimes. Obviously, corporations cannot be imprisoned, but they can be fined or denied certain legal privileges (such as a license).

The Model Penal Code provides that a corporation may be convicted of a crime in the following situations:

1. The criminal act by the corporation's agent or employee is within the scope of his or her employment, and the purpose of the statute defining the act as a crime is to impose liability on the corporation.
2. The crime consists of a failure to perform a specific affirmative duty imposed on corporations by law.
3. The crime was authorized, requested, commanded, committed, or recklessly tolerated by one of the corporation's high managerial agents.[7]

As implied by the first statement in the above list, corporate criminal liability is vicarious—the corporation as an entity may be liable for the criminal acts of its employees when the acts are committed within the scope of employment. Thus, a corporation that is found to be criminally responsible for an act committed by an employee can be fined for that offense. Through the fine, stockholders and other employees suffer because of the vicarious liability of the corporation. For such criminal liability to be imposed, the prosecutor must show that the corporation could have prevented the act or that there was authorized consent to or knowledge of the act by persons in supervisory positions within the corporation.

LIABILITY OF CORPORATE OFFICERS AND DIRECTORS

Corporate directors and officers are personally liable for the crimes they commit, regardless of whether the crimes were committed for their private benefit or on the corporation's behalf. Additionally, corporate directors and officers may be held liable for the actions of employees under their supervision. Under what has become known as the "responsible corporate officer" doctrine, a court may impose criminal liability on a corporate officer regardless of whether he or she participated in, directed, or even knew about a given criminal violation.

For example, in *United States v. Park*,[8] the chief executive officer of a national supermarket chain was held personally liable for sanitation violations in corporate warehouses where food was exposed to contamination by rodents. The United States Supreme Court imposed personal liability on the corporate officer not because he intended the crime or even knew about it but rather because he was in a "responsible relationship" to the corporation and had the power to prevent the violation. Since the *Park* decision, courts have applied this "responsible corporate officer" doctrine on a number of occasions to hold corporate officers liable for their employees' statutory violations, including violations of environmental statutes (discussed in Chapter 45).

SECTION 5 | Types of Crimes

Numerous actions are designated as criminal. Federal, state, and local laws provide for the classification and punishment of hundreds of thousands of different criminal acts. Generally, though, criminal acts can be grouped into five broad categories: violent crime (crimes against persons), property crime, public order crime, white-collar crime, and organized crime. Cyber crime—which consists of crimes committed in cyberspace with the use of computers—is, as mentioned earlier in this chapter, less a category of crime than a new way to commit crime. We will examine cyber crime later in this chapter.

VIOLENT CRIME

Some types of crime are called *violent crimes*, or crimes against persons, because they cause others to suffer harm or death. Murder is a violent crime. So is sexual assault, or rape. Assault and battery, which were discussed in Chapter 6 in the context of tort law, are also classified as violent crimes. **Robbery**—defined as the taking of money, personal property, or any other article of value from a person by means of force or fear—is also a violent crime. Typically, states have more

---

7. Model Penal Code Section 2.07.

8. 421 U.S. 658, 95 S.Ct. 1903, 44 L.Ed.2d 489 (1975).

severe penalties for *aggravated robbery—robbery with the use of a deadly weapon.*

Each of these violent crimes is further classified by degree, depending on the circumstances surrounding the criminal act. These circumstances include the intent of the person committing the crime, whether a weapon was used, and (in cases other than murder) the level of pain and suffering experienced by the victim.

PROPERTY CRIME

The most common type of criminal activity is property crime, or those crimes in which the goal of the offender is some form of economic gain or the damaging of property. Robbery is a form of property crime, as well as a violent crime, because the offender seeks to gain the property of another. We look here at a number of other crimes that fall within the general category of property crime.

BURGLARY Traditionally, **burglary** was defined as breaking and entering the dwelling of another at night with the intent to commit a felony. Originally, the definition was aimed at protecting an individual's home and its occupants. Most state statutes have eliminated some of the requirements found in the common law definition. The time at which the breaking and entering occurs, for example, is usually immaterial. State statutes frequently omit the element of breaking, and some states do not require that the building be a dwelling. *Aggravated burglary—which is defined as burglary with the use of a deadly weapon, burglary of a dwelling, or both—incurs a greater penalty.*

LARCENY Any person who wrongfully or fraudulently takes and carries away another individual's personal property is guilty of **larceny.** Larceny includes the fraudulent intent to deprive an owner permanently of property. Many business-related larcenies entail fraudulent conduct. Whereas robbery involves force or fear, larceny does not. Therefore, picking pockets is larceny, not robbery. Similarly, taking company products and supplies home for personal use, if one is not authorized to do so, is larceny.

In most states, the definition of property that is subject to larceny statutes has expanded. For example, stealing computer programs may constitute larceny even though the "property" consists of magnetic impulses. Stealing computer time may also be considered larceny. So, too, may the theft of natural gas.

Intercepting cellular phone calls to obtain another's phone-card number—and then using that number to place long-distance calls, often overseas—is a form of property theft. These types of larceny are covered by "theft of services" statutes in many jurisdictions.

The common law distinguishes between grand and petit larceny depending on the value of the property taken. Many states have abolished this distinction, but in those that have not, grand larceny (theft above a certain amount) is a felony and petit larceny is a misdemeanor.

ARSON The willful and malicious burning of a building (and, in some states, personal property) owned by another is the crime of **arson.** At common law, arson applied only to burning down another person's house. The law was designed to protect human life. Today, arson statutes have been extended to cover the destruction of any building, regardless of ownership, by fire or explosion.

Every state has a special statute that covers the burning of a building for the purpose of collecting insurance. If Shaw owns an insured apartment building that is falling apart and sets fire to it himself or pays someone else to do so, he is guilty not only of arson but also of defrauding insurers, which is an attempted larceny. Of course, the insurer need not pay the claim when insurance fraud is proved.

RECEIVING STOLEN GOODS It is a crime to receive stolen goods. The recipient of such goods need not know the true identity of the owner or the thief. All that is necessary is that the recipient knows or should know that the goods are stolen, which implies an intent to deprive the owner of those goods.

FORGERY The fraudulent making or altering of any writing in a way that changes the legal rights and liabilities of another is **forgery.** If, without authorization, Severson signs Bennett's name to the back of a check made out to Bennett, Severson is committing forgery. Forgery also includes changing trademarks, falsifying public records, counterfeiting, and altering a legal document.

OBTAINING GOODS BY FALSE PRETENSES It is a criminal act to obtain goods by false pretenses—for example, to buy groceries with a check, knowing that one has insufficient funds to cover it. Using another's credit-card number to obtain goods is another example of obtaining goods by false pretenses. Statutes dealing with such illegal activities vary widely from state to state. For example, in some states an intent to defraud must be proved before a person is criminally liable for writing a bad check.

PUBLIC ORDER CRIME

Historically, societies have always outlawed activities that are considered contrary to public values and morals. Today, the most common public order crimes include public drunkenness, prostitution, gambling, and illegal drug use. These crimes are sometimes referred to as *victimless crimes* because they normally harm only the offender. From a broader perspective, however, they are deemed detrimental to society as a whole because they might create an environment that gives rise to property and violent crimes.

WHITE-COLLAR CRIME

Crimes occurring in the business context are popularly referred to as white-collar crimes. Although there is no official definition of **white-collar crime,** the term is commonly used to mean an illegal act or series of acts committed by an individual or business entity using some nonviolent means to obtain a personal or business advantage. Usually, this kind of crime takes place in the course of a legitimate business occupation. The crimes discussed next normally occur only in the business environment and thus fall into the category of white-collar crimes. Note, though, that certain property crimes, such as larceny and forgery, may also fall into this category if they occur within the business context.

EMBEZZLEMENT When a person entrusted with another person's property or funds fraudulently appropriates that property or those funds, **embezzlement occurs.** Typically, embezzlement involves an employee who steals funds from her or his employer. Banks often face this problem, and so do a number of businesses in which corporate officers or accountants "doctor" the books to cover up the fraudulent conversion of funds for their own benefit. Embezzlement is not larceny because the wrongdoer does not *physically* take the property from the possession of another, and it is not robbery because no force or fear is used.

It does not matter whether the accused takes the funds from the victim or from a third person. If, as the

financial officer of a large corporation, Carlson pockets a certain number of checks from third parties that were given to her to deposit into the corporate account, she is embezzling.

Ordinarily, an embezzler who returns what has been taken will not be prosecuted because the owner usually will not take the time to make a complaint, give depositions, and appear in court. That the accused intended eventually to return the embezzled property does not constitute a sufficient defense to the crime of embezzlement, however.

MAIL AND WIRE FRAUD One of the most potent weapons against white-collar criminals is the Mail Fraud Act of 1990.[9] Under this act, it is a federal crime to use the mails to defraud the public. Illegal use of the mails must involve (1) mailing or causing someone else to mail a writing—something written, printed, or photocopied—for the purpose of executing a scheme to defraud and (2) contemplating or organizing a scheme to defraud by false pretenses. If, for example, Johnson advertises by mail the sale of a cure for cancer that he knows to be fraudulent because it has no medical validity, he can be prosecuted for fraudulent use of the mails.

Federal law also makes it a crime (wire fraud) to use wire, radio, or television transmissions to defraud.[10] Violators may be fined up to $1,000, imprisoned for up to twenty years, or both. If the violation affects a financial institution, the violator may be fined up to $1 million, imprisoned for up to thirty years, or both.

BRIBERY Basically, three types of bribery are considered crimes: (1) commercial bribery, (2) bribery of public officials, and (3) bribery of foreign officials. As an element of the crime of bribery, intent must be present and proved. The bribe can be anything the recipient considers to be valuable. Realize that the *crime of bribery occurs when the bribe is offered.* It does not matter whether the person to whom the bribe is offered accepts the bribe or agrees to perform whatever action is desired by the person offering the bribe. *Accepting a bribe* is a separate crime.

Typically, people make commercial bribes to obtain proprietary information, cover up an inferior product, or secure new business. Industrial espionage sometimes involves commercial bribes. For example, a person in one firm may offer an employee in a competing firm

---

9. 18 U.S.C. Sections 1341–1342.
10. 18 U.S.C. Section 1343.

some type of payoff in exchange for trade secrets or pricing schedules. So-called kickbacks, or payoffs for special favors or services, are a form of commercial bribery in some situations.

Bribing foreign officials to obtain favorable business contracts is a crime. This crime was discussed in detail in Chapter 5, along with the Foreign Corrupt Practices Act of 1977, which was passed to curb the use of bribery by American businesspersons in securing foreign contracts.

BANKRUPTCY FRAUD Today, federal bankruptcy law (see Chapter 30) allows individuals and businesses to be relieved of oppressive debt through bankruptcy proceedings. Numerous white-collar crimes may be committed during the many phases of a bankruptcy action. A creditor, for example, may file a false claim against the debtor, which is a crime. Also, a debtor may fraudulently transfer assets to favored parties before or after the petition for bankruptcy is filed. For example, a company-owned automobile may be "sold" at a bargain price to a trusted friend or relative. Closely related to the crime of fraudulent transfer of property is the crime of fraudulent concealment of property, such as the hiding of gold coins.

INSIDER TRADING An individual who obtains "inside information" about the plans of a publicly listed corporation can often make stock-trading profits by using this information to guide decisions relating to the purchase or sale of corporate securities. *Insider trading* is a violation of securities law and will be considered more fully in Chapter 41. At this point, it may be said that one who possesses inside information and who has a duty not to disclose it to outsiders may not profit from the purchase or sale of securities based on that information until the information is available to the public.

THE THEFT OF TRADE SECRETS As discussed in Chapter 8, trade secrets constitute a form of intellectual property that for many businesses can be extremely valuable. The Economic Espionage Act of 1996[11] makes the theft of trade secrets a federal crime. The act also makes it a federal crime to buy or possess another person's trade secrets, knowing that the trade secrets were stolen or otherwise acquired without the owner's authorization.

---

11. 18 U.S.C. Sections 1831–1839.

Violations of the act can result in steep penalties. The act provides that an individual who violates the act can be imprisoned for up to ten years and fined up to $500,000. If a corporation or other organization violates the act, it can be fined up to $5 million. Additionally, the law provides that any property acquired as a result of the violation or used in the commission of the violation is subject to criminal forfeiture—meaning that the government can take the property. A theft of trade secrets conducted via the Internet, for example, could result in the forfeiture of every computer, printer, or other device used to commit or facilitate the violation.

ORGANIZED CRIME

White-collar crime takes place within the confines of the legitimate business world. Organized crime, in contrast, operates *illegitimately* by, among other things, providing illegal goods and services. Traditionally, the preferred markets for organized crime have been gambling, prostitution, illegal narcotics, and loan sharking (lending funds at higher-than-legal interest rates), along with more recent ventures into counterfeiting and credit-card scams.

MONEY LAUNDERING The profits from organized crime and other illegal activities amount to billions of dollars a year, particularly the profits from illegal drug transactions and, to a lesser extent, from racketeering, prostitution, and gambling. Under federal law, banks, savings and loan associations, and other financial institutions are required to report currency transactions involving more than $10,000. Consequently, those who engage in illegal activities face difficulties in depositing their cash profits from illegal transactions.

As an alternative to storing cash from illegal transactions in a safe-deposit box, wrongdoers and racketeers have invented ways to launder "dirty" money to make it "clean." This **money laundering is done through legitimate businesses.** For example, suppose that Harris, a successful drug dealer, becomes a partner with a restaurateur. Little by little, the restaurant shows an increasing profit. As a partner in the restaurant, Harris is able to report the "profits" of the restaurant as legitimate income on which he pays federal and state taxes. He can then spend those after-tax funds without worrying about whether his lifestyle exceeds the level possible with his reported income.

CONCEPT SUMMARY 9.1 | Types of Crimes

CRIME CATEGORY	DEFINITIONS AND EXAMPLES
VIOLENT CRIME	1. *Definition*—Crimes that cause others to suffer harm or death. 2. *Examples*—Murder, assault and battery, sexual assault (rape), and robbery.
PROPERTY CRIME	1. *Definition*—Crimes in which the goal of the offender is some form of economic gain or the damaging of property; the most common form of crime. 2. *Examples*—Burglary, larceny, arson, receiving stolen goods, forgery, and obtaining goods by false pretenses.
PUBLIC ORDER CRIME	1. *Definition*—Crimes contrary to public values and morals. 2. *Examples*—Public drunkenness, prostitution, gambling, and illegal drug use.
WHITE-COLLAR CRIME	1. *Definition*—An illegal act or series of acts committed by an individual or business entity using some nonviolent means to obtain a personal or business advantage; usually committed in the course of a legitimate occupation. 2. *Examples*—Embezzlement, mail and wire fraud, bribery, bankruptcy fraud, insider trading, and the theft of trade secrets.
ORGANIZED CRIME	1. *Definition*—A form of crime conducted by groups operating illegitimately to satisfy the public's demand for illegal goods and services (such as gambling and illegal narcotics). 2. *Money laundering*—The establishment of legitimate enterprises through which "dirty" money (obtained through criminal activities, such as illegal drug trafficking) can be "laundered" (made to appear as legitimate income). 3. *RICO*—The Racketeer Influenced and Corrupt Organizations Act (RICO) of 1970 makes it a federal crime to (a) use income obtained from racketeering activity to purchase any interest in an enterprise, (b) acquire or maintain an interest in an enterprise through racketeering activity, (c) conduct or participate in the affairs of an enterprise through racketeering activity, or (d) conspire to do any of the preceding activities. RICO provides for both civil and criminal liability.

The Federal Bureau of Investigation (FBI) estimates that organized crime has invested tens of billions of dollars in as many as a hundred thousand business establishments in the United States for the purpose of money laundering. Globally, it is estimated that $500 billion in illegal money moves through the world banking system every year.

RICO In 1970, in an effort to curb the apparently increasing entry of organized crime into the legitimate business world, Congress passed the Racketeer Influenced and Corrupt Organizations Act (RICO).[12] The statute, which was enacted as part of the Organized Crime Control Act, makes it a federal crime to (1) use income obtained from racketeering activity to purchase any interest in an enterprise, (2) acquire or maintain an interest in an enterprise through racketeering activity, (3) conduct or participate in the affairs of an enterprise through racketeering activity, or (4) conspire to do any of the preceding activities.

Racketeering activity is not a new type of substantive crime created by RICO; rather, RICO incorporates by reference twenty-six separate types of federal crimes and nine types of state felonies[13] and declares that a person who commits two of these offenses is guilty of "racketeering activity." The act provides for both civil and criminal liability.

---

12. 18 U.S.C. Sections 1961–1968.

13. See 18 U.S.C. Section 1961(1)(A). The crimes listed in this section relate to murder, kidnapping, gambling, arson, robbery, bribery, extortion, money laundering, securities fraud, counterfeiting, dealing in obscene matter, dealing in controlled substances (illegal drugs), and a number of others.

—*Civil Liability under RICO.* The penalties for violations of the RICO statute are harsh. In the event of a violation, the statute permits the government to seek civil penalties, including the divestiture of a defendant's interest in a business (called *forfeiture*) or the dissolution of the business. Perhaps the most controversial aspect of RICO is that in some cases, private individuals are allowed to recover three times their actual losses (treble damages), plus attorneys' fees, for business injuries caused by a violation of the statute.

The broad language of RICO has allowed it to be applied in cases that have little or nothing to do with organized crime, and an aggressive trial attorney may attempt to show that any business fraud constitutes "racketeering activity." In its 1985 decision in *Sedima, S.P.R.L. v. Imrex Co.,*[14] the United States Supreme Court interpreted RICO broadly and set a significant precedent for subsequent applications of the act. Plaintiffs have used the RICO statute in numerous commercial fraud cases because of the inviting prospect of being awarded treble damages if they win. The most frequent targets of civil RICO lawsuits are insurance companies, employment agencies, and commercial banks.

One of the requirements of RICO is that there be more than one offense—there must be a "pattern of racketeering activity." What constitutes a "pattern" has been the subject of much litigation. According to the interpretation of some courts, a pattern must involve, among other things, continued criminal activity. This is known as the "continuity" requirement. Part of this requirement is that the activity occur over a "substantial" period of time.

—*Criminal Liability under RICO.* Many criminal RICO offenses, such as gambling, arson, and extortion, have little, if anything, to do with normal business activities. But securities fraud (involving the sale of stocks and bonds) and mail and wire fraud may also constitute criminal RICO violations, and RICO has become an effective tool in attacking these white-collar crimes in recent years. Under the criminal provisions of RICO, any individual found guilty of a violation is subject to a fine of up to $25,000 per violation, imprisonment for up to twenty years, or both. Additionally, the statute provides that those who violate RICO may be required to forfeit (give up) any assets, in the form of property or cash, that were acquired as a result of the illegal activity or that were "involved in" or an "instrumentality of" the activity.

SECTION 6 | Defenses to Criminal Liability

In certain circumstances, the law may allow a person to be excused from criminal liability because she or he lacks the required mental state. Criminal defendants may also be relieved of criminal liability if they can show that their criminal actions were justified, given the circumstances. Among the most important defenses to criminal liability are infancy, intoxication, insanity, mistake, consent, duress, justifiable use of force, necessity, entrapment, and the statute of limitations. Additionally, in some cases defendants are given *immunity* from prosecution and thus are relieved, at least in part, of criminal liability for their actions. We look next at each of these defenses.

Note that procedural violations (such as obtaining evidence without a valid search warrant) may also operate as defenses because evidence obtained in violation of a defendant's constitutional rights may not be admitted in court. If the evidence is suppressed, then there may be no basis for prosecuting the defendant.

INFANCY

The term *infant,* as used in the law, refers to any person who has not yet reached the age of majority (see Chapter 13). In all states, certain courts handle cases involving children who allegedly have violated the law. In some states, juvenile courts handle children's cases exclusively. In most states, however, courts that handle children's cases also have jurisdiction over other matters, such as traffic offenses.

Originally, juvenile court hearings were informal, and lawyers were rarely present. Since 1967, however, when the United States Supreme Court ordered that a child charged with delinquency must be allowed to consult with an attorney before being committed to a state institution,[15] juvenile court hearings have become more formal. In most states, a child may be treated as an adult and tried in a regular court if he or she is above a certain age (usually fourteen) and is charged with a felony, such as rape or murder.

---

14. 473 U.S. 479, 105 S.Ct. 3275, 87 L.Ed.2d 346 (1985).

15. *In re Gault,* 387 U.S. 1, 87 S.Ct. 1428, 18 L.Ed.2d 527 (1967).

INTOXICATION

The law recognizes two types of intoxication, whether from drugs or from alcohol: involuntary and voluntary. *Involuntary intoxication* occurs when a person either is physically forced to ingest or inject an intoxicating substance or is unaware that such a substance contains drugs or alcohol. Involuntary intoxication is a defense to a crime if its effect was to make a person incapable of understanding that the act committed was wrong or incapable of obeying the law.

Using voluntary drug or alcohol intoxication as a defense is based on the theory that extreme levels of intoxication may negate the state of mind that a crime requires. Many courts are reluctant to allow *voluntary intoxication* as a defense to a crime, however. After all, the defendant, by definition, voluntarily chose to put herself or himself into an intoxicated state.

INSANITY

Just as a child is often judged incapable of the state of mind required to commit a crime, so also may be someone suffering from a mental illness. Thus, insanity may be a defense to a criminal charge. The courts have had difficulty deciding what standards should be used to measure sanity for the purposes of a criminal trial. One of the oldest standards, or tests, for insanity is the *M'Naghten* test,[16] which is still used in about one-third of the states. Under this test, which is sometimes called the "right-wrong" test, a criminal defendant is not responsible if, at the time of the offense, he or she did not know the nature and quality of the act or did not know that the act was wrong.

Several other jurisdictions use the less restrictive "irresistible-impulse" test to determine sanity. Under this test, a person may be found insane even if she or he was aware that a criminal act was wrong, providing that some "irresistible impulse" resulting from a mental deficiency drove her or him to commit the crime.

Today, almost all federal courts and about half of the states use the relatively liberal standard set forth in the Model Penal Code:

> A person is not responsible for criminal conduct if at the time of such conduct as a result of mental disease or defect he lacks *substantial capacity* either to appreciate the wrongfulness of his conduct or to conform his conduct to the requirements of the law.[17] [Emphasis added.]

This "substantial-capacity" standard is considerably easier to meet than the *M'Naghten* test or the irresistible-impulse test.

Under any of these tests, it is extremely difficult to prove insanity. For this reason, the insanity defense is rarely used. It is raised in only about 1 percent of felony cases and is unsuccessful in about three-fourths of those cases.

MISTAKE

Everyone has heard the saying "Ignorance of the law is no excuse." Ordinarily, ignorance of the law or a mistaken idea about what the law requires is not a valid defense. In some states, however, that rule has been modified. People who claim that they honestly did not know that they were breaking a law may have a valid defense if (1) the law was not published or reasonably made known to the public or (2) the people relied on an official statement of the law that was erroneous.

A *mistake of fact,* as opposed to a *mistake of law*, operates as a defense if it negates the mental state necessary to commit a crime. If, for example, Oliver Wheaton mistakenly walks off with Julie Tyson's briefcase because he thinks it is his, there is no theft. Theft requires knowledge that the property belongs to another.

CONSENT

What if a victim consents to a crime or even encourages the person intending a criminal act to commit it? Ordinarily, **consent** does not operate as a bar to criminal liability. In some rare circumstances, however, the law may allow consent to be used as a defense. In each case, the question is whether the law forbids an act committed against the victim's will or forbids the act without regard to the victim's will. The law forbids murder, prostitution, and drug use whether the victim consents or not. Also, if the act causes harm to a third person who has not consented, there is no escape from criminal liability. Consent or forgiveness given after a crime has been committed is not really a defense, although it can affect the likelihood of prosecution.

Normally, consent is a successful defense only in crimes against property. For example, suppose that Barry gives Phong permission to hunt for deer on Barry's land while staying in Barry's lakeside cabin. After observing Phong carrying a gun into the cabin at night, a neighbor calls the police, and an officer subsequently arrests Phong. If charged with burglary (or

---

16. A rule derived from *M'Naghten's Case*, 8 Eng.Rep. 718 (1843).
17. Model Penal Code Section 4.01.

aggravated burglary, because he had a weapon), Phong can assert the defense of consent and will likely succeed in escaping criminal liability because he had obtained Barry's consent to enter the premises.

DURESS

Duress exists when the *wrongful threat* of one person induces another person to perform an act that he or she would not otherwise have performed. In such a situation, duress is said to negate the mental state necessary to commit a crime. For duress to qualify as a defense, the following requirements must be met:

1. The threat must be of serious bodily harm or death.
2. The harm threatened must be greater than the harm caused by the crime.
3. The threat must be immediate and inescapable.
4. The defendant must have been involved in the situation through no fault of his or her own.

One crime that cannot be excused by duress is murder. It is difficult to justify taking a life as a result of duress even if one's own life is threatened.

JUSTIFIABLE USE OF FORCE

Probably the most well-known defense to criminal liability is **self-defense.** Other situations, however, also justify the use of force: the defense of one's dwelling, the defense of other property, and the prevention of a crime. In all of these situations, it is important to distinguish between deadly and nondeadly force. *Deadly force* is likely to result in death or serious bodily harm. *Nondeadly force* is force that reasonably appears necessary to prevent the imminent use of criminal force.

Generally speaking, people can use the amount of nondeadly force that seems necessary to protect themselves, their dwellings, or other property or to prevent the commission of a crime. Deadly force can be used in self-defense if there is a *reasonable belief* that imminent death or grievous bodily harm will otherwise result, if the attacker is using unlawful force (an example of lawful force would be that exerted by a police officer), and if the defender has not initiated or provoked the attack. Deadly force can be used to defend a dwelling only if the unlawful entry is violent and the person believes deadly force is necessary to prevent imminent death or great bodily harm or—in some jurisdictions—if the person believes deadly force is necessary to prevent the commission of a felony in the dwelling.

NECESSITY

Sometimes criminal defendants can be relieved of liability by showing that a criminal act was necessary to prevent an even greater harm. According to the Model Penal Code, the defense of **necessity** is justifiable if "the harm or evil sought to be avoided by such conduct is greater than that sought to be prevented by the law defining the offense charged."[18] For example, in one case a convicted felon was threatened by an acquaintance with a gun. The felon grabbed the gun and fled the scene, but subsequently he was arrested under a statute that prohibits convicted felons from possessing firearms. In this situation, the necessity defense succeeded because the defendant's crime avoided a "greater evil."[19]

ENTRAPMENT

Entrapment is a defense designed to prevent police officers or other government agents from encouraging crimes in order to apprehend persons wanted for criminal acts. In the typical entrapment case, an undercover agent *suggests* that a crime be committed and somehow pressures or induces an individual to commit it. The agent then arrests the individual for the crime. For entrapment to be considered a defense, both the suggestion and the inducement must take place. The defense is not intended to prevent law enforcement agents from setting a trap for an unwary criminal; rather, the intent is to prevent them from pushing the individual into that trap. The crucial issue is whether a person who committed a crime was predisposed to commit the crime or did so because the agent induced it.

STATUTE OF LIMITATIONS

With some exceptions, such as for the crime of murder, statutes of limitations apply to crimes just as they do to civil wrongs. In other words, the state must initiate criminal prosecution within a certain number of years. If a criminal action is brought after the statutory time period has expired, the accused person can raise the statute of limitations as a defense. The running of the time period in a statute of limitations may be tolled—that is, suspended or stopped temporarily—if the defendant is a minor or is not in the jurisdiction.

---

18. Model Penal Code Section 3.02.
19. *United States v. Paolello,* 951 F.2d 537 (3d Cir. 1991).

When the defendant reaches the age of majority or returns to the jurisdiction, the statute revives—that is, its time period begins to run or to run again.

IMMUNITY

At times, the state may wish to obtain information from a person accused of a crime. Accused persons are understandably reluctant to give information if it will be used to prosecute them, and they cannot be forced to do so. The privilege against self-incrimination is granted by the Fifth Amendment to the Constitution, which reads, in part, "nor shall [any person] be compelled in any criminal case to be a witness against himself." In cases in which the state wishes to obtain information from a person accused of a crime, the state can grant *immunity* from prosecution or agree to prosecute for a less serious offense in exchange for the information. Once immunity is given, the person now has an absolute privilege against self-incrimination and therefore can no longer refuse to testify on Fifth Amendment grounds.

Often, a grant of immunity from prosecution for a serious crime is part of the **plea bargaining** between the defending and prosecuting attorneys. The defendant may be convicted of a lesser offense, while the state uses the defendant's testimony to prosecute accomplices for serious crimes carrying heavy penalties.

SECTION 7 | Criminal Procedures

Criminal law brings the force of the state, with all of its resources, to bear against the individual. Criminal procedures are designed to protect the constitutional rights of individuals and to prevent the arbitrary use of power on the part of the government.

The U.S. Constitution provides specific safeguards for those accused of crimes. The United States Supreme Court has ruled that most of these safeguards apply not only in federal but also in state courts by virtue of the due process clause of the Fourteenth Amendment. These safeguards include the following:

1. The Fourth Amendment protection from unreasonable searches and seizures.
2. The Fourth Amendment requirement that no warrant for a search or an arrest be issued without probable cause.
3. The Fifth Amendment requirement that no one be deprived of "life, liberty, or property without due process of law."

4. The Fifth Amendment prohibition against **double jeopardy** (trying someone twice for the same criminal offense).[20]
5. The Fifth Amendment requirement that no person be required to be a witness against (incriminate) himself or herself.
6. The Sixth Amendment guarantees of a speedy trial, a trial by jury, a public trial, the right to confront witnesses, and the right to a lawyer at various stages in some proceedings.
7. The Eighth Amendment prohibitions against excessive bail and fines and cruel and unusual punishment.

THE EXCLUSIONARY RULE

Under what is known as the **exclusionary rule,** all evidence obtained in violation of the constitutional rights spelled out in the Fourth, Fifth, and Sixth Amendments normally is not admissible at trial. All evidence derived from the illegally obtained evidence is known as the "fruit of the poisonous tree," and such evidence normally must also be excluded from the trial proceedings. For example, if a confession is obtained after an illegal arrest, the arrest is the "poisonous tree," and the confession, if "tainted" by the arrest, is the "fruit."

As you will read shortly, under the *Miranda* rule, suspects must be advised of certain constitutional rights when they are arrested. For example, the Sixth Amendment right to counsel is one of the rights of which a suspect must be advised when he or she is arrested. In many cases, a statement that a criminal suspect makes in the absence of counsel is not admissible at trial unless the suspect has knowingly and voluntarily waived this right. In the following case, the United States Supreme Court considered at what point a suspect's right to counsel is triggered during criminal proceedings.

---

20. The prohibition against double jeopardy means that once a criminal defendant is found not guilty of a particular crime, the government may not reindict the person and retry him or her for the same crime. The prohibition against double jeopardy does not preclude a *civil* suit's being brought against the same person by the crime victim to recover damages. For example, a person found not guilty of assault and battery in a criminal case may be sued by the victim in a civil (tort) case for damages. Additionally, a state's prosecution of a crime will not prevent a separate federal prosecution of the same crime, and vice versa. For example, a defendant found not guilty of violating a state law can be tried in federal court for the same act, if the act is also defined as a crime under federal law.

CASE 9.1

Supreme Court of the
United States, 2004.
540 U.S. 519,
124 S.Ct. 1019,
157 L.Ed.2d 1016.

Fellers v. United States

Justice O'CONNOR delivered the opinion of the Court.
* * * *

On February 24, 2000, after a grand jury indicted petitioner [John J. Fellers] for conspiracy to distribute methamphetamine, Lincoln Police Sergeant Michael Garnett and Lancaster County Deputy Sheriff Jeff Bliemeister went to petitioner's home in Lincoln, Nebraska, to arrest him. The officers knocked on petitioner's door and, when petitioner answered, identified themselves and asked if they could come in. Petitioner invited the officers into his living room.

The officers advised petitioner they had come to discuss his involvement in methamphetamine distribution. They informed petitioner that they had a federal warrant for his arrest and that a grand jury had indicted him for conspiracy to distribute methamphetamine. The officers told petitioner that the indictment referred to his involvement with certain individuals, four of whom they named. Petitioner then told the officers that he knew the four people and had used methamphetamine during his association with them.

After spending about 15 minutes in petitioner's home, the officers transported petitioner to the Lancaster County jail. There, the officers advised petitioner for the first time of his [right to counsel under the Sixth Amendment]. Petitioner and the two officers signed a * * * waiver form, and petitioner then reiterated the inculpatory [incriminating] statements he had made earlier, admitted to having associated with other individuals implicated in the charged conspiracy, and admitted to having loaned money to one of them even though he suspected that she was involved in drug transactions.

Before trial, petitioner moved to suppress the inculpatory statements he made at his home and at the county jail. * * *

The District Court suppressed the "unwarned" statements petitioner made at his house but admitted petitioner's jailhouse statements * * * , concluding petitioner had knowingly and voluntarily waived his * * * rights before making the statements.

Following a jury trial at which petitioner's jailhouse statements were admitted into evidence, petitioner was convicted of conspiring to possess with intent to distribute methamphetamine. Petitioner appealed, arguing that his jailhouse statements should have been suppressed as fruits of the statements obtained at his home in violation of the Sixth Amendment. The [U.S.] Court of Appeals [for the Eighth Circuit] affirmed. * * * [T]he Court of Appeals stated: " * * * [T]he officers did not interrogate [petitioner] at his home." * * * [Fellers appealed to the United States Supreme Court.]
* * * *

*The Sixth Amendment right to counsel is triggered at or after the time that judicial proceedings have been initiated * * * whether by way of formal charge, preliminary hearing, indictment, information, or arraignment.* We have held that an accused is denied the basic protections of the Sixth Amendment when there is used against him at his trial evidence of his own incriminating words, which federal agents * * * deliberately elicited from him after he had been indicted and in the absence of his counsel. [Emphasis added.]

We have consistently applied the *deliberate-elicitation standard* in * * * Sixth Amendment cases * * * . [Emphasis added.]

The Court of Appeals erred in holding that the absence of an "interrogation" foreclosed petitioner's claim that the jailhouse statements should have been suppressed as fruits of the statements taken from petitioner [Fellers] at his home. First, there is no question that the officers in this case deliberately elicited information from petitioner. Indeed, the officers, upon arriving at petitioner's house, informed him that their purpose in coming was to discuss his involvement in the distribution of methamphetamine and his association with certain charged co-conspirators. Because the ensuing discussion took place after petitioner had been indicted, outside the presence of counsel, and in the absence of any waiver of petitioner's Sixth Amendment rights, the Court of Appeals erred in holding that the officers' actions did not violate the Sixth Amendment standards * * * .

CONTINUED ▶

CASE 9.1 | Continued

Second, because of its erroneous determination that petitioner was not questioned in violation of Sixth Amendment standards, the Court of Appeals improperly conducted its "fruits" analysis * * * . Specifically, it * * * [held] that the admissibility of the jailhouse statements turns solely on whether the statements were knowingly and voluntarily made. The Court of Appeals did not reach the question whether the Sixth Amendment requires suppression of petitioner's jailhouse statements on the ground that they were the fruits of previous questioning conducted in violation of the Sixth Amendment deliberate-elicitation standard. We have not had occasion to decide whether [such statements should be excluded from trial] when a suspect makes incriminating statements after a knowing and voluntary waiver of his right to counsel notwithstanding earlier police questioning in violation of Sixth Amendment standards. We therefore remand to the Court of Appeals to address this issue in the first instance.

Accordingly, the judgment of the Court of Appeals is reversed, and the case is remanded for further proceedings consistent with this opinion.

It is so ordered.

QUESTIONS

1. Why did Fellers argue on appeal that his "jailhouse statements" should have been excluded from his trial?
2. Should Fellers's "jailhouse statements" have been excluded from his trial? Why or why not?

PURPOSE OF THE EXCLUSIONARY RULE The purpose of the exclusionary rule is to deter police from conducting warrantless searches and from engaging in other misconduct. The rule is sometimes criticized because it can lead to injustice. Many a defendant has "gotten off on a technicality" because law enforcement personnel failed to observe procedural requirements based on the above-mentioned constitutional amendments. Even though a defendant may be obviously guilty, if the evidence of that guilt was obtained improperly (without a valid search warrant, for example), it cannot be used against the defendant in court.

EXCEPTIONS TO THE EXCLUSIONARY RULE Over the last several decades, the United States Supreme Court has diminished the scope of the exclusionary rule by creating some exceptions to its applicability. For example, in 1984 the Court held that if illegally obtained evidence would have been discovered "inevitably" and obtained by the police using lawful means, the evidence will be admissible at trial.[21] In another case decided in the same year, the Court held that a police officer who used a technically incorrect search warrant form to obtain evidence had acted in good faith and therefore the evidence was admissible.

The Court thus created the "good faith" exception to the exclusionary rule.[22] Additionally, the courts can exercise a certain amount of discretion in determining whether evidence has been obtained improperly, which somewhat balances the scales.

THE MIRANDA RULE

In regard to criminal procedure, one of the questions many courts faced in the 1950s and 1960s was not whether suspects had constitutional rights—that was not in doubt—but how and when those rights could be exercised. Could the right to be silent (under the Fifth Amendment's prohibition against self-incrimination) be exercised during pretrial interrogation proceedings, or only during the trial? Were confessions obtained from suspects admissible in court if the suspects had not been advised of their right to remain silent and other constitutional rights?

To clarify these issues, the United States Supreme Court issued a landmark decision in 1966 in *Miranda v. Arizona,* which we present here. Today, the procedural rights required by the Court in this case are familiar to virtually every American.

---

21. *Nix v. Williams,* 467 U.S. 431, 104 S.Ct. 2501, 81 L.Ed.2d 377 (1984).

22. *Massachusetts v. Sheppard,* 468 U.S. 981, 104 S.Ct. 3424, 82 L.Ed.2d 737 (1984).

CASE 9.2

Miranda v. Arizona

Supreme Court of the
United States, 1966.
384 U.S. 436,
86 S.Ct. 1602,
16 L.Ed.2d 694.

BACKGROUND AND FACTS *On March 13, 1963, Ernesto Miranda was arrested at his home for the kidnapping and rape of an eighteen-year-old woman. Miranda was taken to a Phoenix, Arizona, police station and questioned by two officers. Two hours later, the officers emerged from the interrogation room with a written confession signed by Miranda. A paragraph at the top of the confession stated that the confession had been made voluntarily, without threats or promises of immunity, and "with full knowledge of my legal rights, understanding any statement I make may be used against me." Miranda was at no time advised that he had a right to remain silent and a right to have a lawyer present. The confession was admitted into evidence at the trial, and Miranda was convicted and sentenced to prison for twenty to thirty years. Miranda appealed the decision, claiming that he had not been informed of his constitutional rights. The Supreme Court of Arizona held that Miranda's constitutional rights had not been violated and affirmed his conviction. The Miranda case was subsequently reviewed by the United States Supreme Court.*

IN THE LANGUAGE OF THE COURT

Mr. Chief Justice *WARREN* delivered the opinion of the Court.

The cases before us raise questions which go to the roots of our concepts of American criminal jurisprudence; the restraints society must observe consistent with the Federal Constitution in prosecuting individuals for crime. * * *

* * * *

At the outset, if a person in custody is to be subjected to interrogation, he must first be informed in clear and unequivocal terms that he has the right to remain silent. * * *

* * * *

The warning of the right to remain silent must be accompanied by the explanation that anything said can and will be used against the individual in court. This warning is needed in order to make him aware not only of the privilege, *but also of the consequences of forgoing it.* * * * [Emphasis added.]

The circumstances surrounding in-custody interrogation can operate very quickly to overbear the will of one merely made aware of his privilege by his interrogators. Therefore the right to have counsel present at the interrogation is indispensable to the protection of the Fifth Amendment privilege under the system we delineate today.

* * * *

In order fully to apprise a person interrogated of the extent of his rights under this system then, it is necessary to warn him not only that he has the right to consult with an attorney, but also that if he is indigent [without funds] a lawyer will be appointed to represent him. * * * The warning of a right to counsel would be hollow if not couched in terms that would convey to the indigent—the person most often subjected to interrogation—the knowledge that he too has a right to have counsel present.

DECISION AND REMEDY *The Supreme Court held that Miranda could not be convicted of the crime on the basis of his confession because his confession was inadmissible as evidence. For any statement made by a defendant to be admissible, the defendant must be informed of certain constitutional rights prior to police interrogation. If the accused waives his or her rights to remain silent and to have counsel present, the government must demonstrate that the waiver was made knowingly, voluntarily, and intelligently.*

INTERNATIONAL CONSIDERATIONS **The Right to Remain Silent in Great Britain**
The right to remain silent has long been a legal hallmark in Great Britain as well as in the United States. In 1994, however, the British Parliament passed an act that provides a criminal defendant's silence may be interpreted as evidence of the defendant's guilt. British police officers are now required, when making arrests, to inform the suspects, "You do not have to say anything. But if you do not mention now something which you later use in your defense, the court may decide that your failure to mention it now strengthens the case against you. A record will be made of everything you say, and it may be given in evidence if you are brought to trial."

CONTINUED

CASE 9.2 | Continued

IMPACT OF THIS CASE ON TODAY'S LAW

Police officers routinely advise suspects of their "*Miranda* rights" on arrest. When Ernesto Miranda himself was later murdered, the suspected murderer was "read his *Miranda* rights." Despite significant criticisms and later attempts to overrule the *Miranda* decision through legislation, the requirements stated in this case continue to provide the benchmark by which criminal procedures are judged today.

CONGRESS'S RESPONSE TO THE MIRANDA RULING The Supreme Court's *Miranda* decision was controversial, and two years later Congress attempted to overrule it by enacting Section 3501 of the Omnibus Crime Control and Safe Streets Act of 1968.[23] Essentially, Section 3501 reinstated the rule that had been in effect for 180 years before *Miranda*—namely, that statements by defendants can be used against them as long as the statements are made voluntarily. The U.S. Department of Justice immediately refused to enforce Section 3501, however. Although the U.S. Court of Appeals for the Fourth Circuit attempted to enforce the provision in 1999, its decision was reversed by the United States Supreme Court in 2000. The Supreme Court held that the *Miranda* rights enunciated by the Court in the 1966 case were constitutionally based and thus could not be overruled by a legislative act.[24]

EXCEPTIONS TO THE MIRANDA RULE As part of a continuing attempt to balance the rights of accused persons against the rights of society, the Supreme Court has made a number of exceptions to the *Miranda* ruling. In 1984, for example, the Court recognized a "public safety" exception to the *Miranda* rule. The need to protect the public warranted the admissibility of statements made by the defendant (in this case, indicating where he had placed the gun) as evidence at trial, even though the defendant had not been informed of his *Miranda* rights.[25]

In 1986, the Court held that a confession need not be excluded even though the police failed to inform a suspect in custody that his attorney had tried to reach him by telephone.[26] In an important 1991 decision,

the Court stated that a suspect's conviction will not be overturned solely on the ground that the suspect was coerced by law enforcement personnel into making a confession. If the other evidence admitted at trial was strong enough to justify the conviction without the confession, then the fact that the confession was obtained illegally can be, in effect, ignored.[27]

In yet another case, in 1994 the Supreme Court ruled that a suspect must unequivocally and assertively request to exercise his or her right to counsel in order to stop police questioning. Saying, "Maybe I should talk to a lawyer" during an interrogation after being taken into custody is not enough. The Court held that police officers are not required to decipher the suspect's intentions in such situations.[28] In sum, courts today allow confessions that are not unequivocally voluntary to be admitted into evidence against defendants in criminal trials.

RECORDED VIDEO INTERROGATIONS There are no guarantees that *Miranda* will survive indefinitely—particularly in view of the numerous exceptions that are made to the rule. Additionally, law enforcement personnel are increasingly using digital video cameras to record interrogations. According to some scholars, the recording of *all* such interrogations would satisfy the Fifth Amendment's prohibition against coercion and would render the *Miranda* warnings unnecessary.

CRIMINAL PROCESS

As mentioned earlier in this chapter, a criminal prosecution differs significantly from a civil case in several respects. These differences reflect the desire to safeguard the rights of the individual against the state. Exhibit 9–3 summarizes the major steps in processing

23. 42 U.S.C. Section 3789d.

24. *Dickerson v. United States,* 530 U.S. 428, 120 S.Ct. 2326, 147 L.Ed.2d 405 (2000).

25. *New York v. Quarles,* 467 U.S. 649, 104 S.Ct. 2626, 81 L.Ed.2d 550 (1984).

26. *Moran v. Burbine,* 475 U.S. 412, 106 S.Ct. 1135, 89 L.Ed.2d 410 (1986).

27. *Arizona v. Fulminante,* 499 U.S. 279, 111 S.Ct. 1246, 113 L.Ed.2d 302 (1991).

28. *Davis v. United States,* 512 U.S. 452, 114 S.Ct. 2350, 129 L.Ed.2d 362 (1994).

EXHIBIT 9–3 **Major Procedural Steps in a Criminal Case**

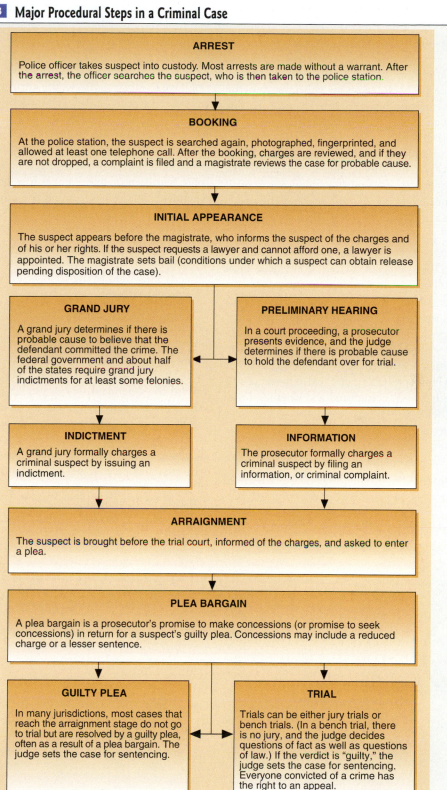

ARREST

Police officer takes suspect into custody. Most arrests are made without a warrant. After the arrest, the officer searches the suspect, who is then taken to the police station.

BOOKING

At the police station, the suspect is searched again, photographed, fingerprinted, and allowed at least one telephone call. After the booking, charges are reviewed, and if they are not dropped, a complaint is filed and a magistrate reviews the case for probable cause.

INITIAL APPEARANCE

The suspect appears before the magistrate, who informs the suspect of the charges and of his or her rights. If the suspect requests a lawyer and cannot afford one, a lawyer is appointed. The magistrate sets bail (conditions under which a suspect can obtain release pending disposition of the case).

GRAND JURY

A grand jury determines if there is probable cause to believe that the defendant committed the crime. The federal government and about half of the states require grand jury indictments for at least some felonies.

PRELIMINARY HEARING

In a court proceeding, a prosecutor presents evidence, and the judge determines if there is probable cause to hold the defendant over for trial.

INDICTMENT

A grand jury formally charges a criminal suspect by issuing an indictment.

INFORMATION

The prosecutor formally charges a criminal suspect by filing an information, or criminal complaint.

ARRAIGNMENT

The suspect is brought before the trial court, informed of the charges, and asked to enter a plea.

PLEA BARGAIN

A plea bargain is a prosecutor's promise to make concessions (or promise to seek concessions) in return for a suspect's guilty plea. Concessions may include a reduced charge or a lesser sentence.

GUILTY PLEA

In many jurisdictions, most cases that reach the arraignment stage do not go to trial but are resolved by a guilty plea, often as a result of a plea bargain. The judge sets the case for sentencing.

TRIAL

Trials can be either jury trials or bench trials. (In a bench trial, there is no jury, and the judge decides questions of fact as well as questions of law.) If the verdict is "guilty," the judge sets the case for sentencing. Everyone convicted of a crime has the right to an appeal.

a criminal case. We now discuss three phases of the criminal process—arrest, indictment or information, and trial—in more detail.

ARREST Before a warrant for arrest can be issued, there must be probable cause for believing that the individual in question has committed a crime. As discussed in Chapter 4, *probable cause* can be defined as a substantial likelihood that the person has committed or is about to commit a crime. Note that probable cause involves a likelihood, not just a possibility. Arrests may sometimes be made without a warrant if there is no time to get one, but the action of the arresting officer is still judged by the standard of probable cause.

INDICTMENT OR INFORMATION Individuals must be formally charged with having committed specific crimes before they can be brought to trial. If issued by a grand jury, such a charge is called an **indictment.**[29] A **grand jury** does not determine the guilt or innocence of an accused party; rather, its function is to determine, after hearing the state's evidence, whether a reasonable basis (probable cause) exists for supposing that a crime has been committed and whether a trial ought to be held.

Usually, grand juries are called in cases involving serious crimes, such as murder. For lesser crimes, an individual may be formally charged with a crime by an **information,** or criminal complaint. An information

---

29. Pronounced in-*dyte*-ment.

will be issued by a government prosecutor if the prosecutor determines that there is sufficient evidence to justify bringing the individual to trial.

TRIAL At a criminal trial, the accused person does not have to prove anything; the entire burden of proof is on the prosecutor (the state). As discussed at the beginning of this chapter, the burden of proof is higher in a criminal case than in a civil case. The prosecution must show that, based on all the evidence, the defendant's guilt is established *beyond a reasonable doubt.* If there is any reasonable doubt as to whether a criminal defendant did, in fact, commit the crime with which she or he has been charged, then the verdict must be "not guilty." Note that giving a verdict of "not guilty" is not the same as stating that the defendant is innocent; it merely means that not enough evidence was properly presented to the court to prove guilt beyond all reasonable doubt.

Courts have complex rules about what types of evidence may be presented and how the evidence may be brought out in criminal cases, especially in jury trials. These rules are designed to ensure that evidence presented at trials is relevant, reliable, and not prejudicial toward the defendant. For example, under the Sixth Amendment, persons accused of a crime have the right to confront, in open court, the witnesses against them. Is a defendant's Sixth Amendment right to confront witnesses violated when, in a jury trial, witnesses who are reluctant to travel consequently testify by way of two-way video teleconferencing? That was the question in the following case.

| CASE 9.3 | **United States v. Yates** |

United States
Court of Appeals,
Eleventh Circuit, 2004.
391 F.3d 1182.

BACKGROUND AND FACTS *Anton Pusztai and Anita Yates were involved in operating an Internet pharmacy based in Clanton, Alabama, called the Norfolk Men's Clinic. They were charged in a federal district court with mail fraud and other crimes, including prescription drug–related offenses, in connection with the pharmacy. The government asked the court to allow two witnesses in Australia to testify at Pusztai and Yates's trial by means of a two-way video teleconference. The witnesses—Paul Christian, who allegedly processed customers' Internet payments for Pusztai and Yates, and Dr. Tibor Konkoly, whose name was allegedly used on Internet drug prescriptions—were "essential witnesses," according to the government. But "they are unwilling to travel to the United States" and "they are beyond the government's subpoena powers." Pusztai and Yates argued that allowing the testimony would violate their Sixth Amendment right to confront witnesses. The court allowed the witnesses to testify. A jury found Pusztai and Yates guilty. The defendants appealed to the U.S. Court of Appeals for the Eleventh Circuit.*

IN THE LANGUAGE OF THE COURT

COX, Circuit Judge.
* * * *

Pusztai and Yates contend that their Sixth Amendment confrontation rights were violated by the admission of testimony by two-way live video teleconference with the witnesses in Australia because it was not necessary to further an important public policy * * * .

* * * *

The Sixth Amendment provides: "In all criminal prosecutions, the accused shall enjoy the right * * * to be confronted with the witnesses against him." This clause, known as the Confrontation Clause, guarantees the defendant a face-to-face meeting with witnesses appearing before the trier of fact. But this guarantee is not without exception.

* * * [A] Maryland rule of criminal procedure * * * allows child victims of abuse to testify by one-way closed circuit television from outside the courtroom. In such a scenario, the defendant [can] see the testifying child witness on a video monitor, but the child witness [can] not see the defendant. * * * *[A] defendant's right to confront accusatory witnesses may be satisfied absent a physical, face-to-face confrontation at trial only where denial of such confrontation is necessary to further an important public policy* * * . [Emphasis added.]

* * * *

In its order, the district court * * * permit[ted] the Australian witnesses to testify by two-way video teleconference before the court in the United States Attorney's Office in Montgomery, Alabama.

* * * [T]he district court ruled that the testimony was necessary to further an important public policy. The court accepted the Government's contention that the testimony would serve the "important public policy of providing the fact-finder with crucial evidence," and found that "the Government also has an interest in expeditiously and justly resolving the case."

We accept the district court's rationale that the witnesses were necessary to the prosecution's case on at least some of the charges, as the record supports the Government's assertion that the testimony was crucial to a successful prosecution of the Defendants and aided expeditious resolution of the case. * * *

But the prosecutor's need for the testimony in order to make a case and expeditiously resolve it are not public policies that are important enough to outweigh a defendant's right to confront an accuser face-to-face. Comparing the public policy behind Maryland's rule—protection of certain children from trauma caused by confronting their attacker—with the policies offered in this case—providing the fact-finder with crucial prosecution evidence and expeditious resolution of the case—leaves us unconvinced that the policy justification in this case meets [the] standard for an important public policy.

The district court made no findings of fact that would support a conclusion that this case is different from any other criminal prosecution in which the Government would find it convenient to present testimony by two-way video teleconference. All criminal prosecutions include at least some evidence crucial to the Government's case, and there is no doubt that many criminal cases could be more expeditiously resolved were it not necessary for witnesses to appear at trial. If we were to approve introduction of testimony in this manner, on this record, every prosecutor could argue that providing crucial prosecution evidence and expeditious resolution of the case are important public policies that support the admission of testimony by two-way video teleconference.

The Sixth Amendment demands more. *The text of the Sixth Amendment does not suggest any open-ended exceptions from the confrontation requirement to be developed by the courts.* We therefore hold that providing the fact-finder with crucial prosecution evidence and expeditious resolution of the case, on the record before us, are not important public policies that justify the denial of actual confrontation between witness and defendant. [Emphasis added.]

CONTINUED

 **Continued**

DECISION AND REMEDY *The U.S Court of Appeals for the Eleventh Circuit reversed the decision of the lower court to allow the overseas witnesses to testify electronically and remanded the case for a new trial. The appellate court reasoned that the admission of the testimony via a live, two-way video teleconference violated the defendants' Sixth Amendment right to confront witnesses.*

WHAT IF THE FACTS WERE DIFFERENT? *Suppose that there was only one essential witness in Australia, Paul Christian, who was asked to attend the trial in the United States. Further suppose that Christian was undergoing an intensive course of chemotherapy and was too sick to travel. How might the fact that a witness is unable (as opposed to unwilling) to attend the trial affect the court's opinion on teleconferencing and the Sixth Amendment?*

FEDERAL SENTENCING GUIDELINES

In the past, persons who committed the same crime might receive very different sentences, depending on the judge hearing the case, the jurisdiction in which it was heard, and many other factors. In 1984, however, Congress passed the Sentencing Reform Act. This act created the U.S. Sentencing Commission, which was charged with the task of standardizing sentences for federal crimes. The commission's guidelines, which became effective in 1987, established a range of possible penalties for each federal crime but *required* the judge to select a sentence from within that range. In other words, the guidelines established a mandatory system because judges were not allowed to deviate from the specified sentencing range.

In 2005, the Supreme Court held that certain provisions of the federal sentencing guidelines were unconstitutional. We look at these guidelines in this chapter's *Emerging Trends* feature on pages 200 and 201.

The U.S. Sentencing Commission has also established guidelines, which went into effect in 1991, that encourage stiffer penalties for white-collar crimes, including mail and wire fraud, commercial bribery and kickbacks, and money laundering. In addition, the commission recommended increased penalties for criminal violations of employment laws (see Chapters 33 and 34), securities laws (see Chapter 41), and antitrust laws (see Chapter 46).[30] The guidelines set forth a number of factors that judges should take into consideration when imposing a sentence for a specified crime. These factors include the defendant company's history of past violations, the extent of management's cooperation with federal investigators, and the extent to which the firm has undertaken spe-

cific programs and procedures to prevent criminal activities by its employees.

SECTION 8 | Cyber Crimes

Some years ago, the American Bar Association defined **computer crime** as any act that is directed against computers and computer parts, that uses computers as instruments of crime, or that involves computers and constitutes abuse. Today, because much of the crime committed with the use of computers occurs in cyberspace, many computer crimes fall under the broad label of **cyber crime.**

As we mentioned earlier, most cyber crimes are not "new" crimes. Rather, they are existing crimes in which the Internet is the instrument of wrongdoing. The challenge for law enforcement is to apply traditional laws—which were designed to protect persons from physical harm or to safeguard their physical property—to crimes committed in cyberspace. Here we look at several types of activity that constitute cyber crimes against persons or property. Other cyber crimes will be discussed in later chapters as they relate to particular topics, such as banking or consumer law.

CYBER THEFT

In cyberspace, thieves are not subject to the physical limitations of the "real" world. A thief can steal data stored in a networked computer with Internet access from anywhere on the globe. Only the speed of the connection and the thief's computer equipment limit the quantity of data that can be stolen.

FINANCIAL CRIMES Computer networks also provide opportunities for employees to commit crimes that can involve serious economic losses. For example, employees of a company's accounting department can

---

30. As required by the Sarbanes-Oxley Act of 2002, the U.S. Sentencing Commission revised its guidelines in 2003 to impose stiffer penalties for corporate securities fraud—see Chapter 41.

transfer funds among accounts with little effort and often with less risk than would be involved in transactions evidenced by paperwork.

Generally, the dependence of businesses on computer operations has left firms vulnerable to sabotage, fraud, embezzlement, and the theft of proprietary data, such as trade secrets or other intellectual property. As noted in Chapter 8, the piracy of intellectual property via the Internet is one of the most serious legal challenges facing lawmakers and the courts today.

IDENTITY THEFT A form of cyber theft that has become particularly troublesome in recent years is **identity theft.** Identity theft occurs when the wrongdoer steals a form of identification—such as a name, date of birth, and Social Security number—and uses the information to access the victim's financial resources. This crime existed to a certain extent before the widespread use of the Internet. Thieves would "steal" calling-card numbers by watching people using public telephones, or they would rifle through garbage to find bank account or credit-card numbers. The identity thieves would then use the calling-card or credit-card numbers or would withdraw funds from the victims' accounts.

The Internet, however, has turned identity theft into perhaps the fastest-growing financial crime in the United States. From the identity thief's perspective, the Internet provides those who steal information offline with an easy medium for using items such as stolen credit-card numbers while remaining protected by anonymity. An estimated 10 million Americans are victims of identity theft each year, and annual losses are estimated to exceed $50 billion.

CYBERSTALKING

California enacted the first stalking law in 1990, in response to the murders of six women—including Rebecca Schaeffer, a television star—by men who had harassed them. The law made it a crime to harass or follow a person while making a "credible threat" that puts that person in reasonable fear for his or her safety or the safety of the person's immediate family.[31] Since then, all other states have enacted some form of stalking laws. In about half of the states these laws require a physical act (following the victim).

Cyberstalkers (stalkers who commit their crimes in cyberspace), however, find their victims through Internet chat rooms, Usenet newsgroups or other bulletin boards, or e-mail. To close this "loophole" in existing stalking laws, more than three-fourths of the states now have laws specifically designed to combat cyberstalking and other forms of online harassment.

Note that cyberstalking can be even more threatening than physical stalking in some respects. While it takes a great deal of effort to physically stalk someone, it is relatively easy to harass a victim with electronic messages. Furthermore, the possibility of personal confrontation may discourage a stalker from actually following a victim. This disincentive is removed in cyberspace. Also, there is always the possibility that a cyberstalker will eventually pose a physical threat to her or his target. Finally, the Internet makes it easier to obtain information about the victim, such as where he or she lives or works, because numerous companies provide online investigation and information services.

HACKING

Persons who use one computer to break into another are sometimes referred to as **hackers.** Hackers who break into computers without authorization often commit cyber theft. Sometimes, however, their principal aim is to prove how smart they are by gaining access to others' password-protected computers and causing random data errors or making toll telephone calls for free.[32]

It is difficult to know just how frequently hackers succeed in breaking into databases across the United States. The FBI estimates that only 25 percent of all corporations that suffer such security breaches report the incident to a law enforcement agency. For one thing, corporations do not want it to become publicly known that the security of their data has been breached. For another, admitting to a breach would be admitting to a certain degree of incompetence, which could damage their reputations.

CYBERTERRORISM

Cyberterrorists are also hackers, but rather than trying to gain attention, they strive to remain undetected so that they can exploit computers to achieve harmful impacts. Just as "real" terrorists destroyed the World Trade Center towers and a portion of the Pentagon in

---

31. Ca. Penal Code Section 646.9.

32. The total cost of crime on the Internet is estimated to be several billion dollars annually, but two-thirds of that total is said to consist of unpaid-for toll calls.

The New Advisory Nature of the Federal Sentencing Guidelines

Until 2005, federal judges were required to consult a 1,800-page book that provided *mandatory* federal sentencing guidelines for hundreds of federal crimes. Congress's intent was to impose uniformity in the punishment aspect of the federal criminal justice system. Additionally, over the last several decades, Congress has wanted to appear "tough on crime."

Some federal judges felt uneasy about imposing long prison sentences on certain criminal defendants, particularly on first-time offenders and in illegal-substances cases involving small quantities of drugs. Consider, for example, the punishment of Weldon Angelos. Angelos, a twenty-four-year-old executive of a music company, had no criminal record. Nonetheless, in November 2004 Angelos was sentenced to fifty-five years in federal prison for selling a total of 1.5 pounds of marijuana to a government informant. Judge Paul Cassell of the U.S. District Court for the District of Utah noted that Angelos's sentence was "far in excess of the sentences imposed for such serious crimes as aircraft hijacking, second-degree murder, espionage, kidnapping, aggravated assault, and rape." Cassell went so far as to urge President George W. Bush to commute the sentence, calling it "unjust, cruel, and irrational." The judge was forced to impose it, though, because of mandatory sentencing rules.[a]

FINDING UNCONSTITUTIONALITY IN STATE SENTENCING GUIDELINES

While federal judges both publicly and privately have complained about federal sentencing guidelines for years, it was not until 2004 that the Supreme Court considered the constitutionality of state mandatory sentencing guidelines. In *Blakely v. Washington*,[b] the defendant, Ralph Blakely, pleaded guilty to kidnapping his estranged wife. According to the Washington state sentencing guidelines, his admission alone supported a maximum sentence of fifty-three months. The judge—but not the jury—learned that he had acted with deliberate cruelty. The sentencing judge therefore imposed a ninety-month sentence because of the cruelty issue, which was a statutorily granted reason to depart from the standard sentencing range. Blakely appealed the sentence. He argued that he had a federal constitutional right to have a jury determine beyond a reasonable doubt all of the facts legally essential to his sentence and that this right had been violated. Ultimately, the United States Supreme Court overturned the sentence. The Court relied on its ruling in a previous case in which it had held that "any fact that increases the penalty for a crime beyond the prescribed statutory minimum must be submitted to a jury and proved beyond a reasonable doubt."[c] Interestingly, the Court in the *Blakely* case specifically noted that it was not ruling on the constitutionality of sentencing guidelines at the federal level—a topic it did not address until the following year.

THE SIXTH AMENDMENT AND UNITED STATES V. BOOKER

The Sixth Amendment to the Constitution guarantees a trial by jury. In 2005, in *United States v. Booker*,[d] the United States Supreme Court held that federal sentencing guidelines are subject to the jury trial requirements of the Sixth Amendment. The case involved Freddie Booker, who was arrested with 92.5 grams of crack cocaine in his possession. During questioning by police, he signed a written statement in which he admitted to selling an additional quantity—566 grams of crack cocaine—elsewhere. That statement was not introduced or used at the trial, though.

---

a. *United States v. Angelos*, 345 F.Supp.2d 1227 (D.Utah 2004).
b. 542 U.S. 296, 124 S.Ct. 2531, 159 L.Ed.2d 403 (2004).

c. *Apprendi v. New Jersey*, 530 U.S. 466, 120 S.Ct. 2348, 147 L.Ed.2d 435 (2000).
d. ___U.S.___, 125 S.Ct. 738, 160 L.Ed.2d 621 (2005).

September 2001, cyberterrorists might explode "logic bombs" to shut down central computer systems. Such activities can pose a danger to national security.

Businesses may also be targeted by cyberterrorists. A hacking operation might engage in a wholesale theft of data, such as a merchant's customer files, or monitor a computer to discover a business firm's plans and transactions. A cyberterrorist might also want to insert false codes or data. For example, by hacking into the processing-control system of a food manufacturer, a cyberterrorist might alter the levels of ingredients so that consumers of the food would become ill. A cyberterrorist attack on a major financial institution, such as the New York Stock Exchange or a large bank, could leave securities or money markets in flux and seriously affect the daily lives of millions of citizens. Similarly, any prolonged disruption of computer, cable, satellite, or telecommunications systems due to the actions of expert hackers would have serious repercussions on business operations—and national security—on a

The jury convicted Booker of possessing and distributing more than 50 grams of crack cocaine based solely on the quantity of drugs in his possession at the time of the arrest. Under the federal sentencing guidelines, this offense carried a minimum sentence of ten years in prison and a maximum sentence of life in prison. At the posttrial sentencing hearing, however, the judge concluded that because Booker had admitted to possessing and selling an additional 566 grams of crack cocaine, he should receive an enhanced penalty. Applying the federal sentencing guidelines to this larger quantity of crack cocaine increased Booker's sentence from twenty-two to thirty years in prison.

The question before the Supreme Court was whether it is constitutionally permissible for the judge, instead of the jury, to make a factual determination that enhances the defendant's sentence under the federal sentencing guidelines. The Court ruled that it was not. "It has been settled throughout our history that the Constitution protects every criminal defendant 'against conviction except upon proof beyond a reasonable doubt of every fact necessary to constitute the crime with which he is charged.'"[e] Because the jury did not find beyond a reasonable doubt that Booker had possessed the additional 566 grams of crack, the court could not use this amount to enhance his sentence.

LOOKING TOWARD THE FUTURE

The ruling in *United States v. Booker* (and in a related case, *United States v. Fanfan*[f]) effectively eliminates the requirement that federal judges adhere precisely to the federal sentencing guidelines when setting criminal sentences. In other words, the guidelines are now just that—guidelines. They are

advisory rather than mandatory. Although trial judges must still consider the guidelines when sentencing criminal defendants, the judges now have more discretion. Depending on the circumstances of the case, a trial judge may depart from the guidelines if he or she believes that it is reasonable to do so. If a trial judge's decision is challenged as unreasonable, it will be up to an appellate court to decide the issue.

---

e. *In re Winship*, 397 U.S. 358, 90 S.Ct. 1068, 25 L.Ed.2d 368 (1970).
f. This case was consolidated with the *Booker* case on appeal before the United States Supreme Court. The lower court's decision in the *Fanfan* case is located at 2004 WL 1723114.

---

global level. Computer viruses are another tool that can be used by cyberterrorists to cripple communications networks.

PROSECUTING CYBER CRIMES

The "location" of cyber crime (cyberspace) has raised new issues in the investigation of crimes and the prosecution of offenders. A threshold issue is, of course, jurisdiction. A person who commits an act against a

business in California, where the act is a cyber crime, might never have set foot in California but might instead reside in New York, or even in Canada, where the act may not be a crime. If the crime was committed via e-mail, the question arises as to whether the e-mail would constitute sufficient "minimum contacts" (see Chapter 2) for the victim's state to exercise jurisdiction over the perpetrator.

Identifying the wrongdoers can also be difficult. Cyber criminals do not leave physical traces, such as fingerprints or DNA samples, as evidence of their crimes. Even electronic "footprints" can be hard to find and follow. For example, e-mail may be sent through a remailer, an online service that guarantees that a message cannot be traced to its source.

For these reasons, laws written to protect physical property are difficult to apply in cyberspace. Nonetheless, governments at both the state and federal levels have taken significant steps toward controlling cyber crime, both by applying existing criminal statutes and by enacting new laws that specifically address wrongs committed in cyberspace.

THE COMPUTER FRAUD AND ABUSE ACT

Perhaps the most significant federal statute specifically addressing cyber crime is the Counterfeit Access Device and Computer Fraud and Abuse Act of 1984 (commonly known as the Computer Fraud and Abuse Act, or CFAA). This act, as amended by the National

Information Infrastructure Protection Act of 1996,[33] provides, among other things, that a person who accesses a computer online, without authority, to obtain classified, restricted, or protected data (or attempts to do so) is subject to criminal prosecution. Such data could include financial and credit records, medical records, legal files, military and national security files, and other confidential information in government or private computers. The crime has two elements: accessing a computer without authority and taking the data.

This theft is a felony if it is committed for a commercial purpose or for private financial gain, or if the value of the stolen data (or computer time) exceeds $5,000. Penalties include fines and imprisonment for up to twenty years. A victim of computer theft can also bring a civil suit against the violator to obtain damages, an injunction, and other relief.

---

33. 18 U.S.C. Section 1030.

REVIEWING CRIMINAL LAW AND CYBER CRIMES

Edward Hanousek worked for Pacific & Arctic Railway and Navigation Company (P&A) as a roadmaster of the White Pass & Yukon Railroad in Alaska. Hanousek was responsible "for every detail of the safe and efficient maintenance and construction of track, structures and marine facilities of the entire railroad," including special projects. One project was a rock quarry, known as "6-mile," above the Skagway River. Next to the quarry, and just beneath the surface, ran a high-pressure oil pipeline owned by Pacific & Arctic Pipeline, Inc., P&A's sister company. When the quarry's backhoe operator punctured the pipeline, an estimated 1,000 to 5,000 gallons of oil were discharged into the river. Hanousek was charged with negligently discharging a harmful quantity of oil into a navigable water of the United States in violation of the criminal provisions of the Clean Water Act (CWA). Using the information presented in the chapter, answer the following questions.

1. | What are the two elements of criminal liability? Are both elements present in this case? Explain.

2. | Under which theory discussed in the chapter might Hanousek be found guilty of a crime?

3. | Could the quarry's backhoe operator who punctured the pipeline also be charged with a crime in this situation? Why or why not?

4. | Suppose that at trial, Hanousek argued that he could not be convicted because he was not aware of the requirements of the Clean Water Act. Would this defense be successful? Why or why not?

5. | If corporate actors were able to avoid responsibility for violations of environmental statutes of which they were unaware, what might result?

6. | Based solely on the facts given, are there any defenses to criminal liability that Hanousek could assert? Explain.

TERMS AND CONCEPTS TO REVIEW

actus reus 181	duress 189	larceny 183
arson 183	embezzlement 184	*mens rea* 181
beyond a reasonable doubt 178	entrapment 189	misdemeanor 180
burglary 183	exclusionary rule 190	money laundering 185
computer crime 198	felony 179	necessity 189
consent 188	forgery 183	petty offense 180
crime 178	grand jury 196	plea bargaining 190
cyber crime 198	hacker 199	robbery 182
cyberstalker 199	identity theft 199	self-defense 189
cyberterrorist 199	indictment 196	white-collar crime 184
double jeopardy 190	information 196	

QUESTIONS AND CASE PROBLEMS

9–1. The following situations are similar (in all of them, Juanita's television set is stolen), yet three different crimes are described. Identify the three crimes, noting the differences among them.

(a) While passing Juanita's house one night, Sarah sees a portable television set left unattended on Juanita's lawn. Sarah takes the television set, carries it home, and tells everyone she owns it.

(b) While passing Juanita's house one night, Sarah sees Juanita outside with a portable television set. Holding Juanita at gunpoint, Sarah forces her to give up the set. Then Sarah runs away with it.

(c) While passing Juanita's house one night, Sarah sees a portable television set in a window. Sarah breaks the front-door lock, enters, and leaves with the set.

9–2. Which, if any, of the following crimes necessarily involves illegal activity on the part of more than one person?

(a) Bribery.
(b) Forgery.
(c) Embezzlement.
(d) Larceny.
(e) Receiving stolen property.

9–3. QUESTION WITH SAMPLE ANSWER

Armington, while robbing a drugstore, shot and seriously injured a drugstore clerk, Jennings. Subsequently, in a criminal trial, Armington was convicted of armed robbery and assault and battery. Jennings later brought a civil (tort) suit against Armington for damages. Armington contended that he could not be tried again

for the same crime, as that would constitute double jeopardy, which is prohibited by the Fifth Amendment to the Constitution. Is Armington correct? Explain.
For a sample answer to this question, go to Appendix I at the end of this text.

9–4. Rafael stops Laura on a busy street and offers to sell her an expensive wristwatch for a fraction of its value. After some questioning by Laura, Rafael admits that the watch is stolen property, although he says he was not the thief. Laura pays for and receives the wristwatch. Has Laura committed any crime? Has Rafael? Explain.

9–5. **FIFTH AMENDMENT.** The federal government was investigating a corporation and its employees. The alleged criminal wrongdoing, which included the falsification of corporate books and records, occurred between 1993 and 1996 in one corporate division. In 1999, the corporation pled guilty and agreed to cooperate in an investigation of the individuals who might have been involved in the improper corporate activities. "Doe I," "Doe II," and "Doe III" were officers of the corporation during the period in which the illegal activities occurred and worked in the division where the wrongdoing took place. They were no longer employed by the corporation, however, when, as part of the subsequent investigation, the government asked them to provide specific corporate documents in their possession. All three asserted the Fifth Amendment privilege against self-incrimination. The government asked a federal district court to order the three to produce the records. Corporate employees can be compelled to produce corporate records in a criminal proceeding because they hold the records as representatives of the corporation, to which the Fifth Amendment privilege against self-incrimination does not apply. Should *former* employees also be compelled to produce corporate records in their possession? Why or why not? [*In re Three Grand Jury Subpoenas* Duces Tecum *Dated January 29, 1999,* 191 F.3d 173 (2d Cir. 1999)]

9–6. COMPUTER FRAUD. The District of Columbia Lottery Board licensed Soo Young Bae, a Washington, D.C., merchant, to operate a terminal that prints and dispenses lottery tickets for sale. Bae used the terminal to generate tickets with a face value of $525,586, for which he did not pay. The winning tickets among these had a total redemption value of $296,153, of which Bae successfully obtained all but $72,000. Bae pleaded guilty to computer fraud, and the court sentenced him to eighteen months in prison. In sentencing a defendant for fraud, a federal court must make a reasonable estimate of the victim's loss. The court determined that the value of the loss due to the fraud was $503,650—the market value of the tickets less the commission Bae would have received from the lottery board had he sold those tickets. Bae appealed, arguing that "[a]t the instant any lottery ticket is printed," it is worth whatever value the lottery drawing later assigns to it; that is, losing tickets have no value. Bae thus calculated the loss at $296,153, the value of his winning tickets. Should the U.S. Court of Appeals for the District of Columbia Circuit affirm or reverse Bae's sentence? Explain your answer. [*United States v. Bae,* 250 F.3d 774 (D.C.Cir. 2001)]

9–7. ⚖ CASE PROBLEM WITH SAMPLE ANSWER

The Sixth Amendment secures to a defendant who faces possible imprisonment the right to counsel at all critical stages of the criminal process, including the arraignment and the trial. In 1996, Felipe Tovar, a twenty-one-year-old college student, was arrested in Ames, Iowa, for operating a motor vehicle while under the influence of alcohol (OWI). Tovar was informed of his right to apply for court-appointed counsel and waived it. At his arraignment, he pleaded guilty. Six weeks later, he appeared for sentencing, again waived his right to counsel, and was sentenced to two days' imprisonment. In 1998, Tovar was convicted of OWI again, and in 2000, he was charged with OWI for a third time. In Iowa, a third OWI offense is a felony. Tovar asked the court not to use his first OWI conviction to enhance the third OWI charge. He argued that his 1996 waiver of counsel was not "intelligent" because the court did not make him aware of "the dangers and disadvantages of self-representation." What determines whether a person's choice in any situation is "intelligent"? What should determine whether a defendant's waiver of counsel is "intelligent" at critical stages of a criminal proceeding? [*Iowa v. Tovar,* 541 U.S. 77, 124 S.Ct. 1379, 158 L.Ed.2d 209 (2004)]

To view a sample answer for this case problem, go to this book's Web site at http://wbl.westbuslaw.com, select "Chapter 9," and click on "Case Problem with Sample Answer."

9–8. THEFT OF TRADE SECRETS. Four Pillars Enterprise Co. is a Taiwanese company owned by Pin Yen Yang. Avery Dennison, Inc., a U.S. corporation, is one of Four Pillars's chief competitors in the manufacture of adhesives. In 1989, Victor Lee, an Avery employee, met Yang and Yang's daughter Hwei Chen. They agreed to pay Lee $25,000 a year to serve as a consultant to Four Pillars. Over the next eight years, Lee supplied the Yangs with confidential Avery reports, including information that Four Pillars used to make a new adhesive that had been developed by Avery. The Federal Bureau of Investigation (FBI) confronted Lee, and he agreed to cooperate in an operation to catch the Yangs. When Lee next met the Yangs, he showed them documents provided by the FBI. The documents bore "confidential" stamps, and Lee said that they were Avery's confidential property. The FBI arrested the Yangs with the documents in their possession. The Yangs and Four Pillars were charged with, among other crimes, the attempted theft of trade secrets. The defendants argued in part that it was impossible for them to have committed this crime because the documents were not actually trade secrets. Should the court acquit them? Why or why not? [*United States v. Yang,* 281 F.3d 534 (6th Cir. 2002)]

9–9. LARCENY. In February 2001, a homeowner hired Jimmy Smith, a contractor claiming to employ a crew of thirty workers, to build a garage. The homeowner paid Smith $7,950 and agreed to make additional payments as needed to complete the project, up to $15,900. Smith promised to start the next day and finish within eight weeks. Nearly a month passed with no work, while Smith lied to the homeowner that materials were on "back order." During a second month, footings were created for the foundation, and a subcontractor poured the concrete slab, but Smith did not return the homeowner's phone calls. After eight weeks, the homeowner confronted Smith, who promised to complete the job, worked on the site that day until lunch, and never returned. Three months later, the homeowner again confronted Smith, who promised to "pay [him] off" later that day but did not do so. In March 2002, the state of Georgia filed criminal charges against Smith. While his trial was pending, he promised to pay the homeowner "next week" but again failed to refund any of the funds paid. The value of the labor performed before Smith abandoned the project was between $800 and $1,000, the value of the materials was $367, and the subcontractor was paid $2,270. Did Smith commit larceny? Explain. [*Smith v. State of Georgia,* 592 S.E.2d 871 (Ga.App. 2004)]

9–10. VIDEO QUESTION

Go to this text's Web site at **http://wbl.westbuslaw.com** and select "Chapter 9." Click on "Video Questions" and view the video titled *Casino.* Then answer the following questions.

(a) In the video, a casino manager, Ace (Robert DeNiro), discusses how politicians "won their 'comp life' when they got elected." "Comps" are the free gifts that casinos give to high-stakes gamblers to keep their business. If an elected official accepts comps, is he or she committing a crime? If so, what type of crime? Explain your answers.

(b) Assume that Ace committed a crime by giving politicians comps. Can the casino, Tangiers Corporation,

be held liable for that crime? Why or why not? How could a court punish the corporation?

(c) Suppose that the Federal Bureau of Investigation wants to search the premises of Tangiers for evidence of criminal activity. If casino management refuses to consent to the search, what constitutional safeguards and criminal procedures, if any, protect Tangiers?

LAW | on the Web

For updated links to resources available on the Web, as well as a variety of other materials, visit this text's Web site at http://wbl.westbuslaw.com.

The Bureau of Justice Statistics in the U.S. Department of Justice offers an impressive collection of statistics on crime at the following Web site:

http://www.ojp.usdoj.gov/bjs

For summaries of famous criminal cases and documents relating to these trials, go to Court TV's Web site at

http://www.courttv.com/index.html

Many state criminal codes are now online. To find your state's code, go to the following home page and select "State" under the link to "Laws: Cases and Codes:"

http://www.findlaw.com

You can learn about some of the constitutional questions raised by various criminal laws and procedures by going to the Web site of the American Civil Liberties Union at

http://www.aclu.org

The following Web site, which is maintained by the U.S. Department of Justice, offers information ranging from the various types of cyber crime to a description of how computers and the Internet are being used to prosecute cyber crime:

http://www.cybercrime.gov

LEGAL RESEARCH EXERCISES ON THE WEB

Go to http://wbl.westbuslaw.com, the Web site that accompanies this text. Select "Chapter 9" and click on "Internet Exercises." There you will find the following Internet research exercises that you can perform to learn more about topics covered in this chapter.

Activity 9–1: **LEGAL PERSPECTIVE**
Revisiting *Miranda*

Activity 9–2: **MANAGEMENT PERSPECTIVE**
Hackers

Activity 9–3: **INTERNATIONAL PERSPECTIVE**
Fighting Cyber Crime Worldwide

Torts and Crimes

Ethical and legal concepts are often closely intertwined. This is because the common law, as it evolved in England and then in America, reflects society's values and customs. This connection between law and ethics is clearly evident in the area of tort law, which provides remedies for harms caused by actions that society has deemed wrongful. Criminal law is also rooted in common law concepts of right and wrong behavior, although common law concepts governing criminal acts are now expressed in, or replaced by, federal, state, and local criminal statutes. The number of torts and crimes has continued to expand as new ways to commit wrongs have been discovered.

The laws governing torts, crimes, and intellectual property—the areas of law covered in the previous unit—constitute an important part of the legal environment of business. In each of these areas, new legal (and ethical) challenges have emerged as a result of developments in technology. Today, we are witnessing some of the challenges posed by the use of new communications networks, particularly the Internet. In this *Focus on Ethics,* we look at the ethical dimensions of selected topics discussed in the preceding chapters, including some issues that are unique to the cyber age.

Privacy Rights in an Online World

Privacy rights are protected under constitutional law, tort law, and various federal and state statutes. How to protect privacy rights in an online world, though, has been a recurring question over the last ten years. One problem is that individuals today often cannot even know what kind of information on their personal lives and preferences is being collected by Internet companies and other online users. Nor can they know how that information will be used. "Cookies" installed in computers may allow users' Web movements to be tracked. Furthermore, any person who wants to purchase goods from online merchants or auctions inevitably must reveal some personal information, including (often) a credit-card number.

The Increased Value of Personal Information One of the major concerns of consumers in recent years has been the increasing value of personal information for online marketers, who are willing to pay a high price to those who collect and sell them such information. Because of these concerns—and the possibility of lawsuits based on privacy laws—businesses marketing goods online need to exercise care. Today, it is commonplace for an online business to create and post on its Web site a privacy policy disclosing how any information obtained from its customers will be used.

The Duty of Care and Personal Information Selling data can bolster a company's profits, which may satisfy the firm's duty to its owners, but when the information is personal, its sale may violate an ethical or legal duty. In what circumstances might a party who sells information about someone else have a duty to that other party with respect to the sale of the information?

Gradually, the courts are providing some answers to this question. In one case, for example, a man contacted an Internet-based investigation and information service and requested information about Amy Boyer. The man provided his name, address, and phone number and paid the fee online using his credit card. In return, the company provided him with Boyer's home address, birth date, Social Security number, and work address. The man then drove to Boyer's workplace and fatally shot her, after which the police discovered that the man maintained a Web site that referred to stalking and killing Boyer. Boyer's mother filed suit against the company for disclosing her daughter's private information without investigating the reason for the request. The state supreme court found that because the threats of stalking and identity theft were sufficiently foreseeable, the company had a duty to exercise reasonable care in disclosing a third person's personal information to a client.[1]

Privacy Rights in the Workplace Another area of concern today is the extent to which employees' privacy rights should be protected in the workplace. Traditionally, employees have been afforded a certain "zone of privacy" in the workplace. For example, the courts have concluded that employees have a reasonable expectation of privacy with respect to personal items contained in their desks or in their lockers. Should this zone of privacy extend to personal e-mail sent via the employer's computer system as well? This question and others relating to employee privacy rights in today's cyber age will be discussed in greater detail in Chapter 33, in the context of employment law.

Should Civil Liberties Be Sacrificed to Control Cyber Crime?

Another issue that has come to the forefront in the cyber age is whether it is possible to control cyber crime without sacrificing some civil liberties. Governments in certain countries, such as Russia, have succeeded in controlling Internet crime to some extent by monitoring the e-mail and other electronic transmissions of users of specific Internet

---

1. *Remsburg v. Docusearch, Inc.,* 149 N.H. 148, 816 A.2d 1001 (2003).

service providers. In the United States, however, any government attempt to monitor Internet use to detect criminal conspiracies or terrorist activities does not sit well with the American people. The traditional attitude has been that civil liberties must be safeguarded to the greatest extent feasible.

After the terrorist attacks in September 2001, Congress enacted legislation, including the USA Patriot Act mentioned in Chapter 4. These statutes gave law enforcement personnel more authority to conduct electronic surveillance, such as monitoring Web sites and e-mail exchanges. For a time, it seemed that the terrorist attacks might have made Americans less reluctant to trade off some of their civil liberties for greater national security. Today, though, many complain that this legislation has gone too far in curbing traditional civil liberties guaranteed by the U.S. Constitution. As the types of Internet crimes and torts continue to expand, determining the degree to which individuals should sacrifice personal freedoms in exchange for greater protection will likely become even more difficult.

Who Should Be Held Liable for Computer Viruses?

As everybody knows, viruses sent into cyberspace can cause significant damage to the computer systems they "infect." To date, adapting tort law to virus-caused damages has been difficult because it is not clear who should be held liable for these damages. For example, who should be held liable for damages caused by the "ILOVEYOU" virus that spread around the globe in 2000 and caused an estimated $10 billion in damage?

Of course, the person who wrote the virus is responsible. But what about the producer of the e-mail software that the virus accessed to spread itself so rapidly? What about the antivirus software companies? Were they negligent in failing to market products that could have identified and disabled the virus before damage occurred? Should the users themselves share part of the blame? After all, even after the virus had received widespread publicity, users continued to open e-mail attachments containing the virus.

Clearly, the courts have yet to determine what tort duties apply in cyberspace and the point at which one of these duties is breached. In the meantime, legal and ethical issues posed by computer viruses will continue to arise.

Do Gun Makers Have a Duty to Warn?

One of the issues facing today's courts is how tort law principles apply to harms caused by guns. Across the nation, many plaintiffs have filed negligence actions against gun manufacturers claiming that gun makers have a duty to warn users of their products of the dangers associated with gun use. Would it be fair to impose such a requirement on gun manufacturers? Some say no, because such dangers are "open and obvious." (Recall from Chapter 7 that manufacturers and

sellers do not have a duty to warn of open and obvious dangers.) Others contend that warnings could prevent numerous gun accidents.

State courts addressing this issue have generally ruled that manufacturers have no duty to warn users of the obvious risks associated with gun use. For example, New York's highest court has held that a gun manufacturer's duty of care does not extend to those who are injured by the illegal use of handguns.[2] Several state courts also have found that makers of BB guns and air rifles have no duty to warn users of the risks.[3] Some courts, however, have held that gun makers whose marketing or sales practices cause a large influx of guns into the illegal secondary market could be liable under a public nuisance theory.[4]

Should the Courts Cancel Existing Trademarks That Are Disparaging?

The Lanham Act prohibits the U.S. Patent and Trademark Office from registering trademarks that are immoral, scandalous, or disparaging (demeaning). Trademark examiners review new proposals and reject any new trademarks that are disparaging by today's standards. But what happens when a trademark that was registered some time ago is perceived as disparaging to a group of people today? Can that registration be canceled? According to a federal district court in 2003, the answer is no. The case involved the Washington Redskins, a professional football team, and six Native Americans (the plaintiffs) who claimed that the term *Redskins* was the most derogatory one used for native people and the trademark should be canceled.

The federal district court held that the plaintiffs had not presented enough evidence to prove that the mark was disparaging. According to the court, the test is not whether the term is disparaging to Native Americans today but whether it was disparaging at the time it was originally registered. At trial, the plaintiffs presented evidence that a number of Native Americans found the term insulting today. The plaintiffs also presented some evidence, including survey results and the testimony of historians and linguists, to suggest that the mark was disparaging when it was first registered in 1967. The court found that this evidence was insufficient, however, and held that the plaintiffs had waited too long to complain about the trademark.[5] Given that what society considers disparaging often changes over time, some have contended that this ruling is unfair.

---

2. *Hamilton v. Beretta U.S.A. Corp.*, 96 N.Y.2d 222, 750 N.E.2d 1055, 727 N.Y.S.2d 7 (2001).
3. *Abney v. Crosman Corp.*, ___So.2d ___ (Ala. 2005); *Marzullo v. Crosman Corp.*, 289 F.Supp.2d 1337 (M.D.Fla. 2003).
4. *City of New York v. Beretta U.S.A. Corp.*, F.Supp.2d 256 (E.D.N.Y. 2004); *Johnson v. Bryco Arms*, 304 F.Supp.2d 383 (E.D.N.Y. 2004); *City of Gary ex rel. King v. Smith & Wessen Corp.*, 801 N.E.2d 1222 (Ind. 2003); *Ileto v. Glock, Inc.*, 349 F.3d 1191 (9th Cir. 2003).
5. *Pro-Football, Inc. v. Harjo*, 284 F.Supp.2d 96 (D.D.C. 2003).

Trademark Protection versus Free Speech Rights

Another legal issue involving questions of fairness pits the rights of trademark owners against the right to free speech. The issue—so-called cybergriping—is unique to the cyber age.

Cybergriping Cybergripers are individuals who complain in cyberspace about corporate products, services, or activities. For trademark owners, the issue becomes particularly thorny when cybergriping sites add the word *sucks* or *stinks* or some other disparaging term to the domain name of the mark's owners. These sites, sometimes referred to collectively as "sucks" sites, are established solely for the purpose of criticizing the products or services sold by the owners of the marks.

The Question of Trademark Infringement A number of companies have sued the owners of such sites for trademark infringement in the hope that a court or an arbitrating panel will order the site owner to cease using the domain name. To date, however, companies have had little success pursuing this alternative.

In one case, for example, Bally Total Fitness Holding Corporation sued Andrew Faber, who had established a "Bally sucks" site for the purpose of criticizing Bally's health clubs and business practices. Bally claimed that Faber had infringed on its trademark. The court did not agree, holding that the "speech"—consumer commentary—on Faber's Web site was protected by the First Amendment. According to the court, "The explosion of the Internet is not without its growing pains. It is an efficient means for businesses to disseminate information, but it also affords critics of those businesses an equally efficient means of disseminating commentary." In short, Bally could not look to trademark law for a remedy against cyber critics.[6]

Generally, the courts have been reluctant to hold that the use of a business's domain name in a "sucks" site infringes on the trademark owner's rights. After all, one of the primary reasons trademarks are protected under U.S. law is to prevent customers from becoming confused over the origins of the goods for sale—and a cybergriping site would certainly not create such confusion. Furthermore, American courts give extensive protection to free speech rights, including the right to express opinions about companies and their products.[7]

Trade Secrets versus Free Speech Rights

Another ongoing issue with ethical dimensions is the point at which free speech rights come into conflict with the right of copyright holders to protect their property by using encryption technology. This issue came before the California Supreme Court in 2003 in the case of *DVD Copy Control Association v. Bunner.*[8] Trade associations in the movie industry (the plaintiffs) sued an Internet Web site operator (the defendant) who had posted the code of a computer program that cracked technology used to encrypt DVDs. This posed a significant threat to the plaintiffs because, by using the code-cracking software, users would be able to duplicate the copyrighted movies stored on the DVDs.

In their suit, the plaintiffs claimed that the defendant had misappropriated trade secrets. The defendant argued that software programs designed to break encryption programs were a form of constitutionally protected speech. When the case reached the California Supreme Court, the court held that although the First Amendment applies to computer code, computer code is not a form of "pure speech" and the courts can therefore protect it to a lesser extent. The court reinstated the trial court's order that enjoined (prevented) the defendant from continuing to post the code.

DISCUSSION QUESTIONS

1. Some observers maintain that privacy rights are quickly becoming a thing of the past. In your opinion, is it possible to protect privacy rights in today's online world?

2. Many argue that the federal government should not be allowed to monitor the Internet activities and e-mail exchanges of its citizens. Yet, such monitoring goes a long way toward keeping Americans safe from terrorism. Where should the line be drawn between justifiable and unjustifiable governmental interference with American citizens' civil liberties?

3. Suppose that it could be documented that a certain computer virus caused $15 million in damages across the nation. Should the person who created and launched the virus (assuming he or she is caught) be held solely responsible for the damages? Should other parties, including companies that market antivirus software and computer users who are careless in preventing virus-caused damages, also be subject to liability under a theory of comparative negligence?

4. In your opinion, should gun manufacturers have a duty to warn gun users of the dangers of using guns? Would such a warning be effective in preventing gun-related accidents?

5. Generally, do you believe that the law has struck a fair balance between the rights of intellectual property owners and the rights of the public?

---

6. *Bally Total Fitness Holding Corp. v. Faber*, 29 F.Supp.2d 1161 (C.D.Cal. 1998).

7. Many businesses have concluded that while they cannot control what people say about them, they can make it more difficult for it to be said. Today, businesses commonly register such insulting domain names before the cybergripers themselves can register them.

---

8. 31 Cal.4th 864, 75 P.3d 1, 4 Cal.Rptr.3d 69 (2003).

UNIT THREE
Contracts and E-Contracts

CONTENTS

Nature and Terminology

The noted legal scholar Roscoe Pound once said that "[t]he social order rests upon the stability and predictability of conduct, of which keeping promises is a large item."[1] Contract law deals with, among other things, the formation and keeping of promises. A **promise** is a person's assurance that the person will or will not do something.

Like other types of law, contract law reflects our social values, interests, and expectations at a given point in time. It shows, for example, to what extent our society allows people to make promises or commitments that are legally binding. It distinguishes between promises that create only *moral* obligations (such as a promise to take a friend to lunch) and promises that are legally binding (such as a promise to pay for merchandise purchased). Contract law also demonstrates what excuses our society accepts for breaking certain types of promises. In addition, it indicates what promises are considered to be contrary to public policy—against the interests of society as a whole—and therefore legally invalid. When the person making a promise is a child or is mentally incompetent, for example, a question will arise as to whether the promise should be enforced. Resolving such questions is the essence of contract law.

SECTION 1 | An Overview of Contract Law

Before we look at the numerous rules that courts use to determine whether a particular promise will be enforced, it is necessary to understand some fundamental concepts of contract law. In this section, we describe the sources and general function of contract law. We also provide the definition of a contract and introduce the objective theory of contracts.

SOURCES OF CONTRACT LAW

The common law governs all contracts except when it has been modified or replaced by statutory law, such as the Uniform Commercial Code (UCC),[2] or by administrative agency regulations. Contracts relating to services, real estate, employment, and insurance, for example, generally are governed by the common law of contracts.

Contracts for the sale and lease of goods, however, are governed by the UCC—to the extent that the UCC has modified general contract law. The relationship between general contract law and the law governing sales and leases of goods will be explored in detail in Chapter 20. In the discussion of general contract law that follows, we indicate in footnotes the areas in which the UCC has significantly altered common law contract principles.

THE FUNCTION OF CONTRACT LAW

The law encourages competent parties to form contracts for lawful objectives. Indeed, no aspect of modern life is entirely free of contractual relationships. Even the ordinary consumer in his or her daily activities acquires rights and obligations based on contract law. You acquire rights and obligations, for example, when you purchase a DVD or when you borrow funds to buy a house. Contract law is designed to provide stability and predictability, as well as certainty, for both buyers and sellers in the marketplace.

Contract law deals with, among other things, the formation and enforcement of agreements between

---

1. R. Pound, *Jurisprudence*, Vol. 3 (St. Paul: West Publishing Co., 1959), p. 162.
2. See Chapters 1 and 20 for further discussions of the significance and coverage of the UCC. The UCC is presented in Appendix C at the end of this book.

parties (in Latin, *pacta sunt servanda*—"agreements shall be kept"). By supplying procedures for enforcing private contractual agreements, contract law provides an essential condition for the existence of a market economy. Without a legal framework of reasonably assured expectations within which to plan and venture, businesspersons would be able to rely only on the good faith of others. Duty and good faith are usually sufficient to obtain compliance with a promise, but when price changes or adverse economic factors make compliance costly, these elements may not be enough. Contract law is necessary to ensure compliance with a promise or to entitle the innocent party to some form of relief.

DEFINITION OF A CONTRACT

A **contract** is "a promise or a set of promises for the breach of which the law gives a remedy, or the performance of which the law in some way recognizes as a duty."[3] Put simply, a contract is a legally binding agreement between two or more parties who agree to perform or to refrain from performing some act now or in the future. Generally, contract disputes arise when there is a promise of future performance. If the contractual promise is not fulfilled, the party who made it is subject to the sanctions of a court (see Chapter 18). That party may be required to pay damages for failing to perform the contractual promise; in limited instances, the party may be required to perform the promised act.

THE OBJECTIVE THEORY OF CONTRACTS

In determining whether a contract has been formed, the element of intent is of prime importance. In contract law, intent is determined by what is called the **objective theory of contracts,** not by the personal or subjective intent, or belief, of a party. The theory is that a party's intention to enter into a legally binding agreement, or contract, is judged by outward, objective facts as interpreted by a *reasonable* person, rather than by the party's own secret, subjective intentions.

Objective facts include (1) what the party said when entering into the contract, (2) how the party acted or appeared (intent may be manifested by conduct as well as by oral or written words), and (3) the circumstances surrounding the transaction. We will look further at the objective theory of contracts in Chapter 11, in the context of contract formation.

SECTION 2 | Elements of a Contract

The many topics that will be discussed in the following chapters on contract law require an understanding of the basic elements of a valid contract and the way in which a contract is created. The topics to be covered in this unit on contracts also require an understanding of the types of circumstances in which even legally valid contracts will not be enforced.

REQUIREMENTS OF A VALID CONTRACT

The following list briefly describes the four requirements that must be met before a valid contract exists. If any of these elements is lacking, no contract will have been formed. (Each requirement will be explained more fully in subsequent chapters.)

1. *Agreement.* An agreement to form a contract includes an *offer* and an *acceptance*. One party must offer to enter into a legal agreement, and another party must accept the terms of the offer.

2. *Consideration.* Any promises made by the parties to the contract must be supported by legally sufficient and bargained-for *consideration* (something of value received or promised, such as money, to convince a person to make a deal).

3. *Contractual capacity.* Both parties entering into the contract must have the contractual *capacity* to do so; the law must recognize them as possessing characteristics that qualify them as competent parties.

4. *Legality.* The contract's purpose must be to accomplish some goal that is legal and not against public policy.

DEFENSES TO THE ENFORCEABILITY OF A CONTRACT

Even if all of the above-listed requirements are satisfied, a contract may be unenforceable if the following requirements are not met. These requirements typically are raised as *defenses* to the enforceability of an otherwise valid contract.

---

3. *Restatement (Second) of Contracts.* The *Restatement of the Law of Contracts* is a nonstatutory, authoritative exposition of the common law of contracts compiled by the American Law Institute in 1932. The *Restatement,* which is now in its second edition (a third edition is being drafted), will be referred to throughout the following chapters on contract law.

1. *Genuineness of assent.* The apparent consent of both parties must be genuine. For example, if a contract was formed as a result of fraud, undue influence, mistake, or duress, the contract may not be enforceable.

2. *Form.* The contract must be in whatever form the law requires; for example, some contracts must be in writing to be enforceable.

SECTION 3 | Types of Contracts

There are many types of contracts. In this section, you will learn that contracts can be categorized based on legal distinctions as to formation, performance, and enforceability.

CONTRACT FORMATION

As you can see in Exhibit 10–1, three classifications, or categories, of contracts are based on how and when a contract is formed. We explain each of these types of contracts in the following subsections.

BILATERAL VERSUS UNILATERAL CONTRACTS

Every contract involves at least two parties. The **offeror** is the party making the offer. The **offeree** is the party to whom the offer is made. Whether the contract is classified as *unilateral* or *bilateral* depends on what the offeree must do to accept the offer and to bind the offeror to a contract.

——*Bilateral Contracts.* If to accept the offer the offeree must only *promise* to perform, the contract is a **bilateral contract.** Hence, a bilateral contract is a "promise for a promise." No performance, such as payment of money or delivery of goods, need take place for a bilateral contract to be formed. The contract comes into existence at the moment the promises are exchanged.

For example, Jeff offers to buy Ann's digital camera for $200. Jeff tells Ann that he will give her the money for the camera next Friday, when he gets paid. Ann accepts Jeff's offer and promises to give him the camera when he pays her on Friday. Jeff and Ann have formed a bilateral contract.

——*Unilateral Contracts.* If the offer is phrased so that the offeree can accept the offer only by completing the contract performance, the contract is a **unilateral contract.** Hence, a unilateral contract is a "promise for an act."[4] In other words, the time of contract formation in a unilateral contract is not at the moment when promises are exchanged but when the contract is *performed.* A classic example of a unilateral contract is as follows: O'Malley says to Parker, "If you carry this package across the Brooklyn Bridge, I'll give you $20." Only on Parker's complete crossing with the package does she fully accept O'Malley's offer to pay $20. If she chooses not to undertake the walk, there are no legal consequences.

Contests, lotteries, and other competitions involving prizes are examples of offers to form unilateral con-

---

4. Clearly, a contract cannot be "one sided," because, by definition, an agreement implies the existence of two or more parties. Therefore, the phrase *unilateral contract,* if read literally, is a contradiction in terms. As traditionally used in contract law, however, the phrase refers to the kind of contract that results when only one promise is being made (the promise made by the offeror in return for the offeree's performance).

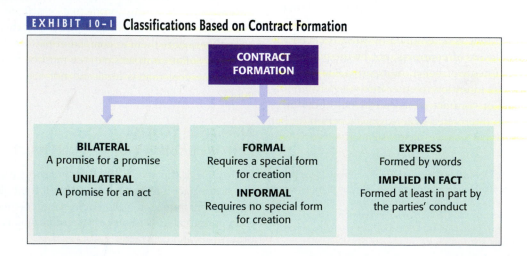

EXHIBIT 10-1 **Classifications Based on Contract Formation**

CONTRACT FORMATION

| BILATERAL A promise for a promise UNILATERAL A promise for an act | FORMAL Requires a special form for creation INFORMAL Requires no special form for creation | EXPRESS Formed by words IMPLIED IN FACT Formed at least in part by the parties' conduct |

tracts. If a person complies with the rules of the contest—such as by submitting the right lottery number at the right place and time—a unilateral contract is formed, binding the organization offering the prize to a contract to perform as promised in the offer.

Can a school's, or an employer's, letter of tentative acceptance to a prospective student, or a possible employee, qualify as a unilateral contract? That was the issue in the following case.

CASE 10.1 — Ardito v. City of Providence

United States District Court, District of Rhode Island, 2003. 263 F.Supp.2d 358.

BACKGROUND AND FACTS *In 2001, the city of Providence, Rhode Island, decided to begin hiring police officers to fill vacancies in its police department. Because only individuals who had graduated from the Providence Police Academy were eligible, the city also decided to conduct two training sessions, the "60th and 61st Police Academies." To be admitted, an applicant had to pass a series of tests and be deemed qualified by members of the department after an interview. The applicants judged most qualified were sent a letter informing them that they had been selected to attend the academy if they successfully completed a medical checkup and a psychological examination. The letter for the applicants to the 61st Academy, dated October 15, stated that it was "a conditional offer of employment." Meanwhile, a new chief of police, Dean Esserman, decided to revise the selection process, which caused some of those who had received the letter to be rejected. Derek Ardito and thirteen other newly rejected applicants—who had all completed the examinations—filed a suit in a federal district court against the city, seeking a halt to the 61st Academy unless they were allowed to attend. They alleged in part that the city was in breach of contract.*

IN THE LANGUAGE OF THE COURT
ERNEST C. TORRES, Chief District Judge.
* * * *

* * * [T]he October 15 letter * * * *is a classic example of an offer to enter into a unilateral contract.* The October 15 letter expressly stated that it was a "conditional offer of employment" and the message that it conveyed was that the recipient would be admitted into the 61st Academy if he or she successfully completed the medical and psychological examinations, requirements that the city could not lawfully impose unless it was making a conditional offer of employment. [Emphasis added.]

Moreover, the terms of that offer were perfectly consistent with what applicants had been told when they appeared [for their interviews]. At that time, [Police Major Dennis] Simoneau informed them that, if they "passed" the [interviews], they would be offered a place in the academy provided that they also passed medical and psychological examinations.

The October 15 letter also was in marked contrast to notices sent to applicants by the city at earlier stages of the selection process. Those notices merely informed applicants that they had completed a step in the process and remained eligible to be considered for admission into the academy. Unlike the October 15 letter, the prior notices did not purport to extend a "conditional offer" of admission.

The plaintiffs accepted the city's offer of admission into the academy by satisfying the specified conditions. Each of the plaintiffs submitted to and passed lengthy and intrusive medical and psychological examinations. In addition, many of the plaintiffs, in reliance on the City's offer, jeopardized their standing with their existing employers by notifying the employers of their anticipated departure, and some plaintiffs passed up opportunities for other employment.

* * * *

The city argues that there is no contract between the parties because the plaintiffs have no legally enforceable right to employment. The city correctly points out that, even if the plaintiffs graduate from the Academy and there are existing vacancies in the department, they would be required to serve a one-year probationary period during which they could be

CONTINUED ▶

CASE 10.1 | **Continued**

terminated without cause * * * . That argument misses the point. The contract that the plaintiffs seek to enforce is not a contract that they will be appointed as permanent Providence police officers; rather, it is a contract that they would be admitted to the Academy if they passed the medical and psychological examinations.

DECISION AND REMEDY   *The court issued an injunction to prohibit the city from conducting the 61st Police Academy unless the plaintiffs were included. The October 15 letter was a unilateral offer that the plaintiffs had accepted by passing the required medical and psychological examinations.*

WHAT IF THE FACTS WERE DIFFERENT?   *Suppose that the October 15 letter had used the phrase* potential offer of employment *instead of using the word* conditional. *Would the court in this case still have considered the letter to be a unilateral contract? Why or why not?*

—Problems with Unilateral Contracts. A problem arises in unilateral contracts when the **promisor** (the one making the promise) attempts to *revoke* (cancel) the offer after the **promisee** (the one to whom the promise was made) has begun performance but before the act has been completed. The promisee can accept the offer only on full performance, and under traditional contract principles, an offer may be revoked at any time before the offer is accepted. The present-day view, however, is that an offer to form a unilateral contract becomes irrevocable—cannot be revoked—once performance has begun. Thus, even though the offer has not yet been accepted, the offeror is prohibited from revoking it for a reasonable time period.

For instance, in the earlier example involving the Brooklyn Bridge, suppose that Parker is walking across the bridge and has only three yards to go when O'Malley calls out to her, "I revoke my offer." Under traditional contract law, O'Malley's revocation would terminate the offer. Under the modern view of unilateral contracts, however, O'Malley will not be able to revoke his offer because Parker has undertaken performance and walked all but three yards of the bridge. In these circumstances, Parker can finish crossing the bridge and bind O'Malley to the contract.

FORMAL VERSUS INFORMAL CONTRACTS

Another classification system divides contracts into formal contracts and informal contracts. **Formal contracts** are contracts that require a special form or method of creation (formation) to be enforceable. One type of formal contract is the **contract under seal,** a formalized writing with a special seal attached. The seal may be actual (made of wax or some other durable substance) or impressed on the paper or indicated simply by the word *seal* or the letters *L.S.* at the

end of the document. *L.S.* stands for *locus sigilli* and means "the place for the seal."[5]

A written contract may be considered sealed if the promisor *adopts* a seal already on it. A standard-form contract purchased at the local office supply store, for example, may have the word *seal* (or something else that qualifies as a seal) printed next to the blanks intended for the signatures. Unless the parties who sign the form indicate a contrary intention, when they sign the form, they adopt the seal.

Informal contracts include all other contracts. Such contracts are also called *simple contracts*. No special form is required (except for certain types of contracts that must be in writing), as the contracts are usually based on their substance rather than their form. Typically, businesspersons put their contracts in writing to ensure that there is some proof of a contract's existence should problems arise.

EXPRESS VERSUS IMPLIED-IN-FACT CONTRACTS

Contracts may also be categorized as *express* or *implied* by the conduct of the parties. We look here at the differences between these two types of contracts.

—Express Contracts. In an **express contract,** the terms of the agreement are fully and explicitly stated in words, oral or written. A signed lease for an apartment or a house is an express written contract. If a classmate calls you on the phone and agrees to buy your textbook from last semester for $45, an express oral contract has been made.

—Implied-in-Fact Contracts. A contract that is implied from the conduct of the parties is called an

---

5. The contract under seal has been almost entirely abolished under such provisions as UCC 2–203 (Section 2–203 of the Uniform Commercial Code). In sales of real estate, however, it is still common to use a seal (or an acceptable substitute).

implied-in-fact contract or an implied contract. This type of contract differs from an express contract in that the *conduct* of the parties, rather than their words, creates and defines the terms of the contract. (Note that a contract may be a mixture of an express contract and an implied-in-fact contract. In other words, a contract may contain some express terms, while others are implied.)

—*Requirements for Implied-in-Fact Contracts.* For an implied-in-fact contract to arise, certain requirements must be met. Normally, if the following conditions exist, a court will hold that an implied contract was formed:

1. The plaintiff furnished some service or property.
2. The plaintiff expected to be paid for that service or property, and the defendant knew or should have known that payment was expected.
3. The defendant had a chance to reject the services or property and did not.

For example, suppose that you need an accountant to complete your tax return this year. You look through the Yellow Pages and find an accountant at an office in your neighborhood, so you drop by to see her. You go into the accountant's office and explain your problem, and she tells you what her fees are. The next day you return and give her administrative assistant all the necessary information and documents—canceled checks, W-2 forms, and so on. You then walk out the door without saying anything expressly to the assistant. In this situation, you have entered into an implied-in-fact contract to pay the accountant the usual and reasonable fees for her services. The contract is implied by your conduct and by hers. She expects to be paid for completing your tax return, and by bringing in the records she will need to do the work, you have implied an intent to pay her.

Many disputes arise between construction contractors and subcontractors. In the following case, the question was whether the subcontractor could receive extra compensation for work that was not listed in the parties' express contract based on the existence of an implied-in-fact contract.

CASE 10.2 | **Gary Porter Construction v. Fox Construction, Inc.**

Court of Appeals of Utah, 2004.
2004 UT App 354,
101 P.3d 371.
http://www.utcourts.gov/opinions[a]

BACKGROUND AND FACTS *The University of Utah contracted with Fox Construction, Inc., to build a women's gymnastics training facility on the university's campus. Fox subcontracted with Gary Porter Construction to do excavation and soil placement work, according to specific sections of the project's plans (the "Included Sections"), for $146,740. Later, Fox asked Porter to do additional work that had not been included in the subcontract (the "Excluded Sections"). Porter did all of the work, but Fox refused to pay more than the amount of the subcontract, claiming that the added work had been mistakenly excluded from it. Porter filed a suit in a Utah state court against Fox, alleging, among other things, breach of an implied-in-fact contract. The court granted Porter's motion for summary judgment. Fox appealed to a state intermediate appellate court.*

IN THE LANGUAGE OF THE COURT

BILLINGS, Presiding Judge.
* * * *
Porter argues that Fox owes additional compensation for work it did under the Excluded Sections based upon a contract implied in fact. To succeed on this claim, Porter must show that (1) Fox requested Porter to perform the work under the Excluded Sections, (2) Porter expected additional compensation from Fox for the work, and (3) Fox knew or should have known that Porter expected additional compensation. The facts provided by Porter satisfy all of these elements and are not properly controverted [opposed] by Fox.

In its [motion for summary judgment] Porter set forth the following facts * * * : (1) Jeff Wood, Fox's project manager, drafted the subcontract which contains only the Included

---

a. In the "Court of Appeals" section, in the "By Date" row, click on "2004." In the list that opens, scroll to the name of the case and click on it to access the opinion. The Utah State Courts, through their Administrative Office of the Court, maintain this Web site.

CONTINUED ▶

CASE 10.2 Continued

Sections; (2) Fox repeatedly asked Porter to perform work outside the subcontract under the Excluded Sections; (3) Porter performed all work identified in the subcontract as well as the requested work under the Excluded Sections; (4) for months, Fox reviewed and paid * * * bills from Porter which identified the work performed, the costs of the work, and the specific section under which the work was done; (5) at times, Fox acknowledged that Porter was performing work outside the subcontract; and (6) the total cost of the work performed by Porter was $296,750.00, and the amount Fox paid Porter was $135,441.62, leaving a balance of $161,309.08.

The additional facts submitted by Fox do not create a material dispute regarding any of the three elements required for Porter's implied-in-fact contract claim. Fox does not dispute that it requested Porter to perform work under the Excluded Sections; and Fox provides no facts to dispute Porter's claim that Porter expected additional compensation for the work under the Excluded Sections. However, Fox does attempt to dispute the third element [in the first paragraph above]—whether Fox knew or should have known that Porter expected additional compensation.

* * * *

* * * [Floyd Cox, Fox's vice president, testified] that one Excluded Section, "section 2300, had been left out of the subcontract"; and Wood [testified] "that there was a section of specifications that was left out of the subcontract by mistake." Neither statement creates a material dispute over whether the Excluded Sections are part of the subcontract because they do not explain how the mistakes occurred despite ordinary diligence on the part of Fox. Also, because Fox presents no evidence that Porter should have known about Fox's mistake either when it entered into the subcontract or after performing, billing for, and being paid for work under the Excluded Sections, *as a matter of law, Fox should have known that Porter expected additional compensation for its work under the Excluded Provisions.* [Emphasis added.]

The facts set forth [by Fox] do not create a material dispute regarding whether (1) Fox requested Porter to perform the work under the Excluded Sections, (2) Porter expected additional compensation from Fox for the work, and (3) Fox knew or should have known that Porter expected additional compensation. Also, Fox does not dispute the amounts provided by Porter regarding the value of the work for which it was uncompensated. Therefore, the trial court did not err when it granted Porter's motion for summary judgment against Fox for $161,309.08.

DECISION AND REMEDY *The state intermediate appellate court affirmed the lower court's summary judgment in favor of Porter. The appellate court concluded that Porter met all of the requirements for establishing an implied-in-fact contract: Porter provided its services at Fox's request, expecting to be paid, which Fox knew or should have known.*

Contract Performance

Contracts are also classified according to the degree to which they have been performed. A contract that has been fully performed on both sides is called an **executed contract.** A contract that has not been fully performed by the parties is called an **executory contract.** If one party has fully performed but the other has not, the contract is said to be executed on the one side and executory on the other, but the contract is still classified as executory.

For example, assume that you agree to buy ten tons of coal from the Northern Coal Company. Further assume that Northern has delivered the coal to your steel mill, where it is now being burned. At this point, the contract is executed on the part of Northern and executory on your part. After you pay Northern for the coal, the contract will be executed on both sides.

Contract Enforceability

A **valid contract** has the elements necessary to entitle at least one of the parties to enforce it in court. Those elements, as mentioned earlier, consist of (1) an agreement consisting of an offer and an acceptance of that offer, (2) supported by legally sufficient consideration, (3) made by parties who have the legal capacity to enter into the contract, and (4) made for a legal purpose. As you can see in Exhibit 10–2, valid contracts may be enforceable, voidable, or unenforceable. Additionally, a contract may be referred to as a *void contract.* We look next at the meaning of the terms *voidable, unenforceable,* and *void* in relation to contract enforceability.

VOIDABLE CONTRACTS A **voidable contract** is a valid contract but one that can be avoided at the

EXHIBIT 10-2 Enforceable, Voidable, Unenforceable, and Void Contracts

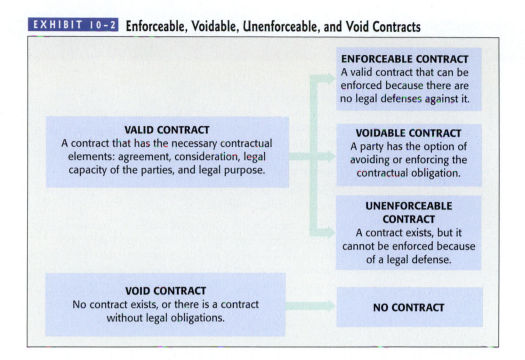

VALID CONTRACT
A contract that has the necessary contractual elements: agreement, consideration, legal capacity of the parties, and legal purpose.

ENFORCEABLE CONTRACT
A valid contract that can be enforced because there are no legal defenses against it.

VOIDABLE CONTRACT
A party has the option of avoiding or enforcing the contractual obligation.

UNENFORCEABLE CONTRACT
A contract exists, but it cannot be enforced because of a legal defense.

VOID CONTRACT
No contract exists, or there is a contract without legal obligations.

NO CONTRACT

option of one or both of the parties. The party having the option can elect either to avoid any duty to perform or to *ratify* (make valid) the contract. If the contract is avoided, both parties are released from it. If it is ratified, both parties must fully perform their respective legal obligations.

As a general rule, but subject to exceptions, contracts made by minors are voidable at the option of the minor (see Chapter 13). Contracts entered into under fraudulent conditions are voidable at the option of the defrauded party. In addition, contracts entered into under duress or undue influence are voidable (see Chapter 14).

UNENFORCEABLE CONTRACTS An **unenforceable contract** is one that cannot be enforced because of certain legal defenses against it. It is not unenforceable because a party failed to satisfy a legal requirement of the contract; rather, it is a valid contract rendered unenforceable by some statute or law. For example, certain contracts must be in writing (see Chapter 15), and if they are not, they will not be enforceable except in certain exceptional circumstances.

VOID CONTRACTS. A **void contract** is no contract at all. The terms *void* and *contract* are contradictory. A void contract produces no legal obligations on any of the parties. For example, a contract can be void because one of the parties was adjudged by a court to

be legally insane (and thus lacked the legal capacity to enter into a contract—see Chapter 13) or because the purpose of the contract was illegal.

SECTION 4 | Quasi Contracts

Quasi contracts, or contracts *implied in law,* are not actual contracts. Whereas express contracts and implied-in-fact contracts are actual contracts formed by the words or conduct of the parties, quasi contracts are fictional contracts created by courts and imposed on parties in the interests of fairness and justice. Quasi contracts are therefore equitable, rather than contractual, in nature. Usually, quasi contracts are imposed to avoid the *unjust enrichment* of one party at the expense of another. Under the doctrine of quasi contract, a plaintiff may recover in **quantum meruit**,[6] a Latin phrase meaning "as much as he deserves." *Quantum meruit* essentially describes the extent of compensation owed under a contract implied in law.

For example, suppose that a vacationing physician is driving down the highway and encounters Potter lying unconscious on the side of the road. The physician renders medical aid that saves Potter's life. Although the injured, unconscious Potter did not solicit the medical aid and was not aware that the aid

---

6. Pronounced *kwahn*-tuhm *mehr*-oo-wit.

CONCEPT SUMMARY 10.1 | Types of Contracts

ASPECT	DEFINITION
FORMATION	1. *Bilateral*—A promise for a promise. 2. *Unilateral*—A promise for an act (acceptance is the completed performance of the act). 3. *Formal*—Requires a special form for creation. 4. *Informal*—Requires no special form for creation. 5. *Express*—Formed by words (oral, written, or a combination). 6. *Implied in fact*—Formed by the conduct of the parties.
PERFORMANCE	1. *Executed*—A fully performed contract. 2. *Executory*—A contract not fully performed.
ENFORCEABILITY	1. *Valid*—The contract has the necessary contractual elements: agreement (offer and acceptance), consideration, legal capacity of the parties, and legal purpose. 2. *Voidable*—One party has the option of avoiding or enforcing the contractual obligation. 3. *Unenforceable*—A contract exists, but it cannot be enforced because of a legal defense. 4. *Void*—No contract exists, or there is a contract without legal obligations.

had been rendered, Potter received a valuable benefit, and the requirements for a quasi contract were fulfilled. In such a situation, the law will impose a quasi contract, and Potter normally will have to pay the physician for the reasonable value of the medical services rendered.

LIMITATIONS ON QUASI-CONTRACTUAL RECOVERY

Although quasi contracts exist to prevent unjust enrichment, the party obtaining the enrichment is not liable in some situations. Basically, a party who has conferred a benefit on someone else unnecessarily or as a result of misconduct or negligence cannot invoke the principle of quasi contract.

Consider the following example: You take your car to the local car wash and ask to have it run through the washer and to have the gas tank filled. While it is being washed, you go to a nearby shopping center for two hours. In the meantime, one of the workers at the car wash has mistaken your car for the one that he is supposed to hand wax. When you come back, you are presented with a bill for a full tank of gas, a wash job, and a hand wax. Clearly, a benefit has been conferred on you. But this benefit has been conferred because of a mistake by the car wash employee. You have not been *unjustly* enriched under these circumstances. People normally cannot be forced to pay for benefits "thrust" on them.

WHEN AN ACTUAL CONTRACT EXISTS

The doctrine of quasi contract generally cannot be used when there is an *actual contract* that covers the matter in controversy. For example, Bateman contracts with Cameron to deliver a furnace to a building owned by Jones. Bateman delivers the furnace, but Cameron never pays Bateman. Jones has been unjustly enriched in this situation, to be sure. Bateman, however, cannot recover from Jones in quasi contract because Bateman had an actual contract with Cameron. Bateman already has a remedy—he can sue for breach of contract to recover the price of the furnace from Cameron. No quasi contract need be imposed by the court in this instance to achieve justice.

SECTION 5 | Interpretation of Contracts

Sometimes parties agree that a contract has been formed but disagree on its meaning or legal effect. One reason this may happen is that one of the parties is not familiar with the legal terminology used in the contract. To an extent, special laws have helped to avoid this difficulty. Today, the federal government and a majority of the states have enacted "plain language" laws to regulate legal writing. Additionally, however, a dispute may arise over the meaning of a contract simply because the rights or obligations under the contract are not expressed clearly—no matter how "plain" the language used.

In this section, we look at some common law rules of contract interpretation. These rules, which have evolved over time, provide the courts with guidelines for deciding disputes over how contract terms or provisions should be interpreted. Exhibit 10–3 provides a brief graphic summary of how these rules are applied.

THE PLAIN MEANING RULE

When a contract's writing is clear and unequivocal, a court will enforce it according to its obvious terms. This is sometimes referred to as the *plain meaning rule*. Under this rule, if a contract's words appear to be clear and unambiguous, a court cannot consider *extrinsic evidence*, which is any evidence not contained in the document itself. If a contract's terms are unclear or ambiguous, however, extrinsic evidence may be admissible to clarify the meaning of the contract. The admissibility of such evidence can significantly affect the court's interpretation of ambiguous contractual provisions and thus the outcome of litigation.

OTHER RULES OF INTERPRETATION

Generally, a court will interpret the language to give effect to the parties' intent as *expressed in their contract*. This is the primary purpose of the rules of interpretation—to determine the parties' intent from the language used in their agreement and to give effect to that intent. Usually, a court will not make or remake a contract, nor will it interpret the language according to what the parties *claim* their intent was when they made it. The courts use the following rules in interpreting contractual terms:

1. Insofar as possible, a reasonable, lawful, and effective meaning will be given to all of a contract's terms.
2. A contract will be interpreted as a whole; individual, specific clauses will be considered subordinate to the contract's general intent. All writings that are a part of the same transaction will be interpreted together.
3. Terms that were the subject of separate negotiation will be given greater consideration than standardized terms and terms that were not negotiated separately.
4. A word will be given its ordinary, commonly accepted meaning, and a technical word or term will be given its technical meaning, unless the parties clearly intended something else.
5. Specific and exact wording will be given greater consideration than general language.
6. Written or typewritten terms will prevail over preprinted ones.
7. Because a contract should be drafted in clear and unambiguous language, a party who uses ambiguous expressions is held to be responsible for the ambiguities. Thus, when the language has more than one meaning, it will be interpreted against the party who drafted the contract.
8. Evidence of trade usage, prior dealing, and course of performance may be admitted to clarify the meaning of an ambiguously worded contract (these terms will be defined and discussed in Chapter 20). When considering custom and usage, a court will look at what is common to the particular business or industry and to the locale where the contract was made or is to be performed.

In the following case, the ordinary meaning of a word was at the heart of a significant dispute.

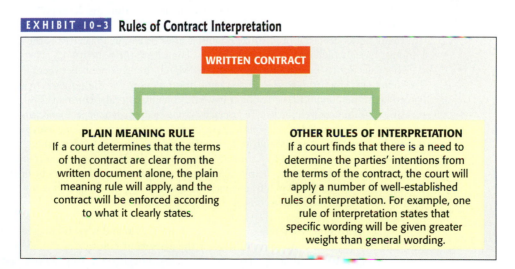

EXHIBIT 10-3 **Rules of Contract Interpretation**

WRITTEN CONTRACT

PLAIN MEANING RULE
If a court determines that the terms of the contract are clear from the written document alone, the plain meaning rule will apply, and the contract will be enforced according to what it clearly states.

OTHER RULES OF INTERPRETATION
If a court finds that there is a need to determine the parties' intentions from the terms of the contract, the court will apply a number of well-established rules of interpretation. For example, one rule of interpretation states that specific wording will be given greater weight than general wording.

Citizens Communications Co. v. Trustmark Insurance

United States
District Court,
District of
Connecticut. 2004.
303 F.Supp.2d 197.

KRAVITZ, D.J. [District Judge]

Citizens Communications ("Plaintiff" or "Citizens") brings this action against Defendants Trustmark Insurance ("Trustmark") [and others] seeking * * * damages [and other relief] stemming from a dispute over Defendants' alleged breach of contractual insurance coverage obligations. * * *

* * * *

* * * Stop-loss insurance is purchased primarily by large corporations that self-insure their employees. The insurance reimburses the corporation for claims paid under its self-funded plan, usually pursuant to a high deductible. * * * Citizens, as the seventh largest telephone company in the United States, with assets of nearly $7 billion (for the year ending Dec. 31, 2000), and with about 5,000 employees, provides health insurance to its employees under such a self-funded health plan (the "Plan"). * * *

* * * *

Trustmark issued a medical stop-loss insurance policy to Citizens, effective January 1, 1999, providing for an individual deductible of $100,000 * * * .

* * * *

* * * Garry Lonquist, a Citizens employee, [underwent heart surgery] on November 30, 1999. * * * [By] December 13 * * * Lonquist was in intensive care * * * .

* * * Meanwhile, * * * Citizens intended to renew the Trustmark stop-loss insurance policy for 2000. * * *

* * * *

On January 12, 2000, * * * Citizens faxed Trustmark an initial notice of Mr. Lonquist's stop-loss claim in the amount of $1,053,657. Mr. Lonquist's medical bills ultimately reached $3.1 million. * * * Trustmark then offered Citizens two options: either Citizens could "accept the rescission [cancellation] of stop-loss coverage beginning January 1, 2000," with all premiums returned, or Trustmark would accept the renewal with the existing terms and conditions * * * and * * * a separate $1 million deductible for Garry Lonquist, effectively removing him from the Plan's coverage * * * . This proviso [condition of renewal] * * * is referred to by the parties as the "Lonquist Laser." * * *

* * * *

On March 3, Citizens accepted Trustmark's [renewal] offer and confirmed its acceptance in a letter dated March 6 * * * .

* * * *

Both parties have moved for summary judgment with regard to the causes of action surrounding the Lonquist claim. Citizens seeks a declaratory judgment [a judgment establishing the rights of the parties] that Mr. Lonquist was included within the 2000 policy subject to a deductible of $100,000, because Citizens argues that the Lonquist Laser was invalid. Trustmark seeks dismissal of all the Lonquist causes of action [in part] on the basis of the Lonquist Laser, which effectively excludes his claims from the policy. * * *

There seems to be no dispute that the March 6 agreement between Citizens and Trustmark, in which the parties agreed upon the premium for the policy renewal and also agreed upon the Lonquist Laser, ordinarily would constitute a valid contract. The standard for creating a contract is well settled. *To form a valid and binding contract in Connecticut, there must be a mutual understanding of the terms that are definite and certain between the parties. * * * If the minds of the parties have not truly met, no enforceable contract exists.* Here, there was an offer by Trustmark, an acceptance by Citizens, intent by the parties to form a contract, a meeting of the minds about its terms, definite terms, and consideration. Under traditional contract principles, therefore, the March 6 agreement unquestionably would qualify as a valid amendment to the existing insurance contract between the parties. [Emphasis added.]

* * * *

* * * Both sides agree that an agreement was reached and what that agreement specifies. The sole point of contention is whether the agreement constitutes a valid amendment under the terms of the insurance policy. * * * Although the policy defines many of its

CASE 10.3 | Continued

terms, it does not define the term "amendment"; nor does anything in the policy specify precisely what an amendment must look like, other than that it must be approved by Trustmark and signed by Citizens, both of which occurred here.

* * * The ordinary meaning of the term "amendment" is "a change made by correction, addition, or deletion" [according to *Webster's Unabridged Dictionary* (Random House 2001)]. That is precisely what occurred here, when the parties knowingly agreed, in return for good and valuable consideration, to alter or change the terms of the original 2000 renewal by deleting or removing the Lonquist claim from the 2000 policy.

* * * *

Accordingly, Plaintiff's Motion for Summary Judgment [on this issue] is DENIED; Trustmark's Motion for Summary Judgment [on this issue] is GRANTED * * * .

QUESTIONS

1. Considering that Citizens did not want Lonquist's claims excluded from its contract with an insurer, what might the company have done instead of renewing the policy with Trustmark?
2. If the parties' insurance contract had defined the term *amendment*, would the result in this case have been the same? Explain.

REVIEWING NATURE AND TERMINOLOGY

Grant Borman, who was engaged in a construction project, leased a crane from Allied Equipment and hired Crosstown Trucking Co. to deliver the crane to the construction site. Crosstown, while the crane was in its possession and without permission from either Borman or Allied Equipment, used the crane to install a transformer for a utility company, which paid Crosstown for the job. Crosstown then delivered the crane to Borman's construction site at the appointed time of delivery. When Allied Equipment learned of the unauthorized use of the crane by Crosstown, it sued Crosstown for damages, seeking to recover the rental value of Crosstown's use of the crane. Using the information presented in the chapter, answer the following questions.

1. What are the four requirements of a valid contract?

2. Did Crosstown have a valid contract with Borman concerning the use of the crane? If so, was it a bilateral or a unilateral contract? Explain.

3. What are the requirements of an implied-in-fact contract? Can Allied Equipment obtain damages from Crosstown based on an implied-in-fact contract? Explain.

4. Should a court impose a quasi contract on the parties in this situation to allow Allied to recover damages from Crosstown? Why or why not?

TERMS AND CONCEPTS TO REVIEW

bilateral contract 212

contract 211

contract under seal 214

executed contract 216

executory contract 216

express contract 214

formal contract 214

implied-in-fact contract 215

informal contract 214

objective theory of contracts 211

offeree 212

offeror 212

promise 210

promisee 214

promisor 214

quantum meruit 217

quasi contract 217

unenforceable contract 217

unilateral contract 212

valid contract 216

void contract 217

voidable contract 216

QUESTIONS AND CASE PROBLEMS

10-1. Suppose that Everett McCleskey, a local businessperson, is a good friend of Al Miller, the owner of a local candy store. Every day on his lunch hour, McCleskey goes into Miller's candy store and spends about five minutes looking at the candy. After examining Miller's candy and talking with Miller, McCleskey usually buys one or two candy bars. One afternoon, McCleskey goes into Miller's candy shop, looks at the candy, and picks up a $1 candy bar. Seeing that Miller is very busy, he waves the candy bar at Miller without saying a word and walks out. Is there a contract? If so, classify it within the categories presented in this chapter.

10-2. ⚖ QUESTION WITH SAMPLE ANSWER

Janine was hospitalized with severe abdominal pain and placed in an intensive care unit. Her doctor told the hospital personnel to order around-the-clock nursing care for Janine. At the hospital's request, a nursing services firm, Nursing Services Unlimited, provided two weeks of in-hospital care and, after Janine was sent home, an additional two weeks of at-home care. During the at-home period of care, Janine was fully aware that she was receiving the benefit of the nursing services. Nursing Services later billed Janine $4,000 for the nursing care, but Janine refused to pay on the ground that she had never contracted for the services, either orally or in writing. In view of the fact that no express contract was ever formed, can Nursing Services recover the $4,000 from Janine? If so, under what legal theory? Discuss.
For a sample answer to this question, go to Appendix I at the end of this text.

10-3. Atencio is confined to his bed. He calls a friend who lives across the street and offers to sell her his watch next week for $100. If his friend wishes to accept, she is to put a red piece of paper in her front window. The next morning, she places a red piece of paper in her front window. Has a bilateral or a unilateral contract been formed? Explain.

10-4. Burger Baby restaurants engaged Air Advertising to fly an advertisement above the Connecticut beaches. The advertisement offered $1,000 to any person who could swim from the Connecticut beaches to Long Island across Long Island Sound in less than a day. At 10:00 A.M. on Saturday, October 10, Air Advertising's pilot flew a sign above the Connecticut beaches that read: "Swim across the Sound and Burger Baby pays $1,000." On seeing the sign, Davison dived in. About four hours later, when he was about halfway across the Sound, Air Advertising flew another sign over the Sound that read: "Burger Baby revokes." Davison completed the swim in another six hours. Is there a contract between Davison and Burger Baby? Can Davison recover anything?

10-5. Zdanis contacts Joe, who does lawn maintenance work, and makes the following offer: "After my lawn is mowed, I'll pay you $25." Joe responds by saying, "I accept your offer." Is there a contract? Is this an offer to form a bilateral or a unilateral contract? What is the legal significance of the distinction?

10-6. TYPES OF CONTRACTS. Professor Dixon was an adjunct professor at Tulsa Community College (TCC) in Tulsa, Oklahoma. Each semester, near the beginning of the term, the parties executed a written contract that always included the following provision: "It is agreed that this agreement may be cancelled by the Administration or the instructor at anytime before the first class session." In the spring semester of Dixon's seventh year, he filed a complaint with TCC alleging that one of his students, Meredith Bhuiyan, had engaged in disruptive classroom conduct. He gave her an "incomplete" grade and asked TCC to require her to apologize as a condition of receiving a final grade. TCC later claimed, and Dixon denied, that he was told to assign Bhuiyan a grade if he wanted to teach in the fall. Toward the end of the semester, Dixon was told which classes he would teach in the fall, but the parties did not sign a written contract. The Friday before classes began, TCC terminated him. Dixon filed a suit in an Oklahoma state court against TCC and others, alleging breach of contract. Did the parties have a contract? If so, did TCC breach it? Explain. [*Dixon v. Bhuiyan*, 10 P.3d 888 (Okla. 2000)]

10-7. ⚖ CASE PROBLEM WITH SAMPLE ANSWER

In December 2000, Nextel South Corp., a communications firm, contacted R. A. Clark Consulting, Ltd., an executive search company, about finding an employment manager for Nextel's call center in Atlanta, Georgia. Over the next six months, Clark screened, evaluated, and interviewed over three hundred candidates. Clark provided Nextel over fifteen candidate summaries, including one for Dan Sax. Nextel hired Sax for the position at an annual salary of $75,000. Sax started work on June 25, 2001, took two weeks' vacation, and quit on July 31 in the middle of a project. Clark spent the next six weeks looking for a replacement, until Nextel asked Clark to stop. Clark billed Nextel for its services, but Nextel refused to pay, asserting in part that the parties had not signed an agreement. Nextel's typical agreement specified payment to an employment agency of 20 percent of an employee's annual salary. Clark filed a suit in a Georgia state court against Nextel to recover in *quantum meruit*. What is *quantum meruit*? What should Clark have to show to recover on this basis? Should the court rule in Clark's favor? Explain. [*Nextel South Corp. v. R. A. Clark Consulting, Ltd.*, 266 Ga.App. 85, 596 S.E.2d 416 (2004)]

To view a sample answer for this case problem, go to this book's Web site at http://wbl.westbuslaw.com, select "Chapter 10," and click on "Case Problem with Sample Answer."

10-8. BILATERAL VERSUS UNILATERAL CONTRACTS. D.L. Peoples Group (D.L.) placed an ad in a Missouri newspaper to recruit admissions representatives, who were hired to recruit Missouri residents to attend D.L.'s college in Florida. Donald Hawley responded to the ad, his interviewer recommended him for the job, and he signed, in Missouri, an "Admissions Representative Agreement," which was mailed to D.L.'s president, who signed it in his office in Florida. The agreement provided in part that Hawley would devote exclusive time and effort to the business in his assigned territory in Missouri and that D.L. would pay Hawley a commission if he successfully recruited students for the school. While attempting to make one of his first calls on his new job, Hawley was accidentally shot and killed. On the basis of his death, a claim was filed in Florida for workers' compensation. (Under Florida law, when an accident occurs outside Florida, workers' compensation benefits are payable only if the employment contract was made in Florida.) Is this admissions representative agreement a bilateral or a unilateral contract? What are the consequences of the distinction in this case? Explain. [*D.L. Peoples Group, Inc. v. Hawley,* 804 So.2d 561 (Fla.App. 1 Dist. 2002)]

10-9. INTERPRETATION OF CONTRACTS. East Mill Associates (EMA) was developing residential "units" in East Brunswick, New Jersey, within the service area of the East Brunswick Sewerage Authority (EBSA). The sewer system required an upgrade to the Ryder's Lane Pumping Station to accommodate the new units. EMA agreed to pay "fifty-five percent (55%) of the total cost" of the upgrade. At the time, the estimated cost to EMA was

$150,000 to $200,000. Impediments to the project arose, however, substantially increasing the cost. Among other things, the pumping station had to be moved to accommodate a widened road nearby. The upgrade was delayed for almost three years. When it was completed, EBSA asked EMA for $340,022.12, which represented 55 percent of the total cost. EMA did not pay. EBSA filed a suit in a New Jersey state court against EMA for breach of contract. What rule should the court apply to interpret these parties' contract? How should that rule be applied? Why? [*East Brunswick Sewerage Authority v. East Mill Associates, Inc.,* 365 N.J.Super, 120, 838 A.2d 494 (A.D. 2004)]

10-10. VIDEO QUESTION

Go to this text's Web site at http://wbl.westbuslaw.com and select "Chapter 10." Click on "Video Questions" and view the video titled *Bowfinger.* Then answer the following questions.

(a) In the video, Renfro (Robert Downey, Jr.) says to Bowfinger (Steve Martin), "You bring me this script and Kit Ramsey and you've got yourself a 'go' picture." Assume for the purposes of this question that their agreement is a contract. Is the contract bilateral or unilateral? Is it express or implied? Is it formal or informal? Is it executed or executory? Explain your answers.

(b) What criteria would a court rely on to interpret the terms of the contract?

(c) Recall from the video that the contract between Bowfinger and the producer was oral. Suppose that a statute requires contracts of this type to be in writing. In that situation, would the contract be void, voidable, or unenforceable? Explain.

LAW | on the Web

For updated links to resources available on the Web, as well as a variety of other materials, visit this text's Web site at http://wbl.westbuslaw.com.

The 'Lectric Law Library provides information on contract law, including a definition of a contract, the elements required for a contract, and so on. Go to

http://www.lectlaw.com/lay.html

Scroll down to the "Other Assorted Items" section and click on "Contracts."

You can keep abreast of recent and planned revisions of the *Restatements of the Law,* including the *Restatement (Second) of Contracts,* by accessing the American Law Institute's Web site at

http://www.ali.org

LEGAL RESEARCH EXERCISES ON THE WEB

Go to **http://wbl.westbuslaw.com**, the Web site that accompanies this text. Select "Chapter 10" and click on "Internet Exercises." There you will find the following Internet research exercises that you can perform to learn more about topics covered in this chapter.

Activity 10–1: **LEGAL PERSPECTIVE**
             Contracts and Contract Provisions

Activity 10–2: **MANAGEMENT PERSPECTIVE**
             Implied Employment Contracts

Activity 10–3: **HISTORICAL PERSPECTIVE**
             Contracts in Ancient Mesopotamia

CHAPTER 11
Agreement

An essential element for contract formation is **agreement**—the parties must agree on the terms of the contract and manifest to each other their **mutual assent** (agreement) to the same bargain. Ordinarily, agreement is evidenced by two events: an *offer* and an *acceptance*. One party offers a certain bargain to another party, who then accepts that bargain. The agreement does not necessarily have to be in writing. Both parties, however, must manifest their assent to the same bargain. Once an agreement is reached, if the other elements of a contract are present (consideration, capacity, and legality—discussed in subsequent chapters), a valid contract is formed, generally creating enforceable rights and duties between the parties.

Note that not all agreements are contracts. John and Kevin may agree to play golf on a certain day, but a court would not hold that their agreement is an enforceable contract. A *contractual* agreement arises only when the terms of the agreement impose legally enforceable obligations on the parties.

In today's world, contracts are frequently formed via the Internet. For a discussion of online offers and acceptances, see Chapter 19, which is devoted entirely to the subject of electronic contracts, or e-contracts.

SECTION 1 | Requirements of the Offer

As mentioned in Chapter 10, the parties to a contract are the *offeror*, the one who makes an offer or proposal to another party, and the *offeree*, the one to whom the offer or proposal is made. An **offer** is a promise or commitment to do or refrain from doing some specified thing in the future. Under the common law, three elements are necessary for an offer to be effective:

1. The offeror must have a serious intention to become bound by the offer.
2. The terms of the offer must be reasonably certain, or definite, so that the parties and the court can ascertain the terms of the contract.
3. The offer must be communicated by the offeror to the offeree, resulting in the offeree's knowledge of the offer.

Once an effective offer has been made, the offeree has the power to accept the offer. If the offeree accepts, an agreement is formed (and thus a contract arises, if other essential elements are present).

INTENTION

The first requirement for an effective offer is a serious intent on the part of the offeror. Serious intent is not determined by the *subjective* intentions, beliefs, and assumptions of the offeror. As discussed in Chapter 10, courts generally adhere to the *objective theory of contracts* in determining whether a contract has been formed. Under this theory, a party's words and conduct are held to mean whatever a reasonable person in the offeree's position would think they meant. The court will give words their usual meanings even if "it were proved by twenty bishops that [the] party . . . intended something else."[1]

Offers made in obvious anger, jest, or undue excitement do not meet the intent test because a reasonable person would realize that a serious offer was not being made. Because these offers are not effective, an offeree's acceptance does not create an agreement. For

---

1. Judge Learned Hand in *Hotchkiss v. National City Bank of New York*, 200 F. 287 (2d Cir. 1911); aff'd 231 U.S. 50, 34 S.Ct. 20, 58 L.Ed. 115 (1913).

example, suppose that you and three classmates ride to school each day in Davina's new automobile, which has a market value of $20,000. One cold morning, the four of you get into the car, but Davina cannot get the car started. She yells in anger, "I'll sell this car to anyone for $500!" You drop $500 in her lap. Given these facts, a reasonable person, taking into consideration Davina's frustration and the obvious difference in worth between the market value of the car and the proposed purchase price, would declare that her offer was not made with serious intent and that you did not have an agreement.

The concept of intention can be further clarified through an examination of the types of expressions and statements that are *not* offers. We look at these expressions and statements in the subsections that follow. In the classic case of *Lucy v. Zehmer*, presented below, the court considered whether an offer made "after a few drinks" met the serious-intent requirement.

CASE 11.1   Lucy v. Zehmer

Supreme Court of
Appeals of Virginia, 1954.
196 Va. 493,
84 S.E.2d 516.

BACKGROUND AND FACTS   *W. O. Lucy and J. C. Lucy, the plaintiffs, filed a suit against A. H. Zehmer and Ida Zehmer, the defendants, to compel the Zehmers to transfer title of their property, known as the Ferguson Farm, to the Lucys for $50,000, as the Zehmers had allegedly agreed to do. Lucy had known Zehmer for fifteen or twenty years and for the last eight years or so had been anxious to buy the Ferguson Farm from Zehmer. One night, Lucy stopped in to visit the Zehmers in the combination restaurant, filling station, and motor court they operated. While there, Lucy tried to buy the Ferguson Farm once again. This time he tried a new approach. According to the trial court transcript, Lucy said to Zehmer, "I bet you wouldn't take $50,000 for that place." Zehmer replied, "Yes, I would too; you wouldn't give fifty." Throughout the evening, the conversation returned to the sale of the Ferguson Farm for $50,000. At the same time, the parties continued to drink whiskey and engage in light conversation. Eventually, Lucy enticed Zehmer to write up an agreement to the effect that Zehmer would sell to Lucy the Ferguson Farm for $50,000 complete. Later, Lucy sued Zehmer to compel him to go through with the sale. Zehmer argued that he had been drunk and that the offer had been made in jest and hence was unenforceable. The trial court agreed with Zehmer, and Lucy appealed.*

IN THE LANGUAGE OF THE COURT

BUCHANAN, J. [Justice] delivered the opinion of the court.

* * * *

In his testimony, Zehmer claimed that he "was high as a Georgia pine," and that the transaction "was just a bunch of two doggoned drunks bluffing to see who could talk the biggest and say the most." That claim is inconsistent with his attempt to testify in great detail as to what was said and what was done. * * *

* * * *

The appearance of the contract, the fact that it was under discussion for forty minutes or more before it was signed; Lucy's objection to the first draft because it was written in the singular, and he wanted Mrs. Zehmer to sign it also; the rewriting to meet that objection and the signing by Mrs. Zehmer; the discussion of what was to be included in the sale, the provision for the examination of the title, the completeness of the instrument that was executed, the taking possession of it by Lucy with no request or suggestion by either of the defendants that he give it back, are facts which furnish persuasive evidence that the execution of the contract was a serious business transaction rather than a casual, jesting matter as defendants now contend.

* * * *

In the field of contracts, as generally elsewhere, *[w]e must look to the outward expression of a person as manifesting his intention rather than to his secret and unexpressed intention. The law imputes to a person an intention corresponding to the reasonable meaning of his words and acts.* [Emphasis added.]

* * * *

Whether the writing signed by the defendants and now sought to be enforced by the complainants was the result of a serious offer by Lucy and a serious acceptance by the defendants, or was a serious offer by Lucy and an acceptance in secret jest by the defendants, in either event it constituted a binding contract of sale between the parties.

CASE 11.1 | Continued

DECISION AND REMEDY *The Supreme Court of Virginia determined that the writing was an enforceable contract and reversed the ruling of the lower court. The Zehmers were required by court order to follow through with the sale of the Ferguson Farm to the Lucys.*

WHAT IF THE FACTS WERE DIFFERENT? *Suppose that the day after Lucy purchased the farm, he decided that he didn't want it after all, and Zehmer sued Lucy to perform the contract. Would this change in the facts alter the court's decision that Lucy and Zehmer had created an enforceable contract?*

IMPACT OF THIS CASE ON TODAY'S LAW

This is a classic case in contract law because it illustrates so clearly the objective theory of contracts with respect to determining whether a serious offer was intended. Today, the objective theory of contracts continues to be applied by the courts, and *Lucy v. Zehmer* is routinely cited as a significant precedent in this area.

EXPRESSIONS OF OPINION An expression of opinion is not an offer. It does not evidence an intention to enter into a binding agreement. Consider an example. Hawkins took his son to McGee, a physician, and asked McGee to operate on the son's hand. McGee said that the boy would be in the hospital three or four days and that the hand would *probably* heal a few days later. The son's hand did not heal for a month, but the father did not win a suit for breach of contract. The court held that McGee had not made an offer to heal the son's hand in a few days. He had merely expressed an opinion as to when the hand would heal.[2]

STATEMENTS OF FUTURE INTENT If Arif says, "I *plan* to sell my stock in Novation, Inc., for $150 per share," a contract is not created if John "accepts" and tenders the $150 per share for the stock. Arif has merely expressed his intention to enter into a future contract for the sale of the stock. If John accepts and tenders the $150 per share, no contract is formed because a reasonable person would conclude that Arif was only *thinking about* selling his stock, not *promising* to sell it.

PRELIMINARY NEGOTIATIONS A request or invitation to negotiate is not an offer. It only expresses a willingness to discuss the possibility of entering into a contract. Included are statements such as "Will you sell Blythe Estate?" or "I wouldn't sell my car for less than $1,000." A reasonable person in the offeree's position would not conclude that these statements evidenced an intention to enter into a binding obliga-

tion. Likewise, when the government or private firms require construction work, they invite contractors to submit bids. The *invitation* to submit bids is not an offer, and a contractor does not bind the government or private firm by submitting a bid. (The bids that the contractors submit are offers, however, and the government or private firm can bind the contractor by accepting the bid.)

AGREEMENTS TO AGREE During preliminary negotiations, the parties may form an agreement to agree to a material term of a contract at some future date. Traditionally, such "agreements to agree" were not considered to be binding contracts. More recent cases illustrate the view that agreements to agree serve valid commercial purposes and can be enforced if the parties clearly intended to be bound by such agreements.

For example, suppose Zahn Consulting leases office space from Leon Properties, Inc. Their lease agreement includes a clause permitting Zahn to extend the lease at an amount of rent to be agreed on at the time the lease is extended. Under the traditional rule, because the amount of rent is not specified in the lease clause itself, the clause would be too indefinite in its terms to enforce. Under the current view, a court could hold that the parties intended the future rent to be a reasonable amount and could enforce the clause.[3] In other words, under the modern view, the emphasis is on the parties' intent rather than on form. (For a further discussion of this issue, see this chapter's *Emerging Trends* feature beginning on the following page.)

---

2. *Hawkins v. McGee*, 84 N.H. 114, 146 A. 641 (1929).

3. *Restatement (Second) of Contracts*, Section 33. See also Sections 2–204 and 2–305 of the Uniform Commercial Code (UCC).

The Enforcement of Preliminary Agreements

Suppose that during protracted contract negotiations, but before a formal contract is drawn up, the parties proclaim that they have "made a deal." Does their agreement mean that an enforceable contract has been formed even though the parties have not signed a formal contract? Or does their agreement simply mean that they have agreed to agree to a contract in the future?

How a court might interpret such a situation can, of course, have significant consequences for the parties. Fluorogas, Ltd., learned this when a federal court held that its preliminary agreement with Fluorine On Call, Ltd., was a binding contract. In that case, executives of the two companies had enjoyed a weekend of yachting in the Florida keys. During the trip, the executives drew up a brief handwritten document stating that Fluorogas would sell to Fluorine the exclusive rights to a technology to build and sell sophisticated semiconductor equipment. When Fluorogas refused to transfer the patents and intellectual property at issue to Fluorine, Fluorine sued for breach of contract. Was there a contract? Yes, according to the court. Because the essential terms of the agreement were included in the handwritten document, the document constituted a contract, not an agreement to agree to form a contract at some point in the future.[a]

THE TEXACO CASE

An important case challenging the traditional notion that preliminary contracts do not bind the parties was *Texaco, Inc. v.*

Pennzoil Co.[b] When the Pennzoil Company discussed with the Getty Oil Company the possible purchase of Getty's stock, a "memorandum of agreement" was drafted to reflect the terms of the conversations. After more negotiations over the price, both companies issued press releases announcing an agreement in principle on the terms of the memorandum. The next day, Texaco, Inc., offered to buy all of Getty's stock at a higher price. Getty accepted Texaco's offer, and the two firms signed a merger agreement. When Pennzoil sued Texaco for tortious (wrongful) interference with its "contractual" relationship with Getty, a jury concluded that Getty and Pennzoil had intended a binding contract before Texaco made its offer and that only the details were left to be worked out. Texaco was held liable for interfering with this contract and had to pay damages in the hundreds of millions of dollars.

TWO TYPES OF PRELIMINARY AGREEMENTS EMERGE

In *Adjustre Systems v. GAB Business Services,*[c] the U.S. Court of Appeals for the Second Circuit set forth some helpful guidelines for distinguishing between an agreement to agree and an enforceable contract. The court pointed out that when the parties contemplate further negotiations and the execution of a formal instrument, a preliminary agreement ordinarily does not create a binding contract. If the parties do not

a. *Fluorine On Call, Ltd. v. Fluorogas Limited,* No. 01-CV-186 (W.D. Tex. 2002). A federal appellate court later affirmed the district court's holding on the contract issue but reversed the award of damages. *Fluorine On Call, Ltd. v. Fluorogas Limited,* 380 F.3d 849 (5th Cir. 2004).

b. 729 S.W.2d 768 (Tex.App.—Houston [1st Dist.] 1987; writ ref'd n.r.e.). (Generally, a complete Texas Court of Appeals citation includes a writ-of-error history showing the Texas Supreme Court's disposition of the case. In this case, *writ ref'd n.r.e.* is an abbreviation for "writ refused, no reversible error," which means that Texas's highest court refused to grant the appellant's request to review the case because the court did not consider there to be any reversible error.) Note that after the *Texaco* decision, Texas enacted legislation that superseded portions of the court's ruling regarding damages.

c. 145 F.3d 543 (2d Cir. 1998).

ADVERTISEMENTS In general, advertisements—including representations made in mail-order catalogues, price lists, and circulars—are treated not as offers to contract but as invitations to negotiate. Suppose that Loeser advertises a used paving machine. The ad is mailed to hundreds of firms and reads, "Used Loeser Construction Co. paving machine. Builds curbs and finishes cement work all in one process. Price: $42,350." If Star Paving calls Loeser and says, "We accept your offer," no contract is formed. Any reasonable person

would conclude that Loeser was not promising to sell the paving machine but rather was soliciting offers to buy it. If such an ad were held to constitute a legal offer, and fifty people accepted the offer, there would be no way for Loeser to perform all fifty of the resulting contracts. He would have to breach forty-nine contracts. Obviously, the law seeks to avoid such unfairness.

Price lists are another form of invitation to negotiate or trade. A seller's price list is not an offer to sell at that price; it merely invites the buyer to offer to buy at

intend to be bound by an agreement until it is in writing and signed, then there is no contract until that event occurs. The Second Circuit recognized, though, that in some circumstances preliminary agreements can create binding obligations. These "binding preliminary agreements" fall into one of two categories—Type I agreements or Type II agreements.

A Type I preliminary agreement is one in which all essential terms have been agreed on and no disputed issues remain to be resolved, as in the Getty-Pennzoil memorandum of agreement. This type of agreement is preliminary only in form and is fully binding. The formal contract to follow is simply that—a writing to satisfy formalities. A Type II preliminary agreement is created when the parties agree on certain major terms but leave other terms open for further negotiation. A Type II preliminary agreement is binding only in the sense that the parties have committed themselves to "negotiate together in good faith in an effort to reach final agreement." A party to a Type II preliminary agreement has no right to demand performance of the proposed contract.

OTHER FACTORS THAT COURTS CONSIDER

The courts have also developed a series of factors to be considered in determining whether the parties to a preliminary agreement intended to be bound in the absence of a final, executed agreement. The first and most important factor is whether the parties expressly stated that they would not be bound by the agreement in the absence of a formal writing.

Another factor to be considered is whether the agreement has been partially performed by either party. Normally, the agreement will be considered partially performed only if one of the parties has given the other something of value and the other party has accepted it. A third factor is whether all of the terms of the alleged contract have been agreed on. If any material terms have not been agreed on, then the third factor is not satisfied. Finally, the courts will consider whether the

agreement at issue is the type of contract that is usually committed to writing. In other words, they will look to what is customary when similar agreements are formed.[d]

IMPLICATIONS FOR THE BUSINESSPERSON

1. When engaging in preliminary negotiations, businesspersons should be aware that if all material terms are agreed on, they may be bound in contract even though they have not yet drawn up a formal contract.

2. Businesspersons should always keep in mind that in determining contractual intent, a court will consider what they say and do during preliminary negotiations—and *not* their subjective intentions.

FOR CRITICAL ANALYSIS

1. In deciding whether an agreement to agree or an enforceable contract has been formed, would it matter whether the parties are experienced business executives or relatively inexperienced businesspersons?

2. Is it fair for a court to hold that parties are bound in contract even though one of the parties claims that he or she did not intend to form a contract? Generally, should the courts give more weight to subjective intent in determining whether a contract has been formed?

RELEVANT WEB SITES

To locate information on the Web concerning the issues discussed in this feature, go to this text's Web site at **http://wbl.westbuslaw.com**, select "Chapter 11," and click on "Emerging Trends."

---

d. For examples of cases in which preliminary agreements did not satisfy these factors, or requirements, see *Novecon, Ltd. v. Bulgarian-American Enterprise Fund*, 190 F.3d 556 (D.C. Cir. 1999); and *Rappaport v. Buske*, 2000 WL 1224828 (S.D.N.Y. 2000).

---

that price. In fact, the seller usually puts "prices subject to change" on the price list. Only in rare circumstances will a price quotation be construed as an offer.[4]

Although most advertisements and the like are treated as invitations to negotiate, this does not mean that an advertisement can never be an offer. If the advertisement makes a promise so definite in character that it is apparent that the offeror is binding

himself or herself to the conditions stated, the advertisement is treated as an offer.[5]

AUCTIONS Sometimes, what appears to be an offer is not sufficient to serve as the basis for contract formation. Particularly problematic in this respect are "offers" to sell goods at auctions. In an auction, a seller "offers" goods for sale through an auctioneer. This is

---

4. See, for example, *Fairmount Glass Works v. Crunden-Martin Woodenware Co.*, 106 Ky. 659, 51 S.W. 196 (1899).

5. See, for example, *Lefkowitz v. Great Minneapolis Surplus Store, Inc.*, 251 Minn. 188, 86 N.W.2d 689 (1957).

not, however, a *contractual* offer (an offer to form a contract). Rather, it is an invitation asking bidders to submit offers. In the context of an auction, a bidder is the offeror, and the auctioneer is the offeree. The offer is accepted when the auctioneer strikes the hammer. Before the fall of the hammer, a bidder may revoke (take back) her or his bid, or the auctioneer may reject that bid or all bids. Typically, an auctioneer will reject a bid that is below the price the seller is willing to accept.

When the auctioneer accepts a higher bid, he or she rejects all previous bids. Because rejection terminates an offer (as will be pointed out later), those bids represent offers that have been terminated. Thus, if the highest bidder withdraws his or her bid before the hammer falls, none of the previous bids is reinstated. If the bid is not withdrawn or rejected, the contract is formed when the auctioneer announces, "Going once, going twice, sold!" (or something similar) and lets the hammer fall.

Traditionally, auctions have been referred to as either "with reserve" or "without reserve." In an auction with reserve, the seller (through the auctioneer) may withdraw the goods at any time before the auctioneer closes the sale by announcement or by the fall of the hammer. All auctions are assumed to be auctions with reserve unless the terms of the auction are explicitly stated to be *without reserve*. In an auction without reserve, the goods cannot be withdrawn by the seller and must be sold to the highest bidder. In auctions with reserve, the seller may reserve the right to confirm or reject the sale even after "the hammer has fallen." In this situation, the seller is obligated to notify those attending the auction that sales of goods made during the auction are not final until confirmed by the seller.[6]

DEFINITENESS OF TERMS

The second requirement for an effective offer involves the definiteness of its terms. An offer must have terms

that are reasonably definite so that, if it is accepted and a contract formed, a court can determine if a breach has occurred and can provide an appropriate remedy. The specific terms required depend, of course, on the type of contract. Generally, a contract must include the following terms, either expressed in the contract or capable of being reasonably inferred from it:

1. The identification of the parties.
2. The identification of the object or subject matter of the contract (also the quantity, when appropriate), including the work to be performed, with specific identification of such items as goods, services, and land.
3. The consideration to be paid.
4. The time of payment, delivery, or performance.

An offer may invite an acceptance to be worded in such specific terms that the contract is made definite. For example, suppose that Marcus Business Machines contacts your corporation and offers to sell "from one to ten MacCool copying machines for $1,600 each; state number desired in acceptance." Your corporation agrees to buy two copiers. Because the quantity is specified in the acceptance, the terms are definite, and the contract is enforceable.

Courts sometimes are willing to supply a missing term in a contract when the parties have clearly manifested an intent to form a contract. If, in contrast, the parties have attempted to deal with a particular term of the contract but their expression of intent is too vague or uncertain to be given any precise meaning, the court will not supply a "reasonable" term because to do so might conflict with the intent of the parties. In other words, the court will not rewrite the contract.[7] The following case illustrates this point.

---

6. These rules apply under both the common law of contracts and the UCC—see UCC 2–328.

7. See Chapter 20 and UCC 2–204. Article 2 of the UCC specifies different rules relating to the definiteness of terms used in a contract for the sale of goods. In essence, Article 2 modifies general contract law by requiring less specificity.

CASE 11.2 · Baer v. Chase

United States
Court of Appeals,
Third Circuit. 2004.
392 F.3d 609.

GREENBERG, Circuit Judge.
* * * *

[David] Chase, who originally was from New Jersey, but relocated to Los Angeles in 1971, is the creator, producer, writer and director of *The Sopranos*. Chase has numerous credits for other television productions as well. * * * Chase had worked on a number of projects involving organized crime activities based in New Jersey, including a script for "a mob boss in therapy," a concept that, in part, would become the basis for *The Sopranos*.

In 1995, Chase was producing and directing a *Rockford Files* "movie-of-the-week" when he met Joseph Urbancyk who was working on the set as a camera operator and temporary director of photography. * * *

CASE 11.2 | Continued

[Through Urbancyk, Chase met Robert] Baer, * * * a New Jersey attorney [who] recently had left his employment in the Union County Prosecutor's Office in Elizabeth, New Jersey, where he had worked for the previous six years.
* * * *

Chase, Urbancyk and Baer met for lunch on June 20, 1995 * * * , with Baer describing his experience as a prosecutor. Baer also pitched the idea to shoot "a film or television shows about the New Jersey Mafia." At that time Baer was unaware of Chase's previous work involving mob activity premised in New Jersey. At the lunch there was no reference to any payment that Chase might make to Baer for the latter's services * * * .

In October 1995, Chase visited New Jersey for three days. During this "research visit" Baer arranged meetings for Chase with Detective Thomas Koczur, Detective Robert A. Jones, and Tony Spirito who provided Chase with information, material and personal stories about their experiences with organized crime. * * * Baer does not dispute that virtually all of the ideas and locations that he "contributed" to Chase existed in the public record.

After returning to Los Angeles, Chase sent Baer a copy of a draft of a *Sopranos* screenplay that he had written, which was dated December 20, 1995. Baer asserts that after he read it he called Chase and made various comments with regard to it. Baer claims that the two spoke at least four times during the following year and that he sent a letter to Chase dated February 10, 1997, discussing *The Sopranos* script. * * *
* * * *

Baer asserts that he and Chase orally agreed on three separate occasions that if the show became a success, Chase would "take care of" Baer, and "remunerate Baer in a manner commensurate to the true value of his services." * * *

Baer claims that on each of these occasions the parties had the same conversation in which Chase offered to pay Baer, stating "you help me; I pay you." Baer always rejected Chase's offer, reasoning that Chase would be unable to pay him "for the true value of the services Baer was rendering." Each time Baer rejected Chase's offer he did so with a counteroffer, "that I would perform the services while assuming the risk that if the show failed Chase would owe me nothing. If, however, the show succeeded he would remunerate me in a manner commensurate to the true value of my services." Baer acknowledges that this counteroffer * * * always was oral and did not include any fixed term of duration or price. * * * In fact, Chase has not paid Baer for his services.

On or about May 15, 2002, Baer filed a * * * complaint against Chase in [a federal] district court * * * [claiming among other things] * * * breach of implied contract. Eventually Chase brought a motion for summary judgment * * * . Chase claimed that the alleged contract * * * [was] too vague, ambiguous and lacking in essential terms to be enforced * * * .

The district court granted Chase's motion * * * .
* * * *

Baer predicates [bases] his contract claim on this appeal on an implied-in-fact contract * * * . The issue with respect to the implied-in-fact contract claim concerns whether Chase and Baer entered into an enforceable contract for services Baer rendered that aided in the creation and production of *The Sopranos*. * * *
* * * *

* * * [A] contract arises from offer and acceptance, and must be sufficiently definite so that the performance to be rendered by each party can be ascertained with reasonable certainty. Therefore parties create an enforceable contract when they agree on its essential terms and manifest an intent that the terms bind them. *If parties to an agreement do not agree on one or more essential terms of the purported agreement, courts generally hold it to be unenforceable.* [Emphasis added.]
* * * *

* * * [The] law deems the price term, *i.e.*, the amount of compensation, an essential term of any contract. An agreement lacking definiteness of price, however, is not unenforceable if the parties specify a practicable method by which they can determine the amount. However, *in the absence of an agreement as to the manner or method of determining compensation*

CONTINUED ▶

CASE 11.2 | Continued

the purported agreement is invalid. Additionally, *the duration of the contract is deemed an essential term and therefore any agreement must be sufficiently definitive to allow a court to determine the agreed upon length of the contractual relationship.* [Emphasis added.]

   *   *   *   *

    The * * * question with respect to Baer's contract claim, therefore, is whether his contract is enforceable in light of the traditional requirement of definitiveness * * * . A contract may be expressed in writing, or orally, or in acts, or partly in one of these ways and partly in others. There is a point, however, at which interpretation becomes alteration. In this case, even when all of the parties' verbal and non-verbal actions are aggregated and viewed most favorably to Baer, we cannot find a contract that is distinct and definitive enough to be enforceable.

    Nothing in the record indicates that the parties agreed on how, how much, where, or for what period Chase would compensate Baer. The parties did not discuss who would determine the "true value" of Baer's services, when the "true value" would be calculated, or what variables would go into such a calculation. There was no discussion or agreement as to the meaning of "success" of *The Sopranos*. There was no discussion how "profits" were to be defined. There was no contemplation of dates of commencement or termination of the contract. And again, nothing in Baer's or Chase's conduct, or the surrounding circumstances of the relationship, shed light on, or answers, any of these questions. The district court was correct in its description of the contract between the parties: "The contract as articulated by the Plaintiff lacks essential terms, and is vague, indefinite and uncertain; no version of the alleged agreement contains sufficiently precise terms to constitute an enforceable contract." We therefore will affirm the district court's rejection of Baer's claim to recover under a theory of implied-in-fact contract.

QUESTIONS

1. Why must the terms of a contract be "sufficiently definite" before a court will enforce the contract?
2. What might a court consider when looking for a "sufficiently definite meaning" to make a contract term enforceable?

COMMUNICATION

A third requirement for an effective offer is communication of the offer to the offeree, resulting in the offeree's knowledge of the offer. Ordinarily, one cannot agree to a bargain without knowing that it exists. Suppose that Estrich advertises a reward for the return of his lost dog. Hoban, not knowing of the reward, finds the dog and returns it to Estrich. Hoban cannot recover the reward, because she did not know it had been offered.[8]

---

8. A few states allow recovery of the reward, but not on contract principles. Because Estrich wanted his dog to be returned and Hoban returned it, these few states would allow Hoban to recover on the basis that it would be unfair to deny her the reward just because she did not know it had been offered.

SECTION 2 | Termination of the Offer

The communication of an effective offer to an offeree gives the offeree the power to transform the offer into a binding, legal obligation (a contract) by an acceptance. This power of acceptance, however, does not continue forever. It can be terminated either by the action of the parties or by operation of law.

TERMINATION BY ACTION OF THE PARTIES

An offer can be terminated by the action of the parties in any of three ways: by revocation, by rejection, or by counteroffer.

REVOCATION OF THE OFFER BY THE OFFEROR

The offeror's act of withdrawing (revoking) an offer is known as **revocation.** Unless an offer is irrevocable (irrevocable offers will be discussed shortly), the offeror usually can revoke the offer (even if he or she has promised to keep it open) as long as the revocation is communicated to the offeree before the offeree accepts. Revocation may be accomplished by express repudiation of the offer (for example, with a statement such as "I withdraw my previous offer of October 17") or by performance of acts that are inconsistent with the existence of the offer and are made known to the offeree.

The general rule followed by most states is that a revocation becomes effective when the offeree or the offeree's agent (a person acting on behalf of the offeree) actually receives it. Therefore, a letter of revocation mailed on April 1 and delivered at the offeree's residence or place of business on April 3 becomes effective on April 3.

An offer made to the general public can be revoked in the same manner that the offer was originally communicated. Suppose that a department store offers a $10,000 reward to anyone providing information leading to the apprehension of the persons who burglarized the store's downtown branch. The offer is published in three local papers and four papers in neighboring communities. To revoke the offer, the store must publish the revocation in all of the seven papers in which it published the offer. The revocation is then accessible to the general public, even if some particular offeree does not know about it.

IRREVOCABLE OFFERS

Although most offers are revocable, some can be made irrevocable—that is, they cannot be revoked, or canceled. An option contract involves one type of irrevocable offer. Increasingly, courts also refuse to allow an offeror to revoke an offer when the offeree has changed position because of justifiable reliance on the offer. (An offer for the sale of goods may also be considered irrevocable if the merchant-offeror gives assurances in a signed writing that the offer will remain open—see the discussion of the "merchant's firm offer" in Chapter 20.)

—Option Contract. An **option contract** is created when an offeror promises to hold an offer open for a specified period of time in return for a payment (consideration) given by the offeree. An option contract takes away the offeror's power to revoke the offer for the period of time specified in the option. If no time is specified, then a reasonable period of time is implied. For example, suppose that you are in the business of writing movie scripts. Your agent contacts the head of development at New Line Cinema and offers to sell New Line your latest movie script. New Line likes your script and agrees to pay you $10,000 for a six-month option. In this situation, you (through your agent) are the offeror, and New Line is the offeree. You cannot revoke your offer to sell New Line your script for the next six months. If after six months no contract has been formed, however, New Line loses the $10,000, and you are free to sell the script to another firm.

—Real Estate Option Contracts. Option contracts are also frequently used in conjunction with the sale or lease of real estate. For example, you might agree with a landowner to lease a home and include in the lease contract a clause stating that you will pay $9,000 for an option to purchase the home within a specified period of time. If you decide not to purchase the home after the specified period has lapsed, you forfeit the $9,000, and the landlord is free to sell the property to another buyer.

Additionally, contracts to lease business premises often include options to renew the leases at certain intervals, such as after five years. Typically, a lease contract containing a renewal option requires notification—that is, the person leasing the premises must notify the property owner of his or her intention to exercise the renewal option within a certain number of days or months before the current lease expires.

—Detrimental Reliance and Promissory Estoppel. When the offeree justifiably relies on an offer to her or his detriment, the court may hold that this *detrimental reliance* makes the offer irrevocable. For example, assume that Angela has rented commercial property from Jake for the past thirty-three years under a series of five-year leases. Under business conditions existing as their seventh lease nears its end, the rental property market is more favorable for tenants than for landlords. Angela tells Jake that she is going to look at other, less expensive properties as possible sites for her business. Wanting Angela to remain a tenant, Jake promises to reduce the rent in their next lease. In reliance on the promise, Angela continues to occupy and do business on Jake's property and does not look at other sites. When they sit down to negotiate a new lease, however, Jake says he has changed his mind and will increase the rent. Can he effectively revoke his promise?

Normally he cannot, because Angela has been relying on his promise to reduce the rent. Had the promise not been made, she would have relocated her business. This is a case of detrimental reliance on a promise, which therefore cannot be revoked. In this situation, the doctrine of **promissory estoppel** comes into play. To **estop** means to bar, impede, or preclude someone from doing something. Thus, promissory estoppel means that the promisor (the offeror) is barred from revoking the offer, in this case because the offeree has already changed her actions in reliance on the offer. We look again at the doctrine of promissory estoppel in Chapter 12 in the context of consideration.

—Detrimental Reliance and Partial Performance.

Detrimental reliance on the part of the offeree can also involve partial performance by the offeree in response to an offer to form a unilateral contract. As discussed in Chapter 10, an offer to form a unilateral contract invites acceptance only by full performance; merely promising to perform does not constitute acceptance. Injustice can result if an offeree expends time and funds in partial performance, only to have the offeror revoke the offer before performance can be completed. Many courts will not allow the offeror to revoke the offer after the offeree has performed some substantial part of his or her duties.[9] In effect, partial performance renders the offer irrevocable, giving the original offeree reasonable time to complete performance. Of course, once the performance is complete, a unilateral contract exists.

REJECTION OF THE OFFER BY THE OFFEREE The offer may be rejected by the offeree, in which case the offer is terminated. Any subsequent attempt by the offeree to accept will be construed as a new offer, giving the original offeror (now the offeree) the power of acceptance. A rejection is ordinarily accomplished by words or conduct evidencing an intent not to accept the offer. As with revocation, rejection of an offer is effective only when it is actually received by the offeror or the offeror's agent.

Merely inquiring about an offer does not constitute rejection. Suppose that a friend offers to buy your CD-ROM library for $300, and you respond, "Is that your best offer?" or "Will you pay me $375 for it?" A reasonable person would conclude that you had not rejected the offer but had merely made an inquiry for further consideration of the offer. You can still accept and bind your friend to the $300 purchase price. When the offeree merely inquires as to the firmness of the offer, there is no reason to presume that he or she intends to reject it.

COUNTEROFFER BY THE OFFEREE A **counteroffer** occurs when the offeree rejects the original offer and simultaneously makes a new offer. Suppose that Duffy offers to sell her Picasso lithograph to Wong for $4,500. Wong responds, "Your price is too high. I'll offer to purchase your lithograph for $4,000." Wong's response is a counteroffer, because it terminates Duffy's offer to sell at $4,500 and creates a new offer by Wong to purchase at $4,000.

At common law, the **mirror image rule** requires the offeree's acceptance to match the offeror's offer exactly—to mirror the offer. Any material change in, or addition to, the terms of the original offer automatically terminates that offer and substitutes the counteroffer. The counteroffer, of course, need not be accepted; but if the original offeror does accept the terms of the counteroffer, a valid contract is created.[10]

TERMINATION BY OPERATION OF LAW

The power of the offeree to transform the offer into a binding, legal obligation can be terminated by operation of law through the occurrence of any of the following events:

1. Lapse of time.
2. Destruction of the specific subject matter of the offer.
3. Death or incompetence of the offeror or the offeree.
4. Supervening illegality of the proposed contract.

LAPSE OF TIME An offer terminates automatically by law when the period of time specified in the offer has passed. For example, suppose Alejandro offers to sell his camper to Kelly if she accepts within twenty days. Kelly must accept within the twenty-day period, or the offer will lapse (terminate). The time period specified in an offer normally begins to run when the offer is actually received by the offeree, not when it is sent or drawn up. When the offer is delayed (through the misdelivery of mail, for example), the period begins to run from the date the offeree would have received the offer, but only if the offeree knows or should know that the offer is delayed.[11]

---

9. *Restatement (Second) of Contracts*, Section 45.

10. The mirror image rule has been greatly modified in regard to sales contracts. Section 2–207 of the UCC provides that a contract is formed if the offeree makes a definite expression of acceptance (such as signing the form in the appropriate location), even though the terms of the acceptance modify or add to the terms of the original offer (see Chapter 20).

11. *Restatement (Second) of Contracts*, Section 49.

If the offer does not specify a time for acceptance, the offer terminates at the end of a *reasonable* period of time. What constitutes a reasonable period of time depends on the subject matter of the contract, business and market conditions, and other relevant circumstances. An offer to sell farm produce, for example, will terminate sooner than an offer to sell farm equipment because farm produce is perishable and subject to greater fluctuations in market value.

DESTRUCTION OF THE SUBJECT MATTER
An offer is automatically terminated if the specific subject matter of the offer is destroyed before the offer is accepted.[12] If Johnson offers to sell his prize greyhound to Rizzo, for example, but the dog dies before Rizzo can accept, the offer is automatically terminated. Johnson does not have to tell Rizzo that the animal has died for the offer to terminate.

DEATH OR INCOMPETENCE OF THE OFFEROR OR OFFEREE
An offeree's power of acceptance is terminated when the offeror or offeree dies or is deprived of legal capacity to enter into the proposed contract. A revocable offer is personal to both parties and cannot pass to the heirs, guardian, or estate of either. Furthermore, this rule applies whether or not the other party had notice of the death or incompetence. If the offer is irrevocable, however, the death of the offeror or offeree does not terminate the offer.[13]

SUPERVENING ILLEGALITY OF THE PROPOSED CONTRACT
When a statute or court decision makes an offer illegal, the offer is automatically terminated.[14] For example, Lee offers to lend Kim $10,000 at an annual interest rate of 12 percent. Before Kim can accept the offer, a law is enacted that prohibits interest rates higher than 10 percent. Lee's offer is automatically terminated. If Kim had accepted the offer before the law was passed, a valid contract would have been formed, because the offer would still have been legal when it was accepted. In some circumstances, such a contract might be unenforceable, however, as when a statute or law is retroactively applied.

12. *Restatement (Second) of Contracts*, Section 36.

13. *Restatement (Second) of Contracts*, Section 48. If the offer is such that it can be accepted by the performance of a series of acts, and those acts began before the offeror died, the offeree's power of acceptance is not terminated.

14. *Restatement (Second) of Contracts*, Section 36.

CONCEPT SUMMARY 11.1 | Methods by Which an Offer Can Be Terminated

METHODS OF TERMINATION	BASIC RULES
BY ACTION OF THE PARTIES	
REVOCATION	1. An offer can be revoked at any time before acceptance without liability unless the offer is irrevocable. 2. Option contracts, merchants' firm offers, and, in some circumstances, the promissory estoppel theory render offers irrevocable. 3. Except for public offers, revocation is not effective until received by the offeree or the offeree's authorized agent.
REJECTION	1. Rejection of an offer is accomplished by words or actions that demonstrate a clear intent not to accept the offer or further consider the offer. Inquiries about an offer do not constitute a rejection. 2. A rejection is not effective until received by the offeror or an authorized agent of the offeror.
COUNTEROFFER	A counteroffer is a rejection of the original offer and the making of a new offer.
BY OPERATION OF LAW	
LAPSE OF TIME	1. If a time period for acceptance is stated in the offer, the offer ends at the stated time. 2. If no time period for acceptance is stated, the offer terminates at the end of a reasonable period.
DESTRUCTION	Destruction of the specific subject matter of the offer terminates the offer.
DEATH OR INCOMPETENCE	Death or incompetence of either the offeror or the offeree terminates an offer, unless the offer is irrevocable.
ILLEGALITY	Supervening illegality terminates an offer.

SECTION 3 | Acceptance

Acceptance is a voluntary act (either words or conduct) by the offeree that shows assent (agreement) to the terms of an offer. The acceptance must be unequivocal and must be communicated to the offeror.

UNEQUIVOCAL ACCEPTANCE

To exercise the power of acceptance effectively, the offeree must accept unequivocally. This is the *mirror image rule* previously discussed. If the acceptance is subject to new conditions or if the terms of the acceptance *materially* change the original offer, the acceptance may be deemed a counteroffer that implicitly rejects the original offer. An acceptance may be unequivocal even though the offeree expresses dissatisfaction with the contract. For example, "I accept the offer, but I wish I could have gotten a better price" is an effective acceptance. So, too, is "I accept, but can you shave the price?" In contrast, the statement "I accept the offer but only if I can pay on ninety days' credit" is not an unequivocal acceptance and operates as a counteroffer, rejecting the original offer.

Certain terms, when added to an acceptance, will not qualify the acceptance sufficiently to constitute rejection of the offer. Suppose that in response to an offer to sell a piano, the offeree replies, "I accept; please send a written contract." The offeree is requesting a written contract but is not making it a condition for acceptance. Therefore, the acceptance is effective without the written contract. If the offeree replies, "I accept if you send a written contract," however, the acceptance is expressly conditioned on the request for a writing, and the statement is not an acceptance but a counteroffer. (Notice how important each word is!)[15]

SILENCE AS ACCEPTANCE

Ordinarily, silence cannot constitute acceptance, even if the offeror states, "By your silence and inaction, you will be deemed to have accepted this offer." This general rule applies because an offeree should not be obligated to act affirmatively to reject an offer when no consideration has passed to the offeree to impose such a duty.

---

15. As noted in footnote 10, in regard to sales contracts the UCC provides that an acceptance may still be valid even if some terms are added. The new terms are simply treated as proposed additions to the contract.

ACCEPTANCE OF OFFERED SERVICES BY SILENCE

In some instances, however, the offeree does have a duty to speak, in which case her or his silence or inaction will operate as an acceptance. For example, silence may be an acceptance when an offeree takes the benefit of offered services even though he or she had an opportunity to reject them and knew that they were offered with the expectation of compensation. Suppose that Sayre watches while a stranger rakes his leaves, even though the stranger has not been asked to rake the yard. Sayre knows the stranger expects to be paid and does nothing to stop her. Here, his silence constitutes an acceptance, and an implied-in-fact contract is created (see Chapter 10). He is bound to pay a reasonable value for the stranger's work. This rule normally applies only when the offeree has received a benefit from the goods or services rendered.

PRIOR DEALINGS AND ACCEPTANCE BY SILENCE

Silence can also operate as acceptance when the offeree has had prior dealings with the offeror. Suppose that a merchant routinely receives shipments from a certain supplier and always notifies the supplier when defective goods are rejected. In this situation, silence regarding a shipment will constitute acceptance.

ACCEPTANCE BY SILENCE OF SOLICITED OFFERS

Additionally, if a person solicits an offer specifying that certain terms and conditions are acceptable, and the offeror makes the offer in response to the solicitation, the offeree has a duty to reject—that is, a duty to tell the offeror that the offer is not acceptable. In this situation, failure to reject (silence) operates as an acceptance.

COMMUNICATION OF ACCEPTANCE

Whether the offeror must be notified of the acceptance depends on the nature of the contract. In a bilateral contract, communication of acceptance is necessary because acceptance is in the form of a promise (not performance) and the contract is formed when the promise is made (rather than when the act is performed). The offeree must communicate the acceptance to the offeror. Communication of acceptance is not necessary, however, if the offer dispenses with the requirement. Additionally, if the offer can be accepted by silence, no communication is necessary.

Because a unilateral contract calls for the full performance of some act, acceptance is usually evident, and notification is therefore unnecessary. Exceptions do exist, however. When the offeror requests notice of acceptance or has no adequate means of determining whether the requested act has been performed, or when the law requires notice of acceptance, then notice is necessary.[16]

MODE AND TIMELINESS OF ACCEPTANCE

Acceptance in bilateral contracts must be timely. The general rule is that acceptance in a bilateral contract is timely if it is made before the offer is terminated. Problems arise, however, when the parties involved are not dealing face to face. In such cases, acceptance takes effect, thus completing formation of the contract, at the time the acceptance is communicated via the mode expressly or impliedly authorized by the offeror. According to the *Restatement (Second) of Contracts*, unless the offeror provides otherwise, "an acceptance made in a manner and by a medium invited by an offer is operative and completes the manifestation of mutual assent as soon as put out of the offeree's possession, without regard to whether it ever reaches the offeror."[17]

This rule traditionally has been referred to as the **mailbox rule,** also called the "deposited acceptance rule," because once an acceptance has been deposited in a mailbox, it is "out of the offeree's possession." Under this rule, if the authorized mode of communication is the mail, then an acceptance becomes valid when it is dispatched by mail (even if it is never received by the offeror). Thus, whereas a revocation becomes effective only when it is received by the offeree, an acceptance becomes effective on *dispatch,* providing that an *authorized* means of communication is used.

AUTHORIZED MEANS OF ACCEPTANCE An authorized means of communication may be either expressly authorized—that is, expressly stipulated in the offer—or impliedly authorized by the facts and circumstances surrounding the situation or by law. When an offeror specifies how acceptance should be made (for example, by overnight delivery), *express authorization* is said to exist, and the contract is not formed unless the offeree uses that specified mode of acceptance. Moreover, both offeror and offeree are bound in contract the moment this means of acceptance is employed. If overnight delivery is expressly authorized as the only means of acceptance, a contract is created as soon as the offeree delivers the message to the express delivery company. The contract would still exist even if the delivery company failed to deliver the message.

—When the Preferred Means of Acceptance Is Not Indicated. Many offerors, for one reason or another, do not indicate their preferred method of acceptance. When the offeror does not specify expressly that the offeree is to accept by a certain means, or that the acceptance will be effective only when received, acceptance of an offer may be made by any medium that is *reasonable under the circumstances*.[18] When two parties are at a distance, for example, mailing is impliedly authorized because it is a customary mode of dispatch.[19]

Several factors determine whether the acceptance was reasonable: the nature of the circumstances existing at the time the offer was made, the means used by the offeror to transmit the offer to the offeree, and the reliability of the offer's delivery. If, for example, an offer was sent by FedEx overnight delivery because an acceptance was urgently required, then the offeree's use of first-class mail (which may take three days or more to deliver) might not be deemed reasonable.[20]

—When the Authorized Means of Acceptance Is Not Used. An acceptance sent by means not expressly or impliedly authorized is normally not effective *until it is received by the offeror.* If an acceptance is timely sent and timely received, however, despite the means by which it is transmitted, it is considered to have been effective on its dispatch.[21] If, in the previous example, the acceptance that was sent by first class mail was actually delivered to the offeror the next day (the same as FedEx overnight delivery), then the court would recognize the acceptance as operative.

These principles are illustrated in the following case in the context of an option to renew a lease.

---

16. Under UCC 2–206(1)(b), an order or other offer to buy goods for prompt shipment may be treated as an offer contemplating either a bilateral or a unilateral contract and may be accepted by either a promise to ship (bilateral contract) or actual shipment (unilateral contract). If the offer is accepted by actual shipment of the goods, the buyer must be notified of the acceptance within a reasonable period of time, or the buyer may treat the offer as having lapsed before acceptance [UCC 2–206(2)]. See also Chapter 20.

17. *Restatement (Second) of Contracts*, Section 63(a).

18. *Restatement (Second) of Contracts*, Section 30. This is also the rule under UCC 2–206(1)(a).

19. *Adams v. Lindsell,* 106 Eng.Rep. 250 (K.B. 1818); *Restatement (Second) of Contracts*, Section 65, Comment c.

20. See, for example, *Defeo v. Amfarms Associates,* 161 A.D.2d 904, 557 N.Y.2d 469 (1990).

21. *Restatement (Second) of Contracts*, Section 67.

CASE 11.3

Osprey L.L.C. v. Kelly-Moore Paint Co.

Supreme Court of
Oklahoma, 1999.
984 P.2d 194.
http://www.oscn.net^a

BACKGROUND AND FACTS *Kelly-Moore Paint Company leased a store in Edmond, Oklahoma, from Osprey L.L.C. The parties signed a fifteen-year lease with two five-year renewal options. The lease required Kelly-Moore to give Osprey written notice of the lessee's intent to renew at least six months before the lease expired. The notice "may be delivered either personally or by depositing the same in United States mail, first class postage prepaid, registered or certified mail, return receipt requested." Six months before the end of the fifteen-year term, Kelly-Moore sent the required notice by certified mail. Five years later, however, at the end of the first five-year term, on the last day of the six-month notification deadline, at 5:28 P.M., Kelly-Moore sent the notice by fax. Phone company records indicated that the fax was transmitted correctly, but Osprey denied receiving it. Osprey filed a suit in an Oklahoma state court to evict Kelly-Moore. Osprey argued that the lease specifically prescribed delivery of the notice personally or by mail. Kelly-Moore countered that the lease's use of the word "may" permitted other means of delivery. The court granted a judgment in favor of Kelly-Moore, and Osprey appealed. The state intermediate appellate court reversed this judgment, and Kelly-Moore appealed to the Oklahoma Supreme Court.*

IN THE LANGUAGE OF THE COURT

 KAUGER, J. [Justice]

* * * *

* * * Although the question tendered is novel in Oklahoma, the sufficiency of the notice given when exercising an option contract or an option to renew or extend a lease has been considered by several jurisdictions. A few have found that delivery of notice by means other than hand delivery or by certified or registered mail was insufficient if the terms of the contract specifically referred to the method of delivery. However, the majority have reached the opposite conclusion. These courts generally recognize that, despite the contention that there must be strict compliance with the notice terms of a lease option agreement, *use of an alternative method does not render the notice defective if the substituted method performed the same function or served the same purpose as the authorized method.* [Emphasis added.]

* * * *

* * * The lease does not appear to be ambiguous. "Shall" is ordinarily construed as mandatory and "may" is ordinarily construed as permissive. * * * The provision for delivery, either personally or by certified or registered mail, uses the permissive "may" and it does not bar other modes of transmission which are just as effective.

* * * The purpose of providing notice by personal delivery or registered mail is to insure the delivery of the notice, and to settle any dispute which might arise between the parties concerning whether the notice was received. A substituted method of notice which performs the same function and serves the same purpose as an authorized method of notice is not defective. Here, the contract provided that time was of the essence. Although Osprey denies that it ever received the fax, the fax activity report and telephone company records confirm that the fax was transmitted successfully, and that it was sent to Osprey's correct facsimile number on the last day of the deadline to extend the lease. The fax provided immediate written communication similar to personal delivery and, like a telegram, would be timely if it were properly transmitted before the expiration of the deadline to renew. Kelly-Moore's use of the fax served the same function and the same purpose as the two methods suggested by the lease and it was transmitted before the expiration of the deadline to renew. Under these facts, we hold that the faxed or facsimile delivery of the written notice to renew the commercial lease was sufficient to exercise timely the renewal option of the lease.

DECISION AND REMEDY *The Oklahoma Supreme Court held that the use of an alternative method to exercise a lease option does not render the notice defective if the substituted notice performs the same function or serves the same purpose as the authorized method. The court vacated the decision of the state intermediate appellate court.*

---

a. This is the Oklahoma Supreme Court Network Web site, which is part of the Oklahoma Supreme Court Information System. In the "QuickCase" box near the top of the page, type "1999 OK 50" and click on "Go" to access the opinion.

EXCEPTIONS There are three basic exceptions to the rule that a contract is formed when an acceptance is sent by authorized means:

1. If the acceptance is not properly dispatched by the offeree (if it was sent to an incorrect address, for example), in most states it will not be effective until it is received by the offeror.[22] For example, if mail is the authorized means for acceptance, the offeree's letter must be properly addressed and have the correct postage. Nonetheless, if the acceptance is timely sent and timely received, despite the offeree's carelessness in sending it, it is still considered to have been effective on dispatch.[23]

2. The offeror can stipulate in the offer that an acceptance will normally not be effective until it is received by the offeror.

3. Sometimes an offeree sends a rejection first, then later changes his or her mind and sends an acceptance. Obviously, this chain of events could cause confusion and even detriment to the offeror, depending on whether the rejection or the acceptance arrives first. To prevent these potential problems, the law cancels the rule of acceptance on dispatch in such situations, and the first communication received by the offeror determines whether a con-

tract is formed. If the rejection arrives first, there is no contract.[24]

SECTION 4 | Technology and Acceptance Rules

Clearly, some of the traditional rules governing acceptance do not seem to apply to an age in which acceptances are commonly delivered via e-mail, fax, or other delivery system, such as FedEx or DHL. For example, the mailbox rule does not apply to online acceptances, which typically are communicated instantaneously to the offeror. Nonetheless, the traditional rules—and the principles that underlie those rules—provide a basis for understanding what constitutes a valid acceptance in today's online environment. This is because, as in other areas of the law, much of the law governing online offers and acceptances has been adapted from traditional law to a new context.

While online offers are not significantly different from traditional offers contained in paper documents, online acceptances have posed some unusual problems for the court. These problems, as well as other aspects of e-contracting, will be discussed in detail in Chapter 19.

---

22. *Restatement (Second) of Contracts*, Section 66.
23. *Restatement (Second) of Contracts*, Section 67.

---

24. *Restatement (Second) of Contracts*, Section 40.

CONCEPT SUMMARY 11.2 | Effective Time of Acceptance

ACCEPTANCE	TIME EFFECTIVE
BY AUTHORIZED MEANS OF COMMUNICATION	Effective at the time communication is sent (deposited in a mailbox or delivered to a courier service) via the mode expressly or impliedly authorized by the offeror (mailbox rule). *Exceptions:* 1. If the acceptance is not properly dispatched, it will not be effective until received by the offeror. 2. If the offeror specifically conditioned the offer on receipt of acceptance, it will not be effective until received by the offeror. 3. If acceptance is sent after rejection, whichever is received first is given effect.
BY UNAUTHORIZED MEANS OF COMMUNICATION	Effective on receipt of acceptance by the offeror (if timely received, it is considered to have been effective on dispatch).

REVIEWING AGREEMENT

Shane Durbin wanted to have a recording studio custom-built in his home. He sent invitations to a number of local contractors to submit bids on the project. Rory Johnson submitted the lowest bid, which was $20,000 less than any of the other bids Durbin received. Durbin called Johnson to find out the type and quality of the materials that were included in the bid and ask if he could substitute a superior brand of acoustic tiles for the same bid price. Johnson said he would have to check into the price difference. The parties also discussed a possible start date for construction. Two weeks later, Durbin changed his mind and decided not to go forward with his plan to build a recording studio. Johnson filed a suit against Durbin for breach of contract. Using the information presented in the chapter, answer the following questions.

1. Who is the offeror and who is the offeree in this scenario?

2. Did Johnson's bid meet the requirements of an offer? Explain.

3. Was there an acceptance of the offer? Why or why not?

4. How is an offer terminated? Assuming that Durbin did not inform Johnson that he was rejecting the offer, was the offer terminated at any time described here? Explain.

5. Suppose that the court determines that the parties did not reach an agreement. Further suppose that Johnson, in anticipation of building Durbin's studio, had purchased materials and refused other jobs so that he would have time in his schedule for Durbin's project. Under what theory discussed in the chapter might Johnson attempt to recover these costs?

TERMS AND CONCEPTS TO REVIEW

acceptance 236

agreement 225

counteroffer 234

estop 234

mailbox rule 237

mirror image rule 234

mutual assent 225

offer 225

option contract 233

promissory estoppel 234

revocation 233

QUESTIONS AND CASE PROBLEMS

11–1. Ball writes Sullivan and inquires how much Sullivan is asking for a specific forty-acre tract of land Sullivan owns. In a letter received by Ball, Sullivan states, "I will not take less than $60,000 for the forty-acre tract as specified." Ball immediately sends Sullivan a telegram stating, "I accept your offer for $60,000 for the forty-acre tract as specified." Discuss whether Ball can hold Sullivan to a contract for the sale of the land.

11–2. QUESTION WITH SAMPLE ANSWER

Schmidt, operating a sole proprietorship, has a large piece of used farm equipment for sale. He offers to sell the equipment to Barry for $10,000. Discuss the legal effects of the following events on the offer:

(a) Schmidt dies prior to Barry's acceptance, and at the time he accepts, Barry is unaware of Schmidt's death.

(b) The night before Barry accepts, fire destroys the equipment.

(c) Barry pays $100 for a thirty-day option to purchase the equipment. During this period, Schmidt dies, and later Barry accepts the offer, knowing of Schmidt's death.

(d) Barry pays $100 for a thirty-day option to purchase the equipment. During this period, Barry dies, and Barry's estate accepts Schmidt's offer within the stipulated time period.

For a sample answer to this question, go to Appendix I at the end of this text.

11–3. Perez sees an advertisement in the newspaper that the ABC Corp. is offering for sale a two-volume set of books, *How to Make Repairs around the House*, for $39.95. All Perez has to do is send in a card requesting delivery of the books for a thirty-day trial period of examination. If he does not ship the books back within thirty days of delivery, ABC will bill him for $39.95. Discuss whether Perez and ABC have a contract under either of the following circumstances:

(a) Perez sends in the card and receives the books in the U.S. mail. He uses the books to make repairs and fails to return them within thirty days.

(b) Perez does not send in the card, but ABC sends him the books anyway through the U.S. mail. Perez uses the books and fails to return them within thirty days.

11–4. On Thursday, Dennis mailed a letter to Tanya's office offering to sell his car to her for $3,000. On Saturday, having changed his mind, Dennis sent a fax to Tanya's office revoking his offer. Tanya did not go to her office over the weekend and thus did not learn about the revocation until Monday morning, just a few minutes after she had mailed a letter of acceptance to Dennis. When Tanya demanded that Dennis sell his car to her as promised, Dennis claimed that no contract existed because he had revoked his offer prior to Tanya's acceptance. Is Dennis correct? Explain.

11–5. AUCTIONS. Ameritrust Co. employed Rosen & Co. to conduct an auction. Included in Rosen's extensive advertisements of the sale was the announcement that the sale was subject to confirmation by Ameritrust. The auctioneer made a similar announcement at the time of the sale. At the auction, the auctioneer first offered the equipment in bulk, but only one bid—from Alpine Co. for $50,000—was received. Then the equipment was offered piecemeal, and total bids of $139,000 were received. Two bids—one from Lawrence Paper Co. and one from American Corrugated Machine Corp. (ACMC)—were accepted, and both companies submitted checks for 25 percent of their bid totals, as requested. Subsequent to the auction, Alpine offered $175,000 for the equipment, and Ameritrust sold the entire lot to Alpine. Lawrence and ACMC sued for breach of contract. Will they succeed in their suit? Why or why not? [*Lawrence Paper Co. v. Rosen & Co.*, 939 F.2d 376 (6th Cir. 1991)]

11–6. INTENTION. Before an employee convention, Nationwide Mutual Insurance Co. created a committee, whose members included Mary Peterson, to select a theme. The committee announced a contest for theme suggestions: "Here's what you could win: His and Hers Mercedes. An all expense paid trip for two around the world. Additional prize to be announced. (All prizes subject to availability.)" David Mears submitted the theme "At the Top and Still Climbing." At a dinner of Nationwide employees, Peterson told Mears that he had won two Mercedes. Mears and others who heard this believed that he had won the cars. Nationwide never gave him the cars, however, and he filed a suit in a federal district court, alleging breach of contract. At the trial, Peterson claimed that she had spoken with a facetious tone and, in reality, had had no intention of awarding the cars. Is Mears entitled to the cars? Why or why not? [*Mears v. Nationwide Mutual Insurance Co.*, 91 F.3d 1118 (8th Cir. 1996)]

11–7. ⚖ **CASE PROBLEM WITH SAMPLE ANSWER**
The Pittsburgh Board of Public Education in Pittsburgh, Pennsylvania, as required by state law, keeps lists of eligible teachers in order of their rank or standing. According to an "Eligibility List" form made available to applicants, no one may be hired to teach whose name is not within the top 10 percent of the names on the list. In 1996, Anna Reed was in the top 10 percent. She was not hired that year, although four other applicants who placed lower on the list—and not within the top 10 percent—were hired. In 1997 and 1998, Reed was again in the top 10 percent, but she was not hired until 1999. Reed filed a suit in a federal district court against the board and others. She argued in part that the state's requirement that the board keep a list constituted an offer, which she accepted by participating in the process to be placed on that list. She claimed that the board breached this contract by hiring applicants who ranked lower than she did. The case was transferred to a Pennsylvania state court. What are the requirements of an offer? Do the circumstances in this case meet those requirements? Why or why not? [*Reed v. Pittsburgh Board of Public Education*, 862 A.2d 131 (Pa.Cmwlth. 2004)]

To view a sample answer for this case problem, go to this book's Web site at http://wbl.westbuslaw.com, select "Chapter 11," and click on "Case Problem with Sample Answer."

11–8. DEFINITENESS OF TERMS. Southwick Homes, Ltd., develops and markets residential subdivisions. William McLinden and Ronald Coco are the primary owners of Southwick Homes. Coco is also the president of Mutual Development Co. Whiteco Industries, Inc., wanted to develop lots and sell homes in Schulien Woods, a subdivision in Crown Point, Indiana. In September 1996, Whiteco sent McLinden a letter enlisting Southwick Homes to be the project manager for the developing and marketing of the finished lots (lots where roads had been built and on which utility installation and connections to water and sewer lines were complete); the letter set out the roles and expectations of each of the parties, including the terms of payment. In October 1997, Whiteco sent Coco a letter naming Mutual Development the developer and general contractor for the houses to be built on the finished lots. A few months later, Coco told McLinden that he would not share the profits from the construction of the houses. McLinden and others filed a suit in an Indiana state court against Coco and others, claiming, in part, a breach of fiduciary duty. The defendants responded that the letter to McLinden lacked such essential terms as to render it unenforceable. What terms must an agreement include to be an enforceable contract? Did the McLinden letter include these terms? In whose favor should the court rule? Explain. [*McLinden v. Coco*, 765 N.E.2d 606 (Ind.App. 2002)]

11–9. INTENTION. Music that is distributed on compact discs and similar media generates income in the form of "mechanical" royalties. Music that is publicly performed, such as when a song is played on a radio, in a movie or commercial, or sampled in another song, produces "performance" royalties. Each of these types of royalties is divided between the songwriter and the song's publisher. Vincent Cusano is a musician and songwriter who performed under the name "Vinnie Vincent" as a guitarist with the group KISS in the early 1980s. Cusano co-wrote three songs entitled "Killer," "I Love It Loud," and "I Still Love You" that KISS recorded and released in 1982 on an album titled *Creatures of the Night*. Cusano left KISS in 1984. Eight years later, Cusano sold to Horipro Entertainment Group "one hundred (100%) percent undivided interest" of his rights in the songs "other than Songwriter's share of performance income." Later, Cusano filed a suit in a federal district court against Horipro, claiming in part that he never intended to sell the writer's share of the mechanical royalties.

Horipro filed a motion for summary judgment. Should the court grant the motion? Explain. [*Cusano v. Horipro Entertainment Group*, 301 F.Supp.2d 272 (S.D.N.Y. 2004)]

11–10.   VIDEO QUESTION

Go to this text's Web site at http://wbl.westbuslaw.com and select "Chapter 11." Click on "Video Questions" and view the video titled *Offer and Acceptance*. Then answer the following questions.

(a) On the video, Vinny indicates that he can't sell his car to Oscar for four thousand dollars and then says, "maybe five . . . ." Discuss whether Vinny has made an offer or a counteroffer.

(b) Oscar then says to Vinny, "Okay, I'll take it. But you gotta let me pay you four thousand now and the other thousand in two weeks." According to the chapter, do Oscar and Vinny have an agreement? Why or why not?

(c) When Maria later says to Vinny, "I'll take it," has she accepted an offer? Why or why not?

LAW | on the Web

For updated links to resources available on the Web, as well as a variety of other materials, visit this text's Web site at http://wbl.westbuslaw.com.

To learn what kinds of clauses are included in typical contracts for certain goods and services, you can explore the collection of contract forms made available by FindLaw at

http://forms.lp.findlaw.com

LEGAL RESEARCH EXERCISES ON THE WEB

Go to http://wbl.westbuslaw.com, the Web site that accompanies this text. Select "Chapter 11" and click on "Internet Exercises." There you will find the following Internet research exercises that you can perform to learn more about topics covered in this chapter.

Activity 11–1: LEGAL PERSPECTIVE
Contract Terms

Activity 11–2: MANAGEMENT PERSPECTIVE
Sample Contracts

Activity 11–3: ETHICAL PERSPECTIVE
Offers and Advertisements

CHAPTER 12
Consideration

The fact that a promise has been made does not mean the promise can or will be enforced. Under Roman law, a promise was not enforceable without some sort of *causa*—that is, a reason for making the promise that was also deemed to be a sufficient reason for enforcing it. Under the common law, a primary basis for the enforcement of promises is consideration. **Consideration** is usually defined as the value (such as money) given in return for a promise (such as the promise to sell a stamp collection on receipt of payment) or in return for a performance.

SECTION 1 | Elements of Consideration

Often, consideration is broken down into two parts: (1) something of *legally sufficient value* must be given in exchange for the promise; and (2) usually, there must be a *bargained-for* exchange.

LEGAL VALUE

The "something of legally sufficient value" may consist of (1) a promise to do something that one has no prior legal duty to do, (2) the performance of an action that one is otherwise not obligated to undertake, or (3) the refraining from an action that one has a legal right to undertake (called a **forbearance**). Consideration in bilateral contracts normally consists of a promise in return for a promise, as explained in Chapter 10. For example, suppose that in a contract for the sale of goods, the seller promises to ship specific goods to the buyer, and the buyer promises to pay for those goods when they are received. Each of these promises constitutes consideration for the contract.

In contrast, unilateral contracts involve a promise in return for a performance. Suppose that Anita says to her neighbor, "When you finish painting the garage, I will pay you $100." Anita's neighbor paints the garage. The act of painting the garage is the consideration that creates Anita's contractual obligation to pay her neighbor $100.

What if, in return for a promise to pay, a person refrains from pursuing harmful habits (a forbearance), such as the use of tobacco and alcohol? Does such forbearance constitute legally sufficient consideration? This was the issue before the court in the following case, which is one of the classics in contract law with respect to consideration.

CASE 12.1 | Hamer v. Sidway

Court of Appeals
of New York,
Second Division, 1891.
124 N.Y. 538,
27 N.E. 256.

BACKGROUND AND FACTS *William E. Story, Sr., was the uncle of William E. Story II. In the presence of family members and guests invited to a family gathering, the elder Story promised to pay his nephew $5,000 ($72,000 in today's dollars) if he would refrain from drinking, using tobacco, swearing, and playing cards or billiards for money until he reached the age of twenty-one. (Note that in 1869, when this contract was formed, it was legal in New York to drink and play cards for money prior to the age of twenty-one.) The nephew agreed and fully performed his part of the bargain. When he reached the age of twenty-one, he wrote and told his uncle that he had kept his part of the agreement and was therefore entitled to $5,000. The uncle replied that he was pleased with his nephew's performance, writing, "I have no doubt but you have, for which you shall have five thousand*

CONTINUED ▶

dollars, as I promised you. I had the money in the bank the day you was twenty-one years old that I intend for you, and you shall have the money certain. . . . P.S. You can consider this money on interest." The nephew received his uncle's letter and thereafter consented that the money should remain with his uncle according to the terms and conditions of the letter. The uncle died about twelve years later without having paid his nephew any part of the $5,000 and interest. The executor of the uncle's estate (Sidway, the defendant in this action) claimed that there had been no valid consideration for the promise and therefore refused to pay the $5,000 (plus interest) to Hamer, a third party to whom the nephew had transferred his rights in the note. The court reviewed the case to determine whether the nephew had given valid consideration under the law.

IN THE LANGUAGE OF THE COURT

PARKER, J. [Justice]
* * * *
* * * Courts will not ask whether the thing which forms the consideration does in fact benefit the promisee or a third party, or is of any substantial value to any one. It is enough that something is promised, done, forborne, or suffered by the party to whom the promise is made as consideration for the promise made to him. *In general a waiver of any legal right at the request of another party is a sufficient consideration for a promise.* Any damage, or suspension, or forbearance of a right will be sufficient to sustain a promise. * * * Now, applying this rule to the facts before us, the promisee used tobacco, occasionally drank liquor, and he had a legal right to do so. That right he abandoned for a period of years upon the strength of the promise of the testator [his uncle] that for such forbearance he would give him $5,000. We need not speculate on the effort which may have been required to give up the use of those stimulants. It is sufficient that he restricted his lawful freedom of action within certain prescribed limits upon the faith of his uncle's agreement * * * . [Emphasis added.]

DECISION AND REMEDY   *The court ruled that the nephew had provided legally sufficient consideration by giving up smoking, drinking, swearing, and playing cards or billiards for money until he reached the age of twenty-one and was therefore entitled to the money.*

WHAT IF THE FACTS WERE DIFFERENT?   *If the nephew had not had a legal right to engage in the behavior that he agreed to forgo, would the result in this case have been different?*

IMPACT OF THIS CASE ON TODAY'S LAW
Although this case was decided over a century ago, the principles enunciated in the case remain applicable to contracts formed today, including online contracts. For a contract to be valid and binding, consideration must be given, and that consideration must be something of legally sufficient value.

BARGAINED-FOR EXCHANGE

The second element of consideration is that it must provide the basis for the bargain struck between the contracting parties. The promise given by the promisor (offeror) must induce the promisee (offeree) to offer a return promise, a performance, or a forbearance, and the promisee's promise, performance, or forbearance must induce the promisor to make the promise.

This element of bargained-for exchange distinguishes contracts from gifts. For example, suppose that Arlene says to her son, "In consideration of the fact that you are not as wealthy as your brothers, I will pay you $500." The fact that the word *consideration* is used does not, by itself, mean that consideration has been given. Indeed, this is not an enforceable promise because the son need not do anything in order to receive the promised $500.[1] The son need not give Arlene something of legal value in return for her promise, and the promised $500 does not involve a bargained-for exchange. Rather, Arlene has simply stated her motive for giving her son a gift.

SECTION 2 | Adequacy of Consideration

Legal sufficiency of consideration involves the requirement that consideration be something of legally sufficient value in the eyes of the law. Adequacy of consideration involves "how much" consideration is given. Essentially, adequacy of consideration concerns the fairness of the bargain. On the surface, fairness would appear to be an issue when the items exchanged are of unequal value. In general, however, a court will not question the adequacy of

---

1. See *Fink v. Cox*, 18 Johns. 145, 9 Am.Dec. 191 (N.Y. 1820).

consideration if the consideration is legally sufficient. Under the doctrine of freedom of contract, parties are normally free to bargain as they wish. If people could sue merely because they had entered into an unwise contract, the courts would be overloaded with frivolous suits.

In extreme cases, a court may consider the adequacy of consideration in terms of its amount or worth because inadequate consideration may indicate that fraud, duress, or undue influence was involved or that the element of bargained-for exchange was lacking. It may also reflect a party's incompetence (for example, an individual might have been too intoxicated or simply too young to make a contract). Suppose that Dylan has a house worth $100,000 and sells it for $50,000. A $50,000 sale could indicate that the buyer unduly pressured Dylan into selling the house at that price or that Dylan was defrauded into selling the house at far below market value. (Of course, it might also indicate that Dylan was in a hurry to sell and that the amount was legally sufficient.)

In the following case, the issue was whether consideration existed in a contract to accept lower payments for medical services than the maximum fees allowed under state regulations.

CASE 12.2 | Seaview Orthopaedics v. National Healthcare Resources, Inc.

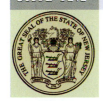

Superior Court
of New Jersey,
Appellate Division, 2004.
366 N.J.Super. 501,
841 A.2d 917.

FISHER, J.A.D. [Judge, Appellate Division]

[Seaview Orthopaedics and the other plaintiffs] are medical service providers who * * * claim * * * Allstate Indemnity Company (Allstate) [through its claims administrator] National Healthcare Resources, Inc. (NHR), wrongfully "under-reimbursed" for treatment plaintiffs rendered to various auto accident victims [who were Allstate's clients]. Allstate * * * reimbursed pursuant to rates set forth in plaintiffs' contract with * * * Consumer Health Network (CHN) and not pursuant to the maximum rate allowed by the PIP [personal injury protection] medical fee schedule set forth in [New Jersey state regulations]. * * *

* * * * *

* * * Because the CHN fee schedule imposes lower rates than the PIP fee schedule set forth in [New Jersey state regulations] plaintiffs filed [this suit in a New Jersey state court against NHR and others], seeking to recover damages * * * representing the monetary difference between the two schedules. [The court issued a summary judgment in favor of the defendants and dismissed the plaintiffs' complaint. The plaintiffs appealed to a state intermediate appellate court.]

CHN claims to be the largest preferred provider organization (PPO) in New Jersey. * * * [I]ts network includes over 11,000 physicians, nearly 14,000 medical services providers (which includes not only physicians but also laboratories and hospitals) and has 950,000 enrollees. CHN provides its clients with a PPO network in three distinct areas: workers' compensation, group health benefits and auto insurance. By entering into a contract with CHN, plaintiffs gained potential access to the numerous enrollees in exchange for accepting reimbursement at lesser rates.

CONTINUED

CASE 12.2 | **Continued**

* * * The CHN contract states in unambiguous terms that it covers policies of automobile insurance. The contract also contains plaintiffs' agreement to be reimbursed, in such circumstances, only when rendering appropriate and necessary treatment, and at rates no greater than those set forth in the CHN fee schedule. Accordingly, on its face, when treating auto accident victims, the CHN contract limits plaintiffs to payments no greater than those permitted by the CHN fee schedule.

Plaintiffs * * * argue that their agreement to be bound to the CHN rates for auto accident victims is not supported by consideration. It is well-settled that contracts are not enforceable in the absence of consideration, i.e., both sides must get something out of the exchange. *Consideration may take many forms and may be based upon either a detriment incurred by the promisee or a benefit received by the promisor.* Courts, however, do not inquire into the adequacy of consideration in determining whether to enforce a contract. *Any inquiry into the presence of consideration does not depend upon the comparative value of the things exchanged.* Instead, when we speak of the need for an exchange of valuable consideration what is meant is that the consideration must merely be valuable in the sense that it is something that is bargained for in fact. [Emphasis added.]

Here, the contract provided benefits to plaintiffs in a variety of ways which either collectively or separately constituted valuable consideration for plaintiffs' promise to accept the CHN rates for reimbursement from auto accident victims (and other types of patients) and not the maximum rate permitted by the PIP fee schedule. Plaintiffs, for example, obtained the benefit of marketing their businesses in a directory of providers utilized by numerous payors in the workers' compensation and health benefits markets and many thousands of potential patients. Payors make the list available to the largest PPO membership network in New Jersey and, in the health and workers' compensation settings, are generally offered substantial financial incentives when those patients use the providers on the list.

Plaintiffs argue that the likelihood of a provider receiving a referral from the CHN network of an auto accident victim "is practically nil." Defendants dispute this, contending that an auto accident victim, who is in a health benefits or workers' compensation plan that utilized the CHN network, may likely use the same provider that was engaged for these other purposes. This point is, perhaps, debatable. But even if plaintiffs' argument is accurate and the actual benefits received by them in the auto insurance area are illusory, plaintiffs received valuable consideration by being in the network and by obtaining or at least gaining access to patients in the workers' compensation and health benefits areas. That the predominant (or even exclusive) benefits for providers may come from workers' compensation or health benefit sources does not render the contract unenforceable for lack of consideration when services provided for auto accident victims are reimbursed at a lesser rate. We need not, as plaintiffs argue, find some specific monetary benefit for plaintiffs when called upon to provide services for auto accident victims so long as the other aspects of the contract provide, or have the potential to provide, a benefit to plaintiffs. *It is the totality of the exchange of promises and benefits that is considered* and, in this case, this exchange was sufficient to create an enforceable contract. [Emphasis added.]

* * * *

* * * [W]e reject plaintiffs' contentions in their entirety and affirm the entry of summary judgment dismissing the complaints in these * * * actions. We * * * also affirm the order imposing costs in favor of defendants and against plaintiffs in each action.

QUESTIONS

1. If a provider could prove that it received no benefit under a contract such as the one at the center of this case, would that be a ground for concluding that there was no consideration?
2. Could a provider successfully claim that the CHN contract lacked consideration if the provider's customary fee was higher than the state's maximum rate?

SECTION 3 | Agreements That Lack Consideration

Sometimes, one of the parties (or both parties) to an agreement may think that consideration has been exchanged when in fact it has not. Here, we look at some situations in which the parties' promises or actions do not qualify as contractual consideration.

PREEXISTING DUTY

Under most circumstances, a promise to do what one already has a legal duty to do does not constitute legally sufficient consideration.[2] The preexisting legal duty may be imposed by law or may arise out of a previous contract. A sheriff, for example, cannot collect a reward for providing information leading to the capture of a criminal if the sheriff already has a legal duty to capture the criminal.

Likewise, if a party is already bound by contract to perform a certain duty, that duty cannot serve as consideration for a second contract. For example, suppose that Bauman-Bache, Inc., begins construction on a seven-story office building and after three months demands an extra $75,000 on its contract. If the extra $75,000 is not paid, it will stop working. The owner of the land, having no one else to complete the construction, agrees to pay the extra $75,000. The agreement is unenforceable because it is not supported by legally sufficient consideration; Bauman-Bache was under a preexisting contract to complete the building.

UNFORESEEN DIFFICULTIES The rule regarding preexisting duty is meant to prevent extortion and the so-called holdup game. What happens, though, when an honest contractor who has contracted with a landowner to construct a building runs into extraordinary difficulties that were totally unforeseen at the time the contract was formed? In the interests of fairness and equity, the courts sometimes allow exceptions to the preexisting duty rule. In the example just mentioned, if the landowner agrees to pay extra compensation to the contractor for overcoming unforeseen difficulties, the court may refrain from applying the preexisting duty rule and enforce the agreement. When the "unforeseen difficulties" that give rise to a contract modification involve the types of risks ordinarily assumed in business, however, the courts will usually assert the preexisting duty rule.[3]

RESCISSION AND NEW CONTRACT The law recognizes that two parties can mutually agree to rescind, or cancel, their contract, at least to the extent that it is executory (still to be carried out). **Rescission**[4] is defined as the unmaking of a contract so as to return the parties to the positions they occupied before the contract was made. When rescission and the making of a new contract take place at the same time, but the duties of both parties remain the same as in their rescinded contract, the courts frequently are given a choice of applying the preexisting duty rule or allowing rescission and letting the new contract stand.

PAST CONSIDERATION

Promises made in return for actions or events that have already taken place are unenforceable. These promises lack consideration in that the element of bargained-for exchange is missing. In short, you can bargain for something to take place now or in the future but not for something that has already taken place. Therefore, **past consideration** is no consideration.

Suppose, for example, that Elsie, a real estate agent, does her friend Judy a favor by selling Judy's house and not charging any commission. Later, Judy says to Elsie, "In return for your generous act, I will pay you $3,000." This promise is made in return for past consideration and is thus unenforceable; in effect, Judy is stating her intention to give Elsie a gift.

Is a party's suggestion that a professional athlete use a certain nickname for marketing products sufficient consideration for the athlete's later promise to pay the party a portion of the profits? That was the question in the following case.

---

2. See *Foakes v. Beer*, 9 App.Cas. 605 (1884).

3. Note that under Article 2 of the Uniform Commercial Code (UCC), an agreement modifying a contract needs no consideration to be binding. See UCC 2–209(1).
4. Pronounced reh-*sih*-zhen.

CASE 12.3

United States
District Court,
Eastern District of
Pennsylvania, 2003.
324 F.Supp.2d 602.

Blackmon v. Iverson

BACKGROUND AND FACTS *Jamil Blackmon became friends with Allen Iverson in 1987 when Iverson was a high school student who showed tremendous promise as an athlete. Blackmon began to provide financial and other support to Iverson and his family. One evening in 1994, Blackmon suggested that Iverson use "The Answer" as a nickname in the summer league basketball tournaments. Blackmon said that Iverson would be "The Answer" to all of the National Basketball Association's woes. Later that night, Iverson said that he would give Blackmon 25 percent of any proceeds from the merchandising of products that used "The Answer" as a logo or a slogan. Blackmon invested time, money, and effort in refining the concept of "The Answer." In 1996, just before Iverson was drafted by the Philadelphia 76ers, Iverson told Blackmon that Iverson intended to use "The Answer" under a contract with Reebok. In 1997, Reebok began to sell, and continues to sell, products bearing "The Answer" slogan. None of the products uses any of Blackmon's designs, however, and Iverson does not share any of his profits with Blackmon. In 1998, Iverson persuaded Blackmon to move to Philadelphia. Blackmon subsequently filed a suit in a federal district court against Iverson, alleging breach of contract, among other things. Iverson filed a motion for summary judgment.*

IN THE LANGUAGE OF THE COURT

MCLAUGHLIN, District Judge.
* * * *

The plaintiff claims that he entered into an express contract with the defendant pursuant to which he was to receive twenty-five percent of the proceeds that the defendant received from marketing products with "The Answer" on them. The defendant argues that there was not a valid contract because * * * there was no consideration alleged.
* * * *

Under [the] law, a plaintiff must present clear and precise evidence of an agreement in which both parties manifested an intent to be bound, for which both parties gave consideration, and which contains sufficiently definite terms.

Consideration confers a benefit upon the promisor or causes a detriment to the promisee and must be an act, forbearance, or return promise bargained for and given in exchange for the original promise. Under [the] law, past consideration is insufficient to support a subsequent promise. [Emphasis added.]
* * * *

The plaintiff has argued that, in exchange for the defendant's promise to pay the twenty-five percent, the plaintiff gave three things as consideration: (1) the plaintiff's idea to use "The Answer" as a nickname to sell athletic apparel; (2) the plaintiff's assistance to and relationship with the defendant and his family; and (3) the plaintiff's move to Philadelphia.

According to the facts alleged by the plaintiff, he made the suggestion that the defendant use "The Answer" as a nickname and for product merchandising one evening in 1994. This was before the defendant first promised to pay; according to the plaintiff, the promise to pay was made later that evening. The disclosure of the idea also occurred before the defendant told the plaintiff that he was going to use the idea in connection with the Reebok contract in 1996, and before the sales of goods bearing "The Answer" actually began in 1997.

Regardless of whether the contract was formed in 1994, 1996, or 1997, the disclosure of "The Answer" idea had already occurred and was, therefore, past consideration insufficient to create a binding contract.
* * * *

According to the complaint, the plaintiff's relationship and support for the defendant, * * * began in 1987, seven years before the first alleged promise to pay was made. There is no allegation that the plaintiff began engaging in this conduct because of any promise by the defendant, or that the plaintiff continued his gratuitous conduct in 1994, 1996, or 1997 in exchange for the promise to pay. These actions are not valid consideration.

The plaintiff also alleged at oral argument that his move to Philadelphia during the 1997–1998 season was consideration for the promise to pay. If the parties reached a mutual

---

CASE 12.3 | Continued agreement in 1994, the plaintiff has not properly alleged that the move was consideration because there is no allegation that the parties anticipated that the plaintiff would move to Philadelphia three or four years later, or that the plaintiff promised to do so in exchange for the defendant's promise to pay.

Nor is there any allegation that the move was part of the terms of any contract created in 1996 or 1997. The complaint states only that the defendant "persuaded" him to move to Philadelphia to "begin seeking the profits from his ideas." Even when the complaint is construed broadly, there is no allegation that the move was required in exchange for any promise by the defendant to pay. In the absence of valid consideration, the plaintiff has no claim for breach of an express contract.

DECISION AND REMEDY *The court granted Iverson's motion to dismiss Blackmon's complaint. The alleged contract between the parties was not supported by sufficient consideration. The disclosure of the idea for the use of "The Answer" as a marketing tool occurred before the formation of a promise to pay for the use of the idea.*

WHAT IF THE FACTS WERE DIFFERENT? *Suppose that only five minutes had elapsed between Blackmon's suggesting that Iverson use "The Answer" as a marketing slogan and Iverson's promising to give Blackmon a percentage of the proceeds. Would the court's ruling in this case have been any different? Why or why not?*

SECTION 4 | Problem Areas Concerning Consideration

Problems concerning consideration usually fall into one of the following categories:

1. Promises exchanged when total performance by the parties is uncertain.
2. Settlement of claims.
3. Promises enforceable without consideration.

The courts' solutions to these types of problems give insight into how the law views the complex concept of consideration.

UNCERTAIN PERFORMANCE

If the terms of the contract express such uncertainty of performance that the promisor has not definitely promised to do anything, the promise is said to be *illusory*—without consideration and unenforceable. For example, suppose that the president of Tuscan Corporation says to her employees, "All of you have worked hard, and if profits continue to remain high, a 10 percent bonus at the end of the year will be given— if management thinks it is warranted." The employees continue to work hard, and profits remain high, but no bonus is given. This is an *illusory promise*, or no promise at all, because performance depends solely on the discretion of the president (the management). There is no bargained-for consideration. The statement declares merely that the management may or may not do something in the future. The president is not obligated (incurs no detriment) now or later.

OPTION-TO-CANCEL CLAUSES Option-to-cancel clauses in term contracts sometimes present problems in regard to consideration. For example, suppose that I contract to hire you for one year at $5,000 per month, reserving the right to cancel the contract at any time. On close examination of these words, you can see that I have not actually agreed to hire you, as I could cancel without liability before you started performance. I have not given up the opportunity of hiring someone else. This contract is therefore illusory. Suppose, however, that I am required to give you thirty days' notice to exercise the option. The thirty days' notice entitles you to at least one month's salary of $5,000, which is consideration. Thus, until I give you notice, you are entitled to $5,000 per month until the contract is terminated at the end of the year.

REQUIREMENTS CONTRACTS AND OUTPUT CONTRACTS Problems with consideration may also arise in other types of contracts because of uncertainty of performance. Uncertain performance is characteristic of requirements and output contracts, for example. In a *requirements contract,* a buyer and a seller agree that the buyer will purchase from the seller all of the goods of a designated type that the buyer needs, or requires. In an *output contract,* the buyer and seller agree that the buyer will purchase from the seller all of what the seller produces, or the seller's output. These types of contracts will be discussed further in Chapter 20.

SETTLEMENT OF CLAIMS

Businesspersons or others can settle legal claims in several ways, and it is important to understand the nature of consideration given in these kinds of settlement agreements, or contracts. In an *accord and satisfaction,* which is a common means of settling a claim, a debtor offers to pay a lesser amount than the creditor purports to be owed. Other methods that are commonly used to settle claims include a *release* and a *covenant not to sue.*

ACCORD AND SATISFACTION The concept of **accord and satisfaction** involves a debtor's offer of payment and a creditor's acceptance of a lesser amount than the creditor originally purported to be owed. The *accord* is defined as the agreement under which one of the parties undertakes to give or perform, and the other to accept, in satisfaction of a claim, something other than that on which the parties originally agreed. *Satisfaction* takes place when the accord is executed. A basic rule is that there can be no satisfaction unless there is first an accord. For accord and satisfaction to occur, the amount of the debt *must be in dispute.*

—*Liquidated Debts.*   If a debt is *liquidated,* accord and satisfaction cannot take place. A liquidated debt is one whose amount has been ascertained, fixed, agreed on, settled, or exactly determined. For example, if Baker signs an installment loan contract with her banker in which she agrees to pay a specified rate of interest on a specified sum of borrowed funds at monthly intervals for two years, that is a liquidated debt. The total obligation is precisely known to both parties, and reasonable persons will not differ over the amount owed.

Suppose that Baker has missed her last two payments on the loan and the creditor demands that she pay the overdue debt. Baker makes a partial payment and states that she believes this payment is all she should have to pay and that, if the creditor accepts the payment, the debt will be satisfied, or discharged. In the majority of states, acceptance of a lesser sum than the entire amount of a liquidated debt is *not* satisfaction, and the balance of the debt is still legally owed. The rationale for this rule is that no consideration is given by the debtor to satisfy the obligation of paying the balance to the creditor—because the debtor has a preexisting legal obligation to pay the entire debt.

—*Unliquidated Debts.*   An *unliquidated debt* is the opposite of a liquidated debt. Here, reasonable persons may differ over the amount owed. It is not settled, fixed, agreed on, ascertained, or determined. In these circumstances, acceptance of payment of the lesser sum operates as satisfaction, or discharge, of the debt. For example, suppose that Devereaux goes to the dentist's office. The dentist tells him that he needs three special types of gold inlays. The price is not discussed, and there is no standard fee for this type of procedure. Devereaux has the work done and leaves the office. At the end of the month, the dentist sends him a bill for $3,000.

Devereaux, believing that this amount is grossly out of proportion with what a reasonable person would believe to be the debt owed, sends a check for $2,000. On the back of the check he writes, "payment in full for three gold inlays." The dentist cashes the check. Because the situation involves an unliquidated debt—the amount has not been agreed on—payment accepted by the dentist normally will eradicate the debt. One argument to support this rule is that the parties give up a legal right to contest the amount in dispute, and thus consideration is given.

RELEASE   A **release** is a contract in which one party forfeits the right to pursue a legal claim against the other party. It bars any further recovery beyond the terms stated in the release. For example, suppose that you are involved in an automobile accident caused by Donovan's negligence. Donovan offers to give you $1,000 if you will release him from further liability resulting from the accident. You believe that this amount will cover your damages, so you agree, in writing, to the release. Later, you discover that it will cost $1,500 to repair your car. Can you collect the balance from Donovan?

The answer is normally no; you are limited to the $1,000 specified in the release because the release represents a valid contract. You and Donovan both assented to the bargain (hence, agreement existed), and sufficient consideration was present. The consideration was the legal detriment you suffered (by releasing Donovan from liability, you forfeited your right to sue to recover damages, should they be more than $1,000).

Clearly, you are better off if you know the extent of your injuries or damages before signing a release. Releases will generally be binding if they are (1) given in good faith, (2) stated in a signed writing (which is required in many states), and (3) accompanied by consideration.[5]

COVENANT NOT TO SUE

A **covenant not to sue** is an agreement to substitute a contractual obligation for some other type of legal action based on a valid claim. Unlike a release, a covenant not to sue does not always bar further recovery. Suppose (continuing the earlier example) that you agree with Donovan not to sue for damages in a tort action if he will pay for the damage to your car. If Donovan fails to pay, you can bring an action against him for breach of contract.

Promises Enforceable without Consideration

There are some exceptions to the rule that only promises supported by consideration are enforceable. The following types of promises may be enforced despite the lack of consideration:

1. Promises to pay debts that are barred by a statute of limitations.
2. Promises that induce detrimental reliance, under the doctrine of promissory estoppel.
3. Promises to make charitable contributions.

PROMISES TO PAY DEBTS BARRED BY A STATUTE OF LIMITATIONS

Statutes of limitations in all states require a creditor to sue within a specified period to recover a debt. If the creditor fails to sue in time, recovery of the debt is barred by the statute of limitations. A debtor who promises to pay a previous debt even though recovery is barred by the statute of limitations makes an enforceable promise. *The promise needs no consideration.* (Some states, however, require that it be in writing.) In effect, the promise extends the limitations period, and the creditor can sue to recover the entire debt, or at least the amount promised. The promise can be implied if the debtor acknowledges the barred debt by making a partial payment.

PROMISSORY ESTOPPEL

As discussed in Chapter 11, under the doctrine of *promissory estoppel* (also called *detrimental reliance*), a person who has reasonably and substantially relied on the promise of another may be able to obtain some measure of recovery. This doctrine is applied in a wide variety of contexts in which a promise is otherwise unenforceable, such as when a promise is not supported by consideration. Under this doctrine, a court may enforce an otherwise unenforceable promise to avoid the injustice that would otherwise result. For the doctrine to be applied, the following elements are required:

1. There must be a clear and definite promise.
2. The promisee must justifiably rely on the promise.
3. The reliance normally must be of a substantial and definite character.
4. Justice will be better served by enforcement of the promise.

If these requirements are met, a promise may be enforced even though it is not supported by consideration. In essence, the promisor will be *estopped* (prevented) from asserting the lack of consideration as a defense. For example, suppose that your uncle tells you, "I'll pay you $150 a week so you won't have to work anymore." In reliance on your uncle's promise, you quit your job, but your uncle refuses to pay you. Under the doctrine of promissory estoppel, you may be able to enforce such a promise.[6] (See this chapter's

---

5. Under the UCC, a written, signed waiver or renunciation by an aggrieved party discharges any further liability for a breach, even without consideration.

6. *Ricketts v. Scothorn,* 57 Neb. 51, 77 N.W. 365 (1898).

Promissory Estoppel and Employment Contracts

Today, approximately 85 percent of American workers have the legal status of "employees at will." Under this common law employment doctrine, which applies in all states except Montana, an employer may fire an employee for any reason or no reason. The at-will doctrine, however, does not apply to any employee who has an employment contract or who falls under the protection of a state or federal statute—which is, of course, a large number of employees. Even when an employee is subject to the employment-at-will doctrine, the courts sometimes make exceptions to the doctrine based on tort theory or contract principles or on the ground that a termination violates an established public policy (see Chapter 33).

These exceptions to the at-will doctrine, however, apply only when a current employee's employment is *terminated*. Should they also apply when a company fails to *hire* a job candidate after promising to do so? Consider an example. Suppose that a job candidate, relying on a company's offer of employment, quits his or her existing job, moves to another city, and rents or buys housing in the new location. Then the company decides not to hire the candidate after all. Given the employee's detrimental reliance on the company's job offer, should the company be prevented from revoking its offer under the doctrine of promissory estoppel? This question has come before a number of courts. As yet, however, the courts have not reached a consensus on the issue. Some jurisdictions allow the doctrine of promissory estoppel to be applied; others do not.

PROMISSORY ESTOPPEL SHOULD NOT BE APPLIED

Many jurisdictions believe that reliance on a prospective employer's promise of at-will employment is unreasonable as a matter of law. Courts in these jurisdictions reason that an employee should know that, even if she or he is hired, the employer could terminate the employment at any time for any reason without liability. According to these courts, it would be contrary to reason to allow an employee who has not yet begun work to recover damages under a theory of promissory estoppel, given that the same employee's job could be terminated without liability one day after beginning work.

Consider a case example. Arlie Thompson had worked for nine years at a hospital as a technician assistant when she was laid off. A year later, the same hospital offered her a clerical position, which she accepted. She was measured for a new uniform, given a security badge, and provided with the password for the computer system. Thompson, who was then working at another job, quit the other position in reliance on the hospital's job offer. Shortly thereafter, the hospital asked her to take a test. When she failed the test, the hospital refused to hire her. Thompson filed a suit claiming that the doctrine of promissory estoppel should prevent the hospital from revoking its offer. The court, however, held that the hospital's promise of employment was not sufficiently "clear and definite" for that doctrine to be applied.[a]

---

a. *Thompson v. Bridgeport Hospital,* 2001 WL 823130 (Conn.Super. 2001).

Contemporary Legal Debates feature for a discussion of the applicability of promissory estoppel to promises of employment.)

CHARITABLE SUBSCRIPTIONS Subscriptions to religious, educational, and charitable institutions are promises to make gifts and are unenforceable on traditional contract grounds because they are not supported by legally sufficient consideration. A gift, after all, is the opposite of bargained-for consideration.

Exceptions to this general rule are occasionally made, however. Some courts have held that a promise to give funds to a charity was supported by consideration. For instance, the promisor may have bargained for and received a promise from the charity that the gift would be used in a specific way or that it would be memorialized with the promisor's name. The modern

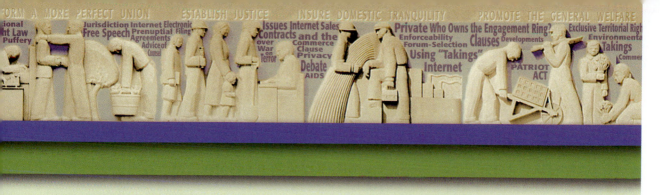

PROMISSORY ESTOPPEL SHOULD BE APPLIED

A number of other jurisdictions have held that an employee can recover damages incurred as a result of resigning from a former job in reliance on an offer of at-will employment. These jurisdictions have determined that when a prospective employer knows or should know that a promise of employment will induce the future employee to leave his or her current job, the employer should be responsible for the prospective employee's damages. After all, without the offer from the prospective employer, the prospective employee would have continued to work in his or her prior position.

This approach is reflected in a case involving Julie Goff-Hamel, who had worked for Hastings Family Planning for eleven years. Her job benefits included six weeks' paid maternity leave, six weeks' vacation time, twelve paid holidays, twelve paid sick days, educational reimbursement, and medical and dental insurance. A women's health group approached her with an offer of employment. Although Goff-Hamel was offered a lower salary than what she was making, she was offered a retirement plan at the end of the second year retroactive to the end of the first year. Goff-Hamel quit her job with Hastings and accepted the offer from the women's health group. The prospective employer gave her uniforms for her new job and a copy of her work schedule. The day before she was supposed to start, however, a representative of the women's health group told her that she need not report to work because the wife of a part-owner of that group opposed hiring her. Goff-Hamel filed a suit, seeking damages in part on the basis of promissory estoppel.

The trial court concluded that because she was to be employed as an at-will employee, she could not seek damages. On appeal, however, the appellate court reversed the trial court's decision, holding that promissory estoppel could be asserted in connection with an offer of at-will employment. The court reasoned that "a cause of action for promissory estoppel is based upon a promise which the promisor should reasonably expect to induce action or forbearance on the part of the promisee [and] which does in fact induce such action or forbearance."[b]

WHERE DO YOU STAND?

Some jurisdictions maintain that it would be irrational to apply the doctrine of promissory estoppel to a promise of at-will employment, given that the employee could be fired after working for only one day on the job. Other jurisdictions, in contrast, conclude that the doctrine should apply because the employer should reasonably expect a job candidate in this situation to act in reliance on the promise. Does one of these two arguments have greater merit than the other? What is your position on this issue?

---

b. *Goff-Hamel v. Obstetricians & Gynecologists, P.C.*, 256 Neb. 19, 588 N.W.2d 798 (1999).

---

view, however, is to make exceptions to the general rule under the doctrine of promissory estoppel on the basis of detrimental reliance or to find consideration simply as a matter of public policy.

For example, suppose that a church solicits and receives pledges (commitments to contribute funds) from church members to erect a new church building. On the basis of these pledges, the church purchases land, employs architects, and makes other contracts that change its position. Because of the church's detrimental reliance, a court may enforce the pledges under the theory of promissory estoppel. Alternatively, a court may find consideration in the fact that each promise was made in reliance on the other promises of support or that the trustees, by accepting the subscriptions, impliedly promised to complete the proposed undertaking.

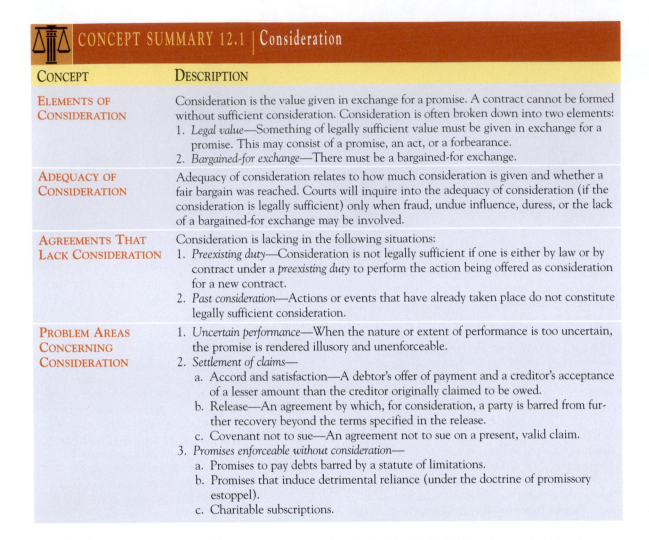

CONCEPT SUMMARY 12.1 | Consideration

CONCEPT	DESCRIPTION
ELEMENTS OF CONSIDERATION	Consideration is the value given in exchange for a promise. A contract cannot be formed without sufficient consideration. Consideration is often broken down into two elements: 1. *Legal value*—Something of legally sufficient value must be given in exchange for a promise. This may consist of a promise, an act, or a forbearance. 2. *Bargained-for exchange*—There must be a bargained-for exchange.
ADEQUACY OF CONSIDERATION	Adequacy of consideration relates to how much consideration is given and whether a fair bargain was reached. Courts will inquire into the adequacy of consideration (if the consideration is legally sufficient) only when fraud, undue influence, duress, or the lack of a bargained-for exchange may be involved.
AGREEMENTS THAT LACK CONSIDERATION	Consideration is lacking in the following situations: 1. *Preexisting duty*—Consideration is not legally sufficient if one is either by law or by contract under a *preexisting duty* to perform the action being offered as consideration for a new contract. 2. *Past consideration*—Actions or events that have already taken place do not constitute legally sufficient consideration.
PROBLEM AREAS CONCERNING CONSIDERATION	1. *Uncertain performance*—When the nature or extent of performance is too uncertain, the promise is rendered illusory and unenforceable. 2. *Settlement of claims*— a. Accord and satisfaction—A debtor's offer of payment and a creditor's acceptance of a lesser amount than the creditor originally claimed to be owed. b. Release—An agreement by which, for consideration, a party is barred from further recovery beyond the terms specified in the release. c. Covenant not to sue—An agreement not to sue on a present, valid claim. 3. *Promises enforceable without consideration*— a. Promises to pay debts barred by a statute of limitations. b. Promises that induce detrimental reliance (under the doctrine of promissory estoppel). c. Charitable subscriptions.

REVIEWING CONSIDERATION

Blair is a college freshman whose uncle is paying her tuition. Toward the end of the second semester, Blair's uncle tells her that if she earns straight As, he will continue paying her tuition, and as a reward, will give her a new Mercedes when she graduates. Blair earns straight As for three years but gets two Bs in her senior year. Her uncle sends her a bill for the entire amount spent on tuition for all four years. Using the information presented in the chapter, answer the following questions.

1. What are the basic elements of consideration? Are these elements present in Blair's uncle's promise to pay her tuition? Why or why not?

2. Did Blair's uncle have a preexisting duty to pay her tuition?

3. Was there adequate consideration to support the uncle's promise of a Mercedes? Why or why not? What is this type of promise called?

4. What principle discussed in the chapter might lead a court to conclude that this agreement lacked consideration?

5. Should a court require Blair to refund all or part of the tuition paid by her uncle? Explain.

6. If Blair had actually received straight As throughout college, would she be entitled to enforce her uncle's promises?

TERMS AND CONCEPTS TO REVIEW

accord and satisfaction 250

consideration 243

covenant not to sue 251

forbearance 243

past consideration 247

release 250

rescission 247

QUESTIONS AND CASE PROBLEMS

12–1. Tabor is a buyer of file cabinets manufactured by Martin. Martin's contract with Tabor calls for delivery of fifty file cabinets at $40 per cabinet in five equal installments. After delivery of two installments (twenty cabinets), Martin informs Tabor that because of inflation, Martin is losing money and will promise to deliver the remaining thirty cabinets only if Tabor will pay $50 per cabinet. Tabor agrees in writing to do so. Discuss whether Martin can legally collect the additional $100 on delivery to Tabor of the next installment of ten cabinets.

12–2. ⚖ QUESTION WITH SAMPLE ANSWER

Bernstein owns a lot and wants to build a house according to a particular set of plans and specifications. She solicits bids from building contractors and receives three bids: one from Carlton for $60,000, one from Friend for $58,000, and one from Shade for $53,000. She accepts Shade's bid. One month after beginning construction of the house, Shade contacts Bernstein and informs her that because of inflation and a recent price hike in materials, he will not finish the house unless Bernstein agrees to pay an extra $3,000. Bernstein reluctantly agrees to pay the additional sum. After the house is finished, however, Bernstein refuses to pay the extra $3,000. Discuss whether Bernstein is legally required to pay this additional amount.

For a sample answer to this question, go to Appendix I at the end of this text.

12–3. Daniel, a recent college graduate, is on his way home for the Christmas holidays from his new job. He gets caught in a snowstorm and is taken in by an elderly couple, who provide him with food and shelter. After the snowplows have cleared the road, Daniel proceeds home. Daniel's father, Fred, is most appreciative of the elderly couple's action and in a letter promises to pay them $500. The elderly couple, in need of funds, accept Fred's offer. Then, because of a dispute between Daniel and Fred, Fred refuses to pay the elderly couple the $500. Discuss whether the couple can hold Fred liable in contract for the services rendered to Daniel.

12–4. Costello hired Sagan to drive his racing car in a race. Sagan's friend Gideon promised to pay Sagan $3,000 if she won the race. Sagan won the race, but Gideon refused to pay the $3,000. Gideon contended that no legally binding contract had been formed because he had received no consideration from Sagan in exchange for his promise to pay the $3,000. Sagan sued Gideon for breach of contract, arguing that winning the race was the consideration given in exchange for Gideon's promise to pay the $3,000. What rule of law discussed in this chapter supports Gideon's claim?

12–5. PAST CONSIDERATION. Rivendell Forest Products, Ltd., had a computer program—the *Quote Screen* system—that allowed it to quote prices to its customers many times faster than its competitors. To keep the *Quote Screen* system a secret, Rivendell insisted that all of its employees, including Timothy Cornwell, sign a confidentiality agreement in 1988. Cornwell was employed by Rivendell from 1987 to 1990, when he left Rivendell to work as a marketing manager for the Georgia-Pacific Corp., a competitor. Cornwell introduced Georgia-Pacific to Rivendell's *Quote Screen* system. Rivendell sued Cornwell for, among other things, breach of the confidentiality agreement. The trial court held that the confidentiality agreement was not a valid contract because Rivendell had failed to provide consideration, such as a salary increase or a promotion, in exchange for Cornwell's promise to keep the *Quote Screen* system a secret. If Cornwell had signed the confidentiality agreement when he was first hired, would the result have been the same? Explain. [*Rivendell Forest Products, Ltd. v. Georgia-Pacific Corp.*, 824 F.Supp. 961 (D.Colo. 1993)]

12–6. ACCORD AND SATISFACTION. E. S. Herrick Co. grows and sells blueberries. Maine Wild Blueberry Co. agreed to buy all of Herrick's 1990 crop under a contract that left the price unliquidated. Herrick delivered the berries, but a dispute arose over the price. Maine Wild sent Herrick a check with a letter that stated the check was the "final settlement." Herrick cashed the check but filed a suit in a Maine state court against Maine Wild, on the ground of breach of contract, alleging that the buyer owed more. What will the court likely decide in this case? Why? [*E. S. Herrick Co. v. Maine Wild Blueberry Co.*, 670 A.2d 944 (Me. 1996)]

12-7. ⚖ CASE PROBLEM WITH SAMPLE ANSWER

As a child, Martha Carr once visited her mother's 108-acre tract of unimproved land in Richland County, South Carolina. In 1968, Betty and Raymond Campbell leased the land. Carr, a resident of New York, was diagnosed as having schizophrenia and depression in 1986, was hospitalized five or six times, and subsequently took prescription drugs for the illnesses. In 1996, Carr inherited the Richland property and, two years later, contacted the Campbells about selling the land. Carr asked Betty about the value of the land, and Betty said that the county tax assessor had determined that the land's *agricultural value* was $54,000. The Campbells knew at the time that the county had assessed the total property value at $103,700 for tax purposes. A real estate appraiser found that the *real market value* of the property was $162,000. On August 6, Carr signed a contract to sell the land to the Campbells for $54,000. Believing the price to be unfair, however, Carr did not deliver the deed. The Campbells filed a suit in a South Carolina state court against Carr, seeking specific performance of the contract. At trial, an expert real estate appraiser testified that the real market value of the property was $162,000 at the time of the contract. Under what circumstances will a court examine the adequacy of consideration? Are those circumstances present in this case? Should the court enforce the contract between Carr and the Campbells? Explain. [*Campbell v. Carr*, 361 S.C. 258, 603 S.E.2d 625 (App. 2004)]

To view a sample answer for this case problem, go to this book's Web site at http://wbl.westbuslaw.com, select "Chapter 12," and click on "Case Problem with Sample Answer."

12-8. PREEXISTING DUTY. New England Rock Services, Inc., agreed to work as a subcontractor on a sewer project on which Empire Paving, Inc., was the general contractor. For drilling and blasting a certain amount of rock, Rock Services was to be paid $29 per cubic yard or on a time-and-materials basis, whichever was less. From the beginning, Rock Services encountered problems. The primary obstacle was a heavy concentration of water, which, according to the custom in the industry, Empire should have controlled but did not. Rock Services was compelled to use more costly and time-consuming methods than anticipated, and it was unable to complete the work on time. The subcontractor asked Empire to pay for the rest of the project on a time-and-materials basis. Empire signed a modification

of the original agreement. On completion of the work, Empire refused to pay Rock Services the balance due under the modification. Rock Services filed a suit in a Connecticut state court against Empire. Empire claimed that the modification lacked consideration and was thus not valid and enforceable. Is Empire right? Why or why not? [*New England Rock Services, Inc. v. Empire Paving, Inc.*, 53 Conn.App. 771, 731 A.2d 784 (1999)]

12-9. CONSIDERATION. In 1995, Helikon Furniture Co. appointed Tom Gaede as its independent sales agent for the sale of its products in parts of Texas. The parties signed a one-year contract that specified, among other things, the commissions that Gaede would receive. Over a year later, although the parties had not signed a new contract, Gaede was still representing Helikon when it was acquired by a third party. Helikon's new management allowed Gaede to continue to perform for the same commissions and sent him a letter stating that it would make no changes in its sales representatives "for at least the next year." Three months later, in December 1997, the new managers sent Gaede a letter proposing new terms for a contract. Gaede continued to sell Helikon products until May 1997, when he received a letter effectively reducing the amount of his commissions. Gaede filed a suit in a Texas state court against Helikon, alleging breach of contract. Helikon argued in part that there was no contract because there was no consideration. In whose favor should the court rule, and why? [*Gaede v. SK Investments, Inc.*, 38 S.W.3d 753 (Tex.App.—Houston [14 Dist.] 2001)]

12-10. SETTLEMENT OF CLAIMS. Shoreline Towers Condominium Owners Association in Gulf Shores, Alabama, authorized Resort Development, Inc. (RDI), to manage Shoreline's property. On Shoreline's behalf, RDI obtained a property insurance policy from Zurich American Insurance Co. In October 1995, Hurricane Opal struck Gulf Shores. RDI filed claims with Zurich regarding damage to Shoreline's property. Zurich determined that the cost of the damage was $334,901. Zurich then subtracted an applicable $40,000 deductible and sent checks to RDI totaling $294,901. RDI disputed the amount. Zurich eventually agreed to issue a check for an additional $86,000 in return for RDI's signing a "Release of All Claims." Later, contending that the deductible had been incorrectly applied and that this was a breach of contract, among other things, Shoreline filed a suit against Zurich in a federal district court. How, if at all, should the agreement reached by RDI and Zurich affect Shoreline's claim? Explain. [*Shoreline Towers Condominium Owners Association, Inc. v. Zurich American Insurance Co.*, 196 F.Supp.2d 1210 (S.D.Ala. 2002)]

LAW | on the Web

For updated links to resources available on the Web, as well as a variety of other materials, visit this text's Web site at http://wbl.westbuslaw.com.

A good way to learn more about how the courts decide such issues as whether consideration was lacking for a particular contract is to look at relevant case law. To find recent cases on contract law decided by the United States Supreme Court and the federal appellate courts, access Cornell University's School of Law site at

http://www.law.cornell.edu/topics/contracts.html

The *New Hampshire Consumer's Sourcebook* provides information on contract law, including consideration, from a consumer's perspective. You can access this site at

http://www.doj.nh.gov/consumer/sourcebook

LEGAL RESEARCH EXERCISES ON THE WEB

Go to http://wbl.westbuslaw.com, the Web site that accompanies this text. Select "Chapter 12" and click on "Internet Exercises." There you will find the following Internet research exercises that you can perform to learn more about topics covered in this chapter.

Activity 12–1: LEGAL PERSPECTIVE
Legal Value of Consideration

Activity 12–2: MANAGEMENT PERSPECTIVE
Promissory Estoppel

Activity 12–3: INTERNATIONAL PERSPECTIVE
Contract Consideration in Canada

CHAPTER 13
Capacity and Legality

In addition to agreement and consideration, for a contract to be deemed valid the parties to the contract must have **contractual capacity**—the legal ability to enter into a contractual relationship. Courts generally presume the existence of contractual capacity, but there are some situations in which capacity is lacking or may be questionable. For example, in many situations, a minor has the capacity to enter into a contract but also has the right to avoid liability under it. Similarly, contracts calling for the performance of an illegal act are illegal and thus void—they are not contracts at all. In this chapter, we examine contractual capacity and some aspects of illegal bargains.

Realize that capacity and legality are not inherently related other than that they are both contract requirements. We treat these topics in one chapter merely for convenience and reasons of space.

SECTION 1 | Contractual Capacity

Historically, the law has given special protection to those who bargain with the inexperience of youth or those who lack the degree of mental competence required by law. A person *adjudged by a court* to be mentally incompetent, for example, cannot form a legally binding contract with another party. In other situations, a party may have the capacity to enter into a valid contract but also have the right to avoid liability under it. For example, minors—or *infants*, as they are commonly referred to in legal terminology—usually are not legally bound by contracts. In this section, we look at the effect of youth, intoxication, and mental incompetence on contractual capacity.

MINORS

Today, in virtually all states, the **age of majority** (when a person is no longer a minor) for contractual purposes is eighteen years.[1] In addition, some states provide for the termination of minority on marriage. Minority status may also be terminated by a minor's **emancipation,** which occurs when a child's parent or legal guardian relinquishes the legal right to exercise control over the child. Normally, a minor who leaves home to support

himself or herself is considered emancipated. Several jurisdictions permit minors to petition a court for emancipation themselves. For business purposes, a minor may petition a court to be treated as an adult.

The general rule is that a minor can enter into any contract that an adult can, provided that the contract is not one prohibited by law for minors (for example, the sale of tobacco or alcoholic beverages). A contract entered into by a minor, however, is voidable at the option of that minor, subject to certain exceptions. To exercise the option to avoid a contract, a minor need only manifest an intention not to be bound by it. The minor "avoids" the contract by disaffirming it.

A MINOR'S RIGHT TO DISAFFIRM The technical definition of **disaffirmance** is the legal avoidance, or setting aside, of a contractual obligation. To disaffirm, a minor must express his or her intent, through words or conduct, not to be bound to the contract. The minor must disaffirm the entire contract, not merely a portion of it. For example, the minor cannot decide to keep part of the goods purchased under a contract and return the remaining goods.

A contract can ordinarily be disaffirmed at any time during minority[2] or for a reasonable period after

---

1. The age of majority may still be twenty-one for other purposes, such as the purchase and consumption of alcohol.

2. In some states, however, a minor who enters into a contract for the sale of land cannot disaffirm the contract until she or he reaches the age of majority.

reaching majority. While two months would probably be considered reasonable, a court, depending on the circumstances, may *not* consider it reasonable to wait a year or more after coming of age to disaffirm. If an individual fails to disaffirm an executed contract within a reasonable time after reaching the age of majority, a court will likely hold that the contract has been ratified (ratification will be discussed shortly).

A MINOR'S OBLIGATIONS ON DISAFFIRMANCE

Although all states' laws permit minors to disaffirm contracts (with certain exceptions), states differ on the extent of a minor's obligations on disaffirmance.

—*Majority Rule.* Courts in a majority of states hold that the minor need only return the goods (or other consideration) subject to the contract, provided the goods are in the minor's possession or control. For example, suppose that Jim Garrison, a seventeen-year-old, purchases a computer from Radio Shack. While transporting the computer to his home, Garrison negligently drops it, breaking the plastic casing. The next day, he returns the computer to Radio Shack and disaffirms the contract. Under the majority view, this return fulfills Garrison's duty even though the computer is now damaged. Garrison is entitled to receive a refund of the purchase price (if paid in cash) or to be relieved of any further obligations under an agreement to purchase the computer on credit.

—*Minority Rule.* An increasing number of states, either by statute or by court decision, place an additional duty on the minor—the duty to restore the adult party to the position that she or he held before the contract was made. Consider an example. Sixteen-year-old Joseph Dodson bought a pickup truck for $4,900 from a used-car dealer. Although the truck developed mechanical problems nine months later, Dodson continued to drive it until the engine blew up and it stopped running. Then Dodson disaffirmed the contract and attempted to return the truck to the dealer for a full refund of the purchase price. The dealer refused to accept the pickup or refund the money. Dodson filed a lawsuit. Ultimately, the Tennessee Supreme Court allowed Dodson to disaffirm the contract but required the seller to be compensated for the depreciated value—not the purchase price—of the pickup.[3] This example illustrates the trend among today's courts to hold a minor responsible for damage,

ordinary wear and tear, and depreciation of goods that the minor used prior to disaffirmance.

EXCEPTIONS TO A MINOR'S RIGHT TO DISAFFIRM

State courts and legislatures have carved out several exceptions to the minor's right to disaffirm. Some contracts cannot be avoided simply as a matter of law, on the ground of public policy. For example, marriage contracts and contracts to enlist in the armed services fall into this category. Other contracts may not be disaffirmed for other reasons, including those discussed here.

—*Misrepresentation of Age.* Suppose that a minor tells a seller that she is twenty-one years old when she is really seventeen. Ordinarily, the minor can disaffirm the contract even though she has misrepresented her age. Moreover, the minor is not liable in certain jurisdictions for the tort of deceit (fraud) for such misrepresentation, the rationale being that such a tort judgment might indirectly force the minor to perform the contract.

Many jurisdictions, however, find circumstances under which a minor can be bound by a contract when the minor has misrepresented his or her age. First, several states have enacted statutes for precisely this purpose. In these states, misrepresentation of age is enough to prohibit disaffirmance. Other statutes prohibit disaffirmance by a minor who has engaged in business as an adult. Second, some courts refuse to allow minors to disaffirm executed (fully performed) contracts unless they can return the consideration received. The combination of the minors' misrepresentation and their unjust enrichment has persuaded these courts to *estop* (prevent) minors from asserting contractual incapacity.

Finally, some courts allow a misrepresenting minor to disaffirm the contract, but they hold the minor liable for damages in tort. Here, the defrauded party may sue the minor for misrepresentation or fraud. A split in authority exists on this point, because some courts, as previously noted, have recognized that allowing a suit in tort is equivalent to indirectly enforcing the minor's contract.

—*Contracts for Necessaries.* A minor who enters into a contract for necessaries may disaffirm the contract but remains liable for the reasonable value of the goods. **Necessaries** are items that fulfill basic needs, such as food, clothing, shelter, and medical services, at a level of value required to maintain the minor's standard of living or financial and social status. Thus,

---

3. *Dodson v. Shrader*, 824 S.W.2d 545 (Tenn. Sup.Ct. 1992).

what will be considered a necessary for one person may be a luxury for another. Additionally, what is considered a necessary depends on whether the minor is under the care or control of his or her parents, who are required by law to provide necessaries for the minor. If a minor's parents provide him or her with shelter, for example, then a contract to lease shelter (such as an apartment) normally will not be classified as a contract for necessaries.

Generally, then, for a contract to qualify as a contract for necessaries, (1) the item contracted for must be necessary to the minor's subsistence, (2) the value of the necessary item must be up to a level required to maintain the minor's standard of living or financial and social status, and (3) the minor must not be under the care of a parent or guardian who is required to supply this item. Unless these three criteria are met, the minor can disaffirm the contract *without* being liable for the reasonable value of the goods used.

—*Insurance and Loans.* Traditionally, insurance has not been viewed as a necessary, so minors can ordinarily disaffirm their insurance contracts and recover all premiums paid. Some jurisdictions, though, prohibit the right to disaffirm insurance contracts—for example, when minors contract for life insurance on their own lives. Financial loans are seldom considered to be necessaries, even if the minor spends the funds borrowed on necessaries. If, however, a lender makes a loan to a minor for the express purpose of enabling the minor to purchase necessaries, and the lender personally makes sure the funds are so spent, the minor normally is obligated to repay the loan.

The issue in the following case was whether a medical service provider could collect from a minor the cost of emergency services rendered to the minor when his mother did not pay.

CASE 13.1   **Yale Diagnostic Radiology v. Estate of Harun Fountain**

Supreme Court of
Connecticut, 2004.
267 Conn. 351,
838 A.2d 179.

BORDEN, J. [Justice]

The sole issue in this appeal is whether a medical service provider that has provided emergency medical services to a minor may collect for those services from the minor when the minor's parents refuse or are unable to make payment. The defendants, the estate of Harun Fountain, an unemancipated [dependent on parents] minor, and Vernetta Turner-Tucker (Tucker) * * * claim that the [appellate] court improperly determined that they are liable to the plaintiff [Yale Diagnostic Radiology] for payment of Fountain's medical expenses. * * *

* * * *

* * * In March, 1996, Fountain was shot in the back of the head at point-blank range by a playmate. As a result of his injuries, including the loss of his right eye, Fountain required extensive lifesaving medical services from a variety of medical services providers, including the plaintiff. The expense of the services rendered by the plaintiff to Fountain totaled $17,694. The plaintiff billed Tucker, who was Fountain's mother, but the bill went unpaid and, in 1999, the plaintiff obtained a collection judgment against her. In January, 2001, however, all of Tucker's debts were discharged pursuant to an order of [a federal bankruptcy court]. Among the discharged debts was the judgment in favor of the plaintiff against Tucker.

During the time between the rendering of medical services and the bankruptcy filing, Tucker * * * initiated a tort action against the boy who had shot him. Among the damages claimed were substantial sums of money expended on medical care and treatment * * * . A settlement was reached, and funds were placed in the estate established on Fountain's behalf * * * .

Following the discharge of Tucker's debts, the plaintiff moved the [state trial court] for payment of the $17,694 from the estate. The [court] denied the motion, reasoning that, * * * parents are liable for medical services rendered to their minor children, and that a parent's refusal or inability to pay for those services does not render the minor child liable. The * * * Court further ruled that minor children are incapable of entering into a legally binding contract or consenting, in the absence of parental consent, to medical treatment. The * * * Court held, therefore, that the plaintiff was barred from seeking payment from the estate.

The plaintiff appealed the decision of the * * * Court to the [state intermediate appellate court]. The [appellate] court sustained the appeal and rendered judgment for the plain-

CASE 13.1 Continued

tiff, holding that, under Connecticut law, minors are liable for payment for their necessaries, even though the provider of those necessaries relies on the parents' credit for payment when the injured child lives with his parents * * * . The [appellate] court reasoned that, although parents are primarily liable, * * * for their child's medical bills, the parents' failure to pay renders the minor secondarily liable. Additionally, the [appellate] court relied on the fact that Fountain had obtained money damages, based in part on the medical services rendered to him by the plaintiff. This appeal followed.

The defendants claim that the [appellate] court improperly determined that a minor may be liable for payment for emergency medical services rendered to him. They further claim that the [appellate] court, in reaching its decision, improperly considered the fact that Fountain had received a settlement, based in part on his medical expenses. * * *

Connecticut has long recognized the common-law rule that a minor child's contracts are voidable. Under this rule, *a minor may, upon reaching majority, choose either to ratify or to avoid contractual obligations entered into during his minority.* The traditional reasoning behind this rule is based on the well established common-law principles that the law should protect children from the detrimental consequences of their youthful and improvident acts, and that children should be able to emerge into adulthood unencumbered [free of] by financial obligations incurred during the course of their minority. The rule is further supported by a policy of protecting children from unscrupulous individuals seeking to profit from their youth and inexperience. [Emphasis added.]

The rule that a minor's contracts are voidable, however, is not absolute. An exception to this rule, eponymously [by name] known as the doctrine of necessaries, is that a minor may not avoid a contract for goods or services necessary for his health and sustenance. Such contracts are binding even if entered into during minority, and *a minor, upon reaching majority, may not, as a matter of law, disaffirm them.* [Emphasis added.]

* * * *

We have not heretofore articulated the particular legal theory underlying the doctrine of necessaries. We therefore take this occasion to do so, and we conclude that the most apt theory is that of an implied in law contract, also sometimes referred to as a quasi-contract. * * *

In distinction to an implied in fact contract, a quasi or implied in law contract is not a contract, but an obligation which the law creates out of the circumstances present, even though a party did not assume the obligation. * * * It is based on equitable principles to operate whenever justice requires compensation to be made * * * . With no other test than what, under a given set of circumstances, is just or unjust, equitable or inequitable, conscionable or unconscionable, it becomes necessary * * * to examine the circumstances and the conduct of the parties and apply this standard. [Emphasis added.]

Thus, when a medical service provider renders necessary medical care to an injured minor, two contracts arise: the primary contract between the provider and the minor's parents; and an implied in law contract between the provider and the minor himself. The primary contract between the provider and the parents is based on the parents' duty to pay for their children's necessary expenses * * * . Such contracts, where not express, may be implied in fact and generally arise both from the parties' conduct and their reasonable expectations. The primacy of this contract means that the provider of necessaries must make all reasonable efforts to collect from the parents before resorting to the secondary, implied in law contract with the minor.

The secondary implied in law contract between the medical services provider and the minor arises from equitable considerations, including the law's disfavor of unjust enrichment. Therefore, where necessary medical services are rendered to a minor whose parents do not pay for them, equity and justice demand that a secondary implied in law contract arise between the medical services provider and the minor who has received the benefits of those services. These principles compel the conclusion that, in the circumstances of the present case, the [defendant is] liable to the plaintiff, under the common-law doctrine of necessaries, for the services rendered by the plaintiff to Fountain.

* * * *

The judgment is affirmed.

QUESTIONS

1. What might have happened in future cases if the court had held that there was no implied-in-law contract between Fountain and Yale Diagnostic Radiology?
2. How does the result in this case encourage payment on contracts for necessaries?

RATIFICATION In contract law, **ratification** is the act of accepting and giving legal force to an obligation that previously was not enforceable. A minor who has reached the age of majority can ratify a contract expressly or impliedly. *Express* ratification takes place when the individual, on reaching the age of majority, states orally or in writing that he or she intends to be bound by the contract. *Implied* ratification takes place when the minor, on reaching the age of majority, evidences an intent to abide by the contract.

For example, suppose that Lin enters a contract to sell her laptop to Arturo, a minor. If, on reaching the age of majority, Arturo writes a letter to Lin stating that he still agrees to buy the laptop, he has *expressly* ratified the contract. If, instead, Arturo takes possession of the laptop as a minor and continues to use it well after reaching the age of majority, he has *impliedly* ratified the contract.

If a minor fails to disaffirm a contract within a reasonable time after reaching the age of majority, then the court must determine whether the conduct constitutes ratification or disaffirmance. Generally, a contract that is *executed* (fully performed by both parties) is presumed to be ratified. A contract that is still *executory* (not yet fully performed by both parties) is normally considered to be disaffirmed.

PARENTS' LIABILITY As a general rule, parents are not liable for contracts made by minor children acting on their own. This is why businesses ordinarily require parents to sign any contract made with a minor. The parents then become personally obligated under the contract to perform the conditions of the contract, even if their child avoids liability.

Generally, minors are personally liable for their own torts. The parents of the minor can *also* be held liable in certain situations. In some states, parents may be liable if they failed to exercise proper parental control over the minor child and they knew or should have known that failure to exercise control posed an unreasonable risk of harm to others. Other states have enacted statutes that impose liability on parents for certain tortious acts, such as those that are willful or grossly negligent, that their children commit.

CONCEPT SUMMARY 13.1 | Contracts by Minors

CONCEPT	DESCRIPTION
GENERAL RULE	Contracts entered into by minors are *voidable* at the option of the minor.
RULES OF DISAFFIRMANCE	A minor may disaffirm the contract at any time while still a minor and within a reasonable time after reaching the age of majority. Most states do not require restitution.
EXCEPTIONS TO BASIC RULES OF DISAFFIRMANCE	1. *Necessaries*—Minors remain liable for the reasonable value of the necessaries (goods and services). 2. *Ratification*—After reaching the age of majority, a person can ratify a contract that he or she formed as a minor, becoming fully liable thereon. 3. *Fraud or misrepresentation*—Misrepresentation of age in many jurisdictions prohibits the right of disaffirmance.

INTOXICATION

Intoxication is a condition in which a person's normal capacity to act or think is inhibited by alcohol or some other drug.[4] A contract entered into by an intoxicated person can be either voidable or valid (and thus enforceable). If the person was sufficiently intoxicated to lack mental capacity, then the transaction may be voidable at the option of the intoxicated person even if the intoxication was purely voluntary. For the contract to be voidable, the person must prove that the intoxication impaired her or his reason and judgment so severely that she or he did not comprehend the legal consequences of entering into the contract.

If, despite intoxication, the person understood these legal consequences, the contract will be enforceable. The fact that the terms of the contract are foolish or obviously favor the other party does not make the contract voidable (unless the other party *fraudulently* induced the person to become intoxicated). As a practical matter, courts rarely permit contracts to be avoided on the ground of intoxication because it is difficult to determine whether a party was sufficiently intoxicated to avoid legal duties. Rather than inquire into the intoxicated person's mental state, many courts prefer to look at objective indications to determine whether the contract is voidable owing to intoxication.[5]

DISAFFIRMANCE If a contract is voidable because of a person's intoxication, that person has the option of disaffirming it—the same option available to a minor. The vast majority of courts, however, require that the intoxicated person make full restitution (fully return any consideration received) as a condition of disaffirmance, except in cases involving necessaries (as previously discussed). For example, suppose that Briller, who is intoxicated, contracts to purchase a set of encyclopedias from Stevens. If the books are delivered, Briller can disaffirm the executed contract and recover the payment made to Stevens only by returning the encyclopedias.

RATIFICATION An intoxicated person, after becoming sober, may ratify a contract expressly or impliedly, just as a minor may do on reaching majority. Implied ratification occurs when a person enters into a contract while intoxicated and fails to disaffirm the contract within a *reasonable* time after becoming sober. Acts or conduct inconsistent with an intent to disaffirm—such as the continued use of property purchased under a voidable contract—will also ratify the contract. In addition, contracts for necessaries are voidable, but the intoxicated person is liable in quasi contract for the reasonable value of the consideration received.

---

4. The lack of contractual capacity of a person intoxicated while the contract is being made differs from the contractual capacity of an alcoholic. If an alcoholic makes a contract while sober, there is no lack of capacity. See *Wright v. Fisher*, 32 N.W. 605 (Mich. 1887).

5. See, for example, Case 11.1 (*Lucy v. Zehmer*) in Chapter 11.

CONCEPT SUMMARY 13.2 | Contracts by Intoxicated Persons

CONCEPT	DESCRIPTION
GENERAL RULES	If a person was sufficiently intoxicated to lack the mental capacity to comprehend the legal consequences of entering into the contract, the contract may be *voidable* at the option of the intoxicated person. If, despite intoxication, the person understood these legal consequences, the contract will be enforceable.
RULES OF DISAFFIRMANCE	An intoxicated person may disaffirm the contract at any time while intoxicated and for a reasonable time after becoming sober but must make full restitution.
EXCEPTIONS TO BASIC RULES OF DISAFFIRMANCE	1. *Necessaries*—Liable for the reasonable value of the necessaries. 2. *Ratification*—After becoming sober, a person can ratify a contract that he or she formed while intoxicated, becoming fully liable thereon.

MENTAL INCOMPETENCE

Contracts made by mentally incompetent persons can be void, voidable, or valid. We look here at the circumstances that determine which of these classifications apply.

WHEN THE CONTRACT WILL BE VOID If a court has previously determined that a person is mentally incompetent and has appointed a guardian to represent the individual, any contract made by the mentally incompetent person is *void*—no contract exists. Only the guardian can enter into binding legal obligations on the incompetent person's behalf.

WHEN THE CONTRACT WILL BE VOIDABLE If a court has not previously judged a person to be mentally incompetent but in fact the person was incompetent at the time the contract was formed, the contract may be *voidable*. A contract is voidable if the person does not know he or she is entering into the contract or lacks the mental capacity to comprehend its nature, purpose, and consequences. In such a situation, the contract is voidable at the option of the mentally incompetent person but not the other party. The contract may then be disaffirmed or ratified (if the person regains mental competence). Like minors and intoxicated persons, mentally incompetent persons are liable (in quasi contract) for the reasonable value of any necessaries they receive.

WHEN THE CONTRACT WILL BE VALID A contract entered into by a mentally incompetent person (whom a court has not previously declared incompetent) may also be *valid*. For example, a person may be able to understand the nature and effect of entering into a certain contract yet simultaneously lack capacity to engage in other activities. In such cases, the contract will be valid, because the person is not legally mentally incompetent for contractual purposes.[6] Similarly, an otherwise mentally incompetent person may have a *lucid interval*—a temporary restoration of sufficient intelligence, judgment, and will to enter into contracts without disqualification—during which she or he will be considered to have full legal capacity.

SECTION 2 | Legality

For a contract to be valid and enforceable, it must be formed for a legal purpose. A contract to do something that is prohibited by federal or state statutory law is illegal and, as such, void from the outset and thus unenforceable. Also, a contract that calls for a tortious act or an action contrary to public policy is illegal and unenforceable. It is important to note that a contract

---

6. Modern courts no longer require a person to be completely irrational to disaffirm contracts on the basis of mental incompetence. A contract may be voidable if, by reason of a mental illness or defect, an individual was unable to act reasonably with respect to the transaction and the other party had reason to know of the condition.

CONCEPT SUMMARY 13.3 | Contracts by Mentally Incompetent Persons

CONCEPT	DESCRIPTION
GENERAL RULES	1. Contracts made by persons who have been adjudged to be mentally incompetent by a court and for whom guardians have been appointed are *void*. 2. Contracts made by persons who lack the mental capacity to comprehend the subject matter, nature, and consequences of their actions, but who have not been adjudged by a court to be mentally incompetent, are *voidable*. 3. Contracts made by persons who understand the nature and effect of entering into a contract, even if they lack capacity to engage in other activities, are *valid*.
RULES OF DISAFFIRMANCE	A mentally incompetent person may disaffirm a voidable contract at any time while mentally incompetent and for a reasonable time after regaining mental competence, but he or she must make full restitution.
EXCEPTIONS TO BASIC RULES OF DISAFFIRMANCE	1. *Necessaries*—Liable for the reasonable value of the necessaries. 2. *Ratification*—After regaining mental competence, an individual can ratify the voidable contract, becoming fully liable thereon.

or a clause in a contract may be illegal even in the absence of a specific statute prohibiting the action promised by the contract.

CONTRACTS CONTRARY TO STATUTE

Statutes often prescribe the terms of contracts. We now examine several ways in which contracts may be contrary to statute and thus illegal.

USURY Virtually every state has a statute that sets the maximum rate of interest that can be charged for different types of transactions, including ordinary loans. A lender who makes a loan at an interest rate above the lawful maximum commits **usury.** The maximum rate of interest varies from state to state.

Although usury statutes place a ceiling on allowable rates of interest, exceptions have been made to facilitate business transactions. For example, many states exempt corporate loans from the usury laws. In addition, almost all states have adopted special statutes allowing much higher interest rates on small loans to help those borrowers who are in need of funds but simply cannot get loans at interest rates below the normal lawful maximum.

The consequences for lenders who make usurious loans vary from state to state. A number of states allow the lender to recover only the principal of a usurious loan along with interest up to the legal maximum. In effect, the lender is denied recovery of the excess interest. In other states, the lender can recover the principal amount of the loan but no interest.

GAMBLING All states have statutes that regulate gambling—defined as any scheme that involves distribution of property by chance among persons who have paid a valuable consideration for the opportunity (chance) to receive the property. Gambling is the creation of risk for the purpose of assuming it. Traditionally, state statutes have deemed gambling contracts to be illegal and thus void.

In several states, however, including Louisiana, Michigan, Nevada, and New Jersey, casino gambling is lawful. In other states, certain forms of gambling are legal. California, for example, has not defined draw poker as a crime, although criminal statutes prohibit numerous other types of gambling games. A number of states allow gambling at horse races, and the majority of the states have legalized state-operated lotteries. Many states also allow gambling on Native American reservations.

Sometimes it is difficult to distinguish a gambling contract from the risk sharing inherent in almost all contracts. Suppose that Isaacson takes out a life insurance policy on Donohue, naming himself as beneficiary under the policy. At first glance, this may seem entirely legal; but further examination shows that Isaacson is simply gambling on how long Donohue will live. To prevent that type of practice, insurance contracts can be entered into only by someone with an *insurable interest* (see Chapter 49).

SABBATH (SUNDAY) LAWS Statutes referred to as Sabbath (Sunday) laws prohibit the formation or performance of certain contracts on a Sunday. Under the common law, such contracts are legal in the absence of this statutory prohibition. According to a few state statutes, all contracts entered into on a Sunday are illegal. Statutes in other states prohibit only the sale of certain types of merchandise, particularly alcoholic beverages, on a Sunday.

These statutes, which date back to colonial times, are often called blue laws. **Blue laws** get their name from the blue paper on which New Haven, Connecticut, printed its Sabbath law in 1781. The ordinance prohibited all work on Sunday and required all shops to close on the "Lord's Day." A number of states enacted laws forbidding the carrying on of "all secular [nonreligious] labor and business on the Lord's Day." Exceptions to Sunday laws permit contracts for necessities (such as food or drugs) and works of charity. A fully performed (executed) contract that was entered into on a Sunday, however, cannot be rescinded (canceled).

Sunday laws are often not enforced, and some of these laws have been held to be unconstitutional on the ground that they are contrary to the freedom of religion. Nonetheless, as a precaution, business owners contemplating doing business in a particular locality should check to see if any Sunday statutes or ordinances will affect their business activities.

LICENSING STATUTES All states require that members of certain professions or occupations obtain licenses allowing them to practice. Physicians, lawyers, real estate brokers, architects, electricians, and stockbrokers are but a few of the people who must be licensed. Some licenses are obtained only after extensive schooling and examinations, which indicate to the public that a special skill has been acquired. Others require only that the particular person be of good moral character and pay a fee.

—The Purpose of Licensing Statutes. Generally, business licenses provide a means of regulating and taxing certain enterprises and protecting the public against actions that could threaten the general welfare. For example, in nearly all states, a stockbroker must be licensed and must file a bond with the state to protect the public from fraudulent stock transactions. Similarly, a plumber must be licensed and bonded to protect the public against incompetent plumbers and to protect the public health. Only persons or businesses possessing the qualifications and complying with the conditions required by statute are entitled to licenses. For example, the owner of a tavern can be required to sell food as a condition of obtaining a license to sell liquor.

—Contracts with Unlicensed Practitioners. When a person enters into a contract with an unlicensed individual, the contract may still be enforceable, depending on the nature of the licensing statute. Some states expressly provide that the lack of a license in certain occupations bars the enforcement of work-related contracts. If the statute does not expressly declare this, one must look to the underlying purpose of the licensing requirements for a particular occupation. If the purpose is to protect the public from unauthorized practitioners, a contract involving an unlicensed individual normally is illegal and unenforceable. If the underlying purpose of the statute is to raise government revenues, however, a contract entered into with an unlicensed practitioner generally is enforceable—although the unlicensed person is usually fined.

CONTRACTS TO COMMIT A CRIME Any contract to commit a crime is a contract in violation of a statute. Thus, a contract to sell an illegal drug (the sale of which is prohibited by statute) is not enforceable. Should the object or performance of the contract be rendered illegal by statute *after* the contract has been entered into, the contract is considered to be discharged by law. (See the discussion under "Impossibility or Impracticability of Performance" in Chapter 17.)

CONTRACTS CONTRARY TO PUBLIC POLICY

Although contracts involve private parties, some are not enforceable because of the negative impact they would have on society. We look here at certain types of business contracts that are often said to be *contrary to public policy.*

CONTRACTS IN RESTRAINT OF TRADE Contracts in restraint of trade (anticompetitive agreements) usually adversely affect the public (which favors competition in the economy) and typically violate one or more federal or state statutes.[7] An exception is recognized when the restraint is reasonable and is contained in an ancillary (subordinate) clause in a contract. Many such exceptions involve a type of restraint called a **covenant not to compete,** or a restrictive covenant.

—Covenants Not to Compete and the Sale of an Ongoing Business. Covenants (promises) not to compete are often contained as ancillary clauses in contracts concerning the sale of an ongoing business. A covenant not to compete is created when a seller agrees not to open a new store in a certain geographic area surrounding the existing store. Such agreements enable the seller to sell, and the purchaser to buy, the goodwill and reputation of an ongoing business. If, for example, a well-known merchant sells his or her store and opens a competing business a block away, many of the customers will likely do business at the well-known merchant's new store. This, in turn, renders less valuable the good name and reputation purchased for a price by the new owner of the old store. If a covenant not to compete is not ancillary to a sales agreement, however, it is void, because it unreasonably restrains trade and is contrary to public policy.

—Covenants Not to Compete in Employment Contracts. Agreements not to compete can also be contained in employment contracts. It is common for people in middle-level and upper-level management positions to agree not to work for competitors or not to start competing businesses for a specified period of time after termination of employment. Such agreements are legal in most states so long as the specified period of time (of restraint) is not excessive in duration and the geographic restriction is reasonable.

Basically, a restriction on competition must protect a legitimate business interest and must not be any greater than necessary to protect that interest. The following case illustrates these requirements.

---

7. Federal statutes include the Sherman Antitrust Act, the Clayton Act, and the Federal Trade Commission Act (see Chapter 46).

CASE 13.2 — Moore v. Midwest Distribution, Inc.

Court of Appeals
of Arkansas, 2002.
76 Ark.App. 397,
65 S.W.3d 490.
http://courts.state.ar.us/
opinions/opinions.html[a]

BACKGROUND AND FACTS *Ronnie Moore began working in the product display business in 1997 for Hubb Group (HG), in Memphis, Tennessee. In 1999, HG terminated his contract. Moore moved to Fort Smith, Arkansas, to work for Midwest Distribution, Inc., which set up product displays as a contractor for HG. Midwest asked Moore to sign a "Service Work for Hire Agreement" under which Moore agreed that, for one year after the termination of his employment, he would not "provide, or solicit or offer to provide to any present or former Customer of Contractor, or become directly or indirectly interested in any person or entity which provides, or solicits or offers to provide, any services to such Customers." The agreement applied "to those geographical areas in which the Contractee [Moore] acts as independent contractor including, but not limited to, the State of Arkansas, Illinois, Iowa, Kansas, Missouri, Nebraska, New Mexico, Oklahoma, Texas, and any other state that Contractor has granted a contract or agreement within." Moore quit this job at Midwest to work for Jay Godwin, who also contracted with HG. Midwest filed a suit in an Arkansas state court against Moore, seeking to enjoin (prevent) him from providing services to Godwin. The court issued a temporary injunction. Moore appealed to a state intermediate appellate court.*

IN THE LANGUAGE OF THE COURT

TERRY CRABTREE, Judge.

* * * *

* * * The test of reasonableness of contracts in restraint of trade is that the restraint imposed upon one party must not be greater than is reasonably necessary for the protection of the other and not so great as to injure a public interest. *Where a covenant not to compete grows out of an employment relationship, the courts have found an interest sufficient to warrant enforcement of the covenant only in those cases where the covenantee provided special training, or made available trade secrets, confidential business information or customer lists, and then only if it is found that the covenantee was able to use information so obtained to gain an unfair competitive advantage.* [Emphasis added.]

In the present case, appellee's [Midwest Distribution's] president, Kevin Barrett, testified that appellant [Moore] had been provided with no special training. In addition, he stated that appellant had not been provided with any trade secrets, confidential business information, or customer lists. Further, Mr. Barrett testified that appellant was not using information he obtained from appellee to gain an unfair advantage over appellee, except how to install "fixtures and stuff." We hold that appellant did not use any information to gain an unfair competitive advantage over appellee. As such, we hold that appellee did not have a legitimate interest to be protected by the agreement.

We are also persuaded that the geographical area included in the agreement is too broad. The geographical area in a covenant not to compete must be limited in order to be enforceable. The restraint imposed upon one party must not be greater than is reasonably necessary for protecting the other party. In determining whether the geographic restriction is reasonable, the trade area of the former employer is viewed. Where a geographic restriction is greater than the trade area, the restriction is too broad and the covenant not to compete is void.

In the case at bar [before the court], the agreement precluded appellant from working in the trade of setting up displays in any of the nine states listed. The agreement included the state of Oklahoma. However, appellee did not conduct any business in Oklahoma. We find that it is not reasonable to restrict appellant from working in a state he never worked in before. By including in the scope of the non-compete agreement's geographic restriction a state that appellant has never worked in, appellee more broadly limited appellant's working than is reasonably necessary to protect appellee's trade area.

---

a. In the "Search Cases by Party Name" section, enter "Moore" in the "Party Name" box and select "Search by Date Range." For the date range, choose "From January 2002" and "To February 2002," and click on "Search." From the list of results, click on the name of the case that includes the word "Reversed" to access the opinion. The Arkansas judiciary maintains this Web site.

CONTINUED ▶

 **Continued**

DECISION AND REMEDY *The state intermediate appellate court reversed the judgment of the lower court. The appellate court concluded that the covenant not to compete was unenforceable because it did not protect a legitimate interest of Midwest Distribution and the geographical scope of the agreement was unreasonably broad.*

WHAT IF THE FACTS WERE DIFFERENT? *Suppose that Midwest Distribution had given Moore special training and provided him with a customer list, which he used when he worked for Godwin. Would the result in this case have been different? If so, how?*

UNCONSCIONABLE CONTRACTS OR CLAUSES

Ordinarily, a court does not look at the fairness or equity of a contract. For example, the courts generally do not inquire into the adequacy of consideration (see Chapter 12). Persons are assumed to be reasonably intelligent, and the courts will not come to their aid just because they have made an unwise or foolish bargain. In certain circumstances, however, bargains are so oppressive that the courts relieve innocent parties of part or all of their duties. Such bargains are deemed **unconscionable** because they are so unscrupulous or grossly unfair as to be "void of conscience."[8] A contract can be unconscionable on either procedural or substantive grounds, as discussed in the following subsections and illustrated graphically in Exhibit 13–1.

—Procedural Unconscionability. *Procedural* unconscionability has to do with how a term becomes part of a contract and relates to factors that make it difficult for a party to know or understand the contract terms due to inconspicuous print, unintelligible language ("legalese"), or the lack of an opportunity to read the contract or to ask questions about its meaning. Procedural unconscionability sometimes relates to purported lack of voluntariness due to a disparity in bargaining power between the two parties. Contracts entered into because of one party's vastly superior bargaining power may be deemed unconscionable. These situations usually involve an **adhesion contract,** which is a contract drafted by the dominant party and then presented to the other—the adhering party—on a take-it-or-leave-it basis.[9]

—Substantive Unconscionability. *Substantive* unconscionability characterizes those contracts, or portions of contracts, that are oppressive or overly harsh. Courts generally focus on provisions that deprive one party of the benefits of the agreement or leave that party without a remedy for nonperformance by the other. For example, suppose that a person with little income and with only a fourth-grade education agrees to purchase a refrigerator for $2,000 and signs a two-year installment contract. The same type of refrigerator usually sells for $600 on the market. Some courts have held this type of contract to be unconscionable—despite the general rule that the courts will not inquire into the adequacy of the consideration—simply because the contract terms are so oppressive as to "shock the conscience" of the court.[10]

EXCULPATORY CLAUSES Closely related to the concept of unconscionability are **exculpatory clauses**—clauses that release a party from liability in the event of monetary or physical injury, no matter who is at fault. Indeed, courts sometimes refuse to enforce such clauses because they are unconscionable. Suppose, for example, that an employer requires its employees to sign contract provisions removing the employer's potential liability for any injuries to those employees. In that situation, a court would usually hold the exculpatory clause to be contrary to public policy.[11] Exculpatory clauses found in rental agreements for commercial property are frequently held to be contrary to public policy, and such clauses are almost always unenforceable in residential property leases.

---

8. The Uniform Commercial Code incorporated the concept of unconscionability in Sections 2–302 and 2A–108. These provisions, which apply to contracts for the sale or lease of goods, will be discussed in Chapter 20.

9. For a classic case involving an adhesion contract, see *Henningsen v. Bloomfield Motors, Inc.*, 32 N.J. 358, 161 A.2d 69 (1960).

10. See, for example, *Jones v. Star Credit Corp.*, 59 Misc.2d 189, 298 N.Y.S.2d 264 (1969). This case is presented in Chapter 20 as Case 20.3.

11. For a case with similar facts, see *Little Rock & Fort Smith Railway Co. v. Eubanks*, 48 Ark. 460, 3 S.W. 808 (1887). Today, this type of exculpatory clause may also be illegal on the basis of a violation of a state workers' compensation law.

EXHIBIT 13-1 **Unconscionability**

UNCONSCIONABLE CONTRACT OR CLAUSE

This is a contract or clause that is void for reasons of public policy.

PROCEDURAL UNCONSCIONABILITY

This occurs if a contract is entered into, or a term becomes part of the contract, because of a party's lack of knowledge or understanding of the contract or its term.

SUBSTANTIVE UNCONSCIONABILITY

This exists when a contract, or one of its terms, is oppressive or overly harsh.

FACTORS THAT COURTS CONSIDER

- Is the print inconspicuous?
- Is the language unintelligible?
- Did one party lack an opportunity to ask questions about the contract?
- Was there a disparity of bargaining power between the parties?

FACTORS THAT COURTS CONSIDER

- Does a provision deprive one party of the benefits of the agreement?
- Does a provision leave one party without a remedy for nonperformance by the other?

Exculpatory clauses may be enforced, however, when the parties seeking their enforcement are private businesses that are not involved in enterprises considered important to the public interest, such as common carriers and banks. Businesses such as health clubs, racetracks, amusement parks, skiing facilities, horse-rental operations, golf-cart concessions, and skydiving organizations frequently use exculpatory clauses to limit their liability for patrons' injuries. Because these services are not essential, the firms offering them are sometimes considered to have no relative advantage in bargaining strength, and anyone contracting for their services is considered to do so voluntarily.

OTHER CONTRACTS CONTRARY TO PUBLIC POLICY Contracts in which a party promises to discriminate on the basis of race, color, national origin, religion, gender, age, or disability are contrary to statute and contrary to public policy. They are also unenforceable.[12] For example, if a property owner

promises in a contract not to sell the property to a member of a particular race, the contract is unenforceable. The public policy underlying these prohibitions is very strong, and the courts are quick to invalidate discriminatory contracts. Contracts that require a party to commit a civil wrong, or tort, have also been held to be contrary to public policy. Remember that a tort is an act that is wrongful to another individual in a private sense, even though it may not necessarily be criminal in nature (an act against society). Contracts that interfere with the duties of a public officer or cause a conflict between a person's official duties and his or her private interests are also contrary to public policy. Exhibit 13–2 on page 272 illustrates the types of contracts that may be illegal because they are contrary to statute or public policy.

Is a private school's regulation concerning the length of hair of its male students an enforceable provision of the school's contract with its students, or does this regulation violate public policy? That was the question in the following case.

---

12. The major federal statute prohibiting discrimination is the Civil Rights Act of 1964, 42 U.S.C. Sections 2000e–2000e-17. For a discussion of this act and other acts prohibiting discrimination in the employment context, see Chapter 34.

CASE 13.3

Rhode Island
Supreme Court, 2004.
853 A.2d 28.

Gorman v. St. Raphael Academy

BACKGROUND AND FACTS   *Saint Raphael Academy is a Catholic, coeducational, college preparatory school for grades nine through twelve in Pawtucket, Rhode Island. Saint Raphael has almost five hundred students and is operated by the Brothers of the Christian Schools with sixty lay faculty and staff members. It traces its educational tradition and mission to 1679, when John Baptist de La Salle opened his first school in Reims, France. As described in the student handbook, the Lasallian heritage is to address the educational needs of an economically diverse student body in a manner that is imbued with Christian spiritual values. In 2000, Russell Gorman III applied for admission to Saint Raphael. He interviewed with school officials. None of the officials commented on Gorman's hair, which was, at the time, six to eight inches below his shirt collar. In January 2001, his application was accepted. Shortly after he started his freshman year in August, the officials demanded that he cut his hair and told him that he would be expelled if he did not. After unsuccessfully attempting to resolve the matter, Gorman filed a suit in a Rhode Island state court, alleging breach of contract. The court issued an injunction against the school, which appealed to the Rhode Island Supreme Court.*

IN THE LANGUAGE OF THE COURT

SUTTELL, Justice.

* * * *

* * * The question now before us is whether the trial justice erroneously granted the permanent injunction. Our review, therefore, must focus on the issue of whether a hair-length rule at a private school is permissible in the context of the educational contract that students enter into each year. This is a question of first impression in our jurisdiction. In fact, we have found no other published case from any other jurisdiction that examines the validity of a hair-length rule in a private educational institution.

* * * *

Because contracts for private education have unique qualities, we must construe them in a manner that leaves the school administration broad discretion to meet its educational and doctrinal responsibilities. *Courts have recognized that implicit in an educational contract is the right to modify disciplinary and academic rules and regulations.* That a student handbook can be a source of the terms defining the reciprocal rights and obligations of a school and its students is also an idea fairly well established in modern case law. Courts normally construe educational contracts to allow the school administration flexibility in meeting its educational responsibilities. [Emphasis added.]

In the case before us, the contractual relationship between a student, his or her parents and Saint Raphael is renewable annually by entering into a distinct and express contract for each academic year. As part of the educational contract, the student and parents agree to abide by the rules and regulations promulgated [published] by the administration. * * *

* * * *

* * * [T]he appropriate inquiry is whether the term at issue in a contract involving a private educational institution is contrary to law or public policy. *It is a general rule of contract law that competent persons shall have the utmost liberty of contracting and that their agreements voluntarily and fairly made shall be held valid and enforced in the courts unless a violation of the law or public policy is clear and certain.* [Emphasis added.]

* * * *

Private schools must have considerable latitude to formulate and enforce their own rules to accomplish their academic and educational objectives. These rules and regulations generally are binding on those who wish to remain members, provided however, that said rules do not conflict with public policy.

In Rhode Island, it is firmly established that a contract term is unenforceable only if it violates public policy. As discussed above, the student/school relationship is a contractual one, and thus we find this rule applicable.

We extend this rule to hold that a contractual rule or regulation of a private school is lawful and enforceable as long as it is not against public policy or law. It is well established that

CASE 13.3 Continued in Rhode Island a contract violates public policy only if it is: [1] injurious to the interests of the public, [2] interferes with the public welfare or safety, [3] is unconscionable, or [4] tends to injustice or oppression. We adopt the same standard to private school contracts to determine whether a promulgated rule or regulation is lawful.

The [plaintiff] did not offer any evidence that a private school rule regulating the length of a student's hair is injurious to the interests of the public, nor that it interferes with the public welfare or safety. This rule clearly does not rise to the level of unconscionable, nor does it tend to injustice or oppression. The [plaintiff] failed to adduce [offer] evidence of a violated contractual right or evidence that the hair-length rule is contrary to public policy of the State of Rhode Island. We hold, therefore, that Saint Raphael's adoption of a regulation concerning the length of hair of male students was a valid exercise of its discretionary authority and an enforceable provision of its educational contract with students.

DECISION AND REMEDY *The Rhode Island Supreme Court reversed the judgment of the lower court. The state supreme court held that a private school's regulation concerning the length of hair of its male students does not violate public policy. The regulation is an enforceable provision of the school's contract with its students, absent any evidence that the regulation is injurious to the interests of the public, interferes with public welfare or safety, is unconscionable, or otherwise "tends to injustice or oppression."*

EFFECT OF ILLEGALITY

In general, an illegal contract is void—that is, the contract is deemed never to have existed, and the courts will not aid either party. In most illegal contracts, both parties are considered to be **in pari delicto**[13] (equally at fault). In such cases, the contract is void. If the contract is executory, neither party can enforce it. If it has been executed, there can be neither contractual nor quasi-contractual recovery.

That one wrongdoer who is a party to an illegal contract is unjustly enriched at the expense of the other is of no concern to the law—except under certain special circumstances that will be discussed below. The major justification for this hands-off attitude is that it is improper to place the machinery of justice at the disposal of a plaintiff who has broken the law by entering into an illegal bargain. Another justification is the hoped-for deterrent effect of this general hands-off rule. A plaintiff who suffers loss because of an illegal bargain should presumably be deterred from entering into similar illegal bargains.

EXCEPTIONS TO THE GENERAL RULE There are some exceptions to the general rule that neither party to an illegal bargain can sue for breach and that neither party can recover for performance rendered.

—Justifiable Ignorance of the Facts. When one of the parties is relatively innocent, that party can often recover any benefits conferred in a partially executed contract. In this situation, the courts will not enforce the contract but will allow the parties to return to their original positions. An innocent party who has fully performed under the contract may sometimes enforce the contract against the guilty party. For example, a trucking company contracts with Gillespie to carry goods to a specific destination for a normal fee of $500. The trucker delivers the goods and later finds out that the contents of the shipped crates were illegal. Although the law specifies that the shipment, use, and sale of the goods were illegal, the trucker, being an innocent party, can still legally collect the $500 from Gillespie.

—Members of Protected Classes. When a statute is clearly designed to protect a certain class of people, a member of that class can enforce a contract in violation of the statute even though the other party cannot. For example, flight attendants and pilots are subject to a federal statute that prohibits them from flying more than a certain number of hours every month. If an attendant or a pilot exceeds the maximum, the airline must nonetheless pay for those extra hours of service.

Other examples of statutes designed to protect particular classes of people include *blue sky laws*—state laws that regulate and supervise investment companies

---

13. Pronounced in *paa*-ree deh-*lick*-tow.

EXHIBIT 13-2 Contract Legality

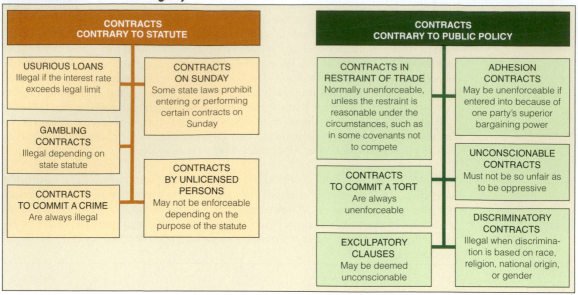

for the protection of the public (see Chapter 41)—and state statutes regulating the sale of insurance. If an insurance company violates a statute when selling insurance, the purchaser can nevertheless enforce the policy and recover from the insurer.

—*Withdrawal from an Illegal Agreement.* If an agreement has been only partly carried out and the illegal portion of the bargain has not yet been performed, the party rendering performance can withdraw from the contract and recover the performance or its value. For example, Sam and Jim decide to wager (illegally) on the outcome of a boxing match. Each deposits money with a stakeholder, who agrees to pay the winner of the bet. At this point, each party has performed part of the agreement, but the illegal element of the agreement will not occur until the funds are paid to the winner. Before such payment occurs, either party is entitled to withdraw from the bargain by giving notice of repudiation to the stakeholder.

—*Contract Illegal through Fraud, Duress, or Undue Influence.* Often, an illegal contract involves one party who is more at fault than the other. When a party has been induced to enter into an illegal bargain by fraud, duress, or undue influence on the part of the

other party to the agreement, that party will be allowed to recover for the performance or its value.

SEVERABLE, OR DIVISIBLE, CONTRACTS A contract that is *severable*, or divisible, consists of distinct parts that can be performed separately, with separate consideration provided for each part. An *indivisible* contract, in contrast, exists when the parties intended that complete performance by each party would be essential, even if the contract contains a number of seemingly separate provisions.

If a contract is divisible into legal and illegal portions, a court may enforce the legal portion but not the illegal one, so long as the illegal portion does not affect the essence of the bargain. This approach of the courts is consistent with the basic policy of enforcing the legal intentions of the contracting parties whenever possible. For example, if an overly broad and thus illegal covenant not to compete was drafted into an employment contract, the court might allow the employment contract to be enforceable but reform the unreasonably broad covenant by converting its terms into reasonable ones. Alternatively, the court could declare the covenant illegal (and thus void) and enforce the remaining employment terms.

REVIEWING CAPACITY AND LEGALITY

Renee Beaver started racing go-karts competitively in 1997, when she was fourteen. Many of the races required her to sign an exculpatory clause to participate, which she or her parents regularly signed. In 2000, she participated in the annual Elkhart Grand Prix, a series of races in Elkhart, Indiana. During the event in which she drove, a piece of foam padding used as a course barrier was torn from its base and ended up on the track. A portion of the padding struck Beaver in the head, and another portion was thrown into oncoming traffic, causing a multikart collision during which she sustained severe injuries. Beaver filed an action against the race organizers for negligence. The organizers could not locate the exculpatory clause that Beaver was supposed to have signed. Race organizers argued that she must have signed one to enter the race, but even if she had not signed one, her actions showed her intent to be bound by its terms. Using the information presented in the chapter, answer the following questions.

1. Did Beaver have the contractual capacity to enter a contract with an exculpatory clause? Why or why not?

2. Assuming that Beaver did, in fact, sign the exculpatory clause, did she later disaffirm or ratify the contract? Explain.

3. Now assume that Beaver had stated that she was eighteen years old at the time that she signed the exculpatory clause. How might this affect Beaver's ability to disaffirm or ratify the contract?

4. If Beaver did not actually sign the exculpatory clause, could a court conclude that she impliedly accepted its terms by participating in the race? Why or why not?

5. Discuss whether it is likely that a court would conclude that the exculpatory clause that Beaver signed was contrary to public policy.

TERMS AND CONCEPTS TO REVIEW

adhesion contract 268	disaffirmance 258	ratification 262
age of majority 258	emancipation 258	unconscionable 268
blue laws 265	exculpatory clause 268	usury 265
contractual capacity 258	*in pari delicto* 271	
covenant not to compete 266	necessaries 259	

QUESTIONS AND CASE PROBLEMS

13–1. After Kira had had several drinks one night, she sold Charlotte a diamond necklace worth thousands of dollars for just $100. The next day, Kira offered the $100 to Charlotte and requested the return of her necklace. Charlotte refused to accept the $100 or return the necklace, claiming that there was a valid contract of sale. Kira explained that she had been intoxicated at the time the bargain was made and thus the contract was voidable at her option. Was Kira correct? Explain.

13–2. ⚖ QUESTION WITH SAMPLE ANSWER

A famous New York City hotel, Hotel Lux, is noted for its food as well as its luxury accommodations. Hotel Lux contracts with a famous chef, Chef Perlee, to become its head chef at $6,000 per month. The contract states that should Perlee leave the employment of Hotel Lux for any reason, he will not work as a chef for any hotel or restaurant in New York, New Jersey, or Pennsylvania for a period of one year. During the first six months of the contract, Hotel Lux substantially advertises Perlee as its head chef, and business at the hotel is excellent. Then a dispute arises between the hotel management and Perlee, and Perlee terminates his employment. One month later, he is hired by a famous New Jersey restaurant just across the New York state line. Hotel Lux learns of Perlee's employment through a large advertisement in a New York City newspaper. It seeks to enjoin (prevent) Perlee from working in that restaurant as a chef for one year. Discuss how successful Hotel Lux will be in its action.

For a sample answer to this question, go to Appendix I at the end of this text.

13–3. Joanne is a seventy-five-year-old widow who survives on her husband's small pension. Joanne has become increasingly forgetful, and her family worries that she may have Alzheimer's disease (a brain disorder that seriously affects a person's ability to carry out daily activities). No physician has diagnosed her, however, and no court has ruled on Joanne's legal competence. One day while she is out shopping, Joanne stops by a store that is having a sale on pianos and enters into a fifteen-year installment contract to buy a grand piano. When the piano arrives the next day, Joanne seems confused and repeatedly asks the deliveryperson why a piano is being delivered. Joanne claims that she does not recall buying a piano. Explain whether this contract is void, voidable, or valid. Can Joanne avoid her contractual obligation to buy the piano? If so, how?

13–4. CONTRACTS BY MINORS. Sergei Samsonov, a Russian, was one of the world's top hockey players in the 1990s. When Samsonov was seventeen years old, he signed a contract to play hockey for two seasons with the Central Sports Army Club, a Russian club known by the abbreviation CSKA. Before the start of the second season, Samsonov learned that because of a dispute between CSKA coaches, he would not be playing in Russia's premier hockey league. Samsonov hired Athletes and Artists, Inc. (A&A), an American sports agency, to make a deal with a U.S. hockey team. Samsonov signed a contract to play for the Detroit Vipers (whose corporate name was, at the time, Arena Associates, Inc.). Neither A&A nor Arena knew about the CSKA contract. CSKA filed a suit in a federal district court against Arena and others, alleging, among other things, wrongful interference with a contractual relationship. What effect will Samsonov's age have on the outcome of this suit? [*Central Sports Army Club v. Arena Associates, Inc.*, 952 F.Supp. 181 (S.D.N.Y. 1997)]

13–5. EXCULPATORY CLAUSE. Norbert Eelbode applied for a job with Travelers Inn in the state of Washington. As part of the application process, Eelbode was sent to Laura Grothe, a physical therapist at Chec Medical Centers, Inc., for a preemployment physical exam. Before the exam, Eelbode signed a document that stated in part, "I hereby release Chec and the Washington Readicare Medical Group and its physicians from all liability arising from any injury to me resulting from my participation in the exam." During the exam, Grothe asked Eelbode to lift an item while bending from the waist using only his back with his knees locked. Eelbode experienced immediate sharp and burning pain in his lower back and down the back of his right leg. Eelbode filed a suit in a Washington state court against Grothe and Chec, claiming that he had been injured because of an improperly administered back torso strength test. Grothe and Chec cited the document that Eelbode signed and filed a motion for summary judgment. Should the court grant the motion? Why or why not? [*Eelbode v. Chec Medical Centers, Inc.*, 984 P.2d 436 (Wash.App. 1999)]

13–6. COVENANTS NOT TO COMPETE. In 1993, Mutual Service Casualty Insurance Co. and its affiliates (collectively, MSI) hired Thomas Brass as an insurance agent. Three years later, Brass entered into a career agent's contract with MSI. This contract contained provisions regarding Brass's activities after termination. These provisions stated that, for a period of not less than one year, Brass could not solicit any MSI customers to "lapse, cancel, or replace" any insurance contract in force with MSI in an effort to take that business to a competitor. If he did, MSI could at any time refuse to pay the commissions that it otherwise owed him. The contract also restricted Brass from working for American National Insurance Co. for three years after termination. In 1998, Brass quit MSI and immediately went to work for American National, soliciting MSI customers. MSI filed a suit in a Wisconsin state court against Brass, claiming that he had violated the noncompete terms of his MSI contract. Should the court enforce the covenant not to compete? Why or why not? [*Mutual Service Casualty Insurance Co. v. Brass*, 625 N.W.2d 648 (Wis.App. 2001)]

13–7. ⚖ CASE PROBLEM WITH SAMPLE ANSWER

Millennium Club, Inc., operates a tavern in South Bend, Indiana. In January 2003, Pamela Avila and other minors gained admission by misrepresenting themselves to be at least twenty-one years old. According to the club's representatives, the minors used false driver's licenses, "fraudulent transfer of a stamp used to gain admission by another patron or other means of false identification." To gain access, the minors also signed affidavits falsely attesting to the fact that they were aged twenty-one or older. When the state filed criminal charges against the club, the club filed a suit in an Indiana state court against Avila and more than two hundred others, seeking damages of $3,000 each for misrepresenting their ages. The minors filed a motion to dismiss the complaint. Should the court grant the motion? What are the competing policy interests in this case? If the club was not careful in checking minors' identification, should it be allowed to recover? If the club reasonably relied on the minors' representations, should the minors be allowed to avoid liability? Discuss. [*Millennium Club, Inc. v. Avila*, 809 N.E.2d 906 (Ind.App. 2004)]

To view a sample answer for this case problem, go to this book's Web site at http://wbl.westbuslaw.com, select "Chapter 13," and click on "Case Problem with Sample Answer."

13–8. **UNCONSCIONABILITY.** Frank Rodziewicz was driving a Volvo tractor-trailer on Interstate 90 in Lake County, Indiana, when he struck a concrete barrier. His tractor-trailer became stuck on the barrier, and the Indiana State Police contacted Waffco Heavy Duty Towing, Inc., to assist in the recovery of the truck. Before beginning work, Waffco told Rodziewicz that it would cost $275 to tow the truck. There was no discussion of labor or any other costs. Rodziewicz told Waffco to take the truck to a local Volvo dealership. Within a few minutes, Waffco pulled the truck off the barrier and towed it to Waffco's nearby towing yard. Rodziewicz was soon notified that, in addition to the $275 towing fee, he would have to pay $4,070 in labor costs and that Waffco would not release the truck until payment was made. Rodziewicz paid the total amount. Disputing the labor charge, however, he filed a suit in an Indiana state court against Waffco, alleging in part breach of contract. Was the towing contract unconscionable? Would it make a difference if the parties had discussed the labor charge before the tow? Explain. [*Rodziewicz v. Waffco Heavy Duty Towing, Inc.*, 763 N.E.2d 491 (Ind.App. 2002)]

13–9. **COVENANT NOT TO COMPETE.** Gary Forsee was an executive officer with responsibility for the U.S. operations of BellSouth Corp., a company providing global telecommunications services. Under a covenant not to compete, Forsee agreed that for a period of eighteen months after termination from employment, he would not "provide services . . . in competition with

[BellSouth] . . . to any person or entity which provides products or services identical or similar to products and services provided by [BellSouth] . . . within the territory." *Territory* was defined to include the geographic area in which Forsee provided services to BellSouth. The *services* included "management, strategic planning, business planning, administration, or other participation in or providing advice with respect to the communications services business." Forsee announced his intent to resign and accept a position as chief executive officer of Sprint Corp., a competitor of BellSouth. BellSouth filed a suit in a Georgia state court against Forsee, claiming in part that his acceptance of employment with Sprint would violate the covenant not to compete. Is the covenant legal? Should it be enforced? Why or why not? [*BellSouth Corp. v. Forsee*, 595 S.E.2d 99 (Ga.App. 2004)]

13–10. **VIDEO QUESTION**

Go to this text's Web site at http://wbl.westbuslaw.com and select "Chapter 13." Click on "Video Questions" and view the video titled *The Money Pit*. Then answer the following questions.

(a) Assume that a valid contract exists between Walter (Tom Hanks) and the plumber. Recall from the video that the plumber had at least two drinks before agreeing to take on the plumbing job. If the plumber was intoxicated, is the contract voidable? Why or why not?

(b) Suppose that state law requires plumbers in Walter's state to have a plumber's license and that this plumber does not have a license. Would the contract be enforceable? Why or why not?

(c) In the video, the plumber suggests that Walter has been "turned down by every other plumber in the valley." Although the plumber does not even look at the house's plumbing, he agrees to do the repairs if Walter gives him a check for $5,000 right away "before he changes his mind." If Walter later seeks to void the contract because it is contrary to public policy, what should he argue?

LAW | on the Web

For updated links to resources available on the Web, as well as a variety of other materials, visit this text's Web site at http://wbl.westbuslaw.com.

For an example of state statutory provisions governing the emancipation of minors, you can view Wyoming's statutory provisions on this topic at

http://legisweb.state.wy.us/statutes/sub14.htm

To read the first "Sunday law" in colonial America and learn about some of the punishments meted out in those days for failing to obey such laws, go to

http://www.natreformassn.org/statesman/99/charactr.html

LEGAL RESEARCH EXERCISES ON THE WEB

Go to http://wbl.westbuslaw.com, the Web site that accompanies this text. Select "Chapter 13" and click on "Internet Exercises." There you will find the following Internet research exercises that you can perform to learn more about topics covered in this chapter.

Activity 13–1: **LEGAL PERSPECTIVE**
　　　　　　　　Covenants Not to Compete

Activity 13–2: **MANAGEMENT PERSPECTIVE**
　　　　　　　　Minors and the Law

Activity 13–3: **SOCIAL PERSPECTIVE**
　　　　　　　　Online Gambling

CHAPTER 14

Genuineness of Assent

A contract has been entered into by two parties, each with full legal capacity and for a legal purpose. The contract is also supported by consideration. The contract thus meets the four requirements for a valid contract that were specified in Chapter 10. Nonetheless, the contract may be unenforceable if the parties have not genuinely assented to its terms. As stated in Chapter 10, lack of **genuineness of assent** (voluntary consent) can be used as a defense to the contract's enforceability. Genuineness of assent may be lacking because of a mistake, misrepresentation, undue influence, or duress—in other words, because there is no true "meeting of the minds." In this chapter, we examine problems relating to genuineness of assent.

SECTION 1 | Mistakes

We all make mistakes, and it is therefore not surprising that mistakes are made when contracts are formed. It is important to distinguish between *mistakes of fact* and *mistakes of value or quality*. Only a mistake of fact may allow a contract to be avoided.

MISTAKES OF FACT

Mistakes of fact occur in two forms—*bilateral* and *unilateral*. A bilateral, or mutual, mistake is made by both of the contracting parties. A unilateral mistake is made by only one of the parties. We look next at these two types of mistakes and illustrate them graphically in Exhibit 14–1.

BILATERAL (MUTUAL) MISTAKES OF FACT A bilateral, or mutual, mistake occurs when both parties are mistaken as to some *material fact*—that is, a fact important to the subject matter of the contract. When a bilateral mistake occurs, the contract can be rescinded, or canceled, by either party.[1] For example, Keeley buys a landscape painting from Umberto's art gallery. Both Umberto and Keeley believe that the

---

1. *Restatement (Second) of Contracts*, Section 152.

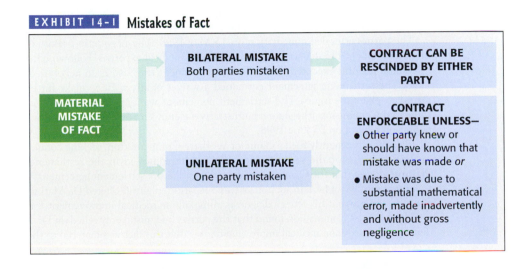

EXHIBIT 14-1 Mistakes of Fact

MATERIAL MISTAKE OF FACT		
BILATERAL MISTAKE Both parties mistaken	→	**CONTRACT CAN BE RESCINDED BY EITHER PARTY**
UNILATERAL MISTAKE One party mistaken	→	**CONTRACT ENFORCEABLE UNLESS—** • Other party knew or should have known that mistake was made *or* • Mistake was due to substantial mathematical error, made inadvertently and without gross negligence

painting is by the artist Vincent van Gogh. Later, Keeley discovers that the painting is a very clever fake. Because neither Umberto nor Keeley was aware of this material fact when they made their deal, Keeley can rescind the contract and recover the purchase price of the painting.

A word or term in a contract may be subject to more than one reasonable interpretation. In that situation, if the parties to the contract attach materially different meanings to the term, their mutual mistake of fact may allow the contract to be rescinded because there has been no "meeting of the minds," or true assent, which is required for a contract to arise.

The classic case on bilateral mistake is *Raffles v. Wichelhaus,*[2] which was decided by an English court in

1864. The defendant, Wichelhaus, paid for a shipment of Surat cotton from the plaintiff, Raffles, "to arrive 'Peerless' from Bombay." Wichelhaus expected the goods to be shipped on the *Peerless,* a ship sailing from Bombay, India, in October. Raffles expected to ship the goods on a different *Peerless,* which sailed from Bombay in December. When the goods arrived and Raffles tried to deliver them, Wichelhaus refused to accept them. The court held for Wichelhaus, concluding that no mutual assent existed because the parties had attached materially different meanings to an essential term of the written contract (the ship that was to transport the goods).

In the following case, an injured worker sought to set aside a settlement agreement entered into with his employer, arguing that a physician's mistaken diagnosis of the worker's injury was a mutual mistake of fact on which the agreement was based.

---

2. 159 Eng.Rep. 375 (1864).

Court of Appeals of
North Carolina. 2004.
592 S.E.2d 215.

CASE 14.1 Roberts v. Century Contractors, Inc.

LEVINSON, Judge.

Plaintiff (Bobby Roberts) suffered a compensable injury by accident on 28 July 1993 when he was struck by a pipe while working for Century Contractors, Incorporated, causing trauma to his neck and back. Defendants admitted liability, and plaintiff sought treatment for his injuries with Dr. James Markworth of Southeastern Orthopaedic Clinic. Dr. Markworth diagnosed plaintiff as having some narrowing of the cervical spinal canal and some degeneration of multiple levels of the cervical disks, with bulging of some of the disks. Dr. Markworth performed an anterior cervical discectomy infusion * * * with bone grafts * * * .

* * * Dr. Markworth subsequently indicated that plaintiff was at maximum medical improvement [MMI] and stopped treating plaintiff. A physician's assistant at Southeastern Orthopaedic Clinic continued to treat plaintiff. Because he was still experiencing pain, plaintiff issued a request for a second medical opinion on 3 April 1998.

On 2 June 1998, plaintiff saw Dr. Allen Friedman for a second medical opinion. Dr. Friedman noted that there was a question [about one of the grafts] and that x-rays needed to be repeated to be sure that the fusion was stable. Dr. Friedman indicated his concern to plaintiff that current x-rays needed to be obtained to be certain as to whether the fusion was solid.

The parties attended a mediation on 13 May 1998. The negotiation resulted in a settlement amount of $125,000 and payment of related medical expenses. Following his visit to Dr. Friedman, plaintiff executed the settlement agreement that had been negotiated on 13 May 1998. The settlement agreement contained a waiver of any right to make further claims in regard to plaintiff's injury. The settlement agreement was approved by the North Carolina Industrial Commission [the state administrative agency empowered to rule on workers' compensation claims] on 25 June 1998.

Plaintiff subsequently filed a claim for Workers' Compensation, seeking compensation and medical benefits for the same injuries which were addressed in the settlement agreement. Plaintiff alleged that the Commission should set aside the settlement agreement * * * due to mutual mistake of fact. In support of this allegation, plaintiff offered Dr. Markworth's deposition testimony that his office's diagnosis of maximum medical improvement was a mistake.

The * * * Commission found that the parties had mistakenly relied on Dr. Markworth's diagnosis of maximum medical improvement and that this fact was material to the settlement

CASE 14.1 | Continued

agreement. The * * * Commission set aside the agreement and awarded plaintiff compensation and medical benefits in an Opinion and Award filed on 18 September 2002. * * *

Defendants appeal [to a North Carolina state intermediate appellate court], contending * * * the * * * Opinion and Award must be reversed because the * * * Commission erred in setting aside the parties' mediated settlement agreement on the basis of mutual mistake of fact * * * .

* * * *

* * * Compromise settlement agreements, including mediated settlement agreements in Workers' Compensation cases, are governed by general principles of contract law.

It is a well-settled principle of contract law that a *valid contract exists only where there has been a meeting of the minds as to all essential terms of the agreement. Therefore, where a mistake is common to both parties and concerns a material past or presently existing fact, such that there is no meeting of the minds, a contract may be avoided.* [Emphasis added.]

To afford relief, the mistake must be of a certain nature. The fact about which the parties are mistaken must be an existing or past fact. The mistaken fact must also be material * * * . It must be as to a fact which enters into and forms the basis of the contract, or in other words, it must be of the essence of the agreement—the *sine qua non*—or, as is sometimes said, the efficient cause of the agreement, and must be such that it animates and controls the conduct of the parties.

Additionally, *relief from a contract due to mistake of fact will be had only where both parties to an agreement are mistaken.* Thus, as a general rule relief will be denied where the party against whom it is sought was ignorant that the other party was acting under a mistake and the former's conduct in no way contributed thereto. Likewise, a party who assumed the risk of a mistaken fact cannot avoid a contract. [Emphasis added.]

A party bears the risk of a mistake when

(a) the risk is allocated to him by agreement of the parties, or
(b) he is aware, at the time the contract is made that he has only limited knowledge with respect to the facts to which the mistake relates but treats his limited knowledge as sufficient, or
(c) the risk is allocated to him by the court on the ground that it is reasonable in the circumstances to do so.

* * * *

* * * The x-rays [examined by Dr. Friedman] after Dr. Markworth or Southern Orthopaedic Clinic had last treated plaintiff [Roberts], indicated Dr. Markworth's diagnosis of maximum medical improvement * * * was a mistake. Dr. Markworth testified * * * that advising plaintiff that he was at maximum medical improvement at that time was a mistake.

* * * *

* * * [T]he finding of maximum medical improvement and the impairment rating given by Dr. Markworth were material to the settlement of this claim and * * * both parties relied on this information in entering into settlement negotiations.

* * * *

* * * [T]he parties believed that plaintiff had reached maximum medical improvement and, further, * * * they materially relied upon this fact in reaching a settlement. Defendants' essential argument on appeal is that because plaintiff either knew that there was a possibility that [he had not reached MMI] or was negligent in not declining to sign the settlement agreement, mutual mistake is a legal impossibility in this case. As the facts * * * support a contrary conclusion, we do not agree.

* * * The plaintiff testified that he based his decision to sign the settlement agreement on Dr. Markworth's diagnosis and that he would not have settled his case if Dr. Friedman had told him that [he had not reached MMI]. Thus, there is competent record evidence to support the * * * findings that the parties were mistaken as to whether plaintiff had reached maximum medical improvement and that this mistaken fact was material. * * *

* * * *

* * * We affirm the * * * Award filed 18 September 2002.

CONTINUED ►

CASE 14.1 | Continued

QUESTIONS

1. Why did the court in this case consider Dr. Markworth's misdiagnosis a bilateral mistake rather than a unilateral mistake?
2. Why are situations such as the one presented in this case often sources of litigation appealed to the states' highest courts?

UNILATERAL MISTAKES OF FACT A unilateral mistake occurs when only one of the contracting parties makes a mistake as to some material fact. The general rule is that a unilateral mistake does not afford the mistaken party any right to relief from the contract. For example, DeVinck intends to sell his motor home for $17,500. When he learns that Benson is interested in buying a used motor home, DeVinck faxes Benson an offer to sell the vehicle to him. When typing the fax, however, DeVinck mistakenly keys in the price of $15,700. Benson immediately sends DeVinck a fax accepting DeVinck's offer. Even though DeVinck intended to sell his motor home for $17,500, his unilateral mistake falls on him. He is bound in contract to sell the motor home to Benson for $15,700.

There are at least two exceptions to this general rule.[3] First, if the *other* party to the contract knows or should have known that a mistake of fact was made, the contract may not be enforceable. In the above example, if Benson knew that DeVinck intended to sell his motor home for $17,500, then DeVinck's unilateral mistake (stating $15,700 in his offer) may render the resulting contract unenforceable. The second exception arises when a unilateral mistake of fact was due to a mathematical mistake in addition, subtraction, division, or multiplication and was made inadvertently and without gross (extreme) negligence. If a contractor's bid was significantly low because he or she made a mistake in addition when totaling the estimated costs, any contract resulting from the bid may be rescinded, or canceled. Of course, in both situations, the mistake must still involve some material fact.

MISTAKES OF VALUE

If a mistake concerns the future market value or quality of the object of the contract, the mistake is one of *value*, and either party can normally enforce the contract. Mistakes of value can be bilateral or unilateral; but either way, they do not serve as a basis for avoid-

ing a contract. For example, suppose that Chi buys a violin from Bev for $250. Although the violin is very old, neither party believes that it is extremely valuable. An antiques dealer later informs the parties, however, that the violin is rare and worth thousands of dollars. Although a mutual mistake has been made, the mistake is not a mistake of *fact* that warrants contract rescission. Similarly, a unilateral mistake of value will not serve as the basis for avoiding a contract.

The reason that mistakes of value or quality have no legal significance is that value is variable. Depending on the time, place, and other circumstances, the same item may be worth considerably different amounts. When parties form a contract, their agreement establishes the value of the object of their transaction—for the moment. Each party is considered to have assumed the risk that the value will change in the future or prove to be different from what he or she thought. Without this rule, almost any party who did not receive what she or he considered a fair bargain could argue mistake.

SECTION 2 | Fraudulent Misrepresentation

Although fraud is a tort (see Chapter 6), it also affects the genuineness of the innocent party's consent to the contract. Thus, the transaction is not voluntary in the sense of involving "mutual assent." When an innocent party is fraudulently induced to enter into a contract, the contract normally can be avoided because that party has not *voluntarily* consented to its terms.[4] Normally, the innocent party can either rescind (cancel) the contract and be restored to his or her original position or enforce the contract and seek damages for any injuries resulting from the fraud.

The word *fraudulent* means many things in the law. Generally, fraudulent misrepresentation refers only to misrepresentation that is consciously false and is intended to mislead another. The perpetrator of the fraudulent misrepresentation knows or believes that

---

3. The *Restatement (Second) of Contracts*, Section 153, liberalizes the general rule to take into account the modern trend of allowing avoidance even though only one party has been mistaken.

4. *Restatement (Second) of Contracts*, Sections 163 and 164.

the assertion is false or knows that she or he does not have a basis (stated or implied) for the assertion.[5] Typically, fraudulent misrepresentation consists of the following elements:

1. A misrepresentation of a material fact must occur.
2. There must be an intent to deceive.
3. The innocent party must justifiably rely on the misrepresentation.

To collect damages, a party must also have been injured. To obtain rescission of a contract, or to defend against the enforcement of a contract on the basis of fraudulent misrepresentation, in most states a party need not have suffered an injury.

MISREPRESENTATION HAS OCCURRED

The first element of proving fraud is to show that misrepresentation of a material fact has occurred. This misrepresentation can occur by words or actions. For example, the statement "This sculpture was created by Michelangelo" is an express misrepresentation of fact if another artist sculpted the statue. The misrepresen-

tation as to the identity of the artist would certainly be a material fact in the formation of this contract.

Representations of future facts (predictions) and statements of opinion are generally not subject to claims of fraud. Every person is expected to exercise care and judgment when entering into contracts, and the law will not come to the aid of one who simply makes an unwise bargain. Statements such as "This land will be worth twice as much next year" or "This car will last for years and years" are statements of opinion, not fact. Contracting parties should recognize them as such and not rely on them. An opinion is usually subject to contrary or conflicting views; a fact is objective and verifiable. Thus, a seller of goods is allowed to use *puffery* to sell his or her wares without liability for fraud.

In certain cases, however, particularly when a naïve purchaser relies on a so-called expert's opinion, the innocent party may be entitled to rescission or reformation. (*Reformation* is an equitable remedy granted by a court in which the terms of a contract are altered to reflect the true intentions of the parties—see Chapter 18.) The issue in the following case was whether the statements made by instructors at a dance school to one of the school's students qualified as statements of opinion or statements of fact.

---

5. *Restatement (Second) of Contracts*, Section 162.

CASE 14.2 | Vokes v. Arthur Murray, Inc.

District Court of
Appeal of Florida,
Second District, 1968.
212 So.2d 906.

COMPANY PROFILE *Arthur Murray, founder of Arthur Murray, Inc. (http://www.arthurmurray .com), began teaching people how to dance in 1919. At the time, social dancing was becoming increasingly popular among young people, in part because so many adults were shocked by the new "jazz dancing." Across America, young people wanted to learn the new steps—the turkey trot, the fox-trot, the kangaroo dip, the chicken scratch, the bunny hug, the grizzly bear, and others. By the 1930s, Murray's instructors were giving lessons on cruise ships, in tourist hotels, and to the employees of New York stores during the employees' lunch breaks. In 1937, Murray founded the Arthur Murray Studios, a chain of franchised dance schools. During the 1950s, Murray sponsored a television show—The Arthur Murray Party—to attract students to the schools. Murray retired in 1964, estimating that he had taught more than twenty million people how to dance.*

BACKGROUND AND FACTS *Audrey E. Vokes, a widow without family, wished to become "an accomplished dancer" and to find "a new interest in life." In 1961, she was invited to attend a "dance party" at J. P. Davenport's "School of Dancing," an Arthur Murray, Inc., franchise. Vokes went to the school and received elaborate praise from her instructor for her grace, poise, and potential as "an excellent dancer." The instructor sold her eight half-hour dance lessons for $14.50 each, to be utilized within one calendar month. Subsequently, over a period of less than sixteen months, Vokes bought a total of fourteen dance courses, which amounted to 2,302 hours of dancing lessons at Davenport's school, for a total cash outlay of $31,090.45 (in 2005, this would amount to more than $128,000). When it became clear to Vokes that she did not, in fact, have the potential to be an excellent dancer, she filed a suit against the school, alleging fraudulent misrepresentation. When the trial court dismissed her complaint, she appealed.*

CONTINUED ▶

CASE 14.2 | Continued

IN THE LANGUAGE OF THE COURT

PIERCE, Judge.
* * * *

[The dance contracts] were procured by defendant Davenport and Arthur Murray, Inc., by false representations to her that she was improving in her dancing ability, that she had excellent potential, that she was responding to instructions in dancing grace, and that they were developing her into a beautiful dancer, whereas in truth and in fact she did not develop in her dancing ability, she had no "dance aptitude," and in fact had difficulty in "hearing the musical beat." * * *
* * * *

It is true that generally a misrepresentation, to be actionable, must be one of fact rather than of opinion. * * * A statement of a party having * * * superior knowledge may be regarded as a statement of fact although it would be considered as opinion if the parties were dealing on equal terms.

It could be reasonably supposed here that defendants had superior knowledge as to whether plaintiff had "dance potential" and as to whether she was noticeably improving in the art of terpsichore [dancing]. And it would be a reasonable inference from the undenied averments [assertions] of the complaint that the flowery eulogiums [praises] heaped upon her by defendants * * * proceeded as much or more from the urge to "ring the cash register" as from any honest or realistic appraisal of her dancing prowess or a factual representation of her progress.
* * * *

* * * [W]hat is plainly injurious to good faith ought to be considered as a fraud sufficient to impeach a contract, and * * * *an improvident [unwise] agreement may be avoided because of surprise, or mistake, want of freedom, undue influence, the suggestion of falsehood, or the suppression of truth.* [Emphasis added.]

DECISION AND REMEDY *Vokes's complaint was reinstated, and the case was returned to the trial court to allow Vokes to prove her case.*

IMPACT OF THIS CASE ON TODAY'S LAW

This case has become a classic in contract law because it clearly illustrates an important principle. The general rule—that a misrepresentation must be one of fact rather than one of opinion to be actionable—does not apply in certain situations, such as when one party misrepresents something about which he or she possesses superior knowledge (Vokes's dancing ability, in this case).

MISREPRESENTATION BY CONDUCT Misrepresentation can also take place through the conduct of a party, such as by the concealment of a fact that is material to the contract.[6] Suppose, for example, that Rakas contracts to buy a new car from Bustamonte, a dealer in new automobiles. The car has been used as a demonstration model for prospective customers to test-drive, but Bustamonte has turned back the odometer. Rakas cannot tell from the odometer reading that the car has been driven nearly one thousand miles, and Bustamonte does not tell Rakas the distance the car

has actually been driven. Bustamonte's concealment constitutes misrepresentation by conduct.

MISREPRESENTATION OF LAW Misrepresentation of law *ordinarily* does not entitle a party to relief from a contract. For example, Camara has a parcel of property that she is trying to sell to Pye. Camara knows that a local ordinance prohibits building anything higher than three stories on the property. Nonetheless, she tells Pye, "You can build a condominium fifty stories high if you want to." Pye buys the land and later discovers that Camara's statement was false. Normally, Pye cannot avoid the contract because at common law people are assumed to know state and local ordi-

---
6. *Restatement (Second) of Contracts*, Section 160.

nances. Additionally, a layperson should not rely on a statement made by a nonlawyer about a point of law.

Exceptions to this rule occur, however, when the misrepresenting party is in a profession that is known to require greater knowledge of the law than the average citizen possesses. The courts are recognizing an increasing number of such professions. For example, the courts recognize that clients expect their real estate brokers to know the law governing real estate sales and land use. If Camara, in the preceding example, had been a lawyer or a real estate broker, her misrepresentation of the area's zoning status would probably have constituted fraud.

MISREPRESENTATION BY SILENCE Ordinarily, neither party to a contract has a duty to come forward and disclose facts. Therefore, a contract cannot be set aside because certain pertinent information is not volunteered. For example, suppose you have an accident that requires extensive bodywork on one side of your car. After the repair, the car's appearance and operation are the same as they were before the accident. One year later you decide to sell your car. You do not need to volunteer this information to a potential buyer. In this situation, silence does not constitute misrepresentation. In contrast, if the purchaser asks you if the car has had extensive bodywork and you lie, you have committed a fraudulent misrepresentation.

Some exceptions to the general rule exist. Generally, if the seller knows of a *serious* defect or a *serious* potential problem that could not reasonably be suspected by the buyer, the seller may have a duty to speak. For example, if a city fails to disclose to bidders subsoil conditions that will cause great expense in constructing a sewer system, the city is guilty of fraud. Also, when the parties are in a *fiduciary relationship* (one of trust, such as the relationship between business partners, physicians and their patients, and attorneys and their clients—see Chapter 31), there is a duty to disclose material facts; failure to do so may constitute fraud.[7] Statutes provide still other exceptions to the general rule of nondisclosure. The Truth-in-Lending Act, for example, requires disclosure of certain facts in financial transactions (see Chapter 44).

A duty to disclose information may also arise in an employment context when the employer either misrepresents or conceals information from a prospective employee during the hiring process. For a further discussion of this issue, see this chapter's *Emerging Trends* feature on the following two pages.

INTENT TO DECEIVE

The second element of fraud is knowledge on the part of the misrepresenting party that facts have been falsely represented. This element, normally called *scienter,*[8] or "guilty knowledge," signifies that there was an *intent to deceive. Scienter* clearly exists if a party knows a fact is not as stated. *Scienter* also exists if a party makes a statement that he or she believes is not true or makes a statement recklessly, without regard to whether it is true or false. Finally, this element is met if a party says or implies that a statement is made on some basis, such as personal knowledge or personal investigation, when it is not.

For example, assume that Meese, a securities broker, offers to sell BIM stock to Packer. Meese assures Packer that BIM shares are blue-chip securities—that is, they are stable, are limited in risk, and yield a good return on investment over time. In fact, Meese knows nothing about the quality of BIM stock and does not believe what he is saying to be true. Meese's statement is thus a misrepresentation. If Packer is induced by Meese's intentional misrepresentation of a material fact to enter into a contract to buy the stock, normally he can avoid his obligations under the contract.

RELIANCE ON THE MISREPRESENTATION

The third element of fraud is reasonably *justifiable reliance* on the misrepresentation of fact. The deceived party must have a justifiable reason for relying on the misrepresentation, and the misrepresentation must be an important factor (but not necessarily the sole factor) in inducing that party to enter into the contract.

Reliance is not justified if the innocent party knows the true facts or relies on obviously extravagant statements. If a used-car dealer tells you, "This old Cadillac will get fifty miles to the gallon," you normally will not be justified in relying on the statement. Or suppose that Kovich, a bank director, induces Mallory, a co-director, to sign a guaranty that the bank's assets will satisfy its liabilities, stating, "We have plenty of assets to satisfy our creditors." If Mallory knows the true facts, he will not be justified in relying on Kovich's statement. If, however, Mallory does not know the

---

7. *Restatement (Second) of Contracts,* Sections 161 and 173.

8. Pronounced sy-en-ter.

Misrepresentation in the Employment Context

Given the fairly dramatic rise in bankruptcies in our economy, there has been a trend among employers to misrepresent the financial status of their companies during the hiring process. In other words, companies that may be experiencing financial difficulties have often sought to avoid discussing such difficulties when interviewing job candidates. Although sometimes these omissions of critical information during the hiring process have been willful, at other times they have been unintentional. After all, many job interviewers may themselves be unaware that their own companies are having financial problems.

THE COURTS REACT TO FRAUDULENT MISREPRESENTATION

Increasingly, courts are reacting negatively to what appears to be fraudulent misrepresentation about a company's financial health during hiring interviews. In one case, a group of men were offered jobs at the El-Jay Division of Cedarapids, Inc. During each of the interviews, the applicants asked about El-Jay's future. They were told that business was growing, that sales were up, and that the future looked promising. In reality, Cedarapids's management had already planned to close the El-Jay facility. Each applicant quit his present job or passed up

other employment opportunities, moved with his family to the new job site, and signed an at-will employment agreement.

When the El-Jay facility closed soon after the men started their new jobs, they filed suit in a federal district court against Cedarapids, alleging, in part, fraudulent misrepresentation, based on the statements made to them during their job interviews. The trial court granted summary judgment in favor of Cedarapids. The appellate court, however, concluded that the case should go to trial because there was sufficient evidence to support a finding of fraud. In the court's view, Cedarapids could be held liable for either failing to disclose material facts or making representations that were misleading because they were in the nature of "half-truth."[a]

THE TREND CONTINUES

In a subsequent case, Philip McConkey, a former New York Giants professional football player, worked as an insurance broker for Ross & Company. While McConkey was working for Ross, representatives of Alexander & Alexander Services, Inc. (A&A), a brokerage firm, offered him a position with their company. McConkey was definitely interested in the offer, but

_____

a. *Meade v. Cedarapids, Inc.*, 164 F.3d 1218 (9th Cir. 1999).

---

true facts *and has no way of discovering them*, he may be justified in relying on Kovich's statement.

The same rule applies to defects in property sold. If the defects are of the kind that would be obvious on inspection, the buyer cannot justifiably rely on the seller's representations. If the defects are hidden or

latent (that is, not apparent on the surface), the buyer is justified in relying on the seller's statements.

The question in the following case was whether an auto lessor was entitled to rescind a lease contract, including its insurance, with a teenager who misrepresented his age to be twenty-two.

CASE 14.3 | ## Fogel v. Enterprise Leasing Co. of Chicago

Appellate Court of Illinois, First District, 2004.
353 Ill.App.3d 165,
817 N.E.2d 1135,
288 Ill.Dec. 485.
http://www.state.il.us/court/
Opinions/AppellateCourt/
2004/default.asp[a]

BACKGROUND AND FACTS *Mehul Thakkar was eighteen years old on November 3, 1997, when he rented a car from Enterprise Leasing Company of Chicago in Hoffman Estates, Illinois. Enterprise's policy was not to rent vehicles to customers under age twenty-one, but Thakkar presented a false California driver's license that showed his picture and the name "Mehul Thak" and indicated his age to be twenty-two. Eight days later, he returned the car and entered into a second lease with Enterprise in Schaumberg, Illinois. As part of this lease, he bought insurance in the amount of $1 million. On November 14, Thakkar was in an accident with a vehicle driven by Michael DeLuca, whose passengers, including Donald Fogel, were injured. Fogel and others filed a suit in an Illinois state court against Enterprise and others, seeking a declaration of the rights and liabilities of the parties with respect to the insurance. Enterprise filed a motion for summary judgment, arguing that it was entitled*

_____

a. In the "First District" section, click on "September." On that list, scroll to the name of the case and click on it to access the opinion. The Administrative Office of the Illinois Courts maintains this Web site.

284

he had already heard rumors that A&A was going to be acquired by another firm. Consequently, during the negotiations that followed, he asked about a possible takeover of the company. He was assured on several occasions that A&A was absolutely not going to be sold to another firm.

McConkey then left his position at Ross and joined A&A. Several months later, contrary to the assurances that he had received prior to his employment, A&A was acquired by Aon Corporation. A short time later, McConkey was fired. Subsequently, he learned that negotiations to sell the firm to Aon were under way long before he was hired.

McConkey sued both companies, alleging that he had been fraudulently induced to leave his former position. The court agreed, concluding that McConkey had reasonably relied on A&A's misrepresentations regarding the status of the company. The court awarded McConkey over $6 million in damages. The decision was affirmed on appeal.[b]

b. *McConkey v. AON Corp.*, 804 A.2d 572 (N.J.Super.A.D. 2002).

IMPLICATIONS FOR THE BUSINESSPERSON

1. During job interviews, interviewers often "promise the moon" to prospective employees and paint their companies' prospects as quite bright. Business owners and managers should be careful, though, to avoid any conduct that could be interpreted by a court as intentionally deceptive.

2. When a prospective employee asks for financial information, the employer must be forthcoming with, at a minimum, any information that is publicly available.

FOR CRITICAL ANALYSIS

1. What are some of the ways that a firm can entice qualified job applicants to come to work for it even when the firm's financial future is in doubt?

2. At what point will a court decide that a company's representation of its financial health to a prospective employee constitutes fraudulent misrepresentation?

RELEVANT WEB SITES

To locate information on the Web concerning the issues discussed in this feature, go to this text's Web site at **http://wbl.westbuslaw.com**, select "Chapter 14," and click on "Emerging Trends."

 **Continued**   *to rescind the rental agreement and the insurance policy based on Thakkar's misrepresentations. The court issued a summary judgment in favor of Enterprise. Fogel appealed this judgment to a state intermediate appellate court.*

IN THE LANGUAGE OF THE COURT

Justice *TULLY* delivered the opinion of the court:
* * * *

In order to establish an equitable claim for rescission on the basis of fraud and misrepresentation, Enterprise must demonstrate: (1) a false statement of material fact; (2) known or believed to be false by the party making it; (3) intended to induce the other party to act; (4) acted upon by the other party in reliance upon the truth of the representations; and (5) damaging to the other party as a result. In this case, each of these elements has been established.

A misrepresentation is material if the party seeking rescission would have acted differently had it been aware of the misrepresentation. Fogel argues that Thakkar's misrepresentation did not relate to a material fact. We disagree. Here, Thakkar made a false statement of material fact which he knew to be false. Thakkar presented a California driver's license that indicated his age was 22. Thakkar knew that he was not 22 years old, but in fact was only 18 years old. Thakkar signed the rental agreement containing this false information. Enterprise had a policy that it did not rent vehicles to persons under the age of 21 * * * . Both of the Enterprise agents who rented vehicles to Thakkar stated that they would not have rented a

CONTINUED ▶

285

CASE 14.3 | Continued

vehicle to him had they been aware of his true age. The facts show that Enterprise would not have rented the vehicle to Thakkar had he not misrepresented his age. We find that the misrepresentation was material. [Emphasis added.]

Fogel further argues that Thakkar did not misrepresent his age intending to induce Enterprise to rent a car to him. Fogel maintains that the evidence establishes Thakkar had no knowledge of Enterprise's age restriction. Again, we disagree. We acknowledge that Thakkar did not admit he used the fictitious license because he knew Enterprise would not rent a vehicle to him unless he was 21 years old. * * * However, Thakkar did admit that he used the fake identification to falsely represent his age to be over 21 in order to gain entry to bars. Further, the evidence shows that Thakkar presented the fictitious California license rather than the valid Illinois driver's license which was in his wallet and which showed his true age of 18 years. The facts show that Thakkar intended to represent his age to be over 21 in order to induce Enterprise to rent a vehicle to him.

We also find that Enterprise relied on Thakkar's misrepresentation when it rented a vehicle to him. Fogel argues that Enterprise's reliance was not justified. Fogel maintains that the name on the fake identification did not match the name on the credit card Thakkar presented and Enterprise had an obligation to investigate these discrepancies and verify the information provided by Thakkar. Further, Fogel contends that Enterprise had a financial incentive to not verify the information and just accept Thakkar's misrepresentations as valid. However, the facts show that Enterprise relied on Thakkar's representation that he was 22 years old. Both Enterprise agents testified that they would not have rented the car to Thakkar had he not been at least 21 years of age. Thakkar presented what appeared to be a valid driver's license and Enterprise had no reason to suspect that it was not valid. Thakkar supported his fraud by telling the agents that he was a student at UCLA. There is nothing in the record to support Fogel's contention that Enterprise was unreasonable in accepting Thakkar's misrepresentation.

Finally, Fogel argues that rescission is not proper because the status quo * * * cannot be restored. Fogel asserts that apart from the issue of the premiums paid by Thakkar, the status quo * * * cannot be restored because of the intervening accident.

Restoration of the status quo initially requires the return of any consideration that has passed to the rescinding party under the contract. Here, Fogel admits that Enterprise tendered a refund of the premiums paid by Thakkar for the rental of the vehicle on November 12, 1997. Fogel's assertion concerning the intervening accident apparently raised the argument that the contract cannot be rescinded because Fogel cannot be restored to the position he was in before the contract. However, * * * Fogel was not a party to the contract. *Restoration of the status quo requires only that the party seeking rescission restore to the other party to the contract the consideration it received under the contract.* [Emphasis added.]

DECISION AND REMEDY *The state intermediate appellate court affirmed the trial court's order granting summary judgment in favor of Enterprise. The appellate court reasoned that an auto lessor may rescind a lease contract, including its insurance, with a teenager when the lessee's misrepresentation of his age is material, is made with the intent to deceive the lessor, and is justifiably relied on by the lessor. Thus, the court concluded that the agreement between Enterprise and Thakkar was properly rescinded in this case.*

WHAT IF THE FACTS WERE DIFFERENT? *Suppose that instead of presenting false identification to the two Enterprise agents who rented the car to him, Thakkar had given them each fifty dollars to allow him to rent the car regardless of his age. How would this have affected the court's decision in this case?*

INJURY TO THE INNOCENT PARTY

Most courts do not require a showing of injury when the action is to rescind (cancel) the contract. These courts hold that because rescission returns the parties to the positions they held before the contract was made, a showing of injury to the innocent party is unnecessary.

For a person to recover damages caused by fraud, proof of an injury is universally required. The measure of damages is ordinarily equal to the property's value had it been delivered as represented, less the actual price paid for the property. In actions based on fraud, courts often award *punitive damages*, or *exemplary damages*, which are granted to a plaintiff over and above the proved, actual compensation for the loss.[9] As discussed in Chapter 6, punitive damages are based on the public-policy consideration of punishing the defendant or setting an example to deter similar wrongdoing by others.

SECTION 3 | Nonfraudulent Misrepresentation

If a plaintiff seeks to rescind a contract on the ground of *fraudulent* misrepresentation, the plaintiff must prove that the defendant had the intent to deceive. Most courts also allow rescission in cases involving *nonfraudulent* misrepresentation—that is, innocent or negligent misrepresentation—if all of the other elements of misrepresentation exist.

INNOCENT MISREPRESENTATION

If a person makes a statement that he or she believes to be true but that actually misrepresents material facts, the person is guilty only of an **innocent misrepresentation,** not of fraud. If an innocent misrepresentation occurs, the aggrieved party can rescind the contract but usually cannot seek damages. For example, Parris tells Roberta that a tract contains 250 acres. Parris is mistaken—the tract of land contains only 215 acres—but Parris does not know that. Roberta is induced by the statement to make a contract to buy the land. Even though the misrepresentation is innocent, Roberta can avoid the contract if the misrepresentation is material.

NEGLIGENT MISREPRESENTATION

Sometimes a party will make a misrepresentation through carelessness, believing the statement is true. This misrepresentation is negligent if the person fails to exercise reasonable care in uncovering or disclosing the facts or does not use the skill and competence that her or his business or profession requires. For example, an operator of a weight scale certifies the weight of

Sneed's commodity, even though the scale's accuracy has not been checked in more than a year. In this situation, the scale operator's lack of action could constitute **negligent misrepresentation.**

In virtually all states, such negligent misrepresentation is equal to *scienter*, or knowingly making a misrepresentation. In effect, negligent misrepresentation is treated as fraudulent misrepresentation, even though the misrepresentation was not purposeful. In negligent misrepresentation, culpable ignorance of the truth supplies the intention to mislead, even if the defendant can claim, "I didn't know."

SECTION 4 | Undue Influence

Undue influence arises from special kinds of relationships in which one party can greatly influence another party, thus overcoming that party's free will. A contract entered into under excessive or undue influence lacks genuine assent and is therefore voidable.[10]

HOW UNDUE INFLUENCE MAY OCCUR

As mentioned, undue influence arises from relationships in which one party may dominate another party, thus unfairly influencing him or her. Minors and elderly people, for example, are often under the influence of guardians (persons who are legally responsible for another). If a guardian induces a young or elderly ward (the person whom the guardian looks after) to enter into a contract that benefits the guardian, undue influence may have been exerted. Undue influence can arise from a number of confidential or fiduciary relationships: attorney-client, physician-patient, guardian-ward, parent-child, husband-wife, or trustee-beneficiary. The essential feature of undue influence is that the party being taken advantage of does not, in reality, exercise free will in entering into a contract.

To determine whether undue influence has been exerted, a court must ask, "To what extent was the transaction induced by domination of the mind or emotions of the person in question?" It follows, then, that the mental state of the person in question will often demonstrate to what extent the persuasion from the outside influence was "unfair."

---

9. See, for example, *Alexander v. Meduna*, 47 P.3d 206 (Wyo. 2002).

10. *Restatement (Second) of Contracts*, Section 177.

THE PRESUMPTION OF UNDUE INFLUENCE

When a contract enriches a party at the expense of another who is in a relationship of trust and confidence with, or who is dominated by, the enriched party, the court will often *presume* that the contract was made under undue influence. For example, if a person challenges a contract made by his or her guardian, the presumption will normally be that the guardian has taken advantage of the ward. To rebut (refute) this presumption successfully, the guardian has to show that full disclosure was made to the ward, that consideration was adequate, and that the ward received, if available, independent and competent advice before completing the transaction.

In a relationship of trust and confidence, such as between an attorney and a client, the dominant party (the attorney) is held to extreme or utmost good faith in dealing with the other party. Suppose that a long-time attorney for an elderly client induces him to sign a contract for the sale of some of his assets to a friend of the attorney at below-market prices. It is presumed that the attorney has not exercised good faith in dealing with the client. Unless this presumption can be rebutted, the contract will be voidable.

SECTION 5 | Duress

Assent to the terms of a contract is not genuine if one of the parties is *forced* into the agreement. Recall from Chapter 9 that forcing a party to do something, including entering into a contract, through fear created by threats is legally defined as *duress*. In addition, blackmail or extortion to induce consent to a contract constitutes duress. Duress is both a defense to the enforcement of a contract and a ground for the rescission of a contract.

THE THREATENED ACT MUST BE WRONGFUL OR ILLEGAL

Generally, for duress to occur the threatened act must be wrongful or illegal. Threatening to exercise a legal right, such as the right to sue someone, ordinarily is not illegal and usually does not constitute duress. For example, suppose that Joan injures Olin in an auto accident. The police are not called. Joan has no automobile insurance, but she has substantial assets. Olin wants to settle the potential claim out of court for $3,000, but Joan refuses. After much arguing, Olin loses his patience and says, "If you don't pay me $3,000 right now, I'm going to sue you for $35,000." Joan is frightened and gives Olin a check for $3,000. Later in the day, Joan stops payment on the check, and Olin later sues her for the $3,000. Although Joan argues that she was the victim of duress, the threat of a civil suit normally is not considered duress. Therefore, a court would not allow Joan to use duress as a defense to the enforcement of her settlement agreement with Olin.

ECONOMIC DURESS

Economic need is generally not sufficient to constitute duress, even when one party exacts a very high price for an item that the other party needs. If the party exacting the price also creates the need, however, *economic duress* may be found.

For example, suppose that the Internal Revenue Service (IRS) assesses a large tax and penalty against Weller. Weller retains Eyman, the accountant who had filed the tax returns on which the assessment was based, to resist the assessment. Two days before the deadline for filing a reply with the IRS, Eyman declines to represent Weller unless he signs a very high contingency-fee agreement for the services. This agreement would be unenforceable. Although Eyman had threatened only to withdraw his services, something that he was legally entitled to do, he was responsible for delaying the withdrawal until the last days before the deadline. Because it would have been impossible at that late date to obtain adequate representation elsewhere, Weller was forced either to sign the contract or to lose his right to challenge the IRS assessment.

SECTION 6 | Adhesion Contracts and Unconscionability

Questions concerning genuineness of assent may arise when the terms of a contract are dictated by a party with overwhelming bargaining power and the signer must agree to those terms or go without the commodity or service in question. As mentioned in Chapter 13, such contracts are often referred to as *adhesion contracts*. An adhesion contract is written *exclusively* by one party (the dominant party, usually the seller or the creditor) and presented to the other party (the adhering party, usually the buyer or the borrower) on a take-it-or-leave-it basis. In other words, the adhering party has no opportunity to negotiate the terms of the contract.

STANDARD-FORM CONTRACTS

Standard-form contracts often contain fine-print provisions that shift a risk naturally borne by one party to the other. A variety of businesses use such contracts. Life insurance policies, residential leases, loan agreements, and employment agency contracts are often standard-form contracts. To avoid enforcement of the contract or of a particular clause, the aggrieved party must show that the parties had substantially unequal bargaining positions and that enforcement would be manifestly unfair or oppressive. If the required showing is made, the contract or particular term is deemed *unconscionable* and is not enforced.

UNCONSCIONABILITY AND THE COURTS

Technically, unconscionability under Section 2–302 of the Uniform Commercial Code (UCC) applies only

---

CONCEPT SUMMARY 14.1 | Genuineness of Assent

PROBLEMS OF ASSENT	RULE
MISTAKES	1. *Unilateral*—Generally, the mistaken party is bound by the contract, unless the other party knows or should have known of the mistake, or in some states, the mistake is an inadvertent mathematical error in addition, subtraction, and so on, that is committed without gross negligence. 2. *Bilateral (mutual)*—If both parties are mistaken about a material fact, such as the identity of the subject matter, either party can avoid the contract. If the mistake relates to the value or quality of the subject matter, either party can enforce the contract.
FRAUDULENT MISREPRESENTATION	Three elements are necessary to establish fraudulent misrepresentation: 1. A misrepresentation of a material fact has occurred. 2. There has been an intent to deceive. 3. The innocent party has justifiably relied on the misrepresentation.
NONFRAUDULENT MISREPRESENTATION	1. *Innocent misrepresentation*—Occurs when a person makes a statement that he or she believes to be true but that actually misrepresents material facts. The aggrieved party can rescind the contract but usually cannot seek damages. 2. *Negligent misrepresentation*—Occurs when a person, through carelessness, makes an untrue statement but believes the statement to be true. Negligent misrepresentation has the same legal effect as fraudulent misrepresentation in virtually all states.
UNDUE INFLUENCE/DURESS	1. *Undue influence*—Arises from special relationships, such as fiduciary relationships, in which one party's free will has been overcome by the undue influence of another. Usually, the contract is voidable. 2. *Duress*—Defined as forcing a party to enter into a contract under fear of threat—for example, the threat of violence or economic pressure. The party forced to enter into the contract can rescind the contract.
ADHESION CONTRACTS AND UNCONSCIONABILITY	Concerns one-sided bargains in which one party has substantially superior bargaining power and can dictate the terms of a contract. Unconscionability typically occurs as a result of the following: 1. Standard-form contracts in which a fine-print provision purports to shift a risk normally borne by one party to the other (for example, a liability disclaimer). 2. Take-it-or-leave-it adhesion contracts in which the buyer has no choice but to agree to the seller's dictated terms if the buyer is to procure certain goods or services.

to contracts for the sale of goods. Many courts, however, have broadened the concept and applied it in other situations.

Although unconscionability was discussed in Chapter 13, it is important to note here that the UCC gives courts a great degree of discretion to invalidate or strike down a contract or clause as being unconscionable. As a result, some states have not adopted Section 2–302 of the UCC. In those states, the legislature and the courts prefer to rely on traditional notions of fraud, undue influence, and duress.

REVIEWING GENUINENESS OF ASSENT

Chelene had been a caregiver for Marta's eighty-year-old mother, Janis, for nine years. Shortly before Janis passed away, Chelene convinced her to buy Chelene's house for her daughter, Marta. The elderly woman died before the papers were signed, however. Four months later, Marta used her inheritance to buy Chelene's house without having it inspected. The house was built in the 1950s, and Chelene said it was in "perfect condition." Nevertheless, one year after the purchase, the basement started leaking. Marta had the paneling removed from the basement walls and discovered that the walls were bowed inward and cracked. Marta then had a civil engineer inspect the basement walls, and he found that the cracks had been caulked and painted over before the paneling was installed. He concluded that the "wall failure" had existed "for at least thirty years" and that the basement walls were "structurally unsound." Using the information presented in the chapter, answer the following questions.

1. Can Marta obtain rescission of the contract based on undue influence? If the sale to Janis had been completed before her death, could Janis have obtained rescission based on undue influence? Explain.

2. Can Marta avoid the contract on the ground that both parties made a mistake about the condition of the house? Explain.

3. Can Marta sue Chelene for fraudulent misrepresentation? Why or why not? What element(s) might be lacking?

4. Now assume that Chelene knew that the basement walls were cracked and bowed and that she had hired someone to install paneling prior to offering to sell the house. Did she have a duty to disclose this defect to Marta? Could a court find that Chelene's silence in this situation constituted misrepresentation? Explain.

5. If Chelene knew about the problem with the walls but did not know that the house was structurally unsound, could she be liable for negligent misrepresentation? Why or why not?

TERMS AND CONCEPTS TO REVIEW

genuineness of assent 277

innocent misrepresentation 287

negligent misrepresentation 287

scienter 283

QUESTIONS AND CASE PROBLEMS

14–1. Juan is an elderly man who lives with his nephew, Samuel. Juan is totally dependent on Samuel's support. Samuel tells Juan that unless he transfers a tract of land he owns to Samuel for a price 35 percent below its market value, Samuel will no longer support and take care of him. Juan enters into the contract. Discuss fully whether Juan can set aside this contract.

14–2. **QUESTION WITH SAMPLE ANSWER**

Grano owns a forty-room motel on Highway 100. Tanner is interested in purchasing the motel. During the course of negotiations, Grano tells Tanner that the motel netted $30,000 during the previous year and that it will net at least $45,000 the next year. The motel books, which Grano turns over to Tanner before the purchase, clearly show that Grano's motel netted only $15,000 the previous year. Also, Grano fails to tell Tanner that a bypass to Highway 100 is being planned that will redirect most traffic away from the front of the motel. Tanner purchases the motel. During the first year under Tanner's operation, the motel nets only $18,000. At this time, Tanner learns of the previous low profitability of the motel and the planned bypass. Tanner wants his money back from Grano. Discuss fully Tanner's probable success in getting his money back.

For a sample answer to this question, go to Appendix I at the end of this text.

14–3. Discuss whether either of the following contracts will be unenforceable on the ground that genuineness of assent is lacking:

(a) Simmons finds a stone in his pasture that he believes to be quartz. Jenson, who also believes that the stone is quartz, contracts to purchase it for $10. Just before delivery, the stone is discovered to be a diamond worth $1,000.

(b) Jacoby's barn is burned to the ground. He accuses Goldman's son of arson and threatens to have the prosecutor bring a criminal action unless Goldman agrees to pay him $5,000. Goldman agrees to pay.

14–4. Lund offered to sell Steck his car and told Steck that the car had been driven only 25,000 miles and had never been in an accident. Steck hired Carvallo, a mechanic, to appraise the condition of the car, and Carvallo said that the car probably had at least 50,000 miles on it and most likely had been in an accident. In spite of this information, Steck still thought the car would be a good buy for the price, so he purchased it. Later, when the car developed numerous mechanical problems, Steck sought to rescind the contract on the basis of Lund's fraudulent misrepresentation of the auto's condition. Will Steck be able to rescind his contract? Explain.

14–5. MISTAKE. Steven Lanci was involved in an automobile accident with an uninsured motorist. Lanci was insured with Metropolitan Insurance Co., although he did not have a copy of the insurance policy. Lanci and Metropolitan entered settlement negotiations, during which Lanci told Metropolitan that he did not have a copy of his policy. Ultimately, Lanci agreed to settle all claims for $15,000, noting in a letter to Metropolitan that $15,000 was the "sum you have represented to be the . . . policy limits applicable to this claim." After signing a release, Lanci learned that the policy limits were actually $250,000, and he refused to accept the settlement proceeds. When Metropolitan sued to enforce the settlement agreement, Lanci argued that the release had been signed as the result of a mistake and therefore was unenforceable. Should the court enforce the contract? Explain. [*Lanci v. Metropolitan Insurance Co.*, 388 Pa.Super. 1, 564 A.2d 972 (1989)]

14–6. MISREPRESENTATION. W. B. McConkey owned commercial property, including a building that, as McConkey knew, had experienced flooding problems for years. McConkey painted the building, replaced damaged carpeting, and sold the property to M&D, Inc., on an "as is" basis. M&D did not ask whether there were flooding problems, and McConkey said nothing about them. M&D leased the property to Donmar, Inc., to operate a pet supply store. Two months after the store opened, the building flooded following heavy rain. M&D and Donmar filed a suit in a Michigan state court against McConkey and others, claiming in part that McConkey had committed misrepresentation by silence. Based on this claim, will the court hold McConkey liable? Why or why not? [*M&D, Inc. v. McConkey*, 585 N.W.2d 33 (Mich.App. 1998)]

14–7. ⚖ CASE PROBLEM WITH SAMPLE ANSWER

The law firm of Traystman, Coric and Keramidas represented Andrew Daigle in a divorce in Norwich, Connecticut. Scott McGowan, an attorney with the firm, handled the two-day trial. After the first day of the trial, McGowan told Daigle to sign a promissory note in the amount of $26,973, which represented the amount that Daigle then owed to the firm, or McGowan would withdraw from the case, and Daigle would be forced to get another attorney or to continue the trial by himself. Daigle said that he wanted another attorney, Martin Rutchik, to see the note. McGowan urged Daigle to sign it and assured him that a copy would be sent to Rutchik. Feeling that he had no other choice, Daigle signed the note. When he did not pay, the law firm filed a suit in a Connecticut state court against him. Daigle asserted that the note was unenforceable because he had signed it under duress. What are the requirements for the use of duress as a defense to a contract? Are the requirements met here? What might the law firm argue in response to Daigle's assertion? Explain. [*Traystman, Coric and Keramidas v. Daigle*, 84 Conn.App. 843, 855 A.2d 996 (2004)]

To view a sample answer for this case problem, go to this book's Web site at http://wbl.westbuslaw.com, select "Chapter 14," and click on "Case Problem with Sample Answer."

14–8. FRAUDULENT MISREPRESENTATION. In 1987, United Parcel Service Co. and United Parcel Service of America, Inc. (together known as UPS), decided to change the parcel delivery business from relying on contract carriers to establishing its own airline. During the transition, which took sixteen months, UPS hired 811 pilots. At the time, UPS expressed a desire to hire pilots who remained throughout that period with its contract carriers, which included Orion Air. A UPS representative met with more than fifty Orion pilots and made promises of future employment. John Rickert, a captain with Orion, was one of the pilots. Orion ceased operation after the UPS transition, and UPS did not hire

Rickert, who obtained employment about six months later as a second officer with American Airlines, but at a lower salary. Rickert filed a suit in a Kentucky state court against UPS, claiming, in part, fraud based on the promises made by the UPS representative. UPS filed a motion for a directed verdict. What are the elements for a cause of action based on fraudulent misrepresentation? In whose favor should the court rule in this case, and why? [*United Parcel Service, Inc. v. Rickert*, 996 S.W.2d 464 (Ky. 1999)]

14-9. NEGLIGENT MISREPRESENTATION. Cleveland Chiropractic College (CCC) promised prospective students that CCC would provide clinical training and experience—a critical part of a chiropractic education and a requirement for graduation and obtaining a license to practice. Specifically, CCC expressly promised that it would provide an ample variety of patients. CCC knew, however, that it did not have the ability to provide sufficient patients, as evidenced by its report to the Council on Chiropractic Education, an accreditation body through which chiropractic colleges monitor and certify themselves. In that report, CCC said that patient recruitment was the "joint responsibility" of the college and the student. During the 1990s, most of the "patients" that students saw were healthy persons whom

the students recruited to be stand-in patients. After graduating and obtaining licenses to practice, Michael Troknya and nineteen others filed a suit in a federal district court against CCC, alleging, among other things, negligent misrepresentation. What are the elements of this cause of action? Are they satisfied in this case? Why or why not? [*Troknya v. Cleveland Chiropractic Clinic*, 280 F.3d 1200 (8th Cir. 2002)]

14-10. VIDEO QUESTION

Go to this text's Web site at <u>http://wbl.westbuslaw.com</u> and select "Chapter 14." Click on "Video Questions" and view the video titled *Mistake*. Then answer the following questions.

(a) What kind of mistake is involved in the dispute shown in the video (mutual or unilateral, mistake of fact or mistake of value)?

(b) According to the chapter, in what two situations would the supermarket be able to rescind a contract to sell peppers to Melnick at the incorrectly advertised price?

(c) Does it matter if the price that was advertised was a reasonable price for the peppers? Why or why not?

LAW | on the Web

For updated links to resources available on the Web, as well as a variety of other materials, visit this text's Web site at <u>http://wbl.westbuslaw.com</u>.

For a discussion of fraudulent misrepresentation, go to the Web site of attorney Owen Katz at

<u>http://www.katzlawoffice.com/misrep.html</u>

For a collection of leading cases on contract law, including cases involving topics covered in this chapter, go to

<u>http://www.lectlaw.com/files/lws49.htm</u>

LEGAL RESEARCH EXERCISES ON THE WEB

Go to <u>http://wbl.westbuslaw.com</u>, the Web site that accompanies this text. Select "Chapter 14" and click on "Internet Exercises." There you will find the following Internet research exercises that you can perform to learn more about topics covered in this chapter.

Activity 14–1: LEGAL PERSPECTIVE
            Negligent Misrepresentation and *Scienter*

Activity 14–2: MANAGEMENT PERSPECTIVE
            Fraudulent Misrepresentation

Activity 14–3: ECONOMIC PERSPECTIVE
            Economic Duress

CHAPTER 15

The Statute of Frauds

As discussed in Chapter 14, a contract that is otherwise valid may still be unenforceable if the parties have not genuinely assented to its terms. An otherwise valid contract may also be unenforceable for another reason—because it is not in the proper form. For example, certain types of contracts are required to be in writing or evidenced by a writing. If a contract is required by law to be in writing or evidenced by a writing and there is no written evidence of the contract, it may not be enforceable. In this chapter, we examine the kinds of contracts that require a writing under what is called the **Statute of Frauds.**

The chapter concludes with a discussion of the *parol evidence rule*, which courts follow when determining whether evidence that is extraneous, or external, to written contracts may be admissible at trial. Though not inherently related to the Statute of Frauds, the parol evidence rule has general application in contract law. We cover these topics within one chapter primarily for reasons of convenience and space.

SECTION 1 | The Origins of the Statute of Frauds

At early common law, parties to a contract were not allowed to testify. This led to the practice of hiring third party witnesses. As early as the seventeenth century, the English recognized the many problems presented by this practice and enacted a statute to help deal with it. The statute, passed by the English Parliament in 1677, was known as "An Act for the Prevention of Frauds and Perjuries." The act established that certain types of contracts, to be enforceable, had to be evidenced by a writing and signed by the party against whom enforcement was sought.

Today, almost every state has a statute, modeled after the English act, that stipulates what types of contracts must be in writing or evidenced by a writing. Although the statutes vary slightly from state to state, all states require certain types of contracts to be in writing or evidenced by a written memorandum signed by the party against whom enforcement is sought, unless certain exceptions apply. (These exceptions will be discussed later in this chapter.) In this text, we refer to these statutes collectively as the Statute of Frauds. The actual name of the Statute of Frauds is misleading because it neither applies to fraud nor invalidates any type of contract. Rather, it denies *enforceability* to certain contracts that do not comply with its requirements.

SECTION 2 | Contracts That Fall within the Statute of Frauds

The following types of contracts are said to fall "within" or "under" the Statute of Frauds and therefore are required to be in writing or evidenced by a written memorandum:

1. Contracts involving interests in land.
2. Contracts that cannot by their terms be performed within one year from the date of formation.
3. Collateral, or secondary, contracts, such as promises to answer for the debt or duty of another and promises by the administrator or executor of an estate to pay a debt of the estate personally—that is, out of her or his own pocket.
4. Promises made in consideration of marriage.
5. Under the Uniform Commercial Code (UCC), contracts for the sale of goods priced at $500 or more ($5,000 or more under the 2003 amendments to the UCC—see Chapter 20).

CONTRACTS INVOLVING INTERESTS IN LAND

A contract calling for the sale of land is not enforceable unless it is in writing or evidenced by a written memorandum. Land is *real property* and includes all physical objects that are permanently attached to the soil, such as buildings, fences, trees, and the soil itself (see Chapter 47). The Statute of Frauds operates as a *defense* to the enforcement of an oral contract for the sale of land. For example, if Sam contracts orally to sell Blackacre to Betty but later decides not to sell,

under most circumstances Betty cannot enforce the contract. The Statute of Frauds also requires all contracts for the transfer of other interests in land, such as mortgages and leases (see Chapter 48), to be in writing, although most state statutes provide for the enforcement of short-term oral leases.

In the following case, the court was asked to enforce a purported purchase clause in an agreement for a lease of commercial property. There was only one problem: no one could provide a copy of the lease.

CASE 15.1   ## Michel v. Bush

Court of Appeals of Ohio,
Ninth District, 2001.
765 N.E.2d 911.

BACKGROUND AND FACTS   *Betty and Frank Bush owned two commercial structures in Doylestown, Ohio: an office building and an unoccupied building. In 1989, Donald Michel, on behalf of himself and Amanda Enterprises, Inc., agreed to lease the unoccupied building to operate a video store and tanning salon. In 1993, Michel asked the Bushes about buying the realty, or property, and they discussed financing arrangements, but Michel failed to present an offer. Three years later, Michel again spoke with the Bushes about the possibility of a sale, but the next year, the Bushes sold the property to a third party, the B&S Group. Michel and Amanda Enterprises filed a suit in an Ohio state court against the Bushes, claiming, among other things, breach of contract. Michel alleged that the lease agreement contained an option to buy the leased property. He testified that the option read, "First right of refusal on purchase of said property." The Bushes denied this allegation. Everyone agreed that the lease agreement had been in writing, but no one could provide a copy of it. The court granted a summary judgment in the Bushes' favor, in part on the ground that the Statute of Frauds barred Michel's claim. Michel appealed to a state intermediate appellate court.*

IN THE LANGUAGE OF THE COURT

WHITMORE, Judge.
* * * *
* * * Michel has claimed that the trial court incorrectly determined that the Statute of Frauds barred the prosecution of his claim. Specifically, he has argued that the Statute of Frauds bars claims based only upon oral agreements regarding the sale of a property interest, and, because the Agreement herein was admittedly in writing, the trial court's determination to that end was in error. This court disagrees.

Ohio's Statute of Frauds is found at [Revised Code Section] 1335.05. That statute provides:

"No action shall be brought whereby to charge the defendant, * * * upon a contract or sale of lands, * * * or interest in or concerning them, * * * unless the agreement upon which such action is brought, or some memorandum or note thereof, is in writing and signed by the party to be charged therewith[.]"

Taking the plain language of the statute, it is clear that a claim regarding any interest in land, [such as] a right of first refusal, cannot be brought, as a matter of law, unless the agreement pertaining thereto was reduced to writing, signed by the party to be charged, and produced.

Moreover, it is important to note * * * [t]his statute serves to ensure that transactions involving a transfer of realty interests are commemorated with sufficient solemnity. *A signed writing provides greater assurance that the parties and the public can reliably know when such a transaction occurs.* It supports the public policy favoring clarity in determining real estate interests and discourages indefinite or fraudulent claims about such interests. [Emphasis added.]

In this case, there is no dispute that an agreement regarding a mere leasehold interest was in writing. However, the present dispute is not over the lease agreement; rather, the issue is

 **Continued** whether an interest, * * * the alleged option/right of first refusal, was reduced to writing. Michel has alleged and sworn that the alleged option/right of first refusal was written in the margins of the Agreement. The Bushes, on the other hand, have argued that no such option/right of first refusal interest was ever created or given in the first place. None of the parties has produced a copy of the Agreement. Without the document or other written evidence, Michel cannot bring a claim to enforce an alleged interest in realty. To hold otherwise would be to defeat the very purpose of the Statute of Frauds.

DECISION AND REMEDY *The state intermediate appellate court affirmed the judgment of the lower court. The appellate court held that when a written agreement relating to an interest in land cannot be produced, an action to enforce a purported term in the agreement cannot be sustained.*

THE ONE-YEAR RULE

A contract that cannot, *by its own terms*, be performed within one year from the date it was formed must be in writing to be enforceable.[1] The one-year period begins to run *the day after the contract is made*. Suppose that Superior University forms a contract with Kimi San stating that San will teach three courses in history during the coming academic year (September 15 through June 15). If the contract is formed in March, it must be in writing to be enforceable—because it cannot be performed within one year. If the contract is not formed until July, however, it will not have to be in writing to be enforceable—because it can be performed within one year.

The test for determining whether an oral contract is enforceable under the one-year rule of the Statute of Frauds is not whether an agreement is *likely* to be performed within a year but whether performance is *possible* within one year. Even if performance takes place more than one year after the date of contract formation, an oral contract is binding as long as performance was possible in less than a year.

For example, suppose that Bankers Life orally contracts to lend $40,000 to Janet Lawrence "as long as Lawrence and Associates operates its financial consulting firm in Omaha, Nebraska." The contract is not within the Statute of Frauds—no writing is required—because Lawrence and Associates could go out of business in one year or less. In this event, the contract would be fully performed within one year.[2] Exhibit 15–1 illustrates graphically the application of the one-year rule.

---

1. *Restatement (Second) of Contracts*, Section 130.

2. See *Warner v. Texas & Pacific Railroad Co.*, 164 U.S. 418, 17 S.Ct. 147, 41 L.Ed. 495 (1896).

EXHIBIT 15-1 **The One-Year Rule**

Under the Statute of Frauds, contracts that by their terms are impossible to perform within one year from the date of contract formation must be in writing to be enforceable. Put another way, if it is at all possible to perform an oral contract within one year from the day after the contract is made, the contract will fall outside the Statute of Frauds and be enforceable. (As you will read in Chapter 20, a 2003 amendment to the Uniform Commercial Code exempts contracts for the sale of goods from the one-year rule.)

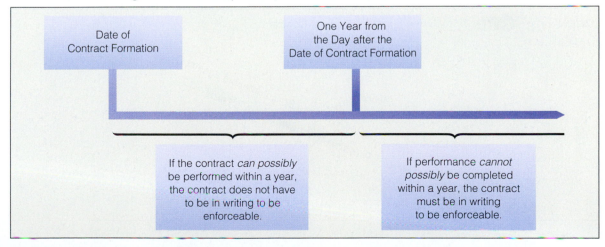

COLLATERAL PROMISES

A **collateral promise,** or secondary promise, is one that is ancillary (subsidiary) to a principal transaction or primary contractual relationship. In other words, a collateral promise is one made by a third party to assume the debts or obligations of a primary party to a contract if that party does not perform. Any collateral promise of this nature falls under the Statute of Frauds and therefore must be in writing to be enforceable. To understand this concept, it is important to distinguish between primary and secondary promises and obligations.

PRIMARY VERSUS SECONDARY OBLIGATIONS

Suppose that Bancroft forms an oral contract with Harmony's Floral Boutique to send his mother a dozen roses for Mother's Day. Bancroft's oral contract with Harmony's Floral Boutique provides that he will pay for the roses when he receives the bill for the flowers. Bancroft is a direct party to this contract and has incurred a *primary* obligation under the contract. Because he is a party to the contract and has a primary obligation to Harmony's Floral Boutique, this contract does *not* fall under the Statute of Frauds and does not have to be in writing to be enforceable.

Now suppose that Bancroft's mother borrows $10,000 from the International Trust Company on a promissory note payable six months later. Bancroft promises the bank officer handling the loan that he will pay the $10,000 *only if his mother does not pay the loan on time.* Bancroft, in this situation, becomes what

is known as a *guarantor* on the loan—that is, he is guaranteeing to the bank that he will pay back the loan if his mother fails to do so—and has incurred a *secondary* obligation. This kind of collateral promise, in which the guarantor states that he or she will become responsible only if the primary party does not perform, must be in writing to be enforceable. Exhibit 15–2 illustrates the concept of a collateral promise. (We will return to the concept of guaranty and the distinction between primary and secondary obligations in Chapter 28, in the context of creditors' rights.)

AN EXCEPTION—THE "MAIN PURPOSE" RULE   A promise to answer for the debt of another is covered by the Statute of Frauds *unless* the guarantor's main purpose in incurring a secondary obligation is to secure a personal benefit. This type of contract need not be in writing.[3] The assumption is that a court can infer from the circumstances of a particular case whether the "leading objective" of the promisor was to secure a personal benefit and thus, in effect, to answer for her or his own debt.

Consider an example. Braswell contracts with Custom Manufacturing Company to have some machines custom-made for Braswell's factory. She promises Newform Materials Supply Company, Custom Manufacturing's supplier, that if Newform continues to deliver the materials to Custom Manufacturing for the production of the custom-made machines, she will guarantee payment. This promise

---

3. *Restatement (Second) of Contracts,* Section 116.

Collateral Promises

A collateral (secondary) promise is one made by a third party (C, in this exhibit) to a creditor (B, in this exhibit) to pay the debt of another (A, in this exhibit), who is primarily obligated to pay the debt. Under the Statute of Frauds, collateral promises must be in writing to be enforceable.

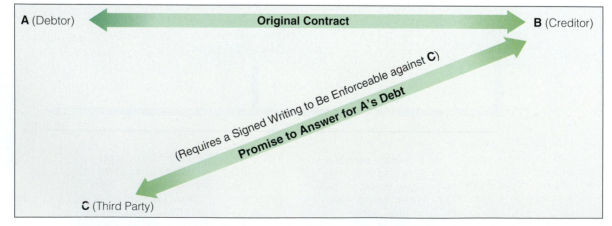

need not be in writing, even though the effect may be to pay the debt of another. This is because Braswell's main purpose in forming the contract is to secure a benefit for herself.

Another typical application of the main purpose rule is the situation in which one creditor guarantees the debtor's debt to another creditor to prevent litigation. This allows the debtor to remain in business long enough to generate profits sufficient to pay both creditors.

PROMISES MADE IN CONSIDERATION OF MARRIAGE

A unilateral promise to pay a sum or to give property in consideration of a promise to marry must be in writing. If Baumann promises to pay Villard $10,000 if Villard promises to marry Baumann's daughter, the promise must be in writing. The same rule applies to **prenuptial agreements**—agreements made before marriage that define each partner's ownership rights in the other partner's property. A couple might make such an agreement if, for example, a prospective wife wishes to limit the amount her prospective husband can obtain if the marriage ends in divorce. Prenuptial agreements must be in writing to be enforceable.[4]

CONSIDERATION GENERALLY REQUIRED Generally, courts tend to give more credence to prenuptial agreements that are accompanied by consideration. For example, assume that Maureen, who has few assets, and Kaiser, who has a net worth of $300 million, plan to marry. Kaiser has several children, and he wants them to receive most of his wealth on his death. The couple form a prenuptial agreement in which Kaiser promises to give Maureen $100,000 a year for the rest of her life should they divorce. Kaiser offers to give Maureen $200,000 if she consents to the agreement. If Maureen consents to the agreement and accepts the $200,000, very likely a court will hold this to be a valid prenuptial agreement should it ever be contested.

Courts have used the same reasoning to require adequate consideration in *postnuptial agreements*

(agreements entered into after the marriage that define each spouse's rights). For example, suppose that one year after a couple married, they entered into an agreement concerning the division of marital assets in the event of divorce. The husband, a medical student, agreed to give the wife one-half of his future earnings if he instigated a divorce. The wife, in turn, promised not to pursue a dental career and not to leave the marriage. Is the agreement enforceable? According to many states' courts, the answer is no. Because the wife in this situation had already given up her career to stay at home and tend to the household, this promise was based on past consideration, which is no consideration. Also, because the parties were not having marital difficulties at the time, she was not giving up anything by promising to stay in the marriage.[5]

MUST BE VOLUNTARILY ENTERED In some circumstances, a prenuptial agreement will not be enforceable even if it is in writing. For example, an agreement is not enforceable if the party against whom enforcement is sought proves that he or she did not sign the agreement voluntarily. (For a further discussion of this topic, see this chapter's *Contemporary Legal Debates* feature beginning on page 298.)

CONTRACTS FOR THE SALE OF GOODS

The Uniform Commercial Code (UCC) contains Statute of Frauds provisions that require written evidence of a contract for the sale of goods priced at $500 or more ($5,000 or more under the 2003 amendments to the UCC—see Chapter 20). A writing that will satisfy the UCC requirement need only state the quantity term; other terms agreed on can be omitted or even stated imprecisely in the writing, as long as they adequately reflect both parties' intentions. The contract will not be enforceable, however, for any quantity greater than that set forth in the writing. In addition, the writing must have been signed by the person to be charged—that is, by the person who refuses to perform or the one being sued. Beyond these two requirements, the writing normally need not designate the buyer or the seller, the terms of payment, or the price. Requirements of the Statute of Frauds under the UCC will be discussed in more detail in Chapter 20.

---

4. To add certainty to the enforceability of prenuptial agreements, the National Conference of Commissioners on Uniform State Laws issued the Uniform Prenuptial Agreements Act (UPAA) in 1983. The act provides that prenuptial agreements must be in writing to be enforceable and that the agreements become effective when the parties marry.

---

5. See, for example, *Bratton v. Bratton*, 136 S.W.3d 595 (Tenn. 2004).

Prenuptial Agreements and Advice of Counsel

The drafting and signing of prenuptial agreements are often at odds with the very concept of marriage. After all, the parties purport to be in love with each other and desirous of sharing all aspects of their lives. Under these circumstances, the thought of involving lawyers in the negotiation of a prenuptial agreement seems inappropriate. Nonetheless, prenuptial agreements are drafted and entered into every day. Cases occasionally come before the courts in which a party to a prenuptial agreement claims that the agreement should not be enforced because one party was not advised to consult his or her own attorney before signing the agreement.

SOME JURISDICTIONS REQUIRE INDEPENDENT COUNSEL

In a growing number of jurisdictions, courts regard the advice of independent counsel as a significant factor in determining whether a party signed a prenuptial agreement voluntarily. In other words, if a prospective spouse did not have the advice of her or his own attorney before signing the agreement, that could indicate that the agreement was not signed voluntarily. In one case, for example, a woman challenged the enforceability of a prenuptial agreement on the ground that her husband's

lawyer, who was hired to draft the agreement, did not advise her to have it reviewed by her own attorney. The Supreme Court of North Dakota held that the agreement could in fact be unenforceable for this reason.[a] In a subsequent case involving similar facts, the Supreme Court of North Dakota reiterated that "adequate legal representation will often be the best evidence that a spouse signed the agreement knowledgeably and voluntarily."[b]

Many courts have been particularly suspicious of prenuptial agreements involving a waiver by the future wife of all spousal support in the event of marriage or divorce. The reasoning has been that any prenuptial support waiver might undermine the permanency of the marital relationship, which would be contrary to public policy.

OTHER JURISDICTIONS DO NOT REQUIRE INDEPENDENT COUNSEL

Other jurisdictions take a different approach. For example, in a highly publicized case involving baseball player Barry Bonds,

---

a. *Estate of Lutz,* 563 N.W.2d 90 (N.Dak. 1997).
b. See *Binek v. Binek,* 673 N.W.2d 594 (N.Dak. 2004).

EXCEPTIONS TO THE APPLICABILITY OF THE STATUTE OF FRAUDS

Exceptions to the applicability of the Statute of Frauds are made in certain circumstances. We look here at these exceptions.

PARTIAL PERFORMANCE In cases involving contracts relating to the transfer of interests in land, if the purchaser has paid part of the price, taken possession, and made permanent improvements to the property and the parties cannot be returned to the positions they occupied before the contract was formed, a court may grant *specific performance* (performance of the contract according to its precise terms). Whether the courts will enforce an oral contract for an interest in land when partial performance has taken place is usually determined by the degree of injury that would be suffered if the court chose not to enforce the oral contract. Under the UCC, an oral contract is enforceable to the extent that a seller accepts payment or a buyer

accepts delivery of the goods (see Chapter 20 for a fuller discussion of this exception).[6]

ADMISSIONS In some states, if a party against whom enforcement of an oral contract is sought "admits" in pleadings, testimony, or otherwise in court that a contract for sale was made, the contract will be enforceable.[7] Thus, in one of these states, if the president of Ashley Corporation admits under oath that an oral agreement was made with Com Best, Inc., to sell certain business premises, the agreement will be enforceable. A contract subject to the UCC will be enforceable, but only to the extent of the quantity admitted.[8]

PROMISSORY ESTOPPEL In some states, an oral contract that would otherwise be unenforceable under the Statute of Frauds may be enforced under the doc-

---

6. UCC 2–201(3)(c).
7. *Restatement (Second) of Contracts,* Section 133.
8. UCC 2–201(3)(b).

the California Supreme Court held that a prenuptial agreement was enforceable even though Bonds's wife was not advised to obtain independent counsel before signing it. The wife, who was Swedish and had little knowledge of English, later stated that she had not understood that by signing the agreement, she would forfeit any right to the earnings and property acquisitions of the parties during their marriage. The court, however, held that the agreement was enforceable. The court concluded that the evidence indicated that the wife had consented to the terms of the agreement.[c]

In another case, just days before the wedding, a man drove his future wife to his attorney's office and asked her to sign a prenuptial agreement as a precondition of their marriage. The agreement provided that each spouse waived his or her rights to the other spouse's property. The attorney advised the woman to obtain independent counsel and gave her an opportunity to review the document before signing it, but she did neither. After her husband's death, she claimed that the agreement was invalid because she had not signed it voluntarily. She stated that she

had been embarrassed by the scene in the attorney's office when she signed the agreement and had just wanted to "get it over with." Nonetheless, the court held that the agreement was valid. The court declared that while the husband's actions were "certainly not laudatory" and could be "fairly characterized as surprise tactics," they did not negate the "voluntary nature of the execution."[d]

Some observers argue that allowing prenuptial agreements to be enforced when both parties did not have the advice of independent counsel unduly burdens the financially weaker party to the marriage, customarily the woman. Others contend that more marriages are encouraged when financially successful future spouses are able to protect their assets.

Clearly, the courts are divided on the issue of whether prenuptial agreements should be upheld despite the lack of independent counsel by both parties. Should the advice of independent counsel be a requirement for a valid prenuptial agreement? What is your position on this issue?

---

c. *In re Marriage of Bonds*, 24 Cal.4th 1, 5 P.3d 815, 99 Cal.Rptr.2d 252 (2000).

d. *In re Estate of Ingmand*, 2001 WL 855406 (Iowa App. 2001).

---

trine of promissory estoppel, based on detrimental reliance. Recall from Chapter 12 that if a promisor makes a promise on which the promisee justifiably relies to his or her detriment, a court may *estop* (prevent) the promisor from denying that a contract exists. Section 139 of the *Restatement (Second) of Contracts* provides that in these circumstances, an oral promise can be enforceable notwithstanding the Statute of Frauds if the reliance was foreseeable to the person making the promise and if injustice can be avoided only by enforcing the promise.

SPECIAL EXCEPTIONS UNDER THE UCC Special exceptions to the applicability of the Statute of Frauds apply to sales contracts. Oral contracts for customized goods may be enforced in certain circumstances. Another exception has to do with oral contracts *between merchants* that have been confirmed in writing. These exceptions and those mentioned above will be examined in greater detail in Chapter 20, when we discuss the UCC provisions regarding the Statute of

Frauds. Exhibit 15–3 on the next page graphically summarizes the types of contracts that fall under the Statute of Frauds and the various exceptions that apply.

SECTION 3 | Sufficiency of the Writing

The Statute of Frauds and the UCC require either a written contract or a written memorandum evidencing an oral contract signed by the party against whom enforcement is sought, except when there is a legally recognized exception, such as partial performance. The signature need not be placed at the end of the document but can be anywhere in the writing. It can even be an initial rather than the full name. Indeed, it can even be some form of electronic signature. (For a discussion of electronic signatures, see Chapter 19.)

A memorandum evidencing the oral contract need only contain the essential terms of the contract. Under the UCC, for contracts evidencing sales of goods, the writing need only name the quantity term

EXHIBIT 15-3 Contracts Subject to the Statute of Frauds

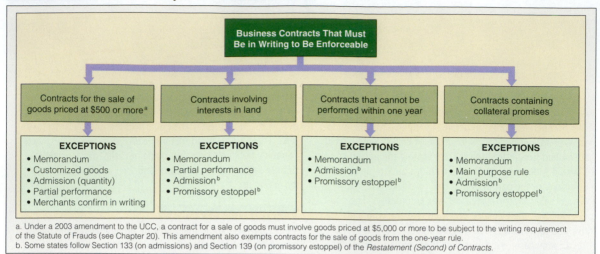

a. Under a 2003 amendment to the UCC, a contract for a sale of goods must involve goods priced at $5,000 or more to be subject to the writing requirement of the Statute of Frauds (see Chapter 20). This amendment also exempts contracts for the sale of goods from the one-year rule.
b. Some states follow Section 133 (on admissions) and Section 139 (on promissory estoppel) of the *Restatement (Second) of Contracts.*

and be signed by the party to be charged. Any confirmation, invoice, sales slip, check, fax, or e-mail—or such items in combination—can constitute a sufficient writing. Under most state Statute of Frauds provisions, the writing must also name the parties, the subject matter, the consideration, and the essential terms with reasonable certainty. In addition, contracts for the sale of land often are required to state the price and describe the property with sufficient clarity to allow them to be determined without reference to outside sources.

In the following case, the court considered whether a fax recap of the parties' oral agreement contained the essential terms of the contract and therefore satisfied the Statute of Frauds.

CASE 15.2

Court of Appeals of Indiana, 2004. 806 N.E.2d 37.

Coca-Cola Co. v. Babyback's International, Inc.

BARNES, Judge.

* * * *

[Babyback's International, Inc., ("Babyback's")] made ready-to-eat barbeque products, which were available in grocery stores. [The Coca-Cola Company ("Coke USA")] owns the formulas to Coca-Cola soft drinks and licenses the rights to manufacture those beverages to various bottling companies, including Coca-Cola Bottling Company Indianapolis, Inc. ("Coke Indy") and [Coca-Cola Enterprises, Inc. ("CCE")]. Coke Indy bottles Coca-Cola products for the Indianapolis [Indiana] area. CCE is a large bottling company whose markets include Louisville [Kentucky] and Atlanta [Georgia].

In January 1997, Babyback's and Coke Indy entered into a written contract, which provided that Coke Indy and Babyback's would co-market their products to 300 area grocery stores. Under the contract, Babyback's made arrangements to provide free-standing double-door coolers to the grocery stores. Coca-Cola products were shelved on one half of the cooler and Babyback's products were shelved on the other half. * * *

In the spring of 1997, Babyback's met with CCE about expanding the co-marketing program to Louisville. Babyback's and CCE's Louisville division entered into an oral agreement to co-market their products in the Louisville area. The terms of the agreement were to be the same as Babyback's contract with Coke Indy. Although this agreement was never reduced to a written contract, Babyback's supplied coolers to area grocery stores and CCE displayed Coca-Cola products in them.

In the fall of 1997, Babyback's and CCE discussed expanding the co-marketing concept to other markets, including Atlanta. Although the parties reached an oral agreement, they never entered into a formal written agreement. Regardless, Babyback's ordered and installed coolers in several Atlanta grocery stores and incurred marketing and placement fees and other expenses. Babyback's also ordered additional coolers, contacted many grocery store chains, and operated at a loss in Atlanta in an attempt to secure the placement of coolers in other areas.

In the meantime, Coke USA began to have concerns about the quality of Babyback's product. * * * Coke USA decided not to continue associating with Babyback's and * * * refused to allow Coke Indy or CCE to bottle Coca-Cola if they continued to associate with Babyback's. Babyback's relationships with CCE and Coke Indy deteriorated, and soon thereafter Babyback's stopped production because of financial difficulties.

On January 4, 1999, Babyback's filed a complaint [alleging breach of contract by CCE]. CCE [filed a motion for] summary judgment. On July 11, 2003, the trial court denied [the motion and CCE appealed.]

* * * *

CCE argues that the trial court improperly denied its motion for summary judgment because the parties' failure to reduce their agreement to writing violates the statute of frauds, rendering it unenforceable. * * *

* * * *

For a writing to satisfy the statute of frauds, it must set out the agreement with such reasonable certainty that its terms may be understood from the writing itself, without recourse to parol [oral] evidence. * * * *All that is required is reasonable certainty in the terms and conditions of the promises made, including by whom and to whom.* [Emphasis added.]

CCE argues that a fax from CCE to Babyback's summarizing a meeting between the two * * * is insufficient to satisfy the statute of frauds. Babyback's responds that the fax contained the essential terms of the contract and satisfied the statute of frauds. The fax provided in part:

> We enjoyed our meeting today with you and believe we have made further strides toward coming to agreement on a "quiet partnership" with your company. * * * As we stated several times, we do agree that the complimentary merchandising of Babyback's with the #1 brand in the world, Coca-Cola, does make sense.
>
> Attached is a recap on the discussion yesterday * * * .

[The "recap" provided in part:]

> • * * * While we are interested in chain supermarkets and other high trafficked accounts, we are not inclined to support placements in small stores.
> * * * *
> • Provided [there are signed customer agreements or their equivalent] CCE will pay Babyback's up front and on an annual basis. * * *
> * * * *
> • Per our conversation today, you are to send CCE * * * a listing of approximately 2000 stores within the territory * * * . The list will provide a date by which the units can be placed. It is further assumed that store contacts have been made by Babyback's to gain store level approval of the cooler.
> • We agreed in principle that CCE would pay $600 per year per unit to Babyback's for these 2000 placements. Payment will be made up front and on an annual basis * * * .

The fax was on Coca-Cola letterhead * * * .

* * * *

CCE contends that the statute of frauds is not satisfied because certain essential terms are missing. These allegedly omitted terms include when performance was to begin; whether Babyback's was to be paid up front and, if so, how much; how long the program would be in effect; the identity and location of the stores in which coolers would be placed; which party would deliver and install the coolers; and how advertising and promotion would be accomplished.

Careful consideration, however, indicates that these questions either are not essential terms of the contract or are addressed by the fax. For example, the fax provides that Babyback's would supply CCE with a list of 2000 stores, indicating when coolers could be placed in those stores. Based on this language, it appears that the parties agreed to place the coolers after Babyback's

CONTINUED ▶

CASE 15.2 | Continued
made arrangements with the stores and provided that information to CCE. The fax twice provides that Babyback's will be paid up front on an annual basis. This language governs when Babyback's was to be paid and indicates that the program would be in effect for more than one year. The fax also provides that CCE will pay Babyback's $600 per year per cooler; thus addressing how much CCE was to pay Babyback's. Contrary to CCE's assertion, the fax also details the type and number of stores in which CCE was interested * * * .

* * * *

* * * [W]e conclude that the fax contains the essential terms of the parties' agreement and satisfies the statute of frauds. * * *

* * * *

Because the fax from CCE to Babyback's satisfies the statute of frauds and there are genuine issues of material facts regarding Babyback's various * * * claims against CCE * * * , the trial court properly denied CCE's * * * [motion] for summary judgment. We affirm.

QUESTIONS

1. Why did this contract fall within or under the Statute of Frauds?
2. How could a party argue successfully that a written "recap" of contract negotiations does not satisfy the Statute of Frauds?

SECTION 4 | The Parol Evidence Rule

Sometimes, a written contract does not include—or contradicts—an oral understanding reached by the parties before or at the time of contracting. For example, suppose that Laura is about to lease an apartment. As she is signing the lease, she asks the landlord whether cats are allowed in the building. The landlord says that they are and that Laura can keep her cat in the apartment. The lease that Laura actually signs, however, contains a provision prohibiting pets. Later, a dispute arises between Laura and the landlord over whether the landlord agreed that Laura could have a cat in the apartment. Will Laura be able to introduce evidence at trial to show that, at the time the written contract was formed, the landlord orally agreed that she could have a cat, or will the written contract absolutely control?

In determining the outcome of contract disputes such as the one between Laura and her landlord, the courts look to a common law rule governing the admissibility in court of oral evidence, or *parol evidence*. Under the **parol evidence rule,** if a court finds that the parties intended their written contract to be a complete and final embodiment of their agreement, a party cannot introduce in court evidence of any oral agreement or promise made prior to the contract's formation or at the time the contract was created.[9]

Did a football team's agreement with its fans to sell "stadium builder licenses" (SBLs) for seats represent the parties' entire contract, or could an SBL brochure vary the agreement? That was the question in the following case.

---

9. *Restatement (Second) of Contracts*, Section 213.

CASE 15.3

Supreme Court of
Pennsylvania. 2004.
578 Pa. 479,
854 A.2d 425.

Yocca v. Pittsburgh Steelers Sports, Inc.

BACKGROUND AND FACTS *In October 1998, Pittsburgh Steelers Sports, Inc., and others (collectively, the Steelers) sent Ronald Yocca a brochure that advertised a new stadium to be built for the Pittsburgh Steelers football team. The brochure publicized the opportunity to buy stadium builder licenses (SBLs), which grant the right to buy annual season tickets to the games. Prices varied depending on the seats' locations, which were indicated by small diagrams. Yocca applied for an SBL, listing his seating preferences. The Steelers sent him a letter notifying him of the section in which his seat was located. A diagram included with the letter detailed the parameters of the section, but it differed from the brochure's diagrams. The Steelers also sent Yocca documents setting out the terms of the SBL and requiring his signature. These documents included a clause that read, "This Agreement*

CASE 15.3 | Continued *contains the entire agreement of the parties." Yocca signed the documents, and the Steelers told him the specific location of his seat. When he arrived at the stadium, however, the seat was not where he expected it to be. Yocca and other SBL buyers filed a suit in a Pennsylvania state court against the Steelers, alleging, among other things, breach of contract. The court ordered the dismissal of the complaint. The plaintiffs appealed to a state intermediate appellate court, which reversed this order. The defendants appealed to the state supreme court.*

IN THE LANGUAGE OF THE COURT

Justice *NIGRO*.

* * * *

* * * Where the parties, without any fraud or mistake, have deliberately put their engagements in writing, the law declares the writing to be not only the best, but the only, evidence of their agreement. All preliminary negotiations, conversations and verbal agreements are merged in and superseded by the subsequent written contract * * * and its terms and agreements cannot be added to nor subtracted from by parol evidence. Therefore, *for the parol evidence rule to apply, there must be a writing that represents the entire contract between the parties*. To determine whether or not a writing is the parties' entire contract, the writing must be looked at and if it appears to be a contract complete within itself, couched in such terms as import a complete legal obligation without any uncertainty as to the object or extent of the parties' engagement, it is conclusively presumed that the writing represents the whole engagement of the parties * * *. An integration[a] clause [a provision stating that all of the terms of the parties' agreement are included in the written contract] * * * is also a clear sign that the writing is meant to be just that and thereby expresses all of the parties' negotiations, conversations, and agreements made prior to its execution. [Emphasis added.]

Once a writing is determined to be the parties' entire contract, the parol evidence rule applies and evidence of any previous oral or written negotiations or agreements involving the same subject matter as the contract is almost always inadmissible to explain or vary the terms of the contract. One exception to this general rule is that parol evidence may be introduced to vary a writing meant to be the parties' entire contract where a party avers [asserts] that a term was omitted from the contract because of fraud, accident, or mistake. In addition, where a term in the parties' contract is ambiguous, parol evidence is admissible to explain or clarify or resolve the ambiguity, irrespective of whether the ambiguity is created by the language of the instrument or by extrinsic or collateral circumstances. [Emphasis added.]

In the instant case, we cannot agree with the [appellate court] that the SBL Brochure represented the terms of the parties' contract concerning the sale of SBLs. Contrary to the [appellate court's] understanding, the SBL Brochure did not represent a promise by the Steelers to sell SBLs to Appellees. Rather, the Brochure was merely an offer by the Steelers to sell Appellees the right to be assigned an unspecified seat in an unspecified section of the new stadium and the right to receive a contract to buy an SBL for that later-assigned seat. Moreover, by sending in their applications * * *, Appellees simply secured their right to be considered for assigned seats and the opportunity to receive a subsequent offer to purchase SBLs for those seats. In this respect, the SBL Brochure was similar to an option contract in that it merely gave Appellees the option to possibly accept an offer for SBLs at some later date.

On the other hand, the SBL Agreement clearly represented the parties' contract concerning the sale of SBLs. Unlike the SBL Brochure, the SBL Agreement reflected a promise by the Steelers to actually sell Appellees a specific number of SBL seats in a specified section. Furthermore, the SBL Agreement detailed all of the terms and conditions of that sale, *i.e.*, the precise number of seats to be sold to the named Licensee, the exact section in which those seats were located (including a visual depiction of that location), the total amounts due for each SBL, the dates those amounts were due, and all of the rights and duties associated with owning an SBL, including the Licensee's right to transfer the SBL. Most importantly, the SBL Agreement explicitly stated that it represented the parties' entire contract regarding the sale of SBLs. Accordingly, we find that the SBL Agreement represented the parties' entire

---

a. Integrated contracts will be discussed later in this chapter.

CONTINUED ▶

CASE 15.3 | Continued   contract with respect to the sale of SBLs and that the parol evidence rule bars the admission of any evidence of previous oral or written negotiations or agreements entered into between the parties concerning the sale of the SBLs, such as the SBL Brochure, to explain or vary those terms expressed in the SBL Agreement.

DECISION AND REMEDY *The Pennsylvania Supreme Court reversed the lower court's judgment. The state supreme court held that the SBL documents constituted the parties' entire contract and under the parol evidence rule could not be supplemented by previous negotiations or agreements. Because the plaintiffs based their complaint on the claim that the defendants violated the terms of the brochure, and the court held that the brochure was not part of the contract, the complaint was properly dismissed.*

WHAT IF THE FACTS WERE DIFFERENT? *Suppose that the Steelers had not sent Yocca a diagram with the letter notifying him of his seat's section and that the SBL documents had not included an integration clause. Would the result have been different?*

EXCEPTIONS TO THE PAROL EVIDENCE RULE

Because of the rigidity of the parol evidence rule, the courts have created the following exceptions:

1. *Contracts subsequently modified.* Evidence of any *subsequent modification* (oral or written) of a written contract can be introduced into court. Keep in mind that the oral modifications may not be enforceable if they come under the Statute of Frauds—for example, if they increase the price of the goods for sale to $500 or more ($5,000 or more under the 2003 amendments) or increase the term for performance to more than one year. Also, oral modifications will not be enforceable if the original contract provides that any modification must be in writing.[10]

2. *Voidable or void contracts.* Oral evidence can be introduced in all cases to show that the contract was voidable or void (for example, induced by mistake, fraud, or misrepresentation). In this case, if deception led one of the parties to agree to the terms of a written contract, oral evidence attesting to the fraud should not be excluded. Courts frown on bad faith and are quick to allow such evidence when it establishes fraud.

3. *Contracts containing ambiguous terms.* When the terms of a written contract are ambiguous, evidence is admissible to show the meaning of the terms.

4. *Incomplete contracts.* When the written contract is incomplete in that it lacks one or more of the essential terms, the courts allow evidence to "fill in the gaps."

5. *Prior dealing, course of performance, or usage of trade.* Under the UCC, evidence can be introduced to explain or supplement a written contract by showing a prior dealing, course of performance, or usage of trade.[11] These terms will be discussed in further detail in Chapter 20, in the context of sales contracts. Here, it is sufficient to say that when buyers and sellers deal with each other over extended periods of time, certain customary practices develop. These practices are often overlooked in the writing of the contract, so courts allow the introduction of evidence to show how the parties have acted in the past.

6. *Contracts subject to orally agreed-on conditions.* The parol evidence rule does not apply if the existence of the entire written contract is subject to an orally agreed-on condition. Proof of the condition does not alter or modify the written terms but affects the *enforceability* of the written contract. For example, suppose that Jackson agrees to purchase Armand's car for $4,000, but only if Jackson's mechanic, Frank, inspects the car and approves of the purchase. Armand agrees to this condition, but because he is leaving town for the weekend and Jackson wants to use the car (if he buys it) before Armand returns, Jackson drafts a contract of sale, and they both sign it. Frank, the mechanic, does not approve of the purchase, and when Jackson does not buy the car, Armand sues him, alleging that he breached the contract. In this case, Jackson's oral agreement did not alter or modify the terms of the written agreement but concerned whether the contract existed at all. Therefore, the parol evidence rule does

---

10. UCC 2–209(2), (3).

11. UCC 1–205, 2–202.

not apply and the oral evidence is admissible to show that there is not an agreement.

7. *Contracts with an obvious or gross clerical (or typographic) error that clearly would not represent the agreement of the parties.* Parol evidence is admissible to correct an obvious typographic error.

INTEGRATED CONTRACTS

The key in determining whether evidence will be allowed basically depends on whether the written contract is intended to be a complete and final embodiment of the terms of the agreement. If it is so intended, it is referred to as an **integrated contract,** and extraneous evidence (evidence derived from sources outside the contract itself) is excluded. If it is only partially integrated, evidence of consistent additional terms is admissible to supplement the written agreement.[12] Exhibit 15–4 illustrates the relationship between integrated contracts and the parol evidence rule.

SECTION 5 | The Statute of Frauds in the International Context

As you will read in Chapter 20, the Convention on Contracts for the International Sale of Goods (CISG) provides rules that govern international sales contracts between citizens of countries that have ratified the convention (agreement). Article 11 of the CISG does not incorporate any Statute of Frauds provisions. Rather, it states that a "contract for sale need not be concluded in or evidenced by writing and is not subject to any other requirements as to form."

Article 11 accords with the legal customs of most nations, which no longer require contracts to meet certain formal or writing requirements to be enforceable. Ironically, even England, the nation that created the original Statute of Frauds in 1677, has repealed all of it except the provisions relating to collateral promises and to transfers of interests in land. Many other countries that once had such statutes have also repealed all or parts of them. Some countries, such as France, have never required certain types of contracts to be in writing.

EXHIBIT 15–4 **Parol Evidence Rule**

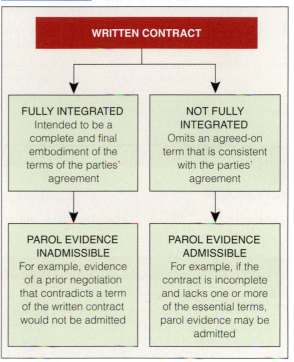

WRITTEN CONTRACT

FULLY INTEGRATED
Intended to be a complete and final embodiment of the terms of the parties' agreement

NOT FULLY INTEGRATED
Omits an agreed-on term that is consistent with the parties' agreement

PAROL EVIDENCE INADMISSIBLE
For example, evidence of a prior negotiation that contradicts a term of the written contract would not be admitted

PAROL EVIDENCE ADMISSIBLE
For example, if the contract is incomplete and lacks one or more of the essential terms, parol evidence may be admitted

---

12. *Restatement (Second) of Contracts*, Section 216.

REVIEWING THE STATUTE OF FRAUDS

Charter Golf, Inc., manufactures and sells golf apparel and supplies. Ken Odin had worked as a Charter sales representative for six months when he was offered a position with a competing firm. Charter's president, Jerry Montieth, offered Odin a 10 percent commission "for the rest of his life" if Ken would turn down the offer and stay on with Charter. He also promised that Odin would not be fired unless he was dishonest. Odin turned down the competitor's offer and stayed with Charter. Three years later, Charter fired Odin for no reason. Odin sued, alleging breach of contract. Using the information presented in the chapter, answer the following questions.

1. Discuss whether this contract falls within the Statute of Frauds.

2. Is an "employment-for-life" contract *capable* of being performed within one year? What if the employee dies within one year of making the agreement? Explain.

3. Suppose that Montieth admits that he orally promised Odin a 10 percent commission for the rest of his life. Will a court enforce Montieth's promise under the doctrine of promissory estoppel? Why or why not? Name any other exceptions discussed in the chapter that might apply.

4. Now suppose that Montieth had taken out a pencil and written on the back of a register receipt, "10 percent for life." Would this satisfy the requirements of the Statute of Frauds? Why or why not?

5. Assume that Odin had signed a written employment contract at the time he was hired to work for Charter and that the agreement did not say that it was integrated. How would the parol evidence rule apply to this situation? Under which theories might the court allow parol evidence of the oral contract?

TERMS AND CONCEPTS TO REVIEW

collateral promise 296   parol evidence rule 302   Statute of Frauds 293
integrated contract 305   prenuptial agreement 297

QUESTIONS AND CASE PROBLEMS

15-1. On May 1, by telephone, Yu offers to hire Benson to perform personal services. On May 5, Benson returns Yu's call and accepts the offer. Discuss fully whether this contract falls under the Statute of Frauds in the following circumstances:

(a) The contract calls for Benson to be employed for one year, with the right to begin performance immediately.

(b) The contract calls for Benson to be employed for nine months, with performance of services to begin on September 1.

(c) The contract calls for Benson to submit a written research report, with a deadline of two years for submission.

15-2. QUESTION WITH SAMPLE ANSWER
Mallory promises a local hardware store that she will pay for a lawn mower that her brother is purchasing on credit if the brother fails to pay the debt. Must this promise be in writing to be enforceable? Why or why not?
For a sample answer to this question, go to Appendix I at the end of this text.

15-3. On January 1, Damon, for consideration, orally promised to pay Gary $300 a month for as long as Gary lived, with the payments to be made on the first day of every month. Damon made the payments regularly for nine months and then made no further payments. Gary claimed that Damon had breached the oral contract and sued Damon for damages. Damon contended that the contract was unenforceable because, under the Statute of Frauds, contracts that cannot be performed within one year must be in writing. Discuss whether Damon will succeed in this defense.

15-4. Jeremy took his mother on a special holiday to Mountain Air Resort. Jeremy was a frequent patron of the resort and was well known by its manager. The resort required each of its patrons to make a large deposit to ensure payment of the room rental. Jeremy asked the manager to waive the requirement for his mother and told the manager that if his mother for any reason failed to pay the resort for her stay there, he would cover the bill. Relying on Jeremy's promise, the manager waived the deposit requirement for Jeremy's mother. After she returned home from her holiday, Jeremy's mother refused to pay the resort bill. The resort manager tried to collect the sum from Jeremy, but Jeremy also refused to pay, stating that his promise was not enforceable under the Statute of Frauds. Is Jeremy correct? Explain.

15-5. THE PAROL EVIDENCE RULE. Glenn Grove bought a 1936 Pontiac from Bernard Stanfield. Stanfield signed the certificate of title, which stated that the car was sold for $1,000. No other terms of sale were mentioned in the certificate, and none were incorporated by reference. Three years later, Stanfield filed a suit against Grove in a Missouri state court, claiming that Grove still owed $9,000 on the price of the car. At the trial, Stanfield testified that he and Grove had an oral agreement by which Grove was to pay $1,000 for the "title document" and $9,000 for the actual car. The court entered a judgment in Stanfield's favor. What will happen on appeal? Explain. [*Stanfield v. Grove*, 924 S.W.2d 611 (Mo.App.Div.4 1996)]

15-6. THE PAROL EVIDENCE RULE. Vision Graphics, Inc., provides printing services to customers such as Milton Bradley Co. To perform its services, Vision agreed to buy or lease from E. I. du Pont de Nemours & Co. parts of a computer software system. Vision needed the system to accept files written in "PostScript," a computer language used in the printing industry. Du Pont orally represented to Vision that with three upgrades, its system would be completely "postscriptable." Promises regarding postscriptability were not included in any of the parties' written contracts. Each contract, however, was an integrated contract explicitly stating that the contract contained the entire agreement of the parties. Before the three upgrades were complete, du Pont determined that for financial reasons, it could no longer support its system and told Vision that the software would not be made postscriptable. Vision lost customers and could not attract new accounts, and its reputation in the industry was damaged. Vision filed a suit in a federal district court against du Pont, alleging, among other things, breach of contract on the basis of the oral promises. Du Pont filed a motion for summary judgment, arguing that whether it breached any oral agreement was "immaterial." Will the court agree? Why or why not? [*Vision Graphics, Inc. v. E. I. du Pont de Nemours & Co.*, 41 F.Supp.2d 93 (D.Mass. 1999)]

15-7. ⚖️ **CASE PROBLEM WITH SAMPLE ANSWER**
Novell, Inc., owned the source code for DR DOS, a computer operating system that Microsoft Corp. targeted

with allegedly anticompetitive practices in the early 1990s. Novell worried that if it filed a suit for unfair practices, Microsoft would retaliate with further alleged unfair practices. Consequently, Novell sold DR DOS to Canopy Group, Inc., a Utah corporation. The purposes of the sale were to obligate Canopy to bring an action against Microsoft and to allow Novell to share in the recovery without revealing its role. Novell and Canopy signed two documents—a contract of sale, obligating Canopy to pay $400,000 for rights to the source code, and a temporary license, obligating Canopy to pay at least $600,000 in royalties, which included a percentage of any recovery from the suit. Canopy settled the dispute with Microsoft, deducted its expenses, and paid Novell the remainder of what was due. Novell filed a suit in a Utah state court against Canopy, alleging breach of contract for Canopy's deduction of expenses. Canopy responded that it could show that the parties had an oral agreement on this point. On what basis might the court refuse to consider this evidence? Is that the appropriate course in this case? Explain. [*Novell, Inc. v. Canopy Group, Inc.*, 2004 UT App 162, 92 P.3d 768 (2004)]
To view a sample answer for this case problem, go to this book's Web site at http://wbl.westbuslaw.com, select "Chapter 15," and click on "Case Problem with Sample Answer."

15-8. ORAL CONTRACTS. Robert Pinto, doing business as Pinto Associates, hired Richard MacDonald as an independent contractor in March 1992. The parties orally agreed on the terms of employment, including payment to MacDonald of a share of the company's income, but they did not put anything in writing. In March 1995, MacDonald quit. Pinto then told MacDonald that he was entitled to $9,602.17—25 percent of the difference between the accounts receivable and the accounts payable as of MacDonald's last day. MacDonald disagreed and demanded more than $83,500—25 percent of the revenue from all invoices, less the cost of materials and outside processing, for each of the years that he worked for Pinto. Pinto refused. MacDonald filed a suit in a Connecticut state court against Pinto, alleging breach of contract. In Pinto's response and at the trial, he testified that the parties had an oral contract under which MacDonald was entitled to 25 percent of the difference between accounts receivable and payable as of the date of MacDonald's termination. Did the parties have an enforceable contract? What should the court rule, and why? [*MacDonald v. Pinto*, 62 Conn.App. 317, 771 A.2d 156 (2001)]

15-9. INTERESTS IN LAND. Sierra Bravo, Inc., and Shelby's, Inc., entered into a written "Waste Disposal Agreement" under which Shelby's allowed Sierra to deposit on Shelby's land waste products, deleterious (harmful) materials, and debris removed by Sierra in the construction of a highway. Later, Shelby's asked Sierra why it had not constructed a waterway and a building pad suitable for a commercial building on the property, as they had orally agreed. Sierra denied any such agreement. Shelby's filed a suit in a Missouri state court against Sierra, alleging breach of contract. Sierra contended that any oral agreement was unenforceable under the Statute of Frauds. Sierra argued that because the right to *remove* minerals from land is considered a contract for the sale of an interest in land to which the Statute of Frauds applies, the Statute of Frauds should apply to the right to *deposit* soil on another person's property. How should the court rule, and why? [*Shelby's, Inc. v. Sierra Bravo, Inc.*, 68 S.W.3d 604 (Mo.App.S.D. 2002)]

15–10. THE PAROL EVIDENCE RULE. Carlin Krieg owned a dairy farm in St. Joe, Indiana, appraised at $154,000 in December 1997. In August 1999, Krieg told Donald Hieber that he intended to sell the farm for $106,000. Hieber offered to buy it. Krieg also told Hieber that he wanted to retain a "right of residency" for life in the farm. In October, Krieg and Hieber executed a purchase agreement that provided Krieg "shall transfer full and complete possession" of the farm "subject to [his] right of residency." The agreement also contained an integration clause that stated "there are no conditions, representations, warranties or agreements not stated in this instrument." In November 2000, the house was burned in a fire, rendering it uninhabitable. Hieber filed an insurance claim for the damage and received the proceeds, but he did not fix the house. Krieg filed a suit in an Indiana state court against Hieber, alleging breach of contract. Is there any basis on which the court can consider evidence regarding the parties' negotiations prior to their agreement for the sale of the farm? Explain. [*Krieg v. Hieber*, 802 N.E.2d 938 (Ind.App. 2004)]

LAW | on the Web

For updated links to resources available on the Web, as well as a variety of other materials, visit this text's Web site at http://wbl.westbuslaw.com.

The online version of UCC Section 2–201 on the Statute of Frauds includes links to definitions of certain terms used in the section. To access this site, go to

http://www.law.cornell.edu/ucc/2/2-201.html

To read a summary of cases concerning whether the exchange of e-mails satisfies the writing requirements of the Statute of Frauds, go to

http://www.phillipsnizer.com/library/topics/statute_frauds.cfm

Professor Eric Talley of the University of Southern California provides an interesting discussion of the history and current applicability of the Statute of Frauds, both internationally and in the United States, at

http://www-bcf.usc.edu/~etalley/frauds.html

LEGAL RESEARCH EXERCISES ON THE WEB

Go to http://wbl.westbuslaw.com, the Web site that accompanies this text. Select "Chapter 15" and click on "Internet Exercises." There you will find the following Internet research exercises that you can perform to learn more about topics covered in this chapter.

Activity 15–1: LEGAL PERSPECTIVE
Promissory Estoppel and the Statute of Frauds

Activity 15–2: MANAGEMENT PERSPECTIVE
"Get It in Writing"

Activity 15–3: HISTORICAL PERSPECTIVE
The English Act for the Prevention of Frauds and Perjuries

CHAPTER 16

Third Party Rights

Once it has been determined that a valid and legally enforceable contract exists, attention can turn to the rights and duties of the parties to the contract. A contract is a private agreement between the parties who have entered into it, and traditionally these parties alone have rights and liabilities under the contract. This principle is referred to as **privity of contract.** A *third party*—one who is not a direct party to a particular contract—normally does not have rights under that contract.

There are exceptions to the rule of privity of contract. For example, privity of contract between a seller and a buyer is no longer a requirement to recover damages under product liability laws (see Chapter 23). In this chapter, we look at two other exceptions. One exception allows a party to a contract to transfer the rights or duties arising from the contract to another person through an *assignment* (of rights) or a *delegation* (of duties). The other exception involves a *third party beneficiary contract*—a contract in which the parties to the contract intend that the contract benefit a third party. We look at both of these exceptions to the rule of privity of contract in this chapter, beginning with the law relating to assignments and delegations.

SECTION 1 | Assignments and Delegations

In a bilateral contract, the two parties have corresponding rights and duties. One party has a *right* to require the other to perform some task, and the other has a *duty* to perform it. The transfer of contractual *rights* to a third party is known as an **assignment.** The transfer of contractual *duties* to a third party is known as a **delegation.** An assignment or a delegation occurs *after* the original contract was made.

ASSIGNMENTS

Assignments are important because they are involved in many types of business financing. Banks, for example, frequently assign the rights to receive payments under their loan contracts to other firms, which pay for those rights. If you obtain a loan from your local bank to purchase a car, you may later receive in the mail a notice from your bank stating that it has transferred (assigned) its rights to receive payments on the

loan to another firm and that, when the time comes to repay your loan, you must make future payments to that other firm.

Financial institutions that make *mortgage loans* (loans to enable prospective home buyers to purchase land or a home) often assign their rights to collect the mortgage payments to a third party, such as GMAC Mortgage Corporation. Following the assignment, the home buyers are notified that they must make future payments *not* to the bank that loaned them the funds but to the third party. Millions of dollars change hands daily in the business world in the form of assignments of rights in contracts. If it were not possible to transfer (assign) contractual rights, many businesses could not continue to operate.

TERMINOLOGY In an assignment, the party assigning the rights to a third party is known as the **assignor,** and the party receiving the rights is the **assignee.** Other traditional terms used to describe the parties in assignment relationships are **obligee** (the person to whom a duty, or obligation, is owed) and **obligor** (the person who is obligated to perform the duty).

THE EFFECT OF AN ASSIGNMENT When rights under a contract are assigned unconditionally, the rights of the assignor are extinguished.[1] The third party (the assignee) has a right to demand performance from the other original party to the contract. The assignee takes only those rights that the assignor originally had, however.

For example, suppose that Brower is obligated by contract to pay Horton $1,000. In this situation, Brower is the obligor because she owes an obligation, or duty, to Horton. Horton is the obligee, the one to whom the obligation, or duty, is owed. Now suppose that Horton assigns his right to receive the $1,000 to Kuhn. Horton is the assignor, and Kuhn is the assignee. Kuhn now becomes the obligee, because Brower owes Kuhn the $1,000. Here, a valid assignment of a debt exists. Kuhn (the assignee-obligee) is entitled to enforce payment in court if Brower (the obligor) does not pay her the $1,000. These concepts are illustrated in Exhibit 16–1.

RIGHTS ASSIGNED ARE SUBJECT TO THE SAME DEFENSES The assignee's rights are subject to the defenses that the obligor has against the assignor. For example, assume that in the preceding scenario,

Brower owed Horton the $1,000 under a contract in which Brower agreed to buy Horton's personal computer. Brower, in deciding to purchase the computer, relied on Horton's fraudulent misrepresentation that the computer's hard drive had a storage capacity of 120 gigabytes. When Brower discovered that the computer could store only 20 gigabytes, she told Horton that she was going to return the computer to him and cancel the contract. Even though Horton had assigned his "right" to receive the $1,000 to Kuhn, Brower need not pay Kuhn the $1,000—Brower can raise the defense of Horton's fraudulent misrepresentation to avoid payment.

FORM OF THE ASSIGNMENT In general, an assignment can take any form, oral or written. Naturally, it is more difficult to prove that an oral assignment occurred, so it is practical to put all assignments in writing. Of course, assignments covered by the Statute of Frauds must be in writing to be enforceable. For example, an assignment of an interest in land must be in writing to be enforceable. In addition, most states require contracts for the assignment of wages to be in writing.[2]

---

1. *Restatement (Second) of Contracts*, Section 317.

2. See, for example, California Labor Code Section 300. There are other assignments that must be in writing as well.

EXHIBIT 16-1 **Assignment Relationships**

In the assignment relationship illustrated here, Horton assigns his *rights* under a contract that he made with Brower to a third party, Kuhn. Horton thus becomes the *assignor* and Kuhn the *assignee* of the contractual rights. Brower, the *obligor* (the party owing performance under the contract), now owes performance to Kuhn instead of Horton. Horton's original contract rights are extinguished after assignment.

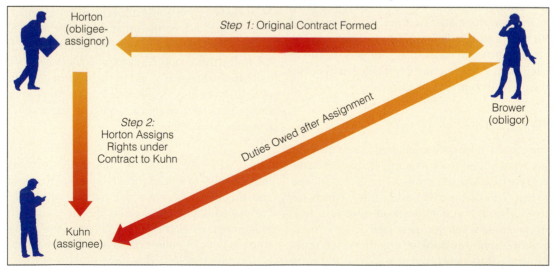

Horton (obligee-assignor)

Step 1: Original Contract Formed

Brower (obligor)

Step 2: Horton Assigns Rights under Contract to Kuhn

Duties Owed after Assignment

Kuhn (assignee)

The circumstances in the following case illustrate some of the problems that can arise with oral assignments. The case also stands for the principle that an assignment, like any contract, must have consideration—in this case, a dance center's assumption of a choreographer's legal and financial duties associated with her choreography.

CASE 16.1

United States
Court of Appeals,
Second Circuit, 2004.
380 F.3d 624.

Martha Graham School and Dance Foundation, Inc. v. Martha Graham Center of Contemporary Dance, Inc.

BACKGROUND AND FACTS *Martha Graham's career as a dancer, dance instructor, and choreographer began in the first third of the twentieth century. In the 1920s, she started a dance company and a dance school and choreographed works on commission. In the 1940s, she founded the Martha Graham Center of Contemporary Dance, Inc. (the Center). She sold her school to the Martha Graham School of Contemporary Dance, Inc. (the School), in 1956. By 1980, the Center had absorbed the School. In 1989, two years before her death, Graham executed a will in which she gave Ronald Protas, the Center's general director, "any rights or interests" in "dance works, musical scores [and] scenery sets." After her death, Protas asserted ownership of all of Graham's dances and related property. In 1999, the Center's board removed Protas and, due to financial problems, suspended operations. Meanwhile, Protas founded the Martha Graham School and Dance Foundation, Inc., and began licensing Graham's dances. When the School reopened in 2001, Protas and his foundation filed a suit in a federal district court against the Center and others to enjoin their use of, among other things, seventy of the dances. The Center responded in part that Graham had assigned the dances to it. The court ruled that twenty-one of the dances had been assigned to the Center. The plaintiffs appealed to the U.S. Court of Appeals for the Second Circuit.*

IN THE LANGUAGE OF THE COURT

JON O. NEWMAN, Circuit Judge.
* * * *
    The Appellants contend that the District Court erred in finding that Graham assigned to the Center 21 dances, * * * which were created before 1956, unpublished at the time of assignment, and not commissioned. We disagree.
* * * *
    Although there is no document memorializing Graham's assignment of copyright in her pre-1956 dances to the Center, the District Court was entitled to find that Graham assigned to the Center, orally or in writing, her copyrights in her noncommissioned pre-1956 dances that were not published at the time she assigned them.
    The District Court relied on several items of evidence to reach its conclusion. For example, Jeannette Roosevelt, former President of the Center's board of directors, testified that Graham had given the dances to the Center prior to 1965 or 1966, when she joined the board. There was additional evidence that the Center acted as the owner of the dances by entering into contracts with third parties, and that Graham was aware of this and did not object. Other evidence showed that the Center received royalties for the dances and treated them as its assets. However, the only evidence that Graham had assigned the entire group of her pre-1956 dances (noncommissioned and unpublished) to the Center are two letters from Lee Leatherman, the Center's Executive Administrator at that time, written in 1968 and 1971. These letters indicated that "[r]ecently Miss Graham assigned performing rights to all of her works to the Martha Graham Center of Contemporary Dance, Inc.," and that "Martha has assigned all rights to all of her works to the Martha Graham Center, Inc." The Appellants contend that these letters are hearsay[a] and were impermissibly considered.
    These two letters, both in existence 20 years or more at the time they were offered as evidence, were authenticated * * * . There was no reason to suspect their authenticity.

---

a. *Hearsay* is testimony given in court about a statement made by someone else, as was discussed in Chapter 3.

CONTINUED

CASE 16.1 | Continued

Moreover, Linda Hodes, a witness with relevant knowledge, testified that the letters were what they purported to be. *The letters were therefore exceptions to the hearsay rule [under which the letters would otherwise be inadmissible].* The District Court did not err in admitting and relying on these letters. [Emphasis added.]

Under New York law, an assignment * * * may be made without writing or delivery of any written statement of the claim assigned, * * * provided only that *the assignment is founded on a valid consideration between the parties.* The District Court was entitled to find that Graham received consideration for the assignment of her pre-1956 dances. Graham benefited from the Center's assumption of the legal and financial duties associated with her choreography; assigning to the Center the copyrights in her dances gave her what she wished—freedom from the responsibilities of copyright registration and renewal, licensing, collection of royalties, and archival tasks. [Emphasis added.]

The District Court was entitled to find that Graham assigned her pre-1956 dances * * * to the Center sometime between 1957 and the mid-1960s.

DECISION AND REMEDY *The U.S. Court of Appeals for the Second Circuit affirmed the lower court's judgment on this issue, "commend[ing] the District Court for its careful rulings on the many issues in this complicated case." The appellate court held that Graham had received consideration for her assignment of certain dances, and although the assignment had been oral, it had been reliably proved by written testimony.*

WHAT IF THE FACTS WERE DIFFERENT? *Suppose that Graham had not benefited from the Center's assumption of the duties associated with her choreography. Would the alleged assignment have been valid? Why or why not?*

RIGHTS THAT CANNOT BE ASSIGNED As a general rule, all rights can be assigned. Exceptions are made, however, under certain circumstances. Some exceptions are described next.

—When a Statute Expressly Prohibits Assignment. When a statute expressly prohibits assignment of a particular right, that right cannot be assigned. Suppose that Quincy is an employee of Specialty Computer, Inc. Specialty Computer is an employer under workers' compensation statutes in this state, and thus Quincy is a covered employee. Quincy is injured on the job and begins to collect monthly workers' compensation checks (see Chapter 33 for a discussion of workers' compensation laws). In need of a loan, Quincy asks Draper to lend her some funds and offers to assign to Draper all of her future workers' compensation benefits. The assignment of future workers' compensation benefits is prohibited by state statute, however, and thus such rights cannot be assigned.

—When a Contract Is Personal in Nature. When a contract is for personal services, the rights under the contract normally cannot be assigned unless all that remains is a money payment.[3] Suppose that Brower signs a contract to be a tutor for Horton's chil-

dren. Horton then attempts to assign to Kuhn his right to Brower's services. Kuhn cannot enforce the contract against Brower. Kuhn's children may be more difficult to tutor than Horton's; thus, if Horton could assign his rights to Brower's services to Kuhn, it would change the nature of Brower's obligation. Because personal services are unique to the person rendering them, rights to receive personal services are likewise unique and cannot be assigned.

—When an Assignment Will Increase or Alter the Risk or Duties of the Obligor. A right cannot be assigned if assignment will materially increase or alter the risk or duties of the obligor.[4] Assume that Horton has a hotel, and to insure it, he takes out a policy with Southeast Insurance. The policy insures against fire, theft, flood, and vandalism. Horton attempts to assign the insurance policy to Kuhn, who also owns a hotel. The assignment is ineffective because it substantially alters Southeast Insurance's *duty of performance.* An insurance company evaluates the particular risk of a certain party and tailors its policy to fit that risk. If the policy is assigned to a third party, the insurance risk is materially altered because the insurance company may have no information on the third party. Therefore, the

---

3. *Restatement (Second) of Contracts,* Sections 317 and 318.

4. Section 2–210(1) of the Uniform Commercial Code (UCC). (This section number reflects the 2003 amendments to the UCC— see Chapter 20.)

assignment will not operate to give Kuhn any rights against Southeast Insurance.

—When the Contract Prohibits Assignment. When a contract specifically stipulates that a right cannot be assigned, then *ordinarily* the right cannot be assigned. Whether an antiassignment clause is effective depends in part on how it is phrased. A contract that states that any assignment is void effectively prohibits any assignment. Note that restraints on the power to assign operate only against the parties themselves. They do not prohibit an assignment by operation of law, such as an assignment pursuant to bankruptcy or death.

There are several exceptions to this rule. First, a contract cannot prevent an assignment of the right to receive money. This exception exists to encourage the free flow of money and credit in modern business settings. Second, the assignment of rights in real estate often cannot be prohibited because such a prohibition is contrary to public policy. Prohibitions of this kind are called restraints against **alienation** (transfer of land ownership). Third, the assignment of *negotiable instruments* (see Chapter 24) cannot be prohibited. Finally, in a contract for the sale of goods, the right to receive damages for breach of contract or payment of an account owed may be assigned even though the sales contract prohibits such assignment.[5]

NOTICE OF ASSIGNMENT Once a valid assignment of rights has been made, the assignee (the third party to whom the rights have been assigned) should notify the obligor (the one owing performance) of the assignment. For instance, in the previously discussed example, when Horton assigns to Kuhn his right to receive the $1,000

from Brower, Kuhn should notify Brower, the obligor, of the assignment. Giving notice is not legally necessary to establish the validity of the assignment: an assignment is effective immediately, whether or not notice is given. Two major problems arise, however, when notice of the assignment is not given to the obligor.

1. If the assignor assigns the same right to two different persons, the question arises as to which one has priority—that is, which one has the right to the performance by the obligor. Although the rule most often observed in the United States is that the first assignment in time is the first in right, some states follow the English rule, which basically gives priority to the first assignee who gives notice.

2. Until the obligor has notice of assignment, the obligor can discharge his or her obligation by performance to the assignor (the obligee), and performance by the obligor to the assignor (obligee) constitutes a discharge to the assignee. Once the obligor receives proper notice, however, only performance to the assignee can discharge the obligor's obligations. In the Horton-Brower-Kuhn example, assume that Brower, the obligor, is not notified of Horton's assignment of his rights to Kuhn. Brower subsequently pays Horton the $1,000. Although the assignment was valid, Brower's payment to Horton discharges the debt. Kuhn's failure to give notice to Brower of the assignment has caused Kuhn to lose the right to collect the money from Brower. If, however, Kuhn had given Brower notice of the assignment, Brower's payment to Horton would not have discharged the debt, and Kuhn would have had a legal right to require payment from Brower.

In the following case, the issue was whether the right to buy advertising space in certain publications at a steep discount was validly assigned from the original owner to companies that he later formed.

5. UCC 2–210(1). (This section number reflects the 2003 amendments to the UCC—see Chapter 20.)

CASE 16.2   Gold v. Ziff Communications Co.

Appellate Court of Illinois,
First District, 2001.
322 Ill.App.3d 32,
748 N.E.2d 198,
254 Ill.Dec. 752.
http://state.il.us/court/
default.htm[a]

BACKGROUND AND FACTS *In 1982, Ziff Communications Company, a publisher of specialty magazines, bought PC Magazine from its founder, Anthony Gold, for more than $10 million. As part of the deal, Ziff gave Gold, or a company that he "controlled," "ad/list rights"—rights to advertise at an 80 percent discount on a limited number of pages in Ziff publications and free use of Ziff's subscriber lists. In 1983, Gold formed Software Communications, Inc. (SCI), a mail-order software business that he wholly owned, to use the ad/list rights. In 1987 and 1988, he formed two new*

a. On this page, click on "Appellate Court of Illinois." On the next page, in the "Appellate Court Documents" section, click on "Appellate Court Opinions." In the result, in the "Appellate Court" section, click on "2001." On the next page, in the "First District" section, click on "March." Finally, scroll to the bottom of the chart and click on the case name to access the opinion. The state of Illinois maintains this Web site.

CONTINUED ▶

CASE 16.2 | Continued

mail-order companies, Hanson & Connors, Inc., and PC Brand, Inc. Gold told Ziff that he was allocating his ad/list rights to Hanson & Connors, which took over most of SCI's business, and to PC Brand, of which Gold owned 90 percent. Ziff's other advertisers complained about this "allocation." As a result, Ziff refused to run large ads for Hanson & Connors or to release its subscriber lists to the company. Ziff also declared PC Brand ineligible for the ad discount because it "was not controlled by Gold." Gold and his companies filed a suit in an Illinois state court against Ziff, alleging breach of contract. The court ordered Ziff to pay the plaintiffs more than $88 million in damages and interest. Ziff appealed to an intermediate state appellate court, arguing in part that Gold had not properly assigned the ad/list rights to Hanson & Connors and PC Brand.

IN THE LANGUAGE OF THE COURT

Justice COUSINS delivered the opinion of the court:

* * * *

Ziff * * * argues that Gold never properly reassigned his rights under the amended ad/list agreement from SCI to PC Brand and Hanson. We agree with plaintiffs that assignments can be implied from circumstances. *No particular mode or form * * * is necessary to effect a valid assignment, and any acts or words are sufficient which show an intention of transferring or appropriating the owner's interest.* [Emphasis added.]

In the instant case, it is undisputed that Gold owned 100% of SCI. In a letter dated May 13, 1988, Gold, as president of SCI, instructed Ziff that he was allocating the ad/list rights to Hanson and PC Brand. Additionally, SCI stopped using the ad/list rights when PC Brand and Hanson were formed. * * * Gold's behavior toward his companies and his conduct toward the obligor, Ziff, implied that the ad/list rights were assigned to PC Brand and Hanson.

DECISION AND REMEDY *The state intermediate appellate court affirmed the lower court's decision on this issue. The appellate court remanded the case, however, for a new trial on the amount of the damages, reasoning that some parts of the award "were not within the reasonable contemplation of the parties."*

WHAT IF THE FACTS WERE DIFFERENT? *Suppose that Gold had not given any notice to Ziff of the assignment of the ad/list rights to Hanson and PC Brand. Would the outcome of the case have been different?*

DELEGATIONS

Just as a party can transfer rights through an assignment, a party can also transfer duties. Duties are not assigned, however; they are *delegated*. Normally, a delegation of duties does not relieve the party making the delegation (the **delegator**) of the obligation to perform in the event that the party to whom the duty has been delegated (the **delegatee**) fails to perform. No special form is required to create a valid delegation of duties. As long as the delegator expresses an intention to make the delegation, it is effective; the delegator need not even use the word *delegate*. Exhibit 16–2 illustrates delegation relationships.

DUTIES THAT CANNOT BE DELEGATED As a general rule, any duty can be delegated. There are, however, some exceptions to this rule. Delegation is prohibited in the circumstances discussed next.

—When the Duties Are Personal in Nature. When special trust has been placed in the obligor or when performance depends on the personal skill or talents of the *obligor* (the person contractually obligated to perform), contractual duties cannot be delegated. For example, suppose that Horton, who is impressed with Brower's ability to perform veterinary surgery, contracts with Brower to have Brower perform surgery on Horton's prize-winning stallion in July. Brower later decides that she would rather spend the summer at the beach, so she delegates her duties under the contract to Kuhn, who is also a competent veterinary surgeon. The delegation is not effective without Horton's consent, no matter how competent Kuhn is, because the contract is for *personal* performance.

In contrast, nonpersonal duties may be delegated. Assume that Brower contracts with Horton to pick up and deliver heavy construction machinery to Horton's property. Brower delegates this duty to Kuhn, who is in

EXHIBIT 16–2 Delegation Relationships

In the delegation relationship illustrated here, Brower delegates her *duties* under a contract that she made with Horton to a third party, Kuhn. Brower thus becomes the *delegator* and Kuhn the *delegatee* of the contractual duties. Kuhn now owes performance of the contractual duties to Horton. Note that a delegation of duties normally does not relieve the delegator (Brower) of liability if the delegatee (Kuhn) fails to perform the contractual duties.

Step 1: Original Contract Formed

Brower
(obligor-delegator)

Horton
(obligee)

Step 2:
Brower
Delegates
Contract Duties
to Kuhn

Performance Owed after Delegation

Kuhn
(delegatee)

the business of delivering heavy machinery. This delegation is effective because the performance required is of a *routine* and *nonpersonal* nature.

—*When Performance by a Third Party Will Vary from That Expected by the Obligee.* When performance by a third party will vary materially from that expected by the obligee (the one to whom performance is owed) under the contract, contractual duties cannot be delegated. For example, suppose that Brower contracts with Horton to tutor Horton in various aspects of financial underwriting and investment banking. Brower, an experienced businessperson known for her expertise in finance, wants to delegate her duties to a third party, Kuhn. This delegation is ineffective because Brower has contracted to render a service that is founded on her expertise. The delegation would change Horton's expectations under the contract. Therefore, Kuhn cannot perform Brower's duties.

—*When the Contract Prohibits Delegation.* When the contract expressly prohibits delegation by including an *antidelegation clause*, the duties cannot be delegated. In some situations, however, when the duties are completely impersonal in nature, courts have held that the duties can be delegated notwithstanding an antidelegation clause.

EFFECT OF A DELEGATION If a delegation of duties is enforceable, the obligee (the one to whom performance is owed) must accept performance from the delegatee (the one to whom the duties have been delegated). Consider again the example in which Brower delegates to Kuhn the duty to pick up and deliver heavy construction machinery to Horton's property. In that situation, Horton (the obligee) must accept performance from Kuhn (the delegatee) because the delegation was effective. The obligee can legally refuse performance from the delegatee only if the duty is one that cannot be delegated.

As noted, a valid delegation of duties does not relieve the delegator of obligations under the contract.[6] Thus, in the above example, if Kuhn (the delegatee) fails to perform, Brower (the delegator) is still liable to Horton (the obligee). The obligee can also hold the delegatee liable if the delegatee made a promise of performance that will directly benefit the obligee. In this situation, there is an "assumption of duty" on the part of the delegatee, and breach of this duty makes the delegatee liable to the obligee. For example, if Kuhn (the delegatee) promises Brower (the delegator), in a contract, to pick up and deliver

---

6. See, for example, *Mehul's Investment Corp. v. ABC Advisors, Inc.*, 130 F.Supp.2d 700 (D.Md. 2001).

the construction equipment to Horton's property but fails to do so, Horton (the obligee) can sue Brower, Kuhn, or both. Although there are many exceptions, the general rule today is that the obligee can sue both the delegatee and the delegator. *Concept Summary 16.1* outlines the basic principles of the laws governing assignments and delegations.

ASSIGNMENT OF "ALL RIGHTS"

When a contract provides for an "assignment of all rights," this wording may create both an assignment of rights and a delegation of duties.[7] Therefore, when general words are used (for example, "I assign the contract" or "I assign all my rights under the contract"), the contract normally is construed as implying both an assignment of the assignor's rights and a delegation of any duties of performance owed by the assignor under the contract being assigned. Thus, the assignor remains liable if the assignee fails to perform the contractual obligations.

---

7. *Restatement (Second) of Contracts*, Section 328; UCC 2–210(3), (4).

SECTION 2 | Third Party Beneficiaries

Another exception to the doctrine of privity of contract arises when the original parties to the contract intend at the time of contracting that the contract performance directly benefit a third person. In this situation, the third person becomes a **third party beneficiary** of the contract. As an **intended beneficiary** of the contract, the third party has legal rights and can sue the promisor directly for breach of the contract.

Who, though, is the promisor? In a bilateral contract, both parties to the contract are promisors because they both make promises that can be enforced. To determine the identity of the promisor in a third party beneficiary contract, the court will ask which party made the promise that benefits the third party—that person is the promisor. Allowing a third party to sue the promisor directly in effect circumvents the "middle person" (the promisee) and thus reduces the burden on the courts. Otherwise, the third party would sue the promisee, who would then sue the promisor.

CONCEPT SUMMARY 16.1 | Assignments and Delegations

WHICH RIGHTS CAN BE ASSIGNED, AND WHICH DUTIES CAN BE DELEGATED?	All rights can be assigned *unless*: 1. A statute expressly prohibits assignment. 2. The contract is for personal services. 3. The assignment will materially alter the obligor's risk or duties. 4. The contract prohibits assignment.	All duties can be delegated *unless*: 1. Performance depends on the obligor's personal skills or talents. 2. Special trust has been placed in the obligor. 3. Performance by a third party will materially vary from that expected by the obligee. 4. The contract prohibits delegation.
WHAT IF THE CONTRACT PROHIBITS ASSIGNMENT OR DELEGATION?	No rights can be assigned *except*: 1. Rights to receive money. 2. Ownership rights in real estate. 3. Rights to negotiable instruments. 4. Rights to sales contract payments or damages for breach of a sales contract.	Generally, no duties can be delegated.
WHAT IS THE EFFECT ON THE ORIGINAL PARTY'S RIGHTS?	On a valid assignment, effective immediately, the original party (assignor) no longer has any rights under the contract.	On a valid delegation, if the delegatee fails to perform, the original party (delegator) is liable to the obligee (who generally may also hold the delegatee liable).

TYPES OF INTENDED BENEFICIARIES

At one time, third party beneficiaries had no legal rights in contracts. Over time, however, the concept developed that a third party for whose benefit a contract was formed could sue the promisor to have the contract enforced.

CREDITOR BENEFICIARIES In a classic case decided in 1859, *Lawrence v. Fox*,[8] the court permitted a third party beneficiary to bring suit directly against a promisor. This case established the rule that a *creditor beneficiary* can sue the promisor directly. A creditor beneficiary is one who benefits from a contract in which one party (the promisor) promises another party (the promisee) to pay a debt that party owes to a third party (the creditor beneficiary). The creditor beneficiary, although not a party to the contract between the debtor and the other person, becomes the intended beneficiary and can thus enforce the promisor's promise to pay the debt.

DONEE BENEFICIARIES Another type of intended beneficiary is a *donee beneficiary*. When a contract is made for the express purpose of giving a gift to a third party, the third party (the donee beneficiary) can sue the promisor directly to enforce the promise.[9] The most common donee beneficiary contract is a life insurance contract. For example, in a typical life insurance contract, Akins (the promisee) pays premiums to Standard Life, a life insurance company, and Standard Life (the promisor) promises to pay a certain amount on Akins's death to anyone Akins designates as a beneficiary. The designated beneficiary is a donee beneficiary under the life insurance policy and can enforce the promise made by the insurance company to pay him or her on Akins's death.

THIRD PARTY BENEFICIARY CONTRACTS: THE MODERN VIEW As the law concerning third party beneficiaries evolved, numerous cases arose in which the third party beneficiary did not fit readily into either the creditor beneficiary or the donee beneficiary category. Thus, the modern view, and the one adopted by the *Restatement (Second) of Contracts*, does not draw such clear lines and distinguishes only between *intended beneficiaries* (who can sue to enforce contracts made for their benefit) and *incidental beneficiaries* (who cannot sue, as will be discussed shortly).

THE VESTING OF AN INTENDED BENEFICIARY'S RIGHTS

An intended third party beneficiary cannot enforce a contract against the original parties until the rights of the third party have *vested*, which means the rights have taken effect and cannot be taken away. Until these rights have vested, the original parties to the contract—the promisor and the promisee—can modify or rescind the contract without the consent of the third party.

When do the rights of third parties vest? Generally, the rights vest when either of the following occurs:

1. When the third party demonstrates manifest assent to the contract, such as by sending a letter or note acknowledging awareness of and consent to a contract formed for her or his benefit.

2. When the third party materially alters his or her position in detrimental reliance on the contract.

If the contract expressly reserves to the contracting parties the right to cancel, rescind, or modify the contract, the rights of the third party beneficiary are subject to any changes that result. In such a situation, the vesting of the third party's rights does not terminate the power of the original contracting parties to alter their legal relationships.[10] This is particularly true in most life insurance contracts, in which the right to change the beneficiary is reserved to the policyholder.

INTENDED VERSUS INCIDENTAL BENEFICIARIES

The benefit that an **incidental beneficiary** receives from a contract between two parties is unintentional. Because the benefit is *unintentional*, an incidental beneficiary cannot sue to enforce the contract.

DETERMINING WHETHER A THIRD PARTY IS AN INTENDED OR AN INCIDENTAL BENEFICIARY In determining whether a third party beneficiary is an intended or an incidental beneficiary, the courts generally use the *reasonable person* test; that is, a beneficiary will be considered an intended beneficiary if a reasonable person in the position of the beneficiary

---

8. 20 N.Y. 268 (1859).

9. *Seaver v. Ransom*, 224 N.Y. 233, 120 N.E. 639 (1918).

10. Defenses against third party beneficiaries are given in the *Restatement (Second) of Contracts*, Section 309.

would believe that the promisee *intended* to confer on the beneficiary the right to bring suit to enforce the contract. The court also looks at some other factors. The presence of one or more of the following factors strongly indicates that the third party is an *intended* (rather than an *incidental*) beneficiary of the contract:

1. Performance is rendered directly to the third party.
2. The third party has the right to control the details of performance.
3. The third party is expressly designated as the beneficiary in the contract.

Exhibit 16–3 graphically illustrates the distinction between intended beneficiaries and incidental beneficiaries.

In the following case, a subcontractor claimed to be an intended beneficiary of the general contractor's contractual promise to obtain property insurance after the construction of an addition to a building was completed. The case illustrates how resolving the issue of whether a beneficiary is intended or incidental can have serious consequences for the beneficiary's liability.

CASE 16.3

Midwestern Indemnity Co. v. Systems Builders, Inc.

Court of Appeals
of Indiana, 2004.
801 N.E.2d 661.

SHARPNACK, JUDGE.

This appeal arises out of a contract for the construction of an addition to an industrial building and the collapse of that addition due to an accumulation of snow on its roof. The plaintiff and appellant is Midwestern Indemnity Company ("Midwestern"), which brought suit [in place] of Louise Litwick and Action Steel, Inc. ("Action Steel"), to recover the amount it paid to its insureds for damage to their property incurred by the collapse of the addition. The defendant and appellee is Varco-Pruden Building ("Varco-Pruden"), a subcontractor of Systems Builders, Inc. ("Systems Builders"), the general contractor for the construction of the building addition. Varco-Pruden designed and erected the addition. * * *

* * * *

* * * Litwick, in her capacity as the owner of Action Steel, entered into a contract with Systems Builders for the construction of an addition to a commercial building. Systems Builders was the general contractor and agreed to erect a building designed and manufactured by Varco-Pruden. * * *

The construction of the building addition was completed in the summer of 1995. On January 16, 1996, a snowstorm hit the Indianapolis area and a portion of the addition collapsed. Action Steel was insured by Midwestern under a policy issued after completion of the construction. Midwestern paid $1,391,818.90 to Action Steel for the loss. * * *

On January 16, 1998, Midwestern [which, because it paid for the loss, stood in the place of] Action Steel, filed an amended complaint for damages to recover what it had paid. The complaint asserted * * * claims against Varco-Pruden * * * .

Varco-Pruden filed [a motion] for summary judgment [arguing in part that it was a third party beneficiary of the waiver clause in the contract between Action Steel and Systems Builders]. * * *

* * * *

The trial court granted Varco-Pruden's * * * motion * * * .

* * * *

Here, the construction contract includes language indicating that if Action Steel obtained property insurance after project completion it would waive its rights against contractors and subcontractors. Specifically, * * * Section 11.3.5 of the construction contract discusses the acquisition of property insurance after project completion and provides that "if after final payment property insurance is to be provided on the completed Project through a policy or policies other than those insuring the Project during the construction period, the Owner shall waive all rights in accordance with the terms of Subparagraph 11.3.7 [the waiver clause]." Further, Section 11.3.1 addresses the extent of property insurance and provides that "[t]his insurance shall include interests of the Owner, the Contractor, Subcontractors and Sub-subcontractors in the Work." Varco-Pruden, as the designer, manufacturer, and supplier of the pre-engineered building system used in the construction of the building addition, was a subcontractor within the meaning of Section 11.3.1 of the construction contract. Moreover, Section 11.3.7 * * * pro-

CASE 16.3 | **Continued** vides that "[t]he Owner and Contractor waive all rights against (1) each other and any of their subcontractors, sub-subcontractors, agents and employees." * * *

* * * *A person or entity who is not a party to a contract may directly enforce that contract as a third party beneficiary if: (1) the parties intend to benefit a third party; (2) the contract imposes a duty on one of the parties in favor of the third party; and (3) the performance of the terms of the contract renders a direct benefit to the third party.* [Emphasis added.]

Varco-Pruden argues that it has satisfied the first element, which requires that the parties intended to benefit a third party. The plain reading of the construction contract indicates that Action Steel intended to benefit Varco-Pruden. * * * Accordingly, the first element is satisfied because when Action Steel purchased property insurance after the project was completed, it intended that subcontractors, such as Varco-Pruden, would benefit from the waiver * * * clause.

Varco-Pruden also argues that it has satisfied the second element, which requires that the contract impose a duty upon one of the parties in favor of the third party. Here, * * * Section 11.3.5 of the construction contract provides that if Action Steel purchased property insurance after project completion, it agreed to waive its right * * * with respect to subcontractors such as Varco-Pruden. Accordingly, the second element is satisfied because the construction contract imposed a duty upon Action Steel in favor of Varco-Pruden.

Finally, Varco-Pruden argues that it has satisfied the final element, which requires that the performance of the terms of the contract render a direct benefit to a third party. Again, the construction contract provides that if Action Steel purchased property insurance after project completion it would waive its right * * * with regard to subcontractors, thereby requiring that it render a direct benefit to those subcontractors, namely Varco-Pruden. Varco-Pruden has satisfied all three elements of the third party beneficiary test. Thus, Varco-Pruden is a third party beneficiary and can enforce the waiver * * * clause contained within the construction contract.

* * * *

For the foregoing reasons, we affirm the judgment of the trial court granting Varco-Pruden's [motion] for summary judgment.

QUESTIONS

1. For what reasons did the state intermediate appellate court uphold the lower court's summary judgment?
2. If the collapse of the building had been due to the negligence of a subcontractor, how might that party argue successfully against recovery?

EXHIBIT 16-3 **Third Party Beneficiaries**

CONTRACT THAT BENEFITS A THIRD PARTY

INTENDED BENEFICIARY
An intended beneficiary is a third party
- To whom performance is rendered directly
- Who has the right to control the details of the performance *or*
- Who is designated a beneficiary in the contract

CAN SUE TO ENFORCE THE CONTRACT

INCIDENTAL BENEFICIARY
An incidental beneficiary is a third party
- Who benefits from a contract but whose benefit was not the purpose for the contract
- Who has no rights in the contract

CANNOT SUE TO ENFORCE THE CONTRACT

TWO EXAMPLES OF INCIDENTAL THIRD PARTY BENEFICIARIES As mentioned, if a third party is deemed an *incidental beneficiary*, she or he has no rights in the contract and cannot enforce it against the promisor. The following are examples of incidental beneficiaries:

1. Escobedo contracts with Monell to build a cottage on Monell's land. Escobedo's plans specify that All-Weather Insulation Company's insulation materials must be used in constructing the house. All-Weather is an incidental beneficiary and cannot enforce the contract against Escobedo by attempting to require that Escobedo purchase its insulation materials.

2. Bollow contracts with Coolidge to build a recreational facility on Coolidge's land. Once the facility is constructed, it will greatly enhance the property values in the neighborhood. If Bollow subsequently refuses to build the facility, Tran, Coolidge's neighbor, cannot enforce the contract against Bollow because Tran is an incidental beneficiary.

REVIEWING THIRD PARTY RIGHTS

Myrtle Jackson owns several commercial buildings that she leases to businesses, one of which is a restaurant. The lease states that tenants are responsible for securing all necessary insurance policies but the landlord is obligated to keep the buildings in good repair. The owner of the restaurant, Joe McCall, tells his restaurant manager to purchase insurance, but the manager never does so. Jackson tells her son-in-law, Rob Dunn, to perform any necessary maintenance for the buildings. Dunn knows that the ceiling in the restaurant needs repair but fails to do anything about it. One day a customer, Ian Fleming, is dining in the restaurant when a chunk of the ceiling falls on his head and fractures his skull. Fleming files suit against the restaurant and discovers that there is no insurance policy in effect. Fleming then files suit against Jackson, arguing that he is an intended third party beneficiary of the lease provision requiring insurance and thus can sue Jackson for failing to enforce the lease (which requires the restaurant to carry insurance). Using the information presented in the chapter, answer the following questions.

1. Can Jackson delegate her duty to maintain the buildings to Dunn? Why or why not?

2. Who can be held liable for Dunn's failure to fix the ceiling, Jackson or Dunn?

3. Was Fleming an intended third party beneficiary of the lease between Jackson and McCall? Why or why not?

4. Suppose that Jackson tells Dan Stryker, a local builder to whom she owes $50,000, that he can collect the rents from the buildings' tenants until the debt is satisfied. Is this a valid assignment? Why or why not? What happens if the tenants are not notified of the assignment and continue to pay rent to Jackson? Have the tenants discharged their obligations? Explain.

TERMS AND CONCEPTS TO REVIEW

alienation 313

assignee 309

assignment 309

assignor 309

delegatee 314

delegation 309

delegator 314

incidental beneficiary 317

intended beneficiary 316

obligee 309

obligor 309

privity of contract 309

third party beneficiary 316

QUESTIONS AND CASE PROBLEMS

16–1. Alexander has been accepted as a freshman at a college two hundred miles from his home for the fall semester. Alexander's wealthy uncle, Michael, decides to give Alexander a car for Christmas. In November, Michael makes a contract with Jackson Auto Sales to purchase a new car for $18,000 to be delivered to Alexander just before the Christmas holidays, in mid-December. The title to the car is to be in Alexander's name. Michael pays the full purchase price, calls Alexander and tells him about the gift, and takes off for a six-month vacation in Europe. Is Alexander an intended third party beneficiary of the contract between Michael and Jackson Auto Sales? Suppose that Jackson Auto Sales never delivers the car to Alexander. Does Alexander have the right to sue Jackson Auto Sales for breaching its contract with Michael? Explain.

16–2. QUESTION WITH SAMPLE ANSWER

Five years ago, Hensley purchased a house. At that time, being unable to pay the full purchase price, she borrowed money from Thrift Savings and Loan, which in turn took a 6.5 percent mortgage on the house. The mortgage contract did not prohibit the assignment of the mortgage. Then Hensley secured a new job in another city and sold the house to Sylvia. The purchase price included payment to Hensley of the value of her equity and the assumption of the mortgage debt still owed to Thrift. At the time the contract between Hensley and Sylvia was made, Thrift did not know about or consent to the sale. On the basis of these facts, if Sylvia defaults in making the house payments to Thrift, what are Thrift's rights? Discuss.

For a sample answer to this question, go to Appendix I at the end of this text.

16–3. Marsala, a college student, signs a one-year lease agreement that runs from September 1 to August 31. The lease agreement specifies that the lease cannot be assigned without the landlord's consent. In late May, Marsala decides not to go to summer school and assigns the balance of the lease (three months) to a close friend, Fred. The landlord objects to the assignment and denies Fred access to the apartment. Marsala claims that Fred is financially sound and should be allowed the full rights and privileges of an assignee. Discuss fully who is correct, the landlord or Marsala.

16–4. Inez has a specific set of plans to build a sailboat. The plans are detailed in nature, and any boatbuilder can construct the boat. Inez secures bids, and the low bid is made by the Whale of a Boat Corp. Inez contracts with Whale to build the boat for $4,000. Whale then receives unexpected business from elsewhere. To meet the delivery date in the contract with Inez, Whale delegates its obligation to build the boat, without Inez's consent, to Quick Brothers, a reputable boatbuilder. When the boat is ready for delivery, Inez learns of the delegation and refuses to accept delivery, even though the boat is built to her specifications. Discuss fully whether Inez is obligated to accept and pay for the boat. Would your answer be any different if Inez had not had a specific set of plans but had instead contracted with Whale to design and build a sailboat for $4,000? Explain.

16–5. ASSIGNMENT. Fox Brothers Enterprises, Inc., agreed to convey to Canfield a lot, Lot 23, in a subdivision known as Fox Estates, together with a one-year option to purchase Lot 24. The agreement did not contain any prohibitions, restrictions, or limitations against assignments. Canfield paid the price of $20,000 and took title to Lot 23. Thereafter, Canfield assigned his option right in Lot 24 to the Scotts. When the Scotts tried to exercise their right to the option, Fox Brothers refused to convey the property to them. The Scotts then brought a suit for specific performance. What was the result? [*Scott v. Fox Brothers Enterprises, Inc.*, 667 P.2d 773 (Colo.App. 1983)]

16–6. ASSIGNMENT. Joseph LeMieux, of Maine, won $373,000 in a lottery operated by the Tri-State Lotto Commission. The lottery is sponsored by the three northern New England states and is administered in Vermont. In accordance with its usual payment plan, Tri-State was to pay the $373,000 to LeMieux in annual installments over a twenty-year period. LeMieux assigned his rights to the lottery payments for the years 1996 through 2006 to Singer Freidlander Corp. for the sum of $80,000. LeMieux and Singer Freidlander (the plaintiffs) sought a court judgment authorizing their assignment agreement despite Tri-State's regulation barring the assignment of lottery proceeds. The trial court granted Tri-State's motion for summary judgment. On appeal, the plaintiffs argued that Tri-State's regulation was invalid. Is it? Discuss fully. [*LeMieux v. Tri-State Lotto Commission*, 666 A.2d 1170 (Vt. 1995)]

16–7. CASE PROBLEM WITH SAMPLE ANSWER

The National Collegiate Athletic Association (NCAA) regulates intercollegiate amateur athletics among the more than 1,200 colleges and universities with whom it contracts. Among other things, the NCAA maintains rules of eligibility for student participation in intercollegiate athletic events. Jeremy Bloom, a high school football and track star, was recruited to play football at the University of Colorado (CU). Before enrolling, he competed in Olympic and professional World Cup skiing events, becoming the World Cup champion in freestyle moguls. During the Olympics, Bloom appeared on MTV and was offered other paid entertainment opportunities, including a chance to host a show on Nickelodeon.

Bloom was also paid to endorse certain ski equipment and contracted to model clothing for Tommy Hilfiger. On Bloom's behalf, CU asked the NCAA to waive its rules restricting student-athlete endorsement and media activities. The NCAA refused, and Bloom quit the activities to play football for CU. He filed a suit in a Colorado state court against the NCAA, however, asserting breach of contract on the ground that its rules permitted these activities if they were needed to support a professional athletic career. The NCAA responded that Bloom did not have standing to pursue this claim. What contract has allegedly been breached in this case? Is Bloom a party to this contract? If not, is he a third party beneficiary of it, and if so, is his status intended or incidental? Explain. [*Bloom v. National Collegiate Athletic Association*, 93 P.3d 621 (Colo.App. 2004)]

To view a sample answer for this case problem, go to this book's Web site at http://wbl.westbuslaw.com, select "Chapter 16," and click on "Case Problem with Sample Answer."

16–8. NOTICE OF ASSIGNMENT. As the building services manager for Fulton County, Georgia, Steve Fullard oversaw custodial services. Fullard determined which services to contract for, received the bids, and recommended the selection of a vendor. After the selection of Total Quality Maintenance of Georgia (TQM) on a particular contract, Fullard supervised TQM's performance and received and processed its invoices. Later, TQM assigned its unpaid invoices to American Factors of Nashville, Inc., which forwarded copies to Fullard with a statement rubber-stamped on each invoice. The statement began with the word "NOTICE" and the name, address, and phone number of American Factors. It also said, "Remittance to other than American Factors of Nashville, Inc., does not constitute payment of this Invoice." Included with each invoice was a certification by TQM's president that the invoice had been assigned to American Factors. Nevertheless, the county paid TQM on these invoices, and American Factors filed a suit in a Georgia state court against the county, claiming that it still owed American Factors. Did the county have sufficient notice of TQM's assignment? Can the county

be required to pay the same invoice twice? Why or why not? [*Fulton County v. American Factors of Nashville, Inc.*, 551 S.E.2d 781 (Ga.App. 2001)]

16–9. THIRD PARTY BENEFICIARY. Acciai Speciali Terni USA, Inc. (AST), hired a carrier to ship steel sheets and coils from Italy to the United States on the *M/V Berane*. The ship's receipt for the goods included a forum-selection clause, which stated that any dispute would be "decided in the country where the carrier has his principal place of business." The receipt also contained a "Himalaya" clause, which extended "every right, exemption from liability, defense and immunity" that the carrier enjoyed to those acting on the carrier's behalf. Transcom Terminals, Ltd., was the U.S. stevedore—that is, Transcom off-loaded the vessel and stored the cargo for eventual delivery to AST. Finding the cargo damaged, AST filed a suit in a federal district court against Transcom and others, charging in part negligence in the off-loading. Transcom filed a motion to dismiss on the basis of the forum-selection clause. Transcom argued that it was an intended third party beneficiary of this provision through the Himalaya clause. Is Transcom correct? What should the court rule? Explain. [*Acciai Speciali Terni USA, Inc. v. M/V Berane*, 181 F.Supp.2d 458 (D.Md. 2002)]

16–10. VIDEO QUESTION

Go to this text's Web site at http://wbl.westbuslaw.com and select "Chapter 16." Click on "Video Questions" and view the video titled *Third Party Beneficiaries*. Then answer the following questions.

(a) Discuss whether a valid contract was formed when Oscar and Vinny bet on the outcome of a football game. Would Vinny be able to enforce the contract in court?

(b) Is the Fresh Air Fund an incidental or intended beneficiary? Why?

(c) Can Maria sue to enforce Vinny's promise to donate Oscar's winnings to the Fresh Air Fund?

LAW | on the Web

For updated links to resources available on the Web, as well as a variety of other materials, visit this text's Web site at http://wbl.westbuslaw.com.

You can find a summary of the law governing assignments, as well as "SmartAgreement" forms that you can use for various types of contracts, including assignments, at

http://www.smartagreements.com

LEGAL RESEARCH EXERCISES ON THE WEB

Go to **http://wbl.westbuslaw.com**, the Web site that accompanies this text. Select "Chapter 16" and click on "Internet Exercises." There you will find the following Internet research exercises that you can perform to learn more about topics covered in this chapter.

Activity 16–1: **LEGAL PERSPECTIVE**
New York's Leading Decisions

Activity 16–2: **MANAGEMENT PERSPECTIVE**
Professional Liability to Third Parties

CHAPTER 17
Performance and Discharge

Just as rules are necessary to determine when a legally enforceable contract exists, so also are they required to determine when one of the parties can justifiably say, "I have fully performed, so I am now discharged from my obligations under this contract." The legal environment of business requires the identification of some point at which the parties can reasonably know that their duties are at an end.

The most common way to **discharge,** or terminate, one's contractual duties is by the **performance** of those duties. For example, a buyer and seller have a contract for the sale of a 2006 Buick for $34,000. This contract will be discharged on the performance by the parties of their obligations under the contract—the buyer's payment of $34,000 to the seller and the seller's transfer of possession of the Buick to the buyer.

The duty to perform under a contract may be *conditioned* on the occurrence or nonoccurrence of a certain event, or the duty may be *absolute*. In the first part of this chapter, we look at conditions of performance and the degree of performance required. We then examine some other ways in which a contract can be discharged, including discharge by agreement of the parties and discharge by operation of law.

SECTION 1 | Conditions

In most contracts, promises of performance are not expressly conditioned or qualified. Instead, they are *absolute promises*. They must be performed, or the parties promising the acts will be in breach of contract. For example, Jerome contracts to sell Alfonso a painting for $3,000. The parties' promises—Jerome's transfer of the painting to Alfonso and Alfonso's payment of $3,000 to Jerome—are unconditional. The payment does not have to be made if the painting is not transferred.

In some situations, however, performance is contingent on the occurrence or nonoccurrence of a certain event. A **condition** is a possible future event, the occurrence or nonoccurrence of which will trigger the performance of a legal obligation or terminate an existing obligation under a contract.[1] If this condition

is not satisfied, the obligations of the parties are discharged. Suppose that Alfonso, in the previous example, offers to purchase Jerome's painting only if an independent appraisal indicates that it is worth at least $3,000. Jerome accepts Alfonso's offer. Their obligations (promises) are conditioned on the outcome of the appraisal. Should the condition not be satisfied (for example, if the appraiser deems the value of the painting to be only $1,500), the parties' obligations to each other are discharged and cannot be enforced.

Three types of conditions can be present in contracts: conditions *precedent*, conditions *subsequent*, and *concurrent* conditions. Conditions are also classified as *express* or *implied*.

CONDITIONS PRECEDENT

A condition that must be fulfilled before a party's performance can be required is called a **condition precedent.** The condition precedes the absolute duty to perform, as in the Jerome-Alfonso example just discussed. Real estate contracts frequently are conditioned on the buyer's ability to obtain financing. For example, Fisher promises to buy Calvin's house if

---

1. The *Restatement (Second) of Contracts*, Section 224, defines a condition as "an event, not certain to occur, which must occur, unless its nonoccurrence is excused, before performance under a contract becomes due."

Salvation Bank approves Fisher's mortgage application. The Fisher-Calvin contract is therefore subject to a condition precedent—the bank's approval of Fisher's mortgage application. If the bank does not approve the application, the contract will fail because the condition precedent was not met. Insurance contracts frequently specify that certain conditions must be met before the insurance company will be obligated to perform under the contract.

CONDITIONS SUBSEQUENT

When a condition operates to terminate a party's absolute promise to perform, it is called a **condition subsequent.** The condition follows, or is subsequent to, the arising of an absolute duty to perform. If the condition occurs, the party need not perform any further. For example, imagine that a law firm hires Koker, a recent law school graduate and newly licensed attorney. Their contract provides that the firm's obligation to continue employing Koker is discharged if Koker fails to maintain her license to practice law. This is a condition subsequent because a failure to maintain the license would discharge a duty that has already arisen.

Generally, conditions precedent are common; conditions subsequent are rare. The *Restatement (Second) of Contracts* does not use the terms *condition subsequent* and *condition precedent* but refers to both simply as conditions.[2]

CONCURRENT CONDITIONS

When each party's absolute duty to perform is conditioned on the other party's absolute duty to perform, there are **concurrent conditions.** Concurrent conditions occur only when the parties expressly or impliedly are to perform their respective duties *simultaneously.* For example, if a buyer promises to pay for goods when they are delivered by the seller, each party's absolute duty to perform is conditioned on the other party's absolute duty to perform. The buyer's duty to pay for the goods does not become absolute until the seller either delivers or tenders the goods. (**Tender** is an unconditional offer to perform by one who is ready, willing, and able to do so.) Likewise, the seller's duty to deliver the goods does not become absolute until the buyer tenders or actually makes payment. Therefore, neither can recover from the other

for breach unless he or she first tenders his or her own performance.

EXPRESS AND IMPLIED-IN-FACT CONDITIONS

Conditions can also be classified as express or implied in fact. *Express conditions* are provided for by the parties' agreement. An express condition is usually prefaced by the word *if, provided, after,* or *when.*

Conditions *implied in fact* are similar to express conditions because they are understood to be part of the agreement, but they are not found in the express language of the agreement. The court infers them from the promises. For example, Wellbuilt Construction builds a house for Kirby under a contract that includes a one-year warranty against defects in materials and construction—that is, Wellbuilt promises to fix or replace anything attributable to its work that goes wrong within a year. Clearly, Wellbuilt could not be required to fix a defect that it did not know existed. Thus, a court would likely conclude that Kirby's notifying Wellbuilt of a defect is an implied-in-fact condition of Wellbuilt's duty to correct the defects.

SECTION 2 | Discharge by Performance

The great majority of contracts are discharged by performance. The contract comes to an end when both parties fulfill their respective duties by performing the acts they have promised. Performance can also be accomplished by *tender.* Therefore, a seller who places goods at the disposal of a buyer has tendered delivery and can demand payment. A buyer who offers to pay for goods has tendered payment and can demand delivery of the goods. Once performance has been tendered, the party making the tender has done everything possible to carry out the terms of the contract. If the other party then refuses to perform, the party making the tender can sue for breach of contract.

TYPES OF PERFORMANCE

There are two basic types of performance—*complete performance* and *substantial performance.* A contract may stipulate that performance must meet the personal satisfaction of either the contracting party or a third party. Such a provision must be considered in determining whether the performance rendered satisfies the contract.

---

2. *Restatement (Second) of Contracts*, Section 224.

COMPLETE PERFORMANCE When a party performs exactly as agreed, there is no question as to whether the contract has been performed. When a party's performance is perfect, it is said to be complete.

Normally, conditions expressly stated in a contract must be fully satisfied for complete performance to take place. For example, most construction contracts require the builder to meet certain specifications. If the specifications are conditions, complete performance is required to avoid material breach (material breach will be discussed shortly). If the conditions are met, the other party to the contract must then fulfill her or his obligation to pay the builder. If the specifications are not conditions and if the builder, without the other party's permission, fails to comply with the specifications, performance is not complete. What effect does such a failure have on the other party's obligation to pay? The answer is part of the doctrine of *substantial performance*.

SUBSTANTIAL PERFORMANCE A party who in good faith performs substantially all of the terms of a contract can enforce the contract against the other party under the doctrine of substantial performance. Note that good faith is required. Intentionally failing to comply with the terms is a breach of the contract.

—Confer Most Benefits Promised in the Contract. Generally, to qualify as substantial, the performance must not vary greatly from the performance promised in the contract, and it must create substantially the same benefits as those promised in the contract. If the omission, variance, or defect in performance is unimportant and can easily be compensated for by awarding damages, a court is likely to hold that the contract has been substantially performed.

Courts decide whether the performance was substantial on a case-by-case basis, examining all of the facts of the particular situation. For example, in a construction contract, a court would look at the intended purpose of the structure and the expense required to bring the structure into complete compliance with the contract. Thus, the exact point at which performance is considered substantial varies.

—Entitles Other Party to Damages. Because substantial performance is not perfect, the other party is entitled to damages to compensate for the failure to comply with the contract. The measure of the damages is the cost to bring the object of the contract into compliance with its terms, if that cost is reasonable under the circumstances. If the cost is unreasonable, the measure of damages is the difference in value between the performance that was rendered and the performance that would have been rendered if the contract had been performed completely.

The following classic case emphasizes that there is no exact formula for deciding when a contract has been substantially performed.

CASE 17.1 **Jacob & Youngs v. Kent**

Court of Appeals
of New York, 1921.
230 N.Y. 239,
129 N.E. 889.

CARDOZO, J. [Judge]

The plaintiff built a country residence for the defendant at a cost of upwards of $77,000, and now sues to recover a balance of $3,483.46, remaining unpaid. The work of construction ceased in June, 1914, and the defendant then began to occupy the dwelling. There was no complaint of defective performance until March, 1915. One of the specifications for the plumbing work provides that—

> All wrought-iron pipe must be well galvanized, lap welded pipe of the grade known as "standard pipe" of Reading manufacture.

The defendant learned in March, 1915, that some of the pipe, instead of being made in Reading, was the product of other factories. The plaintiff was accordingly directed by the architect to do the work anew. The plumbing was then encased within the walls except in a few places where it had to be exposed. Obedience to the order meant more than the substitution of other pipe. It meant the demolition at great expense of substantial parts of the completed structure. The plaintiff left the work untouched, and asked for a certificate that the final payment was due. Refusal of the certificate was followed by this suit [in a New York state court].

The evidence sustains a finding that the omission of the prescribed brand of pipe was neither fraudulent nor willful. It was the result of the oversight and inattention of the plaintiff's subcontractor. Reading pipe is distinguished from Cohoes pipe and other brands only by the name of the manufacturer stamped upon it at intervals of between six and seven feet. Even

CASE 17.1 | Continued

the defendant's architect, though he inspected the pipe upon arrival, failed to notice the discrepancy. The plaintiff tried to show that the brands installed, though made by other manufacturers, were the same in quality, in appearance, in market value, and in cost as the brand stated in the contract—that they were, indeed, the same thing, though manufactured in another place. The evidence was excluded, and a verdict directed for the defendant. The [state intermediate appellate court] reversed, and granted a new trial.

We think the evidence, if admitted, would have supplied some basis for the inference that the defect was insignificant in its relation to the project. The courts never say that one who makes a contract fills the measure of his duty by less than full performance. They do say, however, that *an omission, both trivial and innocent, will sometimes be atoned for by allowance of the resulting damage, and will not always be the breach of a condition* * * * . [Emphasis added.]

* * * Where the line is to be drawn between the important and the trivial cannot be settled by a formula. In the nature of the case precise boundaries are impossible. The same omission may take on one aspect or another according to its setting. Substitution of equivalents may not have the same significance in fields of art on the one side and in those of mere utility on the other. Nowhere will change be tolerated, however, if it is so dominant or pervasive as in any real or substantial measure to frustrate the purpose of the contract. There is no general license to install whatever, in the builder's judgment, may be regarded as "just as good." The question is one of degree, to be answered, if there is doubt, by the triers of the facts, and, if the inferences are certain, by the judges of the law. *We must weigh the purpose to be served, the desire to be gratified, the excuse for deviation from the letter, the cruelty of enforced adherence. Then only can we tell whether literal fulfillment is to be implied by law as a condition.* * * * [Emphasis added.]

In the circumstances of this case, we think the measure of the allowance is not the cost of replacement, which would be great, but the difference in value, which would be either nominal or nothing. Some of the exposed sections might perhaps have been replaced at moderate expense. The defendant did not limit his demand to them, but treated the plumbing as a unit to be corrected from cellar to roof. In point of fact, the plaintiff never reached the stage at which evidence of the extent of the allowance became necessary. The trial court had excluded evidence that the defect was unsubstantial, and in view of that ruling there was no occasion for the plaintiff to go farther with an offer of proof. We think, however, that the offer, if it had been made, would not of necessity have been defective because directed to difference in value. It is true that in most cases the cost of replacement is the measure. The owner is entitled to the money which will permit him to complete, unless the cost of completion is grossly and unfairly out of proportion to the good to be attained. When that is true, the measure is the difference in value. * * * The rule that gives a remedy in cases of substantial performance with compensation for defects of trivial or inappreciable importance has been developed by the courts as an instrument of justice. The measure of the allowance must be shaped to the same end.

The order should be affirmed, and judgment absolute directed in favor of the plaintiff upon the stipulation, with costs in all courts.

QUESTIONS

1. The New York Court of Appeals found that Jacob & Youngs had substantially performed the contract. To what, if any, remedy is Kent entitled?
2. A requirement of substantial performance is good faith. Do you think that Jacob & Youngs substantially performed all of the terms of the contract in good faith? Why or why not?

IMPACT OF THIS CASE ON TODAY'S LAW

At the time of the *Jacob* case, some courts did not apply the doctrine of substantial performance to disputes involving breaches of contract. This landmark decision contributed to a developing trend toward equity and fairness in those circumstances. Today, an unintentional and trivial omission or deviation from the terms of a contract will not prevent its enforcement but will permit an adjustment in the value of its performance.

PERFORMANCE TO THE SATISFACTION OF ONE OF THE PARTIES Contracts often state that completed work must personally satisfy one of the parties. The question then arises whether this satisfaction becomes a condition precedent, requiring actual personal satisfaction or approval for discharge, or whether the test of satisfaction is an absolute promise requiring such performance as would satisfy a *reasonable person* (substantial performance).

—*Personal-Service Contracts.* When the subject matter of the contract is personal, a contract to be performed to the satisfaction of one of the parties is conditioned, and performance must actually satisfy that party. For example, contracts for portraits, works of art, medical or dental work, and tailoring are considered personal. Therefore, only the personal satisfaction of the party will be sufficient to fulfill the condition.

To illustrate: Suppose that Williams agrees to paint a portrait of Hirshon's daughter for $750. The contract provides that Hirshon must be satisfied with the portrait. If Hirshon is not, she will not be required to pay for it. The only requirement imposed on Hirshon is that she behave honestly and in good faith. If Hirshon expresses dissatisfaction only to avoid paying for the portrait, the condition of satisfaction is excused, and her duty to pay becomes absolute. (Of course, the jury, or the judge acting as a jury, will have to decide whether she is acting honestly.)[3]

—*All Other Contracts.* Contracts that involve mechanical fitness, utility, or marketability need only be performed to the satisfaction of a *reasonable* person. For example, construction contracts and manufacturing contracts are usually *not* considered to be personal, so the party's personal satisfaction is normally irrelevant. As long as the performance will satisfy a reasonable person, the contract is fulfilled.[4]

PERFORMANCE TO THE SATISFACTION OF A THIRD PARTY At times, contracts may require performance to the satisfaction of a third party (not a party to the contract). To illustrate: Assume that you contract to pave several city streets. The contract provides that the work will be done "to the satisfaction of Phil Hopper, the supervising engineer." In this situation, the courts are divided.

A few courts require the personal satisfaction of the third party—in this example, Phil Hopper. If Hopper is not satisfied, you will not be paid, even if a reasonable person would be satisfied. Again, the personal judgment must be made honestly, or the condition will be excused.

A majority of courts, however, require the work to be satisfactory to a reasonable person. Thus, even if Hopper is dissatisfied with the paving work, you will be paid, as long as a qualified supervising engineer would have been satisfied. All of the above examples demonstrate the necessity for *clear, specific wording in contracts*.

MATERIAL BREACH OF CONTRACT

A **breach of contract** is the nonperformance of a contractual duty. The breach is *material*[5] when performance is not at least substantial. If there is a material breach, then the nonbreaching party is excused from the performance of contractual duties and has a cause of action to sue for damages resulting from the breach. If the breach is *minor* (not material), the nonbreaching party's duty to perform can sometimes be suspended until the breach has been remedied, but the duty to perform is not entirely excused. Once the minor breach has been cured, the nonbreaching party must resume performance of the contractual obligations undertaken.

Any breach entitles the nonbreaching party to sue for damages, but only a material breach discharges the nonbreaching party from the contract. The policy underlying these rules allows contracts to go forward when only minor problems occur but allows them to be terminated if major difficulties arise.

Under what circumstances is an employer excused from further performance under a contract with an employee? That was the question in the following case.

---

3. For a classic case illustrating this principle, see *Gibson v. Cranage,* 39 Mich. 49 (1878).

4. If, however, the contract specifically states that it is to be fulfilled to the "personal" satisfaction of one or more of the parties, and the parties so intended, the outcome will probably be different.

---

5. *Restatement (Second) of Contracts,* Section 241.

CASE 17.2 — Shah v. Cover-It, Inc.

Appellate Court of
Connecticut. 2004.
86 Conn.App. 71,
859 A.2d 959.

BACKGROUND AND FACTS *In November 1997, Cover-It, Inc., hired Khalid Shah to work as its structural engineering manager. Shah agreed to work a flexible schedule of thirty-five hours per week. In exchange, he would receive an annual salary of $70,000 for five years, a 2 percent commission on the sales of products that he designed, three weeks of paid vacation after one year, a company car, time off to attend to prior professional obligations, and certain other benefits. Either party could terminate the contract with ninety days' written notice, but if Cover-It terminated it, Shah would receive monthly payments for the rest of the five-year term.[a] In June 1998, Shah went on vacation and did not return until September. In mid-October, Brian Goldwitz, Cover-It's owner and president, terminated Shah's contract. Shah filed a suit in a Connecticut state court against Cover-It and others. The court determined that Shah had breached the contract and rendered a judgment in the defendants' favor. Shah appealed to a state intermediate appellate court.*

IN THE LANGUAGE OF THE COURT

SCHALLER, J. [Judge]

* * * *

On appeal, the plaintiff claims that the court improperly found that he had breached the contract or, in the alternative, that any breach was not material. Specifically, the plaintiff argues that the court failed to identify an express term or condition that was breached and instead merely found that certain acts, considered together, demonstrated a material breach prior to the termination of his employment. Therefore, according to the plaintiff, the defendants were not relieved of their obligations, under the terms of the contract, to pay his full salary for ninety days and to pay his post-termination salary pursuant to the schedule set forth in the contract. * * *

* * * *

It is a general rule of contract law that a total breach of the contract by one party relieves the injured party of any further duty to perform further obligations under the contract. [Emphasis added.]

* * * Section 241 of the *Restatement (Second) of Contracts* provides:

In determining whether a failure to render or to offer performance is material, the following circumstances are significant: (a) the extent to which the injured party will be deprived of the benefit which he reasonably expected; (b) the extent to which the injured party can be adequately compensated for the part of that benefit of which he will be deprived; (c) the extent to which the party failing to perform or to offer to perform will suffer forfeiture; (d) the likelihood that the party failing to perform or to offer to perform will cure his failure, taking account of all the circumstances including any reasonable assurances; [and] (e) the extent to which the behavior of the party failing to perform or to offer to perform comports with standards of good faith and fair dealing.

The standards of materiality are to be applied in the light of the facts of each case in such a way as to further the purpose of securing for each party his expectation of an exchange of performances. Section 241 therefore states circumstances, not rules, which are to be considered in determining whether a particular failure is material. [Emphasis added.]

In the present case, the court found that the plaintiff took a ten-week vacation, which exceeded the time authorized. After the plaintiff returned, he reported for work only two or three days per week and spent long periods of time visiting Internet Web sites that were unrelated to his professional duties. Additionally, after being instructed by [Cover-It's] human resources manager to document his attendance by use of a time clock, the plaintiff refused and simply marked his time sheets with a "P" for present. Last, the court found that when Goldwitz asked when certain designs would be completed, the plaintiff responded that he was not sure and that he would take his time in completing them. When reviewing those findings in light

a. The contract provided that for up to two years of service, Shah would be paid $20,000 per year; for three years of service, $30,000 per year; and for four years of service, $40,000 per year.

CONTINUED

CASE 17.2 | Continued of the factors set forth in [Section] 241 of the *Restatement (Second) of Contracts*, we conclude that the court's finding of a material breach was not clearly erroneous.

It is clear from the court's findings that the plaintiff failed to perform under the obligations of the employment contract. * * * One cannot recover upon a contract unless he has fully performed his own obligation under it, has tendered performance or has some legal excuse for not performing. As a result of the material breach by the plaintiff, the defendants were excused from further performance under the contract, and were relieved of the obligation to pay the plaintiff his full salary for ninety days and to pay his post-termination salary pursuant to the schedule set forth in the contract.

DECISION AND REMEDY *The state intermediate appellate court affirmed the judgment of the lower court. The appellate court held that Shah had materially breached his contract with Cover-It and that this breach excused Cover-It from further performance of its contractual duties, relieving the defendant of any obligation to continue paying Shah's salary.*

WHAT IF THE FACTS WERE DIFFERENT? *Suppose that during his ten-week absence Shah was fulfilling prior professional obligations and that on his return he met Cover-It's hours and time-keeping requirements. Further suppose that Shah responded to Goldwitz's questions about his projects with reasonable estimates. Would the outcome of the case have been different? Why or why not?*

ANTICIPATORY REPUDIATION

Before either party to a contract has a duty to perform, one of the parties may refuse to carry out his or her contractual obligations. This is called **anticipatory repudiation**[6] of the contract.

ANTICIPATORY REPUDIATION AND BREACH OF CONTRACT

When one party to a contract informs the other party, prior to the time for performance, that she or he does not intend to perform the contract, this anticipatory repudiation can discharge the nonbreaching party from performance. Until the nonbreaching party treats an early repudiation as a breach, however, the repudiating party can retract her or his anticipatory repudiation by proper notice and restore the parties to their original obligations.[7]

An anticipatory repudiation is treated as a present, material breach for two reasons.

1. The nonbreaching party should not be required to remain ready and willing to perform when the other party has already repudiated the contract.
2. The nonbreaching party should have the opportunity to seek a similar contract elsewhere.[8]

---

6. *Restatement (Second) of Contracts*, Section 253; Section 2–610 of the Uniform Commercial Code (UCC).
7. See UCC 2–611.
8. The doctrine of anticipatory repudiation first arose in the landmark case of *Hochster v. De La Tour*, 2 Ellis and Blackburn Reports 678 (1853), when the English court recognized the delay and expense inherent in a rule requiring a nonbreaching party to wait until the time of performance before suing on an anticipatory repudiation.

ANTICIPATORY REPUDIATION AND MARKET PRICES

Quite often, anticipatory repudiation occurs when performance of the contract would be extremely unfavorable to one of the parties because of a sharp fluctuation in market prices. For example, Martin Corporation contracts to manufacture and sell ten thousand personal computers to ComAge, a retailer of computer equipment that has five hundred outlet stores. Delivery is to be made six months from the date of the contract. The contract price is based on the seller's present costs of purchasing inventory parts from others. One month later, three inventory suppliers raise their prices to Martin.

Based on these prices, if Martin Corporation manufactures and sells the personal computers to ComAge at the contract price, Martin stands to lose $500,000. Martin immediately writes ComAge that it cannot deliver the ten thousand computers at the contract price. Martin's letter is an anticipatory repudiation of the contract. ComAge has the option of treating the repudiation as a material breach of contract and proceeding immediately to pursue remedies, even though the actual contract delivery date is still five months away.

TIME FOR PERFORMANCE

If no time for performance is stated in the contract, a *reasonable time* is implied.[9] If a specific time is stated,

---

9. See UCC 2–204, 2–309(1).

the parties must usually perform by that time. Unless time is expressly stated to be vital, however, a delay in performance will not destroy the performing party's right to payment. When time is expressly stated to be vital, or when it is construed to be "of the essence," the parties normally must perform within the stated time period because the time element becomes a condition.

The court in the following case explained the reasoning behind the requirement that payment be made within a reasonable time.

| CASE 17.3 | **Manganaro Corp. v. HITT Contracting, Inc.** |

United States
District Court,
District of Columbia, 2002.
193 F.Supp.2d 88.

COMPANY PROFILE *Lucent Technologies, Inc. (http://www.lucent.com), makes and sells telecommunications equipment and software, including products to build network infrastructures. Lucent's transmission, switching, wireless, and optical equipment is used in countries around the world. Originally part of AT&T, Inc., Lucent has cut costs over the last decade through massive layoffs and restructured its organization to focus on serving its largest customers, including AT&T.*

BACKGROUND AND FACTS *Lucent Technologies, Inc., engaged HITT Contracting, Inc. (HITT), to act as the general contractor for a construction project at Metropolitan Square in Washington, D.C. In July 1999, HITT hired Manganaro Corporation to perform drywall and ceiling work and to install two specialty ceilings. As the project progressed, Manganaro submitted invoices to HITT for payment to cover finished contract work. On average, HITT paid Manganaro within thirty-six days of each of these invoices. Manganaro was also expected to perform "change order" work, or work in excess of its contract, for which it could seek additional payment. By December 23, after completing all of the work except for the two specialty ceilings and certain punch list items,[a] Manganaro was owed more than $22,000 for unpaid contract work (the most recent invoice had been submitted on November 19) and $64,000 for unpaid change order work. Manganaro notified HITT that it was suspending performance until it was paid. HITT claimed that Manganaro was abandoning the project. HITT therefore terminated their contract and hired another subcontractor to finish the job. Manganaro filed a suit in a federal district court against HITT for breach of contract.*

IN THE LANGUAGE OF THE COURT

 FACCIOLA, United States Magistrate Judge.

* * * *

* * * The first question is * * * when was payment due, since the contract did not specify a date certain.

* * * On an average, Manganaro was being paid within 36 days for its contract work; the median was 34.5 days.

HITT seizes on this fact and asserts that the November 19, 1999, requisition was not past due when Manganaro ceased performance on December 23, 1999. That is, at best, half true. HITT paid for the contract work in a reasonably timely manner. But, HITT never paid for the change order work in a timely manner. * * *

Perhaps more significant is the amount outstanding when viewed absolutely or in relation to the total change order work billed. * * * By December 23, 1999, Manganaro had billed $108,301.28 in change order work * * * but had been paid $34,485.07. That is as unfair as it is unreasonable.

Since HITT's failure to pay the outstanding change order invoices by December 23, 1999, was unreasonable, Manganaro was entitled to suspend performance. * * * *[A] subcontractor who is unreasonably denied payment as he progresses towards completion is justified in suspending performance until he is paid.* * * * There is a special factor to be considered in the case of a building contract, or any other contract the financing of which requires a progressive expenditure in the course of performance. In these cases, one reason for providing for installment

---

a. After a contractor finishes work, the architect or another party inspects it and can demand that the contractor make the repairs that the party details on a *punch list*.

CONTINUED ▶

CASE 17.3 | **Continued**   payments as construction proceeds is to supply the funds necessary for the agreed performance; and failure to pay one or more installments is more likely to cause inconvenience and difficulty to the building contractor. Therefore, a failure to make one of the progress payments, even though the contract is not divisible into pairs of separate equivalents and the installment unpaid is only a small part of the whole consideration, is more likely to justify suspension of performance by the builder, or even total renunciation of further duty. [Emphasis added.]

     * * * [A] subcontractor cannot and should not be expected to finance the project until such time that the prime contractor * * * decides to pay the amount due. If the subcontractor is ordered to perform the work or even required to do so, then the obligation in the absence of an express contract provision falls upon the party so ordering the work to be done to pay a reasonable amount for that work within a reasonable time. To hold otherwise would cast a burden upon the subcontractor which in many cases would be impossible to carry as the subcontractors are usually smaller in size than the prime contractors.

DECISION AND REMEDY *The court held that Manganaro was justified in suspending its performance on its contract with HITT until payment was made after HITT failed to pay the outstanding invoices for change order work in a timely manner.*

WHAT IF THE FACTS WERE DIFFERENT? *Suppose the contract with Manganaro contained a clause that required the subcontractor to wait for HITT to be paid before the subcontractor was paid. If HITT had difficulty obtaining payment from Lucent, how would that have affected the outcome in this case?*

SECTION 3 | Discharge by Agreement

Any contract can be discharged by agreement of the parties. The agreement can be contained in the original contract, or the parties can form a new contract for the express purpose of discharging the original contract.

DISCHARGE BY RESCISSION

As mentioned in previous chapters, *rescission* is the process by which a contract is canceled or terminated and the parties are returned to the positions they occupied prior to forming it. For **mutual rescission** to take place, the parties must make another agreement that also satisfies the legal requirements for a contract. There must be an *offer*, an *acceptance*, and *consideration*. Ordinarily, if the parties agree to rescind the original contract, their promises not to perform the acts stipulated in the original contract will be legal consideration for the second contract (the rescission).

     Agreements to rescind executory contracts (in which neither party has performed) are generally enforceable, even if the agreement is made orally and even if the original agreement was in writing. An exception applies under the Uniform Commercial Code (UCC) to agreements rescinding a contract for the sale of goods, regardless of price, when the contract requires a written rescission.[10] Also, agreements to rescind contracts involving transfers of realty must be evidenced by a writing.

     When one party has fully performed, an agreement to cancel the original contract normally will not be enforceable. Because the performing party has received no consideration for the promise to call off the original bargain, additional consideration is necessary.

DISCHARGE BY NOVATION

A contractual obligation may also be discharged through novation. A **novation** occurs when both of the parties to a contract agree to substitute a third party for one of the original parties. The requirements of a novation are as follows:

1. A previous valid obligation.
2. An agreement by all the parties to a new contract.
3. The extinguishing of the old obligation (discharge of the prior party).
4. A new contract that is valid.

     For example, suppose that Union Corporation contracts to sell its pharmaceutical division to British Pharmaceuticals, Ltd. Before the transfer is completed,

---

10. UCC 2–209(2), (4).

Union, British Pharmaceuticals, and a third company, Otis Chemicals, execute a new agreement to transfer all of British Pharmaceutical's rights and duties in the transaction to Otis Chemicals. As long as the new contract is supported by consideration, the novation will discharge the original contract (between Union and British Pharmaceuticals) and replace it with the new contract (between Union and Otis Chemicals).

A novation expressly or impliedly revokes and discharges a prior contract.[11] The parties involved may expressly state in the new contract that the old contract is now discharged. If the parties do not expressly discharge the old contract, it will be impliedly discharged if the new contract's terms are inconsistent with the old contract's terms.

DISCHARGE BY SUBSTITUTED AGREEMENT

A *compromise*, or settlement agreement, that arises out of a genuine dispute over the obligations under an existing contract will be recognized at law. Such an agreement will be substituted as a new contract, and it will either expressly or impliedly revoke and discharge the obligations under any prior contract. In contrast to a novation, a substituted agreement does not involve a third party. Rather, the two original parties to the contract form a different agreement to substitute for the original one.

DISCHARGE BY ACCORD AND SATISFACTION

For a contract to be discharged by accord and satisfaction, the parties must agree to accept performance that is different from the performance originally promised. As discussed in Chapter 12, an *accord* is a contract to perform some act to satisfy an existing contractual duty.[12] The duty has not yet been discharged. A *satisfaction* is the performance of the accord agreement. An accord and its satisfaction discharge the original contractual obligation.

Once the accord has been made, the original obligation is merely suspended. The obligor (the one owing the obligation) can discharge the obligation by performing either the obligation agreed to in the accord or the original obligation. If the obligor refuses to perform the accord, the obligee (the one to whom performance is owed) can bring action on the original obligation or seek a decree compelling specific performance on the accord.

For example, suppose that Frazer has a judgment against Ling for $8,000. Later, both parties agree that the judgment can be satisfied by Ling's transfer of his automobile to Frazer. This agreement to accept the auto in lieu of $8,000 in cash is the accord. If Ling transfers the car to Frazer, the accord is fully performed, and the debt is discharged. If Ling refuses to transfer the car, the accord is breached. Because the original obligation is merely suspended, Frazer can sue Ling to enforce the original judgment for $8,000 in cash or bring an action for breach of the accord.

SECTION 4 | Discharge by Operation of Law

Under certain circumstances, contractual duties may be discharged by operation of law. These circumstances include material alteration of the contract, the running of the statute of limitations, bankruptcy, and the impossibility or impracticability of performance.

ALTERATION OF THE CONTRACT

To discourage parties from altering written contracts, the law operates to allow an innocent party to be discharged when the other party has materially altered a written contract without consent. For example, contract terms such as quantity or price might be changed without the knowledge or consent of all parties. If so, the party who was not involved in the alteration can treat the contract as discharged or terminated.[13]

---

11. It is this immediate discharge of the prior contract that distinguishes a novation from both an accord and satisfaction, discussed in a later subsection, and an assignment of all rights, discussed in Chapter 16. In an *assignment of all rights*, the original party to the contract (the assignor) remains liable under the original contract if the assignee fails to perform the contractual obligations. In contrast, in a novation, the original party's obligations are completely discharged.

12. *Restatement (Second) of Contracts*, Section 281.

---

13. The contract is voidable, and the innocent party can also treat the contract as in effect, either on the original terms or on the terms as altered. A buyer who discovers that a seller altered the quantity of goods in a sales contract from 100 to 1,000 by secretly inserting a zero can purchase either 100 or 1,000 of the items.

STATUTES OF LIMITATIONS

As mentioned earlier in this text, statutes of limitations restrict the period during which a party can sue on a particular cause of action. After the applicable limitations period has passed, a suit can no longer be brought. For example, the limitations period for bringing suits for breach of oral contracts is usually two to three years; for written contracts, four to five years; and for recovery of amounts awarded in judgments, ten to twenty years, depending on state law. Suits for breach of a contract for the sale of goods generally must be brought within four years after the cause of action has accrued.[14] By their original agreement, the parties can reduce this four-year period to not less than one year, but they cannot agree to extend it.

Technically, the running of a statute of limitations bars access only to *judicial* remedies; it does not extinguish the debt or the underlying obligation. The statute precludes access to the courts for collection. If, however, the party who owes the debt or obligation agrees to perform (that is, makes a new promise to perform), the cause of action barred by the statute of limitations will be revived. For the old agreement to be restored by a new promise in this manner, many states require that the promise be in writing or that there be evidence of partial performance.

BANKRUPTCY

A proceeding in bankruptcy attempts to allocate the assets the debtor owns to the creditors in a fair and equitable fashion. Once the assets have been allocated, the debtor receives a **discharge in bankruptcy.** A discharge in bankruptcy will ordinarily bar enforcement of most of the debtor's contracts by the creditors. Partial payment of a debt *after* discharge in bankruptcy will not revive the debt. (Bankruptcy will be discussed in detail in Chapter 30.)

IMPOSSIBILITY OR IMPRACTICABILITY OF PERFORMANCE

After a contract has been made, performance may become impossible in an objective sense. This is known as **impossibility of performance** and may discharge a contract.[15]

OBJECTIVE IMPOSSIBILITY OF PERFORMANCE *Objective impossibility* ("It can't be done") must be distinguished from *subjective impossibility* ("I'm sorry, I simply can't do it"). Examples of subjective impossibility include the situation in which goods cannot be delivered on time because of freight car shortages and the situation in which payment cannot be made on time because the bank is closed. In effect, the party in each of these situations is saying, "It is impossible for me to perform," not "It is impossible for anyone to perform." Accordingly, such excuses do not discharge a contract, and the nonperforming party is normally held in breach of contract. Three basic types of situations, however, generally qualify as grounds for the discharge of contractual obligations based on impossibility of performance:[16]

1. *When one of the parties to a personal contract dies or becomes incapacitated prior to performance.* For example, Fred, a famous dancer, contracts with Ethereal Dancing Guild to play a leading role in its new ballet. Before the ballet can be performed, Fred becomes ill and dies. His personal performance was essential to the completion of the contract. Thus, his death discharges the contract and his estate's liability for his nonperformance.

2. *When the specific subject matter of the contract is destroyed.* For example, A-1 Farm Equipment agrees to sell Gudgel the green tractor on its lot and promises to have it ready for Gudgel to pick up on Saturday. On Friday night, however, a truck veers off the nearby highway and smashes into the tractor, destroying it beyond repair. Because the contract was for this specific tractor, A-1's performance is rendered impossible owing to the accident.

3. *When a change in law renders performance illegal.* For example, a contract to build an apartment building becomes impossible to perform when the zoning laws are changed to prohibit the construction of residential rental property at the planned location.

COMMERCIAL IMPRACTICABILITY Courts may excuse parties from their performance obligations when the performance becomes much more difficult or

---

14. Section 2–725 of the UCC contains this four-year limitation period. In 2003, amendments to this section of the UCC added a provision that extended the limitation period for up to one additional year to accommodate a discovery of the breach late in the four-year period. No action can be brought after five years, however (see Chapter 20).

15. *Restatement (Second) of Contracts*, Section 261.

16. *Restatement (Second) of Contracts*, Sections 262–266; UCC 2–615.

expensive than originally contemplated at the time the contract was formed. For someone to invoke the doctrine of **commercial impracticability** successfully, however, the anticipated performance must become *extremely* difficult or costly.[17] The added burden of performing not only must be extreme but also *must not have been known by the parties when the contract was made*.

In the following case, a party to a contract for a sale of land argued that the contract should be rescinded because a possible spread of pollution and the potential liability involved made the sale impossible or impracticable.

---

17. *Restatement (Second) of Contracts*, Section 264.

CASE 17.4 — Cape-France Enterprises v. Estate of Peed

Supreme Court
of Montana, 2001.
305 Mont. 513,
29 P.3d 1011.

BACKGROUND AND FACTS *Cape-France Enterprises owns real property in Bozeman, Montana. In 1994, Lola Peed and her granddaughter, Marthe Moore, entered into an agreement with Cape-France to buy five acres of the land on which to build a motel or hotel. To complete the sale, the state required the land to be surveyed, subdivided, and rezoned. To subdivide the property, the state required a well to be drilled and the water to be tested. The parties were aware of underground pollution in Bozeman but believed that Cape-France's property was not affected by the pollution. Montana's Department of Environmental Quality, Water Quality Division (DEQ), however, feared that the water under the land was contaminated. The DEQ warned in letters to Cape-France that if there was pollution, drilling a well could exacerbate (make worse) the problem, treatment of the water would be extensive, and Cape-France would be liable for the cost. When Peed and Moore would not agree to share the risk, Cape-France filed a suit in a Montana state court against Moore and Peed's estate (Peed had since died), seeking to rescind their contract in part on the ground of impossibility or impracticability of performance. The court granted a summary judgment in Cape-France's favor. The defendants appealed to the Montana Supreme Court.*

IN THE LANGUAGE OF THE COURT

Justice JAMES C. NELSON delivered the Opinion of the Court.

* * * *

* * * [T]he doctrine of impossibility is a valid defense not only when performance is impossible, but also when supervening circumstances make performance impracticable. * * *

* * * [A]n act is impracticable when it can only be done at an excessive, unreasonable and unbargained-for cost. *While the doctrine of impossibility or impracticability is not set in stone, it is applied by courts where, aside from the object of the contract being unlawful, the public policy underlying the strict enforcement of contracts is outweighed by the senselessness of requiring performance.* [Emphasis added.]

The doctrine is applicable under the facts in the case at bar. * * * It is undisputed that after the agreement was executed, the state and local regulatory authorities required the completion of water drilling and testing. The parties discussed the situation. Cape-France was unwilling to assume large risks related to this new, unknown and unexpected situation. Peed-Moore was unwilling to [share the risks to a degree] satisfactory to Cape-France. Contamination, if it exists or occurs by reason of well-drilling, could expose Cape-France as landowners to financial liability of an unquantifiable nature. * * *

Peed and Moore argue that the contract should not be rescinded on the basis of impossibility because it is not impossible to drill the well. They point to the [DEQ] letters as evidence that the well could be drilled and that there is no proof that there would be actual groundwater contamination where they would drill. However, Peed and Moore do not argue, and cannot argue, that there is no groundwater contamination, nor can they say that there will not be any in the future. Unfortunately, the only way to determine whether there is and, if so,

CONTINUED ▶

CASE 17.4 | Continued   the extent of groundwater contamination is to drill a well. And that is the precise activity that may exacerbate the contamination problem, to both parties' substantial and unbargained-for economic detriment. Indeed, it is clear that Peed and Moore are unwilling or unable to share in these economic risks.

Moreover, as already noted, while impossibility or impracticability is a high standard, the application of this doctrine is not limited to cases of literal impossibility. Here, the potential for substantial and unbargained-for damage involved in performing the contract is not only of an economic nature. Just as importantly, environmental degradation with consequences extending well beyond the parties' land sale is also a real possibility.

DECISION AND REMEDY   *The Montana Supreme Court affirmed the judgment of the lower court. The state supreme court agreed that rescission of this contract was appropriate, on the ground of impossibility or impracticability, because Cape-France would otherwise be forced to expose itself to substantial and unbargained-for economic risks, to expose the public to potential health risks, and to expose the environment to possible degradation.*

INTERNATIONAL CONSIDERATIONS   **Impossibility of Performance in Germany** *In the United States, when a party alleges that contract performance is impossible or impracticable because of circumstances unforeseen at the time the contract was formed, a court will either discharge the party's contractual obligations or hold the party to the contract. Under German law, however, a court may adjust the terms of a contract in light of economic developments. If an unforeseen event affects the foundation of the agreement, the court can alter the contract's terms in view of the disruption in expectations, thus making the contract fair to the parties.*

FRUSTRATION OF PURPOSE   A theory closely allied with the doctrine of commercial impracticability is the doctrine of **frustration of purpose.** In principle, a contract will be discharged if supervening circumstances make it impossible to attain the purpose both parties had in mind when making the contract.

The origins of the doctrine lie in the old English "coronation cases." A coronation procession was planned for Edward VII when he became king of England following the death of his mother, Queen Victoria. Hotel rooms along the coronation route were rented at exorbitant prices for that day. When the king became ill and the procession was canceled, a flurry of lawsuits resulted. Hotel and building owners sought to enforce the room-rent bills against would-be parade observers, and would-be parade observers sought to be reimbursed for rental monies paid in advance on the rooms. Would-be parade observers were excused from their duty of payment because the purpose of the room contracts had been "frustrated."

TEMPORARY IMPOSSIBILITY   An occurrence or event that makes performance temporarily impossible

operates to suspend performance until the impossibility ceases. Then, ordinarily, the parties must perform the contract as originally planned. If, however, the lapse of time and the change in circumstances surrounding the contract make it substantially more burdensome for the parties to perform the promised acts, the contract is discharged.

The leading case on the subject, *Autry v. Republic Productions*,[18] involved an actor who was drafted into the army in 1942. Being drafted rendered the actor's contract temporarily impossible to perform, and it was suspended until the end of the war. When the actor got out of the army, the value of the dollar had so changed that performance of the contract would have been substantially burdensome to the actor. Therefore, the contract was discharged.

Exhibit 17–1 graphically illustrates the ways in which a contract can be discharged.

_____

18. 30 Cal.2d 144, 180 P.2d 888 (1947).

EXHIBIT 17–1 Contract Discharge

REVIEWING PERFORMANCE AND DISCHARGE

Val's Foods signs a contract to buy 1,500 pounds of basil from Sun Farms, a small organic herb grower, as long as an independent organization inspects and certifies that the crop contains no pesticide or herbicide residue. Val's has a number of contracts with different restaurant chains to supply pesto and intends to use Sun Farms' basil in its pesto to fulfill these contracts. While Sun Farms is preparing to harvest the basil, an unexpected hailstorm destroys half the crop. Sun Farms attempts to purchase additional basil from other farms, but it is late in the season and the price is twice the normal market price. Sun Farms is too small to absorb this cost and immediately notifies Val's that it will not fulfill the contract. Using the information presented in the chapter, answer the following questions.

1. Suppose that the basil does not pass the chemical-residue inspection. Which concept discussed in the chapter might allow Val's to refuse to perform the contract in this situation?

2. Does the notice that Sun Farms sent to Val's constitute an anticipatory repudiation? Why or why not? What rights does this notification give to Val's?

3. Under which legal theory or theories might Sun Farms claim that its obligation under the contract has been discharged by operation of law? Discuss fully.

4. Suppose that Sun Farms contacts every basil grower in the country and buys the last remaining chemical-free basil anywhere. Nevertheless, Sun Farms is only able to ship 1,475 pounds to Val's. Would this fulfill Sun Farms' obligations to Val's? Why or why not?

5. Now suppose that Sun Farms sells its operations to Happy Valley Farms. As a part of the sale, all three parties agree that Happy Valley will provide the basil as stated under the original contract. What is this type of agreement called? Does it discharge the obligations of any of the parties? Explain.

TERMS AND CONCEPTS TO REVIEW

anticipatory repudiation 330

breach of contract 328

commercial impracticability 335

concurrent conditions 325

condition 324

condition precedent 324

condition subsequent 325

discharge 324

discharge in bankruptcy 334

frustration of purpose 336

impossibility of performance 334

mutual rescission 332

novation 332

performance 324

tender 325

QUESTIONS AND CASE PROBLEMS

17–1. The Caplans own a real estate lot, and they contract with Faithful Construction, Inc., to build a house on it for $60,000. The specifications list "all plumbing bowls and fixtures . . . to be Crane brand." The Caplans leave on vacation, and during their absence Faithful is unable to buy and install Crane plumbing fixtures. Instead, Faithful installs Kohler brand fixtures, an equivalent in the industry. On completion of the building contract, the Caplans inspect the work, discover the substitution, and refuse to accept the house, claiming Faithful has breached the conditions set forth in the specifications. Discuss fully the Caplans' claim.

17–2. ⚖ **QUESTION WITH SAMPLE ANSWER**

Junior owes creditor Iba $1,000, which is due and payable on June 1. Junior has been in a car accident, has missed a great deal of work, and consequently will not have the funds on June 1. Junior's father, Fred, offers to pay Iba $1,100 in four equal installments if Iba will discharge Junior from any further liability on the debt. Iba accepts. Is this transaction a novation or an accord and satisfaction? Explain.

For a sample answer to this question, go to Appendix I at the end of this text.

17–3. ABC Clothiers, Inc., has a contract with Taylor & Sons, a retailer, to deliver one thousand summer suits to Taylor's place of business on or before May 1. On April 1, Taylor senior receives a letter from ABC informing him that ABC will not be able to make the delivery as scheduled. Taylor is very upset, as he had planned a big ad campaign. He wants to file a suit against ABC immediately (on April 2). Taylor's son Tom tells his father that filing a lawsuit is not proper until ABC actually fails to deliver the suits on May 1. Discuss fully who is correct, Taylor or Tom.

17–4. In the following situations, certain events take place after the formation of contracts. Discuss which of these contracts are discharged because the events render the contracts impossible to perform.

(a) Jimenez, a famous singer, contracts to perform in your nightclub. He dies prior to performance.

(b) Raglione contracts to sell you her land. Just before title is to be transferred, she dies.

(c) Oppenheim contracts to sell you one thousand bushels of apples from her orchard in the state of Washington. Because of a severe frost, she is unable to deliver the apples.

(d) Maxwell contracts to lease a service station for ten years. His principal income is from the sale of gasoline. Because of an oil embargo by foreign oil-producing nations, gasoline is rationed, cutting sharply into Maxwell's gasoline sales. He cannot make his lease payments.

17–5. Murphy contracts to purchase six cases of French champagne from Lone Star Liquors for $1,200. The contract states that delivery is to be made at the Murphy residence "on or before June 1, to be used for daughter's wedding reception on June 2." Lone Star regularly carries the champagne in stock. On June 1, Lone Star's delivery van is involved in an accident, and the champagne is not delivered that day. On the morning of June 2, Murphy discovers the nondelivery. Unable to reach Lone Star because its line is busy, Murphy purchases the champagne from another dealer. That afternoon, just before the wedding reception, Lone Star tenders delivery of the champagne at Murphy's residence. Murphy refuses tender, and Lone Star sues for breach of contract. Discuss fully the result.

17–6. CONDITIONS. Heublein, Inc., makes wines and distilled spirits. Tarrant Distributors, Inc., agreed to distribute Heublein brands. When problems arose, the parties entered mediation. Under a settlement agreement, Heublein agreed to pay Tarrant the amount of its "net loss" as determined by Coopers & Lybrand, an accounting firm, according to a specified formula. The parties agreed that Coopers & Lybrand's calculation would be "final and binding." Heublein disagreed with Coopers & Lybrand's calculation, however, and refused to pay. The parties asked a federal district court to rule on the dispute. Heublein argued that the settlement agreement included an implied condition precedent that Coopers & Lybrand would correctly apply the specified formula before Heublein would be obligated to pay.

Tarrant pointed to the clause that the calculation would be "final and binding." With whom will the court agree, and why? [*Tarrant Distributors, Inc. v. Heublein, Inc.*, 127 F.3d 375 (5th Cir. 1997)]

17-7. ⚖ CASE PROBLEM WITH SAMPLE ANSWER

Train operators and other railroad personnel use signaling systems to ensure safe train travel. Reading Blue Mountain & Northern Railroad Co. (RBMN) and Norfolk Southern Railway Co. entered into a contract for the maintenance of a signaling system that serviced a stretch of track near Jim Thorpe, Pennsylvania. The system included a series of poles, similar to telephone poles, suspending wires above the tracks. The contract provided that "the intent of the parties is to maintain the existing . . . facilities" and split the cost equally. In December 2002, a severe storm severed the wires and destroyed most of the poles. RBMN and Norfolk discussed replacing the old system, which they agreed was antiquated, inefficient, dangerous to rebuild, and expensive, but they could not agree on an alternative. Norfolk installed an entirely new system and filed a suit in a federal district court against RBMN to recover half of the cost. RBMN filed a motion for summary judgment, asserting in part the doctrine of frustration of purpose. What is this doctrine? Does it apply in this case? How should the court rule on RBMN's motion? Explain. [*Norfolk Southern Railway Co. v. Reading Blue Mountain & Northern Railroad Co.*, 364 F.Supp.2d 270 (M.D.Pa. 2004)]

To view a sample answer for this case problem, go to this book's Web site at http://wbl.westbuslaw.com, select "Chapter 17," and click on "Case Problem with Sample Answer."

17-8. PERFORMANCE. In May 1996, O'Brien-Shiepe Funeral Home, Inc., in Hempstead, New York, hired Teramo & Co. to build an addition to O'Brien's funeral home. The parties' contract did not specify a date for the completion of the work. The city of Hempstead issued a building permit for the project on June 14, and Teramo began work about two weeks later. There was some delay in construction because O'Brien asked that no construction be done during funeral services, but by the end of March 1997, the work was substantially complete. The city of Hempstead issued a "Certificate of Completion" on April 15. During the construction, O'Brien made periodic payments to Teramo, but there was a balance due of $17,950, which O'Brien did not pay. To recover this amount, Teramo filed a suit in a New York state court against O'Brien. O'Brien filed a counterclaim to recover lost profits for business allegedly lost due to the time Teramo took to build the addition and for $6,180 spent to correct problems caused by poor craftsmanship. Which, if any, party is entitled to an award in this case? Explain. [*Teramo & Co. v. O'Brien-Shiepe Funeral Home, Inc.*, 725 N.Y.S.2d 87 (A.D. 2 Dept. 2001)]

17-9. SUBSTANTIAL PERFORMANCE. Adolf and Ida Krueger contracted with Pisani Construction, Inc., to erect a metal building as an addition to an existing structure. The two structures were to share a common wall, and the frames and panel heights of the new building were to match those of the existing structure. Shortly before completion of the project, however, it was apparent that the roofline of the new building was approximately three inches higher than that of the existing structure. Pisani modified the ridge caps of the buildings to blend the rooflines. The discrepancy had other consequences, however, including misalignment of the gutters and windows of the two buildings, which resulted in an icing problem in the winter. The Kruegers occupied the new structure, but refused to make the last payment under the contract. Pisani filed a suit in a Connecticut state court to collect. Did Pisani substantially perform its obligations? Should the Kruegers be ordered to pay? Why or why not? [*Pisani Construction, Inc. v. Krueger*, 68 Conn.App. 361, 791 A.2d 634 (2002)]

17-10. ⚖ A QUESTION OF ETHICS

Steven McPheters, a house builder and developer, hired Terry Tentinger, a painting contractor, to do some touching up and repainting on one of McPheters's new houses. Tentinger worked two days, billed McPheters $420 (for a three-man crew for fourteen hours at $30 per hour), and offered to return to the house to remedy any defects in his workmanship at no cost. McPheters objected to the number of hours on the bill—although he did not express dissatisfaction with the work—and offered Tentinger $250. Tentinger refused to accept this sum and filed a suit in an Idaho state court to collect the full amount. McPheters filed a counterclaim, alleging that Tentinger had failed to perform the job in a workmanlike manner because there was paint overspray on a redwood deck and inadequate paint coverage on portions of the rain gutter. McPheters sought $3,000 in damages to cover the costs of repairs that he claimed were necessary. In view of these facts, consider the following questions. [*Tentinger v. McPheters*, 132 Idaho 620, 977 P.2d 234 (Idaho App. 1999)]

(a) The court in this case stated that a contract has been substantially performed if one party provided the "important and essential benefits of the contract" to the other. Did Tentinger substantially perform his part of the bargain (touching up and repainting)?

(b) Given that McPheters failed to complain about Tentinger's workmanship at the time and did not give Tentinger a chance to remedy the defects, would it be fair to allow him to recover repair costs from Tentinger? Why or why not?

(c) What is the underlying policy for the general rule that substantial performance discharges a party's contractual obligations?

LAW | on the Web

For updated links to resources available on the Web, as well as a variety of other materials, visit this text's Web site at **http://wbl.westbuslaw.com**.

For a summary of how contracts may be discharged and other principles of contract law, go to

http://www.rnoon.com/lawlaymen/contracts/performance.html

LEGAL RESEARCH EXERCISES ON THE WEB

Go to **http://wbl.westbuslaw.com**, the Web site that accompanies this text. Select "Chapter 17" and click on "Internet Exercises." There you will find the following Internet research exercises that you can perform to learn more about topics covered in this chapter.

Activity 17–1: LEGAL PERSPECTIVE
　　　　　　　　　　Anticipatory Repudiation

Activity 17–2: MANAGEMENT PERSPECTIVE
　　　　　　　　　　Commercial Impracticability

CHAPTER 18
Breach of Contract and Remedies

When one party breaches a contract, the other party—the nonbreaching party—can choose one or more of several remedies. A *remedy* is the relief provided for an innocent party when the other party has breached the contract. It is the means employed to enforce a right or to redress an injury.

The most common remedies available to a nonbreaching party include damages, rescission and restitution, specific performance, and reformation. As discussed in Chapter 1, a distinction is made between *remedies at law* and *remedies in equity*. Today, the remedy at law is normally money damages, which are discussed in the first part of this chapter. Equitable remedies include rescission and restitution, specific performance, and reformation, all of which will be examined later in the chapter. Usually, a court will not award an equitable remedy unless the remedy at law is inadequate. Special legal doctrines and concepts relating to remedies will be discussed in the final pages of this chapter.

SECTION 1 | Damages

A breach of contract entitles the nonbreaching party to sue for money (damages). As discussed in Chapter 6, damages are designed to compensate a party for harm suffered as a result of another's wrongful act. In the context of contract law, damages compensate the nonbreaching party for the loss of the bargain. Often, courts say that innocent parties are to be placed in the position they would have occupied had the contract been fully performed.[1]

Realize at the outset, though, that to collect damages through a court judgment means litigation, which can be expensive and time consuming. Also keep in mind that court judgments are often difficult to enforce, particularly if the breaching party does not have sufficient assets to pay the damages awarded (as discussed in Chapter 3). For these reasons, the majority of actions for damages (or other remedies) are settled by the parties before trial.

---
1. *Restatement (Second) of Contracts*, Section 347; Section 1–106(1) of the Uniform Commercial Code (UCC).

TYPES OF DAMAGES

There are basically four broad categories of damages:

1. Compensatory (to cover direct losses and costs).
2. Consequential (to cover indirect and foreseeable losses).
3. Punitive (to punish and deter wrongdoing).
4. Nominal (to recognize wrongdoing when no monetary loss is shown).

Compensatory and punitive damages were discussed in Chapter 6 in the context of tort law. Here, we look at these types of damages, as well as consequential and nominal damages, in the context of contract law.

COMPENSATORY DAMAGES Damages compensating the nonbreaching party for the *loss of the bargain* are known as *compensatory damages*. These damages compensate the injured party only for damages actually sustained and proved to have arisen directly from the loss of the bargain caused by the breach of contract. They simply replace what was lost because of the wrong or damage. The standard measure of compensatory damages is the difference between the value of the breaching party's promised performance under the contract and the value of her or his actual performance. This amount is reduced by any loss that the injured party has avoided, however.

To illustrate: Wilcox contracts to perform certain services exclusively for Hernandez during the month of March for $4,000. Hernandez cancels the contract and is in breach. Wilcox is able to find another job during the month of March but can earn only $3,000. He can sue Hernandez for breach and recover $1,000 as compensatory damages. Wilcox can also recover from Hernandez the amount that he spent to find the other job. Expenses that are caused directly by a breach of contract—such as those incurred to obtain performance from another source—are known as **incidental damages.**

The measurement of compensatory damages varies by type of contract. Certain types of contracts deserve special mention. They are contracts for the sale of goods, land contracts, and construction contracts.

—Sale of Goods. In a contract for the sale of goods, the usual measure of compensatory damages is an amount equal to the difference between the contract price and the market price.[2] For example, suppose that Chrylon Corporation contracts to buy ten model UTS 400 network servers from an XEXO Corporation dealer for $8,000 each. The dealer, however, fails to deliver the ten servers to Chrylon. The market price of the servers at the time the buyer learns of the breach is $8,150. Chrylon's measure of damages is therefore $1,500 (10 × $150) plus any incidental damages (expenses) caused by the breach. In a situation in which the buyer breaches and the seller has not yet produced the goods, compensatory damages normally equal lost profits on the sale, not the difference between the contract price and the market price.

—Sale of Land. Ordinarily, because each parcel of land is unique, the remedy for a seller's breach of a contract for a sale of real estate is specific performance—that is, the buyer is awarded the parcel of property for which she or he bargained (specific performance is discussed more fully later in this chapter). When this remedy is unavailable (for example, when the seller has sold the property to someone else), or when the breach is on the part of the buyer, the measure of damages is ordinarily the same as in contracts

for the sale of goods—that is, the difference between the contract price and the market price of the land. The majority of states follow this rule.

A minority of states follow a different rule when the seller breaches the contract and the breach is not deliberate.[3] In this situation, these states allow the prospective purchaser to recover any down payment plus any expenses incurred (such as fees for title searches, attorneys, and escrows). This minority rule effectively places purchasers in the position they occupied prior to the sale.

—Construction Contracts. The measure of damages in a building or construction contract varies depending on which party breaches and when the breach occurs. The owner can breach at three different stages of the construction:

1. Before performance has begun.
2. During performance.
3. After performance has been completed.

If the owner breaches *before performance has begun,* the contractor can recover only the profits that would have been made on the contract (that is, the total contract price less the cost of materials and labor). If the owner breaches *during performance,* the contractor can recover the profits plus the costs incurred in partially constructing the building. If the owner breaches *after the construction has been completed,* the contractor can recover the entire contract price, plus interest.

When the construction contractor breaches the contract either by failing to undertake construction or by stopping work partway through the project, the measure of damages is the cost of completion, which includes reasonable compensation for any delay in performance. If the contractor finishes late, the measure of damages is the loss of use. These rules concerning the measurement of damages in breached construction contracts are summarized in Exhibit 18–1.

—Construction Contracts and Economic Waste. If the contractor substantially performs, the courts may use the cost-of-completion formula, but only if there is no unreasonable economic waste in requiring completion. Economic waste occurs when the cost of repairing or completing the performance as required

---

2. In other words, the amount is the difference between the contract price and the market price at the time and place at which the goods were to be delivered or tendered. See UCC 2–708 and 2–713.

3. "Deliberate" breaches include the seller's failure to convey the land because the market price has gone up. "Nondeliberate" breaches include the seller's failure to convey the land because an unknown easement (another's right of use over the property) has rendered title unmarketable. See Chapter 48.

EXHIBIT 18-1 Measurement of Damages—Breach of Construction Contracts

PARTY IN BREACH	TIME OF BREACH	MEASUREMENT OF DAMAGES
Owner	Before construction has begun	Profits (contract price less cost of materials and labor)
Owner	During construction	Profits, plus costs incurred up to time of breach
Owner	After construction is completed	Contract price, plus interest
Contractor	Before construction has begun	Cost above contract price to complete work
Contractor	Before construction is completed	Generally, all costs incurred by owner to complete work

by the contract greatly outweighs the benefit to the owner. For example, suppose that a contractor discovers that it will cost $20,000 to move a large coral rock eleven inches as specified in the contract. Because changing the rock's position will alter the appearance of the project only a trifle, a court would likely conclude that full completion would involve economic waste. Thus, the contractor will not be required to pay the full $20,000 to complete performance.

CONSEQUENTIAL DAMAGES Foreseeable damages that result from a party's breach of contract are called **consequential damages,** or *special damages*. They differ from compensatory damages in that they are caused by special circumstances beyond the contract itself. They flow from the consequences, or results, of a breach.

For example, if a seller fails to deliver goods, and the seller knows that a buyer is planning to resell these goods immediately, consequential damages will be awarded for the loss of profit from the planned resale.

The buyer will also recover compensatory damages for the difference between the contract price and the market price of the goods.

To recover consequential damages, the breaching party must know (or have reason to know) that special circumstances will cause the nonbreaching party to suffer an additional loss. This rule was enunciated in the classic case of *Hadley v. Baxendale*, which is presented next. In reading this decision, it is helpful to understand that it was customary in the mid-1800s in England for large flour mills to have more than one crankshaft in the event that the main crankshaft broke and had to be repaired. Also, in those days it was common knowledge that flour mills did indeed have spare crankshafts. It is against this background that the parties in the case presented here argued their respective positions on whether the damages resulting from the loss of profits while the crankshaft was repaired were reasonably foreseeable.

CASE 18.1   Hadley v. Baxendale

Court of Exchequer, 1854.
156 Eng.Rep. 145.

BACKGROUND AND FACTS *The Hadleys (the plaintiffs) ran a flour mill in Gloucester. The crankshaft attached to the steam engine in the mill broke, causing the mill to shut down. The shaft had to be sent to a foundry located in Greenwich so that the new shaft could be made to fit the other parts of the engine. Baxendale, the defendant, was a common carrier that transported the shaft from Gloucester to Greenwich. The freight charges were collected in advance, and Baxendale promised to deliver the shaft the following day. It was not delivered for a number of days, however. As a consequence, the mill was closed for several days. The Hadleys sued to recover the profits lost during that time. Baxendale contended that the loss of profits was "too remote" to be recoverable. The court held for the plaintiffs, and the jury was allowed to take into consideration the lost profits. The defendant appealed.*

IN THE LANGUAGE OF THE COURT

ALDERSON, B.

* * * *

* * * Where two parties have made a contract which one of them has broken, the damages which the other party ought to receive in respect of such breach of contract

CONTINUED ▶

CASE 18.1 | Continued

should be such as may fairly and reasonably be considered either arising naturally, *i.e.*, according to the usual course of things, from such breach of contract itself, or such as may reasonably be supposed to have been in the contemplation of both parties, at the time they made the contract, as the probable result of the breach of it. Now, if the special circumstances under which the contract was actually made were communicated by the plaintiffs to the defendants, and thus known to both parties, the damages resulting from the breach of such a contract, *which they would reasonably contemplate*, would be the amount of injury which would ordinarily follow from a breach of contract under these special circumstances so known and communicated. * * * Now, in the present case, if we are to apply the principles above laid down, we find that the only circumstances here communicated by the plaintiffs to the defendants at the time the contract was made, were, that the article to be carried was the broken shaft of a mill, and that the plaintiffs were the millers of that mill. * * * [S]pecial circumstances were here never communicated by the plaintiffs to the defendants. It follows, therefore, that the loss of profits here cannot reasonably be considered such a consequence of the breach of contract as could have been fairly and reasonably contemplated by both the parties when they made this contract. [Emphasis added.]

DECISION AND REMEDY *The Court of Exchequer ordered a new trial. According to the court, to collect consequential damages, the plaintiffs would have to have given express notice of the special circumstances that caused the loss of profits.*

IMPACT OF THIS CASE ON TODAY'S LAW

This case established the rule that when damages are awarded, compensation is given only for those injuries that the defendant could reasonably have foreseen as a probable result of the usual course of events following a breach. Today, the rule enunciated by the court in this case still applies. To recover consequential damages, the plaintiff must show that the defendant had reason to know or foresee that a particular loss or injury would occur.

PUNITIVE DAMAGES Punitive, or exemplary, damages are generally not awarded in an action for breach of contract. Punitive damages are designed to punish a guilty party and to make an example of the party to deter similar conduct in the future. Such damages have no legitimate place in contract law because they are, in essence, penalties, and a breach of contract is not unlawful in a criminal sense. A contract is simply a civil relationship between the parties. The law may compensate one party for the loss of the bargain, no more and no less.

In a few situations, a person's actions can constitute both a breach of contract and a tort. For example, the parties may establish by contract a certain reasonable standard or duty of care. Failure to live up to that standard is a breach of contract, and the act itself may constitute negligence. Additionally, some intentional torts, such as fraud, may be tied to a breach of the terms of a contract. In such cases, it is possible for the nonbreaching party to recover punitive damages for the commission of the tort, in addition to compensatory and consequential damages for breach of contract.

NOMINAL DAMAGES When no actual damage or financial loss results from a breach of contract and only a technical injury is involved, the court may award **nominal damages** to the innocent party. Awards of nominal damages are often trifling, such as a dollar, but they do establish that the defendant acted wrongfully. Most lawsuits for nominal damages are brought as a matter of principle under the theory that a breach has occurred and some damages must be imposed regardless of actual loss.

For example, suppose that Jackson contracts to buy potatoes from Stanley at fifty cents a pound. Stanley breaches the contract and does not deliver the potatoes. In the meantime, the price of potatoes has fallen. Jackson is able to buy them in the open market at half the price he contracted for with Stanley. He is clearly better off because of Stanley's breach. Thus, in a suit for breach of contract, Jackson may be awarded only nominal damages for the technical injury he sustained, because no monetary loss was involved.

MITIGATION OF DAMAGES

In most situations, when a breach of contract occurs, the innocent injured party is held to a duty to mitigate, or reduce, the damages that he or she suffers. Under this doctrine of **mitigation of damages,** the duty owed depends on the nature of the contract.

For example, some states require a landlord to use reasonable means to find a new tenant if a tenant abandons the premises and fails to pay rent. If an acceptable tenant becomes available, the landlord is required to lease the premises to this tenant to mitigate the damages recoverable from the former tenant. The former tenant is still liable for the difference between the amount of the rent under the original lease and the rent received from the new tenant. If the landlord has not used the reasonable means necessary to find a new tenant, presumably a court can reduce the award made by the amount of rent the landlord could have received had such reasonable means been used.

In the majority of states, persons whose employment has been wrongfully terminated owe a duty to mitigate damages suffered because of their employers' breach of the employment contract. In other words, wrongfully terminated employees have a duty to take similar jobs if they are available. If the employees fail to do this, the damages they are awarded will be equivalent to their salaries less the incomes they would have received in similar jobs obtained by reasonable means. The employer has the burden of proving that such a job existed and that the employee could have been hired. Normally, the employee is under no duty to take a job of a different type and rank, however.

LIQUIDATED DAMAGES PROVISIONS

A **liquidated damages** provision in a contract specifies that a certain dollar amount is to be paid in the event of a *future* default or breach of contract. (*Liquidated* means determined, settled, or fixed.) For example, a provision requiring a construction contractor to pay $300 for every day he or she is late in completing the construction is a liquidated damages provision. Liquidated damages provisions are frequently used in construction contracts because it is difficult to estimate the amount of damages that would be caused by a delay in completing construction. These clauses are also common in contracts for the sale of goods, and Section 2–718(1) of the Uniform Commercial Code (UCC) specifically authorizes the use of liquidated damages clauses.[4]

LIQUIDATED DAMAGES VERSUS PENALTIES When a contract specifies a sum to be paid for nonperformance, the issue becomes whether the amount should be treated as liquidated damages or as a penalty. Liquidated damages provisions are enforceable; penalty provisions are not. Generally, if the amount stated is excessive and the clause is designed to *penalize* the breaching party, a court will consider it a **penalty.** If the amount specified is a reasonable estimation of actual damages, a court may enforce it as a liquidated damages provision.

FACTORS COURTS CONSIDER To determine if a particular provision is for liquidated damages or for a penalty, two questions must be answered:

1. When the contract was entered into, was it apparent that damages would be difficult to estimate in the event of a breach?

2. Was the amount set as damages a reasonable estimate and not excessive?[5]

If the answers to both questions are yes, the provision normally will be enforced. If either answer is no, the provision normally will not be enforced. For example, in a case involving a sophisticated business contract to lease computer equipment, the court held that a liquidated damages provision that valued computer equipment at more than four times its market value was a reasonable estimate. According to the court, the amount of actual damages was difficult to ascertain at the time the contract was formed because of the "speculative nature of the value of computers at termination of lease schedules."[6]

In the following case, the court considered a liquidated damages provision in the context of an agreement for the lease of a hotel.

---

4. Note that in 2003, this section was amended (see Chapter 20). Under the revised version of the statute, only in consumer contracts must the amount of damages be difficult to estimate and a reasonable forecast. In contracts between merchants, it is no longer required that the damages be difficult to estimate. See Official Comment 2.

5. *Restatement (Second) of Contracts,* Section 356(1).

6. *Winthrop Resources Corporation v. Eaton Hydraulics, Inc.,* 361 F.3d 465 (8th Cir. 2004).

CASE 18.2   Green Park Inn, Inc. v. Moore

North Carolina
Court of Appeals, 2002.
562 S.E.2d 53.
http://www.nccourts.org[a]

COMPANY PROFILE *Green Park Inn (http://www.greenparkinn.com) is one of the oldest hotels in the United States. Established in 1882 and listed on the National Register of Historic Places, it is located in the Blue Ridge Mountains near Blowing Rock, North Carolina. Eminent guests have included Annie Oakley, Herbert Hoover, Eleanor Roosevelt, Margaret Mitchell, Calvin Coolidge, and John D. Rockefeller. Green Park Inn is a full-service, first class hotel and restaurant.*

BACKGROUND AND FACTS *Allen and Pat McCain own Green Park Inn, Inc., which operates the Green Park Inn. In 1996, they leased the Inn to GMAFCO, LLC, which is owned by Gary and Gail Moore. The lease agreement provided that, in case of a default by GMAFCO, Green Park, Inc., would be entitled to $500,000 as "liquidated damages." GMAFCO defaulted on the February 2000 rent. Green Park Inn, Inc., gave GMAFCO an opportunity to cure the default, but GMAFCO made no further payments and returned possession of the property to the lessor. When Green Park Inn, Inc., sought the "liquidated damages," the Moores refused to pay. Green Park Inn, Inc., filed a suit in a North Carolina state court against the Moores, GMAFCO, and their bank to obtain the $500,000. The defendants contended in part that the lease clause requiring payment of "liquidated damages" was an unenforceable penalty provision. The court ordered the defendants to pay Green Park Inn, Inc. The defendants appealed to a state intermediate appellate court.*

IN THE LANGUAGE OF THE COURT

HUDSON, Judge.

* * * *

The parties agreed to the following in the liquidated damages clause of the Lease Agreement:

> Allen and Pat McCain, the only two shareholders of lessor, have actively worked in the day to day operation of the hotel for the past fourteen years, and have steadily built up the clientele, reputation and physical plant of the hotel, and, correspondingly, the revenues/profits of the hotel. In addition, Allen and Pat McCain are 64 and 55 years old respectively, and both retired from the business after this lease was agreed to. The McCains have retired to Florida, and would have to relocate back to Blowing Rock for extended periods of time if they are forced out of retirement to take over operation of the hotel. The parties agree to the following items which will be included in lessor's damages:
>
> (a) restoration of the physical plant;
> (b) lost lease payments owed to lessor which will not be paid because of lessee's breach with due consideration having been given to lessor's obligation to mitigate damages;
> (c) harm to the reputation of the hotel, which will have to be remedied by lessor;
> (d) interruption of business damages caused by the necessity of lessor having to hire new employees to recommence operations.

While some of the items listed in the liquidated damages provision are not indefinite or uncertain, others, such as the harm to the hotel's reputation or the cost to the McCains of being forced out of retirement, clearly would have been difficult to ascertain at the time the Lease Agreement was signed. * * *

Whether a liquidated damages amount is a reasonable estimate of the damages that would likely result from a default is a question of fact. * * * [McCain] stated that, after he and his wife were forced out of retirement and back to Blowing Rock to operate the hotel, "[t]he estimate of $500,000.00 as the fair and reasonable estimate to measure the damages suffered by us in the event of default has proven to be just that fair and reasonable." Additionally, the Lease Agreement states that "[t]he parties have agreed that the sum of Five Hundred Thousand Dollars ($500,000.00) represents a fair and reasonable estimate and measure of the damages to be suffered by lessor in the event of default by lessee." Defendants have proffered [offered] no evidence to show the liquidated damages amount was unreasonable. [Emphasis added.]

a. Select the link to "Court Opinions," enter "Green Park" in the box labeled "Keywords," and click on "Search." Select the name of the case from the resulting list to access the opinion. The North Carolina Appellate Division Reporter maintains this Web site.

 **CASE 18.2** | **Continued**   **DECISION AND REMEDY** *The state intermediate appellate court affirmed the decision of the lower court. The lease provision satisfied the two-part test for liquidated damages. The amount of the damages would have been difficult to determine at the time that the lease was signed, and the estimate of the damages was reasonable.*

WHAT IF THE FACTS WERE DIFFERENT? *If the lease had specified $3 million in damages, would the result in this case have been different? If so, in what way?*

SECTION 2 | Rescission and Restitution

As discussed in Chapter 17, *rescission* is essentially an action to undo, or terminate, a contract—to return the contracting parties to the positions they occupied prior to the transaction.[7] When fraud, a mistake, duress, undue influence, misrepresentation, or lack of capacity to contract is present, unilateral rescission is available. Rescission may also be available by

statute.[8] The failure of one party to perform entitles the other party to rescind the contract. The rescinding party must give prompt notice to the breaching party.

RESTITUTION

Generally, to rescind a contract, both parties must make **restitution** to each other by returning goods, property, or funds previously conveyed.[9] If the physical

---

7. The rescission discussed here is *unilateral* rescission, in which only one party wants to undo the contract. In mutual rescission, both parties agree to undo the contract (see Chapter 17). Mutual rescission discharges the contract; unilateral rescission is generally available as a remedy for breach of contract.

8. The Federal Trade Commission and many states have rules or statutes allowing consumers to unilaterally rescind contracts made at home with door-to-door salespersons. Rescission is allowed within three days for any reason or for no reason at all. See, for example, California Civil Code Section 1689.5.

9. *Restatement (Second) of Contracts*, Section 370.

CONCEPT SUMMARY 18.1 | Damages

REMEDY	AVAILABILITY	RESULT
COMPENSATORY DAMAGES	A party sustains and proves an injury arising directly from the loss of the bargain.	The injured party is compensated for the loss of the bargain.
CONSEQUENTIAL DAMAGES	Special circumstances, of which the breaching party is aware or should be aware, cause the injured party additional loss.	The injured party is given the *entire* benefit of the bargain.
PUNITIVE DAMAGES	Damages are normally available only when a tort is also involved.	The wrongdoer is punished, and others are deterred from committing similar acts.
NOMINAL DAMAGES	There is no financial loss.	Wrongdoing is established without actual damages being suffered. The plaintiff is awarded a nominal amount (such as $1) in damages.
LIQUIDATED DAMAGES	A contract provides a specific amount to be paid as damages in the event that the contract is later breached.	The nonbreaching party is paid the amount stipulated in the contract for the breach, unless the amount is construed as a penalty.

property or goods can be returned, they must be. If the goods or property have been consumed, restitution must be made in an equivalent amount of money.

Essentially, restitution refers to the plaintiff's recapture of a benefit conferred on the defendant through which the defendant has been unjustly enriched. For example, Katie pays $10,000 to Bob in return for Bob's promise to design a house for her. The next day Bob calls Katie and tells her that he has taken a position with a large architectural firm in another state and cannot design the house. Katie decides to hire another architect that afternoon. Katie can obtain restitution of the $10,000.

RESTITUTION IS NOT LIMITED TO RESCISSION CASES

Restitution may be appropriate when a contract is rescinded, but the right to restitution is not limited to rescission cases. Restitution may be sought in actions for breach of contract, tort actions, and other actions at law or in equity. Usually, restitution can be obtained when funds or property has been transferred by mistake or because of fraud. An award in a case may include restitution of funds or property obtained through embezzlement, conversion, theft, copyright infringement, or misconduct by a party in a confidential or other special relationship.

SECTION 3 | Specific Performance

The equitable remedy of **specific performance** calls for the performance of the act promised in the contract. This remedy is quite attractive to the nonbreaching party for three reasons:

1. The nonbreaching party need not worry about collecting the money damages awarded by a court (see the discussion in Chapter 3 of some of the difficulties that may arise when trying to enforce court judgments).
2. The nonbreaching party need not spend time seeking an alternative contract.
3. The performance is more valuable than the money damages.

Normally, however, specific performance will not be granted unless the party's legal remedy (money damages) is inadequate.[10] For this reason, contracts for the sale of goods rarely qualify for specific performance. The legal remedy—money damages—is ordinarily adequate in such situations because substantially identical goods can be bought or sold in the market. Only if the goods are unique will a court grant specific performance. For example, paintings, sculptures, or rare books or coins are so unique that money damages will not enable a buyer to obtain substantially identical substitutes in the market.

SALE OF LAND

Specific performance is granted to a buyer in a contract for the sale of land. The legal remedy for breach of a land sales contract is inadequate because every parcel of land is considered to be unique. Money damages will not compensate a buyer adequately because the same land in the same location obviously cannot be obtained elsewhere. Only when specific performance is unavailable (for example, when the seller has sold the property to someone else) will money damages be awarded instead.

CONTRACTS FOR PERSONAL SERVICES

Personal-service contracts require one party to work personally for another party. Courts normally refuse to grant specific performance of personal-service contracts. If a contract is not deemed personal, the remedy at law may be adequate if substantially identical service (for example, lawn mowing) is available from other persons.

In individually tailored personal-service contracts, courts will not order specific performance by the party who was to be employed because public policy strongly discourages involuntary servitude.[11] Moreover, the courts do not want to have to monitor a continuing service contract if supervision would be difficult—as it would be if the contract required the exercise of personal judgment or talent. For example, if you contracted with a brain surgeon to perform brain surgery on you and the surgeon refused to perform, the court would not compel (and you certainly would not want) the surgeon to perform under those circumstances. A court cannot assure meaningful performance in such a situation.[12]

---

10. *Restatement (Second) of Contracts*, Section 359.

11. The Thirteenth Amendment to the U.S. Constitution prohibits involuntary servitude, and thus a court will not order a person to perform under a personal-service contract. A court may grant an order (injunction) prohibiting that person from engaging in similar contracts in the future for a period of time, however.
12. Similarly, courts often refuse to order specific performance of construction contracts because courts are not set up to operate as construction supervisors or engineers.

SECTION 4 | Reformation

Reformation is an equitable remedy used when the parties have *imperfectly* expressed their agreement in writing. Reformation allows a court to rewrite the contract to reflect the parties' true intentions.

WHEN FRAUD OR MUTUAL MISTAKE IS PRESENT

Reformation occurs most often when fraud or mutual mistake (for example, a clerical error) is present. It is almost always sought so that some other remedy may then be pursued. For example, if Keshan contracts to buy a certain parcel of land from Malboa but their contract mistakenly refers to a parcel of land different from the one being sold, the contract does not reflect the parties' intentions. Accordingly, a court can reform the contract so that it conforms to the parties' intentions and accurately refers to the parcel of land being sold. Keshan can then, if necessary, show that Malboa has breached the contract as reformed. She can at that time request an order for specific performance.

ORAL CONTRACTS AND COVENANTS NOT TO COMPETE

There are two other situations in which the courts frequently reform contracts. The first involves two parties who have made a binding oral contract. They further agree to put the oral contract in writing, but in doing so, they make an error in stating the terms. Normally, the courts will allow into evidence the cor-

rect terms of the oral contract, thereby reforming the written contract.

The second situation is when the parties have executed a written covenant not to compete (discussed in Chapter 13). If the covenant is for a valid and legitimate purpose (such as the sale of a business) but the area or time restraints of the covenant are unreasonable, some courts will reform the restraints by making them reasonable and will enforce the entire contract as reformed. Other courts, however, will throw out the entire restrictive covenant as illegal.

Exhibit 18–2 graphically summarizes the remedies, including reformation, that are available to the nonbreaching party.

SECTION 5 | Recovery Based on Quasi Contract

Recall from Chapter 10 that quasi contract is a legal theory under which an obligation is imposed in the absence of an agreement. The courts use this theory to prevent unjust enrichment. Hence, quasi contract provides a basis for relief when no enforceable contract exists. Generally, when one party has conferred a benefit on another party, justice requires the party receiving the benefit to pay the reasonable value for it. The party conferring the benefit can recover in *quantum meruit*, which means "as much as he [or she] deserves" (see Chapter 10).

WHEN QUASI CONTRACTS ARE USED

Quasi-contractual recovery is often granted when one party has partially performed under a contract that is

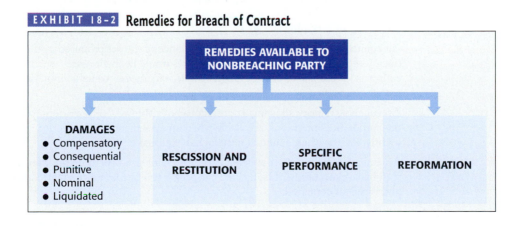

EXHIBIT 18-2 Remedies for Breach of Contract

REMEDIES AVAILABLE TO NONBREACHING PARTY

DAMAGES
- Compensatory
- Consequential
- Punitive
- Nominal
- Liquidated

RESCISSION AND RESTITUTION

SPECIFIC PERFORMANCE

REFORMATION

unenforceable. It provides an alternative to suing for damages and allows the party to recover the reasonable value of the partial performance, measured in some cases according to the benefit received and in others according to the detriment suffered.

For example, suppose that Watson contracts to build two oil derricks for Energy Industries. The derricks are to be built over a period of three years, but the parties do not make a written contract. The Statute of Frauds will thus bar the enforcement of the contract.[13] After Watson completes one derrick, Energy Industries informs him that it will not pay for the derrick. Watson can sue Energy Industries under the theory of quasi contract.

THE REQUIREMENTS OF QUASI CONTRACT

To recover under the theory of quasi contract, the party seeking recovery must show the following:

1. The party has conferred a benefit on the other party.
2. The party conferred the benefit with the reasonable expectation of being paid.
3. The party did not act as a volunteer in conferring the benefit.

---

13. Contracts that by their terms cannot be performed within one year must be in writing to be enforceable. See Chapter 15.

4. The party receiving the benefit would be unjustly enriched by retaining the benefit without paying for it.

In the example just given, Watson can sue in quasi contract because all of the conditions for quasi-contractual recovery have been fulfilled. Watson conferred a benefit on Energy Industries with the reasonable expectation of being paid. The derrick conferred an obvious benefit on Energy Industries. Allowing Energy Industries to retain the derrick without paying Watson would enrich the company unjustly. Therefore, Watson should be able to recover in *quantum meruit* the reasonable value of the oil derrick, which is ordinarily equal to its fair market value.

SECTION 6 | Election of Remedies

In many cases, a nonbreaching party has several remedies available. When the remedies are inconsistent with one another, the common law of contracts requires the party to choose which remedy to pursue. This is called *election of remedies*.

THE PURPOSE OF THE DOCTRINE

The purpose of the doctrine of election of remedies is to prevent double recovery. Suppose, for example, that McCarthy agrees in writing to sell his land to Tally.

CONCEPT SUMMARY 18.2 | Equitable Remedies

REMEDY	DESCRIPTION
RESCISSION AND RESTITUTION	1. *Rescission*—A remedy whereby a contract is canceled and the parties are restored to the original positions that they occupied prior to the transaction. 2. *Restitution*—When a contract is rescinded, both parties must make restitution to each other by returning the goods, property, or money previously conveyed.
SPECIFIC PERFORMANCE	An equitable remedy calling for the performance of the act promised in the contract. Only available when monetary damages would be inadequate—such as in contracts for the sale of land or unique goods—and never available in personal-service contracts.
REFORMATION	An equitable remedy allowing a contract to be "reformed," or rewritten, to reflect the parties' true intentions. Available when an agreement is imperfectly expressed in writing, such as when a mutual mistake has occurred.
RECOVERY BASED ON QUASI CONTRACT	An equitable theory under which a party who confers a benefit on another with the reasonable expectation of being paid can seek a court order for the fair market value of the benefit conferred.

Then McCarthy changes his mind and repudiates the contract. Tally can sue for compensatory damages *or* for specific performance. If Tally could seek compensatory damages in addition to specific performance, she would recover twice for the same breach of contract. The doctrine of election of remedies requires Tally to choose the remedy she wants, and it eliminates any possibility of double recovery. In other words, the election doctrine represents the legal embodiment of the adage "You can't have your cake and eat it, too."

The doctrine has often been applied in a rigid and technical manner, leading to some harsh results. For example, suppose that Beacham is fraudulently induced to buy a parcel of land for $150,000. He spends an additional $10,000 moving onto the land and then discovers the fraud. Instead of suing for damages, Beacham sues to rescind the contract. The court allows Beacham to recover only the purchase price of $150,000 in restitution, but not the additional $10,000 in moving expenses (because the seller did not receive this money, he or she will not be required to return it). So Beacham suffers a net loss of $10,000 on the transaction. If Beacham had elected to sue for damages instead of seeking the remedy of rescission and restitution, he could have recovered the $10,000 as well as the $150,000.

THE UCC'S REJECTION OF THE DOCTRINE

Because of the many problems associated with the doctrine of election of remedies, the UCC expressly rejects it.[14] As will be discussed in Chapter 22, remedies under the UCC are not exclusive but cumulative in nature and include all the available remedies for breach of contract.

PLEADING IN THE ALTERNATIVE

Although the parties must ultimately elect which remedy to pursue, modern court procedures do allow plaintiffs to plead their cases "in the alternative" (pleadings were discussed in Chapter 2). In other words, when the plaintiff originally files a lawsuit, he or she can ask the court to order either rescission (and restitution) or damages, for example. Then, as the case progresses to trial, the parties can elect which remedy

---

14. See UCC 2–703 and 2–711.

is most beneficial or appropriate, or the judge can order one remedy and not another. This process still prevents double recovery because the party can only be awarded one of the remedies that was requested.

SECTION 7 | Waiver of Breach

Under certain circumstances, a nonbreaching party may be willing to accept a defective performance of the contract. This knowing relinquishment of a legal right (that is, the right to require satisfactory and full performance) is called a **waiver.**

CONSEQUENCES OF A WAIVER OF BREACH

When a waiver of a breach of contract occurs, the party waiving the breach cannot take any later action on it. In effect, the waiver erases the past breach; the contract continues as if the breach had never occurred. Of course, the waiver of breach of contract extends only to the matter waived and not to the whole contract.

REASONS FOR WAIVING A BREACH

Businesspersons often waive breaches of contract to get whatever benefit is still possible out of the contract. For example, a seller contracts with a buyer to deliver to the buyer ten thousand tons of coal on or before November 1. The contract calls for the buyer to pay by November 10 for coal delivered. Because of a coal miners' strike, coal is hard to find. The seller breaches the contract by not tendering delivery until November 5. The buyer may be well advised to waive the seller's breach, accept delivery of the coal, and pay as contracted.

WAIVER OF BREACH AND SUBSEQUENT BREACHES

Ordinarily, the waiver by a contracting party will not operate to waive subsequent, additional, or future breaches of contract. This is always true when the subsequent breaches are unrelated to the first breach. For example, an owner who waives the right to sue for late completion of a stage of construction does not waive the right to sue for failure to comply with engineering specifications on the same job. A waiver will be extended to subsequent defective performance, however, if a reasonable person would conclude that similar defective performance in the future will be acceptable. Therefore, a *pattern of conduct* that waives a number of successive breaches will operate as a continued waiver. To change this result, the nonbreaching party should give notice to the breaching party that full performance will be required in the future.

The party who has rendered defective or less-than-full performance remains liable for the damages caused by the breach of contract. In effect, the waiver operates to keep the contract going. The waiver prevents the nonbreaching party from calling the contract to an end or rescinding the contract. The contract continues, but the nonbreaching party can recover damages caused by defective or less-than-full performance.

SECTION 8 | Contract Provisions Limiting Remedies

A contract may include provisions stating that no damages can be recovered for certain types of breaches or that damages must be limited to a maximum amount. The contract may also provide that the only remedy for breach is replacement, repair, or refund of the purchase price. Provisions stating that no damages can be recovered are called *exculpatory clauses* (see

Chapter 13). Provisions that affect the availability of certain remedies are called *limitation-of-liability clauses*.

THE UCC ALLOWS SALES CONTRACTS TO LIMIT REMEDIES

The UCC provides that in a contract for the sale of goods, remedies can be limited. We will examine the UCC provisions on limited remedies in Chapter 22, in the context of the remedies available on the breach of a contract for the sale or lease of goods.[15]

ENFORCEABILITY OF LIMITATION-OF-LIABILITY CLAUSES

Whether these contract provisions and clauses will be enforced depends on the type of breach that is excused by the provision. For example, a provision excluding liability for fraudulent or intentional injury will not be enforced. Likewise, a clause excluding liability for illegal acts or violations of law will not be enforced. A clause excluding liability for negligence may be enforced in certain cases, however. When an exculpatory clause for negligence is contained in a contract made between parties who have roughly equal bargaining positions, the clause usually will be enforced.

At issue in the following case was the enforceability of a limitation-of-liability clause in a contract for a home inspection.

15. See UCC 2–719(1).

CASE 18.3	**Lucier v. Williams**

Superior Court
of New Jersey,
Appellate Division, 2004.
366 N.J.Super. 485,
851 A.2d 62.

LISA, J.A.D. [Judge, Appellate Division]
    *   *   *   *

Plaintiffs Eric Lucier and Karen A. Haley, a young married couple, were first-time home-buyers. They contracted with *   *   * Angela M. Williams and James B. Williams, to purchase a single-family residence in Berlin Township [New Jersey] for $128,500. Lucier and Haley engaged the services of Cambridge Associates, Ltd. (CAL) to perform a home inspection. *   *   * [Al] Vasys performed the inspection and issued the home inspection report *   *   * .

The home inspection agreement contains this provision *   *   * :

    *   *   * CAL's total liability *   *   * shall not exceed *   *   * $500, or 50% of fees actually paid to CAL by Client, whichever sum is smaller. Such causes include, but are not limited to, CAL's negligence *   *   * [or] breach of contract *   *   * .

    *   *   * [W]hen [Lucier] began to read the agreement, in Vasys' presence, he felt some of the language was unfair and confusing [but he signed the contract]. *   *   *
    *   *   * The fee for the home inspection contract was $385 *   *   * .
    *   *   *   *

Lucier and Haley went to settlement and obtained title to the property from the Williams[es]. Shortly after settlement, plaintiffs noticed leaks in the house. They *   *   * engaged the services of a roofing contractor. Plaintiffs contend the roof was defective because of a lack of flashing, which they contend Vasys should have observed and reported to them. *   *   * They contend the cost of repair was about $8,000 to $10,000.

Plaintiffs brought suit [in a New Jersey state court] against * * * CAL [and others] seeking damages to compensate them for the loss occasioned by the alleged defect. * * * CAL * * * moved for * * * summary judgment seeking a declaration that the limit of [its] liability in the action, if any, was one-half the contract price, or $192.50. On January 5, 2001, the motion for * * * summary judgment was granted * * * .
* * * *

Lucier and Haley then filed this appeal * * * .
* * * *

We begin our analysis of the enforceability of the limitation of liability clause with the fundamental proposition that contracts will be enforced as written. Ordinarily, courts will not rewrite contracts to favor a party, for the purpose of giving that party a better bargain. However, courts have not hesitated to strike limited liability clauses that are unconscionable or in violation of public policy.

There is no hard and fast definition of unconscionability. * * * *[U]nconscionability is an amorphous [vague] concept obviously designed to establish a broad business ethic. The standard of conduct that the term implies is a lack of good faith, honesty in fact and observance of fair dealing.* [Emphasis added.]

In determining whether to enforce the terms of a contract, we look not only to its adhesive nature,[a] but also to the subject matter of the contract, the parties' relative bargaining positions, the degree of economic compulsion motivating the adhering party, and the public interests affected by the contract. Where the provision limits a party's liability, we pay particular attention to any inequality in the bargaining power and status of the parties, as well as the substance of the contract.
* * * *

Applying these principles to the home inspection contract before us, we find the limitation of liability provision unconscionable. We do not hesitate to hold it unenforceable for the following reasons: (1) the contract, prepared by the home inspector, is one of adhesion; (2) the parties, one a consumer and the other a professional expert, have grossly unequal bargaining status; and (3) the substance of the provision eviscerates the contract and its fundamental purpose because the potential damage level is so nominal that it has the practical effect of avoiding almost all responsibility for the professional's negligence. * * *
* * * *

The foisting [forcing] of a contract of this type in this setting on an inexperienced consumer clearly demonstrates a lack of fair dealing by the professional. * * *
* * * If, upon the occasional dereliction, the home inspector's only consequence is the obligation to refund a few hundred dollars (the smaller of fifty percent of the inspection contract price or $500), there is no meaningful incentive to act diligently in the performance of home inspection contracts. To compound the problem, such excessively restricted damage allowance is grossly disproportionate to the potential loss to the homebuyer if a substantial defect is negligently overlooked. * * *
* * * *

Of course, we express no comment on whether or not Vasys or CAL breached any duty to Lucier and Haley under their agreement. Our holding here is only that if they are liable, the extent of any damages for which they should be liable is not limited by the terms of the contract.
* * * The order of [the trial court] is reversed. The matter is remanded for further proceedings.

QUESTIONS

1. What is the difference between the limitation-of-liability clause in this case and an exculpatory clause (discussed in Chapter 13)?
2. Why do limitation-of-liability clauses seem especially unfavorable in cases involving professionals?

---

a. *Adhesion contracts* are those drafted by one party and presented to the other party on a take-it-or-leave-it basis. See Chapter 14.

REVIEWING BREACH OF CONTRACT AND REMEDIES

Suppose that Kyle Bruno enters into a contract with X Entertainment to be a stuntman in a movie that is being produced. Bruno is widely known as the best motorcycle stuntman in the business, and the movie to be produced, *Xtreme Riders*, has numerous scenes involving high-speed freestyle street-bike stunts. Filming is set to begin August 1 and end by December 1 so that the film can be released the following summer. Both parties to the contract have stipulated that the filming must end on time to capture the profits from the summer movie market. The contract states that Bruno will be paid 10 percent of the royalties from the movie for his stunts. The contract also includes a liquidated damages provision, which specifies that if Bruno breaches the contract, he will owe X Entertainment one million dollars. In addition, the contract includes a limitation-of-liability clause stating that if Bruno is injured during filming, X Entertainment's liability is limited to nominal damages. Using the information presented in the chapter, answer the following questions.

1. | One day, while Bruno is preparing for a difficult maneuver, he gets into an argument with the director and refuses to perform any stunts at all. Can X Entertainment seek specific performance of the contract? Why or why not?

2. | Suppose that while performing a high-speed wheelie on a motorcycle, Bruno is injured by the intentionally reckless act of an X Entertainment employee. Will a court be likely to enforce the limitation-of-liability clause? Why or why not? If the court allows Bruno to seek damages, what types of damages would he be able to obtain?

3. | What factors would a court consider to determine whether the one-million-dollar liquidated damages provision is valid or constitutes a penalty?

4. | Suppose that there was no liquidated damages provision (or the court refused to enforce it) and X Entertainment breached the contract. The breach caused the release of the film to be delayed until the fall. Could Bruno seek consequential (special) damages for lost profits in that situation? Explain.

TERMS AND CONCEPTS TO REVIEW

consequential damages 343	nominal damages 344	specific performance 348
incidental damages 342	penalty 345	waiver 351
liquidated damages 345	reformation 349	
mitigation of damages 345	restitution 347	

QUESTIONS AND CASE PROBLEMS

18–1. Cohen contracts to sell his house and lot to Windsor for $100,000. The terms of the contract call for Windsor to pay 10 percent of the purchase price as a deposit toward the purchase price, or a down payment. The terms further stipulate that should the buyer breach the contract, the deposit will be retained by Cohen as liquidated damages. Windsor pays the deposit, but because her expected financing of the $90,000 balance falls through, she breaches the contract. Two weeks later Cohen sells the house and lot to Ballard for $105,000. Windsor demands her $10,000 back, but Cohen refuses, claiming that Windsor's breach and the contract terms entitle him to keep the deposit. Discuss who is correct.

18–2. QUESTION WITH SAMPLE ANSWER

In which of the following situations would specific performance be an appropriate remedy? Discuss fully.

(a) Thompson contracts to sell her house and lot to Cousteau. Then, on finding another buyer willing to pay a higher purchase price, she refuses to deed the property to Cousteau.

(b) Amy contracts to sing and dance in Fred's nightclub for one month, beginning May 1. She then refuses to perform.

(c) Hoffman contracts to purchase a rare coin owned by Erikson, who is breaking up his coin collection. At the last minute, Erikson decides to keep his coin collection intact and refuses to deliver the coin to Hoffman.

(d) ABC Corp. has three shareholders: Panozzo, who owns 48 percent of the stock; Chang, who owns another 48 percent; and Ryan, who owns 4 percent. Ryan contracts to sell her 4 percent to Chang. Later, Ryan refuses to transfer the shares to Chang.

For a sample answer to this question, go to Appendix I at the end of this text.

18–3. Ken owns and operates a famous candy store and makes most of the candy sold in the store. Business is particularly heavy during the Christmas season. Ken contracts with Sweet, Inc., to purchase ten thousand pounds of sugar to be delivered on or before November 15. Ken has informed Sweet that this particular order is to be used for the Christmas season business. Because of problems at the refinery, the sugar is not tendered to Ken until December 10, at which time Ken refuses it as being too late. Ken has been unable to purchase the quantity of sugar needed to meet his Christmas orders and has had to turn down numerous regular customers, some of whom have indicated that they will purchase candy elsewhere in the future. What sugar Ken has been able to purchase has cost him 10 cents per pound above the price contracted for with Sweet. Ken sues Sweet for breach of contract, claiming as damages the higher price paid for sugar from others, lost profits from this year's lost Christmas sales, future lost profits from customers who have indicated that they will discontinue doing business with him, and punitive damages for failure to meet the contracted delivery date. Sweet claims Ken is limited to compensatory damages only. Discuss who is correct, and why.

18–4. Wallechinsky purchases a used automobile from Anderson Motors, paying $1,000 down and agreeing to pay off the balance in thirty-six monthly payments of $200 each. The terms of the agreement call for Wallechinsky to make a payment on or before the first of each month. During the first six months, Anderson receives a $200 payment before the first of each month. During the next six months, Wallechinsky's payment is never made until the fifth of the month. Anderson accepts and cashes the payment check each time. When Wallechinsky tenders the thirteenth payment on the fifth of the next month, Anderson refuses to accept the check, claiming that Wallechinsky is in breach of contract. Anderson demands the entire balance owed. Wallechinsky claims that Anderson cannot hold her in breach. Discuss the result in detail.

18–5. MITIGATION OF DAMAGES. Vuylsteke, a single mother with three children, lived in Portland, Oregon. Cynthia Broan also lived in Oregon until she moved to New York City to open and operate an art gallery. Broan contacted Vuylsteke and invited her to manage the gallery under a one-year contract for an annual salary of $72,000. To begin work, Vuylsteke relo-

cated to New York. As part of the move, Vuylsteke transferred custody of her children to her husband, who lived in London, England. In accepting the job, Vuylsteke also forfeited her husband's alimony and child-support payments, including unpaid amounts of nearly $30,000. Before Vuylsteke started work, Broan repudiated the contract. Unable to find employment for more than an annual salary of $25,000, Vuylsteke moved to London to be near her children. Vuylsteke filed a suit in an Oregon state court against Broan, seeking damages for breach of contract. Should the court hold, as Broan argued, that Vuylsteke did not take reasonable steps to mitigate her damages? Why or why not? [*Vuylsteke v. Broan*, 172 Or.App. 74, 17 P.3d 1072 (2001)]

18–6. MITIGATION OF DAMAGES. William West, an engineer, worked for Bechtel Corp., an organization of about 150 engineering and construction companies, which is headquartered in San Francisco, California, and operates worldwide. Except for a two-month period in 1985, Bechtel employed West on long-term assignments or short-term projects for thirty years. In October 1997, West was offered a position on a project with Saudi Arabian Bechtel Co. (SABCO), which West understood would be for two years. In November, however, West was terminated for what he believed was his "age and lack of display of energy." After his return to California, West received numerous offers from Bechtel for work that suited his abilities and met his salary expectations, but he did not accept any of them and did not look for other work. Three months later, he filed a suit in a California state court against Bechtel, alleging in part breach of contract and seeking the salary he would have earned during two years with SABCO. Bechtel responded in part that, even if there had been a breach, West had failed to mitigate his damages. Is Bechtel correct? Discuss. [*West v. Bechtel Corp.*, 96 Cal.App.4th 966, 117 Cal.Rptr.2d 647 (1 Dist. 2002)]

18–7. CASE PROBLEM WITH SAMPLE ANSWER

Tyna Ek met Russell Peterson in Seattle, Washington. Peterson persuaded Ek to buy a boat that he had once owned, the *O'Hana Kai*, which was in Juneau, Alaska. Ek paid $43,000 for the boat, and in January 2000, the parties entered into a contract. In the contract, Peterson agreed to make the vessel seaworthy so that within one month it could be transported to Seattle, where he would pay its moorage costs. He would also renovate the boat at his own expense in return for a portion of the profit on its resale in 2001. At the time of the resale, Ek would recover her costs, after which she would reimburse Peterson for his expenses. Ek loaned Peterson her cell phone so that they could communicate while he prepared the vessel for the trip to Seattle. In March, Peterson, who was still in Alaska, borrowed $4,000 from Ek. Two months later, Ek began to receive unanticipated, unauthorized bills for vessel parts and moorage, the use of her phone, and charges on her credit card. She went to Juneau to take possession of the boat. Peterson moved it to Petersburg, Alaska, where he registered it under a false name, and then to Taku Harbor, where the police seized it. Ek filed a suit in an Alaska state court against Peterson, alleging breach of contract and seeking damages. If the court finds in Ek's favor, what should her damages include? Discuss. [*Peterson v. Ek*, 93 P.3d 458 (Alaska 2004)]

To view a sample answer for this case problem, go to this book's Web site at http://wbl.westbuslaw.com, select "Chapter 18," and click on "Case Problem with Sample Answer."

18–8. LIQUIDATED DAMAGES VERSUS PENALTIES. Every homeowner in the Putnam County, Indiana, subdivision of Stardust Hills must be a member of the Stardust Hills Owners Association, Inc., and must pay annual dues of $200 for the maintenance of common areas and other community services. Under the association's rules, dues paid more than ten days late "shall bear a delinquent fee at a rate of $2.00 per day." Phyllis Gaddis owned a Stardust Hills lot on which she failed to pay the dues. Late fees began to accrue. Nearly two months later, the association filed a suit in an Indiana state court to collect the unpaid dues and the late fees. Gaddis argued in response that the delinquent fee was an unenforceable penalty. What questions should be considered in determining the status of this fee? Should the association's rule regarding assessment of the fee be enforced? Explain. [*Gaddis v. Stardust Hills Owners Association, Inc.*, 804 N.E.2d 231 (Ind.App. 2004)]

18–9. A QUESTION OF ETHICS

Julio Garza was employed by the Texas Animal Health Commission (TAHC) as a health inspector in 1981. His responsibilities included tagging cattle, vaccinating and tattooing calves, and working livestock markets. Garza was injured on the job in 1988 and underwent surgery in January 1989. When his paid leave was exhausted, he asked TAHC for light-duty work, specifically the job of tick inspector, but his supervisor refused the request. In September, TAHC notified Garza that he was fired. Garza sued TAHC and others, alleging in part wrongful termination, and an important issue before the court was whether Garza had mitigated his damages. The court found that in the seven years between his termination and his trial date, Garza had held only one job—an

unpaid job on his parents' ranch. When asked how often he had looked for work during that time, Garza responded that he did not know, but he had looked in "several" places. The last time he had looked for work was three or four months before the trial. That effort was merely an informal inquiry to his neighbors about working on their ranch. In view of these facts, consider the following questions. [*Texas Animal Health Commission v. Garza*, 27 S.W.3d 54 (Tex.App.—San Antonio 2000)]

(a) The court in this case stated that the "general rule as to mitigation of damages in breach of employment suits is that the discharged employee must use reasonable diligence to mitigate damages by seeking other employment." In your opinion, did Garza fulfill this requirement? If you were the judge, how would you rule in this case?

(b) Assume for the moment that Garza had indeed been wrongfully terminated. In this situation, would it be fair to Garza to require him to mitigate his damages? Why or why not?

(c) Generally, what are the ethical underpinnings of the rule that employees seeking damages for breach of employment contracts must mitigate their damages?

18–10. VIDEO QUESTION

Go to this text's Web site at http://wbl.westbuslaw.com and select "Chapter 18." Click on "Video Questions" and view the video titled *Midnight Run*. Then answer the following questions.

(a) In the video, Eddie (Joe Pantoliano) and Jack (Robert DeNiro) negotiate a contract for Jack to find the Duke, a mob accountant who embezzled funds, and bring him back for trial. Assume that the contract is valid. If Jack breaches the contract by failing to bring in the Duke, what kinds of remedies, if any, can Eddie seek? Explain your answer.

(b) Would the equitable remedy of specific performance be available to either Jack or Eddie in the event of a breach? Why or why not?

(c) Now assume that the contract between Eddie and Jack is unenforceable. Nevertheless, Jack performs his side of the bargain (brings in the Duke). Does Jack have any legal recourse in this situation? Why or why not?

LAW | on the Web

For updated links to resources available on the Web, as well as a variety of other materials, visit this text's Web site at **http://wbl.westbuslaw.com**.

For a summary of how contracts may be breached and other information on contract law, go to Lawyers.com's "Business Needs" Web page at

http://www.lawyers.com/lawyers/P~B~General+Business~LDC.html

Then click on "Contracts" and review your options under the "Get Info" section.

The following sites offer information on contract law, including breach of contract and remedies:

http://www.nolo.com/Chunkcm/CM9.html

http://www.law.cornell.edu/topics/contracts.html

LEGAL RESEARCH EXERCISES ON THE WEB

Go to **http://wbl.westbuslaw.com**, the Web site that accompanies this text. Select "Chapter 18" and click on "Internet Exercises." There you will find the following Internet research exercises that you can perform to learn more about topics covered in this chapter.

Activity 18–1: LEGAL PERSPECTIVE
Contract Damages and Contract Theory

Activity 18–2: MANAGEMENT PERSPECTIVE
The Duty to Mitigate

CHAPTER 19
E-Contracts

The basic principles of contract law that were covered in the previous chapters evolved over an extended period of time. Certainly, they were formed long before cyberspace and electronic contracting became realities. Therefore, new legal theories, new adaptations of existing laws, and new laws are needed to govern **e-contracts,** or contracts entered into electronically. To date, however, most courts have adapted traditional contract law principles and, when applicable, provisions of the Uniform Commercial Code (UCC) to cases involving e-contract disputes. (As you will read in Chapter 20, Articles 2 and 2A of the UCC, which cover the sale and lease of goods, were amended in 2003 to accommodate electronic commerce.)

In the first part of this chapter, we look at how traditional laws are being applied to contracts formed online. We then examine some new laws that have been created to apply in situations in which traditional laws governing contracts have sometimes been thought inadequate. For example, traditional laws governing signature and writing requirements are not easily adapted to contracts formed in the online environment. Thus, new laws have been created to address these issues.

SECTION 1 | Online Contract Formation

Today, numerous contracts are being formed online. Although the medium through which these contracts are generated has changed, the age-old problems attending contract formation have not. Disputes concerning contracts formed online continue to center around contract terms and whether the parties voluntarily assented to those terms.

Note that online contracts may be formed not only for the sale of goods and services but also for the purpose of *licensing*. For example, as you will learn later in this chapter, the "sale" of software generally involves a license, or a right to use the software, rather than the passage of title (ownership rights) from the seller to the buyer. As you read through the following pages, keep in mind that although we typically refer to the offeror and offeree as a *seller* and a *buyer*, in many transactions these parties would be more accurately described as a *licensor* and a *licensee*.

ONLINE OFFERS

Sellers doing business via the Internet can protect themselves against contract disputes and legal liability by creating offers that clearly spell out the terms that will govern their transactions if the offers are accepted. Significant terms should be conspicuous and easy to view.

An important rule to keep in mind is that the offeror controls the offer and thus the resulting contract. Therefore, the seller (offeror) should anticipate the terms that he or she wants to include in a contract and provide for them in the offer. At a minimum, an online offer should include the following provisions:

1. A provision specifying the remedies available to the buyer if the goods turn out to be defective or if the contract is otherwise breached. Any limitation of remedies should be clearly spelled out.
2. A clause that clearly indicates what will constitute the buyer's agreement to the terms of the offer.
3. A provision specifying how payment for the goods or services and for any applicable taxes must be made.

4. A statement of the seller's refund and return policies.

5. Disclaimers of liability for certain uses of the goods. For example, an online seller of business forms may add a disclaimer that the seller does not accept responsibility for the buyer's reliance on the forms rather than on an attorney's advice.

6. A statement explaining how the information gathered about the buyer will be used by the seller.

DISPUTE-SETTLEMENT PROVISIONS In addition to the above provisions, many online offers include provisions relating to dispute settlement. For example, an arbitration clause might be included, indicating that any dispute arising under the contract will be arbitrated in a specified forum.

Many online contracts also contain a **forum-selection clause**—a clause indicating the forum, or location, for the resolution of any dispute arising under the contract. For a discussion of forum-selection clauses in online contracts, see this chapter's *Contemporary Legal Debates* feature on the next two pages.

DISPLAYING THE OFFER The seller's Web site should include a hypertext link to a page containing the full contract so that potential buyers are made aware of the terms to which they are assenting. The contract generally must be displayed online in a readable format such as a twelve-point typeface. All provisions should be reasonably clear. For example, if a seller is offering certain goods priced according to a complex price schedule, that schedule must be fully provided and explained.

INDICATING HOW THE OFFER CAN BE ACCEPTED An online offer should also include some mechanism by which the customer may accept the offer. Typically, online sellers include boxes containing the words "I agree" or "I accept the terms of the offer" that offerees can click on to indicate acceptance. The agreement resulting from such an acceptance is often called a **click-on agreement.**

ONLINE ACCEPTANCES

In many ways, click-on agreements are the Internet equivalents of *shrink-wrap agreements* (or *shrink-wrap licenses*, as they are sometimes called). Because similar legal problems have arisen with respect to both shrink-wrap and click-on agreements, we look first at how the law has been applied to shrink-wrap agreements.

SHRINK-WRAP AGREEMENTS A **shrink-wrap agreement** is an agreement whose terms are expressed inside a box in which the goods are packaged. (The term *shrink-wrap* refers to the plastic that covers the box.) Usually, the party who opens the box is told that she or he agrees to the terms by keeping whatever is in the box. Similarly, when the purchaser opens a software package, he or she agrees to abide by the terms of the limited license agreement. For example, suppose that John orders a new computer from a national company, which ships the computer to John. Along with the computer, the box contains an agreement setting forth the terms of the sale, including what remedies are available. The document also states that John's retention of the computer for longer than thirty days will be construed as an acceptance of the terms.

In most instances, a shrink-wrap agreement is not between a retailer and a buyer, but between the manufacturer of the hardware or software and the ultimate buyer-user of the product. The terms generally concern warranties, remedies, and other issues associated with the use of the product.

—Shrink-Wrap Agreements and Enforceable Contract Terms. The *Restatement (Second) of Contracts*—a compilation of common law contract principles—states that parties may agree to a contract "by written or spoken words or by other action or by failure to act."[1] The Uniform Commercial Code (UCC)—the law governing sales contracts—has a similar provision. Section 2–204 of the UCC states that any contract for the sale of goods "may be made in any manner sufficient to show agreement, including conduct by both parties which recognizes the existence of such a contract." The courts have used these provisions to conclude that a binding contract can be created by conduct, including conduct accepting the terms in either a shrink-wrap agreement or a click-on agreement. Thus, a buyer's failure to object to terms contained within a shrink-wrapped software package (or an online offer) may constitute an acceptance of the terms by conduct.[2]

In many cases, the courts have enforced the terms of shrink-wrap agreements, reasoning that shrink-wrap

---

1. *Restatement (Second) of Contracts*, Section 19.
2. For a leading case on this issue, see *ProCD, Inc. v. Zeidenberg*, 86 F.3d 1447 (7th Cir. 1996).

The Enforceability of Forum-Selection Clauses

Parties to contracts frequently include clauses in their contracts indicating how any disputes that arise may be resolved. For example, as noted elsewhere in this chapter, contracts often contain arbitration clauses stipulating that any dispute will be resolved through arbitration proceedings rather than through litigation. A contract may also include a *forum-selection clause*, specifying the forum (such as the court or jurisdiction) in which the dispute will be resolved.

As you will read in Chapter 20, forum-selection clauses are routinely included in contracts for the international sale of goods because the parties to such contracts are often quite distant from one another geographically. Determining the forum where any dispute arising under a contract will be settled is thus normally part of the bargaining process when the contract is being formed.

FORUM SELECTION AND ONLINE CONTRACTS

Because parties to contracts formed online may be located at physically distant sites, online sellers of goods and services normally include forum-selection clauses in their contracts. These clauses can help online sellers avoid having to appear in court in many distant jurisdictions when customers are dissatisfied with their purchases. (Recall from Chapter 2 that under a state long arm statute, a state court may exercise jurisdiction over an out-of-state defendant if the defendant has "minimum contacts" with the state.)

For example, suppose that a California buyer purchases defective goods sold online by a company located in New York. Unable to obtain a refund or adequate replacement goods from the seller, the California buyer files suit against the seller in a California state court. If the New York seller meets the "minimum-contacts" requirement for the California court to exercise jurisdiction over the dispute, the New York seller will need to travel to California to defend against the lawsuit. Forum-selection clauses in online contracts offer a way for sellers to avoid this problem.

ARE FORUM-SELECTION CLAUSES FAIR TO ONLINE PURCHASERS?

Clearly, those who sell goods and services online benefit from including forum-selection clauses in their contracts. Yet what about the purchasers of these goods and services? Continuing with the above example, suppose that the seller's contract includes a forum-selection clause specifying New York as the forum where any disputes under the contract must be resolved. An individual in California may not have the resources to travel to New York to initiate proceedings against the seller in a New York court. In effect, the clause deprives the buyer of the ability to easily sue the seller in the buyer's home state.

Nonetheless, normally the courts will enforce clauses or contracts to which parties have voluntarily agreed, and this principle extends to forum-selection clauses in online contracts as well. As one court held (in a case challenging the enforceability of the forum-selection clause in Microsoft Network's online agreement), "If a forum-selection clause is terms should be treated the same as the terms of other contracts. Some courts have concluded that by including the terms with the product, the seller proposes a contract that the buyer can accept by using the product after having an opportunity to read the terms. Additionally, it seems practical from a business's point of view to enclose a full statement of the legal terms of a sale with the product rather than to read the statement over the phone, for example, when a buyer calls in an order for the product.

—*Shrink-Wrap Terms That May Not Be Enforced.* Courts do not enforce all of the terms included in shrink-wrap agreements. An important consideration is whether the parties form their contract before or after the seller communicates the terms of the shrink-wrap agreement to the buyer. If a court finds that the buyer learned of the shrink-wrap terms *after* the parties entered into a contract, the court may conclude that those terms were proposals for additional terms and were not part of the contract unless the buyer expressly agreed to them.[3]

---

3. See, for example, *Klocek v. Gateway, Inc.*, 104 F.Supp.2d 1332 (D.Kans. 2000).

clear in its purport [meaning] and has been presented to the party to be bound in a fair and forthright fashion, no . . . policies or principles have been violated."[a]

FORUM-SELECTION CLAUSES ARE NOT ALWAYS ENFORCED

Depending on the jurisdiction, however, a court may make an exception to the rule that forum-selection clauses in online contracts should be enforced. Consider a case decided by a California appellate court in 2001. The case was brought against America Online, Inc. (AOL), by Al Mendoza and other former AOL subscribers living in California. The plaintiffs, who sought compensatory and punitive damages, claimed that AOL had continued to debit their credit cards for monthly service fees, without authorization, for some time after they had terminated their subscriptions. AOL moved to dismiss the action on the basis of the forum-selection clause in its "Terms of Service" agreement with subscribers. That clause required all lawsuits under the agreement to be brought in Virginia, AOL's home state. At issue in the case was whether the clause was enforceable.

A California trial court held that it was not. The court based its conclusion on the finding that the clause, among other things, was contained in a standard form and was not readily identifiable by subscribers because of its small type and

location at the end of the agreement. According to the court, the clause was "unfair and unreasonable," and public policy was best served by denying enforceability to the clause. A California appellate court affirmed the lower court's ruling and also gave another reason why the clause should not be enforced. The appellate court noted that Virginia law provides "significantly less" consumer protection than California law, and therefore enforcing the forum-selection clause would violate the "strong California public policy" expressed in the state's consumer protection statutes.[b]

WHERE DO YOU STAND?

The case just discussed may mark an exception to the rule that forum-selection clauses in online contracts are generally enforceable. Yet different courts have reached varying conclusions on this issue, which continues to elicit debate. On the one hand, online sellers do need to protect themselves from the possibility of having to travel to distant states time and again to resolve disputes. Also, it is a general principle of contract law that clauses voluntarily entered into by the parties should be enforced. On the other hand, in some instances forum-selection clauses clearly impose an unfair burden on those who purchase goods or services from online vendors. What is your position on this issue? Can you think of a solution that is fair to all parties and consistent with contract law principles?

---

a. *Caspi v. MSN, Inc.*, 323 N.J.Super. 118, 732 A.2d 528 (1999). For another example, see *DeJohn v. The .TV Corp. International*, 245 F.Supp.2d 913 (2003).

b. *America Online, Inc. v. Superior Court*, 90 Cal.App.4th 1, 108 Cal.Rptr.2d 699 (2001).

CLICK-ON AGREEMENTS As described earlier, a click-on agreement (also sometimes called a *click-on license* or *click-wrap agreement*) arises when a buyer, completing a transaction on a computer, indicates assent to be bound by the terms of an offer by clicking on a button that says, for example, "I agree." The terms may be contained on a Web site through which the buyer is obtaining goods or services, or they may appear on a computer screen when software is loaded. Exhibit 19–1 on page 363 contains the language of a click-on agreement that accompanies a package of software made and marketed by Microsoft.

Generally, under the law governing contracts, including sales and lease contracts covered by the UCC, there is no requirement that all of the terms in a contract must actually have been read by all of the parties to be effective. For example, clicking on a button or box that states "I agree" to certain terms can be enough.

In the following case, the court considered the enforceability of a click-on (click-wrap) software licensing agreement that included a forum-selection clause.

CASE 19.1

United States
District Court,
District of Kansas, 2004.
__ F.Supp.2d __.

Mortgage Plus, Inc. v. DocMagic, Inc.

BACKGROUND AND FACTS *In 1997, Mortgage Plus, Inc., a mortgage lender in Kansas, asked DocMagic, Inc., a California firm, for software to prepare and manage loan documents and for document preparation services. DocMagic sent Mortgage Plus a CD-ROM containing the software, which had to be loaded onto a computer. Before it could be installed, however, a window displayed a "Software License and User Agreement" on the screen. The agreement asked, "Do you accept all terms of the preceding License Agreement? If you choose No, Setup will close." A click on a "Yes" button was needed to continue. The agreement also included a clause designating California as the venue for the resolution of any disputes. To prepare loan documents, the software asked for certain information, which it used to create a worksheet. The worksheet was e-mailed to DocMagic, which completed the documents and returned them via e-mail. Over the next six years, Mortgage Plus borrowers filed claims against the firm, alleging that the firm had made mistakes that cost the borrowers $150,000 to resolve. Mortgage Plus filed a suit in a federal district court against DocMagic, alleging that its software failed to produce documents that met certain legal requirements. The defendant filed a motion to transfer the suit to a federal court in California based on the clause in the click-on agreement.*

IN THE LANGUAGE OF THE COURT

WAXSE, Magistrate J. [Judge]
* * * *

Mortgage Plus argues the purported license agreement is invalid, as it improperly attempts to supplement and/or modify the terms of the parties' original contractual agreement. In support of this argument, Mortgage Plus maintains that prior to the subject license agreement, Mortgage Plus and DocMagic negotiated and entered into a contract whereby Mortgage Plus agreed to pay specific amounts to DocMagic in exchange for document preparation services. Mortgage Plus submits that when DocMagic shipped the software necessary to utilize these services, the parties entered into a binding contract and that neither during these negotiations nor in the resulting agreement did the parties discuss a venue where a potential dispute between the parties would have to be filed and resolved.

* * * *

* * * Mortgage Plus argues it is not bound by the Software Licensing Agreement because the license was not an "agreed-to" modification of the original agreement between the parties. The Court is not persuaded by this argument.

First, Mortgage Plus has failed to present evidence to establish existence of the phantom "original contract," including but not limited to the date the contract was formed, the terms and conditions of the contract (other than pricing) or documents memorializing the agreement. The Court cannot find the software licensing agreement improperly altered the terms and conditions of the original contractual agreement when there is no evidence that an original contractual agreement ever existed.

* * * *

Mortgage Plus next contends that even in the absence of an original agreement, it simply was not aware of and never accepted any version of the Software Licensing Agreement. In support of its contention, Mortgage Plus states * * * a click-wrap agreement consisting of a window entitled "Software Licensing Agreement" appearing prior to installation of software cannot be construed as a legally binding contract * * * .

* * * *

A license is a form of contract and is objectionable on grounds applicable to contracts in general. *By the terms of the license here, installation and use of the software with the license attached constituted acceptance of the license terms.* The license was "bundled" with the DocMagic software, meaning that the software required users to accept the terms by clicking through a series of screens before they could access and subsequently install the software. This type of license is known as a "click-wrap" license agreement. Such agreements are common on websites that sell or distribute software programs. *The term "click-wrap" agreement is borrowed from the idea of "shrink-wrap agreements," which are generally license agreements placed inside the cellophane*

CASE 19.1 Continued *"shrink-wrap" of computer software boxes that, by their terms, become effective once the "shrink-wrap" is opened. Courts have found both types of licenses valid and enforceable. * * * [Emphasis added.]*

    *   *   *   *

    *   *   * *[I]t is undisputed between the parties in this case that Mortgage Plus had to affirmatively click the "Yes" button in assenting to the Software Licensing Agreement as a prerequisite to installing the DocMagic software. It further is undisputed that the software would not be installed if Mortgage Plus did not accept the terms and conditions of the Software Licensing Agreement. Plaintiff had a choice as to whether to download the software and utilize the related services; thus, under the specific facts presented here, installation and use of the software with the attached license constituted an affirmative acceptance of the license terms by Mortgage Plus and the licensing agreement became effective upon this affirmative assent. The Court finds the click-wrap agreement here is a valid contract.*

DECISION AND REMEDY *The court concluded that the software licensing agreement was a valid contract because a user had to agree to its terms before the software could be installed and used. The forum-selection clause was thus enforceable, and the court ordered the suit to be transferred to a federal district court in California.*

WHAT IF THE FACTS WERE DIFFERENT? *Suppose that the individual who clicked on the "Yes" button and installed the software was not authorized to do so. Would the result have been different?*

BROWSE-WRAP TERMS Like the terms of a click-on agreement, **browse-wrap terms** can occur in a transaction conducted over the Internet. Unlike a click-on agreement, however, browse-wrap terms do not require an Internet user to assent to the terms before, say, downloading or using certain software. In other words, a person can install the software without clicking "I agree" to the terms of a license. Offerors of browse-wrap terms generally assert that the terms are binding without the user's active consent.

EXHIBIT 19-1 **A Click-On Agreement**

This exhibit illustrates an online offer to form a contract. To accept the offer, the user simply scrolls down the page and clicks on the "Accept" box.

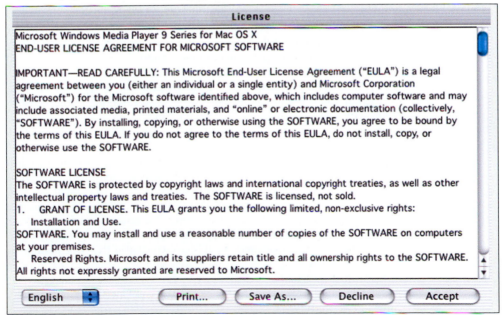

Critics contend that browse-wrap terms are not enforceable because they do not satisfy the basic elements of contract formation. It has been suggested that to form a valid contract online, a user must at least be presented with the terms before indicating assent.[4]

With respect to a browse-wrap term, this would require that a user navigate past it and agree to it before being able to obtain whatever is being granted.

The following case involved the enforceability of a clause in an agreement that the court characterized as a browse-wrap license.

---

4. American Bar Association Committee on the Law of Cyberspace, "Click-Through Agreements: Strategies for Avoiding Disputes on the Validity of Assent" (document presented at the annual American Bar Association meeting in August 2001).

CASE 19.2 — Specht v. Netscape Communications Corp.

United States
Court of Appeals,
Second Circuit, 2002.
306 F.3d 17.

BACKGROUND AND FACTS *Netscape Communications Corporation's "SmartDownload" software makes it easier for users to download files from the Internet without losing progress if they pause to do some other task or their Internet connection is interrupted. Netscape offers SmartDownload free of charge on its Web site to those who indicate by clicking in a designated box that they wish to obtain it. John Gibson clicked in the box and downloaded the software. On the Web site's download page is a reference to a license agreement that is visible only by scrolling to the next screen. Affirmatively indicating assent to the agreement is not required to download the software. The agreement provides that any disputes arising from use of the software are to be submitted to arbitration in California. Believing that the use of SmartDownload transmits private information about its users, Gibson and others filed a suit in a federal district court in New York against Netscape, alleging violations of federal law. Netscape asked the court to order the parties to arbitration in California, as specified in the license agreement. The court denied the request, and Netscape appealed.*

IN THE LANGUAGE OF THE COURT

SOTOMAYER, Circuit Judge.

*   *   *   *

Whether governed by the common law or by Article 2 of the Uniform Commercial Code ("UCC"), a transaction, in order to be a contract, requires a manifestation of agreement between the parties. *Mutual manifestation of assent, whether by written or spoken word or by conduct, is the touchstone of contract.* Although an onlooker observing the disputed transactions in this case would have seen each of the user plaintiffs click on the SmartDownload "Download" button, a consumer's clicking on a download button does not communicate assent to contractual terms if the offer did not make clear to the consumer that clicking on the download button would signify assent to those terms. *   *   * . [Emphasis added.]

*   *   *   *

*   *   * It is true that a party cannot avoid the terms of a contract on the ground that he or she failed to read it before signing. But *   *   * [a]n exception to this general rule exists when the writing does not appear to be a contract and the terms are not called to the attention of the recipient. In such a case, no contract is formed with respect to the undisclosed term.

*   *   *   *

*   *   * Plaintiffs were responding to an offer that did not carry an immediately visible notice of the existence of license terms or require unambiguous manifestation of assent to those terms. Thus, plaintiffs' apparent manifestation of *   *   * consent was to terms contained in a document whose contractual nature was not obvious. Moreover, the fact that, given the position of the scroll bar on their computer screens, plaintiffs may have been aware that an unexplored portion of the Netscape webpage remained below the download button does not mean that they reasonably should have concluded that this portion contained a notice of license terms. *   *   *

*   *   * [I]n circumstances such as these, *   *   * a reference to the existence of license terms on a submerged screen is not sufficient to place consumers on *   *   * notice of those

 **Continued**   terms. The SmartDownload webpage screen was printed in such a manner that it tended to conceal the fact that it was an express acceptance of Netscape's rules and regulations. Internet users may have, as defendants put it, "as much time as they need" to scroll through multiple screens on a webpage, but there is no reason to assume that viewers will scroll down to subsequent screens simply because screens are there.

DECISION AND REMEDY   *The U.S. Court of Appeals for the Second Circuit affirmed the judgment of the lower court. The appellate court held that the plaintiffs had not received reasonable notice of the license terms and had not agreed to those terms before acting on the invitation to download the software. Thus, the plaintiffs were not subject to the arbitration clause.*

SECTION 2 | E-Signatures

In many instances, a contract cannot be enforced unless it is signed by the party against whom enforcement is sought. In the days when many people could not write, documents were signed with an "X." Then handwritten signatures became common, followed by typed signatures, printed signatures, and, most recently, digital signatures that are transmitted electronically. Throughout the evolution of signature technology, the question of what constitutes a valid signature has arisen frequently, and with good rea-

son—without some consensus on what constitutes a valid signature, little business or legal work could be accomplished. In this section, we look at how electronic signatures, or **e-signatures,** can be created and verified on e-contracts, as well as how the parties can enter into agreements that prevent disputes concerning e-signatures.

E-SIGNATURE TECHNOLOGIES

Today, numerous technologies allow electronic documents to be signed. These include digital signatures and alternative technologies.

CONCEPT SUMMARY 19.1 | Online Contract Formation

CONCEPT	DESCRIPTION
ONLINE OFFERS	Generally, the terms of an online offer should be just as inclusive as the terms in an offer made in a written (paper) document. All possible contingencies should be anticipated and provided for in the offer. 1. *Special provisions*—It is particularly important to include dispute-settlement provisions and forum-selection clauses in online offers to prevent jurisdictional issues. 2. *Display of the offer*—The offer should be displayed in such a way as to be easily readable and clear. 3. *Method of acceptance*—An online offer should also include some mechanism, such as an "I agree" or "I accept" box, by which the customer can accept the offer.
ONLINE ACCEPTANCES	1. *Click-on (or click-wrap) agreement*—Online offers may be accepted by clicking on an "I agree" or "I accept" box, resulting in what is often called a "click-on" or "click-wrap" agreement. The terms of the agreement may appear on the Web site through which the buyer is obtaining goods or services, or they may appear on a computer screen when software is downloaded. 2. *Enforceability of click-on agreements*—The courts have enforced click-on agreements, holding that by clicking "I agree," the offeree has indicated acceptance by conduct. Browse-wrap terms (terms in a license that an Internet user does not have to read prior to downloading the product, such as software), however, may not be enforced on the ground that the user is not made aware that he or she is entering into a contract.

DIGITAL SIGNATURES The most common e-signature technology is the *asymmetric cryptosystem,* which creates a digital signature using two different (asymmetric) cryptographic "keys," one private and one public. With this system, a person attaches a digital signature to a document using a private key, or code. The key has a publicly available counterpart. Anyone with the appropriate software can use the public key to verify that the digital signature was made using the private key. A **cybernotary,** or legally recognized certification authority, issues the key pair, identifies the owner of the keys, and certifies the validity of the public key. The cybernotary also serves as a repository for public keys.

SIGNATURE DYNAMICS With another type of signature technology, known as *signature dynamics,* a sender's signature is captured using a stylus and an electronic digitizer pad. A computer program takes the signature's measurements, the sender's identity, the time and date of the signature, and the identity of the hardware. This information is then placed in an encrypted *biometric token* attached to the document being transmitted. To verify the authenticity of the signature, the recipient of the document compares the measurements of the signature with the measurements in the token. When this type of e-signature is used, it is not necessary to have a third party verify the signer's identity.

OTHER E-SIGNATURE FORMS Still other forms of e-signatures have been—or are now being—developed as well. For example, some e-signatures use "smart cards." A *smart card* is a device the size of a credit card that is embedded with code and other data. Like credit and debit cards, a smart card can be inserted into computers to transfer information. Unlike those other cards, however, a smart card could be used to establish a person's identity as validly as a signature on a piece of paper. In addition, technological innovations now under way will allow an e-signature to be evidenced by an image of a person's retina, fingerprint, or face that is scanned by a computer and then matched to a numeric code. The scanned image and the numeric code are registered with security companies that maintain files on an accessible server that can be used to authenticate a transaction.

STATE LAWS GOVERNING E-SIGNATURES

Most states have laws governing e-signatures. The problem is that state e-signature laws are not uniform.

Some states—California is a notable example—prohibit many types of documents from being signed with e-signatures, whereas other states are more permissive. Additionally, some states recognize only digital signatures as valid, while others permit other types of e-signatures.

In an attempt to create more uniformity among the states, in 1999 the National Conference of Commissioners on Uniform State Laws and the American Law Institute promulgated the Uniform Electronic Transactions Act (UETA). To date, the UETA has been adopted, at least in part, by forty-eight states. Among other things, the UETA declares that a signature may not be denied legal effect or enforceability solely because it is in electronic form.[5] (We will look more closely at the provisions of the UETA later in the chapter.)

FEDERAL LAW ON E-SIGNATURES AND E-DOCUMENTS

In 2000, Congress enacted the Electronic Signatures in Global and National Commerce Act (E-SIGN Act),[6] which provides that no contract, record, or signature may be "denied legal effect" solely because it is in an electronic form. In other words, under this law, an electronic signature is as valid as a signature on paper, and an e-document can be as enforceable as a paper one.

For an e-signature to be enforceable, the contracting parties must have agreed to use electronic signatures. For an electronic document to be valid, it must be in a form that can be retained and accurately reproduced.

The E-SIGN Act does not apply to all types of documents, however. Contracts and documents that are exempt include court papers, divorce decrees, evictions, foreclosures, health-insurance terminations, prenuptial agreements, and wills. Also, the only agreements governed by the UCC that fall under this law are those covered by Articles 2 and 2A and UCC 1–107 and 1–206. Despite these limitations, the E-SIGN Act significantly expanded the possibilities for contracting online without the need for delivering, signing, and returning paper documents.

At issue in the following case was whether an exchange of e-mail between the representatives of a seller and a buyer constituted a "writing."

---

5. The 2003 amendments to UCC Article 2 include a similar provision in UCC 2–211.
6. 15 U.S.C. Sections 7001 *et seq.*

CASE 19.3

In re Cafeteria Operators, L.P.

United States
Bankruptcy Court,
Northern District
of Texas, 2003.
299 Bankr. 411.

HARLIN D. HALE, Bankruptcy Judge.
   *   *   *   *

The Perishable Agricultural Commodities Act was enacted in 1930 to regulate the sale of perishable commodities and promote fair dealing in the sale of fruits and vegetables. *   *   * Pursuant to PACA regulations, payment for shipment of perishable commodities is due within ten days after delivery unless the parties agree to extend the payment term *   *   * in writing *   *   * . The maximum time for payment *   *   * under [the PACA] is 30 days *   *   * .
   *   *   *   *

*   *   * [Cherrco, Inc.,] is a Michigan corporation engaged in the business of wholesale food distribution. *   *   * [Cafeteria Operators, Limited Partnership, and other buyers (collectively the Debtor)] placed orders with Cherrco in the ordinary course of business for cherries *   *   * . These orders were placed through Tim Dent ("Dent") of George E. Dent Sales, Inc. *   *   * . Cherrco [bought the fruit from Peterson Farms, Inc., and others] and made delivery of all of the items ordered, and the Debtor accepted delivery. The invoices sent in connection with the transactions at issue provided for terms of payment [within] 30 days. The Debtor failed to pay *   *   * within the thirty days *   *   * . Dent *   *   * and Gene Baldwin ("Baldwin"), the representative of the Debtor, began negotiating a payment plan that would pay Cherrco's claim over time. *   *   * On January 3, 2003, however, [the Debtor] filed its petition for relief in this bankruptcy case. The amount owing on the claim as of the petition date was $25,269.12. *   *   * Cherrco asserts that [it is entitled to the full amount under the PACA.] The Debtor has refused to pay *   *   * on the basis that Cherrco waived its rights to the PACA *   *   * claim [in e-mail between Dent and Baldwin. Cherrco argues that the e-mail was not a "writing."]
   *   *   *   *

*   *   * The Debtor argues *   *   * that a post-default series of e-mails between Dent and Baldwin, the representative of the Debtor, constituted a "written agreement" extending the original payment terms beyond thirty days such that Cherrco lost its ability to assert its PACA rights against the Debtor. Apparently, after the Debtor defaulted in the payment of the amounts due Cherrco, *   *   * Baldwin and Dent, as agent for Cherrco, began negotiating a payment schedule that would satisfy Cherrco so that Cherrco would defer enforcement of its PACA rights. A payment schedule was sent to Dent, who then forwarded the payment schedule *   *   * to Sarah Peterson-Schlukebir, a representative of Peterson Farms, Inc. In an e-mail dated October 10, 2002, Ms. Peterson-Schlukebir wrote to *   *   * Dent the following:

> *   *   * As discussed verbally on 10/10/02, both Peterson Farms and Cherrco are not willing to sign the *   *   * Release dated 10/4/02 from Gene Baldwin *   *   * . If we sign the release, we are no longer covered by PACA. *   *   *

On that same day, Dent sent an e-mail to Baldwin, with the above e-mail as an attachment *   *   * .
   *   *   *   *

On October 11, 2002, Baldwin wrote an e-mail to Dent in which he stated:

> *   *   * [W]e do not need a formal [contract]. We will just start making the payments starting today. All we really want is the agreement from them that the payment plan is ok. We don't want to lose them as a supplier. We know we will have to pay up front for our orders until we get thru this situation. *   *   *

   *   *   *   *

This Court rejects Cherrco's argument that the e-mails do not constitute a "writing" because this issue was resolved by Congress with the passage, in June, 2000, of the Electronic Signatures in Global and National Commerce Act (the "E-Sign Act"). The E-Sign Act, which had an effective date of October 1, 2000, provides, in pertinent part, at Section 7001:

CONTINUED

CASE 19.3 | Continued

(a) In general

Notwithstanding any statute, regulation, or other rule of law * * * , with respect to any transaction in or affecting interstate or foreign commerce—

(1) a signature, contract, or other record relating to such transaction may not be denied legal effect, validity, or enforceability solely because it is in electronic form; and

(2) a contract relating to such transaction may not be denied legal effect, validity, or enforceability solely because an electronic signature or electronic record was used in its formation. * * *

Thus, *in transactions involving interstate commerce, e-mails constitute "writings."* The transactions between Cherrco and the Debtor occurred in 2002, and clearly qualify for the requirement in Section 7001(a) that the transaction is in or affects interstate commerce. Thus, the e-mails between the parties satisfy the writing requirement, to the extent that one is required under [the] PACA. [Emphasis added.]

   *   *   *   *

For [other] reasons, [however,] the Court grants Cherrco's motion to compel the payment of its PACA * * * claim.

QUESTIONS

1. Did the e-mail between Dent and Baldwin constitute an agreement between the parties to extend the original payment terms beyond thirty days? Why or why not?
2. If Cherrco or Dent, on Cherrco's behalf, had not responded to Baldwin's last e-mail, how might this "silence" have affected the outcome of this case? Could this "silence" be construed as an acceptance of the proposed new payment schedule?

PARTNERING AGREEMENTS

One way that online sellers and buyers can prevent disputes over signatures, as well as disputes over the terms and conditions of their e-contracts, is to form partnering agreements. In a **partnering agreement,** a seller and a buyer who frequently do business with each other agree in advance on the terms and conditions that will apply to all transactions subsequently conducted electronically. The partnering agreement can also establish special access and identification codes to be used by the parties when transacting business electronically.

A partnering agreement reduces the likelihood that disputes will arise under the contract because the buyer and the seller have agreed in advance to the terms and conditions that will accompany each sale. Furthermore, if a dispute does arise, a court or arbitration forum will be able to refer to the partnering agreement when determining the parties' intent with respect to subsequent contracts. Of course, even with a partnering agreement fraud remains a possibility. If an unauthorized person uses a purchaser's designated access number and identification code, it may be some time before the problem is discovered.

SECTION 3 | The Uniform Electronic Transactions Act

As noted earlier, the Uniform Electronic Transactions Act (UETA) was promulgated in 1999. The UETA represented one of the first comprehensive efforts to create uniform laws pertaining to e-commerce.

The primary purpose of the UETA is to remove barriers to e-commerce by giving the same legal effect to electronic records and signatures as is currently given to paper documents and signatures. The UETA broadly defines an *e-signature* as "an electronic sound, symbol, or process attached to or logically associated with a record and executed or adopted by a person with the intent to sign the record."[7] E-signatures include encrypted digital signatures, names (intended

---

7. UETA 102(8).

as signatures) at the ends of e-mail messages, and "clicks" on a Web page if the click includes the identification of the person. A **record** is "information that is inscribed on a tangible medium or that is stored in an electronic or other medium and is retrievable in perceivable [visual] form."[8]

THE SCOPE AND APPLICABILITY OF THE UETA

The UETA does not create new rules for electronic contracts but rather establishes that records, signatures, and contracts may not be denied enforceability solely due to their electronic form. The UETA does not apply to all writings and signatures but only to electronic records and electronic signatures *relating to a transaction*. A *transaction* is defined as an interaction between two or more people relating to business, commercial, or governmental activities.[9]

The act specifically does not apply to laws governing wills or testamentary trusts (see Chapter 50), the UCC (other than Articles 2 and 2A), or the Uniform Computer Information Transactions Act (discussed later in this chapter).[10] In addition, the provisions of the UETA allow the states to exclude its application to other areas of law.

As described earlier, Congress passed the E-SIGN Act in 2000, a year after the UETA was presented to the states for adoption. Thus, a significant issue is whether and to what extent the federal E-SIGN Act preempts the UETA as adopted by the states.

THE FEDERAL E-SIGN ACT AND THE UETA

The E-SIGN Act refers explicitly to the UETA and provides that if a state has enacted the uniform version of the UETA, it is not preempted by the E-SIGN Act.[11] In other words, if the state has enacted the UETA without modification, state law will govern. The problem is that many states have enacted nonuniform (modified) versions of the UETA, largely for the purpose of excluding other areas of state law from the UETA's terms. The E-SIGN Act specifies

that those exclusions will be preempted to the extent that they are inconsistent with the E-SIGN Act's provisions.

The E-SIGN Act, however, explicitly allows the states to enact alternative procedures or requirements for the use or acceptance of electronic records or electronic signatures, *if* certain conditions are met. Generally, the procedures or requirements must be consistent with the provisions of the E-SIGN Act, and the state must not give greater legal status or effect to one specific type of technology. Additionally, if a state enacted alternative procedures or requirements *after* the E-SIGN Act was adopted, the state law must specifically refer to the E-SIGN Act. The relationship between the UETA and the E-SIGN Act is illustrated in Exhibit 19–2 on the following page.

HIGHLIGHTS OF THE UETA

We look next at selected provisions of the UETA. Our discussion is, of course, based on the act's uniform provisions. Keep in mind that the states that have enacted the UETA may have adopted slightly different versions.

THE PARTIES MUST AGREE TO CONDUCT TRANSACTIONS ELECTRONICALLY The UETA will not apply to a transaction unless each of the parties has agreed to conduct transactions by electronic means. The agreement need not be explicit, however, and it may be implied by the conduct of the parties and the surrounding circumstances.[12] In the comments that accompany the UETA, the drafters stated that it may be reasonable to infer that a person who gives out a business card with an e-mail address on it has consented to transact business electronically.[13] The party's agreement may also be inferred from a letter or other writing, as well as from some verbal communication. Nothing in the UETA requires that the agreement to conduct transactions electronically be made electronically.

A person who has previously agreed to an electronic transaction can also withdraw his or her consent and refuse to conduct further business electronically. Additionally, the act expressly gives parties the power

---

8. UETA 102(15).
9. UETA 2(12) and 3.
10. UETA 3(b).
11. 15 U.S.C. Section 7002(2)(A)(i).

12. UETA 5(b).
13. UETA 5, Comment 4B.

EXHIBIT 19-2 The E-SIGN Act and the UETA

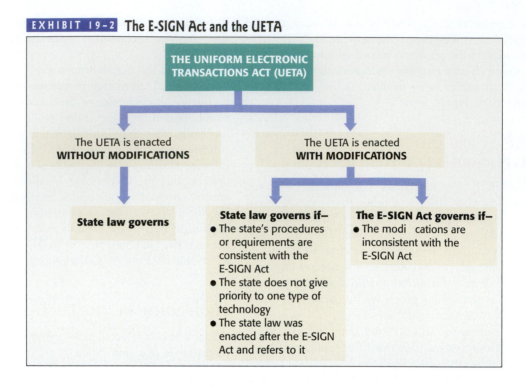

to vary the UETA's provisions by contract. In other words, *parties can opt out of all or some of the terms of the UETA.* If the parties do not opt out of the terms of the UETA, however, the UETA will govern their electronic transactions.

ATTRIBUTION In the context of electronic transactions, the term *attribution* refers to the procedures that may be used to ensure that the person sending an electronic record is the same person whose e-signature accompanies the record. Under the UETA, if an electronic record or signature was the act of a particular person, the record or signature may be attributed to that person. If a person types her or his name at the bottom of an e-mail purchase order, that name will qualify as a "signature" and be attributed to the person whose name appears. Just as in paper contracts, one may use any relevant evidence to prove that the record or signature is or is not the act of the person.[14]

Note that even if an individual's name does not appear on a record (a voice-mail message, for exam-

ple), the UETA states that the effect of the record is to be determined from the context and surrounding circumstances. In other words, a record may have legal effect even if no one has signed it. For instance, a fax that contains a letterhead identifying the sender may, depending on the circumstances, be attributed to that sender.

The UETA does not contain any express provisions about what constitutes fraud or whether an agent (a person who acts on behalf of another—see Chapter 31) is authorized to enter into a contract. Under the UETA, other state laws control if any issues relating to agency, authority, forgery, or contract formation arise.

NOTARIZATION If a document is required to be notarized under existing state law, the UETA provides that this requirement is satisfied by the electronic signature of a notary public or other person authorized to verify signatures. For example, if a person intends to accept an offer to purchase real estate via e-mail, the requirement is satisfied if a notary public is present to verify the person's identity and affix an electronic signature to the e-mail acceptance.

---

14. UETA 9.

THE EFFECT OF ERRORS The UETA encourages, but does not require, the use of security procedures (such as encryption) to verify changes to electronic documents and to correct errors. Section 10 of the UETA provides that if the parties have agreed to a security procedure and one party fails to detect an error because he or she did not follow the procedure, the conforming party can legally avoid the effect of the change or error. If the parties have not agreed to use a security procedure, then other state laws (including contract law governing mistakes—see Chapter 14) will determine the effect of the error on the parties' agreement.

To avoid the effect of errors, a party must take certain steps. First, the party must promptly notify the other party of the error and of her or his intent not to be bound by the error. Second, the party must take reasonable steps to return any benefit or consideration received. Parties cannot avoid a transaction from which they have benefited. For example, if as a result of the error a party received access to valuable information, the transaction may be unavoidable because the party obviously cannot give back the benefit of access to valuable information. In all other situations in which a change or error occurs in an electronic record (and the parties' agreement does not specifically address errors), the UETA states that the traditional law governing mistakes will control.

TIMING Section 15 of the UETA sets forth provisions relating to the sending and receiving of electronic records. These provisions apply unless the parties agree to different terms. Under Section 15, an electronic record is considered *sent* when it is properly directed to the intended recipient in a form readable by the recipient's computer system. Once the electronic record leaves the control of the sender or comes under the control of the recipient, the UETA deems it to have been sent. An electronic record is considered *received* when it enters the recipient's processing system in a readable form—*even if no individual is aware of its receipt*.

Additionally, the UETA provides that, unless otherwise agreed, an electronic record is to be sent from or received at the party's principal place of business. If a party has no place of business, the provision then authorizes the place of sending or receipt to be the party's residence. If a party has multiple places of business, the record should be sent from or received at the location that has the closest relationship to the underlying transaction.

SECTION 4 | The Uniform Computer Information Transactions Act

The National Conference of Commissioners on Uniform State Laws (NCCUSL) promulgated the Uniform Computer Information Transactions Act (UCITA) in 1999. The primary purpose of the UCITA is to validate e-contracts to license or purchase software, or contracts that give access to—or allow the distribution of—computer information.[15] The UCITA is controversial, and only two states (Maryland and Virginia) have adopted it, while four states (Iowa, North Carolina, Vermont, and West Virginia) have passed anti-UCITA provisions. In 2003, the NCCUSL withdrew its support of the UCITA. Although the UCITA remains a legal resource, the NCCUSL will no longer seek its adoption by the states, which are thus unlikely to consider it further.

---

15. *Computer information* is "information in an electronic form obtained from or through use of a computer, or that is in digital or an equivalent form capable of being processed by a computer" [UCITA 102(10)].

REVIEWING E-CONTRACTS

Ted and Betty Hyatt live in California, a state that has extensive statutory protection for consumers. The Hyatts decided to buy a computer so that they could use e-mail to stay in touch with their grandchildren, who live in another state. Over the phone, they ordered a computer from CompuEdge, Inc. When the box arrived, it was sealed with a brightly colored sticker warning that the terms enclosed within the box would govern the sale unless the customer returned the computer within thirty days. Among those terms was a clause that required any disputes to be resolved in a Tennessee state court. The Hyatts then signed up for Internet service through CyberTool, an Internet service provider. They downloaded CyberTool's software and clicked on the "quick install" button that allowed them to bypass CyberTool's "Terms of Service" page. It was possible to read this page by scrolling to the next screen, but the Hyatts did not realize this. The terms included a clause that stated that all disputes were to be submitted to a Virginia state court. As soon as the Hyatts attempted to e-mail their grandchildren, they experienced problems using CyberTool's e-mail service, which continually stated that the network was busy. They also were unable to receive the photos sent by their grandchildren. Using the information presented in the chapter, answer the following questions.

1. | Did the list of contract terms included in the computer box constitute an offer that the Hyatts could accept or reject? Did the Hyatts accept the terms? If so, at what point did acceptance occur?

2. | What legal term used in the chapter describes the type of agreement the Hyatts formed with CompuEdge? How does the UCC describe the way acceptance can occur in such contracts?

3. | Suppose that the Hyatts experienced trouble with the computer's components after they had used the computer for two months. What factors will a court consider in deciding whether to enforce the forum-selection clause? Would a court be likely to enforce the clause in this contract? Why or why not?

4. | Are the Hyatts bound by the contract terms specified on CyberTool's "Terms of Service" page that they had not read? Which of the required elements for contract formation might the Hyatts claim was lacking? How might a court rule on this issue?

TERMS AND CONCEPTS TO REVIEW

browse-wrap terms 363	e-contract 358	partnering agreement 368
click-on agreement 359	e-signature 365	record 369
cybernotary 366	forum-selection clause 359	shrink-wrap agreement 359

QUESTIONS AND CASE PROBLEMS

19-1. Paul is a financial analyst for King Investments, Inc., a brokerage firm. He uses the Internet to investigate the background and activities of companies that might be good investments for King's customers. While visiting the Web site of Business Research, Inc., Paul sees on his screen a message that reads, "Welcome to businessresearch.com. By visiting our site, you have been entered as a subscriber to our e-publication, *Companies Unlimited*. This publication will be sent to you daily at a cost of $7.50 per week. An invoice will be included with *Companies Unlimited* every four weeks. You may cancel your subscription at any time." Has Paul entered into an enforceable contract to pay for *Companies Unlimited*? Why or why not?

19-2. ⚖ QUESTION WITH SAMPLE ANSWER

Anne is a reporter for *Daily Business Journal*, a print publication consulted by investors and other businesspersons. She often uses the Internet to perform research for the articles that she writes for the publication. While visiting the Web site of Cyberspace Investments Corp., Anne reads a pop-up window that states, "Our business newsletter, *E-Commerce Weekly,* is available at a one-year subscription rate of $5 per issue. To subscribe, enter your e-mail address below and click 'SUBSCRIBE.' By subscribing, you agree to the terms of the subscriber's agreement. To read this agreement, click 'AGREEMENT.'" Anne enters her e-mail address, but does not click on "AGREEMENT" to read the terms. Has Anne entered into an enforceable contract to pay for *E-Commerce Weekly?* Explain.

For a sample answer to this question, go to Appendix I at the end of this text.

19-3. Bob, a sales representative for Central Computer Co., occasionally uses the Internet to obtain information about his customers and to look for new sales leads. While visiting the Web site of Marketing World, Inc., Bob is presented with an on-screen message that offers, "To improve your ability to make deals, read our monthly online magazine, *Sales Genius,* available at a subscription rate of $15 a month. To subscribe, fill in your name, company name, and e-mail address below, and click 'YES!' By clicking 'YES!' you agree to the terms of the subscription contract. To read this contract, click 'TERMS.'" Among those terms is a clause that allows Marketing World to charge interest for subscription bills not paid within a certain time. The terms also prohibit subscribers from copying or distributing part or all of *Sales Genius* in any form. Bob subscribes without reading the terms. Marketing World later files a suit against Bob based on his failure to pay for his subscription. Should the court hold that Bob is obligated to pay interest on the amount? Explain.

19-4. LICENSE AGREEMENTS. Management Computer Controls, Inc. (known as "MC 2"), is a Tennessee corporation in the business of selling software. Charles Perry Construction, Inc., a Florida corporation, entered into two contracts with MC 2 to buy software designed to perform estimating and accounting functions for construction firms. Each contract was printed on a standard order form containing a paragraph that referred to a license agreement. The license agreement included a choice-of-forum and choice-of-law provision: "Agreement is to be interpreted and construed according to the laws of the State of Tennessee. Any action, either by you or MC 2, arising out of this Agreement shall be initiated and prosecuted in the Court of Shelby County, Tennessee, and nowhere else." Each of the software packages arrived with the license agreement affixed to the outside of the box. Additionally, the boxes were sealed with an orange sticker bearing the following warning: "By opening this packet, you indicate your acceptance of the MC 2 license agreement." Alleging that the software was not suitable for use with Windows NT, Perry filed a suit against MC 2 in a Florida state court. MC 2 filed a motion to dismiss the complaint on the ground that the suit should be heard in Tennessee. How should the court rule? Why?

[*Management Computer Controls, Inc. v. Charles Perry Construction, Inc.,* 743 So.2d 627 (Fla.App. 1 Dist. 1999)]

19-5. BROWSE-WRAP TERMS. Ticketmaster Corp. operates a Web site that allows customers to buy tickets to concerts, ball games, and other events. On the site's home page are instructions and an index to internal pages (one page per event). Each event page provides basic information (a short description of the event, with the date, time, place, and price) and a description of how to order tickets over the Internet, by telephone, by mail, or in person. The home page contains—if a customer scrolls to the bottom—"terms and conditions" that proscribe, among other things, linking to Ticketmaster's internal pages. A customer need not view these terms to go to an event page. Tickets.Com, Inc., operates a Web site that also publicizes special events. Tickets.Com's site includes links to Ticketmaster's internal events pages. These links bypass Ticketmaster's home page. Ticketmaster filed a suit in a federal district court against Tickets.Com, alleging in part breach of contract on the ground that Tickets.Com's linking violated Ticketmaster's terms and conditions. Tickets.Com filed a motion to dismiss. Was Tickets.Com bound by the terms and conditions posted on Ticketmaster's home page? Why or why not? How should the court rule on the motion? [*Ticketmaster Corp. v. Tickets.Com, Inc.,* ___ F.Supp.2d ___ (C.D.Cal. 2000)]

19-6. SHRINK-WRAP AGREEMENTS. 1-A Equipment Co. signed a sales order to lease Accware 10 User NT software, which is made and marketed by ICode, Inc. Just above the signature line, the order stated: "Thank you for your order. No returns or refunds will be issued for software license and/or services. All sales are final. Please read the End User License and Service Agreement." The software was delivered in a sealed envelope inside a box. On the outside of the envelope, an "End User Agreement" provided in part, "BY OPENING THIS PACKAGING, CLICKING YOUR ACCEPTANCE OF THE AGREEMENT DURING DOWNLOAD OR INSTALLATION OF THIS PRODUCT, OR BY USING ANY PART OF THIS PRODUCT, YOU AGREE TO BE LEGALLY BOUND BY THE TERMS OF THE AGREEMENT. . . . This agreement will be governed by the laws in force in the Commonwealth of Virginia . . . and exclusive venue for any litigation shall be in Virginia." Later, dissatisfied with the software, 1-A filed a suit in a Massachusetts state court against ICode, alleging breach of contract and misrepresentation. ICode asked the court to dismiss the case on the basis of the "End User Agreement." Is the agreement enforceable? Should the court dismiss the suit? Why or why not? [*1-A Equipment Co. v. ICode, Inc.,* 43 UCC Rep.Serv.2d 807 (Mass.Dist. 2000)]

19-7. **CASE PROBLEM WITH SAMPLE ANSWER**

Stewart Lamle invented "Farook," a board game similar to "Tic Tac Toe." In May 1996, Lamle began negotiating with Mattel, Inc., to license "Farook" for distribution outside the United States. On June 11, 1997, the parties met and agreed on many terms, including a three-year duration, the geographic scope of the agreement, a schedule for payment, and a royalty percentage. Mike Bucher, a Mattel employee, sent Lamle an e-mail titled "Farook Deal" on June 26 that repeated these terms and added that they "ha[ve] been agreed [to] . . . by . . . Mattel subject to contract. . . . Best regards Mike Bucher." Lamle faxed Mattel a more formal draft of the terms, but Mattel did not sign it. Mattel displayed Farook at its Pre-Toy Fair in August. After the fair, Mattel faxed Lamle that it no longer wished to license his game. Lamle filed a suit in a federal district court against Mattel, asserting in part breach of contract. One of the issues was whether the parties had entered into a contract. Could Bucher's name on the June 26 e-mail be considered a valid signature under the Uniform Electronic Transactions Act (UETA)? Could it be considered a valid signature outside the UETA? Why or why not? [*Lamle v. Mattel, Inc.*, 394 F.3d 1355 (Fed.Cir. 2005)]

To view a sample answer for this case problem, go to this book's Web site at http://wbl.westbuslaw.com, select "Chapter 19," and click on "Case Problem with Sample Answer."

19-8. CLICK-ON AGREEMENTS. America Online, Inc. (AOL), provided e-mail service to Walter Hughes and other members under a click-on agreement titled "Terms of Service." This agreement consisted of three parts: a "Member Agreement," "Community Guidelines," and a "Privacy Policy." The member agreement included a forum-selection clause that read, "You expressly agree that exclusive jurisdiction for any claim or dispute with AOL or relating in any way to your membership or your use of AOL resides in the courts of Virginia." When Officer Thomas McMenamon of the Methuen, Massachusetts, Police Department received threatening e-mail sent from an AOL account, he requested and obtained from AOL Hughes's name and other personal information. Hughes filed a suit in a federal district court against AOL, which filed a motion to dismiss on the basis of the forum-selection clause. Considering that the clause was a click-on provision, is it enforceable? Explain. [*Hughes v. McMenamon*, 204 F.Supp.2d 178 (D.Mass. 2002)]

19-9. SHRINK-WRAP AGREEMENTS AND BROWSE-WRAP TERMS. Mary DeFontes bought a computer and a service contract from Dell Computers Corp. DeFontes was charged $950.51, of which $13.51 was identified on the invoice as "tax." This amount was paid to the state of Rhode Island. DeFontes and other Dell customers filed a suit in a Rhode Island state court against Dell, claiming that Dell was overcharging its customers by collecting a tax on service contracts and transportation costs. Dell asked the court to order DeFontes to submit the dispute to arbitration. Dell cited its "Terms and Conditions Agreement," which provides in part that by accepting delivery of Dell's products or services, a customer agrees to submit any dispute to arbitration. Customers can view this agreement through an *inconspicuous* link at the bottom of Dell's Web site, and Dell encloses a copy with each order when it is shipped. Dell argued that DeFontes accepted these terms by failing to return her purchase within thirty days, although the agreement did not state this. Is DeFontes bound to the "Terms and Conditions Agreement"? Should the court grant Dell's request? Why or why not? [*DeFontes v. Dell Computers Corp.*, __ A.2d __ (R.I. 2004)]

19-10. VIDEO QUESTION

Go to this text's Web site at http://wbl.westbuslaw.com and select "Chapter 19." Click on "Video Questions" and view the video titled *E-Contracts: Agreeing Online.* Then answer the following questions.

(a) According to the instructor in the video, what is the key factor in determining whether a particular term in an online agreement is enforceable?

(b) Suppose that you click on "I accept" in order to download software from the Internet. You do not read the terms of the agreement before accepting it, even though you know that such agreements often contain forum-selection and arbitration clauses. The software later causes irreparable harm to your computer system, and you want to sue. When you go to the Web site and view the agreement, however, you discover that a choice-of-law clause in the contract specifies that the law of Nigeria controls. Is this term enforceable? Is it a term that should be reasonably expected in an online contract?

(c) Does it matter what the term actually says if it is a type of term that one could reasonably expect to be in the contract? What arguments can be made for and against enforcing a choice-of-law clause in an online contract?

LAW | on the Web

For updated links to resources available on the Web, as well as a variety of other materials, visit this text's Web site at http://wbl.westbuslaw.com.

You can access the UCC, including Article 2, at the Web site of the University of Pennsylvania Law School. Go to

http://www.law.upenn.edu/bll/ulc/ulc.htm

The Web site of the law firm of Baker & McKenzie offers articles and other resources on e-commerce, including summaries of the UETA and the E-SIGN Act of 2000. Go to

http://www.baker.com/ecommerce.htm

The Web site of the National Conference of Commissioners on Uniform State Laws provides the draft and final versions of the UETA, lists the states that have adopted it, and offers information on why states should adopt it, at

http://www.nccusl.org

LEGAL RESEARCH EXERCISES ON THE WEB

Go to http://wbl.westbuslaw.com, the Web site that accompanies this text. Select "Chapter 19" and click on "Internet Exercises." There you will find the following Internet research exercises that you can perform to learn more about topics covered in this chapter.

Activity 19–1: **LEGAL PERSPECTIVE**
E-Contract Formation

Activity 19–2: **MANAGEMENT PERSPECTIVE**
E-Signatures

Contract Law and the Application of Ethics

Generally, as you read in Chapter 5, a responsible business manager will evaluate a business transaction on the basis of three criteria—legality, profitability, and ethics. But what does acting ethically mean in the area of contracts? If an individual with whom you enter into a contract fails to look after her or his own interests, is that your fault? Should you be doing something about it? If the contract happens to be to your advantage and to the other party's detriment, do you have a responsibility to correct the situation?

For example, assume that a neighbor whom you rarely see places a "for sale" sign on her car, offering to sell it for $6,000. You learn that she is moving to another state and needs the extra cash to help finance the move. You know that she could easily get $10,000 for the car, and you are considering purchasing it and then reselling it at a profit. But you also discover that your neighbor is completely unaware that she has priced the car significantly below its *Blue Book* value. Are you ethically obligated to tell her that she is essentially giving away $4,000 if she sells you the car for only $6,000?

This kind of situation, transplanted into the world of commercial transactions, raises an obvious question: At what point should the sophisticated businessperson cease looking after his or her own economic welfare and become "his brother's keeper," so to speak?

Freedom of Contract and Freedom from Contract

The answer to the question just raised is not simple. On the one hand, a common ethical assumption in our society is that individuals should be held responsible for the consequences of their own actions, including their contractual promises. This principle is expressed in the legal concept of freedom of contract. On the other hand, another common assumption in our society is that individuals should not harm one another by their actions. This is the basis of both tort law and criminal law.

In the area of contract law, ethical behavior often involves balancing these principles. In the above example, if you purchased the car and the neighbor later learned its true value and sued you for the difference, very likely no court of law would find that the contract should be rescinded. At times, however, courts will hold that the principle of freedom *of* contract should give way to the principle of freedom *from* contract, a doctrine based on the assumption that people should not be harmed by the actions of others. We look next at some examples of how parties to contracts may be excused from performance to prevent injustice.

Impossibility of Performance The doctrine of impossibility of performance is based to some extent on the ethical question of whether one party should suffer economic loss when it is impossible to perform a contract. The rule that one is "bound by his or her contracts" is not followed when performance is made impossible. This doctrine, however, is applied only when the parties themselves did not consciously assume the risk of the events that rendered performance impossible. Furthermore, this doctrine rests on the assumption that the party claiming the defense of impossibility has acted ethically.

A contract is discharged, for example, if it calls for the delivery of a particular car and, through no fault of either party, this car is stolen and completely demolished in an accident. Yet the impossibility doctrine will not excuse performance if the party agreeing to sell the car causes the car's destruction by her or his negligence.

Prior to the late nineteenth century, courts were reluctant to discharge a contract even when it appeared that performance was literally impossible. Just as society's ethics changes with the passage of time, however, the law also changes to reflect society's new perceptions of ethical behavior.[1] Today, courts are much more willing to discharge a contract when its performance has become literally impossible. Holding a party in breach of contract, when performance has become literally impossible through no fault of the party claiming the defense of impossibility, no longer coincides with society's notions of fairness.

Unconscionability The doctrine of unconscionability is a good example of how the law attempts to enforce ethical behavior. Under this doctrine, a contract may be deemed to be so unfair to one party as to be unenforceable—even though that party voluntarily agreed to the contract's terms. Unconscionable action, like unethical action, is incapable of precise definition. Information about the particular facts and specific circumstances surrounding the contract is essential. For example, the courts might find that a contract made with a marginally literate consumer was unfair and unenforceable but might uphold the same contract made with a major business firm.

Section 2–302 of the Uniform Commercial Code, which incorporates the common law concept of unconscionability, similarly does not define the concept with any precision. Rather, it leaves it to the courts to determine when a contract is

---

1. A leading English case in which the court held that a defendant was discharged from the duty to perform due to impossibility of performance is *Taylor v. Caldwell*, 122 Eng.Rep. 309 (K.B. [King's Bench] 1863).

so one sided and unfair to one party as to be unconscionable and thus unenforceable.

Usually, courts will do all they can to save contracts rather than render them unenforceable. Only in extreme situations, as when a contract or clause is so one sided as to "shock the conscience" of the court, will a court hold a contract or contractual clause unconscionable.

Exculpatory Clauses In some situations, courts have also refused to enforce exculpatory clauses on the ground that they are unconscionable or that they are contrary to public policy. An *exculpatory clause* attempts to excuse a party from liability in the event of monetary or physical injury, no matter who is at fault. In some situations, such clauses are upheld. For example, a health club can require its members to sign a clause releasing the club from any liability for injuries the members might incur while using the club's equipment and facilities. The law permits parties to assume, by express agreement, the risks inherent in certain activities. In such situations, exculpatory clauses make it possible for a firm's owner to stay in business—by shifting some of the liability risks from the business to the customer.

Nonetheless, some jurisdictions take a dubious view of exculpatory agreements, particularly when the agreement is between parties with unequal bargaining power, such as a landlord and a tenant or an employer and an employee. An exculpatory clause that attempts to exempt an employer from *all* liability for negligence toward its employees frequently is held to be against public policy and thus void.[2] The courts reason that disparity in bargaining power and economic necessity force the employee to accept the employer's terms.

Covenants Not to Compete

In today's complicated, technological business world, knowledge learned on the job, including trade secrets, has become a valuable commodity. To prevent this knowledge from falling into the hands of competitors, more and more employers are requiring their employees to sign covenants not to compete. The increasing number of lawsuits over noncompete clauses in employment contracts has caused numerous courts to reconsider the reasonableness of these covenants.

Should Courts Reform Unreasonable Noncompete Covenants? In a number of jurisdictions, if a court finds that a restraint in a noncompete covenant is not reasonable in light of the circumstances, it will reform the unreasonable provision and then enforce it. In other words, rather than void such a covenant, a court will rewrite the unreasonable restriction (by reducing the time period during which a former employee cannot compete from three years to one

year, for example) and then enforce the reformed agreement.[3]

Other jurisdictions are not so "employer friendly." As one observer noted, the farther west you go from the Mississippi River, the harder it is to enforce a covenant not to compete. Under California law, covenants not to compete are illegal, and other western states tend to regard such covenants with suspicion. For example, in 2004 the Supreme Court of the state of Washington refused to reform (and then enforce) a noncompete covenant that it deemed to be unreasonable and lacking in consideration.[4]

In 2002, an Arizona state court reached a similar conclusion, even though the covenant not to compete itself had included a clause permitting a court to reform the covenant if necessary. The court reasoned that noncompete agreements tend to have a threatening effect on employees, even when the covenants are so unreasonable as to be unenforceable. If the courts modified and then enforced such covenants, this would only encourage employers to continue to create unreasonable covenants—for two reasons: (1) most noncompete covenants are never challenged in court, and (2) if a covenant were contested, the worst that could happen is that the court would modify, and then enforce, the covenant.[5]

Do Noncompete Covenants Stifle Innovation? One of the reasons that the courts usually look closely at covenants not to compete and evaluate them on a case-by-case basis is the strong public policy favoring competition in this country. Even so, claim some scholars, covenants not to compete, regardless of their "reasonability," may stifle competition and innovation.

Consider, for example, the argument put forth by Ronald Gilson, a Stanford University professor of law and business. He contends that California's prohibition on covenants not to compete may help to explain why technological innovation and economic growth have skyrocketed in California's Silicon Valley, while technological development along Massachusetts's Route 128 has languished. According to Gilson, "The different legal rules governing postemployment covenants not to compete in California and Massachusetts help explain the difference in employee job mobility and therefore the knowledge transfer that [is] a critical factor in explaining the differential performance of Silicon Valley and Route 128."[6] Because of this and for other reasons, some scholars contend that covenants not to compete may not survive the cyber age.[7] Certainly, such covenants

---

2. See, for example, *Health Net of California, Inc. v. Department of Health Services,* 113 Cal.App.4th 224, 6 Cal.Rptr.3d 235 (2003).

3. See, for example, *National Café Services, Ltd. v. Podaras,* 148 S.W.3d 194 (Tex.App.—Waco 2004). Also, for a Florida court's reformation and enforcement of a covenant not to compete, see *Health Care Enterprises, Inc. v. Levy,* 715 So.2d 341 (Fla.App.4th 1998).

4. *Labriola v. Pollard Group, Inc.,* 152 Wash.2d 828, 100 P.3d 791 (2004).

5. *Varsity Gold, Inc. v. Porzio,* 202 Ariz. 355, 45 P.3d 352 (2002).

6. Ronald J. Gilson, "The Legal Infrastructure of High Technology Industrial Districts: Silicon Valley, Route 128, and Covenants Not to Compete," 575 *New York University Law Review* 579 (June 1999).

7. See, for example, Robert C. Welsh, Larry C. Drapkin, and Samantha C. Grant, "Are Noncompete Clauses Kaput?" *The National Law Journal,* August 14, 2000, pp. B13–B14.

present new types of challenges for the courts in deciding what restrictions are reasonable in the context of the Internet.[8]

Oral Contracts and Promissory Estoppel

Oral contracts are made every day. Many—if not most—of them are carried out, and no problems arise. Occasionally, however, oral contracts are not performed, and one party decides to sue the other. Sometimes, to prevent injustice, the courts will enforce oral contracts under the theory of promissory estoppel if detrimental reliance can be shown. The court may even use this theory to remove a contract from the Statute of Frauds—that is, render the oral contract enforceable.

In addition, ethical standards certainly underlie the doctrine of *promissory estoppel,* under which a person who has reasonably relied on the promise of another to his or her detriment can often obtain some measure of recovery. Essentially, promissory estoppel allows a variety of promises to be enforced even though they lack what is formally regarded as consideration.

An oral promise made by an insurance agent to a business owner, for example, may be binding if the owner relies on that promise to her or his detriment. Employees who rely to their detriment on an employer's promise may be able to recover under the doctrine of promissory estoppel.[9] A contractor who, when bidding for a job, relies on a subcontractor's promise to perform certain construction work at a certain price may be able to recover, on the basis of promissory estoppel, any damages sustained because of the subcontractor's failure to perform. These are but a few of the many examples in which the courts, in the interests of fairness and justice, have estopped a promisor from denying that a contract existed.

Oral Contracts and the Statute of Frauds

As you learned in Chapter 15, the Statute of Frauds was originally instituted in England in 1677. The act was intended to prevent harm to innocent parties by requiring written evidence of agreements concerning important transactions.

Until the Statute of Frauds was passed, the English courts had enforced oral contracts on the strength of oral testimony by witnesses. It was not too difficult, therefore, to evade justice by procuring "convincing" witnesses to support the claim that a contract had been created and then breached. The possibility of fraud in such actions was enhanced by the fact that in seventeenth-century England, courts did not allow oral testimony to be given by the parties to a lawsuit—or by any parties with an interest in the litigation, such as husbands or wives. Defense against actions for breach of contract was thus limited to written evidence or the testimony of third parties.

Detrimental Reliance Under the Statute of Frauds, if a contract is oral when it is required to be in writing, it will not, as a rule, be enforced by the courts. An exception to this rule is made if a party has reasonably relied, to his or her detriment, on the oral contract. Enforcing an oral contract on the basis of a party's reliance arguably undercuts the essence of the Statute of Frauds. The reason that such an exception is made is to prevent the statute—which was created to avert injustice—from being used to promote injustice. Nevertheless, this use of the doctrine is controversial—as is the Statute of Frauds itself.

Criticisms of the Statute of Frauds Since its inception more than three hundred years ago, the statute has been criticized by some because, although it was created to protect the innocent, it can also be used as a technical defense by a party breaching a genuine, mutually agreed-on oral contract—if the contract falls within the Statute of Frauds. For this reason, some legal scholars believe the act has caused more injustice than it has prevented. Thus, exceptions are sometimes made—such as under the doctrine of promissory estoppel—to prevent unfairness and inequity. Generally, the courts are slow to apply the statute if doing so will result in obvious injustice. In some instances, this has required a good deal of inventiveness on the part of the courts.

DISCUSSION QUESTIONS

1. Suppose that you contract to purchase steel at a fixed price per ton. Before the contract is performed, a lengthy steelworkers' strike causes the price of steel to triple from the price specified in the contract. If you demand that the supplier fulfill the contract, the supplier will go out of business. What are your ethical obligations in this situation? What are your legal rights?

2. Many countries have no Statute of Frauds, and even England, the country that created the original act, has repealed it. Should the United States do likewise? What are some of the costs and benefits to society of the Statute of Frauds?

3. In determining whether an exculpatory clause should be enforced, why does it matter whether the contract containing the clause involves essential services (such as transportation) or nonessential services (such as skiing or other leisure-time activities)?

4. Employers often include covenants not to compete in employment contracts to protect their trade secrets. What effect, if any, will the growth in e-commerce have on the reasonableness of covenants not to compete?

---

8. For an example of one dispute in the Internet context, see *EarthWeb v. Schlack,* 71 F.Supp.2d 299 (S.D.N.Y. 1999).

9. Note, though, at least one court has held that an employer's oral promise not to fire an at-will employee was not enforceable under the doctrine of promissory estoppel. *Balmer v. Elan Corp.,* 278 Ga. 227, 599 S.E.2d 158 (2004).

UNIT FOUR

Domestic and International Sales and Lease Contracts

CHAPTER 20

The Formation of Sales and Lease Contracts

When we turn to contracts for the sale and lease of goods, we move away from common law principles and into the area of statutory law. State statutory law governing sales and lease transactions is based on the Uniform Commercial Code (UCC), which, as mentioned in Chapter 1, has been adopted as law by all of the states.[1]

We open this chapter with a discussion of the historical development of sales and lease law and the UCC's significance as a legal landmark. We then look at the scope of the UCC's Article 2 (on sales) and Article 2A (on leases) as a background to the topic of this chapter, which is the formation of contracts for the sale and lease of goods. Because international sales transactions are increasingly commonplace in the business world, we conclude the chapter with an examination of the United Nations Convention on Contracts for the International Sale of Goods (CISG), which governs international sales contracts.

The UCC was amended in 2003 to update its provisions to accommodate electronic commerce. To date, the amendments to Article 2 and 2A have not been adopted by any state.[2] Throughout this chapter and the chapters that follow, however, any amendments that significantly change the UCC provisions currently in effect in most states will be discussed in footnotes. (Excerpts from the 2003 amendments appear in Appendix C, which presents the full text of the UCC.)

SECTION 1 | The Uniform Commercial Code

In the early years of this nation, sales law varied from state to state, and this lack of uniformity complicated the formation of multistate sales contracts. The problems became especially troublesome in the late nineteenth century as multistate contracts became the norm. For this reason, numerous attempts were made to produce a uniform body of laws relating to commercial transactions. The National Conference of Commissioners on Uniform State Laws (NCCUSL) drafted two uniform ("model") acts that were widely adopted by the states: the Uniform Negotiable Instruments Law (1896) and the Uniform Sales Act (1906). Several other proposed uniform acts followed, although most were not as widely adopted.

In the 1940s, the need to integrate the half dozen or so uniform acts covering commercial transactions into a single, comprehensive body of statutory law was recognized. The NCCUSL developed the Uniform Commercial Code (UCC) to serve that purpose. First issued in 1949, the UCC facilitates commercial transactions by making the laws governing sales and lease contracts clearer, simpler, and more readily applicable to the numerous difficulties that can arise during such transactions.

COMPREHENSIVE COVERAGE OF THE UCC

The UCC is the single most comprehensive codification of the broad spectrum of laws involved in a total commercial transaction. The UCC views the entire "commercial transaction for the sale of and payment for goods" as a single legal occurrence having numerous facets.

You can gain an idea of the comprehensiveness of the UCC by looking at the titles of the articles of the UCC in Appendix C. As you will note, Article 1,

---

1. Louisiana has not adopted Articles 2 and 2A, however.
2. Legislation to adopt these amendments is pending in Kansas (House Bill 2454) and Nevada (Senate Bill 200).

titled "General Provisions," sets forth definitions and general principles applicable to commercial transactions, including an obligation to perform in "good faith" all contracts falling under the UCC [UCC 1–203]. Article 1 thus provides the basic groundwork for the remaining articles, each of which focuses on a particular aspect of commercial transactions.

A SINGLE, INTEGRATED FRAMEWORK FOR COMMERCIAL TRANSACTIONS An example will help to clarify how several articles of the UCC can be applied to a single commercial transaction. Suppose that a consumer—a person who purchases goods primarily for personal or household use—buys a deluxe, side-by-side refrigerator with ice maker from an appliance store. The consumer agrees to pay for the refrigerator on an installment plan.

Because there is a contract for the sale of goods, Article 2 will apply. If the consumer gives a check as the down payment on the purchase price, it will be negotiated and ultimately passed through one or more banks for collection. This process is the subject matter of Article 3, Negotiable Instruments, and Article 4, Bank Deposits and Collections. If the appliance store extends credit to the consumer through an installment plan, and if it retains a lien (a legal right or interest) on the refrigerator (the collateral, which is the property pledged as security against a debt), then Article 9, Secured Transactions, will be applicable. (Secured transactions will be discussed in detail in Chapter 29.)

Suppose, in addition, that the appliance company must obtain the refrigerator from the manufacturer's warehouse before shipping it by common carrier to the consumer. The storage and shipment of goods are the subject matter of Article 7, Documents of Title. To pay the manufacturer, which is located in another state, for the refrigerator supplied, the appliance company may use a letter of credit—the subject matter of Article 5. Thus, the UCC attempts to provide a consistent and integrated framework of rules to deal with all the phases *ordinarily arising* in a commercial sales transaction from start to finish.

ARTICLES 6 AND 8 Two articles of the UCC seem not to apply to an "ordinary" commercial sales transaction. Article 6, Bulk Transfers, involves merchants who sell off the major part of their inventory (sometimes leaving creditors unpaid). Because bulk sales ordinarily do not arise in a commercial sales transaction, most states have repealed Article 6 entirely,

although some states have adopted the revised version of Article 6 (see Appendix C).

Article 8, Investment Securities, deals with transactions involving certain negotiable securities (stocks and bonds), which do not involve a sale of (or payment for) *goods*. Nevertheless, the UCC's drafters considered the subject matter of Articles 6 and 8 related *sufficiently* to commercial transactions to warrant the inclusion of these articles in the UCC.

PERIODIC REVISIONS OF THE UCC

Various articles and sections of the UCC are periodically changed or supplemented to clarify certain rules or to establish new rules when changes in business customs have rendered the existing UCC provisions inapplicable. For example, because of the increasing importance of leases of goods in the commercial context, Article 2A, governing leases, was added to the UCC. To clarify the rights of parties to commercial fund transfers, particularly electronic fund transfers, Article 4A was issued.

Articles 3 and 4, covering negotiable instruments and banking, underwent a significant revision in the 1990s, as did Articles 5, 8, and 9. Because of other changes in business and in the law, the NCCUSL has recommended the repeal of Article 6 and has offered a revised Article 6 to those states that prefer not to repeal it. Article 1 was revised in 2001, and the NCCUSL approved amendments to Articles 3 and 4 in 2002. In 2003, the NCCUSL approved amendments to Articles 2 and 2A, which have now been proposed to the states for adoption.

THE AMENDMENTS TO ARTICLES 2 AND 2A

For the most part, the 2003 amendments to Articles 2 and 2A mark an attempt by the NCCUSL to update the UCC to accommodate electronic commerce. Among other things, the amendments include revised definitions of various terms to make the definitions consistent with those given in the Uniform Electronic Transactions Act (UETA) and the federal Electronic Signatures in Global and National Commerce Act (E-SIGN Act) of 2000. (These acts were discussed in Chapter 19.) Throughout the amendments, for example, the word *record* replaces the word *writing*, and the definition of *sign* has been modified to include electronic signatures. Provisions governing electronic contracts, including contracts formed by electronic agents, have also been added.

In addition, the amendments include a number of new protections for buyers, some of which apply only to buyers who are consumers. Other new or revised provisions relate to contract formation (offer and acceptance), the Statute of Frauds, the parol evidence rule, and a number of other miscellaneous topics. Exhibit 20–1 summarizes the most significant changes made by the 2003 amendments. As mentioned earlier,

we include excerpts from the 2003 amendments to Article 2 in Appendix C for further reference.

SECTION **2** │ The Scope of Article 2— The Sale of Goods

Article 2 of the UCC governs **sales contracts,** or contracts for the sale of goods. To facilitate commercial transactions, Article 2 modifies some of the common

EXHIBIT 20–1 **The 2003 Amendments to UCC Article 2: Selected Provisions***

GENERAL CHANGES

- *Electronic contracting*—The 2003 amendments reflect the rise of electronic contracting (for example, the word *record* is substituted for the word *writing*) and the provisions of the federal law governing e-signatures (see Chapter 19).
- *New protections for buyers*—There are some new protections for buyers, and some provisions are applicable only to buyers who qualify as consumers. For example, specific language is required to disclaim implied warranties (see Chapter 23).
- *Remedies*—The amendments in UCC 2–703 and UCC 2–711 give a complete list of the remedies available to buyers and sellers, respectively, on a breach of contract (see Chapter 22).

SOME IMPORTANT SPECIFIC CHANGES

- *Shipping and delivery terms*—Entirely eliminated are UCC Sections 2–319 through 2–324, which deal with shipping and delivery terms (F.O.B., C.I.F., and others listed in Chapter 21 in Exhibit 21–1). Additionally, risk of loss relating to goods to be delivered without movement (see Chapter 22) now passes on the buyer's receipt of the goods regardless of the seller's status as a merchant or nonmerchant.
- *New sections on express warranties*—With respect to *new goods only*, two new sections extend express warranties made by a seller or lessor in an advertisement or in a record accompanying goods to remote purchasers (see Chapter 23).
- *Remedial promises*—Although not an express warranty, added to the sections on express warranties is a seller's obligation to honor a "remedial promise"—defined as a promise to repair, replace, or refund all or part of the price on the happening of a specified event (see Chapter 23).
- *The seller's right to cure*—This right has been extended (except in consumer contracts) to allow sellers, in some circumstances, to cure even after the time for performance has expired (see Chapter 22).
- *Contract formation*—Under the 2003 amendments, the terms of the contract, subject to the parol evidence rule, are (a) the terms that appear in the records of both parties, (b) the terms to which both parties agree, and (c) the terms supplied or incorporated under UCC Article 2.

MISCELLANEOUS CHANGES

- *Statute of Frauds*—The Statute of Frauds threshold amount increases from $500 to $5,000, and the one-year rule is repealed for contracts for the sale of goods [UCC 2–201].
- *Assignment and delegation*—Rules governing assignment and delegation [UCC 2–210] have been modified to conform to revised Article 9, which deals with secured transactions (see Chapter 29).
- *Buyer's acceptance of nonconforming goods*—When a buyer has accepted nonconforming goods [UCC 2–607(3)], the failure of the buyer to notify the seller of the breach no longer will operate as a bar to further recovery. Failure to give timely notice will bar a remedy "only to the extent that the seller is prejudiced by the failure" (see Chapters 22 and 23).
- *Consequential damages*—A seller can now recover consequential damages resulting from a buyer's breach under UCC 2–710. Under existing law, the seller is limited to incidental damages (see Chapter 22).
- *Statute of limitations*—The statute of limitations [UCC 2–725] has been modified to, among other things, clarify when a breach or cause of action accrues and to provide added protection for consumers (see Chapter 23).

*This exhibit lists only selected changes made by the 2003 amendments. As of this writing, the amendments have not been adopted by any state.

law contract requirements that were discussed in the previous chapters. To the extent that it has not been modified by the UCC, however, the common law of contracts also applies to sales contracts. For example, the common law requirements for a valid contract—agreement (offer and acceptance), consideration, capacity, and legality—that were summarized in Chapter 10 and discussed at length in Chapters 11 through 13 are also applicable to sales contracts. Thus, you should reexamine these common law principles when studying the law of sales.

In general, the rule is that whenever a conflict arises between a common law contract rule and the UCC, the UCC controls. In other words, when a UCC provision addresses a certain issue, the UCC governs; when the UCC is silent, the common law governs. The relationship between general contract law and the law governing sales of goods is illustrated in Exhibit 20–2.

In regard to Article 2, you should keep two things in mind. First, Article 2 deals with the sale of *goods*; it does not deal with real property (real estate), services, or intangible property such as stocks and bonds. Thus, if the subject matter of a dispute is goods, the UCC governs. If it is real estate or services, the common law applies. Second, in some cases, the rules may vary quite a bit, depending on whether the buyer or the seller is a *merchant*. We look now at how the UCC defines a *sale*, *goods*, and *merchant status*.

WHAT IS A SALE?

Section 2–102 of the UCC states that Article 2 "applies to transactions in goods." This implies a broad scope—covering gifts, bailments (temporary deliveries of personal property, discussed in Chapter 47), and purchases of goods. In this chapter, however, we treat Article 2 as being applicable only to an actual sale (as would most authorities and courts). The UCC defines a **sale** as "the passing of title [evidence of ownership rights] from the seller to the buyer for a price," where *title* refers to the formal right of ownership of property [UCC 2–106(1)]. The price may be payable in money or in other goods, services, or realty (real estate).

WHAT ARE GOODS?

To be characterized as a *good*, an item of property must be *tangible*, and it must be *movable*.[3] **Tangible property** has physical existence—it can be touched or seen.

---

3. The 2003 amendments to Article 2 change this phrase slightly to reduce the importance of movability. The new section states that "goods must be both *existing* and *identified* before any interest in them may pass" [Amended UCC 2–105(1)].

EXHIBIT 20-2 **The Law Governing Contracts**

This exhibit graphically illustrates the relationship between general contract law and statutory law (UCC Articles 2 and 2A) governing contracts for the sale and lease of goods. Sales contracts are not governed exclusively by Article 2 of the UCC but are also governed by general contract law whenever it is relevant and has not been modified by the UCC.

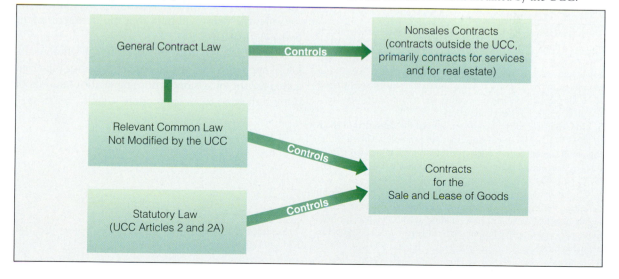

Intangible property—such as corporate stocks and bonds, patents and copyrights, and ordinary contract rights—has only conceptual existence and thus does not come under Article 2.[4] A *movable* item can be carried from place to place. Hence, real estate is excluded from Article 2.

Two areas of dispute arise in determining whether the object of a contract is goods and thus whether Article 2 is applicable. One problem concerns *goods associated with real estate*, such as crops or timber, and the other concerns contracts involving a combination of *goods and services*.

GOODS ASSOCIATED WITH REAL ESTATE Goods associated with real estate often fall within the scope of Article 2. Section 2–107 provides the following rules:

1. A contract for the sale of minerals or the like (including oil and gas) or a structure (such as a building) is a contract for the sale of goods if *severance, or separation, is to be made by the seller*. If the *buyer* is to sever (separate) the minerals or structures from the land, the contract is considered to be a sale of real estate governed by the principles of real property law, not the UCC.

2. A sale of growing crops[5] or timber to be cut is a contract for the sale of goods *regardless of who severs them*.

3. Other "things attached" to realty but capable of severance without material harm to the land are considered to be goods *regardless of who severs them*.[6]

Examples of "things attached" that are severable without harm to realty are a window air conditioner in a house and tables and stools in a restaurant. Thus, removal of these things would be considered a sale of goods. The test is whether removal will cause substantial harm to the real property to which the item is attached.

GOODS AND SERVICES COMBINED In cases in which goods and services are combined, courts disagree. For example, is the furnishing of blood to a patient during an operation a "sale of goods" or the "performance of a medical service"? Some courts say it is a good; others say it is a service. The UCC does stipulate, however, that serving food or drink to be consumed either on or off restaurant premises is a "sale of goods," at least for the purpose of an implied warranty of merchantability (to be explained in Chapter 23) [UCC 2–314(1)]. Other special cases are also explicitly characterized as goods by the UCC, including unborn animals and rare coins.

Whether the transaction in question involves the sale of goods or services is important because the majority of courts treat services as being excluded by the UCC. If the transaction is not covered by the UCC, then UCC provisions, including those relating to implied warranties, will not apply. For example, suppose that an Indiana company contracts to purchase customized software from Dharma Systems. The contract states that half of the purchase price is for Dharma Systems' professional services and the other half is for the goods (the software). If the court determines that the contract is predominantly for the software, rather than the services to customize the software, the court will hold that the transaction falls under Article 2.[7]

The question in the following case was whether the UCC applied to an agreement for a sale of pigs that called for the provision of housing facilities and labor to raise the pigs to an appropriate weight.

---

4. The 2003 amendments specifically exclude "information" that is not associated with goods [Amended UCC 2–103(1)(k)]. Nevertheless, Article 2 *may* apply to transactions involving both goods and information when a sale involves "smart goods" (for example, a toy or automobile that contains computer programs). It is up to the courts to determine whether and to what extent Article 2 should be applied to such transactions.

5. Note that the 2003 amendments moved the definition of goods to UCC 2–103(k), but growing crops are expressly included within the definition of *goods*. Contracts to sell timber, minerals, or structures to be removed from the land will continue to be controlled by UCC 2–107(1).

6. The UCC avoids the term *fixtures* here because of the numerous definitions of the word. A fixture is anything so firmly or permanently attached to land or to a building as to become a part of it. Once personal property becomes a fixture, real estate law governs. See Chapter 47.

---

7. See *Micro Data Base Systems, Inc. v. Dharma Systems, Inc.*, 148 F.3d 649 (7th Cir. 1998).

CASE 20.1 — Lohman v. Wagner

Court of Special Appeals
of Maryland, 2004.
160 Md.App. 122,
862 A.2d 1042.

BACKGROUND AND FACTS *Charles Lohman operated a farrow-to-finish pig-raising oper-*
ation[a] at his farm in Washington County, Maryland. In late 1997, John Wagner proposed establishing
a network of pork producers and discussed Lohman's becoming a weaner-pig[b] producer. To convert
his existing operation into a weaner-pig facility, Lohman needed to provide more gestation space,
reduce his feeder-pig inventory, and increase his number of sows. In July 1998, Lohman sought
financing from First National Bank of Mercersburg to fund the conversion. The bank asked to see
Lohman's weaner-pig purchase agreement with Wagner's network. At Lohman's request, Wagner
signed a retyped copy of an old agreement but left blank the space to state a quantity of pigs. He
faxed this to Lohman, who signed it and faxed it to the bank. The same month, Lohman began pro-
ducing only weaner pigs and shipping them to Wagner at $28 per head. In October, Wagner said he
was reducing the price to $18 per head because of a drop in market prices for pork. At this price,
Lohman was out of business by March 1999. He filed a suit in a Maryland state court against Wagner
alleging breach of contract and seeking damages. The court entered a judgment against Lohman,
who appealed to a state intermediate appellate court.

IN THE LANGUAGE OF THE COURT

MEREDITH, J. [Judge]
* * * *

Lohman asserts that the trial court erred in finding the * * * Uniform
Commercial Code applies to the alleged contract in this case. Lohman contends the agreement with Wagner was a contract for the provision of services, not a contract for the sale of
goods, and therefore, the UCC does not apply. Lohman argues that the language of the agreement "was carefully crafted to avoid a sales transaction" by requiring the "Producer"
(Lohman) to furnish housing facilities, labor, utilities, and production supplies in producing
and raising weaner pigs. Additionally, Lohman notes that the agreement gave Wagner the
authority to access Lohman's facility and to oversee various aspects of breeding and raising the
pigs. Lohman contends the agreement is therefore one for the provision of services by him,
and not a contract for the sale of weaner pigs.

* * * *

* * * *The definition of the goods that are subject to Article 2 of the UCC covers young ani-*
mals and even the unborn young of animals. The definition of goods would cover the weaner pigs
that were raised by Lohman. [Emphasis added.]

Other courts have found that contracts for the sale of pigs are governed by the UCC.

Lohman is correct that the alleged weaner pig purchase agreement involves providing certain services. However, as the trial court correctly observed, the UCC may apply to contracts
involving both services and the delivery of goods. * * *

* * * *

* * * *The cases presenting mixed contracts of this type are legion [numerous]. The test*
for inclusion or exclusion is not whether they are mixed, but, granting that they are mixed, whether
their predominant factor, their thrust, their purpose, reasonably stated, is the rendition of service, with
goods incidentally involved (e.g., contract with artist for painting) or is a transaction of sale, with

---

a. A *farrow-to-finish pig-raising operation* involves the breeding, gestation, and raising of pigs to a weight of 50
pounds so that they can be transferred to a finishing floor, where they continue to mature until they reach a market weight of 250 to 300 pounds.

b. *Weaner pigs* are young pigs in the developmental stage from the time of their birth until they are weaned from
their mothers at a weight of seven to fourteen pounds, after which they are known as *feeder pigs* until they reach a
weight of fifty pounds.

CONTINUED

CASE 20.1 | Continued

labor incidentally involved ([such as the] installation of a water heater in a bathroom). * * * [Emphasis added.]

* * * *

* * * Courts have generally looked principally to the language of the parties' agreement and the circumstances surrounding its making in determining the predominant thrust of the transaction. Moreover, in analyzing the parties' agreement, it is appropriate to look to the terminology used therein to determine whether it is peculiar to sales or service contracts.

In this case, the trial court expressly applied [this] analysis to the alleged contract and concluded that the predominant purpose of the document captioned "Weaner Pig Purchase Agreement" was a sale of goods. * * *

The evidence supports the trial court's conclusion that although the agreement called for Lohman to provide certain services, those services were all incidental to the eventual delivery of the specified pigs and did not constitute the main thrust or predominant purpose of the agreement. The predominant purpose of the agreement was the purchase and sale of young pigs. Therefore, the alleged agreement is governed by the UCC.

DECISION AND REMEDY *The state intermediate appellate court affirmed the lower court's judgment. The parties' agreement contemplated predominantly a sale of goods—young pigs. The agreement also called for Lohman to provide certain services, but those services were incidental to the delivery of the pigs. The UCC therefore applied.*

WHAT IF THE FACTS WERE DIFFERENT? *Suppose that the agreement between Lohman and Wagner had called for Lohman to raise pigs that Wagner supplied. Would the court have held that this agreement fell under the UCC? Explain.*

WHO IS A MERCHANT?

Article 2 governs the sale of goods in general. It applies to sales transactions between all buyers and sellers. In a limited number of instances, though, the UCC presumes that special business standards ought to be imposed because of the merchants' relatively high degree of commercial expertise.[8] Such standards do not apply to the casual or inexperienced seller or buyer ("consumer"). Section 2–104 sets forth three ways in which merchant status can arise:

1. A merchant is a person who *deals in goods of the kind* involved in the sales contract. Thus, a retailer, a wholesaler, or a manufacturer is a merchant of those goods sold in the business. A merchant for one type of goods is not necessarily a merchant for another type. For example, a sporting goods retailer is a merchant when selling tennis rackets but not when selling a used computer.

2. A merchant is a person who, by occupation, holds himself or herself out as having knowledge and skill unique to the practices or goods involved in the transaction. This broad definition may include banks or universities as merchants.

3. A person who *employs a merchant as a broker, agent, or other intermediary* has the status of merchant in that transaction. Hence, if a "gentleman farmer" who ordinarily does not run the farm hires a broker to purchase or sell livestock, the farmer is considered a merchant in the transaction.

In summary, a person is a **merchant** when she or he, acting in a mercantile capacity, possesses or uses an expertise specifically related to the goods being sold. This basic distinction is not always clear-cut. For example, state courts appear to be split on whether farmers should be considered merchants.[9] In some states, including Illinois, Michigan, Missouri, North Carolina, New York, Texas, and Wisconsin, courts have held that farmers are merchants. In other states, such as Alabama, Arkansas, Iowa, Kansas, New

---

8. The provisions that apply only to merchants deal principally with the Statute of Frauds, firm offers, confirmatory memoranda, warranties, and contract modification. These special rules reflect expedient business practices commonly known to merchants in the commercial setting. They will be discussed later in this chapter.

9. See the court's discussion of this issue in *R. F. Cunningham & Co. v. Driscoll,* 7 Misc.3d 234, 790 N.Y.S.2d 368 (2005).

Mexico, South Dakota, and Utah, the courts have determined that the drafters of the UCC did not intend to include farmers as merchants.

SECTION 3 | The Scope of Article 2A—Leases

In the past few decades, leases of goods have become increasingly common. Consumers and business firms lease automobiles, industrial equipment, items for use in the home (such as floor polishers), and many other types of goods. Article 2A of the UCC was created to fill the need for uniform guidelines in this area. Article 2A covers any transaction that creates a lease of goods or a sublease of goods [UCC 2A–102, 2A–103(k)]. Article 2A is essentially a repetition of Article 2, except that it applies to leases of goods rather than sales of goods and only varies to reflect differences between sales and lease transactions. As previously mentioned, Article 2A was also amended in 2003, and these amendments have been recommended to the states for adoption.

DEFINITION OF A LEASE

Article 2A defines a **lease agreement** as the bargain of the lessor and lessee, as found in their language and as implied by other circumstances [UCC 2A–103(k)]. A **lessor** is one who sells the right to the possession and use of goods under a lease [UCC 2A–103(p)]. A **lessee** is one who acquires the right to the possession and use of goods under a lease [UCC 2A–103(o)]. In other words, the lessee is the party who is leasing the goods from the lessor. Article 2A applies to all types of leases of goods. Special rules apply to certain types of leases, however, including consumer leases and finance leases.

CONSUMER LEASES

A *consumer lease* involves three elements: (1) a lessor who regularly engages in the business of leasing or selling; (2) a lessee (except an organization) who leases the goods "primarily for a personal, family, or household purpose"; and (3) total lease payments that are less than $25,000 [UCC 2A–103(1)(e)].[10] In the

interest of providing special protection for consumers, certain provisions of Article 2A apply only to consumer leases. For example, one provision states that a consumer may recover attorneys' fees if a court determines that a term in a consumer lease contract is unconscionable [UCC 2A–108(4)(a)].

FINANCE LEASES

A *finance lease* involves a lessor, a lessee, and a supplier. The lessor buys or leases goods from a supplier and leases or subleases them to the lessee [UCC 2A–103(g)]. Typically, in a finance lease, the lessor is simply financing the transaction. For example, suppose that Marlin Corporation wants to lease a crane for use in its construction business. Marlin's bank agrees to purchase the equipment from Jennco, Inc., and lease the equipment to Marlin. In this situation, the bank is the lessor-financer, Marlin is the lessee, and Jennco is the supplier.

Article 2A, unlike ordinary contract law, makes the lessee's obligations under a finance lease irrevocable and independent from the financer's obligations [UCC 2A–407]. In other words, the lessee must perform and continue to make lease payments even if the leased equipment turns out to be defective. The lessee must look almost entirely to the supplier for any recovery.

For example, in one case American Transit Insurance Company (ATIC) arranged to lease telephone equipment through a finance lease. Siemens Credit Corporation obtained the equipment from the manufacturer and then leased the equipment to ATIC for a five-year term at $2,314 per month. When the equipment turned out to be defective, ATIC stopped making the lease payments. Siemens then sued ATIC for the lease payments due. ATIC alleged, among other things, that it was unconscionable to require it to make payments on defective equipment. According to the court, though, the lease clearly qualified as a finance lease under Article 2A, and thus ATIC was obligated to make all payments due under the lease regardless of the condition or performance of the leased equipment. The court stated that ATIC's claims could be brought only against the manufacturer, not against the lessor (Siemens).[11]

---

10. The 2003 amendments to Article 2A define a consumer lease in UCC 2A–103(1)(f). The amended section leaves it up to the states whether or not to place a dollar limitation on the total lease payments.

---

11. *Siemens Credit Corp. v. American Transit Insurance Co.*, 2001 WL 40775 (S.D.N.Y. 2001).

SECTION 4 | The Formation of Sales and Lease Contracts

In regard to the formation of sales and lease contracts, the UCC modifies the common law in several ways. We look here at how Article 2 and Article 2A of the UCC modify common law contract rules. Remember that parties to sales contracts are free to establish whatever terms they wish. The UCC comes into play when the parties fail to provide in their contract for a contingency that later gives rise to a dispute. The UCC makes this very clear time and again by its use of such phrases as "unless the parties otherwise agree" and "absent a contrary agreement by the parties."

OFFER

In general contract law, the moment a definite offer is met by an unqualified acceptance, a binding contract is formed. In commercial sales transactions, the verbal exchanges, correspondence, and actions of the parties may not reveal exactly when a binding contractual obligation arises. The UCC states that an agreement sufficient to constitute a contract can exist even if the moment of its making is undetermined [UCC 2–204(2), 2A–204(2)].

OPEN TERMS According to contract law, an offer must be definite enough for the parties (and the courts) to ascertain its essential terms when it is accepted. The UCC states that a sales or lease contract will not fail for indefiniteness even if one or more terms are left open as long as (1) the parties intended to make a contract and (2) there is a reasonably certain basis for the court to grant an appropriate remedy [UCC 2–204(3), 2A–204(3)].

For example, Mike agrees to lease from CompuQuik a highly specialized computer station. Mike and one of CompuQuik's sales representatives sign a lease agreement that leaves some of the details blank, to be "worked out" the following week, when the leasing manager will be back from her vacation. In the meantime, CompuQuik obtains the necessary equipment from one of its suppliers and spends several days modifying the equipment to suit Mike's needs. When the leasing manager returns, she calls Mike and tells him that his work station is ready. Mike says he is no longer interested in the work station, as he has arranged to lease the same equipment for a

lower price from another firm. CompuQuik sues Mike to recover its costs in obtaining and modifying the equipment, and one of the issues before the court is whether the parties had an enforceable contract. The court will likely hold that they did, based on their intent and conduct, despite the blanks in their written agreement.

Relative to the common law of contracts, the UCC has radically lessened the requirement of definiteness of terms. Keep in mind, though, that if too many terms are left open, a court may find that the parties did not intend to form a contract.

—Open Price Term. If the parties have not agreed on a price, the court will determine a "reasonable price at the time for delivery" [UCC 2–305(1)]. If either the buyer or the seller is to determine the price, the price is to be fixed in good faith [UCC 2–305(2)]. Under the UCC, good faith means honesty in fact and the observance of reasonable commercial standards of fair dealing in the trade [UCC 2–103(1)(b)].[12] The concepts of *good faith* and *commercial reasonableness* permeate the UCC.

Sometimes, the price fails to be fixed through the fault of one of the parties. In that case, the other party can treat the contract as canceled or fix a reasonable price. For example, Perez and Merrick enter into a contract for the sale of goods and agree that Perez will fix the price. Perez refuses to fix the price. Merrick can either treat the contract as canceled or set a reasonable price [UCC 2–305(3)].

—Open Payment Term. When parties do not specify payment terms, payment is due at the time and place at which the buyer is to receive the goods [UCC 2–310(a)]. The buyer can tender payment using any commercially normal or acceptable means, such as a check or credit card. If the seller demands payment in cash, however, the buyer must be given a reasonable time to obtain it [UCC 2–511(2)]. This is especially important when the contract states a definite and final time for performance.

—Open Delivery Term. When no delivery terms are specified, the buyer normally takes delivery at the seller's place of business [UCC 2–308(a)]. If the seller has no place of business, the seller's residence is used.

---

12. The 2003 amendments retain this definition of good faith, although it appears in 2–103(j). Many of the section numbers and subparts in Articles 2 and 2A change slightly under the amendments.

When goods are located in some other place and both parties know it, delivery is made there. If the time for shipment or delivery is not clearly specified in the sales contract, then the court will infer a "reasonable" time for performance [UCC 2–309(1)].

—Duration of an Ongoing Contract. A single contract might specify successive performances but not indicate how long the parties are required to deal with each other. In this situation, either party may terminate the ongoing contractual relationship. Nevertheless, principles of good faith and sound commercial practice call for reasonable notification before termination so as to give the other party sufficient time to seek a substitute arrangement [UCC 2–309(2), (3)].

—Options and Cooperation Regarding Performance. When specific shipping arrangements have not been made but the contract contemplates shipment of the goods, the *seller* has the right to make these arrangements in good faith, using commercial reasonableness in the situation [UCC 2–311]. (The obligations of good faith and commercial reasonableness in sales and lease contracts will be discussed in detail in Chapter 22.)

When terms relating to the assortment of goods are omitted from a sales contract, the buyer can specify the assortment. For example, Harley and Babcock contract for the sale of one thousand pens. The pens come in a variety of colors, but the contract is silent as to which colors are ordered. Babcock, the buyer, has the right to take whatever colors he wishes. Babcock, however, must exercise good faith and commercial reasonableness in making the selection [UCC 2–311].

—Open Quantity Term. Normally, if the parties do not specify a quantity, a court will have no basis for determining a remedy. The UCC recognizes two exceptions in requirements and output contracts [UCC 2–306(1)].

In a **requirements contract,** the buyer agrees to purchase and the seller agrees to sell all or up to a stated amount of what the buyer *needs* or *requires*. There is implicit consideration in a requirements contract because the buyer gives up the right to buy from any other seller, and this forfeited right creates a legal detriment. Requirements contracts are common in the business world and are normally enforceable. If, however, the buyer promises to purchase only if the buyer *wishes* to do so, or if the buyer reserves the right to buy the goods from someone other than the seller, the

promise is illusory (without consideration) and unenforceable by either party.

In an **output contract,** the seller agrees to sell and the buyer agrees to buy all or up to a stated amount of what the seller *produces*. Again, because the seller essentially forfeits the right to sell goods to another buyer, there is implicit consideration in an output contract.

The UCC imposes a *good faith limitation* on requirements and output contracts. The quantity under such contracts is the amount of requirements or the amount of output that occurs during a *normal* production period. The actual quantity purchased or sold cannot be unreasonably disproportionate to normal or comparable prior requirements or output [UCC 2–306].

MERCHANT'S FIRM OFFER Under regular contract principles, an offer can be revoked at any time before acceptance. The major common law exception is an *option contract* (discussed in Chapter 11), in which the offeree pays consideration for the offeror's irrevocable promise to keep the offer open for a stated period. The UCC creates a second exception, which applies only to firm offers for the sale or lease of goods made by a merchant (regardless of whether or not the offeree is a merchant).

—When a Merchant's Firm Offer Arises. A **firm offer** arises when a merchant-offeror gives *assurances in a signed writing* that the offer will remain open. The merchant's firm offer is irrevocable without the necessity of consideration[13] for the stated period or, if no definite period is stated, a reasonable period (neither to exceed three months) [UCC 2–205, 2A–205].

To illustrate: Osaka, a used-car dealer, writes a letter to Bennett on January 1 stating, "I have a used 2005 Pontiac on the lot that I'll sell you for $10,500 any time between now and January 31." By January 18, Osaka has heard nothing from Bennett, so he sells the Pontiac to another person. On January 23, Bennett tenders $10,500 to Osaka and asks for the car. When Osaka tells him the car has already been sold, Bennett claims that Osaka has breached a valid contract. Bennett is right. Osaka is a merchant of used cars and assured Bennett in a signed writing that he would keep his offer open until the end of January. Bennett's acceptance on January 23 thus created a contract, which Osaka breached.

---

13. If the offeree pays consideration, then an option contract (not a merchant's firm offer) is formed.

—The Offer Must Be in Writing and Signed by the Offeror.   It is necessary that the offer be both *written* and *signed* by the offeror.[14] When a firm offer is contained in a form contract prepared by the offeree, the offeror must also sign a separate firm-offer assurance. This requirement ensures that the offeror will be made aware of the offer. If the firm offer is buried amid copious language in one of the pages of the offeree's form contract, the offeror may inadvertently sign the contract without realizing that it contains a firm offer, thus defeating the purpose of the rule—which is to give effect to a merchant's deliberate intent to be bound to a firm offer.

ACCEPTANCE

The following sections examine the UCC's provisions governing acceptance. As you will see, acceptance of an offer to buy, sell, or lease goods generally may be made in any reasonable manner and by any reasonable means.

METHODS OF ACCEPTANCE   The general common law rule is that an offeror can specify, or authorize, a particular means of acceptance, making that means the only one effective for contract formation. Even an unauthorized means of communication is effective, however, as long as the acceptance is received by the specified deadline. For example, suppose that the offer states, "Answer by fax within five days." If the offeree, nonetheless, sends a letter, but the offeror receives it within five days, a valid contract is still formed. (For a review of the requirements relating to mode and timeliness of acceptance, see Chapter 11.)

—Any Reasonable Means.   When the offeror does not specify a means of acceptance, the UCC provides that acceptance can be made by any means of communication that is reasonable under the circumstances [UCC 2–206(1), 2A–206(1)]. This is also the basic rule under the common law of contracts (see Chapter 11).

For example, Anodyne Corporation writes a letter to Bethlehem Industries offering to lease $5,000 worth of goods. The offer states that Anodyne will keep the offer open for only ten days from the date of the letter. Before the ten days have lapsed, Bethlehem sends Anodyne an acceptance by fax. The fax is misdirected by someone at Anodyne's offices and does not reach the right person at Anodyne until after the ten-day deadline has passed. Is a valid contract formed? The answer is probably yes, because acceptance by fax appears to be a commercially reasonable medium of acceptance under the circumstances. Acceptance would be effective on Bethlehem's transmission of the fax, which occurred before the offer lapsed.

—Promise to Ship or Prompt Shipment.   The UCC permits acceptance of an offer to buy goods "either by a prompt promise to ship or by the prompt or current shipment of conforming or nonconforming goods" [UCC 2–206(1)(b)]. *Conforming* goods are goods that accord with the contract's terms; *nonconforming* goods do not. The seller's prompt shipment of *nonconforming goods* constitutes both an *acceptance* (a contract) and a *breach* of that contract. This rule does not apply if the seller **seasonably** (within a reasonable amount of time) notifies the buyer that the nonconforming shipment is offered only as an *accommodation*, or as a favor. The notice of accommodation must clearly indicate to the buyer that the shipment does not constitute an acceptance and that therefore no contract has been formed.

Suppose that Barrymore orders one thousand *black* fans from Stroh. Stroh ships one thousand *blue* fans to Barrymore, notifying Barrymore that because Stroh has only blue fans in stock, these are sent as an accommodation. The shipment of blue fans is not an acceptance but a counteroffer, and a contract will be formed only if Barrymore accepts the blue fans. If, however, Stroh ships one thousand blue fans instead of black *without* notifying Barrymore that the goods are being shipped as an accommodation, Stroh's shipment acts as both an acceptance of Barrymore's offer and a breach of the resulting contract. Barrymore may sue Stroh for any appropriate damages.

COMMUNICATION OF ACCEPTANCE   Under the common law, because a unilateral offer invites acceptance by performance, the offeree need not notify the offeror of performance unless the offeror would not otherwise know about it. The UCC is more stringent than the common law, stating that when the begin-

---

14. "Signed" includes any symbol executed or adopted by a party with a present intention to authenticate a writing [UCC 1–201(39)]. A complete signature is not required. Therefore, initials, a thumbprint, a trade name, or any mark used in lieu of a written signature will suffice, regardless of its location on the document. Under the 2003 amendments to UCC Articles 2 and 2A, the definition of *sign* is broad enough to cover any record that contains an e-signature.

ning of the requested performance is a reasonable mode of acceptance, an offeror who is not notified of acceptance within a reasonable time may treat the offer as having lapsed before acceptance [UCC 2–206(2), 2A–206(2)].

ADDITIONAL TERMS Under the common law, if Alderman makes an offer to Beale, and Beale in turn accepts but adds some slight modification, there is no contract. Recall from Chapter 11 that the so-called mirror image rule requires that the terms of the acceptance exactly match those of the offer. The UCC, however, dispenses with the mirror image rule. The UCC generally takes the position that if the offeree's response indicates a *definite* acceptance of the offer, a contract is formed, even if the acceptance includes terms additional to or different from those contained in the offer [UCC 2–207(1)]. What happens to these additional terms? The answer to this question depends, in part, on whether the parties are nonmerchants or merchants.[15]

—Rules When One Party or Both Parties Are Nonmerchants. If one (or both) of the parties is a *nonmerchant*, the contract is formed according to the terms of the original offer and not according to the additional terms of the acceptance [UCC 2–207(2)]. For example, Tolsen offers in writing to sell his personal computer and Zip drive to Valdez for $1,500. Valdez e-mails a reply to Tolsen, stating, "I accept your offer to purchase your computer and Zip drive for $1,500. I *would like* twenty Zip disks to be included in the purchase price." Valdez has given Tolsen a definite expression of acceptance (creating a contract), even though the acceptance also suggests an added term for the offer. Because Tolsen is not a merchant, the additional term is merely a proposal (suggestion), and Tolsen is not legally obligated to comply with that term.

—Rules When Both Parties Are Merchants. In contracts *between merchants*, the additional terms automatically become part of the contract unless (1) the original offer expressly limited acceptance to

its terms, (2) the new or changed terms materially alter the contract, or (3) the offeror objects to the new or changed terms within a reasonable period of time [UCC 2–207(2)].

What constitutes a material alteration of the contract is frequently a question of fact that only a court can decide. Generally, if the modification involves no unreasonable element of surprise or hardship for the offeror, the court will hold that the modification did not materially alter the contract. For example, suppose that Woolf has ordered meat from Tupman sixty-four times over a two-year period. Each time, Woolf placed the order over the phone, and Tupman mailed a confirmation form, and then an invoice, to Woolf. Tupman's confirmation form and invoice have always included an arbitration clause. If Woolf places another order and fails to pay for the meat, the court will likely hold that the additional term—the arbitration provision—did not materially alter the contract, because Woolf should not have been surprised by the term.[16]

—Conditioned on Offeror's Assent. Regardless of merchant status, the UCC provides that the offeree's expression cannot be construed as an acceptance if it contains additional or different terms that are expressly *conditioned* on the offeror's assent to those terms [UCC 2–207(1)]. For example, Philips offers to sell Hundert 650 pounds of turkey thighs at a specified price and with specified delivery terms. Hundert responds, "I accept your offer for 650 pounds of turkey thighs *on the condition that you agree that the weight will be evidenced by a city scale weight certificate*." Hundert's response will be construed not as an acceptance but as a counteroffer, which Philips may or may not accept.

—Additional Terms May Be Stricken. The UCC provides yet another option for dealing with conflicting terms in the parties' writings. Section 2–207(3) states that conduct by both parties that recognizes the existence of a contract is sufficient to establish a contract for sale even though the writings of the parties do not otherwise establish a contract. In this situation, "the terms of the particular contract will consist of those terms on which the writings of the parties agree, together with any supplementary terms incorporated under any other provisions of this Act." In a dispute over contract terms, this provision allows a court simply to strike from the contract those terms on which the parties do not agree.

---

15. The 2003 amendments to UCC Article 2 do not distinguish between merchants and others in setting out rules for the effect of additional terms in sales contracts. Instead, a court is directed to determine whether (1) the terms appear in the records of both parties, (2) both parties agree to the terms even if they are not in a record, or (3) the terms are supplied or incorporated under another provision of Article 2 [Amended UCC 2–207]. Basically, the amendments give the courts more discretion to include or exclude certain terms.

16. *Tupman Thurlow Co. v. Woolf International Corp.*, 43 Mass.App. 334, 682 N.E.2d 1378 (1997).

CONSIDERATION

The common law rule that a contract requires consideration also applies to sales and lease contracts. Unlike the common law, however, the UCC does not require a contract modification to be supported by new consideration. The UCC states that an agreement modifying a contract for the sale or lease of goods "needs no consideration to be binding" [UCC 2–209(1), 2A–208(1)].

MODIFICATIONS MUST BE MADE IN GOOD FAITH

Of course, any contract modification must be made in good faith [UCC 1–203]. For example, Allied agrees to lease certain goods to Louise for a stated price. Subsequently, a sudden shift in the market makes it difficult for Allied to lease the items to Louise at the given price without suffering a loss. Allied tells Louise of the situation, and she agrees to pay an additional sum for the goods. Later, Louise reconsiders and refuses to pay more than the original price. Under the UCC, Louise's promise to modify the contract needs no consideration to be binding. Hence, Louise is bound by the modified contract.

In this example, a shift in the market is a *good faith* reason for contract modification. What if there really was no shift in the market, however, and Allied knew that Louise needed the goods immediately but refused to deliver them unless Louise agreed to pay an additional amount? This sort of extortion of a modification without a legitimate commercial reason would violate the duty of good faith, and Allied would not be permitted to enforce the higher price.

WHEN CONTRACT MODIFICATION WITHOUT CONSIDERATION REQUIRES A WRITING

In some situations, modification of a sales or lease contract without consideration must be in writing to be enforceable. For example, if the contract itself prohibits any changes to the contract unless they are in a signed writing, only those changes agreed to in a signed writing are enforceable. If a consumer (non-merchant buyer) is dealing with a merchant and the merchant supplies the form that contains the prohibition against oral modification, the consumer must sign a separate acknowledgment of the clause [UCC 2–209(2), 2A–208(2)].

Also, under Article 2, any modification that brings a sales contract under the Statute of Frauds must usually be in writing to be enforceable. Thus, if an oral contract for the sale of goods priced at $400 (or $4,000 under the amended UCC) is modified so that the contract goods are priced at $600 (or $6,000 under the amended UCC), the modification must be in writing—because sales contracts for goods priced at $500 or more ($5,000 or more under the 2003 amendments) must be in writing to be enforceable, as you will read shortly. Nevertheless, if the buyer accepts delivery of the goods after the modification, he or she may still be bound to pay the modified price on the theory that he or she waived the right to complain that it violated the Statute of Frauds [UCC 2–209]. (Note that the provisions governing modifications of leases in Article 2A do not say whether a lease as modified needs to satisfy the Statute of Frauds [UCC 2A–208].)

THE STATUTE OF FRAUDS

As discussed in Chapter 15, the Statute of Frauds requires that certain types of contracts, to be enforceable, must be in writing or evidenced by a writing.[17] The UCC contains Statute of Frauds provisions covering sales and lease contracts. Under these provisions, sales contracts for goods priced at $500 or more and lease contracts requiring total payments of $1,000 or more must be in writing to be enforceable [UCC 2–201(1), 2A–201(1)].[18]

SUFFICIENCY OF THE WRITING   The UCC has greatly relaxed the requirements for the sufficiency of a writing to satisfy the Statute of Frauds. A writing or a memorandum will be sufficient as long as it indicates that the parties intended to form a contract and as long as it is signed by the party (or agent of the party) against whom enforcement is sought. The contract normally will not be enforceable beyond the quantity of goods shown in the writing, however. All other terms can be proved in court by oral testimony. For leases, the writing must reasonably identify and describe the goods leased and the lease term.

SPECIAL RULES FOR CONTRACTS BETWEEN MERCHANTS   Once again, the UCC provides a special rule for merchants. The rule, however, applies

---

17. Under the common law, a contract that by its own terms cannot be performed within one year from the day after the date of its formation must be in writing to be enforceable. The 2003 amendments to UCC Articles 2 and 2A repeal the one-year rule in sales and lease contracts [Amended UCC 2–201(4), 2A–201(6)].

18. Note that a 2003 amendment significantly increased the price of goods that will fall under the Statute of Frauds. Under the amended UCC 2–201(1), goods must be priced at $5,000 or more to be subject to the record (writing) requirement.

only to sales (under Article 2); there is no corresponding rule that applies to leases (under Article 2A).[19] Merchants can satisfy the requirements of a writing for the Statute of Frauds if, after the parties have agreed orally, one of the merchants sends a signed written confirmation to the other merchant. The communication must indicate the terms of the agreement, and the merchant receiving the confirmation must have reason to know of its contents. Unless the merchant who receives the confirmation gives written notice of objection to its contents within ten days after receipt, the writing is sufficient against the receiving merchant, even though she or he has not signed anything [UCC 2–201(2)].

For example, Alfonso is a merchant-buyer in Cleveland. He contracts over the telephone to purchase $6,000 worth of goods from Goldstein, a New York City merchant-seller. Two days later, Goldstein sends written confirmation detailing the terms of the oral contract, and Alfonso subsequently receives it. If Alfonso does not give Goldstein written notice of objection to the contents of the written confirmation within ten days of receipt, Alfonso cannot raise the Statute of Frauds as a defense against the enforcement of the oral contract.

EXCEPTIONS The UCC defines three exceptions to the writing requirements of the Statute of Frauds. An oral contract for the sale of goods priced at $500 or more ($5,000 or more under the 2003 amendments) or the lease of goods involving total payments of $1,000 or more will be enforceable despite the absence of a writing in the circumstances described next [UCC 2–201(3), 2A–201(4)]. These exceptions and other ways in which sales law differs from general contract law are summarized in Exhibit 20–3.

—Specially Manufactured Goods. An oral contract is enforceable if (1) it is for goods that are specially manufactured for a particular buyer or specially manufactured or obtained for a particular lessee, (2) these

---

19. According to the Comments accompanying UCC 2A–201 (Article 2A's Statute of Frauds), the "between merchants" provision was not included because "the number of such transactions involving leases, as opposed to sales, was thought to be modest." Also, as mentioned in footnote 17, the 2003 amendments repeal the one-year rule in contracts for the lease of goods.

EXHIBIT 20-3 **Major Differences between Contract Law and Sales Law**

	CONTRACT LAW	SALES LAW
Contract Terms	Contract must contain all material terms.	Open terms are acceptable if parties intended to form a contract, but contract is not enforceable beyond quantity term.
Acceptance	Mirror image rule applies. If additional terms are added in acceptance, counteroffer is created.	Additional terms will not negate acceptance unless acceptance is expressly conditioned on assent to the additional terms.
Contract Modification	Modification requires consideration.	Modification does not require consideration.
Irrevocable Offers	Option contracts (with consideration).	Merchants' firm offers (without consideration).
Statute of Frauds Requirements	All material terms must be included in the writing.	Writing is required only for sale of goods of $500[a] or more, but contract is not enforceable beyond quantity specified. *Exceptions:* 1. Specially manufactured goods. 2. Admissions by party against whom enforcement is sought. 3. Partial performance. 4. Confirmatory memorandum (between merchants).

a. Under a 2003 amendment to the UCC, a writing (record) is required only for the sale of goods priced at $5,000 or more.

goods are not suitable for resale or lease to others in the ordinary course of the seller's or lessor's business, and (3) the seller or lessor has substantially started to manufacture the goods or has made commitments for the manufacture or procurement of the goods. In these situations, once the seller or lessor has taken action, the buyer or lessee cannot repudiate the agreement claiming the Statute of Frauds as a defense.

For example, suppose Womach orders custom-made draperies for her new boutique. The price is $6,000, and the contract is oral. When the merchant-seller manufactures the draperies and tenders delivery to Womach, she refuses to pay for them even though the job has been completed on time. Womach claims that she is not liable because the contract was oral. Clearly, if the unique style and color of the draperies make it improbable that the seller can find another buyer, Womach is liable to the seller. Note that the seller must have made a substantial beginning in manufacturing the specialized item prior to the buyer's repudiation. (Here, the manufacture was completed.) Of course, the court must still be convinced by evidence of the terms of the oral contract.

—Admissions.

An oral contract for the sale or lease of goods is enforceable if the party against whom enforcement is sought admits in pleadings, testimony, or other court proceedings that a sales or lease contract was made.[20] In this situation, the contract will be enforceable even though it was oral, but enforceability will be limited to the quantity of goods admitted.

For example, Lane and Salazar negotiate an agreement over the telephone. During the negotiations, Lane requests a delivery price for five hundred gallons of gasoline and a separate price for seven hundred gallons of gasoline. Salazar replies that the price would be the same, $2.10 per gallon. Lane orally orders five hundred gallons. Salazar honestly believes that Lane ordered seven hundred gallons and tenders that amount. Lane refuses the shipment of seven hundred gallons, and Salazar sues for breach. In his pleadings and testimony, Lane admits that an oral contract was made, but only for five hundred gallons. Because Lane admits the existence of the oral contract, Lane cannot plead the Statute of Frauds as a defense. The contract is enforceable, however, only to the extent of the quantity admitted (five hundred gallons).

—Partial Performance.

An oral contract for the sale or lease of goods is enforceable if payment has been made and accepted or goods have been received and accepted. This is the "partial performance" exception. The oral contract will be enforced at least to the extent that performance *actually* took place.

Suppose that Allan orally contracts to lease Opus ten thousand chairs at $1 each to be used during a one-day rock concert. Before delivery, Opus sends Allan a check for $5,000, which Allan cashes. Later, when Allan attempts to deliver the chairs, Opus refuses delivery, claiming the Statute of Frauds as a defense, and demands the return of his $5,000. Under the UCC's partial performance rule, Allan can enforce the oral contract by tender of delivery of five thousand chairs for the $5,000 accepted. Similarly, if Opus had made no payment but had accepted the delivery of five thousand chairs from Allan, the oral contract would have been enforceable against Opus for $5,000, the lease payment due for the five thousand chairs delivered.

PAROL EVIDENCE

If the parties to a contract set forth its terms in a confirmatory memorandum (a writing expressing offer and acceptance of the deal) or in a writing intended as their final expression, the terms of the contract cannot be contradicted by evidence of any prior agreements or contemporaneous oral agreements. As discussed in Chapter 15, this principle of law is known as the parol evidence rule. The terms of a contract may, however, be explained or supplemented by *consistent additional terms* or by *course of dealing, usage of trade, or course of performance* [UCC 2–202, 2A–202].[21]

AMBIGUOUS TERMS If the court finds an ambiguity in a writing that is supposed to be a final expression of the agreement between the parties, it may accept evidence of *consistent* additional terms to clarify or remove the ambiguity. The court will not, however, accept evidence of contradictory terms. This is the rule under the common law of contracts.

---

20. Any admission under oath, including one not made in a court, satisfies UCC 2–201(3)(b) and 2A–201(4) under the 2003 amendments to Articles 2 and 2A.

21. The 2003 amendments to this section substitute the term *record* for *writing* and add the stipulation that the "terms in a record may be explained by evidence of course of performance, course of dealing, or usage of trade without a preliminary determination by the court that the language used is ambiguous" [Amended UCC 2–202(2)].

COURSE OF DEALING AND USAGE OF TRADE

Under the UCC, the meaning of any agreement, evidenced by the language of the parties and by their actions, must be interpreted in light of commercial practices and other surrounding circumstances. In interpreting a commercial agreement, the court will assume that the *course of prior dealing* between the parties and the *usage of trade* were taken into account when the agreement was phrased.

A **course of dealing** is a sequence of previous actions and communications between the parties to a particular transaction that establishes a common basis for their understanding [UCC 1–205(1)]. A course of dealing is restricted to the sequence of conduct between the parties in their transactions previous to the agreement.

Usage of trade is defined as any practice or method of dealing having such regularity of observance in a place, vocation, or trade as to justify an expectation that it will be observed with respect to the transaction in question [UCC 1–205(2)]. Further, the express terms of an agreement and an applicable course of dealing or usage of trade will be construed to be consistent with each other whenever reasonable. When such a construction is *unreasonable*, however, the express terms in the agreement will prevail [UCC 1–205(4)].

In the following case, the question was whether a clause in the seller's invoice was part of a contract between the parties according to the usage of trade in their industry and the course of dealing between them.

CASE 20.2

Supreme Court of Washington, 2002.
146 Wash.2d 428,
47 P.3d 940.
http://www.legalwa.org[a]

Puget Sound Financial, LLC v. Unisearch, Inc.

BACKGROUND AND FACTS *Puget Sound Financial, LLC, lends money to businesses.*[b] *In 1993, Puget hired Unisearch, Inc., to search the public records in the state of Washington to locate existing liens on potential borrowers' assets. Puget would request a search under a particular name. Unisearch would send a report and an invoice for $25 to Puget. Every invoice contained the statement "Liability Limited to Amount of Fee." In July 1996, Puget requested a search for "The Benefit Group, Inc." Unisearch reported that there were no liens. Puget loaned The Benefit Group $100,000, with payment guaranteed by the firm's assets. When The Benefit Group failed to pay, Puget discovered that another lender had priority to the assets under a previous lien filed in the public records under the name "The Benefits Group, Inc." Puget filed a suit in a Washington state court against Unisearch, alleging in part breach of contract. Unisearch argued that if it was liable, the amount of damages would be limited to $25 under the invoices' limitation-of-liability clause, which was part of its contract with Puget according to the usage of trade in the search industry and the course of dealing between the parties. The court ruled in favor of Unisearch on this issue. Puget appealed to a state intermediate appellate court, which reversed the judgment. Unisearch appealed to the Washington Supreme Court.*

IN THE LANGUAGE OF THE COURT

BRIDGE, J. [Justice]
* * * *

Section 222 of the *Restatement [(Second) of Contracts]* pertaining to trade usage states:

(1) A usage of trade is a usage having such regularity of observance in a place, vocation, or trade as to justify an expectation that it will be observed with respect to a particular agreement. * * *

---

a. Click on "Washington State Supreme and Appellate Court Decisions." In the "Search" box, type "Unisearch," select "Search case titles only," and click on "Search." Click on the case name in the resulting list to access the opinion. Municipal Research and Services Center, which is funded by the state of Washington, maintains this Web site.

b. Before making a loan, a lender normally wants to know whether the property that will guarantee the potential borrower's payment of the loan is already being used to guarantee the payment of other debts of the borrower. If the borrower were to default on payment of the loan, the property's value might not be sufficient to pay all creditors. Loans guaranteed, or secured, by a debtor's personal property are known as secured transactions, which are discussed more fully in Chapter 29.

CONTINUED ▶

CASE 20.2 | Continued

Unisearch has presented numerous examples of liability exclusions on invoices from other states as evidence of trade usage. Unisearch has also presented examples of search firms who [sic] claimed that they would reimburse the search fees paid, if they made a mistake. Additionally, Unisearch produced an expert who declared that, "It is a standard practice in the * * * search industry to disclaim any liability resulting from the use of the information provided, and to provide a limitation of damages equal to the fee paid for the service." Furthermore, * * * the National Public Records Research Association notes:

> The industry practice is to place liability limitations on the invoices accompanying search results. This practice is born of customers' need for searches to be completed as quickly as possible. With customers expecting search results within the day and companies processing a multitude of searches, companies simply do not have time to negotiate the terms of all search orders received.

We find this * * * evidence persuasive of trade usage, supporting the inclusion of the limiting language in the contract between [Puget] and Unisearch.

Section 223 of the *Restatement* regarding course of dealing states:

> (1) A course of dealing is a sequence of previous conduct between the parties to an agreement which is fairly to be regarded as establishing a common basis of understanding for interpreting their expressions and other conduct. * * *

Unisearch sent 47 search results and invoices to [Puget] prior to the transaction before this court. Unisearch contends that, after the first invoice was sent and [Puget] did not reject it, a course of dealing was established. We need not determine the impact of the first invoice to decide that, after 48 transactions, a course of dealing was clearly established.

DECISION AND REMEDY *The Washington Supreme Court reversed the appellate court's decision and affirmed the trial court's judgment limiting Unisearch's liability, if any, to the amount of its fee. The state supreme court held that the limitation-of-liability clause in Unisearch's invoices was part of the contract between Puget and Unisearch according to the usage of trade in the industry and the parties' course of dealing.*

COURSE OF PERFORMANCE The conduct that occurs under the terms of a particular agreement is called a **course of performance.** Presumably, the parties themselves know best what they meant by their words, and the course of performance actually undertaken under their agreement is the best indication of what they meant [UCC 2–208(1), 2A–207(1)].[22]

For example, suppose that Janson's Lumber Company contracts with Barrymore to sell Barrymore a specified number of two-by-fours. The lumber in fact does not measure 2 inches by 4 inches but rather 1⅞ inches by 3¾ inches. Janson's agrees to deliver the lumber in five deliveries, and Barrymore, without objection, accepts the lumber in the first three deliveries. On the fourth delivery, however, Barrymore objects that the two-by-fours do not measure 2 inches by 4 inches.

The course of performance in this transaction—that is, the fact that Barrymore accepted three deliveries without objection under the agreement—is relevant in determining that here a "two-by-four"

actually means a "1⅞-by-3¾." Janson's can also prove that two-by-fours need not be exactly 2 inches by 4 inches by applying usage of trade, course of dealing, or both. Janson's can, for example, show that in previous transactions, Barrymore took 1⅞-inch-by-3¾-inch lumber without objection. In addition, Janson's can show that in the trade, two-by-fours are commonly 1⅞ inches by 3¾ inches.

RULES OF CONSTRUCTION The UCC provides *rules of construction* for interpreting contracts. Express terms, course of performance, course of dealing, and usage of trade are to be construed together when they do not contradict one another. When such a construction is unreasonable, however, the following order of priority controls: (1) express terms, (2) course of performance, (3) course of dealing, and (4) usage of trade [UCC 1–205(4), 2–208(2), 2A–207(2)].[23]

---

22. UCC 2–208 and UCC 2A–207 were deleted from the UCC in the 2003 amendments. Course of performance is, however, expressly mentioned in the context of parol evidence. See UCC 2–202.

23. Note that there is no section establishing rules of priority in the 2003 amendments, which omit UCC 2–208 and 2A–207. Instead, amended UCC 2–207 provides that the terms of a contract are to be interpreted from (a) the records of both parties, (b) the terms to which both parties agree, and (c) the terms supplied or incorporated by UCC provisions.

UNCONSCIONABILITY

As discussed in Chapter 13, an unconscionable contract is one that is so unfair and one sided that it would be unreasonable to enforce it. The UCC allows the court to evaluate a contract or any term in a contract, and if the court deems it to have been unconscionable *at the time it was made*, the court can do any of the following [UCC 2–302, 2A–108]:

1. Refuse to enforce the contract.
2. Enforce the remainder of the contract without the unconscionable part.
3. Limit the application of the unconscionable term to avoid an unconscionable result.

The inclusion of Sections 2–302 and 2A–108 in the UCC reflects an increased sensitivity to certain realities of modern commercial activities. Classical contract theory holds that a contract is a bargain in which the terms have been worked out *freely* between parties that are equals. In many modern commercial transactions, this premise is invalid. Standard-form contracts and leases are often signed by consumer-buyers who understand few of the terms used and who often do not even read them. Virtually all of the terms are advantageous to the party supplying the standard-form contract or lease. The UCC's unconscionability provisions give the courts a powerful weapon for policing such transactions, as the following classic case illustrates.

CASE 20.3

Supreme Court
of New York,
Nassau County, 1969.
59 Misc.2d 189,
298 N.Y.S.2d 264.

Jones v. Star Credit Corp.

SOL M. WACHTLER, Justice.

On August 31, 1965 the plaintiffs, who are welfare recipients, agreed to purchase a home freezer unit for $900 as the result of a visit from a salesman representing Your Shop At Home Service, Inc. With the addition of the time credit charges, credit life insurance, credit property insurance, and sales tax, the purchase price totaled $1,234.80. Thus far the plaintiffs have paid $619.88 toward their purchase. The defendant claims that with various added credit charges paid for an extension of time there is a balance of $819.81 still due from the plaintiffs. The uncontroverted proof at the trial established that the freezer unit, when purchased, had a maximum retail value of approximately $300. The question is whether this transaction and the resulting contract could be considered unconscionable within the meaning of section 2–302 of the Uniform Commercial Code * * * .

* * * *

There was a time when the shield of *caveat emptor* ["let the buyer beware"] would protect the most unscrupulous in the marketplace—a time when the law, in granting parties unbridled latitude to make their own contracts, allowed exploitive and callous practices which shocked the conscience of both legislative bodies and the courts.

* * * *

The law is beginning to fight back against those who once took advantage of the poor and illiterate without risk of either exposure or interference. * * *

* * * *

Section 2–302 of the Uniform Commercial Code enacts the moral sense of the community into the law of commercial transactions. It authorizes the court to find, as a matter of law, that a contract or a clause of a contract was "unconscionable at the time it was made," and upon so finding the court may refuse to enforce the contract, excise the objectionable clause or limit the application of the clause to avoid an unconscionable result. The principle * * * is one of the prevention of oppression and unfair surprise. It permits a court to accomplish directly what heretofore was often accomplished by construction of language, manipulations of fluid rules of contract law and determinations based upon a presumed public policy.

* * * *

Fraud, in the instant case, is not present; nor is it necessary under the statute. The question which presents itself is whether or not, under the circumstances of this case, the sale of a freezer unit having a retail value of $300 for $900 ($1,439.69 including credit charges and $18 sales tax) is unconscionable as a matter of law. The court believes it is.

CONTINUED ▶

CASE 20.3 Continued

*   *   *   *

Concededly, deciding [this case] is substantially easier than explaining it. No doubt, the mathematical disparity between $300, which presumably includes a reasonable profit margin, and $900, which is exorbitant on its face, carries the greatest weight. Credit charges alone exceed by more than $100 the retail value of the freezer. These alone may be sufficient to sustain the decision. Yet, a caveat [warning] is warranted lest we reduce the import of Section 2–302 solely to a mathematical ratio formula. It may, at times, be that; yet it may also be much more. The very limited financial resources of the purchaser, known to the sellers at the time of the sale, is entitled to weight in the balance. Indeed, the value disparity itself leads inevitably to the felt conclusion that knowing advantage was taken of the plaintiffs. In addition, *the meaningfulness of choice essential to the making of a contract can be negated by a gross inequality of bargaining power.* [Emphasis added.]

There is no question about the necessity and even the desirability of installment sales and the extension of credit. Indeed, there are many, including welfare recipients, who would be deprived of even the most basic conveniences without the use of these devices. Similarly, the retail merchant selling on installment or extending credit is expected to establish a pricing factor which will afford a degree of protection commensurate with the risk of selling to those who might be default prone. However, neither of these accepted premises can clothe the sale of this freezer with respectability.

*   *   *   *

Having already [been] paid more than $600 toward the purchase of this $300 freezer unit, it is apparent that the defendant has already been amply compensated. In accordance with the statute, the application of the payment provision should be limited to amounts already paid by the plaintiffs and the contract be reformed and amended by changing the payments called for therein to equal the amount of payment actually so paid by the plaintiffs.

QUESTIONS

1. Why would the seller's knowledge of the buyers' limited resources support a finding of unconscionability? Explain.
2. Why didn't the court rule that the Joneses, as adults, had made a decision of their own free will and therefore were bound by the terms of the contract, regardless of the difference between the freezer's contract price and its retail value?

IMPACT OF THIS CASE ON TODAY'S LAW

This early case illustrates the approach that many courts today take when deciding whether a sales contract is unconscionable—an approach that focuses on "excessive" price and unequal bargaining power. Most of the litigants who have used UCC 2–302 successfully have been consumers who are poor or otherwise at a disadvantage (for example, Spanish-speaking consumers who sign a contract written in English that requires them to pay an excessive amount for items).

SECTION 5 | Contracts for the International Sale of Goods

International sales contracts between firms or individuals located in different countries may be governed by the 1980 United Nations Convention on Contracts for the International Sale of Goods (CISG). The CISG governs international contracts only if the countries of the parties to the contract have ratified the CISG and if the parties have not agreed that some other law will govern their contract. As of 2005, sixty-two countries had ratified, acceded to, or approved the CISG, including the United States, Canada, Mexico, some Central and South American countries, and most European nations. That means that the CISG is the uniform international sales law of countries that account for over two-thirds of all world trade.

CONCEPT SUMMARY 20.1	The Formation of Sales and Lease Contracts
CONCEPT	**DESCRIPTION**

OFFER AND ACCEPTANCE	1. *Offer—*
	  a. Not all terms have to be included for a contract to be formed.
	  b. The price does not have to be included for a contract to be formed.
	  c. Particulars of performance can be left open.
	  d. An offer by a merchant in a signed writing with assurances that the offer will not be withdrawn is irrevocable without consideration (for up to three months).
	2. *Acceptance—*
	  a. Acceptance may be made by any reasonable means of communication; it is effective when dispatched.
	  b. The acceptance of a unilateral offer can be made by a promise to ship or by the shipment of conforming or nonconforming goods.
	  c. Acceptance by performance requires notice within a reasonable time; otherwise, the offer can be treated as lapsed.
	  d. A definite expression of acceptance creates a contract even if the terms of the acceptance modify the terms of the offer.

CONSIDERATION	A modification of a contract for the sale of goods does not require consideration.

REQUIREMENTS UNDER THE STATUTE OF FRAUDS	1. All contracts for the sale of goods priced at $500 or more ($5,000 or more under the 2003 amendments to the UCC) must be in writing. A writing is sufficient as long as it indicates a contract between the parties and is signed by the party against whom enforcement is sought. A contract is not enforceable beyond the quantity shown in the writing.
	2. When written confirmation of an oral contract between merchants is not objected to in writing by the receiver within ten days, the oral contract is enforceable.
	3. Exceptions to the requirement of a writing exist in the following situations:
	  a. When the oral contract is for specially manufactured or obtained goods not suitable for resale or lease to others and the seller or lessor has made commitments for the manufacture or procurement of the goods.
	  b. If the defendant admits in pleadings, testimony, or other court proceedings that an oral contract for the sale or lease of goods was made, then the contract will be enforceable to the extent of the quantity of goods admitted.
	  c. The oral agreement will be enforceable to the extent that payment has been received and accepted or to the extent that goods have been received and accepted.

PAROL EVIDENCE RULE	1. The terms of a clearly and completely worded written contract cannot be contradicted by evidence of prior agreements or contemporaneous oral agreements.
	2. Evidence is admissible to clarify the terms of a writing in the following situations:
	  a. If the contract terms are ambiguous.
	  b. If evidence of course of dealing, usage of trade, or course of performance is necessary to learn or to clarify the intentions of the parties to the contract.

APPLICABILITY OF THE **CISG**

Essentially, the CISG is to international sales contracts what Article 2 of the UCC is to domestic sales contracts. As discussed in this chapter, in domestic transactions the UCC applies when the parties to a contract for a sale of goods have failed to specify in writing some important term concerning price, delivery, or the like. Similarly, whenever the parties to international transactions have failed to specify in writing the precise terms of a contract, the CISG will be applied. Unlike the UCC, the CISG does not apply to consumer sales, and neither the UCC nor the CISG applies to contracts for services.

Businesspersons must take special care when drafting international sales contracts to avoid problems caused by distance, including language differences and differences in national laws. The appendix just following this chapter shows an actual international sales contract used by Starbucks Coffee Company. The contract illustrates many of the special terms and clauses that are typically contained in international contracts for the sale of goods. Annotations in the appendix explain the meaning and significance of specific clauses in the contract. (See Chapter 52 for a discussion of other laws that frame global business transactions.)

A COMPARISON OF CISG AND UCC PROVISIONS

The provisions of the CISG, although similar for the most part to those of the UCC, differ from them in some respects. In the event that the CISG and the UCC are in conflict, the CISG applies (because it is a treaty of the national government and therefore is supreme—see the discussion of the supremacy clause of the U.S. Constitution in Chapter 4).

The major differences between the CISG and the UCC in regard to contract formation concern the mirror image rule, irrevocable offers, the Statute of Frauds, the price term, and the time of contract formation. We discuss these differences in the subsections that follow. CISG provisions relating to risk of loss, performance, remedies, and warranties will be discussed in the following chapters as those topics are examined.

THE MIRROR IMAGE RULE   Under the UCC, a definite expression of acceptance that contains additional terms can still result in the formation of a contract, unless the additional terms are conditioned on the assent of the offeror. In other words, the UCC does away with the mirror image rule in domestic sales contracts.

Article 19 of the CISG provides that a contract can be formed even though the acceptance contains additional terms, unless the additional terms materially alter the contract. Under the CISG, however, the definition of a "material alteration" includes virtually any change in the terms. If an additional term relates to payment, quality, quantity, price, time and place of delivery, extent of one party's liability to the other, or

the settlement of disputes, the CISG considers the added term a material alteration. In effect, then, the CISG requires that the terms of the acceptance mirror those of the offer.

Therefore, as a practical matter, businesspersons undertaking international sales transactions should not use the sale or purchase forms that they customarily use for transactions within the United States. Instead, they should draft specific forms to suit the needs of the particular transactions.

IRREVOCABLE OFFERS   UCC 2–205 requires that an irrevocable offer without consideration be in writing. In contrast, Article 16(2) of the CISG provides that an offer will be irrevocable if the offeror simply states orally that the offer is irrevocable or if the offeree reasonably relies on the offer as being irrevocable. In both of these situations, the offer will be irrevocable even without a writing and without consideration.

THE STATUTE OF FRAUDS   As mentioned previously, the UCC states that contracts for the sale of goods priced at $500 or more ($5,000 or more in the 2003 amendments) must be in writing [UCC 2–201]. The writing must be signed by the party against whom enforcement is sought and must be sufficient to show that a contract has been made. Article 11 of the CISG, however, states that a contract of sale "need not be concluded in or evidenced by writing and is not subject to any other requirements as to form. It may be proved by any means, including witnesses."

Article 11 of the CISG accords with the legal customs of most nations, which no longer require contracts to meet certain formal or writing requirements to be enforceable. Ironically, even England, the nation that created the original Statute of Frauds in 1677, has repealed all of it except the provisions relating to collateral promises and to transfers of interests in land. Many other countries that once had such a statute have also repealed all or parts of it. Some countries, such as France, never had a writing requirement.

THE NECESSITY OF A PRICE TERM   Under the UCC, if the parties to a contract have not agreed on a price, the contract will not fail if the parties intended to form a contract (had a "meeting of the minds"). If the price term is left open, the court will determine "a reasonable price at the time for delivery" [UCC 2–305(1)]. Under the CISG, however, the price term must be specified, or provisions for its specification must be included in the agreement; otherwise, normally no contract will exist. For example, if the contract states that the price of wheat to be delivered in two months will be its spot price at the Chicago Board of Trade on that day, that is a sufficient price term under the CISG.

TIME OF CONTRACT FORMATION Under the common law of contracts, an acceptance is effective on dispatch, so a contract is created when the acceptance is transmitted. The UCC does not alter this so-called mailbox rule. Under the CISG, however, a contract is created not at the time the acceptance is transmitted but only on its *receipt* by the offeror. (The offer becomes *irrevocable*, however, when the acceptance is sent.) Article 18(2) states that an acceptance by return promise "becomes effective at the moment the indication of assent reaches the offeror." Under Article 18(3), the offeree may also bind the offeror by performance even without giving any notice to the offeror. The acceptance becomes effective "at the moment the act is performed." Thus, the rule is that it is the offeree's reliance, rather than the communication of acceptance to the offeror, that creates the contract.

SPECIAL PROVISIONS IN INTERNATIONAL CONTRACTS

Language and legal differences among nations can create special problems for parties to international contracts when disputes arise. It is possible to avoid these problems by including in a contract special provisions relating to choice of language, choice of forum, choice of law, and the types of events that may excuse the parties from performance.

CHOICE OF LANGUAGE A deal struck between a U.S. company and a company in another country normally involves two languages. One party may not understand complex contractual terms that are written in the other party's language. Translating the terms poses its own problems, as typically many phrases are not readily translatable into another language. To make sure that no disputes arise out of this language problem, an international sales contract should have a **choice-of-language clause** designating the official language by which the contract will be interpreted in the event of disagreement. The clause might also specify that the agreement is to be translated into, say, Spanish; that the translation is to be ratified by both parties; and that the foreign company can rely on the translation. If arbitration is anticipated, an additional clause must be added to indicate that the arbitration proceeding will be conducted in, say, English, Spanish, or French.

CHOICE OF FORUM As discussed in Chapter 19, a forum-selection clause designates the *forum* (place, or court) in which any disputes that arise under the contract will be litigated. Including a forum-selection clause in an international contract is especially important because when several countries are involved, litigation may be sought in courts in different nations. There are no universally accepted rules regarding the jurisdiction of a particular court over subject matter or parties to a dispute. A forum-selection clause should indicate the specific court that will have jurisdiction. The forum does not necessarily have to be within the geographic boundaries of either party's nation.

Under certain circumstances, a forum-selection clause will not be valid. Specifically, if the clause denies one party an effective remedy, is the product of fraud or unconscionable conduct, causes substantial inconvenience to one of the parties to the contract, or violates public policy, the clause will not be enforced.

CHOICE OF LAW A contractual provision designating the applicable law, called a **choice-of-law clause,** is typically included in every international contract. At common law (and in European civil law systems—see Chapter 52), parties are allowed to choose the law that will govern their contractual relationship, provided that the law chosen is the law of a jurisdiction that has a substantial relationship to the parties and to the business transaction.

Under UCC 1–105, parties may choose the law that will govern the contract as long as the choice is "reasonable." Article 6 of the CISG, however, imposes no limitation on the parties in their choice of what law will govern the contract, and the 1986 Hague Convention on the Law Applicable to Contracts for the International Sale of Goods—often referred to as the Choice-of-Law Convention—allows unlimited autonomy in the choice of law. Whenever a choice of law is not specified in a contract, the Hague Convention indicates that the law of the country where the seller's place of business is located will govern.

FORCE MAJEURE CLAUSE Every contract, and particularly those involving international transactions, should have a *force majeure* **clause.** The meaning of the French term *force majeure* is "impossible or irresistible force"—sometimes loosely defined as "an act of God." *Force majeure* clauses commonly stipulate that in addition to acts of God, a number of other eventualities (such as governmental orders or regulations, embargoes, or shortages of materials) may excuse a party from liability for nonperformance.

REVIEWING THE FORMATION OF SALES AND LEASE CONTRACTS

Guy Holcomb owns and operates Oasis Goodtime Emporium, an adult entertainment establishment. Holcomb wanted to create an adult Internet system for Oasis that would offer customers adult theme videos and "live" chat room programs using performers at the club. On May 10, Holcomb signed a work order authorizing Thomas Consulting Group (TCG) "to deliver a working prototype of a customer chat system, demonstrating the integration of live video and chatting in a Web browser." In exchange for creating the prototype, Holcomb agreed to pay TCG $64,697. On May 20, Holcomb signed an additional work order in the amount of $12,943 for TCG to install a customized firewall system. The work orders stated that Holcomb would make monthly installment payments to TCG, and both parties expected the work would be finished by September. Due to unforeseen problems largely attributable to system configuration and software incompatibility, completion of the project required more time than anticipated. By the end of the summer, the Web site was still not ready, and Holcomb had fallen behind in his payments to TCG. TCG was threatening to cease work and file suit for breach of contract unless the bill was paid. Rather than making further payments, Holcomb wanted to abandon the Web site project. Using the information presented in the chapter, answer the following questions.

1. Is the transaction between Holcomb and TCG covered by the Uniform Commercial Code (UCC)? Why or why not? Discuss whether the predominant purpose of the contract in this scenario involved goods or services. What is the significance of this distinction?

2. Would a court be likely to consider Holcomb a merchant under the UCC? Why or why not?

3. Did the parties have a valid contract under the UCC? Were any terms left open in the contract? If so, which terms? How would a court deal with open terms?

4. Suppose that Holcomb and TCG meet in October in an attempt to resolve their problems. At that time, the parties reach an oral agreement that TCG will continue to work without demanding full payment of the past-due amounts and Holcomb will pay TCG $5,000 per week. Assuming the contract falls under the UCC, is the oral agreement enforceable? Why or why not? If TCG continues to work and completes the prototype, can TCG enforce the agreement?

5. If the parties end up taking their dispute before a court, will they be allowed to present parol evidence of their course of dealing and course of performance? Explain.

TERMS AND CONCEPTS TO REVIEW

QUESTIONS AND CASE PROBLEMS

20–1. A. B. Zook, Inc., is a manufacturer of washing machines. Over the telephone, Zook offers to sell Radar Appliances one hundred model Z washers at a price of $150 per unit. Zook agrees to keep this offer open for ninety days. Radar tells Zook that the offer appears to be a good one and that it will let Zook know of its acceptance within the next two to three weeks. One week later, Zook sends and Radar receives notice that Zook has withdrawn its offer. Radar immediately thereafter telephones Zook and accepts the $150-per-unit offer. Zook claims, first, that no sales contract was ever formed between it and Radar and, second, that if there is a contract, the contract is unenforceable. Discuss Zook's contentions.

20–2. QUESTION WITH SAMPLE ANSWER

Flint, a retail seller of television sets, orders one hundred Color-X sets from manufacturer Martin. The order specifies the price and that the television sets are to be shipped by Hummingbird Express on or before October 30. Martin receives the order on October 5. On October 8, Martin writes Flint a letter indicating that the order was received and that the sets will be shipped as directed, at the specified price. Flint receives this letter on October 10. On October 28, Martin, in preparing the shipment, discovers it has only ninety Color-X sets in stock. Martin ships the ninety Color-X sets and ten television sets of a different model, stating clearly on the invoice that the ten are being shipped only as an accommodation. Flint claims Martin is in breach of contract. Martin claims that the shipment was not an acceptance and therefore no contract was formed. Explain who is correct, and why.

For a sample answer to this question, go to Appendix I at the end of this text.

20–3. Shane has a requirements contract with Sky that obligates Sky to supply Shane with all the gasoline Shane needs for his delivery trucks for one year at $2.30 per gallon. A clause inserted in small print in the contract by Shane, and not noticed by Sky, states, "The buyer reserves the right to reject any shipment for any reason without liability." For six months, Shane orders and Sky delivers under the contract without any controversy. Then, because of a war in the Middle East, the price of gasoline to Sky increases substantially. Sky contacts Shane and tells Shane he cannot possibly fulfill the requirements contract unless Shane agrees to pay $2.50 per gallon. Shane, in need of the gasoline, agrees in writing to modify the contract. Later that month, Shane learns he can buy gasoline at $2.40 per gallon from Collins. Shane refuses delivery of his most recent order from Sky, claiming, first, that the contract allows him to do so without liability and, second, that he is required to pay only $2.30 per gallon if he accepts the delivery. Discuss fully Shane's contentions.

20–4. Strike offers to sell Bailey one thousand shirts for a stated price. The offer declares that shipment will be made by the Dependable Truck Line. Bailey replies, "I accept your offer for one thousand shirts at the price quoted. Delivery to be by Yellow Express Truck Line." Both Strike and Bailey are merchants. Three weeks later, Strike ships the shirts by the Dependable Truck Line, and Bailey refuses shipment. Strike sues for breach of contract. Bailey claims, first, that there never was a contract because the reply, which included a modification of carriers, did not constitute an acceptance and, second, that even if there had been a contract, Strike would have been in breach owing to having shipped the shirts by Dependable, contrary to the contract terms. Discuss fully Bailey's claims.

20–5. THE STATUTE OF FRAUDS. SNK, Inc., makes video arcade games and sells them to distributors, including Entertainment Sales, Inc. (ESI). Most sales between SNK and ESI were phone orders. Over one four-month period, ESI phoned in several orders for Samurai Showdown games. SNK did not fill the orders. ESI filed a suit against SNK and others, alleging, among other things, breach of contract. There was no written contract covering the orders. ESI claimed that it had faxed purchase orders for the games to SNK but did not offer proof that the faxes had been sent or received. SNK filed a motion for summary judgment. In whose favor will the court rule, and why? [*Entertainment Sales Co. v. SNK, Inc.,* 232 Ga.App. 669, 502 S.E.2d 263 (1998)]

20–6. OPEN TERMS. In 1988, International Business Machines Corp. (IBM) and American Shizuki Corp. (ASC) signed an agreement for "future purchase by IBM" of plastic film capacitors made by ASC to be used in IBM computers. The agreement stated that IBM was not obligated to buy from ASC and that future purchase orders "shall be [ASC]'s only authorization to manufacture Items." In February 1989, IBM wrote to ASC about "the possibility of IBM purchasing 15,000,000 Plastic Capacitors per two consecutive twelve (12) months periods. . . . This quantity is a forecast only, and represents no commitment by IBM to purchase these quantities during or after this time period." ASC said that it wanted greater assurances. In a second letter, IBM re-expressed its "intent to order" from ASC 30 million capacitors over a minimum period of two years, contingent on the condition "[t]hat IBM's requirements for these capacitors continue." ASC spent about $2.6 million on equipment to make the capacitors. By 1997, the need for plastic capacitors had dissipated with the advent of new technology, and IBM told ASC that it would no longer buy them. ASC filed a suit in a federal district court against IBM, seeking $8.5 million in damages. On what basis might the court rule in favor of IBM?

Explain fully. [*American Shizuki Corp. v. International Business Machines Corp.*, 251 F.3d 1206 (8th Cir. 2001)]

20–7. **CASE PROBLEM WITH SAMPLE ANSWER**
Propulsion Technologies, Inc., a Louisiana firm doing business as PowerTech Marine Propellers, markets small steel boat propellers that are made by a unique tooling method. Attwood Corp., a Michigan firm, operated a foundry (a place where metal is cast) in Mexico. In 1996, Attwood offered to produce castings of the propellers. Attwood promised to maintain quality, warrant the castings against defects, and obtain insurance to cover liability. In January 1997, the parties signed a letter that expressed these and other terms—Attwood was to be paid per casting, and twelve months' notice was required to terminate the deal—but the letter did not state a quantity. PowerTech provided the tooling. Attwood produced rough castings, which PowerTech refined by checking each propeller's pitch; machining its interior; grinding, balancing, and polishing the propeller; and adding serial numbers and a rubber clutch. In October, Attwood told PowerTech that the foundry was closing. PowerTech filed a suit in a federal district court against Attwood, alleging in part breach of contract. One of the issues was whether their deal was subject to Article 2 of the Uniform Commercial Code (UCC). What type of transactions does Article 2 cover? Does the arrangement between PowerTech and Attwood qualify? Explain. [*Propulsion Technologies, Inc. v. Attwood Corp.*, 369 F.3d 896 (5th Cir. 2004)]

To view a sample answer for this case problem, go to this book's Web site at http://wbl.westbuslaw.com, select "Chapter 20," and click on "Case Problem with Sample Answer."

20–8. GOODS ASSOCIATED WITH REAL ESTATE.
Heatway Radiant Floors and Snowmelting Corp. sells parts for underground radiant heating systems. These systems circulate warm fluid under indoor flooring as an alternative to conventional heating systems or under driveways and sidewalks to melt snow and ice. Goodyear Tire and Rubber Co. made and sold a hose, Entran II, that Heatway used in its radiant systems. Between 1989 and 1993, 25 million feet of Entran II was made by Goodyear and installed by Heatway. In 1992, homeowners began complaining about hardening of the hose and leaks in the systems. Linda Loughridge and other homeowners filed a suit in a federal district court against Goodyear and Heatway, alleging a variety of contract breaches under Colorado's version of the Uniform Commercial Code (UCC). Goodyear filed a motion for summary judgment, arguing in part that because Entran II was used in the construction of underground systems that were covered by flooring or cement, the hose was not a "good" and thus the UCC did not apply. Should the court agree with this interpretation of the scope of Article 2? Explain. [*Loughridge v. Goodyear Tire and Rubber Co.*, 192 F.Supp.2d 1175 (D.Colo. 2002)]

20–9. STATUTE OF FRAUDS. Quality Pork International is a Nebraska firm that makes and sells custom pork products. Rupari Food Services, Inc., buys and sells food products from and to retail operations and food brokers. In November 1999, Midwest Brokerage arranged an oral contract between Quality and Rupari, under which Quality would ship three orders to Star Food Processing, Inc., and Rupari would pay for the products. Quality shipped the goods to Star and sent invoices to Rupari. In turn, Rupari billed Star for all three orders but paid Quality only for the first two (for $43,736.84 and $47,467.80, respectively), not for the third. Quality filed a suit in a Nebraska state court against Rupari, alleging breach of contract, to recover $44,051.98, the cost of the third order. Rupari argued that there was nothing in writing, as required by the Uniform Commercial Code (UCC) Section 2–201, and thus there was no enforceable contract. What are the exceptions to the UCC's writing requirement? Do any of those exceptions apply here? Explain. [*Quality Pork International v. Rupari Food Services, Inc.*, 267 Neb. 474, 675 N.W.2d 642 (2004)]

20–10. VIDEO QUESTION
Go to this text's Web site at http://wbl.westbuslaw.com and select "Chapter 20." Click on "Video Questions" and view the video titled *Sales and Lease Contracts: Price as a Term*. Then answer the following questions.

(a) Is Anna correct in assuming that a contract can exist even though the sales price for the computer equipment was not specified? Explain.

(b) According to the Uniform Commercial Code (UCC), what conditions must be satisfied in order for a contract to be formed when certain terms are left open? What terms (in addition to price) can be left open?

(c) Are the e-mail messages that Anna refers to sufficient proof of the contract? Would parol evidence be admissible?

(d) How do the 2003 amendments to Article 2 of the UCC improve Anna's position?

LAW | on the Web

For updated links to resources available on the Web, as well as a variety of other materials, visit this text's Web site at **http://wbl.westbuslaw.com**.

To view the text of the Uniform Commercial Code (UCC)—and keep up to date on its various revisions—go to the Web site of the National Conference of Commissioners on Uniform State Laws (NCCUSL) at

> **http://www.nccusl.org**

Cornell University's Legal Information Institute also offers online access to the UCC, as well as to UCC articles as enacted by particular states and proposed revisions to articles, at

> **http://straylight.law.cornell.edu/ucc/ucc.table.html**

The Pace University School of Law's Institute of International Commercial Law maintains a Web site that contains the full text of the CISG, as well as relevant cases and discussions of the law. Go to

> **http://cisgw3.law.pace.edu/cisg/text/treaty.html**

LEGAL RESEARCH EXERCISES ON THE WEB

Go to **http://wbl.westbuslaw.com**, the Web site that accompanies this text. Select "Chapter 20" and click on "Internet Exercises." There you will find the following Internet research exercises that you can perform to learn more about topics covered in this chapter.

Activity 20–1: LEGAL PERSPECTIVE
　　　　　　　Is It a Contract?

Activity 20–2: MANAGEMENT PERSPECTIVE
　　　　　　　A Checklist for Sales Contracts

1 OVERLAND COFFEE IMPORT CONTRACT
OF THE
GREEN COFFEE ASSOCIATION
OF
NEW YORK CITY, INC.*

2

Contract Seller's No.: **504617**
Buyer's No.: **P9264**
Date: **10/11/06**

SOLD BY: **XYZ Co.**
TO: **Starbucks**

3 QUANTITY: **Five Hundred** (**500**) Tons of (Bags) **Mexican** coffee
weighing about **152.117 lbs.** per bag.

PACKAGING: Coffee must be packed in clean sound bags of uniform size made of sisal, henequen, jute, burlap, or
4 similar woven material, without inner lining or outer covering of any material properly sewn by hand
and/or machine.
Bulk shipments are allowed if agreed by mutual consent of Buyer and Seller.

DESCRIPTION: **High grown Mexican Altura**
5

PRICE: At **Ten/$10.00 dollars** U.S. Currency, per **lb.** net, (U.S. Funds)
Upon delivery in Bonded Public Warehouse at **Laredo, TX**
(City and State)

PAYMENT: **Cash against warehouse receipts**
6

Bill and tender to DATE when all import requirements and governmental regulations have been satisfied,
and coffee delivered or discharged (as per contract terms). Seller is obliged to give the Buyer two (2)
calendar days free time in Bonded Public Warehouse following but not including date of tender.

ARRIVAL: During **December** via **truck**
7 (Period) (Method of Transportation)
from **Mexico** for arrival at **Laredo, TX, USA**
(Country of Exportation) (Country of Importation)
Partial shipments permitted.

ADVICE OF
ARRIVAL: Advice of arrival with warehouse name and location, together with the quantity, description, marks and
place of entry, must be transmitted directly, or through Seller's Agent/Broker, to the Buyer or his Agent/
Broker. Advice will be given as soon as known but not later than the fifth business day following arrival
at the named warehouse. Such advice may be given verbally with written confirmation to be sent the
same day.

WEIGHTS: (1) DELIVERED WEIGHTS: Coffee covered by this contract is to be weighed at location named in
8 tender. Actual tare to be allowed.
(2) SHIPPING WEIGHTS: Coffee covered by this contract is sold on shipping weights. Any loss in
weight exceeding **1/2** percent at location named in tender is for account of Seller at contract price.
(3) Coffee is to be weighed within fifteen (15) calendar days after tender. Weighing expenses, if any, for
account of **Seller** (Seller or Buyer)

MARKINGS: Bags to be branded in English with the name of Country of Origin and otherwise to comply with laws
and regulations of the Country of Importation, in effect at the time of entry, governing marking of import
merchandise. Any expense incurred by failure to comply with these regulations to be borne by
9 Exporter/Seller.

RULINGS: The "Rulings on Coffee Contracts" of the Green Coffee Association of New York City, Inc., in effect on
the date this contract is made, is incorporated for all purposes as a part of this agreement, and together
herewith, constitute the entire contract. No variation or addition hereto shall be valid unless signed by
the parties to the contract.
10 Seller guarantees that the terms printed on the reverse hereof, which by reference are made a part hereof,
are identical with the terms as printed in By-Laws and Rules of the Green Coffee Association of New
York City, Inc., heretofore adopted.
Exceptions to this guarantee are:

ACCEPTED: COMMISSION TO BE PAID BY:
XYZ Co. **Seller**

BY _____*DM*_____ Seller
11 Agent

Starbucks
Buyer
BY _____ **ABC Brokerage**
12 Agent Broker(s)
When this contract is executed by a person acting for another, such person hereby represents that he is
13 fully authorized to commit his principal.

---

* Reprinted with permission of The Green Coffee Association of New York City, Inc.

1 This is a contract for a sale of coffee to be *imported* internationally. If the parties have their principal places of business located in different countries, the contract may be subject to the United Nations Convention on Contracts for the International Sale of Goods (CISG). If the parties' principal places of business are located in the United States, the contract may be subject to the Uniform Commercial Code (UCC).

2 Quantity is one of the most important terms to include in a contract. Without it, a court may not be able to enforce the contract. See Chapter 20.

3 Weight per unit (bag) can be exactly stated or approximately stated. If it is not so stated, usage of trade in international contracts determines standards of weight.

4 Packaging requirements can be conditions for acceptance and payment. Bulk shipments are not permitted without the consent of the buyer.

5 A description of the coffee and the "Markings" constitute express warranties. Warranties in contracts for domestic sales of goods are discussed generally in Chapter 23. International contracts rely more heavily on descriptions and models or samples.

6 Under the UCC, parties may enter into a valid contract even though the price is not set. Under the CISG, a contract must provide for an exact determination of the price.

7 The terms of payment may take one of two forms: credit or cash. Credit terms can be complicated. A cash term can be simple, and payment can be made by any means acceptable in the ordinary course of business (for example, a personal check or a letter of credit). If the seller insists on actual cash, the buyer must be given a reasonable time to get it. See Chapter 22.

8 *Tender* means the seller has placed goods that conform to the contract at the buyer's disposition. What constitutes a valid tender is explained in Chapter 22. This contract requires that the coffee meet all import regulations and that it be ready for pickup by the buyer at a "Bonded Public Warehouse." (A *bonded warehouse* is a place in which goods can be stored without paying taxes until the goods are removed.)

9 The delivery date is significant because, if it is not met, the buyer may hold the seller in breach of the contract. Under this contract, the seller can be given a "period" within which to deliver the goods, instead of a specific day, which could otherwise present problems. The seller is also given some time to rectify goods that do not pass inspection (see the "Guarantee" clause on page two of the contract). For a discussion of the remedies of the buyer and seller, see Chapter 22.

10 As part of a proper tender, the seller (or its agent) must inform the buyer (or its agent) when the goods have arrived at their destination. The responsibilities of agents are set out in Chapters 31 and 32.

11 In some contracts, delivered and shipped weights can be important. During shipping, some loss can be attributed to the type of goods (spoilage of fresh produce, for example) or to the transportation itself. A seller and buyer can agree on the extent to which either of them will bear such losses. See Chapter 47 for a discussion of the liability of common carriers for loss during shipment.

12 Documents are often incorporated in a contract by reference, because including them word for word can make a contract difficult to read. If the document is later revised, the entire contract might have to be reworked. Documents that are typically incorporated by reference include detailed payment and delivery terms, special provisions, and sets of rules, codes, and standards.

13 In international sales transactions, and for domestic deals involving certain products, brokers are used to form the contracts. When so used, the brokers are entitled to a commission. See Chapter 31.   *(Continued)*

TERMS AND CONDITIONS

ARBITRATION: All controversies relating to, in connection with, or arising out of this contract, its modification, making or the authority or obligations of the signatories hereto, and whether involving the principals, agents, brokers, or others who actually subscribe hereto, shall be settled by arbitration in accordance with the "Rules of Arbitration" of the Green Coffee Association of New York City, Inc., as they exist at the time of the arbitration (including provisions as to payment of fees and expenses). Arbitration is the sole remedy hereunder, and it shall be held in accordance with the law of New York State, and judgment of any award may be entered in the courts of that State, or in any other court of competent jurisdiction. All notices or judicial service in reference to arbitration or enforcement shall be deemed given if transmitted as required by the aforesaid rules.

GUARANTEE: (a) If all or any of the coffee is refused admission into the country of importation by reason of any violation of governmental laws or acts, which violation existed at the time the coffee arrived at Bonded-Public Warehouse, seller is required, as to the amount not admitted and as soon as possible, to deliver replacement coffee in conformity to all terms and conditions of this contract, excepting only the Arrival terms, but not later than thirty (30) days after the date of the violation notice. Any payment made and expenses incurred for any coffee denied entry shall be refunded within ten (10) calendar days of denial of entry, and payment shall be made for the replacement delivery in accordance with the terms of this contract. Consequently, if Buyer removes the coffee from the Bonded Public Warehouse, Seller's responsibility as to such portion hereunder ceases.

(b) Contracts containing the overstamp "No Pass-No Sale" on the face of the contract shall be interpreted to mean: If any or all of the coffee is not admitted into the country of Importation in its original condition by reason of failure to meet requirements of the government's laws or Acts, the contract shall be deemed null and void as to that portion of the coffee which is not admitted in its original condition. Any payment made and expenses incurred for any coffee denied entry shall be refunded within ten (10) calendar days of denial of entry.

CONTINGENCY: This contract is not contingent upon any other contract.

CLAIMS: Coffee shall be considered accepted as to quality unless within _fifteen_ (15) calendar days after delivery at Bonded Public Warehouse or within _fifteen_ (15) calendar days after all Government clearances have been received, whichever is later, either:
(a) Claims are settled by the parties hereto, or,
(b) Arbitration proceedings have been filed by one of the parties in accordance with the provisions hereof.
(c) If neither (a) nor (b) has been done in the stated period or if any portion of the coffee has been removed from the Bonded Public Warehouse before representative sealed samples have been drawn by the Green Coffee Association of New York City, Inc., in accordance with its rules, Seller's responsibility for quality claims ceases for that portion so removed.
(d) Any question of quality submitted to arbitration shall be a matter of allowance only, unless otherwise provided in the contract.

DELIVERY: (a) No more than three (3) chops may be tendered for each lot of 250 bags.
(b) Each chop of coffee tendered is to be uniform in grade and appearance. All expense necessary to make coffee uniform shall be for account of seller.
(c) Notice of arrival and/or sampling order constitutes a tender, and must be given not later than the fifth business day following arrival at Bonded Public Warehouse stated on the contract.

INSURANCE: Seller is responsible for any loss or damage, or both, until Delivery and Discharge of coffee at the Bonded Public Warehouse in the Country of Importation.

All Insurance Risks, costs and responsibility are for Seller's Account until Delivery and Discharge of coffee at the Bonded Public Warehouse in the Country of Importation.

Buyer's insurance responsibility begins from the day of importation or from the day of tender, whichever is later.

FREIGHT: Seller to provide and pay for all transportation and related expenses to the Bonded Public Warehouse in the Country of Importation.

EXPORT DUTIES/TAXES: Exporter is to pay all Export taxes, duties or other fees or charges, if any, levied because of exportation.

IMPORT DUTIES/TAXES: Any Duty or Tax whatsoever, imposed by the government or any authority of the Country of Importation, shall be borne by the Importer/Buyer.

INSOLVENCY OR FINANCIAL FAILURE OF BUYER OR SELLER: If, at any time before the contract is fully executed, either party hereto shall meet with creditors because of inability generally to make payment of obligations when due, or shall suspend such payments, fail to meet his general trade obligations in the regular course of business, shall file a petition in bankruptcy or, for an arrangement, shall become insolvent, or commit an act of bankruptcy, then the other party may at his option, expressed in writing, declare the aforesaid to constitute a breach and default of this contract, and may, in addition to other remedies, decline to deliver further or make payment or may sell or purchase for the defaulter's account, and may collect damage for any injury or loss, or shall account for the profit, if any, occasioned by such sale or purchase.

This clause is subject to the provisions of (11 USC 365 (e) 1) if invoked.

BREACH OR DEFAULT OF CONTRACT: In the event either party hereto fails to perform, or breaches or repudiates this agreement, the other party shall subject to the specific provisions of this contract be entitled to the remedies and relief provided for by the Uniform Commercial Code of the State of New York. The computation and ascertainment of damages, or the determination of any other dispute as to relief, shall be made by the arbitrators in accordance with the Arbitration Clause herein.

Consequential damages shall not, however, be allowed.

⑭ Arbitration is the settling of a dispute by submitting it to a disinterested party (other than a court) that renders a decision. The procedures and costs can be provided for in an arbitration clause or incorporated through other documents. To enforce an award rendered in an arbitration, the winning party can "enter" (submit) the award in a court "of competent jurisdiction." For a general discussion of arbitration and other forms of dispute resolution (other than courts), see Chapter 2.

⑮ When goods are imported internationally, they must meet certain import requirements before being released to the buyer. Because of this, buyers frequently want a guaranty clause that covers the goods not admitted into the country and that either requires the seller to replace the goods within a stated time or allows the contract for those goods not admitted to be void. See Chapter 17.

⑯ In the "Claims" clause, the parties agree that the buyer has a certain time within which to reject the goods. The right to reject is a right by law and does not need to be stated in a contract. If the buyer does not exercise the right within the time specified in the contract, the goods will be considered accepted. See Chapter 22.

⑰ Many international contracts include definitions of terms so that the parties understand what they mean. Some terms are used in a particular industry in a specific way. Here, the word *chop* refers to a unit of like-grade coffee bean. The buyer has a right to inspect ("sample") the coffee. If the coffee does not conform to the contract, the seller must correct the nonconformity. See Chapter 22.

⑱ The "Delivery," "Insurance," and "Freight" clauses, with the "Arrival" clause on page one of the contract, indicate that this is a destination contract. The seller has the obligation to deliver the goods to the destination, not simply deliver them into the hands of a carrier. Under this contract, the destination is a "Bonded Public Warehouse" in a specific location. The seller bears the risk of loss until the goods are delivered at their destination. Typically, the seller will have bought insurance to cover the risk. See Chapter 21 for a discussion of delivery terms and the risk of loss and Chapter 49 for a general discussion of insurance.

⑲ Delivery terms are commonly placed in all sales contracts. Such terms determine who pays freight and other costs and, in the absence of an agreement specifying otherwise, who bears the risk of loss. International contracts may use these delivery terms or they may use INCOTERMS, which are published by the International Chamber of Commerce. For example, the INCOTERM DDP (delivered duty paid) requires the seller to arrange shipment, obtain and pay for import or export permits, and get the goods through customs to a named destination.

⑳ Exported and imported goods are subject to duties, taxes, and other charges imposed by the governments of the countries involved. International contracts spell out who is responsible for these charges.

㉑ This clause protects a party if the other party should become financially unable to fulfill the obligations under the contract. Thus, if the seller cannot afford to deliver, or the buyer cannot afford to pay, for the stated reasons, the other party can consider the contract breached. This right is subject to "11 USC 365(e)(1)," which refers to a specific provision of the U.S. Bankruptcy Code dealing with executory contracts. Bankruptcy provisions are covered in Chapter 30.

㉒ In the "Breach or Default of Contract" clause, the parties agreed that the remedies under this contract are the remedies (except for consequential damages) provided by the UCC, as in effect in the state of New York. The amount and "ascertainment" of damages, as well as other disputes about relief, are to be determined by arbitration. Breach of contract and contractual remedies in general are explained in Chapter 22. Arbitration is discussed in Chapter 2.

㉓ Three clauses frequently included in international contracts (see Chapter 20) are omitted here. There is no choice-of-language clause designating the official language to be used in interpreting the contract terms. There is no choice-of-forum clause designating the place in which disputes will be litigated, except for arbitration (law of New York State). Finally, there is no *force majeure* clause relieving the sellers or buyers from nonperformance due to events beyond their control.

CHAPTER 21

Title, Risk, and Insurable Interest

Before the creation of the Uniform Commercial Code (UCC), *title*—the right of ownership—was the central concept in sales law, controlling all issues of rights and remedies of the parties to a sales contract. There were numerous problems with this concept, however. For example, it was frequently difficult to determine when title actually passed from seller to buyer, and therefore it was also difficult to predict which party a court would decide had title at the time of a loss. Because of such problems, the UCC divorced the question of title as completely as possible from the question of the rights and obligations of buyers, sellers, and third parties (such as subsequent purchasers, creditors, or the tax collector).

In some situations, title is still relevant under the UCC, and the UCC has special rules for locating title. These rules will be discussed in the sections that follow. In most situations, however, the UCC has replaced the concept of title with three other concepts: (1) identification, (2) risk of loss, and (3) insurable interest.

In lease contracts, of course, title to the goods is retained by the lessor-owner of the goods. Hence, the UCC's provisions relating to passage of title do not apply to leased goods. Other concepts discussed in this chapter, though, including identification, risk of loss, and insurable interest, relate to lease contracts as well as to sales contracts.

SECTION 1 | Identification

Before any interest in specific goods can pass from the seller or lessor to the buyer or lessee, the goods must be (1) in existence and (2) identified as the specific goods designated in the contract. **Identification** is a designation of goods as the subject matter of a sales or lease contract. Title and risk of loss cannot pass to the buyer from the seller unless the goods are identified to the contract [UCC 2–105(2)]. Identification is significant because it gives the buyer or lessee the right to insure (or obtain an insurable interest in) the goods and the right to recover from third parties who damage the goods.

Once the goods are in existence, the parties can agree in their contract on when identification will take place. If they do not so specify, however, the Uniform Commercial Code (UCC) will determine when identification takes place [UCC 2–501(1), 2A–217].

EXISTING GOODS

If the contract calls for the sale or lease of specific and ascertained goods that are already in existence, identification takes place at the time the contract is made. For example, you contract to purchase or lease a fleet of five cars by the serial numbers listed for the cars.

FUTURE GOODS

If a sale involves unborn animals to be born within twelve months after contracting, identification takes place when the animals are conceived. If a sale involves crops that are to be harvested within twelve months (or the next harvest season occurring after contracting, whichever is longer), identification takes place when the crops are planted or begin to grow. In a sale or lease of any other future goods, identification occurs when the goods are shipped, marked, or otherwise designated by the seller or lessor as the goods to which the contract refers.

GOODS THAT ARE PART OF A LARGER MASS

Goods that are part of a larger mass are identified when the goods are marked, shipped, or somehow designated by the seller or lessor as the particular goods to pass under the contract. Suppose that a buyer orders 1,000 cases of beans from a 10,000-case lot. Until the seller separates the 1,000 cases of beans from the 10,000-case lot, title and risk of loss remain with the seller.

A common exception to this rule deals with fungible goods. **Fungible goods** are goods that are alike naturally, by agreement, or by trade usage. Typical examples are specific grades or types of wheat, oil, and wine, usually stored in large containers. If the owners of these goods hold title as tenants in common (owners having shares undivided from the entire mass—see Chapter 47), a seller-owner can pass title and risk of loss to the buyer without actually separating the goods. The buyer replaces the seller as an owner in common [UCC 2–105(4)].

For example, Anselm, Braudel, and Carpenter are farmers. They deposit, respectively, 5,000 bushels, 3,000 bushels, and 2,000 bushels of grain of the same grade and quality in a bin. The three become owners in common, with Anselm owning 50 percent of the 10,000 bushels, Braudel 30 percent, and Carpenter 20 percent. Anselm could contract to sell her 5,000 bushels of grain to Treyton and, because the goods are fungible, pass title and risk of loss to Treyton without physically separating the 5,000 bushels. Treyton now becomes an owner in common with Braudel and Carpenter.

SECTION 2 | When Title Passes

Once goods exist and are identified, the provisions of UCC 2–401 apply to the passage of title. Unless the parties explicitly agree,[1] title passes to the buyer at the time and the place the seller performs the *physical*

delivery of the goods [UCC 2–401(2)]. For example, suppose that a person is buying cattle at a livestock auction. In that situation, title will pass when the cattle are physically delivered to the buyer (unless, of course, the parties agree otherwise).[2]

SHIPMENT AND DESTINATION CONTRACTS

In the absence of an agreement, delivery arrangements can determine when title passes from the seller to the buyer. In a **shipment contract,** the seller is required or authorized to ship goods by carrier, such as a trucking company. Under a shipment contract, the seller is required only to deliver the goods into the hands of a carrier, and title passes to the buyer at the time and place of shipment [UCC 2–401(2)(a)]. *Generally, all contracts are assumed to be shipment contracts if nothing to the contrary is stated in the contract.*

In a **destination contract,** the seller is required to deliver the goods to a particular destination, usually directly to the buyer, although sometimes the buyer designates that the goods should be delivered to another party. Title passes to the buyer when the goods are *tendered* at that destination [UCC 2–401(2)(b)]. A tender of delivery occurs when the seller places or holds conforming goods at the buyer's disposition (with any necessary notice), enabling the buyer to take delivery [UCC 2A–503(1)].

DELIVERY WITHOUT MOVEMENT OF THE GOODS

When the contract of sale does not call for the seller's shipment or delivery of the goods (when the buyer is to pick up the goods), the passage of title depends on whether the seller must deliver a **document of title,** such as a bill of lading or a warehouse receipt, to the buyer. A *bill of lading* is a receipt for goods that is signed by a carrier and that serves as a contract for the transportation of the goods. A *warehouse receipt* is a receipt issued by a warehouser for goods stored in a warehouse.

When a document of title is required, title passes to the buyer *when and where the document is delivered.* Thus, if the goods are stored in a warehouse, title passes to the buyer when the appropriate documents are delivered to the buyer. The goods never move. In

---

1. In many sections of the UCC, the words "unless otherwise explicitly agreed" appear, meaning that any explicit agreement between the buyer and the seller determines the rights, duties, and liabilities of the parties, including when title passes.

2. See, for example, *In re Stewart,* 274 Bankr. 503 (2002).

fact, the buyer can choose to leave the goods at the same warehouse for a period of time, and the buyer's title to those goods will be unaffected.

When no documents of title are required, and delivery is made without moving the goods, title passes at the time and place the sales contract is made, if the goods have already been identified. If the goods have not been identified, title does not pass until identification occurs. For example, Juan sells lumber to Bodan. They agree that Bodan will pick up the lumber at the yard. If the lumber has been identified (segregated, marked, or in any other way distinguished from all other lumber), title passes to Bodan when the contract is signed. If the lumber is still in large storage bins at the mill, title does not pass to Bodan until the particular pieces of lumber to be sold under this contract are identified [UCC 2–401(3)].

SALES OR LEASES BY NONOWNERS

Problems occur when persons who acquire goods with imperfect titles attempt to sell or lease them. Sections 2–402 and 2–403 of the UCC deal with the rights of two parties who lay claim to the same goods sold with imperfect titles. Generally, a buyer acquires at least whatever title the seller has to the goods sold.

These same UCC sections also protect lessees. Obviously, a lessee does not acquire whatever title the lessor has to the goods; rather, the lessee acquires a right to possess and use the goods—that is, a *leasehold interest*. A lessee acquires whatever leasehold interest the lessor has or has the power to transfer, subject to the lease contract [UCC 2A–303, 2A–304, 2A–305].

VOID TITLE   A buyer may unknowingly purchase goods from a seller who is not the owner of the goods. If the seller is a thief, the seller's title is void—legally, no title exists. Thus, the buyer acquires no title, and the real owner can reclaim the goods from the buyer. If the goods were leased instead, the same result would occur because the lessor would have no leasehold interest to transfer.

For example, if Jim steals goods owned by Maren, Jim has a *void title* to those goods. If Jim sells the goods to Shidra, Maren can reclaim them from Shidra even though Shidra acted in good faith and honestly was not aware that the goods were stolen. Article 2A contains similar provisions for leases.

VOIDABLE TITLE   A seller has a *voidable title* if the goods that he or she is selling were obtained by fraud, paid for with a check that is later dishonored, purchased from a minor, or purchased on credit when the seller was *insolvent*. (Under the UCC, a person is **insolvent** when that person ceases to pay "his [or her] debts in the ordinary course of business or cannot pay his [or her] debts as they become due or is insolvent within the meaning of federal bankruptcy law" [UCC 1–201(23)].)

—Good Faith Purchasers.   In contrast to a seller with void title, a seller with voidable title has the power to transfer good title to a good faith purchaser for value. A **good faith purchaser** is one who buys without knowledge of circumstances that would make a person of ordinary prudence inquire about the validity of the seller's title to the goods. One who purchases *for value* gives legally sufficient consideration (value) for the goods purchased. The real owner normally cannot recover goods from a good faith purchaser for value [UCC 2–403(1)].[3] If the buyer of the goods is not a good faith purchaser for value, then the actual owner of the goods can reclaim them from the buyer (or from the seller, if the goods are still in the seller's possession).

—Voidable Title and Leases.   The same rules apply to leases. A lessor with voidable title has the power to transfer a valid leasehold interest to a good faith lessee for value. The real owner cannot recover the goods, except as permitted by the terms of the lease. The real owner can, however, receive all proceeds arising from the lease, as well as a transfer of all rights, title, and interest as the lessor under the lease, including the lessor's interest in the return of the goods when the lease expires [UCC 2A–305(1)].

THE ENTRUSTMENT RULE   According to Section 2–403(2), entrusting goods to a merchant *who deals in goods of that kind* gives the merchant the power to transfer all rights to a *buyer in the ordinary course of business*. This is known as the **entrustment** rule. A buyer in the ordinary course of business is a person who, in good faith and without knowledge that the sale violates the ownership rights or security interest of a third party, buys in ordinary course from a merchant (other than a pawnbroker) in the business of selling goods of that kind [UCC 1–201(9)].

—As Applied to Sales Contracts.   The entrustment rule basically allows innocent buyers to obtain title to goods purchased from merchants even if the merchants do not have good title. Consider an example. Jan leaves her watch with a jeweler to be repaired.

---

3. The real owner could, of course, sue the person who initially obtained voidable title to the goods.

The jeweler sells both new and used watches. The jeweler sells Jan's watch to Kim, a customer who does not know that the jeweler has no right to sell it. Kim, as a good faith buyer, gets good title against Jan's claim of ownership.[4] Kim, however, obtains only those rights held by the person entrusting the goods (here, Jan). Suppose that in this example, Jan had stolen the watch from Greg and then left it with the jeweler to be repaired. The jeweler then sold it to Kim. Kim would obtain good title against Jan, who entrusted the watch to the jeweler, but not against Greg (the real owner), who neither entrusted the watch to Jan nor authorized Jan to entrust it.

—As Applied to Lease Contracts. Article 2A provides a similar rule for leased goods. If a lessor entrusts goods to a lessee-merchant who deals in goods of that kind, and the lessee-merchant transfers the goods to a buyer or sublessee in the ordinary course of business, the buyer or sublessee acquires all of the rights that the lessor had in the goods [UCC 2A–305(2)].[5]

The following case illustrates an application of the entrustment rule to the purchase of a Mercedes convertible that had previously been leased to another party.

---

4. Jan, of course, can sue the jeweler for the tort of conversion (or trespass to personal property) to obtain damages equivalent to the value of the watch (see Chapter 6).

---

5. This rule is consistent with the common law of bailments (see Chapter 47).

CASE 21.1   Bank One, N.A.[a] v. Amercani

Court of Appeals
of Georgia. 2005.
271 Ga.App. 483,
610 S.E.2d 103.

BACKGROUND AND FACTS *In January 2001, Alicia Fox leased a Mercedes Benz CLK 430 convertible from Luxury Cars of Palm Beach, Inc. (LCPB), in Florida. Fox financed her lease through Bank One, N.A. Without immediately telling Bank One, Fox consigned the car to LCPB for resale in May 2002. She continued to make payments on the lease until September but did not tell Bank One of the consignment until a few weeks later. Meanwhile, in June, Khalid Amercani of Atlanta, Georgia, bought the car from LCPB for $56,500. Of the purchase price, $39,000 came from the trade-in of his 1999 Mercedes convertible. LCPB sold this car for $42,500 in a deal also financed by Bank One. The lender credited the amount to LCPB without checking whether Fox's lease had been paid off. Although Amercani had been told that he would receive the title to Fox's old car within two weeks, LCPB went out of business without paying off Fox's old lease, and because the lease was not paid, Bank One did not forward the car's title to Amercani. He filed a suit in a Georgia state court against Bank One to, among other things, obtain the title. The court ruled in a summary judgment that he was entitled to the car. Bank One appealed this ruling to a state intermediate appellate court.*

IN THE LANGUAGE OF THE COURT

MILLER, Judge.

*   *   *   *

This case pits a lienholder against a purchaser in the ordinary course of business in the absence of both the original owner and the middleman who vanished with the purchaser's payment. *   *   * [T]he Uniform Commercial Code governs, and reads in relevant part:

(1) A purchaser of goods acquires all title which her or his transferor had or had power to transfer except that a purchaser of a limited interest acquires rights only to the extent of the interest purchased. A person with voidable title has power to transfer a good title to a good faith purchaser for value. *   *   *

(2) Any entrusting of possession of goods to a merchant who deals in goods of that kind gives the merchant power to transfer all rights of the entruster to a buyer in ordinary course of business.

(3) "Entrusting" includes any delivery and any acquiescence in [consenting to the] retention of possession regardless of any condition expressed between the parties to the delivery or acquiescence and regardless of whether the procurement of the entrusting or the possessor's disposition of the goods have been such as to be larcenous under the criminal law.

---

a. The initials *N.A.* stand for National Association.

CONTINUED

CASE 21.1 | Continued

(4) The rights of other purchasers of goods and of lien creditors are governed by [other] chapters. *   *   *

Though [UCC 2–403(1)] begins with a version of the old rule that no one can transfer a title greater than she possesses, the statute proceeds to detail the exception to that rule whereby a person with voidable title can transfer good title to a good faith purchaser for value: specifically, that *when an owner entrusts goods to a merchant, and that merchant sells to a good faith purchaser for value, that purchaser takes good title, even if the owner and entruster's title is subject to a security interest and the merchant converted the goods by selling them.* As the Comment to the Uniform Commercial Code puts it, "[t]he many particular situations in which a buyer in ordinary course of business from a dealer has been protected against reservation of property or other hidden interest" have been gathered in subsections (2) and (3) into "a single principle protecting persons who buy in ordinary course out of inventory." [Emphasis added.]

The undisputed facts in this case are that Fox was the owner of the car, subject to Bank One's security interest; that she entrusted the car to LCPB for the purpose of selling it; that Bank One knew of the practice of allowing lease customers to consign cars in this way; and that Amercani did not know about Bank One's security interest in the car. As such, Amercani is just the kind of good faith buyer in the ordinary course for whom [UCC 2–403(2)] was written.

Bank One argues that since it was never informed of Fox's transfer of her car to LCPB, it cannot be held to have "acquiesced" to that transfer or any of its consequences. However, *   *   * the practice of allowing lessees to consign their vehicle to a dealership is a common one, and *   *   * nothing in the lease agreement barred Fox from doing so. Moreover, Bank One considers being cheated by an unscrupulous dealer "a risk in this business," and one taken voluntarily by it and "and every other lender in the country." Whether or not it should have checked whether LCPB had applied the proceeds from the consignment sale to clear the title, then, Bank One acquiesced to Fox's entrusting of her car to LCPB and cannot achieve [a] *   *   * position superior to Amercani as a purchaser in the ordinary course.

The trial court thus properly granted summary judgment to Amercani as to ownership of and title to the 2001 Mercedes convertible.

DECISION AND REMEDY   *The state intermediate appellate court affirmed the lower court's judgment. As the appellate court stated, "when an owner entrusts goods to a merchant, and that merchant sells to a good faith purchaser for value, that purchaser takes good title." In this case, Fox entrusted her car to LCPB, which sold it to Amercani, who bought it in good faith and without knowledge of Bank One's interest. Amercani thus was entitled to the title to the car.*

WHAT IF THE FACTS WERE DIFFERENT?   *Would it have made any difference in the outcome if Bank One had not known of the practice of allowing lease customers to consign cars as was done in this case? Why or why not?*

SECTION 3 | Risk of Loss

Under the UCC, risk of loss does not necessarily pass with title. When risk of loss passes from a seller or lessor to a buyer or lessee is generally determined by the contract between the parties. Sometimes, the contract states expressly when the risk of loss passes. At other times, it does not, and a court must interpret the existing terms to ascertain whether the risk has passed. When no provision in the contract indicates when risk passes, the UCC provides special rules, based on delivery terms, to guide the courts, as will be discussed shortly.

DELIVERY WITH MOVEMENT OF THE GOODS

When the agreement does not specify when risk passes, the following rules apply in situations involving movement of the goods (so-called carrier cases).

CONTRACT TERMS   Specific terms in the contract can help determine when risk of loss passes to the buyer. These terms, which are listed and defined in Exhibit 21–1, relate generally to the determination of which party will bear the costs of delivery, as well as which party will bear the risk of loss.

EXHIBIT 21-1 **Contract Terms—Definitions**

The contract terms listed and defined in this exhibit help to determine which party will bear the costs of delivery and when risk of loss will pass from the seller to the buyer (although the terms will not appear in the UCC once a state has adopted the 2003 amendments).

F.O.B. (free on board)—Indicates that the selling price of goods includes transportation costs to the specific F.O.B. place named in the contract. The seller pays the expenses and carries the risk of loss to the F.O.B. place named [UCC 2–319(1)]. If the named place is the place from which the goods are shipped (for example, the seller's city or place of business), the contract is a shipment contract. If the named place is the place to which the goods are to be shipped (for example, the buyer's city or place of business), the contract is a destination contract.

F.A.S. (free alongside)—Requires that the seller, at his or her own expense and risk, deliver the goods alongside the carrier before risk passes to the buyer [UCC 2–319(2)].

C.I.F. or **C.&F.** (cost, insurance, and freight or just cost and freight)—Requires, among other things, that the seller "put the goods in possession of a carrier" before risk passes to the buyer [UCC 2–320(2)]. (These are basically pricing terms, and the contracts remain shipment contracts, not destination contracts.)

Delivery ex-ship (delivery from the carrying vessel)—Means that risk of loss does not pass to the buyer until the goods are properly unloaded from the ship or other carrier [UCC 2–322].

Note that the 2003 amendments to UCC Article 2 omit these terms because they are "inconsistent with modern commercial practice." Until most states adopt the amended version of Article 2, however, these terms will remain in use.

SHIPMENT CONTRACTS In a shipment contract, if the seller or lessor is required or authorized to ship goods by carrier (but not required to deliver them to a particular destination), risk of loss passes to the buyer or lessee when the goods are duly delivered to the carrier [UCC 2–509(1)(a), 2A–219(2)(a)].

For example, a seller in Texas sells five hundred cases of grapefruit to a buyer in New York, F.O.B. Houston (free on board in Houston, which means that the buyer pays the transportation charges from Houston—see Exhibit 21–1). The contract authorizes shipment by carrier; it does not require that the seller tender the grapefruit in New York. Risk passes to the buyer when conforming goods are properly placed in

the possession of the carrier. If the goods are damaged in transit, the loss is the buyer's. (Actually, buyers have recourse against carriers, subject to certain limitations, and they may insure the goods from the time the goods leave the seller.)

DESTINATION CONTRACTS In a destination contract, the risk of loss passes to the buyer or lessee when the goods are tendered to the buyer or lessee at the specified destination [UCC 2–509(1)(b), 2A–219(2)(b)]. In the preceding example, if the contract had been a destination contract, F.O.B. New York (see Exhibit 21–1), risk of loss during transit to New York would have been the seller's and would not have passed to the buyer until the carrier tendered the goods to the buyer in New York.

Whether a contract is a shipment contract or a destination contract can have significant consequences for the parties, as illustrated by the following case.

CASE 21.2

United States
Court of Appeals,
Second Circuit, 1999.
177 F.3d 114.

Windows, Inc. v. Jordan Panel Systems Corp.

LEVAL, Circuit Judge:
* * * *

Windows, Inc. ("Windows" or "the seller") is a fabricator and seller of windows, based in South Dakota. Jordan [Panel] Systems, Inc. ("Jordan" or "the buyer") is a construction subcontractor, which contracted to install window wall panels at an air cargo facility at John F. Kennedy Airport in New York City. Jordan ordered custom-made windows from Windows. The purchase contract specified that the windows were to be shipped properly packaged for cross country motor freight transit and "delivered to New York City."

CONTINUED

CASE 21.2 | Continued

Windows constructed the windows according to Jordan's specifications. It arranged to have them shipped to Jordan by a common carrier, Consolidated Freightways Corp. ("Consolidated" or "the carrier"), and delivered them to Consolidated intact and properly packaged. During the course of shipment, however, the goods sustained extensive damage. Much of the glass was broken and many of the window frames were gouged and twisted. Jordan's president signed a delivery receipt noting that approximately two-thirds of the shipment was damaged due to "load shift." Jordan, seeking to stay on its contractor's schedule, directed its employees to disassemble the window frames in an effort to salvage as much of the shipment as possible.

Jordan made a claim with Consolidated for damages it had sustained as a result of the casualty, including labor costs from its salvage efforts and other costs from Jordan's inability to perform its own contractual obligations on schedule. Jordan also ordered a new shipment from Windows, which was delivered without incident.

Jordan did not pay Windows for either the first shipment of damaged windows or the second, intact shipment. Windows filed suit to recover payment from Jordan for both shipments in the Supreme Court of the State of New York, Suffolk County. Jordan counterclaimed, seeking incidental and consequential damages resulting from the damaged shipment. Windows then brought a * * * claim against Consolidated, which removed the suit to the United States District Court for the Eastern District of New York.

Windows settled its claims against Consolidated. Windows later withdrew its claims against Jordan. The only remaining claim is Jordan's counterclaim against Windows for incidental and consequential damages.

The district court granted Windows' motion for summary judgment. [Jordan appealed to the U.S. Court of Appeals for the Second Circuit.] * * *

* * * *

* * * A destination contract is covered by [UCC 2–503(3)]; it arises where "the seller is required to deliver at a particular destination." In contrast, a shipment contract arises [under UCC 2–504] where "the seller is required * * * to send the goods to the buyer and the contract does not require him to deliver them at a particular destination." Under a shipment contract, the seller must "put the goods in the possession of such a carrier and make such a contract for their transportation as may be reasonable having regard to the nature of the goods and other circumstances of the case."

Where the terms of an agreement are ambiguous, there is a strong presumption under the U.C.C. favoring shipment contracts. Unless the parties expressly specify that the contract requires the seller to deliver to a particular destination, the contract is generally construed as one for shipment. [Emphasis added.]

* * * *

To overcome the presumption favoring shipment contracts, the parties must have explicitly agreed to impose on Windows the obligation to effect delivery at a particular destination. The language of this contract does not do so. Nor did Jordan use any commonly recognized industry term indicating that a seller is obligated to deliver the goods to the buyer's specified destination.

Given the strong presumption favoring shipment contracts, and the absence of explicit terms satisfying both requirements for a destination contract, we conclude that the contract should be deemed a shipment contract.

Under the terms of its contract, Windows thus satisfied its obligations to Jordan when it put the goods, properly packaged, into the possession of the carrier for shipment. Upon Windows' proper delivery to the carrier, Jordan assumed the risk of loss, and cannot recover incidental or consequential damages from the seller caused by the carrier's negligence.

This allocation of risk is confirmed by the terms of [UCC 2–509(1)(a)] entitled "Risk of Loss in the Absence of Breach." It provides that where the contract "does not require [the seller] to deliver [the goods] at a particular destination, the risk of loss passes to the buyer when the goods are duly delivered to the carrier." * * * Jordan does not contest the court's finding that Windows duly delivered conforming goods to the carrier. Accordingly, as Windows had already fulfilled its contractual obligations at the time the goods were damaged

CASE 21.2 | **Continued** | and Jordan had assumed the risk of loss, there was no "seller's breach" as is required for a buyer to claim incidental and consequential damages. Summary judgment for Windows was therefore proper.

QUESTIONS

1. Under the contract between Windows, Inc., and Jordan, it was Windows' responsibility to pack the windows properly and ship them to New York City. Why was Jordan unable to recover from Windows, Inc., for damage to the windows that occurred in transit?
2. What would be necessary for the court to rule that this contract was a destination contract?

DELIVERY WITHOUT MOVEMENT OF THE GOODS

The UCC also addresses situations in which the seller or lessor is required neither to ship nor to deliver the goods. Frequently, the buyer or lessee is to pick up the goods from the seller or lessor, or the goods are to be held by a bailee. A *bailment* is a temporary delivery of personal property, without passage of title, into the care of another, called a *bailee*. Under the UCC, a bailee is a party who—by a bill of lading, warehouse receipt, or other document of title—acknowledges possession of goods and contracts to deliver them. A warehousing company, for example, or a trucking company that normally issues documents of title for the goods it receives is a bailee.[6]

GOODS HELD BY THE SELLER   If the goods are held by the seller, a document of title is usually not used. If the seller is a merchant, risk of loss to goods held by the seller passes to the buyer when the buyer *actually takes physical possession of the goods* [UCC 2–509(3)]. If the seller is not a merchant, the risk of loss to goods held by the seller passes to the buyer on tender of delivery [UCC 2–509(3)].

In respect to leases, the risk of loss passes to the lessee on the lessee's receipt of the goods if the lessor—or supplier, in a finance lease (see Chapter 20)—is a merchant. Otherwise, the risk passes to the lessee on tender of delivery [UCC 2A–219(c)].[7]

The following case illustrates the consequences of the passage of the risk of loss under these principles.

---

6. See Chapter 47 for a detailed discussion of the law of bailments.

7. Under the 2003 amendments to UCC 2–509(3) and 2A–219(c), the risk of loss passes to the buyer or the lessee on that party's receipt of the goods regardless of whether the seller or the lessor is a merchant.

CASE 21.3   **Ganno v. Lanoga Corp.**

Court of Appeals of Washington, Division 2, 2003. 119 Wash.App. 310, 80 P.3d 180.
http://www.legalwa.org[a]

BACKGROUND AND FACTS   *Henry Ganno went to the Lumbermen's Building Center store in Fife, Washington, where he bought a twelve-foot beam weighing one hundred pounds. In the lumberyard, a store employee approached Ganno, took his receipt, and used a forklift to place the beam in the open bed of Ganno's truck. The beam projected about four feet from the end of the truck. The employee asked Ganno if he wanted the beam flagged. Ganno said, "Yes," and the employee flagged the beam. The employee did not tie down or otherwise secure the beam, however. A sign in the lumberyard stated Lumbermen's policy not to secure loads for customers. Ganno, who did not get out of the truck or check the load to make sure that it was secure, drove out of the lumberyard onto a public street. When he turned a corner, the beam fell off the truck. As Ganno attempted to retrieve*

---

a. Click on the "Washington State Supreme and Appellate Court Decisions" link. Type "Ganno" in the search box, select "Search case titles only," choose "Washington Appellate Reports" in the "Limit search to:" column, and click on "Search." In the result, click on the name of the case to access the opinion. Municipal Research and Services Center of Washington maintains this Web site.

CONTINUED ▶

CASE 21.3 | Continued   *the beam, another vehicle hit it, causing it to strike Ganno's leg and shatter his kneecap. Ganno filed a suit in a Washington state court against Lanogo Corporation, which owned the Fife Lumbermen's store, alleging negligence in failing to secure the beam. The court granted a judgment in Lanoga's favor. Ganno appealed to a state intermediate appellate court.*

IN THE LANGUAGE OF THE COURT

HUNT, C.J. [Chief Judge]

* * * *

Ganno * * * asserts that Lumbermen's duty of care did not end when he drove off Lumbermen's property. * * * [W]e disagree.

[Revised Code of Washington Section 62A.2-509(3), the state of Washington's version of Section 2–509(3)] of the Uniform Commercial Code declares that where the seller is a merchant, the risk of loss passes to the buyer on receipt of goods. Accordingly, Lumbermen's duty of care ended when it placed the beam into Ganno's truckbed.

* * * Ganno received the beam from Lumbermen's in good condition at the merchant's place of business. * * *

In the absence of a legal duty to secure a customer's load, as here, there is no liability to a customer once he is in possession of the goods. The risk of loss passed to Ganno when Lumbermen's loaded the beam into his truck. Again, Lumbermen's is not liable for the ensuing damage after Ganno took possession and left Lumbermen's property.

* * * *

We hold that there are no issues of material fact and that the trial court properly granted Lumbermen's motion for summary judgment as a matter of law. Thus, we affirm.

DECISION AND REMEDY   *The state intermediate appellate court affirmed the lower court's judgment, holding that it was Ganno's duty, not Lumbermen's, to make sure the load was secure before Ganno drove onto the public streets. In other words, the risk had passed to Ganno, the buyer, before the loss.*

GOODS HELD BY A BAILEE   When a bailee is holding goods for a person who has contracted to sell them and the goods are to be delivered without being moved, the goods are usually represented by a negotiable or nonnegotiable document of title (a bill of lading or a warehouse receipt).[8] Risk of loss passes to the buyer when (1) the buyer receives a negotiable document of title for the goods, (2) the bailee acknowledges the buyer's right to possess the goods, or (3) the buyer receives a nonnegotiable document of title or a writing (record) directing the bailee *and* has had a *reasonable time* to present the document to the bailee and demand the goods. Obviously, if the bailee refuses to honor the document, the risk of loss remains with the seller [UCC 2–503(4)(b), 2–509(2)].

With respect to leases, if goods held by a bailee are to be delivered without being moved, the risk of loss passes to the lessee on acknowledgment by the bailee

of the lessee's right to possession of the goods [UCC 2A–219(2)(b)].

CONDITIONAL SALES

Buyers and sellers sometimes form sales contracts that are conditioned either on the buyer's approval of the goods or on the buyer's resale of the goods. Under such contracts, the buyer is in possession of the goods, and disputes sometimes arise as to which party should bear the loss if, for example, the goods are damaged or stolen.

SALE OR RETURN   A **sale or return** is a type of contract by which the buyer (usually a merchant) purchases goods primarily for resale but has the right to return all or part of the goods (undo the sale) in lieu of payment if the goods fail to be resold. Basically, a sale or return is the present sale of goods, which may be undone at the buyer's option within a specified time period. When the buyer receives possession at the time of sale, title and risk of loss pass to the buyer. Title and risk of loss remain

---

8. A negotiable document of title actually stands for the goods it covers, so that any transfer of the goods requires the surrender of the document. In contrast, a nonnegotiable document of title merely serves as evidence of the goods' existence.

with the buyer until the buyer returns the goods to the seller within the time period specified. If the buyer fails to return the goods within this time period, the sale is finalized. The return of the goods is made at the buyer's risk and expense. Goods held under a sale-or-return contract are subject to the claims of the buyer's creditors while they are in the buyer's possession.

The UCC treats a **consignment** as a sale or return. Under a consignment, the owner of goods (the *consignor*) delivers them to another (the *consignee*) for the consignee to sell or to keep. If the consignee sells the goods, the consignee must pay the consignor for them. If the consignee does not sell or keep the goods, they may simply be returned to the consignor. While the goods are in the possession of the consignee, the consignee holds title to them, and creditors of the consignee will prevail over the consignor in any action to repossess the goods [UCC 2–326(3)].[9]

SALE ON APPROVAL When a seller offers to sell goods to a buyer and sends the goods to the buyer on a trial basis, a **sale on approval** is made. Essentially, the

seller in such contracts delivers the goods primarily so that the prospective buyer (usually not a merchant) can use the goods and be convinced of their appearance or performance. The term *sale* here is misleading, however, because only an *offer* to sell has been made, along with a bailment created by the buyer's possession.

Therefore, title and risk of loss (from causes beyond the buyer's control) remain with the seller until the buyer accepts (approves) the offer. Acceptance can be made expressly, by any act inconsistent with the *trial* purpose or the seller's ownership, or by the buyer's election not to return the goods within the trial period. If the buyer does not wish to accept, the buyer may notify the seller of that fact within the trial period, and the return is made at the seller's expense and risk [UCC 2–327(1)]. Goods held on approval are not subject to the claims of the buyer's creditors until acceptance.

RISK OF LOSS WHEN A SALES OR LEASE CONTRACT IS BREACHED

There are many ways to breach a sales or lease contract, and the transfer of risk operates differently depending on which party breaches. Generally, the party in breach bears the risk of loss.

---

9. This provision is omitted from the 2003 amendments to UCC Article 2. Consignments are to be covered by UCC Article 9. See, for example, UCC 9–103(d), 9–109(a)(4), and 9–319.

CONCEPT SUMMARY 21.1 | Delivery without Movement of the Goods

CONCEPT	DESCRIPTION
GOODS NOT REPRESENTED BY A DOCUMENT OF TITLE	Unless otherwise agreed, if the goods are not represented by a document of title, title and risk pass as follows: 1. Title passes on the formation of the contract [UCC 2–401(3)(b)]. 2. If the seller or lessor (or supplier, in a finance lease) is a merchant, risk passes to the buyer or lessee on the buyer's or lessee's receipt of the goods. If the seller or lessor is a nonmerchant, risk passes to the buyer or lessee on the seller's or lessor's *tender* of delivery of the goods [UCC 2–509(3), 2A–219(c)].[a]
GOODS REPRESENTED BY A DOCUMENT OF TITLE	Unless otherwise agreed, if the goods are represented by a document of title, title and risk pass to the buyer when: 1. The buyer receives a negotiable document of title for the goods, or 2. The bailee acknowledges the buyer's right to possess the goods, or 3. The buyer receives a nonnegotiable document of title or a writing (record) directing the bailee and has had a reasonable time to present the document to the bailee and demand the goods [UCC 2–503(4)(b), 2–509(2)].
LEASED GOODS HELD BY A BAILEE	If leased goods held by a bailee are to be delivered without being moved, the risk of loss passes to the lessee on acknowledgment by the bailee of the lessee's right to possession of the goods [UCC 2A–219(2)(b)].

a. Under the 2003 amendments to UCC 2–509(3) and 2A–219(c), the risk of loss passes to the buyer or the lessee on that party's receipt of the goods regardless of whether the seller or the lessor is a merchant.

WHEN THE SELLER OR LESSOR BREACHES If the goods are so nonconforming that the buyer has the right to reject them, the risk of loss does not pass to the buyer until the defects are *cured* (that is, until the goods are repaired, replaced, or discounted in price by the seller—see Chapter 22) or until the buyer accepts the goods in spite of their defects (thus waiving the right to reject). For example, a buyer orders blue file cabinets from a seller, F.O.B. seller's plant. The seller ships black file cabinets instead. The black cabinets (nonconforming goods) are damaged in transit. The risk of loss falls on the seller. Had the seller shipped blue cabinets (conforming goods) instead, the risk would have fallen on the buyer [UCC 2–510(1)].

If a buyer accepts a shipment of goods and later discovers a defect, acceptance can be revoked. The revocation allows the buyer to pass the risk of loss back to the seller, at least to the extent that the buyer's insurance does not cover the loss [UCC 2–510(2)].

In regard to leases, Article 2A states a similar rule. If the tender or delivery of goods is so nonconforming that the lessee has the right to reject them, the risk of loss remains with the lessor (or the supplier) until cure or acceptance [UCC 2A–220(1)(a)]. If the lessee, after acceptance, rightfully revokes her or his acceptance of the goods, the risk of loss passes back to the lessor or supplier to the extent that the lessee's insurance does not cover the loss [UCC 2A–220(1)(b)].

WHEN THE BUYER OR LESSEE BREACHES The general rule is that when a buyer or lessee breaches a contract, the risk of loss *immediately* shifts to the buyer or lessee. This rule has three important limitations [UCC 2–510(3), 2A–220(2)]:

1. The seller or lessor must already have identified the contract goods.

2. The buyer or lessee bears the risk for only a *commercially reasonable time* after the seller or lessor has learned of the breach.

3. The buyer or lessee is liable only to the extent of any deficiency in the seller's or lessor's insurance coverage.

SECTION 4 ｜ Insurable Interest

Parties to sales and lease contracts often obtain insurance coverage to protect against damage, loss, or destruction of goods. Any party purchasing insurance, however, must have a sufficient interest in the insured item to obtain a valid policy. Insurance laws—not the UCC—determine sufficiency. The UCC is helpful, however, because it contains certain rules regarding insurable interests in goods.

INSURABLE INTEREST OF THE BUYER OR LESSEE

A buyer or lessee has an **insurable interest** in identified goods. The moment the contract goods are *identified* by the seller or lessor, the buyer or lessee has a special property interest that allows the buyer or lessee to obtain necessary insurance coverage for those goods even before the risk of loss has passed [UCC 2–501(1),

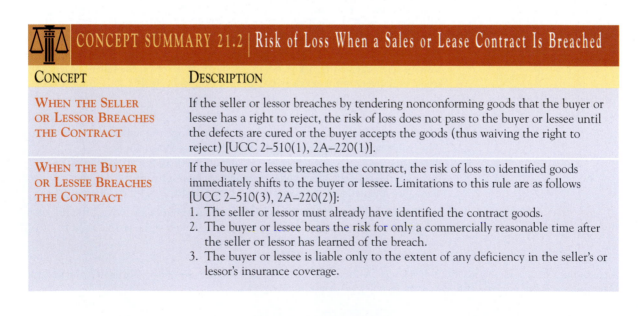

CONCEPT SUMMARY 21.2 ｜ Risk of Loss When a Sales or Lease Contract Is Breached	
CONCEPT	DESCRIPTION
WHEN THE SELLER OR LESSOR BREACHES THE CONTRACT	If the seller or lessor breaches by tendering nonconforming goods that the buyer or lessee has a right to reject, the risk of loss does not pass to the buyer or lessee until the defects are cured or the buyer accepts the goods (thus waiving the right to reject) [UCC 2–510(1), 2A–220(1)].
WHEN THE BUYER OR LESSEE BREACHES THE CONTRACT	If the buyer or lessee breaches the contract, the risk of loss to identified goods immediately shifts to the buyer or lessee. Limitations to this rule are as follows [UCC 2–510(3), 2A–220(2)]: 1. The seller or lessor must already have identified the contract goods. 2. The buyer or lessee bears the risk for only a commercially reasonable time after the seller or lessor has learned of the breach. 3. The buyer or lessee is liable only to the extent of any deficiency in the seller's or lessor's insurance coverage.

2A–218(1)]. Identification can be made at any time and in any manner agreed to by the parties. If the parties do not explicitly agree on identification, then the UCC provisions apply.

For example, in March a farmer sells a cotton crop she hopes to harvest in October. If the contract does not specify otherwise, the buyer acquires an insurable interest in the crop when it is planted because the goods (the cotton crop) are identified to the sales contract. The rule stated in UCC 2–501(1)(c) is that the buyer obtains an insurable interest in crops when the crops are planted or otherwise become growing crops, provided that the crops will "be harvested within twelve months or the next normal harvest season after contracting, whichever is longer."

INSURABLE INTEREST OF THE SELLER OR LESSOR

A seller has an insurable interest in goods as long as he or she retains title to the goods. Even after title passes to a buyer, a seller who has a security interest in the goods (a right to secure payment—see Chapter 29) still has an insurable interest and can insure the goods [UCC 2–501(2)]. Thus, both the buyer and the seller can have an insurable interest in identical goods at the same time. Of course, the buyer or seller must sustain an actual loss to have the right to recover from an insurance company. In regard to leases, the lessor retains an insurable interest in leased goods until an option to buy has been exercised by the lessee and the risk of loss has passed to the lessee [UCC 2A–218(3)].

SECTION 5 | Bulk Transfers

Article 6 of the UCC covers bulk transfers. A *bulk transfer* is defined as any transfer of a major part of the transferor's material, supplies, merchandise, or other inventory *not made in the ordinary course of the transferor's business* [UCC 6–102(1)]. Article 6 was designed to prevent certain difficulties with such transfers—such as when a business sold a substantial part of its equipment and inventories to a buyer and then failed to pay its creditors. Today, changes in the business and legal contexts in which bulk sales are conducted have largely made their regulation unnecessary. For this reason, the vast majority of the states have repealed Article 6. Those states that have not repealed the article follow either the original version of Article 6 or its alternative (see Appendix C).

REVIEWING TITLE, RISK, AND INSURABLE INTEREST

In December, Mendoza agreed to buy the broccoli grown on 100 acres of Willow Glen's 1,000-acre broccoli farm. The sales contract specified F.O.B. Willow Glen's field by Falcon Trucking. The broccoli was to be planted in February and harvested in March of the following year. Using the information presented in the chapter, answer the following questions.

1. At what point is a crop of broccoli identified to the contract under the UCC? Explain. Why is identification significant?

2. When does title to the broccoli pass from Willow Glen to Mendoza under the terms of this contract? Why?

3. Suppose that while in transit, Falcon's truck overturned and spilled the entire load. Who bears the loss, Mendoza or Willow Glen? At what point would Mendoza have acquired an insurable interest? Discuss.

4. Suppose that instead of buying fresh broccoli, Mendoza had contracted with Willow Glen to purchase 1,000 cases of frozen broccoli from Willow Glen's processing plant. The highest grade of broccoli is packaged under the "FreshBest" label, and everything else is packaged under the "FamilyPac" label. Further suppose that although the contract had specified that Mendoza was to receive FreshBest broccoli, Willow Glen delivered FamilyPac broccoli to the carrier. What rights would Mendoza have under the UCC in that situation?

5. Now suppose that the FamilyPac broccoli delivered to the carrier was stolen and sold to DeVry, who had no knowledge of the theft. Does DeVry have title to the goods? Why or why not?

TERMS AND CONCEPTS TO REVIEW

consignment 419

destination contract 411

document of title 411

entrustment 412

fungible goods 411

good faith purchaser 412

identification 410

insolvent 412

insurable interest 420

sale on approval 419

sale or return 418

shipment contract 411

QUESTIONS AND CASE PROBLEMS

21–1. Mackey orders from Pride one thousand cases of Greenie brand peas from lot A at list price to be shipped F.O.B. Pride's city via Fast Freight Lines. Pride receives the order and immediately sends Mackey an acceptance of the order with a promise to ship promptly. Pride later separates the one thousand cases of Greenie peas and prints Mackey's name and address on each case. The peas are placed on Pride's dock, and Fast Freight is notified to pick up the shipment. The night before the pickup by Fast Freight, through no fault of Pride's, a fire destroys the one thousand cases of peas. Pride claims that title passed to Mackey at the time the contract was made and that risk of loss passed to Mackey when the goods were marked with Mackey's name and address. Discuss Pride's contentions.

21–2. **QUESTION WITH SAMPLE ANSWER**

On May 1, Sikora goes into Carson's retail clothing store to purchase a suit. Sikora finds a suit he likes for $190 and buys it. The suit needs alterations. Sikora is to pick up the altered suit at Carson's store on May 10. Consider the following separate sets of circumstances:

(a) One of Carson's major creditors obtains a judgment on the debt Carson owes and has the court issue a writ of execution (a court order to seize a debtor's property to satisfy a debt) to collect on that judgment all clothing in Carson's possession. Discuss Sikora's rights in the suit under these circumstances.

(b) On May 9, through no fault of Carson's, the store burns down, and all contents are a total loss. Between Carson and Sikora, who suffers the loss of the suit destroyed by the fire? Explain.

For a sample answer to this question, go to Appendix I at the end of this text.

21–3. Zeke, who sells lawn mowers, tells Stasio, a regular customer, about a special promotional campaign. On receipt of a $50 down payment, Zeke will sell Stasio a new Universal lawn mower for $200, even though it normally sells for $350. Zeke further states to Stasio that if Stasio does not like the performance of the lawn mower, he can return it within thirty days, and Zeke will refund the $50 down payment. Stasio pays the $50 and takes the mower. On the tenth day, the lawn mower is stolen through no fault of Stasio's. Stasio calls Zeke and demands the return of his $50. Zeke claims that Stasio should suffer the risk of loss and that he still owes Zeke the remainder of the purchase price, $150. Discuss who is correct, Stasio or Zeke.

21–4. In the following situations, two parties lay claim to the same goods sold. Discuss which of the parties would prevail in each instance.

(a) Toscano steals Dean's television set and sells the set to Bosky, an innocent purchaser, for value. Dean learns Bosky has the set and demands its return.

(b) Kerr takes her television set for repair to Unger, a merchant who sells new and used television sets. By accident, one of Unger's employees sells the set to Gale, an innocent purchaser-customer, who takes possession. Kerr wants her set back from Gale.

21–5. SHIPMENT AND DESTINATION CONTRACTS. Roderick Cardwell owns Ticketworld, which sells tickets (a sale of goods, according to the court) to entertainment and sporting events to be held at locations throughout the United States. Ticketworld's Massachusetts office sold tickets to an event in Connecticut to Mary Lou Lupovitch, a Connecticut resident, for $125 per ticket, although each ticket had a fixed price of $32.50. There was no agreement that Ticketworld would bear the risk of loss until the tickets were delivered to a specific location. Ticketworld gave the tickets to a carrier in Massachusetts, who delivered the tickets to Lupovitch in Connecticut. The state of Connecticut brought an action against Cardwell in a Connecticut state court, charging in part a violation of a state statute that prohibited the sale of a ticket for more than $3 over its fixed price. Cardwell contended in part that the statute did not apply because the sale to Lupovitch involved a shipment contract that was formed outside the state. Is Cardwell correct? How will the court rule? Why? [*State v. Cardwell*, 246 Conn. 721, 718 A.2d 954 (1998)]

21–6. RISK OF LOSS. H.S.A. II, Inc., made parts for motor vehicles. Under an agreement with Ford Motor Co., Ford provided steel to H.S.A. to make Ford parts. Ford's purchase orders for the parts contained the term

"FOB Carrier Supplier's [Plant]." GMAC Business Credit, L.L.C., loaned money to H.S.A. under terms that guaranteed payment would be made—if the funds were not otherwise available—from H.S.A.'s inventory, raw materials, and finished goods. H.S.A. filed for bankruptcy on February 2, 2000, and ceased operations on June 20, when it had in its plant more than $1 million in finished goods for Ford. Ford sent six trucks to H.S.A. to pick up the goods. GMAC halted the removal. The parties asked the bankruptcy court to determine whose interest had priority. GMAC contended in part that Ford did not have an interest in the goods because there had not yet been a sale. Ford responded that under its purchase orders, title and risk of loss transferred on completion of the parts. In whose favor should the court rule, and why? [*In re H.S.A. II, Inc.*, 271 Bankr. 534 (E.D.Mich. 2002)]

21-7. CASE PROBLEM WITH SAMPLE ANSWER

National Hydro-Vac Industrial Services, L.L.C., based in Houston, Texas, bought some of the assets of Freemyer Co. The assets included three industrial, trailer-mounted vacuum units made by Guzzler Manufacturing, Inc., with which National had an account. National offered to trade in the three used units to Guzzler in exchange for one new one and shipped the used units to Guzzler in Birmingham, Alabama, in the spring of 2000. Guzzler inspected the units and refurbished two, which it then sold to Vac-Tech, a company in Australia, for $110,000 each. Meanwhile, the trade-in deal with National fell through, and in May or June, Guzzler offered to pay National for the units sold to Vac-Tech. Bills of sale dated August 1 stated the price as $75,000 each, but Guzzler credited National's account with only $130,000 for both. National filed a claim in a federal bankruptcy court against Guzzler and others, seeking damages. Was there a sale of the units from National to Guzzler? If so, when did title to the units pass? Discuss. [*In re National Hydro-Vac Industrial Services, L.L.C.*, 314 Bankr. 753 (E.D.Ark. 2004)]

To view a sample answer for this case problem, go to this book's Web site at http://wbl.westbuslaw.com, select "Chapter 21," and click on "Case Problem with Sample Answer."

21-8. CONDITIONAL SALES.

Corvette Collection of Boston, Inc. (CCB), was a used-Corvette dealership located (despite its name) in Pompano Beach, Florida. In addition to selling used Corvettes, CCB serviced Corvettes and sold Corvette parts. CCB owned some of its inventory and held the rest on consignment, although there were no signs indicating the consignments. In November 2001, CCB filed a petition for bankruptcy in a federal district court. At the time, CCB possessed six Corvettes that were consigned by Chester Finley and The Corvette Experience, Inc. (TCE), neither of which had a security interest in the goods. Robert Furr, on CCB's behalf, asked the court to declare that CCB held the goods under a contract for a sale or return. Finley and TCE asserted that the goods were held under a contract for a sale on approval. What difference does it make? Under what circumstances would the court rule in favor of Finley and TCE? How should the court rule under the facts as stated? Why? [*In re Corvette Collection of Boston, Inc.*, 294 Bankr. 409 (S.D.Fla. 2003)]

21-9. A QUESTION OF ETHICS

Toby and Rita Kahr accidentally included a small bag containing their sterling silver in a bag of used clothing that they donated to Goodwill Industries, Inc. The silverware, which was valued at over $3,500, had been given to them twenty-seven years earlier by Rita's father as a wedding present and had great sentimental value for them. The Kahrs realized what had happened shortly after Toby returned from Goodwill, but when Toby called Goodwill, he was told that the silver had immediately been sold to a customer, Karon Markland, for $15. Although Goodwill called Markland and asked her to return the silver, Markland refused to return it. The Kahrs then brought an action against Markland to regain the silver, claiming that Markland did not have good title to it. In view of these circumstances, discuss the following issues. [*Kahr v. Markland*, 187 Ill.App.3d 603, 543 N.E.2d 579, 135 Ill.Dec. 196 (1989)]

(a) Did Karon Markland act wrongfully in any way by not returning the silver to Goodwill Industries when requested to do so? What would you have done in her position?

(b) Goodwill argued that the entrustment rule should apply. Why would Goodwill want the rule to be applied? How might Goodwill justify its argument from an ethical point of view?

21-10. VIDEO QUESTION

Go to this text's Web site at **http://wbl.westbuslaw.com** and select "Chapter 21." Click on "Video Questions" and view the video titled *Risk of Loss*. Then answer the following questions.

(a) Does Oscar have a right to refuse the shipment because the lettuce is wilted? Why or why not? What type of contract is involved in this video?

(b) Does Oscar have a right to refuse the shipment because the lettuce is not organic butter crunch lettuce? Why or why not?

(c) Assume that you are in Oscar's position—that is, you are buying produce for a supermarket. What different approaches might you take to avoid having to pay for a delivery of wilted produce?

LAW | on the Web

For updated links to resources available on the Web, as well as a variety of other materials, visit this text's Web site at http://wbl.westbuslaw.com.

To find information on the UCC, including the UCC provisions discussed in this chapter, refer to the Web sites listed in the *Law on the Web* feature in Chapter 20.

Publications on current commercial law topics, including some of the topics discussed in this chapter, are available at the Web site of the law firm, Wilmer Cutler Pickering Hale and Dorr. Go to

http://www.wilmerhale.com

For an overview of bills of lading, access the following Web site:

http://straylight.law.cornell.edu/ucc/7/overview.html

LEGAL RESEARCH EXERCISES ON THE WEB

Go to http://wbl.westbuslaw.com, the Web site that accompanies this text. Select "Chapter 21" and click on "Internet Exercises." There you will find the following Internet research exercises that you can perform to learn more about topics covered in this chapter.

Activity 21–1: **LEGAL PERSPECTIVE**
The Entrustment Rule

Activity 21–2: **MANAGEMENT PERSPECTIVE**
Passage of Title

CHAPTER 22

Performance and Breach of Sales and Lease Contracts

The performance that is required of the parties under a sales or lease contract consists of the duties and obligations each party has under the terms of the contract. Keep in mind that "duties and obligations" under the terms of the contract include those specified by the agreement, by custom, and by the Uniform Commercial Code (UCC). In performing a sales or lease contract, the basic obligation of the seller or lessor is to *transfer and deliver conforming goods*. The basic obligation of the buyer or lessee is to *accept and pay for conforming goods* in accordance with the contract [UCC 2–301, 2A–516(1)]. Overall performance of a sales or lease contract is controlled by the agreement between the parties. When the contract is unclear and disputes arise, the courts look to the UCC.

Sometimes, circumstances make it difficult for a person to carry out the promised performance, leading to a breach of the contract. When a breach occurs, the aggrieved party looks for remedies. The UCC provides a range of possible remedies, from retaining the goods to requiring the breaching party's performance under the contract. Generally, these remedies are designed to put the aggrieved party "in as good a position as if the other party had fully performed." Note that in contrast to the common law of contracts, remedies under the UCC are *cumulative* in nature. In other words, an innocent party to a breached sales or lease contract is not limited to one exclusive remedy.

In this chapter, after first scrutinizing the general requirement of good faith, we examine the basic performance obligations of the parties under a sales or lease contract. We discuss the remedies available under the UCC in the second half of the chapter.

SECTION 1 | The Good Faith Requirement

The obligations of good faith and commercial reasonableness underlie every sales and lease contract falling within the purview of the UCC. These obligations can form the basis for a suit for breach of contract later on.

THE UCC'S GOOD FAITH PROVISION

The UCC's good faith provision, which can never be disclaimed, reads as follows: "Every contract or duty within this Act imposes an obligation of good faith in its performance or enforcement" [UCC 1–203]. *Good faith* means honesty in fact. In the case of a merchant, it means honesty in fact and the observance of reasonable commercial standards of fair dealing in the trade

[UCC 2–103(1)(b)]. In other words, in those states that have not adopted the 2003 amendments, merchants are held to a higher standard of performance or duty than are nonmerchants.[1]

GOOD FAITH AND CONTRACT PERFORMANCE

Good faith can mean that one party must not take advantage of the other party by manipulating contract terms. Good faith applies to both parties, even the nonbreaching party. The principle of good faith applies through both the performance and the enforcement of all agreements or duties under a contract. Good faith is a question of fact for the jury.

---

1. The 2003 amendments to UCC Articles 2 and 2A apply this definition of good faith to all parties, merchants and nonmerchants alike [Amended UCC 2–103(1)(j), 2A–103(1)(m)].

The standards of good faith and commercial reasonableness provide the framework within which the parties are to specify particulars of performance. If a sales contract leaves open some particulars of performance and permits one of the parties to specify them, "[a]ny such specification must be made in good faith and within limits set by commercial reasonableness" [UCC 2–311(1)]. Thus, when one party delays specifying particulars of performance for an unreasonable period of time or fails to cooperate with the other party, the innocent party is excused from any resulting delay in performance. In addition, the innocent party can proceed to perform in any reasonable manner.[2]

SECTION 2 | Obligations of the Seller or Lessor

The major obligation of the seller or lessor under a sales or lease contract is to tender conforming goods to the buyer or lessee. **Tender of delivery** requires that the seller or lessor have and hold *conforming goods* at the disposal of the buyer or lessee and give the buyer or lessee whatever notification is reasonably necessary to enable the buyer or lessee to take delivery [UCC 2–503(1), 2A–508(1)]. **Conforming goods** are goods that conform exactly to the description of the goods in the contract.

Tender must occur at a *reasonable hour* and in a *reasonable manner*. For example, a seller cannot call the buyer at 2:00 A.M. and say, "The goods are ready. I'll give you twenty minutes to get them." Unless the parties have agreed otherwise, the goods must be tendered for delivery at a reasonable hour and kept available for a reasonable period of time to enable the buyer to take possession of them [UCC 2–503(1)(a)].

All goods called for by a contract must be tendered in a single delivery unless the parties agree otherwise [UCC 2–612, 2A–510] or the circumstances are such that either party can rightfully request delivery in lots [UCC 2–307]. Hence, an order for 1,000 shirts cannot be delivered two shirts at a time. If, however, the seller and the buyer contemplate that the shirts will be delivered in 4 orders of 250 each, as they are produced (for summer, fall, winter, and spring stock), and the price can be apportioned accordingly, it may be commercially reasonable to deliver the shirts in this way.

PLACE OF DELIVERY

The UCC provides for the place of delivery pursuant to a contract if the contract does not do so. Of course, the parties may agree on a particular destination, or their contract's terms or the circumstances may indicate the place.

NONCARRIER CASES   If the contract does not designate the place of delivery for the goods, and the buyer is expected to pick them up, the place of delivery is the *seller's place of business* or, if the seller has none, the *seller's residence* [UCC 2–308]. If the contract involves the sale of *identified goods*, and the parties know when they enter into the contract that these goods are located somewhere other than at the seller's place of business (such as at a warehouse), then the *location of the goods* is the place for their delivery [UCC 2–308].

For example, Li Wan and Boyd both live in San Francisco. In San Francisco, Li Wan contracts to sell Boyd five used trucks, which both parties know are located in a Chicago warehouse. If nothing more is specified in the contract, the place of delivery for the trucks is Chicago. The seller may tender delivery either by giving the buyer a negotiable or nonnegotiable document of title or by obtaining the bailee's (warehouser's) acknowledgment that the buyer is entitled to possession.[3]

CARRIER CASES   In many instances, attendant circumstances or delivery terms in the contract make it apparent that the parties intend that a carrier be used to move the goods. A seller can complete performance of the obligation to deliver the goods in carrier cases in two ways: through a shipment contract or through a destination contract.

—Shipment Contracts.   Recall from Chapter 21 that a *shipment contract* requires or authorizes the seller to ship goods by a carrier. The contract does not require that the seller deliver the goods at a particular destination [UCC 2–319, 2–509].[4] Unless otherwise agreed, the seller must do the following:

---

2. See the *Focus on Ethics* feature following Chapter 23 for a further discussion of the UCC's emphasis on good faith and commercial reasonableness.

3. If the seller delivers a nonnegotiable document of title or merely instructs the bailee in a writing (record) to release the goods to the buyer without the bailee's acknowledgment of the buyer's rights, this is also a sufficient tender, unless the buyer objects [UCC 2–503(4)]. Risk of loss, however, does not pass until the buyer has had a reasonable amount of time in which to present the document or the instructions. See Chapter 21.

4. As mentioned in Chapter 21, UCC 2–319 was omitted from the 2003 amendments to Article 2.

1. Place the goods into the hands of the carrier.
2. Make a contract for their transportation that is reasonable according to the nature of the goods and their value. (For example, certain types of goods need refrigeration in transit.)
3. Obtain and promptly deliver or tender to the buyer any documents necessary to enable the buyer to obtain possession of the goods from the carrier.
4. Promptly notify the buyer that shipment has been made [UCC 2–504].

If the seller fails to notify the buyer of the shipment or fails to make a proper contract for transportation, the buyer can reject the goods, but only if a *material loss* of the goods or a significant *delay* results. Of course, the parties can agree that a loss that is not necessarily "material" or a delay that is not "significant"—that is, any loss—will be grounds for rejection.

—Destination Contracts. In a *destination contract*, the seller agrees to deliver conforming goods to the buyer at a particular destination. The goods must be tendered at a reasonable hour and held at the buyer's disposal for a reasonable length of time. The seller must also give the buyer appropriate notice. In addition, the seller must provide the buyer with any documents of title necessary to enable the buyer to obtain delivery from the carrier. Sellers often do this by tendering the documents through ordinary banking channels [UCC 2–503].

THE PERFECT TENDER RULE

As previously noted, the seller or lessor has an obligation to ship or tender *conforming goods,* which the buyer or lessee is then obligated to accept and pay for according to the terms of the contract. Under the common law, the seller was obligated to deliver goods that conformed with the terms of the contract in every detail. This was called the **perfect tender rule.** The UCC preserves the perfect tender doctrine by stating that if goods or tender of delivery fails *in any respect* to conform to the contract, the buyer or lessee has the right to accept the goods, reject the entire shipment, or accept part and reject part [UCC 2–601, 2A–509].

For example, a lessor contracts to lease fifty Comclear computers to be delivered at the lessee's place of business on or before October 1. On September 28, the lessor discovers that it has only thirty Comclear computers in inventory but will have another twenty Comclear computers within the next

two weeks. The lessor tenders delivery of the thirty Comclear computers on October 1, with the promise that the other computers will be delivered within three weeks. Because the lessor has failed to make a perfect tender of fifty Comclear computers, the lessee has the right to reject the entire shipment and hold the lessor in breach.

EXCEPTIONS TO THE PERFECT TENDER RULE

Because of the rigidity of the perfect tender rule, several exceptions to the rule have been created, some of which we discuss here.

AGREEMENT OF THE PARTIES Exceptions to the perfect tender rule may be established by agreement. If the parties have agreed, for example, that defective goods or parts will not be rejected if the seller or lessor is able to repair or replace them within a reasonable period of time, the perfect tender rule does not apply.

CURE The UCC does not specifically define the term **cure,** but it refers to the right of the seller or lessor to repair, adjust, or replace defective or nonconforming goods [UCC 2–508, 2A–513]. When any tender of delivery is rejected because of nonconforming goods and the time for performance has not yet expired, the seller or lessor can notify the buyer or lessee promptly of the intention to cure and can then do so *within the contract time for performance* [UCC 2–508(1), 2A–513(1)]. Once the time for performance under the contract has expired, the seller or lessor can still exercise the right to cure if he or she has *reasonable grounds to believe that the nonconforming tender will be acceptable to the buyer or lessee* [UCC 2–508(2), 2A–513(2)].[5]

—Reasons for Tendering Nonconforming Goods. A seller or lessor will sometimes tender nonconforming goods with some type of price allowance, although

---

5. The 2003 amendments to UCC Articles 2 and 2A expressly exempt consumer contracts and consumer leases from these provisions [Amended UCC 2–508, 2A–508]. In other words, cure is not available as a matter of right after a justifiable revocation of acceptance under a consumer contract or lease. The new provisions also abandon the "reasonable grounds to believe" test, thus expanding the seller's right to cure after the time for performance has expired. Although this test has been abandoned, the requirement that the initial tender be made in good faith prevents a seller from deliberately tendering goods that the seller knows the buyer cannot use.

this is not required under the UCC. The allowance serves as the "reasonable grounds" for the seller or lessor to believe that the nonconforming tender will be acceptable to the buyer or lessee. A seller or lessor might also have other reasons for assuming that a buyer or lessee will accept a nonconforming tender. For example, if in the past a buyer frequently accepted a particular substitute for a good when the good ordered was not available, the seller has reasonable grounds to believe the buyer will again accept the substitute. Even if the buyer rejects the substitute good on a particular occasion, the seller nonetheless had reasonable grounds to believe that the substitute would be acceptable. Therefore, the seller can cure within a *reasonable time*, even though conforming delivery will occur after the time limit for performance allowed under the contract.

—A Restriction on the Buyer's or Lessee's Right of Rejection. The right to cure substantially restricts the right of the buyer or lessee to reject goods. For example, if a lessee refuses a tender of goods as nonconforming but does not disclose the nature of the defect to the lessor, the lessee cannot later assert the defect as a defense if the defect is one that the lessor could have cured. Generally, buyers and lessees must act in good faith and state specific reasons for refusing to accept goods [UCC 2–605, 2A–514].[6]

SUBSTITUTION OF CARRIERS When an agreed-on manner of delivery (such as the use of a particular carrier to transport the goods) becomes impracticable or unavailable through no fault of either party, but a commercially reasonable substitute is available, this substitute performance is sufficient tender to the buyer and must be used [UCC 2–614(1)]. For example, a sales contract calls for the delivery of a large piece of machinery to be shipped by ABC Truck Lines on or before June 1. The contract terms clearly state the importance of the delivery date. The employees of ABC Truck Lines go on strike. The seller must make a reasonable substitute tender, perhaps by rail, if it is available. Note that the seller here normally is responsible for any additional shipping costs, unless contrary arrangements have been made in the sales contract.

INSTALLMENT CONTRACTS An **installment contract** is a single contract that requires or authorizes delivery in two or more separate lots to be accepted and paid for separately. Under an installment contract, a buyer or lessee can reject an installment *only if the nonconformity substantially impairs the value* of the installment and cannot be cured [UCC 2–307, 2–612(2), 2A–510(1)].[7]

The entire installment contract is breached only when one or more nonconforming installments *substantially* impair the value of the *whole contract*. If the buyer or lessee subsequently accepts a nonconforming installment and fails to notify the seller or lessor of the cancellation, however, the contract is reinstated [UCC 2–612(3), 2A–510(2)].

—When Is the Value of the Whole Contract Substantially Impaired? A major issue to be determined is what constitutes substantial impairment of the "value of the whole contract." For example, consider an installment contract for the sale of twenty carloads of plywood. The first carload does not conform to the contract because 9 percent of the plywood deviates from the thickness specifications. The buyer cancels the contract, and immediately thereafter the second and third carloads of plywood arrive at the buyer's place of business. If a lawsuit ensues, the court will have to grapple with the question of whether the nonconforming plywood, comprising 9 percent of one carload, substantially impaired the value of the whole.

A more clear-cut example is an installment contract that involves parts of a machine. Suppose that the first part is delivered and is irreparably defective but is necessary for the operation of the machine. The failure of this first installment will be a breach of the whole contract. Even when the defect in the first shipment gives the buyer only a "reasonable apprehension" about the ability or willingness of the seller to complete the other installments properly, the breach on the first installment may be regarded as a breach of the whole.

---

6. The 2003 amendments to UCC 2–605 and 2A–514 change this restriction in three ways. First, a buyer's or lessee's failure to disclose the nature of the defect affects only the right to reject or revoke acceptance, not the right to establish a breach. Second, the new sections expressly require that the seller or lessor must have had a right to cure, as well as the ability to cure. Finally, these sections extend to include not only rejection but also revocation of acceptance.

---

7. The 2003 amendments make it clear that the buyer's or lessee's right to reject an installment depends on whether there has been a substantial impairment of the value of the installment to the buyer or lessee and not on the ability of the seller or lessor to cure [Amended UCC 2–612(2), 2A–510(2)].

—Effectively Limits the Buyer's or Lessee's Right of Rejection. The point to remember is that the UCC significantly alters the right of the buyer or lessee to reject the entire contract if the contract requires delivery to be made in several installments. The UCC strictly limits rejection to cases of *substantial* nonconformity (unless the parties agree that breach of an installment constitutes a breach of the entire contract).

COMMERCIAL IMPRACTICABILITY As stated in Chapter 17, occurrences unforeseen by either party when a contract was made may make performance commercially impracticable. When this occurs, the rule of perfect tender no longer holds. According to UCC 2–615(a) and 2A–405(a), delay in delivery or nondelivery in whole or in part is not a breach when performance has been made impracticable "by the occurrence of a contingency the nonoccurrence of which was a basic assumption on which the contract was made." The seller or lessor must, however, notify the buyer or lessee as soon as practicable that there will be a delay or nondelivery.

—Foreseeable versus Unforeseeable Contingencies. An increase in cost resulting from inflation does not in and of itself excuse performance, as this kind of risk is ordinarily assumed by a seller or lessor conducting business. The unforeseen contingency must be one that would have been impossible to contemplate in a given business situation [UCC 2–615, 2A–405].

For example, a major oil company that receives its supplies from the Middle East has a contract to supply a buyer with 100,000 gallons of oil. Because of an oil embargo by the Organization of Petroleum Exporting Countries (OPEC), the seller is prevented from securing oil supplies to meet the terms of the contract. Because of the same embargo, the seller cannot secure oil from any other source. This situation comes fully under the commercial impracticability exception to the perfect tender doctrine.

Can unanticipated increases in a seller's costs that make performance "impracticable" constitute a valid defense to performance on the basis of commercial impracticability? The court dealt with this question in the following case.

CASE 22.1

Maple Farms, Inc. v. City School District of Elmira

Supreme Court
of New York, 1974.
76 Misc.2d 1080,
352 N.Y.S.2d 784.

BACKGROUND AND FACTS *On June 15, 1973, Maple Farms, Inc., formed an agreement with the city school district of Elmira, New York, to supply the school district with milk for the 1973–1974 school year. The agreement was in the form of a requirements contract, under which Maple Farms would sell to the school district all the milk the district required at a fixed price—which was the June market price of milk. By December 1973, the price of raw milk had increased by 23 percent over the price specified in the contract. This meant that if the terms of the contract were fulfilled, Maple Farms would lose $7,350. Because it had similar contracts with other school districts, Maple Farms stood to lose a great deal if it was held to the price stated in the contracts. When the school district would not agree to release Maple Farms from its contract, Maple Farms brought an action in a New York state court for a declaratory judgment (a determination of the parties' rights under a contract). Maple Farms contended that the substantial increase in the price of raw milk was an event not contemplated by the parties when the contract was formed and that, given the increased price, performance of the contract was commercially impracticable.*

IN THE LANGUAGE OF THE COURT

CHARLES B. SWARTWOOD, Justice.

    * * * *

    * * * [The doctrine of commercial impracticability requires that] a contingency—something unexpected—must have occurred. Second, the risk of the unexpected occurrence must not have been allocated either by agreement or by custom. * * *

    * * * [H]ere we find that the contingency causing the increase of the price of raw milk was not totally unexpected. The price from the low point in the year 1972 to the price on the

CONTINUED ▶

CASE 22.1 | **Continued** date of the award of the contract in June 1973 had risen nearly 10%. And *any businessman should have been aware of the general inflation in this country during the previous years * * *.* [Emphasis added.]

* * * Here the very purpose of the contract was to guard against fluctuation of price of half pints of milk as a basis for the school budget. Surely had the price of raw milk fallen substantially, the defendant could not be excused from performance. We can reasonably assume that the plaintiff had to be aware of escalating inflation. It is chargeable with knowledge of the substantial increase of the price of raw milk from the previous year's low. * * * It nevertheless entered into this agreement with that knowledge. It did not provide in the contract any exculpatory clause to excuse it from performance in the event of a substantial rise in the price of raw milk. On these facts the risk of a substantial or abnormal increase in the price of raw milk can be allocated to the plaintiff.

DECISION AND REMEDY *The New York trial court ruled that inflation and fluctuating prices did not render performance impracticable in this case and granted summary judgment in favor of the school district.*

WHAT IF THE FACTS WERE DIFFERENT? *Suppose that the court had ruled in the plaintiff's favor. How might that ruling have affected the plaintiff's contracts with other parties?*

IMPACT OF THIS CASE ON TODAY'S LAW

This case is a classic illustration of the UCC's commercial impracticability doctrine as courts still apply it today. Under this doctrine, increased cost alone does not excuse performance unless the rise in cost is due to some unforeseen contingency that alters the essential nature of the performance.

—*Partial Performance.* Sometimes, the unforeseen event only *partially* affects the capacity of the seller or lessor to perform. When the seller or lessor can *partially* fulfill the contract but cannot tender total performance, the seller or lessor is required to allocate in a fair and reasonable manner any remaining production and deliveries among its regular customers and those to whom it is contractually obligated to deliver the goods [UCC 2–615(b), 2A–405(b)]. The buyer or lessee must receive notice of the allocation and has the right to accept or reject it [UCC 2–615(c), 2A–405(c)].

For example, a Florida orange grower, Best Citrus, Inc., contracts to sell this season's production to a number of customers, including Martin's grocery chain. Martin's contracts to purchase two thousand crates of oranges. Best Citrus has sprayed *some* of its orange groves with a chemical called Karmoxin. The U.S. Department of Agriculture discovers that persons who eat products sprayed with Karmoxin may develop cancer and issues an order prohibiting the sale of these products. Best Citrus picks all the oranges not sprayed with Karmoxin, but the quantity is insufficient to meet all the contracted-for deliveries. In this situation,

Best Citrus is required to allocate its production, so it notifies Martin's that it cannot deliver the full quantity agreed on in the contract and specifies the amount it will be able to deliver under the circumstances. Martin's can either accept or reject the allocation, but Best Citrus has no further contractual liability.

DESTRUCTION OF IDENTIFIED GOODS Sometimes, an unexpected event, such as a fire, totally destroys goods through no fault of either party and before risk passes to the buyer or lessee. In such a situation, *if the goods were identified at the time the contract was formed,* the parties are excused from performance [UCC 2–613, 2A–221]. If the goods are only partially destroyed, however, the buyer or lessee can inspect them and either treat the contract as void or accept the damaged goods with a reduction in the contract price.

Consider an example. Atlas Sporting Equipment agrees to lease to River Bicycles sixty bicycles of a particular model that has been discontinued. No other bicycles of that model are available. River specifies that it needs the bicycles to rent to tourists. Before Atlas can deliver the bikes, they are destroyed by a fire. In this situation, Atlas is not liable to River for failing to deliver the bikes. Through no fault of either party, the goods were destroyed before the risk of loss passed to the lessee. The loss was total, so the contract is avoided. Clearly, Atlas has no obligation to tender the bicycles, and River has no obligation to pay for them.

ASSURANCE AND COOPERATION Two other exceptions to the perfect tender doctrine apply equally to parties to sales and lease contracts: the right of assurance and the duty of cooperation.

—The Right of Assurance. The UCC provides that if one of the parties to a contract has "reasonable grounds" to believe that the other party will not perform as contracted, she or he may *in writing* "demand adequate assurance of due performance" from the other party. Until such assurance is received, she or he may "suspend" further performance without liability. What constitutes "reasonable grounds" is determined by commercial standards. If such assurances are not forthcoming within a reasonable time (not to exceed thirty days), the failure to respond may be treated as a *repudiation* of the contract [UCC 2–609, 2A–401].

For example, Zena has contracted to ship Jenkins one hundred shirts on or before October 1, with Jenkins's payment due within thirty days of delivery. Zena has made two previous shipments, but Jenkins has paid for neither of them. On September 20, Zena demands in writing certain assurances of payment (including payment for the last two orders to bring the account up to date) before she will ship the shirts. If these desired assurances are reasonable, Zena can suspend shipment of the shirts without liability pending Jenkins's compliance. If Jenkins does not provide the assurances within a reasonable time (no longer than thirty days), Zena can hold Jenkins in breach of contract without having made the contracted-for third shipment.

—The Duty of Cooperation. Sometimes, the performance of one party depends on the cooperation of the other. The UCC provides that when such cooperation is not forthcoming, the other party can suspend his or her own performance without liability and hold the uncooperative party in breach or proceed to perform the contract in any reasonable manner [UCC 2–311(3)(b)].

For example, Amati is required by contract to deliver twelve hundred model Z washing machines to locations in the state of California to be specified later by Farrell. Deliveries are to be made on or before October 1. Amati has repeatedly requested the delivery locations, but Farrell has not responded. The twelve hundred model Z machines are ready for shipment on October 1, but Farrell still refuses to give Amati delivery locations. Amati does not ship on October 1. Can Amati be held liable? The answer is no. Amati is excused for any resulting delay of performance because of Farrell's failure to cooperate.

SECTION 3 | Obligations of the Buyer or Lessee

Once the seller or lessor has adequately tendered delivery, the buyer or lessee is obligated to accept the goods and pay for them according to the terms of the contract.

PAYMENT

In the absence of any specific agreements, the buyer or lessee must make payment at the time and place the goods are *received* [UCC 2–310(a), 2A–516(1)]. When a sale is made on credit, the buyer is obliged to pay according to the specified credit terms (for example, 60, 90, or 120 days), not when the goods are received. The credit period usually begins on the *date of shipment* [UCC 2–310(d)]. Under a lease contract, a lessee must make the lease payment specified in the contract [UCC 2A–516(1)].

Payment can be made by any means agreed on between the parties—cash or any other method generally acceptable in the commercial world. If the seller demands cash when the buyer offers a check, credit card, or the like, the seller must permit the buyer reasonable time to obtain legal tender [UCC 2–511].

RIGHT OF INSPECTION

Unless the parties otherwise agree, or for C.O.D. (collect on delivery) transactions, the buyer or lessee has an absolute right to inspect the goods. This right allows the buyer or lessee to verify, before making payment, that the goods tendered or delivered are what were contracted for or ordered. If the goods are not as ordered, the buyer or lessee has no duty to pay. *An opportunity for inspection is therefore a condition precedent to the right of the seller or lessor to enforce payment* [UCC 2–513(1), 2A–515(1)].

Unless the parties otherwise agree, inspection can take place at any reasonable place and time and in any reasonable manner. Generally, what is reasonable is determined by custom of the trade, past practices of the parties, and the like. The buyer bears the costs of inspecting the goods but can recover the costs from the seller if the goods do not conform and are rejected [UCC 2–513(2)].

ACCEPTANCE

A buyer or lessee can manifest assent to the delivered goods in the following ways, each of which constitutes acceptance:

1. If, after having had a reasonable opportunity to inspect the goods, the buyer or lessee signifies to the seller or lessor that the goods either are conforming or are acceptable in spite of their nonconformity [UCC 2–606(1)(a), 2A–515(1)(a)].

2. If the buyer or lessee has had a reasonable opportunity to inspect the goods and has failed to reject them within a reasonable period of time, then acceptance is presumed [UCC 2–602(1), 2–606(1)(b), 2A–515(1)(b)].

3. In sales contracts, if the buyer performs any act inconsistent with the seller's ownership, then the buyer will be deemed to have accepted the goods. For

CONCEPT SUMMARY 22.1 | Performance of Sales and Lease Contracts

CONCEPT	DESCRIPTION
OBLIGATIONS OF THE SELLER OR LESSOR	1. The seller or lessor must tender *conforming* goods to the buyer or lessee at a *reasonable hour* and in a *reasonable manner*. Under the perfect tender doctrine, the seller or lessor must tender goods that exactly conform to the terms of the contract [UCC 2–503(1), 2A–508(1)]. 2. If the seller or lessor tenders nonconforming goods and the buyer or lessee rejects them, the seller or lessor may *cure* (repair or replace the goods) within the contract time for performance [UCC 2–508(1), 2A–513(1)]. Even if the time for performance under the contract has expired, the seller or lessor has a reasonable time to substitute conforming goods without liability if the seller or lessor has reasonable grounds to believe the nonconforming tender will be acceptable to the buyer or lessee [UCC 2–508(2), 2A–513(2)]. 3. If the agreed-on means of delivery becomes impracticable or unavailable, the seller must substitute an alternative means (such as a different carrier) if a reasonable one is available [UCC 2–614(1)]. 4. If a seller or lessor tenders nonconforming goods in any one installment under an installment contract, the buyer or lessee may reject the installment only if the nonconformity substantially impairs its value and cannot be cured. The entire installment contract is breached only when one or more installments *substantially* impair the value of the *whole* contract [UCC 2–612, 2A–510]. 5. When performance becomes commercially impracticable owing to circumstances unforeseen when the contract was formed, the perfect tender rule no longer holds [UCC 2–615, 2A–405].
OBLIGATIONS OF THE BUYER OR LESSEE	1. On tender of delivery by the seller or lessor, the buyer or lessee must pay for the goods at the time and place the goods are *received*, unless the sale is made on credit. Payment can be made by any method generally acceptable in the commercial world, but the seller can demand cash [UCC 2–310, 2–511]. 2. Unless otherwise agreed or in C.O.D. shipments, the buyer or lessee has an absolute right to inspect the goods before acceptance [UCC 2–513(1), 2A–515(1)]. 3. The buyer or lessee can manifest acceptance of delivered goods in words or by conduct, such as by failing to reject the goods after having had a reasonable opportunity to inspect them. A buyer will be deemed to have accepted goods if he or she performs any act inconsistent with the seller's ownership [UCC 2–606(1), 2A–515(1)].

example, any use or resale of the goods—except for the limited purpose of testing or inspecting the goods—generally constitutes an acceptance [UCC 2–606(1)(c)].

PARTIAL ACCEPTANCE

If some of the goods delivered do not conform to the contract and the seller or lessor has failed to cure, the buyer or lessee can make a *partial* acceptance [UCC 2–601(c), 2A–509(1)]. The same is true if the nonconformity was not reasonably discoverable before acceptance. (In the latter situation, the buyer or lessee may be able to revoke the acceptance, as will be discussed later in this chapter.)

A buyer or lessee cannot accept less than a single commercial unit, however. The UCC defines a *commercial unit* as a unit of goods that, by commercial usage, is viewed as a "single whole" for purposes of sale, and division of which would materially impair the character of the unit, its market value, or its use [UCC 2–105(6), 2A–103(c)]. A commercial unit can be a single article (such as a machine), a set of articles (such as a suite of furniture or an assortment of sizes), a quantity (such as a bale, a gross, or a carload), or any other unit treated in the trade as a single whole.

SECTION 4 | Anticipatory Repudiation

What if, before the time for contract performance, one party clearly communicates to the other the intention *not* to perform? Such an action is a breach of the contract by *anticipatory repudiation*.[8]

SUSPENSION OF PERFORMANCE OBLIGATIONS

When anticipatory repudiation occurs, the non-breaching party has a choice of two responses. One option is to treat the repudiation as a final breach by pursuing a remedy; the other is to wait and hope that the repudiating party will decide to honor her or his obligations under the contract despite the avowed intention to renege [UCC 2–610, 2A–402]. (In either situation, the nonbreaching party may suspend performance.)

The following case illustrates the concept of anticipatory repudiation.

---

8. Refer back to Chapter 17 for a discussion of the common law origins and application of the doctrine of anticipatory repudiation.

CASE 22.2 | **Banco International, Inc. v. Goody's Family Clothing**

United States District Court, Eastern District of Tennessee, 1999. 54 F.Supp.2d 765.

MURRIAN, United States Magistrate Judge.
* * * *

In April, 1994, [Banco International, Inc., and Goody's Family Clothing] entered into a series of purchase orders for the development and delivery of custom made, private label boys and girls windsuits (jogging suits). The contracts were for a total of 62,748 windsuits at a total contract price of $749,103.60. The first shipment of 26,640 windsuits had to be at Goody's distribution center in Knoxville, Tennessee, by September 30, 1994, or the order was subject to cancellation.

Goody's orally canceled the entire contract (all six purchase orders) at approximately 3:00 P.M., Knoxville, Tennessee, time on August 23, 1994. This was accomplished by a telephone call to Banco's headquarters in Humble, Texas. This notice was then immediately passed along to Muhammed Akhtar, the president and owner of Banco, who was in Bangladesh where the windsuits were to be manufactured. Bangladesh time is 12 hours ahead of Eastern Daylight Time and so Mr. Akhtar received notice of the cancellation around 3:00 A.M. in Bangladesh on August 24, 1994. Mr. Akhtar called Tom Baatz, Goody's boy's wear buyer, and asked if the contract was indeed canceled. Mr. Baatz told him it was due to Banco's dispute with its subcontractor. * * * Mr. Akhtar represented that although Banco was behind schedule, it could meet the September 30, 1994, delivery date for the first shipment if it shipped by air freight, it could meet the October 5 deadline for the second shipment if it shipped by air freight, and it could meet the delivery deadline for the third shipment by shipping by sea. Shipping by air freight was over six times more expensive than shipping by sea and Banco would have to absorb the cost.

CONTINUED ▶

CASE 22.2 | Continued

Goody's did not accept Banco's assurances of performance and formally confirmed cancellation of the entire contract by letter dated August 29, 1994. [Banco then filed a suit in a federal district court against Goody's, alleging breach of contract. Goody's argued there was an anticipatory repudiation, or breach, of the contract by Banco.]

*   *   *   *

At the inception of this contract, Mr. Akhtar had led Goody's to believe that the windsuits would be produced in Banco's factory. Goody's was not aware that production was going to be subcontracted to Attune or City Apparel. It therefore came as a shock and surprise when the Managing Director of Attune, Towhid Islam Ratan, spoke by telephone with Randy Hodge at Goody's on August 23, 1994, and told Hodge that Attune was in possession of all the fabric and other raw materials for the contract; that Attune and Banco were in a dispute over an alleged $70,000 debt Banco had to Attune; that Attune would not ship Goody's order through Banco; that the shipment had been "momentarily delayed"; but that Attune was willing to produce the garments for Goody's under certain conditions, including [payment to Attune] by Goody's. *   *   *

*   *   *   *

*   *   * *It is not necessary for [anticipatory] repudiation that performance be made literally and utterly impossible. Repudiation can result from action which reasonably indicates a rejection of the continuing obligation.* [Emphasis added.]

Banco's failure to start actual production of the windsuits prior to cancellation of the contract on August 23, 1994, Banco's apparent inability to gain possession and control of the fabric and other raw materials necessary to perform the contract, Banco's false representations about production, and Banco's failure to give Goody's adequate assurances that it could perform the contract in a timely manner during the days following cancellation are the primary actions by Banco which reasonably indicated to Goody's that Banco had rejected its continuing obligation under the contract. These actions justified Goody's suspension of its own performance and cancellation of the contract.

In all contracts governed by Article 2 of the Uniform Commercial Code there is a continuing obligation of good faith and reasonableness. In this case, Goody's came to realize by August 23, 1994, that Mr. Akhtar had not been truthful with Goody's about the status of production of the windsuits; Goody's had reason to believe that the production samples were not production samples at all; Banco did not have possession of the fabric and raw materials to perform the contract; and, as far as Goody's knew, Banco had no prospects of obtaining possession and control of those raw materials. In the days subsequent to the cancellation, Banco's proffered [offered] "reasonable assurances" consisted of more promises from Mr. Akhtar (whose credibility had been severely damaged) but without an explanation of just how Banco proposed to perform because Mr. Akhtar believed it was "none of Goody's business."

*   *   * It was this apparent inability to perform without a substantial breach of the contract that justified Goody's in canceling the contract and in refusing Banco's proffered "reasonable assurances" of performance.

I find that Goody's was justified in reasonably concluding that Banco could not deliver the windsuits to it by the date set in the first purchase order between the parties. Additionally, the failure to deliver the goods by that date would have substantially impaired the value of those goods to Goody's. *   *   * Therefore, Goody's is not liable for canceling those remaining deliveries.

For the reasons indicated, judgment will enter in Goody's favor and Banco will take nothing on its claim.

QUESTIONS

1. What did Banco International do or fail to do that "reasonably indicated a rejection" of its contractual obligation to Goody's?
2. If Banco International assured Goody's that it could have the shipments to Goody's on time, why did the court not accept this as a reasonable assurance of performance?

REPUDIATION MAY BE RETRACTED

The UCC permits the breaching party (subject to some limitations) to "retract" his or her repudiation. This can be done by any method that clearly indicates the party's intent to perform. Once retraction is made, the rights of the repudiating party under the contract are reinstated. The breaching party cannot retract the repudiation, however, if since the time of the repudiation the other party has canceled or materially changed position or otherwise indicated that the repudiation is final [UCC 2–611, 2A–403].

For example, assume that Cora, who owns a small inn, purchases a suite of furniture from Horton's Furniture Warehouse on April 1. The contract states that "delivery must be made on or before May 1." On April 10, Horton informs Cora that he cannot make delivery until May 10 and asks her to consent to the modified delivery date. In this situation, Cora has the option of either treating Horton's notice of late delivery as a final breach of contract and pursuing a remedy or agreeing to the later delivery date. Suppose that Cora does neither for two weeks. On April 24, Horton informs Cora that he will be able to deliver the furniture by May 1 after all. In effect, Horton has retracted his repudiation, reinstating the rights and obligations of the parties under the original contract. Note that if Cora had indicated after Horton's repudiation that she was canceling the contract, Horton would not have been able to retract his repudiation.

SECTION 5 | Remedies of the Seller or Lessor

Numerous remedies are available under the UCC to a seller or lessor when the buyer or lessee is in breach. Generally, the remedies available to the seller or lessor depend on the circumstances existing at the time of the breach, such as which party has possession of the goods, whether the goods are in transit, whether the buyer or lessee has rejected or accepted the goods, and so on.

WHEN THE GOODS ARE IN THE POSSESSION OF THE SELLER OR LESSOR

Under the UCC, if the buyer or lessee breaches the contract before the goods have been delivered to her or him, the seller or lessor has the right to pursue the remedies discussed here.

THE RIGHT TO CANCEL THE CONTRACT One of the options available to a seller or lessor when the buyer or lessee breaches the contract is simply to cancel the contract [UCC 2–703(f), 2A–523(1)(a)]. The seller or lessor must notify the buyer or lessee of the cancellation, and at that point all remaining obligations of the seller or lessor are discharged. The buyer or lessee is not discharged from all remaining obligations, however; he or she is in breach, and the seller or lessor can pursue remedies available under the UCC for breach.

THE RIGHT TO WITHHOLD DELIVERY In general, sellers and lessors can withhold or discontinue performance of their obligations under sales or lease contracts when the buyers or lessees are in breach. If a buyer or lessee has wrongfully rejected or revoked acceptance of contract goods (rejection and revocation of acceptance will be discussed later in this chapter), failed to make proper and timely payment, or repudiated a part of the contract, the seller or lessor can withhold delivery of the goods in question [UCC 2–703(a), 2A–523(1)(c)]. If the breach results from the buyer's or the lessee's insolvency (inability to pay debts as they become due), the seller or lessor can refuse to deliver the goods unless the buyer or lessee pays in cash [UCC 2–702(1), 2A–525(1)].

THE RIGHT TO RESELL OR DISPOSE OF THE GOODS When a buyer or lessee breaches or repudiates the contract while the seller or lessor is still in possession of the goods, the seller or lessor can resell or dispose of the goods, holding the buyer or lessee liable for any loss [UCC 2–703(d), 2–706(1), 2A–523(1)(e), 2A–527(1)].[9]

---

9. Under the 2003 amendments to UCC Articles 2 and 2A, this loss includes consequential damages, except that a seller or lessor cannot recover consequential damages from a consumer under a consumer contract or lease [Amended UCC 2–706(1), 2–710, 2A–527(2), 2A–530]. Consequential damages may also be recovered, except from a consumer under a consumer contract or lease, when a seller or lessor has a right to recover the purchase price or lease payments due or to recover other damages [Amended UCC 2–708(1), 2–709(1), 2–710, 2A–528(1), 2A–529(1), 2A–530]. Subtracted from these amounts, of course, would be any expenses saved as a consequence of the buyer's or lessee's breach.

—Unfinished Goods. When the goods contracted for are unfinished at the time of breach, the seller or lessor can do one of two things: (1) cease manufacturing the goods and resell them for scrap or salvage value or (2) complete the manufacture and resell or dispose of the goods, holding the buyer or lessee liable for any deficiency. In choosing between these two alternatives, the seller or lessor must exercise reasonable commercial judgment in order to mitigate the loss and obtain maximum value from the unfinished goods [UCC 2–704(2), 2A–524(2)]. Any resale of the goods must be made in good faith and in a commercially reasonable manner.

In sales transactions, the seller can recover any deficiency between the resale price and the contract price, along with *incidental damages*, defined as those costs to the seller resulting from the breach [UCC 2–706(1), 2–710]. The resale can be private or public, and the goods can be sold as a unit or in parcels.

—Requirements Related to Resales. The seller must give the original buyer reasonable notice of the resale, unless the goods are perishable or will rapidly decline in value [UCC 2–706(2), (3)]. A good faith purchaser in a resale takes the goods free of any of the rights of the original buyer, even if the seller fails to comply with this requirement [UCC 2–706(5)]. The UCC encourages the resale of the goods because although the buyer is liable for any deficiency, the seller is not accountable to the buyer for any profits made on the resale [UCC 2–706(6)].

—Leased Goods. In lease transactions, the lessor may lease the goods to another party and recover from the original lessee, as damages, any unpaid lease payments up to the beginning date of the lease term under the new lease. The lessor can also recover any deficiency between the lease payments due under the original lease contract and those under the new lease contract, along with incidental damages [UCC 2A–527(2)].

THE RIGHT TO RECOVER THE PURCHASE PRICE OR LEASE PAYMENTS DUE Under the UCC, an unpaid seller or lessor who is unable to resell or dispose of the goods can bring an action to recover the purchase price or the payments due under the lease contract, plus incidental damages [UCC 2–709(1),

2A–529(1)]. If a seller or lessor sues under these circumstances, the goods must be held for the buyer or lessee. The seller or lessor can resell or dispose of the goods at any time prior to collection of the judgment from the buyer or lessee, but in that situation the net proceeds from the sale must be credited to the buyer or lessee. This illustrates the duty to mitigate damages.

For example, suppose that Southern Realty contracts with Gem Point, Inc., to purchase one thousand pens with Southern Realty's name inscribed on them. Gem Point delivers the pens, but Southern Realty refuses to pay for them. In this situation, Gem Point has, as a proper remedy, an action for the purchase price. Gem Point has delivered conforming goods, and Southern Realty, because it has failed to pay, is in breach. Gem Point obviously cannot sell pens that are in the hands of the buyer. Also, because the pens are inscribed with the buyer's business name, Gem Point could not sell them to anyone else, so this situation falls under UCC 2–709.

THE RIGHT TO RECOVER DAMAGES If a buyer or lessee repudiates a contract or wrongfully refuses to accept the goods, a seller or lessor can maintain an action to recover the damages sustained. Ordinarily, the amount of damages equals the difference between the contract price or lease payments and the market price or lease payments at the time and place of tender of the goods, plus incidental damages [UCC 2–708(1), 2A–528(1)]. The time and place of tender are frequently given by such terms as F.O.B., F.A.S., C.I.F.,[10] and the like, which determine whether there is a shipment or a destination contract.

If the difference between the contract price or payments due under the lease contract and the market price or lease payments is too small to place the seller or lessor in the position that he or she would have been in if the buyer or lessee had fully performed, the proper measure of damages is the lost profits of the seller or lessor, including a reasonable allowance for overhead and other expenses [UCC 2–708(2), 2A–528(2)].

In the following case, the issue had to do with the proper measure of damages after a buyer had breached a sales contract.

---

10. See Exhibit 21–1 in Chapter 21 for a definition of these contract terms, which are eliminated in the 2003 amendments to Article 2 [Amended UCC 2–319 through 2–324].

CASE 22.3 — Utica Alloys, Inc. v. Alcoa, Inc.

United States
District Court,
Northern District
of New York. 2004.
303 F.Supp.2d 247.

BACKGROUND AND FACTS *Alcoa, Inc., through its business, generates scrap metal. Utica Alloys, Inc., buys and processes this type of scrap and sells it to its only buyer, General Electric Company (GE), which uses it in land-based power turbines. In July 2001, Utica agreed to buy all of Alcoa's scrap through August 2003. Their contract indexed the monthly price of the scrap to the monthly market price of nickel but contemplated that the parties would review this price semiannually. In November, GE reduced its production of turbines, which lowered the market value of the scrap. This change was not reflected in Alcoa's arrangement with Utica, however, because the price in their contract was based on the market value of nickel. In January 2002, the opportunity arose to review the scrap's price, and the parties began to negotiate while they continued to ship and process it. Unable to agree on a price, Alcoa stated in May that the contract was terminated and retrieved the scrap processed after January, which Alcoa then sold to another party. Utica filed a suit in a federal district court against Alcoa, alleging in part unjust enrichment. Alcoa counterclaimed for breach of contract, asking for damages based on the difference between the contract price for the unprocessed scrap and the price for which the processed scrap was sold after it was retrieved.*

IN THE LANGUAGE OF THE COURT

HURD, District Judge.

* * * *

* * * Defendant claims its measure of damages is the difference between the purchase agreement price of the scrap and the price for which it sold the processed scrap it retrieved from plaintiff.

This, however, would serve as a double penalty to Utica Alloys, Inc. for processing the scrap. Absent the purchase agreement, Alcoa Inc. would have sold the scrap at the unprocessed market price. Because of the purchase agreement, it is entitled to the higher purchase agreement price. The processed feature of the scrap, as Alcoa Inc. points out numerous times, was not part of the agreement between the parties and actually decreased its value because of the demand reduction in the market for such scrap. However, Alcoa Inc. accepted return of the processed scrap from Utica Alloys, Inc. when it elected to terminate the purchase agreement in May 2002. It has also refused to pay plaintiff for processing the scrap. Defendant cannot be permitted in one breath to denounce processing as irrelevant to the contractual relationship, while in another embrace the market change of processed scrap as the yardstick for measuring its damages under the contract.

Therefore, *the proper measure of damages is the difference between the purchase price of the unprocessed scrap, as such is calculated under the purchase agreement, and the market value of unprocessed scrap.* The market value of unprocessed scrap is not to be determined solely from the amount for which Alcoa Inc. was able to sell the scrap in May of 2002. *Rather, because the purchase agreement called for monthly shipments and prices, damages will have to be ascertained for three different time periods.* The following determinations will therefore need to be made, for each of the months from February to April of 2002, before the proper amount of total damages can be calculated: (1) the amount, *in pounds*, of scrap shipped during each of the relevant months; (2) the per pound purchase agreement price, calculated *using the formula in the agreement*, for each of the relevant months; and (3) the per pound *fair market value of unprocessed scrap* for each of the three months. The damages will be calculated for each of the three months, and will then be added together to determine defendant's total damages for plaintiff's failure to pay for the scrap it was shipped. The parties will be permitted to submit * * * *only* the three *figures*, as well as any facts/figures supporting the same, required *for each month*. [Emphasis added.]

* * * *

CONTINUED

CASE 22.3 | Continued   * * * Defendant is * * * entitled to judgment on its counterclaim, and may receive as damages for plaintiff's failure to pay for scrap shipped and received under the purchase agreement the difference between the monthly purchase agreement price for such scrap and the monthly fair market value of unprocessed scrap. * * *

DECISION AND REMEDY *The federal district court entered a judgment for the defendant and awarded damages based on the difference between the contract's monthly price for the unprocessed scrap and the monthly fair market value of unprocessed scrap.*

WHEN THE GOODS ARE IN TRANSIT

When the seller or lessor has delivered the goods to a carrier or a bailee but the buyer or lessee has not yet received them, the goods are said to be *in transit*. If, while the goods are in transit, the seller or lessor learns that the buyer or lessee is insolvent, the seller or lessor can stop the carrier or bailee from delivering the goods, regardless of the quantity of goods shipped. If the buyer or lessee is in breach but is not insolvent, the seller or lessor can stop the goods in transit only if the quantity shipped is at least a carload, a truckload, a planeload, or a larger shipment [UCC 2–705(1), 2A–526(1)].[11]

To stop delivery, the seller or lessor must *timely notify* the carrier or other bailee that the goods are to be returned or held for the seller or lessor. If the carrier has sufficient time to stop delivery, the goods must be held and delivered according to the instructions of the seller or lessor, who is liable to the carrier for any additional costs incurred [UCC 2–705(3), 2A–526(3)].

The seller or lessor has the right to stop delivery of the goods under UCC 2–705(2) and 2A–526(2) until the time when:

1. The buyer or lessee receives the goods.
2. The carrier or the bailee acknowledges the rights of the buyer or lessee in the goods (by reshipping or holding the goods for the buyer or lessee, for example).
3. A negotiable document of title covering the goods has been properly transferred to the buyer in sales transactions, giving the buyer ownership rights in the goods [UCC 2–705(2)].

WHEN THE GOODS ARE IN THE POSSESSION OF THE BUYER OR LESSEE

When the buyer or lessee breaches a sales or lease contract and the goods are in her or his possession, the UCC gives the seller or lessor the right to choose among various remedies.

THE RIGHT TO RECOVER THE PURCHASE PRICE OR THE PAYMENTS DUE UNDER THE LEASE CONTRACT If the buyer or lessee has accepted the goods but refuses to pay for them, the seller or lessor can sue for the purchase price of the goods or for the lease payments due, plus incidental damages [UCC 2–709(1), 2A–529(1)].

THE RIGHT TO RECLAIM GOODS In a sales transaction, if a seller discovers that the buyer has received goods on credit and is insolvent, the seller can demand return of the goods. Ordinarily, the demand must be made within ten days of the buyer's receipt of the goods. The seller can demand and reclaim the goods at any time, though, if the buyer misrepresented his or her solvency in writing within three months prior to the delivery of the goods [UCC 2–702(2)].[12] The seller's right to reclaim the goods is subject to the rights of a good faith purchaser or other subsequent buyer in the ordinary course of business who purchases the goods from the buyer before the seller reclaims them.

Under the UCC, a seller seeking to exercise the right to reclaim goods receives preferential treatment over the buyer's other creditors—the seller need only demand the return of the goods within ten days after the buyer has received them.[13] Because of this preferential treatment, the UCC provides that successful reclamation (reclaiming) of goods excludes all other remedies with respect to those goods [UCC 2–702(3)].

In regard to lease contracts, if the lessee is in default (fails to make payments that are due, for example) the lessor may reclaim the leased goods that are in the lessee's possession [UCC 2A–525(2)].

---

11. The 2003 amendments to UCC Articles 2 and 2A omit the restriction that prohibits the stoppage of less than "a carload, truckload, planeload, or larger shipments" because carriers can now identify a shipment as small as a single package [Amended UCC 2–705(1), 2A–526(1)].

12. The 2003 amendments to UCC Article 2 omit the ten-day limitation and the three-month exception to the ten-day limitation, referring instead to "a reasonable time" [Amended UCC 2–702(2)].
13. A seller who has delivered goods to an insolvent buyer also receives preferential treatment if the buyer enters into bankruptcy proceedings (discussed in Chapter 30).

SECTION 6 | Remedies of the Buyer or Lessee

Under the UCC, numerous remedies are available to the buyer or lessee when the seller or lessor breaches the contract. Like the remedies available to sellers and lessors, the remedies available to buyers and lessees depend on the circumstances existing at the time of the breach.

WHEN THE SELLER OR LESSOR REFUSES TO DELIVER THE GOODS

If the seller or lessor refuses to deliver the goods to the buyer or lessee, the remedies available to the buyer or lessee include those discussed here.

THE RIGHT TO CANCEL THE CONTRACT When a seller or lessor fails to make proper delivery or repudiates the contract, the buyer or lessee can cancel, or rescind, the contract. On giving notice of cancellation, the buyer or lessee is relieved of any further obligations under the contract but retains all rights to other remedies against the seller or lessor [UCC 2–711(1), 2A–508(1)(a)]. (The right to cancel the contract is also available to a buyer or lessee who has rightfully rejected goods or revoked acceptance, as will be discussed shortly.)

THE RIGHT TO RECOVER THE GOODS If a buyer or lessee has made a partial or full payment for goods that remain in the possession of the seller or lessor, the buyer or lessee can recover the goods if the seller or lessor becomes insolvent within ten days after receiving the first payment and if the goods are identified to the contract. To exercise this right, the buyer or lessee must tender to the seller or lessor any unpaid balance of the purchase price or lease payments [UCC 2–502, 2A–522].[14]

THE RIGHT TO OBTAIN SPECIFIC PERFORMANCE
A buyer or lessee can obtain specific performance when the goods are unique or when the remedy at law is inadequate [UCC 2–716(1), 2A–521(1)].[15] Ordinarily, an award of money damages is sufficient to place a buyer or lessee in the position she or he would have occupied if the seller or lessor had fully performed. When the contract is for the purchase of a particular work of art or a similarly unique item, however, money damages may not be sufficient. Under these circumstances, equity requires that the seller or lessor perform exactly by delivering the particular goods identified to the contract (the remedy of specific performance).

THE RIGHT OF COVER In certain situations, buyers and lessees can protect themselves by obtaining **cover**—that is, by buying or leasing substitute goods for those that were due under the contract. This option is available when the seller or lessor repudiates the contract or fails to deliver the goods.[16]

In obtaining cover, the buyer or lessee must act in good faith and without unreasonable delay [UCC 2–712, 2A–518]. After purchasing or leasing substitute goods, the buyer or lessee can recover from the seller or lessor the difference between the cost of cover and the contract price (or lease payments), plus incidental and consequential damages, less the expenses (such as delivery costs) that were saved as a result of the breach [UCC 2–712, 2–715, 2A–518]. Consequential damages are any losses suffered by the buyer or lessee that the seller or lessor could have foreseen (had reason to know about) at the time of contract formation and any injury to the buyer's or lessee's person or property proximately resulting from the contract's breach [UCC 2–715(2), 2A–520(2)].

Buyers and lessees are not required to cover, and failure to do so will not bar them from using any other remedies available under the UCC. A buyer or lessee who fails to cover, however, risks not being able to collect consequential damages that could have been avoided had he or she purchased or leased substitute goods.

THE RIGHT TO REPLEVY GOODS Buyers and lessees also have the right to replevy goods. **Replevin**[17]

---

14. The 2003 amendments to UCC Articles 2 and 2A create a new right to recover goods identified to a contract when a consumer buyer or lessee makes a down payment and the seller or lessor then repudiates the contract or lease or fails to deliver the goods [Amended UCC 2–502(1)(a), 2A–522].

15. The 2003 amendments to UCC Articles 2 and 2A provide that in nonconsumer contracts and leases, the parties can explicitly agree that specific performance will be available as a remedy unless the breaching party's only remaining obligation is the payment of money [Amended 2–716(1), 2A–507].

16. The right to obtain cover is also available to a buyer or lessee who has rightfully rejected goods or revoked acceptance. Rejection and revocation of acceptance will be discussed shortly.

17. Pronounced ruh-*pleh*-vun.

is an action to recover identified goods in the hands of a party who is unlawfully withholding them. Outside the UCC, the term *replevin* refers to a prejudgment process (a proceeding that takes place prior to a court's judgment) involving the seizure of specific personal property in which a party claims a right or an interest. Under the UCC, a buyer or lessee can replevy goods subject to the contract if the seller or lessor has repudiated or breached the contract. To maintain an action to replevy goods, buyers and lessees must usually show that they were unable to cover for the goods after making a reasonable effort [UCC 2–716(3), 2A–521(3)].

THE RIGHT TO RECOVER DAMAGES   If a seller or lessor repudiates the contract or fails to deliver the goods, the buyer or lessee can sue for damages. The measure of recovery is the difference between the contract price (or lease payments) and the market price of the goods (or lease payments that could be obtained for the goods) at the time the buyer (or lessee) *learned* of the breach.[18] The market price or market lease payments are determined at the place where the seller or lessor was supposed to deliver the goods. The buyer or lessee can also recover incidental and consequential damages less the expenses that were saved as a result of the breach [UCC 2–713, 2A–519].

Consider an example. Schilling orders 10,000 bushels of wheat from Valdone for $5.00 a bushel, with delivery due on June 14 and payment due on June 20. Valdone does not deliver on June 14. On June 14, the market price of wheat is $5.50 per bushel. Schilling chooses to do without the wheat. He sues Valdone for damages for nondelivery. Schilling can recover $0.50 × 10,000, or $5,000, plus any expenses the breach has caused him. The measure of damages is the market price on the day Schilling was to have received delivery less the contract price. (Any expenses Schilling saved by the breach would be deducted from the damages.)

WHEN THE SELLER OR LESSOR DELIVERS NONCONFORMING GOODS

When the seller or lessor delivers nonconforming goods, the buyer or lessee has several remedies available under the UCC.

THE RIGHT TO REJECT THE GOODS   If either the goods or the tender of the goods by the seller or lessor fails to conform to the contract in any respect, the buyer or lessee can reject the goods in whole or in part [UCC 2–601, 2A–509]. If the buyer or lessee rejects the goods, she or he may then obtain cover or cancel the contract, just as if the seller or lessor had refused to deliver the goods (see the earlier discussion of these remedies).

—Timeliness and Reason for Rejection Required. The buyer or lessee must reject the goods within a reasonable amount of time after delivery or tender of delivery and must seasonably (timely) notify the seller or lessor [UCC 2–602(1), 2A–509(2)]. If the buyer or lessee fails to reject the goods within a reasonable amount of time, acceptance will be presumed. The buyer or lessee must also designate defects that are ascertainable by reasonable inspection. Failure to do so precludes the buyer or lessee from using such defects to justify rejection or to establish breach when the seller or lessor could have cured the defects if they had been disclosed seasonably [UCC 2–605, 2A–514].[19]

—Duties of Merchant Buyers and Lessees When Goods Are Rejected. Suppose that a *merchant buyer* or *lessee* rightfully rejects goods and the seller or lessor has no agent or business at the place of rejection. What should the buyer or lessee do in that situation? Under the UCC, the merchant buyer or lessee has a good faith obligation to follow any reasonable instructions received from the seller or lessor with respect to the goods [UCC 2–603, 2A–511]. The buyer or lessee is entitled to be reimbursed for the care and cost entailed in following the instructions. The same requirements hold if the buyer or lessee rightfully revokes her or his acceptance of the goods at some later time [UCC 2–608(3), 2A–517(5)]. (Revocation of acceptance will be discussed shortly.)

If no instructions are forthcoming and the goods are perishable or threaten to decline in value quickly, the buyer or lessee can resell the goods in good faith, taking appropriate reimbursement and a selling commission (not to exceed 10 percent of the gross proceeds) from the proceeds [UCC 2–603(1), (2);

---

18. The 2003 amendments to UCC Article 2 change the rule that the time for measuring damages is the time that the buyer learned of the breach. In a case not involving repudiation, the buyer's damages are to be based on the market price at the time for tender [Amended UCC 2–713(1)(a)].

19. The 2003 amendments to UCC 2–605 and 2A–514 change this restriction. Under the amendments, a buyer's or lessee's failure to disclose the nature of the defect affects only the right to reject or revoke acceptance, not the right to establish a breach. The new sections expressly require that the seller or lessor have had a right to cure, as well as the ability to cure.

2A–511(1)]. If the goods are not perishable, the buyer or lessee may store them for the seller or lessor or reship them to the seller or lessor [UCC 2–604, 2A–512].[20]

—*Buyer's Security Interest in the Goods.* Buyers who rightfully reject goods (or who justifiably revoke acceptance of goods—discussed next) that remain in their possession or control have a *security interest* in the goods (basically, a legal claim to the goods to the extent necessary to recover expenses, costs, and the like—see Chapter 29). The security interest encompasses any payments the buyer has made for the goods, as well as any expenses incurred with regard to inspection, receipt, transportation, care, and custody of the goods [UCC 2–711(3)]. A buyer with a security interest in the goods has the same rights as an unpaid seller. Thus, the buyer can resell, withhold delivery of, or stop delivery of the goods. A buyer who chooses to resell must account to the seller for any amounts received in excess of the security interest [UCC 2–706(6), 2–711].

REVOCATION OF ACCEPTANCE Acceptance of the goods precludes the buyer or lessee from exercising the right of rejection, but it does not necessarily preclude the buyer or lessee from pursuing other remedies (discussed later in this chapter). Additionally, in certain circumstances, a buyer or lessee is permitted to *revoke* his or her acceptance of the goods. Acceptance of a lot or a commercial unit can be revoked if the nonconformity *substantially* impairs the value of the lot or unit and if one of the following factors is present:

1. Acceptance was predicated on the reasonable assumption that the nonconformity would be cured, and it has not been cured within a reasonable period of time [UCC 2–608(1)(a), 2A–517(1)(a)].[21]

2. The buyer or lessee did not discover the nonconformity before acceptance, either because it was difficult to discover before acceptance or because assurances made by the seller or lessor that the goods were conforming kept the buyer or lessee from inspecting the goods [UCC 2–608(1)(b), 2A–517(1)(b)].

Revocation of acceptance is not effective until notice is given to the seller or lessor. Notice must occur within a reasonable time after the buyer or lessee either discovers or *should have discovered* the grounds for revocation. Additionally, revocation must occur before the goods have undergone any substantial change (such as spoilage) not caused by their own defects [UCC 2–608(2), 2A–517(4)]. Once acceptance is revoked, the buyer or lessee can pursue remedies, just as if the goods had been rejected.

THE RIGHT TO RECOVER DAMAGES FOR ACCEPTED GOODS A buyer or lessee who has accepted nonconforming goods may also keep the goods and recover for any loss "resulting in the ordinary course of events . . . as determined in any manner which is reasonable" [UCC 2–714(1), 2A–519(3)]. The buyer or lessee, however, must notify the seller or lessor of the breach within a reasonable time after the defect was or should have been discovered. Otherwise, the buyer or lessee cannot recover from the seller or lessor damages caused by defects in the goods [UCC 2–607(3), 2A–516(3)].[22] In addition, the parties to a sales or lease contract can insert a provision requiring that the buyer or lessee give notice of any defects in the goods within a prescribed period.

When the goods delivered are not as warranted, the measure of damages equals the difference between the value of the goods as accepted and their value if they had been delivered as warranted, unless special circumstances show proximately caused damages of a different amount [UCC 2–714(2), 2A–519(4)]. The buyer or lessee is also entitled to incidental and consequential damages when appropriate [UCC 2–714(3), 2A–519]. The UCC further permits the buyer or lessee, with proper notice to the seller or lessor, to deduct all or any part of the damages from the price or lease payments still due under the contract [UCC 2–717, 2A–516(1)].

Is two years after a sale of goods a reasonable time period in which to discover a defect in those goods and notify the seller or lessor of a breach? That was the question in the following case.

---

20. Under the 2003 amendments to UCC 2–608(4) and 2A–517(6), use of the goods by the buyer or lessee following rejection or revocation of acceptance is not wrongful if the use is reasonable in the circumstances, as it would be, for example, in an attempt to mitigate damages. Of course, the buyer or lessee must compensate the seller or lessor for the value of the use.
21. Under the 2003 amendments to UCC 2–508 and 2A–513, cure after a justifiable revocation of acceptance is *not* available as a matter of right in a consumer contract or lease.

---

22. Under the 2003 amendments to UCC Articles 2 and 2A, a buyer or lessee who fails to give timely notice is barred from recovery for the breach but only "to the extent that the seller is prejudiced by the failure." In other words, if the seller is not harmed by the buyer's failure to notify, the buyer may still recover [Amended UCC 2–607(3)(a), 2A–516(3)(a)].

CASE 22.4   Fitl v. Strek

Supreme Court
of Nebraska, 2005.
269 Neb. 51,
690 N.W.2d 605.
http://www.findlaw.com/
11stategov/ne/neca.html [a]

BACKGROUND AND FACTS *Over the Labor Day weekend in 1995, James Fitl attended a sports-card show in San Francisco, California, where he met Mark Strek, doing business as Star Cards of San Francisco, an exhibitor at the show. Later, on Strek's representation that a certain 1952 Mickey Mantle Topps baseball card was in near-mint condition, Fitl bought the card from Strek for $17,750. Strek delivered it to Fitl in Omaha, Nebraska, where Fitl placed it in a safe-deposit box. In May 1997, Fitl sent the card to Professional Sports Authenticators (PSA), a sports-cards grading service. PSA told Fitl that the card was ungradable because it had been discolored and doctored. Fitl complained to Strek, who replied that Fitl should have initiated a return of the card within "a typical grace period for the unconditional return of a card, . . . 7 days to 1 month" of its receipt. In August, Fitl sent the card to ASA Accugrade, Inc. (ASA), another grading service, for a second opinion on its value. ASA also concluded that the card had been refinished and trimmed. Fitl filed a suit in a Nebraska state court against Strek, seeking damages. The court awarded Fitl $17,750, plus his court costs. Strek appealed to the Nebraska Supreme Court.*

IN THE LANGUAGE OF THE COURT

WRIGHT, J. [Justice]
        * * * *
        Strek claims that the [trial] court erred in determining that notification of the defective condition of the baseball card 2 years after the date of purchase was timely pursuant to [UCC] 2–607(3)(a).
        * * * The [trial] court found that Fitl had notified Strek within a reasonable time after discovery of the breach. Therefore, our review is whether the [trial] court's finding as to the reasonableness of the notice was clearly erroneous.
        Section 2–607(3)(a) states: "Where a tender has been accepted * * * the buyer must within a reasonable time after he discovers or should have discovered any breach notify the seller of breach or be barred from any remedy." [Under UCC 1–204(2)] *"[w]hat is a reasonable time for taking any action depends on the nature, purpose and circumstances of such action."* [Emphasis added.]
        The notice requirement set forth in Section 2–607(3)(a) serves three purposes. * * *
        * * * The most important one is to enable the seller to make efforts to cure the breach by making adjustments or replacements in order to minimize the buyer's damages and the seller's liability. A second policy is to provide the seller a reasonable opportunity to learn the facts so that he may adequately prepare for negotiation and defend himself in a suit. A third policy * * * is the same as the policy behind statutes of limitation: to provide a seller with a terminal point in time for liability.
        * * * *[A] party is justified in relying upon a representation made to the party as a positive statement of fact when an investigation would be required to ascertain its falsity.* In order for Fitl to have determined that the baseball card had been altered, he would have been required to conduct an investigation. We find that he was not required to do so. Once Fitl learned that the baseball card had been altered, he gave notice to Strek. [Emphasis added.]
        * * * [O]ne of the most important policies behind the notice requirement * * * is to allow the seller to cure the breach by making adjustments or replacements to minimize the buyer's damages and the seller's liability. However, even if Fitl had learned immediately upon taking possession of the baseball card that it was not authentic and had notified Strek at that time, there is no evidence that Strek could have made any adjustment or taken any action that would have minimized his liability. In its altered condition, the baseball card was worthless.
        * * * Earlier notification would not have helped Strek prepare for negotiation or defend himself in a suit because the damage to Fitl could not be repaired. Thus, the policies

---

a. In the "Supreme Court Opinions" section, in the "2005" row, click on "January." In the result, click on the appropriate link next to the name of the case to access the opinion.

CASE 22.4 | Continued

behind the notice requirement, to allow the seller to correct a defect, to prepare for negotiation and litigation, and to protect against stale claims at a time beyond which an investigation can be completed, were not unfairly prejudiced by the lack of an earlier notice to Strek. Any problem Strek may have had with the party from whom he obtained the baseball card was a separate matter from his transaction with Fitl, and an investigation into the source of the altered card would not have minimized Fitl's damages.

DECISION AND REMEDY *The state supreme court affirmed the decision of the lower court. In the circumstances of this case, notice of a defect in the goods two years after their purchase was reasonable. The buyer had reasonably relied on the seller's representation that the goods were "authentic" (which they were not), and when their defects were discovered, the buyer had given a timely notice.*

WHAT IF THE FACTS WERE DIFFERENT? *Suppose that Fitl and Strek had included in their agreement a clause requiring Fitl to give notice of any defect in the card within "7 days to 1 month" of its receipt. Would the result have been different? Why or why not?*

SECTION 7 | Additional Provisions Affecting Remedies

The parties to a sales or lease contract can vary their respective rights and obligations by contractual agreement. For example, a seller and buyer can expressly provide for remedies in addition to those provided in the UCC. They can also specify remedies in lieu of those provided in the UCC, or they can change the measure of damages. As under the common law of contracts, they may also include clauses in their contracts providing for liquidated damages in the event of a breach or a delay in performance (see Chapter 18).

Additionally, a seller can stipulate that the buyer's only remedy on the seller's breach will be repair or replacement of the item, or the seller can limit the buyer's remedy to return of the goods and refund of the purchase price. In sales and lease contracts, an agreed-on remedy is in addition to those provided in the UCC unless the parties expressly agree that the remedy is exclusive of all others [UCC 2–719(1), 2A–503(1)]. State "lemon-law" statutes also furnish additional remedies to buyers in contracts involving the sales of automobiles.

EXCLUSIVE REMEDIES

If the parties state that a remedy is *exclusive*, then it is the sole remedy. For example, suppose that Standard Tool Company agrees to sell a pipe-cutting machine to United Pipe & Tubing Corporation. The contract limits United's remedy exclusively to repair or replacement of any defective parts. Thus, repair or replacement of defective parts is the buyer's exclusive remedy under this contract.

When circumstances cause an exclusive remedy to fail in its essential purpose, however, it is no longer exclusive [UCC 2–719(2), 2A–503(2)]. In the example just given, suppose that Standard Tool Company was unable to repair a defective part, and no replacement parts were available. In this situation, because the exclusive remedy failed in its essential purpose, the buyer could pursue other remedies available under the UCC.

CONSEQUENTIAL DAMAGES

As discussed in Chapter 18, *consequential damages* are special damages that compensate for indirect losses (such as lost profits) resulting from a breach of contract. For the nonbreaching party to recover consequential damages, however, these damages must have been reasonably foreseeable at the time the breach occurred.

Under the UCC, parties to a contract can limit or exclude consequential damages, provided the limitation is not unconscionable. When the buyer or lessee is a consumer, any limitation of consequential damages for personal injuries resulting from consumer goods is *prima facie* (presumptively) unconscionable. The limitation of consequential damages is not necessarily unconscionable when the loss is commercial in nature—for example, lost profits and property damage [UCC 2–719(3), 2A–503(3)].

LEMON LAWS

Some purchasers of defective automobiles—called "lemons"—found that the remedies provided by the UCC, after limitations had been imposed by the seller, were inadequate. In response to the frustration of these buyers, all of the states and the District of Columbia have enacted *lemon laws*. Basically, lemon laws provide that if an automobile under warranty possesses a defect that significantly affects the vehicle's value or use, and the defect has not been remedied by the seller within a specified number of opportunities (usually three or four), the buyer is entitled to a new car, replacement of defective parts, or return of all consideration paid.

In most states, lemon laws require an aggrieved new-car owner to notify the dealer or manufacturer of the problem and to provide the dealer or manufacturer with an opportunity to solve it. If the problem remains, the owner must then submit complaints to the arbitration program specified in the manufacturer's warranty before taking the case to court. Decisions by arbitration panels are binding on the manufacturer (that is, cannot be appealed by the manufacturer to the courts) but usually are not binding on the purchaser. All arbitration boards must meet state and/or federal standards of impartiality, and some states have established mandatory government-sponsored arbitration programs for lemon-law disputes.

SECTION 8 | Dealing with International Contracts

Because buyers and sellers (or lessees and lessors) engaged in international business transactions may be separated by thousands of miles, special precautions are often taken to ensure performance under international contracts. Sellers and lessors want to avoid delivering goods for which they might not be paid. Buyers and lessees desire the assurance that sellers and lessors will not be paid until there is evidence that the goods have been shipped. Thus, **letters of credit** are frequently used to facilitate international business transactions.

ELEMENTS OF A LETTER-OF-CREDIT TRANSACTION

In a simple letter-of-credit transaction, the *issuer* (a bank) agrees to issue a letter of credit and to ascertain whether the *beneficiary* (seller or lessor) performs certain acts. In return, the *account party* (buyer or lessee) promises to reimburse the issuer for the amount paid to the beneficiary. The transaction may also involve an *advising bank* that transmits information and a *paying bank* that expedites payment under the letter of credit. See Exhibit 22–1 for an illustration of a letter-of-credit transaction.

Under a letter of credit, the issuer is bound to pay the beneficiary (seller or lessor) when the beneficiary has complied with the terms and conditions of the letter of credit. The beneficiary looks to the issuer, not to the account party (buyer or lessee), when it presents the documents required by the letter of credit. Typically, the letter of credit will require that the beneficiary deliver a *bill of lading* to prove that shipment has been made. Letters of credit assure beneficiaries (sellers or lessors) of payment while at the same time assuring account parties (buyers or lessees) that payment will not be made until the beneficiaries have complied with the terms and conditions of the letter of credit.

THE LETTER OF CREDIT AND THE UNDERLYING CONTRACT

The basic principle behind letters of credit is that payment is made against the documents presented by the beneficiary and not against the facts that the documents purport to reflect. Thus, in a letter-of-credit transaction, the issuer does not police the underlying contract; a letter of credit is independent of the underlying contract between the buyer and the seller. Eliminating the need for the bank (issuer) to inquire into whether actual conditions have been satisfied greatly reduces the cost of a letter of credit. Moreover, the use of a letter of credit protects all parties to a transaction.

REMEDIES FOR BREACH OF INTERNATIONAL SALES CONTRACTS

The United Nations Convention on Contracts for the International Sale of Goods (CISG) provides

EXHIBIT 22-1 **A Letter-of-Credit Transaction**

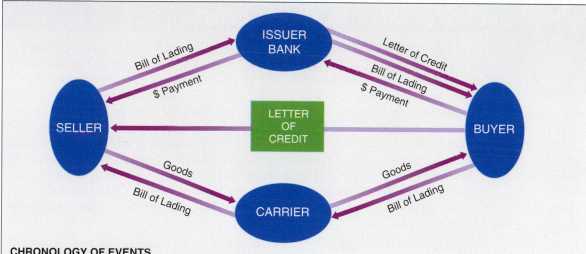

CHRONOLOGY OF EVENTS

1. Buyer contracts with issuer bank to issue a letter of credit; this sets forth the bank's obligation to pay on the letter of credit and buyer's obligation to pay the bank.

2. Letter of credit is sent to seller informing seller that on compliance with the terms of the letter of credit (such as presentment of necessary documents—in this example, a bill of lading), the bank will issue payment for the goods.

3. Seller delivers goods to carrier and receives a bill of lading.

4. Seller delivers the bill of lading to issuer bank and, if the document is proper, receives payment.

5. Issuer bank delivers the bill of lading to buyer.

6. Buyer delivers the bill of lading to carrier.

7. Carrier delivers the goods to buyer.

8. Buyer settles with issuer bank.

international sellers and buyers with remedies very similar to those available under the UCC. Article 74 of the CISG provides for money damages, including foreseeable consequential damages, on a contract's breach. As under the UCC, the measure of damages is normally the difference between the contract price and the market price of the goods. Under Article 49, the buyer is permitted to avoid obligations under the contract if the seller breaches the contract or fails to deliver the goods during the time specified in the contract or later agreed on by the parties. Similarly, under Article 64, the seller can avoid obligations under the contract if the buyer breaches the contract, fails to accept delivery of the goods, or fails to pay for the goods.

The CISG also allows for specific performance as a remedy under Article 28, which provides that "one party is entitled to require performance of any obligation by the other party." This statement is then qualified, however. Article 28 goes on to state that a court may grant specific performance as a remedy only if it would do so "under its own law in respect of similar contracts of sale not governed by this Convention." As already discussed, in the United States the equitable remedy of specific performance will normally be granted only if no adequate remedy at law (money damages) is available and the goods are unique in nature. In other countries, however, such as Germany, specific performance is a commonly granted remedy for breach of contract.

REVIEWING PERFORMANCE AND BREACH OF SALES AND LEASE CONTRACTS

GFI, Inc., a Hong Kong company, makes audio decoder chips, one of the essential components used in the manufacture of MP3 players. Egan Electronics contracts with GFI to buy 10,000 chips on an installment contract, with 2,500 chips to be shipped every three months, F.O.B. Hong Kong via Air Express. At the time for the first delivery, GFI delivers only 2,400 chips but explains to Egan that while the shipment is less than 5 percent short, the chips are of a higher quality than those specified in the contract and are worth 5 percent more than the contract price. Egan accepts the shipment and pays GFI the contract price. At the time for the second shipment, GFI makes a shipment identical to the first. Egan again accepts and pays for the chips. At the time for the third shipment, GFI ships 2,400 of the same chips, but this time GFI sends them via Hong Kong Air instead of Air Express. While in transit, the chips are destroyed. When it is time for the fourth shipment, GFI again sends 2,400 chips, but this time Egan rejects the chips without explanation. Using the information presented in the chapter, answer the following questions.

1. | Based on Egan's acceptance of the first short shipment, does GFI have a legitimate reason to expect that Egan will accept the subsequent short shipments? Why or why not?

2. | How does the substitution of carriers in the third shipment affect the contract between Egan and GFI? Does the substitution of carriers constitute a breach of the contract by GFI?

3. | Suppose that the silicon used for the chips becomes unavailable for a period of time and that GFI cannot manufacture enough chips to fulfill the contract. Does this lack of availability of silicon release GFI from its obligations under the contract? Explain.

4. | Suppose that Egan knows that silicon is not available but hears nothing from GFI. Does Egan have a right to ask GFI about its intentions to fulfill the contract? If so, does GFI have an obligation to respond? Explain.

5. | Under the UCC, does Egan have a right to reject the fourth shipment? Why or why not?

TERMS AND CONCEPTS TO REVIEW

conforming goods 426

cover 439

cure 427

installment contract 428

letter of credit 444

perfect tender rule 427

replevin 439

tender of delivery 426

QUESTIONS AND CASE PROBLEMS

22–1. Ames contracts to ship to Curley one hundred model Z television sets. The terms of delivery are F.O.B. Ames's city, by Green Truck Lines, with delivery on or before April 30. On April 15, Ames discovers that because of an error in inventory control, all model Z sets have been sold, and the stock has not been replenished. Ames has model X, a similar but slightly more expensive unit, in stock. On April 16, Ames ships one hundred model X sets, with notice that Curley will be charged the model Z price. Curley (in a proper manner) rejects the model X sets when they are tendered on April 18. Ames does not wish to be held in breach of contract, even though he has tendered nonconforming goods. Discuss Ames's options.

22–2. QUESTION WITH SAMPLE ANSWER

Topken has contracted to sell Lorwin five hundred washing machines of a certain model at list price. Topken is to ship the goods on or before December 1. Topken produces one thousand washing machines of this model but has not yet prepared Lorwin's shipment. On

November 1, Lorwin repudiates the contract. Discuss the remedies available to Topken.

For a sample answer to this question, go to Appendix I at the end of this text.

22–3. Lehor collects antique cars. He contracts to purchase spare parts for a 1938 engine from Beem. These parts are not made anymore and are scarce. To obtain the contract with Beem, Lehor agrees to pay 50 percent of the purchase price in advance. On May 1, Lehor sends the payment, which is received on May 2. On May 3, Beem, having found another buyer willing to pay substantially more for the parts, informs Lehor that he will not deliver as contracted. That same day, Lehor learns that Beem is insolvent. Discuss fully any possible remedies available to Lehor to enable him to take possession of these parts.

22–4. Moore contracted in writing to sell her 1997 Ford Taurus to Hammer for $8,500. Moore agreed to deliver the car on Wednesday, and Hammer promised to pay the $8,500 on the following Friday. On Tuesday, Hammer informed Moore that he would not be buying the car after all. By Friday, Hammer had changed his mind again and tendered $8,500 to Moore. Moore, although she had not sold the car to another party, refused the tender and refused to deliver the car. Hammer claimed that Moore had breached their contract. Moore contended that Hammer's repudiation had released her from her duty to perform under the contract. Who is correct, and why?

22–5. Gibson contracts to deliver one hundred model X color television sets to a new retail customer, Beaver, on May 1, with payment to be made on delivery. Gibson tenders delivery in her own truck. Beaver notices that one or two cartons have scrape marks on them. He asks Gibson whether the sets might have been damaged as they were being loaded. Gibson assures Beaver that the sets are in perfect condition. Beaver tenders Gibson a check, but Gibson refuses the check, claiming that the first delivery to new customers is always for cash. Beaver promises to have the cash within two days. Gibson leaves the sets with Beaver, who stores them in a warehouse pending a "grand opening sale" date. Two days later, Beaver opens some of the cartons and discovers that a number of the televisions are damaged beyond ordinary repair. Gibson claims Beaver has accepted the sets and is in breach by not paying on delivery. Discuss fully Gibson's claims.

22–6. RIGHT TO CURE. Metro-North Commuter Railroad Co. decided to install a fall-protection system for elevated walkways, roof areas, and interior catwalks in Grand Central Terminal, in New York City. The system was needed to ensure the safety of Metro-North employees when they worked at great heights on the interior and exterior of the terminal. Sinco, Inc., proposed a system called "Sayfglida," which involved a harness worn by the worker, a network of cables, and metal clips or sleeves called "Sayflinks" that connected the harness to the cables. Metro-North agreed to pay $197,325 for the installation of this system by June 26, 1999. Because the system's reliability was crucial, the

contract required certain quality control processes. During a training session for Metro-North employees on June 29, the Sayflink sleeves fell apart. Within two days, Sinco manufactured and delivered two different types of replacement clips without subjecting them to the contract's quality control process, but Metro-North rejected them. Sinco suggested other possible solutions, which Metro-North did not accept. In September, Metro-North terminated its contract with Sinco and awarded the work to Surety, Inc., at a price of about $348,000. Sinco filed a suit in a federal district court, alleging breach of contract. Metro-North counterclaimed for its cost of cover. In whose favor should the court rule, and why? [*Sinco, Inc. v. Metro-North Commuter Railroad Co.,* 133 F.Supp.2d 308 (S.D.N.Y. 2001)]

22–7. ⚖ CASE PROBLEM WITH SAMPLE ANSWER

Eaton Corp. bought four air-conditioning units from Trane Co., an operating division of American Standard, Inc., in 1998. The contract stated in part, "NEITHER PARTY SHALL BE LIABLE FOR . . . CONSEQUENTIAL DAMAGES." Trane was responsible for servicing the units. During the last ten days of March 2003, Trane's employees serviced and inspected the units, changed the filters and belts, and made a material list for repairs. On April 3, a fire occurred at Eaton's facility, extensively damaging the units and the facility, although no one was hurt. Alleging that the fire started in the electric motor of one of the units, and that Trane's faulty servicing of the units caused the fire, Eaton filed a suit in a federal district court against Trane. Eaton asserted a breach of contract, among other claims, seeking consequential damages. Trane filed a motion for summary judgment, based on the limitation-of-remedies clause. What are consequential damages? Can these be limited in some circumstances? Is the clause valid in this case? Explain. [*Eaton Corp. v. Trane Carolina Plains,* 350 F.Supp.2d 699 (D.S.C. 2004)]

To view a sample answer for this case problem, go to this book's Web site at http://wbl.westbuslaw.com, select "Chapter 22," and click on "Case Problem with Sample Answer."

22–8. REMEDIES OF THE BUYER OR LESSEE. Mississippi Chemical Corp. (MCC) produces ammonia at its fertilizer plant in Yazoo City, Mississippi. The production of ammonia involves the compression of gas in special equipment called a compressor train. In 1989, MCC bought from Dresser-Rand Co. a specially designed train that included a "high-case compressor" and a "low-case compressor." The contract expressly guaranteed that the train would be free from defects and would conform to certain technical specifications, but it did not work as promised. When the high-case compressor broke in 1990, MCC wrote to Dresser, "This letter constitutes notice by MCC that [Dresser] is in breach" of the contract. The same defects caused the low-case compressor to break in 1993 and 1996. In 1997, MCC filed a suit in a federal district court against Dresser, asserting a number of claims based on the contract. Dresser argued in part that it had never received written notice of the defects in the low-case compressor and thus was entitled to judgment as a matter of law. Was there sufficient notice to Dresser for MCC to recover for damages caused by defects in the train? Discuss. [*Mississippi Chemical Corp. v. Dresser-Rand Co.*, 287 F.3d 359 (5th Cir. 2002)]

22–9. ACCEPTANCE. In April 1996, Excalibur Oil Group, Inc., applied for credit and opened an account with Standard Distributors, Inc., to obtain snack foods and other items for Excalibur's convenience stores. For three months, Standard delivered the goods and Excalibur paid the invoices. In July, Standard was dissolved and its assets were distributed to J. F. Walker Co. Walker continued to deliver the goods to Excalibur, which continued to pay the invoices until November, when the firm began to experience financial difficulties. By January 1997, Excalibur owed Walker $54,241.77. Walker then dealt with Excalibur solely on a collect-on-delivery basis until Excalibur's stores closed in 1998. Walker filed a suit in a Pennsylvania state court against Excalibur and its owner to recover amounts due on the unpaid invoices. To successfully plead its case, Walker had to show that there was a contract between the parties. One question was whether Excalibur had manifested acceptance of the goods delivered by Walker. How does a buyer manifest acceptance? Was there an accep-

tance in this case? In whose favor should the court rule, and why? [*J. F. Walker Co. v. Excalibur Oil Group, Inc.*, 792 A.2d 1269 (Pa.Super. 2002)]

22–10. PERFECT TENDER. Advanced Polymer Sciences, Inc. (APS), based in Ohio, makes polymers and resins for use as protective coatings in industrial applications. APS also owns the technology for equipment used to make certain composite fibers. *SAVA gumarska in kemijska industria d.d.* (SAVA), based in Slovenia, makes rubber goods. In 1999, SAVA and APS contracted to form *SAVA Advanced Polymers proizvodno podjetje d.o.o.* (SAVA AP) to make and distribute APS products in Eastern Europe. Their contract provided for, among other things, the alteration of a facility to make the products using specially made equipment to be sold by APS to SAVA. Disputes arose between the parties, and in August 2000, SAVA stopped work on the new facility. APS then notified SAVA that it was stopping the manufacture of the equipment and "insist[ed] on knowing what is SAVA's intention towards this venture." In October, SAVA told APS that it was canceling their contract. In subsequent litigation, SAVA claimed that APS had repudiated the contract when it stopped making the equipment. What might APS assert in its defense? How should the court rule? Explain. [*SAVA gumarska in kemijska industria d.d. v. Advanced Polymer Sciences, Inc.*, 128 S.W.3d 304 (Tex.App.—Dallas 2004)]

LAW | on the Web

For updated links to resources available on the Web, as well as a variety of other materials, visit this text's Web site at **http://wbl.westbuslaw.com**.

To find information on the UCC, including the UCC provisions discussed in this chapter, refer to the Web sites listed in the *Law on the Web* section in Chapter 20.

To obtain information on performance requirements in relation to contracts for the international sale of goods, you can access the Institute of International Commercial Law at Pace University at

http://cisgw3.law.pace.edu

LEGAL RESEARCH EXERCISES ON THE WEB

Go to **http://wbl.westbuslaw.com**, the Web site that accompanies this text. Select "Chapter 22" and click on "Internet Exercises." There you will find the following Internet research exercises that you can perform to learn more about topics covered in this chapter.

Activity 22–1: LEGAL PERSPECTIVE
International Performance Requirements

Activity 22–2: SOCIAL PERSPECTIVE
Lemon Laws

Activity 22–3: MANAGEMENT PERSPECTIVE
The Right to Reject Goods

CHAPTER 23
Warranties and Product Liability

Warranty is an age-old concept. In sales and lease law, a warranty is an assurance by one party of the existence of a fact on which the other party can rely. Article 2 (on sales) and Article 2A (on leases) of the Uniform Commercial Code (UCC) designate several types of warranties that can arise in a sales or lease contract. These warranties include warranties of title, express warranties, and implied warranties. We examine each of these types of warranties in this chapter.

Because a warranty imposes a duty on the seller or lessor, a breach of warranty is a breach of the seller's or lessor's promise. Assuming that the parties have not agreed to limit or modify the remedies available, if the seller or lessor breaches a warranty, the buyer or lessee can sue to recover damages from the seller or lessor. Under some circumstances, a breach of warranty can allow the buyer or lessee to rescind (cancel) the agreement.[1]

Product liability encompasses the contract theory of warranty, as well as the tort theories of negligence, misrepresentation, and strict liability (discussed in Chapters 6 and 7). We examine product liability in the latter part of the chapter. Warranty law is also part of the broad body of consumer protection law that will be discussed in Chapter 44.

SECTION 1 | Types of Warranties

Most goods are covered by some type of warranty designed to protect buyers. Articles 2 and 2A of the UCC designate several types of warranties that can arise in a sales or lease contract, including warranties of title, express warranties, and implied warranties. We discuss these types of warranties in the following subsections, as well as a federal statute that is designed to prevent deception and make warranties more understandable.

WARRANTIES OF TITLE

Title warranty arises automatically in most sales contracts. UCC 2–312 imposes the three types of warranties of title discussed here.

GOOD TITLE In most cases, sellers warrant that they have good and valid title to the goods sold and that

transfer of the title is rightful [UCC 2–312(1)(a)].[2] For example, Alice steals goods from Henry and sells them to Ona, who does not know that they are stolen. If Henry discovers that Ona has the goods, then he has the right to reclaim them from Ona. When Alice sold Ona the goods, Alice *automatically* warranted to Ona that the title conveyed was valid and that its transfer was rightful. Because a thief has no title to stolen goods, Alice breached the warranty of title imposed by UCC 2–312(1)(a) and became liable to the buyer for appropriate damages. (See Chapter 21 for a detailed discussion of sales by nonowners.)

NO LIENS A second warranty of title provided by the UCC protects buyers who are *unaware* of any encumbrances (claims, charges, or liabilities—usually called

---

1. *Rescission* restores the parties to the positions they were in before the contract was made.

2. Under the 2003 amendments to UCC 2–312(1)(a), good title also includes the warranty that the sale "shall not unreasonably expose the buyer to litigation because of any colorable [legitimate or reasonable] claim to or interest in the goods." Thus, the buyer is entitled not only to a good title but also to a marketable title that is free of "colorable claims." Amendments to UCC Article 2A also provide for the doctrine of marketable title in the context of leases [Amended UCC 2A–211(1), (2)].

liens[3]) against goods at the time the contract is made [UCC 2–312(1)(b)]. This warranty protects buyers who, for example, unknowingly purchase goods that are subject to a creditor's security interest (see Chapter 29). If a creditor legally repossesses the goods from a buyer *who had no actual knowledge of the security interest*, the buyer can recover from the seller for breach of warranty. (A buyer who has *actual knowledge of a security interest* has no recourse against a seller.)

Consider an example. Henderson buys a used boat from Loring for cash. A month later, Barish proves that she has a valid security interest in the boat and that Loring, who has missed five payments, is in default. Barish then repossesses the boat from Henderson. Henderson demands his cash back from Loring. Under Section 2–312(1)(b), Henderson has legal grounds to recover from Loring because the seller of goods warrants that the goods are delivered free from any security interest or other lien of which the buyer has no knowledge.

Article 2A affords similar protection for lessees. Section 2A–211(1) provides that during the term of the lease, no claim of any third party will interfere with the lessee's enjoyment of the leasehold interest.

NO INFRINGEMENTS   A merchant-seller is also deemed to warrant that the goods delivered are free from any copyright, trademark, or patent claims of a third person[4] [UCC 2–312(3), 2A–211(2)]. If this warranty is breached and the buyer is sued by the party holding copyright, trademark, or patent rights in the goods, the buyer *must notify the seller* of the litigation within a reasonable time to enable the seller to decide whether to defend the lawsuit. If the seller states in a writing (or record) that she or he has decided to defend and agrees to bear all expenses, then the buyer must turn over control of the litigation to the seller; otherwise, the buyer is barred from any remedy against the seller for liability established by the litigation [UCC 2–607(3)(b), 2–607(5)(b)].

Article 2A provides for the same notice of litigation in situations that involve leases rather than sales [UCC 2A–516(3)(b), 2A–516(4)(b)]. An exception is made for leases made by individual consumers for personal, family, or household purposes. A consumer who fails to notify the lessor within a reasonable time does not lose his or her remedy against the lessor for any liability established in the litigation [UCC 2A–516(3)(b)].

DISCLAIMER OF TITLE WARRANTY   In an ordinary sales transaction, the title warranty can be disclaimed or modified only by *specific language* in a contract. For example, sellers may assert that they are transferring only such rights, title, and interest as they have in the goods. In a lease transaction, the disclaimer must "be specific, be by a writing, and be conspicuous" [UCC 2A–214(4)].

In certain situations, the circumstances surrounding the sale are sufficient to indicate clearly to a buyer that no assurances as to title are being made. The classic example is a sheriff's sale; in this situation, buyers know that the goods have been seized to satisfy debts and that the sheriff cannot guarantee title [UCC 2–312(2)].

EXPRESS WARRANTIES

A seller or lessor can create an **express warranty** by making representations concerning the quality, condition, description, or performance potential of the goods. Under UCC 2–313 and 2A–210, express warranties arise when a seller or lessor indicates any of the following:

1. That the goods conform to any *affirmation* (declaration) of fact or *promise* that the seller or lessor makes to the buyer or lessee about the goods. Such affirmations or promises are usually made during the bargaining process. Statements such as "these drill bits will *easily* penetrate stainless steel—and without dulling" are express warranties.[5]

2. That the goods conform to any *description* of them. For example, a label that reads "Crate contains one 150-horsepower diesel engine" or a contract that calls for the delivery of a "wool coat" creates an express warranty that the content of the goods sold conforms to the description.

---

3. Pronounced *leens*. Liens will be discussed in detail in Chapter 28.
4. Recall from Chapter 20 that a *merchant* is defined in UCC 2–104(1) as a person who deals in goods of the kind involved in the sales contract or who, by occupation, presents himself or herself as having knowledge or skill peculiar to the goods involved in the transaction.

5. The 2003 amendments to UCC Article 2 introduce the term *remedial promise*, which is "a promise by the seller to repair or replace the goods or to refund all or part of the price on the happening of a specified event" [Amended UCC 2–103(1)(n), 2–313(4)]. A remedial promise is not an express warranty, so a right of action for its breach accrues not at the time of tender, as with warranties, but if the promise is *not* performed when due [Amended UCC 2–725(2)(c)].

3. That the goods conform to any *sample or model* of the goods shown to the buyer or lessee.

Express warranties can be found in a seller's or lessor's advertisement, brochure, or promotional materials, in addition to being made orally or in an express warranty provision in a sales or lease contract. To create an express warranty, a seller or lessor does not have to use formal words such as *warrant* or *guarantee*. It is only necessary that a reasonable buyer or lessee would regard the representation as part of the basis of the bargain [UCC 2–313(2), 2A–210(2)].[6]

BASIS OF THE BARGAIN The UCC requires that for an express warranty to be created, the affirmation, promise, description, or sample must become part of the "basis of the bargain" [UCC 2–313(1), 2A–210(1)]. Just what constitutes the basis of the bargain is hard to say. The UCC does not define the concept, and it is a question of fact in each case whether a representation was made at such a time and in such a way that it induced the buyer or lessee to enter into the contract. Therefore, if an express warranty is not intended, the marketing agent or salesperson should not promise too much.

STATEMENTS OF OPINION AND VALUE Statements of fact create express warranties. If the seller or lessor merely makes a statement that relates to the value or worth of the goods, or makes a statement of opinion or recommendation about the goods, the seller or lessor is not creating an express warranty [UCC 2–313(2), 2A–210(2)].

For example, a seller claims that "this is the best used car to come along in years; it has four new tires and a 250-horsepower engine just rebuilt this year." The seller has made several *affirmations of fact* that can create a warranty: the automobile has an engine, it has a 250-horsepower engine, the engine was rebuilt this year, there are four tires on the automobile, and the tires are new. The seller's *opinion* that the vehicle is "the best used car to come along in years," however, is known as "puffing" and creates no warranty. (*Puffing*

is an expression of opinion by a seller or lessor that is not made as a representation of fact.) A statement relating to the value of the goods, such as "it's worth a fortune" or "anywhere else you'd pay $10,000 for it," usually does not create a warranty.

—An Exception for Statements of Opinion by Experts. Although an ordinary seller or lessor can give an opinion that is not a warranty, if the seller or lessor is an expert and gives an opinion as an expert to a layperson, then a warranty may be created. For example, Saul is an art dealer and an expert in eighteenth-century paintings. If Saul states to Lauren, a purchaser, that in his opinion a particular painting is a Rembrandt, Saul has warranted the accuracy of his opinion.

—Puffery versus Express Warranties. It is not always easy to determine what constitutes an express warranty and what constitutes puffing. The reasonableness of the buyer's or lessee's reliance appears to be the controlling criterion in many cases. For example, a salesperson's statements that a ladder will "never break" and will "last a lifetime" are so clearly improbable that no reasonable buyer should rely on them. Additionally, the context in which a statement is made may be relevant in determining the reasonableness of a buyer's or lessee's reliance. A reasonable person is more likely to rely on a written statement made in an advertisement than on a statement made orally by a salesperson.

For example, in one case a tobacco farmer had read an ad stating that Chlor-O-Pic was a chemical fumigant that would suppress black shank disease, a fungal disease that destroys tobacco crops. The ad specifically indicated how much of the product should be applied per acre and stated that, if applied as directed, Chlor-O-Pic would give "season-long control with application in fall, winter, or spring." The farmer bought eight thousand pounds of Chlor-O-Pic and applied it as directed to 143 acres of his tobacco crop. Nonetheless, the crop developed black shank disease, resulting in an estimated loss of three thousand pounds of tobacco per acre. When the farmer sued the manufacturer of Chlor-O-Pic, he argued that he had purchased the product in reliance on what he assumed to be a "strong promise" of "season-long control." In this case, the jury agreed with the farmer. The manufacturer had indeed made a strong promise—one that created an express warranty.[7]

---

6. The 2003 amendments to the UCC distinguish between immediate buyers (those who enter into contracts with sellers) and remote purchasers (those who buy or lease goods from immediate buyers) and extend sellers' obligations regarding new goods to remote purchasers. For example, suppose that a manufacturer sells packaged goods to a retailer, who resells the goods to a consumer. If a reasonable person in the position of the consumer would believe that a description on the package creates an obligation, the manufacturer is liable for its breach. (See Amended UCC 2–313, 2–313A, and 2–313B.)

7. *Triple E, Inc. v. Hendrix & Dail, Inc.,* 344 S.C. 186, 543 S.E.2d 245 (2001).

IMPLIED WARRANTIES

An **implied warranty** is one that *the law derives* by inference from the nature of the transaction or the relative situations or circumstances of the parties. Under the UCC, merchants impliedly warrant that the goods they sell or lease are merchantable and, in certain circumstances, fit for a particular purpose. In addition, an implied warranty may arise from a course of dealing or usage of trade. We examine these three types of implied warranties in the following subsections.

IMPLIED WARRANTY OF MERCHANTABILITY

Every sale or lease of goods made by a merchant who deals in goods of the kind sold or leased automatically gives rise to an **implied warranty of merchantability** [UCC 2–314, 2A–212]. Thus, a merchant who is in the business of selling ski equipment makes an implied warranty of merchantability every time the merchant sells a pair of skis, but a neighbor selling his or her skis at a garage sale does not.

—Merchantable Goods. To be *merchantable*, goods must be "reasonably fit for the ordinary purposes for which such goods are used." They must be of at least average, fair, or medium-grade quality. The quality must be comparable to quality that will pass without objection in the trade or market for goods of the same description. To be merchantable, the goods must also be adequately packaged and labeled as provided by the agreement, and they must conform to the promises or affirmations of fact made on the container or label, if any.

It makes no difference that the merchant did not know or could not have discovered that a product was defective (not merchantable). For example, Khalil buys an ax at Enrique's Hardware Store. No express

warranties are made. The first time Khalil chops wood with the ax the handle breaks, and he is injured. He immediately notifies Enrique. Examination shows that the wood of the handle was rotten inside—a fact that could not have been detected by either Enrique or Khalil. Nonetheless, Enrique is responsible for Khalil's injuries because a merchant-seller of goods warrants that the goods he or she sells are fit for the ordinary purposes for which such goods are used. This ax was obviously not fit for those purposes.

Of course, merchants are not absolute insurers against *all* accidents arising in connection with the goods. For example, a bar of soap is not unmerchantable merely because a user could slip and fall by stepping on it.

—Merchantable Food. The UCC recognizes the serving of food or drink to be consumed on or off the premises as a sale of goods subject to the implied warranty of merchantability [UCC 2–314(1)]. "Merchantable" food is food that is fit to eat on the basis of consumer expectations. For example, the courts assume that consumers should reasonably expect to find on occasion bones in fish fillets, cherry pits in cherry pie, a nutshell in a package of shelled nuts, and so on—because such substances are natural to the ingredients or the finished food product. In contrast, consumers would not reasonably expect to find an inchworm in a can of peas or a piece of glass in a soft drink—because these substances are *not* natural to the food product.[8] In the following classic case, the court had to determine whether one should reasonably expect to find a fish bone in fish chowder.

---

8. See, for example, *Mexicali Rose v. Superior Court*, 1 Cal.4th 617, 822 P.2d 1292, 4 Cal.Rptr.2d 145 (1992).

CASE 23.1

Supreme Judicial Court
of Massachusetts, 1964.
347 Mass. 421,
198 N.E.2d 309.

Webster v. Blue Ship Tea Room, Inc.

BACKGROUND AND FACTS *Blue Ship Tea Room, Inc., was located in Boston in an old building overlooking the ocean. Webster, who had been born and raised in New England, went to the restaurant and ordered fish chowder. The chowder was milky in color. After three or four spoonfuls, she felt something lodged in her throat. As a result, she underwent two esophagoscopies; in the second esophagoscopy, a fish bone was found and removed. Webster filed a suit against the restaurant in a Massachusetts state court for breach of the implied warranty of merchantability. The jury rendered a verdict for Webster, and the restaurant appealed to the state's highest court.*

IN THE LANGUAGE OF THE COURT

 REARDON, Justice.

[The plaintiff] ordered a cup of fish chowder. Presently, there was set before her "a small bowl of fish chowder." * * * After 3 or 4 [spoonfuls] she was aware that

CASE 23.1 | Continued

something had lodged in her throat because she "couldn't swallow and couldn't clear her throat by gulping and she could feel it." This misadventure led to two esophagoscopies [procedures in which a telescope-like instrument is used to look into the throat] at the Massachusetts General Hospital, in the second of which, on April 27, 1959, a fish bone was found and removed. The sequence of events produced injury to the plaintiff which was not insubstantial.

We must decide whether a fish bone lurking in a fish chowder, about the ingredients of which there is no other complaint, constitutes a breach of implied warranty under applicable provisions of the Uniform Commercial Code * * * . As the judge put it in his charge [jury instruction], "Was the fish chowder fit to be eaten and wholesome? * * * [N]obody is claiming that the fish itself wasn't wholesome. * * * But the bone of contention here—I don't mean that for a pun—but was this fish bone a foreign substance that made the fish chowder unwholesome or not fit to be eaten?"

* * * *

[We think that it] is not too much to say that a person sitting down in New England to consume a good New England fish chowder embarks on a gustatory [taste-related] adventure which may entail the removal of some fish bones from his bowl as he proceeds. We are not inclined to tamper with age-old recipes by any amendment reflecting the plaintiff's view of the effect of the Uniform Commercial Code upon them. We are aware of the heavy body of case law involving foreign substances in food, but we sense a strong distinction between them and those relative to unwholesomeness of the food itself, [such as] tainted mackerel, and a fish bone in a fish chowder. * * * [W]e consider that the joys of life in New England include the ready availability of fresh fish chowder. We should be prepared to cope with the hazards of fish bones, the occasional presence of which in chowders is, it seems to us, to be anticipated, and which, in the light of a hallowed tradition, do not impair their fitness or merchantability.

DECISION AND REMEDY *The Supreme Judicial Court of Massachusetts "sympathized with a plaintiff who has suffered a peculiarly New England injury" but entered a judgment for the defendant, Blue Ship Tea Room. A fish bone in fish chowder is not a breach of the implied warranty of merchantability.*

IMPACT OF THIS CASE ON TODAY'S LAW
This classic case, phrased in memorable language, was an early application of the UCC's implied warranty of merchantability to food products. The case established the rule that consumers should expect to find, on occasion, elements of food products that are natural to the product (such as fish bones in fish chowder). Courts today still apply this rule.

IMPLIED WARRANTY OF FITNESS FOR A PARTICULAR PURPOSE The **implied warranty of fitness for a particular purpose** arises when any *seller or lessor* (merchant or nonmerchant) knows the particular purpose for which a buyer or lessee will use the goods *and* knows that the buyer or lessee is relying on the skill and judgment of the seller or lessor to select suitable goods [UCC 2–315, 2A–213].

—*Particular versus Ordinary Purpose.* A "particular purpose" of the buyer or lessee differs from the "ordinary purpose for which goods are used" (merchantability). Goods can be merchantable but unfit for a particular purpose. For example, suppose that you need a gallon of paint to match the color of

your living room walls—a light shade somewhere between coral and peach. You take a sample to your local hardware store and request a gallon of paint of that color. Instead, you are given a gallon of bright blue paint. Here, the salesperson has not breached any warranty of implied merchantability—the bright blue paint is of high quality and suitable for interior walls—but she or he has breached an implied warranty of fitness for a particular purpose.

—*Knowledge and Reliance Requirements.* A seller or lessor need not have actual knowledge of the buyer's or lessee's particular purpose. It is sufficient if a seller or lessor "has reason to know" the purpose. The buyer or lessee, however, must have *relied* on the skill or judgment of the seller or lessor in selecting or furnishing suitable goods for an implied warranty to be created.

For example, Bloomberg leases a computer from Future Tech, a lessor of technical business equipment. Bloomberg tells the clerk that she wants a computer that will run a complicated new engineering graphics program at a realistic speed. Future Tech leases Bloomberg an Architex One computer with a CPU speed of only 2 gigahertz, even though a speed of at least 3.2 gigahertz would be required to run Bloomberg's graphics program at a "realistic speed." After discovering that it takes forever to run her program, Bloomberg wants a full refund. Here, because Future Tech has breached the implied warranty of fitness for a particular purpose, Bloomberg normally will be able to recover. The clerk knew specifically that Bloomberg wanted a computer with enough speed to run certain software. Furthermore, Bloomberg relied on the clerk to furnish a computer that would fulfill this purpose. Because Future Tech did not do so, the warranty was breached.

OTHER IMPLIED WARRANTIES Implied warranties can also arise (or be excluded or modified) as a result of course of dealing or usage of trade [UCC 2–314(3), 2A–212(3)]. In the absence of evidence to the contrary, when both parties to a sales or lease contract have knowledge of a well-recognized trade custom, the courts will infer that both parties intended for that custom to apply to their contract. For example, if it is an industry-wide custom to lubricate a new car before it is delivered and a dealer fails to do so, the dealer can be held liable to a buyer for damages resulting from the breach of an implied warranty. (This, of course, would also be negligence on the part of the dealer.)

MAGNUSON-MOSS WARRANTY ACT

The Magnuson-Moss Warranty Act of 1975[9] was designed to prevent deception in warranties by making them easier to understand. The Federal Trade Commission (FTC) primarily enforces the act (the FTC's role in protecting consumers is discussed in Chapter 44). Additionally, the attorney general or a consumer who has been injured can enforce the act if informal procedures for settling disputes prove to be ineffective. The act modifies UCC warranty rules to

some extent when *consumer* transactions are involved. The UCC, however, remains the primary codification of warranty rules for industrial and commercial transactions.

No seller is *required* to give a written warranty for consumer goods sold under the Magnuson-Moss Warranty Act. If a seller chooses to make an express written warranty, however, and the cost of the consumer goods is more than $10, the warranty must be labeled as either "full" or "limited." In addition, if the cost of the goods is more than $15, by FTC regulation the warrantor must make certain disclosures fully and conspicuously in a single document in "readily understood language." These disclosures state the names and addresses of the warrantor(s), what specifically is warranted, procedures for enforcement of the warranty, any limitations on warranty relief, and that the buyer has legal rights.

FULL WARRANTY Although a *full warranty* may not cover every aspect of the consumer product sold, what it covers ensures some type of consumer satisfaction in the event that the product is defective. A full warranty requires free repair or replacement of any defective part; if the product cannot be repaired within a reasonable time, the consumer has the choice of either a refund or a replacement without charge. There is frequently no time limit on a full warranty. Any limitation on consequential damages must be *conspicuously* stated. Additionally, the warrantor need not perform warranty services if the problem with the product was caused by damage to the product or unreasonable use by the consumer.

LIMITED WARRANTY A *limited warranty* arises when the written warranty fails to meet one of the minimum requirements of a full warranty. The fact that only a limited warranty is being given must be conspicuously disclosed. If the only difference between a limited warranty and a full warranty is a time limitation, the Magnuson-Moss Warranty Act allows the warrantor to identify the warranty as a full warranty by such language as "full twelve-month warranty."

IMPLIED WARRANTIES Implied warranties are not covered under the Magnuson-Moss Warranty Act; they continue to be created according to UCC provisions. When an express warranty is made, it may not, under the Magnuson-Moss Warranty Act, include disclaimers or modifications of the implied warranties of merchantability and fitness for a particular purpose. A

---

9. 15 U.S.C. Sections 2301–2312.

CONCEPT SUMMARY 23.1 | Types of Warranties

CONCEPT	DESCRIPTION
WARRANTIES OF TITLE	The UCC provides for the following warranties of title [UCC 2–312, 2A–211]: 1. *Good title*—A seller warrants that he or she has the right to pass good and rightful title to the goods. 2. *No liens*—A seller warrants that the goods sold are free of any encumbrances (claims, charges, or liabilities—usually called *liens*). A lessor warrants that the lessee will not be disturbed in her or his possession of the goods by the claims of a third party. 3. *No infringements*—A merchant-seller warrants that the goods are free of infringement claims (claims that a patent, trademark, or copyright has been infringed) by third parties. Lessors make similar warranties.
EXPRESS WARRANTIES	An express warranty arises under the UCC when a seller or lessor indicates any of the following as part of the sale or bargain [UCC 2–313, 2A–210]: a. An affirmation or promise of fact. b. A description of the goods. c. A sample or model shown as conforming to the contract goods.
IMPLIED WARRANTY OF MERCHANTABILITY	When a seller or lessor is a merchant who deals in goods of the kind sold or leased, the seller or lessor warrants that the goods sold or leased are properly packaged and labeled, are of proper quality, and are reasonably fit for the ordinary purposes for which such goods are used [UCC 2–314, 2A–212].
IMPLIED WARRANTY OF FITNESS FOR A PARTICULAR PURPOSE	An implied warranty of fitness for a particular purpose arises when the buyer's or lessee's purpose or use is known by the seller or lessor, and the buyer or lessee purchases or leases the goods in reliance on the seller's or lessor's selection [UCC 2–315, 2A–213].
OTHER IMPLIED WARRANTIES	Other implied warranties can arise as a result of course of dealing or usage of trade [UCC 2–314(3), 2A–212(3)].
MAGNUSON-MOSS WARRANTY ACT	Express written warranties covering consumer goods priced at more than $10, *if made*, must be labeled as either a full warranty or a limited warranty. A full warranty requires free repair or replacement of defective parts and refund or replacement for goods that cannot be repaired in a reasonable time. A limited warranty arises when less than a full warranty is being offered.

warrantor can impose a time limit on the duration of an implied warranty, but it must correspond to the duration of the express warranty.[10]

SECTION 2 | Overlapping Warranties

Sometimes, two or more warranties are made in a single transaction. An implied warranty of merchantability, an implied warranty of fitness for a particular purpose, or both can exist in addition to an express warranty. For example, when a sales contract for a new car states that "this car engine is warranted to be free from defects for 36,000 miles or thirty-six months, whichever occurs first," there is an express warranty against all defects, as well as an implied warranty that the car will be fit for normal use.

WHEN THE WARRANTIES ARE CONSISTENT

The rule under the UCC is that express and implied warranties are construed as *cumulative* if they are consistent with one another [UCC 2–317, 2A–215]. In other words, courts interpret two or more warranties as being in agreement with each other unless this construction is unreasonable. If a court determines that it

---

10. This time limit must, of course, be reasonable, conscionable, and set forth in clear and conspicuous language on the face of the warranty.

is unreasonable for the two warranties to be consistent, then the court looks at the intention of the parties to determine which warranty is dominant.

CONFLICTING WARRANTIES

If the warranties are *inconsistent*, the courts usually apply the following rules to interpret which warranty is most important:

1. *Express* warranties displace inconsistent *implied* warranties, except implied warranties of fitness for a particular purpose.
2. Samples take precedence over inconsistent general descriptions.
3. Exact or technical specifications displace inconsistent samples or general descriptions.

In the example presented earlier, suppose that when Bloomberg leases the computer at Future Tech, the contract contains an express warranty concerning the speed of the CPU and the application programs that the computer is capable of running. Bloomberg does not realize that the speed expressly warranted in the contract is insufficient for her needs until she tries to run the software and the computer slows to a crawl. Bloomberg claims that Future Tech has breached the implied warranty of fitness for a particular purpose because she made it clear that she was leasing the computer to perform certain tasks. In this situation, the express warranty would not take precedence over an implied warranty of fitness for a particular purpose (though it would take precedence over any implied warranty of merchantability). Bloomberg therefore has a good claim against Future Tech for breaching the implied warranty of fitness for a particular purpose.

SECTION 3 | Warranty Disclaimers and Limitations on Liability

The UCC generally permits warranties to be disclaimed or limited by specific and unambiguous language, provided that this is done in a manner that protects the buyer or lessee from surprise. We examine here the specific requirements for disclaiming warranties and several UCC provisions that limit liability for breach of warranty.

WARRANTY DISCLAIMERS

Because each type of warranty is created in a special way, the manner in which a seller or lessor can disclaim warranties varies with the type of warranty.

EXPRESS WARRANTIES As already stated, any affirmation of fact or promise, description of the goods, or use of samples or models by a seller or lessor creates an express warranty. Obviously, then, express warranties can be excluded if the seller or lessor carefully refrains from making any promise or affirmation of fact relating to the goods, describing the goods, or using a sample or model. In addition, a written disclaimer in language that is clear and conspicuous, and called to a buyer's or lessee's attention, could negate all oral express warranties not included in the written sales or lease contract [UCC 2–316(1), 2A–214(1)]. This allows the seller or lessor to avoid false allegations that oral warranties were made, and it ensures that only representations made by properly authorized individuals are included in the bargain.

Note, however, that a buyer or lessee must be made aware of any warranty disclaimers or modifications *at the time the contract is formed*. In other words, any oral or written warranties—or disclaimers—made during the bargaining process cannot be modified at a later time by the seller or lessor without the consent of the buyer or lessee.

IMPLIED WARRANTIES Generally speaking, unless circumstances indicate otherwise, the implied warranties of merchantability and fitness are disclaimed by the expressions "as is," "with all faults," and other similar phrases that in common understanding for *both* parties call the buyer's or lessee's attention to the fact that there are no implied warranties [UCC 2–316(3)(a), 2A–214(3)(a)]. The UCC also permits a seller or lessor to specifically disclaim an implied warranty either of merchantability or of fitness [UCC 2–316(2), 2A–214(2)].

—Disclaimer of the Implied Warranty of Merchantability. A merchantability disclaimer must specifically mention *merchantability*. It need not be written; but if it is, the writing must be conspicuous [UCC 2–316(2), 2A–214(4)].[11] Under the UCC, a term or clause is conspicuous when it is written or displayed in such a way that a reasonable person would notice it. For example, a heading in capitals or a clause that appears in a larger font or in a different

---

11. Under the 2003 amendments to UCC Articles 2 and 2A, if a *consumer* contract or lease is set forth in a writing (physical or electronic), the implied warranty of merchantability can be disclaimed only by language also set forth conspicuously in the record [Amended UCC 2–316(3) and 2A–214(3)].

color from the surrounding text would be considered conspicuous.

—Disclaimer of the Implied Warranty of Fitness. To disclaim an implied warranty of fitness for a particular purpose, the disclaimer must be in writing and be conspicuous. The word *fitness* does not have to be mentioned in the writing; it is sufficient if, for example, the disclaimer states, "THERE ARE NO WARRANTIES THAT EXTEND BEYOND THE DESCRIPTION ON THE FACE HEREOF."

BUYER'S OR LESSEE'S EXAMINATION OF THE GOODS

Under the UCC, if a buyer or lessee actually examines the goods (or a sample or model) as fully as desired before entering into a contract, or refuses to examine the goods on the seller's or lessor's demand that he or she do so, *there is no implied warranty with respect to defects that a reasonable examination would reveal or defects that are found on examination* [UCC 2–316(3)(b), 2A–214(2)(b)].

For example, suppose that Joplin buys an ax at Gershwin's Hardware Store. No express warranties are made. Joplin, even after Gershwin suggests it, refuses to inspect the ax before buying it. Had she done so, she would have noticed that the handle of the ax was obviously cracked. If Joplin is later injured by the defective ax, she normally will not be able to hold Gershwin liable for breach of the warranty of merchantability because she would have spotted the defect during an inspection.

UNCONSCIONABILITY

The UCC sections dealing with warranty disclaimers do not refer specifically to unconscionability as a factor. Ultimately, however, the courts will test warranty disclaimers with reference to the UCC's unconscionability standards [UCC 2–302, 2A–108]. Such things as lack of bargaining position, "take-it-or-leave-it" choices, and a buyer's or lessee's failure to understand or know of a warranty disclaimer will be relevant to the issue of unconscionability.

STATUTE OF LIMITATIONS

An action for breach of contract under the UCC must be commenced *within four years after the cause of action accrues*—that is, within four years after the breach

occurs.[12] In addition to filing a suit within the four-year period, the aggrieved party usually must notify the breaching party of the breach within a reasonable time, or the aggrieved party is barred from pursuing any remedy [UCC 2–607(3)(a), 2A–516(3)].[13] By agreement in the contract, the parties can reduce this period to not less than one year, but they *cannot* extend it beyond four years [UCC 2–725(1), 2A–506(1)].[14]

The statute of limitations begins to run when a cause of action accrues (becomes an enforceable right). A cause of action for breach of warranty accrues when the seller or lessor *tenders* delivery, even if the aggrieved party is unaware that the cause of action has accrued [UCC 2–725(2), 2A–506(2)].[15] For example, Hoover purchases a central air-conditioning unit for his restaurant. The unit is warranted specifically to keep the temperature below a certain level during the summer months. The unit is installed in the winter, but when summer comes, the restaurant does not stay cool. Because discovery of the warranty's breach is, of necessity, made in the summer and not when the unit is delivered in the winter, the statute of limitations does not begin to run until the summer.

SECTION 4 | Product Liability

Manufacturers, sellers, and lessors of goods can be held liable to consumers, users, and bystanders for physical harm or property damage that is caused by the goods. This is called **product liability.** Because one particular product may cause harm to a number of consumers, product liability actions are sometimes filed by a group of plaintiffs acting together. (For a discussion of a new

---

12. A 2003 amendment to UCC 2–725(1) adjusts this limit by permitting a cause of action to be brought within the later of four years after the right of action accrues or one year after a breach is or should have been discovered, but no later than five years after the time that the right accrued. The amendments to Article 2 include specific rules for determining when rights accrue for breaches of certain obligations [Amended UCC 2–725(2), (3)].

13. Under the 2003 amendments to the UCC, failure to give timely notice bars a buyer or lessee from a remedy only to the extent that the seller or lessor is prejudiced by the failure [Amended UCC 2–607(3)(a), 2A–516(3)(a)].

14. Under the 2003 amendments to the UCC, the four-year period cannot be reduced in a consumer contract or lease [Amended UCC 2–725(1), 2A–506(1)].

15. Under the 2003 amendments to UCC Article 2, the seller is also required to have completed any agreed-on installation or assembly of the goods [Amended UCC 2–725(3)(a)].

Class Actions and Product Liability Lawsuits

Many product liability actions are class actions. A *class action* is a lawsuit in which a single person or a small group of people represents the interests of a larger group. Women allegedly injured by silicone breast implants, for example, sued the manufacturers as a class, as did many of those allegedly injured by asbestos and tobacco. The idea behind class actions is that they allow the average person to participate in complex litigation in an attempt to hold large corporations accountable for their allegedly wrongful acts and harmful products. Because an individual might not have the financial means to pursue the case alone, class actions allow them to pool resources with other injured parties and obtain competent legal counsel to represent them as a group.

Federal procedure has always had specific requirements for maintaining a class action. For example, the class must be so large that individual suits would be impracticable, and there must be legal or factual issues common to all members of the class. Until 2005, however, any state or federal court could hear and decide class actions.

THE CLASS ACTION FAIRNESS ACT OF 2005

The Class Action Fairness Act (CAFA) of 2005[a] significantly changes the way class-action cases are tried. The CAFA was primarily designed to shift large, interstate product liability and tort class-action suits from the state courts to the federal courts (although it affects all class-action claims). The act grants federal courts original, or trial, jurisdiction over any

_____

a. Pub. L. No. 109-2, 119 St. 4 (February 18, 2005).

civil action involving plaintiffs from multiple states in which the damages sought are $5 million or more.

Under the CAFA, a state court can retain jurisdiction over a case *only* if more than two-thirds of the plaintiffs and at least one principal defendant are citizens of the state and the injuries were incurred in the state. If the number of plaintiffs that live in a state is greater than one-third but less than two-thirds, the act gives federal judges the discretion to decide (based on specified considerations) whether the trial should be held in the state or federal court system. The CAFA applies only to actions filed after February 18, 2005.

Another provision in the act increases a defendant's ability to remove (transfer) a case that was filed in a state court to a federal court, even if the defendant also resides in the state where the action was filed. In cases involving multiple defendants, it also allows one defendant to remove the case to federal court without the consent of all defendants (as was previously required). In sum, the act encourages all class actions to be heard by federal court judges, who have historically been less sympathetic to consumers with product liability claims.

GOALS OF THE ACT

One of the main goals of the CAFA is to prevent plaintiffs' lawyers from shopping around for a state court that is predisposed to be sympathetic to their clients' cause. Corporate lawyers and business groups have been complaining for years that the plaintiffs' lawyers shop for local courts in which judges and juries have a reputation for awarding large verdicts in class-action suits. According to proponents, the new law

law that affects claims filed by a large group of plaintiffs, see this chapter's *Emerging Trends* feature.)

Product liability may be based on the warranty theories just discussed, as well as on the theories of negligence, misrepresentation, and strict liability. We look here at product liability based on negligence and based on misrepresentation.

PRODUCT LIABILITY BASED ON NEGLIGENCE

In Chapter 7, *negligence* was defined as the failure to exercise the degree of care that a reasonable, prudent person would have exercised under the circumstances. If a manufacturer fails to exercise "due care" to make a product safe, a person who is injured by the product may sue the manufacturer for negligence.

DUE CARE MUST BE EXERCISED   Due care must be exercised in designing the product, in selecting the materials, in using the appropriate production process, in assembling and testing the product, and in placing adequate warnings on the label informing the user of dangers of which an ordinary person might not be aware. The duty of care also extends to the inspection

will prevent such practices and help cut down on frivolous lawsuits, ultimately benefiting the business community. According to President George W. Bush, the act marks a critical step toward ending the "lawsuit culture in our country."[b] The CAFA represents only the first step in the growing trend toward tort reform. Next on the agenda is litigation involving asbestos (a product liability action) and medical malpractice claims.

POTENTIAL PROBLEMS WITH THE ACT

Some claim that the end result of the CAFA will be bad for consumers. According to critics, the practical effect of the CAFA will be that many cases will never make it to court. Litigating in federal court is a costly ordeal, and federal courts have more procedural rules than state courts. For this reason, many plaintiffs' attorneys might leave class-action practice, and injured persons with legitimate claims may not be able to obtain the representation they need. In addition, the federal court system is already overburdened. The number of civil cases filed in the federal courts during 2004 rose substantially, while budget cuts forced a 6 percent reduction in staffing.[c] Some commentators suggest that the federal courts are especially unfamiliar and uncomfortable with consumer and product liability claims. Overall, federal courts are expected to allow fewer large class-action suits to go forward. Also, cer-

tain aspects of the CAFA are likely to complicate its application. For example, how will a court determine whether one-third or two-thirds of the plaintiffs are from a particular state without substantial analysis of the class members?

---

b. Presidential press release titled "President Signs Class Action Fairness Act of 2005," February 18, 2005.

c. Administrative Office of the U.S. Courts press release, March 15, 2005.

---

and testing of any purchased components that are used in the product sold by the manufacturer.

PRIVITY OF CONTRACT NOT REQUIRED A product liability action based on negligence does not require the injured plaintiff and the negligent defendant-manufacturer to be in **privity of contract.** In other words, the plaintiff and the defendant need not be directly involved in a contractual relationship. A manufacturer is liable for its failure to exercise due care to *any person* who sustains an injury proximately caused by a negligently made (defective) product.

Relative to the long history of the common law, this exception to the privity requirement is a fairly recent development, dating to the early part of the twentieth century.[16]

PRODUCT LIABILITY BASED ON MISREPRESENTATION

When a fraudulent misrepresentation has been made to a user or consumer and that misrepresentation

---

16. A landmark case in this respect is *MacPherson v. Buick Motor Co.*, 217 N.Y. 382, 111 N.E. 1050 (1916).

ultimately results in an injury, the basis of liability may be the tort of fraud. In this situation, the misrepresentation must have been made knowingly or with reckless disregard for the facts. For example, the intentional mislabeling of packaged cosmetics and the intentional concealment of a product's defects would constitute fraudulent misrepresentation.

NONFRAUDULENT MISREPRESENTATION Nonfraudulent misrepresentation, which occurs when a merchant *innocently* misrepresents the character or quality of goods, can also provide a basis of liability. In this situation, the plaintiff does not have to prove that the misrepresentation was made knowingly. For example, suppose that a pharmaceutical company innocently indicates to the medical profession that a certain drug that it markets is not physically addictive. The company's statement is supported by fairly extensive studies of the medication, none of which revealed any evidence of addictive qualities. Based on the company's information, a physician prescribes the medication to a patient, who develops an addiction that turns out to be fatal. Even though the addiction was a highly uncommon reaction resulting from the victim's unusual susceptibility to this product, the drug company may still be held liable.

THE MISREPRESENTATION MUST BE OF A MATERIAL FACT Whether fraudulent or nonfraudulent, the misrepresentation must be of a material fact (a fact concerning the quality, nature, or appropriate use of the product on which a normal buyer may be expected to rely). There must also have been an intent to induce the buyer's reliance on the misrepresentation. Misrepresentation on a label or advertisement is enough to show an intent to induce the reliance of anyone who may use the product. In addition, the buyer must have relied on the misrepresentation. If the buyer was not aware of the misrepresentation or if it did not influence the transaction, there is normally no liability.

SECTION 5 | Strict Product Liability

Under the doctrine of *strict liability* (discussed in Chapter 7), people may be liable for the results of their acts regardless of their intentions or their exercise of reasonable care. In the 1960s, courts applied the doctrine of strict liability in several landmark cases involving manufactured goods, and it has since become a common method of holding manufacturers liable. Some states, however, including Massachusetts and Virginia, have refused to recognize strict product liability. Additionally, some courts limit the application of the doctrine to cases involving personal injuries (not property damage).

STRICT PRODUCT LIABILITY AND PUBLIC POLICY

The law imposes strict product liability as a matter of public policy. This public policy rests on the threefold assumption that (1) consumers should be protected against unsafe products; (2) manufacturers and distributors should not escape liability for faulty products simply because they are not in privity of contract with the ultimate user of those products; and (3) manufacturers, sellers, and lessors of products are in a better position to bear the costs associated with injuries caused by their products—costs that they can ultimately pass on to all consumers in the form of higher prices.

California was the first state to impose strict product liability in tort on manufacturers. In a landmark 1962 decision, *Greenman v. Yuba Power Products, Inc.*,[17] the California Supreme Court set out the reason for applying tort law rather than contract law (including laws governing warranties) in cases involving consumers who were injured by defective products. According to the *Greenman* court, the "purpose of such liability is to [e]nsure that the costs of injuries resulting from defective products are borne by the manufacturers . . . rather than by the injured persons who are powerless to protect themselves."

THE REQUIREMENTS FOR STRICT PRODUCT LIABILITY

The courts often look to the *Restatements of the Law* for guidance, even though the *Restatements* are not binding authorities. Section 402A of the *Restatement (Second) of Torts*, which was originally issued in 1964, has become a widely accepted statement of the liabilities of sellers of goods (including manufacturers, processors, assemblers, packagers, bottlers, wholesalers, distributors, retailers, and lessors).

The bases for an action in strict liability as set forth in Section 402A of the *Restatement (Second) of Torts*,

---

17. 59 Cal.2d 57, 377 P.2d 897, 27 Cal.Rptr. 697 (1962).

and as the doctrine came to be commonly applied, can be summarized as a series of six requirements, which are listed here.

1. The product must be in a *defective condition* when the defendant sells it.
2. The defendant must normally be engaged in the *business of selling* (or otherwise distributing) that product.
3. The product must be *unreasonably dangerous* to the user or consumer because of its defective condition (in most states).
4. The plaintiff must incur *physical harm* to self or property by use or consumption of the product.
5. The defective condition must be the *proximate cause* of the injury or damage.
6. The *goods must not have been substantially changed* from the time the product was sold to the time the injury was sustained.

Depending on the jurisdiction, if these requirements were met, a manufacturer's liability to an injured party could be virtually unlimited.

PROVING A DEFECTIVE CONDITION   Under these requirements, in any action against a manufacturer, seller, or lessor the plaintiff need not show why or in what manner the product became defective. The plaintiff does, however, have to prove that the product was defective at the time it left the hands of the seller or lessor and that this defective condition makes it "unreasonably dangerous" to the user or consumer. Unless evidence can be presented that will support the conclusion that it was defective when it was sold or leased, the plaintiff normally will not succeed. If the product was delivered in a safe condition and subsequent mishandling made it harmful to the user, the seller or lessor is not strictly liable.

UNREASONABLY DANGEROUS PRODUCTS   The *Restatement* recognizes that many products cannot possibly be made entirely safe for all uses, and thus only holds sellers or lessors liable for products that are *unreasonably* dangerous. A court could consider a product so defective as to be an **unreasonably dangerous product** in either of the following situations:

1. The product was dangerous beyond the expectation of the ordinary consumer.
2. A less dangerous alternative was *economically* feasible for the manufacturer, but the manufacturer failed to produce it.

As will be discussed next, a product may be unreasonably dangerous due to a flaw in the manufacturing process, a design defect, or an inadequate warning.

PRODUCT DEFECTS

Because Section 402A of the *Restatement (Second) of Torts* did not clearly define such terms as *defective* and *unreasonably dangerous*, these terms have been subject to different interpretations by different courts. In 1997, to address these concerns, the American Law Institute (ALI) issued the *Restatement (Third) of Torts: Products Liability*. This *Restatement* defines the three types of product defects that have traditionally been recognized in product liability law—manufacturing defects, design defects, and warning defects.

MANUFACTURING DEFECTS   According to Section 2(a) of the *Restatement* concerning product liability, a product "contains a manufacturing defect when the product departs from its intended design even though all possible care was exercised in the preparation and marketing of the product." Basically, a manufacturing defect is a departure from a product unit's design specifications. Defective products include those that are physically flawed, damaged, or incorrectly assembled. A glass bottle that is made too thin and explodes in a consumer's face is an example of a manufacturing defect. Liability is imposed on the manufacturer (and possibly on the wholesaler and retailer) regardless of whether the manufacturer's quality control efforts were "reasonable." The idea behind holding defendants strictly liable for manufacturing defects is to encourage greater investment in product safety and stringent quality control standards.

DESIGN DEFECTS   In contrast to a manufacturing defect (in which the product fails to meet the manufacturer's design specifications), a design defect relates to the product's actual design and to claims that it created an unreasonable risk to the user. A product "is defective in design when the foreseeable risks of harm posed by the product could have been reduced or avoided by the adoption of a reasonable alternative design by the seller or other distributor, or a predecessor in the commercial chain of distribution, and the omission of the alternative design renders the product not reasonably safe."[18]

---

18. *Restatement (Third) of Torts: Products Liability*, Section 2(b).

—Test for Design Defects. To successfully assert a design defect, a plaintiff has to show that a reasonable alternative design was available and that the defendant's failure to adopt the alternative design rendered the product not reasonably safe. In other words, a manufacturer or other defendant is liable only when the harm was reasonably preventable. In one case, for example, Gillespie, who cut off several of his fingers while operating a table saw, alleged that the blade guards on the saw were defectively designed. At trial, however, an expert testified that the alternative design for blade guards used for table saws could not have been used for the particular cut that Gillespie was performing at the time he was injured. The court found that Gillespie's claim about defective blade guards must fail because there was no proof that the "better" design of guard would have prevented his injury.[19]

—Factors to Be Considered. According to the Official Comments accompanying the *Restatement*, a court can consider a broad range of factors, including the magnitude and probability of the foreseeable risks, and the relative advantages and disadvantages of the product as it was designed and as it could have been designed. For example, suppose that four-year-old Andrea suffers serious burns when she gets out of bed one night to go to the bathroom, trips on the electric cord connected to a hot-water vaporizer, and falls on the vaporizer heating unit. Andrea's parents file a suit against the manufacturer alleging that the vaporizer was defectively designed because the top-heating unit is not secured to the jar that holds the hot water. A court would likely consider the following factors as relevant: (1) the foreseeability that the vaporizer might be accidentally tipped over, (2) the overall safety provided by an alternative design that secures the heating unit to the receptacle holding the water, (3) consumer knowledge or lack of knowledge that the water in the glass jar is scalding hot, (4) the added cost of the safer alternative design, and (5) the relative convenience of a vaporizer with a lift-off cap. If the plaintiff offers sufficient evidence for a reasonable person to conclude that the harm was reasonably preventable, then the manufacturer could be held liable.

WARNING DEFECTS A product may also be deemed defective because of inadequate instructions or warn-

ings. A product "is defective because of inadequate instructions or warnings when the foreseeable risks of harm posed by the product could have been reduced or avoided by the provision of reasonable instructions or warnings by the seller or other distributor, or a predecessor in the commercial chain of distribution, and the omission of the instructions or warnings renders the product not reasonably safe."[20]

Important factors for a court to consider under the *Restatement (Third) of Torts: Products Liability* include the risks of a product, the "content and comprehensibility" and "intensity of expression" of warnings and instructions, and the "characteristics of expected user groups."[21] For example, children would likely respond readily to bright, bold, simple warning labels, whereas educated adults might need more detailed information.

—Obvious Risks. There is no duty to warn about risks that are obvious or commonly known. Warnings about such risks do not add to the safety of a product and could even detract from it by making other warnings seem less significant. The obviousness of a risk and a user's decision to proceed in the face of that risk may be a defense in a product liability suit based on a warning defect. (Defenses to product liability will be discussed later in the chapter.)

—Foreseeable Misuses. Generally, a seller must warn those who purchase its product of the harm that can result from the foreseeable misuse of the product as well. The key is the foreseeability of the misuse. According to the Official Comments accompanying the *Restatement (Third) of Torts: Products Liability*, sellers "are not required to foresee and take precautions against every conceivable mode of use and abuse to which their products might be put."

MARKET-SHARE LIABILITY

Generally, in cases involving product liability, a plaintiff must prove that the defective product that caused his or her injury was the product of a specific defendant. In a few situations, however, courts have dropped this requirement when plaintiffs could not

---

19. *Gillespie v. Sears, Roebuck & Co.,* 386 F.3d 21 (1st Cir. 2004).

20. *Restatement (Third) of Torts: Products Liability,* Section 2(c).
21. *Restatement (Third) of Torts: Products Liability,* Section 2, Comment h.

prove which of many distributors of a harmful product supplied the particular product that caused the injuries. For example, in one case a plaintiff who was a hemophiliac received injections of a blood protein known as antihemophiliac factor (AHF) concentrate. The plaintiff later tested positive for the AIDS (acquired immune deficiency syndrome) virus. Because it was not known which manufacturer was responsible for the particular AHF received by the plaintiff, the court held that all of the manufacturers of AHF could be held liable under the theory of **market-share liability.**[22] Many jurisdictions, however, do not apply this theory, believing that it deviates too significantly from traditional legal principles.[23]

OTHER APPLICATIONS OF STRICT PRODUCT LIABILITY

Strict product liability also applies to suppliers of component parts. For example, suppose that General Motors buys brake pads from a subcontractor and puts them in Chevrolets without changing their composition. If those pads are defective, both the supplier of the brake pads and General Motors will be held strictly liable for the damages caused by the defects.[24]

Although the drafters of Section 402A of the *Restatement (Second) of Torts* did not take a position on bystanders, all courts extend the strict liability of manufacturers and other sellers to injured bystanders. For example, in one case, an automobile manufacturer was held liable for injuries caused by the explosion of a car's motor. A cloud of steam resulting from the explosion caused multiple collisions because other drivers could not see well.[25]

SECTION 6 | Defenses to Product Liability

Defendants in product liability suits can raise a number of defenses. One defense, of course, is to show that there is no basis for the plaintiff's claim. For example,

in a product liability case based on negligence, if a defendant can show that the plaintiff has *not* met the requirements (such as causation) for an action in negligence, generally the defendant will not be liable. In regard to strict product liability, a defendant can claim that the plaintiff failed to meet one of the requirements for an action in strict liability. For example, if the defendant establishes that the goods have been subsequently altered, normally the defendant will not be held liable.[26] Defendants may also assert the defenses discussed next.

ASSUMPTION OF RISK

Assumption of risk can sometimes be used as a defense in a product liability action. To establish such a defense, the defendant must show that (1) the plaintiff knew and appreciated the risk created by the product defect and (2) the plaintiff voluntarily assumed the risk, even though it was unreasonable to do so. For example, if a buyer failed to heed a seller's product recall, the buyer may be deemed to have assumed the risk of the product defect that the seller offered to cure. (See Chapter 7 for a more detailed discussion of assumption of risk.)

PRODUCT MISUSE

Similar to the defense of voluntary assumption of risk is that of **product misuse.** Here, the injured party *does not know that the product is dangerous for a particular use* (contrast this with assumption of risk), but the use is not the one for which the product was designed. The courts have severely limited this defense. For example, even if the injured party does not know about the inherent danger of using the product in a wrong way, if the misuse is reasonably foreseeable, the seller must take measures to guard against it.

Does a manufacturer have a duty to prevent a criminal misuse of its product, particularly if that use is entirely foreign to the purpose for which the product was intended? That was the question in the following case.

---

22. *Smith v. Cutter Biological, Inc.*, 72 Haw. 416, 823 P.2d 717 (1991). See also *Sutowski v. Eli Lilly & Co.*, 82 Ohio St.3d 347, 696 N.E.2d 187 (1998).

23. For the Illinois Supreme Court's position on market-share liability, see *Smith v. Eli Lilly Co.*, 137 Ill.2d 222, 560 N.E.2d 324 (1990).

24. See *Restatement (Third) of Torts: Products Liability*, Section 5.

25. *Giberson v. Ford Motor Co.*, 504 S.W.2d 8 (Mo. 1974).

26. Under some state laws, the failure to properly maintain a product may constitute a subsequent alteration. See, for example, *LaPlante v. American Honda Motor Co.*, 27 F.3d 731 (1st Cir. 1994).

CASE 23.2

United States
District Court,
District of
New Jersey, 2004.
341 F.Supp.2d 499.
http://lawlibrary.rutgers.
edu/fed/search.shtml [a]

Ward v. Arm & Hammer

BACKGROUND AND FACTS *Church & Dwight Company manufactures Arm & Hammer Baking Soda, which features five warnings on its package. George Ward used the baking soda with cocaine to make crack cocaine. After a conviction in March 1995 on criminal charges for distribution of the illegal drug, Ward was sentenced to a two-hundred-month prison term in the low-security Federal Correctional Institution in Petersburg, Virginia. In 2003, Ward filed a suit pro se* [b] *in a federal district court against Church & Dwight, asserting that the manufacturer failed to include a certain sixth warning on its product's package. According to Ward, the package should have included a description of the consequences of criminally misusing baking soda to make crack cocaine. He argued, "I feel [that] if I was forewarned by this company that I'd never [have] used this product like I was charged with." Church & Dwight filed a motion to dismiss the complaint.*

IN THE LANGUAGE OF THE COURT

CHESLER, District Judge.
* * * *

DISCUSSION

A. *Motion to Dismiss Standard*

In deciding a motion to dismiss * * * all allegations in the complaint must be taken as true and viewed in the light most favorable to the plaintiff. * * * *If, after viewing the allegations in the complaint in the light most favorable to the plaintiff, it appears beyond doubt that no relief could be granted under any set of facts which could prove consistent with the allegations, a court shall dismiss a complaint for failure to state a claim.* [Emphasis added.]

In the case of a *pro se* litigant, the court must find that it is clear beyond doubt that the plaintiff can prove no set of facts in support of his claim which would entitle him to relief.

B. *Duty to Warn of the Consequences of Criminal Misuse of Products*

Nowhere in his complaint or response brief does Plaintiff assert that he was unaware that distribution of crack cocaine was unlawful or that ingestion of crack cocaine was harmful. Indeed, Plaintiff in his response brief implies that it is common knowledge that misuse of baking soda with cocaine may be harmful. Furthermore, under [the applicable state] law, citizens are charged with knowledge of the law, including the criminal laws. It follows that Church & Dwight had no duty to warn Plaintiff of that which he knew, and that which the law already charged him with knowing.

Additionally, *the law is clear that manufacturers have no duty to warn of the potential consequences for criminal misuse of their products.* * * * [M]anufacturers have no duty to prevent a criminal misuse of their products which is entirely foreign to the purpose for which the product was intended. Plaintiff himself acknowledges and concedes that "baking soda is not a product that * * * is intended for the production for illegal drug use or distribution." Plaintiff contends, though, that "it cannot be said that the use of this product to make Crack Cocaine is *foreign* anymore, this is well established knowledge * * *." However, * * * the manufacturer of a raw material or component part that is not itself dangerous has no legal duty to prevent a buyer from incorporating the material or part into another device that is or may be dangerous. [Emphasis added.]

To require Church & Dwight to warn customers of potential criminal consequences for the intentional misuse of baking soda would be analogous to requiring that all automobile manufacturers place warnings on their products to the effect that you may be subject to punishment

---

a. In the "Find Decisions by Docket Number" section, select "Civil Case," enter "03-6113" in the "Enter Docket Number" boxes, and click on "Submit Form." In the result, click the appropriate link to access the opinion. Rutgers University Law School in Camden, New Jersey, maintains this Web site.

b. *Pro se* means that Ward filed his suit and argued his case without an attorney.

CASE 23.2 | **Continued**

if you use the cars for illegal drag-racing. Although the manufacturers in both instances may be aware of the products' potential for misuse, this itself does not give rise to a duty to warn of the criminal consequences of such unintended activities.

CONCLUSION

Having taken into account the fact that Plaintiff is proceeding in this matter *pro se,* the Court is satisfied nonetheless that it is clear beyond doubt that the plaintiff can prove no set of facts in support of his claim which would entitle him to relief. For the foregoing reasons, the Court will grant Defendant's Motion to Dismiss Plaintiff's claim *   *   *   .

DECISION AND REMEDY   *The court granted Church & Dwight's motion to dismiss Ward's complaint. The court held that the manufacturer of Arm & Hammer Baking Soda had no duty to warn that the use of its product with illegal drugs was prohibited and punishable by law.*

WHAT IF THE FACTS WERE DIFFERENT?   *Suppose that Ward had not been aware that misuse of baking soda with cocaine is harmful. Would the result in this case have been different?*

COMPARATIVE NEGLIGENCE (FAULT)

Developments in the area of comparative negligence, or fault (discussed in Chapter 7), have also affected the doctrine of strict liability—the most extreme theory of product liability. Whereas previously the plaintiff's conduct was not a defense to strict liability, today many jurisdictions, when apportioning liability and damages, consider the negligent or intentional actions of both the plaintiff and the defendant. This means that even if the plaintiff misused the products, she or he may nonetheless be able to recover at least some damages for injuries caused by the defendant's defective product. For example, Dan Smith, a mechanic in Alaska, was not wearing a hard hat at work when he was asked to start the diesel engine of an air compressor. Because the compressor was an older model, he had to prop open a door to start it. When he got the engine started, the door fell from its position and hit Smith's head, which resulted in his suffering from seizures and epilepsy. Smith sued the manufacturer, claiming that the engine was defectively designed. The Alaska Supreme Court ruled that a defendant in a product liability action can raise the plaintiff's ordinary negligence as a defense.[27]

COMMONLY KNOWN DANGERS

The dangers associated with certain products (such as matches and sharp knives) are so commonly known that, as already mentioned, manufacturers need not

warn users of those dangers. If a defendant succeeds in convincing the court that a plaintiff's injury resulted from a *commonly known danger,* the defendant will not be liable.

A classic case on this issue involved a plaintiff who was injured when an elastic exercise rope she had purchased slipped off her foot and struck her in the eye, causing a detachment of the retina. The plaintiff claimed that the manufacturer should be liable because it had failed to warn users that the exerciser might slip off a foot in such a manner. The court stated that to hold the manufacturer liable in these circumstances "would go beyond the reasonable dictates of justice in fixing the liabilities of manufacturers." After all, stated the court, "[a]lmost every physical object can be inherently dangerous or potentially dangerous in a sense. . . . A manufacturer cannot manufacture a knife that will not cut or a hammer that will not mash a thumb or a stove that will not burn a finger. The law does not require [manufacturers] to warn of such common dangers."[28]

A related defense is the *knowledgeable user* defense. If a particular danger is or should be commonly known by particular users of a product, the manufacturer need not warn these users of the danger. In the following case, the plaintiffs alleged that McDonald's, the well-known fast-food chain, should be held liable for failing to warn customers of the adverse health effects of eating its food products.

---

27. *Smith v. Ingersoll-Rand Co.,* 14 P.3d 990 (Alaska 2000).

28. *Jamieson v. Woodward & Lothrop,* 247 F.2d 23 (D.C. 1957).

CASE 23.3

United States
District Court,
Southern District
of New York, 2003.
237 F.Supp.2d 512.

Pelman v. McDonald's Corp.

SWEET, J. [Judge]

This action presents unique and challenging issues. The plaintiffs have alleged that the practices of [McDonald's Corporation and McDonald's of New York—collectively, McDonald's] in making and selling their products are deceptive and that this deception has caused the minors who have consumed McDonald's products to injure their health by becoming obese. Questions of personal responsibility, common knowledge and public health are presented * * * .

* * * *

This opinion is guided by the principle that *legal consequences should not attach to the consumption of hamburgers and other fast food fare unless consumers are unaware of the dangers of eating such food.* * * * [K]nowledge is power. Following from this aphorism, one important principle in assigning legal responsibility is the common knowledge of consumers. If consumers know (or reasonably should know) the potential ill health effects of eating at McDonald's, they cannot blame McDonald's if they, nonetheless, choose to satiate their appetite with a surfeit of supersized McDonald's products. On the other hand, consumers cannot be expected to protect against a danger that was solely within McDonald's knowledge. Thus, one necessary element of any potentially viable claim must be that McDonald's products involve a danger that is not within the common knowledge of consumers. * * * [Emphasis added.]

* * * Americans now spend more than $110 billion on fast food each year, and on any given day in the United States, almost one in four adults visits a fast food restaurant. * * *

* * * *

The plaintiffs commenced suit on August 22, 2002, in the State Supreme Court of New York, Bronx County. Defendants removed the action to [the federal district court for] the Southern District of New York on September 30, 2002 * * * .

McDonald's filed [a] motion to dismiss plaintiffs' complaint (the "Complaint") on October 7, 2002. * * *

* * * *

Ashley Pelman, a minor, and her mother and natural guardian Roberta Pelman are residents of the Bronx, New York.

* * * *

[Ashley and other teenagers] are consumers who have purchased and consumed the defendants' products and * * * have become overweight and have developed diabetes, coronary heart disease, high blood pressure, elevated cholesterol intake, and/or other detrimental and adverse health effects * * * .

* * * Ashley and Roberta Pelman purchased and consumed food products at the Bruckner Boulevard [McDonald's] outlet. * * * All products, ingredients, promotions and advertisements sold, provided, utilized, advertised and promoted by the * * * Bruckner Boulevard [outlet] were authorized by McDonald's Corp. and McDonald's of New York.

* * * *

Obese individuals have a 50 to 100 percent increased risk of premature death from all causes. Approximately 300,000 deaths a year in the United States are currently associated with overweight and obesity. * * * [L]eft unabated, overweight and obesity may soon cause as much preventable disease and death as cigarette smoking.

* * * *

[Among other things, the plaintiffs assert] that McDonald's failed to post nutritional labeling on the products and at points of purchase. * * *

* * * *

* * * Plaintiffs admit that McDonald's has made its nutritional information available online and do not contest that such information is available upon request. Unless McDonald's

CASE 23.3 | **Continued**

has specifically promised to provide nutritional information on all its products and at all points of purchase, plaintiffs do not state a claim.

* * * *

[Or] in order to state a claim, the Complaint must allege either that the attributes of McDonald's products are so extraordinarily unhealth[ful] that they are outside the reasonable contemplation of the consuming public or that the products are so extraordinarily unhealth[ful] as to be dangerous in their intended use. The Complaint—which merely alleges that the foods contain high levels of cholesterol, fat, salt and sugar, and that the foods are therefore unhealth[ful]—fails to reach this bar. It is well-known that fast food in general, and McDonald's products in particular, contain high levels of cholesterol, fat, salt, and sugar, and that such attributes are bad for one.

* * * If a person knows or should know that eating copious orders of supersized McDonald's products is unhealth[ful] and may result in weight gain (and its concomitant [associated] problems) because of the high levels of cholesterol, fat, salt and sugar, it is not the place of the law to protect them from their own excesses. Nobody is forced to eat at McDonald's. (Except, perhaps, parents of small children who desire McDonald's food, toy promotions or playgrounds and demand their parents' accompaniment.) Even more pertinent, nobody is forced to supersize their meal or choose less health[ful] options on the menu.

As long as a consumer exercises free choice with appropriate knowledge, liability * * * *will not attach to a manufacturer.* It is only when that free choice becomes but a chimera [illusion]—for instance, by the masking of information necessary to make the choice, such as the knowledge that eating McDonald's with a certain frequency would irrefragably [indisputably] cause harm—that manufacturers should be held accountable. Plaintiffs have failed to allege in the Complaint that their decisions to eat at McDonald's several times a week were anything but a choice freely made and which now may not be pinned on McDonald's. [Emphasis added.]

* * * *

For the forgoing reasons, the Complaint is dismissed in its entirety.

QUESTIONS

1. On what reasoning did the court base its dismissal of the plaintiffs' complaint?
2. What might the plaintiffs have alleged (and substantiated with proof) to succeed in their suit?

STATUTES OF LIMITATIONS AND REPOSE

As discussed in Chapter 1, *statutes of limitations* restrict the time within which an action may be brought. A typical statute of limitations provides that an action must be brought within a specified period of time after the cause of action accrues. Generally, a cause of action is held to accrue when some damage occurs. Sometimes, the running of the prescribed period is *tolled* (that is, suspended) until the party suffering an injury has discovered it or should have discovered it.

Many states have passed laws, called **statutes of repose,** placing outer time limits on some claims so that the defendant will not be left vulnerable to law-suits indefinitely. These statutes may limit the time within which a plaintiff can file a product liability suit. Typically, a statute of repose begins to run at an earlier date and runs for a longer time than a statute of limitations. For example, a statute of repose may require that claims must be brought within twelve years from the date of sale or manufacture of the defective product. It is immaterial that the product is defective or causes an injury if the injury occurs *after* this statutory period has lapsed. In addition, some of these legislative enactments have limited the application of the doctrine of strict liability to only new goods.

REVIEWING WARRANTIES AND PRODUCT LIABILITY

Shalene Kolchek bought a Great Lakes spa from Val Porter, a dealer who was selling spas at the state fair. Porter told Kolchek that Great Lakes spas are "top of the line" and "the Cadillac of spas" and indicated that the spa she was buying was "fully warranted for three years." Kolchek signed an installment contract; then Porter handed her the manufacturer's paperwork and arranged for the spa to be delivered and installed for her. Three months later, Kolchek noticed that one corner of the spa was leaking onto her new deck and causing damage. She complained to Porter, but he did nothing about the problem. Kolchek's family continued to use the spa. Using the information presented in the chapter, answer the following questions.

1. Describe any express or implied warranties that applied to this sale. Were any of these warranties breached?

2. Did Porter's statement that the spa was "top of the line" and "the Cadillac of spas" create any type of warranty? Why or why not?

3. If the paperwork provided to Kolchek after her purchase indicated that the spa had no warranty, would this be an effective disclaimer under the UCC? Explain.

4. One night, Kolchek's six-year-old daughter, Litisha, was in the spa with her mother. Litisha's hair became entangled in the spa's drain and she was sucked down and held underwater for a prolonged period, causing her to suffer brain damage. Under which theory or theories of product liability can Kolchek sue Porter to recover for Litisha's injuries?

5. If Kolchek had negligently left Litisha alone in the spa prior to the incident described in the previous question, what defense to liability might Porter assert?

TERMS AND CONCEPTS TO REVIEW

express warranty 450

implied warranty 452

implied warranty of fitness
   for a particular purpose 453

implied warranty of
   merchantability 452

market-share liability 463

privity of contract 459

product liability 457

product misuse 463

statute of repose 467

unreasonably dangerous
   product 461

QUESTIONS AND CASE PROBLEMS

23–1. Moon, a farmer, needs to install a two-thousand-pound piece of equipment in his barn. This will require lifting the equipment thirty feet up into a hayloft. Moon goes to Davidson Hardware and tells Davidson that he needs some heavy-duty rope to be used on his farm. Davidson recommends a one-inch-thick nylon rope, and Moon purchases two hundred feet of it. Moon ties the rope around the piece of equipment; puts the rope through a pulley; and, with a tractor, lifts the equipment off the ground. Suddenly the rope breaks. The equipment crashes to the ground and is severely damaged. Moon files suit against Davidson for breach of the implied warranty of fitness for a particular purpose. Discuss how successful Moon will be in his suit.

23–2. QUESTION WITH SAMPLE ANSWER

Colt manufactures a new pistol. The firing of the pistol depends on an enclosed high-pressure device. The pistol has been thoroughly tested in two laboratories in the Midwest, and its design and manufacture are in accord with current technology. Wayne purchases one of the new pistols from Hardy's Gun and Rifle Emporium. When he uses the pistol in the high altitude of the Rockies, the difference in pressure causes the pistol to misfire, resulting in serious injury to Wayne. Colt can prove that all due care was used in the manufacturing process, and it refuses to pay for Wayne's injuries. Discuss Colt's liability in tort.

For a sample answer to this question, go to Appendix I at the end of this text.

23–3. Darrow purchases a new car from Slippery Motors. The retail installment sales contract states immediately above the buyer's signature in large, bold type: "There are no warranties that extend beyond the description on the face hereof" and "There are no express warranties that accompany this sale unless expressly written in this contract." Before purchasing the car, Darrow specifically informed Slippery's salesperson that he wanted a car that could be driven in a dusty area without needing mechanical repairs. Slippery's salesperson told Darrow, "Nothing will go wrong with this car, but if it does, return it to us, and we will repair it without cost to you." Neither this statement nor any similar statement appears in the retail sales contract. Darrow drives the car into a dust storm. The air filter gets plugged up and the car engine overheats, causing motor damage. Slippery Motors refuses to repair the engine under any warranty. Darrow claims that Slippery is liable for breach of the implied warranty of fitness for a particular purpose, that the Magnuson-Moss Warranty Act prohibits disclaiming this implied warranty, and that the salesperson's express warranty has also been breached. Discuss Darrow's claims.

23–4. Baxter manufactures electric hair dryers. Julie purchases a Baxter dryer from her local Ace Drugstore. Cox, a friend and guest in Julie's home, has taken a shower and wants to dry her hair. Julie tells Cox to use the new Baxter hair dryer that she has just purchased. As Cox plugs in the dryer, sparks fly out from the motor, and sparks continue to fly as she operates it. Despite this, Cox begins drying her hair. Suddenly, the entire dryer ignites into flames, severely burning Cox's scalp. Cox sues Baxter on the basis of negligence and strict liability in tort. Baxter admits that the dryer was defective but denies liability, particularly because Cox was not the person who purchased the dryer. In other words, Cox had no contractual relationship with Baxter. Discuss the validity of Baxter's defense. Are there any other defenses that Baxter might assert to avoid liability? Discuss fully.

23–5. EXPRESS WARRANTIES. Ronald Anderson, Jr., a self-employed construction contractor, went to a Home Depot store to buy lumber for a construction project. It was raining, so Anderson bought a tarp to cover the bed of his pickup truck. To secure the tarp, Anderson bought a bag of cords made by Bungee International Manufacturing Corp. The printed material on the Bungee bag included the words "Made in the U.S.A." and "Premium Quality." To secure the tarp at the rear of

the passenger's side, Anderson put one hook into the eyelet of the tarp, stretched the cord over the utility box, and hooked the other end in the drainage hole in the bottom of the box. As Anderson stood up, the upper hook dislodged and hit him in the left eye. Anderson filed a suit in a federal district court against Bungee and others, alleging in part breach of express warranty. Anderson alleged that the labeling on the bag of cords was an express warranty that "played some role in [his] decision to purchase this product." Bungee argued that, in regard to the cords' quality, the statements were puffery. Bungee filed a motion for summary judgment on this issue. Will the court grant the motion? Why or why not? [*Anderson v. Bungee International Manufacturing Corp.*, 44 F.Supp.2d 534 (S.D.N.Y. 1999)]

23–6. DESIGN DEFECT. In May 1995, Ms. McCathern and her daughter, together with McCathern's cousin, Ms. Sanders, and her daughter, were riding in Sanders's 1994 Toyota 4Runner. Sanders was driving, McCathern was in the front passenger seat, and the children were in the backseat. Everyone was wearing a seat belt. While the group was traveling south on Oregon State Highway 395 at a speed of approximately fifty miles per hour, an oncoming vehicle veered into Sanders's lane of travel. When Sanders tried to steer clear, the 4Runner rolled over and landed upright on its four wheels. During the rollover, the roof over the front passenger seat collapsed, and as a result, McCathern sustained serious, permanent injuries. McCathern filed a suit in an Oregon state court against Toyota Motor Corp. and others, alleging in part that the 1994 4Runner "was dangerously defective and unreasonably dangerous in that the vehicle, as designed and sold, was unstable and prone to rollover." What is the test for product liability based on a design defect? What would McCathern have to prove to succeed under that test? [*McCathern v. Toyota Motor Corp.*, 332 Or. 59, 23 P.3d 320 (2001)]

23–7. CASE PROBLEM WITH SAMPLE ANSWER

Mary Jane Boerner began smoking in 1945 at the age of fifteen. For a short time, she smoked Lucky Strikes (a brand of cigarettes) before switching to the Pall Mall brand, which she smoked until she quit altogether in 1981. Pall Malls had higher levels of carcinogenic tar than other cigarettes and lacked effective filters, which would have reduced the amount of tar inhaled into the lungs. In 1996, Mary Jane developed lung cancer. She and her husband, Henry Boerner, filed a suit in a federal district court against Brown & Williamson Tobacco Co., the maker of Pall Malls. The Boerners claimed, among other things, that Pall Malls contained a design defect. Mary Jane died in 1999. According to Dr. Peter Marvin, her treating physician, she died from the effects of cigarette smoke. Henry continued the suit, offering evidence that Pall Malls featured a filter that actually increased the amount of tar taken into the body. When is a product defective in design? Does this product meet the requirements? Why or why not? [*Boerner v. Brown & Williamson Tobacco Co.*, 394 F.3d 594 (8th Cir. 2005)]

To view a sample answer for this case problem, go to this book's Web site at http://wbl.westbuslaw.com, select "Chapter 23," and click on "Case Problem with Sample Answer."

23–8. IMPLIED WARRANTIES. Shalom Malul contracted with Capital Cabinets, Inc., in August 1999 for new kitchen cabinets made by Holiday Kitchens. The price was $10,900. On Capital's recommendation, Malul hired Barry Burger to install the cabinets for $1,600. Burger finished the job in March 2000, and Malul contracted for more cabinets at a price of $2,300, which Burger installed in April. Within a couple of weeks, the doors on several of the cabinets began to "melt"—the laminate (surface covering) began to pull away from the substrate (the material underneath the surface). Capital replaced several of the doors, but the problem occurred again, involving a total of six out of thirty doors. A Holiday Kitchens representative inspected the cabinets and concluded that the melting was due to excessive heat, the result of the doors being placed too close to the stove. Malul filed a suit in a New York state court against Capital alleging, among other things, a breach of the implied warranty of merchantability. Were these goods "merchantable"? Why or why not? [*Malul v. Capital Cabinets, Inc.*, 191 Misc.2d 399, 740 N.Y.S.2d 828 (N.Y.City Civ.Ct. 2002)]

23–9. PRODUCT LIABILITY. In January 1999, John Clark of Clarksdale, Mississippi, bought a paintball gun. Clark practiced with the gun and knew how to screw in the CO_2 cartridge, pump the gun, and use its safety and trigger. He hunted and had taken a course in hunter safety education. He knew that protective eyewear was available for purchase, but he chose not to buy it. Clark also understood that it was "common sense" not to shoot anyone in the face. Chris Rico, another Clarksdale resident, owned a paintball gun made by Brass Eagle, Inc. Rico was similarly familiar with the gun's use and its risks. At that time and place, Clark, Rico, and their friends played a game that involved shooting paintballs at cars whose occupants also had the guns. One night, while Clark and Rico were cruising with their guns, Rico shot at Clark's car but hit Clark in the eye. Clark filed a suit in a Mississippi state court against Brass Eagle to recover for the injury, alleging in part that its gun was defectively designed. During the trial, Rico testified that his gun "never malfunctioned." In whose favor should the court rule? Why? [*Clark v. Brass Eagle, Inc.*, 866 So.2d 456 (Miss. 2004)]

23–10.   VIDEO QUESTION

Go to this text's Web site at **http://wbl.westbuslaw.com** and select "Chapter 23." Click on "Video Questions" and view the video titled *Warranties*. Then answer the following questions.

(a) Discuss whether the grocery store's label of a "Party Platter for Twenty" creates an express warranty under the UCC that the platter will actually serve twenty people.
(b) List and describe any implied warranties discussed in the chapter that apply to this scenario.
(c) How would a court determine whether Oscar had breached any express or implied warranties concerning the quantity of food on the platter?

LAW | on the Web

For updated links to resources available on the Web, as well as a variety of other materials, visit this text's Web site at **http://wbl.westbuslaw.com**.

The Federal Trade Commission posts *A Businessperson's Guide to Federal Warranty Law* at

http://www.ftc.gov/bcp/conline/pubs/buspubs/warranty.htm

For information on the *Restatements of the Law*, including the *Restatement (Second) of Torts* and the *Restatement (Third) of Torts: Products Liability*, go to the Web site of the American Law Institute at

http://www.ali.org

For information on product liability suits against tobacco companies, go to the Web site of the Library & Center for Knowledge Management, which is maintained by the University of California, San Francisco, at

http://library.ucsf.edu/tobacco/litigation

LEGAL RESEARCH EXERCISES ON THE WEB

Go to **http://wbl.westbuslaw.com**, the Web site that accompanies this text. Select "Chapter 23" and click on "Internet Exercises." There you will find the following Internet research exercises that you can perform to learn more about topics covered in this chapter.

Activity 23–1: **LEGAL PERSPECTIVE**
Product Liability Litigation

Activity 23–2: **MANAGEMENT PERSPECTIVE**
The Duty to Warn

Activity 23–3: **SOCIAL PERSPECTIVE**
Warranties

Domestic and International Sales and Lease Contracts

Transactions involving the sale or lease of goods make up a great deal of the business activity in the commercial and manufacturing sectors of our economy. Articles 2 and 2A of the Uniform Commercial Code (UCC) govern the sale or lease of goods in every state except Louisiana. Many of the UCC's provisions express our ethical standards. As noted in Chapter 20, in 2003 UCC Articles 2 and 2A were amended to bring them into line with modern commercial practices, including electronic contracting.

Good Faith and Commercial Reasonableness

The concepts of good faith and commercial reasonableness permeate the UCC and help to prevent unethical behavior by businesspersons. These two key concepts are read into every contract and impose certain duties on all parties. Additionally, reasonability in the formation, performance, and termination of contracts underlies virtually all of the UCC's provisions.

As an example of the UCC's approach, consider Section 2–311(1), which states that when parties leave the particulars of performance—a term—to be specified by one of the parties, "[a]ny such specification must be made in good faith and within limits set by commercial reasonableness." The requirement of commercial reasonableness means that the term subsequently supplied by one party should not come as a surprise to the other. The party filling in the missing term may not take advantage of the opportunity to add a term that will be beneficial to himself or herself (and detrimental to the other party) and then demand contractual performance of the other party that was totally unanticipated. Under the UCC, the party filling in the missing term is not allowed to deviate from what is commercially reasonable in the context of the transaction. Courts frequently look to course of dealing, usage of trade, and the surrounding circumstances in determining what is commercially reasonable in a given situation.

Good Faith in Output and Requirements Contracts The obligation of good faith is particularly important in so-called output and requirements contracts. UCC 2–306 states that "quantity" in these contracts "means such actual output or requirements as may occur in good faith." For example, suppose that Mandrow's Machines has fifty employees assembling personal computers. Mandrow's has a requirements contract with Advanced Tech Circuit Boards, under which Advanced Tech is to supply Mandrow's with all of the circuit boards it needs. If Mandrow's suddenly quadruples the size of its business, it cannot insist that Advanced Tech supply it with all of its requirements, as specified in the original contract.

Consider another example. Assume that the market price of the goods subject to a requirements contract rises rapidly and dramatically because of a shortage of materials necessary to their production. The buyer could claim that her or his needs are equivalent to the entire output of the seller. Then, after buying all of the seller's output at the contract price (which is substantially below the market price), the buyer could turn around and sell the goods that she or he does not need at the higher market price. Under the UCC, this type of unethical behavior is prohibited, even though the buyer in this instance has not technically breached the contract.

Bad Faith Not Required A party can breach the obligation of good faith under the UCC even if the party did not show "bad faith"—that is, even when there is no proof that the party was dishonest. For example, in one case a large manufacturer of recreational boats, Genmar Holdings, Inc., purchased Horizon, a small company that produced a particular type of "deep-V" fishing boat. Genmar bought Horizon to expand into the southern boat market and to prevent Horizon from becoming a potential future competitor. At the time of the sale, Genmar executives promised that Horizon boats would be the "champion" of the facility and vowed to keep Horizon's key employees (including the founder and his family) on as managers. The contract required Genmar to pay Horizon a lump sum in cash as well as paying "earn-out consideration" under a specified formula for five years. The "earn-out" amount depended on the number of Horizon brand boats sold and on the annual gross revenues of the facility.

One year after the sale, Genmar renamed the Horizon brand of boats "Nova" and told employees at the facility to give priority to producing the original Genmar brand of boats over the Nova boats. Because the Genmar boats were more difficult and time consuming to make than the Nova boats, the facility's gross revenues and production decreased, and Genmar was not required to pay the "earn-out" amounts. Eventually, Genmar fired the former Horizon employees and stopped manufacturing the Nova brand of boats entirely. The former employees filed a suit alleging that Genmar had breached the implied covenant of good faith and fair dealing. The defendants argued that they could not have violated good faith because there was no proof that they had engaged in fraud, deceit, or misrepresentation. The court held for the plaintiffs, however, and the decision was affirmed on appeal.[1] It is possible for a party to breach its good

1. *O'Tool v. Genmar Holdings, Inc.,* 387 F.3d 1188 (10th Cir. 2004).

faith obligations under the UCC even if the party did not engage in fraud, deceit, or misrepresentation.

Commercial Reasonableness Under the UCC, the concept of good faith is closely linked to commercial reasonableness. All commercial actions—including the performance and enforcement of contract obligations—must display commercial reasonableness. A merchant is expected to act in a reasonable manner according to reasonable commercial customs.

The concept of commercial reasonableness is clearly expressed in the doctrine of commercial impracticability. Under this doctrine, which is related to the common law doctrine of impossibility of performance, a party's nonperformance of a contractual obligation may be excused when, because of unforeseen circumstances, performance of the contract becomes impracticable. The courts make clear, however, that before performance will be excused under this doctrine, the nonperforming party must have made every reasonable effort to fulfill his or her obligations.

The General Requirement of Reasonability

The requirement of reasonability is expressed numerous times in the UCC. If you examine the UCC in Appendix C, you will see that the word *reasonable* appears again and again in its pages. Who decides what is "reasonable"? Generally, when the parties disagree over the issue, this decision is left up to the courts. Often, as already indicated, reasonability requires the parties to a contract to avoid unfairly surprising one another with their actions.

Businesspersons who fail to take the requirement of reasonability seriously may be forced to do so by a court, and sometimes at a high cost. Consider an example. Maytronics, Ltd., a manufacturer of pool products, contracted to sell its robotic pool cleaners to Aqua Vac Systems, Inc. (AVS), a distributor of pool products. The contract, although renewable automatically on an annual basis, was terminable at will. A few years later, AVS developed its own pool cleaner and terminated the contract. Maytronics sued AVS for breach of contract, alleging that AVS had failed to give Maytronics adequate prior notice of termination. As a result, Maytronics asserted, it faced serious losses because it had stocked up on materials and made commitments to suppliers. AVS responded that it had not breached the contract because the contract was terminable at will.

The court cited UCC 2–309, which requires that when one party terminates a contract, even a contract that is terminable at will, the other party must be given "reasonable notification" of the termination. The court held that in this case "reasonable notice" meant at least six months. Because AVS had not given reasonable notice, it had breached the contract and was ordered to pay Maytronics more than $700,000 in damages (including lost profits).[2]

---

2. *Maytronics, Ltd. v. Aqua Vac Systems, Inc.*, 277 F.3d 1317 (11th Cir. 2002).

Clearly, AVS could have prevented this lawsuit—and the payment of significant damages—by informing Maytronics that it was developing its own pool cleaner and giving Maytronics sufficient notice that it was terminating their contract. As it was, AVS did neither of these things—and suffered the consequences.

The Concept of the Good Faith Purchaser

The concept of the good faith purchaser reflects the UCC's emphasis on protecting innocent parties. Suppose, for example, that you innocently and in good faith purchase a boat from someone who appears to have good title and who demands and receives from you a fair market price. The UCC believes that you should be protected from the possibility that the real owner—from whom the seller may have fraudulently obtained the boat—will later appear and demand his or her boat back. (Nothing, however, prevents the true owner from bringing suit against the party who defrauded him or her.)

Ethical questions arise, however, when the purchaser is not quite so innocent. Suppose that the purchaser has reason to suspect that the seller may not have good title to the goods being sold but nonetheless lets the transaction go forward because it is a "good deal." At what point does the buyer, in this situation, cross over the boundary that separates the good faith purchaser from one who purchases in bad faith? This boundary is a significant one in the law of sales because the UCC will not be a refuge for those who purchase in bad faith. The term *good faith purchaser* means just that— one who enters into a contract for the purchase of goods without knowing, or having any reason to know, that there is anything shady or illegal about the deal.

Unconscionability

The doctrine of unconscionability represents a good example of how the law attempts to enforce ethical behavior. This doctrine suggests that some contracts may be so unfair to one party as to be unenforceable, even though that party originally agreed to the contract's terms. Section 2–302 of the UCC provides that a court will consider the fairness of contracts and may hold that a contract or any clause of a contract was unconscionable at the time it was made. If so, the court may refuse to enforce the contract, enforce the contract without the unconscionable clause, or limit the application of the clause so as to avoid an unconscionable result.

The Test for Unconscionability The UCC does not define the term *unconscionability*. The drafters of the UCC, however, have added explanatory comments to the relevant sections, and these comments serve as guidelines for applying the UCC. Comment 1 to Section 2–302 suggests that the basic test for unconscionability is whether, under the circumstances existing at the time of the contract's formation, the clause in question was so one sided as to be unconscionable. This test is to be applied against the general commercial background of the contract. For example, a court might find that a contract between a merchant-seller and a marginally literate consumer was unfair and unenforceable, but the court might uphold the same contract when it was made between two merchants.

Unconscionability—A Case Example

In one case applying Section 2–302, a New York appellate court held that an arbitration clause was unconscionable and refused to enforce it. Gateway 2000, Inc., which sells computers and software directly to consumers, included in its retail agreements a clause specifying that any dispute arising out of the contract had to be arbitrated in Chicago, Illinois, in accordance with the arbitration rules of the International Chamber of Commerce (ICC).

A number of consumers who had purchased Gateway products became incensed when they learned that ICC rules governing arbitration required advance fees of $4,000 (more than the cost of most Gateway products), of which the $2,000 registration fee was nonrefundable—even if the consumer prevailed at the arbitration. Additionally, the consumers would have to pay travel expenses to Chicago. In the class-action litigation against Gateway that followed, the New York court agreed with the consumers that the "egregiously oppressive" arbitration clause was unconscionable: "Barred from resorting to the courts by the arbitration clause in the first instance, the designation of a financially prohibitive forum effectively bars consumers from this forum as well; consumers are thus left with no forum at all in which to resolve a dispute."[3]

Warranties

A seller or lessor has not only a legal obligation to provide safe products but also an ethical one. When faced with the possibility of increasing safety at no extra cost, every ethical businessperson will certainly opt for a safer product. An ethical issue arises, however, when producing a safer product means higher costs. To some extent, our warranty laws serve to protect consumers from sellers who may be tempted to neglect ethical concerns if what they are doing is both legal and profitable.

Express and Implied Warranties

Both express and implied warranties are recognized by the UCC. Under UCC 2–314 and 2A–212, goods sold by a merchant or leased by a lessor must be fit for the ordinary purposes for which such goods are used, be of proper quality, and be properly labeled and packaged. A description of goods is an express warranty, and hence a seller or lessor of goods may be held to have breached a contract if the goods fail to conform to the description. The UCC injects greater fairness into contractual

situations by recognizing descriptions as express warranties. The UCC acknowledges that a buyer or lessee may often reasonably believe that a seller or lessor is warranting his or her product, even though the seller or lessor may not use a formal word such as *warrant* or *guarantee*. Thus, the law imposes an ethical obligation on sellers and lessors in a statutory form.

Warranty Disclaimers

The UCC requirement that warranty disclaimers be sufficiently conspicuous to catch the eye of a reasonable purchaser is based on the ethical premise that sellers of goods should not take advantage of unwary consumers, who may not—in the excitement of making a new purchase—always read the "fine print" on standard purchase-order forms. As discussed in Chapter 23, if a seller or lessor, when attempting to disclaim warranties, fails to meet the specific requirements imposed by the UCC, the warranties will not be effectively disclaimed. Before the UCC was adopted by the states, in contrast, purchasers of automobiles frequently signed standard-form purchase agreements drafted by the auto manufacturer without learning until later the meaning of all the fine print.

Freedom of Contract versus Freedom from Contract—Revisited

Although freedom of contract reflects a basic ethical principle in our society, courts have made it clear that when such freedom leads to gross unfairness, it should be curbed. (Several examples of the exceptions to freedom of contract that courts will make were offered in the *Focus on Ethics* feature at the end of Unit Three.) Nonetheless, before the UCC was in effect, courts generally would not intervene in cases involving warranty disclaimers in fine print or otherwise "hidden" in a standard purchase-order form. Exceptions were made only when the resulting unfairness "shocked the conscience" of the court. By obligating sellers and lessors to meet specific requirements when disclaiming warranties, the UCC has made dealing fairly with buyers and lessees—already an ethical obligation of all sellers and lessors of goods—a legal obligation as well.

Today, if a warranty disclaimer unfairly "surprises" a purchaser or a lessee, chances are that the disclaimer was not sufficiently conspicuous. In this situation, the unfairness of the bargain need not be so great as to "shock the court's conscience" before a remedy will be granted.

The Battle of the Forms

UCC Section 2–207 provides that a contract can be entered into even though the acceptance includes additional terms. Conflicts often arise because whether a form is defined as an offer or an acceptance can have significant consequences for the parties. Indeed, one of the results of Section 2–207 is that buyers and sellers go to great lengths to draft their responses as "offers" or "counteroffers" (instead of acceptances) so that

---

3. *Brower v. Gateway 2000, Inc.*, 246 A.D.2d 246, 676 N.Y.S.2d 659 (1998).

their terms will control any resulting contracts. Remember that under UCC 2–207(2), between merchants additional terms in an acceptance that materially alter the contract do not become part of the contract—the terms of the offer control.[4]

Some courts have taken a different approach in resolving contract disputes when the parties are in fundamental disagreement over a material term. Rather than looking to UCC 2–207(2), they apply the rule expressed in UCC 2–207(3). This rule provides that when the parties' conduct and communications clearly indicate that a contract was formed, any conflicting material terms may simply be stricken from the contract. This rule is sometimes referred to, aptly enough, as the "knock-out rule." Thus, this UCC provision leaves it to the discretion of the courts to determine whether,

under the circumstances, a contract has been formed and what the terms of the contract are—which will be the terms on which the parties agree.

DISCUSSION QUESTIONS

1. Review the UCC provisions that apply to the topics discussed in Chapters 20 through 23. Discuss fully how various UCC provisions, excluding the provisions discussed above, reflect social values and ethical standards.

2. How can a court objectively measure good faith and commercial reasonableness?

3. Generally, it is left to the courts to determine what constitutes "reasonable" behavior in disputes between contract parties over this issue. Should the UCC be more specific in defining what will be deemed reasonable in specific circumstances so that the courts do not have to decide the issue? Why or why not?

4. Why does the UCC protect innocent persons (good faith purchasers) who buy goods from sellers with voidable title but not innocent persons who buy goods from sellers with void title?

---

4. As noted in Chapter 20, the 2003 amendments to UCC 2–207 do not distinguish between a merchant and others in setting out rules for determining the terms in a contract for a sale of goods, nor is preference given to the first or the last terms to be stated. Under those amendments, the terms of a contract, subject to the UCC's parol evidence rule, are (1) the terms that appear in the records of both parties; (2) the terms to which both parties agree, whether or not they appear in a record; and (3) the terms supplied or incorporated under any provision of Article 2.

UNIT FIVE
Negotiable Instruments

CONTENTS

CHAPTER 24

The Function and Creation of Negotiable Instruments

A **negotiable instrument** is a signed writing (or record) that contains an unconditional promise or order to pay an exact amount of money, either on demand or at a specific future time. The checks you write to pay for groceries, rent, your monthly car payment, insurance premiums, and other items are negotiable instruments.

Most commercial transactions that take place in the modern business world would be inconceivable without negotiable instruments. A negotiable instrument can function as a substitute for cash or as an extension of credit. For example, when a buyer writes a check to pay for goods, the check serves as a substitute for cash. When a buyer gives a seller a promissory note in which the buyer promises to pay the seller the purchase price within sixty days, the seller has essentially extended credit to the buyer for a sixty-day period. For a negotiable instrument to operate *practically* as either a substitute for cash or a credit device, or both, it is essential that the instrument be *easily transferable without danger of being uncollectible*. This is a fundamental function of negotiable instruments. Each rule described in the following pages can be examined in light of this function.

The law governing negotiable instruments grew out of commercial necessity. In the medieval world, merchants engaging in foreign trade used *bills of exchange* to finance and conduct their affairs, rather than risk transporting gold or coins. Because the English king's courts of those times did not recognize the validity of these bills of exchange, the merchants developed their own set of rules, which were enforced by "fair" or "borough" courts. Eventually, the decisions of these courts became a distinct set of laws known as the *Lex Mercatoria* (Law Merchant). The Law Merchant was codified in England in the Bills of Exchange Act of 1882. In 1896, in the United States, the National Conference of Commissioners on Uniform State Laws (NCCUSL) drafted the Uniform Negotiable Instruments Law. This law was the forerunner of Article 3 of the Uniform Commercial Code (UCC).

SECTION 1 | Articles 3 and 4 of the UCC

Negotiable instruments are governed by Articles 3 and 4 of the UCC. In this chapter and in Chapters 25 and 26, we will focus on the law as established by Article 3. You will learn about the different types of negotiable instruments, the requirements that all negotiable instruments must meet, the process of *negotiation* (transferring an instrument from one party to another), and the responsibilities of parties to negotiable instruments. Note that UCC 3–104(b) defines an *instrument* as a "negotiable instrument." For that reason, whenever the term *instrument* is used in this book, it refers to a negotiable instrument. Article 4 governs bank deposits and collections as well as bank-customer relationships—topics that we will examine in Chapter 27.

THE 1990 REVISION OF ARTICLES 3 AND 4

In 1990, a revised version of Article 3 was issued for adoption by the states. Many of the changes to Article 3 simply clarified old sections; some, however, significantly altered the former provisions. As of this writing, all of the states except New York and South Carolina have adopted the revised article. Therefore, all references to Article 3 in this chapter and in the following chapters are to the *revised* Article 3. When the revisions to Article 3 have made important changes in the law, however, we discuss the previous law in footnotes. Article 4 was also revised in 1990. In part, these changes were necessary because the changes in Article 3 affected Article 4 provisions. The revised Articles 3 and 4 are included in their entirety in Appendix C.

THE 2002 AMENDMENTS TO ARTICLES 3 AND 4

In 2002, the NCCUSL and the American Law Institute approved a number of amendments to Articles 3 and 4 of the UCC. One of the purposes of the amendments was to update the law with respect to e-commerce. For example, the amended versions of the articles implement the policy of the Uniform Electronic Transactions Act (see Chapter 19) by removing unnecessary obstacles to electronic communications. Additionally, the word *writing* has been replaced with the term *record* throughout the articles. Other amendments relate to such topics as telephone-generated checks and the payment and discharge of negotiable instruments.

Most states have not yet adopted these amendments. Therefore, in this text we provide footnotes to the amendments only if they will significantly alter

existing law. Keep in mind, however, that even when the changes are not substantive, some of the section numbers may change slightly once a state has adopted the amendments to Article 3 (subsection 9 may become subsection 12, for example).

SECTION 2 | Types of Negotiable Instruments

The UCC specifies four types of negotiable instruments: *drafts, checks, notes,* and *certificates of deposit* (CDs). These instruments, which are summarized briefly in Exhibit 24–1, are frequently divided into the two classifications that we will discuss in the following subsections: *orders to pay* (drafts and checks) and *promises to pay* (promissory notes and CDs).

Negotiable instruments may also be classified as either demand instruments or time instruments. A *demand instrument* is payable on demand—that is, it is payable immediately after it is issued and thereafter for a reasonable period of time.[1] **Issue** is "the first delivery

---

1. "A promise or order is 'payable on demand' if it (i) states that it is payable on demand or at sight, or otherwise indicates that it is payable at the will of the holder, or (ii) does not state any time of payment" [UCC 3–108(a)]. The UCC defines a *holder* as "the person in possession if the instrument is payable to bearer or, in the cases of an instrument payable to an identified person, if the identified person is in possession" [see UCC 1–201(20)]. The term *bearer* is defined later in this chapter.

EXHIBIT 24–1 **Basic Types of Negotiable Instruments**

INSTRUMENTS	CHARACTERISTICS	PARTIES
ORDERS TO PAY		
Draft	An order by one person to another person or to bearer [UCC 3–104(e)].	Drawer—The person who signs or makes the order to pay [UCC 3–103(a)(3)].
Check	A draft drawn on a bank and payable on demand [UCC 3–104(f)].[a] (With certain types of checks, such as cashier's checks, the bank is both the drawer and the drawee—see Chapter 27 for details.)	Drawee—The person to whom the order to pay is made [UCC 3–103(a)(2)]. Payee—The person to whom payment is ordered.
PROMISES TO PAY		
Promissory note	A promise by one party to pay money to another party or to bearer [UCC 3–104(e)].	Maker—The person who promises to pay [UCC 3–103(a)(5)]. Payee—The person to whom the promise is made.
Certificate of deposit	A note made by a bank acknowledging a deposit of funds made payable to the holder of the note [UCC 3–104(j)].	

a. Under UCC 4–105(1), banks include savings banks, savings and loan associations, credit unions, and trust companies.

of an instrument by the maker or drawer . . . for the purpose of giving rights on the instrument to any person" [UCC 3–105].[2] All checks are demand instruments, because by definition, they must be payable on demand. A *time instrument* is payable at a future date.

DRAFTS AND CHECKS (ORDERS TO PAY)

A **draft** (bill of exchange) is an unconditional written order that involves *three parties*. The party creating the draft (the **drawer**) orders another party (the **drawee**) to pay money, usually to a third party (the **payee**). The most common type of draft is a check.

TIME DRAFTS AND SIGHT DRAFTS A *time draft* is payable at a definite future time. A *sight draft* (or demand draft) is payable on sight—that is, when it is presented for payment. A sight draft may be payable on acceptance. **Acceptance** is the drawee's written promise to pay the draft when it comes due. The usual manner of accepting an instrument is by writing the word *accepted* across the face of the instrument, followed by the date of acceptance and the signature of the drawee. A draft can be both a time and a sight draft; such a draft is payable at a stated time after sight.

Exhibit 24–2 shows a typical time draft. For the drawee to be obligated to honor the order, the drawee must be obligated to the drawer either by agreement or

_____
2. Under the unrevised UCC 3–102(1)(a), *issue* was limited to "the first delivery of an instrument to a holder or remitter."

through a debtor-creditor relationship. For example, on January 16, Ourtown Real Estate orders $1,000 worth of office supplies from Eastman Supply Company, with payment due April 16. Also on January 16, Ourtown sends Eastman a draft drawn on its account with the First National Bank of Whiteacre as payment. In this scenario, the drawer is Ourtown, the drawee is Ourtown's bank (First National Bank of Whiteacre), and the payee is Eastman Supply Company. First National Bank is obligated to honor the draft because of its account agreement with Ourtown Real Estate.

TRADE ACCEPTANCES A trade acceptance is a type of draft that is frequently used in the sale of goods. In a **trade acceptance,** the seller of the goods is both the drawer and the payee. Essentially, the draft orders the buyer to pay a specified amount of money to the seller, usually at a stated time in the future.

For example, Midwestern Style Fabrics sells $50,000 worth of fabric to D & F Clothiers, Inc., each spring on terms requiring payment to be made in ninety days. One year, Midwestern Style needs cash, so it draws a *trade acceptance* that orders D & F to pay $50,000 to the order of Midwestern Style Fabrics ninety days hence. Midwestern Style presents the draft to D & F, which *accepts* the draft by signing and dating the face of the instrument. D & F then returns the draft to Midwestern Style Fabrics. D & F's acceptance creates an enforceable promise to pay the draft when it comes due in ninety days. Midwestern Style can now sell the

EXHIBIT 24–2 **A Typical Time Draft**

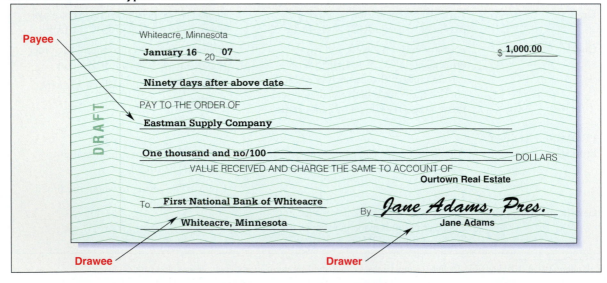

EXHIBIT 24-3 A Typical Trade Acceptance

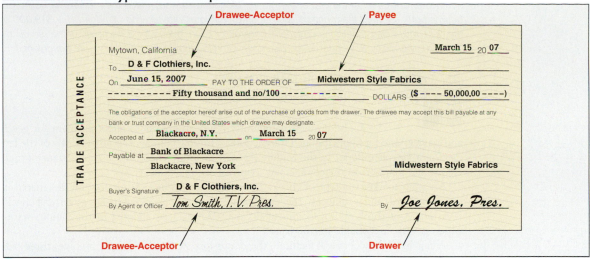

trade acceptance in the *commercial money market* (a financial market dealing in instruments that have a maturity date shorter than one year) to obtain the cash it needs. Trade acceptances are the standard credit instruments in sales transactions (see Exhibit 24–3).

When the draft is drawn by a seller on the buyer's bank for acceptance, it is called a banker's acceptance. A **banker's acceptance** is commonly used in international trade.

CHECKS As mentioned, the most commonly used type of draft is a **check.** The writer of the check is the drawer, the bank on which the check is drawn is the drawee, and the person to whom the check is made payable is the payee. As stated earlier, checks, because they are payable on demand, are demand instruments.

Checks will be discussed more fully in Chapter 27, but it should be noted here that with certain types of checks, such as *cashier's checks*, the bank is both the drawer and the drawee. The bank customer purchases a cashier's check from the bank—that is, pays the bank the amount of the check—and indicates to whom the check should be made payable. The bank, not the customer, is the drawer of the check, as well as the drawee. The idea behind a cashier's check is that it functions the same as cash, so there is no question of whether the check will be paid—the bank has committed itself to paying the stated amount on demand.

The following case arose from a party's petition for the discharge of a gambling debt in bankruptcy. Is a casino marker (by which the casino extends credit to a customer) the equivalent of a check? Can a "bad" check, without more, constitute the making of a false statement (fraud is a ground for denying a discharge in bankruptcy)? The court in this case considered these questions.

CASE 24.1   In re Miller

United States
Bankruptcy Court,
Central District
of California, 2004.
310 Bankr. 185.

BACKGROUND AND FACTS *Obtaining credit at the Mandalay Bay casino in Las Vegas, Nevada, is a four-step process. First, the customer applies for credit. Second, the casino verifies that the customer has funds in a bank account to cover the amount. Third, the casino approves the request. Fourth, the customer signs and delivers a marker to the casino to draw money against the account and buy gambling chips. Richard Miller gambled at Mandalay Bay on at least four occasions in 1999 and 2000. Each time, he obtained credit—for $10,000, $20,000, $30,000, and $25,000, respectively—and each time, he repaid as much of the credit as he used. On his fifth trip, in August 2000, Mandalay Bay granted him $50,000 in credit and accepted four markers—three for*

 CONTINUED

CASE 24.1 | Continued *$10,000 and one for $20,000—based on the amount in his account with Wells Fargo Bank in Southgate, California. At the end of the month, Mandalay Bay submitted the markers for collection, but the bank returned them unpaid. More than a year later, after paying Mandalay Bay $19,000 of the debt, Miller filed a petition in a federal bankruptcy court, asking for a discharge of the remaining $31,000. Mandalay Bay opposed the discharge, claiming that Miller's markers were fraudulent.*

IN THE LANGUAGE OF THE COURT

SAMUEL L. BUFFORD, Bankruptcy Judge.

* * * *

* * * The business community relies on checks to effect payment for goods and services and for financing such transactions. This law is ancient: it arose as part of the law merchant *(lex mercatoria)* in the Middle Ages to facilitate the business transactions of merchants and mariners in the commercial countries of the world.

A casino marker is a type of check, drawn on the customer's bank account designated in the instrument, and is subject to the legal regime governing checks. The law governing checks is Article 3 of the Uniform Commercial Code ("UCC"), as adopted in the various states, which governs negotiable instruments.

A few basic concepts will facilitate the discussion. A check typically involves three parties, (1) the "drawer" who writes the check, (2) the "payee" to whose order the check is made out, and (3) the "drawee" or "payor bank," the bank which has the drawer's checking account from which the check is to be paid. In form, a check is an order to the drawee bank to pay the face amount of the check "to the order of" the payee. After receiving the check, the payee typically indorses it on the back, and then deposits it in the payee's account in a different bank, the "depositary bank." The depositary bank credits the check to the payee's account, and sends the check through the check clearing system to the payor bank for ultimate payment from the drawer's account.[a]

A check is a species of documents called "commercial paper," "instruments" or "negotiable instruments."

* * * *

Article 3 divides instruments into two categories—notes and drafts. A note is a promise to pay a fixed amount of money (usually plus interest), and a draft is an order to pay a fixed amount of money. A check * * * is a draft payable on demand and drawn on a bank. *Thus a check is an order to a bank, payable on demand of the payee or transferee, to pay a fixed sum of money.* [Emphasis added.]

If a draft (including a check) is paid by a bank, the payment on the draft is completed and the drawer is discharged. If an unaccepted check is dishonored by the bank, the drawer is obliged to pay it according to its terms at the time it was issued.

* * * *

* * * Depositing checks that [are] not supported by sufficient funds * * * [does] not involve making a false statement * * * because a check is literally not a statement * * * .

* * * [D]elivery of a check involves no representation.

Business transactions frequently involve statements. However, these statements are found elsewhere in a business transaction, and not in the check.

* * * *

* * * To prevail on a claim for actual fraud, Mandalay must show that Miller made an untrue or false statement of fact when issuing his markers in exchange for casino chips.

Mandalay has offered no evidence of anything Miller said or wrote when obtaining his markers. Mandalay offers only the markers themselves, the legal equivalent of checks.

* * * *[T]he presentation of a marker, just like a check, does not involve the making of a false statement.* [Emphasis added.]

Therefore, Miller did not make a false statement or representation by delivering the markers to Mandalay.

---

a. The terms and concepts outlined in this paragraph will be discussed more fully in Chapters 25 and 27.

CASE 24.1 Continued

DECISION AND REMEDY *The court discharged the rest of Miller's debt to Mandalay Bay. A casino marker is the equivalent of a check. The delivery of a check alone does not involve the making of a false statement, although this delivery may be part of a larger transaction in which a debtor does make false representations. Here, however, Mandalay Bay did not show any representation that Miller made apart from the delivery of the markers.*

WHAT IF THE FACTS WERE DIFFERENT? *Suppose that Mandalay Bay had proved the debt represented by Miller's markers was induced by fraud. Would the result have been different?*

PROMISSORY NOTES AND CDs (PROMISES TO PAY)

A **promissory note** is a written promise made by one person (the **maker** of the promise to pay) to another (usually a payee). A promissory note, which is often referred to simply as a *note*, can be made payable at a definite time or on demand. It can name a specific payee or merely be payable to bearer (bearer instruments are discussed later in this chapter). For example, on April 30, Laurence and Margaret Roberts sign a writing unconditionally promising to pay "to the order of" the First National Bank of Whiteacre $3,000 (with 8 percent interest) on or before June 29. This writing is a promissory note. A typical promissory note is shown in Exhibit 24–4.

Promissory notes are used in a variety of credit transactions. Often a promissory note will carry the name of the transaction involved. For example, suppose that a note is secured by personal property, such as an automobile. This type of note is referred to as a

collateral note, because the property pledged as security for the satisfaction of the debt is called *collateral*.[3] A note payable in installments, such as installment payments for a large-screen television over a twelve-month period, is called an *installment note*.

A **certificate of deposit (CD)** is a type of note. A CD is issued when a party deposits funds with a bank, and the bank promises to repay the funds, with interest, on a certain date [UCC 3–104(j)]. The bank is the maker of the note, and the depositor is the payee. For example, on February 15, Sara Levin deposits $5,000 with the First National Bank of Whiteacre. The bank promises to repay the $5,000, plus 3.25 percent annual interest, on August 15.

---

3. To minimize the risk of loss when making a loan, a creditor often requires the debtor to provide some *collateral*, or security, beyond a promise that the debt will be repaid. When this security takes the form of personal property (such as a motor vehicle), the creditor has an interest in the property known as a *security interest*. Security interests will be discussed in Chapter 29.

EXHIBIT 24-4 **A Typical Promissory Note**

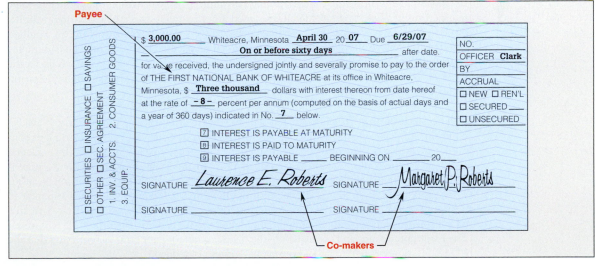

EXHIBIT 24-5 **A Typical Small Certificate of Deposit**

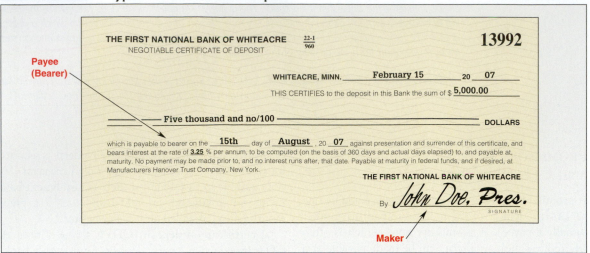

Certificates of deposit in small denominations (for amounts up to $100,000) are often sold by savings and loan associations, savings banks, commercial banks, and credit unions. Certificates of deposit for amounts greater than $100,000 are referred to as large or jumbo CDs. Exhibit 24–5 shows a typical small CD.

The treatment of a CD, as a note under the UCC, is explained and illustrated in the following case.

CASE 24.2

United States
Court of Appeals,
Fifth Circuit, 2003.
82 Fed.Appx. 126.

In re Premier Interval Resorts, Inc.

PER CURIAM [By the whole court].
  * * * *

Premier [Interval Resorts, Inc.] * * * borrowed $42 million from Meralex, secured by a Deed of Trust on the property to be purchased with the $42 million, a casino named the Maxim. In addition, Premier made two deposits at Bank West in the form of two CDs, one for $2.5 million and one for $350,000. These CDs served as collateral * * * to put Premier in compliance with Nevada's workers' compensation laws.

Shortly after securing this funding, Premier filed for * * * bankruptcy [and the CDs were returned to Premier]. * * * Meralex assigned all of its interest to a newly-created, wholly-owned subsidiary, Revanche. * * * [Revanche claimed] that the remains of the $2.5 million CD that was returned to Premier was cash collateral under the Deed of Trust. The bankruptcy court [ruled in] Revanche's [favor], finding that the CD did qualify as cash collateral under the Deed of Trust. The district court affirmed the bankruptcy court's order and final judgment. Premier timely appealed [to the U.S. Court of Appeals for the Fifth Circuit]. * * *
  * * * *

The Deed of Trust stipulates that it will be governed by the laws of Nevada. Nevada's Uniform Commercial Code statutorily defines a "certificate of deposit" as "an instrument containing an acknowledgment by a bank that a sum of money has been received by the bank and *a promise* by the bank *to repay* the sum of money." In the same statutory section, a note is defined as a promise of payment. * * * By *definition* * * * *a CD is a promise of payment; a promise of payment, in turn, is a note.* Further, the Uniform Commercial Code Comment to Section 104.3104 makes clear that, while the former version of Nevada's Article 3 treated CDs as instruments separate from notes and drafts, the revised Article 3 treats CDs as notes. The bankruptcy court, and consequently the district court, did not err in determining that the CD in question was a note under Nevada law. [Emphasis added.]

* * * *

Neither party disputes that * * * the Deed of Trust expressly grants a security interest in certain items to Meralex, which Meralex transferred to Revanche. Specifically, Premier granted

to [Revanche] (as Creditor and Secured Party) as security for the payment of the Note * * * secured by this Deed of Trust a security interest in all the following described property * * * relating to or arising from the [Maxim]: * * * any * * * property * * * listed in any "Financing Statement" * * * .

Premier claims that this language is ambiguous.

Under Nevada law, a contract is ambiguous if it is reasonably susceptible to more than one interpretation. *Only if the contract is ambiguous may parol evidence be introduced.* * * * [T]here is no ambiguity in the contract such that we would permit the introduction of parol evidence. The contract clearly states that items listed in a financing statement are the subject of Revanche's security interest. We must therefore determine whether the Financing Statement lists Premier's returned CD. [Emphasis added.]

The * * * Financing Statement * * * identifies the following items: "instruments, documents, notes, [and] drafts * * * , which arise from or relate to construction on the Land or to any business now or later to be conducted on it * * * ." Nevada law, as discussed above, includes CDs in its definition of "notes."

Because the CD is a note, and notes are listed in the Financing Statement, the CD is subject to Revanche's security interest if it "relate[s] to * * * any business now or later to be conducted" on the land. We conclude that this CD is related to the business of the Maxim. The CD would not have been purchased had it not been necessary for the running of the Maxim. More importantly, once the Maxim was no more, the CD was returned.

* * * *

Because the CD in question is listed in the * * * Financing Statement, * * * the district court did not err in concluding that the Deed of Trust granted Revanche a security interest in the CD and the proceeds therefrom. Accordingly, the ruling of the district court is AFFIRMED.

QUESTIONS

1. What difference did it make to the result in the *Premier* case whether a CD qualifies as a note under the UCC?
2. How did the CD in the *Premier* case "relate to the business of the Maxim"?

SECTION 3 | Requirements for Negotiability

For an instrument to be negotiable, it must meet the following requirements:

1. Be in writing.
2. Be signed by the maker or the drawer.
3. Be an unconditional promise or order to pay.
4. State a fixed amount of money.
5. Be payable on demand or at a definite time.
6. Be payable to order or to bearer, unless it is a check.

WRITTEN FORM

Negotiable instruments must be in written form [UCC 3–103(a)(6)].[4] Clearly, an oral promise can create the danger of fraud or make it difficult to determine liability. Negotiable instruments must possess the quality of certainty that only formal, written expression can give. The writing must have the following qualities:

---

4. UCC Section 3–104, which defines negotiable instruments, does not explicitly require a writing. The writing requirement comes from the definitions of *order* (as a written instruction) and *promise* (as a written undertaking) in UCC 3–103(a)(6), (9). In the unrevised Article 3, UCC 3–104(1) refers directly to "[a]ny writing."

1. The writing must be on material that lends itself to *permanence*. Instruments carved in blocks of ice or recorded on other impermanent surfaces would not qualify as negotiable instruments. Suppose Shanda writes in the sand, "I promise to pay $500 to the order of Jason." This is not a negotiable instrument, because, although it is in writing, it lacks permanence.

2. The writing must also have *portability*. Although the UCC does not explicitly state this requirement, if an instrument is not movable, it obviously cannot meet the requirement that it be freely transferable. For example, Cullen writes on the side of a cow, "I, Cullen, promise to pay to Merrill or her order $500 on demand." Technically, this meets the requirements of a negotiable instrument, but because a cow cannot easily be transferred in the ordinary course of business, the "instrument" is nonnegotiable.

SIGNATURES

For an instrument to be negotiable, it must be signed by (1) the maker if it is a note or a certificate of deposit or (2) the drawer if it is a draft or a check [UCC 3–103(a)(3), (5)]. If a person signs an instrument as an authorized *agent* for the maker or drawer, the maker or drawer has effectively signed the instrument. (Agents' signatures will be discussed in Chapter 26.)

SIGNATURE REQUIREMENTS   The UCC grants extreme latitude in regard to what constitutes a signature. UCC 1–201(39) provides that a **signature** may include "any symbol executed or adopted by a party with present intention to authenticate a writing." UCC 3–401(b) expands on this by stating that a "signature may be made (i) manually or by means of a device or machine, and (ii) by the use of any name, including a trade or assumed name, or by a word, mark, or symbol executed or adopted by a person with present intention to authenticate a writing." Thus, initials, an X (if the writing is also signed by a witness), or a thumbprint will suffice as a signature. A trade name or an assumed name is also sufficient. Signatures that are placed onto instruments by means of rubber stamps are permitted and frequently used in the business world. If necessary, parol evidence (discussed in Chapter 15) is admissible to identify the signer. When the signer is identified, the signature becomes effective.

There are virtually no limitations on the manner in which a signature can be made, but one should be careful about receiving an instrument that has been signed in an unusual way. Furthermore, an unusual signature clearly decreases the *marketability* of an instrument because it creates uncertainty.

PLACEMENT OF THE SIGNATURE   The location of the signature on the document is unimportant, though the usual place is the lower right-hand corner. A *handwritten* statement on the body of the instrument, such as "I, Kammie Orlik, promise to pay Janel Tan," is sufficient to act as a signature.

UNCONDITIONAL PROMISE OR ORDER TO PAY

The terms of the promise or order must be included in the writing on the face of a negotiable instrument. The terms must also be *unconditional*—that is, they cannot be conditioned on the occurrence or nonoccurrence of some other event or agreement [UCC 3–104(a)].

PROMISE OR ORDER   For an instrument to be negotiable, it must contain an express promise or order to pay. A mere acknowledgment of the debt, such as an I.O.U. ("I owe you"), might logically *imply* a promise, but it is not sufficient under the UCC. This is because the UCC requires that a promise be an *affirmative* (express) undertaking [UCC 3–103(a)(9)]. If such words as "to be paid on demand" or "due on demand" are added to an I.O.U., however, the need for an express promise is satisfied. Thus, if a buyer executes a promissory note using the words "I promise to pay $1,000 to the order of the seller for the purchase of X goods," then this requirement for a negotiable instrument is satisfied.

A certificate of deposit is exceptional in this respect. No express promise is required in a CD because the bank's acknowledgment of the deposit and the other terms of the instrument clearly indicate a promise by the bank to repay the sum of money [UCC 3–104(j)].

An *order* is associated with three-party instruments, such as trade acceptances, checks, and drafts. An order directs a third party to pay the instrument as drawn. In the typical check, for example, the word *pay* (to the order of a payee) is a command to the drawee bank to pay the check when presented, and thus it is an order. A command, such as "pay," is mandatory even if it is accompanied by courteous words, as in "Please pay" or "Kindly pay." Generally, the language used must indicate that a command, or order, is being given. Stating "I wish you would pay" does not fulfill this requirement. An order may be addressed to one person or to more than one person, either jointly ("to A *and* B") or alternatively ("to A *or* B") [UCC 3–103(a)(6)].

UNCONDITIONALITY OF PROMISE OR ORDER A negotiable instrument's utility as a substitute for money or as a credit device would be dramatically reduced if it had conditional promises attached to it. Investigating the conditional promises would be time consuming and expensive, and therefore the transferability of the negotiable instrument would be greatly restricted. Suppose that Granados promises in a note to pay McGraw $10,000 only if a certain ship reaches port. No one could safely purchase the promissory note without first investigating whether the ship had arrived. Even then, the facts disclosed by the investigation might be incorrect. To avoid such problems, the UCC provides that only instruments with *unconditional* promises or orders can be negotiable [UCC 3–104(a)].

A promise or order is conditional (and *not* negotiable) if it states (1) an express condition to payment, (2) that the promise or order is subject to or governed by another writing, or (3) that the rights or obligations with respect to the promise or order are stated in another writing. A mere *reference* to another writing, however, does not of itself make the promise or order conditional [UCC 3–106(a)]. For example, including the phrase "as per contract" or "This debt arises from the sale of goods X and Y" does not render an instrument nonnegotiable.

—Payment Out of a Particular Fund. Similarly, a statement in the instrument that payment can be made only out of a particular fund or source will not render the instrument nonnegotiable [UCC 3–106(b)(ii)].[5] Thus, for example, terms in a note that include the condition that payment will be made out of the proceeds of next year's cotton crop will not make the note nonnegotiable. (The payee of such a note, however, may find the note commercially unacceptable and refuse to take it.)

—Note Secured by a Mortgage. Finally, a simple statement in an otherwise negotiable note indicating that the note is secured by a mortgage does not destroy its negotiability [UCC 3–106(b)(i)]. Actually, such a statement might even make the note more acceptable in commerce. Realize, though, that the statement that a note is secured by a mortgage must not stipulate that the maker's promise to pay is *subject to* the terms and conditions of the mortgage [UCC 3–106(a)(ii)].

A FIXED AMOUNT OF MONEY

Negotiable instruments must state with certainty a fixed amount of money to be paid at any time the instrument is payable [UCC 3–104(a)]. This requirement ensures that the value of the instrument can be determined with clarity and certainty.

FIXED AMOUNT The term *fixed amount* means an amount that is ascertainable from the face of the instrument. A demand note payable with 10 percent interest meets the requirement of a fixed amount because its amount can be determined at the time it is payable [UCC 3–104(a)].

The rate of interest may also be determined with reference to information that is not contained in the instrument if that information is readily ascertainable by reference to a formula or a source described in the instrument [UCC 3–112(b)]. For example, an instrument that is payable at the *legal rate of interest* (a rate of interest fixed by statute) is negotiable. Mortgage notes tied to a variable rate of interest (a rate that fluctuates as a result of market conditions) can also be negotiable.

PAYABLE IN MONEY UCC 3–104(a) provides that a fixed amount is to be *payable in money*. The UCC defines money as "a medium of exchange authorized or adopted by a domestic or foreign government as a part of its currency" [UCC 1–201(24)].

Suppose that the maker of a note promises "to pay on demand $1,000 in U.S. gold." Because gold is not a medium of exchange adopted by the U.S. government, the note is not payable in money. The same result occurs if the maker promises "to pay $1,000 and fifty magnums of 1994 Chateau Lafite-Rothschild wine" because the instrument is not payable *entirely* in money. An instrument payable in government bonds or in shares of IBM stock is not negotiable, because neither is a medium of exchange recognized by the U.S. government. The statement "Payable in $1,000 U.S. currency or an equivalent value in gold" would render the instrument nonnegotiable if the maker reserved the option of paying in money *or* gold. If the option were left to the payee, some legal scholars argue that

---

5. Section 3–105(2) of the unrevised Article 3 provided just the opposite: a term providing that payment could be made only out of a particular fund or source rendered the instrument nonnegotiable.

the instrument would be negotiable. Any instrument payable in the United States with a face amount stated in a foreign currency can be paid in the foreign money or in the equivalent in U.S. dollars [UCC 3–107].

PAYABLE ON DEMAND OR AT A DEFINITE TIME

A negotiable instrument must "be payable on demand or at a definite time" [UCC 3–104(a)(2)]. Clearly, to ascertain the value of a negotiable instrument, it is essential to know when the maker, drawee, or *acceptor* is required to pay (an **acceptor** is a drawee who has accepted, or agreed to pay, an instrument when it is presented later for payment). It is also necessary to know when the obligations of secondary parties, such as *indorsers*,[6] will arise. Furthermore, it is necessary to know when an instrument is due in order to calculate when the statute of limitations may apply [UCC 3–118(a)]. Finally, with an interest-bearing instrument, it is necessary to know the exact interval during which the interest will accrue to determine the instrument's value at the present time.

PAYABLE ON DEMAND   Instruments that are payable on demand include those that contain the words "Payable at sight" or "Payable upon presentment." **Presentment** occurs when a person presents an instrument to the party liable on the note to collect payment; presentment also occurs when a person presents an instrument to a drawee for acceptance—see the discussion of trade acceptances earlier in this chapter.

The very nature of the instrument may indicate that it is payable on demand. For example, a check, by definition, is payable on demand [UCC 3–104(f)]. If no time for payment is specified and the person responsible for payment must pay on the instrument's presentment, the instrument is payable on demand [UCC 3–108(a)].

PAYABLE AT A DEFINITE TIME   If an instrument is not payable on demand, to be negotiable it must be payable at a definite time. An instrument is payable at

a definite time if it states that it is payable (1) on a specified date, (2) within a definite period of time (such as thirty days) after being presented for payment, or (3) on a date or time readily ascertainable at the time the promise or order is issued [UCC 3–108(b)]. The maker or drawee is under no obligation to pay until the specified time.

Suppose that an instrument dated June 1, 2005, states, "One year after the death of my grandfather, Jeremy Adams, I promise to pay to the order of Lucy Harmon $5,000. [Signed] Jacqueline Wells." This instrument is nonnegotiable. Because the date of the grandfather's death is uncertain, the instrument is not payable at a definite time, even though the event is bound to occur or has already occurred. Similarly, if the "date" blanks on a promissory note were not filled in with the date on which the note was payable, the note would not meet the requirements of a negotiable instrument.[7]

When an instrument is payable on or before a stated date, it is clearly payable at a definite time, although the maker has the option of paying before the stated maturity date. This uncertainty does not violate the definite-time requirement. Suppose that John gives Ernesto an instrument dated May 1, 2005, that indicates on its face that it is payable on or before May 1, 2007. This instrument satisfies the requirement. In contrast, an instrument that is undated and made payable "one month after date" is clearly nonnegotiable. There is no way to determine the maturity date from the face of the instrument.

ACCELERATION CLAUSE   An **acceleration clause** allows a payee or other holder of a time instrument to demand payment of the entire amount due, with interest, if a certain event occurs, such as a default in payment of an installment when due. (Under the UCC, a **holder** is any person in the possession of a negotiable instrument that is payable either to the bearer or to an identified person that is the person in possession [UCC 1–201(20)].)

Assume that Martin lends $1,000 to Ruth. Ruth makes a negotiable note promising to pay $100 per month for eleven months. The note contains an acceleration provision that permits Martin or any holder to demand at once all the payments plus the interest owed to date if Ruth fails to pay an installment in any

---

6. We should note that because the UCC uses the spelling *indorse* (*indorsement,* and so on), rather than the more common spelling *endorse* (*endorsement,* and so on), we adopt the UCC's spelling here and in other chapters in this text. Indorsers will be discussed in Chapter 25.

7. *Barclays Bank PLC v. Johnson,* 129 N.C.App. 370, 499 S.E.2d 768 (1998).

given month. If, for example, Ruth fails to make the third payment and Martin accelerates the unpaid balance, the note will be due and payable in full. Ruth will owe Martin the remaining principal plus any unpaid interest to that date.

Under the UCC, instruments that include acceleration clauses are negotiable, regardless of the reason for the acceleration, because (1) the exact value of the instrument can be ascertained and (2) the instrument will be payable on a specified date if the event allowing acceleration does not occur [UCC 3–108(b)(ii)]. Thus, the specified date is the outside limit used to determine the value of the instrument.

EXTENSION CLAUSE   The reverse of an acceleration clause is an **extension clause,** which allows the date of maturity to be extended into the future [UCC 3–108(b)(iii), (iv)]. To keep the instrument negotiable, the interval of the extension must be specified if the right to extend it is given to the maker or the drawer of the instrument. If, however, the holder of the instrument can extend it, the extended maturity date need not be specified.

Suppose that Alek executes a note that reads, "The maker has the right to postpone the time of payment of this note beyond its definite maturity date of January 1, 2008. This extension, however, shall be for no more than a reasonable time." A note with this language is not negotiable because it does not satisfy the definite-time requirement. The right to extend is the maker's, and the maker has not indicated when the note will become due after the extension.

In contrast, suppose that Alek's note reads, "The holder of this note at the date of maturity, January 1, 2008, can extend the time of payment until the following June 1 or later, if the holder so wishes." This note is a negotiable instrument. The length of the extension does not have to be specified because the option to extend is solely that of the holder. After January 1, 2008, the note is, in effect, a demand instrument.

PAYABLE TO ORDER OR TO BEARER

Because one of the functions of a negotiable instrument is to serve as a substitute for money, freedom to transfer is essential. To assure a proper transfer, the instrument must be "payable to order or to bearer" at the time it is issued or first comes into the possession of the holder [UCC 3–104(a)(1)]. An instrument is not negotiable unless it meets this requirement.

ORDER INSTRUMENTS   An **order instrument** is an instrument that is payable (1) "to the order of an identified person" or (2) "to an identified person or order" [UCC 3–109(b)]. An identified person is the person "to whom the instrument is initially payable" as determined by the intent of the maker or drawer [UCC 3–110(a)]. The identified person, in turn, may transfer the instrument to whomever he or she wishes. Thus, the maker or drawer is agreeing to pay either the person specified on the instrument or whomever that person might designate. In this way, the instrument retains its transferability. Suppose an instrument states, "Payable to the order of James Crawford" or "Pay to James Crawford or order." Clearly, the maker or drawer has indicated that a payment will be made to Crawford or to whomever Crawford designates. The instrument is negotiable.

Except for bearer instruments (explained in the following subsection), the person specified must be named with *certainty* because the transfer of an order instrument requires an indorsement. An **indorsement** is a signature placed on an instrument, such as on the back of a check, generally for the purpose of transferring one's ownership rights in the instrument. Indorsements will be discussed at length in Chapter 25.

If an instrument states, "Payable to the order of my kissing cousin," the instrument is nonnegotiable because a holder could not be sure that the person who indorsed the instrument was actually the "kissing cousin" who was supposed to have indorsed it.

BEARER INSTRUMENTS   A **bearer instrument** is an instrument that does not designate a specific payee [UCC 3–109(a)]. The term **bearer** refers to a person in possession of an instrument that is payable to bearer or indorsed in blank (with a signature only, as will be discussed in Chapter 25) [UCC 1–201(5), 3–109(a), 3–109(c)]. This means that the maker or drawer agrees to pay anyone who presents the instrument for payment. Any instrument containing terms such as the following is a bearer instrument:

1. "Payable to the order of bearer."
2. "Payable to Simon Reed or bearer."
3. "Payable to bearer."
4. "Pay cash."
5. "Pay to the order of cash."

In addition, an instrument that "indicates that it is not payable to an identified person" is a bearer instrument [UCC 3–109(a)(3)]. Thus, an instrument that is

CONCEPT SUMMARY 24.1 | Requirements for Negotiability

REQUIREMENTS	BASIC RULES
MUST BE IN WRITING UCC 3–103(6), (9)	A writing can be on anything that is readily transferable and that has a degree of permanence. [See also UCC 1–201(46).]
MUST BE SIGNED BY THE MAKER OR DRAWER UCC 1–201(39) UCC 3–103(a)(3), (5) UCC 3–401(b) UCC 3–402	1. The signature can be anywhere on the face of the instrument. 2. It can be in any form (such as a word, mark, or rubber stamp) that purports to be a signature and authenticates the writing. 3. A signature may be made in a representative capacity.
MUST BE A DEFINITE PROMISE OR ORDER UCC 3–103(a)(6), (9) UCC 3–104(a)	1. A promise must be more than a mere acknowledgment of a debt. 2. The words "I/We promise" or "Pay" meet this criterion.
MUST BE UNCONDITIONAL UCC 3–106	1. Payment cannot be expressly conditional on the occurrence of an event. 2. Payment cannot be made subject to or governed by another agreement.
MUST BE AN ORDER OR PROMISE TO PAY A FIXED AMOUNT UCC 3–104(a) UCC 3–112(b)	An amount may be considered a fixed sum even if payable in installments, with a fixed or variable rate of interest, at a stated discount, or at a foreign exchange rate.
MUST BE PAYABLE IN MONEY UCC 3–104(a)(3) UCC 3–107	1. Any medium of exchange recognized as the currency of a government is money. 2. The maker or drawer cannot retain the option to pay the instrument in money or something else.
MUST BE PAYABLE ON DEMAND OR AT A DEFINITE TIME UCC 3–104(a)(2) UCC 3–108(a), (b), (c)	1. Any instrument that is payable on sight, presentation, or issue or that does not state any time for payment is a demand instrument. 2. An instrument is still payable at a definite time, even if it is payable on or before a stated date or within a fixed period after sight or if the drawer or maker has an option to extend the time for a definite period. 3. Acceleration clauses do not affect the negotiability of the instrument.
MUST BE PAYABLE TO ORDER OR TO BEARER UCC 3–104(a)(1), (c) UCC 3–109 UCC 3–110(a)	1. An order instrument must identify the payee with reasonable certainty. 2. An instrument whose terms intend payment to no particular person is payable to bearer. 3. Checks are not required to be payable to order or bearer.

"payable to X" can be negotiated as a bearer instrument, as though it were payable to cash. An instrument that is "payable to the order of the Camrod Company," however, when no such company exists, is neither an order instrument nor a bearer instrument—and is thus not a negotiable instrument [UCC 3–109, Comment 2].

SECTION 4 | Factors Not Affecting Negotiability

Certain ambiguities or omissions will not affect the negotiability of an instrument. Article 3's rules for interpreting ambiguous terms include the following:

1. Unless the date of an instrument is necessary to determine a definite time for payment, the fact that an instrument is undated does not affect its negotiability. A typical example is an undated check. If a check is not dated, under the UCC its date is the date of its issue, meaning the date on which the drawer first delivers the check to another person to give that person rights on the check [UCC 3–113(b)]. Therefore, an undated check is still negotiable.

2. Antedating or postdating an instrument does not affect its negotiability [UCC 3–113(a)]. *Antedating* occurs when a party puts a date on the instrument that precedes the actual calendar date. *Postdating* occurs when a party puts a date on the instrument that is after the actual date. For example, Crenshaw draws a check on his account at First Bank, payable to Sung Imports. Crenshaw postdates the check by fifteen days. Sung Imports can immediately negotiate the check, and, unless Crenshaw tells First Bank otherwise, can charge the amount of the check to Crenshaw's account [UCC 4–401(c)].

3. Handwritten terms outweigh typewritten and printed terms (preprinted terms on forms, for example), and typewritten terms outweigh printed terms [UCC 3–114]. For example, if your check is printed "Pay to the order of," and in handwriting you insert in the blank "Anita Delgado or bearer," the check is a bearer instrument.

4. Words outweigh figures unless the words are ambiguous [UCC 3–114]. This is important when the numerical amount and the written amount on a check differ. Suppose that Paruzzo issues a check payable to Cheaper Appliance Company. For the amount, he fills in the number "$100" but writes out the words "One thousand and 00/100" dollars. The check is payable in the amount of $1,000.

5. When an instrument simply states "with interest" and does not specify a particular interest rate, the interest rate is the judgment rate of interest (a rate of interest fixed by statute that is applied to a monetary judgment awarded by a court until the judgment is paid or terminated) [UCC 3–112(b)].

6. A check is negotiable even if there is a notation on it stating that it is "nonnegotiable" or "not governed by Article 3." Any other instrument, however, can be made nonnegotiable by the maker's or drawer's conspicuously noting on it that it is "nonnegotiable" or "not governed by Article 3" [UCC 3–104(d)].[8]

8. This is not true under the unrevised Article 3.

REVIEWING THE FUNCTION AND CREATION OF NEGOTIABLE INSTRUMENTS

Regent Corporation, U.S.A., an import company in New York, contracted with Azmat Bangladesh, Ltd., a textile firm in Bangladesh, for the purchase of bedsheets and pillowcases for import and resale in the United States. An essential condition of the sale was that the goods be manufactured in Bangladesh. The contract required payment by Regent within ninety days of the date on the bill of lading (a document indicating the receipt of goods for shipment), and Regent issued promissory notes that indicated this term. After the goods were shipped, Azmat's bank presented drafts drawn against Regent to Regent's banks. Like the notes, each draft indicated that payment was to be made "at 90 days deferred from bill of lading date." The drafts were accompanied by dated bills of lading. On delivery of the goods, U.S. Customs refused to allow their entry because they had been partially manufactured in Pakistan. Regent filed a suit in a New York state court against its banks, and Azmat, to stop payment on the drafts. Using the information presented in the chapter, answer the following questions.

1. Describe what type of instruments the promissory notes and drafts are, using the categories discussed in this chapter.

2. Review the requirements for negotiability. Were the promissory notes and drafts in this case unconditional? Why or why not?

3. One of the questions here is whether the notes and drafts were "payable at a definite time." How should the court rule on this issue? Explain fully.

4. Suppose that on the original promissory notes, Regent had included handwritten notations that the notes were "not subject to Article 3." What would be the legal significance of this notation?

TERMS AND CONCEPTS TO REVIEW

QUESTIONS AND CASE PROBLEMS

24–1. A college student, Maynard Keynes, wished to purchase a new DVD burner from Friedman Electronics, Inc. Because Keynes did not have the cash to pay for the equipment, he offered to sign a note promising to pay $150 per month for the next six months. Friedman Electronics, eager to sell the burner to Keynes, agreed to accept the promissory note, which read, "I, Maynard Keynes, promise to pay to Friedman Electronics or its order the sum of $150 per month for the next six months." The note was signed by Maynard Keynes. About a week later, Friedman Electronics, which was badly in need of cash, signed the back of the note and sold it to the First National Bank of Halston. Give the specific designation of each of the three parties on this note.

24–2. **QUESTION WITH SAMPLE ANSWER**

Juan Sanchez writes the following note on the back of an envelope: "I, Juan Sanchez, promise to pay Kathy Martin or bearer $500 on demand." Is this a negotiable instrument? Discuss fully.

For a sample answer to this question, go to Appendix I at the end of this text.

24–3. Sabrina Runyan writes the following note on a sheet of paper: "I, the undersigned, do hereby acknowledge that I owe Leo Woo one thousand dollars, with interest, payable out of the proceeds of the sale of my horse, Lightning, next month. Payment is to be made on or before six months from date." Discuss specifically why this is not a negotiable instrument.

24–4. Adam's checks are imprinted with the words "Pay to the order of" followed by a blank. Adam fills in an amount on one of the checks and signs it, but he does not write anything in the blank following the "Pay to the order of" language. Adam gives this check to Beth. On another of the checks, Adam writes in the blank "Carl or bearer." Which, if either, of these checks are bearer instruments, and why?

24–5. **WORDS VERSUS FIGURES.** Eugene Kindy, a seller of diesel engine parts, agreed to buy four diesel engines from Tony Hicks for $13,000. Kindy transferred $6,500 by wire to Hicks's bank and issued a check for the remainder. Kindy placed two different amounts on the check because he did not want the check honored until Hicks had delivered the engine parts. Using a check-imprinting machine, Kindy imprinted $5,500 on the check in the space where the dollar amount is normally written in words, but he wrote $6,500 in figures in the box usually reserved for numbers. An employee of Galatia Community State Bank, noticing the discrepancy, altered the figures to read "$5,500," initialed the change, and accepted the check. The check was returned to Galatia by First National Bank at Kindy's request because Hicks had not delivered the engine parts. In the litigation that followed, a key issue was whether the machine-imprinted figure took precedence over the handwritten figure. What should the court decide on this issue? Discuss. [*Galatia Community State Bank v. Kindy*, 307 Ark. 467, 821 S.W.2d 765 (1991)]

24–6. **FIXED AMOUNT OF MONEY.** William Bailey and William Vaught, as officers for Bailey, Vaught, Robertson, and Co. (BVR), signed a promissory note to borrow $34,000 from the Forestwood National Bank. The interest rate was variable: "the lender's published prime rate" plus 1 percent. Forestwood went out of business, and ultimately the note was acquired by

Remington Investments, Inc. When BVR failed to make payments, Remington filed a suit in a Texas state court against BVR. BVR contended in part that the note was not negotiable because after Forestwood closed, there was no "published lender's prime rate" to use to calculate the interest. Did the note provide for payment of a "fixed amount of money"? Discuss fully. [*Bailey, Vaught, Robertson, and Co. v. Remington Investments, Inc.*, 888 S.W.2d 860 (Tex.App.—Dallas 1994)]

24-7. ⚖ CASE PROBLEM WITH SAMPLE ANSWER

In July 1981, Southeast Bank in Miami, Florida, issued five cashier's checks, totaling $450,000, to five payees, including Roberto Sanchez. Two months later, in Colombia, South America, Sanchez gave the checks to Juan Diaz. In 1991, Southeast failed. Under federal law, notice must be mailed to a failed bank's depositors, who then have eighteen months to file a claim for their funds. Under an "Assistance Agreement," First Union National Bank agreed to assume Southeast's liability for outstanding cashier's checks and other items. First Union received funds to pay these items but was required to return the funds if, within eighteen months after Southeast's closing, payment for any item had not been claimed. In 1996, in Colombia, with the five cashier's checks that Diaz had received from Sanchez, Diaz paid a debt to John Acevedo. In 2001, Acevedo tendered these checks to First Union for payment. Does First Union have to pay? Would it make any difference if the required notice had not been mailed? Why or why not? [*Acevedo v. First Union National Bank*, 357 F.3d 1244 (11th Cir. 2004)]

To view a sample answer for this case problem, go to this book's Web site at http://wbl.westbuslaw.com, select "Chapter 24," and click on "Case Problem with Sample Answer."

24-8. NEGOTIABILITY.

In October 1998, Somerset Valley Bank notified Alfred Hauser, president of Hauser Co., that the bank had begun to receive what appeared to be Hauser Co. payroll checks. None of the payees were Hauser Co. employees, however, and Hauser had not written the checks or authorized anyone to sign them on his behalf. Automatic Data Processing, Inc., provided payroll services for Hauser Co. and used a facsimile signature on all its payroll checks. Hauser told the bank not to cash the checks. In early 1999, Robert Triffin, who deals in negotiable instruments, bought eighteen of the checks, totaling more than $8,800, from various check-cashing agencies. The agencies stated that they had cashed the checks expecting the bank to pay them. Each check was payable to a bearer for a fixed amount, on demand, and did not state any undertaking by the person promising payment other than the payment of money. Each check bore a facsimile drawer's signature stamp identical to Hauser Co.'s authorized stamp.

Each check had been returned to an agency marked "stolen check" and stamped "do not present again." When the bank refused to cash the checks, Triffin filed a suit in a New Jersey state court against Hauser Co. Were the checks negotiable instruments? Why or why not? [*Triffin v. Somerset Valley Bank*, 777 A.2d 993 (N.J. Super. App.Div. 2001)]

24-9. NEGOTIABILITY.

In October 1996, Robert Hildebrandt contracted with Harvey and Nancy Anderson to find a tenant for the Andersons' used-car lot. The Andersons agreed to pay Hildebrandt "a commission equal in amount to five percent up to first three years of lease." On December 12, Paramount Automotive, Inc., agreed to lease the premises for three years at $7,500 per month, and the Andersons signed a promissory note, which stated that they would pay Hildebrandt $13,500, plus interest, in consecutive monthly installments of $485 until the total sum was paid. The note contained an acceleration clause. In a separate agreement, Paramount promised to pay $485 of its monthly rent directly to Hildebrandt. Less than a year later, Paramount stopped making payments to all parties. To enforce the note, Hildebrandt filed a suit in an Oregon state court against the Andersons. One issue in the case was whether the note was a negotiable instrument. The Andersons claimed that it was not, because it was not "unconditional," arguing that their obligation to make payments on the note was conditioned on their receipt of rent from Paramount. Are the Andersons correct? Explain. [*Hildebrandt v. Anderson*, 180 Or.App. 192, 42 P.3d 355 (2002)]

24-10. VIDEO QUESTION

Go to this text's Web site at http://wbl.westbuslaw.com and select "Chapter 24." Click on "Video Questions" and view the video titled *Negotiable Instruments*. Then answer the following questions.

(a) Who is the maker of the promissory note discussed in the video?

(b) Is the note in the video payable on demand or at a definite time?

(c) Does the note contain an unconditional promise or order to pay?

(d) If the note does not meet the requirements of negotiability, can Onyx assign the note (assignment was discussed in Chapter 16) to the bank in exchange for cash?

LAW | on the Web

For updated links to resources available on the Web, as well as a variety of other materials, visit this text's Web site at http://wbl.westbuslaw.com.

The National Conference of Commissioners on Uniform State Laws, in association with the University of Pennsylvania Law School, now offers an official site for in-process and final drafts of uniform and model acts. For an index of final acts, including UCC Articles 3 and 4, go to

http://www.law.upenn.edu/bll/ulc/ulc_final.htm

Cornell University's Legal Information Institute offers online access to the UCC, as well as to UCC articles as enacted by particular states and proposed revisions to articles, at

http://www.law.cornell.edu/ucc/ucc.table.html

LEGAL RESEARCH EXERCISES ON THE WEB

Go to http://wbl.westbuslaw.com, the Web site that accompanies this text. Select "Chapter 24" and click on "Internet Exercises." There you will find the following Internet research exercises that you can perform to learn more about topics covered in this chapter.

Activity 24–1: LEGAL PERSPECTIVE
              Overview of Negotiable Instruments

Activity 24–2: MANAGEMENT PERSPECTIVE
              Banks and Bank Accounts

CHAPTER 25

Transferability and Holder in Due Course

Once issued, a negotiable instrument can be transferred to others by *assignment* or by *negotiation*. Recall from Chapter 16 that an assignment is a transfer of rights under a contract. Under general contract principles, a transfer by assignment to an assignee gives the assignee only those rights that the assignor possessed. Any defenses that can be raised against an assignor can normally be raised against the assignee. This same principle applies when an instrument, such as a promissory note, is transferred by assignment. The transferee is then an *assignee* rather than a *holder*.

Negotiation is the transfer of an instrument in such form that the transferee (the person to whom the instrument is transferred) becomes a holder [UCC 3–201(a)]. Under the Uniform Commercial Code (UCC), a holder receives, at the very least, the rights of the previous possessor [UCC 3–203(b), 3–305]. Unlike an assignment, a transfer by negotiation can make it possible for a holder to receive *more* rights in the instrument than the prior possessor had [UCC 3–305]. A holder who receives greater rights is known as a *holder in due course*, a concept we discuss in this chapter. First, though, we look at the requirements for negotiation and examine the various types of *indorsements* that are used when order instruments are negotiated.

SECTION 1 | Negotiation

There are two methods of negotiating an instrument so that the receiver becomes a holder. The method used depends on whether the instrument is an *order instrument* or a *bearer instrument*.

NEGOTIATING ORDER INSTRUMENTS

An order instrument contains the name of a payee capable of indorsing, as in "Pay to the order of Elliot Goodseal." If an instrument is an order instrument, it is negotiated by delivery with any necessary indorsements. For example, the Carrington Corporation issues a payroll check "to the order of Elliot Goodseal." Goodseal takes the check to the bank, signs his name on the back (an indorsement), gives it to the teller (a delivery), and receives cash. Goodseal has negotiated the check to the bank [UCC 3–201(b)].

Negotiating order instruments requires both delivery and indorsement. If Goodseal had taken the check to the bank and delivered it to the teller without sign-ing it, the transfer would not qualify as a negotiation. In that situation, the transfer would be treated as an assignment, and the bank would become an assignee rather than a holder.

NEGOTIATING BEARER INSTRUMENTS

If an instrument is payable to bearer, it is negotiated by delivery—that is, by transfer into another person's possession. Indorsement is not necessary [UCC 3–201(b)]. The use of bearer instruments thus involves a greater risk of loss or theft than the use of order instruments.

Assume that Alan Tyson writes a check payable to "cash," thus creating a bearer instrument. Tyson then hands the check to Blaine Parrington (a delivery). Parrington places the check in his wallet, which is subsequently stolen. The thief has possession of the check. At this point, the thief has no rights in the check. If the thief "delivers" the check to an innocent third person, however, negotiation will be complete. All rights to the check will be passed *absolutely* to that third person, and Parrington will lose all right to recover the proceeds of the check from that person [UCC 3–306]. Of course, Parrington can recover his funds from the thief if the thief can be found.

SECTION **2** | Indorsements

An indorsement is required whenever an instrument being negotiated is classified as an order instrument. An *indorsement* is a signature with or without additional words or statements. It is most often written on the back of the instrument itself. If there is no room on the instrument, the indorsement can be written on a separate piece of paper, called an **allonge.**[1] The allonge must be "so firmly affixed [to the instrument] as to become a part thereof" [UCC 3–204(a)]. Pins or paper clips will not suffice. Most courts hold that staples are sufficient.

A person who transfers a note or a draft by signing (indorsing) it and delivering it to another person is an **indorser.** The person to whom the check is indorsed and delivered is the **indorsee.** For example, Luisa Parks receives a graduation check for $100. She can transfer the check to her mother (or to anyone) by signing it on the back. Luisa is an indorser. If Luisa indorses the check by writing "Pay to Aretha Parks," Aretha Parks is the indorsee.

We examine here four categories of indorsements: blank indorsements, special indorsements, qualified indorsements, and restrictive indorsements.

BLANK INDORSEMENTS

A **blank indorsement** specifies no particular indorsee and can consist of a mere signature [UCC 3–205(b)]. Hence, a check payable "to the order of Mark Deitsch" can be indorsed in blank simply by having Deitsch's signature written on the back of the check. Exhibit 25–1 shows a blank indorsement.

EXHIBIT 25–1   **A Blank Indorsement**

An instrument payable to order and indorsed in blank becomes a bearer instrument and can be negotiated by delivery alone [UCC 3–205(b)]. In other

words, as will be discussed later, a blank indorsement converts an order instrument to a bearer instrument, which anybody can cash. If Rita Chou indorses in blank a check payable to her order and then loses it on the street, Coker can find it and sell it to Duncan for value without indorsing it. This constitutes a negotiation because Coker has made delivery of a bearer instrument (which was an order instrument until it was indorsed in blank).

SPECIAL INDORSEMENTS

A **special indorsement** identifies the person to whom the indorser intends to make the instrument payable; that is, it names the indorsee [UCC 3–205(a)]. For example, words such as "Pay to the order of Clay" or "Pay to Clay," followed by the signature of the indorser, are sufficient. When an instrument is indorsed in this way, it is an order instrument.

To avoid the risk of loss from theft, a holder may convert a blank indorsement to a special indorsement. This changes the bearer instrument back to an order instrument. A holder may "convert a blank indorsement that consists only of a signature into a special indorsement by writing, above the signature of the indorser, words identifying the person to whom the instrument is made payable" [UCC 3–205(c)].

For example, a check is made payable to Hal Cohen. He indorses his name by blank indorsement on the back of the check and negotiates the check to William Hunter. Hunter, not wishing to cash the check immediately, wants to avoid any risk should he lose the check. He therefore writes "Pay to William Hunter" above Cohen's blank indorsement. In this manner, Hunter has converted Cohen's blank indorsement into a special indorsement. Further negotiation now requires William Hunter's indorsement, plus delivery. Exhibit 25–2 shows a special indorsement.

EXHIBIT 25–2   **A Special Indorsement**

QUALIFIED INDORSEMENTS

Generally, an indorser, *merely by indorsing,* impliedly promises to pay the holder, or any subsequent indorser, the amount of the instrument in the event that the

---

1. Pronounced uh-*lohnj*.

drawer or maker defaults on the payment [UCC 3–415(a)]. Usually, then, indorsements are *unqualified indorsements*. In other words, the indorser is guaranteeing payment of the instrument in addition to transferring title to it. An indorser who does not wish to be liable on an instrument can use a **qualified indorsement** to disclaim this liability [UCC 3–415(b)]. The notation "without recourse" is commonly used to create a qualified indorsement.

Suppose that a check is made payable to the order of Sarah Jacobs. Sarah wants to negotiate the check to Allison Jong but does not want to assume liability for the check's payment. Sarah could create a qualified indorsement by indorsing the check as follows: "Pay to Allison Jong, without recourse [Signed] Sarah Jacobs" (see Exhibit 25–3).

EXHIBIT 25-3 A Qualified Indorsement

> Pay to Allison Jong,
> without recourse
> Sarah Jacobs

THE EFFECT OF QUALIFIED INDORSEMENTS

Qualified indorsements are often used by persons acting in a representative capacity. For example, insurance agents sometimes receive checks payable to them that are really intended as payment to the insurance company. The agent is merely indorsing the payment through to the insurance company and should not be required to make good on a check if it is later dishonored. The "without recourse" indorsement relieves the agent from any liability on the check. If the instrument is dishonored, the holder cannot obtain recovery from the agent who indorsed "without recourse" unless the indorser has breached one of the transfer warranties that will be discussed in Chapter 26. These warranties relate to good title, authorized signature, no material alteration, and other requirements.

SPECIAL VERSUS BLANK QUALIFIED INDORSEMENTS

A qualified indorsement ("without recourse") can be accompanied by either a special indorsement or a blank indorsement. A special qualified indorsement includes the name of the indorsee as well as the words "without recourse," as in Exhibit 25–3. The special indorsement makes the instrument an order instrument, and it requires an indorsement plus delivery for

negotiation. A blank qualified indorsement makes the instrument a bearer instrument, and only delivery is required for negotiation. In either situation, the instrument still transfers title to the indorsee and can be further negotiated.

RESTRICTIVE INDORSEMENTS

A **restrictive indorsement** requires the indorsee to comply with certain instructions regarding the funds involved but does not prohibit further negotiation of the instrument [UCC 3–206(a)]. Restrictive indorsements come in many forms, some of which we discuss here.

INDORSEMENTS PROHIBITING FURTHER INDORSEMENT

An indorsement such as "Pay to Julie Thrush only, [signed] Thomas Fasulo" does not destroy negotiability. Thrush can negotiate the paper to a holder just as if it had read "Pay to Julie Thrush [Signed] Thomas Fasulo" [UCC 3–206(a)]. If the holder gives value, this type of restrictive indorsement has the same legal effect as a special indorsement.

CONDITIONAL INDORSEMENTS

When payment depends on the occurrence of some event specified in the indorsement, the instrument has a conditional indorsement [UCC 3–204(a)]. For example, suppose that Ken Barton indorses a check as follows: "Pay to Lars Johansen if he completes the renovation of my kitchen by June 1, 2007, [signed] Ken Barton." Article 3 states that an indorsement conditioning the right to receive payment "does not affect the right of the indorsee to enforce the instrument" [UCC 3–206(b)]. A person paying or taking an instrument for value (*taking for value* will be discussed later in the chapter) can disregard the condition without liability.[2]

A conditional indorsement does not prevent further negotiation of the instrument. If conditional language appears on the *face* of an instrument, however, the instrument is not negotiable because it does not meet the requirement that a negotiable instrument must contain an unconditional promise to pay.

---

2. Under Section 3–206(3) of the unrevised Article 3, the indorsement was enforceable (except against *intermediary banks*, which will be defined in Chapter 27), and neither the indorsee nor any subsequent holder had the right to enforce payment against that indorser on the instrument before the condition was met.

INDORSEMENTS FOR DEPOSIT OR COLLECTION

A common type of restrictive indorsement makes the indorsee (almost always a bank) a collecting agent of the indorser [UCC 3–206(c)]. Exhibit 25–4 illustrates this type of indorsement on a check payable and issued to Marcel Dumont. In particular, the indorsements "For deposit only" and "For collection only" have the effect of locking the instrument into the bank collection process. Only a bank can acquire the rights of a holder following one of these indorsements until the item has been specially indorsed by a bank to a person who is not a bank [UCC 3–206(c), 4–201(b)]. A bank's liability for payment of an instrument with a restrictive indorsement of this kind will be discussed in Chapter 27.

EXHIBIT 25–4 "For Deposit" and "For Collection" Indorsements

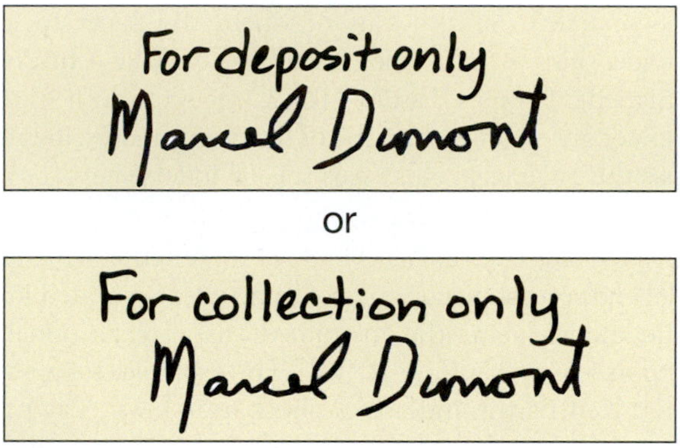

For deposit only
Marcel Dumont

or

For collection only
Marcel Dumont

TRUST INDORSEMENTS Indorsements to persons who are to hold or use the funds for the benefit of the indorser or a third party are called **trust indorsements** (also known as *agency indorsements*) [UCC 3–206(d), (e)]. For example, assume that Ralph Zimmer asks his accountant, Stephanie Contento, to pay some bills for him while he is out of the country. He indorses a check, drawn by a friend, to Stephanie Contento "as agent for Ralph Zimmer." This trust (agency) indorsement obligates Contento to use the funds from his friend's check only for the benefit of Zimmer.

The result of a trust indorsement is that legal rights in the instrument are transferred to the original indorsee. To the extent that the original indorsee pays or applies the proceeds consistently with the indorsement (for example, in an indorsement stating "Pay to Ellen Cook in trust for Roger Callahan"), the indorsee is a holder and can become a holder in due course (a status that will be described shortly).

Sample trust (agency) indorsements are shown in Exhibit 25–5.

EXHIBIT 25–5 Trust (Agency) Indorsements

Pay to Stephanie Contento
as Agent for Ralph Zimmer
Ralph Zimmer

or

Pay to Ellen Cook
in trust for Roger Callahan
Roger Callahan

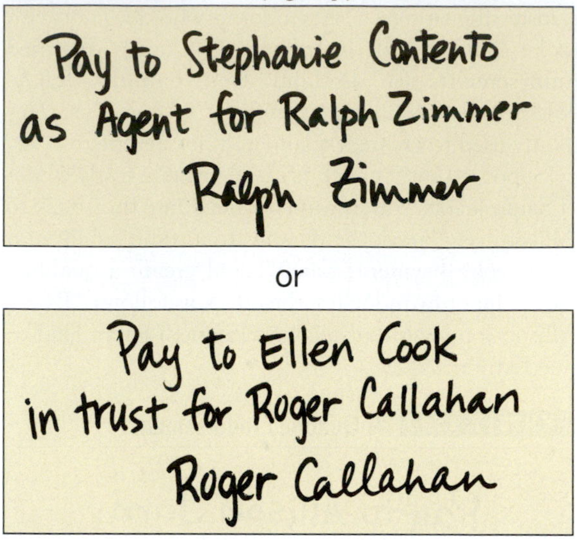

The fiduciary restrictions—restrictions mandated by a relationship involving trust and loyalty—on the instrument do not reach beyond the original indorsee [UCC 3–206(d), (e)]. Any subsequent purchaser can qualify as a holder in due course unless he or she has actual notice that the instrument was negotiated in breach of a fiduciary duty.

HOW INDORSEMENTS CAN CONVERT ORDER INSTRUMENTS TO BEARER INSTRUMENTS AND VICE VERSA

As mentioned previously, order instruments and bearer instruments are negotiated differently. The method used for negotiation depends on the character of the instrument *at the time the negotiation takes place*. Indorsement can convert an order instrument into a bearer instrument. For example, a check originally payable to "cash" but subsequently indorsed with the words "Pay to Arnold" must be negotiated as an order instrument (by indorsement and delivery), even though it was previously a bearer instrument [UCC 3–205(a)].

An instrument payable to the order of a named payee and indorsed in blank (by the holder's signature only, as discussed previously) becomes a bearer instrument [UCC 3–205(b)]. For example, a check made payable to the order of Jessie Arnold is issued to

Arnold, and Arnold indorses it by signing her name on the back. The instrument, which is now a bearer instrument, can be negotiated by delivery without indorsement. Arnold can negotiate the check to whomever she wishes merely by delivery, and that person can negotiate by delivery without indorsement. If Arnold loses the check after she indorses it, then a finder can negotiate it further.

Similarly, a bearer instrument can be converted into an order instrument through indorsement. Suppose that Arnold negotiates, by delivery, the check that she indorsed in blank (now a bearer instrument) to Jonas Tolling. Tolling indorses the check "Pay to Mark Hyatt [Signed] Jonas Tolling." By adding this special indorsement, Tolling has converted the check into an order instrument. The check can be further negotiated only by indorsement (by Mark Hyatt) and delivery [UCC 3–205(b)]. Exhibit 25–6 illustrates how an indorsement can convert an order instrument into a bearer instrument and vice versa.

SECTION 3 | Miscellaneous Indorsement Problems

Of course, a significant problem occurs when an indorsement is forged or unauthorized. The UCC rules concerning unauthorized or forged signatures and indorsements will be discussed in Chapter 26 in the context of signature liability. These rules will be examined again in Chapter 27 in the context of the bank's liability for payment of an instrument containing an unauthorized signature. Here we look at some other difficulties that may arise with indorsements.

MISSPELLED NAMES

An indorsement should be identical to the name that appears on the instrument. A payee or indorsee whose name is misspelled can indorse with the misspelled name, the correct name, or both [UCC 3–204(d)]. For example, if Marie Ellison receives a check payable to the order of Mary Ellison, she can indorse the check either "Marie Ellison" or "Mary Ellison." The usual practice is to indorse with the name as it appears on the instrument and follow it by the correct name.

INSTRUMENTS PAYABLE TO LEGAL ENTITIES

A negotiable instrument can be drawn payable to a legal entity such as an estate, a partnership, or an organization. In this situation, an authorized representative of the entity can negotiate the instrument. For example, a check may read "Pay to the order of the Red Cross." An authorized representative of the Red Cross can negotiate this check. Similarly, negotiable

EXHIBIT 25–6 | Converting an Order Instrument to a Bearer Instrument and Vice Versa

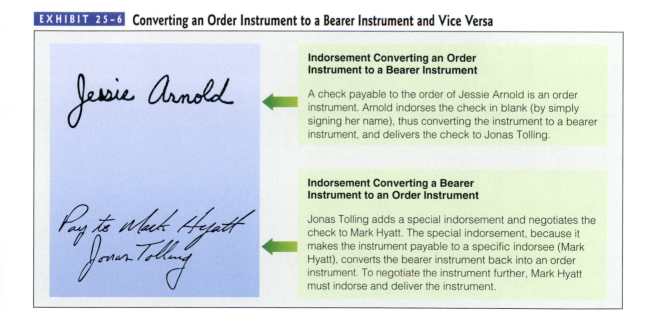

Indorsement Converting an Order Instrument to a Bearer Instrument

A check payable to the order of Jessie Arnold is an order instrument. Arnold indorses the check in blank (by simply signing her name), thus converting the instrument to a bearer instrument, and delivers the check to Jonas Tolling.

Indorsement Converting a Bearer Instrument to an Order Instrument

Jonas Tolling adds a special indorsement and negotiates the check to Mark Hyatt. The special indorsement, because it makes the instrument payable to a specific indorsee (Mark Hyatt), converts the bearer instrument back into an order instrument. To negotiate the instrument further, Mark Hyatt must indorse and deliver the instrument.

paper can be payable to a public officer. For example, checks reading "Pay to the order of the County Tax Collector" or "Pay to the order of Larry White, Receiver of Taxes" can be negotiated by whoever holds the office [UCC 3–110(c)].

ALTERNATIVE OR JOINT PAYEES

An instrument payable to two or more persons *in the alternative* (for example, "Pay to the order of Ying or Mifflin") requires the indorsement of only one of the payees [UCC 3–110(d)]. If, however, an instrument is made payable to two or more persons *jointly* (for example, "Pay to the order of Bridgette and Tony Van Horn"), all of the payees' indorsements are necessary for negotiation. If an instrument payable to two or more persons does not clearly indicate whether it is payable in the alternative or payable jointly, then "the instrument is payable to the persons alternatively" [UCC 3–110(d)]. The same principles apply to special indorsements that identify more than one person to whom the indorser intends to make the instrument payable [UCC 3–205(a)]. These principles were applied in the following case.

CASE 25.1   ## Hyatt Corp. v. Palm Beach National Bank

District Court
of Appeal of Florida,
Third District, 2003.
840 So.2d 300.

LEVY, Judge.
* * * *
* * * Skyscraper Building Maintenance, LLC [limited liability company—see Chapter 37], had a contract with Hyatt [Corporation] to perform maintenance work for various Hyatt hotels in South Florida. Skyscraper entered into [an] agreement with J & D [Financial Corporation]. As part of the * * * agreement, J & D requested Hyatt to make checks payable for maintenance services to Skyscraper and J & D. Of the many checks issued by Hyatt to Skyscraper and J & D, two were negotiated by [Palm Beach National Bank] but endorsed only by Skyscraper. They were made payable as follows:

1. Check No. 1-78671 for $22,531 payable to:
J & D Financial Corp. Skyscraper Building Maint[enance] * * *

2. Check No. 1-75723 for $21,107 payable to:
Skyscraper Building Maint[enance] J & D Financial Corp. * * *

Only one of the payees, Skyscraper, endorsed these two checks. The bank cashed the checks. According to J & D, it did not receive the benefit of these two payments.

J & D filed a complaint [in a Florida state court] against * * * Hyatt and the bank [and others]. J & D sought damages * * * against Hyatt and the bank for negotiation of the two checks. * * *

The bank argued that the checks were payable to J & D and Skyscraper alternatively, and thus the bank could properly negotiate the checks based upon the [indorsement] of either of the two payees. * * *

Hyatt's position was that the checks were not ambiguous, were payable jointly and not alternatively, and thus * * * the checks could only be negotiated by [indorsement] of both of the payees. J & D similarly argued that the checks were payable jointly. The trial court granted Summary Judgment in favor of the bank * * * . Hyatt appealed. J & D filed a cross-appeal.
* * * *
In 1990, Article 3 of the UCC was revised, and the language of UCC Section 3–116 was added to UCC Section 3–110 and became subsection (d). Revised UCC Section 3–110(d), which added language to follow former 3–116(a) and (b), states, "If an instrument payable to two or more persons is ambiguous as to whether it is payable to the persons alternatively, the instrument is payable to the persons alternatively." The net effect of the amendment was to change the presumption. What was unambiguous before is now ambiguous.

Turning to our jurisdiction, Florida has adopted the statutory revision to UCC 3–110, with its enactment of Section 673.1101, Florida Statutes. Section 673.1101(4) now provides the following:

CASE 25.1 | Continued

(4) If an instrument is payable to two or more persons alternatively, it is payable to any of them and may be negotiated, discharged, or enforced by any or all of them in possession of the instrument. If an instrument is payable to two or more persons not alternatively, it is payable to all of them and may be negotiated, discharged, or enforced only by all of them. If an instrument payable to two or more persons is ambiguous as to whether it is payable to the persons alternatively, the instrument is payable to the persons alternatively.

*   *   *   *

*   *   * [T]he predecessor statute provided that if an ambiguity existed as to whether multiple payees were intended as joint or alternative payees, they were deemed joint payees, while the amended statute applicable to this case reverses the prior rule.

*   *   *   *

We conclude that based on the 1990 amendment to the Uniform Commercial Code, *when a check lists two payees without the use of the word "and" or "or," the nature of the payee is ambiguous as to whether they are alternative payees or joint payees.* Therefore, the UCC amendment prevails and they are to be treated as alternative payees, thus requiring only one of the payees' signatures. Consequently, the bank could negotiate the check when it was [indorsed] by only one of the two payees, thereby escaping liability. [Emphasis added.]

*   *   * As the parties correctly point out, this is a case of first impression in Florida appellate courts. *   *   *

*   *   * [W]e hold that the trial court was correct in granting the Summary Final Judgment. *Affirmed.*

QUESTIONS

1. Other than negotiation, what is the significance of the provision of the UCC at issue in this case?
2. If a stacked-payee designation was considered unambiguous and payable jointly before the amendment of this provision of the UCC, should that same payee designation be considered unambiguous after the amendment?

SECTION 4 | Holder versus Holder in Due Course

The rules contained in Article 3 of the UCC govern a party's right to payment of a check, draft, note, or certificate of deposit.[3] Problems arise when a holder seeking payment of a negotiable instrument learns that a defense to payment exists or that another party has a prior claim to the instrument. In such situations, it becomes important for the person seeking payment to have the rights of a *holder in due course* (HDC). An HDC takes a negotiable instrument free of all claims and most defenses of other parties.

STATUS OF AN ORDINARY HOLDER

As pointed out in Chapter 24, the UCC defines a *holder* as a person in possession of an instrument "if the instrument is payable to bearer or, in the cases of an instrument payable to an identified person, if the identified person is in possession" [UCC 1–201(20)]. An ordinary holder obtains only those rights that the transferor had in the instrument. In this respect, a holder has the same status as an assignee (see Chapter 16). A holder normally is subject to the same defenses that could be asserted against the transferor, just as an assignee is subject to the defenses that could be asserted against the assignor.

STATUS OF A HOLDER IN DUE COURSE (HDC)

In contrast, a **holder in due course (HDC)** is a holder who, by meeting certain acquisition requirements (to be discussed shortly), takes the instrument free of most of the defenses and claims to which the transferor was

---

3. The rights and liabilities on checks, drafts, notes, and certificates of deposit are determined under Article 3 of the UCC. Other kinds of documents, such as stock certificates, bills of lading, and other documents of title, meet the requirements of negotiable instruments, but the rights and liabilities of the parties on these documents are covered by Articles 7 and 8 of the UCC. See Chapter 47, on bailments, for information about Article 7.

CONCEPT SUMMARY 25.1 | Types of Indorsements and Their Consequences

Words Constituting the Indorsement	Type of Indorsement	Indorser's Signature Liability[a]
"Mark Deitsch"	Blank	Unqualified signature liability on proper presentment and notice of dishonor.[b]
"Pay to William Hunter, Hal Cohen"	Special	Unqualified signature liability on proper presentment and notice of dishonor.
"Without recourse, Sarah Jacobs"	Qualified (blank for further negotiation)	No signature liability. Transfer warranty liability if breach occurs.[c]
"Pay to Allison Jong, without recourse, Sarah Jacobs"	Qualified (special for further negotiation)	No signature liability. Transfer warranty liability if breach occurs.
"For deposit only, Marcel Dumont"	Restrictive—for deposit (blank for further negotiation within the banking system)	Signature liability only on Dumont's having amount deposited in his account. If deposit is made, signature liability on proper presentment and notice of dishonor.
"Pay to Ellen Cook in trust for Roger Callahan, Roger Callahan"	Restrictive—trust (special for further negotiation)	Signature liability to original indorsee only on payment to Ellen Cook for Roger Callahan's benefit. Regardless of whether restriction is met, signature liability to subsequent indorsers on proper presentment and notice of dishonor.

a. *Signature liability* refers to the liability of a party who signs an instrument. Signature liability will be discussed in more detail in Chapter 26.
b. When an instrument is dishonored—that is, when, for example, a drawer's bank refuses to cash the drawer's check on proper presentment—an indorser of the check may be liable on it if he or she is given proper notice of dishonor. Dishonor and notice of dishonor will be discussed in Chapter 26.
c. The transferor of an instrument makes certain warranties to the transferee and subsequent holders, and thus, even if the transferor's signature does not render him or her liable on the instrument, he or she may be liable for breach of a transfer warranty. Transfer warranties will be discussed in Chapter 26. See also UCC 3–416.

subject. Stated another way, an HDC can normally acquire a higher level of immunity than can an ordinary holder in regard to defenses against payment on the instrument or ownership claims to the instrument by other parties.

An example will help to clarify the distinction between the rights of an ordinary holder and the rights of an HDC. Debby Morrison signs a $1,000 note payable to Alex Jerrod in payment for goods. Jerrod negotiates the note to Beverly Larson, who promises to pay Jerrod for it in thirty days. During the next month, Larson learns that Jerrod has breached his contract with Morrison by delivering defective goods and that, for this reason, Morrison will not honor the $1,000 note. Whether Larson can hold Morrison liable on the note depends on whether Larson has met the requirements for HDC status. If Larson has met

these requirements and thus has HDC status, she is entitled to payment on the note. If Larson has not met these requirements, she has the status of an ordinary holder, and Morrison's defense against payment to Jerrod will also be effective against Larson.

SECTION 5 | Requirements for HDC Status

The basic requirements for attaining HDC status are set forth in UCC 3–302. An HDC must first be a holder of a negotiable instrument and must have taken the instrument (1) for value; (2) in good faith; and (3) without notice that it is overdue, that it has been dishonored, that any person has a defense against it or a claim to it, or that the instrument contains unauthorized signatures or alterations or is so irregular or incomplete as to call into question its authenticity. We now examine each of these requirements.

TAKING FOR VALUE

An HDC must have given value for the instrument [UCC 3–302(a)(2)(i), 3–303]. A person who receives an instrument as a gift or inherits it has *not* met the requirement of value. In these situations, the person normally becomes an ordinary holder and does not possess the rights of an HDC.

HOW AN INSTRUMENT IS TAKEN FOR VALUE

Under UCC 3–303(a), a holder can take an instrument for value in one of five ways:

1. By performing the promise for which the instrument was issued or transferred.

2. By acquiring a security interest or other lien in the instrument (other than a lien obtained by a judicial proceeding).[4]

3. By taking an instrument in payment of, or as security for, an antecedent (preexisting) claim.

4. By giving a negotiable instrument as payment.

5. By giving an irrevocable commitment as payment.

---

4. Security interests will be discussed in Chapter 29. Other liens will be discussed in Chapter 28.

THE CONCEPT OF VALUE IN NEGOTIABLE INSTRUMENTS LAW The concept of value in the law of negotiable instruments is not the same as the concept of consideration in the law of contracts. An executory promise (a promise to give value in the future) is clearly valid consideration to support a contract [UCC 1–201(44)]. It does not, however, normally constitute value sufficient to make one an HDC. UCC 3–303(a)(1) provides that a holder takes the instrument for value only to the extent that the promise has been performed. Therefore, if the holder plans to pay for the instrument later or plans to perform the required services at some future date, the holder has not yet given value. In that situation, the holder is not yet a holder in due course.

In the Morrison-Jerrod-Larson example presented earlier, Larson is not an HDC because she did not take the instrument (Morrison's note) for value—she had not yet paid Jerrod for the note. Thus, Morrison's defense of breach of contract is valid not only against Jerrod but also against Larson. If Larson had paid Jerrod for the note at the time of transfer (which would mean she had given value for the instrument), she would be an HDC. As an HDC, she could hold Morrison liable on the note even though Morrison has a valid defense against Jerrod on the basis of breach of contract. Exhibit 25–7 illustrates these concepts.

ANTECEDENT CLAIM When an instrument is given in payment of—or as security for—an **antecedent claim** (a preexisting claim), the value requirement is

---

EXHIBIT 25-7 Taking for Value

By exchanging defective goods for the note, Jerrod breached his contract with Morrison. Morrison could assert this defense if Jerrod presented the note to her for payment. Jerrod exchanged the note for Larson's promise to pay in thirty days, however. Because Larson did not take the note for value, she is not a holder in due course. Thus, Morrison can assert against Larson the defense of Jerrod's breach when Larson submits the note to Morrison for payment. If Larson had taken the note for value, Morrison could not assert that defense and would be liable to pay the note.

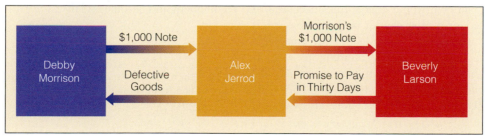

met [UCC 3–303(a)(3)]. Here again, the UCC's Article 3 and contract law produce different results. An antecedent claim is not valid consideration under general contract law, but it does constitute value sufficient to satisfy the requirement for HDC status under the UCC. To illustrate: Cary owes Dwyer $2,000 on a past-due account. If Cary negotiates a $2,000 note signed by Gordon to Dwyer and Dwyer accepts it to discharge the overdue account balance, Dwyer has given value for the instrument.

NEGOTIABLE INSTRUMENT AS VALUE UCC 3–303(a)(4) provides that a holder takes the instrument for value if "the instrument is issued or transferred in exchange for a negotiable instrument." Suppose that Martin has issued a $500 negotiable promissory note to Paula. The note is due six months from the date issued. Paula's financial circumstances are such that she does not want to wait for the maturity date to collect. Therefore, she negotiates the note to her friend Susan, who pays her $200 in cash and writes her a check—a negotiable instrument—for the balance of $300. Susan has given full value for the note by paying $200 in cash and issuing Paula the check for $300. Note that a negotiable instrument has value when it is issued, not when the underlying obligation is finally paid.

CHECK DEPOSITS AND WITHDRAWALS Occasionally, a commercial bank becomes an HDC when honoring other banks' checks for its own customers. In this situation, the bank is an "involuntary" HDC, in that at the time of giving value, the bank has no intention of becoming an HDC.

Assume that on Monday morning at the end of the month, Pat Stoven has $400 in her checking account at the First National Bank. That morning, Stoven deposits her payroll check for $300, drawn by her employer on the Second Interstate Bank. During her lunch hour, she issues a check to her landlord for $425. The landlord cashes the check at the First National Bank. Later, the Second Interstate Bank returns the payroll check marked "insufficient funds." In most cases, First National would charge this check against Stoven's account. If that cannot be done, however, is the First National Bank an HDC of the employer's check? The answer is yes. According to what is referred to as the *first-money-in, first-money-out rule,* First National Bank has paid to the landlord $25 of its own funds [UCC 4–210(b)]. Therefore, First National

is an HDC to the extent that it has given value— $25—and can seek recovery of $25 from the employer (the drawer of the check).

SPECIAL SITUATIONS In a few exceptional circumstances, a holder can take an instrument for value but still not be accorded HDC status. UCC 3–302(c) specifies that in the following situations, the rights of the holder will be limited to those of an ordinary holder:

1. Purchase at a judicial sale (for example, a bankruptcy sale) or acquisition by taking under legal process.
2. Acquisition when taking over an estate (as an administrator).
3. Purchase as part of a bulk transfer (as when a corporation buys the assets of another corporation).

TAKING IN GOOD FAITH

The second requirement for HDC status is that the holder take the instrument in *good faith* [UCC 3–302(a)(2)(ii)]. Under Article 3, *good faith* is defined as "honesty in fact and the observance of reasonable commercial standards of fair dealing" [UCC 3–103(a)(4)].[5] The good faith requirement applies only to the *holder.* It is immaterial whether the transferor acted in good faith. Thus, a person who in good faith takes a negotiable instrument from a thief may become an HDC.

Because of the good faith requirement, one must ask whether the purchaser, when acquiring the instrument, honestly believed that the instrument was not defective. If a person purchases a $10,000 note for $300 from a stranger on a street corner, the issue of good faith can be raised on the grounds of both the suspicious circumstances and the grossly inadequate consideration (value). The UCC does not provide clear guidelines to determine good faith, so each situation must be examined separately. In the following case, the court considered whether a bank observed "reasonable commercial standards of fair dealing" to fulfill the good faith requirement and become an HDC.

---

5. Before the revision of Article 3, the applicable definition of *good faith* was "honesty in fact in the conduct or transaction concerned" [UCC 1–201(19)].

CASE 25.2

Mid Wisconsin Bank v. Forsgard Trading, Inc.

Wisconsin Court
of Appeals, 2003.
266 Wis.2d 685,
668 N.W.2d 830,
2003 WI App. 186.
http://www.wisbar.org/
WisCtApp/index.html[a]

BACKGROUND AND FACTS *Forsgard Trading, Inc., opened an account at Mid Wisconsin Bank in July 1999. The account agreement stated, "Any items, other than cash, accepted for deposit * * * will be given provisional credit only until collection is final." Mid Wisconsin's practice is to give immediate credit on deposits, but an employee may place a hold on a check if, for example, there is reasonable doubt about it. On May 7, 2001, Lakeshore Truck and Equipment Sales, Inc., wrote a check payable to Forsgard in the amount of $18,500. On May 8, Forsgard deposited the check in its account at Mid Wisconsin, which gave Forsgard immediate credit. The same day, Lakeshore issued a stop-payment order (an order to its bank not to pay the check—see Chapter 27). When Mid Wisconsin received notice on May 16 that payment had been stopped, it deducted the $18,500 from Forsgard's account. Because of transfers from the account between May 8 and May 16, the deduction resulted in a negative balance. Before this incident, Forsgard had overdrawn the account twenty-four times but, on each occasion, had deposited money to cover the overdraft. Forsgard did not do so this time. Mid Wisconsin filed a suit in a Wisconsin state court against Forsgard, Lakeshore, and others to recover the loss. The court issued a summary judgment in Mid Wisconsin's favor. Lakeshore appealed to a state intermediate appellate court.*

IN THE LANGUAGE OF THE COURT

PETERSON, J. [Judge]
* * * *

Lakeshore claims Mid Wisconsin was not a holder in due course of the check Forsgard deposited. *Wisconsin Statutes Section 403.305 [Wisconsin's version of UCC 3–305] gives a holder in due course the right to recover from a drawer who places a stop-payment order on a check.* According to Wis. Stat. Sec. 403.302(1) [UCC 3–302(a)], a holder in due course is one who takes an instrument for value and in good faith. There is no dispute Mid Wisconsin took the check for value. Lakeshore argues, however, that Mid Wisconsin did not take the check in good faith. Wis. Stat. Sec. 403.103(1)(d) [UCC 3–103(a)(4)] defines good faith as "honesty in fact and the observance of reasonable commercial standards of fair dealing." Lakeshore concedes that Mid Wisconsin took the check with honesty in fact, but contends Mid Wisconsin did not observe reasonable commercial standards of fair dealing. [Emphasis added.]

First, Lakeshore contends that Mid Wisconsin's banking agreement with Forsgard did not allow it to give immediate credit, so that the Bank was not observing reasonable commercial standards when it granted the credit. The banking agreement states, "Any items, other than cash, accepted for deposit (including items drawn 'on us') will be given provisional credit only until collection is final * * * ." Lakeshore contends that this means Mid Wisconsin could not grant immediate credit. Lakeshore misinterprets the agreement. In fact, Mid Wisconsin complied with the agreement. Mid Wisconsin gave Forsgard provisional credit, which the agreement allows. When Lakeshore stopped payment on the check, the Bank deducted the amount of the check from Forsgard's account. This also was in accordance with the agreement. However, Forsgard did not cover the negative balance that resulted from the deduction.

Next, Lakeshore maintains that under the circumstances, reasonable commercial standards of fair dealing should have led Mid Wisconsin to place a hold on the check instead of giving immediate credit. Lakeshore notes that * * * Forsgard's account had been overdrawn many times in the past.

To begin with, Wisconsin courts have approved of the practice of extending immediate credit on deposited checks. * * * *[E]xtending immediate credit is consistent with reasonable banking standards.* * * * [Emphasis added.]

---

a. Click on "Simple Search" and then type the docket number, "03-0123," in the "Keywords" box. The State Bar of Wisconsin maintains this Web site.

CONTINUED

 **Continued**

> * * * *It would hinder commercial transactions if depository banks refused to permit the withdrawal prior to the clearance of checks.* * * * [B]anking practice is to the contrary. It is clear that the Uniform Commercial Code was intended to permit the continuation of this practice and to protect banks who have given credit on deposited items prior to notice of a stop payment order* * * * . [Emphasis added.]

DECISION AND REMEDY *The state appellate court affirmed the lower court's judgment that Mid Wisconsin had observed reasonable commercial standards of fair dealing and was an HDC of the check.*

WHAT IF THE FACTS WERE DIFFERENT? *Suppose that Forsgard's account at Mid Wisconsin had been overdrawn when the check was deposited. How might the result in this case have been different?*

TAKING WITHOUT NOTICE

The final requirement for HDC status involves notice [UCC 3–302]. A person will not be afforded HDC protection if she or he acquires an instrument and is *on notice* (knows or has reason to know) that it is defective in any one of the following ways [UCC 3–302(a)]:

1. It is overdue.
2. It has been dishonored.
3. There is an uncured (uncorrected) default with respect to another instrument issued as part of the same series.
4. The instrument contains an unauthorized signature or has been altered.
5. There is a defense against the instrument or a claim to the instrument.
6. The instrument is so irregular or incomplete as to call into question its authenticity.[6]

WHAT CONSTITUTES NOTICE? Notice of a defective instrument is given whenever the holder (1) has actual knowledge of the defect; (2) has received a notice of the defect (such as a bank's receipt of a letter listing the serial numbers of stolen bearer instruments); or (3) has reason to know that a defect exists, given all the facts and circumstances known at the time in question [UCC 1–201(25)]. The holder must also have received the notice "at a time and in a manner that gives a reasonable opportunity to act on it" [UCC 3–302(f)]. A purchaser's knowledge of certain facts, such as insolvency proceedings against the

maker or drawer of the instrument, does not constitute notice that the instrument is defective [UCC 3–302(b)].

OVERDUE INSTRUMENTS What constitutes notice that an instrument is overdue depends on whether it is a demand instrument (payable on demand) or a time instrument (payable at a definite time).

—Demand Instruments. A purchaser has notice that a *demand instrument* is overdue if he or she either takes the instrument knowing that demand has been made or takes the instrument an unreasonable length of time after its date. A "reasonable time" for the presentment of a check is ninety days after its date, but for other demand instruments, what will be considered a reasonable time depends on the circumstances [UCC 3–304(a)].

—Time Instruments. Anyone who holds a *time instrument* and takes the instrument at any time after its expressed due date is on notice that it is overdue [UCC 3–304(b)]. Nonpayment by the due date should indicate to any purchaser that the instrument may be defective. Thus, a promissory note due on May 15 must be acquired before midnight on May 15. If it is purchased on May 16, the purchaser will be an ordinary holder, not an HDC. In some instances, a time instrument reads, "Payable in thirty days." To count thirty days, you *exclude* the first day and count the last day. Therefore, a note dated December 1 that is payable in thirty days is due by midnight on December 31. If the payment date falls on a Sunday or holiday, the instrument is payable on the next business day.

If a debt is to be paid in installments or through a series of notes, the maker's default on any one installment or on any one note of the series will constitute

---

6. Section 302(1)(c) of the unrevised Article 3 provided that HDC protection is lost if a holder has notice that an instrument is overdue or has been dishonored or if there is a claim to or a defense against it.

notice to the purchaser that the instrument is overdue [UCC 3–304(b)].

An instrument does not become overdue if there is a default on a payment of interest only [UCC 3–304(c)]. Most installment notes provide that any payment by the maker shall be applied first to interest and the balance to the principal. This serves as notice that any installment payment for less than the full amount results in a default on an installment payment toward the principal.

—A Series of Notes with Successive Maturity Dates.

Also, when a series of notes with successive maturity dates is issued at a single time for a single indebtedness, a default on any one note of the series will constitute overdue notice for the entire series. In this way, prospective purchasers know that they cannot qualify as HDCs [UCC 3–302(a)(2)(iii)].

Suppose that a note reads, "Payable May 15, but may be accelerated if the holder feels insecure." A purchaser, unaware that a prior holder has elected to accelerate the due date on the instrument, buys the instrument before May 15. UCC 3–304(b)(3) provides that an instrument becomes overdue on the day after the accelerated due date. The purchaser may still qualify as an HDC, however, because he or she has no reason to know that acceleration has occurred [UCC 3–302(a)(2)(iii)].

DISHONORED INSTRUMENTS

An instrument is *dishonored* when the party to which the instrument is presented refuses to pay it. If a holder has actual knowledge that an instrument has been dishonored or has knowledge of facts that would lead her or him to suspect that an instrument has been dishonored, the holder is on notice [UCC 3–302(a)(2)]. Thus, a person who takes a check clearly stamped "insufficient funds" is put on notice.

For example, Schultz holds a demand note dated September 1 on Apex, Inc., a local business firm. On September 17, she demands payment, and Apex refuses (that is, dishonors the instrument). On September 22, Schultz negotiates the note to Brenner, a purchaser who lives in another state. Brenner does not know, and has no reason to know, that the note has been dishonored. Because Brenner is *not* put on notice, Brenner can become an HDC.

NOTICE OF CLAIMS OR DEFENSES

A holder cannot become an HDC if he or she has notice of any claim to the instrument or defense against it [UCC

3–302(a)(2)(v), (vi)]. Knowledge of claims or defenses can be imputed (attributed) to the purchaser if these claims or defenses are apparent on the face of the instrument—if the instrument is incomplete or irregular in any way, for example—or if the purchaser otherwise had reason to know of them from facts surrounding the transaction.[7]

—Incomplete Instruments.

A purchaser cannot expect to become an HDC of an instrument so incomplete on its face that an element of negotiability is lacking (for example, the amount is not filled in) [UCC 3–302(a)(1)]. Minor omissions (such as the omission of the date—see Chapter 24) are permissible because these do not call into question the validity of the instrument [UCC 3–113(b)].

Similarly, when a person accepts an instrument that has been completed without knowing that it was incomplete when issued, the person can take it as an HDC [UCC 3–115(b), 3–302(a)(1)]. Even if an instrument that is originally incomplete is later completed in an unauthorized manner, the unauthorized completion is not a good defense against an HDC, who can enforce the instrument as completed [UCC 3–407(c)].

To illustrate: Peyton asks Brittany to buy a textbook for him when she goes to the campus book store. Peyton writes a check payable to the campus store, leaves the amount blank, and tells Brittany to fill in the price of the textbook. The cost of the textbook is $85. If Brittany fills in the check for $150 before she gets to the book store, the book store cashier sees only a properly completed instrument. Therefore, because the book store had no notice that the check was incomplete when it was issued, the book store can take the check for $150 and become an HDC. (Material alterations will be discussed in Chapter 26.)

—Irregular Instruments.

Any irregularity on the face of an instrument that calls into question its validity or terms of ownership or that creates an ambiguity as to the party to pay will bar HDC status. A difference between the handwriting used in the body of a check and that used in the signature will not in and of itself make an instrument irregular. Antedating or postdating a check or stating the amount in digits but

---

7. If an instrument contains a statement required by a statute or an administrative rule to the effect that the rights of a holder or transferee are subject to the claims or defenses that the issuer could assert against the original payee, the instrument is negotiable, but there cannot be an HDC of the instrument. See UCC 3–106(d) and the discussion of federal limitations on HDC rights in the next chapter.

failing to write out the numbers will not make a check irregular [UCC 3–113(a)]. Visible evidence of forgery of a maker's or drawer's signature, however, or alterations to material elements of negotiable instruments will disqualify a purchaser from HDC status. Conversely, a good forgery of a maker's or drawer's signature or a careful alteration can go undetected by reasonable examination; therefore, the purchaser can qualify as an HDC [UCC 3–302(a)(1)].

Losses that result from well-crafted forgeries usually fall on the party to whom the forger transferred the instrument (assuming, of course, that the forger cannot be found). Also, a forged indorsement (see Chapter 26) does not transfer title; thus, a person obtaining an instrument that has a forged indorsement of a name necessary to good title normally cannot become a holder or an HDC.

The following case raised questions concerning the potential liability of a bank that accepted three checks for deposit despite apparent evidence on the faces of the checks that they were irregular.

CASE 25.3   Firstar Bank, N.A. v. First Star Title Agency, Inc.

Court of Appeals of Ohio, First District, Hamilton County, 2004. __ Ohio App.3d __, __ N.E.2d __.

BACKGROUND AND FACTS *On January 22, 2002, as part of a real estate transaction, First Service Title Agency (FSTA) issued three checks drawn on its account with Key Bank. The first check was for $850.00 and was paid to the order of "Richard G. Knostman, Atty. and Mark F. Foster, Atty. and Resa Kermani & Badri Kermani." The second check was for $36,295.80 and was made payable to "JD Properties and Reza Kermani & Badri Kermani." The third was for $4,010.00 and was made payable to "Knab Mortgage." The next day, FSTA learned that the real estate transaction had been fraudulent and put stop-payment orders on all three checks. Meanwhile, Randall Davis, who had accounts at Firstar Bank, N.A., presented the checks to Firstar. Firstar paid the checks even though Davis was not a party to any of them, they included multiple indorsements that appeared to be in the same handwriting, and they were marked "for deposit only." Key Bank returned the checks to Firstar with the notation "Payment Stopped." Firstar filed a suit in an Ohio state court against FSTA, seeking damages for the failure to pay the checks. The court granted a summary judgment in FSTA's favor. Firstar Bank appealed to a state intermediate appellate court, claiming that it was entitled to payment as an HDC.*

IN THE LANGUAGE OF THE COURT

PER CURIAM [By the whole court].
    *   *   *   *

A holder becomes a holder in due course if the holder takes the instrument (1) for value; (2) in good faith; (3) and without notice of any claims or defenses otherwise available to the person obligated on the instrument or of various defects in the instrument. A person has notice of a fact when (1) the person has actual knowledge of it; (2) the person has received a notice or notification of it; or (3) from all the facts and circumstances known to the person at the time in question, the person has reason to know that it exists. Additionally, *an instrument, when issued or negotiated to the holder, cannot bear evidence of forgery or alteration that is so apparent, or cannot otherwise be so irregular or incomplete, as to call into question its authenticity.* [Emphasis added.]

The trial court held that Firstar was not a holder in due course because it "failed to exercise ordinary care having knowledge that the checks were forged or otherwise deficient." The issue of whether a holder is a holder in due course is generally a question of fact. But the record in this case presents no genuine issue of fact. The checks in question bore evidence of forgery and were so irregular on their face as to call into question their authenticity and to give notice to a reasonably prudent person exercising ordinary care of defects in the checks.

Firstar relies upon [Ohio Revised Code Section] 1303.01(A)(9) [Ohio's version of UCC 3–103(1)(a)(7)], which defines "ordinary care" in the context of negotiable instruments. It provides that " 'ordinary care' in the case of a person engaged in business means observance of the reasonable commercial standards that are prevailing in the area in which the person is located with respect to the business in which the person is engaged. In the case of a bank that

CASE 25.3 | Continued

takes an instrument for processing for collection or payment by automated means, reasonable commercial standards do not require the bank to examine the instrument if the failure to examine does not violate the bank's prescribed procedures, and the bank's procedures do not vary unreasonably from general banking usage * * * ."

* * * *

In this case, Firstar presented no evidence showing that it had followed its own procedures or that those procedures did not vary unreasonably from general banking usage. Consequently, it failed to meet its burden to show that a genuine issue of fact existed for trial.

Since Firstar had notice that the checks were irregular and that claims and defenses existed, it was not a holder in due course. Consequently, FSTA, as the maker of the checks, could assert all valid claims and defenses.

[Ohio Revised Code Section] 1303.50(B) [UCC 3–407(b)] states that "except as provided in division (C) of this section, an alteration fraudulently made discharges a party whose obligation is affected by the alteration unless that party assents or is precluded from asserting the alteration." [Ohio Revised Code Section] 1303.50(C) [UCC 3–407(c)] states that "a payor bank or drawee paying a fraudulently altered instrument or a person taking it for value, in good faith and without notice of the alteration, may enforce rights with respect to the instrument according to its original terms."

FSTA placed a stop-payment order on the checks * * * as soon as it discovered fraud in the underlying transaction, and it notified the parties and the payees of the stop-payment orders. Consequently, it did not assent to the alteration of the forged endorsements. Firstar, on the other hand, had notice of the alterations because of the irregularities on the faces of the three checks. Consequently, the alterations discharged FSTA of its obligation to pay the instruments pursuant to their terms.

* * * Construing the evidence most strongly in Firstar's favor, we hold that reasonable minds could come to but one conclusion—Firstar was not a holder in due course and FSTA was not liable to pay Firstar on the checks. FSTA was entitled to judgment as a matter of law, and the trial court did not err in granting summary judgment in its favor.

DECISION AND REMEDY *The state intermediate appellate court affirmed the lower court's judgment. Firstar was not an HDC of the checks because it had failed to exercise ordinary care as to whether they were forged or otherwise deficient. FSTA could, therefore, successfully assert its defenses to Firstar's demand for payment.*

WHAT IF THE FACTS WERE DIFFERENT? *Would the result in this case have been different if Davis, Firstar's account holder who presented the checks for payment, had been a party to all of the checks; if the checks' indorsements had not all appeared to be in the same handwriting; and if the checks had not been marked "for deposit only"?*

—Voidable Obligations. It stands to reason that a purchaser cannot be an HDC if she or he knows that a party to an instrument has a defense that entitles that party to avoid the obligation. For example, a potential purchaser who knows that the maker of a note has breached the underlying contract with the payee cannot thereafter purchase the note as an HDC.

Knowledge of one defense precludes a holder from asserting HDC status in regard to all other defenses. For example, Litton, knowing that the note he has taken has a forged indorsement, presents it to the maker for payment. The maker refuses to pay on the ground of breach of the underlying contract. The maker can assert this defense against Litton even though Litton had no knowledge of the breach, because Litton's knowledge of the forgery alone prevents him from being an HDC in *all* circumstances.

Knowledge that a fiduciary has wrongfully negotiated an instrument is sufficient notice of a claim against the instrument to preclude HDC status. Suppose that O'Banion, a university trustee, improperly writes a check on the university trust account to pay a personal debt. Lewis knows that the check has been improperly drawn on university funds, but she accepts it anyway. Lewis cannot claim to be an HDC. When a purchaser knows that a fiduciary is acting in breach of duty, HDC status is denied [UCC 3–307(b)].

CONCEPT SUMMARY 25.2 | Rules and Requirements for HDC Status

BASIC REQUIREMENTS	RULES
MUST BE A HOLDER	A *holder* is defined as a person in possession of an instrument "if the instrument is payable to bearer or, in the cases of an instrument payable to an identified person, if the identified person is in possession" [UCC 1–201(20)].
MUST TAKE FOR VALUE	A holder gives *value* by doing any of the following [UCC 3–303]: 1. Performing the promise for which the instrument was issued or transferred. 2. Acquiring a security interest or other lien in the instrument (other than a lien obtained by a judicial proceeding). 3. Taking the instrument in payment of, or as security for, an antecedent debt. 4. Giving a negotiable instrument as payment. 5. Giving an irrevocable commitment as payment.
MUST TAKE IN *GOOD FAITH*	*Good faith* is defined for purposes of revised Article 3 as "honesty in fact and the observance of reasonable commercial standards of fair dealing" [UCC 3–103(a)(4)].
MUST TAKE WITHOUT NOTICE	A holder must not be *on notice* that the instrument is defective in any of the following ways [UCC 3–302, 3–304]: 1. The instrument is overdue. 2. The instrument has been dishonored. 3. There is an uncured (uncorrected) default with respect to another instrument issued as part of the same series. 4. The instrument contains an unauthorized signature or has been altered. 5. There is a defense against the instrument or a claim to the instrument. 6. The instrument is so irregular or incomplete as to call into question its authenticity.
SHELTER PRINCIPLE— HOLDER THROUGH A HOLDER IN DUE COURSE	A holder who cannot qualify as an HDC has the rights of an HDC if he or she derives title through a holder in due course [UCC 3–203(b)].
SPECIAL SITUATIONS IN WHICH PURCHASERS ARE NOT HDCs	The following acquisitions cannot result in a holder's having HDC status [UCC 3–302(c)]: 1. Purchase at a judicial sale. 2. Acquisition as part of an estate. 3. Purchase as part of a bulk transfer.

SECTION 6 | Holder through an HDC

A person who does not qualify as an HDC but who derives his or her title through an HDC can acquire the rights and privileges of an HDC. This rule is sometimes called the **shelter principle.** According to UCC 3–203(b):

> Transfer of an instrument, whether or not the transfer is a negotiation, vests in the transferee any right of the transferor to enforce the instrument, including any right as a holder in due course, but the transferee cannot acquire rights of a holder in due course by a transfer, directly or indirectly, from a holder in due course if the transferee engaged in fraud or illegality affecting the instrument.

THE PURPOSE OF THE SHELTER PRINCIPLE

The shelter principle seems counter to the basic HDC philosophy. It is, however, in line with the concept of marketability and free transferability of negotiable instruments, as well as with contract law, which provides that assignees acquire the rights of assignors. The shelter principle extends the benefits of HDC status and is designed to aid the HDC in readily disposing of the instrument. Anyone, no matter how far removed from an HDC, who can ultimately trace her or his title back to an HDC comes within the shelter principle. Normally, a person who acquires an instrument from an HDC or from someone with HDC rights receives HDC rights on the legal theory that the transferee of an instrument receives at least the rights that the transferor had.

LIMITATIONS ON THE SHELTER PRINCIPLE

There are some limitations, however, on the shelter principle. Certain persons who formerly held instruments cannot improve their positions by later reac- quiring the instruments from HDCs [UCC 3–203(b)]. Therefore, if a holder was a party to fraud or illegality affecting the instrument or if, as a prior holder, he or she had notice of a claim or defense against the instrument, that holder is not allowed to improve his or her status by repurchasing the instrument from a later HDC.

To illustrate: Matthew and Carla collaborate to defraud Lorena. Lorena is induced to give Carla a negotiable note payable to Carla's order. Carla then specially indorses the note for value to Larry, an HDC. Matthew and Carla split the proceeds. Larry negoti- ates the note to Stuart, another HDC. Stuart then negotiates the note for value to Matthew. Matthew, even though he obtained the note through an HDC, is not a holder through an HDC, because he partici- pated in the original fraud and can never acquire HDC rights in this note.

REVIEWING TRANSFERABILITY AND HOLDER IN DUE COURSE

The Brown family owns several companies, including the J. H. Stevedoring Company and Penn Warehousing and Distribution, Inc. The companies are intertwined in many of their operations and management. Dennis Bishop began working for J. H. and Penn in 1994. By 2003, Bishop was financial controller at J. H., where he was responsible for approving invoices for payment and reconciling the corporate checkbook. In December, Bishop began stealing from Penn and J. H. by writing checks on the corporate accounts and using the funds for his own benefit (committing the crime of embezzlement). Several members of the Brown family signed the checks for Bishop without hesi- tation because he was a longtime, trusted employee. Over the next two years, Bishop embezzled $1,209,436, of which $670,632 was used to buy horses from the Fasig-Tipton Company and Fasig-Tipton Midlantic, Inc., with Penn and J. H. checks made payable to those firms. When Bishop's fraud was revealed, J. H. and Penn filed a suit in a federal district court against the Fasig-Tipton firms (the defendants) to recover the amounts of the checks made payable to them. Using the information presented in the chapter, answer the following questions.

1. What method was most likely used to negotiate the instruments described here?

2. Suppose that all of the checks issued to the defendants were made payable to "Fasig-Tipton Co., Fasig-Tipton Midlantic, Inc." Under the UCC, were the instruments payable jointly or in the alternative? Why is this significant?

3. In situations involving fraudulent instruments, it is very important to determine whether a holder is an ordinary holder or a holder in due course (HDC). Why?

4. Do the defendants in this situation (the two Fasig-Tipton firms) meet the requirements of an HDC? Why or why not?

5. In whose favor should the court rule, and why?

TERMS AND CONCEPTS TO REVIEW

allonge 496

antecedent claim 503

blank indorsement 496

holder in due course (HDC) 501

indorsee 496

indorser 496

negotiation 495

qualified indorsement 497

restrictive indorsement 497

shelter principle 510

special indorsement 496

trust indorsement 498

QUESTIONS AND CASE PROBLEMS

25–1. A check drawn by Cullen for $500 is made payable to the order of Jordan and issued to Jordan. Jordan owes his landlord $500 in rent and transfers the check to his landlord with the following indorsement: "For rent paid, [signed] Jordan." Jordan's landlord has contracted to have Deborah do some landscaping on the property. When Deborah insists on immediate payment, the landlord transfers the check to Deborah without indorsement. Later, to pay for some palm trees purchased from Better-Garden Nursery, Deborah transfers the check with the following indorsement: "Pay to Better-Garden Nursery, without recourse, [signed] Deborah." Better-Garden Nursery sends the check to its bank indorsed "For deposit only, [signed] Better-Garden Nursery."

(a) Classify each of these indorsements.

(b) Was the transfer from Jordan's landlord to Deborah, without indorsement, an assignment or a negotiation? Explain.

25–2. ⚖ QUESTION WITH SAMPLE ANSWER

Celine issues a ninety-day negotiable promissory note payable to the order of Hayden. The amount of the note is left blank, pending a determination of the amount of money Hayden will need to purchase a used car for Celine. Celine authorizes any amount not to exceed $2,000. Hayden, without authority, fills in the note in the amount of $5,000 and thirty days later sells the note to First National Bank of Oklahoma for $4,850. Hayden does not buy the car and leaves the state. First National Bank has no knowledge that the instrument was incomplete when issued or that Hayden had no authority to complete the instrument in the amount of $5,000.

(a) Does the bank qualify as a holder in due course? If so, for what amount? Explain.

(b) If Hayden had sold the note to a stranger in a bar for $500, would the stranger qualify as a holder in due course? Explain.

For a sample answer to this question, go to Appendix I at the end of this text.

25–3. Through negotiation, Emilio has received from dishonest payees two checks with the following histories:

(a) The drawer issued a check to the payee for $9. The payee cleverly altered the numeral on the check from $9 to $90 and the written word from "nine" to "ninety."

(b) The drawer issued a check to the payee without filling in the amount. The drawer authorized the payee to fill in the amount for no more than $90. The payee filled in the amount of $900.

Discuss whether Emilio, by giving value to the payees, can qualify as a holder in due course of these checks.

25–4. Bertram writes a check for $200 payable to "cash." He puts the check in his pocket and drives to the bank to cash the check. As he gets out of his car in the bank's parking lot, the check slips out of his pocket and falls to the pavement. Jerrod walks by moments later, picks up the check, and later that day delivers it to Amber, to whom he owes $200. Amber indorses the check "For deposit only, [signed] Amber Dowel" and deposits it into her checking account. In light of these circumstances, answer the following questions:

(a) Is the check a bearer instrument or an order instrument?

(b) Did Jerrod's delivery of the check to Amber constitute a valid negotiation? Why or why not?

(c) What type of indorsement did Amber make?

(d) Does Bertram have a right to recover the $200 from Amber? Explain.

25–5. INDORSEMENTS. Universal Premium Acceptance Corp. issued more than $1 million in drafts, intending the payee to be Great American Insurance Co. When the drafts were issued, they were nonnegotiable instruments. Walter Talbot, an insurance agent, intercepted the drafts, forged Great American's indorsements in blank, and deposited the drafts in a phony account at York Bank & Trust Co. After Talbot was caught and convicted, Universal filed a suit in a federal district court against York to recover some of its losses.

One of the issues in the case was whether Talbot's indorsements converted the nonnegotiable drafts into negotiable bearer instruments. Did they? Why or why not? [*Universal Premium Acceptance Corp. v. York Bank & Trust Co.*, 69 F.3d 695 (3d Cir. 1995)]

25-6. REQUIREMENTS FOR HDC STATUS. In February 2001, New York Linen Co., a party rental company, agreed to buy 550 chairs from Elite Products. On delivery of the chairs, New York Linen issued a check (dated February 27) for $13,300 to Elite. Elite's owner, Meir Shmeltzer, transferred the check to General Credit Corp., a company in the business of buying instruments from payees for cash. Meanwhile, after recounting the chairs, New York Linen discovered that delivery was not complete and stopped payment of the check. The next day, New York Linen drafted a second check, reflecting an adjusted payment of $11,275, and delivered it to Elite. A notation on the second check indicated that it was a replacement for the first check. When the first check was dishonored, General Credit filed a suit in a New York state court against New York Linen to recover the amount. New York Linen argued in part that General Credit was not a holder in due course because of the notation on the second check. In whose favor should the court rule? Why? [*General Credit Corp. v. New York Linen Co.*, __ Misc.2d __ (N.Y. City Civ.Ct. 2002)]

25-7. ⚖ **CASE PROBLEM WITH SAMPLE ANSWER**

Harford Mutual Insurance Co. issued a check for $60,150 payable to "Andrew Michael Bogdan, Jr., Crystal Bogdan, Oceanmark Bank FSB, Goodman-Gable-Gould Company." The check was to pay a claim related to the Bogdans' commercial property. Besides the Bogdans, the payees were the mortgage holder (Oceanmark) and the insurance agent who adjusted the claim. The Bogdans and the agent indorsed the check and cashed it at Provident Bank of Maryland. Meanwhile, Oceanmark sold the mortgage to Pelican National Bank, which asked Provident to pay it the amount of the check. Provident refused. Pelican filed a suit in a Maryland state court against Provident, arguing that the check had been improperly negotiated. Was this check payable jointly or in the alternative? Whose indorsements were required to cash it? In whose favor should the court rule? Explain. [*Pelican National Bank v. Provident Bank of Maryland*, 381 Md. 327, 849 A.2d 475 (2004)]

To view a sample answer for this case problem, go to this book's Web site at http://wbl.westbuslaw.com, select "Chapter 25," and click on "Case Problem with Sample Answer."

25-8. TRANSFER OF INSTRUMENTS. In July 1988, Chester Crow executed a promissory note payable "to the order of THE FIRST NATIONAL BANK OF SHREVE-PORT or BEARER" in the amount of $21,578.42 at an interest rate of 3 percent per year above the "prime rate in effect at The First National Bank of Shreveport" in Shreveport, Louisiana, until paid. The note was a standard preprinted promissory note. In 1999, Credit Recoveries, Inc., filed a suit in a Louisiana state court against Crow, alleging that he owed $7,222.57 on the note, plus interest. Crow responded that the debt represented by the note had been canceled by the bank in September 1994, contending that, in any event, to collect on the note Credit Recoveries had to prove its legitimate ownership of it. When no evidence of ownership was forthcoming, Crow filed a motion to dismiss the suit. Is the note an order instrument or a bearer instrument? How might it have been transferred to Credit Recoveries? With this in mind, should the court dismiss the suit on the basis of Crow's contention? [*Credit Recoveries, Inc. v. Crow*, 862 So.2d 1146 (La.App. 2 Cir. 2003)]

25-9. ⚖ **A QUESTION OF ETHICS**

Richard Caliendo, an accountant, prepared tax returns for various clients. To satisfy their tax liabilities, the clients issued checks payable to various state taxing entities and gave them to Caliendo. Between 1977 and 1979, Caliendo forged indorsements on these checks, deposited them into his own bank account, and subsequently withdrew the proceeds. In 1983, after learning of these events and after Caliendo's death, the state brought an action against Barclays Bank of New York, N.A., the successor to Caliendo's bank, to recover the amount of the checks. Barclays moved for dismissal on the ground that because the checks had never been delivered to the state, the state never acquired the status of holder and therefore never acquired any rights in the instruments. The trial court held for the state, but the appellate court reversed. The state then appealed the case to the state's highest court. That court ruled that the state could not recover the amount of the checks from the bank because, although the state was the named payee on the checks, the checks had never been delivered to the payee. [*State v. Barclays Bank of New York, N.A.*, 561 N.Y.2d 533, 563 N.E.2d 11, 76 N.Y.S.2d 697 (1990)]

(a) If you were deciding this case, would you make an exception to the rule and let the state collect the funds from Barclays Bank? Why or why not? What ethical policies must be balanced in this situation?

(b) Under agency law, which will be discussed in Chapters 31 and 32, delivery to the agent of a given individual or entity constitutes delivery to that person or entity. The court deemed that Caliendo was an agent of the taxpayers, not of the state. Does it matter that the taxpayers may not have known this principle of agency law and might have thought that, by delivering their checks to Caliendo, they were delivering them to the state? Discuss fully.

25–10. VIDEO QUESTION

Go to this text's Web site at http://wbl.westbuslaw.com and select "Chapter 25." Click on "Video Questions" and view the video titled *Negotiability & Transferability: Indorsing Checks*. Then answer the following questions.

(a) According to the instructor in the video, what are the two reasons why banks generally require a person to indorse a check that is made out to cash (a bearer instrument), even when the check is signed in the presence of the teller?

(b) Suppose that your friend makes out a check payable to cash, signs it, and hands it to you. You take the check to your bank and indorse the check with your name and the words "without recourse." What type of indorsement is this? How does this indorsement affect the bank's rights?

(c) Now suppose that you go to your bank and write a check on your account payable to cash for $500. The teller gives you the cash without asking you to indorse the check. After you leave, the teller slips the check into his pocket. Later, the teller delivers it (without an indorsement) to his friend Carol in payment for a gambling debt. Carol takes your check to her bank, indorses it, and deposits the money. Discuss whether Carol is a holder in due course.

LAW | on the Web

For updated links to resources available on the Web, as well as a variety of other materials, visit this text's Web site at http://wbl.westbuslaw.com.

To find information on the UCC, including the Article 3 provisions discussed in this chapter, refer to the Web sites listed in the *Law on the Web* section in Chapter 24.

LEGAL RESEARCH EXERCISES ON THE WEB

Go to http://wbl.westbuslaw.com, the Web site that accompanies this text. Select "Chapter 25" and click on "Internet Exercises." There you will find the following Internet research exercises that you can perform to learn more about topics covered in this chapter.

Activity 25–1: LEGAL PERSPECTIVE
Electronic Negotiable Instruments

Activity 25–2: MANAGEMENT PERSPECTIVE
Holder in Due Course

CHAPTER 26

Liability, Defenses, and Discharge

Two kinds of liability are associated with negotiable instruments: signature liability and warranty liability. *Signature liability* relates to signatures on instruments. Those who sign negotiable instruments are potentially liable for payment of the amount stated on the instrument. *Warranty liability*, in contrast, extends to both signers and nonsigners. A breach of warranty can occur when the instrument is transferred or presented for payment.

Note that the focus is on liability *on the instrument itself or on warranties connected with transfer or presentment of the instrument* as opposed to liability on any underlying contract. Suppose, for example, that Donald agrees to buy one thousand compact discs from Luis and issues a check to Luis in payment. The liability discussed in this chapter does not relate directly to the contract (for instance, whether the compact discs are of proper quality or fit for the purpose for which they are intended). The liability discussed here relates to liability arising in connection with the *check* (such as what recourse Luis will have if Donald's bank refuses to pay the check due to insufficient funds in Donald's account or Donald's order to his bank to stop payment on the check).

The first part of this chapter covers the liability of the parties who sign instruments—for example, drawers of drafts and checks, makers of notes and certificates of deposit, and indorsers. It also covers the liability of accommodation parties and the warranty liability of those who transfer instruments and present instruments for payment. The chapter then examines the defenses that can be raised to avoid liability on an instrument. The final section in the chapter looks at some of the ways in which parties can be *discharged* from liability on negotiable instruments.

SECTION 1 | Signature Liability

The key to liability on a negotiable instrument is a signature. As discussed in Chapter 24, the Uniform Commercial Code (UCC) broadly defines a signature as any name, word, mark, or symbol executed or adopted by a person with present intention to authenticate a writing [UCC 1–209(39), 3–401(b)]. A signature can be handwritten, typed, or printed; it can also be made by mark, by thumbprint, by machine, or in virtually any other manner.

The general rule is as follows: "A person is not liable on an instrument unless (i) the person signed the instrument, or (ii) the person is represented by an agent or representative who signed the instrument and the signature is binding on the represented person" [UCC 3–401(a)]. Essentially, this means that every

party, except a qualified indorser,[1] who signs a negotiable instrument is either primarily or secondarily liable for payment of that instrument when it comes due. The following subsections discuss these two types of liability, as well as the conditions that must be met before liability can arise.

PRIMARY LIABILITY

A person who is primarily liable on a negotiable instrument is absolutely required to pay the instrument—unless, of course, he or she has a valid defense to payment [UCC 3–305]. The primary party's liability is

---

1. A qualified indorser—one who indorses "without recourse"—undertakes no obligation to pay [UCC 3–415(b)]. A qualified indorser merely assumes warranty liability, which will be discussed later in this chapter.

immediate when the instrument is signed or issued and effective when the instrument becomes due. No action by the holder of the instrument is required. *Makers* and *acceptors* are primarily liable [UCC 3–412, 3–413].

MAKERS The maker of a promissory note promises to pay the note. It is the maker's promise to pay that renders the note a negotiable instrument. The words "I promise to pay" embody the maker's obligation to pay the instrument according to the terms as written at the time of the signing or issue. If the instrument was incomplete when the maker signed it, then the maker is obligated to pay it according to its stated terms or according to terms that were agreed on and later filled in to complete the instrument [UCC 3–115, 3–407, 3–412]. For example, Tristan executes a preprinted promissory note to Sharon, without filling in the due-date blank. If Sharon does not complete the form by adding the date, the note will be payable on demand. If Sharon subsequently writes in a due date that Tristan authorized, the note is payable on the stated due date. In either situation, Tristan (the maker) is obligated to pay the note.

ISSUERS The issuer of a cashier's check or other draft drawn on the drawer is also primarily liable on the instrument [UCC 3–412]. Any "draft drawn on the drawer" refers to an instrument similar to a cashier's check, on which there are really only two parties. The first party is the payee, and the second party is a bank, which is both the drawer and the drawee. Of course, there is a third party—the person who pays the funds to the bank for the check—but she or he is not a party to the instrument. Some courts view a bank money order as a "draft drawn on the drawer."

ACCEPTORS An *acceptor* is a drawee that promises to pay an instrument when it is presented later for payment, as mentioned in Chapter 24. When a drawee *accepts* a draft, the drawee becomes primarily liable to all subsequent holders of the instrument. In other words, the drawee's acceptance places the drawee in virtually the same position as the maker of a promissory note [UCC 3–413]. A drawee that refuses to accept a draft that requires the drawee's acceptance (such as a trade acceptance) has dishonored the instrument. (**Dishonor** of an instrument occurs when payment or acceptance of the instrument, whichever is required, is refused even though the instrument is presented in a timely and proper manner.)

Acceptance of a check is called *certification*, as will be discussed in Chapter 27. Certification is not necessary on checks, and a bank is under no obligation to certify checks. On certification, however, the drawee bank occupies the position of an acceptor and is primarily liable on the check to any holder [UCC 3–409(d)].

SECONDARY LIABILITY

Drawers and *indorsers* have secondary liability. On a negotiable instrument, secondary liability is similar to the liability of a guarantor in a simple contract (described in Chapter 28) in the sense that it is *contingent liability*. In other words, a drawer or an indorser will be liable only if the party that is responsible for paying the instrument refuses to do so (dishonors the instrument). In regard to drafts and checks, a drawer's secondary liability does not arise until the drawee fails to pay or to accept the instrument, whichever is required. In regard to notes, an indorser's secondary liability does not arise until the maker, who is primarily liable, has defaulted on the instrument [UCC 3–412, 3–415].

Dishonor of an instrument thus triggers the liability of parties who are secondarily liable on the instrument—that is, the drawer and *unqualified* indorsers. For example, Lamar writes a check for $1,000 on her account at Western Bank payable to the order of Carerra. Carerra indorses and delivers the check, for value, to Deere. Deere deposits the check into his account at Universal Bank, but the bank returns the check to Deere marked "insufficient funds," thus dishonoring the check. The question for Deere is whether the drawer (Lamar) or the indorser (Carerra) can be held liable on the check after the bank has dishonored it. The answer to the question depends on whether certain conditions for secondary liability have been satisfied.

According to the UCC, parties who are secondarily liable on a negotiable instrument, such as Lamar and Carerra in our example, promise to pay on that instrument only if the following events occur:[2]

---

2. An instrument can be drafted to provide a waiver of the presentment and notice of dishonor requirements [UCC 3–504]. Presume, for simplicity's sake, that such waivers have *not* been incorporated into the instruments described in this chapter.

1. The instrument is properly and timely presented.
2. The instrument is dishonored.
3. Timely notice of dishonor is given.[3]

PROPER PRESENTMENT As discussed in Chapter 24, *presentment* occurs when a person presents an instrument to the party liable on the note to collect payment. Presentment also occurs when a person presents an instrument to a drawee for acceptance.

—*What Constitutes a Proper Presentment?* The UCC requires that a holder present the instrument to the appropriate party, in a timely fashion, and in a proper manner (providing reasonable identification if necessary) [UCC 3–414(f), 3–415(e), 3–501]. The party to whom the instrument must be presented depends on the type of instrument involved. A note or certificate of deposit (CD) must be presented to the maker for payment. A draft is presented by the holder to the drawee for acceptance, payment, or both, whichever is required. A check is presented to the drawee (bank) for payment [UCC 3–501(a), 3–502(b)].

Presentment can be made by any commercially reasonable means, including oral, written, or electronic communication [UCC 3–501(b)]. It can also be made at the place specified in the instrument. It is ordinarily effective when the demand for payment or acceptance is received (unless presentment takes place after an established cutoff hour).

—*The Importance of Timeliness.* One of the most crucial criteria for proper presentment is timeliness [UCC 3–414(f), 3–415(e), 3–501(b)(4)]. Failure to present on time is the most common reason for improper presentment and consequent discharge of unqualified indorsers from secondary liability.

Suppose, for example, that Deere does not deposit Lamar's check into his account until two months after Carerra indorsed it. If the bank dishonors the check, Deere cannot hold Carerra liable and risks not being able to hold Lamar liable because the check was not presented for payment within the time frame specified by the UCC. For domestic checks, the holder must present the check for payment or collection within thirty days of its *date* to hold the drawer secondarily liable and within thirty days after an indorsement to hold the indorser secondarily liable [UCC 3–414(f), 3–415(e)].[4] The time for proper presentment for different types of instruments is shown in Exhibit 26–1.

DISHONOR As mentioned earlier, an instrument is dishonored when presentment is properly and timely made and the required acceptance or payment is refused or cannot be obtained within the prescribed time. An instrument is also dishonored when the required presentment is excused (as it would be, for example, if the maker had died) and the instrument is not properly accepted or paid [UCC 3–502(e)].

In certain situations, a postponement of payment or a refusal to pay an instrument will *not* dishonor the instrument. We look next at some of these situations.

—*Presentment after an Established Cutoff Hour.* Payment can be postponed without dishonoring the instrument if presentment is made after an established cutoff hour (not earlier than 2:00 P.M.), but payment cannot be postponed beyond the close of the next business day after the day of presentment [UCC

---

3. Note that these requirements are necessary for a secondarily liable party to have *signature* liability on a negotiable instrument, but they are not necessary for a secondarily liable party to have *warranty* liability (to be discussed later in this chapter).

4. Section 3–503(2) of the unrevised UCC *presumes* these periods to be thirty days after the date or issue of the instrument with respect to a drawer's liability and seven days after indorsement for an indorser's liability.

EXHIBIT 26–1 **Time for Proper Presentment**

Type of Instrument	For Acceptance	For Payment
Time	On or before due date.	On due date.
Demand	Within a reasonable time (after date of issue or after secondary party becomes liable on the instrument).	Within a reasonable time.
Check	Not applicable.	Within thirty days of its date, to hold drawer secondarily liable. Within thirty days of indorsement, to hold indorser secondarily liable.

3–501(b)(4)]. Banks frequently establish cutoff hours, after which payment will be postponed until the next business day (see Chapter 27).

—The Holder's Failure to Comply with Certain Requests.   In addition, the party to whom presentment is made may refuse payment without dishonoring the instrument if the holder refuses to exhibit the instrument, to give reasonable identification and/or authority to receive payment, or to sign on the instrument as a receipt for any payment made [UCC

3–501(b)(2)]. For example, suppose that Deere, instead of depositing Lamar's check into his bank account, demands payment from Universal Bank in cash. The bank requests identification, which Deere refuses to provide. In this situation, the bank would be within its rights to refuse payment to Deere, and the bank's refusal to pay would not dishonor the check.

Some banks require a check holder who does not have an account at the bank to provide a thumbprint before the bank will honor the check. The issue in the following case was whether this practice is lawful.

CASE 26.1   Messing v. Bank of America, N.A.

Maryland Court of Appeals, 2003. 373 Md. 672, 821 A.2d 22.

HARRELL, Judge.
* * * *
At some point in time prior to 3 August 2000, [Jeff Messing] came into possession of a check in the amount of $976.00 (the check) from Toyson J. Burruss, the drawer, doing business as Prestige Auto Detail Center. * * * Petitioner elected to present the check for payment at a branch of Mr. Burruss' bank, Bank of America, the drawee. On 3 August 2000, Petitioner [Messing] approached a teller * * * and asked to cash the check. * * *

* * * She asked if the Petitioner was a customer of Bank of America. The Petitioner stated that he was not. The teller returned the check to Petitioner and requested, consistent with bank policy when cashing checks for non-customers, that Petitioner place his thumbprint on the check [using an inkless fingerprinting device]. Petitioner refused and the teller informed him that she would be unable to complete the transaction without his thumbprint.

Petitioner requested, and was referred to, the branch manager. * * * The branch manager examined the check and returned it to the Petitioner, informing him that, because Petitioner was a non-customer, Bank of America would not cash the check without Petitioner's thumbprint * * * .

* * * Petitioner, two months later, on 10 October 2000, filed a declaratory judgment action against Bank of America (the Bank) in [a Maryland state court]. * * * Petitioner asked the trial court to declare [in part] that * * * under [Maryland Code Section 3–501(b)(2) of the state's Commercial Law Article—Maryland's version of UCC 3–501(b)(2)] a thumbprint is not reasonable identification * * * .

* * * [The court] entered summary judgment in favor of the Bank * * * .

Petitioner appealed [to a state intermediate appellate court, which] concluded that the * * * decision in favor of the Bank was * * * correct * * * .

Petitioner [appealed to the Maryland Court of Appeals, the state's highest court] * * * .
* * * *
The question is whether requiring a thumbprint constitutes a request for "reasonable identification" under Section 3-501(b)(2)(ii). If it is "reasonable," then under Section 3–501(b)(3)(ii), the refusal of the Bank to accept the check from Petitioner did not constitute dishonor. If, however, requiring a thumbprint is not "reasonable" under Section 3–501(b)(2)(ii), then the refusal to accept the check may constitute dishonor under Section 3–501(b)(2). The issue of dishonor is arguably relevant because Petitioner [Messing] has no cause of action against any party, including the drawer, until the check is dishonored.
* * * *
* * * According to Petitioner, the purpose of requiring "reasonable identification" is to allow the drawee bank to determine that the presenter is the proper person to be paid on the

CASE 26.1 | Continued

instrument. Because a thumbprint does not provide that information at the time presentment and payment are made, Petitioner argues that a thumbprint cannot be read to fall within the meaning of "reasonable identification" for the purposes of Section 3-501(b)(2)(ii).

Bank of America argues that the requirement of a thumbprint * * * is a reasonable and necessary industry response to the growing problem of check fraud. * * *

* * * We agree with Petitioner that a thumbprint cannot be used, in most instances, to confirm the identity of a non-account checkholder at the time that the check is presented for cashing, as his or her thumbprint is usually not on file with the drawee at that time. We disagree, however, with Petitioner's conclusion that a thumbprint signature is therefore not "reasonable identification" for purposes of Section 3-501(b)(2).

*Nowhere does the language of Section 3-501(b)(2) suggest that "reasonable identification" is limited to information Respondent can authenticate at the time presentment is made. Rather, all that is required is that the person making presentment must * * * give reasonable identification.* While providing a thumbprint signature does not necessarily confirm identification of the checkholder at presentment—unless of course the drawee bank has a duplicate thumbprint signature on file—it does assist in the identification of the checkholder should the check later prove to be bad. It therefore serves as a powerful deterrent to those who might otherwise attempt to pass a bad check. That one method provides identification at the time of presentment and the other identification after the check may have been honored, does not prevent the latter from being "reasonable identification" for purposes of Section 3-501(b)(2). * * * [Emphasis added.]

* * * *

As a result of this conclusion, Bank of America in the present case did not dishonor the check when it refused to accept it over the counter. Under Section 3-501(b)(3)(ii), Bank of America "refused payment or acceptance for failure of the presentment to comply with * * * other applicable law or rule." The rule not complied with by the Petitioner-presenter was Section 3-501(b)(2)(ii) in that he refused to give what we have determined to be reasonable identification. Therefore, there was no dishonor of the check by Bank of America's refusal to accept it. * * *

* * * *

JUDGMENT OF THE COURT OF SPECIAL APPEALS AFFIRMED.

QUESTIONS

1. Why might a customer be reluctant to provide a thumbprint to a bank, even if he or she is presenting a valid check?
2. Could the thumbprint requirement in this case be considered an invasion of the customer's privacy? Explain your answer.

—*Lack of Proper Indorsement.* The UCC provides, in accordance with general banking practices, that returning an instrument because it lacks a proper indorsement also is not a dishonor [UCC 3–501(b)(3)(i)]. Assume that Carerra does not indorse Lamar's check before delivering it to Deere. Because at this point the check is an order instrument—payable to Carerra or his order—Carerra's indorsement is required for further negotiation. If Deere indorses the check "For deposit only" into his account, the bank may return the check on the ground that it was not properly indorsed. In this situation, the return of the check is not a dishonor.

PROPER NOTICE The third requirement to hold secondary parties liable on an instrument is that those parties be properly notified of the dishonor. In our example, Deere would have to notify Carerra or Lamar of the dishonor to hold either party liable for the $1,000 payment. Again, the UCC specifies time frames for proper notice. A bank must give any necessary notice before its midnight deadline (midnight of the next banking day after receipt) [UCC 3–503(c)]. Any party other than a bank, such as Deere, must give notice within thirty days following the day on which the person receives notice of dishonor [UCC 3–503(c)].[5]

—Manner of Notice. Except for the dishonor of foreign drafts, notice may be given in any reasonable manner. This includes oral notice, written notice, electronic notice (notice by fax, e-mail, and the like), and notice written or stamped on the instrument itself [UCC 3–503(b)]. To give notice of dishonor of a foreign draft (a draft drawn in one country and payable in another country), a formal notice called a *protest* is required [UCC 3–505(b)]. In our example, Deere could telephone Lamar and inform her of the dishonor. Lamar, as the drawer, would then become liable for the check's payment. Similarly, Deere could notify Carrera, who indorsed the check, of the dishonor and request payment from Carrera.

—Notice to Indorsers. Notice operates for the benefit of all parties who have rights in an instrument against the party notified [UCC 3–503(b)]. For example, assume that there are four indorsers on a note that its maker dishonors, and the holder gives timely notice to indorsers 1 and 4. If the holder collects payment from indorser 4, indorser 4 need not give notice to indorser 1 again to collect from indorser 1. (Indorsers 2 and 3 are not liable to indorser 4 because they were not given timely notice.) It is important to remember that if more than one indorsement appears on an instrument, each indorser is liable for the full amount to any subsequent indorser or to any holder.

ACCOMMODATION PARTIES

In addition to the parties to instruments already discussed, accommodation parties may also be primarily or secondarily liable on instruments. An **accommodation party** is one who signs an instrument for the purpose of lending his or her name as credit to another party on the instrument [UCC 3–419(a)].

THE ROLE OF ACCOMMODATION PARTIES
Accommodation parties are one form of security against nonpayment on a negotiable instrument.

Consider an example. A bank about to make a loan wants some reasonable assurance that the debt will be paid. If the prospective borrower's financial condition is uncertain, the bank may be reluctant to rely solely on the borrower's ability to pay. To reduce the risk of nonpayment, the bank can require that a third person join as an accommodation party on the borrower's promissory note. When one person (such as a parent) cosigns a promissory note with the maker (such as the parent's son or daughter), the cosigner is an accommodation party.[6]

If an accommodation party pays the instrument, she or he has a right of recourse against the party accommodated [UCC 3–419(e)]. If the *accommodated party* pays the instrument, however, he or she does not have a right of recourse (contribution) against the *accommodation party*.[7]

ACCOMMODATION MAKERS VERSUS ACCOMMODATION INDORSERS
If the accommodation party signs on behalf of the *maker*, he or she is an *accommodation maker* and is primarily liable on the instrument. For example, if Abe takes out a loan to purchase a car and has his uncle cosign the note, the uncle becomes primarily liable on the instrument. If, however, the accommodation party signs on behalf of a *payee or other holder* (usually to make the instrument more marketable), she or he is an *accommodation indorser* and, as an indorser, is secondarily liable. For example, if Abe's lender (who has possession of the note) has Mary sign the note so that Todd will buy it, Mary is an accommodation indorser and her liability is secondary.

AUTHORIZED AGENTS' SIGNATURES

Questions often arise as to the liability on an instrument signed by an agent. An **agent** is a person who agrees to represent or act for another, called the **principal.** Agents can sign negotiable instruments, just as they can sign contracts, and thereby bind their principals [UCC 3–401(a)(ii), 3–402(a)]. Without such a rule, all corporate commercial business would stop, as

---

5. Under Section 3–508(2) of the unrevised Article 3, notice by a person other than a bank must be given "before midnight of the third business day after dishonor or receipt of notice of dishonor."

6. A 2002 amendment to UCC Article 3 expressly provides that an accommodation party is primarily liable if the party indicates on the instrument that he or she guarantees payment or "does not unambiguously indicate an intention to guarantee collection rather than payment" [Amended UCC 3–419(e)]. Recall from Chapter 24, however, that as yet only a few states have adopted the 2002 amendments to Article 3.

7. See, for example, *Quality Wash Group V, Ltd. v. Shawkat Hallak,* 58 Cal.Rptr.2d 592 (1996).

every corporation can and must act through its agents. (Agency law will be covered in detail in Chapters 31 and 32.)

Certain requirements must be met, however, before the principal becomes liable on the instrument. A basic requirement to hold the principal liable on the instrument is that the agent be *authorized* to sign the instrument on the principal's behalf. We will assume here, for purposes of discussion, that such authority exists (unauthorized signatures will be dealt with shortly). Additionally, the UCC imposes certain requirements regarding the way in which the agent signs the instrument.

LIABILITY OF THE PRINCIPAL Generally, an authorized agent binds a principal on an instrument if the agent *clearly names* the principal in the signature (by writing, mark, or some symbol). In this situation, the UCC presumes that the signature is authorized and genuine [UCC 3–308(a)]. The agent may or may not add his or her own name, but if the signature shows clearly that it is made on behalf of the principal, the agent is not liable on the instrument [UCC 3–402(b)(1)]. For example, either of the following signatures by Sandra Binney as agent for Bob Aronson would bind Aronson on the instrument:

1. Aronson, by Binney, agent.
2. Aronson.

LIABILITY OF THE AGENT What happens if an authorized agent signs just her or his own name on the instrument (such as "Binney") and does not name the principal? In this situation, normally the agent will be *personally* liable to a holder in due course who has no notice that the original parties did not intend the agent to be liable. With respect to ordinary holders, the agent can escape liability if the agent proves that the original parties did not intend the agent to be liable [UCC 3–402(a), (b)(2)].[8] In either situation, the principal is bound if the party entitled to enforce the instrument can prove the agency relationship.

—When an Agent May Be Held Personally Liable. An authorized agent may be held personally liable on a negotiable instrument in two other situations. When an instrument is signed in both the agent's name and

the principal's name ("Sandra Binney, Bob Aronson" or "Aronson, Binney") but nothing on the instrument indicates the agency relationship (so the agent cannot be distinguished from the principal), the agent may be held personally liable. An agent may also be held personally liable if the agent indicates agency status in signing a negotiable instrument but fails to name the principal ("Sandra Binney, agent") [UCC 3–402(b)(2)]. Because these forms of signing are ambiguous, however, parol evidence is admissible to prove the agency relationship.

—An Exception. An important exception to the above rules is made for checks that are signed by agents. If an agent signs his or her own name on a check that is payable from the account of the principal, and the principal is identified on the check, the agent will not be personally liable on the check [UCC 3–402(c)]. For example, suppose that Binney, who is *authorized* to draw checks on Aronson Company's account, signs a check that is preprinted with Aronson Company's name. The signature reads simply "Sandra Binney." In this situation, Binney will not be personally liable on the check.

UNAUTHORIZED SIGNATURES

People normally are not liable to pay on negotiable instruments unless their signatures appear on the instruments. The general rule is that an unauthorized signature is wholly inoperative and will not bind the person whose name is forged. Assume, for example, that Pablo finds Veronica's checkbook lying on the street, writes out a check to himself, and forges Veronica's signature. If a bank negligently fails to ascertain that Veronica's signature is not genuine and cashes the check for Pablo, the bank will generally be liable to Veronica for the amount. (The liability of banks for paying instruments with forged signatures will be discussed further in Chapter 27.)

Similarly, if an agent has no authority to sign the principal's name, the "unauthorized signature is ineffective except as the signature of the unauthorized signer" [UCC 3–403(a)]. Assume that Maya Campbell is the principal and Lena Shem is her agent. Shem, without authority, signs a promissory note as follows: "Maya Campbell, by Lena Shem, agent." Because Maya Campbell's "signature" is unauthorized, Campbell cannot be held liable, but Shem is liable to a holder of the note. This would be true even if Shem had signed the note "Maya Campbell," without indicating any

---

8. See UCC 3–402, Comment 1. Under Section 3–401(1) of the unrevised UCC, the principal is not liable on an instrument unless his or her signature appears on it, even if the parties are aware of the agency relationship.

agency relationship. In either situation, the unauthorized signer, Shem, is liable on the instrument.

EXCEPTIONS TO THE GENERAL RULE

There are two exceptions to the general rule that an unauthorized signature will not bind the person whose name is signed:

1. An exception is made when the person whose name is signed *ratifies* (affirms) the signature [UCC 3–403(a)]. For example, a principal can ratify an unauthorized signature made by an agent, either expressly (by affirming the validity of the signature) or impliedly (by other conduct, such as keeping any benefits received in the transaction or failing to repudiate the signature). The parties involved need not be principal and agent. For example, a mother may ratify her daughter's forgery of the mother's name so that the daughter will not be prosecuted for forgery.

2. Moreover, a person whose name is forged may be precluded from denying the effectiveness of the signature if the person's own negligence substantially contributed to the forgery. For example, Rob, the owner of a business, leaves his signature stamp and a blank check on an office counter. An employee, using the stamp, fills in and cashes the check. Rob can be estopped (prevented), on the basis of his negligence, from denying liability for payment of the check [UCC 3–115, 3–406, 4–401(d)(2)]. Whatever loss occurs may be allocated, however, between certain parties on the basis of *comparative negligence* [UCC 3–406(b)].[9] If Rob, in this example, can demonstrate that the bank was negligent in paying the check, the bank may bear a portion of the loss. The liability of the parties in this type of situation will be discussed further in Chapter 27.

WHEN THE HOLDER IS A HOLDER IN DUE COURSE

An unauthorized signature operates as the signature of the unauthorized signer in favor of a holder in due course, or HDC [UCC 3–403(a)]. For example, if Michel Vuillard signs "Paul Richaud" without Richaud's authorization, Vuillard is personally liable just as if he had signed his own name. Vuillard's liability is limited, however, to persons who take or pay the instrument in good faith. One who knew the signature was unauthorized would not qualify as an HDC and thus could not recover from Vuillard on the instrument. (The defenses that are effective against ordinary holders versus HDCs will be discussed in detail later in this chapter.)

SPECIAL RULES FOR UNAUTHORIZED INDORSEMENTS

Generally, when an indorsement is forged or unauthorized, the burden of loss falls on the first party to take the instrument with the forged or unauthorized indorsement. This general rule is premised on the concept that the first party to take an instrument is in the best position to prevent the loss.

For example, suppose that a check drawn on Universal Bank and payable to the order of Inga Leed is stolen by Jenny Nilson. Nilson indorses the check "Inga Leed" and presents the check to Universal Bank for payment. The bank, without asking Nilson for identification, pays the check, and Nilson disappears. In this situation, Leed will not be liable on the check because her indorsement was forged. The bank will bear the loss, which it might have avoided if it had requested identification from Nilson.

There are two important exceptions to this general rule. These exceptions arise when an indorsement is made by an imposter or by a fictitious payee. We look at these two situations here.

IMPOSTERS

An **imposter** is one who, by her or his personal appearance or use of the mail, telephone, or other communication, induces a maker or drawer to issue an instrument in the name of an impersonated payee. If the maker or drawer believes the imposter to be the named payee at the time of issue, the indorsement by the imposter is not treated as unauthorized when the instrument is transferred to an innocent party. This is because the maker or drawer *intended* the imposter to receive the instrument. In this situation, under the UCC's *imposter rule*, the imposter's indorsement will be effective—that is, not considered a forgery—insofar as the drawer or maker is concerned [UCC 3–404(a)].

For example, suppose that Kayla impersonates Donna and induces Edward to write a check payable to the order of Donna. Kayla, continuing to impersonate Donna, negotiates the check to First National Bank. As the drawer of the check, Edward is liable for its amount to First National.

The comparative negligence standard mentioned previously also applies in situations involving imposters [UCC 3–404(d)].[10] Thus, if a bank fails to exercise ordinary care in cashing a check made out to an imposter—for example, if the bank fails to check

---

9. Section 3–406 of the unrevised Article 3 does not provide for an allocation of such a loss on a comparative negligence basis.

10. Section 3–405 of the unrevised Article 3 does not provide for an allocation of loss on a comparative negligence basis.

the identity of the holder-payee and this failure substantially contributes to the drawer's loss—the drawer may have a cause of action against the bank and be able to recover a portion of the loss.

FICTITIOUS PAYEES An unauthorized indorsement will also be effective when a person causes an instrument to be issued to a payee who will have *no interest* in the instrument [UCC 3–404(b), 3–405]. In this situation, the payee is referred to as a **fictitious payee.** Situations involving fictitious payees most often arise when (1) a dishonest employee deceives the employer into signing an instrument payable to a party with no

right to receive payment on the instrument or (2) a dishonest employee or agent has the authority to issue an instrument on behalf of the employer and issues a check to a party who has no interest in the instrument. Under the UCC's *fictitious payee rule*, the payee's indorsement is not treated as a forgery, and the employer can be held liable on the instrument by an innocent holder.

—An Example of How a Fictitious Payee Can Be Created. Assume that Goldstar Aviation, Inc., gives its bookkeeper, Leslie Rose, general authority to issue checks in the company name drawn on First State Bank so that Rose can pay employees' wages and other

CONCEPT SUMMARY 26.1 | Signature Liability

CONCEPT	DESCRIPTION

PRIMARY AND SECONDARY LIABILITY	Every party (except a qualified indorser) who signs a negotiable instrument is either primarily or secondarily liable for payment of the instrument when it comes due.
	1. *Primary liability*—Makers and acceptors are primarily liable [UCC 3–409, 3–412, 3–413].
	2. *Secondary liability*—Drawers and indorsers are secondarily liable [UCC 3–414, 3–415, 3–501, 3–502, 3–503]. Parties who are secondarily liable on an instrument promise to pay on that instrument only if the following events occur:
	  a. The instrument is properly and timely presented.
	  b. The instrument is dishonored.
	  c. Timely notice of dishonor is given.

ACCOMMODATION PARTIES	An accommodation party is one who signs an instrument for the purpose of lending his or her name as credit to another party on the instrument [UCC 3–419]. Accommodation *makers* are primarily liable; accommodation *indorsers* are secondarily liable.
AGENTS' SIGNATURES	An *agent* is a person who agrees to represent or act for another, called the *principal*. Agents can sign negotiable instruments and thereby bind their principals. Liability on the instrument depends on whether the agent is authorized and on whether the agent's representative capacity and the principal's identity are both indicated on the instrument [UCC 3–401, 3–402, 3–403]. Agents need not indicate their representative capacity on *checks*—provided the checks clearly identify the principal and are drawn on the principal's account.
UNAUTHORIZED SIGNATURES	An unauthorized signature is wholly inoperative as the signature of the person whose name is signed *unless*: 1. The person whose name is signed ratifies (affirms) it or is precluded from denying it [UCC 3–115, 3–403, 3–406, 4–401]. 2. The instrument has been negotiated to a holder in due course [UCC 3–403].
SPECIAL RULES FOR UNAUTHORIZED INDORSEMENTS	An unauthorized indorsement will not bind the maker or drawer of the instrument except in the following circumstances: 1. When an imposter induces the maker or drawer of an instrument to issue it to the imposter (*imposter rule*) [UCC 3–404(a)]. 2. When a person causes an instrument to be issued to a payee who will have *no interest* in the instrument (*fictitious payee rule*) [UCC 3–404(b), 3–405].

corporate bills. Rose decides to cheat Goldstar out of $10,000 by issuing a check payable to the Del Rey Company, a supplier of aircraft parts. Rose does not intend Del Rey to receive any of the funds, nor is Del Rey entitled to the payment. Rose indorses the check in Del Rey's name and deposits the check in an account that she opened in West National Bank in the name "Del Rey Co." West National Bank accepts the check and collects payment from the drawee bank, First State Bank. First State Bank charges Goldstar's account $10,000. Rose transfers $10,000 out of the Del Rey account and closes the account. Goldstar discovers the fraud and demands that the account be recredited.

—Who Bears the Loss? Who bears the loss? Because Rose's indorsement in the name of a payee with no interest in the instrument is "effective," there is no "forgery" [UCC 3–404(b)(2)]. Under this provision, West National Bank is protected in paying on the check, and the drawee bank is protected in charging Goldstar's account. Thus, the employer-drawer, Goldstar, will bear the loss. Of course, Goldstar has recourse against Rose, if Rose has not absconded with the funds. Additionally, if Goldstar can prove that the bank's failure to exercise reasonable care contributed substantially to the loss, the bank may be required to bear a proportionate share of the loss under the UCC's comparative negligence standard [UCC 3–404(d)]. Thus, West National Bank could be liable for a portion of the loss if it failed to exercise ordinary care in its dealings with Rose.

Whether a dishonest employee actually signs the check or merely supplies his or her employer with names of fictitious creditors (or with true names of creditors having fictitious debts), the result is the same under the UCC. Assume that Dan Symes draws up the payroll list from which employees' salary checks are written. He fraudulently adds the name Penny Trip (a friend not entitled to payment) to the payroll, thus causing checks to be issued to her. Trip cashes the checks and shares the proceeds with Symes. Again, it is the employer-drawer who bears the loss.

SECTION 2 | Warranty Liability

In addition to the signature liability discussed in the preceding section, transferors make certain implied warranties regarding the instruments that they are negotiating. Liability under these warranties is not subject to the conditions of proper presentment, dis-

honor, and notice of dishonor. These warranties arise even when a transferor does not indorse the instrument (as in delivery of a bearer instrument). Warranty liability is particularly important when a holder cannot hold a party liable on her or his signature.

Warranties fall into two categories: those that arise from the *transfer* of a negotiable instrument and those that arise on *presentment* [UCC 3–416, 3–417]. Both transfer and presentment warranties attempt to shift liability back to a wrongdoer or to the person who dealt face to face with the wrongdoer and thus was in the best position to prevent the wrongdoing.

TRANSFER WARRANTIES

For **transfer warranties** to arise, an instrument must be transferred for *consideration*. For example, Quality Products Corporation sells goods to Royal Retail Stores, Inc., and receives in payment Royal Retail's note. Quality then sells the note, for value, to Superior Finance Company. In this situation, the instrument has been transferred for consideration. One who transfers an instrument for consideration makes transfer warranties to all subsequent transferees and holders who take the instrument in good faith (with some exceptions, as will be noted shortly). There are five transfer warranties [UCC 3–416]:

1. The transferor is entitled to enforce the instrument.

2. All signatures are authentic and authorized.

3. The instrument has not been altered.

4. The instrument is not subject to a defense or claim of any party that can be asserted against the transferor.[11]

5. The transferor has no knowledge of any insolvency proceedings against the maker, the acceptor, or the drawer of the instrument.[12]

---

11. Under Section 3–417(3) of the unrevised UCC, a qualified indorser who indorses an instrument "without recourse" limits this warranty to a warranty that he or she has "no knowledge" of such a defense rather than that there *is* no defense. This limitation does not apply under the revised Article 3.

12. A 2002 amendment to UCC 3–416(a) adds a sixth warranty: "with respect to a remotely created consumer item, that the person on whose account the item is drawn authorized the issuance of the item in the amount for which the item is drawn." For example, a telemarketer submits an instrument to a bank for payment, claiming that the consumer on whose account the instrument purports to be drawn authorized it over the phone. Under this amendment, a bank that accepts and pays the instrument warrants to the next bank in the collection chain that the consumer authorized the item in that amount.

PARTIES TO WHOM WARRANTY LIABILITY EXTENDS The manner of transfer and the negotiation that is used determine how far and to whom a transfer warranty will run. Transfer of an order instrument by indorsement and delivery extends warranty liability to any subsequent holder who takes the instrument in good faith. The warranties of a person who, for consideration, transfers *without indorsement* (by delivery of bearer paper), however, will extend only to the immediate transferee [UCC 3–416(a)].

Suppose that Wylie forges Kim's name as a maker of a promissory note. The note is made payable to Wylie. Wylie indorses the note in blank, negotiates it for consideration to Bret, and then leaves the country. Bret, without indorsement, delivers the note for consideration to Fern. Fern, also without indorsement, delivers the note for consideration to Rick. On Rick's presentment of the note to Kim, the forgery is discovered. Rick can hold Fern (the immediate transferor) liable for breach of the warranty that all signatures are genuine. Rick cannot hold Bret liable because Bret is not Rick's immediate transferor; rather, Bret is a prior nonindorsing transferor.

Note that if Wylie had added a special indorsement ("Payable to Bret") instead of a blank indorsement, the instrument would have remained an order instrument. In that situation, Bret would have had to indorse the instrument to negotiate it to Fern, and his transfer warranties would extend to all subsequent holders, including Rick. This example shows the importance of the distinction between transfer by indorsement and delivery (of an order instrument) and transfer by delivery only, without indorsement (of a bearer instrument).

RECOVERY FOR BREACH OF WARRANTY A transferee or holder who takes an instrument in good faith can sue on the basis of breach of warranty as soon as he or she has reason to know of the breach [UCC 3–416(d)]. Notice of a claim for breach of warranty must be given to the warrantor within thirty days after the transferee or holder has reason to know of the breach and the identity of the warrantor, or the warrantor is not liable for any loss caused by a delay [UCC 3–416(c)]. The transferee or holder can recover damages for the breach in an amount equal to the loss suffered (but not more than the amount of the instrument), plus expenses and any loss of interest caused by the breach [UCC 3–416(b)].

These warranties can be disclaimed with respect to any instrument except a check [UCC 3–416(c)]. In the check-collection process, banks rely on these warranties. For all other instruments, the immediate parties can agree to a disclaimer, and an indorser can disclaim by including in the indorsement such words as "without warranties."

PRESENTMENT WARRANTIES

Any person who presents an instrument for payment or acceptance makes the following **presentment warranties** to any other person who in good faith pays or accepts the instrument [UCC 3–417(a), (d)]:

1. The person obtaining payment or acceptance is entitled to enforce the instrument or is authorized to obtain payment or acceptance on behalf of a person who is entitled to enforce the instrument. (This is, in effect, a warranty that there are no missing or unauthorized indorsements.)

	CONCEPT SUMMARY 26.2	Transfer Warranty Liability for Transferors Who Receive Consideration
TRANSFERORS	**TRANSFEREES TO WHOM WARRANTIES EXTEND IF CONSIDERATION IS RECEIVED**
INDORSERS WHO RECEIVE CONSIDERATION	Five transfer warranties extend to *all* subsequent holders: 1. The transferor is entitled to enforce the instrument. 2. All signatures are authentic and authorized. 3. The instrument has not been altered. 4. The instrument is not subject to a defense or claim of any party that can be asserted against the transferor. 5. The transferor has no knowledge of insolvency proceedings against the maker, acceptor, or drawer of the instrument.
NONINDORSERS WHO RECEIVE CONSIDERATION	Same as for indorsers, but warranties extend *only* to the *immediate transferee*.

2. The instrument has not been altered.

3. The person obtaining payment or acceptance has no knowledge that the signature of the drawer of the instrument is unauthorized.[13]

These warranties are referred to as *presentment warranties* because they protect the person to whom the instrument is presented. The second and third warranties do not apply in certain cases (to certain parties). It is assumed, for example, that a drawer will recognize her or his own signature and that a maker or an acceptor will recognize whether an instrument has been materially altered.

Presentment warranties cannot be disclaimed with respect to checks, and a claim for breach must be given to the warrantor within thirty days after the claimant knows or has reason to know of the breach and the identity of the warrantor, or the warrantor is not liable for any loss caused by a delay [UCC 3–417(e)].

SECTION 3 | Defenses

Depending on whether a holder or a holder in due course (HDC)—or a holder through an HDC—makes the demand for payment, certain defenses can bar collection from persons who would otherwise be liable on an instrument. There are two general categories of defenses—*universal defenses* and *personal defenses*.

UNIVERSAL DEFENSES

Universal defenses (also called *real defenses*) are valid against *all* holders, including HDCs and holders through HDCs. Universal defenses include those described in the following subsections.

FORGERY   Forgery of a maker's or drawer's signature cannot bind the person whose name is used unless that person ratifies (approves or validates) the signature or is precluded from denying it (because the forgery was made possible by the maker's or drawer's negligence, for example) [UCC 3–401(a), 3–403(a)]. Thus, when a person forges an instrument, the person whose name is used has no liability to pay any holder or any HDC the value of the forged instrument. In addition, a principal can assert the defense of unauthorized signature against any holder or HDC when an agent exceeds his

or her authority to sign negotiable paper on behalf of the principal [UCC 3–403].

Contrast this type of forgery with an imposter's indorsement. An imposter's indorsement is effective against the maker or drawer because the maker or drawer intended the imposter to receive the instrument, whereas a person whose name is forged has no such intent.

FRAUD IN THE EXECUTION   If a person is deceived into signing a negotiable instrument, believing that she or he is signing something other than a negotiable instrument (such as a receipt), *fraud in the execution* (or inception) is committed against the signer. For example, a consumer unfamiliar with the English language signs a paper presented by a salesperson. The salesperson states that the paper is a request for an estimate, but it is in fact a promissory note. Even if the note is negotiated to an HDC, the consumer has a valid defense against payment [UCC 3–305(a)(1)(iii)].

This defense cannot be raised, however, if a reasonable inquiry would have revealed the nature and terms of the instrument.[14] Thus the signer's age, experience, and intelligence are relevant because they frequently determine whether the signer should have understood the nature of the transaction before signing.

MATERIAL ALTERATION   An alteration is *material* if it changes the contract terms between two parties *in any way*. Examples of material alterations include completing an instrument, adding words or numbers, or making any other change in an unauthorized manner that relates to a party's obligation [UCC 3–407(a)]. Any change in the amount, the date, or the rate of interest—even if the change is only one penny, one day, or 1 percent—is material. It is not a material alteration, however, to correct the maker's address, to draw a red line across the instrument to indicate that an auditor has checked it, or to correct the total final payment due when a mathematical error is discovered in the original computation. If the alteration is not material, any holder is entitled to enforce the instrument according to its original terms.

Material alteration is a *complete defense* against an ordinary holder but only a *partial defense* against an HDC. An ordinary holder can recover nothing on an instrument that has been materially altered [UCC 3–407(b)]. In contrast, when the holder is an HDC

---

13. The warranty added by a 2002 amendment to UCC 3–416(a), "with respect to a remotely created consumer item" (discussed earlier in this chapter in footnote 12), is also added by the 2002 amendments as a fourth warranty to UCC 3–417(a).

14. *Burchett v. Allied Concord Financial Corp.*, 74 N.M. 575, 396 P.2d 186 (1964).

and an original term, such as the monetary amount payable, has been *altered*, the HDC can enforce the instrument against the maker or drawer according to the original terms but not for the altered amount [UCC 3–407(c)(i)]. If the instrument was originally incomplete and was later completed in an unauthorized manner, alteration can no longer be claimed as a defense against an HDC, and the HDC can enforce the instrument as completed [UCC 3–407(b), (c)]. This is because a drawer or maker who has issued an incomplete instrument will normally be held responsible for such an alteration, which could have been avoided by the exercise of greater care. If the alteration is readily apparent, then obviously the holder has notice of some defect or defense and therefore cannot be an HDC [UCC 3–302(a)(1), (2)(iv)].

DISCHARGE IN BANKRUPTCY Discharge in bankruptcy (see Chapter 30) is an absolute defense on any instrument regardless of the status of the holder, because the purpose of bankruptcy is to finally settle all of the insolvent party's debts [UCC 3–305(a)(1)(iv)].

MINORITY Minority, or infancy, is a universal defense only to the extent that state law recognizes it as a defense to a simple contract. Because state laws on minority vary, so do determinations of whether minority is a universal defense against an HDC [UCC 3–305(a)(1)(i)]. (See Chapter 13 for a further discussion of the contractual liability of minors.)

ILLEGALITY When the law declares that an instrument is void because it has been executed in connection with illegal conduct, the defense is universal—that is, effective against both an ordinary holder and an HDC. If the law merely makes the instrument voidable—as in the personal (rather than the universal) defense of illegality, discussed later—then it is still a defense against a holder, but not against an HDC. The courts are sometimes prone to treat the word *void* in a statute as meaning *voidable* to protect an HDC [UCC 3–305(a)(1)(ii)].

MENTAL INCAPACITY If a person has been declared by a court to be mentally incompetent, then any instrument thereafter issued by that person is void. The instrument is void *ab initio* (from the beginning) and unenforceable by any holder or HDC [UCC 3–305(a)(1)(ii)]. Mental incapacity in these circumstances is thus a universal defense. (If a person has *not* been declared mentally incompetent by state proceed-

ings, mental incapacity is a personal, rather than a universal, defense.)

EXTREME DURESS When a person signs and issues a negotiable instrument under such extreme duress as an immediate threat of force or violence (for example, at gunpoint), the instrument is void and unenforceable by any holder or HDC [UCC 3–305(a)(1)(ii)]. (Ordinary duress is a personal, rather than a universal, defense.)

PERSONAL DEFENSES

Personal defenses, such as those described next, are used to avoid payment to an ordinary holder of a negotiable instrument. Remember that an ordinary holder is a holder who has not met the requirements for HDC status.

BREACH OF CONTRACT OR BREACH OF WARRANTY When there is a breach of the underlying contract for which the negotiable instrument was issued, the maker of a note can refuse to pay it, or the drawer of a check can stop payment. Breach of warranty can also be claimed as a defense to liability on the instrument.

For example, Elias purchases two dozen pairs of athletic shoes from De Soto. The shoes are to be delivered in six weeks. Elias gives De Soto a promissory note for $1,000, which is the price of the shoes. The shoes arrive, but many of them are stained, and the soles of several pairs are coming apart. Elias has a defense to liability on the note on the basis of breach of contract and breach of warranty. (Recall from Chapter 23 that a seller impliedly promises that the goods being sold are at least merchantable.) If, however, the note is no longer in the hands of the payee-seller (De Soto) but is presented for payment by an HDC, the maker-buyer (Elias) will not be able to plead breach of contract or warranty as a defense against liability on the note.

LACK OR FAILURE OF CONSIDERATION The absence of consideration may be a successful defense in some instances [UCC 3–303(b), 3–305(a)(2)]. For example, Tony gives Cleo, as a gift, a note that states, "I promise to pay you $100,000," and Cleo accepts the note. No consideration is given in return for Tony's promise, and a court will not enforce the promise.

Similarly, if delivery of goods becomes impossible, a party who has issued a draft or note under the contract has a defense for not paying it. Thus, in the hypothetical athletic-shoe transaction described previously, if delivery of the shoes became impossible due to their loss in an accident, De Soto could not subsequently enforce Elias's promise to pay the $1,000 promissory note. If the note was in the hands of an HDC, however, Elias's defense would not be available against the HDC.

FRAUD IN THE INDUCEMENT (ORDINARY FRAUD)

A person who issues a negotiable instrument based on false statements by the other party will be able to avoid payment on that instrument, unless the holder is an HDC. To illustrate: Gerhard agrees to purchase Carla's used tractor for $26,500. Carla, knowing her statements to be false, tells Gerhard that the tractor is in good working order and that it has been used for only one harvest. In addition, she tells Gerhard that she owns the tractor free and clear of all claims. Gerhard pays Carla $4,500 in cash and issues a negotiable promissory note for the balance. As it turns out, Carla still owes the original seller $10,000 on the purchase of the tractor, and the tractor is subject to a valid security interest (discussed in Chapter 29). In addition, the tractor is three years old and has been used in three harvests.

In this situation, Gerhard can refuse to pay the note if it is held by an ordinary holder. If, however, Carla has negotiated the note to an HDC, Gerhard must pay the HDC. Of course, Gerhard can then sue Carla to recover the money.

ILLEGALITY

As mentioned, if a statute provides that an illegal transaction is void, a universal defense exists. If, however, the statute provides that an illegal transaction is voidable, the defense is personal. For example, a state may make gambling contracts illegal and void but be silent on the payment of gambling debts. Thus, an instrument given in payment of a gambling debt becomes voidable and is a personal defense.

MENTAL INCAPACITY

As mentioned, if a maker or drawer has been declared by a court to be mentally incompetent, mental incapacity is a universal defense [UCC 3–305(a)(1)(ii)]. If a maker or drawer issues a negotiable instrument while mentally incompetent but before a formal court hearing has declared him or her to be so, however, the instrument is voidable. In this situation, mental incapacity can serve only as a personal defense.

OTHER PERSONAL DEFENSES

A number of other personal defenses can be used to avoid payment to an ordinary holder, but not an HDC, of a negotiable instrument, including the following:

1. Discharge by payment or cancellation [UCC 3–601(b), 3–602(a), 3–603, 3–604].
2. Unauthorized completion of an incomplete instrument [UCC 3–115, 3–302, 3–407, 4–401(d)(2)].
3. Nondelivery of the instrument [UCC 1–201(14), 3–105(b), 3–305(a)(2)].
4. Ordinary duress or undue influence rendering the contract voidable [UCC 3–305(a)(1)(ii)].

FEDERAL LIMITATIONS ON HDC RIGHTS

Because of the sometimes harsh effects of the HDC doctrine on consumers, the federal government limits HDC rights in certain circumstances. To understand the punitive effects of the doctrine, consider an example. A consumer purchases a used car under an express warranty from an automobile dealer. The consumer pays $3,000 down and signs a promissory note to the dealer for the remaining $7,000 due on the car. The dealer sells the bank this promissory note, which is a negotiable instrument, and the bank then becomes the creditor, to whom the consumer makes payments.

The car, however, does not perform as warranted. The consumer returns the car and requests a refund of the down payment and cancellation of the contract. Even if the dealer refunds the $3,000, however, under the traditional HDC rule, the consumer would normally still owe the remaining $7,000 because the consumer's claim of breach of warranty is a personal defense and the bank is an HDC.

Thus, the traditional HDC rule leaves consumers who have purchased defective products liable to HDCs. To protect consumers, in 1976 the Federal Trade Commission (FTC) issued Rule 433,[15] which effectively abolished the HDC doctrine in consumer credit transactions.

REQUIREMENTS OF FTC RULE 433

FTC Rule 433, entitled "Preservation of Consumers' Claims and Defenses," limits the rights of an HDC in an instru-

---

15. 16 C.F.R. Section 433.2. The rule was enacted in 1976 pursuant to the FTC's authority under the Federal Trade Commission Act, 15 U.S.C. Sections 41–58.

CONCEPT SUMMARY 26.3 | Valid Defenses against Holders of Negotiable Instruments

DEFENSES	TYPES
UNIVERSAL (REAL) DEFENSES Valid against all holders, including holders in due course and holders with the rights of holders in due course (through the shelter principle) [UCC 3–305, 3–401, 3–403, 3–407].	1. Forgery. 2. Fraud in the execution. 3. Material alteration. 4. Discharge in bankruptcy. 5. Minority, if the contract is voidable. 6. Illegality, incapacity, or duress, if the contract is void under state law.
PERSONAL DEFENSES Valid against ordinary holders but not against holders in due course or holders with the rights of holders in due course [UCC 3–105, 3–115, 3–302, 3–305, 3–306, 3–407, 3–601, 3–602, 3–603, 3–604, 4–401].	1. Breach of contract (including breach of contract warranties). 2. Lack or failure of consideration. 3. Fraud in the inducement (ordinary fraud). 4. Illegality, incapacity (other than minority), or duress, if the contract is voidable. 5. Previous payment or cancellation of the instrument. 6. Unauthorized completion of an incomplete instrument. 7. Nondelivery of the instrument.

ment that evidences a debt arising out of a consumer credit transaction. The rule attempts to prevent a consumer from being required to make payment for a defective product to a third party (the bank, in the previous example) who is an HDC of a promissory note that formed part of the contract with the dealer who sold the defective good.

FTC Rule 433 applies to any seller of goods or services who takes or receives a consumer credit contract. The rule also applies to a seller who accepts as full or partial payment for a sale the proceeds of any purchase-money loan[16] made in connection with any consumer credit contract. Under this rule, these parties must include in the consumer credit contract the following provision:

NOTICE

ANY HOLDER OF THIS CONSUMER CREDIT CONTRACT IS SUBJECT TO ALL CLAIMS AND DEFENSES WHICH THE DEBTOR COULD ASSERT AGAINST THE SELLER OF GOODS OR SERVICES OBTAINED PURSUANT HERETO OR WITH THE PROCEEDS HEREOF. RECOVERY HEREUNDER BY THE DEBTOR SHALL NOT EXCEED AMOUNTS PAID BY THE DEBTOR HEREUNDER.

EFFECT OF THE RULE FTC Rule 433 allows a consumer who is a party to a consumer credit transaction to bring any defense she or he has against the seller of a product against a subsequent holder as well. In essence, the rule places an HDC of the instrument in the position of a contract assignee. The rule makes the buyer's duty to pay conditional on the seller's full performance of the contract. Both the seller and the creditor are responsible for the seller's misconduct. The rule also clearly reduces the degree of transferability of negotiable instruments resulting from consumer credit contracts. An instrument that contains this notice or a similar statement required by law may remain negotiable, but there cannot be an HDC of such an instrument [UCC 3–106(d)].

What if the seller does not include the notice in a promissory note and then sells the note to a third party, such as a bank? Although the seller has violated the rule, the bank has not. Because the FTC rule does not prohibit third parties from purchasing notes or

---

16. A *purchase-money loan* is one in which a seller or lessor advances funds to a buyer or lessee through a credit contract to purchase or lease the goods, as will be discussed in Chapter 29.

credit contracts that do *not* contain the required rule, the third party does not become subject to the buyer's defenses against the seller. Thus, some consumers remain unprotected by the FTC rule.[17]

SECTION 4 | Discharge

Discharge from liability on an instrument can occur in several ways, including by payment, by cancellation, and, as previously discussed, by material alteration. Discharge can also occur if a party reacquires an instrument, if a holder impairs another party's right of recourse, or if a holder surrenders collateral without consent.

DISCHARGE BY PAYMENT OR TENDER OF PAYMENT

All parties to a negotiable instrument will be discharged when the party primarily liable on it pays to a holder the amount due in full [UCC 3–602, 3–603].[18] The same is true if the drawee of an unaccepted draft or check makes payment in good faith to the holder. In these situations, all parties on the instruments are usually discharged. In contrast, such payment made by any other party (for example, an indorser) will discharge only that party and subsequent parties on the instrument. The party making such a payment still has the right to recover on the instrument from any prior parties.[19]

A party will not be discharged when paying in bad faith to a holder who acquired the instrument by theft or who obtained the instrument from someone else who acquired it by theft (unless, of course, the person has the rights of an HDC) [UCC 3–602(b)(2)].

If a tender of payment is made to a person entitled to enforce the instrument and the tender is refused, indorsers and accommodation parties with a right of recourse against the party making the tender are discharged to the extent of the amount of the tender [UCC 3–603(b)]. If a tender of payment of an amount due on an instrument is made to a person entitled to enforce the instrument, the obligor's obligation to pay interest after the due date on the amount tendered is discharged [UCC 3–603(c)].

DISCHARGE BY CANCELLATION OR SURRENDER

Intentional cancellation of an instrument discharges the liability of all parties [UCC 3–604]. Intentionally writing "Paid" across the face of an instrument cancels it. Intentionally tearing up an instrument cancels it. If a holder intentionally crosses out a party's signature, that party's liability and the liability of subsequent indorsers who have already indorsed the instrument are discharged. Materially altering an instrument may discharge the liability of all parties, as previously discussed [UCC 3–407(b)]. (An HDC may be able to enforce a materially altered instrument against its maker or drawer according to the instrument's *original* terms, however.)

Destruction or mutilation of a negotiable instrument is considered cancellation only if it is done with the intention of eliminating obligation on the instrument [UCC 3–604(a)(i)]. Thus, if destruction or mutilation occurs by accident, the instrument is not discharged, and the original terms can be established by parol evidence [UCC 3–309].

A note's holder may also discharge the obligation by surrendering the note to the person to be discharged [UCC 3–604(a)(i)]. The question in the following case was whether a lender's surrender of a note marked "PAID" was sufficient to show an intent to cancel and thereby discharge the note.

---

17. Under a 2002 amendment to UCC 3–305(e), a third party holder in possession of a note or other instrument that is required to include this notice would be subject to a buyer's defenses against a seller even if the instrument did not include the notice.

18. This is true even if the payment is made with knowledge of a claim to the instrument by another person unless the payor knows that "payment is prohibited by injunction or similar process of a court of competent jurisdiction" or, in most cases, "the party making payment accepted, from a person having a claim to the instrument, indemnity against loss resulting from refusal to pay the person entitled to enforce the instrument" [UCC 3–602(a), (b)(1)].

19. Under a 2002 amendment to UCC 3–602(b), when a party entitled to enforce an instrument transfers it without giving notice to parties obligated to pay it, and one of those parties pays the transferor, that payment is effective. For example, suppose that Roberto borrows $5,000 from Consumer Finance Company on a note payable to the lender. Consumer Finance transfers the note to Delta Investment Corporation but continues to collect payments from Roberto. Under this amendment, those payments effectively discharge Roberto to the extent of their amount.

CASE 26.2

Court of Appeals
of Ohio,
Fourth District,
Highland County, 2004.
__ Ohio App.3d __,
__ N.E.2d __.

Huntington National Bank v. Mark

BACKGROUND AND FACTS *In July 1998, Edith Mark bought a 1997 Ford F150 pickup truck. Mark signed a loan agreement with Huntington National Bank of Ohio for $19,072.05 to finance the purchase, granting the bank a lien*[a] *on the truck. She had made twenty of the sixty-six required monthly payments on the loan when she received in the mail the original agreement stamped "PAID" and her truck's certificate of title stamped "Lien Cancelled." She stopped making the payments. Huntington filed a suit in an Ohio state court against Mark to recover $14,876.83—the unpaid amount of the loan. Robert Smith, the bank's litigation specialist, testified that the loan agreement had been stamped "PAID" and had been returned together with the title certificate "due to a mistake of fact and clerical error." The court issued a judgment in favor of the bank. Mark appealed to a state intermediate appellate court.*

IN THE LANGUAGE OF THE COURT

ABELE, J. [Judge]
* * * *

* * * [A]ppellant asserts that the trial court erred in finding that appellee's surrender of the loan document did not constitute a valid cancellation of the lien. Appellant contends, citing [Ohio Revised Code Section] 1303.69 [Ohio's version of UCC 3–604], that "appellee's employee, either at the direction or under the direct supervision" of appellee, cancelled the lien on the vehicle. Appellant notes that she did not request this action and that appellee "did it on their own volition, voluntarily." Thus, appellant reasons, "the fact that the document was stamped with the official stamp at the direction of or by an employee under the direct supervision of the [appellee] demonstrates the intent to discharge the debt." * * *

Appellee argues that the record supports the trial court's conclusion that it "inadvertently released the lien on the Certificate of Title and forwarded the original personal loan agreement marked 'PAID' by mistake." Appellee contends that its lack of care should not permit the appellant to retain the benefits resulting from appellee's mistake and that restitution [restoring the parties to their original position in which the lien is valid until the balance of the loan is paid] is the appropriate remedy. * * *

The promissory note at issue in the case at bar [this case] is an instrument that falls within the scope of [Ohio Revised Code] Chapter 1303 [UCC Article 3]. A party may be discharged from liability on a promissory note by * * * payment * * * or cancellation * * * [among other methods]. *In order for a valid discharge to occur, however, an intent to discharge is required.* [Emphasis added.]
* * * *

In the case at bar, appellant asserts that the evidence adduced [put forth] at trial does not support the trial court's conclusion that the note's surrender resulted from inadvertence [carelessness] or mistake rather than appellee's intent to discharge the obligation. Appellant contends that "the fact that the document was mailed to the proper person and address demonstrates the requisite intent to surrender." Appellant notes that appellee's witness [Smith] testified that he had reviewed the file involved in this matter, but that he possessed no firsthand knowledge of the facts. Appellant castigates [sharply criticizes] appellee [for] its failure to "produce the employee who allegedly mistakenly discharged the lien or stamped the note 'paid.'"

The appellee notes that Smith provided unrebutted testimony that he had reviewed the records and accounts and that the lien's discharge resulted from a mistake or clerical error, not bank policy or a decision to forgive the amount due under the note. The appellee further asserts that * * * appellant presented no evidence of payment or explanation of why the lien would have been marked "paid" when payment in full was never made * * * .
* * * *

* * * [W]e believe that the record contains sufficient competent, credible evidence to support the trial court's judgment. The trial court determined that the surrender of the note

---

a. A *lien* is a claim against specific property to satisfy a debt. See Chapters 28 and 29.

CONTINUED ▶

CASE 26.2 | Continued

and the release of the lien occurred through a clerical error or a mistake. Thus, the court concluded that the surrender of the note did not constitute a valid discharge of the obligation in view of the fact that the appellee lacked the necessary intent to discharge the obligation. After our review of the evidence, we find no error with the trial court's conclusion. Robert Smith testified that the surrender occurred through a mistake or a clerical error. His testimony * * * provides an adequate basis for the trial court's finding.

DECISION AND REMEDY *The state intermediate appellate court affirmed the judgment of the lower court in favor of the bank. Smith's testimony that the surrender of the note stamped "PAID" was due to a clerical error or a mistake was sufficient to show that the bank did not intend to discharge the note. Thus, its surrender did not constitute a valid cancellation.*

WHAT IF THE FACTS WERE DIFFERENT? *Suppose that the trial court had not found Smith's testimony to be credible and had issued a judgment in Mark's favor. Would the result on appeal have been different?*

DISCHARGE BY REACQUISITION

A person who reacquires an instrument that he or she held previously discharges all intervening indorsers against subsequent holders who do not qualify as HDCs [UCC 3–207]. Of course, the person reacquiring the instrument may be liable to subsequent holders if the instrument is dishonored.

DISCHARGE BY IMPAIRMENT OF RECOURSE

Discharge can also occur when a party's right of recourse is impaired [UCC 3–605]. A *right of recourse* is a right to seek reimbursement. Ordinarily, when a holder collects the amount of an instrument from an indorser, the indorser has a right of recourse against prior indorsers, the maker or drawer, and accommodation parties. If the holder has adversely affected the indorser's right to seek reimbursement from these other parties, however, the indorser is not liable on the instrument (to the extent that the indorser's right of recourse is impaired). This occurs when, for example, the holder releases or agrees not to sue a party against whom the indorser has a right of recourse. It also occurs when a holder agrees to an extension of the instrument's due date or to some other material modification that results in a loss to the indorser with respect to the right of recourse [UCC 3–605(c), (d)].[20]

---

20. The 2002 amendments to UCC 3–605 essentially apply the principles of suretyship and guaranty (to be discussed in Chapter 28) to circumstances that involve the impairment of the right of recourse of "secondary obligors," which include indorsers and accommodation parties. One important difference from the principles of suretyship and guaranty, however, is that under amended UCC 3–605(a), the release of a principal obligor by a person entitled to enforce a check grants a complete discharge to an indorser of the check without requiring proof of harm.

DISCHARGE BY IMPAIRMENT OF COLLATERAL

Sometimes, a party to an instrument gives collateral to secure that her or his performance will occur. When a holder "impairs the value" of that collateral without the consent of the parties who would benefit from the collateral in the event of nonpayment, those parties to the instrument are discharged to the extent of the impairment [UCC 3–605(e), (f)].

For example, suppose that Jerome and Myra sign a note as co-makers, putting up Jerome's property as collateral. The note is payable to Montessa. Montessa is required by law to file a financing statement with the state to put others on notice of her interest in Jerome's property as collateral for the note. If Montessa fails to file the statement and Jerome goes through bankruptcy—which results in his property's being sold to pay other debts and leaves him unable to pay anything on the note—Montessa has impaired the value of the collateral to Myra, who is discharged to the extent of that impairment.

In other words, when Jerome goes through bankruptcy, Montessa's earlier failure to file the statement prevents her from taking possession of the collateral, selling it, and crediting the amount owed on the note. Myra, as co-maker, is then responsible only for any remaining indebtedness, instead of the entire unpaid balance. Thus, Myra is discharged to the extent that the proceeds from the sale of the collateral would have discharged her liability on the note.

REVIEWING LIABILITY, DEFENSES, AND DISCHARGE

Nancy Mahar was the office manager at Golden Years Nursing Home, Inc. She was given a signature stamp to issue checks to the nursing home's employees for up to $100 as advances on their pay. The checks were drawn on Golden Years' account at the First National Bank. Over a seven-year period, Mahar wrote a number of checks to employees exclusively for the purpose of embezzling funds for herself. She forged the employees' indorsements on the checks, signed her name as a second indorser, and deposited the checks in her personal account at Star Bank. The employees whose names were on the checks never actually requested them. When the scheme was uncovered, Golden Years filed a suit against Mahar, Star Bank, and others to recover the funds. Using the information presented in the chapter, answer the following questions.

1. With regard to signature liability, which UCC provision discussed in this chapter applies to this scenario?

2. What is the rule set forth by that provision?

3. Under the UCC, which party, Golden Years or Star Bank, must bear the loss in this situation? Why?

4. Describe any transfer or presentment warranties that Mahar might have violated based on these facts.

TERMS AND CONCEPTS TO REVIEW

accommodation party 520

agent 520

dishonor 516

fictitious payee 523

imposter 522

personal defense 527

presentment warranty 525

principal 520

transfer warranty 524

universal defense 526

QUESTIONS AND CASE PROBLEMS

26–1. What are the exceptions to the rule that a bank will be liable for paying a check over an unauthorized indorsement?

26–2. Waldo makes out a negotiable promissory note payable to the order of Grace. Grace indorses the note by writing on it "Without recourse, Grace" and transfers the note for value to Adam. Adam, in need of cash, negotiates the note to Keith by indorsing it with the words "Pay to Keith, Adam." On the due date, Keith presents the note to Waldo for payment, only to learn that Waldo has filed for bankruptcy and will have all debts (including the note) discharged. Discuss fully whether Keith can hold Waldo, Grace, or Adam liable on the note.

26–3. QUESTION WITH SAMPLE ANSWER
Niles sold Kennedy a small motorboat for $1,500, maintaining to Kennedy that the boat was in excellent condition. Kennedy gave Niles a check for $1,500, which

Niles indorsed and gave to Frazier for value. When Kennedy took the boat for a trial run, she discovered that the boat leaked, needed to be painted, and required a new motor. Kennedy stopped payment on her check, which had not yet been cashed. Niles has disappeared. Can Frazier recover from Kennedy as a holder in due course? Discuss.

For a sample answer to this question, go to Appendix I at the end of this text.

26–4. Williams purchased a used car from Stein for $1,000. Williams paid for the car with a check (written in pencil) payable to Stein for $1,000. Stein, through careful erasures and alterations, changed the amount on the check to read $10,000 and negotiated the check to Boz. Boz took the check for value, in good faith, and without notice of the alteration and thus met the UCC requirements for the status of a holder in due course. Can Williams successfully raise the universal (real) defense of material alteration to avoid payment on the check? Explain.

26–5. Gil makes out a $900 negotiable promissory note payable to Ben. By special indorsement, Ben transfers the note for value to Jess. By blank indorsement, Jess transfers the note for value to Pam. By special indorsement, Pam transfers the note for value to Adrien. In need of cash, Adrien transfers the instrument for value by blank indorsement back to Jess. When told that Ben has left the country, Jess strikes out Ben's indorsement. Later she learns that Ben is a wealthy restaurant owner in Baltimore and that Gil is financially unable to pay the note. Jess contends that, as a holder in due course, she can hold Ben, Pam, or Adrien liable on the note. Discuss fully Jess's contentions.

26–6. DISCHARGE. Mary Ann McClusky and her husband, Curtis, borrowed $75,000 and signed a note payable to Francis and Thomas Gardner. As collateral, Mary Ann gave the Gardners a mortgage on a farm owned in her name only. After the McCluskys divorced, Mary Ann found, in a file in the basement of her house, the note with the word "Paid" written across it. When the Gardners refused to cancel the mortgage, she filed a suit in an Indiana state court against them. During the trial, she testified that she did not know how the note came to be in her basement or who wrote "Paid" across it. The Gardners testified that they had not surrendered it. Should the court presume that the note had been discharged, given that it was in Mary Ann's possession and had the word "Paid" written across it? Discuss. [*Gardner v. McClusky,* 647 N.E.2d 1 (Ind.App. 1995)]

26–7. ⚖ **CASE PROBLEM WITH SAMPLE ANSWER**

Ameripay, LLC, is a payroll services company that, among other things, issues payroll checks to the employees of its clients. In July 2002, Nu Tribe Radio Networks, Inc. (NTRN), based in New York City, hired Ameripay. Under their agreement, Ameripay set up an account on NTRN's behalf at Commerce Bank. NTRN agreed to deposit funds in the account to cover its payroll obligations. Arthur Piacentini, an owner of Ameripay, was an authorized signatory on the account. On the checks, NTRN was the only identified company, and Piacentini's signature appeared without indicating his status. At the end of the month, four NTRN employees cashed their payroll checks, which Piacentini had signed, at A-1 Check Cashing Emporium, Inc. The checks were returned dishonored. Ameripay had stopped their payment because it had not received the funds from NTRN. A-1 assigned its interest in the checks to Robert Triffin, who filed a suit in a New Jersey state court against Ameripay. What principles determine who, between a principal and an agent, is liable for the amount of an unpaid instrument? How do those principles apply in this case? Is Ameripay liable? Why or why not? [*Triffin v. Ameripay, LLC,* 368 N.J.Super. 587, 847 A.2d 628 (App.Div. 2004)]

To view a sample answer for this case problem, go to this book's Web site at http://wbl.westbuslaw.com, select "Chapter 26," and click on "Case Problem with Sample Answer."

26–8. UNAUTHORIZED INDORSEMENTS. Telemedia Publications, Inc., publishes *Cablecast* magazine, a weekly guide to the listings of the cable television programming in Baton Rouge, Louisiana. Cablecast hired Jennifer Pennington as a temporary employee. Pennington's duties included indorsing subscription checks received in the mail with the Cablecast deposit stamp, preparing the deposit slip, and taking the checks to be deposited to City National Bank. John McGregor, the manager of Cablecast, soon noticed shortages in revenues coming into Cablecast. When he learned that Pennington had taken checks payable to Cablecast and deposited them into her personal account at Premier Bank, N.A., he confronted her. She admitted to taking $7,913.04 in Cablecast checks. Cablecast filed a suit in a Louisiana state court against Premier Bank. The bank responded in part that Cablecast was solely responsible for losses caused by the fraudulent indorsements of its employees. At trial, Cablecast failed to prove that Premier Bank had not acted in good faith or that it had not exercised ordinary care in its handling of the checks. What rule should the court apply here? Why? [*Cablecast Magazine v. Premier Bank, N.A.,* 729 So.2d 1165 (La.App. 1 Cir. 1999)]

26–9. AGENTS' SIGNATURES. Robert Helmer and Percy Helmer, Jr., were authorized signatories on the corporate checking account of Event Marketing, Inc. The Helmers signed a check drawn on Event Marketing's account and issued to Rumarson Technologies, Inc. (RTI), in the amount of $24,965. The check was signed on July 13, 1998, but dated August 14. When RTI presented the check for payment, it was dishonored due to insufficient funds. RTI filed a suit in a Georgia state court against the Helmers to collect the amount of the check. Claiming that the Helmers were personally liable on Event Marketing's check, RTI filed a motion for summary judgment. Can an authorized signatory on a corporate account be held personally liable for corporate checks returned for insufficient funds? Are the Helmers liable in this case? Discuss. [*Helmer v. Rumarson Technologies, Inc.,* 538 S.E.2d 504 (Ga.App. 2000)]

26–10. DEFENSES. On September 13, 1979, Barbara Shearer and Barbara Couvion signed a note for $22,500, with interest at 11 percent, payable in monthly installments of $232.25 to Edgar House and Paul Cook. House and Cook assigned the note to Southside Bank in Kansas City, Missouri. In 1997, the note was assigned to Midstates Resources Corp., which assigned the note to The Cadle Co. in 2000. According to the payment history that Midstates gave to Cadle, the interest rate on the note was 12 percent. A Cadle employee noticed the discrepancy and recalculated the payments at 11 percent. When Shearer and Couvion refused to make further payments on the note, Cadle filed a suit in a Missouri state court against them to collect. Couvion and Shearer responded that they had made timely payments on the note, that Cadle and the previous holders had failed to accurately apply the payments to the reduction of principal and interest, and that the note "is either paid in full and satisfied or very close to being paid in full and satisfied." Is the makers' answer sufficient to support a verdict in their favor? If so, on what ground? If not, why not? [*The Cadle Co. v. Shearer*, 69 S.W.3d 122 (Mo.App. W.D. 2002)]

LAW | on the Web

For updated links to resources available on the Web, as well as a variety of other materials, visit this text's Web site at **http://wbl.westbuslaw.com**.

To find information on the UCC, including the Article 3 provisions discussed in this chapter, refer to the Web sites listed in the *Law on the Web* section in Chapter 24.

LEGAL RESEARCH EXERCISES ON THE WEB

Go to **http://wbl.westbuslaw.com**, the Web site that accompanies this text. Select "Chapter 26" and click on "Internet Exercises." There you will find the following Internet research exercises that you can perform to learn more about topics covered in this chapter.

Activity 26–1: **LEGAL PERSPECTIVE**
Fictitious Payees

Activity 26–2: **MANAGEMENT PERSPECTIVE**
FTC Rule 433

CHAPTER 27

Checks, the Banking System, and E-Money

Checks are the most common type of negotiable instruments governed by the Uniform Commercial Code (UCC). Issues relating to checks are governed by Article 3 and Article 4 of the UCC. As noted in the preceding chapters, Article 3 establishes the requirements that all negotiable instruments, including checks, must meet. Article 3 also sets forth the rights and responsibilities of parties to negotiable instruments. Article 4 establishes a framework for deposit and checking agreements between a bank and its customers. Article 4 also governs the relationships of banks with one another as they process checks for payment. A check therefore may fall within the scope of Article 3 and yet be subject to the provisions of Article 4 while in the course of collection. If a conflict arises between Article 3 and Article 4, Article 4 controls [UCC 4–102(a)].

In this chapter, we first identify the legal characteristics of checks and the legal duties and liabilities that arise when a check is issued. Then we examine the procedure by which checks deposited into bank accounts move through banking channels, causing the underlying cash dollars to be shifted from one bank account to another. Increasingly, credit cards, debit cards, and other devices and methods for transferring funds electronically are being used to pay for goods and services. In the latter part of this chapter, we look at the law governing electronic fund transfers.

SECTION 1 | Checks

A **check** is a special type of draft that is drawn on a bank, ordering the bank to pay a fixed amount of money on demand [UCC 3–104(f)]. Article 4 defines a *bank* as "a person engaged in the business of banking, including a savings bank, savings and loan association, credit union or trust company" [UCC 4–105(1)].[1] If any other nonbank institution (such as a brokerage firm) handles a check for payment or for collection, the check is not covered by Article 4.

Recall from the preceding chapters that a person who writes a check is called the *drawer*. The drawer is usually a depositor in the bank on which the check is drawn. The person to whom the check is payable is the *payee*. The bank or financial institution on which

the check is drawn is the *drawee*. If Anne Tomas writes a check from her checking account to pay her college tuition, she is the drawer, her bank is the drawee, and her college is the payee.

Between the time a check is drawn and the time it reaches the drawee, the effectiveness of the check may be altered by some event—for example, the drawer may die or order payment not to be made, or the account on which the check is drawn may be depleted. To avoid this problem, a payee may insist on payment by an instrument that has already been accepted by the drawee. Such an instrument may be a cashier's check, a traveler's check, or a certified check.

CASHIER'S CHECKS

Checks are usually three-party instruments, but on certain types of checks, the bank can serve as both the drawer and the drawee. For example, when a bank draws a check on itself, the check is called a **cashier's check** and is a negotiable instrument on issue (see Exhibit 27–1) [UCC 3–104(g)]. Normally, a cashier's check indicates a specific payee. In effect, with a cashier's check, the bank assumes responsibility for

---

1. The unrevised Article 4 does not define the term *bank*, except to distinguish among banks that deposit, collect, and pay instruments. The term was generally considered to include only commercial banks, which at the time the unrevised Article 4 was written were the only banks that could offer checking accounts. Revised Article 4's definition makes it clear that other depositary institutions now have the authority to issue and otherwise deal with checks.

EXHIBIT 27-1 **A Cashier's Check**

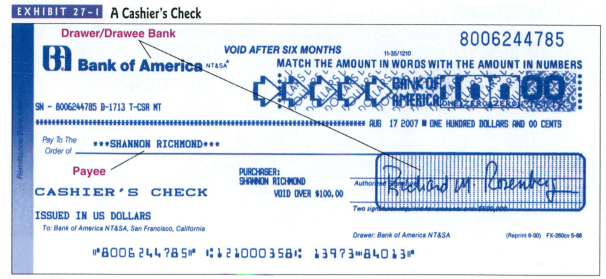

*The abbreviation *NT&SA* stands for National Trust and Savings Association. The Bank of America NT&SA is a subsidiary of BankAmerica Corporation, which is engaged in financial services, insurance, investment management, and other businesses.

paying the check, thus making the check more readily acceptable in commerce.

For example, Blake needs to pay a moving company $7,000 for moving his household goods to a new home in another state. The moving company requests payment in the form of a cashier's check. Blake goes to a bank (he need not have an account at the bank) and purchases a cashier's check, payable to the moving company, in the amount of $7,000. Blake has to pay the bank the $7,000 for the check, plus a small service fee. He then gives the check to the moving company.

Cashier's checks are sometimes used in the business community as nearly the equivalent of cash. Except in very limited circumstances, the issuing bank must honor its cashier's checks when they are presented for payment. If a bank wrongfully dishonors a cashier's check, a holder can recover from the bank all expenses incurred, interest, and consequential damages [UCC 3–411]. This same rule applies if a bank wrongfully dishonors a certified check (to be discussed shortly) or a teller's check. (A **teller's check** is usually drawn by a bank on another bank; when drawn on a nonbank, it is payable at or through a bank [UCC 3–104(h)].)

TRAVELER'S CHECKS

A **traveler's check** is an instrument that is payable on demand, drawn on or payable at a bank, and designated as a traveler's check. The issuing institution is directly obligated to accept and pay its traveler's check accord-

ing to the check's terms. The purchaser is required to sign the check at the time it is purchased and again at the time it is used [UCC 3–104(i)]. Most major banks today do not issue traveler's checks; rather, they purchase and issue American Express traveler's checks for their customers (see Exhibit 27–2 on the next page).

CERTIFIED CHECKS

A **certified check** is a check that has been drawn by a depositor and then *accepted* by the bank on which it is drawn [UCC 3–409(d)]. When a drawee bank agrees to certify a check, it immediately charges the drawer's account with the amount of the check and transfers those funds to its own certified-check account. In effect, the bank is agreeing in advance to accept that check when it is presented for payment and to make payment from those funds reserved in the certified-check account. Essentially, certification prevents the bank from denying liability. It is a promise that sufficient funds are on deposit and *have been set aside* to cover the check.

A drawee bank is not obligated to certify a check, and failure to do so is not a dishonor of the check [UCC 3–409(d)]. If a bank does certify a check, however, the bank should write on the check the amount that it will pay. If the certification does not state an amount, and the amount is later fraudulently increased and the instrument negotiated to a holder in due course (HDC), the obligation of the certifying

EXHIBIT 27-2 An American Express Traveler's Check

bank is the amount of the instrument when it was taken by the HDC [UCC 3–413(b)]. If a certifying bank wrongfully refuses to pay a certified check, "the person asserting the right to enforce the check is entitled to compensation for expenses and loss of interest" and may also recover consequential damages [UCC 3–411(b)].

Certification may be requested by a holder (to ensure that the check will not be dishonored for insufficient funds) or by the drawer. In either circumstance, on certification the drawer and any prior indorsers are completely discharged from liability on the instrument [UCC 3–414(c), 3–415(d)].[2]

LOST, DESTROYED, OR STOLEN CASHIER'S, TELLER'S, AND CERTIFIED CHECKS

What happens if a cashier's, teller's, or certified check is lost? Under UCC 3–312, the **remitter** (the check's purchaser) or the payee of a cashier's check or a teller's check—and the drawer of a certified check—can obtain a refund of the amount of the check from the bank by asking for it before the check is paid. The

bank may require that the claimant provide reasonable identification.[3]

The claim becomes enforceable ninety days after the date of the check [UCC 3–312(b)(1)]. If a person entitled to enforce the check presents it for payment within that ninety days and the bank pays, the bank is discharged [UCC 3–312(b)(2)]. If the claim becomes enforceable and no one entitled to enforce the check has presented it for payment, the bank's refund to the claimant discharges the bank—even if the claim was false [UCC 3–312(b)(4)]. (This is because a person who asks for a refund warrants to the bank, and to anybody else who might have a right to enforce the check, that the check was in fact lost, stolen, or destroyed. If it was not lost, stolen, or destroyed, a holder who cannot obtain payment on the check can sue the claimant for breach of warranty.)

SECTION **2** | The Bank-Customer Relationship

The bank-customer relationship begins when the customer opens a checking account and deposits funds that the bank will use to pay for checks written by the customer. The rights and duties of the bank and the customer are contractual and depend on the nature of

---

2. Under Section 3–411 of the unrevised Article 3, the legal liability of a drawer varies according to whether certification is requested by the drawer or a holder. The drawer who obtains certification remains secondarily liable on the instrument if the certifying bank does not honor the check when it is presented for payment. If the check is certified at the request of a holder, the drawer and anyone who indorses the check before certification are completely discharged.

3. The bank cannot require that the claimant post a bond. Under UCC 3–309, however, a court can refuse to enter a judgment in favor of a person seeking enforcement unless it finds that the person required to pay the instrument is "adequately protected" against a claim by another person to enforce the instrument.

the transaction. Essentially, three types of relationships come into being, as discussed next.

CREDITOR-DEBTOR RELATIONSHIP

A creditor-debtor relationship is created between a customer and a bank when, for example, the customer makes cash deposits into a checking account. When a customer makes a deposit, the customer becomes a creditor, and the bank a debtor, for the amount deposited.

AGENCY RELATIONSHIP

An agency relationship also arises between the customer and the bank when the customer writes a check on his or her account. In effect, the customer is ordering the bank to pay the amount specified on the check to the holder when the holder presents the check to the bank for payment. In this situation, the bank becomes the customer's agent and is obligated to honor the customer's request. Similarly, if the customer deposits a check into his or her account, the bank, as the customer's agent, is obligated to collect payment on the check from the bank on which the check was drawn. To transfer checkbook dollars among different banks, each bank acts as the collection agent for its customer [UCC 4–201(a)].

CONTRACTUAL RELATIONSHIP

Whenever a bank-customer relationship is established, certain contractual rights and duties arise. The rights and duties of the bank and the customer are contractual and depend on the nature of the transaction. The respective rights and duties of banks and their customers are discussed in detail in the following pages.

SECTION 3 | Honoring Checks

When a banking institution provides checking services, it agrees to honor the checks written by its customers, with the usual stipulation that sufficient funds must be available in the account to pay each check. When a drawee bank *wrongfully* fails to honor a check, it is liable to its customer for damages resulting from its refusal to pay. The UCC does not attempt to specify the theory under which the customer may recover for wrongful dishonor; it merely states that the drawee is liable [UCC 4–402(b)].

The customer's agreement with the bank includes a general obligation to keep sufficient funds on deposit to cover all checks written. The customer is liable to the payee or to the holder of a check in a civil suit if a check is not honored. If intent to defraud can be proved, the customer can also be subject to criminal prosecution for writing a bad check.

When the bank properly dishonors a check for insufficient funds, it has no liability to the customer. The bank may rightfully refuse payment on a customer's check in other circumstances as well. We look here at the rights and duties of both the bank and its customers in relation to specific situations.

OVERDRAFTS

When the bank receives an item properly payable from its customer's checking account but the account contains insufficient funds to cover the amount of the check, the bank has two options. It can either (1) dishonor the item or (2) pay the item and charge the customer's account, thus creating an **overdraft,** providing that the customer has authorized the payment and the payment does not violate any bank-customer agreement [UCC 4–401(a)].[4] The bank can subtract the difference from the customer's next deposit because the check carries with it an enforceable implied promise to reimburse the bank.

When a check "bounces," a holder can resubmit the check, hoping that at a later date sufficient funds will be available to pay it. The holder must notify any indorsers on the check of the first dishonor, however; otherwise, they will be discharged from their signature liability, as discussed in Chapter 26.

A bank can expressly agree with a customer to accept overdrafts through what is sometimes called an "overdraft protection agreement." If such an agreement is formed, any failure of the bank to honor a check because it would create an overdraft breaches this agreement and is treated as wrongful dishonor [UCC 4–402(a), (b)].

POSTDATED CHECKS

A bank may also charge a postdated check against a customer's account, unless the customer notifies the

---

4. With a joint account, the bank cannot hold any joint-account customer liable for payment of an overdraft unless the customer has signed the check or has benefited from the proceeds of the check [UCC 4–401(b)].

bank, in a timely manner, not to pay the check until the stated date. The notice of postdating must be given in time to allow the bank to act on the notice before committing itself to pay on the check. The UCC states that the bank should treat the notice like a stop-payment order (to be discussed shortly). If the bank fails to act on the customer's notice and charges the customer's account before the date on the post-dated check, the bank may be liable for any damages incurred by the customer. Damages include those that result from the dishonor of checks that are subsequently presented for payment and are dishonored for insufficient funds [UCC 4–401(c)].

STALE CHECKS

Commercial banking practice regards a check that is presented for payment more than six months from its date as a **stale check.** A bank is not obligated to pay an uncertified check presented more than six months from its date [UCC 4–404]. When receiving a stale check for payment, the bank has the option of paying or not paying the check. If a bank pays a stale check in good faith without consulting the customer, the bank has the right to charge the customer's account for the amount of the check.

DEATH OR INCOMPETENCE OF A CUSTOMER

Neither death nor incompetence revokes the bank's authority to pay an item until the bank knows of the situation and has had reasonable time to act on the notice [UCC 4–405]. Thus, if, at the time a check is issued or its collection has been undertaken, a bank does not know that the customer who wrote the check has been declared incompetent, the item can be paid and the bank will not incur liability. Even when a bank knows of the death of its customer, for ten days after the *date of death* it can pay or certify checks drawn on or before the date of death. An exception to this rule is made if a person claiming an interest in that account, such as an heir or an executor of the estate (see Chapter 50), orders the bank to stop payment. Without this provision, banks would constantly be required to verify the continued life and competence of their drawers.

STOP-PAYMENT ORDERS

A **stop-payment order** is an order by a customer to her or his bank not to pay a certain check.[5] Only a customer or a "person authorized to draw on the account" can order the bank not to pay the check when it is presented for payment [UCC 4–403(a)]. A customer has no right to stop payment on a check that has already been certified (or accepted) by a bank, however. Also, a stop-payment order must be received within a reasonable time and in a reasonable manner to permit the bank to act on it [UCC 4–403(a)]. Although a stop-payment order can be given orally, usually by phone, the order is binding on the bank for only fourteen calendar days unless confirmed in writing.[6] A written stop-payment order (see Exhibit 27–3) or an oral order confirmed in writing is effective for six months, at which time it must be renewed in writing [UCC 4–403(b)].

BANK'S LIABILITY FOR WRONGFUL PAYMENT If the bank pays the check over the customer's properly instituted stop-payment order, the bank will be obligated to recredit the customer's account, but only to the extent of the actual loss suffered by the drawer because of the wrongful payment [UCC 4–403(c)].

Assume that Toshio Murano orders one hundred cellular telephones from Advanced Communications, Inc., at $50 each. Murano pays in advance for the phones with a check for $5,000. Later that day, Advanced Communications tells Murano that it will not deliver the phones as arranged. Murano immediately calls the bank and stops payment on the check. Two days later, in spite of this stop-payment order, the bank inadvertently honors Murano's check to Advanced Communications for the undelivered phones. The bank will be liable to Murano for the full $5,000.

The result would be different, however, if Advanced Communications had delivered and Murano had accepted ninety-nine phones. Because Murano would have owed Advanced Communications $4,950 for the goods delivered, Murano's actual loss would be only

---

5. Note that although this discussion is focused on checks, the right to stop payment is not limited to checks; it extends to any item payable by any bank. See Official Comment 3 to UCC 4–403.

6. Some states do not recognize oral stop-payment orders; the orders must be in writing.

EXHIBIT 27–3 **A Stop-Payment Order**

BankAmerica Bank of America

Checking Account Stop-Payment Order

To: Bank of America NT&SA
I want to stop payment on the following check(s).

ACCOUNT NUMBER: ☐☐☐☐☐☐ — ☐☐☐☐☐☐☐

SPECIFIC STOP

*ENTER DOLLAR AMOUNT: _____ *CHECK NUMBER: _____

THE CHECK WAS SIGNED BY: _____

THE CHECK IS PAYABLE TO: _____

THE REASON FOR THIS STOP PAYMENT IS: _____

STOP RANGE (Use for lost or stolen check(s) only.)

DOLLAR AMOUNT: 000

*ENTER STARTING CHECK NUMBER: _____   *END CHECK NUMBER: _____

THE REASON FOR THIS STOP PAYMENT IS: _____

I agree that this order (1) is effective only if the above check(s) has (have) not yet been cashed or paid against my account, (2) will end six months from the date it is delivered to you unless I renew it in writing, and (3) is not valid if the check(s) was (were) accepted on the strength of my Bank of America courtesy-check guarantee card by a merchant participating in that program. I also agree (1) to notify you immediately to cancel this order if the reason for the stop payment no longer exists or (2) that closing the account on which the check(s) is (are) drawn automatically cancels this order.

IF ANOTHER BRANCH OF THIS BANK OR ANOTHER PERSON OR ENTITY BECOMES A "HOLDER IN DUE COURSE" OF THE ABOVE CHECK, I UNDERSTAND THAT PAYMENT MAY BE ENFORCED AGAINST THE CHECK'S MAKER (SIGNER).

*I CERTIFY THE AMOUNT AND CHECK NUMBER(S) ABOVE ARE CORRECT.
☐ I have written a replacement check (number and date of check).

(Optional—please circle one: Mr., Ms., Mrs., Miss) CUSTOMER'S SIGNATURE **X** _____ DATE _____

BANK USE ONLY

TRANCODE:
☐ 21—ENTER STOP PAYMENT (SEE OTHER SIDE TO REMOVE)

NON READS: _____
UNPROC. STMT HIST: _____
PRIOR STMT CYCLE: _____
HOLDS ON COOLS: _____
REJECTED CHKS: _____
LARGE ITEMS: _____
FEE COLLECTED: _____
DATE ACCEPTED: _____
TIME ACCEPTED: _____

$50. Consequently, the bank would be liable to Murano for only $50.

CUSTOMER'S LIABILITY FOR WRONGFUL STOP-PAYMENT ORDER A stop-payment order has its risks for a customer. The drawer must have a *valid legal ground* for issuing such an order; otherwise, the holder can sue the drawer for payment. Moreover, defenses sufficient to refuse payment against a payee may not be valid grounds to prevent payment against a subsequent holder in due course [UCC 3–305, 3–306]. A person who wrongfully stops payment on a check not only will be liable to the payee for the amount of the check but also may be liable for consequential damages incurred by the payee as a result of the wrongful stop-payment order.

CHECKS BEARING FORGED SIGNATURES

When a bank pays a check on which the drawer's signature is forged, generally the bank suffers the loss.[7] A

bank may be able to recover at least some of the amount of the loss, however, from a customer whose negligence substantially contributed to the forgery, from the forger of the check, or from a holder who presented the check for payment (if the holder knew that the signature was forged).

THE GENERAL RULE A forged signature on a check has no legal effect as the signature of a drawer [UCC 3–403(a)]. For this reason, banks require a signature card from each customer who opens a checking account so that the bank can determine whether the signature on a customer's check is genuine. The general rule is that the bank must recredit the customer's account when it pays on a forged signature. (Note that banks today normally verify signatures only on checks that exceed a certain threshold, such as $1,000, $2,500, or some higher amount. Even though a bank sometimes incurs liability costs when it has paid forged checks, the costs involved in verifying the signature on every check would be much higher.)

Note that a bank may contractually shift to the customer the risk of forged checks created by the use of facsimile or other nonmanual signatures. For example, the contract might stipulate that the customer is solely

---

7. Each year, check fraud costs banks many billions of dollars— more than the combined losses from credit-card fraud, theft from automated teller machines, and armed robberies.

responsible for maintaining security over any device affixing a signature. The contract might also provide that any nonmanual signature is effective as the customer's signature regardless of whether the person who affixed the signature was authorized to do so.[8]

CUSTOMER NEGLIGENCE When a customer's negligence substantially contributes to a forgery, the bank normally will not be obligated to recredit the customer's account for the amount of the check [UCC 3–406(a)]. A customer's liability may be reduced, however, by the amount of a loss caused by negligence on the part of a bank (or other "person") paying the instrument or taking it for value or for collection if the negligence substantially contributes to the loss [UCC 3–406(b)].[9]

Suppose that CompuNet, Inc., uses a check-writing machine to write its payroll and business checks. A CompuNet employee uses the machine to create himself a check for $10,000, and CompuNet's bank subsequently honors it. CompuNet requests the bank to recredit $10,000 to its account for incorrectly paying on a forged check. If the bank can show that CompuNet failed to take reasonable care in controlling access to the check-writing equipment, the bank will not be required to recredit its account for the amount of the forged check. If CompuNet can show that negligence on the part of the bank (or another person) contributed substantially to the loss, however, then CompuNet's liability may be reduced proportionately.

In the following case, a bank that had paid a forged check claimed that the account holder's negligence had contributed to the forgery. Specifically, the bank alleged that the account holder had failed to exercise ordinary care to prevent his wife from forging a check on the account.

---

8. *Lor-Mar/Toto, Inc. v. 1st Constitution Bank*, 871 A.2d 110 (N.J. Super. 2005).
9. The unrevised Article 3 does not include a similar provision.

CASE 27.1   **Nesper v. Bank of America**

Court of Appeals
of Ohio, Sixth District,
Ottawa County, 2004.
__ Ohio App.3d __,
__ N.E.2d __.

BACKGROUND AND FACTS *Robert Nesper knew his wife, Patricia Nesper, had engaged in financial misconduct both before and during their marriage. The misconduct included forging Robert's name on applications for credit cards and a contract to buy a vehicle. The couple continued to live together, but Robert kept a bank account solely in his name at Bank of America. He kept the unused checks for the account hidden in their house in a room that could be locked, although the room was not kept locked all of the time. In early 2002, he became aware that Patricia had forged his name to the account's check number 275 in the amount of $2,000. Robert filed a suit in an Ohio state court against the bank, seeking the return of the $2,000 to his account. Robert argued that banks have a responsibility to refuse to honor forged checks, regardless of the marital status of the forger. The court ruled in Robert's favor. The bank appealed to a state intermediate appellate court.*

IN THE LANGUAGE OF THE COURT
KNEPPER, J. [Judge]
* * * *
* * * Bank of America argues that the trial court ignored evidence of appellee's [Robert's] negligence, as well as evidence that appellee ratified his wife's forgery. Bank of America further argues that * * * allowing appellee to recover in this case would cause banks to be reluctant to cash any checks between a husband and wife "because of the potential problem of abuse."
* * * *
* * * [A] check that bears a forged drawer's signature is not properly payable and, if the bank pays a check under such circumstances, the bank is generally liable to its customer. Nevertheless, Bank of America seeks to show that appellee should be held responsible for his wife's forgery pursuant to [Revised Code (R.C.)] Section 1303.49 [Ohio's version of UCC 3–406(a)] which states, in relevant part, that:

"(A) A person whose failure to exercise ordinary care substantially contributes to an alteration of an instrument or to the making of a forged signature on an instrument is precluded from asserting the

CASE 27.1 Continued

alteration or the forgery against a person who, in good faith, pays the instrument or takes it for value or for collection. * * * "

* * * *

The relationship between a bank and its customer is based on both statutory and contractual principles. The definition of "ordinary care" on the part of a bank is statutorily defined in R.C. Section 1303.01(A)(9) [UCC 3–103(7)] as the observance of "reasonable commercial standards that are prevailing in the area * * * ." In contrast, "ordinary care" on the part of a bank's customer, while not statutorily defined, has been described by Ohio courts as the duty of the customer to perform his or her obligations to the bank with care, skill, reasonable expedience, and faithfulness * * * . This duty has been applied in cases where a party who has notice that his signature has been forged in the past is negligent in failing to prevent further forgeries by the same person.

In addition to its statutory remedies, Bank of America seeks to invoke the common-law defense of ratification. *Ratification occurs when a party, by his conduct, affirms a prior act which did not bind him but which was done or professedly done on his account whereby the act, * * * is given effect as if it was originally authorized by him.* Affirmance can be established by showing that the party had knowledge of the facts and manifested his intent to approve the transaction. [Emphasis added.]

As to the issue of ordinary care, the record demonstrates that appellee knew his wife was capable of financial misconduct, including forgery. The record also shows that appellee attempted to keep his wife from having access to his checkbooks by keeping them hidden in a room that was usually, although not always, locked. * * * Mrs. Nesper refused to respond when she was confronted * * * about the forgery. The record contains no evidence as to how Mrs. Nesper actually obtained the blank checks.

As to the issue of ratification, Bank of America directs our attention to that portion of the record which shows that appellee unsuccessfully attempted to discuss the forgery with his wife. The rest of the record shows that appellee notified [the bank] and the police of his wife's actions, filled out police reports, and filed the complaint herein seeking return of his funds. * * *

This court has reviewed the entire record of proceedings in this case and, upon consideration thereof, we cannot say that the trial court abused its discretion by finding that the record contains insufficient evidence to show that appellee's failure to exercise ordinary care substantially contributed to the forging of his signature on check no. 275, or by not finding that appellee ratified his wife's forgery. * * *

The judgment of the [lower court] is affirmed.

DECISION AND REMEDY *The state intermediate appellate court affirmed the judgment of the lower court. The bank failed to successfully prove that Robert had not exercised ordinary care with respect to Patricia's forgery of his signature on check number 275. Consequently, the bank was obliged to recredit its customer's account for the amount of the check.*

WHAT IF THE FACTS WERE DIFFERENT? *If the bank had shown that Robert had failed to take reasonable care in controlling access to the blank checks for his account, would the outcome in this case have been different? Why or why not?*

—Timely Examination of Bank Statements Required. Banks typically send or make available to their customers monthly statements detailing the activity of the customers' checking accounts. Banks are not obligated to include the original canceled checks themselves with the statement sent to the customer. If the bank does not send the original canceled checks, however, it must provide the customer with information (check number, amount, and date of payment) on the statement that will allow the customer to reasonably identify each check that the bank has paid [UCC 4–406(a), (b)]. Sometimes, banks send photocopies of the canceled checks with the statement. If the bank retains the canceled checks, it must keep the checks— or legible copies of them—for seven years [UCC 4–406(b)]. The customer may obtain a canceled check (or a copy of the check) from the bank during this time period.

The customer has a duty to examine bank statements (and canceled checks or photocopies, if they are included with the statements) promptly and with reasonable care when the statements are received or made available, and to report any alterations or forged signatures promptly [UCC 4–406(c)]. This includes forged signatures of indorsers (to be discussed later). If the customer fails to fulfill this duty and the bank suffers a loss as a result, the customer will be liable for the loss [UCC 4–406(d)]. Even if the customer can prove that he or she took reasonable care against forgeries, the UCC provides that the customer must discover the forgeries and give notice to the bank within a specific time frame in order to require the bank to recredit his or her account.

—Consequences of Failing to Detect Forgeries. When a series of forgeries by the same wrongdoer has taken place, the UCC provides that the customer, to recover for all of the forged items, must have discovered and reported the first forged check to the bank within thirty calendar days of the receipt or availability of the bank statement (and canceled checks or copies, if they are included) [UCC 4–406(d)(2)]. Failure to notify the bank within this time period discharges the bank's liability for all forged checks that it pays prior to notification. In the following case, the court was asked to apply this rule.

CASE 27.2

Court of Appeal
of California,
First District,
Division 1, 2002.
100 Cal.App.4th 525,
124 Cal.Rptr.2d 549.

Espresso Roma Corp. v. Bank of America, N.A.

BACKGROUND AND FACTS *Espresso Roma Corporation is a privately held company that owns a chain of coffeehouses as well as a number of other businesses and real properties (including university dormitories). David Boyd is the president of Espresso Roma and runs Hillside Residence Hall on the Berkeley campus of the University of California. Espresso Roma and the other businesses had checking accounts with Bank of America, N.A. All of the businesses employed Joseph Montanez, whose duties included bookkeeping. As an employee, Montanez learned how to generate company checks on the computer and had access to blank company checks. In October 1997, Montanez began to steal blank checks and, using stolen company computer programs, to print company checks on his home computer. He forged the checks in amounts totaling more than $330,000. When the bank statements containing the forged checks arrived in the mail, Montanez sorted through the statements and removed the checks. Boyd discovered the forgeries and reported them to the bank in May 1999. Boyd and the businesses filed a suit in a California state court against the bank, alleging, among other things, unauthorized payment of the checks. The bank filed a motion for summary judgment in its favor, in part on the ground that UCC 4–406(d) precluded the claims. The court granted the motion, and the plaintiffs appealed to a state intermediate appellate court.*

IN THE LANGUAGE OF THE COURT

STEIN, Acting P.J. [Presiding Judge]
* * * *

Pursuant to [UCC 4–406(d)] the customer is precluded from making a claim against the bank for unauthorized payment unless the customer notified the bank no more than 30 days after the *first* forged item was included in the monthly statement or canceled checks and should have been discovered.

According to the complaint, the forged checks were presented for payment between October 1997, and May 1999, but appellants [Boyd and the businesses] did not discover, or report them until on, or about, May 15, 1999. To establish its [contention] that * * * [UCC 4–406(d)] applied, the Bank presented the deposition testimony of Boyd, that it made monthly account statements and canceled checks available to appellants shortly after the closing period of each statement. Boyd testified that he received statements on a monthly basis, and they included canceled checks. When Boyd began to suspect unauthorized checks were being written and reviewed the statements and checks in May 1999, he was able to identify, and reported, the forgery. This evidence supports the inference that the first monthly

CASE 27.2 | Continued

statement that would have reflected the forgery by Montanez would have been in November 1997. Yet, despite having the means to discover the forgeries, more than a year and a half elapsed before appellants discovered and reported any of them, far beyond the 30 days specified in [UCC 4–406(d)].

Appellants argue * * * that Boyd's testimony did not support the Bank's assertion that it made monthly checks or statements available because Boyd also testified that there were some instances in which the statements or checks did not arrive through the mail in a timely fashion. Boyd, however, acknowledged that when this occurred he was able to pick up the statement, or a duplicate at the [Bank]. Nothing in Boyd's testimony contradicts the Bank's assertion that it made monthly statements available to appellants in accordance with [UCC 4–406(a)]. * * *

Appellants also suggest that the Bank was required to establish, with respect to *each forged check*, exactly *when* it made the monthly statement including the forged check available, thereby providing the means by which appellants should have discovered the forgery, and triggering the 30-day notification period. To the contrary, *where as here, the forgeries are all committed by the same person, it is the failure to report the first forged item within 30 days that precludes the customer from asserting the subsequent forgeries.* Regardless of the exact date the first monthly statement after October 1997 was made available to appellant, the evidence the Bank submitted established that it made statements and checks available on a monthly basis, yet the first forgery was not reported until mid-May 1999, long after the 30-day period expired. [Emphasis added.]

DECISION AND REMEDY *The state intermediate appellate court affirmed the judgment of the lower court. Because the bank's customers did not report the first forged check to the bank within the thirty-day period of UCC 4–406(d), the bank's liability for payment of the checks was discharged.*

—When the Bank Is Also Negligent. There is one situation in which a bank customer can escape liability, at least in part, for failing to notify the bank of forged or altered checks within the required thirty-day period. If the customer can prove that the bank was also negligent—that is, that the bank failed to exercise ordinary care—then the bank will also be liable, and the loss will be allocated between the bank and the customer on the basis of comparative negligence [UCC 4–406(e)]. In other words, even though a customer may have been negligent, the bank may still have to recredit the customer's account for a portion of the loss if the bank failed to exercise ordinary care.

Section 3–103(a)(7) of the UCC defines *ordinary care* to mean the "observance of reasonable commercial standards, prevailing in the area in which [a] person is located, with respect to the business in which that person is engaged." As mentioned earlier, it is customary in the banking industry to manually examine signatures only on checks over a certain amount (such as $1,000, $2,500, or some higher amount). Thus, if a bank, in accordance with prevailing banking standards, fails to examine a signature on a particular check, the bank may or may not have breached its duty to exercise ordinary care.[10]

Regardless of the degree of care exercised by the customer or the bank, the UCC places an absolute time limit on the liability of a bank for paying a check with a forged customer signature. A customer who fails to report her or his forged signature within one year from the date that the statement was made available for inspection loses the legal right to have the bank recredit her or his account [UCC 4–406(f)].

OTHER PARTIES FROM WHOM THE BANK MAY RECOVER As noted earlier, a forged signature on a check has no legal effect as the signature of a drawer; a forged signature, however, is effective as the signature of the unauthorized signer [UCC 3–403(a)]. Therefore, when a bank pays a check on which the

---

10. Prior to the 1990 revision of Article 3, courts differed in their interpretation of what constituted ordinary care on the part of a bank. Some courts held that a bank had a duty to examine every signature on the checks it paid; other courts disagreed. The revised Article 3 put an end to the problem by clarifying the meaning of ordinary care in the context of today's banking system.

drawer's signature is forged, the bank has a right to recover from the party who forged the signature.

The bank may also have a right to recover from a party (its customer or a collecting bank) who transferred a check bearing a forged drawer's signature and received a settlement. A customer or collecting bank guarantees that "all signatures on the item are authentic and authorized" [UCC 4–207(a)(2)]. If a drawee bank pays or accepts a check in the mistaken belief that the drawer's signature was authorized, the bank may recover the amount of the check from "the person to whom or for whose benefit payment was made" [UCC 3–418(a)(ii)].

This right is limited, however. A drawee bank cannot recover from "a person who took the instrument in good faith and for value or who in good faith changed position in reliance on the payment or acceptance" [UCC 3–418(c)]. This means that, in most circumstances, a drawee bank will not recover from the person paid because usually that person took the check in good faith and for value or in good faith changed position in reliance on the payment or acceptance.

Checks Bearing Forged Indorsements

A bank that pays a customer's check bearing a forged indorsement must recredit the customer's account or be liable to the customer (drawer) for breach of contract. Suppose that Carlo issues a $500 check "to the order of Sophia." Marcello steals the check, forges Sophia's indorsement, and cashes the check. When the check reaches Carlo's bank, the bank pays it and debits Carlo's account. The bank must recredit Carlo's account for the $500 because it failed to carry out Carlo's order to pay "to the order of Sophia" [UCC 4–401(a)]. (Carlo's bank will in turn recover—under the principles of breach of warranty—from the bank that cashed the check [UCC 4–207(a)(2)].)

Eventually, the loss usually falls on the first party to take the instrument bearing the forged indorsement because, as discussed in Chapter 26, a forged indorsement does not transfer title. Thus, whoever takes an instrument with a forged indorsement cannot become a holder.

The customer, in any event, has a duty to report forged indorsements promptly on discovery or notice. Failure to report forged indorsements within a three-year period after the forged items have been made

available to the customer relieves the bank of liability [UCC 4–111].[11]

Altered Checks

The customer's instruction to the bank is to pay the exact amount on the face of the check to the holder. The bank has an implicit duty to examine checks before making final payments. If it fails to detect an alteration, it is liable to its customer for the loss because it did not pay as the customer ordered. The loss is the difference between the original amount of the check and the amount actually paid. Suppose that a check written for $11 is raised to $111. The customer's account will be charged $11 (the amount the customer ordered the bank to pay). The bank will normally be responsible for the $100 [UCC 4–401(d)(1)].

CUSTOMER NEGLIGENCE   As in a situation involving a forged drawer's signature, a customer's negligence can shift the loss when payment is made on an altered check. A common example occurs when a person carelessly writes a check, leaving large gaps around the numbers and words so that additional numbers and words can be inserted (see Exhibit 27–4).

Similarly, a person who signs a check and leaves the dollar amount for someone else to fill in is barred from protesting when the bank unknowingly and in good faith pays whatever amount is shown [UCC 4–401(d)(2)]. Finally, if the bank can trace its loss on successive altered checks to the customer's failure to discover the initial alteration, then the bank can reduce its liability for reimbursing the customer's account [UCC 4–406].[12] The law governing the customer's duty to examine monthly statements and canceled checks, and to discover and report alterations to the bank, is the same as that applied to a forged drawer's signature.

---

11. The unrevised Article 4 limits this three-year period to the reporting of unauthorized indorsements. The revised Article 4 expands the limitation to cover any "action to enforce an obligation, duty, or right arising under this Article" [UCC 4–111]. In other words, under the revised Article 4, this is a general statute of limitations; it provides that any lawsuit must be begun within three years of the time that the cause of action takes place.

12. The bank's defense is the same whether the successive payments were made on a forged drawer's signature or on altered checks. The bank must prove that prompt notice would have prevented its loss. For example, notification might have alerted the bank not to pay further items or might have enabled it to catch the forger.

EXHIBIT 27-4 **A Poorly Filled-Out Check**

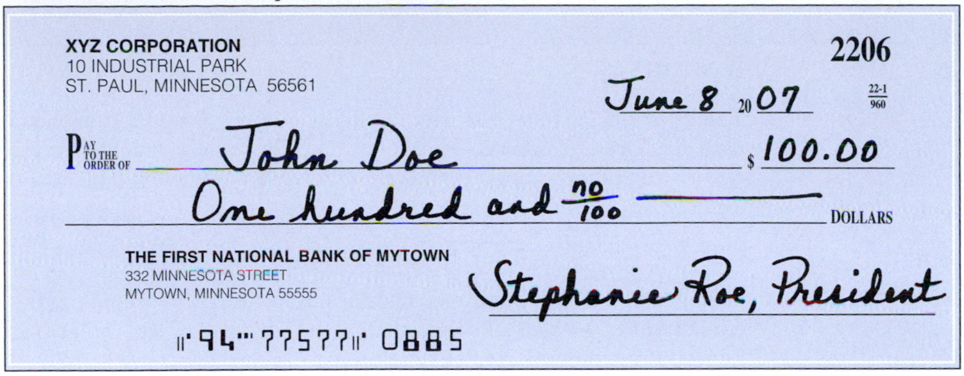

XYZ CORPORATION
10 INDUSTRIAL PARK
ST. PAUL, MINNESOTA 56561

2206

June 8 20 07   22-1/960

PAY TO THE ORDER OF   John Doe $ 100.00

One hundred and no/100 ————— DOLLARS

THE FIRST NATIONAL BANK OF MYTOWN
332 MINNESOTA STREET
MYTOWN, MINNESOTA 55555

Stephanie Roe, President

⑆94⑆77577⑆ 0885

In every situation involving a forged drawer's signature or an alteration, a bank must observe reasonable commercial standards of care in paying on a customer's checks [UCC 4–406(e)]. The customer's contributory negligence can be asserted only if the bank has exercised ordinary care.

OTHER PARTIES FROM WHOM THE BANK MAY RECOVER The bank is entitled to recover the amount of loss (including expenses and any loss of interest) from the transferor who, by presenting the check for payment, warrants that the check has not been altered.[13]

There are two exceptions dealing with accepted drafts, however. If the bank is the drawer (as it is on a cashier's check and a teller's check), it cannot recover on this ground from the presenting party if the party is a holder in due course (HDC) acting in good faith [UCC 3–417(a)(2), 4–208(a)(2)]. The reason is that an instrument's drawer is in a better position than an HDC to know whether the instrument has been altered.

Similarly, an HDC, acting in good faith in presenting a certified check for payment, does not warrant to the check's certifier that the check was not altered before the HDC acquired it [UCC 3–417(a)(2), 4–208(a)(2)]. Consider an example. Alan, the drawer, draws a check for $500 payable to Pam, the payee. Pam alters the amount to $5,000. The National City Bank, the drawee, certifies the check for $5,000. Pam

negotiates the check to Don, an HDC. The drawee bank pays Don $5,000. On discovering the mistake, the bank cannot recover from Don the $4,500 paid by mistake, even though the bank was not in a superior position to detect the alteration. This is in accord with the purpose of certification, which is to obtain the definite obligation of a bank to honor a definite instrument.

SECTION 4 | Accepting Deposits

A bank has a duty to its customer to accept the customer's deposits of cash and checks. When checks are deposited, the bank must make the funds represented by those checks available within certain time frames. A bank also has a duty to collect payment on any checks payable or indorsed to its customer and deposited by the customer into his or her account. Cash deposits made in U.S. currency are received into the customer's account without being subject to further collection procedures.

AVAILABILITY SCHEDULE FOR DEPOSITED CHECKS

The Expedited Funds Availability Act of 1987[14] and Regulation CC,[15] which was issued by the Federal Reserve Board of Governors (the Federal Reserve System will be discussed shortly) to implement the act, require that any local check deposited must be available for withdrawal by check or as cash within one

---

13. Usually, the party presenting an instrument for payment is the payee, a holder, a bank customer, or a collecting bank. A bank's customers include its account holders, which may include other banks [UCC 4–104(a)(5)]. As will be discussed later in this chapter, a collecting bank is any bank handling an item for collection except the bank on which the check is drawn [UCC 4–105(5)].

14. 12 U.S.C. Sections 4001–4010.

15. 12 C.F.R. Sections 229.1–229.42.

CONCEPT SUMMARY 27.1 | Honoring Checks

SITUATION	BASIC RULES
WRONGFUL DISHONOR [UCC 4–402]	The bank is liable to its customer for actual damages proved if it wrongfully dishonors a check due to mistake. Damages can include those proximately caused by subsequent arrest or prosecution of the drawer, as well as other consequential damages.
OVERDRAFT [UCC 4–401]	The bank has a right to charge a customer's account for any item properly payable, even if the charge results in an overdraft.
POSTDATED CHECK [UCC 4–401]	A bank may charge a postdated check against a customer's account, unless the customer notifies the bank of the postdating in time to allow the bank to act on the notice before the bank commits itself to pay on the check.
STALE CHECK [UCC 4–404]	The bank is not obligated to pay an uncertified check presented more than six months after its date, but the bank may do so in good faith without liability.
DEATH OR INCOMPETENCE OF A CUSTOMER [UCC 4–405]	So long as the bank does not know of the death or incompetence of a customer, the bank can pay an item without liability. Even with knowledge of a customer's death, a bank can honor or certify checks (in the absence of a stop-payment order) for ten days after the date of the customer's death.
STOP-PAYMENT ORDER [UCC 4–403]	The customer (or a "person authorized to draw on the account") must make a stop-payment order in time for the bank to have a reasonable opportunity to act. Oral orders are binding for only fourteen days unless they are confirmed in writing. Written orders are effective for only six months, unless renewed in writing. The bank is liable for wrongful payment over a timely stop-payment order to the extent that the customer suffers a loss. A customer has no right to stop payment on a certified check or an accepted draft and can be held liable for stopping payment on any check without a valid legal ground.
UNAUTHORIZED SIGNATURE OR ALTERATION [UCC 4–406]	The customer has a duty to examine account statements with reasonable care on receipt and to notify the bank promptly of any unauthorized signatures or alterations. On a series of unauthorized signatures or alterations by the same wrongdoer, examination and report must be made within thirty calendar days of receipt of the statement. Failure to comply releases the bank from liability unless the bank failed to exercise reasonable care, in which case liability may be apportioned according to a comparative negligence standard. Regardless of care or lack of care, the customer is *estopped* (prevented) from holding the bank liable after one year for unauthorized customer signatures or alterations and after three years for unauthorized indorsements.

business day from the date of deposit. A check is classified as a local check if the first bank to receive the check for payment and the bank on which the check is drawn are located in the same check-processing region (check-processing regions are designated by the Federal Reserve Board of Governors). For nonlocal checks, the funds must be available for withdrawal within not more than five business days.

ADDITIONAL REQUIREMENTS In addition to the above requirements, the Expedited Funds Availability Act requires the following:

1. That funds be available on the next business day for cash deposits and wire transfers, government checks, the first $100 of a day's check deposits, cashier's checks, certified checks, and checks for which the banks receiving and paying the checks are branches of the same institution.

2. That the first $100 of any deposit be available for cash withdrawal on the opening of the *next business day* after deposit. If a local check is deposited, the next $400 is to be available for withdrawal by no later than 5 P.M. the next business day. If, for example, you deposit a local check for $500 on Monday, you can withdraw $100 in cash at the opening of the business day on Tuesday, and an additional $400 must be available for withdrawal by no later than 5 P.M. on Wednesday.

EXCEPTIONS A different availability schedule applies to deposits made at *nonproprietary* automated teller machines (ATMs). These are ATMs that are not owned or operated by the bank receiving the deposits. Basically, a five-day hold is permitted on all deposits, including cash deposits, that are made at nonproprietary ATMs.

Other exceptions also exist. A banking institution has eight days to make funds available in new accounts (those open less than thirty days). It has an extra four days on deposits over $5,000 (except deposits of government and cashier's checks), on accounts with repeated overdrafts, and on checks of questionable collectibility (if the institution tells the depositor it suspects fraud or insolvency).

INTEREST-BEARING ACCOUNTS

Under the Truth-in-Savings Act (TISA) of 1991[16] and Regulation DD,[17] the act's implementing regulation, banks must pay interest based on the full balance of a customer's interest-bearing account each day. For example, Vogel has an interest-bearing checking account with the First National Bank. Vogel keeps a $500 balance in the account for most of the month but withdraws all but $50 the day before the bank posts the interest. The bank cannot pay interest on just the $50. The interest must be adjusted to account for the entire month, including those days when Vogel's balance was higher.

Before opening a deposit account, new customers must be provided certain information in a brochure, pamphlet, or other handout. The information, which must also appear in all advertisements, includes the following:

1. The minimum balance required to open an account and to be paid interest.
2. The interest, stated in terms of the annual percentage yield on the account.
3. How interest is calculated.
4. Any fees, charges, and penalties and how they are calculated.

Also, under the TISA and Regulation DD, a customer's monthly statement must declare the interest earned on the account, any fees that were charged, how the fees were calculated, and the number of days that the statement covers.

THE TRADITIONAL COLLECTION PROCESS

Usually, deposited checks involve parties who do business at different banks, but sometimes checks are written between customers of the same bank. Either situation brings into play the bank collection process as it operates within the statutory framework of Article 4 of the UCC. Note that the check-collection process described in the following subsections likely will be modified in the future as the banking industry implements the Check Clearing in the 21st Century Act,[18] also known as the Check 21 Act. For a discussion of the Check 21 Act, which went into effect in late 2004, see this chapter's *Emerging Trends* feature on pages 552–553.

DESIGNATIONS OF BANKS INVOLVED IN THE COLLECTION PROCESS The first bank to receive a check for payment is the **depositary bank.**[19] For example, when a person deposits a tax-refund check from the Internal Revenue Service into a personal checking account at the local bank, that bank is the depositary bank. The bank on which a check is drawn (the drawee bank) is called the **payor bank.** Any bank except the payor bank that handles a check during some phase of the collection process is a **collecting bank.** Any bank except the payor bank or the depositary bank to which an item is transferred in the course of this collection process is called an **intermediary bank.**

During the collection process, any bank can take on one or more of the various roles of depositary, payor, collecting, or intermediary bank. To illustrate: A buyer in New York writes a check on her New York bank and sends it to a seller in San Francisco. The seller deposits the check in her San Francisco bank account. The seller's bank is both a *depositary bank* and a *collecting bank*. The buyer's bank in New York is the *payor bank*. As the check travels from San Francisco to New York, any *collecting bank* handling the item in the collection process (other than the ones acting as depositary bank and payor bank) is also called an

---

16. 12 U.S.C. Sections 4301–4313.
17. 12 C.F.R. Sections 230.1–230.9.

18. 12 U.S.C. Sections 5001–5018.
19. All definitions in this section are found in UCC 4–105. The terms *depositary* and *depository* have different meanings in the banking context. A depository bank refers to a physical place (a bank or other institution) in which deposits or funds are held or stored.

intermediary bank. Exhibit 27–5 illustrates how various banks function in the collection process.

CHECK COLLECTION BETWEEN CUSTOMERS OF THE SAME BANK

An item that is payable by the depositary bank that receives it (which in this situation is also the payor bank) is called an "on-us item." If the bank does not dishonor the check by the opening of the second banking day following its receipt, the check is considered paid [UCC 4–215(e)(2)]. For example, Oswald and Martin both have checking accounts at First State Bank. On Monday morning, Martin deposits into his own checking account a $300 check from Oswald. That same day, the bank issues Martin a "provisional credit" for $300. When the bank opens on Wednesday, Oswald's check is considered honored, and Martin's provisional credit becomes a final payment.

CHECK COLLECTION BETWEEN CUSTOMERS OF DIFFERENT BANKS

Once a depositary bank receives a check, it must arrange to present the check, either directly or through intermediary banks, to the appropriate payor bank. Each bank in the collection chain must pass the check on before midnight of the next banking day following its receipt [UCC 4–202(b)].[20] A "banking day" is any part of a day that the bank is open to carry on substantially all of its banking functions. Thus, if a bank has only its drive-through facilities open, a check deposited on Saturday would not trigger a bank's midnight deadline until the following Monday. When the check reaches the payor bank, that bank is liable for the face amount of the check, unless the payor bank dishonors the check or returns it by midnight of the next banking day following receipt [UCC 4–302].[21]

---

20. A bank may take a "reasonably longer time," such as when the bank's computer system is down because of a power failure [UCC 4–202(b)].

21. Most checks are cleared by a computerized process, and communication and computer facilities may fail because of weather, equipment malfunction, or other conditions. If such conditions arise and a bank fails to meet its midnight deadline, the bank is "excused" from liability if the bank has exercised "such diligence as the circumstances require" [UCC 4–109(d)].

EXHIBIT 27-5 **The Check-Collection Process**

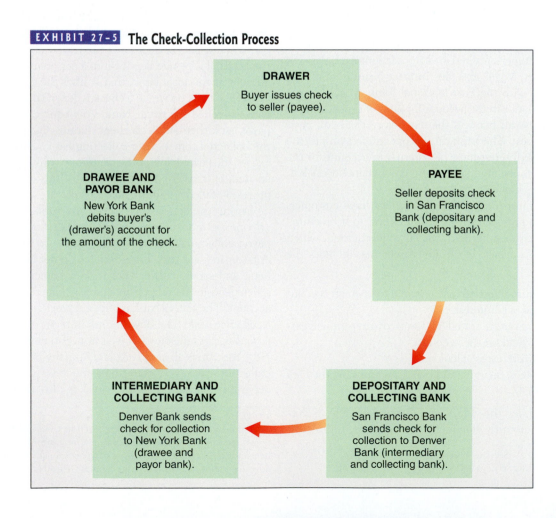

DRAWER
Buyer issues check to seller (payee).

PAYEE
Seller deposits check in San Francisco Bank (depositary and collecting bank).

DEPOSITARY AND COLLECTING BANK
San Francisco Bank sends check for collection to Denver Bank (intermediary and collecting bank).

INTERMEDIARY AND COLLECTING BANK
Denver Bank sends check for collection to New York Bank (drawee and payor bank).

DRAWEE AND PAYOR BANK
New York Bank debits buyer's (drawer's) account for the amount of the check.

Because of this deadline and because banks need to maintain an even work flow in the many items they handle daily, the UCC permits what is called *deferred posting*. According to UCC 4–108, "a bank may fix an afternoon hour of 2 P.M. or later as a cutoff hour for the handling of money and items and the making of entries on its books." Any checks received after that hour "may be treated as being received at the opening of the next banking day." Thus, if a bank's "cutoff hour" is 3 P.M., a check received by a payor bank at 4 P.M. on Monday will be deferred for posting until Tuesday. In this situation, the payor bank's deadline will be midnight Wednesday.

HOW THE FEDERAL RESERVE SYSTEM CLEARS CHECKS The **Federal Reserve System** is a network of twelve district banks, which are located around the country and headed by the Federal Reserve Board of Governors. Most banks in the United States have Federal Reserve accounts. The Federal Reserve System has greatly simplified the check-collection process by acting as a **clearinghouse**—a system or a place where banks exchange checks and drafts drawn on each other and settle daily balances.

Suppose that Pamela Moy of Philadelphia writes a check to Jeanne Sutton of San Francisco. When Jeanne receives the check in the mail, she deposits it in her bank. Her bank then deposits the check in the Federal Reserve Bank of San Francisco, which transfers it to the Federal Reserve Bank of Philadelphia. That Federal Reserve bank then sends the check to Moy's bank, which deducts the amount of the check from Moy's account. Exhibit 27–6 illustrates this process.

EXHIBIT 27-6 **How a Check Is Cleared**

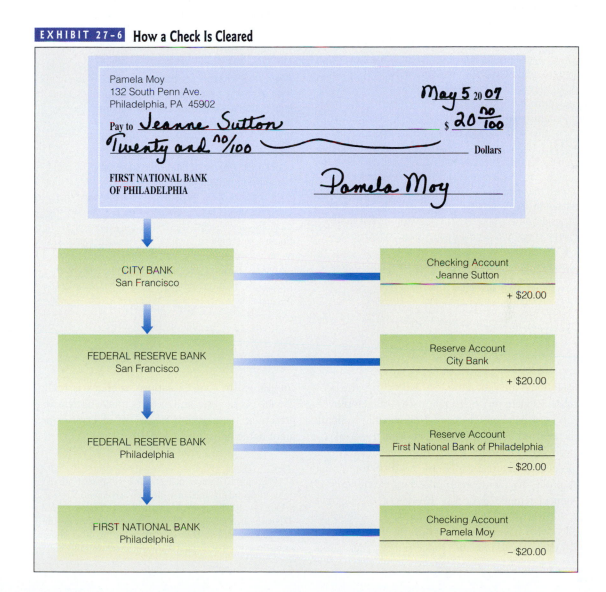

Check 21's Impact on the Nation's Check-Processing System

In the age of electronic payments, e-commerce, and the extensive use of the Internet, an anomaly occurs every night. This anomaly is the physical transportation of paper checks across town and across the country. As you learned in this chapter, checks usually must be physically transported before they can be cleared. Certainly, this physical transportation is costly and time consuming. In an effort to improve the overall efficiency of this nation's payment system, Congress passed the Check Clearing in the 21st Century Act (Check 21),[a] which went into effect on October 28, 2004.

PHYSICAL VERSUS ELECTRONIC PRESENTMENT

Prior to the implementation of Check 21, banks had to present the original paper check for payment in the absence of an agreement for acceptance of presentment in some other form. While the UCC authorizes banks to use other means of presentment, such as electronic presentment, there has been no broad-based adoption of electronic presentment because it has required agreements among individual banks.[b] Check 21 has changed this. It has created a new negotiable instrument called a *substitute check*. While the act does not require that any bank change its current check-collection practices, the creation of a substitute check will certainly facilitate the use of electronic check processing over time.

Consider an example. A depositary bank in Oregon receives a check drawn on a Rhode Island bank. Prior to Check 21, the Oregon bank had to send the original paper check for collection to an intermediary collecting bank or a

Federal Reserve bank. That bank, in turn, had to send the original check to the drawee bank in Rhode Island for collection (unless the particular banks had electronic presentment agreements in place). Now, under Check 21, all banks are required to accept presentment of the *substitute* check just as if it were an original check. Instead of processing and transferring the original paper check across the entire country, the Oregon bank can transmit the information electronically to an intermediary bank in Rhode Island, for example. That bank can then use the digital image to create a substitute check for collection and, using only local Rhode Island transportation, present it to the Rhode Island bank on which the check was drawn.

WHAT IS A SUBSTITUTE CHECK?

A *substitute check* is a paper reproduction of the front and back of an original check that contains all of the same information required on checks for automated processing. Banks create a substitute check from a *digital image* of an original check. Every substitute check must include the following statement somewhere on it: "This a legal copy of your check. You can use it in the same way you would use the original check."

In essence then, those financial institutions that exchange digital images of checks do not have to send the original paper checks. They can simply transmit the information electronically and replace the original checks with paper reproductions—substitute checks. Banks that do not exchange checks electronically are required to accept substitute checks in the same way that they are required to accept original checks.

---

a. 12 U.S.C. 5001, Pub. L. No. 108-100.
b. UCC Sections 3–501(b)(2) and 4–110.

ELECTRONIC CHECK PRESENTMENT In the past, most checks were processed manually—the employees of each bank in the collection chain would physically handle each check that passed through the bank for collection or payment. Today, however, most checks are processed electronically. In contrast to manual check processing, which can take days, *electronic check presentment* can be done on the day of the deposit. With electronic check presentment, items may be encoded with information (such as the amount of the check) that can be read and processed by other banks'

computers. In some situations, a check is retained at its place of deposit, and only its image or description is presented for payment under an electronic presentment agreement [UCC 4–110].[22]

---

22. UCC 4–110 assumes that no bank will participate in an electronic presentment program without an agreement. See Comment 2 to UCC 4–110. For example, two banks that frequently do business with each other might enter into an agreement allowing the depositary bank to send an electronic image to the other bank for presentment instead of sending the physical check.

THE GRADUAL ELIMINATION OF ORIGINAL PAPER CHECKS

Because financial institutions must accept substitute checks as if they were original checks, the original checks no longer need to exist after their digital substitutes have been created. Clearly, though, at least for quite a while, not all checks will be converted to substitute checks. That means if your bank returns canceled checks to you at the end of each month, some of those returned checks may be substitute checks and some may be original canceled paper checks.

Once a substitute check has been created, the original check, in all likelihood, will be destroyed. This is because after a substitute check has been created, the financial system will tend to eliminate the original check in order to prevent the check from being paid twice. Also, eliminating original checks and retaining only digital images will reduce the expense of storage and retrieval.

Since the passage of Check 21, financial institution customers can no longer demand original canceled checks. Check 21 is a federal law and applies to all financial institutions, other businesses, and individuals in the United States. In other words, no customers can opt out of Check 21 and demand that their original canceled checks be returned with their monthly statements. Also, businesses and individuals must accept a substitute check as proof of payment because it is the legal equivalent of the original check.

A MORE EFFICIENT CHECK-PROCESSING SYSTEM MEANS REDUCED "FLOAT"

Sometimes individuals and businesses write checks on their accounts even though the accounts contain insufficient funds to cover those checks. They are relying on "float." *Float* is the time between when a drawer writes a check and when it is presented for payment at the drawer's financial institution.

The Expedited Funds Availability Act requires that the Federal Reserve Board reduce the maximum hold times on checks to correspond to reductions in check-processing times. Therefore, as Check 21 is implemented, the speed of check processing will increase. The Federal Reserve Board will thus reduce maximum hold times on deposited checks. Consequently, float time will be reduced.

IMPLICATIONS FOR THE BUSINESSPERSON

1. As more financial institutions make agreements to transfer digital images of checks, the check-processing system will become more efficient and therefore less costly, affecting banking fees everywhere.

2. Businesses will be increasingly less able to rely on banking float when they are low on current funds.

FOR CRITICAL ANALYSIS

1. How might Check 21 affect the potential for banking fraud?

2. Are there any circumstances in which you can now demand a copy of your original canceled paper check? Discuss.

RELEVANT WEB SITES

To locate information on the Web concerning the issues discussed in this feature, go to this text's Web site at **http://wbl.westbuslaw.com**, select "Chapter 27," and click on "Emerging Trends."

A person who encodes information on an item after the item has been issued warrants to any subsequent bank or payor that the encoded information is correct [UCC 4–209]. This is also true for a person who retains an item while transmitting its image or information describing it as presentation for payment. This person warrants that the retention and presentment of the item comply with a Federal Reserve or other agreement.

Regulation CC provides that a returned check must be encoded with the routing number of the depositary bank, the amount of the check, and other information and adds that this "does not affect a paying bank's responsibility to return a check within the deadlines required by the U.C.C." What happens when a payor bank fails to properly encode an item and thereby causes the check to be returned to the depositary bank after the required deadline? That was the question in the following case.

CASE 27.3

NBT Bank, N.A. v. First National Community Bank

United States
Court of Appeals,
Third Circuit, 2004.
393 F.3d 404.

SMITH, Circuit Judge.

*   *   *   *

*   *   * [A] small group of Pennsylvania business entities arranged to write checks on one account, drawing on non-existent funds, and then cover these overdrafts with checks drawn on another account that also lacked sufficient funds. *   *   * The scheme collapsed when three checks initially deposited at [NBT Bank, N.A.] and subsequently presented for payment to [First National Community Bank (FNCB)] were discovered by FNCB to have been drawn on an FNCB account that lacked sufficient funds. There is no dispute between the parties that two of these three checks were properly returned by FNCB to the [Federal Reserve Bank of Philadelphia] prior to the applicable midnight deadline.

The Disputed Check (i.e., the third check, for $706,000) was drawn on an FNCB account and drafted by an entity called Human Services Consultants, Inc. On March 8, 2001, the Disputed Check was proffered [handed over] for deposit at NBT by an entity called Human Services Consultants Management, Inc., [doing business as] "PA Health." *   *   *

*   *   *   *

After the Disputed Check was presented for deposit at NBT, the bank gave provisional credit to the depositor, PA Health, for the amount of the Disputed Check. NBT also transmitted the Disputed Check to the Reserve Bank for presentment to FNCB. *   *   * The Reserve Bank then forwarded the Disputed Check to FNCB, and FNCB received it on March 12, 2001. *   *   *

*   *   *   *

On March 13, 2001, FNCB determined it would not pay the Disputed Check because of the absence of sufficient funds in the account on which the check was drawn. That same day, FNCB sought to return the Disputed Check to NBT through the Reserve Bank. *   *   * [T]he Disputed Check was physically delivered to the Reserve Bank prior to 11:59 P.M. on March 13. *   *   * FNCB also sent a notice of dishonor to NBT *   *   * in which FNCB indicated that it did not intend to pay the Disputed Check. NBT received this notice prior to the close of business on March 13. *   *   *

*   *   *   *

When FNCB sent the Disputed Check to the Reserve Bank on March 13, 2001, FNCB *   *   * erroneously encoded [it] with the routing number for PNC Bank instead of the routing number for NBT [Bank].

*   *   * Because the Disputed Check was improperly encoded, NBT did not receive it back *   *   * until March 16, 2001. *   *   * NBT suffered no damages or actual loss as a result of the encoding error *   *   * .

*   *   *   *

NBT instituted this action [in a federal district court] against FNCB on May 25, 2001. *   *   * NBT claimed that FNCB's encoding error meant FNCB had failed to return the Disputed Check prior to the midnight deadline as required by the UCC, and that FNCB was therefore accountable to NBT for the full amount of the Disputed Check. *   *   *

The District Court granted FNCB's motion [for summary judgment]. NBT appeals.

*   *   *   *

*   *   * Federal law forms part of the legal framework within which check-processing activities take place. Of particular relevance to this appeal are the 1988 regulations adopted by the Federal Reserve implementing the Expedited Funds Availability Act. These regulations, referred to collectively as "Regulation CC," complement but do not necessarily replace the requirements of Article 4 of the UCC.

*   *   *   *

*   *   * Regulation CC indisputably binds the parties, pursuant to both its own terms, as well as [13 Pennsylvania Consolidated Statutes Annotated Section 4103 (Pennsylvania's version of UCC 4–103)], which indicates that "Federal Reserve regulations" are to be treated as agreements that may vary the terms of the UCC. *   *   *

CASE 27.3 | **Continued**

Because Regulation CC * * * is binding on the parties, and because Regulation CC is the source of the encoding requirement invoked by NBT, the extent of FNCB's liability for its encoding error must be measured by the standards set forth in Regulation CC. *Regulation CC states that a bank that fails to exercise ordinary care in complying with the [encoding] provisions of * * * Regulation CC * * * "may be liable" to the depositary bank.* Then, in broad, unrestricted language, Regulation CC states:

> The measure of damages for failure to exercise ordinary care is the amount of the loss incurred, up to the amount of the check, reduced by the amount of the loss that the [plaintiff bank] would have incurred even if the [defendant] bank had exercised ordinary care.

This provision does not provide an exception to this standard for measuring damages in instances where noncompliance with Regulation CC is alleged to have resulted in noncompliance with the UCC's midnight deadline rule. Here, the parties have stipulated that NBT suffered no loss as a result of FNCB's encoding error. Thus, under the plain language of Regulation CC, NBT may not recover from FNCB for the amount of the Disputed Check. [Emphasis added.]
* * * *
Accordingly, * * * we affirm the order of the District Court * * * .

QUESTIONS

1. How might the result in this case have been different if NBT had committed the encoding error and FNCB had suffered the loss?
2. If a bank warrants that the information it encoded on an item is correct and FNCB committed an error in encoding, then why did the court not hold FNCB liable for the amount of the check?

SECTION 5 | Electronic Fund Transfers

The application of computer technology to banking, in the form of *electronic fund transfer systems,* has helped to relieve banking institutions of the burden of having to move mountains of paperwork to process fund transfers. An **electronic fund transfer (EFT)** is a transfer of funds made by the use of an electronic terminal, a telephone, a computer, or magnetic tape. The law governing EFTs depends on the type of transfer involved. Consumer fund transfers are governed by the Electronic Fund Transfer Act (EFTA) of 1978.[23] Commercial fund transfers are governed by Article 4A of the UCC.

TYPES OF EFT SYSTEMS

Most banks today offer EFT services to their customers. The four most common types of EFT systems used by bank customers are listed below.

1. *Automated teller machines* (ATMs)—Machines connected online to the bank's computers. To access an account through an ATM, the bank customer uses a plastic card, known as a **debit card,** issued to him or her by the bank, plus a secret *personal identification number* (PIN).
2. *Point-of-sale systems*—Online terminals that allow consumers to transfer funds to merchants to pay for purchases using debit cards.
3. *Direct deposits and withdrawals*—Customers can authorize the bank to allow another party, such as the government or an employer, to make direct deposits into their accounts. Similarly, a customer can request the bank to make automatic payments to a third party at regular, recurrent intervals from the customer's funds (insurance premiums or loan payments, for example).
4. *Pay-by-Internet systems*—A financial institution may permit its customers to access the institution's computer system via the Internet and direct a transfer of funds between accounts or pay a particular bill, such as, for example, a utility bill.

---

23. 15 U.S.C. Sections 1693–1693r. The EFTA amended Title IX of the Consumer Credit Protection Act.

CONSUMER FUND TRANSFERS

The Electronic Fund Transfer Act (EFTA) provides a basic framework for the rights, liabilities, and responsibilities of users of EFT systems. Additionally, the act gave the Federal Reserve Board authority to issue rules and regulations to help implement the act's provisions. The Federal Reserve Board's implemental regulation is called **Regulation E.** The EFTA governs financial institutions that offer electronic transfers of funds involving customer accounts. The types of accounts covered include checking accounts, savings accounts, and any other asset accounts established for personal, family, or household purposes.

DISCLOSURE REQUIREMENTS The EFTA is essentially a disclosure law benefiting consumers. The act requires financial institutions to inform consumers of their rights and responsibilities, including those listed here, with respect to EFT systems.

1. If a customer's debit card is lost or stolen and used without her or his permission, the customer may be required to pay no more than $50. The customer, however, must notify the bank of the loss or theft within two days of learning about it. Otherwise, the customer's liability increases to $500. The customer may be liable for more than $500 if she or he does not report the unauthorized use within sixty days after it appears on the customer's statement.

2. The customer has sixty days to discover and notify the bank of any error on the monthly statement. The bank then has ten days to investigate and must report its conclusions to the customer in writing. If the bank takes longer than ten days to do so, it must return the disputed amount to the customer's account until it finds the error. If there is no error, however, the customer must return the funds to the bank.

3. The bank must furnish receipts for transactions made through computer terminals, but it is not obligated to do so for telephone transfers.

4. The bank must provide a monthly statement for every month in which there is an electronic transfer of funds. Otherwise, the bank must provide a statement every quarter. The statement must show the amount and date of the transfer, the names of the retailers or other third parties involved, the location or identification of the terminal, and the fees. Additionally, the statement must give an address and a phone number for inquiries and error notices.

5. Any preauthorized payment for utility bills and insurance premiums can be stopped three days before the scheduled transfer if the customer notifies the financial institution orally or in writing. (The institution may require the customer to provide written confirmation within fourteen days of an oral notification.)

STOPPING PAYMENT AND REVERSIBILITY As just mentioned, a customer may cancel a preauthorized transfer before the transfer is made, just as a drawer—the person who signs a check—may stop payment on a check before it is paid. For other EFT transactions, however, the EFTA does not provide for the reversal of an electronic transfer of funds once the transfer has occurred. This is because, unlike checks, the instantaneous nature of an EFT provides no "float time" (the time between a check's issuance and final payment) during which an effective reversal of an order to pay can be made.

UNAUTHORIZED TRANSFERS Because of the vulnerability of EFT systems to fraudulent activities, the EFTA of 1978 clearly defined what constitutes an unauthorized transfer. Under the act, a transfer is unauthorized if (1) it is initiated by a person who has no actual authority to initiate the transfer, (2) the consumer receives no benefit from it, and (3) the consumer did not furnish the person "with the card, code, or other means of access" to his or her account. Unauthorized access to an EFT system constitutes a federal felony, and those convicted may be sentenced to a fine of up to $10,000 and up to ten years' imprisonment.

VIOLATIONS AND DAMAGES Banks are held to strict compliance with the terms of the EFTA. If they fail to adhere to the letter of the law of the EFTA, they will be held liable for violation. For a bank's violation of the EFTA, a consumer may recover both actual damages (including attorneys' fees and costs) and punitive damages of not less than $100 and not more than $1,000. In a class-action suit, the punitive-damages award can be up to $500,000 or 1 percent of the institution's net worth. (Unlike actual damages, punitive damages are assessed to punish a defendant or to set an example for similar wrongdoers.) Failure to investigate an error in good faith makes the bank liable for treble damages (three times the amount of damages).

COMMERCIAL FUND TRANSFERS

Funds are also transferred electronically "by wire" between commercial parties. In fact, the dollar volume of payments made via wire transfers is more than $1 trillion a day—an amount that far exceeds the dollar volume of payments made by other means. The two major wire payment systems are the Federal Reserve wire transfer network (Fedwire) and the New York Clearing House Interbank Payments Systems (CHIPS).

Commercial wire transfers are governed by Article 4A of the UCC, which has been adopted by most of the states. As an example of the type of fund transfer covered by Article 4A, assume that American Industries, Inc., owes $5 million to Chandler Corporation. Instead of sending Chandler a check or some other instrument that would enable Chandler to obtain payment, American Industries tells its bank, North Bank, to credit $5 million to Chandler's account in South Bank. North Bank debits American Industries' North Bank account and wires $5 million to South Bank with instructions to credit $5 million to Chandler's South Bank account. In more complex transactions, additional banks would be involved.

In these and similar circumstances, ordinarily a financial institution's instruction is transmitted electronically. Any means may be used, however, including first class mail. To reflect this fact, Article 4A uses the term *funds transfer* rather than *wire transfer* to describe the overall payment transaction. The full text of Article 4A is presented in Appendix C, following the revised Article 4 of the UCC.

SECTION 6 | E-Money and Online Banking

New forms of electronic payments (e-payments) have the potential to replace *physical* cash—coins and paper currency—with *virtual* cash in the form of electronic impulses. This is the unique promise of **digital cash,** which consists of funds stored on microchips and other computer devices.

Various forms of electronic money, or **e-money,** are emerging. The simplest kind of e-money system uses *stored-value cards*. These are plastic cards embossed with magnetic strips containing magnetically encoded data. A person can use a stored-value card to purchase specific goods and services offered by the card issuer. For example, university libraries typically have copy machines that students operate by inserting a stored-value card. Each time a student makes copies, the machine deducts the per-copy fee from the card.

Another form of e-money is the smart card. **Smart cards** are plastic cards containing computer microchips that can hold much more information than magnetic strips. A smart card carries and processes security programming. This capability gives smart cards a technical advantage over stored-value cards. The microprocessors on smart cards can also authenticate the validity of transactions. Retailers can program electronic cash registers to confirm the authenticity of a smart card by examining a unique digital signature stored on its microchip. (Digital signatures were discussed in Chapter 19.)

ONLINE BANKING SERVICES

Most online bank customers currently use three kinds of services. One of the most popular is bill consolidation and payment. Another is transferring funds among accounts (which may often also be accomplished by phone). The third is applying for loans, which many banks permit customers to do via the Internet. Customers typically must appear in person to finalize the terms of a loan, however.

Two important banking activities generally are not yet available online: depositing and withdrawing funds. With smart cards, people could transfer funds on the Internet, thereby effectively transforming their personal computers into ATMs. Many observers believe that people will eventually be introduced to e-money and smart cards through online banking.

Since the late 1990s, several banks have operated exclusively on the Internet. These "virtual banks" have no physical branch offices. Because few individuals are equipped to send funds to virtual banks via smart-card technology, the virtual banks have accepted deposits through physical delivery systems, such as the U.S. Postal Service and FedEx.

REGULATORY COMPLIANCE

Banks have an interest in promoting the widespread use of online banking because it has significant potential for reducing costs and thus increasing profits. As in other areas of cyberspace, however, determining how laws apply to online banking activities can be difficult.

The Home Mortgage Disclosure Act[24] and the Community Reinvestment Act (CRA) of 1977,[25] for example, require a bank to define its market area and also to provide information about its deposits and loans. Under the CRA, banks establish market areas contiguous to their branch offices. The banks map these areas using boundaries defined by counties or standard metropolitan areas and annually review the maps. The purpose of these requirements is to prevent discrimination in lending practices.

How does a successful "cyberbank" delineate its community? If, for example, Bank of Internet becomes a tremendous success, does it really have any physical communities? Will the Federal Reserve Board simply allow a written description of a cybercommunity for Internet customers? Such regulatory issues are new, challenging, and certain to become more complicated as Internet banking widens its scope internationally.

PRIVACY PROTECTION

At present, it is not clear which, if any, laws apply to the security of e-money payment information and e-money issuers' financial records. This is partly because it is not clear whether e-money issuers fit within the traditional definition of a financial institution.

E-MONEY PAYMENT INFORMATION The Federal Reserve has decided not to impose Regulation E, which governs certain electronic fund transfers, on e-money transactions. Federal laws prohibiting unauthorized access to electronic communications might apply, however. For example, the Electronic Communications Privacy Act of 1986[26] prohibits any person from knowingly divulging to any other person the contents of an electronic communication while that communication is in transmission or in electronic storage.

E-MONEY ISSUERS' FINANCIAL RECORDS Under the Right to Financial Privacy Act of 1978,[27] before a financial institution may give financial information about you to a federal agency, you must explicitly consent. If you do not, a federal agency wishing to obtain your financial records must obtain a warrant. A digital

cash issuer may be subject to this act if that issuer is deemed to be (1) a bank by virtue of its holding customer funds or (2) any entity that issues a physical card similar to a credit or debit card.

CONSUMER FINANCIAL DATA In 1999, Congress passed the Financial Services Modernization Act,[28] also known as the Gramm-Leach-Bliley Act, in an attempt to delineate how financial institutions can treat customer data. In general, the act and its rules[29] place restrictions and obligations on financial institutions to protect consumer data and privacy. Every financial institution must provide its customers with information on its privacy policies and practices. No financial institution can disclose nonpublic personal information about a consumer to an unaffiliated third party unless the act's disclosure and opt-out requirements are met.

SECTION 7 | The Uniform Money Services Act

Over the past few years, many states have enacted various regulations that apply to money services in a rather haphazard fashion. At the same time, e-money services that operate on the Internet—which, of course, cuts across jurisdictional lines—have been asking that these regulations be made more predictable.

In 2001, the National Conference of Commissioners on Uniform State Laws recommended to state legislatures a new uniform act that would subject both traditional money services and online and e-money services to the same regulations that apply to traditional financial service businesses. This law, which is known as the Uniform Money Services Act (UMSA), has been adopted in a few states.[30]

TRADITIONAL MONEY SERVICES

Money service businesses (MSBs) have not been subject to regulation to the same extent as other financial service businesses. Unlike banks, MSBs do not accept deposits. They do, however, issue money orders, traveler's checks, and stored-value cards; exchange foreign currency; and cash checks. Immigrants often use these businesses to send funds to their relatives in other

---

24. 12 U.S.C. Sections 2801–2810.
25. 12 U.S.C. Sections 2901–2908.
26. 18 U.S.C. Sections 2510–2521.
27. 12 U.S.C. Sections 3401 et seq.

28. 12 U.S.C. Sections 24a, 248b, 1820a, 1828b, and others.
29. 12 C.F.R. Part 40.
30. To date, the UMSA has been adopted in Iowa, Vermont, and Washington, as well as in the U.S. Virgin Islands.

countries. Because MSBs often do not have continuing relationships with their customers, the customers have sometimes evaded federal law with respect to large currency transactions or used the services to launder money (see Chapter 9). This has been particularly true with respect to financing terrorist activities.

The UMSA applies to persons engaged in funds transmission, check cashing, or currency exchange. The uniform act requires an MSB involved in these activities to obtain a license from a state, to be examined by state officials, to report on its activities to the state, and to comply with certain record-keeping requirements. Each of these subjects has its provisions and exceptions. Safety and soundness measures—such as annual examinations, surety bonds (to guarantee financial soundness), and permissible investments—are also mandated by the act.

INTERNET-BASED MONEY SERVICES

Under the UMSA, Internet-based money services, as well as other types of e-money services, would be treated the same as other money services.[31] The drafters of the UMSA ensured that it would cover these services by referring to *monetary value* instead of simply *money* [UMSA 1–102(c)(11)].

Internet-based monetary value systems subject to the new law may include:

1. *E-money and Internet payment mechanisms.* Money, or its substitute, that is stored as data on a chip or a personal computer so that it can be transferred over the Internet or an intranet.

2. *Internet scrip.* Monetary value that can be exchanged over the Internet but can also be redeemed for cash.

3. *Stored-value products.* Smart cards, prepaid cards, or value-added cards [UMSA 1–102(c)(21)].

---

31. The UMSA does not apply to state governments, the federal government, securities dealers, banks, businesses that incidentally transport currency and instruments in the normal course of business, payday loan businesses, and others [UMSA 1–103].

REVIEWING CHECKS, THE BANKING SYSTEM, AND E-MONEY

RPM Pizza, Inc., issued a $96,000 check to Systems Marketing for an advertising campaign. A few days later, RPM decided not to go through with the deal and placed a written stop-payment order on the check. RPM and Systems had no further contact for many months. Three weeks after the stop-payment order expired, however, Toby Rierson, an employee at Systems, cashed the check. Bank One Cambridge, RPM's bank, paid the check with funds from RPM's account. Because of the amount of the check, and because the check was more than six months old (stale), the signature on the check should have been specially verified according to standard banking procedures and Bank One's own policies, but it was not. RPM filed a suit in a federal district court against Bank One to recover the amount of the check. Using the information presented in the chapter, answer the following questions.

1. How long is a written stop-payment order effective? What else could RPM have done to prevent this check from being cashed?

2. What would happen if it turned out that RPM did not have a legitimate reason for stopping payment on the check?

3. What are a bank's obligations with respect to stale checks? Should Bank One have contacted RPM before paying the check? Why or why not?

4. RPM claimed that Bank One violated its duty to act with ordinary care when it failed to verify the signature on the check. Do you agree? Why or why not?

5. Suppose that Toby Rierson, the employee at Systems who cashed the check, had altered the face amount of the check from $96,000 to $196,000 and Bank One had cashed it. How might this affect the outcome of the case? Which party normally would be responsible for the $100,000 difference (Bank One, RPM, or Systems)?

TERMS AND CONCEPTS TO REVIEW

QUESTIONS AND CASE PROBLEMS

27–1. Checks are usually three-party instruments. On what type of check, however, does a bank serve as both the drawer and the drawee? What type of check does a bank agree in advance to accept when the check is presented for payment?

27–2. QUESTION WITH SAMPLE ANSWER
Gary goes grocery shopping and carelessly leaves his checkbook in his shopping cart. His checkbook, with two blank checks remaining, is stolen by Dolores. On May 5, Dolores forges Gary's name on a check for $10 and cashes the check at Gary's bank, Citizens Bank of Middletown. Gary has not reported the loss of his blank checks to his bank. On June 1, Gary receives his monthly bank statement and copies of canceled checks from Citizens Bank, including the forged check, but he does not examine the canceled checks. On June 20, Dolores forges Gary's last check. This check is for $1,000 and is cashed at Eastern City Bank, a bank with which Dolores has previously done business. Eastern City Bank puts the check through the collection process, and Citizens Bank honors it. On July 1, on receipt of his bank statement and canceled checks covering June transactions, Gary discovers both forgeries and immediately notifies Citizens Bank. Dolores cannot be found. Gary claims that Citizens Bank must recredit his account for both checks, as his signature was forged. Discuss fully Gary's claim.
For a sample answer to this question, go to Appendix I at the end of this text.

27–3. On January 5, Brian drafts a check for $3,000 drawn on the Southern Marine Bank and payable to his assistant, Shanta. Brian puts last year's date on the check by mistake. On January 7, before Shanta has had a chance to go to the bank, Brian is killed in an automobile accident. The Southern Marine Bank is aware of Brian's death. On January 10, Shanta presents the check to the bank, and the bank honors the check by payment to Shanta. Later, Brian's widow, Joyce, claims that the bank wrongfully paid Shanta, because it knew of Brian's death and also because the check was by date over one year old. Joyce, as executor of Brian's estate and sole heir by his will, demands that Southern Marine Bank recredit Brian's estate for the check paid to Shanta. Discuss fully Southern Marine's liability in light of Joyce's demand.

27–4. Yannuzzi has a checking account at Texas Bank. She frequently uses her access card to obtain money from the bank's automated teller machines. She always withdraws $50 when she makes a withdrawal, but she never withdraws more than $50 in any one day. When she received the April statement on her account, she noticed that on April 13 two withdrawals for $50 each had been made from the account. Believing this to be a mistake, she went to her bank on May 10 to inform it of the error. A bank officer told her that the bank would investigate and advise her as to the result. On May 26, the bank officer called her and said that bank personnel were having trouble locating the error but would continue to try to find it. On June 20, the bank sent her a full written report telling her that no error had been made. Yannuzzi, unhappy with the bank's explanation, filed suit against the bank, alleging that it had violated the Electronic Fund Transfer Act. What was the outcome of the suit? Would it matter if the bank could show that on the day in question it deducted $50 from Yannuzzi's account to cover a check that cleared the bank on that day—a check that Yannuzzi had written to a local department store?

27–5. STALE CHECKS. On July 15, 1986, IBP, Inc., issued to Meyer Land & Cattle Co. a check for $135,234.18 payable to both Meyer and Sylvan State Bank for the purchase of cattle. IBP wrote the check on its account at Mercantile Bank of Topeka. Someone at the Meyer firm misplaced the check. In the fall of 1995, Meyer's president, Tim Meyer, found the check behind a desk drawer. Jana Huse, Meyer's office manager, presented the check for deposit at Sylvan, which accepted it. After Mercantile received the instrument and its computers noted the absence of any stop-payment order, it paid the check with funds from IBP's checking account. IBP insisted that Mercantile credit IBP's account. Mercantile refused. IBP filed a suit in a federal district court against Mercantile and others, claiming, among other things, that Mercantile had not acted in good faith because it had processed the check by automated means, without examining it manually. Mercantile responded that its check-processing procedures adhered to its own policies, as well as to reasonable commercial standards of fair dealing in the banking industry. Mercantile filed a motion for summary judgment. Should the court grant the motion? Why or why not? [*IBP, Inc. v. Mercantile Bank of Topeka*, 6 F.Supp.2d 1258 (D.Kan. 1999)]

27–6. DEBIT CARDS. On April 20, 1999, while visiting her daughter and her son-in-law, Michael Dowdell, Carol Farrow asked Dowdell to fix her car. She gave him her car keys, attached to which was a small wallet containing her debit card. Dowdell repaired her car and returned the keys. Two days later, Farrow noticed that her debit card was missing and contacted Auburn Bank, which had issued the card. Farrow reviewed her automated teller machine (ATM) transaction record and noticed that a large amount of cash had been withdrawn from her checking account on April 22 and April 23. When Farrow reviewed the photos taken by the ATM cameras at the time of the withdrawals, she recognized Dowdell as the person using her debit card. Dowdell was convicted in an Alabama state court of the crime of fraudulent use of a debit card. What procedures are involved in a debit-card transaction? What problems with debit-card transactions are apparent from the facts of this case? How might these problems be prevented? [*Dowdell v. State*, 790 So.2d 359 (Ala.Crim.App. 2000)]

27–7. ⚖️ **CASE PROBLEM WITH SAMPLE ANSWER**

In December 1999, Jenny Triplett applied for a bookkeeping position with Spacemakers of America, Inc., in Atlanta, Georgia. Spacemakers hired Triplett and delegated to her all responsibility for maintaining the company checkbook and reconciling it with the monthly statements from SunTrust Bank. Triplett also handled invoices from vendors. Spacemakers' president, Dennis Rose, reviewed the invoices and signed the checks to pay them, but no other employee checked Triplett's work. By the end of her first full month of employment, Triplett had forged six checks totaling more than $22,000, all payable to Triple M Entertainment (a company owned by Triplett's husband), which was not a Spacemakers vendor. By October 2000, Triplett had forged fifty-nine more checks, totaling more than $475,000. A SunTrust employee became suspicious of an item that required sight inspection under the bank's fraud detection standards, which exceeded those of other banks in the area. Triplett was arrested. Spacemakers filed a suit in a

Georgia state court against SunTrust. The bank filed a motion for summary judgment. On what basis could the bank avoid liability? In whose favor should the court rule, and why? [*Spacemakers of America, Inc. v. SunTrust Bank*, 271 Ga.App. 335, 609 S.E.2d 683 (2005)]

To view a sample answer for this case problem, go to this book's Web site at http://wbl.westbuslaw.com, select "Chapter 27," and click on "Case Problem with Sample Answer."

27–8. CHECK COLLECTION. Robert Santoro was the manager of City Check Cashing, Inc., a check-cashing service in New Jersey, and Peggyann Slansky was the clerk. On July 14, Misir Koci presented Santoro with a $290,000 check signed by Melvin Green and drawn on Manufacturers Hanover Trust Co. (a bank). The check was stamped with a Manufacturers certification stamp. The date on the check had clearly been changed from August 8 to July 7. Slansky called the bank to verify the check and was told that the serial number "did not sound like one belonging to the bank." Slansky faxed the check to the bank with a query about the date but received no reply. Slansky also called Green, who stated that the date on the check had been altered before the check was certified. Check Cashing cashed and deposited the check within two hours. The drawee bank found the check to be invalid and timely returned it unpaid. Check Cashing filed a suit in a New Jersey state court against Manufacturers and others, asserting that the bank should have responded to the fax before the midnight deadline in UCC 4–302. Did the bank violate the midnight-deadline rule? Explain. [*City Check Cashing, Inc. v. Manufacturers Hanover Trust Co.*, 166 N.J. 49, 764 A.2d 411 (2001)]

27–9. FORGED SIGNATURES. Visiting Nurses Association of Telfair County, Inc. (VNA), maintained a checking account at Security State Bank in Valdosta, Georgia. Wanda Williamson, a VNA clerk, was responsible for making VNA bank deposits, but she was not a signatory on the association's account. Over a four-year period, Williamson embezzled more than $250,000 from VNA by forging its indorsement on checks, cashing them at the bank, and keeping a portion of the proceeds. Williamson was arrested, convicted, sentenced to a prison term, and ordered to pay restitution. VNA filed a suit in a Georgia state court against the bank, alleging, among other things, negligence. The bank filed a motion for summary judgment on the ground that VNA was precluded by UCC 4–406(f) from recovering on checks with forged indorsements. Should the court grant the motion? Explain. [*Security State Bank v. Visiting Nurses Association of Telfair County, Inc.*, 568 S.E.2d 491 (Ga.App. 2002)]

27–10. FORGED SIGNATURES. Cynthia Stafford worked as an administrative professional at Gerber & Gerber, P.C. (professional corporation), a law firm, for more than two years. During that time, she stole ten checks payable to Gerber & Gerber (G&G), which she indorsed in blank by forging one of the attorney's signatures. She then indorsed the forged checks in her name and deposited them in her account at Regions Bank. Over the same period, G&G deposited in its accounts at Regions Bank thousands of checks amounting to $300 million to $400 million. Each G&G check was indorsed with a rubber stamp for deposit into the G&G account. The thefts were made possible in part because G&G kept unindorsed checks in an open file accessible to all employees and Stafford was sometimes the person assigned to stamp the checks. When the thefts were discovered, G&G filed a suit in a Georgia state court against Regions Bank to recover the stolen funds, alleging in part negligence. Regions Bank filed a motion for summary judgment. What principles apply to attribute liability between these parties? How should the court rule on the bank's motion? Explain. [*Gerber & Gerber, P.C. v. Regions Bank*, 596 S.E.2d 174 (Ga.App. 2004)]

LAW | on the Web

For updated links to resources available on the Web, as well as a variety of other materials, visit this text's Web site at http://wbl.westbuslaw.com.

You can obtain extensive information on banking regulation from the Federal Deposit Insurance Corporation (FDIC) at

http://www.fdic.gov

Additional information about banking can be obtained from the Federal Reserve System at

http://www.federalreserveonline.org

The American Bankers Association is the largest banking trade association in the United States. To learn more about the banking industry, go to

http://www.aba.com

LEGAL RESEARCH EXERCISES ON THE WEB

Go to **http://wbl.westbuslaw.com**, the Web site that accompanies this text. Select "Chapter 27" and click on "Internet Exercises." There you will find the following Internet research exercises that you can perform to learn more about topics covered in this chapter.

Activity 27–1: LEGAL PERSPECTIVE
Smart Cards

Activity 27–2: MANAGEMENT PERSPECTIVE
Check Fraud

Negotiable Instruments

Articles 3 and 4 of the Uniform Commercial Code (UCC), which deal with negotiable instruments, constitute an important part of the law governing commercial transactions. These articles reflect several fundamental ethical principles. One principle is that individuals should be protected against harm caused by the misuse of negotiable instruments. Another basic principle—and one that underlies the entire concept of negotiable instruments—is that the laws governing the use of negotiable instruments should be practical and reasonable to encourage the free flow of commerce.

In the following pages, we look first at some of the ethical implications of the concept of a holder in due course (HDC). We then examine some other ethical issues that frequently arise in relation to these instruments.

Ethics, the HDC Concept, and *Ort v. Fowler*

The drafters of Article 3 did not create the HDC concept out of thin air. Indeed, under the common law, courts had often restricted the extent to which defenses could successfully be raised against a good faith holder of a negotiable instrument. As an example, consider a classic 1884 case, *Ort v. Fowler.*[1]

Case Background Ort, a farmer who was working alone in his field one day, was approached by a stranger who claimed to be the statewide agent for a manufacturer of iron posts and wire fencing. The two men conversed for some time, and eventually the stranger persuaded the farmer to act as an area representative for the manufacturer. The stranger then completed two documents for Ort to sign, telling him that they were identical copies of an agreement in which Ort agreed to represent the manufacturer.

Because the farmer did not have his glasses with him and could read only with great difficulty, he asked the stranger to read what the document said. The stranger then purported to read the document to Ort, not mentioning that it was a promissory note. Both men signed each document. The stranger later negotiated the promissory note he had fraudulently obtained from Ort to a party that today we would refer to as an HDC. When this party brought suit against him, Ort attempted to defend on the basis of fraud in the execution.

The Court's Decision The Kansas court deciding the issue entertained three possible views. One was that because Ort never *intended* to execute a note, he should not be held liable for doing so. A second view was that the jury should decide,

as a question of fact, whether Ort was guilty of negligence under the circumstances. The third view was that because Ort possessed all of his faculties and was able to read the English language, signing a promissory note solely in reliance on a stranger's assurances that it was a different instrument constituted negligence.

This third view was the one adopted by the court in 1884. The court held that Ort's negligence had contributed to the fraud and that such negligence precluded Ort from raising fraud as a defense against payment on the note. Today, the UCC expresses essentially the same reasoning: fraud is a defense against an HDC only if the injured party signed the instrument "with neither knowledge nor a reasonable opportunity to learn of its character or its essential terms" [UCC 3–305(a)(1)(iii)].

The Reasoning Underlying the HDC Concept Although it may not seem fair that an innocent victim should have to suffer the consequences of another's fraudulent act, the UCC assumes that it would be even less fair if an HDC could not collect payment. The reasoning behind this assumption is that an HDC, as a third party, is less likely to have been responsible for—or to have had an opportunity to protect against—the fraud in the underlying transaction.

In general, the HDC doctrine, like other sections of the UCC, reflects the philosophy that when two or more innocent parties are at risk, the burden should fall on the party that was in the best position to prevent the loss. For businesspersons, the HDC doctrine means that caution must be exercised in issuing and accepting commercial paper in order to protect against the risk of loss through fraud.

Good Faith in Negotiable Instruments Law

Clearly, the principle of good faith reflects ethical principles. The most notable application of the good faith requirement in negotiable instruments law is, of course, the HDC doctrine. Traditionally, to acquire the protected status of an HDC, a holder must have acquired an instrument in good faith. Yet other transactions subject to Articles 3 and 4 also require good faith—as, indeed, do all transactions governed by the UCC.

The Importance of Good Faith A party that acts in bad faith may be precluded from seeking shelter under UCC provisions that would otherwise apply. This point was emphasized by a Pennsylvania court's decision with respect to the fictitious payee rule. The bank in this case had accepted 882 payroll checks generated and indorsed by Dorothy Heck, a payroll clerk employed by Pavex, Inc. The checks were made

---

1. 31 Kan. 478, 2 P. 580 (1884).

payable to various current and former Pavex employees, indorsed by Heck with the payees' names, and deposited into Heck's personal checking account at her bank.

In spite of its policy that indorsements on checks must match exactly the names of the payees, the bank never refused any of Heck's deposited checks on which the indorsements did not match the payees' names. Furthermore, even though bank personnel discussed among themselves Heck's check-depositing activities on more than one occasion, they never contacted her employer to see if Heck was authorized to deposit third party payroll checks.

The court held that to assert the fictitious payee rule, "the bank must have acted in good faith when paying the instrument." In this case, the bank's failure to question perceived irregularities in Heck's transactions led the court to conclude that the bank had acted in bad faith and was therefore liable for approximately $170,000 of the $250,000 loss suffered by Pavex.[2]

How Should Good Faith Be Tested? From an early time, there has been a division of opinion with respect to how good faith should be measured, or tested. At one end of the spectrum of views is the position that the test of good faith should be subjective in nature. In other words, as long as a person acts honestly, no matter how negligent or foolish the conduct may be, that person is acting in good faith. At the other end of the spectrum is the "objective" test of good faith. Under this test, honesty in itself is not enough. A party must also act reasonably under the circumstances. Whereas a fool might pass the subjective test, he or she would not meet the objective test.

Over time, the pendulum seems to have swung from one end of the spectrum to the other. When the UCC was initially drafted, the definition of *good faith* set forth in UCC 1–201(19) was adopted for use throughout the UCC. That section established a subjective test for good faith by defining good faith as "honesty in fact in the conduct or transaction concerned." The only UCC article that incorporated a more objective test for good faith was Article 2. Section 2–103(1)(b) defined good faith as both honesty in fact *and* the observance of reasonable commercial standards of fair dealing in the trade. Under this definition of good faith, a person who acts honestly in fact but does not observe reasonable commercial standards of fair dealing will not meet the good faith requirement.

This more objective measure of good faith has since been incorporated into other articles of the UCC, including Articles 3, 4, and 4A. The 1990 revision of Article 3, for example, defines good faith as requiring not only honesty in fact but also "reasonable commercial standards of fair dealing"—see UCC 3–103(a)(4).

Criticisms of the Objective Standard Some critics claim that while the subjective test of "honesty in fact" is manageable, the objective test that requires the "observance of reasonable commercial standards" opens the door to potentially endless litigation. After all, it is difficult to determine what is commercially reasonable in a given context until you hear what others in that commercial situation have to say. Thus, parties to a dispute can nearly always make some kind of good faith argument, and any time the issue is raised, litigation can result.

How Good Faith Standards Can Affect HDC Status To illustrate the impact of the objective versus subjective standards of good faith on HDC status, consider an example. Mitchell was a farmer who operated a multistate farming operation on leased property. Runnells, a grain broker, had sold Mitchell's 2001 crop of grain. Out of the crop proceeds, Mitchell instructed Runnells to draw checks payable to Mitchell's various landlords in payment of his rent obligations. The checks totaled over $153,000. The landlords accepted the checks in payment of the farmer's rent—completely unaware that Mitchell had already pledged the proceeds from the sale of his crops as collateral for a loan from Agriliance (security interests will be discussed in Chapter 29). Agriliance filed a lawsuit in a federal court against Runnells and the various landlords for conversion (wrongful taking of personal property—see Chapter 6).

According to the UCC, an HDC takes a negotiable instrument free of any claim to the instrument, including claims of prior secured parties. Thus, the outcome of the case depended on whether Runnells and the landlords were HDCs. Under the subjective standard (and prior to the 1990 revision of the UCC), the landlords would be HDCs because they had taken the checks without actual knowledge of Agriliance's claim to the crop proceeds. The objective standard, however, dictated a different result. Because it is common for farmers to put their crops up as collateral for loans, the court held that reasonable commercial standards of fair dealing required Mitchell's creditors (Runnells and the landlords) to conduct a search of the public records. Such a search would have revealed the existence of Agriliance's prior secured claim. Runnells and the landlords in this case could not be HDCs because they failed to meet the objective element of good faith. The court, therefore, ruled that Agriliance was entitled to the crop proceeds.[3]

Efficiency versus Due Care

A major problem faced by today's banking institutions is how to verify customer signatures on the billions of checks that are processed by the banking system each month. If a bank fails to verify a signature on a check it receives for payment and

2. *Pavex, Inc. v. York Federal Savings and Loan Association,* 716 A.2d 640 (Pa.Super.Ct. 1998).

3. *Agriliance, L.L.C. v. Runnells Grain Elevator, Inc.,* 272 F.Supp.2d 800 (S.D. Iowa 2003).

the check turns out to be forged, the bank will normally be held liable to its customer for the amount paid. But how can banks possibly examine, item by item, each signature on every check that they pay?

The Banks' Solution to the Problem The banks' solution to this problem is simply to not examine all signatures. Instead, computers are programmed to verify signatures only on checks exceeding a certain threshold amount, such as $1,000 or $2,500 or perhaps some higher figure. Checks for less than the threshold amount are selected for signature verification only on a random basis. In other words, serious attention is restricted to serious matters. The result is that many, if not most, checks are paid without signature verification. This practice, which has become an acceptable standard within today's banking industry, is economically efficient for banks. Even though liability costs are sometimes incurred—when forged checks are paid—the total costs involved in verifying the authenticity of each and every signature would be far higher.

Some people have alleged that banks using such procedures are not exercising due care in handling their customers' accounts. Under the UCC, banks are held to a standard of "ordinary care." At one time in the banking industry, ordinary care normally was interpreted to mean that a bank had a duty to inspect *all* signatures on checks. The question is, what constitutes ordinary care in the context of today's world? Does a bank exercise ordinary care if it follows the prevailing industry practice of examining signatures on only a few, randomly selected checks payable for under a certain amount? Or does ordinary care still mean that a bank should examine each signature?

The Unrevised versus the Revised Article 3 Under the unrevised Article 3, a number of courts have held that banks do not breach their duty of care by establishing and adhering to a practice that is cost-effective and customary within the industry. Other courts, however, have reasoned that banks are supposed to verify all signatures on all checks, and thus banks are not exercising ordinary care when they fail to do so.

The revised Article 3 specifically addressed this problem in UCC 3–103(a)(7). That section states that "[i]n the case of a bank that takes an instrument for processing for collection or payment by automated means, reasonable commercial standards do not require the bank to examine the instrument if failure to examine does not violate the bank's prescribed procedures and the bank's procedures do not vary unreasonably from the general banking usage."

Technology and Banking

Electronic banking practices have posed legal—and ethical—issues, just as electronic transactions have created problems in other areas of the law, such as torts and crimes. We look here at some of these concerns.

Electronic Fund Transfers From the time they were first used, electronic fund transfers (EFTs) have given rise to evidentiary issues. In other words, because an EFT leaves no "paper trail," it is difficult for either the customer or the bank to prove what really happened when a dispute arises. For example, if you obtain cash via an automated teller machine (ATM), the only evidence of the transaction is the ATM receipt that you receive and the bank's computerized record of the transaction. There is nothing on the ATM receipt or in the bank's computer files to indicate that you authorized the transaction. If someone else used your personal identification number (PIN) and withdrew the cash from your account—or if a withdrawal from your account was simply due to a computer error—there would be no paper trail, no signatures, and no other evidence that could be used as proof.

Although the Electronic Fund Transfer Act (EFTA) addressed many issues concerning the customer's liability with respect to EFTs and the bank's duty of care to the customer, not all issues have been resolved—particularly those that involve disagreement between the customer and the bank's computer. Suppose that Kevin, a bank customer, states that he did not make a specific withdrawal reflected on his bank statement. He also states that he was at work at the time of the withdrawal—as several co-workers will testify. Furthermore, no one else could have used his card because he keeps it with him at all times and no one else knows his PIN. If the dispute comes before a court, the bank will argue that, clearly, someone must have used Kevin's card and PIN to withdraw the funds. Kevin will argue, and have witnesses testify, that there was no way he could have withdrawn the funds.

Which party should the court believe? Often, the courts side with the banks in these situations. In at least one case, however, the court opted to believe the customer.[4]

Unauthorized Wire Transfers As discussed in Chapter 27, a "wire" transfer is an electronic fund transfer between commercial parties covered by UCC Article 4A. Wire transfers usually involve large amounts and, if unauthorized, can cause significant loss. Who should take the loss on unauthorized wire transfers? The answer is not always clear and often raises issues of fairness and equity. Although under UCC 4A–202 the bank normally bears the loss of any unauthorized fund transfer, this rule is subject to an important exception. If the bank and its customer have an agreed-upon commercially reasonable security procedure to guard against unauthorized transfers, and if the bank follows that procedure in good faith, then the customer bears the loss. A court must therefore determine if there was an agreed-upon security procedure in place, if it was commercially reasonable, and if the bank complied with the procedure in good faith. All three issues are fraught with potential for litigation.

---

4. *Judd v. Citibank*, 107 Misc.2d 526, 435 N.Y.S.2d 210 (1980); see also *Porter v. Citibank, N.A.*, 123 Misc.2d 28, 474 N.Y.S.2d 582 (1984).

Can the One-Year Period for Reporting Unauthorized Wire Transfers Be Varied by Agreement?

Under UCC 4A–505, a customer has one year after receiving notice of the payment order (wire transfer) to notify the bank that the fund transfer was unauthorized. If the customer does not notify the bank within this time, the customer is precluded from asserting that the bank wrongfully transferred the funds. Article 4A of the UCC does not specify whether this one-year period can be varied by agreement, however, which creates another layer of confusion for the courts in determining who takes the loss on unauthorized fund transfers.

In one case, for example, Regatos, a citizen of Brazil, regularly wire-transferred funds out of his Commercial Bank of New York (CBNY) account. His usual practice was to sign and fax a payment order to a designated representative of CBNY in Brazil, then follow up with a phone call confirming the bank's receipt of the payment order. CBNY accepted two allegedly unauthorized wire transfers that drained over half of the assets ($600,000) from Regatos's account. Because Regatos, like most other Brazilian customers of CBNY, had given the bank permission to retain his bank statements, he did not find out about the unauthorized transfers until several months after they occurred. When CBNY refused to refund the amount of the transfers, Regatos filed a lawsuit. CBNY argued that Regatos should bear the loss because he had signed an account agreement stating that he had only fifteen calendar days after his bank statement became available to complain that a payment order was unauthorized. According to the court in that case, however, the bank was not allowed to vary the one-year time limit for objecting to a fund transfer that was specified by UCC 4A–505.[5]

Digital Banking

Another technological development with ethical implications is the use of *e-money*, or digital cash. The increasing use of e-money poses many legal (and ethical) problems. For one thing, the traditional definition of money will certainly no longer hold. E-cash moves along completely outside the network of banks, checks, and paper currency. Thus, e-cash—at least as yet—is not subject to government regulation. Furthermore, e-cash may create difficulties if it is stored in computer systems. What if the systems crash? Additionally, electronic counterfeiting may be a serious problem. Computer hackers who break into an e-cash system might be able to steal funds from thousands or even hundreds of thousands of individuals at once. Finally, e-cash may allow for more tax evasion and money laundering.

DISCUSSION QUESTIONS

1. Because the UCC offers special protection to HDCs, innocent makers of notes or drawers of checks in fraudulent transactions often have no legal recourse. From an ethical standpoint, how could you justify to the "losers" in such situations the provisions of the UCC that fail to protect them? Can you think of a way in which such problems could be handled more fairly or ethically than they are under the UCC?

2. What do you think would result if a change in the law allowed personal defenses to be successfully raised against HDCs? Who would lose, and who would gain? How would such a change in the law affect the flow of commerce in this country?

3. Under Article 4, banks may choose to send their customers only a monthly itemized checking-account statement listing the check numbers, amounts, dates, and so on. Banks may include the canceled checks, but if the checks are not included, the banks must keep them for seven years in case customers wish to examine them [UCC 4–406(a), (b)]. What implications does this provision have for bank customers in terms of liability for unauthorized signatures and indorsements?

4. Do you think that the UCC's provisions have struck an appropriate balance between the interests of banks and those of bank customers?

5. What are some of the implications of the growing use of electronic banking and e-money?

---

5. *Regatos v. North Fork Bank*, 257 F.Supp.2d 632 (2003). Because this case presents important state law issues of first impression that will undoubtedly recur in other cases, the U.S. Court of Appeals for the Second Circuit has certified this case for appeal in a New York state court, and the state court has agreed to hear the appeal. See 396 F.3d 493 (C.A. N.Y. 2005); and 4 N.Y.3d 776, 825 N.E.2d 1090 (2005).

CHAPTER 28

Creditors' Rights and Remedies

Normally, creditors have no problem collecting the debts owed to them. When disputes arise over the amount owed, however, or when the debtor simply cannot or will not pay, what happens? What remedies are available to creditors when a debtor **defaults** (fails to pay as promised)? In this chapter, we focus on some basic laws that assist the debtor and creditor in resolving their dispute without the debtor's having to resort to bankruptcy—a topic to be discussed in Chapter 30. In Chapter 29, we will discuss the remedies that are only available to secured creditors (those whose loans are supported or backed by collateral) under Article 9 of the Uniform Commercial Code (UCC).

SECTION 1 | Laws Assisting Creditors

Both the common law and statutory laws other than Article 9 of the UCC create various rights and remedies for creditors. We discuss here some of these rights and remedies, including liens, garnishment, creditors' composition agreements, mortgage foreclosure, and a debtor's assignment of assets for the benefit of creditors.

LIENS

A **lien** is a claim against a debtor's property that must be satisfied before the property (or its proceeds) is available to satisfy the claims of other creditors. As mentioned, liens may arise under the common law or under statutory law. Statutory liens include *mechanic's liens*. Liens created at common law include *artisan's liens* and *innkeeper's liens*. *Judicial liens* include those that represent a creditor's efforts to collect on a debt before or after a judgment is entered by a court. Liens are a very important tool for creditors because they generally take priority over other claims against the same property (priority of claims will be discussed in depth in Chapter 29).

MECHANIC'S LIENS When a person contracts for labor, services, or materials to be furnished for the purpose of making improvements on real property but does not immediately pay for the improvements, the creditor can place a **mechanic's lien** on the property. This creates a special type of debtor-creditor relationship in which the real estate itself becomes security for the debt.

For example, a painter agrees to paint a house for a homeowner for an agreed-on price to cover labor and materials. If the homeowner cannot pay or pays only a portion of the charges, a mechanic's lien against the property can be created. The painter is the lienholder, and the real property is encumbered with a mechanic's lien for the amount owed. If the homeowner does not pay the lien, the property can be sold to satisfy the debt. Notice of the *foreclosure* (the enforcement of the lien) must be given to the debtor in advance, however.

Note that state law governs the procedures that must be followed to create a mechanic's lien. Generally, the lienholder has to file a written notice of lien against the particular property involved. The notice of lien must be filed within a specific time period, measured from the last date on which materials or labor were provided (usually within 60 to 120 days). If the property owner fails to pay the debt, the lienholder is entitled to foreclose on the real estate on which the improvements were made and to sell it to satisfy the amount of the debt. Of course, as mentioned, the lienholder is required by statute to give notice to the owner of the property prior to foreclosure and sale. The sale proceeds are used to pay the debt and the costs of the legal proceedings; the surplus, if any, is paid to the former owner.

ARTISAN'S LIENS An **artisan's lien** is a device created at common law through which a creditor can recover payment from a debtor for labor and materials furnished in the repair of personal property. For example, Whitney leaves her diamond ring at the jewelry shop to be repaired and to have her initials engraved on the band. In the absence of an agreement, the jeweler can keep the ring until Whitney pays for the services that the jeweler provides. Should Whitney fail to pay, the jeweler has a lien on Whitney's ring for the amount of the bill and can sell the ring in satisfaction of the lien.

—A Possessory Lien. In contrast to a mechanic's lien, an artisan's lien is *possessory*. The lienholder ordinarily must have retained possession of the property and have expressly or impliedly agreed to provide the services on a cash, not a credit, basis. The lien remains in existence as long as the lienholder maintains possession, and the lien is terminated once possession is voluntarily surrendered—unless the surrender is only temporary. With a temporary surrender, there must be an agreement that the property will be returned to the lienholder. Even with such an agreement, if a third party obtains rights in that property while it is out of the possession of the lienholder, the lien is lost.

—Notice of Foreclosure and Sale Required. Modern statutes permit the holder of an artisan's lien to foreclose and sell the property subject to the lien to satisfy payment of the debt. As with a mechanic's lien, the lienholder is required to give notice to the owner of the property prior to foreclosure and sale. In some states, holders of artisan's liens must give notice to title lienholders of automobiles prior to foreclosure. The sale proceeds are used to pay the debt and the costs of the legal proceedings, and the surplus, if any, is paid to the former owner. An artisan's lien has priority over both a filed statutory lien (such as a title lien on an automobile or a lien filed under Article 9 of the UCC) and a bailee's lien (such as a storage lien).

INNKEEPER'S LIENS An **innkeeper's lien** is another type of lien created at common law. An innkeeper's lien is placed on the personal property (baggage) of guests for any agreed-on hotel charges that remain unpaid. If no express agreement has been made on the amount of those charges, then the lien will be for the reasonable value of the accommodations furnished. The innkeeper's lien is terminated either by the guest's payment of the hotel bill or by the innkeeper's surrender of the baggage to the guest, unless the surrender is temporary. Most state statutes permit the innkeeper to satisfy the debt by means of a public sale of the guest's baggage. Some jurisdictions require that the guest first be given an impartial judicial hearing.

JUDICIAL LIENS When a debt is past due, a creditor can bring a legal action against the debtor to collect the debt. If the creditor is successful in the action, the court awards the creditor a judgment against the debtor (usually for the amount of the debt plus any interest and legal costs incurred in obtaining the judgment). Frequently, however, the creditor is unable to collect the awarded amount.

To ensure that a judgment in the creditor's favor will be collectible, creditors are permitted to request that certain nonexempt property of the debtor be seized to satisfy the debt. (As will be discussed later in this chapter, under state or federal statutes, some kinds of property are exempt from attachment by creditors.) If the court orders the debtor's property to be seized prior to a judgment in the creditor's favor, the court's order is referred to as a *writ of attachment*. If the court orders the debtor's property to be seized following a judgment in the creditor's favor, the court's order is referred to as a *writ of execution*.

—Attachment. In the context of judicial liens, **attachment** refers to a court-ordered seizure and taking into custody of property prior to the securing of a judgment for a past-due debt. (As you will read in Chapter 29, in the context of secured transactions this word has a different meaning. *Attachment* under UCC 9–203 refers to the process through which a security interest becomes effective and enforceable against a debtor with respect to the debtor's collateral.) Normally, attachment is a *prejudgment* remedy, occurring either at the time a lawsuit is filed or immediately thereafter. In order to attach *before* a judgment, a creditor must comply with the specific state's statutory restrictions and the requirements of the due process clause of the Fourteenth Amendment to the U.S. Constitution (see Chapter 4).

The creditor must have an enforceable right to payment of the debt under law and must follow certain procedures. Otherwise, the creditor can be liable for damages for wrongful attachment. Typically, the creditor must file with the court an *affidavit* (a written or printed statement, made under oath or sworn to) stating that the debtor has failed to pay and delineating the statutory grounds under which attachment is sought. The creditor must also post a bond to cover at least the court costs, the value of the loss of use of the good suffered by the debtor, and the value of the property attached. When the court is satisfied that all the requirements have been met, it issues a **writ of attachment,** which directs the sheriff or other officer to seize nonexempt property. If the creditor prevails at trial, the seized property can be sold to satisfy the judgment.

—*Writ of Execution.*   If a creditor obtains a judgment against the debtor and the debtor will not or cannot pay the judgment, the creditor is entitled to go back to the court and request a **writ of execution.** A writ of execution is an order that directs the sheriff to seize (levy) and sell any of the debtor's nonexempt real or personal property that is within the court's geographic jurisdiction (usually the county in which the courthouse is located). The proceeds of the sale are used to pay off the judgment, accrued interest, and the costs of the sale. Any excess is paid to the debtor.

The debtor can pay the judgment and redeem the nonexempt property at any time before the sale takes place. Because of exemption laws (discussed later in this chapter) and bankruptcy laws (discussed in Chapter 30), however, many judgments are virtually uncollectible.

GARNISHMENT

An order for **garnishment** permits a creditor to collect a debt by seizing property of the debtor that is being held by a third party. In a garnishment proceeding, the third party—the person or entity on whom the garnishment judgment is served—is called the *garnishee*. Typically, a garnishee is the debtor's employer. A creditor may seek a garnishment judgment against the debtor's employer so that part of the debtor's usual paycheck will be paid to the creditor. In some situations, however, the garnishee is a third party that holds funds belonging to the debtor (such as a bank) or a third party who has possession of, or exercises control over, funds or other types of property belonging to the debtor. Almost all types of property can be garnished, including tax refunds, pensions, and trust funds—so long as the property is not exempt from garnishment and is in the possession of a third party.

GARNISHMENT PROCEEDINGS   The legal proceeding for a garnishment action is governed by state law. As a result of a garnishment proceeding, as noted, a third party (such as the debtor's employer) is ordered by the court to turn over property owned by the debtor (such as wages) to pay the debt. Garnishment can be a prejudgment remedy, requiring a hearing before a court, or a postjudgment remedy. According to the laws in some states, the judgment creditor needs to obtain only one order of garnishment, which will then continuously apply to the judgment debtor's weekly wages until the entire debt is paid. In other states, the judgment creditor must go back to court for a separate order of garnishment for each pay period.

LAWS LIMITING THE AMOUNT OF WAGES SUBJECT TO GARNISHMENT   Both federal and state laws limit the amount that can be taken from a debtor's weekly take-home pay through garnishment proceedings.[1] Federal law provides a minimal framework to protect debtors from losing all their income to pay judgment debts.[2] State laws also provide dollar exemptions, and these amounts are often larger than those provided by federal law. State and federal statutes can be applied together to create a pool of funds sufficient to enable a debtor to continue to provide for family needs while also paying the judgment debt in a reasonable manner. Under federal law, an employer cannot dismiss an employee because his or her wages are being garnished for one indebtedness.

In the following case, the issue was whether, for purposes of a garnishment order, an employee's wages included the tips that the employee received directly from her employer's customers.

---

1. A few states (for example, Texas) do not permit garnishment of wages by private parties except under a child-support order.
2. For example, the federal Consumer Credit Protection Act, 15 U.S.C. Sections 1601–1693r, provides that a debtor can retain either 75 percent of his or her disposable earnings per week or the sum equivalent to thirty hours of work paid at federal minimum wage rates, whichever is greater.

CASE 28.1

Court of Appeals
of Maryland, 2001.
364 Md. 538,
774 A.3d 411.

Shanks v. Lowe

BACKGROUND AND FACTS *Laura Shanks won a judgment in a Maryland state court against Susan Lowe for $6,000. Shanks obtained a garnishment order and served it on Lowe's employer, Kibby's Restaurant & Lounge, which was ordered to withhold her attachable wages to pay the judgment and other costs. Exempt, under Maryland statutes, was one of two amounts, whichever was greater: (1) $154.50 multiplied by the number of weeks in which wages due were earned or (2) 75 percent of disposable wages ("the part of wages that remain after deduction of any amount required to be withheld by law").[a] Kibby's responded that Lowe's gross wages averaged $95 per week and that her "disposable income average per week is approx $35–$40," which was less than the allowable exemption of $154.50. Kibby's added that Lowe also earned tips, which Kibby's included in her wages for tax purposes,[b] but claimed that the tips were not wages for garnishment purposes because they were never in Kibby's possession—restaurant patrons paid them directly to Lowe. The court agreed and dismissed the garnishment. Shanks appealed to a state intermediate appellate court, which affirmed the dismissal. Shanks appealed to the Maryland Court of Appeals, the state's highest court.*

IN THE LANGUAGE OF THE COURT

WILNER, Judge:

The issue before us is whether tips earned by a waitress (or other person who earns tips) constitute "wages" for purposes of the Maryland wage garnishment law * * * . Principally at issue is whether tips fall within the definition of "wages" in [Maryland Code Section] 15–601(c): "all monetary remuneration paid to any employee for his employment." * * *

* * * * *

* * * Maryland Code [Section] 3–413(1) * * * requires each employer in Maryland to pay its employees the minimum wage required by the Federal Fair Labor Standards Act. The term "wage" is defined in [Section] 3–401(e) as "all compensation that is due to an employee for employment" * * * . Section 3–419 takes specific account of tips and, as to any employee who regularly receives more than $30/month in tips, * * * provides, in relevant part, that an employer may include, "as part of the wage of an employee to whom this section applies," an amount that the employer sets to represent the tips of the employee, up to $2.77/hour. This is consistent with the Federal law, which defines a "tipped employee" as an employee engaged in an occupation in which he or she customarily and regularly receives more than $30/month in tips and, in relevant part, calculates the required minimum wage for such an employee as the actual cash wage paid by the employer plus an additional amount on account of tips equal to the difference between that actual cash wage and the minimum wage * * * . Thus, for purposes of the State and Federal minimum wage laws, tips are regarded as part of wages.

Significantly, tips are included within the meaning of wages for purposes of the unemployment insurance and workers' compensation laws, each of which provide benefits based on the employee's wages. Were Ms. [Lowe] to file a claim for either unemployment insurance or workers' compensation benefits, any benefits to which she might be entitled would be determined on the basis of the aggregate amounts she received from both Kibby's and its customers.

* * * * *

---

a. See Maryland Code Sections 15–601 through 15–607.

b. For example, in one week, Kibby's reported to the federal and state governments $92.44 in wages due to Lowe and $153.50 in tips, for total taxable wages of $245.94. From that amount, Kibby's deducted $29.25 in federal taxes, $18.82 in Social Security taxes, and $13.87 in state taxes, leaving $30.50 owed to Lowe over the amount of her tips.

CONTINUED ▶

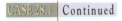 **Continued**

These statutes illustrate a consistent view by the General Assembly [Maryland's legislature] that, in using terms such as "wage" or "wages," it intended to include all forms of remuneration, whether or not paid directly by the employer, except to the extent specifically excluded. When it desired to limit the scope of a statute to the remuneration paid in the form of a salary or other periodic payment by an employer, it made that intent clear.

DECISION AND REMEDY *The Maryland Court of Appeals reversed the judgment of the lower court and remanded the case for further proceedings. The state's highest court held that under state law, for purposes of a garnishment order, tips constitute "monetary remuneration paid to any employee for his employment" and are therefore part of the employee's wages.*

WHAT IF THE FACTS WERE DIFFERENT? *Suppose that the dispute in this case had involved a bonus that Lowe received from her employer rather than the amount she received in tips. Would the court still have concluded the bonus was part of Lowe's wages? Why or why not?*

CREDITORS' COMPOSITION AGREEMENTS

Creditors may contract with the debtor for discharge of the debtor's liquidated debts (debts that are definite, or fixed, in amount) on payment of a sum less than that owed. These agreements are referred to as *composition agreements* or **creditors' composition agreements** and are usually held to be enforceable unless they are formed under duress.

MORTGAGES

A **mortgage** is a written instrument giving a creditor an interest in (lien on) the debtor's real property as security for the payment of a debt. Financial institutions grant mortgage loans for the purchase of property—usually a dwelling (real property is discussed in Chapter 48). Given the relatively large sums that many individuals borrow to purchase a home, defaults are not uncommon. Mortgages are recorded with the county in the state where the property is located. Recording ensures that the creditor is officially on record as holding an interest in the property. As a further precaution, most creditors require mortgage insurance for debtors who do not pay at least 20 percent of the purchase price as a down payment at the time of the transaction.

MORTGAGE FORECLOSURE Mortgage holders have the right to foreclose on mortgaged property in the event of a debtor's default. The usual method of foreclosure is by judicial sale of the property, although the statutory methods of foreclosure vary from state to state. If the proceeds of the foreclosure sale are sufficient to cover both the costs of the foreclosure and the mortgaged debt, any surplus goes to the debtor. If the sale proceeds are insufficient to cover the foreclosure costs and the mortgaged debt, however, the **mortgagee** (the creditor-lender) can seek to recover the difference from the **mortgagor** (the debtor) by obtaining a *deficiency judgment* representing the difference between the mortgaged debt plus foreclosure costs and the amount actually received from the proceeds of the foreclosure sale.

The creditor obtains a deficiency judgment in a separate legal action that is pursued subsequent to the foreclosure action. The deficiency judgment entitles the creditor to recover from other property owned by the debtor. Some states do not permit deficiency judgments for some types of real estate interests.

REDEMPTION RIGHTS Before the foreclosure sale, a defaulting mortgagor can redeem the property by paying the full amount of the debt, plus any interest and costs that have accrued. This right is known as the **equity of redemption.** In some states, a mortgagor may even redeem the property within a certain period of time—called a **statutory period of redemption**—after the sale. In these states, the deed to the property usually is not delivered to the purchaser until the statutory period has expired.

ASSIGNMENT FOR THE BENEFIT OF CREDITORS

Both common law and statutes may provide for a debtor's assignment of assets to a trustee or assignee for the benefit of the debtor's creditors. In these situations, the debtor voluntarily transfers title to assets owned to a trustee or assignee, who in turn sells or liquidates these assets, tendering payment to the debtor's creditors on a pro rata (proportionate) basis. Each creditor may accept the tender (and discharge the debt

CONCEPT SUMMARY 28.1 | Remedies Available to Creditors

REMEDY	DESCRIPTION

LIENS	1. *Mechanic's lien*—A lien filed on an owner's real estate for labor, services, or materials furnished for improvements made to the realty.
	2. *Artisan's lien*—A lien on an owner's personal property for labor performed or value added to the personal property.
	3. *Innkeeper's lien*—A lien on a hotel guest's baggage for hotel charges that remain unpaid.
	4. *Judicial liens*—
	  a. Attachment—A court-ordered seizure of property prior to a court's final determination of the creditor's rights to the property. Creditors must strictly comply with applicable state statutes to obtain a writ of attachment.
	  b. Writ of execution—A court order directing the sheriff to seize (levy) and sell a debtor's nonexempt real or personal property to satisfy a court's judgment in the creditor's favor.

GARNISHMENT	A collection remedy that allows the creditor to attach a debtor's funds (such as wages owed or bank accounts) and property that are held by a third person.
CREDITORS' COMPOSITION AGREEMENT	A contract between a debtor and his or her creditors by which the debtor's debts are discharged by payment of a sum less than the sum that is actually owed.
MORTGAGE FORECLOSURE	On the debtor's default, the entire mortgage debt is due and payable, allowing the creditor to foreclose on the realty by selling it to satisfy the debt.
ASSIGNMENT FOR THE BENEFIT OF CREDITORS	The debtor's assignment of certain assets to a trustee or assignee, who sells or liquidates the assets and pays the creditors on a pro rata basis. Acceptance of the payment by a creditor discharges the debt.

owed to her or him) or reject it (and attempt to collect the debt in another way).

The flexibility and informality of an assignment for the benefit of creditors may save creditors time and expense and result in better prices when a debtor's property is liquidated. Nevertheless, creditors may decide that this option does not adequately protect their rights. Under bankruptcy law, creditors may be able to force the debtor into involuntary bankruptcy, depending on the amount of their claims against the debtor and other factors (see Chapter 30). Thus, a debtor's bankruptcy may supersede an assignment for the benefit of creditors—even if a creditor initiated the bankruptcy.

SECTION 2 | Suretyship and Guaranty

When a third person promises to pay a debt owed by another in the event the debtor does not pay, either a *suretyship* or a *guaranty* relationship is created. Exhibit 28–1 on the next page illustrates these relationships.

The third person's credit becomes the security for the debt owed.

SURETYSHIP

A contract of strict **suretyship** is a promise made by a third person to be responsible for the debtor's obligation. It is an express contract between the **surety** and the creditor. The surety in the strictest sense is primarily liable for the debt of the principal. The creditor can demand payment from the surety from the moment that the debt is due. A suretyship contract is not a form of indemnity; that is, it is not merely a promise to make good any loss that a creditor may incur as a result of the debtor's failure to pay. The creditor need not exhaust all legal remedies against the principal debtor before holding the surety responsible for payment. Moreover, a surety agreement does not have to be in writing to be enforceable, although usually such agreements are in writing.

For example, Jason Oller wants to borrow funds from the bank to buy a used car. Because Jason is still

EXHIBIT 28-1 **Suretyship and Guaranty Parties**

In a suretyship or guaranty arrangement, a third party promises to be responsible for a debtor's obligations. A third party who agrees to be responsible for the debt even if the primary debtor does not default is known as a surety; a third party who agrees to be *secondarily* responsible for the debt—that is, responsible only if the primary debtor defaults—is known as a guarantor. As noted in Chapter 15, normally a promise of guaranty (a collateral, or secondary, promise) must be in writing to be enforceable.

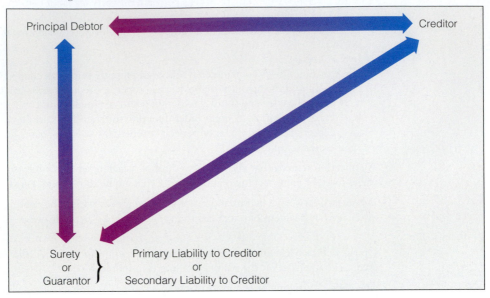

in college, the bank will not lend him the funds unless his father, Stuart Oller, who has dealt with the bank before, will cosign the note (add his signature to the note, thereby becoming jointly liable for payment of the debt). When Mr. Oller cosigns the note, he becomes primarily liable to the bank. On the note's due date, the bank can seek payment from Jason Oller, Stuart Oller, or both jointly.

GUARANTY

A guaranty contract is similar to a suretyship contract in that it includes a promise to answer for the debt or default of another. There are some significant differences between these two types of contracts, however.

SURETYSHIP VERSUS GUARANTY With a suretyship arrangement, the surety is *primarily* liable for the debtor's obligation. With a guaranty arrangement, the **guarantor**—the third person making the guaranty—is *secondarily* liable. The guarantor can be required to pay the obligation only after the principal debtor defaults, and usually only after the creditor has made an attempt to collect from the debtor.

For example, a corporation, BX Enterprises, needs to borrow money to meet its payroll. The bank is skeptical about the creditworthiness of BX and requires Dawson, its president, who is a wealthy businessperson and owner of 70 percent of BX Enterprises, to sign an agreement making himself personally liable for payment if BX does not pay off the loan. As a guarantor of the loan, Dawson cannot be held liable until BX Enterprises is in default.

Another difference between suretyship and guaranty has to do with the Statute of Frauds. Whereas a surety agreement can be oral, the Statute of Frauds generally requires that a contract between a guarantor and a creditor be in writing to be enforceable.[3]

In the following case, the issue was whether a guaranty of a lease signed by the officer of a corporation was enforceable against the officer personally even though he claimed to have signed the guaranty only as a representative of the corporation.

---

3. This general rule is enforced *unless* the *main purpose exception* applies. Briefly, this exception provides that if the main purpose of the guaranty agreement is to benefit the guarantor, then the contract need not be in writing to be enforceable. (See Chapter 15 for a more detailed discussion of this exception.)

CASE 28.2

Court of Appeals
of Indiana, 2003.
794 N.E.2d 555.

JSV, Inc. v. Hene Meat Co., Inc.

BARNES, Judge.

* * * *

On August 30, 1999, JSV, Inc. ("JSV") signed a lease to rent a portion of a building in Indianapolis from Hene [Meat Company. Mark] Kennedy signed the lease on behalf of JSV as one of that corporation's officers. In addition, Kennedy signed a document simply denominated [described] "GUARANTY." The document indicated that it was "an absolute and unconditional guaranty" of the lease's performance by JSV * * * . Kennedy's printed name and signature on the document are not followed by any corporate officer designation.

JSV stopped paying rent to Hene in September 2000. On June 5, 2001, Hene sued both JSV under the lease and Kennedy under the guaranty [in an Indiana state court]. * * *

On April 16, 2002, Hene moved for summary judgment. * * * On September 9, 2002, * * * the trial court * * * granted Hene's summary judgment motion and entered judgment against both JSV and Kennedy personally for the sum of $75,041.07. Kennedy alone now appeals.

* * * *

The * * * argument of Kennedy's that we address is whether the trial court erred in granting summary judgment in favor of Hene on its claim that Kennedy was personally liable under the guaranty he executed. * * *

The interpretation of a guaranty is governed by the same rules applicable to other contracts. *Absent ambiguity, the terms of a contract will be given their plain and ordinary meaning and will not be considered ambiguous solely because the parties dispute the proper interpretation of the terms.* * * * [Emphasis added.]

We conclude that the guaranty Kennedy executed was unambiguously a personal guaranty * * * . It is axiomatic [clear] under Indiana law that a guaranty agreement must consist of three parties: the obligor, the obligee, and the surety or guarantor. Here, Hene as landlord under the lease was the obligee and JSV as the tenant was the obligor; the disputed issue is the identity of the guarantor. Kennedy claims he signed both the lease *and* the guaranty as an officer of JSV.

However, *there would have been no point in Hene's obtaining Kennedy's guaranty of the lease if he was doing so only in his official capacity as an officer of JSV.* Such an action would have been equivalent to JSV guaranteeing JSV's performance of the lease and to JSV being both the obligor under the lease and the guarantor under the guaranty. * * * [S]uch a result would be paradoxical and untenable. In [a different case] we concluded that where a corporate officer executed a guaranty with respect to credit extended to the corporation, the guaranty was a personal one and the officer personally was the guarantor despite the fact that the officer placed his corporate title after his signature on the guaranty. We further concluded that this was apparent as a matter of law and summary judgment on the issue was appropriate. In this case, the guaranty is even more clearly a personal one * * * because Kennedy's signature thereon is not followed by any corporate officer designation. The trial court did not err in concluding that the guaranty Kennedy executed was a personal one as a matter of law and in granting summary judgment against Kennedy personally. [Emphasis added.]

* * * *

The trial court * * * properly concluded that Kennedy was personally liable to Hene on the guaranty he executed for any breach of the underlying lease by JSV. We affirm.

QUESTIONS

1. How significant should the court have found the omission of the word *personal* from the guaranty?
2. What effect might it have had on the result in this case if Hene had misled Kennedy into believing he was signing the guaranty only in his capacity as an officer of JSV?

THE EXTENT AND TIME OF THE GUARANTOR'S LIABILITY

The guaranty contract terms determine the extent and time of the guarantor's liability. For example, the guaranty can be *continuing*, designed to cover a series of transactions by the debtor. Also, the guaranty can be *unlimited* or *limited* as to time and amount. In addition, the guaranty can be *absolute* or *conditional*. With a conditional guaranty, the guarantor becomes liable only on the happening of a certain event. When a guaranty is absolute, the guarantor becomes liable immediately on the debtor's default.

DEFENSES OF THE SURETY AND THE GUARANTOR

The defenses of the surety and the guarantor are basically the same. Therefore, the following discussion applies to both, although it refers only to the surety.

ACTIONS RELEASING THE SURETY Certain actions will release the surety from the obligation. For example, making any material modification in the terms of the original contract between the principal debtor and the creditor, including the awarding of a binding extension of time for making payment, without first obtaining the consent of the surety will discharge a gratuitous surety (one who receives no consideration in return for acting as a surety) completely. A surety who is compensated will be discharged to the extent that the surety suffers a loss.

Naturally, if the principal obligation is paid by the debtor or by another person on behalf of the debtor, the surety is discharged from the obligation. Similarly, if valid tender of payment is made, and the creditor for some reason rejects it with knowledge of the surety's existence, then the surety is released from any obligation on the debt.

DEFENSES OF THE PRINCIPAL DEBTOR Generally, any defenses available to the principal debtor can be used by the surety to avoid liability on the obligation to the creditor. Defenses available to the principal debtor that the surety *cannot* use include the principal debtor's incapacity or bankruptcy and the statute of limitations. The ability of the surety to assert any defenses the debtor may have against the creditor is the most important concept in suretyship, because most of the defenses available to the surety are also those of the debtor.

SURRENDER OR IMPAIRMENT OF COLLATERAL In addition, if a creditor surrenders or impairs the debtor's collateral while knowing of the surety and without the surety's consent, the surety is released to the extent of any loss suffered from the creditor's actions. The primary reason for this is to protect the surety who agreed to become obligated only because the debtor's collateral was in the possession of the creditor.

OTHER DEFENSES Obviously, a surety may also have his or her own defenses—for example, incapacity or bankruptcy. If the creditor fraudulently induced the surety to guarantee the debt, the surety can assert fraud as a defense. In most states, the creditor has a legal duty to inform the surety, prior to the formation of the suretyship contract, of material facts known by the creditor that would substantially increase the surety's risk. Failure to so inform is fraud and makes the suretyship obligation voidable.

RIGHTS OF THE SURETY AND THE GUARANTOR

Generally, when the surety or guarantor pays the debt owed to the creditor, the surety or guarantor is entitled to certain rights. Because the rights of the surety and the guarantor are basically the same, the following discussion applies to both.

THE RIGHT OF SUBROGATION First, the surety has the legal **right of subrogation.** Simply stated, this means that any right the creditor had against the debtor now becomes the right of the surety. Included are creditor rights in bankruptcy, rights to collateral possessed by the creditor, and rights to judgments obtained by the creditor. In short, the surety now stands in the shoes of the creditor and may pursue any remedies that were available to the creditor against the debtor.

THE RIGHT OF REIMBURSEMENT Second, the surety has a right to be reimbursed by the debtor. This **right of reimbursement** may stem either from the suretyship contract or from equity. Basically, the surety is entitled to receive from the debtor all outlays made on behalf of the suretyship arrangement. Such outlays can include expenses incurred, as well as the actual amount of the debt paid to the creditor.

THE RIGHT OF CONTRIBUTION Third, in the case of **co-sureties** (two or more sureties on the same obligation owed by the debtor), the **right of contribution** allows a surety who pays more than his or her proportionate share on a debtor's default to recover from the co-sureties the amount paid above the surety's obligation. Generally, a co-surety's liability either is determined by agreement or, in the absence of agreement, is set at the maximum liability under the suretyship contract.

For example, assume that two co-sureties are obligated under a suretyship contract to guarantee the debt of a debtor. Together, the sureties' maximum liability is $25,000. Surety A's maximum liability is $15,000, and surety B's is $10,000. The debtor owes $10,000 and is in default. Surety A pays the creditor the entire $10,000. In the absence of agreement, surety A can recover $4,000 from surety B ($10,000/$25,000 × $10,000 = $4,000, surety B's obligation).

SECTION 3 | Protection for Debtors

The law protects debtors, as well as creditors. Certain property of the debtor, for example, is exempt under state law from creditors' actions. Consumer protection statutes (see Chapter 44) also protect debtors' rights. Of course, bankruptcy laws, which will be discussed in Chapter 30, are designed specifically to assist debtors in need of help.

In most states, certain types of real and personal property are exempt from execution or attachment. State exemption statutes usually include both real and personal property.

EXEMPTED REAL PROPERTY

Probably the most familiar exemption is the **homestead exemption.** Each state permits the debtor to retain the family home, either in its entirety or up to a specified dollar amount, free from the claims of unsecured creditors or trustees in bankruptcy. (As of 2005, new federal bankruptcy laws override state exemptions for debtors in bankruptcy and place limitations and

restrictions on debtors seeking to use state homestead exemptions—see Chapter 30 for details.) Suppose that Beere owes Veltman $40,000. The debt is the subject of a lawsuit, and the court awards Veltman a judgment of $40,000 against Beere. Beere's homestead is valued at $50,000, and the homestead exemption is $25,000. There are no outstanding mortgages or other liens on his homestead. To satisfy the judgment debt, Beere's family home is sold at public auction for $45,000. The proceeds of the sale are distributed as follows:

1. Beere is given $25,000 as his homestead exemption.
2. Veltman is paid $20,000 toward the judgment debt, leaving a $20,000 deficiency judgment (that is, "leftover debt") that can be satisfied from any other nonexempt property (personal or real) that Beere may own, if allowed by state law.

In a few states, statutes allow the homestead exemption only if the judgment debtor has a family. The policy behind this type of statute is to protect the family; if a judgment debtor does not have a family, a creditor may be entitled to collect the full amount realized from the sale of the debtor's home.

EXEMPTED PERSONAL PROPERTY

Personal property that is most often exempt from satisfaction of judgment debts includes the following:

1. Household furniture up to a specified dollar amount.
2. Clothing and certain personal possessions, such as family pictures or a Bible.
3. A vehicle (or vehicles) for transportation (at least up to a specified dollar amount).
4. Certain classified animals, usually livestock but including pets.
5. Equipment that the debtor uses in a business or trade, such as tools or professional instruments, up to a specified dollar amount.

REVIEWING CREATORS' RIGHTS AND REMEDIES

Air Ruidoso, Ltd., operated a commuter airline and air charter service between Ruidoso, New Mexico, and airports in Albuquerque and El Paso. Executive Aviation Center, Inc., provided services for airlines at the Albuquerque International Airport. When Air Ruidoso failed to pay more than $10,000 that it owed for fuel, oil, and oxygen, Executive Aviation took possession of Air Ruidoso's plane, claiming that it had a lien on the plane. Using the information presented in the chapter, answer the following questions.

1. Can Executive Aviation establish an artisan's lien on the plane? Do supplies such as fuel, oil, and oxygen qualify as "materials" for the purpose of creating an artisan's lien? Why or why not?

(Continued)

REVIEWING CREDITORS' RIGHTS AND REMEDIES (continued)

2. | Suppose that Executive Aviation files a lawsuit in court against Air Ruidoso for the $10,000 past-due debt. What two methods discussed in this chapter would allow the court to seize Air Ruidoso's plane to satisfy the debt? What is the difference between these two remedies?

3. | Suppose that Executive Aviation discovers that Air Ruidoso has sufficient assets in one of its bank accounts to pay the past-due amount. How might Executive Aviation attempt to obtain access to these funds?

4. | Suppose that a clause in the contract between Air Ruidoso and Executive Aviation provides that "if the airline becomes insolvent, Braden Fasco, the CEO of Air Ruidoso, agrees to cover its outstanding debts." Is this a suretyship or a guaranty agreement? Considering the facts given above, can Executive Aviation go after Braden Fasco for the amount due? Why or why not?

TERMS AND CONCEPTS TO REVIEW

artisan's lien 569

attachment 569

co-surety 576

creditors' composition
    agreement 572

default 568

equity of redemption 572

garnishment 570

guarantor 574

homestead exemption 577

innkeeper's lien 569

lien 568

mechanic's lien 568

mortgage 572

mortgagee 572

mortgagor 572

right of contribution 576

right of reimbursement 576

right of subrogation 576

statutory period of
    redemption 572

surety 573

suretyship 573

writ of attachment 570

writ of execution 570

QUESTIONS AND CASE PROBLEMS

28–1. Sylvia takes her car to Caleb's Auto Repair Shop. A sign in the window states that all repairs must be paid for in cash unless credit is approved in advance. Sylvia and Caleb agree that Caleb will repair Sylvia's car engine and put in a new transmission. No mention is made of credit. Because Caleb is not sure how much engine repair will be necessary, he refuses to give Sylvia an estimate. He repairs the engine and puts in a new transmission. When Sylvia comes to pick up her car, she learns that the bill is $2,500. Sylvia is furious, refuses to pay Caleb that amount, and demands possession of her car. Caleb insists on payment. Discuss the rights of both parties in this matter.

28–2. **QUESTION WITH SAMPLE ANSWER**
Kanahara is employed by the Cross-Bar Packing Corp. and earns take-home pay of $400 per week. He is $2,000 in debt to the Holiday Department Store for goods purchased on credit over the past eight months. Most of this property is nonexempt and is currently located in Kanahara's apartment. Kanahara is in default on his payments to Holiday. Holiday learns that Kanahara has a girlfriend in another state and that he plans on giving her most of this property for Christmas. Discuss what actions are available and should be taken by Holiday to collect the debt owed by Kanahara.
For a sample answer to this question, go to Appendix I at the end of this text.

28–3. Natalie is a student at Slippery Stone University. In need of funds to pay for tuition and books, she asks West Bank for a short-term loan. The bank agrees to make a loan if Natalie will have someone who is financially responsible guarantee the loan payments. Sheila, a well-known businessperson and a friend of Natalie's family, calls the bank and agrees to pay the loan if Natalie cannot. Because of Sheila's reputation, the loan is made. Natalie is making the payments, but because of illness she is unable to work for one month. She requests that

West Bank extend the loan for three months. West Bank agrees, raising the interest rate for the extended period. Sheila is not notified of the extension (and thus does not consent to it). One month later, Natalie drops out of school. All attempts to collect from Natalie fail. West Bank wants to hold Sheila liable. Discuss the validity of West Bank's claim against Sheila.

28–4. Grant is the owner of a relatively old home valued at $45,000. He notices that the bathtubs and fixtures in both bathrooms are leaking and need to be replaced. He contracts with Jane's Plumbing to replace the bathtubs and fixtures. Jane replaces them, and on June 1 she submits her bill of $4,000 to Grant. Because of financial difficulties, Grant does not pay the bill. Grant's only asset is his home, but his state's homestead exemption is $40,000. Discuss fully Jane's remedies in this situation.

28–5. RIGHT OF SUBROGATION. Levinson and Johnson, who had both signed a promissory note, did not pay the note when it was due. Instead, American Thermex, Inc., a corporation in which Johnson had a controlling interest, voluntarily paid the note. American Thermex later brought suit against Levinson, seeking reimbursement for the payment. American Thermex argued, among other things, that because it had paid the note, it had the legal right of subrogation against the note's co-maker, Levinson. Will the court agree that American Thermex has a legal right of subrogation? Why or why not? [*Levinson v. American Thermex, Inc.*, 196 Ga.App. 291, 396 S.E.2d 252 (1990)]

28–6. GUARANTY. In 1988, Jamieson-Chippewa Investment Co. entered into a five-year commercial lease with TDM Pharmacy, Inc., for certain premises in Ellisville, Missouri, on which TDM intended to operate a small drugstore. Dennis and Tereasa McClintock ran the pharmacy business. The lease granted TDM three additional five-year options to renew. The lease was signed by TDM and by the McClintocks individually as guarantors. The lease did not state that the guaranty was continuing; in fact, there were no words of guaranty in the lease other than the single word "Guarantors" on the signature page. In 1993, Dennis McClintock, acting as the president of TDM, exercised TDM's option to renew the lease for one term. Three years later, when the pharmacy failed, TDM defaulted on the lease. Jamieson-Chippewa filed a suit in a Missouri state court against the McClintocks for the rent for the rest of the term, based on their guaranty. The McClintocks filed a motion for summary judgment, contending that they had not guaranteed any rent payments beyond the initial five-year term. How should the court rule? Why? [*Jamieson-Chippewa Investment Co. v. McClintock*, 996 S.W.2d 84 (Mo.App.E.D. 1999)]

28–7. ⚖ **CASE PROBLEM WITH SAMPLE ANSWER**
Karen and Gerald Baldwin owned property in Rapid City, South Dakota, which they leased to Wyoming Alaska Corp. (WACO) for use as a gas station and convenience store. The lease obligated the Baldwins to maintain the property, but WACO was authorized to make necessary repairs. After seventeen years, the property had become dilapidated; the store's customers were tripping over chunks of concrete in the parking lot, and an underground gasoline storage tank was leaking. The store's manager hired Duffield Construction, Inc., to install a new tank and make other repairs. The Baldwins saw the new tank sitting on the property before the work began. When WACO paid only a small portion of the cost of the repairs, Duffield filed a mechanic's lien and asked a South Dakota state court to foreclose on the property. The Baldwins disputed the lien, arguing that they had not requested the work. What is the purpose of a mechanic's lien? Should property owners who do not contract for improvements be liable for the financial obligations under such a lien? How might property owners protect themselves against a lien for work that they do not request? Explain. [*Duffield Construction, Inc. v. Baldwin*, 679 N.W.2d 477 (S.D. 2004)]

To view a sample answer for this case problem, go to this book's Web site at http://wbl.westbuslaw.com, select "Chapter 28," and click on "Case Problem with Sample Answer."

28–8. GARNISHMENT. Susan Guinta is a real estate salesperson. Smythe Cramer Co. obtained in an Ohio state court a garnishment order to attach Guinta's personal earnings. The order was served on Russell Realtors to attach sales commissions that Russell owed to Guinta. Russell objected, arguing that commissions are not personal earnings and are therefore exempt from attachment under a garnishment of personal earnings. An Ohio statute defines *personal earnings* as "money, or any other consideration or thing of value, that is paid or due to a person in exchange for work, labor, or personal services provided by the person to an employer." An *employer* is "a person who is required to withhold taxes out of payments of personal earnings made to a judgment debtor." Russell does not withhold taxes from its salespersons' commissions. Under a federal statute, *earnings* means "compensation paid or payable for personal services, whether denominated as wages, salary, commission, bonus, or otherwise." Where the federal definition is more restrictive and results in a smaller garnishment, that definition is controlling. Property other than personal earnings may be subject to garnishment without limits. How should the court rule regarding Russell's objection? Why? [*Smythe Cramer Co. v. Guinta*, 762 N.E.2d 1083 (Ohio Mun. 2001)]

28–9. GUARANTY. In 1981, in Troy, Ohio, Willis and Mary Jane Ward leased a commercial building to Buckeye Pizza Corp. to operate a pizza parlor. Two years later, Buckeye assigned its interest in the building to Ohio, Ltd. In 1985, Ohio sold its pizza business, including its lease of the Wards' building, to NR Dayton Mall, Inc., an Indiana corporation and a subsidiary of Noble Roman's, Inc. As part of the deal, Noble Roman's agreed that it "unconditionally guarantees the performance by N.R. DAYTON MALL, INC., of all its obligations under the . . . Assumption Undertaking." In the "Assumption Undertaking," NR agreed to accept assignment of the Ward lease and to pay Buckeye's and Ohio's expenses if they were sued under it. A dozen years later, NR defaulted on the lease and abandoned the premises. The Wards filed a suit in an Indiana state court against Noble Roman's and others, contending that the firm was liable for NR's default. Noble Roman's argued that it had guaranteed only to indemnify Buckeye and Ohio. The Wards filed a motion for summary judgment. Should the court grant the motion? Explain. [*Noble Roman's, Inc. v. Ward*, 760 N.E.2d 1132 (Ind.App. 2002)]

28–10.  A QUESTION OF ETHICS

Herpel, Inc., agreed to make a stone fireplace mantel for a house owned by Straub Capital Corp. When the mantel was first delivered, Straub was not satisfied, so Herpel took the mantel back, refinished it, and redelivered it five weeks later. The mantel was installed, but Straub did not pay. Herpel filed a mechanic's lien 113 days after the first delivery but less than 90 days after the second delivery. Herpel then filed an action in a Florida district court to foreclose on the lien. The trial court ruled in favor of Straub because the lien had been filed more than 90 days

from the time the mantel was first delivered. The appellate court reversed, noting that although the time for filing a lien is not extended by repair, corrective, or warranty work, "work done in fulfillment of the contract will extend the time for filing of the claim of lien." In view of these events, consider the following questions. [*Herpel, Inc. v. Straub Capital Corp.*, 682 So.2d 661 (S.D.Fla. 1996)]

(a) The court's ruling hinges on the fact that Herpel took the fireplace mantel back, attempted to cure the alleged defects, and then offered it again for acceptance by Straub. Do you agree that this work was "in fulfillment of the contract," rather than to correct the defects?

(b) Would the outcome of this case have been different if the fireplace mantel had been left with the buyer at the time of delivery and the seller had attempted to make repairs to it while it was in the buyer's possession? Why or why not?

(c) Generally, do you think that it is fair for the court to consider who was in possession of the mantel at the time of repair when determining whether the lien was filed within the statutory time period?

LAW | on the Web

For updated links to resources available on the Web, as well as a variety of other materials, visit this text's Web site at **http://wbl.westbuslaw.com**.

The Legal Information Institute at Cornell University offers a collection of law materials concerning debtor-creditor relationships, including federal statutes and recent Supreme Court decisions on this topic, at

> **http://spraylight.law.cornell.edu/topics/debtor_creditor.html**

The U.S. Department of Labor's Web site contains a page on garnishment and employees' rights in relation to garnishment proceedings at

> **http://www.dol.gov/asp/programs/handbook/garnish.htm**

LEGAL RESEARCH EXERCISES ON THE WEB

Go to **http://wbl.westbuslaw.com**, the Web site that accompanies this text. Select "Chapter 28" and click on "Internet Exercises." There you will find the following Internet research exercises that you can perform to learn more about topics covered in this chapter.

Activity 28–1: LEGAL PERSPECTIVE
Debtor-Creditor Relations

Activity 28–2: MANAGEMENT PERSPECTIVE
Mechanic's Liens

CHAPTER 29
Secured Transactions

Whenever the payment of a debt is guaranteed, or *secured,* by personal property owned by the debtor or in which the debtor has a legal interest, the transaction becomes known as a **secured transaction.** The concept of the secured transaction is as basic to modern business practice as the concept of credit. Logically, sellers and lenders do not want to risk nonpayment, so they usually will not sell goods or lend funds unless the promise of payment is somehow guaranteed. Indeed, business as we know it could not exist without laws permitting and governing secured transactions.

Article 9 of the Uniform Commercial Code (UCC) governs secured transactions as applied to personal property, *fixtures* (certain property that is attached to land—see Chapter 47), accounts, instruments, commercial assignments of $1,000 or more, *chattel paper* (any writing evidencing a debt secured by personal property), agricultural liens, and what are called general intangibles (such as patents and copyrights). Article 9 does not cover the creditor devices, such as liens and mortgages that were discussed in Chapter 28. Because the revised version of Article 9 has now been adopted by all of the states, we base this chapter's discussion of secured transactions entirely on the provisions of the revised version.

In this chapter, we first look at the terminology of secured transactions. We then discuss how the rights and duties of creditors and debtors are created and enforced under Article 9. As will become evident, the law of secured transactions tends to favor the rights of creditors; to a lesser extent, however, it offers debtors some protections as well.

SECTION 1 | The Terminology of Secured Transactions

The UCC's terminology is now uniformly adopted in all documents used in situations involving secured transactions. A brief summary of the UCC's definitions of terms relating to secured transactions follows.

1. A **secured party** is any creditor who has a *security interest* in the *debtor's collateral.* This creditor can be a seller, a lender, a cosigner, and even a buyer of accounts or chattel paper [UCC 9–102(a)(72)].
2. A **debtor** is the party who *owes payment* or other performance of a secured obligation [UCC 9–102(a)(28)].
3. A **security interest** is the *interest* in the collateral (such as personal property, fixtures, or accounts) that *secures payment or performance of an obligation* [UCC 1–201(37)].

4. A **security agreement** is an *agreement* that *creates* or provides for a *security interest* [UCC 9–102(a)(73)].
5. **Collateral** is the *subject* of the *security interest* [UCC 9–102(a)(12)].
6. A **financing statement**—referred to as the UCC-1 form—is the *document that is normally filed* to give *public notice* to *third parties* of the *secured party's security interest* [UCC 9–102(a)(39)].

Together, these basic definitions form the concept under which a debtor-creditor relationship becomes a secured transaction relationship (see Exhibit 29–1 on the next page).

SECTION 2 | Creating a Security Interest

A creditor has two main concerns if the debtor defaults: (1) Can the debt be satisfied through the

EXHIBIT 29-1 Secured Transactions—Concept and Terminology

In a security agreement, a debtor and a creditor agree that the creditor will have a security interest in collateral in which the debtor has rights. In essence, the collateral secures the loan and ensures the creditor of payment should the debtor default.

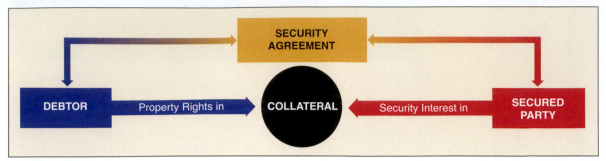

possession and (usually) sale of the collateral? (2) Will the creditor have priority over any other creditors or buyers who may have rights in the same collateral? These two concerns are met through the creation and perfection of a security interest. We begin by examining how a security interest is created.

To become a secured party, the creditor must obtain a security interest in the collateral of the debtor. Three requirements must be met for a creditor to have an enforceable security interest:

1. Either (a) the collateral must be in the possession of the secured party in accordance with an agreement, or (b) there must be a written or authenticated security agreement that describes the collateral subject to the security interest and is signed or authenticated by the debtor.
2. The secured party must give the debtor something of value.
3. The debtor must have rights in the collateral.

Once these requirements have been met, the creditor's rights are said to *attach* to the collateral. **Attachment** gives the creditor an enforceable security interest in the collateral [UCC 9–203].[1]

WRITTEN OR AUTHENTICATED SECURITY AGREEMENT

When the collateral is *not* in the possession of the secured party, the security agreement must be either written or authenticated, and it must describe the col-

lateral. Note here that **authentication** means to sign, execute, or adopt any symbol on an electronic record verifying that the person signing has the intent to adopt or accept the record [UCC 9–102(a)(7)]. If the security agreement is in writing or authenticated, *only the debtor's signature or authentication* is required to create the security interest. The reason authentication is acceptable is to provide for electronic filing (the filing process will be discussed later).

A security agreement must contain a description of the collateral that reasonably identifies it. Generally, such words as "all the debtor's personal property" or "all the debtor's assets" would *not* constitute a sufficient description [UCC 9–108(c)].

SECURED PARTY MUST GIVE VALUE

The secured party must give the debtor something of value. Under the UCC, value can take any of several forms, including a binding commitment to extend credit and, in general, any consideration sufficient to support a simple contract [UCC 1–201 (44)]. Normally, the value given by a secured party involves a direct loan or a commitment to sell goods on credit.

DEBTOR MUST HAVE RIGHTS IN THE COLLATERAL

The debtor must have rights in the collateral; that is, the debtor must have some ownership interest or right to obtain possession of that collateral. The debtor's rights can represent either a current or a future legal interest in the collateral. For example, a retail seller–debtor can give a secured party a security interest not only in existing inventory owned by the retailer but also in *future* inventory to be acquired by the retailer.

---

1. Note that the term *attachment* has a different meaning in secured transactions than it does in the context of judicial liens, as was mentioned in Chapter 28. In the context of judicial liens, attachment refers to a court-ordered seizure and taking into custody of property prior to the securing of a court judgment for a past-due debt.

One common misconception about having rights in the collateral is that the debtor must hold title to it. This is not a requirement. A beneficial interest in a trust, even though the trustee holds title to the trust property, can be the subject of a security interest for a loan that a creditor makes to the beneficiary.

SECTION 3 | Perfecting a Security Interest

Perfection is the legal process by which secured parties protect themselves against the claims of third parties who may wish to have their debts satisfied out of the same collateral. Perfection is usually accomplished by filing a financing statement with the office of the appropriate government official. In some circumstances, however, a security interest becomes perfected without the filing of a financing statement.

Where or how to perfect a security interest sometimes depends on the classification or definition of the collateral. Collateral is generally divided into two classifications: *tangible collateral* (collateral that can be seen, felt, and touched) and *intangible collateral* (collateral that consists of or generates rights). Exhibit 29–2 summarizes the various classifications of collateral and the methods of perfecting a security interest in collateral falling within each of those classifications.[2]

---

2. There are additional classifications, such as agricultural liens, commercial tort claims, and investment property. For definitions of these types of collateral, see UCC 9–102(a)(5), (a)(13), and (a)(49).

EXHIBIT 29–2 **Types of Collateral and Methods of Perfection**

TANGIBLE COLLATERAL All things that are movable at the time the security interest attaches (such as livestock) or that are attached to the land, including timber to be cut and growing crops.		METHOD OF PERFECTION
1. **Consumer Goods** [UCC 9–301, 9–303, 9–309(1), 9–310(a), 9–313(a)]	Goods used or bought primarily for personal, family, or household purposes—for example, household furniture [UCC 9–102(a)(23)].	For purchase-money security interest, attachment (that is, the creation of a security interest) is sufficient; for boats, motor vehicles, and trailers, filing or compliance with a certificate-of-title statute is required; for other consumer goods, general rules of filing or possession apply.
2. **Equipment** [UCC 9–301, 9–310(a), 9–313(a)]	Goods bought for or used primarily in business (and not part of inventory or farm products)—for example, a delivery truck [UCC 9–102(a)(33)].	Filing or (rarely) possession by secured party.
3. **Farm Products** [UCC 9–301, 9–310(a), 9–313(a)]	Crops (including aquatic goods), livestock, or supplies produced in a farming operation—for example, ginned cotton, milk, eggs, and maple syrup [UCC 9–102(a)(34)].	Filing or (rarely) possession by secured party.
4. **Inventory** [UCC 9–301, 9–310(a), 9–313(a)]	Goods held by a person for sale or under a contract of service or lease; raw materials held for production and work in progress [UCC 9–102(a)(48)].	Filing or (rarely) possession by secured party.
5. **Accessions** [UCC 9–301, 9–310(a), 9–313(a)]	Personal property that is so attached, installed, or fixed to other personal property (goods) that it becomes a part of these goods—for example, a DVD player installed in an automobile [UCC 9–102(a)(1)].	Filing or (rarely) possession by secured party (same as personal property being attached).

(Continued)

EXHIBIT 29-2 Types of Collateral and Methods of Perfection *(continued)*

INTANGIBLE COLLATERAL Nonphysical property that exists only in connection with something else.		METHOD OF PERFECTION
1. Chattel Paper [UCC 9–301, 9–310(a), 9–312(a), 9–313(a), 9–314(a)]	A writing or writings (records) that evidence both a monetary obligation and a security interest in goods and software used in goods—for example, a security agreement or a security agreement and promissory note. *Note:* If the record or records consist of information stored in an electronic medium, the collateral is called *electronic chattel paper.* If the information is inscribed on a tangible medium, it is called *tangible chattel paper* [UCC 9–102(a)(11), (a)(31), and (a)(78)].	Filing or possession or control by secured party.
2. Instruments [UCC 9–301, 9–309(4), 9–310 (a), 9–312(a) and (e), 9–313(a)]	A negotiable instrument, such as a check, note, certificate of deposit, or draft, or other writing that evidences a right to the payment of money and is not a security agreement or lease but rather a type that can ordinarily be transferred (after indorsement, if necessary) by delivery [UCC 9–102(a)(47)].	Except for temporary perfected status, filing or possession. For the sale of promissory notes, perfection can be by attachment (automatically on the creation of the security interest).
3. Accounts [UCC 9–301, 9–309(2) and (5), 9–310(a)]	Any right to receive payment for the following: (a) any property, real or personal, sold, leased, licensed, assigned, or otherwise disposed of, including intellectual licensed property; (b) services rendered or to be rendered, such as contract rights; (c) policies of insurance; (d) secondary obligations incurred; (e) use of a credit card; (f) winnings of a government-sponsored or government-authorized lottery or other game of chance; and (g) health-care insurance receivables, defined as an interest or claim under a policy of insurance to payment for health-care goods or services provided [UCC 9–102(a)(2) and (a)(46)].	Filing required except for certain assignments that can be perfected by attachment (automatically on the creation of the security interest).
4. Deposit Accounts [UCC 9–104, 9–304, 9–312(b), 9–314(a)]	Any demand, time, savings, passbook, or similar account maintained with a bank [UCC 9–102(a)(29)].	Perfection by control, such as when the secured party is the bank in which the account is maintained or when the parties have agreed that the secured party can direct the disposition of funds in a particular account.
5. General Intangibles [UCC 9–301, 9–309(3), 9–310(a) and (b)(8)]	Any personal property (or debtor's obligation to make payments on such) other than that defined above [UCC 9–102(a)(42)], including software that is independent from a computer or other good [UCC 9–102(a)(44), (a)(61), and (a)(75)].	Filing only (for copyrights, with the U.S. Copyright Office), except a sale of a payment intangible by attachment (automatically on the creation of the security interest).

PERFECTION BY FILING

The most common means of perfection is by filing a *financing statement*—a document that gives public notice to third parties of the secured party's security interest—with the office of the appropriate government official. The security agreement itself can also be filed to perfect the security interest. The financing statement must provide the names of the debtor and the secured party and must indicate the collateral covered by the financing statement. There is now a uniform financing statement form. This uniform financing statement is shown in Exhibit 29–3.

Communication of the financing statement to the appropriate filing office, together with the correct

EXHIBIT 29–3 The Uniform Financing Statement

UCC FINANCING STATEMENT

FOLLOW INSTRUCTIONS (front and back) CAREFULLY

A. NAME & PHONE OF CONTACT AT FILER (optional)

B. SEND ACKNOWLEDGEMENT TO: (Name and Address)

THE ABOVE SPACE IS FOR FILING OFFICE USE ONLY

1. DEBTOR'S EXACT FULL LEGAL NAME - Insert only one debtor name (1a or 1b) - do not abbreviate or combine names

1a. ORGANIZATION'S NAME				
OR 1b. INDIVIDUAL'S LAST NAME	FIRST NAME	MIDDLE NAME		SUFFIX
1c. MAILING ADDRESS	CITY	STATE	POSTAL CODE	COUNTRY
1d. TAX ID# SSN OR EIN / ADD'L INFO RE ORGANIZATION DEBTOR / 1e. TYPE OF ORGANIZATION	1f. JURISDICTION OR ORGANIZATION	1g. ORGANIZATIONAL ID #, if any		☐ NONE

2. ADDITIONAL DEBTOR'S EXACT FULL LEGAL NAME - Insert only one debtor name (2a or 2b) - do not abbreviate or combine names

2a. ORGANIZATION'S NAME				
OR 2b. INDIVIDUAL'S LAST NAME	FIRST NAME	MIDDLE NAME		SUFFIX
2c. MAILING ADDRESS	CITY	STATE	POSTAL CODE	COUNTRY
2d. TAX ID# SSN OR EIN / ADD'L INFO RE ORGANIZATION DEBTOR / 2e. TYPE OF ORGANIZATION	2f. JURISDICTION OR ORGANIZATION	2g. ORGANIZATIONAL ID #, if any		☐ NONE

3. SECURED PARTY'S NAME - (or NAME of TOTAL ASSIGNOR S/P) Insert only one secured party name (3a or 3b)

3a. ORGANIZATION'S NAME				
OR 3b. INDIVIDUAL'S LAST NAME	FIRST NAME	MIDDLE NAME		SUFFIX
3c. MAILING ADDRESS	CITY	STATE	POSTAL CODE	COUNTRY

4. This FINANCING STATEMENT covers the following collateral:

5. ALTERNATIVE DESIGNATION (if applicable) ☐ LESSEE/LESSOR ☐ CONSIGNEE/CONSIGNOR ☐ BAILEE/BAILOR ☐ SELLER/BUYER ☐ AG. LIEN ☐ NON-UCC FILING

6. ☐ This FINANCING STATEMENT is to be filed [for record] (or recorded) in the REAL ESTATE RECORDS. Attach Addendum (if applicable)

7. Check to REQUEST SEARCH REPORT(S) on Debtor(s) (ADDITIONAL FEE) (optional) ☐ All Debtors ☐ Debtor 1 ☐ Debtor 2

OPTIONAL FILER REFERENCE DATA

NATIONAL UCC FINANCING STATEMENT (FORM UCC1) REV. 07/29/98)

filing fee, or the acceptance of the financing statement by the filing officer constitutes a filing [UCC 9–516(a)]. The word *communication* means that the filing can be accomplished electronically [UCC 9–102(a)(18)]. Once completed, filings are indexed in the name of the debtor so that they can be located by subsequent searchers. A financing statement may be filed even before a security agreement is made or a security interest attaches [UCC 9–502(d)].

THE DEBTOR'S NAME The UCC requires that a financing statement be filed under the name of the debtor [UCC 9–502(a)(1)]. If the debtor is identified by the correct name at the time of the filing of a financing statement, the secured party's interest retains its priority even if the debtor's name later changes. Because most states use electronic filing systems, UCC 9–503 sets out detailed rules for determining when the debtor's name as it appears on a financing statement is sufficient.

—Corporate Debtors. For corporations, which are organizations that have registered with the state, the debtor's name on the financing statement must be "the name of the debtor indicated on the public record of the debtor's jurisdiction of organization" [UCC 9–503(a)(1)]. Slight variations in a name normally will not be considered misleading if a search of the filing office's records, using a standard computer search engine routinely used by that office, would disclose the filings [UCC 9–506(c)].

—Trusts, Individuals, and Organizations. If the debtor is a trust, or a trustee with respect to property held in trust, this information must be disclosed on the filed financing statement, and the statement must provide the name of the trust as specified in its official documents [UCC 9–503(a)(3)]. For all others, the filed financing statement must disclose "the individual or organizational name of the debtor" [UCC 9–503(a)(4)(A)]. As used here, the word *organization* includes unincorporated associations, such as clubs and some churches, as well as joint ventures and general partnerships, even when these organizations are created without formal certificates of formation. Note that if an organizational debtor does not have a group name, the names of all of the individuals that make up the group must be listed.

—Trade Names. In general, providing only the debtor's trade name (or a fictitious name) in a financing statement is not sufficient for perfection [UCC 9–503(c)]. Assume that a loan is being made to a sole proprietorship owned by Peter Jones. The trade (or fictitious) name is Pete's Plumbing. A financing statement cannot use the trade name Pete's Plumbing; rather, it must be filed under the name of the actual debtor, who in this instance is Peter Jones. The reason for this rule is that a sole proprietorship is not a legal entity distinct from the person who owns it. The rule also furthers an important goal of Article 9—to ensure that the debtor's name on a financing statement is one that prospective lenders can locate and recognize in future searches.

CHANGES IN THE DEBTOR'S NAME A problem arises when the debtor subject to a filed perfected security interest changes his or her (or its) name. What happens if a subsequent creditor extends credit to the debtor and perfects its security interest under the debtor's new name? Obviously, a search by this subsequent creditor for filed security interests under the debtor's changed name may not disclose the previously filed security interest.

The UCC's revised Article 9 attempts to prevent potential conflicts caused by changes in the debtor's name if the debtor goes into default. First, UCC 9–503 states specifically what constitutes the "sufficiency" of the debtor's name in a financing statement. Second, if the debtor's name is insufficient, the filing is considered seriously misleading *unless* a search of records using the debtor's correct name by the filing officer's search engine would disclose the security interest [UCC 9–506(b) and (c)]. Third, even if the change of name renders the financing statement misleading, the financing statement is effective as a perfection of a security interest in collateral acquired by the debtor before or within four months after the name change. Unless an amendment is filed within this four-month period, collateral acquired by the debtor after the four-month period is unperfected [UCC 9–507(b) and (c)].

The following case illustrates some of the complications that arose from a debtor's use of several names to do business—including a change of one of those names—and two creditors' assertions of claims under those different names to the same collateral.

CASE 29.1

Cabool State Bank v. Radio Shack, Inc.

Missouri Court
of Appeals,
Southern District,
Division One, 2002.
65 S.W.3d 613.
http://www.osca.state.mo.us [a]

COMPANY PROFILE *In 1921, Theodore and Milton Deutschmann opened a one-store retail and mail-order operation in Boston, Massachusetts, under the name "Radio Shack," which was a term for a small, wooden structure housing a ship's radio equipment. Today, Radio Shack, Inc. (http://www.radioshack.com), a division of Tandy Corporation, is based in Fort Worth, Texas, and has more than 7,200 stores across the United States. Radio Shack is a consumer electronics retailer of wireless communications equipment and other electronic parts, batteries, and accessories, including digital products and services.*

BACKGROUND AND FACTS *In June 1995, Michael and Debra Boudreaux, doing business as D & J Enterprises, Inc., bought from Van Pamperien a retail electronics store operated under a franchise from Radio Shack. To pay for the business, the Boudreauxes borrowed funds from Cabool State Bank in Springfield, Missouri. The loan documents included a financing statement. On the statement's signature lines, the only capacity identified for the Boudreauxes' signatures was that of "Debtors." Elsewhere on the form, the bank listed "D & J Enterprises, Inc., Radio Shack, Dealer, Debra K. Boudreaux, Michael C. Boudreaux" as "Debtors." The statement covered, in part, the store inventory. Before the end of the year, the Boudreauxes changed the name of their business to Tri-B Enterprises, Inc. In January 1998, the store closed. The next month, Radio Shack terminated the franchise and, despite the lack of a security interest, took possession of the inventory, claiming the Boudreauxes and Tri-B owed Radio Shack $6,394.73. The bank filed a suit in a Missouri state court against Radio Shack, claiming a perfected security interest in the inventory with priority over Radio Shack's claim. The court entered a judgment for $15,529.43 in the bank's favor. Radio Shack appealed to a state intermediate appellate court.*

IN THE LANGUAGE OF THE COURT

KENNETH W. SHRUM, Presiding Judge.

* * * *

* * * Radio Shack argues that the so-called change of name was seriously misleading * * *, the inventory that Radio Shack took from the store was acquired exclusively by Tri-B more than four months after the so-called name change; Bank never filed a new financing statement within four months of the so-called name change, and therefore, Bank's original * * * filings were ineffective to perfect a security interest in the inventory against Radio Shack.

* * * *

First and foremost, the argument thus advanced is based on flagrant mischaracterizations about what the record shows. Contrary to Radio Shack's * * * assertions that after November 1995 it only did business with Tri-B and the inventory taken from the closed store had been sold exclusively to the corporate entity, Radio Shack *stipulated* it had sold the subject inventory to Tri-B Enterprises *and* Boudreauxes, and it took the inventory *from both parties*—not just Tri-B Enterprises—after the store closed. Radio Shack confirmed that it recognized and treated Michael [Boudreaux], in his individual capacity, as having an ownership interest in the franchise and dealership after November 1995 when it stipulated that Tri-B *and* Boudreauxes "ceased business operations in January 1998[,]" and "[o]n February 25, 1998, Mr. Boudreaux *and* Tri-B * * * were given official notice * * * that the [franchise] agreement * * * was terminated." * * *

* * * [T]he record does show, without contradiction or conflict, that (1) Boudreauxes bought the original inventory in their individual names, (2) Boudreauxes gave Bank a security

---

a. In the "Court of Appeals" pull-down menu, select "Southern District" and click on "Go!" On that page, click on "Opinions and Orders." Scroll to "01/30/2002" and click on the name of the case to access the opinion. The Missouri Judiciary maintains this Web site.

CASE 29.1 | **Continued**

interest in the original inventory and "all inventory purchased or replaced," (3) Bank perfected its security interest in existing and future inventory owned by Boudreauxes by filing * * * financing statements that listed Boudreauxes and D & J Enterprises, Inc., as "Debtors," (4) Radio Shack had actual knowledge of the loan transaction between Bank and Boudreauxes, and (5) the subject inventory was sold to both the Boudreauxes and Tri-B. * * *

* * * From the outset, Bank listed Boudreauxes (who admittedly had an ownership interest in the inventory) as "Debtors" on the [UCC] filings. Because the financing statement was filed under the true name of at least one debtor/owner, there was no possibility the Bank's financing statement could seriously have misled Radio Shack.

DECISION AND REMEDY *The state intermediate appellate court affirmed the judgment of the lower court. Radio Shack had not been misled by the debtors' change of their business name because the financing statement had been filed under the "true name" of at least one of the debtors with whom Radio Shack admitted doing business. Radio Shack also had actual knowledge of the bank loan.*

DESCRIPTION OF THE COLLATERAL The UCC requires that both the security agreement and the financing statement contain a description of the collateral in which the secured party has a security interest. The security agreement must include a description of the collateral because no security interest in goods can exist unless the parties agree on which goods are subject to the security interest. The financing statement must include a description of the collateral to provide public notice of the fact that certain goods of the debtor are subject to a security interest. Other parties who might later wish to lend funds to the debtor or buy the collateral can thus learn of the security interest by checking with the state or local office in which a financing statement for that type of collateral would be filed. For land-related security interests, a legal description of the realty is also required [UCC 9–502(b)].

Sometimes, the descriptions in the two documents vary, with the description in the security agreement being more precise than the description in the financing statement (which is allowed to be more general). For example, a security agreement for a commercial loan to a manufacturer may list all of the manufacturer's equipment subject to the loan by serial number, whereas the financing statement may simply state "all equipment owned or hereafter acquired." The UCC permits broad, general descriptions in the financing statement, such as "all assets" or "all personal property." Usually, whenever the description in a financing statement accurately describes the agreement between the secured party and the debtor, the description is sufficient [UCC 9–504].

WHERE TO FILE In most states, a financing statement must be filed centrally in the appropriate state office, such as the office of the secretary of state, in the state where the debtor is located. Filing in the county where the collateral is located is required only when the collateral consists of timber to be cut; fixtures; or items to be extracted, such as oil, coal, gas, and minerals [UCC 9–301(3) and (4), 9–502(b)].

The state in which a financing statement should be filed depends on the *debtor's location,* not the location of the collateral (as was required under the unrevised Article 9) [UCC 9–301]. The debtor's location is determined as follows [UCC 9–307]:

1. For *individual debtors,* it is the state of the debtor's principal residence.
2. For an organization registered with the state (such as a corporation), it is the state in which the organization is registered. For example, if a debtor is incorporated in Maryland, and has its chief executive office in New York, a secured party would file the financing statement in Maryland, which is the state of the debtor's organizational formation.
3. For all other entities, it is the state where the business is located or, if more than one, the state where the chief executive office is located.

CONSEQUENCES OF AN IMPROPER FILING Any improper filing renders the secured party unperfected and reduces the secured party's claim in bankruptcy to that of an unsecured creditor. For example, if the debtor's name on the financing statement is inaccurate or if the collateral is not sufficiently described on the filing statement, the filing may not be effective.

PERFECTION WITHOUT FILING

In two types of situations, security interests can be perfected without filing a financing statement. The first occurs when the collateral is transferred into the possession of the secured party. The second occurs when the security interest is one of a limited number under the UCC that can be perfected on attachment (without a filing and without having to possess the goods) [UCC 9–309]. The phrase *perfected on attachment* means that these security interests are automatically perfected at the time of their creation. Two of the most common security interests that are perfected on attachment are a *purchase-money security interest* in consumer goods (defined and explained below) and an assignment of a beneficial interest in a decedent's estate [UCC 9–309(1) and (13)].

PERFECTION BY POSSESSION In the past, one of the most frequently used means of obtaining financing under the common law was to **pledge** certain collateral as security for the debt and transfer the collateral into the creditor's possession. When the debt was paid, the collateral was returned to the debtor. Although the debtor usually entered into a written security agreement, oral security agreements were also enforceable as long as the secured party possessed the collateral. Article 9 of the UCC retained the common law pledge and the principle that the security agreement need not be in writing to be enforceable if the collateral is transferred to the secured party [UCC 9–310, 9–312(b), 9–313].

For most collateral, possession by the secured party is impractical because it denies the debtor the right to use or derive income from the property to pay off the debt. For example, suppose that a farmer takes out a loan to finance the purchase of a piece of heavy farm equipment needed to harvest crops and uses the equipment as collateral. Clearly, the purpose of the purchase would be defeated if the farmer transferred the collateral into the creditor's possession. Certain items, however, such as stocks, bonds, instruments, and jewelry, are commonly transferred into the creditor's possession when they are used as collateral for loans.

PERFECTION BY ATTACHMENT—THE PURCHASE-MONEY SECURITY INTEREST IN CONSUMER GOODS Under the UCC, thirteen types of security interests are perfected automatically at the time they are created [UCC 9–309]. The most common of these is the **purchase-money security interest (PMSI).** A PMSI in consumer goods is created when a person buys goods primarily for personal, family, or household purposes, and the seller or lender agrees to extend credit for part or all of the purchase price of the goods.

The entity that extends the credit and obtains the PMSI can be either the seller (a store, for example) or a financial institution that lends the buyer the funds with which to purchase the goods [UCC 9–102(a)(2)].

—Automatic Perfection. A PMSI in consumer goods is perfected automatically at the time of a credit sale—that is, at the time the PMSI is created. For example, suppose that Jamie wants to purchase a new large-screen television set from ABC Television, Inc. The purchase price is $2,500. Not being able to pay the entire amount in cash, Jamie signs a purchase agreement to pay $1,000 down and $100 per month until the balance plus interest is fully paid. ABC is to retain a security interest in the purchased goods until full payment has been made. Because the security interest was created as part of the purchase agreement, it is a PMSI. ABC need do nothing more to perfect its security interest.

—Exceptions to the Rule of Automatic Perfection. There are two exceptions to this rule of automatic perfection for PMSIs. First, certain types of security interests that are subject to other federal or state laws may require additional steps to be perfected [UCC 9–311]. For example, many jurisdictions have certificate-of-title statutes that establish perfection requirements for security interests in certain goods, including automobiles, trailers, boats, mobile homes, and farm tractors. If a consumer in these jurisdictions purchases a boat, for example, the secured party will need to file a certificate of title with the appropriate state official to perfect the PMSI. The second exception occurs when the sale is to a business or entity that is not considered a consumer under Article 9. *Nonconsumer* PMSIs usually involve a business's inventory or livestock, and Article 9 provides special rules to deal with these types of security interests (discussed later in this chapter in the context of priorities) [UCC 9–324].

EFFECTIVE TIME DURATION OF PERFECTION

A financing statement is effective for five years from the date of filing [UCC 9–515]. If a **continuation statement** is filed within six months *prior to* the expiration date, the effectiveness of the original statement is continued for another five years, starting with the expiration date of the first five-year period [UCC 9–515(d) and (e)]. The effectiveness of the statement can be continued in the same manner indefinitely.

CONCEPT SUMMARY 29.1 | Creating and Perfecting a Security Interest

CONCEPT	DESCRIPTION
CREATING A SECURITY INTEREST	1. Unless the creditor has possession of the collateral, there must be a written or authenticated security agreement signed or authenticated by the debtor and describing the collateral subject to the security interest. 2. The secured party must give value to the debtor. 3. The debtor, with some exceptions, must have rights in the collateral—some ownership interest or right to obtain possession of the specified collateral.
PERFECTING A SECURITY INTEREST	1. *Perfection by filing*—The most common method of perfection is by filing a financing statement containing the names of the secured party and the debtor and indicating the collateral covered by the financing statement. 　a. Communication of the financing statement to the appropriate filing office, together with the correct filing fee, constitutes a filing. 　b. The financing statement must be filed under the name of the debtor; fictitious (trade) names normally are not accepted. 　c. The classification of collateral determines whether filing is necessary and where to file. 2. *Perfection without filing*— 　a. By transfer of collateral—The debtor can transfer possession of the collateral to the secured party. For example, a *pledge* is this type of transfer. 　b. By attachment—A limited number of security interests are perfected by attachment, such as a purchase-money security interest (PMSI) in consumer goods. If the secured party has a PMSI in consumer goods (bought for personal, family, or household purposes), the secured party's security interest is perfected automatically.

Any attempt to file a continuation statement outside the six-month window will render the continuation ineffective, and the perfection will lapse at the end of the five-year period.

If a financing statement lapses, the security interest that had been perfected by the filing now becomes unperfected. It is as if the security interest had never been perfected as against a purchaser for value [UCC 9–515(c)].

SECTION 4 | The Scope of a Security Interest

In addition to covering collateral already in the debtor's possession, a security agreement can cover various other types of property, including the proceeds of the sale of collateral, after-acquired property, and future advances.

PROCEEDS

Proceeds include whatever is received when collateral is sold or disposed of in some other way [UCC 9–102(a)(64)]. A secured party's security interest in the collateral includes a security interest in the proceeds of the sale of that collateral. For example, suppose that a bank has a perfected security interest in the inventory of a retail seller of heavy farm machinery. The retailer sells a tractor out of this inventory to a farmer, who is by definition *a buyer in the ordinary course of business*. The farmer agrees, in a security agreement, to make monthly payments to the retailer for a period of twenty-four months. If the retailer should go into default on the loan from the bank, the bank is entitled to the remaining payments the farmer owes to the retailer as proceeds.

A security interest in proceeds perfects automatically on the *perfection* of the secured party's security interest in the original collateral and remains perfected for twenty days after receipt of the proceeds by the debtor. One way to extend the twenty-day automatic perfection period is to provide for such extended coverage in the original security agreement [UCC 9–315(c) and (d)]. This is typically done when the collateral is the type that is likely to be sold, such as a retailer's inventory—for example, of computers or DVD players. The UCC also permits a security interest in identifiable cash proceeds to remain perfected after twenty days [UCC 9–315(d)(2)].

AFTER-ACQUIRED PROPERTY

After-acquired property is property that the debtor acquired after the execution of the security agreement. The security agreement may provide for a security interest in after-acquired property [UCC 9–204(1)]. This is particularly useful for inventory financing arrangements because a secured party whose security interest is in existing inventory knows that the debtor will sell that inventory, thereby reducing the collateral subject to the security interest.

Generally, the debtor will purchase new inventory to replace the inventory sold. The secured party wants this newly acquired inventory to be subject to the original security interest. Thus, the after-acquired property clause continues the secured party's claim to any inventory acquired thereafter. This is not to say that the original security interest will be superior to the rights of all other creditors with regard to this after-acquired inventory, as will be discussed later.

To illustrate: Amato buys factory equipment from Bronson on credit, giving as security an interest in all of her equipment—both what she is buying and what she already owns. The security agreement with Bronson contains an after-acquired property clause. Six months later, Amato pays cash to another seller of factory equipment for additional equipment. Six months after that, Amato goes out of business before she has paid off her debt to Bronson. Bronson has a security interest in all of Amato's equipment, even the equipment bought from the other seller.

FUTURE ADVANCES

Often, a debtor will arrange with a bank to have a *continuing line of credit* under which the debtor can borrow funds intermittently. Advances against lines of credit can be subject to a properly perfected security interest in certain collateral. The security agreement may provide that any future advances made against that line of

credit are also subject to the security interest in the same collateral [UCC 9–204(c)]. Future advances need not be of the same type or otherwise related to the original advance to benefit from this type of **cross-collateralization.**[3] Cross-collateralization occurs when an asset that is not the subject of a loan is used to collateralize that loan.

For example, Stroh is the owner of a small manufacturing plant with equipment valued at $1 million. He has an immediate need for $40,000 of working capital, so he obtains a loan from Midwestern Bank and signs a security agreement, putting up all of his equipment as security. The bank properly perfects its security interest. The security agreement provides that Stroh can borrow up to $500,000 in the future, using the same equipment as collateral for any future advances. In this situation, Midwestern Bank does not have to execute a new security agreement and perfect a security interest in the collateral each time an advance is made, up to a cumulative total of $500,000. For priority purposes, each advance is perfected as of the date of the *original* perfection.

THE FLOATING-LIEN CONCEPT

A security agreement that provides for a security interest in proceeds, in after-acquired property, or in collateral subject to future advances by the secured party (or in all three) is often characterized as a **floating lien.** This type of security interest continues in the collateral or proceeds even if the collateral is sold, exchanged, or disposed of in some other way.

A FLOATING LIEN IN INVENTORY Floating liens commonly arise in the financing of inventories. A creditor is not interested in specific pieces of inventory, which are constantly changing, so the lien "floats" from one item to another, as the inventory changes.

Consider an example. Suppose that Cascade Sports, Inc., a corporation formed in Oregon, operates as a cross-country ski dealer and has a line of credit with Portland First Bank to finance an inventory of cross-country skis. Cascade and Portland First enter into a security agreement that provides for coverage of proceeds, after-acquired inventory, present inventory, and future advances. This security interest in inventory is perfected by filing centrally (with the office of the secretary of state in Oregon). One day, Cascade sells a new pair of the latest cross-country skis and

---

3. See Official Comment 5 to UCC 9–204.

receives a used pair in trade. That same day, Cascade purchases two new pairs of cross-country skis from a local manufacturer for cash. Later that day, Cascade borrows $8,000 from Portland First Bank under the security agreement to meet its payroll.

Portland First gets a perfected security interest in the used pair of skis under the proceeds clause, has a perfected security interest in the two new pairs of skis purchased from the local manufacturer under the after-acquired property clause, and has the new amount of funds advanced to Cascade secured on all of the above collateral by the future-advances clause. All of this is accomplished under the original perfected security interest. The various items in the inventory have changed, but Portland First still has a perfected security interest in Cascade's inventory. Hence, it has a floating lien on the inventory.

A FLOATING LIEN IN A SHIFTING STOCK OF GOODS The concept of the floating lien can also apply to a shifting stock of goods. The lien can start with raw materials; follow them as they become finished goods and inventories; and continue as the goods are sold and are turned into accounts receivable, chattel paper, or cash.

SECTION 5 | Priorities

The importance of perfection to a secured party cannot be overemphasized, particularly when another party is claiming an interest in the same collateral covered by the perfected secured party's security agreement.

THE GENERAL RULE

The general rule is that a perfected secured party's interest has priority over the interests of the following parties [UCC 9–317, 9–322]:

1. An unsecured creditor.
2. An unperfected secured party.
3. A subsequent lien creditor, such as a judgment creditor who acquires a lien on the collateral by *execution and levy*—a process discussed later in this chapter.
4. A trustee in bankruptcy (see Chapter 30)—at least, the perfected secured party has priority to the proceeds from the sale of the collateral by the trustee.

5. Most buyers who *do not* purchase the collateral in the ordinary course of a seller's business.

In addition, whether a secured party's interest is perfected or unperfected may have serious consequences for the secured party if the debtor defaults on the debt or files for bankruptcy. For example, what if the debtor has borrowed from two different creditors, using the same property as collateral for both loans? If the debtor defaults on both loans, which of the two creditors has first rights to the collateral? In this situation, the creditor with a perfected security interest will prevail.

BUYERS OF THE COLLATERAL

Sometimes, the conflict is between a perfected secured party and a buyer of the collateral. The question then arises as to which party has priority to the collateral.

TYPES OF BUYERS The UCC recognizes that there are five types of buyers whose interest in purchased goods could conflict with those of a perfected secured party on the debtor's default. These five types are:

1. Buyers in the ordinary course of business (this type of buyer will be discussed in detail shortly).
2. Buyers of consumer goods purchased outside the ordinary course of business.
3. Buyers of chattel paper [UCC 9–330].
4. Buyers of instruments, documents, or securities [UCC 9–330(d), 9–331(a)].
5. Buyers of farm products.[4]

BUYERS IN THE ORDINARY COURSE OF BUSINESS Because buyers should not be required to find out if there is an outstanding security interest in, for example, a merchant's inventory, the UCC also provides that a person who buys "in the ordinary course of business" will take the goods free from any security interest created by the seller in the purchased collateral. This is so even if the security interest is perfected and *even if the buyer knows of its existence* [UCC

---

4. Under the Food Security Act of 1985, buyers in the ordinary course of business include buyers of farm products from a farmer. Under this act, these buyers are protected from prior perfected security interests unless the secured parties perfected centrally by filing a special form called an *effective financing statement* or the buyers received proper notice of the secured party's security interest.

9–320(a)].[5] The UCC defines a *buyer in the ordinary course of business* as any person who in good faith, and without knowledge that the sale is in violation of the ownership rights or security interest of a third party in the goods, buys in ordinary course from a person in the business of selling goods of that kind [UCC 1–201(9)].

For example, on August 1 West Bank has a perfected security interest in all of ABC Television's existing inventory and any inventory thereafter acquired. On September 1, Carla, a student at Central University, purchases one of the television sets in ABC's inventory. If, on December 1, ABC goes into default, can West Bank repossess the television set sold to Carla? The answer is no, because Carla is a buyer in the ordinary course of business (ABC is in the business of selling goods of that kind) and takes the television free and clear of West Bank's perfected security interest.

CREDITORS OR SECURED PARTIES

Generally, the following UCC rules apply when more than one creditor claims rights in the same collateral:

1. *Conflicting perfected security interests.* When two or more secured parties have perfected security interests in the same collateral, generally the first to perfect (file or take possession of the collateral) has priority, unless the state's statute provides otherwise [UCC 9–322(a)(1)].
2. *Conflicting unperfected security interests.* When two conflicting security interests are unperfected, the first to attach (be created) has priority [UCC 9–322(a)(3)]. This is sometimes called the "first-in-time" rule.
3. *Conflicting perfected security interests in commingled or processed goods.* When goods to which two or more perfected security interests attach are so manufactured or commingled that they lose their identities into a product or mass, the perfected parties' security interests attach to the new product or mass "according to the ratio that the cost of goods to which each interest originally attached bears to the cost of the total product or mass" [UCC 9–336].

Under some circumstances, on the debtor's default, the perfection of a security interest will not protect a secured party against certain other third parties having claims to the collateral. For example, the UCC provides that in some instances a PMSI, properly perfected,[6] will prevail over another security interest in after-acquired collateral, even though the other was perfected first. Exhibit 29–4 on the next page summarizes the rules regarding the priority of claims.

AN EXCEPTION TO THE FIRST-IN-TIME RULE— THE PMSI An important exception to the first-in-time rule involves certain types of collateral, such as equipment, in which one of the perfected security parties has a PMSI [UCC 9–324(a)]. For example, suppose that Smith borrows funds from West Bank, signing a security agreement in which she puts up all of her present and after-acquired equipment as security. On May 1, West Bank perfects this security interest (which is not a PMSI). On July 1, Smith purchases a new piece of equipment from XYZ Company on credit, signing a security agreement.

XYZ Company thus has a PMSI in the new equipment. The delivery date for the new equipment is August 1. If Smith defaults on her payments to both West Bank and XYZ, which of them has priority with regard to the new piece of equipment? Generally, West Bank would have priority because its interest perfected first in time. In this situation, however, XYZ has a PMSI, and if it perfects its interest by filing before Smith takes possession on August 1, or within twenty days after that date, XYZ has priority.

ANOTHER EXCEPTION TO THE FIRST-IN-TIME RULE—SECURITY INTEREST IN INVENTORY Another important exception to the first-in-time rule has to do with security interests in inventory [UCC 9–324(b)]. For example, on May 1, ABC borrows funds from West Bank. ABC signs a security agreement, putting up all of its present inventory and any inventory thereafter acquired as collateral. West Bank perfects its interest (not a PMSI) on that date. On June 10, ABC buys new inventory from Martin, Inc., a manufacturer, to use for its Fourth of July sale. ABC makes a down payment for the new inventory and signs a security agreement giving Martin a PMSI in the new inventory as collateral for the remaining debt.

---

5. Remember that, generally, there are three methods of perfection: by filing, by possession, and by attachment.

6. Recall that, with some exceptions (such as motor vehicles), a PMSI in *consumer goods* is automatically perfected—no filing is necessary. A PMSI that is not in consumer goods must still be perfected, however.

EXHIBIT 29-4 **Priority of Claims to a Debtor's Collateral**

Unperfected Secured Party	An unperfected secured party prevails over unsecured creditors and creditors who have obtained judgments against the debtor but who have not begun the legal process to collect on those judgments [UCC 9–201(a)].

Purchaser of Debtor's Collateral	1. *Goods purchased in the ordinary course of the seller's business*—Buyer prevails over a secured party's security interest, even if the security interest is perfected and even if the buyer knows of the security interest [UCC 9–320(a)].
	 2. *Consumer goods purchased outside the ordinary course of business*—Buyer prevails over a secured party's interest, even if it is perfected by attachment, providing buyer purchased as follows:
	   a. For value.
	   b. Without actual knowledge of the security interest.
	   c. For use as a consumer good.
	   d. Prior to secured party's perfection by *filing* [UCC 9–320(b)].
	 3. *Buyers of chattel paper*—Buyer prevails if the buyer:
	   a. Gave new value in making the purchase.
	   b. Took possession in the ordinary course of the buyer's business.
	   c. Took without knowledge of the security interest [UCC 9–330].
	 4. *Buyers of instruments, documents, or securities*—Buyers who are holders in due course, holders to whom negotiable documents have been duly negotiated, or bona fide purchasers of securities have priority over a previously perfected security interest [UCC 9–330(d), 9–331(a)].
	 5. *Buyers of farm products*—Buyers from a farmer take free and clear of perfected security interests unless, where permitted, a secured party files centrally an effective financing statement (EFS) or the buyer receives proper notice of the security interest before the sale.

Perfected Secured Parties to the Same Collateral	1. *The general rule*—Between two perfected secured parties in the same collateral, the first in time of perfection is first in right to the collateral [UCC 9–322(a)(1)].
	 2. *Exception: Purchase-money security interest (PMSI)*—A PMSI, even if second in time of perfection, has priority providing that the following conditions are met:
	   a. Inventory—A PMSI is perfected and proper written or authenticated notice is given to the other security-interest holder *on* or *before* the time that debtor takes possession [UCC 9–324(b)].
	   b. Other collateral—A PMSI has priority, providing it is perfected within twenty days after debtor receives possession [UCC 9–324(a)].
	   c. Software—A PMSI arises in software only if the debtor acquires its interest in the software for the principal purpose of using the software in goods subject to a PMSI. In that situation, the PMSI in the software has the same priority as the PMSI in the goods in which the software was acquired for use [UCC 9–103(c), 9–324(f)].

Martin delivers the inventory to ABC on June 28. Because of a hurricane in the area, ABC's Fourth of July sale is a disaster, and most of its inventory remains unsold. In August, ABC defaults on its payments to both West Bank and Martin.

Does West Bank or Martin have priority with respect to the new inventory delivered to ABC on June 28? If Martin has not perfected its security interest by June 28, West Bank's after-acquired collateral clause has priority because it was the first to be perfected. If, however, Martin has perfected *and* gives proper notice of its security interest to West Bank before ABC takes possession of the goods on June 28, Martin has priority.

The following case illustrates how the first-in-time rule and its exceptions apply to determining the priority of conflicting security interests on a debtor's default.

CASE 29.2

In re Rebel Rents, Inc.

United States
Bankruptcy Court,
Central District
of California, 2004.
307 Bankr. 171.

PETER H. CARROLL, Bankruptcy Judge.

* * * *

[Rebel Rents, Inc. and Perris Valley Rentals, Inc. (collectively, "Rebel") comprise] the largest independent equipment rental company in Southern California. * * *

* * * *

Sometime prior to September 14, 2000, Rebel executed a Distributor Security Agreement with Snorkel International, Inc. ("Snorkel") in conjunction with the purchase of certain inventory for use in its equipment rental business. * * *

On September 14, 2000, Rebel executed a "Finance Plan" and "Wholesale Security Agreement" with Textron [Financial Corporation] to finance its purchase of the inventory from Snorkel, and granted Textron a security interest in the following collateral * * * :

> All equipment and inventory, wherever located, in which Debtor now or hereafter has rights, financed or refinanced by Secured Party for Debtor, including * * * the proceeds * * * .

* * * *

On December 29, 2000, Rebel obtained a $23,000,000 revolving line of credit ("Line of Credit") and a $2,000,000 term loan ("Term Loan") from [General Electric Capital Corporation ("GECC")]. * * * Rebel executed a Security Agreement dated December 29, 2000, granting GECC a security interest in substantially all of Rebel's assets, including * * * inventory, * * * together with all "[p]roceeds * * * ." On January 5, 2001, GECC filed a financing statement with the California Secretary of State to perfect its security interest in the collateral.

* * * *

On September 23, 2002, Rebel filed a [bankruptcy] petition * * * .

* * * *

On September 19, 2003, Rebel surrendered the [Snorkel] Equipment to Textron pursuant to * * * [this court's] order.

On September 19, 2003, Textron filed its motion alleging that Rebel received gross income of approximately $430,661 attributable to its rental of the Equipment between September 23, 2002 and September 19, 2003, and that such funds were "proceeds" subject to its lien. * * *

* * * *

[Bankruptcy law] places the burden on the secured creditor to establish the validity, priority and extent of its interest in property. * * * [A] party seeking to establish the "extent" of its interest in property under [bankruptcy law] must satisfy a two-prong test: First, as a preliminary matter, the party must prove that it holds a perfected security interest in post-petition revenues to which its liens [security interests] still rightly attach. Second, a party must prove the amount of money to which its liens attach.

In this case, Textron failed to meet its burden under [bankruptcy law] to establish a valid, duly perfected lien on rental income attributable to the Equipment. Textron produced evidence that Rebel generated revenue of $430,661 from leases of the Equipment between September 22, 2002 through September 19, 2003. However, Textron submitted no direct evidence in support of the motion establishing the validity, extent and priority of its lien on such revenue. Through confirmation of [Rebel's bankruptcy] Plan, Textron repeatedly pointed to its Finance Plan, Wholesale Security Agreement, Rental Inventory Addendum, and financing statement filed on January 16, 2001, as evidence of its secured claim in this case. * * *

* * * Textron's Finance Plan, Wholesale Security Agreement, Rental Inventory Addendum, and financing statement fail to establish that Textron's lien had priority over GECC's lien on the Equipment rental income. Under California law, *conflicting security interests rank according to the priority in time of filing or perfection. A purchase-money lender's security interest in equipment is entitled to priority over conflicting interests in the same collateral only if the purchase-money security interest is perfected at the time the debtor receives possession of the collateral* * * * . [Emphasis added.]

CONTINUED

CASE 29.2 Continued

There is no evidence that Textron perfected its security interest [at the time] Rebel received possession of the Equipment. Indeed, the documents reveal that Textron's security interest attached on September 14, 2000, but was not perfected until January 16, 2001. Given that GECC's financing statement was filed on January 5, 2001, and preceded the filing of Textron's financing statement by eleven days, GECC's security interest was senior to Textron's and entitled to priority over Textron's security in the same collateral.

* * * *

In summary, Textron has failed * * * to establish the validity, extent and priority of its lien on the $430,661 in Equipment lease revenues claimed as cash collateral. * * * Textron's security interest * * * on "proceeds" [does not] defeat GECC's senior lien on rental income attributable to Rebel's lease of the Equipment to its customers. * * * Textron's motion is denied.

QUESTIONS

1. What could Textron have done to avoid the result in this case?
2. For purposes of determining the perfection of a purchase-money security interest in inventory, when should a debtor be considered to "receive possession" of goods delivered in stages or goods that require assembly and testing?

SECTION 6 | Rights and Duties of Debtors and Creditors

The security agreement itself determines most of the rights and duties of the debtor and the secured party. The UCC, however, imposes some rights and duties that are applicable in the absence of a valid security agreement that states the contrary.

INFORMATION REQUESTS

Under UCC 9–523(a), a secured party has the option, when making the filing, of furnishing a *copy* of the financing statement being filed to the filing officer and requesting that the filing officer make a note of the file number, the date, and the hour of the original filing on the copy. The filing officer must send this copy to the person designated by the secured party or to the debtor, if the debtor makes the request. Under UCC 9–523(c) and (d), a filing officer must also give information to a person who is contemplating obtaining a security interest from a prospective debtor. The filing officer must issue a certificate that provides information on possible perfected financing statements with respect to the named debtor. The filing officer will charge a fee for the certification and for any information copies provided [UCC 9–525(d)].

RELEASE, ASSIGNMENT, AND AMENDMENT

A secured party can release all or part of any collateral described in the filing, thereby terminating its security interest in that collateral. The release is recorded by filing a uniform amendment form [UCC 9–512, 9–521(b)]. A secured party can assign all or part of the security interest to a third party (the assignee). The assignee can become the secured party of record if the assignment is filed by use of a uniform amendment form [UCC 9–514, 9–521(a)].

If the debtor and secured parties so agree, they can amend the filing by adding new collateral, for example—by filing a uniform amendment form that indicates by file number the initial financing statement [UCC 9–512(a)]. The amendment does not extend the time period of perfection. If, however, the amendment adds collateral, the perfection date (for priority purposes) for the new collateral begins on the date of the filing of the amendment [UCC 9–512(b) and (c)].

CONFIRMATION OR ACCOUNTING REQUEST BY DEBTOR

The debtor may believe that the unpaid debt amount or the listing of the collateral subject to the security interest is inaccurate. The debtor has the right to request a confirmation of the unpaid debt or listing of collateral. The secured party must either approve or correct this confirmation request [UCC 9–210].

The secured party must comply with the debtor's confirmation request by authenticating and sending to the debtor an accounting within fourteen days after the request is received. Otherwise, the secured party will be held liable for any loss suffered by the debtor, plus $500 [UCC 9–210, 9–625(f)].

The debtor is entitled to one request without charge every six months. For any additional requests, the secured party is entitled to the payment of a statutory fee of up to $25 per request [UCC 9–210(f)].

TERMINATION STATEMENT

When the debtor has fully paid the debt, if the secured party perfected the collateral by filing, the debtor is entitled to have a termination statement filed. Such a statement demonstrates to the public that the filed perfected security interest has been terminated [UCC 9–513].

Whenever consumer goods are involved, the secured party *must* file a termination statement (or, in the alternative, a release) within one month of the final payment or within twenty days of receipt of the debtor's authenticated demand, whichever is earlier [UCC 9–513(b)].

When the collateral is other than consumer goods, on an authenticated demand by the debtor, the secured party must either send a termination statement to the debtor or file such a statement within twenty days [UCC 9–513(c)]. Otherwise, when the collateral is other than consumer goods, the secured party is not required to file or to send a termination statement. Whenever a secured party fails to file or send the termination statement as requested, the debtor can recover $500 plus any additional loss suffered [UCC 9–625(e)(4) and (f)].

SECTION 7 | Default

Article 9 defines the rights, duties, and remedies of the secured party and of the debtor on the debtor's default. Should the secured party fail to comply with his or her duties, the debtor is afforded particular rights and remedies.

The topic of default is one of great concern to secured lenders and to the lawyers who draft security

agreements. What constitutes *default* is not always clear. In fact, Article 9 does not define the term. Consequently, parties are encouraged in practice—and by the UCC—to include in their security agreements certain standards to be applied in determining when default has actually occurred. In so doing, parties can stipulate the conditions that will constitute a default [UCC 9–601, 9–603]. Often, these critical terms are shaped by the creditor in an attempt to provide the maximum protection possible. The ultimate terms, however, cannot go beyond the limitations imposed by the good faith requirement and the unconscionability provisions of the UCC.

Although any breach of the terms of the security agreement can constitute default, default occurs most commonly when the debtor fails to meet the scheduled payments that the parties have agreed on or when the debtor becomes bankrupt.

BASIC REMEDIES

The rights and remedies of secured parties under Article 9 are *cumulative* [UCC 9–601(c)]. Therefore, if a creditor is unsuccessful in enforcing rights by one method, she or he can pursue another method.[7] Generally, a secured party's remedies can be divided into the two basic categories discussed next.

REPOSSESSION OF THE COLLATERAL On the debtor's default, a secured party can take peaceful or judicial possession of the collateral covered by the security agreement [UCC 9–609(b)]. This provision, because it allows the secured party to take peaceful possession of the collateral without the use of the judicial process, is often referred to as the "self-help" provision of Article 9. This provision has been controversial, largely because the UCC does not define what constitutes *peaceful possession*. The general rule, however, is that the collateral has been taken peacefully if the secured party has taken it without committing (1) trespass onto realty, (2) assault and/or battery, or (3) breaking and entering. On taking possession, the secured party may either retain the collateral for satisfaction of the debt [UCC 9–620] or resell the goods and apply the proceeds toward the debt [UCC 9–610].

---

7. See James J. White and Robert S. Summers, *Uniform Commercial Code,* 4th ed. (St. Paul: West Publishing Co., 1995), pp. 908–909.

JUDICIAL REMEDIES A secured party can relinquish a security interest and use any judicial remedy available, such as obtaining a judgment on the underlying debt, followed by execution and levy. (**Execution** is the implementation of a court's decree or judgment. **Levy** is the obtaining of funds by legal process through the seizure and sale of nonsecured property, usually done after a writ of execution has been issued. These writs were discussed in Chapter 28.) Execution and levy are rarely undertaken unless the collateral is no longer in existence or has declined so much in value that it is worth substantially less than the amount of the debt and the debtor has other assets available that may be legally seized to satisfy the debt [UCC 9–601(a)].[8]

DISPOSITION OF COLLATERAL

Once default has occurred and the secured party has obtained possession of the collateral, the secured party may retain the collateral in full satisfaction of the debt (subject to limitations, discussed next) or may sell, lease, or otherwise dispose of the collateral in any commercially reasonable manner [UCC 9–602(7), 9–603, 9–610(a), 9–620]. Any sale is always subject to procedures established by state law.

RETENTION OF COLLATERAL BY THE SECURED PARTY The UCC acknowledges that parties are sometimes better off if they do not sell the collateral. Therefore, a secured party may retain the collateral unless it consists of consumer goods and the debtor has paid 60 percent or more of the purchase price in a PMSI or debt in a non-PMSI (as will be discussed shortly) [UCC 9–620(e)].

This general right, however, is subject to several conditions. The secured party must send notice of the proposal to the debtor if the debtor has not signed a statement renouncing or modifying her or his rights *after default* [UCC 9–620(a), 9–621]. If the collateral is consumer goods, the secured party does not need to give any other notice. In all other situations, the secured party must also send notice to any other secured party from whom the secured party has received written or authenticated notice of a claim of interest in the collateral in question. The secured party must also send notice to any other **junior lienholder** (one holding a lien that is subordinate to one or more other liens on the same property) who has

filed a statutory lien (such as a mechanic's lien—see Chapter 28) or a security interest in the collateral ten days before the debtor consented to the retention [UCC 9–621].

If, within twenty days after the notice is sent, the secured party receives an objection sent by a person entitled to receive notification, the secured party must sell or otherwise dispose of the collateral in accordance with the provisions of UCC 9–602, 9–603, 9–610, and 9–613 (disposition procedures will be discussed shortly). If no such written objection is forthcoming, the secured party may retain the collateral in full or partial satisfaction of the debtor's obligation [UCC 9–620(a), 9–621].

CONSUMER GOODS When the collateral is consumer goods and the debtor has paid 60 percent of the purchase price on a PMSI, or 60 percent of the debt on a non-PMSI, the secured party must sell or otherwise dispose of the repossessed collateral within ninety days [UCC 9–620(e) and (f)]. Failure to comply opens the secured party to an action for conversion or other liability under UCC 9–625(b) and (c) unless the consumer-debtor signed a written statement *after default* renouncing or modifying the right to demand the sale of the goods [UCC 9–624].

DISPOSITION PROCEDURES A secured party who does not choose to retain the collateral or who is required to sell it must resort to the disposition procedures prescribed under UCC 9–602(7), 9–603, 9–610(a), and 9–613. The UCC allows a great deal of flexibility with regard to disposition. UCC 9–610(a) states that after default, a secured party may sell, lease, license, or otherwise dispose of any or all of the collateral in its present condition or following any commercially reasonable preparation or processing. The secured party may also purchase the collateral at a public sale, but it may not do so at a private sale—unless the collateral is of a kind customarily sold on a recognized market or is the subject of widely distributed standard price quotations [UCC 9–610(c)].

—The Sale Must Be Accomplished in a Commercially Reasonable Manner. One of the major limitations with respect to the disposition of collateral is that it be accomplished in a commercially reasonable manner. UCC 9–610(b) states as follows:

> Every aspect of a disposition of collateral, including the method, manner, time, place, and other terms, must be commercially reasonable. If commercially reasonable, a

---

8. Some assets are exempt from creditors' claims under state statutes (see Chapter 28) or bankruptcy laws (see Chapter 30).

secured party may dispose of collateral by public or private proceedings, by one or more contracts, as a unit or in parcels, and at any time and place and on any terms.

The issue in the following case was whether it was commercially reasonable on a debtor's default for the creditor to delay in selling the debtor's stock, which served as the collateral for the parties' loan. Between the time of the default and the sale of the stock, the stock's market value declined significantly.

CASE 29.3

United States
Court of Appeals,
Sixth Circuit, 2005.
395 F.3d 271.

Layne v. Bank One, Kentucky, N.A.

BACKGROUND AND FACTS *Charles Johnson was the chief executive officer of PurchasePro.com, Inc. Geoff Layne was the company's marketing director. Johnson and Layne entered into two separate loan agreements with Bank One, Kentucky, N.A., and Banc One Securities Corporation (collectively, Bank One), secured by their shares of PurchasePro.com stock. Layne's agreement included a loan-to-value (LTV) ratio of 50 percent. This meant that the market value of the stock had to be at least twice the outstanding balance on the loan. Johnson's agreement had a 40 percent LTV ratio, which meant that the stock's market value had to be two and a half times the balance. If the market value dropped, Layne and Johnson had five days to provide more collateral or pay off the loans. Otherwise, they would be in default and Bank One could sell the stock. In February 2001, the price of the stock fell below these limits. After months of unsuccessful negotiations, Bank One sold Johnson's shares in July, recovering $524,757.39 in proceeds to pay down his debt, leaving an unpaid balance of approximately $2.2 million. Layne and Johnson filed a suit in a federal district court against Bank One, alleging in part breach of contract. Bank One filed counterclaims against Johnson and Layne, seeking payment on the loans. The court issued a summary judgment in Bank One's favor. Johnson appealed to the U.S. Court of Appeals for the Sixth Circuit.*

IN THE LANGUAGE OF THE COURT

MOORE, Circuit Judge.
* * * *
Johnson's * * * argument raised on appeal is that Bank One violated Kentucky law by failing to dispose of the PurchasePro stock in a commercially reasonable manner. * * * [Kentucky Revised Statutes Annotated Section 355.9-610 (Kentucky's version of UCC 9–610)] requires that "[e]very aspect of a disposition of collateral, including the method, manner, time, place, and other terms, must be commercially reasonable." *The purpose of the provision is to protect the debtor's interest by ensuring he will receive the market price of his collateral.* [Kentucky Revised Statutes Annotated Section 355.9-627(2) (UCC 9–627(b)] also provides a "recognized market" safe harbor, which states that: [Emphasis added.]

> [A] disposition of collateral is made in a commercially reasonable manner if the disposition is made:
> (a) In the usual manner on any recognized market;
> (b) At the price current in any recognized market at the time of disposition; or
> (c) Otherwise in conformity with reasonable commercial practices among dealers in the type of property that was the subject of the disposition.

* * * [A] "recognized market" [is] one in which the items sold are fungible [commercially interchangeable] and prices are not subject to individual negotiation. For example, the New York Stock Exchange is a recognized market. Sales on a recognized market are commercially reasonable because the price on the recognized market represents the fair market value of the collateral from day to day. Therefore, where the collateral is sold in a recognized market, Kentucky courts have found the transaction to be commercially reasonable as a matter of law. Courts in other states have held similarly that a sale on a recognized market is *per se* commercially reasonable. Moreover, [Kentucky Revised Statutes Annotated Section 355.9-627(1) (UCC 9–627(a)] provides that "[t]he fact that a greater amount could have been obtained by * * * disposition * * * at a different time or in a different method from that selected

CONTINUED ▶

CASE 29.3 | **Continued**

by the secured party is not of itself sufficient to preclude the secured party from establishing that the * * * disposition * * * was made in a commercially reasonable manner."

Applying the U.C.C. provisions to this case, the district court was correct to find that Bank One's disposition of the PurchasePro shares through a sale on the NASDAQ [National Association of Securities Dealers Automated Quotations[a]] national market was commercially reasonable. Johnson * * * [argues] that delaying the sale of the pledged stock from February was commercially unreasonable. Johnson's argument, however, misinterprets the statute. *Section 9-610 does not impose an obligation on a lender to liquidate and sell the collateral stock at a specific time during the life of the loan.* Put another way, Section 9-610 does not address *whether* a lender should dispose of its collateral, but rather once that decision has been made, *how* the disposition should occur. When Johnson's loan fell below the LTV ratio, Bank One attempted to restructure the loan and secure additional collateral rather than sell the shares. Under the [loan] agreement and Kentucky law, Bank One was not under any obligation to sell the stock at that point. In late May, after repeated negotiations with Johnson fell through, Bank One decided to begin the liquidation process, which was completed by July. The sale of the stock was on the NASDAQ, a recognized market, and thus ensured that Johnson received the fair market value for his stock shortly after the decision to liquidate was made, which is all that Section 9-610 requires. Therefore, we conclude that the sale of Johnson's PurchasePro stock was commercially reasonable and the district court's grant of summary judgment on this issue is affirmed. [Emphasis added.]

DECISION AND REMEDY *The U.S. Court of Appeals for the Sixth Circuit affirmed the judgment of the lower court. Bank One was not liable for the depreciation in the value of the PurchasePro.com shares that it held as collateral for the loan to Johnson. Also, by selling the stock on a national stock exchange, Bank One acted in a commercially reasonable manner in disposing of the collateral.*

WHAT IF THE FACTS WERE DIFFERENT? *If Bank One had refused to negotiate with Johnson and Layne, and had sold their stock as soon as their loans were in default, would the result in this case have been different?*

---

a. NASDAQ is an automated information system that gives price quotations on publicly traded securities, including stock traded among stockbrokers and others.

—*Notification Requirements.* Unless the collateral is perishable or will decline rapidly in value or is a type customarily sold on a recognized market, a secured party must send to the debtor and other identified persons "a reasonable authenticated notification of disposition" [UCC 9–611(b) and (c)]. The debtor may waive the right to receive this notice, but only after default [UCC 9–624(a)].

PROCEEDS FROM DISPOSITION Proceeds from the disposition of collateral after default on the underlying debt are distributed in the following order:

1. Expenses incurred by the secured party in repossessing, storing, and reselling the collateral.
2. Balance of the debt owed to the secured party.
3. Junior lienholders who have made written or authenticated demands.

4. Unless the collateral consists of accounts, payment intangibles, promissory notes, or chattel paper, any surplus goes to the debtor [UCC 9–608(a), 9–615(a) and (e)].

NONCASH PROCEEDS Whenever the secured party receives noncash proceeds from the disposition of collateral after default, the secured party must make a value determination and apply this value in a commercially reasonable manner [UCC 9–608(a)(3), 9–615(c)].

DEFICIENCY JUDGMENT Often, after proper disposition of the collateral, the secured party still has not collected all that the debtor owes. Unless otherwise agreed, the debtor is liable for any deficiency, and the creditor can obtain a **deficiency judgment**

from a court to collect the deficiency. Note, however, that if the underlying transaction was, for example, a sale of accounts or of chattel paper, the debtor is entitled to any surplus or is liable for any deficiency only if the security agreement so provides [UCC 9–615(d) and (e)].

Whenever the secured party fails to conduct a disposition in a commercially reasonable manner or to give proper notice, the amount that the debtor still owes is reduced to the extent that such failure affected the price received at the disposition [UCC 9–626(a)(3)].

REDEMPTION RIGHTS At any time before the secured party disposes of the collateral or enters into a contract for its disposition, or before the debtor's obligation has been discharged through the secured party's retention of the collateral, the debtor or any other secured party can exercise the right of *redemption* of the collateral. The debtor or other secured party can do this by tendering performance of all obligations secured by the collateral and by paying the expenses reasonably incurred by the secured party in retaking and maintaining the collateral [UCC 9–623].

CONCEPT SUMMARY 29.2 | Remedies of the Secured Party on the Debtor's Default

CONCEPT	DESCRIPTION

REPOSSESSION OF THE COLLATERAL	The secured party may take possession (peacefully or by court order) of the collateral covered by the security agreement and then pursue one of two alternatives:
	1. Retain the collateral (unless the collateral is consumer goods and the debtor has paid 60 percent of the selling price on a PMSI or 60 percent of the debt on a non-PMSI). To retain the collateral, the secured party must—
	  a. Give notice to the debtor if the debtor has not signed a statement renouncing or modifying his or her rights after default. With consumer goods, no other notice is necessary.
	  b. Send notice to any other secured party who has given written or authenticated notice of a claim to the same collateral or who has filed a security interest or a statutory lien ten days before the debtor consented to the retention. If an objection is received within twenty days from the debtor or any other secured party given notice, the creditor must dispose of the collateral according to the requirements of UCC 9–602, 9–603, 9–610, and 9–613. Otherwise, the creditor may retain the collateral in full or partial satisfaction of the debt.
	2. Dispose of the collateral in accordance with the requirements of UCC 9–602(7), 9–603, 9–610(a), and 9–613. To do so, the secured party must—
	  a. Dispose of (sell, lease, or license) the goods in a commercially reasonable manner.
	  b. Notify the debtor and (except in sales of consumer goods) other identified persons, including those who have given notice of claims to the collateral to be sold (unless the collateral is perishable or will decline rapidly in value).
	  c. Apply the proceeds in the following order:
	    (1) Expenses incurred by the secured party in repossessing, storing, and reselling the collateral.
	    (2) The balance of the debt owed to the secured party.
	    (3) Junior lienholders who have made written or authenticated demands.
	    (4) Surplus to the debtor (unless the collateral consists of accounts, payment intangibles, promissory notes, or chattel paper).

JUDICIAL REMEDIES	The secured party may relinquish the security interest and proceed with any judicial remedy available, such as obtaining a judgment on the underlying debt, followed by execution and levy on the nonexempt assets of the debtor.

REVIEWING SECURED TRANSACTIONS

Paul Barton owned a small property management company, doing business as Brighton Homes. In October, Barton went on a spending spree. First, he bought a Bose surround-sound system for his home from KDM Electronics. The next day, he purchased a Wilderness Systems kayak and roof rack from Outdoor Outfitters, and the day after that he bought a new Toyota 4-Runner financed through Bridgeport Auto. Two weeks later, Barton purchased six new iMac computers for his office, also from KDM Electronics. Barton bought each of these items under installment sales contracts. Six months later, Barton's property management business went bankrupt, and he could not make the payments due on any of these purchases and thus defaulted on the loans. Using the information presented in the chapter, answer the following questions.

1. | Explain how a security interest was likely created for each of Barton's purchases (the surround-sound system, the kayak and roof rack, the 4-Runner, and the six iMacs).

2. | For which of these purchases would the creditor need to file a financing statement to perfect its security interest?

3. | Suppose that Barton's contract for the office computers mentioned only the name Brighton Homes. What would be the consequences if KDM Electronics filed a financing statement that listed only Brighton Homes as the debtor's name?

4. | Which of these purchases would qualify as a PMSI in consumer goods? Would the security interest in each of these goods be automatically perfected? Why or why not? What else might a creditor have to do to perfect the security interest?

5. | Suppose that after KDM Electronics repossesses the surround-sound system, it decides to keep it rather than to sell it. Could KDM do this under Article 9? Explain.

TERMS AND CONCEPTS TO REVIEW

after-acquired property 591

attachment 582

authentication 582

collateral 581

continuation statement 589

cross-collateralization 591

debtor 581

deficiency judgment 600

execution 598

financing statement 581

floating lien 591

junior lienholder 598

levy 598

perfection 583

pledge 589

proceeds 590

purchase-money security interest (PMSI) 589

secured party 581

secured transaction 581

security agreement 581

security interest 581

QUESTIONS AND CASE PROBLEMS

29–1. Redford is a seller of electric generators. He purchases a large quantity of generators from a manufacturer, Mallon Corp., by making a down payment and signing an agreement to make the balance of payments over a period of time. The agreement gives Mallon Corp. a security interest in the generators and the proceeds. Mallon Corp. properly files a financing statement on its security interest. Redford receives the generators and immediately sells one of them to Garfield on an installment contract, with payment to be made in twelve equal installments. At the time of the sale, Garfield knows of Mallon's security interest. Two months later, Redford goes into default on his payments to Mallon. Discuss Mallon's rights against Garfield in this situation.

29–2. Marsh has a prize horse named Arabian Knight. Marsh is in need of working capital. She borrows $50,000 from Mendez, who takes possession of Arabian Knight as security for the loan. No written agreement is signed. Discuss whether, in the absence of a written agreement, Mendez has a security interest in Arabian Knight. If Mendez does have a security interest, is it a perfected security interest?

29–3. QUESTION WITH SAMPLE ANSWER

Delgado is a retail seller of television sets. He sells a color television set to Cummings for $600. Cummings cannot pay cash, so she signs a security agreement, paying $100 down and agreeing to pay the balance in twelve equal installments of $50 each. The security agreement gives Delgado a security interest in the television set sold. Cummings makes six payments on time; then she goes into default because of unexpected financial problems. Delgado repossesses the set and wants to keep it in full satisfaction of the debt. Discuss Delgado's rights and duties in this matter.

For a sample answer to this question, go to Appendix I at the end of this text.

29–4. Edward owned a retail sporting goods shop. A new ski resort was being built in his area, and to take advantage of the potential business, Edward decided to expand his operations. He borrowed a large sum from his bank, which took a security interest in his present inventory and any after-acquired inventory as collateral for the loan. The bank properly perfected the security interest by filing a financing statement. Edward's business was profitable, so he doubled his inventory. A year later, just a few months after the ski resort had opened, an avalanche destroyed the ski slope and lodge. Edward's business consequently took a turn for the worse, and he defaulted on his debt to the bank. The bank then sought possession of his entire inventory, even though the inventory was now twice as large as it had been when the loan was made. Edward claimed that the bank had rights to only half of his inventory. Is Edward correct? Explain.

29–5. **FINANCING STATEMENT.** In 1994, SouthTrust Bank, N.A., loaned funds to Environmental Aspecs, Inc. (EAI), and its subsidiary, EAI of NC. SouthTrust perfected its security interest by filing financing statements that listed only EAI as the debtor, described only EAI's assets as collateral, and were signed only on EAI's behalf. SouthTrust believed that both companies were operating as a single business represented by EAI. In 1996, EAI of NC borrowed almost $300,000 from Advanced Analytics Laboratories, Inc. (AAL). AAL filed financing statements that listed the assets of EAI of NC as collateral but identified the debtor as EAI. The statements referred, however, to attached copies of the security agreements, which were signed by the president of EAI of NC and identified the debtor as EAI of NC. One year later, EAI and EAI of NC renegotiated their loan with SouthTrust, and the bank filed financing statements listing both companies as debtors. In 1998, EAI and EAI of NC filed for bankruptcy. One of the issues was the priority of the security interests of SouthTrust and AAL.

AAL contended that its failure to identify, on its financing statements, EAI of NC as the debtor did not give SouthTrust priority. Is AAL correct? Why or why not? [*In re Environmental Aspecs, Inc.,* 235 Bankr. 378 (E.D.N.C., Raleigh Div. 1999)]

29–6. **PURCHASE-MONEY SECURITY INTEREST.** When a customer opens a credit-card account with Sears, Roebuck & Co., the customer fills out an application and sends it to Sears for review; if the application is approved, the customer receives a Sears card. The application contains a security agreement, a copy of which is also sent with the card. When a customer buys an item using the card, the customer signs a sales receipt that describes the merchandise and contains language granting Sears a purchase-money security interest (PMSI) in the merchandise. Dayna Conry bought a variety of consumer goods from Sears on her card. When she did not make payments on her account, Sears filed a suit against her in an Illinois state court to repossess the goods. Conry filed for bankruptcy and was granted a discharge. Sears then filed a suit against her to obtain possession of the goods through its PMSI, but it could not find Conry's credit-card application to offer into evidence. Is a signed Sears sales receipt sufficient proof of its security interest? In whose favor should the court rule? Explain. [*Sears, Roebuck & Co. v. Conry,* 321 Ill.App.3d 997, 748 N.E.2d 1248, 255 Ill.Dec. 178 (3 Dist. 2001)]

29–7. CASE PROBLEM WITH SAMPLE ANSWER

In St. Louis, Missouri, in August 2000, Richard Miller orally agreed to loan Jeff Miller $35,000 in exchange for a security interest in a 1999 Kodiak dump truck. The Millers did not put anything in writing concerning the loan, its repayment terms, or Richard's security interest or rights in the truck. Jeff used the amount of the loan to buy the truck, which he kept in his possession. In June 2004, Jeff filed a petition to obtain a discharge of his debts in bankruptcy. Richard claimed that he had a security interest in the truck and thus was entitled to any proceeds from its sale. What are a creditor's main concerns on a debtor's default? How does a creditor satisfy these concerns? What are the requirements for a creditor to have an enforceable security interest? Have these requirements been met in this case? Considering these points, what is the court likely to rule with respect to Richard's claim? [*In re Miller,* 320 Bankr. 911 (E.D.Mo. 2005)]

To view a sample answer for this case problem, go to this book's Web site at http://wbl.westbuslaw.com, select "Chapter 29," and click on "Case Problem with Sample Answer."

29–8. **PLEDGE.** On April 14, 1992, David and Myrna Grossman borrowed $10,000 from Brookfield Bank in Brookfield, Connecticut, and signed a note to repay the principal with interest. As collateral, the Grossmans gave the bank possession of stock certificates representing 123 shares in General Electric Co. The note was nonnegotiable and thus was not subject to UCC Article 3.

On May 8, the bank closed its doors. The Grossmans did not make any payments on the note and refused to permit the sale of the stock to apply against the debt. The Grossmans' note and collateral were assigned to Premier Capital, Inc., which filed a suit in a Connecticut state court against them, seeking to collect the principal and interest due. The Grossmans responded in part that they were entitled to credit for the value of the stock that secured the note. By the time of the trial, the stock certificates had been lost. What should be the duty of a creditor toward collateral that is transferred into the creditor's possession as security for a loan? How should the court rule, and why? [*Premier Capital, Inc. v. Grossman*, 68 Conn.App. 51, 789 A.2d 565 (2002)]

29–9. PRIORITIES. PC Contractors, Inc., was an excavating business in Kansas City, Missouri. Union Bank made loans to PC, subject to a perfected security interest in its equipment and other assets, including "after-acquired property." In late 1997, PC leased heavy construction equipment from Dean Machinery Co. The lease agreements required monthly payments, which PC often made late or missed completely. After eighteen months, Dean demanded that PC either return the equipment or buy it. While attempting to obtain financing for the purchase, PC continued to make monthly payments. In November 2000, Dean, which had not filed a financing statement to cover the transaction, demanded full payment of the amount due. Before paying the price, PC went out of business and surrendered its assets to Union, which prepared to sell them. Dean

filed a suit in a Missouri state court against Union to recover the equipment, claiming in part that the bank's security interest had not attached to the equipment because PC had not paid for it. In whose favor should the court rule, and why? [*Dean Machinery Co. v. Union Bank*, 106 S.W.3d 510 (Mo.App.W.D. 2003)]

29–10. VIDEO QUESTION

Go to this text's Web site at <u>http://wbl.westbuslaw.com</u> and select "Chapter 29." Click on "Video Questions" and view the video titled *Secured Transactions*. Then answer the following questions.

(a) This chapter lists three requirements for creating a security interest. In the video, which requirement does Laura assert has not been met?

(b) What, if anything, must the bank have done to perfect its interest in the editing equipment?

(c) If the bank exercises its self-help remedy to repossess Onyx's editing equipment, does Laura have any chance of getting it back? Explain.

(d) Assume that the bank had a perfected security interest and repossessed the editing equipment. Also assume that the purchase price (and the loan amount) for the equipment was $100,000, of which Onyx has paid $65,000. Discuss the rights and duties of the bank with regard to the collateral in this situation.

LAW | on the Web

For updated links to resources available on the Web, as well as a variety of other materials, visit this text's Web site at <u>http://wbl.westbuslaw.com</u>.

To find Article 9 of the UCC as modified by a particular state on adoption, go to

<u>http://straylight.law.cornell.edu/ucc/ucc.table.html</u>

For an overview of secured transactions law and links to UCC provisions and case law on this topic, go to

<u>http://straylight.law.cornell.edu/topics/secured_transactions.</u>html

LEGAL RESEARCH EXERCISES ON THE WEB

Go to <u>http://wbl.westbuslaw.com</u>, the Web site that accompanies this text. Select "Chapter 29" and click on "Internet Exercises." There you will find the following Internet research exercises that you can perform to learn more about topics covered in this chapter.

Activity 29–1: LEGAL PERSPECTIVE
          Repossession

Activity 29–2: MANAGEMENT PERSPECTIVE
          Filing Financial Statements

CHAPTER 30
Bankruptcy Law

Historically, debtors had few rights. Today, in contrast, debtors have numerous rights. Some of these rights were discussed in Chapters 28 and 29. In this chapter, we look at another significant right of debtors: the right to petition for bankruptcy relief under federal law. Article I, Section 8, of the U.S. Constitution gave Congress the power to establish "uniform Laws on the subject of Bankruptcies throughout the United States."

Bankruptcy law in the United States has two goals—to protect a debtor by giving him or her a fresh start, free from creditors' claims, and to ensure equitable treatment to creditors who are competing for a debtor's assets. Federal bankruptcy legislation was first enacted in 1898 and has undergone several modifications since that time.

Bankruptcy law prior to 2005 was based on the Bankruptcy Reform Act of 1978, as amended—hereinafter called the Bankruptcy Code, or more simply, the Code (not to be confused with the Uniform Commercial Code, which is also sometimes called the Code). In 2005, Congress enacted a new Bankruptcy Reform Act, which became effective six months after President George W. Bush signed the act into law.[1] As you will read throughout this chapter, the 2005 act significantly overhauled certain provisions of the Bankruptcy Code—for the first time in twenty-five years. One of the major goals of the new act is to require consumers to pay as many of their debts as they possibly can instead of having those debts fully discharged in bankruptcy. The law was passed, in part, in response to businesses' concerns about the rise in personal bankruptcy filings, which have increased every year since 1980 (from fewer than 300,000 to over 1.6 million per year).

SECTION 1 | Bankruptcy Proceedings

Bankruptcy proceedings are held in federal bankruptcy courts, which are under the authority of the U.S. district courts, and rulings from bankruptcy courts can be appealed to the district courts. Although bankruptcy law is federal law, state laws on secured transactions, liens, judgments, and exemptions also play a role in federal bankruptcy proceedings.

THE ROLE OF THE BANKRUPTCY COURTS

Essentially, a bankruptcy court fulfills the role of an administrative court for the federal district court concerning matters in bankruptcy. The bankruptcy court holds proceedings dealing with the procedures required to administer the estate of the debtor in bankruptcy. A bankruptcy court can conduct a jury trial if the appropriate district court has authorized it and the parties to the bankruptcy consent. Bankruptcy court judges are federally appointed for fourteen-year terms. The 2005 Bankruptcy Reform Act created a section entitled the Bankruptcy Judgeship Act of 2005, which enlarged the number of bankruptcy judges by twenty-eight (four for the Delaware District).

---

1. The full title of the act is the Bankruptcy Abuse Prevention and Consumer Protection Act of 2005, Pub. L. No. 109-8, 119 Stat. 23 (April 20, 2005). The bulk of the act became effective 180 days after being signed by the president on April 20, 2005. Thus, the new provisions took effect in October 2005. (Bankruptcy petitions that were filed before the act became effective continued to be administered and governed by the 1978 Reform Act, as amended.)

TYPES OF BANKRUPTCY RELIEF

Title 11 of the *United States Code* encompasses the Bankruptcy Code, which has eight chapters. Chapters 1, 3, and 5 of the Code contain general definitional provisions, as well as provisions governing case administration, creditors, the debtor, and the estate. These three chapters apply generally to all kinds of bankruptcies. The next five chapters of the Code set forth the different types of relief that debtors may seek. Chapter 7 provides for **liquidation** proceedings (the selling of all nonexempt assets and the distribution of the proceeds to the debtor's creditors). Chapter 9 governs the adjustment of a municipality's debts. Chapter 11 governs reorganizations. Chapters 12 and 13 provide for the adjustment of debts by parties with regular incomes (family farmers and family fishermen under Chapter 12 and individuals under Chapter 13).[2] A debtor (except for a municipality) need not be insolvent[3] to file for bankruptcy relief under any chapter of the Bankruptcy Code. Anyone obligated to a creditor can declare bankruptcy.

SPECIAL TREATMENT OF CONSUMER-DEBTORS

To fully inform a consumer-debtor of the various types of relief available, the Code requires that the clerk of the court provide certain information to all consumer-debtors prior to the commencement of a bankruptcy filing. (Recall from Chapter 29 that a consumer-debtor is a debtor whose debts result primarily from the purchase of goods for personal, family, or household use.) First, the clerk must give consumer-debtors written notice of the general purpose, benefits, and costs of each chapter of the Bankruptcy Code under which they might proceed. Second, under the 2005 act, the clerk must provide consumer-debtors with informational materials on the types of services available from credit counseling agencies.

In this chapter, we deal first with liquidation proceedings under Chapter 7 of the Code. We then examine the procedures required for Chapter 11 reorganizations and Chapter 12 and 13 plans. (The latter three chapters of the Code are known as "rehabilitation" chapters.)

SECTION 2 | Liquidation Proceedings

Liquidation under Chapter 7 of the Bankruptcy Code is generally the most familiar type of bankruptcy proceeding and is often referred to as an *ordinary*, or *straight*, *bankruptcy*. Put simply, a debtor in a liquidation bankruptcy turns all assets over to a **trustee.** The trustee sells the nonexempt assets and distributes the proceeds to creditors. With certain exceptions, the remaining debts are then **discharged** (extinguished), and the debtor is relieved of the obligation to pay the debts.

Any "person"—defined as including individuals, partnerships, and corporations[4]—may be a debtor in a liquidation proceeding. Railroads, insurance companies, banks, savings and loan associations, investment companies licensed by the Small Business Administration, and credit unions cannot be debtors in a liquidation bankruptcy, however. Other chapters of the Bankruptcy Code or federal or state statutes apply to them.

A straight bankruptcy may be commenced by the filing of either a voluntary or an involuntary **petition in bankruptcy**—the document that is filed with a bankruptcy court to initiate bankruptcy proceedings. If a debtor files the petition, it is a voluntary bankruptcy. If one or more creditors file a petition to force the debtor into bankruptcy, it is called an involuntary bankruptcy. We discuss both voluntary and involuntary bankruptcy proceedings under Chapter 7 in the following subsections.

VOLUNTARY BANKRUPTCY

To bring a voluntary petition in bankruptcy, the debtor files official forms designated for that purpose in the bankruptcy court. The Bankruptcy Reform Act of 2005 specifies that before debtors can file a petition, they must receive credit counseling from an approved

---

2. There are no Chapters 2, 4, 6, 8, or 10 in Title 11. Such "gaps" are not uncommon in the *United States Code*. This is because chapter numbers (or other subdivisional unit numbers) are sometimes reserved for future use when a statute is enacted. (A gap may also appear if a law has been repealed.)

3. The inability to pay debts as they become due is known as *equitable* insolvency. A *balance sheet* insolvency, which exists when a debtor's liabilities exceed assets, is not the test. Thus, it is possible for debtors to voluntarily petition for bankruptcy or to be thrown into involuntary bankruptcy even though their assets far exceed their liabilities. This may occur when a debtor's cash flow problems become severe.

---

4. The definition of *corporation* includes unincorporated companies and associations. It also covers labor unions.

nonprofit agency within the 180-day period preceding the date of filing. The act provides detailed criteria for the *U.S. Trustee* to approve nonprofit budget and counseling agencies and requires that a list of approved agencies be made publicly available.[5] A debtor filing a Chapter 7 petition must include a certificate proving that he or she received an individual or group briefing from an approved counseling agency within the last 180 days (roughly six months).

The Code requires a consumer-debtor who has opted for liquidation bankruptcy proceedings to confirm the accuracy of the petition's contents. The debtor must also state in the petition, at the time of filing, that he or she understands the relief available under other chapters of the Code and has chosen to proceed under Chapter 7. If an attorney is representing the consumer-debtor, the attorney must file an affidavit stating that she or he has informed the debtor of the relief available under each chapter of the Bankruptcy Code. In addition, the 2005 act requires the attorney to reasonably attempt to verify the accuracy of the consumer-debtor's petition and schedules (described below). Failure to do so is considered perjury.

CHAPTER 7 SCHEDULES The voluntary petition must contain the following schedules:

1. A list of both secured and unsecured creditors, their addresses, and the amount of debt owed to each.
2. A statement of the financial affairs of the debtor.
3. A list of all property owned by the debtor, including property that the debtor claims is exempt.
4. A list of current income and expenses.
5. A certificate from an approved credit counseling agency (as discussed previously).
6. Proof of payments received from employers within sixty days prior to the filing of the petition.
7. A statement of the amount of monthly income, itemized to show how the amount is calculated.
8. A copy of the debtor's federal income tax return (or a transcript of such a return) for the most recent year ending immediately before the filing of the petition.

As previously noted, the official forms must be completed accurately, sworn to under oath, and signed by the debtor. To conceal assets or knowingly supply false information on these schedules is a crime under the bankruptcy laws.

—Additional Information May Be Required. At the request of the court, the **U.S. Trustee** (a government official who performs appointment and other administrative tasks that a bankruptcy judge would otherwise have to perform), or any party in interest, the debtor must file tax returns at the end of each tax year while the case is pending and provide copies to the court. This requirement also applies to Chapter 11 and 13 bankruptcies (discussed later in this chapter). Also, if requested by the U.S. Trustee or bankruptcy trustee, the debtor must provide a photo document establishing his or her identity (such as a driver's license or passport) or other personal identifying information.

—Time Period for Filing Schedules. With the exception of tax returns, failure to file the required schedules within forty-five days after the filing of the petition (unless an extension of up to forty-five days is granted) will result in an automatic dismissal of the petition. The debtor has up to seven days before the date of the first creditors' meeting to provide a copy of the most recent tax returns to the trustee.

SUBSTANTIAL ABUSE Prior to 2005, a bankruptcy court could dismiss a Chapter 7 petition for relief (discharge of debts) if the use of Chapter 7 would constitute a "substantial abuse" of that chapter. The Bankruptcy Reform Act of 2005 established a new system of "means testing" (the debtor's income) to determine whether a debtor's petition is presumed to be a "substantial abuse" of Chapter 7.

—When Abuse Will Be Presumed. If the debtor's family income is greater than the median family income in the state in which the petition is filed, the trustee or any party in interest (such as a creditor) can bring a motion to dismiss the Chapter 7 petition. State median incomes vary from state to state and are calculated and reported by the U.S. Bureau of the Census.[6]

The debtor's current monthly income is calculated using the last six months' average income, less certain "allowed expenses" reflecting the basic needs of the

---

5. The Bankruptcy Reform Act of 2005 also required the director of the Executive Office for the U.S. Trustees to develop a curriculum for financial-management training and create materials that can be used to educate individual debtors on how to better manage their finances.

6. For example, in 2004 the median family income in Kentucky was $53,319, and in West Virginia it was $49,470, according to statistics prepared by the Bureau of the Census and reported for each state annually in the *Federal Register*.

debtor.[7] The monthly amount is then multiplied by twelve. If the resulting income exceeds the state median income by $6,000 or more,[8] abuse is presumed, and the trustee or any creditor can file a motion to dismiss the petition. A debtor can rebut (refute) the presumption of abuse "by demonstrating special circumstances that justify additional expenses or adjustments of current monthly income for which there is no reasonable alternative." (One example might be anticipated medical costs not covered by health insurance.) These additional expenses or adjustments must be itemized and their accuracy attested to under oath by the debtor.

7. Section 707 of the Bankruptcy Reform Act of 2005 describes the means test and provides a detailed listing of the expenses allowed under the act.

8. This amount ($6,000) is the equivalent of $100 per month for five years, indicating that the debtor could pay at least $100 per month under a Chapter 13 five-year repayment plan.

—When Abuse Will Not Be Presumed. If the debtor's income is below the state median (or if the debtor has successfully rebutted the means-test presumption), abuse will not be presumed. In these situations, the court may still find substantial abuse, but the creditors will not have standing (see Chapter 2) to file a motion to dismiss. Basically, this leaves intact the prior law on substantial abuse, allowing the court to consider such factors as the debtor's bad faith or circumstances indicating substantial abuse. The following case illustrates how a court determined whether granting a Chapter 7 discharge to the debtor would constitute substantial abuse by applying the "totality-of-the-circumstances" test. Although the case was decided before the 2005 reforms were enacted, a court could take the same approach under the new law (if, for example, the means test did not require substantial abuse to be presumed).

CASE 30.1 **In re Lamanna**

United States Court of Appeals, First Circuit, 1998. 153 F.3d 1. http://www.law.emory.edu/1circuit [a]

BACKGROUND AND FACTS In 1996, Richard Lamanna was living with his parents. For this reason, his monthly expenses were only $580. His monthly income was $1,350.96, leaving a difference of $770.96, the amount of his disposable income.[b] He had no plans to move out of his parents' house. During four weeks in October and November, he charged $9,994.45 on credit cards. In February 1997, when his total unsecured debt was $15,911.96, he filed a voluntary petition in a federal bankruptcy court to declare bankruptcy under Chapter 7 of the Bankruptcy Code. The court noted that Lamanna was capable of paying all of his debts under a Chapter 13 repayment plan and dismissed the case. The U.S. Bankruptcy Appellate Panel (BAP)[c] for the First Circuit affirmed the dismissal, and Lamanna appealed to the U.S. Court of Appeals for the First Circuit. Lamanna argued in part that if he did not live with his parents, he would not have as much disposable income, and that thus he was being penalized for living with his parents.

IN THE LANGUAGE OF THE COURT

LYNCH, Circuit Judge.
* * * *
The question of whether allowing Lamanna's bankruptcy petition would constitute "substantial abuse" of Chapter 7 under Section 707(b) contains two components: first, the proper test by which "substantial abuse" is measured; second, whether, applying that test, the BAP [Bankruptcy Appellate Panel] correctly decided the issue. * * *
* * * *
* * * Although tests employed by various courts of appeals do not employ precisely the same language, they share common elements. First and foremost, it is agreed that *a consumer debtor's ability to repay his debts out of future disposable income is strong evidence of "substantial*

---

a. This Web site is maintained by Emory University School of Law. In the "Listing by Month of Decision" section, click on "August" in the row for "1998" cases. When the list of cases appears, click on the case name to access the opinion.

b. *Disposable income* is income "not reasonably necessary to be expended for the maintenance or support of the debtor or a dependent of the debtor," according to 11 U.S.C. Section 1325(b)(2).

c. A *bankruptcy appellate panel* has jurisdiction, with the consent of the parties, to hear appeals from final judgments, orders, and decrees of bankruptcy judges.

CASE 30.1 | Continued *abuse.*" * * * In determining whether to apply Section 707(b) to an individual debtor, * * * a court should ascertain from the totality of the circumstances whether he is merely seeking an advantage over his creditors, or is "honest," * * * and whether he is "needy" in the sense that his financial predicament warrants the discharge of his debts in exchange for liquidation of his assets. * * * [T]he "totality of the circumstances" test demands a comprehensive review of the debtor's current and potential financial situation. [Emphasis added.]
* * * *

Applying the "totality of the circumstances" test to Lamanna's case results in affirmance of the dismissal of his Chapter 7 petition for "substantial abuse." Lamanna's schedules showed that he has sufficient disposable income to repay his debts under a Chapter 13 repayment plan in three to five years. There is no evidence that Lamanna's living situation was unstable or likely to change in the near future. There is no evidence of other factors that cast doubt on the stability of Lamanna's future income and expenses. Although Lamanna's expenses are particularly low because he lives with his parents, this state of affairs, as the BAP noted, "is not artificial; it is actual." The court properly based its decision on the current and foreseeable facts. If Lamanna's circumstances dramatically change, he is free to seek relief anew.

Lamanna's argument that the court penalized him for living with his parents (and thus having exceptionally low monthly expenses) boils down to the notion that Section 707 requires the bankruptcy court to impute a minimum cost of living to a debtor and then measure the debtor's actual income against the higher of the imputed minimum and the debtor's actual expenses. Section 707 does not contain such an implicit requirement, and this court will not write such a requirement into the statute.

DECISION AND REMEDY *The U.S. Court of Appeals for the First Circuit affirmed the decision of the lower court and held that granting Lamanna's petition would constitute substantial abuse of Chapter 7. The appellate court looked at the "totality of the circumstances" to reach its conclusion.*

WHAT IF THE FACTS WERE DIFFERENT? *If the debtor in this case had not been able to pay his debts as they came due, would the result in the case have been different?*

ADDITIONAL GROUNDS FOR DISMISSAL As noted, a debtor's voluntary petition for Chapter 7 relief may be dismissed for substantial abuse or for failing to provide the necessary documents (such as schedules and tax returns) within the specified time. In addition, a motion to dismiss a Chapter 7 filing might be granted in two other situations under the Bankruptcy Reform Act of 2005. First, if the debtor has been convicted of a violent crime or a drug-trafficking offense, the victim can file a motion to dismiss the voluntary petition.[9] Second, if the debtor fails to pay postpetition domestic-support obligations (which include child and spousal support), the court may dismiss the debtor's Chapter 7 petition.

ORDER FOR RELIEF If the voluntary petition for bankruptcy is found to be proper, the filing of the petition will itself constitute an **order for relief.** (An order

for relief is a court's grant of assistance to a complainant.) Once a consumer-debtor's voluntary petition has been filed, the clerk of the court or other appointee must give the trustee and creditors notice of the order for relief by mail not more than twenty days after entry of the order. A husband and wife may file jointly for bankruptcy under a single petition.

INVOLUNTARY BANKRUPTCY

An involuntary bankruptcy occurs when the debtor's creditors force the debtor into bankruptcy proceedings. An involuntary case cannot be commenced against a farmer[10] or a charitable institution. For an involuntary action to be filed against other debtors, the following requirements must be met: If the debtor

---

9. Note that the court may not dismiss a case on this ground if the debtor's bankruptcy is necessary to satisfy a claim for a domestic-support obligation.

10. The definition of *farmer* includes persons who receive more than 50 percent of their gross income from farming operations, such as tilling the soil, dairy farming, ranching, or the production or raising of crops, poultry, or livestock. Corporations and partnerships may qualify under certain conditions.

has twelve or more creditors, three or more of these creditors having unsecured claims totaling at least $12,300 must join in the petition. If a debtor has fewer than twelve creditors, one or more creditors having a claim of $12,300 may file.

If the debtor challenges the involuntary petition, a hearing will be held, and the bankruptcy court will enter an order for relief if it finds either of the following:

1. The debtor is generally not paying debts as they become due.
2. A general receiver, assignee, or custodian took possession of, or was appointed to take charge of, substantially all of the debtor's property within 120 days before the filing of the petition.

If the court grants an order for relief, the debtor will be required to supply the same information in the bankruptcy schedules as in a voluntary bankruptcy.

An involuntary petition should not be used as an everyday debt-collection device, and the Code provides penalties for the filing of frivolous petitions against debtors. Judgment may be granted against the petitioning creditors for the costs and attorneys' fees incurred by the debtor in defending against an involuntary petition that is dismissed by the court. If the petition is filed in bad faith, damages can be awarded for injury to the debtor's reputation. Punitive damages may also be awarded.

Automatic Stay

The moment a petition, either voluntary or involuntary, is filed, an **automatic stay,** or suspension, of virtually all actions by creditors against the debtor or the debtor's property normally goes into effect. In other words, once a petition has been filed, creditors cannot contact the debtor by phone or mail or start any legal proceedings to recover debts or to repossess property. A secured creditor or other party in interest, however, may petition the bankruptcy court for relief from the automatic stay. The Code provides that if a creditor knowingly violates the automatic stay (a willful violation), any party injured, including the debtor, is entitled to recover actual damages, costs, and attorneys' fees and may be entitled to recover punitive damages as well.

Underlying the Code's automatic-stay provision for a secured creditor is a concept known as *adequate protection*. The **adequate protection doctrine,** among other things, protects secured creditors from losing their security as a result of the automatic stay. The bankruptcy court can provide adequate protection by requiring the debtor or trustee to make periodic cash payments or a one-time cash payment (or to provide additional collateral or replacement liens) to the extent that the stay may actually cause the value of the property to decrease. Alternatively, the court may grant other relief that protects the secured party's interest in the property, such as a guaranty by a solvent third party to cover losses suffered by the secured party as a result of the stay.

EXCEPTIONS TO THE AUTOMATIC STAY The 2005 Bankruptcy Reform Act provides several exceptions to the automatic stay. A new exception is created for domestic-support obligations, which include any debt owed to or recoverable by a spouse, former spouse, child of the debtor, a child's parent or guardian, or a governmental unit. In addition, proceedings against the debtor related to divorce, child custody or visitation, domestic violence, and support enforcement are not stayed. Also excepted are investigations by a securities regulatory agency, the creation or perfection of statutory liens for property taxes or special assessments on real property, eviction actions on judgments obtained prior to filing the petition, and withholding from the debtor's wages for repayment of a retirement account loan.

LIMITATIONS ON THE AUTOMATIC STAY Under the new Code, if a creditor or other party in interest requests relief from the stay, the stay will automatically terminate sixty days after the request, unless the court grants an extension[11] or the parties agree otherwise. Also, the automatic stay on secured debts (see Chapter 29) will terminate thirty days after the petition is filed if the debtor had filed a bankruptcy petition that was dismissed within the prior year. (This is true unless the dismissal was based on the means test and the current petition was filed under a different chapter.) Any party in interest can request the court to extend the stay by showing that the filing is in good faith.

If two or more bankruptcy petitions were dismissed during the prior year, the Code presumes bad faith and the automatic stay does not go into effect until the court determines that the filing was made in good faith. In addition, if the petition is subsequently dismissed because the debtor failed to file the required

---

11. The court might grant an extension, for example, on a motion by the trustee that the property is of value to the estate.

documents within thirty days of filing, for example, the stay is terminated. Finally, the automatic stay on secured property terminates forty-five days after the creditors' meeting (to be discussed shortly) unless the debtor redeems or reaffirms certain debts (reaffirmation is discussed later in this chapter). In other words, the debtor cannot keep the secured property (such as a financed automobile), even if she or he continues to make payments on it, without reinstating the rights of the secured party to collect on the debt.

PROPERTY OF THE ESTATE

On the commencement of a liquidation proceeding under Chapter 7, an *estate in property* is created. The estate consists of all the debtor's legal and equitable interests in property currently held, wherever located, together with community property, property transferred in a transaction voidable by the trustee, proceeds and profits from the property of the estate, and certain after-acquired property. Interests in certain property—such as gifts, inheritances, property settlements (from divorce), and life insurance death proceeds—to which the debtor becomes entitled *within 180 days after filing* may also become part of the estate. Under the 2005 act, withholdings for employee benefit plan contributions are excluded from the estate. Generally, though, the filing of a bankruptcy petition fixes a dividing line: property acquired prior to the filing of the petition becomes property of the estate, and property acquired after the filing of the petition, except as just noted, remains the debtor's.

CREDITORS' MEETING AND CLAIMS

Within a reasonable time after the order for relief has been granted (not less than twenty days or more than forty days), the trustee must call a meeting of the creditors listed in the schedules filed by the debtor. The bankruptcy judge does not attend this meeting.

DEBTOR'S PRESENCE REQUIRED The debtor is required to attend the meeting (unless excused by the court) and to submit to examination under oath by the creditors and the trustee. Failing to appear when required or making false statements under oath may result in the debtor's being denied a discharge in bankruptcy. At the meeting, the trustee ensures that the debtor is aware of the potential consequences of bankruptcy and of his or her ability to file for bankruptcy under a different chapter of the Bankruptcy Code.

CREDITORS' CLAIMS To be entitled to receive a portion of the debtor's estate, each creditor normally files a *proof of claim* with the bankruptcy court clerk within ninety days of the creditors' meeting.[12] The proof of claim lists the creditor's name and address, as well as the amount that the creditor asserts is owed to the creditor by the debtor. A creditor need not file a proof of claim if the debtor's schedules list the creditor's claim as liquidated (exactly determined) and the creditor does not dispute the amount of the claim. A proof of claim is necessary if there is any dispute concerning the claim. If a creditor fails to file a proof of claim, the bankruptcy court or trustee may file the proof of claim on the creditor's behalf but is not obligated to do so.

Generally, any legal obligation of the debtor is a claim (except claims for breach of employment contracts or real estate leases for terms longer than one year). When a claim is disputed, or unliquidated, the bankruptcy court will set the value of the claim. Any creditor holding a debtor's obligation can file a claim against the debtor's estate. These claims are automatically allowed unless contested by the trustee, the debtor, or another creditor. A creditor who files a false claim commits a crime.

EXEMPTIONS

The trustee takes control over the debtor's property, but an individual debtor is entitled to exempt certain property from the bankruptcy. The Bankruptcy Code exempts the following property:[13]

1. Up to $18,450 in equity in the debtor's residence and burial plot (the homestead exemption).
2. Interest in a motor vehicle up to $2,950.
3. Interest, up to $475 for a particular item, in household goods and furnishings, wearing apparel, appliances, books, animals, crops, and musical instruments (the aggregate total of all items is limited, however, to $9,850).
4. Interest in jewelry up to $1,225.
5. Interest in any other property up to $975, plus any unused part of the $18,450 homestead exemption up to $9,250.

---

12. This ninety-day rule applies in Chapter 12 and Chapter 13 bankruptcies as well.

13. The dollar amounts stated in the Bankruptcy Code are adjusted automatically every three years on April 1 based on changes in the Consumer Price Index. The adjusted amounts are rounded to the nearest $25. The amounts stated in this chapter are in accordance with those computed on April 1, 2004.

6. Interest in any tools of the debtor's trade up to $1,850.

7. Any unmatured life insurance contract owned by the debtor.

8. Certain interests in accrued dividends and interest under life insurance contracts owned by the debtor, not to exceed $9,850.

9. Professionally prescribed health aids.

10. The right to receive Social Security and certain welfare benefits, alimony and support, certain retirement funds and pensions, and education savings accounts held for specific periods of time.

11. The right to receive certain personal-injury and other awards up to $18,450.

Individual states have the power to pass legislation precluding debtors from using the federal exemptions within the state; a majority of the states have done this (see Chapter 28). In those states, debtors may use only state, not federal, exemptions. In the rest of the states, an individual debtor (or a husband and wife filing jointly) may choose either the exemptions provided under state law or the federal exemptions.[14]

Note also that the 2005 Bankruptcy Reform Act clarified specifically what is included in "household goods and furnishings" (referred to in number 3 in the above list). For example, the category includes one computer, one radio, one television, one videocassette recorder, educational materials or equipment primarily for use by minor dependent children, and furniture that is used exclusively by a minor dependent (or by an elderly or disabled dependent). Other items, such as works of art; electronic entertainment equipment with a fair market value of over $500; antiques and jewelry (except wedding rings) valued at more than $500; and motor vehicles, tractors, lawn mowers, watercraft, and aircraft are not included in household goods.

THE HOMESTEAD EXEMPTION

The 2005 Bankruptcy Reform Act significantly changed the law for those debtors seeking to use state homestead exemption statutes (which were discussed in Chapter 28). In six states, among them Florida and Texas, homestead exemptions allow debtors petitioning for bankruptcy to shield unlimited amounts of equity in their homes from creditors. The prior Bankruptcy Code required that the debtor must have been domiciled in the state for at least six months to apply any of the state exemptions. Under the 2005 act, however, the domicile period is now two years. In other words, the debtor must have lived in the state for two years prior to filing the petition to be able to use the state homestead exemption.

In addition, if the homestead is acquired within three and a half years preceding the date of filing, the maximum equity exempted is $125,000, even if the state law would permit a higher amount. (This does not apply to equity that has been rolled over during the specified period from the sale of a previous homestead in the same state.) Also, if the debtor owes a debt arising from a violation of securities law or if the debtor committed certain criminal or tortious acts in the previous five years that indicate the filing was substantial abuse, the debtor may not exempt any amount of equity.[15]

THE TRUSTEE

Promptly after the order for relief in the liquidation proceeding has been entered, an interim, or provisional, trustee is appointed by the U.S. Trustee. The interim, or provisional, trustee presides over the debtor's property until the first meeting of creditors. At this first meeting, either a permanent trustee is elected, or the interim trustee becomes the permanent trustee.

The basic duty of the trustee is to collect the debtor's available estate and reduce it to cash for distribution, preserving the interests of both the debtor and unsecured creditors. This requires that the trustee be accountable for administering the debtor's estate. To enable the trustee to accomplish this duty, the Code gives the trustee certain powers, stated in both general and specific terms. These powers must be exercised within two years of the order for relief.

NEW DUTIES UNDER THE 2005 ACT The Bankruptcy Reform Act of 2005 imposes new duties on trustees (and bankruptcy administrators) with

---

14. State exemptions may or may not be limited with regard to value. Under state exemption laws, a debtor may enjoy an unlimited value exemption on a motor vehicle, for example, even though the federal bankruptcy scheme exempts a vehicle only up to a value of $2,950. A state's law may also define the property coming within an exemption differently than the federal law or may exclude, or except, specific items from an exemption, making it unavailable to a debtor who fits within the exception.

15. Specifically, the debtor may not claim the homestead exemption if the debtor has committed any criminal act, intentional tort, or willful or reckless misconduct that caused serious physical injury or death to another individual in the preceding five years. Also, if the debtor has been convicted of a felony, he or she may not be able to claim the exemption.

regard to means testing all debtors who file Chapter 7 petitions. Under the new law, the U.S. Trustee or bankruptcy administrator is required to promptly review all materials filed by the debtor. Not later than ten days after the first meeting of the creditors, the trustee must file a statement as to whether the case is presumed to be an abuse under the means test. The trustee must then provide a copy of this statement concerning abuse to all creditors within five days. Not later than forty days after the first creditors' meeting, the trustee must either file a motion to dismiss the petition (or convert it to a Chapter 13 case) or file a statement setting forth the reasons why the motion would not be appropriate.

The trustee also has new duties under the 2005 act designed to protect domestic-support creditors (those to whom a domestic-support obligation is owed). The trustee is required to provide written notice of the bankruptcy to the claim holder (a former spouse who is owed child support, for example). The notice must also include certain information, such as the debtor's address, the name and address of the debtor's last known employer, and the address and phone number of the state child-support enforcement agency. (Note that these requirements are not limited to Chapter 7 bankruptcies, and the trustee may have additional duties in other types of bankruptcy to collect assets for distribution to the domestic-support creditor.)

THE TRUSTEE'S POWERS The general powers of the trustee are described by the statement that the trustee occupies a position *equivalent* in rights to that of certain other parties. For example, the trustee has the same rights as a *lien creditor* who could have obtained a judicial lien on the debtor's property or who could have levied execution on the debtor's property. This means that a trustee has priority over an unperfected secured party to the debtor's property. This right of a trustee, equivalent to that of a lien creditor, is known as the *strong-arm power*. A trustee also has power equivalent to that of a *bona fide purchaser* of real property from the debtor.

Nevertheless, in most states a creditor with a non-consumer purchase-money security interest may prevail against a trustee if the creditor files within ten days (twenty days, in many states) of the debtor's receipt of the collateral, even if the bankruptcy petition is filed before the creditor perfects. For example, Baker loaned Newbury $20,000 on January 1, taking a security interest in the machinery that Newbury purchased with the $20,000 and that was delivered on

that same date. On January 27, before Baker had perfected her security interest, Newbury filed for bankruptcy. The trustee can invalidate Baker's security interest because it was unperfected when Newbury filed the bankruptcy petition. Baker can assert a claim only as an unsecured creditor. But if Newbury had filed for bankruptcy on January 7, and Baker had perfected her security interest on January 8, she would have prevailed, because she would have perfected her purchase-money security interest within ten days of Newbury's receipt of the machinery.

THE RIGHT TO POSSESSION OF THE DEBTOR'S PROPERTY The trustee has the power to require persons holding the debtor's property at the time the petition is filed to deliver the property to the trustee. (A trustee usually does not take actual possession of a debtor's property. Instead, a trustee's possession is constructive. For example, to obtain control of a debtor's business inventory, a trustee might change the locks on the doors to the business and hire a security guard.)

AVOIDANCE POWERS The trustee also has specific powers of *avoidance*—that is, the trustee can set aside a sale or other transfer of the debtor's property, taking it back as a part of the debtor's estate. These powers include any voidable rights available to the debtor, preferences, certain statutory liens, and fraudulent transfers by the debtor. Each of these powers is discussed in more detail below.

The debtor shares most of the trustee's avoidance powers. Thus, if the trustee does not take action to enforce one of the rights mentioned above, the debtor in a liquidation bankruptcy can nevertheless enforce that right.[16]

Note that under the 2005 act, the trustee no longer has the power to avoid any transfer that was a bona fide payment of a domestic-support debt.

VOIDABLE RIGHTS A trustee steps into the shoes of the debtor. Thus, any reason that a debtor can use to obtain the return of her or his property can be used by the trustee as well. These grounds include fraud, duress, incapacity, and mutual mistake.

For example, Ben sells his boat to Tara. Tara gives Ben a check, knowing that she has insufficient funds

---

16. Under a Chapter 11 bankruptcy (to be discussed later), for which no trustee other than the debtor generally exists, the debtor has the same avoidance powers as a trustee under Chapter 7. Under Chapters 12 and 13 (also to be discussed later), a trustee must be appointed.

in her bank account to cover the check. Tara has committed fraud. Ben has the right to avoid that transfer and recover the boat from Tara. Once an order for relief under Chapter 7 of the Code has been entered for Ben, the trustee can exercise the same right to recover the boat from Tara, and the boat becomes a part of the debtor's estate.

PREFERENCES   A debtor is not permitted to transfer property or to make a payment that favors—or gives a **preference** to—one creditor over others. The trustee is allowed to recover payments made both voluntarily and involuntarily to one creditor in preference over another. If a **preferred creditor** (one who has received a preferential transfer from the debtor) has sold the property to an innocent third party, the trustee cannot recover the property from the innocent party. The preferred creditor, however, generally can be held accountable for the value of the property.

To have made a preferential payment that can be recovered, an *insolvent* debtor generally must have transferred property, for a *preexisting* debt, within *ninety days* prior to the filing of the petition in bankruptcy. The transfer must give the creditor more than the creditor would have received as a result of the bankruptcy proceedings. The trustee need not prove insolvency, as the Code provides that the debtor is presumed to be insolvent during this ninety-day period.

—Preferences to Insiders.   Sometimes, the creditor receiving the preference is an **insider**—an individual, a partner, a partnership, a corporation, or an officer or a director of a corporation (or a relative of one of these) who has a close relationship with the debtor. In this situation, the avoidance power of the trustee is extended to transfers made within *one year* before filing; however, the *presumption* of insolvency is confined to the ninety-day period. Therefore, the trustee must prove that the debtor was insolvent at the time of a transfer that occurred prior to the ninety-day period.

—Transfers That Do Not Constitute Preferences. Not all transfers are preferences. To be a preference, the transfer must be made for something other than current consideration. Most courts generally assume that payment for services rendered within ten to fifteen days prior to the payment of the current consideration is not a preference. If a creditor receives payment in the ordinary course of business from an individual or business debtor, such as payment of last month's telephone bill, the payment cannot be recovered by the trustee in bankruptcy. To be recoverable, a preference must be a transfer for an antecedent (preexisting) debt, such as a year-old printing bill. In addition, the Code permits a consumer-debtor to transfer any property to a creditor up to a total value of $5,000, without the transfer's constituting a preference (this amount was increased from $600 to $5,000 by the 2005 act). Payment of domestic-support debts does not constitute a preference. Also, transfers that were made as part of an alternative repayment schedule negotiated by an approved credit counseling agency are not preferences.

LIENS ON DEBTOR'S PROPERTY   The trustee has the power to avoid certain statutory liens against the debtor's property, such as a landlord's lien for unpaid rent. The trustee can avoid statutory liens that first became effective against the debtor when the bankruptcy petition was filed or when the debtor became insolvent. The trustee can also avoid any lien against a bona fide purchaser that was not perfected or enforceable on the date of the bankruptcy filing. Under the 2005 act, the trustee cannot avoid certain warehouser's liens (see Chapter 47), however.

FRAUDULENT TRANSFERS   The trustee may avoid fraudulent transfers or obligations if they are made within two years of the filing of the petition or if they are made with actual intent to hinder, delay, or defraud a creditor. Transfers made for less than a reasonably equivalent consideration are also vulnerable if by making them, the debtor became insolvent, was left engaged in business with an unreasonably small amount of capital, or intended to incur debts that he or she could not pay. When a fraudulent transfer is made outside the Code's two-year limit, creditors may seek alternative relief under state laws. State laws often allow creditors to recover for transfers made up to three years prior to the filing of a petition.

DISTRIBUTION OF PROPERTY

The Code provides specific rules for the distribution of the debtor's property to secured and unsecured creditors. (We will examine these distributions shortly.) If any amount remains after the priority classes of creditors have been satisfied, it is turned over to the debtor. Exhibit 30–1 illustrates graphically the collection and distribution of property in most voluntary bankruptcies.

EXHIBIT 30-1 **Collection and Distribution of Property in Most Voluntary Bankruptcies**

This exhibit illustrates the property that might be collected in a debtor's voluntary bankruptcy and how it might be distributed to creditors. Involuntary bankruptcies and some voluntary bankruptcies could include additional types of property and other creditors.

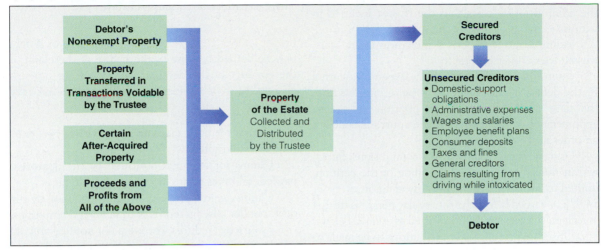

In a bankruptcy case in which the debtor has no assets,[17] creditors are notified of the debtor's petition for bankruptcy but are instructed not to file a claim. In such a case, the unsecured creditors will receive no payment, and most, if not all, of these debts will be discharged.

DISTRIBUTION TO SECURED CREDITORS The rights of perfected secured creditors were discussed in Chapter 29. The Code provides that a consumer-debtor, either within thirty days of filing a liquidation petition or before the date of the first meeting of the creditors (whichever is first), must file with the clerk a statement of intention with respect to the secured collateral. The statement must indicate whether the debtor will redeem the collateral (make a single payment equal to the current value of the property), reaffirm the debt (continue making payments on the debt), or surrender the property to the secured party.[18] The trustee is obligated to enforce the debtor's statement within forty-five days after the meeting of the creditors. As noted previously, failure of the debtor to redeem or reaffirm within forty-five days terminates the automatic stay.

If the collateral is surrendered to the perfected secured party, the secured creditor can enforce the security interest either by accepting the property in full satisfaction of the debt or by foreclosing on the collateral and using the proceeds to pay off the debt. Thus, the perfected secured party has priority over unsecured parties as to the proceeds from the disposition of the collateral. Indeed, the Code provides that if the value of the collateral exceeds the perfected secured party's claim and if the security agreement so provides, the secured party also has priority as to the proceeds in an amount that will cover reasonable fees and costs incurred because of the debtor's default. Fees include reasonable attorneys' fees. Any excess over this amount is used by the trustee to satisfy the claims of unsecured creditors. Should the collateral be insufficient to cover the secured debt owed, the secured creditor becomes an unsecured creditor for the difference.

DISTRIBUTION TO UNSECURED CREDITORS Bankruptcy law establishes an order of priority for classes of debts owed to *unsecured* creditors, and they are paid in the order of their priority. Each class must be fully paid before the next class is entitled to any of the remaining proceeds. If there are insufficient proceeds to pay fully all the creditors in a class, the proceeds are distributed *proportionately* to the creditors in that class, and classes lower in priority receive nothing. The new bankruptcy law elevated domestic-support obligations to the highest priority of unsecured claims. The order

17. This type of bankruptcy is called a "no-asset" case.
18. Also, if applicable, the debtor must specify whether the collateral will be claimed as exempt property.

of priority among classes of unsecured creditors is as follows:

1. Claims for domestic-support obligations, such as child support and alimony (subject to the priority of the administrative costs that the trustee incurred in administering assets to pay the obligations).

2. Administrative expenses including court costs, trustee fees, and attorneys' fees.

3. In an involuntary bankruptcy, expenses incurred by the debtor in the ordinary course of business from the date of the filing of the petition up to the appointment of the trustee or the court's issuance of an order for relief.

4. Unpaid wages, salaries, and commissions earned within ninety days prior to the filing of the petition, limited to $4,925 per claimant. Any claim in excess of $4,925 or earned before the ninety-day period is treated as a claim of a general creditor (listed as item 10 below).

5. Unsecured claims for contributions to be made to employee benefit plans, limited to services performed during the 180-day period prior to the filing of the bankruptcy petition and $4,925 per employee.

6. Claims by farmers and fishermen, up to $4,925, against debtor-operators of grain storage or fish storage or processing facilities.

7. Consumer deposits of up to $2,225 given to the debtor before the petition was filed in connection with the purchase, lease, or rental of property or purchase of services that were not received or provided. Any claim in excess of $2,225 is treated as a claim of a general creditor (listed as item 10 below).

8. Certain taxes and penalties due to government units, such as income and property taxes.

9. Claims for death or personal injury resulting from the operation of a motor vehicle or vessel if such operation was unlawful because the debtor was intoxicated as a result of using alcohol, a drug, or another substance. (This provision was added by the 2005 act.)

10. Claims of general creditors.

DISCHARGE

From the debtor's point of view, the primary purpose of liquidation is to obtain a fresh start through a discharge of debts.[19] As mentioned earlier, once the debtor's assets have been distributed to creditors as permitted by the Code, the debtor's remaining debts

are then discharged, meaning that the debtor is not obligated to pay them. Certain debts, however, are not dischargeable in bankruptcy. Also, certain debtors may not qualify to have all debts discharged in bankruptcy. These situations are discussed below.

EXCEPTIONS TO DISCHARGE Discharge of a debt may be denied because of the nature of the claim or the conduct of the debtor. Claims that are not dischargeable in a liquidation bankruptcy include the following:

1. Claims for back taxes accruing within two years prior to bankruptcy.

2. Claims for amounts borrowed by the debtor to pay federal taxes or any nondischargeable taxes.

3. Claims against property or funds obtained by the debtor under false pretenses or by false representations.

4. Claims by creditors who were not notified and did not know of the bankruptcy; these claims did not appear on the schedules the debtor was required to file.

5. Claims based on fraud or misuse of funds by the debtor while he or she was acting in a fiduciary capacity or claims involving the debtor's embezzlement or larceny.

6. Domestic-support obligations and property settlements as provided for in a separation agreement or divorce decree.

7. Claims for amounts due on a retirement account loan.

8. Claims based on willful or malicious conduct by the debtor toward another or the property of another.

9. Certain government fines and penalties, which under the 2005 act also include penalties imposed under federal election laws.

10. Certain student loans or obligations to repay funds received as an educational benefit, scholarship, or stipend—unless payment of the loans imposes an undue hardship on the debtor and the debtor's dependents.

11. Consumer debts of more than $500 for luxury goods or services owed to a single creditor incurred within ninety days of the order for relief. (Prior to the passage of the 2005 act, the amount was $1,150 and the period was sixty days.) This denial of discharge is a rebuttable presumption (that is, the denial may be challenged by the debtor), however, and any debts reasonably incurred to support the debtor or dependents are not classified as luxuries.

12. Cash advances totaling more than $750 that are extensions of open-end consumer credit obtained by the debtor within seventy days of the order for relief.

---

19. Discharges are granted under Chapter 7 only to individuals, not to corporations or partnerships. The latter may use Chapter 11, or they may terminate their existence under state law.

(The prior law allowed $1,150 in cash advances that were obtained within sixty days.) A denial of discharge of these debts is also a rebuttable presumption.
13. Judgments or consent decrees against a debtor as a result of the debtor's operation of a motor vehicle or any vessel or aircraft while intoxicated.
14. Fees or assessments arising from a lot in a home-owners' association, as long as the debtor retained an interest in the lot.

15. Failure of the debtor to provide required or requested tax documents. (This exception to discharge also applies to Chapter 11 and Chapter 13 bankruptcies.)

In the following case, the court considered whether to order the discharge of a debtor's student loan obligations. Is it "undue hardship" if, to repay the loans, a debtor has to forgo her son's private school tuition?

CASE 30.2	In re Savage

United States
Bankruptcy
Appellate Panel,
First Circuit, 2004.
311 Bankr. 835.

BACKGROUND AND FACTS *Brenda Savage attended college in the mid-1980s—taking out five student loans—but she did not graduate. In 2003, at the age of forty-one, single, and in good health, she lived with her fifteen-year-old son in an apartment in Boston, Massachusetts. Her son attended Boston Trinity Academy, a private school. Savage worked 37.5 hours per week for Blue Cross/Blue Shield of Massachusetts. Her monthly gross wages were $3,079.79. Her employment provided health insurance, dental insurance, life insurance, a retirement savings plan, and paid vacations and personal days. She also received monthly child-support income of $180.60. After deductions, her total net monthly income was $2,030.72. Her monthly expenses included, among other things, $607 for rent, $221 for utilities, $76 for phone, $23.99 for an Internet connection, $430 for food, $75 for clothing, $12.50 for laundry and dry cleaning, $23 for medical expenses, $95.50 for transportation, $193.50 for charitable contributions, $43 for entertainment, $277.50 for her son's tuition, and $50 for his books. In February, Savage filed a petition in bankruptcy, seeking to discharge her student loan obligations to Educational Credit Management Corporation (ECMC). At the time, she owed $32,248.45. The court ordered a discharge of all but $3,120. ECMC appealed to the U.S. Bankruptcy Appellate Panel for the First Circuit.*

IN THE LANGUAGE OF THE COURT

HAINES, Bankruptcy Judge.
* * * *
Under 11 U.S.C. Section 523(a)(8), debtors are not permitted to discharge educational loans unless excepting the loans from discharge will impose an undue hardship on the debtor and the debtor's dependents. * * *
* * * *
Under "totality of the circumstances" analysis, a debtor seeking discharge of student loans must prove by a preponderance of evidence that (1) her past, present, and reasonably reliable future financial resources; (2) her and her dependents' reasonably necessary living expenses, and; (3) other relevant facts or circumstances unique to the case prevent her from paying the student loans in question while still maintaining a minimal standard of living, even when aided by a discharge of other pre-petition debts.
* * * *
The debtor must show not only that her current income is insufficient to pay her student loans, but also that her prospects for increasing her income in the future are too limited to afford her sufficient resources to repay the student loans and provide herself and her dependents with a minimal (but fair) standard of living. [Emphasis added.]
Ms. Savage has not demonstrated that her current level of income and future prospects warrant discharge of her loans. Her present income may be insufficient to pay her student loans and still maintain precisely the standard of living she now has. But * * * it would

CONTINUED ▶

CASE 30.2 | **Continued**

enable her to repay the loans without undue hardship. Moreover, the record plainly establishes that her prospects for a steady increase in income over time are promising. She has been steadily employed at the same job and regularly receives annual raises. Nothing indicates change is in the wind. Moreover, Ms. Savage currently works 37½ hours a week, leaving time for some part-time work (or longer hours at her present job) * * * .

* * * *

To prove undue hardship for purposes of Section 523(a)(8), a debtor must show that her necessary and reasonable expenses leave her with too little to afford repayment. * * * [Emphasis added.]

* * * *

Private school tuition is not *generally* considered a reasonably necessary expense in bankruptcy cases * * * . Although compelling circumstances may distinguish a given case, the [courts] uniformly hold that a debtor's mere preference for private schooling is insufficient to qualify the attendant expense as necessary and reasonable.

Ms. Savage did not demonstrate a satisfactory reason why her son needs to attend private school at a monthly cost of $277.50 (plus $50 for books). When asked to explain why she did so, she testified:

> There were a lot of fights, a lot of swearing, a lot of other things going on. I mean he would wake up every morning crying because he didn't want to go to school. * * * So I had to find a school to put him in * * * where he was going to—I mean, he didn't do well that whole year. I had to keep going down to the school several times. He was just a mess the whole school year. * * * So I had to find another school.

Although we understand why Ms. Savage prefers that her son attend private school, she has not demonstrated that the public school system cannot adequately meet her son's educational needs. Her preference appears sincere, but that alone is not sufficient to sustain the bankruptcy court's implicit conclusion that forgoing this expense would constitute undue hardship * * * .

* * * *

Given the fact that at least $322.50 (private school tuition and books) in expense can be eliminated from Ms. Savage's budget without creating undue hardship, her student loans cannot be discharged under Section 523(a)(8). It is worth noting, as well, that Ms. Savage's son will reach majority in just a few years, a consequence that will reduce her required expenses considerably.

DECISION AND REMEDY   *The U.S. Bankruptcy Appellate Panel for the First Circuit reversed the order of the bankruptcy court and remanded the case for the entry of a judgment in ECMC's favor. The appellate panel was "satisfied" that "Ms. Savage has now (and will increasingly have) the ability to repay her five student loans without undue hardship."*

WHAT IF THE FACTS WERE DIFFERENT?   *Suppose that Savage's son had a learning disability that only a private school could accommodate and treat. Would the result in this case have been different?*

OBJECTIONS TO DISCHARGE In addition to the exceptions to discharge previously listed, a bankruptcy court may also deny the discharge of the *debtor* (as opposed to the debt). In the latter situation, the assets of the debtor are still distributed to the creditors, but the debtor remains liable for the unpaid portion of all claims. Grounds for the denial of discharge of the debtor include the following:

1. The debtor's concealment or destruction of property with the intent to hinder, delay, or defraud a creditor.

2. The debtor's fraudulent concealment or destruction of financial records.

3. The granting of a discharge to the debtor within eight years of the filing of the petition. (This period was increased from six to eight years by the 2005 act.)

4. Failure of the debtor to complete the required consumer education course (unless such a course is unavailable). (This ground for denial was provided for by the 2005 act and also applies to Chapter 13 petitions.)

5. Proceedings in which the debtor could be found guilty of a felony (basically, the 2005 act states that a court may not discharge any debt until the completion of felony proceedings against the debtor).

The purpose of denying a discharge on these or other grounds is to prevent a debtor from avoiding, through bankruptcy, the consequences of his or her wrongful conduct. In the following case, a creditor had asked the bankruptcy court to deny a discharge to debtors whose alleged indebtedness arose from their misconduct. The court's decision ultimately came before the United States Supreme Court.

CASE 30.3	Archer v. Warner

Supreme Court of the
United States, 2003.
538 U.S. 314,
123 S.Ct. 1462,
155 L.Ed.2d 454.

Justice *BREYER* delivered the opinion of the Court.

The Bankruptcy Code provides that a debt shall not be dischargeable in bankruptcy "to the extent" it is "for money * * * obtained by * * * false pretenses, a false representation, or actual fraud." Can this language cover a debt embodied in a settlement agreement that settled a creditor's earlier claim "for money * * * obtained by * * * fraud"? * * *

* * * *

* * * In late 1991, Leonard and Arlene Warner bought the Warner Manufacturing Company for $250,000. About six months later they sold the company to Elliott and Carol Archer for $610,000. A few months after that the Archers sued the Warners in [a] North Carolina state court for (among other things) fraud connected with the sale.

In May 1995, the parties settled the lawsuit. The settlement agreement specified that the Warners would pay the Archers "$300,000.00 less legal and accounting expenses" * * * . It added that the Archers would "execute releases to any and all claims * * * arising out of this litigation * * * ." The Warners paid the Archers $200,000 and executed a promissory note for the remaining $100,000. The Archers executed releases "discharg[ing]" the Warners "from any and every right, claim, or demand" that the Archers "now have or might otherwise hereafter have against" them, "excepting only obligations under" the promissory note * * * . A few days later the Archers voluntarily dismissed the state-court lawsuit * * * .

In November 1995, the Warners failed to make the first payment on the $100,000 promissory note. The Archers sued for the payment in state court. The Warners filed for bankruptcy. The [U.S.] Bankruptcy Court ordered liquidation under Chapter 7 of the Bankruptcy Code. And the Archers brought the present claim, asking the Bankruptcy Court to find the $100,000 debt nondischargeable * * * .

The Bankruptcy Court, finding the promissory note debt dischargeable, denied the Archers' claim. [A federal] District Court affirmed the Bankruptcy Court. And the [U.S.] Court of Appeals for the Fourth Circuit * * * affirmed the District Court. * * *

We granted the Archers' petition for *certiorari*. * * *

* * * *

* * * [T]he Court of Appeals for the Fourth Circuit * * * reasoned that the settlement agreement, releases, and promissory note had worked a kind of "novation." This novation replaced (1) an original potential debt to the Archers for money obtained by fraud with (2) a new debt. The new debt was not for money obtained by fraud. It was for money promised in a settlement contract. And it was consequently dischargeable in bankruptcy.

* * * *

We agree * * * that "[t]he settlement agreement and promissory note here, coupled with the broad language of the release, completely addressed and released each and every underlying state law claim." That agreement left only one relevant debt: a debt for money promised in the settlement agreement itself. To recognize that fact, however, does not end our inquiry. We must decide whether that same debt can also amount to a debt for money obtained by fraud * * * .

* * * *

As a matter of logic, * * * the Fourth Circuit's novation theory cannot be right. * * *

* * * *[T]he mere fact that a conscientious creditor has previously reduced his claim to [settlement] should not bar further inquiry into the true nature of the debt.* * * * [Emphasis added.]

CONTINUED

CASE 30.3 | Continued

* * * [T]he Bankruptcy Code's nondischargeability provision had originally covered only judgments sounding in [evidencing] fraud. Congress later changed the language so that it covered all such liabilities. This change indicated that *Congress intended the fullest possible inquiry to ensure that all debts arising out of fraud are excepted from discharge, no matter what their form.* Congress also intended to allow the relevant determination (whether a debt arises out of fraud) to take place in bankruptcy court, not to force it to occur earlier in state court at a time when nondischargeability concerns are not directly in issue and neither party has a full incentive to litigate them. [Emphasis added.]

* * * The dischargeability provision applies to all debts that arise out of fraud. A debt embodied in the settlement of a fraud case arises no less out of the underlying fraud than a debt embodied in a stipulation and consent decree [which occurred in a previous case, in which we held that a debt originating in fraud was not dischargeable]. Policies that favor the settlement of disputes, like those that favor repose, are neither any more nor any less at issue here than in [the previous case]. * * * [W]hat has *not* been established here * * * is that the parties meant to resolve the *issue* of fraud or, more narrowly, to resolve that issue for purposes of a later claim of nondischargeability in bankruptcy. In a word, we can find no significant difference between [the previous case] and the case now before us.

* * * *

We conclude that the Archers' settlement agreement and releases may have worked a kind of novation, but that fact does not bar the Archers from showing that the settlement debt arose out of "false pretenses, a false representation, or actual fraud," and consequently is nondischargeable. We reverse the Court of Appeals' judgment to the contrary. And we remand this case for further proceedings consistent with this opinion.

QUESTIONS

1. Why did the Supreme Court conclude that the lower court's novation theory could not be right?
2. How might the result in this case affect a party's decision to sign a release on a fraud claim and accept a note in payment of the debt?

EFFECT OF DISCHARGE The primary effect of a discharge is to void any judgment on a discharged debt and enjoin any action to collect a discharged debt. A discharge does not affect the liability of a co-debtor.

REVOCATION OF DISCHARGE On petition by the trustee or a creditor, the bankruptcy court can, within one year, revoke the discharge decree. The discharge decree will be revoked if it is discovered that the debtor acted fraudulently or dishonestly during the bankruptcy proceedings. The revocation renders the discharge void, allowing creditors not satisfied by the distribution of the debtor's estate to proceed with their claims against the debtor.

REAFFIRMATION OF DEBT

An agreement to pay a debt dischargeable in bankruptcy is called a **reaffirmation agreement.** A debtor may wish to pay a debt—such as, for example, a debt owed to a family member, physician, bank, or some other creditor—even though the debt could be discharged in bankruptcy. Also, as noted previously, under the new Code a debtor cannot retain secured property while continuing to pay without entering into a reaffirmation agreement.

To be enforceable, reaffirmation agreements must be made before the debtor is granted a discharge. The agreement must be signed and filed with the court (along with the original disclosure documents, as you will read shortly). Court approval is required unless the debtor is represented by an attorney during the negotiation of the reaffirmation and submits the proper documents and certifications. Nevertheless, court approval may be required even if the debtor is represented by an attorney when it appears that the reaffirmation will result in undue hardship on the debtor. When court approval is required, a separate hearing will take place. The court will approve the reaffirmation only if it finds that the agreement will not result in undue hardship to the debtor and that the reaffirmation is consistent with the debtor's best interests.

PRESUMPTION OF UNDUE HARDSHIP Under the provisions of the 2005 act, if the debtor's monthly income minus the debtor's monthly expenses as shown on her or his completed and signed statement is less than the scheduled payments on the reaffirmed debt, undue hardship will be presumed. A presumption of undue hardship can be rebutted, however. The debtor can file a written statement with the court that includes an explanation identifying additional sources of funds from which to make the agreed-on payments. If the court is not satisfied with the written explanation, it may disapprove of the reaffirmation or hold a hearing. The debtor may also rebut the presumption of undue hardship by explaining to the court in person at the hearing how she or he will be able to make future payments on the debt.

If the debtor has an attorney, the attorney must certify in writing that he or she has fully advised the debtor of the legal effect and consequences of reaffirmation. In addition, to rebut the presumption of undue hardship, the attorney must certify that, in the attorney's opinion, the debtor is able to make the payments.

NEW REAFFIRMATION DISCLOSURES To discourage creditors from engaging in abusive reaffirmation practices, the 2005 act added new requirements for reaffirmation. The Code now provides the specific language for several pages of disclosures that must be given to debtors entering reaffirmation agreements.[20] Among other things, these disclosures explain that the debtor is not required to reaffirm any debt, but that liens on secured property, such as mortgages and cars, will remain in effect even if the debt is not reaffirmed. The reaffirmation agreement must disclose the amount of the debt reaffirmed, the rates of interest, the date payments begin, and the right to rescind. The disclosures also caution the debtor, "Only agree to reaffirm a debt if it is in your best interest. Be sure you can afford the payments you agree to make." The original disclosure documents must be signed by the debtor, certified by the debtor's attorney, and filed with the court at the same time as the reaffirmation agreement. A reaffirmation agreement that is not accompanied by the original signed disclosures will not be effective.

If the debtor is represented by an attorney and no presumption of undue hardship arises, then the reaffirmation becomes effective immediately on filing with the court. If the debtor is not represented, the reaffirmation is not effective until the court approves it. The debtor can rescind, or cancel, the agreement at any time before the court enters a discharge order, or within sixty days of the filing of the agreement, whichever is *later*.

SECTION 3 | Reorganizations

The type of bankruptcy proceeding most commonly used by corporate debtors is the Chapter 11 *reorganization*. In a reorganization, the creditors and the debtor formulate a plan under which the debtor pays a portion of the debts and is discharged of the remainder. The debtor is allowed to continue in business. Although this type of bankruptcy is generally a corporate reorganization, any debtors (including individuals but excluding stockbrokers and commodities brokers)[21] who are eligible for Chapter 7 relief are eligible for relief under Chapter 11.[22] In 1994, Congress established a "fast-track" Chapter 11 procedure for small-business debtors whose liabilities do not exceed $2 million and who do not own or manage real estate. This allows for bankruptcy proceedings without the appointment of committees and can save time and costs.

The same principles that govern the filing of a liquidation (Chapter 7) petition apply to reorganization (Chapter 11) proceedings. The case may be brought either voluntarily or involuntarily. The same guidelines govern the entry of the order for relief. The automatic-stay and adequate protection provisions are applicable in reorganizations as well. The 2005 Bankruptcy Reform Act's exceptions to the automatic stay also apply to Chapter 11 proceedings, as do the new provisions regarding substantial abuse and additional grounds for dismissal (or conversion) of bankruptcy petitions. Also, the 2005 act contains specific rules and limitations for individual debtors who file a Chapter 11 petition. For example, an individual debtor's postpetition acquisitions and earnings become the property of the bankruptcy estate.

---

20. Note that credit unions are exempted from these disclosure requirements.

21. In *Toibb v. Radloff*, 501 U.S. 157, 111 S.Ct. 2197, 115 L.Ed.2d 145 (1991), the United States Supreme Court ruled that a nonbusiness debtor may petition for relief under Chapter 11.
22. In addition, railroads are eligible for Chapter 11 relief.

MUST BE IN THE BEST INTERESTS OF THE CREDITORS

Under Section 305(a) of the Bankruptcy Code, a court, after notice and a hearing, may dismiss or suspend all proceedings in a case at any time if dismissal or suspension would better serve the interests of the creditors. Section 1112 also allows a court, after notice and a hearing, to dismiss a case under reorganization "for cause." Cause includes the absence of a reasonable likelihood of rehabilitation, the inability to effect a plan, and an unreasonable delay by the debtor that is prejudicial to (may harm the interests of) creditors.[23]

WORKOUTS

In some instances, creditors may prefer private, negotiated adjustments of creditor-debtor relations, also known as **workouts,** to bankruptcy proceedings. Often, these out-of-court workouts are much more flexible and thus more conducive to a speedy settlement. Speed is critical because delay is one of the most costly elements in any bankruptcy proceeding. Another advantage of workouts is that they avoid the various administrative costs of bankruptcy proceedings.

DEBTOR IN POSSESSION

On entry of the order for relief, the debtor generally continues to operate the business as a **debtor in possession (DIP).** The court, however, may appoint a trustee (often referred to as a *receiver*) to operate the debtor's business if gross mismanagement of the business is shown or if appointing a trustee is in the best interests of the estate.

The DIP's role is similar to that of a trustee in a liquidation. The DIP is entitled to avoid prepetition preferential payments made to creditors and prepetition fraudulent transfers of assets. The DIP has the power to decide whether to cancel or assume prepetition executory contracts (those that are not yet performed) or unexpired leases.

Under the strong-arm clause[24] of the Bankruptcy Code, a DIP can avoid any obligation or any transfer of property of the debtor that could be avoided by certain parties. These parties include (1) a creditor who

extended credit to the debtor at the time of bankruptcy (petition) and who consequently obtained a lien on the debtor's property; (2) a creditor who extended credit to the debtor at the time of bankruptcy and who consequently obtained a writ of execution against the debtor that was returned unsatisfied; and (3) a bona fide purchaser of real property from the debtor, if at the time of the bankruptcy the transfer was perfected.

COLLECTIVE BARGAINING AGREEMENTS

After the Bankruptcy Reform Act of 1978 was enacted, questions arose as to whether a reorganization debtor could reject a recently negotiated collectively bargained labor contract. In *National Labor Relations Board v. Bildisco and Bildisco*,[25] the United States Supreme Court held that a collective bargaining agreement subject to the National Labor Relations Act of 1935 (see Chapter 33) is an "executory contract" and thus is subject to *rejection* by a debtor in possession. The Court emphasized, though, that such a rejection should not be permitted unless there is a finding that the policy of Chapter 11 (successful rehabilitation of debtors) would be served by the action. Hence, when the bankruptcy court determines that rejection of a collective bargaining agreement should be permitted, it must make a reasoned finding *on the record* as to why it has determined that the rejection should be permitted.

The Code attempts to reconcile federal policies favoring collective bargaining with the need to allow a debtor company to reject executory labor contracts while trying to reorganize. The Code sets forth standards and procedures under which collective bargaining contracts can be assumed or rejected under a reorganization filing. In general, a collective bargaining contract can be rejected if the debtor has first proposed necessary contractual modifications to the union and the union has failed to adopt them without *good cause*. The company is required (1) to provide the union with the relevant information needed to evaluate this proposal and (2) to confer in *good faith* in attempting to reach a mutually satisfactory agreement on the modifications.

CREDITORS' COMMITTEES

As soon as practicable after the entry of the order for relief, a creditors' committee of unsecured creditors is appointed. If the debtor has filed a plan accepted by

---

23. See 11 U.S.C. Section 1112(b). Debtors are not prohibited from filing successive petitions, however. A debtor whose petition is dismissed, for example, can file a new Chapter 11 petition (which may be granted unless it is filed in bad faith).

24. 11 U.S.C. Section 544(a).

25. 465 U.S. 513, 104 S.Ct. 1188, 79 L.Ed.2d 482 (1984).

the creditors, however, the trustee may decide not to call a meeting of the creditors. The committee may consult with the trustee or the DIP concerning the administration of the case or the formulation of the plan. Additional creditors' committees may be appointed to represent special interest creditors. Under the 2005 act, a court may order the trustee to change the membership of a committee or to increase the number of committee members to include a small-business concern if the court deems it necessary to ensure adequate representation of the creditors.

Orders affecting the estate generally will be entered only with the consent of the committee or after a hearing in which the judge is informed of the position of the committee. As mentioned earlier, businesses with debts of less than $2 million that do not own or manage real estate can avoid creditors' committees. In these cases, orders can be entered without a committee's consent.

THE REORGANIZATION PLAN

A reorganization plan to rehabilitate the debtor is a plan to conserve and administer the debtor's assets in the hope of an eventual return to successful operation and solvency.

FILING THE PLAN   Only the debtor may file a plan within the first 120 days after the date of the order for relief. Under the 2005 act, the 120-day period may be extended but not beyond 18 months from the date of the order for relief. If the debtor does not meet the 120-day deadline or obtain an extension, and if the debtor fails to procure the required creditor consent (discussed below) within 180 days, any party may propose a plan up to 20 months from the date of the order for relief. (In other words, the 180-day period cannot be extended beyond 20 months past the date of the order for relief.) For a small-business debtor, the time for the debtor's filing is 180 days.

The plan must be fair and equitable and must do the following:

1. Designate classes of claims and interests.
2. Specify the treatment to be afforded the classes. (The plan must provide the same treatment for all claims in a particular class.)
3. Provide an adequate means for execution. (The 2005 Bankruptcy Reform Act requires individual debtors to utilize postpetition assets as necessary to execute the plan.)

4. Provide for payment of tax claims over a five-year period.

ACCEPTANCE AND CONFIRMATION OF THE PLAN
Once the plan has been developed, it is submitted to each class of creditors for acceptance. Each class must accept the plan unless the class is not adversely affected by it. A class has accepted the plan when a majority of the creditors, representing two-thirds of the amount of the total claim, vote to approve it. Confirmation is conditioned on the debtor certifying that all postpetition domestic-support obligations have been paid in full. For small-business debtors, if the plan meets the listed requirements, the court must confirm the plan within forty-five days (unless this period is extended).

Even when all classes of creditors accept the plan, the court may refuse to confirm it if it is not "in the best interests of the creditors."[26] A former spouse or child of the debtor can block the plan if it does not provide for payment of her or his claims in cash. Under the 2005 act, if an unsecured creditor objects to the plan, specific rules apply to the value of property to be distributed under the plan. The plan can also be modified on the request of the debtor, trustee, U.S. Trustee, or holder of the unsecured claim. Tax claims must be paid over a five-year period.

Even if only one class of creditors has accepted the plan, the court may still confirm the plan under the Code's so-called **cram-down provision.** In other words, the court may confirm the plan over the objections of a class of creditors. Before the court can exercise this right of cram-down confirmation, it must be demonstrated that the plan does not discriminate unfairly against any creditors and that the plan is fair and equitable.

DISCHARGE   The plan is binding on confirmation; however, the Bankruptcy Reform Act of 2005 provides that confirmation of a plan does not discharge an individual debtor. For individual debtors, plan completion is required prior to discharge, unless the court orders otherwise. For all other debtors, the court may order discharge at any time after the plan is confirmed. The debtor is given a reorganization discharge from all claims not protected under the plan. This discharge does not apply to any claims that would be denied discharge under liquidation.

---

26. The plan need not provide for full repayment to unsecured creditors. Instead, creditors receive a percentage of each dollar owed to them by the debtor.

CONTEMPORARY LEGAL DEBATES

Who Benefits from the 2005 Bankruptcy Reform Act?

When Congress enacted the Bankruptcy Reform Act of 1978, many claimed that the new act made it too easy for debtors to file for bankruptcy protection. Certainly, the facts cannot be denied: from 1978 to 2005, personal bankruptcy filings increased ninefold, reaching a peak of 1,613,097 in the year ending June 30, 2003. By the early 2000s, various business groups—including credit-card companies, banks, and firms providing loans for automobile purchases—were claiming that the bankruptcy process was being abused and that reform was necessary. As Mallory Duncan of the National Retail Federation put it, bankruptcy had gone from being a "stigma" to a "financial planning tool" for many.[a] Not surprisingly, the 2005 Bankruptcy Reform Act's full title is the Bankruptcy Abuse Prevention and Consumer Protection Act.

While lenders in general supported the bankruptcy reform bill, consumer groups fought it. According to Travis B. Plunkett, legislative director of the Consumer Federation of America, "The big winners under the new law will be the special interests that literally wrote it, particularly the credit-card industry. This is particularly ironic because reckless and abusive lending practices by credit-card companies have driven many Americans to the brink of bankruptcy."[b]

As with all contemporary legal debates, both sides have strong supporting arguments. In this feature, we examine a few of the major points of controversy.

HAS THE RISE IN BANKRUPTCIES BEEN DUE TO RISING MEDICAL COSTS?

Those who contend that the Bankruptcy Reform Act is anticonsumer and "mean spirited" point to several studies that link rising bankruptcy rates to high medical costs. Researchers at Harvard's medical and law schools conducted extensive interviews of almost two thousand bankruptcy filers in California, Illinois, Pennsylvania, Tennessee, and Texas. Illness and medical bills were cited as a cause in 46.2 percent of the personal bankruptcies under study. The lead author of the study, Dr. David Himmelstein, stated, "Most of the medical bankruptcies [involved] average Americans who happened to get sick."[c]

Judge Richard Posner of the U.S. Court of Appeals for the Seventh Circuit offers an alternative view about so-called medical bankruptcies. He points out that "[w]hether one is forced into bankruptcy by a medical expense (or by an interruption of employment as a result of a medical problem) depends on one's other borrowing. If one has already borrowed to the hilt, an unexpected medical expense may indeed force one over the edge. But knowing that medical expenses are a risk in our society, prudent people avoid loading themselves to the hilt with non-medical debt."[d]

CREATING MORE HARDSHIPS FOR THE POOR

Prior to the Bankruptcy Reform Act of 2005, only about 20 percent of personal bankruptcies were filed under Chapter 13.

---

a. As cited in Nedra Pickler, "Bush Signs Big Rewrite of Bankruptcy Law," *The Los Angeles Times,* April 20, 2005.
b. "Statement of Travis B. Plunkett, Legislative Director of the Consumer Federation of America, on the New Bankruptcy Law," press release by the Consumer Federation of America, April 20, 2005.

c. David Himmelstein *et al.,* "Illness and Injury as Contributors to Bankruptcy," *Health Affairs,* February 2, 2005.
d. Richard Posner, "The Bankruptcy Reform Act," March 27, 2005. You can access this article online by going to **http://www.becker-posner-blog.com** and selecting "March 2005" in the "Archives" column.

SECTION 4 | Bankruptcy Relief under Chapter 13 and Chapter 12

In addition to bankruptcy relief through liquidation and reorganization, the Code also provides for individuals' repayment plans (Chapter 13), and family-farmer and family-fishermen debt adjustments (Chapter 12). As noted previously, the 2005 Bankruptcy Reform Act includes provisions for converting Chapter 7 bankruptcies into Chapter 13 repayment plans. It is therefore likely that there will be an increase in Chapter 13 bankruptcies as a result, because those debtors who have some ability to pay their obligations will file under Chapter 13. There has been a great deal of controversy over the practical effect of the 2005 act. This chapter's *Contemporary Legal Debates* feature provides details on some of the issues in dispute.

INDIVIDUALS' REPAYMENT PLAN

Chapter 13 of the Bankruptcy Code provides for "Adjustment of Debts of an Individual with Regular Income." Individuals (not partnerships or corpora-

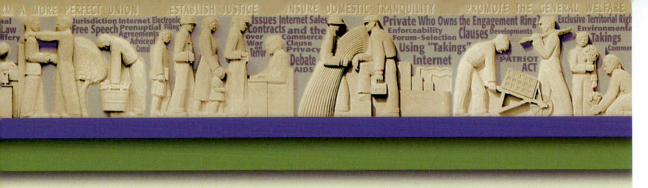

The remaining bankruptcies were filed under Chapter 7. The distinction has been important for all creditors. Given that most individuals who declared personal bankruptcy had few durable assets, Chapter 7 essentially "stiffed" the bankrupt's creditors. Under the new law, as previously indicated in this chapter, whenever a debtor has an annual income in excess of the mean income in that debtor's state of residence, the debtor may be forced into a Chapter 13 plan and make periodic payments over a period of five years to his or her creditors.

Critics of the 2005 Bankruptcy Reform Act point out that it will be more costly to declare personal bankruptcy in the future than it has been in the past. In part, this is because a much higher percentage of bankruptcy petitioners will now have to agree to a Chapter 13 repayment plan—and thus repay a portion of their debts. Additionally, the new law requires that each debtor's attorney certify the accuracy of all factual allegations in the bankruptcy petition and schedules or be subject to sanctions. Further, the bankruptcy attorney may also be responsible for the legal fees of the trustee or bankruptcy administrator who contests a Chapter 7 discharge. Finally, the debtor's attorney must certify the debtor's ability to make payments under any reaffirmation agreement. As a result, many bankruptcy attorneys have indicated that the certification requirements will force them to hire private investigators, appraisers, and auditors. According to attorney Mark Stern, the certification requirements will drive up the cost of filing a bankruptcy when using a lawyer.[e]

WILL CREDITORS REALLY BENEFIT?

Interestingly, forcing more debtors into Chapter 13 plans may not be all that beneficial to creditors. Consider that not all debtors who have filed under Chapter 13 actually complete their plans. According to David Stone, president of Nevada Association Services (a collection agency for about one thousand homeowners' associations statewide), about 80 percent of debtors default on their Chapter 13 plans. "In theory, if everyone complied with their Chapter 13 plans, [the new law] would be an improvement. But the fact of the matter is that most people fail to comply with Chapter 13 plans and therefore the case is dismissed," he asserts.[f]

WHERE DO YOU STAND?

The Bankruptcy Reform Act of 2005 subjects a large class of individuals in the United States to increased financial risk. Supporters of the new law contend that it will curb abuse by deterring financially troubled debtors from looking at bankruptcy as a mere "planning tool" instead of as a last resort. Critics of the act argue that the reform legislation will make it difficult for debtors to obtain a "fresh start" financially—one of the goals of bankruptcy law in the United States. What is your position on this issue? Do you believe that the 2005 act adequately balances the interests of creditors and debtors? Why or why not?

---

e. As cited in Marcia Coyle, "Debtor's Attorneys See Red in Senate Bill: Bankruptcy Judges More Burdened Also," *The National Law Journal*, March 14, 2005.

f. Steven Mihailovich, "Bankruptcy Law Could Make Problems in Nevada," *Las Vegas Business Press*, May 5, 2005.

---

tions) with regular income who owe fixed unsecured debts of less than $307,675 or fixed secured debts of less than $922,975 may take advantage of bankruptcy repayment plans. Among those eligible are salaried employees; sole proprietors; and individuals who live on welfare, Social Security, fixed pensions, or investment income. Many small-business debtors have a choice of filing a plan for reorganization or for repayment. Repayment plans offer several advantages, however. One benefit is that they are less expensive and less complicated than reorganization proceedings or, for that matter, even liquidation proceedings.

FILING THE PETITION   A repayment plan case can be initiated only by the filing of a voluntary petition by the debtor or by the conversion of a Chapter 7 petition (because of a finding of substantial abuse under the means test, for example). Certain liquidation and reorganization cases may be converted to repayment plan cases with the consent of the debtor.[27] A trustee, who will make payments under the plan, must be

---

27. A Chapter 13 case may be converted to a Chapter 7 case either at the request of the debtor or, under certain circumstances, "for cause" by a creditor. A Chapter 13 case may be converted to a Chapter 11 case after a hearing.

appointed. On the filing of a repayment plan petition, the automatic stay previously discussed takes effect. Although the stay applies to all or part of the debtor's consumer debt, it does not apply to any business debt incurred by the debtor. The automatic stay also does not apply to domestic-support obligations.

THE REPAYMENT PLAN   A plan of rehabilitation by repayment must provide for the following:

1. The turnover to the trustee of such future earnings or income of the debtor as is necessary for execution of the plan.
2. Full payment in deferred cash payments of all claims entitled to priority.[28]
3. Identical treatment of all claims within a particular class. (The Code permits the debtor to list co-debtors, such as guarantors or sureties, as a separate class.)

—*Filing the Plan.*   Only the debtor may file for a repayment plan. This plan may provide either for payment of all obligations in full or for payment of a lesser amount.[29] Prior to the 2005 act, the time for repayment was usually three years unless the court approved an extension for up to five years. Under the new Code, the length of the payment plan (three or five years) is determined by the debtor's median family income. If the debtor's family income is greater than the state median family income under the means test (previously discussed), the proposed plan must be for five years.[30] The term may not exceed five years, however.

The Code requires the debtor to make "timely" payments from the debtor's disposable income, and the trustee must ensure that the debtor commences these payments. The plan cannot materially alter terms of repayment on a retirement loan account, however. These payment amounts must take into consideration the scheduled payments to lessors of personal property, and must provide adequate protection to secured cred-

itors of personal property. Proof of adequate insurance on personal property is required. The debtor must begin making payments under the proposed plan within thirty days after the plan has been *filed.*

If the plan has not been confirmed, the trustee is instructed to retain the payments until the plan is confirmed and then distribute them accordingly. If the plan is denied, the trustee will return the payments to the debtor less any costs. Failure of the debtor to make timely payments or to commence payments within the thirty-day period will allow the court to convert the case to a liquidation bankruptcy or to dismiss the petition.

—*Confirmation of the Plan.*   After the plan is filed, the court holds a confirmation hearing, at which interested parties (such as creditors) may object to the plan. Under the 2005 act, the hearing must be held at least twenty days, but no more than forty-five days, after the meeting of the creditors. Confirmation of the plan is dependent on the debtor's certification that postpetition domestic-support obligations have been paid in full, and all prepetition tax returns have been filed. The court will confirm a plan with respect to each claim of a secured creditor under any of the following circumstances:

1. If the secured creditors have accepted the plan.
2. If the plan provides that secured creditors retain their liens until there is payment in full or until the debtor receives a discharge.
3. If the debtor surrenders the property securing the claims to the creditors.

In addition, for confirmation, the plan must provide that a creditor with a purchase-money security interest (PMSI—see Chapter 29) retains its lien until payment of the entire debt for a motor vehicle purchased within 910 days before filing the petition. For PMSIs on other personal property, the payment plan must cover debts incurred within a one-year period preceding the filing.

—*Objection to the Plan.*   Unsecured creditors do not have the power to confirm a repayment plan, but they can object to it. The court can approve a plan over the objection of the trustee or any unsecured creditor only in either of the following situations:

1. When the value of the property (replacement value as of the date of filing) to be distributed under the plan is at least equal to the amount of the claims.

---

28. As with a Chapter 11 reorganization plan, full repayment of all claims is not always required.
29. Under the 2005 act, a plan under Chapter 13 or Chapter 12 (to be discussed shortly) might propose to pay less than 100 percent of prepetition domestic-support obligations that had been assigned, but only if disposable income is dedicated to a five-year plan. Disposable income is also redefined to exclude the amounts reasonably necessary to pay current domestic-support obligations.
30. See 11 U.S.C. Section 1322(d) for details on when the court will find that the Chapter 13 plan should extend to a five-year period.

2. When all of the debtor's projected disposable income to be received during the plan period will be applied to making payments. Disposable income is all income received less amounts needed to pay domestic-support obligations and/or amounts needed to meet ordinary expenses to continue the operation of a business. The 2005 act also excludes from disposable income charitable contributions up to 15 percent of the debtor's gross income, and the reasonable and necessary costs for health insurance for the debtor and his or her dependents.

—Modification of the Plan. Prior to completion of payments, the plan may be modified at the request of the debtor, the trustee, or an unsecured creditor. If any interested party objects to the modification, the court must hold a hearing to determine whether the modified plan will be approved.

DISCHARGE After completion of all payments, the court grants a discharge of all debts provided for by the repayment plan. Except for allowed claims not provided for by the plan, certain long-term debts provided for by the plan, certain tax claims, payments on retirement accounts, and claims for domestic-support obligations, all other debts are dischargeable. Under prior law, a discharge of debts under a Chapter 13 repayment plan was sometimes referred to as a "superdischarge" because it allowed the discharge of fraudulently incurred debt and claims resulting from malicious or willful injury.

The 2005 Bankruptcy Reform Act, however, deleted most of the "superdischarge" provisions, especially for debts based on fraud. Today, debts for trust fund taxes, taxes for which returns were never filed or filed late (within two years of filing), domestic-support payments, student loans, and injury or property damage from driving under the influence of alcohol or drugs are nondischargeable. The new law also excludes fraudulent tax obligations, criminal fines and restitution, fraud by a person acting in a fiduciary capacity, and restitution for willfully and maliciously causing personal injury or death.

Even if the debtor does not complete the plan, a hardship discharge may be granted if failure to complete the plan was due to circumstances beyond the debtor's control and if the value of the property distributed under the plan was greater than what would have been paid in a liquidation. A discharge can be revoked within one year if it was obtained by fraud.

FAMILY FARMERS AND FISHERMEN

In 1986, to help relieve economic pressure on small farmers, Congress created Chapter 12 of the Bankruptcy Code. In 2005, Congress extended this protection to family fishermen,[31] modified its provisions somewhat, and made it a permanent chapter in the Bankruptcy Code (previously the statutes authorizing Chapter 12 had to be periodically renewed by Congress).

DEFINITIONS For purposes of Chapter 12, a *family farmer* is one whose gross income is at least 50 percent farm dependent and whose debts are at least 50 percent farm related. The total debt for a family farmer must not exceed $3.237 million. (Prior law required a farmer's debts to be 80 percent farm related and not to exceed $1.5 million.) A partnership or closely held corporation (at least 50 percent owned by the farm family) can also qualify as a family farmer.

A *family fisherman* is defined by the 2005 act as one whose gross income is at least 50 percent dependent on commercial fishing operations[32] and whose debts are at least 80 percent related to commercial fishing. The total debt for a family fisherman must not exceed $1.5 million. As with family farmers, a partnership or closely held corporation can also qualify.

FILING THE PETITION The procedure for filing a family-farmer or family-fishermen bankruptcy plan is very similar to the procedure for filing a repayment plan under Chapter 13. The debtor must file a plan not later than ninety days after the order for relief. The filing of the petition acts as an automatic stay against creditors' and co-obligors' actions against the estate.

A farmer or fisherman who has already filed a reorganization or repayment plan may convert it to a Chapter 12 plan. The debtor may also convert a Chapter 12 plan to a liquidation plan.

CONTENT AND CONFIRMATION OF THE PLAN The content of a plan under Chapter 12 is basically the same as that of a Chapter 13 repayment plan. The plan

---

31. Although the Code uses the terms *fishermen* and *fisherman*, Chapter 12 provisions apply equally to men and women.
32. Commercial fishing operations include catching, harvesting, or aquaculture raising fish, shrimp, lobsters, urchins, seaweed, shellfish, or other aquatic species or products.

CONCEPT SUMMARY 30.1 | Forms of Bankruptcy Relief Compared

ISSUE	CHAPTER 7	CHAPTER 11	CHAPTERS 12 AND 13
PURPOSE	Liquidation.	Reorganization.	Adjustment.
WHO CAN PETITION	Debtor (voluntary) or creditors (involuntary).	Debtor (voluntary) or creditors (involuntary).	Debtor (voluntary) only.
WHO CAN BE A DEBTOR	Any "person" (including partnerships, corporations, and municipalities) except railroads, insurance companies, banks, savings and loan institutions, investment companies licensed by the Small Business Administration, and credit unions. Farmers and charitable institutions also cannot be involuntarily petitioned. If the court finds the petition to be a substantial abuse of the use of Chapter 7, the debtor may be required to convert to a Chapter 13 repayment plan.	Any debtor eligible for Chapter 7 relief; railroads are also eligible. Individuals have specific rules and limitations.	*Chapter 12*—Any family farmer (one whose gross income is at least 50 percent farm dependent and whose debts are at least 50 percent farm related) or family fisherman (one whose gross income is at least 50 percent dependent on commercial fishing operations and whose debts are at least 80 percent related to commercial fishing) or any partnership or closely held corporation at least 50 percent owned by a family farmer or fisherman, when total debt does not exceed a specified amount ($3.237 million for farmers and $1.5 million for fishermen). *Chapter 13*—Any individual (not partnerships or corporations) with regular income who owes fixed unsecured debts of less than $307,675 or fixed secured debts of less than $922,975.
PROCEDURE LEADING TO DISCHARGE	Nonexempt property is sold with proceeds to be distributed (in order) to priority groups. Dischargeable debts are terminated.	Plan is submitted; if it is approved and followed, debts are discharged.	Plan is submitted and must be approved if the value of the property to be distributed equals the amount of the claims or if the debtor turns over disposable income for a three-year or five-year period; if the plan is followed, debts are discharged.
ADVANTAGES	On liquidation and distribution, most debts are discharged, and the debtor has an opportunity for a fresh start.	Debtor continues in business. Creditors can either accept the plan, or it can be "crammed down" on them. The plan allows for the reorganization and liquidation of debts over the plan period.	Debtor continues in business or possession of assets. If the plan is approved, most debts are discharged after the plan period.

can be modified by the debtor but, except for cause, must be confirmed or denied within forty-five days of filing.

Court confirmation of the plan is the same as for a repayment plan. In summary, the plan must provide for payment of secured debts at the value of the collateral. If the secured debt exceeds the value of the collateral, the remaining debt is unsecured. For unsecured debtors, the plan must be confirmed if either the value of the property to be distributed under the plan equals the amount of the claim or the plan provides that all of the debtor's disposable income to be received in a three-year period (or longer, by court approval) will be applied to making payments. Disposable income is all income received less amounts needed to support the farmer or fisherman and his or her family and to continue the farming or commercial fishing operation. Completion of payments under the plan discharges all debts provided for by the plan.

REVIEWING BANKRUPTCY LAW

Three months ago, Janet Hart's husband of twenty years died of cancer. Although he had medical insurance, he left Janet with outstanding medical bills of more than $50,000. Janet has worked at the local library for the past ten years, earning $1,700 per month. Since her husband's death, Janet also receives $1,500 in Social Security benefits and $1,100 in life insurance proceeds every month, which leaves her with a monthly income of $4,300. After she pays the monthly mortgage payment of $1,500 and the monthly amounts due on other debts, Janet barely has enough left over to buy groceries for her family. (She has two teenage daughters at home.) She decides to file for Chapter 7 bankruptcy, hoping for a fresh start. Using the information presented in the chapter, answer the following questions.

1. Under the Bankruptcy Code after the enactment of the 2005 revisions, what must Janet do prior to filing a petition for relief under Chapter 7?

2. What schedules must Janet include with her voluntary petition, and how long does she have to file these schedules? Must anyone verify the information contained in these schedules? Explain.

3. Assume that Janet files a petition under Chapter 7. Further assume that the median family income in the state in which Janet lives is $49,300. Describe the steps a court would take to determine whether Janet's petition is presumed to be "substantial abuse" using the means test.

4. Suppose that the court determines that no *presumption* of substantial abuse applies in Janet's case. Nevertheless, the court finds that Janet does have the ability to repay at least a portion of the amount due on the medical bills out of her disposable income. What would the court likely order in that situation?

5. Suppose that Janet, who is not represented by an attorney, decides to enter into a reaffirmation agreement with the mortgage lender to keep the family home. Describe the procedure that would need to be followed.

TERMS AND CONCEPTS TO REVIEW

QUESTIONS AND CASE PROBLEMS

30–1. Burke has been a rancher all her life, raising cattle and crops. Her ranch is valued at $500,000, almost all of which is exempt under state law. Burke has eight creditors and a total indebtedness of $70,000. Two of her largest creditors are Oman ($30,000 owed) and Sneed ($25,000 owed). The other six creditors have claims of less than $5,000 each. A drought has ruined all of Burke's crops and forced her to sell many of her cattle at a loss. She cannot pay off her creditors.

(a) Under the Bankruptcy Code, can Burke, with a $500,000 ranch, voluntarily petition herself into bankruptcy? Explain.

(b) Could either Oman or Sneed force Burke into involuntary bankruptcy? Explain.

30–2. Sam is a retail seller of television sets. He sells Gracen a $900 set on a retail installment security agreement in which she pays $100 down and agrees to pay the balance in equal installments. Sam retains a security interest in the set, and he perfects that interest by filing a financing statement centrally. Two months later, Gracen is in default on her payments to Sam and is involuntarily petitioned into bankruptcy by her creditors. Sam wants to repossess the television set, as provided for in the security agreement, and he wants to have priority over the trustee in bankruptcy as to any proceeds from the disposal of the set. Discuss fully Sam's right to repossess and whether he has priority over the trustee in bankruptcy as to any proceeds from the disposal of the set.

30–3. ⚖ **QUESTION WITH SAMPLE ANSWER**

Peaslee is not known for his business sense. He started a greenhouse and nursery business two years ago, and because of his lack of experience, he soon was in debt to a number of creditors. On February 1, Peaslee borrowed $5,000 from his father to pay some of these creditors. On May 1, Peaslee paid back the $5,000, depleting his entire working capital. One creditor, the Cool Springs Nursery Supply Corp., extended credit to Peaslee on numerous purchases. Cool Springs pressured Peaslee for payment, and on July 1, Peaslee paid Cool Springs half the money owed. On September 1, Peaslee voluntarily petitioned himself into bankruptcy. The trustee in bankruptcy claimed that both Peaslee's father and Cool Springs must turn over to the debtor's estate the amounts Peaslee paid to them. Discuss fully the trustee's claims.

For a sample answer to this question, go to Appendix I at the end of this text.

30–4. Montoro petitioned himself into voluntary bankruptcy. There were three major claims against his estate. One was made by Carlton, a friend who held Montoro's negotiable promissory note for $2,500; one was made by Elmer, an employee who was owed three months' back wages of $4,500; and one was made by the United Bank of the Rockies on an unsecured loan of $5,000. In addition, Dietrich, an accountant retained by the trustee, was owed $500, and property taxes of $1,000 were owed to Rock County. Montoro's nonexempt property was liquidated, with proceeds of $5,000. Discuss fully what amount each party will receive, and why.

30–5. East Bank was a secured party on a $5,000 loan it made to Kirksey. Kirksey experienced financial difficulty, and creditors other than East Bank petitioned her into involuntary bankruptcy. The value of the secured collateral had substantially decreased in value. On its sale, the debt to East Bank was reduced to $2,500. Kirksey's estate consisted of $100,000 in exempt assets and $2,000 in nonexempt assets. After the bankruptcy costs and back wages to Kirksey's employees had been paid, nothing was left for unsecured creditors. Kirksey received a discharge in bankruptcy. Later, she decided to go back into business. By selling a few exempt assets and getting a small loan, she would be able to buy a small but profitable restaurant. She went to East Bank for the loan. East Bank claimed that the balance of its secured debt had not been discharged in bankruptcy. Kirksey signed an agreement to pay East Bank the $2,500, as the bank had not been a party to petitioning her into bankruptcy. Because of this, East Bank made the new unsecured loan to Kirksey.

(a) Discuss East Bank's claim that the balance of its secured debt had not been discharged in bankruptcy.

(b) Discuss the legal effect of Kirksey's agreement to pay East Bank $2,500 after the discharge in bankruptcy.

(c) If one year after buying the restaurant, Kirksey went into voluntary bankruptcy, what effect would the bankruptcy proceedings have on the new unsecured loan?

30–6. AUTOMATIC STAY. David Sisco had about $600 in an account in Tinker Federal Credit Union. Sisco owed DPW Employees Credit Union a little more than $1,100. To collect on the debt, DPW obtained a garnishment judgment and served it on Tinker. The next day, Sisco filed a bankruptcy petition. Tinker then told DPW that because of the bankruptcy filing, it could not pay the garnishment. DPW objected, and Tinker asked an Oklahoma state court to resolve the issue. What effect, if any, does Sisco's bankruptcy filing have on DPW's garnishment action? [*DPW Employees Credit Union v. Tinker Federal Credit Union*, 925 P.2d 93 (Okla.App.4th 1996)]

30-7. ⚖ CASE PROBLEM WITH SAMPLE ANSWER

Between 1980 and 1987, Craig Hanson borrowed funds from Great Lakes Higher Education Corp. to finance his education at the University of Wisconsin. Hanson defaulted on the debt in 1989, and Great Lakes obtained a judgment against him for $31,583.77. Three years later, Hanson filed a bankruptcy petition under Chapter 13. Great Lakes timely filed a proof of claim in the amount of $35,531.08. Hanson's repayment plan proposed to pay $135 monthly to Great Lakes over sixty months, which in total was only 19 percent of the claim, but said nothing about discharging the remaining balance. The plan was confirmed without objection. After Hanson completed the payments under the plan, without any additional proof or argument being offered, the court granted a discharge of his student loans. In 2003, Educational Credit Management Corp. (ECMC), which had taken over Great Lakes' interest in the loans, filed a motion for relief from the discharge. What is the requirement for the discharge of a student loan obligation in bankruptcy? Did Hanson meet this requirement? Should the court grant ECMC's motion? Discuss. [*In re Hanson*, 397 F.3d 482 (7th Cir. 2005)]

To view a sample answer for this case problem, go to this book's Web site at http://wbl.westbuslaw.com, select "Chapter 30," and click on "Case Problem with Sample Answer."

30-8. DISCHARGE IN BANKRUPTCY.

Jon Goulet attended the University of Wisconsin in Eau Claire and Regis University in Denver, Colorado, from which he earned a bachelor's degree in history in 1972. Over the next ten years, he worked as a bartender and restaurant manager. In 1984, he became a life insurance agent and his income ranged from $20,000 to $30,000. In 1989, however, his agent's license was revoked for insurance fraud, and he was arrested for cocaine possession. From 1991 to 1995, Goulet was again at the University of Wisconsin, working toward, but failing to obtain, a master's degree in psychology. To pay for his studies, he took out student loans totaling $76,000. Goulet then returned to bartending and restaurant management and tried real estate sales. His income for the year 2000 was $1,490, and his expenses, excluding a child-support obligation, were $5,904. When the student loans came due, Goulet filed a petition for bankruptcy. On what ground might the loans be dischargeable? Should the court grant a discharge on this ground? Why or why not? [*Goulet v.*

Educational Credit Management Corp., 284 F.3d 773 (7th Cir. 2002)]

30-9. AUTOMATIC STAY.

On January 22, 2001, Marlene Moffett bought a used 1998 Honda Accord from Hendrick Honda in Woodbridge, Virginia. Moffett agreed to pay $20,024.25, with interest, in sixty monthly installments, and Hendrick retained a security interest in the car. (As discussed in Chapter 29, Hendrick thus had the right to repossess the car in the event of default, subject to Moffett's right of redemption.) Hendrick assigned its rights under the sales agreement to Tidewater Finance Co., which perfected its security interest. The car was Moffett's only means of traveling the forty miles from her home to her workplace. In March and April 2002, Moffett missed two monthly payments. On April 25, Tidewater repossessed the car. On the same day, Moffett filed a Chapter 13 plan in a federal bankruptcy court. Moffett asked that the car be returned to her, in part under the Bankruptcy Code's automatic-stay provision. Tidewater asked the court to terminate the automatic stay so that it could sell the car. How can the interests of both the debtor and the creditor be fully protected in this case? What should the court rule? Explain. [*In re Moffett*, 356 F.3d 518 (4th Cir. 2004)]

30-10. VIDEO QUESTION

Go to this text's Web site at http://wbl.westbuslaw.com and select "Chapter 30." Click on "Video Questions" and view the video titled *The River*. Then answer the following questions.

(a) In the video, a crowd (including Mel Gibson) is gathered at a farm auction in which a neighbor's (Jim Antonio's) farming goods are being sold. The people in the crowd, who are upset because they believe that the bank is selling out the farmer, begin chanting "no sale, no sale." In an effort to calm the group, the farmer tells the crowd that "they've already foreclosed" on his farm. What does he mean?

(b) Assume that the auction is a result of Chapter 7 bankruptcy proceedings. Was the farmer's petition for bankruptcy voluntary or involuntary? Explain.

(c) Suppose that the farmer purchased the homestead three years prior to filing a petition for bankruptcy and that the current market value of the farm is $215,000. What is the maximum amount of equity the farmer could claim as exempt under the 2005 Bankruptcy Reform Act?

(d) Compare the results of a Chapter 12 bankruptcy as opposed to a Chapter 7 bankruptcy for the farmer in the video.

LAW | on the Web

For updated links to resources available on the Web, as well as a variety of other materials, visit this text's Web site at http://wbl.westbuslaw.com.

The U.S. Bankruptcy Code is online at

http://www.law.cornell.edu:80/uscode/11

For information and news on bankruptcy reform legislation, go to the site maintained by Bankruptcy Media at

http://www.bankruptcyfinder.com/bankruptcyreformnews.html

Another good resource for bankruptcy information is the American Bankruptcy Institute (ABI) at

http://www.abiworld.org

LEGAL RESEARCH EXERCISES ON THE WEB

Go to http://wbl.westbuslaw.com, the Web site that accompanies this text. Select "Chapter 30" and click on "Internet Exercises." There you will find the following Internet research exercises that you can perform to learn more about topics covered in this chapter.

Activity 30–1: LEGAL PERSPECTIVE
Bankruptcy

Activity 30–2: MANAGEMENT PERSPECTIVE
Bankruptcy Alternatives

Creditors' Rights and Bankruptcy

We have certainly come a long way from the period in our history when debtors' prisons existed. Today, debtors are in a much more favorable position—they can file for protection under bankruptcy law. Indeed, after the Bankruptcy Reform Act of 1978 was passed, some claimed that we had gone too far toward protecting debtors and had made it too easy for them to avoid paying what they legally owe. Critics of the 2005 Bankruptcy Reform Act are concerned that the pendulum has swung too far in the opposite direction— favoring creditors' interests and making it too difficult for debtors to obtain a fresh start. Clearly, it is hard to protect the rights of both debtors and creditors at the same time, and laws governing debtor-creditor relationships have traditionally been perceived, by one group or another, as being unfair.

It is obviously not possible for the law to protect both debtors and creditors at all times under all circumstances. Attempts to balance the rights of both groups necessarily raise questions of fairness and justice. In this *Focus on Ethics* feature, we look at several aspects of debtor-creditor relationships that frequently involve issues of fairness, and we examine the ethical ramifications of the 2005 Bankruptcy Reform Act on debtors and creditors.

"Self-Help" Repossession

Section 9–503 of the Uniform Commercial Code (UCC) states that "[u]nless otherwise agreed, a secured party has on default the right to take possession of the collateral. In taking possession, a secured party may proceed without judicial process if this can be done without breach of the peace." The underlying rationale for this "self-help" provision of Article 9 is that it simplifies the process of repossession for creditors and reduces the burden on the courts. Because the UCC does not define "breach of the peace," however, it is not always easy to predict what behavior will constitute such a breach.

The debtor may not always realize what is happening when agents of the creditor show up to repossess the collateral. Often, to avoid confrontation with the debtor and any potential violence or breach of the peace, a secured creditor will arrange to have the collateral repossessed during the night or in the early-morning hours, when the repossession effort is least likely to be observed. For the debtor, repossession can therefore be very stressful. A debtor may awaken in the night and see his or her car being towed away—without realizing that it is being repossessed.

At the same time, repossession can be risky for the creditor; if the repossession results in a breach of the peace, the creditor may be liable for substantial damages. Inevitably, repossession attempts will occasionally result in confrontations with the debtor. Indeed, some contend that the self-help provision encourages violence by providing an incentive for debtors to induce creditors to breach the peace, which may entitle the debtors to damages.

Ethics and Bankruptcy

As we have seen, the first goal of bankruptcy law is to provide relief and protection to debtors. Society has generally concluded that everyone should be given the chance to start over. But how far should society go in allowing debtors to avoid obligations that they voluntarily incurred? This question has been debated for some time, and it is certainly at the forefront of the 2005 Bankruptcy Reform Act.

Consider the concept of bankruptcy from the point of view of the creditor. The creditor has extended a transfer of purchasing power from himself or herself to the debtor. That transfer of purchasing power represents a transfer of an asset for an asset. The debtor obtains the asset of money, goods, or services, and the creditor obtains the asset called a *secured* or *unsecured* legal obligation to pay. Once the debtor is in bankruptcy, voluntarily or involuntarily, the asset that the creditor owns most often has a diminished value. Indeed, in many circumstances, that asset has no value. Yet the easier it becomes for debtors to discharge their debts under bankruptcy laws, the greater will be the incentive for debtors to use such laws to avoid payment of legally owed sums of money.

Clearly, bankruptcy law is a balancing act between providing a second chance for debtors and ensuring that creditors are given reasonable protection. Understandably, ethical issues arise in the process.

Bankruptcy and Economics

Among other things, the increasing number of bankruptcies since the early 1990s means that creditors incur higher risks in making loans, because bankruptcy shifts the cost of the debt from the debtor to the creditor. To compensate for these higher risks, creditors will take one or more of the following actions: increase the interest rates charged to everyone, require additional security (collateral), or be more selective in the granting of credit. Thus, with more lenient bankruptcy laws, debtors who find themselves in bankruptcy will be better off, but those debtors who will never be in bankruptcy will be worse off. Ethical concerns regarding this trade-off must be matched with the economic concerns of other groups of individuals affected by the law.

Consequences of Bankruptcy Under the 2005 Bankruptcy Reform Act, filing for personal bankruptcy (particularly under Chapter 7) has become more difficult. Although it is true that there is less of a stigma attached to bankruptcy today than there once was, bankruptcy is never easy for debtors. Many debtors feel a sense of shame and failure when they petition for bankruptcy. After all, bankruptcy is a matter of public record, and there is no way to avoid a certain amount of publicity. In one case, for example, a couple who filed for Chapter 7 bankruptcy wanted to use their attorney's mailing address in another town on their bankruptcy schedules in an effort to prevent an elderly parent and one of their employers from learning about the bankruptcy. The court, however, held that debtors are not entitled to be protected from publicity surrounding the filing of their cases.[1]

Bankruptcy also has other consequences for debtors, including blemished credit ratings for up to ten years and higher interest charges for new debts, such as those incurred through the purchase of cars or homes. Some private employers may even refuse to hire a job applicant who has filed for bankruptcy. The courts provide little relief for applicants who are denied a job for this reason.[2]

Thus, bankruptcy can have adverse effects for both debtors and creditors. Because of the consequences of bankruptcy, debtors do not always get the fresh start promised by bankruptcy law. At the same time, creditors rarely are able to recover all of the money owed them once a debtor petitions for bankruptcy.

Is It Fair to Increase the Costs for Debtors Seeking Bankruptcy Relief? The 2005 Bankruptcy Reform Act will increase the costs of filing for bankruptcy. Although the filing fee for Chapter 7 bankruptcies has been increased from $155 to $200, filing fees do not constitute the major expense for bankruptcy filings. Rather, attorneys' fees loom large for many potential bankruptcy filers.

As mentioned in Chapter 30, the 2005 act requires that each debtor's attorney certify the accuracy of all factual allegations in the bankruptcy petition and schedules under penalty of perjury. In other words, attorneys may be subject to sanctions (fines) if there are any factual inaccuracies. This change alone may convince many attorneys not to represent debtors in bankruptcy. Those that do continue to represent debtors will undoubtedly charge higher attorneys' fees than they did before the 2005 act because they will be assuming greater risk.

In addition, if the attorney will be held accountable for factual inaccuracies, then she or he will most likely want to independently investigate the truth of the facts stated in the petition and schedules. This means hiring private investigators, appraisers, and auditors for assistance in accounting for all of the debtors' income and assets. The attorney must also certify that the debtor is capable of making the payments due under a reaffirmation agreement for that agreement to be enforceable. This entails another round of investigations before an attorney will sign such a certification. Obviously, the debtor is the one who will ultimately end up paying these costs. Does making it more expensive and difficult to file for bankruptcy defeat the primary purpose of bankruptcy laws—to protect debtors by giving them a fresh start? After all, if debtors can't afford to pay their monthly bills, then how can they possibly afford to file for bankruptcy given the increased cost of hiring an attorney under the new act?

DISCUSSION QUESTIONS

1. Do you think that the law favors debtors at the expense of creditors, or vice versa? Is there any way to achieve a better balance between the interests of creditors and those of debtors?

2. So long as a breach of the peace does not result, a lender may repossess goods on the debtor's default under the self-help provision of Article 9. Do you think that debtors have a right to be told in advance about a planned repossession? Some observers argue that the self-help remedy under Article 9 should be abolished. Do you agree? Why or why not?

3. Is it unethical to avoid paying one's debts by going into bankruptcy? Does a person have a moral responsibility to pay his or her debts?

4. Will borrowers be better off as a result of the 2005 Bankruptcy Reform Act? Why or why not?

---

1. *In the Matter of Laws*, 223 Bankr. 714 (D.Neb. 1998).
2. See, for example, *Pastore v. Medford Savings Bank*, 186 Bankr. 553 (D.Mass. 1995).

UNIT SEVEN
Agency and Employment

CONTENTS

CHAPTER 31

Agency Formation and Duties

One of the most common, important, and pervasive legal relationships is that of **agency.** As discussed in Chapter 26, in an agency relationship between two parties, one of the parties, called the *agent*, agrees to represent or act for the other, called the *principal*. The principal has the right to control the agent's conduct in matters entrusted to the agent. By using agents, a principal can conduct multiple business operations simultaneously in various locations. Thus, for example, contracts that bind the principal can be made at different places with different persons at the same time.

A familiar example of an agent is a corporate officer who serves in a representative capacity for the owners of the corporation. In this capacity, the officer has the authority to bind the principal (the corporation) to a contract. Indeed, agency law is essential to the existence and operation of a corporate entity, because only through its agents can a corporation function and enter into contracts.

Most employees are also considered to be agents for their employers. Thus, some of the concepts that you will learn about in Chapters 33 and 34, on employment law, are based on agency law. Generally, agency relationships permeate the business world. For that reason, an understanding of the law of agency is crucial to understanding business law.

SECTION 1 | Agency Relationships

Section 1(1) of the *Restatement (Second) of Agency*[1] defines *agency* as "the fiduciary relation [that] results from the manifestation of consent by one person to another that the other shall act in his [or her] behalf and subject to his [or her] control, and consent by the other so to act." The term **fiduciary** is at the heart of agency law. The term can be used both as a noun and as an adjective. When used as a noun, it refers to a person having a duty created by his or her undertaking to act primarily for another's benefit in matters connected with the undertaking. When used as an adjective, as in the phrase "fiduciary relationship," it means that the relationship involves trust and confidence.

Agency relationships commonly exist between employers and employees. Agency relationships may sometimes also exist between employers and independent contractors who are hired to perform special tasks or services.

EMPLOYER-EMPLOYEE RELATIONSHIPS

Normally, all employees who deal with third parties are deemed to be agents. A salesperson in a department store, for instance, is an agent of the store's owner (the principal) and acts on the owner's behalf. Employment laws (state and federal) apply only to the employer-employee relationship. Statutes governing Social Security, withholding taxes, workers' compensation, unemployment compensation, workplace safety, employment discrimination, and other aspects of employment (see Chapters 33 and 34) are applicable only when an employer-employee relationship exists. *These laws do not apply to an independent contractor.*

---

1. The *Restatement (Second) of Agency* is an authoritative summary of the law of agency and is often referred to by judges in their decisions and opinions.

Because employees may be deemed agents of their employers, agency law and employment law overlap considerably. Agency relationships, though, as will become apparent, can exist outside an employer-employee relationship and thus have a broader reach than employment laws do.

EMPLOYER–INDEPENDENT CONTRACTOR RELATIONSHIPS

Independent contractors are not employees because, by definition, those who hire them have no control over the details of their work performance. Section 2 of the *Restatement (Second) of Agency* defines an **independent contractor** as follows:

> [An independent contractor is] a person who contracts with another to do something for him [or her] but who is not controlled by the other nor subject to the other's right to control with respect to his [or her] physical conduct in the performance of the undertaking. He [or she] may or may not be an agent.

Building contractors and subcontractors are independent contractors, and a property owner does not control the acts of either of these professionals. Truck drivers who own their equipment and hire out on a per-job basis are independent contractors, but truck drivers who drive company trucks on a regular basis are usually employees.

The relationship between a principal and an independent contractor may or may not involve an agency relationship. To illustrate: An owner of real estate who hires a real estate broker to negotiate the sale of her property not only has contracted with an independent contractor (the real estate broker) but also has established an agency relationship for the specific purpose of selling the property. Another example is an insurance agent, who is both an independent contractor and an agent of the insurance company for which he or she sells policies. (Note that an insurance *broker*, in contrast, normally is an agent of the person obtaining insurance and not of the insurance company.)

DETERMINING EMPLOYEE STATUS

The courts are frequently asked to determine whether a particular worker is an employee or an independent contractor. How a court decides this issue can have a significant effect on the rights and liabilities of the parties. For example, employers are required to pay certain taxes, such as Social Security and unemployment taxes, for employees but not for independent contractors.

CRITERIA USED BY THE COURTS In deciding whether a worker is categorized as an employee or an independent contractor, courts often consider the following questions:

1. How much control can the employer exercise over the details of the work? (If an employer can exercise considerable control over the details of the work and the day-to-day activities of the worker, this indicates employee status. This is perhaps the most important factor weighed by the courts in determining employee status.)
2. Is the worker engaged in an occupation or business distinct from that of the employer? (If so, this points to independent-contractor, not employee, status.)
3. Is the work usually done under the employer's direction or by a specialist without supervision? (If the work is usually done under the employer's direction, this indicates employee status.)
4. Does the employer supply the tools at the place of work? (If so, this indicates employee status.)
5. For how long is the person employed? (If the person is employed for a long period of time, this indicates employee status.)
6. What is the method of payment—by time period or at the completion of the job? (Payment by time period, such as once every two weeks or once a month, indicates employee status.)
7. What degree of skill is required of the worker? (If a great degree of skill is required, this may indicate that the person is an independent contractor hired for a specialized job and not an employee.)

Sometimes, it may be advantageous to have independent-contractor status—for tax purposes, for example. At other times, it is advantageous for a worker to have employee status—to take advantage of laws protecting employees, for example. As stated above, federal statutes governing employment discrimination apply only when an employer-employee relationship exists. The question in the following case was whether, for the purpose of applying one of these statutes, a television show's co-host was an employee or an independent contractor.

CASE 31.1   Alberty-Vélez v. Corporación de Puerto Rico

United States
Court of Appeals,
First Circuit, 2004.
361 F.3d 1.
http://www.ca1.uscourts.gov[a]

BACKGROUND AND FACTS *In July 1993, Victoria Lis Alberty-Vélez (Alberty) began to co-host a new television show,* Desde Mi Pueblo, *on WIPR, a television station in Puerto Rico. The show profiled Puerto Rican cities and towns. Instead of signing a single contract, Alberty signed a new contract for each episode. Each contract obligated her to work a certain number of days. She was not obliged to do other work for WIPR, and WIPR was not obliged to contract with her for other work. During the filming, Alberty was responsible for providing her own clothing, shoes, accessories, hairstylist, and other services and materials. She was paid a lump sum, ranging from $400 to $550, for each episode. WIPR did not withhold income or Social Security taxes and did not provide health insurance, life insurance, a retirement plan, paid sick leave, maternity leave, or vacation pay. Alberty became pregnant, and after November 1994, WIPR stopped contracting with her. She filed a suit in a federal district court against WIPR's owner, Corporación de Puerto Rico para la Difusión Pública, alleging in part discrimination on the basis of her pregnancy in violation of a federal statute. The court issued a judgment in the defendant's favor. Alberty appealed to the U.S. Court of Appeals for the First Circuit.*

IN THE LANGUAGE OF THE COURT

HOWARD, Circuit Judge.

* * * *

* * * We * * * will apply the common law test to determine whether Alberty was WIPR's employee or an independent contractor.

Under the common law test, a court must consider * * * *the hiring party's right to control the manner and means by which the product is accomplished.* Among other factors relevant to this inquiry are the skills required; the source of the instrumentalities and tools; the location of the work; the duration of the relationship between the parties; whether the hiring party has the right to assign additional projects to the hired party; the extent of the hired party's discretion over when and how long to work; the method of payment; * * * whether the work is part of the regular business of the hiring party; whether the hiring party is in business; the provision of employee benefits; and the tax treatment of the hired party. * * * [Emphasis added.]

* * * *

Several factors favor classifying Alberty as an independent contractor. First, a television actress is a skilled position requiring talent and training not available on-the-job. In this regard, Alberty possesses a master's degree in public communications and journalism; is trained in dance, singing, and modeling; taught within the drama department at the University of Puerto Rico; and acted in several theater and television productions prior to her affiliation with "Desde Mi Pueblo."

Second, Alberty provided the tools and instrumentalities necessary for her to perform. Specifically, she provided, or obtained sponsors to provide, the costumes, jewelry, and other image-related supplies and services necessary for her appearance. * * *

Third, WIPR could not assign Alberty work in addition to filming "Desde Mi Pueblo." * * *

Fourth, the method of payment favors independent-contractor status. Alberty received a lump sum fee for each episode. Her compensation was based on completing the filming, not the time consumed. If she did not film an episode she did not get paid.

Fifth, WIPR did not provide Alberty with benefits. * * *

Sixth, Alberty's tax treatment suggests independent-contractor status. * * *

Despite these factors favoring independent-contractor status, Alberty argues that she was WIPR's employee because WIPR controlled the manner of her work by directing her during filming, dictated the location of her work by selecting the filming sites, and determined the hours of her work * * * . *While "control" over the manner, location, and hours of work is often critical to the independent contractor/employee analysis, it must be considered in light of the work performed and the industry at issue.* Considering the tasks that an actor performs, we do not believe that the sort of control identified by Alberty necessarily indicates employee status. [Emphasis added.]

---

a. In the right-hand column, click on "Opinions." When that page opens, under "General Search," type "02-2187" in the "Opinion Number begins with" box, and click on "Submit Query." In the result, click on the appropriate link to access the opinion. The U.S. Court of Appeals for the First Circuit maintains this Web site.

CASE 31.1 Continued

* * * *

* * * Alberty's work on "Desde Mi Pueblo" required her to film at the featured sites at the required times and to follow the instructions of the director. WIPR could only achieve its goal of producing its program by having Alberty follow these directions. Just as an orchestra musician is subject to the control of the conductor during concerts and rehearsals, an actor is subject to the control of the director during filming. * * *

* * * *

While no one factor is dispositive [determines the outcome], it is clear, based on the parties' entire relationship, that a reasonable fact finder could only conclude that Alberty was an independent contractor. * * * Accordingly, we conclude that Alberty was an independent contractor as a matter of law and therefore cannot maintain [this] action against WIPR.

DECISION AND REMEDY *The U.S. Court of Appeals for the First Circuit affirmed the lower court's judgment in WIPR's favor. The court stated, "The parties structured their relationship through the use of set length contracts that permitted Alberty the freedom to pursue other opportunities and assured WIPR that it would not have to pay Alberty for the weeks that it was not filming. Further, the lack of benefits, the method of payment, and the parties' own description of their relationship in tax documents all indicate independent-contractor status."*

WHAT IF THE FACTS WERE DIFFERENT? *Suppose that Alberty had been a full-time, hourly worker and that such status was common among television hosts, but WIPR had manipulated the benefits and tax-treatment factors to favor independent-contractor status. How might the result have been different?*

CRITERIA USED BY THE IRS Businesspersons should be aware that the Internal Revenue Service (IRS) has established its own criteria for determining whether a worker is an independent contractor or an employee. Although the IRS once considered twenty factors in determining a worker's status, guidelines that took effect in 1997 encourage IRS examiners to look closely at just one of those factors—the degree of control the business exercises over the worker.

The IRS tends to scrutinize closely a firm's classification of a worker as an independent contractor rather than an employee because employers can avoid certain tax liabilities by hiring independent contractors instead of employees. Even when the firm has classified a worker as an independent contractor, if the IRS decides that the worker is actually an employee, then the employer will be responsible for paying any applicable Social Security, withholding, and unemployment taxes. For example, in one widely publicized case, Microsoft Corporation was ordered to pay back payroll taxes for hundreds of temporary workers who had contractually agreed to work for Microsoft as independent contractors.[2]

In contrast, when a worker is a corporate officer, the exercise of control may be the opposite of the usual situation involving an employer and an employee. In that circumstance, the question may concern the degree of control that the officer (the employee) exercises over the corporation (the employer). In the following case, the issue was whether a corporate officer was an employee of the corporation.

2. *Vizcaino v. U.S. District Court for the Western District of Washington,* 173 F.3d 713 (9th Cir. 1999).

CASE 31.2

United States
Court of Appeals,
Third Circuit, 2004.
356 F.3d 290.

Nu-Look Design, Inc. v. Commissioner of Internal Revenue

BACKGROUND AND FACTS *Nu-Look Design, Inc., is a home-improvement company involved in carpentry, siding installation, and general residential construction services. During 1996, 1997, and 1998, Ronald Stark was Nu-Look's president, manager, and sole shareholder. He solicited business for the company, performed the bookkeeping, handled the firm's finances, and hired and supervised its workers. Instead of paying Stark a salary or wages, Nu-Look distributed its income to him "as Mr. Stark's needs arose." Nu-Look reported on its tax returns for those years net income of $10,866.14, $14,216.37, and $7,103.60, respectively. Stark reported the same amounts as income*

CONTINUED ▶

CASE 31.2 Continued

on his tax returns. In 2001, the Internal Revenue Service (IRS) classified Stark as Nu-Look's employee and assessed federal employment taxes for 1996, 1997, and 1998. Nu-Look filed a suit in the U.S. Tax Court against the commissioner of the IRS, seeking relief from this liability. Nu-Look contended in part that Stark was not an employee because Nu-Look did not control Stark—Stark controlled Nu-Look. The court ruled against the firm, which appealed to the U.S. Court of Appeals for the Third Circuit.

IN THE LANGUAGE OF THE COURT

SMITH, Circuit Judge.

This appeal challenges the determination by the United States Tax Court that the Internal Revenue Service ("IRS") appropriately classified Ronald A. Stark, who was an officer and the sole shareholder of Nu-Look Design, Inc. ("Nu-Look"), as an employee of Nu-Look. That determination resulted in Nu-Look's liability for certain employment taxes under the Federal Insurance Contributions Act ("FICA") and the Federal Unemployment Tax Act ("FUTA"). * * *

* * * *

Nu-Look contends that the Tax Court erred in determining that Stark was an employee under the FICA and the FUTA. We begin by looking to the statutory language. Where the statutory language is plain and unambiguous, further inquiry is not required * * * .

Both the FICA and the FUTA impose taxes on employers based on the wages paid to individuals in their employ. "Wages," *as defined by both Acts, includes, with certain exceptions not applicable here,* "all remuneration for employment * * * ." *Employment is* "any service of whatever nature, performed * * * by an employee for the person employing him * * * ." *Employee is defined by the FICA [to include]* * * * *any officer of a corporation* * * * . Under the FUTA, the term *employee*, with certain exceptions not relevant here, has the same meaning * * * . [Under the IRS regulations] there is an exception for an "officer of a corporation who as such does not perform any services or performs only minor services and who neither receives nor is entitled to receive, directly or indirectly, any remuneration." [Emphasis added.]

* * * *

Mindful of these statutory provisions and Stark's status as a corporate officer, the Tax Court appropriately focused on the nature of the services Stark rendered and whether the distributions Nu-Look paid were remuneration for those services. It found that Stark performed more than minor services and that the distributions Stark received were, in fact, remuneration for his services. Those findings led the Tax Court to conclude that Stark was an employee for purposes of the FICA and the FUTA.

We agree. The record establishes that Stark was a corporate officer and that he single-handedly managed Nu-Look's entire operation. The services that Stark rendered for Nu-Look were, therefore, substantial and the Tax Court appropriately concluded that Stark was an employee * * * .

* * * *

In sum, we conclude that Stark was properly classified by the IRS as an employee of Nu-Look and that Nu-Look lacked a reasonable basis for failing to treat Stark as an employee. We will affirm the decision of the Tax Court that Nu-Look is liable for certain employment taxes under the FICA and the FUTA for calendar years 1996, 1997 and 1998.

DECISION AND REMEDY *The U.S. Court of Appeals for the Third Circuit affirmed the ruling of the lower court. For federal tax purposes, Stark was to be considered an employee of Nu-Look, in light of the nature of the services that he rendered to the company and the income that the firm distributed to him as payment for those services.*

EMPLOYEE STATUS AND "WORKS FOR HIRE"

Under the Copyright Act of 1976, any copyrighted work created by an employee within the scope of her or his employment at the request of the employer is a "work for hire," and the employer owns the copyright to the work. In contrast, when an employer hires an independent contractor—a freelance artist, writer, or computer programmer, for example—the independent contractor normally owns the copyright. In this situation, the employer can own the copyright only if the parties agree in writing that the work is a "work for hire" and the work falls into one of nine specific categories, including audiovisual and other works.

In one case, for example, Graham marketed CD-ROM discs containing compilations of software programs that are available free to the public. Graham hired James to create a file-retrieval program that allowed users to access the software on the CDs. James built into the final version of the program a notice stating that he was the author of the program and owned the copyright. Graham removed the notice. When James sold the program to another CD-ROM publisher, Graham filed a suit claiming that James's program was a "work for hire" and that Graham owned the copyright to the file-retrieval program. The court, however, decided that James—who was a skilled computer programmer who controlled the manner and method of his work—was an independent contractor and not an employee for hire. Thus, James owned the copyright to the file-retrieval program.[3]

SECTION 2 | Formation of the Agency Relationship

Agency relationships normally are *consensual*; in other words, they come about by voluntary consent and agreement between the parties. Generally, the agreement need not be in writing,[4] and consideration is not required.

A principal must have contractual capacity.[5] A person who cannot legally enter into contracts directly should not be allowed to do so indirectly through an agent. Any person can be an agent, however, regardless of whether he or she has the capacity to contract. Because an agent derives the authority to enter into

contracts from the principal and because a contract made by an agent is legally viewed as a contract of the principal, it is immaterial whether the agent personally has the legal capacity to make that contract. Thus, even a minor or a person who is legally incompetent can be appointed as an agent.

An agency relationship can be created for any legal purpose. An agency relationship created for a purpose that is illegal or contrary to public policy is unenforceable. If LaSalle (as principal) contracts with Burke (as agent) to sell illegal narcotics, the agency relationship is unenforceable because selling illegal narcotics is a felony and is contrary to public policy. It is also illegal for physicians and other licensed professionals to employ unlicensed agents to perform professional actions.

Generally, an agency relationship can arise in four ways: by agreement of the parties, by ratification, by estoppel, and by operation of law. We look here at each of these possibilities.

AGENCY BY AGREEMENT

Most agency relationships are based on an express or implied agreement that the agent will act for the principal and that the principal agrees to have the agent so act. An agency agreement can take the form of an express written contract. For example, Henchen enters into a written agreement with Vogel, a real estate agent, to sell Henchen's house. An agency relationship exists between Henchen and Vogel for the sale of the house and is detailed in a document that both parties sign.

Many express agency relationships are created by oral agreement and are not based on a written contract. If Henchen asks Grace, a gardener, to contract with others for the care of his lawn on a regular basis, and Grace agrees, an agency relationship exists between Henchen and Grace for the lawn care.

An agency agreement can also be implied by conduct. For example, a hotel expressly allows only Hans Cooper to park cars, but Hans has no employment contract there. The hotel's manager tells Hans when to work, as well as where and how to park the cars. The hotel's conduct amounts to a manifestation of its willingness to have Hans park its customers' cars, and Hans can infer from the hotel's conduct that he has authority to act as a parking valet. It can be inferred that Hans is an agent for the hotel, his purpose being to provide valet parking services for hotel guests.

---

3. *Graham v. James*, 144 F.3d 229 (2d Cir. 1998).

4. There are two main exceptions to the statement that agency agreements need not be in writing. An agency agreement must be in writing (1) whenever agency authority empowers the agent to enter into a contract that the Statute of Frauds requires to be in writing (this is called the *equal dignity rule*, to be discussed in the next chapter) and (2) whenever an agent is given power of attorney.

5. Note that some states allow a minor to be a principal. When a minor is permitted to be a principal, however, any resulting contracts will be voidable by the minor principal but *not* by the adult third party.

AGENCY BY RATIFICATION

On occasion, a person who is in fact not an agent may make a contract on behalf of another (a principal). If the principal approves or affirms that contract by word or by action, an agency relationship is created by ratification. Ratification involves a question of intent, and intent can be expressed by either words or conduct. The basic requirements for ratification will be discussed in Chapter 32.

AGENCY BY ESTOPPEL

When a principal causes a third person to believe that another person is the principal's agent, and the third person acts to his or her detriment in reasonable reliance on that belief, the principal is "estopped to deny" the agency relationship. In such a situation, the principal's actions have created the *appearance* of an agency that does not in fact exist. The third person must prove that he or she *reasonably* believed that an agency relationship existed, however.[6]

Suppose that Jerry accompanies Grant, a seed sales representative, to call on a customer, Palko, who is the proprietor of the Neighborhood Seed Store. Jerry has performed independent sales work but has never signed an employment agreement with Grant. Grant boasts to Palko that he wishes he had three more assistants "just like Jerry." By making this representation,

Grant creates the impression that Jerry is his agent and has authority to solicit orders. Palko has reason to believe from Grant's statements that Jerry is an agent for Grant. Palko then places seed orders with Jerry.

If Grant does not correct the impression that Jerry is an agent, Grant will be bound to fill the orders just as if Jerry were really Grant's agent. The acts or declarations of a purported agent in and of themselves do not create an agency by estoppel. Rather, it is the deeds or statements *of the principal* that create an agency by estoppel. If Jerry walked into Palko's store and claimed to be Grant's agent, when in fact he was not, and Grant had no knowledge of Jerry's representations, Grant would not be bound to any deal struck by Jerry and Palko.

AGENCY BY OPERATION OF LAW

The courts may find an agency relationship in the absence of a formal agreement in other situations as well. This may occur in family relationships. For example, suppose one spouse purchases certain basic necessaries (such as food or clothing—see Chapter 13) and charges them to the other spouse's charge account. The courts will often rule that the latter is liable for payment of the necessaries, either because of a social policy of promoting the general welfare of the spouse or because of a legal duty to supply necessaries to family members.

Agency by operation of law may also occur in emergency situations, when the agent's failure to act outside the scope of her or his authority would cause the principal substantial loss. If the agent is unable to con-

---

6. These concepts also apply when a person who is in fact an agent undertakes an action that is beyond the scope of her or his authority, as will be discussed in Chapter 32.

CONCEPT SUMMARY 31.1 | Formation of the Agency Relationship

METHOD OF FORMATION	DESCRIPTION
BY AGREEMENT	Agency relationship is formed through express consent (oral or written) or implied by conduct.
BY RATIFICATION	Principal either by act or by agreement ratifies conduct of a person who is not in fact an agent.
BY ESTOPPEL	Principal causes a third person to believe that another person is the principal's agent, and the third person acts to his or her detriment in reasonable reliance on that belief.
BY OPERATION OF LAW	Agency relationship is based on a social duty (such as the need to support family members) or formed in emergency situations when the agent is unable to contact the principal.

tact the principal, the courts will often grant this emergency power. For example, a railroad engineer may contract on behalf of his or her employer for medical care for an injured motorist hit by the train.

SECTION 3 | Duties of Agents and Principals

Once the principal-agent relationship has been created, both parties have duties that govern their conduct. As discussed previously, the principal-agent relationship is *fiduciary*—one of trust. In a fiduciary relationship, each party owes the other the duty to act with the utmost good faith. In this section, we examine the various duties of agents and principals.

AGENT'S DUTIES TO THE PRINCIPAL

Generally, the agent owes the principal five duties—performance, notification, loyalty, obedience, and accounting.

PERFORMANCE An implied condition in every agency contract is the agent's agreement to use reasonable diligence and skill in performing the work. When an agent fails to perform his or her duties, liability for breach of contract may result. The degree of skill or care required of an agent is usually that expected of a reasonable person under similar circumstances. Generally, this is interpreted to mean ordinary care. If an agent has represented herself or himself as possessing special skills, however, the agent is expected to exercise the degree of skill or skills claimed. Failure to do so constitutes a breach of the agent's duty.

Not all agency relationships are based on contract. In some situations, an agent acts gratuitously—that is, without payment. A gratuitous agent cannot be liable for breach of contract, as there is no contract; he or she is subject only to tort liability. Once a gratuitous agent has begun to act in an agency capacity, he or she has the duty to continue to perform in that capacity in an acceptable manner and is subject to the same standards of care and duty to perform as other agents.

For example, Bower's friend Alcott is a real estate broker. Alcott offers to sell Bower's farm at no charge. If Alcott never attempts to sell the farm, Bower has no legal cause of action to force her to do so. If Alcott does find a buyer, however, but negligently fails to follow through with the sales contract, causing the buyer

to seek other property, then Bower can sue Alcott for negligence.

NOTIFICATION An agent is required to notify the principal of all matters that come to her or his attention concerning the subject matter of the agency. This is the *duty of notification*, or the duty to inform. For example, suppose that Lang, an artist, is about to negotiate a contract to sell a series of paintings to Barber's Art Gallery for $25,000. Lang's agent learns that Barber is insolvent and will be unable to pay for the paintings. Lang's agent has a duty to inform Lang of this knowledge because it is relevant to the subject matter of the agency—the sale of Lang's paintings. Generally, the law assumes that the principal is aware of any information acquired by the agent that is relevant to the agency—regardless of whether the agent actually passes on this information to the principal.

LOYALTY Loyalty is one of the most fundamental duties in a fiduciary relationship. Basically stated, the agent has the duty to act *solely for the benefit of his or her principal* and not in the interest of the agent or a third party. For example, an agent cannot represent two principals in the same transaction unless both know of the dual capacity and consent to it. The duty of loyalty also means that any information or knowledge acquired through the agency relationship is confidential. It would be a breach of loyalty to disclose such information either during the agency relationship or after its termination. Typical examples of confidential information are trade secrets and customer lists compiled by the principal (see Chapters 8 and 13).

In short, the agent's loyalty must be undivided. The agent's actions must be strictly for the benefit of the principal and must not result in any secret profit for the agent. For example, suppose that Remington contracts with Averly, a real estate agent, to sell Remington's property. Averly knows that he can find a buyer who will pay substantially more for the property than Remington is asking. If Averly were to secretly purchase Remington's property, however, and sell it at a profit to another buyer, Averly would breach his duty of loyalty as Remington's agent. Averly has a duty to act in Remington's best interests and can only become the purchaser in this situation with Remington's knowledge and approval.[7]

---

7. For a further discussion of the duty of loyalty and some of the challenges it can present for agent-employees, see the *Focus on Ethics* feature following Chapter 34.

The following case involved a real estate agent who discovered, while working for a principal, that the property owner would only sell the property as a package deal with another parcel. If the agent buys the property to resell it to the principal, does the agent breach the duty of loyalty? That was one of the issues in the following case.

CASE 31.3

Court of Appeal
of Louisiana,
Fifth Circuit, 2003.
844 So.2d 860.

Cousins v. Realty Ventures, Inc.

MARION F. EDWARDS, Judge.

* * * *

* * * Don Cousins acted as the representative/agent for Eagle Ventures [Inc.] * * * to find a real estate investment for the corporation to purchase. To do so, Mr. Cousins engaged the services of Leo Hodgins, a real estate agent/broker and owner of Realty Ventures, Inc. ("RVI").

* * * *

In March of 1991, Leo Hodgins learned that 3330 Lake Villa Drive, an 8,000-square-foot office building [in Metairie, Louisiana], owned by Westinghouse Credit Corporation, was being sold for $125,000 * * * . In June 1991, Leo Hodgins first brought 3330 Lake Villa to Mr. Cousins' attention. * * * [Cousins] asked [Hodgins] to submit an offer to Westinghouse on [behalf of] Eagle Ventures, Inc. for $90,000.00 * * * . Mr. Hodgins submitted the offer to Westinghouse * * * .

* * * Westinghouse * * * was unable to sell the property at the time because it was having difficulties with Tonti Management, which was managing some of its local commercial holdings * * * .

In October 1991, Leo Hodgins resubmitted Eagle Ventures' June 1991 offer * * * . Hodgins [learned] that Westinghouse was ready to sell 3330 Lake Villa, but only as part of a package deal with its neighboring property, 4141 Veterans Boulevard * * * .

* * * *

In April 1992, Mr. Hodgins and his brother, Paul, created a * * * partnership, known as 4141 Vets Limited Partnership, to purchase the property * * * . On May 7, 1992, Westinghouse sold 3330 Lake Villa to 4141 Vets Limited Partnership for $65,000.00 and sold 4141 Veterans to the same * * * partnership for $355,000.00. [Hodgins then offered to sell 3330 Lake Villa to Eagle Ventures for $175,000.]

* * * [P]laintiffs, Don Cousins [and others] filed the instant suit against defendants, * * * Realty Ventures, Inc. [and others]. Plaintiffs' suit alleged that defendants breached their fiduciary duties to them * * * .

* * * [T]he jury returned a verdict in favor of plaintiffs * * * and awarded damages in the amount of $1,750,000 * * * .

Defendants filed this * * * appeal. Plaintiffs answered the appeal.

* * * *

The precise duties of a real estate broker must be determined by an examination of the nature of the task the real estate agent undertakes to perform and the agreements he makes with the involved parties. In the instant case, Leo Hodgins accepted Mr. Cousins' request to find commercial real estate for Eagle Ventures to purchase by turning his attention to 3330 Lake Villa. * * * The [common law] * * * sets forth the types of duties expected of a real estate agent. For example, a real estate agent may be found liable where he or she does not timely communicate an offer and that failure to communicate results in damages to the client. *Similarly, a real estate broker has been found to have a duty to communicate to his principal all offers received and may be liable in damages for failure to do so.* Moreover, a [R]ealtor has a duty to relay accurate information about property, a duty which extends to both vendor and purchaser, and may be held liable if such duty is breached. [Emphasis added.]

* * * *

Plaintiffs argued at trial that Leo Hodgins committed a breach of his fiduciary duty to them in several respects [including] * * * failing to communicate Westinghouse's response to their

CASE 31.3 | Continued offer * * * . Defendants argue they owed no further duty to plaintiffs after the June purchase offer for 3330 Lake Villa was submitted to Westinghouse. Once Westinghouse responded that it could not sell the property due to the property management agreement * * * , Leo Hodgins relayed this information to Don Cousins. Plaintiffs contend that the agent/client relationship persisted far beyond that point based on Leo Hodgins' resubmission of Eagle Ventures' offer in October. They argue that the information regarding the package sale of 3330 Lake Villa and 4141 Veterans Boulevard constituted a counter-offer by Westinghouse that should have been communicated to Mr. Cousins. * * *

In our opinion, * * * as late as February or March of 1992, Mr. Cousins was still communicating with Leo Hodgins regarding the status of his offer and Leo Hodgins was still discussing Eagle Ventures' offer with Westinghouse as late as January 1992. We believe Mr. Cousins acted consistently with his belief that Leo Hodgins was acting as his agent with Westinghouse at that time, while Leo Hodgins did nothing to dispel that belief. * * * During some of that time, Leo Hodgins was armed with the information that 3330 Lake Villa was only for sale as a package with 4141 Veterans Boulevard and was covertly planning to acquire the property himself. * * * [Hodgins] never told Don Cousins or anyone else associated with Eagle Ventures about Westinghouse's decision to sell the properties together prior to March 1992. *Leo Hodgins' failure to communicate the package sale to plaintiffs the moment he learned of it constituted a breach of his fiduciary duties to them.* Leo Hodgins' duty was to give plaintiffs the information that Westinghouse rejected their offer for a single property sale and allow them to decide whether they wished to purchase both properties. [Emphasis added.]

* * * [W]e conclude the jury's finding that the defendants fraudulently breached their fiduciary duty to plaintiffs is not manifestly erroneous.

* * * *

Accordingly, the judgment is * * * affirmed.

QUESTIONS

1. Suppose that the agent was not aware that his actions breached a fiduciary duty owed to his principal. Would the agent's lack of awareness have affected the outcome in this case? Why or why not?
2. Do the facts in the *Cousins* case indicate steps that an investor might want to consider when dealing through an agent?

OBEDIENCE When an agent is acting on behalf of the principal, a duty is imposed on that agent to follow all lawful and clearly stated instructions of the principal. Any deviation from such instructions is a violation of this duty. During emergency situations, however, when the principal cannot be consulted, the agent may deviate from the instructions without violating this duty. Whenever instructions are not clearly stated, the agent can fulfill the duty of obedience by acting in good faith and in a manner reasonable under the circumstances.

ACCOUNTING Unless an agent and a principal agree otherwise, the agent has the duty to keep and make available to the principal an account of all property and funds received and paid out on behalf of the principal. The agent has a duty to maintain separate accounts for the principal's funds and the agent's personal funds, and no intermingling of these accounts is allowed. Whenever a licensed professional (such as an attorney) violates this duty to account, he or she may be subject to disciplinary proceedings carried out by the appropriate regulatory institution (such as the state bar association) in addition to being liable to the principal (the professional's client) for failure to account.

PRINCIPAL'S DUTIES TO THE AGENT

The principal also has certain duties to the agent. These duties relate to compensation, reimbursement and indemnification, cooperation, and safe working conditions.

COMPENSATION In general, when a principal requests certain services from an agent, the agent reasonably expects payment. The principal therefore has a duty to pay the agent for services rendered. For example, when an accountant or an attorney is asked to act as an agent, an agreement to compensate the agent for this service is implied. The principal also has a duty to pay that compensation in a timely manner. Except in a gratuitous agency relationship, in which the agent does not act for money, the principal must pay the agreed-on value for the agent's services. If no amount has been expressly agreed on, then the principal owes the agent the customary compensation for such services.

REIMBURSEMENT AND INDEMNIFICATION Whenever an agent disburses sums of money to fulfill the request of the principal or to pay for necessary expenses in the course of a reasonable performance of her or his agency duties, the principal has the duty to reimburse the agent for these payments.[8] Agents cannot recover for expenses incurred by their own misconduct or negligence, however.

Subject to the terms of the agency agreement, the principal has the duty to *indemnify* (compensate) an agent for liabilities incurred because of authorized and lawful acts and transactions. For example, if the agent, on the principal's behalf, forms a contract with a third party, and the principal fails to perform the contract, the third party may sue the agent for damages. In this situation, the principal is obligated to compensate the agent for any costs incurred by the agent as a result of the principal's failure to perform the contract. Additionally, the principal must indemnify the agent for the value of benefits that the agent confers on the principal. The amount of indemnification is usually specified in the agency contract. If it is not, the courts will look to the nature of the business and the type of loss to determine the amount.

COOPERATION A principal has a duty to cooperate with the agent and to assist the agent in performing his or her duties. The principal must do nothing to prevent such performance. For example, when a principal grants an agent an exclusive territory, creating an *exclusive agency*, the principal cannot compete with the agent or appoint or allow another agent to so compete in violation of the exclusive agency. If the principal did so, she or he would be exposed to liability for the agent's lost sales or profits.

SAFE WORKING CONDITIONS The common law requires the principal to provide safe working premises, equipment, and conditions for all agents and employees. The principal has a duty to inspect working areas and to warn agents and employees about any unsafe situations. When the agent is an employee, the employer's liability is frequently covered by state workers' compensation insurance, and federal and state statutes often require the employer to meet certain safety standards (see Chapter 33).

SECTION 4 | Rights and Remedies of Agents and Principals

It is said that every wrong has its remedy. In business situations, disputes between agents and principals may arise out of either contract or tort laws and carry corresponding remedies. These remedies include monetary damages, termination of the agency relationship, injunction, and required accountings.

AGENT'S RIGHTS AND REMEDIES AGAINST THE PRINCIPAL

For every duty of the principal, the agent has a corresponding right. Therefore, the agent has the right to be compensated, reimbursed, and indemnified and to work in a safe environment. An agent also has the right to perform agency duties without interference by the principal.

TORT AND CONTRACT REMEDIES Remedies of the agent for breach of duty by the principal follow normal contract and tort remedies. For example, suppose that Aaron Hart, a builder who has just completed construction on a new house, contracts with a real estate agent, Fran Boller, to sell the house. The contract calls for the agent to have an exclusive, ninety-day listing and to receive 6 percent of the selling price when the home is sold. Boller holds several

---

8. This principle applies to acts by gratuitous agents as well. If a finder of a dog that becomes sick takes the dog to a veterinarian and pays the required fees for the veterinarian's services, the agent is entitled to be reimbursed by the owner of the dog for those fees.

open houses and shows the home to a number of potential buyers. One month before the ninety-day listing terminates, Hart agrees to sell the house to another buyer—not one to whom Boller has shown the house—after the ninety-day listing expires. Hart and the buyer agree that Hart will reduce the price of the house by 3 percent, because he will sell it directly and thus will not have to pay Boller's commission. In this situation, if Boller learns of Hart's actions, she can terminate the agency relationship and sue Hart for damages—including the 6 percent commission she should have earned on the sale of the house.

DEMAND FOR AN ACCOUNTING An agent can also withhold further performance and demand that the principal give an accounting. For example, a sales agent may demand an accounting if the agent and principal disagree on the amount of commissions the agent should have received for sales made during a specific period of time.

NO RIGHT TO SPECIFIC PERFORMANCE In a situation in which the principal-agent relationship is not contractual, an agent has no right to specific performance. An agent can recover for past services and future damages but cannot force the principal to allow him or her to continue acting as an agent.

PRINCIPAL'S RIGHTS AND REMEDIES AGAINST THE AGENT

In general, a principal has contract remedies for an agent's breach of fiduciary duties. The principal also has tort remedies if the agent commits misrepresentation, negligence, deceit, libel, slander, or trespass. In addition, any breach of a fiduciary duty by an agent may justify the principal's termination of the agency. The main actions available to the principal are constructive trust, avoidance, and indemnification.

CONSTRUCTIVE TRUST Anything that an agent obtains by virtue of the employment or agency relationship belongs to the principal. An agent commits a breach of fiduciary duty if he or she secretly retains benefits or profits that, by right, belong to the principal. For example, Andrews, a purchasing agent, receives cash rebates from a customer. If Andrews keeps the rebates, he violates his fiduciary duty to his

principal, Metcalf. On finding out about the cash rebates, Metcalf can sue Andrews and recover them.

An agent is also prohibited from taking advantage of the agency relationship to obtain goods or property that the principal wants to purchase. For example, Peterson (the principal) wants to purchase property in the suburbs. Cox, Peterson's agent, learns that a valuable tract of land has just become available. Cox cannot buy the land for herself. Peterson gets the right of first refusal. If Cox purchases the land for her own benefit, the courts will impose a *constructive trust* on the land; that is, the land will be held for, and on behalf of, the principal despite the fact that the agent attempted to buy it in her own name.

AVOIDANCE When an agent breaches the agency agreement or agency duties under a contract, the principal has a right to avoid any contract entered into with the agent. This right of avoidance is at the election of the principal.

INDEMNIFICATION In certain situations, when a principal is sued by a third party for an agent's negligent conduct, the principal can sue the agent for an equal amount of damages. This is called *indemnification*. The same holds true if the agent violates the principal's instructions. For example, Parke (the principal) tells his agent Moore, who is a used-car salesperson, to make no warranties for the used cars. Moore is eager to make a sale to Walters, a third party, and adds a 50,000-mile warranty for the car's engine. Parke may still be liable to Walters for engine failure, but if Walters sues Parke, Parke normally can then sue Moore for indemnification for violating his instructions.

Sometimes, it is difficult to distinguish between instructions of the principal that limit an agent's authority and those that are merely advice. For example, Gutierrez (the principal) owns an office supply company; Logan (the agent) is the manager. Gutierrez tells Logan, "Don't purchase any more inventory this month." Gutierrez goes on vacation. A large order comes in from a local business, and the present inventory is insufficient to meet it. What is Logan to do? In this situation, Logan probably has the inherent authority to purchase more inventory despite Gutierrez's command. It is unlikely that Logan would be required to indemnify Gutierrez in the event that the local business subsequently canceled the order.

REVIEWING AGENCY FORMATION AND DUTIES

James Blatt hired Marilyn Scott to sell insurance for the Massachusetts Mutual Life Insurance Co. Their contract stated, "Nothing in this contract shall be construed as creating the relationship of employer and employee." The contract was terminable at will by either party. Scott financed her own office and staff, was paid according to performance, had no taxes withheld from her checks, and could legally sell products of Massachusetts Mutual's competitors. But when Blatt learned that Scott was simultaneously selling insurance for Perpetual Life Insurance Corp., one of Massachusetts Mutual's fiercest competitors, Blatt withheld client contact information from Scott that would have assisted her insurance sales for Massachusetts Mutual. Scott complained to Blatt that he was inhibiting her ability to sell insurance for Massachusetts Mutual. Blatt subsequently terminated their contract. Scott filed a suit in a New York state court against Blatt and Massachusetts Mutual. Scott claimed that she had lost sales for Massachusetts Mutual—and her commissions—as a result of Blatt's withholding contact information from her. Using the information presented in the chapter, answer the following questions.

1. | Who is the principal and who is the agent in this scenario? By which method was an agency relationship formed between Scott and Blatt?

2. | What criteria would the court consider to determine whether Scott was an employee or an independent contractor?

3. | How would the IRS decide Scott's employee status?

4. | What four duties did Blatt owe Scott in their agency relationship? Which, if any, of those duties has been breached?

5. | What five duties did Scott owe Blatt? Did Scott breach any of her duties by selling insurance for Perpetual Life? Explain.

TERMS AND CONCEPTS TO REVIEW

agency 636   fiduciary 636   independent contractor 637

QUESTIONS AND CASE PROBLEMS

31–1. Paul Gett is a well-known, wealthy financial expert living in the city of Torris. Adam Wade, Gett's friend, tells Timothy Brown that he is Gett's agent for the purchase of rare coins. Wade even shows Brown a local newspaper clipping mentioning Gett's interest in coin collecting. Brown, knowing of Wade's friendship with Gett, contracts with Wade to sell a rare coin valued at $25,000 to Gett. Wade takes the coin and disappears with it. On the payment due date, Brown seeks to collect from Gett, claiming that Wade's agency made Gett liable. Gett does not deny that Wade was a friend, but he claims that Wade was never his agent. Discuss fully whether an agency was in existence at the time the contract for the rare coin was made.

31–2. QUESTION WITH SAMPLE ANSWER

Peter hires Alice as an agent to sell a piece of property he owns. The price is to be at least $30,000. Alice discovers

that because a shopping mall is planned for the area where Peter's property is located, the fair market value of the property will be at least $45,000 and could be higher. Alice forms a real estate partnership with her cousin Carl, and she prepares for Peter's signature a contract for the sale of the property to Carl for $32,000. Peter signs the contract. Just before closing and passage of title, Peter learns about the shopping mall and the increased fair market value of his property. Peter refuses to deed the property to Carl. Carl claims that Alice, as agent, solicited a price above that agreed on when the agency was created and that the contract is therefore binding and enforceable. Discuss fully whether Peter is bound to this contract.
For a sample answer to this question, go to Appendix I at the end of this text.

31–3. John Paul Corp. made the following contracts:

(a) A contract with Able Construction to build an addition to the corporate office building.

(b) A contract with a certified public accountant (CPA), a recent college graduate, to head the cost-accounting division.

(c) A contract with a salesperson to solicit orders (contracts) for the corporation in a designated territory.

Able contracts with Apex for materials for the addition; the CPA hires an experienced accountant to advise her on certain accounting procedures; and the salesperson contracts to sell a large order to Green, agreeing to deliver the goods in person within twenty days. Later, Able refuses to pick up the materials, the CPA is in default in paying the hired consultant, and the salesperson does not deliver on time. Apex, the accountant, and Green claim John Paul Corp. is liable under agency law. Discuss fully whether an agency relationship was created by John Paul with Able, the CPA, or the salesperson.

31–4. Ankir is hired by Jamison as a traveling salesperson. Ankir not only solicits orders but also delivers the goods and collects payments from his customers. Ankir places all payments in his private checking account and at the end of each month draws sufficient cash from his bank to cover the payments made. Jamison is totally unaware of this procedure. Because of a slowdown in the economy, Jamison tells all his salespeople to offer 20 percent discounts on orders. Ankir solicits orders, but he offers only 15 percent discounts, pocketing the extra 5 percent paid by customers. Ankir has not lost any orders by this practice, and he is rated one of Jamison's top salespersons. Jamison learns of Ankir's actions. Discuss fully Jamison's rights in this matter.

31–5. EMPLOYEE VERSUS INDEPENDENT CONTRACTOR. Stephen Hemmerling was a driver for the Happy Cab Co. Hemmerling paid certain fixed expenses and abided by a variety of rules relating to the use of the cab, the hours that could be worked, the solicitation of fares, and so on. Rates were set by the state. Happy Cab did not withhold taxes from Hemmerling's pay. While driving a cab, Hemmerling was injured in an accident and filed a claim against Happy Cab in a Nebraska state court for workers' compensation benefits. Such benefits are not available to independent contractors. On what basis might the court hold that Hemmerling is an employee? Explain. [*Hemmerling v. Happy Cab Co.*, 247 Neb. 919, 530 N.W.2d 916 (1995)]

31–6. AGENT'S DUTIES TO PRINCIPAL. Ana Barreto and Flavia Gugliuzzi asked Ruth Bennett, a real estate salesperson who worked for Smith Bell Real Estate, to list for sale their house in the Pleasant Valley area of Underhill, Vermont. Diana Carter, a California resident, visited the house as a potential buyer. Bennett worked under the supervision of David Crane, an officer of Smith Bell. Crane knew, but did not disclose to Bennett or Carter, that the house was subject to frequent and severe winds, that a window had blown in years earlier, and that other houses in the area had suffered wind damage. Crane knew of this because he lived in the Pleasant Valley area, had sold a number of nearby properties, and had been Underhill's zoning officer. Many valley residents, including Crane, had wind gauges on their homes to measure and compare wind speeds with their neighbors. Carter bought the house, and several months later, high winds blew in a number of windows and otherwise damaged the property. Carter filed a suit in a Vermont state court against Smith Bell and others, alleging fraud. She argued in part that Crane's knowledge of the winds was imputable to Smith Bell. Smith Bell responded that Crane's knowledge was obtained outside the scope of employment. What is the rule regarding how much of an agent's knowledge a principal is assumed to know? How should the court rule in this case? Why? [*Carter v. Gugliuzzi*, 168 Vt. 48, 716 A.2d 17 (1998)]

31–7. ⚖️ **CASE PROBLEM WITH SAMPLE ANSWER**

Sam and Theresa Daigle decided to build a home in Cameron Parish, Louisiana. To obtain financing, they contacted Trinity United Mortgage Co. At a meeting with Joe Diez on Trinity's behalf, on July 18, 2001, the Daigles signed a temporary loan agreement with Union Planters Bank. Diez assured them that they did not need to make payments on this loan until their house was built and that permanent financing had been secured. Because the Daigles did not make payments on the Union loan, Trinity declined to make the permanent loan. Meanwhile, Diez left Trinity's employ. On November 1, the Daigles moved into their new house. They tried to contact Diez at Trinity but were told that he was unavailable and would get back to them. Three weeks later, Diez came to the Daigles' home and had them sign documents that they believed were to secure a permanent loan but that were actually an application with Diez's new employer. Union filed a suit in a Louisiana state court against the Daigles for failing to pay on its loan. The Daigles paid Union, obtained permanent financing through another source, and filed a suit against Trinity to recover the cost. Who should have told the Daigles that Diez was no longer Trinity's agent? Could Trinity be liable to the Daigles on this basis? Explain. [*Daigle v. Trinity United Mortgage, L.L.C.*, 890 So.2d 583 (La.App. 3 Cir. 2004)]

To view a sample answer for this case problem, go to this book's Web site at http://wbl.westbuslaw.com, select "Chapter 31," and click on "Case Problem with Sample Answer."

31–8. AGENCY FORMATION. Ford Motor Credit Co. is a subsidiary of Ford Motor Co. with its own offices, officers, and directors. Ford Credit buys contracts and leases of automobiles entered into by dealers and consumers. Ford Credit also provides inventory financing for dealers' purchases of Ford and non-Ford vehicles and makes loans to Ford and non-Ford dealers. Dealers and consumers are not required to finance their purchases or leases of Ford vehicles through Ford Credit. Ford Motor is not a party to the agreements between Ford Credit and its customers and does not directly receive any payments under those agreements. Also, Ford Credit is not subject to any agreement with Ford Motor "restricting or conditioning" its ability to finance the dealers' inventories or the consumers' purchases or leases of vehicles. A number of plaintiffs filed a product liability suit in a Missouri state court against Ford Motor. Ford Motor claimed that the court did not have venue. The plaintiffs asserted that Ford Credit, which had an office in the jurisdiction, acted as Ford's "agent for the transaction of its usual and customary business" there. Is Ford Credit an agent of Ford Motor? Discuss. [*State ex rel. Ford Motor Co. v. Bacon*, 63 S.W.3d 641 (Mo. 2002)]

31–9. PRINCIPAL'S DUTIES TO AGENT. Josef Boehm was an officer and the majority shareholder of Alaska Industrial Hardware, Inc. (AIH), in Anchorage, Alaska. In August 2001, Lincolnshire Management, Inc., in New York, created AIH Acquisition Corp. to buy AIH. The three firms signed a "commitment letter" to negotiate "a definitive stock purchase agreement" (SPA). In September, Harold Snow and Ronald Braley began to work, on Boehm's behalf, with Vincent Coyle, an agent for AIH Acquisition, to produce an SPA. They exchanged many drafts and dozens of e-mails. Finally, in February 2002, Braley told Coyle that Boehm would sign the SPA "early next week." That did not occur, however, and at the end of March, after more negotiations and drafts, Boehm demanded more money. AIH Acquisition agreed and, following more work by the agents, another

SPA was drafted. In April, the parties met in Anchorage. Boehm still refused to sign. AIH Acquisition and others filed a suit in a federal district court against AIH. Did Boehm violate any of the duties that principals owe to their agents? If so, which duty, and how was it violated? Explain. [*AIH Acquisition Corp., LLC v. Alaska Industrial Hardware, Inc.*, __ F.Supp.2d __ (S.D.N.Y. 2004)]

31–10. VIDEO QUESTION

Go to this text's Web site at http://wbl.westbuslaw.com and select "Chapter 31." Click on "Video Questions" and view the video titled *Fast Times at Ridgemont High.* Then answer the following questions.

(a) Recall from the video that Brad (Judge Reinhold) is told to deliver an order of Captain Hook Fish and Chips to IBM. Is Brad an employee or an independent contractor? Why?

(b) Assume that Brad is an employee and agent of Captain Hook Fish and Chips. What duties does he owe Captain Hook Fish and Chips? What duties does Captain Hook Fish and Chips, as principal, owe Brad?

(c) In the video, Brad throws part of his uniform and several bags of the food that he is supposed to deliver out of his car window while driving. Assuming Brad is an agent-employee of Captain Hook Fish and Chips, did these actions violate any of his duties as an agent? Explain.

LAW | on the Web

For updated links to resources available on the Web, as well as a variety of other materials, visit this text's Web site at http://wbl.westbuslaw.com.

An excellent source for information on agency law, including court cases involving agency concepts, is the Legal Information Institute (LII) at Cornell University. You can access the LII's Web page on this topic at

http://www.law.cornell.edu/topics/agency.html

LEGAL RESEARCH EXERCISES ON THE WEB

Go to http://wbl.westbuslaw.com, the Web site that accompanies this text. Select "Chapter 31" and click on "Internet Exercises." There you will find the following Internet research exercises that you can perform to learn more about topics covered in this chapter.

Activity 31–1: LEGAL PERSPECTIVE
Employees or Independent Contractors?

Activity 31–2: MANAGEMENT PERSPECTIVE
Problems with Using Independent Contractors

CHAPTER 32

Liability to Third Parties and Termination

As discussed in the previous chapter, the law of agency focuses on the special relationship that exists between a principal and an agent—how the relationship is formed and the duties the principal and agent assume once the relationship is established. This chapter deals with another important aspect of agency law—the liability of principals and agents to third parties.

We first look at the liability of principals for contracts formed by agents with third parties. Generally, the liability of the principal will depend on whether the agent was authorized to form the contracts. The second part of the chapter deals with an agent's liability to third parties in contract and tort and the principal's liability to third parties because of an agent's torts. The chapter concludes with a discussion of how agency relationships are terminated.

SECTION 1 | Scope of Agent's Authority

A principal's liability in a contract with a third party arises from the authority given the agent to enter into legally binding contracts on the principal's behalf. An agent's authority can be either *actual* (express or implied) or *apparent*.

EXPRESS AUTHORITY

Express authority is embodied in that which the principal has engaged the agent to do. Express authority can be given orally or in writing.

THE EQUAL DIGNITY RULE   The **equal dignity rule** in most states requires that if the contract being executed is or must be in writing, then the agent's authority must also be in writing. Failure to comply with the equal dignity rule can make a contract voidable *at the option of the principal*. The law regards the contract at that point as a mere offer. If the principal decides to accept the offer, acceptance must be ratified, or affirmed, in writing.

Assume that Pattberg (the principal) orally asks Austin (the agent) to sell a ranch that Pattberg owns. Austin finds a buyer and signs a sales contract (a contract for an interest in realty must be in writing) on

behalf of Pattberg to sell the ranch. The buyer cannot enforce the contract unless Pattberg subsequently ratifies Austin's agency status in writing. Once the contract is ratified, either party can enforce rights under the contract.

Modern business practice allows an exception to the equal dignity rule. An executive officer of a corporation, when acting for the corporation in an ordinary business situation, is not required to obtain written authority from the corporation. In addition, the equal dignity rule does not apply when an agent acts in the presence of a principal or when the agent's act of signing is merely perfunctory. Thus, if Healy (the principal) negotiates a contract but is called out of town the day it is to be signed and orally authorizes Scougall to sign, the oral authorization is sufficient.

POWER OF ATTORNEY   Giving an agent a **power of attorney** confers express authority.[1] The power of attorney is a written document and is usually notarized. (A document is notarized when a **notary public**—a public official authorized to attest to the authenticity of signatures—signs and dates the document and imprints it with her or his seal of authority.) Most states have statutory provisions for creating a power of attorney. A power of attorney can be special

---

1. An agent who holds the power of attorney is called an *attorney-in-fact* for the principal. The holder does not have to be an attorney-at-law (and often is not).

(permitting the agent to perform specified acts only), or it can be general (permitting the agent to transact all business for the principal). Because of the extensive authority granted to an agent by a general power of attorney (see Exhibit 32–1), it should be used with great caution and usually only in exceptional circumstances. Ordinarily, a power of attorney terminates on the incapacity or death of the person giving the power.[2]

---

2. A *durable* power of attorney, however, continues to be effective despite the principal's incapacity. An elderly person, for example, might grant a durable power of attorney to provide for the handling of property and investments or specific health-care needs should he or she become incompetent (see Chapter 50).

IMPLIED AUTHORITY

Implied authority is conferred by custom, can be inferred from the position the agent occupies, or is implied by virtue of being reasonably necessary to carry out express authority. For example, Carlson is employed by Packard Grocery to manage one of its stores. Packard has not expressly stated that Carlson has authority to contract with third persons. In this situation, though, authority to manage a business implies authority to do what is reasonably required (as is customary or can be inferred from a manager's position) to operate the business. This includes making contracts for hiring personnel, for buying mer-

EXHIBIT 32-1 A Sample General Power of Attorney

GENERAL POWER OF ATTORNEY

Know All Men by These Presents:

That I, _____ , hereinafter referred to as PRINCIPAL, in the County of _____
State of _____ , do(es) appoint _____ as my true and lawful attorney.

In principal's name, and for principal's use and benefit, said attorney is authorized hereby;

(1) To demand, sue for, collect, and receive all money, debts, accounts, legacies, bequests, interest, dividends, annuities, and demands as are now or shall hereafter become due, payable, or belonging to principal, and take all lawful means, for the recovery thereof and to compromise the same and give discharges for the same;
(2) To buy and sell land, make contracts of every kind relative to land, any interest therein or the possession thereof, and to take possession and exercise control over the use thereof;
(3) To buy, sell, mortgage, hypothecate, assign, transfer, and in any manner deal with goods, wares and merchandise, choses in action, certificates or shares of capital stock, and other property in possession or in action, and to make, do, and transact all and every kind of business of whatever nature;
(4) To execute, acknowledge, and deliver contracts of sale, escrow instructions, deeds, leases including leases for minerals and hydrocarbon substances and assignments of leases, covenants, agreements and assignments of agreements, mortgages and assignments of mortgages, conveyances in trust, to secure indebtedness or other obligations, and assign the beneficial interest thereunder, subordinations of liens or encumbrances, bills of lading, receipts, evidences of debt, releases, bonds, notes, bills, requests to reconvey deeds of trust, partial or full judgments, satisfactions of mortgages, and other debts, and other written instruments of whatever kind and nature, all upon such terms and conditions as said attorney shall approve.

GIVING AND GRANTING to said attorney full power and authority to do all and every act and thing whatsoever requisite and necessary to be done relative to any of the foregoing as fully to all intents and purposes as principal might or could do if personally present.

All that said attorney shall lawfully do or cause to be done under the authority of this power of attorney is expressly approved.

Dated: _____   /s/_____

State of California
   County of _____ } SS.
On _____ , before me, the undersigned, a Notary Public in and for said
State, personally appeared _____
_____

known to me to be the person _____ whose name _____ subscribed
to the within instrument and acknowledged that _____ executed the same.

Witness my hand and official seal.   (Seal) _____
                                     Notary Public in and for said State.

chandise and equipment, and even for advertising the products sold in the store.

Because implied authority is conferred on the basis of custom, it is important for third persons to be familiar with the custom of the particular trade. Courts have developed rules to determine what authority is implied based on custom or on the agent's position. In general, implied authority is authority customarily associated with the position occupied by the agent or authority that can be inferred from the express authority given to the agent to fully perform his or her duties.

For example, an agent who has authority to solicit orders for goods sold by the principal generally has no authority to collect payments for the goods unless the agent possesses the goods. The test is whether it was reasonable for the agent to believe that she or he had the authority to enter into the contract in question.

APPARENT AUTHORITY AND ESTOPPEL

Actual authority (express or implied) arises from what the principal manifests *to the agent*. An agent has **apparent authority** when the principal, by either word or action, causes a *third party* reasonably to believe that the agent has authority to act, even though the agent has no express or implied authority. If the third party changes his or her position in reliance on the principal's representations, the principal may be *estopped* (prevented) from denying that the agent had authority.

APPARENT AUTHORITY THROUGH A PATTERN OF CONDUCT

When a principal's actions over time lead a third party to believe that an agency relationship exists, an *agency by estoppel* may arise based on apparent authority. For example, assume that Adam is a traveling sales agent for a pesticide company. Adam neither possesses the goods ordered nor delivers them, and he has no express or implied authority to collect payments from customers. Now assume that a customer, Ling, pays Adam for a solicited order. Adam then takes the payment to the principal's accounting department. An accountant accepts the payment and sends Ling a receipt. This procedure is thereafter followed for other orders solicited by Adam and paid for by Ling. Later, Adam solicits an order, and Ling pays Adam as before. This time, however, Adam absconds with the money.

Can Ling claim that the payment to Adam was authorized and thus, in effect, was a payment to the principal? The answer is yes, because the principal's *repeated* acts of accepting Ling's payments through Adam led Ling reasonably to believe that Adam had authority to receive payments for goods solicited. Although Adam did not have express or implied authority, the principal's conduct gave Adam apparent authority to collect the payments.

APPARENT AUTHORITY THROUGH AN AGENT'S POSSESSION OF PROPERTY

An agency by estoppel may also arise in other situations based on apparent authority. If, for example, the principal has "clothed the agent" with both possession and apparent ownership of the principal's property, the agent has very broad powers and can deal with the property as if she or he were the true owner. For example, to deceive certain creditors, Sikora (the principal) and Hunter (the agent) agree verbally that Hunter will hold certain bearer bonds for Sikora. Because the bonds are bearer paper (that is, they do not require indorsement to be transferred—see Chapter 25), Hunter's possession and apparent ownership of the bonds are such strong indications of ownership that a reasonable person would conclude that Hunter was the actual owner. If Hunter negotiates the bonds to a third person, Sikora will be estopped from denying Hunter's authority to transfer the bonds.

When land is involved, courts have held that possession alone is not a sufficient indication of ownership (see Chapter 48 for details). If, however, the agent also possesses the deed to the property and sells the property against the principal's wishes to an unsuspecting buyer, the principal normally cannot cancel the sale or assert a claim to the title.

EMERGENCY POWERS

When an unforeseen emergency demands action by the agent to protect or preserve the property and rights of the principal, but the agent is unable to communicate with the principal, the agent has emergency power.

For example, Fulsom is an engineer for Pacific Railroad. While Fulsom is acting within the scope of his employment, he falls under the train many miles from home and is severely injured. Dudley, the conductor, directs Thompson, a physician, to give medical aid to Fulsom and to charge Pacific for the medical services. Dudley, an agent, has no express or implied authority to bind the principal, Pacific Railroad, for Thompson's services. Because of the emergency situation, however, the law recognizes Dudley as having authority to act appropriately under the circumstances.

RATIFICATION

Ratification occurs when the principal affirms an agent's *unauthorized* act. When ratification occurs the principal is bound to the agent's act, and the act is treated as if it had been authorized by the principal *from the outset*. Ratification can be either express or implied.

If the principal does not ratify the contract, the principal is not bound, and the third party's agreement with the agent is merely an unaccepted offer. Because the third party's agreement is an unaccepted offer, the third party can revoke it any time, without liability, before the principal ratifies the contract. The agent, however, may be liable to the third party for misrepresenting his or her authority.

REQUIREMENTS FOR RATIFICATION
The requirements for ratification can be summarized as follows:

1. The agent must act on behalf of an identified principal who subsequently ratifies the action.
2. The principal must affirm the agent's act in its entirety.
3. The principal's affirmance must occur before the third party withdraws from the transaction.
4. The principal must have the legal capacity to authorize the transaction at the time the agent engages in the act and at the time the principal ratifies. The third party must also have the legal capacity to engage in the transaction.
5. The principal must know all of the material facts involved in the transaction.

PRINCIPAL'S KNOWLEDGE OF THE FACTS
Regarding the last requirement in the above list, if a principal ratifies a contract *without knowing* all of the facts, the principal can rescind (cancel) the ratification. If the third party has changed position in reliance on the apparent contract, however, the principal can rescind but must reimburse the third party for any costs.

For example, suppose that an agent, without authority, contracts with a third person on behalf of a principal for repair work on the principal's office building. The principal learns of the contract and agrees to "some repair work," thinking that it will involve only patching and painting the building's exterior. In fact, the contract includes resurfacing the parking lot, which the principal does not want done. On learning of the additional provision, the principal rescinds the contract. If the third party has made preparations to do the work (such as purchasing materials, hiring additional employees, or renting equipment) in reliance on the principal's apparent ratification, the principal must reimburse the third party for the cost of those preparations.

SECTION 2 | Liability for Contracts

Liability for contracts formed by an agent depends on how the principal is classified and on whether the actions of the agent were authorized or unauthorized. Principals are classified as disclosed, partially disclosed, or undisclosed.[3]

A **disclosed principal** is a principal whose identity is known by the third party at the time the contract is made by the agent. A **partially disclosed principal** is a principal whose identity is not known by the third party, but the third party knows that the agent is or may be acting for a principal at the time the contract is made. An **undisclosed principal** is a principal whose identity is totally unknown by the third party, and the third party has no knowledge that the agent is acting in an agency capacity at the time the contract is made.

AUTHORIZED ACTS

If an agent acts within the scope of her or his authority, normally the principal is obligated to perform the contract regardless of whether the principal was disclosed, partially disclosed, or undisclosed. Whether the agent may also be held liable under the contract, however, depends on the disclosed, partially disclosed, or undisclosed status of the principal.

DISCLOSED OR PARTIALLY DISCLOSED PRINCIPAL
A disclosed or partially disclosed principal is liable to a third party for a contract made by the agent. If the principal is disclosed, an agent has no contractual liability for the nonperformance of the principal or the third party. If the principal is partially disclosed, in most states the agent is also treated as a party to the contract, and the third party can hold the agent liable for contractual nonperformance.[4] The following case illustrates the rules that apply to contracts signed by agents on behalf of fully disclosed principals.

---

3. *Restatement (Second) of Agency*, Section 4.
4. *Restatement (Second) of Agency*, Section 321.

CASE 32.1	McBride v. Taxman Corp.

Appellate Court
of Illinois,
First District, 2002.
327 Ill.App.3d 992,
765 N.E.2d 51,
262 Ill.Dec. 225.
http://state.il.us/court/
default.htm[a]

BACKGROUND AND FACTS *Walgreens Company entered into a lease with Taxman Corporation to operate a drugstore in Kedzie Plaza, a shopping center in Chicago, Illinois, owned by Kedzie Plaza Associates; Taxman was the center's property manager. The lease required the "Landlord" to promptly remove snow and ice from the center's sidewalks. Taxman also signed, on behalf of Kedzie Associates, an agreement with Arctic Snow and Ice Control, Inc., to remove ice and snow from the sidewalks surrounding the Walgreens store. On January 27, 1996, Grace McBride, a Walgreens employee, slipped and fell on snow and ice outside the entrance to the store. McBride filed a suit in an Illinois state court against Taxman and others alleging, among other things, that Taxman had negligently failed to remove the accumulation of ice and snow.[b] Taxman filed a motion for summary judgment in its favor, which the court granted. McBride appealed to a state intermediate appellate court.*

IN THE LANGUAGE OF THE COURT

Justice CERDA delivered the opinion of the court.

 *   *   *   *

On October 10, 1995, Taxman signed, on behalf of the owner, Arctic's one-page "Snow Removal Proposal & Contract" (although dated August 7, 1995), for the term November 15, 1995, through April 15, 1996, for the shopping center where this Walgreens store was located. *   *   *

Also on October 10, 1995, Arctic and Taxman signed a multi-page document dated October 3, 1995, that was apparently drafted by Taxman. The document was not given a title but contained several pages of terms concerning snow removal "per contract(s) attached." *   *   *

 *   *   *   *

Plaintiff argues that the contract between Taxman and Arctic created a duty of Taxman to remove ice and snow for the benefit of plaintiff. *   *   *

 *   *   *   *

The Arctic proposal and contract was signed "Kedzie Associates by the Taxman." The Taxman-drafted portion of the contract contained a line above the signature of Taxman's director of property management stating "The Taxman Corporation, agent for per contracts attached." The latter document specifically stated that the contract was not an obligation of Taxman and that all liabilities were those of the owner and not Taxman. We conclude that Taxman was the management company for the property owner and entered into the two contracts for snow and ice removal only as the owner's agent.

Taxman did not assume a contractual obligation to remove snow or ice; it merely retained Arctic as a contractor on behalf of the owner.

DECISION AND REMEDY *The state intermediate appellate court affirmed the judgment of the lower court. The appellate court held that Taxman entered into the snow removal contracts only as the agent of the owner, whose identity was fully disclosed. As agent for a disclosed principal, Taxman had no liability for the nonperformance of the principal or the third party to the contract.*

WHAT IF THE FACTS WERE DIFFERENT? *Suppose that the Arctic contract had not identified Kedzie as the principal. How might the court's decision in this case have been different?*

a. On this page, click on "Appellate Court of Illinois." On the page that opens, in the "Appellate Court Documents" section, click on "Appellate Court Opinions." In the result, in the "Appellate Court" section, click on "2002." On the next page, in the "First District" section, click on "January." Finally, scroll to the bottom of the chart and click on the case name to access the opinion. The state of Illinois maintains this Web site.
b. McBride included in her suit complaints against Walgreens and Kedzie Associates but settled those complaints before trial.

UNDISCLOSED PRINCIPAL When neither the fact of an agency relationship nor the identity of the principal is disclosed, the undisclosed principal is fully bound to perform just as if the principal had been fully disclosed at the time the contract was made.

When a principal's identity is undisclosed and the agent is forced to pay the third party, the agent is entitled to be *indemnified* (compensated) by the principal. The principal had a duty to perform, even though his or her identity was undisclosed,[5] and failure to do so will make the principal ultimately liable. Once the undisclosed principal's identity is revealed, the third party generally can elect to hold either the principal or the agent liable on the contract.

Conversely, the undisclosed principal can require the third party to fulfill the contract, *unless* (1) the undisclosed principal was expressly excluded as a party in the written contract, (2) the contract is a negotiable instrument signed by the agent with no indication of signing in a representative capacity,[6] or (3) the performance of the agent is personal to the contract, allowing the third party to refuse the principal's performance.

UNAUTHORIZED ACTS

If an agent has no authority but nevertheless contracts with a third party, the principal cannot be held liable on the contract. It does not matter whether the principal was disclosed, partially disclosed, or undisclosed. The agent is liable, however. For example, Scammon signs a contract for the purchase of a truck, purportedly acting as an agent under authority granted by Johnson. In fact, Johnson has not given Scammon any such authority. Johnson refuses to pay for the truck, claiming that Scammon had no authority to purchase it. The seller of the truck is entitled to hold Scammon liable for payment.

If the principal is disclosed or partially disclosed, the agent is liable as long as the third party relied on the agency status. The agent's liability here is based on the theory of breach of implied warranty of authority, not on breach of the contract itself.[7] The agent's implied warranty of authority can be breached intentionally or by a good faith mistake.[8] If the third party knows at the time the contract is made that the agent is mistaken about the extent of her or his authority, though, the agent is not liable. Similarly, if the agent indicates to the third party *uncertainty* about the extent of the authority, the agent is not personally liable.

ACTIONS BY E-AGENTS

An electronic agent, or **e-agent,** is not a person but a semiautonomous computer program that is capable of executing specific tasks. E-agents used in e-commerce include software that can search through many databases and retrieve only relevant information for the user. Although in the past, standard agency principles have applied only to *human* agents, today these same agency principles are being applied to e-agents.

The Uniform Electronic Transactions Act (UETA), which was discussed in detail in Chapter 19, sets forth provisions relating to the principal's liability for the actions of e-agents. Provisions of the act have been adopted in the majority of the states. Section 15 of the UETA states that e-agents may enter into binding agreements on behalf of their principals. For example, if you place an order over the Internet, the company (principal) whose system took the order via an e-agent cannot claim that it did not receive your order. The UETA establishes that e-agents generally have the authority to bind the principal in contract—at least in those states that have adopted the act.

The UETA also stipulates that if an e-agent does not provide an opportunity to prevent errors at the time of the transaction, the other party to the transaction can avoid the transaction. If an e-agent fails to provide an on-screen confirmation of a purchase or sale, for instance, the other party can avoid the effect of any errors. For example, suppose that Finig wants to purchase three each of three different items (a total of nine items). The e-agent mistakenly records an order for thirty-three of a single item and does not provide an on-screen verification of the order. If thirty-three items are then sent to Finig, he can avoid the contract to purchase them.

ACTIONS OF SUBAGENTS

If an agent is authorized to hire subagents for the principal to perform simple and definite duties, when it is the business custom or for unforeseen emergencies, then the principal is liable for the acts of the subagents.

---

5. If the agent is a gratuitous agent, and the principal accepts the benefits of the agent's contract with a third party, then the principal will be liable to the agent on the theory of quasi contract (see Chapter 10).

6. Under the Uniform Commercial Code (UCC), only the agent is liable if the instrument neither names the principal nor shows that the agent signed in a representative capacity [UCC 3–402(b)(2)].

7. The agent is not liable on the contract because the agent was never intended personally to be a party to the contract.

8. If the agent intentionally misrepresents his or her authority, then the agent can also be liable in tort for fraud.

CONCEPT SUMMARY 32.1 | Authority of Agent to Bind Principal and Third Party

AUTHORITY OF AGENT	DEFINITION	EFFECT ON PRINCIPAL AND THIRD PARTY
EXPRESS AUTHORITY	Authority expressly given by the principal to the agent.	Principal and third party are bound in contract.
IMPLIED AUTHORITY	Authority implied (1) by custom, (2) from the position in which the principal has placed the agent, or (3) because such authority is necessary if the agent is to carry out expressly authorized duties and responsibilities.	Principal and third party are bound in contract.
APPARENT AUTHORITY	Authority created when the conduct of the principal leads a third party to believe that the principal's agent has authority.	Principal and third party are bound in contract.
UNAUTHORIZED ACTS	Acts committed by an agent that are outside the scope of his or her express, implied, or apparent authority.	Principal and third party are not bound in contract—*unless* the principal ratifies prior to the third party's withdrawal.

The result is slightly different if the agent hires subagents for an undisclosed principal. In that situation, the *agent* is responsible for the subagent in contract law for such things as wages. An agent's unauthorized hiring of a subagent generally does not create any legal relationship between the principal and the subagent.

SECTION 3 | Liability for Torts and Crimes

Obviously, any person, including an agent, is liable for his or her own torts and crimes. Whether a principal can also be held liable for an agent's torts and crimes depends on several factors, which we examine here. In some situations, a principal may be held liable not only for the torts of an agent but also for the torts committed by an independent contractor.

PRINCIPAL'S TORTIOUS CONDUCT

A principal conducting an activity through an agent may be liable for harm resulting from the principal's own negligence or recklessness. Thus, a principal may be liable for giving improper instructions, authorizing the use of improper materials or tools, or establishing improper rules that result in the agent's committing a tort. For instance, if Jack knows that Lucy cannot drive but nevertheless tells her to use the company truck to deliver some equipment to a customer, he will be liable for his own negligence to anyone injured by her negligent driving.

PRINCIPAL'S AUTHORIZATION OF AGENT'S TORTIOUS CONDUCT

Similarly, a principal who authorizes an agent to commit a tort may be liable to persons or property injured thereby, because the act is considered to be the principal's. For example, Selkow directs his agent, Warren, to cut the corn on specific acreage, which neither of them has the right to do. The harvest is therefore a trespass (a tort), and Selkow is liable to whoever owns the corn.

Note that an agent acting at the principal's direction can be liable as a *tortfeasor* (one who commits a wrong, or tort), along with the principal, for committing the tortious act even if the agent was unaware of the wrongfulness of the act. Assume in the above example that Warren, the agent, did not know that Selkow had no right to harvest the corn. Warren can still be held liable to the owner of the field for damages, along with Selkow, the principal.

LIABILITY FOR AGENT'S MISREPRESENTATION

A principal is exposed to tort liability whenever a third person sustains a loss due to the agent's misrepresentation. The principal's liability depends on whether the agent was actually or apparently authorized to make representations and whether such representations were made within the scope of the agency. The principal is always directly responsible for an agent's misrepresentation made within the scope of the agent's authority.

Assume that Bassett is a demonstrator for Moore's products. Moore sends Bassett to a home show to demonstrate the products and to answer questions from consumers. Moore has given Bassett authority to make statements about the products. If Bassett makes only true representations, all is fine; but if he makes false claims, Moore will be liable for any injuries or damages sustained by third parties in reliance on Bassett's false representations.

APPARENT IMPLIED AUTHORITY When a principal has placed an agent in a position of apparent authority—making it possible for the agent to defraud a third party—the principal may also be liable for the agent's fraudulent acts. For example, Frendak is a loan officer at First Security Bank. In the ordinary course of the job, Frendak approves and services loans and has access to the credit records of all customers. Frendak

falsely represents to a borrower, McMillan, that the bank feels insecure about McMillan's loan and intends to call it in unless McMillan provides additional collateral, such as stocks and bonds. McMillan gives Frendak numerous stock certificates, which Frendak keeps in her own possession and later uses to make personal investments. The bank is liable to McMillan for losses sustained on the stocks even though the bank was unaware of the fraudulent scheme.

If, in contrast, Frendak had been a recently hired junior bank teller rather than a loan officer when she told McMillan that the bank required additional security for the loan, McMillan would not have been justified in relying on Frendak's representation. In that situation, the bank normally would not be held liable to McMillan for the losses sustained.

The following case focused on a partner's potential liability for claims against the partnership arising from the torts of its manager. The partner argued that he could not be liable because the manager did not have the apparent authority to commit torts. Among those with claims against the firm was the partner's mother.

CASE 32.2 In re Selheimer & Co.

United States District Court, Eastern District of Pennsylvania, 2005. 319 Bankr. 395.

BACKGROUND AND FACTS *Selheimer & Company was formed as a partnership in 1967 to act as a securities broker-dealer, buying and selling stocks and bonds and providing other financial services, in Pennsylvania. In 1994, during an investigation by the Securities and Exchange Commission (SEC), the firm closed.[a] Perry Selheimer, the managing partner, was charged with various crimes and pleaded guilty to mail fraud. Other partners, including Edward Murphy, and the firm's clients, including Murphy's mother, Jeanne Murphy, filed claims with the Securities Investor Protection Corporation (SIPC) to be reimbursed for their losses. The SIPC advanced over $250,000 to pay these claims. With more than $1 million in claims outstanding, the SIPC petitioned the firm into involuntary bankruptcy in 2002. Because the firm had few assets, the SIPC asked the court to rule that the personal assets of the individual partners could be used to cover the liability. The SIPC filed a motion for summary judgment on this issue. Edward Murphy opposed the request.*

IN THE LANGUAGE OF THE COURT

STEPHEN RASLAVICH, Bankruptcy Judge.

* * * *

* * * [I]n Pennsylvania a partner is jointly and severally liable for certain torts *chargeable to the partnership [if those torts are committed within the ordinary course of the partnership business].* * * * [Emphasis added.]

* * * *

Murphy maintains that he is not * * * liable for Selheimer's acts because the record does not show that such conduct was within the ordinary course of business of the partnership * * * .

---

a. The SEC is a federal agency that regulates the activities of securities brokers and others. See Chapter 41.

 Continued

The record demonstrates that Selheimer & Co. perpetrated its fraud under the guise of operating a brokerage firm. The partnership was a registered securities broker-dealer that accepted money from clients for investment purposes. Instead, Selheimer embezzled those funds. Selheimer's criminal acts were performed within the normal operation of this partnership's business. Put another way, at the time Selheimer was defrauding clients, it was acting in the ordinary course of the partnership's business. The partnership is therefore liable for those acts of Mr. Selheimer. And if the partnership is liable for those debts, then individual partners, including Murphy, are jointly and severally liable as well.

* * * *

Alternatively, Murphy argues that there is no evidence of partnership liability * * * because there is nothing to indicate that Selheimer was acting within the scope of his apparent authority when defrauding customers. In this Commonwealth, the doctrine of apparent authority has been incorporated into the principles of agency law. Apparent authority has been defined [in the *Restatement (Second) of Agency*, Section 8] as "the power to affect the legal relations of another person by transactions with third persons, professedly as agent for the other, arising from and in accordance with the other's manifestations to third persons." [According to the *Restatement (Second) of Agency*, Section 27, the] general rule governing the creation of apparent authority is:

> Except for the execution of instruments under seal or for the conduct of transactions required by statute to be authorized in a particular way, apparent authority to do an act is created as to a third person by written or spoken words or any other conduct of the principal which, reasonably interpreted, causes the third person to believe that the principal consents to have the act done on his behalf by the person purporting to act for him.

Apparent authority exists when a principal, by words or conduct, leads people with whom the alleged agent deals to believe the principal has granted the agent authority he or she purports to exercise. *Apparent authority may result when a principal permits an agent to occupy a position [in] which, according to the ordinary experience and habits of mankind, it is usual for that occupant to have authority of a particular kind.* The nature and extent of an agent's apparent authority is a question of fact for the fact-finder. [Emphasis added.]

Murphy misinterprets agency law when he argues that Selheimer lacked authority, express or apparent, to defraud clients. His argument operates from the erroneous premise that the record must show that Selheimer & Co., as principal, gave Perry Selheimer, as agent, license to steal. If that were so, then the doctrine of apparent authority would be eviscerated [gutted]. What matters is whether Selheimer & Co. was authorized to accept client funds for investment. And the record shows that it certainly was: Selheimer & Co. was a broker-dealer registered with the SEC. Mr. Selheimer formally admitted—pleaded guilty, in fact—to having committed "an abuse of trust" as to his clients. Client confidence would not have been placed in him unless he held himself out as an honest broker-dealer of financial investments; otherwise, clients simply would have taken their business elsewhere. There is thus sufficient proof to support a finding that Selheimer was acting within his apparent authority when defrauding clients. That, in turn, supports a finding of liability as to the partnership which may by assessed against Murphy.

DECISION AND REMEDY *The court found that "Selheimer & Co. is deficient; that Murphy was a partner of Selheimer & Co.; and that he is indirectly liable under Pennsylvania law for the acts of Perry Selheimer which are chargeable to Selheimer & Co." on a theory of apparent authority. The court issued a summary judgment "in a liquidated amount for the $251,158.12 in claims advanced by [the] SIPC and an additional $840,667 for the customer claim of Jeanne Murphy."*

WHAT IF THE FACTS WERE DIFFERENT? *If Selheimer & Company had not had the authority to accept funds for investment, did not authorize its manager to accept such funds, and did not represent that the manager or the firm had this authority, would the outcome in this case have been different? Explain.*

INNOCENT MISREPRESENTATION Tort liability based on fraud requires proof that a material misstatement was made knowingly and with the intent to deceive. An agent's innocent mistakes occurring in a contract transaction or involving a warranty contained in the contract can provide grounds for the third party's rescission of the contract and the award of damages. Moreover, justice dictates that when a principal knows that an agent is not accurately advised of facts but does not correct either the agent's or the third party's impressions, the principal is directly responsible to the third party for resulting damages. The point is that the principal is always directly responsible for an agent's misrepresentation made within the scope of authority.

LIABILITY FOR AGENT'S NEGLIGENCE

Under the doctrine of **respondeat superior,**[9] the principal-employer is liable for any harm caused to a third party by an agent-employee within the scope of employment. This doctrine imposes **vicarious liability,** or indirect liability, on the employer—that is, liability without regard to the personal fault of the employer for torts committed by an employee in the course or scope of employment.[10] Third persons injured through the negligence of an employee can sue either the employee who was negligent or the employer, if the employee's negligent conduct occurred while the employee was acting within the scope of employment.

RATIONALE UNDERLYING THE DOCTRINE OF RESPONDEAT SUPERIOR At early common law, a servant (employee) was viewed as the master's (employer's) property. The master was deemed to have absolute control over the servant's acts and was held strictly liable for them no matter how carefully the master supervised the servant. The rationale for the doctrine of *respondeat superior* is based on the principle of social duty that requires every person to manage his or her affairs, whether accomplished by the person or through agents, so as not to injure another. Liability is imposed on employers because they are deemed to be in a better financial position to bear the loss. The

superior financial position carries with it the duty to be responsible for damages.

Generally, public policy requires that an injured person be afforded effective relief, and recovery from a business enterprise often provides far more effective relief than recovery from an individual employee. Employers normally carry liability insurance to protect themselves against such lawsuits. They are also able to spread the cost of risk over the entire business enterprise.

The doctrine of *respondeat superior,* which the courts have applied for nearly two centuries, continues to have practical implications in all situations involving principal-agent (employer-employee) relationships. Today, the small-town grocer with one clerk and the multinational corporation with thousands of employees are equally subject to the doctrinal demand of "let the master respond." (Keep this principle in mind as you read through Chapters 33 and 34.)

DETERMINING THE SCOPE OF EMPLOYMENT As mentioned, for the employer to be liable under the doctrine of *respondeat superior,* the employee's injury-causing act must have occurred within the course and scope of her or his employment. The *Restatement (Second) of Agency,* Section 229, outlines the following general factors that courts will consider in determining whether a particular act occurred within the course and scope of employment:

1. Whether the employee's act was authorized by the employer.
2. The time, place, and purpose of the act.
3. Whether the act was one commonly performed by employees on behalf of their employers.
4. The extent to which the employer's interest was advanced by the act.
5. The extent to which the private interests of the employee were involved.
6. Whether the employer furnished the means or instrumentality (for example, a truck or a machine) by which an injury was inflicted.
7. Whether the employer had reason to know that the employee would perform the act in question and whether the employee had done it before.
8. Whether the act involved the commission of a serious crime.

EMPLOYEE TRAVEL TIME An employee going to and from work or to and from meals is usually considered to be outside the scope of employment. In con-

---

9. Pronounced ree-*spahn*-dee-uht soo-*peer*-ee-your. The doctrine of *respondeat superior* applies not only to employer-employee relationships but also to other principal-agent relationships in which the principal has the right of control over the agent.
10. The theory of *respondeat superior* is similar to the theory of strict liability covered in Chapter 7.

trast, all travel time of traveling salespersons or others whose jobs require them to travel is normally considered to be within the scope of employment for the duration of the business trip, including the return trip home, unless there is a significant departure from the employer's business.

NOTICE OF DANGEROUS CONDITIONS The employer is charged with knowledge of any dangerous conditions discovered by an employee and pertinent to the employment situation. Suppose that Brad, a maintenance employee in Tartin's apartment building, notices a lead pipe protruding from the ground in the building's courtyard. The employee neglects either to fix it or to inform the employer of the danger. John falls on the pipe and is injured. The employer is charged with knowledge of the dangerous condition regardless of whether Brad actually informed the employer. That knowledge is imputed to the employer by virtue of the employment relationship.

THE DISTINCTION BETWEEN A "DETOUR" AND A "FROLIC" A useful insight into the concept of the "scope of employment" may be gained from Judge Baron Parke's classic distinction between a "detour" and a "frolic" in the case of *Joel v. Morison* (1834).[11] In this case, the English court held that if a servant merely took a detour from his master's business, the master will be responsible. If, however, the servant was on a "frolic of his own" and not in any way "on his master's business," the master will not be liable.

Consider an example. Mandel, a traveling salesperson, while driving the employer's vehicle to call on

11. 6 Car. & P. 501, 172 Eng. Rep. 1338 (1834).

a customer, decides to stop at the post office—which is one block off his route—to mail a personal letter. As Mandel approaches the post office, he negligently runs into a parked vehicle owned by Chan. In this situation, because Mandel's detour from the employer's business is not substantial, he is still acting within the scope of employment, and the employer is liable. The result would be different, though, if Mandel had decided to pick up a few friends for cocktails in another city and in the process had negligently run his vehicle into Chan's. In that circumstance, the departure from the employer's business would be substantial, and the employer normally would not be liable to Chan for damages. Mandel would be considered to have been on a "frolic" of his own.

BORROWED SERVANTS Employers can lend the services of their employees to other employers. Suppose that an employer leases ground-moving equipment to another employer and sends along an employee to operate the machinery. Who is liable for injuries caused by the employee's negligent actions on the job site? Liability turns on *which employer had the primary right to control* the employee at the time the injuries occurred. Generally, the employer who rents out the equipment is presumed to retain control over her or his employee. If the rental is for a relatively long period of time, however, control may be deemed to pass to the employer who is renting the equipment and presumably controlling and directing the employee.

The following case illustrates the two-pronged test that courts often use to determine liability in situations in which one employer loans an employee to another company for a particular project.

CASE 32.3

Supreme Court of
New Jersey, 2004.
179 N.J. 462,
846 A.2d 1215.

Galvao v. G. R. Robert Construction Co.

Justice *LaVECCHIA* delivered the opinion of the Court.
* * * *

On October 27, 1998, plaintiff, Sergio Galvao, was injured while working on the Route 21 Viaduct Replacement Project (the Project) in Newark [New Jersey]. Specifically, a rebar cage used for the pouring of concrete failed and plaintiff fell twenty feet onto another rebar cage. Employees of [G. R. Robert Construction Company (Robert)] had constructed the defective rebar cage. * * * George Harms Excavating Company (Excavating), * * * [was] the payor of plaintiff's salary. * * *

Robert and Excavating are wholly owned subsidiaries of George Harms Construction Company (GHCC) * * *.

Robert and Excavating serve as payroll companies that supply employees to GHCC and receive reimbursement from GHCC for their respective payroll expenses. * * *

 CONTINUED

CASE 32.3 | Continued

* * * [W]hen plaintiff was injured, GHCC was performing construction and related services on the Project pursuant to a contract (the Contract) with the New Jersey Department of Transportation (DOT). * * *

In respect of the performance of work on the Project, GHCC controlled the direction and supervision of all workers, which necessarily included all employees of Robert and Excavating. * * *

In May 1999, plaintiffs filed this * * * action [in a New Jersey state court] against Robert, asserting liability under the doctrine of *respondeat superior* for the alleged negligent construction of the rebar cage by Robert's employees. Plaintiffs already had filed a workers' compensation claim against GHCC and received benefits. The trial court dismissed the complaint on Robert's motion for summary judgment. * * *

* * * [A state intermediate appellate court] affirmed * * * . [The New Jersey Supreme Court] granted plaintiffs' petition for certification.

* * * *

* * * [T]he test * * * for determining whether a general employer (i.e. Robert) may be held vicariously liable for the alleged negligence of its special employee loaned to a special employer (i.e. GHCC) necessarily contains two parts. The threshold inquiry is whether the general employer controlled the special employee. By "control," we mean control in the fundamental *respondeat superior* sense, which * * * [is] the right to direct the manner in which the business shall be done, as well as the result to be accomplished, or in other words, not only what shall be done, but how it shall be done. In addition to evidence of direct or "on-spot" control over the means by which the task is accomplished, *we will infer an employer's control based on the method of payment, who furnishes the equipment, and the right of termination*. The retention of either on-spot, or broad, control by a general employer would satisfy this first prong. [Emphasis added.]

If a general employer is not found to exercise either on-spot, or broad, control over a special employee, then the general employer cannot be held vicariously liable for the alleged negligence of that employee. If the general employer did exercise such control, however, then it must be ascertained whether the special employee furthered the business of the general employer. A special employee is furthering the business of the general employer if the work being done by the special employee is within the general contemplation of the general employer, and the general employer derives an economic benefit by loaning its employee. If the answer to the second question is in the affirmative, the general employer may be held vicariously liable for the alleged negligence of a special employee. [Emphasis added.]

* * * *

In this matter, we are confident that plaintiffs cannot satisfy either prong necessary to hold Robert vicariously liable under the doctrine of *respondeat superior*. In respect of the first prong concerning control, * * * Robert did not have the type of broad influence over the Project from which we might infer the right to control, such as paying plaintiff's salary, furnishing construction materials or equipment for the Project, or retaining the right to hire forepersons and assign employees to particular aspects of the Project. Nor is there is any evidence that Robert had on-spot control of the special employees. Robert did not direct the on-site work, design the rebar cages, or have any responsibility for safety. Thus, under the facts of this matter, Robert did not control the Project or the activities on the Project. For that reason alone, we conclude that Robert cannot be held vicariously liable under *respondeat superior* for plaintiff's injuries.

Although the lack of control ends the inquiry, for completeness we add the following analysis of the second prong. Robert did not derive any economic benefit by providing special employees to GHCC. Robert's only income was reimbursement from GHCC for its payroll expenses, a pass-through transaction. Any benefit derived from the use of Robert's employees on the Project, economic or otherwise, was GHCC's alone. It was GHCC that created Robert and Excavating * * * , and it was GHCC that entered the contract with, and was paid by, DOT for completing the Project. The only beneficiaries of the contract between DOT and GHCC, other than the principals themselves, were the employees who received remuneration

**Continued**   for their services. Therefore, as with the control prong, plaintiff failed to meet the business-furtherance prong to demonstrate that Robert may be held vicariously liable for the alleged negligence of the special employees here.

* * * *

The judgment of the [state intermediate appellate court] is affirmed.

QUESTIONS

1. What are the two "prongs" of the test for liability for injuries caused by the negligence of borrowed servants (employees) under the doctrine of *respondeat superior,* according to the court in the *Galvao* case?
2. How does the basis for the second "prong" of this test resemble the basis for the imposition of strict liability in other cases?

LIABILITY FOR AGENT'S INTENTIONAL TORTS

Most intentional torts that employees commit have no relation to their employment; thus, their employers will not be held liable. Nevertheless, under the doctrine of *respondeat superior,* the employer can be liable for intentional torts of the employee that are committed within the course and scope of employment, just as the employer is liable for negligence. For example, an employer is liable when an employee (such as a "bouncer" at a nightclub or a security guard at a department store) commits assault and battery or false imprisonment while acting within the scope of employment.

In addition, an employer who knows or should know that an employee has a propensity for committing tortious acts is liable for the employee's acts even if they would not ordinarily be considered within the scope of employment. For example, if the employer hires a bouncer knowing that he has a history of arrests for assault and battery, the employer may be liable if the employee viciously attacks a patron in the parking lot after hours.

An employer is also liable for permitting an employee to engage in reckless actions that can injure others. For example, an employer observes an employee smoking while filling containerized trucks with highly flammable liquids. Failure to stop the employee will cause the employer to be liable for any injuries that result if a truck explodes. Needless to say, most employers purchase liability insurance to cover their potential liability for employee conduct in many situations (see Chapter 49).

LIABILITY FOR INDEPENDENT CONTRACTOR'S TORTS

Generally, an employer is not liable for physical harm caused to a third person by the negligent act of an independent contractor in the performance of the contract. This is because the employer does not have *the right to control* the details of an independent contractor's performance. Exceptions to this rule are made in certain situations, though, such as when unusually hazardous activities are involved. Typical examples of such activities include blasting operations, the transportation of highly volatile chemicals, or the use of poisonous gases. In these situations, an employer cannot be shielded from liability merely by using an independent contractor. Strict liability is imposed on the employer-principal as a matter of law. Also, in some states, strict liability may be imposed by statute.

LIABILITY FOR AGENT'S CRIMES

An agent is liable for his or her own crimes. A principal or employer is not liable for an agent's or employee's crime simply because the agent or employee committed the crime while otherwise acting within the scope of authority or employment. An exception to this rule is made when the principal or employer participated in the crime by conspiracy or other action. In some jurisdictions, under specific statutes, a principal may be liable for an agent's violating, in the course and scope of employment, such regulations as those governing sanitation, prices, weights, and the sale of liquor.

SECTION 4 | Termination of an Agency

Agency law is similar to contract law in that both an agency and a contract may be terminated by an act of the parties or by operation of law. Once the relationship between the principal and the agent has ended, the agent no longer has *actual* authority to bind the principal—that is, she or he lacks the principal's consent to act on the principal's behalf. Generally, however, if the agency is terminated by an act of the parties, the principal can still be bound by the agent's acts if the agent has acted within the scope of his or her *apparent* authority. To terminate the agent's apparent authority, third parties must be notified of the agency termination—as will be discussed later.

TERMINATION BY ACT OF THE PARTIES

An agency relationship may be terminated by act of the parties in a number of ways, including those discussed here.

LAPSE OF TIME An agency agreement may specify the time period during which the agency relationship will exist. If so, the agency ends when that time expires. For example, Akers signs an agreement of agency with Janz "beginning January 1, 2005, and ending December 31, 2006." The agency is automatically terminated on December 31, 2006. Of course, the parties can agree to continue the relationship; if they do, the same terms will apply. If no definite time is stated, then the agency continues for a reasonable time and can be terminated at will by either party. What constitutes a reasonable time depends on the circumstances and the nature of the agency relationship.

PURPOSE ACHIEVED An agent can be employed to accomplish a particular objective, such as the purchase of stock for a cattle rancher. In that situation, the agency automatically ends after the cattle have been purchased. If more than one agent is employed to accomplish the same purpose, such as the sale of real estate, the first agent to complete the sale automatically terminates the agency relationship for all the others.

OCCURRENCE OF A SPECIFIC EVENT An agency can be created to terminate on the happening of a certain event. For example, Janz asks Akers to handle her business affairs while she is away. When Janz returns, the agency automatically terminates.

Sometimes, one aspect of the agent's authority terminates on the occurrence of a particular event, but the agency relationship itself does not terminate. For example, Janz, a banker, permits Akers, the credit manager, to grant a credit line of $5,000 to certain depositors who maintain a balance of $5,000 in a savings account. If any customer's savings account balance falls below $5,000, Akers can no longer make the credit line available to that customer. Akers, however, continues to have the right to extend credit to the other customers maintaining the minimum balance.

MUTUAL AGREEMENT Recall from basic contract law that parties can rescind (cancel) a contract by mutually agreeing to terminate the contractual relationship. The same holds true in agency law, regardless of whether the agency contract is in writing or whether it is for a specific duration. For example, Janz no longer wishes Akers to be her agent, and Akers does not want to work for Janz anymore. Either party can communicate to the other the intent to terminate the relationship. Agreement to terminate effectively relieves each of the rights, duties, and powers inherent in the relationship.

TERMINATION BY ONE PARTY As a *general* rule, either party can terminate the agency relationship. The agent's act is said to be a *renunciation* of authority. The principal's act is a *revocation* of authority. Although both parties may have the *power* to terminate—because agency is a consensual relationship, and thus neither party can be compelled to continue in the relationship—they may not possess the *right* to terminate and may therefore be liable for breach of contract.

—Wrongful Termination. Wrongful termination can subject the canceling party to a suit for damages. For example, Akers has a one-year employment contract with Janz to act as Janz's agent for $35,000. Janz can discharge Akers before the contract period expires (Janz has the *power* to breach the contract). Janz, though, will be liable to Akers for money damages, because Janz has no *right* to breach the contract.

Even in an agency at will (that is, an agency that either party may terminate at any time), the principal who wishes to terminate must give the agent *reasonable* notice—that is, at least sufficient notice to allow the agent to recoup his or her expenses and, in some situations, to make a normal profit.

—Agency Coupled with an Interest. A special rule applies in an *agency coupled with an interest.* This type of agency is not an agency in the usual sense because it is created for the agent's benefit instead of for the principal's benefit. For example, suppose that Julie borrows $5,000 from Rob, giving Rob some of her jewelry and signing a letter authorizing him to sell the jewelry as her agent if she fails to repay the loan. After Julie receives the funds from Rob, she attempts to revoke his authority to sell the jewelry. Julie will not succeed in this attempt because a principal cannot revoke an agency created for the agent's benefit.

An agency coupled with an interest should not be confused with a situation in which the agent merely derives proceeds or profits from the sale of the subject matter. For example, an agent who merely receives a commission from the sale of real property does not have a beneficial interest in the property itself. Likewise, an attorney whose fee is a percentage of the recovery (a *contingency fee*—see Chapter 3) merely has an interest in the proceeds. These agency relationships are revocable by the principal, subject to any express contractual arrangements between the principal and the agent.

NOTICE OF TERMINATION When an agency has been terminated by act of the parties, it is the principal's duty to inform any third parties who know of the existence of the agency that it has been terminated (although notice of the termination may be given by others).

—Agent's Authority Continues until Notified. An agent's authority continues until the agent receives some notice of termination. As previously mentioned, notice to third parties follows the general rule that an agent's *apparent authority* continues until the third party receives notice (from any source of information) that the authority has been terminated. The principal is expected to notify *directly* any third party who the principal knows has dealt with the agent. For third parties who have heard about the agency but have not dealt with the agent, *constructive notice* is sufficient.[12]

—Form of Notice. No particular form is required for notice of termination of the principal-agent relationship to be effective. The principal can actually notify the agent, or the agent can learn of the termi-

nation through some other means. For example, Manning bids on a shipment of steel, and Stone is hired as an agent to arrange transportation of the shipment. When Stone learns that Manning has lost the bid, Stone's authority to make the transportation arrangement terminates.

If the agent's authority is written, it must be revoked in writing, and the writing must be shown to all people who saw the original writing that established the agency relationship. Sometimes, a written authorization (such as a power of attorney) contains an expiration date. If the authorization has expired that will be sufficient notice of termination.

TERMINATION BY OPERATION OF LAW

Certain events will terminate agency authority automatically because their occurrence makes it impossible for the agent to perform or improbable that the principal would continue to want performance. We look at these events here. Note that when an agency terminates by operation of law, there is no duty to notify third persons—unless the agent's authority is coupled with an interest.[13]

DEATH OR INSANITY The general rule is that the death or insanity of either the principal or the agent automatically and immediately terminates an ordinary agency relationship. Knowledge of the death or insanity is not required. For example, Janz sends Arlen to Japan to purchase a rare book. Before Arlen makes the purchase, Janz dies. Arlen's agent status is terminated at the moment of Janz's death, even though Arlen does not know that Janz has died. (Some states, however, have changed the common law by statute to make knowledge of the principal's death a requirement for agency termination.)

An agent's transactions that occur after the death of the principal are not binding on the principal's estate. Assume that Arlen is hired by Janz to collect a debt from Cochran (a third party). Janz dies, but Arlen, not knowing of Janz's death, still collects the debt from Cochran. Cochran's payment to Arlen is no

---

12. With *constructive notice* of a fact, knowledge of the fact is imputed by law to a person if he or she could have discovered the fact by proper diligence. Constructive notice is often accomplished by publication in a newspaper.

13. There is an exception to this rule in banking. UCC 4–405 provides that the bank, as agent, can continue to exercise specific types of authority even after the customer's death or insanity unless it has knowledge of the death or insanity. When the bank has knowledge of the customer's death, it has authority for ten days after the death to pay checks (but not notes or drafts) drawn by the customer unless it receives a stop-payment order from someone who has an interest in the account, such as an heir.

CONCEPT SUMMARY 32.2 | Termination of an Agency

METHOD OF TERMINATION	RULES	NOTICE OF TERMINATION
ACT OF THE PARTIES		
1. Lapse of time	Automatic at end of stated time.	**NOTICE TO THIRD PARTIES REQUIRED—**
2. Purpose achieved	Automatic on completion of purpose.	
3. Occurrence of a specific event	Normally automatic on the happening of the event.	
4. Mutual agreement	Mutual consent required.	1. Direct to those who have dealt with agency.
5. Termination by one party (revocation, if by principal; renunciation, if by agent)	At-will agencies—generally no breach. Specified-time agencies—breach unless there is legal cause. Cannot revoke an agency coupled with an interest.	2. Constructive to all others.
OPERATION OF LAW		
1. Death or insanity	Automatic on death or insanity of either principal or agent (except when agency is coupled with an interest).	
2. Impossibility—destruction of the specific subject matter	Applies any time agency cannot be performed because of event beyond parties' control.	**NO NOTICE REQUIRED—**
3. Changed circumstances	Events so unusual that it would be inequitable to allow agency to continue to exist.	Automatic on the happening of the event.
4. Bankruptcy	Bankruptcy decree (not mere insolvency) usually terminates agency.	
5. War between principal's country and agent's country	Automatically suspends or terminates agency—no way to enforce legal rights.	

longer legally sufficient to discharge the debt to Janz because Arlen no longer has Janz's authority to collect the funds. If Arlen absconds with the funds, Cochran must pay the debt again to Janz's estate.

IMPOSSIBILITY When the specific subject matter of an agency is destroyed or lost, the agency terminates. For example, Janz employs Arlen to sell Janz's house. Prior to any sale, the house is destroyed by fire. Arlen's agency and authority to sell the house terminate. Similarly, when it is impossible for the agent to perform the agency lawfully because of war or a change in the law, the agency terminates.

CHANGED CIRCUMSTANCES When an event occurs that has such an unusual effect on the subject matter of the agency that the agent can reasonably infer that the principal will not want the agency to continue, the agency terminates. Suppose that Janz hires Arlen to sell a tract of land for $40,000.

Subsequently, Arlen learns that there is oil under the land and that the land is therefore worth $1 million. The agency and Arlen's authority to sell the land for $40,000 are terminated.

BANKRUPTCY If either the principal or the agent petitions for bankruptcy, the agency is *usually* terminated. In certain circumstances, as when the agent's financial status is irrelevant to the purpose of the agency, the agency relationship may continue. *Insolvency* (defined as the inability to pay debts when they become due or when liabilities exceed assets), as distinguished from bankruptcy, does not necessarily terminate the relationship.

WAR When the principal's country and the agent's country are at war with each other, the agency is terminated. In this situation, the agency is automatically suspended or terminated because there is no way to enforce the legal rights and obligations of the parties.

REVIEWING LIABILITY TO THIRD PARTIES AND TERMINATION

Lynne Meyer, on her way to a business meeting and in a hurry, stopped at a Buy-Mart store for a new pair of nylons to wear to the meeting. There was a long line at one of the checkout counters, but a cashier, Valerie Watts, opened another counter and began loading the cash drawer. Meyer told Watts that she was in a hurry and asked Watts to work faster. Watts, however, only slowed her pace. At this point, Meyer hit Watts. It is not clear from the record whether Meyer hit Watts intentionally or, in an attempt to retrieve the nylons, hit her inadvertently. In response, Watts grabbed Meyer by the hair and hit her repeatedly in the back of the head, while Meyer screamed for help. Management personnel separated the two women and questioned them about the incident. Watts was immediately fired for violating the store's no-fighting policy. Meyer subsequently sued Buy-Mart, alleging that the store was liable for the tort (assault and battery) committed by its employee. Using the information presented in the chapter, answer the following questions.

1. Why would Meyer sue Buy-Mart and not Watts in this scenario?

2. Did Watts's behavior constitute an intentional tort or a tort of negligence? Is this distinction important in this case? Why or why not?

3. Under what doctrine discussed in this chapter might Buy-Mart be held liable for the tort committed by Watts? What is the key factor in determining whether Buy-Mart is liable under this doctrine?

4. Suppose that Watts was an independent contractor who worked for a temporary employment agency instead of a Buy-Mart employee. Could Buy-Mart be held liable for Watts's conduct in that situation? Why or why not?

5. Now suppose that when Watts applied for the job at Buy-Mart, she disclosed in her application that she had previously been convicted of felony assault and battery. Nevertheless, Buy-Mart hired Watts as a cashier. How might this fact affect Buy-Mart's liability for Watts's actions?

TERMS AND CONCEPTS TO REVIEW

apparent authority 653	implied authority 652	*respondeat superior* 660
disclosed principal 654	notary public 651	undisclosed principal 654
e-agent 656	partially disclosed principal 654	vicarious liability 660
equal dignity rule 651	power of attorney 651	
express authority 651	ratification 654	

QUESTIONS AND CASE PROBLEMS

32–1. Adam is a traveling salesperson for Peter Petri Plumbing Supply Corp. Adam has express authority to solicit orders from customers and to offer a 5 percent discount if payment is made within thirty days of delivery. Petri has said nothing to Adam about extending credit. Adam calls on a new prospective customer, John's Plumbing Firm. John tells Adam that he will place a large order for Petri products if Adam will give him a 10 percent discount with payment due in equal installments thirty, sixty, and ninety days from delivery. Adam says he has authority to make such a contract. John calls Petri and asks if Adam is authorized to make contracts giving a discount. No mention is made of payment terms. Petri replies that Adam has authority to make discounts on purchase orders. On the basis of this information, John orders $10,000 worth of plumbing supplies and fixtures. The goods are delivered and are being sold. One week later, John receives a bill for $9,500, due in thirty days. John insists he owes only $9,000 and can pay it in three equal installments, at thirty, sixty, and ninety days from delivery. Discuss the liability of Petri and John only.

32–2. **QUESTION WITH SAMPLE ANSWER**
Alice Adams is a purchasing agent-employee for the A & B Coal Supply partnership. Adams has authority to purchase the coal needed by A & B to satisfy the needs of its customers. While Adams is leaving a coal mine from

which she has just purchased a large quantity of coal, her car breaks down. She walks into a small roadside grocery store for help. While there, she runs into Will Wilson. Wilson owns 360 acres back in the mountains with all mineral rights. Wilson, in need of money, offers to sell Adams the property at $1,500 per acre. On inspection of the property, Adams forms the opinion that the subsurface contains valuable coal deposits. Adams contracts to purchase the property for A & B Coal Supply, signing the contract "A & B Coal Supply, Alice Adams, agent." The closing date is August 1. Adams takes the contract to the partnership. The managing partner is furious, as A & B is not in the property business. Later, just before closing, both Wilson and the partnership learn that the value of the land is at least $15,000 per acre. Discuss the rights of A & B and Wilson concerning the land contract.

For a sample answer to this question, go to Appendix I at the end of this text.

32–3. Paula Enterprises hires Able to act as its agent to purchase a 1,000-acre tract of land from Thompson for $1,000 per acre. Paula Enterprises does not wish Thompson to know that it is the principal or that Able is its agent. Paula wants the land for a new country housing development, and Thompson may not sell the land for that purpose or may demand a premium price. Able makes the contract for the purchase, signing only his name as purchaser and not disclosing to Thompson the agency relationship. The closing and transfer of deed are to take place on September 1.

(a) If Thompson learns of Paula's identity on August 1, can Thompson legally refuse to deed the property on September 1? Explain.

(b) Paula gives Able the funds for the closing, but Able absconds with the funds, causing a breach of Able's contract at the date of closing. Thompson then learns of Paula's identity and wants to enforce the contract. Discuss fully Thompson's rights under these circumstances.

32–4. ABC Tire Corp. hires Arnez as a traveling salesperson and assigns him a geographic area and time schedule in which to solicit orders and service customers. Arnez is given a company car to use in covering the territory. One day, Arnez decides to take his personal car to cover part of his territory. It is 11:00 A.M., and Arnez has just finished calling on all customers in the city of Tarrytown. His next appointment is in the city of Austex, twenty miles down the road, at 2:00 P.M. Arnez starts out for Austex, but halfway there he decides to visit a former college roommate who runs a farm ten miles off the main highway. Arnez is enjoying his visit with his former roommate when he realizes that it is 1:45 P.M. and that he will be late for the appointment in Austex. Driving at a high speed down the country road to reach the main highway, Arnez crashes his car into Thomas's tractor, severely injuring Thomas, a farmer. Thomas claims he can hold the ABC Tire Corp. liable for his injuries. Discuss fully ABC's liability in this situation.

32–5. *RESPONDEAT SUPERIOR.* Justin Jones suffered from genital herpes and sought treatment from Dr. Steven Baisch of Region West Pediatric Services. Jeni Hallgren, a nurse's assistant who was a Region West employee, told her friends and some of Jones's friends about Jones's condition. This was a violation of the Region West employee handbook, which required employees to maintain the confidentiality of patients' records. Jones filed a suit in a federal district court against Region West, among others, alleging that Region West should be held liable for its employee's actions on the basis of *respondeat superior*. On what basis might the court hold that Region West was not liable for Hallgren's acts? Discuss fully. [*Jones v. Baisch, M.D.*, 40 F.3d 252 (8th Cir. 1994)]

32–6. UNDISCLOSED PRINCIPAL. John Dunning was the sole officer of the R. B. Dunning Co. and was responsible for the management and operation of the business. When the company rented a warehouse from Samuel and Ruth Saliba, Dunning did not say that he was acting for the firm. The parties did not have a written lease. Business faltered, and the firm stopped paying rent. Eventually, it went bankrupt and vacated the property. The Salibas filed a suit in a Maine state court against Dunning personally, seeking to recover the unpaid rent. Dunning claimed the debt belonged to the company because he had been acting only as its agent. Who is liable for the rent, and why? [*Estate of Saliba v. Dunning*, 682 A.2d 224 (Me. 1996)]

32–7. ⚖ **CASE PROBLEM WITH SAMPLE ANSWER**

In 1998, William Larry Smith signed a lease for certain land in Chilton County, Alabama, owned by Sweet Smitherman. The lease stated that it was between "Smitherman, and WLS, Inc., d/b/a [doing business as] S & H Mobile Homes" and the signature line identified the lessee as "WLS, Inc. d/b/a S & H Mobile Homes . . . By: William Larry Smith, President." The amount of the rent was $5,000, payable by the tenth of each month. All of the checks that Smitherman received for the rent identified the owner of the account as "WLS Corporation d/b/a S & H Mobile Homes." Nearly four years later, Smitherman filed a suit in an Alabama state court against William Larry Smith, alleging that he owed $26,000 in unpaid rent. Smith responded in part that WLS was the lessee and that he was not personally responsible for the obligation to pay the rent. Is Smith a principal, an agent, both a principal and an agent, or neither? In any event, in the lease, is the principal disclosed, partially disclosed, or undisclosed? With the answers to these questions in mind, who is liable for the unpaid rent, and why? Discuss. [*Smith v. Smitherman*, 887 So.2d 285 (Ala.Civ.App. 2004)]

To view a sample answer for this case problem, go to this book's Web site at http://wbl.westbuslaw.com, select "Chapter 32," and click on "Case Problem with Sample Answer."

32–8. LIABILITY FOR EMPLOYEE'S ACTS. Federated Financial Reserve Corp. leases consumer and business equipment. As part of its credit-approval and debt-collection practices, Federated hires credit collectors and authorizes them to obtain credit reports on its customers. Janice Caylor, a Federated collector, used this authority to obtain a report on Karen Jones, who was not a Federated customer but who was the former wife of Caylor's roommate, Randy Lind. When Jones discovered that Lind had her address and how he had obtained it, she filed a suit in a federal district court against Federated and the others. Jones claimed in part that they had violated the Fair Credit Reporting Act, the goal of which is to protect consumers from the improper use of credit reports. Under what theory might an employer be held liable for an employee's violation of a statute? Does that theory apply in this case? Explain. [*Jones v. Federated Financial Reserve Corp.*, 144 F.3d 961 (6th Cir. 1998)]

32-9. LIABILITY FOR EMPLOYEE'S NEGLIGENCE. Lend Lease Trucks, Inc., employed Thomas Jones as an interstate truck driver. While on an assignment, Jones parked on the shoulder of U.S. Highway 301 near Kenly, North Carolina, and crossed the highway to the Dry Dock Lounge. In the lounge, Jones drank enough liquor for his blood-alcohol level to rise dramatically above the level at which he could legally drive his truck. After a few hours, Jones left the lounge. As he started across the highway to his truck, he darted into the path of a motor-cycle driven by Edward McNair. In the collision, Jones and McNair were killed. McNair's wife, Catherine, filed a suit in a North Carolina state court against Lend Lease Trucks, Inc., and others, claiming in part that Jones was acting within the scope of employment at the time of the accident. The case was removed to a federal district court. Lend Lease filed a motion to dismiss, the court granted the motion, and Catherine appealed. Was Jones acting within the scope of employment? Explain. [*McNair v. Lend Lease Trucks, Inc.*, 62 F.3d 651 (4th Cir. 1995)]

32-10. LIABILITY FOR INDEPENDENT CONTRACTOR'S TORTS. Greif Brothers Corp., a steel drum manufacturer, owned and operated a manufacturing plant in Youngstown, Ohio. In 1987, Lowell Wilson, the plant superintendent, hired Youngstown Security Patrol, Inc. (YSP), a security company, to guard Greif property and "deter thieves and vandals." Some YSP security guards, as Wilson knew, carried firearms. Eric Bator, a YSP security guard, was not certified as an armed guard but nevertheless took his gun, in a briefcase, to work. While working at the Greif plant on August 12, 1991, Bator fired his gun at Derrell Pusey, in the belief that Pusey was an intruder. The bullet struck and killed Pusey. Pusey's mother filed a suit in an Ohio state court against Greif and others, alleging in part that her son's death was the result of YSP's negligence, for which Greif was responsible. Greif filed a motion for a directed verdict. What is the plaintiff's best argument that Greif is responsible for YSP's actions? What is Greif's best defense? Explain. [*Pusey v. Bator*, 94 Ohio St.3d 275, 762 N.E.2d 968 (2002)]

LAW | on the Web

For updated links to resources available on the Web, as well as a variety of other materials, visit this text's Web site at http://wbl.westbuslaw.com.

An excellent source for information on agency law, including court cases involving agency concepts, is the Legal Information Institute (LII) at Cornell University. You can access the LII's Web page on this topic at

http://www.law.cornell.edu/topics/agency.html

There are now numerous "shopping bots" (e-agents) that will search the Web to obtain the best prices for specified products. You can obtain the latest reviews on the merits of various shopping bots by going to

http://www.botspot.com

LEGAL RESEARCH EXERCISES ON THE WEB

Go to http://wbl.westbuslaw.com, the Web site that accompanies this text. Select "Chapter 32" and click on "Internet Exercises." There you will find the following Internet research exercises that you can perform to learn more about topics covered in this chapter.

Activity 32–1: LEGAL PERSPECTIVE
Power of Attorney

Activity 32–2: MANAGEMENT PERSPECTIVE
Liability in Agency Relationships

CHAPTER 33

Employment and Labor Law

In the United States, employment relationships traditionally have been governed primarily by the common law. Before the industrial revolution, workers and employers enjoyed relatively equal bargaining power. Today, the workplace is regulated extensively by federal and state statutes. Recall from Chapter 1 that common law doctrines apply only to areas *not* covered by statutory law. Common law doctrines have thus been displaced to a significant extent by statutory law.

In this chapter, we look at the most significant laws regulating employment relationships. We examine other important laws regulating the workplace—those prohibiting employment discrimination—in the next chapter.

SECTION 1 | Employment at Will

Traditionally, employment relationships have generally been governed by the common law doctrine of **employment at will.** Other common law rules governing employment relationships—including rules under contract, tort, and agency law—have already been discussed at length in previous chapters of this text.

Given that many employees (those who deal with third parties) are normally deemed agents of an employer, agency concepts are especially relevant in the employment context. The distinction under agency law between employee status and independent-contractor status is also relevant to employment relationships. Generally, the laws discussed in this chapter and in Chapter 34 apply only to the employer-employee relationship; they do not apply to independent contractors.

APPLICATION OF THE EMPLOYMENT-AT-WILL DOCTRINE

Under the employment-at-will doctrine, either party may terminate an employment contract at any time and for any reason, unless the contract specifically provides to the contrary. As discussed in the *Contemporary Legal Debates* feature in Chapter 12, the legal status of the majority of American workers is

"employee at will." In other words, this common law doctrine is still in widespread use, and only one state (Montana) does not apply the doctrine. Nonetheless, as mentioned in the chapter introduction, federal and state statutes governing employment relationships prevent the doctrine from being applied in a number of circumstances. Today, an employer is not permitted to fire an employee if to do so would violate a federal or state employment statute, such as one prohibiting employment termination for discriminatory reasons (see Chapter 34).

EXCEPTIONS TO THE EMPLOYMENT-AT-WILL DOCTRINE

Under the employment-at-will doctrine, as mentioned, an employer may hire and fire employees at will (regardless of the employees' performance) without liability, unless the decision violates the terms of an employment contract or statutory law. Because of the harsh effects of the employment-at-will doctrine for employees, courts have carved out various exceptions to this doctrine. These exceptions are based on contract theory, tort theory, and public policy.

EXCEPTIONS BASED ON CONTRACT THEORY
Some courts have held that an *implied* employment contract exists between the employer and the employee. If the employee is fired outside the terms of

the implied contract, he or she may succeed in an action for breach of contract even though no written employment contract exists.

For example, an employer's manual or personnel bulletin may state that, as a matter of policy, workers will be dismissed only for good cause. If the employee is aware of this policy and continues to work for the employer, a court may find that there is an implied contract based on the terms stated in the manual or bulletin. Generally, the key consideration in determining whether an employment manual creates an implied contractual obligation is the employee's reasonable expectations.

Oral promises that an employer makes to employees regarding discharge policy may also be considered part of an implied contract. If the employer fires a worker in a manner contrary to what was promised, a court may hold that the employer has violated the implied contract and is liable for damages. Most state courts will consider this claim and judge it by traditional contract standards. In some cases, courts have held that an implied employment contract exists even though employees agreed in writing to be employees at will.[1] A few states have gone further and held that all employment contracts contain an implied covenant of good faith. In those states, if an employer fires an employee for an arbitrary or unjustified reason, the employee can claim that the covenant of good faith was breached and the contract violated.

EXCEPTIONS BASED ON TORT THEORY

In some situations, the discharge of an employee may give rise to an action for wrongful discharge under tort theories. Abusive discharge procedures may result in intentional infliction of emotional distress or defamation, and some courts have permitted workers to sue their employers under the tort theory of fraud. Under this theory, an employer may be held liable for making false promises to a prospective employee if the employee detrimentally relies on the employer's representations by taking the job.

For example, suppose that an employer induces a prospective employee to leave a lucrative position and move to another state by offering "a long-term job with a thriving business." In fact, the employer is having significant financial problems. Furthermore, the employer is planning a merger that will result in the elimination of the position offered to the prospective

employee. If the employee takes the job in reliance on the employer's representations and is laid off shortly thereafter, the employee may be able to bring an action against the employer for fraud.[2]

EXCEPTIONS BASED ON PUBLIC POLICY

The most widespread common law exception to the employment-at-will doctrine is that made on the basis of public policy. Courts may apply this exception when an employer fires a worker for reasons that violate a fundamental public policy of the jurisdiction.

—Requirements for the Public-Policy Exception.

Generally, the courts require that the public policy involved be expressed clearly in the statutory law governing the jurisdiction. The public policy against employment discrimination, for example, is expressed clearly in federal and state statutes. Thus, if a worker is fired for discriminatory reasons but has no cause of action under statutory law (because, for example, the workplace has too few employees to be covered by the statute), that worker may succeed in a suit against the employer for wrongful discharge in violation of public policy.[3]

—Whistleblowing.

Sometimes, an employer will direct an employee to perform an illegal act and fire the employee if he or she refuses to do so. At other times, employers will fire or discipline employees who "blow the whistle" on the employer's wrongdoing. **Whistleblowing** occurs when an employee tells a government official, upper-management authorities, or the press that her or his employer is engaged in some unsafe or illegal activity. Whistleblowers on occasion have been protected from wrongful discharge for reasons of public policy.

Today, whistleblowers have some protection under statutory law. For example, most states have enacted so-called whistleblower statutes that protect whistleblowers from subsequent retaliation on the part of employers. On the federal level, the Whistleblower Protection Act of 1989[4] protects federal employees

---

1. See, for example, *Kuest v. Regent Assisted Living, Inc.*, 111 Wash.App. 36, 43 P.3d 23 (2002).

2. See, for example, *Lazar v. Superior Court of Los Angeles Co.*, 12 Cal.4th 631, 909 P.2d 981, 49 Cal.Rptr.2d 377 (1996); and *McConkey v. AON Corp.*, 804 A.2d 572 (N.J.Super.A.D. 2002), which was discussed in the *Emerging Trends* feature presented in Chapter 14.

3. See, for example, *Molesworth v. Brandon*, 341 Md. 621, 672 A.2d 608 (1996); and *Wholey v. Sears Roebuck*, 370 Md. 38, 803 A.2d 482 (2002).

4. 5 U.S.C. Section 1201.

who blow the whistle on their employers from their employers' retaliatory actions. Whistleblower statutes may also provide an incentive to disclose information by providing the whistleblower with a monetary reward. For example, the federal False Claims Reform Act of 1986[5] requires that a whistleblower who has disclosed information relating to a fraud perpetrated against the U.S. government receive between 15 and 25 percent of the proceeds if the government brings suit against the wrongdoer.

WRONGFUL DISCHARGE

Whenever an employer discharges an employee in violation of an employment contract or a statutory law protecting employees, the employee may bring an action for **wrongful discharge.** If an employer's actions do not violate any express employment contract or statute, then the question is whether the employer may be subject to liability under a common law doctrine, such as a tort theory or agency. For example, suppose that an employer discharges a female employee and publicly discloses private facts about her sex life to her co-workers. In that situation, the employee could bring a wrongful discharge claim against the employer based on the tort of invasion of privacy (see Chapter 6).

SECTION 2 | Wage-Hour Laws

In the 1930s, Congress enacted several laws regulating the wages and working hours of employees. In 1931, Congress passed the Davis-Bacon Act,[6] which requires the payment of "prevailing wages" to employees of contractors and subcontractors working on government construction projects. In 1936, the Walsh-Healey Act[7] was passed. This act requires that a minimum wage, as well as overtime pay of time and a half, be paid to employees of manufacturers or suppliers entering into contracts with agencies of the federal government.

In 1938, with the passage of the Fair Labor Standards Act[8] (FLSA), Congress extended wage-hour requirements to cover all employers engaged in interstate commerce or engaged in the production of goods for interstate commerce. We examine here the

FLSA's provisions in regard to child labor, maximum hours, and minimum wages.

CHILD LABOR

The FLSA prohibits oppressive child labor. Children under fourteen years of age are allowed to do certain types of work, such as deliver newspapers, work for their parents, and be employed in the entertainment and (with some exceptions) agricultural areas. Children who are fourteen or fifteen years of age are allowed to work, but not in hazardous occupations. There are also numerous restrictions on how many hours per day and per week they can work. For example, minors under the age of sixteen cannot work during school hours, for more than three hours on a school day (or eight hours on a nonschool day), for more than eighteen hours during a school week (or forty hours during a nonschool week), or before 7 A.M. or after 7 P.M. (9 P.M. during the summer). Most states require persons under sixteen years of age to obtain work permits.

Persons who are between the ages of sixteen and eighteen do not face such restrictions on working times and hours, but they cannot be employed in hazardous jobs or in jobs detrimental to their health and well-being. Those over the age of eighteen are not affected by any of the above-mentioned restrictions.

HOURS AND WAGES

The FLSA provides that a **minimum wage** of a specified amount ($5.15 per hour, as of this writing) must be paid to employees in covered industries. Congress periodically revises the amount of the minimum wage.[9] Under the FLSA, the term *wages* includes the reasonable costs of the employer in furnishing employees with board, lodging, and other facilities if they are customarily furnished by that employer.

Under the FLSA, any employee who agrees to work more than forty hours per week must be paid no less than one and a half times her or his regular pay for all hours over forty. Note that the FLSA overtime provisions apply only after an employee has worked more than forty hours per *week.* Thus, employees who work for ten hours a day, four days per week, are not entitled to overtime pay because they do not work more than forty hours a week.

---

5. 31 U.S.C. Sections 3729–3733. This act amended the False Claims Act of 1863.
6. 40 U.S.C. Sections 276a–276a-5.
7. 41 U.S.C. Sections 35–45.
8. 29 U.S.C. Sections 201–260.

---

9. Note that many state and local governments also have minimum-wage laws; these laws provide for higher minimum-wage rates than that required by the federal government.

OVERTIME EXEMPTIONS

Certain employees are exempt from the overtime provisions of the act. These exemptions typically include employees whose jobs are categorized as executive, administrative, or professional, as well as outside salespersons and computer employees. In the past, to fall into one of these categories, an employee had to earn more than a specified salary threshold and devote a certain percentage of work time to the performance of specific types of duties. Because the salary limits were low and the duties tests were complex and confusing, over the last twenty years some employers have been able to avoid paying overtime wages to their employees. This prompted the U.S. Department of Labor to substantially revise the regulations pertaining to overtime for the first time in over fifty years.

NEW OVERTIME RULES In August 2004, new rules were implemented that expand the number of workers eligible for overtime by nearly tripling the salary threshold.[10] Under the new provisions, workers earning less than $23,660 a year are guaranteed overtime pay for working more than forty hours per week (the previous ceiling was $8,060). Employers can continue to pay overtime to ineligible employees if they want to do so, but cannot waive or reduce the overtime requirements of the FLSA.

The exemptions to payment of overtime by employers do not apply to manual laborers or other "blue-collar" workers who perform tasks involving repetitive operations with their hands (such as production-line employees who are not part of management, for example). The exemptions also do not apply to police, firefighters, licensed nurses, and other public-safety workers. White-collar workers who earn more than $100,000 a year, computer programmers, dental hygienists, and insurance adjusters are typically exempt—though they must also meet certain other criteria.

JOB TITLES ALONE ARE INSUFFICIENT TO ESTABLISH EXEMPTIONS Under the new provisions, an employer cannot deny overtime wages to an employee based only on the employee's job title. For example, in one case an employer refused to pay overtime wages to a computer maintenance worker. The court held that the worker, who performed troubleshooting on individual computers but did not engage in systems analysis or design, was not exempt as a "computer professional" under the rules.[11]

SECTION 3 | Labor Unions

In the 1930s, in addition to wage-hour laws, the government enacted several other laws. These laws protect employees' rights to join labor unions, to bargain with management over the terms and conditions of employment, and to conduct strikes.

FEDERAL LABOR LAWS

Federal labor laws governing union-employer relations have developed considerably since the first law was enacted in 1932. Initially, the laws were concerned with protecting the rights and interests of workers. Subsequent legislation placed some restraints on unions and granted rights to employers. We look here at four major federal statutes regulating union-employer relations.

NORRIS-LAGUARDIA ACT Congress protected peaceful strikes, picketing, and boycotts in 1932 in the Norris-LaGuardia Act.[12] The statute restricted the power of federal courts to issue injunctions against unions engaged in peaceful strikes. In effect, this act declared a national policy permitting employees to organize.

NATIONAL LABOR RELATIONS ACT One of the foremost statutes regulating labor is the National Labor Relations Act (NLRA) of 1935.[13] This act established the rights of employees to engage in collective bargaining and to strike. The NLRA also specifically defined a number of employer practices as unfair to labor:

1. Interference with the efforts of employees to form, join, or assist labor organizations or to engage in concerted activities for their mutual aid or protection.
2. An employer's domination of a labor organization or contribution of financial or other support to it.
3. Discrimination in the hiring of or the awarding of tenure to employees for reason of union affiliation.

---

11. *Martin v. Indiana Michigan Power Co.*, 381 F.3d 574 (6th Cir. 2004).
12. 29 U.S.C. Sections 101–110, 113–115.
13. 20 U.S.C. Sections 151–169.

---

10. 29 C.F.R. Section 541.

4. Discrimination against employees for filing charges under the act or giving testimony under the act.

5. Refusal to bargain collectively with the duly designated representative of the employees.

—The National Labor Relations Board. The purpose of the NLRA was to secure for employees the rights to organize; to bargain collectively through representatives of their own choosing; and to engage in concerted activities for organizing, collective bargaining, and other purposes. To aid in achieving these goals, the act created the National Labor Relations Board (NLRB) to oversee union elections and to prevent employers from engaging in unfair and illegal union-related activities and unfair labor practices.

The NLRB has the authority to investigate employees' charges of unfair labor practices and to file complaints against employers in response to these charges. The NLRB may also issue **cease-and-desist orders**—orders compelling employers to cease engaging in the unfair practices—when violations are found. Cease-and-desist orders can be enforced by a circuit court of appeals if necessary. Arguments over alleged unfair labor practices are first decided by the NLRB and may then be appealed to a federal court.

—Workers Protected by the NLRA. To be protected under the NLRA, an individual must be an *employee*, as that term is defined in the statute. Courts have long held that job applicants fall within that definition (otherwise, the NLRA's ban on "discrimination in regard to hire" would mean little). Additionally, the United States Supreme Court has held that individuals who are hired by a union to organize a company are to be considered employees of the company for NLRA purposes.[14]

LABOR-MANAGEMENT RELATIONS ACT The Labor-Management Relations Act (LMRA) of 1947[15] was passed to proscribe certain unfair union practices, such as the *closed shop*. A **closed shop** is a firm that requires union membership of its workers as a condition of employment. Although the act made the closed shop illegal, it preserved the legality of the union shop. A **union shop** does not require membership as a prerequisite for employment but can, and usually does, require that workers join the union after a specified amount of time on the job.

The act also prohibited unions from refusing to bargain with employers, engaging in certain types of picketing, and *featherbedding* (causing employers to hire more employees than necessary). In addition, the act allowed individual states to pass their own **right-to-work laws**—laws making it illegal for union membership to be required for *continued* employment in any establishment. Thus, union shops are technically illegal in the twenty-three states that have right-to-work laws.

LABOR-MANAGEMENT REPORTING AND DISCLOSURE ACT The Labor-Management Reporting and Disclosure Act (LMRDA) of 1959[16] established an employee bill of rights and reporting requirements for union activities. The act strictly regulates unions' internal business procedures. Union elections, for example, are regulated by the LMRDA, which requires that regularly scheduled elections of officers occur and that secret ballots be used. Former convicts are prohibited from holding union office. Moreover, union officials are accountable for union property and funds. Members have the right to attend and to participate in union meetings, to nominate officers, and to vote in most union proceedings.

The act also outlawed **hot-cargo agreements**—agreements in which employers voluntarily agree with unions not to handle, use, or deal in goods of other employers produced by nonunion employees. The act made all such boycotts (called **secondary boycotts**) illegal.

UNION ORGANIZATION

Suppose that the workers of a particular firm want to join a union. How is a union formed? Typically, the first step in the process is to have the workers sign authorization cards. An authorization card usually states that the worker desires to have a certain union, such as the American Federation of Labor and Congress of Industrial Organizations (AFL-CIO), represent the workforce. If those in favor of the union can obtain authorization cards from a majority of the workers, they may present the cards to the employer and ask the employer to recognize the union formally. If the employer refuses to do so, the unionizers can petition the NLRB for an election.

---

14. *National Labor Relations Board v. Town & Country Electric, Inc.*, 516 U.S. 85, 116 S.Ct. 450, 133 L.Ed.2d 371 (1995).

15. 29 U.S.C. Sections 141 *et seq.*

16. 29 U.S.C. Sections 401 *et seq.*

UNION ELECTIONS For an election to be held, the unionizers must demonstrate that at least 30 percent of the workers to be represented support a union or an election on unionization. The NLRB supervises the election and ensures that the voting is secret and that the voters are eligible. If the election is a fair one and if the proposed union receives majority support, the NLRB certifies the union as the bargaining representative for the employees.

UNION ELECTION CAMPAIGNS Many disputes between labor and management arise during union election campaigns. Generally, the employer has control over unionizing activities that take place on company property and during working hours. Employers may thus limit the campaign activities of union supporters as long as the employer has a legitimate business reason for doing so. For example, suppose that a union is seeking to organize clerks at a department store owned by Amanti Enterprises. Amanti can prohibit all union solicitation in areas of the store open to the public because it could seriously interfere with the store's business. Amanti may not, however, discriminate in its prohibition against solicitation in the workplace by prohibiting union solicitation but allowing solicitation for charitable causes. If the activity is conducted outside working hours, though, such as during lunch hours or coffee breaks, employers cannot prevent union-related solicitation in employee lunchrooms and break areas.

An employer may also campaign among its workers against the union, but the NLRB carefully monitors and regulates the campaign tactics of management. Otherwise, management might use its economic power to coerce the workers to vote not to unionize. If the employer issues threats ("If the union wins, you'll all be fired") or engages in other unfair labor practices, the NLRB may certify the union even though it lost the election. Alternatively, the NLRB may ask a court to order a new election.

Like an employer, a union and its supporters may not engage in unfair labor practices during a union election campaign. In the following case, the court considered the impact of a union proponent's allegedly unfair labor practice on the outcome of an election.

CASE 33.1 | **Associated Rubber Co. v. National Labor Relations Board**

United States
Court of Appeals,
Eleventh Circuit, 2002.
296 F.3d 1055.
http://www.law.emory.edu/
11circuit[a]

BACKGROUND AND FACTS *Associated Rubber Company owns three rubber-production plants in Tallapoosa, Georgia. In June 1999, the United Steelworkers of America, AFL-CIO-CLC, filed a petition with the National Labor Relations Board (NLRB), seeking an election to obtain certification as the collective bargaining representative of maintenance workers, truck drivers, and mechanics employed at Associated Rubber's plants. During the election campaign, Leroy Brown, an Associated Rubber employee and a union supporter, threatened Tim Spears, an employee and a union opponent. Three days before the election, Brown speeded up the rate at which heavy, scalding batches of rubber compound were mixed and sent to Spears. Barely able to handle the speed, Spears told his foreman that if the union won the election, he would quit his job out of fear that the incident would be repeated. Other employees were aware of Brown's threat and the "Banbury incident" (Banbury was the brand name of the compound mixer). The union won the election by a vote of 53 to 50. Associated Rubber filed an objection on the basis of Brown's conduct. The NLRB concluded that the election was not tainted, certified the union, and ordered Associated Rubber to bargain. Associated Rubber appealed the order to the U.S. Court of Appeals for the Eleventh Circuit.*

IN THE LANGUAGE OF THE COURT
CARNES, Circuit Judge:
* * * *

When the union itself engages in objectionable misconduct, the Board will overturn the election if the conduct interfered with the employees' exercise of free choice to such an extent that it materially affected the results of the election. If, however, a third party engages in misconduct,

---

a. In the "Listing by Month of Decision" section, in the "2002" row, click on "July." In the result, click on the name of the case to access the opinion. Emory University School of Law in Atlanta, Georgia, maintains this Web site.

CONTINUED

the party objecting to the election has the burden of showing that the misconduct was so aggravated as to create a general atmosphere of fear and reprisal rendering a free election impossible. * * * [Emphasis added.]

* * * *

Applying these legal standards to the record in this case convinces us that the Board's conclusion that the Banbury mixer incident did not warrant overturning the election should itself be overturned. To begin with, the record shows that Brown accelerated the mixer in retaliation for Spears' refusal to accept union literature. Brown threatened to make Spears "pay" for refusing to accept union literature, and he did so. Seven or eight days after the threat, and as the election drew near, Brown accelerated the Banbury mixer during Spears' shift as mill operator, causing the hot 450-pound batches of rubber compound to drop at a faster rate, a rate that made things more difficult and more dangerous than would have been the case but for Brown's malicious behavior. * * *

* * * *

* * * No employee ought to be subjected to any increased danger because of his position in a union certification election, and an increased risk of injury can itself be enough to have a chilling effect on the employees' right to freely decide whether they wish to be represented by a union.

* * * *

Importantly, the incident occurred only three days before the election took place. That fact makes the incident worse and increases the impact it had on the election. * * *

* * * *

In sum, the fact that Spears was threatened and then retaliated against in a way that placed him in personal danger would reasonably create fear in the minds of employees who were voting in the certification election. Although there apparently is no evidence that Spears' own vote was affected, at least seven people, including Spears, knew of the incident and connected it to Brown's earlier threat, and the election results turned on two votes.

DECISION AND REMEDY *The U.S. Court of Appeals for the Eleventh Circuit set aside the NLRB's order. The court held that given the seriousness of the incident, the degree to which news of it was disseminated before the election, its proximity to the election, and the closeness of the vote, the NLRB should have ordered a new election.*

WHAT IF THE FACTS WERE DIFFERENT? *If Brown's conduct in the "Banbury incident" had been motivated by something other than his support for the union and Spears's refusal to accept union literature, would the result in this case have been different? Explain.*

COLLECTIVE BARGAINING

If a fair election is held and the union wins, the NLRB will certify the union as the *exclusive bargaining representative* of the workers. The central legal right of a union is to engage in collective bargaining on the members' behalf. **Collective bargaining** can be defined as the process by which labor and management negotiate the terms and conditions of employment, including wages, benefits, working conditions, and other matters. Through collective bargaining, union representatives elected by union members speak on behalf of the members at the bargaining table.

When a union is officially recognized, it may demand to bargain with the employer and negotiate new terms or conditions of employment. In collective bargaining, as in most other business negotiations,

each side uses its economic power to pressure or persuade the other side to grant concessions.

Bargaining does not mean that one side must give in to the other or that compromises must be made. It does mean that a demand to bargain with the employer must be taken seriously and that both sides must bargain in "good faith." Good faith bargaining requires that management, for example, must be willing to meet with union representatives and consider the union's wishes when negotiating a contract. Examples of bad faith bargaining on the part of management include engaging in a campaign among workers to undermine the union, constantly shifting positions on disputed contract terms, and sending bargainers who lack authority to commit the company to a contract. If an employer (or a union) refuses to bargain in good faith without justification, it has committed an unfair labor practice, and the other party may petition the NLRB for an order requiring good faith bargaining.

STRIKES

Even when labor and management have bargained in good faith, they may be unable to reach a final agreement. When extensive collective bargaining has been conducted and an impasse results, the union may call a strike against the employer to pressure it into making concessions. A **strike** occurs when the unionized employees leave their jobs and refuse to work. The workers also typically picket the plant, standing outside the facility with signs that complain of management's unfairness.

A strike is an extreme action. Striking workers lose their right to be paid, and management loses production and may lose customers, whose orders cannot be filled. Labor law regulates the circumstances and conduct of strikes. Most strikes are "economic strikes," which are initiated because the union wants a better contract. A union may also strike when the employer has engaged in unfair labor practices.

THE RIGHT TO STRIKE The right to strike is guaranteed by the NLRA, within limits, and strike activities, such as picketing, are protected by the free speech guarantee of the First Amendment to the U.S. Constitution. Nonworkers have a right to participate in picketing an employer. The NLRA also gives workers the right to refuse to cross a picket line of fellow workers who are engaged in a lawful strike. Employers are permitted to hire replacement workers to substitute for the striking workers.

THE RIGHTS OF STRIKERS AFTER A STRIKE ENDS
An important issue concerns the rights of strikers after a strike ends. In a typical economic strike over working conditions, the strikers have no right to return to their jobs. If satisfactory replacement workers have been found, the strikers may find themselves out of work. The law does prohibit the employer from discriminating against former strikers, however. Employers must give former strikers preferential rights to any new vacancies that arise and also allow them to retain their seniority rights. Different rules apply when a union strikes because the employer has engaged in unfair labor practices. In this situation, the employer may still hire replacements but must give the strikers back their jobs once the strike is over.

SECTION 4 | Worker Health and Safety

Under the common law, employees injured on the job had to rely on tort law or contract law theories in suits they brought against their employers. Additionally, workers had some recourse under the common law governing agency relationships (discussed in Chapters 31 and 32), which imposes a duty on a principal-employer to provide a safe workplace for an agent-employee. Today, numerous state and federal statutes protect employees from the risk of accidental injury, death, or disease resulting from their employment. This section discusses the primary federal statute governing health and safety in the workplace, along with state workers' compensation acts.

THE OCCUPATIONAL SAFETY AND HEALTH ACT

At the federal level, the primary legislation protecting employees' health and safety is the Occupational Safety and Health Act of 1970.[17] Congress passed this act in an attempt to ensure safe and healthful working conditions for practically every employee in the country. The act provides for specific standards that employers must meet, plus a general duty to keep workplaces safe.

ENFORCEMENT AGENCIES Three federal agencies develop and enforce the standards set by the Occupational Safety and Health Act. The Occupational Safety and Health Administration (OSHA) is part of the Department of Labor and has the authority to promulgate standards, make inspections, and enforce the act. OSHA has issued safety standards governing many workplace details, such as the structural stability of ladders and the requirements for railings. OSHA also establishes standards that protect employees against exposure to substances that may be harmful to their health.

The National Institute for Occupational Safety and Health is part of the Department of Health and Human Services. Its main duty is to conduct research on safety and health problems and to recommend standards for OSHA to adopt. Finally, the Occupational Safety and Health Review Commission is an independent agency set up to handle appeals from actions taken by OSHA administrators.

---

17. 29 U.S.C. Sections 553, 651–678.

PROCEDURES AND VIOLATIONS OSHA compliance officers may enter and inspect facilities of any establishment covered by the Occupational Safety and Health Act.[18] Employees may also file complaints of violations. Under the act, an employer cannot discharge an employee who files a complaint or who, in good faith, refuses to work in a high-risk area if bodily harm or death might result.

Employers with eleven or more employees are required to keep occupational injury and illness records for each employee. Each record must be made available for inspection when requested by an OSHA inspector. Whenever a work-related injury or disease occurs, employers must make reports directly to OSHA. Whenever an employee is killed in a work-related accident or when five or more employees are hospitalized in one accident, the employer must notify the Department of Labor within forty-eight hours. If the company fails to do so, it will be fined. Following the accident, a complete inspection of the premises is mandatory.

Criminal penalties for willful violation of the Occupational Safety and Health Act are limited. Employers may be prosecuted under state laws, however. In other words, the act does not preempt state and local criminal laws.[19]

STATE WORKERS' COMPENSATION LAWS

State **workers' compensation laws** establish an administrative procedure for compensating workers injured on the job. Instead of suing, an injured worker files a claim with the administrative agency or board that administers the local workers' compensation claims.

EMPLOYEES COVERED BY WORKERS' COMPENSATION Most workers' compensation statutes are similar. No state covers all employees. Typically excluded are domestic workers, agricultural workers, temporary employees, and employees of common carriers (companies that provide shipping and transportation services to the public). Generally, the statutes cover minors. Usually, the statutes allow employers to purchase insurance from a private insurer or a state fund to pay workers' compensation benefits in the event of a claim. Most states also allow employers to be *self-insured*—that is, employers who show an ability to pay claims do not need to buy insurance.

REQUIREMENTS FOR RECEIVING WORKERS' COMPENSATION In general, the right to recover benefits is predicated wholly on the existence of an employment relationship and the fact that the worker's injury was *accidental* and *occurred on the job or in the course of employment*, regardless of fault. Intentionally inflicted self-injury, for example, would not be considered accidental and hence would not be covered. If an injury occurs while an employee is commuting to or from work, it usually will not be considered to have occurred on the job or in the course of employment and hence will not be covered.

An employee must notify his or her employer of an injury promptly (usually within thirty days of the injury's occurrence). Generally, an employee also must file a workers' compensation claim with the appropriate state agency or board within a certain period (sixty days to two years) from the time the injury is first noticed, rather than from the time of the accident.

WORKERS' COMPENSATION VERSUS LITIGATION An employee's acceptance of workers' compensation benefits bars the employee from suing for injuries caused by the employer's negligence. By barring lawsuits for negligence, workers' compensation laws also bar employers from raising common law defenses to negligence, such as contributory negligence. For example, an employer can no longer raise such defenses as contributory negligence or assumption of risk to avoid liability for negligence. A worker may sue an employer who *intentionally* injures the worker, however.

SECTION 5 | Income Security, Pension, and Health Plans

Federal and state governments participate in insurance programs designed to protect employees and their families by covering the financial impact of retirement, disability, death, hospitalization, and unemployment. The key federal law on this subject is the Social Security Act of 1935.[20]

---

18. In 1978, the United States Supreme Court held that warrantless inspections violated the warrant clause of the Fourth Amendment to the U.S. Constitution. See *Marshall v. Barlow's, Inc.*, 436 U.S. 307, 98 S.Ct. 1816, 56 L.Ed.2d 305 (1978). Although this case has not been overruled, the Supreme Court subsequently indicated that statutory inspection programs can provide a constitutionally adequate substitute for a warrant. See *Donovan v. Dewey*, 452 U.S. 594, 101 S.Ct. 2534, 69 L.Ed.2d 262 (1981).
19. *Pedraza v. Shell Oil Co.*, 942 F.2d 48 (1st Cir. 1991); *cert.* denied, 502 U.S. 1082, 112 S.Ct. 993, 117 L.Ed.2d 154 (1992). See also *In re Welding Fume Products Liability Litigation*, 364 F.Supp.2d 669 (N.D. Ohio 2005).

20. 42 U.S.C. Sections 301–1397e.

SOCIAL SECURITY

The Social Security Act of 1935 provides for old-age (retirement), survivors, and disability insurance. The act is therefore often referred to as OASDI. Both employers and employees must "contribute" under the Federal Insurance Contributions Act (FICA)[21] to help pay for the employees' loss of income on retirement.

The basis for the employee's and the employer's contribution is the employee's annual wage base—the maximum amount of the employee's wages that are subject to the tax. The employer withholds the employee's FICA contribution from the employee's wages and then matches this contribution. The annual wage base increases each year to take into account the rising cost of living. In 2005, employers were required to withhold 6.2 percent of each employee's wages, up to a maximum amount of $90,000, and to match this contribution.

Retired workers are eligible to receive monthly payments from the Social Security Administration, which administers the Social Security Act. Social Security benefits are fixed by statute but increase automatically with increases in the cost of living.

MEDICARE

Medicare, a federal government health-insurance program, is administered by the Social Security Administration for people sixty-five years of age and older and for some under age sixty-five who are disabled. It has two parts, one pertaining to hospital costs and the other to nonhospital medical costs, such as visits to physicians' offices. People who have Medicare hospital insurance can obtain additional federal medical insurance if they pay small monthly premiums, which increase as the cost of medical care rises.

As with Social Security contributions, both the employer and the employee contribute to Medicare. For 2005, employees paid 1.45 percent of their income on *all* wages and salaries, and employers contributed a matching percentage (1.45 percent). This resulted in a total contribution to Medicare (from both employer and employee) that is equal to 2.9 percent of the wages of each employee. Persons who were self-employed contributed 2.9 percent of their total income toward Medicare.

Unlike Social Security contributions (which have a limit each year), there is no cap on the amount of wages subject to the Medicare tax. In other words, for the first $90,000 of income (in 2005), both the

employer and the employee paid 7.65 percent each in contributions to finance Medicare and Social Security (a combined total of 15.3 percent). After this maximum taxable income, employees and employers only paid the Medicare portion of the total tax.

PRIVATE PENSION PLANS

Significant legislation has been enacted to regulate employee retirement plans set up by employers to supplement Social Security benefits. The major federal act covering these retirement plans is the Employee Retirement Income Security Act (ERISA) of 1974.[22] This statute empowers the Labor Management Services Administration of the Department of Labor to enforce its provisions governing employers who have private pension funds for their employees. ERISA does not require an employer to establish a pension plan. When a plan exists, however, ERISA establishes standards for its management.

A key provision of ERISA concerns vesting. **Vesting** gives an employee a legal right to receive pension benefits at some future date when she or he stops working. Before ERISA was enacted, some employees who had worked for companies for as long as thirty years received no pension benefits when their employment terminated because those benefits had not vested. ERISA establishes complex vesting rules. Generally, however, all employee contributions to pension plans vest immediately, and employee rights to employer pension-plan contributions vest after five years of employment.

In an attempt to prevent mismanagement of pension funds, ERISA has established rules on how they must be invested. Pension managers must be cautious in choosing investments and must diversify the plan's investments in order to minimize the risk of large losses. ERISA also contains detailed record-keeping and reporting requirements.

UNEMPLOYMENT COMPENSATION

To ease the financial impact of unemployment, the United States has a system of unemployment insurance. The Federal Unemployment Tax Act of 1935[23] created a state-administered system that provides unemployment compensation to eligible individuals. Under this system, employers pay into a fund, and the proceeds are paid out to qualified unemployed workers. The FUTA and state laws require employers

---

21. 26 U.S.C. Sections 3101–3125.

22. 29 U.S.C. Sections 1001 *et seq.*

23. 26 U.S.C. Sections 3301–3310.

that fall under the provisions of the act to pay unemployment taxes at regular intervals.

COBRA

Federal legislation also addresses the issue of health insurance for workers whose jobs have been terminated and who are thus no longer eligible for group health-insurance plans. The Consolidated Omnibus Budget Reconciliation Act (COBRA) of 1985[24] prohibits the elimination of a worker's medical, optical, or dental insurance coverage on the voluntary or involuntary termination of the worker's employment. The act applies to most workers who have either lost their jobs or had their hours decreased so that they are no longer eligible for coverage under the employer's health plan. Only workers fired for gross misconduct are excluded from protection.

APPLICATION OF COBRA The worker has sixty days (beginning with the date that the group coverage would stop) to decide whether to continue with the employer's group insurance plan. If the worker chooses to discontinue the coverage, then the employer has no further obligation. If the worker chooses to continue coverage, though, the employer is obligated to keep the policy active for up to eighteen months. If the worker is disabled, the employer must extend coverage for up to twenty-nine months. The coverage provided must be the same as that enjoyed by the worker prior to the termination or reduction of employment. If family members were originally included, for example, COBRA prohibits their exclusion. The worker does not receive a free ride, however. To receive continued benefits, he or she may be required to pay the entire premium, as well as a 2 percent administrative charge.

EMPLOYERS' OBLIGATIONS UNDER COBRA Employers, with some exceptions, must comply with COBRA if they employ twenty or more workers and provide a benefit plan to those workers. An employer must inform an employee of COBRA's provisions when that worker faces termination or a reduction of hours that would affect her or his eligibility for coverage under the plan. An employer that fails to comply with COBRA risks substantial penalties, such as a tax of up to 10 percent of the annual cost of the group plan or $500,000, whichever is less.

An employer is relieved of the responsibility to provide benefit coverage if the employer completely eliminates its group benefit plan. An employer is also relieved of responsibility when the worker becomes eligible for Medicare, falls under a spouse's health plan, becomes insured under a different plan (with a new employer, for example), or fails to pay the premium.

EMPLOYER-SPONSORED GROUP HEALTH PLANS

The Health Insurance Portability and Accountability Act (HIPAA),[25] which was discussed in Chapter 4 in the context of its privacy protections, contains provisions that affect employer-sponsored group health plans. HIPAA does not require employers to provide health insurance, but it does establish requirements for those that do provide such coverage. For example, under HIPAA, an employer's ability to exclude persons from coverage for "preexisting conditions" is strictly limited to the previous six months. The act defines preexisting conditions as those for which medical advice, diagnosis, care, or treatment was recommended or received within the previous six months (excluding pregnancy).

In addition, employers who are plan sponsors have significant responsibilities regarding the manner in which they collect, use, and disclose the health information of employees and their families. Essentially, the act requires employers to comply with a number of administrative, technical, and procedural safeguards (such as training employees, designating privacy officials, and distributing privacy notices) to ensure that employees' health information is not disclosed to unauthorized parties. Failure to comply with HIPAA regulations can result in civil penalties of up to $100 per person per violation (with a cap of $25,000 per year). The employer is also subject to criminal prosecution for certain types of HIPAA violations and can face up to $250,000 in criminal fines and imprisonment for up to ten years if convicted.

SECTION 6 | Family and Medical Leave

In 1993, Congress passed the Family and Medical Leave Act (FMLA)[26] to protect employees who need time off work for family or medical reasons. A majority of the states also have legislation allowing for a leave from employment for family or medical reasons, and many employers maintain private family-leave plans for their workers.

---

24. 29 U.S.C. Sections 1161–1169.

25. 29 U.S.C.A. Sections 1181 *et seq.*
26. 29 U.S.C. Sections 2601, 2611–2619, 2651–2654.

COVERAGE AND APPLICATION OF THE FMLA

The FMLA requires employers who have fifty or more employees to provide an employee with up to twelve weeks of family or medical leave during any twelve-month period. Generally, an employee may take family leave to care for a newborn baby, an adopted child, or a foster child, and medical leave when the employee or the employee's spouse, child, or parent has a "serious health condition" requiring care.[27] The act does not apply to part-time or newly hired employees (those who have worked for less than one year).

For most absences, the employee must demonstrate that the health condition requires continued treatment by a health-care provider and includes a period of incapacity of more than three days. Employees suffering from certain chronic health conditions such as asthma and diabetes, as well as those who are pregnant, however, may take FMLA leave for their own incapacities that require absences of less than three days.

PROTECTS EMPLOYEE'S JOB AND HEALTH BENEFITS The employer cannot interfere with, restrain, or deny an employee from exercising or attempting to exercise his or her rights under the FMLA, nor can the employer discharge or discriminate against an employee for taking leave. The employer must continue the worker's health-care coverage and guarantee employment in the same or a comparable position when the employee returns to work. In addi-

tion, the employer is required to immediately reinstate the employee after the leave, provided that the worker can perform the essential functions of the position.[28]

An important exception to the FMLA, however, allows the employer to avoid reinstating a *key employee*—defined as an employee whose pay falls within the top 10 percent of the firm's workforce. If reinstating a highly paid key employee would cause "substantial and grievous economic injury" to the employer, the employer is not required to restore the employee's position after the leave. The employer must continue to maintain health benefits for the key employee during the leave, however. This exception is to be used only in specified and limited circumstances, and the employer is required to follow certain procedures. For example, the employer must notify the employee of her or his status as a key employee as soon as possible and must offer the employee the option of returning to work immediately rather than risk losing her or his position.

APPLIES TO BOTH PUBLIC- AND PRIVATE-SECTOR EMPLOYERS The FMLA expressly covers private and public (government) employees. Nevertheless, some states argued that public employees could not sue their state employers in federal courts to enforce their FMLA rights unless the states consented to be sued.[29] This argument came before the United States Supreme Court in the following case.

---

27. The foster care must be state sanctioned before such an arrangement falls within the coverage of the FMLA.

28. See, for example, *Hoge v. Honda of America Manufacturing, Inc.*, 384 F.3d 238 (6th Cir. 2004).

29. Under the Eleventh Amendment to the U.S. Constitution, a state is immune from suit in a federal court unless the state agrees to be sued.

| CASE 33.2 | Nevada Department of Human Resources v. Hibbs |

Supreme Court of the United States, 2003. 538 U.S. 721, 123 S.Ct. 1972, 155 L.Ed.2d 953.

Chief Justice *REHNQUIST* delivered the opinion of the Court.
* * * *

Petitioners include the Nevada Department of Human Resources (Department) * * *. Respondent William Hibbs (hereinafter respondent) worked for the Department's Welfare Division. In April and May 1997, he sought leave under the FMLA to care for his ailing wife, who was recovering from a car accident and neck surgery. The Department granted his request for the full 12 weeks of FMLA leave and authorized him to use the leave intermittently as needed between May and December 1997. Respondent did so until August 5, 1997, after which he did not return to work. In October 1997, the Department informed respondent that he had exhausted his FMLA leave, that no further leave would be granted, and that he must report to work by November 12, 1997. Respondent failed to do so and was terminated.

CONTINUED ▶

CASE 33.2 Continued

Respondent sued petitioners in [a] United States District Court * * * . The District Court awarded petitioners summary judgment on the grounds that the FMLA claim was barred by the [U.S. Constitution's] Eleventh Amendment * * * . Respondent appealed * * * . The Ninth Circuit reversed.

We granted *certiorari* * * * .

* * * *

The history of the many state laws limiting women's employment opportunities is chronicled in—and, until relatively recently, was sanctioned by—this Court's own opinions. For example, in [previous cases] the Court upheld state laws prohibiting women from practicing law and tending bar * * * . State laws frequently subjected women to distinctive restrictions, terms, conditions, and benefits for those jobs they could take. In [one case] for example, this Court approved a state law limiting the hours that women could work for wages, and observed that 19 States had such laws at the time. Such laws were based on the related beliefs that (1) woman is, and should remain, the center of home and family life, and (2) a proper discharge of a woman's maternal functions—having in view not merely her own health, but the well-being of the race—justifies legislation to protect her from the greed as well as the passion of man. Until [1971] it remained the prevailing doctrine that government, both federal and state, could withhold from women opportunities accorded men so long as any basis in reason—such as the above beliefs—could be conceived for the discrimination.

Congress responded to this history of discrimination by abrogating [revoking] States' sovereign immunity in Title VII of the Civil Rights Act of 1964 * * * .[a] But state gender discrimination did not cease. * * * According to evidence that was before Congress when it enacted the FMLA, States continue[d] to rely on invalid gender stereotypes in the employment context, specifically in the administration of leave benefits. * * *

* * * *

Congress * * * heard testimony that parental leave for fathers * * * is rare. Even * * * where child-care leave policies do exist, men, both in the public and private sectors, receive notoriously discriminatory treatment in their requests for such leave. Many States offered women extended "maternity" leave that far exceeded the typical 4- to 8-week period of physical disability due to pregnancy and childbirth, but very few States granted men a parallel benefit: Fifteen States provided women up to one year of extended maternity leave, while only four provided men with the same. This and other differential leave policies were not attributable to any differential physical needs of men and women, but rather to the pervasive sex-role stereotype that caring for family members is women's work.

* * * *

* * * Because employers continued to regard the family as the woman's domain, they often denied men similar accommodations or discouraged them from taking leave. These mutually reinforcing stereotypes created a self-fulfilling cycle of discrimination that forced women to continue to assume the role of primary family caregiver, and fostered employers' stereotypical views about women's * * * value as employees. * * *

* * * *

By creating an across-the-board, routine employment benefit for all eligible employees, Congress sought to ensure that family-care leave would no longer be stigmatized as an inordinate drain on the workplace caused by female employees, and that employers could not evade leave obligations simply by hiring men. *By setting a minimum standard of family leave for all eligible employees, irrespective of gender, the FMLA attacks the formerly state-sanctioned stereotype that only women are responsible for family caregiving, thereby reducing employers' incentives to engage in discrimination by basing hiring and promotion decisions on stereotypes.* [Emphasis added.]

* * * *

* * * [T]he FMLA is narrowly targeted at the fault line between work and family—precisely where sex-based overgeneralization has been and remains strongest—and affects only one aspect of the employment relationship.

* * * *

---

a. This statute will be discussed in detail in Chapter 34.

CASE 33.2 | Continued For the above reasons, we conclude that [the FMLA] is congruent [harmonious] and proportional to its remedial object, and can be understood as responsive to, or designed to prevent, unconstitutional behavior. The judgment of the Court of Appeals [holding that the Eleventh Amendment did not bar the plaintiff's suit] is therefore *Affirmed*.

QUESTIONS

1. What did the Court hold with respect to the primary issue in this case?
2. How might a law foster discrimination even when the law is not obviously discriminatory?

REMEDIES FOR VIOLATIONS OF THE FMLA

Remedies for violations of the FMLA include (1) damages for unpaid wages (or salary), lost benefits, denied compensation, and actual monetary losses (such as the cost of providing for care of the family member) up to an amount equivalent to the employee's wages for twelve weeks; (2) job reinstatement; and (3) promotion. The successful plaintiff is entitled to court costs, attorneys' fees, and—in cases involving bad faith on the part of the employer—double damages. Supervisors may also be subject to personal liability, as employers, for violations of the act.[30]

Department of Labor (DOL) regulations impose additional sanctions on employers who fail to comply with certain rules relating to notice requirements. For example, employers are required to designate leave as FMLA qualifying and to notify the employee of the designation within two business days (absent extenuating circumstances). If an employer fails to provide this notice, then the employer may not be able to count the FMLA leave against the sick leave normally provided by the employer.[31] Note, however, that the United States Supreme Court has held that an employer cannot be sanctioned for failing to provide notice under DOL regulations unless the employee was injured or prejudiced by the lack of notice.[32]

INTERACTION WITH OTHER LAWS

The FMLA does not affect any other federal or state law that prohibits discrimination. Nor does it supersede any state or local law that provides more generous family- or medical-leave protection. For example, if a

California state law allows employees who are disabled by pregnancy to take up to four months of unpaid leave, an employer in California would have to comply with that law (in addition to the provisions of the FMLA). Also, an employer who is obligated to provide greater leave rights under a collective bargaining agreement must do so, regardless of the FMLA.

SECTION 7 | Employee Privacy Rights

In the last twenty-five years, concerns about the privacy rights of employees have arisen in response to the sometimes invasive tactics used by employers to monitor and screen workers. Perhaps the greatest privacy concern in today's employment arena has to do with electronic performance monitoring. Clearly, employers need to protect themselves from liability for their employees' online activities. They also have a legitimate interest in monitoring the productivity of their workers. At the same time, employees expect to have a certain zone of privacy in the workplace. Indeed, many lawsuits have involved allegations that employers' intrusive monitoring practices violate employees' privacy rights.

ELECTRONIC MONITORING IN THE WORKPLACE

According to a survey by the American Management Association, more than two-thirds of employers engage in some form of electronic monitoring of their employees. Types of monitoring include reviewing employees' e-mail and computer files, video recording of employee job performance, and recording and reviewing telephone conversations and voice mail.

A variety of specially designed software products have made it easier for an employer to track employees' Internet use. For example, software is now available that allows an employer to track virtually every move made using the Internet, including the specific Web

---

30. See, for example, *Rupnow v. TRC, Inc.*, 999 F.Supp. 1047 (N.D. Ohio 1998).
31. See, for example, *Sims v. Schultz*, 305 F.Supp.2d 838 (N.D.Ill. 2004).
32. *Ragsdale v. Wolverine World Wide, Inc.*, 535 U.S. 81, 122 S.Ct. 1155, 152 L.Ed.2d 167 (2002).

sites visited and the time spent surfing the Web. Filtering software, which was discussed in Chapter 4, can also be used to prevent access to certain Web sites, such as sites containing pornographic or sexually explicit images. Other filtering software may be used to screen incoming e-mail for viruses and to block junk e-mail (spam).

Although the use of filtering software by public employers (government agencies) has led to charges that blocking access to Web sites violates employees' rights to free speech, this issue does not arise in private businesses. This is because the First Amendment's protection of free speech applies only to *government* restraints on speech, not restraints imposed in the private sector.

LAWS PROTECTING EMPLOYEE PRIVACY RIGHTS

A number of laws protect privacy rights. We look here at laws that apply in the employment context.

—*Protection under Constitutional and Tort Law.*

Recall from Chapter 4 that the Supreme Court has inferred a personal right to privacy from the constitutional guarantees provided by the First, Third, Fourth, Fifth, and Ninth Amendments to the Constitution. Tort law (see Chapters 6 and 7), state constitutions, and a number of state and federal statutes also provide for privacy rights.

—*The Electronic Communications Privacy Act.*

The major statute with which employers must comply is the Electronic Communications Privacy Act (ECPA) of 1986.[33] This act amended existing federal wiretapping law to cover electronic forms of communications, such as communications via cellular telephones or e-mail. The ECPA prohibits the intentional interception of any wire or electronic communication or the intentional disclosure or use of the information obtained by the interception. Excluded from coverage, however, are any electronic communications through devices that are "furnished to the subscriber or user by a provider of wire or electronic communication service" and that are being used by the subscriber or user, or by the provider of the service, "in the ordinary course of its business."

This "business-extension exception" to the ECPA permits an employer to monitor employee electronic communications in the ordinary course of business. It does not, however, permit an employer to monitor employees' personal communications. Under another exception to the ECPA, however, an employer may avoid liability under the act if the employees consent to having their electronic communications intercepted by the employer. Thus, an employer may be able to avoid liability under the ECPA by simply requiring employees to sign forms indicating that they consent to such monitoring.

Although the law clearly allows employers to engage in electronic monitoring in the workplace, there are some limits on how far an employer can go in monitoring employee communications.

FACTORS CONSIDERED BY THE COURTS IN EMPLOYEE PRIVACY CASES When determining whether an employer should be held liable for violating an employee's privacy rights, the courts generally weigh the employer's interests against the employee's reasonable expectation of privacy. Generally, if employees are informed that their communications are being monitored, they cannot reasonably expect those communications to be private. If employees are not informed that certain communications are being monitored, however, the employer may be held liable for invading their privacy.

In one case, for example, an employer secretly recorded conversations among his four employees by placing a tape recorder in their common office. The conversations were of a highly personal nature and included harsh criticisms of the employer. The employer immediately fired two of the employees because of their comments on the tape. In the ensuing suit, the court held that the employees had a reasonable expectation of privacy in these circumstances and granted summary judgment in their favor. The employees clearly would not have criticized their boss if they had not assumed that their conversations were private.[34] (For a discussion of employee privacy rights and e-mail systems, see this chapter's *Contemporary Legal Debates* feature.)

OTHER TYPES OF MONITORING

In addition to monitoring their employees' online activities, employers also engage in other types of employee screening and monitoring practices. The practices discussed below have often been challenged as violations of employee privacy rights.

---

33. 18 U.S.C. Sections 2510–2521.

34. *Dorris v. Absher*, 179 F.3d 420 (6th Cir. 1999).

Employee Privacy Rights and E-Mail

Business owners and managers today routinely provide their employees with e-mail access to facilitate the performance of job duties. Sometimes, however, an employee may be using e-mail to spread rumors or make sexually explicit and unprofessional comments about other employees. Clearly, an employer has both a legal and an ethical obligation to prevent harassment and discrimination in the workplace, as well as a practical interest in avoiding liability for such actions. Other uses of e-mail by employees—such as to send important trade secrets to unauthorized persons—have also caused employers to be concerned about their employees' use of company e-mail systems.

For these and other reasons, many employers today monitor their employees' electronic communications. As stated elsewhere in this chapter, the Electronic Communications Privacy Act (ECPA) prohibits the intentional interception or disclosure of any wire or electronic communication. Nevertheless, under the "business-extension exception" to the ECPA, an employer can monitor an employee's e-mail as long as the messages being monitored involve business rather than personal concerns. This exception is based on the assumption that when the employer furnishes e-mail services to an employee, that employee has no reasonable expectation of privacy. Not surprisingly, disputes over employers' monitoring of employees' e-mail messages continue to be the subject of debate in courts across the United States.

PRIVACY EXPECTATIONS AND E-MAIL SYSTEMS

Generally, the courts have tended to side with employers on this issue and hold that employees have no reasonable expectation of privacy in e-mail. This is true even when employees are not informed that their e-mail will be monitored. Consider, for example, the case of *Smyth v. Pillsbury Co.*[a] In that case, Michael Smyth, a regional operations manager for Pillsbury, was fired for his e-mail response to a message from his supervisor. In his e-mail, Smyth had little positive to say about the company's sales staff and referred to an upcoming office party as the "Jim Jones Kool-Aid affair" (alluding to a mass suicide). Despite Pillsbury's stated policy that it would not intercept the e-mail transmissions of its employees, it did intercept this message and fired Smyth on the ground that his comments were unprofessional and inappropriate.

Smyth sued the company for wrongful discharge, claiming that Pillsbury's actions had violated his right to privacy. The federal district court held that Smyth had no reasonable expectation of privacy in the e-mail communications that he voluntarily made to his supervisor over the company's e-mail system. It did not matter that Smyth actually sent the e-mail from his home computer because it still went through the company's e-mail system.

MAY PASSWORD-PROTECTED FILES BE MONITORED?

Courts are reluctant to hold that employees' privacy interests have been violated even if employers access employees' password-protected files. In one case, for example, Microsoft Corporation had suspended an employee pending an investigation into accusations of sexual harassment and other misconduct. During the suspension, Microsoft read his e-mail, which was stored in "personal folders" and protected by a password. After Microsoft fired the employee, he sued the company for invasion of privacy, claiming that the e-mail was his personal property. The court, however, reasoned that because the company gave the employee the computer to enable him to do his job and provided him with the e-mail application, the e-mail on his computer was "merely an inherent part of the office environment."[b]

MONITORING INDEPENDENT CONTRACTORS' E-MAIL

What happens when an employer makes e-mail services available to an independent contractor who is working from a separate location? Does the independent contractor have a reasonable expectation of privacy in his or her e-mail, or can the employer legally monitor that person's electronic communications? This issue came before a federal appellate court in a case brought by Richard Fraser, an independent insurance agent who had entered into an agreement to sell insurance policies exclusively for Nationwide Mutual Insurance Company. As an independent contractor, Fraser served as an agent for Nationwide but was not an employee (because Nationwide did not control his work performance).

Fraser worked from his own office in Pennsylvania, but Nationwide provided Fraser with an e-mail address and server. When Nationwide found out that Fraser had written two letters to its competitors (inquiring about insurance policies), Nationwide became concerned about his loyalty. Nationwide then searched its main file server, on which all of Fraser's e-mail was logged. The company concluded that Fraser had

---

a. 914 F.Supp. 97 (E.D.Pa. 1996).

b. *McLaren v. Microsoft Corp.*, 1999 WL 339015 (Tex.App.—Dallas 1999).

(Continued)

Employee Privacy Rights and E-Mail (*continued*)

been disloyal and terminated his contract. In the lawsuit that followed, the trial court ruled that Nationwide had not violated the ECPA.

The appellate court found two reasons to affirm the lower court's decision—neither of which was contingent on Fraser's status as an independent contractor. First, the court looked at the ECPA's definition of *intercept* and concluded that an intercept must occur "contemporaneously with transmission"— that is, at the same time that it is sent. Because Nationwide had looked at Fraser's e-mail *after* it had already been sent, the court held that Nationwide had not intercepted the e-mail within the meaning of the act. Second, the court found that Nationwide was authorized under the ECPA to access the e-mail because Nationwide was the entity that provided the e-mail service. The fact that Fraser was an independent contractor was irrelevant, in the court's view, if the employer provided the e-mail service and accessed stored messages.[c]

WHERE DO YOU STAND?

The courts have issued diverse opinions regarding employee drug testing, medical testing, and screening procedures. In contrast, the courts have predominantly sided with the employer with respect to the electronic monitoring of employees' e-mail. Do you think that the courts fairly balance the rights of employers and employees in regard to these monitoring practices? Should employees have a right to expect that their personal e-mail messages will remain private? What is your position on this issue, which continues to be debated?

c. *Fraser v. Nationwide Mutual Insurance Co.*, 352 F.3d 107 (3d Cir. 2004).

LIE-DETECTOR TESTS   At one time, many employers required employees or job applicants to take polygraph examinations (lie-detector tests). To protect the privacy interests of employees and job applicants, in 1988 Congress passed the Employee Polygraph Protection Act.[35] The act prohibits employers from (1) requiring or causing employees or job applicants to take lie-detector tests or suggesting or requesting that they do so; (2) using, accepting, referring to, or asking about the results of lie-detector tests taken by employees or applicants; and (3) taking or threatening negative employment-related action against employees or applicants based on results of lie-detector tests or on their refusal to take the tests.

Employers excepted from these prohibitions include federal, state, and local government employers; certain security service firms; and companies manufacturing and distributing controlled substances. Other employers may use polygraph tests when investigating losses attributable to theft, including embezzlement and the theft of trade secrets.

DRUG TESTING   In the interests of public safety and to reduce unnecessary costs, many employers, including the government, require their employees to submit to drug testing. State laws relating to the privacy rights and drug testing of private-sector employees vary from state to state. Many states have statutes that allow drug testing by private employers but place restrictions on when the testing is appropriate and how it is performed. A collective bargaining agreement may also provide protection against drug testing. In some instances, employees have brought an action against the employer for the tort of invasion of privacy (discussed in Chapter 6).

Government employers, of course, are constrained in drug testing by the Fourth Amendment of the U.S. Constitution, which prohibits unreasonable searches and seizures (see Chapter 4). When there was a reasonable basis for suspecting government employees of using drugs, however, or when drug use in a particular job could threaten public safety, testing has been upheld.[36] The Fourth Amendment does not apply to drug testing conducted by private employers.[37]

The permissibility of a private employee's drug test often hinges on whether the employer's testing was reasonable. Is a private employer's substance abuse policy that denies a "second chance" to employees who test positive for drugs reasonable? That was the question in the following case.

---

35. 29 U.S.C. Sections 2001 *et seq.*

36. *International Brotherhood of Electrical Workers Local 1245 v. Skinner*, 913 F.2d 1454 (9th Cir. 1990).
37. See *Chandler v. Miller*, 520 U.S. 305, 117 S.Ct. 1295, 137 L.Ed.2d 513 (1997).

CASE 33.3

United States
Court of Appeals,
Third Circuit, 2004.
385 F.3d 809.

CITGO Asphalt Refining Co. v. Paper, Allied-Industrial, Chemical, and Energy Workers International Union Local No. 2-991

BACKGROUND AND FACTS *CITGO Petroleum Corporation (CITGO) operates more than sixty oil-refining facilities, including CITGO Asphalt Refining Company (CARCO) in Paulsboro, New Jersey. Paper, Allied-Industrial, Chemical, and Energy Workers International Union (PACE) represents some of CITGO's workers. Under an agreement between CITGO and PACE, the company has the right to "make and enforce rules for the maintenance of discipline and safety." In December 1998, CITGO implemented a new substance abuse policy, which included a zero-tolerance provision. The local chapter 2-991 of PACE challenged the policy at CARCO. During arbitration on the dispute, PACE representatives testified that policies at smaller facilities owned by other companies—Motiva and Sun Oil—did not include zero-tolerance provisions. John DeLeon, a CITGO manager, testified that Tosco, Marathon, and Exxon, three major companies in the industry, had zero-tolerance polices. He also testified that CITGO's safety record is the best in the industry. The arbitrator ruled that CITGO should modify its policy to allow a rehabilitation opportunity, or "second chance." CARCO filed a suit in a federal district court against PACE, challenging the arbitrator's ruling. The court issued an order to enforce the award. CARCO appealed to the U.S. Court of Appeals for the Third Circuit.*

IN THE LANGUAGE OF THE COURT

McKEE, Circuit Judge.

* * * *

* * * [T]he only issue before us is the propriety of the arbitrator's determination that CITGO's zero tolerance policy is unreasonable. CITGO * * * contends that the arbitrator's determination that the zero tolerance policy is unreasonable is not supported by the record. * * *

* * * *

The arbitrator relied only on two "facts" to support his determination that the zero tolerance policy was unreasonable. First, the arbitrator noted that neither Motiva nor Sun Oil have zero tolerance policies at their refineries. However, the fact that two companies with safety records that are inferior to CITGO's do not have zero tolerance policies does not establish that CITGO acted unreasonably in adopting a zero tolerance policy. In fact, considering the stipulated catastrophic repercussions of a safety lapse at the Paulsboro plant, and CITGO's superior safety record, one could just as readily conclude that it was unreasonable for Sun Oil and Motiva not to have a zero tolerance policy. Moreover, the arbitrator's finding of the unreasonableness of the zero tolerance policy completely ignores DeLeon's * * * testimony that the three largest companies in the industry—Exxon, Marathon and Tosco—have zero tolerance policies exactly like CITGO's. The undisputed fact that the three largest companies in the industry have zero tolerance policies certainly casts doubt upon the arbitrator's focus on Motiva and Sun Oil, and the arbitrator never explained why he elevated the importance of Motiva and Sun Oil refineries over larger ones with better safety records.

The arbitrator also relied upon provisions of the Omnibus Transportation Employee Testing Act of 1991 and the [U.S.] Department of Transportation regulations promulgated under it. *That Act and its regulations allow employees a second chance for rehabilitation. However, that does not mean that a decision to the contrary is unreasonable.* This is especially true when we consider the hazardous nature of CITGO's facilities, the need for prompt and unimpaired action in the event of an emergency, and the exception for employees who step forward seeking help for a substance abuse problem that CITGO has included in its policy. Indeed, * * * the statute and the regulations at issue leave it to the parties to define appropriate discipline. * * * When promulgating these regulations, DOT decided not to require employers either to provide rehabilitation or to hold a job open for a driver who has tested positive, on the basis that such decisions should be left to management/driver negotiation. That determination reflects basic

CONTINUED ▶

CASE 33.3 | Continued

background labor law principles, which caution against interference with labor-management agreements about appropriate employee discipline. The arbitrator's award here ignores that caution as well as the express reservation of the employer's prerogatives as set forth in [the agreement between CITGO and PACE]. [Emphasis added.]

Thus, the fact that Motiva and Sun Oil do not have zero tolerance policies and the fact that a particular federal statute and its implementing regulations allow a second chance are not sufficient to support a finding that CITGO's zero tolerance policy is unreasonable. This is especially true given the undisputed evidence that the Paulsboro facility is a hazardous work environment susceptible to explosions, Local 2-991 members are employed in safety-sensitive positions there, and that impaired employees pose a threat to co-workers, the work place, the environment and to the public at large.

Since the Managements Rights Clause of the [agreement between CITGO and PACE] expressly gives CITGO the right "to make and enforce rules for the maintenance of discipline and safety" * * * , we are hard-pressed to understand how the arbitrator could have concluded that the zero tolerance policy is unreasonable without substituting his own judgment for CITGO's and ignoring CITGO's expressly reserved right * * * .

DECISION AND REMEDY *The U.S. Court of Appeals for the Third Circuit reversed the lower court's order and remanded the case for an order vacating the arbitrator's award. That other, smaller companies "do not have zero tolerance policies" and that "a particular federal statute and its implementing regulations allow a second chance" are not sufficient to support a finding that CITGO's zero-tolerance policy is unreasonable. The "safety-sensitive positions" of CITGO's workers and the firm's right under its agreement with PACE outweigh these facts.*

WHAT IF THE FACTS WERE DIFFERENT? *Suppose that CITGO's safety record was not the oil-refining industry's "best," but its "worst." Would the result have been different?*

AIDS TESTING A number of employers test their workers for acquired immune deficiency syndrome (AIDS). Some state laws restrict or ban AIDS testing, and federal statutes offer some protection to employees or job applicants who have AIDS or have tested positive for the AIDS virus. The federal Americans with Disabilities Act of 1990[38] (discussed in Chapter 34), for example, prohibits discrimination against persons with disabilities, and the term *disability* has been broadly defined to include those individuals with diseases such as AIDS. HIPPA, which was discussed earlier in this chapter, would also require employers to follow procedures to safeguard a person's protected medical information—the test results—from disclosure to other employees. As a rule, although the law may not prohibit AIDS testing, it may prohibit the discharge of employees based on the results of those tests and prohibit the employer from disclosing the test results to unauthorized parties.

GENETIC TESTING A serious privacy issue arose when some employers began conducting genetic testing

of employees or prospective employees in an effort to identify individuals who might develop significant health problems in the future. To date, however, only a few cases have come before the courts on this matter. In one case, the Lawrence Berkeley Laboratory screened prospective employees for the gene that causes sickle-cell anemia, although the applicants were not informed of this. In a lawsuit subsequently brought by the prospective employees, a federal appellate court held that they had a cause of action for violation of their privacy rights.[39] The case was later settled for $2.2 million.

In another case, the Equal Employment Opportunity Commission (EEOC), the federal agency in charge of administering laws prohibiting employment discrimination, brought an action against a railroad company that had genetically tested its employees. The EEOC contended that the genetic testing violated the Americans with Disabilities Act of 1990. In 2002, this case was settled out of court, also for $2.2 million.[40]

---

38. 42 U.S.C. Sections 12102–12118.

39. *Norman-Bloodsaw v. Lawrence Berkeley Laboratory*, 135 F.3d 1260 (9th Cir. 1998).

40. For a discussion of this settlement, see David Hechler, "Railroad to Pay $2.2 Million over Genetic Testing," *The National Law Journal*, May 13, 2002, p. A22.

SCREENING PROCEDURES Preemployment screening procedures are another area of concern to potential employees. What kinds of questions are permissible on an employment application or a preemployment test? What kinds of questions invade the potential employee's privacy? Is it an invasion of privacy, for example, to ask questions about the potential employee's sexual orientation or religious convictions? Although an employer may believe that such information is relevant to the job, the applicant may feel differently. Generally, questions on an employment application must have a reasonable nexus, or connection, with the job for which an applicant is applying.

SECTION 8 | Employment-Related Immigration Laws

The most important immigration laws governing employment relationships are the Immigration Reform and Control Act of 1986[41] and the Immigration Act of 1990.[42]

---

41. 29 U.S.C. Section 1802.
42. This act amended various provisions of the Immigration and Nationality Act of 1952, 8 U.S.C. Sections 1101 *et seq.*

IMMIGRATION REFORM AND CONTROL ACT

The Immigration Reform and Control Act (IRCA), which is administered by the U.S. Bureau of Citizenship and Immigration Services, prohibits employers from hiring illegal immigrants. Employers must complete a special form—called Form I-9—for each employee and indicate on it that the employer has verified that the employee is either a U.S. citizen or is otherwise entitled to work in this country.

IMMIGRATION ACT

The Immigration Act of 1990 limits the number of legal immigrants entering the United States by capping the number of visas (entry permits) that are issued each year. Under the act, employers recruiting employees from other countries must complete a certification process and satisfy the Department of Labor that there is a shortage of qualified U.S. workers capable of performing the work. The employer must also establish that bringing immigrants into this country will not adversely affect the existing labor market in that particular area. In this way, the act attempts to serve two purposes: encouraging skilled workers to enter this country and at the same time restricting competition for American jobs.

REVIEWING EMPLOYMENT AND LABOR LAW

Akito Ichimura accepted a job as an assembly technician at an appliance manufacturing plant. The employer required Ichimura to join the union within sixty days after her start date, which Ichimura reluctantly did. Ichimura's work required her to look upward at an overhead monitor for prolonged periods. After working four months, Ichimura developed acute neck pain as a result of looking at the monitor. Ichimura saw a doctor and e-mailed her concerns about the placement of the monitor to the union representative. The next day, Ichimura's supervisor asked her if she intended to file a workers' compensation claim. Ichimura realized that the supervisor had read her e-mail without her consent—which violated the policy stated in the employer's manual. Ichimura complained to management that her supervisor had invaded her privacy. Before Ichimura files a workers' compensation claim, she is fired from her job.

1. Can an employer legally require a person to join a union as a condition of employment? Why or why not? Is this union practice considered a closed shop, an open shop, or a union shop? Explain.

2. Suppose that Ichimura works in a state with a right-to-work law. How might this affect the legality of a company requiring union membership?

(Continued)

REVIEWING EMPLOYMENT AND LABOR LAW (continued)

3. | Can Ichimura file a state workers' compensation claim for her injury? If so, how long does she have to notify her employer about her neck injury?

4. | Suppose that Ichimura files a lawsuit against the employer alleging that her privacy rights were violated when the supervisor read her e-mail. How would a court be likely to rule on this issue? What factors would the court consider?

5. | Assume that Ichimura was an "employee at will" and wants to bring an action for wrongful discharge. Which of the three exceptions discussed in the chapter (contract, tort, or public policy) would provide her with the best argument? Explain your answer.

TERMS AND CONCEPTS TO REVIEW

cease-and-desist order 674
closed shop 674
collective bargaining 676
employment at will 670
hot-cargo agreement 674

minimum wage 672
right-to-work law 674
secondary boycott 674
strike 677
union shop 674

vesting 679
whistleblowing 671
workers' compensation law 678
wrongful discharge 672

QUESTIONS AND CASE PROBLEMS

33–1. Calzoni Boating Co. is an interstate business engaged in manufacturing and selling boats. The company has five hundred nonunion employees. Representatives of these employees are requesting a four-day, ten-hours-per-day workweek, and Calzoni is concerned that this would require paying time and a half after eight hours per day. Which federal act is Calzoni thinking of that might require this? Will the act in fact require paying time and a half for all hours worked over eight hours per day if the employees' proposal is accepted? Explain.

33–2. **QUESTION WITH SAMPLE ANSWER**
Denton and Carlo were employed at an appliance plant. Their job required them to perform occasional maintenance work while standing on a wire mesh twenty feet above the plant floor. Other employees had fallen through the mesh, and one of them had been killed by the fall. When Denton and Carlo were asked by their supervisor to perform tasks that would likely require them to walk on the mesh, they refused because of their fear of bodily harm or death. Because of their refusal to do the requested work, the two employees were fired from their jobs. Was their discharge wrongful? If so,

under what federal employment law? To what federal agency or department should they turn for assistance?
For a sample answer to this question, go to Appendix I at the end of this text.

33–3. Suppose that Consolidated Stores is undergoing a unionization campaign. Prior to the union election, management states that the union is unnecessary to protect workers. Management also provides bonuses and wage increases to the workers during this period. The employees reject the union. Union organizers protest that the wage increases during the election campaign unfairly prejudiced the vote. Should these wage increases be regarded as an unfair labor practice? Discuss.

33–4. HOURS AND WAGES. Richard Ackerman was an advance sales representative and account manager for Coca-Cola Enterprises, Inc. His primary responsibility was to sell Coca-Cola products to grocery stores, convenience stores, and other sales outlets. Coca-Cola also employed merchandisers, who did not sell Coca-Cola products but performed tasks associated with their distribution and promotion, including restocking shelves, filling vending machines, and setting up displays. The account managers, who serviced the smaller accounts themselves, regularly worked between fifty-five and seventy-two hours each week. Coca-Cola paid them a salary, bonuses, and commissions, but it did not pay them—as it did the merchandisers—additional compensation for the overtime. Ackerman and the other account managers filed a suit in a federal district court against Coca-Cola, alleging that they were entitled to overtime compensation. Coca-Cola responded that because of an exemption under the Fair Labor Standards Act, it was not required to pay them overtime. Is Coca-Cola correct? Explain. [*Ackerman v. Coca-Cola Enterprises, Inc.*, 179 F.3d 1260 (10th Cir. 1999)]

33–5. PERFORMANCE MONITORING. Patience Oyoyo worked as a claims analyst in the claims management department of Baylor Healthcare Network, Inc. When questions arose about Oyoyo's performance on several occasions, department manager Debbie Outlaw met with Oyoyo to discuss, among other things, Oyoyo's personal use of a business phone. Outlaw reminded Oyoyo that company policy prohibited excessive personal calls and that these would result in the termination of her employment. Outlaw began to monitor Oyoyo's phone usage, noting lengthy outgoing calls on several occasions, including some long-distance calls. Eventually, Outlaw terminated Oyoyo's employment, and Oyoyo filed a suit in a federal district court against Baylor. Oyoyo asserted in part that in monitoring her phone calls, the employer had invaded her privacy. Baylor asked the court to dismiss this claim. In whose favor should the court rule, and why? [*Oyoyo v. Baylor Healthcare Network, Inc.*, __ F.Supp.2d __ (N.D.Tex. 2000)]

33–6. UNFAIR LABOR PRACTICE. The New York Department of Education's e-mail policy prohibits the use of the e-mail system for unofficial purposes. An exception allows officials of the New York Public Employees Federation (PEF), the union representing state employees, to use the system for some limited communications, including the scheduling of union meetings and activities. In 1998, Michael Darcy, an elected PEF official, began sending mass, union-related e-mails to employees, including a summary of a union delegates' convention, a union newsletter, a criticism of proposed state legislation, and a criticism of the state governor and the Governor's Office of Employee Relations. Richard Cate, the department's chief operating officer, met with Darcy and reiterated the department's e-mail policy. When Darcy refused to stop his use of the e-mail system, Cate terminated his access to it. Darcy filed a complaint with the New York Public Employment Relations Board, alleging an unfair labor practice. Do the circumstances support Cate's action? Why or why not? [*Benson v. Cuevas*, 293 A.D.2d 927, 741 N.Y.S.2d 310 (3 Dept. 2002)]

33–7. ⚖ **CASE PROBLEM WITH SAMPLE ANSWER**
The Touch of Class Lounge is in a suburban shopping plaza, or strip mall, in Omaha, Nebraska. Patricia Bauer, the Lounge's owner, does not own the parking lot, which

is provided for the common use of all of the businesses in the plaza. Stephanie Zoucha was a bartender at the Lounge. Her duties ended when she locked the door after closing. On June 4, 2001, at 1:15 A.M., Zoucha closed the bar and locked the door from the inside. An hour later, she walked to her car in the parking lot, where she was struck with "[l]ike a tire iron on the back of my head." Zoucha sustained a skull fracture and other injuries, including significant cognitive damage (impairment of speech and thought formation). Her purse, containing her tip money, was stolen. She identified her attacker as William Nunez, who had been in the Lounge earlier that night. Zoucha filed a petition in a Nebraska state court to obtain workers' compensation. What are the requirements for receiving workers' compensation? Should Zoucha's request be granted or denied? Why? [*Zoucha v. Touch of Class Lounge*, 269 Neb. 89, 690 N.W.2d 610 (2005)]

To view a sample answer for this case problem, go to this book's Web site at http://wbl.westbuslaw.com, select "Chapter 33," and click on "Case Problem with Sample Answer."

33–8. COLLECTIVE BARGAINING. Verizon New York, Inc. (VNY), provides telecommunications services. VNY and the Communications Workers of America (CWA) are parties to collective bargaining agreements covering installation and maintenance employees. At one time, VNY supported annual blood drives. VNY, CWA, and charitable organizations jointly set dates, arranged appointments, and adjusted work schedules for the drives. For each drive, about a thousand employees, including managers, spent up to four hours traveling to a donor site, giving blood, recovering, and returning to their jobs. Employees received full pay for the time. In 2001, VNY told CWA that it would no longer allow employees to participate "on Company time," claiming that it experienced problems meeting customer requests for service during the drives. CWA filed a complaint with the National Labor Relations Board (NLRB), asking that VNY be ordered to bargain over the decision. Did VNY commit an unfair labor practice? Should the NLRB grant CWA's request? Why or why not? [*Verizon New York, Inc. v. National Labor Relations Board*, 360 F.3d 206 (D.C. Cir. 2004)]

33–9. ⚖ **A QUESTION OF ETHICS**
Keith Cline worked for Wal-Mart Stores, Inc., as a night maintenance supervisor. When he suffered a recurrence of a brain tumor, he took a leave from work, which was covered by the Family and Medical Leave Act (FMLA) of 1993 and authorized by his employer. When he returned to work, his employer refused to allow him to continue his supervisory job and demoted him to the status of a regular maintenance worker. A few weeks later, the company fired him, ostensibly because he "stole" company time by clocking in thirteen minutes early for a company meeting. Cline sued Wal-Mart, alleging,

among other things, that Wal-Mart had violated the FMLA by refusing to return him to his prior position when he returned to work. In view of these facts, answer the following questions. [*Cline v. Wal-Mart Stores, Inc.*, 144 F.3d 294 (4th Cir. 1998)]

(a) Did Wal-Mart violate the FMLA by refusing to return Cline to his prior position when he returned to work?

(b) From an ethical perspective, the FMLA has been viewed as a choice on the part of society to shift to the employer family burdens caused by changing economic and social needs. What "changing" needs does the act meet? In other words, why did Congress feel that workers should have the right to family and medical leave in 1993, but not in 1983, or 1973, or earlier?

(c) "Congress should amend the FMLA, which currently applies to employers with fifty or more employees, so that it applies to employers with twenty-five or more employees." Do you agree with this statement? Why or why not?

33–10. VIDEO QUESTION

Go to this text's Web site at **http://wbl.westbuslaw.com** and select "Chapter 33." Click on "Video Questions" and view the video titled *Employment at Will*. Then answer the following questions.

(a) In the video, Laura asserts that she can fire Ray "for any reason; for no reason." Is this true? Explain your answer.

(b) What exceptions to the employment-at-will doctrine are discussed in the chapter? Does Ray's situation fit into any of these exceptions?

(c) Would Ray be protected from wrongful discharge under whistleblowing statutes? Why or why not?

(d) Assume that you are the employer in this scenario. What arguments can you make that Ray should not be able to sue for wrongful discharge in this situation?

LAW | on the Web

For updated links to resources available on the Web, as well as a variety of other materials, visit this text's Web site at **http://wbl.westbuslaw.com**.

A good Web site for information on employee benefits, including the full text of the FMLA, COBRA, other relevant statutes and case law, and current articles, is BenefitsLink. Go to

http://benefitslink.com/index.html

The American Federation of Labor–Congress of Industrial Organizations (AFL-CIO) provides links to a broad variety of labor-related resources at

http://www.aflcio.org

The National Labor Relations Board is online at

http://www.nlrb.gov

LEGAL RESEARCH EXERCISES ON THE WEB

Go to **http://wbl.westbuslaw.com**, the Web site that accompanies this text. Select "Chapter 33" and click on "Internet Exercises." There you will find the following Internet research exercises that you can perform to learn more about topics covered in this chapter.

Activity 33–1: LEGAL PERSPECTIVE
Workers' Compensation

Activity 33–2: MANAGEMENT PERSPECTIVE
Workplace Monitoring and Surveillance

Activity 33–3: HISTORICAL PERSPECTIVE
Labor Unions and Labor Law

CHAPTER 34

Employment Discrimination

Out of the 1960s civil rights movement to end racial and other forms of discrimination grew a body of law protecting employees against discrimination in the workplace. This protective legislation further eroded the employment-at-will doctrine, which was discussed in Chapter 33. In the past several decades, judicial decisions, administrative agency actions, and legislation have restricted the ability of employers, as well as unions, to discriminate against workers on the basis of race, color, religion, national origin, gender, age, or disability. A class of persons defined by one or more of these criteria is known as a **protected class.**

Several federal statutes prohibit **employment discrimination** against members of protected classes. The most important statute is Title VII of the Civil Rights Act of 1964.[1] Title VII prohibits employment discrimination on the basis of race, color, religion, national origin, and gender. The Age Discrimination in Employment Act of 1967[2] and the Americans with Disabilities Act of 1990[3] prohibit discrimination on the basis of age and disability, respectively. The protections afforded under these laws extend to U.S. citizens who are working abroad for U.S. firms or for companies that are controlled by U.S. firms—*unless* to do so would violate the laws of the countries in which their workplaces are located. This "foreign laws exception" allows employers to avoid being subjected to conflicting laws.

This chapter focuses on the kinds of discrimination prohibited by these federal statutes. Note, however, that discrimination against employees on the basis of any of the above-mentioned criteria may also violate state human rights statutes or other state laws prohibiting discrimination.

SECTION 1 | Title VII of the Civil Rights Act of 1964

Title VII of the Civil Rights Act of 1964 and its amendments prohibit job discrimination against employees, applicants, and union members on the basis of race, color, national origin, religion, and gender at any stage of employment. Title VII applies to employers affecting interstate commerce with fifteen or more employees, labor unions with fifteen or more members, labor unions that operate hiring halls (to which members go regularly to be rationed jobs as they become available), employment agencies, and state and local governing units or agencies. A special section of the act prohibits discrimination in most federal government employment.

1. 42 U.S.C. Sections 2000e–2000e-17.
2. 29 U.S.C. Sections 621–634.
3. 42 U.S.C. Sections 12102–12118.

PROCEDURES UNDER TITLE VII

Compliance with Title VII is monitored by the Equal Employment Opportunity Commission (EEOC). A victim of alleged discrimination, before bringing a suit against the employer, must first file a claim with the EEOC. The EEOC may investigate the dispute and attempt to obtain the parties' voluntary consent to an out-of-court settlement. If voluntary agreement cannot be reached, the EEOC may then file a suit against the employer on the employee's behalf. If the EEOC decides not to investigate the claim, the victim may bring his or her own lawsuit against the employer.

The EEOC does not investigate every claim of employment discrimination; rather, it investigates only "priority cases." Generally, priority cases are cases that affect many workers, cases involving retaliatory discharge (firing an employee in retaliation for submitting a claim with the EEOC), and cases involving types of discrimination that are of particular concern to the EEOC.

INTENTIONAL AND UNINTENTIONAL DISCRIMINATION

Title VII of the Civil Rights Act of 1964 prohibits both intentional and unintentional discrimination.

INTENTIONAL DISCRIMINATION

Intentional discrimination by an employer against an employee is known as **disparate-treatment discrimination.** Because intent may sometimes be difficult to prove, courts have established certain procedures for resolving disparate-treatment cases. Suppose that a woman applies for employment with a construction firm and is rejected. If she sues on the basis of disparate-treatment discrimination in hiring, she must show that (1) she is a member of a protected class, (2) she applied and was qualified for the job in question, (3) she was rejected by the employer, and (4) the employer continued to seek applicants for the position or filled the position with a person not in a protected class.

If the woman can meet these relatively easy requirements, she makes out a **prima facie** case of illegal discrimination. Making out a *prima facie* case of discrimination means that the plaintiff has met her initial burden of proof and will win in the absence of a legally acceptable employer defense (defenses to claims of employment discrimination will be discussed later in this chapter). The burden then shifts to the employer-defendant, who must articulate a legal reason for not hiring the plaintiff. For example, the employer might say that the plaintiff was not hired because she lacked sufficient experience or training. To prevail, the plaintiff must then show that the employer's reason is a *pretext* (not the true reason) and that discriminatory intent actually motivated the employer's decision.

UNINTENTIONAL DISCRIMINATION

Employers often find it necessary to use interviews and testing procedures to choose from among a large number of applicants for job openings. Minimum educational requirements are also common. Employer practices, such as those involving educational requirements, may have an unintended discriminatory impact on a protected class. **Disparate-impact discrimination** occurs when an employer's practices, procedures, or tests, which do not seem to be discriminatory, adversely impact a protected group of people. In a disparate-impact discrimination case, the complaining party must first show statistically that the employer's practices, procedures, or tests are discriminatory in effect. Once the plaintiff has made out a *prima facie* case, the burden of proof shifts to the employer to show that the practices or procedures in question were justified. There are two ways of proving that disparate impact exists, as discussed below.

—Pool of Applicants. A plaintiff can prove a disparate impact by comparing the employer's workforce to the pool of qualified individuals available in the local labor market. The plaintiff must show that, as a result of educational or other job requirements or hiring procedures, an employer's workforce does not reflect the percentage of nonwhites, women, or members of other protected classes that characterizes the pool of qualified individuals available. If a person challenging an employment practice having a discriminatory effect can show a connection between the practice and the disparity, she or he makes out a *prima facie* case and need not provide evidence of discriminatory intent.

—Rate of Hiring. Disparate-impact discrimination can also occur when an educational or other job requirement or hiring procedure excludes members of a protected class from an employer's workforce at a substantially higher rate than nonmembers, regardless of the racial balance in the employer's workforce. This "rates analysis" compares the selection rate for whites with that for nonwhites (or other members of a protected class). It does not require the plaintiff to prove what percentage of qualified nonwhite persons are available in the local labor market.

The EEOC has devised a test, called the "four-fifths rule" or the "80 percent rule," to determine whether an employment examination is discriminatory on its face. Under this rule, a selection rate for protected classes that is less than four-fifths, or 80 percent, of the rate for the group with the highest rate will generally be regarded as evidence of disparate impact. To illustrate: One hundred majority applicants take an employment test, and fifty pass the test and are hired. One hundred minority applicants take the test, and twenty pass the test and are hired. Because twenty is less than four-fifths (80 percent) of fifty, the test would be considered discriminatory under the EEOC guidelines.

DISCRIMINATION BASED ON RACE, COLOR, AND NATIONAL ORIGIN

Title VII prohibits employers from discriminating against employees or job applicants on the basis of race, color, or national origin. This prohibition extends to both intentional (disparate-treatment) and unintentional (disparate-impact) discrimination. If a company's standards or policies for selecting or promoting employees have the effect of discriminating against employees or job applicants on the basis of race, color, or national origin, they are illegal—unless (except for race) they have a substantial, demonstrable relationship to realistic qualifications for the job in question. Discrimination against these protected classes in regard to employment conditions and benefits is also illegal.

Note that victims of racial or ethnic discrimination may also have a cause of action under 42 U.S.C. Section 1981. This section, which was enacted as part of the Civil Rights Act of 1866, prohibits discrimination on the basis of race or ethnicity in the formation or enforcement of contracts. Although Section 1981 remained a "dead letter" on the books for over a century, since the 1970s many plaintiffs have succeeded in Section 1981 cases against their employers. Unlike Title VII, Section 1981 does not place a cap on damages (see the discussion of Title VII remedies later in this chapter). Thus, if an employee can prove that he or she was discriminated against in the formation or enforcement of a contract, the employee may be able to obtain a greater amount of damages under Section 1981 than under Title VII.

DISCRIMINATION BASED ON RELIGION

Title VII of the Civil Rights Act of 1964 also prohibits government employers, private employers, and unions from discriminating against persons because of their religion. An employer must "reasonably accommodate" the religious practices of its employees, unless to do so would cause undue hardship to the employer's business. For example, if an employee's religion prohibits him from working on a certain day of the week or at a certain type of job, the employer must make a reasonable attempt to accommodate these religious requirements. Employers must reasonably accommodate an employee's religious belief even if the belief is not based on the tenets or dogma of a particular church, sect, or denomination. The only requirement is that the belief be sincerely held by the employee.[4]

DISCRIMINATION BASED ON GENDER

Under Title VII, as well as under other federal acts, employers are forbidden from discriminating against employees on the basis of gender. Employers are pro-

hibited from classifying jobs as male or female and from advertising in help-wanted columns that are designated male or female unless the employer can prove that the gender of the applicant is essential to the job. Furthermore, employers cannot have separate male and female seniority lists. Generally, to succeed in a suit for gender discrimination, a plaintiff must demonstrate that gender was a determining factor in the employer's decision to hire, fire, or promote him or her. Typically, this involves looking at all of the surrounding circumstances.

The Pregnancy Discrimination Act of 1978,[5] which amended Title VII, expanded the definition of gender discrimination to include discrimination based on pregnancy. Women affected by pregnancy, childbirth, or related medical conditions must be treated—for all employment-related purposes, including the provision of benefits under employee benefit programs—the same as other persons not so affected but similar in ability to work.

CONSTRUCTIVE DISCHARGE

The majority of Title VII complaints involve unlawful discrimination in decisions to hire or fire employees. In some situations, however, employees who leave their jobs voluntarily can claim that they were "constructively discharged" by the employer. **Constructive discharge** refers to a situation in which the employer causes the employee's working conditions to be so intolerable that a reasonable person in the employee's position would feel compelled to quit.

PROVING CONSTRUCTIVE DISCHARGE The plaintiff must present objective proof of intolerable working conditions, which the employer knew or had reason to know about yet failed to correct within a reasonable time period. Courts generally also require the employee to show causation—that the employer's unlawful discrimination caused the working conditions to be intolerable. Put a different way, the employee's resignation must be a foreseeable result of the employer's discriminatory action.

For example, Khalil, who was born in Iraq, is humiliated in front of his co-workers at the time that his employer informs him that he is being demoted to an inferior position. Co-workers continue to insult and harass Khalil and make derogatory remarks about his national origin. The employer is aware of this

---

4. *Frazee v. Illinois Department of Employment Security*, 489 U.S. 829, 109 S.Ct. 1514, 103 L.Ed.2d 914 (1989).

5. 42 U.S.C. Section 2000e(k).

discriminatory treatment but does nothing to remedy the situation, despite repeated complaints from Khalil. After several months, Khalil quits his job and files a Title VII claim. In this situation, Khalil would likely have sufficient evidence to maintain an action for constructive discharge in violation of Title VII. Although courts weigh the facts on a case-by-case basis, employee demotion is one of the most frequently cited reasons for a finding of constructive discharge, particularly when the employee was subjected to humiliation.

CAN BE APPLIED TO ANY TYPE OF TITLE VII DISCRIMINATION Note that constructive discharge is a theory that plaintiffs can use to establish any type of discrimination claims under Title VII, including race, color, national origin, religion, gender, pregnancy, and sexual harassment. Constructive discharge

has also been successfully used in situations that involve discrimination based on age or disability (both of which will be discussed later in this chapter). Constructive discharge is most commonly asserted in cases involving sexual harassment, however.

When constructive discharge is claimed, the employee can pursue damages for loss of income, including back pay. These damages would not ordinarily be available to an employee who left a job voluntarily.

The following case involved an employee's claim that she was constructively discharged from her job for refusing to participate in a scheme to discriminate against male co-workers and supervisors. The question for the court was whether the employer should have been aware of the employee's mistreatment and purported unbearable working conditions and done something about it.

CASE 34.1   Conway-Jepsen v. Small Business Administration

United States
District Court,
District of Montana, 2004.
303 F.Supp.2d 1155.

LOVELL, Senior District Judge.

* * * *

Plaintiff Mary Conway-Jepsen, an Assistant District Director for the Helena, Montana, office of the United States [Small] Business Administration (the "Helena SBA") from December 26, 1993, to August 6, 1997, complains that she was retaliated against in violation of Title VII * * * .

* * * *

Shortly after August, 1992, Jo Alice Mospan came to Helena, Montana, as the new District Director ("DD") of the Helena SBA. * * *

* * * *

* * * [T]here were no females above a [certain pay level] in the Helena SBA office and * * * most of the senior employees and supervisors were male.

* * * *

Mospan * * * mete[d] out discipline frequently to SBA employees, but particularly to certain male SBA employees. * * * She was described, in today's parlance, as an "in your face" type micro-manager.

* * * *

* * * [Mospan's] express purpose [was] harassing and ultimately firing certain male career SBA employees, * * * so that they could be replaced by females.

* * * *

* * * When Mospan arrived in 1992, the top layer of supervisors and program directors in the Helena SBA office was male * * * . When Mospan left in 2000, none of these men was employed by the SBA. * * *

* * * *

In 1993, Mospan * * * recruited Conway-Jepsen. * * *

In the Fall of 1994, * * * [I]t dawned on Conway-Jepsen that the promotion of women by Mospan would be "on the backs of the guys * * * ".

* * * Conway-Jepsen told Mospan that what she was doing * * * was wrong. * * * In response, Mospan became angry with Conway-Jepsen. * * *

* * * *

Mospan's [subsequent] harassment of Conway-Jepsen ranged from * * * program-irrelevant work assignments * * * [to] counterproductive actions in Plaintiff's projects * * * .

CASE 34.1 Continued

* * * *

* * * [Conway-Jepsen] eventually sought help from her physician, who * * * recommended that she quit her job. * * *

A few months before Plaintiff did resign, however, she * * * request[ed] that she be transferred to another SBA office or program. Notably, [no SBA official] responded to Plaintiff's request for a transfer * * * .

* * * *

Title VII prohibits an employer from discriminating against any employee because he or she has opposed * * * an unlawful employment practice * * * . In order to prove retaliation, Plaintiff must show that (1) she opposed an unlawful employment practice, (2) she suffered an adverse employment action, and (3) a causal connection existed between the adverse employment action and the protected activity or opposition. * * *

*Among the unlawful employment practices forbidden by Title VII is the rule that employers must not * * * discharge any individual, or otherwise * * * discriminate against any individual with respect to his compensation, terms, conditions, or privileges of employment, because of such individual's race, color, religion, sex, or national origin.* * * * [Emphasis added.]

* * * *

In order to meet her burden of proving that she was constructively discharged, Plaintiff must show that a reasonable person in her position would have felt compelled to resign because of intolerable working conditions. * * *

In addition, Plaintiff must show that the intolerable working conditions were created by the very conduct that constituted a violation of Title VII (in this case, e.g., the retaliation) and that her resignation resulted from the intolerable working conditions.

* * * *

* * * [T]he Court concludes that Plaintiff reasonably found her hostile working conditions intolerable, that the intolerable working conditions were created by conduct that constituted a violation of Title VII, and that Plaintiff's resignation resulted from the hostile and intolerable working conditions. The Court concludes that Plaintiff was a diligent and competent SBA employee who was constructively discharged from her position by Mospan's lengthy, continuous, and pervasive pattern of retaliatory treatment for the reason that she had objected to employment practices which were unlawful under Title VII.

* * * *

IT IS HEREBY ORDERED AND ADJUDGED * * * as follows:

1. Defendant * * * shall pay to Plaintiff back pay * * * .
2. Defendant * * * shall reinstate Plaintiff in a non-hostile work environment * * * .
3. Defendant * * * shall pay to Plaintiff * * * compensatory damages for emotional pain, suffering, inconvenience, mental anguish, loss of enjoyment of life, and other nonpecuniary losses.
4. Defendant * * * shall pay Plaintiff's reasonable attorney's fee.

QUESTIONS

1. What message does the outcome in this case send to employers covered by Title VII?
2. What conclusion might be drawn from the facts and result in this case with respect to diversity among employees as a goal for employers?

SEXUAL HARASSMENT

Title VII also protects employees against **sexual harassment** in the workplace. Sexual harassment can take two forms: *quid pro quo* harassment and hostile-environment harassment. *Quid pro quo* is a Latin phrase that is often translated to mean "something in exchange for something else." *Quid pro quo* harass- ment occurs when job opportunities, promotions, salary increases, and the like are given in return for sexual favors. According to the United States Supreme Court, hostile-environment harassment occurs when "the workplace is permeated with discriminatory intimidation, ridicule, and insult, that is sufficiently severe or pervasive to alter the conditions of the victim's employment and create an abusive working environment."[6]

Generally, the courts apply this Supreme Court guideline on a case-by-case basis. Some courts have held that just one incident of sexually offensive conduct—such as a sexist remark by a co-worker or a photo on an employer's desk of his bikini-clad wife—can create a hostile environment.[7] Other courts, however, require more than one instance of sexually offensive conduct to find an abusive working environment exists. According to some employment specialists, employers should assume that hostile-environment harassment has occurred if an employee claims that it has.

HARASSMENT BY SUPERVISORS What if an employee is harassed by a manager or supervisor of a large firm, and the firm itself (the "employer") is not aware of the harassment? Should the employer be held liable for the harassment nonetheless? For some time, the courts were in disagreement on this issue. Typically, employers were held liable for Title VII violations by the firm's managerial or supervisory personnel in *quid pro quo* harassment cases regardless of whether the employer knew about the harassment. In hostile-environment cases, in contrast, the majority of courts tended to hold employers liable only if the employer knew or should have known of the harassment and failed to take prompt remedial action.

—Tangible Employment Action. For an employer to be held liable for a supervisor's sexual harassment, the supervisor must have taken a *tangible employment action* against the employee. A **tangible employment action** is a significant change in employment status, such as firing or failing to promote an employee; reassigning the employee to a position with significantly different responsibilities; or effecting a significant change in employment benefits.

Only a supervisor, or another person acting with the authority of the employer, can cause this sort of injury. A co-worker can sexually harass another employee, and anyone who has regular contact with an employee can inflict psychological injuries by offensive conduct. A co-worker cannot dock another's pay, demote her or him, or set conditions for continued employment, however.

—Supreme Court Guidelines. In 1998, in two separate cases, the United States Supreme Court issued some significant guidelines relating to the liability of employers for their supervisors' harassment of employees in the workplace. In *Faragher v. City of Boca Raton,*[8] the Court held that an employer (a city) could be held liable for a supervisor's harassment of employees even though the employer was unaware of the behavior. The Court reached this conclusion primarily because, although the city had a written policy against sexual harassment, the policy had not been distributed to city employees. Additionally, the city had not established any procedures that could be followed by employees who felt that they were victims of sexual harassment. In *Burlington Industries, Inc. v. Ellerth,*[9] the Court ruled that a company could be held liable for the harassment of an employee by one of its vice presidents even though the employee suffered no adverse job consequences.

In these two cases, the Court set forth some commonsense guidelines on liability for harassment in the workplace that are helpful to employers and employees alike. On the one hand, employees benefit by the ruling that employers may be held liable for their supervisors' harassment even though the employers were unaware of the actions and even though the employees suffered no adverse job consequences. On the other hand, the Court made it clear in both decisions that employers have an affirmative defense against liability for their supervisors' harassment of employees if the employers can show the following:

1. That they have taken "reasonable care to prevent and correct promptly any sexually harassing behavior" (by establishing effective harassment policies and complaint procedures, for example).
2. That the employee suing for harassment failed to follow these policies and procedures.

In 2004 the Supreme Court further clarified the tangible employment action requirement in the following case. The Court had to decide how the guidelines apply to a state police employee's constructive discharge caused by her supervisors' sexual harassment. Does a constructive discharge count as a tangible employment action and preclude the employer's assertion of the affirmative defense? That was the issue before the Court.

---

6. *Harris v. Forklift Systems,* 510 U.S. 17, 114 S.Ct. 367, 126 L.Ed.2d 295 (1993).
7. For other examples, see *Radtke v. Everett,* 442 Mich. 368, 501 N.W.2d 155 (1993); and *Nadeau v. Rainbow Rugs, Inc.,* 675 A.2d 973 (Me. 1996).

---

8. 524 U.S. 775, 118 S.Ct. 2275, 141 L.Ed.2d 662 (1998).
9. 524 U.S. 742, 118 S.Ct. 2257, 141 L.Ed.2d 633 (1998).

CASE 34.2

Supreme Court of the
United States, 2004.
542 U.S. 129,
124 S.Ct. 2342,
159 L.Ed.2d 204.
*http://www.findlaw.com/
casecode/supreme.html*[a]

Pennsylvania State Police v. Suders

BACKGROUND AND FACTS *In March 1998, the Pennsylvania State Police (PSP) hired Nancy Suders to work as a communications operator. Suders's supervisors—Sergeant Eric Easton, Corporal William Baker, and Corporal Eric Prendergast—subjected her to a continuous barrage of sexual harassment. In June, Suders told Officer Virginia Smith-Elliott, whom PSP had designated as its equal employment opportunity officer, that Suders might need help. Two months later, again to Smith-Elliott, Suders reported that she was being harassed and was afraid. Smith-Elliott told Suders to file a complaint, but did not tell her how to obtain the necessary form. Two days later, Suders's supervisors arrested her for the theft of her own computer-skills exam paper, which she had removed after they reported falsely that she had failed the exam. Suders resigned and filed a suit in a federal district court against PSP, alleging, in part, sexual harassment. The court issued a summary judgment in PSP's favor. Suders appealed to the U.S. Court of Appeals for the Third Circuit, which reversed the judgment and remanded the case for trial, holding that the* Ellerth/Faragher *affirmative defense is never available in constructive discharge cases. PSP appealed to the United States Supreme Court.*

IN THE LANGUAGE OF THE COURT

Justice *GINSBURG* delivered the opinion of the Court.

* * * *

This case concerns an employer's liability for * * * constructive discharge resulting from sexual harassment, or hostile work environment, attributable to a supervisor. Our starting point is the framework [the] *Ellerth* and *Faragher* [decisions, discussed previously in this chapter] established to govern employer liability for sexual harassment by supervisors. * * * [T]hose decisions delineate two categories of hostile work environment claims: (1) harassment that culminates in a tangible employment action, for which employers are strictly liable, and (2) harassment that takes place in the absence of a tangible employment action, to which employers may assert an affirmative defense * * * .

* * * *

Suders' claim is of the same genre as the hostile work environment claims the Court analyzed in [the] *Ellerth* and *Faragher* [decisions]. Essentially, Suders presents a "worse case" harassment scenario, harassment ratcheted up to the breaking point. Like the harassment considered in our pathmarking decisions, harassment so intolerable as to cause a resignation may be effected through co-worker conduct, unofficial supervisory conduct, or official company acts. Unlike an actual termination, which is *always* effected through an official act of the company, a constructive discharge need not be. A *constructive discharge involves both an employee's decision to leave and precipitating conduct: The former involves no official action; the latter, like a harassment claim without any constructive discharge assertion, may or may not involve official action.* [Emphasis added.]

To be sure, a constructive discharge is functionally the same as an actual termination in [some] respects. * * * [B]oth end the employer-employee relationship, and both inflict * * * direct economic harm. But when an official act does not underlie the constructive discharge, the *Ellerth* and *Faragher* analysis, we here hold, calls for extension of the affirmative defense to the employer. As those leading decisions indicate, official directions and declarations are the acts most likely to be brought home to the employer, the measures over which the employer can exercise greatest control. Absent an official act of the enterprise as the last straw, the employer ordinarily would have no particular reason to suspect that a resignation is not the typical kind daily occurring in the work force. And as [the] *Ellerth* and *Faragher* [decisions] further point out, an official act reflected in company records—a demotion or a reduction in compensation, for example—shows beyond question that the supervisor has used his managerial or controlling position to the employee's disadvantage. *Absent such an official act, the extent to which the supervisor's misconduct has been aided by the [employment] relation is less*

---

a. In the "Browsing" section, click on "2004 Decisions." When that page opens, click on the name of the case to access the opinion.

CONTINUED ▶

CASE 34.2 | **Continued**   *certain. That uncertainty * * * justifies affording the employer the chance to establish, through the Ellerth/Faragher affirmative defense, that it should not be held vicariously liable. [Emphasis added.]*

*   *   *   *

We agree with the Third Circuit that the case, in its current posture, presents genuine issues of material fact concerning Suders' hostile work environment and constructive discharge claims. We hold, however, that the Court of Appeals erred in declaring the affirmative defense described in [the] *Ellerth* and *Faragher* [decisions] never available in constructive discharge cases. Accordingly, we vacate the Third Circuit's judgment and remand the case for further proceedings consistent with this opinion.

DECISION AND REMEDY *The United States Supreme Court vacated the lower court's judgment and remanded the case for further proceedings. To establish constructive discharge, a plaintiff alleging sexual harassment must show that the work environment became so intolerable that resignation was a fitting response. An employer may then assert the* Ellerth/Faragher *affirmative defense unless the plaintiff quit in reasonable response to a tangible employment action.*

WHAT IF THE FACTS WERE DIFFERENT? *If the plaintiff had filed a complaint with the employer's equal employment opportunity officer, how might the result have been different?*

HARASSMENT BY CO-WORKERS AND NON-EMPLOYEES Often, employees alleging harassment complain that the actions of co-workers, not supervisors, are responsible for creating a hostile working environment. In such cases, the employee still has a cause of action against the employer. Generally, though, the employer will be held liable only if it knew or should have known about the harassment and failed to take immediate remedial action.

Employers may also be liable for harassment by *nonemployees* under certain conditions. For example, if a restaurant owner or manager knows that a particular customer repeatedly harasses a waitress and permits the harassment to continue, the restaurant owner may be liable under Title VII even though the customer is not an employee of the restaurant. The issue turns on the control that the employer exerts over a nonemployee. In one case, the owner of a Pizza Hut franchise was held liable for the harassment of a waitress by two male customers because no steps were taken to prevent the harassment.[10]

SAME-GENDER HARASSMENT The courts have also had to address the issue of whether men who are harassed by other men, or women who are harassed by other women, are also protected by laws that prohibit gender-based discrimination in the workplace. For example, what if the male president of a firm demands sexual favors from a male employee? Does this action qualify as sexual harassment? For some time, the courts were widely split on this question. In 1998, in *Oncale*

v. Sundowner Offshore Services, Inc.,[11] the Supreme Court resolved the issue by holding that Title VII protection extends to situations in which individuals are harassed by members of the same gender.

It can be difficult to prove that the harassment in same-gender harassment cases is "based on sex." Suppose that a gay man is harassed by another man at the workplace. The harasser is not a homosexual and does not treat all men with hostility—just this one man. Does the victim in this situation have a cause of action under Title VII? A court may find that this does not qualify as sexual harassment under Title VII because the harasser's conduct was not "because of sex," but because of sexual orientation.[12]

Although Title VII does not prohibit discrimination or harassment based on a person's sexual orientation, a growing number of companies are voluntarily establishing nondiscrimination policies that include sexual orientation. According to one study, at the end of 2004, 410 companies on the Fortune 500 had procedures in place to specifically protect gay, lesbian, bisexual, and transgender (those transitioning from one gender to another) employees from workplace discrimination and harassment.[13]

11. 523 U.S. 75, 118 S.Ct. 998, 140 L.Ed.2d 207 (1998).

12. See, for example, *McCown v. St. John's Health System,* 349 F.3d 540 (8th Cir. 2003); and *Rene v. MGM Grand Hotel, Inc.,* 305 F.3d 1061 (9th Cir. 2002).

13. Amy Joyce, "Workplace Improves for Gay, Transgender Employees, Rights Group Says," *The Washington Post,* June 6, 2005, reporting a study conducted by the Human Rights Campaign Foundation, "The State of the Workplace for Lesbian, Gay, Bisexual, and Transgender Americans 2004."

10. *Lockard v. Pizza Hut, Inc.,* 162 F.3d 1062 (10th Cir. 1998).

ONLINE HARASSMENT

Employees' online activities can create a hostile working environment in many ways. Racial jokes, ethnic slurs, or other comments contained in e-mail may become the basis for a claim of hostile-environment harassment or other forms of discrimination. A worker who sees sexually explicit images on a co-worker's computer screen may find the images offensive and claim that they create a hostile working environment.

Nevertheless, employers may be able to avoid liability for online harassment by taking prompt remedial action. For example, in one case Angela Daniels, an employee under contract to WorldCom, received racially harassing e-mailed jokes from another employee. After receiving the jokes, Daniels complained to WorldCom managers. Shortly afterward, the company issued a warning to the offending employee about the proper use of the e-mail system and held two meetings to discuss company policy on the use of the system. In Daniels's suit against WorldCom for racial discrimination, a federal district court concluded that the employer was not liable for its employee's racially harassing e-mails because the employer took prompt remedial action.[14]

REMEDIES UNDER TITLE VII

Employer liability under Title VII may be extensive. If the plaintiff successfully proves that unlawful discrimination occurred, he or she may be awarded reinstatement, back pay, retroactive promotions, and damages.[15] Compensatory damages are available only in cases of intentional discrimination. Punitive damages may be recovered against a private employer only if the employer acted with malice or reckless indifference to an individual's rights. The statute limits the total amount of compensatory and punitive damages that the plaintiff can recover from specific employers (ranging from $50,000 against employers with one hundred or fewer employees to $300,000 against employers with more than five hundred employees).

---

14. *Daniels v. WorldCom Corp.*, 1998 WL 91261 (N.D.Tex. 1998). Also see *Musgrove v. Mobil Oil Corp.*, 2003 WL 21653125 (N.D. Tex. 2003).

15. Damages were not available under Title VII until 1991. The Civil Rights Act of that year amended Title VII to provide for both compensatory and punitive damages, as well as for jury trials.

SECTION 2 | Equal Pay Act of 1963

The Equal Pay Act of 1963 was enacted as an amendment to the Fair Labor Standards Act of 1938. Basically, the act prohibits gender-based discrimination in the wages paid for similar work. For the equal pay requirements to apply, the male and female workers must be employed at the same establishment.

A person alleging wage discrimination in violation of the Equal Pay Act may sue her or his employer. To determine whether the act has been violated, a court will look to the primary duties of the two jobs—it is job content rather than job description that controls in all cases. The jobs of a barber and a beautician, for example, are considered essentially equal. So, too, are those of a tailor and a seamstress. Small differences in job content do not legally justify higher pay for one gender. An employer will *not* be found liable for violating the act if it can show that the wage differential for equal work was based on (1) a seniority system, (2) a merit system, (3) a system that pays according to quality or quantity of production, or (4) any factor other than gender.

SECTION 3 | Discrimination Based on Age

Age discrimination is potentially the most widespread form of discrimination, because anyone—regardless of race, color, national origin, or gender—could be a victim at some point in life. The Age Discrimination in Employment Act (ADEA) of 1967, as amended, prohibits employment discrimination on the basis of age against individuals forty years of age or older. The act also prohibits mandatory retirement for nonmanagerial workers. For the act to apply, an employer must have twenty or more employees, and the employer's business activities must affect interstate commerce. The EEOC administers the ADEA, but the act also permits private causes of action against employers for age discrimination.

PROCEDURES UNDER THE ADEA

The burden-shifting procedure under the ADEA is similar to that under Title VII. If a plaintiff can establish that he or she (1) was a member of the protected age group, (2) was qualified for the position from which he or she was discharged, and (3) was discharged under circumstances that give rise to an inference of discrimination, the plaintiff has established a *prima facie* case of unlawful age discrimination. The burden then shifts to the employer, who must articulate a legitimate reason for the discrimination. If the plaintiff can prove that the employer's reason is only a pretext and that the plaintiff's age was a determining factor in the employer's decision, the employer will be held liable under the ADEA.

REPLACING OLDER WORKERS WITH YOUNGER WORKERS

Numerous cases of alleged age discrimination have been brought against employers who, to cut costs, replaced older, higher-salaried employees with younger, lower-salaried workers. Whether a firing is discriminatory or simply part of a rational business decision to prune the company's ranks is not always clear. Companies generally defend a decision to discharge a worker by asserting that the worker could no longer perform her or his duties or that the worker's skills were no longer needed. The employee must prove that the discharge was motivated, at least in part, by age bias. Proof that qualified older employees are generally discharged before employees who are younger or that co-workers continually made unflattering age-related comments about the discharged worker may be enough. The plaintiff need not prove that she or he was replaced by a person outside the protected class—that is, by a person under the age of forty years.[16] Rather, the issue in all ADEA cases turns on whether age discrimination has, in fact, occurred, regardless of the age of the replacement worker.

A SPECIAL CASE—STATE EMPLOYEES

Under the Eleventh Amendment to the U.S. Constitution, as that amendment has been interpreted by the United States Supreme Court, states are immune from lawsuits brought by private individuals in federal court, unless the state consents to the suit. In a number of age-discrimination cases brought in the late 1990s, state agencies that were sued by state employees for age discrimination sought to have the suits dismissed on this ground.

STATE EMPLOYEES NOT COVERED BY THE ADEA
In two Florida cases, professors and librarians contended that their employers—two Florida state universities—denied them salary increases and other benefits because they were getting old and their successors could be hired at lower cost. The universities

claimed that as agencies of a sovereign state, they could not be sued without the state's consent. Because the courts were rendering conflicting opinions in these cases, the United States Supreme Court agreed to address the issue. In *Kimel v. Florida Board of Regents*,[17] decided in 2000, the Court held that the sovereign immunity granted the states by the Eleventh Amendment precluded suits against them by private parties alleging violations of the ADEA.

STATE IMMUNITY IS NOT ABSOLUTE
In 2004 the Supreme Court clarified that state immunity under the Eleventh Amendment is not absolute. The case was brought under the Americans with Disabilities Act (ADA), which will be discussed shortly, alleging that disabled individuals were denied access to the courts. The Court held that in some situations, such as when fundamental rights are at stake, Congress has the power to abrogate (abolish) state immunity to private suits through legislation that unequivocally shows Congress's intent to subject states to private suits.[18]

Generally, though, the Court has found that state employers are immune from private suits brought by employees under the ADEA (for age discrimination, as noted above), the ADA[19] (for disability discrimination), and the Fair Labor Standards Act[20] (FLSA, which relates to wages and hours—see Chapter 33), but are not immune from the requirements of the Family Medical Leave Act[21] (FMLA—see Chapter 33).

SECTION 4 | Discrimination Based on Disability

The Americans with Disabilities Act (ADA) of 1990 is designed to eliminate discriminatory employment practices that prevent otherwise qualified workers with disabilities from fully participating in the national labor force. Prior to 1990, the major federal law providing protection to those with disabilities was the Rehabilitation Act of 1973. That act protected only federal government employees and those employed

---

16. *O'Connor v. Consolidated Coin Caterers Corp.*, 517 U.S. 308, 116 S.Ct. 1307, 134 L.Ed.2d 433 (1996).

17. 528 U.S. 62, 120 S.Ct. 631, 145 L.Ed.2d 522 (2000).

18. *Tennessee v. Lane*, 541 U.S. 509, 124 S.Ct. 1978, 158 L.Ed.2d 820 (2004).

19. *Board of Trustees of the University of Alabama v. Garrett*, 531 U.S. 356, 121 S.Ct. 955, 148 L.Ed.2d 866 (2001).

20. *Alden v. Maine*, 527 U.S. 706, 119 S.Ct. 2240, 144 L.Ed.2d 636 (1999).

21. *Nevada Department of Human Resources v. Hibbs*, 538 U.S. 721, 123 S.Ct. 1972, 155 L.Ed.2d 953 (2003). This case was presented in Chapter 33 as Case 33.2.

under federally funded programs. The ADA extends federal protection against disability-based discrimination to all workplaces with fifteen or more workers (with the exception of state government employers, who are generally immune under the Eleventh Amendment, as was just discussed). Basically, the ADA requires that employers "reasonably accommodate" the needs of persons with disabilities unless to do so would cause the employer to suffer an "undue hardship."

PROCEDURES UNDER THE ADA

To prevail on a claim under the ADA, a plaintiff must show that he or she (1) has a disability, (2) is otherwise qualified for the employment in question, and (3) was excluded from the employment solely because of the disability. As in Title VII cases, a claim alleging violation of the ADA may be commenced only after the plaintiff has pursued the claim through the EEOC, which administers the provisions of the act relating to disability-based discrimination in the employment context. The EEOC may decide to investigate and perhaps even sue the employer on behalf of the employee. If the EEOC decides not to sue, then the employee is entitled to sue.

Significantly, the United States Supreme Court held in 2002 that the EEOC could bring a suit against an employer for disability-based discrimination even though the employee had agreed to submit any job-related disputes to arbitration (see Chapter 2). The Court reasoned that because the EEOC was not a party to the arbitration agreement, the agreement was not binding on the EEOC.[22]

Plaintiffs in lawsuits brought under the ADA may seek many of the same remedies that are available under Title VII. These include reinstatement, back pay, a limited amount of compensatory and punitive damages (for intentional discrimination), and certain other forms of relief. Repeat violators may be ordered to pay fines of up to $100,000.

WHAT IS A DISABILITY?

The ADA broadly defines *persons with disabilities* as persons with physical or mental impairments that "substantially limit" their everyday activities. More specifically, the ADA defines a *disability* as "(1) a physical or mental impairment that substantially limits one or more of the major life activities of such individuals; (2) a record of such impairment; or (3) being regarded as having such an impairment."

Health conditions that have been considered disabilities under federal law include blindness, alcoholism, heart disease, cancer, muscular dystrophy, cerebral palsy, paraplegia, diabetes, acquired immune deficiency syndrome (AIDS), and morbid obesity (which exists when an individual's weight is more than two times what it should be).[23] In 1998, the Supreme Court held that a person who is infected with the human immunodeficiency virus (HIV) but who has no symptoms of AIDS is protected under the ADA.[24] The ADA excludes from coverage certain conditions, such as kleptomania (the obsessive desire to steal).

In a series of cases decided in the last several years, the courts have been significantly narrowing the scope of the ADA through their interpretation of what constitutes a disability under the act. For a discussion of these cases, see this chapter's *Emerging Trends* feature beginning on the following page.

REASONABLE ACCOMMODATION

If a job applicant or an employee with a disability can perform essential job functions with reasonable accommodation, the employer must make the accommodation. Required modifications may include installing ramps for a wheelchair, establishing flexible working hours, creating or modifying job assignments, and designing or improving training materials and procedures.

Generally, employers should give primary consideration to employees' preferences in deciding what accommodations should be made. If an applicant or employee fails to let the employer know how his or her disability can be accommodated, the employer may avoid liability for failing to hire or retain the individual on the ground that the individual has failed to meet the "otherwise qualified" requirement.[25]

Employers should be cautious in making this assumption in situations involving mental illness, though. For example, in one case, an employee was held to have a cause of action against his employer under the ADA even though the employee never explicitly told the employer how his disability could be accommodated.[26]

---

22. *EEOC v. Waffle House, Inc.,* 534 U.S. 279, 122 S.Ct. 754, 151 L.Ed.2d 755 (2002).

23. *Cook v. Rhode Island Department of Mental Health,* 10 F.3d 17 (1st Cir. 1993).

24. *Bragdon v. Abbott,* 524 U.S. 624, 118 S.Ct. 2196, 141 L.Ed.2d 540 (1998).

25. See, for example, *Beck v. University of Wisconsin Board of Regents,* 75 F.3d 1130 (7th Cir. 1996); and *White v. York International Corp.,* 45 F.3d 357 (10th Cir. 1995).

26. *Bultemeyer v. Fort Wayne Community Schools,* 100 F.3d 1281 (7th Cir. 1996).

Narrowing the Definition of "Disability"

The Americans with Disabilities Act (ADA) does not precisely define what constitutes a disability under the act. Thus, deciding which disabilities qualify under the ADA has largely been left to the courts. Clearly, how the courts interpret the act has significant implications for both employers and employees. When a court holds that a person's impairment does not "substantially limit" a major life activity, that person will not be considered to have a disability under the ADA. Employers benefit from such a holding because they will not be required to accommodate persons with similar disabilities. In contrast, of course, individuals suffering from similar disabilities will not be able to obtain the protections afforded by the ADA.

Starting in 1999, the United States Supreme Court has issued a series of decisions narrowing the definition of what constitutes a disability under the act. In other words, the Court's decisions represent a trend toward limiting the scope of the ADA.

CORRECTABLE CONDITIONS

In 1999, in *Sutton v. United Airlines, Inc.,*[a] the Supreme Court reviewed a case raising the issue of whether severe myopia, or nearsightedness, which can be corrected with eyeglasses or contact lenses, qualified as a disability under the ADA. The Supreme Court ruled that it did not. The determination of whether a person is substantially limited in a

major life activity is based on how the person functions when taking medication or using corrective devices, not on how the person functions without these measures.

In a similar case in 2002, a federal appellate court held that a pharmacist suffering from diabetes, which could be corrected by insulin, had no cause of action against his employer under the ADA.[b] In other cases decided in the early 2000s, the courts have held that plaintiffs with bipolar disorder, epilepsy, and other such conditions do *not* fall under the ADA's protections if the conditions can be corrected.

THE TOYOTA CASE

In 2002, the Supreme Court further limited the scope of the ADA by its broad interpretation of what constitutes a substantially limiting impairment of a major life activity. The case before the Court involved Ella Williams, an employee of Toyota Motor Manufacturing in Kentucky. Williams's use of tools on an engine fabrication assembly line eventually caused pain in her hands, wrists, and arms. For the following two years, she held modified-duty jobs to avoid repetitive physical activity. Nonetheless, she started to experience pain in her neck and shoulders and was finally placed on a no-work-of-any-kind restriction. Toyota then terminated her employment.

The Supreme Court had to decide whether her condition, generally referred to as carpal tunnel syndrome, constituted a disability under the ADA. The Court unanimously held that it

---

a. 527 U.S. 471, 119 S.Ct. 2139, 144 L.Ed.2d 450 (1999).

b. *Orr v. Wal-Mart Stores, Inc.,* 297 F.3d 720 (8th Cir. 2002).

UNDUE HARDSHIP Employers who do not accommodate the needs of persons with disabilities must demonstrate that the accommodations would cause *undue hardship*. Generally, the law offers no uniform standards for identifying what is an undue hardship other than the imposition of a "significant difficulty or expense" on the employer.

Usually, the courts decide whether an accommodation constitutes an undue hardship on a case-by-case basis. In one case, the court decided that paying for a parking space near the office for an employee with a disability was not an undue hardship.[27] In another case, the court held that accommodating the request of an employee with diabetes for indefinite leave until his disease was under control would create an undue hard-

ship for the employer, because the employer would not know when the employee was returning to work. The court stated that reasonable accommodation under the ADA means accommodation so that the employee can perform the job now or "in the immediate future" rather than at some unspecified distant time.[28]

JOB APPLICATIONS AND PREEMPLOYMENT PHYSICAL EXAMS Employers must modify their job-application process so that those with disabilities can compete for jobs with those who do not have disabilities. A job announcement that has only a phone number, for example, would discriminate against potential job applicants with hearing impairments. Thus, the job announcement must also provide an address.

---

27. See *Lyons v. Legal Aid Society,* 68 F.3d 1512 (2d Cir. 1995).

28. *Myers v. Hose,* 50 F.3d 278 (4th Cir. 1995).

did not. The Court stated that although the employee could not perform the manual tasks associated with her job, the condition did not constitute a disability under the ADA because it did not "substantially limit" the major life activity of performing manual tasks. For the fired worker, Williams, to prevail, her carpal tunnel syndrome would have had to be so severe that it prevented or severely restricted activities that were of central importance to her daily life, not just work-related activities.[c]

FURTHER LIMITING THE SCOPE OF THE ADA

In a 2001 case, the Supreme Court also limited the applicability of the ADA by holding that lawsuits under the ADA cannot be brought against state government employers. The Court concluded that states, as sovereigns, are immune from lawsuits brought against them by private parties under the federal ADA.[d]

The Court went on to further limit the scope of the ADA by supporting Equal Employment Opportunity Commission regulations that permit an employer to refuse to hire a person when the job would pose a threat to that person's health.[e]

---

c. *Toyota Motor Manufacturing, Kentucky, Inc. v. Williams,* 534 U.S. 184, 122 S.Ct. 681, 151 L.Ed.2d 615 (2002).
d. *Board of Trustees of the University of Alabama v. Garrett,* 531 U.S. 356, 121 S.Ct. 955, 148 L.Ed.2d 866 (2001).
e. *Chevron USA, Inc. v. Echazabal,* 536 U.S. 73, 122 S.Ct. 2045, 153 L.Ed.2d 82 (2002).

Employers are restricted in the kinds of questions they may ask on job-application forms and during pre-employment interviews. Furthermore, employers cannot require persons with disabilities to submit to preemployment physicals unless such exams are required of all other applicants. Employers can condition an offer of employment on the applicant's successfully passing a medical examination, but can disqualify the applicant only if the medical problems they discover would render the applicant unable to perform the job.

DANGEROUS WORKERS Employers are not required to hire or retain workers who, because of their disabilities, pose a "direct threat to the health or safety" of their co-workers. (As mentioned in this chapter's *Emerging Trends* feature, employers may also refuse to hire persons with disabilities if the job would pose a threat to their own health.)

In the wake of the AIDS epidemic, many employers became concerned about hiring or continuing to employ workers who have AIDS under the assumption that they might pose a direct threat to the health or safety of others in the workplace. Courts have generally held, however, that AIDS is not so contagious as to disqualify employees from most jobs. Therefore, employers must reasonably accommodate job applicants or employees who have AIDS or who test positive for HIV, the virus that causes AIDS.

SUBSTANCE ABUSERS Drug addiction is a disability under the ADA because drug addiction is a substantially limiting impairment. Those who are currently using illegal drugs are not protected by the act, however. The ADA only protects persons with *former* drug addictions—those who have completed a supervised drug-rehabilitation program or who are currently participating in a supervised rehabilitation program. Individuals who have used drugs casually in the past are not protected under the act. They are not considered addicts and therefore do not have a disability (addiction).

People suffering from alcoholism are protected by the ADA. Employers cannot legally discriminate against employees simply because they are living with alcoholism and must treat them the same way other employees are treated. For example, an employee with alcoholism who comes to work late because she or he was drinking the night before cannot be disciplined any differently than an employee who comes to work late for another reason. Of course, employers have the right to prohibit the use of alcohol in the workplace and can require that employees not be under the influence of alcohol while working. Employers can also fire or refuse to hire a person with alcoholism if he or she poses a substantial risk of harm either to himself or herself or to others and the risk cannot be reduced by reasonable accommodation.

HEALTH-INSURANCE PLANS Workers with disabilities must be given equal access to any health insurance provided to other employees. Employers can exclude from coverage preexisting health conditions and certain types of diagnostic or surgical procedures, however. An employer can also put a limit, or cap, on health-care payments under its particular group health policy as long as the cap is "applied equally to all insured employees" and does not "discriminate on the basis of disability." Whenever a group health-care plan makes a disability-based distinction in its benefits, the plan violates the ADA. The employer must then be able to justify the distinction by proving one of the following:

1. That limiting coverage of certain ailments is required to keep the plan financially sound.
2. That coverage of certain ailments would cause a significant increase in premium payments or their equivalent, making the plan unappealing to a significant number of employees.
3. That the disparate treatment is justified by the risks and costs associated with a particular disability.

HOSTILE-ENVIRONMENT CLAIMS UNDER THE ADA

As discussed earlier in this chapter, under Title VII of the Civil Rights Act of 1964, an employee may base certain types of employment-discrimination causes of action on a hostile-environment theory. Using this theory, a worker may successfully sue her or his employer, even if the worker was not fired or otherwise discriminated against.

Can a worker file a suit founded on a hostile-environment claim under the ADA? The ADA does not expressly provide for such suits, but some courts have allowed them. Others have assumed that the claim was possible without deciding whether the ADA allowed it.[29] To succeed, such a claim would likely have to be based on conduct that a reasonable person would find so offensive that it would change the conditions of the person's employment.

Whether a worker with a disability who was harassed by her co-workers could successfully sue her employer for a hostile environment was the issue in the following case.

29. See, for example, *Steele v. Thiokol Corp.*, 241 F.3d 1248 (10th Cir. 2001).

CASE 34.3   **Flowers v. Southern Regional Physician Services, Inc.**

United States Court of Appeals, Fifth Circuit. 2001. 247 F.3d 229. http://www.ca5.uscourts.gov/opinions.aspx[a]

BACKGROUND AND FACTS *Beginning in September 1993, Sandra Flowers worked for Southern Regional Physician Services, Inc., as a medical assistant to Dr. James Osterberger. In March 1995, Margaret Hallmark, Flowers's immediate supervisor, discovered that Flowers was infected with the human immunodeficiency virus (HIV). Suddenly Flowers, who had received only excellent performance reviews, was the subject of several negative disciplinary reports. Also, she was required to take four drug tests in one week. Previously, she had been asked to take only one. Hallmark stopped socializing with Flowers, her co-workers began avoiding her, and the president of the hospital refused to*

a. In the "Docket number is:" box, enter "99-31354" and click on "Search." Then click on the docket number again to access the opinion.

CASE 34.3 | Continued *shake her hand. In November 1995, after being put on probation twice, Flowers was fired. She filed a suit in a federal district court against Southern Regional under the ADA, arguing in part that she had been subjected to a hostile environment on the basis of her disability. The court entered a judgment in her favor and awarded her $100,000. Southern Regional appealed to the U.S. Court of Appeals for the Fifth Circuit.*

IN THE LANGUAGE OF THE COURT

KING, Chief Judge:
* * * *

The ADA provides that no employer covered by the Act "shall discriminate against a qualified individual with a disability because of the disability of such individual in regard to * * * *terms, conditions, and privileges of employment.*" In almost identical fashion, Title VII provides that it is unlawful for an employer "to fail or refuse to hire or to discharge any individual, or otherwise to discriminate against any individual with respect to his compensation, *terms, conditions, or privileges of employment*, because of such individual's race, color, religion, sex, or national origin[.]"

It is evident, after a review of the ADA's language, purpose, and remedial framework, that Congress's intent in enacting the ADA was, *inter alia* [among other things], to eradicate disability-based harassment in the workplace. First, as a matter of statutory interpretation, * * * the [United States] Supreme Court interpreted Title VII, which contains language similar to that in the ADA, to provide a cause of action for harassment which is sufficiently severe or pervasive to alter the conditions of the victim's employment and create an abusive working environment * * * because it affects a term, condition, or privilege of employment. We conclude that the language of Title VII and [of] the ADA dictates a consistent reading of the two statutes. Therefore, following the Supreme Court's interpretation of the language contained in Title VII, we interpret the phrase "terms, conditions, and privileges of employment," as it is used in the ADA, to strike at harassment in the workplace.

Not only are Title VII and the ADA similar in their language, they are also alike in their purposes and remedial structures. *Both Title VII and the ADA are aimed at the same evil—employment discrimination against individuals of certain classes.* Moreover, this court has recognized that the ADA is part of the same broad remedial framework as * * * Title VII, and that all the anti-discrimination acts have been subjected to similar analysis. Furthermore, other courts of appeals have noted the correlation between the two statutes. We conclude, therefore, that the purposes and remedial frameworks of the two statutes also command our conclusion that the ADA provides a cause of action for disability-based harassment. [Emphasis added.]

DECISION AND REMEDY *The U.S. Court of Appeals for the Fifth Circuit held that the right to bring a hostile-environment claim can be inferred because the ADA is similar in language, purpose, and "remedial structure" to Title VII. (The court added that Flowers was entitled only to nominal damages, however, because she did not prove that she actually suffered emotional injury.)*

SECTION 5 | Defenses to Employment Discrimination

The first line of defense for an employer charged with employment discrimination is, of course, to assert that the plaintiff has failed to meet his or her initial burden of proof—proving that discrimination in fact occurred. As noted, plaintiffs bringing cases under the ADA may find it difficult to meet this initial burden because they must prove that their alleged disabilities are disabilities covered by the ADA. Furthermore, plaintiffs in ADA cases must prove that they were otherwise qualified for the job.

Once a plaintiff succeeds in proving that discrimination occurred, then the burden shifts to the employer to justify the discriminatory practice. Often, employers attempt to justify the discrimination by claiming that it was the result of a business necessity, a bona fide occupational qualification, a seniority system, or employee misconduct.

BUSINESS NECESSITY

An employer may defend against a claim of *disparate-impact* discrimination by asserting that a practice that has a discriminatory effect is a **business necessity.** If requiring a high school diploma, for example, is shown to have a discriminatory effect, an employer might argue that a high school education is required for workers to perform the job at a required level of competence. If the employer can demonstrate to the court's satisfaction that a definite connection exists between a high school education and job performance, then the employer will succeed in this business necessity defense.

BONA FIDE OCCUPATIONAL QUALIFICATION

Another defense applies when discrimination against a protected class is essential to a job—that is, when a particular trait is a **bona fide occupational qualification (BFOQ).** For example, a women's clothing boutique might legitimately hire only female attendants if part of an attendant's job involves assisting clients in the boutique's dressing rooms. Similarly, the Federal Aviation Administration can legitimately impose age limits for airline pilots.

Race, color, and national origin, however, can never be justified as a BFOQ. Generally, courts have restricted the BFOQ defense to instances in which the employee's gender or religion is essential to the job.

SENIORITY SYSTEMS

An employer with a history of discrimination may have no members of protected classes in upper-level positions. Even if the employer now seeks to be unbiased, it may face a lawsuit seeking an order that members of protected classes be promoted ahead of schedule to compensate for past discrimination. If no present intent to discriminate is shown, however, and if promotions or other job benefits are distributed according to a fair **seniority system** (in which workers with more years of service are promoted first or laid off last), the employer has a good defense against the suit.

According to the United States Supreme Court, this defense may also apply to alleged discrimination under the ADA. If an employee with a disability requests an accommodation (such as an assignment to a particular position) that conflicts with an employer's seniority system, the accommodation will generally not be considered "reasonable" under the act.[30]

AFTER-ACQUIRED EVIDENCE OF EMPLOYEE MISCONDUCT

In some situations, employers have attempted to avoid liability for employment discrimination on the basis of "after-acquired evidence" of an employee's misconduct. For example, suppose that an employer fires a worker, who then sues the employer for employment discrimination. During pretrial investigation, the employer learns that the employee made material misrepresentations on his employment application—misrepresentations that, had the employer known about them, would have served as a ground to fire the individual. Can this after-acquired evidence be used as a defense?

According to the United States Supreme Court, after-acquired evidence of wrongdoing cannot be used to shield an employer entirely from liability for employment discrimination. It may, however, be used to limit the amount of damages for which the employer is liable.[31]

SECTION 6 | Affirmative Action

The laws discussed in this chapter were designed to reduce or eliminate discriminatory practices with respect to hiring, retaining, and promoting employees. **Affirmative action** programs go a step further and attempt to "make up" for past patterns of discrimination by giving members of protected classes preferential treatment in hiring or promotion. During the 1960s, all federal and state government agencies, private companies that contract to do business with the federal government, and institutions that receive federal funding were required to implement affirmative action policies.

Title VII of the Civil Rights Act of 1964 neither requires nor prohibits affirmative action. Thus, most private companies and organizations have not been required to implement affirmative action policies, though many have done so voluntarily.

Affirmative action programs have caused much controversy over the last forty years, particularly when they result in what is frequently called "reverse

---

30. *U.S. Airways, Inc. v. Barnett,* 535 U.S. 391, 122 S.Ct. 1516, 152 L.Ed.2d 589 (2002).
31. *McKennon v. Nashville Banner Publishing Co.*, 513 U.S. 352, 115 S.Ct. 879, 130 L.Ed.2d 852 (1995).

discrimination"—discrimination against "majority" workers, such as white males. At issue is whether affirmative action programs, because of their inherently discriminatory nature, violate employee rights or the equal protection clause of the Fourteenth Amendment to the U.S. Constitution.

THE BAKKE CASE

An early case addressing this issue outside the employment context, *Regents of the University of California v. Bakke*,[32] involved an affirmative action program implemented by the University of California at Davis. Allan Bakke, who had been turned down for medical school at the Davis campus, sued the university for reverse discrimination after he discovered that his academic record was better than the records of some of the minority applicants who had been admitted to the program.

The United States Supreme Court held that affirmative action programs were subject to intermediate scrutiny. Recall from the discussion of the equal protection clause in Chapter 4 that any law or action evaluated under a standard of intermediate scrutiny, to be constitutionally valid, must be substantially related to important government objectives. Applying this standard, the Court held that the university could give favorable weight to minority applicants as part of a plan to increase minority enrollment so as to achieve a more culturally diverse student body. The Court stated, however, that the use of a quota system, in which a certain number of places are explicitly reserved for minority applicants, violated the equal protection clause of the Fourteenth Amendment.

THE ADARAND CASE

Although the *Bakke* case and later court decisions alleviated the harshness of the quota system, today's courts are going even further in questioning the constitutional validity of affirmative action programs. In 1995, in its landmark decision in *Adarand Constructors, Inc. v. Peña*,[33] the United States Supreme Court held that any federal, state, or local affirmative action program that uses racial or ethnic classifications as the basis for making decisions is subject to strict scrutiny by the courts.

In effect, the Court's ruling in *Adarand* means that an affirmative action program is constitutional only if

it attempts to remedy past discrimination and does not make use of quotas or preferences. Furthermore, once such a program has succeeded in the goal of remedying past discrimination, it must be changed or dropped. Since then, other federal courts have followed the Supreme Court's lead by declaring affirmative action programs invalid unless they attempt to remedy past or current discrimination.[34]

THE HOPWOOD CASE

In 1996, in *Hopwood v. State of Texas*,[35] the Court of Appeals for the Fifth Circuit held that an affirmative action program at the University of Texas School of Law in Austin violated the equal protection clause. In that case, two white law school applicants sued the university when they were denied admission. The court decided that the affirmative action policy unlawfully discriminated in favor of minority applicants. In its decision, the court directly challenged the *Bakke* decision by stating that the use of race even as a means of achieving diversity on college campuses "undercuts the Fourteenth Amendment." The United States Supreme Court declined to hear the case, thus letting the lower court's decision stand. Federal appellate court decisions since then have been divided on whether such programs are constitutional.[36]

SUBSEQUENT COURT DECISIONS

In 2003, the United States Supreme Court reviewed two cases involving issues similar to that in the *Hopwood* case. Both cases involved admissions programs at the University of Michigan. In *Gratz v. Bollinger*,[37] two white applicants who were denied undergraduate admission to the university alleged reverse discrimination. The school's policy gave each applicant a score based on a number of factors, including grade point average, standardized test scores, and personal achievements. The system *automatically* awarded every "underrepresented" minority (African American, Hispanic, and Native American) applicant twenty points—one-fifth of the points needed to

---

32. 438 U.S. 265, 98 S.Ct. 2733, 57 L.Ed.2d 750 (1978).
33. 515 U.S. 200, 115 S.Ct. 2097, 132 L.Ed.2d 158 (1995).
34. See, for example, *Taxman v. Board of Education of the Township of Piscataway*, 91 F.3d 1547 (3d Cir. 1996); and *Schurr v. Resorts International Hotel, Inc.*, 196 F.3d 486 (3d Cir. 1999).
35. 84 F.3d 720 (5th Cir. 1996).
36. See, for example, *Johnson v. Board of Regents of the University of Georgia*, 263 F.3d 1234 (11th Cir. 2001); and *Smith v. University of Washington School of Law*, 233 F.3d 1188 (9th Cir. 2000).
37. 539 U.S. 244, 123 S.Ct. 2411, 156 L.Ed.2d 257 (2003).

guarantee admission. The Court held that this policy violated the equal protection clause.

In contrast, in *Grutter v. Bollinger*,[38] the Court held that the University of Michigan Law School's admission policy was constitutional. In that case, the Court concluded that "[u]niversities can, however, consider race or ethnicity more flexibly as a 'plus' factor in the context of individualized consideration of each and every applicant." The significant difference between the two admissions policies, in the Court's view, was that the law school's approach did not apply a mechanical formula giving "diversity bonuses" based on race or ethnicity.

SECTION 7 | State Laws Prohibiting Discrimination

Although the focus of this chapter is on federal legislation, most states also have statutes that prohibit employment discrimination. Generally, the same kinds of discrimination are prohibited under federal and state legislation. In addition, state statutes often provide

---

38. 539 U.S. 306, 123 S.Ct. 2325, 156 L.Ed.2d 304 (2003).

protection for certain individuals who are not protected under federal laws. For example, a New Jersey appellate court held that anyone over the age of eighteen was entitled to sue for age discrimination under the state law, which specified no threshold age limit.[39]

Furthermore, state laws prohibiting discrimination may apply to firms with fewer employees than the threshold number required under federal statutes, thus offering protection to a greater number of workers. Even when companies are too small to be covered by state statutes, state courts may uphold employees' rights against discrimination in the workplace for public-policy reasons.[40] State laws may also provide for additional damages, such as damages for emotional distress, that are not provided for under federal statutes. Finally, some states, such as California and Washington, have passed laws that end affirmative action programs in those states or modify admission policies at state-sponsored universities.

---

39. *Bergen Commercial Bank v. Sisler*, 307 N.J.Super. 333, 704 A.2d 1017 (1998).

40. See, for example, *Roberts v. Dudley, D.V.M.*, 92 Wash.App. 652, 966 P.2d 377 (1998); and *Insignia Residential Corp. v. Ashton*, 359 Md. 560, 755 A.2d 1080 (2000).

REVIEWING EMPLOYMENT DISCRIMINATION

Amaani Lyle, an African American woman, took a job as a scriptwriters' assistant at Warner Brothers Television Productions working for the writers of *Friends*, a popular, adult-oriented television series. One of her essential job duties was to type detailed notes for the scriptwriters during brainstorming sessions in which they discussed jokes dialogue, and story lines. The writers then combed through Lyle's notes after the meetings for script material. During these meetings, the three male scriptwriters told lewd and vulgar jokes, and made sexually explicit comments and gestures. They often talked about their personal sexual experiences and fantasies, and some of these conversations were then used in episodes of *Friends*.

Lyle never complained that she found the writers' conduct during the meetings offensive. After four months, Lyle was fired because she could not type fast enough to keep up with the writers' conversations during the meetings. She filed a suit against Warner Brothers, alleging sexual harassment and claiming that her termination was based on racial discrimination. Using the information presented in the chapter, answer the following questions.

1. Explain whether Lyle's claim of racial discrimination would be for intentional (disparate-treatment) or unintentional (disparate-impact) discrimination.

2. Can Lyle establish a *prima facie* case of racial discrimination? Why or why not?

3. Lyle was told when she was hired that typing speed was extremely important to her position. At the time, she maintained that she could type eighty words per minute, so she was not given a typing test. It later turned out that Lyle could type only fifty words per minute. What impact might typing speed have on Lyle's lawsuit?

(Continued)

REVIEWING EMPLOYMENT DISCRIMINATION *(continued)*

4. | Lyle's sexual-harassment claim is based on the hostile work environment created by the writers' sexually offensive conduct at meetings that she was required to attend. The writers, however, argue that their behavior was essential to the "creative process" of writing for *Friends*, a show that routinely contains sexual innuendos and adult humor. Which defense discussed in the chapter might Warner Brothers assert using this argument?

5. | Suppose that Warner Brothers was completely unaware of the writers' sexually explicit banter and conduct during the meetings. Can Lyle still hold Warner Brothers liable for the writers' conduct? Why or why not?

TERMS AND CONCEPTS TO REVIEW

affirmative action 708

bona fide occupational qualification (BFOQ) 708

business necessity 708

constructive discharge 695

disparate-impact discrimination 694

disparate-treatment discrimination 694

employment discrimination 693

prima facie case 694

protected class 693

seniority system 708

sexual harassment 697

tangible employment action 698

QUESTIONS AND CASE PROBLEMS

34–1. Discuss fully whether any of the following actions would constitute a violation of Title VII of the 1964 Civil Rights Act, as amended:

(a) Tennington, Inc., is a consulting firm and has ten employees. These employees travel on consulting jobs in seven states. Tennington has an employment record of hiring only white males.

(b) Novo Films is making a movie about Africa and needs to employ approximately one hundred extras for this picture. Novo advertises in all major newspapers in Southern California for the hiring of these extras. The ad states that only African Americans need apply.

34–2. **QUESTION WITH SAMPLE ANSWER**

Tavo Jones had worked since 1974 for Westshore Resort, where he maintained golf carts. During the first decade, he received positive job evaluations and numerous merit pay raises. He was promoted to the position of supervisor of golf-cart maintenance at three courses. Then a new employee, Ben Olery, was placed in charge of the golf courses. He demoted Jones, who was over the age of forty, to running one of the three cart facilities, and he froze Jones's salary indefinitely. Olery also demoted five other men over the age of forty. Another cart facility was placed under the supervision of Blake Blair. Later, the cart facilities for the three courses were again consolidated, but Blair—not Jones—was put in charge. At the time, Blair was in his twenties. Jones overheard Blair say that "we are going to have to do away with these . . . old and senile" men. Jones quit and sued Westshore for employment discrimination. Should he prevail? Explain. **For a sample answer to this question, go to Appendix I at the end of this text.**

34–3. DISCRIMINATION BASED ON DISABILITY. When the University of Maryland Medical System Corp. learned that one of its surgeons was HIV positive, the university offered him transfers to positions that did not involve surgery. The surgeon refused, and the university terminated him. The surgeon filed a suit in a federal district court against the university, alleging in part a violation of the Americans with Disabilities Act. The surgeon claimed that he was "otherwise qualified" for his former position. What does he have to prove to win his case? Should he be reinstated? [*Doe v. University of Maryland Medical System Corp.*, 50 F.3d 1261 (4th Cir. 1995)]

34–4. RELIGIOUS DISCRIMINATION. Mary Tiano, a devout Roman Catholic, worked for Dillard Department Stores, Inc. (Dillard's), in Phoenix, Arizona. Dillard's considered Tiano a productive employee because her sales exceeded $200,000 a year. At the time, the store gave its managers the discretion to grant unpaid leave to employees but prohibited vacations or leave during the holiday season (October through December). Tiano felt that she had a "calling" to go on a "pilgrimage" in October 1988 to Medjugorje, Yugoslavia, where some persons claimed to have had visions of the Virgin Mary.

The Catholic Church had not designated the site an official pilgrimage site, the visions were not expected to be stronger in October, and tours were available at other times. The store managers denied Tiano's request for leave, but she had a nonrefundable ticket and left anyway. Dillard's terminated her employment. For a year, Tiano searched for a new job and did not attain the level of her Dillard's salary for four years. She filed a suit in a federal district court against Dillard's, alleging religious discrimination in violation of Title VII. Can Tiano establish a *prima facie* case of religious discrimination? Explain. [*Tiano v. Dillard Department Stores, Inc.,* 139 F.3d 679 (9th Cir. 1998)]

34-5. DISCRIMINATION BASED ON DISABILITY. Vaughn Murphy was first diagnosed with hypertension (high blood pressure) when he was ten years old. Unmedicated, his blood pressure is approximately 250/160. With medication, however, he can function normally and engage in the same activities as anyone else. In 1994, United Parcel Service, Inc. (UPS), hired Murphy to be a mechanic, a position that required him to drive commercial motor vehicles. To get the job, Murphy had to meet a U.S. Department of Transportation (DOT) regulation that a driver have "no current clinical diagnosis of high blood pressure likely to interfere with his/her ability to operate a commercial vehicle safely." At the time, Murphy's blood pressure was measured at 186/124, but he was erroneously certified and started work. Within a month, the error was discovered and he was fired. Murphy obtained another mechanic's job—one that did not require DOT certification—and filed a suit in a federal district court against UPS, claiming discrimination under the Americans with Disabilities Act. UPS filed a motion for summary judgment. Should the court grant UPS's motion? Explain. [*Murphy v. United Parcel Service, Inc.,* 527 U.S. 516, 119 S.Ct. 2133, 144 L.Ed.2d 484 (1999)]

34-6. DISCRIMINATION BASED ON DISABILITY. PGA Tour, Inc., sponsors professional golf tournaments. A player may enter in several ways, but the most common method is to compete successfully in a three-stage qualifying tournament known as the "Q-School." Anyone may enter the Q-School by submitting two letters of recommendation and paying $3,000 to cover greens fees and the cost of a golf cart, which is permitted during the first two stages, but is prohibited during the third stage. The rules governing the events include the "Rules of Golf," which apply at all levels of amateur and professional golf and do not prohibit the use of golf carts, and the "hard card," which applies specifically to the PGA tour and requires the players to walk the course during most of a tournament. Casey Martin is a talented golfer with a degenerative circulatory disorder that prevents him from walking golf courses. Martin entered the Q-School and asked for permission to use a cart during the third stage. PGA refused. Martin filed a suit in a federal district court against PGA, alleging a violation of the Americans with Disabilities Act. Is a golf cart in these circumstances a "reasonable accommodation" under the

ADA? Why or why not? [*PGA Tour, Inc. v. Martin,* 531 U.S. 1049, 121 S.Ct. 652, 148 L.Ed.2d 556 (2001)]

34-7. ⚖ CASE PROBLEM WITH SAMPLE ANSWER
Kimberly Cloutier began working at the Costco store in West Springfield, Massachusetts, in July 1997. Cloutier had multiple earrings and four tattoos, but no facial piercings. In June 1998, Costco promoted Cloutier to cashier. Over the next two years, she engaged in various forms of body modification, including facial piercing and cutting. In March 2001, Costco revised its dress code to prohibit all facial jewelry, aside from earrings. Cloutier was told that she would have to remove her facial jewelry. She asked for a complete exemption from the code, asserting that she was a member of the Church of Body Modification and her eyebrow piercing was part of her religion. She was told to remove the jewelry, cover it, or go home. She went home and was later discharged for her absence. Cloutier filed a suit in a federal district court against Costco, alleging religious discrimination in violation of Title VII. Does an employer have any obligation to accommodate its employees' religious practices? If so, to what extent? How should the court rule in this case? Discuss. [*Cloutier v. Costco Wholesale Corp.,* 390 F.3d 126 (1st Cir. 2004)]

To view a sample answer for this case problem, go to this book's Web site at http://wbl.westbuslaw.com, select "Chapter 34," and click on "Case Problem with Sample Answer."

34-8. DISCRIMINATION BASED ON RACE. The hiring policy of Phillips Community College of the University of Arkansas (PCCUA) is to conduct an internal search for qualified applicants before advertising outside the college. Steven Jones, the university's chancellor, determines the application and appointment process for vacant positions, however, and is the ultimate authority in hiring decisions. Howard Lockridge, an African American, was PCCUA's Technical and Industrial Department Chair. Between 1988 and 1998, Lockridge applied for several different positions, some of which were unadvertised, some of which were unfilled for years, and some of which were filled with less qualified persons from outside the college. In 1998, when Jones advertised an opening for the position of Dean of Industrial Technology and Workforce Development, Lockridge did not apply for the job. Jones hired Tracy McGraw, a white male. Lockridge filed a suit in a federal district court against the university under Title VII. The university filed a motion for summary judgment in its favor. What are the elements of a *prima facie* case of disparate-treatment discrimination? Can Lockridge pass this test, or should the court issue a judgment in the university's favor? Explain. [*Lockridge v. Board of Trustees of the University of Arkansas,* 315 F.3d 1005 (8th Cir. 2003)]

34-9. DISCRIMINATION BASED ON AGE. The United Auto Workers (UAW) is the union that represents the employees of General Dynamics Land Systems,

Inc. In 1997, a collective bargaining agreement between UAW and General Dynamics eliminated the company's obligation to provide health insurance to employees who retired after the date of the agreement, except for current workers at least fifty years of age. Dennis Cline and 194 other employees over the age of forty, but under age fifty, objected to this term. They complained to the Equal Employment Opportunity Commission, claiming that the agreement violated the Age Discrimination in Employment Act (ADEA) of 1967. The ADEA forbids discriminatory preference for the "young" over the "old." Does the ADEA also prohibit favoring the old over the young? How should the court rule? Explain. [*General Dynamics Land Systems, Inc. v. Cline,* 540 U.S. 581, 124 S.Ct. 1236, 157 L.Ed.2d 1094 (2004)]

34–10. VIDEO QUESTION

Go to this text's Web site at http://wbl.westbuslaw.com and select "Chapter 34." Click on "Video Questions"

and view the video titled *Parenthood*. Then answer the following questions.

(a) In the video, Gil (Steve Martin) threatens to leave his job when he discovers that his boss is promoting another person to partner instead of him. His boss (Dennis Dugan) laughs and tells him that the threat is not realistic because if Gil leaves, he will be competing for positions with workers who are younger than he is and willing to accept lower salaries. If Gil takes his employer's advice and stays in his current position, can he sue his boss for age discrimination based on the boss's statements? Why or why not?

(b) Suppose that Gil leaves his current position and applies for a job at another firm. The prospective employer refuses to hire him based on his age. What would Gil have to prove to establish a *prima facie* case of age discrimination? Explain your answer.

(c) What defenses might Gil's current employer raise if Gil sues for age discrimination?

LAW | on the Web

For updated links to resources available on the Web, as well as a variety of other materials, visit this text's Web site at http://wbl.westbuslaw.com.

The law firm of Arent Fox posts articles on current issues in the area of employment law, including sexual harassment, on its Web site at

http://www.arentfox.com

An abundance of helpful information on disability-based discrimination, including the text of the Americans with Disabilities Act of 1990, can be found at the following Web site:

http://janweb.icdi.wvu.edu/kinder

An excellent source for information on various forms of employment discrimination is the Equal Employment Opportunity Commission's Web site at

http://www.eeoc.gov

LEGAL RESEARCH EXERCISES ON THE WEB

Go to http://wbl.westbuslaw.com, the Web site that accompanies this text. Select "Chapter 34" and click on "Internet Exercises." There you will find the following Internet research exercises that you can perform to learn more about topics covered in this chapter.

Activity 34–1: LEGAL PERSPECTIVE
Americans with Disabilities

Activity 34–2: MANAGEMENT PERSPECTIVE
Equal Employment Opportunity

Activity 34–3: SOCIAL PERSPECTIVE
Religious and National-Origin Discrimination

Agency and Employment

Ethical principles—and challenging ethical issues—pervade the areas of agency and employment. As you read in Chapter 31, when one person agrees to act on behalf of another, as an agent does in an agency relationship, that person assumes certain ethical responsibilities. Similarly, the principal also assumes certain ethical duties. In essence, agency law gives legal force to the ethical duties arising in an agency relationship. Although agency law also focuses on the rights of agents and principals, those rights are framed by the concept of duty— that is, an agent's duty becomes a right for the principal, and vice versa. Significantly, many of the duties of the principal and agent are negotiable when they form their contract. In forming a contract, the principal and the agent can extend or abridge many of the ordinary duties owed in such a relationship.

Employees who deal with third parties are also deemed to be agents and thus share the ethical (and legal) duties imposed under agency law. In the employment context, however, it is not always possible for an employee to negotiate favorable employment terms. Often, an employee who is offered a job either accepts the job on the employer's terms or looks elsewhere for a position. Although numerous federal and state statutes protect employees, in some situations employees still have little recourse against their employers. At the same time, employers complain that statutes regulating employment relationships impose so many requirements that they find it hard to exercise a reasonable amount of control over their workplaces.

In the following pages, we focus on the ethical dimensions of selected issues in agency and employment law.

The Agent's Duty to the Principal

The very nature of the principal-agent relationship is one of trust, which we call a fiduciary relationship. Because of the nature of this relationship, an agent is considered to owe certain duties to the principal. These duties include being loyal and obedient, informing the principal of important facts concerning the agency, accounting to the principal for property or funds received, and performing with reasonable diligence and skill.

Thus, ethical conduct would prevent an agent from representing two principals in the same transaction, making a secret profit from the agency relationship, or failing to disclose the agent's interest in property being purchased by the principal. The expected ethical conduct of the agent has evolved into rules that, if breached, cause the agent to be held legally liable.

But does an agent's obligation extend beyond the duty to the principal and include a duty to society as well? Consider,

for example, the situation faced by an employee who knows that her employer is engaging in an unethical—or even illegal—practice, such as marketing an unsafe product. Does the employee's duty to the principal include keeping silent about this practice, which may harm users of the product? Does the employee have a duty to protect consumers by disclosing this information to the public, even if she loses her job as a result? Some scholars have argued that many of the greatest evils in the past thirty years have been accomplished in the name of duty to the principal.

The Principal's Duty to the Agent

Just as agents owe certain fiduciary duties to their principals, so do principals owe ethical duties to their agents, such as compensation and reimbursement for job-related expenses. Principals also owe their agents a duty of cooperation. One might expect most principals to cooperate with their agents out of self-interest, but this is not universally the case. Suppose that a principal hires an agent on commission to sell a building, and the agent puts considerable time and expense into the process. If the principal changes his mind and decides to retain the building, he might want to prevent the agent from completing a sale. Is such action ethical? Does it violate the principal's duty of cooperation? What alternatives would the principal have?

Although a principal is legally obligated to fulfill certain duties to the agent, these duties do not include any specific duty of loyalty. Some argue that the lack of employers' loyalty to their employees has resulted in a reduction in employee loyalty to employers. After all, they maintain, why should an employee be loyal to an employer's interests over the years when the employee knows that the employer has no corresponding legal duty to be loyal to the employee's interests? Employers who do show a sense of loyalty to employees—for example, by not laying off longtime, faithful employees when business is slow or when those employees could be replaced by younger workers at lower cost— base that sense of loyalty primarily on ethical, not legal, considerations.

Apparent Authority and Agency by Estoppel

Agency law is designed to enforce the ethical or fiduciary duties that arise once an agency relationship is established. To perhaps an even greater extent, agency law is designed to protect third parties—people outside the agency relationship. The doctrines of apparent authority and agency by estoppel stem primarily from ethical considerations that arise when third parties suffer a loss from an apparent agency relationship.

Sometimes, for example, a third party may be led by the actions of the principal to believe that an individual is acting in the capacity of an agent, when in fact the individual is not an agent at all. For instance, a patient treated by a physician in a hospital's emergency room (ER) may assume that the physician is an agent of the hospital, even though the physician is an independent contractor and has no agency relationship with the hospital. If the patient suffers harm because of the physician's negligence and sues the hospital, some courts may hold the hospital liable under a theory of apparent agency.[1]

Respondeat Superior

Another legal concept that addresses the effect of agency relationships on third parties is the doctrine of *respondeat superior*. The doctrine raises a significant ethical question: Why should innocent employers be required to assume responsibility for the tortious, or wrongful, actions of their agent-employees? Again, the answer has to do with the courts' perception that when one of two innocent parties must suffer a loss, the party in the best position to prevent that loss should bear the burden. In an employment relationship, for example, the employer has more control over the employee's behavior than a third party to the relationship does.

Another reason for retaining the doctrine of *respondeat superior* in our laws is based on the employer's assumed ability to pay any damages that are incurred by a third party. Our society's collection of shared beliefs suggests that an injured party should be afforded the most effective relief possible. Thus, even though an employer may be absolutely innocent, the employer has "deeper pockets" than the employee and will be more likely to have the funds necessary to make the injured party whole.

Employee versus Independent Contractor

An aspect of agency law that has troubled employers and employees alike on numerous occasions has to do with a worker's declared status as an independent contractor. Not surprisingly, many employers prefer to designate certain workers as independent contractors rather than as employees. Yet the courts increasingly are holding that certain workers who are designated as independent contractors are, in fact, employees if the employer exercises a significant degree of control over their performance. In one case, for example, a group of drivers for a delivery service signed contracts explicitly agreeing to work as independent contractors and to use their own cars to make deliveries. Nonetheless, a court held that the workers qualified as employees because they were dependent for their business on the employer. The

delivery service "procured the customers, set the delivery prices, made the delivery assignments, billed the customers, set the commission rate, and paid the drivers."[2]

Why should a court interfere if a worker agrees to be classified as an independent contractor? The answer is, at least in part, that issues of fairness may be involved. For most types of work—especially work that does not require great expertise—the employee may have very limited power to negotiate favorable contract terms with the employer. If an employer states that a worker will be hired as an independent contractor, generally the worker has only two options—accept the arrangement or forfeit the job. Certainly, that was the choice faced by many workers at Microsoft Corporation when that company, to save costs, required employees to agree to become independent contractors if they wished to continue to work for Microsoft (this case was mentioned in Chapter 31).

Designating workers as independent contractors has several advantages for employers. An independent contractor must pay all Social Security taxes, is not entitled to employer-provided benefits, and does not receive the legal protections afforded to employees under such laws as those prohibiting employment discrimination (discussed in Chapter 34). For these reasons, the courts will sometimes intervene to determine whether workers designated as independent contractors should more appropriately be designated as employees.

Should an Employee Who Participates in Fraud Be Rewarded for Whistleblowing?

Many whistleblowing statutes reward employees who report their employers' wrongdoing with a percentage of the funds recovered after a lawsuit. In other words, employees have a strong financial incentive to offer up their employers for civil litigation. But what if the employee is somehow involved in the wrongdoing? Should the employee still receive a share of the proceeds?

Consider, for example, the largest Medicaid fraud settlement in U.S. history, involving a deal between Bayer Corporation and Kaiser Permanente, a health-maintenance organization. As one of Bayer's biggest customers, Kaiser demanded a discount price on Cipro, an antibiotic manufactured by Bayer. By law, however, Bayer could not sell the antibiotic to Kaiser for less than it sold Cipro to the federal government for use in the Medicaid program. (Medicaid helps low-income persons pay for necessary medical services.) If Bayer lowered the price of Cipro to Kaiser, it would have to refund millions of dollars to Medicaid. Therefore, Bayer "privately labeled" the same antibiotic using a different name and sold it to Kaiser at a 40 percent discount. Ironically, the person who blew the whistle on the fraudulent scheme—George Couto—was the marketing

---

1. See, for example, *Arrington v. Galen-Med, Inc.*, 838 So.2d 895 (La.App. 2003); and *Campbell v. Hospital Service Dist. No. 1*, 768 So.2d 803 (La.App. 2000).

2. *AFM Messenger Service, Inc. v. The Department of Employment Security*, 198 Ill.2d 380, 763 N.E.2d 272 (2001).

manager who actually negotiated the private labeling deal with Kaiser. Although Couto did not initiate the labeling scheme, he was instrumental in its success—despite the fact that he had suspected that the practice was illegal. Even though Couto had been a prime mover in the fraudulent scheme on behalf of Bayer, he was given 24 percent of the government's share of the $257 million settlement.[3]

Whistleblower statutes exist to encourage employees to report the wrongdoing of their employers with the ultimate objective of inhibiting such wrongdoing. But is it fair for an employee who participates in the employer's wrongdoing to benefit financially to such a large degree? Will this practice effectively inhibit, or could it even encourage, wrongful acts?

At-Will Employment

Because of the extensive array of statutory protections for workers, it is easy to lose sight of the fact that the majority of workers in the United States have the legal status of "employees at will" (see Chapter 33). An employer may fire at-will employees for any reason or no reason if they do not have employment contracts—unless, of course, the employees are protected under a state or federal statute.

Statutes Do Not Protect All Employees A problem faced by many at-will employees is that federal and state statutes regulating the workplace do not apply to all employers. As mentioned previously, the Family and Medical Leave Act applies only to employers that have fifty or more workers. Additionally, the major federal law prohibiting employment discrimination applies only to firms that have twenty-five or more employees and are engaged in interstate commerce. Similarly, state laws apply only to firms with a threshold number of employees, such as eight or ten employees. Even if an employer is subject to such statutes, these laws do not apply to many types of employment disputes, such as whether an employment contract was formed.

Exceptions to the At-Will Doctrine Sometimes, the only hope for plaintiffs in many employment disputes is that a court will make an exception to the at-will doctrine—on the basis of public policy, for example. The public-policy exception, though, remains just that—an exception. Often, courts are reluctant to make such an exception unless it can be justified by a clearly expressed public policy.

Consider an example. William Jenkins had worked for AKZO, a North Carolina company that manufactured coatings for furniture and wood products, for over twenty years when he was asked to take a position that required him to move to Singapore. Jenkins accepted the position on the condition that he would have a job with AKZO when he returned to the United States. Jenkins and AKZO entered into a written

contract that included this condition, and the contract was extended several times while Jenkins was living in Singapore. When the last extension expired, Jenkins's supervisor assured him that they would "just continue under those terms." Jenkins repeatedly asked his superiors if he could go back to the United States, and was told that he would be transferred as soon as a job became available for him and a replacement was found for him in Singapore. Nevertheless, AKZO terminated Jenkins the following year, citing poor performance as its reason.

Jenkins sued AKZO, claiming that he was wrongfully discharged in breach of an employment contract. He also alleged that AKZO had committed fraud by promising that he would be sent back to the United States as soon as a position became available. The federal district court that heard the case noted that North Carolina is an employment-at-will state and that Jenkins, whose contract with AKZO had expired, was an employee at will and could not maintain an action based on the public-policy exception to the employment-at-will doctrine.[4]

DISCUSSION QUESTIONS

1. How much obedience and loyalty does an agent-employee owe to an employer? What if the employer engages in an activity—or requests that the employee engage in an activity—that violates the employee's ethical standards but does not necessarily violate any public policy or law? In such a situation, does an employee's duty to abide by her or his own ethical standards override the employee's duty of loyalty to the employer?

2. If an agent injures a third party during the course of employment, under the doctrine of *respondeat superior*, the employer may be held liable for the agent's actions even though the employer did not authorize the action and was not even aware of it. Do you think that it is fair to hold employers liable in such situations? Do you think that it would be more equitable to hold that the employee alone should bear the responsibility for his or her tortious (legally wrongful) actions to third parties, even when the actions are committed within the scope of employment?

3. Should an employee who is involved in but later "blows the whistle" on an employer's wrongdoing be allowed to collect a financial reward under whistleblower statutes? Why or why not?

4. Should the courts be more willing to grant public-policy exceptions to the employment-at-will doctrine? Should the doctrine be abandoned entirely in favor of a doctrine under which all employment arrangements constitute implied-in-fact contracts under which employees can be discharged only for cause?

---

3. Peter Aronson, "A Rogue to Catch a Rogue," *The National Law Journal*, August 18–25, 2003.

4. *Jenkins v. AKZO Noble Coatings, Inc.*, 2002 WL 1020698, citing the North Carolina case precedent of *Kurtzman v. Applied Analytical Industries, Inc.*, 347 N.C. 329, 493 S.E.2d 420 (1997).

UNIT EIGHT
Business Organizations

CHAPTER 35
Sole Proprietorships and Franchises

A basic question facing anyone who wishes to start a business is which of the several forms of business organization available will be most appropriate for the business endeavor. In deciding this question, the **entrepreneur** (one who initiates and assumes the financial risk of a new enterprise) needs to consider a number of factors. Four important factors are (1) ease of creation, (2) the liability of the owners, (3) tax considerations, and (4) the need for capital. In studying this unit on business organizations, keep these factors in mind as you read about the various business organizational forms available to entrepreneurs. You might also find it helpful to refer to Exhibit 40–4 near the end of Chapter 40 for a comparison of the major business forms in use today with respect to formation, liability of owners, management, taxation, and other factors.

Traditionally, entrepreneurs have used three major forms to structure their business enterprises—the sole proprietorship, the partnership, and the corporation. In this chapter, we examine the sole proprietorship as well as franchises. Although the franchise is not really a business organizational form, it is widely used today by entrepreneurs seeking to make profits. In Chapter 36, we will examine the second major traditional business form, the partnership, as well as some newer variations on partnerships. The third major traditional form—the corporation—will be discussed in detail in Chapters 38 through 41. We will also look at the limited liability company (LLC), a relatively new and increasingly popular form of business enterprise, and other special forms of business in Chapter 37. We conclude the unit with a chapter (Chapter 42) discussing practical legal information that all businesspersons should know, particularly those operating small businesses.

SECTION 1 | Sole Proprietorships

The simplest form of business is a **sole proprietorship.** In this form, the owner is the business; thus, anyone who does business without creating a separate business organization has a sole proprietorship. Over two-thirds of all American businesses are sole proprietorships. They are usually small enterprises—about 99 percent of the sole proprietorships in the United States have revenues of less than $1 million per year. Sole proprietors can own and manage any type of business from an informal, home-office undertaking to a large restaurant or construction firm.

ADVANTAGES OF THE SOLE PROPRIETORSHIP

A major advantage of the sole proprietorship is that the proprietor receives all of the profits (because she or he assumes all of the risk). In addition, it is often easier and less costly to start a sole proprietorship than to start any other kind of business, as few legal formalities are involved. This type of business organization also provides more flexibility than does a partnership or a corporation. The sole proprietor is free to make any decision he or she wishes concerning the business—whom to hire, when to take a vacation, what kind of business to pursue, and so on. A sole proprietor pays only personal income taxes on the business's profits, which are reported as personal income on the proprietor's personal income tax return. Sole proprietors are also allowed to establish tax-exempt retirement accounts in the form of Keogh plans.[1]

---

1. A *Keogh plan* is a retirement program designed for self-employed persons. A person can contribute a certain percentage of income to the plan, and interest earnings will not be taxed until funds are withdrawn from the plan.

DISADVANTAGES OF THE SOLE PROPRIETORSHIP

The major disadvantage of the sole proprietorship is that, as sole owner, the proprietor alone bears the burden of any losses or liabilities incurred by the business enterprise. In other words, the sole proprietor has unlimited liability, or legal responsibility, for all obligations that arise in doing business. This unlimited liability is a major factor to be considered in choosing a business form. The sole proprietorship also has the disadvantage of lacking continuity on the death of the proprietor. When the owner dies, so does the business—it is automatically dissolved. If the business is transferred to family members or other heirs, a new proprietorship is created.

Another disadvantage is that the proprietor's opportunity to raise capital is limited to personal funds and the funds of those who are willing to make loans to him or her. If the owner wishes to expand the business significantly, one way to raise more capital to finance the expansion is to join forces with another entrepreneur and establish a partnership or form a corporation.

The Internet has expanded the ability of sole proprietorships to market their products worldwide without greatly increasing their costs. Does this mean that sole proprietorships should now, for some purposes, be considered the equivalent of corporations and other associational business forms? That was the question in the following case.

CASE 35.1

United States District Court, Southern District of New York, 2000. 138 F.Supp.2d 449.

Hsin Ten Enterprise USA, Inc. v. Clark Enterprises

BACKGROUND AND FACTS *Clark Enterprises is a Kansas company with its only established offices in Salina, Kansas. Clark is a sole proprietorship owned and operated by Clifford Clark, who lives in Salina. Through representatives and trade shows, Clark sells "The Exercise Machine," an aerobic exercise device. The Exercise Machine can also be purchased through Clark's Web site. Clark markets the Exercise Machine in direct competition with "The Chi Machine," another aerobic exercise product. The Chi Machine is manufactured and sold by Hsin Ten Enterprise USA, Inc., a corporation with its principal place of business in Farmingdale, New York. Hsin Ten also makes and sells other products under the "Chi" trademark, which it owns. One of Clark's Web sites uses the name "Chi Exerciser 2000" to promote Clark's Exercise Machine, and the term Chi is frequently used on the Web site to refer to the product. Hsin Ten filed a suit in a federal district court in New York against Clark, asserting trademark infringement and other claims. Clark filed a motion to dismiss the trademark claim in part on the ground that the court did not have venue under 28 U.S.C. Section 1391(c), the applicable statute.[a] That section provides, "For purposes of venue . . . , a defendant that is a corporation shall be deemed to reside in any judicial district in which it is subject to personal jurisdiction." Hsin Ten argued that although Clark is an unincorporated sole proprietorship with its offices in Kansas, it should be deemed a "corporation" for venue purposes.*

IN THE LANGUAGE OF THE COURT

SCHEINDLIN, D.J. [District Judge]

* * * *

On its face, Section 1391(c) applies only to corporations. However, the [United States] Supreme Court has held that it also applies to unincorporated associations. Since then, other courts have held that Section 1391(c) is applicable to partnerships and foreign trusts.

* * * [C]ourts have been unwilling to expand the definition of "corporation" beyond [these] general categories * * * . In fact, at least two other federal courts have declined to extend Section 1391(c) to include sole proprietorships such as Clark.

Hsin Ten argues that Clark is unlike other sole proprietorships because it does business in forty-seven states. Plaintiff contends that Clark "resembles a national corporation in all respects except its choice of legal structure * * * . An entity such as Clark * * * ,

---

a. As explained in Chapter 2, *venue* concerns the most appropriate location for a trial.

CONTINUED

which obviously enjoys the benefits of doing business on a national scale, should not be granted preferential treatment in venue determinations simply because it chose not to incorporate." Plaintiff's argument is unconvincing.

First, broad geographic distribution does not convert a small sole proprietorship into a corporation. With the advent of the Internet and e-commerce, a sole proprietorship can distribute its products throughout the United States with only a relatively minor investment of resources. Moreover, although Clark does business in forty-seven states, it still is not the type of unincorporated business entity that has been included in the definition of corporation. For instance, * * * [t]he defendant partnership in [one case] was one of only four snowmobile manufacturers in the world [and] had annual sales of over $240 million * * * . By contrast, between July 8, 1999 and October 17, 2000, Clark sold 1,855 Exercise Machines. Although this is impressive for a sole proprietorship, it is hardly remarkable. Nor does it convert Clark to the functional equivalent of a corporation.

Second, expanding the definition of "corporation" would greatly burden sole proprietors. Unlike corporations, partnerships and unincorporated associations—all of which are associations of two or more persons—a sole proprietorship is owned and controlled by a single person. *Venue is primarily a question of convenience for litigants and witnesses and venue provisions should be treated in practical terms.* In practical terms, expanding the definition of "corporation" to include sole proprietorships would be overly burdensome and inconvenient to sole proprietors, most of whom would be unable to afford the expense of litigating in distant states. [Emphasis added.]

DECISION AND REMEDY *The court agreed with Clark that it should not be deemed a "corporation" for venue purposes. The court denied Clark's motion to dismiss other parts of Hsin Ten's complaint, however, and ordered the case to proceed to trial.*

SECTION 2 | Franchises

A **franchise** is defined as any arrangement in which the owner of a trademark, a trade name, or a copyright licenses others to use the trademark, trade name, or copyright in the selling of goods or services. A **franchisee** (a purchaser of a franchise) is generally legally independent of the **franchisor** (the seller of the franchise). At the same time, the franchise is economically dependent on the franchisor's integrated business system. In other words, a franchisee can operate as an independent businessperson but still obtain the advantages of a regional or national organization. Today, it is estimated that franchising companies and their franchisees account for about 40 percent of all retail sales in this country. Well-known franchises include McDonald's, 7-Eleven, and Burger King.

TYPES OF FRANCHISES

Because the franchising industry is so extensive and so many different kinds of businesses sell franchises, it is difficult to summarize the many types of franchises that now exist. Generally, though, franchises fall into one of the following three classifications: distributor-

ships, chain-style business operations, and manufacturing or processing-plant arrangements.

DISTRIBUTORSHIP A *distributorship* arises when a manufacturing concern (franchisor) licenses a dealer (franchisee) to sell its product. Often, a distributorship covers an exclusive territory. An example is an automobile dealership.

CHAIN-STYLE BUSINESS OPERATION In a *chain-style business operation*, a franchise operates under a franchisor's trade name and is identified as a member of a select group of dealers that engage in the franchisor's business. The franchisee is generally required to follow standardized or prescribed methods of operation. Often, the franchisor insists that the franchisee maintain certain standards of performance. In addition, sometimes the franchisee is obligated to deal exclusively with the franchisor to obtain materials and supplies. Examples of this type of franchise are McDonald's and most other fast-food chains.

MANUFACTURING OR PROCESSING-PLANT ARRANGEMENT With a *manufacturing* or *processing-plant arrangement*, the franchisor transmits to the franchisee the essential ingredients or formula to make a particular product. The franchisee then markets the product either at wholesale or at retail in accordance with the franchisor's standards. Examples of this type of franchise are Coca-Cola and other soft-drink bottling companies.

LAWS GOVERNING FRANCHISING

Because a franchise relationship is primarily a contractual relationship, it is governed by contract law. If the franchise exists primarily for the sale of products manufactured by the franchisor, the law governing sales contracts as expressed in Article 2 of the Uniform Commercial Code applies (see Chapters 20 through 23). Additionally, the federal government and most states have enacted laws governing certain aspects of franchising. Generally, these laws are designed to protect prospective franchisees from dishonest franchisors and to prohibit franchisors from terminating franchises without good cause.

FEDERAL PROTECTION FOR FRANCHISEES Automobile dealership franchisees are protected from automobile manufacturers' bad faith termination of their franchises by the Automobile Dealers' Franchise Act—also known as the Automobile Dealers' Day in Court Act—of 1965.[2] If a manufacturer-franchisor terminates a franchise because of a dealer-franchisee's failure to comply with unreasonable demands (for example, failure to attain an unrealistically high sales quota), the manufacturer may be liable for damages.

Another federal statute is the Petroleum Marketing Practices Act (PMPA) of 1979,[3] which prescribes the grounds and conditions under which a franchisor may terminate or decline to renew a gasoline station franchise. Federal antitrust laws (discussed in Chapter 46), which prohibit certain types of anticompetitive agreements, may also apply in certain circumstances.

Additionally, the Franchise Rule of the Federal Trade Commission (FTC) requires franchisors to disclose material facts that a prospective franchisee needs to make an informed decision concerning the purchase of a franchise. The rule was designed to enable potential franchisees to weigh the risks and benefits of an investment. The rule requires numerous written disclosures, plus a personal meeting between the franchisor and the prospective franchisee at least ten business days before the franchise agreement is signed or any payment is made in connection with the purchase of the franchise.[4]

STATE PROTECTION FOR FRANCHISEES State legislation tends to be similar to federal statutes and the FTC regulations. For example, to protect franchisees, a state law might require the disclosure of information that is material to making an informed decision regarding the purchase of a franchise. This could include such information as the actual costs of operation, recurring expenses, and profits to be earned, along with facts substantiating these figures. State deceptive trade practices acts may also prohibit certain types of actions on the part of franchisors.

For example, the Illinois Franchise Disclosure Act prohibits any untrue statement of a material fact in connection with the offer or sale of any franchise. If Miyamoto, a franchisor of bagel stores, underestimates the start-up cost and exaggerates the anticipated yearly profits from operating a bagel shop to a franchisee, he has violated state law.[5]

In response to the need for a uniform franchise law, the National Conference of Commissioners on Uniform State Laws drafted a model law that standardizes the various state franchise regulations. Because the uniform legislation represents a compromise of so many diverse interests, however, it has not been adopted as law by many states.

THE FRANCHISE CONTRACT

The franchise relationship is defined by a contract between the franchisor and the franchisee. The franchise contract specifies the terms and conditions of the franchise and spells out the rights and duties of the franchisor and the franchisee. If either party fails to perform its contractual duties, that party may be subject to a lawsuit for breach of contract. Furthermore, if a franchisee is induced to enter into a franchise contract by the franchisor's fraudulent misrepresentation, the franchisor may be liable for damages. Generally, the statutory law and the case law governing franchising tend to emphasize the importance of good faith and fair dealing in franchise relationships.

Because each type of franchise relationship has its own characteristics, it is difficult to describe the broad range of details a franchising contract may include.

2. 15 U.S.C. Sections 1221 et seq.
3. 15 U.S.C. Sections 2801 et seq.
4. 16 C.F.R. Section 436.1.
5. *Bixby's Food Systems, Inc. v. McKay*, 193 F.Supp.2d 1053 (N.D. Ill. 2002).

Exclusive Territorial Rights and the Internet

Many franchise lawsuits involve disputes over territorial rights—an aspect of franchising that often involves an implied covenant of good faith and fair dealing. For example, suppose that the franchise contract does not give the franchisee exclusive territorial rights or is silent on the issue. If the franchisor allows a competing franchise to be established nearby, the franchisee may suffer a significant loss in profits. In this situation, a court may hold that the franchisor's actions breached an implied covenant of good faith and fair dealing.

If, in contrast, the franchisee has been given exclusive territorial rights to serve a specific area, then the matter is more straightforward. If the franchisor allows a competing franchise to be established in the vicinity, the contract has been breached. Yet how do these rules apply in a cyber age, when a franchisor may offer its products for sale via its Web site?

ENTER THE INTERNET

With the growth of inexpensive and easy online marketing, it was inevitable that cyberturf conflicts would eventually arise between franchisors and franchisees. Suppose, for example,

that a franchise contract does grant to the franchisee exclusive rights to sell the franchised product within a certain territory. What happens if the franchisor then begins to sell the product from its Web site to anyone anywhere in the world, including in the franchisee's territory? Does this constitute a breach of the franchise contract?

This is a relatively new issue to come before the courts, and how the question is resolved has important implications for both franchisors and franchisees. From the franchisor's perspective, it would seem unfair to deprive it of the ability to market its goods, efficiently and inexpensively, from its Web site. From the franchisee's perspective, it would seem only fair (and consistent with the franchise contract's guarantee of exclusive territorial rights) to have the exclusive right to market the franchisor's product within its area.

DRUG EMPORIUM'S "ELECTRONIC ENCROACHMENT"

The issue of "electronic encroachment" came before a panel of arbitrators in an American Arbitration Association (AAA) proceeding. (As you learned in Chapter 2, the AAA is a

---

We look next at some of the major issues that typically are addressed in a franchise contract.

PAYMENT FOR THE FRANCHISE The franchisee ordinarily pays an initial fee or lump-sum price for the franchise license (the privilege of being granted a franchise). This fee is separate from the various products that the franchisee purchases from or through the franchisor. In some industries, the franchisor relies heavily on the initial sale of the franchise for realizing a profit. In other industries, the continued dealing between the parties brings profit to both. In most situations, the franchisor will receive a stated percentage of the annual sales or annual volume of business done by the franchisee. The franchise agreement may also require the franchisee to pay a percentage of the franchisor's advertising costs and certain administrative expenses.

BUSINESS PREMISES The franchise agreement may specify whether the premises for the business must be

leased or purchased outright. In some cases, a building must be constructed to meet the terms of the agreement. Certainly, the agreement will specify whether the franchisor supplies equipment and furnishings for the premises or whether this is the responsibility of the franchisee.

LOCATION OF THE FRANCHISE Typically, the franchisor will determine the territory to be served. Some franchise contracts will give the franchisee exclusive rights, or "territorial rights," to a certain geographic area. Other franchise contracts, while they define the territory allotted to a particular franchise, either specifically state that the franchise is nonexclusive or are silent on the issue of territorial rights.

In today's online world, franchisees face a problem when franchisors attempt to sell their products themselves via their Web sites. For a discussion of this issue, see this chapter's *Contemporary Legal Debates* feature.

leading provider of arbitration services.) The proceeding involved franchise contracts between Drug Emporium, Inc., and several of its franchisees. The contracts provided that each franchisee had the exclusive right to conduct business in a specific geographic area. The franchisees claimed that Drug Emporium had breached its contractual obligation to honor their territories by using its Web site to sell directly to customers within the franchisees' territories.

Ultimately, in what is believed to be the first ruling by a court or arbitrating panel on the issue of electronic encroachment, the arbitrating panel decided in favor of the franchisees. The panel ordered Drug Emporium to cease marketing its goods from its Web site to potential customers who were physically located within the franchisees' territories.[a]

WHERE DO YOU STAND?

Although the AAA panel held in favor of the franchisees, there is no way to know how other arbitrating panels or courts will

---

a. *Emporium Drug Mart, Inc. of Shreveport v. Drug Emporium, Inc.*, No. 71-114-0012600 (American Arbitration Association, September 2, 2000).

decide this issue.[b] On the one hand, a valid contract that grants exclusive territorial rights to a franchisee deserves to be enforced, just as any contract does if the parties have voluntarily agreed to its terms. On the other hand, the Internet offers franchisors an inexpensive marketing vehicle, which, according to some, they should be able to utilize. If franchisors are prevented from any direct competition with their franchisees via the Web, franchisors may stop granting exclusive territorial rights to any of their franchisees—which, of course, could also be detrimental to franchisees. Where do you stand on this issue? Should a franchisor be able to market goods on the Internet, even though customers in its franchisees' exclusive territories may purchase the goods directly from the franchisor's Web site? Why or why not?

---

b. For an article discussing two subsequent arbitrations involving similar facts and issues, but in which the arbitrator concluded that the franchisor's sales activities over the Internet did not violate the franchise contract, see Rupert M. Barkoff, "Encroachment Issues Persist," *The National Law Journal*, April 19, 2004.

BUSINESS ORGANIZATION   The business organization of the franchisee is of great concern to the franchisor. Depending on the terms of the franchise agreement, the franchisor may specify particular requirements for the form and capital structure of the business. The franchise agreement may also provide that standards of operation—relating to such aspects of the business as sales quotas, quality, and record keeping—be met by the franchisee. Furthermore, a franchisor may wish to retain stringent control over the training of personnel involved in the operation and over administrative aspects of the business.

QUALITY CONTROL   Although the day-to-day operation of the franchise business is normally left up to the franchisee, the franchise agreement may provide for the amount of supervision and control agreed on by the parties. When the franchise is a service operation, such as a motel, the contract often provides that the franchisor will establish certain standards for the facil-

ity to protect the franchise's name and reputation. Typically, the contract will state that the franchisor is permitted to make periodic inspections to ensure that the standards are being maintained.

As a general rule, the validity of a provision permitting the franchisor to establish and enforce certain quality standards is unquestioned. Because the franchisor has a legitimate interest in maintaining the quality of the product or service to protect its name and reputation, it can exercise greater control in this area than would otherwise be tolerated. Increasingly, however, franchisors are finding that if they exercise too much control over the operations of their franchisees, they may incur vicarious (indirect) liability under agency theory for the acts of their franchisees' employees. The actual exercise of control, or at least the right to control, is the key consideration. If the franchisee controls the day-to-day operations of the business to a significant degree, the franchisor may be able to avoid liability, as the following case illustrates.

CASE 35.2

Kerl v. Dennis Rasmussen, Inc.

Wisconsin Supreme
Court, 2004.
273 Wis.2d 106,
682 N.W.2d 328.

DIANE S. SYKES, J. [Justice]
* * * *

* * * [On June 11, 1999] Harvey Pierce ambushed and shot Robin Kerl and her fiancé David Jones in the parking lot of a Madison [Wisconsin] Wal-Mart where Kerl and Jones worked. Kerl was seriously injured in the shooting, and Jones was killed. Pierce, who was Kerl's former boyfriend, then shot and killed himself. At the time of the shooting, Pierce was a work-release inmate at the Dane County jail who was employed at a nearby Arby's [Inc.] restaurant operated by Dennis Rasmussen, Inc. ("DRI"). Pierce had left work without permission at the time of the attempted murder and murder/suicide.

Kerl and Jones' estate sued DRI and Arby's, Inc. [in a Wisconsin state court.] * * * [T]he plaintiffs alleged that Arby's is vicariously liable, as DRI's franchisor, for DRI's negligent supervision of Pierce. The * * * court granted summary judgment in favor of Arby's, concluding that there was no basis for vicarious liability. The [state intermediate] court of appeals affirmed. [The plaintiffs appealed to the Wisconsin Supreme Court.]

Vicarious liability under the doctrine of *respondeat superior* depends upon the existence of a master/servant agency relationship. Vicarious liability under *respondeat superior* is a form of liability without fault—the imposition of liability on an innocent party for the tortious conduct of another based upon the existence of a particularized agency relationship. As such, it is an exception to our fault-based liability system, and is imposed only where the principal has control or the right to control the physical conduct of the agent such that a master/servant relationship can be said to exist.

A franchise is a business format typically characterized by the franchisee's operation of an independent business pursuant to a license to use the franchisor's trademark or trade name. A franchise is ordinarily operated in accordance with a detailed franchise or license agreement designed to protect the integrity of the trademark by setting uniform quality, marketing, and operational standards applicable to the franchise.

The rationale for vicarious liability becomes somewhat attenuated [weak] when applied to the franchise relationship, and vicarious liability premised upon the existence of a master/servant relationship is conceptually difficult to adapt to the franchising context. If the operational standards included in the typical franchise agreement for the protection of the franchisor's trademark were broadly construed as capable of meeting the "control or right to control" test that is generally used to determine *respondeat superior* liability, then franchisors would almost always be exposed to vicarious liability for the torts of their franchisees. We see no justification for such a broad rule of franchisor vicarious liability. If vicarious liability is to be imposed against franchisors, a more precisely focused test is required. [Emphasis added.]
* * * *

Applying these principles here, we conclude that Arby's did not have control or the right to control the day-to-day operation of the specific aspect of DRI's business that is alleged to have caused the plaintiffs' harm, that is, DRI's supervision of its employees. We note first that the license agreement between Arby's and DRI contains a provision that disclaims any agency relationship. * * *

The license agreement contains a plethora [a large number] of general controls on the operation of DRI's restaurant * * *.

These provisions in the license agreement are consistent with the quality and operational standards commonly contained in franchise agreements to achieve product and marketing uniformity and to protect the franchisor's trademark. They are insufficient to establish a master/servant relationship. More particularly, they do not establish that Arby's controlled or had the right to control DRI's hiring and supervision of employees, which is the aspect of DRI's business that is alleged to have caused the plaintiffs' harm.

The agreement's provisions regarding the specific issue of personnel are broad and general. * * *

By the terms of this agreement, DRI has sole control over the hiring and supervision of its employees. Arby's could not step in and take over the management of DRI's employees.

 | Continued

* * * Accordingly, we agree with the court of appeals and the [trial] court that there is no genuine issue of material fact as to whether DRI is Arby's servant for purposes of the plaintiffs' *respondeat superior* claim against Arby's: clearly it is not. Arby's cannot be held vicariously liable for DRI's alleged negligent supervision of Pierce.

* * * *

We conclude that the quality, marketing, and operational standards and inspection and termination rights commonly included in franchise agreements do not establish the close supervisory control or right of control over a franchisee necessary to support imposing vicarious liability against the franchisor for all purposes or as a general matter. We hold that *a franchisor may be subject to vicarious liability for the tortious conduct of its franchisee only if the franchisor had control or a right of control over the daily operation of the specific aspect of the franchisee's business that is alleged to have caused the harm*. Because Arby's did not have control or a right of control over DRI's supervision of its employees, there was no master/servant relationship between Arby's and DRI for purposes of the plaintiffs' *respondeat superior* claim against Arby's. Arby's cannot be held vicariously liable for DRI's negligent supervision of Pierce. [Emphasis added.]

The decision of the court of appeals is affirmed.

QUESTIONS

1. Should a franchisor be allowed to control the operation of its franchisee without liability for the franchisee's conduct? Explain your answer.
2. What would constitute the "right to control" under a franchise contract?

PRICING ARRANGEMENTS Franchises provide the franchisor with an outlet for the firm's goods and services. Depending on the nature of the business, the franchisor may require the franchisee to purchase certain supplies from the franchisor at an established price.[6] A franchisor cannot, however, set the prices at which the franchisee will resell the goods because such price setting may be a violation of state or federal antitrust laws, or both. A franchisor can suggest retail prices but cannot mandate them.

SECTION 3 | Franchise Termination

The duration of the franchise is a matter to be determined between the parties. Generally, a franchise relationship starts with a short trial period, such as a year, so that the franchisee and the franchisor can determine whether they want to stay in business with one another. Usually, the franchise agreement specifies that termination must be "for cause," such as the death or disability of the franchisee, insolvency of the fran-

chisee, breach of the franchise agreement, or failure to meet specified sales quotas. Most franchise contracts provide that notice of termination must be given. If no set time for termination is specified, then a reasonable time, with notice, is implied. A franchisee must be given reasonable time to wind up the business—that is, to do the accounting and return the copyright or trademark or any other property of the franchisor.

WRONGFUL TERMINATION

Because a franchisor's termination of a franchise often has adverse consequences for the franchisee, much franchise litigation involves claims of wrongful termination. Generally, the termination provisions of contracts are more favorable to the franchisor than the franchisee. This means that the franchisee, who normally invests a substantial amount of time and financial resources in the franchise operation to make it successful, may receive little or nothing for the business on termination. The franchisor owns the trademark and hence the business.

It is in this area that statutory and case law become important. The federal and state laws discussed earlier attempt, among other things, to protect franchisees from the arbitrary or unfair termination of their franchises by the franchisors. Generally, both statutory and case law emphasize the importance of good faith and fair dealing in terminating a franchise relationship.

---

6. Although a franchisor can require franchisees to purchase supplies from it, requiring a franchisee to purchase exclusively from the franchisor may violate federal antitrust laws (see Chapter 46). For two landmark cases in these areas, see *United States v. Arnold, Schwinn & Co.*, 388 U.S. 365, 87 S.Ct. 1956, 18 L.Ed.2d 1249 (1967); and *Fortner Enterprises, Inc. v. U.S. Steel Corp.*, 394 U.S. 495, 89 S.Ct. 1252, 22 L.Ed.2d 495 (1969).

THE IMPORTANCE OF GOOD FAITH AND FAIR DEALING

In determining whether a franchisor has acted in good faith when terminating a franchise agreement, the courts generally try to balance the rights of both parties. If a court perceives that a franchisor has arbitrarily or unfairly terminated a franchise, the franchisee will be provided with a remedy for wrongful termina-tion. If a franchisor's decision to terminate a franchise was made in the normal course of the franchisor's business operations, however, and reasonable notice of termination was given to the franchisee, normally a court will not consider the termination wrongful.

At issue in the following case was whether General Motors Corporation acted wrongfully in terminating its franchise with a motor vehicle dealer in Connecticut.

CASE 35.3

United States District Court, District of Connecticut, 2005. 352 F.Supp.2d 251.

Chic Miller's Chevrolet, Inc. v. General Motors Corp.

BACKGROUND AND FACTS *Chapin Miller began work as a mail clerk with General Motors Acceptance Corporation (GMAC). By 1967, Miller had succeeded sufficiently within the organization to acquire Chic Miller's (no relation) Chevrolet, a General Motors Corporation (GM) dealership, in Bristol, Connecticut. As part of its operations, Chic Miller's entered into lending agreements, commonly known as* floor plan financing, *to enable it to buy new vehicles from GM. At first, the dealership had floor financing through GMAC. In 2001, however, Miller felt that GMAC was charging interest "at an inappropriately high rate" and negotiated a lower rate from Chase Manhattan Bank. In November 2002, Chase declined to provide further financing. Unable to obtain a loan from any other lender, Chic Miller's contacted GMAC, which also refused to make a deal. Under the parties' "Dealer Sales and Service Agreement," GM could terminate a dealership for "Failure of Dealer to maintain the line of credit." GM sent several notices of termination, but Chic Miller's remained open until March 2004, when it closed for seven days. GM sent a final termination notice. Chic Miller's filed a suit in a federal district court against GM, alleging in part a failure to act in good faith in terminating the franchise. GM filed a motion for summary judgment.*

IN THE LANGUAGE OF THE COURT
ARTERTON, District Judge.
* * * *

* * * [T]here is no dispute of material fact concerning Chic Miller's lack of floor plan financing after November 2002. * * * [T]he dealership contract unambiguously places the burden on the dealer to find and maintain floor plan financing. Without floor plan financing, the plaintiff was in clear breach of * * * the dealership contract, justifying GM's termination of the contract * * * .
* * * *

In order to lawfully terminate a franchise under the Connecticut [Franchise Act, which applies in this case], a franchisor must: provide notice that complies with statutory requirements; have "good cause" for the termination; and act "in good faith." [Emphasis added.]

"Good cause" exists [under the statute] if "[t]here is a failure by the dealer to comply with a provision of the franchise which is both reasonable and of material significance to the franchise relationship * * * ." According to James Ragsdale, Northeast Region Zone Manager for GM, floor plan financing is a material aspect of a dealership agreement because "without floor plan financing, a dealership is unable to purchase motor vehicle inventory, which, in turn, severely limits a dealership's ability to earn income from vehicle sales. * * * If a dealership is without floor plan financing for an extended period of time, it will eventually lose its ability to generate revenues and become financially insolvent, and will not be able to conduct customary sales and service operations." Miller does not dispute that floor plan financing is a material term of his franchise contract with GM. As discussed above, GM was justified under the contract in terminating Miller's franchise for failure to maintain floor plan financing. Because that term is material to the agreement, GM had "good cause" under the Connecticut dealer statute for terminating the franchise because of Miller's uncured breach.

CASE 35.3 | Continued

GM also had good cause to terminate the contract because it has shown that Chic Miller's Chevrolet failed to conduct customary sales and service operations between March 1 and March 8, 2004. A sign posted on the door of the dealership during that time stated: "CHIC MILLER'S CHEVROLET IS CLOSED. Please bring your vehicle to the dealer of your choice. Thank you for your past patronage." Although Miller asserts that the dealership was only temporarily closed for repair, the sign does not say that the dealership would reopen, and the phrases "bring your vehicle to the dealer of your choice" and "thank you for your past patronage" certainly suggest permanent closure * * * . [T]he dealership contract permits GM to terminate the agreement for "[f]ailure of the Dealer to conduct customary sales and service operations during customary business hours for seven consecutive business days." Since that term is material to the agreement, GM had "good cause" under the Connecticut dealer statute for terminating the franchise because of Plaintiff's breach.

Chic Miller's Chevrolet alleges that by "prematurely seeking the ultimate remedy of termination of the dealership franchise, the Defendant has not acted in good faith * * * ." The undisputed record shows that GM extended the period several times for Miller to try to obtain replacement floor plan financing after his arrangement with Chase ended. GM first notified Plaintiff of its breach of the dealership contract on December 20, 2002, with an amended notice on January 2, 2003 * * * . [O]n March 7, 2003, GM extended the deadline until March 31, and when Miller was still unable to find a lender, GM gave him another extension until July 1. * * * While Miller may have expected, based on GM's past practices, more than GM provided to him, Miller has not offered evidence to show that GM was acting "prematurely" or in bad faith during the course of the dealings recounted above.
* * * *

Because Plaintiff has not offered evidence from which a factfinder could conclude that GM acted without good cause or good faith, GM is entitled to judgment as a matter of law on Plaintiff's claims under the Connecticut Franchise Act.

DECISION AND REMEDY *The court granted GM's motion for summary judgment. GM acted in good faith, with good cause under the applicable state statute to terminate Chic Miller's franchise. The dealer failed to maintain floor plan financing, a material requirement under the franchise agreement. The dealer also failed to conduct sales and service operations for seven consecutive business days, another material requirement under the parties' contract.*

WHAT IF THE FACTS WERE DIFFERENT? *Suppose that in March 2004, Chic Miller's had placed one newspaper ad promoting its services and had sold one car. Would the result have been different?*

REVIEWING SOLE PROPRIETORSHIPS AND FRANCHISES

Carlos Del Rey decided to open a Mexican fast-food restaurant and signed a franchise contract with a national chain called *La Grande Enchilada*. The contract required the franchisee to strictly follow the franchisor's operating manual and stated that failure to do so would be grounds for terminating the franchise contract. The manual set forth detailed operating procedures and safety standards, and provided that a *La Grande* representative would inspect the restaurant monthly to ensure compliance. Nine months after Del Rey began operating his restaurant, a spark from the grill ignited an oily towel in the kitchen. No one was injured, but by the time firefighters were able to put out the fire, the kitchen had sustained extensive damage. The cook told the fire department that the towel was "about two feet from the grill" when it caught fire, which was in compliance with the franchisor's manual that required towels be placed at least one foot from the grills. Nevertheless, the next day *La Grande* notified Del Rey that his franchise would terminate in thirty days for failure to follow the prescribed safety procedures. Using the information presented in the chapter, answer the following questions.

1. | What type of franchise was Del Rey's *La Grande Enchilada* restaurant?

(Continued)

REVIEWING SOLE PROPRIETORSHIPS AND FRANCHISES *(continued)*

2. | The franchise agreement stipulates that Del Rey will purchase the building and that *La Grande Enchilada* will supply the equipment. Del Rey operates the restaurant as a sole proprietorship. Who bears the loss for the damaged kitchen? Explain.

3. | Assume that Del Rey operates the restaurant as a sole proprietorship. In the event of his death, can his daughter take over the business? Why or why not?

4. | Now assume that Del Rey files a lawsuit against *La Grande Enchilada,* claiming that his franchise was wrongfully terminated. What factors would a court consider in determining whether the franchise was wrongfully terminated? How would a court be likely to rule?

5. | Suppose that it turns out that the fire was actually caused by a defective grill supplied by *La Grande* (rather than by a spark igniting a towel). Would this affect a court's decision on wrongful termination? Should it? Explain.

TERMS AND CONCEPTS TO REVIEW

entrepreneur 718	franchisee 720	sole proprietorship 718
franchise 720	franchisor 720	

QUESTIONS AND CASE PROBLEMS

35–1. Maria, Pablo, and Vicky are recent college graduates who would like to go into business for themselves. They are considering purchasing a franchise. If they enter into a franchising arrangement, they would have the support of a large company that could answer any questions they might have. Also, a firm that has been in business for many years would be experienced in dealing with some of the problems that novice businesspersons might encounter. These and other attributes of franchises can lessen some of the risks of the marketplace. What other aspects of franchising—positive and negative—might Maria, Pablo, and Vicky want to consider before committing themselves to a particular franchise?

35–2. **QUESTION WITH SAMPLE ANSWER**

National Foods, Inc., sells franchises to its fast-food restaurants, known as Chicky-D's. Under the franchise agreement, franchisees agree to hire and train employees strictly according to Chicky-D's standards. Chicky-D's regional supervisors are required to approve all job candidates before they are hired and all general policies affecting those employees. Chicky-D's reserves the right to terminate a franchise for violating the franchisor's rules. In practice, however, Chicky-D's regional supervisors routinely approve new employees and individual franchisees' policies. After several incidents of racist comments and conduct by Tim, a recently hired assistant manager at a Chicky-D's, Sharon, a counterperson at the restaurant, resigns. Sharon files a suit in a federal district court against National. National files a motion for summary judgment, arguing that it is not liable for harassment by franchise employees. Will the court grant National's motion? Why or why not?

For a sample answer to this question, go to Appendix I at the end of this text.

35–3. Otmar has secured a particular high-quality ice cream franchise. The franchise agreement calls for Otmar to sell the ice cream only at a specific location; to buy all the ice cream from the franchisor; to order and sell all the flavors produced by the franchisor; and to refrain from selling any ice cream stored for more than two weeks after delivery by the franchisor, as the quality of the ice cream declines after that period of time. After two months of operation, Otmar believes that he can increase his profits by moving the store to another part of the city. He refuses to order even a limited quantity of the "fruit delight" flavor because of its higher cost, and he has sold ice cream that has been stored longer than two weeks without customer complaint. Otmar maintains that the franchisor has no right to restrict him in these practices. Discuss his claims.

35–4. Omega Computers, Inc., is a franchisor that grants exclusive physical territories to its franchisees with retail locations, including Pete's Digital Products. Omega sells over two hundred franchises before establishing an interactive Web site. On the site, a customer can order Omega's products directly from the franchisor. When Pete's sets up a Web site through which a customer can also order Omega's products, Omega and Pete's file suits against each other, each alleging that the other is in violation of the franchise relationship. To decide this issue, what factors should the court consider? How might the parties have avoided this conflict? Discuss.

35–5. FRANCHISE TERMINATION. C. B. Management Co. operated McDonald's restaurants in Cleveland, Ohio, under a franchise agreement with McDonald's Corp. The agreement required C. B. to make monthly payments of, among other things, certain percentages of the gross sales to McDonald's. If any payment was more than thirty days late, McDonald's had the right to terminate the franchise. The agreement stated, "No waiver by [McDonald's] of any breach . . . shall constitute a waiver of any subsequent breach." McDonald's sometimes accepted C. B.'s late payments, but when C. B. defaulted on the payments in July 1997, McDonald's gave notice of thirty days to comply or surrender possession of the restaurants. C. B. missed the deadline. McDonald's demanded that C. B. vacate the restaurants. C. B. refused. McDonald's filed a suit in a federal district court against C. B., alleging violations of the franchise agreement. C. B. counterclaimed in part that McDonald's had breached the implied covenant of good faith and fair dealing. McDonald's filed a motion to dismiss C. B.'s counterclaim. On what did C. B. base its claim? Will the court agree? Why or why not? [*McDonald's Corp. v. C. B. Management Co.*, 13 F.Supp.2d 705 (N.D.Ill. 1998)]

35–6. FRANCHISE TERMINATION. Heating & Air Specialists, Inc., doing business as A/C Service Co., marketed heating and air-conditioning products. A/C contracted with Lennox Industries, Inc., to be a franchised dealer of Lennox products. The parties signed a standard franchise contract drafted by Lennox. The contract provided that either party could terminate the agreement with or without cause on thirty days' notice and that the agreement would terminate immediately if A/C opened another facility at a different location. At the time, A/C operated only one location in Arkansas. A few months later, A/C opened a second location in Tulsa, Oklahoma. Lennox's district sales manager gave A/C oral authorization to sell Lennox products in Tulsa, at least on a temporary basis, but nothing was put in writing. Several of Lennox's other dealers in Tulsa complained to Lennox about A/C's presence. Lennox gave A/C notice that it was terminating A/C's Tulsa franchise. Meanwhile, A/C had failed to keep its Lennox account current and owed the franchisor more than $200,000. Citing this delinquency, Lennox notified A/C that unless it paid its account within ten days, Lennox

would terminate both franchises. A/C did not pay, and Lennox terminated the franchises. A/C filed a suit in a federal district court against Lennox, alleging in part breach of the franchise agreement for terminating the Tulsa franchise. Should A/C prevail? Explain. [*Heating & Air Specialists, Inc. v. Jones*, 180 F.3d 923 (8th Cir. 1999)]

35–7. ⚖ **CASE PROBLEM WITH SAMPLE ANSWER**
Walik Elkhatib, a Palestinian Arab, emigrated to the United States in 1971 and became an American citizen. Eight years later, Elkhatib bought a Dunkin' Donuts, Inc., franchise in Bellwood, Illinois. Dunkin' Donuts began offering breakfast sandwiches with bacon, ham, or sausage through its franchises in 1984, but Elkhatib refused to sell these items at his store on the ground that his religion forbade the handling of pork. In 1995, Elkhatib opened a second franchise in Berkeley, Illinois, at which he also refused to sell pork products. The next year, at both locations, Elkhatib began selling meatless sandwiches. In 1998, Elkhatib opened a third franchise in Westchester, Illinois. When he proposed to relocate this franchise, Dunkin' Donuts refused to approve the new location and added that it would not renew any of his franchise agreements because he did not carry the full sandwich line. Elkhatib filed a suit in a federal district court against Dunkin' Donuts and others. The defendants filed a motion for summary judgment. Did Dunkin' Donuts act in good faith in its relationship with Elkhatib? Explain. [*Elkhatib v. Dunkin' Donuts, Inc.*, __ F.Supp.2d __ (N.D.Ill. 2004)]
To view a sample answer for this case problem, go to this book's Web site at http://wbl.westbuslaw.com, select "Chapter 35," and click on "Case Problem with Sample Answer."

35–8. FRANCHISE TERMINATION. In 1985, Bruce Byrne, with his sons Scott and Gordon, opened Lone Star R.V. Sales, Inc., a motor home dealership in Houston, Texas. In 1994, Lone Star became a franchised dealer for Winnebago Industries, Inc., a manufacturer of recreational vehicles. The parties renewed the franchise in 1995, but during the next year, their relationship began to deteriorate. Lone Star did not maintain a current inventory, its sales did not meet goals agreed to between the parties, and Lone Star disparaged Winnebago products to consumers and otherwise failed to actively promote them. Several times, the Byrnes subjected Winnebago employees to verbal abuse. During one phone conversation, Bruce threatened to throw a certain Winnebago sales manager off Lone Star's lot if he appeared at the dealership. Bruce was physically incapable of carrying out the threat, however. In 1998, Winnebago terminated the franchise, claiming, among many other things, that it was concerned for the safety of its employees. Lone Star filed a protest with the Texas Motor Vehicle Board. Did Winnebago have good cause to terminate Lone Star's franchise? Discuss. [*Lone Star R.V. Sales, Inc. v. Motor Vehicle Board of the*

Texas Department of Transportation, 49 S.W.3d 492 (Tex.App.—Austin 2001)]

35–9. FRANCHISE TERMINATION. In the automobile industry, luxury-car customers are considered the most demanding segment of the market with respect to customer service. Jaguar Cars, a division of Ford Motor Co., is the exclusive U.S. distributor of Jaguar luxury cars. Jaguar Cars distributes its products through franchised dealers. In April 1999, Dave Ostrem Imports, Inc., an authorized Jaguar dealer in Des Moines, Iowa, contracted to sell its dealership to Midwest Automotive III, LLC. A Jaguar franchise generally cannot be sold without Jaguar Cars' permission. Jaguar Cars asked Midwest Auto to submit three years of customer satisfaction index (CSI) data for all franchises with which its owners had been associated. (CSI data are intended to measure how well dealers treat their customers and satisfy their customers' needs. Jaguar Cars requires above-average CSI ratings for its dealers.) Most of Midwest Auto's scores fell below the national average. Jaguar Cars rejected Midwest Auto's application and sought to terminate the franchise, claiming that a transfer of the dealership would be "substantially detrimental" to the distribution of Jaguar vehicles in the community. Was Jaguar Cars'

attempt to terminate this franchise reasonable? Why or why not? [*Midwest Automotive III, LLC v. Iowa Department of Transportation,* 646 N.W.2d 417 (Iowa 2002)]

35–10. THE FRANCHISE CONTRACT. On August 23, 1995, Climaco Guzman entered into a commercial janitorial services franchise agreement with Jan-Pro Cleaning Systems, Inc., in Rhode Island for a franchise fee of $3,285. In the agreement, Jan-Pro promised to furnish Guzman with "one (1) or more customer account(s) . . . amounting to $8,000.00 gross volume per year. . . . No portion of the franchise fee is refundable except and to the extent that the Franchisor, within 120 business days following the date of execution of the Franchise Agreement, fails to provide accounts." By February 19, Guzman had not received any accounts and demanded a full refund. Jan-Pro then promised "two accounts grossing $12,000 per year in income." Despite its assurances, Jan-Pro did not have the ability to furnish accounts that met the stated requirements. In September, Guzman filed a suit in a Rhode Island state court against Jan-Pro, alleging in part fraudulent misrepresentation. Should the court rule in Guzman's favor? Why or why not? [*Guzman v. Jan-Pro Cleaning Systems, Inc,.* 839 A.2d 504 (R.I. 2003)]

LAW | on the Web

For updated links to resources available on the Web, as well as a variety of other materials, visit this text's Web site at **http://wbl.westbuslaw.com**.

To learn how the U.S. Small Business Administration assists in forming, financing, and operating businesses, go to

http://www.sbaonline.sba.gov

For information about FTC regulations on franchising, as well as state laws regulating franchising, go to

http://www.ftc.gov/bcp/franchise/netfran.htm

A good source of information on the purchase and sale of franchises is Franchising.org, which is online at

http://www.franchising.org

LEGAL RESEARCH EXERCISES ON THE WEB

Go to **http://wbl.westbuslaw.com**, the Web site that accompanies this text. Select "Chapter 35" and click on "Internet Exercises." There you will find the following Internet research exercises that you can perform to learn more about topics covered in this chapter.

Activity 35–1: LEGAL PERSPECTIVE
　　　　　　　Starting a Business

Activity 35–2: MANAGEMENT PERSPECTIVE
　　　　　　　Franchises

CHAPTER 36
Partnerships and Limited Liability Partnerships

Traditionally, one of the most common forms of business organization selected by two or more persons is the *partnership*. A **partnership** arises from an agreement, express or implied, between two or more persons to carry on a business for a profit. Partners are co-owners of a business and have joint control over its operation and the right to share in its profits. In this chapter we examine several forms of partnership.

We begin the chapter with an examination of ordinary partnerships, or *general partnerships*, and the rights and duties of partners in this traditional business entity. We then examine some special forms of partnerships known as *limited partnerships* and *limited liability partnerships*, which receive a different treatment under the law.

SECTION 1 | Basic Partnership Concepts

Partnerships are governed both by common law concepts (in particular, those relating to agency) and by statutory law. As in so many other areas of business law, the National Conference of Commissioners on Uniform State Laws has drafted uniform laws for partnerships, and these have been widely adopted by the states.

AGENCY CONCEPTS AND PARTNERSHIP LAW

When two or more persons agree to do business as partners, they enter into a special relationship with one another. To an extent, their relationship is similar to an agency relationship because each partner is deemed to be the agent of the other partners and of the partnership. The agency concepts that were discussed in Chapters 31 and 32 thus apply—specifically, the imputation of knowledge of, and responsibility for, acts carried out within the scope of the partnership relationship. In their relationship to one another, partners are also bound by the fiduciary ties that bind an agent and principal under agency law.

Partnership law is distinct from agency law in one significant way, however. A partnership is based on a voluntary contract between two or more competent persons who agree to place some or all of their funds or other assets, labor, and skills in a business with the understanding that profits and losses will be shared. In a nonpartnership agency relationship, the agent usually does not have an ownership interest in the business, nor is he or she obligated to bear a portion of ordinary business losses.

THE UNIFORM PARTNERSHIP ACT

The Uniform Partnership Act (UPA) governs the operation of partnerships *in the absence of express agreement* and has done much to reduce controversies in the law relating to partnerships. Except for Louisiana, all of the states, as well as the District of Columbia, have adopted the UPA. The majority of states have enacted the most recent version of the UPA, which was adopted in 1994 and amended in 1997 to provide limited liability for partners in a limited liability partnership.[1] Excerpts from the latest version of the UPA, including the 1997 amendments, are presented in Appendix E.

---

1. At the time this book went to press, over half of the states had adopted the UPA with the 1997 amendments, including the District of Columbia, Puerto Rico, and the U.S. Virgin Islands. We therefore base our discussion of the UPA on the 1997 version of the act and refer to older versions of the UPA in footnotes if necessary.

DEFINITION OF PARTNERSHIP

Parties commonly find themselves in conflict over whether their business enterprise is a legal partnership, especially in the absence of a formal, written partnership agreement. The UPA defines the term *partnership* as "an association of two or more persons to carry on as co-owners a business for profit" [UPA 101(6)]. The *intent* to associate is a key element of a partnership, and one cannot join a partnership unless all other partners consent [UPA 401(i)].

PARTNERSHIP STATUS

In resolving disputes over whether partnership status exists, courts usually look for the following three essential elements of partnership implicit in the UPA's definition:

1. A sharing of profits or losses.
2. A joint ownership of the business.
3. An equal right in the management of the business.

If the evidence in a particular case is insufficient to establish all three factors, the UPA provides a set of guidelines to be used. For example, the sharing of profits and losses from a business creates a presumption that a partnership exists. No presumption is made, however, if the profits were received as payment of any of the following [UPA 202(c)(3)]:

1. A debt by installments or interest on a loan.
2. Wages of an employee or for the services of an independent contractor.
3. Rent to a landlord.
4. An annuity to a surviving spouse or representative of a deceased partner.
5. A sale of the goodwill of a business or property.

To illustrate: Suppose that a debtor owes a creditor $5,000 on an unsecured debt. To repay the debt, the debtor agrees to pay (and the creditor, to accept) 10 percent of the debtor's monthly business profits until the loan with interest has been paid. Although the creditor is sharing profits from the business, the debtor and creditor are not presumed to be partners.

When one of the parties disputes whether a partnership was created, the courts frequently look to other factors, such as the conduct of the parties, to determine partnership status. In the following case, the parties met and discussed buying and developing a commercial site. Using some of one party's funds, another party bought the site solely in the name of his business. The buyer refused to share ownership of the property, claiming that he had only entered into an unenforceable agreement to form a partnership and was not a partner.

| CASE 36.1 | Cap Care Group, Inc. v. McDonald |

North Carolina
Court of Appeals, 2002.
149 N.C.App. 817,
561 S.E.2d 578.
http://www.aoc.state.nc.us/
www/public/html/
opinions.htm[a]

BACKGROUND AND FACTS *Cap Care Group, Inc., PWPP Partners, and C & M Investments of High Point, Inc., buy and develop commercial real estate. Ronnel Parker is president of Cap Care and PWPP. Wayne McDonald owns and controls C & M. In November 1996, Parker and Daniel Greene, another Cap Care officer, met McDonald to discuss buying and renovating a commercial site in High Point, North Carolina. Cap Care later claimed that at the meeting the parties (Parker on behalf of Cap Care and PWPP, and McDonald on behalf of C & M) agreed that they would be partners in the purchase and development of the property, and that McDonald would make an offer to the seller on the partnership's behalf. In February 1997, McDonald signed a contract to buy the site, using PWPP funds as half of the earnest money.[b] McDonald and Greene (of Cap Care) then discussed jointly owning the property as partners. In March, McDonald bought the property in the name of C & M only. Cap Care demanded that McDonald contribute the property to the partnership, but he refused. Cap Care filed a suit in a North Carolina state court against McDonald and C & M, alleging in part breach of contract. McDonald argued that he and Parker had merely entered into an unenforceable agreement to form a partnership. The court awarded Cap Care $477,511, plus interest and fees. The defendants appealed to a state intermediate appellate court.*

---

a. In the "Court of Appeals Opinions" section, click on "2002." On the next page, scroll to the "16 April 2002" section and click on the name of the case to access the opinion.
b. *Earnest money* is a deposit of funds that usually accompanies an offer to buy real estate to show that the offer is earnest, or serious.

CASE 36.1 | Continued

IN THE LANGUAGE OF THE COURT

THOMAS, Judge.

* * * *

* * * [D]efendants argue the trial court should have granted their motions for directed verdict and judgment notwithstanding the verdict on the issue of the breach of an agreement to enter into a partnership. We disagree.

* * * *

A partnership is defined as an association of two or more persons to carry on as co-owners a business for profit. *A partnership can be formed orally or implied by the parties' conduct.* [Emphasis added.]

McDonald's wife, Wendy McDonald, who is also an officer of C & M, testified that she knew McDonald had a deal with plaintiffs and that Parker had agreed to fund half of the earnest money to get the property. McDonald himself testified that his account would have been overdrawn had he not deposited Parker's checks and that the $20,000 earnest money was part of the purchase price of the property. There was substantial evidence that the parties had reached an agreement to jointly purchase and develop the property. Further, defendants never informed plaintiffs that they were not acting as partners until after the purchase of the property.

An enforceable agreement requires an offer, acceptance and consideration.

Here, the offer to form a partnership is not contested. Defendants argue they never accepted the offer. However, defendants did accept the consideration of $10,000 from plaintiffs to pay for the property. They also precisely carried out the joint plan of the parties until *after* the purchase of the property. There was never any indication during that process that the parties were not operating in unison, as partners. The general law of partnership applies to a partnership formed for the purpose of dealing in land. *An acceptance by conduct is a valid acceptance.* [Emphasis added.]

Defendants contend there was no meeting of the minds because how the property would be managed was not clear. However, it is well established * * * that a failure to agree on some issues does not invalidate the underlying agreement.

We therefore hold that there was a valid agreement among the parties to form a partnership to purchase the property and that defendants breached that agreement.

DECISION AND REMEDY *The state intermediate appellate court affirmed the lower court's judgment. The defendants had entered into, and breached, an oral partnership contract to buy real estate, as evidenced by the parties' discussions, the defendants' acceptance of a partner's funds, and the defendants' acting according to the parties' plan until after the purchase of the property.*

JOINT PROPERTY OWNERSHIP AND PARTNERSHIP STATUS

Joint ownership of property, obviously, does not in and of itself create a partnership. Therefore, the fact that, say, MacPherson and Bunker own real property as joint tenants or as tenants in common (a form of joint ownership that will be discussed in Chapter 47) does not by itself establish a partnership. In fact, the sharing of gross returns and even profits from such ownership "does not by itself establish a partnership" [UPA 202(c)(1) and (2)]. Thus, if MacPherson and Bunker jointly own a piece of rural property and lease the land to a farmer for a share of the profits from the farming operation in lieu of set rental payments, the sharing

of the profits ordinarily will not make MacPherson, Bunker, and the farmer partners.

Note, though, that although the sharing of profits from ownership of property does not prove the existence of a partnership, sharing *both profits and losses* usually does. For example, two sisters, Zoe and Cienna, buy a restaurant together, open a joint bank account from which they pay for supplies and expenses, and share the proceeds that the restaurant generates. Zoe manages the restaurant and Cienna handles the bookkeeping. After eight years, Cienna stops keeping the books and does no other work for the restaurant. Zoe, who is now operating the restaurant by herself, no longer wants to share the profits with Cienna. She offers to buy her sister out, but the two cannot agree on a fair price. When Cienna files a lawsuit, a question arises as to whether the two sisters were partners in the restaurant. In this situation, a court would find that a partnership existed because the sisters shared management responsibilities, had joint accounts, and shared the profits and the losses of the restaurant equally.

ENTITY VERSUS AGGREGATE

A partnership is sometimes called a *company* or a *firm*, terms that suggest that the partnership is an entity separate and apart from its aggregate members. The law of partnership recognizes the independent entity for most purposes but may treat the partnership as a composite of its individual partners for some purposes.

PARTNERSHIP AS AN ENTITY At common law, a partnership was never treated as a separate legal entity. Thus, a common law suit could never be brought by or against the firm in its own name; each individual partner had to sue or be sued. Today, most states provide specifically that a partnership can be treated as an entity for certain purposes. These usually include the capacity to sue or be sued, to collect judgments, and to have all accounting procedures carried out in the name of the partnership. In addition, the UPA clearly states, "A partnership is an entity" and "A partnership may sue and be sued in the name of the partnership" [UPA 201 and 307(a)]. As an entity, a partnership may hold the title to real or personal property in its name rather than in the names of the individual partners. Finally, federal procedural laws frequently permit a partnership to be treated as an entity in such matters as lawsuits in federal courts, bankruptcy proceedings, and the filing of federal information tax returns.

PARTNERSHIP AS AN AGGREGATE In one circumstance, the partnership is not regarded as a separate legal entity, but is treated as an aggregate of the individual partners. For federal income tax purposes, a partnership is not a taxpaying entity. The income and losses it incurs are "passed through" the partnership framework and attributed to the partners on their individual tax returns. The partnership itself has no tax liability and is responsible only for filing an **information return** with the Internal Revenue Service. In other words, the firm itself pays no taxes. A partner's profit from the partnership (whether distributed or not) is taxed as individual income to the individual partner.

SECTION 2 | Partnership Formation

As a general rule, agreements to form a partnership can be *oral, written*, or *implied by conduct*. Some partnership agreements, however, must be in writing to be legally enforceable within the Statute of Frauds (see Chapter 15 for details). For example, a partnership agreement that authorizes the partners to deal in transfers of real property must be evidenced by a sufficient writing (or record).

THE PARTNERSHIP AGREEMENT

A partnership agreement, called **articles of partnership,** can include virtually any terms that the parties wish, unless they are illegal or contrary to public policy or statute [UPA 103]. The terms commonly included in a partnership agreement are listed in Exhibit 36–1. (Notice that this list includes an arbitration clause, which is often included in a partnership agreement.)

DURATION OF THE PARTNERSHIP

The partnership agreement can specify the duration of the partnership by stating that it will continue until a designated date or until the completion of a particular project. This is called a *partnership for a term*. If this type of partnership is dissolved (broken up) without the consent of all the partners prior to the expiration of the partnership term, the dissolution constitutes a breach of the agreement. The responsible partner can be held liable for any resulting losses.

If no fixed duration is specified, the partnership is a *partnership at will*. Any partner can dissolve this type of partnership at any time without violating the agreement and without incurring liability for losses to other partners that result from the termination.

A CORPORATION AS PARTNER

In a general partnership, the partners are personally liable for the debts incurred by the partnership. If one of the general partners is a corporation, however, what does personal liability mean? Basically, the capacity of corporations to contract is a question of corporate law. At one time, many states had restrictions on corporations becoming partners, although such restrictions have become less common over the years.

The Revised Model Business Corporation Act (see Appendix G) allows corporations generally to make contracts and incur liabilities. The UPA specifically permits a corporation to be a partner. By definition, "a partnership is an association of two or more persons," and the UPA defines *person* as including corporations [UPA 101(10)].

PARTNERSHIP BY ESTOPPEL

Persons who are not partners may nevertheless hold themselves out as partners and make representations that third parties rely on in dealing with them. In such a situation, a court may conclude that a **partnership by estoppel** exists and impose liability—but not partnership *rights*—on the alleged partner or partners.

TWO ASPECTS OF LIABILITY There are two aspects of liability under a theory of partnership by estoppel. The person representing that she or he is a partner in an actual or alleged partnership is liable to any third person who extends credit in good faith reliance on such representations. Similarly, a person who expressly or impliedly consents to the misrepresentation of an alleged partnership relationship is also liable to third parties who extend credit in good faith reliance. When this occurs, the nonpartner is regarded as an agent whose acts are binding on the partnership [UPA 308].

For example, Moreno owns a small shop. Knowing that Midland Bank will not make a loan on his credit alone, Moreno represents that Loman, a financially secure businesswoman, is a partner in Moreno's business. Loman knows of Moreno's misrepresentation but fails to correct it. Midland Bank, relying on the strength of Loman's reputation and credit, extends a loan to Moreno. Moreno will be liable to the bank for the loan repayment. In many states, Loman would also be held liable to the bank. Loman has impliedly consented to the misrepresentation and will normally be estopped from denying that she is Moreno's partner. She will be regarded as if she were in fact a partner in Moreno's business insofar as this loan is concerned.

EXHIBIT 36–1 Terms Commonly Included in a Partnership Agreement

Basic Structure	1. Name of the partnership. 2. Names of the partners. 3. Location of the business and the state law under which the partnership is organized. 4. Purpose of the partnership. 5. Duration of the partnership.
Capital Contributions	1. Amount of capital that each partner is contributing. 2. The agreed-on value of any real or personal property that is contributed instead of cash. 3. How losses and gains on contributed capital will be allocated, and whether contributions will earn interest.
Sharing of Profits and Losses	1. Percentage of the profits and losses of the business that each partner will receive. 2. When distributions of profit will be made and how net profit will be calculated.
Management and Control	1. How management responsibilities will be divided among the partners. 2. Name of the managing partner or partners, and whether other partners have voting rights.
Accounting and Partnership Records	1. Name of the bank in which the partnership will maintain its business and checking accounts. 2. Statement that an accounting of partnership records will be maintained and that any partner or her or his agent can review these records at any time. 3. The dates of the partnership's fiscal year and when the annual audit of the books will take place.
Dissolution	1. Events that will dissolve the partnership, such as the retirement, death, or incapacity of any partner. 2. How partnership property will be valued and apportioned on dissolution. 3. Whether an arbitrator will determine the value of partnership property on dissolution and whether that determination will be binding.
Miscellaneous	Whether arbitration is required for any dispute relating to the partnership agreement.

WHEN A NONPARTNER IS REPRESENTED AS A MEMBER OF AN EXISTING PARTNERSHIP When a real partnership exists and a partner represents that a nonpartner is a member of the firm, the nonpartner is regarded as an agent whose acts are binding on the partner (but normally *not* on the partnership). For example, Middle Earth Movers has three partners—Jansen, Mahar, and Harran. Mahar represents to the business community that Tully is also a partner. If Tully negotiates a contract in the name of Middle Earth Movers, the contract will be binding on Mahar but normally not on Jansen and Harran (unless, of course, they knew about, and consented to, Mahar's representation about Tully). Again, partnership by estoppel requires that a third person reasonably and detrimentally rely on the representation that a person was part of the partnership.

SECTION 3 | Partnership Operation

The rights and duties of partners are governed largely by the specific terms of their partnership agreement. In the absence of provisions to the contrary in the partnership agreement, the law imposes the rights and duties discussed in the following subsections. The character and nature of the partnership business generally influence the application of these rights and duties.

RIGHTS OF PARTNERS

The rights of partners in a partnership relate to the following areas: management, interest in the partnership, compensation, inspection of books, accounting, and property.

MANAGEMENT In a general partnership, "All partners have equal rights in the management and conduct of partnership business" [UPA 401(f)]. Unless the partners agree otherwise, each partner has one vote in management matters *regardless of the proportional size of his or her interest in the firm*. Often, in a large partnership partners will agree to delegate daily management responsibilities to a management committee made up of one or more of the partners.

The majority rule controls decisions on ordinary matters connected with partnership business, unless otherwise specified in the agreement. Decisions that significantly affect the nature of the partnership or that are not apparently for carrying on the ordinary course of the partnership business, or business of the kind, however, require the *unanimous* consent of the partners [UPA 301(2), 401(i), 401(j)]. Unanimous consent is likely to be required for a decision to undertake any of the following actions:[2]

1. To alter the essential nature of the firm's business as expressed in the partnership agreement or to alter the capital structure of the partnership.
2. To admit new partners or to engage in a completely new business.
3. To assign partnership property to a trust for the benefit of creditors.
4. To dispose of the partnership's goodwill.
5. To confess judgment against the partnership or submit partnership claims to arbitration. (A **confession of judgment** is an act by a debtor permitting a judgment to be entered against him or her by a creditor, for an agreed sum, without the institution of legal proceedings.)
6. To undertake any act that would make further conduct of partnership business impossible.
7. To amend the terms of the partnership agreement.

INTEREST IN THE PARTNERSHIP Each partner is entitled to the proportion of business profits and losses that is designated in the partnership agreement. If the agreement does not apportion profits (indicate how the profits will be shared), the UPA provides that profits will be shared equally. If the agreement does not apportion losses, losses will be shared in the same ratio as profits [UPA 401(b)].

For example, assume that Rico and Brett form a partnership. The partnership agreement provides for capital contributions of $60,000 from Rico and $40,000 from Brett, but it is silent as to how they will share profits or losses. In this situation, they will share both profits and losses equally. If their partnership agreement had provided that they would share profits in the same ratio as capital contributions, however, 60 percent of the profits would go to Rico, and 40 percent of the profits would go to Brett. If the agreement was silent as to losses, losses would be shared in the same ratio as profits (60 percent to 40 percent).

---

2. The previous version of the UPA specifically listed most of these actions as requiring unanimous consent. The current version of the UPA omits the list entirely to allow the courts more flexibility. The Official Comments explain that most of these acts, except for submitting a claim to arbitration, will likely still remain outside the apparent authority of a partner.

COMPENSATION Devoting time, skill, and energy to partnership business is a partner's duty and generally is not a compensable service. Partners can, of course, agree otherwise. For example, the managing partner of a law firm often receives a salary in addition to her or his share of profits for performing special administrative duties in office and personnel management.

UPA 401(h) provides that a partner is entitled to compensation for services in winding up partnership affairs (and reimbursement for expenses incurred in the process) above and apart from his or her share in the partnership profits.

INSPECTION OF BOOKS Partnership books and records must be kept accessible to all partners. Each partner has the right to receive (and the corresponding duty to produce) full and complete information concerning the conduct of all aspects of partnership business [UPA 403]. Each firm retains books for recording and securing such information. Partners contribute the information, and a bookkeeper typically has the duty to preserve it. The books must be kept at the firm's principal business office (unless the partners agree otherwise). Every partner, whether active or inactive, is entitled to inspect all books and records on demand and can make copies of the materials. The personal representative of a deceased partner's estate has the same right of access to partnership books and records that the decedent would have had [UPA 403].

ACTIONS FOR ACCOUNTING AGAINST THE PARTNERSHIP AND AMONG THE PARTNERS An accounting of partnership assets or profits is required to determine the value of each partner's share in the partnership. An accounting can be performed voluntarily, or it can be compelled by court order. Under UPA 405(b), a partner has the right to bring an action for an accounting during the term of the partnership, as well as on the firm's dissolution and winding up.[3] A partner also has the right to bring an action against the partnership or another partner, with or without a formal accounting, in the following situations:

1. To enforce the partner's rights under the partnership agreement.
2. To enforce the partner's rights under the UPA.

3. To enforce the partner's rights and interests arising independently of the partnership relationship.

PROPERTY RIGHTS A partner has two basic property rights. First, a partner has an interest in the partnership (which includes a share of the profits and losses and the right to participate in management). Second, a partner has a right in specific partnership property. Note, however, that a partner is not the co-owner of partnership property and cannot transfer his or her interest in partnership property, either voluntarily or involuntarily [UPA 501].

—Partner's Interest in the Firm. A partner's interest in the firm is a personal asset consisting of a proportionate share of the profits earned [UPA 502] and a return of capital on the partnership's termination. A partner's interest is subject to assignment or to a judgment creditor's lien (a lien obtained through the judicial process). Judgment creditors can attach a partner's interest by petitioning the court that entered the judgment to grant the creditors a **charging order.** This order entitles the judgment creditors to the profits of the partner and to any assets available to the partner on dissolution [UPA 504]. Neither an assignment nor a court's charging order will cause the dissolution of the firm [UPA 503].

—Partnership Property. Property acquired *by* a partnership is the property of the partnership and not of the partners individually [UPA 203]. Property acquired *in the name of* the partnership or a partner is partnership property if the person's capacity as a partner or the existence of the partnership is indicated in the instrument transferring title. If the transferring instrument refers to neither of these, the property is still presumed to be partnership property when it is acquired with partnership funds [UPA 204].[4]

In all other circumstances, the property is presumed to be the property of an individual partner, even if it is used in the partnership business. Ultimately, in those situations, it is the intention of the partners that determines whether property belongs to the partnership or to a partner in his or her individual capacity [UPA 204(d)].

---

3. Under the previous version of the UPA, a partner could bring an action for an accounting only if the partnership agreement provided for it, the partner was wrongfully excluded from the business or its property or books, another partner was in breach of his or her fiduciary duty, or other circumstances rendered it "just and reasonable."

4. *Partnership property* was defined in the previous version of the UPA as "all property originally brought into the partnership's stock or subsequently acquired, by purchase or otherwise, on account of the partnership" [UPA 8(1)]. This definition, unlike the one in the current UPA, did not provide any guidance concerning when property is "acquired by" a partnership.

A partner may use or possess partnership property only on behalf of the partnership [UPA 401(g)]. A partner is not a co-owner of partnership property and has no interest in the property that can be transferred, either voluntarily or involuntarily [UPA 501]. In other words, partnership property is owned by the partnership as an entity and not by the individual partners.[5]

DUTIES AND LIABILITIES OF PARTNERS

The duties and liabilities of partners that we examine here are basically derived from agency law. Each partner is an agent of every other partner and acts as both a principal and an agent in any business transaction within the scope of the partnership agreement. Each partner is also a general agent of the partnership in carrying out the usual business of the firm "or business of the kind carried on by the partnership" [UPA 301(1)]. Thus, every act of a partner concerning partnership business and "business of the kind" and every contract signed in the partnership's name bind the firm. The UPA affirms general principles of agency law that pertain to the authority of a partner to bind a partnership in contract or tort.

FIDUCIARY DUTIES   The only fiduciary duties a partner owes to the partnership and the other partners are the duty of loyalty and the duty of care, according to UPA 404(a). A partner's duty of loyalty is limited to accounting to the partnership for "any property, profit, or benefit" derived by the partner in the conduct of the partnership business or from a use of its property, and to refrain from dealing with the firm as an adverse party or competing with it in the conduct of partnership business [UPA 404(b)]. A partner's duty of care is limited to refraining from "grossly negligent or reckless conduct, intentional misconduct, or a knowing violation of law" [UPA 404(c)].[6]

These duties may not be waived or eliminated in the partnership agreement, and in fulfilling them each partner must act consistently with the obligation of good faith and fair dealing, which applies to all contracts, including partnership agreements [UPA 103(b) and 404(d)].

A partner may pursue his or her own interests, however, without automatically violating these duties [UPA 404(e)]. For example, a partner who owns a shopping mall may vote against a partnership proposal to open a competing mall.

AUTHORITY OF PARTNERS   The UPA affirms general principles of agency law that pertain to the authority of a partner to bind a partnership in contract. Under the same principles, a partner may also subject a partnership to liability in tort. When a partner is apparently carrying on partnership business or business of the kind with third parties in the usual way, both the partner and the firm share liability. The partnership will not be liable, however, if the third parties *know* that the partner has no such authority. For example, Patricia, a partner in the partnership of Heise, Green, and Stevens, applies for a loan on behalf of the partnership without authorization from the other partners. The bank manager knows that Patricia has no authority to do so. If the bank manager grants the loan, Patricia will be personally bound, but the firm will not be liable.

Under UPA 105 and 303, a partnership may file in a designated state office a "statement of partnership authority" to limit the capacity of a partner to act as the firm's agent or transfer property on its behalf. Any limit on a partner's authority, however, does not affect a third party who does not know about the statement—unless the statement of partnership authority is filed with the appropriate state office that records real property transfers (see Chapter 48). Statements limiting the partners' authority to transfer real property that are filed with the appropriate state records office will bind third parties, regardless of their knowledge of the limitation.

The agency concepts relating to apparent authority, actual authority, and ratification that were discussed in Chapter 32 also apply to partnerships. The extent of *implied authority* is generally broader for partners than for ordinary agents, however.

—The Scope of Implied Powers.   The character and scope of the partnership business and the customary nature of the particular business operation determine the implied powers of partners. For example, each partner in a trading partnership—essentially, any partnership business that has goods in inventory and makes profits buying and selling those goods—has a wide range of implied powers, such as to advertise products, to hire employees, and to extend the firm's credit by issuing or indorsing instruments.

---

5. Under the previous version of the UPA, partners were *tenants in partnership*. This meant that every partner was a co-owner with all other partners of the partnership property. The current UPA does not recognize this concept.

6. The previous version of the UPA touched only briefly on the duty of loyalty and left the details of the partners' fiduciary duties to be developed under the law of agency.

In an ordinary partnership, firm members can exercise all implied powers reasonably necessary and customary to carry on that particular business. Some customarily implied powers include the authority to make warranties on goods in the sales business, the power to convey (transfer) real property in the firm name when such conveyances are part of the ordinary course of partnership business, and the power to enter into contracts consistent with the firm's regular course of business.

—Authorized versus Unauthorized Actions. If a partner acts within the scope of authority, the partnership is legally bound to honor the partner's commitments to third parties. For example, a partner's authority to sell partnership products carries with it the implied authority to transfer title and to make usual warranties. Hence, in a partnership that operates a retail tire store, any partner negotiating a contract with a customer for the sale of a set of tires can warrant that "each tire will be warranted for normal wear for 40,000 miles."

This same partner, however, does not have the authority to sell office equipment, fixtures, or the partnership office building without the consent of all of the other partners. In addition, because partnerships are formed for profit, a partner generally does not have the authority to make charitable contributions without the consent of the other partners. No such action is binding on the partnership unless it is ratified by all of the other partners.

LIABILITY OF PARTNERS One significant disadvantage associated with a traditional partnership is that partners are *personally* liable for the debts of the partnership. Moreover, the liability is essentially unlimited, because the acts of one partner in the ordinary course of business subject the other partners to personal liability [UPA 305]. The following subsections explain the rules on a partner's liability.

—Joint Liability. Under the prior version of the UPA, which is still in effect in some states, partners were subject to **joint liability** on partnership debts and contracts, but not on partnership debts arising from torts.[7] Joint liability means the liability is shared between the partners, but each partner is liable for the full amount. If, for example, a third party sues a partner on a partnership contract, the partner has the right to demand that the other partners be sued with her or him. In fact, if the third party does not sue all of the partners, those partners sued cannot be required to pay a judgment, and the assets of the partnership cannot be used to satisfy the judgment. (Similarly, a third party's release of one partner releases all partners.) In other words, to bring a successful claim against the partnership on a debt or contract, a plaintiff must name all of the partners as defendants.

—Joint and Several Liability. In the majority of the states, under UPA 306(a), partners are jointly and severally (separately, or individually) liable for partnership obligations, including contracts, torts, and breaches of trust.[8] **Joint and several liability** means that a third party may sue all of the partners together (jointly) or one or more of the partners separately (severally) or at his or her option. This is true even if the partner did not participate in, ratify, or know about whatever it was that gave rise to the cause of action.

Generally, under UPA 307(d), however, a creditor cannot bring an action to collect a partnership debt from any partner of a nonbankrupt partnership without first attempting to collect from the partnership, or convincing a court that the attempt would be unsuccessful.

A judgment against one partner on her or his several (separate) liability does not extinguish the others' liability. (Similarly, a release of one partner does not discharge the partners' several liability.) Thus, those not sued in the first action may be sued subsequently. The first action, however, may have been conclusive on the question of liability. If, for example, in an action against one partner, the court held that the partnership was in no way liable, the third party cannot bring an action against another partner and succeed on the issue of the partnership's liability.

If the third party is successful in a suit against a partner or partners, he or she may collect on the judgment only against the assets of those partners named as defendants. A partner who commits a tort is required to indemnify (reimburse) the partnership for any damages it pays. The question in the following case was whether a partnership must indemnify a partner for liability that results from negligent conduct occurring in the ordinary course of the partnership's business.

7. Joint liability was the rule stated in the previous version of the UPA [see UPA 15(b)]. For a case applying joint liability to partnerships, see *Shar's Cars, LLC v. Elder*, 97 P.3d 724 (Utah App. 2004).

8. As noted, under the previous version of the UPA, partners' liability for torts was joint and several, while their liability for contracts was joint but not several.

CASE 36.2

Minnesota Court
of Appeals, 2004.
679 N.W.2d 165.
http://www.lawlibrary.state.
mn.us/archive/cap1st.html[a]

Moren v. Jax Restaurant

BACKGROUND AND FACTS *"Jax Restaurant" is a partnership that operates Jax Restaurant in Foley, Minnesota. One afternoon in October 2000, Nicole Moren, one of the partners, finished her shift at the restaurant at 4:00 P.M. and picked up her two-year-old son Remington from day care. About 5:30 P.M., Moren returned to the restaurant with Remington after Amy Benedetti, the other partner and Moren's sister, asked for help. Moren's husband, Martin, offered to pick up Remington in twenty minutes. Because Moren did not want Remington running around the restaurant, she brought him into the kitchen with her, set him on top of the counter, and began rolling out pizza dough using a dough-pressing machine. While she was making pizzas, Remington reached his hand into the dough press. His hand was crushed, causing permanent injuries. Through his father, Remington filed a suit in a Minnesota state court against the partnership, alleging negligence. The partnership filed a complaint against Moren, arguing that it was entitled to indemnity (compensation or reimbursement) from Moren for her negligence. The court issued a summary judgment in favor of Moren on the complaint. The partnership appealed this judgment to a state intermediate appellate court.*

IN THE LANGUAGE OF THE COURT

CRIPPEN, Judge

* * * *

Under Minnesota's Uniform Partnership Act [the most recent version of the UPA], a partnership is an entity distinct from its partners, and as such, a partnership may sue and be sued in the name of the partnership. [Under the UPA] *"[a] partnership is liable for loss or injury caused to a person * * * as a result of a wrongful act or omission, or other actionable conduct, of a partner acting in the ordinary course of business of the partnership or with authority of the partnership."* Accordingly, a "partnership shall * * * indemnify [reimburse] a partner for liabilities incurred by the partner in the ordinary course of the business of the partnership * * * ." Stated conversely, an "act of a partner which is not apparently for carrying on in the ordinary course the partnership business or business of the kind carried on by the partnership binds the partnership only if the act was authorized by the other partners." Thus, under the plain language of the UPA, *a partner has a right to indemnity from the partnership, but the partnership's claim of indemnity from a partner is not authorized or required.* [Emphasis added.]

The [lower] court correctly concluded that Nicole Moren's conduct was in the ordinary course of business of the partnership and, as a result, indemnity by the partner to the partnership was inappropriate. It is undisputed that one of the cooks scheduled to work that evening did not come in, and that Moren's partner asked her to help in the kitchen. It also is undisputed that Moren was making pizzas for the partnership when her son was injured. Because her conduct at the time of the injury was in the ordinary course of business of the partnership, under the UPA, her conduct bound the partnership and it owes indemnity to her for her negligence.

* * * *

Appellant * * * claims that because Nicole Moren's action of bringing Remington into the kitchen was partly motivated by personal reasons, her conduct was outside the ordinary course of business. Because it has not been previously addressed, there is no Minnesota authority regarding this issue. * * * [W]e conclude that the conduct of Nicole Moren was no less in the ordinary course of business because it also served personal purposes. It is undisputed that Moren was acting for the benefit of the partnership by making pizzas when her son was injured, and even though she was simultaneously acting in her role as a mother, her conduct remained in the ordinary course of the partnership business.

DECISION AND REMEDY *The state intermediate appellate court affirmed the lower court's judgment. "Minnesota law requires a partnership to indemnify its partners for the result of their negligence." The appellate court also reasoned that "the conduct of a partner may be partly moti-*

---

a. In the "Published" section, click on "M–O." On that page, scroll to the name of the case and click on the docket number to access the opinion. The Minnesota State Law Library maintains this Web site.

CASE 36.2 | Continued *vated by personal reasons and still occur in the ordinary course of business of the partnership." Thus "[l]iability for Nicole Moren's negligence rested with the partnership, even if the partner's conduct partly served her personal interests."*

WHAT IF THE FACTS WERE DIFFERENT? *Suppose that Moren's predominant motive in bringing her son to the restaurant had been to benefit herself because she wanted to feed him free pizza. Would the result have been different? Why or why not?*

—Liability of Incoming Partners. A partner newly admitted to an existing partnership normally has limited liability for whatever debts and obligations the partnership incurred prior to the new partner's admission. The new partner's liability can be satisfied only from partnership assets [UPA 306(b)]. This means that the new partner usually has no personal liability for these debts and obligations, but any capital contribution that he or she made to the partnership is subject to these debts.

SECTION 4 | Partnership Dissociation

Dissociation occurs when a partner ceases to be associated in the carrying on of the partnership business. Dissociation normally entitles the partner to have his or her interest purchased by the partnership, and terminates his or her authority to act for the partnership and to participate with the partners in running the business. Otherwise, the partnership continues to do business without the dissociating partner.[9]

EVENTS CAUSING DISSOCIATION

Under UPA 601, a partner can be dissociated from a partnership in any of the following ways.

1. By voluntarily giving notice of "express will to withdraw."

2. By the occurrence of an event agreed to in the partnership agreement.

3. By a unanimous vote of the other partners under certain circumstances, such as when a partner transfers substantially all of his or her interest in the partnership, or when it becomes unlawful to carry on partnership business with that partner.

4. By order of a court or arbitrator if the partner has engaged in wrongful conduct that affects the partnership business, breached the partnership agreement or violated a duty owed to the partnership or the other partners, or engaged in conduct that makes it "not reasonably practicable to carry on the business in partnership with the partner" [UPA 601(5)].

5. By declaring bankruptcy, assigning his or her interest in the partnership for the benefit of creditors, becoming physically or mentally incapacitated, or by death. Note that although the bankruptcy or death of a partner represents that partner's "dissociation" from the partnership, it is not an *automatic* ground for the partnership's dissolution (dissolution will be discussed shortly).

WRONGFUL DISSOCIATION

A partner has the power to dissociate from a partnership at any time, but a partner's dissociation can be wrongful in a few circumstances [UPA 602]. For example, if dissociation is in breach of a partnership agreement, it is wrongful. Also, in the case of a partnership for a definite term or a particular undertaking, dissociation that occurs before the expiration of the term or the completion of the undertaking can be wrongful if the partner withdraws by express will, is expelled by a court or an arbitrator, or declares bankruptcy.

A partner who wrongfully dissociates is liable to the partnership and to the other partners for damages caused by the dissociation. This liability is in addition to any other obligation of the partner to the partnership or to the other partners. For example, a dissociating partner would be liable for any damage caused by a breach of a partnership agreement. The partner would also be liable to the partnership for costs incurred to replace the partner's expertise or obtain new financing.

EFFECTS OF DISSOCIATION

Dissociation terminates some of the rights of the dissociated partner, creates a mandatory duty for the

---

9. Under the previous version of the UPA, when a partner withdrew from a partnership, the partnership was considered dissolved, its business had to be wound up, and the proceeds had to be distributed to creditors and among partners. The new UPA provisions dramatically change the law governing partnership breakups and dissolution by no longer requiring that the partnership end if one partner dissociates.

partnership, and alters the liability of both parties to third parties.

RIGHTS AND DUTIES On a partner's dissociation, his or her right to participate in the management and conduct of the partnership business terminates [UPA 603]. The partner's duty of loyalty also ends. A partner's other fiduciary duties, including the duty of care, continue only with respect to events that occurred before dissociation, unless the partner participates in winding up the partnership's business (discussed later in this chapter). Thus, a partner who leaves an accounting firm, for example, may immediately compete with the firm for new clients, but must exercise care in completing ongoing client transactions and must account to the firm for any fees received from the old clients on account of those transactions.

After a partner's dissociation, his or her interest in the partnership must be purchased according to the rules in UPA 701. The **buyout price** is based on the amount that would have been distributed to the partner if the partnership were wound up on the date of dissociation. Offset against the price are amounts owed by the partner to the partnership, including damages for wrongful dissociation.

LIABILITY TO THIRD PARTIES For two years after a partner dissociates from a continuing partnership, the partnership may be bound by the acts of the dissociated partner based on apparent authority [UPA 702]. In other words, the partnership may be liable to a third party with whom a dissociated partner enters into a transaction if the third party reasonably believed that the dissociated partner was still a partner. Similarly, a dissociated partner may be liable for partnership obligations entered into during a two-year period following dissociation [UPA 703].

To avoid this possible liability, a partnership should notify its creditors, and customers or clients, of a partner's dissociation and file a statement of dissociation in the appropriate state office to limit the partner's authority to ninety days after the filing [UPA 704]. A dissociated partner should also file a statement of dissociation with the state to limit his or her potential liability to ninety days.

SECTION 5 | Partnership Termination

Some changes in the relations of the partners that demonstrate unwillingness or inability to carry on the partnership business dissolve the partnership, resulting

in termination [UPA 801]. If any partner wishes to continue the business, she or he is free to reorganize into a new partnership with the remaining partners.

The termination of a partnership has two stages—*dissolution* and *winding up*. Both stages must take place before termination is complete. **Dissolution** occurs when any partner (or partners) initiates proceedings to terminate the partnership or when an event specified in the partnership agreement occurs. **Winding up** is the actual process of collecting and distributing the partnership's assets. When winding up is complete, the partnership's *legal* existence is terminated.

DISSOLUTION

Dissolution of a partnership can be brought about by acts of the partners, by operation of law, or by judicial decree.

DISSOLUTION BY ACTS OF THE PARTNERS Dissolution of a partnership may come about through the acts of the partners in several ways. First, any partnership can be dissolved by the partners' agreement. For example, when a partnership agreement states a fixed term or a particular business objective to be accomplished, the passing of the date or the accomplishment of the objective dissolves the partnership.

Second, because a partnership at will is a voluntary association, a partner has the power to dissociate himself or herself from the partnership at any time and perhaps dissolve the partnership by giving notice of "express will to withdraw" [UPA 801(1)]. If, after dissolution, none of the partners, including the withdrawing partner, wants the partnership wound up, the remaining partners may continue the business [UPA 802(b)].[10]

Third, a partnership for a definite term or a particular undertaking can be dissolved if, within ninety days of a partner's dissociation caused by bankruptcy, incapacity, or death, at least half of the remaining partners decide in favor of dissolution [UPA 801(2)].

DISSOLUTION BY OPERATION OF LAW Any event that makes it unlawful for the partnership to continue its business will result in dissolution [UPA 801(4)]. Note, however, that if the illegality of the partnership business is a cause for dissolution, within ninety days,

---

10. Any change in a partnership caused by the withdrawal of a partner or the admission of a new partner resulted in dissolution under the previous version of the UPA. If the remaining or new partners continued the firm's business, a new partnership arose.

the partners can decide to change the nature of their business and continue in the partnership.[11]

DISSOLUTION BY JUDICIAL DECREE A partner can request a court to dissolve a partnership by judicial decree. A court may dissolve the partnership if it determines that the partnership can only be operated at a loss, if one partner has perpetrated a fraud on the other partners, or when dissension among the partners undermines the ability of the partnership to conduct business [UPA 801(5)].

NOTICE OF DISSOLUTION A partner must communicate her or his intent to dissolve or to withdraw from the firm to each of the other partners. A partner can express this notice of intent by either words (*actual notice*) or actions (*constructive notice*). All partners will share liability for the acts of any partner who continues to conduct business for the firm without knowledge that the partnership has been dissolved.

For example, suppose that Alzor, Jennifer, and Carla have a partnership. Alzor tells Jennifer of her intent to withdraw. Before Carla learns of Alzor's intentions, she enters into a contract with a third party. The contract is equally binding on Alzor, Jennifer, and Carla. Unless the other partners have notice, the withdrawing partner will continue to be bound as a partner to all contracts created for the firm.

To avoid liability for obligations a partner incurs after dissolution of a partnership, the firm must give notice to all affected third parties [UPA 804(2)]. After dissolution, one of the partners can file a statement of dissolution with the appropriate state office, declaring that the partnership has dissolved and is winding up its business. Ninety days after this statement is filed, creditors and other nonpartners are deemed to have notice of the dissolution [UPA 805].[12]

WINDING UP AND DISTRIBUTION OF ASSETS

Once dissolution has occurred and the partners have been notified, they cannot create new obligations on behalf of the partnership. Their only authority is to complete transactions begun but not finished at the time of dissolution and to wind up the business of the partnership [UPA 803, 804(1)]. Winding up includes collecting and preserving partnership assets, discharging liabilities (paying debts), and accounting to each partner for the value of his or her interest in the partnership.

Both creditors of the partnership and creditors of the individual partners can make claims on the partnership's assets. In general, partnership creditors share proportionately with the partners' individual creditors in the assets of the partners' estates, which include their interests in the partnership. A partnership's assets are distributed according to the following priorities [UPA 807]:

1. Payment of debts, including those owed to partner and nonpartner creditors.
2. Return of capital contributions and distribution of profits to partners.[13]

If the partnership's liabilities are greater than its assets, the partners bear the losses—in the absence of a contrary agreement—in the same proportion in which they shared the profits (rather than, for example, in proportion to their contributions to the partnership's capital). Partners continue in their fiduciary relationship until the winding-up process is completed.

PARTNERSHIP BUY-SELL AGREEMENTS

Usually, when people enter into partnerships, they are getting along with one another. To prepare for the possibility that the situation might change and they may become unable to work together amicably, the partners should make express arrangements during the formation of the partnership to provide for its smooth dissolution. A **buy-sell agreement,** sometimes called simply a *buyout agreement*, provides for one or more partners to buy out the other or others, should the situation warrant. Agreeing beforehand on who buys what, under what circumstances, and, if possible, at what price may eliminate costly negotiations or litigation later. Alternatively, the agreement may specify that one or more partners will determine the value of the interest being sold and that the other or others will decide whether to buy or sell.

Under UPA 701(a), if a partner's dissociation does not result in a dissolution of the partnership, a buyout of the partner's interest is mandatory. The UPA

---

11. A partner's death or bankruptcy, or an event that made it illegal for the partner to carry on, also dissolved the partnership by operation of law under the previous version of the UPA.

12. Different types of notice were necessary under the previous version of the UPA, depending on the relationship of an outside party to the firm and the circumstances of dissolution, For example, partnership creditors had to receive notice personally unless dissolution resulted from an operation of law, in which case no notice was required.

13. Under the previous version of the UPA, creditors of the partnership had priority over creditors of the individual partners. Also, in distributing partnership assets, third party creditors were paid before partner creditors, and capital contributions were returned before profits.

contains an extensive set of buyout rules. Basically, a withdrawing partner receives the same amount through a buyout that he or she would receive if the business were winding up [UPA 701(b)].

SECTION 6 | Limited Liability Partnerships

The **limited liability partnership (LLP)** is a hybrid form of business designed mostly for professionals who normally do business as partners in a partnership. The major advantage of the LLP is that it allows a partnership to continue as a pass-through entity for tax purposes but limits the personal liability of the partners.

The first state to enact an LLP statute was Texas, in 1991. Other states quickly followed suit, and by 1997, virtually all of the states had enacted LLP statutes. LLPs must be formed and operated in compliance with state statutes, which may include provisions of the UPA. The appropriate form must be filed with a central state agency, usually the secretary of state's office, and the business's name must include either "Limited Liability Partnership" or "LLP" [UPA 1001, 1002]. In addition, LLPs must file annual reports with the state to remain qualified as an LLP in that state [UPA 1003]. In most states, it is relatively easy to convert a traditional partnership into an LLP because the firm's basic organizational structure remains the same. Additionally, all of the statutory and common law rules governing partnerships still apply (apart from those modified by the LLP statute). Normally, LLP statutes are simply amendments to a state's already existing partnership law.

The LLP is especially attractive for two categories of enterprises: professional services and family businesses. Professional service firms include law firms and accounting firms. *Family limited liability partnerships* (discussed later in this chapter) are basically business organizations in which the majority of the partners are related to each other.

LIABILITY IN AN LLP

Many professionals, such as attorneys and accountants, work together using the partnership business form. As stated previously in this chapter, a major disadvantage of the general partnership is the unlimited personal liability of its owner-partners. Partners are also subject to joint and several (individual) liability for partnership obligations. For example, suppose that a group of accountants is operating as a general part-

nership. A client sues one of the accountants for malpractice and wins a large judgment, and the firm's malpractice insurance is insufficient to cover the obligation. When the accountant's personal assets are exhausted, the personal assets of the other, innocent partners can be used to satisfy the judgment.

The LLP allows professionals to avoid personal liability for the malpractice of other partners. Although LLP statutes vary from state to state, generally each state statute limits the liability of partners in some way. For example, Delaware law protects each innocent partner from the "debts and obligations of the partnership arising from negligence, wrongful acts, or misconduct." In North Carolina, Texas, and Washington, D.C., the statutes protect innocent partners from obligations arising from "errors, omissions, negligence, incompetence, or malfeasance." The UPA more broadly exempts partners from personal liability for any partnership obligation, "whether arising in contract, tort, or otherwise" [UPA 306(c)]. Although the language of these statutes may seem to apply specifically to attorneys, virtually any group of professionals can use the LLP.

Questions remain, however, concerning the exact limits of this exemption from liability. One issue is whether limits on liability apply outside the state in which the LLP was formed. Another inquiry involves whether liability should be imposed to some extent on a negligent partner's supervising partner.

LIABILITY OUTSIDE THE STATE OF FORMATION Some states require that when an LLP formed in one state wants to do business in another state, the LLP must first register in the other state—for example, by filing a statement of foreign qualification [UPA 1102]. Because state LLP statutes are not uniform, a question arises in this situation. If the LLP statutes in the two states provide different liability protection, which law applies? Most states apply the law of the state in which the LLP was formed, even when the firm does business in another state, which is also the rule under UPA 1101.

SUPERVISING PARTNER'S LIABILITY A partner who commits a wrongful act, such as negligence, is liable for the results of the act. Also liable is the partner who supervises the party who commits a wrongful act. This is generally true for all types of partners and partnerships, including LLPs.

When the partners are members of an LLP and more than one member is negligent, there is a question as to how liability is to be shared. Is each partner jointly and severally liable for the entire result, as a general partner would be in most states? Some states provide for proportionate liability—that is, for separate determinations of the negligence of the partners.[14] The American Institute of Certified Public Accountants supports the enactment of proportionate liability statutes.[15]

For example, suppose that accountants Don and Jane are partners in an LLP, with Don supervising Jane. Jane negligently fails to file tax returns for their client, Centaur Tools. Centaur files a suit against Don and Jane. In a state that does not allow for proportionate liability, Don can be held liable for the entire loss. Under a proportionate liability statute, Don will be liable for no more than his portion of the responsibility for the missed tax deadline. (Even if Jane settles the case quickly, Don will still be liable for his portion.)

FAMILY LIMITED LIABILITY PARTNERSHIPS

A **family limited liability partnership (FLLP)** is a limited liability partnership in which the majority of the partners are persons related to each other, essentially as spouses, parents, grandparents, siblings, cousins, nephews, or nieces. A person acting in a fiduciary capacity for persons so related can also be a partner. All of the partners must be natural persons or persons acting in a fiduciary capacity for the benefit of natural persons.

Probably the most significant use of the FLLP form of business organization is in agriculture. Family-owned farms sometimes find this form to their benefit. The FLLP offers the same advantages as other LLPs with certain additional advantages, such as, in Iowa, an exemption from real estate transfer taxes when partnership real estate is transferred among partners.[16]

SECTION 7 | Limited Partnerships

We now look at a business organizational form that limits the liability of *some* of its owners—the **limited partnership.** Limited partnerships originated in medieval Europe and have been existence in the United States since the early 1800s. In many ways, limited partnerships are like the general partnerships discussed at the beginning of this chapter, but they differ from general partnerships in several ways. Because of this, they are sometimes referred to as *special partnerships*.

A limited partnership consists of at least one **general partner** and one or more **limited partners.** A general partner assumes management responsibility for the partnership and thus has full responsibility for the partnership and for all its debts. A limited partner contributes cash or other property and owns an interest in the firm but does not undertake any management responsibilities and is not personally liable for partnership debts beyond the amount of his or her investment. A limited partner can forfeit limited liability by taking part in the management of the business. A comparison of the characteristics of general partnerships and limited partnerships appears in Exhibit 36–2 on page 746.[17]

Until 1976, the law governing limited partnerships in all states except Louisiana was the Uniform Limited Partnership Act (ULPA). Since 1976, most states and the District of Columbia have adopted the revised version of the ULPA, known as the Revised Uniform Limited Partnership Act (RULPA). Because the RULPA is the dominant law governing limited partnerships in the United States, we will refer to the RULPA in the following discussion.

FORMATION OF A LIMITED PARTNERSHIP

In contrast to the informal, private, and voluntary agreement that usually suffices for a general partnership, the formation of a limited partnership is a public and formal proceeding that must follow statutory requirements.[18] In this regard, a limited partnership resembles a corporation more than it does a general partnership. A limited partnership must have at least one general partner and one limited partner, as mentioned previously. Additionally, the partners must sign a **certificate of limited partnership,** which requires information similar to that found in a corporate charter (see Chapter 38). The certificate must be filed with the designated state official—under the RULPA, the secretary of state. The certificate is usually open to public inspection.

---

14. See, for example, Colorado Revised Statutes Annotated Section 13-21-111.5(1) and Utah Code Annotated Section 78-27-39.
15. Public Oversight Board of the SEC Practice Section, AICPA, *In the Public Interest: Issues Confronting the Accounting Profession* (New York: AICPA, March 5, 1993), Recommendation I-1.
16. Iowa Statutes Section 428A.2.

17. Under the UPA, a general partnership can be converted into a limited partnership and vice versa [UPA 902, 903]. The UPA also provides for the merger of a general partnership with one or more general or limited partnerships [UPA 905].
18. For a case illustrating the importance of complying with these statutory requirements, see *Miller v. Department of Revenue, State of Oregon,* 327 Or. 129, 958 P.2d 833 (1998).

EXHIBIT 36-2 A Comparison of General Partnerships and Limited Partnerships

CHARACTERISTIC	GENERAL PARTNERSHIP (UPA)	LIMITED PARTNERSHIP (RULPA)
Creation	By agreement of two or more persons to carry on a business as co-owners for profit.	By agreement of two or more persons to carry on a business as co-owners for profit. Must include one or more general partners and one or more limited partners. Filing of a certificate with the secretary of state is required.
Sharing of Profits and Losses	By agreement; or, in the absence of agreement, profits are shared equally by the partners, and losses are shared in the same ratio as profits.	Profits are shared as required in the certificate agreement, and losses are shared likewise, up to the amount of the limited partners' capital contributions. In the absence of a provision in the certificate agreement, profits and losses are shared on the basis of percentages of capital contributions.
Liability	Unlimited personal liability of all partners.	Unlimited personal liability of all general partners; limited partners liable only to the extent of their capital contributions.
Capital Contribution	No minimum or mandatory amount; set by agreement.	Set by agreement.
Management	By agreement; or, in the absence of agreement, all partners have an equal voice.	General partners by agreement, or else each has an equal voice. Limited partners have no voice or else are subject to liability as general partners (but only if a third party has reason to believe that the limited partner is a general partner). A limited partner may act as an agent or employee of the partnership and vote on amending the certificate or on the sale or dissolution of the partnership.
Duration	Terminated by agreement of the partners, but (in many states) can continue to do business even when a partner dissociates from the partnership.	By agreement in the certificate or by retirement, death, or mental incompetence of a general partner in the absence of the right of the other general partners to continue the partnership. Death of a limited partner, unless he or she is the only remaining limited partner, does not terminate the partnership.
Distribution of Assets on Liquidation— Order of Priorities	1. Payment of debts, including those owed to partner and nonpartner creditors. 2. Return of capital contributions and distribution of profit to partners.	1. Outside creditors and partner creditors. 2. Partners and former partners entitled to distributions of partnership assets. 3. Unless otherwise agreed, return of capital contributions and distribution of profit to partners.

RIGHTS AND LIABILITIES OF PARTNERS

General partners, unlike limited partners, are personally liable to the partnership's creditors; thus, at least one general partner is necessary in a limited partnership so that someone has personal liability. This policy can be circumvented in states that allow a corporation to be the general partner in a partnership.

Because the corporation has limited liability by virtue of corporation statutes, if a corporation is the general partner, no one in the limited partnership has personal liability.

RIGHTS OF LIMITED PARTNERS Subject to the limitations that will be discussed shortly, limited partners have essentially the same rights as general partners, including the right of access to partnership books and the right to other information regarding partnership business. On dissolution of the partnership, limited partners are entitled to a return of their contributions in accordance with the partnership certificate [RULPA 201(a)(10)]. They can also assign their interests subject to the certificate [RULPA 702, 704].

The RULPA provides that a limited partner has the right to sue an outside party on behalf of the firm if the general partners with authority to do so have refused to file suit [RULPA 1001].[19] In addition, investor protection legislation, such as securities laws (discussed in Chapter 41), may give some protection to limited partners.

LIABILITIES OF LIMITED PARTNERS In contrast to the personal liability of general partners, the liability of a limited partner is limited to the capital that she or he contributes or agrees to contribute to the partnership [RULPA 502].

A limited partnership is formed by good faith compliance with the requirements for signing and filing the certificate, even if it is incomplete or defective. When a limited partner discovers a defect in the formation of the limited partnership, he or she can avoid future liability by causing an appropriate amendment or certificate to be filed or by renouncing an interest in the profits of the partnership [RULPA 304]. If the lim-

ited partner takes neither of these actions on discovery of the defect, however, the partner can be held personally liable by the firm's creditors. Liability for false statements in a partnership certificate runs in favor of persons relying on the false statements and against partners who know of the falsity but still sign the certificate [RULPA 207].

LIMITED PARTNERS AND MANAGEMENT Limited partners enjoy limited liability so long as they do not participate in management [RULPA 303]. A limited partner who participates in management will be just as liable as a general partner to any creditor who transacts business with the limited partnership and believes, based on the limited partner's conduct, that the limited partner is a general partner [RULPA 303]. How much actual review and advisement a limited partner can engage in before being exposed to liability is an unsettled question.[20] A limited partner who knowingly permits his or her name to be used in the name of the limited partnership is liable to creditors who extend credit to the limited partnership without knowledge that the limited partner is not a general partner [RULPA 102, 303(d)].

Although limited partners cannot participate in management, this does not mean that the general partners are totally free of restrictions in running the business. The general partners in a limited partnership have fiduciary obligations to the partnership and to the limited partners, as the following case illustrates.

---

19. For a case from a jurisdiction that does *not* follow the RULPA in this respect, see *Energy Investors Fund, L.P. v. Metric Constructors, Inc.*, 351 N.C. 331, 525 S.E.2d 441 (2000).

20. The question is unsettled partly because state laws differ on this issue. Factors to be considered under the RULPA are listed in RULPA 303(b), (c).

CASE 36.3 — Smith v. Fairfax Realty, Inc.

Supreme Court
of Utah, 2003.
82 P.3d 1064.

PARRISH, Justice:

* * * *

* * * In 1984, Price [Development Company] purchased a thirty-three-acre parcel of property in Clovis, New Mexico, from [Armand and Virginia Smith]. As part of the transaction, the Smiths received a 15% limited partnership interest in each of two partnerships formed to build and operate [the North Plains Mall] on the property. Price became the general partner * * * .

* * * *

In July 1993, Price informed the Smiths that * * * [it] wanted to include the North Plains Mall in [a real estate investment trust (REIT)] and told the Smiths that if the mall were included, the Smiths would have three distinct options for handling their 15% interest in the mall.

* * * Then, without further communication with the Smiths on the matter, Price proceeded to * * * transfer the mall property into the REIT, despite provisions in the partnership agreements that required the Smiths' consent for such transactions. * * *

CONTINUED

CASE 36.3 Continued

In the ensuing months, the Smiths repeatedly requested information regarding the status of their interests in the mall, but Price failed to disclose its unilateral decision to contribute the mall property to the REIT. Instead, Price fielded the Smiths' questions regarding the three options previously given to the Smiths, leading them to believe the options were still open, even though Price knew that its unilateral action had left the Smiths with no options. When the Smiths inquired as to the possible value of their holdings should the mall be included in the REIT, Price sent various conflicting estimates * * * .

* * * *

The Smiths brought suit [in a Utah state court] against Price * * * .

* * * [T]he jury reached a verdict in favor of the Smiths, finding that Price had breached * * * its fiduciary duty to the Smiths * * * . The jury awarded the Smiths $410,000 in compensatory damages, * * * $690,000 * * * in prejudgment interest * * * [and] punitive damages in the sum of $5,500,000 against Price [now doing business as Fairfax Realty, Inc. Price appealed to the Utah Supreme Court].

* * * *

* * * [We] analyze Price's misconduct in terms of maliciousness, reprehensibility, and wrongfulness. * * * [C]ertain wrongdoings are more egregious and blameworthy than others so as to justify larger awards. Deliberate false statements, acts of affirmative misconduct, and concealment of evidence of improper motive support more substantial awards, as do acts involving trickery and deceit. * * * *[E]conomic injury, especially when done intentionally through affirmative acts of misconduct, or when the target is financially vulnerable, can warrant a substantial penalty.* [Emphasis added.]

* * * [The trial] court detailed Price's prolonged, deliberate failure to inform the Smiths of the execution of the [transfer] agreements and the resulting unavailability of the three options that Price originally gave the Smiths regarding how their interests could be handled in the REIT transaction. The court also detailed Price's conflicting and "intentionally misleading" calculations of the value of the Smiths' interests in the mall property in the REIT. The calculations given to the Smiths differed significantly from the company's own calculations, which the company did not reveal until six years of litigation had ensued. Additionally, the court detailed Price's acts of financial misconduct, including payment of excessive fees to itself as general partner, commingling funds from different Price-owned properties, and accruing interest to itself on its own capital contributions while denying the Smiths interest on their contributions.

We agree with the trial court that Price's actions amount to affirmative misconduct showing deliberate misrepresentation and disregard of the rights of the Smiths. Price's actions accordingly support a substantial award * * * .

* * * *

* * * Throughout the creation of the REIT, Price was aware of its fiduciary obligations to the Smiths and of the consent clause written into the partnership agreements. Price consciously disregarded its obligations.

* * * *

With respect to Price's failure to disclose its dealings with the partnership property to the Smiths, Price asserts without elaboration that it avoided responding to the Smiths' inquiries on the advice of legal counsel. * * * [S]ubstantial evidence was presented at trial that Price did not want the Smiths to interfere with the REIT's formation by filing an adverse claim or a lawsuit * * * . Thus, Price's self-interested actions, made in the face of known fiduciary obligations, support a substantial * * * award.

* * * *

* * * *The fiduciary relationship of a general partner to a limited partner is one of loyalty, trust, disclosure, and confidence, calling for the utmost good faith and permitting no unfair benefits to the general partner as against the limited partner.* * * * [Emphasis added.]

Price failed as a fiduciary to deal fairly with the Smiths and their partnership interests. * * * The Smiths rightly expected a greater degree of candor and loyalty than they received. * * *

* * * *

We affirm * * * the jury's award * * * . We remand to the [lower] court for a determination of the proper amount of the [interest on the award and of the costs and attorneys' fees required by the partnership agreements].

CASE 36.3 | Continued

1. Why does the law impose fiduciary obligations on general partners?
2. What is the motivation for a general partner to breach its fiduciary obligations to the limited partners?

DISSOLUTION

A limited partnership is dissolved in much the same way as an ordinary partnership. The retirement, death, or mental incompetence of a general partner can dissolve the partnership, but not if the business can be continued by one or more of the other general partners in accordance with their certificate or by the consent of all of the members [RULPA 801]. The death or assignment of interest of a limited partner does not dissolve the limited partnership [RULPA 702, 704, 705]. A limited partnership can be dissolved by court decree [RULPA 802].

Bankruptcy or the withdrawal of a general partner dissolves a limited partnership. Bankruptcy of a limited partner, however, does not dissolve the partnership unless it causes the bankruptcy of the limited partnership. The retirement of a general partner causes a dissolution unless the members consent to a continuation by the remaining general partners or unless this contingency is provided for in the certificate.

On dissolution, creditors' rights, including those of partners who are creditors, take first priority. After that, partners and former partners receive unpaid distributions of partnership assets and, except as otherwise agreed, amounts representing returns on their contributions and amounts proportionate to their shares of the distributions [RULPA 804].

LIMITED LIABILITY LIMITED PARTNERSHIPS

A **limited liability limited partnership (LLLP)** is a type of limited partnership. An LLLP differs from a limited partnership in that a general partner in an LLLP has the same liability as a limited partner; that is, the liability of all partners is limited to the amount of their investments in the firm.

A few states provide expressly for LLLPs.[21] In states that do not provide for LLLPs but do allow for limited partnerships and limited liability partnerships, a limited partnership should probably still be able to register with the state as an LLLP.

---

21. See, for example, Colorado Revised Statutes Annotated Section 7-62-109. Other states that provide expressly for limited liability limited partnerships include Delaware, Florida, Missouri, Pennsylvania, Texas, and Virginia.

REVIEWING PARTNERSHIPS AND LIMITED LIABILITY PARTNERSHIPS

Grace Tarnavsky and her sons, Manny and Jason, bought a ranch known as the Cowboy Palace in March 2002, and the three verbally agreed to share the business for five years. Grace contributed 50 percent of the investment and each son contributed 25 percent. Manny agreed to handle the livestock and Jason agreed to handle the bookkeeping. The Tarnavskys took out joint loans and opened a joint bank account into which they deposited the ranch's proceeds and from which they made payments toward property, cattle, equipment, and supplies. In September 2004, Manny severely injured his back while baling hay and became permanently unable to handle livestock. Manny therefore hired additional laborers to tend the livestock, causing the Cowboy Palace to incur significant debt. In September 2005, Al's Feed Barn filed a lawsuit against Jason to collect $12,400 in unpaid debts. Using the information presented in the chapter, answer the following questions.

1. Was the relationship among Grace and her sons a partnership for a term or a partnership at will?
2. Under the current Uniform Partnership Act (UPA), how would the profits and losses from the Cowboy Palace be shared?

(Continued)

REVIEWING PARTNERSHIPS AND LIMITED LIABILITY PARTNERSHIPS *(continued)*

3. Did Manny have the authority to hire additional laborers to work at the ranch after his injury? Discuss the scope of his powers as a partner.

4. Under the current UPA, can Al's Feed Barn bring an action against Jason individually for the Cowboy Palace's debt? Why or why not? How is joint liability different from joint and several liability in this regard?

5. Suppose that after his back injury, Manny sent his mother and brother a notice indicating his intent to withdraw from the partnership. Does that mean he could not be held liable for the debt to Al's Feed Barn? Why or why not? For how long is a partnership liable to third parties for the acts of a dissociated partner under the UPA?

TERMS AND CONCEPTS TO REVIEW

articles of partnership 734

buyout price 742

buy-sell agreement 743

certificate of limited partnership 745

charging order 737

confession of judgment 736

dissociation 741

dissolution 742

family limited liability partnership (FLLP) 745

general partner 745

information return 734

joint and several liability 739

joint liability 739

limited liability limited partnership (LLLP) 749

limited liability partnership (LLP) 744

limited partner 745

limited partnership 745

partnership 731

partnership by estoppel 735

winding up 742

QUESTIONS AND CASE PROBLEMS

36–1. Daniel is the owner of a chain of shoe stores. He hires Rubya to be the manager of a new store, which is to open in Grand Rapids, Michigan. Daniel, by written contract, agrees to pay Rubya a monthly salary and 20 percent of the profits. Without Daniel's knowledge, Rubya represents himself to Classen as Daniel's partner, showing Classen the agreement to share profits. Classen extends credit to Rubya. Rubya defaults. Discuss whether Classen can hold Daniel liable as a partner.

36–2. 🝀 QUESTION WITH SAMPLE ANSWER

Dorinda, Luis, and Elizabeth form a limited partnership. Dorinda is a general partner, and Luis and Elizabeth are limited partners. Consider each of the separate events below, and discuss fully which event(s) constitute(s) a dissolution of the limited partnership.

(a) Luis assigns his partnership interest to Ashley.

(b) Elizabeth is petitioned into involuntary bankruptcy.

(c) Dorinda dies.

For a sample answer to this question, go to Appendix I at the end of this text.

36–3. Meyer, Knapp, and Cavanna establish a partnership to operate a window-washing service. Meyer contributes $10,000 to the partnership, and Knapp and Cavanna contribute $1,000 each. The partnership agreement is silent as to how profits and losses will be shared. One month after the partnership begins operation, Knapp and Cavanna vote, over Meyer's objection, to purchase another truck for the firm. Meyer believes that because he contributed $10,000, the partnership cannot make any major commitment to purchase over his objection. In addition, Meyer claims that in the absence of any provision in the agreement, profits must be divided in the same ratio as capital contributions. Discuss Meyer's contentions.

36-4. LIMITED LIABILITY PARTNERSHIPS. Mudge Rose Guthrie Alexander & Ferdon, a law firm, was organized as a general partnership but converted into a limited liability partnership (LLP). Mudge's principal place of business was New York, where it was organized, but some of its members were citizens of Maryland. The firm filed a suit in a federal district court to recover unpaid legal fees from Robert Pickett and other citizens of Maryland. The defendants filed a motion to dismiss on the ground that there was not complete diversity of citizenship, because some of the LLP members were Maryland citizens as well. Mudge argued that an LLP was like a corporation, and therefore the citizenship of the firm's members was irrelevant. How should the court rule? Explain. [*Mudge Rose Guthrie Alexander & Ferdon v. Pickett*, 11 F.Supp.2d 449 (S.D.N.Y. 1998)]

36-5. LIABILITY OF PARTNERS. Frank Kolk was the manager of Triples American Grill, a sports bar and restaurant. Kolk and John Baines opened bank accounts in the name of the bar, each signing the account signature cards as "owner." Baines was often at the bar and had free access to its office. Baines told others that he was "an owner" and "a partner." Kolk told Steve Mager, the president of Cheesecake Factory, Inc., that Baines was a member of a partnership that owned Triples. On this basis, Cheesecake delivered its goods to Triples on credit. In fact, the bar was owned by a corporation. When the unpaid account totaled more than $20,000, Cheesecake filed a suit in a New Mexico state court against Baines to collect. On what basis might Baines be liable to Cheesecake? What does Cheesecake have to show to win its case? [*Cheesecake Factory, Inc. v. Baines*, 964 P.2d 183 (N.M.App. 1998)]

36-6. INDICATIONS OF PARTNERSHIP. In August 1998, Jea Yu contacted Cameron Eppler, president of Design88, Ltd., to discuss developing a Web site that would cater to investors and provide services to its members for a fee. Yu and Patrick Connelly invited Eppler and Ha Tran, another member of Design88, to a meeting to discuss the site. The parties agreed that Design88 would perform certain Web design, implementation, and maintenance functions for 10 percent of the profits from the site, which would be called "The Underground Trader." They signed a "Master Partnership Agreement," which was later amended to include Power Uptik Productions, LLC (PUP). The parties often referred to themselves as partners. From Design88's offices in Virginia, Design88 designed and hosted the site, solicited members through Internet and national print campaigns, processed member applications, provided technical support, monitored access to the site, and negotiated and formed business alliances on the site's behalf. When relations among the parties soured, PUP withdrew. Design88 filed a suit against PUP and the others. Did a partnership exist among these parties? Explain. [*Design88 Ltd. v. Power Uptik Productions, LLC*, 133 F.Supp.2d 873 (W.D.Va. 2001)]

36-7. ⚖️ **CASE PROBLEM WITH SAMPLE ANSWER**

At least six months before the 1996 Summer Olympic Games in Atlanta, Georgia, Stafford Fontenot, Steve Turner, Mike Montelaro, Joe Sokol, and Doug Brinsmade agreed to sell Cajun food at the Games and began making preparations. Calling themselves "Prairie Cajun Seafood Catering of Louisiana," on May 19 the group applied for a license with the Fulton County, Georgia, Department of Public Health–Environmental Health Services. Later, Ted Norris received for the sale of a mobile kitchen an $8,000 check drawn on the "Prairie Cajun Seafood Catering of Louisiana" account and two promissory notes, one for $12,000 and the other for $20,000. The notes, which were dated June 12, listed only Fontenot "d/b/a [doing business as] Prairie Cajun Seafood" as the maker. On July 31, Fontenot and his friends signed a partnership agreement, which listed specific percentages of profits and losses. They drove the mobile kitchen to Atlanta, but business was "disastrous." When the notes were not paid, Norris filed a suit in a Louisiana state court against Fontenot, seeking payment. What are the elements of a partnership? Was there a partnership among Fontenot and the others? Who is liable on the notes? Explain. [*Norris v. Fontenot*, 867 So.2d 179 (La.App. 3 Cir. 2004)]

To view a sample answer for this case problem, go to this book's Web site at http://wbl.westbuslaw.com, select "Chapter 36," and click on "Case Problem with Sample Answer."

36-8. FIDUCIARY DUTIES. Charles Chaney and Lawrence Burdett were equal partners in a partnership in Georgia known as BMW Partners. Their agreement was silent as to the effect of a partner's death on the firm. The partnership's sole asset was real property, which the firm leased in 1987 to a corporation that the partners co-owned. Under the lease, the corporation was to pay the partnership $8,000 per month, but after a few years, the corporation began paying $9,000 per month. Chaney died on April 15, 1998. Burdett wanted to continue the partnership business and offered to buy Chaney's estate's interest in it. Meanwhile, claiming that the real property's fair rental value was $4,500 (not $9,000) and that the corporation had overpaid the rent by $80,000, Burdett adjusted the rental payments to recoup this amount. Bonnie Chaney, Charles's widow and his estate's legal representative, filed a suit in a Georgia state court against Burdett, alleging in part that he had breached his fiduciary duty by adjusting the amount of the rent. Did Burdett's fiduciary duty expire on Chaney's death? Explain. [*Chaney v. Burdett*, 274 Ga. 805, 560 S.E.2d 21 (2002)]

36-9. PARTNERSHIP STATUS. Charlie Waugh owned and operated an auto parts junkyard in Georgia. Charlie's son, Mack, started working in the business part-time as a child and full-time when he left school at the age of sixteen. Mack oversaw the business's finances, depositing the profits in a bank. Charlie gave Mack a one-half interest in the business, telling him that if "something happened" to Charlie, the entire business would be his. In 1994, Charlie and his wife, Alene, transferred to Mack the land on which the junkyard was located. Two years later, however, Alene and her daughters, Gail and Jewel, falsely convinced Charlie, whose mental competence had deteriorated, that Mack had cheated him. Mack was ordered off the land. Shortly thereafter, Charlie died. Mack filed a suit in a Georgia state court against the rest of the family, asserting in part that he and Charlie had been partners and that he was entitled to Charlie's share of the business. Was the relationship between Charlie and Mack a partnership? Is Mack entitled to Charlie's "share"? Explain. [*Waugh v. Waugh*, 265 Ga.App. 799, 595 S.E.2d 647 (2004)]

36–10. ⚖️ **A QUESTION OF ETHICS**

Sandra Lerner was one of the original founders of Cisco Systems. When she sold her interest in Cisco, she received a substantial amount of money, which she invested, and she became extremely wealthy. Patricia Holmes met Lerner at Holmes's horse training facility, and they became friends. One evening in Lerner's mansion, while applying nail polish, Holmes layered a raspberry color over black to produce a new color, which Lerner liked. Later, the two created other colors with names such as "Bruise," "Smog,"

and "Oil Slick," and titled their concept "Urban Decay." Lerner and Holmes started a firm to produce and market the polishes but never discussed the sharing of profits and losses. They agreed to build the business and then sell it. Together, they did market research, experimented with colors, worked on a logo and advertising, obtained capital from an investment firm, and hired employees. Then Lerner began working to edge Holmes out of the firm. Several months later, when Holmes was told not to attend meetings of the firm's officers, she filed a suit in a California state court against Lerner, claiming, among other things, a breach of their partnership agreement. [*Holmes v. Lerner*, 74 Cal.App.4th 442, 88 Cal.Rptr.2d 130 (1 Dist. 1999)]

(a) Lerner claimed that there was no partnership agreement because there was no agreement to divide profits. Was Lerner right? Why or why not? How should the court rule?

(b) Suppose that Lerner, but not Holmes, had contributed a significant amount of personal funds to developing and marketing the new nail polish. Would this entitle Lerner to receive more of the profits? Should it? Explain.

(c) What ethical considerations are involved in the rule that partners have a fiduciary duty to be loyal to one another and to account for all partnership profits? Did Lerner violate her fiduciary duty in this case?

LAW | on the Web

For updated links to resources available on the Web, as well as a variety of other materials, visit this text's Web site at http://wbl.westbuslaw.com.

For some of the advantages and disadvantages of doing business as a partnership, go to the following page, which is part of the U.S. Small Business Administration's Web site. Then scroll down to "Partnerships."

http://www.sba.gov/starting_business/legal/forms.html

LEGAL RESEARCH EXERCISES ON THE WEB

Go to http://wbl.westbuslaw.com, the Web site that accompanies this text. Select "Chapter 36" and click on "Internet Exercises." There you will find the following Internet research exercises that you can perform to learn more about topics covered in this chapter.

Activity 36–1: **LEGAL PERSPECTIVE**
Liability of Dissociated Partners

Activity 36–2: **ECONOMIC PERSPECTIVE**
Taxation of Partnerships

Activity 36–3: **MANAGEMENT PERSPECTIVE**
Limited Partnerships and Limited Liability Partnerships

CHAPTER 37

Limited Liability Companies and Special Business Forms

In the preceding chapters, we have examined sole proprietorships, partnerships, and several forms of limited partnerships. Before we move on to discuss corporations, one of the most prevalent business forms, we pause to examine a relatively new form of business organization called the **limited liability company (LLC).** The LLC is a hybrid form that combines the limited liability aspects of the corporation and the tax advantages of a partnership. Increasingly, LLCs are becoming an organizational form of choice among businesspersons—a trend encouraged by state statutes permitting their use.

In this chapter, we begin by examining the LLC. After looking at the LLC form of business in some detail, we describe a number of business forms that can be used for special types of business ventures.

SECTION 1 | Limited Liability Companies

Limited liability companies (LLCs) are governed by state LLC statutes. These laws vary, of course, from state to state. In an attempt to create more uniformity among the states in this respect, in 1995 the National Conference of Commissioners on Uniform State Laws issued the Uniform Limited Liability Company Act (ULLCA). To date, less than one-fourth of the states have adopted the ULLCA, and thus the law governing LLCs remains far from uniform. Some provisions are common to most state statutes, however, and we base our discussion of LLCs in this section on these common elements.

EVOLUTION OF THE LLC

In 1977, Wyoming became the first state to pass legislation authorizing the creation of an LLC. Although LLCs emerged in the United States only in 1977, they have been in existence for over a century in other areas, including several European and South American nations. For example, the South American *limitada* is a form of business organization that operates more or less as a partnership but provides limited liability for the owners.

TAXATION OF THE LLC   In the United States, after Wyoming's adoption of an LLC statute, it still was not known how the Internal Revenue Service (IRS) would treat the LLC for tax purposes. In 1988, however, the IRS ruled that Wyoming LLCs would be taxed as partnerships instead of corporations, providing that certain requirements were met. Prior to this ruling, only one other state—Florida, in 1982—had authorized LLCs. The 1988 ruling encouraged other states to enact LLC statutes, and in less than a decade, all states had done so.

IRS rules that went into effect on January 1, 1997, encouraged even more widespread use of LLCs in the business world. These rules provide that any unincorporated business will automatically be taxed as a partnership unless it indicates otherwise on the tax form. The exceptions involve publicly traded companies, companies formed under a state incorporation statute, and certain foreign-owned companies. If a business chooses to be taxed as a corporation, it can indicate this preference by checking a box on the IRS form.

FOREIGN ENTITIES MAY BE LLC MEMBERS   Part of the impetus behind creating LLCs in this country is that foreign investors are allowed to become LLC members. Generally, in an era increasingly characterized by global business efforts and investments, the LLC offers U.S. firms and potential investors from other countries flexibility and opportunities that allow for limited liability and increased tax benefits.

THE NATURE OF THE LLC

LLCs share many characteristics with corporations. Like corporations, LLCs are creatures of the state. In other words, they must be formed and operated in compliance with state law. Like shareholders in a corporation, members of an LLC enjoy limited liability [ULLCA 303].[1] Also like corporations, LLCs are legal entities apart from their owners, who are called

---

1. Members of an LLC can also bring derivative actions, which you will read about in Chapter 39, on behalf of the LLC [ULLCA 101]. As with a corporate shareholder's derivative suit, any damages recovered go to the LLC, not to the members personally. See, for example, *PacLink Communications International, Inc. v. Superior Court*, 90 Cal.App.4th 958, 109 Cal.Rptr.2d 436 (2001).

members. As a legal person, the LLC can sue or be sued, enter into contracts, and hold title to property [ULLCA 201]. The terminology used to describe LLCs formed in other states or nations is also similar to that used in corporate law. For example, an LLC formed in one state but doing business in another state is referred to in the second state as a *foreign LLC*.

As you will read in Chapter 38, on occasion the courts will disregard the corporate entity ("pierce the corporate veil") and hold a shareholder personally liable for corporate obligations. At issue in the following case was whether this same principle should be extended to an LLC. Could the managing member of an LLC be held personally liable for property damage caused by the LLC?

CASE 37.1

Kaycee Land and Livestock v. Flahive

Wyoming Supreme Court, 2002.
2002 WY 73,
46 P.3d 323.

BACKGROUND AND FACTS *Roger Flahive is the managing member of Flahive Oil & Gas LLC. To exercise mineral rights beneath certain real property, Flahive Oil & Gas entered into a contract with Kaycee Land and Livestock in Johnson County, Wyoming, allowing Flahive Oil & Gas to use the surface of Kaycee's land. Later, alleging environmental contamination to its property, Kaycee filed a suit in a Wyoming state court against Flahive and his LLC. On discovering that Flahive Oil & Gas had no assets as of the time of the suit, Kaycee asked the court to disregard the LLC entity and hold Flahive personally liable for the contamination. Before issuing a judgment in the case, the court submitted this question to the Wyoming Supreme Court: "[I]s a claim to pierce the Limited Liability entity veil or disregard the Limited Liability Company entity in the same manner as a court would pierce a corporate veil or disregard a corporate shield, an available remedy" against an LLC? Unlike some states' statutes, Wyoming's LLC provisions do not address this issue.*

IN THE LANGUAGE OF THE COURT

KITE, Justice.

* * * *

* * * Every state that has enacted LLC piercing legislation has chosen to follow corporate law standards and not develop a separate LLC standard. Statutes [that] create corporations and LLCs have the same basic purpose—to limit the liability of individual investors with a corresponding benefit to economic development. Statutes created the legal fiction of the corporation being a completely separate entity which could act independently from individual persons. If the corporation were created and operated in conformance with the statutory requirements, the law would treat it as a separate entity and shelter the individual shareholders from any liability caused by corporate action, thereby encouraging investment. However, courts throughout the country have consistently recognized certain unjust circumstances can arise if immunity from liability shelters those who have failed to operate a corporation as a separate entity. *Consequently, when corporations fail to follow the statutorily mandated formalities, co-mingle funds, or ignore the restrictions in their articles of incorporation regarding separate treatment of corporate property, the courts deem it appropriate to disregard the separate identity and do not permit shareholders to be sheltered from liability to third parties for damages caused by the corporations' acts.* [Emphasis added.]

We can discern no reason, in either law or policy, to treat LLCs differently than we treat corporations. If the members and officers of an LLC fail to treat it as a separate entity as con-

CASE 37.1 | Continued templated by statute, they should not enjoy immunity from individual liability for the LLC's acts that cause damage to third parties. * * *

Certainly, the various factors which would justify piercing an LLC veil would not be identical to the corporate situation for the obvious reason that many of the organizational formalities applicable to corporations do not apply to LLCs. The LLC's operation is intended to be much more flexible than a corporation's. Factors relevant to determining when to pierce the corporate veil have developed over time in a multitude of cases. It would be inadvisable in this case * * * to attempt to articulate all the possible factors to be applied to LLCs in Wyoming in the future. For guidance, we direct attention to commentators who have opined on the appropriate factors to be applied in the LLC context.

DECISION AND REMEDY *The Wyoming Supreme Court held that the LLC entity could be disregarded. The court concluded that there was no reason to treat an LLC differently than a corporation when considering whether to disregard the legal entity and hold its members personally liable. The court remanded the case for a determination as to whether piercing the LLC veil was appropriate under these circumstances.*

WHAT IF THE FACTS WERE DIFFERENT? *Suppose that Flahive had scrupulously followed all statutorily mandated formalities, had not commingled personal and LLC funds, and had always treated LLC property as separate and distinct from his personal property. Would the decision in this case likely have been different? Why or why not?*

LLC FORMATION

To form an LLC, **articles of organization** must be filed with a central state agency—usually the secretary of state's office [ULLCA 202]. Typically, the articles are required to include such information as the name of the business, the business's principal address, the name and address of a registered agent, the names of the owners, and information on how the LLC will be managed [ULLCA 203]. The business's name must include the words *Limited Liability Company* or the initials *LLC* [ULLCA 105(a)]. In addition to filing the articles of organization, a few states require that a notice of the intention to form an LLC be published in a local newspaper.

About one-fourth of the states specifically require LLCs to have at least two owners, or members. The rest of the states usually permit one-member LLCs, although some LLC statutes are silent on this issue.

JURISDICTIONAL REQUIREMENTS

One of the significant differences between LLCs and corporations has to do with federal jurisdictional requirements. The federal jurisdiction statute provides that a corporation is deemed to be a citizen of the state where it is incorporated and maintains its principal place of business. The statute does not mention the state citizenship of partnerships, LLCs, and other unincorporated associations, but the courts have tended to regard these entities as citizens of every state in which their members are citizens.

The state citizenship of LLCs may come into play when a party sues an LLC based on diversity of citizenship. Remember from Chapter 2 that in some circumstances, such as when parties to a lawsuit are from different states, a federal court can exercise diversity jurisdiction in cases in which the amount in controversy exceeds $75,000. *Total* diversity of citizenship must exist, however. For example, Fong is a citizen of New York who wishes to bring suit against Skycel, an LLC formed under the laws of Connecticut. One of Skycel's members also lives in New York. Fong will not be able to bring a suit against Skycel in federal court on the basis of diversity jurisdiction because the defendant LLC is also a citizen of New York. The same would be true if Fong was bringing suit against multiple defendants and one of the defendants lived in New York.

ADVANTAGES AND DISADVANTAGES OF THE LLC

Although the LLC offers many advantages to businesspersons, it also has some disadvantages. We look now at some of the advantages and disadvantages of the LLC.

ADVANTAGES OF THE LLC A key advantage of the LLC is that the liability of members is limited to the amount of their investments. Another advantage is the flexibility that the LLC offers in regard to business operations and management (as will be discussed shortly).

An additional benefit is that an LLC with two or more members can choose to be taxed either as a partnership or as a corporation. As will be discussed in Chapter 38, a corporate entity must pay income taxes on its profits, and the shareholders pay personal income taxes on profits distributed as dividends. An LLC that wants to distribute profits to the members may prefer to be taxed as a partnership to avoid the "double taxation" characteristic of the corporate entity. Unless an LLC indicates that it wishes to be taxed as a corporation, the IRS automatically taxes it as a partnership. This means that the LLC as an entity pays no taxes; rather, as in a partnership, profits are "passed through" the LLC to the members, who then personally pay taxes on the profits. If LLC members want to reinvest profits in the business, however, rather than distribute the profits to members, they may prefer to be taxed as a corporation. Corporate income tax rates are often lower than personal tax rates. Part of the attractiveness of the LLC is this flexibility with respect to taxation.

For federal income tax purposes, one-member LLCs are automatically taxed as sole proprietorships unless they indicate that they wish to be taxed as corporations. With respect to state taxes, most states follow the IRS rules.

DISADVANTAGES OF THE LLC The disadvantages of the LLC are relatively few. Although initially there was uncertainty over how LLCs would be taxed, that disadvantage no longer exists. One remaining drawback is that state LLC statutes are not yet uniform. Until all of the states have adopted the ULLCA, an LLC in one state will have to check the rules in the other states in which the firm does business to ensure that it retains its limited liability. Generally, though, most—if not all—states apply to a foreign LLC (an LLC formed in another state) the law of the state where the LLC was formed.

Still another disadvantage is the lack of case law dealing with LLCs. How the courts interpret statutes provides important guidelines for businesses. Given the relative newness of the LLC as a business form in the United States, there is not, as yet, a substantial body of case law to provide this kind of guidance.

SECTION 2 | Management and Operation of an LLC

As mentioned, one of the advantages of the LLC form of business is that it provides a substantial degree of flexibility in terms of operation and management. The members get to choose who will participate in the management and operation of their business, and how other issues will be resolved. We discuss the various options available to members in the following subsections.

THE LLC OPERATING AGREEMENT

In an LLC, the members themselves can decide how to operate the many aspects of the business by forming an **operating agreement** [ULLCA 103(a)]. Operating agreements typically contain provisions relating to management, how profits will be divided, the transfer of membership interests, whether the LLC will be dissolved on the death or departure of a member, and other important issues.

An operating agreement need not be in writing and indeed need not even be formed for an LLC to exist. Generally, though, LLC members should protect their interests by forming a written operating agreement. As with any business arrangement, disputes may arise over any number of issues. If there is no agreement covering the topic under dispute, such as how profits will be divided, the state LLC statute will govern the outcome. For example, most LLC statutes provide that if the members have not specified how profits will be divided, they will be divided equally among the members.

Generally, when an issue is not covered by an operating agreement or by an LLC statute, the principles of partnership law are applied. The following case illustrates what can happen in the absence of a written operating agreement when one of the members of the LLC has a "bad intent."

| CASE 37.2 | **Kuhn v. Tumminelli** |

Superior Court
of New Jersey,
Appellate Division, 2004.
366 N.J.Super. 431,
841 A.2d 496.
http://lawlibrary.rutgers.
edu/search.shtml#party[a]

BACKGROUND AND FACTS *Clifford Kuhn, Jr., and Joseph Tumminelli formed Touch of Class Limousine Service under the New Jersey Limited Liability Company Act in 1999, doing business as Touch of Elegance Limousine Service. They did not sign a written operating agreement, but orally agreed that Kuhn would provide the financial backing and procure customers, and Tumminelli would manage the day-to-day operations of the company. Tumminelli embezzled $283,000 from the company after cashing customers' checks at Quick Cash, Inc., a local check-cashing service. Quick Cash deposited the checks in its bank account with First Union National Bank, N.A., which collected on the checks from the drawee banks, Bank of America Corporation and Chase Manhattan Bank, N.A. Kuhn filed a suit in a New Jersey state court against Tumminelli, the banks, and others to recover the embezzled funds. The court ordered Tumminelli to pay Kuhn and to transfer his interest in Touch of Class to Kuhn, but issued a summary judgment in favor of the other defendants. Kuhn appealed to a state intermediate appellate court, arguing in part that Quick Cash and the banks were liable because Tumminelli did not have the authority to cash the company's checks and convert the funds.*

IN THE LANGUAGE OF THE COURT

LEFELT, J.A.D. [Judge, Appellate Division]
* * * *
New Jersey enacted the Limited Liability Company Act in 1994. Its purpose was to enable members and managers of LLCs to take advantage of both the limited liability afforded to shareholders and directors of corporations and the pass-through tax advantages available to partnerships.

Under the LLC Act, *when a limited liability company is managed by its members, unless otherwise provided in the operating agreement, each member shall have the authority to bind the limited liability company.* Moreover, except as otherwise provided in an operating agreement, a member or manager may lend money to, borrow money from, act as a surety, guarantor or endorser for, * * * an LLC. [Emphasis added.]

In the absence of a written operating agreement providing to the contrary, Tumminelli as a 50% owner of the LLC had broad authority to bind the LLC * * * and specific authority * * * to endorse and presumably cash checks payable to the LLC. If more limited authority was desired, Kuhn and Tumminelli had to so provide in a written operating agreement.
* * * *
* * * [T]he LLC Act contemplates that its provisions will control unless the members agree otherwise in an operating agreement. *When executing an operating agreement, which must be written if the LLC has more than one member, the members are free to structure the company in a variety of ways and are free to restrict and expand the rights, responsibilities and authority of its managers and members.* [Emphasis added.]

The LLC Act is, therefore, quite flexible and permits the LLC members great discretion to establish the company structure and procedures, with the statute controlling in the absence of a contrary operating agreement. The legislative intent is revealed by the directive that the LLC Act is to be liberally construed to give the maximum effect to the principle of freedom of contract and to the enforceability of operating agreements.
* * * *
Tumminelli was authorized under the LLC Act to endorse the checks. In fact, considering Tumminelli's position at the LLC, his responsibilities, and daily functions along with the

---

a. In the "Which courts do you want to search?" section, click on the small box next to "Appellate Division." In the "Enter Names Here" section, in the "First Name:" box, type "Kuhn"; in the "Second Name:" box, type "Tumminelli"; then click on "Submit Form." In the result, click on the appropriate link to access the opinion. Rutgers University School of Law in Camden, New Jersey, maintains this Web site.

CONTINUED

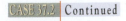

CASE 37.2 | Continued

statutory grant of authority, it can be inferred that Tumminelli had actual authority to receive the checks, endorse the checks, and cash them at Quick Cash, especially because Kuhn knew that Tumminelli was paying business expenses in cash.

* * * Under Kuhn's argument, even if a person had been authorized to endorse and cash a check, if that person converts the funds to an unauthorized use, a depository bank would be liable, as if the check had been paid on a forged endorsement. * * *

We disagree that an authorized endorsement can become unauthorized by a subsequent unauthorized use of the funds. Rather, we view the circumstances as constituting two acts, the endorsement necessary to obtain the funds and the subsequent use of the funds. These acts are not inseparable. *The misappropriation of the funds is unauthorized, but does not convert an authorized endorsement into a forgery.* [Emphasis added.]

It defies reason to allow an event that occurs after the endorsement to affect the validity of the endorsement. The use to which the agent later puts the check does not affect the agent's authorization to endorse it. The validity of an endorsement does not depend upon the agent's subjective motivation at the time of the endorsement. * * * [H]ow can a bank or anyone else protect themselves against someone's bad intent?

If the agent is otherwise authorized * * * the fact that the agent had an improper purpose in making or endorsing the instrument in the authorized form does not prevent a bona fide purchaser in due course, or a subsequent transferee from one, from having the same rights in the instrument and against the principal as if the agent's act were authorized.

DECISION AND REMEDY *The state intermediate appellate court affirmed the lower court's judgment in favor of Quick Cash and the banks. Tumminelli had the authority to accept, indorse, and cash checks on behalf of Touch of Class, under the LLC Act and in the absence of a written operating agreement, which might have specified otherwise. His "bad intent" to convert the funds to his own use did not affect this authority.*

WHAT IF THE FACTS WERE DIFFERENT? *Suppose that Kuhn and Tumminelli had signed a written operating agreement that required both members' indorsements when cashing customers' checks. Assuming that Quick Cash would have known of this requirement, would the result in this case have been different?*

MANAGEMENT OF AN LLC

Basically, the members have two options for managing an LLC—the members may decide in their operating agreement to be either a "member-managed" LLC or a "manager-managed" LLC. Most LLC statutes and the ULLCA provide that unless the articles of organization specify otherwise, an LLC is assumed to be member managed [ULLCA 203(a)(6)].

PARTICIPATION IN MANAGEMENT In a *member-managed* LLC, all of the members participate in management, and decisions are made by majority vote [ULLCA 404(a)]. In a *manager-managed* LLC, the members designate a group of persons to manage the firm. The management group may consist of only members, both members and nonmembers, or only nonmembers. Managers in a manager-managed LLC owe fiduciary duties to the LLC and its members, including the duty of loyalty and the duty of care

[ULLCA 409(a), 409(h)], just as corporate directors and officers owe fiduciary duties to the corporation and its shareholders.

OPERATING PROCEDURES The members of an LLC can include provisions governing decision-making procedures in their operating agreement. For example, the agreement can include procedures for choosing or removing managers. Although most LLC statutes are silent on this issue, the ULLCA provides that members may choose and remove managers by majority vote [ULLCA 404(b)(3)]. The members can also include in the agreement provisions designating when and for what purposes members' meetings will be held, although in contrast to corporate laws, most state LLC statutes do not require formal meetings.

Members may also specify in their agreement how voting rights will be apportioned. If they do not, LLC statutes in most states provide that voting rights are apportioned according to each member's capital contributions. Some states provide that, in the absence of an agreement to the contrary, each member has one vote.

SECTION 3 | Special Business Forms

In addition to the LLC and the other traditional business forms discussed in this unit, several other forms can be used to organize a business. For the most part, these special business forms are hybrid organizations—that is, they have characteristics similar to those of partnerships or corporations, or combine features of both. These forms include joint ventures, syndicates, joint stock companies, business trusts, and cooperatives.

JOINT VENTURE

A **joint venture** is an undertaking by two or more persons or business entities engaged in a single defined project or a series of related transactions. Unless otherwise agreed, joint venturers share profits and losses equally and have an equal voice in controlling the project. Joint ventures range in size from very small activities to huge, multimillion-dollar joint actions undertaken by some of the world's largest corporations. Large organizations often investigate new markets or new ideas by forming joint ventures with other enterprises. For example, Apple entered into a joint venture with Hewlett-Packard (HP) to install software compatible with Apple's iPod, the world's leading digital music player, on HP computers.

SIMILARITIES TO PARTNERSHIPS The joint venture resembles a partnership and is taxed like a partnership. The main difference is that a joint venture typically involves the pursuit of a single project or series of transactions, whereas a partnership usually (though not always) concerns an ongoing business. For this reason, most courts apply the same principles to joint ventures as they apply to partnerships. For instance, the joint venturers owe to each other the same fiduciary duties, including the duty of loyalty, that partners owe each other.

Like partners, the joint venturers have equal rights to manage the activities of the enterprise. Control of the operation may be given to one of the members, however, without affecting the status of the relationship. The following case illustrates one factor that courts consider in determining whether a joint venture exists.

CASE 37.3 | **PGI, Inc. v. Rathe Productions, Inc.**

Supreme Court
of Virginia, 2003.
265 Va. 334,
576 S.E.2d 438.

Opinion by Justice *DONALD W. LEMONS*.
　　* * * *

　　PGI, Inc. ("PGI") specializes in the marketing and production of various events including exhibitions, conferences, and corporate meetings. Rathe Productions, Inc. ("Rathe") is a specialty producer of museum displays. Beginning in 1997, both PGI and Rathe provided a range of services to the Smithsonian Institute ("Smithsonian") for the management and production of "America's Smithsonian Exposition," a traveling museum that displayed a variety of historical and cultural exhibits (the "Exposition"). * * * * [A]fter touring just five cities, the Smithsonian's funding was depleted. The Smithsonian solicited bids for private operation, financing, and management of the Exposition.

　　PGI and Rathe ("PGI/Rathe") submitted a joint proposal to manage and operate the Exposition, which the Smithsonian accepted. * * *

　　* * * [After a three-city tour] the Smithsonian hired PGI/Rathe for $250,000 to conduct a market study (the "Market Study") to investigate the feasibility of producing and touring a self-sustaining international Exposition. * * * After the Market Study was completed, PGI, on behalf of PGI/Rathe * * * , submitted an invoice to the Smithsonian for the previous management of the Exposition and for conducting the Market Study. The Smithsonian did not immediately pay the amounts invoiced * * * .

　　* * * On July 20, 2000, Rathe entered into a settlement agreement with the Smithsonian to satisfy the Market Study and management invoices in exchange for $250,000. Rathe failed * * * to distribute any of the proceeds to [PGI]. * * *

　　[PGI filed a suit in a Virginia state court against Rathe, alleging in part conversion.]

CONTINUED ▶

* * * *

* * * The trial court * * * entered judgment in favor of Rathe. PGI appeals the adverse judgment of the trial court.

* * * *

* * * A review of the trial court's * * * opinion reveals [the] reasons for the trial court's action: * * * PGI did not present evidence at trial to establish that a [joint venture] existed between the parties * * * [and] PGI did not present credible evidence to support its claim for conversion.

* * * *

* * * A *joint venture exists where two or more parties enter into a special combination for the purpose of a specific business undertaking, jointly seeking a profit, gain, or other benefit, without any actual partnership or corporate designation* * * * *[and] each is to have a voice in its control and management.* [Emphasis added.]

* * * On the theory of conversion, the [court] had to find that a joint venture existed in order to reach [a] verdict in favor of PGI. * * *

* * * In a letter from the Smithsonian dated May 12, 1997, to PGI and Rathe, referred to as a "Notice to Proceed," the following "understandings" are evident:

> [T]he Smithsonian is confident that Rathe/PGI, together with its proposed team, will provide the management and production expertise needed to bring new levels of success to [America's Smithsonian Exposition] and to launch a similar and even more successful international exhibition.
>
> This letter serves to formally notify Rathe/PGI that it has been chosen as the exclusive contractor of the [Smithsonian] for management and production of the remainder of [the America's Smithsonian Exposition]. * * * This letter also authorizes Rathe/PGI * * * as the exclusive producer of a similar international tour * * * .

The "Notice to Proceed" letter is replete with references to PGI and Rathe in a joint capacity, namely "PGI/Rathe," for a limited purpose. The letter is signed "ACCEPTED AND AGREED" by representatives of PGI and Rathe. The exhibits introduced at trial include a "Proposed International Tour Feasibility Study" submitted to the Smithsonian as "A Joint Venture Report by Rathe/PGI." Finally, the testimony overwhelmingly supports the finding of a joint venture and includes the testimony of Cynthia Engel, President and Chief Operating Officer of PGI, that the relationship with Rathe was "a joint venture and that all expenses would be paid and if there was a profit, it would be split." The evidence reveals that Rathe and PGI created a joint venture with shared management responsibilities and the expectation of shared profits. * * *

* * * *

* * * Upon completion of the objective of the joint venture, all that remained was the collection of accounts receivable from the Smithsonian * * * . When difficulties arose in the collection of sums due to the joint venture from the Smithsonian, a further agreement was reached between the joint venturers to authorize Rathe to negotiate and settle the claim. Thereafter, Rathe wrote the Smithsonian indicating that a compromised settlement figure "will allow PGI [and Rathe] to receive a reduced final payment." A settlement was reached with Rathe executing the settlement agreement on behalf of its co-venturer, PGI. Rathe received $250,000 from the Smithsonian but refused to pay any of the proceeds to PGI * * * , contrary to its express agreement to do so.

* * * *

* * * [T]he trial court erred in * * * entering judgment for Rathe. We * * * remand to the trial court with directions to enter judgment [in PGI's favor] and empanel a jury to * * * decide PGI's claim for punitive damages.

QUESTIONS

1. On what basis should Rathe be held liable for conversion?
2. Could PGI successfully sue Rathe for breach of contract? Why or why not?

DIFFERENCES FROM PARTNERSHIPS Joint ventures differ from partnerships in several important ways. The members of a joint venture have less implied and apparent authority than the partners in a partnership. As discussed in Chapter 36, each partner is treated as an agent of the other partners. Because the activities of a joint venture are more limited than the business of a partnership, the members of a joint venture are presumed to have less power to bind their co-venturers. In addition, the death of a joint venturer ordinarily does not terminate a joint venture, unlike the death of a partner. A joint venture normally terminates when the project or the transaction for which it was formed has been completed, though the members can specify how long the relationship will last.

SYNDICATE

A group of individuals getting together to finance a particular project, such as the building of a shopping center or the purchase of a professional basketball franchise, is called a **syndicate,** or an *investment group*. The form of such groups varies considerably. A syndicate may exist as a corporation or as a general or limited partnership. In some cases, the members merely own property jointly and have no legally recognized business arrangement.

JOINT STOCK COMPANY

A **joint stock company** is a true hybrid of a partnership and a corporation. It has many characteristics of a corporation in that (1) its ownership is represented by transferable shares of stock, (2) it is usually managed by directors and officers of the company or association, and (3) it can have a perpetual existence. Most of its other features, however, are more characteristic of a partnership, and it is usually treated like a partnership. As with a partnership, a joint stock company is formed by agreement (not statute); property is usually held in the names of the members; shareholders have personal liability; and generally the company is not treated as a legal entity for purposes of a lawsuit. In a joint stock company, however, shareholders are not considered to be agents of each other, as would be the case if the company were a true partnership.

BUSINESS TRUST

A **business trust** is created by a written trust agreement that sets forth the interests of the beneficiaries and the obligations and powers of the trustees. With a business trust, legal ownership and management of the property of the business stay with one or more of the trustees, and the profits are distributed to the beneficiaries.

The business trust form of business was started in Massachusetts in an attempt to obtain the limited liability advantage of corporate status while avoiding certain restrictions on a corporation's ownership and development of real property. A business trust resembles a corporation in many respects. Beneficiaries of the trust, for example, are not personally responsible for the trust's debts or obligations. In fact, in a number of states, business trusts must pay corporate taxes.

COOPERATIVE

A **cooperative** is an association that is organized to provide an economic service to its members (or shareholders); it may or may not be incorporated. Most cooperatives are governed by state statutes for cooperatives, general business incorporation statutes, or LLC statutes. Generally, an incorporated cooperative will distribute dividends, or profits, to its owners on the basis of their transactions with the cooperative rather than on the basis of the amount of capital they contributed. Members of incorporated cooperatives have limited liability, as do shareholders of corporations or members of LLCs. Cooperatives that are unincorporated are often treated like partnerships. The members have joint liability for the cooperative's acts.

The cooperative form of business is generally adopted by groups of individuals who wish to pool their resources to gain some advantage in the marketplace. Consumer purchasing co-ops are formed to obtain lower prices through quantity discounts. Seller marketing co-ops are formed to control the market and thereby obtain higher retail prices from consumers. Co-ops range in size from small, local consumer cooperatives to national businesses such as Ace Hardware and Land O' Lakes, the well-known producer of dairy products.

REVIEWING LIMITED LIABILITY COMPANIES AND SPECIAL BUSINESS FORMS

The city of Papagos, Arizona, had a deteriorating bridge in need of repair on a prominent public roadway. The city posted notices seeking proposals for an artistic bridge design and reconstruction. Davidson Masonry, LLC, which was owned and managed by Carl Davidson and his wife, Marilyn Rowe, decided to submit a bid for a decorative concrete project that incorporated artistic metalwork. They contacted Shana Lafayette, a local sculptor who specialized in large-scale metal designs, to help them design the bridge. The city selected their bridge design and awarded them the contract for a commission of $184,000. Davidson Masonry and Lafayette then entered into an agreement to work together on the bridge project. Davidson Masonry agreed to install and pay for concrete and structural work, and Lafayette agreed to install the metalwork at her expense. They agreed that overall profits would be split, with 25 percent to Lafayette and 75 percent to Davidson Masonry. Lafayette designed numerous metal sculptures of salmon that were incorporated into colorful decorative concrete forms designed by Rowe, while Davidson performed the structural engineering. The group worked together successfully until the project was completed. Using the information presented in the chapter, answer the following questions.

1. Would Davidson Masonry automatically be taxed as a partnership or a corporation?

2. What are the advantages and disadvantages of the limited liability company business form?

3. Is Davidson Masonry member managed or manager managed?

4. Would the project agreement between Davidson Masonry and Lafayette be considered a cooperative, a business trust, a joint stock company, a syndicate, or a joint venture? Explain.

5. What principles that apply to partnerships would not apply to the business arrangement between Davidson Masonry and Lafayette?

TERMS AND CONCEPTS TO REVIEW

articles of organization 755

business trust 761

cooperative 761

joint stock company 761

joint venture 759

limited liability company (LLC) 753

member 754

operating agreement 756

syndicate 761

QUESTIONS AND CASE PROBLEMS

37–1. John, Lesa, and Tabir form a limited liability company. John contributes 60 percent of the capital, and Lesa and Tabir each contribute 20 percent. Nothing is decided about how profits will be divided. John assumes that he will be entitled to 60 percent of the profits, in accordance with his contribution. Lesa and Tabir, however, assume that the profits will be divided equally. A dispute over the question arises, and ultimately a court has to decide the issue. What law will the court apply? In most states, what will result? How could this dispute have been avoided in the first place? Discuss fully.

37–2. QUESTION WITH SAMPLE ANSWER

Assume that Bateson Corp. is considering entering into two contracts—one with a joint stock company that distributes home products east of the Mississippi River and the other with a business trust formed by a number of sole proprietors who are sellers of home products on the West Coast. Both contracts involve large capital outlays for Bateson to supply the businesses with restaurant equipment. In both business organizations, at least two shareholders or beneficiaries are personally wealthy, but both organizations have limited financial resources. The owner-managers of Bateson are not familiar with either form of business organization. Because each form resembles a corporation, they are concerned with potential limits on liability in the event that either business organization breaches the contract by failing to pay for the equipment. Discuss fully Bateson's concern.

For a sample answer to this question, go to Appendix I at the end of this text.

37-3. Joe, a resident of New Jersey, wants to open a restaurant. He asks Kay, his friend, an experienced attorney and a New Yorker, for her business and legal advice in exchange for a 20 percent ownership interest in the restaurant. Kay helps Joe negotiate a lease for the restaurant premises and advises Joe to organize the business as a limited liability company (LLC). Joe forms Café Olé, LLC, and with Kay's help, obtains financing. Then, the night before the restaurant opens, Joe tells Kay that he is "cutting her out of the deal." The restaurant proves to be a success. Kay wants to file a suit in a federal district court against Joe and the LLC. Can a federal court exercise jurisdiction over the parties based on diversity of citizenship? Explain.

37-4. FOREIGN LIMITED LIABILITY COMPANIES. Page, Scrantom, Sprouse, Tucker & Ford, a Georgia law firm, entered into a lease of office equipment in Georgia. The lessor assigned the lease to Danka Funding Co. (DFC), a New York limited liability company (LLC) with its principal place of business in New Jersey. DFC was registered as a foreign LLC in New Jersey for almost two years before the registration lapsed or was withdrawn. Under the applicable statute, a foreign LLC "may not maintain any action . . . in this State until it has registered." When Page defaulted on the lease, DFC filed a complaint in a New Jersey state court against Page for more than $100,000. In its response, Page pointed out that DFC was not registered as a foreign LLC. DFC reregistered. Asserting that DFC had not been registered when it filed its suit, Page asked a federal district court to dismiss the suit. Should the court grant this request? Why or why not? [*Danka Funding, L.L.C. v. Page, Scrantom, Sprouse, Tucker & Ford, P.C.*, 21 F.Supp.2d 465 (D.N.J. 1998)]

37-5. JOINT VENTURES. Frank Hartman, Jr., and Robert Wiesner visited the site of a derailment of a Burlington Northern (BN) train to bid on lumber carried on the train. Hartman was to provide the salvage expertise, and Wiesner was to provide the know-how to sell the lumber. They submitted a bid of $113,663, which BN accepted. To make the payment, Hartman and Wiesner contacted Dave Anderson, who contacted Doug Feller, the managing partner of BBD Partnership. Hartman, Wiesner, Anderson, and Feller agreed to share profits from the sale of the lumber. BBD then borrowed the money to pay BN. BBD, through Feller, had promised to get involved only if it could own the lumber, however. Thus on the bill of sale, BN entered the names "Hartman Construction" and "Feller Associates," a sole proprietorship owned by Feller. BBD later sold its interest in the deal to another party. Two years later, Hartman, Wiesner, BBD, and Feller became involved in a lawsuit over the funds that BBD had borrowed. Was the deal among the parties a joint venture or simply a loan from BBD to Hartman and the others? Discuss fully. [*Wiesner v. BBD Partnership*, 845 P.2d 120 (Mont. 1993)]

37-6. LIMITED LIABILITY COMPANIES. Gloria Duchin, a Rhode Island resident, was the sole shareholder and chief executive officer of Gloria Duchin, Inc. (Duchin, Inc.), which manufactured metallic Christmas ornaments and other novelty items. The firm was incor-

porated in Rhode Island. Duchin Realty, Inc., also incorporated in Rhode Island, leased real estate to Duchin, Inc. The Duchin entities hired Gottesman Co. to sell Duchin, Inc., and to sign with the buyer a consulting agreement for Gloria Duchin and a lease for Duchin Realty's property. Gottesman negotiated a sale, a consulting agreement, and a lease with Somerset Capital Corp. James Mitchell, a resident of Massachusetts, was the chairman and president of Somerset, and Mary Mitchell, also a resident of Massachusetts, was the senior vice president. The parties agreed that to buy Duchin, Inc., Somerset would create a new limited liability company, JMTR Enterprises, L.L.C., in Rhode Island, with the Mitchells as its members. When the deal fell apart, JMTR filed a suit in a Massachusetts state court against the Duchin entities, alleging, among other things, breach of contract. When the defendants tried to remove the case to a federal district court, JMTR argued that the court did not have jurisdiction because there was no diversity of citizenship between the parties: all of the plaintiffs and defendants were citizens of Rhode Island. Is JMTR correct? Why or why not? [*JMTR Enterprises, L.L.C. v. Duchin*, 42 F.Supp.2d 87 (D.Mass. 1999)]

37-7. CASE PROBLEM WITH SAMPLE ANSWER

Westbury Properties, Inc., and others (collectively, the Westbury group) owned, managed, and developed real property. Jerry Stoker and The Stoker Group, Inc. (the Stokers), also developed real property. The Westbury group entered into agreements with the Stokers concerning a large tract of property in Houston County, Georgia. The parties formed limited liability companies (LLCs), including Bellemeade, LLC (the LLC group), to develop various parcels of the tract for residential purposes. The operating agreements provided that "no Member shall be accountable to the [LLC] or to any other Member with respect to [any other] business or activity even if the business or activity competes with the [LLC's] business." The Westbury group entered into agreements with other parties to develop additional parcels within the tract in competition with the LLC group. The Stokers filed a suit in a Georgia state court against the Westbury group, alleging, among other things, breach of fiduciary duty. What duties do the members of an LLC owe to each other? Under what principle might the terms of an operating agreement alter these duties? In whose favor should the court rule? Discuss. [*Stoker v. Bellemeade, LLC*, 272 Ga.App. 817, __ S.E.2d __ (2005)]

To view a sample answer for this case problem, go to this book's Web site at http://wbl.westbuslaw.com, select "Chapter 37," and click on "Case Problem with Sample Answer."

37-8. FOREIGN LIMITED LIABILITY COMPANIES. Walter Matjasich and Cary Hanson organized Capital Care, LLC, in Utah. Capital Care operated, and Matjasich and Hanson managed, Heartland Care Center in Topeka, Kansas. LTC Properties, Inc., held a mortgage on the Heartland facilities. When Heartland failed as a business, its residents were transferred to other facilities. Heartland employees who provided care to the residents for five days during the transfers were not paid wages. The employees filed claims with the Kansas Department of Human Resources for the unpaid wages. Kansas state law provides that a *corporate* officer or manager may be liable for a firm's unpaid wages, but protects limited liability company (LLC) members from personal liability generally and states that an LLC cannot be construed as a corporation. Under Utah state law, the members of an LLC can be personally liable for wages due the LLC's employees, however. Should Matjasich and Hanson be held personally liable for the unpaid wages? Explain. [*Matjasich v. State, Department of Human Resources*, 271 Kan. 246, 21 P.3d 985 (2001)]

37–9. LIMITED LIABILITY COMPANIES. Michael Collins entered into a three-year employment contract with E-Magine, LLC. In business for only a brief time, E-Magine lost a considerable sum of money. In terminating operations, which ceased before the term of the contract with Collins expired, E-Magine also terminated Collins's services. Collins signed a "final payment agreement," which purported to be a settlement of any claims that he might have against E-Magine in exchange for a payment of $24,240. Collins filed a suit in a New York state court against E-Magine, its members and managers, and others, alleging, among other things, breach of his employment contract. Collins claimed that signing the "final payment agreement" was the only means for him to obtain what he was owed for past sales commissions and asked the court to impose personal liability on the members and managers of E-Magine for breach of contract. Should the court grant this request? Why or why not? [*Collins v. E-Magine, LLC*, 291 A.D.2d 350, 739 N.Y.S.2d 121 (1 Dept. 2002)]

37–10. JOINT VENTURES. In 1993, TOG Acquisition Co. attempted to acquire the Orleander Group, a manufacturer of bicycle accessories, but failed for lack of financing. Orleander then granted to Herrick Co. an exclusive right to negotiate for the sale of the business. In August, representatives of TOG, Herrick, and SCS Communications, Inc., signed a letter under which they agreed "to work together to acquire the business of the Orleander Group." The "letter agreement" provided that the parties would contribute "equal amounts of capital" and that all of the terms of the acquisition required the approval of each party. On November 19, TOG and SCS told Herrick that it was out of the deal and, ten days later, acquired Orleander without Herrick. Herrick filed a suit in a federal district court against SCS and others, alleging, among other things, that the "letter agreement" was a contract to establish a joint venture, which TOG and SCS had breached. The defendants filed a motion for summary judgment. In whose favor should the court rule? Why? [*SCS Communications, Inc. v. Herrick Co.*, 360 F.3d 329 (2d Cir. 2004)]

LAW | on the Web

For updated links to resources available on the Web, as well as a variety of other materials, visit this text's Web site at http://wbl.westbuslaw.com.

In the "Business & Human Resources" section of its home page, Nolo Press provides information on LLCs. Go to

http://www.nolo.com/chapter/RUNS/RUNS_toc.html

You can find information on filing fees for LLCs at

http://www.bizcorp.com

LEGAL RESEARCH EXERCISES ON THE WEB

Go to http://wbl.westbuslaw.com, the Web site that accompanies this text. Select "Chapter 37" and click on "Internet Exercises." There you will find the following Internet research exercises that you can perform to learn more about topics covered in this chapter.

Activity 37–1: LEGAL PERSPECTIVE
        Limited Liability Companies

Activity 37–2: MANAGEMENT PERSPECTIVE
        Joint Ventures

CHAPTER 38

CORPORATIONS—
Formation and Financing

The corporation is a creature of statute. A corporation is an artificial being, existing in law only and neither tangible nor visible. Its existence depends generally on state law, although some corporations, especially public organizations, can be created under federal law. Each state has its own body of corporate law, and these laws are not entirely uniform.

The Model Business Corporation Act (MBCA) is a codification of modern corporation law that has been influential in the codification of state corporation statutes. Today, the majority of state statutes are guided by the most recent version of the MBCA, often referred to as the Revised Model Business Corporation Act (RMBCA). Excerpts from the RMBCA are included in Appendix G of this text. You should keep in mind, however, that there is considerable variation among the regulations of the states that have used the MBCA or the RMBCA as a basis for their statutes, and several states do not follow either act. Because of this, individual state corporation laws should be relied on to determine corporate law rather than the MBCA or RMBCA.

In this chapter, we examine the nature of the corporate form of business enterprise and the various classifications of corporations. We then discuss the formation and financing of today's corporation.

SECTION 1 | The Nature of the Corporation

A corporation can consist of one or more *natural persons* (as opposed to the artificial *legal person* of the corporation) identified under a common name. The corporation substitutes itself for its shareholders in conducting corporate business and in incurring liability, yet its authority to act and the liability for its actions are separate and apart from the individuals who own it. (In certain limited situations, the "corporate veil" can be pierced; that is, liability for the corporation's obligations can be extended to shareholders, a topic to be discussed later in this chapter.)

CORPORATE PERSONNEL

Responsibility for the overall management of the corporation is entrusted to a board of directors, which is elected by the shareholders. The board of directors hires corporate officers and other employees to run the daily business operations of the corporation.

When an individual purchases a share of stock in a corporation, that person becomes a shareholder and an owner of the corporation. Unlike the members in a partnership, the body of shareholders can change constantly without affecting the continued existence of the corporation. A shareholder can sue the corporation, and the corporation can sue a shareholder. Additionally, under certain circumstances, a shareholder can sue on behalf of a corporation. The rights and duties of all corporate personnel will be examined in Chapter 39.

CORPORATE TAXATION

Corporate profits are taxed by various levels of government. Corporations can do one of two things with corporate profits—retain them or pass them on to shareholders in the form of dividends. The corporation normally receives no tax deduction for dividends distributed to shareholders. Dividends are again taxable (except when they represent distributions of capital) to the shareholder receiving them. This double-taxation feature of the corporation is one of its major disadvantages.

NEW DIVIDEND RULE   The Jobs Growth Tax Relief Reconciliation Act of 2003[1] mitigates this double-taxation feature of corporations to some extent. Under this law, certain qualified dividends receive preferential federal tax treatment because the dividends are taxed at the same rate as a person's net capital gains (10 to 15 percent) rather than being taxed at the higher rate of the shareholder's ordinary income (up to 35 percent in 2005). To qualify for this reduced rate, the stock on which the dividends are paid must have been held for more than 60 days during the 120-day period beginning 60 days before the dividend is paid.[2] This rule does not apply to certain dividends from foreign corporations, dividends from tax-exempt entities, and dividends that do not satisfy the holding-period requirement. In addition, the law contains "sunset provisions" stipulating that the reduced tax rates will not be available on dividends paid after 2008.

RETAINED EARNINGS   Profits that are not distributed are retained by the corporation. These **retained earnings,** if invested properly, will yield higher corporate profits in the future and thus cause the price of the company's stock to rise. Individual shareholders can then reap the benefits of the retained earnings in the capital gains they receive when they sell their shares.

CONSTITUTIONAL RIGHTS OF CORPORATIONS

A corporation is recognized under state and federal law as a "person," and it enjoys many of the same rights and privileges that natural persons who are U.S. citizens enjoy. The Bill of Rights guarantees persons certain protections, and corporations are considered persons in most instances. Accordingly, a corporation as an entity has the same right of access to the courts and can sue or be sued. It also has the right of due process before denial of life, liberty, or property, as well as freedom from unreasonable searches and seizures and from double jeopardy.

Under the First Amendment, corporations are entitled to freedom of speech. As we pointed out in Chapter 4, however, commercial speech (such as advertising) and political speech (such as contribu-tions to political causes or candidates) receive significantly less protection than noncommercial speech.

Only the corporation's individual officers and employees possess the Fifth Amendment right against self-incrimination. Additionally, the privileges and immunities clause of the Constitution (Article IV, Section 2) does not protect corporations, nor does it protect unincorporated associations. This clause requires each state to treat citizens of other states equally with respect to certain rights, such as access to courts and travel rights. This constitutional clause does not apply to corporations because corporations are legal persons only, not natural citizens.

TORTS AND CRIMINAL ACTS

A corporation is liable for the torts committed by its agents or officers within the course and scope of their employment. This principle applies to a corporation exactly as it applies to the ordinary agency relationships discussed in Chapter 32. It follows the doctrine of *respondeat superior.*

Under modern criminal law, a corporation may also be held liable for the criminal acts of its agents and employees, provided the punishment is one that can be applied to the corporation. Obviously, corporations cannot be imprisoned, but they can be fined. (Of course, corporate directors and officers can be imprisoned, and in recent years, many have faced criminal penalties for their own actions or for the actions of employees under their supervision. The criminal liability of corporate directors and officers was examined in Chapter 9.)

CORPORATE SENTENCING GUIDELINES

Recall from Chapter 9 that the U.S. Sentencing Commission created standardized sentencing guidelines for federal crimes. These guidelines went into effect in 1987. The commission subsequently created the Federal Organizational Corporate Sentencing Guidelines, which consist of specific sentencing guidelines for crimes committed by corporate employees (white-collar crimes).[3] The net effect of the guidelines has been a significant increase in criminal penalties for crimes committed by corporate personnel.

---

1. Pub. L. No. 108-27, May 28, 2003, codified at 26 U.S.C.A. Sections 1, 24, 55, 57 note, 63, 163, 168, 179, 301, 306, 341, 338, 467, 531, 541, 584, 702, 854, 1255, 1257, 1400, 1445, 6429, 7518; and at 42 U.S.C.A. Sections 801, 1396d.
2. 26 U.S.C.A. Section 1(h)(11).

---

3. Note that the Sarbanes-Oxley Act of 2002 increased the penalties for certain types of corporate crime and ordered the U.S. Sentencing Commission to revise the sentencing guidelines accordingly—see Chapter 41.

CRIMINAL OFFENSES AND PUNISHMENTS The corporate sentencing guidelines cover thirty-two levels of offenses. The punishment for each offense depends on such matters as the seriousness of the charge, the amount of money concerned, and the extent to which top company executives are involved. Under the sentencing guidelines, corporate lawbreakers face sanctions and fines that can be as high as hundreds of millions of dollars. The guidelines allow judges to ease up on penalties, however, when companies have taken substantial steps to prevent, investigate, and punish wrongdoing. Additionally, if firms cooperate with government investigators, the penalties may be less severe.

FORMULA FOR DETERMINING PENALTIES The guidelines present judges with a complicated formula for determining penalties for businesses based on the seriousness of the offense and the degree of the company's guilt. A company's so-called culpability score depends on the role that senior management played in the alleged wrongdoing as well as the company's history of past violations and the extent of management's cooperation with federal investigators. Additionally, the effectiveness of the firm's compliance program is important. A company can earn "credits" against potential penalties by undertaking the following measures:

1. The firm must establish and put in writing crime prevention standards and procedures for all employees and agents, and these standards must be communicated to all employees and agents in writing, through training programs, or by both methods.
2. The standards must be enforced by high-level employees.
3. When an employee has demonstrated an apparent propensity to engage in criminal activities, the company must prevent that employee from exercising discretionary authority.
4. All anticrime standards of the company must include methods of detecting as well as preventing crimes.
5. Whistleblowers must be protected from reprisals.

SECTION 2 | Corporate Powers

Under modern law, a corporation generally can engage in any act and enter into any contract available to a natural person in order to accomplish the purposes for which it was formed. When a corporation is created, the express and implied powers necessary to achieve its purpose also come into existence.

EXPRESS AND IMPLIED POWERS

Corporations possess both express and implied powers. We look next at each of these types of powers.

EXPRESS POWERS The express powers of a corporation are found in its **articles of incorporation** (a document containing information about the corporation, including its organization and functions), in the law of the state of incorporation, and in the state and federal constitutions. Corporate **bylaws** (internal rules of management adopted by the corporation at its first organizational meeting) and the resolutions of the corporation's board of directors also grant or restrict certain powers.

The following order of priority is used when conflicts arise among documents involving corporations:

1. U.S. Constitution.
2. State constitutions.
3. State statutes.
4. Articles of incorporation.
5. Bylaws.
6. Resolutions of the board of directors.

IMPLIED POWERS Certain implied powers arise when a corporation is created. Barring express constitutional, statutory, or charter prohibitions, the corporation has the implied power to perform all acts reasonably appropriate and necessary to accomplish its corporate purposes. For this reason, a corporation has the implied power to borrow funds within certain limits, to lend funds, and to extend credit to those with whom it has a legal or contractual relationship.

To borrow funds, the corporation acts through its board of directors to authorize the loan. Most often, the president or chief executive officer of the corporation will execute the necessary papers on behalf of the corporation. Corporate officers such as these have the implied power to bind the corporation in matters directly connected with the *ordinary* business affairs of the enterprise. A corporate officer does not have the authority to bind the corporation to an action that will greatly affect the corporate purpose or undertaking, such as the sale of substantial corporate assets, however.

ULTRA VIRES DOCTRINE

The term **ultra vires** means "beyond the powers." In corporate law, acts of a corporation that are beyond its express or implied powers are *ultra vires* acts. A majority of cases dealing with *ultra vires* acts have involved contracts made for unauthorized purposes. For example, Suarez is the chief executive officer of SOS Plumbing, Inc. He enters into a contract with Carlini for the purchase of ten cases of brandy. It is difficult to see how this contract is reasonably related to the conduct and furtherance of the corporation's stated purpose of providing plumbing installation and services. Hence, a court would probably find such a contract to be *ultra vires*.

In some states, when a contract is entirely executory (not yet performed by either party), either party can use a defense of *ultra vires* to prevent enforcement of the contract. When an *ultra vires* contract is partially or fully executed at the time of challenge, courts may enforce, or uphold, the contract if the circumstances are such that it would be inequitable to allow one party to assert the defense of *ultra vires*.

Under Section 3.04 of the RMBCA, the following remedies are available for *ultra vires* acts:

1. The shareholders may sue on behalf of the corporation to obtain an injunction (to prohibit the corporation from engaging in the *ultra vires* transactions) or to obtain damages for the harm caused by the transactions.

2. The corporation itself can sue the officers and directors who were responsible for the *ultra vires* transactions to recover damages.

3. The attorney general of the state may institute a proceeding to obtain an injunction against the *ultra vires* transactions or to institute dissolution proceedings against the corporation for *ultra vires* acts.

SECTION 3 | Classification of Corporations

The classification of a corporation normally depends on its location, purpose, and ownership characteristics.

DOMESTIC, FOREIGN, AND ALIEN CORPORATIONS

A corporation is known as a **domestic corporation** in its home state (the state in which it incorporates). A corporation that is formed in one state but is doing business in another is referred to in that other state as a **foreign corporation.** A corporation formed in another country (say, Mexico) but doing business in the United States is referred to in the United States as an **alien corporation.**

A corporation does not have an automatic right to locate a business in a state other than its state of incorporation. A corporation normally is required to obtain a *certificate of authority* in any state in which it plans to do business. Once the certificate has been issued, the powers conferred on the corporation by its home state generally can be exercised in the other state. If a foreign corporation does business in a state without obtaining a certificate of authority, the state can impose substantial fines and sanctions on the corporation, and sometimes even on its officers, directors, or agents.[4]

PUBLIC AND PRIVATE CORPORATIONS

A public corporation is one formed by the government to meet some political or governmental purpose. Cities and towns that incorporate are common examples. In addition, many federal government organizations, such as the U.S. Postal Service, the Tennessee Valley Authority, and AMTRAK, are public corporations. Note that a public corporation is not the same as a *publicly held* corporation (often called a *public company*). A publicly held corporation is any corporation whose shares are publicly traded in securities markets, such as the New York Stock Exchange or the over-the-counter market.

In contrast to public corporations, private corporations are created either wholly or in part for private benefit. Most corporations are private. Although they may serve a public purpose, as a public utility does, they are owned by private persons rather than by the government.

NONPROFIT CORPORATIONS

Corporations formed for purposes other than making a profit are called *nonprofit* or *not-for-profit* corporations. Nonprofit corporations are usually (although not

---

4. Note that most state statutes specify certain activities, such as soliciting orders via the Internet, that are not considered doing business within the state. Thus, a certificate of authority is not normally required for a foreign corporation to sell goods or services via the Internet or by mail.

necessarily) private corporations. Private hospitals, educational institutions, charities, religious organizations, and the like are frequently organized as nonprofit corporations. The nonprofit corporation is a convenient form of organization that allows various groups to own property and to form contracts without exposing the individual members to personal liability.

CLOSE CORPORATIONS

A **close corporation** is one whose shares are held by members of a family or by relatively few persons. Close corporations are also referred to as *closely held, family,* or *privately held* corporations. Usually, the members of the small group constituting a close corporation are personally known to one another. Because the number of shareholders is so small, there is no trading market for the shares. In practice, a close corporation is often operated like a partnership. Some states recognize this similarity and have enacted special statutory provisions that cover close corporations. These provisions expressly permit close corporations to depart significantly from certain formalities required by traditional corporation law.[5]

Additionally, Section 7.32 of the RMBCA—a provision added to the RMBCA in 1991 and adopted in several states—gives close corporations a substantial amount of flexibility in determining the rules by which they will operate. Under Section 7.32, if all of the shareholders of a corporation agree in writing, the corporation can operate without directors, bylaws, annual or special shareholders' or directors' meetings, stock certificates, or formal records of shareholders' or directors' decisions.[6]

MANAGEMENT OF CLOSE CORPORATIONS A close corporation has a single shareholder or a closely knit group of shareholders, who usually hold the positions of directors and officers. Management of a close corporation resembles that of a sole proprietorship or a partnership. As a corporation, however, the firm must meet all specific legal requirements set forth in state statutes.

To prevent a majority shareholder from dominating a close corporation, the corporation may specify that approval of more than a simple majority of the directors is needed before the board can take action. Typically, this would be required only for extraordinary measures, such as changing the amount of dividends or dismissing an employee-shareholder—not for ordinary business decisions. Additionally, in some cases courts have held that majority shareholders owe a fiduciary duty to minority shareholders (see Chapter 39 for a further discussion of the duties of majority shareholders).

TRANSFER OF SHARES IN CLOSE CORPORATIONS By definition, a close corporation has a small number of shareholders. The transfer of one shareholder's shares to someone else can thus cause serious management problems. The other shareholders may find themselves required to share control with someone they do not know or like.

Consider an example. Three brothers, Terry, Damon, and Henry Johnson, are the only shareholders of Johnson's Car Wash, Inc. Henry wants to sell his shares to an unknown third person. Terry and Damon object to Henry's idea, and a dispute ensues. What could they have done to avoid this situation?

—Restrictions in the Articles of Incorporation. The articles of incorporation could have restricted the transferability of shares to outside persons by stipulating that shareholders offer their shares to the corporation or other shareholders before selling them to an outside purchaser. In fact, a few states have statutes under which close corporation shares cannot be transferred unless certain persons—including shareholders, family members, and the corporation—are first given the opportunity to purchase the shares for the same price.

—Restrictions through a Shareholder Agreement. Another way that control of a close corporation can be stabilized is through the use of a shareholder agreement. A shareholder agreement can provide that when one of the original shareholders dies, her or his shares of stock in the corporation will be divided in such a way that the proportionate holdings of the survivors, and thus their proportionate control, will be maintained. Courts are generally reluctant to interfere with private agreements, including shareholder agreements. The effect of a close corporation's stock transfer restriction was at the heart of the following case.

---

5. For example, in some states (such as Maryland), a close corporation need not have a board of directors.

6. Shareholders cannot agree, however, to eliminate certain shareholder rights, such as the right to inspect corporate books and records or the right to bring derivative actions (lawsuits on behalf of the corporation—see Chapter 39).

Salt Lake Tribune Publishing Co. v. AT&T Corp.

United States
Court of Appeals,
Tenth Circuit, 2003.
320 F.3d 1081.
*http://www.kscourts.org/
ca10/wordsrch.htm*[a]

EBEL, Circuit Judge:

* * * *

* * * *The Salt Lake Tribune* was owned by the Kearns-Tribune Corporation, the principal shareholders of which were members of the Kearns-McCarthey family. * * * In April 1997, * * * the shareholders * * * decided to sell Kearns-Tribune Corporation to cable company Tele-Communications, Inc. ("TCI"), while receiving an option to repurchase the assets of *The Tribune* at a later date. [The family formed Salt Lake Tribune Publishing Company (Tribune Publishing) to own the option.] * * *

* * * *

* * * In 1999, TCI merged with AT&T Corporation, giving AT&T control over Kearns-Tribune Corporation [which became Kearns-Tribune Limited Liability Company, or KTLLC], * * * Tribune Publishing * * * [filed] a complaint against AT&T in the United States District Court for the District of Utah in December 2000 [to enforce the option]. * * *

* * * *

* * * Tribune Publishing moved for a preliminary injunction * * * . The district court denied that motion * * * . Tribune Publishing [appealed to the U.S. Court of Appeals for the Tenth Circuit] * * * .

* * * *

In 1952, Deseret News and the predecessor in interest of KTLLC entered into the Joint Operating Agreement ("JOA"), the purpose of which was to share overhead expenses related to the production of *The Salt Lake Tribune* and the *Deseret News*. The JOA created the Newspaper Agency Corporation (NAC) to be the agent of KTLLC and Deseret News. * * * KTLLC and Deseret News each own 50% of the stock in the NAC * * * .

* * * [T]he JOA * * * [prohibits] the transfer by KTLLC or Deseret News of their ownership of the NAC stock to anyone else. * * *

* * * *

* * * [T]he district court * * * ruled that the stock transfer restriction is an obstacle to Tribune Publishing's claim for specific performance of the Option Agreement * * * .

* * * *

* * * Section 16-10a-627 of the Utah Code states:

* * * [A] corporation may impose restrictions on the transfer or registration of transfer of shares of the corporation * * * for any * * * reasonable purpose.

* * * Through the statute, Utah plainly embraces the validity of stock transfer restrictions. * * * *The only issue we must resolve * * * is whether the stock transfer restriction contained in * * * the JOA is designed to serve a reasonable purpose.* [Emphasis added.]

* * * *

The desire to limit the participation of outsiders in a close corporation like the NAC has long been recognized as a reasonable purpose for a share transfer restriction. * * * The particular significance of the "close" character of a corporation * * * lies very clearly in the fact that such a share transfer restriction is inherently more "reasonable" when applied to the stock of a corporation having only a few shareholders who are generally active in the business * * * than when imposed upon the stock of a corporation which has numerous shareholders who * * * do not participate actively in the day-to-day management and conduct of the corporation's affairs. [Emphasis added.]

* * * *

Finding unpersuasive Tribune Publishing's arguments that * * * the JOA is invalid, we conclude that the stock transfer restriction is valid and enforceable.

---

a. Type "Salt Lake Tribune Publishing Co." in the box and click on "Search." In the result, scroll to the name of the case and click on it to access the opinion. Washburn University School of Law Library in Topeka, Kansas, maintains this Web site.

CASE 38.1 | **Continued**

*   *   *   *

With regard to ownership of the Tribune Assets, we disagree with and reverse the district court's ruling *   *   * .

*   *   * The district court concluded that Tribune Publishing had a clear entitlement under the Option Agreement to receive "all, and not less than all" of the Tribune Assets upon exercise of the option. It felt, however, that it could not fashion the relief requested by Tribune Publishing: a decree of specific performance requiring the transfer of all of the Tribune Assets.

We find that the district court read too narrowly the relief sought by Tribune Publishing in its complaint. *   *   * We read Tribune Publishing's complaint as seeking whatever combination of equitable and legal relief the court may award to remedy a refusal by KTLLC to perform under the Option Agreement, including a failure to transfer to Tribune Publishing the NAC stock. It is a venerable [long-standing and respected] principle of our law that *for the violation of every right there should be a remedy,* and we should not lightly put down our obligation to determine whether appropriate remedies exist. [Emphasis added.]

*   *   *   *

Accordingly, the district court's order denying Tribune Publishing's motion for a preliminary injunction is **AFFIRMED** in part and **REVERSED** in part and the matter **REMANDED** for further proceedings.

QUESTIONS

1. What is the relationship between NAC and its shareholders, and how is that relationship different from the usual relationship between a corporation and its shareholders?
2. The plaintiff in this case argued in part that the stock transfer restriction was a "restraint on alienation (transfer of ownership)," constituting "an unreasonable incursion on the free flow of commerce." How do the facts of this case show that this is not a valid argument?

S CORPORATIONS

A close corporation that meets the qualifying requirements specified in Subchapter S of the Internal Revenue Code can operate as an **S corporation.** If a corporation has S corporation status, it can avoid the imposition of income taxes at the corporate level while retaining many of the advantages of a corporation, particularly limited liability.

QUALIFICATION REQUIREMENTS FOR S CORPORATIONS Among the numerous requirements for S corporation status, the following are the most important:

1. The corporation must be a domestic corporation.
2. The corporation must not be a member of an affiliated group of corporations.
3. The shareholders of the corporation must be individuals, estates, or certain trusts. Nonqualifying trusts and partnerships cannot be shareholders. Corporations can be shareholders under certain circumstances.
4. The corporation must have no more than one hundred shareholders.
5. The corporation must have only one class of stock, although not all shareholders need have the same voting rights.
6. No shareholder of the corporation may be a nonresident alien.

BENEFITS OF S CORPORATIONS At times, it is beneficial for a regular corporation to elect S corporation status. Benefits include the following:

1. When the corporation has losses, the S election allows the shareholders to use the losses to offset other income.
2. When the stockholder's tax bracket is lower than the tax bracket for regular corporations, the S election causes the corporation's entire income to be taxed in the shareholder's bracket (because it is taxed as personal income), whether or not it is distributed. This is particularly attractive when the corporation wants to accumulate earnings for some future business purpose.

Because of these tax benefits, many close corporations opted for S corporation status in the past. Today, however, the limited liability partnership and the limited liability company (discussed in Chapters 36 and 37, respectively) offer similar advantages plus additional benefits, including more flexibility in forming and operating the business. Hence, the S corporation is losing some of its significance.

PROFESSIONAL CORPORATIONS

Professionals such as physicians, lawyers, dentists, and accountants can incorporate. Professional corporations are typically identified by the letters *P.C.* (professional corporation), *S.C.* (service corporation), or *P.A.* (professional association). In general, the laws governing professional corporations are similar to those governing ordinary business corporations, but there are a few differences with regard to liability that deserve mention.

First, there is generally no limitation on liability for acts of malpractice or obligations incurred because of a breach of duty to a client or patient of the professional corporation. In other words, each shareholder in a professional corporation can be held liable for any malpractice liability incurred by the others within the scope of the corporate business. The reason for this rule is that professionals, in contrast to shareholders in other types of corporations, should not be allowed to avoid liability for their wrongful acts simply by virtue of incorporating. Second, under many states' statutes, professional persons are fully liable not only for their own negligent or wrongful acts, but also for the misconduct of any person under their direct supervision who is rendering professional services on behalf of the corporation. Third, a shareholder in a professional corporation is generally protected from contractual liability and liability arising from the tortious acts of other professionals that are unrelated to malpractice or breach of a duty to clients or patients.

CONCEPT SUMMARY 38.1 | Classification of Corporations

CLASSIFICATION	DESCRIPTION
DOMESTIC, FOREIGN, AND ALIEN CORPORATIONS	A corporation is referred to as a *domestic corporation* in its home state (the state in which it incorporates). A corporation formed in one state but doing business in another is referred to in that other state as a *foreign corporation*. A corporation formed in another country but doing business in the United States is referred to in the United States as an *alien corporation*.
PUBLIC AND PRIVATE CORPORATIONS	A *public corporation* is one formed by government (for example, a city or town that incorporates). A *private corporation* is one formed wholly or in part for private benefit. Most corporations are private corporations.
NONPROFIT CORPORATION	A corporation formed for purposes other than profit (for example, charitable, educational, and religious organizations and hospitals).
CLOSE CORPORATION	A corporation owned by a family or a relatively small number of individuals; transfer of shares is usually restricted so that the corporation cannot make a public offering of its securities.
S CORPORATION	A small domestic corporation (must have no more than one hundred shareholders) that, under Subchapter S of the Internal Revenue Code, is given special tax treatment. S corporations allow shareholders to enjoy the limited legal liability of the corporate form but avoid its double-taxation feature (a single tax is imposed at individual income tax rates at the shareholder level, and the S corporation is not taxed separately).
PROFESSIONAL CORPORATION	A corporation formed by professionals (for example, physicians or lawyers) to obtain the advantages of incorporation (such as tax benefits and some limited liability). In most situations, the professional corporation is treated like other corporations, but the courts will hold professionals liable for the malpractice of other professionals in the corporation.

SECTION 4 | Corporate Formation

Corporations generally come into existence through two steps: (1) preliminary organizational and promotional undertakings (particularly, obtaining capital for the future corporation) and (2) the legal process of incorporation.

PROMOTIONAL ACTIVITIES

Before a corporation becomes a reality, people invest in the proposed corporation as subscribers, and contracts are frequently made by promoters on behalf of the future corporation. **Promoters** are those who, for themselves or others, take the preliminary steps in organizing a corporation. One of the tasks of the promoter is to issue a **prospectus,** which is a document required by federal or state securities laws (see Chapter 41) that describes the financial operations of the corporation, thus allowing an investor to make an informed decision. The promoter also secures the corporate charter.

In addition, a promoter may purchase or lease property with a view toward selling it to the corporation when the corporation is formed. A promoter may also enter into contracts with attorneys, accountants, architects, and other professionals whose services will be needed in planning for the proposed corporation. Finally, a promoter induces people to purchase stock in the corporation.

PROMOTER'S LIABILITY As a general rule, a promoter is held personally liable on preincorporation contracts. Courts simply hold that promoters are not agents when a corporation has yet to come into existence. If, however, the promoter secures the contracting party's agreement to hold only the corporation (not the promoter) liable on the contract, the promoter will not be liable in the event of any breach.

Once the corporation is formed, the promoter remains personally liable until the corporation assumes the preincorporation contract by *novation* (see Chapter 16). Novation releases the promoter and makes the corporation liable for performing the contractual obligations. In some cases, the corporation adopts the promoter's contract by undertaking to perform it. Most courts hold that adoption in and of itself does not discharge the promoter from contractual liability. A corporation normally cannot ratify a preincorporation contract, as no principal was in existence at the time the contract was made.

SUBSCRIBERS AND SUBSCRIPTIONS Prior to the actual formation of the corporation, the promoter can contact potential individual investors, and they can agree to purchase shares of stock in the future corporation. This agreement is often referred to as a *subscription agreement,* and the potential investor is called a *subscriber.* Depending on state law, subscribers become shareholders as soon as the corporation is formed or as soon as the corporation accepts the agreement. This way, if corporation X becomes insolvent, the trustee in bankruptcy (see Chapter 30) can collect the consideration for any unpaid stock from a preincorporation subscriber.

Most courts view preincorporation subscriptions as continuing offers to purchase corporate stock. On or after its formation, the corporation can choose to accept the offer to purchase stock. Many courts also treat a subscription as a contract between the subscribers, making it irrevocable except with the consent of all of the subscribers. Under the RMBCA, a subscription is irrevocable for a period of six months unless the subscription agreement provides otherwise or unless all the subscribers agree to the revocation of the subscription [RMBCA 6.20]. In other jurisdictions, the preincorporation subscriber can revoke the offer to purchase before acceptance without liability, however.

INCORPORATION PROCEDURES

The exact procedures for incorporation differ among the states, but the basic requirements are similar.

STATE CHARTERING The first step in the incorporation procedure is to select a state in which to incorporate. Because state incorporation laws differ, individuals may look for the states that offer the most advantageous tax or incorporation provisions. Delaware has historically had the least restrictive laws. Consequently, many corporations, including a number of the largest, have incorporated there. Delaware's statutes permit firms to incorporate in Delaware and carry out their business and locate their operating headquarters elsewhere. (Most other states now permit this as well.) Closely held corporations, however, particularly those of a professional nature, generally incorporate in the state in which their principal stockholders live and work.

In the following case, the state had revoked a corporation's **corporate charter** (the document issued by a state agency or authority—usually the secretary of state—that grants a corporation legal existence and the right to function) because of the corporation's failure to pay certain taxes. The issue before the court was whether a shareholder who had assumed an obligation of the corporation after revocation of its charter could be held personally liable for the unsatisfactory performance of the contract.

CASE 38.2   ## Bullington v. Palangio

Arkansas Supreme
Court, 2001.
345 Ark. 320.
45 S.W.3d 834.
http://courts.state.ar.us/
opinions/opinions.html[a]

BACKGROUND AND FACTS *Jerry Bullington, doing business as Bullington Builders, Inc. (BBI), entered into a contract with Helen Palangio for the construction of a new house in Damascus, Arkansas. Bullington signed the contract "Jerry Bullington, d/b/a Bullington Builders, Inc.," but did not indicate any official capacity as a corporate officer. BBI had been incorporated in 1993. Its only shareholders were Bullington, who managed the business, and his wife. About one and a half months before Palangio's house was completed, BBI's charter was revoked for failure to pay Arkansas franchise taxes,[b] and it was not reinstated. Bullington finished the house, but Palangio was not satisfied with the work or with Bullington's attempts to address her complaints. More than a year later, Palangio hired another builder to remedy the alleged defects. Palangio then filed a suit in an Arkansas state court against Bullington, alleging, in part, breach of contract and asserting that the corporate entity did not shield him from personal liability. The court held Bullington liable to Palangio for $19,000. Bullington appealed to the Arkansas Supreme Court.*

IN THE LANGUAGE OF THE COURT

  RAY THORNTON, Justice.

* * * *

* * * [Arkansas Code Section] 26-54-104(a) provides, in relevant part:

(a) Every corporation shall file an annual franchise tax report and pay an annual franchise tax, unless exempted * * * .

Additionally, [Arkansas Code Section] 26-54-111(a) provides:

(a) On or before January 1 of each year, the Secretary of State shall issue a proclamation proclaiming as forfeited the corporate charters * * * of all corporations, both domestic and foreign which, according to his records, are delinquent in the payment of the annual franchise tax for any prior year.

* * * Reading these statutory provisions together, it is clear that *our statutory law imposes an affirmative duty on the corporation to file franchise tax forms and pay the corresponding fees in order to maintain its corporate status.* [Emphasis added.]

In addition to our statutory law, we have well-established case law regarding the issue of whether personal liability attaches for liabilities that arise if a corporate charter * * * is revoked. * * * [T]o exempt any association of persons from personal liability for the debts of a proposed corporation, they must comply fully with the [law] under which the corporation is created and that partial compliance with the [law] is not sufficient.

* * * [T]he reasoning behind cases holding officers and stockholders individually liable for obligations that arise during the operation of a corporation when the corporate charter has been revoked for nonpayment of franchise taxes is that they ought not be allowed to avoid personal liability because of their nonfeasance [failure to comply with the law].

* * * *

---

a. In the "Search Cases by Party Name" box, enter "Bullington." In the page showing search results, scroll down the list to 6/21/2001 and click on the case name to access the opinion. The Arkansas judiciary maintains this Web site.

b. A *franchise tax* is an annual tax imposed for the privilege of doing business in a state.

CASE 38.2 | Continued In the instant case, it is undisputed that the corporate charter of Bullington Builders, Inc., was revoked for failure to pay franchise taxes approximately one and one-half months prior to the completion of construction, and the charter was not reinstated. After the corporate charter was revoked, appellant individually assumed the performance of the contract. * * * [W]e hold that appellant was personally liable for any liabilities that resulted from faulty or incomplete performance of the contract, including those arising as breaches of express or implied warranties.

DECISION AND REMEDY *The Arkansas Supreme Court affirmed the lower court's judgment, holding Bullington personally liable for the unsatisfactory performance of the contract with Palangio.*

WHAT IF THE FACTS WERE DIFFERENT? *If there had been no express warranties and all implied warranties had been disclaimed, could Bullington have avoided liability?*

ARTICLES OF INCORPORATION The primary document needed to begin the incorporation process is called the *articles of incorporation* (see Exhibit 38–1 on the next page). The articles include basic information about the corporation and serve as a primary source of authority for its future organization and business functions. The person or persons who execute the articles are called *incorporators* and will be discussed shortly. Generally, the information indicated below should be included in the articles of incorporation.

—Corporate Name. The choice of a corporate name is subject to state approval to ensure against duplication or deception. State statutes usually require that the secretary of state run a check on the proposed name in the state of incorporation. Some states require the incorporators to run a check on the proposed name at their own expense. Once cleared, a name can be reserved for a short time (for a fee), pending the completion of the articles of incorporation. All corporate statutes require the corporation name to include the word *Corporation, Incorporated, Company,* or *Limited* or an abbreviation of one of these terms [RMBCA 4.01, 4.02].

The new corporation's name may not be the same as, or deceptively similar to, the name of an existing corporation doing business in the state. For example, if an existing corporation is named General Dynamics, Inc., the state will not allow another corporation to be called General Dynamic, Inc., because that name is deceptively similar to the first and would impliedly transfer part of the goodwill established by the first corporate user to the second corporation. (See the discussion of trade names in Chapter 8.)

—Nature and Purpose. The articles must specify the intended business activities of the corporation,

and naturally, these activities must be lawful. Stating a general corporate purpose is usually sufficient to give rise to all of the powers necessary or convenient to the purpose of the organization. The articles can state, for example, that the corporation is organized "to engage in the production and sale of agricultural products." There is a trend toward allowing corporate charters to state that the corporation is organized for "any legal business," with no mention of specifics, to avoid the need for future amendments to the corporate articles [RMBCA 2.02(b)(2)(i), 3.01].

Some states prohibit certain licensed professionals, such as physicians or lawyers, from forming a general business corporation and require them instead to incorporate as a professional corporation (discussed previously).[7] Also, in some states, businesses in certain industries—such as banks, insurance companies, or public utilities—cannot be operated in the general corporate form and are governed by special incorporation statutes.

—Duration. A corporation can have perpetual existence under the corporate statutes of most states. A few states, however, prescribe a maximum duration, after which the corporation must formally renew its existence.

—Capital Structure. The articles generally set forth the capital structure of the corporation. A few state statutes require a very small capital investment for ordinary business corporations but a greater capital investment for those engaged in insurance or banking. The articles must also indicate the number of shares of stock the corporation is authorized to issue and may

---

7. See, for example, New Jersey Statutes Annotated Title 14A:17-1 *et seq.*

EXHIBIT 38-1   Articles of Incorporation

ARTICLE ONE

The name of the corporation is _____ .

ARTICLE TWO

The period of its duration is _____ (may be "perpetual," a number of years, or until a certain date).

ARTICLE THREE

The purpose (or purposes) for which the corporation is organized is (are) _____ _____ .

ARTICLE FOUR

The aggregate number of shares that the corporation shall have authority to issue is _____ of the par value of _____ dollar(s) each (or "without par value").

ARTICLE FIVE

The corporation will not commence business until it has received for the issuance of its shares consideration of the value of _____ (can be any sum not less than $1,000).

ARTICLE SIX

The address of the corporation's registered office is _____ , and the name of its registered agent at such address is _____ _____ .
(Use the street or building or rural address of the registered office, not a post office box number.)

ARTICLE SEVEN

The number of initial directors is _____ , and the names and addresses of the directors are _____ _____ .

ARTICLE EIGHT

The name and address of the incorporator is _____ _____ .

                (signed) _____
                                       Incorporator

Sworn to on _____ by the above-named incorporator.
               (date)

                                   _____
                                           Notary Public
(Notary Seal)

include other information, such as the valuation of the shares and the types or classes of stock authorized for issuance [RMBCA 2.02(a)].

—Internal Organization. The articles should describe the internal management structure of the corporation, although this can be included in bylaws adopted after the corporation is formed [RMBCA 2.02]. The articles of incorporation commence the corporation; the bylaws are formed after commence-

ment by the board of directors. Bylaws are subject to, and cannot conflict with, the incorporation statute or the corporation's charter [RMBCA 2.06].

Under the RMBCA, the shareholders may amend or repeal bylaws. The board of directors may also amend or repeal bylaws unless the articles of incorporation or provisions of the incorporation statute reserve that power to the shareholders exclusively [RMBCA 10.20]. Typical bylaw provisions describe voting procedures and requirements for shareholders, the election of the board of directors, the methods of replacing directors, and the manner and scheduling of shareholders' meetings and board meetings (these procedures will be discussed in Chapter 39).

—*Registered Office and Agent.* The corporation must indicate the location and address of its registered office within the state [RMBCA 2.02(a)(3)]. Usually, the registered office is also the principal office of the corporation. The corporation must give the name and address of a specific person who has been designated as an agent and who can receive legal documents on behalf of the corporation. These legal documents include service of process (the delivery of a court order requiring an appearance in court).

—*Incorporators.* Each incorporator must be listed by name and must also indicate an address [RMBCA 2.02(a)(4)]. An incorporator is a person— often, the corporate promoter—who applies to the state on behalf of the corporation to obtain its corporate charter. The incorporator need not be a subscriber and need not have any interest at all in the corporation. Many states do not impose residency or age requirements for incorporators. States vary as to the required number of incorporators; it can be as few as one or as many as three. Incorporators are required to sign the articles of incorporation when they are submitted to the state; often, this is the incorporators' only duty. In some states, they participate at the first organizational meeting of the corporation.

CERTIFICATE OF INCORPORATION Once the articles of incorporation have been prepared, signed, and authenticated by the incorporators, they are sent to the appropriate state official, usually the secretary of state, along with the appropriate filing fee. In many states, the secretary of state will then issue a **certificate of incorporation** representing the state's authorization for the corporation to conduct business. (This may also be called the *corporate charter.*) The certificate and a copy of the articles are returned to the incorporators. The incorporators then hold the initial organizational meeting, which completes the details of incorporation [RMBCA 2.03].

FIRST ORGANIZATIONAL MEETING The first organizational meeting is often provided for in the articles of incorporation but is not held until after the charter is actually granted. At this meeting, the incorporators elect the first board of directors and complete the routine business of incorporation (pass bylaws, issue stock, and so forth). Sometimes, the meeting is held after the election of the board of directors, and the business to be transacted depends on the requirements of the state's incorporation statute, the nature of the business, the provisions made in the articles, and the desires of the promoters [RMBCA 2.05].

Adoption of bylaws—the internal rules of management for the corporation—is probably the most important function of the first organizational meeting. The shareholders, directors, and officers must abide by the bylaws in conducting corporate business. Corporate employees and third persons dealing with the corporation are not bound by the bylaws, however, unless they have reason to be familiar with them.

SECTION 5 | Improper Incorporation

The procedures for incorporation are very specific. If they are not followed precisely, others may be able to challenge the existence of the corporation. Errors in incorporation procedures can become important when, for example, a third person who is attempting to enforce a contract or bring suit for a tort injury fortuitously learns of them. On the basis of improper incorporation, the plaintiff could seek to make the would-be shareholders personally liable. Also, when the corporation attempts to enforce a contract against a defaulting party, if the defaulting party learns of a defect in the incorporation procedures, he or she may be able to avoid liability on that ground.

To prevent injustice, the courts will sometimes attribute corporate existence to an improperly formed corporation by holding it to be a *de jure* corporation or a *de facto* corporation, as discussed below. In some circumstances, corporation by estoppel may also occur.

DE JURE AND DE FACTO CORPORATIONS

In the event of substantial compliance with all conditions precedent to incorporation, a corporation is said to have *de jure* existence in law. In most states and under RMBCA 2.03(b), the certificate of incorporation is viewed as conclusive evidence that all mandatory statutory provisions have been met. This means that the corporation is properly formed, and only the state, not a third party, can attack its existence. If, for example, an incorporator's address was incorrectly listed, the corporation was improperly formed. The law, however, does not regard such inconsequential procedural defects as detracting from substantial compliance, and courts will uphold the *de jure* status of the corporate entity.

Sometimes, there is a defect in complying with statutory mandates—for example, the corporate charter may have expired. Under these circumstances, the corporation may have *de facto* status, meaning that its existence cannot be challenged by third parties (except the state). The following elements are required for *de facto* status:

1. There must be a state statute under which the corporation can be validly incorporated.
2. The parties must have made a good faith attempt to comply with the statute.
3. The enterprise must already have undertaken to do business as a corporation.

CORPORATION BY ESTOPPEL

If an association that is neither an actual corporation nor a *de facto* or *de jure* corporation holds itself out as being a corporation, it will be estopped from denying corporate status in a lawsuit by a third party. This situation usually arises when a third party contracts with a business entity that claims to be a corporation but does not hold a certificate of incorporation. When justice requires, the courts treat an alleged corporation as if it were an actual corporation for the purpose of determining the rights and liabilities in particular circumstances. Corporation by estoppel is thus determined by the situation. The recognition of corporate status does not extend beyond the resolution of the problem at hand.

SECTION 6 | Disregarding the Corporate Entity

Occasionally, the owners use a corporate entity to perpetrate a fraud, circumvent the law, or in some other way accomplish an illegitimate objective. In these situations, the court will ignore the corporate structure and **pierce the corporate veil,** thus exposing the shareholders to personal liability [RMBCA 2.04]. In other words, when the facts show that great injustice would result from the use of a corporation to avoid individual responsibility, a court will look behind the corporate structure to the individual stockholder.

The following are some of the factors that frequently cause the courts to pierce the corporate veil:

1. A party is tricked or misled into dealing with the corporation rather than the individual.
2. The corporation is set up never to make a profit or always to be insolvent, or it is too "thinly" capitalized—that is, it has insufficient capital at the time it is formed to meet its prospective debts or potential liabilities.
3. Statutory corporate formalities, such as holding required corporation meetings, are not followed.
4. Personal and corporate interests are mixed together, or **commingled,** to the extent that the corporation has no separate identity.

As the next case illustrates, sometimes more than one of these factors is present.

CASE 38.3 | **In re Flutie New York Corp.**

United States Bankruptcy Court, Southern District of New York, 2004. 310 Bankr. 31.

BACKGROUND AND FACTS *In 1990, Michael Flutie created MFME Model Management Company (MFME), doing business as "Company Management," to represent fashion models for all purposes, including the entertainment business. MFME's offices were in New York City, New York. In 1995, Michael transferred MFME's assets to Flutie New York Corporation (Flutie N.Y.), a company that Michael and his mother Victoria had created one year earlier. Flutie N.Y. performed the same services for the same models at the same address, and also did business as Company Management. Michael's father, Albert, was the sole shareholder and president of Flutie N.Y., but Michael was responsible for all major decisions involving the company. Flutie N.Y. did not follow any corporate formalities—there were no board meetings, shareholders' meetings, or shareholder votes—but did pay Albert's and Michael's personal expenses. In 2001, Michael transferred the assets of Flutie N.Y. to Flutie Media Corporation, a firm that he and Albert had created in 1999. The next year, Flutie N.Y. filed a petition in a federal bankruptcy court to declare bankruptcy. David Kittay, the court-appointed trustee, filed a suit against Michael, in part seeking to pierce the corporate veil and hold him liable for all of Flutie N.Y.'s debts, including more than $2.7 million in creditors' claims.*

IN THE LANGUAGE OF THE COURT

BURTON R. LIFLAND, Bankruptcy Judge.

* * * *

Here, the elements present warrant a finding of individual liability under [a theory that personal and corporate business were commingled] against Michael Flutie. Evidence reflects that Michael Flutie was using Flutie N.Y. and then later Flutie Media, to suit his own needs, and was using corporate funds for his own personal use. It is clear that Michael Flutie had exclusive control over the operations of Flutie N.Y., and with this control he committed wrongful acts which resulted in significant losses by Flutie N.Y.

* * * I find that the transfers to Michael Flutie, as well as the transfers to Albert Flutie on behalf of Michael, were made without fair consideration to Flutie N.Y. The facts are clear that Michael Flutie abused the corporate form and thereby, harmed Flutie N.Y.

Further, there is sufficient evidence that Flutie Media acted as the alter ego of Flutie N.Y. Flutie N.Y. fraudulently transferred model management contracts and/or its arrangements for the services of the models it represented to Flutie Media for no consideration. Flutie Media, under the control of Michael Flutie, continued to operate a modeling agency, continued to represent themselves to the public as Company Management and continued to earn commissions on the work performed by the former Flutie N.Y. models.

Sufficient factors are also present to warrant the piercing of the corporate veil and a finding that Michael Flutie is liable for any and all damages suffered by Flutie N.Y. It is clear from the evidence adduced [provided] during discovery that no corporate formalities were followed. There were no board of directors' meetings, no board meetings or votes, and stock certificates were never issued.

Several entities shared common office space with Flutie N.Y. without paying rent, including Flutie Media * * * .

Another factor to consider when determining whether to pierce the corporate veil is inadequate capitalization. It is clear from the books and records of Flutie N.Y. that from at least December 31, 1997 through December 31, 2000, the company's liabilities exceeded its assets. In addition, the company had income losses on its income statements in 1995, 1996, 1997, 1998, and 2000. These factors illustrate that from the beginning of the corporation, the business was undercapitalized. [Emphasis added.]

Michael Flutie looted Flutie N.Y. and used the corporate veil as a sham through which to engage in conduct intended to deprive the Debtor's legitimate creditors of assets of the Debtor. * * *

* * * *

Based on the facts alleged, the Trustee has provided the Court with the requisite proof to support a claim for alter ego against Michael Flutie, and Michael Flutie is, therefore, personally responsible for all of the debts of the Debtor's Estate.

DECISION AND REMEDY *The court pierced the corporate veil and held Michael liable for all of Flutie N.Y.'s debts. The firm was too thinly capitalized, failed to follow corporate formalities, and was used as a "sham" to deprive its creditors of amounts that they were owed. Michael behaved as though the firm's assets were his, and ignored the effect of his actions on the firm and its creditors.*

WHAT IF THE FACTS WERE DIFFERENT? *If the corporation had observed corporate formalities, including board meetings, shareholders' meetings, and shareholder votes, would the result have been different? Explain.*

THE COMMINGLING OF PERSONAL AND CORPORATE ASSETS

To elaborate on the fourth factor in the preceding list, consider a close corporation that is formed according to law by a single person or by a few family members. In such a situation, the corporate entity and the sole stockholder (or family-member stockholders) must carefully preserve the separate status of the corporation and its owners. Certain practices invite trouble for the one-person or family-owned corporation: the commingling of corporate and personal funds; the failure to remit taxes, including payroll and sales taxes; and the shareholders' continuous personal use of corporate property (for example, vehicles).

LOANS TO THE CORPORATION

Corporation laws usually do not specifically prohibit a stockholder from lending funds to her or his corporation. When an officer, director, or majority shareholder lends the corporation funds and takes back security in the form of corporate assets, however, the courts will scrutinize the transaction closely. Any such transaction must be made in good faith and for fair value.

PERSONAL LIABILITY TO CREDITORS

When the corporate privilege is abused for personal benefit and the corporate business is treated in such a careless manner that the corporation and the shareholder in control are no longer separate entities, the court usually will require the shareholder to assume personal liability to creditors for the corporation's debts.

SECTION **7** | Corporate Financing

Corporations are financed by the issuance and sale of corporate securities. **Securities** (stocks and bonds) evidence the obligation to pay funds or the right to participate in earnings and the distribution of corporate assets. **Stocks,** or *equity securities*, represent the purchase of ownership in the business firm. **Bonds** (debentures), or *debt securities*, represent the borrowing of funds by firms (and governments). Of course, not all debt is in the form of debt securities. For example, some debt is in the form of accounts payable and notes payable. Accounts and notes payable are typically short-term debts. Bonds are simply a way for a corporation to split up its long-term debt so that it can market the debt more easily.

BONDS

Bonds are issued by business firms and by governments at all levels as evidence of the funds they are borrowing from investors. Bonds almost always have a designated *maturity date*—the date when the principal, or face amount, of the bond (or loan) is returned to the investor—and are sometimes referred to as *fixed-income securities* because their owners receive fixed-dollar interest payments during the period of time prior to maturity.

The characteristics of corporate bonds vary widely, in part because corporations differ in their ability to generate the earnings and cash flow necessary to make interest payments and to repay the principal amount of the bonds at maturity. Furthermore, corporate bonds are only a part of the total debt and the overall financial structure of corporate business. The various types of corporate bonds are described in Exhibit 38–2.

STOCKS

Issuing stocks is another way for corporations to obtain financing [RMBCA 6.01]. The ways in which stocks differ from bonds are summarized in Exhibit 38–3. Basically, stocks represent ownership in a business firm, whereas bonds represent borrowing by the firm.

Exhibit 38–4 offers a summary of the types of stocks issued by corporations. The two major types are *common stock* and *preferred stock*.

COMMON STOCK   The true ownership of a corporation is represented by **common stock.** It provides a proportionate interest in the corporation with regard to (1) control, (2) earnings, and (3) net assets. A shareholder's interest is generally in proportion to the

EXHIBIT 38–2 **Types of Corporate Bonds**

TYPE	DEFINITION
Debenture Bonds	Bonds for which no specific assets of the corporation are pledged as backing. Rather, the bonds are backed by the general credit rating of the corporation, plus any assets that can be seized if the corporation allows the debentures to go into default.
Mortgage Bonds	Bonds that pledge specific property. If the corporation defaults on the bonds, the bondholders can foreclose on the property.
Convertible Bonds	Bonds that can be exchanged for a specified number of shares of stock under certain conditions.
Callable Bonds	Bonds that may be called in and the principal repaid at specified times or under conditions stipulated in the bond when it is issued.

EXHIBIT 38-3 **How Do Stocks and Bonds Differ?**

STOCKS	BONDS
1. Stocks represent ownership.	1. Bonds represent debt.
2. Stocks (common) do not have a fixed dividend rate.	2. Interest on bonds must always be paid, whether or not any profit is earned.
3. Stockholders can elect the board of directors, which controls the corporation.	3. Bondholders usually have no voice in or control over management of the corporation.
4. Stocks do not have a maturity date; the corporation usually does not repay the stockholder.	4. Bonds have a maturity date, when the corporation is to repay the bondholder the face value of the bond.
5. All corporations issue or offer to sell stocks. This is the usual definition of a corporation.	5. Corporations do not necessarily issue bonds.
6. Stockholders have a claim against the property and income of a corporation after all creditors' claims have been met.	6. Bondholders have a claim against the property and income of a corporation that must be met before the claims of stockholders.

number of shares owned out of the total number of shares issued.

Any person who purchases shares acquires voting rights—one vote per share held. Voting rights in a corporation apply to the election of the firm's board of directors and to any proposed changes in the ownership structure of the firm. For example, a holder of common stock generally has the right to vote in a decision on a proposed merger, as mergers can change the proportion of ownership. State corporation law specifies the types of actions for which shareholder approval must be obtained.

Holders of common stock are investors who assume a *residual* position in the overall financial structure of the business. In terms of receiving returns on their investments, they are last in line. They are entitled to earnings only after the corporation pays all other groups—suppliers, employees, managers, bankers, governments, bondholders, and holders of preferred stock—what is due them. Once those groups are paid, the owners of common stock may be entitled to *all* the remaining earnings. But the board of directors normally is not under any duty to declare the remaining earnings as dividends.

PREFERRED STOCK **Preferred stock** is stock with *preferences*. Usually, this means that holders of preferred stock have priority over holders of common

EXHIBIT 38-4 **Types of Stocks**

TYPE	DEFINITION
Common Stock	Voting shares that represent ownership interest in a corporation. Common stock has the lowest priority with respect to payment of dividends and distribution of assets on the corporation's dissolution.
Preferred Stock	Shares of stock that have priority over common-stock shares as to payment of dividends and distribution of assets on dissolution. Dividend payments are usually a fixed percentage of the face value of the share. Preferred shares may or may not be nonvoting shares.
Cumulative Preferred Stock	Preferred shares for which required dividends not paid in a given year must be paid in a subsequent year before any common-stock dividends can be paid.
Participating Preferred Stock	Preferred shares entitling the owner to receive (1) the preferred-stock dividend and (2) additional dividends after the corporation has paid dividends on common stock.
Convertible Preferred Stock	Preferred shares entitling the owner to convert his or her shares into a specified number of common shares either in the issuing corporation or, sometimes, in another corporation.
Redeemable, or Callable, Preferred Stock	Preferred shares issued with the express condition that the issuing corporation has the right to repurchase the shares as specified.

stock as to dividends and to payment on dissolution of the corporation. Preferred stockholders may or may not have the right to vote (the trend is toward giving preferred stockholders the right to vote).

From an investment standpoint, preferred stock is more similar to bonds than to common stock. Preferred shareholders receive periodic dividend payments, usually established as a fixed percentage of the face amount of each preferred share. A share of 6 percent preferred stock with a face amount of $100 per share would pay its owner a $6 dividend each year. Payment of these dividends is not a legal obligation on the part of the firm. Technically, preferred stock is equity, so it is not included among the liabilities of a business. Like other equity securities, preferred shares have no fixed maturity date on which they must be retired by the firm. Although occasionally firms retire preferred stock, they are not legally obligated to do so.

LOCATING POTENTIAL INVESTORS ONLINE

Today, the Internet allows promoters and others to access, easily and inexpensively, a large number of potential investors. A number of online "matching services" are available to match potential investors with companies or future companies that are seeking investors. Online matching services enable entrepreneurs to reach a wide group of potential investors quickly and with relatively little effort. A corporate promoter or a small company seeking capital investment can pay a fee to one of these services, which will then include a description of the company in a list that it makes available to investors, also for a fee.

Although matching services are not new, what is new is that service providers are now online and many of them have significantly expanded the geographic scope of their operations. Some services specialize in matching entrepreneurs in specific industries with potential investors. Other services might focus on matching start-up companies with foreign investors, or restrict their operations to firms within a certain region, such as the Pacific Northwest. These companies sometimes also assist businesspersons in creating effective business plans or managing financial issues.

REVIEWING CORPORATIONS— FORMATION AND FINANCING

William Sharp was the sole shareholder and manager of Chickasaw Club, Inc., an S corporation that operated a popular nightclub of the same name in Columbus, Georgia. Sharp maintained a corporate checking account, but paid the club's employees, suppliers, and entertainers in cash out of the club's proceeds. Sharp owned the property on which the club was located and rented it to the club, but made mortgage payments out of the club's proceeds and often paid other personal expenses with Chickasaw corporate funds. At 12:45 A.M. on July 31, 2005, eighteen-year-old Aubrey Lynn Pursley, who was already intoxicated, entered the Chickasaw Club. A city ordinance prohibited individuals under the age of twenty-one from entering nightclubs, but Chickasaw employees did not check Pursley's identification to verify her age. Pursley drank more alcohol at Chickasaw and was visibly intoxicated when she left the club at 3:00 A.M. with a beer in her hand. Shortly afterward, Pursley lost control of her car, struck a tree, and was killed. Joseph Dancause, Pursley's stepfather, filed a tort lawsuit in a Georgia state court against Chickasaw Club, Inc., and William Sharp, seeking damages. Using the information presented in the chapter, answer the following questions.

1. Under what theory might a court in this case make an exception to the limited liability of shareholders and hold Sharp personally liable for the damages? What factors would be relevant to the court's decision?

2. Suppose that Chickasaw's articles of incorporation failed to describe the corporation's purpose or management structure as required by state law. Would a court be likely to rule that Sharp is personally liable to Dancause on that basis?

3. Suppose that the club extended credit to its regular patrons in an effort maintain a loyal clientele, although neither the articles of incorporation nor the corporate bylaws authorized this practice. Would the corporation likely have the power to engage in this activity? Explain.

REVIEWING CORPORATIONS—FORMATION AND FINANCING (*continued*)

4. | How would the court classify the Chickasaw Club corporation—domestic or foreign, public or private?

5. | Suppose that Chickasaw Club, Inc., wants to obtain additional funds. Discuss the options available.

TERMS AND CONCEPTS TO REVIEW

alien corporation 768

articles of incorporation 767

bond 780

bylaw 767

certificate of incorporation 777

close corporation 769

commingle 778

common stock 780

corporate charter 774

domestic corporation 768

foreign corporation 768

pierce the corporate veil 778

preferred stock 781

promoter 773

prospectus 773

retained earnings 766

S corporation 771

securities 780

stock 780

ultra vires 768

QUESTIONS AND CASE PROBLEMS

38–1. Jonathan, Gary, and Ricardo are active members of a partnership called Swim City. The partnership manufactures, sells, and installs outdoor swimming pools in the states of Arkansas and Texas. The partners want to continue to be active in management and to expand the business into other states as well. They also are concerned about rather large recent judgments entered against swimming pool companies throughout the United States. Based on these facts only, discuss whether the partnership should incorporate.

38–2. 🏛 **QUESTION WITH SAMPLE ANSWER**

Cummings, Okawa, and Taft are recent college graduates who want to form a corporation to manufacture and sell personal computers. Peterson tells them he will set in motion the formation of their corporation. First, Peterson makes a contract with Owens for the purchase of a piece of land for $20,000. Owens does not know of the prospective corporate formation at the time the contract is signed. Second, Peterson makes a contract with Babcock to build a small plant on the property being purchased. Babcock's contract is conditional on the corporation's formation. Peterson secures all necessary subscription agreements and capitalization, and he files the articles of incorporation. A charter is issued.

(a) Discuss whether the newly formed corporation, Peterson, or both are liable on the contracts with Owens and Babcock.

(b) Discuss whether the corporation is automatically liable to Babcock on formation.

For a sample answer to this question, go to Appendix I at the end of this text.

38–3. Oya Paka and two business associates formed a corporation called Paka Corp. for the purpose of selling computer services. Oya, who owned 50 percent of the corporate shares, served as the corporation's president. Oya wished to obtain a personal loan from her bank for $250,000, but the bank required the note to be cosigned by a third party. Oya cosigned the note in the name of the corporation. Later, Oya defaulted on the note, and the bank sued the corporation for payment. The corporation asserted, as a defense, that Oya had exceeded her authority when she cosigned the note on behalf of the corporation. Had she? Explain.

38–4. DISREGARDING THE CORPORATE ENTITY. Steven and Janis Gimbert leased a warehouse to a manufacturing business owned by Manzar Zuberi. Zuberi signed the lease as the purported representative of "ATM Manufacturing, Inc.," which was a nonexistent corporation. Zuberi was actually the president of two existing corporations, ATM Enterprises, Inc., and Ameri-Pak International. Under the Ameri-Pak name, Zuberi manufactured a household cleaning product in the Gimberts' warehouse. The hydrochloric acid used in the operations severely damaged the premises, and the Gimberts filed a suit in a Georgia state court against Zuberi personally to collect for the damage. On what basis might Zuberi be held personally liable? Discuss fully. [*Zuberi v. Gimbert*, 230 Ga.App. 471, 496 S.E.2d 741 (1998)]

38-5. S CORPORATIONS. James, Randolph, and Judith Agley, and Michael and Nancy Timmis were shareholders in F & M Distributors, Inc., Venture Packaging, Inc., and Diamond Automations, Inc. James Agley was also a shareholder in Middletown Aerospace. All of the firms were S corporations organized and located in Michigan and doing business in Ohio. None of the shareholders was a resident of Ohio, and none of them personally did business in Ohio. Between 1988 and 1992, the Agleys and the Timmises included their prorated share of the S corporations' income on Ohio personal income tax returns. They believed, however, that out-of-state shareholders should not be taxed in Ohio on the income they received from an S corporation doing business in Ohio. They contended that the income was earned by the S corporation, not by the shareholders. They also emphasized that none of them personally did business in the state. Finally, they asked the Ohio Tax Commissioner for refunds for those years. Should the state grant their request? Why or why not? [*Agley v. Tracy*, 87 Ohio St.3d 265, 719 N.E.2d 951 (1999)]

38-6. TORTS AND CRIMINAL ACTS. Greg Allen is an employee, shareholder, director, and the president of Greg Allen Construction Co. In 1996, Daniel and Sondra Estelle hired Allen's firm to renovate a home they owned in Ladoga, Indiana. To finance the cost, they obtained a line of credit from Banc One, Indiana, which required periodic inspections to disburse funds. Allen was on the job every day and supervised all of the work. He designed all of the structural changes, including a floor system for the bedroom over the living room, the floor system of the living room, and the stairway to the second floor. He did all of the electrical, plumbing, and carpentry work and installed all of the windows. He did most of the drywall taping and finishing and most of the painting. The Estelles found much of this work to be unacceptable, and the bank's inspector agreed that it was of poor quality. When Allen failed to act on the Estelles' complaints, they filed a suit in an Indiana state court against Allen Construction and Allen personally, alleging in part that his individual work on the project was negligent. Can both Allen and his corporation be held liable for this tort? Explain. [*Greg Allen Construction Co. v. Estelle*, 798 N.E.2d 171 (Ind. 2004)]

38-7. ⚖ **CASE PROBLEM WITH SAMPLE ANSWER**

Thomas Persson and Jon Nokes founded Smart Inventions, Inc., in 1991 to market household consumer products. The success of their first product, the Smart Mop, continued with later products, which were sold through infomercials and other means. Persson and Nokes were the firm's officers and equal shareholders, with Persson responsible for product development and Nokes in charge of day-to-day operations. By 1998, they had become dissatisfied with each other's efforts. Nokes represented the firm as financially "dying," "in a grim state, . . . worse than ever," and offered to buy all of Persson's shares for $1.6 million. Persson accepted. On the day that they signed the agreement to transfer the shares, Smart Inventions began marketing a new product—the Tap Light—which was an instant success, generating millions of dollars in revenues. In negotiating with Persson, Nokes had intentionally kept the Tap Light a secret. Persson filed a suit in a California state court against Smart Inventions and others, asserting fraud and other claims. Under what principle might Smart Inventions be liable for Nokes's fraud? Is Smart Inventions liable in this case? Explain. [*Persson v. Smart Inventions, Inc.*, 125 Cal.App.4th 1141, 23 Cal.Rptr.3d 335 (2 Dist. 2005)]

To view a sample answer for this case problem, go to this book's Web site at http://wbl.westbuslaw.com, select "Chapter 38," and click on "Case Problem with Sample Answer."

38-8. CORPORATE POWERS. InterBel Telephone Cooperative, Inc., is a Montana corporation organized under the Montana Rural Electric and Telephone Cooperative Act. This statute limits the purposes of such corporations to providing "adequate telephone service," but adds that this "enumeration . . . shall not be deemed to exclude like or similar objects, purposes, powers, manners, methods, or things." Mooseweb Corp. is an Internet service provider that has been owned and operated by Fred Weber since 1996. Mooseweb provides Web site hosting, modems, computer installation, technical support, and dial-up access to customers in Lincoln County, Montana. InterBel began to offer Internet service in 1999, competing with Mooseweb in Lincoln County. Weber filed a suit in a Montana state court against InterBel, alleging that its Internet service was *ultra vires*. Both parties filed motions for summary judgment. In whose favor should the court rule, and why? [*Weber v. InterBel Telephone Cooperative, Inc.*, 318 Mont. 295, 80 P.3d 88, 2003 MT 320 (2003)]

38-9. ⚖ **A QUESTION OF ETHICS**

In 1990, American Design Properties, Inc. (ADP), leased premises at 8604 Olive Boulevard in St. Louis County, Missouri. Under the lease agreement, ADP had the right to terminate the lease on 120 days' written notice, but it did not have the right to sublease the premises without the lessor's (landowner's) consent. ADP had no bank account, no employees, and no money. ADP had never filed an income tax return or held a directors' or shareholders' meeting. In fact, ADP's only business was to collect and pay the exact amount of rent due under the lease. American Design Group, Inc. (ADG), a wholesale distributor of jewelry and other merchandise, actually occupied 8604 Olive Boulevard. J. H. Blum owned ADG and was an officer and director of both ADG and ADP. Blum's husband, Marvin, was an officer of ADG and signed the lease as an officer of ADP.

Marvin's former son-in-law, Matthew Smith, was a salaried employee of ADG, an officer of ADG, and an officer and director of ADP. In 1995, Nusrala Four, Inc. (later known as Real Estate Investors Four, Inc.), purchased the property at 8604 Olive Boulevard and became the lessor. No one told Nusrala that ADG was the occupant of the premises leased by ADP. ADP continued to pay the rent until November 1998 when Smith paid with a check drawn on ADG's account. No more payments were made. On February 26, 1999, Marvin sent Nusrala a note that read, "We have vacated the property at 8604 Olive," which, Nusrala discovered, had been damaged. Nusrala filed a suit in a Missouri state court against ADG and ADP, seeking payment for the damage. In view of these facts, consider the following questions. [*Real Estate Investors Four, Inc. v. American Design Group, Inc.*, 46 S.W.3d 51 (Mo.App. E.D. 2001)]

(a) Given that ADG had not signed the lease and was not rightfully a sublessee, could ADG be held liable, at least in part, for the damage to the premises? Under what theory might the court ignore the separate corporate identities of ADG and ADP? If you were the judge, how would you rule in this case?

(b) Assuming that ADP had few, if any, corporate assets, would it be fair to preclude Nusrala from recovering payment for the damage from ADG?

(c) Is it ever appropriate for a court to ignore the corporate structure? Why or why not?

38-10. VIDEO QUESTION

Go to this text's Web site at http://wbl.westbuslaw.com and select "Chapter 38." Click on "Video Questions" and view the video titled *Corporation or LLC: Which Is Better?* Then answer the following questions.

(a) Compare the liability that Anna and Caleb would be exposed to as shareholders/owners of a corporation versus as members of a limited liability company (LLC).

(b) How are corporations taxed differently than LLCs?

(c) Given that Anna and Caleb conduct their business (Wizard Internet) over the Internet, can you think of any drawbacks to forming an LLC?

(d) If you were in the position of Anna and Caleb, would you choose to create a corporation or an LLC? Why?

LAW | on the Web

For updated links to resources available on the Web, as well as a variety of other materials, visit this text's Web site at http://wbl.westbuslaw.com.

Cornell University's Legal Information Institute has links to state corporation statutes at

http://www.law.cornell.edu/topics/state_statutes.html

The Center for Corporate Law at the University of Cincinnati College of Law is a good source of information on corporate law. Go to

http://www.law.uc.edu/CCL

LEGAL RESEARCH EXERCISES ON THE WEB

Go to http://wbl.westbuslaw.com, the Web site that accompanies this text. Select "Chapter 38" and click on "Internet Exercises." There you will find the following Internet research exercises that you can perform to learn more about topics covered in this chapter.

Activity 38–1: LEGAL PERSPECTIVE
Corporate Law

Activity 38–2: MANAGEMENT PERSPECTIVE
Online Incorporation

CHAPTER 39
CORPORATIONS—
Directors, Officers, and Shareholders

A corporation joins the efforts and resources of a large number of individuals for the purpose of producing greater returns than those persons could have obtained individually. Corporate directors, officers, and shareholders all play different roles within the corporate entity. Sometimes, actions that may benefit the corporation as a whole do not coincide with the separate interests of the individuals making up the corporation. In such situations, it is important to know the rights and duties of all participants in the corporate enterprise. This chapter focuses on these rights and duties and the ways in which conflicts among corporate participants are resolved.

SECTION 1 | Roles of Directors and Officers

Every corporation is governed by a board of directors. A director occupies a position of responsibility unlike that of other corporate personnel. Directors are sometimes inappropriately characterized as *agents* because they act on behalf of the corporation. No individual director, however, can act as an agent to bind the corporation; and as a group, directors collectively control the corporation in a way that no agent is able to control a principal. Directors are also sometimes incorrectly characterized as *trustees* because they occupy positions of trust and control over the corporation. Unlike trustees, however, they do not own or hold title to property for the use and benefit of others.

Few legal requirements exist concerning directors' qualifications. Only a handful of states impose minimum age and residency requirements. A director is sometimes a shareholder, but this is not a necessary qualification—unless, of course, statutory provisions or corporate articles or bylaws require ownership.

ELECTION OF DIRECTORS

Subject to statutory limitations, the number of directors is set forth in the corporation's articles or bylaws. Historically, the minimum number of directors has been three, but today many states permit fewer. Indeed, the Revised Model Business Corporation Act

(RMBCA), in Section 8.01, permits corporations with fewer than fifty shareholders to eliminate the board of directors.

INITIAL BOARD OF DIRECTORS Normally, the incorporators appoint the first board of directors at the time the corporation is created, or the corporation itself names the directors in the articles. The initial board serves until the first annual shareholders' meeting. Subsequent directors are elected by a majority vote of the shareholders.

TERM OF OFFICE A director usually serves for a term of one year—from annual meeting to annual meeting. Longer and staggered terms are permissible under most state statutes. A common practice is to elect one-third of the board members each year for a three-year term. In this way, there is greater management continuity.

REMOVAL OF DIRECTORS A director can be removed *for cause* (that is, for failing to perform a required duty), either as specified in the articles or bylaws or by shareholder action. Even the board of directors itself may be given power to remove a director for cause, subject to shareholder review. In most states, unless the shareholders have reserved the right at the time of election, a director cannot be removed without cause.

VACANCIES ON THE BOARD OF DIRECTORS Vacancies can occur on the board of directors because of death or resignation or when a new position is created through amendment of the articles or bylaws. In these situations, either the shareholders or the board itself can fill the position, depending on state law or on the provisions of the bylaws.

In the following case, a board increased the number of its directors to diminish the influence that subsequently elected directors would have on the board's decisions. This may have been "legal" according to the firm's bylaws, but was it valid under Delaware law?

CASE 39.1

Delaware Supreme
Court, 2003.
813 A.2d 1118.

MM Companies, Inc. v. Liquid Audio, Inc.

COMPANY PROFILE *Liquid Audio, Inc. (http://www.liquidaudio.com), is a Delaware corporation, with its principal place of business in Redwood City, California. Liquid Audio provides software and services for the delivery of music over the Internet. Formed in 1996, Liquid Audio offered the first digital music-commerce system featuring copy protection and copyright management, as well as the first and largest digital music-distribution network. Liquid Audio's catalogue of secure music downloads is one of the world's largest.*

BACKGROUND AND FACTS *MM Companies, Inc., a Delaware corporation with its principal place of business in New York City, New York, owned 7 percent of Liquid Audio's stock. In October 2001, MM sent a letter to Liquid Audio's board of directors offering to buy all of the company's stock for about $3 per share. The board rejected the offer. Liquid Audio's bylaws provide for a board of five directors divided into three classes. One class is elected each year. The next election, at which two directors would be chosen, was set for September 2002. By mid-August, it appeared that MM's nominees, Seymour Holtzman and James Mitarotonda, would win the election. The board amended the bylaws to increase the number of directors to seven, and appointed Judith Frank and James Somes to fill the new positions. In September, MM's nominees were elected to the board, but their influence was diminished because there were now seven directors. MM filed a suit in a Delaware state court against Liquid Audio and others, challenging the board's actions. The court ruled in favor of the defendants. MM appealed to the Delaware Supreme Court.*

IN THE LANGUAGE OF THE COURT

HOLLAND, Justice:

*   *   *   *

The most fundamental principles of corporate governance are a function of the allocation of power within a corporation between its stockholders and its board of directors. The stockholders' power is the right to vote on specific matters, in particular, in an election of directors. The power of managing the corporate enterprise is vested in the shareholders' duly elected board representatives. *   *   *

*Maintaining a proper balance in the allocation of power between the stockholders' right to elect directors and the board of directors' right to manage the corporation is dependent upon the stockholders' unimpeded right to vote effectively in an election of directors. *   *   * [Emphasis added.]*

*   *   *   *

When the *primary purpose* of a board of directors' [action] is to interfere with or impede the effective exercise of the shareholder franchise [voting rights] in a contested election for directors, the board must first demonstrate a compelling justification for such action as a condition precedent to any judicial consideration of reasonableness and proportionality. *   *   * [S]uch *   *   * actions by a board need not actually prevent the shareholders from attaining any success in seating one or more nominees in a contested election for directors and the election contest need not involve a challenge for outright control of the board of directors. *   *   * [T]he *   *   * actions of the board only need to be taken for the primary purpose of interfering with or impeding the effectiveness of the stockholder vote in a contested election for directors.

*   *   *   *

*   *   * [In this case, the directors] amended the bylaws to provide for a board of seven and appointed two additional members of the Board for the primary purpose of diminishing the

(CONTINUED)

CASE 39.1 | Continued

influence of MM's two nominees * * * . That * * * action * * * compromised the essential role of corporate democracy in maintaining the proper allocation of power between the shareholders and the Board, because that action was taken in the context of a contested election for successor directors. Since the * * * Defendants did not demonstrate a compelling justification for that * * * action, the bylaw amendment that expanded the size of the Liquid Audio board, and permitted the appointment of two new members on the eve of a contested election, should have been invalidated.

DECISION AND REMEDY *The Delaware Supreme Court reversed the judgment of the lower court and remanded the case for further proceedings. The state supreme court concluded that the board's amending the bylaws to increase the number of directors and filling the new positions with appointments was invalid, because the board acted primarily to impede the shareholders' right to vote in an impending election for successor directors.*

BOARD OF DIRECTORS' MEETINGS

The board of directors conducts business by holding formal meetings with recorded minutes. The dates of regular meetings are usually established in the articles or bylaws or by board resolution, and no further notice is customarily required. Special meetings can be called, with notice sent to all directors.

Quorum requirements vary among jurisdictions. (A **quorum** is the minimum number of members of a body of officials or other group that must be present for business to be validly transacted.) Many states leave the decision as to quorum requirements to the corporate articles or bylaws. In the absence of specific state statutes, most states provide that a quorum is a majority of the number of directors authorized in the articles or bylaws.

Voting is normally done in person (unlike voting at shareholders' meetings, which can be done by proxy, as discussed later in this chapter).[1] The rule is one vote per director. Ordinary matters generally require a simple majority vote; certain extraordinary issues may require a greater-than-majority vote. Today, the corporation laws of most states—including California, Delaware, New York, and Texas—expressly permit telephone conferences for board of directors' meetings as long as the participants can hear one another. Section 8.20 of the RMBCA also allows directors' meetings to be held by telephone conference. California permits board of directors' meetings to be held by electronic video screen communication or similar means, as long as certain conditions are satisfied.

RIGHTS OF DIRECTORS

A director of a corporation has a number of rights, including the rights of participation, inspection, compensation, and indemnification.

PARTICIPATION AND INSPECTION A corporate director must have certain rights to function properly in that position. The main right is one of participation—meaning that the director must be notified of board of directors' meetings so as to participate in them. As pointed out earlier in this chapter, regular board meetings are usually established by the bylaws or by board resolution, and no notice of these meetings is required. If special meetings are called, however, notice is required unless waived by the director.

A director must have access to all of the corporate books and records to make decisions and to exercise the necessary supervision over corporate officers and employees. This right of inspection is virtually absolute and cannot be restricted.

COMPENSATION AND INDEMNIFICATION Directors are often paid nominal sums as honorariums. In many corporations, directors are also chief corporate officers (president or chief executive officer, for example) and receive compensation in their managerial positions. Most directors also gain through indirect benefits, such as business contacts, prestige, and other rewards. There is a trend toward providing more than nominal compensation for directors, especially in large corporations in which directorships can be burdensome in terms of time, work, effort, and risk. Many states permit the corporate articles or bylaws to authorize compensation for directors, and sometimes the board can set its own compensation unless the articles or bylaws provide otherwise.

---

1. Except in Louisiana, which allows a director to vote by proxy under certain circumstances.

Corporate directors may become involved in lawsuits by virtue of their positions and their actions as directors. Most states (and RMBCA 8.51) permit a corporation to indemnify (guarantee reimbursement to) a director for legal costs, fees, and judgments involved in defending corporation-related suits. Many states specifically permit a corporation to purchase liability insurance for the directors and officers to cover indemnification. When the statutes are silent on this matter, the authority to purchase such insurance is usually considered to be part of the corporation's implied power.

DIRECTORS' MANAGEMENT RESPONSIBILITIES

Directors have responsibility for all policymaking decisions necessary to the management of all corporate affairs. Just as shareholders cannot act individually to bind the corporation, the directors must act as a body in carrying out routine corporate business. Each director has one vote, and customarily the majority rules. The general areas of responsibility of the board of directors include the following:

1. Authorization for major corporate policy decisions—for example, the initiation of negotiations for the sale or lease of corporate assets outside the regular course of business, the determination of new product lines, and the oversight of major contract negotiations and major management-labor negotiations.
2. Appointment, supervision, and removal of corporate officers and other managerial employees and determination of their compensation.
3. Financial decisions, such as the declaration and payment of dividends to shareholders and the issuance of authorized shares and bonds.

Most states permit the board of directors to elect an executive committee from among the directors to handle the interim management decisions between board of directors' meetings, as provided for in the bylaws. The executive committee is limited to making management decisions about ordinary business matters. The board of directors can also delegate some of its functions to corporate officers. In doing so, the board is not relieved of its overall responsibility for directing the affairs of the corporation, but corporate officers and managerial personnel are empowered to make decisions relating to ordinary, daily corporate activities within well-defined guidelines.

CORPORATE OFFICERS AND EXECUTIVES

Officers and other executive employees are hired by the board of directors or, in rare instances, by the shareholders. In addition to carrying out the duties articulated in the bylaws, corporate and managerial officers act as agents of the corporation, and the ordinary rules of agency (discussed in Chapters 31 and 32) normally apply to their employment. The qualifications required of officers and executive employees are determined at the discretion of the corporation and are included in the articles or bylaws. In most states, a person can hold more than one office and can be both an officer and a director of the corporation.

Corporate officers and other high-level managers are employees of the company, so their rights are defined by employment contracts. The board of directors, though, normally can remove corporate officers at any time with or without cause and regardless of the terms of the employment contracts—although, in so doing, the corporation may be liable for breach of contract. The duties of corporate officers are the same as those of directors because both groups are involved in decision making and are in similar positions of control. Hence, officers and directors are viewed as having the same fiduciary duties of care and loyalty in their conduct of corporate affairs, a subject to which we now turn.

SECTION 2 | Duties and Liabilities of Directors and Officers

Directors and officers are deemed to be fiduciaries of the corporation because their relationship with the corporation and its shareholders is one of trust and confidence. As fiduciaries, directors and officers owe ethical—and legal—duties to the corporation and the shareholders. These fiduciary duties include the duty of care and the duty of loyalty.

DUTY OF CARE

Directors and officers must exercise due care in performing their duties. The standard of *due care* has been variously described in judicial decisions and codified in many corporation codes. Generally, a director or officer is expected to act in good faith, to exercise the care that an ordinarily prudent person would exercise in similar circumstances, and to act in what he or she

CONCEPT SUMMARY 39.1 | Roles of Directors and Officers

ASPECT	DESCRIPTION
ELECTION OF DIRECTORS	The incorporators usually appoint the first board of directors; thereafter, shareholders elect the directors. Directors usually serve a one-year term, although the term can be longer. Few qualifications are required; a director can be a shareholder but is not required to be. Compensation is usually specified in the corporate articles or bylaws.
BOARD OF DIRECTORS' MEETINGS	The board of directors conducts business by holding formal meetings with recorded minutes. The dates of regular meetings are usually established in the corporate articles or bylaws; special meetings can be called, with notice sent to all directors. Quorum requirements vary from state to state; usually, a quorum is a majority of the corporate directors. Voting must usually be done in person, and in ordinary matters, only a majority vote is required.
RIGHTS OF DIRECTORS	Directors' rights include the rights of participation, inspection, compensation, and indemnification.
DIRECTORS' MANAGEMENT RESPONSIBILITIES	Directors are responsible for authorizing major corporate decisions; appointing, supervising, and removing corporate officers and other managerial employees; determining employees' compensation; making financial decisions necessary to the management of corporate affairs; and issuing authorized shares and bonds. Directors may delegate some of their responsibilities to executive committees and corporate officers and executives.
ROLE OF CORPORATE OFFICERS AND EXECUTIVES	The board of directors normally hires the corporate officers and other executive employees. In most states, a person can hold more than one office and can be both an officer and a director of a corporation. The rights of corporate officers and executives are defined by employment contracts.

considers to be the best interests of the corporation [RMBCA 8.30(a)]. Directors and officers who have not exercised the required duty of care can be held liable for the harms suffered by the corporation as a result of their negligence.

DUTY TO MAKE INFORMED AND REASONABLE DECISIONS Directors and officers are expected to be informed on corporate matters. To be informed, a director or officer must do what is necessary to become informed: attend presentations, ask for information from those who have it, read reports, and review other written materials. In other words, directors and officers must carefully study a situation and its alternatives before making a decision. Depending on the nature of the business, directors and officers are often expected to act in accordance with their own knowledge and training. Nevertheless, most states—and Section 8.30(b) of the RMBCA—allow a director to make decisions in reliance on information furnished by competent officers or employees, professionals such as attorneys and accountants, or even an executive committee of the board without being accused of acting in bad faith or failing to exercise due care if such information turns out to be faulty.

Directors are also expected to make reasonable decisions. For example, a director should not accept a *tender offer* (an offer to purchase shares in the company that is made by another company directly to the shareholders—see Chapter 40) with only a moment's consideration and on the sole basis of the price per share that is being offered.

DUTY TO EXERCISE REASONABLE SUPERVISION Directors are also expected to exercise a reasonable amount of supervision when they delegate work to corporate officers and employees. For example, suppose that a corporate bank director fails to attend any board of directors' meetings for five years, never inspects any of the corporate books or records, and generally neglects to supervise the efforts of the bank president and the loan committee. Meanwhile, a corporate officer, the bank president, makes various improper loans and permits large overdrafts. In this situation, the corporate director may be held liable to the corporation for losses resulting from the unsupervised actions of the bank president and the loan committee.

DISSENTING DIRECTORS Directors are expected to attend board of directors' meetings, and their votes should be entered into the minutes of corporate meetings. Unless a dissent is entered, the director is presumed to have assented. Directors who dissent are rarely held individually liable for mismanagement of the corporation. For this reason, a director who is absent from a given meeting sometimes registers with the secretary of the board a dissent to actions taken at the meeting.

DUTY OF LOYALTY

Loyalty can be defined as faithfulness to one's obligations and duties. In the corporate context, the duty of loyalty requires directors and officers to subordinate their personal interests to the welfare of the corporation.

For example, directors may not use corporate funds or confidential corporate information for personal advantage. Similarly, they must refrain from putting their personal interests above those of the corporation. For instance, a director should not oppose a transaction that is in the corporation's best interest simply because accepting it may cost the director her or his position. Cases dealing with fiduciary duty typically involve one or more of the following:

1. Competing with the corporation.
2. Usurping (taking personal advantage of) a corporate opportunity.
3. Having an interest that conflicts with the interest of the corporation.
4. Engaging in *insider trading* (using information that is not public to make a profit trading securities, as discussed in Chapter 41).
5. Authorizing a corporate transaction that is detrimental to minority shareholders.
6. Selling control over the corporation.

CONFLICTS OF INTEREST

Corporate directors often have many business affiliations, and a director can sit on the board of more than one corporation. Of course, directors are precluded from entering into or supporting businesses that operate in direct competition with corporations on whose boards they serve. Their fiduciary duty requires them to make a full disclosure of any potential conflicts of interest that might arise in any corporate transaction [RMBCA 8.60].

DISCLOSURE REQUIREMENTS Sometimes, a corporation enters into a contract or engages in a transaction in which an officer or director has a personal interest. The director or officer must make a *full disclosure* of that interest and must abstain from voting on the proposed transaction.

For example, Ballo Corporation needs office space. Stephan Colson, one of its five directors, owns the building adjoining the corporation's headquarters. He negotiates a lease with Ballo for the space, making a full disclosure to Ballo and the other four directors. The lease arrangement is fair and reasonable, and it is unanimously approved by the other members of the corporation's board of directors. Under these circumstances, the contract is valid. The rule is one of reason; otherwise, directors would be prevented from ever having financial dealings with the corporations they serve.

State statutes contain different standards, but a contract will generally not be voidable if it was fair and reasonable to the corporation at the time it was made, if there was a full disclosure of the interest of the officers or directors involved in the transaction, and if the contract was approved by a majority of the disinterested directors or shareholders [RMBCA 8.62].

CORPORATIONS WITH COMMON DIRECTORS Often, contracts are negotiated between corporations having one or more directors who are members of both boards. Such transactions require great care, as they are closely scrutinized by the courts. (As will be discussed in Chapter 46, in certain circumstances—if two large corporations are competing with each other, for example—having a director sit on the boards of both companies may constitute a violation of antitrust laws.)

LIABILITY OF DIRECTORS AND OFFICERS

Directors and officers are exposed to liability on many fronts. Corporate directors and officers may be held liable for the crimes and torts committed by themselves or by corporate employees under their supervision, as discussed in Chapters 9 and 38. Additionally, if shareholders perceive that the corporate directors are not acting in the best interests of the corporation, they may sue the directors, in what is called a *shareholder's derivative suit,* on behalf of the corporation.

(This type of action is discussed later in this chapter, in the context of shareholders' rights.)

THE BUSINESS JUDGMENT RULE A corporate director or officer may be able to avoid liability to the corporation or to its shareholders for poor business judgments under the **business judgment rule.** Directors and officers are expected to exercise due care and to use their best judgment in guiding corporate management, but they are not insurers of business success. Honest mistakes of judgment and poor business decisions on their part do not automatically make them liable for resulting damages.

The business judgment rule generally immunizes directors and officers from liability for the consequences of a decision that is within managerial authority, as long as the decision complies with management's fiduciary duties and as long as acting on the decision is within the powers of the corporation. Consequently, if there is a reasonable basis for a business decision, a court is unlikely to interfere with that decision, even if the corporation suffers as a result.

REQUIREMENTS FOR THE BUSINESS JUDGMENT RULE TO APPLY To benefit from the business judgment rule, directors and officers must act in good faith, in what they consider to be the best interests of the corporation, and with the care that an ordinarily prudent person in a similar position would exercise in like circumstances. This requires an informed decision, with a rational basis, and with no conflict between the decision maker's personal interests and the interests of the corporation.

SECTION 3 | The Role of Shareholders

The acquisition of a share of stock makes a person an owner of and a shareholder in a corporation. Shareholders thus own the corporation. Although they have no legal title to corporate property vested in the corporation, such as buildings and equipment, they do have an *equitable* (ownership) interest in the firm.

As a general rule, shareholders have no responsibility for the daily management of the corporation, although they are ultimately responsible for choosing the board of directors, which does have such control. Ordinarily, corporate officers and other employees owe no direct duty to individual stockholders. Their duty is to the corporation as a whole. A director, however, is in a fiduciary relationship with the corporation and therefore serves the interests of the shareholders in general. Ordinarily, there is no legal relationship between shareholders and creditors of the corporation.

CONCEPT SUMMARY 39.2	Duties and Liabilities of Directors and Officers
ASPECT	**DESCRIPTION**
DUTIES OF DIRECTORS AND OFFICERS	1. *Duty of care*—Directors and officers are obligated to act in good faith, to use prudent business judgment in the conduct of corporate affairs, and to act in the corporation's best interests. If a director or officer fails to exercise this duty of care, he or she may be answerable to the corporation and to the shareholders for breaching the duty. 2. *Duty of loyalty*—Directors and officers have a fiduciary duty to subordinate their own interests to those of the corporation in matters relating to the corporation. 3. *Conflicts of interest*—To fulfill their duty of loyalty, directors and officers must make a full disclosure of any potential conflicts between their personal interests and those of the corporation.
LIABILITY OF DIRECTORS AND OFFICERS	Corporate directors and officers are personally liable for their own torts and crimes; additionally, they may be held personally liable for the torts and crimes committed by corporate personnel under their direct supervision (see Chapters 9 and 38). The *business judgment rule* immunizes a director from liability for a corporate decision as long as it was within the powers of the corporation and the authority of the director to make and was an informed, reasonable, and loyal decision.

Shareholders can, in fact, be creditors of the corporation and have the same rights of recovery against the corporation as any other creditor.

In this section, we look at the powers, rights, and liabilities of shareholders, which may be established in the articles of incorporation and under the state's general corporation law.

Shareholders' Powers

Shareholders must approve fundamental changes affecting the corporation before the changes can be implemented. Hence, shareholders are empowered to amend the articles of incorporation (charter) and bylaws, approve a merger or the dissolution of the corporation, and approve the sale of all or substantially all of the corporation's assets. Some of these powers are subject to prior board approval.

Election and removal of the board of directors are accomplished by a vote of the shareholders. The first board of directors is either named in the articles of incorporation or chosen by the incorporators to serve until the first shareholders' meeting. From that time on, selection and retention of directors are exclusively shareholder functions.

Directors usually serve their full terms; if they are not satisfactory, they are simply not reelected. Shareholders have the inherent power, however, to remove a director from office *for cause* (breach of duty or misconduct) by a majority vote.[2] Some state statutes (and some corporate charters) even permit removal of directors without cause by the vote of a majority of the holders of outstanding shares entitled to vote.[3]

Shareholders' Meetings

Shareholders' meetings must occur at least annually. In addition, special meetings can be called to deal with urgent matters.

NOTICE OF MEETINGS Shareholders are notified of the date and hour of a shareholders' meeting in a written announcement that is sent a reasonable length of time prior to the date of the meeting.[4] Notices of special meetings must include a statement of the purpose of the meeting; business transacted at a special meeting is limited to that purpose.

PROXIES Because it usually is not practical for owners of only a few shares of stock of publicly traded corporations to attend a shareholders' meeting, such stockholders normally give third parties written authorization to vote their shares at the meeting. This authorization is called a **proxy** (from the Latin *procurare*, "to manage, take care of"). Proxies are often solicited by management, but any person can solicit proxies to concentrate voting power. Proxies have been used by groups of shareholders as a device for taking over a corporation (corporate takeovers will be discussed in Chapter 40). Proxies are normally revocable (that is, they can be withdrawn), unless they are specifically designated as irrevocable. Under RMBCA 7.22(c), proxies last for eleven months, unless the proxy agreement mandates a longer period.

PROXY MATERIALS AND SHAREHOLDER PROPOSALS When shareholders want to change a company policy, they can put their ideas up for a shareholder vote. They do this by submitting a shareholder proposal to the board of directors and asking the board to include the proposal in the proxy materials that are sent to all shareholders before meetings.

The Securities and Exchange Commission (SEC), which regulates the purchase and sale of securities (see Chapter 41), has special provisions relating to proxies and shareholder proposals. SEC Rule 14a-8 requires that when a company sends proxy materials to its shareholders, it must also include whatever proposals will be considered at the meeting and provide shareholders with the opportunity to vote on the proposals by marking and returning their proxy cards. SEC Rule 14a-8 provides that all shareholders who own stock worth at least $1,000 are eligible to submit proposals for inclusion in corporate proxy materials.

---

2. A director can often demand court review of removal for cause, however.

3. Most states allow *cumulative voting* (which will be discussed shortly) for directors. If cumulative voting is authorized, a director may not be removed if the number of votes sufficient to elect him or her under cumulative voting is voted against his or her removal. See, for example, California Corporate Code Section 303A. Also see Section 8.08(c) of the RMBCA.

---

4. The shareholder can waive the requirement of written notice by signing a waiver form [RMBCA 7.06]. A shareholder who does not receive written notice but who learns of the meeting and attends without protesting the lack of notice is said to have waived notice by such conduct. State statutes and corporate bylaws typically set forth the time within which notice must be sent, what methods can be used, and what the notice must contain.

SHAREHOLDER VOTING

Shareholders exercise ownership control through the power of their votes. Corporate business matters are presented in the form of resolutions, which shareholders vote to approve or disapprove. Each common shareholder is entitled to one vote per share, although the voting techniques discussed below all enhance the power of the shareholder's vote. The articles of incorporation can exclude or limit voting rights, particularly to certain classes of shares. For example, owners of preferred shares are usually denied the right to vote [RMBCA 7.21]. If a state statute requires specific voting procedures, the corporation's articles or bylaws must be consistent with the statute.

QUORUM REQUIREMENTS   For shareholders to act during a meeting, a quorum must be present. Generally, this condition is met when shareholders holding more than 50 percent of the outstanding shares are in attendance. In some states, obtaining the unanimous written consent of shareholders is a permissible alternative to holding a shareholders' meeting [RMBCA 7.25].

Once a quorum is present, voting can proceed. A majority vote of the shares represented at the meeting is usually required to pass resolutions. Assume that Novo Pictures, Inc., has 10,000 outstanding shares of voting stock. Its articles of incorporation set the quorum at 50 percent of outstanding shares and provide that a majority vote of the shares present is necessary to pass ordinary matters. Therefore, for this firm, at the shareholders' meeting a quorum of stockholders representing 5,000 outstanding shares must be present to conduct business, and a vote of at least 2,501 of those shares is needed to pass ordinary resolutions. If 6,000 shares are represented, a vote of 3,001 will be necessary, and so on.

At times, more than a simple majority vote will be required either by statute or by corporate charter. Extraordinary corporate matters, such as a merger, a consolidation, or the dissolution of the corporation (see Chapter 40), require approval by a higher percentage of the representatives of all corporate shares entitled to vote, not just a majority of those present at that particular meeting [RMBCA 7.27].

VOTING LISTS   The corporation prepares a voting list before each shareholders' meeting. Persons whose names appear on the corporation's stockholder records as owners are the ones ordinarily entitled to vote.[5] The voting list contains the name and address of each shareholder as shown on the corporate records on a given cutoff date, or *record date*. (Under RMBCA 7.07, the record date may be as much as seventy days before the meeting.) The voting list also includes the number of voting shares held by each owner. The list is usually kept at the corporate headquarters and is available for shareholder inspection [RMBCA 7.20].

CUMULATIVE VOTING   Most states permit or require shareholders to elect directors by *cumulative voting*, a method of voting designed to allow minority shareholders to have representation on the board of directors.[6] With cumulative voting, the number of board members to be elected is multiplied by the number of voting shares a shareholder owns. The result equals the number of votes the shareholder has, and this total can be cast for one or more nominees for director. All nominees stand for election at the same time. When cumulative voting is not required by statute or under the articles, the entire board can be elected by a majority of shares at a shareholders' meeting.

Suppose, for example, that a corporation has 10,000 shares issued and outstanding. The minority shareholders hold 3,000 shares, and the majority shareholders hold the other 7,000 shares. Three members of the board are to be elected. The majority shareholders' nominees are Alomon, Beasley, and Caravel. The minority shareholders' nominee is Dovrik. Can Dovrik be elected to the board by the minority shareholders?

If cumulative voting is allowed, the answer is yes. The minority shareholders have 9,000 votes among them (the number of directors to be elected times the number of shares equals 3 times 3,000, which equals 9,000 votes). All of these votes can be cast to elect Dovrik. The majority shareholders have 21,000 votes (3 times 7,000 equals 21,000 votes), but these votes must be distributed among their three nominees. The principle of cumulative voting is that no matter how the majority shareholders cast their 21,000 votes, they will not be able to elect all three directors if the minority shareholders cast all of their 9,000 votes for Dovrik, as illustrated in Exhibit 39–1.

---

5. When the legal owner is deceased, bankrupt, mentally incompetent, or in some other way under a legal disability, his or her vote can be cast by a person designated by law to control and manage the owner's property.

6. See, for example, California Corporate Code Section 708. Under RMBCA 7.28, however, no cumulative voting rights exist unless the articles of incorporation so provide.

EXHIBIT 39–1 Results of Cumulative Voting

BALLOT	MAJORITY SHAREHOLDER VOTES			MINORITY SHAREHOLDER VOTES	DIRECTORS ELECTED
	Alomon	*Beasley*	*Caravel*	*Dovrik*	
1	10,000	10,000	1,000	9,000	Alomon, Beasley, Dovrik
2	9,001	9,000	2,999	9,000	Alomon, Beasley, Dovrik
3	6,000	7,000	8,000	9,000	Beasley, Caravel, Dovrik

OTHER VOTING TECHNIQUES A group of shareholders can agree in writing prior to a shareholders' meeting, in a *shareholder voting agreement,* to vote their shares together in a specified manner. Such agreements usually are held to be valid and enforceable. A shareholder can also appoint a voting agent and vote by proxy. As mentioned previously, a proxy is a written authorization to cast the shareholder's vote, and a person can solicit proxies from a number of shareholders in an attempt to concentrate voting power [RMBCA 7.22, 7.31].

Another technique is for shareholders to enter into a **voting trust,** which is an agreement (a trust contract) under which legal title (recorded ownership on the corporate books) is transferred to a trustee who is responsible for voting the shares. The agreement can specify how the trustee is to vote, or it can allow the trustee to use his or her discretion. The trustee takes physical possession of the stock certificate and in return gives the shareholder a *voting trust certificate*. The shareholder retains all of the rights of ownership (for example, the right to receive dividend payments) except the power to vote the shares [RMBCA 7.30].

SECTION 4 | Rights of Shareholders

Shareholders possess numerous rights. A significant right—the right to vote their shares—has already been discussed. We now look at some additional rights of shareholders in the following subsections.

STOCK CERTIFICATES

A **stock certificate** is a certificate issued by a corporation that evidences ownership of a specified number of shares in the corporation. In jurisdictions that require the issuance of stock certificates, shareholders have the right to demand that the corporation issue certificates and record their names and addresses in the corporate stock record books. In most states (and under RMBCA 6.26), the board of directors may provide that shares of stock will be uncertificated (that is, no actual, physical stock certificates will be issued). When shares are uncertificated, the corporation may be required to send each shareholder a letter or some other form of notice containing the same information that is required to be included on the face of stock certificates.

Stock is intangible personal property, and the ownership right exists independently of the certificate itself. If a stock certificate is lost or destroyed, ownership is not destroyed with it. A new certificate can be issued to replace the one that has been lost or destroyed.[7] Notice of shareholders' meetings, dividends, and operational and financial reports are all distributed according to the recorded ownership listed in the corporation's books, not on the basis of possession of the certificate.

PREEMPTIVE RIGHTS

A **preemptive right** is a common law concept under which a shareholder is given a preference over all other purchasers to subscribe to or purchase a prorated share of a new issue of stock. This right does not apply to **treasury shares**—shares that are authorized but have not been issued.

THE PURPOSE OF PREEMPTIVE RIGHTS Preemptive rights allow the shareholder to maintain her or his portion of control, voting power, or financial interest in the corporation. Most statutes either (1) grant preemptive rights but allow them to be negated in the corporation's articles or (2) deny

---

7. For a lost or destroyed certificate to be reissued, a shareholder normally must furnish an *indemnity bond,* which is a written promise to reimburse the holder for any actual or claimed loss caused by the issuer's or some other person's conduct. The bond protects the corporation against potential loss should the original certificate reappear at some future time in the hands of a bona fide purchaser [UCC 8–302, 8–405(2)].

preemptive rights except to the extent that they are granted in the articles [RMBCA 6.30]. The result is that the articles of incorporation determine the existence and scope of preemptive rights. Generally, preemptive rights apply only to additional, newly issued stock sold for cash and must be exercised within a specified time period (such as thirty days).

For example, Tron Corporation authorizes and issues 1,000 shares of stock, and Omar Loren purchases 100 shares, making him the owner of 10 percent of the company's stock. Subsequently, Tron, by vote of its shareholders, authorizes the issuance of another 1,000 shares (by amending the articles of incorporation). This increases its capital stock to a total of 2,000 shares. If preemptive rights have been provided, Loren can purchase one additional share of the new stock being issued for each share he already owns—or 100 additional shares. Thus, he can own 200 of the 2,000 shares outstanding, and his relative position as a shareholder will be maintained. If preemptive rights are not reserved, his proportionate control and voting power will be diluted from that of a 10 percent shareholder to that of a 5 percent shareholder because the additional 1,000 shares were issued.

PREEMPTIVE RIGHTS IN CLOSE CORPORATIONS
Preemptive rights are the most important for shareholders in close corporations because these corporations have a relatively small number of shareholders and each shareholder controls a substantial interest in the corporation. Without preemptive rights, it would be possible for a shareholder to lose his or her proportionate control over the firm.

STOCK WARRANTS

Usually, when preemptive rights exist and a corporation is issuing additional shares, each shareholder is given **stock warrants,** which are transferable options to acquire a given number of shares from the corporation at a stated price. Warrants are often publicly traded on securities exchanges. When the option to purchase is in effect for a short period of time, the stock warrants are usually referred to as *rights*.

DIVIDENDS

A **dividend** is a distribution of corporate profits or income *ordered by the directors* and paid to the shareholders in proportion to their respective shares in the corporation. Dividends can be paid in cash, property,

stock of the corporation that is paying the dividends, or stock of other corporations.[8]

State laws vary, but every state determines the general circumstances and legal requirements under which dividends are paid. State laws also control the sources of revenue to be used; only certain funds are legally available for paying dividends. Once declared, a cash dividend becomes a corporate debt enforceable at law like any other debt. Depending on state law, dividends may be paid from the following sources:

1. *Retained earnings.* All state statutes allow dividends to be paid from the undistributed net profits earned by the corporation, including capital gains from the sale of fixed assets. The undistributed net profits are called *retained earnings*.
2. *Net profits.* A few state statutes allow dividends to be issued from current net profits without regard to deficits in prior years.
3. *Surplus.* A number of state statutes allow dividends to be paid out of any kind of surplus.

ILLEGAL DIVIDENDS Sometimes, dividends are improperly paid from an unauthorized account, or their payment causes the corporation to become insolvent. Generally, in such situations, shareholders must return illegal dividends only if they knew that the dividends were illegal when they received them. A dividend paid while the corporation is insolvent is automatically an illegal dividend, and shareholders may be liable for returning the payment to the corporation or its creditors. In all instances of illegal and improper dividends, the board of directors can be held personally liable for the amount of the payment. When directors can show that a shareholder knew a dividend was illegal when it was received, however, the directors are entitled to reimbursement from the shareholder.

DIRECTORS' FAILURE TO DECLARE A DIVIDEND When directors fail to declare a dividend, shareholders can ask a court of equity for an injunction to compel the directors to meet and declare a dividend. For the injunction to be granted, the shareholders must show that the directors have acted so unreasonably in withholding the dividend that their conduct is an abuse of their discretion.

Often, a corporation accumulates large cash reserves for a bona fide purpose, such as expansion, research, or some other legitimate corporate use. The

---

8. On one occasion, a distillery declared and paid a "dividend" in bonded whiskey.

mere fact that the firm has sufficient earnings or surplus available to pay a dividend is not enough to compel the directors to distribute funds that, in the board's opinion, should not be distributed.[9] The courts are hesitant to interfere with corporate operations and will not compel directors to declare dividends unless abuse of discretion is clearly shown.

INSPECTION RIGHTS

Shareholders in a corporation enjoy both common law and statutory inspection rights. The shareholder's right of inspection is limited, however, to the inspection and copying of corporate books and records for a *proper purpose*, provided the request is made in advance. The shareholder can inspect in person, or an attorney, accountant, or other authorized assistant can do so as the shareholder's agent. The RMBCA requires

---

9. A striking exception to this rule was made in *Dodge v. Ford Motor Co.*, 204 Mich. 459, 170 N.W. 668 (1919), when Henry Ford, the president and major stockholder of Ford Motor Company, refused to declare a dividend notwithstanding the firm's large capital surplus. The court, holding that Ford had abused his discretion, ordered the company to declare a dividend.

the corporation to maintain an alphabetical voting list of shareholders with addresses and number of shares owned; this list must be kept open at the annual meeting for inspection by any shareholder of record [RMBCA 7.20].

The power of inspection is fraught with potential abuses, and the corporation is allowed to protect itself from them. For example, a shareholder can properly be denied access to corporate records to prevent harassment or to protect trade secrets or other confidential corporate information. Some states require that a shareholder must have held her or his shares for a minimum period of time immediately preceding the demand to inspect or must hold a minimum number of outstanding shares. The RMBCA provides that every shareholder is entitled to examine specified corporate records [RMBCA 16.02]. A shareholder who is denied the right of inspection can seek a court order to compel the inspection.

The question in the following case was whether a shareholder who obtains access to corporate books and records that the company regards as confidential should be free to publicly disseminate information in those documents.

CASE 39.2	### Disney v. Walt Disney Co.

Court of
Chancery of
Delaware, 2004.
857 A.2d 444.

BACKGROUND AND FACTS *Roy Disney is a shareholder of Walt Disney Company, a Delaware corporation with its principal offices in Burbank, California. Disney was a director of the company until he resigned in November 2003. After his resignation, Roy Disney began a campaign to encourage other shareholders to vote "no" on the reelection of Michael Eisner and three other members of the board of directors at the company's March 2004 annual meeting. As part of this effort, in January, Disney sought access to corporate books and records related to compensation for the company's five senior executives. Before honoring this request, the company designated some of the information "confidential" and asked Disney not to publicly disseminate it. He agreed only to hold it in "strict confidence." On review of the material, however, Disney objected to the confidentiality designation. He filed a suit in a Delaware state court against the company, asking the court to order that the designation of the information as "confidential" was inappropriate.*

IN THE LANGUAGE OF THE COURT

LAMB, Vice Chancellor
* * * *
* * * Section 220 of the Delaware General Corporation Law provides every stockholder of a Delaware corporation acting for a proper purpose a powerful right to inspect the company's books and records. * * *
* * * *
* * * [T]he production of nonpublic corporate books and records to a stockholder making a demand pursuant to Section 220 should be conditioned upon a reasonable confidentiality order. * * * Counterposed to the duty to protect the rights of the stockholder, the court has the duty to safeguard the rights and legitimate interests of the corporation. * * * It

CONTINUED ▶

 **Continued**

follows that *the Court of Chancery is empowered to protect the corporation's legitimate interests and to prevent possible abuse of the shareholder's right of inspection by placing such reasonable restrictions and limitations as its deems proper on the exercise of the right. * * * In fact, it is often the case* that the Court of Chancery will condition its judgment in Section 220 cases on the entry of a reasonable confidentiality order to prevent the dissemination of confidential business information to "curiosity seekers." [Emphasis added.]

* * * *

Mr. Disney argues eloquently and forcefully for a * * * novel use of a Section 220 books and records demand—that of ferreting out [extracting] information for use in an ongoing public relations campaign challenging the truthfulness or completeness of a corporation's routine public disclosures, especially its disclosures relating to executive compensation. He argues that disclosure of the information at issue here will serve the best interests of the Company's stockholders "who, given the supposedly incomplete and misleading disclosures made by the Company, have under Delaware law an important right to receive a full and fair disclosure of facts." This is particularly true, he stresses, "where, as here, the disclosure pertains to the bases for a compensation committee's decisions to award enormous compensation packages to a public company's top executives."

In support of this argument, Mr. Disney * * * suggests that the stockholders' need to "know the whole truth" is especially urgent in this case because "there exists a 'crisis of confidence' in executive compensation in the United States that reflects a 'mistrust of the system.'" Thus, he argues, "requiring disclosure of the bases for senior executive compensation decisions in the context of a Section 220 case promotes good public policy."

* * * *

The court is unable to accept this expansive reading of Section 220. To begin with, despite Mr. Disney's invitation to do so, there is no basis in the language of the statute to limit the proposed use of Section 220 to executive compensation issues. Instead, the court would have to recognize a right to make a books and records demand for the purpose of investigating any well-grounded suspicion of mismanagement and then publicly disclosing information discovered from that investigation. In addition, the expansion for which Mr. Disney argues would extend equally to any single stockholder, not only to those thought to adequately represent the interests of the corporation or the stockholders as a whole. Moreover, a stockholder seeking to disclose non-public information in those circumstances would not be under the same fiduciary obligation as the corporation to make complete or candid disclosures. Instead, as is evident in this case, the disclosure sought to be made would likely relate to snippets of information gleaned from a few e-mails or internal memoranda that the stockholder contends are inconsistent with the corporation's public disclosures. Undoubtedly, any decision that permitted the public disclosure of that information would lead the corporation to disclose even more otherwise non-public information in order to put the stockholder's disclosures in what the corporation believes to be the proper context. All in all, this is not a process that promises to advance the best interests of the corporation or its stockholders.

DECISION AND REMEDY *The court denied Roy Disney's request to remove the confidentiality designation from the documents on which the company had imposed it, and dismissed the case. Opening the confidentiality limit in this case would lead to the disclosure of nonpublic information in other cases, which would not "advance the best interests of the corporation or its stockholders."*

WHAT IF THE FACTS WERE DIFFERENT? *If the information that Disney sought to disseminate publicly—via a Web site, for example—had been previously disclosed in a limited manner (such as in a company newsletter), would the result have been different?*

TRANSFER OF SHARES

Corporate stock represents an ownership right in intangible personal property. The law generally recognizes the right of an owner to transfer property to another person unless there are valid restrictions on its transferability. Although stock certificates are negotiable and freely transferable by indorsement and delivery, transfer of stock in closely held corporations (see Chapter 38) is usually restricted. Restrictions may be found in the bylaws, stamped on the stock certificate, or stated in a shareholder agreement. The existence of any restrictions on transferability must always be noted on the face of the stock certificate, and these restrictions must be reasonable.

Sometimes, corporations or their shareholders restrict transferability by reserving the option to purchase any shares offered for resale by a shareholder. This **right of first refusal** remains with the corporation or the shareholders for only a specified duration or a reasonable period of time. Variations on the purchase option are possible. For example, a shareholder might be required to offer the shares to other shareholders or to the corporation first.

When shares are transferred, a new entry is made in the corporate stock book to indicate the new owner. Until the corporation is notified and the entry is complete, all rights—including voting rights, notice of shareholders' meetings, and the right to dividend distributions—remain with the current record owner.

RIGHTS ON DISSOLUTION

When a corporation is dissolved and its outstanding debts and the claims of its creditors have been satisfied, the remaining assets are distributed on a pro rata basis among the shareholders. If no class of stock has been given preferences in the distribution of assets on liquidation, all of the stockholders share the remaining assets.

Shareholders also have the right to petition the court to dissolve the corporation in some situations. Suppose that a minority shareholder knows that the board of directors is mishandling corporate assets or is permitting a deadlock to threaten or irreparably injure the corporation's finances. The minority shareholder is not powerless to intervene. He or she can petition a court to appoint a **receiver** who will wind up corporate affairs and liquidate the business assets of the corporation. The RMBCA permits any shareholder to initiate such an action in any of the following circumstances [RMBCA 14.30]:

1. The directors are deadlocked in the management of corporate affairs, shareholders are unable to break that deadlock, and irreparable injury to the corporation is being suffered or threatened.
2. The acts of the directors or those in control of the corporation are illegal, oppressive, or fraudulent.
3. Corporate assets are being misapplied or wasted.

4. The shareholders are deadlocked in voting power and have failed, for a specified period (usually two annual meetings), to elect successors to directors whose terms have expired or would have expired with the election of successors.

THE SHAREHOLDER'S DERIVATIVE SUIT

When those in control of a corporation—the corporate directors—fail to sue in the corporate name to redress a wrong suffered by the corporation, shareholders are permitted to do so "derivatively" in what is known as a **shareholder's derivative suit.** Before a derivative suit can be brought, some wrong must have been done to the corporation, and the shareholders must have stated their complaint to the board of directors. Only if the directors fail to solve the problem or to take appropriate action can the derivative suit go forward.

The right of shareholders to bring a derivative action is especially important when the wrong suffered by the corporation results from the actions of corporate directors. This is because the directors and officers would probably be unwilling to take any action against themselves [RMBCA 7.40–7.47].

The shareholder's derivative suit is unusual in that those suing are not pursuing rights or benefits for themselves personally but are acting as guardians of the corporate entity. Therefore, any damages recovered by the suit normally go into the corporation's treasury, not to the shareholders personally.

SECTION 5 | Liability of Shareholders

One of the hallmarks of the corporate organization is that shareholders are not personally liable for the debts of the corporation. If the corporation fails, shareholders can lose their investments, but that is generally the limit of their liability. As discussed in Chapter 38, however, in certain instances of fraud, undercapitalization, or careless observance of corporate formalities, a court will pierce the corporate veil (disregard the corporate entity) and hold the shareholders individually liable. These situations are the exception, not the rule, however.

There are certain other, albeit rare, instances in which a shareholder can be personally liable. One relates to illegal dividends, which were discussed previously. Two others relate to *stock subscriptions* and *watered stock.* Finally, in some instances, a majority shareholder who engages in oppressive conduct or attempts to exclude minority shareholders from receiving certain benefits can sometimes be held personally liable.

STOCK-SUBSCRIPTION AGREEMENTS

As discussed earlier, sometimes stock-subscription agreements—written contracts to buy capital stock of a corporation—exist prior to incorporation. Normally, these agreements are treated as continuing offers and are irrevocable (for up to six months under RMBCA 6.20). Once the corporation has been formed, it can sell shares to investors. In either situation, once the subscription agreement or stock offer is accepted, a binding contract is formed. Any refusal to pay will

constitute a breach and result in the personal liability of the shareholder.

Shares of stock can be paid for with property or services rendered instead of cash. (Shares cannot be purchased with promissory notes, however.) The general rule is that for **par-value shares** (shares that have a specific face value, or formal cash-in value, written on them, such as one penny or one dollar), the corporation must receive a value at least equal to the par-value amount. For **no-par shares** (shares without a par value), the corporation must receive the fair market value of the shares as determined by the board or the shareholders. For either par-value or no-par shares, the value is set based on the same factors: tax

CONCEPT SUMMARY 39.3	Role of Shareholders	
ASPECT	**DESCRIPTION**
SHAREHOLDERS' POWERS	Shareholders' powers include approval of all fundamental changes affecting the corporation and election of the board of directors.
SHAREHOLDERS' MEETINGS	Shareholders' meetings must occur at least annually; special meetings can be called when necessary. Notice of the time and place of a meeting (and its purpose, if the meeting is specially called) must be sent to shareholders. Voting requirements and procedures are as follows: 1. A minimum number of shareholders (a quorum—generally, shareholders representing more than 50 percent of shares held) must be present at a meeting; resolutions are normally passed by majority vote. 2. A voting list of shareholders of record must be prepared by the corporation prior to each shareholders' meeting. 3. Cumulative voting may or may not be required or permitted so as to give minority shareholders a better chance to be represented on the board of directors. 4. Shareholders' voting agreements to vote their shares together are usually held to be valid and enforceable. 5. A shareholder may appoint a proxy (substitute) to vote his or her shares. 6. A shareholder may enter into a voting trust agreement by which title (ownership of record) of her or his shares is given to a trustee, and the trustee votes the shares in accordance with the trust agreement.
SHAREHOLDERS' RIGHTS	Shareholders have numerous rights, which may include the following: 1. Voting rights. 2. The right to receive stock certificates (depending on the jurisdiction). 3. Preemptive rights (depending on the corporate charter). 4. The right to receive dividends (at the discretion of the directors). 5. The right to inspect the corporate records. 6. The right to transfer shares (this right may be restricted in close corporations). 7. The right to receive a share of corporate assets when the corporation is dissolved. 8. The right to sue on behalf of the corporation (bring a shareholder's derivative suit) when the directors fail to do so.
SHAREHOLDERS' LIABILITY	Shareholders may be liable for the retention of illegal dividends, for breach of a stock-subscription agreement, and for watered stock. In certain situations, majority shareholders may be regarded as having a fiduciary duty to minority shareholders and will be liable if that duty is breached.

rates, whether the corporation needs capital surplus, and what the corporation will receive for the shares (money, property, or services).

WATERED STOCK

When shares are issued by the corporation for less than their fair market value, the shares are referred to as **watered stock.**[10] In most instances, the shareholder who receives watered stock must pay the difference to the corporation (the shareholder is personally liable). In some states, the shareholder who receives watered stock may be liable to creditors of the corporation for unpaid corporate debts.

To illustrate: Suppose that during the formation of a corporation, Gomez, one of the incorporators, transfers his property, Sunset Beach, to the corporation for 10,000 shares of stock at a par value of $100 per share for a total price of $1 million. After the property is transferred and the shares are issued, Sunset Beach is carried on the corporate books at a value of $1 million. On appraisal, it is discovered that the market value of the property at the time of transfer was only $500,000. The shares issued to Gomez are therefore watered stock, and he is liable to the corporation for the difference between the value of the shares and the value of the property.

---

10. The phrase *watered stock* was originally used to describe cattle that were kept thirsty during a long drive and then were allowed to drink large quantities of water just prior to their sale. The increased weight of the "watered stock" allowed the seller to reap a higher profit.

DUTIES OF MAJORITY SHAREHOLDERS

In some instances, a majority shareholder is regarded as having a fiduciary duty to the corporation and to the minority shareholders. This occurs when a single shareholder (or a few shareholders acting in concert) owns a sufficient number of shares to exercise *de facto* (actual) control over the corporation. In these situations, majority shareholders owe a fiduciary duty to minority shareholders.

Consider an example. Three brothers, Alfred, Carl, and Eugene, each owned a one-third interest in a corporation and had worked for the corporation for most of their adult lives. When a dispute arose concerning discrepancies in the corporation's accounting records, Carl and Eugene fired Alfred and told the company's employees that Alfred had had a nervous breakdown, which was not true. Alfred sued Carl and Eugene, alleging, among other things, that they had breached their fiduciary duties. The brothers argued that because there was no diminution in the value of the corporation or the value of Alfred's shares in the company, they had not breached their fiduciary duties. The court, however, held that the brothers' conduct, which was unfairly prejudicial toward Alfred, supported a finding of breach of fiduciary duty.[11]

Such a breach of fiduciary duties by those who control a closely held corporation normally constitutes what is known as *oppressive conduct.* The court in the following case examined a pattern of conduct by those in control to determine whether that conduct was oppressive.

---

11. *Pedro v. Pedro,* 489 N.W.2d 798 (Minn.App. 1992).

CASE 39.3   Robbins v. Sanders

Alabama Supreme Court, 2004.
890 So.2d 998.

PER CURIAM. [By the whole court.]
* * * *

In 1988, James Bailey and his wife, Mary Bailey, owned approximately 53 acres of real property in Birmingham [Alabama]. This property was mortgaged to SouthTrust Bank for $400,000; an individual had a second mortgage on the property in the amount of $50,000. The Baileys generated income by renting several buildings located on the property and by using a part of the land as a landfill. An underground fire developed on the portion of the property used as a landfill * * * .

* * * [O]n June 1, 1988, James Bailey, Mary Bailey, and [Pete] Robbins entered into [an] agreement * * * .

The June 1 agreement provided that Robbins would extinguish the underground fire on the Baileys' property. In addition, the June 1 agreement provided that the parties would form a corporation; that the corporation would acquire the 53 acres owned by the Baileys; * * * that Robbins would assume personal liability on the mortgage debt; that the corporation

CONTINUED ▶

would issue 1,000 shares of stock, and Robbins would receive 500 of those shares, and James Bailey and Mary Bailey would each receive 250 shares * * * .

* * * *

Pursuant to the June 1, 1988, agreement, Corridor Enterprises, Inc., was formed in October 1988. * * *

* * * *

On October 24, 1991, the Baileys and Robbins entered into a stock-purchase agreement. In this agreement, the Baileys agreed to sell their stock in Corridor Enterprises to Robbins for $500 per share * * * at the rate of at least two shares per month.

James Bailey died on February 9, 1997; he was 91 years old at the time of his death. Mary Bailey died on April 27, 1997; she was 85 years old. On September 11, 1997, Terrill Sanders was appointed as administrator of Mary Bailey's estate. On September 27, 1997, Sanders was appointed as administrator of James Bailey's estate.

[Over the next twelve months, Sanders had difficulty obtaining information from Robbins and uncovered discrepancies in Corridor's corporate records. On the estates' behalf, Sanders filed a suit in an Alabama state court, alleging, among other things, oppression of minority shareholders.]

* * * *

The trial court awarded Corridor Enterprises and the estates of James Bailey and Mary Bailey a total of $3,269,125.91 in compensatory damages and $750,000 in punitive damages. * * *

* * * *

Robbins appeals * * * .

* * * *

Robbins argues that the claims asserted by the estates * * * are barred by the two-year statute of limitations found in [Alabama Code] Section 6-2-38. He argues that the "undisputed evidence" presented at trial established that, more than two years before this action was filed, the Baileys had "such knowledge * * * sufficient to provoke inquiry in reasonable minds which would have led to the facts on which the claims in this action are based." We reject this argument.

* * * *

The estates of James Bailey and Mary Bailey became minority shareholders in Corridor Enterprises in 1997, after James and Mary died. The evidence established that Robbins engaged in * * * oppression * * * and that he attempted to squeeze out the minority shareholders after the estates became the minority shareholders in Corridor Enterprises. For example, in 1998, Robbins used funds of Corridor Enterprises to purchase real estate in his own name, to invest in other businesses in his own name, and to purchase personal property for himself; he refused to provide an accounting of the corporate finances when he was requested to do so; he failed to pay the corporate property and income taxes, failed to have tax returns prepared and filed, and failed to maintain proper corporate records; he entered into a contract to sell property belonging to Corridor Enterprises without notice to or approval of the minority shareholders; and he failed to declare dividends during the entire time the estates were shareholders while he paid himself an exorbitant salary and drained the corporate funds.

The minority shareholders filed their complaint on August 4, 1998, within approximately a year of becoming shareholders and in the same year that many of the above-described activities occurred. *Therefore, the estates' claims of * * * oppression were not time-barred to the extent those claims sought to recover damages for injuries occurring to the estates * * * .* [Emphasis added.]

* * * *

Because each award of damages was made jointly to the corporation and to the minority shareholders, the manner in which the trial court structured its damages award is improper. * * * [W]e find * * * no error in the trial court's determination that Robbins is liable for oppression and attempting to squeeze out the minority shareholders (the estates). We simply find that the trial court's order, as it pertains to damages, is improper.

* * * [W]e reverse the judgment and remand this case on the issue of damages. On remand, we instruct the trial court to clarify its order and, if necessary, to correct the amount of damages awarded. * * * We express no opinion on these issues; we simply point them out for the trial court's consideration.

CASE 39.3 | Continued

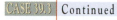

QUESTIONS

1. What should be the basis for determining the specific amount of damages to be awarded to the minority shareholders in this case?
2. How much might the minority shareholders be entitled to recover in a shareholder's derivative suit, based on, among other things, Robbins's breach of his duty of loyalty?

REVIEWING CORPORATIONS— DIRECTORS, OFFICERS, AND SHAREHOLDERS

David Brock is on the board of directors of Firm Body Fitness, Inc., which owns a string of fitness clubs in New Mexico. Brock owns 15 percent of the Firm Body stock and he is also employed as a tanning technician at one of the fitness clubs. After the January financial report showed that Firm Body's tanning division was operating at a substantial net loss, the board of directors, led by Marty Levinson, discussed the possibility of terminating the tanning operations. Brock successfully convinced a majority of the board that the tanning division was necessary to market the clubs' overall fitness package. By April, the tanning division's financial losses had risen. The board hired a business analyst, who conducted surveys and determined that the tanning operations did not significantly increase membership. A shareholder, Diego Peñada, discovered that Brock owned stock in Sunglow, Inc., the company from which Firm Body purchased its tanning equipment. Peñada notified Levinson, who privately reprimanded Brock. Shortly thereafter Brock and Mandy Vail, who owned 37 percent of Firm Body stock and also held shares of Sunglow, voted to replace Levinson on the board of directors. Using the information presented in the chapter, answer the following questions.

1. What duties did Brock, as a director, owe to Firm Body? Has Brock breached any of these duties? Explain.
2. Does the fact that Brock owned shares in Sunglow establish a conflict of interest? Why or why not? What would the law require Brock to do in this situation?
3. Discuss whether Peñada could bring a shareholder's derivative suit based on these facts.
4. Suppose that Firm Body brought an action against Brock claiming that he had breached the duty of loyalty by not disclosing his interest in Sunglow to the other directors. What theory might Brock use in his defense?
5. Did Brock and Vail do anything wrong when they voted to replace Levinson as director? Why or why not?

 ## TERMS AND CONCEPTS TO REVIEW

business judgment rule 792   proxy 793   stock certificate 795

dividend 796   quorum 788   stock warrant 796

no-par share 800   receiver 799   treasury share 795

par-value share 800   right of first refusal 799   voting trust 795

preemptive rights 795   shareholder's derivative suit 799   watered stock 801

 ## QUESTIONS AND CASE PROBLEMS

39–1. Oxy Corp. is negotiating with the Wick Construction Co. for the renovation of the Oxy corporate headquarters. Wick, owner of the Wick Construction Co., is also one of the five members of the board of directors of Oxy. The contract terms are standard for this type of contract. Wick has previously informed two of the other directors of his interest in the construction company. The contract is approved by Oxy's board on a three-to-two vote, with Wick voting with the majority. Discuss whether this contract is binding on the corporation.

39-2. ⚖ QUESTION WITH SAMPLE ANSWER

AstroStar, Inc., has a board of directors consisting of three members (Eckhart, Dolan, and Macero) and has approximately five hundred shareholders. At a regular board meeting, the board selects Galiard as president of the corporation by a two-to-one vote, with Eckhart dissenting. The minutes of the meeting do not register Eckhart's dissenting vote. Later, an audit discovers that Galiard is a former convict and has embezzled $500,000 from the corporation that is not covered by insurance. Can the corporation hold directors Eckhart, Dolan, and Macero personally liable? Discuss.

For a sample answer to this question, go to Appendix I at the end of this text.

39-3. Superal Corp. authorized 100,000 shares and issued all of them during its first six months in operation. Avril purchased 10,000 of the shares (10 percent). Later, Superal reacquired 10,000 of the shares it originally issued. With shareholder approval, Superal has now amended its articles so as to authorize and issue another 100,000 shares. It has also, by a resolution of the board of directors, made plans to reissue the 10,000 shares of treasury stock (the shares reacquired by the corporation). The corporate articles do not include a provision dealing with shareholders' preemptive rights. Because of her ownership of 10 percent of Superal, Avril claims that she has the preemptive right to purchase 10,000 shares of the new issue and 1,000 shares of the stock being reissued. Discuss her claims.

39-4. Lucia has acquired one share of common stock of a multimillion-dollar corporation with over 500,000 shareholders. Lucia's ownership interest is so small that she is questioning what her rights are as a shareholder. For example, she wants to know whether this one share entitles her to (1) attend and vote at shareholders' meetings, (2) inspect the corporate books, and (3) receive yearly dividends. Discuss Lucia's rights in these three matters.

39-5. Riddle has made a preincorporation subscription agreement to purchase 500 shares of a newly formed corporation. The shares have a par value of $100 per share. The corporation is formed, and Riddle's subscription is accepted by the corporation. Riddle transfers a piece of land he owns to the corporation, and the corporation issues 250 shares for it. One year later, with the corporation in serious financial difficulty, the board declares and pays a dividend of $5 per share. It is now learned that the land transferred by Riddle had a market value of $18,000 at the time of transfer. Discuss Riddle's potential liability to the corporation or its creditors.

39-6. BUSINESS JUDGMENT RULE. Charles Pace and Maria Fuentez were shareholders of Houston Industries, Inc. (HII), and employees of Houston Lighting & Power, a subsidiary of HII, when they lost their jobs because of a company-wide reduction in its workforce. Pace, as a shareholder, three times wrote to

HII, demanding that the board of directors terminate certain HII directors and officers and file a suit to recover damages for breach of fiduciary duty. Three times, the directors referred the charges to board committees and an outside law firm, which found that the facts did not support the charges. The board also received input from federal regulatory authorities about the facts behind some of the charges. The board notified Pace that it would refuse his demands. In response, Pace and Fuentez filed a shareholder's derivative suit in a Texas state court against Don Jordan and the other HII directors, contending that the board's investigation was inadequate. The defendants filed a motion for summary judgment, arguing that the suit was barred by the business judgment rule. Are the defendants right? How should the court rule? Why? [*Pace v. Jordan*, 999 S.W.2d 615 (Tex.App.—Houston [1 Dist.] 1999)]

39-7. ⚖ CASE PROBLEM WITH SAMPLE ANSWER

In 1978, David Brandt and Dean Somerville incorporated Posilock Puller, Inc. (PPI), to make and market bearing pullers. Each received half of the stock. Initially operating out of McHenry, North Dakota, PPI moved to Cooperstown, North Dakota, in 1984 into a building owned by Somerville. After the move, Brandt's participation in PPI diminished, and Somerville's increased. In 1998, Somerville formed PL MFG as his own business to make components for the bearing pullers and sell the parts to PPI. The start-up costs included a $450,000 loan from Sheyenne Valley Electric Cooperative. PPI executed the loan documents and indorsed the check. The proceeds were deposited into an account for PL MFG, which did not sign a promissory note payable to PPI until 2000. When Brandt learned of PL MFG and the loan, he filed a suit in a North Dakota state court against Somerville, alleging in part a breach of fiduciary duty. What fiduciary duty does a director owe to his or her corporation? What does this duty require? Should the court hold Somerville liable? Why or why not? [*Brandt v. Somerville*, 692 N.W.2d 144, 2005 ND 35 (N.D. 2005)]

To view a sample answer for this case problem, go to this book's Web site at http://wbl.westbuslaw.com, select "Chapter 39," and click on "Case Problem with Sample Answer."

39-8. DUTIES OF MAJORITY SHAREHOLDERS. Atlas Food Systems & Services, Inc., based in South Carolina, was a food vending service that provided refreshments to factories and other businesses. Atlas was a closely held corporation. John Kiriakides was a minority shareholder of Atlas. Alex Kiriakides was the majority shareholder. Throughout most of Atlas's history, Alex was the chairman of the board, which included John as a director. In 1995, while John was the president of the firm, the board and shareholders decided to convert Atlas to an S corporation. A few months later, however, Alex, without calling a vote, decided that the firm would not convert. In 1996, a dispute arose over Atlas's contract to buy certain property. John and others decided not to buy it. Without consulting anyone, Alex elected to go through with the sale. Within a few days, Alex refused to allow John to stay on as president. Two months later, Atlas offered to buy John's interest in the firm for almost $2 million. John refused, believing the offer was too low. John filed a suit in a South Carolina state court against Atlas and Alex, seeking, among other things, to force a buyout of John's shares. On what basis might the court grant John's request? Discuss. [*Kiriakides v. Atlas Food Systems & Services, Inc.*, 343 S.C. 587, 541 S.E.2d 257 (2001)]

39–9. INSPECTION RIGHTS. Craig Johnson founded Distributed Solutions, Inc. (DSI), in 1991 to make software and provide consulting services, including payroll services for small companies. Johnson was the sole officer and director and the majority shareholder. Jeffrey Hagen was a minority shareholder. In 1993, Johnson sold DSI's payroll services to himself and a few others and set up Distributed Payroll Solutions, Inc. (DPSI). In 1996, DSI had revenues of $739,034 and assets of $541,168. DSI's revenues in 1997 were $934,532. Within a year, however, all of DSI's assets were sold, and Johnson told Hagen that he was dissolving the firm because, in part, it conducted no business and had no prospects for future business. Hagen asked for corporate records to determine the value of DSI's stock, DSI's financial condition, and "whether unauthorized and oppressive acts had occurred in connection with the operation of the corporation which impacted the value of" the stock. When there was no response, Hagen filed a suit in an Illinois state court against DSI and Johnson, seeking an order to compel the inspection. The defendants filed a motion to dismiss, arguing that Hagen had failed to plead a proper purpose. Should the court grant Hagen's request? Discuss. [*Hagen v. Distributed Solutions, Inc.*, 328 Ill.App.3d 132, 764 N.E.2d 1141, 262 Ill.Dec. 24 (1 Dist. 2002)]

39–10. DUTY OF LOYALTY. Digital Commerce, Ltd., designed software to enable its clients to sell their products or services over the Internet. Kevin Sullivan served as a Digital vice president until 2000, when he became president. Sullivan was dissatisfied that his compensation did not include stock in Digital, but he was unable to negotiate a deal that included equity (that is, shares of ownership in the company). In May, Sullivan solicited ASR Corp.'s business for Digital while he investigated employment opportunities with ASR for himself. When ASR would not include an "equity component" in a job offer, Sullivan refused to negotiate further on Digital's behalf. A few months later, Sullivan began to form his own firm to compete with Digital, conducting organizational and marketing activities on Digital's time, including soliciting ASR's business. Sullivan had all e-mail pertaining to the new firm deleted from Digital's computers in August, and then resigned. ASR signed a contract with Sullivan's new firm and paid it $400,000 for work through October 2001. Digital filed a suit in a federal district court against Sullivan, claiming that he usurped a corporate opportunity. Did Sullivan breach his fiduciary duty to Digital? Explain. [*In re Sullivan*, 305 Bankr. 809 (W.D.Mich. 2004)]

LAW | on the Web

For updated links to resources available on the Web, as well as a variety of other materials, visit this text's Web site at http://wbl.westbuslaw.com.

One of the best sources on the Web for information on corporations, including their directors, is the EDGAR database of the Securities and Exchange Commission (SEC) at

http://www.sec.gov/edgar.shtml

You can find definitions of terms used in corporate law, as well as court decisions and articles on corporate law topics, at

http://www.law.com

LEGAL RESEARCH EXERCISES ON THE WEB

Go to http://wbl.westbuslaw.com, the Web site that accompanies this text. Select "Chapter 39" and click on "Internet Exercises." There you will find the following Internet research exercises that you can perform to learn more about topics covered in this chapter.

Activity 39–1: LEGAL PERSPECTIVE
Liability of Directors and Officers

Activity 39–2: MANAGEMENT PERSPECTIVE
D&O Insurance

CHAPTER 40
CORPORATIONS—Merger, Consolidation, and Termination

A corporation typically extends its operations by combining with another corporation through a merger, a consolidation, a purchase of assets, or a purchase of a controlling interest in the other corporation. This chapter examines these four types of corporate expansion. Dissolution and liquidation are the combined processes by which a corporation terminates its existence. The last part of this chapter discusses some of the typical reasons for terminating a corporation's existence and the methods used in the termination process.

SECTION 1 | Merger and Consolidation

The terms *merger* and *consolidation* are often used interchangeably, but they refer to two legally distinct proceedings. Whether a combination is a merger or a consolidation, however, the rights and liabilities of shareholders, the corporation, and the corporation's creditors are the same.

MERGER

A **merger** involves the legal combination of two or more corporations. After a merger, only one of the corporations continues to exist. Consider an example. Corporation A and Corporation B decide to merge. It is agreed that A will absorb B; so after the merger, B ceases to exist as a separate entity, and A continues as the **surviving corporation.** This process is illustrated in Exhibit 40–1.

After the merger, A is recognized as a single corporation possessing all the rights, privileges, and powers of itself and B. A automatically acquires all of B's property and assets without the necessity of formal transfer. A also becomes liable for all of B's debts and obligations.[1] Finally, A's articles of incorporation are deemed amended to include any changes that are stated in the *articles of merger.*

In a merger, the surviving corporation is vested with the disappearing corporation's preexisting legal rights and obligations. For example, if the disappearing corporation had a right of action against a third party, the surviving corporation can bring suit after the merger to recover the disappearing corporation's damages. The

EXHIBIT 40–1 Merger

In this illustration, Corporations A and B decide to merge. They agree that A will absorb B; so, on merging, B ceases to exist as a separate entity, and A continues as the surviving corporation.

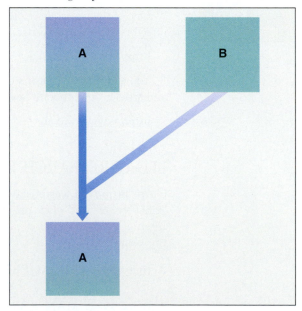

---

1. A corporation that is subject to a lawsuit in some jurisdictions cannot avoid liability by merging with a corporation that could not otherwise have been sued in those jurisdictions. See, for example, *In re Silicone Gel Breast Implants Product Liability Litigation*, 837 F.Supp. 1123 (N.D.Ala. 1993).

common law similarly recognizes that following a merger, a right to bring an action to enforce a property right will vest with the successor (surviving) corporation, and no right of action will remain with the disappearing corporation. The principles regarding successor liability were applied in the following case.

CASE 40.1 Rodriguez v. Tech Credit Union Corp.

Court of Appeals
of Indiana, 2005.
824 N.E.2d 442.
http://www.findlaw.com/
11stategov/in/inca.html[a]

BACKGROUND AND FACTS *Catalina Rodriguez became the general manager of LTV Steel Employees Federal Credit Union in East Chicago, Indiana, in January 2000, subject to an employment contract. At the time, LTV was in poor financial condition, with a large number of delinquent and unpaid loans. In January 2002, LTV's board of directors terminated Rodriguez's employment for, among other things, extending loan payment periods for individuals with whom she had personal relationships and directing some of LTV's insurance business to Airey Insurance and Financial Services, Inc., a brokerage for which her son worked as a sales representative. On April 27, Tech Credit Union Corporation acquired LTV. The "Agreement of Merger" stated, "The LTV Steel Employees Federal Credit Union shall be merged into Tech Credit Union under the name and charter of Tech Credit Union." The agreement was silent as to whether Tech acquired LTV's liabilities. LTV dissolved. Later, Rodriguez filed a suit in an Indiana state court against Tech and others, alleging in part breach of contract. Tech filed a motion for summary judgment, which the court granted. Rodriguez appealed to a state intermediate appellate court.*

IN THE LANGUAGE OF THE COURT

BAKER, Judge.

* * * *

Rodriguez argues that summary judgment was improper * * * . Specifically, she argues that Tech was responsible for LTV's alleged breach of her employment contract because it acquired LTV through a merger * * * .

* * * *

* * * Generally, only a party to the contract can be held liable for its breach because contractual obligations are personal in nature. Nevertheless, *following a merger, the surviving corporation succeeds to all the rights, powers, liabilities and obligations of the merging corporation.* However, where one corporation purchases the assets of another, the buyer does not assume the debts and liabilities of the seller. * * * Generally recognized exceptions to this rule include (1) an implied or express agreement to assume the obligation; (2) a fraudulent sale of assets done for the purpose of escaping liability; (3) a purchase that is a *de facto* consolidation or merger; or (4) instances where the purchaser is a mere continuation of the seller. Successor in assets liability, under these exceptions, takes place only when the predecessor corporation no longer exists, such as when a corporation dissolves or liquidates in bankruptcy. [Emphasis added.]

Rodriguez contends that Tech succeeded to LTV's liabilities because it acquired LTV through a merger, while Tech asserts that it merely purchased the assets of LTV, which would mean that Tech did not acquire LTV's liabilities. We find Tech's argument to be rather disingenuous, considering the document under which Tech acquired LTV is entitled, "Agreement of Merger." Moreover, the Agreement repeatedly refers to the transaction as a merger. Thus, Tech, as the surviving corporation, succeeded to LTV's liabilities. Even if we were to find that Tech purchased LTV's assets, the transaction would fit under the exception to the rule that a buyer does not acquire the liabilities of the seller because this would be a *de facto* merger, inasmuch as LTV, the predecessor corporation, no longer exists.

This does not end the question * * * . [W]e must determine if LTV would have been entitled to summary judgment. We do so by addressing the issue of whether the Board Members acted within the scope of their authority in terminating Rodriguez because if the Board Members, as agents of LTV, committed no wrongdoing, then LTV committed no wrongdoing.

a. In the "Court of Appeals" section, in the "2005" row, click on "March." In the result, scroll to the name of the case and click on "html" to access the opinion.

CONTINUED ▶

CASE 40.1 | **Continued**

[An Indiana statute] immunizes * * * *directors from civil liability for an action taken as a director, or for failure to take an action, unless they have not exercised their business judgment in good faith, with the care of an ordinarily prudent person, in a manner reasonably believed to be in the best interests of the corporation, and the breach or failure to perform constitutes willful misconduct or recklessness. [Emphasis added.]*

The record demonstrates that LTV was failing financially when Rodriguez became the general manager but that things did not improve on her watch. Questionable loans and extensions were made and collections efforts were ineffective. In addition, Rodriguez signed a contract with Airey, then presented it to the Board of Directors as a proposal rather than as an existing contract. Although Rodriguez may have informed the original Board of Directors of her son's employment with Airey, she did not give the new Board of Directors the same information after the election. * * * Furthermore, Rodriguez directly contravened orders of the Board that LTV perform its own collections work * * * . This evidence, when taken together, demonstrates that the Board Members exercised their business judgment in good faith and acted in the best interest of the corporation. Thus, the Board Members committed no wrongdoing and are immune from civil liability. As such, LTV committed no wrongdoing, and the trial court did not err in granting summary judgment * * * .

DECISION AND REMEDY *The state intermediate appellate court affirmed the judgment of the lower court. Tech acquired the liabilities of LTV in their merger. Because neither LTV nor its board acted wrongfully with respect to Rodriguez, however, there was no basis for assessing liability against Tech.*

WHAT IF THE FACTS WERE DIFFERENT? *Suppose that the document under which Tech acquired LTV was not titled "Agreement of Merger" and that it did not refer to the transaction as a merger. Would the result have been different? Explain.*

CONSOLIDATION

In a **consolidation,** two or more corporations combine so that each corporation ceases to exist and a new one emerges. Corporation A and Corporation B consolidate to form an entirely new organization, Corporation C. In the process, A and B both terminate. C comes into existence as an entirely new entity. This process is illustrated in Exhibit 40–2.

The results of a consolidation are essentially the same as the results of a merger. C is recognized as a new corporation and a single entity; A and B cease to exist. C accedes to all the rights, privileges, and powers previously held by A and B. Title to any property and assets owned by A and B passes to C without formal transfer. C assumes liability for all debts and obligations owed by A and B. The *articles of consolidation* take the place of A's and B's original corporate articles and are thereafter regarded as C's corporate articles.

When a merger or a consolidation takes place, the surviving corporation or newly formed corporation will issue shares or pay some fair consideration to the shareholders of the corporation that ceases to exist.

EXHIBIT 40-2 **Consolidation**

In this illustration, Corporations A and B consolidate to form an entirely new organization, Corporation C. In the process, A and B terminate, and C comes into existence as an entirely new entity.

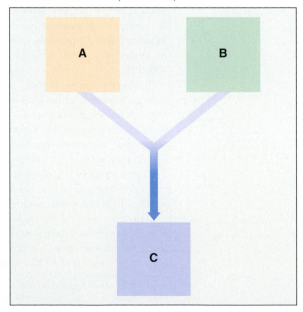

MERGER AND CONSOLIDATION PROCEDURES

All states have statutes authorizing mergers and consolidations for domestic (in-state) corporations, and most states allow the combination of domestic and foreign (out-of-state) corporations. Although the procedures vary somewhat among jurisdictions, the basic requirements set forth in the Revised Model Business Corporation Act (RMBCA) are as outlined below [RMBCA 11.01–11.07].

1. The board of directors of *each* corporation involved must approve a merger or consolidation plan.[2]

2. The shareholders of *each* corporation must vote to approve of the plan at a shareholders' meeting. Most state statutes require the approval of two-thirds of the outstanding shares of voting stock, although some states require only a simple majority, and others require a four-fifths vote. Frequently, statutes require that each class of stock approve the merger; thus, the holders of nonvoting stock must also approve. A corporation's bylaws can dictate a stricter requirement.

3. Once approved by the directors and the shareholders of both corporations, the plan (articles of merger or consolidation) is filed, usually with the secretary of state.

4. When state formalities are satisfied, the state issues a certificate of merger to the surviving corporation or a certificate of consolidation to the newly consolidated corporation.

SHORT-FORM MERGERS RMBCA 11.04 provides a simplified procedure for the merger of a substantially

owned subsidiary corporation into its parent corporation. Under these provisions, a **short-form merger**—also referred to as a **parent-subsidiary merger**—can be accomplished *without* the approval of the shareholders of either corporation. The short-form merger can be used only when the parent corporation owns at least 90 percent of the outstanding shares of each class of stock of the subsidiary corporation. The simplified procedure requires that the board of directors of the parent corporation approve a plan for the merger before it is filed with the state. A copy of the merger plan must be sent to each shareholder of record of the subsidiary corporation.

APPRAISAL RIGHTS What if a shareholder disapproves of a merger or a consolidation but is outvoted by the other shareholders? The law recognizes that a dissenting shareholder should not be forced to become an unwilling shareholder in a corporation that is new or different from the one in which the shareholder originally invested. The shareholder has the right to dissent and may be entitled to be paid the fair value for the number of shares held on the date of the merger or consolidation. This right is referred to as the shareholder's **appraisal right.** If a shareholder is dissatisfied with the price received for the stock, she or he cannot sue the corporation on the ground of fraud or other illegal conduct; appraisal rights are the exclusive remedy.

Appraisal rights are available only when a state statute specifically provides for them. State laws vary on whether appraisal rights are available in close corporations. Appraisal rights normally extend to regular mergers, consolidations, short-form mergers, and sales of substantially all of the corporate assets not in the ordinary course of business.

In a short-form merger, is the exercise of an appraisal right a minority shareholder's only remedy when he or she dissents from the merger? That was the question in the following case.

---

2. When a corporation undertakes a transaction that will cause a change in corporate control or that will break up the corporate entity, the directors have an obligation "to seek the best value reasonably available to the stockholders." See, for example, *Paramount Communications, Inc., v. QVC Network, Inc.*, 637 A.2d 34 (Del. 1994).

CASE 40.2 ## Glassman v. Unocal Exploration Corp.

Delaware Supreme Court, 2001.
777 A.2d 242.

BERGER, Justice.
* * * *

I. Factual and Procedural Background

Unocal Corporation is an earth resources company primarily engaged in the exploration for and production of crude oil and natural gas. At the time of the merger at issue, Unocal owned approximately 96% of the stock of Unocal Exploration Corporation ("UXC"), an oil

CONTINUED ▶

CASE 40.2 | Continued

and gas company operating in and around the Gulf of Mexico. In 1991, low natural gas prices caused a drop in both companies' revenues and earnings. Unocal investigated areas of possible cost savings and decided that, by eliminating the UXC minority, it would reduce taxes and overhead expenses.

In December 1991 the boards of Unocal and UXC appointed special committees to consider a possible merger. The UXC committee consisted of three directors who, although also directors of Unocal, were not officers or employees of the parent company. The UXC committee retained financial and legal advisors and met four times before agreeing to a merger exchange ratio of .54 shares of Unocal stock for each share of UXC. Unocal and UXC announced the merger on February 24, 1992, and it was effected, pursuant to 8 [Delaware Code Section] 253, on May 2, 1992. The Notice of Merger and Prospectus stated the terms of the merger and advised the former UXC stockholders of their appraisal rights.

Plaintiffs filed this * * * action [in a Delaware state court], on behalf of UXC's minority stockholders, on the day the merger was announced. They asserted, among other claims, that Unocal and its directors breached their fiduciary duties of entire fairness and full disclosure. The Court * * * held that: (i) the Prospectus did not contain any material misstatements or omissions; (ii) the entire fairness standard does not control in a short-form merger; and (iii) plaintiffs' exclusive remedy in this case was appraisal. * * *

II. Discussion

* * * In its current form, * * * 8 Del. C. [Section] 253 provides * * * :

(a) In any case in which at least 90 percent of the outstanding shares of each class of the stock of a corporation * * * is owned by another corporation * * * , the corporation having such stock ownership may * * * merge the other corporation * * * into itself * * * by executing, acknowledging and filing * * * a certificate of such ownership and merger setting forth a copy of the resolution of its board of directors to so merge and the date of the adoption; provided, however, that in case the parent corporation shall not own all the outstanding stock of * * * the subsidiary corporation[ ], * * * the resolution * * * shall state the terms and conditions of the merger * * * . * * * *

(d) In the event that all of the stock of a subsidiary Delaware corporation * * * is not owned by the parent corporation immediately prior to the merger, the stockholders of the subsidiary Delaware corporation party to the merger shall have appraisal rights * * * .

* * * *

* * * [W]e must decide whether a minority stockholder may challenge a short-form merger by seeking equitable relief through an entire fairness claim. Under settled principles, *a parent corporation and its directors undertaking a short-form merger are self-dealing fiduciaries who should be required to establish entire fairness, including fair dealing and fair price.* The problem is that [Section] 253 authorizes a summary procedure that is inconsistent with any reasonable notion of fair dealing. In a short-form merger, there is no agreement of merger negotiated by two companies; there is only a unilateral act—a decision by the parent company that its 90% owned subsidiary shall no longer exist as a separate entity. The minority stockholders receive no advance notice of the merger; their directors do not consider or approve it; and there is no vote. Those who object are given the right to obtain fair value for their shares through appraisal. [Emphasis added.]

The equitable claim plainly conflicts with the statute. If a corporate fiduciary follows the truncated [shortened] process authorized by [Section] 253, it will not be able to establish the fair dealing prong of entire fairness. If, instead, the corporate fiduciary sets up negotiating committees, hires independent financial and legal experts, etc., then it will have lost the very benefit provided by the statute—a simple, fast and inexpensive process for accomplishing a merger. * * * In order to serve its purpose, [Section] 253 must be construed to obviate [avoid] the requirement to establish entire fairness.

Thus, we * * * hold that, absent fraud or illegality, appraisal is the exclusive remedy available to a minority stockholder who objects to a short-form merger. * * * The determination of fair value must be based on *all* relevant factors, including damages and elements of future value, where appropriate. So, for example, if the merger was timed to take advantage of a depressed market, or a low point in the company's cyclical earnings, or to precede an

CASE 40.2 | Continued anticipated positive development, the appraised value may be adjusted to account for those factors. * * *

Although fiduciaries are not required to establish entire fairness in a short-form merger, the duty of full disclosure remains, in the context of this request for stockholder action. Where the only choice for the minority stockholders is whether to accept the merger consideration or seek appraisal, they must be given all the factual information that is material to that decision. * * *

III. Conclusion

Based on the foregoing, we affirm the [lower] Court * * * and hold that plaintiffs' only remedy in connection with the short-form merger of UXC into Unocal was appraisal.

QUESTIONS

1. Why were the minority shareholders barred from challenging the "entire fairness" of the merger?
2. Besides appraisal rights, do the shareholders of the subsidiary corporation have any other rights when it comes to a short-form merger? Explain.

—*Appraisal Rights Procedures.* Shareholders may lose their appraisal rights if they do not follow precisely the elaborate procedures prescribed by statute. When they lose the right to an appraisal, dissenting shareholders must go along with the transaction despite their objections. The dissenting shareholders usually are required to file a written notice of dissent prior to the shareholders' vote on the proposed transaction. This notice of dissent basically serves as a notice to all shareholders of the costs that dissenting shareholders may impose on the corporation should the merger or consolidation be approved. In addition, after approval, the dissenting shareholders must make a written demand for payment and for the fair value of their shares.

—*Appraisal Rights and Shareholder Status.* Once a dissenting shareholder elects appraisal rights under a statute, in some jurisdictions the shareholder loses shareholder status. Without that status, a shareholder cannot vote, receive dividends, or sue to enjoin whatever action prompted dissent. In some of those jurisdictions, statutes provide or courts have held that shareholder status may be reinstated during the appraisal process (for example, if the shareholder decides to withdraw from the process and the corporation approves). In other jurisdictions, shareholder status may not be reinstated until the appraisal is concluded. Even when shareholder status is lost, courts may allow the individual to sue on the ground of fraud or other illegal conduct associated with the merger.

—*Valuation of Shares.* Valuation of shares is often a point of contention between the dissenting shareholder and the corporation. RMBCA 13.01 provides that the "fair value of shares" normally is the value on the day prior to the date on which the vote was taken. The corporation must make a written offer to purchase a dissenting shareholder's stock, accompanying the offer with a current balance sheet and income statement for the corporation. If the shareholder and the corporation do not agree on the fair value, a court will determine it.

SECTION 2 | Purchase of Assets

When a corporation acquires all or substantially all of the assets of another corporation by direct purchase, the corporation purchasing the assets—the *acquiring corporation*—simply extends its ownership and control over more physical assets. Because no change in the legal entity occurs, the acquiring corporation need not obtain shareholder approval for the purchase.[3]

---

3. If the acquiring corporation plans to pay for the assets with its own corporate stock and not enough authorized unissued shares are available, the shareholders must vote to approve the issuance of additional shares by amendment of the corporate articles. Also, acquiring corporations whose stock is traded on a national stock exchange can be required to obtain their own shareholders' approval if they plan to issue a significant number of shares, such as a number equal to 20 percent or more of the outstanding shares.

ANTITRUST IMPLICATIONS

Although the acquiring corporation may not be required to obtain the shareholders' approval, the U.S. Department of Justice has issued guidelines that significantly constrain and often prohibit mergers that could result from a purchase of assets. These guidelines are part of the federal antitrust laws to enforce Section 7 of the Clayton Act (discussed in Chapter 46).

SALES OF CORPORATE ASSETS

Note that the corporation that is *selling* all its assets is substantially changing its business position and perhaps its ability to carry out its corporate purposes. For that reason, the corporation whose assets are *acquired* must obtain approval from both its board of directors and its shareholders. In most states and under the RMBCA, a dissenting shareholder of the selling corporation can demand appraisal rights.

POTENTIAL LIABILITY IN PURCHASES OF ASSETS

Generally, a corporation that purchases the assets of another corporation is not responsible for the liabilities of the selling corporation. Exceptions to this rule are made in the following circumstances:

1. When the purchasing corporation impliedly or expressly assumes the seller's liabilities.
2. When the sale amounts to what in fact is a merger or a consolidation.
3. When the purchaser continues the seller's business and retains the same personnel (same shareholders, directors, and officers).
4. When the sale is fraudulently executed to escape liability.

In any of these situations, the acquiring corporation will be held to have assumed both the assets and the liabilities of the selling corporation.

SECTION 3 | Purchase of Stock

An alternative to the purchase of another corporation's assets is the purchase of a substantial number of the voting shares of its stock. This enables the acquiring corporation to gain control of the acquired corporation, or **target corporation.** The process of acquiring control over a corporation in this way is commonly referred to as a corporate **takeover.** The acquiring corporation deals directly with the shareholders in seeking to purchase the shares they hold.

TENDER OFFERS

When the acquiring corporation makes a public offer to all shareholders of the target corporation, it is called a **tender offer.** The price offered is generally higher than the market price of the target stock prior to the announcement of the tender offer. The higher price induces shareholders to tender (offer to sell) their shares to the acquiring firm. The tender offer can be conditioned on the receipt of a specified number of outstanding shares by a certain date. The offering corporation can make an *exchange* tender offer in which it offers target stockholders its own securities in exchange for their target stock. In a cash tender offer, the offering corporation offers cash in exchange for the target stock.

Federal securities laws strictly control the terms, duration, and circumstances under which most tender offers are made. In addition, a majority of states have passed takeover statutes that impose additional regulations on tender offers.

RESPONSES TO TENDER OFFERS

A firm may respond to a tender offer in numerous ways. Sometimes, a target firm's board of directors will see a tender offer as favorable and will recommend to the shareholders that they accept it. In contrast, to resist a takeover, a target company may make a *self-tender*, which is an offer to acquire stock from its own shareholders and thereby retain corporate control. Alternatively, a target corporation might resort to one of several other tactics to resist a takeover (see Exhibit 40–3 on page 814). In one commonly used tactic, known as the "poison pill," a target company gives its shareholders rights to purchase additional shares at low prices when there is a takeover attempt. The use of poison pills prevents takeovers by making them prohibitively expensive.

TAKEOVERS AND ANTITRUST LAW

Sometimes, a target corporation will seek an injunction against an aggressor on the ground that the attempted takeover violates antitrust laws. This defense may succeed if a court finds that the takeover

CONCEPT SUMMARY 40.1 | Methods of Expanding Corporate Operations and Interests

METHOD	DESCRIPTION

MERGER AND CONSOLIDATION	1. *Merger*—The legal combination of two or more corporations, with the result that the surviving corporation acquires all the assets and obligations of the other corporation, which then ceases to exist.
	2. *Consolidation*—The legal combination of two or more corporations, with the result that each corporation ceases to exist and a new one emerges. The new corporation assumes all the assets and obligations of the former corporations.
	3. *Procedure*—Determined by state statutes. Basic requirements are the following:
	  a. The board of directors of each corporation involved must approve the merger or consolidation plan.
	  b. The shareholders of each corporation must approve the merger or consolidation plan at a shareholders' meeting.
	  c. Articles of merger or consolidation (the plan) must be filed, usually with the secretary of state.
	  d. The state issues a certificate of merger (or consolidation) to the surviving (or newly consolidated) corporation.
	4. *Short-form merger (parent-subsidiary merger)*—Possible when the parent corporation owns at least 90 percent of the outstanding shares of each class of stock of the subsidiary corporation.
	  a. Shareholder approval is not required.
	  b. The merger must be approved only by the board of directors of the parent corporation.
	  c. A copy of the merger plan must be sent to each shareholder of record.
	  d. The merger plan must be filed with the state.
	5. *Appraisal rights*—Rights of shareholders (given by state statute) to receive the *fair value* for their shares when a merger or consolidation takes place. If the shareholder and the corporation do not agree on the fair value, a court will determine it.

PURCHASE OF ASSETS	A purchase of assets occurs when one corporation acquires all or substantially all of the assets of another corporation. 1. *Acquiring corporation*—The acquiring (purchasing) corporation is not required to obtain shareholder approval; the corporation is merely increasing its assets, and no fundamental business change occurs. 2. *Acquired corporation*—The acquired (purchased) corporation is required to obtain the approval of both its directors and its shareholders for the sale of its assets, because this creates a substantial change in the corporation's business position.
PURCHASE OF STOCK	A purchase of stock occurs when one corporation acquires a substantial number of the voting shares of the stock of another (target) corporation. 1. *Tender offer*—A public offer to all shareholders of the target corporation to purchase its stock at a price generally higher than the market price of the target stock prior to the announcement of the tender offer. Federal and state securities laws strictly control the terms, duration, and circumstances under which most tender offers are made. 2. *Target responses*—Ways in which target corporations respond to takeover bids. These include self-tender (the target firm's offer to acquire its own shareholders' stock) and numerous other strategies (see Exhibit 40–3 on the next page).

would result in a substantial increase in the acquiring corporation's market power. Because antitrust laws are designed to protect competition rather than competi-tors, incumbent managers who are able to avoid a takeover by resorting to the use of private antitrust actions are unintended beneficiaries of the laws.

EXHIBIT 40-3 The Terminology of Takeover Defenses

Type	Definition
Crown Jewel	When threatened with a takeover, management makes the company less attractive to the raider by selling to a third party the company's most valuable asset (the "crown jewel").
Golden Parachute	When a takeover is successful, top management is usually changed. With this in mind, a company may establish special termination or retirement benefits that must be paid to top managers if they are "retired." In other words, a departing high-level manager's parachute will be "golden" when he or she is forced to "bail out" of the company.
Greenmail	To regain control, a target company may pay a higher-than-market price to repurchase the stock bought by the acquiring corporation. When a takeover is attempted through a gradual accumulation of target stock rather than a tender offer, the intent may be to get the target company to buy back the shares at a premium price—a concept similar to blackmail.
Pac-Man	Named after the Atari video game, this is an aggressive defense in which the target corporation attempts its own takeover of the acquiring corporation.
Poison Pill	The target corporation issues to its stockholders rights to purchase additional shares at low prices when there is a takeover attempt. This makes the takeover undesirably or even prohibitively expensive for the acquiring corporation.
White Knight	The target corporation solicits a merger with a third party, which then makes a better (often simply a higher) tender offer to the target's shareholders. The third party that "rescues" the target is the "white knight."

As will be discussed in Chapter 46, antitrust challenges to mergers may also be brought by the government rather than by private parties. Hence, the antitrust considerations involved in a proposed takeover can exist apart from the consideration of defense tactics.

SECTION 4 | Termination

Termination of a corporate life, like termination of a partnership, has two phases—dissolution and liquidation. **Dissolution** is the legal death of the artificial "person" of the corporation. **Liquidation** is the process by which corporate assets are converted into cash and distributed among creditors and shareholders according to specific rules of preference.[4]

DISSOLUTION

Dissolution can be brought about voluntarily by the directors and shareholders or involuntarily by the state or through a court's order. Once a corporation is dissolved, either voluntarily or involuntarily, its corporate existence is ended except for the process of winding up corporate affairs and distributing corporate assets.

VOLUNTARY DISSOLUTION Once a corporation has issued shares and commenced business operations it can be voluntarily dissolved in basically two ways.[5] First, the shareholders can initiate corporate dissolution proceedings by a unanimous vote to dissolve the corporation.[6] Second, the directors can propose that the corporation be dissolved and submit the proposal to the shareholders for a vote at the shareholders' annual meeting or a specially called shareholders' meeting.

Under RMBCA 14.03, once a decision is reached to dissolve the corporation, the corporation must file *articles of dissolution* with the secretary of state. These articles must include the name of the corporation, the date on which the dissolution was authorized, and how the dissolution was authorized. The effective date of dissolution will be the date of the articles of dissolution. The corporation must also establish a date (at least 120 days following the date of dissolution) by which all claims against the corporation must be received [RMBCA 14.06].

INVOLUNTARY DISSOLUTION As explained earlier, corporations are creatures of statute. Just as the

---

4. On dissolution, the liquidated assets are first used to pay creditors. Any remaining assets are distributed to shareholders according to their respective stock rights; preferred stock has priority over common stock, generally by charter.

5. If the corporation was formed but has not yet undertaken any business or issued any shares, a majority of the incorporators can dissolve the corporation relatively simply—by filing articles of dissolution with the secretary of state's office, which will then issue a certificate of dissolution.

6. Delaware Code Section 275(c).

state can allow a corporation to come into existence, so can the state end that existence. The state, in an action brought by the secretary of state or the state attorney general, can dissolve a corporation for any of the following reasons [RMBCA 14.20]:

1. Failure of the corporation to comply with administrative requirements (such as failure to pay annual taxes, submit an annual report, or have a designated registered agent).
2. Procurement of a corporate charter through fraud or misrepresentation on the state.
3. Abuse of corporate powers (*ultra vires* acts).
4. Violation of the state criminal code after a demand to discontinue the violation has been made by the secretary of state.
5. Failure to commence business operations.
6. Abandonment of operations before starting up.

In some states, statutory provisions provide that the articles of incorporation of a close corporation can empower any shareholder to dissolve the corporation at will or on the occurrence of a specified event—such as the death of another shareholder. This provides a shareholder in a close corporation with the same power to dissolve the business organization as a partner in a partnership.

Shareholders can also petition a court for corporate dissolution in some circumstances. For example, when the board of directors is deadlocked, an involuntary dissolution of a corporation may be necessary. Courts hesitate to order involuntary dissolution unless there is specific statutory authorization to do so, but if the shareholders cannot resolve the deadlock and if it will irreparably injure the corporation, the court will proceed with an involuntary dissolution. Courts can also dissolve a corporation for mismanagement [RMBCA 14.30].

The court in the following case was asked to dissolve a corporation on the basis of allegedly illegal, oppressive, and fraudulent conduct.

| CASE 40.3 | **Colt v. Mt. Princeton Trout Club, Inc.** |

Colorado Court
of Appeals,
Division I, 2003.
78 P.3d 1115.

BACKGROUND AND FACTS *Mt. Princeton Trout Club, Inc. (MPTC), was formed in 1965 to own land in Colorado and provide fishing and other recreational benefits to its shareholders. MPTC's capital consisted of eight shares of stock with voting rights. The shareholders constituted the board of directors under the articles of incorporation, which prohibited MPTC from selling or leasing "any of the property and assets of the corporation" without a majority vote of the directors. Despite this provision, MPTC officers entered into leases—including a lease of the corporate lodge, which some of the shareholders opposed—and contracts to sell corporate property without notice to, or a meeting of, the directors. After MPTC officers engaged in further questionable activities, Sam Colt, one of the original eight shareholders, filed a suit in a Colorado state court against MPTC and others to dissolve the corporation. The plaintiff alleged that the corporation committed illegal, oppressive, and fraudulent acts. The court ordered dissolution. MPTC appealed to a state intermediate appellate court.*

IN THE LANGUAGE OF THE COURT

Opinion by Judge GRAHAM.

* * * *

The trial court found: (1) the officers of MPTC failed to file federal tax returns; (2) the officers and directors failed to collect, in a timely fashion, shareholder assessments [for local property taxes] to the detriment of MPTC; (3) leases and contracts were entered into without notice to the shareholders and without a formal meeting of the officers, directors, or shareholders; (4) funds of the corporation were not properly accounted for; (5) minutes of corporate meetings inexplicably were missing or withheld from shareholders; (6) an officer of the corporation entered into agreements listing corporate property for sale without authorization or resolution of the corporation; and (7) there existed a "consistent undercurrent of dealing corporate interests without notice to the shareholders and all directors."

* * * *

[Under Colorado Statutes Section 7-114-301(2)(b),] *a corporation may be dissolved judicially in a proceeding brought by a shareholder if "[t]he directors or those in control of the corporation have acted, are acting, or will act in a manner that is illegal, oppressive, or fraudulent."* [Emphasis added.]

* * * *

CONTINUED ▶

CASE 40.3 | Continued

* * * [F]or the purposes of this statute, oppressive conduct is generally defined as:

[B]urdensome, harsh and wrongful conduct; a lack of probity and fair dealing in the affairs of the company to the prejudice of some of its members; or a * * * departure from the standards of fair dealing, and a violation of fair play on which every shareholder who entrusts his money to a company is entitled to rely.

Here, in support of its dissolution order, the [trial] court specifically found that "MPTC * * * breached its fiduciary duty to all of its shareholders. It has acted in an oppressive manner."
* * * *

The [trial] court * * * determined as a general matter that "there has been a consistent undercurrent of dealing corporate interests without notice to the shareholders and all directors." Self-dealing and failure to comply with rules of corporate governance include, of necessity, elements of unlawful conduct * * * .

Here, the record amply supports the trial court's finding * * * .
* * * *

These acts * * * might be properly characterized as illegal, oppressive, or fraudulent.
* * *
* * * *

Evidence presented at trial established that implicit in the formation of MPTC was the idea that the shareholders could pursue their fishing hobby with reasonable and unfettered access to the land and reap the rewards of appreciation when the land was ultimately sold. The shareholders also reasonably could expect that the corporation would be managed in a proper manner for their mutual benefit.
* * * *

Here, the primary reason for corporate existence has disappeared. MPTC no longer serves the interests of all the shareholders, and under this and other circumstances enumerated in the record, a sufficient showing was made to justify dissolution.

DECISION AND REMEDY *The state intermediate appellate court affirmed the order of the lower court. Under the circumstances, it was proper to dissolve the corporation on the basis of MPTC's illegal, oppressive, and fraudulent activities.*

LIQUIDATION

When dissolution takes place by voluntary action, the members of the board of directors act as trustees of the corporate assets. As trustees, they are responsible for winding up the affairs of the corporation for the benefit of corporate creditors and shareholders. This makes the board members personally liable for any breach of their fiduciary trustee duties.

Liquidation can be accomplished without court supervision unless the members of the board do not wish to act in this capacity or unless shareholders or creditors can show cause to the court why the board should not be permitted to assume the trustee function. In either case, the court will appoint a receiver to wind up the corporate affairs and liquidate corporate assets. A receiver is always appointed when the dissolution is involuntary.

SECTION 5 | Major Business Forms Compared

When deciding which form of business organization would be most appropriate, businesspersons nor-

mally take several factors into consideration. As discussed previously, these factors include ease of creation, the liability of the owners, tax considerations, and the need for capital. Each major form of business organization offers distinct advantages and disadvantages with respect to these and other factors.

For example, the sole proprietorship has the advantage of being easily and inexpensively established, but the owner faces personal liability for business obligations as well as restrictions on obtaining capital for additional financing. The partnership is relatively easy to set up and provides a way for the business to obtain capital (from partners' contributions). It enjoys tax benefits as well. The partnership also has a major disadvantage: the personal liability of the partners. One of the advantages of the corporate form is that capital for expansion can be obtained by the issuance of shares of stock. Another advantage is the limited liability of the shareholder-owners. The limited liability company and the limited liability partnership increasingly are becoming forms of choice because of the many advantages they offer with respect to both the liability of the owners and taxation.

Exhibit 40–4 summarizes the essential advantages and disadvantages of each of the forms of business organization discussed in Chapters 35 through 40.

EXHIBIT 40–4 **Major Forms of Business Compared**

CHARACTERISTIC	SOLE PROPRIETORSHIP	PARTNERSHIP	CORPORATION
Method of Creation	Created at will by owner.	Created by agreement of the parties.	Charter issued by state—created by statutory authorization.
Legal Position	Not a separate entity; owner is the business.	Is a separate legal entity in most states.	Always a legal entity separate and distinct from its owners—a legal fiction for the purposes of owning property and being a party to litigation.
Liability	Unlimited liability.	Unlimited liability.	Limited liability of shareholders—shareholders are not liable for the debts of the corporation.
Duration	Determined by owner; automatically dissolved on owner's death.	Terminated by agreement of the partners, but in most states can continue to do business even when a partner dissociates from the partnership.	Can have perpetual existence.
Transferability of Interest	Interest can be transferred, but individual's proprietorship then ends.	Although partnership interest can be assigned, assignee does not have full rights of a partner.	Shares of stock can be transferred.
Management	Completely at owner's discretion.	Each general partner has a direct and equal voice in management unless expressly agreed otherwise in the partnership agreement.	Shareholders elect directors, who set policy and appoint officers.
Taxation	Owner pays personal taxes on business income.	Each partner pays pro rata share of income taxes on net profits, whether or not they are distributed.	Double taxation—corporation pays income tax on net profits, with no deduction for dividends, and shareholders pay taxes on the dividends they receive (at the same rate either as their income tax or as their capital gains tax for qualified dividends).
Organizational Fees, Annual License Fees, and Annual Reports	None.	None.	All required.
Transaction of Business in Other States	Generally no limitation.	Generally no limitation.[a]	Normally must qualify to do business and obtain certificate of authority.

a. A few states have enacted statutes requiring that foreign partnerships qualify to do business there.   *(Continued)*

EXHIBIT 40-4   Major Forms of Business Compared *(continued)*

CHARACTERISTIC	LIMITED PARTNERSHIP	LIMITED LIABILITY COMPANY	LIMITED LIABILITY PARTNERSHIP
Method of Creation	Created by agreement to carry on a business for a profit. At least one party must be a general partner and the other(s) limited partner(s). Certificate of limited partnership is filed. Charter must be issued by the state.	Created by an agreement of member-owners of the company. Articles of organization are filed. Charter must be issued by the state.	Created by agreement of the partners. A statement of qualification for the limited liability partnership is filed.
Legal Position	Treated as a legal entity.	Treated as a legal entity.	Generally, treated the same as a general partnership.
Liability	Unlimited liability of all general partners; limited partners are liable only to the extent of capital contributions.	Member-owners' liability is limited to the amount of capital contributions or investments.	Varies, but under the UPA, liability of a partner for acts committed by other partners is limited.
Duration	By agreement in certificate, or by termination of the last general partner (retirement, death, and the like) or last limited partner.	Unless a single-member LLC, can have perpetual existence (same as a corporation).	Remains in existence until cancellation or revocation.
Transferability of Interest	Interest can be assigned (same as general partnership), but if assignee becomes a member with consent of other partners, certificate must be amended.	Member interests are freely transferable.	Interest can be assigned same as in a general partnership.
Management	General partners have equal voice or by agreement. Limited partners may not retain limited liability if they actively participate in management.	Member-owners can fully participate in management, or management is selected by member-owners who manage on behalf of the members.	Same as a general partnership.
Taxation	Generally taxed as a partnership.	LLC is not taxed, and members are taxed personally on profits "passed through" the LLC.	Same as a general partnership.
Organizational Fees, Annual License Fees, and Annual Reports	Organizational fee required; usually not others.	Organizational fee required; others vary with states.	Fees are set by each state for filing statements of qualification, foreign qualification, and annual reports.
Transaction of Business in Other States	Generally, no limitations.	Generally, no limitation but may vary depending on state.	Must file a statement of foreign qualification before doing business in another state.

REVIEWING CORPORATIONS— MERGER, CONSOLIDATION, AND TERMINATION

In November 1999, Mario Bonsetti and Rico Sanchez incorporated Gnarly Vulcan Gear, Inc. (GVG), to manufacture windsurfing equipment. Bonsetti owned 60 percent and Sanchez owned 40 percent of the corporation's stock, and both men served on the board of directors. In January 2003, Hula Boards, Inc., owned solely by Mai Jin Li, made a public offer to Bonsetti and Sanchez to buy GVG stock. Hula offered 30 percent more than the market price per share for the GVG stock, and Bonsetti and Sanchez each sold 20 percent of their stock to Hula. Jin Li became the third member of the GVG board of directors. In April 2005, an irreconcilable dispute arose between Bonsetti and Sanchez over design modifications of their popular Baked Chameleon board. Sanchez and Jin Li voted to merge GVG with Hula Boards under the latter name, despite Bonsetti's dissent. Gnarly Vulcan Gear was dissolved and production of the Baked Chameleon ceased. Using the information presented in the chapter, answer the following questions.

1. What rights does Bonsetti have (in most states) as a minority shareholder dissenting to the merger of GVG and Hula Boards?

2. Could the parties have used a short-form merger procedure in this situation? Why or why not?

3. What is the term used for Hula's offer to purchase GVG stock? By what method did Hula acquire control over GVG?

4. Suppose that after the merger, a person who was injured on a Baked Chameleon board sued Hula (the surviving corporation). Can Hula be held liable for an injury? Why or why not?

5. Suppose that GVG was organized as a limited partnership (see Chapter 36) rather than a corporation. Further suppose that Bonsetti was the only general partner, and Sanchez and Hula Boards, Inc., were limited partners. How would the dispute over the design of the Baked Chameleon board be resolved in that situation? How would the partners' liability for injuries to third parties be different?

TERMS AND CONCEPTS TO REVIEW

appraisal right 809

consolidation 808

dissolution 814

liquidation 814

merger 806

parent-subsidiary merger 809

short-form merger 809

surviving corporation 806

takeover 812

target corporation 812

tender offer 812

QUESTIONS AND CASE PROBLEMS

40-1. Gretz is chairperson of the board of directors of Faraday, Inc., and Williams is chairperson of the board of directors of Firebrand, Inc. Faraday is a manufacturing corporation, and Firebrand is a transportation corporation. Gretz and Williams meet to consider the possibility of combining their corporations and activities into a single corporate entity. They consider two alternative courses of action: (1) acquisition by Faraday of all the stock and assets of Firebrand and (2) combination of the two corporations to form a new corporation, Farabrand, Inc. Both chairpersons are concerned about the necessity of formal transfer of property, liability for existing debts, and the need to amend the articles of incorporation. Explain what the two proposed combinations are called, and discuss the legal effect each has on the transfer of property, the liabilities of the combined corporations, and the need to amend the articles of incorporation.

40–2. ⚖ QUESTION WITH SAMPLE ANSWER

Alir owns 10,000 shares of Ajax Corp. Her shares represent a 10 percent ownership in Ajax. Zeta Corp. is interested in acquiring Ajax in a merger, and the board of directors of each corporation has approved the merger. The shareholders of Zeta have already approved the acquisition, and Ajax has called for a shareholders' meeting to approve the merger. Alir disapproves of the merger and does not want to accept Zeta shares for the Ajax shares she holds. The market price of Ajax shares is $20 per share the day before the shareholder vote and drops to $16 on the day the shareholders of Ajax approve the merger. Discuss Alir's rights in this matter, beginning with the notice of the proposed merger.

For a sample answer to this question, go to Appendix I at the end of this text.

40–3. Green Corp. wants to acquire all the assets of Red Dot Corp. Green plans to pay for the assets by issuing its own corporate stock. Green's board of directors has already approved the merger. Discuss whether shareholder approval is required for this merger.

40–4. Alitech Corp. is a small midwestern business that owns a valuable patent. Alitech has approximately 1,000 shareholders with 100,000 authorized and outstanding shares. Block Corp. would like to have the use of the patent, but Alitech refuses to give Block a license. Block has tried to acquire Alitech by purchasing Alitech's assets, but Alitech's board of directors has refused to approve the acquisition. Alitech's shares are currently selling for $5 per share. Discuss how Block Corp. might proceed to gain the control and use of Alitech's patent.

40–5. Saunders Corp. has been losing money for several years but still has valuable fixed assets. The shareholders see little hope that the corporation will ever make a profit. Another corporation, Topway Corp., has failed to pay state taxes for several years or to file annual reports as required by statute. In addition, Topway is accused of committing gross and persistent *ultra vires* acts. Discuss whether these corporations will be terminated and how the assets of each would be handled on dissolution.

40–6. **DISSOLUTION.** In 1988, Farad Mohammed and Syed Parveen formed Hina Pharmacy, Health & Beauty Aids, Inc., to operate a pharmacy in New York. Parveen, an experienced pharmacist, contributed his expertise and $7,000. Mohammed contributed $120,000. Each took 50 percent of the Hina stock. Mohammed assigned his shares to his brother Azam, and Syed assigned his to his wife Aisha. A dispute soon arose over the disparity in capital contributions. The parties held only one shareholders' meeting, and they never attempted to elect directors. Syed later claimed that Azam, who exercised sole control over the daily management of Hina, kept 80 percent of the profits. Azam argued that Syed had agreed to work for 20 percent of the profits plus a salary. Syed stopped working at the pharmacy in 1994. Aisha filed a petition in a New York state court to dissolve Hina.

Could the court grant the petition? If so, on what basis? If not, why not? [*In re Parveen*, 259 A.D.2d 389, 687 N.Y.S.2d 90 (1 Dept. 1999)]

40–7. ⚖ CASE PROBLEM WITH SAMPLE ANSWER

In January 1999, General Star Indemnity Co. agreed to insure Indianapolis Racing League (IRL) race cars against damage during on-track accidents. In connection with the insurance, General Star deposited $400,000 with G Force LLC (GFCO), a Colorado firm, to enable it to buy and provide, without delay, parts for damaged cars. GFCO agreed to return any unspent funds. Near the end of the season, Elan Motorsports Technologies (EMT) acquired GFCO. In 2000, EMT incorporated G Force LLC in Georgia (GFGA), and GFCO ceased to exist. GFGA renewed the arrangement with General Star and engaged in the same operations as GFCO, but EMT employees conducted GFGA's business at EMT's offices. In 2002, EMT assumed ownership of GFGA's assets and continued the business. EMT also assumed GFGA's liabilities, except for the obligation to return General Star's unspent funds. General Star filed a suit in a Georgia state court against EMT, seeking to recover its deposit. What is the rule concerning the liability of a corporation that buys the assets of another? Are there exceptions? Which principles apply in this case? Explain. [*General Star Indemnity Co. v. Elan Motorsports Technologies, Inc.*, 356 F.Supp.2d 1333 (N.D.Ga. 2004)]

To view a sample answer for this case problem, go to this book's Web site at http://wbl.westbuslaw.com, select "Chapter 40," and click on "Case Problem with Sample Answer."

40–8. **SUCCESSOR LIABILITY.** In 1996, Robert McClellan, a licensed contractor doing business as McClellan Design and Construction, entered into a contract with Peppertree North Condominium Association, Inc., to do earthquake repair work on Peppertree's seventy-six-unit condominium complex in Northridge, California. McClellan completed the work, but Peppertree failed to pay. In an arbitration proceeding against Peppertree to collect the amount due, McClellan was awarded $141,000, plus 10 percent interest, attorneys' fees, and costs. McClellan filed a suit in a California state court against Peppertree to confirm the award. Meanwhile, the Peppertree board of directors filed articles of incorporation for Northridge Park Townhome Owners Association, Inc., and immediately transferred Peppertree's authority, responsibilities, and assets to the new association. Two weeks later, the court issued a judgment against Peppertree. When McClellan learned about the new association, he filed a motion asking the court to add Northridge as a debtor to the judgment. Should the court grant the motion? Why or why not? [*McClellan v. Northridge Park Townhome Owners Association, Inc.*, 89 Cal.App.4th 746, 107 Cal.Rptr.2d 702 (2 Dist. 2001)]

40–9. **CORPORATE DISSOLUTION.** Trans-System, Inc. (TSI), is an interstate trucking business. In 1994, to provide a source of well-trained drivers, TSI formed Northwestern Career Institute, Inc., a school for persons interested in obtaining a commercial driver's license. Tim Scott, who had worked for TSI since 1987, was named chief administrative officer and director. Scott, a Northwestern shareholder, disagreed with James Williams, the majority shareholder of both TSI and Northwestern, over four equipment leases between the two firms under which the sum of the payments exceeded the value of the equipment by not more than $3,000. Under four other leases, payments were $40,000 less than the value of the equipment. Scott also disputed TSI's one-time use, for purposes unrelated to the driving school, of $125,000 borrowed by Northwestern. Scott was terminated in 1998. He filed a suit in a Washington state court against TSI, seeking, among other things, the dissolution of Northwestern on the ground that the directors of the two firms had acted in an oppressive manner and misapplied corporate assets. Should the court grant this relief? If not, what remedy might be appropriate? Discuss. [*Scott v. Trans-System, Inc.*, 148 Wash.2d 701, 64 P.3d 1 (2003)]

40-10. PURCHASE OF ASSETS. Paradise Pools, Inc. (PPI), also known as "Paradise Pools and Spas," was incorporated in 1981. In 1994, PPI entered into a contract with Bromanco, Inc., to build a pool in Vicksburg, Mississippi, as part of a Days Inn Hotel project being developed by Amerihost Development, Inc. PPI built the pool, but Bromanco, the general contractor, defaulted on other parts of the project, and Amerihost completed the construction itself. Litigation ensued in Mississippi state courts, and Amerihost was awarded $12,656.46 against PPI. Meanwhile, Paradise Corp. (PC) was incorporated in 1995 with the same management as PPI, but different shareholders. PC acquired PPI's assets in 1996, without assuming its liabilities, and soon became known as "Paradise Pools and Spas." Amerihost obtained a writ of garnishment against PC to enforce the judgment against PPI. PC filed a motion to dismiss the writ on the basis that it was "not a party to the proceeding." Should the court dismiss the case? Why or why not? [*Paradise Corp. v. Amerihost Development, Inc.*, 848 So.2d 177 (Miss. 2003)]

LAW | on the Web

For updated links to resources available on the Web, as well as a variety of other materials, visit this text's Web site at **http://wbl.westbuslaw.com**.

The court opinions of Delaware's Court of Chancery, which is widely considered to be the nation's premier trial court for corporate law, are now available on the Web in a searchable database offered by the Delaware Corporate Law Clearinghouse. The site also offers valuable links to other sites dealing with corporate law and litigation. Go to

http://corporate-law.widener.edu

Ballard, Spahr, Andrews & Ingersoll, LLP, a law firm in Philadelphia, offers an eight-step guide on how to uncover company information that may be of interest to shareholders and others. Go to

http://www.virtualchase.com/coinfo/index.htm

LEGAL RESEARCH EXERCISES ON THE WEB

Go to **http://wbl.westbuslaw.com**, the Web site that accompanies this text. Select "Chapter 40" and click on "Internet Exercises." There you will find the following Internet research exercises that you can perform to learn more about topics covered in this chapter.

Activity 40–1: LEGAL PERSPECTIVE
Mergers

Activity 40–2: MANAGEMENT PERSPECTIVE
Golden Parachutes

CHAPTER 41

CORPORATIONS—
Securities Law and
Corporate Governance

The stock market crash of October 29, 1929, and the ensuing economic depression caused the public to focus on the importance of securities markets for the economic well-being of the nation. Congress was pressured to regulate securities trading, and the result was the Securities Act of 1933[1] and the Securities Exchange Act of 1934.[2] Both acts were designed to provide investors with more information to help them make buying and selling decisions about securities—generally defined as any documents evidencing corporate ownership (stock) or debts (bonds)—and to prohibit deceptive, unfair, and manipulative practices in the purchase and sale of securities.

This chapter discusses the nature of federal securities regulation and its effect on the business world. We begin by looking at the federal administrative agency that regulates securities transactions, the Securities and Exchange Commission. Next, we examine the major traditional laws governing securities offerings and trading. We then discuss corporate governance and the Sarbanes-Oxley Act, which was passed by Congress in 2002 and significantly affects certain types of securities transactions. In the concluding pages of this chapter, we look at how securities laws are being adapted to the online environment.

SECTION 1 | The Securities and Exchange Commission

The 1934 act created the Securities and Exchange Commission (SEC) as an independent regulatory agency whose function was to administer the 1933 and 1934 acts. The SEC plays a key role in interpreting the provisions of these acts (and their amendments) and in creating regulations governing the purchase and sale of securities.

THE BASIC FUNCTIONS OF THE SEC

The SEC regulates the securities industry by undertaking the following activities:

1. Requiring disclosure of facts concerning offerings of securities listed on national securities exchanges and offerings of certain securities traded over the counter (OTC).

2. Regulating the trade in securities on the national and regional securities exchanges and in the OTC markets.

3. Investigating securities fraud.

4. Requiring the registration of securities brokers, dealers, and investment advisers and regulating their activities.

5. Supervising activities conducted by mutual funds companies.

6. Recommending administrative sanctions, injunctive remedies, and criminal prosecution in cases involving violations of securities laws. (The Fraud Section of the Criminal Division of the U.S. Department of Justice prosecutes violations of federal securities laws.)

THE EXPANDING REGULATORY POWERS OF THE SEC

Since its creation, the SEC's regulatory functions have gradually been increased by legislation granting it authority in different areas. For example, to further curb securities fraud, the Securities Enforcement

---

1. 15 U.S.C. Sections 77a–77aa.
2. 15 U.S.C. Sections 78a–78mm.

Remedies and Penny Stock Reform Act of 1990[3] allowed SEC administrative law judges to hear many more types of securities violation cases and expanded the SEC's enforcement options. The act also gave courts the power to prevent persons who have engaged in securities fraud from serving as officers and directors of publicly held corporations. The Securities Acts Amendments of 1990 authorized the SEC to seek sanctions against those who violate foreign securities laws.[4] The Market Reform Act of 1990 gave the SEC authority to suspend trading in securities in the event that prices rise and fall excessively in a short period of time.[5]

The National Securities Markets Improvement Act of 1996 allowed the SEC to exempt persons, securities, and transactions from the requirements of the securities laws.[6] The act also limited the authority of the states to regulate certain securities transactions, as well as particular investment advisory firms.[7] The Sarbanes-Oxley Act of 2002,[8] which will be discussed shortly, further expanded the authority of the SEC by directing the agency to issue new rules relating to corporate disclosure requirements and by creating an SEC oversight board.

STREAMLINING THE REGULATORY PROCESS

For years, Congress and the SEC have been attempting to streamline the regulatory process generally. The goal is to make the process more efficient and more relevant to today's securities trading practices. Another goal is to create more oversight over securities transactions and accounting practices. As the number and types of online securities frauds increase, the SEC is trying to keep pace by expanding its online fraud division.

SECTION 2 | The Securities Act of 1933

The Securities Act of 1933 governs initial sales of stock by businesses. The act was designed to prohibit various forms of fraud and to stabilize the securities industry by requiring that all essential information concerning the issuance of securities be made available to the investing public. Basically, the purpose of this act is to require disclosure.

WHAT IS A SECURITY?

Section 2(1) of the Securities Act states that securities include the following:

> [A]ny note, stock, treasury stock, bond, debenture, evidence of indebtedness, certificate of interest or participation in any profit-sharing agreement, collateral-trust certificate, preorganization certificate or subscription, transferable share, investment contract, voting-trust certificate, certificate of deposit for a security, fractional undivided interest in oil, gas, or other mineral rights, or, in general, any interest or instrument commonly known as a "security," or any certificate of interest or participation in, temporary or interim certificate for, receipt for, guarantee of, or warrant or right to subscribe to or purchase, any of the foregoing.[9]

The courts have interpreted the act's definition of what constitutes a *security*[10] to include investment contracts. An investment contract is any transaction in which a person (1) invests (2) in a common enterprise (3) reasonably expecting profits (4) derived *primarily* or *substantially* from others' managerial or entrepreneurial efforts.[11]

For our purposes, it is probably most convenient to think of securities in their most common form—stocks and bonds issued by corporations. Bear in mind, though, that securities can take many forms and have been held to include interests in whiskey, cosmetics, worms, beavers, boats, vacuum cleaners, muskrats, and cemetery lots, as well as investment contracts in condominiums, franchises, limited partnerships, oil or gas or other mineral rights, and farm animals accompanied by care agreements. Businesspersons usually require the advice of an attorney to determine whether a given transaction involves securities.

REGISTRATION STATEMENT

Section 5 of the Securities Act of 1933 broadly provides that if a security does not qualify for an exemption, that security must be *registered* before it is offered

---

3. 15 U.S.C. Section 77g.
4. 15 U.S.C. Section 78a.
5. 15 U.S.C. Section 78i(h).
6. 15 U.S.C. Sections 77z-3, 78mm.
7. 15 U.S.C. Section 80b-3a.
8. H.R. 3762. This act became effective on August 29, 2002.

9. 15 U.S.C. Section 77b(1). Amendments in 1982 added stock options.
10. See 15 U.S.C. Section 77b(a)(1).
11. *SEC v. W. J. Howey Co.*, 328 U.S. 293, 66 S.Ct. 1100, 90 L.Ed. 1244 (1946).

to the public either through the mails or through any facility of interstate commerce, including securities exchanges. Issuing corporations must file a *registration statement* with the SEC. Investors must be provided with a prospectus that describes the security being sold, the issuing corporation, and the risk attaching to the security. In principle, the registration statement and the prospectus supply sufficient information to enable unsophisticated investors to evaluate the financial risk involved.

CONTENTS OF THE REGISTRATION STATEMENT

The registration statement must include the following:

1. A description of the significant provisions of the security offered for sale, including the relationship between that security and the other securities of the registrant. Also, the corporation must disclose how it intends to use the proceeds of the sale.

2. A description of the corporation's properties and business.

3. A description of the management of the corporation; its security holdings; and its remuneration and other benefits, including pensions and stock options. Any interests of directors or officers in any material transactions with the corporation must be disclosed.

4. A financial statement certified by an independent public accounting firm.

5. A description of pending lawsuits.

OTHER REQUIREMENTS Before filing the registration statement and the prospectus with the SEC, the corporation is allowed to obtain an underwriter who will monitor the distribution of the new issue. There is a twenty-day waiting period (which can be accelerated by the SEC) after registration before the sale can take place. During this period, oral offers between interested investors and the issuing corporation concerning the purchase and sale of the proposed securities may take place, and very limited written advertising is allowed. At this time, what is known as a **red herring** prospectus may be distributed. The name comes from the red legend printed across it stating that the registration statement has been filed but has not yet become effective.

After the waiting period, the SEC allows the registration statement to become "effective." The registered securities can then be legally bought and sold. Written advertising is initially allowed in the form of a **tombstone ad,** so named because historically the format resembled a tombstone. Such ads simply tell

the investor where and how to obtain a prospectus. Normally, any other type of advertising is prohibited until the registration becomes effective.

EXEMPT SECURITIES

A number of specific securities are exempt from the registration requirements of the Securities Act of 1933. These securities—which can also generally be resold without being registered—include the following:[12]

1. All bank securities sold prior to July 27, 1933.

2. Commercial paper, if the maturity date does not exceed nine months.

3. Securities of charitable organizations.

4. Securities resulting from a corporate reorganization issued for exchange with the issuer's existing security holders and certificates issued by trustees, receivers, or debtors in possession under the bankruptcy laws (bankruptcy was discussed in Chapter 30).

5. Securities issued exclusively for exchange with the issuer's existing security holders, provided no commission is paid (for example, stock dividends and stock splits).

6. Securities issued to finance the acquisition of railroad equipment.

7. Any insurance, endowment, or annuity contract issued by a state-regulated insurance company.

8. Government-issued securities.

9. Securities issued by banks, savings and loan associations, farmers' cooperatives, and similar institutions subject to supervision by governmental authorities.

10. In consideration of the "small amount involved,"[13] an issuer's offer of up to $5 million in securities in any twelve-month period.

For the last exemption, under Regulation A,[14] the issuer must file with the SEC a notice of the issue and an offering circular, which must also be provided to investors before the sale. This is a much simpler and less expensive process than the procedures associated with full registration. Companies are allowed to "test the waters" for potential interest before preparing the offering circular. (To *test the waters* means to determine potential interest without actually selling any securities or requiring any commitment on the part of those who are interested.) Small-business issuers (companies with annual revenues of less than $25 million and less than

---

12. 15 U.S.C. Section 77c.
13. 15 U.S.C. Section 77c(b).
14. 17 C.F.R. Sections 230.251–230.263.

$25 million in outstanding voting stock) can also utilize an integrated registration and reporting system that uses simpler forms than the full registration procedure.

Exhibit 41–1 summarizes the securities and transactions (discussed next) that are exempt from the registration requirements under the Securities Act of 1933 and SEC regulations.

EXEMPT TRANSACTIONS

An issuer of securities that are not exempt under any of the categories listed above can avoid the high cost and complicated procedures associated with registration by taking advantage of certain *exempt transactions*. These exemptions are very broad, and thus many sales occur without registration. Because the exemptions overlap somewhat, an offering may qualify for more than one.

SMALL OFFERINGS—REGULATION D   The SEC's Regulation D contains four separate exemptions from registration requirements for limited offers (offers that either involve a small amount of money or are made in a limited manner). Regulation D provides that any of these offerings made during any twelve-month period are exempt from the registration requirements.

—*Rule 504.* Noninvestment company offerings up to $1 million in any twelve-month period are exempt.[15] In contrast to investment companies

---

15. 17 C.F.R. Section 230.504. Rule 504 is the exemption used by most small businesses, but that could change under the new SEC Rule 1001. This rule permits, under certain circumstances, "testing the waters" for offerings of up to $5 million *per transaction*. These offerings, however, can be made only to "qualified purchasers" (knowledgeable, sophisticated investors).

EXHIBIT 41–1   **Exemptions under the 1933 Act for Securities Offerings by Businesses**

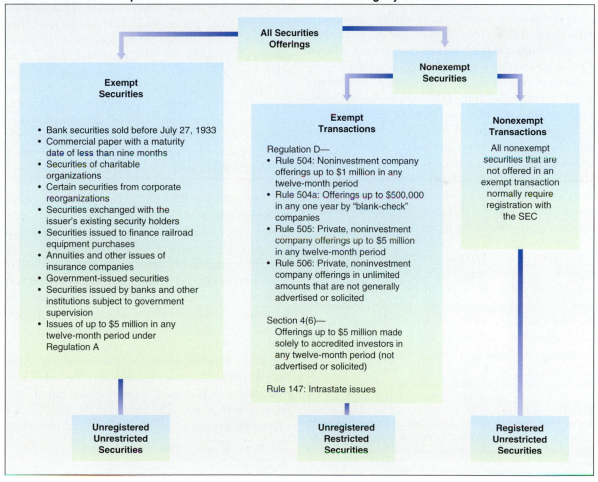

(discussed later in this chapter), noninvestment companies are firms that are not engaged primarily in the business of investing or trading in securities.

—*Rule 504a.* Offerings up to $500,000 in any one year by so-called blank-check companies—companies with no specific business plans except to locate and acquire as yet unidentified businesses or opportunities—are exempt if no general solicitation or advertising is used; the SEC is notified of the sales; and precaution is taken against nonexempt, unregistered resales.[16] The limits on advertising and unregistered resales do not apply if the offering is made solely in states that provide for registration and disclosure and the securities are sold in compliance with those provisions.[17]

—*Rule 505.* Private, noninvestment company offerings up to $5 million in any twelve-month period are exempt, regardless of the number of **accredited investors** (banks, insurance companies, investment companies, the issuer's executive officers and directors, and persons whose income or net worth exceeds a certain threshold), so long as there are no more than thirty-five unaccredited investors; no general solicitation or advertising is used; the SEC is notified of the sales; and precaution is taken against nonexempt, unregistered resales. If the sale involves *any* unaccredited investors, *all* investors must be given material information about the offering company, its business, and the securities before the sale. Unlike Rule 506 (discussed next), Rule 505 includes no requirement that the issuer believe each unaccredited investor "has such knowledge and experience in financial and business matters that he [or she] is capable of evaluating the merits and the risks of the prospective investment."[18]

—*Rule 506.* Private offerings in unlimited amounts that are not generally solicited or advertised are exempt if the SEC is notified of the sales; precaution is taken against nonexempt, unregistered resales; and the issuer believes that each unaccredited investor has sufficient knowledge or experience in financial matters to be capable of evaluating the investment's

merits and risks. There may be no more than thirty-five unaccredited investors, although there may be an unlimited number of accredited investors. If there are any unaccredited investors, the issuer must provide to all purchasers material information about itself, its business, and the securities before the sale.[19]

This exemption is perhaps the most important one for those firms that want to raise funds through the sale of securities without registering them. It is often referred to as the *private placement* exemption because it exempts "transactions not involving any public offering."[20] This provision applies to private offerings to a limited number of persons who are sufficiently sophisticated and able to assume the risk of the investment (and who thus have no need for federal registration protection). It also applies to private offerings to similarly sophisticated institutional investors.

SMALL OFFERINGS—SECTION 4(6) Under Section 4(6) of the Securities Act of 1933, an offer made *solely* to accredited investors is exempt if its amount is not more than $5 million. Any number of accredited investors may participate, but no unaccredited investors may do so. No general solicitation or advertising may be used; the SEC must be notified of all sales; and precaution must be taken against nonexempt, unregistered resales. Precaution is necessary because these are *restricted* securities and may be resold only by registration or in an exempt transaction.[21] (The securities purchased and sold by most people who handle stock transactions are called, in contrast, *unrestricted* securities.)

INTRASTATE ISSUES—RULE 147 Also exempt are intrastate transactions involving purely local offerings.[22] This exemption applies to most offerings that are restricted to residents of the state in which the issuing company is organized and doing business. For nine months after the last sale, virtually no resales may be made to nonresidents, and precautions must be taken against this possibility. These offerings remain subject to applicable laws in the state of issue.

RESALES Most securities can be resold without registration (although some resales may be subject to restrictions, as discussed above in connection with specific exemptions). The Securities Act of 1933 provides exemptions for resales by most persons other

---

16. Precautions to be taken against nonexempt, unregistered resales include asking the investor whether he or she is buying the securities for others; before the sale, disclosing to each purchaser in writing that the securities are unregistered and thus cannot be resold, except in an exempt transaction, without first being registered; and indicating on the certificates that the securities are unregistered and restricted.

17. 17 C.F.R. Section 230.504a.

18. 17 C.F.R. Section 230.505.

19. 17 C.F.R. Section 230.506.

20. 15 U.S.C. Section 77d(2).

21. 15 U.S.C. Section 77d(6).

22. 15 U.S.C. Section 77c(a)(11); 17 C.F.R. Section 230.147.

than issuers or underwriters. The average investor who sells shares of stock need not file a registration statement with the SEC. Resales of restricted securities acquired under Rule 504a, Rule 505, Rule 506, or Section 4(6), however, trigger the registration requirements unless the party selling them complies with Rule 144 or Rule 144A. These rules are sometimes referred to as "safe harbors."

—Rule 144. Rule 144 exempts restricted securities from registration on resale if there is adequate current public information about the issuer, the person selling the securities has owned them for at least one year, they are sold in certain limited amounts in unsolicited brokers' transactions, and the SEC is given notice of the resale.[23] "Adequate current public information" consists of the reports that certain companies are required to file under the Securities Exchange Act of 1934. A person who has owned the securities for at least two years is subject to none of these requirements, unless the person is an affiliate. An *affiliate* is one who controls, is controlled by, or is in common control with the issuer.

—Rule 144A. Securities that at the time of issue are not of the same class as securities listed on a national securities exchange or quoted in a U.S. automated interdealer quotation system may be resold under Rule 144A.[24] They may be sold only to a qualified institutional buyer (an institution, such as an insurance company, an investment company, or a bank, that owns and invests at least $100 million in securities). The seller must take reasonable steps to ensure that the buyer knows that the seller is relying on the exemption under Rule 144A. A sample restricted stock certificate is shown in Exhibit 41–2.

VIOLATIONS OF THE 1933 ACT

It is a violation of the Securities Act of 1933 to intentionally defraud investors by misrepresenting or omitting facts in a registration statement or prospectus. Liability is also imposed on those who are negligent for not discovering the fraud. Selling securities before the effective date of the registration statement or under an exemption for which the securities do not qualify results in liability.

---

23. 17 C.F.R. Section 230.144.

24. 17 C.F.R. Section 230.144A.

EXHIBIT 41–2 **A Sample Restricted Stock Certificate**

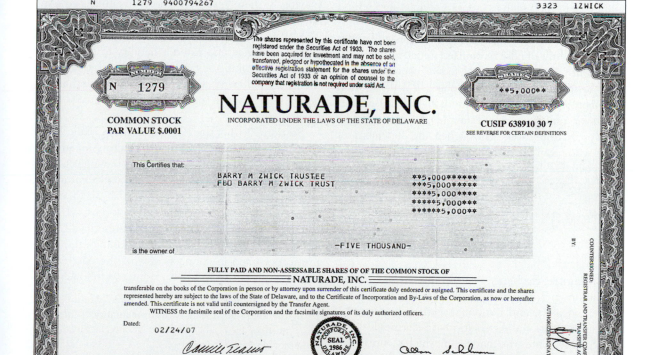

DEFENSES There are three basic defenses to charges of violations under the 1933 act. Even if a statement was not true or a fact was left out of the registration statement, a defendant can avoid liability if he or she can prove that the statement or omission was not material. A defendant can also avoid liability by proving that the plaintiff knew about the misrepresentation and bought the stock anyway.

Any defendant, except the issuer of the stock, can also assert what is called the *due diligence* defense. To make this defense, a person must prove that she or he reasonably believed, at the time the registration statement became effective, that the statements in it were true and there were no omissions of material facts. (This defense is discussed in further detail in Chapter 51, in the context of the liability of accountants.)

CRIMINAL PENALTIES The U.S. Department of Justice brings criminal actions against those who willfully violate the 1933 act. Violators may be penalized by fines up to $10,000, imprisonment up to five years, or both.

CIVIL SANCTIONS The SEC is authorized to impose civil sanctions against those who willfully violate the 1933 act. It can request an injunction to prevent further sales of the securities involved or ask a court to grant other relief, such as ordering a violator to refund profits.

Private parties who purchase securities and suffer harm as a result of false or omitted statements or other violations may bring a suit in a federal court to recover their losses and additional damages. If a registration statement or a prospectus contains material false statements or omissions, for example, damages may be recovered from those who signed the statement or those who provided information used in preparing the statement (such as accountants and other experts— see Chapter 51).

SECTION 3 | The Securities Exchange Act of 1934

The Securities Exchange Act of 1934 provides for the regulation and registration of securities exchanges, brokers, dealers, and national securities associations, such as the National Association of Securities Dealers. The SEC regulates the markets in which securities are traded by maintaining a continuous disclosure system for all corporations with securities on the national securities exchanges and for those companies that have assets in excess of $10 million and five hundred or more shareholders. These corporations are referred to as Section 12 companies, as they are required to file a registration application with the SEC for their securities under Section 12 of the 1934 act.

The act regulates proxy solicitation for voting (see Chapter 39), and it allows the SEC to engage in market surveillance to regulate certain market practices such as fraud, market manipulation, misrepresentation, and stabilization. (*Stabilization* is a commonly used technique in which securities underwriters bid for securities to stabilize their prices during their issuance.)

SECTION 10(b), SEC RULE 10b-5, AND INSIDER TRADING

Section 10(b) is one of the most important sections of the Securities Exchange Act of 1934. This section prohibits the use of any manipulative or deceptive device in violation of SEC rules and regulations.

One of the major goals of Section 10(b) and SEC Rule 10b-5 is to prevent so-called **insider trading.** Because of their positions, corporate directors and officers often obtain advance inside information that may affect the future market value of the corporate stock. Obviously, their "inside" positions give them a trading advantage over the general public and shareholders. The 1934 Securities Exchange Act defines the term *inside information* and extends liability to officers and directors for taking advantage of such information in their personal transactions when they know that it is unavailable to the persons with whom they are dealing.

Section 10(b) of the 1934 act and SEC Rule 10b-5 cover not only corporate officers, directors, and majority shareholders but also any persons having access to or receiving information of a nonpublic nature on which trading is based.

SEC RULE 10b-5 Among the rules prescribed by the SEC is **SEC Rule 10b-5,** which prohibits the commission of fraud in connection with the purchase or sale of any security. Rule 10b-5 states as follows:

It shall be unlawful for any person, directly or indirectly, by the use of any means or instrumentality of interstate commerce, or of the mails or of any facility of any national securities exchange,

(a) To employ any device, scheme, or artifice to defraud,

(b) To make any untrue statement of a material fact or to omit to state a material fact necessary in order to make the statements made, in the light of the circumstances under which they were made, not misleading, or

(c) To engage in any act, practice, or course of business which operates or would operate as a fraud or deceit upon any person, in connection with the purchase or sale of any security.[25]

APPLICABILITY OF SEC RULE 10b-5 SEC Rule 10b-5 applies in virtually all situations involving the trading of securities, whether on organized exchanges, in over-the-counter markets, or in private transactions. The rule covers notes, bonds, certificates of interest and participation in any profit-sharing agreement, agreements to form a corporation, and joint-venture agreements; in short, the rule covers just about any form of security. Whether a firm has securities registered under the 1933 act has no bearing on whether the 1934 act applies.

SEC Rule 10b-5 is applicable only when the requisites of federal jurisdiction (such as the use of the mails, of stock exchange facilities, or of any instrumentality of interstate commerce) are present. Virtually no commercial transaction, however, can be completed without such contact. In addition, the states have corporate securities laws, many of which include provisions similar to SEC Rule 10b-5.

DISCLOSURE REQUIREMENTS UNDER SEC RULE 10b-5 Any material omission or misrepresentation of

25. 17 C.F.R. Section 240.10b-5.

material facts in connection with the purchase or sale of a security may violate Section 10(b) and SEC Rule 10b-5. The key to liability (which can be civil or criminal) under this rule is whether the information omitted or misrepresented is *material*.

—Examples of Material Facts Calling for Disclosure. The following are some examples of material facts calling for disclosure under the rule:

1. Fraudulent trading in the company stock by a broker-dealer.
2. A dividend change (whether up or down).
3. A contract for the sale of corporate assets.
4. A new discovery, a new process, or a new product.
5. A significant change in the firm's financial condition.
6. Potential litigation against the company.

Note that none of these facts, in itself, is *automatically* a material fact. Rather, it will be regarded as a material fact if it is significant enough that it will likely affect an investor's decision to purchase or sell certain securities.

The case that follows is a landmark decision interpreting SEC Rule 10b-5. The SEC sued several of Texas Gulf Sulphur Company's directors, officers, and employees under SEC Rule 10b-5 after they purchased large amounts of the company's stock prior to the announcement of a rich ore discovery by the corporation. At issue was whether the ore discovery was a material fact that had to be disclosed under Rule 10b-5.

CASE 41.1 — SEC v. Texas Gulf Sulphur Co.

United States
Court of Appeals,
Second Circuit, 1968.
401 F.2d 833.

BACKGROUND AND FACTS *Texas Gulf Sulphur Company (TGS) conducted aerial geophysical surveys over more than 15,000 square miles of eastern Canada. The operations indicated concentrations of commercially exploitable minerals. At one site near Timmins, Ontario, TGS drilled a hole that appeared to yield a core with an exceedingly high mineral content. TGS kept secret the results of the core sample. Officers and employees of the company made substantial purchases of TGS's stock or accepted stock options after learning of the ore discovery, even though further drilling was necessary to establish whether there was enough ore to be mined commercially. Several months later, TGS announced that the strike was expected to yield at least 25 million tons of ore. Subsequently, the price of TGS stock rose substantially. The Securities and Exchange Commission (SEC) brought a suit against the officers and employees of TGS for violating SEC Rule 10b-5. The officers and employees argued that the information on which they had traded had not been material at the time of their trades because the mine had not then been commercially proved. The trial court held that most of the defendants had not violated SEC Rule 10b-5, and the SEC appealed.*

CONTINUED ▶

CASE 41.1 Continued

IN THE LANGUAGE OF THE COURT

WATERMAN, Circuit Judge.

* * * *

* * * [W]hether facts are material within Rule 10b-5 when the facts relate to a particular event and are undisclosed by those persons who are knowledgeable thereof *will depend at any given time upon a balancing of both the indicated probability that the event will occur and the anticipated magnitude of the event in light of the totality of the company activity.* Here, * * * knowledge of the possibility, which surely was more than marginal, of the existence of a mine of the vast magnitude indicated by the remarkably rich drill core located rather close to the surface (suggesting mineability by the less expensive openpit method) within the confines of a large anomaly (suggesting an extensive region of mineralization) might well have affected the price of TGS stock and would certainly have been an important fact to a reasonable, if speculative, investor in deciding whether he should buy, sell, or hold. [Emphasis added.]

* * * *

* * * [A] major factor in determining whether the * * * discovery was a material fact is the importance attached to the drilling results by those who knew about it. * * * [T]he timing by those who knew of it of their stock purchases * * *—purchases in some cases by individuals who had never before purchased * * * TGS stock—virtually compels the inference that the insiders were influenced by the drilling results.

DECISION AND REMEDY *The appellate court ruled in favor of the SEC. All of the trading by insiders who knew of the mineral find before its true extent had been publicly announced violated SEC Rule 10b-5.*

IMPACT OF THIS CASE ON TODAY'S LAW

This landmark case affirmed the principle that the test of whether information is "material," for SEC Rule 10b-5 purposes, is whether it would affect the judgment of reasonable investors. The corporate insiders' purchases of stock and stock options (rights to purchase stock) indicated that they were influenced by the drilling results and that the information about the drilling results was material. The courts continue to cite this case when applying SEC Rule 10b-5 to cases of alleged insider trading.

—The Private Securities Litigation Reform Act of 1995. Ironically, one of the effects of SEC Rule 10b-5 was to deter disclosure of forward-looking information. To understand why, consider an example. A company announces that its projected earnings in a certain time period will be X amount. It turns out that the forecast is wrong. The earnings are in fact much lower, and the price of the company's stock is affected—negatively. The shareholders then bring a class-action suit against the company, alleging that the directors violated SEC Rule 10b-5 by disclosing misleading financial information.

In an attempt to rectify this problem and promote disclosure, Congress passed the Private Securities Litigation Reform Act of 1995. Among other things, the act provides a "safe harbor" for publicly held companies that make forward-looking statements, such as financial forecasts. Those who make such statements are protected against federal liability for securities

fraud as long as the statements are accompanied by "meaningful cautionary statements identifying important factors that could cause actual results to differ materially from those in the forward-looking statement."[26]

After the 1995 act was passed, a number of class-action suits involving securities were filed in state courts to skirt the requirements of the 1995 federal act. In response to this problem, Congress passed the Securities Litigation Uniform Standards Act of 1998. The act placed stringent limits on the ability of plaintiffs to bring class-action suits in state courts against firms whose securities are traded on national stock exchanges.

OUTSIDERS AND SEC RULE 10b-5 The traditional insider-trading case involves true insiders—corporate

---

26. 15 U.S.C. Sections 77z-2, 78u-5.

officers, directors, and majority shareholders who have access to (and trade on) inside information. Increasingly, however, liability under Section 10(b) of the 1934 act and SEC Rule 10b-5 has been extended to include certain "outsiders"—those who trade on inside information acquired indirectly. Two theories have been developed under which outsiders may be held liable for insider trading: the *tipper/tippee theory* and the *misappropriation theory*.

—Tipper/Tippee Theory. Anyone who acquires inside information as a result of a corporate insider's breach of his or her fiduciary duty can be liable under SEC Rule 10b-5. This liability extends to **tippees** (those who receive "tips" from insiders) and even remote tippees (tippees of tippees).

The key to liability under this theory is that the inside information must be obtained as a result of someone's breach of a fiduciary duty to the corporation whose shares are traded. The tippee is liable under this theory only if (1) there is a breach of a duty not to disclose inside information, (2) the disclosure is in exchange for personal benefit, and (3) the tippee

knows (or should know) of this breach and benefits from it.[27]

—Misappropriation Theory. Liability for insider trading may also be established under the misappropriation theory. This theory holds that if an individual wrongfully obtains (misappropriates) inside information and trades on it for her or his personal gain, then the individual should be held liable because, in essence, the individual stole information rightfully belonging to another.

The misappropriation theory has been controversial because it significantly extends the reach of SEC Rule 10b-5 to outsiders who ordinarily would not be deemed fiduciaries of the corporations in whose stock they trade. In the following case, the United States Supreme Court addressed the issue of whether liability under SEC Rule 10b-5 can be based on the misappropriation theory.

---

27. See, for example, *Chiarella v. United States*, 445 U.S. 222, 100 S.Ct. 1108, 63 L.Ed.2d 348 (1980); and *Dirks v. SEC*, 463 U.S. 646, 103 S.Ct. 3255, 77 L.Ed.2d 911 (1983).

CASE 41.2 — United States v. O'Hagan

Supreme Court of the
United States, 1997.
521 U.S. 642,
117 S.Ct. 2199,
138 L.Ed.2d 724.
http://straylight.law.cornell.
edu/supct/index.htm[a]

BACKGROUND AND FACTS *James O'Hagan was a partner in the law firm of Dorsey & Whitney. Grand Metropolitan PLC (Grand Met) hired Dorsey & Whitney to assist in a takeover of the Pillsbury Company. Before Grand Met made its tender offer, O'Hagan bought shares of Pillsbury stock. When the tender offer was announced, the price of Pillsbury stock increased more than 35 percent. O'Hagan sold his shares for a profit of more than $4 million. The Securities and Exchange Commission (SEC) prosecuted O'Hagan for, among other things, securities fraud in violation of Rule 10b-5 under the misappropriation theory. The SEC contended that O'Hagan breached fiduciary duties he owed to his law firm and Grand Met. When O'Hagan was convicted, he appealed to the U.S. Court of Appeals for the Eighth Circuit, which reversed the conviction. The SEC appealed to the United States Supreme Court.*

IN THE LANGUAGE OF THE COURT

Justice GINSBURG delivered the opinion of the Court.

* * * *

The "misappropriation theory" holds that a person commits fraud "in connection with" a securities transaction, and thereby violates [Section]10(b) * * *, when he misappropriates confidential information for securities trading purposes, in breach of a duty owed to the source of the information. Under this theory, a fiduciary's undisclosed, self-serving use of a principal's information to purchase or sell securities, in breach of a duty of loyalty and confidentiality, defrauds the principal of the exclusive use of that information. *In lieu of premising liability on a fiduciary relationship between company insider and purchaser or seller of the company's stock, the misappropriation theory premises liability on a fiduciary-turned-trader's deception of those who entrusted him with access to confidential information.* [Emphasis added.]

---

a. In the "Search" box, type in the *O'Hagan* case name and click on "Search" to access the Court's opinion.

CONTINUED ▶

CASE 41.2 | Continued

   *   *   * [M]isappropriation *   *   * satisfies [Section] 10(b)'s requirement that chargeable conduct involve a "deceptive device or contrivance" used "in connection with" the purchase or sale of securities. *   *   * [M]isappropriators *   *   * deal in deception. A fiduciary who pretends loyalty to the principal while secretly converting the principal's information for personal gain dupes or defrauds the principal.

   *   *   *   *

   *   *   * [T]he fiduciary's fraud is consummated [brought to fruition, fulfilled] *   *   * when, without disclosure to his principal, he uses the information to purchase or sell securities. *   *   *

   *   *   *   *

   *   *   * An investor's informational disadvantage vis-à-vis a misappropriator with material, nonpublic information stems from contrivance, not luck; it is a disadvantage that cannot be overcome with research or skill.

DECISION AND REMEDY *The United States Supreme Court held that liability under Rule 10b-5 can be based on the misappropriation theory, reversed the lower court's judgment, and remanded the case.*

WHAT IF THE FACTS WERE DIFFERENT? *Suppose that O'Hagan had disclosed to Dorsey & Whitney and Grand Met that he was going to trade on the nonpublic information. Would he have been liable for misappropriation? Why or why not?*

INSIDER REPORTING AND TRADING—SECTION 16(b)

Officers, directors, and certain large stockholders of Section 12 corporations (stockholders owning 10 percent of the class of equity securities registered under Section 12 of the 1934 act) are required to file reports with the SEC concerning their ownership and trading of the corporation's securities.[28] To discourage such insiders from using nonpublic information about their companies to their personal benefit in the stock market, Section 16(b) of the 1934 act provides for the recapture by the corporation of all profits realized by the insider on any purchase and sale or sale and purchase of the corporation's stock within any six-month period. It is irrelevant whether the insider actually uses inside information; *all such short-swing profits must be returned to the corporation.*

   Section 16(b) applies not only to stock but also to warrants, options, and securities convertible into stock. In addition, the courts have fashioned complex rules for determining profits. Note that the SEC exempts a number of transactions under Rule 16b-3.[29] For all of these reasons, corporate insiders are wise to seek specialized counsel prior to trading in the corpo-

ration's stock. Exhibit 41–3 compares the effects of SEC Rule 10b-5 and Section 16(b).

PROXY STATEMENTS

Section 14(a) of the Securities Exchange Act of 1934 regulates the solicitation of proxies (see Chapter 39) from shareholders of Section 12 companies. The SEC regulates the content of proxy statements, which are statements sent to shareholders by corporate managers and others who are requesting authority to vote on behalf of the shareholders in a particular election on specified issues.

   Whoever solicits a proxy must fully and accurately disclose in the proxy statement all of the facts that are pertinent to the matter on which the shareholders are to vote. SEC Rule 14a-9 is similar to the antifraud provisions of SEC Rule 10b-5. Remedies for violations are extensive, ranging from injunctions to prevent a vote from being taken to monetary damages.

VIOLATIONS OF THE 1934 ACT

As mentioned earlier, violations of Section 10(b) and Rule 10b-5 of the Securities Exchange Act of 1934 include insider trading. This is a criminal offense, with criminal penalties. Violators of these laws may also be subject to civil liability. For any sanctions to be imposed, however, there must be *scienter*—the violator

---

28. 15 U.S.C. Section 78*l*. Note that Section 403 of the Sarbanes-Oxley Act of 2002 speeds up the reporting deadlines specified in Section 16(b).

29. 17 C.F.R. Section 240.16b-3.

EXHIBIT 41-3 **Comparison of Coverage, Application, and Liability under SEC Rule 10b-5 and Section 16(b)**

AREA OF COMPARISON	SEC RULE 10b-5	SECTION 16(b)
What is the subject matter of the transaction?	Any security (does not have to be registered).	Any security (does not have to be registered).
What transactions are covered?	Purchase or sale.	Short-swing purchase and sale or short-swing sale and purchase.
Who is subject to liability?	Virtually anyone with inside information under a duty to disclose—including officers, directors, controlling stockholders, and tippees.	Officers, directors, and certain 10 percent stockholders.
Is omission or misrepresentation necessary for liability?	Yes.	No.
Are there any exempt transactions?	No.	Yes, there are a variety of exemptions.
Is direct dealing with the party necessary?	No.	No.
Who may bring an action?	A person transacting with an insider, the SEC, or a purchaser or seller damaged by a wrongful act.	A corporation or a shareholder by derivative action.

must have had an intent to defraud or knowledge of his or her misconduct (see Chapter 14). *Scienter* can be proved by showing that a defendant made false statements or wrongfully failed to disclose material facts.

Violations of Section 16(b) include the sale by insiders of stock acquired less than six months before the time of sale. These violations are subject to civil sanctions. Liability under Section 16(b) is strict liability. Neither *scienter* nor negligence is required.

CRIMINAL PENALTIES For violations of Section 10(b) and Rule 10b-5, an individual may be fined up to $5 million, imprisoned for up to twenty years, or both. A partnership or a corporation may be fined up to $25 million. Under Section 807 of the Sarbanes-Oxley Act of 2002, for a willful violation of the 1934 act the violator may, in addition to being subject to a fine, be imprisoned for up to twenty-five years.

In a criminal prosecution under the securities laws, a jury is not allowed to speculate on whether a defendant acted willfully—in other words, there can be no reasonable doubt that the defendant knew he or she was acting wrongfully. The issue in the following case was whether, in light of this principle, there was enough evidence that Martha Stewart, founder of a well-known media and homemaking empire, intended to deceive other investors to present the matter to a jury.

CASE 41.3 **United States v. Stewart**

United States
District Court,
Southern District
of New York, 2004.
305 F.Supp.2d 368.

CEDARBAUM, District Judge.

* * * *

The criminal charges [in this case] against [Martha] Stewart * * * arose from Stewart's December 27, 2001 sale of 3,928 shares of stock in ImClone Systems, Inc. ("ImClone"). ImClone is a biotechnology company whose then–chief executive officer, Samuel Waksal, was a friend of Stewart's and a client of Stewart's stockbroker * * * [Peter] Bacanovic. On December 28, * * * ImClone announced that the Food and Drug Administration had rejected the company's application for approval of Erbitux, a cancer-fighting drug that ImClone had previously described as its lead product.

CONTINUED ▶

CASE 41.3 | Continued

The Indictment alleges that on the morning of December 27, 2001, * * * Bacanovic learned that Waksal * * * [was] selling or attempting to sell * * * ImClone shares. Bacanovic allegedly instructed his assistant, Douglas Faneuil, to inform Stewart of the * * * trading activity, and she sold her shares in response to that information.

According to the Indictment, [Stewart] then lied about the real reason for Stewart's sale in order to cover up what was possibly an illegal trade and to deflect attention from Stewart in the ensuing investigations into suspicious ImClone trading in advance of the Erbitux announcement. [Stewart] claimed that [she] had a standing agreement * * * [to] sell her position in ImClone if the stock fell to $60 per share.

* * * *

* * * [T]he Indictment charges Stewart, the CEO of [Martha Stewart Living Omnimedia (MSLO)] with fraud in connection with the purchase and sale of MSLO securities * * * . The [charge] is based on three repetitive public statements she made in June of 2002 [at a conference attended by investment professionals and investors] after the media began reporting investigations of her ImClone trades * * * .

* * * *

* * * *"[S]cienter," or intent, in the civil securities fraud context, indicates a mental state embracing intent to deceive, manipulate, or defraud, and is a required element of any claim of securities fraud.* In a criminal prosecution, the Government must also prove that the defendant acted willfully, that is, with a realization that she was acting wrongfully. * * * The issue at hand is * * * whether, taking into account the heightened standard of proof in criminal cases, there is sufficient evidence of Stewart's intent to deceive investors to present the matter to the jury. [Emphasis added.]

* * * *

The Government contends that a reasonable jury could draw inferences from the evidence * * * that would permit it to find beyond a reasonable doubt that Stewart intended to deceive investors with her statements. Specifically, the Government argues that the evidence supports the inferences that Stewart was aware of the impact of the negative publicity about her ImClone trade on the market value of MSLO securities * * * and that Stewart deliberately directed her statements to investors in MSLO securities.

* * * I hold that a reasonable juror could not, without resorting to speculation and surmise, find beyond a reasonable doubt that Stewart's purpose was to influence the market in MSLO securities.

* * * *

With respect to the June * * * statement, the Government contends that Stewart's awareness that she was speaking to analysts and investors, her prefatory statement that she was embarking upon a topic about which her audience was "probably interested," and the timing of the statement, which occurred as the stock continued to fall, are sufficient * * * to permit the jury to infer that she intended to deceive investors in MSLO securities when she made the statement.

* * * [T]he fact that the * * * statement was read to an audience of analysts and investors * * * cannot be viewed in isolation—the entire context of the statement must be considered. Thus, any inference to be drawn from the makeup of the audience must also take into account the fact that Stewart was only one of several representatives of MSLO, and that MSLO was only one of several corporations making presentations at the conference. The evidence does not show that the conference was organized by Stewart or her company. There is no evidence that the negative publicity about ImClone influenced Stewart's decision to attend and take advantage of a platform from which to reach investors directly. To the contrary, her statement—a very brief portion of a much longer presentation—indicates otherwise. The Government argues that her statement indicating an awareness that the audience was "probably interested" in what she had to say about the ImClone trade is meaningful. Yet her remarks at the close of the statement—"I have nothing to add on this matter today. And I'm here to talk about our terrific company * * * "—support an inference that she wanted to dispose of the issue and begin to address the subjects of the conference.

* * * *

 **Continued**

For the forgoing reasons, defendant Stewart's motion for a judgment of acquittal on [this charge] is granted.[a]

QUESTIONS

1. How does the *scienter*, or intent, requirement in the context of criminal securities fraud differ from its counterpart in the context of civil securities fraud?
2. When a criminal securities fraud case is tried by a jury, as the *Stewart* case was, what is the judge's role with respect to issues to be presented to the jury?

---

a. Stewart was later convicted on other charges related to her sale of ImClone stock, including obstruction of justice and lying to federal officials, and was sentenced and served five months in prison and five months and three weeks of house arrest. She is appealing the decision in an attempt to clear her name.

CIVIL SANCTIONS The SEC can bring a suit in a federal district court against anyone violating, or aiding in a violation of, the 1934 act or SEC rules by purchasing or selling a security while in the possession of material nonpublic information.[30] The violation must occur on or through the facilities of a national securities exchange or from or through a broker or dealer.[31] The court may assess as a penalty as much as triple the profits gained or the loss avoided by the guilty party. Profit or loss is defined as "the difference between the purchase or sale price of the security and the value of that security as measured by the trading price of the security at a reasonable period of time after public dissemination of the nonpublic information."[32]

The Insider Trading and Securities Fraud Enforcement Act of 1988 enlarged the class of persons who may be subject to civil liability for insider-trading violations. This act also gave the SEC authority to award **bounty payments** (rewards given by government officials for acts beneficial to the state) to persons providing information leading to the prosecution of insider-trading violations.[33]

Private parties may also sue violators of Section 10(b) and Rule 10b-5. A private party may obtain rescission of a contract to buy securities or damages to the extent of the violator's illegal profits. Those found liable have a right to seek contribution from those who share responsibility for the violations, including accountants, attorneys, and corporations.[34] (The liability of accountants and attorneys for violations of the securities laws is discussed in Chapter 51.) For violations of Section 16(b), a corporation can bring an action to recover the short-swing profits.

SECTION 4 | Corporate Governance

Corporate governance can be narrowly defined as the relationship between a corporation and its shareholders. The Organization of Economic Cooperation and Development (OECD) provides a broader definition:

> Corporate governance is the system by which business corporations are directed and controlled. The corporate governance structure specifies the distribution of rights and responsibilities among different participants in the corporation, such as the board of directors, managers, shareholders, and other stakeholders, and spells out the rules and procedures for making decisions on corporate affairs.[35]

While this definition has no true legal value, it does set the tone for the ways in which modern corporations should be governed. In other words, effective corporate governance requires more than compliance with laws and regulations.

---

30. 15 U.S.C. Section 78u(d)(2)(A).
31. Transactions pursuant to a public offering by an issuer of securities are exempted.
32. 15 U.S.C. Section 78u(d)(2)(C).
33. 15 U.S.C. Section 78u-1.

34. Note that a private cause of action under Section 10(b) and SEC Rule 10b-5 cannot be brought against accountants, attorneys, and others who "aid and abet" violations of the act. Only the SEC can bring actions against so-called aiders and abettors. See *SEC v. Fehn*, 97 F.3d 1276 (9th Cir. 1996).
35. *Governance in the 21st Century: Future Studies*, OECD, 2001.

THE NEED FOR GOOD CORPORATE GOVERNANCE

The need for effective corporate governance arises in large corporations because corporate ownership (by shareholders) is separated from corporate control (by officers and managers). In the real world, officers and managers are tempted to advance their own interests, even when such interests conflict with those of the shareholders. The reason for concern about managerial opportunism can be illustrated by the recent well-publicized scandals in the corporate world.

ATTEMPTS AT ALIGNING THE INTERESTS OF SHAREHOLDERS WITH THOSE OF OFFICERS

Some corporations have sought to align the financial interests of their officers with those of the company's shareholders. Thus, many officers have been provided with **stock options** for the corporation, which could be exercised at a set price and sold for a profit above that per-share price. When a corporation's share value grows, these options become more valuable for the officers, thereby giving them a financial stake in the share price.

Options have turned out to be an imperfect device for controlling governance, however. Executives in some companies have been tempted to "cook" the company's books in order to keep share prices higher so that they could exercise their options for a profit. Executives in other corporations experienced no losses when share prices dropped; instead, some had their options "repriced" so that they did not suffer from the share price decline and could still profit from future increases above the lowered share price. Although stock options theoretically can motivate officers to protect shareholder interests, stock option plans became a way for officers to take advantage of shareholders.

Because of numerous headline-making scandals within major corporations, there has been an outcry for more "outside" directors—the theory is that independent directors will more closely monitor the actions of corporate officers. Today, we see more boards with outside directors (those with no formal employment affiliation with the company). Note, though, that outside directors may not be truly independent of corporate officers; they may be friends or business associates of the leading officers. A study of board appointments found that the best way to increase one's probability of appointment was to "suck up" to the chief executive officer.[36]

CORPORATE GOVERNANCE AND CORPORATE LAW

Good corporate governance standards are designed to address problems (such as those briefly discussed above) and to motivate officers to make decisions to promote the financial interests of the company's shareholders. Generally, corporate governance entails corporate decision-making structures that monitor employees (particularly officers) to ensure that they are acting for the benefit of the shareholders. Thus, corporate governance involves, at a minimum:

1. The audited reporting of financial conditions at the corporation, so that managers can be evaluated.
2. Legal protections for shareholders, so that violators of the law, who attempt to take advantage of shareholders, can be punished for misbehavior and victims may recover damages for any associated losses.

THE PRACTICAL SIGNIFICANCE OF GOOD CORPORATE GOVERNANCE Effective corporate governance may have considerable practical significance. A study by researchers at Harvard University and the Wharton School of Business found that firms providing greater shareholder rights had higher profits, higher sales growth, higher firm value, and other economic advantages.[37] Better corporate governance in the form of greater accountability to investors may therefore offer the opportunity to enhance considerably institutional wealth.

GOVERNANCE AND CORPORATION LAW Corporate governance is the essential purpose of corporation law in the United States. These statutes set up the legal framework for corporate governance. Under the corporate law of Delaware, where most major companies incorporate, all corporations must have in place certain structures of corporate governance. The key structure of corporate law is, of course, the board of directors. Directors make the most important decisions about the future of the corporation and monitor

---

36. Jennifer Reingold, "Suck Up and Move Fast," *Fast Company*, January 2005, p. 34.
37. Paul A. Gompers, Joy L. Ishii, and Andrew Metrick, "Corporate Governance and Equity Prices," *Quarterly Journal of Economics*, Vol. 118, (2003), p. 107.

the actions of corporate officers. Directors are elected by shareholders to look out for their best interests.

THE BOARD OF DIRECTORS Some argue that shareholder democracy is key to improving corporate governance. If shareholders could vote on major corporate decisions, shareholders could presumably have more control over the corporation. Essential to shareholder democracy is the concept of electing the board of directors, usually at the corporation's annual meeting. Under corporate law, a corporation must have a board of directors elected by shareholders. Virtually anyone can become a director, though some organizations, such as the New York Stock Exchange, require certain standards of service for directors of their listed corporations.

Directors have the responsibility of ensuring that officers are operating wisely and in the exclusive interest of shareholders. Directors receive reports from the officers and give them managerial directions. The board in theory controls the compensation of officers (presumably tied to performance). The reality, though, is that corporate directors devote a relatively small amount of time to monitoring officers.

Ideally, shareholders would monitor the directors' supervision of officers. As one leading board monitor stated, "Boards of directors are like subatomic particles—they behave differently when they are observed." Consequently, monitoring directors, and holding them responsible for corporate failings, can induce the directors to do a better job of monitoring officers and ensuring that the company is being managed in the interest of shareholders. While the directors can be sued for failing to effectively do their jobs, directors are rarely held personally liable.

IMPORTANCE OF THE AUDIT COMMITTEE One crucial board committee is known as the *audit committee*. Members of the audit committee oversee the corporation's accounting and financial reporting processes, including both internal and outside auditors. These audit committee members must, however, have sufficient expertise and be willing to spend the time necessary to examine carefully the corporation's bookkeeping methods. Otherwise, the audit committee may be ineffective.

The audit committee also oversees the corporation's "internal controls." These are the measures taken to ensure that reported results are accurate; they are carried out largely by the company's internal auditing staff. As an example, these controls help to determine whether a corporation's debts are collectible. If the debts are not collectible, it is up to the audit committee to make sure that the corporation's financial officers cannot simply pretend that payment will eventually be made.

THE COMPENSATION COMMITTEE Another important committee of the board of directors is the *compensation committee*. This committee monitors and determines the compensation to be paid to a company's officers. In the process, it has the responsibility for assessing officers' performance, and its members may try to design compensation systems that encourage better performance by officers on behalf of shareholders.

THE SARBANES-OXLEY ACT OF 2002

As discussed in Chapter 5, in 2002, following a series of corporate scandals, Congress passed the Sarbanes-Oxley Act (see Appendix H for excerpts and explanatory comments). The act separately addresses certain issues relating to corporate governance. Generally, the act attempts to increase corporate accountability by imposing strict disclosure requirements and harsh penalties for violations of securities laws. Among other things, the act requires chief corporate executives to take responsibility for the accuracy of financial statements and reports that are filed with the SEC. Chief executive officers and chief financial officers personally must certify that the statements and reports are accurate and complete.

Additionally, the new rules require that certain financial and stock-transaction reports must be filed with the SEC earlier than was required under the previous rules. The act also mandates SEC oversight over a new entity, called the Public Company Accounting Oversight Board, that regulates and oversees public accounting firms. Other provisions of the act created new private civil actions and expanded the SEC's remedies in administrative and civil actions.

Because of the importance of this act for those dealing with securities transactions, we present some of the act's key provisions relating to corporate accountability in Exhibit 41–4 on the next page. We also discuss the act and its effect on corporate governance procedures in this chapter's *Emerging Trends* feature beginning on page 840. (Provisions of the act that relate to public accounting firms and accounting practices will be discussed in Chapter 51, in the context of the liability of accountants.)

EXHIBIT 41-4 Some Key Provisions of the Sarbanes-Oxley Act of 2002 Relating to Corporate Accountability

Certification Requirements—Under Section 906 of the Sarbanes-Oxley Act, the chief executive officers (CEOs) and chief financial officers (CFOs) of most major companies listed on public stock exchanges must now certify financial statements that are filed with the SEC. For virtually all filed financial reports, CEOs and CFOs have to certify that such reports "fully comply" with SEC requirements and that all of the information reported "fairly represents in all material respects, the financial conditions and results of operations of the issuer."

Under Section 302 of the act, for each quarterly and annual filing with the SEC, CEOs and CFOs of reporting companies are required to certify that a signing officer reviewed the report and that it contains no untrue statements of material fact. Also, the signing officer or officers must certify that they have established an internal control system to identify all material information, and that any deficiencies in the system were disclosed to the auditors.

Loans to Directors and Officers—Section 402 prohibits any reporting company, as well as any private company that is filing an initial public offering, from making personal loans to directors and executive officers (with a few limited exceptions, such as for certain consumer and housing loans).

Protection for Whistleblowers—Section 806 protects "whistleblowers"—those employees who report ("blow the whistle" on) securities violations by their employers—from being fired or in any way discriminated against by their employers.

Blackout Periods—Section 306 prohibits certain types of securities transactions during "blackout periods"—periods during which the issuer's ability to purchase, sell, or otherwise transfer funds in individual account plans (such as pension funds) is suspended.

Enhanced Penalties for—
- *Violations of Section 906 Certification Requirements*—A CEO or CFO who certifies a financial report or statement filed with the SEC knowing that the report or statement does not fulfill all of the requirements of Section 906 will be subject to criminal penalties of up to $1 million in fines, ten years in prison, or both. *Willful* violators of the certification requirements may be subject to $5 million in fines, twenty years in prison, or both.
- *Violations of the Securities Exchange Act of 1934*—Penalties for securities fraud under the 1934 act were also increased (as discussed earlier in this chapter). Individual violators may be fined up to $5 million, imprisoned for up to twenty years, or both. *Willful* violators may be imprisoned for up to twenty-five years in addition to being fined.
- *Destruction or Alteration of Documents*—Anyone who alters, destroys, or conceals documents or otherwise obstructs any official proceeding will be subject to fines, imprisonment for up to twenty years, or both.
- *Other Forms of White-Collar Crime*—The act stiffened the penalties for certain criminal violations, such as federal mail and wire fraud, and ordered the U.S. Sentencing Commission to revise the sentencing guidelines for white-collar crimes (see Chapter 9).

Statute of Limitations for Securities Fraud—Section 804 provides that a private right of action for securities fraud may be brought no later than two years after the discovery of the violation or five years after the violation, whichever is earlier.

SECTION 5 | Regulation of Investment Companies

Investment companies, and mutual funds in particular, grew rapidly after World War II. **Investment companies** act on behalf of many smaller shareholders/owners by buying a large portfolio of securities and managing that portfolio professionally. A **mutual fund** is a specific type of investment company that continually buys or sells to investors shares of ownership in a portfolio. Such companies are regulated by the Investment Company Act of 1940,[38] which pro-

vides for SEC regulation of their activities. The 1940 act was expanded by the Investment Company Act Amendments of 1970. Further minor changes were made in the Securities Acts Amendments of 1975 and in later years.

DEFINITION OF AN INVESTMENT COMPANY

For the purposes of the act, an *investment company* is defined as any entity that (1) "is . . . engaged primarily . . . in the business of investing, reinvesting, or trading in securities" or (2) is engaged in such business and more than 40 percent of the company's assets consist

---

38. 15 U.S.C. Sections 80a-1 to 80a-64.

of investment securities. Excluded from coverage by the act are banks, insurance companies, savings and loan associations, finance companies, oil and gas drilling firms, charitable foundations, tax-exempt pension funds, and other special types of institutions, such as closely held corporations.

REGISTRATION AND REPORTING REQUIREMENTS

The 1940 act requires that every investment company register with the SEC by filing a notification of registration. Registered investment companies must also file annual reports with the SEC. To safeguard company assets, all securities must be held in the custody of a bank or stock exchange member, and that bank or stock exchange member must follow strict procedures established by the SEC.

RESTRICTIONS ON INVESTMENT COMPANIES

The 1940 act also imposes restrictions on the activities of investment companies and persons connected with them. For example, investment companies are not allowed to purchase securities on the margin (pay only part of the total price, borrowing the rest), sell short (sell shares not yet owned), or participate in joint trading accounts. Additionally, no dividends may be paid from any source other than accumulated, undistributed net income.

SECTION 6 | State Securities Laws

Today, all states have their own corporate securities laws, or **blue sky laws,** that regulate the offer and sale of securities within individual state borders. (The phrase *blue sky laws* dates to a 1917 United States Supreme Court decision in which the Court declared that the purpose of such laws was to prevent "speculative schemes which have no more basis than so many feet of 'blue sky.' "[39]) Article 8 of the Uniform Commercial Code, which has been adopted by all of the states, also imposes various requirements relating to the purchase and sale of securities.

REQUIREMENTS UNDER STATE SECURITIES LAWS

Despite some differences in philosophy, all state blue sky laws have certain features. Typically, state laws have disclosure requirements and antifraud provisions, many of which are patterned after Section 10(b) of the Securities Exchange Act of 1934 and SEC Rule 10b-5. State laws also provide for the registration or qualification of securities offered or issued for sale within the state and impose disclosure requirements. Unless an exemption from registration is applicable, issuers must register or qualify their stock with the appropriate state official, often called a *corporations commissioner.* Additionally, most state securities laws regulate securities brokers and dealers. The Uniform Securities Act, which has been adopted in part by several states, was drafted to be acceptable to states with differing regulatory philosophies.

CONCURRENT REGULATION

State securities laws apply mainly to intrastate transactions. Since the adoption of the 1933 and 1934 federal securities acts, the state and federal governments have regulated securities concurrently. Issuers must comply with both federal and state securities laws, and exemptions from federal law are not necessarily exemptions from state laws.

The dual federal and state system has not always worked well, particularly during the early 1990s, when there was considerable expansion of the securities markets. In response, Congress passed the National Securities Markets Improvement Act of 1996, which preempted significant areas of state power to duplicate federal regulation. The National Conference of Commissioners on Uniform State Laws then substantially revised the Uniform Securities Act and recommended it to the states for adoption in 2002. Unlike the previous version of this law, the new act is designed to coordinate state and federal securities regulation and enforcement efforts. Since 2002, nine states have adopted the Uniform Securities Act, and several other states are considering adoption.[40]

---

39. *Hall v. Geiger-Jones Co.*, 242 U.S. 539, 37 S.Ct. 217, 61 L.Ed. 480 (1917).

40. At the time this book went to press, the 2002 version of the Uniform Securities Act had been adopted in Idaho, Iowa, Kansas, Maine, Missouri, Oklahoma, South Carolina, South Dakota, and Vermont, as well as in the U.S. Virgin Islands. Adoption legislation was pending in Alabama, Alaska, Hawaii, and Nebraska. You can find current information on state adoptions at **http://www.nccusl.org**.

Corporate Governance and the Sarbanes-Oxley Act

Traditionally, securities law has not been considered a central part of corporate governance considerations. Rather, securities law primarily requires disclosures of corporate financial results and other corporate actions; it does not directly regulate those actions. Practically, though, securities law may be a valuable tool for enhancing good corporate governance. Securities law is intended to make sure that companies accurately disclose their activities and financial results, such as audited statements. Such accurate disclosure better enables shareholders and directors to monitor the job done by the corporate officers. The securities laws also govern accountants who audit public companies, setting standards for their performance.

THE TREND TOWARD MORE INTERNAL CONTROLS AND ACCOUNTABILITY WITHIN PUBLIC COMPANIES

As already noted, in 2002, Congress passed the Sarbanes-Oxley Act, which was intended to improve corporate governance in the United States. This statute includes some traditional securities law provisions but also introduces direct *federal* corporate governance requirements for public companies (companies whose shares are traded in the public securities markets). The law addresses many of the corporate governance procedures discussed in this chapter and creates new requirements in an attempt to make the system work more effectively. The requirements deal with independent monitoring of company officers by both the board of directors and auditors.

Sections 302 and 404 of Sarbanes-Oxley require high-level managers (the most senior officers) to establish and maintain an effective system of internal controls. Moreover, senior management must reassess the system's effectiveness on an annual basis. Some companies already had strong and effective internal control systems in place before the passage of the act, but others had to take expensive steps to bring their internal controls up to the new federal standard. These include "disclosure controls and procedures" to ensure that company financial reports are accurate and timely. Assessment must involve the documenting of financial results and accounting policies before reporting them. By the end of 2005, hundreds of companies had reported that they had identified and corrected shortcomings in their internal control systems.

THE CERTIFICATION AND MONITORING REQUIREMENTS OF SARBANES-OXLEY

Section 906 requires that chief executive officers (CEOs) and chief financial officers (CFOs) certify that the corporate financial statements "fairly present, in all material respects, the financial condition and results of operation of the issuer." These corporate officers are subject to both civil and criminal penalties for violation of this section. This requirement makes officers directly accountable for the accuracy of their financial reporting and avoids any "ignorance defense" if shortcomings are later discovered.

Sarbanes-Oxley also adopts requirements to improve directors' monitoring of officers' activities. All members of the corporate audit committee for public companies must be

---

SECTION 7 | Online Securities Offerings and Disclosures

The Spring Street Brewing Company, headquartered in New York, made history when it became the first company to attempt to sell securities via the Internet. Through its online *initial public offering* (IPO), which ended in early 1996, Spring Street raised about $1.6 million—without having to pay any commissions to brokers or underwriters. The offering was made pursuant to Regulation A, which, as mentioned earlier in this chapter, allows small-business issuers to use a simplified registration procedure.

Such online IPOs are particularly attractive to small companies and start-up ventures that may find it difficult to raise capital from institutional investors or through underwriters. By making the offering online under Regulation A, the company can avoid both commissions and the costly and time-consuming filings required for a traditional IPO under federal and state law.

Clearly, technological advances have affected the securities industry—and securities law—just as they have affected other areas of the law. Investors can now use the Internet to access information that can help them make informed decisions. The SEC's EDGAR (Electronic Data Gathering, Analysis, and Retrieval)

outside directors. The New York Stock Exchange (NYSE) has a similar rule that also extends to the board's compensation committee. The audit committee must have a written charter that sets out its duties and provides for performance appraisal. At least one "financial expert" must serve on the audit committee, which must hold executive meetings without company officers being present. The audit committee must establish procedures for "whistleblowers." In addition to reviewing the internal controls, the committee also monitors the actions of the outside auditor.

THE SEPARATION OF AUDIT AND NONAUDIT SERVICES

The law includes other provisions to improve accounting accuracy. Auditors are prohibited from providing substantial nonaudit services for a company of any kind that might compromise the auditors' independence. The lead audit partner and reviewing partner must rotate off each assignment every five years. This rotation is aimed at preventing them from establishing unduly close relationships with the management officers they are auditing. Other rules apply to lawyers representing public companies and require them to blow the whistle on their clients when they determine a client is engaged in illegal behavior.

CORPORATE ETHICAL CODES

Sarbanes-Oxley also contains provisions for corporate ethical codes. A company regulated by the SEC must report whether it has established an ethical code governing high-level offi-

cers. The contents of that code must be publicly available. The NYSE similarly requires that each listed company adopt a code of conduct and ethics for its officers and post it on the company's Web site. This code of conduct and ethics must specifically prohibit self-dealing at the expense of shareholders. Of course, the code must also prohibit violations of the law.

IMPLICATIONS FOR THE BUSINESSPERSON

1. As more publicly traded corporations adopt internal control systems, persons working for public companies should be aware that their actions could be subjected to multiple levels of scrutiny, from both inside and outside the corporation.

2. Attorneys hired by public companies now have a duty to report their own clients' illegal conduct.

FOR CRITICAL ANALYSIS

1. Do you believe that audit and compensation committees will be effective in enhancing the directors' ability to monitor officers' actions? Why or why not?

2. How will the new requirements for certified financial disclosures be likely to affect who is selected to be an officer of the corporation?

RELEVANT WEB SITES

To locate information on the Web concerning the issues discussed in this feature, go to this text's Web site at **http://wbl.westbuslaw.com**, select "Chapter 41," and click on "Emerging Trends."

database includes IPOs, proxy statements, annual corporate reports, registration statements, and other documents that have been filed with the commission. (See this chapter's *Law on the Web* section for instructions on how to access the EDGAR database.)

REGULATIONS GOVERNING ONLINE SECURITIES OFFERINGS

One of the early questions posed by online offerings was whether the delivery of securities *information* via the Internet met the requirements of the 1933 Securities Act, which traditionally were applied to the delivery of paper documents. In an interpretative

release issued in 1995, the SEC stated that "[t]he use of electronic media should be at least an equal alternative to the use of paper-based media" and that anything that can be delivered in paper form under the current securities laws might also be delivered in electronic form.[41] For example, a prospectus in downloadable form will meet SEC requirements.

---

41. "Use of Electronic Media for Delivery Purposes," Securities Act Release No. 33-7233 (October 6, 1995). The rules governing the use of electronic transmissions for delivery purposes were subsequently confirmed in Securities Act Release No. 33-7289 (May 9, 1996) and expanded in Securities Act Release No. 33-7856 (April 28, 2000).

Basically, there has been no change in the substantive law of disclosure; only the delivery vehicle has changed. When the Internet is used to deliver a prospectus, the same rules apply as for the delivery of a paper prospectus. Once the following three requirements have been satisfied, the prospectus has been successfully delivered.

1. *Timely and adequate notice of the delivery of information is required.* Hosting a prospectus on a Web site does not constitute adequate notice, but separate e-mails or even postcards will satisfy the SEC's notice requirements.

2. *The online communication system must be easily accessible.* This is very simple to do today because virtually anyone interested in purchasing securities has access to the Web.

3. *Some evidence of delivery must be created.* This requirement is relatively easy to satisfy. Those making online offerings can require an e-mail return receipt verification of any materials sent electronically.

POTENTIAL LIABILITY CREATED BY ONLINE OFFERING MATERIALS

All printed prospectuses indicate that only the information given in the prospectuses can be used to make an investment decision about the securities offered. The same wording, of course, appears on Web-based offerings. Those who create such Web-based offerings may be tempted to go one step further—they may include hyperlinks to other sites that have analyzed the future prospects of the company, the products and services sold by the company, or the offering itself. To avoid potential liability, however, online offerors (the entities making the offerings) need to exercise caution when including such hyperlinks.

Suppose that a hyperlink goes to an analyst's Web page on which there are optimistic statements concerning the financial outlook of the offering company. Further suppose that after the IPO, the stock price falls. By including the hyperlink on its Web site, the offering company is impliedly supporting the information presented on the linked page. In such a situation, the company may be liable under federal securities laws.[42]

Potential problems may also occur with some Regulation D offerings, if the offeror places the offering circular on its Web site for general consumption by anybody on the Internet. Because Regulation D offerings are private placements, general solicitation is restricted. If anyone can have access to the offering circular on the Web, the Regulation D exemption may be disqualified.

ONLINE SECURITIES OFFERINGS BY FOREIGN COMPANIES

Online securities offerings by foreign companies may also present difficulties. Traditionally, foreign companies have been unable to offer new shares to the U.S. public unless they first register them with the SEC. Today, however, anybody in the world can offer shares of stock globally via the Web.

The SEC asks that foreign issuers on the Internet implement measures to warn U.S. investors. For example, a foreign company offering shares of stock on the Internet must include a disclaimer on its Web site stating that it has not gone through the registration procedure in the United States. If the SEC believes that a Web site's offering of foreign securities has been targeted at U.S. residents, it will pursue that company in an attempt to require it to register in the United States.[43]

ONLINE SECURITIES FRAUD

The Internet, of course, has also been used to commit fraud. A major problem facing the SEC today is how to enforce the antifraud provisions of the securities laws in the online environment. In 1999, in the first cases involving illegal online securities offerings, the SEC filed suit against three individuals for illegally offering securities on an Internet auction site.[44] In essence, all three indicated that their companies would soon go public and attempted to sell unregistered securities via the Web auction site. All of these actions were in violation of Sections 5, 17(a)(1), and 17(a)(3) of the 1933 Securities Act. Since then, the SEC has brought a variety of Internet-related fraud cases, including cases involving investment scams and the manipulation of stock prices in Internet chat rooms.

INVESTMENT SCAMS An ongoing concern for the SEC is how to curb investment scams. One fraudulent

---

42. See, for example, *In re Syntec Corp. Securities Litigation,* 95 F.3d 922 (9th Cir. 1996).

43. International Series Release No. 1125 (March 23, 1998).

44. *In re Davis,* SEC Administrative File No. 3-10080 (October 20, 1999); *In re Haas,* SEC Administrative File No. 3-10081 (October 20, 1999); and *In re Sitaras,* SEC Administrative File No. 3-10082 (October 20, 1999).

investment scheme involved twenty thousand investors, who lost, in all, more than $3 million. Some cases have involved false claims about the earnings potential of home-business programs, such as the claim that one could "earn $4,000 or more each month." Others have concerned claims of "guaranteed credit repair."

USING CHAT ROOMS TO MANIPULATE STOCK PRICES "Pumping and dumping" occurs when a person who has purchased a particular stock heavily promotes ("pumps up") that stock—thereby creating a great demand for it and driving up its price—and then sells ("dumps") it. The practice of pumping up a stock and then dumping it is quite old. In the online world, however, the process can occur much more quickly and efficiently.

The most famous case in this area involved Jonathan Lebed, a fifteen-year-old stock trader and Internet user from New Jersey. Lebed was the first minor ever charged with securities fraud by the SEC,

but he is unlikely to be the last. The SEC charged that Lebed bought thinly traded stocks. After purchasing a stock, he would flood stock-related chat rooms, particularly at Yahoo's finance boards, with messages touting the stock's virtues. He used numerous false names so that no one would know that a single person was posting the messages. He would say that the stock was the most "undervalued stock in history" and that its price would jump by 1,000 percent "very soon." When other investors bought the stock, the price would go up quickly, and Lebed would sell out. The SEC forced the teenager to repay almost $300,000 in gains plus interest. He was allowed, however, to keep about $500,000 of the profits he made trading small-company stocks that he also touted on the Internet.

The SEC has been bringing an increasing number of cases against those who manipulate stock prices in this way. Consider that in 1995, such fraud resulted in only six SEC cases. By 2005, the SEC had brought over two hundred actions against online perpetrators of fraudulent stock-price manipulation.

REVIEWING CORPORATIONS— SECURITIES LAW AND CORPORATE GOVERNANCE

Dale Emerson served as the chief financial officer for Reliant Electric Co., a distributor of electricity serving portions of Montana and North Dakota. Reliant was in the final stages of planning a takeover of Dakota Gasworks, Inc., a natural gas distributor that operated solely within North Dakota. Emerson went on a weekend fishing trip with his uncle, Ernest Wallace. Emerson mentioned to Wallace that he had been putting in a lot of extra hours at the office planning a takeover of Dakota Gasworks. On returning from the fishing trip, Wallace met with a broker from Chambers Investments and purchased $20,000 of Reliant stock. Three weeks later, Reliant made a tender offer to Dakota Gasworks stockholders and purchased 57 percent of Dakota Gasworks stock. Over the next two weeks, the price of Reliant stock rose 72 percent before leveling out. Wallace then sold his Reliant stock for a gross profit of $14,400. Using the information presented in the chapter, answer the following questions.

1. Would registration with the SEC be required for Dakota Gasworks securities? Why or why not? List three types of transactions that would qualify as exempt from SEC registration.

2. Did Emerson violate any of the laws discussed in this chapter? Why or why not? Did he violate any legal duty? If so, to whom did he owe a duty?

3. Which securities law or laws might Wallace have violated? According to what theory? Explain.

4. Under the Sarbanes-Oxley Act of 2002, who would be required to certify the accuracy of financial statements filed with the SEC? What penalty could be imposed for wrongful certification?

5. Suppose that Reliant's directors chose to offer its stock for sale via the Internet. What would be some advantages of this procedure? How might an investor go about accessing information about Reliant's stock via the Internet?

TERMS AND CONCEPTS TO REVIEW

accredited investor 826	insider trading 828	SEC Rule 10b-5 828
blue sky laws 839	investment company 838	stock options 836
bounty payment 835	mutual fund 838	tippee 831
corporate governance 835	red herring 824	tombstone ad 824

QUESTIONS AND CASE PROBLEMS

41–1. A corporation incorporated and doing business in Florida, Estrada Hermanos, Inc., decides to sell $1 million worth of its no-par-value common stock to the public. The stock will be sold only within the state of Florida. José Estrada, the chairman of the board, says the offering need not be registered with the Securities and Exchange Commission. His brother, Gustavo, disagrees. Who is right? Explain.

41–2. **QUESTION WITH SAMPLE ANSWER**

Huron Corp. has 300,000 common shares outstanding. The owners of these outstanding shares live in several different states. Huron has decided to split the 300,000 shares two for one. Will Huron Corp. have to file a registration statement and prospectus on the 300,000 new shares to be issued as a result of the split? Explain.

For a sample answer to this question, go to Appendix I at the end of this text.

41–3. **SEC RULE 10B-5.** Louis Ferraro was the chairman and president of Anacomp, Inc. In June 1988, Ferraro told his good friend Michael Maio that Anacomp was negotiating a tender offer for stock in Xidex Corp. Maio passed on the information to Patricia Ladavac, a friend of both Ferraro and Maio. Maio and Ladavac immediately purchased shares in Xidex stock. On the day that the tender offer was announced—an announcement that caused the price of Xidex shares to increase—Maio and Ladavac sold their Xidex stock and made substantial profits (Maio made $211,000 from the transactions, and Ladavac gained $78,750). The Securities and Exchange Commission (SEC) brought an action against the three individuals, alleging that they had violated, among other laws, SEC Rule 10b-5. Maio and Ladavac claimed that they had done nothing illegal. They argued that they had no fiduciary duty either to Anacomp or to Xidex, and therefore they had no duty to disclose or abstain from trading in the stock of those corporations. Had Maio and Ladavac violated SEC Rule 10b-5? Discuss fully. [*SEC v. Maio*, 51 F.3d 623 (7th Cir. 1995)]

41–4. **SECTION 10(B).** Joseph Jett worked for Kidder, Peabody & Co., a financial services firm owned by General Electric Co. (GE). Over a three-year period, Jett allegedly engaged in a scheme to generate false profits at Kidder, Peabody to increase his performance-based bonuses. When the scheme was discovered, Daniel Chill and other GE shareholders who had bought stock in the previous year filed a suit in a federal district court against GE. The shareholders alleged that GE had engaged in securities fraud in violation of Section 10(b). They claimed that GE's interest in justifying its investment in Kidder, Peabody gave GE "a motive to willfully blind itself to facts casting doubt on Kidder's purported profitability." On what basis might the court dismiss the shareholders' complaint? Discuss fully. [*Chill v. General Electric Co.*, 101 F.3d 263 (2d Cir. 1996)]

41–5. **SEC RULE 10B-5.** Grand Metropolitan PLC (Grand Met) planned to make a tender offer as part of an attempted takeover of the Pillsbury Company. Grand Met hired Robert Falbo, an independent contractor, to complete electrical work as part of security renovations to its offices to prevent leaks of information concerning the planned tender offer. Falbo was given a master key to access the executive offices. When an executive secretary told Falbo that a takeover was brewing, he used his key to access the offices and eavesdrop on conversations to learn that Pillsbury was the target. Falbo bought thousands of shares of Pillsbury stock for less than $40 per share. Within two months, Grand Met made an offer for all outstanding Pillsbury stock at $60 per share and ultimately paid up to $66 per share. Falbo made over $165,000 in profit. The Securities and Exchange Commission (SEC) filed a suit in a federal district court against Falbo and others for alleged violations of, among other things, SEC Rule 10b-5. Under what theory might Falbo be liable? Do the circumstances of this case meet all of the requirements for liability under that theory? Explain. [*SEC v. Falbo*, 14 F.Supp.2d 508 (S.D.N.Y. 1998)]

41–6. **DEFINITION OF A SECURITY.** In 1997, Scott and Sabrina Levine formed Friendly Power Co. (FPC) and Friendly Power Franchise Co. (FPC-Franchise). FPC obtained a license to operate as a utility company in California. FPC granted FPC-Franchise the right to pay commissions to "operators" who converted residential customers to FPC. Each operator paid for a "franchise"—a geographic area, determined by such factors as the number of households and competition from other utilities. In exchange for 50 percent of FPC's net profits on sales to residential customers in its territory, each franchise was required to maintain a 5 percent market share of power customers in that territory. Franchises were sold to telemarketing firms, which solicited customers. The telemarketers sold interests in each franchise to between fifty and ninety-four "partners," each of whom invested funds. FPC began supplying electricity to its customers in May 1998. Less than three months later, the Securities and Exchange Commission (SEC) filed a suit in a federal district court against the Levines and others, alleging that the "franchises" were unregistered securities offered for sale to the public in violation of the Securities Act of 1933. What is the definition of a security? Should the court rule in favor of the SEC? Why or why not? [*SEC v. Friendly Power Co., LLC*, 49 F.Supp.2d 1363 (S.D.Fla. 1999)]

41-7. CASE PROBLEM WITH SAMPLE ANSWER

Scott Ginsburg was chief executive officer (CEO) of Evergreen Media Corp., which owned and operated radio stations. In 1996, Evergreen became interested in acquiring EZ Communications, Inc., which also owned radio stations. To initiate negotiations, Ginsburg met with EZ's CEO, Alan Box, on Friday, July 12. Two days later, Scott phoned his brother Mark, who, on Monday, bought 3,800 shares of EZ stock. Mark discussed the deal with their father Jordan, who bought 20,000 EZ shares on Thursday. On July 25, the day before the EZ bid was due, Scott phoned his parents' home, and Mark bought another 3,200 EZ shares. The same routine was followed over the next few days, with Scott periodically phoning Mark or Jordan, both of whom continued to buy EZ shares. Evergreen's bid was refused, but on August 5, EZ announced its merger with another company. The price of EZ stock rose 30 percent, increasing the value of Mark and Jordan's shares by $664,024 and $412,875, respectively. The Securities and Exchange Commission (SEC) filed a civil suit in a federal district court against Scott. What was the most likely allegation? What is required to impose sanctions for this offense? Should the court hold Scott liable? Why or why not? [*SEC v. Ginsburg*, 362 F.3d 1292 (11th Cir. 2004)]

To view a sample answer for this case problem, go to this book's Web site at http://wbl.westbuslaw.com, select "Chapter 41," and click on "Case Problem with Sample Answer."

41-8. VIOLATIONS OF THE 1934 ACT.

2TheMart.com, Inc., was conceived in January 1999 to launch an auction Web site to compete with eBay, Inc. On January 19, 2TheMart announced that its Web site was in its "final development" stages and expected to be active by the end of July as a "preeminent" auction site, and that the company had "retained the services of leading Web site design and architecture consultants to design and construct" the site. Based on the announcement, investors rushed to buy 2TheMart's stock, causing a rapid increase

in the price. On February 3, 2TheMart entered into an agreement with IBM to take preliminary steps to plan the site. Three weeks later, 2TheMart announced that the site was "currently in final development." On June 1, 2TheMart signed a contract with IBM to design, build, and test the site, with a target delivery date of October 8. When 2TheMart's site did not debut as announced, Mary Harrington and others who had bought the stock filed a suit in a federal district court against the firm's officers, alleging violations of the Securities Exchange Act of 1934. The defendants responded, in part, that any alleged misrepresentations were not material and asked the court to dismiss the suit. How should the court rule, and why? [*In re 2TheMart.com, Inc. Securities Litigation*, 114 F.Supp.2d 955 (C.D.Ca. 2000)]

41-9. INSIDER REPORTING AND TRADING.

Ronald Bleakney, an officer at Natural Microsystems Corp. (NMC), a Section 12 corporation, directed NMC sales in North America, South America, and Europe. In November 1998, Bleakney sold more than 7,500 shares of NMC stock. The following March, Bleakney resigned from the firm, and the next month, he bought more than 20,000 shares of its stock. NMC provided some guidance to employees concerning the rules of insider trading, and with regard to Bleakney's transactions, the corporation said nothing about potential liability. Richard Morales, an NMC shareholder, filed a suit against NMC and Bleakney to compel recovery, under Section 16(b) of the Securities Exchange Act of 1934, of Bleakney's profits from the purchase and sale of his shares. (When Morales died, his executor Deborah Donoghue became the plaintiff.) Bleakney argued that he should not be liable because he relied on NMC's advice. Should the court order Bleakney to disgorge his profits? Explain. [*Donoghue v. Natural Microsystems Corp.*, 198 F.Supp.2d 487 (S.D.N.Y. 2002)]

41-10. VIDEO QUESTION

Go to this text's Web site at **http://wbl.westbuslaw.com** and select "Chapter 41." Click on "Video Questions" and view the video titled *Mergers and Acquisitions*. Then answer the following questions.

(a) Was the purchase of Onyx Advertising a material fact that the Quigley Company had a duty to disclose under SEC Rule 10b-5? Why or why not?

(b) Does it matter whether Quigley knew about or authorized the company spokesperson's statements? Why or why not?

(c) Which case discussed in the chapter presented issues that are very similar to those presented in the video? Under the holding of that case, would Onyx Advertising be able to maintain a suit against the Quigley Company for violation of SEC Rule 10b-5?

(d) Who else might be able to bring a suit against the Quigley Company for insider trading under SEC Rule 10b-5?

LAW | on the Web

For updated links to resources available on the Web, as well as a variety of other materials, visit this text's Web site at http://wbl.westbuslaw.com.

To access the SEC's EDGAR database, go to

http://www.sec.gov/edgar.shtml

The Center for Corporate Law at the University of Cincinnati College of Law examines many of the laws discussed in this chapter, including the Securities Act of 1933 and the Securities Exchange Act of 1934. Go to

http://www.law.uc.edu/CCL

LEGAL RESEARCH EXERCISES ON THE WEB

Go to http://wbl.westbuslaw.com, the Web site that accompanies this text. Select "Chapter 41" and click on "Internet Exercises." There you will find the following Internet research exercises that you can perform to learn more about topics covered in this chapter.

Activity 41–1: LEGAL PERSPECTIVE
Electronic Delivery

Activity 41–2: MANAGEMENT PERSPECTIVE
The SEC's Role

CHAPTER 42
Law for Small Businesses

Small businesses are responsible for creating much of the wealth and many of the new jobs in the United States. Yet while some new companies, such as Microsoft Corporation and Dell, Inc., have become highly successful, many small businesses fail. A lack of understanding of legal issues and how to respond to them is one of the reasons for such failures. Understanding business law and the legal environment has also been crucial to great business successes. Consider that Microsoft's success is grounded to some extent in the smart contract law decisions the company made in its early days.

For the most part, the underlying laws of interest to small-business owners are the same general business laws covered throughout this text, and this chapter provides a review of some of those laws. In this chapter, we examine a number of the options and legal requirements faced by those who wish to start up their own small businesses. We also indicate how the general legal principles discussed throughout this book apply in the context of a small-business enterprise. Because of the importance of legal compliance in the success of any such venture, we begin the chapter with a discussion of the importance of obtaining legal counsel.

SECTION 1 | The Importance of Legal Counsel

Nearly everyone who starts up a business enterprise faces the following question: "Do I need an attorney?" The answer to this question will likely be "yes." Today, nonexperts find that it is virtually impossible to keep up with the myriad rules and regulations that govern the way in which business can be conducted in the United States. Indeed, businesspersons sometimes incur penalties for violating laws or regulations of which they are totally unaware, as noted in Chapter 5. Obtaining competent legal counsel can help a small business avoid a number of pitfalls. An attorney may be very helpful when undertaking certain types of transactions, including the following:

- Negotiating a franchise agreement.
- Creating corporate forms, such as purchase orders and contract confirmations.
- Buying or selling real property or a business.
- Negotiating agreements to license intellectual property rights.
- Obtaining new outside investors.

Relevant questions thus include how to find the right attorney for your needs and how to hold down legal costs as much as possible.

Although attorneys may seem expensive, the cautious business owner will make sure that he or she is not "penny wise and pound foolish." The consultation fee paid to an attorney may be a drop in the bucket compared with the potential liability facing a business-person for violating a statutory law or regulation. Also, outside legal help may be essential for certain tasks associated with forming a new business, such as drafting and filing the documents necessary for incorporation. Failure to comply with specific state incorporation requirements may subject the owners of the new enterprise to personal liability for contracts or other obligations. Exhibit 42–1 on the next page provides estimated average attorneys' fees for a few basic small-business transactions. Of course, these amounts will vary depending on the complexity of the job and the geographic area where the business is located.

FINDING AN ATTORNEY

In selecting an attorney, most businesspersons rely on referrals from friends, business associates, and other

EXHIBIT 42-1   Average Attorneys' Fees for Selected Small-Business Transactions

LEGAL TASK	FEE RANGE
Partnership creation	$450–$1,000
Lease-option contract	$250–$350
Trademark application	$250–$450
Employee handbook analysis	$750–$1,000

local entities. Business networks, such as chambers of commerce and bar organizations, may also help identify knowledgeable attorneys. Attorneys and their areas of specialty are often listed in the Yellow Pages of the telephone book. A good source of information is the *Martindale-Hubbell Law Directory*, which can be found at most law libraries. (It is also accessible online at **http://www.martindale.com**.) This directory lists the names, addresses, telephone numbers, areas of legal practice, and other data for more than 900,000 attorneys and law firms in the United States. A number of lawyers specialize in small-business law. Many states now have certification programs that identify specialists in various legal areas.

INTERVIEWING AND EVALUATING ATTORNEYS

After you have obtained a list of possibilities, conduct interviews with the attorneys whom you have selected and evaluate them. In assessing a particular attorney, think about the following questions: Did the attorney seem knowledgeable about what you need to do to start up your business? Did she or he seem willing to investigate the laws relevant to your business plans? Did you communicate well with each other? Did the attorney perceive what issues were of foremost concern to you and address those issues to your satisfaction? Did the attorney "speak your language" when explaining the legal implications of those issues?

RETAINING AN ATTORNEY

Retaining an experienced attorney will yield benefits beyond the resolution of legal problems. Many attorneys have valuable contacts, including potential investors in your enterprise. An attorney may also have valuable business expertise. Furthermore, because the law protects the confidentiality of attorney-client communications, an attorney provides a useful sounding board for business plans.

At the start-up stage, you may not have the financial resources to pay a lawyer, especially one who charges a high hourly rate. Attorneys have responded to this situation by offering innovative fee arrangements, especially in such hotbeds of entrepreneurship as Silicon Valley, south of San Francisco. Most attorneys will not charge for an initial consultation, and some will provide a substantial amount of service in exchange for a promise of future legal business after the venture is established. Some attorneys may accept an equity (ownership) stake in the new business in lieu of a cash payment. As a client, you often have the opportunity to negotiate your attorney's compensation system to suit your needs.

Some small-business owners keep an attorney on **retainer.** This means that the client pays the attorney a fixed amount every month, and the attorney handles all necessary legal business that arises during the month. The amount of the retainer is negotiated with an eye toward expected legal needs, so this approach probably will not save money overall. A retainer arrangement, however, has the benefit of making your legal costs stable and predictable over time.

RETAINING AN ACCOUNTANT

In a new business, the proper management of accounts receivable and accounts payable is critical. There are software accounting programs to handle the job, but many small businesses hire professional accountants to do their bookkeeping. Although it is more expensive, having an accountant adds to your credibility with investors and lenders. Bookkeeping accuracy is also legally important, as errors often provoke litigation.

SECTION 2 | Selecting an Appropriate Business Form

The various forms of business organization available to businesspersons were discussed in detail in Chapters 35 through 41; we will review them here in the context of small businesses. In the earliest stages, a small business may operate as a sole proprietorship, which requires few legal formalities. The law considers all new, single-owner businesses to be sole proprietorships unless the owner affirmatively adopts some other form. Once business is under way, however, the sole proprietorship form may become problematic if additional investors are needed or the personal financial risks of the business become too great. You and the additional investors (owners) may then want to establish a more formal organization, such as a limited partnership, a corporation, an S corporation, a limited liability company, or a limited liability partnership.

Each business form has its own particular advantages and disadvantages. Factors to consider when choosing a business form include liability, taxation, continuity of life, and the legal formalities and costs associated with starting up the business.

LIMITATIONS ON LIABILITY

A key consideration in starting up a business is whether the business form chosen will limit one's personal liability for business debts and obligations. If you form a limited liability entity, such as a corporation, you can normally avoid personal liability if, say, a customer slips and breaks his ankle in your store, sues your store, and is awarded damages by a court. Although the business entity may be liable for damages, you and other owners often will not be personally liable beyond the extent of your contribution to the firm. Legal limited liability is generally necessary for those who wish to raise outside capital.

All corporate business forms offer limited liability to the shareholder-owners. In a general partnership, however, there is no limited liability—each partner is personally liable for the debts and obligations of the partnership. In a limited partnership, the limited partners have limited liability. A limited partnership requires at least one general partner, however, who remains personally liable for the partnership's obligations. Note that limited personal liability does not obviate the need to obtain insurance for significant business liability risks (see Chapter 49). Limited liability organizations protect only personal assets, and a substantial uninsured liability can bankrupt the business and cause the owner to lose her or his entire investment.

All states now permit businesspersons to conduct their business operations as limited liability companies (LLCs), and a growing number of states permit single-owner LLCs. Also, many states now provide for limited liability partnerships (LLPs). These increasingly popular business forms also offer the advantage of limited personal liability for business debts and obligations (see Chapters 36 and 37 for a more detailed discussion of this aspect of LLCs and LLPs). LLCs often offer tax advantages for start-up companies, and this business form seems to be the vehicle of choice for most small enterprises. LLC owners are called "members," and they choose whether they will also be the "managers" of the entity. The LLC structure is defined by an "operating agreement." The law as applied to LLCs is still in development, though, and is somewhat uncertain, as illustrated by the following case.

CASE 42.1   Haley v. Talcott

Court of
Chancery of Delaware,
New Castle County, 2004.
864 A.2d 86.

STRINE, Vice Chancellor.

* * * *

* * * In 2001, [Matthew] Haley found the location for what would become the Redfin Grill. [Gregory] Talcott contributed substantial start-up money and Haley managed the Redfin Grill without drawing a salary for the first year.

* * * Haley and Talcott chose to create and operate the Redfin Grill as an entity solely owned by Talcott, with Haley's rights and obligations being defined by a series of contracts * * * [that included] an Agreement regarding an option to purchase real estate (the "Real Estate Agreement").

* * * *

* * * In that agreement, Talcott granted Haley the right to participate in an option to purchase the property where the Redfin Grill was situated which is located at 1111 Highway One in Bethany Beach, Delaware (the "Property"). * * * The agreement provided that if the option were exercised, Haley would shoulder 50% of the burden of the purchase, and would be either a 50% owner of the land or a 50% owner of the entity formed to hold the land.

From late 2001 into 2003, under Haley's supervision, the Redfin Grill grew into a successful business. By the second year of its existence, the start-up money had been repaid to Talcott with interest, both parties were drawing salaries * * * , and the parties each received approximately $150,000 in profit sharing.

CONTINUED ▶

In 2003, the parties formed Matt & Greg Real Estate, LLC, to take advantage of the option to purchase the Property that was the subject of the Real Estate Agreement. The option price was $720,000 and the new LLC took out a mortgage from County Bank in Rehoboth Beach, Delaware, for that amount, exercised the option, and obtained the deed to the Property on or about May 23, 2003. Importantly, both Haley and Talcott, individually, signed personal guaranties for the entire amount of the mortgage in order to secure the loan. * * * Thus by mid-2003, the parties appeared poised to reap the fruits of their labors; unfortunately, at that point their personal relationship began to deteriorate.

* * * On or about October 27, 2003, the conflict that had been brewing between the parties led to some kind of confrontation. As a result, Talcott * * * [forbid Haley] to enter the premises of the Redfin Grill.

* * * *

In [response] Haley * * * [voted] that the Property be put up for sale on the open market.

Of course, as a 50% member, Haley could not force the LLC to take action on [this proposal] because Talcott opposed [it]. * * * In short, * * * Haley is stuck, unless he chooses to avail himself of the exit mechanism provided in the LLC Agreement.

That exit mechanism * * * would provide Haley with his share of the fair market value of the LLC, including the Property. Section 18 of the LLC Agreement provides that upon written notice of election to "quit" the company, the remaining member may elect, in writing, to purchase the departing member's interest for fair market value. * * *

* * * *

Rather than use the exit mechanism, Haley [filed a suit in a Delaware state court against Talcott, seeking] * * * dissolution of the LLC * * * .

* * * *

The Delaware LLC Act is grounded on principles of freedom of contract. * * * *When the agreement itself provides a fair opportunity for the dissenting member who disfavors the * * * status quo to exit and receive the fair market value of her interest, it is at least arguable that the limited liability company may still proceed to operate practicably under its contractual charter because the charter itself provides an equitable way to break the impasse.* [Emphasis added.]

Here, that reasoning might be thought apt because Haley has already "voted" as an LLC member to sell the LLC's only asset, the Property * * * . Given that reality, * * * it arguably makes sense for this court to stay its hand in an LLC case and allow the contract itself to solve the problem.

* * * *

* * * But * * * forcing Haley to exercise the contractual exit mechanism would not permit the LLC to proceed in a practicable way that accords with the LLC Agreement, but would instead permit Talcott to penalize Haley without express contractual authorization.

Why? Because the parties agree that the exit mechanism in the LLC Agreement would not relieve Haley of his obligation under the personal guaranty that he signed to secure the mortgage from County Bank. If Haley is forced to use the exit mechanism, Talcott and he both believe that Haley would still be left holding the bag on the guaranty. * * *

* * * *

For the reasons discussed above, I find that it is not reasonably practicable for the LLC to continue to carry on business in conformity with the LLC Agreement. The parties shall confer and, within four weeks, submit a plan for the dissolution of the LLC. The plan shall include a procedure to sell the Property owned by the LLC within a commercially reasonable time frame. Either party may, of course, bid on the Property.

IT IS SO ORDERED.

QUESTIONS

1. In what circumstance would it be equitable to force a member to exercise a provision in an LLC agreement that includes an "exit mechanism," such as the one at the center of the dispute in the *Haley* case?
2. What might the parties in the *Haley* case have provided in an LLC agreement so that their deadlock and the resulting litigation could have been avoided?

TAX CONSIDERATIONS

Taxes are another critical factor to be considered in choosing a small-business form. A sole proprietorship is not a separate legal entity, and the owner pays taxes on business income as an individual. All revenues are taxable, but business expenses can be deducted, so the owner is taxed only once on the business's profits. Partnerships are taxed in the same fashion, with income and deductions apportioned among the partners.

All corporations must pay certain state and local taxes—such as **franchise taxes** (annual taxes imposed for the privilege of doing business in a state), property taxes, and the like—but the key consideration involves income taxes. The corporate form entails what is known as *double taxation*. The company must pay a corporate income tax on its profits, and the shareholder-owners must also pay individual income tax on any distributions of remaining profits that they receive from the corporation. The double taxation is limited to distributions of profits, though, so corporations are taxed only once on retained earnings. (See Chapter 38 for a complete discussion of corporate taxation, including the new dividend rule that mitigates this double-taxation feature of corporations to some extent.)

The S corporation was created to allow certain small businesses to take advantage of "pass-through" taxation, in which profits are taxed only once on the owners' individual returns and are not taxed at the business level. Government restrictions on qualifying for S corporation status limit corporate flexibility, however. LLCs and LLPs allow small businesses to avoid these restrictions and limitations on flexibility and at the same time reap the tax benefits of the S corporation form.

CONTINUITY OF LIFE

Continuity of life is another concern in selecting a business form. Businesses may fail to prepare for the possibility that an owner may die, resign, be expelled, or become incapacitated. Corporations have continuity of life—that is, they survive their owners—except in the unusual event that the corporate documents provide otherwise. On the death of a corporate shareholder-owner, normally that shareholder's ownership interest simply passes to his or her heirs.

In a partnership in many states, the death or withdrawal of a partner does not cause the termination of the partnership, unless the partners have expressly provided otherwise. (In those states that have not adopted the most recent version of the Uniform Partnership Act, however, the death of a partner will automatically dissolve the partnership—see Chapter 36.) By definition, a sole proprietorship terminates with the death of the sole proprietor.

LEGAL FORMALITY AND EXPENSE

Businesspersons also need to consider the legal formalities and expenses involved in starting up a business. The requirements and costs associated with forming and operating as a corporation can be considerable. Some minor costs are associated with qualifying as an S corporation. The expense of establishing a limited partnership may also be significant. For these reasons, some individuals initially undertake business operations as sole proprietorships or general partnerships—and run considerable financial risk because of the personal liability associated with each of these business forms. Start-up formalities and costs are generally less extensive for LLCs than for corporations or limited partnerships.

REQUIREMENTS FOR ALL BUSINESSES Although sole proprietorships and general partnerships avoid the legal formalities associated with incorporating or creating a limited partnership, sole proprietors and partners must still comply with many laws. Any business, whatever its form, has to meet a variety of legal requirements, which typically relate to the following:

- Business name registration.
- Occupational licensing.
- State tax registration (for example, to obtain permits for collecting and remitting sales taxes).
- Health and environmental permits.
- Zoning and building codes.
- Import/export regulations.

If the business has employees, the owner must also comply with a host of laws governing the workplace. (We will look at many of these laws in the final section of this chapter.)

FORMALIZING THE BUSINESS The owner should not overlook the potential benefits that may be gained by establishing a more formal business arrangement than a sole proprietorship. Consider a family business that is owned and operated by a husband and wife. At the outset, the spouses should consider the possibility that they may have a falling-out in the future. If they run their enterprise as a sole proprietorship, it may be difficult to establish their respective ownership rights in the business should a dispute arise.

If they form a partnership, however, they can specify in a written partnership agreement how profits and losses will be shared, as well as the extent of each partner's ownership interest in the partnership. Alternatively, the spouses could incorporate and draw up a shareholder agreement providing for various eventualities (shareholder agreements are discussed later in this chapter) and permitting the company's continuation. Formalizing the business is critical to its potential expansion as well.

SECTION 3 | Creating the Business Entity

In this section, we discuss procedures for creating a new small business. There are no special legal requirements for creating a sole proprietorship, and a general partnership requires only an agreement between the partners. LLCs involve slightly more legal work, and some states require them to advertise their formation. Forming a limited partnership is even more complicated. The limited partnership agreement, often called a certificate of limited partnership, must be prepared and recorded with the appropriate governmental authority. State laws also regulate the names of limited partnerships, require certain record keeping, and govern other aspects of the business.

CHOOSING A CORPORATE NAME

To incorporate, you first must choose a corporate name and file it with the appropriate state office, usually the office of the secretary of state. The name must be different from those used by existing businesses (even unincorporated businesses). Although private databases can be used to check names, the secretary of state's office should have all of the information necessary. The name of your new company should also include the word *Corporation*, *Company*, or *Incorporated* (abbreviated *Corp.*, *Co.*, and *Inc.*, respectively).

Note that filing a name with the appropriate state official will protect the name as a trade name only within the state. Therefore, businesspersons who anticipate doing business nationally—via the Internet, for example—will want to make sure that their trade names will be protected under trademark law (to be discussed shortly).

ARTICLES OF INCORPORATION, BYLAWS, AND INITIAL MEETINGS

The second key step in incorporation is preparing and filing the articles of incorporation. Other steps involve drafting the corporate bylaws and holding the initial board of directors' meeting.

ARTICLES OF INCORPORATION As discussed in Chapter 38, state requirements vary with respect to what provisions must be included in the articles. For example, you may be required to have a minimum number of incorporators, a minimum number of directors, a minimum capital contribution, and so on. As mentioned, entrepreneurs typically enlist the services of an attorney to help them draft and file the documents necessary to incorporate, including the articles of incorporation.

If the incorporators want to obtain the tax benefits provided by S corporation status, the new company must qualify for that status under Subchapter S of the Internal Revenue Code. The new company must file additional forms with the Internal Revenue Service and, in most states, with the appropriate state agency. If a company does not file its form with the state agency by the prescribed deadline, it may lose the state tax benefits of S corporation status.

DRAFTING CORPORATE BYLAWS An important step in the incorporation process is drafting the corporation's bylaws, which become the company's governing rules. The bylaws include provisions for the dates on which annual meetings will be held, terms for voting quorums, and other rules. The articles of incorporation should not include all of the corporate rules because the articles are relatively difficult to change. Bylaws are binding rules, but they are more easily modified. Usually, bylaws can be changed by a majority vote of the shareholders; in some states, the bylaws can be modified by the board of directors.

HOLDING THE INITIAL BOARD OF DIRECTORS' MEETING The corporation should then hold its first board of directors' meeting. The initial corporate directors are designated in the articles of incorporation. The directors can adopt the agreed-on bylaws, appoint corporate officers and define their respective authority, issue stock, open a bank account, and take other necessary actions. The directors will continue to meet periodically and must stand for election at annual shareholders' meetings.

CREATING A CORPORATE RECORDS BOOK

The next step is to establish a corporate records book in which the corporation's important documents, such as the articles of incorporation, minutes of directors' and shareholders' meetings, and other documents, will be kept. You will also need to create stock certificates for distribution to owners. A special corporate seal may be important, because banks and other institutions may require that seals be placed on certain types of documents. Again, an attorney typically handles these tasks as part of the incorporation process.

SECTION 4 | Intellectual Property

Protecting rights in intellectual property is the central concern for some businesses. For example, software companies depend on their copyrights and patents to protect their investments in the research and development required to create new programs. If copyright or patent protection could not be obtained for this type of intellectual property, a competitor or a customer could simply copy the software. Laws governing rights in intellectual property were discussed in detail in Chapter 8. Here, we examine some aspects of intellectual property law that individuals should consider at the outset of any business venture.

CHOOSING AND PROTECTING YOUR TRADEMARK

Choosing a trademark or service mark and making sure that it can be protected under trademark law can be crucial to the success of a new business venture. One of the factors to consider in choosing a name for your business entity is whether you want to use your business name as a trademark. Assume that you plan to incorporate your business. When the firm is incorporated, the secretary of state (or other state agency with which the business name is filed) approves your company's name only as a trade name—the name that you can use on checks, invoices, and letterhead stationery. You have legal permission to own your trade name only in your own state.

If you decide to use your business (trade) name as a trademark, then you need to follow the principles of trademark law. The general rule is that you cannot use a trademark that is the same as or quite similar to another's distinctive or famous mark or that might lead a customer to think that your product was produced by someone else.

Historically, the first business to use a trademark owned it. The way to qualify as a first user was to be the first company to actually employ the trademark in the marketplace. Today, for national trademark protection, the business must be the first to register the trademark with the U.S. Patent and Trademark Office (PTO) in Washington, D.C. First use still takes some precedence over federal registration, however. For example, suppose that you have used a particular trademark for two years but have not registered the mark with the PTO. If another company then registers the same mark with the PTO, you will probably have the traditional common law right to continue using that mark but only in the geographic region in which you have been operating. Outside that region, the federal registrant will own the mark.

CHOOSING YOUR TRADEMARK In deciding on a trademark, you need to make sure that the mark is distinctive. Use of your name or a mere description of your product will probably receive, at most, only weak protection. If you have started a new online company, you cannot call it "Internet" and expect to receive protection. While it is tempting to make up a slight twist on the word, this may lead to confusion—thousands of companies already have the word *net* as part of their names. A distinctive made-up word (such as *Exxon* or *Kodak*) may be a good choice.

UNDERTAKING A TRADEMARK SEARCH Once you have chosen a mark, you should do a trademark search to ensure that the mark is not too similar to existing marks. You can examine the Yellow Pages in any area in which you do business and consult the *Gale Trade Names Directory* in your local library. You can look at the federal trademark register, as well as the trademark register in your state. (You can go to **http://www.uspto.gov** to check the PTO's online federal trademark register.) You can access other trademark databases, such as TrademarkScan, on the Internet as well. Finally, you can hire a trademark search firm to do the search for you.

REGISTERING YOUR TRADEMARK After selecting a trademark that appears to be available and that is not confusingly similar to an existing mark, you should register the mark with both the state government and the federal government. As explained earlier, registration is not required for you to have a right to the mark, but if you do not register, your protection may be limited to the area in which you do business. Federal registration gives your trademark nationwide protection, provided that the trademark is currently being used or will be used within six months. Even if your current business is only local, registration for national protection is important to protect long-term corporate growth.

—Registration Procedures. To register your trademark, you must submit a form to the government. You will be asked to provide a specimen (picture) of your trademark, a list of marked goods and/or services, the date on which you first used the trademark, and other information. You may want to register more than one mark. If your logo consists of a distinctive name as well as a graphic, you can register each item independently. For example, Apple Computer, Inc., uses a rainbow-colored apple as a registered logo and the name *Apple* as a trademark. The apple logo and the Apple name could be registered separately to get independent protection. The government has supplanted its traditional written forms with online filing through the Trademark Electronic Application System, available at **http://www.uspto.gov/teas**.

—Amending the Trademark Application. After applying for registration, you may hear nothing for several months. You may then receive an action letter from the PTO indicating that there is a problem with your application. The problem may be technical, such as a failure to fill in the form properly, or the PTO may consider your trademark too similar to an existing trademark or too general. In that event, you will need to change your trademark. The government thus gives you a chance to amend your application before sending you a final rejection or approval notice.

PROTECTING YOUR TRADEMARK After registering your trademark, you must take care of it. If your mark is federally registered, you may use the symbol ® along with your mark; this puts others on notice of your registration. Even if you have not registered, you can use the symbol ™ along with your mark. Five years after you initially register your mark, you should file the appropriate forms with the PTO to renew your registration. Thereafter, you can renew your registration at ten-year intervals. Filing for renewal informs the government that your mark is still in use and enhances its strength—others cannot contest the validity of your mark.

The trademark owner should also keep alert to possible trademark infringement. If another company uses your trademark or a mark extremely similar to yours, you should take prompt action by sending that company a letter of complaint and considering the possibility of filing a lawsuit for trademark infringement. If you ignore the problem, you may lose rights in your trademark. If, for example, a media outlet improperly refers to your trademark as if it were a generic word, send a letter of correction and keep a copy in your files. You may at some point need to demonstrate that you have consistently sought to enforce your rights in the mark, or it may be deemed abandoned.

Not all uses of a term similar to a trademarked name constitute infringement, however, as the following case illustrates.

CASE 42.2

Playmakers, LLC v. ESPN, Inc.

United States
Court of Appeals,
Ninth Circuit, 2004.
376 F.3d 894.

BACKGROUND AND FACTS *Four lawyers in Seattle set up a new sports agency as a limited liability company (LLC) in 1997 and named the firm Playmakers, LLC. ESPN began promoting and airing a dramatic series called* Playmakers *that involved professional football players who were sometimes engaged in such activities as illegal drug use and domestic abuse. The LLC filed a suit to enjoin (prevent) the release of the series on video and DVD. The LLC contended that the show devalued the goodwill of its business, as clients might think that the LLC was affiliated with the show (called a "reverse confusion" claim). The district court refused to enjoin the release of the series on video and DVD, and the LLC appealed.*

IN THE LANGUAGE OF THE COURT

PREGERSON, Circuit Judge.

* * * *

The ultimate question in a reverse confusion case is "whether consumers doing business with the senior user might mistakenly believe they are dealing with the junior user."

* * *

CASE 42.2 | Continued  * * * Like the district court, we are persuaded that, despite the marks' similarities, the commonness of the term "playmaker," the remoteness of the parties' lines of business, the differences in their choices of marketing channels, and the degree of care professional and aspiring professional athletes are likely to exercise before choosing an agent strongly suggest that LLC's prospective clients are not likely to be confused.

DECISION AND REMEDY *The court affirmed the judgment denying the LLC's requested injunction.*

PROTECTING TRADE SECRETS

Much of the value of a business may lie in its trade secrets. As discussed in Chapter 8, trade secrets are business secrets that have value and might be appropriated by another company, such as a competitor. Trade secrets may include information concerning product development, production processes and techniques, or customer lists.

Trade secrets must be divulged to key employees, and thus any business runs the risk that those employees might disclose the secrets to competitors—or even set up competing businesses themselves. Generally, protecting against the possibility that valuable trade secrets will fall into the hands of others, especially competitors, presents an ongoing challenge for businesses, including new enterprises.

NONDISCLOSURE AND NONCOMPETE AGREEMENTS To protect their trade secrets, companies may require employees who have access to trade secrets to agree in their employment contracts never to divulge those secrets. A company may also include a covenant not to compete in an employment contract. A noncompete covenant will help to protect against the possibility that a key employee may go to work for a competitor or set up a competing business—situations in which the company's trade secrets will likely be disclosed. (Covenants not to compete will be discussed later in the chapter.)

MISAPPROPRIATION OF TRADE SECRETS As discussed in Chapter 8, trade secrets are protected under the common law.[1] Thus, a company can sue an individual or a firm that has misappropriated its trade secrets. In one case, for example, two engineers developed new software products for an established company. A new, small firm then hired the engineers. After the engineers developed a similar product for their new employer, the established company sued for infringement of trade secrets and prevailed in court. The new company was prohibited from selling any of the contested products for three years.[2]

SECTION 5 | Raising Financial Capital

Raising financial capital is critical to the growth of most small businesses. In the very early days of a business, the sole proprietor or partners may be able to contribute only very limited amounts of capital. If the business becomes successful, the owner or owners may want to raise capital from external sources to expand the business. They can do this in several ways. One way is to borrow funds. Another is to exchange equity (ownership rights) in the company in return for funds, either through private arrangements or through public stock offerings.

LOANS

A business can raise capital through a bank loan, but this option may not be available for some businesses. Banks are usually reluctant to lend significant sums to businesses that are not yet established. Even if a bank is willing to make such a loan, it may require personal guaranty contracts from the owners, putting their personal assets at risk (see Chapter 28).

The small business may find it beneficial to obtain a bank loan if one is available because raising capital in this way allows the founder to retain full ownership and control of the business (though the loan itself may place some restrictions on future business decisions). Loans with desirable terms may be available from the federal Small Business Administration (SBA). One SBA program provides loans of up to $25,000 to businesspersons who are women, low-income individuals, or members of minority groups. Be aware that the SBA requires business owners to put some of their own funds at risk in the business. Some entrepreneurs have even used their credit cards to obtain initial capital.

---

1. The theft of trade secrets is also a federal crime under the Economic Espionage Act of 1996 (see Chapter 9).

2. *Scully Signal Co. v. Joyal*, 881 F.Supp. 727 (D.R.I. 1995).

VENTURE CAPITAL

Many new businesses raise needed capital by exchanging certain ownership rights (equity) in the firm for **venture capital.** In other words, an outsider contributes funds in exchange for an ownership interest in the company. **Venture capitalists,** often organized into major firms, seek out promising enterprises and fund them in exchange for equity stakes. Akin to venture capitalists are individuals, known as "angels," who typically invest somewhat smaller sums in new businesses.

According to the U.S. National Venture Capital Association, U.S. venture capitalists raised nearly $215 billion in over two thousand deals in 2004. The average investment in a company by a venture capitalist is around $5 million to $10 million. In addition to making needed financing available, venture capitalists offer other advantages for businesses. Venture capitalists are often experienced managers who can provide invaluable assistance to entrepreneurs with respect to strategic business decisions, marketing, and important business contacts. Obtaining this assistance may be crucial to a new company's success. The disadvantage is that a venture capitalist with a substantial equity stake will demand a corresponding degree of operational control over the company and a similar proportion of future profits.

To attract outside venture capital, you will need a **business plan.** The plan should be relatively concise (less than fifty pages). It should describe the company, its products, and its anticipated future performance. After considering your plan, a venture capitalist may decide to investigate your venture further. This step may require you to disclose trade secrets, and you should insist that the potential investor sign a confidentiality agreement. If all goes well, you will then negotiate the terms of financing. A key point to be negotiated is how much ownership and control the venture capitalist will receive in exchange for the capital contribution. Exhibit 42–2 summarizes some key issues involved in venture capital negotiations.

SECURITIES REGULATION

Securities regulation is an area of significant concern to those raising capital. Many small-business owners raise funds from friends or business acquaintances instead of from venture capitalists. Whatever method is used, the investor exchanges capital for an interest in the enterprise. If this interest consists of shares of stock (or otherwise qualifies as a security under federal or state law), the business may become subject to extraordinarily detailed regulatory requirements. It may be necessary to register the securities with the Securities and Exchange Commission (SEC) or with the state in which the offering is made, unless the offering falls within an exemption to the securities laws.

EXHIBIT 42-2 **Venture Capital Issues**

Type and Quantity of Stock	The venture capitalists will negotiate the *amount of stock* (which will determine their ownership share of the enterprise) and the *type of stock* (which will usually be preferred stock).
Stock Preferences	If the venture capitalists receive preferred shares, the shares will generally (1) provide for an annual per-share dividend to be paid before common stockholders receive any dividends and (2) give the venture capitalists priority among shareholders in the event of the firm's liquidation.
Conversion and Antidilution Rights	The preferred shares will be convertible into common stock at the option of the venture capitalists, and the company will be restrained from issuing new stock in an amount that would materially dilute the venture capitalists' ownership interests.
Board of Directors	The venture capitalists will define their proportionate representation on the board of directors.
Registration Rights	Should the company conduct a public offering or register its shares at a later date, the venture capitalists will have the right to have their shares registered also ("piggybacked"), making those shares more marketable.
Representations and Warranties	The owner will be required to make representations about the firm's capital structure, its possession of necessary government authorizations, its financial statements, and other material facts.

PRIVATE OFFERINGS In certain circumstances, legal exemptions are available so that the businessperson need not worry about full registration or compliance with all of the securities regulations. (Securities regulations and exemptions were discussed in detail in Chapter 41.) In short, the exemptions permit you to raise a limited amount of funds from a limited number of investors in what is sometimes called a private offering. If your offering qualifies, you need not register your shares as securities with the SEC. States have separate regulatory schemes and different terms for their exemptions from registration. Raising capital in this manner is typically done through a private placement memorandum distributed to selected potential investors.

PUBLIC OFFERINGS A public offering may be made if your business proves especially successful. A public offering makes a certain number of your shares available for purchase by members of the public at a price that you have set. Public offerings are highly regulated, but they may allow you to raise very large amounts of capital. Securities issued through public offerings must be registered with the SEC and applicable state regulatory agencies.

Full registration is complex, but the states and the SEC have jointly created a simplified securities registration process for small businesses. The Small Corporate Offering Registration (SCOR) involves a form with only fifty questions that can be used for small offerings. Forty-three states use the SCOR offering, but the states have varying laws relating to use of the form.

SECTION 6 | Buy-Sell Agreements and Key-Person Insurance

In the excitement of forming a new business, it is easy to overlook the possibility that partners or shareholders may die or become disabled or that disputes among partners or shareholders may make business decision making impossible. At the outset of any enterprise involving two or more owners, provisions can and should be made—and put in writing—to establish how such problems will be resolved.

SHAREHOLDER AGREEMENTS

Even if only two individuals start up a new company, they should have a shareholder agreement that defines their relative ownership rights and interests. Such agreements are vital for small, closely held companies, in large part because shares in such entities cannot be readily sold to outsiders. This means that an owner may be locked into the investment against her or his will with little return.

BUY-SELL AGREEMENTS One key aspect of the shareholder agreement is a *buy-sell agreement*. (This type of agreement was discussed in Chapter 36 in the context of a partnership agreement.) In a corporate shareholder agreement, a buy-sell agreement provides for the buyout of a shareholder and establishes criteria for the price to be paid for that shareholder's ownership interest. A buy-sell agreement might be triggered by the death of a shareholder, enabling the decedent's heirs to cash out the investment. Other common triggering events include a shareholder's bankruptcy, a shareholder's divorce, and the legal attachment of a shareholder's shares for other reasons.

PROVISIONS IN BUY-SELL AGREEMENTS Buy-sell agreements can also resolve serious deadlocks that may develop between co-owners as the business grows. One owner may have a contract option to buy out the others in the event that such a deadlock occurs. Alternatively, all co-owners might submit sealed bids to buy each other out, with the highest bidder being allowed to buy out the others.

A buy-sell agreement might also include a provision for a *right of first refusal* (see Chapter 39). Such a provision will prevent an owner from selling to a third party without first giving the other owners a right to buy out his or her interest. An alternative to the right of first refusal is a provision for a "take-along right," which allows an investor to participate in any sale of shares to a third party. This right can protect relatively passive investors from the possibility that managing shareholders may "bail out" of the corporation by selling their shares to third parties.

KEY-PERSON INSURANCE

Much of the value of a small enterprise may rest in the skills of one or a few employees (such as a software designer or a top management executive). To protect against the risk that these key persons may become disabled or die, business enterprises typically obtain *key-person insurance* (see Chapter 49). The proceeds of a key-person insurance policy can help cover the losses caused by the death or disability of essential employees. Venture capitalists or other investors may require that the company take out a key-person insurance policy as a condition of investing in the corporation.

SECTION 7 | Contract Law and Small Businesses

Small businesses are subject to the common law of contracts, which was covered in detail in Chapters 10 through 19. Any business venture will require that contracts be formed and signed. For example, if you lease business premises, you will need to sign a lease contract. Any equipment that you purchase or sell will also involve contracts. A review of basic contract law principles can help to ensure that any contracts you form will be valid and enforceable. As a general rule, you should make sure that any contractual agreement is in writing. Then, should a dispute arise, there will be written evidence of the contract's terms. Additionally, as discussed in Chapter 15, some contracts—such as contracts for the sale of goods priced at $500 or more[3]—fall under the Statute of Frauds, which means that they must be evidenced by a writing to be enforceable.

_____

3. This amount has been raised to $5,000 or more by the 2003 amendments to Article 2 of the Uniform Commercial Code—see Chapter 20.

CREATING CONTRACT FORMS

Small-business owners often consult with their attorneys in creating contract forms for specific purposes. For example, a business may wish to provide a warranty for its products but also limit the scope of that warranty. This decision is best made through the mutual judgment of the businessperson and her or his attorney to ensure that both business and legal concerns are addressed.

AVOIDING POTENTIAL PERSONAL LIABILITY

Contract law contains traps of which the businessperson should be aware. If you incorporate, you will want to enter contracts as an agent of the corporation, not in your individual capacity. Otherwise, you may be personally liable on the contracts. This principle applies to negotiable instruments as well. For example, if you sign a promissory note on behalf of the corporation, you should indicate that you are signing in a representative capacity (see Chapter 26 for further details on signature liability with respect to negotiable instruments). The same advice applies to partners and partnerships. The following case illustrates these principles.

CASE 42.3 | **Instant Print Centers, Inc. v. Crowley**

Court of Appeal
of Louisiana,
First Circuit, 2002.
814 So.2d 69.

BACKGROUND AND FACTS *John Lee Smith approached David Doucet, the owner of Instant Print Centers, Inc. (IPC). Smith said that he worked for the Gregory Advertising Group (GAG) and that he wanted IPC to do "some work for him." Doucet then met with Bruce Crowley, GAG's president and sole owner. IPC did several jobs over nine months for GAG and sent it twenty invoices (which stated, "Sold To: The Gregory Advertising Group"). GAG paid five of the invoices. IPC sued GAG and Crowley in a Louisiana state court for the unpaid charges, amounting to $15,333.46. The trial court dismissed the claims against Crowley, holding that he was not individually liable on the contracts. IPC appealed.*

IN THE LANGUAGE OF THE COURT

WHIPPLE, Judge.
* * * *

Here, Crowley made Smith vice president and authorized him to contract on behalf of GAG, Inc. Smith contracted with IPC, identifying himself as an agent of GAG, and identifying Crowley as the owner of GAG. Smith failed to disclose that GAG was a corporation, however, and there was insufficient proof of Doucet's knowledge of sufficient indicia [indications] of the agency relationship as to have put him on notice that Smith (and Crowley) were acting on behalf of a corporate entity. * * * Crowley personally communicated with Doucet on at least three occasions in reference to IPC's work for GAG and Crowley and failed to advise Doucet that GAG was incorporated. According to Doucet, he never learned that Crowley was seeking to avoid liability for the unpaid balances on the basis of doing business solely in a corporate status until shortly before trial.

CASE 42.3 | Continued **DECISION AND REMEDY** *The appellate court reversed the lower court's holding and rendered judgment for IPC for the sum of $15,333.46 plus legal interest, reasonable attorneys' fees, and all costs.*

WHAT IF THE FACTS WERE DIFFERENT? *Suppose that Smith and Crowley had sent faxes and other correspondence to IPC using GAG's letterhead. The letterhead showed the company name as "Gregory Advertising Group, Inc." How might the reviewing court have decided the case with this set of facts?*

SECTION 8 | Credit and Payment

Businesses commonly attempt to maintain a positive cash flow, which requires that customers make their payments fairly promptly. Many businesses give their customers thirty to sixty days to pay or extend short-term credit in other ways. A number of customers will fail to pay during this extended period, however, and this can create a substantial problem for the new business.

To give customers an incentive to pay on time, companies may assess late-payment fees. A company may also charge interest on overdue balances, but such a policy entails some legal complications. For consumer sales, the Truth-in-Lending Act (TILA) requires that certain disclosures be made, such as how the interest will be calculated. (The TILA and other consumer protection laws will be discussed in Chapter 44.)

METHODS OF ENCOURAGING PROMPT PAYMENT

There are a variety of devices available to businesses that may be used to encourage prompt payment. For consumer sales, some businesses offer free shipping with prepayment. A company may choose to offer price discounts for prompt payment. The sales contract may also contain a provision making the buyer responsible for all costs involved in collecting overdue payments. Companies frequently run credit checks on consumers or other contract parties before extending credit to them.

COLLECTION EFFORTS

If a problem with late payments persists, you will need to undertake collection efforts. In so doing, you must comply with the laws governing debt-collection practices. Federal law prohibits the use of abusive collection efforts, such as calling individuals frequently at home at inconvenient times or at work. Typically, state laws also prohibit such practices. Certain threats and harassment are also commonly proscribed.

SECTION 9 | Employment Issues

Small businesses are exempt from some employment laws. For example, businesses with fewer than fifteen employees are exempt from federal laws prohibiting employment discrimination and certain other federal acts, such as the Family and Medical Leave Act of 1993.[4] Some state statutes have similar exemptions for small businesses. A knowledge of employment law is crucial for entrepreneurs starting up businesses, however, because even the smallest businesses are subject to many employment laws.

For example, the rather detailed regulations of the federal Occupational Safety and Health Administration have no small-business exemptions. It may be true that small businesses are less likely to be inspected for violations. If enforcement and penalties are applied, however, they can be far more disastrous for start-up companies than for larger, established firms that are in a better position to absorb these costs. Similarly, just one successful lawsuit against a small business can mean bankruptcy for the business, as indicated earlier in this chapter.

HIRING EMPLOYEES

Hiring good employees can be crucial to business success. You should keep several legal issues in mind during this process.

- Be sure that the person you hire will not be disclosing any protected trade secrets of his or her former employer.
- Do not make promises of job security unless you are sure you can keep them. If you promise an employee that her or his job will be permanent and the employee relies on your assurances, you may find it difficult to fire her or him.

---

4. 29 U.S.C. Sections 2601, 2611–2619, 2651–2654.

- Determine what screening tests are appropriate for the job. In some circumstances, you may be able to require the applicant to take a drug test.
- Comply with all of the requirements imposed by federal immigration laws with respect to verifying whether workers are U.S. citizens and whether employees who are not citizens are authorized to work in this country.

EMPLOYMENT CONTRACTS   Generally, you should put all employment agreements in writing. An employment contract might specify that the contract is for at-will employment (see Chapter 33), meaning that you can fire the employee at any time for any reason, providing that no employment laws are violated. In new businesses, an employee might want stock or options in lieu of part of his or her salary. Although this saves scarce cash, granting equity to an employee dilutes the other owners' interests. For high-level employees at least, you would be wise to consult with an attorney regarding what contractual provisions should be included before awarding an equity interest in the firm.

VERIFYING APPLICANTS' CREDENTIALS AND JOB EXPERIENCE   It goes without saying that you should consult with former employers of job applicants and verify the applicants' credentials and job experience. You should also make sufficient inquiries to avoid a negligent-hiring lawsuit. Suppose that you hire a person who has been convicted twice for criminal assault. If that employee attacks a customer, the customer could sue your business for negligence in screening the worker's background during the hiring process. You therefore should check to see if a job applicant has any history of criminal conduct. You should also check a job applicant's driving record if the job involves driving a vehicle for business purposes. Additionally, actions of dishonest employees can cause a small business to suffer substantial economic losses. Thorough screening procedures will help you to avoid such problems.

EMPLOYEE COMPENSATION

Compensation for employees is governed by the Fair Labor Standards Act (FLSA) of 1938.[5] This law applies to all businesses that have $500,000 or more in sales or that are engaged in interstate commerce. The

---

5. 29 U.S.C. Sections 201–260.

FLSA requires that employees be paid at least the minimum wage plus time and a half for overtime. The law also requires that employers keep detailed records of wages paid and hours worked. Executives and professionals are exempt from the minimum-pay and overtime requirements, as are independent contractors. State laws that govern the workplace may require meal breaks or rest breaks for employees.

WORKERS' COMPENSATION

Most states require that employers carry workers' compensation insurance. If one of your employees is injured in the course of employment, the employee will be compensated for the injury by the state workers' compensation fund. That employee generally cannot sue you for further damages.

Workers' compensation insurance premiums are often high, and they may constitute one of a small business's greatest expenses. Premiums are initially based on the size of your payroll and the amount of risk involved in the business that you operate. After some time, your rates may be raised or lowered, depending on the safety record of your company. The fewer claims made against you, the lower your workers' compensation insurance costs will be.

UNEMPLOYMENT COMPENSATION

Unemployment compensation (see Chapter 33) is another expense that new businesses must consider. Unemployment compensation tax rates are based in part on the size of your payroll. Your liability is also affected by the number of claimants from your business. The fewer people you fire, the lower your required payments. Employees are not entitled to unemployment compensation, however, if they voluntarily terminated their employment or if they were fired for misconduct or malfeasance, such as theft.

FIRING EMPLOYEES

At one time or another, a small-business owner will probably find it necessary to fire a worker. Unless otherwise specified in employment contracts, your employees are presumptively at-will employees, and you can fire them without having to give any reason for doing so. It is nevertheless generally advisable to document good cause for terminating a worker—otherwise, he or she may succeed in a lawsuit against you for unlawful discrimination or some other legal violation.

EMPLOYEE FILES Generally, you should keep a file on each employee in which you include the employee's application, performance reviews, and other relevant information. If you fire the employee, full documentation of why she or he was fired should also be added to the file. Realize, though, that nearly half of the states have laws that allow employees to have access to their personnel records.

SEVERANCE PAY If you fire a worker, you might want to offer the worker **severance pay,** which is a payment in addition to the employee's wages owed on termination. Severance pay may be especially appropriate if the termination is not the employee's fault. Normally, you are not required to give severance pay (unless you have previously promised to do so or a union contract requires it). Most states have laws governing when you must provide the employee with his or her final paycheck, however. Moreover, a severance pay package may be conditioned on receipt of a release promising not to sue from the employee.

WRONGFUL DISCHARGE Some states recognize a legal action for wrongful discharge, but these actions are generally limited to terminations in bad faith. You must be aware of any promises you made to an employee in a written contract, in an employee handbook, or even orally. These promises may prevent you from firing the employee without due process, good cause, or whatever else you may have promised.

LIABILITY FOR DEFAMATION OR MISREPRESENTATION Employers may also be liable for defamation if they make false statements to others about the reason for an employee's termination. You should also be cautious in what you say to a prospective employer who asks you for a job reference for a former employee. Do not be tempted to do your former employee a favor by giving him or her an undeserved glowing reference. If the person or company to whom you give the reference hires your former employee and suffers harm as a result, you may be liable for misrepresentation.

COVENANTS NOT TO COMPETE

Covenants not to compete can be very important in the small-business context. As mentioned earlier, many employers include such covenants, or clauses, in their employment contracts with workers. A typical covenant not to compete might require the worker to agree not to work for or establish a competing business

within the same area of the state for six months or one year after his or her employment is terminated. You may want to require your workers to sign such an agreement to prevent them from leaving your business and setting up a competing operation. When hiring new workers, you also need to be alert to the possibility that they may be violating such a clause in their contract with a former employer.

As discussed in Chapter 13, covenants not to compete in employment contracts are generally enforceable in most states so long as they are not unreasonably restrictive in terms of the time period covered or the geographic area involved. A covenant not to compete that restricts an employee from working for a competitor for five years or "anywhere in the world" normally will not be enforced.

USING INDEPENDENT CONTRACTORS

Independent contractors are not considered to be employees. As stated in Chapter 31, according to the *Restatement (Second) of Agency,* an independent contractor is "a person who contracts with another to do something for him [or her] but who is not controlled by the other nor subject to the other's right to control with respect to his [or her] physical conduct in the performance of the undertaking."

BENEFITS OF USING INDEPENDENT CONTRACTORS The use of independent contractors offers many advantages to small businesses. For one thing, you need not withhold income taxes and Social Security and Medicare taxes from payments made to independent contractors, as you are required to do when you pay wages to employees. Furthermore, you need not match the amount withheld for Social Security and Medicare taxes, which can be costly for an employer. Additionally, you need not pay premiums for workers' compensation insurance or unemployment insurance with respect to independent contractors.

Another important benefit of hiring workers as independent contractors rather than employees is that you are not subject to laws governing employment relationships, including laws prohibiting discrimination. Normally, a court will not permit an independent contractor to bring a suit against you for age discrimination, for example, or for any other type of discrimination prohibited by federal or state laws governing employment relationships—because these laws only protect *employees,* not independent contractors.

LIABILITY FOR MISCLASSIFICATION OF WORKERS

Of course, the trade-off in using independent contractors is that you cannot exercise a significant amount of control over how they perform their work. If you do, the Internal Revenue Service (IRS) or another government agency may decide that they are, in fact, employees and not independent contractors. Misclassification of an employee as an independent contractor can subject you to considerable tax liability, including penalties.

Microsoft Corporation certainly realized the potential seriousness of misclassification in 1999. In a tax audit, the IRS concluded that Microsoft exercised significant control over workers who had been designated by the company as independent contractors. The IRS reclassified them as employees. The company accepted the ruling and paid overdue employment taxes. Then several hundred independent contractors sued the company to recover the benefits that Microsoft had made available to its employees but not to the independent contractors. The court held that the workers were entitled to participate in Microsoft's stock-purchase plan and other employee benefits—benefits worth millions of dollars.[6]

6. *Vizcaino v. U.S. District Court for the Western District of Washington,* 173 F.3d 713 (9th Cir. 1999). This case was also mentioned in Chapter 31 in the discussion of the IRS criteria for determining when an agent is an employee.

REVIEWING LAW FOR SMALL BUSINESSES

APC, Inc., is a venture capital firm that invests in new businesses to help them grow. Wyatt Newmark owns and serves as a chef at a restaurant called "Earp's" with a Western design, which he operates as a sole proprietorship. Newmark has five employees at his restaurant—three servers, another chef, and a janitor. Newmark has had great success and hopes to expand or franchise the business. Newmark, who had not even retained an attorney for his small business, approached APC for an investment. Using the information presented in the chapter, answer the following questions.

1. | What approaches may APC take in order to invest in the restaurant, and what are the legal implications of each approach?

2. | If APC takes an equity interest, the restaurant will need a new legal organizational form. What form would you recommend? Why?

3. | In order to preserve the opportunity for growth and a possible franchise, what legal filings should Newmark's entity undertake?

4. | What is the difference between employee status and independent-contractor status? Which form of employment relationship would be more advantageous to Newmark? Why should employers be cautious when designating workers as independent contractors?

TERMS AND CONCEPTS TO REVIEW

business plan 856	**retainer** 848	**venture capital** 856
franchise taxes 851	**severance pay** 861	**venture capitalist** 856

QUESTIONS AND CASE PROBLEMS

42–1. George Overton has plans for establishing a new business with Elena Costanza. They will both be managers, and each will take an annual salary of $50,000. The company will have other expenses of $175,000. They expect to take in $375,000 in the first year of operation and share the profits equally. George and Elena have not yet decided whether to incorporate the new business or run it as a partnership. What are the tax differences between the two approaches?

42–2. QUESTION WITH SAMPLE ANSWER
Amy forms Best Properties, LLC (BP), to own real estate as a long-term investment. BP acquires a 40,000-square-foot warehouse for $500,000, with the financing arranged for, and guaranteed by, Amy. Later, Carl and Dave become BP members. They sign a "member's agreement," which states, "Amy shall own a 50 percent interest in the capital, profits, and losses of BP and shall have 50 percent of

the voting rights. Carl and Dave, collectively, shall own a 50 percent interest in the capital, profits, and losses of BP and shall have 50 percent of the voting rights." BP's sole asset is the warehouse. When relations among the members become strained, Amy executes a deed transferring the warehouse to Excel, LLC, for $500,000. Excel has two members—Amy, with a 60 percent interest, and Carl, with 40 percent. Neither Amy nor Carl discuss the warehouse transfer with Dave, but Amy mails him a check that purports to represent his 25 percent interest in the warehouse. Dave files a suit against Amy and Carl, alleging that the transfer was unfair. On what basis might the court rule in favor of the defendants? Why might the court decide in Dave's favor? Explain.

For a sample answer to this question, go to Appendix I at the end of this text.

42–3. SHAREHOLDER AGREEMENTS. Herman Fryar was a shareholder in a small company, Bryan-Barber Realty, Inc. Fryar's ownership was subject to a shareholder agreement stating that he could not sell or otherwise dispose of his stock without the permission of the other shareholders. In divorce proceedings, the court directed Herman to transfer the stock to his wife, Judith. Bryan-Barber subsequently obtained a judgment against Herman and sought to recover his shares. The company claimed that Herman was still the owner of the shares because the shareholder agreement prohibited the transfer of his shares to anyone else, including Judith, without the permission of the other shareholders. Discuss whether this claim should succeed. [*Bryan-Barber Realty, Inc. v. Fryar*, 461 S.E.2d 29 (N.C.App. 1995)]

42–4. HIRING AND FIRING. Lori McKenzie worked as a personnel director for Renberg's, Inc. She warned the company president that Renberg's was going to be sued for specific violations of the Fair Labor Standards Act. After this encounter, the president stopped speaking to her and fired her sixteen days later. McKenzie sued the company for wrongful discharge. The company claimed that she had been fired for improperly and negligently notarizing a "contract" between two other workers for sexual favors. The jury ruled that she had been improperly fired, but the trial court overruled this finding, holding that the company had adequate legal grounds for firing her. McKenzie appealed. Discuss whether the trial court's ruling should be upheld. [*McKenzie v. Renberg's Inc.*, 94 F.3d 1478 (10th Cir. 1996)]

42–5. OWNER LIABILITY. Gregory and Dale Stires and Stanley Hall owned and operated the Elk Valley Game Ranch as partners. Hall bought thirty-eight head of elk from Martin Carelli and signed a promissory note agreeing to pay $36,000. Hall also signed a security agreement identifying the elk as collateral. Both the note and the security agreement referred to Hall but not to the Stireses. The elk were kept at the ranch. After Hall quit the partnership, the Stireses continued to operate the ranch. When the note was not paid, Carelli filed a suit in a Montana state court against Hall and the Stireses. The court ruled in Carelli's favor. The Stireses appealed, claiming that Hall was personally liable and

they were not. What will the appellate court decide? Why? [*Carelli v. Hall*, 926 P.2d 756 (Mont. 1996)]

42–6. OWNER LIABILITY. Harry Lipson was the president of The Folktree Concertmakers, Inc. To obtain concert advertising in the *Boston Globe*, Lipson completed the newspaper's "Standard Application for Credit." He signed the application "Harry Lipson as President of Folktree Concertmakers, Inc." The application package also contained a form called a Guaranty, which he signed simply as "Harry Lipson." Between 1970 and 1995, Folktree placed about $67,000 in advertising with the paper but failed to pay bills totaling $8,556.55. The Boston Globe Newspaper Co. sued both Folktree and Lipson, and the trial court granted summary judgment for the newspaper. Lipson appealed on the ground that he was not personally liable for the debt. Can Lipson be held personally liable for the debt? What should the appellate court decide? Discuss fully. [*The Boston Globe Newspaper Co. v. The Folktree Concertmakers, Inc.*, 1998 Mass.App.Div. 206 (1998)]

42–7. ⚖ **CASE PROBLEM WITH SAMPLE ANSWER**

Carol Anstett was a salaried, at-will employee of the Plastics Division of Eagle-Picher Industries, Inc. The Plastics Division had an express severance policy under which "[s]alaried employees terminated other than for cause or voluntary separation" were entitled to certain benefits. In July 1997, Eagle-Picher sold the Plastics Division to Cambridge Industries, Inc. Eagle-Picher notified the Plastics Division employees of what was happening to their health insurance and retirement benefits on "termination of service." Cambridge immediately reemployed nearly all of the Plastics Division personnel, including Anstett. The employees believed that the sale of the division triggered an application of the severance policy and asked Eagle-Picher to pay. The company refused, claiming that the employees had not been terminated. Anstett and others filed a suit in a federal district court against Eagle-Picher, seeking the separation benefits. Eagle-Picher responded that the policy was intended only to cover employees who suffered a loss of income, not to cover a corporate asset sale in which the purchaser immediately rehired the employees. How should the court rule? Explain. [*Anstett v. Eagle-Picher Industries, Inc.*, 203 F.3d 501 (7th Cir. 2000)]

To view a sample answer for this case problem, go to this book's Web site at http://wbl.westbuslaw.com, select "Chapter 42," and click on "Case Problem with Sample Answer."

42–8. TRADE SECRETS. J. K. Harris & Co. was a small business that was established to help taxpayers settle delinquent accounts. Harris hired Vicki Dye on February 6, 2001. After several weeks, she was given a "Confidentiality/Non-Disclosure, Non-Solicitation and Non-Compete Agreement" to sign. The company fired Dye on October 2, 2001. Dye subsequently went to work for another small tax-resolution business and sent multiple letters to her former clients. Harris informed Dye that her actions were a serious breach of the confidentiality and noncompete agreement and later filed a suit against her in a federal district court. Harris sought an injunction preventing Dye from contacting former clients and offering tax-resolution services. How would you settle this dispute? Explain. [*J. K. Harris & Co., LLC v. Dye*, 2001 WL 1464728 (D.Minn. 2001)]

42–9. TRADEMARKS. National Distillers Products Co. was founded to market and sell a vodka called *Teton Glacier,* and the company registered this mark with the U.S. Patent and Trademark Office. National Distillers sought to market the product as an ultrapremium vodka, but it was not very successful. Within a year, Refreshment Brands, Inc. (RBI), began advertising that it would be selling a new vodka product called *Glacier Bay.* After RBI produced the product, National Distillers sued for trademark infringement. Should the plaintiff prevail? [*National Distillers Products Co., L.L.C v. Refreshment Brands, Inc.,* 198 F.Supp.2d 474 (S.D.N.Y. 2002)]

42–10. EMPLOYEE COMPENSATION. Between June 10 and September 23, 1998, Jerry Gieg worked for DDR, Inc., doing business as Courtesy Ford in Portland, Oregon. Gieg was a finance and insurance manager. His duties included verifying information in the deals between customers and the sales staff and completing the required forms. He also sold credit-insurance policies, extended warranties, alarm systems, and paint and fabric protection packages. Paid exclusively through commissions on the products he sold, not from the sales or leases of vehicles, Gieg earned $24,025.16, which exceeded one and a half times the minimum wage. Seeking overtime pay, Gieg filed a suit in a federal district court against DDR. The Fair Labor Standards Act exempts employers from paying overtime to "any employee of a retail or service establishment" if the employee's regular rate of pay is more than one and a half times the minimum wage and if "more than half his compensation . . . represents commissions on goods or services." Gieg claimed in part that he was not subject to this provision because he was not engaged in Courtesy's "retail" activity. How should the court rule? Why? [*Gieg v. DDR, Inc.,* 407 F.3d 1038 (9th Cir. 2005)]

LAW | on the Web

For updated links to resources available on the Web, as well as a variety of other materials, visit this text's Web site at http://wbl.westbuslaw.com.

A number of Web sites can provide valuable assistance for a small business. Lawyers.com maintains a site with helpful advice on various subjects, such as hiring an attorney, at

> http://lawyers.com

Court TV and FindLaw jointly operate a wide-ranging site, including a small-business law center that includes legal forms and guidance, at

> http://www.courttv.findlaw.com

Answers to many basic legal questions about running a small business and brief guidance documents can be found at

> http://business-law.freeadvice.com

To obtain tax information and forms, go to the Web site of the Internal Revenue Service at

> http://www.irs.gov

LEGAL RESEARCH EXERCISES ON THE WEB

Go to http://wbl.westbuslaw.com, the Web site that accompanies this text. Select "Chapter 42" and click on "Internet Exercises." There you will find the following Internet research exercises that you can perform to learn more about topics covered in this chapter.

Activity 42–1: LEGAL PERSPECTIVE
The Entrepreneur's Options

Activity 42–2: MANAGEMENT PERSPECTIVE
Financing a Business

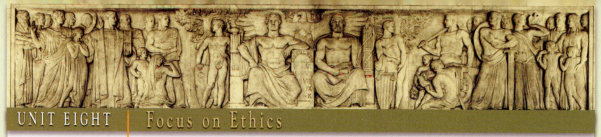

Business Organizations

Every now and then, scandals in the business world rock the nation. Certainly, this was true in the early 2000s when the activities of Enron Corporation and a number of other companies came to light. In response, the public pressured Congress to take action to prevent further such abuses by corporate leaders. As noted in several chapters in this unit, Congress responded in 2002 by passing the Sarbanes-Oxley Act, which imposed stricter requirements on corporations with respect to accounting practices and statements made in documents filed with the Securities and Exchange Commission. The lesson for the business world is, of course, that if business leaders do not behave ethically (and legally), the government will create new laws and regulations that force them to do so. We offered suggestions on how business decision makers can create an ethical workplace in Chapter 5. Here, we look at selected areas in which the relationships within specific business organizational forms may raise ethical issues.

The Emergence of Corporate Governance

The well-publicized corporate abuses that took place in the last ten years have fueled the impetus for businesspersons to create their own internal rules for corporate governance (discussed in Chapter 41). In a few situations, officers have blatantly stolen from the corporation and its shareholders. More frequently, though, officers receive benefits or "perks" of office that are excessive. To illustrate: Tyco International bought a $6,000 shower curtain and a $15,000 umbrella stand for its CEO's apartment.

Corporate officers may be given numerous benefits that they may or may not deserve. A leading corporate officer can receive compensation of $50 million or more even when her or his company's share price is actually declining. Even if corporate officers are scrupulously honest and have modest personal tastes, their behavior may still raise concerns: they may not be good managers, and they may make incompetent corporate choices. They may be a little lazy and fail to do the hard work necessary to investigate corporate decisions. Alternatively, officers may simply fail to appreciate the concerns of shareholders on certain matters, such as maximizing short-term versus long-term results.

Corporate governance controls are meant to ensure that officers receive only the benefits they earn. Governance monitors the actions taken by officers to make sure they are wise and in the best interests of the company. In this way, the corporation can be confident that it is acting ethically toward its shareholders.

Fiduciary Duties Revisited

The law of agency, as outlined in Chapters 31 and 32, permeates virtually all relationships within any partnership or corporation. An important duty that arises in the law of agency, and applies to all partners and corporate directors, officers, and management personnel, is the duty of loyalty. As caretakers of the shareholders' wealth, corporate directors and officers also have a fiduciary duty to exercise care when making decisions affecting the corporate enterprise.

The Duty of Loyalty Every individual has his or her own personal interests, which may at times conflict with the interests of the partnership or corporation with which he or she is affiliated. In particular, a partner or a corporate director may face a conflict between personal interests and the interests of the business entity. Corporate officers and directors may find themselves in a position to acquire assets that would also benefit the corporation if acquired in the corporation's name. If an officer does purchase the asset without offering the opportunity to the corporation, however, she or he may be liable for usurping a corporate opportunity.[1]

The Duty of Care In addition to the duty of loyalty, every corporate director or officer owes a duty of care. *Due care* means that officers and directors must keep themselves informed and make businesslike judgments. Officers have a duty to disclose material information that shareholders need for competent decision making. Corporate law also creates other structures to protect shareholder interests, such as the right to inspect books and records.

Although traditionally the duty of care did not require directors to monitor the behavior of corporate employees to detect and prevent wrongdoing, the tide may be changing. Since the corporate sentencing guidelines were issued in 1991, courts have the power to impose substantial penalties on corporations and corporate directors for criminal wrongdoing. The guidelines allow these penalties to be mitigated, though, if a company can show that it has an effective compliance program in place to detect and prevent wrongdoing by corporate personnel. Furthermore, in 1996 a Delaware chancery (trial) court suggested that corporate directors have a *duty* to implement such programs.

The case involved criminal behavior on the part of a company's middle- and lower-level employees, and the question was whether the directors, who were apparently

---

1. For a landmark case on this issue, see *Guth v. Loft, Inc.,* 5 A.2d 503 (Del. 1939).

unaware of this activity, had breached their oversight duties. Under the traditional rule, as mentioned, directors had no duty to detect and "ferret out" wrongdoing. According to the court in this case, however, the corporate sentencing guidelines have changed this standard. The court stated that "a director's obligation includes a duty to attempt in good faith to assure that a corporation information and reporting system, which the board concludes is adequate, exists."[2] Subsequent decisions by courts applying Delaware law have recognized that directors may be held liable for failing to exercise proper oversight.[3]

Fiduciary Duties to Creditors It is a long-standing principle that corporate directors ordinarily owe fiduciary duties only to a corporation's shareholders. This is because directors are, in a sense, the trustees of the shareholders' property. The true owners of the corporation—the shareholders—entrust the directors with the control and management of the business. The law thus imposes on directors fiduciary duties to shareholders, including the duty of loyalty and the duty of care. Directors who favor the interests of other corporate "stakeholders," such as creditors, over those of the shareholders have been held liable for breaching these duties.

The picture changes, however, when a corporation approaches insolvency. At this point, the shareholders' equity interests in the corporation may be worthless, while the interests of creditors become paramount. In this situation, do the fiduciary duties of loyalty and care extend to the corporation's creditors as well as to the shareholders? The answer to this question, according to many courts, is yes. In a leading case on this issue, a Delaware court noted that "[t]he possibility of insolvency can do curious things to incentives, exposing creditors to risks of opportunistic behavior and creating complexities for directors." The court held that when a corporation is on the brink of insolvency, the directors assume a fiduciary duty to other stakeholders that sustain the corporate entity, including creditors.[4] Some courts have even found that the directors' duties to creditors apply not only when the corporation is technically insolvent, but also when the corporation operates in the "vicinity or zone of insolvency."[5]

Online Chat Rooms and Securities Fraud

The Securities and Exchange Commission (SEC) typically claims that fraud occurs when a false statement of fact is made. Many

statements about stock, however, such as "this stock is headed for $20," are simply opinions. Opinions can never be labeled true or false at the time they are made; otherwise, they would not be opinions. As long as a person has a "genuine belief" that an opinion is true, then presumably no fraud is involved. Yet what if negative "opinions" about a certain company cause the price of its stock to drop? Does the company have any legal recourse against those expressing the opinions?

The Problem Facing GTMI Consider the problem facing Global Telemedia International, Inc. (GTMI). In March 2000, GTMI's stock was trading at $4.70 per share. That month, persons using various aliases began to post messages in the GTMI chat room on the Raging Bull Web site. (Raging Bull is a financial service Web site that organizes chat rooms dedicated to publicly traded companies.) The messages were critical of GTMI and its officers. Over the next six months, GTMI's stock price declined significantly—by October, the stock was closing at $0.25 a share. In an attempt to recoup damages, GTMI sued the "John Does" for defamation (see Chapter 6).

Had Defamation Occurred? The court noted that defamation of a publicly traded company requires a "false statement of fact made with malice that caused damage." The defendants (those who posted the messages) asserted that their online statements were not actionable because they were statements of opinion, not statements of fact. Ultimately, the court agreed with the defendants.

In reaching its decision, the court looked at the "totality of the circumstances," including the context and format of the statements, as well as the expectations of the audience in that particular situation. Here, said the court, the context and format of the statements—anonymous postings "in the general cacophony of an Internet chat room in which about 1,000 messages a week are posted about GTMI"— strongly suggested that the postings constituted opinion, not fact.[6]

Insider Trading

As you learned in Chapter 41, SEC Rule 10b-5 has broad applicability. The rule covers not only corporate insiders but even "outsiders" who trade on tips received from insiders. Investigating and prosecuting violations of SEC Rule 10b-5 is costly, both for the government and for those accused of insider trading. Some people doubt that such extensive regulation is necessary and even contend that insider trading should be legal. Would there be any benefit from the legalization of insider trading?

To evaluate this question, review the facts in *SEC v. Texas Gulf Sulphur Co.* (Case 41.1 in Chapter 41). If insider trading were legal, the discovery of the ore sample would probably have caused many more company insiders to purchase stock. Consequently, the price of Texas Gulf's stock would

---

2. *In re Caremark International, Inc. Derivative Litigation,* 698 A.2d 959 (Del.Ch. [Delaware Chancery Court] 1996).

3. See, for example, *McCall v. Scott,* 239 F.3d 808 (6th Cir. 2001); *Guttman v. Huang,* 823 A.2d 492 (2003); *Landy v. D'Alessandro,* 316 F.Supp.2d 49 (D.Mass. 2004); and *Miller v. U.S. Foodservice, Inc.,* 361 F.Supp.2d 470 (D.Md. 2005).

4. *Credit Lyonnais Bank Nederland N.V. v. Pathe Communications Corp.,* 1991 WL 277613 (Del.Ch. 1991). See also *Production Resources Group, LLC v. NCT Group, Inc.,* 863 A.2d 772 (2004).

5. See, for example, *Gladstone v. Stuart Cinemas, Inc.,* 2005 WL 678506.

6. *Global Telemedia International, Inc. v. Does,* 132 F.Supp.2d 1261 (C.D.Cal. 2001).

have increased fairly quickly. These increases presumably would have attracted the attention of outside investors, who would have realized sooner that something positive had happened to the company and would thus have purchased the stock. The higher demand for the stock would have more quickly translated into higher prices for the stock and hence, perhaps, a more efficient capital market. Nonetheless, the SEC and the courts have routinely upheld the rule that insider trading is illegal.

The Sarbanes-Oxley Act and Insider Trading

The attorney-client privilege generally prevents lawyers from disclosing confidential client information—even when the client has committed an unlawful act. The idea is to encourage clients to be open and honest with their attorneys to ensure competent representation. The Sarbanes-Oxley Act of 2002, however, requires attorneys to report any material violations of securities laws to the corporation's highest authority.[7] The act does not require that the lawyer break client confidences, though, because the lawyer is still reporting to officials within the corporation.

In August 2003, the SEC went one step further than the Sarbanes-Oxley Act to mandate a "noisy withdrawal"—that is, the SEC requires attorneys whose corporate clients are violating securities laws to publicly withdraw from representing the corporation and notify the SEC. This rule is controversial and has been the subject of much debate. Should the SEC be able to force lawyers to disclose privileged client information? Is it fair to the corporation? The American Bar Association (ABA) modified its ethics rules in 2003 to allow—but not require—attorneys to break confidence with a client to report possible corporate fraud. Nonetheless, compliance with the SEC rule is mandatory. In the SEC's view, lawyers owe a duty to the corporation and its investors, not to the individual officers and directors.[8]

Franchise Relationships

Franchise relationships present several ethical issues. One issue concerns the franchisor's quality control over the franchisee's activities. On the one hand, if the franchisor ignores the problem of quality control, the reputation of the franchisor's business may suffer. On the other hand, if a franchisor's control over the operations of the franchisee is too extensive, the franchisor may be liable for the torts of the franchisee's employees under agency theory.[9] Even when an independent business entity purchases a franchise and the franchise agreement specifies that no agency relationship exists, the courts may find otherwise.

Another issue today is how to adapt certain protections for franchisees to the online world. This issue has become increasingly important as more and more prospective franchisees are going online to find information about particular franchises.

Franchisees Held to Be Employees   In a series of cases over the last fifteen years, courts have even held franchisees to be employees of the franchisor, notwithstanding their franchise contracts. For example, in one case a franchisee of a commercial sanitation company was deemed to be an employee of the company even though he was designated as a franchisee in a franchise contract with the company.[10]

In another case, the National Labor Relations Board ruled that some five hundred drivers for a New York company that provided limousine services should be considered employees for labor law purposes, despite their franchise contracts with the company.[11] In these and other cases, the decisions were based on the extensive control exercised by the companies over the activities of the franchisees.

Traditional Franchising Rules and the Internet   Recall from Chapter 35 that the Franchise Rule of the Federal Trade Commission (FTC) imposes certain disclosure requirements on franchisors. In 1978, when this rule was issued, most people had not even heard of the Internet. Today, adapting the rule to the online environment has proved difficult. For example, suppose that a franchisor has a Web site with downloadable information for prospective franchisees. Is this the equivalent of an offer that requires compliance with the FTC's Franchise Rule? Further, does the franchisor have to comply with fifty different state franchise regulations? Generally, how can the interests of franchisees be protected in the cyber environment?

In view of these problems, the FTC is now in the process of amending its Franchise Rule. One proposed change would require that the franchisor provide a prospective franchisee with a proper disclosure document at least fourteen days before the signing of any franchise agreement or any payment to the franchisor. In addition, to give the franchisee more time to consider the franchise contract, the franchisor would have to provide the franchisee with a copy of the contract five calendar days before the agreement is to be signed.

Another proposed rule would require online franchisors to state very clearly that franchisees would not be entitled to exclusive territorial rights. Notwithstanding these changes, however, one problem would remain: given the speed with which online franchises can be created, it may be difficult—if not impossible—for the FTC to effectively regulate these relationships.

---

7. See Section 307 of the Sarbanes-Oxley Act.

8. See 17 C.F.R. Part 205.

9. See, for example, *Parker v. Domino's Pizza, Inc.,* 629 So.2d 1026 (Fla.App. 1993); and *Font v. Stanley Steemer International, Inc.,* 849 So.2d 1214 (Fla.App. 2003).

---

10. *Claim of Francis,* 246 A.D.2d 751, 668 N.Y.S.2d 55 (N.Y.Sup.Ct. App.Div. 1998).

11. *In re Elite Limousine Plus, Inc.,* 324 NLRB No. 182 (November 6, 1997).

DISCUSSION QUESTIONS

1. Three decades ago, corporations and corporate directors were rarely prosecuted for crimes, and penalties for corporate crimes were relatively light. Today, this is no longer true. Under the corporate sentencing guidelines and the Sarbanes-Oxley Act, corporate wrongdoers can receive strict penalties. Do these developments mean that corporations are committing more crimes today than in the past? Will stricter laws be effective in curbing corporate criminal activity? How can a company avoid liability for crimes committed by its employees?

2. Some people contend that SEC Rule 10b-5 against insider trading is being applied too broadly when it is used to prosecute "outsiders"—those who are not corporate insiders but trade securities based on tips from insiders or misappropriated information. Others argue that insider trading should be made legal. Does liability under SEC Rule 10b-5 extend too far? Would there be any benefit if insider trading were legalized?

3. Do you agree that when a corporation is approaching insolvency, the directors' fiduciary obligations should extend to the corporation's creditors as well as to the shareholders? In this situation, should the fiduciary duties owed to creditors take priority over the duties to shareholders? Why or why not?

4. As explained, if a franchisor exercises too much control over a franchisee's business operations, a court may deem the franchisor to be liable as an employer for the torts committed by the franchisee's employees. How can holding franchisors liable in such circumstances be squared with the doctrine of freedom of contract?

5. "When opinions about a company's reputation are exchanged in Internet chat rooms and those opinions cause the price of the company's stock to decline, the company may have a cause of action for defamation." How would you argue in favor of this proposition? How would you argue against it?

UNIT NINE
Government Regulation

CHAPTER 43
Administrative Law

Government agencies established to administer the law have a tremendous impact on the day-to-day operations of the government and the economy. Administrative agencies issue rules covering virtually every aspect of a business's activities. At the federal level, the Securities and Exchange Commission regulates a firm's capital structure and financing, as well as its financial reporting. The National Labor Relations Board oversees relations between a firm and any unions with which it may deal. The Equal Employment Opportunity Commission also regulates employer-employee relationships. The Environmental Protection Agency and the Occupational Safety and Health Administration affect the way a firm manufactures its products, and the Federal Trade Commission influences the way it markets those products.

Added to this layer of federal regulation is a second layer of state regulation that, when not preempted by federal legislation, may cover many of the same activities or regulate independently those activities not covered by federal regulation. Finally, agency regulations at the county or municipal level also affect certain types of business activities.

The rules, orders, and decisions of administrative agencies make up the body of *administrative law*. You were introduced briefly to some of the main principles of administrative law in Chapter 1. In the following pages, we look at these principles in much greater detail.

SECTION 1 | Agency Creation and Powers

Because Congress cannot possibly oversee the actual implementation of all the laws it enacts, it must delegate such tasks to others, particularly when highly technical areas, such as air and water pollution, are involved. By delegating some of its authority to make and implement laws to administrative agencies, Congress can monitor indirectly a particular area in which it has passed legislation without becoming bogged down in the details of enforcement—details that are often best left to specialists.

To create an administrative agency, Congress passes **enabling legislation,** which specifies the name, purposes, functions, and powers of the agency being created. Federal administrative agencies may exercise only those powers that Congress has delegated to them in enabling legislation. Through similar enabling acts, state legislatures create state administrative agencies.

ENABLING LEGISLATION—AN EXAMPLE

Consider the enabling legislation for the Federal Trade Commission (FTC). The enabling statute for this agency is the Federal Trade Commission Act of 1914.[1] The act prohibits unfair methods of competition and deceptive trade practices. It also describes the procedures that the FTC must follow to charge persons or organizations with violations of the act, and it provides for judicial review of agency orders. The act grants the FTC the power to do the following:

1. Create "rules and regulations for the purpose of carrying out the Act."
2. Conduct investigations of business practices.
3. Obtain reports from interstate corporations concerning their business practices.
4. Investigate possible violations of federal antitrust statutes.[2]

---

1. 15 U.S.C. Sections 41–58.
2. The FTC shares enforcement of the Clayton Act with the Antitrust Division of the U.S. Department of Justice.

5. Publish findings of its investigations.

6. Recommend new legislation.

7. Hold trial-like hearings to resolve certain kinds of trade disputes that involve FTC regulations or federal antitrust laws.

AGENCY ORGANIZATION AND STRUCTURE—AN EXAMPLE

The FTC can also serve as an example of the organization and structure of a federal administrative agency. The commission that heads the FTC is composed of five members; each is appointed by the president, with the advice and consent of the Senate, for a term of seven years. The president designates one of the commissioners to be chairperson. Various offices and bureaus within the FTC undertake different administrative activities for the agency. Exhibit 43–1 illustrates the organization of the FTC.

TYPES OF AGENCIES

As discussed in Chapter 1, there are two basic types of administrative agencies: executive agencies and independent regulatory agencies. Federal *executive agencies* include the cabinet departments of the executive branch, which were formed to assist the president in carrying out executive functions, and the subagencies within the cabinet departments. The Occupational Safety and Health Administration, for example, is a subagency within the Department of Labor. Exhibit 43–2 (page 872) lists the cabinet departments and some of their most important subagencies.

All administrative agencies are part of the executive branch of government, but *independent regulatory* agencies are outside the major executive departments. The Federal Trade Commission and the Securities and Exchange Commission are examples of independent regulatory agencies. These and other selected independent regulatory agencies, as well as their principal functions, are listed in Exhibit 43–3 on page 873.

The accountability of the regulators is the most significant difference between the two types of agencies. Agencies that are considered part of the executive branch are subject to the authority of the president, who has the power to appoint and remove federal officers. In theory, this power is less pronounced in regard to independent agencies, whose officers serve for fixed terms and cannot be removed without just cause. In practice, however, the president's ability to exert influence over independent agencies is often considerable.

AGENCY POWERS AND THE CONSTITUTION

Administrative agencies occupy an unusual niche in the U.S. legal scheme because they exercise powers that are normally divided among the three branches of government. Notice that in the FTC's enabling legislation, discussed earlier, the FTC's grant of power incorporates functions associated with the legislative branch (rulemaking), the executive branch (enforcement of the rules), and the courts (**adjudication,** or the formal resolution of disputes).

LEGISLATIVE RULES As you learned in Chapter 4, the constitutional principle of checks and balances allows each branch of government to act as a check on the actions of the other two branches. Furthermore,

EXHIBIT 43-1 **Organization of the Federal Trade Commission**

EXHIBIT 43-2 Executive Departments and Important Subagencies

DEPARTMENT AND DATE FORMED	SELECTED SUBAGENCIES
State (1789)	Passport Office; Bureau of Diplomatic Security; Foreign Service; Bureau of Human Rights and Humanitarian Affairs; Bureau of Consular Affairs; Bureau of Intelligence and Research
Treasury (1789)	Internal Revenue Service; U.S. Mint
Interior (1849)	U.S. Fish and Wildlife Service; National Park Service; Bureau of Indian Affairs; Bureau of Land Management
Justice (1870)[a]	Federal Bureau of Investigation; Drug Enforcement Administration; Bureau of Prisons; U.S. Marshals Service
Agriculture (1889)	Soil Conservation Service; Agricultural Research Service; Food Safety and Inspection Service; Forest Service
Commerce (1913)[b]	Bureau of the Census; Bureau of Economic Analysis; Minority Business Development Agency; U.S. Patent and Trademark Office; National Oceanic and Atmospheric Administration
Labor (1913)[b]	Occupational Safety and Health Administration; Bureau of Labor Statistics; Employment Standards Administration; Office of Labor-Management Standards; Employment and Training Administration
Defense (1949)[c]	National Security Agency; Joint Chiefs of Staff; Departments of the Air Force, Navy, Army; service academies
Housing and Urban Development (1965)	Office of Community Planning and Development; Government National Mortgage Association; Office of Fair Housing and Equal Opportunity
Transportation (1967)	Federal Aviation Administration; Federal Highway Administration; National Highway Traffic Safety Administration; Federal Transit Administration
Energy (1977)	Office of Civilian Radioactive Waste Management; Office of Nuclear Energy; Energy Information Administration
Health and Human Services (1980)[d]	Food and Drug Administration; Centers for Medicare and Medicaid Services; Centers for Disease Control; National Institutes of Health
Education (1980)[d]	Office of Special Education and Rehabilitation Services; Office of Elementary and Secondary Education; Office of Postsecondary Education; Office of Vocational and Adult Education
Veterans' Affairs (1989)	Veterans Health Administration; Veterans Benefits Administration; National Cemetery System
Homeland Security (2002)	Bureau of Citizenship and Immigration Services; Directorate of Border and Transportation Services; U.S. Coast Guard; Federal Emergency Management Agency

a. Formed from the Office of the Attorney General (created in 1789).
b. Formed from the Department of Commerce and Labor (created in 1903).
c. Formed from the Department of War (created in 1789) and the Department of the Navy (created in 1798).
d. Formed from the Department of Health, Education, and Welfare (created in 1953).

the U.S. Constitution authorizes only the legislative branch to create laws. Yet administrative agencies, to which the Constitution does not specifically refer, make **legislative rules,** or *substantive rules,* that are as legally binding as laws passed by Congress.

THE DELEGATION DOCTRINE Courts generally hold that Article I of the U.S. Constitution authorizes delegating such powers to administrative agencies. In fact, courts generally hold that Article I is the

basis for all administrative law. Section 1 of that article grants all legislative powers to Congress and requires Congress to oversee the implementation of all laws. Article I, Section 8, gives Congress the power to make all laws necessary for executing its specified powers. The courts interpret these passages, under what is referred to as the **delegation doctrine,** as granting Congress the power to establish administrative agencies that can create rules for implementing those laws.

EXHIBIT 43-3 Selected Independent Regulatory Agencies

Name and Date Formed	Principal Duties
Federal Reserve System Board of Governors (Fed) (1913)	Determines policy with respect to interest rates, credit availability, and the money supply.
Federal Trade Commission (FTC) (1914)	Prevents businesses from engaging in unfair trade practices; stops the formation of monopolies in the business sector; protects consumer rights.
Securities and Exchange Commission (SEC) (1934)	Regulates the nation's stock exchanges, in which shares of stock are bought and sold; enforces the securities laws, which require full disclosure of the financial profiles of companies that wish to sell stock and bonds to the public.
Federal Communications Commission (FCC) (1934)	Regulates all communications by telegraph, cable, telephone, radio, satellite, and television.
National Labor Relations Board (NLRB) (1935)	Protects employees' rights to join unions and bargain collectively with employers; attempts to prevent unfair labor practices by both employers and unions.
Equal Employment Opportunity Commission (EEOC) (1964)	Works to eliminate discrimination in employment based on religion, gender, race, color, disability, national origin, or age; investigates claims of discrimination.
Environmental Protection Agency (EPA) (1970)	Undertakes programs aimed at reducing air and water pollution; works with state and local agencies to help fight environmental hazards. (It has been suggested recently that its status be elevated to that of a department.)
Nuclear Regulatory Commission (NRC) (1975)	Ensures that electricity-generating nuclear reactors in the United States are built and operated safely; regularly inspects operations of such reactors.

The three branches of government exercise certain controls over agency powers and functions, as will be discussed later in this chapter, but in many ways administrative agencies function independently. For this reason, administrative agencies, which constitute the **bureaucracy,** are sometimes referred to as the "fourth branch" of the U.S. government.

SECTION 2 | Administrative Process

The three functions mentioned previously—rulemaking, enforcement, and adjudication—make up what is known as the **administrative process.** Administrative process involves the administration of law by administrative agencies, in contrast to **judicial process,** which comprises the administration of law by the courts.

All federal agencies must follow specific procedural requirements in their rulemaking, adjudication, and other functions. Sometimes, Congress specifies certain procedural requirements in an agency's enabling legislation. In the absence of any directives from Congress concerning a particular agency procedure, the Administrative Procedure Act (APA) of 1946[3] applies. The APA is such an integral part of the administrative

process that its application will be considered as we examine the basic functions carried out by administrative agencies. In addition, agency procedures are guided indirectly by the courts' interpretation of APA requirements.

RULEMAKING

A major function of an administrative agency is **rulemaking**—the formulation of new regulations. In an agency's enabling legislation, Congress confers the agency's power to make legislative rules, as already mentioned. For example, the Occupational Safety and Health Act of 1970 authorized the Occupational Safety and Health Administration (OSHA) to develop and issue rules governing safety in the workplace. In formulating any new legislative rule, OSHA must follow specific rulemaking procedures required under the APA.

In addition to making legislative rules, administrative agencies also make *interpretive rules.* These rules are not legally binding on the public but simply indicate how an agency plans to interpret and enforce its statutory authority. For example, the Equal Employment Opportunity Commission periodically issues interpretive rules, usually referred to as enforcement guidelines, indicating how it plans to interpret

---

3. 5 U.S.C. Sections 551–706.

and apply a provision of a certain statute, such as the Americans with Disabilities Act. When making interpretive rules, an agency need not follow the requirements of the APA.

The most commonly used rulemaking procedure is called **notice-and-comment rulemaking.** This procedure involves three basic steps: notice of the proposed rulemaking, a comment period, and the final rule.

NOTICE OF THE PROPOSED RULEMAKING When a federal agency decides to create a new rule, the agency publishes a notice of the proposed rulemaking proceedings in the *Federal Register,* a daily publication of the executive branch that prints government orders, rules, and regulations. The notice states where and when the proceedings will be held, the agency's legal authority for making the rule (usually its enabling legislation), and the terms or subject matter of the proposed rule.

COMMENT PERIOD Following the publication of the notice of the proposed rulemaking proceedings, the agency must allow ample time for persons to comment in writing on the proposed rule. The purpose of this comment period is to give interested parties the oppor-

tunity to express their views on the proposed rule in an effort to influence agency policy. The comments may be in writing or, if a hearing is held, may be given orally.

The agency need not respond to all comments, but it must respond to any significant comments that bear directly on the proposed rule. The agency responds by either modifying its final rule or explaining, in a statement accompanying the final rule, why it did not make any changes. In some circumstances, particularly when the procedure being used in a specific instance is less formal, an agency may accept comments after the comment period is closed. The agency should summarize these *ex parte* (private, "off-the-record") comments in the record for possible review.

THE FINAL RULE After the agency reviews the comments, it drafts the final rule and publishes it in the *Federal Register.* The final rule is later compiled along with the rules and regulations of other federal administrative agencies in the *Code of Federal Regulations* (C.F.R.). Final rules have binding legal effect unless the courts later overturn them.

The court in the following case considered whether to enforce rules that were issued outside of the rulemaking procedure.

CASE 43.1   **Hemp Industries Association v. Drug Enforcement Administration**

United States
Court of Appeals,
Ninth Circuit, 2004.
357 F.3d 1012.

BACKGROUND AND FACTS *The members of the Hemp Industries Association (HIA) import and distribute sterilized hemp seed and oil and cake derived from hemp seed, and make and sell food and cosmetic products made from hemp seed and oil. These products contain only nonpsychoactive trace amounts of tetrahydrocannabinols (THC).[a] On October 9, 2001, the U.S. Drug Enforcement Administration (DEA) published an interpretive rule declaring that "any product that contains any amount of THC is a Schedule I controlled substance."[b] On the same day, the DEA proposed two legislative rules. One rule—DEA-205F—amended the listing of THC in "Schedule I" to include natural, as well as synthetic, THC. The second rule—DEA-206F—exempted from control nonpsychoactive hemp products that contain trace amounts of THC not intended to enter the human body. On March 21, 2003, without following formal rulemaking procedures, the DEA declared that these rules were final. This effectively banned the possession and sale of the food products of the HIA's members. The HIA petitioned the U.S. Court of Appeals for the Ninth Circuit to review the rules, asserting that they could not be enforced.*

IN THE LANGUAGE OF THE COURT
BETTY B. FLETCHER, Circuit Judge.
 * * * *
 * * * Appellants * * * argue that DEA-205F is a scheduling action—placing nonpsychoactive hemp in Schedule I for the first time—that fails to follow the procedures for such actions required by the Controlled Substances Act ("CSA"). * * *

---

a. A *nonpsychoactive substance* is one that does not affect a person's mind or behavior. Nonpsychoactive hemp is derived from industrial hemp plants grown in Canada and in Europe, the flowers of which contain only a trace amount of the THC contained in marijuana varieties grown for psychoactive use.
b. A *controlled substance* is a drug whose availability is restricted by law.

*   *   *   *

Under 21 U.S.C. [Section] 811(a) [of the CSA]:

the Attorney General may by rule—
(1) add to *   *   * a schedule *   *   * any drug or other substance if he—
*   *   *

(B) makes with respect to such drug or other substance the findings prescribed by subsection (b) of [S]ection 812 of this title *   *   * .

Rules of the Attorney General under this subsection shall be made on the record after opportunity for a hearing pursuant to the rulemaking procedures prescribed by [the Administrative Procedure Act (APA).]

*   *   * *Formal rulemaking requires hearings on the record, and [the APA] invites parties to submit proposed findings and oppose the stated bases of tentative agency decisions, and requires the agency to issue formal rulings on each finding, conclusion, or exception on the record.* We will not reproduce the entirety of the [APA] here; it suffices to say that the DEA did not and does not claim to have followed formal rulemaking procedures. [Emphasis added.]

In addition, the DEA did not comply with [Section] 811(a)(1)(B), because the findings required by [Section] 812(b) were not made. Section 812(b) states:

(b) Placement on schedules; findings required. *   *   * [A] drug or other substance may not be placed in any schedule unless the findings required for such schedule are made with respect to such drug or other substance.

*   *   *   *

The DEA does not purport to have met the requirements for placement of nonpsychoactive hemp on Schedule I *   *   * . Instead, the DEA argues that naturally occurring THC in those parts of the hemp plant excluded from the definition of "marijuana" have always been included under the listing for "THC" *   *   * .

*   *   *   *

Two CSA provisions are relevant to determining whether Appellants' hemp products were banned before [DEA-205F and DEA-206F]: the definition of THC and the definition of marijuana. Both are unambiguous *   *   * : Appellants' products do not contain the "synthetic" "substances or derivatives" that are covered by the definition of THC, and nonpsychoactive hemp is explicitly excluded from the definition of marijuana.

*   *   *   *

Under 21 U.S.C. [Section] 802(16) [of the CSA]:

The term "marihuana" means all parts of the plant Cannabis sativa L. *   *   * . Such term does not include the mature stalks of such plant, fiber produced from such stalks, oil or cake made from the seeds of such plant, any other compound, manufacture, salt, derivative, mixture, or preparation of such mature stalks (except the resin extracted therefrom), fiber, oil, or cake, or the sterilized seed of such plant which is incapable of germination.

The nonpsychoactive hemp in Appellants' products is derived from the "mature stalks" or is "oil and cake made from the seeds" of the *Cannabis* plant, and therefore fits within the plainly stated exception to the CSA definition of marijuana.

*   *   * Congress knew what it was doing, and its intent to exclude nonpsychoactive hemp from regulation is entirely clear.

DECISION AND REMEDY *The U.S. Court of Appeals for the Ninth Circuit held that DEA-205F and DEA-206F "are inconsistent with the unambiguous meaning of the CSA definitions of marijuana and THC," and the DEA did not follow the proper administrative procedures required to schedule a substance. The court issued an injunction against the enforcement of the rules with respect to nonpsychoactive hemp or products containing it.*

WHAT IF THE FACTS WERE DIFFERENT? *Suppose that the statutory definitions of THC and marijuana covered naturally occurring THC and nonpsychoactive hemp. Would the result in this case have been different?*

INVESTIGATION

Administrative agencies conduct investigations of the entities that they regulate. One type of agency investigation occurs during the rulemaking process to obtain information about a certain individual, firm, or industry. The purpose of such an investigation is to ensure that the rule issued is based on a consideration of relevant factors and is not arbitrary and capricious. After final rules are issued, agencies conduct investigations to monitor compliance with those rules. A typical agency investigation of this kind might begin when a citizen reports a possible violation.

INSPECTIONS Many agencies gather information through on-site inspections. Sometimes, inspecting an office, a factory, or some other business facility is the only way to obtain the evidence needed to prove a regulatory violation. Administrative inspections and tests cover a wide range of activities, including safety inspections of underground coal mines, safety tests of commercial equipment and automobiles, and environmental monitoring of factory emissions. An agency may also ask a firm or individual to submit certain documents or records to the agency for examination.

Normally, business firms comply with agency requests to inspect facilities or business records because it is in any firm's interest to maintain a good relationship with regulatory bodies. In some instances, however, such as when a firm thinks an agency's request is unreasonable and may be detrimental to the firm's interest, the firm may refuse to comply with the request. In such situations, an agency may resort to the use of a subpoena or a search warrant.

SUBPOENAS There are two basic types of subpoenas. The subpoena *ad testificandum* ("to testify") is an ordinary subpoena. It is a writ, or order, compelling a witness to appear at an agency hearing. The subpoena *duces tecum*[4] ("bring it with you") compels an individual or organization to hand over books, papers, records, or documents to the agency. An administrative agency may use either type of subpoena to obtain testimony or documents.

There are limits on what information an agency can demand. To determine whether an agency is abusing its discretion in its pursuit of information as part of an investigation, a court may consider such factors as the following:

1. The purpose of the investigation. An investigation must have a legitimate purpose. Harassment is an example of an improper purpose. An agency may not issue an administrative subpoena to inspect business records if the agency's motive is to harass or pressure the business into settling an unrelated matter.

2. The relevance of the information being sought. Information is relevant if it reveals that the law is being violated or if it assures the agency that the law is not being violated.

3. The specificity of the demand for testimony or documents. A subpoena must, for example, adequately describe the material being sought.

4. The burden of the demand on the party from whom the information is sought. In responding to a request for information, a party must bear the costs of, for example, copying the documents that must be handed over; a business is generally protected from revealing such information as trade secrets, however.

In addition, a subpoena might not be enforced when the subject matter of an investigation is not within the authority of the agency to investigate. The issue in the following case was whether the subject matter of certain subpoenas issued by the Federal Trade Commission had exceeded the agency's statutory authority.

---

4. Pronounced *doo*-cheez *tee*-kum.

Federal Trade Commission v. Ken Roberts Co.

United States
Court of Appeals,
District of Columbia
Circuit, 2001.
276 F.3d 583.

BACKGROUND AND FACTS *Ken Roberts Company, Ken Roberts Institute, Inc., United States Chart Company, and Ted Warren Corporation (collectively, Roberts) sell instructional materials that claim to teach would-be investors how to make money investing. In 1999, the Federal Trade Commission (FTC) began investigating whether a variety of online businesses were engaged in deceptive marketing practices in violation of the Federal Trade Commission Act. Aiming at high-risk, high-yield investment activity and suspicious Internet advertising, the FTC soon focused on Roberts. The FTC issued subpoenas that required Roberts to produce documents and answer written questions relating to the companies' business practices. Roberts refused to respond to most of the requests. The FTC asked a federal district court to enforce the subpoenas. When the court ordered Roberts to comply, Roberts appealed to the U.S. Court of Appeals for the District of Columbia Circuit. Roberts argued that*

CASE 43.2 | Continued *its companies were subject only to other federal agencies, whose authority under, in part, the Investment Advisers Act (IAA) preempted the FTC's authority to investigate Roberts's practices.*

IN THE LANGUAGE OF THE COURT

HARRY T. EDWARDS, Circuit Judge:

* * * *

Subpoena enforcement power is not limitless * * * . *[A] subpoena is proper only where the inquiry is within the authority of the agency, the demand is not too indefinite and the information sought is reasonably relevant.* Accordingly, there is no doubt that a court asked to enforce a subpoena will refuse to do so if the subpoena exceeds an express statutory limitation on the agency's investigative powers. Thus, a court must assure itself that the subject matter of the investigation is within the statutory jurisdiction of the subpoena-issuing agency. * * * [Emphasis added.]

* * * *

On its own terms, the FTC Act gives the FTC ample authority to investigate and, if deceptive practices are uncovered, to regulate appellants' advertising practices. Therefore, the FTC is entitled to have its subpoenas enforced unless some other source of law patently [clearly] undermines these broad powers. * * *

* * * *

[Appellants], whose businesses involve securities * * * , assert that the comprehensive scope of the Investment Advisers Act of 1940 preempts the FTC's jurisdiction to regulate the fraudulent practices of "investment advisers" such as themselves. * * *

* * * [T]he IAA contains no express exclusive jurisdiction provision. * * * [But] where intended by Congress, a precisely drawn, detailed statute preempts more general remedies. This can occur either where the two enactments are in irreconcilable conflict or where the latter was clearly meant to serve as a substitute for the former. Appellants contend that the antifraud provision of the IAA, which prohibits investment advisers from engaging "in any transaction, practice, or course of business which operates as a fraud or deceit upon any client or prospective client," stands as just such a specific remedy that displaces the more general coverage of the FTC Act.

* * * *

Because we live in an age of overlapping and concurring regulatory jurisdiction, a court must proceed with the utmost caution before concluding that one agency may not regulate merely because another may. In this case, while it may be true that the IAA and the FTC Act employ different verbal formulae to describe their antifraud standards, it hardly follows that they therefore impose conflicting or incompatible obligations. Undoubtedly, entities in appellants' position can—and of course should—refrain from engaging in both "unfair and deceptive acts or practices" *and* "any transaction, practice, or course of business which operates as a fraud or deceit upon a client or prospective client." The proscriptions of the IAA are not diminished or confused merely because investment advisers must also avoid that which the FTC Act proscribes. And, because these statutes are capable of co-existence, it becomes the *duty* of this court to regard each as effective—at least absent clear congressional intent to the contrary.

Appellants can point to nothing in the background or history of the IAA that demonstrates (or even hints at) a congressional intent to preempt the antifraud jurisdiction of the FTC over those covered by the new statute. Nor does the subsequent case law interpreting these statutes contain such declarations.

DECISION AND REMEDY *The U.S. Court of Appeals for the District of Columbia Circuit affirmed the lower court's decision. The appellate court held that the FTC was entitled to the enforcement of its subpoenas against Roberts. The Investment Advisers Act does not preempt the FTC's authority to investigate possibly deceptive advertising and marketing practices merely because those practices relate to the investment business.*

SEARCH WARRANTS The Fourth Amendment protects against unreasonable searches and seizures by requiring that in most instances a physical search for evidence must be conducted under the authority of a search warrant. An agency's search warrant is an order directing law enforcement officials to search a specific place for a specific item and present it to the agency. Although it was once thought that administrative inspections were exempt from the warrant requirement, the United States Supreme Court held in *Marshall v. Barlow's, Inc.*,[5] that the requirement does apply to the administrative process.

Agencies can conduct warrantless searches in several situations. Warrants are not required to conduct searches in highly regulated industries. Firms that sell firearms or liquor, for example, are automatically subject to inspections without warrants. Sometimes, a statute permits warrantless searches of certain types of hazardous operations, such as coal mines. Also, a warrantless inspection in an emergency situation is normally considered reasonable.

ADJUDICATION

After conducting an investigation of a suspected rule violation, an agency may begin to take administrative action against an individual or organization. Most administrative actions are resolved through negotiated settlements at their initial stages, without the need for formal adjudication.

NEGOTIATED SETTLEMENTS Depending on the agency, negotiations may take the form of a simple conversation or a series of informal conferences. Whatever form the negotiations take, their purpose is to rectify the problem to the agency's satisfaction and eliminate the need for additional proceedings.

Settlement is an appealing option to firms for two reasons: to avoid appearing uncooperative and to avoid the expense involved in formal adjudication proceedings and in possible later appeals. Settlement is also an attractive option for agencies. To conserve their own resources and avert formal actions, administrative agencies devote a great deal of effort to giving advice and negotiating solutions to problems.

FORMAL COMPLAINTS If a settlement cannot be reached, the agency may issue a formal complaint against the suspected violator. If the Environmental Protection Agency (EPA), for example, finds that a factory is polluting groundwater in violation of federal pollution laws, the EPA will issue a complaint against the violator in an effort to bring the plant into compliance with federal regulations. This complaint is a public document, and a press release may accompany it. The factory charged in the complaint will respond by filing an answer to the EPA's allegations. If the fac-

tory and the EPA cannot agree on a settlement, the case will be adjudicated. Recall from Chapter 1 that agency adjudication may involve a trial-like procedure before an **administrative law judge (ALJ).** The administrative adjudication process is described below and illustrated graphically in Exhibit 43–4.

THE ROLE OF THE ADMINISTRATIVE LAW JUDGE
The ALJ presides over the hearing and has the power to administer oaths, take testimony, rule on questions of evidence, and make determinations of fact. Although technically the ALJ works for the agency prosecuting the case (in our example, the EPA), the law requires an ALJ to be an unbiased adjudicator (judge).

Certain safeguards prevent bias on the part of the ALJ and promote fairness in the proceedings. For example, the Administrative Procedure Act (APA) requires that the ALJ be separate from an agency's

EXHIBIT 43–4 **The Process of Formal Administrative Adjudication**

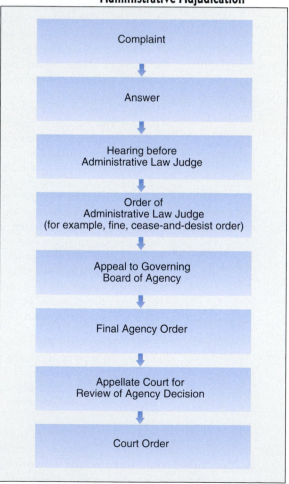

Complaint

↓

Answer

↓

Hearing before Administrative Law Judge

↓

Order of Administrative Law Judge (for example, fine, cease-and-desist order)

↓

Appeal to Governing Board of Agency

↓

Final Agency Order

↓

Appellate Court for Review of Agency Decision

↓

Court Order

5. 436 U.S. 307, 98 S.Ct. 1816, 56 L.Ed.2d 305 (1978).

investigative and prosecutorial staff. The APA also prohibits *ex parte* (private) communications between the ALJ and any party to an agency proceeding, such as the EPA or the factory. Finally, provisions of the APA protect the ALJ from agency disciplinary actions unless the agency can show good cause for such an action.

HEARING PROCEDURES   Hearing procedures vary widely from agency to agency. Administrative agencies generally exercise substantial discretion over the type of procedure that will be used. Frequently, disputes are resolved through informal adjudication proceedings. For example, the parties, their counsel, and the ALJ may simply meet at a table in a conference room to attempt to settle the dispute.

A formal adjudicatory hearing, in contrast, resembles a trial in many respects. Prior to the hearing, the parties are permitted to undertake extensive discovery (involving depositions, interrogatories, and requests for documents or other information, as described in Chapter 3). During the hearing, the parties may give testimony, present other evidence, and cross-examine adverse witnesses. A significant difference between a trial and an administrative agency hearing, though, is that normally much more information, including hearsay (secondhand information), can be introduced as evidence during an administrative hearing.

AGENCY ORDERS   Following a hearing, the ALJ renders an **initial order,** or decision, on the case. Either party can appeal the ALJ's decision to the board or commission that governs the agency. If the factory in the previous example is dissatisfied with the ALJ's decision, it can appeal the decision to the commission that governs the EPA. If the factory is dissatisfied with the commission's decision, it can appeal the decision to a federal court of appeals. If no party appeals the case, the ALJ's decision becomes the **final order** of the agency. The ALJ's decision also becomes final if a party appeals and the commission and the court decline to review the case. If a party appeals and the case is reviewed, the final order comes from the commission's decision or (if that decision is appealed to a federal appellate court) that of the court.

SECTION 3 | Limitations on Agency Powers

Combining the functions normally divided among the three branches of government into an administrative agency concentrates considerable power in a single organization. Because of this concentration of authority, one of the major policy objectives of the government is to control the risks of arbitrariness and overreaching by administrative agencies without hindering the effective use of agency power to deal with particular problem areas, as Congress intends.

The judicial branch of the government exercises control over agency powers through the courts' review of agency actions. The executive and legislative branches of government also exercise control over agency authority.

JUDICIAL CONTROLS

The Administrative Procedure Act provides for judicial review of most agency decisions, as described above. Agency actions are not automatically subject to judicial review, however.

THE RIPENESS DOCTRINE   Under what is known as the *ripeness doctrine*, a court will not review an administrative agency's decision until the case is "ripe for review." Generally, a case is ripe for review if the parties can demonstrate that they have met certain requirements. The party bringing the action must have *standing to sue* the agency (the party must have a direct stake in the outcome of the judicial proceeding), and there must be an *actual controversy* at issue. These are basic judicial requirements that must be met before any court will hear a case, as discussed in Chapter 2. With regard to agency decisions, however, the party must also have *exhausted all possible administrative remedies*. Each agency has its "chain of review," and the party must follow agency appeal procedures before a court will deem that administrative remedies have been exhausted.

The rationale for this doctrine is to prevent courts from entangling themselves in abstract disagreements over administrative policies. The doctrine also protects agencies from judicial interference until an administrative decision has been formalized and its effects are clear. The court can then evaluate both the appropriateness of an issue for judicial decision and the hardship the decision will cause to the challenging party if the court refuses to consider the case.

ISSUES CONSIDERED WHEN REVIEWING AGENCY DECISIONS   Recall from Chapter 2 that appellate courts normally defer to the decisions of trial courts on questions of fact. In reviewing administrative actions, the courts show a similar deference to (reluctance to question) the factual findings of agencies.

In reviewing an administrative agency's decision, a court normally will consider the following types of issues:

1. Whether the agency has exceeded its authority under its enabling legislation.
2. Whether the agency has properly interpreted laws applicable to the agency action under review.
3. Whether the agency has violated any constitutional provisions.
4. Whether the agency has acted in accordance with procedural requirements of the law.
5. Whether the agency's actions were arbitrary, capricious, or an abuse of discretion.
6. Whether any conclusions drawn by the agency are not supported by substantial evidence.

The fifth element in the above list is often referred to as the "arbitrary and capricious" test. An agency action will be deemed arbitrary and capricious if it was taken willfully and unreasonably, and without considering the facts of the case.

EXECUTIVE CONTROLS

The executive branch of government exercises control over agencies both through the president's power to appoint federal officers and through the president's veto power. The president may veto enabling legislation presented by Congress or congressional attempts to modify an existing agency's authority.

LEGISLATIVE CONTROLS

Congress also exercises authority over agency powers. Through enabling legislation, Congress gives power to an agency. Of course, an agency may not exceed the power that Congress has delegated to it. Through subsequent legislation, Congress can take away that power or even abolish an agency altogether. Legislative authority is required to fund an agency, and enabling legislation usually sets certain time and monetary limits on the funding of particular programs. Congress can always revise these limits.

In addition to its power to create and fund agencies, Congress has the authority to investigate the implementation of its laws and the agencies that it has created. Individual legislators may also affect agency policy through their "casework" activities, which

involve attempts to help their constituents deal with agencies.

Congress also has the power to "freeze" the enforcement of most federal regulations before the regulations take effect. Under the Small Business Regulatory Enforcement Fairness Act of 1996,[6] all federal agencies must submit final rules to Congress before the rules become effective. If, within sixty days, Congress passes a joint resolution of disapproval concerning a rule, enforcement of the regulation is frozen while the rule is reviewed by congressional committees.

Another legislative check on agency actions is the Administrative Procedure Act, discussed earlier in this chapter. Additionally, the laws discussed in the next section provide certain checks on the actions of administrative agencies.

SECTION 4 | Public Accountability

As a result of growing public concern over the powers exercised by administrative agencies, Congress passed several laws to make agencies more accountable through public scrutiny. We discuss here the most significant of these laws.

FREEDOM OF INFORMATION ACT

Enacted in 1966, the Freedom of Information Act (FOIA)[7] requires the federal government to disclose certain "records" to "any person" on request, even if no reason is given for the request. The FOIA exempts certain types of records. For other records, though, a request that complies with the FOIA procedures need only contain a reasonable description of the information sought (see Exhibit 43–5). An agency's failure to comply with a request may be challenged in a federal district court. The media, industry trade associations, public-interest groups, and even companies seeking information about competitors rely on these FOIA provisions to obtain information from government agencies.

Under a 1996 amendment to the FOIA, all federal government agencies now must make their records available electronically—on the Internet, on computer disks, and in other electronic formats. As of November 1, 1996, any document created by an

---

6. 5 U.S.C. Sections 801–808.
7. 5 U.S.C. Section 552.

EXHIBIT 43-5 **Sample Letter Requesting Information from an Executive Department or Agency**

Agency Head [or Freedom of Information Act Officer]   Date _____
Name of Agency
Address of Agency
City, State, Zip Code

Re: Freedom of Information Act Request

Dear _____ :

This is a request under the Freedom of Information Act.

I request that a copy of the following documents [or documents containing the following information] be provided to me: [identify the documents or information as specifically as possible].

In order to help to determine my status for purposes of determining the applicability of any fees, you should know that I am [insert a suitable description of the requester and the purpose of the request].

[Optional] I am willing to pay fees for this request up to a maximum of $XX. If you estimate that the fees will exceed this limit, please inform me first.

[Optional] I request a waiver of all fees for this request. Disclosure of the requested information to me is in the public interest because it is likely to contribute significantly to public understanding of the operations or activities of the government and is not primarily in my commercial interest. [Include specific details, including how the requested information will be disseminated by the requester for public benefit.]

[Optional] I request that the information I seek be provided in electronic format, and I would like to receive it on a personal computer disk [or a CD–ROM].

[Optional] I ask that my request receive expedited processing because XXXX. [Include specific details concerning your "compelling need," such as being someone "primarily engaged in disseminating information" and specifics concerning your "urgency to inform the public concerning actual or alleged Federal Government activity."]

[Optional] I also include a telephone number at which I can be contacted during the hours of XXXX, if necessary, to discuss any aspect of my request.

Thank you for your consideration of this request.

Sincerely,
[Signature]
Name
Address
City, State, Zip Code
Telephone number [Optional]

Source: U.S. Congress, House Committee on Government Reform, *A Citizen's Guide on How to Use the Freedom of Information Act and the Privacy Act Requesting Government Documents,* 106th Congress, 1st session, H.R. 106–50, 1999.

agency must be accessible by computer within a year after its creation. Agencies must also provide a clear index to all of their documents.

GOVERNMENT IN THE SUNSHINE ACT

Congress passed the Government in the Sunshine Act,[8] or open meeting law, in 1976. It requires that "every portion of every meeting of an agency" be open to "public observation." The act also requires the establishment of procedures to ensure that the public is provided with adequate advance notice of scheduled meetings and agendas. Like the FOIA, the Sunshine Act contains certain exceptions. Closed meetings are permitted when (1) the subject of the meeting concerns accusing any person of a crime, (2) an open meeting would frustrate the implementation of agency actions, or (3) the subject of the meeting involves matters relating to future litigation or rulemaking. Courts interpret these exceptions to allow open access whenever possible.

8. 5 U.S.C. Section 552b.

REGULATORY FLEXIBILITY ACT

Concern over the effects of regulation on the efficiency of businesses, particularly smaller ones, led Congress to pass the Regulatory Flexibility Act[9] in 1980. Under this act, whenever a new regulation will have a "significant impact upon a substantial number of small entities," the agency must conduct a regulatory flexibility analysis. The analysis must measure the cost that the rule would impose on small businesses and must consider less burdensome alternatives. The act also contains provisions to alert small businesses—through advertising in trade journals, for example—about forthcoming regulations. The act reduces some record-keeping burdens for small businesses, especially with regard to hazardous waste management.

SMALL BUSINESS REGULATORY ENFORCEMENT FAIRNESS ACT

As mentioned above, the Small Business Regulatory Enforcement Fairness Act (SBREFA) of 1996 allows Congress to review new federal regulations for at least sixty days before they take effect. This period gives opponents of the rules time to present their arguments to Congress.

The SBREFA also authorizes the courts to enforce the Regulatory Flexibility Act. This helps to ensure that federal agencies, such as the Internal Revenue Service, will consider ways to reduce the economic impact of new regulations on small businesses. Federal agencies are required to prepare guides that explain in "plain English" how small businesses can comply with federal regulations.

The SBREFA also set up the National Enforcement Ombudsman at the Small Business Administration to receive comments from small businesses about their dealings with federal agencies. Based on these comments, Regional Small Business Fairness Boards rate the agencies and publicize their findings.

Finally, the SBREFA allows small businesses to recover their expenses and legal fees from the government when an agency makes demands for fines or penalties that a court considers excessive.

---

9. 5 U.S.C. Sections 601–612.

SECTION 5 | State Administrative Agencies

Although most of this chapter deals with federal administrative agencies, state agencies play a significant role in regulating activities within the states. Many of the factors that encouraged the proliferation of federal agencies also fostered the expanded presence of state agencies. For example, one reason for the growth of administrative agencies at all levels of government is the inability of Congress and state legislatures to oversee the implementation of their laws. Another is the greater technical competence of the agencies.

PARALLEL AGENCIES

Commonly, a state creates an agency as a parallel to a federal agency to provide similar services on a more localized basis. Such parallel agencies include the federal Social Security Administration and the state welfare agency, the Internal Revenue Service and the state revenue department, and the Environmental Protection Agency and the state pollution-control agency. Not all federal agencies have parallel state agencies, however. For example, the Federal Bureau of Investigation and the Nuclear Regulatory Commission have no parallel agencies at the state level.

CONFLICTS BETWEEN PARALLEL AGENCIES

If the actions of parallel state and federal agencies conflict, the actions of the federal agency will prevail. For example, if the Federal Aviation Administration specifies the hours during which airplanes may land at and depart from airports, a state or local government cannot issue inconsistent laws or regulations governing the same activities. The priority of federal laws over conflicting state laws is based on the supremacy clause of the U.S. Constitution. Remember from Chapter 4 that this clause, which is found in Article VI of the Constitution, states that the Constitution and "the Laws of the United States which shall be made in Pursuance thereof . . . shall be the supreme Law of the Land." The following case illustrates this principle.

CASE 43.3

United States
District Court,
District of
Minnesota, 2004.
290 F.Supp.2d 993.

Vonage Holdings Corp. v. Minnesota Public Utilities Commission

DAVIS, District Court Judge.

* * * *

This case illustrates the impact of emerging technologies evolving ahead of the regulatory scheme intended to address them. The issue before the Court is tied to the evolution of the Internet and the expansion of its capability to transmit voice communications. Despite its continued growth and development, the Internet remains in its infancy, and is an uncharted frontier with vast unknowns left to explore. Congress has expressed a clear intent to leave the Internet free from undue regulation so that this growth and exploration may continue. Congress also differentiated between "telecommunications services," which may be regulated, and "information services," which like the Internet, may not.

* * * *

Vonage [Holdings Corporation] markets and sells Vonage DigitalVoice, a service that permits voice communication via a high-speed ("broadband") Internet connection. Vonage's service uses a technology called Voice over Internet Protocol ("VoIP"), which allows customers to place and receive voice transmissions routed over the Internet.

Traditional telephone companies use circuit-switched technology. * * * Voice communication using the Internet has been called Internet Protocol ("IP") telephony, and rather than using circuit switching, it utilizes "packet switching," a process of breaking down data into packets of digital bits and transmitting them over the Internet.

* * * *

Vonage has approximately 500 customers with billing addresses in Minnesota. * * *

The Minnesota Department of Commerce ("MDOC") investigated Vonage's services and on July 15, 2003, filed a complaint with the [Minnesota Public Utilities Commission (MPUC)]. The complaint alleged that Vonage failed to * * * obtain a proper certificate of authority required to provide telephone service in Minnesota * * * .

Vonage then moved to dismiss the MDOC complaint. * * * The MPUC * * * [concluded] that * * * Vonage was required to comply with Minnesota statutes and rules regarding the offering of telephone service. Vonage then filed a complaint with this Court seeking [an] * * * injunction.

* * * *

The issue before the Court is whether Vonage may be regulated under [a] Minnesota law that requires telephone companies to obtain certification authorizing them to provide telephone service. Vonage asserts that the Communications Act of 1934, as amended by the Communications Act of 1996, preempts the state authority upon which the MPUC's order relies. * * * Vonage asserts that * * * its services are "information services," which are not subject to regulation, rather than "telecommunications services," which may be regulated.

* * *

The Supremacy Clause of Article VI of the Constitution empowers Congress to preempt state law. Preemption occurs when (1) Congress enacts a federal statute that expresses its clear intent to preempt state law; (2) there is a conflict between federal and state law; (3) compliance with both federal and state law is in effect physically impossible; (4) federal law contains an implicit barrier to state regulation; (5) comprehensive congressional legislation occupies the entire field of regulation; or (6) state law is an obstacle to the accomplishment and execution of the full objectives of Congress. *Moreover, a federal agency acting within the scope of its congressionally delegated authority may preempt state regulation.* [Emphasis added.]

* * * *

Examining the statutory language of the Communications Act, the Court concludes that the VoIP service provided by Vonage constitutes an information service because it offers the "capability for generating, acquiring, storing, transforming, processing, retrieving, utilizing, or making available information via telecommunications." * * * Vonage's services are closely tied to the provision of telecommunications services as defined by Congress, the courts and

CONTINUED ▶

CASE 43.3 | Continued

the [Federal Communications Commission (FCC)], but this Court finds that Vonage *uses* telecommunications services, rather than provides them.

* * * *

* * * The Court acknowledges the attractiveness of the MPUC's simplistic "quacks like a duck" argument, essentially holding that because Vonage's customers make phone calls, Vonage's services must be telecommunications services. However, this simplifies the issue to the detriment of an accurate understanding of this complex question. The Court must follow the statutory intent expressed by Congress, and interpreted by the FCC. Short of explicit statutory language, the Court can find no stronger guidance for determining that Vonage's service is an information service * * * .

* * * *

Where federal policy is to encourage certain conduct, state law discouraging that conduct must be preempted. [Emphasis added.]

* * * *

Accordingly, * * * IT IS HEREBY ORDERED that Vonage's motion for * * * [an] injunction * * * is GRANTED.

QUESTIONS

1. How might upholding the state agency's order in the *Vonage* case have affected Vonage?
2. What other consequences might have followed if the court in this case had held that services such as Vonage's could be subject to state regulations enforced by state agencies?

JUDICIAL REVIEW OF STATE AGENCY ACTIONS

Most state agency decisions are subject to judicial review by state courts, provided that the parties seeking that review first meet certain requirements. Once a petition for review is granted, state courts, like their federal counterparts, consider such issues as whether a state or local agency exceeded its authority.

REVIEWING ADMINISTRATIVE LAW

Assume that the Securities and Exchange Commission (SEC) has a rule that it will enforce statutory provisions prohibiting insider trading only when the insiders make monetary profits for themselves. Then the SEC makes a new rule, declaring that it has the statutory authority to bring an enforcement action against an individual even if she or he does not personally profit from the insider trading. In making the new rule, the SEC does not conduct a rulemaking proceeding but simply announces its new decision. A stockbrokerage firm objects and says that the new rule was unlawfully developed without opportunity for public comment. The brokerage firm challenges the rule in an action that ultimately is reviewed by a federal appellate court. Using the information presented in the chapter, answer the following questions.

1. Is the SEC an executive agency or an independent regulatory agency? What is the difference between these two types of government agencies? Does this difference have any bearing on the outcome of this case? Explain.

2. Should the SEC's new rule be invalidated under the Administrative Procedure Act? Why or why not?

3. Is the SEC's new rule a legislative rule or an interpretive rule? Why is this distinction important to the outcome of this case?

4. Generally, what issues will a court consider when reviewing an agency action?

TERMS AND CONCEPTS TO REVIEW

adjudication 871

administrative law judge
  (ALJ) 878

administrative process 873

bureaucracy 873

delegation doctrine 872

enabling legislation 870

final order 879

initial order 879

judicial process 873

legislative rule 872

notice-and-comment
  rulemaking 874

rulemaking 873

QUESTIONS AND CASE PROBLEMS

43–1. For decades, the Federal Trade Commission (FTC) resolved fair trade and advertising disputes through individual adjudications. In the 1960s, the FTC began promulgating rules that defined fair and unfair trade practices. In cases involving violations of these rules, the due process rights of participants were more limited and did not include cross-examination. Although anyone found violating a rule would receive a full adjudication, the legitimacy of the rule itself could not be challenged in the adjudication. Any party charged with violating a rule was almost certain to lose the adjudication. Affected parties complained to a court, arguing that their rights before the FTC were unduly limited by the new rules. What will the court examine to determine whether to uphold the new rules?

43–2. QUESTION WITH SAMPLE ANSWER

Assume that the Food and Drug Administration (FDA), using proper procedures, adopts a rule describing its future investigations. This new rule covers all future circumstances in which the FDA wants to regulate food additives. Under the new rule, the FDA is not to regulate food additives without giving food companies an opportunity to cross-examine witnesses. At a subsequent time, the FDA wants to regulate methylisocyanate, a food additive. The FDA undertakes an informal rulemaking procedure, without cross-examination, and regulates methylisocyanate. Producers protest, saying that the FDA promised them the opportunity for cross-examination. The FDA responds that the Administrative Procedure Act does not require such cross-examination and that it is free to withdraw the promise made in its new rule. If the producers challenge the FDA in court, on what basis would the court rule in their favor?

For a sample answer to this question, go to Appendix I at the end of this text.

43–3. RULEMAKING PROCEDURES. The Atomic Energy Commission (AEC) was engaged in rulemaking proceedings for nuclear reactor safety. An environmental group sued the commission, arguing that its proceedings were inadequate. The commission had carefully complied with all requirements of the Administrative

Procedure Act. The environmentalists argued, however, that the very hazardous and technical nature of the reactor safety issue required elaborate procedures above and beyond those set forth in the act. A federal court of appeals agreed and overturned the AEC rules. The commission appealed the case to the United States Supreme Court. How should the Court rule? Discuss. [*Vermont Yankee Nuclear Power Corp. v. Natural Resources Defense Council, Inc.*, 435 U.S. 519, 98 S.Ct. 1197, 55 L.Ed.2d 460 (1978)]

43–4. ARBITRARY AND CAPRICIOUS TEST. In 1977, the Department of Transportation (DOT) adopted a passive-restraint standard (known as Standard 208) that required new cars to have either air bags or automatic seat belts. By 1981, it had become clear that all of the major auto manufacturers would install automatic seat belts to comply with this rule. The DOT determined that most purchasers of cars would detach their automatic seat belts, rendering them ineffective. Consequently, the department repealed the regulation. State Farm Mutual Automobile Insurance Co. and other insurance companies sued in the District of Columbia Circuit Court of Appeals for a review of the DOT's repeal of the regulation. That court held that the repeal was arbitrary and capricious because the DOT had reversed its rule without sufficient support. The motor vehicle manufacturers, which initially had wanted to avoid the costs associated with implementing Standard 208, then appealed this decision to the United States Supreme Court. What will result? Discuss fully. [*Motor Vehicle Manufacturers Association v. State Farm Mutual Automobile Insurance Co.*, 463 U.S. 29, 103 S.Ct. 2856, 77 L.Ed.2d 443 (1983)]

43–5. JUDICIAL REVIEW. American Message Centers (AMC) provides answering services to retailers. Calls to a retailer are automatically forwarded to AMC, which pays for the calls. AMC obtains telephone service at a discount from major carriers, including Sprint. Sprint's tariff (a public document setting out rates and rules relating to Sprint's services) states that the "subscriber shall be responsible for the payment of all charges for service." When AMC learned that computer hackers had obtained the access code for its lines and had made nearly $160,000 worth of long-distance calls, it asked Sprint to absorb the cost. Sprint refused. AMC filed a complaint with the Federal Communications Commission (FCC), claiming in part that Sprint's tariff was vague and ambiguous, in violation of the Communications Act of 1934 and FCC rules. These laws require that a carrier's tariff "clearly and definitely" specify any "exceptions or conditions which in any way affect the rates named in the tariff." The FCC rejected AMC's complaint. AMC appealed the FCC's decision to a federal appellate court, claiming that the FCC's decision to reject AMC's complaint was arbitrary and capricious. What should the court decide? Discuss fully. [*American Message Centers v. Federal Communications Commission*, 50 F.3d 35 (D.C.Cir. 1995)]

43–6. RULEMAKING. The Occupational Safety and Health Administration (OSHA) is part of the U.S. Department of Labor. OSHA issued a "Directive" under which each employer in selected industries was to be inspected unless it adopted a "Comprehensive Compliance Program (CCP)"—a safety and health program designed to meet standards that in some respects exceeded those otherwise required by law. The Chamber of Commerce of the United States objected to the Directive and filed a petition for review with the U.S. Court of Appeals for the District of Columbia Circuit. The Chamber claimed, in part, that OSHA did not use proper rulemaking procedures in issuing the Directive. OSHA argued that it was not required to follow those procedures because the Directive itself was a "rule of procedure." OSHA claimed that the rule did not "alter the rights or interests of parties, although it may alter the manner in which the parties present themselves or their viewpoints to the agency." What are the steps of the most commonly used rulemaking procedure? Which steps are missing in this case? In whose favor should the court rule, and why? [*Chamber of Commerce of the United States v. U.S. Department of Labor*, 174 F.3d 206 (D.C.Cir. 1999)]

43–7. ⚖ **CASE PROBLEM WITH SAMPLE ANSWER**

Riverdale Mills Corp. makes plastic-coated steel wire products in Northbridge, Massachusetts. Riverdale uses a water-based cleaning process that generates acidic and alkaline wastewater. To meet federal clean-water requirements, Riverdale has a system within its plant to treat the water. It then flows through a pipe that opens into a manhole-covered test pit outside the plant in full view of Riverdale's employees. Three hundred feet away, the pipe merges into the public sewer system. In October 1997, the U.S. Environmental Protection Agency (EPA) sent Justin Pimpare and Daniel Granz to inspect the plant. Without a search warrant and without Riverdale's express consent, the agents took samples from the test pit. Based on the samples, Riverdale and James Knott, the company's owner, were charged with criminal violations of the federal Clean Water Act. The defendants filed a suit in a federal district court against

the EPA agents and others, alleging violations of the Fourth Amendment. What right does the Fourth Amendment provide in this context? This right is based on a "reasonable expectation of privacy." Should the agents be held liable? Why or why not? [*Riverdale Mills Corp. v. Pimpare*, 392 F.3d 55 (1st Cir. 2004)]

To view a sample answer for this case problem, go to this book's Web site at http://wbl.westbuslaw.com, **select "Chapter 43," and click on "Case Problem with Sample Answer."**

43–8. ARBITRARY AND CAPRICIOUS TEST. Lion Raisins, Inc., is a family-owned, family-operated business that grows raisins and markets them to private enterprises. In the 1990s, Lion also successfully bid on more than fifteen contracts awarded by the U.S. Department of Agriculture (USDA). In May 1999, a USDA investigation reported that Lion appeared to have falsified inspectors' signatures, given false moisture content, and changed the grade of raisins on three USDA raisin certificates issued between 1996 and 1998. Lion was subsequently awarded five more USDA contracts. Then, in November 2000, the company was the low bidder on two new USDA contracts for school lunch programs. In January 2001, however, the USDA awarded these contracts to other bidders and, on the basis of the May 1999 report, suspended Lion from participating in government contracts for one year. Lion filed a suit in the U.S. Court of Federal Claims against the USDA, seeking, in part, lost profits on the school lunch contracts on the ground that the USDA's suspension was arbitrary and capricious. What reasoning might the court employ to grant a summary judgment in Lion's favor? [*Lion Raisins Inc. v. United States*, 51 Fed.Cl. 238 (2001)]

43–9. INVESTIGATION. Maureen Droge began working for United Air Lines, Inc. (UAL), as a flight attendant in 1990. In 1995, she was assigned to Paris, France, where she became pregnant. Because UAL does not allow its flight attendants to fly during their third trimester of pregnancy, Droge was placed on involuntary leave. She applied for temporary disability benefits through the French social security system, but her request was denied because UAL does not contribute to the French system on behalf of its U.S.-based flight attendants. Droge filed a charge of discrimination with the U.S. Equal Employment Opportunity Commission (EEOC), alleging that UAL had discriminated against her and other Americans. The EEOC issued a subpoena, asking UAL to detail all benefits received by all UAL employees living outside the United States. UAL refused to provide the information, in part on the grounds that it was irrelevant and compliance would be unduly burdensome. The EEOC filed a suit in a federal district court against UAL. Should the court enforce the subpoena? Why or why not? [*Equal Employment Opportunity Commission v. United Air Lines, Inc.*, 287 F.3d 643 (7th Cir. 2002)]

43–10. JUDICIAL CONTROLS. Under federal law, when accepting bids on a contract, an agency must hold "discussions" with all offerors. An agency may ask a single offeror for "clarification" of its proposal, however, without holding "discussions" with the others. Regulations define *clarifications* as "limited exchanges." In March 2001, the U.S. Air Force asked for bids on a contract. The winning contractor would examine, assess, and develop means of integrating national intelligence assets with the U.S. Department of Defense space systems, to enhance the capabilities of the Air Force's Space Warfare Center. Among the bidders were Information Technology and Applications Corp. (ITAC) and RS Information Systems, Inc. (RSIS). The Air Force asked the parties for more information on their subcontractors but did not allow them to change their proposals. Determining that there were weaknesses in ITAC's bid, the Air Force awarded the contract to RSIS. ITAC filed a suit in the U.S. Court of Federal Claims against the government, contending that the postproposal requests to RSIS, and its responses, were improper "discussions." Should the court rule in ITAC's favor? Why or why not? [*Information Technology & Applications Corp. v. United States*, 316 F.3d 1312 (Fed. Cir. 2003)]

LAW | on the Web

For updated links to resources available on the Web, as well as a variety of other materials, visit this text's Web site at http://wbl.westbuslaw.com.

To view the text of the Administrative Procedure Act of 1946, go to

http://www.fda.gov/opacom/laws/adminpro.html

The Internet Law Library contains links to federal and state regulatory materials, including the *Code of Federal Regulations*. This page can be found at

http://www.lawguru.com/ilawlib

LEGAL RESEARCH EXERCISES ON THE WEB

Go to http://wbl.westbuslaw.com, the Web site that accompanies this text. Select "Chapter 43" and click on "Internet Exercises." There you will find the following Internet research exercises that you can perform to learn more about topics covered in this chapter.

Activity 43–1: **LEGAL PERSPECTIVE**
The Freedom of Information Act

Activity 43–2: **MANAGEMENT PERSPECTIVE**
Agency Inspections

CHAPTER 44
Consumer Law

All statutes, agency rules, and common law judicial decisions that serve to protect the interests of consumers are classified as **consumer law.** Traditionally, in disputes involving consumers, it was assumed that the freedom to contract carried with it the obligation to live by the deal made. Over time, this attitude has changed considerably. Today, myriad federal and state laws protect consumers from unfair trade practices, unsafe products, discriminatory or unreasonable credit requirements, and other problems related to consumer transactions. Nearly every agency and department of the federal government has an office of consumer affairs, and most states have one or more such offices to help consumers. Also, typically the attorney general's office assists consumers at the state level.

In this chapter, we examine some of the major laws and regulations protecting consumers. Because of the wide variation among state consumer protection laws, our primary focus in this chapter is on federal legislation. Exhibit 44–1 indicates some of the types of consumer transactions that are regulated by federal laws.

SECTION 1 | Deceptive Advertising

One of the earliest federal consumer protection laws—and still one of the most important—was the Federal Trade Commission Act of 1914.[1] As mentioned in the preceding chapter, the act created the Federal Trade Commission (FTC) to carry out the broadly stated goal of preventing unfair and deceptive trade practices, including deceptive advertising.[2]

DECEPTIVE ADVERTISING DEFINED

Advertising will be deemed deceptive if a consumer would be misled by the advertising claim. Vague generalities and obvious exaggerations are permissible. These claims are known as *puffing*. When a claim takes on the appearance of literal authenticity, however, it may create problems. Advertising that *appears* to be based on factual evidence but in fact is not will be deemed deceptive.

Some advertisements contain "half-truths," meaning that the presented information is true but incomplete and therefore leads consumers to a false conclusion. For example, the makers of Campbell's soups advertised that "most" Campbell's soups were low in fat and cholesterol and thus were helpful in fighting heart disease. What the ad did not say was that Campbell's soups are high in sodium, and high-sodium diets may increase the risk of heart disease. The FTC ruled that Campbell's claims were thus deceptive. Advertising that contains an endorsement by a celebrity may be deemed deceptive if the celebrity does not actually use the product.

BAIT-AND-SWITCH ADVERTISING

The FTC has issued rules that govern specific advertising techniques. One of the most important rules is contained in the FTC's "Guides Against Bait Advertising,"[3] issued in 1968. The rule seeks to prevent **bait-and-switch advertising**—that is, advertising a very low price for a particular item that will likely be unavailable to the consumer, who will then be encouraged to purchase a more expensive item. The low price is the "bait" to lure the consumer into the store. The salesperson is instructed to "switch" the consumer to a

---

1. 15 U.S.C. Sections 41–58.
2. 15 U.S.C. Section 45.
3. 16 C.F.R. Part 238.

EXHIBIT 44-1 Selected Areas of Consumer Law Regulated by Statutes

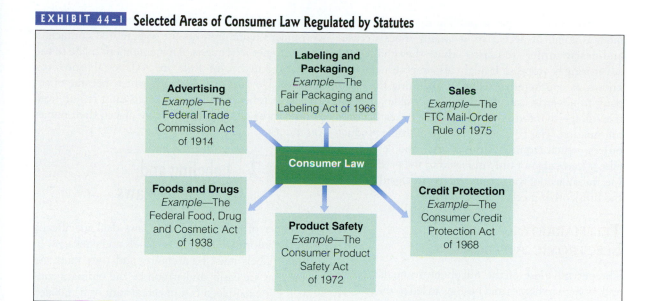

different, more expensive item. Under the FTC guidelines, bait-and-switch advertising occurs if the seller refuses to show the advertised item, fails to have a reasonable quantity of the item in stock, fails to promise to deliver the advertised item within a reasonable time, or discourages employees from selling the item.

ONLINE DECEPTIVE ADVERTISING

Deceptive advertising may occur in the online environment as well. For several years, the FTC has been quite active in monitoring online advertising and has identified hundreds of Web sites that have made false or deceptive advertising claims. These claims have concerned products ranging from medical treatments for various diseases to exercise equipment and weight-loss aids.

In 2000, the FTC issued new guidelines to help online businesses comply with existing laws prohibiting deceptive advertising.[4] The guidelines did not set forth new rules but rather described how existing laws apply to online advertising. Under the rules, generally any ads—online or offline—must be truthful and not misleading, and any claims made in an ad must be substantiated. Additionally, ads cannot be "unfair," defined in the guidelines as "caus[ing] or . . . likely to cause substantial consumer injury that consumers could not reasonably avoid and that is not outweighed by the benefit to consumers or competition."

The guidelines also call for "clear and conspicuous" disclosure of any qualifying or limiting information. The FTC suggests that advertisers should assume that consumers will not read an entire Web page. Therefore, to satisfy the "clear and conspicuous" requirement, online advertisers should place the disclosure as close as possible to the claim being qualified or include the disclosure within the claim itself. If such placement is not feasible, the next-best placement is on a section of the page to which a consumer can easily scroll. Generally, hyperlinks to a disclosure are recommended only for lengthy disclosures or for disclosures that must be repeated in a variety of locations on the Web page.

FTC ACTIONS AGAINST DECEPTIVE ADVERTISING

The FTC receives complaints from many sources, including competitors of alleged violators, consumers, consumer organizations, trade associations, Better Business Bureaus, government organizations, and state and local officials. If enough consumers complain and the complaints are widespread, the FTC will investigate the problem. If the FTC concludes that a given advertisement is unfair or deceptive, it drafts a formal complaint, which is sent to the alleged offender. The company may agree to settle the complaint without further proceedings, or the FTC can conduct a hearing in which the company can present its defense (see Chapter 43).

4. *Advertising and Marketing on the Internet: Rules of the Road*, September 2000.

If the FTC succeeds in proving that an advertisement is unfair or deceptive, it usually issues a **cease-and-desist order** requiring that the challenged advertising be stopped. It might also impose a sanction known as **counteradvertising** by requiring the company to advertise anew—in print, on radio, and on television—to inform the public about the earlier misinformation. The FTC may institute **multiple product orders,** which require a firm to cease and desist from false advertising not only in regard to the product that was the subject of the action but also in regard to all of the firm's other products.

TELEMARKETING AND ELECTRONIC ADVERTISING

The pervasive use of the telephone to market goods and services to homes and businesses led to the passage in 1991 of the Telephone Consumer Protection Act (TCPA).[5] The act prohibits telephone solicitation using an automatic telephone dialing system or a prerecorded voice. Most states also have laws regulating telephone solicitation. The TCPA also makes it illegal to transmit ads via fax without first obtaining the recipient's permission. (Similar issues have arisen with respect to junk e-mail, called "spam"—see Chapter 6.)

The act is enforced by the Federal Communications Commission and also provides for a private right of action. Consumers can recover any actual monetary loss resulting from a violation of the act or receive $500 in damages for each violation, whichever is greater. If a court finds that a defendant willfully or knowingly violated the act, the court has the discretion to treble (triple) the damages awarded.

The Telemarketing and Consumer Fraud and Abuse Prevention Act of 1994[6] directed the FTC to establish rules governing telemarketing and to bring actions against fraudulent telemarketers. The FTC's Telemarketing Sales Rule of 1995[7] requires a telemarketer, before making a sales pitch, to inform the recipient that the call is a sales call and to identify the seller's name and the product being sold. The rule makes it illegal for telemarketers to misrepresent information (including facts about their goods or services, for example). Additionally, telemarketers must inform the people they call of the total cost of the goods being sold, any restrictions on obtaining or using the goods, and whether a sale will be considered to be final and

nonrefundable. A telemarketer must also remove a consumer's name from its list of potential contacts if the customer so requests. An amendment made to the Telemarketing Sales Rule in 2002 established the national Do Not Call Registry, which became effective in October 2003. Telemarketers must refrain from calling those consumers who have placed their names on the list.

SECTION 2 | Labeling and Packaging Laws

A number of federal and state laws deal specifically with the information given on labels and packages. In general, labels must be accurate, and they must use words that are easily understood by the ordinary consumer. For example, a box of cereal cannot be labeled "giant" if that would exaggerate the amount of cereal contained in the box. In some instances, labels must specify the raw materials used in the product, such as the percentage of cotton, nylon, or other fiber used in a garment. In other instances, the product must carry a warning. Cigarette packages and advertising, for example, must include one of several warnings about the health hazards associated with smoking.[8] Some cigar manufacturers also have agreed to put warnings on the cigars they produce that are similar to what appears on cigarette packages.

FEDERAL STATUTES

Federal laws regulating the labeling and packaging of products include the Wool Products Labeling Act of 1939,[9] the Fur Products Labeling Act of 1951,[10] the Flammable Fabrics Act of 1953,[11] the Fair Packaging and Labeling Act of 1966,[12] the Comprehensive Smokeless Tobacco Health Education Act of 1986,[13] and the Nutrition Labeling and Education Act of 1990.[14] The Comprehensive Smokeless Tobacco Health Education Act, for example, requires that producers, packagers, and importers of smokeless tobacco label their product with one of several warnings about the health hazards associated with the use of smokeless

---

5. 47 U.S.C. Sections 227 *et seq.*

6. 15 U.S.C. Sections 6101–6108.

7. 16 C.F.R. Sections 310.1–310.8.

8. 15 U.S.C. Sections 1331–1341.

9. 15 U.S.C. Section 68.

10. 15 U.S.C. Section 69.

11. 15 U.S.C. Section 1191.

12. 15 U.S.C. Sections 1451 *et seq.*

13. 15 U.S.C. Sections 4401–4408.

14. 21 U.S.C. Section 343-1.

tobacco; the warnings are similar to those contained on other tobacco product packages.

FOOD LABELING

The Fair Packaging and Labeling Act requires that products carry labels that identify the product; the net quantity of the contents, as well as the quantity of servings, if the number of servings is stated; the manufacturer; and the packager or distributor. The act also authorizes requirements concerning words used to describe packages, terms that are associated with savings claims, information disclosures for ingredients in nonfood products, and standards for the partial filling of packages.

Food products must bear labels detailing nutritional content, including how much fat the food contains and what kind of fat it is. These restrictions are enforced by the Department of Health and Human Services, as well as the FTC. The Nutrition Labeling and Education Act of 1990 requires standard nutrition facts (including fat content) on food labels; regulates the use of such terms as *fresh* and *low fat;* and, subject to the federal Food and Drug Administration's approval, authorizes certain health claims.

SECTION 3 | Sales

Many of the laws that protect consumers concern the disclosure of certain terms in sales transactions and provide rules governing various forms of sales, such as door-to-door sales, mail-order sales, referral sales, and the unsolicited receipt of merchandise. Much of the federal regulation of sales is conducted by the FTC under its regulatory authority to curb unfair trade practices. Other federal agencies, however, are involved to various degrees. For example, the Federal Reserve Board of Governors has issued **Regulation Z**,[15] which governs credit provisions associated with sales contracts.

Many states have also enacted laws governing consumer sales transactions. Moreover, states have protected consumers to a certain extent through adopting the Uniform Commercial Code and, in some states, the Uniform Consumer Credit Code.

DOOR-TO-DOOR SALES

Door-to-door sales are singled out for special treatment in the laws of most states, in part because of the nature of the sales transaction. Repeat purchases are not as likely as they are in stores, so the seller has less incentive to cultivate the goodwill of the purchaser. Furthermore, the seller is unlikely to present alternative products and their prices. Thus, a number of states have passed "cooling-off" laws that permit the buyers of goods sold door to door to cancel their contracts within a specified period of time, usually two to three days after the sale.

An FTC regulation also requires sellers to give consumers three days to cancel any door-to-door sale. Because this rule applies in addition to the relevant state statutes, consumers are given the most favorable benefits of the FTC rule and their own state statutes. In addition, the FTC rule requires that consumers be notified in Spanish of this right if the oral negotiations for the sale were in that language.

TELEPHONE AND MAIL-ORDER SALES

Sales made by either telephone or mail order are the greatest source of complaints to the nation's Better Business Bureaus. To a certain extent, consumers are protected under federal laws prohibiting mail fraud, which were discussed in Chapter 9, and under state consumer protection laws that parallel and supplement the federal laws.

The FTC Mail or Telephone Order Merchandise Rule of 1993, which amended the FTC Mail-Order Rule of 1975,[16] provides specific protections for consumers who purchase goods via phone lines or through the mails. The 1993 rule extended the 1975 rule to include sales in which orders are transmitted by computer, fax machine, or some similar means involving telephone lines. Among other things, the rule requires mail-order merchants to ship orders within the time promised in their catalogues or advertisements, to notify consumers when orders cannot be shipped on time, and to issue a refund within a specified period of time when a consumer cancels an order.

In addition, the Postal Reorganization Act of 1970[17] provides that *unsolicited* merchandise sent by U.S. mail may be retained, used, discarded, or disposed of in any manner deemed appropriate, without the recipient's incurring any obligation to the sender.

ONLINE SALES

In recent years, the Internet has become a vehicle for a wide variety of business-to-consumer (B2C) sales transactions. Protecting consumers from fraudulent

---

15. 12 C.F.R. Sections 226.1–226.30.

16. 16 C.F.R. Sections 435.1–435.2.
17. 39 U.S.C. Section 3009.

and deceptive sales practices conducted via the Internet has proved to be a challenging task. Nonetheless, the FTC and other federal agencies have brought a number of enforcement actions against those who perpetrate online fraud. Additionally, the laws mentioned earlier, such as the federal statute prohibiting wire fraud, apply to online transactions.

Some states have amended their consumer protection statutes to cover Internet transactions as well. For example, the California legislature revised its Business and Professions Code to include transactions conducted over the Internet or by "any other electronic means of communication." Previously, that code covered only telephone, mail-order catalogue, radio, and television sales. Now any entity selling over the Internet in California must explicitly create an on-screen notice indicating its refund and return policies, where its business is physically located, its legal name, and a number of other details. Various states are also setting up information sites to help consumers protect themselves.

SECTION 4 | Credit Protection

Because of the extensive use of credit by American consumers, credit protection has become an especially important area regulated by consumer protection legislation. One of the most significant statutes regulating the credit and credit-card industries is Title I of the Consumer Credit Protection Act (CCPA),[18] which is commonly referred to as the Truth-in-Lending Act (TILA).

THE TRUTH-IN-LENDING ACT

The TILA is basically a *disclosure law*. It is administered by the Federal Reserve Board and requires sellers and lenders to disclose credit terms or loan terms so that individuals can shop around for the best financing arrangements. TILA requirements apply only to persons who, in the ordinary course of business, lend funds, sell on credit, or arrange for the extension of credit. Thus, sales or loans made between two consumers do not come under the protection of the act. Additionally, only debtors who are natural persons (as opposed to the artificial "person" of a corporation) are protected by this law; other legal entities are not.

The disclosure requirements are contained in Regulation Z, which, as mentioned earlier in this chapter, was promulgated by the Federal Reserve Board. If the contracting parties are subject to the TILA, the requirements of Regulation Z apply to any transaction involving an installment sales contract in which payment is to be made in more than four installments. Transactions subject to Regulation Z typically include installment loans, retail and installment sales, car loans, home-improvement loans, and certain real estate loans if the amount of financing is less than $25,000.

Under the provisions of the TILA, all of the terms of a credit instrument must be clearly and conspicuously disclosed. The TILA provides for contract rescission (cancellation) if a creditor fails to follow *exactly* the procedures required by the act.[19] TILA requirements are strictly enforced.

EQUAL CREDIT OPPORTUNITY In 1974, the Equal Credit Opportunity Act (ECOA)[20] was enacted as an amendment to the TILA. The ECOA prohibits the denial of credit solely on the basis of race, religion, national origin, color, gender, marital status, or age. The act also prohibits credit discrimination on the basis of whether an individual receives certain forms of income, such as public-assistance benefits.

Under the ECOA, a creditor may not require the signature of an applicant's spouse, other than as a joint applicant, on a credit instrument if the applicant qualifies under the creditor's standards of creditworthiness for the amount and terms of the credit request. Creditors are permitted to ask for any information from a credit applicant except information that could be used for the type of discrimination covered in the act or its amendments.

CREDIT-CARD RULES The TILA also contains provisions regarding credit cards. One provision limits the liability of a cardholder to $50 per card for unauthorized charges made before the creditor is notified that the card has been lost. Another provision prohibits a credit-card company from billing a consumer for any unauthorized charges if the credit card was improperly issued by the company; for example, if a consumer receives an unsolicited credit card in the mail and the

---

18. 15 U.S.C. Sections 1601–1693r.

19. Note, however, that amendments to the TILA enacted in 1995 prevent borrowers from rescinding loans for minor clerical errors in closing documents [15 U.S.C. Sections 1605, 1631, 1635, 1640, and 1641].

20. 15 U.S.C. Sections 1691–1691f.

card is later stolen and used by the thief to make purchases, the consumer to whom the card was sent will not be liable for the unauthorized charges.

Further provisions of the act concern billing disputes related to credit-card purchases. If a debtor thinks that an error has occurred in billing or wishes to withhold payment for a faulty product purchased by credit card, the act outlines specific procedures for both the consumer and the credit-card company to follow in settling the dispute.

CONSUMER LEASES The Consumer Leasing Act (CLA) of 1988[21] amended the TILA to provide protection for consumers who lease automobiles and other goods. The CLA applies to those who lease or arrange to lease consumer goods in the ordinary course of their business. The act applies only if the goods are priced at $25,000 or less and if the lease term exceeds four months. The CLA and its implementing regulation, Regulation M,[22] require lessors to disclose in writing all of the material terms of the lease.

THE FAIR CREDIT REPORTING ACT

In 1970, to protect consumers against inaccurate credit reporting, Congress enacted the Fair Credit Reporting Act (FCRA).[23] The act provides that consumer credit reporting agencies may issue credit reports to users only for specified purposes, including the extension of credit, the issuance of insurance policies, compliance with a court order, and in response to a consumer's request for a copy of his or her own credit report. The act further provides that whenever a consumer is denied credit or insurance on the basis of her or his

21. 15 U.S.C. Sections 1667–1667e.
22. 12 C.F.R. Part 213.
23. 15 U.S.C. Sections 1681–1681t.

credit report, or is charged more than others ordinarily would be for credit or insurance, the consumer must be notified of that fact and of the name and address of the credit reporting agency that issued the credit report.

CONSUMER ACCESS TO INFORMATION Under the FCRA, consumers may request the source of any information being given out by a credit agency, as well as the identity of anyone who has received an agency's report. Consumers are also permitted to access information about them contained in a credit reporting agency's files. If a consumer discovers that an agency's files contain inaccurate information about his or her credit standing, the agency, on the consumer's written request, must investigate the matter and delete any unverifiable or erroneous information within a reasonable period of time.

An agency that fails to comply with the act is liable for actual damages, plus additional damages not to exceed $1,000 and attorneys' fees.[24] Damages are also available from anyone who uses a credit report for an improper purpose, as well as from banks and other companies that report information to credit agencies and do not respond adequately to customer complaints.

REPORTING AGENCY MUST INVESTIGATE DISPUTED INFORMATION The agency's investigation should include contacting the creditor whose information a consumer disputes; the creditor, after receiving notice of the dispute, normally should conduct a "reasonable investigation" of its records to determine whether the disputed information can be verified. The question in the following case was exactly what constitutes a "reasonable investigation" by the creditor.

24. 15 U.S.C. Section 1681n.

United States
Court of Appeals,
Fourth Circuit. 2004.
357 F.3d 426.

CASE 44.1

Johnson v. MBNA America Bank, N.A.

WILLIAM W. WILKINS, Chief Judge:

MBNA America Bank, N.A. (MBNA) appeals a judgment entered against it following a jury verdict in favor of Linda Johnson in her action alleging that MBNA violated a provision of the Fair Credit Reporting Act (FCRA) by failing to conduct a reasonable investigation of Johnson's dispute concerning an MBNA account appearing on her credit report. * * *

* * * *

The account at issue, an MBNA MasterCard account, was opened in November 1987. The parties disagree regarding who applied for this account and therefore who was legally obligated to pay amounts owed on it. It is undisputed that one of the applicants was Edward N. Slater, whom Johnson married in March 1991. MBNA contends that Johnson was a co-applicant

CONTINUED

CASE 44.1 | Continued with Slater, and thus a co-obligor on the account. Johnson claims, however, that she was merely an authorized user and not a co-applicant.

In December 2000, Slater filed for bankruptcy, and MBNA promptly removed his name from the account. That same month, MBNA contacted Johnson and informed her that she was responsible for the approximately $17,000 balance on the account. * * * Johnson disputed the MBNA account with [consumer] credit reporting agencies. In response, each credit reporting agency [notified] MBNA * * * . In response * * * , MBNA * * * verified that the disputed information was correct. Based on MBNA's responses * * * , the credit reporting agencies continued reporting the MBNA account on Johnson's credit report.

Johnson subsequently sued MBNA [in a federal district court] * * * . [A] jury found that MBNA had negligently failed to comply with the FCRA, and it awarded Johnson $90,300 in actual damages. * * *

* * * *

MBNA argues that the language of [the FCRA] requiring furnishers of credit information to "conduct an investigation" regarding disputed information, imposes only a minimal duty on creditors to briefly review their records to determine whether the disputed information is correct. Stated differently, MBNA contends that this provision does not contain any qualitative component that would allow courts or juries to assess whether the creditor's investigation was reasonable. By contrast, Johnson asserts [the FCRA] requires creditors to conduct a reasonable investigation. * * *

* * * *

The key term at issue here, "investigation," is defined [in dictionaries] as "a detailed inquiry or systematic examination." Thus, the plain meaning of "investigation" clearly requires some degree of careful inquiry by creditors. Further, [the FCRA] uses the term "investigation" in the context of articulating a creditor's duties in the consumer dispute process * * * . It would make little sense to conclude that, in creating a system intended to give consumers a means to dispute—and, ultimately, correct—inaccurate information on their credit reports, Congress used the term "investigation" to include superficial, *unreasonable inquiries by creditors. We therefore hold that *[the FCRA] requires creditors, after receiving notice of a consumer dispute from a credit reporting agency, to conduct a reasonable investigation of their records to determine whether the disputed information can be verified.* [Emphasis added.]

* * * *

MBNA next contends that even if [the FCRA] requires creditors to conduct reasonable investigations of consumer disputes, no evidence here supports a determination * * * that MBNA's investigation of Johnson's dispute was unreasonable. * * *

* * * MBNA was notified of the specific nature of Johnson's dispute—namely, her assertion that she was not a co-obligor on the account. Yet MBNA's agents testified that their investigation was primarily limited to (1) confirming that the name and address listed on the [correspondence from the credit reporting agencies] were the same as the name and address contained in [MBNA's database] and (2) noting that the [database] contained a code indicating that Johnson was the sole responsible party on the account. The MBNA agents also testified that, in investigating consumer disputes generally, they do not look beyond the information contained in the [database] and never consult underlying documents such as account applications. Based on this evidence, a [court] could reasonably conclude that MBNA acted unreasonably in failing to verify the accuracy of the information contained in the [database].

* * * *

Additionally, MBNA argues that Johnson failed to establish that MBNA's allegedly inadequate investigation was the proximate cause of her damages because there were no other records MBNA could have examined that would have changed the results of its investigation. In particular, MBNA relies on testimony that * * * the original account application was no longer in MBNA's possession. Even accepting this testimony, however, a [court] could reasonably conclude that if the MBNA agents had investigated the matter further and determined that MBNA no longer had the application, they could have at least informed the credit reporting agencies that MBNA could not conclusively verify that Johnson was a co-obligor.

* * * *

For the reasons set forth above, we affirm the judgment of the district court.

CASE 44.1 | **Continued**

1. What should a consumer do, before applying for credit, to avoid disputes such as the confrontation that arose in the *Johnson* case?
2. What costs should be weighed in determining whether a creditor's investigation of a consumer's dispute is reasonable under the FCRA?

FAIR AND ACCURATE CREDIT TRANSACTIONS ACT

In an effort to combat identity theft (discussed in Chapter 9), Congress passed the Fair and Accurate Credit Transactions Act (FACT Act) of 2003.[25] The act established a national fraud alert system so that consumers who suspect that they have been or may be victimized by identity theft can place an alert on their credit files. The act also requires the major credit reporting agencies to provide consumers with a free copy of their own credit report every twelve months. Another provision requires account numbers on credit-card receipts to be shortened ("truncated") so that merchants, employees, or others who may have access to the receipts do not have access to the consumers' names and full credit-card numbers. The act further mandates that financial institutions work with the Federal Trade Commission to identify "red flag" indicators of identity theft and to develop rules on how to dispose of sensitive credit information.

The FACT Act gives consumers who have been victimized by identity theft some assistance in rebuilding their credit reputations. For example, credit reporting agencies must stop reporting allegedly fraudulent account information once the consumer establishes that identify theft has occurred. Business owners and creditors are required to provide consumers with copies of any records that can help the consumer prove that the particular account or transaction is fraudulent (a forged signature, for example). In addition, the act allows consumers to report the accounts affected by identity theft directly to creditors in order to help prevent the spread of erroneous credit information.

THE FAIR DEBT COLLECTION PRACTICES ACT

In 1977, Congress enacted the Fair Debt Collection Practices Act (FDCPA)[26] in an attempt to curb what were perceived to be abuses by collection agencies. The act applies only to specialized debt-collection agencies that regularly attempt to collect debts on behalf of someone else, usually for a percentage of the amount owed. Creditors attempting to collect debts are not covered by the act unless, by misrepresenting themselves, they cause debtors to believe they are collection agencies.

REQUIREMENTS UNDER THE ACT   The act explicitly prohibits a collection agency from using any of the following tactics:

1. Contacting the debtor at the debtor's place of employment if the debtor's employer objects.
2. Contacting the debtor during inconvenient or unusual times (for example, calling the debtor at three o'clock in the morning) or at any time if the debtor is being represented by an attorney.
3. Contacting third parties other than the debtor's parents, spouse, or financial adviser about payment of a debt unless a court authorizes such action.
4. Using harassment or intimidation (for example, using abusive language or threatening violence) or employing false or misleading information (for example, posing as a police officer).
5. Communicating with the debtor at any time after receiving notice that the debtor is refusing to pay the debt, except to advise the debtor of further action to be taken by the collection agency.

The FDCPA also requires a collection agency to include a **validation notice** whenever it initially contacts a debtor for payment of a debt or within five days of that initial contact. The notice must state that the debtor has thirty days within which to dispute the debt and to request a written verification of the debt from the collection agency. The debtor's request for debt validation must be in writing.

ENFORCEMENT OF THE ACT   The enforcement of the FDCPA is primarily the responsibility of the Federal Trade Commission. The act provides that a debt collector who fails to comply with the act is liable for actual damages, plus additional damages not to exceed $1,000[27] and attorneys' fees.

---

25. Pub. L. No. 108-159, 117 Stat. 1952 (December 4, 2003).
26. 15 U.S.C. Section 1692.

27. According to the U.S. Court of Appeals for the Sixth Circuit, the $1,000 limit on damages applies to each lawsuit, not to each violation. See *Wright v. Finance Service of Norwalk, Inc.*, 22 F.3d 647 (6th Cir. 1994).

Cases brought under the FDCPA often raise questions as to who qualifies as a debt collector or debt-collection agency subject to the act. For example, for several years it was not clear whether attorneys who attempted to collect debts owed to their clients were subject to the FDCPA's provisions. In 1995, the United States Supreme Court addressed this issue to resolve conflicting opinions in the lower courts. The Court held that an attorney who regularly tries to obtain payment of consumer debts through legal proceedings meets the FDCPA's definition of "debt collector."[28]

GARNISHMENT OF WAGES

Despite the increasing number of protections afforded debtors, creditors are not without means of securing payment on debts. One of these is the right to garnish a debtor's wages after the debt has gone unpaid for a prolonged period. Recall from Chapter 28 that *garnishment* is the legal procedure by which a creditor may collect on a debt by directly attaching, or seizing, a portion of the debtor's assets (such as wages) that are in the possession of a third party (such as an employer).

State law provides the basis for a process of garnishment, but the law varies among the states as to how easily garnishment can be obtained. Indeed, a few states, such as Texas, prohibit garnishment of wages except for child support and court-approved spousal maintenance. Constitutional due process and federal legislation under the TILA also provide certain protections against abuse.[29] In general, the debtor is entitled to notice and an opportunity to be heard in a process of garnishment. Moreover, wages cannot be garnished beyond 25 percent of the debtor's after-tax earnings, and the garnishment must leave the debtor with at least a specified minimum income.

SECTION 5 | Consumer Health and Safety

Laws discussed earlier regarding the labeling and packaging of products go a long way toward promoting consumer health and safety. But there is a significant distinction between regulating the information dispensed about a product and regulating the content of the product itself. The classic example is tobacco products. Tobacco products have not been altered by regu-lation or banned outright despite their obvious hazards. What has been regulated are the warnings that producers are required to give consumers about the hazards of tobacco.[30] This section focuses on laws that regulate the actual products made available to consumers.

THE FEDERAL FOOD, DRUG AND COSMETIC ACT

The first federal legislation regulating food and drugs was enacted in 1906 as the Pure Food and Drugs Act. That law, as amended in 1938, exists currently as the Federal Food, Drug and Cosmetic Act (FFDCA).[31] The act protects consumers against adulterated and misbranded foods and drugs. More recent amendments have added substantive and procedural requirements to the act. In its present form, the act establishes food standards, specifies safe levels of potentially hazardous food additives, and sets classifications of food and food advertising.

Most of these statutory requirements are monitored and enforced by the Food and Drug Administration (FDA). Under an extensive set of procedures established by the FDA, drugs must be shown to be effective as well as safe before they may be marketed to the public, and the use of some food additives suspected of being carcinogenic is prohibited. A 1976 amendment to the FFDCA[32] authorizes the FDA to regulate medical devices, such as pacemakers and other health devices and equipment, and to withdraw from the market any such device that is mislabeled.

THE CONSUMER PRODUCT SAFETY ACT

Consumer product-safety legislation began in 1953 with the passage of the Flammable Fabrics Act, which prohibits the sale of highly flammable clothing or materials. Over the next two decades, Congress enacted legislation regarding the design or composition of specific classes of products. Then, in 1972, Congress, by enacting the Consumer Product Safety Act,[33] created a comprehensive scheme of regulation over matters of consumer safety. The act also established the Consumer Product Safety Commission (CPSC), which has far-reaching authority over consumer safety.

---

28. *Heintz v. Jenkins*, 514 U.S. 291, 115 S.Ct. 1489, 131 L.Ed.2d 395 (1995).

29. 15 U.S.C. Sections 1671–1677.

30. We are ignoring recent civil litigation concerning the liability of tobacco product manufacturers for injuries that arise from the use of tobacco.

31. 21 U.S.C. Sections 301–393.

32. 21 U.S.C. Sections 352(o), 360(j), 360(k), and 360c–360k.

33. 15 U.S.C. Sections 2051–2083.

THE CPSC'S AUTHORITY The CPSC conducts research on the safety of individual consumer products, and it maintains a clearinghouse of information on the risks associated with various products. The Consumer Product Safety Act authorizes the CPSC to set standards for consumer products and to ban the manufacture and sale of any product that it deems to be potentially hazardous to consumers. The CPSC also has authority to remove from the market any products it believes to be imminently hazardous and to require manufacturers to report on any products already sold or intended for sale if the products have proved to be dangerous. The CPSC also has authority to administer other product-safety legislation, such as the Child Protection and Toy Safety Act of 1969[34] and the Federal Hazardous Substances Act of 1960.[35]

The CPSC's authority is sufficiently broad to allow it to ban any product that it believes poses an "unreasonable risk" to consumers. Some of the products that the CPSC has banned include various types of fireworks, cribs, and toys, as well as many products containing asbestos or vinyl chloride.

NOTIFICATION REQUIREMENTS The Consumer Product Safety Act requires the distributors of consumer products to notify immediately the CPSC on receipt of information that a product "contains a defect which . . . creates a substantial risk to the public" or "an unreasonable risk of serious injury or death." The following case illustrates the consequences of failing to fulfill this requirement.

---

34. This act consists of amendments to 15 U.S.C. Sections 1261, 1262, and 1274.

35. 15 U.S.C. Sections 1261–1277.

CASE 44.2 — United States v. Mirama Enterprises, Inc.

United States
Court of Appeals,
Ninth Circuit, 2004.
387 F.3d 983.

BACKGROUND AND FACTS *Mirama Enterprises, Inc., began operations in 1996 and today does business as Aroma Housewares Company from its headquarters in San Diego, California. Aroma imports a variety of electric kitchen appliances from China and Taiwan and distributes them to retailers in the United States and abroad. From 1996 until 1998, Aroma distributed a juice extractor, or juicer, made by a company in Taiwan, to retail stores throughout the United States. In early January 1998, Aroma received a complaint from a consumer whose juicer had broken. In February, consumer Richard Norton wrote Aroma to report that his juicer had shattered. In capital letters, Norton stated that the juicer*

> *SUDDENLY EXPLODED, THROWING WITH GREAT VIOLENCE PIECES OF THE CLEAR PLASTIC COVER AND SHREDS OF THE RAZOR-SHARP SEPARATOR SCREEN AS FAR AS EIGHT FEET IN MY KITCHEN. * * **

Over the next months, twenty-three complaints about exploding juicers, some of which caused injuries, were made by consumers including Jan Griffin, who added, "I feel that this juicer should be recalled, as it is very unsafe. The injuries that I suffered could have been a lot worse." In August, consumer Sylvia Mendoza filed a suit against Aroma, alleging injuries caused by a shattering juicer. On November 16, Aroma filed a report with the CPSC, which recalled the juicer on June 30, 1999. The federal government filed a suit against Mirama, seeking damages for its alleged failure to notify the CPSC of the danger earlier. The government filed a motion for summary judgment. The court ruled in the government's favor. Mirama appealed to the U.S. Court of Appeals for the Ninth Circuit.

IN THE LANGUAGE OF THE COURT

KOZINSKI, Circuit Judge:

* * * *

* * * [T]he [lower] court held that Aroma's failure to report each potentially dangerous product sold or distributed for sale to consumers was a separate offense, bringing the total number of offenses to somewhere between 30,000 and 40,000. The court ordered the company to pay $300,000 * * * .

Aroma does not contest liability; it challenges only the penalty * * * .

CONTINUED ▶

CASE 44.2 | **Continued**

* * * *

* * * Aroma suggests there is a single violation because only one product line is involved, albeit one of which there were numerous identical units sold. Alternatively, Aroma argues that it violated the reporting requirement at most twenty-three times—once for each failure to report a juicer that a consumer claimed had exploded. * * *

Initially, we consider Aroma's suggestion that "consumer product" in [the Consumer Product Safety Act (CPSA)] refers to the juicer model rather than to the individual units sold. This interpretation is problematic in view of the CPSA's penalty scheme, which imposes a small fine for each violation, capped at a much larger amount in the aggregate. The statutory cap necessarily contemplates that a single defect may affect a large number of products: Regardless of adjustments for inflation, the penalty caps out only after 250 violations. Aroma's interpretation would effectively render the cap meaningless. While a few product lines may share a common defect, it is almost inconceivable that 250 separate lines would possess the same defect. We will not presume that Congress adopted a statutory maximum that could never be reached.

Interpreting "consumer product" to refer to the product line also conflicts with the CPSA's definition of consumer product as "any *article*, or component part thereof, produced or distributed" for sale to or use by a consumer. The ordinary meaning of "article" refers to an individual member of a class (such as a unit of Aroma's juicer line), rather than the class (or product line) itself. *[The CPSA] thus requires that distributors report each individual unit about which they receive information that "reasonably supports the conclusion that such product * * * contains a defect which could create a substantial product hazard * * * or * * * creates an unreasonable risk of serious injury or death."* Accordingly [the CPSA's] provision that violations "shall constitute a separate offense with respect to each consumer product involved" means that a company commits a separate offense for every potentially dangerous unit it fails to report. [Emphasis added.]

* * * Aroma received consumer complaints for only twenty-three units. But the fact that some two dozen units malfunctioned in precisely the same way is evidence that those units share a common defect, which may affect each of the thousands of identical units Aroma distributed. Indeed, it would make little sense to focus only on the particular units discovered to be defective rather than those others that may possess the same flaw. * * *

Our interpretation is supported by the fact that consumer complaints are not the only source of information that can trigger [the CPSA's] reporting requirement. [Consumer Product Safety] Commission regulations note that "[s]uch information can include reports from experts, test reports, product liability lawsuits or claims, * * * quality control data, scientific or epidemiological studies, reports of injury, information from other firms or government entities, and other relevant information." Aroma's proposed reading would squeeze much of the juice out of the statute: Companies would have no incentive to report information that they obtained through their own testing or any source other than consumer complaints, even if it clearly suggested a risk of serious injury or death, because they would face no penalties for failing to report.

DECISION AND REMEDY *The U.S. Court of Appeals for the Ninth Circuit affirmed the lower court's judgment. "Aroma was required to report not merely the twenty-three juicers that shattered, but the 30,000 to 40,000 juicers in the stream of commerce that might well pose an unreasonable risk of serious injury to consumers. When it failed to do so, Aroma committed 30,000 to 40,000 reporting offenses."*

SECTION 6 | State Consumer Protection Laws

Thus far, our primary focus has been on federal legislation. State laws, however, often provide more sweeping and significant protections for the consumer than do federal laws. The warranty and unconscionability provisions of the Uniform Commercial Code (UCC—discussed in Chapters 20 through 23) offer important protections for consumers against unfair practices on the part of sellers and lessors. The Magnuson-Moss Warranty Act, which was discussed in Chapter 23, supplements the UCC provisions in cases involving both a consumer transaction of at least $10 and an express written warranty.

Far less widely adopted than the UCC is the Uniform Consumer Credit Code (UCCC). The UCCC has provisions concerning truth in lending, maximum credit ceilings, door-to-door sales, fine-print clauses, and other practices affecting consumer transactions.

Virtually all states have specific consumer protection acts, often titled "deceptive trade practices acts." Although these statutes vary widely, a common thread runs through most of them. Typically, state consumer protection laws are directed at deceptive trade practices, such as a seller's provision of false or misleading information to consumers. As just mentioned, some of the legislation provides broad protection for consumers. A prime example is the Texas Deceptive Trade Practices Act of 1973, which forbids a seller from selling to a buyer anything that the buyer does not need or cannot afford.

In California, in the 1950s, unscrupulous promoters were misrepresenting their services to exact unjustified payments from property owners for real estate transactions. Therefore, in 1959 the state restricted the collection of "advance fees" to those with state-issued licenses, except for "newspapers of general circulation," which were found not to have engaged in any fraud. In the following case, the court considered whether this interpretation could be applied to an out-of-state, Internet-based service.

CASE 44.3   ForSaleByOwner.com v. Zinnemann

United States
District Court,
Eastern District
of California, 2004.
347 F.Supp.2d 868.

BACKGROUND AND FACTS *ForSaleByOwner.com (FSBO) advertises residential real property for sale. FSBO charges a flat fee to owners to advertise their homes. The Web site lists the properties in a nationwide database that prospective buyers can view at no charge. FSBO also provides information about home sales, crime, schools, costs of living in specific locales, mortgage payments, and interest rates. To providers of related services (home-improvement contractors and others), FSBO sells listings in an online directory. FSBO is not a real estate agent, and proclaims on its site that it is "legally prohibited from taking part in the actual sales transaction of any of the properties." Under California Business and Professions Code Section 10130, it is unlawful for any person or company to act as a real estate broker without first obtaining a state license. Sections 10026, 10131, and 10131.2 define* real estate broker *to include anyone—except newspapers—who, for an "advance fee," lists residential real property for sale. FSBO filed a suit in a federal district court against Paula Zinnemann, Commissioner of the California Department of Real Estate, and others, claiming that this statute violated FSBO's rights under the First Amendment to the U.S. Constitution. FSBO filed a motion for summary judgment.*

IN THE LANGUAGE OF THE COURT

ENGLAND, District Judge.
 *   *   *   *

FSBO argues that California's real estate licensing laws *   *   * "single out" publishers of real estate advertising and information, like FSBO, for a burden the state places on no other speech and is directed only at works with a specified content. FSBO contends that publishers of other sales magazines or websites for different products (like automobiles, jewelry or boats, for instance) are not required to be licensed, and even more significantly argues that newspapers *   *   * are exempt from real estate licensing requirements despite the fact that they offer services virtually identical to those provided by FSBO. According to FSBO, this *differential treatment is unconstitutional unless the State's regulation is necessary to serve a compelling state interest and is narrowly drawn to achieve that end.* [Emphasis added.]

FSBO's argument that [the statute] unconstitutionally discriminates based on media type is persuasive. The Court agrees that California's real estate licensing scheme impermissibly differentiates between certain types of publications carrying the same basic content. *   *   * Given the uncontroverted fact that FSBO's activities are virtually identical to those pursued online by California newspapers, the distinction drawn between the two publishing mediums appears wholly arbitrary.

 *   *   *   *

CONTINUED ▶

CASE 44.3 | Continued

* * * Indeed, given the fact that the online newspaper services and the FSBO website are virtually identical, there appears to be no justification whatsoever for any distinction between the two mediums. Even if a distinction was warranted in 1959, when the statute was amended to include the newspaper exemption, that does not mean that the same rationale for exempting newspapers remains viable in 2004, given the vast advances in technology that have occurred in the meantime.

As FSBO points out, if use of the Internet itself justifies state regulation, that would logically suggest that both online newspaper services and websites like FSBO's should be equally restricted. Instead, however, online newspaper advertising for real property is not subject to licensing, whereas the very same information disseminated by FSBO requires a real estate broker's license. That license entails substantial coursework requirements as well as passage of a rigorous broker's exam. Defendants have simply shown no compelling need why such requirements must be satisfied in the case of FSBO but need not be adhered to by newspapers.

* * * Defendants suggest that FSBO accepts fees from mortgage brokers for business generated through a website referral process, despite the fact that no such referral service is even available on the FSBO website for users in California. The only other specific activity targeted by Defendants concerns referral fees paid by FSBO for customers directed through other websites.

Defendants have not demonstrated that these arrangements are improper, or that licensing will do anything to prevent or regulate any resulting improprieties. Defendants make no effort to show how regulating such activities constitutes a compelling state interest, not to mention whether requiring FSBO to obtain a broker's license is a remedy narrowly tailored to address such an interest. Otherwise, while Defendants vaguely attempt to paint newspapers as geographically situated and relatively more stable than Internet companies, they have not established why this should require websites like FSBO's to obtain a California broker's license as a prerequisite to listing properties for sale, when online services doing exactly the same thing are not subject to any licensing requirement so long as they are operated by a "newspaper." Defendants provide no reasonable explanation whatsoever for this differential treatment, let alone a compelling interest to justify it.

DECISION AND REMEDY   *The court granted FSBO's motion for summary judgment. The court reasoned that the California statute, as applied to FSBO, was unconstitutional, based on the "disparity of treatment" between newspapers and Web sites such as that of FSBO. The defendants failed to show "any compelling state interest" for requiring FSBO to obtain a broker's license, while identical online services were exempt if newspapers operated them.*

WHAT IF THE FACTS WERE DIFFERENT?   *If newspapers published real estate listings only in print and did not provide the same services as FSBO online, would the result have been different?*

REVIEWING CONSUMER LAW

Tonja Sage saw a local motorcycle dealer's newspaper advertisement for a MetroRider EZ electric scooter for $1,699. When she met the salesperson at the dealership, however, she learned that the EZ model had been sold out. The salesperson told Sage that he still had the higher-end MetroRider FX model in stock for $2,199 and would offer her one for $1,999. Sage was disappointed but decided to purchase the FX model. Sage told the sales representative that she wished to purchase the scooter on credit and was directed to the dealer's credit department. As she filled out the credit forms, the clerk told Sage, an African American female, that she would need a cosigner to obtain a loan. Sage could not understand why she would need a cosigner and asked to speak to the store manager. The manager apologized, told her that the clerk was mistaken, and said that he would "speak to"

REVIEWING CONSUMER LAW *(continued)*

the clerk about that. The manager completed Sage's credit application, and Sage then rode the scooter home. Seven months later, Sage received a letter from the manufacturer informing her that a flaw had been discovered in the scooter's braking system and that the model had been recalled. Using the information presented in the chapter, answer the following questions.

1. Had the dealer engaged in deceptive advertising? If so, what form of deceptive advertising was involved? What may the Federal Trade Commission (FTC) order the dealer to do if the ad proved deceptive?

2. Suppose that Sage had ordered the scooter through the dealer's Web site but the dealer had been unable to deliver it by the date promised. What would the merchant be required to do, and what FTC regulation requires the merchant to do it?

3. Assuming that the clerk had required a cosigner based on Sage's race or gender, what act prohibits such credit discrimination?

4. The safety of the scooter is regulated by what organization? How?

TERMS AND CONCEPTS TO REVIEW

bait-and-switch advertising 888

cease-and-desist order 890

consumer law 888

counteradvertising 890

multiple product orders 890

Regulation Z 891

validation notice 895

QUESTIONS AND CASE PROBLEMS

44–1. Andrew, a resident of California, received an advertising circular in the U.S. mail announcing a new line of regional cookbooks distributed by the Every-Kind Cookbook Co. Andrew didn't want any books and threw the circular away. Two days later, Andrew received in the mail an introductory cookbook entitled *Lower Mongolian Regional Cookbook,* as announced in the circular, on a "trial basis" from Every-Kind. Andrew was not interested but did not go to the trouble to return the cookbook. Every-Kind demanded payment of $20.95 for the *Lower Mongolian Regional Cookbook.* Discuss whether Andrew can be required to pay for the book.

44–2. Maria Ochoa receives two new credit cards on May 1. She had solicited one of them from Midtown Department Store, and the other arrived unsolicited from High-Flying Airlines. During the month of May, Ochoa makes numerous credit-card purchases from Midtown Department Store, but she does not use the High-Flying Airlines card. On May 31, a burglar breaks into Ochoa's home and steals both credit cards, along with other items. Ochoa notifies the Midtown Department Store of the theft on June 2, but she fails to notify High-Flying Airlines. Using the Midtown credit

card, the burglar makes a $500 purchase on June 1 and a $200 purchase on June 3. The burglar then charges a vacation flight on the High-Flying Airlines card for $1,000 on June 5. Ochoa receives the bills for these charges and refuses to pay them. Discuss Ochoa's liability in these situations.

44–3. QUESTION WITH SAMPLE ANSWER

On June 28, a salesperson for Renowned Books called on the Gonchars at their home. After a very persuasive sales pitch by the agent, the Gonchars agreed in writing to purchase a twenty-volume set of historical encyclopedias from Renowned Books for a total of $299. A down payment of $35 was required, with the remainder of the cost to be paid in monthly payments over a one-year period. Two days later the Gonchars, having second thoughts, contacted the book company and stated that they had decided to rescind the contract. Renowned Books said this would be impossible. Has Renowned Books violated any consumer law by not allowing the Gonchars to rescind their contract? Explain.

For a sample answer to this question, go to Appendix I at the end of this text.

44–4. EQUAL CREDIT OPPORTUNITY. The Riggs National Bank of Washington, D.C., loaned more than $11 million to Samuel Linch and Albert Randolph. To obtain the loan, Linch and Randolph provided personal financial statements. Linch's statement included substantial assets that he owned jointly with his wife, Marcia. As a condition of the loan, Riggs required that Marcia, as well as Samuel and Albert, sign a personal guaranty for repayment. When the borrowers defaulted, Riggs filed a suit in a federal district court to recover its funds, based on the personal guaranties. The court ruled against the borrowers, who appealed. On what basis might the borrowers argue that Riggs violated the Equal Credit Opportunity Act? [*Riggs National Bank of Washington, D.C. v. Linch*, 36 F.3d 370 (4th Cir. 1994)]

44–5. DEBT COLLECTION. Equifax A.R.S., a debt-collection agency, sent Donna Russell a notice about one of her debts. The front of the notice stated that "[i]f you do not dispute this claim (see reverse side) and wish to pay it within the next 10 days we will not post this collection to your file." The reverse side set out Russell's rights under the Fair Debt Collection Practices Act (FDCPA), including that she had thirty days to decide whether to contest the claim. Russell filed a suit in a federal district court against Equifax. The court ruled against Russell, who appealed. On what basis might Russell argue that Equifax violated the FDCPA? [*Russell v. Equifax A.R.S.*, 74 F.3d 30 (2d Cir. 1996)]

44–6. FAIR DEBT COLLECTION. CrossCheck, Inc., provides check-authorization services to retail merchants. When a customer presents a check, the merchant contacts CrossCheck, which estimates the probability that the check will clear the bank. If the check is within an acceptable statistical range, CrossCheck notifies the merchant. If the check is dishonored, the merchant sends it to CrossCheck, which pays it. CrossCheck then attempts to redeposit the check. If this fails, CrossCheck takes further steps to collect the amount. CrossCheck attempts to collect on more than two thousand checks per year and spends $2 million on these efforts, which involve about 7 percent of its employees and 6 percent of its total expenses. William Winterstein took his truck to C&P Auto Service Center, Inc., for a tune-up and paid for the service with a check. C&P contacted CrossCheck and, on its recommendation, accepted the check. When the check was dishonored, C&P mailed it to CrossCheck, which reimbursed C&P and sent a letter to Winterstein requesting payment. Winterstein filed a suit in a federal district court against CrossCheck, asserting that the letter violated the Fair Debt Collection Practices Act. CrossCheck filed a motion for summary judgment. On what ground might the court grant the motion? Explain. [*Winterstein v. CrossCheck, Inc.*, 149 F.Supp.2d 466 (N.D.Ill. 2001)]

44–7. ⚖ **CASE PROBLEM WITH SAMPLE ANSWER**

Source One Associates, Inc., is based in Poughquag, New York. Peter Easton, Source One's president, is responsible for its daily operations. Between 1995 and 1997, Source One received requests from persons in Massachusetts seeking financial information about individuals and businesses. To obtain this information, Easton first obtained the targeted individuals' credit reports through Equifax Consumer Information Services by claiming the reports would be used only in connection with credit transactions involving the consumers. From the reports, Easton identified financial institutions at which the targeted individuals held accounts and then called the institutions to learn the account balances by impersonating either officers of the institutions or the account holders. The information was then provided to Source One's customers for a fee. Easton did not know why the customers wanted the information. The state ("Commonwealth") of Massachusetts filed a suit in a Massachusetts state court against Source One and Easton, alleging, among other things, violations of the Fair Credit Reporting Act (FCRA). Did the defendants violate the FCRA? Explain. [*Commonwealth v. Source One Associates, Inc.*, 436 Mass. 118, 763 N.E.2d 42 (2002)]

To view a sample answer for this case problem, go to this book's Web site at http://wbl.westbuslaw.com, select "Chapter 44," and click on "Case Problem with Sample Answer."

44–8. DECEPTIVE ADVERTISING. "Set up & Ready to Make Money in Minutes Guaranteed!" the ads claimed. "The Internet Treasure Chest (ITC) will give you everything you need to start your own exciting Internet business including your own worldwide website all for the unbelievable price of only $59.95." The ITC "contains virtually everything you need to quickly and easily get your very own worldwide Internet business up, running, stocked with products, able to accept credit cards and ready to take orders almost immediately." What ITC's marketers—Damien Zamora and end70 Corp.—did not disclose were the significant additional costs required to operate the business: domain name registration fees, monthly Internet access and hosting charges, monthly fees to access the ITC product warehouse, and other "upgrades." The Federal Trade Commission filed a suit in a federal district court against end70 and Zamora, seeking an injunction and other relief. Are the defendants' claims "deceptive advertising"? If so, what might the court order the defendants to do to correct any misrepresentations? [*Federal Trade Commission v. end70 Corp.*, __ F.Supp.2d __ (N.D.Tex. 2003)]

44–9. ⚖ **A QUESTION OF ETHICS**

One of the products that McDonald's Corp. sells is the Happy Meal®, which consists of a McDonald's food entree, a small order of French fries, a small drink, and a toy. In the early 1990s, McDonald's began to aim its Happy Meal® marketing at children aged one to three. In 1995, McDonald's began making nutritional information for its food products available in documents known as "McDonald's Nutrition Facts." Each document lists each food item that the restaurant serves and provides a nutritional breakdown, but the Happy Meal® is not included. Marc Cohen filed a suit in an Illinois state court against McDonald's, alleging in part that the defendant violated a state law prohibiting consumer fraud and deceptive business practices by failing to adhere to the Nutrition Labeling and Education Act of 1990 (NLEA). The court dismissed the suit, and Cohen appealed to a state intermediate appellate court, which affirmed the dismissal, holding that the NLEA preempted the plaintiff's claims. In view of these facts, consider the following questions. [*Cohen v. McDonald's Corp.*, 347 Ill.App.3d 627, 808 N.E.2d 1, 283 Ill.Dec. 451 (1 Dist. 2004)]

(a) What does the NLEA provide? Under these provisions, the NLEA sets out different requirements for products specifically intended for children under the age of four. Does this make sense? Is this ethical? Why or why not?

(b) Because the federal government has not established certain requirements for children under age four,

there are no regulations under the NLEA for reporting these requirements. Should a state court impose such regulations? Explain.

44–10. VIDEO QUESTION

Go to this text's Web site at **http://blt.westbuslaw.com** and select "Chapter 44." Click on "Video Questions" and view the video titled *Advertising Communication Law: Bait and Switch*. Then answer the following questions.

(a) Is the auto dealership's advertisement for the truck in the video deceptive? Why or why not?

(b) Is the advertisement for the truck an offer to which the dealership is bound? Does it matter if Betty detrimentally relied on the advertisement?

(c) Is Tony committed to buying Betty's trade-in truck for $3,000 because that is what he told her over the phone?

LAW | on the Web

For updated links to resources available on the Web, as well as a variety of other materials, visit this text's Web site at **http://wbl.westbuslaw.com**.

For a government-sponsored Web site containing reports on consumer issues, go to

http://www.consumer.com

The FTC's Web site offers extensive information on consumer protection laws, consumer problems, enforcement issues, and other topics relevant to consumer law. Go to

http://www.ftc.gov

and click on "Consumer Protection."

To learn more about the FTC's "cooling-off" rule, you can access it directly by going to the following URL:

http://www.ftc.gov/bcp/conline/pubs/buying/cooling.htm

LEGAL RESEARCH EXERCISES ON THE WEB

Go to **http://wbl.westbuslaw.com**, the Web site that accompanies this text. Select "Chapter 44" and click on "Internet Exercises." There you will find the following Internet research exercises that you can perform to learn more about topics covered in this chapter.

Activity 44–1: LEGAL PERSPECTIVE
The Food and Drug Administration

Activity 44–2: MANAGEMENT PERSPECTIVE
Internet Advertising and Marketing

CHAPTER 45
Environmental Law

Concerns over the degradation of the environment have increased over time in response to the environmental effects of population growth, urbanization, and industrialization. Environmental protection is not without a price, however. For many businesses, the costs of complying with environmental regulations are high, and for some they are too high. A constant tension exists between the desire to increase profits and productivity and the need to protect the environment. In this chapter, we discuss **environmental law,** which consists of all laws and regulations designed to protect and preserve our environmental resources.

SECTION 1 | Common Law Actions

Common law remedies against environmental pollution originated centuries ago in England. Those responsible for operations that created dirt, smoke, noxious odors, noise, or toxic substances were sometimes held liable under common law theories of nuisance or negligence. Today, injured individuals continue to rely on the common law to obtain damages and injunctions against business polluters.

NUISANCE

Under the common law doctrine of **nuisance,** persons may be held liable if they use their property in a manner that unreasonably interferes with others' rights to use or enjoy their own property. In these situations, courts commonly balance the equities between the harm caused by the pollution and the costs of stopping it.

Courts have often denied injunctive relief on the ground that the hardships that would be imposed on the polluter and on the community are greater than the hardships suffered by the plaintiff. For example, a factory that causes neighboring landowners to suffer from smoke, dirt, and vibrations may be left in operation if it is the core of a local economy. The injured parties may be awarded only money damages. These damages may include compensation for the decline in the value of their property as a result of the factory's operation.

A property owner may be given relief from pollution if he or she can identify a distinct harm separate from that affecting the general public. This harm is referred to as a "private" nuisance. Under the common law, citizens were denied standing (access to the courts—see Chapter 2) unless they suffered a harm distinct from the harm suffered by the public at large. Some states still require this. For example, in one case a group of individuals who made their living by commercial fishing in a major river in New York filed a suit seeking damages and an injunction against a company that was polluting the river. The New York court found that the plaintiffs had standing because they were particularly harmed by the pollution in the river.[1] A public authority (such as a state's attorney general), however, can sue to abate a "public" nuisance.

NEGLIGENCE AND STRICT LIABILITY

An injured party may sue a business polluter in tort under the negligence and strict liability theories discussed in Chapters 6 and 7. The basis for a negligence action is a business's alleged failure to use reasonable care toward a party whose injury was foreseeable and was caused by the lack of reasonable care. For example, employees might sue an employer whose failure to use proper pollution controls contaminated the air, causing the employees to suffer respiratory illnesses. A developing area of tort law involves **toxic torts**—actions against toxic polluters.

---

1. *Lee v. General Electric Co.,* 538 N.Y.S.2d 844, 145 A.D.2d 291 (1989).

Businesses that engage in ultrahazardous activities—such as the transportation of radioactive materials—are strictly liable for whatever injuries the activities cause. In a strict liability action, the injured party need not prove that the business failed to exercise reasonable care.

SECTION 2 | Federal, State, and Local Regulation

All levels of government in the United States regulate some aspect of the environment. In this section, we look at some of the ways in which the federal, state, and local governments control business activities and land use in the interests of environmental preservation and protection.

FEDERAL REGULATION

Congress has passed a number of statutes to control the impact of human activities on the environment. Exhibit 45–1 lists and summarizes the major federal environmental statutes discussed in this chapter. Some of these statutes were passed in an attempt to improve air and water quality. Others specifically regulate toxic chemicals, including pesticides, herbicides, and hazardous wastes.

EXHIBIT 45–1 Major Federal Environmental Statutes

POPULAR NAME	PURPOSE	STATUTE REFERENCE
Rivers and Harbors Appropriations Act (1899)	To prohibit ships and manufacturers from discharging and depositing refuse in navigable waterways.	33 U.S.C. Sections 401–418.
Federal Insecticide, Fungicide, and Rodenticide Act (1947)	To control the use of pesticides and herbicides.	7 U.S.C. Sections 136–136y.
Federal Water Pollution Control Act (1948)	To eliminate the discharge of pollutants from major sources into navigable waters.	33 U.S.C. Sections 1251–1387.
Clean Air Act (1963)	To control air pollution from mobile and stationary sources.	42 U.S.C. Sections 7401–7671q.
National Environmental Policy Act (1969)	To limit environmental harm from federal government activities.	42 U.S.C. Sections 4321–4370d.
Endangered Species Act (1973)	To protect species that are threatened with extinction.	16 U.S.C. Sections 1531–1544.
Safe Drinking Water Act (1974)	To regulate pollutants in public drinking water systems.	42 U.S.C. Sections 300f to 300j-25.
Resource Conservation and Recovery Act (1976)	To establish standards for hazardous waste disposal.	42 U.S.C. Sections 6901–6986.
Toxic Substances Control Act (1976)	To regulate toxic chemicals and chemical compounds.	15 U.S.C. Sections 2601–2692.
Comprehensive Environmental Response, Compensation, and Liability Act (1980)	To regulate the clean-up of hazardous waste–disposal sites.	42 U.S.C. Sections 9601–9675.
Oil Pollution Act (1990)	To establish liability for the clean-up of navigable waters after oil-spill disasters.	33 U.S.C. Sections 2701–2761.
Small Business Liability Relief and Brownfields Revitalization Act (2002)	To allow developers who comply with state voluntary clean-up programs to avoid federal liability for the properties that they decontaminate and develop.	42 U.S.C. Section 9628.

REGULATORY AGENCIES The most well known of the federal agencies regulating environmental law is the Environmental Protection Agency (EPA), which was created in 1970 to coordinate federal environmental responsibilities. Other federal agencies with authority for regulating specific environmental matters include the Department of the Interior, the Department of Defense, the Department of Labor, the Food and Drug Administration, and the Nuclear Regulatory Commission. These regulatory agencies—and all other agencies of the federal government—must take environmental factors into consideration when making significant decisions.

Most federal environmental laws provide that citizens can sue to enforce environmental regulations if government agencies fail to do so—or can sue to protest agency enforcement actions if they believe that these actions go too far. Typically, a threshold hurdle in such suits is meeting the requirements for standing to sue (see Chapter 2).

State and local regulatory agencies also play a significant role in carrying out federal environmental legislation. Typically, the federal government relies on state and local governments to implement federal environmental statutes and regulations such as those regulating air quality.

ENVIRONMENTAL IMPACT STATEMENTS The National Environmental Policy Act (NEPA) of 1969[2] requires that an **environmental impact statement (EIS)** be prepared for every major federal action that significantly affects the quality of the environment. An EIS must analyze (1) the impact on the environment that the action will have, (2) any adverse effects on the environment and alternative actions that might be taken, and (3) irreversible effects the action might generate.

An action qualifies as "major" if it involves a substantial commitment of resources (monetary or otherwise). An action is "federal" if a federal agency has the power to control it. Construction by a private developer of a ski resort on federal land, for example, may require an EIS. Building or operating a nuclear plant, which requires a federal permit, or constructing a dam as part of a federal project requires an EIS. If an agency decides that an EIS is unnecessary, it must issue a statement supporting this conclusion. EISs have become instruments for private citizens, consumer interest groups, businesses, and others to challenge federal agency actions on the basis that the actions improperly threaten the environment.

STATE AND LOCAL REGULATION

Many states regulate the degree to which the environment may be polluted. Thus, for example, even when state zoning laws permit a business's proposed development, the proposal may have to be altered to lessen the development's impact on the environment. State laws may restrict a business's discharge of chemicals into the air or water or regulate its disposal of toxic wastes. States may also regulate the disposal or recycling of other wastes, including glass, metal, and plastic containers and paper. Additionally, states may restrict the emissions from motor vehicles.

City, county, and other local governments oversee certain aspects of the environment. For instance, local zoning laws control some land use. These laws may be designed to inhibit or direct the growth of cities and suburbs or to protect the natural environment. In the interest of safeguarding the environment, such laws may prohibit certain land uses. One of the issues subject to ongoing debate is whether landowners should be compensated when restrictions are placed on the use of their property.

Other aspects of the environment may also be subject to local regulation. Methods of waste and garbage removal and disposal, for example, can have a substantial impact on a community. The appearance of buildings and other structures, including advertising signs and billboards, may affect traffic safety, property values, or local aesthetics. Noise generated by a business or its customers may be annoying, disruptive, or damaging to its neighbors. The location and condition of parks, streets, and other public uses of land subject to local control affect the environment and can also affect business.

SECTION 3 | Air Pollution

Federal involvement with air pollution goes back to the 1950s, when Congress authorized funds for air-pollution research. In 1963, the federal government passed the Clean Air Act,[3] which focused on multi-state air pollution and provided assistance to the states. Various amendments, particularly in 1970,

2. 42 U.S.C. Sections 4321–4370d.

3. 42 U.S.C. Sections 7401–7671q.

1977, and 1990, strengthened the government's authority to regulate air quality. These laws provide the basis for issuing regulations to control pollution coming primarily from mobile sources (such as automobiles) and stationary sources (such as electric utilities and industrial plants).

MOBILE SOURCES

Automobiles and other vehicles are referred to as mobile sources of pollution. The EPA has issued regulations specifying standards for mobile sources of pollution, as well as for service stations. The agency periodically updates these standards in light of new developments and data.

MOTOR VEHICLES Regulations governing air pollution from automobiles and other mobile sources specify pollution standards and time schedules for meeting these standards. For example, the 1990 amendments to the Clean Air Act required automobile manufacturers to cut new automobiles' exhaust emissions of nitrogen oxide by 60 percent and emissions of other pollutants by 35 percent. By 1998, all new automobiles had to meet this standard. Regulations that became effective beginning with 2004 model cars called for nitrogen oxide tailpipe emissions to be cut by nearly 10 percent by 2007. For the first time, sport utility vehicles (SUVs) and light trucks were required to meet the same emission standards as automobiles.

UPDATING POLLUTION-CONTROL STANDARDS As mentioned, the EPA attempts to update pollution-control standards when new scientific information becomes available. For example, some studies conducted in the 1990s claimed that very small particles (2.5 microns, or millionths of a meter) of soot affect our health as significantly as larger particles. Based on this evidence, the EPA issued new particulate standards for motor vehicle exhaust systems and other sources of pollution in 1996. The EPA also set a more rigorous acceptable standard for ozone, which is formed when sunlight combines with pollutants from cars and other sources. Ozone is the basic ingredient of smog.

The EPA's particulate standards and ozone standard were challenged in court by a number of business groups. These groups contended that the EPA had exceeded its authority under the Clean Air Act by issuing the stricter rules. Additionally, the groups claimed that the EPA had to take economic costs into

account when developing new regulations. In 2000, however, the United States Supreme Court upheld the EPA's authority under the Clean Air Act to issue the standards. The Court also held that the EPA did not have to take economic costs into account when creating new rules.[4]

STATIONARY SOURCES

The Clean Air Act also authorizes the EPA to establish air-quality standards for stationary sources (such as manufacturing plants) but recognizes that the primary responsibility for implementing these standards rests with state and local governments. The EPA sets primary and secondary levels of ambient standards—that is, the maximum levels of certain pollutants—and the states formulate plans to achieve those standards.

DIFFERENT STANDARDS MAY APPLY Different standards apply to sources of pollution in clean areas and those in polluted ones. Different standards also apply to existing sources of pollution and major new sources. Major new sources include existing sources modified by a change in a method of operation that increases emissions. Performance standards for major sources require use of the *maximum achievable control technology*, or MACT, to reduce emissions from the combustion of fossil fuels (coal and oil). As mentioned, the EPA issues guidelines as to what equipment meets this standard.

CURBING ACID RAIN AND GROUND-LEVEL POLLUTION Under the 1990 amendments to the Clean Air Act, 110 of the oldest coal-burning power plants in the United States had to cut their emissions by 40 percent by the year 2001 to reduce acid rain. Utilities were granted "credits" to emit certain amounts of sulfur dioxide, and those that emit less than the allowed amounts can sell their credits to other polluters. The amendments also required an end to the production of chlorofluorocarbons, carbon tetrachloride, and methyl chloroform, which are used in air-conditioning, refrigeration, and insulation and have been linked to depletion of the ozone layer.

The relationship between the Clean Air Act's 1990 amendments and a New York state law was at issue in the following case.

---

4. *Whitman v. American Trucking Associations*, 531 U.S. 457, 121 S.Ct. 903, 149 L.Ed.2d 1 (2000).

| CASE 45.1 | **Clean Air Markets Group v. Pataki** |

United States
District Court,
Northern District
of New York, 2002.
194 F.Supp.2d 147.

BACKGROUND AND FACTS *Acid rain consists of atmospheric sulfates and nitrates, which are formed from sulfur dioxide (SO_2) and nitrogen oxides (NOx). By 1999, some scientists were contending that SO_2 emissions at the rates permitted by the Clean Air Act would not allow for the environmental restoration of parts of the state of New York. Additional reductions in SO_2 emissions would be required. George Pataki, the governor of New York, ordered New York utilities to cut SO_2 emissions to half of the amount permitted by the Clean Air Act by January 2, 2007. By doing this, the New York utilities would have additional SO_2 credits to sell. In May 2000, the New York state legislature enacted the Air Pollution Mitigation Law (APML), under which most sums received for the sale or trade of SO_2 allowances to polluters in Upwind States—fourteen midwestern, eastern, and southern states that significantly contributed to acid rain in New York—would be forfeited to the New York Public Service Commission (PSC), which regulates New York utilities. This effectively lowered the market value of credits originating with New York utilities. Clean Air Markets Group (CAMG) filed a suit in a federal district court against Pataki and others, claiming in part that the APML was preempted under the U.S. Constitution's supremacy clause.[a] All parties filed motions for summary judgment.*

IN THE LANGUAGE OF THE COURT

HURD, District Judge.

* * * *

* * * [The APML] creates an obstacle to the accomplishment and execution of the full purposes and objectives of Congress. [The Clean Air Act] provides that SO_2 allowances "may be transferred among designated representatives of the owners or operators of [covered units (utilities)] and any other person who holds such allowances." [The APML's] restrictions on transferring allowances to units in the Upwind States is contrary to the federal provision that allowances be tradeable to any other person. Additionally, Congress considered geographically restricted allowance transfers and rejected it. The EPA, in setting regulations to implement [the Clean Air Act], also considered geographically restricted allowance trading and rejected it * * *. *The rejection of a regionally restricted allowance trading system illustrates the Congressional objective of having a nationwide trading market for SO_2 allowances. New York's regional restrictions on SO_2 allowance trading by New York units [are] an obstacle to the execution of that objective.* [Emphasis added.]

Pataki argues that the Air Pollution Mitigation Law * * * imposes a more stringent requirement for air pollution control or abatement, as expressly permitted. However, * * * the Air Pollution Mitigation Law sets no emissions requirements. It sets no requirements for air pollution control or abatement at all. Rather, the New York law is a state regulation of federally allocated SO_2 allowances. Further, it is a restriction on the nationwide trading system for which the Clean Air Act provides. It is insufficient to merely say that it imposes requirements for air pollution control, or that the goal is air pollution control or abatement. New York's Air Pollution Mitigation Law is preempted because it interferes with the Clean Air Act's method for achieving the goal of air pollution control: a cap and nationwide SO_2 allowance trading system.

In addition to interfering with the nationwide trading of SO_2 allowances, the Air Pollution Mitigation Law would result in decreased availability of SO_2 allowances in the Upwind States. Restricted availability of SO_2 allowances could indirectly reduce emissions in the Upwind States. No doubt the New York legislators had this in mind when the Air Pollution Mitigation Law was enacted. However, the Clean Air Act permits restrictions on emissions by a state in that state, but it does not permit one state to control emissions in

---

a. As explained in Chapter 4, if federal law has not supplanted an entire field of state law, state law is preempted to the extent that it actually conflicts with federal law. A conflict between state and federal law occurs when compliance with both is physically impossible or when the state law is an obstacle to accomplishing the objective of the federal law.

another state. Thus, the inevitable result of laws such as New York's Air Pollution Mitigation Law would be the indirect regulation of allowance trading and emissions in other states, which could not be done directly.

DECISION AND REMEDY *The court granted CAMG's motion for summary judgment, holding that New York's Air Pollution Mitigation Law is preempted, under the supremacy clause, by the Clean Air Act because it interferes with that law's methods for achieving air-pollution control. The court enjoined the enforcement of the state law.*

WHAT IF THE FACTS WERE DIFFERENT? *Suppose that the APML also provided for a subsidy to those who claimed that the value of their pollution credits had been reduced. Would this have affected the outcome of the case?*

HAZARDOUS AIR POLLUTANTS

Hazardous air pollutants are those likely to cause an increase in mortality or in serious irreversible or incapacitating illness. In all, there are 189 of these pollutants, including asbestos, benzene, beryllium, cadmium, mercury, and vinyl chloride. These pollutants may cause cancer as well as neurological and reproductive damage. They are emitted from stationary sources by a variety of business activities, including smelting (melting ore to produce metal), dry cleaning, house painting, and commercial baking. Instead of establishing specific emissions standards for each hazardous air pollutant, the 1990 amendments to the Clean Air Act require industry to use pollution-control equipment that represents the maximum achievable control technology, or MACT, to limit emissions. The EPA issues guidelines as to what equipment meets this standard.

In 1996, the EPA issued a rule to regulate hazardous air pollutants emitted by landfills. The rule required landfills constructed after May 30, 1991, that emit more than a specified amount of pollutants to install landfill gas collection and control systems. The rule also required the states to impose the same requirements on landfills constructed before May 30, 1991, if they accepted waste after November 8, 1987.[5]

VIOLATIONS OF THE CLEAN AIR ACT

For violations of emission limits under the Clean Air Act, the EPA can assess civil penalties of up to $25,000 per day. Additional fines of up to $5,000 per day can be assessed for other violations, such as failing to maintain the required records. To penalize those who find it more cost-effective to violate the act than

to comply with it, the EPA is authorized to impose a penalty equal to the violator's economic benefits from noncompliance. Persons who provide information about violators may be paid up to $10,000. Private citizens can also sue violators.

Those who knowingly violate the act may be subject to criminal penalties, including fines of up to $1 million and imprisonment for up to two years (for false statements or failures to report violations). Corporate officers are among those who may be subject to these penalties.

SECTION 4 | Water Pollution

Water pollution stems mostly from industrial, municipal, and agricultural sources. Pollutants entering streams, lakes, and oceans include organic wastes, heated water, sediments from soil runoff, nutrients (including detergents, fertilizers, and human and animal wastes), and toxic chemicals and other hazardous substances. We look here at laws and regulations governing water pollution.

NAVIGABLE WATERS

Federal regulations governing water pollution can be traced back to the Rivers and Harbors Appropriations Act of 1899.[6] These regulations prohibited ships and manufacturers from discharging or depositing refuse in navigable waterways. Once limited to waters actually used for navigation, the term *navigable waters* is today interpreted to include intrastate lakes and streams used by interstate travelers and industries, as well as coastal and freshwater wetlands (*wetlands* will be defined shortly).

---

5. 40 C.F.R. Sections 60.750–759.

6. 33 U.S.C. Sections 401–418.

THE CLEAN WATER ACT AND ITS AMENDMENTS

In 1948, Congress passed the Federal Water Pollution Control Act (FWPCA),[7] but its regulatory system and enforcement powers proved to be inadequate. In 1972, amendments to the FWPCA—known as the Clean Water Act—established the following goals: (1) make waters safe for swimming, (2) protect fish and wildlife, and (3) eliminate the discharge of pollutants into the water. The amendments required that municipal and industrial polluters apply for permits before discharging wastes into navigable waters. The Clean Water Act also set specific schedules, which were extended by amendment in 1977 and by the Water Quality Act of 1987.[8] Under these schedules, the EPA establishes limitations for discharges of various types of pollutants based on the technology available for controlling them. The 1972 act also requires municipal and industrial polluters to apply for permits before discharging wastes into navigable waters.

STANDARDS FOR EQUIPMENT   Regulations, for the most part, specify that the *best available control technology*, or BACT, be installed. The EPA issues guidelines as to what equipment meets this standard; essentially, the guidelines require the most effective pollution-control equipment available. New sources must install BACT equipment before beginning operations. Existing sources are subject to timetables for the installation of BACT equipment. These sources must immediately install equipment that utilizes the *best practical control technology*, or BPCT. The EPA also issues guidelines as to what equipment meets this standard.

WETLANDS   The Clean Water Act prohibits the filling or dredging of wetlands unless a permit is obtained from the Army Corps of Engineers. The EPA defines **wetlands** as "those areas that are inundated or saturated by surface or ground water at a frequency and duration sufficient to support, and that under normal circumstances do support, a prevalence of vegetation typically adapted for life in saturated soil conditions." In recent years, the broad interpretation of what constitutes a wetland subject to the regulatory authority of the federal government has generated substantial controversy.

Perhaps one of the most controversial regulations was the "migratory-bird rule" issued by the Army Corps of Engineers. Under this rule, any bodies of water that could affect interstate commerce, including seasonal ponds or waters "used or suitable for use by migratory birds" that fly over state borders, were "navigable waters" subject to federal regulation under the Clean Water Act as wetlands. The rule was challenged in a case brought by a group of communities in the Chicago suburbs that wanted to build a landfill in a tract of land northwest of Chicago that had once been used as a strip mine. Over time, areas that were once pits in the mine became ponds used by a variety of migratory birds. The Army Corps of Engineers, claiming that the shallow ponds formed a habitat for migratory birds, refused to grant a permit for the landfill.

Ultimately, the United States Supreme Court held that the Army Corps of Engineers had exceeded its authority under the Clean Water Act. The Court stated that it was not prepared to hold that isolated and seasonable ponds, puddles, and "prairie potholes" become "navigable waters of the United States" simply because they serve as a habitat for migratory birds.[9]

VIOLATIONS OF THE CLEAN WATER ACT   Under the Clean Water Act, violators are subject to a variety of civil and criminal penalties. Depending on the violation, civil penalties range from a maximum of $10,000 per day, and not more than $25,000 per violation, to as much as $25,000 per day. Criminal penalties, which apply only if an act was intentional, range from a fine of $2,500 per day and imprisonment for up to one year to a fine of $1 million and fifteen years' imprisonment. Injunctive relief and damages can also be imposed. The polluting party can be required to clean up the pollution or pay for the cost of doing so.

DRINKING WATER

Another statute governing water pollution is the Safe Drinking Water Act.[10] Passed in 1974, this act requires the EPA to set maximum levels for pollutants in public water systems. Operators of public water supply systems must come as close as possible to meeting the EPA's standards by using the best available technology that is economically and technologically feasible. The EPA is particularly concerned with contamination from underground sources. Pesticides and

---

7. 33 U.S.C. Sections 1251–1387.
8. This act amended 33 U.S.C. Section 1251.

9. *Solid Waste Agency of Northern Cook County v. U.S. Army Corps of Engineers*, 531 U.S. 159, 121 S.Ct. 675, 148 L.Ed.2d 576 (2001).
10. 42 U.S.C. Sections 300f to 300j-25.

wastes leaked from landfills or disposed of in underground injection wells are among the more than two hundred pollutants known to exist in groundwater used for drinking in at least thirty-four states. Many of these substances are associated with cancer and damage to the central nervous system, liver, and kidneys.

The act was amended in 1996 to give the EPA greater flexibility in setting regulatory standards governing drinking water. Prior to the 1996 amendments, the EPA had to set standards for twenty-five different drinking water contaminants every three years, which it had largely failed to do. Under the 1996 amendments, the EPA can move at whatever rate it deems necessary to control the contaminants of greatest concern to the public health. The 1996 amendments also imposed new requirements on suppliers of drinking water. Each supplier must send to every household it provides with water an annual statement describing the source of its water, the level of any contaminants contained in the water, and any possible health concerns associated with the contaminants.

OCEAN DUMPING

The Marine Protection, Research, and Sanctuaries Act of 1972[11] (known popularly as the Ocean Dumping Act) regulates the transportation and dumping of material into ocean waters. (The term *material* is synonymous with the term *pollutant* as used in the Federal Water Pollution Control Act.) The Ocean Dumping Act prohibits entirely the ocean dumping of radiological, chemical, and biological warfare agents and high-level radioactive waste.

The act establishes a permit program for transporting and dumping other materials. There are specific exemptions—materials subject to the permit provisions of other pollution legislation, wastes from structures regulated by other laws (for example, offshore oil exploration and drilling platforms), sewage, and other wastes. The Ocean Dumping Act also authorizes the designation of marine sanctuaries for "preserving or restoring such areas for their conservation, recreational, ecological, or esthetic values."

Each violation of any provision or permit may result in a civil penalty of not more than $50,000 or revocation or suspension of the permit. A knowing violation is a criminal offense that may result in a $50,000 fine, imprisonment for not more than a year, or both. An injunction may also be imposed.

OIL POLLUTION

The Oil Pollution Act of 1990[12] provides that any onshore or offshore oil facility, oil shipper, vessel owner, or vessel operator that discharges oil into navigable waters or onto an adjoining shore may be liable for clean-up costs, as well as damages. The act created a $1 billion oil clean-up and economic compensation fund and decreed that by the year 2011, oil tankers using U.S. ports must be double hulled to limit the severity of accidental spills.

Under the act, damage to natural resources, private property, and the local economy, including the increased cost of providing public services, is compensable. The penalties range from $2 million to $350 million, depending on the size of the vessel and depending on whether the oil spill came from a vessel or an offshore facility. The party held responsible for the clean-up costs can bring a civil suit for contribution from other potentially liable parties.

SECTION 5 | Toxic Chemicals

Originally, most environmental clean-up efforts were directed toward reducing smog and making water safe for fishing and swimming. Over time, however, control of toxic chemicals has become an important part of environmental law.

PESTICIDES AND HERBICIDES

The Federal Insecticide, Fungicide, and Rodenticide Act (FIFRA) of 1947[13] regulates pesticides and herbicides. Under the FIFRA, pesticides and herbicides must be (1) registered before they can be sold, (2) certified and used only for approved applications, and (3) used in limited quantities when applied to food crops. If a substance is identified as harmful, the EPA can cancel its registration after a hearing. If the harm is imminent, the EPA can suspend registration pending the hearing. The EPA, or state officers or employees, may also inspect factories where these chemicals are manufactured.

Under 1996 amendments to the Federal Food, Drug and Cosmetic Act, for a pesticide to remain on the market, there must be a "reasonable certainty of no harm" to people from exposure to the pesticide.[14] This

---

11. 16 U.S.C. Sections 1401–1445.

12. 33 U.S.C. Sections 2701–2761.
13. 7 U.S.C. Sections 136–136y.
14. 21 U.S.C. Section 346a.

means that there must be no more than a one-in-a-million risk to people of developing cancer from exposure in any way, including eating food that contains residues from the pesticide. Nearly all fruits and vegetables and processed foods contain some pesticide residues. Under the 1996 amendments, the EPA must distribute to grocery stores brochures on high-risk pesticides that are in food, and the stores must display these brochures for consumers.

Can a state regulate the sale and use of federally registered pesticides? Tort suits against pesticide manufacturers were common long before the enactment of the FIFRA in 1947 and continued to be a feature of the legal landscape at the time the FIFRA was amended. Until it heard the following case, however, the United States Supreme Court had never considered whether that statute preempts claims arising under state law.

CASE 45.2 — Bates v. Dow Agrosciences, LLC

Supreme Court of the
United States, 2005.
__ U.S. __,
125 S.Ct. 1788,
161 L.Ed.2d 687.
http://www.findlaw.com/
casecode/supreme.html [a]

BACKGROUND AND FACTS *The Environmental Protection Agency (EPA) conditionally registered Strongarm, a new weed-killing pesticide, on March 8, 2000.*[b] *Dow Agrosciences, LLC, immediately sold Strongarm to Texas peanut farmers, who normally plant their crops around May 1. The label stated, "Use of Strongarm is recommended in all areas where peanuts are grown." When the farmers applied Strongarm to their fields, the pesticide damaged their crops while failing to control the growth of weeds. After unsuccessfully attempting to negotiate with Dow, the farmers announced their intent to sue Strongarm's maker for violations of Texas state law. Dow filed a suit in a federal district court against the peanut farmers, asserting that the FIFRA preempted their claims. The court issued a summary judgment in Dow's favor. The farmers appealed to the U.S. Court of Appeals for the Fifth Circuit, which affirmed the lower court's judgment. The farmers appealed to the United States Supreme Court.*

IN THE LANGUAGE OF THE COURT

Justice STEVENS delivered the opinion of the Court.

* * * *

Under FIFRA * * *, [a] pesticide is misbranded if its label contains a statement that is false or misleading in any particular, including a false or misleading statement concerning the efficacy of the pesticide. *A pesticide is also misbranded if its label does not contain adequate instructions for use, or if its label omits necessary warnings or cautionary statements.* [Emphasis added.]

* * * *

* * * [Section] 136v provides:

"(a) * * * A State may regulate the sale or use of any federally registered pesticide or device in the State, but only if and to the extent the regulation does not permit any sale or use prohibited by [FIFRA].

"(b) * * * Such State shall not impose or continue in effect any requirements for labeling or packaging in addition to or different from those required under [FIFRA]. * * * "

* * * *

* * * *Nothing in the text of FIFRA would prevent a State from making the violation of a federal labeling or packaging requirement a state offense,* thereby imposing its own sanctions on pesticide manufacturers who violate federal law. The imposition of state sanctions for violating state rules that merely duplicate federal requirements is equally consistent with the text of [Section] 136v. [Emphasis added.]

* * * *

* * * For a particular state rule to be preempted, it must satisfy two conditions. First, it must be a requirement "for labeling or packaging"; rules governing the design of a product, for example, are not preempted. Second, it must impose a labeling or packaging requirement that

---

a. In the "Browsing" section, click on "2005 Decisions." In the result, click on the name of the case to access the opinion.

b. Strongarm might more commonly be called a herbicide, but the FIFRA classifies it as a pesticide.

is "in addition to or different from those required under [FIFRA]." A state regulation requiring the word "poison" to appear in red letters, for instance, would not be preempted if an EPA regulation imposed the same requirement.

* * * Rules that require manufacturers to design reasonably safe products, to use due care in conducting appropriate testing of their products, to market products free of manufacturing defects, and to honor their express warranties or other contractual commitments plainly do not qualify as requirements for "labeling or packaging." None of these common-law rules requires that manufacturers label or package their products in any particular way. Thus, petitioners' claims for defective design, defective manufacture, negligent testing, and breach of express warranty are not preempted.

* * * *

Dow * * * argues that [this] "parallel requirements" reading of [Section] 136v(b) would "give juries in 50 States the authority to give content to FIFRA's misbranding prohibition, establishing a crazy-quilt of anti-misbranding requirements * * * ." Conspicuously absent from the submissions by Dow * * * is any plausible alternative interpretation of "in addition to or different from" that would give that phrase meaning. Instead, they appear to favor reading those words out of the statute * * * . This amputated version of [Section] 136v(b) would no doubt have clearly and succinctly commanded the preemption of all state requirements concerning labeling. *That Congress added the remainder of the provision is evidence of its intent to draw a distinction between state labeling requirements that are preempted and those that are not.* [Emphasis added.]

* * * *

In sum, under our interpretation, [Section] 136v(b) * * * preempts competing state labeling standards—imagine 50 different labeling regimes prescribing the color, font size, and wording of warnings—that would create significant inefficiencies for manufacturers. The provision also preempts any statutory or common-law rule that would impose a labeling requirement that diverges from those set out in FIFRA * * * . It does not, however, preempt any state rules that are fully consistent with federal requirements.

DECISION AND REMEDY *The United States Supreme Court vacated the lower court's judgment. A state can regulate the sale and use of federally registered pesticides to the extent that it does not permit anything that the FIFRA prohibits, but a state cannot impose any requirements for labeling or packaging in addition to or different from those that the FIFRA requires. The Court remanded the case, however, for further proceedings subject to this standard, concerning certain state law claims "on which we have not received sufficient briefing."*

WHAT IF THE FACTS WERE DIFFERENT? *Suppose that the FIFRA required Strongarm's label to include the word CAUTION, and the Texas peanut farmers filed their claims under a state regulation that required the label to use the word DANGER. Would the result have been different?*

VIOLATIONS OF THE FIFRA It is a violation of the FIFRA to sell a pesticide or herbicide that is unregistered, a pesticide or herbicide with a registration that has been canceled or suspended, or a pesticide or herbicide with a false or misleading label. For example, it is an offense to sell a substance that is adulterated (that has a chemical strength different from the concentration declared on the label). It is also an offense to destroy or deface any labeling required under the act. The act's labeling requirements include directions for the use of the pesticide or herbicide, warnings to protect human health and the environment, a statement of treatment in the case of poisoning, and a list of the ingredients.

A private party can petition the EPA to suspend or cancel the registration of a pesticide or herbicide. If the EPA fails to act, the private party can petition a federal court to review the EPA's lack of action.

PENALTIES FOR VIOLATIONS Penalties for registrants and producers for violating the FIFRA include imprisonment for up to one year and a fine of no more than $50,000. Penalties for commercial dealers include imprisonment for up to one year and a fine of no more than $25,000. Farmers and other private users of pesticides or herbicides who violate the act are subject to a $1,000 fine and incarceration for up to thirty days.

TOXIC SUBSTANCES

The first comprehensive law covering toxic substances was the Toxic Substances Control Act of 1976.[15] The act was passed to regulate chemicals and chemical compounds that are known to be toxic—such as asbestos and polychlorinated biphenyls, popularly known as PCBs—and to institute investigation of any possible harmful effects from new chemical compounds. The regulations authorize the EPA to require that manufacturers, processors, and other organizations planning to use chemicals first determine their effects on human health and the environment. The EPA can regulate substances that may pose an imminent hazard or an unreasonable risk of injury to health or the environment. The EPA may require special labeling, limit the use of a substance, set production quotas, or prohibit the use of a substance altogether.

SECTION 6 | Hazardous Wastes

Some industrial, agricultural, and household wastes pose more serious threats than others. If not properly disposed of, these toxic chemicals may present a substantial danger to human health and the environment. If released into the environment, they may contaminate public drinking water resources.

RESOURCE CONSERVATION AND RECOVERY ACT

In 1976, Congress passed the Resource Conservation and Recovery Act (RCRA)[16] in reaction to an ever-increasing concern about the effects of hazardous waste materials on the environment. The RCRA required the EPA to establish regulations to monitor and control hazardous waste disposal and to determine which forms of solid waste should be considered hazardous and thus subject to regulation. The act authorized the EPA to promulgate various technical requirements for some types of facilities for storage and treatment of hazardous waste. The act also requires all producers of hazardous waste materials to label and package properly any hazardous waste to be transported.

AMENDMENTS TO THE RCRA The RCRA was amended in 1984 and 1986 to decrease the use of land containment in the disposal of hazardous waste. The amendments also require compliance with the act by some generators of hazardous waste—such as those generating less than 1,000 kilograms (2,200 pounds) a month—that had previously been excluded from regulation under the RCRA.

PENALTIES UNDER THE RCRA Under the RCRA, a company may be assessed a civil penalty based on the seriousness of the violation, the probability of harm, and the extent to which the violation deviates from RCRA requirements. The assessment may be up to $25,000 for each violation. Criminal penalties include fines up to $50,000 for each day of violation, imprisonment for up to two years (in most instances), or both. In addition, if a person knowingly violates the RCRA requirements and endangers the life of another, he or she may be imprisoned for up to fifteen years and fined up to $250,000. Criminal fines and the time of imprisonment can also be doubled for certain repeat offenders.

SUPERFUND

In 1980, Congress passed the Comprehensive Environmental Response, Compensation, and Liability Act (CERCLA),[17] commonly known as Superfund. The basic purpose of Superfund is to attempt to regulate the clean-up of disposal sites in which hazardous waste is leaking into the environment. A special federal fund was created for that purpose.

POTENTIALLY RESPONSIBLE PARTIES Superfund provides that when a release or a threatened release of hazardous chemicals from a site occurs, the EPA can clean up the site and recover the cost of the clean-up from the following persons: (1) the person who generated the wastes disposed of at the site, (2) the person who transported the wastes to the site, (3) the person who owned or operated the site at the time of the disposal, or (4) the current owner or operator. A person falling within one of these categories is referred to as a **potentially responsible party (PRP).** In the following case, the issue was the meaning of *disposal* as that term is used in the provision of CERCLA that lists PRPs.

15. 15 U.S.C. Sections 2601–2692.
16. 42 U.S.C. Sections 6901–6986.
17. 42 U.S.C. Sections 9601–9675.

United States
Court of Appeals,
Ninth Circuit, 2001.
270 F.3d 863.

CASE 45.3 — Carson Harbor Village, Ltd. v. Unocal Corp.

McKEOWN, Circuit Judge:

* * * *

Carson Harbor [Village Limited] owns and operates a mobile home park on seventy acres in the City of Carson, California. From 1977 until 1983, prior to Carson Harbor's ownership, defendant Carson Harbor Village Mobile Home Park, a general partnership controlled by defendants Braley and Smith (the "Partnership Defendants"), owned the property. They, like Carson Harbor, operated a mobile home park on the property. Beginning over thirty years earlier, however, from 1945 until 1983, Unocal Corporation held a leasehold interest in the property and used it for petroleum production, operating a number of oil wells, pipelines, above-ground storage tanks, and production facilities.

An undeveloped open-flow wetlands area covers approximately seventeen acres of the site. * * *

While attempting to refinance the property in 1993, Carson Harbor discovered hazardous substances on the site. The prospective lender commissioned an environmental assessment, which revealed tar-like and slag materials in the wetlands area of the property. Subsequent investigation revealed that the materials were a waste or by-product of petroleum production and that they had been on the property for several decades prior to its development as a mobile home park.

* * * The material and surrounding soils contained elevated levels of petroleum hydrocarbons (measured in "total petroleum hydrocarbons" or "TPH") and lead * * * .

* * * *

In 1997, Carson Harbor brought suit [in a federal district court] against the Partnership Defendants [and others] seeking relief under federal environmental statutes, [including] CERCLA * * * . Carson Harbor sought to recover the costs of its cleanup (which totaled approximately $285,000) as well as damages arising from its inability to refinance the property. * * *

* * * The district court granted the defendants' [motion for summary judgment]. * * *

* * * *

Carson Harbor appealed the district court's rulings on the CERCLA claim [to the U.S. Court of Appeals for the Ninth Circuit] * * * .

* * * *

CERCLA defines "disposal" * * * with reference to the definition of "disposal" in RCRA, which in turn defines "disposal" as follows:

> The term "disposal" means the discharge, deposit, injection, dumping, spilling, leaking, or placing of any solid waste or hazardous waste into or on any land or water so that such solid waste or hazardous waste or any constituent thereof may enter the environment or be emitted into the air or discharged into any waters, including ground waters.

Under this definition, for the Partnership Defendants to be PRPs [potentially responsible parties], there must have been a "discharge, deposit, injection, dumping, spilling, leaking, or placing" of contaminants on the property during their ownership.

* * * *

Examining the facts of this case, we hold that the gradual passive migration of contamination through the soil that allegedly took place during the Partnership Defendants' ownership was not a "discharge, deposit, injection, dumping, spilling, leaking, or placing" and, therefore, was not a "disposal" within the meaning of [CERCLA]. The contamination on the property included tar-like and slag materials. The tar-like material was highly viscous and uniform, without any breaks or stratification. The slag material had a vesicular structure and was more porous and rigid than the tar-like material. There was some evidence that the tar-like material moved through the soil and that lead and/or TPH may have moved from that material into the soil. If we try to characterize this passive soil migration in plain English, a

CONTINUED ►

CASE 45.3 Continued

number of words come to mind, including gradual "spreading," "migration," "seeping," "oozing," and possibly "leaching." But certainly none of those words fits within the plain and common meaning of "discharge, * * * injection, dumping, * * * or placing." Although these words generally connote active conduct, even if we were to infuse passive meanings, these words simply do not describe the passive migration that occurred here. Nor can the gradual spread here be characterized as a "deposit," because there was neither a deposit by someone, nor does the term "deposit" encompass the gradual spread of contaminants. The term "spilling" is likewise inapposite. Nothing spilled out of or over anything. Unlike the spilling of a barrel or the spilling over of a holding pond, movement of the tar-like and slag materials was not a spill.

Of the terms defining "disposal," the only one that might remotely describe the passive soil migration here is "leaking." But under the plain and common meaning of the word, we conclude that there was no "leaking." The circumstances here are not like that of the leaking barrel or underground storage tank envisioned by Congress, or a vessel or some other container that would connote "leaking." Therefore, there was no "disposal," and the Partnership Defendants are not PRPs. On this basis, we affirm the district court's grant of summary judgment to the Partnership Defendants on the CERCLA claim.

QUESTIONS

1. Why not interpret the term *disposal* to include all subsoil passive migration of hazardous substances, and thus hold any owner of contaminated property liable for the cost of its clean-up?
2. Is it possible to objectively determine how clean-up costs for hazardous waste sites should be apportioned among the responsible parties?

JOINT AND SEVERAL LIABILITY Liability under Superfund is usually joint and several—that is, a PRP who generated only a fraction of the hazardous waste disposed of at the site may nevertheless be liable for all of the clean-up costs. CERCLA authorizes a party who has incurred clean-up costs to bring a "contribution action" against any other person who is liable or potentially liable for a percentage of the costs.

REVIEWING ENVIRONMENTAL LAW

In the late 1980s, various residents of Lake Caliopa, Minnesota, began noticing an unusually high number of lung ailments among their population. A group of concerned local citizens pooled their resources and commissioned a study of the frequency of these health conditions per capita as compared to national averages. The study concluded that Lake Caliopa had four to seven times the usual frequency of asthma, bronchitis, and emphysema when compared to national data. During the study period, citizens began expressing concerns about the large volumes of smog emitted by the Cotton Design apparel manufacturing plant on the outskirts of town. The plant had opened its production facility two miles east of town beside the Tawakoni River in 1977 and employed seventy full-time workers by 1991. Just downstream on the Tawakoni River, the city of Lake Caliopa operated a public water works facility, which supplied all city residents with water. In August 1991, the Minnesota Pollution Control Agency required Cotton Design to install new equipment to control air and water pollution. In May 1992, thirty citizens brought a class-action lawsuit in a Minnesota state court against Cotton Design for various respiratory ailments allegedly caused or compounded by smog from Cotton Design's factory. Using the information presented in the chapter, answer the following questions.

1. Under the common law, what would each plaintiff be required to identify in order to be given relief by the court?
2. Are air-quality regulations typically overseen by federal, state, or local governments? Which agency establishes these regulations?

REVIEWING ENVIRONMENTAL LAW (continued)

3. | The equipment to control air pollution has to meet what standard for limiting emissions from Cotton Design? To what requirements relating to water pollution would Cotton Design be subject?

4. | What information must the city send to every household that the city supplies with water?

5. | In what ways can the Environmental Protection Agency regulate organizations, such as Cotton Design, that use toxic substances?

TERMS AND CONCEPTS TO REVIEW

environmental impact statement (EIS) 906

environmental law 904

nuisance 904

potentially responsible party (PRP) 914

toxic tort 904

wetlands 910

QUESTIONS AND CASE PROBLEMS

45–1. Some scientific knowledge indicates that there is no safe level of exposure to a cancer-causing agent. In theory, even one molecule of such a substance has the potential for causing cancer. Section 112 of the Clean Air Act requires that all cancer-causing substances be regulated to ensure a margin of safety. Some environmental groups have argued that all emissions of such substances must be eliminated to attain such a margin of safety. Total elimination would likely shut down many major U.S. industries. Should the Environmental Protection Agency totally forbid all emissions of cancer-causing chemicals? Discuss.

45–2. **QUESTION WITH SAMPLE ANSWER**

Fruitade, Inc., is a processor of a soft drink called Freshen Up. Fruitade uses returnable bottles, which it cleans with a special acid to allow for further beverage processing. The acid is diluted with water and then allowed to pass into a navigable stream. Fruitade crushes its broken bottles and throws the crushed glass into the stream. Discuss fully any environmental laws that Fruitade has violated.

For a sample answer to this question, go to Appendix I at the end of this text.

45–3. Moonbay is a home-building corporation that primarily develops retirement communities. Farmtex owns a number of feedlots in Sunny Valley. Moonbay purchased 20,000 acres of farmland in the same area and began building and selling homes on this acreage. In the meantime, Farmtex continued to expand its feedlot business, and eventually only 500 feet separated the two operations. Because of the odor and flies from the feed-

lots, Moonbay found it difficult to sell the homes in its development. Moonbay wants to enjoin (prevent) Farmtex from operating its feedlot in the vicinity of the retirement home development. Under what common law theory would Moonbay file this action? Has Farmtex violated any federal environmental laws? Discuss.

45–4. **TOXIC CHEMICALS.** The Environmental Protection Agency canceled the registration of the pesticide diazinon for use on golf courses and sod farms because of concerns over the effects of diazinon on birds. The Federal Insecticide, Fungicide, and Rodenticide Act authorizes cancellation of the registration of products that "generally cause unreasonable adverse effects on the environment." The statute further defines "unreasonable adverse effects on the environment" to mean "any unreasonable risk to man or the environment, taking into account the . . . costs and benefits." Thus, in determining whether a pesticide should continue to be used, it is necessary to balance the risks and benefits of the use of the pesticide. Does this mean that, to prohibit the pesticide's use, a judge must find that the pesticide kills birds more often than not, or is it sufficient to find that the use of the pesticide results in recurrent bird kills? [*Ciba-Geigy Corp. v. Environmental Protection Agency*, 874 F.2d 277 (5th Cir. 1989)]

45–5. **WATER POLLUTION.** Taylor Bay Protective Association is a nonprofit corporation established for the purpose of restoring and improving the water quality of Taylor Bay. Local water districts began operating a flood-control project in the area. As part of the project, a pumping station was developed. Testimony at trial revealed that the pumps were operated contrary to the instructions provided in the operation and maintenance manual. The pumps acted as vacuums, sucking up silt and depositing the silt in Taylor Bay. Thus, the project resulted in sedimentation and turbidity (a condition of having dense, stirred-up particles) problems in the downstream watercourse of Taylor Bay. The association sued the local water districts, alleging that the pumping operations created a nuisance. Do the pumping operations qualify as a common law nuisance? Who should be responsible for the clean-up costs? Discuss both questions fully. [*Taylor Bay Protective Association v. Environmental Protection Agency,* 884 F.2d 1073 (8th Cir. 1989)]

45–6. CLEAN WATER ACT. Attique Ahmad owned the Spin-N-Market, a convenience store and gas station. The gas pumps were fed by underground tanks, one of which had a leak at its top that allowed water to enter. Ahmad emptied the tank by pumping its contents into a storm drain and a sewer system. Through the storm drain, gasoline flowed into a creek, forcing the city to clean the water. Through the sewer system, gasoline flowed into a sewage treatment plant, forcing the city to evacuate the plant and two nearby schools. Ahmad was charged with discharging a pollutant without a permit, which is a criminal violation of the Clean Water Act. The act provides that a person who "knowingly violates" the act commits a felony. Ahmad claimed that he had believed he was discharging only water. Did Ahmad commit a felony? Why or why not? Discuss fully. [*United States v. Ahmad,* 101 F.3d 386 (5th Cir. 1996)]

45–7. ⚖ **CASE PROBLEM WITH SAMPLE ANSWER**
William Gurley was the president and majority stockholder in Gurley Refining Co. (GRC). GRC bought used oil, treated it, and sold it. The refining process created a by-product residue of oily waste. GRC disposed of this waste by dumping it at, among other locations, a landfill in West Memphis, Arkansas. In February 1992, after detecting hazardous chemicals at the site, the Environmental Protection Agency (EPA) asked Gurley about his assets, the generators of the material disposed of at the landfill, site operations, and the structure of GRC. Gurley refused to respond, except to suggest that the EPA ask GRC. In October, the EPA placed the site on its clean-up list and again asked Gurley for information. When he still refused to respond, the EPA filed a suit in a federal district court against him, asking the court to impose a civil penalty. In February 1999, Gurley finally answered the EPA's questions. Under CERCLA, a court may impose a civil penalty "not to exceed $25,000 for each day of noncompliance against any person who unreasonably fails to comply" with an information request. Should the court assess a penalty in this case? Why or why not? [*United States v. Gurley,* 384 F.3d 316 (6th Cir. 2004)]
To view a sample answer for this case problem, go to this book's Web site at http://wbl.westbuslaw.com,

select "Chapter 45," and click on "Case Problem with Sample Answer."

45–8. ENVIRONMENTAL IMPACT STATEMENT. Greers Ferry Lake is in Arkansas, and its shoreline is under the management of the U.S. Army Corps of Engineers, which is part of the U.S. Department of Defense (DOD). The Corps's 2000 Shoreline Management Plan (SMP) rezoned numerous areas along the lake, authorized the Corps to issue permits for the construction of new boat docks in the rezoned areas, increased by 300 percent the area around habitable structures that could be cleared of vegetation, and instituted a Wildlife Enhancement Permit to allow limited modifications of the shoreline. In relation to the SMP's adoption, the Corps issued a Finding of No Significant Impact, which declared that no environmental impact statement (EIS) was necessary. The Corps issued thirty-two boat dock construction permits under the SMP before Save Greers Ferry Lake, Inc., filed a suit in a federal district court against the DOD, asking the court to, among other things, stop the Corps from acting under the SMP and order it to prepare an EIS. What are the requirements for an EIS? Is an EIS needed in this case? Explain. [*Save Greers Ferry Lake, Inc. v. Department of Defense,* 255 F.3d 498 (8th Cir. 2001)]

45–9. CERCLA. Beginning in 1926, Marietta Dyestuffs Co. operated an industrial facility in Marietta, Ohio, to make dyes and other chemicals. In 1944, Dyestuffs became part of American Home Products Corp. (AHP), which sold the Marietta facility to American Cyanamid Co. in 1946. In 1950, AHP sold the rest of the Dyestuffs assets and all of its stock to Goodrich Co., which immediately liquidated the acquired corporation. Goodrich continued to operate the dissolved corporation's business, however. Cyanamid continued to make chemicals at the Marietta facility, and in 1993, it created Cytec Industries, Inc., which expressly assumed all environmental liabilities associated with Cyanamid's ownership and operation of the facility. Cytec spent nearly $25 million on clean-up costs and filed a suit in a federal district court against Goodrich to recover, under CERCLA, a portion of the costs attributable to the clean-up of hazardous wastes that may have been discarded at the site between 1926 and 1946. Cytec filed a motion for summary judgment in its favor. Should the court grant Cytec's motion? Explain. [*Cytec Industries, Inc. v. B. F. Goodrich Co.,* 196 F.Supp.2d 644 (S.D. Ohio 2002)]

45–10. ⚖ **A QUESTION OF ETHICS**
The Endangered Species Act of 1973 makes it unlawful for any person to "take" endangered or threatened species. The act defines *take* to mean to "harass, harm, pursue," "wound," or "kill." The secretary of the interior (Bruce Babbitt) issued a regulation that further defined *harm* to include "significant habitat modification or degradation where it actually kills or injures wildlife." A group of businesses and individuals involved in the timber industry brought an action against the secretary of

the interior and others. The group complained that the application of the "harm" regulation to the red-cockaded woodpecker and the northern spotted owl had injured the group economically because it prevented logging operations (habitat modification) in Pacific Northwest forests containing these species. The group challenged the regulation's validity, contending that Congress did not intend the word *take* to include habitat modification. The case ultimately reached the United States Supreme Court, which held that the secretary reasonably construed Congress's intent when he defined *harm* to include habitat modification. [*Babbitt v. Sweet Home Chapter of Communities for a Great Oregon*, 515 U.S. 687, 115 S.Ct. 2407, 132 L.Ed.2d 597 (1995)]

(a) Traditionally, the term *take* has been used to refer to the capture or killing of wildlife, usually for private gain. Is the secretary's regulation prohibiting habitat modification consistent with this definition?

(b) One of the issues in this case was whether Congress intended to protect existing generations of species or future generations. How do the terms *take* and *habitat modification* relate to this issue?

(c) Three dissenting Supreme Court justices contended that construing the act as prohibiting habitat modification "imposes unfairness to the point of financial ruin—not just upon the rich, but upon the simplest farmer who finds his land conscripted to national zoological use." Should private parties be required to bear the burden of preserving habitats for wildlife?

(d) Generally, should the economic welfare of private parties be taken into consideration when creating and applying environmental statutes and regulations?

LAW | on the Web

For updated links to resources available on the Web, as well as a variety of other materials, visit this text's Web site at **http://wbl.westbuslaw.com**.

For information on the EPA's standards, guidelines, and regulations, go to the EPA's Web site at

http://www.epa.gov

To learn about the RCRA's "buy-recycled" requirements and other steps that the federal government has taken toward "greening the environment," go to

http://www.epa.gov/cpg

The Law Library of the Indiana University School of Law provides numerous links to online environmental law sources. Go to

http://www.law.indiana.edu/library/services/onl_env.shtml

LEGAL RESEARCH EXERCISES ON THE WEB

Go to **http://wbl.westbuslaw.com**, the Web site that accompanies this text. Select "Chapter 45" and click on "Internet Exercises." There you will find the following Internet research exercises that you can perform to learn more about topics covered in this chapter.

Activity 45–1: LEGAL PERSPECTIVE
Nuisance Law

Activity 45–2: MANAGEMENT PERSPECTIVE
Complying with Environmental Regulation

Activity 45–3: ETHICAL PERSPECTIVE
Environmental Justice

CHAPTER 46
Antitrust Law

Today's antitrust laws are the direct descendants of common law actions intended to limit **restraints on trade** (agreements between firms that have the effect of reducing competition in the marketplace). Concern over monopolistic practices arose following the Civil War with the growth of large corporate enterprises and their attempts to reduce or eliminate competition. They did this by legally tying themselves together in a *business trust,* a type of business entity described in Chapter 37. The participants in the most famous trust—the Standard Oil trust in the late 1800s—transferred their stock to a trustee and received trust certificates in exchange. The trustee then made decisions fixing prices, controlling production, and determining the control of exclusive geographic markets for all of the oil companies that were in the Standard Oil trust. Some argued that the trust wielded so much economic power that corporations outside the trust could not compete effectively.

Many states attempted to control such monopolistic behavior by enacting statutes outlawing the use of trusts. That is why all of the laws that regulate economic competition today are referred to as **antitrust laws.** At the national level, the government recognized the problem in 1887 and passed the Interstate Commerce Act,[1] followed by the Sherman Antitrust Act[2] in 1890. In 1914, Congress passed the Clayton Act[3] and the Federal Trade Commission Act[4] to further curb anticompetitive or unfair business practices. Since their passage, the 1914 acts have been amended by Congress to broaden and strengthen their coverage, and they continue to be an important element in the legal environment in which businesses operate. Consider that in 2002, the nation's largest maker of smokeless tobacco suffered a $1.05 billion adverse antitrust judgment for entering exclusive agreements to keep competitors out of its markets and for undertaking other anticompetitive actions.

SECTION 1 | The Sherman Antitrust Act

The author of the Sherman Antitrust Act of 1890, Senator John Sherman, was the brother of the famed Civil War general and a recognized financial authority. He had been concerned for years about the diminishing competition within U.S. industry. He told Congress that the Sherman Act "does not announce a new principle of law, but applies old and well-recognized principles of the common law."[5]

The common law regarding trade regulation was not always consistent. Certainly, it was not very familiar to the legislators of the Fifty-first Congress of the United States in 1890. The public concern over large business integrations and trusts was familiar, however, and in 1890 Congress passed "An Act to Protect Trade and Commerce against Unlawful Restraints and Monopolies"—more commonly referred to as the Sherman Antitrust Act, or simply the Sherman Act.

MAJOR PROVISIONS OF THE SHERMAN ACT

Sections 1 and 2 contain the main provisions of the Sherman Act:

1: Every contract, combination in the form of trust or otherwise, or conspiracy, in restraint of trade or commerce among the several States, or with foreign nations, is hereby declared to be illegal [and is a felony punishable by fine and/or imprisonment].

---

1. 49 U.S.C. Sections 501–526.
2. 15 U.S.C. Sections 1–7.
3. 15 U.S.C. Sections 12–26a.
4. 15 U.S.C. Sections 45–48a.
5. 21 Congressional Record 2456 (1890).

2: Every person who shall monopolize, or attempt to monopolize, or combine or conspire with any other person or persons, to monopolize any part of the trade or commerce among the several States, or with foreign nations, shall be deemed guilty of a felony [and is similarly punishable].

DIFFERENCES BETWEEN SECTION 1 AND SECTION 2

These two sections of the Sherman Act are quite different. Section 1 requires two or more persons, as a person cannot contract, combine, or conspire alone. Thus, the essence of the illegal activity is *the act of joining together.* Section 2 can apply either to an individual person or to to several people, because it refers to "[e]very person." Thus, unilateral conduct can result in a violation of Section 2.

The cases brought to the courts under Section 1 of the Sherman Act differ from those brought under Section 2. Section 1 cases are often concerned with finding an agreement (written or oral) that leads to a restraint of trade. Section 2 cases deal with the structure of a *monopoly* that exists in the marketplace. The term **monopoly** is generally used to describe a market in which there is a single seller. Whereas Section 1 focuses on agreements that are restrictive—that is, agreements that have a wrongful purpose—Section 2 looks at the so-called misuse of **monopoly power** in the marketplace.

Monopoly power exists when a firm has an extreme amount of **market power**—the power to affect the market price of its product. Both Section 1 and Section 2 seek to curtail market industrial practices that result in undesired monopoly pricing and output behavior. For a case to be brought under Section 2, however, it must be one in which the "threshold" or "necessary" amount of monopoly power already exists. We will return to a discussion of these two sections of the Sherman Act after we look at the act's jurisdictional requirements.

JURISDICTIONAL REQUIREMENTS

The Sherman Act applies only to restraints that have a significant impact on interstate commerce. As will be discussed later in this chapter, the Sherman Act also extends to U.S. nationals abroad who are engaged in activities that have an effect on U.S. foreign commerce. State regulation of anticompetitive practices addresses purely local restraints on competition.

Courts have generally held that any activity that substantially affects interstate commerce falls within the scope of the Sherman Act. As discussed in Chapter 4, courts have generally construed the meaning of *interstate commerce* more and more broadly over the years, bringing even local activities within the regulatory power of the national government.

SECTION 2 | Section 1 of the Sherman Act

The underlying assumption of Section 1 of the Sherman Act is that society's welfare is harmed if rival firms are permitted to join in an agreement that consolidates their market power or otherwise restrains competition. To prevent such harm, Section 1 prohibits two broad categories of restraints on trade: *horizontal restraints* and *vertical restraints,* both of which will be discussed shortly. First, though, we look at the rules that the courts may apply when assessing the anticompetitive impact of alleged restraints on trade.

PER SE VIOLATIONS VERSUS THE RULE OF REASON

Some restraints are so blatantly and substantially anticompetitive that they are deemed **per se violations**—illegal *per se* (on their face, or inherently)—under Section 1. Other agreements, however, even though they result in enhanced market power, do not *unreasonably* restrain trade. Under what is called the **rule of reason,** anticompetitive agreements that allegedly violate Section 1 of the Sherman Act are analyzed with the view that they may, in fact, constitute reasonable restraints on trade.

The need for a rule-of-reason analysis of some agreements in restraint of trade is obvious—if the rule of reason had not been developed, virtually any business agreement could conceivably be held to violate the Sherman Act. Justice Louis Brandeis effectively phrased this sentiment in *Chicago Board of Trade v. United States,* a case decided in 1918:

> Every agreement concerning trade, every regulation of trade, restrains. To bind, to restrain, is of their very essence. The true test of legality is whether the restraint imposed is such as merely regulates and perhaps thereby promotes competition or whether it is such as may suppress or even destroy competition.[6]

When analyzing an alleged Section 1 violation under the rule of reason, a court will consider several factors including the purpose of the agreement, the

6. 246 U.S. 231, 38 S.Ct. 242, 62 L.Ed. 683 (1918).

parties' power to implement the agreement to achieve that purpose, and the effect or potential effect of the agreement on competition. The court might also consider whether the parties could have relied on less restrictive means to achieve their purpose.

HORIZONTAL RESTRAINTS

The term **horizontal restraint** is encountered frequently in antitrust law. A horizontal restraint is any agreement that in some way restrains competition between rival firms competing in the same market.

PRICE FIXING Any agreement among competitors to fix prices, or **price-fixing agreement,** constitutes a *per se* violation of Section 1 of the Sherman Act. Perhaps the definitive case regarding price-fixing agreements remains the 1940 case of *United States v. Socony-Vacuum Oil Co.*[7] In that case, a group of independent oil producers in Texas and Louisiana were caught between falling demand due to the Great Depression of the 1930s and increasing supply from newly discovered oil fields in the region. In response to these conditions, a group of the major refining companies agreed to buy "distress" gasoline (excess supplies) from the independents so as to dispose of it in an "orderly manner." Although there was no explicit agreement as to price, it was clear that the purpose of the agreement was to limit the supply of gasoline on the market and thereby raise prices.

There may have been good reasons for the agreement. Nonetheless, the United States Supreme Court recognized the potentially adverse effects that such an agreement could have on open and free competition. The Court held that the reasonableness of a price-fixing agreement is never a defense; any agreement that restricts output or artificially fixes price is a *per se* violation of Section 1. The rationale of the *per se* rule was best stated in what is now the most famous portion of the Court's opinion. In footnote 59, Justice William O. Douglas compared a freely functioning price system to a body's central nervous system, condemning price-fixing agreements as threats to "the central nervous system of the economy."

GROUP BOYCOTTS A **group boycott** is an agreement by two or more sellers to refuse to deal with (boycott) a particular person or firm. Such group boycotts have been held to constitute *per se* violations of Section 1 of the Sherman Act. Section 1 has been violated if it can be demonstrated that the boycott or

joint refusal to deal was undertaken with the intention of eliminating competition or preventing entry into a given market. Some boycotts, such as group boycotts against a supplier for political reasons, may be protected under the First Amendment right to freedom of expression.

HORIZONTAL MARKET DIVISION It is a *per se* violation of Section 1 of the Sherman Act for competitors to divide up territories or customers. For example, manufacturers A, B, and C compete against one another in the states of Kansas, Nebraska, and Iowa. They agree that A will sell products only in Kansas, B only in Nebraska, and C only in Iowa. This concerted action reduces costs and allows each of the three (assuming there is no other competition) to raise the price of the goods sold in its own state. The same violation would take place if A, B, and C simply agreed that A would sell only to institutional purchasers (such as school districts, universities, state agencies and departments, and cities) in the three states, B only to wholesalers, and C only to retailers.

TRADE ASSOCIATIONS Businesses in the same general industry or profession frequently organize trade associations to pursue common interests. Their joint activities may provide for exchanges of information, representation of the members' business interests before governmental bodies, advertising campaigns, and the setting of regulatory standards to govern their industry or profession. Generally, the rule of reason is applied to many of these horizontal actions. For example, if a court finds that a trade association practice or agreement that restrains trade is nonetheless sufficiently beneficial both to the association and to the public, it may deem the restraint reasonable.

Other trade association agreements may have such substantially anticompetitive effects that the court will consider them to be in violation of Section 1 of the Sherman Act. For example, in one case a group of chiropractors sued the American Medical Association (AMA), alleging that the AMA had violated Section 1 of the Sherman Act by conducting an illegal boycott in restraint of trade. The boycott stemmed from a 1966 resolution passed by the AMA that labeled chiropractic an unscientific cult. In effect, this label prevented physicians from associating with chiropractors because one of the principles of the AMA's code of ethical conduct provided that a "physician should practice a method of healing founded on a scientific basis, and should not voluntarily associate with anyone who violates this principle." The court held that

7. 310 U.S. 150, 60 S.Ct. 811, 84 L.E.2d 1129 (1940).

the AMA had violated Section 1 of the Sherman Act because the boycott was intended, at least in part, to destroy a competitor—chiropractors.[8]

JOINT VENTURES Joint ventures undertaken by competitors are also subject to antitrust laws. As discussed in Chapter 37, a *joint venture* is an undertaking by two or more individuals or firms for a specific purpose. If a joint venture does not involve price fixing or market divisions, the agreement will be analyzed under the rule of reason. Whether the venture will then be upheld under Section 1 depends on an overall assessment of the purposes of the venture, a strict analysis of the potential benefits relative to the likely harms, and, in some cases, an assessment of whether there are less restrictive alternatives for achieving the same goals.[9]

VERTICAL RESTRAINTS

A **vertical restraint** of trade results from an agreement between firms at different levels in the manufacturing and distribution process. In contrast to horizontal relationships, which occur at the same level of operation, vertical relationships encompass the entire chain of production: the purchase of inputs, basic manufacturing, distribution to wholesalers, and eventual sale of a product at the retail level. For some products, these distinct phases are carried on by different firms. In other instances, a single firm carries out two or more of the separate functional phases. Such enterprises are considered to be **vertically integrated firms.**

Even though firms operating at different functional levels are not in direct competition with one another, they are in competition with other companies operat-

ing at their own respective levels of operation. Thus, agreements between firms standing in a vertical relationship may affect competition.

TERRITORIAL OR CUSTOMER RESTRICTIONS In arranging for the distribution of its products, a manufacturer often wishes to insulate dealers from direct competition with other dealers selling its products. In this endeavor, the manufacturer may institute territorial restrictions or attempt to prohibit wholesalers or retailers from reselling the products to certain classes of buyers, such as competing retailers.

There may be legitimate reasons for imposing such territorial or customer restrictions. For example, a computer manufacturer may wish to prevent a dealer from reducing costs and undercutting rivals by offering computers without promotion or customer service, while relying on a nearby dealer to provide these services. In this situation, the cost-cutting dealer reaps the benefits (sales of the product) paid for by other dealers who undertake promotion and arrange for customer service. This is an example of the "free rider" problem.[10] By not providing customer service, the cost-cutting dealer may also harm the manufacturer's reputation.

Territorial and customer restrictions are judged under a rule of reason. In the following case, *Continental T.V., Inc. v. GTE Sylvania, Inc.,* the United States Supreme Court overturned its earlier stance, which had been set out in *United States v. Arnold, Schwinn & Co.*[11] In *Schwinn,* the Court had held territorial and customer restrictions to be *per se* violations of Section 1 of the Sherman Act. The *Continental* case that follows has been heralded as one of the most important antitrust cases since the 1940s.

---

8. *Wilk v. American Medical Association,* 895 F.2d 352 (7th Cir. 1990).
9. See, for example, *United States v. Morgan,* 118 F.Supp. 621 (S.D.N.Y. 1953). This case is often cited as a classic example of how to judge joint ventures under the rule of reason.

10. For a discussion of the free rider problem in the context of sports telecasting, see *Chicago Professional Sports Limited Partnership v. National Basketball Association,* 961 F.2d 667 (7th Cir. 1993).
11. 388 U.S. 365, 87 S.Ct. 1856, 18 L.Ed.2d 1249 (1967).

CASE 46.1   Continental T.V., Inc. v. GTE Sylvania, Inc.

Supreme Court of the United States, 1977.
433 U.S. 36,
97 S.Ct. 2549,
53 L.Ed.2d 568.
http://www.findlaw.com/
casecode/supreme.html [a]

BACKGROUND AND FACTS *GTE Sylvania, Inc., a manufacturer of television sets, adopted a franchise plan that limited the number of franchises granted in any given geographic area and that required each franchise to sell only Sylvania products from the location or locations at which it was franchised. Sylvania retained sole discretion to increase the number of retailers in an area, depending on the success or failure of existing retailers in developing their markets. Continental T.V., Inc., was a retailer under Sylvania's franchise plan. Shortly after Sylvania proposed a new franchise that would compete with Continental, Sylvania terminated Continental's franchise, and a suit was brought in a federal district court for money owed. Continental claimed that Sylvania's vertically restrictive franchise system violated Section 1 of the Sherman Act. The district court held for Continental, and Sylvania*

a. In the "Citation Search" section, type "433" in the first box, type "36" in the second box, and click on "Get It" to access the case.

CONTINUED ▶

CASE 46.1 | Continued *appealed. The appellate court reversed the trial court's decision. Continental appealed to the United States Supreme Court.*

IN THE LANGUAGE OF THE COURT

Mr. Justice *POWELL* delivered the opinion of the Court.

* * * *

Vertical restrictions reduce intrabrand competition by limiting the number of sellers of a particular product competing for the business of a given group of buyers. * * *

Vertical restrictions promote interbrand competition by allowing the manufacturer to achieve certain efficiencies in the distribution of his products. * * * Established manufacturers can use them to induce retailers to engage in promotional activities or to provide service and repair facilities necessary to the efficient marketing of their products. * * * The availability and quality of such services affect a manufacturer's goodwill and the competitiveness of his product. * * * [Emphasis added.]

* * * *

* * * When anticompetitive effects are shown to result from particular vertical restrictions, they can be adequately policed under the rule of reason * * * .

DECISION AND REMEDY *The United States Supreme Court upheld the appellate court's reversal of the district court's decision. Sylvania's vertical system, which was not price restrictive, did not constitute a* per se *violation of Section 1 of the Sherman Act.*

IMPACT OF THIS CASE ON TODAY'S LAW

As noted, this case is generally thought of as one of the most important antitrust cases since the 1940s. It marked a definite shift from rigid characterization of these kinds of vertical restraints to a more flexible, economic analysis of the restraints under the rule of reason. Today's courts still apply the rule of reason to territorial and customer restrictions, following the precedent laid down in this case.

RESALE PRICE MAINTENANCE AGREEMENTS An agreement between a manufacturer and a distributor or retailer in which the manufacturer specifies what the retail prices of its products must be is known as a **resale price maintenance agreement.** While once considered a *per se* violation of Section 1 of the Sherman Act, this type of vertical price-fixing agreement is now judged under the rule of reason because the practice may increase competition and benefit consumers.

REFUSALS TO DEAL As discussed previously, joint refusals to deal (group boycotts) are subject to close scrutiny under Section 1 of the Sherman Act. A single manufacturer acting unilaterally is generally free to deal, or not to deal, with whomever it wishes. In vertical arrangements, however, a manufacturer can refuse to deal with retailers or dealers that cut prices to levels substantially below the manufacturer's suggested retail prices.[12]

In some instances, however, a unilateral refusal to deal violates antitrust laws. These instances involve

offenses proscribed under Section 2 of the Sherman Act and occur only if (1) the firm refusing to deal has—or is likely to acquire—monopoly power and (2) the refusal is likely to have an anticompetitive effect on a particular market.

SECTION 3 | Section 2 of the Sherman Act

Section 1 of the Sherman Act proscribes certain concerted, or joint, activities that restrain trade. In contrast, Section 2 condemns "every person who shall monopolize, or attempt to monopolize." Thus, two distinct types of behavior are subject to sanction under Section 2: *monopolization* and *attempts to monopolize.* A tactic that may be involved in either offense is predatory pricing. **Predatory pricing** occurs when one firm attempts to drive its competitors from the market by selling its product at prices substantially *below* the normal costs of production. Once the competitors are eliminated, the firm will attempt to recapture its losses and go on to earn very high profits by driving up prices far above their competitive levels.

---

12. See, for example, *United States v. Colgate & Co.*, 250 U.S. 300, 39 S.Ct. 465, 63 L.Ed. 992 (1919).

MONOPOLIZATION

In *United States v. Grinnell Corp.*,[13] the United States Supreme Court defined **monopolization** as involving the following two elements: "(1) the possession of monopoly power in the relevant market and (2) the willful acquisition or maintenance of the power as distinguished from growth or development as a consequence of a superior product, business acumen, or historic accident." A violation of Section 2 requires that both these elements—monopoly power and an *intent* to monopolize—be established.

MONOPOLY POWER The Sherman Act does not define *monopoly*. In economic parlance, monopoly refers to control of an entire market by a single entity. It is well established in antitrust law, however, that a firm may be a monopolist even though it is not the sole seller in a market. Additionally, size alone does not determine whether a firm is a monopoly. For example, a "mom and pop" grocery located in an isolated desert town is a monopolist if it is the only grocery serving that particular market. Size in relation to the market is what matters, because monopoly involves the power to affect prices and output.

—*Market Power.* *Monopoly power,* as mentioned earlier in this chapter, exists when a firm has sufficient market power to control prices and exclude competition. As difficult as it is to define market power precisely, it is even more difficult to measure it. Courts often use the so-called **market-share test**[14]—a firm's percentage share of the "relevant market"—in determining the extent of the firm's market power. A firm generally is considered to have monopoly power if its share of the relevant market is 70 percent or more. This is merely a rule of thumb, however; it is not a binding principle of law. In some cases, a smaller share may be held to constitute monopoly power.[15]

—*Relevant Market.* The relevant market consists of two elements: (1) a relevant product market and (2) a relevant geographic market. What should

the relevant product market include? No doubt, it must include all products that, although produced by different firms, have identical attributes, such as sugar. Products that are not identical, however, may sometimes be substituted for one another. Coffee may be substituted for tea, for example. In defining the relevant product market, the key issue is the degree of interchangeability between products. If one product is a sufficient substitute for another, the two products are considered to be part of the same product market.

The second component of the relevant market is the geographic boundaries of the market. For products that are sold nationwide, the geographic boundaries of the market encompass the entire United States. If a producer and its competitors sell in only a limited area (one in which customers have no access to other sources of the product), then the geographic market is limited to that area. A national firm may thus compete in several distinct areas and have monopoly power in one area but not in another.

THE INTENT REQUIREMENT Monopoly power, in and of itself, does not constitute the offense of monopolization under Section 2 of the Sherman Act. The offense also requires an *intent* to monopolize. A dominant market share may be the result of good business judgment or the development of a superior product. It may simply be the result of historical accident. In these situations, the acquisition of monopoly power is not an antitrust violation.

If, however, a firm possesses market power as a result of carrying out some purposeful act to acquire or maintain that power through anticompetitive means, then it is in violation of Section 2. In most monopolization cases, intent may be inferred from evidence that the firm had monopoly power and engaged in anticompetitive behavior.

ATTEMPTS TO MONOPOLIZE

Section 2 also prohibits **attempted monopolization** of a market. Any action challenged as an attempt to monopolize must have been specifically intended to exclude competitors and garner monopoly power. The attempt must also have had a "dangerous" probability of success—only *serious* threats of monopolization are condemned as violations. The probability cannot be dangerous unless the alleged offender possesses some degree of market power. The following case demonstrates how an attempt to monopolize may occur.

---

13. 384 U.S. 563, 86 S.Ct. 1698, 16 L.Ed.2d 778 (1966).

14. Other measures of market power have been devised, but the market-share test is the most widely used.

15. This standard was first articulated by Judge Learned Hand in *United States v. Aluminum Co. of America*, 148 F.2d 416 (2d Cir. 1945). A 90 percent share was held to be clear evidence of monopoly power. Anything less than 64 percent, said Judge Hand, made monopoly power doubtful, and anything less than 30 percent was clearly not monopoly power.

United States
District Court,
District of Colorado, 2004.
311 F.Supp.2d 1048.

CASE 46.2

Nobody in Particular Presents, Inc. v. Clear Channel Communications, Inc.

BACKGROUND AND FACTS *Nobody in Particular Presents, Inc. (NIPP), is a music concert promoter in the Denver, Colorado, area and has promoted concerts by Beck, Pearl Jam, the Neville Brothers, and many others in a number of cities. Clear Channel Communications (CCC) is one of the largest radio and entertainment conglomerates in the world. Through its wholly owned subsidiaries, Clear Channel has holdings in radio stations, concert venues, and the concert promotions industry. Clear Channel has four rock-format radio stations in the Denver area and is a major area concert promoter, controlling about 47 percent of the local market. Clear Channel's market share in terms of advertising revenue for rock music may be as high as 87.3 percent. NIPP filed an action against Clear Channel, complaining that Clear Channel used its position in rock-format radio to intimidate and coerce rock artists and their record labels into signing with Clear Channel subsidiaries for concert pro- motion. The defendant (Clear Channel) allegedly informed artists that local radio stations would not play their music or even accept their advertising unless they signed up for Clear Channel promotion. Those who did sign up for Clear Channel concert promotion received additional airtime and free pro- motions. NIPP alleged that this was an attempt to monopolize the market in violation of Section 2 of the Sherman Act. Clear Channel moved for summary judgment.*

IN THE LANGUAGE OF THE COURT

NOTTINGHAM, J.

* * * *

Here, NIPP has presented sufficient evidence that Clear Channel's refusal to accept paid advertising is founded upon an intention to create monopoly power for itself in the rock concert promotions market. As shown earlier in electronic mail messages, Michael O'Connor asked his station personnel to refuse advertising for promoters competing with SFX/Clear Channel Entertainment and/or Radio festivals. This refusal to deal may not be in the commercial best interest of Clear Channel's radio stations because, as O'Connor himself testified, providing radio advertising and radio promotional support benefits the radio stations. * * * *Assuming that the refusal to deal is not in the best commercial interests of the radio stations, an inference could be made that the refusal supports other, more sinister motives, such as the creation of a monopoly.* * * * Finally, NIPP has demonstrated evidence of marketwide injury by showing an increase in ticket prices and a decreasing market share for all of Clear Channel's competitors in the rock concert market * * *. [Emphasis added.]

DECISION AND REMEDY *The defendant's motion for summary judgment on attempted monopolization claims was denied, but the court granted the motion on actual monopolization claims, because the defendant did not have a large enough market share of the concert promotion business to qualify as an actual monopolist.*

SECTION 4 | The Clayton Act

In 1914, Congress enacted the Clayton Act. The Clayton Act was aimed at specific anticompetitive or monopolistic practices that the Sherman Act did not cover. The substantive provisions of the act deal with four distinct forms of business behavior, which are declared illegal but not criminal. For each of the four provisions, the act states that the behavior is illegal only if it tends to substantially lessen competition or

to create monopoly power. The major offenses under the Clayton Act are set out in Sections 2, 3, 7, and 8 of the act.

PRICE DISCRIMINATION

Price discrimination, which occurs when a seller charges different prices to competing buyers for iden- tical goods or services, is prohibited by Section 2 of the Clayton Act. Because businesses frequently circum- vented Section 2 of the act, Congress strengthened this section by amending it with the passage of the Robinson-Patman Act in 1936.

As amended, Section 2 prohibits price discrimination that cannot be justified by differences in production costs, transportation costs, or cost differences due to other reasons. To violate Section 2, the seller must be engaged in interstate commerce, and the effect of the price discrimination must be to substantially lessen competition or to create a competitive injury.

In other words, a seller is prohibited from reducing a price to one buyer below the price charged to that buyer's competitor. An exception is made if the seller can justify the price reduction by demonstrating (1) that the seller charged the lower price temporarily and in good faith to meet another seller's equally low price to the buyer's competitor or (2) that a particular buyer's purchases saved the seller costs in producing and selling the goods (called *cost justification*). To violate the Clayton Act, a seller's pricing policies must also include a reasonable prospect of the seller's recouping its losses.[16]

EXCLUSIONARY PRACTICES

Under Section 3 of the Clayton Act, sellers or lessors cannot sell or lease goods "on the condition, agreement or understanding that the . . . purchaser or lessee thereof shall not use or deal in the goods . . . of a competitor or competitors of the seller." In effect, this section prohibits two types of vertical agreements involving exclusionary practices—exclusive-dealing contracts and tying arrangements.

EXCLUSIVE-DEALING CONTRACTS Under an **exclusive-dealing contract,** a seller forbids a buyer to purchase products from the seller's competitors. A seller is prohibited from making an exclusive-dealing contract under Section 3 if the effect of the contract is "to substantially lessen competition or tend to create a monopoly."

The leading exclusive-dealing decision was made by the United States Supreme Court in the case of *Standard Oil Co. of California v. United States.*[17] In this case, the then-largest gasoline seller in the nation made exclusive-dealing contracts with independent stations in seven western states. The contracts involved 16 percent of all retail outlets, whose sales were approximately 7 percent of all retail sales in that market. The Court noted that the market was substantially concentrated because the seven largest gasoline suppliers all used exclusive-dealing contracts with their independent retailers and together controlled 65 percent of the market. Looking at market conditions after the arrangements were instituted, the Court found that market shares were extremely stable, and entry into the market was apparently restricted. Thus, the Court held that the Clayton Act had been violated because competition was "foreclosed in a substantial share" of the relevant market.

TYING ARRANGEMENTS In a **tying arrangement,** or *tie-in sales agreement,* a seller conditions the sale of a product (the tying product) on the buyer's agreement to purchase another product (the tied product) produced or distributed by the same seller. The legality of a tie-in agreement depends on many factors, particularly the purpose of the agreement and the agreement's likely effect on competition in the relevant markets (the market for the tying product and the market for the tied product).

In 1936, for example, the Supreme Court held that International Business Machines and Remington Rand had violated Section 3 of the Clayton Act by requiring the purchase of their own machine cards (the tied product) as a condition to the leasing of their tabulation machines (the tying product). Because only these two firms sold completely automated tabulation machines, the Court concluded that each possessed market power sufficient to "substantially lessen competition" through the tying arrangements.[18]

Section 3 of the Clayton Act has been held to apply only to commodities, not to services. Tying arrangements, however, can also be considered agreements that restrain trade in violation of Section 1 of the Sherman Act. Thus, cases involving tying arrangements of services have been brought under Section 1 of the Sherman Act. Traditionally, the courts have held tying arrangements examined under the Sherman Act to be illegal *per se*. In recent years, however, courts have shown a willingness to look at factors that are important in a rule-of-reason analysis.

---

16. See, for example, *Brooke Group, Ltd. v. Brown & Williamson Tobacco Corp.,* 509 U.S. 209, 113 S.Ct. 2578, 125 L.Ed.2d 168 (1993), in which the Supreme Court held that a seller's price-cutting policies could not be predatory "[g]iven the market's realities"—the size of the seller's market share, expanding output by other sellers, and other factors.

17. 337 U.S. 293, 69 S.Ct. 1051, 93 L.Ed. 1371 (1949).

18. *International Business Machines Corp. v. United States,* 298 U.S. 131, 56 S.Ct. 701, 80 L.Ed. 1085 (1936).

MERGERS

Under Section 7 of the Clayton Act, a person or business organization cannot hold stock or assets in more than one business when "the effect . . . may be to substantially lessen competition." Section 7 is the statutory authority for preventing mergers that could result in monopoly power or a substantial lessening of competition in the marketplace. Section 7 applies to three types of mergers: horizontal mergers, vertical mergers, and conglomerate mergers. We discuss each type of merger in the following subsections.

A crucial consideration in most merger cases is **market concentration.** Determining market concentration involves allocating percentage market shares among the various companies in the relevant market. When a small number of companies share a large part of the market, the market is concentrated. For example, if the four largest grocery stores in Chicago accounted for 80 percent of all retail food sales, the market clearly would be concentrated in those four firms. Competition is not necessarily diminished solely as a result of market concentration, however, and other factors must be considered to determine if a merger violates Section 7. Another important factor is whether the merger will make it more difficult for *potential* competitors to enter the relevant market.

HORIZONTAL MERGERS Mergers between firms that compete with each other in the same market are called **horizontal mergers.** If a horizontal merger creates an entity with a resulting significant market share, the merger may be presumed illegal. This is because of the United States Supreme Court's interpretation that Congress, in amending Section 7 of the Clayton Act in 1950, intended to prevent mergers that increase market concentration.[19] Three other factors that the courts also consider in analyzing the legality of a horizontal merger are the overall concentration of the relevant market, the relevant market's history of tending toward concentration, and whether the merger is apparently designed to establish market power or restrict competition.

The Federal Trade Commission (FTC) and the U.S. Department of Justice (DOJ) have established guidelines indicating which mergers will be challenged. Under the guidelines, the first factor to be considered in determining whether a merger will be contested is the degree of concentration in the relevant market. This is done by comparing the premerger market concentration with the anticipated postmerger market concentration. The FTC and the DOJ will also consider other factors, including the ease of entry into the relevant market, economic efficiency, the financial condition of the merging firms, and the nature and price of the product or products involved. When a leading firm is involved—one having a share that is at least 35 percent of the market and is twice that of the next leading firm—any merger with another firm will be closely scrutinized.

VERTICAL MERGERS A **vertical merger** occurs when a company at one stage of production acquires a company at a higher or lower stage of production. An example of a vertical merger is a company merging with one of its suppliers or retailers. Courts in the past have almost exclusively focused on "foreclosure" in assessing vertical mergers. Foreclosure occurs when competitors of the merging firms lose opportunities to either sell products to or buy products from the merging firms.

In one early case, for example, du Pont was challenged for acquiring a considerable amount of General Motors (GM) stock. In holding that the transaction was illegal, the United States Supreme Court noted that acquiring the stock would enable du Pont to foreclose other sellers of fabrics and finishes from selling to GM.[20]

Today, whether a vertical merger will be deemed illegal generally depends on several factors, including market concentration, barriers to entry into the market, and the apparent intent of the merging parties. Mergers that do not prevent competitors of either of the merging firms from competing in a segment of the market will not be condemned as foreclosing competition and are legal.

CONGLOMERATE MERGERS There are three general types of **conglomerate mergers:** market-extension, product-extension, and diversification mergers. A market-extension merger occurs when a firm seeks to sell its product in a new market by merging with a firm already established in that market. A product-extension merger occurs when a firm seeks to add a closely related product to its existing line by merging

---

19. *Brown Shoe v. United States,* 370 U.S. 294, 82 S.Ct. 1502, 8 L.Ed.2d 510 (1962).

20. *United States v. E. I. du Pont de Nemours & Co.,* 353 U.S. 586, 77 S.Ct. 872, 1 L.Ed.2d 1057 (1957).

with a firm already producing that product. For example, a manufacturer might seek to extend its line of household products to include floor wax by acquiring a leading manufacturer of floor wax. Diversification occurs when a firm merges with another firm that offers a product or service wholly unrelated to the first firm's existing activities, such as when an automobile manufacturer acquires a motel chain.

INTERLOCKING DIRECTORATES

Section 8 of the Clayton Act deals with *interlocking directorates*—that is, the practice of having individuals serve as directors on the boards of two or more competing companies simultaneously. Specifically, no person may be a director for two or more competing corporations at the same time if either of the corporations has capital, surplus, or undivided profits aggregating more than $21,327,000 or competitive sales of $2,132,700 or more. The threshold amounts are adjusted each year by the Federal Trade Commission. (The amounts given here are those announced by the commission in 2005.)

SECTION 5 | Enforcement of Antitrust Laws

The federal agencies that enforce the federal antitrust laws are the U.S. Department of Justice (DOJ) and the Federal Trade Commission (FTC). The FTC was established by the Federal Trade Commission Act of 1914. Section 5 of that act is its sole substantive provision. Section 5 provides, in part, as follows: "Unfair methods of competition in or affecting commerce, and unfair or deceptive acts or practices in or affecting commerce are hereby declared illegal." Section 5 condemns all forms of anticompetitive behavior that are not covered under other federal antitrust laws.

Only the DOJ can prosecute violations of the Sherman Act as either criminal or civil violations. Violations of the Clayton Act are not crimes, and either the DOJ or the FTC can enforce that statute through civil proceedings. The DOJ or the FTC may ask the courts to impose various remedies including **divestiture** (making a company give up one or more of its operations) and dissolution. A group of meat packers, for example, might be forced to divest itself of control or ownership of butcher shops.

The FTC has sole authority to enforce violations of Section 5 of the Federal Trade Commission Act. FTC actions are effected through administrative orders, but if a firm violates an FTC order, the FTC can seek court sanctions for the violation.

PRIVATE ACTIONS

A private party who allegedly has been injured as a result of a violation of the Sherman Act or the Clayton Act can sue for damages and attorneys' fees. In some instances, private parties may also seek injunctive relief to prevent antitrust violations. The courts have determined that the ability to sue depends on the directness of the injury suffered by the would-be plaintiff. Thus, a person wishing to sue under the Sherman Act must prove (1) that the antitrust violation either caused or was a substantial factor in causing the injury that was suffered and (2) that the unlawful actions of the accused party affected business activities of the plaintiff that were protected by the antitrust laws.

TREBLE DAMAGES

In recent years, more than 90 percent of all antitrust actions have been brought by private plaintiffs. One reason for this is that successful plaintiffs may recover treble damages—three times the damages that they have suffered as a result of the violation. Such recoveries by private plaintiffs for antitrust violations have been rationalized as encouraging people to act as "private attorneys general" who will vigorously pursue antitrust violators on their own initiative. In a situation involving a price-fixing agreement, normally each competitor is jointly and severally liable for the total amount of any damages, including treble damages if they are imposed.

SECTION 6 | Exemptions from Antitrust Law

There are many legislative and constitutional limitations on antitrust enforcement. Most statutory and judicially created exemptions to the antitrust laws apply to the following areas or activities:

1. *Labor.* Section 6 of the Clayton Act generally permits labor unions to organize and bargain without

violating antitrust laws. Section 20 of the Clayton Act specifies that strikes and other labor activities are not violations of any law of the United States. A union can lose its exemption, however, if it combines with a nonlabor group rather than acting simply in its own self-interest.

2. *Agricultural associations and fisheries.* Section 6 of the Clayton Act (along with the Cooperative Marketing Associations Act of 1922[21]) exempts agricultural cooperatives from the antitrust laws. The Fisheries Cooperative Marketing Act of 1976 exempts from antitrust legislation individuals in the fishing industry who collectively catch, produce, and prepare their products for market. Both exemptions allow members of such co-ops to combine and set prices for a particular product but do not allow them to engage in exclusionary practices or restraints of trade directed at competitors.

3. *Insurance.* The McCarran-Ferguson Act of 1945[22] exempts the insurance business from the antitrust laws whenever state regulation exists. This exemption does not cover boycotts, coercion, or intimidation on the part of insurance companies.

4. *Foreign trade.* Under the provisions of the 1918 Webb-Pomerene Act,[23] U.S. exporters may engage in cooperative activity to compete with similar foreign associations. This type of cooperative activity may not, however, restrain trade within the United States or injure other U.S. exporters. The Export Trading Company Act of 1982[24] broadened the Webb-Pomerene Act by permitting the Department of Justice to certify properly qualified export trading companies. Any activity within the scope described by the certificate is exempt from public prosecution under the antitrust laws.

5. *Professional baseball.* In 1922, the United States Supreme Court held that professional baseball was not within the reach of federal antitrust laws because it did not involve "interstate commerce."[25] Some of the effects of this decision, however, were modified by the Curt Flood Act of 1998. Essentially, the act allows players the option of suing team owners for anti-

competitive practices if, for example, the owners collude to "blacklist" players, hold down players' salaries, or force players to play for specific teams.

6. *Oil marketing.* The 1935 Interstate Oil Compact allows states to determine quotas on oil that will be marketed in interstate commerce.

7. *Cooperative research and production.* Cooperative research among small business firms is exempt under the Small Business Act of 1958.[26] Research or production of a product, process, or service by joint ventures consisting of competitors is exempt under special federal legislation, including the National Cooperative Research Act of 1984,[27] as amended.

8. *Joint efforts by businesspersons to obtain legislative or executive action.* This is often referred to as the *Noerr-Pennington* doctrine.[28] For example, DVD producers might jointly lobby Congress to change the copyright laws without being held liable for attempting to restrain trade. Though selfish rather than purely public-minded conduct is permitted, there is an exception: an action will not be protected if it is clear that the action is "objectively baseless in the sense that no reasonable [person] could reasonably expect success on the merits" and it is an attempt to make anticompetitive use of government processes.[29]

9. *Other exemptions.* Other activities exempt from antitrust laws include activities approved by the president in furtherance of the defense of our nation (under the Defense Production Act of 1950[30]); state actions, when the state policy is clearly articulated and the policy is actively supervised by the state; and activities of regulated industries (such as the transportation, communication, and banking industries) when federal agencies (such as the Federal Communications Commission) have primary regulatory authority.

The following case concerns the first exemption in the above list.

---

21. 7 U.S.C. Sections 291–292.
22. 15 U.S.C. Sections 1011–1015.
23. 15 U.S.C. Sections 61–66.
24. 15 U.S.C. Sections 4001–4003.
25. *Federal Baseball Club of Baltimore, Inc. v. National League of Professional Baseball Clubs,* 259 U.S. 200, 42 S.Ct. 465, 66 L.Ed. 898 (1922).

26. 15 U.S.C. Sections 631–657.
27. 15 U.S.C. Sections 4301–4306.
28. See *United Mine Workers of America v. Pennington,* 381 U.S. 657, 85 S.Ct. 1585, 14 L.Ed.2d 626 (1965); and *Eastern Railroad Presidents Conference v. Noerr Motor Freight, Inc.,* 365 U.S. 127, 81 S.Ct. 523, 5 L.Ed.2d 464 (1961).
29. *Professional Real Estate Investors, Inc. v. Columbia Pictures Industries, Inc.,* 508 U.S. 49, 113 S.Ct. 1920, 123 L.Ed.2d 611 (1993).
30. 50 App.U.S.C. Sections 2061–2171.

Clarett v. National Football League

SOTOMAYOR, Circuit Judge.

* * * *

[Maurice] Clarett, former running back for Ohio State University ("OSU") and Big Ten Freshman of the Year, is an accomplished and talented amateur football player. After gaining national attention as a high school player, Clarett became the first college freshman since 1943 to open as a starter at the position of running back for OSU. He led that team through an undefeated season, even scoring the winning touchdown in a double-overtime victory in the 2003 Fiesta Bowl to claim the national championship. * * * Clarett is now interested in turning professional by entering the [National Football League ("NFL" or "the League")] draft. Clarett is precluded from so doing, however, under the NFL's current rules governing draft eligibility.

* * * The eligibility rules * * * permit a player to enter the draft three full seasons after that player's high school graduation.

Clarett graduated high school on December 11, 2001, two-thirds of the way through the 2001 NFL season and is a season shy of the three necessary to qualify under the draft's eligibility rules. Unwilling to forgo the prospect of a year of lucrative professional play or run the risk of a career-compromising injury were his entry into the draft delayed until next year, Clarett filed this suit [in a federal district court] alleging that the NFL's draft eligibility rules are an unreasonable restraint of trade in violation of Section 1 of the Sherman Act and Section 4 of the Clayton Act.

* * * [T]he major source of the parties' * * * disputes is the relationship between the challenged eligibility rules and the current collective bargaining agreement governing the terms and conditions of employment for NFL players * * * . The current collective bargaining agreement between the NFL and its players union was negotiated between the NFL Management Council ("NFLMC"), which is the NFL member clubs' multi-employer bargaining unit, and the NFL Players Association ("NFLPA"), the NFL players' exclusive bargaining representative. * * *

* * * *

* * * On February 5, 2004, the district court granted summary judgment in favor of Clarett and ordered him eligible to enter this year's draft. * * * [The NFL appealed to this court.]

* * * *

* * * *[T]o accommodate the collective bargaining process, certain concerted activity among and between labor and employers [is] held to be beyond the reach of the antitrust laws.* * * * [Emphasis added.]

* * * *

Although the NFL has maintained draft eligibility rules in one form or another for much of its history, the inception of a collective bargaining relationship between the NFL and its players union some thirty years ago irrevocably altered the governing legal regime. * * * [P]rospective players no longer have the right to negotiate directly with the NFL teams over the terms and conditions of their employment. That responsibility is instead committed to the NFL and the players union to accomplish through the collective bargaining process, and throughout that process the NFL and the players union are to have the freedom to craft creative solutions to their differences in light of the economic imperatives of their industry. Furthermore, the NFL teams are permitted to engage in joint conduct with respect to the terms and conditions of players' employment as a multi-employer bargaining unit without risking antitrust liability. * * *

* * * *

Clarett's argument that antitrust law should permit him to circumvent this scheme established by federal labor law starts with the contention that the eligibility rules do not constitute

CONTINUED ▶

CASE 46.3 | **Continued** a mandatory subject of collective bargaining and thus cannot fall within the protection of the * * * exemption. * * * [H]owever, we find that the eligibility rules are mandatory bargaining subjects. Though tailored to the unique circumstance of a professional sports league, the eligibility rules for the draft represent a quite literal condition for initial employment and for that reason alone might constitute a mandatory bargaining subject. But moreover, the eligibility rules constitute a mandatory bargaining subject because they have tangible effects on the wages and working conditions of current NFL players. Because the unusual economic imperatives of professional sports raise numerous problems with little or no precedent in standard industrial relations, * * * many of the arrangements in professional sports that, at first glance, might not appear to deal with wages or working conditions are indeed mandatory bargaining subjects. * * *

Furthermore, by reducing competition in the market for entering players, the eligibility rules also affect the job security of veteran players. Because the size of NFL teams is capped, the eligibility rules diminish a veteran player's risk of being replaced by either a drafted rookie or a player who enters the draft and, though not drafted, is then hired as a rookie free agent. Consequently, * * * we find that to regard the NFL's eligibility rules as merely permissive bargaining subjects would ignore the reality of collective bargaining in sports.
* * * *

For the forgoing reasons, the judgment of the district court is REVERSED and the case REMANDED with instructions to enter judgment in favor of the NFL. The order of the district court designating Clarett eligible to enter this year's NFL draft is VACATED [set aside, rendered void].

QUESTIONS

1. Why are the NFL's member clubs permitted to agree that a player will not be hired until three full football seasons after the player's high school graduation?
2. Why couldn't the NFL's eligibility rules be eliminated from the list of mandatory subjects for the parties' collective bargaining agreement?

SECTION 7 | U.S. Antitrust Laws in the Global Context

U.S. antitrust laws have a broad application. Not only may persons in foreign nations be subject to their provisions, but they may also be applied to protect foreign consumers and competitors from violations committed by U.S. business firms. Consequently, *foreign persons*, a term that by definition includes foreign governments, may sue under U.S. antitrust laws in U.S. courts.

THE EXTRATERRITORIAL APPLICATION OF U.S. ANTITRUST LAWS

Section 1 of the Sherman Act of 1890 provides for the extraterritorial effect of the U.S. antitrust laws. The United States is a major proponent of free competition in the global economy, and thus any conspiracy that has a *substantial effect* on U.S. commerce is within the reach of the Sherman Act. The violation may even occur outside the United States, and foreign governments as well as individuals can be sued for violation of U.S. antitrust laws. Before U.S. courts will exercise jurisdiction and apply antitrust laws, it must be shown that the alleged violation had a substantial effect on U.S. commerce. U.S. jurisdiction is automatically invoked, however, when a *per se* violation occurs.

If a domestic firm, for example, joins a foreign cartel to control the production, price, or distribution of goods, and this cartel has a *substantial effect* on U.S. commerce, a *per se* violation may exist. Hence, both the domestic firm and the foreign cartel could be sued for violation of the U.S. antitrust laws. Likewise, if a foreign firm doing business in the United States enters into a price-fixing or other anticompetitive agreement to control a portion of U.S. markets, a *per se* violation may exist.

THE APPLICATION OF FOREIGN ANTITRUST LAWS

The need for large U.S. companies to worry about the application of foreign antitrust laws is increasing as well. The European Union (EU), for example, has laws that are in many respects stricter than those of the

United States. The EU blocked a bid by General Electric Company to acquire Honeywell International, Inc., in 2001. The EU entered into its own antitrust settlement with Microsoft Corporation, with remedies (including a potential fine of $665 million) that went beyond those imposed in the United States. The EU has also threatened additional fines for Microsoft's alleged failure to comply with requirements that it offer Windows without its private Media Player video and music applications.

REVIEWING ANTITRUST LAW

The Internet Corporation for Assigned Names and Numbers (ICANN) is a nonprofit entity organizing Internet domain names. It is governed by a board of directors elected by various groups with commercial interests in the Internet. One of ICANN's functions is to authorize an entity as a registry for certain "Top Level Domains" (TLDs). ICANN entered into an agreement with VeriSign to serve as registry for the ".com" TLD to provide registry services in accordance with ICANN's specifications. VeriSign complained that ICANN was restricting the services that it could make available as a registrar and blocking new services, imposing unnecessary conditions on those services, and setting prices at which the services were offered. VeriSign claimed that ICANN's control of the registry services for domain names violated Section 1 of the Sherman Act.

1. Should ICANN's actions be judged under the rule of reason or deemed a *per se* violation of Section 1 of the Sherman Act?

2. Should ICANN's actions be viewed as a horizontal or a vertical restraint of trade?

3. Does it matter that ICANN's leadership is chosen by those with a commercial interest in the Internet?

4. If judged under the rule of reason, what might be ICANN's defense for having a standardized set of registry services that must be used?

TERMS AND CONCEPTS TO REVIEW

antitrust law 920

attempted monopolization 925

conglomerate merger 928

divestiture 929

exclusive-dealing contract 927

group boycott 922

horizontal merger 928

horizontal restraint 922

market concentration 928

market power 921

market-share test 925

monopolization 925

monopoly 921

monopoly power 921

per se violation 921

predatory pricing 924

price discrimination 926

price-fixing agreement 922

resale price maintenance agreement 924

restraint on trade 920

rule of reason 921

tying arrangement 927

vertical merger 928

vertical restraint 923

vertically integrated firm 923

QUESTIONS AND CASE PROBLEMS

46-1. Allitron, Inc., and Donovan, Ltd., are interstate competitors selling similar appliances, principally in the states of Indiana, Kentucky, Illinois, and Ohio. Allitron and Donovan agree that Allitron will no longer sell in Ohio and Indiana and that Donovan will no longer sell in Kentucky and Illinois. Have Allitron and Donovan violated any antitrust law? If so, which law? Explain.

46-2.  QUESTION WITH SAMPLE ANSWER

The partnership of Alvarado and Parish is engaged in the oil-wellhead service industry in the states of New Mexico and Colorado. The firm has about 40 percent of the market for this service. Webb Corp. competes with the Alvaredo-Parish partnership in the same states.

Webb has approximately 35 percent of the market. Alvaredo and Parish acquire the stock and assets of Webb Corp. Do the antitrust laws prohibit the type of action undertaken by Alvaredo and Parish? Discuss fully. **For a sample answer to this question, go to Appendix I at the end of this text.**

46–3. Jorge's Appliance Corp. was a new retail seller of appliances in Sunrise City. Because of its innovative sales techniques and financing, Jorge's caused the appliance department of No-Glow Department Store, a large chain store with a great deal of buying power, to lose a substantial amount of sales. No-Glow told a number of appliance manufacturers from whom it made large-volume purchases that if they continued to sell to Jorge's, No-Glow would stop buying from them. The manufacturers immediately stopped selling appliances to Jorge's. Jorge's filed a suit against No-Glow and the manufacturers, claiming that their actions constituted an antitrust violation. No-Glow and the manufacturers were able to prove that Jorge's was a small retailer with a small market share. They claimed that because the relevant market was not substantially affected, they were not guilty of restraint of trade. Discuss fully whether there was an antitrust violation.

46–4. Instant Foto Corp. is a manufacturer of photography film. At the present time, Instant Foto has approximately 50 percent of the market. Instant Foto advertises that the purchase price for Instant Foto film includes photo processing by Instant Foto Corp. Instant Foto claims that its film processing is specially designed to improve the quality of photos taken with Instant Foto film. Is Instant Foto's combination of film sales and film processing an antitrust violation? Explain.

46–5. RESTRAINT OF TRADE. The National Collegiate Athletic Association (NCAA) coordinates the intercollegiate athletic programs of its members by issuing rules and setting standards governing, among other things, the coaching staff. The NCAA set up a cost-reduction committee to consider ways to cut the costs of intercollegiate athletics while maintaining competition. The committee included financial aid personnel, intercollegiate athletic administrators, college presidents, university and faculty members, and a university chancellor. It was felt that "only a collaborate effort could reduce costs while maintaining a level playing field." The committee proposed a rule to restrict the annual compensation of certain coaches to $16,000. The NCAA adopted the rule. Basketball coaches affected by the rule filed a suit in a federal district court against the NCAA, alleging a violation of Section 1 of the Sherman Act. Is the rule a *per se* violation of the Sherman Act, or should it be evaluated under the rule of reason? If it is subject to the rule of reason, is it an illegal restraint of trade? Discuss fully. [*Law v. National Collegiate Athletic Association*, 134 F.3d 1010 (10th Cir. 1998)]

46–6. ⚖ **CASE PROBLEM WITH SAMPLE ANSWER**

Dentsply International, Inc., is one of a dozen manufacturers of artificial teeth for dentures and other restorative devices. Dentsply sells its teeth to twenty-three dealers of dental products. The dealers supply the teeth to dental laboratories, which fabricate dentures for sale to dentists. There are hundreds of other dealers who compete with each other on the basis of price and service. Some manufacturers sell directly to the laboratories. There are also thousands of laboratories that compete with each other on the basis of price and service. Because of advances in dental medicine, however, artificial tooth manufacturing is marked by low growth potential, and Dentsply dominates the industry. Dentsply's market share is greater than 75 percent and is about fifteen times larger than that of its next-closest competitor. Dentsply prohibits its dealers from marketing competitors' teeth unless they were selling the teeth before 1993. The federal government filed a suit in a federal district court against Dentsply, alleging in part a violation of Section 2 of the Sherman Act. What must the government show to succeed in its suit? Are those elements present in this case? What should the court rule? Explain. [*United States v. Dentsply International, Inc.*, 399 F.3d 181 (3d Cir. 2005)]

To view a sample answer for this case problem, go to this book's Web site at http://wbl.westbuslaw.com, select "Chapter 46," and click on "Case Problem with Sample Answer."

46–7. TYING ARRANGEMENT. Public Interest Corp. (PIC) owned and operated television station WTMV-TV in Lakeland, Florida. MCA Television, Ltd., owns and licenses syndicated television programs. The parties entered into a licensing contract with respect to several television shows. MCA conditioned the license on PIC's agreeing to take another show, *Harry and the Hendersons*. PIC agreed to this arrangement, although it would not have chosen to license *Harry* if it had not had to do so to secure the licenses for the other shows. More than two years into the contract, a dispute arose over PIC's payments, and negotiations failed to resolve the dispute. In a letter, MCA suspended PIC's broadcast rights for all of its shows and stated that "[a]ny telecasts of MCA programming by WTMV-TV . . . will be deemed unauthorized and shall constitute an infringement of MCA's copyrights." PIC nonetheless continued broadcasting MCA's programs, with the exception of *Harry*. MCA filed a suit in a federal district court against PIC, alleging breach of contract and copyright infringement. PIC filed a counterclaim, contending in part that MCA's deal was an illegal tying arrangement. Is PIC correct? Explain. [*MCA Television, Ltd. v. Public Interest Corp.*, 171 F.3d 1265 (11th Cir. 1999)]

46–8. ATTEMPTED MONOPOLIZATION. In 1995, to make personal computers (PCs) easier to use, Intel Corp. and other companies developed a standard, called the Universal Serial Bus (USB) specification, to enable the easy attachment of peripherals (printers and other hardware) to PCs. Intel and others formed the Universal Serial Bus Implementers Forum (USB-IF) to promote USB technology and products. Intel, however, makes relatively few USB products and does not make any USB interconnect devices. Multivideo Labs, Inc. (MVL), designed and distributed active extension cables (AECs) to connect peripheral devices to each other or to a PC. The AECs were not USB compliant, a fact that Intel employees told other USB-IF members. Asserting that this caused a "general cooling of the market" for AECs, MVL filed a suit in a federal district court against Intel, claiming in part attempted monopolization in violation of the Sherman Act. Intel filed a motion for summary judgment. How should the court rule, and why? [*Multivideo Labs, Inc. v. Intel Corp.*, __ F.Supp.2d __ (S.D.N.Y. 2000)]

46–9. MONOPOLIZATION. Moist snuff is a smokeless tobacco product sold in small round cans from racks, which include point-of-sale (POS) ads. POS ads are critical because tobacco advertising is restricted and the number of people who use smokeless tobacco products is relatively small. In the moist snuff market in the United States, there are only four competitors, including U.S. Tobacco Co. and its affiliates (USTC) and Conwood Co. In 1990, USTC, which held 87 percent of the market, began to convince major retailers, including Wal-Mart Stores, Inc., to use USTC's "exclusive racks" to display its products and those of all other snuff makers. USTC agents would then destroy competitors' racks. USTC also began to provide retailers with false sales data to convince them to maintain its poor-selling items and drop competitors' less expensive products. Conwood's Wal-Mart market share fell from 12 percent to 6.5 percent. In stores in which USTC did not have rack exclusivity,

however, Conwood's market share increased to 25 percent. Conwood filed a suit in a federal district court against USTC, alleging in part that USTC used its monopoly power to exclude competitors from the moist snuff market. Should the court rule in Conwood's favor? What is USTC's best defense? Discuss. [*Conwood Co., L.P. v. U.S. Tobacco Co.*, 290 F.3d 768 (6th Cir. 2002)]

46–10. RESTRAINT OF TRADE. Visa U.S.A., Inc., MasterCard International, Inc., American Express (Amex), and Discover are the four major credit- and charge-card networks in the United States. Visa and MasterCard are joint ventures, owned by the thousands of banks that are their members. The banks issue the cards, clear transactions, and collect fees from the merchants who accept the cards. By contrast, Amex and Discover themselves issue cards to customers, process transactions, and collect fees. Since 1995, Amex has asked banks to issue its cards. No bank has been willing to do so, however, because it would have to stop issuing Visa and MasterCard cards under those networks' rules barring member banks from issuing cards on rival networks. The U.S. Department of Justice filed a suit in a federal district court against Visa and MasterCard, alleging in part that the rules were illegal restraints of trade under the Sherman Act. Do the rules harm competition? If so, how? What relief might the court order to stop any anticompetitiveness? [*United States v. Visa U.S.A., Inc.*, 344 F.3d 229 (2d Cir. 2003)]

LAW | on the Web

For updated links to resources available on the Web, as well as a variety of other materials, visit this text's Web site at http://wbl.westbuslaw.com.

You can access the Antitrust Division of the U.S. Department of Justice online at

http://www.usdoj.gov

To see the American Bar Association's Web page on antitrust law, go to

http://www.abanet.org/antitrust

The Federal Trade Commission offers an abundance of information on antitrust law, including *A Plain English Guide to Antitrust Laws*, which is available at

http://www.ftc.gov/bc/compguide/index.html

LEGAL RESEARCH EXERCISES ON THE WEB

Go to http://wbl.westbuslaw.com, the Web site that accompanies this text. Select "Chapter 46" and click on "Internet Exercises." There you will find the following Internet research exercises that you can perform to learn more about topics covered in this chapter.

Activity 46–1: LEGAL PERSPECTIVE
    The Standard Oil Trust

Activity 46–2: MANAGEMENT PERSPECTIVE
    Avoiding Antitrust Problems

Government Regulation

If this text had been written a hundred years ago, it would have had little to say about federal government regulation. Today, in contrast, virtually every area of economic activity is regulated by the government. Ethical issues in government regulation arise because regulation, by its very nature, means that some traditional rights and freedoms must be given up to ensure that other rights and freedoms are protected. Essentially, government regulation brings two ethical principles into conflict. On the one hand, deeply embedded in American culture is the idea that the government should play a limited role in directing our lives. Indeed, this nation was founded so that Americans could be free from the "heavy hand of government" experienced by the colonists under British rule. On the other hand, one of the basic functions of government is to protect the welfare of individuals and the environment in which they live.

Ultimately, virtually every law or rule regulating business represents a decision to give up certain rights in order to protect other perceived rights. In this *Focus on Ethics* feature, we look at some of the ethical aspects of government regulation.

Telemarketing and Free Speech

A good example of the conflict between the rights of one group and that of another is the debate over the Do Not Call Registry. As noted in Chapter 44, in 2002 the Federal Trade Commission (FTC) amended the Telemarketing Sales Rule to establish a national "do-not-call" list. The rule became effective in 2003. The do-not-call list offered telephone users the option of registering their names with the FTC to protect themselves from unwanted phone solicitations.

Consumers versus Telemarketers Consumers, who had long complained about receiving unsolicited sales calls, welcomed the Do Not Call Registry and the reduced number of sales calls that they have received as a result. Indeed, respondents in one survey indicated that after the rule was implemented, their unwanted phone calls decreased from an average of thirty calls per month to only six calls per month.

Telemarketers, in contrast, have strongly objected to the new rule. Business has sagged for numerous companies, causing jobs to be lost. Many firms have continued to contact individuals on the registry, making themselves vulnerable to fines of up to $11,000 for each phone number that they dial on the list.

The Free Speech Issue Soon after the do-not-call regulations became effective, a number of telemarketing firms filed lawsuits

against the FTC. The firms claimed that the new rules abridged their commercial speech, which is protected under the First Amendment (see Chapter 4). A federal district court judge sided with the telemarketers, ruling that the FTC's rules were unconstitutional on First Amendment grounds.

On appeal, however, the U.S. Court of Appeals for the Tenth Circuit overturned the decision and outlined four reasons why the do-not-call list was consistent with First Amendment requirements. First, the registry restricts only "core commercial speech," such as sales calls. Second, the court stated that an individual's home is a personal sanctuary. Because the do-not-call list specifically targets speech that invades the privacy of the home, there is no breach of First Amendment rights. Third, the registry is an optional program that places the right to restrict commercial speech in the hands of consumers, not the government. Finally, the court concluded that the Do Not Call Registry "materially furthers the government's interests in combating the danger of abusive telemarketing and preventing the invasion of consumer privacy."[1]

Credit Reporting Agencies and "Blacklisting"

Today, some consumer credit reporting agencies will also investigate and report a person's litigation history online. Physicians and landlords frequently use such services to learn whether prospective patients or tenants have a prior history of suing their physicians or their landlords. One service, for example, allows physicians, for a fee, to perform over two hundred online name searches to find out if a person was a plaintiff in a previous malpractice suit.

Users say that these services are an ideal way to screen out undesirable patients and applicants and reduce the risk of being sued. Consumer rights advocates, however, claim that the sale of such information is akin to "blacklisting"—discriminating against potential patients or tenants on the basis of previous litigation history. Moreover, some agencies do not provide consumers with access to the reports. This means that physicians and landlords may obtain information about individuals' involvement in prior court proceedings without allowing the information to be challenged. In the last decade, these practices have led to complaints of unfairness as well as lawsuits against reporting agencies.

By and large, though, consumers have had little recourse if what is being reported about them is accurate. If the information being disseminated about a person by a reporting

---

1. *Mainstream Marketing Services, Inc. v. Federal Trade Commission*, 358 F.3d 1228 (10th Cir. 2004).

agency is false, however, that person will likely have a cause of action against the agency. Under the Fair Credit Reporting Act (FCRA) of 1970, companies that sell consumer information must report the information accurately and must provide a remedy for consumers who seek to dispute the information. If no remedy is provided, the agency will be in violation of the FCRA.[2]

Environmental Law

Questions of fairness inevitably arise in regard to environmental law. Has the government gone too far—or not far enough—in regulating businesses in the interest of protecting the environment? At what point do the costs of environmental regulations become too burdensome for society to bear?

Consider the problem of toxic waste. Although everybody is in favor of cleaning up America's toxic waste dumps, nobody has the slightest idea what this task will ultimately cost. Much of the problem in determining the eventual costs of the Comprehensive Environmental Response, Compensation, and Liability Act (CERCLA), commonly known as Superfund (see Chapter 45), stems from the difficulty of estimating the costs of cleaning up a site. Moreover, there is no agreed-on standard as to how clean a site must be before it no longer poses any threat. Must 100 percent of the contamination be removed, or would removal of some lesser amount achieve a reasonable degree of environmental quality?

Global Environmental Issues

Pollution does not respect geographic borders. Indeed, one of the reasons that the federal government became involved in environmental protection was that state regulation alone apparently could not solve the problem of air or water pollution. Pollutants generated in one state move in the air and water to other states. Neither does pollution respect national borders. Environmental issues, perhaps more than any others, bring home to everyone the fact that the world today is truly a global community. What one country does or does not do with respect to environmental preservation may be felt by citizens in countries thousands of miles away.

Cross-Border Pollution One issue that has come to the fore in recent years is cross-border pollution. On numerous occasions, beaches in San Diego, California, have been closed because of pollution originating in Mexico. Canada has complained for years about air pollution in that nation caused by sulfuric acid generated by coal-burning power plants in the United States. Examples similar to these can be found everywhere in the world. Countries have made various

2. See, for example, *Decker v. U.D. Registry, Inc.*, 105 Cal.App.4th 1382, 129 Cal.Rptr.2d 892 (2003).

attempts to reduce cross-border pollution through treaties or other agreements, but it remains a challenging issue for virtually all nations.

Global Warming Another challenging—and controversial—issue is potential global warming. The fear is that emissions, largely from combustion of fossil fuels, will remain in the atmosphere and create a "greenhouse effect" by preventing heat from radiating outward. Concerns over this issue have led to many attempts to force all world polluters to "clean up their acts." For example, leaders of 160 nations have already agreed to reduce greenhouse emissions in their respective countries. They did this when they ratified the Kyoto Protocol, which was drawn up at a world summit meeting held in Kyoto, Japan, in 1997. The Kyoto Protocol, which is often referred to as the global warming treaty, established different rates of reduction in greenhouse emissions for different countries or regions. Most nations, however, including the United States, will not meet the treaty's objectives. Indeed, the Bush administration told the world in early 2001 that the treaty was a dead letter because it did not address the problem of curbing greenhouse gases from most of the developing world.

Is Economic Development the Answer? Economists have shown that economic development is the quickest way to reduce pollution worldwide. After a nation reaches a certain per capita income level, the more economic growth the nation experiences, the lower the pollution output. This occurs because richer nations have the resources to pay for pollution reduction. For example, the United States pollutes much less per unit of output than do developing nations—because we are willing to pay for pollution abatement.

Antitrust Law—The Baseball Exemption

The fact that, until relatively recently, baseball remained totally exempt from the antitrust laws not only seemed unfair to many but also defied logic. Why was an exemption made for baseball but not for other professional sports? The answer to this perfectly reasonable question has always been the same: baseball was exempt because the United States Supreme Court, in 1922, said that it was. The Court held that baseball was a sport played only locally by local players. Because the activity purportedly did not involve interstate commerce, it did not meet the requirements for federal jurisdiction.

The exemption was challenged in the early 1970s, but the Supreme Court ruled that it was up to Congress, not the Court, to overturn the exemption. In 1998, Congress did address the issue and passed the Curt Flood Act—named for the St. Louis Cardinals' star outfielder who challenged the exemption in the early 1970s. The act, however, did not invalidate the 1922 Supreme Court decision but only limited some of the effects of baseball's exempt status. Essentially, the act allows players the option of suing team owners for anticompetitive practices if, for example, the owners collude to "blacklist" players, hold down players' salaries, or force players to play for specific teams.

Baseball is still not subject to antitrust laws to the extent that football, basketball, and other professional sports are. Critics of the exemption argue that it should be completely abolished because it makes no sense to continue to treat an enterprise generating revenues of $3 billion a year as a "local" activity.

DISCUSSION QUESTIONS

1. If 90 percent of the toxic waste at a given site can be removed for $50,000, but removing the last 10 percent will cost $2 million, is it reasonable to require that the last 10 percent be removed? How would you address this question?

2. Assume that removing all asbestos from all public buildings in the nation would save ten lives per year and that the cost of the asbestos removal would be $250 billion (or $25 billion per life saved). Is this too high of a price to pay? Should cost ever be a consideration when human lives are at stake?

3. Will the national Do Not Call Registry affect the way that business is conducted in this country? What types of businesses do you think will be the most adversely affected by the registry in the long run?

4. Should credit reporting agencies be prohibited from releasing an individual's prior litigation history to a prospective physician or landlord? Even if such information is true and available in public court records, should the government restrict Web access to this information via reporting agencies? Why or why not?

UNIT TEN
Property

CONTENTS

CHAPTER 47

Personal Property and Bailments

Property consists of the legally protected rights and interests a person has in anything with an ascertainable value that is subject to ownership. **Real property** (sometimes called *realty* or *real estate*) means the land and everything permanently attached to it, including structures and anything attached permanently to the structures. Everything else is **personal property** (sometimes referred to as *personalty* or **chattel**).

Personal property can be tangible or intangible. Tangible personal property, such as a television set, heavy construction equipment, or a car, has physical substance. Intangible personal property represents some set of rights and interests, but it has no real physical existence. Stocks and bonds are intangible personal property. So, too, are patents, trademarks, and copyrights, as discussed in Chapter 8.

In the beginning of this chapter, we examine the ways in which ownership rights in both personal property and real property can be held, as well as issues relating to various types of property. The remainder of the chapter focuses on bailment relationships. A *bailment* is created when property is temporarily delivered into the care of another without a transfer of title. For example, taking your clothes to the dry cleaner gives rise to a bailment of the clothes. The distinguishing characteristic of a bailment compared with a sale or a gift is that there is no passage of title and no intent to transfer title.

SECTION 1 | Fixtures

Certain personal property can become so closely associated with the real property to which it is attached that the law views it as real property. Such property is known as a **fixture**—a thing affixed to realty. A thing is affixed to realty when it is attached to the realty by roots; embedded in it; or permanently attached by means of cement, plaster, bolts, nails, or screws. The fixture can be physically attached to real property or attached to another fixture; it can even be an item, such as a statue, that is not physically attached to the land, as long as the owner *intends* the property to be a fixture.

Fixtures are included in the sale of land if the sales contract does not provide otherwise. The sale of a house includes the land and the house and garage on it, as well as the cabinets, plumbing, and windows. Because these are permanently affixed to the property, they are considered to be a part of it. Unless otherwise agreed, however, the curtains and throw rugs are not included. Items such as drapes and window-unit air conditioners

are difficult to classify. Thus, a contract for the sale of a house or commercial property should indicate which items of this sort are included in the sale.

The issue of whether an item is a fixture (and thus real estate) or not a fixture (and thus personal property) often arises with respect to land sales, real property taxation, insurance coverage, and divorces. How the issue is resolved can have important consequences for the parties involved. Generally, when the courts need to determine whether a certain item is a fixture, they examine several factors. An important factor is the intention of the party who placed the object on the real property.

THE ROLE OF INTENT

Generally, if the facts indicate that the person intended the item to be a fixture, then it will be considered a fixture. When the intent of the party who placed the fixture on the realty is in dispute, the courts usually determine intent based on either or both of the following factors:

1. If the property attached cannot be removed without causing substantial damage to the remaining realty, it is usually deemed to be a fixture.

2. If the property attached is so adapted to the rest of the realty as to become a part of it, the property is usually deemed to be a fixture.

Certain items can only be attached to property permanently; such items are fixtures—it is assumed that the owner intended them to be fixtures because they had to be permanently attached to the property. A tile floor, cabinets, and carpeting are examples. Also, items that are custom-made for installation on real property, such as storm windows, are usually classified as fixtures.

TRADE FIXTURES

Trade fixtures are an exception to the rule that fixtures are a part of the real property. A trade fixture is personal property that is installed for a commercial purpose by a tenant (one who rents real property from the owner, or landlord). Trade fixtures remain the property of the tenant, unless removal would irreparably damage the building or realty. A walk-in cooler, for example, purchased and installed by a tenant who uses the premises for a restaurant, is a trade fixture. The tenant can remove the cooler from the premises when the lease terminates but ordinarily must repair any damage that the removal causes or compensate the landlord for the damage.

SECTION 2 | Property Ownership

Property ownership can be viewed as a bundle of rights, including the right to possess the property and to dispose of it—by sale, gift, lease, and other means.

FEE SIMPLE

A person who holds the entire bundle of rights is said to be the owner in **fee simple.** The owner in fee simple is entitled to use, possess, and dispose of the property as he or she chooses during his or her lifetime; and on death, the owner's interest in the property descends to his or her heirs. We will look further at ownership in fee simple in Chapter 48, in the context of real property ownership.

CONCURRENT OWNERSHIP

Persons who share ownership rights simultaneously in particular property are said to be concurrent owners. There are two principal types of **concurrent ownership:** *tenancy in common* and *joint tenancy.* Other types of concurrent ownership include tenancy by the entirety and community property.

TENANCY IN COMMON The term **tenancy in common** refers to a form of co-ownership in which each of two or more persons owns an undivided interest in the property. The interest is undivided because each tenant has rights in the *whole* property. For example, Rosa and Chad own a rare stamp collection together as tenants in common. This does not mean that Rosa owns some particular stamps and Chad others. Rather, it means that Rosa and Chad each have rights in the entire collection. (If each person had rights in specific items of property, then the interest would be divided.)

On the death of a tenant in common, that tenant's interest in the property passes to her or his heirs. For example, should Rosa die before Chad, a one-half interest in the stamp collection would become the property of Rosa's heirs. If Rosa sold her interest to Fred before she died, Fred and Chad would be co-owners as tenants in common.

How should the value of the property owned by two tenants in common be apportioned when neither tenant has died but both agree that their interests should be divided? That was the question in the following case.

| CASE 47.1 | Clark v. Dady |

Missouri
Court of Appeals,
Western District, 2004.
131 S.W.3d 382.

EDWIN H. SMITH, Judge.
 * * * *

In 1998, [John Dady and Mary Clark] purchased a Holly Park mobile home [in Missouri] for approximately $35,848, [putting] $4,000 down with the balance being financed by Greentree Financial. The debt to Greentree was evidenced by a promissory note that was jointly executed by the parties. * * *

 * * * Sometime in August 2001, the appellant [Dady] voluntarily moved out of the mobile home. The respondent [Clark], who then enjoyed exclusive possession of the mobile

CONTINUED

home, made the note payments, as well as monthly lot rental payments * * * and monthly utility payments.

On January 22, 2002, the respondent [Clark] filed a petition in [a Missouri state court] * * * asking [in part] that * * * [she] "be found to be the rightful owner of said personal property due to the care and amount of money that she has contributed to the purchase of said property." * * *

* * * The respondent * * * testified that there was a balance of $31,964.19 due on the note financing the mobile home. * * * [The appellant, Dady] testified that he had improved the mobile home by adding a $10,000 deck and mud room, a $1,500 barn, and $2,000 worth of landscaping, plus contributing "hours of painting," for which he was requesting reimbursement * * * .

On July 26, 2002, the trial court entered a judgment awarding the mobile home to the respondent "as her sole property * * * free and clear of any lien, claim, right or demand of the appellant." * * * In addition, the judgment recited that the respondent "is entitled to reimbursement, from [the appellant] of $3,050 representing one-half of the lot payments and one-half of the loan payments which [the respondent] made on the [mobile home] since August, 2001."

This appeal [to a state intermediate appellate court] followed.

* * * *

* * * [I]n determining whether the trial court, here, erred in determining the respective interests of the parties in partitioning the mobile home, we begin with the rebuttable presumption that they held equal shares. And, thus, unless the record supports rebuttal of the presumption, the trial court erred in partitioning the mobile home by ordering that the respondent [Clark] be awarded the whole in kind.

In partition, *the presumption of equal shares of tenants in common may be rebutted by proof of a disproportionate contribution of each party toward the acquisition of the property * * * .* Contribution toward the acquisition of property includes not only any cash down payment, but any liability incurred in financing the balance of the purchase price. [Emphasis added.]

At trial, the parties agreed that they purchased the mobile home for $35,848, with $4,000 down. However, they disagree as to who made the down payment. The appellant [Dady] contended that he contributed to the down payment; the respondent [Clark] contended that she paid the full amount. The trial court was free to believe the respondent's testimony, which it did. Thus, with respect to the down payment only, the record supports a finding that the appellant did not contribute anything to the acquisition of the mobile home.

As to the balance of the purchase price of the mobile home, the parties agreed at trial that they jointly obligated themselves for payment of the balance by executing a promissory note in favor of Greentree Financial for $31,848 ($35,848 – $4,000). As a result of the appellant's being jointly obligated on the note, he is considered to have contributed $15,924 to the acquisition of the mobile home ($31,848/2). Hence, * * * the appellant [Dady] would have a 44.42% ($15,924/$35,848) share in the mobile home, for purposes of partition. And, thus, the trial court erred in awarding the mobile home, in kind and in its entirety, to the respondent, requiring us to reverse.

* * * [I]f we find that the trial court's judgment was in error, we are, if possible, to finally dispose of the case, including, where appropriate, giving such judgment as the trial court ought to give. * * * [W]e can only do so where the record permits, and here, the record is not sufficiently developed on the issue in question to allow us to enter judgment with any degree of confidence in its reasonableness, fairness, and accuracy. Here, given the nature of a partition suit, we cannot make a determination of whether to enter judgment disposing of the case or remanding it for further proceedings without first addressing whether the parties are entitled to reimbursement for various expenditures they allegedly made on the property. Both parties made various claims below for reimbursement for expenditures * * * .

* * * *

The record indicates that the issues of the various expenditures claimed by the parties for reimbursement in partition were left undecided by the trial court. * * * Consequently, we are compelled to reverse and remand for further proceedings consistent with this opinion.

CASE 47.1 Continued

JOINT TENANCY In a **joint tenancy,** each of two or more persons owns an undivided interest in the property, and a deceased joint tenant's interest passes to the surviving joint tenant or tenants. The rights of a surviving joint tenant to inherit a deceased joint tenant's ownership interest—which are referred to as *survivorship rights*—distinguish the joint tenancy from the tenancy in common. A joint tenancy can be terminated before a joint tenant's death by gift or by sale, in which situation the person who receives the property as a gift or who purchases the property becomes a tenant in common, not a joint tenant.

To illustrate: In the preceding example, if Rosa and Chad held their stamp collection in a joint tenancy and if Rosa died before Chad, the entire collection would become Chad's property; Rosa's heirs would receive absolutely no interest in the collection. If Rosa, while living, sold her interest to Fred, however, the sale would terminate the joint tenancy, and Fred and Chad would become owners as tenants in common.

Additionally, a joint tenancy can be transferred by *partition;* that is, the tenants can physically divide the property into equal parts. A joint tenant's interest can also be levied against (seized by court order) to satisfy the tenant's judgment creditors.

Generally, it is presumed that a co-tenancy is a tenancy in common unless there is a clear intention to establish a joint tenancy. Thus, language such as "to Jerrold and Eva as joint tenants with right of survivorship, and not as tenants in common" would be necessary to create a joint tenancy.

If one joint tenant uses the property to commit a crime, can the government successfully insist that *all* of the property be forfeited? Or can the innocent joint tenant who paid nearly the entire purchase price for it successfully claim that *none* of the property should be forfeited? These were the questions before the court in the following case.

CASE 47.2 <span></span> **United States v. Wendling**

United States
District Court,
District of
North Dakota, 2005.
359 F.Supp.2d 850.
http://www.ndd.uscourts.
gov/DNDOpinions/
PreDefined.htm[a]

BACKGROUND AND FACTS *In 1999, Steven and Sonya Stramer sold a parcel of real estate in Ashby, Minnesota, to Brian Wendling and his mother, Marjorie Wendling, as joint tenants. Of the $30,000 price, Marjorie paid $25,000, and Brian agreed to pay $5,000 in monthly installments, but when he fell behind on the payments, Marjorie paid the balance. Both parties paid the taxes. Brian handled all of the maintenance and repairs, and lived on the property. Marjorie visited three or four times. In 2004, Brian was arrested and pleaded guilty in a federal district court to criminal charges of conspiring to grow marijuana on the Ashby parcel. As part of his plea, he agreed to forfeit his interest in it. Marjorie, who did not know about the marijuana, filed a petition with the court, claiming that Brian "has no interest in this property even though [the] deed placed the title in both of our names." The government filed a motion for summary judgment, seeking forfeiture of the entire parcel.*

IN THE LANGUAGE OF THE COURT

ERICKSON, District Judge.

* * * *

Under 21 U.S.C. Section 853(a), *any person convicted of a crime, such as a felony conspiracy to manufacture marijuana,* "shall forfeit * * * any of the person's property used, or intended to be used, in any manner or part, to commit, or to facilitate the commission of, such violation." However, Section 853(n) permits a third party to challenge an order of criminal

---

a. In the "Judge Erickson" row, click on "Any Date." In the result, scroll down the list to the name of the case and click on it to access the opinion. The U.S. District Court for the District of North Dakota maintains this Web site.

CONTINUED

CASE 47.2 | Continued

forfeiture by showing, by a preponderance of the evidence, that * * * the petitioner had a vested or superior legal right, title or interest in the property at the time the criminal activity took place * * * . Ms. Wendling has petitioned under Section 853(n)(6)(B) that she has a vested or superior legal right, title or interest in the property. [Emphasis added.]

Criminal forfeiture is an *in personam* action because the statute provides for forfeiture of only the criminal defendant's property, and therefore *the forfeiture cannot extend to an innocent owner's interest in the property. Accordingly, Defendant [Brian] can only forfeit to the United States his interest in the Ashby Property.* [Emphasis added.]

* * * *

* * * [T]here is a long-standing presumption that joint tenants have an equal interest in the land. However, the presumption is not conclusive, and may be rebutted with evidence of true interest. * * * [A] joint tenant in real property [may] * * * bring an action to partition his or her interest in the property or to sell the property if it appears that a partition cannot be had without great prejudice to the owners. Actual possession or a right to *actual possession is not necessary for a joint tenant to bring an action for partition*. [Emphasis added.]

* * * Ms. Wendling, as a joint tenant of the Ashby Property, has a right to retain her half of the property and her lack of actual possession of the property does not defeat her interests in the property. However, under the same analysis, she cannot argue that she is the only owner of the property based on the fact that she paid for the property. Despite paying nearly the entire purchase price, Ms. Wendling allowed her son's name on the title as a joint tenant and permitted him to live exclusively on the property. Further, Defendant made two loan payments on the property, paid for part of the taxes on the property, and took care of repairs and the maintenance of the property. Thus, neither Ms. Wendling nor the United States, acting on behalf of Mr. Wendling, has rebutted the presumption that each joint tenant has an undivided equal interest in the property.

* * * *

The plain language of 21 U.S.C. Section 853 does not preclude partial forfeitures. An alternative to partial forfeitures would be to give the United States a windfall and deny an innocent owner her valid property interest. The United States concedes that Ms. Wendling was not involved in the criminal activities of her son. Ms. Wendling testified, and the United States has not refuted, that she had no knowledge that her son was growing marijuana at the Ashby Property, and she would not have agreed with it if she had found out prior to her son's arrest.

The intent of Congress in enacting the forfeiture statute is to punish, deter and disempower criminals. Giving the United States an innocent owner's share does not further the purpose of this penalty. * * *

* * * This Court also finds that 21 U.S.C. Section 853 allows for partial forfeitures of real property.

* * * *

* * * Accordingly, the United States may take a fifty percent interest in the Ashby Property, with Marjorie Wendling remaining a joint tenant of the property.

DECISION AND REMEDY *The court held that neither the government nor Marjorie successfully rebutted the presumption that joint tenants of real property have equal interests in the property. The court also held that the forfeiture statute at issue in this case allowed for the partial forfeiture of a criminal defendant's property. Thus, the court allowed the forfeiture of 50 percent of the Ashby property, with Marjorie, as joint tenant, to hold the remaining 50 percent.*

WHAT IF THE FACTS WERE DIFFERENT? *If Marjorie had paid the entire price for the Ashby property, and Brian's name had not been included on the deed, would the result have been different?*

TENANCY BY THE ENTIRETY A **tenancy by the entirety** is a less common form of ownership that typically is created by a conveyance (transfer) of real property to a husband and wife. It is distinguished from a joint tenancy by the inability of either spouse to transfer separately his or her interest during his or her lifetime without the consent of the other spouse. In some states where statutes give the wife the right to

CONCEPT SUMMARY 47.1 | Common Types of Property Ownership

CONCEPT	DESCRIPTION
FEE SIMPLE	Owners of property in fee simple have the fullest ownership rights in property. They have the right to use, possess, or dispose of the property as they choose during their lifetimes and to pass on the property to their heirs at death.
CONCURRENT OWNERSHIP	Concurrent ownership of property can take the following forms: 1. *Tenancy in common*—Co-ownership in which two or more persons own an undivided interest in property; on one tenant's death, the property interest passes to his or her heirs. 2. *Joint tenancy*—Co-ownership in which two or more persons own an undivided interest in property; on the death of a joint tenant, the property interest transfers to the remaining tenant(s), not to the heirs of the deceased. 3. *Tenancy by the entirety*—A form of co-ownership between a husband and wife that is similar to a joint tenancy, except that a spouse cannot transfer separately her or his interest during her or his lifetime. 4. *Community property*—A form of co-ownership between a husband and wife in which each spouse technically owns an undivided one-half interest in property acquired during the marriage. This type of ownership occurs in only a few states.

convey her property, this form of concurrent ownership has been effectively abolished. A divorce, either spouse's death, or mutual agreement will terminate a tenancy by the entirety.

COMMUNITY PROPERTY Only a limited number of states[1] allow property to be owned by a married couple as **community property.** If property is held as community property, each spouse technically owns an undivided one-half interest in the property. This type of ownership applies to most property acquired by the husband or the wife during the course of the marriage. It generally does not apply to property acquired prior to the marriage or to property acquired by gift or inheritance during the marriage. After a divorce, community property is divided equally in some states and according to the discretion of the court in other states.

SECTION 3 | Acquiring Ownership of Personal Property

Ownership of personal property can be acquired through purchase, possession, production, gift, will or inheritance, accession, and confusion. Purchasing personal property, which was discussed in Chapters 20

through 23, is one of the most common ways to acquire or transfer personalty. The other forms of acquisition are discussed below.

POSSESSION

One example of acquiring ownership through possession is the capture of wild animals. Wild animals belong to no one in their natural state, and the first person to take possession of a wild animal normally owns it. The killing of a wild animal amounts to assuming ownership of it. Merely being in hot pursuit does not give title, however. There are two exceptions to this basic rule. First, any wild animals captured by a trespasser are the property of the landowner, not the trespasser. The fish in a pond on a farmer's land, for example, are the farmer's property, not the property of a trespasser who fishes for and catches them. Second, if wild animals are captured or killed in violation of wild game statutes, the state, not the capturer, obtains title to the animals.

Those who find lost or abandoned property can also acquire ownership rights through mere possession of the property, as will be discussed later in this chapter. (Real property can also be acquired through *adverse possession*—to be discussed in Chapter 48.)

PRODUCTION

Production is another means of acquiring ownership of personal property. As discussed in Chapter 8,

---

1. These states include Alaska, Arizona, California, Idaho, Louisiana, Nevada, New Mexico, Texas, Washington, and Wisconsin. Puerto Rico allows property to be owned as community property as well.

writers, inventors, manufacturers, and others who produce personal property may thereby acquire title to it. (In some situations, though, as when a researcher is hired to invent a new product or technique, the researcher may not own what is produced—see Chapter 31.)

GIFT

A **gift** is another fairly common means of acquiring or transferring ownership of property. A gift is essentially a *voluntary* transfer of property ownership. It is not supported by legally sufficient consideration (see Chapter 12) because the very essence of a gift is giving without consideration. Gifts can be made during a person's lifetime or in a last will and testament. A gift made by will is called a *testamentary* gift.

There are three requirements for an effective gift—delivery, donative intent on the part of the *donor* (the one giving the gift), and acceptance by the *donee* (the one receiving the gift). Each of these requirements is discussed below. Until these three requirements are met, no effective gift has been made. For example, suppose that your aunt tells you that she is going to give you a new Mercedes-Benz for your next birthday. This is simply a promise to make a gift. It is not considered a gift until the Mercedes-Benz is delivered.

DELIVERY   The gift must be delivered to the donee. Delivery is obvious in most cases, but some objects cannot be relinquished physically. Then the question of delivery depends on the surrounding circumstances.

—Constructive Delivery.   When the physical object itself cannot be delivered, a symbolic delivery, or **constructive delivery,** will be sufficient. Constructive delivery does not confer actual possession of the object in question. It is a general term for all those acts that the law holds to be equivalent to acts of real delivery.

Suppose that you want to make a gift of various old rare coins that you have stored in a safe-deposit box at your bank. You certainly cannot deliver the box itself to the donee, and you do not want to take the coins out of the bank. Instead, you can simply deliver the key to the box to the donee and authorize the donee's access to the box and its contents. This constitutes symbolic, or constructive, delivery of the contents of

the box. Delivery of intangible personal property, such as stock-ownership rights, must be accomplished by symbolic or constructive delivery, such as by the delivery of a stock certificate.

—Relinquishing Dominion and Control.   An effective delivery also requires giving up *complete dominion*[2] *and control* over the subject matter of the gift. The outcome of disputes often turns on whether control has actually been relinquished. The Internal Revenue Service closely scrutinizes transactions between relatives when one has given income-producing property to the other. A relative who does not relinquish complete control over a piece of property will have to pay taxes on the income from that property.

—Delivery by Agents.   Delivery can be accomplished by means of a third person who is acting as an agent for either the donor or the donee. If the person is the agent of the donor, the gift is effective when the agent delivers the property to the donee. If the third person is the agent of the donee, the gift is effective when the donor delivers the property to the donee's agent.[3] Naturally, no delivery is necessary if the gift is already in the hands of the donee. All that is necessary to complete the gift in such a case is the required intent and acceptance by the donee.

DONATIVE INTENT   Donative intent (the intent to make a gift) is determined from the language of the donor and the surrounding circumstances. When a gift is challenged in court, for example, the court may look at the relationship between the parties and the size of the gift in relation to the donor's other assets. A court might question donative intent when the gift was made to an archenemy. Similarly, when a person has given away a large portion of her or his assets, the court will carefully scrutinize the transactions to determine whether the donor was mentally competent or whether fraud or duress was involved. In the following case, the court looked at the intent of the donor and the question of delivery.

---

2. The term *dominion* in this sense refers to absolute ownership rights in, and control over, property. One who has dominion over property both possesses and has title to the property.
3. *Bickford v. Mattocks,* 95 Me. 547, 50 A. 894 (1901).

CASE 47.3 In re Estate of Piper

Missouri Court
of Appeals, 1984.
676 S.W.2d 897.

BACKGROUND AND FACTS *Gladys Piper died intestate (without a will). At the time of her death, she owned personal property consisting of household goods, two old automobiles, farm machinery, and "miscellaneous" items totaling $5,150. This did not include jewelry or cash. When Piper died, she had $206.75 in cash and her two diamond rings, known as the "Andy Piper" rings, in her purse. The contents of Piper's purse were taken by her niece, Wanda Brown, on Piper's death, allegedly to preserve them for the estate. Clara Kauffman, a friend of Gladys Piper, filed a claim against the estate for $4,800. For several years before Piper's death, Kauffman had taken Piper to the doctor, beauty salon, and grocery store; written her checks to pay her bills; and helped her care for her home. Kauffman maintained that Piper had promised to pay her for these services and that Piper had intended the diamond rings to be a gift to her. The trial court denied Kauffman's request for payment of $4,800 on the basis that the services had been voluntary. Kauffman then filed a petition for delivery of personal property (the rings), which was granted by the trial court. The defendants—Piper's heirs and the administrator of Piper's estate—appealed.*

IN THE LANGUAGE OF THE COURT

GREENE, JUDGE.

* * * *

While no particular form is necessary to effect a delivery, and while the delivery may be actual, constructive, or symbolical, there must be some evidence to support a delivery theory. What we have here, at best, * * * was an intention on the part of Gladys, at some future time, to make a gift of the rings to Clara. Such an intention, no matter how clearly expressed, which has not been carried into effect, confers no ownership rights in the property in the intended donee. *Language written or spoken, expressing an intention to give, does not constitute a gift, unless the intention is executed by a complete and unconditional delivery of the subject matter, or delivery of a proper written instrument evidencing the gift.* There is no evidence in this case to prove delivery, and, for such reason, the trial court's judgment is erroneous. [Emphasis added.]

DECISION AND REMEDY *The judgment of the trial court was reversed. No effective gift of the rings had been made because Piper had never delivered the rings to Kauffman.*

WHAT IF THE FACTS WERE DIFFERENT? *Suppose that Gladys had told Clara that she was giving the rings to Clara but wished to keep them in her possession for a few more days. Would this have affected the court's decision in this case?*

ACCEPTANCE The final requirement of a valid gift is acceptance by the donee. This rarely presents any problems because most donees readily accept their gifts. The courts generally assume acceptance unless shown otherwise.

GIFTS *INTER VIVOS* AND GIFTS *CAUSA MORTIS* A gift made during the donor's lifetime is called a **gift *inter vivos.*** A gift ***causa mortis*** is made in contemplation of imminent death. To be effective, a gift *causa mortis* must meet the three requirements of delivery, intent, and acceptance. Gifts *causa mortis* do not become absolute until the donor dies from the contemplated illness or disease. A gift *causa mortis* is rev-

ocable at any time up to the death of the donor and is automatically revoked if the donor recovers.

Suppose that Steck is to be operated on for a cancerous tumor. Before the operation, he delivers an envelope to a close business associate. The envelope contains a letter saying, "I realize my days are numbered, and I want to give you this check for $1 million in the event that this operation causes my death." The business associate cashes the check. The surgeon performs the operation and removes the tumor. Steck recovers fully. Several months later, Steck dies from a heart attack that is totally unrelated to the operation. If Steck's personal representative (the party charged with administering Steck's estate) tries to recover the

$1 million, normally she will succeed. The gift *causa mortis* is automatically revoked if the donor recovers. The *specific event* that was contemplated in making the gift was death caused by a particular operation. Because Steck's death was not the result of this event, the gift is revoked, and the $1 million passes to Steck's estate.[4]

WILL OR INHERITANCE

Ownership of property may be transferred by will or by inheritance under state statutes. These types of transfers will be dealt with at length in Chapter 50.

ACCESSION

Accession means "something added." It occurs when someone adds value to a piece of personal property by use of either labor or materials. Generally, there is no dispute about who owns the property after accession has occurred, especially when the accession is accomplished with the owner's consent. For example, a Corvette-customizing specialist comes to Hoshi's house. Hoshi has all the materials necessary to do the job. The customizing specialist uses them to add a unique bumper to Hoshi's Corvette. Hoshi simply pays the customizer for the value of the labor, obviously retaining title to the property.

WHEN A PARTY WRONGFULLY CAUSES THE ACCESSION
When accession occurs without the owner's consent, the courts tend to favor the owner over the improver—the one who improved the property—provided the accession was done in bad faith. This is true even if the accession increased the value of the property substantially. In addition, many courts will deny the improver (wrongdoer) any compensation for the value added; for example, a car thief who puts new tires on the stolen car will obviously not be compensated for the value of the new tires.

INCREASED PROPERTY VALUE DUE TO A GOOD FAITH ACCESSION
If the accession is performed in good faith, however, even without the owner's consent, ownership of the improved item most often depends on whether the accession has increased the value of the property or changed its identity. The greater the increase, the more likely that ownership will pass to the improver. Obviously, when this occurs, the improver must compensate the original owner for the value the property had prior to the accession. If the increase in value is not sufficient for ownership to be passed to the improver, most courts require the owner to compensate the improver for the value added.

CONFUSION

Confusion is the commingling of goods so that one person's personal property cannot be distinguished from another's. It frequently involves goods that are fungible.[5] *Fungible goods* are goods consisting of identical particles, such as grain or oil. For example, if two farmers put their number 2 grade winter wheat into the same silo, confusion will occur.

When goods are confused due to a wrongful and willful act and the wrongdoer is unable to prove what percentage of the confused goods belongs to him or her, then the innocent party ordinarily acquires title to the whole. If confusion occurs as a result of agreement, honest mistake, or the act of some third party, the owners all share ownership as tenants in common. Suppose that you enter into a cooperative arrangement with five other farmers in a small Iowa community. Each fall, everyone harvests the same amount of number 2 yellow corn and stores it in silos that are held by the cooperative. Each of you owns one-sixth of the total corn in the silos and will bear the risk of loss in equal proportions of one-sixth. If, however, one farmer harvests and stores more corn than the others in the cooperative and wants to claim a greater ownership interest, that farmer must keep careful records. Otherwise, the courts will presume that each of you has an equal interest in the corn.

SECTION 4 | Mislaid, Lost, and Abandoned Property

As already noted, one of the methods of acquiring ownership of property is to possess it. Simply finding something and holding onto it, however, does not *necessarily* entitle the finder to it. Different rules apply, depending on whether the property was mislaid, lost, or abandoned.

MISLAID PROPERTY

Property that has been voluntarily placed somewhere by the owner and then inadvertently forgotten is **mislaid property.** Suppose that you go to a movie

---

4. *Brind v. International Trust Co.*, 66 Colo. 60, 179 P. 148 (1919).

5. See Section 1–201(17) of the Uniform Commercial Code (UCC).

CONCEPT SUMMARY 47.2 | Acquisition of Personal Property

TYPE OF ACQUISITION	HOW ACQUISITION OCCURS
BY PURCHASE OR BY WILL	The most common means of acquiring ownership in personal property is by purchasing it (see Chapters 20 through 23). Another way in which personal property is often acquired is by will or inheritance (see Chapter 50).
POSSESSION	Ownership may be acquired by possession if no other person has ownership title (for example, capturing wild animals or finding abandoned property).
PRODUCTION	Any product or item produced by an individual (with minor exceptions) becomes the property of that individual.
GIFT	An effective gift is made when the following three requirements are met: 1. *Delivery*—The gift is delivered (physically or constructively) to the donee or the donee's agent. 2. *Intent*—There is evidence of *intent* to make a gift of the property in question. 3. *Acceptance*—The gift is accepted by the donee or the donee's agent.
ACCESSION	When someone adds value to a piece of property by use of labor or materials, the added value generally becomes the property of the owner of the original property (when accessions are made in bad faith or wrongfully). Good faith accessions that substantially increase the property's value or change the identity of the property may cause title to pass to the improver.
CONFUSION	In the case of fungible goods, if a person wrongfully and willfully commingles goods with those of another in order to render them indistinguishable, the innocent party acquires title to the whole. Otherwise, the owners become tenants in common of the commingled goods.

theater and leave your cell phone at the concession stand. The phone is mislaid property, and the theater owner is entrusted with the duty of reasonable care for the goods. When mislaid property is found, the finder does not obtain title to the goods.[6] Instead, the owner of the place where the property was mislaid becomes the caretaker of the property because it is highly likely that the true owner will return.[7]

LOST PROPERTY

Property that is *involuntarily* left is **lost property.** A finder of lost property can claim title to the property against the whole world, *except the true owner*. If the true owner demands that the lost property be returned, the finder must return it. If a third party attempts to take possession of lost property from a finder, the third party cannot assert a better title than the finder.

CONVERSION OF LOST PROPERTY When a finder of lost property knows the true owner and fails to return the property to that person, the finder is guilty of a tort known as *conversion* (see Chapter 6). Many states require the finder to make a reasonably diligent search to locate the true owner of lost property.

Suppose Kamal works in a large library at night. After work, as he is walking through the courtyard of the library, he finds a piece of gold jewelry that contains several apparently precious stones. If Kamal knows that the jewelry belongs to Geneva and does not return it to her, he is guilty of conversion. Now suppose instead that Kamal does not know who owns the jewelry and decides to take it to a jewelry store to have it appraised. While pretending to weigh the piece, an employee of the jeweler removes several of the stones. If Kamal brings an action to recover the stones from the jeweler, he will win because, as a finder of lost property, he holds valid title against everyone except the true owner. Because the property was lost and not mislaid, the owner of the library is not the caretaker of the jewelry. Instead, Kamal acquires

---

6. The finder is an *involuntary bailee*—see the discussion of bailments later in this chapter.

7. The owner of the place where property is mislaid is a bailee with right of possession against all except the true owner.

title that is good against the whole world (except the true owner).[8]

ESTRAY STATUTES Many states have **estray statutes** to encourage and facilitate the return of property to its true owner and to reward the finder for honesty if the property remains unclaimed. Such statutes provide an incentive for finders to report their discoveries by making it possible for them, after passage of a specified period of time, to acquire legal title to the property they have found if the property remains unclaimed.

The statutes usually require the county clerk to advertise the property in an attempt to help the owner recover what has been lost. Some preliminary questions must always be resolved before the estray statute can be employed. The item must be lost property, not mislaid or abandoned property. When the situation indicates that the property was probably lost and not mislaid or abandoned, loss is presumed, as a matter of public policy, and the estray statute applies.

ABANDONED PROPERTY

Property that has been *discarded* by the true owner, who has *no intention* of claiming title to it, is referred to as **abandoned property.** Someone who finds abandoned property acquires title to it, and such title is good against the whole world, *including the original*

---

8. See *Armory v. Delamirie,* 93 Eng.Rep. 664 (K.B. [King's Bench] 1722). If Kamal had found the jewelry during the course of his employment, however, his employer would be an involuntary bailee. Further, many courts now say that when lost property is recovered in a private place, the owner of the place, not the finder, becomes the bailee (even if the finder is not a trespasser).

owner. The owner of lost property who eventually gives up any further attempt to find it is frequently held to have abandoned the property.

For example, assume that Aleka is driving with the windows down in her car. Somewhere along her route, a valuable scarf blows out the window. She retraces her route and searches for the scarf but cannot find it. She finally decides that further search is futile and proceeds to her destination five hundred miles away. Six months later, Frye, a hitchhiker, finds the scarf. Frye has acquired title, which is good even against Aleka. By completely giving up her search, Aleka abandoned the scarf just as effectively as if she had intentionally discarded it.

ABANDONED PROPERTY FOUND BY TRESPASSERS A trespasser who finds an item of abandoned personal property does not acquire title to it; the owner of the real property on which it was found does. The same rule applies if the property was lost. If a landowner employs a crew to install an underground septic tank, for example, and the crew digs up a cache of valuable pioneer relics, the landowner has first claim to the relics because they were buried in his or her ground.

TREASURE TROVE If money, gold, silver, and bullion are found, the property may be classified as a **treasure trove** (treasure that is found). In the example just given, for example, if the crew unearths money, gold, silver, or bullion (instead of pewter dishes, tin cups, brass buttons, and old muskets), the find may be deemed a treasure trove, and the crew may be able to keep it. In the United States, in the absence of a statute, a finder normally has title to a treasure trove against all but the true owner. Generally, to constitute

CONCEPT SUMMARY 47.3	Mislaid, Lost, and Abandoned Property	
CONCEPT	**DESCRIPTION**
MISLAID PROPERTY	Property that is placed somewhere voluntarily by the owner and then inadvertently forgotten. A finder of mislaid property will not acquire title to the goods, and the owner of the place where the property was mislaid becomes a caretaker of the mislaid property.
LOST PROPERTY	Property that is involuntarily left and forgotten. A finder of lost property can claim title to the property against the whole world *except the true owner.*
ABANDONED PROPERTY	Property that has been discarded by the true owner, who has no intention of claiming title to the property in the future. A finder of abandoned property can claim title to it against the whole world, *including the original owner.*

a treasure trove, the property owner must be unknown, and its finders must not have been trespassing.

SECTION 5 | Bailments

A **bailment** is formed by the delivery of personal property, without transfer of title, by one person (called a **bailor**) to another (called a **bailee**), usually under an agreement for a particular purpose—for example, to loan, lease, store, repair, or transport the property. On completion of the purpose, the bailee is obligated to return the bailed property in the same or better condition to the bailor or a third person or to dispose of it as directed.

Most bailments are created by agreement, but not necessarily by contract, because in many bailments not all of the elements of a contract (such as mutual assent and consideration) are present. For example, if you loan your business law text to a friend, a bailment is created, but not by contract, because there is no consideration. Most commercial bailments, such as the delivery of your suit to the cleaners for dry cleaning, are based on contract, however. A bailment differs from a sale or a gift in that possession is transferred without passage of title or intent to transfer title. In a sale or a gift, title is transferred from the seller or donor to the buyer or donee.

ELEMENTS OF A BAILMENT

Not all transactions involving the delivery of property from one person to another create a bailment. For such a transfer to become a bailment, the following three elements must be present:

1. Personal property.
2. Delivery of possession (without title).
3. Agreement that the property will be returned to the bailor or otherwise disposed of according to its owner's directions.

PERSONAL PROPERTY REQUIREMENT Only personal property is bailable; there can be no bailment of persons. Although a bailment of your luggage is created when it is transported by an airline, as a passenger you are not the subject of a bailment. Also, you cannot bail realty; thus, leasing your house to a tenant is not a bailment. Although bailments commonly involve *tangible* items—jewelry, cattle, automobiles, and the like—*intangible* personal property, such as

promissory notes and shares of corporate stock, may also be bailed.

DELIVERY OF POSSESSION *Delivery of possession* means transfer of possession of the property to the bailee.

—*Requirements for Delivery of Possession.* Two requirements must be met for delivery of possession to occur:

1. The bailee must be given exclusive possession and control over the property.
2. The bailee must *knowingly* accept the personal property.[9] In other words, the bailee must *intend* to exercise control over it.

If either delivery of possession or knowing acceptance is lacking, there is no bailment relationship. For example, suppose that Sudi is in a hurry to catch his plane. He has a package he wants to check at the airport. He arrives at the airport check-in station, but the person in charge has gone on a coffee break. Sudi decides to leave the package on the counter. Even though there has clearly been a physical transfer of the package, the person in charge of the check-in station has not knowingly accepted the personal property. Therefore, there has been no effective delivery.

The result is the same if, for example, Delacroix goes to a restaurant and checks her coat, leaving a $20,000 diamond necklace in the coat pocket. In accepting the coat, the bailee does not *knowingly* also accept the necklace.

—*Physical versus Constructive Delivery.* Either *physical* or *constructive* delivery will result in the bailee's exclusive possession of and control over the property. Physical delivery, as the phrase implies, occurs when the property is physically transferred to the bailee. For example, if a restaurant patron checks a coat with an attendant, the property has been physically delivered to the bailee. As discussed earlier, in the context of gifts, constructive delivery is a substitute, or symbolic, delivery. What is delivered to the bailee is not the actual property bailed (such as a car)

---

9. We are dealing here with *voluntary bailments*. Under some circumstances, regardless of whether a person intentionally accepts possession of someone else's personal property, the law imposes on him or her the obligation to redeliver it. For example, if property is accidentally left in another's possession without negligence on the part of its owner, the person in whose possession it has been left may be responsible for its return. This is referred to as an *involuntary bailment*.

but something so related to the property (such as the car keys) that the requirement of delivery is satisfied.

—*Involuntary Bailments.* In certain unique situations, a bailment is found despite the apparent lack of the requisite elements of control and knowledge. One example of such a situation occurs when the bailee acquires the property accidentally or by mistake—as in finding someone else's lost or mislaid property. A bailment is created even though the bailor did not voluntarily deliver the property to the bailee. Such bailments are referred to as *constructive* or *involuntary* bailments (see footnote 9).

THE BAILMENT AGREEMENT

A bailment agreement can be *express* or *implied*. Although no written agreement is required for bailments of less than one year (that is, the Statute of Frauds does not apply—see Chapter 15), it is a good idea to have a written agreement, especially when valuable property is involved.

The bailment agreement expressly or impliedly provides for the return of the bailed property to the bailor, or to a third person, or provides for disposal by the bailee. The agreement presupposes that the bailee will return the identical goods originally given by the bailor. In certain types of bailments, though, such as bailments of fungible goods,[10] only equivalent property must be returned.

SECTION **6** | Ordinary Bailments

Bailments are either *ordinary* or *special (extraordinary)*. There are three types of ordinary bailments. The distinguishing feature among them is which party receives a benefit from the bailment. Ultimately, the courts may use this factor to determine the standard of care required of the bailee while in possession of the personal property, and this factor will dictate the rights and liabilities of the parties. The three types of ordinary bailments are:

1. *Bailment for the sole benefit of the bailor.* This is a type of gratuitous bailment (one that involves no consideration) for the convenience and benefit of the bailor. The bailee is liable only for gross negligence. (Negligence is discussed in Chapter 7.)

2. *Bailment for the sole benefit of the bailee.* This is typically a loan of an article to a person (the bailee)

solely for that person's convenience and benefit. The bailee is liable for even slight negligence.

3. *Bailment for the mutual benefit of the bailee and the bailor.* This is the most common kind of bailment and involves some form of compensation for storing items or holding property. It is a contractual bailment and is often referred to as a *bailment for hire*. The bailee is liable for ordinary negligence, or the failure to observe ordinary care, which is the care that a reasonably prudent person would use under the circumstances.

RIGHTS OF THE BAILEE

Certain rights are implicit in the bailment agreement. Generally, the bailee has the right to take possession, to utilize the property for accomplishing the purpose of the bailment, to receive some form of compensation (unless the bailment is intended to be gratuitous), and to limit his or her liability for the bailed goods. These rights of the bailee are present (with some limitations) in varying degrees in all bailment transactions.

RIGHT OF POSSESSION A hallmark of the bailment agreement is that the bailee acquires the *right to control and possess the property temporarily*. The meaning of *temporary* depends on the terms of the bailment agreement. If the bailment agreement specifies a particular period, then the bailment is continuous for that time period. Earlier termination by the bailor is a breach of contract (if the bailment involves consideration), and the bailee can recover damages from the bailor. If no duration is specified, the bailment ends when either the bailor or the bailee so demands and possession of the bailed property is returned to the bailor.

A bailee's right of possession, even though temporary, permits the bailee to recover damages from any third persons for damage or loss to the property. For example, No-Spot Dry Cleaners sends all suede leather garments to Cleanall Company for special processing. If Cleanall loses or damages any leather goods, No-Spot has the right to recover against Cleanall.

RIGHT TO USE BAILED PROPERTY Naturally, the extent to which bailees can use the personal property entrusted to them depends on the terms of the bailment contract. When no provision is made, the extent of use depends on how necessary it is for the goods to be at the bailee's disposal for the ordinary purpose of the bailment to be carried out. When leasing drilling machinery, for example, the bailee is expected to use the equipment to drill. In contrast, when providing

---

10. As mentioned earlier, *fungible goods* are goods that consist of identical particles, such as wheat. Fungible goods are defined in UCC 1–201(17).

long-term storage for a car, the bailee is not expected to use the car because the ordinary purpose of a storage bailment does not include use of the property (unless an emergency dictates such use to protect the car).

RIGHT OF COMPENSATION   A bailee has a right to be compensated as provided for in the bailment agreement, to be reimbursed for costs and services rendered in the keeping of the bailed property, or both. In mutual-benefit bailments, the amount of compensation is often expressed in the bailment contract. For example, in the rental (bailment) of a car, the contract provides for charges on the basis of time, mileage, or a combination of the two, plus other possible charges.

—Gratuitous Bailments.   Even in a gratuitous bailment, a bailee has a right to be reimbursed or compensated for costs incurred in the keeping of the bailed property. For example, Hetta loses her pet dog, which is found by Jesse. Jesse takes Hetta's dog to his home and feeds it. Even though he takes good care of the dog, it becomes ill, and he takes it to a veterinarian. Jesse pays the bill for the veterinarian's services and the medicine. He is normally entitled to be reimbursed by Hetta for these reasonable costs incurred in the keeping of her dog.

—The Bailee's Lien.   To enforce the right of compensation, the bailee has a right to place a *possessory lien* (claim) on the specific bailed property until she or he has been fully compensated. This lien on specific bailed property is sometimes referred to as a **bailee's lien,** or *artisan's lien.* The lien is effective only so long as the bailee has not agreed to extend credit to the bailor and the bailee retains possession over the bailed property.

If the bailor refuses to pay or cannot pay the charges (compensation), the bailee is entitled in most states to foreclose on the lien. This means that the bailee can sell the property and be paid the amount owed for the bailment out of the proceeds, returning any excess to the bailor.

For example, Sarito takes his car to the garage to be stored while he is out of the country. He pays storage fees for two months in advance. When he returns six months later, the garage tenders Sarito his car, but because of unexpected expenses, he cannot pay the garage. The garage has a right to retain possession of Sarito's car, exercising a bailee's lien. If Sarito cannot make arrangements for payment, the garage will normally be entitled to sell the car to be compensated for the storage costs.

RIGHT TO LIMIT LIABILITY   In ordinary bailments, bailees have the right to limit their liability by type of risk, by monetary amount, or both, as long as (1) the limitations are called to the attention of the bailor and (2) the limitations are not against public policy. It is essential that the bailor be notified of the limitation in some way.

Although the bailee is not required to verbally notify the bailor, a small sign posted in an obscure location at the bailee's business is probably not sufficient notice to the bailor. The same holds true with limitations placed on the back of identification receipts (stubs) for parked cars, checked coats, or stored bailed goods.

Even if the bailor has received notice, certain types of disclaimers of liability are considered to be against public policy and therefore illegal. Clauses that limit a person's liability for his or her own wrongful acts, called *exculpatory clauses,* are carefully scrutinized by the courts, and in bailments they are often held to be illegal. A bailee cannot exclude liability for the bailee's own negligence. For example, a receipt from a parking garage that disclaims liability for any damage to parked cars, regardless of the cause, is generally unenforceable because it is against public policy. This is especially true in the case of bailees providing quasi-public services, such as warehousers (which will be discussed later in this chapter).

DUTIES OF THE BAILEE

The bailee has two basic responsibilities: (1) to take appropriate care of the property and (2) to surrender or dispose of the property at the end of the bailment. The bailee's duties are based on a mixture of tort law and contract law.

THE DUTY OF CARE   The bailee must exercise reasonable care in preserving the bailed property. (The duty of care was discussed in Chapter 7.) What constitutes reasonable care in a bailment situation normally depends on the nature and specific circumstances of the bailment.

Traditionally, courts have determined the appropriate standard of care on the basis of the type of bailment involved. In a bailment for the sole benefit of the bailor, for example, the bailee need exercise only a slight degree of care. In a bailment for the sole benefit of the bailee, however, the bailee must exercise great care. In a mutual-benefit bailment, courts normally impose a reasonable standard of care—that is, the bailee must exercise the degree of care that a reasonable

EXHIBIT 47-1 Degree of Care Required of a Bailee

Bailment for the Sole Benefit of the Bailor	Mutual-Benefit Bailment	Bailment for the Sole Benefit of the Bailee
	DEGREE OF CARE	
SLIGHT	REASONABLE	GREAT

and prudent person would exercise in the same circumstances. Exhibit 47–1 illustrates these concepts.

Determining whether a bailee exercised an appropriate degree of care is usually a question of fact for the jury or judge (in a nonjury trial). A bailee's failure to exercise appropriate care in handling the bailor's property results in tort liability.

DUTY TO RETURN BAILED PROPERTY At the end of the bailment, the bailee normally must relinquish the identical undamaged property (unless it is fungible) to either the bailor or someone the bailor designates or must otherwise dispose of it as directed. This is usually a *contractual* duty arising from the bailment agreement (contract). Failure to give up possession at the time the bailment ends is a breach of contract and could result in the tort of conversion.

Generally, the bailee has a duty to return the bailed goods to the bailor. A bailee may be liable if the goods being held or delivered are given to the wrong person. Hence, a bailee must be satisfied that a person (other than the bailor) to whom the goods are being delivered is the actual owner or has authority from the owner to take possession of the goods. Should the bailee deliver in error, then the bailee may be liable for conversion or misdelivery.

PRESUMPTION OF NEGLIGENCE Sometimes, the duty of care and the duty to return bailed property are combined to determine the bailee's liability. At the

end of the bailment, a bailee has the duty to return the bailor's property in the condition in which it was received (allowing for ordinary wear and aging).

In some cases, the bailor can sue the bailee in tort for damage to or loss of goods on the theory of negligence or conversion. At times, though, it is not possible for the bailor to discover and prove what specific acts of negligence or conversion committed by the bailee caused damage or loss to the property.[11] Thus, the law of bailments recognizes a rule whereby a *presumption* that the bailee is guilty of negligence or conversion will be made if the bailee fails to return the property or dispose of it in accordance with the bailor's instructions or if the bailee returns the property in a damaged condition. Once this is shown, the bailee must prove that he or she was not at fault. A bailee who is able to *rebut* (contradict) the presumption is not liable to the bailor.

When damage to goods is of the type that normally results only from someone's negligence, and when the bailee had full control of the goods, it is more likely than not that the damage was caused by the bailee's negligence. Therefore, the bailee's negligence is presumed. The following case illustrates how the presumption applies.

---

11. The basic formula for finding negligence requires proof that (1) a duty exists, (2) a breach of that duty occurred, (3) the breach is the proximate cause of damage or loss, and (4) actual loss or damage resulted.

CASE 47.4 Lembaga Enterprises, Inc. v. Cace Trucking & Warehouse, Inc.

Superior Court
of New Jersey,
Appellate Division, 1999.
320 N.J.Super. 501,
727 A.2d 1026.

BACKGROUND AND FACTS *Lembaga Enterprises, Inc., is an importer and distributor of toiletries and cosmetics. Cace Trucking & Warehouse, Inc., is a common carrier and warehouser. Lembaga and Cace had a business relationship for several years. Cace would pick up shipment containers for Lembaga, store them in its warehouse, and deliver them. The area where Cace parked its trucks was surrounded by an eight-foot-high, barbed-wire fence. The two gates were locked at night and the truck trailers were locked at all times with pin locks. One afternoon, Cace picked up two containers of perfume for Lembaga. When the containers arrived at the warehouse, Lembaga's president told Cace's vice president not to unload the containers until the next day. The next day, the first container was brought into the warehouse and unloaded. When a driver went to retrieve the second*

CASE 47.4 **Continued**

container, it had disappeared. Part of a broken pin lock was found on the ground where the container had been. Lembaga filed a suit in a New Jersey state court against Cace for the loss of its cargo valued at $366,879.53, alleging, among other things, negligence and conversion. Lembaga filed a motion for a directed verdict, arguing that Cace was presumed to have converted the container because it disappeared mysteriously from Cace's warehouse. The court denied the motion, the jury found in Cace's favor, and Lembaga appealed to a state intermediate appellate court.

IN THE LANGUAGE OF THE COURT

RODRIGUEZ, A. A., J.A.D. [Judge, Appellate Division]

* * * [W]e hold that proof of damage to or loss of goods while in the custody of a bailee gives rise to a presumption of conversion by the bailee. The bailee may rebut the presumption by proof that the bailee did not intentionally or negligently convert the goods and that it was not negligent in preventing third parties from causing the loss or damage. However, the burden of proof that the bailee converted the goods rests with the bailor at all times.

Therefore, in a conversion action, the bailor [Lembaga] has the burden to prove that the bailee [Cace] has unlawfully converted the goods. When goods are delivered to a bailee in good condition and then are lost or damaged, the law presumes a conversion and casts upon the bailee the burden of going forward with the evidence to show that the loss did not occur through his negligence or if he cannot affirmatively do this, that he exercised a degree of care sufficient to rebut the presumption of it. * * *

* * * *

Here, the thrust of Cace's defense was that it had adequate security to prevent a theft of the container by third parties. It did not present evidence to rebut the presumption that Cace, its agents or employees had converted the container. Thus, a jury question was presented on the conversion cause of action. * * * [C]onversion is a broader concept than theft. *A conversion can occur even when a bailee has not stolen the merchandise but has acted negligently in permitting the loss of the merchandise from its premises.* [Emphasis added.]

Therefore, here, the judge should have instructed the jury that if Lembaga established that the container had disappeared while in the care of Cace, there is a rebuttable presumption [an assumption that may be disproved by evidence] of conversion based either on Cace's negligent conduct in permitting third parties to steal the container, or by the negligent or intentional conduct of Cace's employees or agents. The burden to prove conversion, however, rests at all times with Lembaga.

Accordingly, we reverse and remand to the [lower court] for a new trial. * * *

DECISION AND REMEDY *The state intermediate appellate court reversed the judgment of the lower court and remanded the case for a new trial. Proof of loss of or injury to the goods while in the custody of the bailee establishes a prima facie case against the bailee, who must then rebut the presumption.*

RIGHTS AND DUTIES OF THE BAILOR

A bailee's duties and a bailor's rights are complementary. In other words, the rights of the bailor are essentially the same as the duties of a bailee, and vice versa.

RIGHTS OF THE BAILOR   A bailor has the right to expect the following:

1. The property will be protected with reasonable care while in the possession of the bailee.
2. The bailee will utilize the property as agreed in the bailment agreement (or not at all).

3. The property will be relinquished at the conclusion of the bailment according to the directions given by the bailor.
4. The bailee will not convert (alter) the goods except as agreed.
5. The bailor will not be bound by any limitations on the bailee's liability unless these limitations are known and are enforceable by law.
6. Repairs or service on the property will be completed without defective workmanship.

DUTIES OF THE BAILOR   Obviously, a bailor has a duty to compensate the bailee either as agreed or as reimbursement for costs incurred by the bailee in keeping the bailed property. A bailor also has an all-encompassing duty to provide the bailee with goods or chattel that are free from hidden defects that could injure the bailee.

—*Bailor's Duty to Reveal Defects.* The bailor's duty to reveal defects to the bailee translates into two rules:

1. In a *mutual-benefit bailment*, the bailor must notify the bailee of all known defects and any hidden defects that the bailor knows of or could have discovered with reasonable diligence and proper inspection.
2. In a *bailment for the sole benefit of the bailee*, the bailor must notify the bailee of any known defects.

The bailor's duty to reveal defects is based on a negligence theory of tort law. A bailor who fails to give the appropriate notice is liable to the bailee and to any other person who might reasonably be expected to come into contact with the defective article.

—*Warranty Liability for Defective Goods.* A bailor can also incur warranty liability based on contract law (see Chapter 23) for injuries resulting from the bailment of defective articles. Property leased by a bailor must be *fit for the intended purpose of the bailment.* The bailor's knowledge of or ability to discover any defects is immaterial. Warranties of fitness arise by law in sales and lease contracts.[12]

TERMINATION OF BAILMENTS

Bailments for a specific term end when the stated period lapses. When no duration is specified, the bailment can be terminated at any time by the following events:

1. The mutual agreement of both parties.
2. A demand by either party.
3. The completion of the purpose of the bailment.
4. An act by the bailee that is inconsistent with the terms of the bailment.
5. The operation of law.

SECTION 7 | Special Types of Bailments

Most of this discussion of bailments has concerned ordinary bailments, or bailments in which bailees are expected to exercise ordinary care in the handling of

bailed property. Some bailment transactions warrant special consideration. These include bailments in which the bailee's duty of care is extraordinary—that is, the bailee's liability for loss or damage to the property is absolute—as is generally true in cases involving common carriers and innkeepers. Warehouse companies have the same duty of care as ordinary bailees; but like carriers, they are subject to extensive federal and state laws, including the UCC's Article 7.

DOCUMENTS OF TITLE AND ARTICLE 7

A shipment or storage of goods may be covered by a *bill of lading*, a *warehouse receipt*, or a *delivery order*. These documents of title are subject to Article 7 of the UCC.[13] To be a **document of title,** a document "must purport to be issued by or addressed to a bailee and purport to cover goods in the bailee's possession which are either identified or are fungible portions of an identified mass."[14]

A **bill of lading** is a document verifying the receipt of goods for shipment issued by a person engaged in the business of transporting or forwarding goods.[15] A **warehouse receipt** is a receipt issued by a person engaged in the business of storing goods for hire.[16] A **delivery order** is a written order to deliver goods directed to a warehouser, carrier, or other person who, in the ordinary course of business, issues warehouse receipts or bills of lading.[17]

Simply put, a document of title is a receipt for goods in the charge of a bailee-carrier or a bailee-warehouser and a contract for the shipment or storage of identified goods.

NEGOTIABILITY OF DOCUMENTS OF TITLE

Negotiability is a concept that applies to documents of title when they contain the words "bearer" or "to the

---

12. UCC 2A–212, 2A–213.

13. Of course, when applicable, federal law takes priority [see UCC 7–103]. For example, the Federal Bills of Lading Act [49 U.S.C. Sections 81–124], enacted in 1916, applies to bills of lading issued by common carriers for goods shipped in interstate or foreign commerce, and the United States Warehouse Act [7 U.S.C. Sections 241–243], also enacted in 1916, applies to receipts covering agricultural products stored for interstate or foreign commerce.
14. UCC 1–201(15), 7–102(1)(e); see also UCC 7–401.
15. UCC 1–201(6).
16. UCC 1–201(45); see also UCC 7–201 and 7–202. UCC 7–102(h) defines the person engaged in the storing of goods for hire as a *warehouseman*.
17. UCC 7–102(1)(d).

order of."[18] If a document of title is negotiable—that is, if it specifies that the goods are to be delivered to bearer or to the order of a named person—the following are also possible:

1. The possessor of the document of title is entitled to receive, hold, and dispose of the document and the goods it covers.

2. A good faith purchaser of the document may acquire greater rights to the document and the goods it covers than the transferor had or had the authority to convey (that is, a good faith purchaser may take free of the claims and defenses of prior parties).

If a document of title is nonnegotiable—that is, if it is not made payable to the order of any named person or to bearer—it may be transferred by assignment but not by negotiation.[19]

DUE NEGOTIATION The concepts of negotiability under Articles 3 and 7 of the UCC are similar. There are important distinctions between them, however. For example, Article 7 refers to the negotiation process as due negotiation. **Due negotiation** requires that the purchaser of a document of title take it in good faith, for value, without notice of a defense against or a claim to it, in the regular course of business or financing, and not in the settlement or payment of a money obligation.[20] In other words, even if all other requirements are met, transfer of a negotiable document of title to a nonbusinessperson is not due negotiation. In such situations, the transferee acquires only those rights the transferor had or had the authority to convey.[21]

On due negotiation, however, a transferee can acquire greater rights in a document of title than the transferor had. The transferee obtains title to the document and to the goods, including rights to goods delivered to the bailee after the document was issued, and takes free of all prior claims and defenses of which he or she had no notice. The document's issuer remains obligated to store or deliver the goods according to the document's terms.[22] Under this provision, business-persons can extend credit on documents of title without concern for adverse claims of third parties.

RECEIVING AND DELIVERING GOODS To prevent a thief or a finder of goods from defeating the rights of the true owner (by, for example, taking them to a warehouse and subsequently negotiating the warehouse receipt to a third party who would otherwise take the goods free of the claims of others), the goods must be delivered to the issuer of the document of title by their owner or the owner's agent.[23] Otherwise, the document does not represent title to the goods. Even if the document does not represent title, however, the bailee will not be liable if she or he acts in good faith and observes reasonable commercial standards in receiving and delivering the goods.[24]

In other words, a carrier or warehouser who receives goods from a thief or finder and delivers them according to that individual's instructions is not liable to the goods' true owner. The reason for this rule is that carriers and warehousers simply furnish a service necessary to trade and commerce; they are not links in the chain of title and do not represent the owner in transactions affecting title.

COMMON CARRIERS

Common carriers are publicly licensed to provide transportation services to the general public. They are distinguished from private carriers, which operate transportation facilities for a select clientele. A private carrier is not bound to provide service to every person or company making a request. A common carrier, however, must arrange carriage for all who apply, within certain limitations.[25]

STRICT LIABILITY OF COMMON CARRIERS A common carrier's contract for transportation creates a *mutual-benefit bailment.* Unlike the bailee in an ordinary mutual-benefit bailment, however, the common carrier is held to a standard of care based on *strict liability,* rather than a standard of reasonable care, in protecting the bailed personal property. Except for the five exceptions to be discussed shortly, the common carrier is liable for any damage to goods in shipment,

---

18. UCC 7–104(1). Negotiability is a concept that also applies in situations involving negotiable instruments.
19. UCC 7–104(2).
20. UCC 7–501(4).
21. UCC 7–504. Until the bailee is notified of the transfer, the transferee's rights may be defeated by certain creditors of the transferor; by a buyer from the transferor in the ordinary course of business, if the bailee has delivered the goods to the buyer; or by the bailee who has dealt with the transferor in good faith.
22. UCC 7–502.

23. UCC 7–503(1).
24. UCC 7–404.
25. A common carrier is not required to take any and all property anywhere in all instances. Public regulatory agencies govern common carriers, and carriers may be restricted to geographic areas. They may also be limited to carrying certain kinds of goods or to providing only special types of transportation equipment.

CONCEPT SUMMARY 47.4 | Rights and Duties of the Bailee and the Bailor

CONCEPT	DESCRIPTION
RIGHTS OF A BAILEE (DUTIES OF A BAILOR)	1. The right of possession allows actions against third parties who damage or convert the bailed property and allows actions against the bailor for wrongful breach of the bailment. 2. A bailee has the right to be compensated or reimbursed for keeping bailed property. This right is based in contract or quasi contract. 3. Unpaid compensation or reimbursement entitles the bailee to a possessory lien on the bailed property and the right of foreclosure. 4. A bailee has the right to limit his or her liability. An ordinary bailee can limit the types of risk, monetary amount, or both, provided proper notice is given and the limitation is not against public policy. In special bailments, limitations on the types of risk are usually not allowed, but limitations on the monetary amount of loss are permitted by regulation.
DUTIES OF A BAILEE (RIGHTS OF A BAILOR)	1. A bailee must exercise reasonable care over property entrusted to her or him. A common carrier (special bailee) is held to a standard of care based on strict liability unless the bailed property is lost or destroyed due to (a) an act of God, (b) an act of a public enemy, (c) an act of a government authority, (d) an act of the shipper, or (e) the inherent nature of the goods. 2. Bailed goods in a bailee's possession must be returned to the bailor or be disposed of according to the bailor's directions. Failure to return the property gives rise to a presumption of negligence. 3. A bailee cannot use or profit from bailed goods except by agreement or in situations in which the use is implied to further the bailment purpose.

even that caused by the willful acts of third persons or by sheer accident.

The UCC retained the common law liability of common carriers in UCC 7–309. Common carriers are treated as if they are absolute insurers for the safe delivery of goods to the destination, even though they are not. They cannot contract away this liability for damaged goods. They are permitted to limit their dollar liability to an amount stated on the shipment contract, however, subject to government regulations.[26]

EXCEPTIONS TO STRICT LIABILITY There are five common law exceptions to the rule that a common carrier is strictly liable for any damages to goods that are shipped:

1. An act of God.
2. An act of a public enemy.
3. An order of a public authority.
4. An act of the shipper.
5. The inherent nature of the goods.

Thus, a common-carrier trucking company moving cargo is liable for acts of vandalism, mechanical defects in refrigeration units, or a dam bursting, if any of these acts results in damage to the cargo. But if the damage is caused by acts of God—an earthquake or lightning, for example—or any other exception listed above, the shipper bears the loss.

SHIPPER'S LOSS The shipper bears any loss occurring through its own faulty or improper crating or packaging procedures. For example, if a bird dies because its crate was poorly ventilated, the shipper, not the carrier, bears the loss.

CONNECTING CARRIERS A bill of lading that specifies one or more connecting carriers is called a *through bill of lading*. When connecting carriers are involved in transporting goods under a through bill of lading, the shipper can recover from the original carrier or any connecting carrier.[27] Normally, the *last* carrier is presumed to have received the goods in satisfactory condition.

---

26. Federal laws require common carriers to offer shippers the opportunity to obtain higher dollar limits for loss by paying a higher fee for the transport.

27. UCC 7–302.

WAREHOUSE COMPANIES

Warehousing is the business of providing storage of property for compensation. Like ordinary bailees, warehouse companies are liable for loss or damage to property resulting from *negligence*. A warehouser must "exercise such care . . . as a reasonably careful [person] would exercise under like circumstances but unless otherwise agreed he [or she] is not liable for damages which could not have been avoided by the exercise of such care."[28] A warehouse company can limit the dollar amount of liability, but the bailor must be given the option of paying an increased storage rate for an increase in the liability limit.[29]

INNKEEPERS

At common law, innkeepers, hotel owners, and similar operators were held to the same strict liability as common carriers with respect to property brought into the rooms by guests. Today, only those who provide lodging to the public for compensation as a *regular* business

28. UCC 7–204(1).
29. UCC 7–204(2).

are covered under this rule of strict liability. Moreover, the rule applies only to those who are *guests*, as opposed to *lodgers*. A lodger is a permanent resident of the hotel or inn, whereas a guest is a traveler.

In many states, innkeepers can avoid strict liability for loss of guests' valuables and cash by providing a safe in which to keep them. Each guest must be clearly notified of the availability of such a safe. Statutes often limit the liability of innkeepers with regard to articles that are not kept in the safe or are of such a nature that they are not ordinarily kept in a safe. These statutes may limit the amount of monetary damages or even provide that the innkeeper incurs no liability in the absence of negligence. Commonly, hotels notify guests of the state laws governing the liability of innkeepers by posting a notice on the inside of the door of the hotel room or in some other prominent place within the room.

Normally, the innkeeper assumes no responsibility for the safety of a guest's automobile because the guest usually retains possession and control. If, however, the innkeeper provides parking facilities, and the guest's car is entrusted to the innkeeper or to an employee, the rules governing ordinary bailments will apply.

REVIEWING PERSONAL PROPERTY AND BAILMENTS

Vanessa Denai purchased forty acres of land in rural Louisiana with a 1,600-square-foot house on it and a metal barn near the house. Seven months later, Denai met Lance Finney, who had been seeking a small plot of rural property to rent. After several meetings, Denai invited Finney to live on a corner of her property in exchange for Finney's assistance in cutting wood and tending her property. Denai agreed to store Finney's sailboat in her barn. With Denai's consent, Finney constructed a concrete and oak foundation on Denai's property. Finney then purchased a 190-square-foot dome from Dome Baja for $3,395. The dome was shipped by Doty Express, a transportation company licensed to serve the public. When he received it, Finney installed the dome frame and fabric exterior so that the dome was detachable from the foundation. A year after Finney installed the dome, Denai wrote Finney a note stating, "I've decided to give you four acres of land surrounding your dome as drawn on this map." This gift violated no local land-use restrictions. Using the information presented in the chapter, answer the following questions.

1. Is the dome real property or personal property? Explain the distinction.

2. What factors would a court normally consider in determining whether the dome was a fixture?

3. Is the gift of land from Denai to Finney a testamentary gift, a gift *causa mortis*, or a gift *inter vivos*?

4. Did the storage of the boat constitute a bailment? If so, who was the bailor, and who was the bailee, and what are the rights and duties of each party to the bailment relationship? What three elements are required for a bailment to arise?

5. Would Doty Express be considered a common carrier or a private carrier? Does the standard of reasonable care apply to the dome shipment by Doty Express?

TERMS AND CONCEPTS TO REVIEW

abandoned property 950

accession 948

bailee 951

bailee's lien 953

bailment 951

bailor 951

bill of lading 956

chattel 940

community property 945

concurrent ownership 941

confusion 948

constructive delivery 946

delivery order 956

document of title 956

due negotiation 957

estray statute 950

fee simple 941

fixture 940

gift 946

gift *causa mortis* 947

gift *inter vivos* 947

joint tenancy 943

lost property 949

mislaid property 948

personal property 940

property 940

real property 940

tenancy by the entirety 944

tenancy in common 941

trade fixture 941

treasure trove 950

warehouse receipt 956

QUESTIONS AND CASE PROBLEMS

47-1. Jaspal has a serious heart attack and is taken to the hospital. He is aware that he is not expected to live. Because he is a bachelor with no close relatives nearby, Jaspal gives his car keys to his close friend, Friedrich, telling Friedrich that he is expected to die and that the car is Friedrich's. Jaspal survives the heart attack, but two months later he dies from pneumonia. Jaspal's uncle, Sam, the executor of Jaspal's estate, wants Friedrich to return the car. Friedrich refuses, claiming that the car was given to him by Jaspal as a gift. Discuss whether Friedrich will be required to return the car to Jaspal's estate.

47-2. QUESTION WITH SAMPLE ANSWER

Curtis is an executive on a business trip to the West Coast. He has driven his car on this trip and checks into the Hotel Ritz. The hotel has a guarded underground parking lot. Curtis gives his car keys to the parking lot attendant but fails to notify the attendant that his wife's $10,000 fur coat is in a box in the trunk. The next day, on checking out, he discovers that his car has been stolen. Curtis wants to hold the hotel liable for both the car and the coat. Discuss the probable success of his claim.

For a sample answer to this question, go to Appendix I at the end of this text.

47-3. Bill Heise is a janitor for the First Mercantile Department Store. While walking to work, Bill finds an expensive watch lying on the curb. Bill gives the watch to his son, Otto. Two weeks later, Martin Avery, the true owner of the watch, discovers that Bill found the watch and demands it back from Otto. Explain who is entitled to the watch, and why.

47-4. Discuss the standard of care required from the bailee for the bailed property in the following situations, and determine whether the bailee breached that duty.

(a) Benedetto borrows Tom's lawn mower because his own lawn mower needs repair. Benedetto mows his front yard. To mow the backyard, he needs to move some hoses and lawn furniture. He leaves the mower in front of his house while doing so. When he returns, he discovers that the mower has been stolen.

(b) Atka owns a valuable speedboat. She is going on vacation and asks her neighbor, Regina, to store the boat in one stall of Regina's double garage. Regina consents, and the boat is moved into the garage. Regina, in need of some grocery items for dinner, drives to the store. When doing so, she leaves the garage door open, as is her custom. While she is at the store, the speedboat is stolen.

47-5. Orlando borrows a gasoline-driven lawn edger from his neighbor, Max. Max has not used the lawn edger for two years. Orlando has never owned a lawn edger and is not familiar with its use. Max previously used this edger often, and if he had made a reasonable inspection, he would have discovered that the blade was loose. Orlando is injured when the blade becomes detached while he is edging his yard.

(a) Can Orlando hold Max liable for his injuries?

(b) Would your answer be different if Orlando had rented the edger from Max and paid a fee? Explain.

47–6. GIFTS *INTER VIVOS*. Thomas Stafford owned four promissory notes. Payments on the notes were deposited into a bank account in the names of Stafford and his daughter, June Zink, "as joint tenants with right of survivorship." Stafford kept control of the notes and would not allow Zink to spend any of the proceeds. He also kept the interest on the account. On one note, Stafford indorsed "Pay to the order of Thomas J. Stafford or June S. Zink, or the survivor." The payee on each of the other notes was "Thomas J. Stafford and June S. Zink, or the survivor." When Stafford died, Zink took possession of the notes, claiming that she had been a joint tenant of the notes with her father. Stafford's son, also Thomas, filed a suit in a Virginia state court against Zink, claiming that the notes were partly his. Thomas argued that their father had not made a valid gift *inter vivos* of the notes to Zink. In whose favor will the court rule? Why? [*Zink v. Stafford*, 509 S.E.2d 833 (Va. 1999)]

47–7. CASE PROBLEM WITH SAMPLE ANSWER
Louis Hennefeld served in the U.S. Air Force between 1952 and 1968, and received an honorable discharge. During his service, Hennefeld suffered a "wartime service-connected disability" that, according to the U.S. Veterans Administration, "was totally disabling." Hennefeld and Blair O'Dell began living together in 1975, and ten years later, they bought a house in Montclair, Essex County, New Jersey. The two men took title to the house as joint tenants with right of survivorship. Under a New Jersey state statute, they received a "disabled veteran's exemption" from the payment of 50 percent of the taxes on the property. In 2004, they attempted to reconvey the house to themselves as tenants by the entirety and filed a claim with Essex County for a 100 percent tax exemption, which is normally granted to qualified veterans in "traditional" marriages. What distinguishes a tenancy by the entirety from a joint tenancy with a right of survivorship? Should the "reconveyance" be considered effective in this case? Discuss. [*Hennefeld v. Township of Montclair*, 22 N.J.Tax 166 (2005)]

To view a sample answer for this case problem, go to this book's Web site at http://wbl.westbuslaw.com, select "Chapter 47," and click on "Case Problem with Sample Answer."

47–8. FOUND PROPERTY. A. D. Lock owned Lock Hospitality, Inc., which in turn owned the Best Western Motel in Conway, Arkansas. Joe Terry and David Stocks were preparing the motel for renovation. As they were removing the ceiling tiles in room 118, with Lock present in the room, a dusty cardboard box was noticed near the heating and air-supply vent where it had apparently

been concealed. Terry climbed a ladder to reach the box, opened it, and handed it to Stocks. The box was filled with more than $38,000 in old currency. Lock took possession of the box and its contents. Terry and Stocks filed a suit in an Arkansas state court against Lock and his corporation to obtain the money. Should the money be characterized as lost, mislaid, or abandoned property? To whom should the court award it? Explain. [*Terry v. Lock*, 37 S.W.3d 202 (Ark. 2001)]

47–9. CONCURRENT OWNERSHIP. Vincent Slavin was a partner of Cantor Fitzgerald Securities in the World Trade Center (WTC) in New York City. In 1998, Slavin and Anna Baez became engaged and started living together. They placed both of their names on three accounts at Chase Manhattan Bank according to the bank's terms, which provided that "accounts with multiple owners are joint, payable to either owner or the survivor." Slavin arranged for the direct deposit of his salary and commissions into one of the accounts. On September 11, 2001, Slavin died when two planes piloted by terrorists crashed into the WTC towers, causing their collapse. At the time, the balance in the three accounts was $656,944.36. On September 14, Cantor Fitzgerald deposited an additional $58,264.73 into the direct-deposit account. Baez soon withdrew the entire amount from all of the accounts. Mary Jelnek, Slavin's mother, filed a suit in a New York state court against Baez to determine the ownership of the funds that had been in the accounts. In what form of ownership were the accounts held? Who is entitled to which of the funds, and why? [*In re Jelnek*, 3 Misc.2d 725, 777 N.Y.S.2d 871 (Sur. 2004)]

47–10. VIDEO QUESTION
Go to this text's Web site at http://wbl.westbuslaw.com and select "Chapter 47." Click on "Video Questions" and view the video titled *Personal Property and Bailments*. Then answer the following questions.

(a) What type of bailment is discussed in the video?

(b) What were Vinny's duties with regard to the rug-cleaning machine? What standard of care should apply?

(c) Did Vinny exercise the appropriate degree of care? Why or why not? How would a court decide this issue?

LAW | on the Web

For updated links to resources available on the Web, as well as a variety of other materials, visit this text's Web site at http://wbl.westbuslaw.com.

To learn about whether a married person has ownership rights in a gift received by his or her spouse, go to Scott Law Firm's Web page at

http://www.scottlawfirm.com/property.htm

For a discussion of the origins of the term *bailment* and how bailment relationships have been defined, go to

http://www.lectlaw.com/def/b005.htm

LEGAL RESEARCH EXERCISES ON THE WEB

Go to http://wbl.westbuslaw.com, the Web site that accompanies this text. Select "Chapter 47" and click on "Internet Exercises." There you will find the following Internet research exercises that you can perform to learn more about topics covered in this chapter.

Activity 47–1: **LEGAL PERSPECTIVE**
Lost Property

Activity 47–2: **MANAGEMENT PERSPECTIVE**
Bailments

CHAPTER 48

Real Property and Landlord-Tenant Relationships

From the earliest times, property has provided a means for survival. Primitive peoples lived off the fruits of the land, eating the vegetation and wildlife. Later, as the wildlife was domesticated and the vegetation cultivated, property provided pastures and farmland. In the twelfth and thirteenth centuries, the power of feudal lords was exemplified by the amount of land that they held. After the age of feudalism passed, property continued to be an indicator of family wealth and social position. In the Western world, the protection of an individual's right to his or her property has become one of our most important rights.

In this chapter, we first look at the nature of ownership rights in real property. We then examine the legal requirements involved in the transfer of real property, including the kinds of rights that are transferred by various types of deeds; the procedures used in the sale of real estate; and a way in which real property can, under certain conditions, be transferred merely by possession. Realize that real property rights are never absolute. There is a higher right—that of the government to take, for compensation, private land for public use. This chapter discusses this right, as well as other restrictions on the ownership of property. We conclude the chapter with a discussion of landlord-tenant relationships.

SECTION 1 | The Nature of Real Property

As discussed in Chapter 47, *real property* consists of land and the buildings, plants, and trees that it contains. Personal property is movable; real property is immovable. Real property usually means land (and structures), but it also includes air space and subsurface rights, plant life and vegetation, and fixtures.

LAND

Land includes the soil on the surface of the earth and the natural products or artificial structures that are attached to it. Land further includes all the waters contained on or under its surface and the air space above it (subject, of course, to legal use by pilots). In other words, unless a statute or case law holds otherwise, a landowner has the right to everything existing permanently below the surface of her or his property to the center of the earth and above it to the heavens.

AIR SPACE AND SUBSURFACE RIGHTS

The owner of real property has relatively exclusive rights to both the air space above the land and the soil and minerals underneath it. Significant limitations, called *encumbrances*, on either air rights or subsurface rights normally must be indicated on the document transferring title at the time of purchase. The ways in which ownership rights in real property can be limited are examined in detail later in this chapter.

AIR RIGHTS Until one hundred years ago, the right to use the air space over an owner's property was not too significant. Early cases involving air rights dealt with such matters as whether a telephone wire could be run across a person's property when the wire did not touch any of the property[1] and whether a bullet shot over a person's land constituted trespass.[2]

Today, cases involving air rights present questions such as the right of commercial and private planes to fly over property and the right of individuals and governments to seed clouds and produce artificial rain. Flights over private land do not normally violate the

---

1. *Butler v. Frontier Telephone Co.*, 186 N.Y. 486, 79 N.E. 716 (1906). Stringing a wire across someone's property violates the air rights of that person. Leaning walls and projecting eave spouts and roofs also violate the air rights of the property owner.
2. *Herrin v. Sutherland*, 74 Mont. 587, 241 P. 328 (1925). Shooting over a person's land normally constitutes trespass.

property owners' rights unless the flights are low and frequent, causing a direct interference with the enjoyment and use of the land.

SUBSURFACE RIGHTS   Ownership of the surface of land can be separated from ownership of its subsurface. Subsurface rights can be extremely valuable when minerals, oil, or natural gas is located beneath the surface. But a subsurface owner's rights would be of little value if he or she could not use the surface to exercise those rights. Hence, a subsurface owner will have a right (called a *profit*, discussed later in this chapter) to go onto the surface of the land to, for example, find and remove minerals.

Of course, conflicts may arise between surface and subsurface owners when attempts are made to excavate below the surface. At common law, a landowner has the right to have the land supported in its natural condition by the owners of the interests under the surface. If the owners of the subsurface rights excavate, they are absolutely liable if their excavation causes the surface to collapse. Depending on the circumstances, the excavators may also be liable for any damage to structures on the land. Many states have statutes that extend excavators' liability to include damage to structures on the property. Typically, these statutes provide exact guidelines as to the requirements for excavations of various depths.

PLANT LIFE AND VEGETATION

Plant life, both natural and cultivated, is also considered to be real property. In many instances, natural vegetation, such as trees, adds greatly to the value of realty. When a parcel of land is sold and the land has growing crops on it, the sale includes the crops, unless otherwise specified in the sales contract. When crops are sold by themselves, however, they are considered to be personal property or goods. Consequently, the sale of crops is a sale of goods and thus is governed by the Uniform Commercial Code (UCC) rather than by real property law.

SECTION 2 | Ownership Interests in Real Property

Ownership of property is an abstract concept that cannot exist independently of the legal system. No one can actually possess, or *hold*, a piece of land, the air above, the earth below, and all the water contained on it. One can only possess *rights* in real property. Numerous rights are involved in real property ownership. As discussed in Chapter 47, one who holds the entire bundle of rights owns the property in *fee simple*. Here we look first at the fee simple and then at some common examples of how an owner in fee simple can part with some, but not all, of her or his rights in real property.

FEE SIMPLE

In a **fee simple absolute,** the owner has the greatest aggregation of rights, privileges, and power possible. The owner can give the property away, sell the property for a price, or transfer the property by will to another. The fee simple absolute is limited to a person and his or her heirs and is assigned forever without limitation or condition.

The rights that accompany a fee simple absolute include the right to use the land for whatever purpose the owner sees fit, subject to laws that prevent the owner from unreasonably interfering with another person's land and subject to applicable zoning laws. Furthermore, the owner has the right of *exclusive* possession of the property. A fee simple is potentially infinite in duration and can be disposed of by deed or by will (by selling or giving it to another). When there is no will, the fee simple passes to the owner's legal heirs.

LIFE ESTATES

A **life estate** is an estate that lasts for the life of some specified individual. A **conveyance,** or transfer of real property, "to A for his life" creates a life estate.[3] In a life estate, the life tenant's ownership rights cease to exist on the life tenant's death. The life tenant has the right to use the land, provided no **waste** (injury to the land) is committed. In other words, the life tenant cannot use the land in a manner that would adversely affect its value. The life tenant can use the land to harvest crops or, if mines and oil wells are already on the land, can extract minerals and oil from it, but the life tenant cannot exploit the land by creating new wells or mines.

The life tenant has the right to mortgage the life estate and create liens, easements, and leases; but none can extend beyond the life of the tenant. In addition, with few exceptions, the owner of a life estate has an exclusive right to possession during his or her lifetime.

---

3. A less common type of life estate is created by the conveyance "to A for the life of B." This is known as an estate *pur autre vie*, or an estate for the duration of the life of another.

Along with these rights, the life tenant also has some duties—to keep the property in repair and to pay property taxes. In sum, the owner of the life estate has the same rights as a fee simple owner except that she or he must maintain the value of the property during her or his tenancy, less the decrease in value resulting from the normal use of the property allowed by the life tenancy.

LEASEHOLD ESTATES

A **leasehold estate** is created when a real property owner or lessor (landlord) agrees to convey the right to possess and use the property to a lessee (tenant) for a certain period of time. In every leasehold estate, the tenant has a *qualified* right to exclusive possession (qualified by the right of the landlord to enter on the premises to assure that waste is not being committed). The tenant can use the land—for example, by harvesting crops—but cannot injure the land by such activities as cutting down timber for sale or extracting oil. The respective rights and duties of the landlord and tenant that arise under a lease agreement will be discussed in greater detail later in this chapter. Here, we look at the types of leasehold estates, or tenancies, that can be created when real property is leased.

TENANCY FOR YEARS A **tenancy for years** is created by an express contract (which can sometimes be oral) under which property is leased for a specified period of time, such as a month, a year, or a period of years. For example, signing a one-year lease to occupy an apartment creates a tenancy for years. At the end of the period specified in the lease, the lease ends (without notice), and possession of the apartment returns to the lessor. If the tenant dies during the period of the lease, the lease interest passes to the tenant's heirs as personal property. Often, leases include renewal or extension provisions.

PERIODIC TENANCY A **periodic tenancy** is created by a lease that does not specify how long it is to last but does specify that rent is to be paid at certain intervals. This type of tenancy is automatically renewed for another rental period unless properly terminated. For example, a periodic tenancy is created by a lease that states, "Rent is due on the tenth day of every month." This provision creates a tenancy from month to month. A week-to-week or year-to-year tenancy can also be created. A periodic tenancy sometimes arises when a landlord allows a tenant under a tenancy for years to *hold over* (retain possession after the lease term ends) and continue paying monthly or weekly rent.

At common law, to terminate a periodic tenancy, the landlord or tenant must give one period's notice to the other party. If the tenancy is month to month, for example, one month's notice must be given. State statutes often require a different period for notice of termination in a periodic tenancy, however.

TENANCY AT WILL Suppose that a landlord rents an apartment to a tenant "for as long as both agree." Here, the tenant receives a leasehold estate known as a **tenancy at will.** Under the common law, either party can terminate a tenancy at will without notice (that is, "at will"). This type of estate usually arises when a tenant who has been under a tenancy for years retains possession after the termination date of that tenancy with the landlord's consent. Before the tenancy has been converted into a periodic tenancy (by the periodic payment of rent), it is a tenancy at will. Once the tenancy is treated as a periodic tenancy, termination notice must conform to the requirements already discussed. The death of either party or the voluntary commission of waste by the tenant will terminate a tenancy at will.

TENANCY AT SUFFERANCE The possession of land without right is called a **tenancy at sufferance.** A tenancy at sufferance is created when a tenant *wrongfully* retains possession of property. It is not a true tenancy for that reason. For example, when a tenancy for years or a periodic tenancy ends and the tenant continues to retain possession of the premises without the owner's permission, a tenancy at sufferance is created.

NONPOSSESSORY INTERESTS

Some interests in land do not include any rights of possession. These interests, known as nonpossessory interests, include *easements, profits,* and *licenses.* Because easements and profits are similar and the same rules apply to both, we discuss them together.

EASEMENTS AND PROFITS An **easement** is the right of a person to make limited use of another person's real property without taking anything from the property. An easement, for example, can be the right to walk across another's property. In contrast, a **profit** is the right to go onto land in possession of another and take away some part of the land itself or some product of the land. For example, Mack, the owner of Sandy View, gives Ann the right to go there and remove all the sand and gravel that she needs for her cement business. Ann has a profit. Easements and profits can be classified as either appurtenant or in gross.

An easement or profit *appurtenant* arises when the owner of one piece of land has a right to go onto (or remove things from) an adjacent piece of land owned by another. Suppose Owen has a right to drive his car across Green's land, which is adjacent to Owen's property. This right-of-way over Green's property is an easement appurtenant to Owen's land and can be used only by Owen. Owen can convey the easement when he conveys his property.

With an easement or profit *in gross*, the right to use or take things from another's land exits exists even though the owner of the easement or profit does not own an adjacent tract of land. When a utility company is granted an easement to run its power lines across another's property, it obtains an easement in gross. An easement or profit in gross requires the existence of only one parcel of land, which must be owned by someone other than the owner of the easement or profit in gross.

—Creation of an Easement or Profit.   Easements and profits can be created by deed or will, contract, implication, necessity, or prescription. Creation by deed or will simply involves the delivery of a *deed* or a transfer by *will* by the owner of an easement stating that the grantee (the person receiving the profit or easement) is granted the rights that the grantor had in the easement or profit. Easements or profits can also be created by *contract*, with the contract terms defining the extent and length of time of use.

An easement or profit may arise by *implication* when the circumstances surrounding the division of a parcel of property imply its creation. If Barrow divides a par-cel of land that has only one well for drinking water and conveys the half without a well to Dan, a profit by implication arises because Dan needs drinking water.

An easement may also be created by necessity. An easement by *necessity* does not require division of property for its existence. A person who rents an apartment, for example, has an easement by necessity in the private road leading up to the dwelling.

An easement arises by *prescription* when one person exercises an easement, such as a right-of-way, on another person's land without the landowner's consent, and the use is apparent and continues for a period of time equal to the applicable statute of limitations. In much the same way, title to property may be obtained by adverse possession, discussed later in this chapter.

—Effect of a Sale of Property.   When a parcel of land that is *benefited* by an easement or profit appurtenant is sold, the property carries the easement or profit along with it. Thus, if Owen sells his property to Thomas and includes the appurtenant right-of-way across Green's property in the deed to Thomas, Thomas will own both the property and the easement that benefits it.

When a parcel of land that has the *burden* of an easement or profit appurtenant is sold, the new owner must recognize its existence only if he or she knew or should have known of it or if it was recorded in the appropriate office of the county. Thus, if Owen records his easement across Green's property in the appropriate county office before Green conveys the land, the new owner of Green's property will have to allow Owen, or any subsequent owner of Owen's property, to continue to use the path across the land formerly owned by Green.

Whether an easement accompanied a sale of property was at issue in the following case.

CASE 48.1   Webster v. Ragona

New York
Supreme Court,
Appellate Division,
Third Department, 2004.
7 A.D.3d 850,
776 N.Y.S.2d 347.

BACKGROUND AND FACTS   *Walter Peeters owned two commercial buildings at 26 and 32 Main Street in Oneonta, New York. The tenants at both addresses used a common driveway for access to a parking lot behind the buildings. In 1992, Gerard Webster leased 26 Main Street and opened a restaurant on the premises. The same year, Giacinto and Antoinette Ragona began leasing 32 Main Street to operate a video store. In September 1994, the Ragonas bought their building. The contract of sale conditioned transfer of title on "the granting of any necessary permanent easement for parking in the rear of the premises." The parties signed an agreement to transfer an easement in the driveway, which the Ragonas agreed to insure and to maintain. That winter, they used the driveway, repaired it, and cleared it of snow. In May 1995, Webster bought 26 Main Street, which included the driveway. The deed did not mention the Ragonas' easement. Six years later, Webster and his associates filed a suit in a New York state court against the Ragonas, arguing in part that their easement in the driveway was extinguished on Peeters's sale of 26 Main Street. The court issued a summary judgment in the defendants' favor. The plaintiffs appealed to a state intermediate appellate court.*

CASE 48.1 | Continued

IN THE LANGUAGE OF THE COURT
SPAIN, J. [Justice]
* * * *

An easement appurtenant is created when such easement is (1) conveyed in writing, (2) subscribed by the person creating the easement and (3) burdens the servient estate for the benefit of the dominant estate. The easement agreement fulfills all of these elements. Plaintiffs nevertheless argue that an easement appurtenant was not created, relying on the fact that the instrument does not expressly state that the easement is permanent * * * .

While it is true that *whether an easement is appurtenant or merely a personal, non-inheritable and non-assignable right depends upon the intent of the parties to the instrument in which the right-of-way was granted,* as with any contract, where possible such intent should be gleaned solely from the language of the instrument creating the easement. It is only when language used in a conveyance is susceptible of more than one interpretation that the courts will look into surrounding circumstances, the situation of the parties, etc. In our view, the easement agreement at issue here can only be interpreted to convey an easement appurtenant. That the easement did not employ the term "permanent" or include an express reference binding Peeters' heirs and assigns is not dispositive [controlling]. The grant of such an easement need not include language expressly describing the easement as "permanent" because *an easement appurtenant, once created, necessarily runs with the land.* Indeed, the clear purpose of the agreement was to convert an informal right-of-way which was already in existence into a legally binding easement which would burden Peeters' estate at 26 Main Street for the benefit of 32 Main Street, the Ragonas' dominant estate. Significantly, the instrument did not contain any language restricting the easement or retaining any right of revocation. Accordingly, we need not look beyond the easement agreement itself to ascertain that the easement created thereby is binding upon Peeters' successors in interest, provided they had notice of the easement when they took title—which brings us to plaintiffs' remaining contentions. [Emphasis added.]
* * * *

In the complaint, plaintiffs [Webster and his associates] allege that they were unaware, prior to purchasing 26 Main Street, that the property was encumbered by an easement or subject to use by the Ragonas. In their answer, the Ragonas allege that plaintiffs had both actual and constructive notice of their claim to the easement, claiming, among other things, that their conduct in maintaining the disputed property would have caused a reasonable person to inquire about the status of that property. * * *

Notably, plaintiffs have not denied any of the specific allegations which would have put them on notice that the Ragonas were using the property in question * * * . Instead, plaintiffs rely on the claim that they lacked notice that the easement was permanent and binding upon them as subsequent purchasers. [The] Supreme Court correctly found that this claim is insufficient to preclude summary judgment in favor of the Ragonas because plaintiffs' knowledge that the Ragonas were enjoying use of the property was sufficient to charge plaintiffs with the duty to inquire about the nature and status of the right-of-way.

DECISION AND REMEDY *The state intermediate appellate court affirmed the judgment of the lower court. The Ragonas had a "permanent" easement appurtenant in the driveway between 26 and 32 Main Street. "[A]n easement appurtenant, once created, necessarily runs with the land."*

WHAT IF THE FACTS WERE DIFFERENT? *What might the result in this case have been if Peeters had told Webster when he bought 26 Main Street that the Ragonas did not have a "permanent" easement in the driveway?*

—*Termination of an Easement or Profit.* An easement or profit can be terminated or extinguished in several ways. The simplest way is to deed it back to the owner of the land that is burdened by it. Also, if the owner of an easement or profit becomes the owner of the property burdened by it, then it is merged into

the property. Another way is to abandon it with the intent to relinquish the right to use it.

LICENSES In the context of real property, a **license** is the revocable right of a person to come onto another person's land. It is a personal privilege that arises from

CONCEPT SUMMARY 48.1 | Interests in Real Property

TYPE OF INTEREST	DESCRIPTION
OWNERSHIP INTERESTS	1. *Fee simple absolute*—The most complete form of ownership. 2. *Life estate*—An estate that lasts for the life of a specified individual; ownership rights in a life estate are subject to the rights of the future-interest holder. 3. *Concurrent interests*—Exist when title to property is held by two or more persons. Co-ownership can take the form of a tenancy in common, a joint tenancy, a tenancy by the entirety, or community property (see Chapter 47 for a description of concurrent ownership).
LEASEHOLD INTERESTS	A leasehold interest, or estate, is an interest in real property that is held only for a limited period of time, as specified in the lease agreement. Types of tenancies relating to leased property include the following: 1. *Tenancy for years*—Tenancy for a period of time stated by express contract. 2. *Periodic tenancy*—Tenancy for a period determined by the frequency of rent payments; automatically renewed unless proper notice is given. 3. *Tenancy at will*—Tenancy for as long as both parties agree; no notice of termination is required. 4. *Tenancy at sufferance*—Possession of land without legal right.
NONPOSSESSORY INTERESTS	Interests that involve the right to use real property but not to possess it. Easements, profits, and licenses are nonpossessory interests.

the consent of the owner of the land and can be revoked by the owner. A ticket to attend a movie at a theater is an example of a license. Assume that a Broadway theater owner issues to Roxanna a ticket to see a play. If Roxanna is refused entry because she is improperly dressed, she has no right to force her way into the theater. The ticket is only a revocable license, not a conveyance of an interest in property.

SECTION 3 | Transfer of Ownership

Ownership of real property can pass from one person to another in a number of ways. Ownership rights in real property are commonly transferred through sale of the property or by will or inheritance. Real property ownership can also be transferred by gift, by possession, or (as will be discussed later in the chapter) by eminent domain. When ownership rights in real property are transferred, the type of interest being transferred and the conditions of the transfer normally are set forth in a *deed* executed by the one who is conveying the property.

DEEDS

Possession and title to land are passed from person to person by means of a **deed**—the instrument of con-

veyance of real property. A deed is a writing signed by an owner of real property by which title to it is transferred to another. Deeds must meet certain requirements. Unlike a contract, a deed need not be supported by legally sufficient consideration. Gifts of real property are common, and they require deeds even though there is no consideration for the gift. The necessary components of a valid deed are the following:

1. The names of the *grantor* (the giver or seller) and the *grantee* (the donee or buyer).
2. Words evidencing an intent to convey (for example, "I hereby bargain," "I hereby sell," "I hereby grant," or "I hereby give").
3. A legally sufficient description of the land.
4. The grantor's (and usually his or her spouse's) signature.
5. Delivery of the deed.

WARRANTY DEED The **warranty deed** makes the greatest number of warranties and thus provides the most extensive protection against defects of title. In most states, special language is required to make a warranty deed. If a contract calls for a "warranty deed" without specifying the covenants to be included in the deed, or if a deed states that the seller is providing the "usual covenants," most courts will infer from this language that the following covenants are being made: a covenant that the grantor has the title to, and the power to convey, the property; a covenant of quiet enjoyment (a warranty that the buyer will not be disturbed in her or his possession of the land); and a covenant that transfer of the property is made without knowledge of adverse claims of third parties. Generally, the warranty deed makes the grantor liable for all defects of title by the grantor and previous titleholders.

SPECIAL WARRANTY DEED

In contrast to the warranty deed, the **special warranty deed,** which is frequently referred to as a *limited warranty deed,* warrants only that the grantor or seller held good title during his or her ownership of the property. In other words, the grantor is not warranting that there were no defects of title when the property was held by previous owners.

If the special warranty deed discloses all liens or other encumbrances, the seller will not be liable to the buyer if a third person subsequently interferes with the buyer's ownership. If the third person's claim arises out of, or is related to, some act of the seller, however, the seller will be liable to the buyer for damages.

QUITCLAIM DEED

A **quitclaim deed** warrants less than any other deed. Essentially, it simply conveys to the grantee whatever interest the grantor had. In other words, if the grantor had nothing, then the grantee receives nothing. Naturally, if the grantor had a defective title or no title at all, a conveyance by warranty deed or special warranty deed would not cure the defects. Such deeds, however, will give the buyer a cause of action to sue the seller.

A quitclaim deed can and often does serve as a release of the grantor's interest in a particular parcel of property. For instance, suppose Sandor owns a strip of waterfront property on which he wants to build condominiums. Lanz has an easement on a portion of the property, which might interfere with Sandor's plans for the development. Sandor can negotiate with Lanz to deed the easement back to Sandor. Lanz's signing of a quitclaim deed would constitute such a transfer.

GRANT DEED

With a **grant deed,** the grantor simply states, "I grant the property to you" or "I convey, or bargain and sell, the property to you." By state statute, grant deeds may carry with them an implied warranty that the grantor owns the property being transferred and has not previously encumbered it or conveyed it to someone else.

SHERIFF'S DEED

A **sheriff's deed** is a document giving ownership rights to a buyer at a sheriff's sale, which is a sale held by a sheriff to pay a court judgment against the owner of the property. Typically, the property was subject to a mortgage or tax payments and the owner defaulted on the payments. After a statutory period of time during which the defaulting owner can redeem the property (see Chapter 28), the deed is delivered to the purchaser.

RECORDING STATUTES

Every jurisdiction has **recording statutes,** which allow deeds to be recorded. Recording a deed involves a fee. The grantee typically pays this fee because he or she is the one who will be protected by recording the deed.

Recording a deed gives notice to the public that a certain person is now the owner of a particular parcel of real estate. Thus, prospective buyers can check the public records for transactions creating interests or rights in specific parcels of real property. Placing everyone on notice as to the true owner is intended to prevent the previous owners from fraudulently conveying the land to other purchasers. Deeds are generally recorded in the county in which the property is located. Many state statutes require that the grantor sign the deed in the presence of two witnesses before it can be recorded.

CONTRACTS FOR THE SALE OF REAL ESTATE

Transfers of ownership interests in real property are frequently accomplished by means of a sale. The sale of real estate is similar to the sale of goods because it involves a transfer of ownership, often with specific warranties. In the sale of real estate, however, certain formalities are observed that are not required in the sale of goods. For example, to meet legal requirements, a deed must be signed and delivered.[4]

Exhibit 48–1 on the next page summarizes the steps involved in any sale of real property. The first step is the formation of the land sales contract. A title search (to verify that the seller has good title to the property and that no other claims to the property exist) follows, along with (usually) negotiations to obtain financing for the purchase. Unless the buyer pays cash for the property, the buyer must obtain financing through a

---

4. The phrase *signed, sealed, and delivered* once referred to the requirements for transferring title to real property by deed. The seal has fallen from use, but signature and delivery are still required.

EXHIBIT 48-1　Steps Involved in the Sale of Real Estate

BUYER'S PURCHASE OFFER
Buyer offers to purchase Seller's property. The offer may be conditioned on Buyer's ability to obtain financing, on satisfactory inspections of the premises, on title examination, and so on. Included with the offer is earnest money, which will be placed in an escrow account.

SELLER'S RESPONSE
If Seller accepts Buyer's offer, then a contract is formed. Seller could also reject the offer or make a counteroffer that modifies Buyer's terms. Buyer may accept or reject Seller's counteroffer or make a counteroffer that modifies Seller's terms.

PURCHASE AND SALE AGREEMENT
Once an offer or a counteroffer is accepted, a purchase and sale agreement is formed.

TITLE EXAMINATION AND INSURANCE
Title examiner investigates and verifies Seller's rights in the property and discloses any claims or interests held by others. Buyer (and/or Seller) may purchase title insurance to protect against a defect in title.

FINANCING
Buyer may seek a mortgage loan to finance the purchase. Buyer agrees to grant lender an interest in the property as security for Buyer's indebtedness.

INSPECTION
Buyer has the property inspected for any physical problems, such as major structural or mechanical defects and insect infestation.

ESCROW
Buyer's purchase money (including earnest money) is held in an escrow account by an escrow agent (such as a title company or a bank). The agent holds the deed transferring title received from Seller and any money received from Buyer until all conditions of the sale have been met.

CLOSING
The escrow agent transfers the deed to Buyer and the proceeds of the sale to Seller. The proceeds are the purchase price less any amount already paid by Buyer and any closing costs to be paid by Seller. Included in the closing costs are fees charged for services performed by the lender, escrow agent, and title examiner. The purchase and sale of the property is complete.

---

mortgage loan. (A **mortgage** is a loan made by an individual or institution, such as a banking institution or trust company, for which the property is given as security.) Normally, the buyer will also have the premises inspected for physical or mechanical defects and for insect infestation. The final step is the *closing*.

Deposits toward the purchase price normally are held in a special account, called an **escrow account,** until all of the conditions of sale have been met and the closing takes place, at which time the money is transferred to the seller. The *escrow agent*, which may be a title company, bank, or special escrow company, acts as a neutral party in the sales transaction and facilitates the sale by allowing the buyer and seller to close the transaction without having to exchange documents and funds.

WARRANTY OF HABITABILITY The common law rule of *caveat emptor* ("let the buyer beware") held that

the seller of a home made no warranties with respect to its soundness or fitness unless such a warranty was specifically included in the deed or contract of sale. Today, there is a strong trend against this rule and in favor of an **implied warranty of habitability.** Under this approach, which is the law in the majority of states, the seller of a house warrants that it will be fit for human habitation regardless of whether any such warranty is included in the deed or contract of sale. This warranty is similar to the UCC's implied warranty of merchantability for sales of personal property.

Essentially, the seller is warranting that the house is in reasonable working order and is of reasonably sound construction. To recover damages for breach of the implied warranty of habitability, the purchaser of the house is required to prove only that it is somehow defective and that the damages were caused by the defect. Thus, under this theory, the seller of a new home is in effect a guarantor of the home's fitness. In some states, the warranty protects not only the first purchaser but any subsequent purchaser as well.

SELLER'S DUTY TO DISCLOSE In most jurisdictions, courts have placed on sellers a duty to disclose any known defect that materially affects the value of the property and that the buyer could not reasonably discover. Under these circumstances, nondisclosure is similar to representing that the defect does not exist, and the buyer may have grounds for a successful lawsuit based on fraud or misrepresentation.

For example, Nick sells Nora a house that he knows has roof problems. Nick does not tell Nora about these problems. During the first rain after the sale, water gushes from the house's ceilings and light fixtures. Nora contacts a roofing contractor, who tells her that she needs a completely new roof. Nora might sue Nick for breach of contract, fraud, and misrepresentation, seeking rescission of their contract and a return of whatever amount she paid Nick toward the purchase price of the house.

TRANSFER BY INHERITANCE

Property that is transferred on an owner's death is passed either by will or by inheritance laws. If the owner of land dies with a will, that land passes according to the terms of the will. If the owner dies without a will, state statutes prescribe how and to whom the property will pass. The transfer of property by inheritance will be discussed in Chapter 50.

ADVERSE POSSESSION

Adverse possession is a means of obtaining title to land without delivery of a deed. Essentially, when one person possesses the property of another for a certain statutory period of time (three to thirty years, with ten years being most common), that person, called the *adverse possessor*, acquires title to the land and cannot be removed from it by the original owner. For property to be held adversely, four elements must be satisfied:

1. Possession must be actual and exclusive; that is, the possessor must take sole physical occupancy of the property.

2. The possession must be open, visible, and notorious, not secret or clandestine. The possessor must occupy the land for all the world to see.

3. Possession must be continuous and peaceable for the required period of time. This requirement means that the possessor must not be interrupted in the occupancy by the true owner or by the courts.

4. Possession must be hostile and adverse. In other words, the possessor must claim the property as against the whole world. He or she cannot be living on the property with the permission of the owner.

There are a number of public-policy reasons for the adverse possession doctrine. These include society's interest in resolving boundary disputes, in quieting (determining) title when title to property is in question, and in assuring that real property remains in the stream of commerce. More fundamentally, policies behind the doctrine include punishing owners who do not take action when they see adverse possession and rewarding possessors for putting land to productive use.

In the following case, the question before the court was whether a couple had obtained title to a certain piece of land by *acquisitive prescription* (Louisiana's term for adverse possession).

CASE 48.2 **Otwell v. Diversified Timber Services, Inc.**

Court of Appeal
of Louisiana.
Third Circuit. 2005.
896 So.2d 222.

BACKGROUND AND FACTS *In 1807, the eastern boundary of a parcel of land known as the "Charles McBride Riquet No. 39" was described as "the waters of Hemphill's Creek" in LaSalle Parish, Louisiana. In the 1930s, a curve in the creek was straightened, moving the bed to the west of its original path. In 1955, E. E. Jones sold 16 acres of land to Jesse Moffett under a deed that described the tract's western boundary as the "East line of the Charles McBride Riquet No. 39." In the late 1960s, Terry Brown and Margaret Otwell granted Bessie Sanders—their granddaughter and daughter, respectively—and William Sanders, Bessie's husband, title to a portion of 24 acres known as the "Terry Brown Estate." This included 3.12 acres between Hemphill's Creek and the "old slough," a natural feature that appeared to have been the creek's original bed. In 2001, Moffett sold the timber on the 3.12 acres to B & S Timber, Inc. The Sanderses filed a suit in a Louisiana state court against Moffett and others, seeking damages for "timber trespass." The court held that the plaintiffs failed to prove "just title" to the disputed land when they could not establish that the creek had flowed through*

CONTINUED ▶

CASE 48.2 | Continued

the old slough in 1807, but ruled that the plaintiffs proved title through acquisitive prescription (adverse possession), and awarded damages and costs of more than $68,000. The defendants appealed to a state intermediate appellate court.

IN THE LANGUAGE OF THE COURT

SULLIVAN, Judge.

* * * *

* * * Defendants argue that the trial court erred in finding sufficient corporeal [physical] possession to establish ownership by thirty years acquisitive prescription.

Ownership of immovable property may be acquired by the prescription of thirty years without the need of just title or possession in good faith. Corporeal possession sufficient to confer prescriptive title must be continuous, uninterrupted, peaceable, public, and unequivocal. For purposes of acquisitive prescription without title, possession extends only to that which has been actually possessed. Actual possession must be either inch-by-inch possession or possession within enclosures. According to well-settled Louisiana jurisprudence, an enclosure is any natural or artificial boundary. [Emphasis added.]

* * * [T]he concept of possession is neither simple nor precise. * * *

Whether a party has possessed property for purposes of thirty-year acquisitive prescription is a factual determination by the trial court and will not be disturbed on appeal unless it is clearly wrong.

Mr. Sanders testified that his wife acquired title from her grandfather to the land between the present channel and the old slough and that he began timber management on this property, as well as on other lands, at her request. It is undisputed that sometime in 1967, Mr. Sanders began marking trees on the perimeter and throughout the disputed property, some of which were inscribed with his wife's registered brand, the initials "BO" over a half-moon. Other trees were inscribed with the initials "CM," designating those trees that Mr. Sanders set aside for another individual, Chris Moss. Mr. Sanders explained that he "hacked trees for a long period of time" so that "anyone passing through there [would] know that this land was occupied by somebody" and that he wanted to let anyone "without knowledge of the boundary [to] know that this property was occupied by someone with apparent brand or someone with initials." He testified that, in no uncertain terms, he told Mr. Moffett that the boundary between their lands was the old creek bed, around which he found old generations of fencing, even though the land was not fenced recently. In addition to marking trees, Mr. Sanders ran off trespassers, cut an existing fence to make a riding trail, shot hogs, hunted wood ducks, and harvested berries. He testified that he placed the property in a hunting club that posted signs and erected deer stands. He also took an interest in the property as "heritage property," searching for Indian artifacts and investigating old sites such as a mill believed to have been burned during the Civil War. According to Mr. Sanders, he has never been "run off" the property, and the only evidence of another's possession occurred when his original markings on the trees were painted over with blue-green paint. He then hired someone to apply red paint over the blue-green paint. Charles Moffett, the son of Mr. Jesse Moffett, testified that the painting over Mr. Sanders' markings would have occurred between his retirement in 1999 and the cutting of the timber in 2001.

In commenting on the number and frequency [of] the trees marked, the trial court stated: "I find as a fact that it was many, many trees. If it was 200 trees that wouldn't be an underestimate of how many trees had marks on 'em. And with that many marks on that many trees on that small a piece of land, you knew that somebody was laying claim to it." The trial court's finding regarding the number of trees marked is supported, in part, by the testimony of Mr. Moffett, who stated that there was "paint on everything," not only by the borders but also "everywhere else." * * *

* * * *

* * * Mr. Moffett testified that he knew as early as 1966 that Mr. and Mrs. Sanders intended to claim the property east of the present creek bed, based upon a conversation that he had with Mrs. Sanders' father, John Otwell. Although he believed that his title extended to the present creek bed, he also knew how long Mr. Sanders had been marking trees on the property. Additionally, Mr. Moffett recalled informing the owner of B & S Timber, Ronnie Jameson, that there would be a controversy about the cutting of the timber. Based upon this record, we cannot conclude that the trial court erred * * * .

CASE 48.2 | Continued

DECISION AND REMEDY *The state intermediate appellate court affirmed the lower court's judgment in the plaintiffs' favor. The circumstances established the Sanderses' ownership of the disputed land. They assertedly acquired title from Bessie's grandfather, managed and marked the timber, ran off trespassers, cut a fence to make a trail, shot hogs, hunted ducks, harvested berries, and placed the property in a hunting club that posted signs and erected deer stands.*

WHAT IF THE FACTS WERE DIFFERENT? *Suppose that the Sanderses had done nothing involving the disputed land except to claim title. Would the result have been different?*

SECTION 4 | Limitations on the Rights of Property Owners

No ownership rights in real property can ever really be absolute; that is, an owner of real property cannot always do whatever she or he wishes on or with the property. Nuisance and environmental laws, for example, restrict certain types of activities. Holding the property is also conditional on the payment of property taxes. Zoning laws and building permits frequently restrict one's use of the realty. In addition, if a property owner fails to pay debts, the property may be seized to satisfy judgment creditors. In short, the rights of every property owner are subject to certain conditions and limitations. We look here at some of the important ways in which owners' rights in real property can be limited.

EMINENT DOMAIN

Even if ownership in real property is in fee simple absolute, there is still a superior ownership that limits the fee simple absolute. Just as the king was the ultimate landowner in medieval England, so in the United States the government has ultimate ownership rights in all land. This right is called **eminent domain,** and it allows the government to take land, from a small parcel of property to a large tract of land, for public use. Eminent domain gives the government the right to acquire possession of real property in the manner directed by the U.S. Constitution and the laws of the state whenever the public interest requires it. The Constitution allows property to be taken only for public use, not for private benefit.

For example, when a new public highway is to be built, the government decides where to build it and how much land to condemn. The power of eminent domain is generally invoked through **condemnation** proceedings—thus, the power of eminent domain is sometimes referred to as the *condemnation power* of government. After the government determines that a particular parcel of land is needed for public use, it brings a judicial proceeding to obtain title to the land. Then, in another proceeding, the court determines the *fair value* of the land, which is usually approximately equal to its market value.

When the government takes land owned by a private party for public use, it is referred to as a **taking,** and the government must compensate the private party. Under the so-called *takings clause* of the Fifth Amendment to the U.S. Constitution, the government may not take private property for public use without "just compensation." State constitutions contain similar provisions. (For a discussion of a current controversy involving the takings clause, see this chapter's *Contemporary Legal Debates* feature beginning on the next page.)

RESTRICTIVE COVENANTS

A private restriction on the use of land is known as a **restrictive covenant.** If the restriction is binding on the party who purchases the property originally and on subsequent purchasers as well, it is said to "run with the land."

COVENANTS RUNNING WITH THE LAND A restrictive covenant that runs with the land goes with the land and cannot be separated from it. Consider an example. Owen is the owner of Grasslands, a twenty-acre estate whose northern half contains a small reservoir. Owen wishes to convey the northern half to Arid City, but before he does, he digs an irrigation ditch connecting the reservoir with the lower ten acres, which he uses as farmland. When Owen conveys the northern ten acres to Arid City, he enters into an agreement with the city. The agreement, which is contained in the deed, states, "Arid City, its heirs and assigns, promises not to remove more than five thousand gallons of water per day from the Grasslands reservoir." Owen has created a restrictive covenant running with the land. Under this covenant, Arid City and all future owners of the northern ten acres of Grasslands are limited as to the amount of water they can draw from its reservoir.

Using "Takings" for Private Developments

Government takings of private property for public use are often controversial. This is understandable, given that landowners whose property is taken may have more than a monetary interest at stake in condemnation proceedings. For example, suppose that the state decides to condemn your home to build a new highway. Although the state's purpose in condemning the property may be rational and in the public interest, you may not want to give up your home for sentimental reasons. Many people who have found themselves in just this situation have learned that they can do little about it—their property will be taken, provided that the government's purpose in condemning the property is rational, the public will benefit from the action, and the property owners are given "just compensation."

But suppose that a city government decides that it is in the public interest to have a manufacturing plant located in the city to create more jobs. To further this interest, the government may condemn certain existing housing or business property and then sell the land to the owner of the manufacturing plant. Although the public may ultimately benefit from these actions, is it constitutional to take property from one private party only to transfer it to another private entity? Even if the government pays the owner just compensation for the land, shouldn't the taking be for *public* ownership and use? Such questions have elicited controversy in today's legal arena.

PRIVATE OR PUBLIC USE?

For some time, state and local governments have been using the power of eminent domain to transfer property to private developers. Government officials claim that this use of eminent domain helps bring in private developers and businesses that provide jobs and increase tax revenues, thus revitalizing communities. Eminent domain is also commonly being used to encourage redevelopment—in blighted (run down, devastated) areas of a city, for example. Critics, however, contend that when eminent domain is used in this way, essentially one group of private owners is replaced by another group of private owners. In other words, the land is not being taken for "public" use, as required by the U.S. Constitution.

Generally, when takings for development or redevelopment are challenged on constitutional grounds, the courts focus on whether the proposed use of the land is genuinely in the public interest or is mainly to further private interests. By and large, the courts have supported the government agencies in these cases, although there have been exceptions. In fact, the ill-fated World Trade Center in New York City came close to never being built because of a challenge to a condemnation action for redevelopment purposes. The trial court held that the taking was permissible, but an appellate court reversed this decision and dismissed the condemnation action. The New York Court of Appeals (that state's highest court) then reversed the appellate court's decision, thus allowing the project to go forward. According to the state's highest court, the concept of a World Trade Center was a public purpose even though, to raise revenue, some of the building space to be erected would be leased to private tenants with a remote connection to world trade.[a]

---

a. *Courtesy Sandwich Shop, Inc. v. Port of New York Authority,* 12 N.Y.2d 379, 190 N.E.2d 402, 240 N.Y.S.2d 1 (1963).

—Requirements for Enforceability. Four requirements must be met for a covenant running with the land to be enforceable. If they are not met, the covenant will apply to the two original parties to a contract only and will not run with the land to future owners. The requirements are as follows:

1. The covenant running with the land must be created in a written agreement (covenant). It is usually contained in the document that conveys the land.

2. The parties must intend that the covenant run with the land. In other words, the instrument that contains the covenant must state not only that the promisor is bound by the terms of the covenant but that all the promisor's "successors, heirs, or assigns" will be bound.

3. The covenant must *touch* and *concern* the land. This means that the limitations on the activities of the owner of the burdened land must have some connection with the land. For example, a purchaser of land cannot be bound by a covenant requiring him or her to drive only Ford pickups because such a restriction has no relation to the land purchased.

4. The successors to the original parties to the covenant must have notice of the covenant.

—Notice May Be Actual or Constructive. To satisfy the last requirement listed above, the notice may

974

RM A MORE PERFECT UNION   ESTABLISH JUSTICE   INSURE DOMESTIC TRANQUILITY   PROMOTE THE GENERAL WELFARE

nal
Law
ffery

Jurisdiction Internet Electronic
Free Speech Prenuptial Filing
Agreements
Advice of
Counsel

Issues Internet Sales
Contracts and the
over Commerce
War Clause
on Privacy
Terror
Debate
AIDS

Private Who Owns the Engagement Ring?
Enforceability
Forum-Selection Clauses Developments
Using "Takings"
Internet

PATRIOT
ACT

Exclusive Territorial Righ
Environmenta
Takings
Commer

THE SUPREME COURT WEIGHS IN

After contradictory rulings by state courts nationwide in recent years, the Supreme Court agreed to hear an eminent domain case in 2005. The case involved a condemnation proceeding, in which private property was to be taken through eminent domain and subsequently handed over to private developers. In *Kelo v. New London, Conn.*,[b] the New London Development Corporation, a public entity, sought ninety acres of a middle-class neighborhood along the Thames River in Connecticut. The city of New London argued that taking the land was justified because the property could generate jobs and greater tax revenue if turned over to developers. City officials claimed that economic development satisfied the "public use" requirement of the Fifth Amendment.

In a five-to-four decision, the Supreme Court narrowly sided with the city of New London. The majority opinion, written by Justice John Paul Stevens, offered a broad interpretation of public use. Cities, not federal judges, Stevens claimed, were best suited to make decisions regarding eminent domain takings in the public interest. Economic development is a valid public use, even if carried out by a private party. New London had "carefully formulated an economic development that it believes will provide appreciable benefits to the community," he wrote. Justice Sandra Day O'Connor, however, strongly dissented, contending that "any property may now be taken for the benefit of another private party." The beneficiaries, she suggested, "are likely to be those citizens with disproportionate

influence and power in the political process, including large corporations and development firms."

The *Kelo* decision reversed a trend in the lower courts toward a stricter interpretation of public use. Numerous courts had ruled in favor of property owners whose land had been threatened in the name of economic development.

STATES REACT TO THE SUPREME COURT'S DECISION

The majority decision in the *Kelo* case recognized "that nothing in our opinion precludes any State from placing further restrictions on its exercise of the takings power." Individual states can pass laws that prohibit takings for economic development. A number of states, including Connecticut, have proposed legislation that would either place restrictions on such takings or forbid them entirely. One plan being widely considered would only authorize the use of eminent domain power for economic development if an area suffered from blight—an idea the Supreme Court considered in *Kelo*, but dismissed, due to its inherent subjectivity. State governments will likely find defining blight similarly confounding, thus opening the possibility for court battles on the state level.

WHERE DO YOU STAND?

The national implications of the Supreme Court's decision in the *Kelo* case are as yet unknown, but the legal debate over takings may not be closed. Given the Court's close decision, do you think that the issue may be revisited by the nation's highest court at some point in the future? Should it be? Why or why not?

b. __U.S.__, 125 S.Ct. 1241, 160 L.Ed.2d 1093 (2005).

---

be actual or constructive. For example, in the course of developing a fifty-lot suburban subdivision, Levitt records a declaration of restrictions that effectively limits construction on each lot to one single-family house. In each lot's deed is a reference to the declaration with a provision that the purchaser and her or his successors are bound to those restrictions. Thus, each purchaser assumes ownership with notice of the restrictions. If an owner attempts to build a duplex (or any structure that does not comply with the restrictions) on a lot, the other owners may obtain a court order enjoining the construction.

In fact, Levitt might simply have included the restrictions on the subdivision's map, filed the map in

the appropriate public office, and included a reference to the map in each deed. In this way, each owner would also have been held to have constructive notice of the restrictions.

ILLEGAL RESTRICTIVE COVENANTS Restrictive covenants have sometimes been used to perpetuate neighborhood segregation, and in these cases they have been invalidated by the courts. In the case of *Shelley v. Kraemer*,[5] the United States Supreme Court held that restrictive covenants proscribing resale to members of minority groups were unconstitutional. In addition, the Civil Rights Act of 1968 (also known as

5. 334 U.S. 1, 68 S.Ct. 836, 92 L.Ed. 1161 (1948).

the Fair Housing Act) prohibits all discrimination based on race, color, religion, gender, familial status, or national origin in the sale and leasing of housing.

SECTION 5 | Landlord-Tenant Relationships

Anyone who rents housing or rents space for commercial purposes becomes subject to the laws governing landlord-tenant relationships. The owner of the property is the landlord, or **lessor;** the party assuming temporary possession is the tenant, or **lessee;** and their rental agreement is the lease contract, or, more simply, the **lease.** The property interest involved in a landlord-tenant relationship is known as a *leasehold estate*, as discussed earlier in this chapter. The *temporary* nature of possession, under a lease, is what distinguishes a tenant from a purchaser, who acquires title to the property. The *exclusivity* of possession distinguishes a tenant from a licensee, who acquires the temporary right to a *nonexclusive* use, such as sitting in a theater seat.

In the past century—and particularly in the past three decades—landlord-tenant relationships have become much more complex than they once were, as have the laws governing them. Generally, the law has come to apply contract doctrines, such as those providing for implied warranties and unconscionability, to the landlord-tenant relationship. Increasingly, landlord-tenant relationships have become subject to specific state and local statutes and ordinances as well. In 1972, in an effort to create more uniformity in the law governing landlord-tenant relationships, the National Conference of Commissioners on Uniform State Laws approved the Uniform Residential Landlord and Tenant Act (URLTA) for adoption by the states. Over one-fourth of the states have adopted variations of the URLTA.

CREATION OF THE LANDLORD-TENANT RELATIONSHIP

A landlord-tenant relationship is established by a lease contract, which may be oral or written. As is the case with most oral agreements, however, a party who seeks to enforce an oral lease may have difficulty proving its existence. In all states, statutes mandate that leases be in writing for some tenancies (such as those exceeding one year).

FORM OF THE LEASE   To create a landlord-tenant relationship, a contract must do the following:

1. Express an intent to establish the relationship.
2. Provide for transfer of the property's possession to the tenant at the beginning of the term.
3. Provide for the landlord's *reversionary* (future) interest, which entitles the property owner to retake possession at the end of the term.
4. Describe the property—for example, give its street address.
5. Indicate the length of the term, the amount of the rent, and how and when it is to be paid.

In drafting commercial leases, sound business practice dictates that the leases be written carefully and that the parties' rights and obligations be clearly defined in the lease agreements.

ILLEGALITY   State or local law often dictates permissible lease terms. The URLTA, for example, prohibits the inclusion in a lease agreement of a clause under which the tenant agrees to pay the landlord's attorneys' fees in a suit to enforce the lease. A statute or ordinance may prohibit leasing a structure that is in disrepair or is not in compliance with local building codes. Similarly, a statute may prohibit the leasing of property for a particular purpose, such as gambling.

A property owner cannot legally discriminate against prospective tenants on the basis of race, color, religion, national origin, or gender.[6] Similarly, a tenant cannot legally promise to do something counter to laws prohibiting discrimination. A commercial tenant, for example, cannot legally promise to do business only with members of a particular race.

PARTIES' RIGHTS AND DUTIES

The rights and duties of landlords and tenants generally pertain to four broad areas of concern—the possession, use, maintenance, and, of course, rent of leased property.

POSSESSION   A landlord is obligated to give a tenant possession of the property that the tenant has agreed to lease. Whether the landlord must provide actual physical possession (making sure that the previous tenant leaves) or the legal right to possession (so that the tenant would have to oust a previous tenant) depends on the particular state. After obtaining possession, the tenant retains the property exclusively until the lease expires, unless the lease states otherwise.

---

6. See, for example, *Osborn v. Kellogg*, 4 Neb.App. 594, 547 N.W.2d 504 (1996).

The covenant of quiet enjoyment mentioned previously also applies to leased premises. Under this covenant, the landlord promises that during the lease term, neither the landlord nor anyone having a superior title to the property will disturb the tenant's use and enjoyment of the property. This covenant forms the essence of the landlord-tenant relationship, and if it is breached, the tenant can terminate the lease and sue for damages.

If the landlord deprives the tenant of possession of the leased property or interferes with the tenant's use or enjoyment of it, an **eviction** occurs. An eviction occurs, for instance, when the landlord changes the lock and refuses to give the tenant a new key. A **constructive eviction** occurs when the landlord wrongfully performs or fails to perform any of the duties the lease requires, thereby making the tenant's further use and enjoyment of the property exceedingly difficult or impossible. Examples of constructive eviction include a landlord's failure to provide heat in the winter, light, or other essential utilities.

USE AND MAINTENANCE OF THE PREMISES If the parties do not limit by agreement the uses to which the property may be put, the tenant may make any use of it, as long as the use is legal and reasonably relates to the purpose for which the property is adapted or ordinarily used and does not injure the landlord's interest.

The tenant is responsible for any damages to the premises that he or she causes, intentionally or negligently, and the tenant may be held liable for the cost of returning the property to the physical condition it was in at the lease's inception. Also, the tenant is not entitled to create a *nuisance* by substantially interfering with others' quiet enjoyment of their property rights (the tort of nuisance was discussed in Chapter 45). The tenant is not usually responsible for ordinary wear and tear and the property's consequent depreciation in value. In some jurisdictions, landlords of residential property are required by statute to maintain the premises in good repair. Landlords must also comply with applicable state statutes and city ordinances regarding maintenance and repair of commercial buildings.

IMPLIED WARRANTY OF HABITABILITY The implied warranty of habitability requires a landlord who leases residential property to furnish premises that are in a habitable condition—that is, in a condition that is safe and suitable for people to live in. Also, the landlord must make repairs to maintain the premises in that condition for the lease's duration. Some state

legislatures have enacted this warranty into law. In other jurisdictions, courts have based the warranty on the existence of a landlord's statutory duty to keep leased premises in good repair, or they have simply applied it as a matter of public policy.

Generally, this warranty applies to major, or *substantial,* physical defects that the landlord knows or should know about and has had a reasonable time to repair—for example, a large hole in the roof. An unattractive or annoying feature, such as a crack in the wall, may be unpleasant, but unless the crack is a structural defect or affects the residence's heating capabilities, it is probably not sufficiently substantial to make the place uninhabitable.

RENT *Rent* is the tenant's payment to the landlord for the tenant's occupancy or use of the landlord's real property. Usually, the tenant must pay the rent even if she or he refuses to occupy the property or moves out, as long as the refusal or the move is unjustifiable and the lease is in force. Under the common law, if the leased premises were destroyed by fire or flood, the tenant still had to pay rent. Today, however, most state's statutes provide that if an apartment building burns down, tenants are not required to continue to pay rent.

In some situations, such as when a landlord breaches the implied warranty of habitability, a tenant may be allowed to withhold rent as a remedy. When rent withholding is authorized under a statute, the tenant must usually put the amount withheld into an *escrow account.* This account is held in the name of the depositor (the tenant) and an *escrow agent* (usually the court or a government agency), and the funds are returnable to the depositor if the third person (the landlord) fails to make the premises habitable. Generally, the tenant may withhold an amount equal to the amount by which the defect rendering the premises unlivable reduces the property's rental value. How much that is may be determined in different ways, and the tenant who withholds more than is legally permissible is liable to the landlord for the excessive amount withheld.

TRANSFERRING RIGHTS TO LEASED PROPERTY

Either the landlord or the tenant may wish to transfer her or his rights to the leased property during the term of the lease.

TRANSFERRING THE LANDLORD'S INTEREST Just as any other real property owner can sell, give away, or otherwise transfer his or her property, so can a landlord—who is, of course, the leased property's owner. If complete title to the leased property is transferred, the tenant becomes the tenant of the new owner. The new owner may collect subsequent rent but must abide by the terms of the existing lease agreement.

TRANSFERRING THE TENANT'S INTEREST The tenant's transfer of his or her entire interest in the leased property to a third person is an *assignment of the lease*. The tenant's transfer of all or part of the premises for a period shorter than the lease term is a *sublease*.

—*Assignment.* A lease assignment is an agreement to transfer all rights, title, and interest in the lease to the assignee. It is a complete transfer. Many leases require that the assignment have the landlord's written consent. An assignment that lacks consent can be avoided (nullified) by the landlord. State statutes may specify that the landlord may not unreasonably withhold such consent, though. Also, a landlord who knowingly accepts rent from the assignee may be held to have waived the consent requirement.

When an assignment is valid, the assignee acquires all of the tenant's rights under the lease. But an assignment does not release the assigning tenant from the obligation to pay rent should the assignee default. Also, if the assignee exercises an option under the original lease to extend the term, the assigning tenant remains liable for the rent during the extension, unless the landlord agrees otherwise.

—*Subleases.* As mentioned, the tenant's transfer of all or part of the premises for a period shorter than the lease term is a **sublease.** The same restrictions that apply to an assignment of the tenant's interest in leased property apply to a sublease. If the landlord's consent is required, a sublease without such permission is ineffective. Also, a sublease does not release the tenant from her or his obligations under the lease any more than an assignment does.

For example, Derek, a student, leases an apartment for a two-year period. Although Derek had planned on attending summer school, he is offered a job in Europe for the summer months and he accepts. Because he does not wish to pay three months' rent for an unoccupied apartment, Derek subleases the apartment to Adva, who becomes a sublessee. (Derek may have to obtain his landlord's consent for this sublease if the lease requires it.) Adva is bound by the same terms of the lease as Derek. As in a lease assign-

ment, the landlord can hold Derek liable if Adva violates the lease terms.

TERMINATION OF THE LEASE

Usually, a lease terminates when its term ends. The tenant surrenders the property to the landlord, who retakes possession. If the lease states the time it will end, the landlord is not required to give the tenant notice. The lease terminates automatically. In contrast, a *periodic tenancy* (a tenancy from month to month, for example) will renew automatically unless one of the parties gives timely notice (usually, one rental period) of termination. If the lease does not contain an option for renewal and the parties have not agreed that the tenant may stay on, the tenant has no right to remain. If the lease is renewable and the tenant decides to exercise the option, the tenant must comply with any conditions requiring notice to the landlord of the tenant's decision.

A lease may also be terminated in several other ways. For example, the landlord may agree that the tenant will purchase the leased property during the term or at its end, thus terminating the lease. The parties may agree to end a tenancy before it would otherwise terminate. The tenant may also *abandon* the premises—move out completely with no intention of returning before the lease term expires.

At common law and in many states, when a tenant abandons leased property, the tenant remains obligated to pay the rent for the remainder of the lease term—however long that might be. The landlord may refuse to lease the premises to an acceptable new tenant and let the property stand vacant. In a growing number of jurisdictions, however, the landlord is required to *mitigate* his or her damages—that is, the landlord is required to make a reasonable attempt to lease the property to another party. In these jurisdictions, the tenant's liability for unpaid rent is restricted to the period of time that the landlord would reasonably need to lease the property to another tenant. Damages may also be allowed for the landlord's costs in leasing the property again.[7] What is considered a reasonable period of time with respect to leasing the property to another party varies with the type of lease and the location of the leased premises.

Whether a landlord of commercial property has a duty to mitigate damages when a tenant abandons leased premises was at issue in the following case.

---

7. For a fuller discussion of mitigation of damages, see Chapter 17.

| CASE 48.3 | **Frenchtown Square Partnership v. Lemstone, Inc.** |

Ohio Supreme
Court, 2003.
99 Ohio St.3d 254,
791 N.E.2d 417.

O'CONNOR, J. [Justice]

* * * *

[Frenchtown Square Partnership, with offices in Youngstown, Ohio] owns Frenchtown Square Shopping Center, a mall located in Monroe, Michigan. Lemstone [Inc.] is an Illinois corporation doing business as a Christian bookstore. On June 3, 1989, Frenchtown leased store space in its mall to Lemstone for a period of ten years.

Frenchtown leased other mall space to Alpha Gifts, a business that, in 1998, began to sell items similar or identical to products sold by Lemstone. Lemstone argues that competition from Alpha Gifts reduced its profitability to the point where it could no longer meet its rent obligations under the lease. Approximately six months prior to lease expiration, Lemstone ceased conducting business at Frenchtown Square and abandoned its store space. For the balance of the lease's term, Lemstone did not pay rent to Frenchtown, and Frenchtown did not relet the property.

Frenchtown sued Lemstone [in an Ohio state court] for rent due * * * . [T]he trial court granted summary judgment in Frenchtown's favor on all issues.

* * * [A state intermediate appellate] court affirmed the trial court's judgment in part but held that Frenchtown, as a commercial lessor, had a duty to mitigate damages when Lemstone abandoned the leasehold. Accordingly, the appeals court remanded the case to the trial court to determine whether Frenchtown had properly mitigated its damages.

From [this] judgment, Frenchtown filed the instant appeal [to the Ohio Supreme Court].

* * *

* * * *

* * * Lessees are potentially liable for rents coming due under the [lease] agreement as long as the property remains unrented. The important corollary to that is *that landlords have a duty, as all parties to contracts do, to mitigate their damages caused by a breach. Landlords mitigate by attempting to rerent the property.* * * * [Emphasis added.]

* * * [T]he narrow issue before us is whether the duty to mitigate is applicable to commercial leases.

Frenchtown argues that failing to exempt commercial leases would create an incentive for tenants to abandon property, thereby encouraging vandalism and punishing the injured party. These are long-standing arguments against treating leases as contracts but do nothing to distinguish commercial leases from other types of leases. Further, there is merit to Lemstone's argument that a rule that permits landlords to "stand by and do nothing" while still reaping the benefit of its lease agreement would encourage vacant properties at least as much as a rule disfavoring mitigation. In fact, if Frenchtown did not take reasonable steps to relet its Frenchtown Square property following Lemstone's abandonment, then it contributed to the problem it asks us to prevent.

In an attempt to distinguish commercial leases from other types of leases, Frenchtown argues that the overall mix of shopping-center tenants is a material aspect of the bargained-for performance in a shopping-center lease. Essentially, by employing contract-law principles, Frenchtown argues that a proper mix of tenants creates a synergistic effect, and a rule that encourages abandonment will detrimentally affect not only the lessor, but also the other tenants. While we acknowledge that where two or more shops adjoin, a symbiotic relationship may exist, we decline to create a rule of law that distinguishes between single- and multi-shop commercial settings. *The duty to mitigate arises in all commercial leases of real property, just as it exists in all other contracts.* [Emphasis added.]

We emphasize that our holding does not require a lessor to accept just any available lessee. The duty to mitigate requires only reasonable efforts. Thus, the tenant mix may reasonably factor into a lessor's decisions to relet. Finally, whether the breaching tenant caused damages beyond the failure to pay rent is a measure of damages. Our holding that contract principles apply to the calculation of damages extends to all damages provable by the lessor. If the

CONTINUED ▶

CASE 48.3 | Continued

breaching tenant caused harm such that the lessor's profitability is affected, then that harm is compensable to the extent it is proved. * * *

* * * *

* * * [L]andlords owe a duty to mitigate their damages caused by a breaching tenant. That rule flows from the premise that modern leases are more than simply property-interest transfers; rather, *leases possess contractual qualities that often include myriad covenants and duties and arise from a bargained-for relationship. In a practical sense, lessors and lessees contract for the use of property. Accordingly, barring contrary contract provisions, a duty to mitigate damages applies to all leases.* [Emphasis added.]

We see no valid reason to exempt commercial leases from the duty to mitigate. A lessor has a duty to mitigate damages caused by a lessee's breach of a commercial lease if the lessee abandons the leasehold. * * *

Accordingly, we affirm the appeals court's decision and remand this case to the trial court * * * for a determination of damages.

QUESTIONS

1. Why, if a lease is viewed as a transfer of a property interest rather than a contract, could it be held that a landlord does not have a duty to mitigate damages?
2. Under the principles of contract law, what is the rationale for a duty to mitigate damages?

REVIEWING REAL PROPERTY AND LANDLORD-TENANT RELATIONSHIPS

Vern Shoepke purchased a two-story home on a one-acre lot in the town of Roche, Maine, from Walter and Eliza Bruster. The warranty deed that effected the transfer did not specify what covenants would be included in the conveyance. The property was adjacent to a public park that included a popular Frisbee golf course. (Frisbee golf is a sport similar to golf but using Frisbees.) Wayakichi Creek ran along the north end of the park and along Shoepke's property as part of a two-mile public trail system. The deed allowed Roche citizens the right to walk across a five-foot-wide section of the lot beside Wayakichi Creek. Two months after moving into his Roche home, Shoepke signed a lease agreement with Lauren Slater under which Slater agreed to rent the second floor for $645 per month for nine months. (The lease did not specify that Shoepke's consent would be required to sublease the second floor.) Teenagers regularly threw Frisbee golf discs from the walking path behind Shoepke's property over his yard to the adjacent park. Shoepke habitually shouted and cursed at the teenagers, demanding that they not throw objects over his yard. After three months of tenancy, Slater sublet the second floor to a local artist, Javier Indalecio. Over the remaining six months, Indalecio's use of oil paints damaged the carpeting in Shoepke's home. Using the information presented in the chapter, answer the following questions.

1. Would the throwing of Frisbees over Shoepke's land constitute trespass?

2. What is the term for the right of Roche citizens to walk across Shoepke's land on the trail? Is this right classified as appurtenant or in gross?

3. In the warranty deed effecting the transfer of the property from the Brusters to Shoepke, what covenants would be inferred by most courts?

4. Was Slater's nine-month lease a tenancy for years, a periodic tenancy, a tenancy at will, or a tenancy at sufferance?

5. Was Shoepke's consent required for Slater to sublease the second floor even though the lease did not specify this?

6. Would Slater have been responsible for payment to Shoepke for the carpeting damaged by Indalecio?

TERMS AND CONCEPTS TO REVIEW

adverse possession 971

condemnation 973

constructive eviction 977

conveyance 964

deed 968

easement 965

eminent domain 973

escrow account 970

eviction 977

fee simple absolute 964

grant deed 969

implied warranty of
   habitability 970

lease 976

leasehold estate 965

lessee 976

lessor 976

license 967

life estate 964

mortgage 970

periodic tenancy 965

profit 965

quitclaim deed 969

recording statute 969

restrictive covenant 973

sheriff's deed 969

special warranty deed 969

sublease 978

taking 973

tenancy at sufferance 965

tenancy at will 965

tenancy for years 965

warranty deed 968

waste 964

QUESTIONS AND CASE PROBLEMS

48–1. Madison owned a tract of land, but he was not sure that he had full title to the property. When Rafael expressed an interest in buying the land, Madison sold it to Rafael and executed a quitclaim deed. Rafael properly recorded the deed immediately. Several months later, Madison learned that he had had full title to the tract of land. He then sold the land to Linda by warranty deed. Linda knew of the earlier purchase by Rafael but took the deed anyway and later sued to have Rafael evicted from the land. Linda claimed that because she had a warranty deed, her title to the land was better than that conferred by Rafael's quitclaim deed. Will Linda succeed in claiming title to the land? Explain.

48–2. James owns a three-story building. He leases the ground floor to Juan's Mexican restaurant. The lease is to run for a five-year period and contains an express covenant of quiet enjoyment. One year later, James leases the top two stories to the Upbeat Club, a discotheque. The club's hours run from 5:00 P.M. to 11:00 P.M. The noise from the Upbeat Club is so loud that it is driving customers away from Juan's restaurant. Juan has notified James of the interference and has called the police on a number of occasions. James refuses to talk to the owners of the Upbeat Club or to do anything to remedy the situation. Juan abandons the premises. James files suit for breach of the lease agreement and for the rental payments still due under the lease. Juan claims that he was constructively evicted and files a countersuit for damages. Discuss who will be held liable.

48–3. **QUESTION WITH SAMPLE ANSWER**
Wilfredo and Patricia are neighbors. Wilfredo's lot is extremely large, and his present and future use of it will not involve the entire area. Patricia wants to build a single-car garage and driveway along the present lot boundary. Because ordinances require buildings to be set back fifteen feet from an owner's property line, however, the placement of Patricia's existing structures prevents her from building the garage. Patricia contracts to purchase ten feet of Wilfredo's property along their boundary line for $3,000. Wilfredo is willing to sell but will give Patricia only a quitclaim deed, whereas Patricia wants a warranty deed. Discuss the differences between these deeds as they would affect the rights of the parties if the title to this ten feet of land later proves to be defective.
For a sample answer to this question, go to Appendix I at the end of this text.

48–4. Sarah has rented a house from Frank. The house is only two years old, but the roof leaks every time it rains. The water that has accumulated in the attic has caused plaster to fall off ceilings in the upstairs bedrooms, and one ceiling has started to sag. Sarah has complained to Frank and asked him to have the roof repaired. Frank says that he has caulked the roof, but the roof still leaks. Frank claims that because Sarah has sole control of the leased premises, she has the duty to repair the roof. Sarah insists that the repair of the roof is Frank's responsibility. Discuss fully who is responsible for repairing the roof and, if the responsibility belongs to Frank, what remedies are available to Sarah.

48–5. Glenn is the owner of a lakeside house and lot. He deeds the house and lot "to my wife, Livia, for life, then to my daughter, Sarina." Given this information, answer these questions: What is Livia's interest called? Is there any limitation on her rights to use the property as she wishes? Discuss.

48–6. WARRANTY OF HABITABILITY. Three-year-old Nkenge Lynch fell from the window of her third-floor apartment and suffered serious and permanent injuries. There were no window stops or guards on the window. The use of window stops, even if installed, is at the tenant's option. Stanley James owned the apartment building. Zsa Zsa Kinsey, Nkenge's mother, filed a suit on Nkenge's behalf in a Massachusetts state court against James, alleging in part a breach of an implied warranty of habitability. The plaintiff did not argue that the absence of stops or guards made the apartment unfit for human habitation but that their absence "endangered and materially impaired her health and safety," and therefore the failure to install them was a breach of warranty. Should the court rule that the absence of window stops breached a warranty of habitability? Should the court mandate that landlords provide window guards? Why or why not? [*Lynch v. James*, 44 Mass.App.Ct. 448, 692 N.E.2d 81 (1998)]

48–7. ⚖ **CASE PROBLEM WITH SAMPLE ANSWER**
The Wallens family owned a cabin on Lummi Island in the state of Washington. A driveway ran from the cabin across their property to South Nugent Road. In 1952, Floyd Massey bought the adjacent lot and built a cabin. To gain access to his property, he used a bulldozer to extend the driveway, without the Wallenses' permission but also without their objection. In 1975, the Wallenses sold their property to Wright Fish Co. Massey continued to use and maintain the driveway without permission or objection. In 1984, Massey sold his property to Robert Drake. Drake and his employees continued to use and maintain the driveway without permission or objection, although Drake knew it was located largely on Wright's property. In 1997, Wright sold its lot to Robert Smersh. The next year, Smersh told Drake to stop using the driveway. Drake filed a suit in a Washington state court against Smersh, claiming an easement by prescription (which is created by meeting the same requirements as adverse possession). Does Drake's use of the driveway meet all of the requirements? What should the court rule? Explain. [*Drake v. Smersh*, 122 Wash.App. 147, 89 P.3d 726 (Div. 1 2004)]

To view a sample answer for this case problem, go to this book's Web site at http://wbl.westbuslaw.com, select "Chapter 48," and click on "Case Problem with Sample Answer."

48–8. REAL ESTATE SALES. In 1999, Stephen and Linda Kailin bought from Perry Armstrong the Monona Center, a mall in Madison, Wisconsin, for $760,000. The contract provided, "Seller represents to Buyer that as of the date of acceptance Seller had no notice or knowledge of conditions affecting the Property or transaction" other than certain items disclosed at the time of the offer. Armstrong told the Kailins of the Center's eight tenants, their lease expiration dates, and the monthly and annual rent due under each lease. One of the lessees, Ring's All-American Karate, occupied about a third of the Center's space under a five-year lease. Because of Ring's financial difficulties, Armstrong had agreed to reduce its rent for nine months in 1997, and by the time of the sale to the Kailins, Ring owed $13,910 in unpaid rent, but Armstrong did not disclose this to the Kailins, who did not ask. Ring continued to fail to pay rent and finally vacated the Center. The Kailins filed a suit in a Wisconsin state court against Armstrong and others, alleging, among other things, misrepresentation. Did Armstrong have a duty to disclose Ring's delinquency and default? Explain. [*Kailin v. Armstrong*, 252 Wis.2d 676, 643 N.W.2d 132 (2002)]

48–9. COMMERCIAL LEASE TERMS. Metropolitan Life Insurance Co. leased space in its Trail Plaza Shopping Center in Florida to Winn-Dixie Stores, Inc., to operate a supermarket. Under the lease, the landlord agreed not to permit "any [other] property located within the shopping center to be used for or occupied by any business dealing in or which shall keep in stock or sell for off-premises consumption any staple or fancy groceries" in more than "500 square feet of sales area." In 1999, Metropolitan leased 22,000 square feet of space in Trail Plaza to 99 Cent Stuff-Trail Plaza, LLC, under a lease that prohibited it from selling "groceries" in more than 500 square feet of "sales area." Shortly after 99 Cent Stuff opened, it began selling food and other products, including soap, matches, and paper napkins. Alleging that these sales violated the parties' leases, Winn-Dixie filed a suit in a Florida state court against 99 Cent Stuff and others. The defendants argued in part that the groceries provision covered only food and the 500-square-foot restriction included only shelf space, not store aisles. How should these lease terms be interpreted? Should the court grant an injunction in Winn-Dixie's favor? Explain. [*Winn-Dixie Stores, Inc. v. 99 Cent Stuff-Trail Plaza, LLC*, 811 So.2d 719 (Fla.App. 3 Dist. 2002)]

48–10. ⚖ **A QUESTION OF ETHICS**
John and Terry Hoffius own property in Jackson, Michigan, which they offered to rent. Kristal McCready and Keith Kerr responded to the Hoffiuses' ad about the property. The Hoffiuses refused to rent to McCready and Kerr, however, when they learned that the two were single and intended to live together. John Hoffius told all prospective tenants that unmarried cohabitation violated his religious beliefs. McCready and others filed a suit in a Michigan state court against the Hoffiuses. They alleged in part that the Hoffiuses' actions violated the plaintiffs' civil rights under a state law that prohibits

discrimination on the basis of "marital status." The Hoffiuses responded in part that forcing them to rent to unmarried couples in violation of the Hoffiuses' religious beliefs would be unconstitutional. [*McCready v. Hoffius*, 586 N.W.2d 723 (Mich. 1998)]

(a) Was it the plaintiffs' "marital status" or their conduct to which the defendants objected? Did the defendants violate the plaintiffs' civil rights? Explain.

(b) Should a court, in the interest of preventing discrimination in housing, compel a landlord to violate his or her conscience? In other words, whose rights should prevail in this case? Why?

(c) Is there an objective rule that determines when civil rights or religious freedom, or any two similarly important principles, should prevail? If so, what is it? If not, should there be?

LAW | on the Web

For updated links to resources available on the Web, as well as a variety of other materials, visit this text's Web site at http://wbl.westbuslaw.com.

For links to numerous sources relating to real property, go to

http://www.findlaw.com/01topics/index.html

and click on "Property Law & Real Estate."

For information on condemnation procedures and rules under one state's (California) law, go to

http://www.eminentdomainlaw.net/propertyguide.html

LEGAL RESEARCH EXERCISES ON THE WEB

Go to http://wbl.westbuslaw.com, the Web site that accompanies this text. Select "Chapter 48" and click on "Internet Exercises." There you will find the following Internet research exercises that you can perform to learn more about topics covered in this chapter.

Activity 48–1: **LEGAL PERSPECTIVE**
Eminent Domain

Activity 48–2: **MANAGEMENT PERSPECTIVE**
Fair Housing

Activity 48–3: **SOCIAL PERSPECTIVE**
The Rights of Tenants

Property

Property rights have long been given extensive legal protection under both English and U.S. law. In the United States, the right to own property is closely associated with liberty, the pursuit of happiness, and other concepts that have played an integral role in American life. At the same time, conflicts often arise over who owns what and over how property should be used. In this *Focus on Ethics* feature, we explore some of the ethical dimensions of property laws and disputes over property ownership rights.

Are Domain Names Property?

Technology often leads to new legal questions, many of which have ethical ramifications as well. One such question arose in a case involving an attempted garnishment of a debtor's assets. Recall from Chapter 28 that garnishment occurs when a creditor is permitted, by court order, to collect a debt by seizing property of the debtor that is being held by a third party. Typically, garnishment involves obtaining from the debtor's employer a portion of the debtor's wages or obtaining from the debtor's bank the funds in the debtor's bank account.

Are Domain Names Subject to Garnishment? The question before the court in *Network Solutions, Inc. v. Umbro International, Inc.,*[1] was whether domain names were "property" subject to garnishment. A federal district court had awarded Umbro International, Inc., nearly $24,000 in a lawsuit over rights to the domain name umbro.com. Because the defendants in the suit had no assets in the United States to satisfy the judgment, Umbro instituted a garnishment proceeding against Network Solutions, Inc. (NSI), with which the defendants had registered more than twenty other domain names. Clearly, domain names have value, and they are commonly purchased and sold in today's marketplace. Thus, Umbro sought to force a judicial sale of those names to help recover some of the debt.

Domain Names Cannot Be Separated from Domain Name Services NSI objected to the garnishment, arguing that domain names cannot function on the Internet in the absence of the services provided by a domain name registrar such as NSI. The court agreed with NSI, holding that the right to use a domain name was inextricably bound to the domain name services that NSI provided—and NSI's services were not subject to garnishment. The court stated that even though the Internet is a "new avenue of commerce," it could not "extend established legal principles beyond their statutory parameters."

1. 259 Va. 759, 529 S.E.2d 80 (2000).

Finders' Rights

The children's adage "finders keepers, losers weepers" is actually written into law—provided that the loser (the rightful owner) cannot be found, that is. A finder may acquire good title to found personal property against everyone *except the true owner*. A number of landmark cases have made this principle clear.

The *Armory* Case An early English case, *Armory v. Delamirie,*[2] is a landmark in Anglo-American jurisprudence concerning actions in *trover*—an early form of recovery of damages for the conversion of property. The plaintiff in this case was Armory, a chimney sweep who found a jewel in its setting during the course of his work. He took the jewel to a goldsmith to have it appraised. The goldsmith refused to return the jewel to Armory, claiming that Armory was not the rightful owner of the property. The court held that the finder, as prior possessor of the item, had rights to the jewel superior to those of all others except the rightful owner. The court said, "The finder of a jewel, though he does not by such finding acquire an absolute property or ownership, yet . . . has such a property as will enable him to keep it against all but the rightful owner, and consequently maintain trover."

The *Armory* case illustrates the doctrine of the *relativity of title*. Under this doctrine, if two contestants, neither of whom can claim absolute title to the property, are before the court, the one who can claim prior possession will likely have established sufficient rights to the property to win the case.

The Treasure Trove Doctrine Recall also from Chapter 47 that a *treasure trove* is found property that consists of money or precious metals (gold and silver, for example). A finder of goods that are classified as a treasure trove can claim good title to the property against all but the true owner. This rule normally holds even if the finder is a trespasser on the property where the treasure trove is discovered.

Some courts have refused to apply the treasure trove doctrine, in part because they consider it unfair. For example, in one case an Idaho court ruled that a construction worker who found four pounds of gold coins while digging a driveway could not keep the coins. Rather, said the court, they belonged to the person who owned the land on which they were found. The court commented that although the treasure trove doctrine "may make good theater, it's not good law." Among other reasons, the court objected to the doctrine because it gave priority to the discoverers of precious metals even if they were trespassers.[3]

2. 93 Eng.Rep. 664 (K.B. [King's Bench] 1722).
3. *Corliss v. Wenner*, 136 Idaho 417, 34 P.3d 1100 (2001).

Bailee's Duty of Care

The standard of care expected of a bailee clearly illustrates how property law reflects ethical principles. For example, suppose that a friend asks to borrow your business law text for the weekend. You agree to loan your friend the book. In this situation, which is a bailment for the sole benefit of the bailee (your friend), most people would agree that your friend has an ethical obligation to take great care of your book. After all, if your friend lost your book, you would incur damages. You would have to purchase another one, and if you could not, you might find it difficult to do well on your homework assignments, examinations, and so on.

The situation would be different if you had loaned your book to your friend totally for your own benefit. For example, suppose that you are leaving town during the summer, and a friend offers to store several boxes of books for you until you return in the fall. In this situation, a bailment for the sole benefit of the bailor (you) exists. If your books are destroyed through the bailee's (your friend's) negligence and you sue the bailee for damages, a court will likely take into consideration the fact that the bailee was essentially doing you a favor by storing the books. Although bailees generally have a duty to exercise reasonable care over bailed property, what constitutes reasonable care in a specific situation normally depends on the surrounding circumstances, including the reason for the bailment and who stood to benefit from the arrangement.

Bailee's Liability

The law of bailments also clearly expresses ethical principles in its rules governing the liability of bailees. On the one hand, the law permits bailees to limit their liability for bailed goods by monetary amount or type of risk, as explained in Chapter 47. On the other hand, the law does not permit bailees to exclude liability for harm caused by their own negligence. Exculpatory clauses in bailment contracts that attempt to relieve the bailee of liability for negligence will normally be closely scrutinized by the courts, particularly if the contract is between a member of the public and a bailee providing quasi-public services, such as a warehouser. Normally, courts will hold exculpatory clauses in such contracts to be contrary to public policy and refuse to enforce them.

Consider an example. Lisa Gonzalez leased short-term storage space from a warehouser and placed an assortment of electronic equipment, furniture, family memorabilia, and other items in the space. Seven weeks later, when she returned to retrieve her property, she discovered that the space had been inundated with water and that her stored possessions had been either destroyed or damaged. When she sued the warehouser for negligence, the warehouser pointed to the exculpatory clause in the bailment (rental) contract. The lengthy clause stated, among other things, that the owner (warehouser) "shall not be liable to Occupant for any loss or damage that may be occasioned by or through Owner's acts, omissions to act, or negligence." The court, stating that the exculpatory clause was "outrageous," deemed it unconscionable and thus void and unenforceable.[4]

Fair Housing versus Religious Freedom

Numerous restraints are imposed on landlords by federal and state antidiscrimination laws, but sometimes these laws conflict with other constitutional rights, such as freedom of religion. For example, suppose that a landlord feels that it would violate his religious principles to rent an apartment to an unmarried couple. Should the law, in the interest of preventing discrimination in housing, compel the landlord to violate his conscience?

This issue brings into conflict two fundamental ethical principles—one promoting freedom from discrimination and the other promoting freedom of religion. It is simply not possible to develop an objective rule to determine which principle should prevail in all cases, and the courts have reached different conclusions.

In one case, for example, the Minnesota Supreme Court held that a landlord had a right to refuse, for religious reasons, to rent a house to a woman who planned to share the house with her fiancé. The court concluded that the landlord's right to exercise his religion outweighed the tenant's interest in cohabiting on the property with her fiancé prior to their marriage.[5] In a case with similar facts, however, the California Supreme Court held that a landlord's refusal to rent commercial property to an unmarried couple for religious reasons violated a state statute that prohibited discrimination based on "marital status." The court stated that enforcing the law would not "substantially burden" the landlord's freedom of religion under either the U.S. Constitution or the California state constitution.[6]

Land-Use Regulations and the "Takings Clause"

Regulations to control land use, including environmental regulations, are prevalent throughout the United States. Generally, these laws reflect the public's interest in preserving natural resources and habitats for wildlife. At times, their goal is to enable the public to have access to and enjoy limited natural resources, such as coastal areas. Although few would disagree with the rationale underlying these laws, the owners of the private property directly affected by the laws often feel that they should be compensated for the limitations imposed on their right to do as they wish with their land.

Remember from Chapter 48 that the Fifth Amendment to the U.S. Constitution gives the government the power to

---

4. *Gonzalez v. A-1 Self Storage, Inc.,* 350 N.J.Super. 403, 795 A.2d 885 (2000).
5. *State by Cooper v. French,* 460 N.W.2d 2 (Minn. 1990).
6. *Smith v. Fair Employment and Housing Commission,* 12 Cal.4th 1143, 913 P.2d 909, 51 Cal.Rptr.2d 700 (1996).

"take" private property for public use. The Fifth Amendment attaches an important condition to this power, however: when private land is taken for public use, the landowner must be given "just compensation."

No General Rule In cases alleging that a "regulatory taking" has occurred, the courts have largely decided the issue on a case-by-case basis. In other words, there is no general rule that one can cite to indicate whether a specific situation will be deemed a taking. In one case, the city of Monterey, California, in the interests of protecting various forms of coastal wildlife, would not allow an owner of oceanfront property to build a residential development. In effect, the city's actions meant that the entire property had to be left in its natural state, thus making the owner's planned use of the land impossible. When the landowner challenged the city's action as an unconstitutional taking without compensation, the United States Supreme Court ultimately agreed, and the landowner had to be compensated.[7]

In another case, however, the Supreme Court held for the regulators. In an attempt to curb pollution in Lake Tahoe, located on the California-Nevada border, a regional government planning agency issued a moratorium on (a temporary suspension of) the construction of housing in certain areas around the lake. The moratorium was extended time and again until, some twenty years later, a number of landowners sued the agency. The landowners claimed that a regulatory taking had occurred for which they should be compensated. The Supreme Court disagreed. Because the agency's actions had not deprived the owners of their property for too long a time, no taking had occurred. How long was too long? The Court said that no categorical rule could be stated; the answer always depended on "the facts presented."[8]

A Question of Fairness The question of whether private landowners should be compensated when their land is essentially "taken" for public use by environmental and land-use regulations clearly involves issues of fairness. On the one hand, states, cities, and other local governments want to preserve their natural resources and need some authority

to regulate land use to achieve this goal. On the other hand, private property owners complain that they alone should not have to bear the costs of creating a benefit, such as environmental preservation, given that all members of the public enjoy that benefit.

Discrimination in Housing

The Fair Housing Act also presents issues of fairness. The act prohibits mortgage lenders from refusing to lend funds for the purchase of homes in certain areas. Prohibiting this practice, known as *redlining*, severely restricts lenders' ability to choose freely where (or where not) to invest their money. Should lenders be coerced by law into lending funds toward the purchase of homes that are located in neighborhoods where criminal activity is on the rise and property values are rapidly declining? The lender is in business to make a profit on its loan; it is not a charitable organization. The public policy expressed in the Fair Housing Act protects disadvantaged borrowers, in this context, by making more housing available to them. Lenders, however, are forced to extend credit in areas that may increase their risk of loss.

DISCUSSION QUESTIONS

1. Do you believe that the law strikes a fair balance between the rights of parties with respect to found property? Do you believe that the treasure trove doctrine is unethical in any way because it allows trespassers to hold good title to treasure troves that they discover?

2. Why do different standards of care apply to bailed goods? Do these standards reflect underlying ethical values? If so, how? Should bailees be able to contract away liability for their own negligence with respect to bailed goods? Why or why not?

3. In your opinion, has the government gone too far in protecting tenants' rights? Or should tenants have even greater protection? When tenants' rights, such as the right to be free of discrimination, conflict with a landlord's constitutionally protected rights, such as the free exercise of religion, which rights should prevail?

4. Do you believe that the law strikes a fair balance between the rights of landowners and the right of governments to control land use in the public interest? Why or why not?

---

7. *City of Monterey v. Del Monte Dunes at Monterey, Ltd.,* 526 U.S. 687, 119 S.Ct. 1624, 143 L.Ed.2d 882 (1999). For a more recent case in which a court held that a taking had occurred, see *Vulcan Materials Co. v. The City of Tehuacana,* 369 F.3d 882 (5th Cir. 2004).

8. *Tahoe-Sierra Preservation Council v. Tahoe Regional Planning Agency,* 535 U.S. 302, 122 S.Ct. 1465, 152 L.Ed.2d 517 (2002).

UNIT ELEVEN
Special Topics

CHAPTER 49

Insurance

Many precautions can be taken to protect against the hazards of life. For example, an individual can wear a seat belt to protect against automobile-accident injuries or install smoke detectors to guard against the risk of harm from fires. Of course, no one can predict whether an accident or a fire will ever occur, but individuals and businesses must establish plans to protect their personal and financial interests should some event threaten to undermine their security.

Insurance is a contract by which the insurance company (the insurer) promises to pay a sum of money or give something of value to another (either the insured or the beneficiary) to compensate the other for a particular, stated loss. Insurance protection may provide for compensation for the injury or death of the insured or another, for damage to the insured's property, or for other types of losses, such as those resulting from lawsuits. Basically, insurance is an arrangement for *transferring and allocating risk*. In general, **risk** can be described as a prediction concerning potential loss based on known and unknown factors. Insurance, however, involves much more than a game of chance.

Risk management normally involves the transfer of certain risks from the individual to the insurance company by a contractual agreement. We examine the insurance contract and its provisions in this chapter. First, however, we look at some basic insurance terminology and concepts.

SECTION 1 | Insurance Terminology and Concepts

Like other legal areas, insurance has its own special concepts and terminology, a knowledge of which is essential to an understanding of insurance law.

trast, an insurance agent is an agent of the insurance company, not an agent of the applicant. As a general rule, the insurance company is bound by the acts of its agents when they act within the scope of the agency relationship (see Chapters 31 and 32). In most situations, state law determines the status of all parties writing or obtaining insurance.

INSURANCE TERMINOLOGY

An insurance contract is called a **policy;** the consideration paid to the insurer is called a **premium;** and the insurance company is sometimes called an **underwriter.** The parties to an insurance policy are the *insurer* (the insurance company) and the *insured* (the person covered by its provisions).

Insurance contracts are usually obtained through an *agent,* who normally works for the insurance company, or through a *broker,* who is ordinarily an independent contractor. When a broker deals with an applicant for insurance, the broker is, in effect, the applicant's agent (and not an agent of the insurance company). In con-

CLASSIFICATIONS OF INSURANCE

Insurance is classified according to the nature of the risk involved. For example, fire insurance, casualty insurance, life insurance, and title insurance apply to different types of risk. Furthermore, policies of these types protect different persons and interests. This is reasonable because the types of losses that are expected and the types that are foreseeable or unforeseeable vary with the nature of the activity. Exhibit 49–1 provides a list of various insurance classifications. (For a discussion of how insurance coverage may be obtained for the loss of computerized information, see this chapter's *Emerging Trends* feature beginning on page 990.)

EXHIBIT 49-1 **Insurance Classifications**

TYPE OF INSURANCE	COVERAGE
Accident	Covers expenses, losses, and suffering incurred by the insured because of accidents causing physical injury and any consequent disability; sometimes includes a specified payment to heirs of the insured if death results from an accident.
All-risk	Covers all losses that the insured may incur except those resulting from fraud on the part of the insured.
Automobile	May cover damage to automobiles resulting from specified hazards or occurrences (such as fire, vandalism, theft, or collision); normally provides protection against liability for personal injuries and property damage resulting from the operation of the vehicle.
Casualty	Protects against losses incurred by the insured as a result of being held liable for personal injuries or property damage sustained by others.
Credit	Pays to a creditor the balance of a debt on the disability, death, insolvency, or bankruptcy of the debtor; often offered by lending institutions.
Decreasing-term life	Provides life insurance; requires uniform payments over the life (term) of the policy, but with a decreasing face value (amount of coverage).
Employer's liability	Insures employers against liability for injuries or losses sustained by employees during the course of their employment; covers claims not covered under workers' compensation insurance.
Fidelity or guaranty	Provides indemnity against losses in trade or losses caused by the dishonesty of employees, the insolvency of debtors, or breaches of contract.
Fire	Covers losses to the insured caused by fire.
Floater	Covers movable property, as long as the property is within the territorial boundaries specified in the contract.
Group	Provides individual life, medical, or disability insurance coverage but is obtainable through a group of persons, usually employees; the policy premium is paid either entirely by the employer or partially by the employer and partially by the employee.
Health	Covers expenses incurred by the insured resulting from physical injury or illness and other expenses relating to health and life maintenance.
Homeowners'	Protects homeowners against some or all risks of loss to their residences and the residences' contents or liability arising from the use of the property.
Key-person	Protects a business in the event of the death or disability of a key employee.
Liability	Protects against liability imposed on the insured resulting from injuries to the person or property of another.
Life	Covers the death of the policyholder. On the death of the insured, an amount specified in the policy is paid by the insurer to the insured's beneficiary.
Major medical	Protects the insured against major hospital, medical, or surgical expenses.
Malpractice	Protects professionals (doctors, lawyers, and others) against malpractice claims brought against them by their patients or clients; a form of liability insurance.
Marine	Covers movable property (including ships, freight, and cargo) against certain perils or navigation risks during a specific voyage or time period.
Mortgage	Covers a mortgage loan; the insurer pays the balance of the mortgage to the creditor on the death or disability of the debtor.
No-fault auto	Covers personal injuries and (sometimes) property damage resulting from automobile accidents. The insured submits his or her claims to his or her own insurance company, regardless of who was at fault. A person may sue the party at fault or that party's insurer only in cases involving serious medical injury and consequent high medical costs. Governed by state "no-fault" statutes.
Term life	Provides life insurance for a specified period of time (term) with no cash surrender value; usually renewable.
Title	Protects against any defects in title to real property and any losses incurred as a result of existing claims against or liens on the property at the time of purchase.

Risk Management in Cyberspace

Over the past decade, hackers have spread numerous viruses that cause computer systems to fail. In today's economy, when a business's computer system fails, the damage is often extensive. Customer service may come to a standstill, and data may be lost. If so, it may take hours or even days to put the data back into the computer and get the system up and running again. Computer systems may fail for other reasons as well.

Traditional business insurance policies, however, usually do not specifically cover the losses resulting from computer "downtime" or other risks associated with doing business online. Typically, business insurance covers only "physical loss," and a number of courts have held that computer information is not physical.[a] Only in rare circumstances have courts held that general business insurance policies cover the loss of computerized information.[b]

INSURANCE COVERAGE FOR WEB-RELATED RISKS

Not surprisingly, a growing number of companies are now offering policies designed to cover Web-related risks. Consider

---

a. See, for example, *America Online, Inc. v. St. Paul Mercury Insurance Co.*, 207 F.Supp.2d 459 (E.D.Va. 2002).
b. *Lambrecht & Associates, Inc. v. State Farm Lloyd's*, 119 S.W.3d 16 (Tex.App. 2003).

the types of coverage offered by Net Secure, a venture undertaken by IBM, several insurance companies, and a New York broker. Net Secure provides insurance protection against losses resulting from programming errors; network and Web site disruptions; the theft of electronic data and assets, including intellectual property; Web-related defamation, copyright infringement, and false advertising; and the violation of users' privacy rights.

InsureTrust.com, an insurer affiliated with three leading insurance companies—American International Group, Lloyd's of London, and Reliance National—offers similar coverage. Existing insurers, such as Lloyd's of London, Hartford Insurance, and the Chubb Group of Insurance Companies, are also adding insurance for Web-related perils to their offerings. Clearly, the market for these new types of insurance coverage is rapidly evolving, and new policies will continue to appear.

CUSTOMIZED POLICIES

Unlike traditional insurance policies, which are generally drafted by insurance companies and presented to insurance applicants on a take-it-or-leave-it basis, Internet-specific policies are usually customized to provide protection against risks faced by a particular type of business. For example,

---

INSURABLE INTEREST

A person can insure anything in which she or he has an **insurable interest.** Without this insurable interest, there is no enforceable contract, and a transaction to purchase insurance coverage would have to be treated as a wager. The existence of an insurable interest is a primary concern in determining liability under an insurance policy.

LIFE INSURANCE In regard to life insurance, one must have a reasonable expectation of benefit from the continued life of another to have an insurable interest in that person's life. The insurable interest must exist *at the time the policy is obtained.* The benefit may be pecuniary (related to money), or it may be founded on the relationship between the parties (by

blood or affinity). Close family relationships give a person an insurable interest in the life of another. Generally, blood or marital relationships fit this category. A husband can take out an insurance policy on his wife and vice versa; parents can take out life insurance policies on their children; brothers and sisters, on each other; and grandparents, on grandchildren—as all these are close family relationships. A policy that a person takes out on his or her spouse remains valid even if they divorce, unless a specific provision in the policy calls for its termination on divorce.

KEY-PERSON LIFE INSURANCE *Key-person insurance* is insurance obtained by an organization on the life of a person who is important to that organization. Because the organization expects to receive some

an Internet service provider will face different risks than an online merchant, and a banking institution will face different risks than a law firm. The specific business-related risks are taken into consideration when determining the policy premium.

pecuniary gain from the continuation of the key person's life or some financial loss from the key person's death, the organization has an insurable interest. Typically, a partnership will insure the life of each partner, because the death of any one partner will cause some degree of loss to the partnership. Similarly, a corporation has an insurable interest in the life expectancy of a key executive whose death would result in financial loss to the company. If a firm insures a key person's life and then that person leaves the firm and subsequently dies, the firm can collect on the insurance policy, provided it continued to pay the premiums.

PROPERTY INSURANCE   In regard to real and personal property, an insurable interest exists when the insured derives a pecuniary benefit from the preserva-

tion and continued existence of the property. In other words, one has an insurable interest in property when one would sustain a pecuniary loss from its destruction. Both a mortgagor and a mortgagee, for example, have an insurable interest in the mortgaged property. So do a landlord and a tenant in leased property, a secured party in the property in which he or she has a security interest, a partner in partnership property, and a stockholder in corporate property. John or Jane Doe, however, cannot obtain fire insurance on the White House.

The existence of an insurable interest is a primary concern in determining liability under an insurance policy. The insurable interest in property must exist when the loss occurs. Whether a party had an insurable interest in property was at issue in the following case.

CASE 49.1

United States
Court of Appeals,
Second Circuit, 2005.
397 F.3d 158.

Zurich American Insurance Co. v. ABM Industries, Inc.

CARDAMONE, Circuit Judge:

The terrorist attack on the World Trade Center complex in lower Manhattan on September 11, 2001 brought about a harvest of bitter distress and loss. Of the complex, one stone was not left on another, it was all thrown down, bringing about, in addition to human casualties, the loss and destruction of businesses. It is the loss of one business that is the focus of this appeal.

* * * *

ABM [Industries, Inc.] provided extensive janitorial, lighting, and engineering services at the World Trade Center. It operated the heating, ventilating, and air-conditioning (HVAC) systems for the entire WTC, essentially running the physical plant. ABM serviced the common areas of the complex pursuant to contracts with the owners Silverstein Properties and the Port Authority of New York and New Jersey.

Under these contracts ABM had office and storage space in the complex and had access to janitorial closets and * * * sinks located on every floor of the WTC buildings. ABM also had effective control over the freight elevators. At the time of the attacks, it employed more than 800 people at the WTC, and its exclusive and significant presence at the complex allowed it to secure service contracts with nearly all of the WTC's tenants. * * *

In order to handle these enormous responsibilities at the WTC, ABM created and manned a call center to which tenants reported problems. ABM's engineering department took complaints at the call center and dispatched its employees to remedy problems as they arose. Additionally, ABM developed complex preventative maintenance schedules through state-of-the-art software that tracked the equipment in the WTC. These procedures allowed ABM to repair equipment before it malfunctioned.

* * * *

ABM procured insurance coverage from Zurich [American Insurance Company] * * * . [T]he policy covers loss or damage to "real and personal property, including but not limited to property owned, controlled, used, leased, or intended for use by the Insured" (Insurable Interest provision). * * * [The policy includes business interruption (BI) coverage. Zurich filed a suit in a federal district court * * * against ABM to determine the extent of Zurich's liability for ABM's claims under the policy.]

* * * *

ABM's claims * * * arise out of the complete destruction of the WTC by the terrorist attacks of September 11, 2001. ABM declares it has lost, as a result of these events, all income that it derived from its operations at the WTC. * * *

* * * *

On May 28, 2003 the district court granted Zurich's motion for partial summary judgment * * * . The district court held that ABM could obtain BI coverage only for the income it lost resulting from "the destruction of the World Trade Center space that ABM itself occupied or caused by the destruction of ABM's own supplies and equipment located in the World Trade Center." The court reasoned that the policy restricts BI coverage to "insured property at an insured location," and that the common areas and the tenants' premises in the WTC did not constitute insured property as that term is defined in the policy. Specifically, the court held that ABM neither "used" nor "controlled" these areas in a manner that sufficed for the creation of a "legally cognizable [recognizable] interest in the property." * * *

* * * *

* * * This appeal followed.

* * * We believe that ABM's activities at the World Trade Center created an insurable interest cognizable under New York law, and that this insurable interest falls within the scope of the policy's coverage. * * *

* * * *

* * * In light of ABM's substantial influence over, and availment of, the WTC infrastructure to develop its business, it is difficult to imagine what would constitute a "legally

CASE 49.1 | Continued cognizable interest in the property," apart from ownership or tenancy. The terms of the insurance policy, however, do not limit coverage to property owned or leased by the insured. To the contrary, *the policy's scope expressly includes real or personal property that the insured "used," "controlled," or "intended for use."* [Emphasis added.]

The district court's imposition of the "legally cognizable interest in the property" requirement is an impermissible hurdle to insurance coverage, contemplated by neither the parties nor the New York legislature. *The only prerequisite to coverage mandated by New York law is that an entity have an "insurable interest" in the property it insures. New York law embraces the sui generis [unique or particular] nature of an "insurable interest" and statutorily defines this term to include "any lawful and substantial economic interest in the safety or preservation of property from loss, destruction or pecuniary [monetary] damage."* ABM's income stream is dependent upon the common areas and leased premises in the WTC complex, and thus ABM meets New York's requirement of having an "insurable interest" in that property. [Emphasis added.]

* * * *

* * * We reverse the district court's May 28, 2003 order granting summary judgment in favor of Zurich and award summary judgment in favor of ABM * * * . Further, we vacate [declare the lower court's decision void] and remand the remaining issues * * * to the district court for further proceedings not inconsistent with this opinion.

QUESTIONS

1. On what issue was the court asked to rule in this case?
2. On what did the court base its reasoning for its ruling on this issue?

SECTION 2 | The Insurance Contract

An insurance contract is governed by the general principles of contract law, although the insurance industry is heavily regulated by the states.[1] Customarily, a party offers to purchase insurance by submitting an insurance application to the insurance company. The company can either accept or reject the offer. Sometimes, the insurance company's acceptance is conditional—on the results of a life insurance applicant's medical examination, for example. For the insurance contract to be binding, consideration (in the form of a premium) must be given, and the parties forming the contract must have the required contractual capacity to do so.

APPLICATION FOR INSURANCE

The filled-in application form for insurance is usually attached to the policy and made a part of the insurance contract. Thus, an insurance applicant is bound by any false statements that appear in the application (subject to certain exceptions). Because the insurance company

evaluates the risk factors based on the information included in the insurance application, misstatements or misrepresentations can void a policy, especially if the insurance company can show that it would not have extended insurance if it had known the facts.

EFFECTIVE DATE

The effective date of an insurance contract—that is, the date on which the insurance coverage begins—is important. In some instances, the insurance applicant is not protected until a formal written policy is issued. In other situations, the applicant is protected between the time the application is received and the time the insurance company either accepts or rejects it. Generally, coverage on an insurance policy can begin when a binder is written (to be discussed shortly); when the policy is issued; or, depending on the terms of the contract, after a certain period of time has elapsed or a specified condition is met.

BROKERS VERSUS AGENTS   A broker is the agent of an applicant. Therefore, if the broker fails to procure a policy, the applicant normally is not insured. According to general principles of agency law, if the broker fails to obtain policy coverage and the applicant

---

1. The states were given authority to regulate the insurance industry by the McCarran-Ferguson Act of 1945, 15 U.S.C. Sections 1011–1015.

is harmed as a result, then the broker is liable to the harmed applicant-principal for the loss.

BINDERS A person who seeks insurance from an insurance company's agent is usually protected from the moment the application is made, provided—in the case of life insurance—that some form of premium has been paid. Between the time the application is received and the time it is either rejected or accepted, the applicant is covered (possibly subject to certain conditions, such as passing a physical examination). Usually, the agent will write a memorandum, or **binder,** indicating that a policy is pending and stating its essential terms.

CONDITIONS AGREED TO BY THE PARTIES If the parties agree that the policy will be issued and delivered at a later time, the contract is not effective until the policy is issued and delivered or sent to the applicant, depending on the agreement. Thus, any loss sustained between the time of application and the delivery of the policy is not covered. An insurance contract may also include a clause stating that the applicant must be "still insurable" on the effective date of the policy.[2]

Parties may agree that a life insurance policy will be binding at the time the insured pays the first premium, or the policy may be expressly contingent on the applicant's passing a physical examination. If the applicant pays the premium and passes the examination, then the policy coverage is continuously in effect. If the applicant pays the premium but dies before having the physical examination, then in order to collect, the applicant's estate normally must show that the applicant would have passed the examination had he or she not died.

PROVISIONS AND CLAUSES

Some of the important provisions and clauses contained in insurance contracts are defined and discussed in the following subsections.

PROVISIONS MANDATED BY STATUTE If a statute mandates that a certain provision be included in insurance contracts, a court will deem that an insurance policy contains the provision regardless of whether the parties actually included it in the language of their con-

tract. If a statute requires that any limitations regarding coverage be stated in the contract, a court will not allow an insurer to avoid liability for a claim through reliance on an unexpressed restriction.

INCONTESTABILITY CLAUSES Statutes commonly require that a life or health insurance policy provide that after the policy has been in force for a specified length of time—often two or three years—the insurer cannot contest statements made in the application. This is known as an *incontestability clause*. Once a policy becomes incontestable, the insurer cannot later avoid a claim on the basis of, for example, fraud on the part of the insured, unless the clause provides an exception for that circumstance. The clause does not prevent an insurer from refusing or reducing payment for a claim due to nonpayment of premiums, failure to file proof of death within a certain period, or lack of an insurable interest.

COINSURANCE CLAUSES Often, when taking out fire insurance policies, property owners insure their property for less than full value because most fires do not result in a total loss. To encourage owners to insure their property for an amount as close to full value as possible, fire insurance policies generally include a coinsurance clause. Typically, a *coinsurance clause* provides that if the owner insures the property up to a specified percentage—usually 80 percent—of its value, she or he will recover any loss up to the face amount of the policy. If the insurance is for less than the fixed percentage, the owner is responsible for a proportionate share of the loss.

Coinsurance applies only in instances of partial loss. For example, if the owner of property valued at $100,000 took out a policy in the amount of $40,000 and suffered a loss of $30,000, the recovery would be $15,000. The formula for calculating the recovery amount is as follows:

$$\frac{\text{amount of insurance } (\$40{,}000)}{\text{coinsurance percentage } (80\%) \times \text{property value } (\$100{,}000)} = \frac{\text{recovery percentage } (50\%)}{}$$

recovery percentage (50%) × amount of loss ($30,000) = recovery amount ($15,000)

If the owner had taken out a policy in the amount of $80,000, then according to the same formula, the full loss would have been recovered.

---

2. See, for example, *Life Insurance Co. of North America v. Cichowlas*, 659 So.2d 1333 (Fla.App.4th 1995).

APPRAISAL AND ARBITRATION CLAUSES Most fire insurance policies provide that if the parties cannot agree on the amount of a loss covered under the policy or on the value of the property lost, an *appraisal* can be demanded. An appraisal is an estimate of the property's value determined by suitably qualified individuals who have no interest in the property. Typically, two appraisers are used, one being appointed by each party. A third party, or umpire, may be called on to resolve differences. Other types of insurance policies also contain provisions for appraisal and arbitration when the insured and insurer disagree on the value of a loss.

MULTIPLE INSURANCE COVERAGE If an insured has *multiple insurance coverage*—that is, policies with several companies covering the same insurable interest—and the amount of coverage exceeds the loss, the insured can collect from each insurer only the company's proportionate share of the liability, relative to the total amount of insurance. Many fire insurance policies include a pro rata clause, which requires that any loss be shared proportionately by all carriers. For example, if Grumbling insured $50,000 worth of property with two companies, each of whose policies had a liability limit of $40,000, then on the property's total destruction Grumbling could collect only $25,000 from each insurer.

ANTILAPSE CLAUSES A life insurance policy may provide, or a statute may require a policy to provide, that it will not automatically lapse if no payment is made on the date due. Ordinarily, under an *antilapse provision,* the insured has a *grace period* of thirty or thirty-one days within which to pay an overdue premium. If the insured fails to pay a premium altogether, there are alternatives to cancellation:

1. The insurer may be required to extend the insurance for a period of time.
2. The insurer may issue a policy with less coverage to reflect the amount of the payments made.
3. The insurer may pay to the insured the policy's **cash surrender value**—the amount the insurer has agreed to pay on the policy's cancellation before the insured's death. (In determining this value, the following factors are considered: the period that the policy has already run, the amount of the premium, the insured's age and life expectancy, and amounts to be repaid on any outstanding loans taken out against the policy.)

When the insurance contract states that the insurer cannot cancel the policy, these alternatives are important.

GOOD FAITH OBLIGATIONS

Essentially, the parties to an insurance contract are responsible for the obligations the contract imposes. These include the basic contractual duties discussed in Chapters 10 through 19 of this text, which cover contract law. In addition, both the insured and the insurer have an implied duty to act in good faith.

OBLIGATIONS OF THE INSURED Good faith requires the party who is applying for insurance to reveal everything necessary for the insurer to evaluate the risk. In other words, the applicant must disclose all material facts. *Material facts* include all facts that an insurer would consider in determining whether to charge a higher premium or to refuse to issue a policy altogether.

OBLIGATIONS OF THE INSURER Once the insurer has accepted the risk, and on the occurrence of an event giving rise to a claim, the insurer has a duty to conduct an investigation to determine the facts. When a policy provides insurance against third party claims, the insurer is obligated to make reasonable efforts to settle such a claim. If a settlement cannot be reached, then regardless of the claim's merit, the insurer must defend any suit against the insured. Usually, a policy provides that in this situation the insured must cooperate. A policy provision may expressly require the insured to attend hearings and trials, to help in obtaining evidence and witnesses, and to assist in reaching a settlement.

BAD FAITH ACTIONS Although the law of insurance generally involves contract law, most states now recognize a "bad faith" tort action against insurers. Thus, if an insurer in bad faith denies coverage of a claim, the insured may recover in tort an amount exceeding the policy's coverage limits and may even recover millions of dollars in punitive damages. Some courts have held insurers liable for a bad faith refusal to settle claims for reasonable amounts within the policy limits.

The question in the following case was whether the insurer acted in bad faith in investigating and paying an insured's claim.

CASE 49.2

Supreme Court
of Arkansas, 2002.
347 Ark. 423,
64 S.W.3d 720.
http://courts.state.ar.us/
opinions/opinions.html[a]

Columbia National Insurance Co. v. Freeman

BACKGROUND AND FACTS *Gary and Peggy Freeman owned and operated Circle F Trading Company, a western wear and general store, in Arkansas. The Freemans were insured against losses to the building, its contents, continuing business expenses, and other coverage, under a policy with Columbia National Insurance Company. In October 1997, a fire damaged Circle F's building and destroyed its inventory. The Freemans filed a claim with Columbia, providing an appraisal of the lost merchandise at $107,905.13 and a list of their continuing business expenses. Columbia obtained a second appraisal of $71,231.69 and attempted to find Circle F a building to serve as a temporary office. In December, Columbia paid the Freemans $77,892.28 for inventory, supplies, and lost income. No payment was made for continuing business expenses, and no office was provided. The parties agreed on an amount of $32,725 to cover the cost of the damage to the building, but Columbia offered to pay only 80 percent of this amount. Circle F never reopened. The Freemans filed a suit in an Arkansas state court against Columbia, alleging, among other things, bad faith. A jury returned a verdict for the Freemans, awarding $170,000 in compensatory damages and $200,000 in punitive damages. Columbia filed a motion for a directed verdict, which the court denied. Columbia appealed to the Arkansas Supreme Court.*

IN THE LANGUAGE OF THE COURT

RAY THORNTON, Justice.

* * * *

* * * An insurance company commits the tort of bad faith when it affirmatively engages in dishonest, malicious, or oppressive conduct in order to avoid a just obligation to its insured. *We have defined "bad faith" as dishonest, malicious, or oppressive conduct carried out with a state of mind characterized by hatred, ill will, or a spirit of revenge. Mere negligence or bad judgment is insufficient* * * * . [Emphasis added.]

* * * *

* * * First, appellees [the Freemans] argue that appellant acted in bad faith when it failed to pay appellees' ongoing business expenses. These expenses included utility bills and appellees' mortgage payment. Bill Green, an insurance adjuster who worked for appellant, was responsible for providing appellees money to cover their ongoing business expenses. He testified that he asked appellees to provide him documentation of the ongoing business expenses before he could pay the expenses. Mr. Freeman and Mrs. Freeman each testified that they had made the requested copies of the bills and mailed the documentation to Mr. Green. Mr. Green testified that the only documentation he received from appellees was a handwritten list of bills * * * . There was sufficient evidence for the jury, without resorting to suspicion or conjecture, to determine whether adequate documentation had been provided, and to support a finding that failure to cover appellees' ongoing business expenses, to which they were entitled, was an act of bad faith.

Next, appellees contend that appellant acted in bad faith when it failed to provide appellees with a temporary location for their business. Sufficient evidence was admitted to present to the jury the question of whether appellant's agent agreed to provide a trailer for appellees to use, researched the cost of providing such a service, and then failed to go forward with the agreement.

Additionally, appellees argue that appellant was acting in bad faith when it * * * agreed * * * upon the sum of $32,725 for the cost of repairing the building but * * * tendered only eighty percent of the amount agreed upon. There was sufficient evidence of such an agreement to submit to the jury the question of whether an agreement was entered into by the parties and then breached by appellant.

* * * *

---

a. In the "Search Cases by Party Name" section, enter "Freeman" in the "Party Name" box and select "Search by Date Range." For the date range, choose "From January 2002" and "To February 2002," and click on "Search." From the list of results, click on the name of the case to access the opinion. The Arkansas judiciary maintains this Web site.

CASE 49.2 | Continued   Finally, appellees argue that appellant acted with bad faith when it requested that two appraisals be performed on appellees' inventory and chose to pay appellees based on the lower of the two appraisals.

> **DECISION AND REMEDY** *The Arkansas Supreme Court affirmed the lower court's judgment. The state supreme court concluded that there was substantial evidence to support the jury's verdict that Columbia's actions constituted oppressive conduct carried out with a state of mind characterized by ill will.*

> **WHAT IF THE FACTS WERE DIFFERENT?** *Suppose that after an investigation, Columbia had simply refused to pay the Freemans' claim. Would the result have been the same?*

INTERPRETING PROVISIONS OF AN INSURANCE CONTRACT

The courts are increasingly cognizant of the fact that most people do not have the special training necessary to understand the intricate terminology used in insurance policies. Therefore, when disputes arise, the courts will interpret the words used in an insurance contract according to their ordinary meanings in light of the nature of the coverage involved. When there is an ambiguity in the policy, the provision is interpreted against the insurance company.

When it is unclear whether an insurance contract actually exists because the written policy has not been delivered, the uncertainty is resolved against the insurance company. The court presumes that the policy is in effect unless the company can show otherwise. Similarly, an insurer must take care to verify that the insured is adequately notified of any change in coverage under an existing policy.

The presence of an ambiguity is often a key issue in insurance disputes, as illustrated by the following case.

CASE 49.3   ## Cary v. United of Omaha Life Insurance Co.

Supreme Court
of Colorado, 2005.
108 P.3d 288.

> **BACKGROUND AND FACTS** *Fourteen-year-old Dena Cary shot herself under the chin in an unsuccessful suicide attempt because she suffered a major depressive episode of her diagnosed bipolar disorder. Her injuries required extensive medical treatment. Dena's father, Thomas Cary, sought payment for these costs under his medical insurance covering injury and illness, but the insurer denied the claim. The insurer argued that coverage was excluded under a provision reading: "Injury. Injury means accidental bodily injury which occurs independently of Illness. Injury does not include self-inflicted bodily injury, either while sane or insane." The Carys filed an action in a Colorado state court for bad faith denial of coverage. The trial court found that the injury was covered by the policy, but the state intermediate appellate court reversed. The Carys appealed to the state supreme court.*

IN THE LANGUAGE OF THE COURT

RICE, Justice:

* * * *

* * * One reasonable interpretation of these definitions is * * * [that] the self-inflicted injury limitation in the second sentence of the "injury" definition modifies only the phrase "accidental bodily injury which occurs independently of Illness." As a result, injuries that occur as a result of illness, even if self-inflicted, are defined out of the "injury" definition and are covered by the Plan's promise to provide coverage for "treatment of an Illness."

* * * *

However, an equally reasonable interpretation is that both sentences in the "injury" definition are of like definitional value, that is to say that one does not modify the other. Thus,

CONTINUED ▶

 **Continued** to be covered, an injury must be [an] "accidental bodily injury which occurs independently of Illness" and must not be [a] "self-inflicted bodily injury, either while sane or insane." Accordingly, if an injury is accidental or is the result of an illness, it nonetheless would be excluded from coverage if it is self-inflicted.

* * * Most importantly for our purposes, however, the plan is ambiguous because it is susceptible to each equally reasonable interpretation. * * * Because we resolve ambiguities in favor of coverage, Dena's injuries are covered.

DECISION AND REMEDY *The Colorado Supreme Court reversed the lower appellate court's decision, with instructions to return the case to the trial court for proceedings consistent with this opinion.*

CANCELLATION

The insured can cancel a policy at any time, and the insurer can cancel under certain circumstances. When an insurance company can cancel its insurance contract, the policy or a state statute usually requires that the insurer give advance written notice of the cancellation.[3] The same requirement applies when only part of a policy is canceled. Any premium paid in advance and not yet earned may be refundable on the policy's cancellation. The insured may also be entitled to a life insurance policy's cash surrender value.

The insurer may cancel an insurance policy for various reasons, depending on the type of insurance. For example, automobile insurance can be canceled for nonpayment of premiums or suspension of the insured's driver's license. Property insurance can be canceled for nonpayment of premiums or for other reasons, including the insured's fraud or misrepresentation, gross negligence, or conviction for a crime that increases the hazard insured against. Life and health policies can be canceled because of false statements made by the insured in the application, but cancellation can take place only before the effective date of an **incontestability clause.** An insurer cannot cancel—or refuse to renew—a policy because of the national origin or race of an applicant or because the insured has appeared as a witness in a case brought against the company.

DEFENSES AGAINST PAYMENT

An insurance company can raise any of the defenses that would be valid in any ordinary action on a contract, as well as some defenses that do not apply in ordinary contract actions. If the insurance company can show that the policy was procured through fraud or misrepresentation, for example, it may have a valid defense for not paying on a claim. (The insurance company may also have the right to disaffirm or rescind an insurance contract.) An absolute defense exists if the insurer can show that the insured lacked an insurable interest—thus rendering the policy void from the beginning. Improper actions, such as those that are against public policy or that are otherwise illegal, can also give the insurance company a defense against the payment of a claim or allow it to rescind the contract.

The insurance company can be prevented, or estopped, from asserting some defenses that are normally available. For example, if a company tells an insured that information requested on a form is optional and the insured provides it anyway, the company cannot use the information to avoid its contractual obligation under the insurance contract. Similarly, incorrect statements regarding the age of the insured normally do not provide the insurance company with a way to escape payment on the death of the insured. Also, incontestability clauses prevent the insurer from asserting certain defenses. Some states follow the *concurrent causation doctrine*, which requires that the insurer pay on a claim when the accident was due to more than one cause, at least one of which was covered under the policy.[4]

SECTION 3 | Types of Insurance

There are four general types of insurance coverage: life insurance, fire and homeowners' insurance, automobile insurance, and business liability insurance. We

---

3. At issue in one case was whether a notification of cancellation included on a diskette sent to the insured constituted "written notice" of cancellation. The court held that the computerized document, which could be printed out as "hard copy," constituted written notice. See *Clyburn v. Allstate Insurance Co.*, 826 F.Supp. 955 (D.S.C. 1993).

4. This doctrine was enunciated by the California Supreme Court in *State Farm Mutual Automobile Insurance Co. v. Partridge*, 10 Cal.3d 94, 514 P.2d 123, 109 Cal.Rptr. 811 (1973). Subsequently, a number of other states, particularly in the Midwest, adopted the doctrine. But see *McGill v. Scottsdale Insurance Co.*, 2002 WL 867738, for an example of a Michigan state court that rejects the doctrine.

now examine briefly the coverage available under each of these types of insurance. In the course of our discussion, we point out certain features and provisions as they relate to the law, with special emphasis on life and fire insurance policies.

LIFE INSURANCE

There are five basic types of life insurance:

1. Whole life, sometimes referred to as straight life, ordinary life, or cash-value insurance, provides protection with a cumulated cash surrender value that can be used as collateral for a loan. Premiums are paid by the insured during the insured's entire lifetime, with a fixed payment to the beneficiary on death.

2. Limited-payment life is a type of policy under which premiums are paid for a stated number of years; after that time, the policy is paid up and fully effective during the insured's life. For example, a policy might call for twenty payments. Naturally, premiums are higher than for whole life. This insurance has a cash surrender value.

3. Term insurance is a type of policy for which premiums are paid for a specified term. Payment on the policy is due only if death occurs within the term period. Premiums are lower than for whole life or limited-payment life, and there is usually no cash surrender value. Frequently, this type of insurance can be converted to another type of life insurance.

4. Endowment insurance involves fixed premium payments that are made for a definite term. At the end of the term, a fixed amount is to be paid to the insured or, on the death of the insured during the specified period, to a beneficiary. Thus, this type of insurance represents both term insurance and a form of **annuity** (the right to receive fixed, periodic payments for life or—as in this instance—for a term of years). Endowment insurance has a rapidly increasing cash surrender value, but premiums are high, as payment is required at the end of the term even if the insured is still living.

5. Universal life combines some aspects of term insurance and some of whole life insurance. From every payment, usually called a "contribution," the issuing life insurance company makes two deductions: the first is a charge for term insurance protection; the second is for company expenses and profit. The funds that remain after these deductions earn interest for the policyholder at a rate determined by the company. The interest-earning amount is called the policy's *cash value*, but that term does not mean the same thing as it

does for a traditional whole life insurance policy. With a universal life policy, the cash value grows at a variable interest rate rather than at a predetermined rate.

The rights and liabilities of the parties to life insurance contracts are basically dependent on the specific contract. A few features deserve special attention.

LIABILITY The life insurance contract determines not only the extent of the insurer's liability but, generally, whether the insurer is liable on the death of the insured. Most life insurance contracts exclude liability for death caused by suicide, military action during war, execution by a state or federal government, and even a mishap that occurs while the insured is a passenger in a commercial vehicle. In the absence of contractual exclusion, most courts today construe any cause of death to be one of the insurer's risks.

ADJUSTMENT DUE TO MISSTATEMENT OF AGE The insurance policy constitutes the agreement between the parties. The application for insurance is part of the policy and is usually attached to the policy. When the insured misstates his or her age on the application, an error is introduced, particularly as to the amount of premiums paid. Misstatement of age is not a material error sufficient to allow the insurer to void the policy. Instead, on discovery of the error, the insurer will adjust the premium payments and/or benefits accordingly.

ASSIGNMENT Most life insurance policies allow the insured to change beneficiaries. When this is permitted, in the absence of any prohibition or notice requirement, the insured can assign the rights to the policy (for example, as security for a loan) without the consent of the insurer or the beneficiary. If the beneficiary's right is *vested*—that is, has become absolute, entitling the beneficiary to payment of the proceeds—the policy cannot be assigned without the consent of the beneficiary. For the most part, life insurance contracts permit assignment and require notice only to the insurer to be effective.

CREDITORS' RIGHTS Unless insurance proceeds are exempt under state law, the insured's interest in life insurance is an asset that is subject to the rights of judgment creditors. These creditors generally can reach insurance proceeds payable to the insured's estate, proceeds payable to anyone if the payment of premiums constituted a fraud on creditors, and proceeds payable to a named beneficiary unless the beneficiary's rights have vested. Creditors, however, cannot compel the insured to make available the cash surrender value of the policy or to change the named beneficiary to that of the creditor. Almost all states exempt at least a part of the proceeds of life insurance from creditors' claims.

TERMINATION Although the insured can cancel and terminate the policy, the insurer generally cannot do so. Therefore, termination usually takes place only on the occurrence of the following:

1. Default in premium payments that causes the policy to lapse.
2. Death and payment of benefits.
3. Expiration of the term of the policy.
4. Cancellation by the insured.

FIRE AND HOMEOWNERS' INSURANCE

There are basically two types of insurance policies for a home—standard fire insurance policies and homeowners' policies.

STANDARD FIRE INSURANCE POLICIES The standard fire insurance policy protects the homeowner against fire and lightning, as well as damage from smoke and water caused by the fire or the fire department. Most fire insurance policies are classified according to the type of property covered and the extent (amount) of the issuer's liability. Exhibit 49–2 lists typical fire insurance policies.

As with life insurance, certain features and provisions of fire insurance deserve special mention. In reading the following, it is important to note some basic differences in the treatment of life and fire policies.

—Liability. The insurer's liability is determined from the terms of the policy. Most policies, however, limit recovery to losses resulting from *hostile* fires—basically, those that break out or begin in places where no fire was intended to burn. A *friendly* fire—one burning in a place where it was intended to burn—is not covered. Therefore, smoke from a fireplace is not covered, but smoke from a fire caused by a defective electrical outlet is covered. Sometimes, owners add "extended coverage" to the fire policy to cover losses from "friendly" fires.

If the policy is a *valued* policy (see Exhibit 49–2) and the subject matter is completely destroyed, the insurer is liable for the amount specified in the policy. If it is an *open* policy, then the extent of the actual loss must be determined, and the insurer is liable only for the amount of the loss or for the maximum amount specified in the policy, whichever is less. For partial losses, actual loss must always be determined, and the insurer's liability is limited to that amount. Most insurance policies permit the insurer to either restore or replace the property destroyed or to pay for the loss.

—Proof of Loss. Fire insurance policies require the insured to file with the insurer, within a specified period or immediately (within a reasonable time), a proof of loss as a condition for recovery. Failure to comply *could* allow the insurance carrier to avoid liability. Courts vary somewhat on the enforcement of such clauses.

EXHIBIT 49-2 **Typical Fire Insurance Policies**

TYPE OF POLICY	COVERAGE
Blanket	Covers a class of property rather than specific property, because the property is expected to shift or vary in nature. A policy covering the inventory of a business is an example.
Floater	Usually supplements a specific policy. It is intended to cover property that may change in either location or quantity. To illustrate, if the painting mentioned below under "specific policy" were to be exhibited during the year at numerous locations throughout the state, a floater policy would be desirable.
Open	A policy in which the value of the property insured is not agreed on. The policy usually provides for a maximum liability of the insurer, but payment for loss is restricted to the fair market value of the property at the time of loss or to the insurer's limit, whichever is less.
Specific	Covers a specific item of property at a specific location. An example is a particular painting located in a residence or a piece of machinery located in a factory or business.
Valued	A policy in which, by agreement, a specific value is placed on the subject to be insured to cover the eventuality of its total loss.

—Occupancy Clause. Most standard policies require that the premises be occupied at the time of loss. The relevant clause states that if the premises become vacant or unoccupied for a given period, unless consent by the insurer is given, the coverage is suspended until the premises are reoccupied. Persons going on extended vacations should check their policies regarding this point.

—Assignment. Before a loss has occurred, a fire insurance policy is not assignable without the consent of the insurer. The theory is that the fire insurance policy is a personal contract between the insured and the insurer. The nonassignability of the policy is extremely important in the purchase of a house. The purchaser must procure his or her own insurance. If the purchaser wishes to assume the remaining insurance coverage period of the seller, consent of the insurer is essential.

To illustrate: Ann is selling her home and lot to Jeff. Ann has a one-year fire policy with Ajax Insurance Company, with six months of coverage remaining at the date on which the sale is to close. Ann agrees to assign the balance of her policy, but Ajax has not given its consent. One day after passage of the deed, a fire totally destroys the house. Can Jeff recover from Ajax?

The answer is no, as the policy is actually voided on the closing of the transaction and the deeding of the property. The reason the policy is voided is that Ann no longer has an insurable interest at the time of loss, and Jeff has no rights in a nonassignable policy.

HOMEOWNERS' POLICIES A homeowners' policy provides protection against a number of risks under a single policy, allowing the policyholder to avoid the cost of buying each protection separately. There are two basic types of homeowners' coverage:

1. *Property coverage* includes the garage, house, and other private buildings on the policyholder's lot. It also includes the personal possessions and property of the policyholder at home, while traveling, or at work. It pays additional expenses for living away from home because of a fire or some other covered peril.

2. *Liability coverage* is for personal liability in case someone is injured on the insured's property, the insured damages someone else's property, or the insured injures someone else who is not in an automobile.

—Property Coverage. Perils insured under property coverage often include fire, lightning, wind, hail, vandalism, and theft (of personal property). Personal property that is typically not included under property coverage, in the absence of a specific provision, includes such items as motor vehicles, farm equipment, airplanes, and boats. Coverage for other property, such as jewelry and securities, is usually limited to a specified dollar amount.

—Liability Coverage. Liability coverage under a homeowners' policy applies when others are injured or property is damaged because of the unsafe condition of the policyholder's premises. It also applies when the policyholder is negligent. It normally does not apply, however, if the liability arises from business or professional activities or from the operation of a motor vehicle. These are subjects for separate policies. Also excluded is liability arising from intentional misconduct. Similar to liability coverage is coverage for the medical payments of others who are injured on the policyholder's property and coverage for the property of others that is damaged by a member of the policyholder's family.

—Renters' Policies. Renters also take out insurance policies to protect against losses to personal property. Renters' insurance covers personal possessions against various perils and includes coverage for additional living expenses and liability.

AUTOMOBILE INSURANCE

There are two basic kinds of automobile insurance: liability insurance and collision and comprehensive insurance.

LIABILITY INSURANCE Automobile liability insurance covers liability for bodily injury and property damage. Liability limits are usually described by a series of three numbers, such as 100/300/50. This means that the policy, for one accident, will pay a maximum of $100,000 for bodily injury to one person, a maximum of $300,000 for bodily injury to more than one person, and a maximum of $50,000 for property damage. Many insurance companies offer liability coverage in amounts up to $500,000 and sometimes higher.

Individuals who are dissatisfied with the maximum liability limits offered by regular automobile insurance coverage can purchase separate coverage under an *umbrella policy.* Umbrella limits sometimes go as high as $10 million. Umbrella policies also cover personal liability in excess of the liability limits of a homeowners' policy.

COLLISION AND COMPREHENSIVE INSURANCE

Collision insurance covers damage to the insured's car in any type of collision. Usually, it is not advisable to purchase full collision coverage (otherwise known as *zero deductible*). The price per year is relatively high, because it is likely that some small repair jobs will be required each year. Most people prefer to take out policies with a deductible of $100, $250, or $500, which costs substantially less than zero-deductible coverage.

Comprehensive insurance covers loss, damage, and destruction due to fire, hurricane, hail, vandalism, and theft. It can be obtained separately from collision insurance.

OTHER AUTOMOBILE INSURANCE

Other types of automobile insurance coverage include the following:

1. *Uninsured motorist coverage.* Uninsured motorist coverage insures the driver and passengers against injury caused by any driver without insurance or by a hit-and-run driver. Certain states require that it be included in all auto insurance policies sold.

2. *Accidental death benefits.* Sometimes referred to as *double indemnity*, accidental death benefits provide for a payment of twice the policy's face amount if the policyholder dies in an accident. This coverage generally costs very little, but it may not be necessary if the insured has a sufficient amount of life insurance.

3. *Medical payment coverage.* Medical payment coverage provided by an auto insurance policy pays hospital and other medical bills and sometimes funeral expenses. This type of insurance protects all the passengers in the insured's car when the insured is driving.

4. *Other-driver coverage.* An **omnibus clause,** or *other-driver clause*, protects the vehicle owner who has taken out the insurance and anyone who drives the vehicle with the owner's permission. This coverage may be held to extend to a third party who drives the vehicle with the permission of the person to whom the owner gave permission.

5. *No-fault insurance.* Under no-fault statutes, claims arising from an accident are made against the claimant's own insurer, regardless of whose fault the accident was. In some situations—for example, when injuries require expensive medical treatment—an injured party may seek recovery from another party or insurer. In those instances, the injured party may collect the maximum amount of no-fault insurance and still sue for total damages from the party at fault, although usually, on winning an award, the injured party must reimburse the insurer for its no-fault payments.

BUSINESS LIABILITY INSURANCE

A business may be vulnerable to all sorts of risks. A key employee may die or become disabled; a customer may be injured when using a manufacturer's product; the patron of an establishment selling liquor may leave the premises and injure a third party in an automobile accident; or a professional may overlook some important detail, causing liability for malpractice. Should the first situation arise (for instance, if the company president dies), the firm may have some protection under a key-person insurance policy, discussed earlier. In the other circumstances, other types of insurance may apply.

GENERAL LIABILITY Comprehensive general liability insurance can encompass virtually as many risks as the insurer agrees to cover. For example, among the types of coverage that a business might wish to acquire is protection from liability for injuries arising from on-premises events not otherwise covered, such as company social functions. Some specialized establishments, such as taverns, may be subject to liability in individualized circumstances, and policies can be drafted to meet their needs. In many jurisdictions, for example, statutes impose liability on a seller of liquor when a buyer of the liquor, intoxicated as a result of the sale, injures a third party. Legal protection may extend not only to the immediate consequences of an injury, such as quadriplegia resulting from an automobile accident, but also to the loss of financial support suffered by a family because of the injuries. Insurance can provide coverage for these injuries and financial losses.

PRODUCT LIABILITY Manufacturers may be subject to liability for injuries that their products cause, and product liability insurance can be written to match specific products' risks. Coverage can be procured under a comprehensive general liability policy or under a separate policy. The coverage may include payment for expenses involved in recalling and replacing a product that has proved to be defective. (For a comprehensive discussion of product liability, see Chapter 23.)

PROFESSIONAL MALPRACTICE In recent years, professionals—attorneys, physicians, architects, and engineers, for example—have increasingly become the targets of negligence suits. Professionals may purchase malpractice insurance to protect themselves against such claims. The large judgments in some malpractice suits have received considerable publicity and are sometimes cited in what has been called "the insurance crisis," because they have contributed to a significant increase in malpractice insurance premiums.

WORKERS' COMPENSATION Workers' compensation insurance covers payments to employees who are injured in accidents arising out of and in the course of employment (that is, on the job). Workers' compensation, which was discussed in detail in Chapter 33, is governed by state statutes.

REVIEWING INSURANCE

Provident Insurance, Inc., issued an insurance policy to a company providing an employee, Steve Matlin, with disability insurance. Soon thereafter, Matlin was diagnosed with "panic disorder and phobia of returning to work." He lost his job and sought disability coverage. Provident denied coverage, doubting the diagnosis of disability. Matlin and his employer sued Provident. During pretrial discovery, the insurer learned that Matlin had stated on the policy application that he had never been treated for any "emotional, mental, nervous, urinary, or digestive disorder" or any kind of heart disease. In fact, before Matlin filled out the application he had visited a physician for chest pains and general anxiety, and the physician had prescribed an antidepressant and recommended that Matlin stop smoking. Using the information presented in the chapter, answer the following questions.

1. Did Matlin commit a misrepresentation on his policy application?

2. If there is any ambiguity on the application, should it be resolved in favor of the insured or the insurer?

3. Assuming that the policy is valid, does Matlin's situation fall within the terms of the disability policy?

4. If Matlin is covered by the policy but is also disqualified by his misrepresentation on the application for coverage, might the insurer still be liable for bad faith denial of coverage? Explain.

 ## TERMS AND CONCEPTS TO REVIEW

annuity 999

binder 994

cash surrender value 995

endowment insurance 999

incontestability clause 998

insurable interest 990

insurance 988

limited-payment life 999

omnibus clause 1002

policy 988

premium 988

risk 988

risk management 988

term insurance 999

underwriter 988

universal life 999

whole life 999

 ## QUESTIONS AND CASE PROBLEMS

49–1. Adia owns a house and has an elderly third cousin living with her. Adia decides she needs fire insurance on the house and a life insurance policy on her third cousin to cover funeral and other expenses that will result from her cousin's death. Adia takes out a fire insurance policy from Ajax Insurance Co. and a $10,000 life insurance policy from Beta Insurance Co. on her third cousin. Six months later, Adia sells the house to John and transfers title to him. Adia and her cousin move into an apartment. With two months remaining on the Ajax policy, a fire totally destroys the house; at the same time, Adia's third cousin dies. Both insurance companies tender back premiums but claim they have no liability under the insurance contracts, as Adia did not have an insurable interest. Discuss their claims.

49–2. **QUESTION WITH SAMPLE ANSWER**

Patrick contracts with an Ajax Insurance Co. agent for a $50,000 ordinary life insurance policy. The application form is filled in to show Patrick's age as thirty-two. In addition, the application form asks whether Patrick has ever had any heart ailments or problems. Patrick answers no, forgetting that as a young child he was diagnosed as having a slight heart murmur. A policy is issued. Three years later, Patrick becomes seriously ill. A review of the policy discloses that Patrick was actually thirty-three at the time of application and issuance of the policy and that he erred in answering the question about a history of heart ailments. Discuss whether Ajax can void the policy and escape liability on Patrick's death.

For a sample answer to this question, go to Appendix I at the end of this text.

49–3. Sapata has an ordinary life insurance policy on her life and a fire insurance policy on her house. Both policies have been in force for a number of years. Sapata's life insurance names her son, Rory, as beneficiary. Sapata has specifically removed her right to change beneficiaries, and the life policy is silent on right of assignment. Sapata is going on a one-year European vacation and borrows money from Leonard to finance the trip. Leonard takes an assignment of the life insurance policy as security for the loan, as the policy has accumulated a substantial cash surrender value. Sapata also rents out her house to Leonard and assigns to him her fire insurance policy. Discuss fully whether Sapata's assignment of these policies is valid.

49–4. Fritz has an open fire insurance policy on his home for a maximum liability of $60,000. The policy has a number of standard clauses, including the right of the insurer to restore or rebuild the property in lieu of a monetary payment, and it has a standard coinsurance clause. A fire in Fritz's house virtually destroys a utility room and part of the kitchen. The fire was caused by the overheating of an electric water heater. The total damage to the property is $10,000. The property at the time of loss is valued at $100,000. Fritz files a proof-of-loss claim for $10,000. Discuss the insurer's liability in this situation.

49–5. Lori has a large house. She secures two open fire insurance policies on the house. Her policy with the Ajax Insurance Co. is for a maximum of $100,000, and her policy with the Beta Insurance Co. is for a maximum of $50,000. Lori's house burns to the ground. The value of the house at the time of the loss is $120,000. Discuss the liability of Ajax and Beta to Lori.

49–6. INSURER'S DEFENSES. Jeffrey Duke purchased a life insurance policy on his own life from New England Mutual Life Insurance Co. Duke listed as his beneficiary his lover and business adviser, William Remmelink. On his insurance application, however, Duke described his beneficiary as merely his business partner. After Duke died of acquired immune deficiency syndrome (AIDS), New England Mutual brought an action against William Johnson, the executor of Duke's estate, to rescind (cancel) the insurance contract on the ground that Duke had "materially misrepresented his relationship with his beneficiary." Johnson claimed that New England Mutual's attempt to rescind the contract was in bad faith and asked for both punitive damages and attorneys' fees. During the trial, an underwriter with twenty-four years of experience testified that New England Mutual had never before rescinded a policy because of a misrepresentation regarding the relationship between the beneficiary and the insured. Did Duke mischaracterize his relationship with

his beneficiary? If so, was such a misrepresentation material? How should the court decide? [*New England Mutual Life Insurance Co. v. Johnson,* 155 Misc.2d 680, 589 N.Y.S.2d 736 (1992)]

49–7. INSURER'S DEFENSES. The City of Worcester, Massachusetts, adopted an ordinance in 1990 that required rooming houses to be equipped with automatic sprinkler systems no later than September 25, 1995. In Worcester, James and Mark Duffy owned a forty-eight-room lodging house with two retail stores on the first floor. In 1994, the Duffys applied with General Star Indemnity Co. for an insurance policy to cover the premises. The application indicated that the premises had sprinkler systems. General issued a policy that required, among other safety features, a sprinkler system. Within a month, the premises were inspected on behalf of General. On the inspection form forwarded to the insurer, in the list of safety systems, next to the word *sprinkler* the inspector had inserted only a hyphen. In July 1995, when the premises sustained over $100,000 in fire damage, General learned that there was no sprinkler system. The insurer filed a suit in a federal district court against the Duffys to rescind the policy, alleging misrepresentation in their insurance application about the presence of sprinklers. How should the court rule, and why? [*General Star Indemnity Co. v. Duffy,* 191 F.3d 55 (1st Cir. 1999)]

49–8. ⚖ **CASE PROBLEM WITH SAMPLE ANSWER**
Valley Furniture & Interiors, Inc., bought an insurance policy from Transportation Insurance Co. (TIC). The policy provided coverage of $50,000 for each occurrence of property loss caused by employee dishonesty. An "occurrence" was defined as "a single act or series of related acts." Valley allowed its employees to take pay advances and to buy discounted merchandise, with the advances and the cost of the merchandise deducted from their paychecks. The payroll manager was to notify the payroll company to make the deductions. Over a period of six years, without notifying the payroll company, the payroll manager issued advances to other employees and herself and bought merchandise for herself, in amounts totaling more than $200,000. Valley filed claims with TIC for three "occurrences" of employee theft. TIC considered the acts a "series of related acts" and paid only $50,000. Valley filed a suit in a Washington state court against TIC, alleging, in part, breach of contract. What is the standard for interpreting an insurance clause? How should this court define "series of related acts"? Why? [*Valley Furniture & Interiors, Inc. v. Transportation Insurance Co.,* 107 Wash.App. 104, 26 P.3d 952 (Div. 1 2001)]

To view a sample answer for this case problem, go to this book's Web site at http://wbl.westbuslaw.com, select "Chapter 49," and click on "Case Problem with Sample Answer."

49–9. CANCELLATION. James Mitchell bought a building in Los Angeles, California, in February 2000, and applied to United National Insurance Co. for a fire insurance policy. The application stated, among other things, that the building measured 3,420 square feet, it was to be used as a video production studio, the business would generate $300,000 in revenue, and the building had no uncorrected fire code violations. In fact, the building measured less than 2,000 square feet; it was used to film only one music video over a two-day period; the business generated only $6,500 in revenue; and the city had cited the building for combustible debris, excessive weeds, broken windows, missing doors, damaged walls, and other problems. In November, Mitchell met Carl Robinson, who represented himself as a business consultant. Mitchell gave Robinson the keys to the property to show it to a prospective buyer. On November 22, Robinson set fire to the building and was killed in the blaze. Mitchell filed a claim for the loss. United denied the claim and rescinded the policy. Mitchell filed a suit in a California state court against United. Can an insurer cancel a policy? If so, on what ground might United have justifiably canceled Mitchell's policy? What might Mitchell argue to oppose a cancellation? What should the court rule? Explain. [*Mitchell v. United National Insurance Co.*, 127 Cal.App.4th 457, 25 Cal.Rptr.3d 627 (2 Dist. 2005)]

49–10. VIDEO QUESTION

Go to this text's Web site at http://wbl.westbuslaw.com and select "Chapter 49." Click on "Video Questions"

and view the video titled *Double Indemnity*. Then answer the following questions.

(a) Recall from the video that Mrs. Dietrichson (Barbara Stanwyck) is attempting to take out an "accident insurance" policy (similar to life insurance) on her husband without his knowledge. Does Mrs. Dietrichson have an insurable interest in the life of her husband? Why or why not?

(b) Why would Walter (Fred MacMurray), the insurance agent, refuse to sell Mrs. Deitrichson an insurance policy covering her husband's life without her husband's knowledge?

(c) Suppose that Mrs. Dietrichson contacts a different insurance agent and does not tell the agent that she wants to obtain insurance on her husband without his knowledge. Instead, she asks the agent to leave an insurance application for her husband to sign. Without her husband's knowledge, Mrs. Dietrichson then fills out the application for insurance, which includes a two-year incontestability clause, and forges Mr. Dietrichson's signature. Mr. Dietrichson dies three years after the policy is issued. Will the insurance company be obligated to pay on the policy? Why or why not?

LAW | on the Web

For updated links to resources available on the Web, as well as a variety of other materials, visit this text's Web site at http://wbl.westbuslaw.com.

For a summary of the law governing insurance contracts in the United States, including rules of interpretation, go to

http://www.consumerlawpage.com/article/insureds.shtml

For more information on business insurance, visit AllBusiness.com's Insurance Center Web page at

http://www.allbusiness.com/business_advice/Insurance/index-30.html

LEGAL RESEARCH EXERCISES ON THE WEB

Go to http://wbl.westbuslaw.com, the Web site that accompanies this text. Select "Chapter 49" and click on "Internet Exercises." There you will find the following Internet research exercises that you can perform to learn more about topics covered in this chapter.

Activity 49–1: LEGAL PERSPECTIVE
Disappearing Decisions

Activity 49–2: MANAGEMENT PERSPECTIVE
Risk Management in Cyberspace

CHAPTER 50
Wills, Trusts, and Elder Law

As the old adage states, "You can't take it with you." All of the real and personal property that you own will be transferred on your death to others. A person can direct the passage of his or her property after death by *will*, subject to certain limitations imposed by the state. If no valid will has been executed, the decedent is said to have died **intestate,** and state **intestacy laws** prescribe the distribution of the property among heirs or next of kin. If no heirs or kin can be found, the property will **escheat**[1] (title will be transferred to the state). In addition, a person can transfer property through a *trust.* In a trust arrangement, the owner (who may be called the *grantor* or the *settlor*) of the property transfers legal title to a trustee, who has a duty imposed by law to hold the property for the use or benefit of another (the beneficiary).

Wills and trusts are two basic devices used in the process of **estate planning**—determining in advance how one's property and obligations should be transferred on death. In this chapter, we examine wills and trusts in some detail. Other estate-planning devices include life insurance (discussed in Chapter 49) and joint-tenancy arrangements (described in Chapter 47). Typically, estate planning involves consultations with professionals, including attorneys, accountants, and financial planners.

For many people, a major estate-planning consideration is the possibility of becoming incapacitated, through accident or illness, at some future time or of needing long-term health care. In the final section of this chapter, we look at how individuals can plan in advance for these situations.

SECTION 1 | Wills

A **will** is the final declaration of how a person desires to have her or his property disposed of after death. It is a formal instrument that must follow exactly the requirements of state law to be effective. One who makes a will is known as a **testator** (from the Latin *testari,* "to make a will"). A will is referred to as a *testamentary disposition* of property, and one who dies after having made a valid will is said to have died **testate.**

A will can serve other purposes besides the distribution of property. It can appoint a guardian for minor children or incapacitated adults. It can also appoint a personal representative to settle the affairs of the deceased. An **executor** is a personal representative named in a will. An **administrator** is a personal repre-

sentative appointed by the court for a decedent who dies without a will, who fails to name an executor in the will, who names an executor lacking the capacity to serve, or who writes a will that the court refuses to admit to probate. Exhibit 50–1 presents excerpts from the will of Diana, Princess of Wales, who died in an automobile accident in 1997. Princess Diana left behind a substantial fortune, most of which was bequeathed to her sons, Prince William and Prince Henry, to be held in trust until they reached the age of majority.

LAWS GOVERNING WILLS

Laws governing wills come into play when a will is probated. To **probate** (prove) a will means to establish its validity and carry out the administration of the estate through a process supervised by a probate court. Probate laws vary from state to state. In 1969, how-

---

1. Pronounced ush-*cheet.*

EXHIBIT 50–1 **Excerpts from the Will of Diana, Princess of Wales**

I **DIANA PRINCESS OF WALES** of Kensington Palace London W8 HEREBY REVOKE all former Wills and testamentary dispositions made by me AND DECLARE this to be my last Will which I make this First day of June One thousand nine hundred and ninety three

1 I APPOINT my mother **THE HONOURABLE MRS FRANCES RUTH SHAND KYDD** of Callinesh Isle of Seil Oban Scotland and **COMMANDER PATRICK DESMOND CHRISTIAN JERMY JEPHSON** of St James's Palace London SW1 to be the Executors and Trustees of this my Will

2 I WISH to be buried

3 SHOULD any child of mine be under age at the date of the death of the survivor of myself and my husband I APPOINT my mother and my brother **EARL SPENCER** to be the guardians of that child and I express the wish that should I predecease my husband he will consult with my mother with regard to the upbringing education and welfare of our children

. . . .

5 SUBJECT to the payment or discharge of my funeral testamentary and administration expenses and debts and other liabilities I GIVE all my property and assets of every kind and wherever situate to my Executors and Trustees Upon trust either to retain (if they think fit without being liable for loss) all or any part in the same state as they are at the time of my death or to sell whatever and wherever they decide with power when they consider it proper to invest trust monies and to vary investments in accordance with the powers contained in the Schedule to this my Will and to hold the same UPON TRUST for such of them my children **PRINCE WILLIAM** and **PRINCE HENRY** as are living three months after my death and attain the age of twenty-five years if more than one in equal shares PROVIDED THAT if either child of mine dies before me or within three months after my death and issue of that child are living three months after my death and attain the age of twenty-one years such issue shall take by substitution if more than one in equal shares *per stirpes* the share that the deceased child of mine would have taken had he been living three months after my death but so that no issue shall take whose parent is then living and so capable of taking

. . . .

(Signed by HER ROYAL HIGHNESS)
(in our joint presence and)
(then by us in her presence)

---

ever, the American Bar Association and the National Conference of Commissioners on Uniform State Laws approved the Uniform Probate Code (UPC).

The UPC, which was significantly revised in 1990, codifies general principles and procedures for the resolution of conflicts in settling estates and relaxes some of the requirements for a valid will contained in earlier state laws. Nearly all of the states have enacted some part of the UPC and incorporated it into their own probate codes. For this reason, references to its provisions will be included in this chapter. Nonetheless, succession and inheritance laws vary widely among states, and one should always check the particular laws of the state involved.[2]

---

2. For example, California law differs substantially from the UPC.

GIFTS BY WILL

A gift of real estate by will is generally called a **devise,** and a gift of personal property under a will is called a **bequest,** or **legacy.** The recipient of a gift by will is a *devisee* or a *legatee*, depending on whether the gift was a devise or a legacy.

TYPES OF GIFTS Gifts by will can be specific, general, or residuary. A *specific* devise or bequest (legacy) describes particular property (such as "Eastwood Estate" or "my gold pocket watch") that can be distinguished from the rest of the testator's property. A *general* devise or bequest (legacy) uses less restrictive terminology. For example, "I devise all my lands" is a general devise. A general bequest often specifies a sum of cash instead of a particular item of property, such as a watch or an automobile. For example, "I give to my nephew, Carleton, $30,000" is a general bequest.

Sometimes, a will provides that any assets remaining after specific gifts have been made and debts have been paid—called the *residuary* (or *residuum*) of the estate—are to be given to the testator's spouse, distributed to the testator's descendants, or disposed of in some other way. If the testator has not indicated what party or parties should receive the residuary of the estate, the residuary passes according to state laws of intestacy.

If a gift is conditioned on the commission of an illegal act or an act that is legally impossible to fulfill, the gift will be invalid. For example, in one case a testator made a gift of $29 million to a nursing home on the condition that the funds be used only to help "white" patients. Because this condition was impossible to fulfill without violating laws prohibiting discrimination, the gift was invalidated.[3]

ABATEMENT   If the assets of an estate are insufficient to pay in full all general bequests provided for in the will, an *abatement* takes place, meaning that the legatees receive reduced benefits. For example, Julie's will leaves "$15,000 each to my children, Tamara and Lynn." On Julie's death, only $10,000 is available to honor these bequests. By abatement, each child will receive $5,000. If bequests are more complicated, abatement may be more complex. The testator's intent, as expressed in the will, controls.

LAPSED LEGACIES   If a legatee dies prior to the death of the testator or before the legacy is payable, a *lapsed legacy* results. At common law, the legacy failed. Today, the legacy may not lapse if the legatee is in a certain blood relationship to the testator (such as a child, grandchild, brother, or sister) and has left a child or other surviving descendant.

REQUIREMENTS FOR A VALID WILL

A will must comply with statutory formalities designed to ensure that the testator understood his or her actions at the time the will was made. These formali-

ties are intended to help prevent fraud. Unless they are followed, the will is declared void, and the decedent's property is distributed according to the laws of intestacy of that state. The requirements are not uniform among the jurisdictions. Most states, however, uphold certain basic requirements for executing a will. We now look at these requirements.

TESTAMENTARY CAPACITY AND INTENT   For a will to be valid, the testator must have testamentary capacity—that is, the testator must be of legal age and sound mind *at the time the will is made*. The legal age for executing a will varies, but in most states and under the UPC, the minimum age is eighteen years [UPC 2–501]. Thus, the will of a twenty-one-year-old decedent written when the person was sixteen is invalid if, under state law, the legal age for executing a will is eighteen.

—The "Sound-Mind" Requirement.   The concept of "being of sound mind" refers to the testator's ability to formulate and to comprehend a personal plan for the disposition of property. Generally, a testator must (1) intend the document to be his or her last will and testament, (2) comprehend the kind and character of the property being distributed, and (3) comprehend and remember the "natural objects of his or her bounty" (usually, family members and persons for whom the testator has affection).

—Intent.   A valid will is one that represents the maker's intention to transfer and distribute her or his property. When it can be shown that the decedent's plan of distribution was the result of fraud or of undue influence, the will is declared invalid. Undue influence may be inferred by the court if the testator ignored blood relatives and named as beneficiary a nonrelative who was in constant close contact with the testator and in a position to influence the making of the will. For example, if a nurse or friend caring for the testator at the time of death was named as beneficiary to the exclusion of all family members, the validity of the will might well be challenged on the basis of undue influence.

In the following case, the issue before the court was whether the testator intended his estate to be distributed to his relatives and friends in sixteen equal shares or in fourteen equal shares. The court looked first at the words used by the testator in his will to determine his intent.

---

3. *Home for Incurables of Baltimore City v. University of Maryland Medical System Corp.*, 369 Md. 67, 797 A.2d 746 (2002).

CASE 50.1	In re Estate of Klauzer

Supreme Court
of South Dakota, 2000.
604 N.W.2d 474.
http://www.sdbar.org/
opinions/Indices/sdindex.htm[a]

SABERS, Justice.

* * * *

On March 26, 1993, Frank [Klauzer] was appointed to act as Guardian and Conservator for his brother, John, who had suffered a severe stroke. In this capacity, Frank was required to inventory, account and manage the property of John and provide an annual accounting of John's estate. Frank was compensated for those services.

On September 9, 1996, John passed away. His estate was valued at $1.4 million. Pursuant to John's will, Frank was appointed personal representative of the estate on October 11, 1996. Wade Klauzer, John's nephew, petitioned for supervised administration and [a South Dakota state] trial court ordered the same.

John's will, dated August 30, 1990, disposed of the majority of his estate in the following residuary clause:

> THIRD: I hereby give, devise and bequeath unto my brother, Thomas Klauzer, my sister, Agnes Blake, my sister, Anna Malenovsky Baker, my brother, Raymond Klauzer, my niece, Jenny Culver, my niece, Judy Klauzer, my niece, Bernice Cunningham, my nephew, Wade Klauzer, my nephew, Jim Klauzer, my niece, Debra Klauzer, friends, Douglas Olson and Fern Olson, and my friends, William Hollister and Shirley Hollister, my brother, Frank Klauzer, and my sister-in-law, Patricia Klauzer, all of my property of every kind and character and wheresoever situated, in equal shares, share and share alike. That should any of the individuals above named predecease me, then their share of my estate shall go to their decedents [descendants] surviving.

On December 22, 1998, the trial court ordered that * * * the residuary clause be distributed in sixteen equal shares * * * . Frank appeals * * * in his personal capacity.

* * * *

Frank argues that the twelve Klauzer relatives named in clause number three should take one share each while friends, Doug and Fern Olson and William and Shirley Hollister, should receive one share per couple resulting in a 1/14th division of the estate. He relies heavily on what he terms the "grammatical geometrics" of the clause to support his contention: i.e., (1) the placement of the commas between the names of the devisees and the indication of relationship for the twelve heirs, but not for Olsons and Hollisters; [and] (2) the word "and," which connects the spouses' names, is claimed as evidence that John intended for each couple to receive one share * * * .

On the other hand, Olsons and Hollisters argue that all named individuals should take in equal shares resulting in a 1/16th division of the estate. For support, they point to John's will which: (1) refers to all sixteen heirs as "individuals"; (2) indicates that if any of the "individuals above named" predecease him, their share is to go to their "[descendants] surviving"; and (3) provides that the named parties are to receive his property "in equal shares, share and share alike." * * *

Our goal in interpreting a will is to discern the testator's intent. *If the intent is clear from the language used, that intent controls. However, if * * * doubt remains as to decedent's intent, the language used and the circumstances surrounding the execution of the writing will again be examined in light of pertinent rules of construction. Our inquiry is limited to what the testator meant by what he said, not what we think the testator meant to say.* [Emphasis added.]

* * * *Language is ambiguous when it is reasonably capable of being understood in more than one sense. An ambiguity is not of itself created simply because the parties differ as to the interpretation of the will. * * * *All the words and provisions appearing in a will must be given effect as far as possible, and none should be cast aside as meaningless.* * * * [Emphasis added.]

---

a. In the left column, click on "2000 Opinions." On that page, under "January 2000," scroll down the list to the case and click on the name to access the opinion. This Web site is maintained by the State Bar of South Dakota.

CONTINUED▶

CASE 50.1 | Continued

The third clause in John's will, as set forth above, names each individual followed by their relationship to John. Olsons and Hollisters are referenced as follows: "friends, Douglas Olson and Fern Olson, and my friends, William Hollister and Shirley Hollister * * * ." Each spouse is named as an individual. They are not referred to as "Mr. and Mrs. Olson" nor as "William and Shirley Hollister."

The clause contains other language to support the position that John intended that his estate be divided sixteen ways versus fourteen ways. After naming all sixteen individuals, the clause provides that they should receive his property "in equal shares, share and share alike. That should any of the *individuals* above named predecease me, then their share of my estate shall go to their [descendants] surviving."

First, John refers to his friends as individuals. Second, he requests that they receive his property "in equal shares, share and share alike." Third, he states that if one individual predeceases him, his or her share "shall go to their [descendants] surviving." In this regard, it is important to point out that married couples may have different descendants.

We determine that the testator's intent is clearly expressed within the four corners of the document. We are bound by the unambiguous language of the will. * * *

* * * *

The structure and language of the clause * * * convince us that John intended to leave one share to Douglas Olson, one share to Fern Olson, one share to William Hollister, and one share to Shirley Hollister. Therefore, we affirm the trial court's order to distribute the estate in sixteen equal shares.

QUESTIONS

1. What method of analysis did the court use in resolving the dispute in this case?
2. Would the result in this case have been different if the will referred to the Olsons as "Mr. and Mrs. Olson" instead of "Douglas Olson and Fern Olson"? Explain.

WRITING REQUIREMENTS Generally, a will must be in writing. The writing itself can be informal as long as it substantially complies with the statutory requirements. In some states, a will can be handwritten in crayon or ink. It can be written on a sheet or scrap of paper, on a paper bag, or on a piece of cloth. A will that is completely in the handwriting of the testator is called a **holographic will** (sometimes referred to as an *olographic will*).

A **nuncupative will** is an oral will made before witnesses. It is not permitted in most states. Where authorized by statute, such wills are generally valid only if made during the last illness of the testator and are therefore sometimes referred to as *deathbed wills*. Normally, only personal property can be transferred by a nuncupative will. Statutes frequently permit soldiers and sailors to make nuncupative wills when on active duty.

SIGNATURE REQUIREMENTS A fundamental requirement for a valid will is that the testator's signature appear on the will, generally at the end of the document. Each jurisdiction dictates by statute and court decision what constitutes a signature. Initials, an X or other mark, and words such as "Mom" have all

been upheld as valid when it was shown that the testators *intended* them to be signatures.

WITNESS REQUIREMENTS A will normally must be attested (sworn to) by two, and sometimes three, witnesses. The number of witnesses, their qualifications, and the manner in which the witnessing must be done are generally set out in a statute. A witness may be required to be disinterested—that is, not a beneficiary under the will. The UPC, however, provides that a will is valid even if it is attested by an interested witness [UPC 2–505]. There are no age requirements for witnesses, but witnesses must be mentally competent.

The purpose of witnesses is to verify that the testator actually executed (signed) the will and had the requisite intent and capacity at the time. A witness need not read the contents of the will. Usually, the testator and all witnesses must sign in the sight or the presence of one another, but there are exceptions.[4] The UPC deems it sufficient if the testator acknowledges her or his signature to the witnesses [UPC 2–502]. The UPC

---

4. See, for example, *Slack v. Truitt*, 368 Md. 2, 791 A.2d 129 (2000).

does not require all parties to sign in the presence of one another.

PUBLICATION REQUIREMENTS The maker of a will *publishes* the will by orally declaring to the witnesses that the document they are about to sign is his or her "last will and testament." Publication is becoming an unnecessary formality in most states, and it is not required under the UPC.

REVOCATION OF WILLS

An executed will is revocable by the maker at any time during the maker's lifetime. The maker may revoke a will by a physical act, such as tearing up the will, or by a subsequent writing. Wills can also be revoked by operation of law. Revocation can be partial or complete, and it must follow certain strict formalities.

REVOCATION BY A PHYSICAL ACT OF THE MAKER The testator may revoke a will by intentionally burning, tearing, canceling, obliterating, or destroying it or by having someone else do so in the presence of the maker and at the maker's direction.[5] In some states, partial revocation by physical act of the maker is recognized. Thus, those portions of a will lined out or torn away are dropped, and the remaining parts of the will are valid. At no time, however, can a provision be crossed out and an additional or substitute provision written in. Such altered portions require reexecution (signing again) and reattestation (rewitnessing).

To revoke a will by physical act, it is necessary to follow the mandates of a state statute exactly. When a state statute prescribes the specific methods for revoking a will by physical act, those are the only methods that will revoke the will.

If the original copy of a will cannot be found after the testator's death, it is generally presumed that the testator must have destroyed it with the intent to revoke it. Whether the testator had destroyed the original copy of her will was at issue in the following case.

---

5. The destruction cannot be inadvertent. The maker's intent to revoke must be shown. When a will has been burned or torn accidentally, it is normally recommended that the maker have a new document created so that it will not falsely appear that the maker intended to revoke the will.

CASE 50.2	**In re Estate of Pallister**

Supreme Court of
South Carolina, 2005.
363 S.C. 437.
611 S.E.2d 250.
http://www.judicial.state.
sc.us/opinions/indexPub.cfm[a]

BACKGROUND AND FACTS *Mary Pallister grew up in South Carolina, but spent most of the last two decades of her life in New Mexico, where she executed two wills. The beneficiaries of both wills included her husband's sister, Ruth Diem, and Diem's daughter, Ann Patton. Pallister had been close friends with Diem for more than fifty years, and maintained a similar relationship with Patton. After Pallister's husband died, she moved to Methodist Manor in Florence, South Carolina, near the family of her brother's son, James Reames. In 1999, Pallister executed a new will, expressly revoking the others. The beneficiaries were again Diem and Patton. James was named to inherit the estate if Diem and Patton died before Pallister. Otherwise, he would inherit nothing. In March 2001, Pallister was admitted to a hospital and died the next month, leaving an estate with a value of more than $1.4 million. The original copy of the 1999 will could not be found. Diem and Patton petitioned a South Carolina probate court to accept a copy of the original. James and others opposed the petition, arguing that because the original could not be found, Pallister must have destroyed it with an intent to revoke it.[b] A jury issued a verdict in the petitioners' (Diem and Patton's) favor. The opponents appealed. The South Carolina Supreme Court agreed to review the case.*

IN THE LANGUAGE OF THE COURT

 Justice BURNETT.

* * * *

* * * *The person asserting that an original will was, in fact, valid but mistakenly lost or destroyed by another, bears the burden of presenting clear and convincing evidence to rebut the presumption the testator destroyed the will with an intent to revoke it.* [Emphasis added.]

---

a. In the left-hand column, in the "Supreme Court" section, click on "2005." On the next page, click on "March." In the result, scroll to the name of the case and click on the appropriate link to access the opinion. The South Carolina Judicial Department maintains this Web site.

b. As explained later in this chapter, if there were no will, Pallister's estate would be distributed according to the applicable intestacy laws. In that circumstance, James would inherit part of the estate.

CONTINUED ►

CASE 50.2 | Continued

* * * *

It is undisputed the 1999 will was valid upon execution. The attorney testified she delivered the original will to Testatrix [Pallister] and James testified he saw it in her apartment two to three months before her death. The * * * beneficiaries of the will were the same persons Testatrix had named in her wills since 1983—Diem and Patton. The record contains no evidence Testatrix expressed any desire to change or revoke her will in order not to pass assets to Diem and Patton; nor is there any evidence Testatrix grew unhappy or displeased with them in any way. The record contains clear and convincing evidence upon which the jury may have relied in determining the original will existed at Testatrix's death.

Testatrix previously had kept her wills in a safe deposit box. * * * Testatrix usually was an organized, "by the books" person who regularly maintained files containing current and past financial and investment documents. Some of those documents were transported in a bag to and from the hospital on several occasions in the month preceding her death. Some of her belongings were moved from an independent living unit to an assisted living unit at the Methodist Manor in the last weeks of her life. Diem and Patton found Testatrix's apartment in an unusually disorganized and unkempt state after her death.

In addition, Testatrix regularly had consulted professionals—lawyers, accountants, and stockbrokers—throughout her life when making important decisions and preparing significant documents. The jury may have reasoned that if Testatrix had wanted to revoke her 1999 will, it is not likely she would have torn it up or discarded it. Instead, it is far more likely she would have consulted the lawyer who had drafted the will to make other arrangements. The record contains clear and convincing evidence upon which the jury may have relied in determining the original 1999 will was misplaced or lost during Testatrix's final illness and frequent moves.

Moreover, James knew about the will and admitted he was displeased with its terms. He telephoned Testatrix's attorney to complain about it and accused her of convincing Testatrix to leave everything to Diem and Patton. He had unfettered access to Testatrix's apartment, knew where she kept financial and investment records, and by his own testimony spent days on end there as Testatrix's health worsened. He had access to Testatrix's apartment for eleven days while she was hospitalized shortly before her death.

The mere fact James, who would benefit financially were the will revoked, had access to Testatrix's missing will is not, standing alone, sufficient to rebut the presumption Testatrix herself revoked it by destroying it. However, in addition to the evidence of Testatrix's practice of keeping careful records and consulting professionals, the record reveals more than motive to destroy the will and opportunity to do so by a third party.

* * * James transferred about $713,000 in assets from Decedent to himself on the day she re-entered the hospital—three days before her death—after obtaining her signature on necessary bank and brokerage forms.

James testified several people were in the room during a half-hour signature session. [A Methodist Manor employee who was a] notary public testified only he, James, and Testatrix were present during a five-minute period. When questioned by Diem and Patton about the transfers and the location of Testatrix's original 1999 will after Testatrix's death, James told them he had never seen the will. The record contains clear and convincing evidence upon which the jury may have relied in determining a third party destroyed the will without Testatrix's consent or knowledge.

DECISION AND REMEDY   *The South Carolina Supreme Court affirmed the decision of the lower court, which had accepted for probate a copy of Pallister's will despite the loss of the original. The state supreme court ruled that "clear and convincing" evidence supported the conclusion that the original existed at the time of Pallister's death, and had been lost after her death or destroyed by a third party without her knowledge or consent.*

WHAT IF THE FACTS WERE DIFFERENT?   *Suppose that shortly before Pallister's death, she had asked James to tear up her will, and he had done it. Would the result have been different?*

REVOCATION BY A SUBSEQUENT WRITING A will may also be wholly or partially revoked by a **codicil,** a written instrument separate from the will that amends or revokes provisions in the will. A codicil eliminates the necessity of redrafting an entire will merely to add to it or amend it. A codicil can also be used to revoke an entire will. The codicil must be executed with the same formalities required for a will, and it must refer expressly to the will. In effect, it updates a will because the will is "incorporated by reference" into the codicil.

A new will (second will) can be executed that may or may not revoke the first or a prior will, depending on the language used. To revoke a prior will, the second will must use language specifically revoking other wills, such as, "This will hereby revokes all prior wills." If the second will is otherwise valid and properly executed, it will revoke all prior wills. If the express *declaration of revocation* is missing, then both wills are read together. If any of the dispositions made in the second will are inconsistent with the prior will, the second will controls.

REVOCATION BY OPERATION OF LAW Revocation by operation of law occurs when marriage, divorce or annulment, or the birth of a child takes place after a will has been executed. In most states, when a testator marries after executing a will that does not include the new spouse, on the testator's death the spouse can still receive the amount he or she would have taken had the testator died intestate (how an intestate's property is distributed under state laws will be discussed shortly). In effect, this revokes the will to the point of providing the spouse with an intestate share. The rest of the estate is passed under the will [UPC 2–301, 2–508]. If, however, the new spouse is otherwise provided for in the will (or by transfer of property outside the will), the new spouse will not be given an intestate amount.

At common law and under the UPC, divorce does not necessarily revoke the entire will. A divorce or an annulment occurring after a will has been executed will revoke those dispositions of property made under the will to the former spouse [UPC 2–508].

If a child is born after a will has been executed and if it appears that the deceased parent would have made a provision for the child, then the child is entitled to receive whatever portion of the estate she or he is allowed under state laws providing for the distribution of an intestate's property. Most state laws allow a child to receive some portion of a parent's estate if no pro-

vision is made in the parent's will, unless it appears from the terms of the will that the testator intended to disinherit the child. Under the UPC, the rule is the same.

RIGHTS UNDER A WILL

The law imposes certain limitations on the way a person can dispose of property in a will. For example, a married person who makes a will generally cannot avoid leaving a certain portion of the estate to the surviving spouse. In most states, this is called an elective share, a forced share, or a widow's (or widower's) share, and it is often one-third of the estate or an amount equal to a spouse's share under intestacy laws.

Beneficiaries under a will have rights as well. A beneficiary can renounce (disclaim) his or her share of the property given under a will. Further, a surviving spouse can renounce the amount given under a will and elect to take the forced share when the forced share is larger than the amount of the gift—this is the widow's (or widower's) election, or right of election. State statutes provide the methods by which a surviving spouse accomplishes renunciation. The purpose of these statutes is to allow the spouse to obtain whichever distribution would be more advantageous. The revised UPC gives the surviving spouse an elective right to take a percentage of the total estate determined by the length of time that the spouse and the decedent were married to each other [UPC 2–201].

PROBATE PROCEDURES

Typically, probate procedures vary, depending on the size of the decedent's estate.

INFORMAL PROBATE PROCEEDINGS For smaller estates, most state statutes provide for the distribution of assets without formal probate proceedings. Faster and less expensive methods are then used. For example, property can be transferred by affidavit (a written statement taken in the presence of a person who has authority to affirm it), and problems or questions can be handled during an administrative hearing. In addition, some state statutes provide that title to cars, savings and checking accounts, and certain other property can be passed merely by filling out forms.

A majority of states also provide for family settlement agreements, which are private agreements among the beneficiaries. Once a will is admitted to probate, the family members can agree to settle among themselves the distribution of the decedent's assets. Although a family settlement agreement speeds the settlement process, a court order is still needed to protect the estate from future creditors and to clear title to the assets involved. The use of these and other types of summary procedures in estate administration can save time and money.

FORMAL PROBATE PROCEEDINGS For larger estates, formal probate proceedings are normally undertaken, and the probate court supervises every aspect of the settlement of the decedent's estate. Additionally, in some situations—such as when a guardian for minor children or for an incompetent person must be appointed and a trust has been created to protect the minor or the incompetent person—more formal probate procedures cannot be avoided. Formal probate proceedings may take several months to complete, and as a result, a sizable portion of the decedent's assets (up to perhaps 10 percent) may go toward payment of fees charged by attorneys and personal representatives, as well as court costs.

PROPERTY TRANSFERS OUTSIDE THE PROBATE PROCESS

Commonly, beneficiaries under a will must wait until the probate process is complete—which can take several months if formal probate proceedings are undertaken—to have access to money or other assets received under the will. For this and other reasons, some persons arrange to have property transferred in ways other than by will and outside the probate process.

METHODS OF TRANSFERRING PROPERTY One method of accomplishing a property transfer is by establishing a living trust, as discussed later in this chapter. Another method is through the joint ownership of property. For example, a person can arrange to hold title to certain real or personal property as a joint tenant with a spouse or other person. Recall from Chapter 47 that in a joint tenancy, when one joint tenant dies, the other joint tenant or tenants automatically inherit the deceased tenant's share of the property. This is true even if the deceased tenant has provided otherwise in her or his will.

Yet another way of transferring property outside the probate process is by making gifts to children or others while one is still living. Additionally, to make sure that a spouse, child, or some other dependent is provided for, many people take out life insurance policies. On the death of the policyholder, the proceeds of the policy go directly to the beneficiary and are not involved in the probate process. The balance in an Individual Retirement Account (IRA) may also pass to a named beneficiary without being involved in the probate process.

THE NEED FOR CAUTION In all of these situations, the person who sets up a living trust, arranges for a joint tenancy, takes out an insurance policy, or names a beneficiary for an IRA should pay careful attention to ensure that the arrangement will benefit the intended person. A court will not apply the same principles in reviewing a transfer outside probate as it would apply to a testamentary transfer, as the following case indicates.

CASE 50.3 | **Bielat v. Bielat**

Supreme Court of Ohio, 2000. 87 Ohio St.3d 350, 721 N.E.2d 28.

BACKGROUND AND FACTS *In 1983, Chester Bielat opened an Individual Retirement Account (IRA) with Merrill Lynch, Pierce, Fenner & Smith, Inc. In the "Adoption Agreement" that he signed to open the account, Chester named his sister, Stella, as the beneficiary of the account on his death. Later, Chester executed a will that gave all of his property to his wife, Dorothy, on his death. In 1993, Ohio enacted its version of the Uniform Transfer-on-Death Security Registration Act, which provided that "[a]ny transfer-on-death resulting from a registration in beneficiary form * * * is not testamentary." This exempted such transfers from the formalities that apply to transfers of property under a will. The act applied to registrations in beneficiary forms made "prior to, on, or after the effective date of this section." After Chester's death in 1996, Dorothy discovered that Stella was the beneficiary of the IRA. Dorothy filed a complaint in an Ohio state court against Stella, claiming that Dorothy was entitled to the IRA. She argued in part that because the state constitution prohibited the legislature from passing retroactive laws and protected "vested rights" from "new legislative encroachments," the act did not apply to Chester's IRA beneficiary clause. Dorothy asserted that the court should apply the law in effect when Chester executed his will, which, according to Dorothy, would void*

CASE 50.3 | Continued *the designation of Stella as the beneficiary of the IRA. Stella responded with a motion to dismiss, which the court granted. Dorothy appealed to a state intermediate appellate court, which affirmed the lower court's judgment. Dorothy appealed to the Ohio Supreme Court.*

IN THE LANGUAGE OF THE COURT

COOK, J. [Justice]

* * * *

Dorothy cannot claim a vested right to the proceeds of the IRA under the law of contracts, for she was in no way connected to the IRA Adoption Agreement that Mr. Bielat executed with Merrill Lynch. * * * The Adoption Agreement signed by Mr. Bielat and Merrill Lynch placed valid contractual obligations upon them, with Merrill Lynch bound to pay the IRA balance to the beneficiary that Chester designated. The IRA Adoption Agreement created no rights or obligations for Dorothy. Dorothy thus had no vested contractual right impaired by the retroactive application of the disputed statutes; she had no contractual rights to impair.

Likewise, at the time of the [Uniform Transfer-on-Death Security Registration] Act's effective date, Dorothy had no vested right to the IRA proceeds as the sole beneficiary under Chester's will. * * * *Until a will has been probated, the legatee under such will has no rights whatever. A mere expectation of property in the future is not a vested right.* * * * If Dorothy had no vested rights in the contract that Mr. Bielat executed with Merrill Lynch, and no vested rights in Chester's probate estate until his death, then the Act did not impair any vested rights of hers when it applied retrospectively to validate the pay-on-death beneficiary clause in Chester's preexisting contract with Merrill Lynch. [Emphasis added.]

* * * *

* * * Dorothy [also] submits that to resolve this dispute, we should apply the law in effect at the time Mr. Bielat executed his will, since that is the law that frames the intent of the testator. Dorothy argues that since Chester executed his will prior to the existence of the Act, he must have done so with the expectation that the designation of Stella as the transfer-on-death beneficiary of his IRA was void, since the Act was not yet in place to explicitly validate it. * * * [This argument] represents a correct statement of the law of interpreting wills, but we are not interpreting Chester's will in this case. This is not a will contest action, where the true intent of the testator may be at the heart of the dispute, nor is it a situation where an unclear testamentary provision requires construction by the court. Rather, we are faced with two equally unambiguous acts by Mr. Bielat: (1) the designation of his sister Stella as the beneficiary of his IRA in his contract with Merrill Lynch, and (2) the clause in his will leaving all of his property to Dorothy.

DECISION AND REMEDY *The Ohio Supreme Court affirmed the judgment of the state intermediate appellate court. The state supreme court reasoned that Dorothy's rights were not impaired by the state's version of the Uniform Transfer-on-Death Security Registration Act because she had no right to the IRA proceeds or to Chester's estate before he died. The court also explained that because the case did not involve the interpretation of a will, the principles that govern interpretation of wills did not apply.*

SECTION 2 | Intestacy Laws

Each state regulates by statute how property will be distributed when a person dies intestate (without a valid will). These statutes are called statutes of descent and distribution—or, more simply, intestacy laws, as mentioned in this chapter's introduction. Intestacy laws attempt to carry out the likely intent and wishes of the decedent. These laws assume that deceased persons would have intended that their natural heirs (spouses, children, grandchildren, or other family members) inherit their property. Therefore, intestacy statutes set out rules and priorities under which these heirs inherit the property. If no heirs exist, the state will assume ownership of the property.

The rules of descent vary widely from state to state. It is thus extremely important to refer to the exact

CONCEPT SUMMARY 50.1 | Wills

CONCEPT	DESCRIPTION
TERMINOLOGY	1. *Intestate*—Describes one who dies without a valid will. 2. *Testator*—A person who makes a will. 3. *Personal representative*—A person appointed in a will or by a court to settle the affairs of a decedent. A personal representative named in the will is an *executor*; a personal representative appointed by the court for an intestate decedent is an *administrator*. 4. *Devise*—A gift of real estate by will; may be general or specific. The recipient of a devise is a *devisee*. 5. *Bequest, or legacy*—A gift of personal property by will; may be general or specific. The recipient of a bequest (legacy) is a *legatee*.
REQUIREMENTS FOR A VALID WILL	1. The testator must have testamentary capacity (be of legal age and sound mind at the time the will is made). 2. A will must be in writing (except for nuncupative wills). 3. A will must be signed by the testator; what constitutes a signature varies from jurisdiction to jurisdiction. 4. A nonholographic will normally must be witnessed in the manner prescribed by state statute. 5. A will may have to be *published*—that is, the testator may be required to announce to witnesses that this is his or her "last will and testament." Not required under the UPC.

REVOCATION OF WILLS	1. *By physical act of the maker*—Tearing up, canceling, obliterating, or deliberately destroying part or all of a will.
	2. *By subsequent writing*—
	    a. Codicil—A formal, separate document that amends or revokes an existing will.
	    b. Second will, or new will—A new, properly executed will expressly revoking the existing will.
	3. *By operation of law*—
	    a. Marriage—Generally revokes a will written before the marriage to the extent of providing for the spouse.
	    b. Divorce or annulment—Revokes dispositions of property made to the former spouse under a will made before the divorce or annulment.
	    c. Subsequently born child—It is inferred that the child is entitled to receive the portion of the estate granted under intestacy distribution laws.

PROBATE PROCEDURES	To *probate* a will means to establish its validity and to carry out the administration of the estate through a court process. Probate laws vary from state to state. Probate procedures may be informal or formal, depending on the size of the estate and other factors, such as whether a guardian for minor children must be appointed.

terms of the applicable state statutes when addressing any problem of intestacy distribution.

SURVIVING SPOUSE AND CHILDREN

Usually, state statutes provide for the rights of the surviving spouse and children. In addition, the law provides that first the debts of the decedent must be satisfied out of the estate, and then the remaining assets can pass to the surviving spouse and the chil-dren. A surviving spouse usually receives only a share of the estate—one-half if there is also a surviving child and one-third if there are two or more children. Only if no children or grandchildren survive the decedent will a surviving spouse receive the entire estate.

Assume that Allen dies intestate and is survived by his wife, Betty, and his children, Duane and Tara. Allen's property passes according to intestacy laws. After Allen's outstanding debts are paid, Betty will receive the homestead (either in fee simple or as a life estate) and ordinarily a one-third to one-half interest in all other property. The remaining real and personal property will pass to Duane and Tara in equal portions. Under most state intestacy laws and under the UPC, in-laws do not share in an estate. If a child dies before his or her parents, the child's spouse will not receive an inheritance on the parents' death. For example, if Duane died before his father (Allen), Duane's spouse would not inherit Duane's share of Allen's estate.

When there is no surviving spouse or child, the order of inheritance is grandchildren, then parents of the decedent. These relatives are usually called *lineal descendants*. If there are no lineal descendants, then *collateral heirs*—brothers, sisters, nieces, nephews, aunts, and uncles of the decedent—make up the next group to share. If there are no survivors in any of these groups, most statutes provide for the property to be distributed among the next of kin of the collateral heirs.

STEPCHILDREN, ADOPTED CHILDREN, AND ILLEGITIMATE CHILDREN

Under intestacy laws, stepchildren are not considered kin. Legally adopted children, however, are recognized as lawful heirs of their adoptive parents. Whether an illegitimate child inherits depends on state statutes. In some states, intestate succession between the father and the child can occur only when the child has been "legitimized" by ceremony or "acknowledged" by the father. Under the revised UPC, the same rule applies to intestate succession between the child and the mother [UPC 2–114]. The United States Supreme Court has allowed state illegitimacy statutes to stand, concluding that they serve legitimate state purposes.[6]

DISTRIBUTION TO GRANDCHILDREN

When a person makes a will, usually the will provides for how the decedent's estate will be distributed to descendants of deceased children (grandchildren). If a will does not include such a provision—or if a person dies intestate—then a question arises as to what share the grandchildren of the decedent will receive. Each state designates one of two methods of distributing the assets of intestate decedents.

Under the *per stirpes* method of dividing an intestate share, a class or group of distributees (for example,

grandchildren) take the share that their deceased parent would have been entitled to inherit had that parent lived. Assume that Moffet, a widower, has two children, Scott and Jillian. Scott has two children (Bonita and Holly), and Jillian has one child (Paul). At the time of Moffet's death, Scott and Jillian have already died. If Moffet's estate is distributed *per stirpes*, the following distribution will take place:

1. Bonita and Holly: one-fourth each, taking Scott's share.
2. Paul: one-half, taking Jillian's share.

Exhibit 50–2 on the following page illustrates the *per stirpes* method of distribution.

An estate may also be distributed on a **per capita** basis. This means that each person takes an equal share of the estate. If Moffet's estate is distributed *per capita*, Bonita, Holly, and Paul will each receive a one-third share. Exhibit 50–3 on the next page illustrates the *per capita* method of distribution.

SECTION 3 | Trusts

A **trust** involves any arrangement by which legal title to property is transferred from one person to be administered by a trustee for another's benefit. It can also be defined as a right of property (real or personal) held by one party for the benefit of another. A trust can be created for any purpose that is not illegal or against public policy. As mentioned, trusts are important estate-planning devices for several reasons. These reasons will become clear as you read through this section.

ESSENTIAL ELEMENTS OF A TRUST

The essential elements of a trust are as follows:

1. A designated beneficiary.
2. A designated trustee.
3. A fund sufficiently identified to enable title to pass to the trustee.
4. Actual delivery to the trustee with the intention of passing title.

If Shanahan conveys his farm to First Bank of Minnesota to be held for the benefit of his daughters, Shanahan has created a trust. Shanahan is the settlor, or grantor (the one creating the trust), First Bank of Minnesota is the trustee, and Shanahan's daughters are the beneficiaries. This arrangement is illustrated in Exhibit 50–4 on page 1019.

---

6. In a landmark ruling in *Trimble v. Gordon*, 430 U.S. 762, 97 S.Ct. 1459, 52 L.Ed.2d 31 (1977), however, the United States Supreme Court ruled that an Illinois illegitimacy statute was unconstitutional because it did not bear a rational relationship to a legitimate state purpose.

EXHIBIT 50-2 *Per Stirpes* **Distribution**

Under this method of distribution, an heir takes the share that his or her deceased parent would have been entitled to inherit, had the parent lived. This may mean that a class of distributees—the grandchildren, in this example—will not inherit in equal portions. (Note that Bonita and Holly receive only one-fourth of Moffet's estate, whereas Paul inherits one-half.)

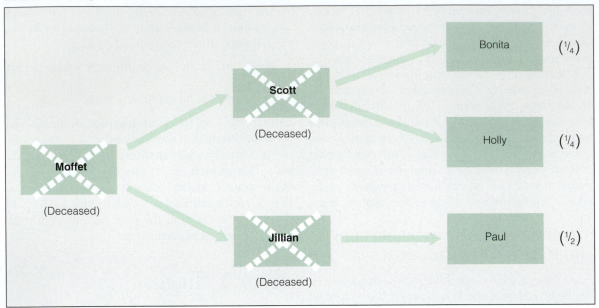

EXHIBIT 50-3 *Per Capita* **Distribution**

Under this method of distribution, all heirs in a certain class—in this case, the grandchildren—inherit equally. Note that Bonita and Holly in this situation each inherit one-third of Moffet's estate (not one-fourth, as they do under the *per stirpes* method of distribution).

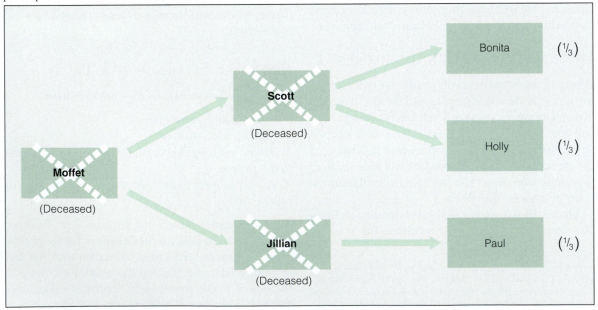

EXHIBIT 50-4 Trust Arrangement

In a trust, there is a separation of interests in the trust property. The trustee takes *legal* title, which appears to be complete ownership and possession but which does not include the right to receive any benefits from the property. The beneficiary takes *equitable* title, which is the right to receive all benefits from the property.

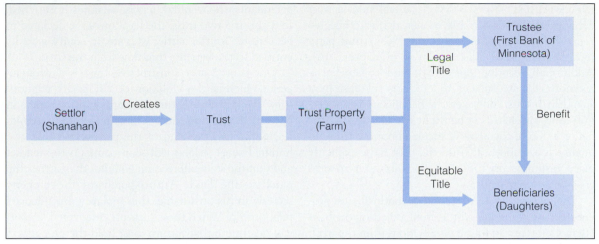

EXPRESS TRUSTS

An express trust is one that is created or declared in explicit terms, usually in writing. There are numerous types of express trusts, each with its own special characteristics.

LIVING TRUSTS   A living trust—or ***inter vivos* trust** (*inter vivos* is Latin for "between or among the living")—is a trust executed by a grantor during her or his lifetime. A living trust may be an attractive estate-planning option because living trusts are not included in the property of a decedent's estate that is probated.

Living trusts can be irrevocable or revocable. The distinction between these two types of trusts is an important one for estate planners. In an *irrevocable* living trust, the grantor permanently gives up control over the property. In a *revocable* living trust, in contrast, the grantor retains control over the trust property during his or her lifetime.

To establish an irrevocable living trust, the grantor executes a trust deed, and legal title to the trust property passes to the named trustee. The trustee has a duty to administer the property as directed by the grantor for the benefit and in the interest of the beneficiaries. The trustee must preserve the trust property; make it productive; and, if required by the terms of the trust agreement, pay income to the beneficiaries, all in accordance with the terms of the trust. Once an irrevocable *inter vivos* trust has been created, the grantor

has, in effect, given over the property for the benefit of the beneficiaries.

To establish a revocable living trust, the grantor deeds the property to the trust but retains the power to amend, alter, or revoke the trust during her or his lifetime. The grantor may also arrange to receive income earned by the trust assets during her or his lifetime. Unless the trust is revoked, the principal of the trust is transferred to the trust beneficiary on the grantor's death.

TESTAMENTARY TRUSTS   A **testamentary trust** is created by will to come into existence on the settlor's death. Although a testamentary trust has a trustee who maintains legal title to the trust property, actions of the trustee are subject to judicial approval. This trustee can be named in the will or appointed by the court. Thus, a testamentary trust does not fail if the will does not name a trustee. The legal responsibilities of the trustee are the same as in an *inter vivos* trust.

If the will setting up a testamentary trust is invalid, then the trust will also be invalid. The property that was supposed to be in the trust will then pass according to intestacy laws, not according to the terms of the trust.

CHARITABLE TRUSTS   A **charitable trust** is designed for the benefit of a segment of the public or the public in general. It differs from other types of trusts in that the identities of the beneficiaries are uncertain. Usually, to be deemed a charitable trust, a trust must be created for charitable, educational, religious, or scientific purposes.

SPENDTHRIFT TRUSTS As a general rule, a trust beneficiary may assign his or her rights to receive the principal or income of a trust to a third party (assignments are discussed in Chapter 16). Additionally, distributions of trust funds to beneficiaries normally are subject to creditors' claims. In a **spendthrift trust,** however, the beneficiary is not permitted to transfer his or her right to the trust's principal or to future payments of income from the trust. To qualify as a spendthrift trust, the trust must explicitly place restraints on the alienation—transfer to others—of the trust funds.

The majority of states enforce spendthrift trust provisions that prohibit creditors from attaching the beneficiary's interest in future distributions from the trust. State laws provide for some exceptions, however. For example, a divorced spouse or a minor child of the beneficiary may be permitted to obtain alimony or child-support payments. Additionally, creditors that have provided *necessaries* (see Chapter 13) to spendthrift trust recipients normally can compel payment from the trust income or principal.

TOTTEN TRUSTS A **Totten trust,**[7] or tentative trust, is a special type of trust that is created when one person deposits funds in her or his own name as a trustee for another. This trust is tentative in that it is revocable at will until the depositor dies or completes the gift in her or his lifetime by some unequivocal act or declaration (for example, delivery of the funds to the intended beneficiary). If the depositor dies before the beneficiary dies and if the depositor has not revoked the trust expressly or impliedly, a presumption arises that an absolute (binding, irrevocable) trust has been created for the benefit of the beneficiary. At the death of the depositor, the beneficiary obtains property rights to the balance on hand.

IMPLIED TRUSTS

Sometimes, a trust is imposed by law, even in the absence of an express trust. Customarily, these implied trusts are characterized as either constructive trusts or resulting trusts.

CONSTRUCTIVE TRUSTS A **constructive trust** arises by operation of law in the interests of equity and fairness. A constructive trust enables plaintiffs to recover property (and sometimes damages) from defendants who would otherwise be unjustly enriched. In a constructive trust, the legal owner is declared to be a trustee for the parties who are, in equity, actually entitled to the benefits that flow from the trust.

One source of a constructive trust is a wrongful action, such as the violation of a fiduciary relationship. To illustrate: Arturo and Spring are partners in buying, developing, and selling real estate. Arturo learns through the staff of the partnership that two hundred acres of land will soon come on the market and that the staff will recommend that the partnership purchase the land. Arturo purchases the property secretly in his own name, thus violating his fiduciary relationship. When these facts are discovered, a court will determine that Arturo must hold the property in trust for the partnership.

RESULTING TRUSTS A **resulting trust** arises from the conduct of the parties. Here, the trust results, or is created, when circumstances raise an inference that the party holding legal title to the property does so for the benefit of another, unless the inference is refuted or the beneficial interest is otherwise disposed of.

To illustrate: Glenda wants to put one acre of land she owns on the market for sale. Because she is going out of the country for two years and will not be available to deed the property to a buyer during that period, she conveys the property to her good friend Oscar. Oscar can then sell and deed the property, with the proceeds to be turned over to Glenda. Because Glenda's intent in deeding the property to Oscar is neither a sale nor a gift, the property will be held in a resulting trust by Oscar (as trustee) for the benefit of Glenda. Therefore, on Glenda's return, Oscar will be required either to deed back the property to Glenda or, if the property has been sold, to turn over the proceeds (held in trust) to her.

THE TRUSTEE

The trustee is the person holding the trust property. Anyone legally capable of holding title to, and dealing in, property can be a trustee. If the settlor of a trust fails to name a trustee, or if a named trustee cannot or will not serve, the trust does not fail—an appropriate court can appoint a trustee.

---

7. This type of trust derives its unusual name from *In the Matter of Totten,* 179 N.Y. 112, 71 N.E. 748 (1904).

CONCEPT SUMMARY 50.2 | Trusts

CONCEPT	DESCRIPTION
DEFINITION AND ESSENTIAL ELEMENTS	A trust is any arrangement by which property is transferred from one person to be administered by a trustee for another's benefit. The essential elements of a trust are (1) a designated beneficiary, (2) a designated trustee, (3) a fund sufficiently identified to enable title to pass to the trustee, and (4) actual delivery to the trustee with the intention of passing title.
TYPES OF TRUSTS	1. *Living (inter vivos) trust*—A trust executed by a grantor during his or her lifetime. A living trust may be revocable or irrevocable. 2. *Testamentary trust*—A trust created by will and coming into existence on the death of the grantor. 3. *Charitable trust*—A trust designed for the benefit of a public group or the public in general. 4. *Spendthrift trust*—A trust created to provide for the maintenance of a beneficiary by allowing only a certain portion of the total amount to be received by the beneficiary at any one time. 5. *Totten trust*—A trust created when one person deposits money in his or her own name as a trustee for another.
IMPLIED TRUSTS	Implied trusts, which are imposed by law in the interests of fairness and justice, include the following: 1. *Constructive trust*—Arises by operation of law whenever a transaction takes place in which the person who takes title to property is, in equity, not entitled to enjoy the beneficial interest therein. 2. *Resulting trust*—Arises from the conduct of the parties when an *apparent intention* to create a trust is present.

TRUSTEE'S DUTIES A trustee must act with honesty, good faith, and prudence in administering the trust and must exercise a high degree of loyalty toward the trust beneficiary. The general standard of care is the degree of care a prudent person would exercise in his or her personal affairs.[8] The duty of loyalty requires that the trustee act in the exclusive interest of the beneficiary.

Among specific duties, a trustee must keep clear and accurate accounts of the trust's administration and furnish complete and correct information to the beneficiary. A trustee must keep trust assets separate from her or his own assets. A trustee has a duty to pay to an income beneficiary the net income of the trust assets at reasonable intervals. A trustee has a duty to distribute the risk of loss from investments by reasonable diversification and a duty to dispose of assets that do not represent prudent investments. Investments in federal, state, or municipal bonds; corporate bonds;

and shares of preferred or common stock may be prudent investments under particular circumstances.

TRUSTEE'S POWERS When a settlor creates a trust, he or she may prescribe the trustee's powers and performance. Generally, state law[9] applies in the absence of specific terms in the trust.[10] When state law does apply, it is most likely to restrict the trustee's investment of trust funds. Typically, statutes confine trustees to investments in conservative debt securities such as government, utility, and railroad bonds and first-mortgage loans on realty. It is common, however, for a settlor to grant a trustee discretionary investment power. In that circumstance, any statute may be considered only advisory, with the trustee's decisions subject in most states to the prudent person rule.

---

8. Revised Uniform Principal and Income Act, Section 2(a)(3); *Restatement (Third) of Trusts*, Section 227. This rule is in force in the majority of states by statute and in a small number of states under the common law.

9. The Uniform Principal and Income Act, which was originally published in 1931, substantially revised in 1962, and amended in 2000, has been adopted in forty-one states. Other uniform acts may also apply—for instance, about a third of the states have enacted the Uniform Trustees' Powers Act, promulgated in 1964, and about ten states have adopted the Uniform Trust Code, set forth in 2000.
10. Revised Uniform Principal and Income Act Section 2(a)(1); *Restatement (Second) of Trusts*, Section 164.

A difficult question concerns the extent of a trustee's discretion to "invade" the principal and distribute it to an income beneficiary, if the income is found to be insufficient to provide for the beneficiary in an appropriate manner. A similar question concerns the extent of a trustee's discretion to retain trust income and add it to the principal, if the income is found to be more than sufficient to provide for the beneficiary in an appropriate manner. Generally, the answer to both questions is that the income beneficiary should be provided with a somewhat predictable annual income, but with a view to the safety of the principal. Thus, a trustee may make individualized adjustments in annual distributions.

Of course, a trustee is responsible for carrying out the purposes of the trust. If the trustee fails to comply with the terms of the trust or the controlling statute, he or she is personally liable for any loss.

ALLOCATIONS BETWEEN PRINCIPAL AND INCOME Frequently, a settlor will provide one beneficiary with a life estate and another beneficiary with the remainder interest in a trust. A farmer, for example, may create a testamentary trust providing that the farm's income be paid to her surviving spouse (the income beneficiary) and that on the surviving spouse's death, the remainder interest (the farm) be given to their children (the principal beneficiaries). Among the income and principal beneficiaries, questions may arise concerning the apportionment of receipts and expenses for the farm's management, as well as the trust's administration between income and principal. Even when the income and principal beneficiaries are the same, these questions may come up.

When a trust instrument does not provide instructions, a trustee must refer to applicable state law. The general rule is that ordinary receipts and expenses are chargeable to the income beneficiary, whereas extraordinary receipts and expenses are allocated to the principal beneficiaries.[11] To illustrate: The receipt of rent from trust realty would be ordinary, as would the expense of paying the property's taxes. The cost of long-term improvements and proceeds from the property's sale, however, would be extraordinary.

TRUST TERMINATION

The terms of a trust should expressly state the event on which the settlor wishes it to terminate—for exam-

ple, the beneficiary's or the trustee's death. If the trust instrument does not provide for termination on the beneficiary's death, the beneficiary's death will not end the trust. Similarly, without an express provision, a trust will not terminate on the trustee's death.

Typically, a trust instrument specifies a termination date. For example, a trust created to educate the settlor's child may provide that the trust ends when the beneficiary reaches the age of twenty-five. If the trust's purpose is fulfilled before that date, a court may order the trust's termination. If no date is specified, a trust will terminate when its purpose has been fulfilled. Of course, if a trust's purpose becomes impossible or illegal, the trust will terminate.

SECTION 4 | Elder Law

In the past, elderly people sought legal assistance primarily for estate-planning purposes, in preparation for their deaths. Today, an increasing percentage of Americans are reaching retirement age, and elderly persons are facing the need to prepare for other possibilities—that they will become incapacitated, for example, or will have to depend on others for their health care and basic needs.

The aging of the U.S. population, a trend that will continue for decades to come, has led to a new legal specialty—elder law. Basically, **elder law** is a legal practice area in which attorneys assist older persons and their families in dealing with such problems as disability, long-term health care, age discrimination, grandparents' visitation rights, and other problems relating to age. Here we look at just two aspects of elder law—planning for disability and Medicaid planning.

Note that all persons can be afflicted by disability. Additionally, care for the elderly often falls on the shoulders of adult children. Thus, elder law addresses the needs of older and younger persons alike.

PLANNING FOR DISABILITY

In 1993, Robert Wendland had a motorcycle accident that essentially brought his life as a functional person to an end. Since then, he has lived in a twilight state. He remains conscious but cannot speak to express his wishes due to serious brain damage and cognitive impairment. He is being kept alive through intravenous injections of nutrients and liquids. His wife and legal guardian, Rose, would like to unhook the feeding tubes and let her husband die. She has stated

---

11. Revised Uniform Principal and Income Act, Sections 3, 6, 8, and 13; *Restatement (Second) of Trusts*, Section 233.

that on two occasions prior to his accident, Robert told her that he never wanted to be kept alive if he was nonfunctional. Robert's mother and one of his sisters disagree. To them, Rose's proposal is equivalent to murder. Other family members have lined up on one side or the other of this dispute. When the case reached the California Supreme Court in 2001, the court refused to grant Rose's request because there was no "clear and convincing evidence" that this is what Robert would have wanted.[12]

Time and again, we hear of stories such as this one in which a person becomes disabled—through the sudden onset of disease or through a car accident, for example—and is unable to make vital health-care decisions for himself or herself. Indeed, in 2005, the issue received nationwide attention when the parents of a Florida woman, Terri Schiavo, who was allegedly in a vegetative state from which she could not recover, did not agree with the husband's decision to end her life. Preparing in advance for such situations can significantly ease the problems faced by family members at such times. Additionally, as more and more individuals live into their eighties and nineties, planning for disability is becoming an important part of preparing for future years when decision making may be difficult or impossible.

POWER OF ATTORNEY An important issue in elder law relates to power of attorney. Adult children need to seek power of attorney from their aging parents, particularly if the parents are becoming mentally incompetent or afflicted by Alzheimer's disease. An elder law attorney may help in arranging for the aging parent to sign a power of attorney and other documents, such as a durable power of attorney or a living will (discussed next), that will enable the adult children to take over the parent's affairs if the parent becomes mentally and perhaps physically incapacitated.

DURABLE POWER OF ATTORNEY One method of providing for future disability is to use a durable power of attorney. A **durable power of attorney** authorizes a person to act on behalf of an incompetent person—write checks, collect insurance proceeds, and otherwise manage the disabled person's affairs, including health care—when she or he becomes incapacitated. A person who is advanced in age may give such a power of attorney to an adult child. Often, younger spouses give each other durable power of attorney as well—in the event that they become incapacitated and cannot make decisions for themselves.

HEALTH-CARE POWER OF ATTORNEY A **health-care power of attorney** designates a person who will have the power to choose what type of and how much medical treatment a person who is unable to make such decisions will receive. The health-care power of attorney is growing in importance as medical technology allows physicians and hospitals to keep people technically alive but in a so-called vegetative state for ever-increasing periods of time.

LIVING WILL A similar power is created by what is referred to as a **living will.** A living will is not a will in the usual sense—that is, it does not appoint an estate representative, dispose of property, establish trusts, and so on. Rather, it allows a person to control what medical treatment may be used after a serious accident or illness. Through a living will, a person can indicate whether he or she wants certain lifesaving procedures to be undertaken in situations in which the treatment will not result in a reasonable quality of life.

Most states have enacted statutes permitting living wills, and it is important that the requirements of state law be followed exactly in creating such wills. Typically, state statutes require physicians to abide by the terms of living wills, and living wills are often included with a patient's medical records.

MEDICAID PLANNING

A serious problem facing older persons is the cost of long-term care—in a nursing home, for example. Suppose that a person can no longer look after her or his own needs and either cannot or does not wish to rely on family or friends to provide full-time care. In all likelihood, this person will end up in an assisted-living facility or a nursing home, and such arrangements are costly. Even those who can afford to spend $60,000 or more per year for nursing-home care might prefer to transfer their assets to others, such as their children, and "go on Medicaid" so that the government will pay for the care. One area of elder law addresses Medicaid planning.

MEDICAID VERSUS MEDICARE Medicaid is not the same as Medicare. As you read in Chapter 33, Medicare is a federal program that is financed through

---

12. *Conservatorship of Wendland,* 26 Cal.4th 519, 28 P.3d 151, 110 Cal.Rptr.2d 412 (2001).

the Social Security system and primarily addresses the needs of the elderly. Medicaid, in contrast, is a cooperative federal-state program that provides health-care services to the poor of all ages. Because the program is administered by state agencies, regulations governing Medicaid vary from state to state. At the federal level, Medicaid is administered by the Health Care Financing Administration.

ADVANCE PLANNING FOR MEDICAID When Medicaid pays for long-term care, all of the person's income must be paid to the state. There are exceptions, though, and this is why Medicaid planning can be important. Some assets—such as a home, an auto-

mobile, and certain other property—up to a threshold dollar amount are exempt from Medicaid accounting. Thus, one strategy is for the elderly person to bring down the total value of all of his or her other assets to less than that threshold amount—by spending funds to fix up his or her house or to buy an expensive new car, for example. This practice is often referred to as "spending down" prior to going on Medicaid.

Assets might also be transferred to others, such as children and friends, before applying for Medicaid. A person who makes uncompensated transfers within a certain number of years before applying for Medicaid, however, faces a "penalty period" during which she or he will not qualify for Medicaid.

REVIEWING WILLS, TRUSTS, AND ELDER LAW

In June 2001, Bernard Ramish set up a $48,000 trust fund through West Plains Credit Union to provide tuition for his nephew, Nathan Covacek, to attend Tri-State Polytechnic Institute. The trust was established under Ramish's control and went into effect that August. In December, Ramish suffered a brain aneurysm that caused frequent, severe headaches with no other symptoms. Shortly thereafter, Ramish met with an attorney to formalize in writing that he wanted no artificial life-support systems to be used should he suffer a serious illness. Ramish designated his cousin, Lizzie Johansen, to act on his behalf, including choosing his medical treatment, should he become incapacitated. Ramish made his neighbor, Hank Talbot, the personal representative of his estate. In August 2003, Ramish developed heatstroke and collapsed on the golf course at La Prima Country Club. After recuperating at the clubhouse, Ramish quickly wrote his will on the back of a wine list. It stated, "My last will and testament: Upon my death, I give all of my personal property to my friend Steve Eshom and my home to Lizzie Johansen." He signed the will at the bottom in the presence of five men in the La Prima clubhouse, and all five men signed as witnesses. A week later, Ramish suffered a second aneurysm and died in his sleep. He was survived by his mother, Dorris Ramish; his son-in-law, Bruce Lupin; and his granddaughter, Tori Lupin. Using the information presented in the chapter, answer the following questions.

1. Was Ramish's testamentary gift to Eshom a devise or a bequest? Was it specific or general?

2. Would Ramish's testament on the back of the wine list have met the requirements for a valid will?

3. What would the order of inheritance have been if Ramish had died intestate?

4. Was the trust to Covacek a living, testamentary, charitable, spendthrift, Totten, constructive, or resulting trust? Explain the distinctions. Was it revocable or irrevocable?

5. What were Talbot's duties as the personal representative of Ramish's estate?

6. Was Johansen granted a power of attorney, a durable power of attorney, or a health-care power of attorney for Ramish? Had Ramish created a living will?

TERMS AND CONCEPTS TO REVIEW

administrator 1006   charitable trust 1019   constructive trust 1020
bequest 1007   codicil 1013   devise 1007

QUESTIONS AND CASE PROBLEMS

50–1. Benjamin is a widower who has two married children, Edward and Patricia. Patricia has two children, Perry and Paul. Edward has no children. Benjamin dies, and his typewritten will leaves all his property equally to his children, Edward and Patricia, and provides that should a child predecease him, the grandchildren are to take *per stirpes*. The will was witnessed by Patricia and by Benjamin's lawyer and was signed by Benjamin in their presence. Patricia has predeceased Benjamin. Edward claims the will is invalid.

(a) Discuss whether the will is valid.
(b) Discuss the distribution of Benjamin's estate if the will is invalid.
(c) Discuss the distribution of Benjamin's estate if the will is valid.

50–2. Gary Mendel drew up a will in which he left his favorite car, a 1966 red Ferrari, to his daughter, Roberta. A year prior to his death, Mendel sold the 1966 Ferrari and purchased a 1969 Ferrari. Discuss whether Roberta will inherit the 1969 Ferrari under the terms of her father's will.

50–3. QUESTION WITH SAMPLE ANSWER

While single, James made out a will naming his mother, Carol, as sole beneficiary. Later, James married Lisa.

(a) If James died while married to Lisa without changing his will, would the estate go to his mother, Carol? Explain.
(b) Assume that James made out a new will on his marriage to Lisa, leaving his entire estate to Lisa. Later, he divorced Lisa and married Mandis, but he did not change his will. Discuss the rights of Lisa and Mandis to his estate after his death.
(c) Assume that James divorced Lisa, married Mandis, and changed his will, leaving his estate to Mandis. Later, a daughter, Claire, was born. James died without having included Claire in his will. Discuss fully whether Claire has any rights in the estate.

For a sample answer to this question, go to Appendix I at the end of this text.

50–4. Merlin Winters had three sons. Merlin and his youngest son, Abraham, had a falling out in 1994 and stopped speaking to each other. Merlin made a formal will in 1996, leaving all his property to the two older sons and deliberately excluding Abraham. Merlin's health began to deteriorate, and by 1997, he was under the full-time care of a nurse, Julia. In 1998, he made a new will expressly revoking the 1996 will and leaving all his property to Julia. On Merlin's death, the two older sons contest the 1998 will, claiming that Julia exercised undue influence over their father. Abraham claims that both wills are invalid because the first will was revoked by the second will, and the second will is invalid on the ground of undue influence. Is Abraham's contention correct? Explain.

50–5. Rohan, an eighty-three-year-old invalid, employs a nurse, Sarah, to care for him. Prior to Sarah's employment, Rohan executed a will leaving his entire estate to his only living relative—his great-grandson, Leon. Sarah convinces Rohan that Leon is dead and gets Rohan to change his will, naming Sarah as his sole beneficiary. After Rohan's death, Leon appears and contests the will. Discuss the probable success of Leon's action.

50–6. ADOPTED CHILDREN. Gail MacCallum was the daughter of Anita Seymour. After the death of Gail's father, Anita had married Richard Seymour, who adopted Gail the next year, when she was seven years old. The same year, Janet Seymour was born to Richard and Anita. Almost forty years later, when Richard's brother Philip died, both Gail and Janet sought to share in the estate. A Vermont state court concluded that Gail could not share in the estate because a state statute prohibited "inheritance between the person adopted . . . and collateral kin of the person or persons making the adoption." Gail appealed, arguing that the statute was unconstitutional. Will the court agree? Discuss fully. [*MacCallum v. Seymour,* 686 A.2d. 935 (Vt. 1996)]

50-7. ⚖ CASE PROBLEM WITH SAMPLE ANSWER

Alma Zeigler, a resident of Georgia, died in June 2001. Zeigler's will named as executor her granddaughter, Stacey Hatchett. Hatchett, who was teaching and attending graduate school in Illinois, filed a petition to probate the will in a Georgia state court, which confirmed her as executor in January 2002. The estate's main asset was a brick, three-bedroom house in Savannah. Hatchett sold the house for $65,000, without obtaining an appraisal, and deposited the proceeds in her personal account. Meanwhile, Zeigler's adopted son took the furnishings from the house and placed them in storage. As of August 2003, Hatchett had not inventoried these items, did not know their location, and knew only that the son lived "somewhere in Florida." Also unaccounted for was a diamond ring that had been on Zeigler's finger at the time of her death and a van that Zeigler had owned. Rita Williams, to whom the will devised certain real property, filed a petition with the court, asking that Hatchett, who had not been in Georgia since filing the petition to probate the will, be removed as executor. What are the duties of an executor, or personal representative? Did Hatchett violate these duties? Explain. [*In re Estate of Zeigler*, __ Ga.App. __, 614 S.E.2d 799 (2005)]

To view a sample answer for this case problem, go to this book's Web site at http://wbl.westbuslaw.com, select "Chapter 50," and click on "Case Problem with Sample Answer."

50-8. REVOCATION OF A WILL.

William Laneer urged his son, also William, to join the family business. The son, who was made partner, became suspicious of the handling of the business's finances. He filed a suit against the business and reported it to the Internal Revenue Service. Laneer then executed a will that disinherited his son, giving him one dollar and leaving the balance of the estate equally to Laneer's four daughters, including Bellinda Barrera. Until his death more than twenty years later, Laneer harbored ill feelings toward his son. After Laneer's death, his original copy of the will could not be found. A photocopy was found in his safe-deposit box, however, and his lawyer's original copy was entered for probate in an Arkansas state court. Barrera, who wanted her brother William to share an equal portion of the inheritance, filed a petition to contest the will. Barrera claimed, among other things, that Laneer had revoked the will, and that was why his original copy of the will could not be found. Was the will revoked? If so, to whom would the estate be distributed? [*Barrera v. Vanpelt*, 332 Ark. 482, 965 S.W.2d 780 (1998)]

50-9. INTESTACY LAWS.

In January 1993, three and a half years after Lauren and Warren Woodward were married, they were informed that Warren had leukemia. At the time, the couple had no children, and the doctors told the Woodwards that the leukemia treatment might leave Mr. Woodward sterile. The couple arranged for Mr. Woodward's sperm to be collected and placed in a sperm bank for later use. In October 1993, Warren Woodward died. Two years later, Lauren Woodward gave birth to twin girls who had been conceived through artificial insemination using Mr. Woodward's sperm. The following year, Mrs. Woodward applied for Social Security survivor benefits for the two children. The Social Security Administration (SSA) rejected her application, on the ground that she had not established that the twins were the husband's children within the meaning of the Social Security Act of 1935. Mrs. Woodward then filed a paternity action in Massachusetts, and the probate court determined that Warren Woodward was the twins' father. Mrs. Woodward resubmitted her application to the SSA but was again refused survivor benefits for the twins. She then filed an action in a federal district court to determine the inheritance rights, under Massachusetts intestacy law, of children conceived from the sperm of a deceased individual and his surviving spouse. How should the court resolve this case? Should children conceived after a parent's death (by means of artificial insemination or *in vitro* fertilization) still inherit under intestate succession laws? Why or why not? [*Woodward v. Commissioner of Social Security*, 435 Mass. 536, 760 N.E.2d 257 (2002)]

50-10. WILLS.

In 1944, Benjamin Feinberg bought a plot in Beth Israel Cemetery in Plattsburgh, New York. A mausoleum was built on the plot to contain six crypts. In 1954, Feinberg's spouse died and was interred in one of the crypts. Feinberg, his only son, one of his two daughters, and the daughter's son, Julian Bergman, began using the mausoleum regularly as a place of prayer and meditation. When Feinberg died, he was interred in the mausoleum. His two daughters were interred in two of the remaining crypts on their deaths. Feinberg's son died in 2001 and was interred in the fifth crypt. His widow Laurie then changed the locks on the mausoleum and refused access to Julian, who filed a suit in a New York state court against her to obtain a key. Feinberg and all of his children died testate, but none of them made a specific bequest of their interest in the plot to anyone. Each person's will included a residuary clause, however. Who owns the plot, who has access to it, and why? [*Bergman v. Feinberg*, 6 A.D.3d 1031, 776 N.Y.S.2d 611 (3 Dept. 2004)]

LAW | on the Web

For updated links to resources available on the Web, as well as a variety of other materials, visit this text's Web site at http://wbl.westbuslaw.com.

The SeniorLaw Web site offers information on a variety of topics, including elder law, estate planning, and trusts. The URL for this site is

http://www.seniorlaw.com

You can find the Uniform Probate Code, as well as links to various state probate statutes, at Cornell University's Legal Information Institute. Go to

http://straylight.law.cornell.edu/uniform/probate.html

A number of tools, including wills and trusts, that can be used in estate planning are described by the National Association of Financial and Estate Planning on its Web site at

http://www.nafep.com

LEGAL RESEARCH EXERCISES ON THE WEB

Go to http://wbl.westbuslaw.com, the Web site that accompanies this text. Select "Chapter 50" and click on "Internet Exercises." There you will find the following Internet research exercises that you can perform to learn more about topics covered in this chapter.

Activity 50–1: LEGAL PERSPECTIVE
                  Wills and Trusts

Activity 50–2: MANAGEMENT PERSPECTIVE
                  Social Security

CHAPTER 51

Professional Liability and Accountability

Professionals such as accountants, attorneys, physicians, architects, and others are increasingly faced with the threat of liability. One of the reasons for this is that the public has become more aware that professionals are required to deliver competent services and are obligated to adhere to standards of performance commonly accepted within their professions.

Certainly, the dizzying collapse of Enron Corporation and the failure of other major companies, including WorldCom, Inc., in the early 2000s called attention to the importance of abiding by professional accounting standards. Arthur Andersen, LLP, one of the world's leading public accounting firms, ended up being indicted on criminal charges for its role in thwarting the government's investigation into Enron's accounting practices.[1] As a result, that company ceased to exist and roughly 85,000 employees lost their jobs. Moreover, under the Sarbanes-Oxley Act of 2002, which Congress passed in response to these events, public accounting firms throughout the nation will feel the effects for years to come. Among other things, the act imposed stricter regulation and oversight on the public accounting industry.

Considering the many potential sources of legal liability that they face, accountants, attorneys, and other professionals should be very aware of their legal obligations. In this chapter, we look at the potential liability of professionals under both the common law and statutory law. We also examine other topics of concern for professionals, such as the increasing use of the limited liability partnership by accountants and other professionals to limit their liability, rights to working papers, and professional client privilege.

SECTION 1 | Common Law Liability to Clients

Under the common law, professionals may be liable to clients for breach of contract, negligence, or fraud.

LIABILITY FOR BREACH OF CONTRACT

Accountants and other professionals face liability for any breach of contract under the common law. A professional owes a duty to her or his client to honor the terms of the contract and to perform the contract within the stated time period. If the professional fails to

perform as agreed in the contract, then she or he has breached the contract, and the client has the right to recover damages from the professional. A professional may be held liable for expenses incurred by her or his client in securing another professional to provide the contracted-for services, for liquidated damages imposed on the client for failure to meet time deadlines, and for any other reasonable and foreseeable monetary losses that arise from the professional's breach.

LIABILITY FOR NEGLIGENCE

Accountants and other professionals may also be held liable under the common law for negligence in the performance of their services. The elements that must be proved to establish negligence on the part of a professional are as follows:

1. A duty of care existed.
2. That duty of care was breached.

---

1. Although Arthur Andersen, LLP, was subsequently convicted in a federal district court on the charge of obstructing justice, the United States Supreme Court reversed and remanded the case in 2005 due to erroneous jury instructions. No final decision has yet been entered on the charges. *Arthur Andersen LLP v. United States*, ___ U.S. ___, 125 S.Ct. 2129, ___ L.Ed.2d ___ (2005).

3. The plaintiff suffered an injury.
4. The injury was proximately caused by the defendant's breach of the duty of care.

All professionals are subject to standards of conduct established by codes of professional standards and ethics, by state statutes, and by judicial decisions. They are also governed by the contracts they enter into with their clients. In their performance of contracts, professionals must exercise the established standards of care, knowledge, and judgment generally accepted by members of their professional group. We look below at the duty of care owed by two groups of professionals that frequently perform services for business firms: accountants and attorneys.

ACCOUNTANT'S DUTY OF CARE Accountants play a major role in a business's financial system. Accountants have the necessary expertise and experience in establishing and maintaining accurate financial records to design, control, and audit record-keeping systems; to prepare reliable statements that reflect an individual's or a business's financial status; and to give tax advice and prepare tax returns.

An *audit* is a systematic inspection, by analyses and tests, of a business's financial records. The purpose of an audit is to provide the auditor with evidence to support an opinion on the reliability of the business's financial statements. A normal audit is not intended to uncover fraud or other misconduct. An accountant may be liable for failing to detect misconduct, however, if a normal audit would have revealed it or if the auditor agreed to examine the records for evidence of fraud or other misconduct that should have been obvious. After performing an audit, the auditor issues an opinion letter stating whether, in his or her opinion, the financial statements fairly present the business's financial position.

—Standard of Care. Generally, an accountant must possess the skills that an ordinarily prudent accountant would have and must exercise the degree of care that an ordinarily prudent accountant would exercise. The level of skill expected of accountants and the degree of care that they should exercise in performing their services are reflected in what are known as **generally accepted accounting principles (GAAP)** and **generally accepted auditing standards (GAAS).** The Financial Accounting Standards Board (FASB, usually pronounced "faz-bee") determines what accounting conventions, rules, and procedures consti-

tute GAAP at a given point in time. GAAS are standards concerning an auditor's professional qualities and the judgment that he or she exercises in auditing financial records. GAAS are established by the American Institute of Certified Public Accountants. GAAP and GAAS are also reflected in the rules established by the Securities and Exchange Commission (see Chapter 41).

As long as an accountant conforms to GAAP and acts in good faith, the accountant normally will not be held liable to the client for a mistake in judgment. An accountant is not required to discover every impropriety, **defalcation**[2] (embezzlement), or fraud in a client's books. If, however, the impropriety, defalcation, or fraud has gone undiscovered because of an accountant's negligence or failure to perform an express or implied duty, the accountant will be liable for any resulting losses suffered by the client and perhaps by third parties. Therefore, an accountant who uncovers suspicious financial transactions and fails to investigate the matter fully or to inform the client of the discovery can be held liable to the client for the resulting loss.

—Violations of GAAP and GAAS. A violation of GAAP and GAAS will be considered *prima facie* evidence of negligence on the part of the accountant. Compliance with GAAP and GAAS, however, does not necessarily relieve an accountant from potential legal liability. An accountant may be held to a higher standard of conduct established by state statute and by judicial decisions. If an accountant is found to have been negligent in the performance of accounting services for a client, the client may collect damages for any losses that arose from the accountant's negligence.

—Defenses to Negligence. Accountants have several defenses available. Possible defenses that an accountant can raise include the following:

1. That the accountant was not negligent.
2. That if the accountant was negligent, this negligence was not the proximate cause of the client's losses.
3. That the client was also negligent (depending on whether state law allows contributory negligence or comparative negligence as a defense—see Chapter 7).

---

2. This term, pronounced deh-ful-*kay*-shun, is derived from the Latin *de* ("off") and *falx* ("sickle"—a tool for cutting grain or tall grass). In law, the term refers to the act of a defaulter or of an embezzler. As used here, it means embezzlement.

The following case involved the second defense in the above list—whether the defendant's negligence was the proximate cause of the plaintiff's loss. The accounting firm claimed that the plaintiff's losses were due to market forces rather than the delay in a public offering of its stock.

CASE 51.1

Oregon
Supreme Court, 2004.
336 Or. 329.
83 P.3d 322.

Oregon Steel Mills, Inc. v. Coopers & Lybrand, LLP

BALMER, J. [Justice]
* * * *
* * * Plaintiff Oregon Steel Mills, Inc., * * * retained defendant Coopers & Lybrand, LLP, for many years to provide accounting and auditing services. In 1994, plaintiff entered into a transaction that involved the sale of stock in one of plaintiff's subsidiaries. Defendant advised plaintiff that the transaction should be reported as a $12.3 million gain on plaintiff's [1994] financial statements and reports. * * *

During late 1995 and early 1996, plaintiff was planning to make a public offering of its stock and debt. Defendant knew of plaintiff's plans * * * . Plaintiff anticipated that it would file the necessary documents with the Securities and Exchange Commission (SEC) on February 27, 1996, and that, * * * the securities would be priced and sold on or about May 2, 1996. * * * [T]he documents that plaintiff filed with the SEC included the 1994 financial statements that defendant had audited.

* * * [T]he SEC concluded that the accounting treatment for the 1994 transaction was incorrect and required plaintiff to restate its 1994 financial statements. Because of the [delay] * * * , the public offering did not occur until June 13, 1996. * * * [T]he price of plaintiff's stock was $13.50 * * * when plaintiff issued the stock on June 13 * * * . On May 2, 1996, the date that plaintiff alleges that it would have issued the stock but for defendant's negligence, plaintiff's stock sold for $16 per share.
* * * *
Plaintiff brought this action in [an Oregon state court], claiming that defendant's negligent conduct caused the delay that resulted in the stock being offered at $13.50 per share, rather than at $16 per share. * * *
* * * *
[The court issued a summary judgment in Coopers' favor.] Plaintiff appealed, and the [state intermediate] Court of Appeals reversed the trial court's summary judgment. * * * [Coopers appealed to the Oregon Supreme Court.]
* * * *
* * * [T]he critical issue is whether plaintiff's [Oregon Steel's] market losses were a reasonably foreseeable result of defendant's wrongful conduct.
* * * The Court of Appeals concluded that the issue of whether plaintiff's damage was "foreseeably" caused by defendant's negligent acts should be tried [by] a jury. The problem with that conclusion is that no one could foresee, at the time of defendant's accounting errors in 1994 and early 1995, the risk that plaintiff would suffer a loss because its securities would be sold at market-determined prices on June 13, 1996, rather than on May 2, 1996. Plaintiff argues that it is foreseeable that stock prices will fluctuate, and that is certainly true. It also is foreseeable * * * that negligent conduct by an accounting firm may harm a client by impairing its ability to raise capital. *With appropriate proof, the client of a negligent accounting firm may recover damages for lost profits or lost business opportunities that result from the accounting firm's negligent acts.* Here, however, plaintiff seeks damages based solely on a decline in the price of plaintiff's stock during the delay that defendant caused in getting the offering to market, yet plaintiff admits that the price decline affected all steel stocks and was unrelated to defendant's misconduct. [Emphasis added.]
* * * *
* * * [D]efendant's conduct caused the delay in the offering that led to an unintended adverse result. However, the intervening action of market forces on the price of plaintiff's stock was the harm-producing force, and defendant's actions did not cause the decline in the stock price so as to support liability for that decline. *As a matter of law, the risk of a decline in*

CASE 51.1 | Continued | *plaintiff's stock price in June 1996 was not a reasonably foreseeable consequence of defendant's negligent acts in 1994 and early 1995.* [Emphasis added.]

That conclusion is similar to the conclusions reached by other courts that have considered whether a client in a professional [negligence] action can recover for losses caused by market forces. * * *

Plaintiff argues that, even if losses due to market forces are not recoverable from a defendant whose negligent behavior did not cause those losses, the losses in this case were foreseeable because defendant knew that plaintiff intended to enter the market and sell its securities at a specific and favorable time. The Court of Appeals relied on that argument, stating that the offering date was timed to take advantage of higher-than-expected first-quarter earnings and favorable market conditions. However, the record does not support plaintiff's assertion or the Court of Appeals' statements. First, * * * [a]lthough defendant knew in 1994 that plaintiff contemplated a public offering at some point, the timing of that offering * * * was known only in the most general sense at the time of defendant's wrongful conduct.

Second, * * * the increase and then decrease in steel company stock prices, including plaintiff's, between April and June 1996 was due to market forces unrelated to plaintiff's financial condition or to defendant's conduct.

* * * *

For the reasons discussed above, we conclude that, although defendant breached its duty to plaintiff by failing to provide competent accounting services, defendant had no duty to protect plaintiff against market fluctuations in plaintiff's stock price. The decline in plaintiff's stock price in June 1996 was, as a matter of law, not reasonably foreseeable, and defendant cannot be liable for damages based on that decline. * * *

The decision of the Court of Appeals is reversed. The judgment of the [trial] court is affirmed.

QUESTIONS

1. What was Coopers's duty to Oregon Steel under the circumstances of this case?
2. Based on the court's reasoning in this case, what damages might Oregon Steel recover for Coopers's negligence?

—*Qualified Opinions and Disclaimers.* In issuing an opinion letter, an auditor may qualify the opinion or include a disclaimer. An auditor will not be held liable for damages resulting from whatever is qualified or disclaimed. An opinion that disclaims any liability for false or misleading financial statements is too general, however. A qualified opinion or a disclaimer must be specific. For example, an auditor might qualify an opinion, in an audit of a corporation, by stating that there is uncertainty about how a lawsuit against the firm will be resolved. The auditor will not be liable if the outcome of the suit is bad for the firm. The auditor could still be liable, however, for failing to discover other problems that an audit in compliance with GAAS and GAAP would have revealed.

—*Unaudited Financial Statements.* Sometimes, accountants are hired to prepare unaudited financial statements. (A financial statement is considered unaudited if incomplete auditing procedures have been used in its preparation or if insufficient procedures have been used to justify an opinion.) Accountants may be subject to liability for failing, in accordance with standard accounting procedures, to designate a balance sheet as "unaudited." An accountant will also be held liable for failure to disclose to a client the facts or circumstances that give reason to believe that misstatements have been made or that a fraud has been committed.

ATTORNEY'S DUTY OF CARE The conduct of attorneys is governed by rules established by each state and by the American Bar Association's Model Rules of Professional Conduct. All attorneys owe a duty to provide competent and diligent representation. Attorneys are required to be familiar with well-settled principles of law applicable to a case and to find law that can be discovered through a reasonable amount of research. The lawyer must also investigate and discover facts that could materially affect the client's legal rights.

—Standard of Care. In judging an attorney's performance, the standard used will normally be that of a reasonably competent general practitioner of ordinary skill, experience, and capacity. If an attorney holds himself or herself out as having expertise in a special area of law (for example, intellectual property), then the attorney's standard of care in that area is higher than for attorneys without such expertise.

—Liability for Malpractice. When an attorney fails to exercise reasonable care and professional judgment, she or he breaches the duty of care and can be held liable for *malpractice* (professional negligence). In malpractice cases—as in all cases involving allegations of negligence—the plaintiff must prove that the attorney's breach of the duty of care actually caused the plaintiff to suffer some injury. For example, if the attorney allows the statute of limitations to lapse on a client's claim, he or she can be held liable for malpractice because the client can no longer file a cause of action in the case and has lost a potential award of damages.

Traditionally, to establish causation, the client normally had to show that "but for" the attorney's negligence, the client would not have suffered the injury. In recent years, however, several courts have held that plaintiffs in malpractice cases need only show that the defendant's negligence was a "substantial factor" in causing the plaintiff's injury.

LIABILITY FOR FRAUD

Recall from Chapter 14 that fraud, or misrepresentation, involves the following elements:

1. A misrepresentation of a material fact has occurred.
2. An intent to deceive exists.
3. The innocent party has justifiably relied on the misrepresentation.
4. For damages, the innocent party must have been injured.

A professional may be held liable for *actual* fraud when he or she intentionally misstates a material fact to mislead a client and the client justifiably relies on the misstated fact to his or her injury. A material fact is one that a reasonable person would consider important in deciding whether to act.

In contrast, a professional may be held liable for *constructive* fraud whether or not he or she acted with fraudulent intent. For example, constructive fraud may be found when an accountant is grossly negligent in the performance of his or her duties. The intentional failure to perform a duty in reckless disregard of the consequences of such a failure will constitute gross negligence on the part of the professional.

LIMITING PROFESSIONALS' LIABILITY

Accountants and other professionals can limit their liability to some extent by disclaiming it. Depending on the circumstances, a disclaimer that does not meet certain requirements will not be effective, however; and in some situations, a disclaimer may not be effective at all.

Professionals may be able to limit their liability for the misconduct of other professionals with whom they work by organizing the business as a professional corporation (P.C.) or a limited liability partnership (LLP). In some states, a professional who is a member of a P.C. is not personally liable for a co-member's misconduct unless she or he participated in it or supervised the member who acted wrongly. The innocent professional is liable only to the extent of his or her interest in the assets of the firm. This is also true for professionals who are partners in an LLP. P.C.s were discussed in more detail in Chapter 38. LLPs were covered in Chapter 36.

SECTION 2 | Liability to Third Parties

Traditionally, an accountant or other professional owed a duty only to those with whom she or he was in *privity of contract*. (Recall from Chapter 16 that privity of contract refers to the relationship that exists between the promisor and the promisee of a contract.) In other words, a professional owed no duty to a third party outside the contractual relationship—a professional's duty was only to his or her client. Violations of statutory laws, fraud, and other intentional or reckless acts of wrongdoing were the only exceptions to this general rule.

Today, numerous third parties—including investors, shareholders, creditors, corporate managers and directors, regulatory agencies, and others—rely on the opinions of auditors (accountants) when making decisions. In view of this extensive reliance, many courts have all but abandoned the privity requirement in regard to accountants' liability to third parties. Like accountants, attorneys may be held liable under the common law to third parties who rely on legal opinions to their detriment. For example, the liability principles stated in Section 552 of the *Restatement (Second) of Torts* (these principles will be discussed shortly) may apply to attorneys just as they apply to accountants. Generally, however, an attorney is not liable to a nonclient unless there is fraud (or malicious conduct) by the attorney.

Understanding an auditor's common law liability to third parties is critical because when a business fails, its independent auditor may be one of the few potentially solvent defendants. The majority of courts now hold that auditors can be held liable to third parties for negligence, but the standard for the imposition of this liability varies. There are generally three different views of accountants' liability to third parties:

1. Accountants should be liable only to those with whom they are in privity or "near privity" of contract (the *Ultramares* rule).

2. Accountants should be liable to foreseen, or known, users of their reports or financial statements (the *Restatement* rule).

3. Accountants should be liable to those whose use of their reports or financial statements is *reasonably foreseeable*.

We discuss each of these views here.

THE ULTRAMARES RULE

The traditional rule regarding an accountant's liability to third parties was enunciated by Chief Judge Benjamin Cardozo in *Ultramares Corp. v. Touche*,[3] a case decided in 1931. In *Ultramares,* Fred Stern & Company hired the public accounting firm of Touche, Niven & Company to review Stern's financial records and prepare a balance sheet for the year ending December 31, 1923.[4] Touche prepared the balance sheet and supplied Stern with thirty-two certified copies. According to the certified balance sheet, Stern had a net worth (assets less liabilities) of $1,070,715.26. In reality, however, Stern was insolvent—the company's records had been falsified by insiders at Stern to reflect a positive net worth. In reliance on the certified balance sheets, a lender, Ultramares Corporation, loaned substantial amounts to Stern. After Stern was declared bankrupt, Ultramares brought an action against Touche for negligence in an attempt to recover damages.

THE REQUIREMENT OF PRIVITY The New York Court of Appeals (that state's highest court) refused to impose liability on Touche and concluded that Touche's accountants owed a duty of care only to those persons for whose "primary benefit" the statements were intended. In this case, the statements were intended only for the primary benefit of Stern. The court held that in the absence of privity or a relationship "so close as to approach that of privity," a party could not recover from an accountant.

MODIFICATION OF THE RULE—THE "NEAR PRIVITY" REQUIREMENT The court's requirement of privity has since been referred to as the *Ultramares* rule, or the New York rule. The rule was restated and somewhat modified in a 1985 New York case, *Credit Alliance Corp. v. Arthur Andersen & Co.*[5] In that case, the court held that if a third party has a sufficiently close relationship or nexus (link or connection) with an accountant, then the *Ultramares* privity requirement may be satisfied without the establishment of an accountant-client relationship. The rule enunciated in *Credit Alliance* is often referred to as the "near privity" rule. Only a minority of states have adopted this rule of accountants' liability to third parties.

Under this rule, does an accountant who is aware that a nonclient might rely on the accountant's work owe the nonclient a duty of care, when preparing reports on that party's financial status for his or her manager? Does the accountant have a duty to advise the nonclient on other financial transactions? These were the questions in the following case.

---

3. 255 N.Y. 170, 174 N.E. 441 (1931).

4. Banks, creditors, stockholders, purchasers, and sellers often rely on balance sheets when making decisions relating to a company's business.

5. 65 N.Y.2d 536, 483 N.E.2d 110 (1985). A "relationship sufficiently intimate to be equated with privity" is enough for a third party to sue another's accountant for negligence.

CASE 51.2

United States
District Court,
Southern District
of New York, 2005.
365 F.Supp.2d 565.

Reznor v. J. Artist Management, Inc.

BACKGROUND AND FACTS *Michael Trent Reznor met John Malm, Jr., a part-time promoter of local rock bands, in Cleveland, Ohio, in 1985. Malm became Reznor's manager and formed J. Artist Management, Inc. (JAM). Reznor became the lead singer in the band Nine Inch Nails (NIN), which performed its first show in 1988. Reznor and Malm signed a management agreement, under which JAM was to receive 20 percent of Reznor's gross compensation. Over the next few years, Reznor and Malm created other companies to sell NIN's merchandise and perform various services. In 1996, Malm hired accountant Richard Szekelyi and his firm, Navigent Group, to provide financial consulting services to JAM and the jointly owned companies. Szekelyi did not provide services to Reznor personally, but his duties included examining Reznor's financial records. Szekelyi discovered that the accounting among the parties was flawed, with Malm, for example, receiving tax benefits that should have gone to Reznor. According to Szekelyi, by 2003, Reznor owed JAM $1.56 million, and the jointly owned companies owed Reznor $5.5 million, which (as later became clear) was unlikely to be repaid. Reznor fired Malm and filed a suit in a federal district court against JAM and others, including Szekelyi and Navigent.*

IN THE LANGUAGE OF THE COURT

JED S. RAKOFF, U.S.D.J. [United States District Judge]

* * * *

* * * [C]o-defendants Szekelyi and Navigent Group (hereinafter, collectively "Szekelyi") seek summary judgment on Reznor's claims against them of negligence, breach of fiduciary duty, and malpractice. There is little distinction between these claims, all of which allege that Szekelyi did not meet the standards of the accounting profession in the performance of professional duties to Reznor.

Since Reznor was not Szekelyi's client, Szekelyi would be liable to Reznor for malpractice only where he was aware that the nonclient would rely on his work for a particular purpose. Szekelyi's presentations to Reznor in 2002 and 2003 meet this standard, and so Szekelyi is liable for any malpractice he may have committed in preparing and presenting these reports of Reznor's financial status. However, there is no evidence that Szekelyi breached any standard of care in preparing and presenting these reports. Reznor does not allege any inaccuracies in these reports; rather, after establishing that Szekelyi owed a duty of care with respect to these reports, he argues that Szekelyi failed to counsel Reznor adequately concerning certain other transactions. Because Szekelyi was not Reznor's accountant or business manager, he owed Reznor in his individual capacity no such duty with respect to other transactions. [Emphasis added.]

* * * Szekelyi (and Navigent) also move for summary judgment with respect to Reznor's claims against them alleging fraud and aiding and abetting fraud. *An accountant can be liable to a nonclient for fraud if he has knowledge of the falsity of his client's statements or acts in reckless disregard of such falsity where the circumstances should cast doubt on the information's veracity [truth] and where the accountant is aware of the plaintiff's reasonable reliance on him.* Here, Reznor alleges that Szekelyi assisted Malm in secretly and illegally diverting Reznor's money into the jointly held companies. However, there is no evidence that, even if Malm were defrauding Reznor by misleading him as to which accounts the loans were coming from, Szekelyi knew or should have known of any impropriety. Indeed, there is no evidence that Szekelyi did anything but attempt to correct the only clearly flawed accounting in evidence, *i.e.,* the improper tax treatment * * * . Accordingly, summary judgment must be granted on the fraud claims, which also means that, given the above-described grant of summary judgment on the other claims against Szekelyi and Navigent, summary judgment is granted as to *all* counts against Szekelyi and Navigent Group. [Emphasis added.]

CASE 51.2 | Continued

DECISION AND REMEDY *The court granted the motion of Szekelyi and Navigent for summary judgment, and dismissed them from the case. Szekelyi did not breach any standard of care in preparing and presenting reports of Reznor's financial status, nor did he fail to counsel Reznor adequately concerning other transactions. "Because Szekelyi was not Reznor's accountant or business manager, he owed Reznor in his individual capacity no such duty."*

WHAT IF THE FACTS WERE DIFFERENT? *If Szekelyi also had been Reznor's accountant, would the result have been different? Why or why not?*

THE RESTATEMENT RULE

Auditors perform much of their work for use by persons who are not parties to the contract; thus, it is asserted that they owe a duty to these third parties. Consequently, there has been an erosion of the *Ultramares* rule, and accountants have increasingly been exposed to potential liability to third parties. The majority of courts have adopted the position taken by the *Restatement (Second) of Torts*, which states that accountants are subject to liability for negligence not only to their clients but also to foreseen, or *known*, users—or classes of users—of their reports or financial statements.

Under Section 552(2) of the *Restatement (Second) of Torts*, an accountant's liability extends to those persons for whose benefit and guidance the accountant "intends to supply the information or knows that the recipient intends to supply it" and to those persons whom the accountant "intends the information to influence or knows that the recipient so intends." In other words, if an accountant prepares a financial statement for a client and knows that the client will submit that statement to a bank to secure a loan, the accountant may be held liable to the bank for negligent misstatements or omissions—because the accountant knew that the bank would rely on the accountant's work product when deciding whether to make the loan.

CONCEPT SUMMARY 51.1 | Common Law Liability of Accountants and Other Professionals

CONCEPT	NATURE OF LIABILITY
LIABILITY TO CLIENTS	1. *Breach of contract*—An accountant or other professional who fails to perform according to his or her contractual obligations can be held liable for breach of contract and resulting damages. 2. *Negligence*—An accountant or other professional, in performance of her or his duties, must use the care, knowledge, and judgment generally used by professionals in the same or similar circumstances. Failure to do so is negligence. An accountant's violation of generally accepted accounting principles and generally accepted auditing standards is *prima facie* evidence of negligence. 3. *Fraud*—Actual intent to misrepresent a material fact to a client, when the client relies on the misrepresentation, is fraud. Gross negligence in performance of duties is constructive fraud.
LIABILITY TO THIRD PARTIES	An accountant may be liable for negligence to any third person the accountant knows or should have known will benefit from the accountant's work. The standard for imposing this liability varies, but generally courts follow one of the following rules: 1. *Ultramares rule*—Liability will be imposed only if the accountant is in privity, or near privity, with the third party. 2. *Restatement rule*—Liability will be imposed only if the third party's reliance is foreseen or known or if the third party is among a class of foreseeable or known users. The majority of courts have adopted this rule. 3. *"Reasonably foreseeable user" rule*—Liability will be imposed if the third party's use was reasonably foreseeable.

LIABILITY TO REASONABLY FORESEEABLE USERS

A small minority of courts hold accountants liable to any users whose reliance on an accountant's statements or reports was *reasonably foreseeable*. This standard has been criticized as extending liability too far because it means that accountants can be liable even in circumstances in which they are unaware of how their opinions will be used.[6]

The majority of courts have concluded that the *Restatement*'s approach is the more reasonable one because it allows accountants to control their exposure to liability. Liability is "fixed by the accountants' particular knowledge at the moment the audit is published," not by the foreseeability of the harm that might occur to a third party after the report is released.[7] Even the California courts, which for years relied on reasonable foreseeability as the standard for determining an auditor's liability to third parties, have changed their position.[8]

SECTION 3 | The Sarbanes-Oxley Act of 2002

As previously mentioned, in 2002 Congress enacted the Sarbanes-Oxley Act, which became effective on August 29, 2002. The act imposes a number of strict requirements on both domestic and foreign public accounting firms that provide auditing services to companies ("issuers") whose securities are sold to public investors. The act defines the term *issuer* as a company that has securities that are registered under Section 12 of the Securities Exchange Act of 1934; that is required to file reports under Section 15(d) of the 1934 act; or that files—or has filed—a registration statement that has not yet become effective under the Securities Act of 1933.

THE PUBLIC COMPANY ACCOUNTING OVERSIGHT BOARD

Among other things, the Sarbanes-Oxley Act calls for an increased degree of government oversight over public accounting practices. To this end, the act created

the Public Company Accounting Oversight Board, which reports to the Securities and Exchange Commission. The board consists of a chair and four other members. The purpose of the board is to oversee the audit of public companies that are subject to securities laws in order to protect public investors and to ensure that public accounting firms comply with the provisions of the Sarbanes-Oxley Act.

APPLICABILITY TO PUBLIC ACCOUNTING FIRMS

Titles I and II of the act set forth the key provisions relating to the duties of the new oversight board and the requirements relating to public accounting firms—defined by the act as firms and associated persons that are "engaged in the practice of public accounting or preparing or issuing audit reports." These provisions are summarized in Exhibit 51–1. (Provisions of the act that are more directly concerned with corporate fraud and the responsibilities of corporate officers and directors were listed and described in Exhibit 41–4 in Chapter 41.)

REQUIREMENTS FOR MAINTAINING WORKING PAPERS

Performing an audit for a client involves an accumulation of **working papers**—the various documents used and developed during the audit. These include notes, computations, memoranda, copies, and other papers that make up the work product of an accountant's services to a client. Under the common law, which in this instance has been codified in a number of states, working papers remain the accountant's property. It is important for accountants to retain such records in the event that they need to defend against lawsuits for negligence or other actions in which their competence is challenged. But because an accountant's working papers reflect the client's financial situation, the client has a right to access them. (On a client's request, an accountant must return to the client any of the client's records or journals, and failure to do so may result in liability.)

Under Section 802(a)(1) of the Sarbanes-Oxley Act, accountants must maintain working papers relating to an audit or review for five years, which has been amended to seven years since the passage of the act, from the end of the fiscal period in which the audit or review was concluded. A knowing violation of this requirement will subject the accountant to a fine, imprisonment for up to ten years, or both.

---

6. See, for example, the North Carolina Supreme Court's criticisms of this rule in *Raritan River Steel Co. v. Cherry, Bekaert & Holland,* 322 N.C. 200, 367 S.E.2d 609 (1988).

7. *Bethlehem Steel Corp. v. Ernst & Whinney,* 822 S.W.2d 592 (Tenn. 1991).

8. *Bily v. Arthur Young & Co.,* 3 Cal.4th 370, 834 P.2d 745, 11 Cal.Rptr.2d 51 (1992).

EXHIBIT 51-1 Key Provisions of the Sarbanes-Oxley Act of 2002 Relating to Public Accounting Firms

DUTIES OF THE PUBLIC COMPANY ACCOUNTING OVERSIGHT BOARD

Title I of the Sarbanes-Oxley Act of 2002 states that the duties of the Public Company Accounting Oversight Board are as follows:

- Generally, to oversee the audit of companies ("issuers") whose securities are sold to public investors in order to protect the interests of investors and further the public interest.
- To register public accounting firms that prepare audit reports for issuers. (A nonregistered firm is prohibited from preparing, or participating in the preparation of, an audit report with respect to an issuer.)
- To establish or adopt standards relating to the preparation of audit reports for issuers.
- To enforce compliance with the Sarbanes-Oxley Act by inspecting registered public accounting firms (RPAFs) and by investigating and disciplining, by appropriate sanctions, firms that violate the act's provisions. (Sanctions range from a temporary or permanent suspension to civil penalties that can be as high as $15 million for intentional violations.)
- To perform any other duties necessary or appropriate to promote high professional standards among RPAFs and improve the quality of audit services offered by those firms.

AUDITOR INDEPENDENCE

To help ensure that auditors remain independent of the firms that they audit, Title II of the Sarbanes-Oxley Act does the following:

- Makes it unlawful for RPAFs to perform both audit and nonaudit services for the same company at the same time. Nonaudit services include the following:
  1. Bookkeeping or other services related to the accounting records or financial statements of the audit client.
  2. Financial information systems design and implementation.
  3. Appraisal or valuation services.
  4. Fairness opinions.
  5. Management functions.
  6. Broker or dealer, investment adviser, or investment banking services.
- Requires preapproval for most auditing services from the issuer's audit committee.
- Requires audit partner rotation by prohibiting RPAFs from providing audit services to an issuer if either the lead audit partner or the audit partner responsible for reviewing the audit has provided such services to the issuer in each of the prior five years.
- Requires RPAFs to make timely reports to the audit committees of the issuers. The report must indicate all critical accounting policies and practices to be used; all alternative treatments of financial information within generally accepted accounting principles that have been discussed with the issuer's management officials, the ramifications of the use of such alternative treatments, and the treatment preferred by the auditor; and other material written communications between the auditor and the issuer's management.
- Makes it unlawful for an RPAF to provide auditing services to an issuer if the issuer's chief executive officer, chief financial officer, chief accounting officer, or controller was previously employed by the auditor and participated in any capacity in the audit of the issuer during the one-year period preceding the date that the audit began.

DOCUMENT RETENTION AND DESTRUCTION

- The Sarbanes-Oxley Act provides that anyone who destroys, alters, or falsifies records with the intent to obstruct or influence a federal investigation or in relation to bankruptcy proceedings can be criminally prosecuted and sentenced to a fine, imprisonment for up to twenty years, or both.
- The act also requires accountants who audit or review publicly traded companies to retain all working papers related to the audit or review for a period of five years (now amended to seven years). Violators can be sentenced to a fine, imprisonment for up to ten years, or both.

SECTION 4 | Liability of Accountants under Securities Laws

Both civil and criminal liability may be imposed on accountants under the Securities Act of 1933, the Securities Exchange Act of 1934, and the Private Securities Litigation Reform Act of 1995.[9]

---

9. Civil and criminal liability may also be imposed on accountants and other professionals under other statutes, including the Racketeer Influenced and Corrupt Organizations Act (RICO). RICO was discussed in Chapter 9.

LIABILITY UNDER THE SECURITIES ACT OF 1933

The Securities Act of 1933 requires registration statements to be filed with the Securities and Exchange Commission (SEC) prior to an offering of securities (see Chapter 41).[10] Accountants frequently prepare and certify the issuer's financial statements that are included in the registration statement.

LIABILITY UNDER SECTION 11   Section 11 of the Securities Act of 1933 imposes civil liability on accountants for misstatements and omissions of material facts in registration statements. An accountant may be held liable if he or she prepared any financial statements included in the registration statement that "contained an untrue statement of a material fact or omitted to state a material fact required to be stated therein or necessary to make the statements therein not misleading."[11]

An accountant may be liable to anyone who acquires a security covered by the registration statement. A purchaser of a security need only demonstrate that she or he has suffered a loss on the security. Proof of reliance on the materially false statement or misleading omission ordinarily is not required, nor is there a requirement of privity between the accountant and the security purchaser.

—The Due Diligence Standard.   Section 11 imposes a duty on accountants to use **due diligence** in the preparation of financial statements included in the filed registration statements. After the purchaser has proved a loss on the security, the accountant bears the burden of showing that he or she exercised due diligence in the preparation of the financial statements. To avoid liability, the accountant must show that he or she had, "after reasonable investigation, reasonable grounds to believe and did believe, at the time such part of the registration statement became effective, that the statements therein were true and that there was no omission of a material fact required to be stated therein or necessary to make the statements therein not misleading."[12] Further, the failure to follow GAAP and GAAS is also proof of a lack of due diligence.

In particular, the due diligence standard places a burden on accountants to verify information furnished by a corporation's officers and directors. The burden of proving due diligence requires an accountant to demonstrate that she or he did not commit negligence or fraud. Accountants may be held liable, for example, for failing to detect danger signals in materials that, under GAAS, required further investigation under the circumstances.[13] Merely asking questions is not always sufficient to satisfy the requirement of due diligence.

—Defenses to Liability.   Besides proving that he or she has acted with due diligence, an accountant may raise the following defenses to Section 11 liability:

1. There were no misstatements or omissions.
2. The misstatements or omissions were not of material facts.
3. The misstatements or omissions had no causal connection to the plaintiff's loss.
4. The plaintiff-purchaser invested in the securities knowing of the misstatements or omissions.

LIABILITY UNDER SECTION 12(2)   Section 12(2) of the Securities Act of 1933 imposes civil liability for fraud on anyone offering or selling a security to any purchaser of the security.[14] Liability is based on communication to an investor, whether orally or in the written prospectus,[15] of an untrue statement or omission of a material fact.

PENALTIES AND SANCTIONS FOR VIOLATIONS
Those who purchase securities and suffer harm as a result of a false or omitted statement, or some other violation, may bring a suit in a federal court to recover their losses and other damages. The U.S. Department of Justice brings criminal actions against those who commit willful violations. The penalties include fines up to $10,000, imprisonment up to five years, or both. The SEC is authorized to seek an injunction against a willful violator to prevent further violations. The SEC can also ask a court to grant other relief, such as an order to a violator to refund profits derived from an illegal transaction.

---

10. Many securities and transactions are expressly exempted from the 1933 act.
11. 15 U.S.C. Section 77k(a).
12. 15 U.S.C. Section 77k(b)(3).

13. See, for example, *Escott v. BarChris Construction Corp.*, 283 F.Supp. 643 (S.D.N.Y. 1968).
14. 15 U.S.C. Section 77l.
15. As discussed in Chapter 38, a *prospectus* contains financial disclosures about the corporation for the benefit of potential investors.

LIABILITY UNDER THE SECURITIES EXCHANGE ACT OF 1934

Under Sections 18 and 10(b) of the Securities Exchange Act of 1934 and Rule 10b-5 of the SEC, an accountant may be found liable for fraud. A plaintiff has a substantially heavier burden of proof under the 1934 act than under the 1933 act. Unlike the 1933 act, which provides that an accountant must prove due diligence to escape liability, the 1934 act relieves an accountant from liability if the accountant acted in "good faith."

LIABILITY UNDER SECTION 18 Section 18 of the 1934 act imposes civil liability on an accountant who makes or causes to be made in any application, report, or document a statement that at the time and in light of the circumstances was false or misleading with respect to any material fact.[16] Under Section 18, a court also has the discretion to assess reasonable costs, including attorneys' fees, against accountants.[17] Sellers and purchasers may maintain a cause of action "within one year after the discovery of the facts constituting the cause of action and within three years after such cause of action accrued."[18]

Liability under Section 18 is narrow in that it applies only to applications, reports, documents, and registration statements filed with the SEC. This remedy is further limited in that it applies only to sellers and purchasers. Under Section 18, a seller or purchaser must prove one of the following:

1. That the false or misleading statement affected the price of the security.
2. That the purchaser or seller relied on the false or misleading statement in making the purchase or sale and was not aware of the inaccuracy of the statement.

—The Good Faith Defense. Even if a purchaser or seller proves these two elements, an accountant can be exonerated of liability by proving good faith in the preparation of the financial statement. To demonstrate good faith, an accountant must show that he or she had no knowledge that the financial statement was false or misleading. Acting in good faith requires the total absence of any intention on the part of the accountant to seek an unfair advantage over, or to

defraud, another party. Proving a lack of intent to deceive, manipulate, or defraud is frequently referred to as proving a lack of *scienter* (knowledge on the part of a misrepresenting party that material facts have been misrepresented or omitted with an intent to deceive).

—Demonstrating the Absence of Good Faith. The absence of good faith can be demonstrated not only by proof of *scienter* but also by the accountant's reckless conduct and gross negligence. (Note that "mere" negligence in the preparation of a financial statement does not constitute liability under the 1934 act. This differs from provisions of the 1933 act, under which an accountant is liable for all negligent actions.) In addition to the good faith defense, the buyer's or seller's knowledge that the financial statement was false or misleading also operates as a defense.

LIABILITY UNDER SECTION 10(b) AND SEC RULE 10b-5 The Securities Exchange Act of 1934 further subjects accountants to potential legal liability in its antifraud provisions. Section 10(b) of the 1934 act and SEC Rule 10b-5 contain these provisions.

Section 10(b) of the 1934 act makes it unlawful for any person, including an accountant, to use, in connection with the purchase or sale of any security, any manipulative or deceptive device or contrivance in contravention of SEC rules and regulations.[19] Rule 10b-5 further makes it unlawful for any person, by use of any means or instrumentality of interstate commerce, to do the following:

1. Employ any device, scheme, or artifice to defraud.
2. Make any untrue statement of a material fact or omit to state a material fact necessary to make the statements made, in light of the circumstances, not misleading.
3. Engage in any act, practice, or course of business that operates or would operate as a fraud or deceit on any person, in connection with the purchase or sale of any security.[20]

—The Scope of Accountants' Liability under Section 10(b) and Rule 10b-5. Accountants may be held liable only to sellers or purchasers under Section 10(b) and Rule 10b-5. The scope of these antifraud provisions is extremely wide. Privity is not necessary

---

16. 15 U.S.C. Section 78r(a).
17. 15 U.S.C. Section 78r(a).
18. 15 U.S.C. Section 78r(c).

19. 15 U.S.C. Section 78j(b).
20. 17 C.F.R. Section 240.10b-5.

for a recovery. Under these provisions, an accountant may be found liable not only for fraudulent misstatements of material facts in written material filed with the SEC but also for any fraudulent oral statements or omissions made in connection with the purchase or sale of any security.

—Requirements for Recovering Damages. To recover from an accountant under the antifraud provisions of the 1934 act, a plaintiff must, in addition to establishing status as a purchaser or seller, prove *scienter,* a fraudulent action or deception, reliance, materiality, and causation. A plaintiff who fails to establish these elements cannot recover damages from an accountant under Section 10(b) or Rule 10b-5.

THE PRIVATE SECURITIES LITIGATION REFORM ACT OF 1995

The Private Securities Litigation Reform Act of 1995 imposed a new statutory obligation on accountants. An auditor must use adequate procedures in an audit to detect any illegal acts of the company being audited. If something illegal is detected, the auditor must disclose it to the company's board of directors, the audit committee, or the SEC, depending on the circumstances.[21] The act also states that aiding and abetting a violation of the Securities Exchange Act of 1934 is a violation in itself. An accountant aids and abets when she or he is generally aware that she or he is participating in an activity that is improper and knowingly assists the activity. Silence may constitute aiding.

In terms of liability, the 1995 act provides that in most situations, a party is liable only for that proportion of damages for which he or she is responsible.[22] For example, if an accountant actually participated in defrauding investors, he or she could be liable for the entire loss. If the accountant was not aware of the fraud, however, his or her liability could be proportionately less.

If an accountant knowingly aids and abets a primary violator, the SEC can seek an injunction or money damages. For example, Smith & Jones, an accounting firm, performs an audit for ABC Sales Company that is so inadequate as to constitute gross negligence. ABC uses the materials provided by Smith & Jones as part of a scheme to defraud investors. When the scheme is uncovered, the SEC can bring an action against Smith & Jones for aiding and abetting on the ground that the firm knew or should have known of the material misrepresentations that were in its audit and on which investors were likely to rely.

SECTION 5 | Potential Criminal Liability of Accountants

An accountant may be found criminally liable for violations of the Securities Act of 1933, the Securities Exchange Act of 1934, the Internal Revenue Code, and state criminal codes.

CRIMINAL VIOLATIONS OF SECURITIES LAWS

Under both the 1933 act and the 1934 act, accountants may be subject to criminal penalties for *willful* violations—imprisonment for up to five years and/or a fine of up to $10,000 under the 1933 act and up to ten years and $100,000 under the 1934 act. Under the Sarbanes-Oxley Act of 2002, for a securities filing that is accompanied by an accountant's false or misleading certified audit statement, the accountant may be fined up to $5 million, imprisoned for up to twenty years, or both.

CRIMINAL VIOLATIONS OF TAX LAWS

The Internal Revenue Code makes aiding or assisting in the preparation of a false tax return a felony punishable by a fine of $100,000 ($500,000 in the case of a corporation) and imprisonment for up to three years.[23] This provision does not apply solely to accountants but to anyone who prepares tax returns for others for compensation.[24] A penalty of $250 per tax return is levied on tax preparers for negligent understatement of the client's tax liability, and a penalty of $1,000 is imposed for willful understatement of tax liability or reckless or intentional disregard of rules or regulations.[25]

A tax preparer may also be subject to penalties for failing to furnish the taxpayer with a copy of the

---

21. 15 U.S.C. Section 78j-1.
22. 15 U.S.C. Section 78u-4(g).

23. 26 U.S.C. Section 7206(2).
24. 26 U.S.C. Section 7701(a)(36).
25. 26 U.S.C. Section 6694.

CONCEPT SUMMARY 51.2 | Statutory Liability of Accountants and Other Professionals

STATUTE	NATURE OF LIABILITY
SARBANES-OXLEY ACT OF 2002	See Exhibit 51–1 on page 1037 for the duties of the Public Company Accounting Oversight Board and the provisions of the act on auditor independence. Additionally, under Section 802(a)(1) of the act, accountants are required, in some circumstances, to maintain working papers relating to an audit or review for five years from the end of the fiscal period in which the audit or review was concluded. A knowing violation of this requirement will subject the accountant to a fine, imprisonment for up to ten years, or both.
SECURITIES ACT OF 1933, SECTIONS 11 AND 12(2)	Under Section 11 of the 1933 Securities Act, an accountant who makes a false statement or omits a material fact in audited financial statements required for registration of securities under the law may be liable to anyone who acquires securities covered by the registration statement. The accountant's defense is basically the use of due diligence and the reasonable belief that the work was complete and correct. The burden of proof is on the accountant. Willful violations of this act may be subject to criminal penalties. Section 12(2) of the 1933 act imposes civil liability for fraud on anyone offering or selling a security to any purchaser of the security.
SECURITIES EXCHANGE ACT OF 1934, SECTIONS 10(b) AND 18	Under Sections 10(b) and 18 of the 1934 Securities Exchange Act, accountants are held liable for false and misleading applications, reports, and documents required under the act. The burden is on the plaintiff, and the accountant has numerous defenses, including good faith and lack of knowledge that what was submitted was false. Willful violations of this act may be subject to criminal penalties.
INTERNAL REVENUE CODE	1. Aiding or assisting in the preparation of a false tax return is a felony. Aiding and abetting an individual's understatement of tax liability is a separate crime. 2. Tax preparers who negligently or willfully understate a client's tax liability or who recklessly or intentionally disregard Internal Revenue rules or regulations are subject to criminal penalties. 3. Tax preparers who fail to provide a taxpayer with a copy of the return, fail to sign the return, or fail to furnish the appropriate tax identification numbers may also be subject to criminal penalties.

return, failing to sign the return, or failing to furnish the appropriate tax identification numbers.[26] In addition, those who prepare tax returns for others may be fined $1,000 per document for aiding and abetting another's understatement of tax liability (the penalty is increased to $10,000 in corporate cases).[27] The tax preparer's liability is limited to one penalty per taxpayer per tax year.

VIOLATION OF STATE CRIMINAL LAWS

In most states, criminal penalties may be imposed for such actions as knowingly certifying false or fraudulent

reports; falsifying, altering, or destroying books of account; and obtaining property or credit through the use of false financial statements.

SECTION 6 | Confidentiality and Privilege

Professionals are restrained by the ethical tenets of their professions to keep all communications with their clients confidential.

ATTORNEY-CLIENT RELATIONSHIPS

The confidentiality of attorney-client communications is protected by law, which confers a *privilege* on

---

26. 26 U.S.C. Section 6695.
27. 26 U.S.C. Section 6701.

such communications. This privilege is granted because of the need for full disclosure to the attorney of the facts of a client's case.

To encourage frankness, confidential attorney-client communications relating to representation are normally held in strictest confidence and protected by law. The attorney and her or his employees may not discuss the client's case with anyone—even under court order—without the client's permission. The client holds the privilege, and only the client may waive it—by disclosing privileged information to someone outside the privilege, for example.

Note, however, that since the Sarbanes-Oxley Act was enacted in 2002, the SEC has implemented new rules requiring attorneys who become aware that a client has violated securities laws to report the violation to the SEC. Reporting a client's misconduct could be a breach of the attorney-client privilege and has caused much controversy in the legal community (see the *Focus on Ethics* feature at the end of Unit 8 for more details).

ACCOUNTANT-CLIENT RELATIONSHIPS

In a few states, accountant-client communications are privileged by state statute. In these states, accountant-client communications may not be revealed even in court or in court-sanctioned proceedings without the client's permission. The majority of states, however, abide by the common law, which provides that, if a court so orders, an accountant must disclose information about his or her client to the court. Physicians and other professionals may similarly be compelled to disclose in court information given to them in confidence by patients or clients.

Communications between professionals and their clients—other than those between an attorney and his or her client—are not privileged under federal law. In cases involving federal law, state-provided rights to confidentiality of accountant-client communications are not recognized. Thus, in those cases, in response to a court order, an accountant must provide the information sought.

REVIEWING PROFESSIONAL LIABILITY AND ACCOUNTABILITY

Superior Wholesale Corp. planned to purchase Regal Furniture, Inc., and wished to determine Regal's net worth. Superior hired Lynette Shuebke, of the accounting firm Shuebke Delgado, to review an audit that had been prepared by Norman Chase, the accountant for Regal. Shuebke advised Superior that Chase had performed a high-quality audit and that Regal's inventory on the audit dates was stated fairly on the general ledger. As a result of these representations, Superior went forward with its purchase of Regal. After the purchase, Superior discovered that the audit by Chase had been materially inaccurate and misleading, primarily because the inventory had been grossly overstated on the balance sheet. Later, a former Regal employee who had begun working for Superior exposed an e-mail exchange between Chase and former Regal chief executive officer Buddy Gantry. The exchange revealed that Chase had cooperated in overstating the inventory and understating Regal's tax liability. Using the information presented in the chapter, answer the following questions.

1. If Shuebke's review was conducted in good faith and conformed to generally accepted accounting principles, could Superior hold Shuebke Delgado liable for negligently failing to detect material omissions in Chase's audit? Why or why not?

2. According to the rule adopted by the majority of courts to determine accountants' liability to third parties, could Chase have been liable to Superior?

3. Generally, what requirements must be met before Superior can recover damages under Section 10(b) of the Securities and Exchange Act of 1934 and SEC Rule 10b-5? Could Superior meet these requirements?

4. Suppose that a court determined that Chase had aided Regal in willfully understating its tax liability. What is the maximum penalty that could be imposed on Chase?

5. How might Shuebke's partner, Carlo Delgado, attempt to limit his liability for any misconduct committed by Shuebke?

TERMS AND CONCEPTS TO REVIEW

defalcation 1029

due diligence 1038

generally accepted accounting
  principles (GAAP) 1029

generally accepted auditing
  standards (GAAS) 1029

working papers 1036

QUESTIONS AND CASE PROBLEMS

51–1. Larkin, Inc., retains Howard Patterson to manage its books and prepare its financial statements. Patterson, a certified public accountant, lives in Indiana and practices there. After twenty years, Patterson has become a bit bored with the format of generally accepted accounting principles (GAAP) and has become creative in his accounting methods. Now, though, Patterson has a problem, as he is being sued by Molly Tucker, one of Larkin's creditors. Tucker alleges that Patterson either knew or should have known that Larkin's financial statements would be distributed to various individuals. Furthermore, she asserts that these financial statements were negligently prepared and seriously inaccurate. What are the consequences of Patterson's failure to adopt GAAP? Under the traditional *Ultramares* rule, can Tucker recover damages from Patterson? Explain.

51–2. **QUESTION WITH SAMPLE ANSWER**

The accounting firm of Goldman, Walters, Johnson & Co. prepared financial statements for Lucy's Fashions, Inc. After reviewing the various financial statements, Happydays State Bank agreed to loan Lucy's Fashions $35,000 for expansion. When Lucy's Fashions declared bankruptcy under Chapter 11 six months later, Happydays State Bank promptly filed an action against Goldman, Walters, Johnson & Co., alleging negligent preparation of financial statements. Assuming that the court has abandoned the *Ultramares* approach, what is the result? What are the policy reasons for holding accountants liable to third parties with whom they are not in privity?

For a sample answer to this question, go to Appendix I at the end of this text.

51–3. In early 1995, Bennett, Inc., offered a substantial number of new common shares to the public. Harvey Helms had a long-standing interest in Bennett because his grandfather had once been president of the company. On receiving a prospectus prepared and distributed by Bennett, Helms was dismayed by the pessimism it embodied. Helms decided to delay purchasing stock in the company. Later, Helms asserted that the prospectus prepared by the accountants was overly pessimistic and contained materially misleading statements. Discuss

fully how successful Helms would be in bringing a cause of action under Rule 10b-5 against the accountants of Bennett, Inc.

51–4. **ACCOUNTANT'S LIABILITY TO THIRD PARTIES.** Toro Co. was a major supplier of equipment and credit to Summit Power Equipment Distributors. Toro required audited reports from Summit to evaluate the distributor's financial condition. Summit supplied Toro with reports prepared by Krouse, Kern & Co., an accounting firm. The reports allegedly contained mistakes and omissions regarding Summit's financial condition. According to Toro, it extended and renewed large amounts of credit to Summit in reliance on the audited reports. Summit was unable to repay these amounts, and Toro brought a negligence action against the accounting firm and the individual accountants. Evidence produced at the trial showed that Krouse knew that the reports it furnished to Summit would be used by Summit to induce Toro to extend credit, but no evidence was produced to show either a contractual relationship between Krouse and Toro or a link between these companies evidencing Krouse's understanding of Toro's actual reliance on the reports. The relevant state law follows the *Ultramares* rule. What was the result? [*Toro Co. v. Krouse, Kern & Co.*, 827 F.2d 155 (7th Cir. 1987)]

51–5. **ATTORNEY'S DUTY OF CARE.** Sheila Simpson and the other two shareholders in H. P. Enterprises Corp. decided to sell the corporation and turned to Ed Oliver, an attorney, for assistance. Oliver formed a corporation, Tide Creek, for a group of investors, and Tide Creek then purchased the assets of H. P. Enterprises for $500,000, $100,000 of which was paid at the time of the sale in November 1983. As security for the sellers, Oliver provided a lien on the stock of Tide Creek and personal guaranties of the buyers on the corporation's $400,000 note to the sellers. Oliver was the sole source of legal advice for both parties. About six months after the sale, a fire destroyed Tide Creek's inventory. In October 1984, Oliver left the law firm in which he had been a partner, and one of the other partners, David James, took over the Simpson and Tide Creek accounts. In January 1985, James advised Simpson that Tide Creek was having financial difficulties and suggested that the note be restructured; this was accomplished. When Simpson asked James what he would do if her interests and those of Tide Creek diverged, James replied, "We would have to support you." Tide Creek later filed for bankruptcy, as did the individuals who had personally guaranteed the note, and Simpson and the others received nothing. Should the sellers succeed in a lawsuit against James for negligence? Discuss fully. [*Simpson v. James*, 903 F.2d 372 (5th Cir. 1990)]

51-6. ACCOUNTANT'S LIABILITY TO THIRD PARTIES. In June 1993, Sparkomatic Corp. agreed to negotiate a sale of its Kenco Engineering division to Williams Controls, Inc. At the end of July, Sparkomatic asked its accountants, Parente, Randolph, Orlando, Carey & Associates, to audit Kenco's financial statements for the previous three years and to certify interim and closing balance sheets to be included with the sale's closing documents. All of the parties knew that these documents would serve as a basis for setting the sale price. Within a few days, Williams signed an "Asset Purchase Agreement" that promised access to Parente's records with respect to Kenco. The sale closed in mid-August. In September, Williams was given the financial statements for Kenco's previous three years and the interim and closing balance sheets, all of which were certified by Parente. Williams's accountant found no errors in the closing balance sheet but did not review any of the other documents. The parties set a final purchase price. Later, however, Williams filed a suit in a federal district court against Parente, claiming negligent misrepresentation, among other things, in connection with Parente's preparation of the financial documents. Parente responded with a motion for summary judgment, asserting that the parties lacked privity. Under the *Restatement (Second) of Torts*, Section 552, how should the court rule? Explain. [*Williams Controls, Inc. v. Parente, Randolph, Orlando, Carey & Associates*, 39 F.Supp.2d 517 (M.D.Pa. 1999)]

51-7. ⚖ CASE PROBLEM WITH SAMPLE ANSWER

In October 1993, Marilyn Greenen, a licensed certified public accountant (CPA), began working at the Port of Vancouver, Washington (the Port), as an account manager. She was not directly engaged in public accounting at the Port, but she oversaw the preparation of financial statements and supervised employees with accounting duties. At the start of her employment, she enrolled her husband for benefits under the Port's medical plan. Her marriage was dissolved in November, but she did not notify the Port of the change. In May 1998 and April 1999, the Port confronted her about the divorce, but she did not update her insurance information. After she was terminated, she reimbursed the Port for the additional premiums it had paid for unauthorized coverage for her former spouse. The Washington State Board of Accountancy imposed sanctions on Greenen for "dishonesty and misleading representations" while, in the words of an applicable state statute, "representing oneself as a CPA." Greenen asked a Washington state court to review the case. What might be an appropriate sanction in this case? What might be Greenen's best argument against the board's action? On what reasoning might the court uphold the decision? [*Greenen v. Washington State Board of Accountancy*, 824 Wash.App. 126, 110 P.3d 224 (Div. 2 2005)]

To view a sample answer for this case problem, go to this book's Web site at http://wbl.westbuslaw.com, select "Chapter 51," and click on "Case Problem with Sample Answer."

51-8. ACCOUNTANT'S LIABILITY. In 1995, JTD Health Systems, Inc., hired Tammy Heiby as accounting coordinator. Apparently overwhelmed by the duties of the position, Heiby failed to make payroll tax payments to the Internal Revenue Service (IRS) in 1995 and 1996. Heiby tried to hide this omission by falsifying journal entries and manually writing three checks out of sequence, totaling $1.7 million and payable to a bank, from JTD's cash account (to dispose of excess funds that should have been paid in taxes). JTD hired Pricewaterhouse Coopers, LLP, to review JTD's internal accounting procedures and audit its financial statements for 1995. Coopers's inexperienced auditor was aware that the cash account had not been balanced in months and knew about the checks but never questioned them. The auditor instead mistakenly explained that the unbalanced account was due to changes in Medicaid/Medicare procedures and recommended no further investigation. In 1996, the IRS asked JTD to remit the unpaid taxes, plus interest and penalties. JTD filed a suit in an Ohio state court against Coopers, alleging common law negligence and breach of contract. Should Coopers be held liable to JTD on these grounds? Why or why not? [*JTD Health Systems, Inc. v. Pricewaterhouse Coopers, LLP*, 141 Ohio App.3d 280, 750 N.E.2d 1177 (Ohio App. 3 Dist. 2001)]

51-9. ACCOUNTANT'S LIABILITY UNDER THE PRIVATE SECURITIES LITIGATION REFORM ACT. Solucorp Industries, Ltd., a corporation headquartered in New York, develops and markets products for use in environmental clean-ups. Solucorp's financial statements for the six months ending December 31, 1997, recognized $1.09 million in license fees payable by Smart International, Ltd. The fees comprised about 50 percent of Solucorp's revenue for the period. At the time, however, the parties had a license agreement only "in principle," and Smart had made only one payment of $150,000. Glenn Ohlhauser, an accountant asked to audit the statements, objected to the inclusion of the fees. In February 1998, Solucorp showed Ohlhauser a license agreement backdated to September 1997 but refused to provide any financial information about Smart. Ohlhauser issued an unqualified opinion on the 1997 statements, which were included with forms filed with the Securities and Exchange Commission (SEC). The SEC filed a suit in a federal district court against Ohlhauser and others. What might be the basis in the Private Securities Litigation

Reform Act for the SEC's suit against Ohlhauser? What might be Ohlhauser's defense? Discuss. [*Securities and Exchange Commission v. Solucorp Industries, Ltd.,* 197 F.Supp.2d 4 (S.D.N.Y. 2002)]

51-10. VIDEO QUESTION

Go to this text's Web site at http://wbl.westbuslaw.com and select "Chapter 51." Click on "Video Questions" and view the video titled *Accountant's Liability.* Then answer the following questions.

(a) Should Ray prepare a financial statement that values a list of assets provided by the advertising firm without verifying that the firm actually owns these assets?

(b) Discuss whether Ray is in privity with the company interested in buying Laura's advertising firm.

(c) Under the *Ultramares* rule, to whom does Ray owe a duty?

(d) Assume that Laura did not tell Ray that she intended to give the financial statement to the potential acquirer. Would this fact change Ray's liability under the *Ultramares* rule? Explain.

LAW | on the Web

For updated links to resources available on the Web, as well as a variety of other materials, visit this text's Web site at http://wbl.westbuslaw.com.

The Web site for the Financial Accounting Standards Board can be found at

http://www.fasb.org

For information on the accounting profession, including links to the Sarbanes-Oxley Act of 2002 and articles concerning the act's impact on the accounting profession, go to the Web site of the American Institute of Certified Public Accountants (AICPA) at

http://aicpa.org/index.htm

LEGAL RESEARCH EXERCISES ON THE WEB

Go to **http://wbl.westbuslaw.com**, the Web site that accompanies this text. Select "Chapter 51" and click on "Internet Exercises." There you will find the following Internet research exercises that you can perform to learn more about topics covered in this chapter.

Activity 51–1: LEGAL PERSPECTIVE
The Sarbanes-Oxley Act of 2002

Activity 51–2: MANAGEMENT PERSPECTIVE
Avoiding Legal Liability

CHAPTER 52

International Law

Since ancient times independent peoples and nations have traded their goods and wares with one another. What is new in our day is the dramatic growth in world trade and the emergence of a global business community. Today, nearly every major business considers the potential of international markets for its products or services. It is no longer uncommon for a U.S. corporation to have investments or manufacturing plants in a foreign country or for a foreign corporation to have operations in the United States. Because the exchange of goods, services, and ideas (intellectual property) on a worldwide level is now routine, students of business law should be familiar with the laws pertaining to international business transactions.

Laws affecting the international legal environment of business include both international law and national law. **International law** can be defined as a body of law—formed as a result of international customs, treaties, and organizations—that governs relations among or between nations. International law may be public, creating standards for the nations themselves; or it may be private, establishing international standards for private transactions that cross national borders. **National law** is the law of a particular nation, such as the United States, Japan, Germany, or Brazil. In this chapter, we examine how both international law and national law frame business operations in the international context.

SECTION 1 | International Law

The major difference between international law and national law is that government authorities can enforce national law. What government, however, can enforce international law? By definition, a *nation* is a sovereign entity—which means that there is no higher authority to which that nation must submit. If a nation violates an international law and persuasive tactics fail, other countries or international organizations have no recourse except to take coercive actions—from severance of diplomatic relations and boycotts to, as a last resort, war—against the violating nation.

In essence, international law is the result of centuries-old attempts to reconcile the traditional need of each country to be the final authority over its own affairs with the desire of nations to benefit economically from trade and harmonious relations with one another. Sovereign nations can, and do, voluntarily agree to be governed in certain respects by international law for the purpose of facilitating international trade and commerce, as well as civilized discourse. As a result, a body

of international law has evolved. In this section, we examine the primary sources and characteristics of that body of law, as well as some important legal principles and doctrines that have been developed over time to facilitate dealings among nations.

SOURCES OF INTERNATIONAL LAW

Basically, there are three sources of international law: international customs, treaties and international agreements, and international organizations and conferences. We look at each of these sources here.

INTERNATIONAL CUSTOMS One important source of international law consists of the international customs that have evolved among nations in their relations with one another. Article 38(1) of the Statute of the International Court of Justice refers to an international custom as "evidence of a general practice accepted as law." The legal principles and doctrines that you will read about shortly are rooted in international customs and traditions that have evolved over time in the international arena.

TREATIES AND INTERNATIONAL AGREEMENTS

Treaties and other explicit agreements between or among foreign nations provide another important source of international law. A **treaty** is an agreement or contract between two or more nations that must be authorized and ratified by the supreme power of each nation. Under Article II, Section 2, of the U.S. Constitution, the president has the power "by and with the Advice and Consent of the Senate, to make Treaties, provided two-thirds of the Senators present concur."

A *bilateral* agreement, as the term implies, is an agreement formed by two nations to govern their commercial exchanges or other relations with one another. A *multilateral* agreement is formed by several nations. For example, regional trade associations such as the European Union (EU) and the trading unit established by the North American Free Trade Agreement (NAFTA), both of which are discussed later in this chapter, are the result of multilateral trade agreements. Other regional trade associations that have been created through multilateral agreements include the Association of Southeast Asian Nations (ASEAN) and the Andean Common Market (ANCOM).

INTERNATIONAL ORGANIZATIONS International organizations and conferences further contribute to international law. In international law, the term **international organization** generally refers to an organization composed mainly of nations' officials and usually established by treaty.

The United States is a member of more than one hundred multilateral and bilateral organizations, including at least twenty through the United Nations (see Exhibit 52–1 on page 1049). These organizations adopt resolutions, declarations, and other types of standards that often require nations to behave in a particular manner. The General Assembly of the United Nations, for example, has adopted numerous nonbinding resolutions and declarations that embody principles of international law. Disputes with respect to these resolutions and declarations may be brought before the International Court of Justice. That court, however, normally has authority to settle legal disputes only when nations voluntarily submit to its jurisdiction.

The United Nations Commission on International Trade Law has made considerable progress in establishing uniformity in international law as it relates to trade and commerce. One of the commission's most significant creations to date is the 1980 Convention on Contracts for the International Sale of Goods (CISG). Recall from Chapters 20 through 23, which cover contracts for the sale of goods, that the CISG is similar to Article 2 of the Uniform Commercial Code in that it is designed to settle disputes between parties to sales contracts. It spells out the duties of international buyers and sellers that will apply if the parties have not agreed otherwise in their contracts. The CISG only governs sales contracts between trading partners in nations that have ratified the CISG, however.

International legal disputes also have unique procedural requirements with which parties must be familiar. The following case provides an example of this necessity.

CASE 52.1 · Brockmeyer v. May

United States Court of Appeals, Ninth Circuit, 2004. 383 F.3d 798.

BACKGROUND AND FACTS *Ronald Brockmeyer owns the trademark <<O>>, under which he distributes adult entertainment media and novelties. He brought suit against a British company, Marquis Publications, Ltd., in a U.S. district court, alleging that Marquis had violated his trademark rights. Brockmeyer sent the summons and complaint to a post office box in England but received no response. He send a second letter by first class mail to the post office box, but Marquis again did not respond. The court entered a default judgment for Brockmeyer, awarding him damages of $410,806.12, plus attorneys' fees and costs. Marquis moved to set aside this judgment for failure of service, contending that international service must be made by certified or registered mail. The district court denied the motion, and Marquis appealed.*

IN THE LANGUAGE OF THE COURT

FLETCHER, Circuit Judge

* * * *

The resolution of this appeal depends on whether Marquis was properly served. Because service of process was attempted abroad, the validity of that service is controlled by [Rule 4(f) of] the Hague Convention. * * *

CONTINUED ▶

CASE 52.1 Continued

* * * *

Today we join the Second Circuit in holding that the Hague Convention allows service of process by international mail. At the same time, we hold that any service by mail in this case was required to be performed in accordance with the requirements of Rule 4(f). Service by international mail is affirmatively authorized by Rule 4(f)(2)(C)(ii), which requires that service be sent by the clerk of the court, using a form of mail requiring a signed receipt. Service by international mail is also affirmatively authorized by Rule 4(f)(3) which requires that the mailing procedure have been specifically directed by the district court. * * * [Plaintiffs] simply dropped the complaint and summons in a mailbox in Los Angeles, to be delivered by ordinary, international first class mail. There is no affirmative authorization for such service in Rule 4(f). The attempted service was therefore ineffective, and the default judgment against Marquis cannot stand.

DECISION AND REMEDY *The U.S. Court of Appeals for the Ninth Circuit reversed the district court's decision and remanded the case to the district court, with instructions to vacate (set aside, treat as void) the judgment against Marquis.*

WHAT IF THE FACTS WERE DIFFERENT? *If Brockmeyer had served Marquis by certified or registered mail, would the result have been different?*

Legal Principles and Doctrines

Over time, a number of legal principles and doctrines have evolved and have been employed—to a greater or lesser extent—by the courts of various nations to resolve or reduce conflicts that involve a foreign element. The three important legal principles discussed below are based primarily on courtesy and respect and are applied in the interests of maintaining harmonious relations among nations.

THE PRINCIPLE OF COMITY   Under what is known as the principle of **comity,** one nation will defer and give effect to the laws and judicial decrees of another country, as long as those laws and judicial decrees are consistent with the law and public policy of the accommodating nation. For example, assume that a Swedish seller and an American buyer have formed a contract, which the buyer breaches. The seller sues the buyer in a Swedish court, which awards damages. The buyer's assets, however, are in the United States and cannot be reached unless the judgment is enforced by a U.S. court of law. In this situation, if a U.S. court determines that the procedures and laws applied in the Swedish court are consistent with U.S. national law and policy, the U.S. court will likely defer to, and enforce, the foreign court's judgment.

One way to understand the principle of comity (and the *act of state doctrine,* which will be discussed shortly) is to consider the relationships among the states in our federal form of government. Each state honors (gives "full faith and credit" to) the contracts, property deeds, wills, and other legal obligations formed in other states, as well as judicial decisions with respect to such obligations. On a worldwide basis, nations similarly attempt to honor judgments rendered in other countries when it is feasible to do so. Of course, a major difference between U.S. federalism and the relationships among nations is that the states within the United States are constitutionally bound to honor other states' actions (see the discussion of the full faith and credit clause in Chapter 4). There is no world constitution, so international doctrines rest primarily on courtesy.

THE ACT OF STATE DOCTRINE   The **act of state doctrine** is a judicially created doctrine that provides that the judicial branch of one country will not examine the validity of public acts committed by a recognized foreign government within its own territory. This doctrine is premised on the theory that the judicial branch should not "pass upon the validity of foreign acts when to do so would vex the harmony of our international relations with that foreign nation."

The act of state doctrine can have important consequences for individuals and firms doing business with, and investing in, other countries. For example, this doctrine is frequently employed in cases involving **expropriation,** which occurs when a government seizes a privately owned business or privately owned goods for a proper public purpose and awards just compensation. When a government seizes private property for an illegal purpose and without just compensation, the taking is referred to as a **confiscation.** The line between these two forms of taking is sometimes blurred because of differing interpretations of what is

EXHIBIT 52-1 Selected Multilateral International Organizations in Which the United States Participates

NAME	PURPOSE
Customs Cooperation Council	Established in 1950. Supervises the application and interpretation of an international code classifying goods and customs tariffs.
International Bank for Reconstruction and Development	Popularly known as the World Bank; a specialized agency of the United Nations since 1947. Promotes growth, trade, and balance of trade by facilitating and providing technical assistance, particularly in agriculture, energy, transportation, and telecommunications.
International Civil Aviation Organization	Established in 1947 and became a specialized agency of the United Nations seven months later. Develops international civil aviation by issuing rules and policies for safe and efficient airports and air navigation.
International Court of Justice (World Court)	Established in 1922 and became one of the principal organs of the United Nations in 1945. Jurisdiction comprises all cases that are referred to it. Decides disputes in accordance with the rules of international law.
International Maritime Organization	Established in 1948. Promotes cooperation in the areas of government regulation, practices and technical matters of all kinds affecting shipping in international trade, the adoption of standards of maritime safety and efficiency, and the abolition of discrimination and unnecessary restrictions.
International Telecommunications Satellite Organization	Established in 1964. Operates an international public communications satellite system on a commercial, nondiscriminatory basis.
Permanent Court of Arbitration	Established in 1899 to facilitate the settlement of international disputes. The court has jurisdiction over all cases that it is requested to arbitrate.
World Intellectual Property Organization	Established in 1967 and became a specialized agency of the United Nations in 1974. Promotes protection of intellectual property throughout the world.
World Trade Organization (WTO)	Established in 1994 during the final round of negotiations of the General Agreement on Tariffs and Trade (GATT). The GATT was created in 1947 and was the first global commercial agreement in history. It became the principal instrument for regulating international trade and limiting tariffs and other barriers to world trade on particular commodities and other items. GATT ceased to exist in 1995, when the WTO came into existence to regulate worldwide trade.

illegal and what constitutes just compensation. To illustrate: Tim Flaherty, an American businessperson, owns a mine in Brazil. The government of Brazil seizes the mine for public use and claims that the profits Tim has already realized from the mine constitute just compensation. Tim disagrees, but the act of state doctrine may prevent Tim's recovery in a U.S. court of law. Note that in a case alleging that a foreign government has wrongfully taken the plaintiff's property, the defendant government has the burden of proving that the taking was an expropriation, not a confiscation.

When applicable, both the act of state doctrine and the doctrine of *sovereign immunity*, which we discuss next, tend to shield foreign nations from the jurisdiction of U.S. courts. As a result, firms or individuals who own property overseas generally have little legal protection against government actions in the countries where they operate.

THE DOCTRINE OF SOVEREIGN IMMUNITY When certain conditions are satisfied, the doctrine of **sovereign immunity** exempts foreign nations from the jurisdiction of the U.S. courts. In 1976, Congress codified this rule in the Foreign Sovereign Immunities Act (FSIA).[1] The FSIA also modified previous applications of the doctrine in certain respects by expanding the rights of plaintiff creditors against foreign nations.

The FSIA exclusively governs the circumstances in which an action may be brought in the United

---

1. 28 U.S.C. Sections 1602–1611.

States against a foreign nation. Section 1605 of the FSIA sets forth the major exceptions to the jurisdictional immunity of a foreign state. A foreign state is not immune from the jurisdiction of U.S. courts when the state has "waived its immunity either explicitly or by implication" or when the state has engaged in actions that are taken "in connection with a commercial activity carried on in the United States by the foreign state" or that have "a direct effect in the United States." The FSIA also contains an exception for torts committed in the United States and for some violations of international law. Generally, because the law is jurisdictional in nature, a plaintiff has the burden of showing that a defendant is not entitled to sovereign immunity.

Questions frequently arise as to whether particular entities fall within the category of foreign state. Under Section 1603 of the FSIA, a *foreign state* is defined to include both a political subdivision of a foreign state and an instrumentality of a foreign state (an agency or entity acting for the state). The specification of a commercial activity has also been the subject of dispute because the act does not spell out the particulars of what constitutes a commercial activity. Rather, it is left to the courts to decide whether a particular activity is governmental or commercial in nature. In the following case, the United States Supreme Court considered whether the principles of the FSIA should apply to a dispute dating back to World War II, before the FSIA had been enacted.

CASE 52.2   Republic of Austria v. Altmann

Supreme Court of the United States, 2004.
541 U.S. 677,
124 S.Ct. 2240,
159 L.Ed.2d 1.

Justice *STEVENS* delivered the opinion of the Court.

In 1998 an Austrian journalist, granted access to the Austrian Gallery's archives [in Vienna, Austria], discovered evidence that certain valuable works in the Gallery's collection had not been donated by their rightful owners but had been seized by the Nazis or expropriated by the Austrian Republic after World War II. The journalist provided some of that evidence to respondent [Maria Altmann], who in turn filed this action [in a U.S. federal district court] to recover possession of six Gustav Klimt paintings. Prior to the Nazi invasion of Austria [in 1938], the paintings had hung in the palatial Vienna home of respondent's uncle, Ferdinand Bloch-Bauer, a Czechoslovakian Jew and patron of the arts. Respondent claims ownership of the paintings under a will executed by her uncle after he fled Austria in 1938. [In the will, he left his estate to Altmann, another niece, and Robert Bentley, a nephew.] She alleges that the Gallery obtained possession of the paintings through wrongful conduct in the years during and after World War II.

The defendants (petitioners here)—the Republic of Austria and the Austrian Gallery (Gallery), an instrumentality of the Republic—filed a motion to dismiss the complaint asserting, among other defenses, a claim of sovereign immunity. [Respondent argued that petitioners are not entitled to immunity because the FSIA exempts from immunity all cases involving "rights in property taken in violation of international law."] The District Court denied the [defendants'] motion, and the [U.S.] Court of Appeals [for the Ninth Circuit] affirmed. We granted *certiorari* limited to the question whether the Foreign Sovereign Immunities Act of 1976 (FSIA or Act) * * * applies to claims that, like respondent's, are based on conduct that occurred before the Act's enactment * * * .

     *   *   *   *

To begin with, the preamble of the FSIA expresses Congress' understanding that the Act would apply to all postenactment claims of sovereign immunity. That section provides:

> Claims of foreign states to immunity should henceforth be decided by courts of the United States and of the States in conformity with the principles set forth in this chapter.

* * * [T]his language is unambiguous: Immunity "claims"—not actions protected by immunity, but assertions of immunity to suits arising from those actions—are the relevant conduct regulated by the Act; those claims are "henceforth" to be decided by the courts. * * * [T]his language suggests *Congress intended courts to resolve all such claims "in conformity with the principles set forth" in the Act, regardless of when the underlying conduct occurred.* [Emphasis added.]

The FSIA's overall structure strongly supports this conclusion. Many of the Act's provisions unquestionably apply to cases arising out of conduct that occurred before 1976. * * * [F]or example, * * * whether an entity qualifies as an "instrumentality" of a "foreign state" for purposes of the FSIA's grant of immunity depends on the relationship between the entity and the state at the time suit is brought rather than when the conduct occurred. * * * [T]here has never been any doubt that the Act's procedural provisions relating to venue, removal, execution, and attachment apply to all pending cases. Thus, the FSIA's preamble indicates that it applies "henceforth," and its body includes numerous provisions that unquestionably apply to claims based on pre-1976 conduct. In this context, *it would be anomalous [irregular, unusual] to presume that an isolated provision (such as the expropriation exception on which respondent relies) is of purely prospective application absent any statutory language to that effect.* [Emphasis added.]

Finally, applying the FSIA to all pending cases regardless of when the underlying conduct occurred is most consistent with two of the Act's principal purposes: clarifying the rules that judges should apply in resolving sovereign immunity claims and eliminating political participation in the resolution of such claims. * * * [T]o accomplish these purposes, Congress established a comprehensive framework for resolving any claim of sovereign immunity: * * * the text and structure of the FSIA demonstrate Congress' intention that the FSIA be the sole basis for obtaining jurisdiction over a foreign state in our courts. * * * *Section 1604 bars federal and state courts from exercising jurisdiction when a foreign state is entitled to immunity, and Section 1330(a) confers jurisdiction on district courts to hear suits brought by United States citizens and by aliens when a foreign state is not entitled to immunity.* * * * [Emphasis added.]

* * * Quite obviously, Congress' purposes in enacting such a comprehensive jurisdictional scheme would be frustrated if, in postenactment cases concerning preenactment conduct, courts were to continue to follow the same ambiguous and politically charged standards that the FSIA replaced.

* * * [W]e affirm the [Court of Appeals'] judgment because the Act * * * clearly applies to conduct, like petitioners' alleged wrongdoing, that occurred prior to 1976 * * * .
* * * *

The judgment of the Court of Appeals is affirmed.
It is so ordered.

QUESTIONS

1. What did the United States Supreme Court hold in this case, and why?
2. How did this case come before the United States Supreme Court, and what is the next step in its journey through the courts?

SECTION 2 | Doing Business Internationally

A U.S. domestic firm can engage in international business transactions in a number of ways. Contracts for the international purchase and sale of goods were discussed earlier in this text, in Chapters 20 through 23. Here, we look at other aspects of international business transactions, including the ways in which businesspersons typically extend their business operations into the international arena, laws regulating international business activities, and dispute settlement in the international context.

TYPES OF INTERNATIONAL BUSINESS OPERATIONS

Most U.S. companies make the initial foray into international business through exporting. There are several other alternatives, however, including those discussed here.

EXPORTING The simplest way to engage in international business operations is to seek out foreign markets for domestically produced products. In other words, U.S. firms can **export** their goods and services to foreign markets. Exporting can take two forms: direct exporting and indirect exporting. In *direct exporting,* a

U.S. company signs a sales contract with a foreign purchaser that provides for the conditions of shipment and payment for the goods. (The use of letters of credit to make payments in international transactions was discussed in Chapter 20.) If business expands sufficiently in a foreign country, a U.S. company may develop a specialized marketing organization in that foreign market by appointing a foreign agent or a foreign distributor. This is called *indirect exporting*.

When a U.S. firm wishes to limit its involvement in an international market, it will typically establish an agency relationship with a foreign firm. In an agency relationship, one person (the agent) agrees to act on behalf of, or instead of, another (the principal) (see Chapter 31). The foreign agent is thereby empowered to enter into contracts in the agent's country on behalf of the U.S. principal.

When a substantial market exists in a foreign country, a U.S. firm may wish to appoint a distributor located in that country. The U.S. firm and the distributor enter into a **distribution agreement,** which is a contract between the seller and the distributor setting out the terms and conditions of the distributorship—for example, price, currency of payment, guaranty of supply availability, and method of payment. The terms and conditions primarily involve contract law. Disputes concerning distribution agreements may involve jurisdictional or other issues, however.

MANUFACTURING ABROAD An alternative to direct or indirect exporting is the establishment of foreign manufacturing facilities. Typically, U.S. firms establish manufacturing plants abroad when they believe that by doing so they will reduce costs—particularly for labor, shipping, and raw materials—and thereby be able to compete more effectively in foreign markets. Apple Computer, IBM, General Motors, and Ford are some of the many U.S. companies that have established manufacturing facilities abroad. Foreign firms have done the same in the United States. Sony, Nissan, and other Japanese manufacturers have established U.S. plants to avoid import duties that the U.S. Congress may impose on Japanese products entering this country.

A U.S. firm can conduct manufacturing operations in other countries in several ways. They include licensing and franchising, as well as investing in a wholly owned subsidiary or a joint venture.

—Licensing. A U.S. firm can obtain business from abroad by licensing a foreign manufacturing company to use its copyrighted, patented, or trademarked intellectual property or trade secrets. Like any other licensing agreement (see Chapters 8 and 19), a licensing agreement with a foreign-based firm calls for a payment of royalties on some basis—such as so many cents per unit produced or a certain percentage of profits from units sold in a particular geographic territory. For example, the Coca-Cola Bottling Company licenses firms worldwide to use (and keep confidential) its secret formula for the syrup used in its soft drink, in return for a percentage of the income gained from the sale of Coca-Cola by those firms.

The licensing of intellectual property rights benefits all parties to the transaction. The firm that receives the license can take advantage of an established reputation for quality. The firm that grants the license receives income from the foreign sales of its products and also establishes a global reputation. Also, once a firm's trademark is known worldwide, the demand for other products manufactured or sold by that firm may increase—obviously, an important consideration.

—Franchising. Franchising is a well-known form of licensing. Recall from Chapter 35 that a franchise is an arrangement in which the owner of a trademark, trade name, or copyright (the franchisor) licenses another (the franchisee) to use the trademark, trade name, or copyright, under certain conditions or limitations, in the selling of goods or services. In return, the franchisee pays a fee, which is usually based on a percentage of gross or net sales. Examples of international franchises include McDonald's, Holiday Inn, Avis, and Hertz.

—Investing in a Wholly Owned Subsidiary or a Joint Venture. Another way to expand into a foreign market is to establish a wholly owned subsidiary firm in a foreign country. A European subsidiary would likely take the form of a *société anonyme* (S.A.), which is similar to a U.S. corporation. In German-speaking nations, it would be called an *Aktiengesellschaft* (A.G.). When a wholly owned subsidiary is established, the parent company, which remains in the United States, retains complete ownership of all the facilities in the foreign country, as well as total authority and control over all phases of the operation.

A U.S. firm can also expand into international markets through a joint venture. In a joint venture, the U.S. company owns only part of the operation; the rest is owned either by local owners in the foreign country or by another foreign entity. All of the firms involved in a joint venture share responsibilities, as well as profits and liabilities. (See Chapter 37 for a more detailed discussion of joint ventures.)

THE REGULATION OF INTERNATIONAL BUSINESS ACTIVITIES

International business transactions can affect the economies, foreign policies, domestic politics, and other national interests of the countries involved. For this reason, nations impose laws to restrict or facilitate international business. Controls may also be imposed by international agreements.

INVESTING Firms that invest in foreign nations face the risk that the foreign government may expropriate the investment property. As mentioned earlier in this chapter, expropriation occurs when property is taken and the owner is paid just compensation for what is taken. This does not violate generally observed principles of international law. Such principles are normally violated, however, when property is confiscated by a government without compensation (or without adequate compensation).

Few remedies are available when property is confiscated by a foreign government. Claims are often resolved by lump-sum settlements after negotiations between the United States and the taking nation. For example, investors whose claims arose out of confiscations following the Russian Revolution in 1917 were offered a lump-sum settlement by the Union of Soviet Socialist Republics in 1974. Still outstanding are $2 billion in claims against Cuba for confiscations that occurred in 1959 and 1960.

To counter the deterrent effect that the possibility of confiscation may have on potential investors, many countries guarantee compensation to foreign investors if property is taken. A guaranty can be in the form of national constitutional or statutory laws or provisions in international treaties. As further protection for foreign investments, some countries provide insurance for their citizens' investments abroad.

EXPORT CONTROLS The U.S. Constitution provides in Article I, Section 9, that "No Tax or Duty shall be laid on Articles exported from any State." Thus, Congress cannot impose any export taxes. Congress can, however, use a variety of other devices to restrict or encourage exports. Congress may set export quotas on various items, such as grain being sold abroad.

IMPORT CONTROLS All nations have restrictions on imports, and the United States is no exception. Restrictions include strict prohibitions, quotas, and tariffs. Under the Trading with the Enemy Act of 1917,[2] for example, no goods may be imported from nations that have been designated enemies of the United States. Other laws prohibit the importation of illegal drugs, books that urge insurrection against the United States, and agricultural products that pose dangers to domestic crops or animals.

—Quotas and Tariffs. Limits on the amounts of goods that can be imported are known as **quotas.** At one time, the United States had legal quotas on the number of automobiles that could be imported from Japan. Today, Japan "voluntarily" restricts the number of automobiles exported to the United States. **Tariffs** are taxes on imports. A tariff is usually a percentage of the value of the import, but it can be a flat rate per unit (such as per barrel of oil). Tariffs raise the prices of goods, causing some consumers to purchase less expensive, domestically manufactured goods.

—Antidumping Duties. The United States has specific laws directed at what it sees as unfair international trade practices. **Dumping,** for example, is the sale of imported goods at "less than fair value." *Fair value* is usually determined by the price of those goods in the exporting country. Dumping is designed to undersell U.S. businesses and obtain a larger share of the U.S. market. To prevent this, an extra tariff—known as an *antidumping duty*—may be assessed on the imports.

The procedure for imposing antidumping duties involves two U.S. government agencies: the International Trade Commission (ITC) and the International Trade Administration (ITA). The ITC is an independent agency that assesses the effects of dumping on domestic businesses and then makes recommendations to the president concerning temporary import restrictions. The ITA, which is part of the Department of Commerce, decides whether imports were sold at less than fair value. The ITA's determination establishes the amount of antidumping duties, which are set to equal the difference between the price charged in the United States and the price charged in the exporting country. A duty may be retroactive to cover past dumping.

---

2. 12 U.S.C. Section 95a.

INTERNATIONAL AGREEMENTS Over the last decade, countries competing for international trade have become more evenly matched than in earlier years. In part, this is due to the increased use and success of international and regional organizations, such as the World Trade Organization, the European Union, and the North American Free Trade Agreement.

—The World Trade Organization. The origins of the World Trade Organization (WTO) date to 1947, when the General Agreement on Tariffs and Trade (GATT) was formed for the purpose of minimizing trade barriers among nations. In subsequent decades, the GATT became the principal instrument for regulating international trade and, over time, negotiated tariff reductions on a broad range of products.

In 1994, in a final round of GATT negotiations, called the "Uruguay Round," representatives from over one hundred nations signed agreements relating to investment policies, dispute resolution, and other topics. One of these agreements, the Trade-Related Aspects of Intellectual Property Rights Agreement (TRIPS), was discussed in Chapter 8. The Uruguay Round also established the WTO, which replaced the GATT beginning in 1995. Each member country of the WTO agreed to grant *most-favored-nation status* to other member countries. This status, now referred to as **normal trade relations (NTR) status,** means that each WTO member must treat other WTO members at least as well as it treats the country that receives its most favorable treatment with regard to imports or exports.

—The European Union (EU). The European Union (EU) arose out of the 1957 Treaty of Rome, which created the Common Market, a free trade zone comprising the nations of Belgium, France, West Germany, Italy, the Netherlands, and Luxembourg. Since 1957, more nations have been added. Today, the EU is a single integrated European trading unit made up of twenty-five European nations.

The EU has its own governing authorities. These include the Council of Ministers, which coordinates economic policies and includes one representative from each nation; a commission, which proposes regulations to the council; and an elected assembly, which oversees the commission. The EU also has its own court, the European Court of Justice, which can review each nation's judicial decisions and is the ultimate authority on EU law.

The EU has gone a long way toward creating a new body of law to govern all of the member nations— although some of its efforts to create uniform laws have been confounded by nationalism. The council and the commission issue regulations, or directives, that define EU law in various areas, and these requirements normally are binding on all member countries. EU directives govern such issues as environmental law, product liability, anticompetitive practices, and laws governing corporations. The EU directive on product liability, for example, states that a "producer of an article shall be liable for damages caused by a defect in the article, whether or not he knew or could have known of the defect." Liability extends to anyone who puts a trademark or other identifying feature on an article, and liability may not be excluded, even by contract.

—The North American Free Trade Agreement (NAFTA). The North American Free Trade Agreement (NAFTA), which was signed in 1993 and became effective on January 1, 1994, created a regional trading unit consisting of Mexico, the United States, and Canada. The primary goal of NAFTA is to eliminate tariffs among these three nations on substantially all goods over a period of fifteen to twenty years.

NAFTA gives the three countries a competitive advantage by retaining tariffs on goods imported from countries outside the NAFTA trading unit. Additionally, NAFTA provides for the elimination of barriers that traditionally have prevented the cross-border movement of services, such as financial and transportation services. For example, NAFTA provides that, with some exceptions, U.S. firms do not have to relocate to Mexico or Canada to provide services in those countries. NAFTA also attempts to eliminate citizenship requirements for the licensing of accountants, attorneys, physicians, and other professionals.

SECTION 3 | National Legal Systems

When doing business in a foreign nation, a company generally will be subject to the jurisdiction and laws of that nation. Therefore, businesspersons will find it helpful to become familiar with the legal systems and laws of foreign nations in which they conduct commercial transactions. In this section, we look at some similarities and differences among national legal systems. We conclude the section with a discussion of international tort law.

Generally, the legal systems of foreign nations differ, in widely varying degrees, from that of the United States. Additionally, a number of nations have specialized commercial law courts to deal with business disputes (in the United States, some jurisdictions are establishing similar courts). France instituted such courts in 1807, and most nations with commercial law codes have done likewise. The United Kingdom also has special commercial courts overseen by judges with expertise in business law.

COMMON LAW AND CIVIL LAW SYSTEMS

Legal systems around the globe generally are divided into *common law* and *civil law* systems.

COMMON LAW SYSTEMS As discussed in Chapter 1, in a common law system, the courts independently develop the rules governing certain areas of law, such as torts and contracts. These common law rules apply to all areas not covered by statutory law. Although the common law doctrine of *stare decisis* obligates judges to follow precedential decisions in their jurisdictions, courts may modify or even overturn precedents when deemed necessary. Additionally, if there is no case law to guide a court, the court may create a new rule of law. Common law systems exist today in countries that were once part of the British Empire (such as Australia, India, and the United States).

CIVIL LAW SYSTEMS In contrast to Great Britain and the other common law countries, most of the European nations base their legal systems on Roman civil law, or "code law." The term *civil law*, as used here, refers not to civil as opposed to criminal law but to *codified* law—an ordered grouping of legal principles enacted into law by a legislature or other governing body. In a **civil law system,** the only official source of law is a statutory code. Courts are required to interpret the code and apply the rules to individual cases, but courts may not depart from the code and develop their own laws. In theory, the law code will set forth all the principles needed for the legal system.

COUNTRIES USING COMMON LAW OR CIVIL LAW SYSTEMS Today, civil law systems are found in most of the continental European countries, as well as in the Latin American, African, and Asian countries that were once colonies of the continental European nations. Japan and South Africa also have civil law

systems. The Islamic courts of predominantly Muslim countries also use elements of the civil law system. In the United States, the state of Louisiana, because of its historical ties to France, has, in part, a civil law system. Exhibit 52–2 lists some of the nations that use civil law systems and some that use common law systems.

LEGAL SYSTEMS COMPARED Common law and civil law systems are not wholly distinct. For example, although the United States has a common law system, crimes are defined by statute as in civil law systems. Civil law systems may also allow considerable room for judges to develop law. There is also some variation within common law and civil law systems. The judges of different common law nations have produced differing common law principles. Although the United States and India both derived their legal traditions from England, for example, the common law principles governing contract law vary in some respects between the two countries.

Similarly, the laws of nations that have civil law systems differ considerably. For example, the French code tends to set forth general principles of law, while the German code is far more specific and runs to thousands of sections. In some Middle Eastern countries, codes are grounded in the religious law of Islam, called **sharia.**[3] The religious basis of these codes makes them far more difficult to alter.

---

3. Pronounced shah-*ree*-uh.

EXHIBIT 52-2 **The Legal Systems of Selected Nations**

CIVIL LAW	COMMON LAW
Argentina	Australia
Austria	Bangladesh
Brazil	Canada
Chile	Ghana
China	India
Egypt	Israel
Finland	Jamaica
France	Kenya
Germany	Malaysia
Greece	New Zealand
Indonesia	Nigeria
Iran	Singapore
Italy	United Kingdom
Japan	United States
Mexico	Zambia
Poland	
South Korea	
Sweden	
Tunisia	
Venezuela	

JUDGES AND PROCEDURES Judges play similar roles in virtually all countries: their primary function is the resolution of litigation. The characteristics and qualifications of judges, which are typically set forth in the nation's constitution, can vary widely, however. In the United States, the judge normally does not actively participate in a trial, but many foreign judges involve themselves closely in the proceedings, such as by questioning witnesses.

The procedures employed in resolving cases also vary substantially from country to country. A knowledge of a nation's legal procedures is important for a person conducting business transactions in that nation. For example, an American businessperson was on trial in Saudi Arabia for assaulting and slandering a co-worker, an offense for which he might have been jailed or deported. He initially was required to present two witnesses to his version of events, but he had only one. Fortunately, he became aware that he could "demand the oath." In this procedure, he swore before God that he had neither kicked nor slandered the complainant. After taking the oath, he was promptly adjudged not guilty, as lying under oath is one of the most serious sins existing under Islamic law. Had he failed to demand the oath, he almost certainly would have been found guilty.

INTERNATIONAL TORTS

The international application of tort liability is growing in significance and controversy. An increasing number of U.S. plaintiffs are suing foreign (or U.S.) entities for torts that these entities have allegedly committed overseas. A number of these cases involve human rights violations by foreign governments. The Alien Tort Claims Act (ATCA),[4] adopted in 1789, allows even foreign citizens to bring civil suits in U.S. courts for injuries caused by violations of the law of nations or a treaty of the United States.

Since 1980, plaintiffs have increasingly used the ATCA to bring actions against companies operating in other countries. In all, over two dozen ATCA cases have been brought against companies doing business in nations such as Colombia, Ecuador, Egypt, Guatemala, India, Indonesia, Nigeria, and Saudi Arabia. Several of these cases have involved alleged environmental destruction. In addition, mineral companies in Southeast Asia have been sued for collaborating with oppressive government regimes, and South African torture victims have filed a multibillion-dollar lawsuit against more than one hundred companies that operated under that nation's apartheid (racially discriminatory) regime. Unocal Corporation recently settled a lawsuit brought because it allowed the army of Myanmar to protect its pipeline through the alleged use of murder and torture.

Of course, U.S. citizens may also file international tort actions in this country, especially when the torts occurred on U.S. soil. The following case addressed litigation arising out of the terrorist attacks of September 11, 2001.

---

4. 28 U.S.C. Section 1350.

CASE 52.3	**In re Terrorist Attacks on September 11, 2001**

United States
District Court,
Southern District
of New York, 2005.
349 F.Supp.2d 765.

BACKGROUND AND FACTS *Insurance carriers as well as thousands of survivors of victims of the terrorist attacks of September 11, 2001, joined in an action under the ATCA and other legal authorities to recover damages for the attacks. Numerous parties were named as defendants, including the terrorist network al Qaeda, the Kingdom of Saudi Arabia, various foreign government officials, charities, and banks. The complaint claimed that the government officials, charities, and banks had provided material support to Osama bin Laden and the al Qaeda terrorists. The individual defendants included Saudi Arabian officials, including Prince Sultan, the nation's minister of defense. The defendants moved to dismiss the complaint on multiple grounds, including lack of jurisdiction under the Foreign Sovereign Immunities Act and the plaintiffs' failure to allege a viable tort claim.*

IN THE LANGUAGE OF THE COURT

CASEY, District Judge.

* * * *

* * * Prince Sultan is alleged to have met with Osama bin Laden after Iraq invaded Kuwait in the summer of 1990. * * * Plaintiffs allege that, at the time of the Gulf War, Prince Sultan "took radical stands against Western countries and publicly supported and funded several Islamic charities that were sponsoring Osama bin Laden and al Qaeda operations." * * *

CASE 52.3 | Continued

Prince Sultan allegedly made personal contributions, totaling $6,000,000 since 1994, to various Islamic charities that plaintiffs claim sponsor or support al Qaeda. * * * According to plaintiffs, with respect to his alleged donations, "[a]t best, Prince Sultan was grossly negligent in the oversight and administration of charitable funds, knowing they would be used to sponsor international terrorism." * * *

* * * *

Both Prince Sultan and Prince Turki claim plaintiffs cannot demonstrate their alleged tortious activity caused plaintiffs' injuries. They argue that plaintiffs ignore that Osama bin Laden also targeted the Saudi royal family. * * * Plaintiffs have pleaded al Qaeda's repeated, public targeting of the United States. They have not, however, pleaded facts to support an inference that the Princes were sufficiently close to the terrorists' illegal activities. * * * The court has reviewed the complaints in their entirety and finds no allegations from which it can infer that the Princes knew the charities to which they donated were fronts for al Qaeda. *The court is not ruling as a matter of law that a defendant cannot be liable for contributions to organizations that are not themselves designated terrorists.* But in such a case, there must be some facts presented to support the allegation that the defendant knew the receiving organization to be a solicitor, collector, supporter, front or launderer for such an entity. [Emphasis added.]

DECISION AND REMEDY *The claims against Prince Sultan and the others were dismissed for failure to state a claim and also for failure to establish personal jurisdiction. Claims were allowed to proceed against some other defendants, including the Saudi National Commercial Bank.*

REVIEWING INTERNATIONAL LAW

Robco, Inc., was a Florida arms dealer. The armed forces of Honduras contracted to purchase weapons from Robco over a six-year period. After the government was replaced and a democracy installed, the Honduran government sought to reduce the size of its military, and its relationship with Robco deteriorated. Honduras refused to go through with the contract and purchase the inventory of arms, which Robco could sell only at a much lower price. Robco filed a suit in a federal district court in the United States to recover damages for this breach of contract by the government of Honduras. Using the information presented in the chapter, answer the following questions.

1. Should the Foreign Sovereign Immunities Act (FSIA) preclude this lawsuit?

2. What exception to the FSIA might apply?

3. If a contract enforcement action had been filed in Honduras, what doctrine of deference would that implicate?

4. Should the act of state doctrine bar this lawsuit?

 ## TERMS AND CONCEPTS TO REVIEW

act of state doctrine 1048

civil law system 1055

comity 1048

confiscation 1048

distribution agreement 1052

dumping 1053

export 1051

expropriation 1048

international law 1046

international organization 1047

national law 1046

normal trade relations (NTR)
   status 1054

quota 1053

sharia 1055

sovereign immunity 1049

tariff 1053

treaty 1047

QUESTIONS AND CASE PROBLEMS

52–1. In 1995, France implemented a law making the use of the French language mandatory in certain legal documents. Documents relating to securities offerings, such as prospectuses, for example, must be written in French. So must instruction manuals and warranties for goods and services offered for sale in France. Additionally, all agreements entered into with French state or local authorities, with entities controlled by state or local authorities, and with private entities carrying out a public service (such as providing utilities) must be written in French. What kinds of problems might this law pose for U.S. businesspersons who wish to form contracts with French individuals or business firms?

52–2. **QUESTION WITH SAMPLE ANSWER**

As China and formerly Communist nations move toward free enterprise, they must develop a new set of business laws. If you could start from scratch, what kind of business law system would you adopt, a civil law system or a common law system? What kind of business regulations would you impose?

For a sample answer to this question, go to Appendix I at the end of this text.

52–3. ACT OF STATE DOCTRINE. W. S. Kirkpatrick & Co. learned that the Republic of Nigeria was interested in contracting for the construction and equipping of a medical center in Nigeria. Kirkpatrick, with the aid of a Nigerian citizen, secured the contract as a result of bribing Nigerian officials. Nigerian law prohibits both the payment and the receipt of bribes in connection with the awarding of government contracts, and the U.S. Foreign Corrupt Practices Act of 1977 expressly prohibits U.S. firms and their agents from bribing foreign officials to secure favorable contracts. Environmental Tectonics Corp., International (ETC), an unsuccessful bidder for the contract, learned of the bribery and sued Kirkpatrick in a federal district court for damages. The district court granted summary judgment for Kirkpatrick on the ground that resolution of the case in favor of ETC would require imputing to foreign officials an unlawful motivation (the obtaining of bribes) and accordingly might embarrass the Nigerian government or interfere with the conduct of U.S. foreign policy. Was the district court correct in assuming that the act of state doctrine barred ETC's action against Kirkpatrick? What should happen on appeal? Discuss fully. [*W. S. Kirkpatrick & Co. v. Environmental Tectonics Corp., International,* 493 U.S. 400, 110 S.Ct. 701, 107 L.Ed.2d 816 (1990)]

52–4. SOVEREIGN IMMUNITY. Nuovo Pignone, Inc., is an Italian company that designs and manufactures turbine systems. Nuovo sold a turbine system to Cabinda Gulf Oil Co. (CABGOC). The system was manufactured, tested, and inspected in Italy, then sent to Louisiana for mounting on a platform by CABGOC's contractor. Nuovo sent a representative to consult on the mounting. The platform went to a CABGOC site off the coast of West Africa. Marcus Pere, an instrument technician at the site, was killed when a turbine within the system exploded. Pere's widow filed a suit in a U.S. federal district court against Nuovo and others. Nuovo claimed sovereign immunity on the ground that its majority shareholder at the time of the explosion was Ente Nazionale Idrocaburi, which was created by the government of Italy to lead its oil and gas exploration and development. Is Nuovo exempt from suit under the doctrine of sovereign immunity? Is it subject to suit under the "commercial activity" exception? Why or why not? [*Pere v. Nuovo Pignone, Inc.,* 150 F.3d 477 (5th Cir. 1998)]

52–5. DUMPING. In response to a petition filed on behalf of the U.S. pineapple industry, the U.S. Commerce Department initiated an investigation of canned pineapple fruit imported from Thailand. The investigation concerned Thai producers of the canned fruit, including The Thai Pineapple Public Co. The Thai producers also turned out products, such as pineapple juice and juice concentrate, outside the scope of the investigation. These products use separate parts of the same fresh pineapple, so they share raw material costs. The Commerce Department had to calculate the Thai producers' cost of production, for the purpose of determining fair value and antidumping duties, and in so doing, it had to allocate a portion of the shared fruit costs to the canned fruit. These allocations were based on the producers' own financial records, which were consistent with Thai generally accepted accounting principles. The result was a determination that more than 90 percent of the canned fruit sales were below the cost of production. The producers filed a suit in the U.S. Court of International Trade against the federal government, challenging this allocation. The producers argued that their records did not reflect actual production costs, which instead should be based on the weight of fresh fruit used to make the products. Did the Commerce Department act reasonably in determining the cost of production? Why or why not? [*The Thai Pineapple Public Co. v. United States,* 187 F.3d 1362 (Fed.Cir. 1999)]

52–6. SOVEREIGN IMMUNITY. Tonoga, Ltd., doing business as Taconic Plastics, Ltd., is a manufacturer incorporated in Ireland with its principal place of business in New York. In 1997, Taconic entered into a contract with a German construction company to supply special material for a tent project designed to shelter religious pilgrims visiting holy sites in Saudi Arabia. Most of the material was made in, and shipped from, New York. The company did not pay Taconic and eventually filed for bankruptcy. Another German firm, Werner Voss Architects and Engineers, acting as an agent for the government of Saudi Arabia, guaranteed the payments due Taconic to induce it to complete the project. When Taconic received all but the final payment, the firm filed a suit in a federal district court against the government of Saudi Arabia, claiming a breach of the guaranty and seeking to collect, in part, about $3 million. The defendant filed a motion to dismiss based, in part, on the doctrine of sovereign immunity. Under what circumstances does this doctrine apply? What are its exceptions? Should this suit be dismissed under the "commercial activity" exception? Explain. [*Tonoga, Ltd. v. Ministry of Public Works and Housing of Kingdom of Saudi Arabia*, 135 F.Supp.2d 350 (N.D.N.Y. 2001)]

52–7. CASE PROBLEM WITH SAMPLE ANSWER

DaimlerChrysler Corp. makes and markets motor vehicles. DaimlerChrysler assembled the 1993 and 1994 model years of its trucks at plants in Mexico. Assembly involved sheet metal components sent from the United States. DaimlerChrysler subjected some of the parts to a complicated treatment process, which included the application of coats of paint to prevent corrosion, to impart color, and to protect the finish. Under federal law, goods or U.S.-made parts that are assembled abroad can be imported tariff free. A federal statute provides that painting is "incidental" to assembly and does not affect the status of the goods. A federal regulation states that "painting primarily intended to enhance the appearance of an article or to impart distinctive features or characteristics" is not incidental. The U.S. Customs Service levied a tariff on the trucks. DaimlerChrysler filed a suit in the U.S. Court of International Trade, challenging the levy. Should the court rule in DaimlerChrysler's favor? Why or why not? [*DaimlerChrysler Corp. v. United States*, 361 F.3d 1378 (Fed.Cir. 2004)]

To view a sample answer for this case problem, go to this book's Web site at http://wbl.westbuslaw.com, select "Chapter 52," and click on "Case Problem with Sample Answer."

52–8. **COMITY.** E&L Consulting, Ltd., is a U.S. corporation that sells lumber products in New York, New Jersey, and Pennsylvania. Doman Industries, Ltd., is a Canadian corporation that also sells lumber products, including green hem-fir, a durable product used for home building. Doman supplies over 95 percent of the green hem-fir for sale in the northeastern United States. In 1990, Doman contracted to sell green hem-fir through E&L, which received monthly payments plus commissions. In 1998, Sherwood Lumber Corp., a New York firm and an E&L competitor, approached E&L about a merger. The negotiations were unsuccessful. According to E&L, Sherwood and Doman then conspired to monopolize the green hem-fir market in the United States. When Doman terminated its contract with E&L, the latter filed a suit in a federal district court against Doman, alleging violations of U.S. antitrust law. Doman filed for bankruptcy in a Canadian court and asked the U.S. court to dismiss E&L's suit in part under the principle of comity. What is the "principle of comity"? On what basis would it apply in this case? What would be the likely result?

Discuss. [*E&L Consulting, Ltd. v. Doman Industries, Ltd.*, 360 F.Supp.2d 465 (E.D.N.Y. 2005)]

52–9. A QUESTION OF ETHICS

Ronald Riley, a U.S. citizen, and Council of Lloyd's, a British insurance corporation with its principal place of business in London, entered into an agreement in 1980 that allowed Riley to underwrite insurance through Lloyd's. The agreement provided that if any dispute arose between Lloyd's and Riley, the courts of England would have exclusive jurisdiction, and the laws of England would apply. Over the next decade, some of the parties insured under policies that Riley underwrote experienced large losses, for which they filed claims. Instead of paying his share of the claims, Riley filed a lawsuit in a U.S. district court against Lloyd's and its managers and directors (all British citizens or entities), seeking, among other things, rescission of the 1980 agreement. Riley alleged that the defendants had violated the Securities Act of 1933, the Securities Exchange Act of 1934, and Rule 10b-5. The defendants asked the court to enforce the forum-selection clause in the agreement. Riley argued that if the clause was enforced, he would be deprived of his rights under the U.S. securities laws. The court held that the parties were to resolve their dispute in England. [*Riley v. Kingsley Underwriting Agencies, Ltd.*, 969 F.2d 953 (10th Cir. 1992)]

(a) Did the court's decision fairly balance the rights of the parties? How would you argue in support of the court's decision in this case? How would you argue against it?

(b) Should the fact that an international transaction may be subject to laws and remedies different from or less favorable than those of the United States be a valid basis for denying enforcement of forum-selection and choice-of-law clauses?

(c) All parties to this litigation other than Riley were British. Should the court consider this fact in deciding this case?

52–10. VIDEO QUESTION

Go to this text's Web site at **http://wbl.westbuslaw.com** and select "Chapter 52." Click on "Video Questions" and view the video titled *International Letter of Credit*. Then answer the following questions.

(a) Do banks always require the same documents to be presented in letter-of-credit transactions? If not, who dictates what documents will be required in the letter of credit?

(b) At what point does the seller receive payment in a letter-of-credit transaction?

(c) What assurances does a letter of credit provide to the buyer and to the seller involved in the transaction?

LAW | on the Web

For updated links to resources available on the Web, as well as a variety of other materials, visit this text's Web site at **http://wbl.westbuslaw.com**.

FindLaw, which is now a part of West Group, includes an extensive array of links to international doctrines and treaties, as well as to the laws of other nations, on its Web site. Go to

http://www.findlaw.com

and click on "International Law."

For information on the legal requirements of doing business internationally, a good source is the Internet Law Library's collection of laws of other countries. You can access this source at

http://www.lawguru.com/ilawlib/index.html

LEGAL RESEARCH EXERCISES ON THE WEB

Go to **http://wbl.westbuslaw.com**, the Web site that accompanies this text. Select "Chapter 52" and click on "Internet Exercises." There you will find the following Internet research exercises that you can perform to learn more about topics covered in this chapter.

Activity 52–1: **LEGAL PERSPECTIVE**
                    The World Trade Organization

Activity 52–2: **MANAGEMENT PERSPECTIVE**
                    Overseas Business Opportunities

Special Topics

Unique situations present particular ethical problems. In this final *Focus on Ethics*, we consider some of the ethical dimensions of the special legal topics discussed in the chapters of this unit.

Insurance

A number of ethical issues arise in the area of insurance, some of which we examine here.

Incontestability Clauses Issues of fairness often arise when insurance companies attempt to avoid payment on policies. Recall from Chapter 49 that policies for life or health insurance commonly include, by statutory requirement, incontestability clauses. An *incontestability clause* provides that after the policy has been in force for a specified length of time—often two or three years—the insurer cannot contest statements made in the application. In other words, the insurer cannot later avoid paying on the policy on the basis of a material misrepresentation made by the insured on the policy application. Nonetheless, an insurer will sometimes attempt to avoid payment, notwithstanding the passage of the time period specified in an incontestability clause.

Consider an example. "John Doe" applied for a disability policy from New England Mutual Life Insurance Company. The application form stated that the policy excluded coverage of preexisting conditions that were not disclosed in the application. The policy also contained an incontestability clause, which stated that after two years, the insurer could no longer contest any statements made in the application. John Doe did not disclose on the application the fact that he had tested positive for HIV (human immunodeficiency virus, the virus that causes AIDS). When he later submitted a claim for benefits under the policy, the insurer argued that it should not be bound by the incontestability clause because the insured knew, at the time that he filled out the application, that he would likely develop AIDS. The court had little sympathy for the insurer, however, stating simply that "once the incontestability period is over, a carrier may not deny coverage" because of a misrepresentation on the application.[1]

Contract Interpretation Recall from Chapter 10 that, when interpreting terms in a contract, the courts apply the "plain meaning" rule. In other words, if the meaning of the terms is clear from the words in the contract, the court will enforce the contract as written. If the contract contains ambiguous terms, however, the courts are guided by several principles.

One of these principles is that the party who created the ambiguous expressions should be held responsible for the ambiguities. In other words, when contract language has more than one meaning, it will be interpreted against the party who drafted the contract.

These principles of contract interpretation, which are clearly rooted in notions of fairness, apply to insurance contracts as well. For example, in one case, a drunk driver crashed his car and died nine days later. His insurance company refused to pay life insurance benefits, citing a clause in the policy that read as follows: "No benefit shall be paid for loss or injury that occurs while the covered person's blood alcohol level is 10 percent . . . or higher." The driver's blood alcohol level was over 10 percent at the time of the accident, but it had dropped by the time he died. The insurer contended that the exclusion stated in the policy applied because the driver's death was caused by injuries incurred while he was intoxicated.

The court disagreed. According to the court, "The language that [the insurer] chose in this particular policy did not cover a situation where an insured sustains injuries while intoxicated, but does not die as a result of those injuries until some time thereafter." In the court's eyes, the insurer "should have written what it meant and not relied on the judicial process to interpret a clearly drafted, carefully thought out, unambiguous insurance policy."[2]

Insurance Agents and Fiduciary Duties When a person applies for insurance coverage through an insurance company's agent, is the agent obligated to advise that person as to what coverage she or he should obtain? If the agent does not advise a client about certain types of coverage, has the agent breached a fiduciary duty owed to the applicant? For example, suppose that a couple applies for auto insurance, and the insurance agent does not advise them that they should obtain uninsured motorist coverage. Later, the couple is involved in an accident with an uninsured motorist, and the insurance company refuses to compensate them for their injuries and losses. The couple claims that the insurance agent was negligent in not advising them to sign up for uninsured motorist coverage. Was the agent negligent? Did the agent breach a duty owed to the client?

The answer to this question is no. As mentioned in Chapter 49, an insurance agent is an agent of the insurer (the insurance company), not of the party who applies for insurance. As such, the agent owes fiduciary duties to the

---

1. *New England Mutual Life Insurance Co. v. Doe*, 93 N.Y.2d 122, 688 N.Y.S.2d 459 (1999).

2. *Burgess v. J. C. Penney Life Insurance Co.*, 167 F.3d 1137 (7th Cir. 1999).

insurer, but not to the insured. The agent's only duties to the insured are contractual in nature. Although this rule may seem unfair to insurance applicants, who may know less about the need for certain types of insurance coverage than the agent does, a contrary rule might create even more unfairness. An insurance agent could be held liable for failure to advise a client of every possible insurance option, and the insured would be relieved of any burden to take care of his or her own financial needs and expectations. Also, as one court noted, if the state legislature does not require such coverage, why should the courts require insurance companies to offer or explain available optional coverage?[3]

Insurance and Computer "Downtime" As noted in Chapter 49, traditional business insurance policies usually do not specifically cover the risks associated with computer "downtime." Thus, in a number of cases, insurers have defended against payment by claiming that these kinds of losses are not covered.

For example, in one case an employment agency's computer system was attacked by a computer virus that caused all data to be lost. The agency's business insurance policy provided coverage for "accidental direct physical loss to business personal property" and for the replacement of valuable "papers or records, including those which exist on electronic or magnetic media." When the agency filed a claim with its insurer, the insurer denied coverage—claiming that the loss was neither "accidental" (because the hacker intended to infect the computer system) nor "physical" (because data are not tangible—capable of being touched). The court, however, concluded that the agency had in no way intentionally caused the computer system to be damaged, and therefore the loss was accidental. The court also noted that the policy expressly covered electronic records and storage media. Therefore, the data loss was "physical" as a matter of law.[4]

In another case, an insurance policy insured against "direct physical loss or damage from any cause" to the "property, business income, and operations." A power outage caused the insured company to lose all of its programming information. The insurer refused to pay for the costs associated with the computer downtime, contending that no "physical loss or damage" had been sustained. Although many courts would likely have agreed with the insurance company, in this case the court sided with the insured. The court concluded that "[a]t a time when computer technology dominates our professional as well as our personal lives," the term should not be "restricted to the physical destruction or harm of computer circuitry" but should also include "loss of access, loss of use, and loss of functionality."[5]

Inheritance Rights

New applications of technology often present thorny issues for the courts, from both a legal and an ethical perspective. A challenging issue has to do with the inheritance rights of posthumously conceived children. Posthumously conceived children are conceived through the use of a decedent's sperm that had been previously collected and stored in a sperm bank. Do such children have inheritance rights under state intestacy laws? Should they?

When this issue came before the Massachusetts Supreme Court, the court ruled that posthumously conceived children do have inheritance rights. The case involved twins who were born two years after the death of their father. The mother applied to the Social Security Administration (SSA) for "survivor's benefits" for the children. When the SSA denied the application, the mother appealed the agency's decision to a court. Ultimately, the Massachusetts Supreme Court held that posthumously conceived children enjoy the same inheritance rights as natural children under intestacy laws. The court did place some conditions on these inheritance rights, however. One condition was that there must be a demonstrable genetic relationship between a child and her or his deceased parent. Another was that the decedent must have consented to the conception. The court placed no time limit on the period within which inheritance rights could be claimed.[6]

Generally, the laws on this issue vary from state to state. Several states (Colorado, Delaware, Texas, Virginia, and Washington) have recently amended their intestacy laws to allow posthumously conceived children to inherit. The amended laws often require conditions such as those imposed by the court in the case just discussed. Courts in two states (Massachusetts and New Jersey) have issued rulings that allow posthumously conceived children to inherit. Only one state (North Dakota) statutorily prohibits such children from inheriting property. Another state (Florida) allows a child who is conceived posthumously to inherit but only if the decedent included the child in his will.[7]

Liability of Accountants

Society has obviously deemed it fair that accountants abide by certain professional standards. This view is reflected in common law principles governing the liability of accountants, as well as in statutory law. Today, accountants face potential liability on many fronts.

Liability of Accountants under the Common Law A long-standing principle under the common law is that

3. *Jones v. Kennedy,* 108 S.W.3d 203 (Mo.App. 2003).
4. *Lambrecht & Associates, Inc. v. State Farm Lloyd's,* 119 S.W.3d 16 (Tex.App. 2003).
5. *American Guarantee & Liability Insurance Co. v. Ingram Micro, Inc.,* ___ F.Supp.2d ___ (D.Ariz. 2000).
6. *Woodward v. Commissioner of Social Security,* 435 Mass. 536, 760 N.E.2d 257 (2002). See also *Gillett-Netting v. Barnhart,* 371 F.3d 593 (9th Cir. 2004).
7. Lindsay Fortado, "Children Born into Legal Limbo," *The National Law Journal,* July 19, 2004, pp. 1, 21.

accountants should be held to a duty of care and that they should stand prepared to compensate clients and others for violating that duty. Still, many consider it unfair that there are no uniform, well-defined limits to the potential liability of accountants. Negligence suits brought against accountants by third parties often raise a question with obvious ethical implications: how far should an accountant's liability extend? As discussed in Chapter 51, courts in different jurisdictions have reached different conclusions on this issue.

At one end of the spectrum are a minority of courts that hold that accountants are liable only to third parties who are in privity or "near privity" with the accountants. At the other end are a minority of courts that have ruled that accountants may be held liable to third parties whose reliance on the accountants' statements or reports was "reasonably foreseeable." In the eyes of many, accountants' liability to third parties is too restricted in the former jurisdictions and too extensive in the latter. For accountants, the courts' varying approaches to liability to third parties pose a significant problem: how can accountants predict, and control, the extent of their liability?

Liability under Statutory Law As you read in Chapter 51, accountants face potential liability under securities laws, under tax laws, and under the Sarbanes-Oxley Act of 2002. This act was passed in response to the public's concerns over the fraudulent and deceptive accounting practices engaged in by Enron Corporation and other companies in the early 2000s. In an attempt to curb such practices, the act created increased public oversight over public accounting firms and imposed heavier penalties on those—including accountants—who violate the provisions of the act.

Further complicating the extent of accountants' statutory liability is the possibility that accountants may be liable to third parties under consumer protection statutes. Consider, for example, a decision by the Texas Supreme Court in which the court held that a third party, as a "consumer," could sue an accounting firm for violations of the state Deceptive Trade Practices Act (DTPA).[8] The Texas DTPA, which is similar to statutes in many other states, allows the successful plaintiff to recover treble damages as well as attorneys' fees. The burden of proof under the DTPA is relatively light for the plaintiff: to recover damages, the plaintiff need only show that there was a "knowing" violation of the statute. The statute also imposes strict liability on defendants.

International Transactions

Conducting business internationally involves unique challenges, including, at times, ethical challenges. This is understandable, given that laws and cultures vary from one country to another. Consider the role of women. In the United States, equal employment opportunity is a fundamental public policy. This policy is clearly expressed in Title VII of the Civil Rights Act of 1964 (discussed in Chapter 34), which prohibits discrimination against women in the employment context. Some other countries, however, largely reject any professional role for women, which may cause difficulties for American women conducting business transactions in those countries. For example, when the World Bank sent a delegation that included women to negotiate with the Central Bank of Korea, the Koreans were surprised and offended. They thought that the presence of women meant that the Koreans were not being taken seriously.

There are also some important ethical differences among nations. In Islamic countries, for example, the consumption of alcohol and certain foods is forbidden by the Islamic religion. Thus, it would be thoughtless and imprudent to invite a Saudi Arabian business contact out for a drink. Additionally, in many foreign nations, gift giving is a common practice between contracting companies or between companies and government officials. To Americans, such gift giving may look suspiciously like an unethical (and possibly illegal) bribe. This has been an important source of friction in international business, particularly after the U.S. Congress passed the Foreign Corrupt Practices Act in 1977 (discussed in Chapter 5). This act prohibits U.S. business firms from offering certain side payments to foreign officials to secure favorable contracts.

DISCUSSION QUESTIONS

1. Suppose that an applicant for insurance knowingly makes a false statement concerning a material fact on the application form. Is it fair to the insurance company to make it later pay out on the policy on the ground that, under the provisions of an incontestability clause, it cannot contest any statements made on the application?

2. Should the courts always apply the "plain meaning" rule when interpreting an insurance contract's terms? Would it be fairer if a court, instead, looked at the circumstances of the particular case to decide what its ruling should be?

3. In your opinion, should the law impose a duty on agents for insurance companies to advise insurance applicants as to what types of coverage would best suit their needs?

4. At one time, most courts held that accountants could not be held liable to third parties in negligence lawsuits. On what contract doctrine was this rule based? Why do the majority of courts today hold that accountants can be held liable to third parties? Generally, what public policies must the courts balance in determining whether third parties can recover from accountants for damages caused by accountants' negligence?

---

8. *Arthur Andersen & Co. v. Perry Equipment Corp.*, 945 S.W.2d 812 (Tex. 1997).

Appendices

CONTENTS

How to Brief Cases and Analyze Case Problems

HOW TO BRIEF CASES

To fully understand the law with respect to business, you need to be able to read and understand court decisions. To make this task easier, you can use a method of case analysis that is called *briefing*. There is a fairly standard procedure that you can follow when you "brief" any court case. You must first read the case opinion carefully. When you feel you understand the case, you can prepare a brief of it.

Although the format of the brief may vary, typically it will present the essentials of the case under headings such as those listed below.

1. Citation. Give the full citation for the case, including the name of the case, the date it was decided, and the court that decided it.

2. Facts. Briefly indicate (a) the reasons for the lawsuit; (b) the identity and arguments of the plaintiff(s) and defendant(s), respectively; and (c) the lower court's decision—if appropriate.

3. Issue. Concisely phrase, in the form of a question, the essential issue before the court. (If more than one issue is involved, you may have two—or even more—questions here.)

4. Decision. Indicate here—with a "yes" or "no," if possible—the court's answer to the question (or questions) in the *Issue* section above.

5. Reason. Summarize as briefly as possible the reasons given by the court for its decision (or decisions) and the case or statutory law relied on by the court in arriving at its decision.

AN EXAMPLE OF A BRIEFED SAMPLE COURT CASE

As an example of the format used in briefing cases, we present here a briefed version of the sample court case that was presented in Chapter 1 in Exhibit 1–6.

D.A.B.E., INC. v. CITY OF TOLEDO
United States Court of Appeals,
Sixth Circuit, 2005.
393 F.3d 692.

FACTS The city of Toledo, Ohio, has regulated smoking in public places since 1987. In 2003, Toledo's city council enacted a new Clean Indoor Air Ordinance. The ordinance restricts the ability to smoke in public places—stores, theaters, courtrooms, libraries, museums, health-care facilities, restaurants, and bars. In enclosed public places, smoking is generally prohibited except in a "separate smoking lounge" that is designated for this purpose. D.A.B.E., Inc., a group consisting of the owners of bars, restaurants, and bowling alleys, filed a suit in a federal district court, claiming that the ordinance constituted a taking of their property in violation of the Fifth Amendment to the U.S. Constitution. The plaintiffs also argued that the ordinance was preempted (prevented from taking effect) by a state statute that regulated smoking "in places of public assembly," excluding restaurants, bowling alleys, and bars. The court ruled in favor of the city. The plaintiffs appealed to the U.S. Court of Appeals for the Sixth Circuit.

ISSUE Does the ordinance deny the plaintiffs "economically viable use of their property," as required to prove a taking? Does a state indoor smoking statute preempt the city ordinance?

DECISION No, to both questions. The U.S. Court of Appeals for the Sixth Circuit affirmed the lower court's ruling. The ordinance did not prevent the beneficial use of the plaintiffs' property, because it did not categorically prohibit smoking, but only regulated it. The state indoor smoking statute did not cover the excluded businesses, and the legislature did not indicate an intent to bar a city from restricting smoking in those places.

REASON The Fifth Amendment provides that private property shall not "be taken for public use, without just compensation." A taking occurs when an ordinance denies an owner economically viable use of his or her property. In this case, the plaintiffs alleged that they lost customers because of the ordinance. The court reasoned that the ordinance's only effect on the plaintiffs' businesses is to restrict the areas in which customers can smoke and the conditions under which smoking is permitted. This might "require some financial investment, but an ordinance does not effect a taking merely because compliance with it requires the expenditure of money." Besides, the owners could elect to make other uses of their property. As for the preemption issue, a state statute takes precedence over a local ordinance when they conflict. In this case, a statute prohibits smoking in certain locations, but "it does not contain the slightest hint that the legislature intended to create a positive right to smoke in all public places where it did not expressly forbid smoking. Nothing in the [statute] is inconsistent with a local jurisdiction's decision to impose greater limits on public smoking."

REVIEW OF SAMPLE COURT CASE

Here we provide a review of the briefed version to indicate the kind of information that is contained in each section.

CITATION The name of the case is *D.A.B.E., Inc. v. City of Toledo*. D.A.B.E. is the plaintiff; Toledo is the defendant. The U.S. Court of Appeals for the Sixth Circuit decided this case in 2005. The citation states that this case can be found in volume 393 the *Federal Reporter, Third Series,* on page 692.

FACTS The *Facts* section identifies the plaintiff and the defendant, describes the events leading up to this suit, the allegations made by the plaintiff in the initial suit, and (because this case is an appellate court decision) the lower court's ruling and the party appealing this ruling. The appellant's contention on appeal is also sometimes included here.

ISSUE The *Issue* section presents the central issue (or issues) decided by the court. In this case, the U.S. Court of Appeals for the Sixth Circuit considers whether the ordinance constitutes a taking in violation of the Fifth Amendment and whether a state statute preempts (or supersedes) the city ordinance.

DECISION The *Decision* section includes the court's decision on the issues before it. The decision reflects the opinion of the judge or justice hearing the case. Decisions by appellate courts are frequently phrased in reference to the lower court's decision; that is, the appellate court may "affirm" the lower court's ruling or "reverse" it. Here, the court determined that the ordinance did not effect a taking because it did not prevent the plaintiffs' beneficial use of their property. The statute did not preempt the ordinance because the legislature did not indicate an intent to prohibit a city from restricting smoking in places excluded from the statute. The court affirmed the lower court's ruling.

REASON The *Reason* section includes references to the relevant laws and legal principles that the court applied in arriving at its conclusion in the case. The relevant law here included the Fifth Amendment, the state indoor smoking statute, and the principles derived from judicial interpretations and applications of those laws. This section also explains the court's application of the law to the facts in this case.

ANALYZING CASE PROBLEMS

In addition to learning how to brief cases, students of business law and the legal environment also find it helpful to know how to analyze case problems. Part of the study of business law and the legal environment usually involves analyzing case problems, such as those included in this text at the end of each chapter.

For each case problem in this book, we provide the relevant background and facts of the lawsuit and the issue before the court. When you are assigned one of these problems, your job will be to determine how the court should decide the issue, and why. In other words, you will need to engage in legal analysis and reasoning. Here we offer some suggestions on how to make this task less daunting. We begin by presenting a sample problem:

> While Janet Lawson, a famous pianist, was shopping in Quality Market, she slipped and fell on a wet floor in one of the aisles. The floor had recently been mopped by one of the store's employees, but there were no signs warning customers that the floor in that area was wet. As a result of the fall, Lawson injured her right arm and was unable to perform piano concerts for the next six months. Had she been able to perform the scheduled concerts, she would have earned approximately $60,000 over that period of time. Lawson sued Quality Market for this amount, plus another $10,000 in medical expenses. She claimed that the store's failure to warn customers of the wet floor constituted negligence and therefore the market was liable for her injuries. Will the court agree with Lawson? Discuss.

UNDERSTAND THE FACTS

This may sound obvious, but before you can analyze or apply the relevant law to a specific set of facts, you must clearly understand those facts. In other words, you should read through the case problem carefully—more than once, if necessary—to make sure you understand the identity of the plaintiff(s) and defendant(s) in the case and the progression of events that led to the lawsuit.

In the sample case just given, the identity of the parties is fairly obvious. Janet Lawson is the one bringing the suit; therefore, she is the plaintiff. Quality Market, against whom she is bringing the suit, is the defendant. Some of the case problems you may work on have multiple plaintiffs or defendants. Often, it is helpful to use abbreviations for the parties. To indicate a reference to a plaintiff, for example, the *pi* symbol—π—is often used, and a defendant is denoted by a *delta*—Δ—a triangle.

The events leading to the lawsuit are also fairly straightforward. Lawson slipped and fell on a wet floor, and she contends that Quality Market should be liable for her injuries because it was negligent in not posting a sign warning customers of the wet floor.

When you are working on case problems, realize that the facts should be accepted as they are given. For example, in our sample problem, it should be accepted that the floor was wet and that there was no sign. In other words, avoid making conjectures, such as "Maybe

the floor wasn't too wet," or "Maybe an employee was getting a sign to put up," or "Maybe someone stole the sign." Questioning the facts as they are presented only adds confusion to your analysis.

LEGAL ANALYSIS AND REASONING

Once you understand the facts given in the case problem, you can begin to analyze the case. Recall from Chapter 1 that the IRAC method is a helpful tool to use in the legal analysis and reasoning process. IRAC is an acronym for Issue, Rule, Application, Conclusion. Applying this method to our sample problem would involve the following steps:

1. First, you need to decide what legal **issue** is involved in the case. In our sample case, the basic issue is whether Quality Market's failure to warn customers of the wet floor constituted negligence. As discussed in Chapter 7, negligence is a *tort*—a civil wrong. In a tort lawsuit, the plaintiff seeks to be compensated for another's wrongful act. A defendant will be deemed negligent if he or she breached a duty of care owed to the plaintiff and the breach of that duty caused the plaintiff to suffer harm.

2. Once you have identified the issue, the next step is to determine what **rule of law** applies to the issue. To make this determination, you will want to review carefully the text of the chapter in which the problem appears to find the relevant rule of law. Our sample case involves the tort of negligence, covered in Chapter 7. The applicable rule of law is the tort law principle that business owners owe a duty to exercise reasonable care to protect their customers ("business invitees"). Reasonable care, in this context, includes either removing—or warning customers of—*foreseeable* risks about which the owner *knew* or *should have known*. Business owners need not warn customers of "open and obvious" risks, however. If a business owner breaches this duty of care (fails to exercise the appropriate degree of care toward customers), and the breach of duty causes a customer to be injured, the business owner will be liable to the customer for the customer's injuries.

3. The next—and usually the most difficult—step in analyzing case problems is the **application** of the relevant rule of law to the specific facts of the case you are studying. In our sample problem, applying the tort law principle just discussed presents few difficulties. An employee of the store had mopped the floor in the aisle where Lawson slipped and fell, but no sign was present indicating that the floor was wet. That a customer might fall on a wet floor is clearly a foreseeable risk. Therefore, the failure to warn customers about the wet floor was a breach of the duty of care owed by the business owner to the store's customers.

4. Once you have completed step 3 in the IRAC method, you should be ready to draw your **conclusion.** In our sample case, Quality Market is liable to Lawson for her injuries, because the market's breach of its duty of care caused Lawson's injuries.

The fact patterns in the case problems presented in this text are not always as simple as those presented in our sample problem. Often, for example, there may be more than one plaintiff or defendant. There also may be more than one issue involved in a case and more than one applicable rule of law. Furthermore, in some case problems the facts may indicate that the general rule of law should not apply. For example, suppose a store employee advised Lawson not to walk on the floor in the aisle because it was wet, but Lawson decided to walk on it anyway. This fact could alter the outcome of the case because the store could then raise the defense of assumption of risk (see Chapter 7). Nonetheless, a careful review of the chapter should always provide you with the knowledge you need to analyze the problem thoroughly and arrive at accurate conclusions.

The Constitution of the United States

PREAMBLE

We the People of the United States, in Order to form a more perfect Union, establish Justice, insure domestic Tranquility, provide for the common defence, promote the general Welfare, and secure the Blessings of Liberty to ourselves and our Posterity, do ordain and establish this Constitution for the United States of America.

ARTICLE I

Section 1. All legislative Powers herein granted shall be vested in a Congress of the United States, which shall consist of a Senate and House of Representatives.

Section 2. The House of Representatives shall be composed of Members chosen every second Year by the People of the several States, and the Electors in each State shall have the Qualifications requisite for Electors of the most numerous Branch of the State Legislature.

No Person shall be a Representative who shall not have attained to the Age of twenty five Years, and been seven Years a Citizen of the United States, and who shall not, when elected, be an Inhabitant of that State in which he shall be chosen.

Representatives and direct Taxes shall be apportioned among the several States which may be included within this Union, according to their respective Numbers, which shall be determined by adding to the whole Number of free Persons, including those bound to Service for a Term of Years, and excluding Indians not taxed, three fifths of all other Persons. The actual Enumeration shall be made within three Years after the first Meeting of the Congress of the United States, and within every subsequent Term of ten Years, in such Manner as they shall by Law direct. The Number of Representatives shall not exceed one for every thirty Thousand, but each State shall have at Least one Representative; and until such enumeration shall be made, the State of New Hampshire shall be entitled to chuse three, Massachusetts eight, Rhode Island and Providence Plantations one, Connecticut five, New York six, New Jersey four, Pennsylvania eight, Delaware one, Maryland six, Virginia ten, North Carolina five, South Carolina five, and Georgia three.

When vacancies happen in the Representation from any State, the Executive Authority thereof shall issue Writs of Election to fill such Vacancies.

The House of Representatives shall chuse their Speaker and other Officers; and shall have the sole Power of Impeachment.

Section 3. The Senate of the United States shall be composed of two Senators from each State, chosen by the Legislature thereof, for six Years; and each Senator shall have one Vote.

Immediately after they shall be assembled in Consequence of the first Election, they shall be divided as equally as may be into three Classes. The Seats of the Senators of the first Class shall be vacated at the Expiration of the second Year, of the second Class at the Expiration of the fourth Year, and of the third Class at the Expiration of the sixth Year, so that one third may be chosen every second Year; and if Vacancies happen by Resignation, or otherwise, during the Recess of the Legislature of any State, the Executive thereof may make temporary Appointments until the next Meeting of the Legislature, which shall then fill such Vacancies.

No Person shall be a Senator who shall not have attained to the Age of thirty Years, and been nine Years a Citizen of the United States, and who shall not, when elected, be an Inhabitant of that State for which he shall be chosen.

The Vice President of the United States shall be President of the Senate, but shall have no Vote, unless they be equally divided.

The Senate shall chuse their other Officers, and also a President pro tempore, in the Absence of the Vice President, or when he shall exercise the Office of President of the United States.

The Senate shall have the sole Power to try all Impeachments. When sitting for that Purpose, they shall be on Oath or Affirmation. When the President of the United States is tried, the Chief Justice shall preside: And no Person shall be convicted without the Concurrence of two thirds of the Members present.

Judgment in Cases of Impeachment shall not extend further than to removal from Office, and disqualification to hold and enjoy any Office of honor, Trust, or Profit under the United States: but the Party convicted shall nevertheless be liable and subject to Indictment, Trial, Judgment, and Punishment, according to Law.

Section 4. The Times, Places and Manner of holding Elections for Senators and Representatives, shall be prescribed in each State by the Legislature thereof; but the Congress may at any time by Law make or alter such Regulations, except as to the Places of chusing Senators.

The Congress shall assemble at least once in every Year, and such Meeting shall be on the first Monday in December, unless they shall by Law appoint a different Day.

Section 5. Each House shall be the Judge of the Elections, Returns, and Qualifications of its own Members, and a Majority of each shall constitute a Quorum to do Business; but a smaller Number may adjourn from day to day, and may be authorized to compel the Attendance of absent Members, in such Manner, and under such Penalties as each House may provide.

Each House may determine the Rules of its Proceedings, punish its Members for disorderly Behavior, and, with the Concurrence of two thirds, expel a Member.

Each House shall keep a Journal of its Proceedings, and from time to time publish the same, excepting such Parts as may in their Judgment require Secrecy; and the Yeas and Nays of the Members of either House on any question shall, at the Desire of one fifth of those Present, be entered on the Journal.

Neither House, during the Session of Congress, shall, without the Consent of the other, adjourn for more than three days, nor to any other Place than that in which the two Houses shall be sitting.

Section 6. The Senators and Representatives shall receive a Compensation for their Services, to be ascertained by Law, and paid out of the Treasury of the United States. They shall in all Cases, except Treason, Felony and Breach of the Peace, be privileged from Arrest during their Attendance at the Session of their respective Houses, and in going to and returning from the same; and for any Speech or Debate in either House, they shall not be questioned in any other Place.

No Senator or Representative shall, during the Time for which he was elected, be appointed to any civil Office under the Authority of the United States, which shall have been created, or the Emoluments whereof shall have been increased during such time; and no Person holding any Office under the United States, shall be a Member of either House during his Continuance in Office.

Section 7. All Bills for raising Revenue shall originate in the House of Representatives; but the Senate may propose or concur with Amendments as on other Bills.

Every Bill which shall have passed the House of Representatives and the Senate, shall, before it become a Law, be presented to the President of the United States; If he approve he shall sign it, but if not he shall return it, with his Objections to the House in which it shall have originated, who shall enter the Objections at large on their Journal, and proceed to reconsider it. If after such Reconsideration two thirds of that House shall agree to pass the Bill, it shall be sent together with the Objections, to the other House, by which it shall likewise be reconsidered, and if approved by two thirds of that House, it shall become a Law. But in all such Cases the Votes of both Houses shall be determined by Yeas and Nays, and the Names of the Persons voting for and against the Bill shall be entered on the Journal of each House respectively. If any Bill shall not be returned by the President within ten Days (Sundays excepted) after it shall have been presented to him, the Same shall be a Law, in like Manner as if he had signed it, unless the Congress by their Adjournment prevent its Return in which Case it shall not be a Law.

Every Order, Resolution, or Vote, to which the Concurrence of the Senate and House of Representatives may be necessary (except on a question of Adjournment) shall be presented to the President of the United States; and before the Same shall take Effect, shall be approved by him, or being disapproved by him, shall be repassed by two thirds of the Senate and House of Representatives, according to the Rules and Limitations prescribed in the Case of a Bill.

Section 8. The Congress shall have Power To lay and collect Taxes, Duties, Imposts and Excises, to pay the Debts and provide for the common Defence and general Welfare of the United States; but all Duties, Imposts and Excises shall be uniform throughout the United States;

To borrow Money on the credit of the United States;

To regulate Commerce with foreign Nations, and among the several States, and with the Indian Tribes;

To establish an uniform Rule of Naturalization, and uniform Laws on the subject of Bankruptcies throughout the United States;

To coin Money, regulate the Value thereof, and of foreign Coin, and fix the Standard of Weights and Measures;

To provide for the Punishment of counterfeiting the Securities and current Coin of the United States;

To establish Post Offices and post Roads;

To promote the Progress of Science and useful Arts, by securing for limited Times to Authors and Inventors the exclusive Right to their respective Writings and Discoveries;

To constitute Tribunals inferior to the supreme Court;

To define and punish Piracies and Felonies committed on the high Seas, and Offenses against the Law of Nations;

To declare War, grant Letters of Marque and Reprisal, and make Rules concerning Captures on Land and Water;

To raise and support Armies, but no Appropriation of Money to that Use shall be for a longer Term than two Years;

To provide and maintain a Navy;

To make Rules for the Government and Regulation of the land and naval Forces;

To provide for calling forth the Militia to execute the Laws of the Union, suppress Insurrections and repel Invasions;

To provide for organizing, arming, and disciplining, the Militia, and for governing such Part of them as may be employed in the Service of the United States, reserving to the States respectively, the Appointment of the Officers, and the Authority of training the Militia according to the discipline prescribed by Congress;

To exercise exclusive Legislation in all Cases whatsoever, over such District (not exceeding ten Miles square) as may, by Cession of particular States, and the Acceptance of Congress, become the Seat of the Government of the United States, and to exercise like Authority over all Places purchased by the Consent of the Legislature of the State in which the Same shall be, for the Erection of Forts, Magazines, Arsenals, dock-Yards, and other needful Buildings;—And

To make all Laws which shall be necessary and proper for carrying into Execution the foregoing Powers, and all other Powers vested by this Constitution in the Government of the United States, or in any Department or Officer thereof.

Section 9.   The Migration or Importation of such Persons as any of the States now existing shall think proper to admit, shall not be prohibited by the Congress prior to the Year one thousand eight hundred and eight, but a Tax or duty may be imposed on such Importation, not exceeding ten dollars for each Person.

The privilege of the Writ of Habeas Corpus shall not be suspended, unless when in Cases of Rebellion or Invasion the public Safety may require it.

No Bill of Attainder or ex post facto Law shall be passed.

No Capitation, or other direct, Tax shall be laid, unless in Proportion to the Census or Enumeration herein before directed to be taken.

No Tax or Duty shall be laid on Articles exported from any State.

No Preference shall be given by any Regulation of Commerce or Revenue to the Ports of one State over those of another: nor shall Vessels bound to, or from, one State be obliged to enter, clear, or pay Duties in another.

No Money shall be drawn from the Treasury, but in Consequence of Appropriations made by Law; and a regular Statement and Account of the Receipts and Expenditures of all public Money shall be published from time to time.

No Title of Nobility shall be granted by the United States: And no Person holding any Office of Profit or Trust under them, shall, without the Consent of the Congress, accept of any present, Emolument, Office, or Title, of any kind whatever, from any King, Prince, or foreign State.

Section 10.   No State shall enter into any Treaty, Alliance, or Confederation; grant Letters of Marque and Reprisal; coin Money; emit Bills of Credit; make any Thing but gold and silver Coin a Tender in Payment of Debts; pass any Bill of Attainder, ex post facto Law, or Law impairing the Obligation of Contracts, or grant any Title of Nobility.

No State shall, without the Consent of the Congress, lay any Imposts or Duties on Imports or Exports, except what may be absolutely necessary for executing its inspection Laws: and the net Produce of all Duties and Imposts, laid by any State on Imports or Exports, shall be for the Use of the Treasury of the United States; and all such Laws shall be subject to the Revision and Controul of the Congress.

No State shall, without the Consent of Congress, lay any Duty of Tonnage, keep Troops, or Ships of War in time of Peace, enter into any Agreement or Compact with another State, or with a foreign Power, or engage in War, unless actually invaded, or in such imminent Danger as will not admit of delay.

ARTICLE II

Section 1.   The executive Power shall be vested in a President of the United States of America. He shall hold his Office during the Term of four Years, and, together with the Vice President, chosen for the same Term, be elected, as follows:

Each State shall appoint, in such Manner as the Legislature thereof may direct, a Number of Electors, equal to the whole Number of Senators and Representatives to which the State may be entitled in the Congress; but no Senator or Representative, or Person holding an Office of Trust or Profit under the United States, shall be appointed an Elector.

The Electors shall meet in their respective States, and vote by Ballot for two Persons, of whom one at least shall not be an Inhabitant of the same State with themselves. And they shall make a List of all the Persons voted for, and of the Number of Votes for each; which List they shall sign and certify, and transmit sealed to the Seat of the Government of the United States, directed to the President of the Senate. The President of the Senate shall, in the Presence of the Senate and House of Representatives, open all the Certificates, and the Votes shall then be counted. The Person having the greatest Number of Votes shall be the President, if such Number be a Majority of the whole Number of Electors appointed; and if there be more than one who have such Majority, and have an equal Number of Votes, then the House of Representatives shall immediately chuse by Ballot one of them for President; and if no Person have a Majority, then from the five highest on the List the said House shall in like Manner chuse the President. But in chusing the President, the Votes shall be taken by States, the Representation from each State having one Vote; A quorum for this Purpose shall consist of a Member or Members from two thirds of the States, and a Majority of all the States shall be necessary to a Choice. In every Case, after the Choice of the President, the Person having the greater Number of Votes of the Electors shall be the Vice President. But if there should remain two or more who have equal Votes, the Senate shall chuse from them by Ballot the Vice President.

The Congress may determine the Time of chusing the Electors, and the Day on which they shall give their Votes; which Day shall be the same throughout the United States.

No person except a natural born Citizen, or a Citizen of the United States, at the time of the Adoption of this Constitution, shall be eligible to the Office of President; neither shall any Person be eligible to that Office who shall not have attained to the Age of thirty five Years, and been fourteen Years a Resident within the United States.

In Case of the Removal of the President from Office, or of his Death, Resignation or Inability to discharge the Powers and Duties of the said Office, the same shall devolve on the Vice President, and the Congress may by Law provide for the Case of Removal, Death, Resignation or Inability, both of the President and Vice President, declaring what Officer shall then act as President, and such Officer shall act accordingly, until the Disability be removed, or a President shall be elected.

The President shall, at stated Times, receive for his Services, a Compensation, which shall neither be increased nor diminished during the Period for which he shall have been elected, and he shall not receive within that Period any other Emolument from the United States, or any of them.

Before he enter on the Execution of his Office, he shall take the following Oath or Affirmation: "I do solemnly swear (or affirm) that I will faithfully execute the Office of President of the United States, and will to the best of my Ability, preserve, protect and defend the Constitution of the United States."

Section 2. The President shall be Commander in Chief of the Army and Navy of the United States, and of the Militia of the several States, when called into the actual Service of the United States; he may require the Opinion, in writing, of the principal Officer in each of the executive Departments, upon any Subject relating to the Duties of their respective Offices, and he shall have Power to grant Reprieves and Pardons for Offenses against the United States, except in Cases of Impeachment.

He shall have Power, by and with the Advice and Consent of the Senate to make Treaties, provided two thirds of the Senators present concur; and he shall nominate, and by and with the Advice and Consent of the Senate, shall appoint Ambassadors, other public Ministers and Consuls, Judges of the supreme Court, and all other Officers of the United States, whose Appointments are not herein otherwise provided for, and which shall be established by Law; but the Congress may by Law vest the Appointment of such inferior Officers, as they think proper, in the President alone, in the Courts of Law, or in the Heads of Departments.

The President shall have Power to fill up all Vacancies that may happen during the Recess of the Senate, by granting Commissions which shall expire at the End of their next Session.

Section 3. He shall from time to time give to the Congress Information of the State of the Union, and recommend to their Consideration such Measures as he shall judge necessary and expedient; he may, on extraordinary Occasions, convene both Houses, or either of them, and in Case of Disagreement between them, with Respect to the Time of Adjournment, he may adjourn them to such Time as he shall think proper; he shall receive Ambassadors and other public Ministers; he shall take Care that the Laws be faithfully executed, and shall Commission all the Officers of the United States.

Section 4. The President, Vice President and all civil Officers of the United States, shall be removed from Office on Impeachment for, and Conviction of, Treason, Bribery, or other high Crimes and Misdemeanors.

ARTICLE III

Section 1. The judicial Power of the United States, shall be vested in one supreme Court, and in such inferior Courts as the Congress may from time to time ordain and establish. The Judges, both of the supreme and inferior Courts, shall hold their Offices during good Behaviour, and shall, at stated Times, receive for their Services a Compensation, which shall not be diminished during their Continuance in Office.

Section 2. The judicial Power shall extend to all Cases, in Law and Equity, arising under this Constitution, the Laws of the United States, and Treaties made, or which shall be made, under their Authority;—to all Cases affecting Ambassadors, other public Ministers and Consuls;—to all Cases of admiralty and maritime Jurisdiction;—to Controversies to which the United States shall be a Party;—to Controversies between two or more States;—between a State and Citizens of another State;—between Citizens of different States;—between Citizens of the same State claiming Lands under Grants of different States, and between a State, or the Citizens thereof, and foreign States, Citizens or Subjects.

In all Cases affecting Ambassadors, other public Ministers and Consuls, and those in which a State shall be a Party, the supreme Court shall have original Jurisdiction. In all the other Cases before mentioned, the supreme Court shall have appellate Jurisdiction, both as to Law and Fact, with such Exceptions, and under such Regulations as the Congress shall make.

The Trial of all Crimes, except in Cases of Impeachment, shall be by Jury; and such Trial shall be held in the State where the said Crimes shall have been committed; but when not committed within any State, the Trial shall be at such Place or Places as the Congress may by Law have directed.

Section 3. Treason against the United States, shall consist only in levying War against them, or, in adhering to their Enemies, giving them Aid and Comfort. No Person shall be convicted of Treason unless on the Testimony of two Witnesses to the same overt Act, or on Confession in open Court.

The Congress shall have Power to declare the Punishment of Treason, but no Attainder of Treason shall work Corruption of Blood, or Forfeiture except during the Life of the Person attainted.

ARTICLE IV

Section 1. Full Faith and Credit shall be given in each State to the public Acts, Records, and judicial Proceedings of every other State. And the Congress may by general Laws prescribe the Manner in which such Acts, Records and Proceedings shall be proved, and the Effect thereof.

Section 2. The Citizens of each State shall be entitled to all Privileges and Immunities of Citizens in the several States.

A Person charged in any State with Treason, Felony, or other Crime, who shall flee from Justice, and be found in another State, shall on Demand of the executive Authority of the State from which he fled, be delivered up, to be removed to the State having Jurisdiction of the Crime.

No Person held to Service or Labour in one State, under the Laws thereof, escaping into another, shall, in Consequence of any Law or Regulation therein, be discharged from such Service or Labour, but shall be delivered up on Claim of the Party to whom such Service or Labour may be due.

Section 3. New States may be admitted by the Congress into this Union; but no new State shall be formed or erected within the Jurisdiction of any other State; nor any State be formed by the Junction of two or more States, or Parts of States, without the Consent of the Legislatures of the States concerned as well as of the Congress.

The Congress shall have Power to dispose of and make all needful Rules and Regulations respecting the Territory or other Property belonging to the United States; and nothing in this Constitution shall be so construed as to Prejudice any Claims of the United States, or of any particular State.

Section 4. The United States shall guarantee to every State in this Union a Republican Form of Government, and shall protect each of them against Invasion; and on Application of the Legislature, or of the Executive (when the Legislature cannot be convened) against domestic Violence.

ARTICLE V

The Congress, whenever two thirds of both Houses shall deem it necessary, shall propose Amendments to this Constitution, or, on the Application of the Legislatures of two thirds of the several States, shall call a Convention for proposing Amendments, which, in either Case, shall be valid to all Intents and Purposes, as part of this Constitution, when ratified by the Legislatures of three fourths of the several States, or by Conventions in three fourths thereof, as the one or the other Mode of Ratification may be proposed by the Congress; Provided that no Amendment which may be made prior to the Year One thousand eight hundred and eight shall in any Manner affect the first and fourth Clauses in the Ninth Section of the first Article; and that no State, without its Consent, shall be deprived of its equal Suffrage in the Senate.

ARTICLE VI

All Debts contracted and Engagements entered into, before the Adoption of this Constitution shall be as valid against the United States under this Constitution, as under the Confederation.

This Constitution, and the Laws of the United States which shall be made in Pursuance thereof; and all Treaties made, or which shall be made, under the Authority of the United States, shall be the supreme Law of the Land; and the Judges in every State shall be bound thereby, any Thing in the Constitution or Laws of any State to the Contrary notwithstanding.

The Senators and Representatives before mentioned, and the Members of the several State Legislatures, and all executive and judicial Officers, both of the United States and of the several States, shall be bound by Oath or Affirmation, to support this Constitution; but no religious Test shall ever be required as a Qualification to any Office or public Trust under the United States.

ARTICLE VII

The Ratification of the Conventions of nine States shall be sufficient for the Establishment of this Constitution between the States so ratifying the Same.

AMENDMENT I [1791]

Congress shall make no law respecting an establishment of religion, or prohibiting the free exercise thereof; or abridging the freedom of speech, or of the press; or the right of the people peaceably to assembly, and to petition the Government for a redress of grievances.

AMENDMENT II [1791]

A well regulated Militia, being necessary to the security of a free State, the right of the people to keep and bear Arms, shall not be infringed.

AMENDMENT III [1791]

No Soldier shall, in time of peace be quartered in any house, without the consent of the Owner, nor in time of war, but in a manner to be prescribed by law.

AMENDMENT IV [1791]

The right of the people to be secure in their persons, houses, papers, and effects, against unreasonable searches and seizures, shall not be violated, and no Warrants shall issue, but upon probable cause, supported by Oath or affirmation, and particularly describing the place to be searched, and the persons or things to be seized.

AMENDMENT V [1791]

No person shall be held to answer for a capital, or otherwise infamous crime, unless on a presentment or indictment of a Grand Jury, except in cases arising in the land or naval forces, or in the Militia, when in actual service in time of War or public danger; nor shall any person be subject for the same offence to be twice put in jeopardy of life or limb; nor shall be compelled in any criminal case to be a witness against himself, nor be deprived of life, liberty, or property, without due process of law; nor shall private property be taken for public use, without just compensation.

AMENDMENT VI [1791]

In all criminal prosecutions, the accused shall enjoy the right to a speedy and public trial, by an impartial jury of the State and district wherein the crime shall have been committed, which district shall have been previously ascertained by law, and to be informed of the nature and cause of the accusation; to be confronted with the witnesses against him; to have compulsory process for obtaining witnesses in his favor, and to have the Assistance of Counsel for his defence.

AMENDMENT VII [1791]

In Suits at common law, where the value in controversy shall exceed twenty dollars, the right of trial by jury shall be preserved, and no fact tried by jury, shall be otherwise re-examined in any Court of the United States, than according to the rules of the common law.

AMENDMENT VIII [1791]

Excessive bail shall not be required, nor excessive fines imposed, nor cruel and unusual punishments inflicted.

AMENDMENT IX [1791]

The enumeration in the Constitution, of certain rights, shall not be construed to deny or disparage others retained by the people.

AMENDMENT X [1791]

The powers not delegated to the United States by the Constitution, nor prohibited by it to the States, are reserved to the States respectively, or to the people.

AMENDMENT XI [1798]

The Judicial power of the United States shall not be construed to extend to any suit in law or equity, commenced or prosecuted against one of the United States by Citizens of another State, or by Citizens or Subjects of any Foreign State.

AMENDMENT XII [1804]

The Electors shall meet in their respective states, and vote by ballot for President and Vice-President, one of whom, at least, shall not be an inhabitant of the same state with themselves; they shall name in their ballots the person voted for as President, and in distinct ballots the person voted for as Vice-President, and they shall make distinct lists of all persons voted for as President, and of all persons voted for as Vice-President, and of the number of votes for each, which lists they shall sign and certify, and transmit sealed to the seat of the government of the United States, directed to the President of the Senate;—The President of the Senate shall, in the presence of the Senate and House of Representatives, open all the certificates and the votes shall then be counted;—The person having the greatest number of votes for President, shall be the President, if such number be a majority of the whole number of Electors appointed; and if no person have such majority, then from the persons having the highest numbers not exceeding three on the list of those voted for as President, the House of Representatives shall choose immediately, by ballot, the President. But in choosing the President, the votes shall be taken by states, the representation from each state having one vote; a quorum for this purpose shall consist of a member or members from two-thirds of the states, and a majority of all states shall be neces-

sary to a choice. And if the House of Representatives shall not choose a President whenever the right of choice shall devolve upon them, before the fourth day of March next following, then the Vice-President shall act as President, as in the case of the death or other constitutional disability of the President.—The person having the greatest number of votes as Vice-President, shall be the Vice-President, if such number be a majority of the whole number of Electors appointed, and if no person have a majority, then from the two highest numbers on the list, the Senate shall choose the Vice-President; a quorum for the purpose shall consist of two-thirds of the whole number of Senators, and a majority of the whole number shall be necessary to a choice. But no person constitutionally ineligible to the office of President shall be eligible to that of Vice-President of the United States.

AMENDMENT XIII [1865]

Section 1. Neither slavery nor involuntary servitude, except as a punishment for crime whereof the party shall have been duly convicted, shall exist within the United States, or any place subject to their jurisdiction.

Section 2. Congress shall have power to enforce this article by appropriate legislation.

AMENDMENT XIV [1868]

Section 1. All persons born or naturalized in the United States, and subject to the jurisdiction thereof, are citizens of the United States and of the State wherein they reside. No State shall make or enforce any law which shall abridge the privileges or immunities of citizens of the United States; nor shall any State deprive any person of life, liberty, or property, without due process of law; nor deny to any person within its jurisdiction the equal protection of the laws.

Section 2. Representatives shall be apportioned among the several States according to their respective numbers, counting the whole number of persons in each State, excluding Indians not taxed. But when the right to vote at any election for the choice of electors for President and Vice President of the United States, Representatives in Congress, the Executive and Judicial officers of a State, or the members of the Legislature thereof, is denied to any of the male inhabitants of such State, being twenty-one years of age, and citizens of the United States, or in any way abridged, except for participation in rebellion, or other crime, the basis of representation therein shall be reduced in the proportion which the number of such male citizens shall bear to the whole number of male citizens twenty-one years of age in such State.

Section 3. No person shall be a Senator or Representative in Congress, or elector of President and Vice President, or hold any office, civil or military, under the United States, or under any State, who having previously taken an oath, as a member of Congress, or as an officer of the United States, or as a member of any State legislature, or as an executive or judicial officer of any State, to support the Constitution of the United States, shall have engaged in insurrection or rebellion against the same, or given aid or comfort to the enemies thereof. But Congress may by a vote of two-thirds of each House, remove such disability.

Section 4. The validity of the public debt of the United States, authorized by law, including debts incurred for payment of pensions and bounties for services in suppressing insurrection or rebellion, shall not be questioned. But neither the United States nor any State shall assume or pay any debt or obligation incurred in aid of insurrection or rebellion against the United States, or any claim for the loss or emancipation of any slave; but all such debts, obligations and claims shall be held illegal and void.

Section 5. The Congress shall have power to enforce, by appropriate legislation, the provisions of this article.

AMENDMENT XV [1870]

Section 1. The right of citizens of the United States to vote shall not be denied or abridged by the United States or by any State on account of race, color, or previous condition of servitude.

Section 2. The Congress shall have power to enforce this article by appropriate legislation.

AMENDMENT XVI [1913]

The Congress shall have power to lay and collect taxes on incomes, from whatever source derived, without apportionment among the several States, and without regard to any census or enumeration.

AMENDMENT XVII [1913]

Section 1. The Senate of the United States shall be composed of two Senators from each State, elected by the people thereof, for six years; and each Senator shall have one vote. The electors in each State shall have the qualifications requisite for electors of the most numerous branch of the State legislatures.

Section 2. When vacancies happen in the representation of any State in the Senate, the executive authority of such State shall issue writs of election to fill such vacancies: *Provided,* That the legislature of any State may empower the executive thereof to make temporary appointments until the people fill the vacancies by election as the legislature may direct.

Section 3. This amendment shall not be so construed as to affect the election or term of any Senator chosen before it becomes valid as part of the Constitution.

AMENDMENT XVIII [1919]

Section 1. After one year from the ratification of this article the manufacture, sale, or transportation of intoxicating liquors within, the importation thereof into, or the exportation thereof from the United States and all territory subject to the jurisdiction thereof for beverage purposes is hereby prohibited.

Section 2. The Congress and the several States shall have concurrent power to enforce this article by appropriate legislation.

Section 3. This article shall be inoperative unless it shall have been ratified as an amendment to the Constitution by the legislatures of the several States, as pro-

vided in the Constitution, within seven years from the date of the submission hereof to the States by the Congress.

AMENDMENT XIX [1920]

Section 1. The right of citizens of the United States to vote shall not be denied or abridged by the United States or by any State on account of sex.

Section 2. Congress shall have power to enforce this article by appropriate legislation.

AMENDMENT XX [1933]

Section 1. The terms of the President and Vice President shall end at noon on the 20th day of January, and the terms of Senators and Representatives at noon on the 3d day of January, of the years in which such terms would have ended if this article had not been ratified; and the terms of their successors shall then begin.

Section 2. The Congress shall assemble at least once in every year, and such meeting shall begin at noon on the 3d day of January, unless they shall by law appoint a different day.

Section 3. If, at the time fixed for the beginning of the term of the President, the President elect shall have died, the Vice President elect shall become President. If the President shall not have been chosen before the time fixed for the beginning of his term, or if the President elect shall have failed to qualify, then the Vice President elect shall act as President until a President shall have qualified; and the Congress may by law provide for the case wherein neither a President elect nor a Vice President elect shall have qualified, declaring who shall then act as President, or the manner in which one who is to act shall be selected, and such person shall act accordingly until a President or Vice President shall have qualified.

Section 4. The Congress may by law provide for the case of the death of any of the persons from whom the House of Representatives may choose a President whenever the right of choice shall have devolved upon them, and for the case of the death of any of the persons from whom the Senate may choose a Vice President whenever the right of choice shall have devolved upon them.

Section 5. Sections 1 and 2 shall take effect on the 15th day of October following the ratification of this article.

Section 6. This article shall be inoperative unless it shall have been ratified as an amendment to the Constitution by the legislatures of three-fourths of the several States within seven years from the date of its submission.

AMENDMENT XXI [1933]

Section 1. The eighteenth article of amendment to the Constitution of the United States is hereby repealed.

Section 2. The transportation or importation into any State, Territory, or possession of the United States for delivery or use therein of intoxicating liquors, in violation of the laws thereof, is hereby prohibited.

Section 3. This article shall be inoperative unless it shall have been ratified as an amendment to the Constitution by conventions in the several States, as provided in the Constitution, within seven years from the date of the submission hereof to the States by the Congress.

AMENDMENT XXII [1951]

Section 1. No person shall be elected to the office of the President more than twice, and no person who has held the office of President, or acted as President, for more than two years of a term to which some other person was elected President shall be elected to the office of President more than once. But this Article shall not apply to any person holding the office of President when this Article was proposed by the Congress, and shall not prevent any person who may be holding the office of President, or acting as President, during the term within which this Article becomes operative from holding the office of President or acting as President during the remainder of such term.

Section 2. This article shall be inoperative unless it shall have been ratified as an amendment to the Constitution by the legislatures of three-fourths of the several States within seven years from the date of its submission to the States by the Congress.

AMENDMENT XXIII [1961]

Section 1. The District constituting the seat of Government of the United States shall appoint in such manner as the Congress may direct:

A number of electors of President and Vice President equal to the whole number of Senators and Representatives in Congress to which the District would be entitled if it were a State, but in no event more than the least populous state; they shall be in addition to those appointed by the states, but they shall be considered, for the purposes of the election of President and Vice President, to be electors appointed by a state; and they shall meet in the District and perform such duties as provided by the twelfth article of amendment.

Section 2. The Congress shall have power to enforce this article by appropriate legislation.

AMENDMENT XXIV [1964]

Section 1. The right of citizens of the United States to vote in any primary or other election for President or Vice President, for electors for President or Vice President, or for Senator or Representative in Congress, shall not be denied or abridged by the United States, or any State by reason of failure to pay any poll tax or other tax.

Section 2. The Congress shall have power to enforce this article by appropriate legislation.

AMENDMENT XXV [1967]

Section 1. In case of the removal of the President from office or of his death or resignation, the Vice President shall become President.

Section 2. Whenever there is a vacancy in the office of the Vice President, the President shall nominate a Vice President who shall take office upon confirmation by a majority vote of both Houses of Congress.

Section 3. Whenever the President transmits to the President pro tempore of the Senate and the Speaker of the House of Representatives his written declaration that he is unable to discharge the powers and duties of his office, and until he transmits to them a written declaration to the contrary, such powers and duties shall be discharged by the Vice President as Acting President.

Section 4. Whenever the Vice President and a majority of either the principal officers of the executive departments or of such other body as Congress may by law provide, transmit to the President pro tempore of the Senate and the Speaker of the House of Representatives their written declaration that the President is unable to discharge the powers and duties of his office, the Vice President shall immediately assume the powers and duties of the office as Acting President.

Thereafter, when the President transmits to the President pro tempore of the Senate and the Speaker of the House of Representatives his written declaration that no inability exists, he shall resume the powers and duties of his office unless the Vice President and a majority of either the principal officers of the executive department or of such other body as Congress may by law provide, transmit within four days to the President pro tempore of the Senate and the Speaker of the House of Representatives their written declaration that the President is unable to discharge the powers and duties of his office. Thereupon Congress shall decide the issue, assembling within forty-eight hours for that purpose if not in session. If the Congress, within twenty-one days after receipt of the latter written declaration, or, if Congress is not in session, within twenty-one days after Congress is required to assemble, determines by two-thirds vote of both Houses that the President is unable to discharge the powers and duties of his office, the Vice President shall continue to discharge the same as Acting President; otherwise, the President shall resume the powers and duties of his office.

AMENDMENT XXVI [1971]

Section 1. The right of citizens of the United States, who are eighteen years of age or older, to vote shall not be denied or abridged by the United States or by any State on account of age.

Section 2. The Congress shall have power to enforce this article by appropriate legislation.

AMENDMENT XXVII [1992]

No law, varying the compensation for the services of the Senators and Representatives, shall take effect, until an election of Representatives shall have intervened.

(Adopted in fifty-two jurisdictions; all fifty States, although Louisiana has adopted only Articles 1, 3, 4, 7, 8, and 9; the District of Columbia; and the Virgin Islands.)

The Code consists of the following articles:

Art.

1. General Provisions
2. Sales
2A. Leases
3. Negotiable Instruments
4. Bank Deposits and Collections
4A. Funds Transfers
5. Letters of Credit
6. Repealer of Article 6—Bulk Transfers and [Revised] Article 6—Bulk Sales
7. Warehouse Receipts, Bills of Lading and Other Documents of Title
8. Investment Securities
9. Secured Transactions
10. Effective Date and Repealer
11. Effective Date and Transition Provisions

Article 1
GENERAL PROVISIONS

Part 1 Short Title, Construction, Application and Subject Matter of the Act

§ 1–101. Short Title.

This Act shall be known and may be cited as Uniform Commercial Code.

§ 1–102. Purposes; Rules of Construction; Variation by Agreement.

(1) This Act shall be liberally construed and applied to promote its underlying purposes and policies.

(2) Underlying purposes and policies of this Act are

(a) to simplify, clarify and modernize the law governing commercial transactions;

(b) to permit the continued expansion of commercial practices through custom, usage and agreement of the parties;

(c) to make uniform the law among the various jurisdictions.

(3) The effect of provisions of this Act may be varied by agreement, except as otherwise provided in this Act and except that the obligations of good faith, diligence, reasonableness and care prescribed by this Act may not be disclaimed by agreement but the parties may by agreement determine the standards by which the performance of such obligations is to be measured if such standards are not manifestly unreasonable.

(4) The presence in certain provisions of this Act of the words "unless otherwise agreed" or words of similar import does not imply that the effect of other provisions may not be varied by agreement under subsection (3).

(5) In this Act unless the context otherwise requires

(a) words in the singular number include the plural, and in the plural include the singular;

(b) words of the masculine gender include the feminine and the neuter, and when the sense so indicates words of the neuter gender may refer to any gender.

§ 1–103. Supplementary General Principles of Law Applicable.

Unless displaced by the particular provisions of this Act, the principles of law and equity, including the law merchant and the law relative to capacity to contract, principal and agent, estoppel, fraud, misrepresentation, duress, coercion, mistake, bankruptcy, or other validating or invalidating cause shall supplement its provisions.

§ 1–104. Construction Against Implicit Repeal.

This Act being a general act intended as a unified coverage of its subject matter, no part of it shall be deemed to be impliedly repealed by subsequent legislation if such construction can reasonably be avoided.

§ 1–105. Territorial Application of the Act; Parties' Power to Choose Applicable Law.

(1) Except as provided hereafter in this section, when a transaction bears a reasonable relation to this state and also to another state or nation the parties may agree that the law either of this state or of such other state or nation shall govern their rights and duties. Failing such agreement this Act applies to transactions bearing an appropriate relation to this state.

(2) Where one of the following provisions of this Act specifies the applicable law, that provision governs and a contrary agreement is effective only to the extent permitted by the law (including the conflict of laws rules) so specified:

Rights of creditors against sold goods. Section 2–402.

Applicability of the Article on Leases. Sections 2A–105 and 2A–106.

Applicability of the Article on Bank Deposits and Collections. Section 4–102.

Governing law in the Article on Funds Transfers. Section 4A–507.

Letters of Credit, Section 5–116.

Bulk sales subject to the Article on Bulk Sales. Section 6–103.

Applicability of the Article on Investment Securities. Section 8–106.

Law governing perfection, the effect of perfection or nonperfection, and the priority of security interests and agricultural liens. Sections 9–301 through 9–307.

As amended in 1972, 1987, 1988, 1989, 1994, 1995, and 1999.

§ 1–106. Remedies to Be Liberally Administered.

(1) The remedies provided by this Act shall be liberally administered to the end that the aggrieved party may be put in as good a position as if the other party had fully performed but neither consequential or special nor penal damages may be had except as specifically provided in this Act or by other rule of law.

(2) Any right or obligation declared by this Act is enforceable by action unless the provision declaring it specifies a different and limited effect.

§ 1–107. Waiver or Renunciation of Claim or Right After Breach.

Any claim or right arising out of an alleged breach can be discharged in whole or in part without consideration by a written waiver or renunciation signed and delivered by the aggrieved party.

§ 1–108. Severability.

If any provision or clause of this Act or application thereof to any person or circumstances is held invalid, such invalidity shall not affect other provisions or applications of the Act which can be given effect without the invalid provision or application, and to this end the provisions of this Act are declared to be severable.

§ 1–109. Section Captions.

Section captions are parts of this Act.

Part 2 General Definitions and Principles of Interpretation

§ 1–201. General Definitions.

Subject to additional definitions contained in the subsequent Articles of this Act which are applicable to specific Articles or Parts thereof, and unless the context otherwise requires, in this Act:

(1) "Action" in the sense of a judicial proceeding includes recoupment, counterclaim, set-off, suit in equity and any other proceedings in which rights are determined.

(2) "Aggrieved party" means a party entitled to resort to a remedy.

(3) "Agreement" means the bargain of the parties in fact as found in their language or by implication from other circumstances including course of dealing or usage of trade or course of performance as provided in this Act (Sections 1–205 and 2–208). Whether an agreement has legal consequences is determined by the provisions of this Act, if applicable; otherwise by the law of contracts (Section 1–103). (Compare "Contract".)

(4) "Bank" means any person engaged in the business of banking.

(5) "Bearer" means the person in possession of an instrument, document of title, or certificated security payable to bearer or indorsed in blank.

(6) "Bill of lading" means a document evidencing the receipt of goods for shipment issued by a person engaged in the business of transporting or forwarding goods, and includes an airbill. "Airbill" means a document serving for air transportation as a bill of lading does for marine or rail transportation, and includes an air consignment note or air waybill.

(7) "Branch" includes a separately incorporated foreign branch of a bank.

(8) "Burden of establishing" a fact means the burden of persuading the triers of fact that the existence of the fact is more probable than its non-existence.

(9) "Buyer in ordinary course of business" means a person that buys goods in good faith, without knowledge that the sale violates the rights of another person in the goods, and in the ordinary course from a person, other than a pawnbroker, in the business of selling goods of that kind. A person buys goods in the ordinary course if the sale to the person comports with the usual or customary practices in the kind of business in which the seller is engaged or with the seller's own usual or customary practices. A person that sells oil, gas, or other minerals at the wellhead or minehead is a person in the business of selling goods of that kind. A buyer in ordinary course of business may buy for cash, by exchange of other property, or on secured or unsecured credit, and may acquire goods or documents of title under a pre-existing contract for sale. Only a buyer that takes possession of the goods or has a right to recover the goods from the seller under Article 2 may be a buyer in ordinary course of business. A person that acquires goods in a transfer in bulk or as security for or in total or partial satisfaction of a money debt is not a buyer in ordinary course of business.

(10) "Conspicuous": A term or clause is conspicuous when it is so written that a reasonable person against whom it is to operate ought to have noticed it. A printed heading in capitals (as: NON-NEGOTIABLE BILL OF LADING) is conspicuous. Language in the body of a form is "conspicuous" if it is in larger or other contrasting type or color. But in a telegram any stated term is "conspicuous". Whether a term or clause is "conspicuous" or not is for decision by the court.

(11) "Contract" means the total legal obligation which results from the parties' agreement as affected by this Act and any other applicable rules of law. (Compare "Agreement".)

(12) "Creditor" includes a general creditor, a secured creditor, a lien creditor and any representative of creditors, including an assignee for the benefit of creditors, a trustee in bankruptcy, a receiver in equity and an executor or administrator of an insolvent debtor's or assignor's estate.

(13) "Defendant" includes a person in the position of defendant in a cross-action or counterclaim.

(14) "Delivery" with respect to instruments, documents of title, chattel paper, or certificated securities means voluntary transfer of possession.

(15) "Document of title" includes bill of lading, dock warrant, dock receipt, warehouse receipt or order for the delivery of goods, and also any other document which in the regular course of business or financing is treated as adequately evidencing that the person in possession of it is entitled to receive, hold and dispose of the document and the goods it covers. To be a document of title a document must purport to be issued by or addressed to a bailee and purport to cover goods in the bailee's possession which are either identified or are fungible portions of an identified mass.

(16) "Fault" means wrongful act, omission or breach.

(17) "Fungible" with respect to goods or securities means goods or securities of which any unit is, by nature or usage of trade, the equivalent of any other like unit. Goods which are not fungible shall be deemed fungible for the purposes of this Act to the extent that under a particular agreement or document unlike units are treated as equivalents.

(18) "Genuine" means free of forgery or counterfeiting.

(19) "Good faith" means honesty in fact in the conduct or transaction concerned.

(20) "Holder" with respect to a negotiable instrument, means the person in possession if the instrument is payable to bearer or, in the cases of an instrument payable to an identified person, if the identified person is in possession. "Holder" with respect to a document of title means the person in possession if the goods are deliverable to bearer or to the order of the person in possession.

(21) To "honor" is to pay or to accept and pay, or where a credit so engages to purchase or discount a draft complying with the terms of the credit.

(22) "Insolvency proceedings" includes any assignment for the benefit of creditors or other proceedings intended to liquidate or rehabilitate the estate of the person involved.

(23) A person is "insolvent" who either has ceased to pay his debts in the ordinary course of business or cannot pay his debts as they become due or is insolvent within the meaning of the federal bankruptcy law.

(24) "Money" means a medium of exchange authorized or adopted by a domestic or foreign government and includes a monetary unit of account established by an intergovernmental organization or by agreement between two or more nations.

(25) A person has "notice" of a fact when

(a) he has actual knowledge of it; or

(b) he has received a notice or notification of it; or

(c) from all the facts and circumstances known to him at the time in question he has reason to know that it exists.

A person "knows" or has "knowledge" of a fact when he has actual knowledge of it. "Discover" or "learn" or a word or phrase of similar import refers to knowledge rather than to reason to know. The time and circumstances under which a notice or notification may cease to be effective are not determined by this Act.

(26) A person "notifies" or "gives" a notice or notification to another by taking such steps as may be reasonably required to inform the other in ordinary course whether or not such other actually comes to know of it. A person "receives" a notice or notification when

(a) it comes to his attention; or

(b) it is duly delivered at the place of business through which the contract was made or at any other place held out by him as the place for receipt of such communications.

(27) Notice, knowledge or a notice or notification received by an organization is effective for a particular transaction from the time when it is brought to the attention of the individual conducting that transaction, and in any event from the time when it would have been brought to his attention if the organization had exercised due diligence. An organization exercises due diligence if it maintains reasonable routines for communicating significant information to the person conducting the transaction and there is reasonable compliance with the routines. Due diligence does not require an individual acting for the organization to communicate information unless such communication is part of his regular duties or unless he has reason to know of the transaction and that the transaction would be materially affected by the information.

(28) "Organization" includes a corporation, government or governmental subdivision or agency, business trust, estate, trust, partnership or association, two or more persons having a joint or common interest, or any other legal or commercial entity.

(29) "Party", as distinct from "third party", means a person who has engaged in a transaction or made an agreement within this Act.

(30) "Person" includes an individual or an organization (See Section 1–102).

(31) "Presumption" or "presumed" means that the trier of fact must find the existence of the fact presumed unless and until evidence is introduced which would support a finding of its non-existence.

(32) "Purchase" includes taking by sale, discount, negotiation, mortgage, pledge, lien, issue or re-issue, gift or any other voluntary transaction creating an interest in property.

(33) "Purchaser" means a person who takes by purchase.

(34) "Remedy" means any remedial right to which an aggrieved party is entitled with or without resort to a tribunal.

(35) "Representative" includes an agent, an officer of a corporation or association, and a trustee, executor or administrator of an estate, or any other person empowered to act for another.

(36) "Rights" includes remedies.

(37) "Security interest" means an interest in personal property or fixtures which secures payment or performance of an obligation. The term also includes any interest of a consignor and a buyer of accounts, chattel paper, a payment intangible, or a promissory note in a transaction that is subject to Article 9. The special property interest of a buyer of goods on identification of those goods to a contract for sale under Section 2–401 is not a "security interest", but a buyer may also acquire a "security interest" by complying with Article 9. Except as otherwise provided in Section 2–505, the right of a seller or lessor of goods under Article 2 or 2A to retain or acquire possession of the goods is not a "security interest", but a seller or lessor may also acquire a "security

interest" by complying with Article 9. The retention or reservation of title by a seller of goods notwithstanding shipment or delivery to the buyer (Section 2–401) is limited in effect to a reservation of a "security interest".

Whether a transaction creates a lease or security interest is determined by the facts of each case; however, a transaction creates a security interest if the consideration the lessee is to pay the lessor for the right to possession and use of the goods is an obligation for the term of the lease not subject to termination by the lessee, and

(a) the original term of the lease is equal to or greater than the remaining economic life of the goods,

(b) the lessee is bound to renew the lease for the remaining economic life of the goods or is bound to become the owner of the goods,

(c) the lessee has an option to renew the lease for the remaining economic life of the goods for no additional consideration or nominal additional consideration upon compliance with the lease agreement, or

(d) the lessee has an option to become the owner of the goods for no additional consideration or nominal additional consideration upon compliance with the lease agreement.

A transaction does not create a security interest merely because it provides that

(a) the present value of the consideration the lessee is obligated to pay the lessor for the right to possession and use of the goods is substantially equal to or is greater than the fair market value of the goods at the time the lease is entered into,

(b) the lessee assumes risk of loss of the goods, or agrees to pay taxes, insurance, filing, recording, or registration fees, or service or maintenance costs with respect to the goods,

(c) the lessee has an option to renew the lease or to become the owner of the goods,

(d) the lessee has an option to renew the lease for a fixed rent that is equal to or greater than the reasonably predictable fair market rent for the use of the goods for the term of the renewal at the time the option is to be performed, or

(e) the lessee has an option to become the owner of the goods for a fixed price that is equal to or greater than the reasonably predictable fair market value of the goods at the time the option is to be performed.

For purposes of this subsection (37):

(x) Additional consideration is not nominal if (i) when the option to renew the lease is granted to the lessee the rent is stated to be the fair market rent for the use of the goods for the term of the renewal determined at the time the option is to be performed, or (ii) when the option to become the owner of the goods is granted to the lessee the price is stated to be the fair market value of the goods determined at the time the option is to be performed. Additional consideration is nominal if it is less than the lessee's reasonably predictable cost of performing under the lease agreement if the option is not exercised;

(y) "Reasonably predictable" and "remaining economic life of the goods" are to be determined with reference to the facts and circumstances at the time the transaction is entered into; and

(z) "Present value" means the amount as of a date certain of one or more sums payable in the future, discounted to the date certain. The discount is determined by the interest rate specified by the parties if the rate is not manifestly unreasonable at the time the transaction is entered into; otherwise, the discount is determined by a commercially reasonable rate that takes into account the facts and circumstances of each case at the time the transaction was entered into.

(38) "Send" in connection with any writing or notice means to deposit in the mail or deliver for transmission by any other usual means of communication with postage or cost of transmission provided for and properly addressed and in the case of an instrument to an address specified thereon or otherwise agreed, or if there be none to any address reasonable under the circumstances. The receipt of any writing or notice within the time at which it would have arrived if properly sent has the effect of a proper sending.

(39) "Signed" includes any symbol executed or adopted by a party with present intention to authenticate a writing.

(40) "Surety" includes guarantor.

(41) "Telegram" includes a message transmitted by radio, teletype, cable, any mechanical method of transmission, or the like.

(42) "Term" means that portion of an agreement which relates to a particular matter.

(43) "Unauthorized" signature means one made without actual, implied or apparent authority and includes a forgery.

(44) "Value". Except as otherwise provided with respect to negotiable instruments and bank collections (Sections 3–303, 4–210 and 4–211) a person gives "value" for rights if he acquires them

(a) in return for a binding commitment to extend credit or for the extension of immediately available credit whether or not drawn upon and whether or not a chargeback is provided for in the event of difficulties in collection; or

(b) as security for or in total or partial satisfaction of a pre-existing claim; or

(c) by accepting delivery pursuant to a preexisting contract for purchase; or

(d) generally, in return for any consideration sufficient to support a simple contract.

(45) "Warehouse receipt" means a receipt issued by a person engaged in the business of storing goods for hire.

(46) "Written" or "writing" includes printing, typewriting or any other intentional reduction to tangible form.

§1–202. Prima Facie Evidence by Third Party Documents.

A document in due form purporting to be a bill of lading, policy or certificate of insurance, official weigher's or inspector's certificate, consular invoice, or any other document authorized or required by the contract to be issued by a third party shall be prima facie evidence of its own authenticity and genuineness and of the facts stated in the document by the third party.

§ 1–203. Obligation of Good Faith.

Every contract or duty within this Act imposes an obligation of good faith in its performance or enforcement.

§ 1–204. Time; Reasonable Time; "Seasonably".

(1) Whenever this Act requires any action to be taken within a reasonable time, any time which is not manifestly unreasonable may be fixed by agreement.

(2) What is a reasonable time for taking any action depends on the nature, purpose and circumstances of such action.

(3) An action is taken "seasonably" when it is taken at or within the time agreed or if no time is agreed at or within a reasonable time.

§ 1–205. Course of Dealing and Usage of Trade.

(1) A course of dealing is a sequence of previous conduct between the parties to a particular transaction which is fairly to be regarded as establishing a common basis of understanding for interpreting their expressions and other conduct.

(2) A usage of trade is any practice or method of dealing having such regularity of observance in a place, vocation or trade as to justify an expectation that it will be observed with respect to the transaction in question. The existence and scope of such a usage are to be proved as facts. If it is established that such a usage is embodied in a written trade code or similar writing the interpretation of the writing is for the court.

(3) A course of dealing between parties and any usage of trade in the vocation or trade in which they are engaged or of which they are or should be aware give particular meaning to and supplement or qualify terms of an agreement.

(4) The express terms of an agreement and an applicable course of dealing or usage of trade shall be construed wherever reasonable as consistent with each other; but when such construction is unreasonable express terms control both course of dealing and usage of trade and course of dealing controls usage trade.

(5) An applicable usage of trade in the place where any part of performance is to occur shall be used in interpreting the agreement as to that part of the performance.

(6) Evidence of a relevant usage of trade offered by one party is not admissible unless and until he has given the other party such notice as the court finds sufficient to prevent unfair surprise to the latter.

§ 1–206. Statute of Frauds for Kinds of Personal Property Not Otherwise Covered.

(1) Except in the cases described in subsection (2) of this section a contract for the sale of personal property is not enforceable by way of action or defense beyond five thousand dollars in amount or value of remedy unless there is some writing which indicates that a contract for sale has been made between the parties at a defined or stated price, reasonably identifies the subject matter, and is signed by the party against whom enforcement is sought or by his authorized agent.

(2) Subsection (1) of this section does not apply to contracts for the sale of goods (Section 2–201) nor of securities (Section 8–113) nor to security agreements (Section 9–203).

As amended in 1994.

§ 1–207. Performance or Acceptance Under Reservation of Rights.

(1) A party who with explicit reservation of rights performs or promises performance or assents to performance in a manner demanded or offered by the other party does not thereby prejudice the rights reserved. Such words as "without prejudice", "under protest" or the like are sufficient.

(2) Subsection (1) does not apply to an accord and satisfaction.

As amended in 1990.

§ 1–208. Option to Accelerate at Will.

A term providing that one party or his successor in interest may accelerate payment or performance or require collateral or additional collateral "at will" or "when he deems himself insecure" or in words of similar import shall be construed to mean that he shall have power to do so only if he in good faith believes that the prospect of payment or performance is impaired. The burden of establishing lack of good faith is on the party against whom the power has been exercised.

§ 1–209. Subordinated Obligations.

An obligation may be issued as subordinated to payment of another obligation of the person obligated, or a creditor may subordinate his right to payment of an obligation by agreement with either the person obligated or another creditor of the person obligated. Such a subordination does not create a security interest as against either the common debtor or a subordinated creditor. This section shall be construed as declaring the law as it existed prior to the enactment of this section and not as modifying it. Added 1966.

Note: *This new section is proposed as an optional provision to make it clear that a subordination agreement does not create a security interest unless so intended.*

Article 2
SALES

Part 1 Short Title, General Construction and Subject Matter

§ 2–101. Short Title.

This Article shall be known and may be cited as Uniform Commercial Code—Sales.

§ 2–102. Scope; Certain Security and Other Transactions Excluded From This Article.

Unless the context otherwise requires, this Article applies to transactions in goods; it does not apply to any transaction which although in the form of an unconditional contract to sell or present sale is intended to operate only as a security transaction nor does this Article impair or repeal any statute regulating sales to consumers, farmers or other specified classes of buyers.

§ 2–103. Definitions and Index of Definitions.

(1) In this Article unless the context otherwise requires

(a) "Buyer" means a person who buys or contracts to buy goods.

(b) "Good faith" in the case of a merchant means honesty in fact and the observance of reasonable commercial standards of fair dealing in the trade.

(c) "Receipt" of goods means taking physical possession of them.

(d) "Seller" means a person who sells or contracts to sell goods.

(2) Other definitions applying to this Article or to specified Parts thereof, and the sections in which they appear are:

"Acceptance". Section 2–606.
"Banker's credit". Section 2–325.
"Between merchants". Section 2–104.
"Cancellation". Section 2–106(4).
"Commercial unit". Section 2–105.
"Confirmed credit". Section 2–325.
"Conforming to contract". Section 2–106.
"Contract for sale". Section 2–106.
"Cover". Section 2–712.
"Entrusting". Section 2–403.
"Financing agency". Section 2–104.
"Future goods". Section 2–105.
"Goods". Section 2–105.
"Identification". Section 2–501.
"Installment contract". Section 2–612.
"Letter of Credit". Section 2–325.
"Lot". Section 2–105.
"Merchant". Section 2–104.
"Overseas". Section 2–323.
"Person in position of seller". Section 2–707.

"Present sale". Section 2–106.

"Sale". Section 2–106.

"Sale on approval". Section 2–326.

"Sale or return". Section 2–326.

"Termination". Section 2–106.

(3) The following definitions in other Articles apply to this Article:

"Check". Section 3–104.

"Consignee". Section 7–102.

"Consignor". Section 7–102.

"Consumer goods". Section 9–109.

"Dishonor". Section 3–507.

"Draft". Section 3–104.

(4) In addition Article 1 contains general definitions and principles of construction and interpretation applicable throughout this Article.

As amended in 1994 and 1999.

§ 2–104. Definitions: "Merchant"; "Between Merchants"; "Financing Agency".

(1) "Merchant" means a person who deals in goods of the kind or otherwise by his occupation holds himself out as having knowledge or skill peculiar to the practices or goods involved in the transaction or to whom such knowledge or skill may be attributed by his employment of an agent or broker or other intermediary who by his occupation holds himself out as having such knowledge or skill.

(2) "Financing agency" means a bank, finance company or other person who in the ordinary course of business makes advances against goods or documents of title or who by arrangement with either the seller or the buyer intervenes in ordinary course to make or collect payment due or claimed under the contract for sale, as by purchasing or paying the seller's draft or making advances against it or by merely taking it for collection whether or not documents of title accompany the draft. "Financing agency" includes also a bank or other person who similarly intervenes between persons who are in the position of seller and buyer in respect to the goods (Section 2–707).

(3) "Between merchants" means in any transaction with respect to which both parties are chargeable with the knowledge or skill of merchants.

§ 2–105. Definitions: Transferability; "Goods"; "Future" Goods; "Lot"; "Commercial Unit".

(1) "Goods" means all things (including specially manufactured goods) which are movable at the time of identification to the contract for sale other than the money in which the price is to be paid, investment securities (Article 8) and things in action. "Goods" also includes the unborn young of animals and growing crops and other identified things attached to realty as described in the section on goods to be severed from realty (Section 2–107).

(2) Goods must be both existing and identified before any interest in them can pass. Goods which are not both existing and identified are "future" goods. A purported present sale of future goods or of any interest therein operates as a contract to sell.

(3) There may be a sale of a part interest in existing identified goods.

(4) An undivided share in an identified bulk of fungible goods is sufficiently identified to be sold although the quantity of the bulk is not determined. Any agreed proportion of such a bulk or any quantity thereof agreed upon by number, weight or other measure may to the extent of the seller's interest in the bulk be sold to the buyer who then becomes an owner in common.

(5) "Lot" means a parcel or a single article which is the subject matter of a separate sale or delivery, whether or not it is sufficient to perform the contract.

(6) "Commercial unit" means such a unit of goods as by commercial usage is a single whole for purposes of sale and division of which materially impairs its character or value on the market or in use. A commercial unit may be a single article (as a machine) or a set of articles (as a suite of furniture or an assortment of sizes) or a quantity (as a bale, gross, or carload) or any other unit treated in use or in the relevant market as a single whole.

§ 2–106. Definitions: "Contract"; "Agreement"; "Contract for Sale"; "Sale"; "Present Sale"; "Conforming" to Contract; "Termination"; "Cancellation".

(1) In this Article unless the context otherwise requires "contract" and "agreement" are limited to those relating to the present or future sale of goods. "Contract for sale" includes both a present sale of goods and a contract to sell goods at a future time. A "sale" consists in the passing of title from the seller to the buyer for a price (Section 2–401). A "present sale" means a sale which is accomplished by the making of the contract.

(2) Goods or conduct including any part of a performance are "conforming" or conform to the contract when they are in accordance with the obligations under the contract.

(3) "Termination" occurs when either party pursuant to a power created by agreement or law puts an end to the contract otherwise than for its breach. On "termination" all obligations which are still executory on both sides are discharged but any right based on prior breach or performance survives.

(4) "Cancellation" occurs when either party puts an end to the contract for breach by the other and its effect is the same as that of "termination" except that the cancelling party also retains any remedy for breach of the whole contract or any unperformed balance.

§ 2–107. Goods to Be Severed From Realty: Recording.

(1) A contract for the sale of minerals or the like (including oil and gas) or a structure or its materials to be removed from realty is a contract for the sale of goods within this

Article if they are to be severed by the seller but until severance a purported present sale thereof which is not effective as a transfer of an interest in land is effective only as a contract to sell.

(2) A contract for the sale apart from the land of growing crops or other things attached to realty and capable of severance without material harm thereto but not described in subsection (1) or of timber to be cut is a contract for the sale of goods within this Article whether the subject matter is to be severed by the buyer or by the seller even though it forms part of the realty at the time of contracting, and the parties can by identification effect a present sale before severance.

(3) The provisions of this section are subject to any third party rights provided by the law relating to realty records, and the contract for sale may be executed and recorded as a document transferring an interest in land and shall then constitute notice to third parties of the buyer's rights under the contract for sale.

As amended in 1972.

Part 2 Form, Formation and Readjustment of Contract

§ 2–201. Formal Requirements; Statute of Frauds.

(1) Except as otherwise provided in this section a contract for the sale of goods for the price of $500 or more is not enforceable by way of action or defense unless there is some writing sufficient to indicate that a contract for sale has been made between the parties and signed by the party against whom enforcement is sought or by his authorized agent or broker. A writing is not insufficient because it omits or incorrectly states a term agreed upon but the contract is not enforceable under this paragraph beyond the quantity of goods shown in such writing.

(2) Between merchants if within a reasonable time a writing in confirmation of the contract and sufficient against the sender is received and the party receiving it has reason to know its contents, its satisfies the requirements of subsection (1) against such party unless written notice of objection to its contents is given within ten days after it is received.

(3) A contract which does not satisfy the requirements of subsection (1) but which is valid in other respects is enforceable

(a) if the goods are to be specially manufactured for the buyer and are not suitable for sale to others in the ordinary course of the seller's business and the seller, before notice of repudiation is received and under circumstances which reasonably indicate that the goods are for the buyer, has made either a substantial beginning of their manufacture or commitments for their procurement; or

(b) if the party against whom enforcement is sought admits in his pleading, testimony or otherwise in court that a contract for sale was made, but the contract is not enforceable under this provision beyond the quantity of goods admitted; or

(c) with respect to goods for which payment has been made and accepted or which have been received and accepted (Sec. 2–606).

§ 2–202. Final Written Expression: Parol or Extrinsic Evidence.

Terms with respect to which the confirmatory memoranda of the parties agree or which are otherwise set forth in a writing intended by the parties as a final expression of their agreement with respect to such terms as are included therein may not be contradicted by evidence of any prior agreement or of a contemporaneous oral agreement but may be explained or supplemented

(a) by course of dealing or usage of trade (Section 1–205) or by course of performance (Section 2–208); and

(b) by evidence of consistent additional terms unless the court finds the writing to have been intended also as a complete and exclusive statement of the terms of the agreement.

§ 2–203. Seals Inoperative.

The affixing of a seal to a writing evidencing a contract for sale or an offer to buy or sell goods does not constitute the writing a sealed instrument and the law with respect to sealed instruments does not apply to such a contract or offer.

§ 2–204. Formation in General.

(1) A contract for sale of goods may be made in any manner sufficient to show agreement, including conduct by both parties which recognizes the existence of such a contract.

(2) An agreement sufficient to constitute a contract for sale may be found even though the moment of its making is undetermined.

(3) Even though one or more terms are left open a contract for sale does not fail for indefiniteness if the parties have intended to make a contract and there is a reasonably certain basis for giving an appropriate remedy.

§ 2–205. Firm Offers.

An offer by a merchant to buy or sell goods in a signed writing which by its terms gives assurance that it will be held open is not revocable, for lack of consideration, during the time stated or if no time is stated for a reasonable time, but in no event may such period of irrevocability exceed three months; but any such term of assurance on a form supplied by the offeree must be separately signed by the offeror.

§ 2–206. Offer and Acceptance in Formation of Contract.

(1) Unless other unambiguously indicated by the language or circumstances

(a) an offer to make a contract shall be construed as inviting acceptance in any manner and by any medium reasonable in the circumstances;

(b) an order or other offer to buy goods for prompt or current shipment shall be construed as inviting acceptance either by a prompt promise to ship or by the prompt or current shipment of conforming or nonconforming goods, but such a shipment of non-conforming goods does not constitute an acceptance if the seller seasonably notifies the buyer that the shipment is offered only as an accommodation to the buyer.

(2) Where the beginning of a requested performance is a reasonable mode of acceptance an offeror who is not notified of acceptance within a reasonable time may treat the offer as having lapsed before acceptance.

§ 2–207. Additional Terms in Acceptance or Confirmation.

(1) A definite and seasonable expression of acceptance or a written confirmation which is sent within a reasonable time operates as an acceptance even though it states terms additional to or different from those offered or agreed upon, unless acceptance is expressly made conditional on assent to the additional or different terms.

(2) The additional terms are to be construed as proposals for addition to the contract. Between merchants such terms become part of the contract unless:

(a) the offer expressly limits acceptance to the terms of the offer;

(b) they materially alter it; or

(c) notification of objection to them has already been given or is given within a reasonable time after notice of them is received.

(3) Conduct by both parties which recognizes the existence of a contract is sufficient to establish a contract for sale although the writings of the parties do not otherwise establish a contract. In such case the terms of the particular contract consist of those terms on which the writings of the parties agree, together with any supplementary terms incorporated under any other provisions of this Act.

§ 2–208. Course of Performance or Practical Construction.

(1) Where the contract for sale involves repeated occasions for performance by either party with knowledge of the nature of the performance and opportunity for objection to it by the other, any course of performance accepted or acquiesced in without objection shall be relevant to determine the meaning of the agreement.

(2) The express terms of the agreement and any such course of performance, as well as any course of dealing and usage of trade, shall be construed whenever reasonable as consistent with each other; but when such construction is unreasonable, express terms shall control course of performance and course of performance shall control both course of dealing and usage of trade (Section 1–205).

(3) Subject to the provisions of the next section on modification and waiver, such course of performance shall be relevant to show a waiver or modification of any term inconsistent with such course of performance.

§ 2–209. Modification, Rescission and Waiver.

(1) An agreement modifying a contract within this Article needs no consideration to be binding.

(2) A signed agreement which excludes modification or rescission except by a signed writing cannot be otherwise modified or rescinded, but except as between merchants such a requirement on a form supplied by the merchant must be separately signed by the other party.

(3) The requirements of the statute of frauds section of this Article (Section 2–201) must be satisfied if the contract as modified is within its provisions.

(4) Although an attempt at modification or rescission does not satisfy the requirements of subsection (2) or (3) it can operate as a waiver.

(5) A party who has made a waiver affecting an executory portion of the contract may retract the waiver by reasonable notification received by the other party that strict performance will be required of any term waived, unless the retraction would be unjust in view of a material change of position in reliance on the waiver.

§ 2–210. Delegation of Performance; Assignment of Rights.

(1) A party may perform his duty through a delegate unless otherwise agreed or unless the other party has a substantial interest in having his original promisor perform or control the acts required by the contract. No delegation of performance relieves the party delegating of any duty to perform or any liability for breach.

(2) Except as otherwise provided in Section 9–406, unless otherwise agreed, all rights of either seller or buyer can be assigned except where the assignment would materially change the duty of the other party, or increase materially the burden or risk imposed on him by his contract, or impair materially his chance of obtaining return performance. A right to damages for breach of the whole contract or a right arising out of the assignor's due performance of his entire obligation can be assigned despite agreement otherwise.

(3) The creation, attachment, perfection, or enforcement of a security interest in the seller's interest under a contract is not a transfer that materially changes the duty of or increases materially the burden or risk imposed on the buyer or impairs materially the buyer's chance of obtaining return performance within the purview of subsection (2) unless, and then only to the extent that, enforcement actually results in a delegation of material performance of the seller. Even in that event, the creation, attachment, perfection, and enforcement of the security interest remain effective, but (i) the seller is liable to the buyer for damages caused by the delegation to the extent that the damages could not reasonably by prevented by the buyer, and (ii) a court having jurisdiction may grant other appropriate relief, including cancellation of the contract for sale or an injunction against enforcement of the security interest or consummation of the enforcement.

(4) Unless the circumstnaces indicate the contrary a prohibition of assignment of "the contract" is to be construed as barring only the delegation to the assignee of the assignor's performance.

(5) An assignment of "the contract" or of "all my rights under the contract" or an assignment in similar general terms is an assignment of rights and unless the language or the circumstances (as in an assignment for security) indicate the contrary, it is a delegation of performance of the duties of the assignor and its acceptance by the assignee constitutes a promise by him to perform those duties. This promise is enforceable by either the assignor or the other party to the original contract.

(6) The other party may treat any assignment which delegates performance as creating reasonable grounds for insecurity and may without prejudice to his rights against the assignor demand assurances from the assignee (Section 2–609).

As amended in 1999.

Part 3 General Obligation and Construction of Contract

§ 2–301. General Obligations of Parties.

The obligation of the seller is to transfer and deliver and that of the buyer is to accept and pay in accordance with the contract.

§ 2–302. Unconscionable Contract or Clause.

(1) If the court as a matter of law finds the contract or any clause of the contract to have been unconscionable at the time it was made the court may refuse to enforce the contract, or it may enforce the remainder of the contract without the unconscionable clause, or it may so limit the application of any unconscionable clause as to avoid any unconscionable result.

(2) When it is claimed or appears to the court that the contract or any clause thereof may be unconscionable the parties shall be afforded a reasonable opportunity to present evidence as to its commercial setting, purpose and effect to aid the court in making the determination.

§ 2–303. Allocations or Division of Risks.

Where this Article allocates a risk or a burden as between the parties "unless otherwise agreed", the agreement may not only shift the allocation but may also divide the risk or burden.

§ 2–304. Price Payable in Money, Goods, Realty, or Otherwise.

(1) The price can be made payable in money or otherwise. If it is payable in whole or in part in goods each party is a seller of the goods which he is to transfer.

(2) Even though all or part of the price is payable in an interest in realty the transfer of the goods and the seller's obligations with reference to them are subject to this Article, but not the transfer of the interest in realty or the transferor's obligations in connection therewith.

§ 2–305. Open Price Term.

(1) The parties if they so intend can conclude a contract for sale even though the price is not settled. In such a case the price is a reasonable price at the time for delivery if

    (a) nothing is said as to price; or

    (b) the price is left to be agreed by the parties and they fail to agree; or

    (c) the price is to be fixed in terms of some agreed market or other standard as set or recorded by a third person or agency and it is not so set or recorded.

(2) A price to be fixed by the seller or by the buyer means a price for him to fix in good faith.

(3) When a price left to be fixed otherwise than by agreement of the parties fails to be fixed through fault of one party the other may at his option treat the contract as cancelled or himself fix a reasonable price.

(4) Where, however, the parties intend not to be bound unless the price be fixed or agreed and it is not fixed or agreed there is no contract. In such a case the buyer must return any goods already received or if unable so to do must pay their reasonable value at the time of delivery and the seller must return any portion of the price paid on account.

§ 2–306. Output, Requirements and Exclusive Dealings.

(1) A term which measures the quantity by the output of the seller or the requirements of the buyer means such actual output or requirements as may occur in good faith, except that no quantity unreasonably disproportionate to any stated estimate or in the absence of a stated estimate to any normal or otherwise comparable prior output or requirements may be tendered or demanded.

(2) A lawful agreement by either the seller or the buyer for exclusive dealing in the kind of goods concerned imposes unless otherwise agreed an obligation by the seller to use best efforts to supply the goods and by the buyer to use best efforts to promote their sale.

§ 2–307. Delivery in Single Lot or Several Lots.

Unless otherwise agreed all goods called for by a contract for sale must be tendered in a single delivery and payment is due only on such tender but where the circumstances give either party the right to make or demand delivery in lots the price if it can be apportioned may be demanded for each lot.

§ 2–308. Absence of Specified Place for Delivery.

Unless otherwise agreed

    (a) the place for delivery of goods is the seller's place of business or if he has none his residence; but

    (b) in a contract for sale of identified goods which to the knowledge of the parties at the time of contracting are in some other place, that place is the place for their delivery; and

    (c) documents of title may be delivered through customary banking channels.

§ 2–309. Absence of Specific Time Provisions; Notice of Termination.

(1) The time for shipment or delivery or any other action under a contract if not provided in this Article or agreed upon shall be a reasonable time.

(2) Where the contract provides for successive performances but is indefinite in duration it is valid for a reasonable time but unless otherwise agreed may be terminated at any time by either party.

(3) Termination of a contract by one party except on the happening of an agreed event requires that reasonable notification be received by the other party and an agreement dispensing with notification is invalid if its operation would be unconscionable.

§ 2–310. Open Time for Payment or Running of Credit; Authority to Ship Under Reservation.

Unless otherwise agreed

(a) payment is due at the time and place at which the buyer is to receive the goods even though the place of shipment is the place of delivery; and

(b) if the seller is authorized to send the goods he may ship them under reservation, and may tender the documents of title, but the buyer may inspect the goods after their arrival before payment is due unless such inspection is inconsistent with the terms of the contract (Section 2–513); and

(c) if delivery is authorized and made by way of documents of title otherwise than by subsection (b) then payment is due at the time and place at which the buyer is to receive the documents regardless of where the goods are to be received; and

(d) where the seller is required or authorized to ship the goods on credit the credit period runs from the time of shipment but post-dating the invoice or delaying its dispatch will correspondingly delay the starting of the credit period.

§ 2–311. Options and Cooperation Respecting Performance.

(1) An agreement for sale which is otherwise sufficiently definite (subsection (3) of Section 2–204) to be a contract is not made invalid by the fact that it leaves particulars of performance to be specified by one of the parties. Any such specification must be made in good faith and within limits set by commercial reasonableness.

(2) Unless otherwise agreed specifications relating to assortment of the goods are at the buyer's option and except as otherwise provided in subsections (1)(c) and (3) of Section 2–319 specifications or arrangements relating to shipment are at the seller's option.

(3) Where such specification would materially affect the other party's performance but is not seasonably made or

where one party's cooperation is necessary to the agreed performance of the other but is not seasonably forthcoming, the other party in addition to all other remedies

(a) is excused for any resulting delay in his own performance; and

(b) may also either proceed to perform in any reasonable manner or after the time for a material part of his own performance treat the failure to specify or to cooperate as a breach by failure to deliver or accept the goods.

§ 2–312. Warranty of Title and Against Infringement; Buyer's Obligation Against Infringement.

(1) Subject to subsection (2) there is in a contract for sale a warranty by the seller that

(a) the title conveyed shall be good, and its transfer rightful; and

(b) the goods shall be delivered free from any security interest or other lien or encumbrance of which the buyer at the time of contracting has no knowledge.

(2) A warranty under subsection (1) will be excluded or modified only by specific language or by circumstances which give the buyer reason to know that the person selling does not claim title in himself or that he is purporting to sell only such right or title as he or a third person may have.

(3) Unless otherwise agreed a seller who is a merchant regularly dealing in goods of the kind warrants that the goods shall be delivered free of the rightful claim of any third person by way of infringement or the like but a buyer who furnishes specifications to the seller must hold the seller harmless against any such claim which arises out of compliance with the specifications.

§ 2–313. Express Warranties by Affirmation, Promise, Description, Sample.

(1) Express warranties by the seller are created as follows:

(a) Any affirmation of fact or promise made by the seller to the buyer which relates to the goods and becomes part of the basis of the bargain creates an express warranty that the goods shall conform to the affirmation or promise.

(b) Any description of the goods which is made part of the basis of the bargain creates an express warranty that the goods shall conform to the description.

(c) Any sample or model which is made part of the basis of the bargain creates an express warranty that the whole of the goods shall conform to the sample or model.

(2) It is not necessary to the creation of an express warranty that the seller use formal words such as "warrant" or "guarantee" or that he have a specific intention to make a warranty, but an affirmation merely of the value of the goods or a statement purporting to be merely the seller's opinion or commendation of the goods does not create a warranty.

§ 2–314. Implied Warranty: Merchantability; Usage of Trade.

(1) Unless excluded or modified (Section 2–316), a warranty that the goods shall be merchantable is implied in a contract for their sale if the seller is a merchant with respect to goods of that kind. Under this section the serving for value of food or drink to be consumed either on the premises or elsewhere is a sale.

(2) Goods to be merchantable must be at least such as

(a) pass without objection in the trade under the contract description; and

(b) in the case of fungible goods, are of fair average quality within the description; and

(c) are fit for the ordinary purposes for which such goods are used; and

(d) run, within the variations permitted by the agreement, of even kind, quality and quantity within each unit and among all units involved; and

(e) are adequately contained, packaged, and labeled as the agreement may require; and

(f) conform to the promises or affirmations of fact made on the container or label if any.

(3) Unless excluded or modified (Section 2–316) other implied warranties may arise from course of dealing or usage of trade.

§ 2–315. Implied Warranty: Fitness for Particular Purpose.

Where the seller at the time of contracting has reason to know any particular purpose for which the goods are required and that the buyer is relying on the seller's skill or judgment to select or furnish suitable goods, there is unless excluded or modified under the next section an implied warranty that the goods shall be fit for such purpose.

§ 2–316. Exclusion or Modification of Warranties.

(1) Words or conduct relevant to the creation of an express warranty and words or conduct tending to negate or limit warranty shall be construed wherever reasonable as consistent with each other; but subject to the provisions of this Article on parol or extrinsic evidence (Section 2–202) negation or limitation is inoperative to the extent that such construction is unreasonable.

(2) Subject to subsection (3), to exclude or modify the implied warranty of merchantability or any part of it the language must mention merchantability and in case of a writing must be conspicuous, and to exclude or modify any implied warranty of fitness the exclusion must be by a writing and conspicuous. Language to exclude all implied warranties of fitness is sufficient if it states, for example, that "There are no warranties which extend beyond the description on the face hereof."

(3) Notwithstanding subsection (2)

(a) unless the circumstances indicate otherwise, all implied warranties are excluded by expressions like "as is", "with all faults" or other language which in common understanding calls the buyer's attention to the exclusion of warranties and makes plain that there is no implied warranty; and

(b) when the buyer before entering into the contract has examined the goods or the sample or model as fully as he desired or has refused to examine the goods there is no implied warranty with regard to defects which an examination ought in the circumstances to have revealed to him; and

(c) an implied warranty can also be excluded or modified by course of dealing or course of performance or usage of trade.

(4) Remedies for breach of warranty can be limited in accordance with the provisions of this Article on liquidation or limitation of damages and on contractual modification of remedy (Sections 2–718 and 2–719).

§ 2–317. Cumulation and Conflict of Warranties Express or Implied.

Warranties whether express or implied shall be construed as consistent with each other and as cumulative, but if such construction is unreasonable the intention of the parties shall determine which warranty is dominant. In ascertaining that intention the following rules apply:

(a) Exact or technical specifications displace an inconsistent sample or model or general language of description.

(b) A sample from an existing bulk displaces inconsistent general language of description.

(c) Express warranties displace inconsistent implied warranties other than an implied warranty of fitness for a particular purpose.

§ 2–318. Third Party Beneficiaries of Warranties Express or Implied.

Note: If this Act is introduced in the Congress of the United States this section should be omitted. (States to select one alternative.)

Alternative A

A seller's warranty whether express or implied extends to any natural person who is in the family or household of his buyer or who is a guest in his home if it is reasonable to expect that such person may use, consume or be affected by the goods and who is injured in person by breach of the warranty. A seller may not exclude or limit the operation of this section.

Alternative B

A seller's warranty whether express or implied extends to any natural person who may reasonably be expected to use, consume or be affected by the goods and who is injured in person by breach of the warranty. A seller may not exclude or limit the operation of this section.

Alternative C

A seller's warranty whether express or implied extends to any person who may reasonably be expected to use, consume or be affected by the goods and who is injured by breach of the warranty. A seller may not exclude or limit the operation of this section with respect to injury to the person of an individual to whom the warranty extends.

As amended 1966.

§ 2–319. F.O.B. and F.A.S. Terms.

(1) Unless otherwise agreed the term F.O.B. (which means "free on board") at a named place, even though used only in connection with the stated price, is a delivery term under which

(a) when the term is F.O.B. the place of shipment, the seller must at that place ship the goods in the manner provided in this Article (Section 2–504) and bear the expense and risk of putting them into the possession of the carrier; or

(b) when the term is F.O.B. the place of destination, the seller must at his own expense and risk transport the goods to that place and there tender delivery of them in the manner provided in this Article (Section 2–503);

(c) when under either (a) or (b) the term is also F.O.B. vessel, car or other vehicle, the seller must in addition at his own expense and risk load the goods on board. If the term is F.O.B. vessel the buyer must name the vessel and in an appropriate case the seller must comply with the provisions of this Article on the form of bill of lading (Section 2–323).

(2) Unless otherwise agreed the term F.A.S. vessel (which means "free alongside") at a named port, even though used only in connection with the stated price, is a delivery term under which the seller must

(a) at his own expense and risk deliver the goods alongside the vessel in the manner usual in that port or on a dock designated and provided by the buyer; and

(b) obtain and tender a receipt for the goods in exchange for which the carrier is under a duty to issue a bill of lading.

(3) Unless otherwise agreed in any case falling within subsection (1)(a) or (c) or subsection (2) the buyer must seasonably give any needed instructions for making delivery, including when the term is F.A.S. or F.O.B. the loading berth of the vessel and in an appropriate case its name and sailing date. The seller may treat the failure of needed instructions as a failure of cooperation under this Article (Section 2–311). He may also at his option move the goods in any reasonable manner preparatory to delivery or shipment.

(4) Under the term F.O.B. vessel or F.A.S. unless otherwise agreed the buyer must make payment against tender of the required documents and the seller may not tender nor the buyer demand delivery of the goods in substitution for the documents.

§ 2–320. C.I.F. and C. & F. Terms.

(1) The term C.I.F. means that the price includes in a lump sum the cost of the goods and the insurance and freight to the named destination. The term C. & F. or C.F. means that the price so includes cost and freight to the named destination.

(2) Unless otherwise agreed and even though used only in connection with the stated price and destination, the term C.I.F. destination or its equivalent requires the seller at his own expense and risk to

(a) put the goods into the possession of a carrier at the port for shipment and obtain a negotiable bill or bills of lading covering the entire transportation to the named destination; and

(b) load the goods and obtain a receipt from the carrier (which may be contained in the bill of lading) showing that the freight has been paid or provided for; and

(c) obtain a policy or certificate of insurance, including any war risk insurance, of a kind and on terms then current at the port of shipment in the usual amount, in the currency of the contract, shown to cover the same goods covered by the bill of lading and providing for payment of loss to the order of the buyer or for the account of whom it may concern; but the seller may add to the price the amount of the premium for any such war risk insurance; and

(d) prepare an invoice of the goods and procure any other documents required to effect shipment or to comply with the contract; and

(e) forward and tender with commercial promptness all the documents in due form and with any indorsement necessary to perfect the buyer's rights.

(3) Unless otherwise agreed the term C. & F. or its equivalent has the same effect and imposes upon the seller the same obligations and risks as a C.I.F. term except the obligation as to insurance.

(4) Under the term C.I.F. or C. & F. unless otherwise agreed the buyer must make payment against tender of the required documents and the seller may not tender nor the buyer demand delivery of the goods in substitution for the documents.

§ 2–321. C.I.F. or C. & F.: "Net Landed Weights"; "Payment on Arrival"; Warranty of Condition on Arrival.

Under a contract containing a term C.I.F. or C. & F.

(1) Where the price is based on or is to be adjusted according to "net landed weights", "delivered weights", "out turn" quantity or quality or the like, unless otherwise agreed the seller must reasonably estimate the price. The payment due on tender of the documents called for by the contract is the amount so estimated, but after final adjustment of the price a settlement must be made with commercial promptness.

(2) An agreement described in subsection (1) or any warranty of quality or condition of the goods on arrival places

upon the seller the risk of ordinary deterioration, shrinkage and the like in transportation but has no effect on the place or time of identification to the contract for sale or delivery or on the passing of the risk of loss.

(3) Unless otherwise agreed where the contract provides for payment on or after arrival of the goods the seller must before payment allow such preliminary inspection as is feasible; but if the goods are lost delivery of the documents and payment are due when the goods should have arrived.

§ 2–322. Delivery "Ex-Ship".

(1) Unless otherwise agreed a term for delivery of goods "ex-ship" (which means from the carrying vessel) or in equivalent language is not restricted to a particular ship and requires delivery from a ship which has reached a place at the named port of destination where goods of the kind are usually discharged.

(2) Under such a term unless otherwise agreed

(a) the seller must discharge all liens arising out of the carriage and furnish the buyer with a direction which puts the carrier under a duty to deliver the goods; and

(b) the risk of loss does not pass to the buyer until the goods leave the ship's tackle or are otherwise properly unloaded.

§ 2–323. Form of Bill of Lading Required in Overseas Shipment; "Overseas".

(1) Where the contract contemplates overseas shipment and contains a term C.I.F. or C. & F. or F.O.B. vessel, the seller unless otherwise agreed must obtain a negotiable bill of lading stating that the goods have been loaded on board or, in the case of a term C.I.F. or C. & F., received for shipment.

(2) Where in a case within subsection (1) a bill of lading has been issued in a set of parts, unless otherwise agreed if the documents are not to be sent from abroad the buyer may demand tender of the full set; otherwise only one part of the bill of lading need be tendered. Even if the agreement expressly requires a full set

(a) due tender of a single part is acceptable within the provisions of this Article on cure of improper delivery (subsection (1) of Section 2–508); and

(b) even though the full set is demanded, if the documents are sent from abroad the person tendering an incomplete set may nevertheless require payment upon furnishing an indemnity which the buyer in good faith deems adequate.

(3) A shipment by water or by air or a contract contemplating such shipment is "overseas" insofar as by usage of trade or agreement it is subject to the commercial, financing or shipping practices characteristic of international deep water commerce.

§ 2–324. "No Arrival, No Sale" Term.

Under a term "no arrival, no sale" or terms of like meaning, unless otherwise agreed,

(a) the seller must properly ship conforming goods and if they arrive by any means he must tender them on arrival but he assumes no obligation that the goods will arrive unless he has caused the non-arrival; and

(b) where without fault of the seller the goods are in part lost or have so deteriorated as no longer to conform to the contract or arrive after the contract time, the buyer may proceed as if there had been casualty to identified goods (Section 2–613).

§ 2–325. "Letter of Credit" Term; "Confirmed Credit".

(1) Failure of the buyer seasonably to furnish an agreed letter of credit is a breach of the contract for sale.

(2) The delivery to seller of a proper letter of credit suspends the buyer's obligation to pay. If the letter of credit is dishonored, the seller may on seasonable notification to the buyer require payment directly from him.

(3) Unless otherwise agreed the term "letter of credit" or "banker's credit" in a contract for sale means an irrevocable credit issued by a financing agency of good repute and, where the shipment is overseas, of good international repute. The term "confirmed credit" means that the credit must also carry the direct obligation of such an agency which does business in the seller's financial market.

§ 2–326. Sale on Approval and Sale or Return; Rights of Creditors.

(1) Unless otherwise agreed, if delivered goods may be returned by the buyer even though they conform to the contract, the transaction is

(a) a "sale on approval" if the goods are delivered primarily for use, and

(b) a "sale or return" if the goods are delivered primarily for resale.

(2) Goods held on approval are not subject to the claims of the buyer's creditors until acceptance; goods held on sale or return are subject to such claims while in the buyer's possession.

(3) Any "or return" term of a contract for sale is to be treated as a separate contract for sale within the statute of frauds section of this Article (Section 2–201) and as contradicting the sale aspect of the contract within the provisions of this Article or on parol or extrinsic evidence (Section 2–202).

As amended in 1999.

§ 2–327. Special Incidents of Sale on Approval and Sale or Return.

(1) Under a sale on approval unless otherwise agreed

(a) although the goods are identified to the contract the risk of loss and the title do not pass to the buyer until acceptance; and

(b) use of the goods consistent with the purpose of trial is not acceptance but failure seasonably to notify the seller of election to return the goods is acceptance, and if the goods conform to the contract acceptance of any part is acceptance of the whole; and

(c) after due notification of election to return, the return is at the seller's risk and expense but a merchant buyer must follow any reasonable instructions.

(2) Under a sale or return unless otherwise agreed

(a) the option to return extends to the whole or any commercial unit of the goods while in substantially their original condition, but must be exercised seasonably; and

(b) the return is at the buyer's risk and expense.

§ 2–328. Sale by Auction.

(1) In a sale by auction if goods are put up in lots each lot is the subject of a separate sale.

(2) A sale by auction is complete when the auctioneer so announces by the fall of the hammer or in other customary manner. Where a bid is made while the hammer is falling in acceptance of a prior bid the auctioneer may in his discretion reopen the bidding or declare the goods sold under the bid on which the hammer was falling.

(3) Such a sale is with reserve unless the goods are in explicit terms put up without reserve. In an auction with reserve the auctioneer may withdraw the goods at any time until he announces completion of the sale. In an auction without reserve, after the auctioneer calls for bids on an article or lot, that article or lot cannot be withdrawn unless no bid is made within a reasonable time. In either case a bidder may retract his bid until the auctioneer's announcement of completion of the sale, but a bidder's retraction does not revive any previous bid.

(4) If the auctioneer knowingly receives a bid on the seller's behalf or the seller makes or procures such as bid, and notice has not been given that liberty for such bidding is reserved, the buyer may at his option avoid the sale or take the goods at the price of the last good faith bid prior to the completion of the sale. This subsection shall not apply to any bid at a forced sale.

Part 4 Title, Creditors and Good Faith Purchasers

§ 2–401. Passing of Title; Reservation for Security; Limited Application of This Section.

Each provision of this Article with regard to the rights, obligations and remedies of the seller, the buyer, purchasers or other third parties applies irrespective of title to the goods except where the provision refers to such title. Insofar as situations are not covered by the other provisions of this Article and matters concerning title became material the following rules apply:

(1) Title to goods cannot pass under a contract for sale prior to their identification to the contract (Section 2–501), and unless otherwise explicitly agreed the buyer acquires by their identification a special property as limited by this Act. Any

retention or reservation by the seller of the title (property) in goods shipped or delivered to the buyer is limited in effect to a reservation of a security interest. Subject to these provisions and to the provisions of the Article on Secured Transactions (Article 9), title to goods passes from the seller to the buyer in any manner and on any conditions explicitly agreed on by the parties.

(2) Unless otherwise explicitly agreed title passes to the buyer at the time and place at which the seller completes his performance with reference to the physical delivery of the goods, despite any reservation of a security interest and even though a document of title is to be delivered at a different time or place; and in particular and despite any reservation of a security interest by the bill of lading

(a) if the contract requires or authorizes the seller to send the goods to the buyer but does not require him to deliver them at destination, title passes to the buyer at the time and place of shipment; but

(b) if the contract requires delivery at destination, title passes on tender there.

(3) Unless otherwise explicitly agreed where delivery is to be made without moving the goods,

(a) if the seller is to deliver a document of title, title passes at the time when and the place where he delivers such documents; or

(b) if the goods are at the time of contracting already identified and no documents are to be delivered, title passes at the time and place of contracting.

(4) A rejection or other refusal by the buyer to receive or retain the goods, whether or not justified, or a justified revocation of acceptance revests title to the goods in the seller. Such revesting occurs by operation of law and is not a "sale".

§ 2–402. Rights of Seller's Creditors Against Sold Goods.

(1) Except as provided in subsections (2) and (3), rights of unsecured creditors of the seller with respect to goods which have been identified to a contract for sale are subject to the buyer's rights to recover the goods under this Article (Sections 2–502 and 2–716).

(2) A creditor of the seller may treat a sale or an identification of goods to a contract for sale as void if as against him a retention of possession by the seller is fraudulent under any rule of law of the state where the goods are situated, except that retention of possession in good faith and current course of trade by a merchant-seller for a commercially reasonable time after a sale or identification is not fraudulent.

(3) Nothing in this Article shall be deemed to impair the rights of creditors of the seller

(a) under the provisions of the Article on Secured Transactions (Article 9); or

(b) where identification to the contract or delivery is made not in current course of trade but in satisfaction of or as security for a pre-existing claim for money, security or the like and is made under circumstances which under any rule of law of the state where the goods are situated would apart from this Article constitute the transaction a fraudulent transfer or voidable preference.

§ 2–403. Power to Transfer; Good Faith Purchase of Goods; "Entrusting".

(1) A purchaser of goods acquires all title which his transferor had or had power to transfer except that a purchaser of a limited interest acquires rights only to the extent of the interest purchased. A person with voidable title has power to transfer a good title to a good faith purchaser for value. When goods have been delivered under a transaction of purchase the purchaser has such power even though

(a) the transferor was deceived as to the identity of the purchaser, or

(b) the delivery was in exchange for a check which is later dishonored, or

(c) it was agreed that the transaction was to be a "cash sale", or

(d) the delivery was procured through fraud punishable as larcenous under the criminal law.

(2) Any entrusting of possession of goods to a merchant who deals in goods of that kind gives him power to transfer all rights of the entruster to a buyer in ordinary course of business.

(3) "Entrusting" includes any delivery and any acquiescence in retention of possession regardless of any condition expressed between the parties to the delivery or acquiescence and regardless of whether the procurement of the entrusting or the possessor's disposition of the goods have been such as to be larcenous under the criminal law.

(4) The rights of other purchasers of goods and of lien creditors are governed by the Articles on Secured Transactions (Article 9), Bulk Transfers (Article 6) and Documents of Title (Article 7).

As amended in 1988.

Part 5 Performance

§ 2–501. Insurable Interest in Goods; Manner of Identification of Goods.

(1) The buyer obtains a special property and an insurable interest in goods by identification of existing goods as goods to which the contract refers even though the goods so identified are non-conforming and he has an option to return or reject them. Such identification can be made at any time and in any manner explicitly agreed to by the parties. In the absence of explicit agreement identification occurs

(a) when the contract is made if it is for the sale of goods already existing and identified;

(b) if the contract is for the sale of future goods other than those described in paragraph (c), when goods are shipped, marked or otherwise designated by the seller as goods to which the contract refers;

(c) when the crops are planted or otherwise become growing crops or the young are conceived if the contract is for the sale of unborn young to be born within twelve months after contracting or for the sale of crops to be harvested within twelve months or the next normal harvest season after contracting whichever is longer.

(2) The seller retains an insurable interest in goods so long as title to or any security interest in the goods remains in him and where the identification is by the seller alone he may until default or insolvency or notification to the buyer that the identification is final substitute other goods for those identified.

(3) Nothing in this section impairs any insurable interest recognized under any other statute or rule of law.

§ 2–502. Buyer's Right to Goods on Seller's Insolvency.

(1) Subject to subsections (2) and (3) and even though the goods have not been shipped a buyer who has paid a part or all of the price of goods in which he has a special property under the provisions of the immediately preceding section may on making and keeping good a tender of any unpaid portion of their price recover them from the seller if:

(a) in the case of goods bought for personal, family, or household purposes, the seller repudiates or fails to deliver as required by the contract; or

(b) in all cases, the seller becomes insolvent within ten days after receipt of the first installment on their price.

(2) The buyer's right to recover the goods under subsection (1)(a) vests upon acquisition of a special property, even if the seller had not then repudiated or failed to deliver.

(3) If the identification creating his special property has been made by the buyer he acquires the right to recover the goods only if they conform to the contract for sale.

As amended in 1999.

§ 2–503. Manner of Seller's Tender of Delivery.

(1) Tender of delivery requires that the seller put and hold conforming goods at the buyer's disposition and give the buyer any notification reasonably necessary to enable him to take delivery. The manner, time and place for tender are determined by the agreement and this Article, and in particular

(a) tender must be at a reasonable hour, and if it is of goods they must be kept available for the period reasonably necessary to enable the buyer to take possession; but

(b) unless otherwise agreed the buyer must furnish facilities reasonably suited to the receipt of the goods.

(2) Where the case is within the next section respecting shipment tender requires that the seller comply with its provisions.

(3) Where the seller is required to deliver at a particular destination tender requires that he comply with subsection (1) and also in any appropriate case tender documents as described in subsections (4) and (5) of this section.

(4) Where goods are in the possession of a bailee and are to be delivered without being moved

(a) tender requires that the seller either tender a negotiable document of title covering such goods or procure acknowledgment by the bailee of the buyer's right to possession of the goods; but

(b) tender to the buyer of a non-negotiable document of title or of a written direction to the bailee to deliver is sufficient tender unless the buyer seasonably objects, and receipt by the bailee of notification of the buyer's rights fixes those rights as against the bailee and all third persons; but risk of loss of the goods and of any failure by the bailee to honor the non-negotiable document of title or to obey the direction remains on the seller until the buyer has had a reasonable time to present the document or direction, and a refusal by the bailee to honor the document or to obey the direction defeats the tender.

(5) Where the contract requires the seller to deliver documents

(a) he must tender all such documents in correct form, except as provided in this Article with respect to bills of lading in a set (subsection (2) of Section 2–323); and

(b) tender through customary banking channels is sufficient and dishonor of a draft accompanying the documents constitutes non-acceptance or rejection.

§ 2–504. Shipment by Seller.

Where the seller is required or authorized to send the goods to the buyer and the contract does not require him to deliver them at a particular destination, then unless otherwise agreed he must

(a) put the goods in the possession of such a carrier and make such a contract for their transportation as may be reasonable having regard to the nature of the goods and other circumstances of the case; and

(b) obtain and promptly deliver or tender in due form any document necessary to enable the buyer to obtain possession of the goods or otherwise required by the agreement or by usage of trade; and

(c) promptly notify the buyer of the shipment.

Failure to notify the buyer under paragraph (c) or to make a proper contract under paragraph (a) is a ground for rejection only if material delay or loss ensues.

§ 2–505. Seller's Shipment under Reservation.

(1) Where the seller has identified goods to the contract by or before shipment:

(a) his procurement of a negotiable bill of lading to his own order or otherwise reserves in him a security interest in the goods. His procurement of the bill to the order of a financing agency or of the buyer indicates in addition only the seller's expectation of transferring that interest to the person named.

(b) a non-negotiable bill of lading to himself or his nominee reserves possession of the goods as security but except in a case of conditional delivery (subsection (2) of Section 2–507) a non-negotiable bill of lading naming the buyer as consignee reserves no security interest even though the seller retains possession of the bill of lading.

(2) When shipment by the seller with reservation of a security interest is in violation of the contract for sale it constitutes an improper contract for transportation within the preceding section but impairs neither the rights given to the buyer by shipment and identification of the goods to the contract nor the seller's powers as a holder of a negotiable document.

§ 2–506. Rights of Financing Agency.

(1) A financing agency by paying or purchasing for value a draft which relates to a shipment of goods acquires to the extent of the payment or purchase and in addition to its own rights under the draft and any document of title securing it any rights of the shipper in the goods including the right to stop delivery and the shipper's right to have the draft honored by the buyer.

(2) The right to reimbursement of a financing agency which has in good faith honored or purchased the draft under commitment to or authority from the buyer is not impaired by subsequent discovery of defects with reference to any relevant document which was apparently regular on its face.

§ 2–507. Effect of Seller's Tender; Delivery on Condition.

(1) Tender of delivery is a condition to the buyer's duty to accept the goods and, unless otherwise agreed, to his duty to pay for them. Tender entitles the seller to acceptance of the goods and to payment according to the contract.

(2) Where payment is due and demanded on the delivery to the buyer of goods or documents of title, his right as against the seller to retain or dispose of them is conditional upon his making the payment due.

§ 2–508. Cure by Seller of Improper Tender or Delivery; Replacement.

(1) Where any tender or delivery by the seller is rejected because non-conforming and the time for performance has not yet expired, the seller may seasonably notify the buyer of his intention to cure and may then within the contract time make a conforming delivery.

(2) Where the buyer rejects a non-conforming tender which the seller had reasonable grounds to believe would be acceptable with or without money allowance the seller may if he seasonably notifies the buyer have a further reasonable time to substitute a conforming tender.

§ 2–509. Risk of Loss in the Absence of Breach.

(1) Where the contract requires or authorizes the seller to ship the goods by carrier

(a) if it does not require him to deliver them at a particular destination, the risk of loss passes to the buyer when the goods are duly delivered to the carrier even though the shipment is under reservation (Section 2–505); but

(b) if it does require him to deliver them at a particular destination and the goods are there duly tendered while in the possession of the carrier, the risk of loss passes to the buyer when the goods are there duly so tendered as to enable the buyer to take delivery.

(2) Where the goods are held by a bailee to be delivered without being moved, the risk of loss passes to the buyer

(a) on his receipt of a negotiable document of title covering the goods; or

(b) on acknowledgment by the bailee of the buyer's right to possession of the goods; or

(c) after his receipt of a non-negotiable document of title or other written direction to deliver, as provided in subsection (4)(b) of Section 2–503.

(3) In any case not within subsection (1) or (2), the risk of loss passes to the buyer on his receipt of the goods if the seller is a merchant; otherwise the risk passes to the buyer on tender of delivery.

(4) The provisions of this section are subject to contrary agreement of the parties and to the provisions of this Article on sale on approval (Section 2–327) and on effect of breach on risk of loss (Section 2–510).

§ 2–510. Effect of Breach on Risk of Loss.

(1) Where a tender or delivery of goods so fails to conform to the contract as to give a right of rejection the risk of their loss remains on the seller until cure or acceptance.

(2) Where the buyer rightfully revokes acceptance he may to the extent of any deficiency in his effective insurance coverage treat the risk of loss as having rested on the seller from the beginning.

(3) Where the buyer as to conforming goods already identified to the contract for sale repudiates or is otherwise in breach before risk of their loss has passed to him, the seller may to the extent of any deficiency in his effective insurance coverage treat the risk of loss as resting on the buyer for a commercially reasonable time.

§ 2–511. Tender of Payment by Buyer; Payment by Check.

(1) Unless otherwise agreed tender of payment is a condition to the seller's duty to tender and complete any delivery.

(2) Tender of payment is sufficient when made by any means or in any manner current in the ordinary course of business unless the seller demands payment in legal tender and gives any extension of time reasonably necessary to procure it.

(3) Subject to the provisions of this Act on the effect of an instrument on an obligation (Section 3–310), payment by instrument on an obligation (Section 3–310), payment by check is conditional and is defeated as between the parties by dishonor of the check on due presentment.

As amended in 1994.

§ 2–512. Payment by Buyer Before Inspection.

(1) Where the contract requires payment before inspection non-conformity of the goods does not excuse the buyer from so making payment unless

(a) the non-conformity appears without inspection; or

(b) despite tender of the required documents the circumstances would justify injunction against honor under this Act (Section 5–109(b)).

(2) Payment pursuant to subsection (1) does not constitute an acceptance of goods or impair the buyer's right to inspect or any of his remedies.

As amended in 1995.

§ 2–513. Buyer's Right to Inspection of Goods.

(1) Unless otherwise agreed and subject to subsection (3), where goods are tendered or delivered or identified to the contract for sale, the buyer has a right before payment or acceptance to inspect them at any reasonable place and time and in any reasonable manner. When the seller is required or authorized to send the goods to the buyer, the inspection may be after their arrival.

(2) Expenses of inspection must be borne by the buyer but may be recovered from the seller if the goods do not conform and are rejected.

(3) Unless otherwise agreed and subject to the provisions of this Article on C.I.F. contracts (subsection (3) of Section 2–321), the buyer is not entitled to inspect the goods before payment of the price when the contract provides

(a) for delivery "C.O.D." or on other like terms; or

(b) for payment against documents of title, except where such payment is due only after the goods are to become available for inspection.

(4) A place or method of inspection fixed by the parties is presumed to be exclusive but unless otherwise expressly agreed it does not postpone identification or shift the place for delivery or for passing the risk of loss. If compliance becomes impossible, inspection shall be as provided in this section unless the place or method fixed was clearly intended as an indispensable condition failure of which avoids the contract.

§ 2–514. When Documents Deliverable on Acceptance; When on Payment.

Unless otherwise agreed documents against which a draft is drawn are to be delivered to the drawee on acceptance of the draft if it is payable more than three days after presentment; otherwise, only on payment.

§ 2–515. Preserving Evidence of Goods in Dispute.

In furtherance of the adjustment of any claim or dispute

(a) either party on reasonable notification to the other and for the purpose of ascertaining the facts and preserving evidence has the right to inspect, test and sample the goods including such of them as may be in the possession or control of the other; and

(b) the parties may agree to a third party inspection or survey to determine the conformity or condition of the goods and may agree that the findings shall be binding upon them in any subsequent litigation or adjustment.

Part 6 Breach, Repudiation and Excuse

§ 2–601. Buyer's Rights on Improper Delivery.

Subject to the provisions of this Article on breach in installment contracts (Section 2–612) and unless otherwise agreed under the sections on contractual limitations of remedy (Sections 2–718 and 2–719), if the goods or the tender of delivery fail in any respect to conform to the contract, the buyer may

(a) reject the whole; or

(b) accept the whole; or

(c) accept any commercial unit or units and reject the rest.

§ 2–602. Manner and Effect of Rightful Rejection.

(1) Rejection of goods must be within a reasonable time after their delivery or tender. It is ineffective unless the buyer seasonably notifies the seller.

(2) Subject to the provisions of the two following sections on rejected goods (Sections 2–603 and 2–604),

(a) after rejection any exercise of ownership by the buyer with respect to any commercial unit is wrongful as against the seller; and

(b) if the buyer has before rejection taken physical possession of goods in which he does not have a security interest under the provisions of this Article (subsection (3) of Section 2–711), he is under a duty after rejection to hold them with reasonable care at the seller's disposition for a time sufficient to permit the seller to remove them; but

(c) the buyer has no further obligations with regard to goods rightfully rejected.

(3) The seller's rights with respect to goods wrongfully rejected are governed by the provisions of this Article on Seller's remedies in general (Section 2–703).

§ 2–603. Merchant Buyer's Duties as to Rightfully Rejected Goods.

(1) Subject to any security interest in the buyer (subsection (3) of Section 2–711), when the seller has no agent or place of business at the market of rejection a merchant buyer is under a duty after rejection of goods in his possession or control to follow any reasonable instructions received from the seller with respect to the goods and in the absence of such instructions to make reasonable efforts to sell them for the seller's account if they are perishable or threaten to decline in value speedily. Instructions are not reasonable if on demand indemnity for expenses is not forthcoming.

(2) When the buyer sells goods under subsection (1), he is entitled to reimbursement from the seller or out of the proceeds for reasonable expenses of caring for and selling them, and if the expenses include no selling commission then to such commission as is usual in the trade or if there is none to a reasonable sum not exceeding ten per cent on the gross proceeds.

(3) In complying with this section the buyer is held only to good faith and good faith conduct hereunder is neither acceptance nor conversion nor the basis of an action for damages.

§ 2–604. Buyer's Options as to Salvage of Rightfully Rejected Goods.

Subject to the provisions of the immediately preceding section on perishables if the seller gives no instructions within a reasonable time after notification of rejection the buyer may store the rejected goods for the seller's account or reship them to him or resell them for the seller's account with reimbursement as provided in the preceding section. Such action is not acceptance or conversion.

§ 2–605. Waiver of Buyer's Objections by Failure to Particularize.

(1) The buyer's failure to state in connection with rejection a particular defect which is ascertainable by reasonable inspection precludes him from relying on the unstated defect to justify rejection or to establish breach

(a) where the seller could have cured it if stated seasonably; or

(b) between merchants when the seller has after rejection made a request in writing for a full and final written statement of all defects on which the buyer proposes to rely.

(2) Payment against documents made without reservation of rights precludes recovery of the payment for defects apparent on the face of the documents.

§ 2–606. What Constitutes Acceptance of Goods.

(1) Acceptance of goods occurs when the buyer

(a) after a reasonable opportunity to inspect the goods signifies to the seller that the goods are conforming or that he will take or retain them in spite of their nonconformity; or

(b) fails to make an effective rejection (subsection (1) of Section 2–602), but such acceptance does not occur until the buyer has had a reasonable opportunity to inspect them; or

(c) does any act inconsistent with the seller's ownership; but if such act is wrongful as against the seller it is an acceptance only if ratified by him.

(2) Acceptance of a part of any commercial unit is acceptance of that entire unit.

§ 2–607. Effect of Acceptance; Notice of Breach; Burden of Establishing Breach After Acceptance; Notice of Claim or Litigation to Person Answerable Over.

(1) The buyer must pay at the contract rate for any goods accepted.

(2) Acceptance of goods by the buyer precludes rejection of the goods accepted and if made with knowledge of a non-conformity cannot be revoked because of it unless the acceptance was on the reasonable assumption that the non-conformity would be seasonably cured but acceptance does not of itself impair any other remedy provided by this Article for non-conformity.

(3) Where a tender has been accepted

(a) the buyer must within a reasonable time after he discovers or should have discovered any breach notify the seller of breach or be barred from any remedy; and

(b) if the claim is one for infringement or the like (subsection (3) of Section 2–312) and the buyer is sued as a result of such a breach he must so notify the seller within a reasonable time after he receives notice of the litigation or be barred from any remedy over for liability established by the litigation.

(4) The burden is on the buyer to establish any breach with respect to the goods accepted.

(5) Where the buyer is sued for breach of a warranty or other obligation for which his seller is answerable over

(a) he may give his seller written notice of the litigation. If the notice states that the seller may come in and defend and that if the seller does not do so he will be bound in any action against him by his buyer by any determination of fact common to the two litigations, then unless the seller after seasonable receipt of the notice does come in and defend he is so bound.

(b) if the claim is one for infringement or the like (subsection (3) of Section 2–312) the original seller may demand in writing that his buyer turn over to him control of the litigation including settlement or else be barred from any remedy over and if he also agrees to bear all expense and to satisfy any adverse judgment, then unless the buyer after seasonable receipt of the demand does turn over control the buyer is so barred.

(6) The provisions of subsections (3), (4) and (5) apply to any obligation of a buyer to hold the seller harmless against infringement or the like (subsection (3) of Section 2–312).

§ 2–608. Revocation of Acceptance in Whole or in Part.

(1) The buyer may revoke his acceptance of a lot or commercial unit whose non-conformity substantially impairs its value to him if he has accepted it

(a) on the reasonable assumption that its nonconformity would be cured and it has not been seasonably cured; or

(b) without discovery of such non-conformity if his acceptance was reasonably induced either by the difficulty of discovery before acceptance or by the seller's assurances.

(2) Revocation of acceptance must occur within a reasonable time after the buyer discovers or should have discovered the ground for it and before any substantial change in condition of the goods which is not caused by their own defects. It is not effective until the buyer notifies the seller of it.

(3) A buyer who so revokes has the same rights and duties with regard to the goods involved as if he had rejected them.

§ 2–609. Right to Adequate Assurance of Performance.

(1) A contract for sale imposes an obligation on each party that the other's expectation of receiving due performance will not be impaired. When reasonable grounds for insecurity arise with respect to the performance of either party the other may in writing demand adequate assurance of due performance and until he receives such assurance may if commercially reasonable suspend any performance for which he has not already received the agreed return.

(2) Between merchants the reasonableness of grounds for insecurity and the adequacy of any assurance offered shall be determined according to commercial standards.

(3) Acceptance of any improper delivery or payment does not prejudice the party's right to demand adequate assurance of future performance.

(4) After receipt of a justified demand failure to provide within a reasonable time not exceeding thirty days such assurance of due performance as is adequate under the circumstances of the particular case is a repudiation of the contract.

§ 2–610. Anticipatory Repudiation.

When either party repudiates the contract with respect to a performance not yet due the loss of which will substantially impair the value of the contract to the other, the aggrieved party may

(a) for a commercially reasonable time await performance by the repudiating party; or

(b) resort to any remedy for breach (Section 2–703 or Section 2–711), even though he has notified the repudiating party that he would await the latter's performance and has urged retraction; and

(c) in either case suspend his own performance or proceed in accordance with the provisions of this Article on the seller's right to identify goods to the contract notwithstanding breach or to salvage unfinished goods (Section 2–704).

§ 2–611. Retraction of Anticipatory Repudiation.

(1) Until the repudiating party's next performance is due he can retract his repudiation unless the aggrieved party has since the repudiation cancelled or materially changed his position or otherwise indicated that he considers the repudiation final.

(2) Retraction may be by any method which clearly indicates to the aggrieved party that the repudiating party intends to perform, but must include any assurance justifiably demanded under the provisions of this Article (Section 2–609).

(3) Retraction reinstates the repudiating party's rights under the contract with due excuse and allowance to the aggrieved party for any delay occasioned by the repudiation.

§ 2–612. "Installment Contract"; Breach.

(1) An "installment contract" is one which requires or authorizes the delivery of goods in separate lots to be separately accepted, even though the contract contains a clause "each delivery is a separate contract" or its equivalent.

(2) The buyer may reject any installment which is nonconforming if the non-conformity substantially impairs the value of that installment and cannot be cured or if the non-conformity is a defect in the required documents; but if the non-conformity does not fall within subsection (3) and the seller gives adequate assurance of its cure the buyer must accept that installment.

(3) Whenever non-conformity or default with respect to one or more installments substantially impairs the value of the whole contract there is a breach of the whole. But the aggrieved party reinstates the contract if he accepts a nonconforming installment without seasonably notifying of cancellation or if he brings an action with respect only to past installments or demands performance as to future installments.

§ 2–613. Casualty to Identified Goods.

Where the contract requires for its performance goods identified when the contract is made, and the goods suffer casualty without fault of either party before the risk of loss passes to the buyer, or in a proper case under a "no arrival, no sale" term (Section 2–324) then

(a) if the loss is total the contract is avoided; and

(b) if the loss is partial or the goods have so deteriorated as no longer to conform to the contract the buyer may nevertheless demand inspection and at his option either treat the contract as voided or accept the goods with due allowance from the contract price for the deterioration or the deficiency in quantity but without further right against the seller.

§ 2–614. Substituted Performance.

(1) Where without fault of either party the agreed berthing, loading, or unloading facilities fail or an agreed type of carrier becomes unavailable or the agreed manner of delivery otherwise becomes commercially impracticable but a commercially reasonable substitute is available, such substitute performance must be tendered and accepted.

(2) If the agreed means or manner of payment fails because of domestic or foreign governmental regulation, the seller may withhold or stop delivery unless the buyer provides a means or manner of payment which is commercially a substantial equivalent. If delivery has already been taken, payment by the means or in the manner provided by the regulation discharges the buyer's obligation unless the regulation is discriminatory, oppressive or predatory.

§ 2–615. Excuse by Failure of Presupposed Conditions.

Except so far as a seller may have assumed a greater obligation and subject to the preceding section on substituted performance:

(a) Delay in delivery or non-delivery in whole or in part by a seller who complies with paragraphs (b) and (c) is not a breach of his duty under a contract for sale if performance as agreed has been made impracticable by the occurrence of a contingency the nonoccurrence of which was a basic assumption on which the contract was made or by compliance in good faith with any applicable foreign or domestic governmental regulation or order whether or not it later proves to be invalid.

(b) Where the causes mentioned in paragraph (a) affect only a part of the seller's capacity to perform, he must allocate production and deliveries among his customers but may at his option include regular customers not then under contract as well as his own requirements for further manufacture. He may so allocate in any manner which is fair and reasonable.

(c) The seller must notify the buyer seasonably that there will be delay or non-delivery and, when allocation is required under paragraph (b), of the estimated quota thus made available for the buyer.

§ 2–616. Procedure on Notice Claiming Excuse.

(1) Where the buyer receives notification of a material or indefinite delay or an allocation justified under the preceding section he may by written notification to the seller as to any delivery concerned, and where the prospective deficiency substantially impairs the value of the whole contract under the provisions of this Article relating to breach of installment contracts (Section 2–612), then also as to the whole,

> (a) terminate and thereby discharge any unexecuted portion of the contract; or

> (b) modify the contract by agreeing to take his available quota in substitution.

(2) If after receipt of such notification from the seller the buyer fails so to modify the contract within a reasonable time not exceeding thirty days the contract lapses with respect to any deliveries affected.

(3) The provisions of this section may not be negated by agreement except in so far as the seller has assumed a greater obligation under the preceding section.

Part 7 Remedies

§ 2–701. Remedies for Breach of Collateral Contracts Not Impaired.

Remedies for breach of any obligation or promise collateral or ancillary to a contract for sale are not impaired by the provisions of this Article.

§ 2–702. Seller's Remedies on Discovery of Buyer's Insolvency.

(1) Where the seller discovers the buyer to be insolvent he may refuse delivery except for cash including payment for all goods theretofore delivered under the contract, and stop delivery under this Article (Section 2–705).

(2) Where the seller discovers that the buyer has received goods on credit while insolvent he may reclaim the goods upon demand made within ten days after the receipt, but if misrepresentation of solvency has been made to the particular seller in writing within three months before delivery the ten day limitation does not apply. Except as provided in this subsection the seller may not base a right to reclaim goods on the buyer's fraudulent or innocent misrepresentation of solvency or of intent to pay.

(3) The seller's right to reclaim under subsection (2) is subject to the rights of a buyer in ordinary course or other good faith purchaser under this Article (Section 2–403). Successful reclamation of goods excludes all other remedies with respect to them.

§ 2–703. Seller's Remedies in General.

Where the buyer wrongfully rejects or revokes acceptance of goods or fails to make a payment due on or before delivery or repudiates with respect to a part or the whole, then with respect to any goods directly affected and, if the breach is of the whole contract (Section 2–612), then also with respect to the whole undelivered balance, the aggrieved seller may

(a) withhold delivery of such goods;

(b) stop delivery by any bailee as hereafter provided (Section 2–705);

(c) proceed under the next section respecting goods still unidentified to the contract;

(d) resell and recover damages as hereafter provided (Section 2–706);

(e) recover damages for non-acceptance (Section 2–708) or in a proper case the price (Section 2–709);

(f) cancel.

§ 2–704. Seller's Right to Identify Goods to the Contract Notwithstanding Breach or to Salvage Unfinished Goods.

(1) An aggrieved seller under the preceding section may

(a) identify to the contract conforming goods not already identified if at the time he learned of the breach they are in his possession or control;

(b) treat as the subject of resale goods which have demonstrably been intended for the particular contract even though those goods are unfinished.

(2) Where the goods are unfinished an aggrieved seller may in the exercise of reasonable commercial judgment for the purposes of avoiding loss and of effective realization either complete the manufacture and wholly identify the goods to the contract or cease manufacture and resell for scrap or salvage value or proceed in any other reasonable manner.

§ 2–705. Seller's Stoppage of Delivery in Transit or Otherwise.

(1) The seller may stop delivery of goods in the possession of a carrier or other bailee when he discovers the buyer to be insolvent (Section 2–702) and may stop delivery of carload, truckload, planeload or larger shipments of express or freight when the buyer repudiates or fails to make a payment due before delivery or if for any other reason the seller has a right to withhold or reclaim the goods.

(2) As against such buyer the seller may stop delivery until

(a) receipt of the goods by the buyer; or

(b) acknowledgment to the buyer by any bailee of the goods except a carrier that the bailee holds the goods for the buyer; or

(c) such acknowledgment to the buyer by a carrier by reshipment or as warehouseman; or

(d) negotiation to the buyer of any negotiable document of title covering the goods.

(3) (a) To stop delivery the seller must so notify as to enable the bailee by reasonable diligence to prevent delivery of the goods.

(b) After such notification the bailee must hold and deliver the goods according to the directions of the seller but the seller is liable to the bailee for any ensuing charges or damages.

(c) If a negotiable document of title has been issued for goods the bailee is not obliged to obey a notification to stop until surrender of the document.

(d) A carrier who has issued a non-negotiable bill of lading is not obliged to obey a notification to stop received from a person other than the consignor.

§ 2–706. Seller's Resale Including Contract for Resale.

(1) Under the conditions stated in Section 2–703 on seller's remedies, the seller may resell the goods concerned or the undelivered balance thereof. Where the resale is made in good faith and in a commercially reasonable manner the seller may recover the difference between the resale price and the contract price together with any incidental damages allowed under the provisions of this Article (Section 2–710), but less expenses saved in consequence of the buyer's breach.

(2) Except as otherwise provided in subsection (3) or unless otherwise agreed resale may be at public or private sale including sale by way of one or more contracts to sell or

of identification to an existing contract of the seller. Sale may be as a unit or in parcels and at any time and place and on any terms but every aspect of the sale including the method, manner, time, place and terms must be commercially reasonable. The resale must be reasonably identified as referring to the broken contract, but it is not necessary that the goods be in existence or that any or all of them have been identified to the contract before the breach.

(3) Where the resale is at private sale the seller must give the buyer reasonable notification of his intention to resell.

(4) Where the resale is at public sale

(a) only identified goods can be sold except where there is a recognized market for a public sale of futures in goods of the kind; and

(b) it must be made at a usual place or market for public sale if one is reasonably available and except in the case of goods which are perishable or threaten to decline in value speedily the seller must give the buyer reasonable notice of the time and place of the resale; and

(c) if the goods are not to be within the view of those attending the sale the notification of sale must state the place where the goods are located and provide for their reasonable inspection by prospective bidders; and

(d) the seller may buy.

(5) A purchaser who buys in good faith at a resale takes the goods free of any rights of the original buyer even though the seller fails to comply with one or more of the requirements of this section.

(6) The seller is not accountable to the buyer for any profit made on any resale. A person in the position of a seller (Section 2–707) or a buyer who has rightfully rejected or justifiably revoked acceptance must account for any excess over the amount of his security interest, as hereinafter defined (subsection (3) of Section 2–711).

§ 2–707. "Person in the Position of a Seller".

(1) A "person in the position of a seller" includes as against a principal an agent who has paid or become responsible for the price of goods on behalf of his principal or anyone who otherwise holds a security interest or other right in goods similar to that of a seller.

(2) A person in the position of a seller may as provided in this Article withhold or stop delivery (Section 2–705) and resell (Section 2–706) and recover incidental damages (Section 2–710).

§ 2–708. Seller's Damages for Non-Acceptance or Repudiation.

(1) Subject to subsection (2) and to the provisions of this Article with respect to proof of market price (Section 2–723), the measure of damages for non-acceptance or repudiation by the buyer is the difference between the market price at the time and place for tender and the unpaid contract price together with any incidental damages pro-

vided in this Article (Section 2–710), but less expenses saved in consequence of the buyer's breach.

(2) If the measure of damages provided in subsection (1) is inadequate to put the seller in as good a position as performance would have done then the measure of damages is the profit (including reasonable overhead) which the seller would have made from full performance by the buyer, together with any incidental damages provided in this Article (Section 2–710), due allowance for costs reasonably incurred and due credit for payments or proceeds of resale.

§ 2–709. Action for the Price.

(1) When the buyer fails to pay the price as it becomes due the seller may recover, together with any incidental damages under the next section, the price

(a) of goods accepted or of conforming goods lost or damaged within a commercially reasonable time after risk of their loss has passed to the buyer; and

(b) of goods identified to the contract if the seller is unable after reasonable effort to resell them at a reasonable price or the circumstances reasonably indicate that such effort will be unavailing.

(2) Where the seller sues for the price he must hold for the buyer any goods which have been identified to the contract and are still in his control except that if resale becomes possible he may resell them at any time prior to the collection of the judgment. The net proceeds of any such resale must be credited to the buyer and payment of the judgment entitles him to any goods not resold.

(3) After the buyer has wrongfully rejected or revoked acceptance of the goods or has failed to make a payment due or has repudiated (Section 2–610), a seller who is held not entitled to the price under this section shall nevertheless be awarded damages for non-acceptance under the preceding section.

§ 2–710. Seller's Incidental Damages.

Incidental damages to an aggrieved seller include any commercially reasonable charges, expenses or commissions incurred in stopping delivery, in the transportation, care and custody of goods after the buyer's breach, in connection with return or resale of the goods or otherwise resulting from the breach.

§ 2–711. Buyer's Remedies in General; Buyer's Security Interest in Rejected Goods.

(1) Where the seller fails to make delivery or repudiates or the buyer rightfully rejects or justifiably revokes acceptance then with respect to any goods involved, and with respect to the whole if the breach goes to the whole contract (Section 2–612), the buyer may cancel and whether or not he has done so may in addition to recovering so much of the price as has been paid

(a) "cover" and have damages under the next section as to all the goods affected whether or not they have been identified to the contract; or

(b) recover damages for non-delivery as provided in this Article (Section 2–713).

(2) Where the seller fails to deliver or repudiates the buyer may also

(a) if the goods have been identified recover them as provided in this Article (Section 2–502); or

(b) in a proper case obtain specific performance or replevy the goods as provided in this Article (Section 2–716).

(3) On rightful rejection or justifiable revocation of acceptance a buyer has a security interest in goods in his possession or control for any payments made on their price and any expenses reasonably incurred in their inspection, receipt, transportation, care and custody and may hold such goods and resell them in like manner as an aggrieved seller (Section 2–706).

§ 2–712. "Cover"; Buyer's Procurement of Substitute Goods.

(1) After a breach within the preceding section the buyer may "cover" by making in good faith and without unreasonable delay any reasonable purchase of or contract to purchase goods in substitution for those due from the seller.

(2) The buyer may recover from the seller as damages the difference between the cost of cover and the contract price together with any incidental or consequential damages as hereinafter defined (Section 2–715), but less expenses saved in consequence of the seller's breach.

(3) Failure of the buyer to effect cover within this section does not bar him from any other remedy.

§ 2–713. Buyer's Damages for Non-Delivery or Repudiation.

(1) Subject to the provisions of this Article with respect to proof of market price (Section 2–723), the measure of damages for non-delivery or repudiation by the seller is the difference between the market price at the time when the buyer learned of the breach and the contract price together with any incidental and consequential damages provided in this Article (Section 2–715), but less expenses saved in consequence of the seller's breach.

(2) Market price is to be determined as of the place for tender or, in cases of rejection after arrival or revocation of acceptance, as of the place of arrival.

§ 2–714. Buyer's Damages for Breach in Regard to Accepted Goods.

(1) Where the buyer has accepted goods and given notification (subsection (3) of Section 2–607) he may recover as damages for any non-conformity of tender the loss resulting in the ordinary course of events from the seller's breach as determined in any manner which is reasonable.

(2) The measure of damages for breach of warranty is the difference at the time and place of acceptance between the value of the goods accepted and the value they would have had if they had been as warranted, unless special circumstances show proximate damages of a different amount.

(3) In a proper case any incidental and consequential damages under the next section may also be recovered.

§ 2–715. Buyer's Incidental and Consequential Damages.

(1) Incidental damages resulting from the seller's breach include expenses reasonably incurred in inspection, receipt, transportation and care and custody of goods rightfully rejected, any commercially reasonable charges, expenses or commissions in connection with effecting cover and any other reasonable expense incident to the delay or other breach.

(2) Consequential damages resulting from the seller's breach include

(a) any loss resulting from general or particular requirements and needs of which the seller at the time of contracting had reason to know and which could not reasonably be prevented by cover or otherwise; and

(b) injury to person or property proximately resulting from any breach of warranty.

§ 2–716. Buyer's Right to Specific Performance or Replevin.

(1) Specific performance may be decreed where the goods are unique or in other proper circumstances.

(2) The decree for specific performance may include such terms and conditions as to payment of the price, damages, or other relief as the court may deem just.

(3) The buyer has a right of replevin for goods identified to the contract if after reasonable effort he is unable to effect cover for such goods or the circumstances reasonably indicate that such effort will be unavailing or if the goods have been shipped under reservation and satisfaction of the security interest in them has been made or tendered. In the case of goods bought for personal, family, or household purposes, the buyer's right of replevin vests upon acquisition of a special property, even if the seller had not then repudiated or failed to deliver.

As amended in 1999.

§ 2–717. Deduction of Damages From the Price.

The buyer on notifying the seller of his intention to do so may deduct all or any part of the damages resulting from any breach of the contract from any part of the price still due under the same contract.

§ 2–718. Liquidation or Limitation of Damages; Deposits.

(1) Damages for breach by either party may be liquidated in the agreement but only at an amount which is reasonable in the light of the anticipated or actual harm caused by the breach, the difficulties of proof of loss, and the inconvenience or nonfeasibility of otherwise obtaining an adequate

remedy. A term fixing unreasonably large liquidated damages is void as a penalty.

(2) Where the seller justifiably withholds delivery of goods because of the buyer's breach, the buyer is entitled to restitution of any amount by which the sum of his payments exceeds

(a) the amount to which the seller is entitled by virtue of terms liquidating the seller's damages in accordance with subsection (1), or

(b) in the absence of such terms, twenty per cent of the value of the total performance for which the buyer is obligated under the contract or $500, whichever is smaller.

(3) The buyer's right to restitution under subsection (2) is subject to offset to the extent that the seller establishes

(a) a right to recover damages under the provisions of this Article other than subsection (1), and

(b) the amount or value of any benefits received by the buyer directly or indirectly by reason of the contract.

(4) Where a seller has received payment in goods their reasonable value or the proceeds of their resale shall be treated as payments for the purposes of subsection (2); but if the seller has notice of the buyer's breach before reselling goods received in part performance, his resale is subject to the conditions laid down in this Article on resale by an aggrieved seller (Section 2–706).

§ 2–719. Contractual Modification or Limitation of Remedy.

(1) Subject to the provisions of subsections (2) and (3) of this section and of the preceding section on liquidation and limitation of damages,

(a) the agreement may provide for remedies in addition to or in substitution for those provided in this Article and may limit or alter the measure of damages recoverable under this Article, as by limiting the buyer's remedies to return of the goods and repayment of the price or to repair and replacement of nonconforming goods or parts; and

(b) resort to a remedy as provided is optional unless the remedy is expressly agreed to be exclusive, in which case it is the sole remedy.

(2) Where circumstances cause an exclusive or limited remedy to fail of its essential purpose, remedy may be had as provided in this Act.

(3) Consequential damages may be limited or excluded unless the limitation or exclusion is unconscionable. Limitation of consequential damages for injury to the person in the case of consumer goods is prima facie unconscionable but limitation of damages where the loss is commercial is not.

§ 2–720. Effect of "Cancellation" or "Rescission" on Claims for Antecedent Breach.

Unless the contrary intention clearly appears, expressions of "cancellation" or "rescission" of the contract or the like shall not be construed as a renunciation or discharge of any claim in damages for an antecedent breach.

§ 2–721. Remedies for Fraud.

Remedies for material misrepresentation or fraud include all remedies available under this Article for non-fraudulent breach. Neither rescission or a claim for rescission of the contract for sale nor rejection or return of the goods shall bar or be deemed inconsistent with a claim for damages or other remedy.

§ 2–722. Who Can Sue Third Parties for Injury to Goods.

Where a third party so deals with goods which have been identified to a contract for sale as to cause actionable injury to a party to that contract

(a) a right of action against the third party is in either party to the contract for sale who has title to or a security interest or a special property or an insurable interest in the goods; and if the goods have been destroyed or converted a right of action is also in the party who either bore the risk of loss under the contract for sale or has since the injury assumed that risk as against the other;

(b) if at the time of the injury the party plaintiff did not bear the risk of loss as against the other party to the contract for sale and there is no arrangement between them for disposition of the recovery, his suit or settlement is, subject to his own interest, as a fiduciary for the other party to the contract;

(c) either party may with the consent of the other sue for the benefit of whom it may concern.

§ 2–723. Proof of Market Price: Time and Place.

(1) If an action based on anticipatory repudiation comes to trial before the time for performance with respect to some or all of the goods, any damages based on market price (Section 2–708 or Section 2–713) shall be determined according to the price of such goods prevailing at the time when the aggrieved party learned of the repudiation.

(2) If evidence of a price prevailing at the times or places described in this Article is not readily available the price prevailing within any reasonable time before or after the time described or at any other place which in commercial judgment or under usage of trade would serve as a reasonable substitute for the one described may be used, making any proper allowance for the cost of transporting the goods to or from such other place.

(3) Evidence of a relevant price prevailing at a time or place other than the one described in this Article offered by one party is not admissible unless and until he has given the other party such notice as the court finds sufficient to prevent unfair surprise.

§ 2–724. Admissibility of Market Quotations.

Whenever the prevailing price or value of any goods regularly bought and sold in any established commodity market is in issue, reports in official publications or trade journals or in newspapers or periodicals of general circulation published as the reports of such market shall be admissible in evidence. The circumstances of the preparation of such a report may be shown to affect its weight but not its admissibility.

§ 2–725. Statute of Limitations in Contracts for Sale.

(1) An action for breach of any contract for sale must be commenced within four years after the cause of action has accrued. By the original agreement the parties may reduce the period of limitation to not less than one year but may not extend it.

(2) A cause of action accrues when the breach occurs, regardless of the aggrieved party's lack of knowledge of the breach. A breach of warranty occurs when tender of delivery is made, except that where a warranty explicitly extends to future performance of the goods and discovery of the breach must await the time of such performance the cause of action accrues when the breach is or should have been discovered.

(3) Where an action commenced within the time limited by subsection (1) is so terminated as to leave available a remedy by another action for the same breach such other action may be commenced after the expiration of the time limited and within six months after the termination of the first action unless the termination resulted from voluntary discontinuance or from dismissal for failure or neglect to prosecute.

(4) This section does not alter the law on tolling of the statute of limitations nor does it apply to causes of action which have accrued before this Act becomes effective.

Article 2 Amendments (Excerpts)[1]

Part 1 Short Title, General Construction and Subject Matter

*   *   *   *

§ 2–103. Definitions and Index of Definitions.

(1) In this article unless the context otherwise requires

*   *   *   *

(b) "Conspicuous", with reference to a term, means so written, displayed, or presented that a reasonable person against which it is to operate ought to have noticed it. A term in an electronic record intended to evoke a response by an electronic agent is conspicuous if it is presented in a form that would enable a reasonably configured electronic agent to take it into account or react to it without review of the record by an individual.

Whether a term is "conspicuous" or not is a decision for the court. Conspicuous terms include the following:

(i) for a person:

(A) a heading in capitals equal to or greater in size than the surrounding text, or in contrasting type, font, or color to the surrounding text of the same or lesser size and;

(B) language in the body of a record or display in larger type than the surrounding text, or in contrasting type, font, or color to the surrounding text of the same size, or set off from surrounding text of the same size by symbols or other marks that call attention to the language; and

(ii) for a person or an electronic agent, a term that is so placed in a record or display that the person or electronic agent cannot proceed without taking action with respect to the particular term.

(c) "Consumer" means an individual who buys or contracts to buy goods that, at the time of contracting, are intended by the individual to be used primarily for personal, family, or household purposes.

(d) "Consumer contract" means a contract between a merchant seller and a consumer.

*   *   *   *

(j) "Good faith" means honesty in fact and the observance of reasonable commercial standards of fair dealing.

(k) "Goods" means all things that are movable at the time of identification to a contract for sale. The term includes future goods, specially manufactured goods, the unborn young of animals, growing crops, and other identified things attached to realty as described in Section 2–107. The term does not include information, the money in which the price is to be paid, investment securities under Article 8, the subject matter of foreign exchange transactions, and choses in action.

*   *   *   *

(m) "Record" means information that is inscribed on a tangible medium or that is stored in an electronic or other medium and is retrievable in perceivable form.

(n) "Remedial promise" means a promise by the seller to repair or replace the goods or to refund all or part of the price upon the happening of a specified event.

*   *   *   *

(p) "Sign" means, with present intent to authenticate or adopt a record,

(i) to execute or adopt a tangible symbol; or

(ii) to attach to or logically associate with the record an electronic sound, symbol, or process.

*   *   *   *

---

1. Additions and new wording are underlined. What follows represents only selected changes made by the 2003 amendments. Although the National Conference of Commissioners on Uniform State Laws and the American Law Institute approved the amendments in May of 2003, as of this writing, they have not as yet been adopted by any state.

Part 2 Form, Formation, Terms and Readjustment of Contract; Electronic Contracting

§ 2–201. Formal Requirements; Statute of Frauds.

(1) A contract for the sale of goods for the price of $5,000 or more is not enforceable by way of action or defense unless there is some record sufficient to indicate that a contract for sale has been made between the parties and signed by the party against which enforcement is sought or by the party's authorized agent or broker. A record is not insufficient because it omits or incorrectly states a term agreed upon but the contract is not enforceable under this subsection beyond the quantity of goods shown in the record.

(2) Between merchants if within a reasonable time a record in confirmation of the contract and sufficient against the sender is received and the party receiving it has reason to know its contents, it satisfies the requirements of subsection (1) against the recipient unless notice of objection to its contents is given in a record within 10 days after it is received.

(3) A contract which does not satisfy the requirements of subsection (1) but which is valid in other respects is enforceable

(a) if the goods are to be specially manufactured for the buyer and are not suitable for sale to others in the ordinary course of the seller's business and the seller, before notice of repudiation is received and under circumstances which reasonably indicate that the goods are for the buyer, has made either a substantial beginning of their manufacture or commitments for their procurement; or

(b) if the party against which enforcement is sought admits in the party's pleading, or in the party's testimony or otherwise under oath that a contract for sale was made, but the contract is not enforceable under this paragraph beyond the quantity of goods admitted; or

(c) with respect to goods for which payment has been made and accepted or which have been received and accepted (Sec. 2–606).

(4) A contract that is enforceable under this section is not rendered unenforceable merely because it is not capable of being performed within one year or any other applicable period after its making.

*   *   *   *

§ 2–207. Terms of Contract; Effect of Confirmation.

Subject to Section 2–202, if (i) conduct by both parties recognizes the existence of a contract although their records do not otherwise establish a contract, (ii) a contract is formed by an offer and acceptance, or (iii) a contract formed in any manner is confirmed by a record that contains terms additional to or different from those in the contract being confirmed, the terms of the contract, are:

(a) terms that appear in the records of both parties;

(b) terms, whether in a record or not, to which both parties agree; and

(c) terms supplied or incorporated under any provision of this Act.

*   *   *   *

Part 3 General Obligation and Construction of Contract

*   *   *   *

§ 2–312. Warranty of Title and Against Infringement; Buyer's Obligation Against Infringement.

(1) Subject to subsection (3) there is in a contract for sale a warranty by the seller that

(a) the title conveyed shall be, good and its transfer rightful and shall not, unreasonably expose the buyer to litigation because of any colorable claim to or interest in the goods; and

(b) the goods shall be delivered free from any security interest or other lien or encumbrance of which the buyer at the time of contracting has no knowledge.

(2) Unless otherwise agreed a seller that is a merchant regularly dealing in goods of the kind warrants that the goods shall be delivered free of the rightful claim of any third person by way of infringement or the like but a buyer that furnishes specifications to the seller must hold the seller harmless against any such claim that arises out of compliance with the specifications.

(3) A warranty under this section may be disclaimed or modified only by specific language or by circumstances that give the buyer reason to know that the seller does not claim title, that the seller is purporting to sell only the right or title as the seller or a third person may have, or that the seller is selling subject to any claims of infringement or the like.

§ 2–313. Express Warranties by Affirmation, Promise, Description, Sample; Remedial Promise.

(1) In this section, "immediate buyer" means a buyer that enters into a contract with the seller.

*   *   *   *

(4) Any remedial promise made by the seller to the immediate buyer creates an obligation that the promise will be performed upon the happening of the specified event.

§ 2–313A. Obligation to Remote Purchaser Created by Record Packaged with or Accompanying Goods.

(1) In this section:

(a) "Immediate buyer" means a buyer that enters into a contract with the seller.

(b) "Remote purchaser" means a person that buys or leases goods from an immediate buyer or other person in the normal chain of distribution.

(2) This section applies only to new goods and goods sold or leased as new goods in a transaction of purchase in the normal chain of distribution.

(3) If in a record packaged with or accompanying the goods the seller makes an affirmation of fact or promise that relates to the goods, provides a description that relates to the goods, or makes a remedial promise, and the seller reasonably expects the record to be, and the record is, furnished to the remote purchaser, the seller has an obligation to the remote purchaser that:

(a) the goods will conform to the affirmation of fact, promise or description unless a reasonable person in the position of the remote purchaser would not believe that the affirmation of fact, promise or description created an obligation; and

(b) the seller will perform the remedial promise.

(4) It is not necessary to the creation of an obligation under this section that the seller use formal words such as "warrant" or "guarantee" or that the seller have a specific intention to undertake an obligation, but an affirmation merely of the value of the goods or a statement purporting to be merely the seller's opinion or commendation of the goods does not create an obligation.

(5) The following rules apply to the remedies for breach of an obligation created under this section:

(a) The seller may modify or limit the remedies available to the remote purchaser if the modification or limitation is furnished to the remote purchaser no later than the time of purchase or if the modification or limitation is contained in the record that contains the affirmation of fact, promise or description.

(b) Subject to a modification or limitation of remedy, a seller in breach is liable for incidental or consequential damages under Section 2–715, but not for lost profits.

(c) The remote purchaser may recover as damages for breach of a seller's obligation arising under subsection (2) the loss resulting in the ordinary course of events as determined in any reasonable manner.

(5) An obligation that is not a remedial promise is breached if the goods did not conform to the affirmation of fact, promise or description creating the obligation when the goods left the seller's control.

§ 2–313B. Obligation to Remote Purchaser Created by Communication to the Public.

(1) In this section:

(a) "Immediate buyer" means a buyer that enters into a contract with the seller.

(b) "Remote purchaser" means a person that buys or leases goods from an immediate buyer or other person in the normal chain of distribution.

(2) This section applies only to new goods and goods sold or leased as new goods in a transaction of purchase in the normal chain of distribution.

(3) If in an advertisement or a similar communication to the public a seller makes an affirmation of fact or promise that relates to the goods, provides a description that relates to the goods, or makes a remedial promise, and the remote purchaser enters into a transaction of purchase with knowledge of and with the expectation that the goods will conform to the affirmation of fact, promise, or description, or that the seller will perform the remedial promise, the seller has an obligation to the remote purchaser that:

(a) the goods will conform to the affirmation of fact, promise or description unless a reasonable person in the position of the remote purchaser would not believe that the affirmation of fact, promise or description created an obligation; and

(b) the seller will perform the remedial promise.

(4) It is not necessary to the creation of an obligation under this section that the seller use formal words such as "warrant" or "guarantee" or that the seller have a specific intention to undertake an obligation, but an affirmation merely of the value of the goods or a statement purporting to be merely the seller's opinion or commendation of the goods does not create an obligation.

(5) The following rules apply to the remedies for breach of an obligation created under this section:

(a) The seller may modify or limit the remedies available to the remote purchaser if the modification or limitation is furnished to the remote purchaser no later than the time of purchase. The modification or limitation may be furnished as part of the communication that contains the affirmation of fact, promise or description.

(b) Subject to a modification or limitation of remedy, a seller in breach is liable for incidental or consequential damages under Section 2–715, but not for lost profits.

(c) The remote purchaser may recover as damages for breach of a seller's obligation arising under subsection (2) the loss resulting in the ordinary course of events as determined in any reasonable manner.

(6) An obligation that is not a remedial promise is breached if the goods did not conform to the affirmation of fact, promise or description creating the obligation when the goods left the seller's control.

* * * *

§ 2–316. Exclusion or Modification of Warranties.

* * * *

(2) Subject to subsection (3), to exclude or modify the implied warranty of merchantability or any part of it in a consumer contract the language must be in a record, be conspicuous, and state "The seller undertakes no responsibility

for the quality of the goods except as otherwise provided in this contract," and in any other contract the language must mention merchantability and in case of a record must be conspicuous. Subject to subsection (3), to exclude or modify the implied warranty of fitness the exclusion must be in a record and be conspicuous. Language to exclude all implied warranties of fitness in a consumer contract must state "The seller assumes no responsibility that the goods will be fit for any particular purpose for which you may be buying these goods, except as otherwise provided in the contract," and in any other contract the language is sufficient if it states, for example, that "There are no warranties that extend beyond the description on the face hereof." Language that satisfies the requirements of this subsection for the exclusion and modification of a warranty in a consumer contract also satisfies the requirements for any other contract.

(3) Notwithstanding subsection (2):

(a) unless the circumstances indicate otherwise, all implied warranties are excluded by expressions like "as is", "with all faults" or other language which in common understanding calls the buyer's attention to the exclusion of warranties, makes plain that there is no implied warranty, and in a consumer contract evidenced by a record is set forth conspicuously in the record; and

(b) when the buyer before entering into the contract has examined the goods or the sample or model as fully as desired or has refused to examine the goods after a demand by the seller there is no implied warranty with regard to defects which an examination ought in the circumstances to have revealed to the buyer; and

(c) an implied warranty can also be excluded or modified by course of dealing or course of performance or usage of trade.

* * * *

§ 2–318. Third Party Beneficiaries of Warranties and Obligations.

(1) In this section:

(a) "Immediate buyer" means a buyer that enters into a contract with the seller.

(b) "Remote purchaser" means a person that buys or leases goods from an immediate buyer or other person in the normal chain of distribution.

Alternative A to subsection (2)

(2) A seller's warranty to an immediate buyer, whether express or implied, a seller's remedial promise to an immediate buyer, or a seller's obligation to a remote purchaser under Section 2–313A or 2–313B extends to any natural person who is in the family or household of the immediate buyer or the remote purchaser or who is a guest in the home of either if it is reasonable to expect that the person may use, consume

or be affected by the goods and who is injured in person by breach of the warranty, remedial promise or obligation. A seller may not exclude or limit the operation of this section.

Alternative B to subsection (2)

(2) A seller's warranty to an immediate buyer, whether express or implied, a seller's remedial promise to an immediate buyer, or a seller's obligation to a remote purchaser under Section 2–313A or 2–313B extends to any natural person who may reasonably be expected to use, consume or be affected by the goods and who is injured in person by breach of the warranty, remedial promise or obligation. A seller may not exclude or limit the operation of this section.

Alternative C to subsection (2)

(2) A seller's warranty to an immediate buyer, whether express or implied, a seller's remedial promise to an immediate buyer, or a seller's obligation to a remote purchaser under Section 2–313A or 2–313B extends to any person that may reasonably be expected to use, consume or be affected by the goods and that is injured by breach of the warranty, remedial promise or obligation. A seller may not exclude or limit the operation of this section with respect to injury to the person of an individual to whom the warranty, remedial promise or obligation extends.

* * * *

Part 5 Performance
* * * *

§ 2–502. Buyer's Right to Goods on Seller's Insolvency.

(1) Subject to subsections (2) and (3) and even though the goods have not been shipped a buyer that has paid a part or all of the price of goods in which the buyer has a special property under the provisions of the immediately preceding section may on making and keeping good a tender of any unpaid portion of their price recover them from the seller if:

(a) in the case of goods bought by a consumer, the seller repudiates or fails to deliver as required by the contract; or

(b) in all cases, the seller becomes insolvent within ten days after receipt of the first installment on their price.

(2) The buyer's right to recover the goods under subsection (1) vests upon acquisition of a special property, even if the seller had not then repudiated or failed to deliver.

(3) If the identification creating the special property has been made by the buyer, the buyer acquires the right to recover the goods only if they conform to the contract for sale.

* * * *

§ 2–508. Cure by Seller of Improper Tender or Delivery; Replacement.

(1) Where the buyer rejects goods or a tender of delivery under Section 2–601 or 2–612 or, except in a consumer con-

tract, justifiably revokes acceptance under Section 2–608(1)(b) and the agreed time for performance has not expired, a seller that has performed in good faith, upon seasonable notice to the buyer and at the seller's own expense, may cure the breach of contract by making a conforming tender of delivery within the agreed time. The seller shall compensate the buyer for all of the buyer's reasonable expenses caused by the seller's breach of contract and subsequent cure.

(2) Where the buyer rejects goods or a tender of delivery under Section 2–601 or 2–612 or except in a consumer contract justifiably revokes acceptance under Section 2–608(1)(b) and the agreed time for performance has expired, a seller that has performed in good faith, upon seasonable notice to the buyer and at the seller's own expense, may cure the breach of contract, if the cure is appropriate and timely under the circumstances, by making a tender of conforming goods. The seller shall compensate the buyer for all of the buyer's reasonable expenses caused by the seller's breach of contract and subsequent cure.

§ 2–509. Risk of Loss in the Absence of Breach.

(1) Where the contract requires or authorizes the seller to ship the goods by carrier

(a) if it does not require the seller to deliver them at a particular destination, the risk of loss passes to the buyer when the goods are delivered to the carrier even though the shipment is under reservation (Section 2–505); but

(b) if it does require the seller to deliver them at a particular destination and the goods are there tendered while in the possession of the carrier, the risk of loss passes to the buyer when the goods are there so tendered as to enable the buyer to take delivery.

(2) Where the goods are held by a bailee to be delivered without being moved, the risk of loss passes to the buyer

(a) on the buyer's receipt of a negotiable document of title covering the goods; or

(b) on acknowledgment by the bailee to the buyer of the buyer's right to possession of the goods; or

(c) after the buyer's receipt of a non-negotiable document of title or other direction to deliver in a record, as provided in subsection (4)(b) of Section 2–503.

(3) In any case not within subsection (1) or (2), the risk of loss passes to the buyer on the buyer's receipt of the goods.

(4) The provisions of this section are subject to contrary agreement of the parties and to the provisions of this Article on sale on approval (Section 2–327) and on effect of breach on risk of loss (Section 2–510).

*   *   *   *

§ 2–513. Buyer's Right to Inspection of Goods.

*   *   *   *

(3) Unless otherwise agreed, the buyer is not entitled to inspect the goods before payment of the price when the contract provides

(a) for delivery on terms that under applicable course of performance, course of dealing, or usage of trade are interpreted to preclude inspection before payment; or

(b) for payment against documents of title, except where such payment is due only after the goods are to become available for inspection.

*   *   *   *

Part 6 Breach, Repudiation and Excuse

*   *   *   *

§ 2–605. Waiver of Buyer's Objections by Failure to Particularize.

(1) The buyer's failure to state in connection with rejection a particular defect or in connection with revocation of acceptance a defect that justifies revocation precludes the buyer from relying on the unstated defect to justify rejection or revocation of acceptance if the defect is ascertainable by reasonable inspection

(a) where the seller had a right to cure the defect and could have cured it if stated seasonably; or

(b) between merchants when the seller has after rejection made a request in a record for a full and final statement in record form of all defects on which the buyer proposes to rely.

(2) A buyer's payment against documents tendered to the buyer made without reservation of rights precludes recovery of the payment for defects apparent on the face of the documents.

*   *   *   *

§ 2–607. Effect of Acceptance; Notice of Breach; Burden of Establishing Breach After Acceptance; Notice of Claim or Litigation to Person Answerable Over.

*   *   *   *

(3) Where a tender has been accepted

(a) the buyer must within a reasonable time after the buyer discovers or should have discovered any breach notify the seller. However, failure to give timely notice bars the buyer from a remedy only to the extent that the seller is prejudiced by the failure and

(b) if the claim is one for infringement or the like (subsection (3) of Section 2–312) and the buyer is sued as a result of such a breach the buyer must so notify the seller within a reasonable time after the buyer receives notice of the litigation or be barred from any remedy over for liability established by the litigation.

*   *   *   *

§ 2–608. Revocation of Acceptance in Whole or in Part.

*   *   *   *

(4) If a buyer uses the goods after a rightful rejection or justifiable revocation of acceptance, the following rules apply:

(a) Any use by the buyer which is unreasonable under the circumstances is wrongful as against the seller and is an acceptance only if ratified by the seller.

(b) Any use of the goods which is reasonable under the circumstances is not wrongful as against the seller and is not an acceptance, but in an appropriate case the buyer shall be obligated to the seller for the value of the use to the buyer.

* * * *

§ 2–612. "Installment Contract"; Breach.

* * * *

(2) The buyer may reject any installment which is non-conforming if the non-conformity substantially impairs the value of that installment to the buyer or if the non-conformity is a defect in the required documents; but if the non-conformity does not fall within subsection (3) and the seller gives adequate assurance of its cure the buyer must accept that installment.

(3) Whenever non-conformity or default with respect to one or more installments substantially impairs the value of the whole contract there is a breach of the whole. But the aggrieved party reinstates the contract if the party accepts a non-conforming installment without seasonably notifying of cancellation or if the party brings an action with respect only to past installments or demands performance as to future installments.

* * * *

Part 7 Remedies

§ 2–702. Seller's Remedies on Discovery of Buyer's Insolvency.

* * * *

(2) Where the seller discovers that the buyer has received goods on credit while insolvent the seller may reclaim the goods upon demand made within a reasonable time after the buyer's receipt of the goods. Except as provided in this subsection the seller may not base a right to reclaim goods on the buyer's fraudulent or innocent misrepresentation of solvency or of intent to pay.

* * * *

§ 2–703. Seller's Remedies in General.

(1) A breach of contract by the buyer includes the buyer's wrongful rejection or wrongful attempt to revoke acceptance of goods, wrongful failure to perform a contractual obligation, failure to make a payment when due, and repudiation.

(2) If the buyer is in breach of contract the seller, to the extent provided for by this Act or other law, may:

(a) withhold delivery of the goods:

(b) stop delivery of the goods under Section 2–705;

(c) proceed under Section 2–704 with respect to goods unidentified to the contract or unfinished;

(d) reclaim the goods under Section 2–507(2) or 2–702(2);

(e) require payment directly from the buyer under Section 2–325(c);

(f) cancel;

(g) resell and recover damages under Section 2–706;

(h) recover damages for nonacceptance or repudiation under Section 2–708(1);

(i) recover lost profits under Section 2–708(2);

(j) recover the price under Section 2–709;

(k) obtain specific performance under Section 2–716;

(l) recover liquidated damages under Section 2–718;

(m) in other cases, recover damages in any manner that is reasonable under the circumstances.

(3) If a buyer becomes insolvent, the seller may:

(a) withhold delivery under Section 2–702(1);

(b) stop delivery of the goods under Section 2–705;

(c) reclaim the goods under Section 2–702(2).

* * * *

§ 2–705. Seller's Stoppage of Delivery in Transit or Otherwise.

(1) The seller may stop delivery of goods in the possession of a carrier or other bailee when the seller discovers the buyer to be insolvent (Section 2–702) or when the buyer repudiates or fails to make a payment due before delivery or if for any other reason the seller has a right to withhold or reclaim the goods.

* * * *

§ 2–706. Seller's Resale Including Contract for Resale.

(1) In an appropriate case involving breach by the buyer, the seller may resell the goods concerned or the undelivered balance thereof. Where the resale is made in good faith and in a commercially reasonable manner the seller may recover the difference between the contract price and the resale price together with any incidental or consequential damages allowed under the provisions of this Article (Section 2–710), but less expenses saved in consequence of the buyer's breach.

* * * *

§ 2–708. Seller's Damages for Non-Acceptance or Repudiation.

(1) Subject to subsection (2) and to the provisions of this Article with respect to proof of market price (Section 2–723)

(a) the measure of damages for non-acceptance by the buyer is the difference between the contract price and the market price at the time and place for tender together with any incidental or consequential damages provided in this Article (Section 2–710), but less expenses saved in consequence of the buyer's breach; and

(b) the measure of damages for repudiation by the buyer is the difference between the contract price and the market price at the place for tender at the expiration of a commercially reasonable time after the seller learned of the repudiation, but no later than the time stated in paragraph (a), together with any incidental or consequential damages provided in this Article (Section 2–710), but less expenses saved in consequence of the buyer's breach.

(2) If the measure of damages provided in subsection (1) or in Section 2–706 is inadequate to put the seller in as good a position as performance would have done then the measure of damages is the profit (including reasonable overhead) which the seller would have made from full performance by the buyer, together with any incidental or consequential damages provided in this Article (Section 2–710).

§ 2–709. Action for the Price.

(1) When the buyer fails to pay the price as it becomes due the seller may recover, together with any incidental or consequential damages under the next section, the price

(a) of goods accepted or of conforming goods lost or damaged within a commercially reasonable time after risk of their loss has passed to the buyer; and

(b) of goods identified to the contract if the seller is unable after reasonable effort to resell them at a reasonable price or the circumstances reasonably indicate that such effort will be unavailing.

* * * *

§ 2–710. Seller's Incidental and Consequential Damages.

(1) Incidental damages to an aggrieved seller include any commercially reasonable charges, expenses or commissions incurred in stopping delivery, in the transportation, care and custody of goods after the buyer's breach, in connection with return or resale of the goods or otherwise resulting from the breach.

(2) Consequential damages resulting from the buyer's breach include any loss resulting from general or particular requirements and needs of which the buyer at the time of contracting had reason to know and which could not reasonably be prevented by resale or otherwise.

(3) In a consumer contract, a seller may not recover consequential damages from a consumer.

* * * *

§ 2–711. Buyer's Remedies in General; Buyer's Security Interest in Rejected Goods.

(1) A breach of contract by the seller includes the seller's wrongful failure to deliver or to perform a contractual obligation, making of a nonconforming tender of delivery or performance, and repudiation.

(2) If a seller is in breach of contract under subsection (1) the buyer, to the extent provided for by this Act or other law, may:

(a) in the case of rightful cancellation, rightful rejection or justifiable revocation of acceptance recover so much of the price as has been paid;

(b) deduct damages from any part of the price still due under Section 2–717;

(c) cancel;

(d) cover and have damages under Section 2–712 as to all goods affected whether or not they have been identified to the contract;

(e) recover damages for non-delivery or repudiation under Section 2–713;

(f) recover damages for breach with regard to accepted goods or breach with regard to a remedial promise under Section 2–714;

(g) recover identified goods under Section 2–502;

(h) obtain specific performance or obtain the goods by replevin or similar remedy under Section 7–716;

(i) recover liquidated damages under Section 2–718;

(j) in other cases, recover damages in any manner that is reasonable under the circumstances.

(3) On rightful rejection or justifiable revocation of acceptance a buyer has a security interest in goods in the buyer's possession or control for any payments made on their price and any expenses reasonably incurred in their inspection, receipt, transportation, care and custody and may hold such goods and resell them in like manner as an aggrieved seller (Section 2–706).

* * * *

§ 2–713. Buyer's Damages for Non-Delivery or Repudiation.

(1) Subject to the provisions of this Article with respect to proof of market price (Section 2–723), if the seller wrongfully fails to deliver or repudiates or the buyer rightfully rejects or justifiably revokes acceptance

(a) the measure of damages in the case of wrongful failure to deliver by the seller or rightful rejection or justifiable revocation of acceptance by the buyer is the difference between the market price at the time for tender under the contract and the contract price together with any incidental or consequential damages provided in this Article (Section 2–715), but less expenses saved in consequence of the seller's <u>breach; and</u>

<u>(b) the measure of damages for repudiation by the seller is the difference between the market price at the expiration of a commercially reasonable time after the buyer learned of the repudiation, but no later than the time stated in paragraph (a), and the contract price together with any incidental or consequential damages provided in this Article (Section 2–715), less expenses saved in consequence of the seller's breach.</u>

* * * *

§ 2–725. Statute of Limitations in Contracts for Sale.

<u>(1)</u> Except as otherwise provided in this section, an action for breach of any contract for sale must be commenced <u>within the later of four years after the right of action has accrued under subsection (2) or (3) or one year after the breach was or should have been discovered, but no longer than five years after the right of action accrued. By the orig</u>inal agreement the parties may reduce the period of limitation to not less than one year <u>but may not extend it. However, in a consumer contract, the period of limitation may not be reduced.</u>

(2) <u>Except as otherwise provided in subsection (3), the fol</u>lowing rules apply:

<u>(a) Except as otherwise provided in this subsection, a right of action for breach of a contract accrues when the breach occurs, even if the aggrieved party did not have knowledge of the breach.</u>

<u>(b) For breach of a contract by repudiation, a right of action accrues at the earlier of when the aggrieved party elects to treat the repudiation as a breach or when a commercially reasonable time for awaiting performance has expired.</u>

<u>(c) For breach of a remedial promise, a right of action accrues when the remedial promise is not performed when performance is due.</u>

<u>(d) In an action by a buyer against a person that is answerable over to the buyer for a claim asserted against the buyer, the buyer's right of action against the person answerable over accrues at the time the claim was orig</u>inally asserted against the buyer.

(3) <u>If a breach of a warranty arising under Section 2–312, 2–313(2), 2–314, or 2–315, or a breach of an obligation, other than a remedial promise, arising under Section 2–313A or 2–313B, is claimed the following rules apply:</u>

<u>(a) Except as otherwise provided in paragraph (c), a right of action for breach of a warranty arising under Section 2–313(2), 2–314 or 2–315 accrues when the seller has tendered delivery to the immediate buyer, as defined in Section 2–313, and has completed perfor</u>mance of any agreed installation or assembly of the goods.

<u>(b) Except as otherwise provided in paragraph (c), a right of action for breach of an obligation other than a remedial promise arising under Section 2–313A or 2–313B accrues when the remote purchaser, as defined in sections 2–313A and 2–313B, receives the goods.</u>

<u>(c) Where a warranty arising under Section 2–313(2) or an obligation, other than a remedial promise, arising under 2–313A or 2–313B explicitly extends to future performance of the goods and discovery of the breach must await the time for performance the right of action accrues when the immediate buyer as defined in Section 2–313 or the remote purchaser as defined in Sections 2–313A and 2–313B discovers or should have discovered the breach.</u>

<u>(d) A right of action for breach of warranty arising under Section 2–312 accrues when the aggrieved party discovers or should have discovered the breach. However, an action for breach of the warranty of non-infringement may not be commenced more than six years after tender of delivery of the goods to the aggrieved party.</u>

* * * *

Article 2A
LEASES

Part 1 General Provisions

§ 2A–101. Short Title.

This Article shall be known and may be cited as the Uniform Commercial Code—Leases.

§ 2A–102. Scope.

This Article applies to any transaction, regardless of form, that creates a lease.

§ 2A–103. Definitions and Index of Definitions.

(1) In this Article unless the context otherwise requires:

(a) "Buyer in ordinary course of business" means a person who in good faith and without knowledge that the sale to him [or her] is in violation of the ownership rights or security interest or leasehold interest of a third party in the goods buys in ordinary course from a person in the business of selling goods of that kind but does not include a pawnbroker. "Buying" may be for cash or by exchange of other property or on secured or unsecured credit and includes receiving goods or documents of title under a pre-existing contract for sale but does not include a transfer in bulk or as security for or in total or partial satisfaction of a money debt.

(b) "Cancellation" occurs when either party puts an end to the lease contract for default by the other party.

(c) "Commercial unit" means such a unit of goods as by commercial usage is a single whole for purposes of lease and division of which materially impairs its character or value on the market or in use. A commercial unit may be a single article, as a machine, or a set of articles, as a suite of furniture or a line of machinery, or a quantity, as a gross or carload, or any other unit treated in use or in the relevant market as a single whole.

(d) "Conforming" goods or performance under a lease contract means goods or performance that are in accordance with the obligations under the lease contract.

(e) "Consumer lease" means a lease that a lessor regularly engaged in the business of leasing or selling makes to a lessee who is an individual and who takes under the lease primarily for a personal, family, or household purpose [, if the total payments to be made under the lease contract, excluding payments for options to renew or buy, do not exceed $_____].

(f) "Fault" means wrongful act, omission, breach, or default.

(g) "Finance lease" means a lease with respect to which:

(i) the lessor does not select, manufacture or supply the goods;

(ii) the lessor acquires the goods or the right to possession and use of the goods in connection with the lease; and

(iii) one of the following occurs:

(A) the lessee receives a copy of the contract by which the lessor acquired the goods or the right to possession and use of the goods before signing the lease contract;

(B) the lessee's approval of the contract by which the lessor acquired the goods or the right to possession and use of the goods is a condition to effectiveness of the lease contract;

(C) the lessee, before signing the lease contract, receives an accurate and complete statement designating the promises and warranties, and any disclaimers of warranties, limitations or modifications of remedies, or liquidated damages, including those of a third party, such as the manufacturer of the goods, provided to the lessor by the person supplying the goods in connection with or as part of the contract by which the lessor acquired the goods or the right to possession and use of the goods; or

(D) if the lease is not a consumer lease, the lessor, before the lessee signs the lease contract, informs the lessee in writing (a) of the identity of the person supplying the goods to the lessor, unless the lessee has selected that person and directed the lessor to acquire the goods or the right to possession and use of the goods from that person, (b) that the lessee is entitled under this Article to any promises and warranties, including those of any third party, provided to the lessor by the person supplying the goods in connection with or as part of the contract by which the lessor acquired the goods or the right to possession and use of the goods, and (c) that the lessee may communicate with the person supplying the goods to the lessor and receive an accurate and complete statement of those promises and warranties, including any disclaimers and limitations of them or of remedies.

(h) "Goods" means all things that are movable at the time of identification to the lease contract, or are fixtures (Section 2A–309), but the term does not include money, documents, instruments, accounts, chattel paper, general intangibles, or minerals or the like, including oil and gas, before extraction. The term also includes the unborn young of animals.

(i) "Installment lease contract" means a lease contract that authorizes or requires the delivery of goods in separate lots to be separately accepted, even though the lease contract contains a clause "each delivery is a separate lease" or its equivalent.

(j) "Lease" means a transfer of the right to possession and use of goods for a term in return for consideration, but a sale, including a sale on approval or a sale or return, or retention or creation of a security interest is not a lease. Unless the context clearly indicates otherwise, the term includes a sublease.

(k) "Lease agreement" means the bargain, with respect to the lease, of the lessor and the lessee in fact as found in their language or by implication from other circumstances including course of dealing or usage of trade or course of performance as provided in this Article. Unless the context clearly indicates otherwise, the term includes a sublease agreement.

(l) "Lease contract" means the total legal obligation that results from the lease agreement as affected by this Article and any other applicable rules of law. Unless the context clearly indicates otherwise, the term includes a sublease contract.

(m) "Leasehold interest" means the interest of the lessor or the lessee under a lease contract.

(n) "Lessee" means a person who acquires the right to possession and use of goods under a lease. Unless the context clearly indicates otherwise, the term includes a sublessee.

(o) "Lessee in ordinary course of business" means a person who in good faith and without knowledge that the lease to him [or her] is in violation of the ownership rights or security interest or leasehold interest of a third party in the goods, leases in ordinary course from a person in the business of selling or leasing goods of that kind but does not include a pawnbroker. "Leasing" may be for cash or by exchange of other property or on secured or unsecured credit and includes receiving goods or documents of title under a pre-existing lease contract but does not include a transfer in bulk or as security for or in total or partial satisfaction of a money debt.

(p) "Lessor" means a person who transfers the right to possession and use of goods under a lease. Unless the context clearly indicates otherwise, the term includes a sublessor.

(q) "Lessor's residual interest" means the lessor's interest in the goods after expiration, termination, or cancellation of the lease contract.

(r) "Lien" means a charge against or interest in goods to secure payment of a debt or performance of an obligation, but the term does not include a security interest.

(s) "Lot" means a parcel or a single article that is the subject matter of a separate lease or delivery, whether or not it is sufficient to perform the lease contract.

(t) "Merchant lessee" means a lessee that is a merchant with respect to goods of the kind subject to the lease.

(u) "Present value" means the amount as of a date certain of one or more sums payable in the future, discounted to the date certain. The discount is determined by the interest rate specified by the parties if the rate was not manifestly unreasonable at the time the transaction was entered into; otherwise, the discount is determined by a commercially reasonable rate that takes into account the facts and circumstances of each case at the time the transaction was entered into.

(v) "Purchase" includes taking by sale, lease, mortgage, security interest, pledge, gift, or any other voluntary transaction creating an interest in goods.

(w) "Sublease" means a lease of goods the right to possession and use of which was acquired by the lessor as a lessee under an existing lease.

(x) "Supplier" means a person from whom a lessor buys or leases goods to be leased under a finance lease.

(y) "Supply contract" means a contract under which a lessor buys or leases goods to be leased.

(z) "Termination" occurs when either party pursuant to a power created by agreement or law puts an end to the lease contract otherwise than for default.

(2) Other definitions applying to this Article and the sections in which they appear are:

"Accessions". Section 2A–310(1).

"Construction mortgage". Section 2A–309(1)(d).

"Encumbrance". Section 2A–309(1)(e).

"Fixtures". Section 2A–309(1)(a).

"Fixture filing". Section 2A–309(1)(b).

"Purchase money lease". Section 2A–309(1)(c).

(3) The following definitions in other Articles apply to this Article:

"Accounts". Section 9–106.

"Between merchants". Section 2–104(3).

"Buyer". Section 2–103(1)(a).

"Chattel paper". Section 9–105(1)(b).

"Consumer goods". Section 9–109(1).

"Document". Section 9–105(1)(f).

"Entrusting". Section 2–403(3).

"General intangibles". Section 9–106.

"Good faith". Section 2–103(1)(b).

"Instrument". Section 9–105(1)(i).

"Merchant". Section 2–104(1).

"Mortgage". Section 9–105(1)(j).

"Pursuant to commitment". Section 9–105(1)(k).

"Receipt". Section 2–103(1)(c).

"Sale". Section 2–106(1).

"Sale on approval". Section 2–326.

"Sale or return". Section 2–326.

"Seller". Section 2–103(1)(d).

(4) In addition Article 1 contains general definitions and principles of construction and interpretation applicable throughout this Article.

As amended in 1990 and 1999.

§ 2A–104. Leases Subject to Other Law.

(1) A lease, although subject to this Article, is also subject to any applicable:

　(a) certificate of title statute of this State: (list any certificate of title statutes covering automobiles, trailers, mobile homes, boats, farm tractors, and the like);

　(b) certificate of title statute of another jurisdiction (Section 2A–105); or

　(c) consumer protection statute of this State, or final consumer protection decision of a court of this State existing on the effective date of this Article.

(2) In case of conflict between this Article, other than Sections 2A–105, 2A–304(3), and 2A–305(3), and a statute or decision referred to in subsection (1), the statute or decision controls.

(3) Failure to comply with an applicable law has only the effect specified therein.

As amended in 1990.

§ 2A–105. Territorial Application of Article to Goods Covered by Certificate of Title.

Subject to the provisions of Sections 2A–304(3) and 2A–305(3), with respect to goods covered by a certificate of title issued under a statute of this State or of another jurisdiction, compliance and the effect of compliance or noncompliance with a certificate of title statute are governed by the law (including the conflict of laws rules) of the jurisdiction issuing the certificate until the earlier of (a) surrender of the certificate, or (b) four months after the goods are removed from that jurisdiction and thereafter until a new certificate of title is issued by another jurisdiction.

§ 2A–106. Limitation on Power of Parties to Consumer Lease to Choose Applicable Law and Judicial Forum.

(1) If the law chosen by the parties to a consumer lease is that of a jurisdiction other than a jurisdiction in which the lessee resides at the time the lease agreement becomes enforceable or within 30 days thereafter or in which the goods are to be used, the choice is not enforceable.

(2) If the judicial forum chosen by the parties to a consumer lease is a forum that would not otherwise have jurisdiction over the lessee, the choice is not enforceable.

§ 2A–107. Waiver or Renunciation of Claim or Right After Default.

Any claim or right arising out of an alleged default or breach of warranty may be discharged in whole or in part without consideration by a written waiver or renunciation signed and delivered by the aggrieved party.

§ 2A–108. Unconscionability.

(1) If the court as a matter of law finds a lease contract or any clause of a lease contract to have been unconscionable at the time it was made the court may refuse to enforce the lease contract, or it may enforce the remainder of the lease contract without the unconscionable clause, or it may so limit the application of any unconscionable clause as to avoid any unconscionable result.

(2) With respect to a consumer lease, if the court as a matter of law finds that a lease contract or any clause of a lease contract has been induced by unconscionable conduct or that unconscionable conduct has occurred in the collection of a claim arising from a lease contract, the court may grant appropriate relief.

(3) Before making a finding of unconscionability under subsection (1) or (2), the court, on its own motion or that of a party, shall afford the parties a reasonable opportunity to present evidence as to the setting, purpose, and effect of the lease contract or clause thereof, or of the conduct.

(4) In an action in which the lessee claims unconscionability with respect to a consumer lease:

(a) If the court finds unconscionability under subsection (1) or (2), the court shall award reasonable attorney's fees to the lessee.

(b) If the court does not find unconscionability and the lessee claiming unconscionability has brought or maintained an action he [or she] knew to be groundless, the court shall award reasonable attorney's fees to the party against whom the claim is made.

(c) In determining attorney's fees, the amount of the recovery on behalf of the claimant under subsections (1) and (2) is not controlling.

§ 2A–109. Option to Accelerate at Will.

(1) A term providing that one party or his [or her] successor in interest may accelerate payment or performance or require collateral or additional collateral "at will" or "when he [or she] deems himself [or herself] insecure" or in words of similar import must be construed to mean that he [or she] has power to do so only if he [or she] in good faith believes that the prospect of payment or performance is impaired.

(2) With respect to a consumer lease, the burden of establishing good faith under subsection (1) is on the party who exercised the power; otherwise the burden of establishing lack of good faith is on the party against whom the power has been exercised.

Part 2 Formation and Construction of Lease Contract

§ 2A–201. Statute of Frauds.

(1) A lease contract is not enforceable by way of action or defense unless:

(a) the total payments to be made under the lease contract, excluding payments for options to renew or buy, are less than $1,000; or

(b) there is a writing, signed by the party against whom enforcement is sought or by that party's authorized agent, sufficient to indicate that a lease contract has been made between the parties and to describe the goods leased and the lease term.

(2) Any description of leased goods or of the lease term is sufficient and satisfies subsection (1)(b), whether or not it is specific, if it reasonably identifies what is described.

(3) A writing is not insufficient because it omits or incorrectly states a term agreed upon, but the lease contract is not enforceable under subsection (1)(b) beyond the lease term and the quantity of goods shown in the writing.

(4) A lease contract that does not satisfy the requirements of subsection (1), but which is valid in other respects, is enforceable:

(a) if the goods are to be specially manufactured or obtained for the lessee and are not suitable for lease or sale to others in the ordinary course of the lessor's business, and the lessor, before notice of repudiation is received and under circumstances that reasonably indicate that the goods are for the lessee, has made either a substantial beginning of their manufacture or commitments for their procurement;

(b) if the party against whom enforcement is sought admits in that party's pleading, testimony or otherwise in court that a lease contract was made, but the lease contract is not enforceable under this provision beyond the quantity of goods admitted; or

(c) with respect to goods that have been received and accepted by the lessee.

(5) The lease term under a lease contract referred to in subsection (4) is:

(a) if there is a writing signed by the party against whom enforcement is sought or by that party's authorized agent specifying the lease term, the term so specified;

(b) if the party against whom enforcement is sought admits in that party's pleading, testimony, or otherwise in court a lease term, the term so admitted; or

(c) a reasonable lease term.

§ 2A–202. Final Written Expression: Parol or Extrinsic Evidence.

Terms with respect to which the confirmatory memoranda of the parties agree or which are otherwise set forth in a writing intended by the parties as a final expression of their agreement with respect to such terms as are included therein may not be contradicted by evidence of any prior agreement or of a contemporaneous oral agreement but may be explained or supplemented:

(a) by course of dealing or usage of trade or by course of performance; and

(b) by evidence of consistent additional terms unless the court finds the writing to have been intended also as a complete and exclusive statement of the terms of the agreement.

§ 2A–203. Seals Inoperative.

The affixing of a seal to a writing evidencing a lease contract or an offer to enter into a lease contract does not render the writing a sealed instrument and the law with respect to sealed instruments does not apply to the lease contract or offer.

§ 2A–204. Formation in General.

(1) A lease contract may be made in any manner sufficient to show agreement, including conduct by both parties which recognizes the existence of a lease contract.

(2) An agreement sufficient to constitute a lease contract may be found although the moment of its making is undetermined.

(3) Although one or more terms are left open, a lease contract does not fail for indefiniteness if the parties have intended to make a lease contract and there is a reasonably certain basis for giving an appropriate remedy.

§ 2A–205. Firm Offers.

An offer by a merchant to lease goods to or from another person in a signed writing that by its terms gives assurance it will be held open is not revocable, for lack of consideration, during the time stated or, if no time is stated, for a reasonable time, but in no event may the period of irrevocability exceed 3 months. Any such term of assurance on a form supplied by the offeree must be separately signed by the offeror.

§ 2A–206. Offer and Acceptance in Formation of Lease Contract.

(1) Unless otherwise unambiguously indicated by the language or circumstances, an offer to make a lease contract must be construed as inviting acceptance in any manner and by any medium reasonable in the circumstances.

(2) If the beginning of a requested performance is a reasonable mode of acceptance, an offeror who is not notified of acceptance within a reasonable time may treat the offer as having lapsed before acceptance.

§ 2A–207. Course of Performance or Practical Construction.

(1) If a lease contract involves repeated occasions for performance by either party with knowledge of the nature of the performance and opportunity for objection to it by the other, any course of performance accepted or acquiesced in without objection is relevant to determine the meaning of the lease agreement.

(2) The express terms of a lease agreement and any course of performance, as well as any course of dealing and usage of trade, must be construed whenever reasonable as consistent with each other; but if that construction is unreasonable, express terms control course of performance, course of performance controls both course of dealing and usage of trade, and course of dealing controls usage of trade.

(3) Subject to the provisions of Section 2A–208 on modification and waiver, course of performance is relevant to show a waiver or modification of any term inconsistent with the course of performance.

§ 2A–208. Modification, Rescission and Waiver.

(1) An agreement modifying a lease contract needs no consideration to be binding.

(2) A signed lease agreement that excludes modification or rescission except by a signed writing may not be otherwise modified or rescinded, but, except as between merchants, such a requirement on a form supplied by a merchant must be separately signed by the other party.

(3) Although an attempt at modification or rescission does not satisfy the requirements of subsection (2), it may operate as a waiver.

(4) A party who has made a waiver affecting an executory portion of a lease contract may retract the waiver by reasonable notification received by the other party that strict performance will be required of any term waived, unless the retraction would be unjust in view of a material change of position in reliance on the waiver.

§ 2A–209. Lessee under Finance Lease as Beneficiary of Supply Contract.

(1) The benefit of the supplier's promises to the lessor under the supply contract and of all warranties, whether express or implied, including those of any third party provided in connection with or as part of the supply contract, extends to the lessee to the extent of the lessee's leasehold interest under a finance lease related to the supply contract, but is subject to the terms warranty and of the supply contract and all defenses or claims arising therefrom.

(2) The extension of the benefit of supplier's promises and of warranties to the lessee (Section 2A–209(1)) does not: (i) modify the rights and obligations of the parties to the supply contract, whether arising therefrom or otherwise, or (ii) impose any duty or liability under the supply contract on the lessee.

(3) Any modification or rescission of the supply contract by the supplier and the lessor is effective between the supplier and the lessee unless, before the modification or rescission, the supplier has received notice that the lessee has entered into a finance lease related to the supply contract. If the modification or rescission is effective between the supplier and the lessee, the lessor is deemed to have assumed, in addition to the obligations of the lessor to the lessee under the lease contract, promises of the supplier to the lessor and warranties that were so modified or rescinded as they existed and were available to the lessee before modification or rescission.

(4) In addition to the extension of the benefit of the supplier's promises and of warranties to the lessee under subsection (1), the lessee retains all rights that the lessee may have against the supplier which arise from an agreement between the lessee and the supplier or under other law.
As amended in 1990.

§ 2A–210. Express Warranties.

(1) Express warranties by the lessor are created as follows:

(a) Any affirmation of fact or promise made by the lessor to the lessee which relates to the goods and becomes part of the basis of the bargain creates an express warranty that the goods will conform to the affirmation or promise.

(b) Any description of the goods which is made part of the basis of the bargain creates an express warranty that the goods will conform to the description.

(c) Any sample or model that is made part of the basis of the bargain creates an express warranty that the whole of the goods will conform to the sample or model.

(2) It is not necessary to the creation of an express warranty that the lessor use formal words, such as "warrant" or "guarantee," or that the lessor have a specific intention to make a warranty, but an affirmation merely of the value of the goods or a statement purporting to be merely the lessor's opinion or commendation of the goods does not create a warranty.

§ 2A–211. Warranties Against Interference and Against Infringement; Lessee's Obligation Against Infringement.

(1) There is in a lease contract a warranty that for the lease term no person holds a claim to or interest in the goods that arose from an act or omission of the lessor, other than a claim by way of infringement or the like, which will interfere with the lessee's enjoyment of its leasehold interest.

(2) Except in a finance lease there is in a lease contract by a lessor who is a merchant regularly dealing in goods of the kind a warranty that the goods are delivered free of the rightful claim of any person by way of infringement or the like.

(3) A lessee who furnishes specifications to a lessor or a supplier shall hold the lessor and the supplier harmless against any claim by way of infringement or the like that arises out of compliance with the specifications.

§ 2A–212. Implied Warranty of Merchantability.

(1) Except in a finance lease, a warranty that the goods will be merchantable is implied in a lease contract if the lessor is a merchant with respect to goods of that kind.

(2) Goods to be merchantable must be at least such as

(a) pass without objection in the trade under the description in the lease agreement;

(b) in the case of fungible goods, are of fair average quality within the description;

(c) are fit for the ordinary purposes for which goods of that type are used;

(d) run, within the variation permitted by the lease agreement, of even kind, quality, and quantity within each unit and among all units involved;

(e) are adequately contained, packaged, and labeled as the lease agreement may require; and

(f) conform to any promises or affirmations of fact made on the container or label.

(3) Other implied warranties may arise from course of dealing or usage of trade.

§ 2A–213. Implied Warranty of Fitness for Particular Purpose.

Except in a finance of lease, if the lessor at the time the lease contract is made has reason to know of any particular purpose for which the goods are required and that the lessee is relying on the lessor's skill or judgment to select or furnish suitable goods, there is in the lease contract an implied warranty that the goods will be fit for that purpose.

§ 2A–214. Exclusion or Modification of Warranties.

(1) Words or conduct relevant to the creation of an express warranty and words or conduct tending to negate or limit a warranty must be construed wherever reasonable as consistent with each other; but, subject to the provisions of Section 2A–202 on parol or extrinsic evidence, negation or

limitation is inoperative to the extent that the construction is unreasonable.

(2) Subject to subsection (3), to exclude or modify the implied warranty of merchantability or any part of it the language must mention "merchantability", be by a writing, and be conspicuous. Subject to subsection (3), to exclude or modify any implied warranty of fitness the exclusion must be by a writing and be conspicuous. Language to exclude all implied warranties of fitness is sufficient if it is in writing, is conspicuous and states, for example, "There is no warranty that the goods will be fit for a particular purpose".

(3) Notwithstanding subsection (2), but subject to subsection (4),

(a) unless the circumstances indicate otherwise, all implied warranties are excluded by expressions like "as is" or "with all faults" or by other language that in common understanding calls the lessee's attention to the exclusion of warranties and makes plain that there is no implied warranty, if in writing and conspicuous;

(b) if the lessee before entering into the lease contract has examined the goods or the sample or model as fully as desired or has refused to examine the goods, there is no implied warranty with regard to defects that an examination ought in the circumstances to have revealed; and

(c) an implied warranty may also be excluded or modified by course of dealing, course of performance, or usage of trade.

(4) To exclude or modify a warranty against interference or against infringement (Section 2A–211) or any part of it, the language must be specific, be by a writing, and be conspicuous, unless the circumstances, including course of performance, course of dealing, or usage of trade, give the lessee reason to know that the goods are being leased subject to a claim or interest of any person.

§ 2A–215. Cumulation and Conflict of Warranties Express or Implied.

Warranties, whether express or implied, must be construed as consistent with each other and as cumulative, but if that construction is unreasonable, the intention of the parties determines which warranty is dominant. In ascertaining that intention the following rules apply:

(a) Exact or technical specifications displace an inconsistent sample or model or general language of description.

(b) A sample from an existing bulk displaces inconsistent general language of description.

(c) Express warranties displace inconsistent implied warranties other than an implied warranty of fitness for a particular purpose.

§ 2A–216. Third-Party Beneficiaries of Express and Implied Warranties.

Alternative A

A warranty to or for the benefit of a lessee under this Article, whether express or implied, extends to any natural person who is in the family or household of the lessee or who is a guest in the lessee's home if it is reasonable to expect that such person may use, consume, or be affected by the goods and who is injured in person by breach of the warranty. This section does not displace principles of law and equity that extend a warranty to or for the benefit of a lessee to other persons. The operation of this section may not be excluded, modified, or limited, but an exclusion, modification, or limitation of the warranty, including any with respect to rights and remedies, effective against the lessee is also effective against any beneficiary designated under this section.

Alternative B

A warranty to or for the benefit of a lessee under this Article, whether express or implied, extends to any natural person who may reasonably be expected to use, consume, or be affected by the goods and who is injured in person by breach of the warranty. This section does not displace principles of law and equity that extend a warranty to or for the benefit of a lessee to other persons. The operation of this section may not be excluded, modified, or limited, but an exclusion, modification, or limitation of the warranty, including any with respect to rights and remedies, effective against the lessee is also effective against the beneficiary designated under this section.

Alternative C

A warranty to or for the benefit of a lessee under this Article, whether express or implied, extends to any person who may reasonably be expected to use, consume, or be affected by the goods and who is injured by breach of the warranty. The operation of this section may not be excluded, modified, or limited with respect to injury to the person of an individual to whom the warranty extends, but an exclusion, modification, or limitation of the warranty, including any with respect to rights and remedies, effective against the lessee is also effective against the beneficiary designated under this section.

§ 2A–217. Identification.

Identification of goods as goods to which a lease contract refers may be made at any time and in any manner explicitly agreed to by the parties. In the absence of explicit agreement, identification occurs:

(a) when the lease contract is made if the lease contract is for a lease of goods that are existing and identified;

(b) when the goods are shipped, marked, or otherwise designated by the lessor as goods to which the lease contract refers, if the lease contract is for a lease of goods that are not existing and identified; or

(c) when the young are conceived, if the lease contract is for a lease of unborn young of animals.

§ 2A–218. Insurance and Proceeds.

(1) A lessee obtains an insurable interest when existing goods are identified to the lease contract even though the goods identified are nonconforming and the lessee has an option to reject them.

(2) If a lessee has an insurable interest only by reason of the lessor's identification of the goods, the lessor, until default or insolvency or notification to the lessee that identification is final, may substitute other goods for those identified.

(3) Notwithstanding a lessee's insurable interest under subsections (1) and (2), the lessor retains an insurable interest until an option to buy has been exercised by the lessee and risk of loss has passed to the lessee.

(4) Nothing in this section impairs any insurable interest recognized under any other statute or rule of law.

(5) The parties by agreement may determine that one or more parties have an obligation to obtain and pay for insurance covering the goods and by agreement may determine the beneficiary of the proceeds of the insurance.

§ 2A–219. Risk of Loss.

(1) Except in the case of a finance lease, risk of loss is retained by the lessor and does not pass to the lessee. In the case of a finance lease, risk of loss passes to the lessee.

(2) Subject to the provisions of this Article on the effect of default on risk of loss (Section 2A–220), if risk of loss is to pass to the lessee and the time of passage is not stated, the following rules apply:

(a) If the lease contract requires or authorizes the goods to be shipped by carrier

(i) and it does not require delivery at a particular destination, the risk of loss passes to the lessee when the goods are duly delivered to the carrier; but

(ii) if it does require delivery at a particular destination and the goods are there duly tendered while in the possession of the carrier, the risk of loss passes to the lessee when the goods are there duly so tendered as to enable the lessee to take delivery.

(b) If the goods are held by a bailee to be delivered without being moved, the risk of loss passes to the lessee on acknowledgment by the bailee of the lessee's right to possession of the goods.

(c) In any case not within subsection (a) or (b), the risk of loss passes to the lessee on the lessee's receipt of the goods if the lessor, or, in the case of a finance lease, the supplier, is a merchant; otherwise the risk passes to the lessee on tender of delivery.

§ 2A–220. Effect of Default on Risk of Loss.

(1) Where risk of loss is to pass to the lessee and the time of passage is not stated:

(a) If a tender or delivery of goods so fails to conform to the lease contract as to give a right of rejection, the risk of their loss remains with the lessor, or, in the case of a finance lease, the supplier, until cure or acceptance.

(b) If the lessee rightfully revokes acceptance, he [or she], to the extent of any deficiency in his [or her] effective insurance coverage, may treat the risk of loss as having remained with the lessor from the beginning.

(2) Whether or not risk of loss is to pass to the lessee, if the lessee as to conforming goods already identified to a lease contract repudiates or is otherwise in default under the lease contract, the lessor, or, in the case of a finance lease, the supplier, to the extent of any deficiency in his [or her] effective insurance coverage may treat the risk of loss as resting on the lessee for a commercially reasonable time.

§ 2A–221. Casualty to Identified Goods.

If a lease contract requires goods identified when the lease contract is made, and the goods suffer casualty without fault of the lessee, the lessor or the supplier before delivery, or the goods suffer casualty before risk of loss passes to the lessee pursuant to the lease agreement or Section 2A–219, then:

(a) if the loss is total, the lease contract is avoided; and

(b) if the loss is partial or the goods have so deteriorated as to no longer conform to the lease contract, the lessee may nevertheless demand inspection and at his [or her] option either treat the lease contract as avoided or, except in a finance lease that is not a consumer lease, accept the goods with due allowance from the rent payable for the balance of the lease term for the deterioration or the deficiency in quantity but without further right against the lessor.

Part 3 Effect of Lease Contract

§ 2A–301. Enforceability of Lease Contract.

Except as otherwise provided in this Article, a lease contract is effective and enforceable according to its terms between the parties, against purchasers of the goods and against creditors of the parties.

§ 2A–302. Title to and Possession of Goods.

Except as otherwise provided in this Article, each provision of this Article applies whether the lessor or a third party has title to the goods, and whether the lessor, the lessee, or a third party has possession of the goods, notwithstanding any statute or rule of law that possession or the absence of possession is fraudulent.

§ 2A–303. Alienability of Party's Interest Under Lease Contract or of Lessor's Residual Interest in Goods; Delegation of Performance; Transfer of Rights.

(1) As used in this section, "creation of a security interest" includes the sale of a lease contract that is subject to Article 9, Secured Transactions, by reason of Section 9–109(a)(3).

(2) Except as provided in subsections (3) and Section 9–407, a provision in a lease agreement which (i) prohibits the voluntary or involuntary transfer, including a transfer by sale, sublease, creation or enforcement of a security interest, or attachment, levy, or other judicial process, of an interest of a party under the lease contract or of the lessor's residual interest in the goods, or (ii) makes such a transfer an event of default, gives rise to the rights and remedies provided in subsection (4), but a transfer that is prohibited or is an event of default under the lease agreement is otherwise effective.

(3) A provision in a lease agreement which (i) prohibits a transfer of a right to damages for default with respect to the whole lease contract or of a right to payment arising out of the transferor's due performance of the transferor's entire obligation, or (ii) makes such a transfer an event of default, is not enforceable, and such a transfer is not a transfer that materially impairs the propsect of obtaining return performance by, materially changes the duty of, or materially increases the burden or risk imposed on, the other party to the lease contract within the purview of subsection (4).

(4) Subject to subsection (3) and Section 9–407:

(a) if a transfer is made which is made an event of default under a lease agreement, the party to the lease contract not making the transfer, unless that party waives the default or otherwise agrees, has the rights and remedies described in Section 2A–501(2);

(b) if paragraph (a) is not applicable and if a transfer is made that (i) is prohibited under a lease agreement or (ii) materially impairs the prospect of obtaining return performance by, materially changes the duty of, or materially increases the burden or risk imposed on, the other party to the lease contract, unless the party not making the transfer agrees at any time to the transfer in the lease contract or otherwise, then, except as limited by contract, (i) the transferor is liable to the party not making the transfer for damages caused by the transfer to the extent that the damages could not reasonably be prevented by the party not making the transfer and (ii) a court having jurisdiction may grant other appropriate relief, including cancellation of the lease contract or an injunction against the transfer.

(5) A transfer of "the lease" or of "all my rights under the lease", or a transfer in similar general terms, is a transfer of rights and, unless the language or the circumstances, as in a transfer for security, indicate the contrary, the transfer is a del-

egation of duties by the transferor to the transferee. Acceptance by the transferee constitutes a promise by the transferee to perform those duties. The promise is enforceable by either the transferor or the other party to the lease contract.

(6) Unless otherwise agreed by the lessor and the lessee, a delegation of performance does not relieve the transferor as against the other party of any duty to perform or of any liability for default.

(7) In a consumer lease, to prohibit the transfer of an interest of a party under the lease contract or to make a transfer an event of default, the language must be specific, by a writing, and conspicuous.

As amended in 1990 and 1999.

§ 2A–304. Subsequent Lease of Goods by Lessor.

(1) Subject to Section 2A–303, a subsequent lessee from a lessor of goods under an existing lease contract obtains, to the extent of the leasehold interest transferred, the leasehold interest in the goods that the lessor had or had power to transfer, and except as provided in subsection (2) and Section 2A–527(4), takes subject to the existing lease contract. A lessor with voidable title has power to transfer a good leasehold interest to a good faith subsequent lessee for value, but only to the extent set forth in the preceding sentence. If goods have been delivered under a transaction of purchase the lessor has that power even though:

(a) the lessor's transferor was deceived as to the identity of the lessor;

(b) the delivery was in exchange for a check which is later dishonored;

(c) it was agreed that the transaction was to be a "cash sale"; or

(d) the delivery was procured through fraud punishable as larcenous under the criminal law.

(2) A subsequent lessee in the ordinary course of business from a lessor who is a merchant dealing in goods of that kind to whom the goods were entrusted by the existing lessee of that lessor before the interest of the subsequent lessee became enforceable against that lessor obtains, to the extent of the leasehold interest transferred, all of that lessor's and the existing lessee's rights to the goods, and takes free of the existing lease contract.

(3) A subsequent lessee from the lessor of goods that are subject to an existing lease contract and are covered by a certificate of title issued under a statute of this State or of another jurisdiction takes no greater rights than those provided both by this section and by the certificate of title statute.

As amended in 1990.

§ 2A–305. Sale or Sublease of Goods by Lessee.

(1) Subject to the provisions of Section 2A–303, a buyer or sublessee from the lessee of goods under an existing lease con-

tract obtains, to the extent of the interest transferred, the lease-hold interest in the goods that the lessee had or had power to transfer, and except as provided in subsection (2) and Section 2A–511(4), takes subject to the existing lease contract. A lessee with a voidable leasehold interest has power to transfer a good leasehold interest to a good faith buyer for value or a good faith sublessee for value, but only to the extent set forth in the preceding sentence. When goods have been delivered under a transaction of lease the lessee has that power even though:

(a) the lessor was deceived as to the identity of the lessee;

(b) the delivery was in exchange for a check which is later dishonored; or

(c) the delivery was procured through fraud punishable as larcenous under the criminal law.

(2) A buyer in the ordinary course of business or a sublessee in the ordinary course of business from a lessee who is a merchant dealing in goods of that kind to whom the goods were entrusted by the lessor obtains, to the extent of the interest transferred, all of the lessor's and lessee's rights to the goods, and takes free of the existing lease contract.

(3) A buyer or sublessee from the lessee of goods that are subject to an existing lease contract and are covered by a certificate of title issued under a statute of this State or of another jurisdiction takes no greater rights than those provided both by this section and by the certificate of title statute.

§ 2A–306. Priority of Certain Liens Arising by Operation of Law.

If a person in the ordinary course of his [or her] business furnishes services or materials with respect to goods subject to a lease contract, a lien upon those goods in the possession of that person given by statute or rule of law for those materials or services takes priority over any interest of the lessor or lessee under the lease contract or this Article unless the lien is created by statute and the statute provides otherwise or unless the lien is created by rule of law and the rule of law provides otherwise.

§ 2A–307. Priority of Liens Arising by Attachment or Levy on, Security Interests in, and Other Claims to Goods.

(1) Except as otherwise provided in Section 2A–306, a creditor of a lessee takes subject to the lease contract.

(2) Except as otherwise provided in subsection (3) and in Sections 2A–306 and 2A–308, a creditor of a lessor takes subject to the lease contract unless the creditor holds a lien that attached to the goods before the lease contract became enforceable.

(3) Except as otherwise provided in Sections 9–317, 9–321, and 9–323, a lessee takes a leasehold interest subject to a security interest held by a creditor of the lessor.

As amended in 1990 and 1999.

§ 2A–308. Special Rights of Creditors.

(1) A creditor of a lessor in possession of goods subject to a lease contract may treat the lease contract as void if as against the creditor retention of possession by the lessor is fraudulent under any statute or rule of law, but retention of possession in good faith and current course of trade by the lessor for a commercially reasonable time after the lease contract becomes enforceable is not fraudulent.

(2) Nothing in this Article impairs the rights of creditors of a lessor if the lease contract (a) becomes enforceable, not in current course of trade but in satisfaction of or as security for a pre-existing claim for money, security, or the like, and (b) is made under circumstances which under any statute or rule of law apart from this Article would constitute the transaction a fraudulent transfer or voidable preference.

(3) A creditor of a seller may treat a sale or an identification of goods to a contract for sale as void if as against the creditor retention of possession by the seller is fraudulent under any statute or rule of law, but retention of possession of the goods pursuant to a lease contract entered into by the seller as lessee and the buyer as lessor in connection with the sale or identification of the goods is not fraudulent if the buyer bought for value and in good faith.

§ 2A–309. Lessor's and Lessee's Rights When Goods Become Fixtures.

(1) In this section:

(a) goods are "fixtures" when they become so related to particular real estate that an interest in them arises under real estate law;

(b) a "fixture filing" is the filing, in the office where a mortgage on the real estate would be filed or recorded, of a financing statement covering goods that are or are to become fixtures and conforming to the requirements of Section 9–502(a) and (b);

(c) a lease is a "purchase money lease" unless the lessee has possession or use of the goods or the right to possession or use of the goods before the lease agreement is enforceable;

(d) a mortgage is a "construction mortgage" to the extent it secures an obligation incurred for the construction of an improvement on land including the acquisition cost of the land, if the recorded writing so indicates; and

(e) "encumbrance" includes real estate mortgages and other liens on real estate and all other rights in real estate that are not ownership interests.

(2) Under this Article a lease may be of goods that are fixtures or may continue in goods that become fixtures, but no lease exists under this Article of ordinary building materials incorporated into an improvement on land.

(3) This Article does not prevent creation of a lease of fixtures pursuant to real estate law.

(4) The perfected interest of a lessor of fixtures has priority over a conflicting interest of an encumbrancer or owner of the real estate if:

(a) the lease is a purchase money lease, the conflicting interest of the encumbrancer or owner arises before the goods become fixtures, the interest of the lessor is perfected by a fixture filing before the goods become fixtures or within ten days thereafter, and the lessee has an interest of record in the real estate or is in possession of the real estate; or

(b) the interest of the lessor is perfected by a fixture filing before the interest of the encumbrancer or owner is of record, the lessor's interest has priority over any conflicting interest of a predecessor in title of the encumbrancer or owner, and the lessee has an interest of record in the real estate or is in possession of the real estate.

(5) The interest of a lessor of fixtures, whether or not perfected, has priority over the conflicting interest of an encumbrancer or owner of the real estate if:

(a) the fixtures are readily removable factory or office machines, readily removable equipment that is not primarily used or leased for use in the operation of the real estate, or readily removable replacements of domestic appliances that are goods subject to a consumer lease, and before the goods become fixtures the lease contract is enforceable; or

(b) the conflicting interest is a lien on the real estate obtained by legal or equitable proceedings after the lease contract is enforceable; or

(c) the encumbrancer or owner has consented in writing to the lease or has disclaimed an interest in the goods as fixtures; or

(d) the lessee has a right to remove the goods as against the encumbrancer or owner. If the lessee's right to remove terminates, the priority of the interest of the lessor continues for a reasonable time.

(6) Notwithstanding paragraph (4)(a) but otherwise subject to subsections (4) and (5), the interest of a lessor of fixtures, including the lessor's residual interest, is subordinate to the conflicting interest of an encumbrancer of the real estate under a construction mortgage recorded before the goods become fixtures if the goods become fixtures before the completion of the construction. To the extent given to refinance a construction mortgage, the conflicting interest of an encumbrancer of the real estate under a mortgage has this priority to the same extent as the encumbrancer of the real estate under the construction mortgage.

(7) In cases not within the preceding subsections, priority between the interest of a lessor of fixtures, including the lessor's residual interest, and the conflicting interest of an encumbrancer or owner of the real estate who is not the lessee is determined by the priority rules governing conflicting interests in real estate.

(8) If the interest of a lessor of fixtures, including the lessor's residual interest, has priority over all conflicting interests of all owners and encumbrancers of the real estate,

the lessor or the lessee may (i) on default, expiration, termination, or cancellation of the lease agreement but subject to the agreement and this Article, or (ii) if necessary to enforce other rights and remedies of the lessor or lessee under this Article, remove the goods from the real estate, free and clear of all conflicting interests of all owners and encumbrancers of the real estate, but the lessor or lessee must reimburse any encumbrancer or owner of the real estate who is not the lessee and who has not otherwise agreed for the cost of repair of any physical injury, but not for any diminution in value of the real estate caused by the absence of the goods removed or by any necessity of replacing them. A person entitled to reimbursement may refuse permission to remove until the party seeking removal gives adequate security for the performance of this obligation.

(9) Even though the lease agreement does not create a security interest, the interest of a lessor of fixtures, including the lessor's residual interest, is perfected by filing a financing statement as a fixture filing for leased goods that are or are to become fixtures in accordance with the relevant provisions of the Article on Secured Transactions (Article 9).

As amended in 1990 and 1999.

§ 2A–310. Lessor's and Lessee's Rights When Goods Become Accessions.

(1) Goods are "accessions" when they are installed in or affixed to other goods.

(2) The interest of a lessor or a lessee under a lease contract entered into before the goods became accessions is superior to all interests in the whole except as stated in subsection (4).

(3) The interest of a lessor or a lessee under a lease contract entered into at the time or after the goods became accessions is superior to all subsequently acquired interests in the whole except as stated in subsection (4) but is subordinate to interests in the whole existing at the time the lease contract was made unless the holders of such interests in the whole have in writing consented to the lease or disclaimed an interest in the goods as part of the whole.

(4) The interest of a lessor or a lessee under a lease contract described in subsection (2) or (3) is subordinate to the interest of

(a) a buyer in the ordinary course of business or a lessee in the ordinary course of business of any interest in the whole acquired after the goods became accessions; or

(b) a creditor with a security interest in the whole perfected before the lease contract was made to the extent that the creditor makes subsequent advances without knowledge of the lease contract.

(5) When under subsections (2) or (3) and (4) a lessor or a lessee of accessions holds an interest that is superior to all interests in the whole, the lessor or the lessee may (a) on default, expiration, termination, or cancellation of the lease contract by the other party but subject to the provisions of the lease contract and this Article, or (b) if necessary to

enforce his [or her] other rights and remedies under this Article, remove the goods from the whole, free and clear of all interests in the whole, but he [or she] must reimburse any holder of an interest in the whole who is not the lessee and who has not otherwise agreed for the cost of repair of any physical injury but not for any diminution in value of the whole caused by the absence of the goods removed or by any necessity for replacing them. A person entitled to reimbursement may refuse permission to remove until the party seeking removal gives adequate security for the performance of this obligation.

§ 2A–311. Priority Subject to Subordination.

Nothing in this Article prevents subordination by agreement by any person entitled to priority.

As added in 1990.

Part 4 Performance of Lease Contract: Repudiated, Substituted and Excused

§ 2A–401. Insecurity: Adequate Assurance of Performance.

(1) A lease contract imposes an obligation on each party that the other's expectation of receiving due performance will not be impaired.

(2) If reasonable grounds for insecurity arise with respect to the performance of either party, the insecure party may demand in writing adequate assurance of due performance. Until the insecure party receives that assurance, if commercially reasonable the insecure party may suspend any performance for which he [or she] has not already received the agreed return.

(3) A repudiation of the lease contract occurs if assurance of due performance adequate under the circumstances of the particular case is not provided to the insecure party within a reasonable time, not to exceed 30 days after receipt of a demand by the other party.

(4) Between merchants, the reasonableness of grounds for insecurity and the adequacy of any assurance offered must be determined according to commercial standards.

(5) Acceptance of any nonconforming delivery or payment does not prejudice the aggrieved party's right to demand adequate assurance of future performance.

§ 2A–402. Anticipatory Repudiation.

If either party repudiates a lease contract with respect to a performance not yet due under the lease contract, the loss of which performance will substantially impair the value of the lease contract to the other, the aggrieved party may:

(a) for a commercially reasonable time, await retraction of repudiation and performance by the repudiating party;

(b) make demand pursuant to Section 2A–401 and await assurance of future performance adequate under the circumstances of the particular case; or

(c) resort to any right or remedy upon default under the lease contract or this Article, even though the aggrieved party has notified the repudiating party that the aggrieved party would await the repudiating party's performance and assurance and has urged retraction. In addition, whether or not the aggrieved party is pursuing one of the foregoing remedies, the aggrieved party may suspend performance or, if the aggrieved party is the lessor, proceed in accordance with the provisions of this Article on the lessor's right to identify goods to the lease contract notwithstanding default or to salvage unfinished goods (Section 2A–524).

§ 2A–403. Retraction of Anticipatory Repudiation.

(1) Until the repudiating party's next performance is due, the repudiating party can retract the repudiation unless, since the repudiation, the aggrieved party has cancelled the lease contract or materially changed the aggrieved party's position or otherwise indicated that the aggrieved party considers the repudiation final.

(2) Retraction may be by any method that clearly indicates to the aggrieved party that the repudiating party intends to perform under the lease contract and includes any assurance demanded under Section 2A–401.

(3) Retraction reinstates a repudiating party's rights under a lease contract with due excuse and allowance to the aggrieved party for any delay occasioned by the repudiation.

§ 2A–404. Substituted Performance.

(1) If without fault of the lessee, the lessor and the supplier, the agreed berthing, loading, or unloading facilities fail or the agreed type of carrier becomes unavailable or the agreed manner of delivery otherwise becomes commercially impracticable, but a commercially reasonable substitute is available, the substitute performance must be tendered and accepted.

(2) If the agreed means or manner of payment fails because of domestic or foreign governmental regulation:

(a) the lessor may withhold or stop delivery or cause the supplier to withhold or stop delivery unless the lessee provides a means or manner of payment that is commercially a substantial equivalent; and

(b) if delivery has already been taken, payment by the means or in the manner provided by the regulation discharges the lessee's obligation unless the regulation is discriminatory, oppressive, or predatory.

§ 2A–405. Excused Performance.

Subject to Section 2A–404 on substituted performance, the following rules apply:

(a) Delay in delivery or nondelivery in whole or in part by a lessor or a supplier who complies with paragraphs (b) and (c) is not a default under the lease contract if performance as agreed has been made impracticable by the occurrence of a contingency the nonoccurrence of which was a basic assumption on which the lease contract was made or by compliance in good faith with any applicable foreign or domestic governmental regulation or order, whether or not the regulation or order later proves to be invalid.

(b) If the causes mentioned in paragraph (a) affect only part of the lessor's or the supplier's capacity to perform, he [or she] shall allocate production and deliveries among his [or her] customers but at his [or her] option may include regular customers not then under contract for sale or lease as well as his [or her] own requirements for further manufacture. He [or she] may so allocate in any manner that is fair and reasonable.

(c) The lessor seasonably shall notify the lessee and in the case of a finance lease the supplier seasonably shall notify the lessor and the lessee, if known, that there will be delay or nondelivery and, if allocation is required under paragraph (b), of the estimated quota thus made available for the lessee.

§ 2A–406. Procedure on Excused Performance.

(1) If the lessee receives notification of a material or indefinite delay or an allocation justified under Section 2A–405, the lessee may by written notification to the lessor as to any goods involved, and with respect to all of the goods if under an installment lease contract the value of the whole lease contract is substantially impaired (Section 2A–510):

  (a) terminate the lease contract (Section 2A–505(2)); or

  (b) except in a finance lease that is not a consumer lease, modify the lease contract by accepting the available quota in substitution, with due allowance from the rent payable for the balance of the lease term for the deficiency but without further right against the lessor.

(2) If, after receipt of a notification from the lessor under Section 2A–405, the lessee fails so to modify the lease agreement within a reasonable time not exceeding 30 days, the lease contract lapses with respect to any deliveries affected.

§ 2A–407. Irrevocable Promises: Finance Leases.

(1) In the case of a finance lease that is not a consumer lease the lessee's promises under the lease contract become irrevocable and independent upon the lessee's acceptance of the goods.

(2) A promise that has become irrevocable and independent under subsection (1):

  (a) is effective and enforceable between the parties, and by or against third parties including assignees of the parties, and

  (b) is not subject to cancellation, termination, modification, repudiation, excuse, or substitution without the consent of the party to whom the promise runs.

(3) This section does not affect the validity under any other law of a covenant in any lease contract making the lessee's promises irrevocable and independent upon the lessee's acceptance of the goods.

As amended in 1990.

Part 5 Default

A. In General

§ 2A–501. Default: Procedure.

(1) Whether the lessor or the lessee is in default under a lease contract is determined by the lease agreement and this Article.

(2) If the lessor or the lessee is in default under the lease contract, the party seeking enforcement has rights and remedies as provided in this Article and, except as limited by this Article, as provided in the lease agreement.

(3) If the lessor or the lessee is in default under the lease contract, the party seeking enforcement may reduce the party's claim to judgment, or otherwise enforce the lease contract by self-help or any available judicial procedure or nonjudicial procedure, including administrative proceeding, arbitration, or the like, in accordance with this Article.

(4) Except as otherwise provided in Section 1–106(1) or this Article or the lease agreement, the rights and remedies referred to in subsections (2) and (3) are cumulative.

(5) If the lease agreement covers both real property and goods, the party seeking enforcement may proceed under this Part as to the goods, or under other applicable law as to both the real property and the goods in accordance with that party's rights and remedies in respect of the real property, in which case this Part does not apply.

As amended in 1990.

§ 2A–502. Notice After Default.

Except as otherwise provided in this Article or the lease agreement, the lessor or lessee in default under the lease contract is not entitled to notice of default or notice of enforcement from the other party to the lease agreement.

§ 2A–503. Modification or Impairment of Rights and Remedies.

(1) Except as otherwise provided in this Article, the lease agreement may include rights and remedies for default in addition to or in substitution for those provided in this Article and may limit or alter the measure of damages recoverable under this Article.

(2) Resort to a remedy provided under this Article or in the lease agreement is optional unless the remedy is expressly agreed to be exclusive. If circumstances cause an exclusive or limited remedy to fail of its essential purpose, or provision for an exclusive remedy is unconscionable, remedy may be had as provided in this Article.

(3) Consequential damages may be liquidated under Section 2A–504, or may otherwise be limited, altered, or excluded unless the limitation, alteration, or exclusion is unconscionable. Limitation, alteration, or exclusion of consequential damages for injury to the person in the case of consumer goods is prima facie unconscionable but limitation, alteration, or exclusion of damages where the loss is commercial is not prima facie unconscionable.

(4) Rights and remedies on default by the lessor or the lessee with respect to any obligation or promise collateral or ancillary to the lease contract are not impaired by this Article.

As amended in 1990.

§ 2A–504. Liquidation of Damages.

(1) Damages payable by either party for default, or any other act or omission, including indemnity for loss or diminution of anticipated tax benefits or loss or damage to lessor's residual interest, may be liquidated in the lease agreement but only at an amount or by a formula that is reasonable in light of the then anticipated harm caused by the default or other act or omission.

(2) If the lease agreement provides for liquidation of damages, and such provision does not comply with subsection (1), or such provision is an exclusive or limited remedy that circumstances cause to fail of its essential purpose, remedy may be had as provided in this Article.

(3) If the lessor justifiably withholds or stops delivery of goods because of the lessee's default or insolvency (Section 2A–525 or 2A–526), the lessee is entitled to restitution of any amount by which the sum of his [or her] payments exceeds:

(a) the amount to which the lessor is entitled by virtue of terms liquidating the lessor's damages in accordance with subsection (1); or

(b) in the absence of those terms, 20 percent of the then present value of the total rent the lessee was obligated to pay for the balance of the lease term, or, in the case of a consumer lease, the lesser of such amount or $500.

(4) A lessee's right to restitution under subsection (3) is subject to offset to the extent the lessor establishes:

(a) a right to recover damages under the provisions of this Article other than subsection (1); and

(b) the amount or value of any benefits received by the lessee directly or indirectly by reason of the lease contract.

§ 2A–505. Cancellation and Termination and Effect of Cancellation, Termination, Rescission, or Fraud on Rights and Remedies.

(1) On cancellation of the lease contract, all obligations that are still executory on both sides are discharged, but any right based on prior default or performance survives, and the cancelling party also retains any remedy for default of the whole lease contract or any unperformed balance.

(2) On termination of the lease contract, all obligations that are still executory on both sides are discharged but any right based on prior default or performance survives.

(3) Unless the contrary intention clearly appears, expressions of "cancellation," "rescission," or the like of the lease contract may not be construed as a renunciation or discharge of any claim in damages for an antecedent default.

(4) Rights and remedies for material misrepresentation or fraud include all rights and remedies available under this Article for default.

(5) Neither rescission nor a claim for rescission of the lease contract nor rejection or return of the goods may bar or be deemed inconsistent with a claim for damages or other right or remedy.

§ 2A–506. Statute of Limitations.

(1) An action for default under a lease contract, including breach of warranty or indemnity, must be commenced within 4 years after the cause of action accrued. By the original lease contract the parties may reduce the period of limitation to not less than one year.

(2) A cause of action for default accrues when the act or omission on which the default or breach of warranty is based is or should have been discovered by the aggrieved party, or when the default occurs, whichever is later. A cause of action for indemnity accrues when the act or omission on which the claim for indemnity is based is or should have been discovered by the indemnified party, whichever is later.

(3) If an action commenced within the time limited by subsection (1) is so terminated as to leave available a remedy by another action for the same default or breach of warranty or indemnity, the other action may be commenced after the expiration of the time limited and within 6 months after the termination of the first action unless the termination resulted from voluntary discontinuance or from dismissal for failure or neglect to prosecute.

(4) This section does not alter the law on tolling of the statute of limitations nor does it apply to causes of action that have accrued before this Article becomes effective.

§ 2A–507. Proof of Market Rent: Time and Place.

(1) Damages based on market rent (Section 2A–519 or 2A–528) are determined according to the rent for the use of the goods concerned for a lease term identical to the remaining lease term of the original lease agreement and prevailing at the times specified in Sections 2A–519 and 2A–528.

(2) If evidence of rent for the use of the goods concerned for a lease term identical to the remaining lease term of the original lease agreement and prevailing at the times or places described in this Article is not readily available, the rent prevailing within any reasonable time before or after the time described or at any other place or for a different lease term which in commercial judgment or under usage of trade

would serve as a reasonable substitute for the one described may be used, making any proper allowance for the difference, including the cost of transporting the goods to or from the other place.

(3) Evidence of a relevant rent prevailing at a time or place or for a lease term other than the one described in this Article offered by one party is not admissible unless and until he [or she] has given the other party notice the court finds sufficient to prevent unfair surprise.

(4) If the prevailing rent or value of any goods regularly leased in any established market is in issue, reports in official publications or trade journals or in newspapers or periodicals of general circulation published as the reports of that market are admissible in evidence. The circumstances of the preparation of the report may be shown to affect its weight but not its admissibility.

As amended in 1990.

B. Default by Lessor

§ 2A–508. Lessee's Remedies.

(1) If a lessor fails to deliver the goods in conformity to the lease contract (Section 2A–509) or repudiates the lease contract (Section 2A–402), or a lessee rightfully rejects the goods (Section 2A–509) or justifiably revokes acceptance of the goods (Section 2A–517), then with respect to any goods involved, and with respect to all of the goods if under an installment lease contract the value of the whole lease contract is substantially impaired (Section 2A–510), the lessor is in default under the lease contract and the lessee may:

    (a) cancel the lease contract (Section 2A–505(1));

    (b) recover so much of the rent and security as has been paid and is just under the circumstances;

    (c) cover and recover damages as to all goods affected whether or not they have been identified to the lease contract (Sections 2A–518 and 2A–520), or recover damages for nondelivery (Sections 2A–519 and 2A–520);

    (d) exercise any other rights or pursue any other remedies provided in the lease contract.

(2) If a lessor fails to deliver the goods in conformity to the lease contract or repudiates the lease contract, the lessee may also:

    (a) if the goods have been identified, recover them (Section 2A–522); or

    (b) in a proper case, obtain specific performance or replevy the goods (Section 2A–521).

(3) If a lessor is otherwise in default under a lease contract, the lessee may exercise the rights and pursue the remedies provided in the lease contract, which may include a right to cancel the lease, and in Section 2A–519(3).

(4) If a lessor has breached a warranty, whether express or implied, the lessee may recover damages (Section 2A–519(4)).

(5) On rightful rejection or justifiable revocation of acceptance, a lessee has a security interest in goods in the lessee's possession or control for any rent and security that has been paid and any expenses reasonably incurred in their inspection, receipt, transportation, and care and custody and may hold those goods and dispose of them in good faith and in a commercially reasonable manner, subject to Section 2A–527(5).

(6) Subject to the provisions of Section 2A–407, a lessee, on notifying the lessor of the lessee's intention to do so, may deduct all or any part of the damages resulting from any default under the lease contract from any part of the rent still due under the same lease contract.

As amended in 1990.

§ 2A–509. Lessee's Rights on Improper Delivery; Rightful Rejection.

(1) Subject to the provisions of Section 2A–510 on default in installment lease contracts, if the goods or the tender or delivery fail in any respect to conform to the lease contract, the lessee may reject or accept the goods or accept any commercial unit or units and reject the rest of the goods.

(2) Rejection of goods is ineffective unless it is within a reasonable time after tender or delivery of the goods and the lessee seasonably notifies the lessor.

§ 2A–510. Installment Lease Contracts: Rejection and Default.

(1) Under an installment lease contract a lessee may reject any delivery that is nonconforming if the nonconformity substantially impairs the value of that delivery and cannot be cured or the nonconformity is a defect in the required documents; but if the nonconformity does not fall within subsection (2) and the lessor or the supplier gives adequate assurance of its cure, the lessee must accept that delivery.

(2) Whenever nonconformity or default with respect to one or more deliveries substantially impairs the value of the installment lease contract as a whole there is a default with respect to the whole. But, the aggrieved party reinstates the installment lease contract as a whole if the aggrieved party accepts a nonconforming delivery without seasonably notifying of cancellation or brings an action with respect only to past deliveries or demands performance as to future deliveries.

§ 2A–511. Merchant Lessee's Duties as to Rightfully Rejected Goods.

(1) Subject to any security interest of a lessee (Section 2A–508(5)), if a lessor or a supplier has no agent or place of business at the market of rejection, a merchant lessee, after rejection of goods in his [or her] possession or control, shall follow any reasonable instructions received from the lessor or the supplier with respect to the goods. In the absence of those instructions, a merchant lessee shall make reasonable efforts to sell, lease, or otherwise dispose of the goods for the lessor's account if they threaten to decline in value speedily.

Instructions are not reasonable if on demand indemnity for expenses is not forthcoming.

(2) If a merchant lessee (subsection (1)) or any other lessee (Section 2A–512) disposes of goods, he [or she] is entitled to reimbursement either from the lessor or the supplier or out of the proceeds for reasonable expenses of caring for and disposing of the goods and, if the expenses include no disposition commission, to such commission as is usual in the trade, or if there is none, to a reasonable sum not exceeding 10 percent of the gross proceeds.

(3) In complying with this section or Section 2A–512, the lessee is held only to good faith. Good faith conduct hereunder is neither acceptance or conversion nor the basis of an action for damages.

(4) A purchaser who purchases in good faith from a lessee pursuant to this section or Section 2A–512 takes the goods free of any rights of the lessor and the supplier even though the lessee fails to comply with one or more of the requirements of this Article.

§ 2A–512. Lessee's Duties as to Rightfully Rejected Goods.

(1) Except as otherwise provided with respect to goods that threaten to decline in value speedily (Section 2A–511) and subject to any security interest of a lessee (Section 2A–508(5)):

(a) the lessee, after rejection of goods in the lessee's possession, shall hold them with reasonable care at the lessor's or the supplier's disposition for a reasonable time after the lessee's seasonable notification of rejection;

(b) if the lessor or the supplier gives no instructions within a reasonable time after notification of rejection, the lessee may store the rejected goods for the lessor's or the supplier's account or ship them to the lessor or the supplier or dispose of them for the lessor's or the supplier's account with reimbursement in the manner provided in Section 2A–511; but

(c) the lessee has no further obligations with regard to goods rightfully rejected.

(2) Action by the lessee pursuant to subsection (1) is not acceptance or conversion.

§ 2A–513. Cure by Lessor of Improper Tender or Delivery; Replacement.

(1) If any tender or delivery by the lessor or the supplier is rejected because nonconforming and the time for performance has not yet expired, the lessor or the supplier may seasonably notify the lessee of the lessor's or the supplier's intention to cure and may then make a conforming delivery within the time provided in the lease contract.

(2) If the lessee rejects a nonconforming tender that the lessor or the supplier had reasonable grounds to believe would be acceptable with or without money allowance, the

lessor or the supplier may have a further reasonable time to substitute a conforming tender if he [or she] seasonably notifies the lessee.

§ 2A–514. Waiver of Lessee's Objections.

(1) In rejecting goods, a lessee's failure to state a particular defect that is ascertainable by reasonable inspection precludes the lessee from relying on the defect to justify rejection or to establish default:

(a) if, stated seasonably, the lessor or the supplier could have cured it (Section 2A–513); or

(b) between merchants if the lessor or the supplier after rejection has made a request in writing for a full and final written statement of all defects on which the lessee proposes to rely.

(2) A lessee's failure to reserve rights when paying rent or other consideration against documents precludes recovery of the payment for defects apparent on the face of the documents.

§ 2A–515. Acceptance of Goods.

(1) Acceptance of goods occurs after the lessee has had a reasonable opportunity to inspect the goods and

(a) the lessee signifies or acts with respect to the goods in a manner that signifies to the lessor or the supplier that the goods are conforming or that the lessee will take or retain them in spite of their nonconformity; or

(b) the lessee fails to make an effective rejection of the goods (Section 2A–509(2)).

(2) Acceptance of a part of any commercial unit is acceptance of that entire unit.

§ 2A–516. Effect of Acceptance of Goods; Notice of Default; Burden of Establishing Default after Acceptance; Notice of Claim or Litigation to Person Answerable Over.

(1) A lessee must pay rent for any goods accepted in accordance with the lease contract, with due allowance for goods rightfully rejected or not delivered.

(2) A lessee's acceptance of goods precludes rejection of the goods accepted. In the case of a finance lease, if made with knowledge of a nonconformity, acceptance cannot be revoked because of it. In any other case, if made with knowledge of a nonconformity, acceptance cannot be revoked because of it unless the acceptance was on the reasonable assumption that the nonconformity would be seasonably cured. Acceptance does not of itself impair any other remedy provided by this Article or the lease agreement for nonconformity.

(3) If a tender has been accepted:

(a) within a reasonable time after the lessee discovers or should have discovered any default, the lessee shall notify the lessor and the supplier, if any, or be barred from any remedy against the party notified;

(b) except in the case of a consumer lease, within a reasonable time after the lessee receives notice of litigation for infringement or the like (Section 2A–211) the lessee shall notify the lessor or be barred from any remedy over for liability established by the litigation; and

(c) the burden is on the lessee to establish any default.

(4) If a lessee is sued for breach of a warranty or other obligation for which a lessor or a supplier is answerable over the following apply:

(a) The lessee may give the lessor or the supplier, or both, written notice of the litigation. If the notice states that the person notified may come in and defend and that if the person notified does not do so that person will be bound in any action against that person by the lessee by any determination of fact common to the two litigations, then unless the person notified after seasonable receipt of the notice does come in and defend that person is so bound.

(b) The lessor or the supplier may demand in writing that the lessee turn over control of the litigation including settlement if the claim is one for infringement or the like (Section 2A–211) or else be barred from any remedy over. If the demand states that the lessor or the supplier agrees to bear all expense and to satisfy any adverse judgment, then unless the lessee after seasonable receipt of the demand does turn over control the lessee is so barred.

(5) Subsections (3) and (4) apply to any obligation of a lessee to hold the lessor or the supplier harmless against infringement or the like (Section 2A–211).

As amended in 1990.

§ 2A–517. Revocation of Acceptance of Goods.

(1) A lessee may revoke acceptance of a lot or commercial unit whose nonconformity substantially impairs its value to the lessee if the lessee has accepted it:

(a) except in the case of a finance lease, on the reasonable assumption that its nonconformity would be cured and it has not been seasonably cured; or

(b) without discovery of the nonconformity if the lessee's acceptance was reasonably induced either by the lessor's assurances or, except in the case of a finance lease, by the difficulty of discovery before acceptance.

(2) Except in the case of a finance lease that is not a consumer lease, a lessee may revoke acceptance of a lot or commercial unit if the lessor defaults under the lease contract and the default substantially impairs the value of that lot or commercial unit to the lessee.

(3) If the lease agreement so provides, the lessee may revoke acceptance of a lot or commercial unit because of other defaults by the lessor.

(4) Revocation of acceptance must occur within a reasonable time after the lessee discovers or should have discovered the ground for it and before any substantial change in condition of the goods which is not caused by the nonconformity. Revocation is not effective until the lessee notifies the lessor.

(5) A lessee who so revokes has the same rights and duties with regard to the goods involved as if the lessee had rejected them.

As amended in 1990.

§ 2A–518. Cover; Substitute Goods.

(1) After a default by a lessor under the lease contract of the type described in Section 2A–508(1), or, if agreed, after other default by the lessor, the lessee may cover by making any purchase or lease of or contract to purchase or lease goods in substitution for those due from the lessor.

(2) Except as otherwise provided with respect to damages liquidated in the lease agreement (Section 2A–504) or otherwise determined pursuant to agreement of the parties (Sections 1–102(3) and 2A–503), if a lessee's cover is by lease agreement substantially similar to the original lease agreement and the new lease agreement is made in good faith and in a commercially reasonable manner, the lessee may recover from the lessor as damages (i) the present value, as of the date of the commencement of the term of the new lease agreement, of the rent under the new lease agreement applicable to that period of the new lease term which is comparable to the then remaining term of the original lease agreement minus the present value as of the same date of the total rent for the then remaining lease term of the original lease agreement, and (ii) any incidental or consequential damages, less expenses saved in consequence of the lessor's default.

(3) If a lessee's cover is by lease agreement that for any reason does not qualify for treatment under subsection (2), or is by purchase or otherwise, the lessee may recover from the lessor as if the lessee had elected not to cover and Section 2A–519 governs.

As amended in 1990.

§ 2A–519. Lessee's Damages for Non-Delivery, Repudiation, Default, and Breach of Warranty in Regard to Accepted Goods.

(1) Except as otherwise provided with respect to damages liquidated in the lease agreement (Section 2A–504) or otherwise determined pursuant to agreement of the parties (Sections 1–102(3) and 2A–503), if a lessee elects not to cover or a lessee elects to cover and the cover is by lease agreement that for any reason does not qualify for treatment under Section 2A–518(2), or is by purchase or otherwise, the measure of damages for non-delivery or repudiation by the lessor or for rejection or revocation of acceptance by the lessee is the present value, as of the date of the default, of the then market rent minus the present value as of the same

date of the original rent, computed for the remaining lease term of the original lease agreement, together with incidental and consequential damages, less expenses saved in consequence of the lessor's default.

(2) Market rent is to be determined as of the place for tender or, in cases of rejection after arrival or revocation of acceptance, as of the place of arrival.

(3) Except as otherwise agreed, if the lessee has accepted goods and given notification (Section 2A–516(3)), the measure of damages for non-conforming tender or delivery or other default by a lessor is the loss resulting in the ordinary course of events from the lessor's default as determined in any manner that is reasonable together with incidental and consequential damages, less expenses saved in consequence of the lessor's default.

(4) Except as otherwise agreed, the measure of damages for breach of warranty is the present value at the time and place of acceptance of the difference between the value of the use of the goods accepted and the value if they had been as warranted for the lease term, unless special circumstances show proximate damages of a different amount, together with incidental and consequential damages, less expenses saved in consequence of the lessor's default or breach of warranty.

As amended in 1990.

§ 2A–520. Lessee's Incidental and Consequential Damages.

(1) Incidental damages resulting from a lessor's default include expenses reasonably incurred in inspection, receipt, transportation, and care and custody of goods rightfully rejected or goods the acceptance of which is justifiably revoked, any commercially reasonable charges, expenses or commissions in connection with effecting cover, and any other reasonable expense incident to the default.

(2) Consequential damages resulting from a lessor's default include:

(a) any loss resulting from general or particular requirements and needs of which the lessor at the time of contracting had reason to know and which could not reasonably be prevented by cover or otherwise; and

(b) injury to person or property proximately resulting from any breach of warranty.

§ 2A–521. Lessee's Right to Specific Performance or Replevin.

(1) Specific performance may be decreed if the goods are unique or in other proper circumstances.

(2) A decree for specific performance may include any terms and conditions as to payment of the rent, damages, or other relief that the court deems just.

(3) A lessee has a right of replevin, detinue, sequestration, claim and delivery, or the like for goods identified to the lease contract if after reasonable effort the lessee is unable

to effect cover for those goods or the circumstances reasonably indicate that the effort will be unavailing.

§ 2A–522. Lessee's Right to Goods on Lessor's Insolvency.

(1) Subject to subsection (2) and even though the goods have not been shipped, a lessee who has paid a part or all of the rent and security for goods identified to a lease contract (Section 2A–217) on making and keeping good a tender of any unpaid portion of the rent and security due under the lease contract may recover the goods identified from the lessor if the lessor becomes insolvent within 10 days after receipt of the first installment of rent and security.

(2) A lessee acquires the right to recover goods identified to a lease contract only if they conform to the lease contract.

C. Default by Lessee

§ 2A–523. Lessor's Remedies.

(1) If a lessee wrongfully rejects or revokes acceptance of goods or fails to make a payment when due or repudiates with respect to a part or the whole, then, with respect to any goods involved, and with respect to all of the goods if under an installment lease contract the value of the whole lease contract is substantially impaired (Section 2A–510), the lessee is in default under the lease contract and the lessor may:

(a) cancel the lease contract (Section 2A–505(1));

(b) proceed respecting goods not identified to the lease contract (Section 2A–524);

(c) withhold delivery of the goods and take possession of goods previously delivered (Section 2A–525);

(d) stop delivery of the goods by any bailee (Section 2A–526);

(e) dispose of the goods and recover damages (Section 2A–527), or retain the goods and recover damages (Section 2A–528), or in a proper case recover rent (Section 2A–529)

(f) exercise any other rights or pursue any other remedies provided in the lease contract.

(2) If a lessor does not fully exercise a right or obtain a remedy to which the lessor is entitled under subsection (1), the lessor may recover the loss resulting in the ordinary course of events from the lessee's default as determined in any reasonable manner, together with incidental damages, less expenses saved in consequence of the lessee's default.

(3) If a lessee is otherwise in default under a lease contract, the lessor may exercise the rights and pursue the remedies provided in the lease contract, which may include a right to cancel the lease. In addition, unless otherwise provided in the lease contract:

(a) if the default substantially impairs the value of the lease contract to the lessor, the lessor may exercise the rights and pursue the remedies provided in subsections (1) or (2); or

(b) if the default does not substantially impair the value of the lease contract to the lessor, the lessor may recover as provided in subsection (2).

As amended in 1990.

§ 2A–524. Lessor's Right to Identify Goods to Lease Contract.

(1) After default by the lessee under the lease contract of the type described in Section 2A–523(1) or 2A–523(3)(a) or, if agreed, after other default by the lessee, the lessor may:

(a) identify to the lease contract conforming goods not already identified if at the time the lessor learned of the default they were in the lessor's or the supplier's possession or control; and

(b) dispose of goods (Section 2A–527(1)) that demonstrably have been intended for the particular lease contract even though those goods are unfinished.

(2) If the goods are unfinished, in the exercise of reasonable commercial judgment for the purposes of avoiding loss and of effective realization, an aggrieved lessor or the supplier may either complete manufacture and wholly identify the goods to the lease contract or cease manufacture and lease, sell, or otherwise dispose of the goods for scrap or salvage value or proceed in any other reasonable manner.

As amended in 1990.

§ 2A–525. Lessor's Right to Possession of Goods.

(1) If a lessor discovers the lessee to be insolvent, the lessor may refuse to deliver the goods.

(2) After a default by the lessee under the lease contract of the type described in Section 2A–523(1) or 2A–523(3)(a) or, if agreed, after other default by the lessee, the lessor has the right to take possession of the goods. If the lease contract so provides, the lessor may require the lessee to assemble the goods and make them available to the lessor at a place to be designated by the lessor which is reasonably convenient to both parties. Without removal, the lessor may render unusable any goods employed in trade or business, and may dispose of goods on the lessee's premises (Section 2A–527).

(3) The lessor may proceed under subsection (2) without judicial process if that can be done without breach of the peace or the lessor may proceed by action.

As amended in 1990.

§ 2A–526. Lessor's Stoppage of Delivery in Transit or Otherwise.

(1) A lessor may stop delivery of goods in the possession of a carrier or other bailee if the lessor discovers the lessee to be insolvent and may stop delivery of carload, truckload, planeload, or larger shipments of express or freight if the lessee repudiates or fails to make a payment due before delivery, whether for rent, security or otherwise under the lease

contract, or for any other reason the lessor has a right to withhold or take possession of the goods.

(2) In pursuing its remedies under subsection (1), the lessor may stop delivery until

(a) receipt of the goods by the lessee;

(b) acknowledgment to the lessee by any bailee of the goods, except a carrier, that the bailee holds the goods for the lessee; or

(c) such an acknowledgment to the lessee by a carrier via reshipment or as warehouseman.

(3) (a) To stop delivery, a lessor shall so notify as to enable the bailee by reasonable diligence to prevent delivery of the goods.

(b) After notification, the bailee shall hold and deliver the goods according to the directions of the lessor, but the lessor is liable to the bailee for any ensuing charges or damages.

(c) A carrier who has issued a nonnegotiable bill of lading is not obliged to obey a notification to stop received from a person other than the consignor.

§ 2A–527. Lessor's Rights to Dispose of Goods.

(1) After a default by a lessee under the lease contract of the type described in Section 2A–523(1) or 2A–523(3)(a) or after the lessor refuses to deliver or takes possession of goods (Section 2A–525 or 2A–526), or, if agreed, after other default by a lessee, the lessor may dispose of the goods concerned or the undelivered balance thereof by lease, sale, or otherwise.

(2) Except as otherwise provided with respect to damages liquidated in the lease agreement (Section 2A–504) or otherwise determined pursuant to agreement of the parties (Sections 1–102(3) and 2A–503), if the disposition is by lease agreement substantially similar to the original lease agreement and the new lease agreement is made in good faith and in a commercially reasonable manner, the lessor may recover from the lessee as damages (i) accrued and unpaid rent as of the date of the commencement of the term of the new lease agreement, (ii) the present value, as of the same date, of the total rent for the then remaining lease term of the original lease agreement minus the present value, as of the same date, of the rent under the new lease agreement applicable to that period of the new lease term which is comparable to the then remaining term of the original lease agreement, and (iii) any incidental damages allowed under Section 2A–530, less expenses saved in consequence of the lessee's default.

(3) If the lessor's disposition is by lease agreement that for any reason does not qualify for treatment under subsection (2), or is by sale or otherwise, the lessor may recover from the lessee as if the lessor had elected not to dispose of the goods and Section 2A–528 governs.

(4) A subsequent buyer or lessee who buys or leases from the lessor in good faith for value as a result of a disposition under this section takes the goods free of the original lease

contract and any rights of the original lessee even though the lessor fails to comply with one or more of the requirements of this Article.

(5) The lessor is not accountable to the lessee for any profit made on any disposition. A lessee who has rightfully rejected or justifiably revoked acceptance shall account to the lessor for any excess over the amount of the lessee's security interest (Section 2A–508(5)).

As amended in 1990.

§ 2A–528. Lessor's Damages for Non-acceptance, Failure to Pay, Repudiation, or Other Default.

(1) Except as otherwise provided with respect to damages liquidated in the lease agreement (Section 2A–504) or otherwise determined pursuant to agreement of the parties (Section 1–102(3) and 2A–503), if a lessor elects to retain the goods or a lessor elects to dispose of the goods and the disposition is by lease agreement that for any reason does not qualify for treatment under Section 2A–527(2), or is by sale or otherwise, the lessor may recover from the lessee as damages for a default of the type described in Section 2A–523(1) or 2A–523(3)(a), or if agreed, for other default of the lessee, (i) accrued and unpaid rent as of the date of the default if the lessee has never taken possession of the goods, or, if the lessee has taken possession of the goods, as of the date the lessor repossesses the goods or an earlier date on which the lessee makes a tender of the goods to the lessor, (ii) the present value as of the date determined under clause (i) of the total rent for the then remaining lease term of the original lease agreement minus the present value as of the same date of the market rent as the place where the goods are located computed for the same lease term, and (iii) any incidental damages allowed under Section 2A–530, less expenses saved in consequence of the lessee's default.

(2) If the measure of damages provided in subsection (1) is inadequate to put a lessor in as good a position as performance would have, the measure of damages is the present value of the profit, including reasonable overhead, the lessor would have made from full performance by the lessee, together with any incidental damages allowed under Section 2A–530, due allowance for costs reasonably incurred and due credit for payments or proceeds of disposition.

As amended in 1990.

§ 2A–529. Lessor's Action for the Rent.

(1) After default by the lessee under the lease contract of the type described in Section 2A–523(1) or 2A–523(3)(a) or, if agreed, after other default by the lessee, if the lessor complies with subsection (2), the lessor may recover from the lessee as damages:

(a) for goods accepted by the lessee and not repossessed by or tendered to the lessor, and for conforming goods lost or damaged within a commercially reasonable time after risk of loss passes to the lessee (Section 2A–219), (i) accrued and unpaid rent as of the date of entry of judg-

ment in favor of the lessor (ii) the present value as of the same date of the rent for the then remaining lease term of the lease agreement, and (iii) any incidental damages allowed under Section 2A–530, less expenses saved in consequence of the lessee's default; and

(b) for goods identified to the lease contract if the lessor is unable after reasonable effort to dispose of them at a reasonable price or the circumstances reasonably indicate that effort will be unavailing, (i) accrued and unpaid rent as of the date of entry of judgment in favor of the lessor, (ii) the present value as of the same date of the rent for the then remaining lease term of the lease agreement, and (iii) any incidental damages allowed under Section 2A–530, less expenses saved in consequence of the lessee's default.

(2) Except as provided in subsection (3), the lessor shall hold for the lessee for the remaining lease term of the lease agreement any goods that have been identified to the lease contract and are in the lessor's control.

(3) The lessor may dispose of the goods at any time before collection of the judgment for damages obtained pursuant to subsection (1). If the disposition is before the end of the remaining lease term of the lease agreement, the lessor's recovery against the lessee for damages is governed by Section 2A–527 or Section 2A–528, and the lessor will cause an appropriate credit to be provided against a judgment for damages to the extent that the amount of the judgment exceeds the recovery available pursuant to Section 2A–527 or 2A–528.

(4) Payment of the judgment for damages obtained pursuant to subsection (1) entitles the lessee to the use and possession of the goods not then disposed of for the remaining lease term of and in accordance with the lease agreement.

(5) After default by the lessee under the lease contract of the type described in Section 2A–523(1) or Section 2A–523(3)(a) or, if agreed, after other default by the lessee, a lessor who is held not entitled to rent under this section must nevertheless be awarded damages for non-acceptance under Sections 2A–527 and 2A–528.

As amended in 1990.

§ 2A–530. Lessor's Incidental Damages.

Incidental damages to an aggrieved lessor include any commercially reasonable charges, expenses, or commissions incurred in stopping delivery, in the transportation, care and custody of goods after the lessee's default, in connection with return or disposition of the goods, or otherwise resulting from the default.

§ 2A–531. Standing to Sue Third Parties for Injury to Goods.

(1) If a third party so deals with goods that have been identified to a lease contract as to cause actionable injury to a party to the lease contract (a) the lessor has a right of action

against the third party, and (b) the lessee also has a right of action against the third party if the lessee:

 (i) has a security interest in the goods;

 (ii) has an insurable interest in the goods; or

 (iii) bears the risk of loss under the lease contract or has since the injury assumed that risk as against the lessor and the goods have been converted or destroyed.

(2) If at the time of the injury the party plaintiff did not bear the risk of loss as against the other party to the lease contract and there is no arrangement between them for disposition of the recovery, his [or her] suit or settlement, subject to his [or her] own interest, is as a fiduciary for the other party to the lease contract.

(3) Either party with the consent of the other may sue for the benefit of whom it may concern.

§ 2A–532. Lessor's Rights to Residual Interest.

In addition to any other recovery permitted by this Article or other law, the lessor may recover from the lessee an amount that will fully compensate the lessor for any loss of or damage to the lessor's residual interest in the goods caused by the default of the lessee.

As added in 1990.

Revised Article 3
NEGOTIABLE INSTRUMENTS

Part 1 General Provisions and Definitions

§ 3–101. Short Title.

This Article may be cited as Uniform Commercial Code–Negotiable Instruments.

§ 3–102. Subject Matter.

(a) This Article applies to negotiable instruments. It does not apply to money, to payment orders governed by Article 4A, or to securities governed by Article 8.

(b) If there is conflict between this Article and Article 4 or 9, Articles 4 and 9 govern.

(c) Regulations of the Board of Governors of the Federal Reserve System and operating circulars of the Federal Reserve Banks supersede any inconsistent provision of this Article to the extent of the inconsistency.

§ 3–103. Definitions.

(a) In this Article:

 (1) "Acceptor" means a drawee who has accepted a draft.

 (2) "Drawee" means a person ordered in a draft to make payment.

 (3) "Drawer" means a person who signs or is identified in a draft as a person ordering payment.

 (4) "Good faith" means honesty in fact and the observance of reasonable commercial standards of fair dealing.

 (5) "Maker" means a person who signs or is identified in a note as a person undertaking to pay.

 (6) "Order" means a written instruction to pay money signed by the person giving the instruction. The instruction may be addressed to any person, including the person giving the instruction, or to one or more persons jointly or in the alternative but not in succession. An authorization to pay is not an order unless the person authorized to pay is also instructed to pay.

 (7) "Ordinary care" in the case of a person engaged in business means observance of reasonable commercial standards, prevailing in the area in which the person is located, with respect to the business in which the person is engaged. In the case of a bank that takes an instrument for processing for collection or payment by automated means, reasonable commercial standards do not require the bank to examine the instrument if the failure to examine does not violate the bank's prescribed procedures and the bank's procedures do not vary unreasonably from general banking usage not disapproved by this Article or Article 4.

 (8) "Party" means a party to an instrument.

 (9) "Promise" means a written undertaking to pay money signed by the person undertaking to pay. An acknowledgment of an obligation by the obligor is not a promise unless the obligor also undertakes to pay the obligation.

 (10) "Prove" with respect to a fact means to meet the burden of establishing the fact (Section 1–201(8)).

 (11) "Remitter" means a person who purchases an instrument from its issuer if the instrument is payable to an identified person other than the purchaser.

(b) [Other definitions' section references deleted.]

(c) [Other definitions' section references deleted.]

(d) In addition, Article 1 contains general definitions and principles of construction and interpretation applicable throughout this Article.

§ 3–104. Negotiable Instrument.

(a) Except as provided in subsections (c) and (d), "negotiable instrument" means an unconditional promise or order to pay a fixed amount of money, with or without interest or other charges described in the promise or order, if it:

 (1) is payable to bearer or to order at the time it is issued or first comes into possession of a holder;

 (2) is payable on demand or at a definite time; and

 (3) does not state any other undertaking or instruction by the person promising or ordering payment to do any act in addition to the payment of money, but the promise or order may contain (i) an undertaking or power to

give, maintain, or protect collateral to secure payment, (ii) an authorization or power to the holder to confess judgment or realize on or dispose of collateral, or (iii) a waiver of the benefit of any law intended for the advantage or protection of an obligor.

(b) "Instrument" means a negotiable instrument.

(c) An order that meets all of the requirements of subsection (a), except paragraph (1), and otherwise falls within the definition of "check" in subsection (f) is a negotiable instrument and a check.

(d) A promise or order other than a check is not an instrument if, at the time it is issued or first comes into possession of a holder, it contains a conspicuous statement, however expressed, to the effect that the promise or order is not negotiable or is not an instrument governed by this Article.

(e) An instrument is a "note" if it is a promise and is a "draft" if it is an order. If an instrument falls within the definition of both "note" and "draft," a person entitled to enforce the instrument may treat it as either.

(f) "Check" means (i) a draft, other than a documentary draft, payable on demand and drawn on a bank or (ii) a cashier's check or teller's check. An instrument may be a check even though it is described on its face by another term, such as "money order."

(g) "Cashier's check" means a draft with respect to which the drawer and drawee are the same bank or branches of the same bank.

(h) "Teller's check" means a draft drawn by a bank (i) on another bank, or (ii) payable at or through a bank.

(i) "Traveler's check" means an instrument that (i) is payable on demand, (ii) is drawn on or payable at or through a bank, (iii) is designated by the term "traveler's check" or by a substantially similar term, and (iv) requires, as a condition to payment, a countersignature by a person whose specimen signature appears on the instrument.

(j) "Certificate of deposit" means an instrument containing an acknowledgment by a bank that a sum of money has been received by the bank and a promise by the bank to repay the sum of money. A certificate of deposit is a note of the bank.

§ 3–105. Issue of Instrument.

(a) "Issue" means the first delivery of an instrument by the maker or drawer, whether to a holder or nonholder, for the purpose of giving rights on the instrument to any person.

(b) An unissued instrument, or an unissued incomplete instrument that is completed, is binding on the maker or drawer, but nonissuance is a defense. An instrument that is conditionally issued or is issued for a special purpose is binding on the maker or drawer, but failure of the condition or special purpose to be fulfilled is a defense.

(c) "Issuer" applies to issued and unissued instruments and means a maker or drawer of an instrument.

§ 3–106. Unconditional Promise or Order.

(a) Except as provided in this section, for the purposes of Section 3–104(a), a promise or order is unconditional unless it states (i) an express condition to payment, (ii) that the promise or order is subject to or governed by another writing, or (iii) that rights or obligations with respect to the promise or order are stated in another writing. A reference to another writing does not of itself make the promise or order conditional.

(b) A promise or order is not made conditional (i) by a reference to another writing for a statement of rights with respect to collateral, prepayment, or acceleration, or (ii) because payment is limited to resort to a particular fund or source.

(c) If a promise or order requires, as a condition to payment, a countersignature by a person whose specimen signature appears on the promise or order, the condition does not make the promise or order conditional for the purposes of Section 3–104(a). If the person whose specimen signature appears on an instrument fails to countersign the instrument, the failure to countersign is a defense to the obligation of the issuer, but the failure does not prevent a transferee of the instrument from becoming a holder of the instrument.

(d) If a promise or order at the time it is issued or first comes into possession of a holder contains a statement, required by applicable statutory or administrative law, to the effect that the rights of a holder or transferee are subject to claims or defenses that the issuer could assert against the original payee, the promise or order is not thereby made conditional for the purposes of Section 3–104(a); but if the promise or order is an instrument, there cannot be a holder in due course of the instrument.

§ 3–107. Instrument Payable in Foreign Money.

Unless the instrument otherwise provides, an instrument that states the amount payable in foreign money may be paid in the foreign money or in an equivalent amount in dollars calculated by using the current bank-offered spot rate at the place of payment for the purchase of dollars on the day on which the instrument is paid.

§ 3–108. Payable on Demand or at Definite Time.

(a) A promise or order is "payable on demand" if it (i) states that it is payable on demand or at sight, or otherwise indicates that it is payable at the will of the holder, or (ii) does not state any time of payment.

(b) A promise or order is "payable at a definite time" if it is payable on elapse of a definite period of time after sight or acceptance or at a fixed date or dates or at a time or times readily ascertainable at the time the promise or order is issued, subject to rights of (i) prepayment, (ii) acceleration, (iii) extension at the option of the holder, or (iv) extension to a further definite time at the option of the maker or acceptor or automatically upon or after a specified act or event.

(c) If an instrument, payable at a fixed date, is also payable upon demand made before the fixed date, the instrument is payable on demand until the fixed date and, if demand for payment is not made before that date, becomes payable at a definite time on the fixed date.

§ 3–109. Payable to Bearer or to Order.

(a) A promise or order is payable to bearer if it:

(1) states that it is payable to bearer or to the order of bearer or otherwise indicates that the person in possession of the promise or order is entitled to payment;

(2) does not state a payee; or

(3) states that it is payable to or to the order of cash or otherwise indicates that it is not payable to an identified person.

(b) A promise or order that is not payable to bearer is payable to order if it is payable (i) to the order of an identified person or (ii) to an identified person or order. A promise or order that is payable to order is payable to the identified person.

(c) An instrument payable to bearer may become payable to an identified person if it is specially indorsed pursuant to Section 3–205(a). An instrument payable to an identified person may become payable to bearer if it is indorsed in blank pursuant to Section 3–205(b).

§ 3–110. Identification of Person to Whom Instrument Is Payable.

(a) The person to whom an instrument is initially payable is determined by the intent of the person, whether or not authorized, signing as, or in the name or behalf of, the issuer of the instrument. The instrument is payable to the person intended by the signer even if that person is identified in the instrument by a name or other identification that is not that of the intended person. If more than one person signs in the name or behalf of the issuer of an instrument and all the signers do not intend the same person as payee, the instrument is payable to any person intended by one or more of the signers.

(b) If the signature of the issuer of an instrument is made by automated means, such as a check-writing machine, the payee of the instrument is determined by the intent of the person who supplied the name or identification of the payee, whether or not authorized to do so.

(c) A person to whom an instrument is payable may be identified in any way, including by name, identifying number, office, or account number. For the purpose of determining the holder of an instrument, the following rules apply:

(1) If an instrument is payable to an account and the account is identified only by number, the instrument is payable to the person to whom the account is payable. If an instrument is payable to an account identified by number and by the name of a person, the instrument is payable to the named person, whether or not that person is the owner of the account identified by number.

(2) If an instrument is payable to:

(i) a trust, an estate, or a person described as trustee or representative of a trust or estate, the instrument is payable to the trustee, the representative, or a successor of either, whether or not the beneficiary or estate is also named;

(ii) a person described as agent or similar representative of a named or identified person, the instrument is payable to the represented person, the representative, or a successor of the representative;

(iii) a fund or organization that is not a legal entity, the instrument is payable to a representative of the members of the fund or organization; or

(iv) an office or to a person described as holding an office, the instrument is payable to the named person, the incumbent of the office, or a successor to the incumbent.

(d) If an instrument is payable to two or more persons alternatively, it is payable to any of them and may be negotiated, discharged, or enforced by any or all of them in possession of the instrument. If an instrument is payable to two or more persons not alternatively, it is payable to all of them and may be negotiated, discharged, or enforced only by all of them. If an instrument payable to two or more persons is ambiguous as to whether it is payable to the persons alternatively, the instrument is payable to the persons alternatively.

§ 3–111. Place of Payment.

Except as otherwise provided for items in Article 4, an instrument is payable at the place of payment stated in the instrument. If no place of payment is stated, an instrument is payable at the address of the drawee or maker stated in the instrument. If no address is stated, the place of payment is the place of business of the drawee or maker. If a drawee or maker has more than one place of business, the place of payment is any place of business of the drawee or maker chosen by the person entitled to enforce the instrument. If the drawee or maker has no place of business, the place of payment is the residence of the drawee or maker.

§ 3–112. Interest.

(a) Unless otherwise provided in the instrument, (i) an instrument is not payable with interest, and (ii) interest on an interest-bearing instrument is payable from the date of the instrument.

(b) Interest may be stated in an instrument as a fixed or variable amount of money or it may be expressed as a fixed or variable rate or rates. The amount or rate of interest may be stated or described in the instrument in any manner and may require reference to information not contained in the instrument. If an instrument provides for interest, but the amount of interest payable cannot be ascertained from the description, interest is payable at the judgment rate in effect at the place of payment of the instrument and at the time interest first accrues.

§ 3–113. Date of Instrument.

(a) An instrument may be antedated or postdated. The date stated determines the time of payment if the instrument is payable at a fixed period after date. Except as provided in Section 4–401(c), an instrument payable on demand is not payable before the date of the instrument.

(b) If an instrument is undated, its date is the date of its issue or, in the case of an unissued instrument, the date it first comes into possession of a holder.

§ 3–114. Contradictory Terms of Instrument.

If an instrument contains contradictory terms, typewritten terms prevail over printed terms, handwritten terms prevail over both, and words prevail over numbers.

§ 3–115. Incomplete Instrument.

(a) "Incomplete instrument" means a signed writing, whether or not issued by the signer, the contents of which show at the time of signing that it is incomplete but that the signer intended it to be completed by the addition of words or numbers.

(b) Subject to subsection (c), if an incomplete instrument is an instrument under Section 3–104, it may be enforced according to its terms if it is not completed, or according to its terms as augmented by completion. If an incomplete instrument is not an instrument under Section 3–104, but, after completion, the requirements of Section 3–104 are met, the instrument may be enforced according to its terms as augmented by completion.

(c) If words or numbers are added to an incomplete instrument without authority of the signer, there is an alteration of the incomplete instrument under Section 3–407.

(d) The burden of establishing that words or numbers were added to an incomplete instrument without authority of the signer is on the person asserting the lack of authority.

§ 3–116. Joint and Several Liability; Contribution.

(a) Except as otherwise provided in the instrument, two or more persons who have the same liability on an instrument as makers, drawers, acceptors, indorsers who indorse as joint payees, or anomalous indorsers are jointly and severally liable in the capacity in which they sign.

(b) Except as provided in Section 3–419(e) or by agreement of the affected parties, a party having joint and several liability who pays the instrument is entitled to receive from any party having the same joint and several liability contribution in accordance with applicable law.

(c) Discharge of one party having joint and several liability by a person entitled to enforce the instrument does not affect the right under subsection (b) of a party having the same joint and several liability to receive contribution from the party discharged.

§ 3–117. Other Agreements Affecting Instrument.

Subject to applicable law regarding exclusion of proof of contemporaneous or previous agreements, the obligation of a party to an instrument to pay the instrument may be modified, supplemented, or nullified by a separate agreement of the obligor and a person entitled to enforce the instrument, if the instrument is issued or the obligation is incurred in reliance on the agreement or as part of the same transaction giving rise to the agreement. To the extent an obligation is modified, supplemented, or nullified by an agreement under this section, the agreement is a defense to the obligation.

§ 3–118. Statute of Limitations.

(a) Except as provided in subsection (e), an action to enforce the obligation of a party to pay a note payable at a definite time must be commenced within six years after the due date or dates stated in the note or, if a due date is accelerated, within six years after the accelerated due date.

(b) Except as provided in subsection (d) or (e), if demand for payment is made to the maker of a note payable on demand, an action to enforce the obligation of a party to pay the note must be commenced within six years after the demand. If no demand for payment is made to the maker, an action to enforce the note is barred if neither principal nor interest on the note has been paid for a continuous period of 10 years.

(c) Except as provided in subsection (d), an action to enforce the obligation of a party to an unaccepted draft to pay the draft must be commenced within three years after dishonor of the draft or 10 years after the date of the draft, whichever period expires first.

(d) An action to enforce the obligation of the acceptor of a certified check or the issuer of a teller's check, cashier's check, or traveler's check must be commenced within three years after demand for payment is made to the acceptor or issuer, as the case may be.

(e) An action to enforce the obligation of a party to a certificate of deposit to pay the instrument must be commenced within six years after demand for payment is made to the maker, but if the instrument states a due date and the maker is not required to pay before that date, the six-year period begins when a demand for payment is in effect and the due date has passed.

(f) An action to enforce the obligation of a party to pay an accepted draft, other than a certified check, must be commenced (i) within six years after the due date or dates stated in the draft or acceptance if the obligation of the acceptor is payable at a definite time, or (ii) within six years after the date of the acceptance if the obligation of the acceptor is payable on demand.

(g) Unless governed by other law regarding claims for indemnity or contribution, an action (i) for conversion of an instrument, for money had and received, or like action based on conversion, (ii) for breach of warranty, or (iii) to enforce an obligation, duty, or right arising under this Article and not governed by this section must be commenced within three years after the [cause of action] accrues.

§ 3–119. Notice of Right to Defend Action.

In an action for breach of an obligation for which a third person is answerable over pursuant to this Article or Article 4, the defendant may give the third person written notice of the litigation, and the person notified may then give similar notice to any other person who is answerable over. If the notice states (i) that the person notified may come in and defend and (ii) that failure to do so will bind the person notified in an action later brought by the person giving the notice as to any determination of fact common to the two litigations, the person notified is so bound unless after seasonable receipt of the notice the person notified does come in and defend.

Part 2 Negotiation, Transfer, and Indorsement

§ 3–201. Negotiation.

(a) "Negotiation" means a transfer of possession, whether voluntary or involuntary, of an instrument by a person other than the issuer to a person who thereby becomes its holder.

(b) Except for negotiation by a remitter, if an instrument is payable to an identified person, negotiation requires transfer of possession of the instrument and its indorsement by the holder. If an instrument is payable to bearer, it may be negotiated by transfer of possession alone.

§ 3–202. Negotiation Subject to Rescission.

(a) Negotiation is effective even if obtained (i) from an infant, a corporation exceeding its powers, or a person without capacity, (ii) by fraud, duress, or mistake, or (iii) in breach of duty or as part of an illegal transaction.

(b) To the extent permitted by other law, negotiation may be rescinded or may be subject to other remedies, but those remedies may not be asserted against a subsequent holder in due course or a person paying the instrument in good faith and without knowledge of facts that are a basis for rescission or other remedy.

§ 3–203. Transfer of Instrument; Rights Acquired by Transfer.

(a) An instrument is transferred when it is delivered by a person other than its issuer for the purpose of giving to the person receiving delivery the right to enforce the instrument.

(b) Transfer of an instrument, whether or not the transfer is a negotiation, vests in the transferee any right of the transferor to enforce the instrument, including any right as a holder in due course, but the transferee cannot acquire rights of a holder in due course by a transfer, directly or indirectly, from a holder in due course if the transferee engaged in fraud or illegality affecting the instrument.

(c) Unless otherwise agreed, if an instrument is transferred for value and the transferee does not become a holder because of lack of indorsement by the transferor, the transferee has a specifically enforceable right to the unqualified indorsement of the transferor, but negotiation of the instrument does not occur until the indorsement is made.

(d) If a transferor purports to transfer less than the entire instrument, negotiation of the instrument does not occur. The transferee obtains no rights under this Article and has only the rights of a partial assignee.

§ 3–204. Indorsement.

(a) "Indorsement" means a signature, other than that of a signer as maker, drawer, or acceptor, that alone or accompanied by other words is made on an instrument for the purpose of (i) negotiating the instrument, (ii) restricting payment of the instrument, or (iii) incurring indorser's liability on the instrument, but regardless of the intent of the signer, a signature and its accompanying words is an indorsement unless the accompanying words, terms of the instrument, place of the signature, or other circumstances unambiguously indicate that the signature was made for a purpose other than indorsement. For the purpose of determining whether a signature is made on an instrument, a paper affixed to the instrument is a part of the instrument.

(b) "Indorser" means a person who makes an indorsement.

(c) For the purpose of determining whether the transferee of an instrument is a holder, an indorsement that transfers a security interest in the instrument is effective as an unqualified indorsement of the instrument.

(d) If an instrument is payable to a holder under a name that is not the name of the holder, indorsement may be made by the holder in the name stated in the instrument or in the holder's name or both, but signature in both names may be required by a person paying or taking the instrument for value or collection.

§ 3–205. Special Indorsement; Blank Indorsement; Anomalous Indorsement.

(a) If an indorsement is made by the holder of an instrument, whether payable to an identified person or payable to bearer, and the indorsement identifies a person to whom it makes the instrument payable, it is a "special indorsement." When specially indorsed, an instrument becomes payable to the identified person and may be negotiated only by the indorsement of that person. The principles stated in Section 3–110 apply to special indorsements.

(b) If an indorsement is made by the holder of an instrument and it is not a special indorsement, it is a "blank indorsement." When indorsed in blank, an instrument becomes payable to bearer and may be negotiated by transfer of possession alone until specially indorsed.

(c) The holder may convert a blank indorsement that consists only of a signature into a special indorsement by writing, above the signature of the indorser, words identifying the person to whom the instrument is made payable.

(d) "Anomalous indorsement" means an indorsement made by a person who is not the holder of the instrument. An anomalous indorsement does not affect the manner in which the instrument may be negotiated.

§ 3–206. Restrictive Indorsement.

(a) An indorsement limiting payment to a particular person or otherwise prohibiting further transfer or negotiation of the instrument is not effective to prevent further transfer or negotiation of the instrument.

(b) An indorsement stating a condition to the right of the indorsee to receive payment does not affect the right of the indorsee to enforce the instrument. A person paying the instrument or taking it for value or collection may disregard the condition, and the rights and liabilities of that person are not affected by whether the condition has been fulfilled.

(c) If an instrument bears an indorsement (i) described in Section 4–201(b), or (ii) in blank or to a particular bank using the words "for deposit," "for collection," or other words indicating a purpose of having the instrument collected by a bank for the indorser or for a particular account, the following rules apply:

(1) A person, other than a bank, who purchases the instrument when so indorsed converts the instrument unless the amount paid for the instrument is received by the indorser or applied consistently with the indorsement.

(2) A depositary bank that purchases the instrument or takes it for collection when so indorsed converts the instrument unless the amount paid by the bank with respect to the instrument is received by the indorser or applied consistently with the indorsement.

(3) A payor bank that is also the depositary bank or that takes the instrument for immediate payment over the counter from a person other than a collecting bank converts the instrument unless the proceeds of the instrument are received by the indorser or applied consistently with the indorsement.

(4) Except as otherwise provided in paragraph (3), a payor bank or intermediary bank may disregard the indorsement and is not liable if the proceeds of the instrument are not received by the indorser or applied consistently with the indorsement.

(d) Except for an indorsement covered by subsection (c), if an instrument bears an indorsement using words to the effect that payment is to be made to the indorsee as agent, trustee, or other fiduciary for the benefit of the indorser or another person, the following rules apply:

(1) Unless there is notice of breach of fiduciary duty as provided in Section 3–307, a person who purchases the instrument from the indorsee or takes the instrument from the indorsee for collection or payment may pay the proceeds of payment or the value given for the instrument to the indorsee without regard to whether the indorsee violates a fiduciary duty to the indorser.

(2) A subsequent transferee of the instrument or person who pays the instrument is neither given notice nor otherwise affected by the restriction in the indorsement unless the transferee or payor knows that the fiduciary dealt with the instrument or its proceeds in breach of fiduciary duty.

(e) The presence on an instrument of an indorsement to which this section applies does not prevent a purchaser of the instrument from becoming a holder in due course of the instrument unless the purchaser is a converter under subsection (c) or has notice or knowledge of breach of fiduciary duty as stated in subsection (d).

(f) In an action to enforce the obligation of a party to pay the instrument, the obligor has a defense if payment would violate an indorsement to which this section applies and the payment is not permitted by this section.

§ 3–207. Reacquisition.

Reacquisition of an instrument occurs if it is transferred to a former holder, by negotiation or otherwise. A former holder who reacquires the instrument may cancel indorsements made after the reacquirer first became a holder of the instrument. If the cancellation causes the instrument to be payable to the reacquirer or to bearer, the reacquirer may negotiate the instrument. An indorser whose indorsement is canceled is discharged, and the discharge is effective against any subsequent holder.

Part 3 Enforcement of Instruments

§ 3–301. Person Entitled to Enforce Instrument.

"Person entitled to enforce" an instrument means (i) the holder of the instrument, (ii) a nonholder in possession of the instrument who has the rights of a holder, or (iii) a person not in possession of the instrument who is entitled to enforce the instrument pursuant to Section 3–309 or 3–418(d). A person may be a person entitled to enforce the instrument even though the person is not the owner of the instrument or is in wrongful possession of the instrument.

§ 3–302. Holder in Due Course.

(a) Subject to subsection (c) and Section 3–106(d), "holder in due course" means the holder of an instrument if:

(1) the instrument when issued or negotiated to the holder does not bear such apparent evidence of forgery or alteration or is not otherwise so irregular or incomplete as to call into question its authenticity; and

(2) the holder took the instrument (i) for value, (ii) in good faith, (iii) without notice that the instrument is overdue or has been dishonored or that there is an uncured default with respect to payment of another instrument issued as part of the same series, (iv) without notice that the instrument contains an unauthorized signature or has been altered, (v) without notice of any claim to the instrument described in Section 3–306, and (vi) without notice that any party has a defense or claim in recoupment described in Section 3–305(a).

(b) Notice of discharge of a party, other than discharge in an insolvency proceeding, is not notice of a defense under subsection (a), but discharge is effective against a person who became a holder in due course with notice of the discharge. Public filing or recording of a document does not of itself constitute notice of a defense, claim in recoupment, or claim to the instrument.

(c) Except to the extent a transferor or predecessor in interest has rights as a holder in due course, a person does not acquire rights of a holder in due course of an instrument taken (i) by legal process or by purchase in an execution, bankruptcy, or creditor's sale or similar proceeding, (ii) by purchase as part of a bulk transaction not in ordinary course of business of the transferor, or (iii) as the successor in interest to an estate or other organization.

(d) If, under Section 3–303(a)(1), the promise of performance that is the consideration for an instrument has been partially performed, the holder may assert rights as a holder in due course of the instrument only to the fraction of the amount payable under the instrument equal to the value of the partial performance divided by the value of the promised performance.

(e) If (i) the person entitled to enforce an instrument has only a security interest in the instrument and (ii) the person obliged to pay the instrument has a defense, claim in recoupment, or claim to the instrument that may be asserted against the person who granted the security interest, the person entitled to enforce the instrument may assert rights as a holder in due course only to an amount payable under the instrument which, at the time of enforcement of the instrument, does not exceed the amount of the unpaid obligation secured.

(f) To be effective, notice must be received at a time and in a manner that gives a reasonable opportunity to act on it.

(g) This section is subject to any law limiting status as a holder in due course in particular classes of transactions.

§ 3–303. Value and Consideration.

(a) An instrument is issued or transferred for value if:

(1) the instrument is issued or transferred for a promise of performance, to the extent the promise has been performed;

(2) the transferee acquires a security interest or other lien in the instrument other than a lien obtained by judicial proceeding;

(3) the instrument is issued or transferred as payment of, or as security for, an antecedent claim against any person, whether or not the claim is due;

(4) the instrument is issued or transferred in exchange for a negotiable instrument; or

(5) the instrument is issued or transferred in exchange for the incurring of an irrevocable obligation to a third party by the person taking the instrument.

(b) "Consideration" means any consideration sufficient to support a simple contract. The drawer or maker of an instrument has a defense if the instrument is issued without consideration. If an instrument is issued for a promise of performance, the issuer has a defense to the extent performance of the promise is due and the promise has not been performed. If an instrument is issued for value as stated in subsection (a), the instrument is also issued for consideration.

§ 3–304. Overdue Instrument.

(a) An instrument payable on demand becomes overdue at the earliest of the following times:

(1) on the day after the day demand for payment is duly made;

(2) if the instrument is a check, 90 days after its date; or

(3) if the instrument is not a check, when the instrument has been outstanding for a period of time after its date which is unreasonably long under the circumstances of the particular case in light of the nature of the instrument and usage of the trade.

(b) With respect to an instrument payable at a definite time the following rules apply:

(1) If the principal is payable in installments and a due date has not been accelerated, the instrument becomes overdue upon default under the instrument for nonpayment of an installment, and the instrument remains overdue until the default is cured.

(2) If the principal is not payable in installments and the due date has not been accelerated, the instrument becomes overdue on the day after the due date.

(3) If a due date with respect to principal has been accelerated, the instrument becomes overdue on the day after the accelerated due date.

(c) Unless the due date of principal has been accelerated, an instrument does not become overdue if there is default in payment of interest but no default in payment of principal.

§ 3–305. Defenses and Claims in Recoupment.

(a) Except as stated in subsection (b), the right to enforce the obligation of a party to pay an instrument is subject to the following:

(1) a defense of the obligor based on (i) infancy of the obligor to the extent it is a defense to a simple contract, (ii) duress, lack of legal capacity, or illegality of the transaction which, under other law, nullifies the obliga-

tion of the obligor, (iii) fraud that induced the obligor to sign the instrument with neither knowledge nor reasonable opportunity to learn of its character or its essential terms, or (iv) discharge of the obligor in insolvency proceedings;

(2) a defense of the obligor stated in another section of this Article or a defense of the obligor that would be available if the person entitled to enforce the instrument were enforcing a right to payment under a simple contract; and

(3) a claim in recoupment of the obligor against the original payee of the instrument if the claim arose from the transaction that gave rise to the instrument; but the claim of the obligor may be asserted against a transferee of the instrument only to reduce the amount owing on the instrument at the time the action is brought.

(b) The right of a holder in due course to enforce the obligation of a party to pay the instrument is subject to defenses of the obligor stated in subsection (a)(1), but is not subject to defenses of the obligor stated in subsection (a)(2) or claims in recoupment stated in subsection (a)(3) against a person other than the holder.

(c) Except as stated in subsection (d), in an action to enforce the obligation of a party to pay the instrument, the obligor may not assert against the person entitled to enforce the instrument a defense, claim in recoupment, or claim to the instrument (Section 3–306) of another person, but the other person's claim to the instrument may be asserted by the obligor if the other person is joined in the action and personally asserts the claim against the person entitled to enforce the instrument. An obligor is not obliged to pay the instrument if the person seeking enforcement of the instrument does not have rights of a holder in due course and the obligor proves that the instrument is a lost or stolen instrument.

(d) In an action to enforce the obligation of an accommodation party to pay an instrument, the accommodation party may assert against the person entitled to enforce the instrument any defense or claim in recoupment under subsection (a) that the accommodated party could assert against the person entitled to enforce the instrument, except the defenses of discharge in insolvency proceedings, infancy, and lack of legal capacity.

§ 3–306. Claims to an Instrument.

A person taking an instrument, other than a person having rights of a holder in due course, is subject to a claim of a property or possessory right in the instrument or its proceeds, including a claim to rescind a negotiation and to recover the instrument or its proceeds. A person having rights of a holder in due course takes free of the claim to the instrument.

§ 3–307. Notice of Breach of Fiduciary Duty.

(a) In this section:

(1) "Fiduciary" means an agent, trustee, partner, corporate officer or director, or other representative owing a fiduciary duty with respect to an instrument.

(2) "Represented person" means the principal, beneficiary, partnership, corporation, or other person to whom the duty stated in paragraph (1) is owed.

(b) If (i) an instrument is taken from a fiduciary for payment or collection or for value, (ii) the taker has knowledge of the fiduciary status of the fiduciary, and (iii) the represented person makes a claim to the instrument or its proceeds on the basis that the transaction of the fiduciary is a breach of fiduciary duty, the following rules apply:

(1) Notice of breach of fiduciary duty by the fiduciary is notice of the claim of the represented person.

(2) In the case of an instrument payable to the represented person or the fiduciary as such, the taker has notice of the breach of fiduciary duty if the instrument is (i) taken in payment of or as security for a debt known by the taker to be the personal debt of the fiduciary, (ii) taken in a transaction known by the taker to be for the personal benefit of the fiduciary, or (iii) deposited to an account other than an account of the fiduciary, as such, or an account of the represented person.

(3) If an instrument is issued by the represented person or the fiduciary as such, and made payable to the fiduciary personally, the taker does not have notice of the breach of fiduciary duty unless the taker knows of the breach of fiduciary duty.

(4) If an instrument is issued by the represented person or the fiduciary as such, to the taker as payee, the taker has notice of the breach of fiduciary duty if the instrument is (i) taken in payment of or as security for a debt known by the taker to be the personal debt of the fiduciary, (ii) taken in a transaction known by the taker to be for the personal benefit of the fiduciary, or (iii) deposited to an account other than an account of the fiduciary, as such, or an account of the represented person.

§ 3–308. Proof of Signatures and Status as Holder in Due Course.

(a) In an action with respect to an instrument, the authenticity of, and authority to make, each signature on the instrument is admitted unless specifically denied in the pleadings. If the validity of a signature is denied in the pleadings, the burden of establishing validity is on the person claiming validity, but the signature is presumed to be authentic and authorized unless the action is to enforce the liability of the purported signer and the signer is dead or incompetent at the time of trial of the issue of validity of the signature. If an action to enforce the instrument is brought against a person as the undisclosed principal of a person who signed the instrument as a party to the instrument, the plaintiff has the burden of establishing that the defendant is liable on the instrument as a represented person under Section 3–402(a).

(b) If the validity of signatures is admitted or proved and there is compliance with subsection (a), a plaintiff producing the instrument is entitled to payment if the plaintiff proves entitlement to enforce the instrument under Section 3–301, unless the defendant proves a defense or claim in recoupment. If a defense or claim in recoupment is proved, the right to payment of the plaintiff is subject to the defense or claim, except to the extent the plaintiff proves that the plaintiff has rights of a holder in due course which are not subject to the defense or claim.

§ 3–309. Enforcement of Lost, Destroyed, or Stolen Instrument.

(a) A person not in possession of an instrument is entitled to enforce the instrument if (i) the person was in possession of the instrument and entitled to enforce it when loss of possession occurred, (ii) the loss of possession was not the result of a transfer by the person or a lawful seizure, and (iii) the person cannot reasonably obtain possession of the instrument because the instrument was destroyed, its whereabouts cannot be determined, or it is in the wrongful possession of an unknown person or a person that cannot be found or is not amenable to service of process.

(b) A person seeking enforcement of an instrument under subsection (a) must prove the terms of the instrument and the person's right to enforce the instrument. If that proof is made, Section 3–308 applies to the case as if the person seeking enforcement had produced the instrument. The court may not enter judgment in favor of the person seeking enforcement unless it finds that the person required to pay the instrument is adequately protected against loss that might occur by reason of a claim by another person to enforce the instrument. Adequate protection may be provided by any reasonable means.

§ 3–310. Effect of Instrument on Obligation for Which Taken.

(a) Unless otherwise agreed, if a certified check, cashier's check, or teller's check is taken for an obligation, the obligation is discharged to the same extent discharge would result if an amount of money equal to the amount of the instrument were taken in payment of the obligation. Discharge of the obligation does not affect any liability that the obligor may have as an indorser of the instrument.

(b) Unless otherwise agreed and except as provided in subsection (a), if a note or an uncertified check is taken for an obligation, the obligation is suspended to the same extent the obligation would be discharged if an amount of money equal to the amount of the instrument were taken, and the following rules apply:

(1) In the case of an uncertified check, suspension of the obligation continues until dishonor of the check or until it is paid or certified. Payment or certification of the check results in discharge of the obligation to the extent of the amount of the check.

(2) In the case of a note, suspension of the obligation continues until dishonor of the note or until it is paid. Payment of the note results in discharge of the obligation to the extent of the payment.

(3) Except as provided in paragraph (4), if the check or note is dishonored and the obligee of the obligation for which the instrument was taken is the person entitled to enforce the instrument, the obligee may enforce either the instrument or the obligation. In the case of an instrument of a third person which is negotiated to the obligee by the obligor, discharge of the obligor on the instrument also discharges the obligation.

(4) If the person entitled to enforce the instrument taken for an obligation is a person other than the obligee, the obligee may not enforce the obligation to the extent the obligation is suspended. If the obligee is the person entitled to enforce the instrument but no longer has possession of it because it was lost, stolen, or destroyed, the obligation may not be enforced to the extent of the amount payable on the instrument, and to that extent the obligee's rights against the obligor are limited to enforcement of the instrument.

(c) If an instrument other than one described in subsection (a) or (b) is taken for an obligation, the effect is (i) that stated in subsection (a) if the instrument is one on which a bank is liable as maker or acceptor, or (ii) that stated in subsection (b) in any other case.

§ 3–311. Accord and Satisfaction by Use of Instrument.

(a) If a person against whom a claim is asserted proves that (i) that person in good faith tendered an instrument to the claimant as full satisfaction of the claim, (ii) the amount of the claim was unliquidated or subject to a bona fide dispute, and (iii) the claimant obtained payment of the instrument, the following subsections apply.

(b) Unless subsection (c) applies, the claim is discharged if the person against whom the claim is asserted proves that the instrument or an accompanying written communication contained a conspicuous statement to the effect that the instrument was tendered as full satisfaction of the claim.

(c) Subject to subsection (d), a claim is not discharged under subsection (b) if either of the following applies:

(1) The claimant, if an organization, proves that (i) within a reasonable time before the tender, the claimant sent a conspicuous statement to the person against whom the claim is asserted that communications concerning disputed debts, including an instrument tendered as full satisfaction of a debt, are to be sent to a designated person, office, or place, and (ii) the instrument or accompanying communication was not received by that designated person, office, or place.

(2) The claimant, whether or not an organization, proves that within 90 days after payment of the instru-

ment, the claimant tendered repayment of the amount of the instrument to the person against whom the claim is asserted. This paragraph does not apply if the claimant is an organization that sent a statement complying with paragraph (1)(i).

(d) A claim is discharged if the person against whom the claim is asserted proves that within a reasonable time before collection of the instrument was initiated, the claimant, or an agent of the claimant having direct responsibility with respect to the disputed obligation, knew that the instrument was tendered in full satisfaction of the claim.

§ 3–312. Lost, Destroyed, or Stolen Cashier's Check, Teller's Check, or Certified Check.*

(a) In this section:

(1) "Check" means a cashier's check, teller's check, or certified check.

(2) "Claimant" means a person who claims the right to receive the amount of a cashier's check, teller's check, or certified check that was lost, destroyed, or stolen.

(3) "Declaration of loss" means a written statement, made under penalty of perjury, to the effect that (i) the declarer lost possession of a check, (ii) the declarer is the drawer or payee of the check, in the case of a certified check, or the remitter or payee of the check, in the case of a cashier's check or teller's check, (iii) the loss of possession was not the result of a transfer by the declarer or a lawful seizure, and (iv) the declarer cannot reasonably obtain possession of the check because the check was destroyed, its whereabouts cannot be determined, or it is in the wrongful possession of an unknown person or a person that cannot be found or is not amenable to service of process.

(4) "Obligated bank" means the issuer of a cashier's check or teller's check or the acceptor of a certified check.

(b) A claimant may assert a claim to the amount of a check by a communication to the obligated bank describing the check with reasonable certainty and requesting payment of the amount of the check, if (i) the claimant is the drawer or payee of a certified check or the remitter or payee of a cashier's check or teller's check, (ii) the communication contains or is accompanied by a declaration of loss of the claimant with respect to the check, (iii) the communication is received at a time and in a manner affording the bank a reasonable time to act on it before the check is paid, and (iv) the claimant provides reasonable identification if requested by the obligated bank. Delivery of a declaration of loss is a warranty of the truth of the statements made in the declaration. If a claim is asserted in compliance with this subsection, the following rules apply:

(1) The claim becomes enforceable at the later of (i) the time the claim is asserted, or (ii) the 90th day fol-

lowing the date of the check, in the case of a cashier's check or teller's check, or the 90th day following the date of the acceptance, in the case of a certified check.

(2) Until the claim becomes enforceable, it has no legal effect and the obligated bank may pay the check or, in the case of a teller's check, may permit the drawee to pay the check. Payment to a person entitled to enforce the check discharges all liability of the obligated bank with respect to the check.

(3) If the claim becomes enforceable before the check is presented for payment, the obligated bank is not obliged to pay the check.

(4) When the claim becomes enforceable, the obligated bank becomes obliged to pay the amount of the check to the claimant if payment of the check has not been made to a person entitled to enforce the check. Subject to Section 4–302(a)(1), payment to the claimant discharges all liability of the obligated bank with respect to the check.

(c) If the obligated bank pays the amount of a check to a claimant under subsection (b)(4) and the check is presented for payment by a person having rights of a holder in due course, the claimant is obliged to (i) refund the payment to the obligated bank if the check is paid, or (ii) pay the amount of the check to the person having rights of a holder in due course if the check is dishonored.

(d) If a claimant has the right to assert a claim under subsection (b) and is also a person entitled to enforce a cashier's check, teller's check, or certified check which is lost, destroyed, or stolen, the claimant may assert rights with respect to the check either under this section or Section 3–309.

Added in 1991.

Part 4 Liability of Parties

§ 3–401. Signature.

(a) A person is not liable on an instrument unless (i) the person signed the instrument, or (ii) the person is represented by an agent or representative who signed the instrument and the signature is binding on the represented person under Section 3–402.

(b) A signature may be made (i) manually or by means of a device or machine, and (ii) by the use of any name, including a trade or assumed name, or by a word, mark, or symbol executed or adopted by a person with present intention to authenticate a writing.

§ 3–402. Signature by Representative.

(a) If a person acting, or purporting to act, as a representative signs an instrument by signing either the name of the represented person or the name of the signer, the represented person is bound by the signature to the same extent

---

*[Section 3–312 was not adopted as part of the 1990 Official Text of Revised Article 3. It was officially approved and recommended for enactment in all states in August 1991 by the National Conference of Commissioners on Uniform State Laws.]

the represented person would be bound if the signature were on a simple contract. If the represented person is bound, the signature of the representative is the "authorized signature of the represented person" and the represented person is liable on the instrument, whether or not identified in the instrument.

(b) If a representative signs the name of the representative to an instrument and the signature is an authorized signature of the represented person, the following rules apply:

(1) If the form of the signature shows unambiguously that the signature is made on behalf of the represented person who is identified in the instrument, the representative is not liable on the instrument.

(2) Subject to subsection (c), if (i) the form of the signature does not show unambiguously that the signature is made in a representative capacity or (ii) the represented person is not identified in the instrument, the representative is liable on the instrument to a holder in due course that took the instrument without notice that the representative was not intended to be liable on the instrument. With respect to any other person, the representative is liable on the instrument unless the representative proves that the original parties did not intend the representative to be liable on the instrument.

(c) If a representative signs the name of the representative as drawer of a check without indication of the representative status and the check is payable from an account of the represented person who is identified on the check, the signer is not liable on the check if the signature is an authorized signature of the represented person.

§ 3–403. Unauthorized Signature.

(a) Unless otherwise provided in this Article or Article 4, an unauthorized signature is ineffective except as the signature of the unauthorized signer in favor of a person who in good faith pays the instrument or takes it for value. An unauthorized signature may be ratified for all purposes of this Article.

(b) If the signature of more than one person is required to constitute the authorized signature of an organization, the signature of the organization is unauthorized if one of the required signatures is lacking.

(c) The civil or criminal liability of a person who makes an unauthorized signature is not affected by any provision of this Article which makes the unauthorized signature effective for the purposes of this Article.

§ 3–404. Impostors; Fictitious Payees.

(a) If an impostor, by use of the mails or otherwise, induces the issuer of an instrument to issue the instrument to the impostor, or to a person acting in concert with the impostor, by impersonating the payee of the instrument or a person authorized to act for the payee, an indorsement of the instrument by any person in the name of the payee is effec-

tive as the indorsement of the payee in favor of a person who, in good faith, pays the instrument or takes it for value or for collection.

(b) If (i) a person whose intent determines to whom an instrument is payable (Section 3–110(a) or (b)) does not intend the person identified as payee to have any interest in the instrument, or (ii) the person identified as payee of an instrument is a fictitious person, the following rules apply until the instrument is negotiated by special indorsement:

(1) Any person in possession of the instrument is its holder.

(2) An indorsement by any person in the name of the payee stated in the instrument is effective as the indorsement of the payee in favor of a person who, in good faith, pays the instrument or takes it for value or for collection.

(c) Under subsection (a) or (b), an indorsement is made in the name of a payee if (i) it is made in a name substantially similar to that of the payee or (ii) the instrument, whether or not indorsed, is deposited in a depositary bank to an account in a name substantially similar to that of the payee.

(d) With respect to an instrument to which subsection (a) or (b) applies, if a person paying the instrument or taking it for value or for collection fails to exercise ordinary care in paying or taking the instrument and that failure substantially contributes to loss resulting from payment of the instrument, the person bearing the loss may recover from the person failing to exercise ordinary care to the extent the failure to exercise ordinary care contributed to the loss.

§ 3–405. Employer's Responsibility for Fraudulent Indorsement by Employee.

(a) In this section:

(1) "Employee" includes an independent contractor and employee of an independent contractor retained by the employer.

(2) "Fraudulent indorsement" means (i) in the case of an instrument payable to the employer, a forged indorsement purporting to be that of the employer, or (ii) in the case of an instrument with respect to which the employer is the issuer, a forged indorsement purporting to be that of the person identified as payee.

(3) "Responsibility" with respect to instruments means authority (i) to sign or indorse instruments on behalf of the employer, (ii) to process instruments received by the employer for bookkeeping purposes, for deposit to an account, or for other disposition, (iii) to prepare or process instruments for issue in the name of the employer, (iv) to supply information determining the names or addresses of payees of instruments to be issued in the name of the employer, (v) to control the disposition of instruments to be issued in the name of the employer, or

(vi) to act otherwise with respect to instruments in a responsible capacity. "Responsibility" does not include authority that merely allows an employee to have access to instruments or blank or incomplete instrument forms that are being stored or transported or are part of incoming or outgoing mail, or similar access.

(b) For the purpose of determining the rights and liabilities of a person who, in good faith, pays an instrument or takes it for value or for collection, if an employer entrusted an employee with responsibility with respect to the instrument and the employee or a person acting in concert with the employee makes a fraudulent indorsement of the instrument, the indorsement is effective as the indorsement of the person to whom the instrument is payable if it is made in the name of that person. If the person paying the instrument or taking it for value or for collection fails to exercise ordinary care in paying or taking the instrument and that failure substantially contributes to loss resulting from the fraud, the person bearing the loss may recover from the person failing to exercise ordinary care to the extent the failure to exercise ordinary care contributed to the loss.

(c) Under subsection (b), an indorsement is made in the name of the person to whom an instrument is payable if (i) it is made in a name substantially similar to the name of that person or (ii) the instrument, whether or not indorsed, is deposited in a depositary bank to an account in a name substantially similar to the name of that person.

§ 3–406. Negligence Contributing to Forged Signature or Alteration of Instrument.

(a) A person whose failure to exercise ordinary care substantially contributes to an alteration of an instrument or to the making of a forged signature on an instrument is precluded from asserting the alteration or the forgery against a person who, in good faith, pays the instrument or takes it for value or for collection.

(b) Under subsection (a), if the person asserting the preclusion fails to exercise ordinary care in paying or taking the instrument and that failure substantially contributes to loss, the loss is allocated between the person precluded and the person asserting the preclusion according to the extent to which the failure of each to exercise ordinary care contributed to the loss.

(c) Under subsection (a), the burden of proving failure to exercise ordinary care is on the person asserting the preclusion. Under subsection (b), the burden of proving failure to exercise ordinary care is on the person precluded.

§ 3–407. Alteration.

(a) "Alteration" means (i) an unauthorized change in an instrument that purports to modify in any respect the obligation of a party, or (ii) an unauthorized addition of words or numbers or other change to an incomplete instrument relating to the obligation of a party.

(b) Except as provided in subsection (c), an alteration fraudulently made discharges a party whose obligation is affected by the alteration unless that party assents or is precluded from asserting the alteration. No other alteration discharges a party, and the instrument may be enforced according to its original terms.

(c) A payor bank or drawee paying a fraudulently altered instrument or a person taking it for value, in good faith and without notice of the alteration, may enforce rights with respect to the instrument (i) according to its original terms, or (ii) in the case of an incomplete instrument altered by unauthorized completion, according to its terms as completed.

§ 3–408. Drawee Not Liable on Unaccepted Draft.

A check or other draft does not of itself operate as an assignment of funds in the hands of the drawee available for its payment, and the drawee is not liable on the instrument until the drawee accepts it.

§ 3–409. Acceptance of Draft; Certified Check.

(a) "Acceptance" means the drawee's signed agreement to pay a draft as presented. It must be written on the draft and may consist of the drawee's signature alone. Acceptance may be made at any time and becomes effective when notification pursuant to instructions is given or the accepted draft is delivered for the purpose of giving rights on the acceptance to any person.

(b) A draft may be accepted although it has not been signed by the drawer, is otherwise incomplete, is overdue, or has been dishonored.

(c) If a draft is payable at a fixed period after sight and the acceptor fails to date the acceptance, the holder may complete the acceptance by supplying a date in good faith.

(d) "Certified check" means a check accepted by the bank on which it is drawn. Acceptance may be made as stated in subsection (a) or by a writing on the check which indicates that the check is certified. The drawee of a check has no obligation to certify the check, and refusal to certify is not dishonor of the check.

§ 3–410. Acceptance Varying Draft.

(a) If the terms of a drawee's acceptance vary from the terms of the draft as presented, the holder may refuse the acceptance and treat the draft as dishonored. In that case, the drawee may cancel the acceptance.

(b) The terms of a draft are not varied by an acceptance to pay at a particular bank or place in the United States, unless the acceptance states that the draft is to be paid only at that bank or place.

(c) If the holder assents to an acceptance varying the terms of a draft, the obligation of each drawer and indorser that does not expressly assent to the acceptance is discharged.

§ 3–411. Refusal to Pay Cashier's Checks, Teller's Checks, and Certified Checks.

(a) In this section, "obligated bank" means the acceptor of a certified check or the issuer of a cashier's check or teller's check bought from the issuer.

(b) If the obligated bank wrongfully (i) refuses to pay a cashier's check or certified check, (ii) stops payment of a teller's check, or (iii) refuses to pay a dishonored teller's check, the person asserting the right to enforce the check is entitled to compensation for expenses and loss of interest resulting from the nonpayment and may recover consequential damages if the obligated bank refuses to pay after receiving notice of particular circumstances giving rise to the damages.

(c) Expenses or consequential damages under subsection (b) are not recoverable if the refusal of the obligated bank to pay occurs because (i) the bank suspends payments, (ii) the obligated bank asserts a claim or defense of the bank that it has reasonable grounds to believe is available against the person entitled to enforce the instrument, (iii) the obligated bank has a reasonable doubt whether the person demanding payment is the person entitled to enforce the instrument, or (iv) payment is prohibited by law.

§ 3–412. Obligation of Issuer of Note or Cashier's Check.

The issuer of a note or cashier's check or other draft drawn on the drawer is obliged to pay the instrument (i) according to its terms at the time it was issued or, if not issued, at the time it first came into possession of a holder, or (ii) if the issuer signed an incomplete instrument, according to its terms when completed, to the extent stated in Sections 3–115 and 3–407. The obligation is owed to a person entitled to enforce the instrument or to an indorser who paid the instrument under Section 3–415.

§ 3–413. Obligation of Acceptor.

(a) The acceptor of a draft is obliged to pay the draft (i) according to its terms at the time it was accepted, even though the acceptance states that the draft is payable "as originally drawn" or equivalent terms, (ii) if the acceptance varies the terms of the draft, according to the terms of the draft as varied, or (iii) if the acceptance is of a draft that is an incomplete instrument, according to its terms when completed, to the extent stated in Sections 3–115 and 3–407. The obligation is owed to a person entitled to enforce the draft or to the drawer or an indorser who paid the draft under Section 3–414 or 3–415.

(b) If the certification of a check or other acceptance of a draft states the amount certified or accepted, the obligation of the acceptor is that amount. If (i) the certification or acceptance does not state an amount, (ii) the amount of the instrument is subsequently raised, and (iii) the instrument is then negotiated to a holder in due course, the obligation of the acceptor is the amount of the instrument at the time it was taken by the holder in due course.

§ 3–414. Obligation of Drawer.

(a) This section does not apply to cashier's checks or other drafts drawn on the drawer.

(b) If an unaccepted draft is dishonored, the drawer is obliged to pay the draft (i) according to its terms at the time it was issued or, if not issued, at the time it first came into possession of a holder, or (ii) if the drawer signed an incomplete instrument, according to its terms when completed, to the extent stated in Sections 3–115 and 3–407. The obligation is owed to a person entitled to enforce the draft or to an indorser who paid the draft under Section 3–415.

(c) If a draft is accepted by a bank, the drawer is discharged, regardless of when or by whom acceptance was obtained.

(d) If a draft is accepted and the acceptor is not a bank, the obligation of the drawer to pay the draft if the draft is dishonored by the acceptor is the same as the obligation of an indorser under Section 3–415(a) and (c).

(e) If a draft states that it is drawn "without recourse" or otherwise disclaims liability of the drawer to pay the draft, the drawer is not liable under subsection (b) to pay the draft if the draft is not a check. A disclaimer of the liability stated in subsection (b) is not effective if the draft is a check.

(f) If (i) a check is not presented for payment or given to a depositary bank for collection within 30 days after its date, (ii) the drawee suspends payments after expiration of the 30-day period without paying the check, and (iii) because of the suspension of payments, the drawer is deprived of funds maintained with the drawee to cover payment of the check, the drawer to the extent deprived of funds may discharge its obligation to pay the check by assigning to the person entitled to enforce the check the rights of the drawer against the drawee with respect to the funds.

§ 3–415. Obligation of Indorser.

(a) Subject to subsections (b), (c), and (d) and to Section 3–419(d), if an instrument is dishonored, an indorser is obliged to pay the amount due on the instrument (i) according to the terms of the instrument at the time it was indorsed, or (ii) if the indorser indorsed an incomplete instrument, according to its terms when completed, to the extent stated in Sections 3–115 and 3–407. The obligation of the indorser is owed to a person entitled to enforce the instrument or to a subsequent indorser who paid the instrument under this section.

(b) If an indorsement states that it is made "without recourse" or otherwise disclaims liability of the indorser, the indorser is not liable under subsection (a) to pay the instrument.

(c) If notice of dishonor of an instrument is required by Section 3–503 and notice of dishonor complying with that section is not given to an indorser, the liability of the indorser under subsection (a) is discharged.

(d) If a draft is accepted by a bank after an indorsement is made, the liability of the indorser under subsection (a) is discharged.

(e) If an indorser of a check is liable under subsection (a) and the check is not presented for payment, or given to a depositary bank for collection, within 30 days after the day the indorsement was made, the liability of the indorser under subsection (a) is discharged.

As amended in 1993.

§ 3–416. Transfer Warranties.

(a) A person who transfers an instrument for consideration warrants to the transferee and, if the transfer is by indorsement, to any subsequent transferee that:

(1) the warrantor is a person entitled to enforce the instrument;

(2) all signatures on the instrument are authentic and authorized;

(3) the instrument has not been altered;

(4) the instrument is not subject to a defense or claim in recoupment of any party which can be asserted against the warrantor; and

(5) the warrantor has no knowledge of any insolvency proceeding commenced with respect to the maker or acceptor or, in the case of an unaccepted draft, the drawer.

(b) A person to whom the warranties under subsection (a) are made and who took the instrument in good faith may recover from the warrantor as damages for breach of warranty an amount equal to the loss suffered as a result of the breach, but not more than the amount of the instrument plus expenses and loss of interest incurred as a result of the breach.

(c) The warranties stated in subsection (a) cannot be disclaimed with respect to checks. Unless notice of a claim for breach of warranty is given to the warrantor within 30 days after the claimant has reason to know of the breach and the identity of the warrantor, the liability of the warrantor under subsection (b) is discharged to the extent of any loss caused by the delay in giving notice of the claim.

(d) A [cause of action] for breach of warranty under this section accrues when the claimant has reason to know of the breach.

§ 3–417. Presentment Warranties.

(a) If an unaccepted draft is presented to the drawee for payment or acceptance and the drawee pays or accepts the draft, (i) the person obtaining payment or acceptance, at the time of presentment, and (ii) a previous transferor of the draft, at the time of transfer, warrant to the drawee making payment or accepting the draft in good faith that:

(1) the warrantor is, or was, at the time the warrantor transferred the draft, a person entitled to enforce the draft or authorized to obtain payment or acceptance of the draft on behalf of a person entitled to enforce the draft;

(2) the draft has not been altered; and

(3) the warrantor has no knowledge that the signature of the drawer of the draft is unauthorized.

(b) A drawee making payment may recover from any warrantor damages for breach of warranty equal to the amount paid by the drawee less the amount the drawee received or is entitled to receive from the drawer because of the payment. In addition, the drawee is entitled to compensation for expenses and loss of interest resulting from the breach. The right of the drawee to recover damages under this subsection is not affected by any failure of the drawee to exercise ordinary care in making payment. If the drawee accepts the draft, breach of warranty is a defense to the obligation of the acceptor. If the acceptor makes payment with respect to the draft, the acceptor is entitled to recover from any warrantor for breach of warranty the amounts stated in this subsection.

(c) If a drawee asserts a claim for breach of warranty under subsection (a) based on an unauthorized indorsement of the draft or an alteration of the draft, the warrantor may defend by proving that the indorsement is effective under Section 3–404 or 3–405 or the drawer is precluded under Section 3–406 or 4–406 from asserting against the drawee the unauthorized indorsement or alteration.

(d) If (i) a dishonored draft is presented for payment to the drawer or an indorser or (ii) any other instrument is presented for payment to a party obliged to pay the instrument, and (iii) payment is received, the following rules apply:

(1) The person obtaining payment and a prior transferor of the instrument warrant to the person making payment in good faith that the warrantor is, or was, at the time the warrantor transferred the instrument, a person entitled to enforce the instrument or authorized to obtain payment on behalf of a person entitled to enforce the instrument.

(2) The person making payment may recover from any warrantor for breach of warranty an amount equal to the amount paid plus expenses and loss of interest resulting from the breach.

(e) The warranties stated in subsections (a) and (d) cannot be disclaimed with respect to checks. Unless notice of a claim for breach of warranty is given to the warrantor within 30 days after the claimant has reason to know of the breach and the identity of the warrantor, the liability of the warrantor under subsection (b) or (d) is discharged to the extent of any loss caused by the delay in giving notice of the claim.

(f) A [cause of action] for breach of warranty under this section accrues when the claimant has reason to know of the breach.

§ 3–418. Payment or Acceptance by Mistake.

(a) Except as provided in subsection (c), if the drawee of a draft pays or accepts the draft and the drawee acted on the mistaken belief that (i) payment of the draft had not been stopped pursuant to Section 4–403 or (ii) the signature of the drawer of the draft was authorized, the drawee may recover the amount of the draft from the person to whom or for whose benefit payment was made or, in the case of acceptance, may revoke the acceptance. Rights of the drawee under this subsection are not affected by failure of the drawee to exercise ordinary care in paying or accepting the draft.

(b) Except as provided in subsection (c), if an instrument has been paid or accepted by mistake and the case is not covered by subsection (a), the person paying or accepting may, to the extent permitted by the law governing mistake and restitution, (i) recover the payment from the person to whom or for whose benefit payment was made or (ii) in the case of acceptance, may revoke the acceptance.

(c) The remedies provided by subsection (a) or (b) may not be asserted against a person who took the instrument in good faith and for value or who in good faith changed position in reliance on the payment or acceptance. This subsection does not limit remedies provided by Section 3–417 or 4–407.

(d) Notwithstanding Section 4–215, if an instrument is paid or accepted by mistake and the payor or acceptor recovers payment or revokes acceptance under subsection (a) or (b), the instrument is deemed not to have been paid or accepted and is treated as dishonored, and the person from whom payment is recovered has rights as a person entitled to enforce the dishonored instrument.

§ 3–419. Instruments Signed for Accommodation.

(a) If an instrument is issued for value given for the benefit of a party to the instrument ("accommodated party") and another party to the instrument ("accommodation party") signs the instrument for the purpose of incurring liability on the instrument without being a direct beneficiary of the value given for the instrument, the instrument is signed by the accommodation party "for accommodation."

(b) An accommodation party may sign the instrument as maker, drawer, acceptor, or indorser and, subject to subsection (d), is obliged to pay the instrument in the capacity in which the accommodation party signs. The obligation of an accommodation party may be enforced notwithstanding any statute of frauds and whether or not the accommodation party receives consideration for the accommodation.

(c) A person signing an instrument is presumed to be an accommodation party and there is notice that the instrument is signed for accommodation if the signature is an anomalous indorsement or is accompanied by words indicating that the signer is acting as surety or guarantor with respect to the obligation of another party to the instrument. Except as provided in Section 3–605, the obligation of an accommodation party to pay the instrument is not affected by the fact that the person enforcing the obligation had notice when the instrument was taken by that person that the accommodation party signed the instrument for accommodation.

(d) If the signature of a party to an instrument is accompanied by words indicating unambiguously that the party is guaranteeing collection rather than payment of the obligation of another party to the instrument, the signer is obliged to pay the amount due on the instrument to a person entitled to enforce the instrument only if (i) execution of judgment against the other party has been returned unsatisfied, (ii) the other party is insolvent or in an insolvency proceeding, (iii) the other party cannot be served with process, or (iv) it is otherwise apparent that payment cannot be obtained from the other party.

(e) An accommodation party who pays the instrument is entitled to reimbursement from the accommodated party and is entitled to enforce the instrument against the accommodated party. An accommodated party who pays the instrument has no right of recourse against, and is not entitled to contribution from, an accommodation party.

§ 3–420. Conversion of Instrument.

(a) The law applicable to conversion of personal property applies to instruments. An instrument is also converted if it is taken by transfer, other than a negotiation, from a person not entitled to enforce the instrument or a bank makes or obtains payment with respect to the instrument for a person not entitled to enforce the instrument or receive payment. An action for conversion of an instrument may not be brought by (i) the issuer or acceptor of the instrument or (ii) a payee or indorsee who did not receive delivery of the instrument either directly or through delivery to an agent or a co-payee.

(b) In an action under subsection (a), the measure of liability is presumed to be the amount payable on the instrument, but recovery may not exceed the amount of the plaintiff's interest in the instrument.

(c) A representative, other than a depositary bank, who has in good faith dealt with an instrument or its proceeds on behalf of one who was not the person entitled to enforce the instrument is not liable in conversion to that person beyond the amount of any proceeds that it has not paid out.

Part 5 Dishonor

§ 3–501. Presentment.

(a) "Presentment" means a demand made by or on behalf of a person entitled to enforce an instrument (i) to pay the instrument made to the drawee or a party obliged to pay the instrument or, in the case of a note or accepted draft payable at a bank, to the bank, or (ii) to accept a draft made to the drawee.

(b) The following rules are subject to Article 4, agreement of the parties, and clearing-house rules and the like:

> (1) Presentment may be made at the place of payment of the instrument and must be made at the place of payment if the instrument is payable at a bank in the United States; may be made by any commercially reasonable means, including an oral, written, or electronic communication; is effective when the demand for payment or acceptance is received by the person to whom present-

ment is made; and is effective if made to any one of two or more makers, acceptors, drawees, or other payors.

(2) Upon demand of the person to whom presentment is made, the person making presentment must (i) exhibit the instrument, (ii) give reasonable identification and, if presentment is made on behalf of another person, reasonable evidence of authority to do so, and (. . .) sign a receipt on the instrument for any payment made or surrender the instrument if full payment is made.

(3) Without dishonoring the instrument, the party to whom presentment is made may (i) return the instrument for lack of a necessary indorsement, or (ii) refuse payment or acceptance for failure of the presentment to comply with the terms of the instrument, an agreement of the parties, or other applicable law or rule.

(4) The party to whom presentment is made may treat presentment as occurring on the next business day after the day of presentment if the party to whom presentment is made has established a cut-off hour not earlier than 2 P.M. for the receipt and processing of instruments presented for payment or acceptance and presentment is made after the cut-off hour.

§ 3–502. Dishonor.

(a) Dishonor of a note is governed by the following rules:

(1) If the note is payable on demand, the note is dishonored if presentment is duly made to the maker and the note is not paid on the day of presentment.

(2) If the note is not payable on demand and is payable at or through a bank or the terms of the note require presentment, the note is dishonored if presentment is duly made and the note is not paid on the day it becomes payable or the day of presentment, whichever is later.

(3) If the note is not payable on demand and paragraph (2) does not apply, the note is dishonored if it is not paid on the day it becomes payable.

(b) Dishonor of an unaccepted draft other than a documentary draft is governed by the following rules:

(1) If a check is duly presented for payment to the payor bank otherwise than for immediate payment over the counter, the check is dishonored if the payor bank makes timely return of the check or sends timely notice of dishonor or nonpayment under Section 4–301 or 4–302, or becomes accountable for the amount of the check under Section 4–302.

(2) If a draft is payable on demand and paragraph (1) does not apply, the draft is dishonored if presentment for payment is duly made to the drawee and the draft is not paid on the day of presentment.

(3) If a draft is payable on a date stated in the draft, the draft is dishonored if (i) presentment for payment is duly made to the drawee and payment is not made on the day the draft becomes payable or the day of presentment, whichever is later, or (ii) presentment for acceptance is

duly made before the day the draft becomes payable and the draft is not accepted on the day of presentment.

(4) If a draft is payable on elapse of a period of time after sight or acceptance, the draft is dishonored if presentment for acceptance is duly made and the draft is not accepted on the day of presentment.

(c) Dishonor of an unaccepted documentary draft occurs according to the rules stated in subsection (b)(2), (3), and (4), except that payment or acceptance may be delayed without dishonor until no later than the close of the third business day of the drawee following the day on which payment or acceptance is required by those paragraphs.

(d) Dishonor of an accepted draft is governed by the following rules:

(1) If the draft is payable on demand, the draft is dishonored if presentment for payment is duly made to the acceptor and the draft is not paid on the day of presentment.

(2) If the draft is not payable on demand, the draft is dishonored if presentment for payment is duly made to the acceptor and payment is not made on the day it becomes payable or the day of presentment, whichever is later.

(e) In any case in which presentment is otherwise required for dishonor under this section and presentment is excused under Section 3–504, dishonor occurs without presentment if the instrument is not duly accepted or paid.

(f) If a draft is dishonored because timely acceptance of the draft was not made and the person entitled to demand acceptance consents to a late acceptance, from the time of acceptance the draft is treated as never having been dishonored.

§ 3–503. Notice of Dishonor.

(a) The obligation of an indorser stated in Section 3–415(a) and the obligation of a drawer stated in Section 3–414(d) may not be enforced unless (i) the indorser or drawer is given notice of dishonor of the instrument complying with this section or (ii) notice of dishonor is excused under Section 3–504(b).

(b) Notice of dishonor may be given by any person; may be given by any commercially reasonable means, including an oral, written, or electronic communication; and is sufficient if it reasonably identifies the instrument and indicates that the instrument has been dishonored or has not been paid or accepted. Return of an instrument given to a bank for collection is sufficient notice of dishonor.

(c) Subject to Section 3–504(c), with respect to an instrument taken for collection by a collecting bank, notice of dishonor must be given (i) by the bank before midnight of the next banking day following the banking day on which the bank receives notice of dishonor of the instrument, or (ii) by any other person within 30 days following the day on which the person receives notice of dishonor. With respect to any other instrument, notice of dishonor must be given within 30 days following the day on which dishonor occurs.

§ 3–504. Excused Presentment and Notice of Dishonor.

(a) Presentment for payment or acceptance of an instrument is excused if (i) the person entitled to present the instrument cannot with reasonable diligence make presentment, (ii) the maker or acceptor has repudiated an obligation to pay the instrument or is dead or in insolvency proceedings, (iii) by the terms of the instrument presentment is not necessary to enforce the obligation of indorsers or the drawer, (iv) the drawer or indorser whose obligation is being enforced has waived presentment or otherwise has no reason to expect or right to require that the instrument be paid or accepted, or (v) the drawer instructed the drawee not to pay or accept the draft or the drawee was not obligated to the drawer to pay the draft.

(b) Notice of dishonor is excused if (i) by the terms of the instrument notice of dishonor is not necessary to enforce the obligation of a party to pay the instrument, or (ii) the party whose obligation is being enforced waived notice of dishonor. A waiver of presentment is also a waiver of notice of dishonor.

(c) Delay in giving notice of dishonor is excused if the delay was caused by circumstances beyond the control of the person giving the notice and the person giving the notice exercised reasonable diligence after the cause of the delay ceased to operate.

§ 3–505. Evidence of Dishonor.

(a) The following are admissible as evidence and create a presumption of dishonor and of any notice of dishonor stated:

(1) a document regular in form as provided in subsection (b) which purports to be a protest;

(2) a purported stamp or writing of the drawee, payor bank, or presenting bank on or accompanying the instrument stating that acceptance or payment has been refused unless reasons for the refusal are stated and the reasons are not consistent with dishonor;

(3) a book or record of the drawee, payor bank, or collecting bank, kept in the usual course of business which shows dishonor, even if there is no evidence of who made the entry.

(b) A protest is a certificate of dishonor made by a United States consul or vice consul, or a notary public or other person authorized to administer oaths by the law of the place where dishonor occurs. It may be made upon information satisfactory to that person. The protest must identify the instrument and certify either that presentment has been made or, if not made, the reason why it was not made, and that the instrument has been dishonored by nonacceptance or nonpayment. The protest may also certify that notice of dishonor has been given to some or all parties.

Part 6 Discharge and Payment

§ 3–601. Discharge and Effect of Discharge.

(a) The obligation of a party to pay the instrument is discharged as stated in this Article or by an act or agreement with the party which would discharge an obligation to pay money under a simple contract.

(b) Discharge of the obligation of a party is not effective against a person acquiring rights of a holder in due course of the instrument without notice of the discharge.

§ 3–602. Payment.

(a) Subject to subsection (b), an instrument is paid to the extent payment is made (i) by or on behalf of a party obliged to pay the instrument, and (ii) to a person entitled to enforce the instrument. To the extent of the payment, the obligation of the party obliged to pay the instrument is discharged even though payment is made with knowledge of a claim to the instrument under Section 3–306 by another person.

(b) The obligation of a party to pay the instrument is not discharged under subsection (a) if:

(1) a claim to the instrument under Section 3–306 is enforceable against the party receiving payment and (i) payment is made with knowledge by the payor that payment is prohibited by injunction or similar process of a court of competent jurisdiction, or (ii) in the case of an instrument other than a cashier's check, teller's check, or certified check, the party making payment accepted, from the person having a claim to the instrument, indemnity against loss resulting from refusal to pay the person entitled to enforce the instrument; or

(2) the person making payment knows that the instrument is a stolen instrument and pays a person it knows is in wrongful possession of the instrument.

§ 3–603. Tender of Payment.

(a) If tender of payment of an obligation to pay an instrument is made to a person entitled to enforce the instrument, the effect of tender is governed by principles of law applicable to tender of payment under a simple contract.

(b) If tender of payment of an obligation to pay an instrument is made to a person entitled to enforce the instrument and the tender is refused, there is discharge, to the extent of the amount of the tender, of the obligation of an indorser or accommodation party having a right of recourse with respect to the obligation to which the tender relates.

(c) If tender of payment of an amount due on an instrument is made to a person entitled to enforce the instrument, the obligation of the obligor to pay interest after the due date on the amount tendered is discharged. If presentment is required with respect to an instrument and the obligor is able and ready to pay on the due date at every place of payment stated in the instrument, the obligor is deemed to have made tender of payment on the due date to the person entitled to enforce the instrument.

§ 3–604. Discharge by Cancellation or Renunciation.

(a) A person entitled to enforce an instrument, with or without consideration, may discharge the obligation of a party to pay the instrument (i) by an intentional voluntary act, such as surrender of the instrument to the party, destruction, mutilation, or cancellation of the instrument, cancellation or striking out of the party's signature, or the addition of words to the instrument indicating discharge, or (ii) by agreeing not to sue or otherwise renouncing rights against the party by a signed writing.

(b) Cancellation or striking out of an indorsement pursuant to subsection (a) does not affect the status and rights of a party derived from the indorsement.

§ 3–605. Discharge of Indorsers and Accommodation Parties.

(a) In this section, the term "indorser" includes a drawer having the obligation described in Section 3–414(d).

(b) Discharge, under Section 3–604, of the obligation of a party to pay an instrument does not discharge the obligation of an indorser or accommodation party having a right of recourse against the discharged party.

(c) If a person entitled to enforce an instrument agrees, with or without consideration, to an extension of the due date of the obligation of a party to pay the instrument, the extension discharges an indorser or accommodation party having a right of recourse against the party whose obligation is extended to the extent the indorser or accommodation party proves that the extension caused loss to the indorser or accommodation party with respect to the right of recourse.

(d) If a person entitled to enforce an instrument agrees, with or without consideration, to a material modification of the obligation of a party other than an extension of the due date, the modification discharges the obligation of an indorser or accommodation party having a right of recourse against the person whose obligation is modified to the extent the modification causes loss to the indorser or accommodation party with respect to the right of recourse. The loss suffered by the indorser or accommodation party as a result of the modification is equal to the amount of the right of recourse unless the person enforcing the instrument proves that no loss was caused by the modification or that the loss caused by the modification was an amount less than the amount of the right of recourse.

(e) If the obligation of a party to pay an instrument is secured by an interest in collateral and a person entitled to enforce the instrument impairs the value of the interest in collateral, the obligation of an indorser or accommodation party having a right of recourse against the obligor is discharged to the extent of the impairment. The value of an interest in collateral is impaired to the extent (i) the value of the interest is reduced to an amount less than the amount of the right of recourse of the party asserting discharge, or (ii) the reduction in value of the interest causes an increase in the amount by which the amount of the right of recourse exceeds the value of the interest. The burden of proving impairment is on the party asserting discharge.

(f) If the obligation of a party is secured by an interest in collateral not provided by an accommodation party and a person entitled to enforce the instrument impairs the value of the interest in collateral, the obligation of any party who is jointly and severally liable with respect to the secured obligation is discharged to the extent the impairment causes the party asserting discharge to pay more than that party would have been obliged to pay, taking into account rights of contribution, if impairment had not occurred. If the party asserting discharge is an accommodation party not entitled to discharge under subsection (e), the party is deemed to have a right to contribution based on joint and several liability rather than a right to reimbursement. The burden of proving impairment is on the party asserting discharge.

(g) Under subsection (e) or (f), impairing value of an interest in collateral includes (i) failure to obtain or maintain perfection or recordation of the interest in collateral, (ii) release of collateral without substitution of collateral of equal value, (iii) failure to perform a duty to preserve the value of collateral owed, under Article 9 or other law, to a debtor or surety or other person secondarily liable, or (iv) failure to comply with applicable law in disposing of collateral.

(h) An accommodation party is not discharged under subsection (c), (d), or (e) unless the person entitled to enforce the instrument knows of the accommodation or has notice under Section 3–419(c) that the instrument was signed for accommodation.

(i) A party is not discharged under this section if (i) the party asserting discharge consents to the event or conduct that is the basis of the discharge, or (ii) the instrument or a separate agreement of the party provides for waiver of discharge under this section either specifically or by general language indicating that parties waive defenses based on suretyship or impairment of collateral.

ADDENDUM TO REVISED ARTICLE 3

Notes to Legislative Counsel

1. If revised Article 3 is adopted in your state, the reference in Section 2–511 to Section 3–802 should be changed to Section 3–310.

2. If revised Article 3 is adopted in your state and the Uniform Fiduciaries Act is also in effect in your state, you may want to consider amending Uniform Fiduciaries Act § 9 to conform to Section 3–307(b)(2)(iii) and (4)(iii). See Official Comment 3 to Section 3–307.

Revised Article 4
BANK DEPOSITS AND COLLECTIONS

Part 1 General Provisions and Definitions

§ 4–101. Short Title.

This Article may be cited as Uniform Commercial Code—Bank Deposits and Collections.

As amended in 1990.

§ 4–102. Applicability.

(a) To the extent that items within this Article are also within Articles 3 and 8, they are subject to those Articles. If there is conflict, this Article governs Article 3, but Article 8 governs this Article.

(b) The liability of a bank for action or non-action with respect to an item handled by it for purposes of present-ment, payment, or collection is governed by the law of the place where the bank is located. In the case of action or non-action by or at a branch or separate office of a bank, its liability is governed by the law of the place where the branch or separate office is located.

§ 4–103. Variation by Agreement; Measure of Damages; Action Constituting Ordinary Care.

(a) The effect of the provisions of this Article may be var-ied by agreement, but the parties to the agreement cannot disclaim a bank's responsibility for its lack of good faith or failure to exercise ordinary care or limit the measure of dam-ages for the lack or failure. However, the parties may deter-mine by agreement the standards by which the bank's responsibility is to be measured if those standards are not manifestly unreasonable.

(b) Federal Reserve regulations and operating circulars, clearing-house rules, and the like have the effect of agree-ments under subsection (a), whether or not specifically assented to by all parties interested in items handled.

(c) Action or non-action approved by this Article or pur-suant to Federal Reserve regulations or operating circulars is the exercise of ordinary care and, in the absence of special instructions, action or non-action consistent with clearing-house rules and the like or with a general banking usage not disapproved by this Article, is prima facie the exercise of ordinary care.

(d) The specification or approval of certain procedures by this Article is not disapproval of other procedures that may be reasonable under the circumstances.

(e) The measure of damages for failure to exercise ordinary care in handling an item is the amount of the item reduced by an amount that could not have been realized by the exer-cise of ordinary care. If there is also bad faith it includes any other damages the party suffered as a proximate consequence. As amended in 1990.

§ 4–104. Definitions and Index of Definitions.

(a) In this Article, unless the context otherwise requires:

(1) "Account" means any deposit or credit account with a bank, including a demand, time, savings, pass-book, share draft, or like account, other than an account evidenced by a certificate of deposit;

(2) "Afternoon" means the period of a day between noon and midnight;

(3) "Banking day" means the part of a day on which a bank is open to the public for carrying on substantially all of its banking functions;

(4) "Clearing house" means an association of banks or other payors regularly clearing items;

(5) "Customer" means a person having an account with a bank or for whom a bank has agreed to collect items, including a bank that maintains an account at another bank;

(6) "Documentary draft" means a draft to be presented for acceptance or payment if specified documents, certifi-cated securities (Section 8–102) or instructions for uncer-tificated securities (Section 8–102), or other certificates, statements, or the like are to be received by the drawee or other payor before acceptance or payment of the draft;

(7) "Draft" means a draft as defined in Section 3–104 or an item, other than an instrument, that is an order;

(8) "Drawee" means a person ordered in a draft to make payment;

(9) "Item" means an instrument or a promise or order to pay money handled by a bank for collection or pay-ment. The term does not include a payment order gov-erned by Article 4A or a credit or debit card slip;

(10) "Midnight deadline" with respect to a bank is midnight on its next banking day following the bank-ing day on which it receives the relevant item or notice or from which the time for taking action commences to run, whichever is later;

(11) "Settle" means to pay in cash, by clearing-house settlement, in a charge or credit or by remittance, or otherwise as agreed. A settlement may be either provi-sional or final;

(12) "Suspends payments" with respect to a bank means that it has been closed by order of the supervi-sory authorities, that a public officer has been appointed to take it over, or that it ceases or refuses to make payments in the ordinary course of business.

(b) [Other definitions' section references deleted.]

(c) [Other definitions' section references deleted.]

(d) In addition, Article 1 contains general definitions and principles of construction and interpretation applicable throughout this Article.

§ 4–105. "Bank"; "Depositary Bank"; "Payor Bank"; "Intermediary Bank"; "Collecting Bank"; "Presenting Bank".

In this Article:

(1) "Bank" means a person engaged in the business of banking, including a savings bank, savings and loan associ-ation, credit union, or trust company;

(2) "Depositary bank" means the first bank to take an item even though it is also the payor bank, unless the item is presented for immediate payment over the counter;

(3) "Payor bank" means a bank that is the drawee of a draft;

(4) "Intermediary bank" means a bank to which an item is transferred in course of collection except the depositary or payor bank;

(5) "Collecting bank" means a bank handling an item for collection except the payor bank;

(6) "Presenting bank" means a bank presenting an item except a payor bank.

§ 4–106. Payable Through or Payable at Bank: Collecting Bank.

(a) If an item states that it is "payable through" a bank identified in the item, (i) the item designates the bank as a collecting bank and does not by itself authorize the bank to pay the item, and (ii) the item may be presented for payment only by or through the bank.

Alternative A

(b) If an item states that it is "payable at" a bank identified in the item, the item is equivalent to a draft drawn on the bank.

Alternative B

(b) If an item states that it is "payable at" a bank identified in the item, (i) the item designates the bank as a collecting bank and does not by itself authorize the bank to pay the item, and (ii) the item may be presented for payment only by or through the bank.

(c) If a draft names a nonbank drawee and it is unclear whether a bank named in the draft is a co-drawee or a collecting bank, the bank is a collecting bank.

As added in 1990.

§ 4–107. Separate Office of Bank.

A branch or separate office of a bank is a separate bank for the purpose of computing the time within which and determining the place at or to which action may be taken or notices or orders shall be given under this Article and under Article 3.

As amended in 1962 and 1990.

§ 4–108. Time of Receipt of Items.

(a) For the purpose of allowing time to process items, prove balances, and make the necessary entries on its books to determine its position for the day, a bank may fix an afternoon hour of 2 P.M. or later as a cutoff hour for the handling of money and items and the making of entries on its books.

(b) An item or deposit of money received on any day after a cutoff hour so fixed or after the close of the banking day may be treated as being received at the opening of the next banking day.

As amended in 1990.

§ 4–109. Delays.

(a) Unless otherwise instructed, a collecting bank in a good faith effort to secure payment of a specific item drawn on a payor other than a bank, and with or without the approval of any person involved, may waive, modify, or extend time limits imposed or permitted by this [act] for a period not exceeding two additional banking days without discharge of drawers or indorsers or liability to its transferor or a prior party.

(b) Delay by a collecting bank or payor bank beyond time limits prescribed or permitted by this [act] or by instructions is excused if (i) the delay is caused by interruption of communication or computer facilities, suspension of payments by another bank, war, emergency conditions, failure of equipment, or other circumstances beyond the control of the bank, and (ii) the bank exercises such diligence as the circumstances require.

§ 4–110. Electronic Presentment.

(a) "Agreement for electronic presentment" means an agreement, clearing-house rule, or Federal Reserve regulation or operating circular, providing that presentment of an item may be made by transmission of an image of an item or information describing the item ("presentment notice") rather than delivery of the item itself. The agreement may provide for procedures governing retention, presentment, payment, dishonor, and other matters concerning items subject to the agreement.

(b) Presentment of an item pursuant to an agreement for presentment is made when the presentment notice is received.

(c) If presentment is made by presentment notice, a reference to "item" or "check" in this Article means the presentment notice unless the context otherwise indicates.

As added in 1990.

§ 4–111. Statute of Limitations.

An action to enforce an obligation, duty, or right arising under this Article must be commenced within three years after the [cause of action] accrues.

As added in 1990.

Part 2 Collection of Items: Depositary and Collecting Banks

§ 4–201. Status of Collecting Bank as Agent and Provisional Status of Credits; Applicability of Article; Item Indorsed "Pay Any Bank".

(a) Unless a contrary intent clearly appears and before the time that a settlement given by a collecting bank for an item is or becomes final, the bank, with respect to an item, is an agent or sub-agent of the owner of the item and any settlement given for the item is provisional. This provision applies regardless of the form of indorsement or lack of indorsement and even though credit given for the item is subject to immediate withdrawal as of right or is in fact withdrawn; but the continuance of ownership of an item by its owner and any rights of the owner to proceeds of the item are subject to rights of a collecting bank, such as those resulting from outstanding advances on the item and rights of recoupment or setoff. If an item is handled by banks for purposes of presentment, payment, collection, or return, the relevant provisions of this Article apply even though action of the parties clearly establishes that a particular bank has purchased the item and is the owner of it.

(b) After an item has been indorsed with the words "pay any bank" or the like, only a bank may acquire the rights of a holder until the item has been:

(1) returned to the customer initiating collection; or

(2) specially indorsed by a bank to a person who is not a bank.

As amended in 1990.

§ 4–202. Responsibility for Collection or Return; When Action Timely.

(a) A collecting bank must exercise ordinary care in:

(1) presenting an item or sending it for presentment;

(2) sending notice of dishonor or nonpayment or returning an item other than a documentary draft to the bank's transferor after learning that the item has not been paid or accepted, as the case may be;

(3) settling for an item when the bank receives final settlement; and

(4) notifying its transferor of any loss or delay in transit within a reasonable time after discovery thereof.

(b) A collecting bank exercises ordinary care under subsection (a) by taking proper action before its midnight deadline following receipt of an item, notice, or settlement. Taking proper action within a reasonably longer time may constitute the exercise of ordinary care, but the bank has the burden of establishing timeliness.

(c) Subject to subsection (a)(1), a bank is not liable for the insolvency, neglect, misconduct, mistake, or default of another bank or person or for loss or destruction of an item in the possession of others or in transit.

As amended in 1990.

§ 4–203. Effect of Instructions.

Subject to Article 3 concerning conversion of instruments (Section 3–420) and restrictive indorsements (Section 3–206), only a collecting bank's transferor can give instructions that affect the bank or constitute notice to it, and a collecting bank is not liable to prior parties for any action taken pursuant to the instructions or in accordance with any agreement with its transferor.

§ 4–204. Methods of Sending and Presenting; Sending Directly to Payor Bank.

(a) A collecting bank shall send items by a reasonably prompt method, taking into consideration relevant instruc-

tions, the nature of the item, the number of those items on hand, the cost of collection involved, and the method generally used by it or others to present those items.

(b) A collecting bank may send:

(1) an item directly to the payor bank;

(2) an item to a nonbank payor if authorized by its transferor; and

(3) an item other than documentary drafts to a nonbank payor, if authorized by Federal Reserve regulation or operating circular, clearing-house rule, or the like.

(c) Presentment may be made by a presenting bank at a place where the payor bank or other payor has requested that presentment be made.

As amended in 1990.

§ 4–205. Depository Bank Holder of Unindorsed Item.

If a customer delivers an item to a depositary bank for collection:

(1) the depositary bank becomes a holder of the item at the time it receives the item for collection if the customer at the time of delivery was a holder of the item, whether or not the customer indorses the item, and, if the bank satisfies the other requirements of Section 3–302, it is a holder in due course; and

(2) the depositary bank warrants to collecting banks, the payor bank or other payor, and the drawer that the amount of the item was paid to the customer or deposited to the customer's account.

As amended in 1990.

§ 4–206. Transfer Between Banks.

Any agreed method that identifies the transferor bank is sufficient for the item's further transfer to another bank.

As amended in 1990.

§ 4–207. Transfer Warranties.

(a) A customer or collecting bank that transfers an item and receives a settlement or other consideration warrants to the transferee and to any subsequent collecting bank that:

(1) the warrantor is a person entitled to enforce the item;

(2) all signatures on the item are authentic and authorized;

(3) the item has not been altered;

(4) the item is not subject to a defense or claim in recoupment (Section 3–305(a)) of any party that can be asserted against the warrantor; and

(5) the warrantor has no knowledge of any insolvency proceeding commenced with respect to the maker or acceptor or, in the case of an unaccepted draft, the drawer.

(b) If an item is dishonored, a customer or collecting bank transferring the item and receiving settlement or other consideration is obliged to pay the amount due on the item (i) according to the terms of the item at the time it was transferred, or (ii) if the transfer was of an incomplete item, according to its terms when completed as stated in Sections 3–115 and 3–407. The obligation of a transferor is owed to the transferee and to any subsequent collecting bank that takes the item in good faith. A transferor cannot disclaim its obligation under this subsection by an indorsement stating that it is made "without recourse" or otherwise disclaiming liability.

(c) A person to whom the warranties under subsection (a) are made and who took the item in good faith may recover from the warrantor as damages for breach of warranty an amount equal to the loss suffered as a result of the breach, but not more than the amount of the item plus expenses and loss of interest incurred as a result of the breach.

(d) The warranties stated in subsection (a) cannot be disclaimed with respect to checks. Unless notice of a claim for breach of warranty is given to the warrantor within 30 days after the claimant has reason to know of the breach and the identity of the warrantor, the warrantor is discharged to the extent of any loss caused by the delay in giving notice of the claim.

(e) A cause of action for breach of warranty under this section accrues when the claimant has reason to know of the breach.

As amended in 1990.

§ 4–208. Presentment Warranties.

(a) If an unaccepted draft is presented to the drawee for payment or acceptance and the drawee pays or accepts the draft, (i) the person obtaining payment or acceptance, at the time of presentment, and (ii) a previous transferor of the draft, at the time of transfer, warrant to the drawee that pays or accepts the draft in good faith that:

(1) the warrantor is, or was, at the time the warrantor transferred the draft, a person entitled to enforce the draft or authorized to obtain payment or acceptance of the draft on behalf of a person entitled to enforce the draft;

(2) the draft has not been altered; and

(3) the warrantor has no knowledge that the signature of the purported drawer of the draft is unauthorized.

(b) A drawee making payment may recover from a warrantor damages for breach of warranty equal to the amount paid by the drawee less the amount the drawee received or is entitled to receive from the drawer because of the payment. In addition, the drawee is entitled to compensation for expenses and loss of interest resulting from the breach. The right of the drawee to recover damages under this subsection is not affected by any failure of the drawee to exercise ordinary care in making payment. If the drawee accepts the draft (i) breach of warranty is a defense to the obligation of the acceptor, and (ii) if the acceptor makes payment with respect to the draft, the acceptor is entitled to recover from a warrantor for breach of warranty the amounts stated in this subsection.

(c) If a drawee asserts a claim for breach of warranty under subsection (a) based on an unauthorized indorsement of the draft or an alteration of the draft, the warrantor may defend by proving that the indorsement is effective under Section 3–404 or 3–405 or the drawer is precluded under Section 3–406 or 4–406 from asserting against the drawee the unauthorized indorsement or alteration.

(d) If (i) a dishonored draft is presented for payment to the drawer or an indorser or (ii) any other item is presented for payment to a party obliged to pay the item, and the item is paid, the person obtaining payment and a prior transferor of the item warrant to the person making payment in good faith that the warrantor is, or was, at the time the warrantor transferred the item, a person entitled to enforce the item or authorized to obtain payment on behalf of a person entitled to enforce the item. The person making payment may recover from any warrantor for breach of warranty an amount equal to the amount paid plus expenses and loss of interest resulting from the breach.

(e) The warranties stated in subsections (a) and (d) cannot be disclaimed with respect to checks. Unless notice of a claim for breach of warranty is given to the warrantor within 30 days after the claimant has reason to know of the breach and the identity of the warrantor, the warrantor is discharged to the extent of any loss caused by the delay in giving notice of the claim.

(f) A cause of action for breach of warranty under this section accrues when the claimant has reason to know of the breach.

As amended in 1990.

§ 4–209. Encoding and Retention Warranties.

(a) A person who encodes information on or with respect to an item after issue warrants to any subsequent collecting bank and to the payor bank or other payor that the information is correctly encoded. If the customer of a depositary bank encodes, that bank also makes the warranty.

(b) A person who undertakes to retain an item pursuant to an agreement for electronic presentment warrants to any subsequent collecting bank and to the payor bank or other payor that retention and presentment of the item comply with the agreement. If a customer of a depositary bank undertakes to retain an item, that bank also makes this warranty.

(c) A person to whom warranties are made under this section and who took the item in good faith may recover from the warrantor as damages for breach of warranty an amount equal to the loss suffered as a result of the breach, plus expenses and loss of interest incurred as a result of the breach.

As added in 1990.

§ 4–210. Security Interest of Collecting Bank in Items, Accompanying Documents and Proceeds.

(a) A collecting bank has a security interest in an item and any accompanying documents or the proceeds of either:

(1) in case of an item deposited in an account, to the extent to which credit given for the item has been withdrawn or applied;

(2) in case of an item for which it has given credit available for withdrawal as of right, to the extent of the credit given, whether or not the credit is drawn upon or there is a right of charge-back; or

(3) if it makes an advance on or against the item.

(b) If credit given for several items received at one time or pursuant to a single agreement is withdrawn or applied in part, the security interest remains upon all the items, any accompanying documents or the proceeds of either. For the purpose of this section, credits first given are first withdrawn.

(c) Receipt by a collecting bank of a final settlement for an item is a realization on its security interest in the item, accompanying documents, and proceeds. So long as the bank does not receive final settlement for the item or give up possession of the item or accompanying documents for purposes other than collection, the security interest continues to that extent and is subject to Article 9, but:

(1) no security agreement is necessary to make the security interest enforceable (Section 9–203(1)(a));

(2) no filing is required to perfect the security interest; and

(3) the security interest has priority over conflicting perfected security interests in the item, accompanying documents, or proceeds.

As amended in 1990 and 1999.

§ 4–211. When Bank Gives Value for Purposes of Holder in Due Course.

For purposes of determining its status as a holder in due course, a bank has given value to the extent it has a security interest in an item, if the bank otherwise complies with the requirements of Section 3–302 on what constitutes a holder in due course.

As amended in 1990.

§ 4–212. Presentment by Notice of Item Not Payable by, Through, or at Bank; Liability of Drawer or Indorser.

(a) Unless otherwise instructed, a collecting bank may present an item not payable by, through, or at a bank by sending to the party to accept or pay a written notice that the bank holds the item for acceptance or payment. The notice must be sent in time to be received on or before the day when presentment is due and the bank must meet any requirement of the party to accept or pay under Section 3–501 by the close of the bank's next banking day after it knows of the requirement.

(b) If presentment is made by notice and payment, acceptance, or request for compliance with a requirement under Section 3–501 is not received by the close of business on the day after maturity or, in the case of demand items, by the close of business on the third banking day after notice was sent, the presenting bank may treat the item as dishonored and charge any drawer or indorser by sending it notice of the facts.

As amended in 1990.

§ 4–213. Medium and Time of Settlement by Bank.

(a) With respect to settlement by a bank, the medium and time of settlement may be prescribed by Federal Reserve regulations or circulars, clearing-house rules, and the like, or agreement. In the absence of such prescription:

(1) the medium of settlement is cash or credit to an account in a Federal Reserve bank of or specified by the person to receive settlement; and

(2) the time of settlement is:

(i) with respect to tender of settlement by cash, a cashier's check, or teller's check, when the cash or check is sent or delivered;

(ii) with respect to tender of settlement by credit in an account in a Federal Reserve Bank, when the credit is made;

(iii) with respect to tender of settlement by a credit or debit to an account in a bank, when the credit or debit is made or, in the case of tender of settlement by authority to charge an account, when the authority is sent or delivered; or

(iv) with respect to tender of settlement by a funds transfer, when payment is made pursuant to Section 4A–406(a) to the person receiving settlement.

(b) If the tender of settlement is not by a medium authorized by subsection (a) or the time of settlement is not fixed by subsection (a), no settlement occurs until the tender of settlement is accepted by the person receiving settlement.

(c) If settlement for an item is made by cashier's check or teller's check and the person receiving settlement, before its midnight deadline:

(1) presents or forwards the check for collection, settlement is final when the check is finally paid; or

(2) fails to present or forward the check for collection, settlement is final at the midnight deadline of the person receiving settlement.

(d) If settlement for an item is made by giving authority to charge the account of the bank giving settlement in the bank receiving settlement, settlement is final when the charge is made by the bank receiving settlement if there are funds available in the account for the amount of the item.

As amended in 1990.

§ 4–214. Right of Charge-Back or Refund; Liability of Collecting Bank: Return of Item.

(a) If a collecting bank has made provisional settlement with its customer for an item and fails by reason of dishonor, suspension of payments by a bank, or otherwise to receive settlement for the item which is or becomes final, the bank may revoke the settlement given by it, charge back the amount of any credit given for the item to its customer's account, or obtain refund from its customer, whether or not it is able to return the item, if by its midnight deadline or within a longer reasonable time after it learns the facts it returns the item or sends notification of the facts. If the return or notice is delayed beyond the bank's midnight deadline or a longer reasonable time after it learns the facts, the bank may revoke the settlement, charge back the credit, or obtain refund from its customer, but it is liable for any loss resulting from the delay. These rights to revoke, charge back, and obtain refund terminate if and when a settlement for the item received by the bank is or becomes final.

(b) A collecting bank returns an item when it is sent or delivered to the bank's customer or transferor or pursuant to its instructions.

(c) A depositary bank that is also the payor may charge back the amount of an item to its customer's account or obtain refund in accordance with the section governing return of an item received by a payor bank for credit on its books (Section 4–301).

(d) The right to charge back is not affected by:

(1) previous use of a credit given for the item; or

(2) failure by any bank to exercise ordinary care with respect to the item, but a bank so failing remains liable.

(e) A failure to charge back or claim refund does not affect other rights of the bank against the customer or any other party.

(f) If credit is given in dollars as the equivalent of the value of an item payable in foreign money, the dollar amount of any charge-back or refund must be calculated on the basis of the bank-offered spot rate for the foreign money prevailing on the day when the person entitled to the charge-back or refund learns that it will not receive payment in ordinary course.

As amended in 1990.

§ 4–215. Final Payment of Item by Payor Bank; When Provisional Debits and Credits Become Final; When Certain Credits Become Available for Withdrawal.

(a) An item is finally paid by a payor bank when the bank has first done any of the following:

(1) paid the item in cash;

(2) settled for the item without having a right to revoke the settlement under statute, clearing-house rule, or agreement; or

(3) made a provisional settlement for the item and failed to revoke the settlement in the time and manner permitted by statute, clearing-house rule, or agreement.

(b) If provisional settlement for an item does not become final, the item is not finally paid.

(c) If provisional settlement for an item between the presenting and payor banks is made through a clearing house or by debits or credits in an account between them, then to the extent that provisional debits or credits for the item are entered in accounts between the presenting and payor banks or between the presenting and successive prior collecting banks seriatim, they become final upon final payment of the item by the payor bank.

(d) If a collecting bank receives a settlement for an item which is or becomes final, the bank is accountable to its customer for the amount of the item and any provisional credit given for the item in an account with its customer becomes final.

(e) Subject to (i) applicable law stating a time for availability of funds and (ii) any right of the bank to apply the credit to an obligation of the customer, credit given by a bank for an item in a customer's account becomes available for withdrawal as of right:

(1) if the bank has received a provisional settlement for the item, when the settlement becomes final and the bank has had a reasonable time to receive return of the item and the item has not been received within that time;

(2) if the bank is both the depositary bank and the payor bank, and the item is finally paid, at the opening of the bank's second banking day following receipt of the item.

(f) Subject to applicable law stating a time for availability of funds and any right of a bank to apply a deposit to an obligation of the depositor, a deposit of money becomes available for withdrawal as of right at the opening of the bank's next banking day after receipt of the deposit.

As amended in 1990.

§ 4–216. Insolvency and Preference.

(a) If an item is in or comes into the possession of a payor or collecting bank that suspends payment and the item has not been finally paid, the item must be returned by the receiver, trustee, or agent in charge of the closed bank to the presenting bank or the closed bank's customer.

(b) If a payor bank finally pays an item and suspends payments without making a settlement for the item with its customer or the presenting bank which settlement is or becomes final, the owner of the item has a preferred claim against the payor bank.

(c) If a payor bank gives or a collecting bank gives or receives a provisional settlement for an item and thereafter suspends payments, the suspension does not prevent or interfere with the settlement's becoming final if the finality occurs automatically upon the lapse of certain time or the happening of certain events.

(d) If a collecting bank receives from subsequent parties settlement for an item, which settlement is or becomes final and the bank suspends payments without making a settlement for the item with its customer which settlement is or becomes final, the owner of the item has a preferred claim against the collecting bank.

As amended in 1990.

Part 3 Collection of Items: Payor Banks

§ 4–301. Deferred Posting; Recovery of Payment by Return of Items; Time of Dishonor; Return of Items by Payor Bank.

(a) If a payor bank settles for a demand item other than a documentary draft presented otherwise than for immediate payment over the counter before midnight of the banking day of receipt, the payor bank may revoke the settlement and recover the settlement if, before it has made final payment and before its midnight deadline, it

(1) returns the item; or

(2) sends written notice of dishonor or nonpayment if the item is unavailable for return.

(b) If a demand item is received by a payor bank for credit on its books, it may return the item or send notice of dishonor and may revoke any credit given or recover the amount thereof withdrawn by its customer, if it acts within the time limit and in the manner specified in subsection (a).

(c) Unless previous notice of dishonor has been sent, an item is dishonored at the time when for purposes of dishonor it is returned or notice sent in accordance with this section.

(d) An item is returned:

(1) as to an item presented through a clearing house, when it is delivered to the presenting or last collecting bank or to the clearing house or is sent or delivered in accordance with clearing-house rules; or

(2) in all other cases, when it is sent or delivered to the bank's customer or transferor or pursuant to instructions.

As amended in 1990.

§ 4–302. Payor Bank's Responsibility for Late Return of Item.

(a) If an item is presented to and received by a payor bank, the bank is accountable for the amount of:

(1) a demand item, other than a documentary draft, whether properly payable or not, if the bank, in any case in which it is not also the depositary bank, retains the item beyond midnight of the banking day of receipt without settling for it or, whether or not it is also the depositary bank, does not pay or return the item or send notice of dishonor until after its midnight deadline; or

(2) any other properly payable item unless, within the time allowed for acceptance or payment of that item, the bank either accepts or pays the item or returns it and accompanying documents.

(b) The liability of a payor bank to pay an item pursuant to subsection (a) is subject to defenses based on breach of a presentment warranty (Section 4–208) or proof that the person seeking enforcement of the liability presented or transferred the item for the purpose of defrauding the payor bank.

As amended in 1990.

§ 4–303. When Items Subject to Notice, Stop-Payment Order, Legal Process, or Setoff; Order in Which Items May Be Charged or Certified.

(a) Any knowledge, notice, or stop-payment order received by, legal process served upon, or setoff exercised by a payor bank comes too late to terminate, suspend, or modify the bank's right or duty to pay an item or to charge its customer's account for the item if the knowledge, notice, stop-payment order, or legal process is received or served and a reasonable time for the bank to act thereon expires or the setoff is exercised after the earliest of the following:

(1) the bank accepts or certifies the item;

(2) the bank pays the item in cash;

(3) the bank settles for the item without having a right to revoke the settlement under statute, clearing-house rule, or agreement;

(4) the bank becomes accountable for the amount of the item under Section 4–302 dealing with the payor bank's responsibility for late return of items; or

(5) with respect to checks, a cutoff hour no earlier than one hour after the opening of the next banking day after the banking day on which the bank received the check and no later than the close of that next banking day or, if no cutoff hour is fixed, the close of the next banking day after the banking day on which the bank received the check.

(b) Subject to subsection (a), items may be accepted, paid, certified, or charged to the indicated account of its customer in any order.

As amended in 1990.

Part 4 Relationship Between Payor Bank and Its Customer

§ 4–401. When Bank May Charge Customer's Account.

(a) A bank may charge against the account of a customer an item that is properly payable from the account even though the charge creates an overdraft. An item is properly payable if it is authorized by the customer and is in accordance with any agreement between the customer and bank.

(b) A customer is not liable for the amount of an overdraft if the customer neither signed the item nor benefited from the proceeds of the item.

(c) A bank may charge against the account of a customer a check that is otherwise properly payable from the account, even though payment was made before the date of the check, unless the customer has given notice to the bank of the postdating describing the check with reasonable certainty. The notice is effective for the period stated in Section

4–403(b) for stop-payment orders, and must be received at such time and in such manner as to afford the bank a reasonable opportunity to act on it before the bank takes any action with respect to the check described in Section 4–303. If a bank charges against the account of a customer a check before the date stated in the notice of postdating, the bank is liable for damages for the loss resulting from its act. The loss may include damages for dishonor of subsequent items under Section 4–402.

(d) A bank that in good faith makes payment to a holder may charge the indicated account of its customer according to:

(1) the original terms of the altered item; or

(2) the terms of the completed item, even though the bank knows the item has been completed unless the bank has notice that the completion was improper.

As amended in 1990.

§ 4–402. Bank's Liability to Customer for Wrongful Dishonor; Time of Determining Insufficiency of Account.

(a) Except as otherwise provided in this Article, a payor bank wrongfully dishonors an item if it dishonors an item that is properly payable, but a bank may dishonor an item that would create an overdraft unless it has agreed to pay the overdraft.

(b) A payor bank is liable to its customer for damages proximately caused by the wrongful dishonor of an item. Liability is limited to actual damages proved and may include damages for an arrest or prosecution of the customer or other consequential damages. Whether any consequential damages are proximately caused by the wrongful dishonor is a question of fact to be determined in each case.

(c) A payor bank's determination of the customer's account balance on which a decision to dishonor for insufficiency of available funds is based may be made at any time between the time the item is received by the payor bank and the time that the payor bank returns the item or gives notice in lieu of return, and no more than one determination need be made. If, at the election of the payor bank, a subsequent balance determination is made for the purpose of reevaluating the bank's decision to dishonor the item, the account balance at that time is determinative of whether a dishonor for insufficiency of available funds is wrongful.

As amended in 1990.

§ 4–403. Customer's Right to Stop Payment; Burden of Proof of Loss.

(a) A customer or any person authorized to draw on the account if there is more than one person may stop payment of any item drawn on the customer's account or close the account by an order to the bank describing the item or account with reasonable certainty received at a time and in a manner that affords the bank a reasonable opportunity to act on it before any action by the bank with respect to the item described in Section 4–303. If the signature of more than one person is required to draw on an account, any of these persons may stop payment or close the account.

(b) A stop-payment order is effective for six months, but it lapses after 14 calendar days if the original order was oral and was not confirmed in writing within that period. A stop-payment order may be renewed for additional six-month periods by a writing given to the bank within a period during which the stop-payment order is effective.

(c) The burden of establishing the fact and amount of loss resulting from the payment of an item contrary to a stop-payment order or order to close an account is on the customer. The loss from payment of an item contrary to a stop-payment order may include damages for dishonor of subsequent items under Section 4–402.

As amended in 1990.

§ 4–404. Bank Not Obliged to Pay Check More Than Six Months Old.

A bank is under no obligation to a customer having a checking account to pay a check, other than a certified check, which is presented more than six months after its date, but it may charge its customer's account for a payment made thereafter in good faith.

§ 4–405. Death or Incompetence of Customer.

(a) A payor or collecting bank's authority to accept, pay, or collect an item or to account for proceeds of its collection, if otherwise effective, is not rendered ineffective by incompetence of a customer of either bank existing at the time the item is issued or its collection is undertaken if the bank does not know of an adjudication of incompetence. Neither death nor incompetence of a customer revokes the authority to accept, pay, collect, or account until the bank knows of the fact of death or of an adjudication of incompetence and has reasonable opportunity to act on it.

(b) Even with knowledge, a bank may for 10 days after the date of death pay or certify checks drawn on or before the date unless ordered to stop payment by a person claiming an interest in the account.

As amended in 1990.

§ 4–406. Customer's Duty to Discover and Report Unauthorized Signature or Alteration.

(a) A bank that sends or makes available to a customer a statement of account showing payment of items for the account shall either return or make available to the customer the items paid or provide information in the statement of account sufficient to allow the customer reasonably to identify the items paid. The statement of account provides sufficient information if the item is described by item number, amount, and date of payment.

(b) If the items are not returned to the customer, the person retaining the items shall either retain the items or, if the items are destroyed, maintain the capacity to furnish legible copies of the items until the expiration of seven years after receipt of the items. A customer may request an item from the bank that paid the item, and that bank must provide in a reasonable time either the item or, if the item has been destroyed or is not otherwise obtainable, a legible copy of the item.

(c) If a bank sends or makes available a statement of account or items pursuant to subsection (a), the customer must exercise reasonable promptness in examining the statement or the items to determine whether any payment was not authorized because of an alteration of an item or because a purported signature by or on behalf of the customer was not authorized. If, based on the statement or items provided, the customer should reasonably have discovered the unauthorized payment, the customer must promptly notify the bank of the relevant facts.

(d) If the bank proves that the customer failed, with respect to an item, to comply with the duties imposed on the customer by subsection (c), the customer is precluded from asserting against the bank:

(1) the customer's unauthorized signature or any alteration on the item, if the bank also proves that it suffered a loss by reason of the failure; and

(2) the customer's unauthorized signature or alteration by the same wrongdoer on any other item paid in good faith by the bank if the payment was made before the bank received notice from the customer of the unauthorized signature or alteration and after the customer had been afforded a reasonable period of time, not exceeding 30 days, in which to examine the item or statement of account and notify the bank.

(e) If subsection (d) applies and the customer proves that the bank failed to exercise ordinary care in paying the item and that the failure substantially contributed to loss, the loss is allocated between the customer precluded and the bank asserting the preclusion according to the extent to which the failure of the customer to comply with subsection (c) and the failure of the bank to exercise ordinary care contributed to the loss. If the customer proves that the bank did not pay the item in good faith, the preclusion under subsection (d) does not apply.

(f) Without regard to care or lack of care of either the customer or the bank, a customer who does not within one year after the statement or items are made available to the customer (subsection (a)) discover and report the customer's unauthorized signature on or any alteration on the item is precluded from asserting against the bank the unauthorized signature or alteration. If there is a preclusion under this subsection, the payor bank may not recover for breach or warranty under Section 4–208 with respect to the unauthorized signature or alteration to which the preclusion applies.

As amended in 1990.

§ 4–407. Payor Bank's Right to Subrogation on Improper Payment.

If a payor has paid an item over the order of the drawer or maker to stop payment, or after an account has been closed, or otherwise under circumstances giving a basis for objection by the drawer or maker, to prevent unjust enrichment and only to the extent necessary to prevent loss to the bank by reason of its payment of the item, the payor bank is subrogated to the rights

(1) of any holder in due course on the item against the drawer or maker;

(2) of the payee or any other holder of the item against the drawer or maker either on the item or under the transaction out of which the item arose; and

(3) of the drawer or maker against the payee or any other holder of the item with respect to the transaction out of which the item arose.

As amended in 1990.

Part 5 Collection of Documentary Drafts

§ 4–501. Handling of Documentary Drafts; Duty to Send for Presentment and to Notify Customer of Dishonor.

A bank that takes a documentary draft for collection shall present or send the draft and accompanying documents for presentment and, upon learning that the draft has not been paid or accepted in due course, shall seasonably notify its customer of the fact even though it may have discounted or bought the draft or extended credit available for withdrawal as of right.

As amended in 1990.

§ 4–502. Presentment of "On Arrival" Drafts.

If a draft or the relevant instructions require presentment "on arrival", "when goods arrive" or the like, the collecting bank need not present until in its judgment a reasonable time for arrival of the goods has expired. Refusal to pay or accept because the goods have not arrived is not dishonor; the bank must notify its transferor of the refusal but need not present the draft again until it is instructed to do so or learns of the arrival of the goods.

§ 4–503. Responsibility of Presenting Bank for Documents and Goods; Report of Reasons for Dishonor; Referee in Case of Need.

Unless otherwise instructed and except as provided in Article 5, a bank presenting a documentary draft:

(1) must deliver the documents to the drawee on acceptance of the draft if it is payable more than three days after presentment, otherwise, only on payment; and

(2) upon dishonor, either in the case of presentment for acceptance or presentment for payment, may seek and

follow instructions from any referee in case of need designated in the draft or, if the presenting bank does not choose to utilize the referee's services, it must use diligence and good faith to ascertain the reason for dishonor, must notify its transferor of the dishonor and of the results of its effort to ascertain the reasons therefor, and must request instructions.

However, the presenting bank is under no obligation with respect to goods represented by the documents except to follow any reasonable instructions seasonably received; it has a right to reimbursement for any expense incurred in following instructions and to prepayment of or indemnity for those expenses.

As amended in 1990.

§ 4–504. Privilege of Presenting Bank to Deal With Goods; Security Interest for Expenses.

(a) A presenting bank that, following the dishonor of a documentary draft, has seasonably requested instructions but does not receive them within a reasonable time may store, sell, or otherwise deal with the goods in any reasonable manner.

(b) For its reasonable expenses incurred by action under subsection (a) the presenting bank has a lien upon the goods or their proceeds, which may be foreclosed in the same manner as an unpaid seller's lien.

As amended in 1990.

Article 4A
FUNDS TRANSFERS

Part 1 Subject Matter and Definitions

§ 4A–101. Short Title.

This Article may be cited as Uniform Commercial Code—Funds Transfers.

§ 4A–102. Subject Matter.

Except as otherwise provided in Section 4A–108, this Article applies to funds transfers defined in Section 4A–104.

§ 4A–103. Payment Order–Definitions.

(a) In this Article:

(1) "Payment order" means an instruction of a sender to a receiving bank, transmitted orally, electronically, or in writing, to pay, or to cause another bank to pay, a fixed or determinable amount of money to a beneficiary if:

(i) the instruction does not state a condition to payment to the beneficiary other than time of payment,

(ii) the receiving bank is to be reimbursed by debiting an account of, or otherwise receiving payment from, the sender, and

(iii) the instruction is transmitted by the sender directly to the receiving bank or to an agent, funds-transfer system, or communication system for transmittal to the receiving bank.

(2) "Beneficiary" means the person to be paid by the beneficiary's bank.

(3) "Beneficiary's bank" means the bank identified in a payment order in which an account of the beneficiary is to be credited pursuant to the order or which otherwise is to make payment to the beneficiary if the order does not provide for payment to an account.

(4) "Receiving bank" means the bank to which the sender's instruction is addressed.

(5) "Sender" means the person giving the instruction to the receiving bank.

(b) If an instruction complying with subsection (a)(1) is to make more than one payment to a beneficiary, the instruction is a separate payment order with respect to each payment.

(c) A payment order is issued when it is sent to the receiving bank.

§ 4A–104. Funds Transfer–Definitions.

In this Article:

(a) "Funds transfer" means the series of transactions, beginning with the originator's payment order, made for the purpose of making payment to the beneficiary of the order. The term includes any payment order issued by the originator's bank or an intermediary bank intended to carry out the originator's payment order. A funds transfer is completed by acceptance by the beneficiary's bank of a payment order for the benefit of the beneficiary of the originator's payment order.

(b) "Intermediary bank" means a receiving bank other than the originator's bank or the beneficiary's bank.

(c) "Originator" means the sender of the first payment order in a funds transfer.

(d) "Originator's bank" means (i) the receiving bank to which the payment order of the originator is issued if the originator is not a bank, or (ii) the originator if the originator is a bank.

§ 4A–105. Other Definitions.

(a) In this Article:

(1) "Authorized account" means a deposit account of a customer in a bank designated by the customer as a source of payment of payment orders issued by the customer to the bank. If a customer does not so designate an account, any account of the customer is an authorized account if payment of a payment order from that account is not inconsistent with a restriction on the use of that account.

(2) "Bank" means a person engaged in the business of banking and includes a savings bank, savings and loan

association, credit union, and trust company. A branch or separate office of a bank is a separate bank for purposes of this Article.

(3) "Customer" means a person, including a bank, having an account with a bank or from whom a bank has agreed to receive payment orders.

(4) "Funds-transfer business day" of a receiving bank means the part of a day during which the receiving bank is open for the receipt, processing, and transmittal of payment orders and cancellations and amendments of payment orders.

(5) "Funds-transfer system" means a wire transfer network, automated clearing house, or other communication system of a clearing house or other association of banks through which a payment order by a bank may be transmitted to the bank to which the order is addressed.

(6) "Good faith" means honesty in fact and the observance of reasonable commercial standards of fair dealing.

(7) "Prove" with respect to a fact means to meet the burden of establishing the fact (Section 1–201(8)).

(b) Other definitions applying to this Article and the sections in which they appear are:

"Acceptance"	Section 4A–209
"Beneficiary"	Section 4A–103
"Beneficiary's bank"	Section 4A–103
"Executed"	Section 4A–301
"Execution date"	Section 4A–301
"Funds transfer"	Section 4A–104
"Funds-transfer system rule"	Section 4A–501
"Intermediary bank"	Section 4A–104
"Originator"	Section 4A–104
"Originator's bank"	Section 4A–104
"Payment by beneficiary's bank to beneficiary"	Section 4A–405
"Payment by originator to beneficiary"	Section 4A–406
"Payment by sender to receiving bank"	Section 4A–403
"Payment date"	Section 4A–401
"Payment order"	Section 4A–103
"Receiving bank"	Section 4A–103
"Security procedure"	Section 4A–201
"Sender"	Section 4A–103

(c) The following definitions in Article 4 apply to this Article:

"Clearing house"	Section 4–104
"Item"	Section 4–104
"Suspends payments"	Section 4–104

(d) In addition, Article 1 contains general definitions and principles of construction and interpretation applicable throughout this Article.

§ 4A–106. Time Payment Order Is Received.

(a) The time of receipt of a payment order or communication cancelling or amending a payment order is determined by the rules applicable to receipt of a notice stated in Section 1–201(27). A receiving bank may fix a cut-off time or times on a funds-transfer business day for the receipt and processing of payment orders and communications cancelling or amending payment orders. Different cut-off times may apply to payment orders, cancellations, or amendments, or to different categories of payment orders, cancellations, or amendments. A cut-off time may apply to senders generally or different cut-off times may apply to different senders or categories of payment orders. If a payment order or communication cancelling or amending a payment order is received after the close of a funds-transfer business day or after the appropriate cut-off time on a funds-transfer business day, the receiving bank may treat the payment order or communication as received at the opening of the next funds-transfer business day.

(b) If this Article refers to an execution date or payment date or states a day on which a receiving bank is required to take action, and the date or day does not fall on a funds-transfer business day, the next day that is a funds-transfer business day is treated as the date or day stated, unless the contrary is stated in this Article.

§ 4A–107. Federal Reserve Regulations and Operating Circulars.

Regulations of the Board of Governors of the Federal Reserve System and operating circulars of the Federal Reserve Banks supersede any inconsistent provision of this Article to the extent of the inconsistency.

§ 4A–108. Exclusion of Consumer Transactions Governed by Federal Law.

This Article does not apply to a funds transfer any part of which is governed by the Electronic Fund Transfer Act of 1978 (Title XX, Public Law 95–630, 92 Stat. 3728, 15 U.S.C. § 1693 et seq.) as amended from time to time.

Part 2 Issue and Acceptance of Payment Order

§ 4A–201. Security Procedure.

"Security procedure" means a procedure established by agreement of a customer and a receiving bank for the purpose of (i) verifying that a payment order or communication amending or cancelling a payment order is that of the customer, or (ii) detecting error in the transmission or the content of the payment order or communication. A security procedure may require the use of algorithms or other codes, identifying words or numbers, encryption, callback procedures, or similar security devices. Comparison of a signature on a payment order or communication with an authorized specimen signature of the customer is not by itself a security procedure.

§ 4A–202. Authorized and Verified Payment Orders.

(a) A payment order received by the receiving bank is the authorized order of the person identified as sender if that person authorized the order or is otherwise bound by it under the law of agency.

(b) If a bank and its customer have agreed that the authenticity of payment orders issued to the bank in the name of the customer as sender will be verified pursuant to a security procedure, a payment order received by the receiving bank is effective as the order of the customer, whether or not authorized, if (i) the security procedure is a commercially reasonable method of providing security against unauthorized payment orders, and (ii) the bank proves that it accepted the payment order in good faith and in compliance with the security procedure and any written agreement or instruction of the customer restricting acceptance of payment orders issued in the name of the customer. The bank is not required to follow an instruction that violates a written agreement with the customer or notice of which is not received at a time and in a manner affording the bank a reasonable opportunity to act on it before the payment order is accepted.

(c) Commercial reasonableness of a security procedure is a question of law to be determined by considering the wishes of the customer expressed to the bank, the circumstances of the customer known to the bank, including the size, type, and frequency of payment orders normally issued by the customer to the bank, alternative security procedures offered to the customer, and security procedures in general use by customers and receiving banks similarly situated. A security procedure is deemed to be commercially reasonable if (i) the security procedure was chosen by the customer after the bank offered, and the customer refused, a security procedure that was commercially reasonable for that customer, and (ii) the customer expressly agreed in writing to be bound by any payment order, whether or not authorized, issued in its name and accepted by the bank in compliance with the security procedure chosen by the customer.

(d) The term "sender" in this Article includes the customer in whose name a payment order is issued if the order is the authorized order of the customer under subsection (a), or it is effective as the order of the customer under subsection (b).

(e) This section applies to amendments and cancellations of payment orders to the same extent it applies to payment orders.

(f) Except as provided in this section and in Section 4A–203(a)(1), rights and obligations arising under this section or Section 4A–203 may not be varied by agreement.

§ 4A–203. Unenforceability of Certain Verified Payment Orders.

(a) If an accepted payment order is not, under Section 4A–202(a), an authorized order of a customer identified as sender, but is effective as an order of the customer pursuant to Section 4A–202(b), the following rules apply:

(1) By express written agreement, the receiving bank may limit the extent to which it is entitled to enforce or retain payment of the payment order.

(2) The receiving bank is not entitled to enforce or retain payment of the payment order if the customer proves that the order was not caused, directly or indirectly, by a person (i) entrusted at any time with duties to act for the customer with respect to payment orders or the security procedure, or (ii) who obtained access to transmitting facilities of the customer or who obtained, from a source controlled by the customer and without authority of the receiving bank, information facilitating breach of the security procedure, regardless of how the information was obtained or whether the customer was at fault. Information includes any access device, computer software, or the like.

(b) This section applies to amendments of payment orders to the same extent it applies to payment orders.

§ 4A–204. Refund of Payment and Duty of Customer to Report with Respect to Unauthorized Payment Order.

(a) If a receiving bank accepts a payment order issued in the name of its customer as sender which is (i) not authorized and not effective as the order of the customer under Section 4A–202, or (ii) not enforceable, in whole or in part, against the customer under Section 4A–203, the bank shall refund any payment of the payment order received from the customer to the extent the bank is not entitled to enforce payment and shall pay interest on the refundable amount calculated from the date the bank received payment to the date of the refund. However, the customer is not entitled to interest from the bank on the amount to be refunded if the customer fails to exercise ordinary care to determine that the order was not authorized by the customer and to notify the bank of the relevant facts within a reasonable time not exceeding 90 days after the date the customer received notification from the bank that the order was accepted or that the customer's account was debited with respect to the order. The bank is not entitled to any recovery from the customer on account of a failure by the customer to give notification as stated in this section.

(b) Reasonable time under subsection (a) may be fixed by agreement as stated in Section 1–204(1), but the obligation of a receiving bank to refund payment as stated in subsection (a) may not otherwise be varied by agreement.

§ 4A–205. Erroneous Payment Orders.

(a) If an accepted payment order was transmitted pursuant to a security procedure for the detection of error and the payment order (i) erroneously instructed payment to a beneficiary not intended by the sender, (ii) erroneously instructed payment in an amount greater than the amount intended by the sender, or (iii) was an erroneously transmitted duplicate of a payment order previously sent by the sender, the following rules apply:

(1) If the sender proves that the sender or a person acting on behalf of the sender pursuant to Section 4A–206 complied with the security procedure and that the error would have been detected if the receiving bank had also complied, the sender is not obliged to pay the order to the extent stated in paragraphs (2) and (3).

(2) If the funds transfer is completed on the basis of an erroneous payment order described in clause (i) or (iii) of subsection (a), the sender is not obliged to pay the order and the receiving bank is entitled to recover from the beneficiary any amount paid to the beneficiary to the extent allowed by the law governing mistake and restitution.

(3) If the funds transfer is completed on the basis of a payment order described in clause (ii) of subsection (a), the sender is not obliged to pay the order to the extent the amount received by the beneficiary is greater than the amount intended by the sender. In that case, the receiving bank is entitled to recover from the beneficiary the excess amount received to the extent allowed by the law governing mistake and restitution.

(b) If (i) the sender of an erroneous payment order described in subsection (a) is not obliged to pay all or part of the order, and (ii) the sender receives notification from the receiving bank that the order was accepted by the bank or that the sender's account was debited with respect to the order, the sender has a duty to exercise ordinary care, on the basis of information available to the sender, to discover the error with respect to the order and to advise the bank of the relevant facts within a reasonable time, not exceeding 90 days, after the bank's notification was received by the sender. If the bank proves that the sender failed to perform that duty, the sender is liable to the bank for the loss the bank proves it incurred as a result of the failure, but the liability of the sender may not exceed the amount of the sender's order.

(c) This section applies to amendments to payment orders to the same extent it applies to payment orders.

§ 4A–206. Transmission of Payment Order through Funds-Transfer or Other Communication System.

(a) If a payment order addressed to a receiving bank is transmitted to a funds-transfer system or other third party communication system for transmittal to the bank, the system is deemed to be an agent of the sender for the purpose of transmitting the payment order to the bank. If there is a discrepancy between the terms of the payment order transmitted to the system and the terms of the payment order transmitted by the system to the bank, the terms of the payment order of the sender are those transmitted by the system. This section does not apply to a funds-transfer system of the Federal Reserve Banks.

(b) This section applies to cancellations and amendments to payment orders to the same extent it applies to payment orders.

§ 4A–207. Misdescription of Beneficiary.

(a) Subject to subsection (b), if, in a payment order received by the beneficiary's bank, the name, bank account number, or other identification of the beneficiary refers to a nonexistent or unidentifiable person or account, no person has rights as a beneficiary of the order and acceptance of the order cannot occur.

(b) If a payment order received by the beneficiary's bank identifies the beneficiary both by name and by an identifying or bank account number and the name and number identify different persons, the following rules apply:

(1) Except as otherwise provided in subsection (c), if the beneficiary's bank does not know that the name and number refer to different persons, it may rely on the number as the proper identification of the beneficiary of the order. The beneficiary's bank need not determine whether the name and number refer to the same person.

(2) If the beneficiary's bank pays the person identified by name or knows that the name and number identify different persons, no person has rights as beneficiary except the person paid by the beneficiary's bank if that person was entitled to receive payment from the originator of the funds transfer. If no person has rights as beneficiary, acceptance of the order cannot occur.

(c) If (i) a payment order described in subsection (b) is accepted, (ii) the originator's payment order described the beneficiary inconsistently by name and number, and (iii) the beneficiary's bank pays the person identified by number as permitted by subsection (b)(1), the following rules apply:

(1) If the originator is a bank, the originator is obliged to pay its order.

(2) If the originator is not a bank and proves that the person identified by number was not entitled to receive payment from the originator, the originator is not obliged to pay its order unless the originator's bank proves that the originator, before acceptance of the originator's order, had notice that payment of a payment order issued by the originator might be made by the beneficiary's bank on the basis of an identifying or bank account number even if it identifies a person different from the named beneficiary. Proof of notice may be made by any admissible evidence. The originator's bank satisfies the burden of proof if it proves that the originator, before the payment order was accepted, signed a writing stating the information to which the notice relates.

(d) In a case governed by subsection (b)(1), if the beneficiary's bank rightfully pays the person identified by number and that person was not entitled to receive payment from the originator, the amount paid may be recovered from that person to the extent allowed by the law governing mistake and restitution as follows:

(1) If the originator is obliged to pay its payment order as stated in subsection (c), the originator has the right to recover.

(2) If the originator is not a bank and is not obliged to pay its payment order, the originator's bank has the right to recover.

§ 4A–208. Misdescription of Intermediary Bank or Beneficiary's Bank.

(a) This subsection applies to a payment order identifying an intermediary bank or the beneficiary's bank only by an identifying number.

(1) The receiving bank may rely on the number as the proper identification of the intermediary or beneficiary's bank and need not determine whether the number identifies a bank.

(2) The sender is obliged to compensate the receiving bank for any loss and expenses incurred by the receiving bank as a result of its reliance on the number in executing or attempting to execute the order.

(b) This subsection applies to a payment order identifying an intermediary bank or the beneficiary's bank both by name and an identifying number if the name and number identify different persons.

(1) If the sender is a bank, the receiving bank may rely on the number as the proper identification of the intermediary or beneficiary's bank if the receiving bank, when it executes the sender's order, does not know that the name and number identify different persons. The receiving bank need not determine whether the name and number refer to the same person or whether the number refers to a bank. The sender is obliged to compensate the receiving bank for any loss and expenses incurred by the receiving bank as a result of its reliance on the number in executing or attempting to execute the order.

(2) If the sender is not a bank and the receiving bank proves that the sender, before the payment order was accepted, had notice that the receiving bank might rely on the number as the proper identification of the intermediary or beneficiary's bank even if it identifies a person different from the bank identified by name, the rights and obligations of the sender and the receiving bank are governed by subsection (b)(1), as though the sender were a bank. Proof of notice may be made by any admissible evidence. The receiving bank satisfies the burden of proof if it proves that the sender, before the payment order was accepted, signed a writing stating the information to which the notice relates.

(3) Regardless of whether the sender is a bank, the receiving bank may rely on the name as the proper identification of the intermediary or beneficiary's bank if the receiving bank, at the time it executes the sender's order, does not know that the name and number identify different persons. The receiving bank need not determine whether the name and number refer to the same person.

(4) If the receiving bank knows that the name and number identify different persons, reliance on either the name or the number in executing the sender's payment order is a breach of the obligation stated in Section 4A–302(a)(1).

§ 4A–209. Acceptance of Payment Order.

(a) Subject to subsection (d), a receiving bank other than the beneficiary's bank accepts a payment order when it executes the order.

(b) Subject to subsections (c) and (d), a beneficiary's bank accepts a payment order at the earliest of the following times:

(1) When the bank (i) pays the beneficiary as stated in Section 4A–405(a) or 4A–405(b), or (ii) notifies the beneficiary of receipt of the order or that the account of the beneficiary has been credited with respect to the order unless the notice indicates that the bank is rejecting the order or that funds with respect to the order may not be withdrawn or used until receipt of payment from the sender of the order;

(2) When the bank receives payment of the entire amount of the sender's order pursuant to Section 4A–403(a)(1) or 4A–403(a)(2); or

(3) The opening of the next funds-transfer business day of the bank following the payment date of the order if, at that time, the amount of the sender's order is fully covered by a withdrawable credit balance in an authorized account of the sender or the bank has otherwise received full payment from the sender, unless the order was rejected before that time or is rejected within (i) one hour after that time, or (ii) one hour after the opening of the next business day of the sender following the payment date if that time is later. If notice of rejection is received by the sender after the payment date and the authorized account of the sender does not bear interest, the bank is obliged to pay interest to the sender on the amount of the order for the number of days elapsing after the payment date to the day the sender receives notice or learns that the order was not accepted, counting that day as an elapsed day. If the withdrawable credit balance during that period falls below the amount of the order, the amount of interest payable is reduced accordingly.

(c) Acceptance of a payment order cannot occur before the order is received by the receiving bank. Acceptance does not occur under subsection (b)(2) or (b)(3) if the beneficiary of the payment order does not have an account with the receiving bank, the account has been closed, or the receiving bank is not permitted by law to receive credits for the beneficiary's account.

(d) A payment order issued to the originator's bank cannot be accepted until the payment date if the bank is the beneficiary's bank, or the execution date if the bank is not the beneficiary's bank. If the originator's bank executes the originator's payment order before the execution date or pays the beneficiary of the originator's payment order before the payment date and the payment order is subsequently cancelled pursuant to Section 4A–211(b), the bank may recover from the beneficiary any payment received to the extent allowed by the law governing mistake and restitution.

§ 4A–210. Rejection of Payment Order.

(a) A payment order is rejected by the receiving bank by a notice of rejection transmitted to the sender orally, electronically, or in writing. A notice of rejection need not use any particular words and is sufficient if it indicates that the receiving bank is rejecting the order or will not execute or pay the order. Rejection is effective when the notice is given if transmission is by a means that is reasonable in the circumstances. If notice of rejection is given by a means that is not reasonable, rejection is effective when the notice is received. If an agreement of the sender and receiving bank establishes the means to be used to reject a payment order, (i) any means complying with the agreement is reasonable and (ii) any means not complying is not reasonable unless no significant delay in receipt of the notice resulted from the use of the noncomplying means.

(b) This subsection applies if a receiving bank other than the beneficiary's bank fails to execute a payment order despite the existence on the execution date of a withdrawable credit balance in an authorized account of the sender sufficient to cover the order. If the sender does not receive notice of rejection of the order on the execution date and the authorized account of the sender does not bear interest, the bank is obliged to pay interest to the sender on the amount of the order for the number of days elapsing after the execution date to the earlier of the day the order is cancelled pursuant to Section 4A–211(d) or the day the sender receives notice or learns that the order was not executed, counting the final day of the period as an elapsed day. If the withdrawable credit balance during that period falls below the amount of the order, the amount of interest is reduced accordingly.

(c) If a receiving bank suspends payments, all unaccepted payment orders issued to it are are deemed rejected at the time the bank suspends payments.

(d) Acceptance of a payment order precludes a later rejection of the order. Rejection of a payment order precludes a later acceptance of the order.

§ 4A–211. Cancellation and Amendment of Payment Order.

(a) A communication of the sender of a payment order cancelling or amending the order may be transmitted to the receiving bank orally, electronically, or in writing. If a security procedure is in effect between the sender and the receiving bank, the communication is not effective to cancel or amend the order unless the communication is verified pursuant to the security procedure or the bank agrees to the cancellation or amendment.

(b) Subject to subsection (a), a communication by the sender cancelling or amending a payment order is effective to cancel or amend the order if notice of the communication is received at a time and in a manner affording the receiving bank a reasonable opportunity to act on the communication before the bank accepts the payment order.

(c) After a payment order has been accepted, cancellation or amendment of the order is not effective unless the receiving bank agrees or a funds-transfer system rule allows cancellation or amendment without agreement of the bank.

> (1) With respect to a payment order accepted by a receiving bank other than the beneficiary's bank, cancellation or amendment is not effective unless a conforming cancellation or amendment of the payment order issued by the receiving bank is also made.

> (2) With respect to a payment order accepted by the beneficiary's bank, cancellation or amendment is not effective unless the order was issued in execution of an unauthorized payment order, or because of a mistake by a sender in the funds transfer which resulted in the issuance of a payment order (i) that is a duplicate of a payment order previously issued by the sender, (ii) that orders payment to a beneficiary not entitled to receive payment from the originator, or (iii) that orders payment in an amount greater than the amount the beneficiary was entitled to receive from the originator. If the payment order is cancelled or amended, the beneficiary's bank is entitled to recover from the beneficiary any amount paid to the beneficiary to the extent allowed by the law governing mistake and restitution.

(d) An unaccepted payment order is cancelled by operation of law at the close of the fifth funds-transfer business day of the receiving bank after the execution date or payment date of the order.

(e) A cancelled payment order cannot be accepted. If an accepted payment order is cancelled, the acceptance is nullified and no person has any right or obligation based on the acceptance. Amendment of a payment order is deemed to be cancellation of the original order at the time of amendment and issue of a new payment order in the amended form at the same time.

(f) Unless otherwise provided in an agreement of the parties or in a funds-transfer system rule, if the receiving bank, after accepting a payment order, agrees to cancellation or amendment of the order by the sender or is bound by a funds-transfer system rule allowing cancellation or amendment without the bank's agreement, the sender, whether or not cancellation or amendment is effective, is liable to the bank for any loss and expenses, including reasonable attorney's fees, incurred by the bank as a result of the cancellation or amendment or attempted cancellation or amendment.

(g) A payment order is not revoked by the death or legal incapacity of the sender unless the receiving bank knows of the death or of an adjudication of incapacity by a court of competent jurisdiction and has reasonable opportunity to act before acceptance of the order.

(h) A funds-transfer system rule is not effective to the extent it conflicts with subsection (c)(2).

§ 4A–212. Liability and Duty of Receiving Bank Regarding Unaccepted Payment Order.

If a receiving bank fails to accept a payment order that it is obliged by express agreement to accept, the bank is liable for breach of the agreement to the extent provided in the agreement or in this Article, but does not otherwise have any duty to accept a payment order or, before acceptance, to take any action, or refrain from taking action, with respect to the order except as provided in this Article or by express agreement. Liability based on acceptance arises only when acceptance occurs as stated in Section 4A–209, and liability is limited to that provided in this Article. A receiving bank is not the agent of the sender or beneficiary of the payment order it accepts, or of any other party to the funds transfer, and the bank owes no duty to any party to the funds transfer except as provided in this Article or by express agreement.

Part 3 Execution of Sender's Payment Order by Receiving Bank

§ 4A–301. Execution and Execution Date.

(a) A payment order is "executed" by the receiving bank when it issues a payment order intended to carry out the payment order received by the bank. A payment order received by the beneficiary's bank can be accepted but cannot be executed.

(b) "Execution date" of a payment order means the day on which the receiving bank may properly issue a payment order in execution of the sender's order. The execution date may be determined by instruction of the sender but cannot be earlier than the day the order is received and, unless otherwise determined, is the day the order is received. If the sender's instruction states a payment date, the execution date is the payment date or an earlier date on which execution is reasonably necessary to allow payment to the beneficiary on the payment date.

§ 4A–302. Obligations of Receiving Bank in Execution of Payment Order.

(a) Except as provided in subsections (b) through (d), if the receiving bank accepts a payment order pursuant to Section 4A–209(a), the bank has the following obligations in executing the order:

(1) The receiving bank is obliged to issue, on the execution date, a payment order complying with the sender's order and to follow the sender's instructions concerning (i) any intermediary bank or funds-transfer system to be used in carrying out the funds transfer, or (ii) the means by which payment orders are to be transmitted in the funds transfer. If the originator's bank issues a payment order to an intermediary bank, the originator's bank is obliged to instruct the intermediary bank according to the instruction of the originator. An intermediary bank in the funds transfer is similarly bound by an instruction given to it by the sender of the payment order it accepts.

(2) If the sender's instruction states that the funds transfer is to be carried out telephonically or by wire transfer or otherwise indicates that the funds transfer is to be carried out by the most expeditious means, the receiving bank is obliged to transmit its payment order by the most expeditious available means, and to instruct any intermediary bank accordingly. If a sender's instruction states a payment date, the receiving bank is obliged to transmit its payment order at a time and by means reasonably necessary to allow payment to the beneficiary on the payment date or as soon thereafter as is feasible.

(b) Unless otherwise instructed, a receiving bank executing a payment order may (i) use any funds-transfer system if use of that system is reasonable in the circumstances, and (ii) issue a payment order to the beneficiary's bank or to an intermediary bank through which a payment order conforming to the sender's order can expeditiously be issued to the beneficiary's bank if the receiving bank exercises ordinary care in the selection of the intermediary bank. A receiving bank is not required to follow an instruction of the sender designating a funds-transfer system to be used in carrying out the funds transfer if the receiving bank, in good faith, determines that it is not feasible to follow the instruction or that following the instruction would unduly delay completion of the funds transfer.

(c) Unless subsection (a)(2) applies or the receiving bank is otherwise instructed, the bank may execute a payment order by transmitting its payment order by first class mail or by any means reasonable in the circumstances. If the receiving bank is instructed to execute the sender's order by transmitting its payment order by a particular means, the receiving bank may issue its payment order by the means stated or by any means as expeditious as the means stated.

(d) Unless instructed by the sender, (i) the receiving bank may not obtain payment of its charges for services and expenses in connection with the execution of the sender's order by issuing a payment order in an amount equal to the amount of the sender's order less the amount of the charges, and (ii) may not instruct a subsequent receiving bank to obtain payment of its charges in the same manner.

§ 4A–303. Erroneous Execution of Payment Order.

(a) A receiving bank that (i) executes the payment order of the sender by issuing a payment order in an amount greater than the amount of the sender's order, or (ii) issues a payment order in execution of the sender's order and then issues a duplicate order, is entitled to payment of the amount of the sender's order under Section 4A–402(c) if that subsection is otherwise satisfied. The bank is entitled to recover from the beneficiary of the erroneous order the excess payment received to the extent allowed by the law governing mistake and restitution.

(b) A receiving bank that executes the payment order of the sender by issuing a payment order in an amount less than the amount of the sender's order is entitled to payment of the amount of the sender's order under Section 4A–402(c) if (i) that subsection is otherwise satisfied and (ii) the bank corrects its mistake by issuing an additional payment order for the benefit of the beneficiary of the sender's order. If the error is not corrected, the issuer of the erroneous order is entitled to receive or retain payment from the sender of the order it accepted only to the extent of the amount of the erroneous order. This subsection does not apply if the receiving bank executes the sender's payment order by issuing a payment order in an amount less than the amount of the sender's order for the purpose of obtaining payment of its charges for services and expenses pursuant to instruction of the sender.

(c) If a receiving bank executes the payment order of the sender by issuing a payment order to a beneficiary different from the beneficiary of the sender's order and the funds transfer is completed on the basis of that error, the sender of the payment order that was erroneously executed and all previous senders in the funds transfer are not obliged to pay the payment orders they issued. The issuer of the erroneous order is entitled to recover from the beneficiary of the order the payment received to the extent allowed by the law governing mistake and restitution.

§ 4A–304. Duty of Sender to Report Erroneously Executed Payment Order.

If the sender of a payment order that is erroneously executed as stated in Section 4A–303 receives notification from the receiving bank that the order was executed or that the sender's account was debited with respect to the order, the sender has a duty to exercise ordinary care to determine, on the basis of information available to the sender, that the order was erroneously executed and to notify the bank of the relevant facts within a reasonable time not exceeding 90 days after the notification from the bank was received by the sender. If the sender fails to perform that duty, the bank is not obliged to pay interest on any amount refundable to the sender under Section 4A–402(d) for the period before the bank learns of the execution error. The bank is not entitled to any recovery from the sender on account of a failure by the sender to perform the duty stated in this section.

§ 4A–305. Liability for Late or Improper Execution or Failure to Execute Payment Order.

(a) If a funds transfer is completed but execution of a payment order by the receiving bank in breach of Section 4A–302 results in delay in payment to the beneficiary, the bank is obliged to pay interest to either the originator or the beneficiary of the funds transfer for the period of delay caused by the improper execution. Except as provided in subsection (c), additional damages are not recoverable.

(b) If execution of a payment order by a receiving bank in breach of Section 4A–302 results in (i) noncompletion of the funds transfer, (ii) failure to use an intermediary bank designated by the originator, or (iii) issuance of a payment order that does not comply with the terms of the payment order of the originator, the bank is liable to the originator for its expenses in the funds transfer and for incidental expenses and interest losses, to the extent not covered by subsection (a), resulting from the improper execution. Except as provided in subsection (c), additional damages are not recoverable.

(c) In addition to the amounts payable under subsections (a) and (b), damages, including consequential damages, are recoverable to the extent provided in an express written agreement of the receiving bank.

(d) If a receiving bank fails to execute a payment order it was obliged by express agreement to execute, the receiving bank is liable to the sender for its expenses in the transaction and for incidental expenses and interest losses resulting from the failure to execute. Additional damages, including consequential damages, are recoverable to the extent provided in an express written agreement of the receiving bank, but are not otherwise recoverable.

(e) Reasonable attorney's fees are recoverable if demand for compensation under subsection (a) or (b) is made and refused before an action is brought on the claim. If a claim is made for breach of an agreement under subsection (d) and the agreement does not provide for damages, reasonable attorney's fees are recoverable if demand for compensation under subsection (d) is made and refused before an action is brought on the claim.

(f) Except as stated in this section, the liability of a receiving bank under subsections (a) and (b) may not be varied by agreement.

Part 4 Payment

§ 4A–401. Payment Date.

"Payment date" of a payment order means the day on which the amount of the order is payable to the beneficiary by the beneficiary's bank. The payment date may be determined by instruction of the sender but cannot be earlier than the day the order is received by the beneficiary's bank and, unless otherwise determined, is the day the order is received by the beneficiary's bank.

§ 4A–402. Obligation of Sender to Pay Receiving Bank.

(a) This section is subject to Sections 4A–205 and 4A–207.

(b) With respect to a payment order issued to the beneficiary's bank, acceptance of the order by the bank obliges the sender to pay the bank the amount of the order, but payment is not due until the payment date of the order.

(c) This subsection is subject to subsection (e) and to Section 4A–303. With respect to a payment order issued to a receiving bank other than the beneficiary's bank, acceptance of the order by the receiving bank obliges the sender to pay the bank the amount of the sender's order. Payment by the sender is not due until the execution date of the sender's order. The obligation of that sender to pay its payment order is excused if the funds transfer is not completed by acceptance by the beneficiary's bank of a payment order instructing payment to the beneficiary of that sender's payment order.

(d) If the sender of a payment order pays the order and was not obliged to pay all or part of the amount paid, the bank receiving payment is obliged to refund payment to the extent the sender was not obliged to pay. Except as provided in Sections 4A–204 and 4A–304, interest is payable on the refundable amount from the date of payment.

(e) If a funds transfer is not completed as stated in subsection (c) and an intermediary bank is obliged to refund payment as stated in subsection (d) but is unable to do so because not permitted by applicable law or because the bank suspends payments, a sender in the funds transfer that executed a payment order in compliance with an instruction, as stated in Section 4A–302(a)(1), to route the funds transfer through that intermediary bank is entitled to receive or retain payment from the sender of the payment order that it accepted. The first sender in the funds transfer that issued an instruction requiring routing through that intermediary bank is subrogated to the right of the bank that paid the intermediary bank to refund as stated in subsection (d).

(f) The right of the sender of a payment order to be excused from the obligation to pay the order as stated in subsection (c) or to receive refund under subsection (d) may not be varied by agreement.

§ 4A–403. Payment by Sender to Receiving Bank.

(a) Payment of the sender's obligation under Section 4A–402 to pay the receiving bank occurs as follows:

(1) If the sender is a bank, payment occurs when the receiving bank receives final settlement of the obligation through a Federal Reserve Bank or through a funds-transfer system.

(2) If the sender is a bank and the sender (i) credited an account of the receiving bank with the sender, or (ii) caused an account of the receiving bank in another bank to be credited, payment occurs when the credit is withdrawn or, if not withdrawn, at midnight of the day on which the credit is withdrawable and the receiving bank learns of that fact.

(3) If the receiving bank debits an account of the sender with the receiving bank, payment occurs when the debit is made to the extent the debit is covered by a withdrawable credit balance in the account.

(b) If the sender and receiving bank are members of a funds-transfer system that nets obligations multilaterally among participants, the receiving bank receives final settlement when settlement is complete in accordance with the rules of the system. The obligation of the sender to pay the amount of a payment order transmitted through the funds-transfer system may be satisfied, to the extent permitted by the rules of the system, by setting off and applying against the sender's obligation the right of the sender to receive payment from the receiving bank of the amount of any other payment order transmitted to the sender by the receiving bank through the funds-transfer system. The aggregate balance of obligations owed by each sender to each receiving bank in the funds-transfer system may be satisfied, to the extent permitted by the rules of the system, by setting off and applying against that balance the aggregate balance of obligations owed to the sender by other members of the system. The aggregate balance is determined after the right of setoff stated in the second sentence of this subsection has been exercised.

(c) If two banks transmit payment orders to each other under an agreement that settlement of the obligations of each bank to the other under Section 4A–402 will be made at the end of the day or other period, the total amount owed with respect to all orders transmitted by one bank shall be set off against the total amount owed with respect to all orders transmitted by the other bank. To the extent of the setoff, each bank has made payment to the other.

(d) In a case not covered by subsection (a), the time when payment of the sender's obligation under Section 4A–402(b) or 4A–402(c) occurs is governed by applicable principles of law that determine when an obligation is satisfied.

§ 4A–404. Obligation of Beneficiary's Bank to Pay and Give Notice to Beneficiary.

(a) Subject to Sections 4A–211(e), 4A–405(d), and 4A–405(e), if a beneficiary's bank accepts a payment order, the bank is obliged to pay the amount of the order to the beneficiary of the order. Payment is due on the payment date of the order, but if acceptance occurs on the payment date after the close of the funds-transfer business day of the bank, payment is due on the next funds-transfer business day. If the bank refuses to pay after demand by the beneficiary and receipt of notice of particular circumstances that will give rise to consequential damages as a result of nonpayment, the beneficiary may recover damages resulting from the refusal to pay to the extent the bank had notice of the damages, unless the bank proves that it did not pay because of a reasonable doubt concerning the right of the beneficiary to payment.

(b) If a payment order accepted by the beneficiary's bank instructs payment to an account of the beneficiary, the bank is obliged to notify the beneficiary of receipt of the order before midnight of the next funds-transfer business day following the payment date. If the payment order does not instruct payment to an account of the beneficiary, the bank is required to notify the beneficiary only if notice is required by the order. Notice may be given by first class mail or any other means reasonable in the circumstances. If the bank fails to give the required notice, the bank is obliged to pay interest to the beneficiary on the amount of the payment order from the day notice should have been given until the day the beneficiary learned of receipt of the payment order by the bank. No other damages are recoverable. Reasonable attorney's fees are also recoverable if demand for interest is made and refused before an action is brought on the claim.

(c) The right of a beneficiary to receive payment and damages as stated in subsection (a) may not be varied by agreement or a funds-transfer system rule. The right of a beneficiary to be notified as stated in subsection (b) may be varied by agreement of the beneficiary or by a funds-transfer system rule if the beneficiary is notified of the rule before initiation of the funds transfer.

§ 4A–405. Payment by Beneficiary's Bank to Beneficiary.

(a) If the beneficiary's bank credits an account of the beneficiary of a payment order, payment of the bank's obligation under Section 4A–404(a) occurs when and to the extent (i) the beneficiary is notified of the right to withdraw the credit, (ii) the bank lawfully applies the credit to a debt of the beneficiary, or (iii) funds with respect to the order are otherwise made available to the beneficiary by the bank.

(b) If the beneficiary's bank does not credit an account of the beneficiary of a payment order, the time when payment of the bank's obligation under Section 4A–404(a) occurs is governed by principles of law that determine when an obligation is satisfied.

(c) Except as stated in subsections (d) and (e), if the beneficiary's bank pays the beneficiary of a payment order under a condition to payment or agreement of the beneficiary giving the bank the right to recover payment from the beneficiary if the bank does not receive payment of the order, the condition to payment or agreement is not enforceable.

(d) A funds-transfer system rule may provide that payments made to beneficiaries of funds transfers made through the system are provisional until receipt of payment by the beneficiary's bank of the payment order it accepted. A beneficiary's bank that makes a payment that is provisional under the rule is entitled to refund from the beneficiary if (i) the rule requires that both the beneficiary and the originator be given notice of the provisional nature of the payment before the funds transfer is initiated, (ii) the beneficiary, the beneficiary's bank, and the originator's bank agreed to be bound by the rule, and (iii) the beneficiary's bank did not receive payment of the payment order that it accepted. If the beneficiary is obliged to refund payment to the beneficiary's bank, acceptance of the payment order by the beneficiary's bank is nullified and no payment by the originator of the funds transfer to the beneficiary occurs under Section 4A–406.

(e) This subsection applies to a funds transfer that includes a payment order transmitted over a funds-transfer system that (i) nets obligations multilaterally among participants, and (ii) has in effect a loss-sharing agreement among participants for the purpose of providing funds necessary to complete settlement of the obligations of one or more participants that do not meet their settlement obligations. If the beneficiary's bank in the funds transfer accepts a payment order and the system fails to complete settlement pursuant to its rules with respect to any payment order in the funds transfer, (i) the acceptance by the beneficiary's bank is nullified and no person has any right or obligation based on the acceptance, (ii) the beneficiary's bank is entitled to recover payment from the beneficiary, (iii) no payment by the originator to the beneficiary occurs under Section 4A–406, and (iv) subject to Section 4A–402(e), each sender in the funds transfer is excused from its obligation to pay its payment order under Section 4A–402(c) because the funds transfer has not been completed.

§ 4A–406. Payment by Originator to Beneficiary; Discharge of Underlying Obligation.

(a) Subject to Sections 4A–211(e), 4A–405(d), and 4A–405(e), the originator of a funds transfer pays the beneficiary of the originator's payment order (i) at the time a payment order for the benefit of the beneficiary is accepted by the beneficiary's bank in the funds transfer and (ii) in an amount equal to the amount of the order accepted by the beneficiary's bank, but not more than the amount of the originator's order.

(b) If payment under subsection (a) is made to satisfy an obligation, the obligation is discharged to the same extent discharge would result from payment to the beneficiary of the same amount in money, unless (i) the payment under subsection (a) was made by a means prohibited by the contract of the beneficiary with respect to the obligation, (ii) the beneficiary, within a reasonable time after receiving notice of receipt of the order by the beneficiary's bank, notified the originator of the beneficiary's refusal of the payment, (iii) funds with respect to the order were not withdrawn by the beneficiary or applied to a debt of the beneficiary, and (iv) the beneficiary would suffer a loss that could reasonably have been avoided if payment had been made by a means complying with the contract. If payment by the originator does not result in discharge under this section, the originator is subrogated to the rights of the beneficiary to receive payment from the beneficiary's bank under Section 4A–404(a).

(c) For the purpose of determining whether discharge of an obligation occurs under subsection (b), if the beneficiary's bank accepts a payment order in an amount equal to the amount of the originator's payment order less charges of one or more receiving banks in the funds transfer, payment to the beneficiary is deemed to be in the amount of the originator's order unless upon demand by the beneficiary the originator does not pay the beneficiary the amount of the deducted charges.

(d) Rights of the originator or of the beneficiary of a funds transfer under this section may be varied only by agreement of the originator and the beneficiary.

Part 5 Miscellaneous Provisions

§ 4A–501. Variation by Agreement and Effect of Funds-Transfer System Rule.

(a) Except as otherwise provided in this Article, the rights and obligations of a party to a funds transfer may be varied by agreement of the affected party.

(b) "Funds-transfer system rule" means a rule of an association of banks (i) governing transmission of payment orders by means of a funds-transfer system of the association or rights and obligations with respect to those orders, or (ii) to the extent the rule governs rights and obligations between banks that are parties to a funds transfer in which a Federal Reserve Bank, acting as an intermediary bank, sends a payment order to the beneficiary's bank. Except as otherwise provided in this Article, a funds-transfer system rule governing rights and obligations between participating banks using the system may be effective even if the rule conflicts with this Article and indirectly affects another party to the funds transfer who does not consent to the rule. A funds-transfer system rule may also govern rights and obligations of parties other than participating banks using the system to the extent stated in Sections 4A–404(c), 4A–405(d), and 4A–507(c).

§ 4A–502. Creditor Process Served on Receiving Bank; Setoff by Beneficiary's Bank.

(a) As used in this section, "creditor process" means levy, attachment, garnishment, notice of lien, sequestration, or similar process issued by or on behalf of a creditor or other claimant with respect to an account.

(b) This subsection applies to creditor process with respect to an authorized account of the sender of a payment order if the creditor process is served on the receiving bank. For the purpose of determining rights with respect to the creditor process, if the receiving bank accepts the payment order the balance in the authorized account is deemed to be reduced by the amount of the payment order to the extent the bank did not otherwise receive payment of the order, unless the creditor process is served at a time and in a manner affording the bank a reasonable opportunity to act on it before the bank accepts the payment order.

(c) If a beneficiary's bank has received a payment order for payment to the beneficiary's account in the bank, the following rules apply:

(1) The bank may credit the beneficiary's account. The amount credited may be set off against an obligation owed by the beneficiary to the bank or may be applied to satisfy creditor process served on the bank with respect to the account.

(2) The bank may credit the beneficiary's account and allow withdrawal of the amount credited unless creditor process with respect to the account is served at a time and in a manner affording the bank a reasonable opportunity to act to prevent withdrawal.

(3) If creditor process with respect to the beneficiary's account has been served and the bank has had a reasonable opportunity to act on it, the bank may not reject the payment order except for a reason unrelated to the service of process.

(d) Creditor process with respect to a payment by the originator to the beneficiary pursuant to a funds transfer may be served only on the beneficiary's bank with respect to the debt owed by that bank to the beneficiary. Any other bank served with the creditor process is not obliged to act with respect to the process.

§ 4A–503. Injunction or Restraining Order with Respect to Funds Transfer.

For proper cause and in compliance with applicable law, a court may restrain (i) a person from issuing a payment order to initiate a funds transfer, (ii) an originator's bank from executing the payment order of the originator, or (iii) the beneficiary's bank from releasing funds to the beneficiary or the beneficiary from withdrawing the funds. A court may not otherwise restrain a person from issuing a payment order, paying or receiving payment of a payment order, or otherwise acting with respect to a funds transfer.

§ 4A–504. Order in Which Items and Payment Orders May Be Charged to Account; Order of Withdrawals from Account.

(a) If a receiving bank has received more than one payment order of the sender or one or more payment orders and other items that are payable from the sender's account, the bank may charge the sender's account with respect to the various orders and items in any sequence.

(b) In determining whether a credit to an account has been withdrawn by the holder of the account or applied to a debt of the holder of the account, credits first made to the account are first withdrawn or applied.

§ 4A–505. Preclusion of Objection to Debit of Customer's Account.

If a receiving bank has received payment from its customer with respect to a payment order issued in the name of the customer as sender and accepted by the bank, and the customer received notification reasonably identifying the order, the customer is precluded from asserting that the bank is not entitled to retain the payment unless the customer notifies the bank of the customer's objection to the payment within one year after the notification was received by the customer.

§ 4A–506. Rate of Interest.

(a) If, under this Article, a receiving bank is obliged to pay interest with respect to a payment order issued to the bank, the amount payable may be determined (i) by agreement of the sender and receiving bank, or (ii) by a funds-transfer system rule if the payment order is transmitted through a funds-transfer system.

(b) If the amount of interest is not determined by an agreement or rule as stated in subsection (a), the amount is calculated by multiplying the applicable Federal Funds rate by the amount on which interest is payable, and then multiplying the product by the number of days for which interest is payable. The applicable Federal Funds rate is the average of the Federal Funds rates published by the Federal Reserve Bank of New York for each of the days for which interest is payable divided by 360. The Federal Funds rate for any day on which a published rate is not available is the same as the published rate for the next preceding day for which there is a published rate. If a receiving bank that accepted a payment order is required to refund payment to the sender of the order because the funds transfer was not completed, but the failure to complete was not due to any fault by the bank, the interest payable is reduced by a percentage equal to the reserve requirement on deposits of the receiving bank.

§ 4A–507. Choice of Law.

(a) The following rules apply unless the affected parties otherwise agree or subsection (c) applies:

(1) The rights and obligations between the sender of a payment order and the receiving bank are governed by the law of the jurisdiction in which the receiving bank is located.

(2) The rights and obligations between the beneficiary's bank and the beneficiary are governed by the law of the jurisdiction in which the beneficiary's bank is located.

(3) The issue of when payment is made pursuant to a funds transfer by the originator to the beneficiary is governed by the law of the jurisdiction in which the beneficiary's bank is located.

(b) If the parties described in each paragraph of subsection (a) have made an agreement selecting the law of a particular jurisdiction to govern rights and obligations between each other, the law of that jurisdiction governs those rights and obligations, whether or not the payment order or the funds transfer bears a reasonable relation to that jurisdiction.

(c) A funds-transfer system rule may select the law of a particular jurisdiction to govern (i) rights and obligations between participating banks with respect to payment orders transmitted or processed through the system, or (ii) the rights and obligations of some or all parties to a funds transfer any part of which is carried out by means of the system. A choice of law made pursuant to clause (i) is binding on participating banks. A choice of law made pursuant to clause (ii) is binding on the originator, other sender, or a receiving bank having notice that the funds-transfer system might be used in the funds transfer and of the choice of law by the system when the originator, other sender, or receiving bank issued or accepted a payment order. The beneficiary of a funds transfer is bound by the choice of law if, when the funds transfer is initiated, the beneficiary has notice that the funds-transfer system might be used in the funds transfer and of the choice of law by the system. The law of a jurisdiction selected pursuant to this subsection may govern, whether or not that law bears a reasonable relation to the matter in issue.

(d) In the event of inconsistency between an agreement under subsection (b) and a choice-of-law rule under subsection (c), the agreement under subsection (b) prevails.

(e) If a funds transfer is made by use of more than one funds-transfer system and there is inconsistency between choice-of-law rules of the systems, the matter in issue is governed by the law of the selected jurisdiction that has the most significant relationship to the matter in issue.

Revised Article 5
LETTERS OF CREDIT

§ 5–101. Short Title.

This article may be cited as Uniform Commercial Code—Letters of Credit.

§ 5–102. Definitions.

(a) In this article:

(1) "Adviser" means a person who, at the request of the issuer, a confirmer, or another adviser, notifies or requests another adviser to notify the beneficiary that a letter of credit has been issued, confirmed, or amended.

(2) "Applicant" means a person at whose request or for whose account a letter of credit is issued. The term includes a person who requests an issuer to issue a letter of credit on behalf of another if the person making the request undertakes an obligation to reimburse the issuer.

(3) "Beneficiary" means a person who under the terms of a letter of credit is entitled to have its complying presentation honored. The term includes a person to whom drawing rights have been transferred under a transferable letter of credit.

(4) "Confirmer" means a nominated person who undertakes, at the request or with the consent of the issuer, to honor a presentation under a letter of credit issued by another.

(5) "Dishonor" of a letter of credit means failure timely to honor or to take an interim action, such as acceptance of a draft, that may be required by the letter of credit.

(6) "Document" means a draft or other demand, document of title, investment security, certificate, invoice, or other record, statement, or representation of fact, law, right, or opinion (i) which is presented in a written or other medium permitted by the letter of credit or, unless prohibited by the letter of credit, by the standard practice referred to in Section 5–108(e) and (ii) which is capable of being examined for compliance with the

terms and conditions of the letter of credit. A document may not be oral.

(7) "Good faith" means honesty in fact in the conduct or transaction concerned.

(8) "Honor" of a letter of credit means performance of the issuer's undertaking in the letter of credit to pay or deliver an item of value. Unless the letter of credit otherwise provides, "honor" occurs

> (i) upon payment,
>
> (ii) if the letter of credit provides for acceptance, upon acceptance of a draft and, at maturity, its payment, or
>
> (iii) if the letter of credit provides for incurring a deferred obligation, upon incurring the obligation and, at maturity, its performance.

(9) "Issuer" means a bank or other person that issues a letter of credit, but does not include an individual who makes an engagement for personal, family, or household purposes.

(10) "Letter of credit" means a definite undertaking that satisfies the requirements of Section 5–104 by an issuer to a beneficiary at the request or for the account of an applicant or, in the case of a financial institution, to itself or for its own account, to honor a documentary presentation by payment or delivery of an item of value.

(11) "Nominated person" means a person whom the issuer (i) designates or authorizes to pay, accept, negotiate, or otherwise give value under a letter of credit and (ii) undertakes by agreement or custom and practice to reimburse.

(12) "Presentation" means delivery of a document to an issuer or nominated person for honor or giving of value under a letter of credit.

(13) "Presenter" means a person making a presentation as or on behalf of a beneficiary or nominated person.

(14) "Record" means information that is inscribed on a tangible medium, or that is stored in an electronic or other medium and is retrievable in perceivable form.

(15) "Successor of a beneficiary" means a person who succeeds to substantially all of the rights of a beneficiary by operation of law, including a corporation with or into which the beneficiary has been merged or consolidated, an administrator, executor, personal representative, trustee in bankruptcy, debtor in possession, liquidator, and receiver.

(b) Definitions in other Articles applying to this article and the sections in which they appear are:

> "Accept" or "Acceptance" Section 3–409
>
> "Value" Sections 3–303, 4–211

(c) Article 1 contains certain additional general definitions and principles of construction and interpretation applicable throughout this article.

§ 5–103. Scope.

(a) This article applies to letters of credit and to certain rights and obligations arising out of transactions involving letters of credit.

(b) The statement of a rule in this article does not by itself require, imply, or negate application of the same or a different rule to a situation not provided for, or to a person not specified, in this article.

(c) With the exception of this subsection, subsections (a) and (d), Sections 5–102(a)(9) and (10), 5–106(d), and 5–114(d), and except to the extent prohibited in Sections 1–102(3) and 5–117(d), the effect of this article may be varied by agreement or by a provision stated or incorporated by reference in an undertaking. A term in an agreement or undertaking generally excusing liability or generally limiting remedies for failure to perform obligations is not sufficient to vary obligations prescribed by this article.

(d) Rights and obligations of an issuer to a beneficiary or a nominated person under a letter of credit are independent of the existence, performance, or nonperformance of a contract or arrangement out of which the letter of credit arises or which underlies it, including contracts or arrangements between the issuer and the applicant and between the applicant and the beneficiary.

§ 5–104. Formal Requirements.

A letter of credit, confirmation, advice, transfer, amendment, or cancellation may be issued in any form that is a record and is authenticated (i) by a signature or (ii) in accordance with the agreement of the parties or the standard practice referred to in Section 5–108(e).

§ 5–105. Consideration.

Consideration is not required to issue, amend, transfer, or cancel a letter of credit, advice, or confirmation.

§ 5–106. Issuance, Amendment, Cancellation, and Duration.

(a) A letter of credit is issued and becomes enforceable according to its terms against the issuer when the issuer sends or otherwise transmits it to the person requested to advise or to the beneficiary. A letter of credit is revocable only if it so provides.

(b) After a letter of credit is issued, rights and obligations of a beneficiary, applicant, confirmer, and issuer are not affected by an amendment or cancellation to which that person has not consented except to the extent the letter of credit provides that it is revocable or that the issuer may amend or cancel the letter of credit without that consent.

(c) If there is no stated expiration date or other provision that determines its duration, a letter of credit expires one year after its stated date of issuance or, if none is stated, after the date on which it is issued.

(d) A letter of credit that states that it is perpetual expires five years after its stated date of issuance, or if none is stated, after the date on which it is issued.

§ 5–107. Confirmer, Nominated Person, and Adviser.

(a) A confirmer is directly obligated on a letter of credit and has the rights and obligations of an issuer to the extent of its confirmation. The confirmer also has rights against and obligations to the issuer as if the issuer were an applicant and the confirmer had issued the letter of credit at the request and for the account of the issuer.

(b) A nominated person who is not a confirmer is not obligated to honor or otherwise give value for a presentation.

(c) A person requested to advise may decline to act as an adviser. An adviser that is not a confirmer is not obligated to honor or give value for a presentation. An adviser undertakes to the issuer and to the beneficiary accurately to advise the terms of the letter of credit, confirmation, amendment, or advice received by that person and undertakes to the beneficiary to check the apparent authenticity of the request to advise. Even if the advice is inaccurate, the letter of credit, confirmation, or amendment is enforceable as issued.

(d) A person who notifies a transferee beneficiary of the terms of a letter of credit, confirmation, amendment, or advice has the rights and obligations of an adviser under subsection (c). The terms in the notice to the transferee beneficiary may differ from the terms in any notice to the transferor beneficiary to the extent permitted by the letter of credit, confirmation, amendment, or advice received by the person who so notifies.

§ 5–108. Issuer's Rights and Obligations.

(a) Except as otherwise provided in Section 5–109, an issuer shall honor a presentation that, as determined by the standard practice referred to in subsection (e), appears on its face strictly to comply with the terms and conditions of the letter of credit. Except as otherwise provided in Section 5–113 and unless otherwise agreed with the applicant, an issuer shall dishonor a presentation that does not appear so to comply.

(b) An issuer has a reasonable time after presentation, but not beyond the end of the seventh business day of the issuer after the day of its receipt of documents:

(1) to honor,

(2) if the letter of credit provides for honor to be completed more than seven business days after presentation, to accept a draft or incur a deferred obligation, or

(3) to give notice to the presenter of discrepancies in the presentation.

(c) Except as otherwise provided in subsection (d), an issuer is precluded from asserting as a basis for dishonor any discrepancy if timely notice is not given, or any discrepancy not stated in the notice if timely notice is given.

(d) Failure to give the notice specified in subsection (b) or to mention fraud, forgery, or expiration in the notice does not preclude the issuer from asserting as a basis for dishonor fraud or forgery as described in Section 5–109(a) or expiration of the letter of credit before presentation.

(e) An issuer shall observe standard practice of financial institutions that regularly issue letters of credit. Determination of the issuer's observance of the standard practice is a matter of interpretation for the court. The court shall offer the parties a reasonable opportunity to present evidence of the standard practice.

(f) An issuer is not responsible for:

(1) the performance or nonperformance of the underlying contract, arrangement, or transaction,

(2) an act or omission of others, or

(3) observance or knowledge of the usage of a particular trade other than the standard practice referred to in subsection (e).

(g) If an undertaking constituting a letter of credit under Section 5–102(a)(10) contains nondocumentary conditions, an issuer shall disregard the nondocumentary conditions and treat them as if they were not stated.

(h) An issuer that has dishonored a presentation shall return the documents or hold them at the disposal of, and send advice to that effect to, the presenter.

(i) An issuer that has honored a presentation as permitted or required by this article:

(1) is entitled to be reimbursed by the applicant in immediately available funds not later than the date of its payment of funds;

(2) takes the documents free of claims of the beneficiary or presenter;

(3) is precluded from asserting a right of recourse on a draft under Sections 3–414 and 3–415;

(4) except as otherwise provided in Sections 5–110 and 5–117, is precluded from restitution of money paid or other value given by mistake to the extent the mistake concerns discrepancies in the documents or tender which are apparent on the face of the presentation; and

(5) is discharged to the extent of its performance under the letter of credit unless the issuer honored a presentation in which a required signature of a beneficiary was forged.

§ 5–109. Fraud and Forgery.

(a) If a presentation is made that appears on its face strictly to comply with the terms and conditions of the letter of credit, but a required document is forged or materially fraudulent, or honor of the presentation would facilitate a material fraud by the beneficiary on the issuer or applicant:

(1) the issuer shall honor the presentation, if honor is demanded by (i) a nominated person who has given

value in good faith and without notice of forgery or material fraud, (ii) a confirmer who has honored its confirmation in good faith, (iii) a holder in due course of a draft drawn under the letter of credit which was taken after acceptance by the issuer or nominated person, or (iv) an assignee of the issuer's or nominated person's deferred obligation that was taken for value and without notice of forgery or material fraud after the obligation was incurred by the issuer or nominated person; and

(2) the issuer, acting in good faith, may honor or dishonor the presentation in any other case.

(b) If an applicant claims that a required document is forged or materially fraudulent or that honor of the presentation would facilitate a material fraud by the beneficiary on the issuer or applicant, a court of competent jurisdiction may temporarily or permanently enjoin the issuer from honoring a presentation or grant similar relief against the issuer or other persons only if the court finds that:

(1) the relief is not prohibited under the law applicable to an accepted draft or deferred obligation incurred by the issuer;

(2) a beneficiary, issuer, or nominated person who may be adversely affected is adequately protected against loss that it may suffer because the relief is granted;

(3) all of the conditions to entitle a person to the relief under the law of this State have been met; and

(4) on the basis of the information submitted to the court, the applicant is more likely than not to succeed under its claim of forgery or material fraud and the person demanding honor does not qualify for protection under subsection (a)(1).

§ 5–110. Warranties.

(a) If its presentation is honored, the beneficiary warrants:

(1) to the issuer, any other person to whom presentation is made, and the applicant that there is no fraud or forgery of the kind described in Section 5–109(a); and

(2) to the applicant that the drawing does not violate any agreement between the applicant and beneficiary or any other agreement intended by them to be augmented by the letter of credit.

(b) The warranties in subsection (a) are in addition to warranties arising under Article 3, 4, 7, and 8 because of the presentation or transfer of documents covered by any of those articles.

§ 5–111. Remedies.

(a) If an issuer wrongfully dishonors or repudiates its obligation to pay money under a letter of credit before presentation, the beneficiary, successor, or nominated person presenting on its own behalf may recover from the issuer the amount that is the subject of the dishonor or repudia-

tion. If the issuer's obligation under the letter of credit is not for the payment of money, the claimant may obtain specific performance or, at the claimant's election, recover an amount equal to the value of performance from the issuer. In either case, the claimant may also recover incidental but not consequential damages. The claimant is not obligated to take action to avoid damages that might be due from the issuer under this subsection. If, although not obligated to do so, the claimant avoids damages, the claimant's recovery from the issuer must be reduced by the amount of damages avoided. The issuer has the burden of proving the amount of damages avoided. In the case of repudiation the claimant need not present any document.

(b) If an issuer wrongfully dishonors a draft or demand presented under a letter of credit or honors a draft or demand in breach of its obligation to the applicant, the applicant may recover damages resulting from the breach, including incidental but not consequential damages, less any amount saved as a result of the breach.

(c) If an adviser or nominated person other than a confirmer breaches an obligation under this article or an issuer breaches an obligation not covered in subsection (a) or (b), a person to whom the obligation is owed may recover damages resulting from the breach, including incidental but not consequential damages, less any amount saved as a result of the breach. To the extent of the confirmation, a confirmer has the liability of an issuer specified in this subsection and subsections (a) and (b).

(d) An issuer, nominated person, or adviser who is found liable under subsection (a), (b), or (c) shall pay interest on the amount owed thereunder from the date of wrongful dishonor or other appropriate date.

(e) Reasonable attorney's fees and other expenses of litigation must be awarded to the prevailing party in an action in which a remedy is sought under this article.

(f) Damages that would otherwise be payable by a party for breach of an obligation under this article may be liquidated by agreement or undertaking, but only in an amount or by a formula that is reasonable in light of the harm anticipated.

§ 5–112. Transfer of Letter of Credit.

(a) Except as otherwise provided in Section 5–113, unless a letter of credit provides that it is transferable, the right of a beneficiary to draw or otherwise demand performance under a letter of credit may not be transferred.

(b) Even if a letter of credit provides that it is transferable, the issuer may refuse to recognize or carry out a transfer if:

(1) the transfer would violate applicable law; or

(2) the transferor or transferee has failed to comply with any requirement stated in the letter of credit or any other requirement relating to transfer imposed by the issuer which is within the standard practice referred to in Section 5–108(e) or is otherwise reasonable under the circumstances.

§ 5–113. Transfer by Operation of Law.

(a) A successor of a beneficiary may consent to amendments, sign and present documents, and receive payment or other items of value in the name of the beneficiary without disclosing its status as a successor.

(b) A successor of a beneficiary may consent to amendments, sign and present documents, and receive payment or other items of value in its own name as the disclosed successor of the beneficiary. Except as otherwise provided in subsection (e), an issuer shall recognize a disclosed successor of a beneficiary as beneficiary in full substitution for its predecessor upon compliance with the requirements for recognition by the issuer of a transfer of drawing rights by operation of law under the standard practice referred to in Section 5–108(e) or, in the absence of such a practice, compliance with other reasonable procedures sufficient to protect the issuer.

(c) An issuer is not obliged to determine whether a purported successor is a successor of a beneficiary or whether the signature of a purported successor is genuine or authorized.

(d) Honor of a purported successor's apparently complying presentation under subsection (a) or (b) has the consequences specified in Section 5–108(i) even if the purported successor is not the successor of a beneficiary. Documents signed in the name of the beneficiary or of a disclosed successor by a person who is neither the beneficiary nor the successor of the beneficiary are forged documents for the purposes of Section 5–109.

(e) An issuer whose rights of reimbursement are not covered by subsection (d) or substantially similar law and any confirmer or nominated person may decline to recognize a presentation under subsection (b).

(f) A beneficiary whose name is changed after the issuance of a letter of credit has the same rights and obligations as a successor of a beneficiary under this section.

§ 5–114. Assignment of Proceeds.

(a) In this section, "proceeds of a letter of credit" means the cash, check, accepted draft, or other item of value paid or delivered upon honor or giving of value by the issuer or any nominated person under the letter of credit. The term does not include a beneficiary's drawing rights or documents presented by the beneficiary.

(b) A beneficiary may assign its right to part or all of the proceeds of a letter of credit. The beneficiary may do so before presentation as a present assignment of its right to receive proceeds contingent upon its compliance with the terms and conditions of the letter of credit.

(c) An issuer or nominated person need not recognize an assignment of proceeds of a letter of credit until it consents to the assignment.

(d) An issuer or nominated person has no obligation to give or withhold its consent to an assignment of proceeds of a letter of credit, but consent may not be unreasonably withheld if the assignee possesses and exhibits the letter of credit and presentation of the letter of credit is a condition to honor.

(e) Rights of a transferee beneficiary or nominated person are independent of the beneficiary's assignment of the proceeds of a letter of credit and are superior to the assignee's right to the proceeds.

(f) Neither the rights recognized by this section between an assignee and an issuer, transferee beneficiary, or nominated person nor the issuer's or nominated person's payment of proceeds to an assignee or a third person affect the rights between the assignee and any person other than the issuer, transferee beneficiary, or nominated person. The mode of creating and perfecting a security interest in or granting an assignment of a beneficiary's rights to proceeds is governed by Article 9 or other law. Against persons other than the issuer, transferee beneficiary, or nominated person, the rights and obligations arising upon the creation of a security interest or other assignment of a beneficiary's right to proceeds and its perfection are governed by Article 9 or other law.

§ 5–115. Statute of Limitations.

An action to enforce a right or obligation arising under this article must be commenced within one year after the expiration date of the relevant letter of credit or one year after the [claim for relief] [cause of action] accrues, whichever occurs later. A [claim for relief] [cause of action] accrues when the breach occurs, regardless of the aggrieved party's lack of knowledge of the breach.

§ 5–116. Choice of Law and Forum.

(a) The liability of an issuer, nominated person, or adviser for action or omission is governed by the law of the jurisdiction chosen by an agreement in the form of a record signed or otherwise authenticated by the affected parties in the manner provided in Section 5–104 or by a provision in the person's letter of credit, confirmation, or other undertaking. The jurisdiction whose law is chosen need not bear any relation to the transaction.

(b) Unless subsection (a) applies, the liability of an issuer, nominated person, or adviser for action or omission is governed by the law of the jurisdiction in which the person is located. The person is considered to be located at the address indicated in the person's undertaking. If more than one address is indicated, the person is considered to be located at the address from which the person's undertaking was issued. For the purpose of jurisdiction, choice of law, and recognition of interbranch letters of credit, but not enforcement of a judgment, all branches of a bank are considered separate juridical entities and a bank is considered to be located at the place where its relevant branch is considered to be located under this subsection.

(c) Except as otherwise provided in this subsection, the liability of an issuer, nominated person, or adviser is governed by any rules of custom or practice, such as the Uniform

Customs and Practice for Documentary Credits, to which the letter of credit, confirmation, or other undertaking is expressly made subject. If (i) this article would govern the liability of an issuer, nominated person, or adviser under subsection (a) or (b), (ii) the relevant undertaking incorporates rules of custom or practice, and (iii) there is conflict between this article and those rules as applied to that undertaking, those rules govern except to the extent of any conflict with the nonvariable provisions specified in Section 5–103(c).

(d) If there is conflict between this article and Article 3, 4, 4A, or 9, this article governs.

(e) The forum for settling disputes arising out of an undertaking within this article may be chosen in the manner and with the binding effect that governing law may be chosen in accordance with subsection (a).

§ 5–117. Subrogation of Issuer, Applicant, and Nominated Person.

(a) An issuer that honors a beneficiary's presentation is subrogated to the rights of the beneficiary to the same extent as if the issuer were a secondary obligor of the underlying obligation owed to the beneficiary and of the applicant to the same extent as if the issuer were the secondary obligor of the underlying obligation owed to the applicant.

(b) An applicant that reimburses an issuer is subrogated to the rights of the issuer against any beneficiary, presenter, or nominated person to the same extent as if the applicant were the secondary obligor of the obligations owed to the issuer and has the rights of subrogation of the issuer to the rights of the beneficiary stated in subsection (a).

(c) A nominated person who pays or gives value against a draft or demand presented under a letter of credit is subrogated to the rights of:

(1) the issuer against the applicant to the same extent as if the nominated person were a secondary obligor of the obligation owed to the issuer by the applicant;

(2) the beneficiary to the same extent as if the nominated person were a secondary obligor of the underlying obligation owed to the beneficiary; and

(3) the applicant to same extent as if the nominated person were a secondary obligor of the underlying obligation owed to the applicant.

(d) Notwithstanding any agreement or term to the contrary, the rights of subrogation stated in subsections (a) and (b) do not arise until the issuer honors the letter of credit or otherwise pays and the rights in subsection (c) do not arise until the nominated person pays or otherwise gives value. Until then, the issuer, nominated person, and the applicant do not derive under this section present or prospective rights forming the basis of a claim, defense, or excuse.

§ 5–118. Security Interest of Issuer or Nominated Person.

(a) An issuer or nominated person has a security interest in a document presented under a letter of credit to the extent that the issuer or nominated person honors or gives value for the presentation.

(b) So long as and to the extent that an issuer or nominated person has not been reimbursed or has not otherwise recovered the value given with respect to a security interest in a document under subsection (a), the security interest continues and is subject to Article 9, but:

(1) a security agreement is not necessary to make the security interest enforceable under Section 9–203(b)(3);

(2) if the document is presented in a medium other than a written or other tangible medium, the security interest is perfected; and

(3) if the document is presented in a written or other tangible medium and is not a certificated security, chattel paper, a document of title, an instrument, or a letter of credit, the security interest is perfected and has priority over a conflicting security interest in the document so long as the debtor does not have possession of the document.

As added in 1999.

Transition Provisions

§ [ ]. Effective Date.

This [Act] shall become effective on _____, 20__.

§ [ ]. Repeal.

This [Act] [repeals] [amends] [insert citation to existing Article 5].

§ [ ]. Applicability.

This [Act] applies to a letter of credit that is issued on or after the effective date of this [Act]. This [Act] does not apply to a transaction, event, obligation, or duty arising out of or associated with a letter of credit that was issued before the effective date of this [Act].

§ [ ]. Savings Clause.

A transaction arising out of or associated with a letter of credit that was issued before the effective date of this [Act] and the rights, obligations, and interests flowing from that transaction are governed by any statute or other law amended or repealed by this [Act] as if repeal or amendment had not occurred and may be terminated, completed, consummated, or enforced under that statute or other law.

Repealer of Article 6
BULK TRANSFERS and [Revised] Article 6 BULK SALES
(States to Select One Alternative)

Alternative A

[§ 1. Repeal

Article 6 and Section 9–111 of the Uniform Commercial Code are hereby repealed, effective _____.

§ 2. Amendment

Section 1–105(2) of the Uniform Commercial Code is hereby amended to read as follows:

(2) Where one of the following provisions of this Act specifies the applicable law, that provision governs and a contrary agreement is effective only to the extent permitted by the law (including the conflict of laws rules) so specified:

Rights of creditors against sold goods. Section 2–402.

Applicability of the Article on Leases. Section 2A–105 and 2A-106.

Applicability of the Article on Bank Deposits and Collections. Section 4–102.

Applicability of the Article on Investment Securities. Section 8–106.

Perfection provisions of the Article on Secured Transactions. Section 9–103.

§ 3. Amendment.

Section 2–403(4) of the Uniform Commercial Code is hereby amended to read as follows:

(4) The rights of other purchasers of goods and of lien creditors are governed by the Articles on Secured Transactions (Article 9) and Documents of Title (Article 7).

§ 4. Savings Clause.

Rights and obligations that arose under Article 6 and Section 9–111 of the Uniform Commercial Code before their repeal remain valid and may be enforced as though those statutes had not been repealed.]

§ 6–101. Short Title.

This Article shall be known and may be cited as Uniform Commercial Code—Bulk Sales.

§ 6–102. Definitions and Index of Definitions.

(1) In this Article, unless the context otherwise requires:

(a) "Assets" means the inventory that is the subject of a bulk sale and any tangible and intangible personal property used or held for use primarily in, or arising from, the seller's business and sold in connection with that inventory, but the term does not include:

(i) fixtures (Section 9–102(a)(41)) other than readily removable factory and office machines;

(ii) the lessee's interest in a lease of real property; or

(iii) property to the extent it is generally exempt from creditor process under nonbankruptcy law.

(b) "Auctioneer" means a person whom the seller engages to direct, conduct, control, or be responsible for a sale by auction.

(c) "Bulk sale" means:

(i) in the case of a sale by auction or a sale or series of sales conducted by a liquidator on the seller's behalf, a sale or series of sales not in the ordinary course of the seller's business of more than half of the seller's inventory, as measured by value on the date of the bulk-sale agreement, if on that date the auctioneer or liquidator has notice, or after reasonable inquiry would have had notice, that the seller will not continue to operate the same or a similar kind of business after the sale or series of sales; and

(ii) in all other cases, a sale not in the ordinary course of the seller's business of more than half the seller's inventory, as measured by value on the date of the bulk-sale agreement, if on that date the buyer has notice, or after reasonable inquiry would have had notice, that the seller will not continue to operate the same or a similar kind of business after the sale.

(d) "Claim" means a right to payment from the seller, whether or not the right is reduced to judgment, liquidated, fixed, matured, disputed, secured, legal, or equitable. The term includes costs of collection and attorney's fees only to the extent that the laws of this state permit the holder of the claim to recover them in an action against the obligor.

(e) "Claimant" means a person holding a claim incurred in the seller's business other than:

(i) an unsecured and unmatured claim for employment compensation and benefits, including commissions and vacation, severance, and sick-leave pay;

(ii) a claim for injury to an individual or to property, or for breach of warranty, unless:

(A) a right of action for the claim has accrued;

(B) the claim has been asserted against the seller; and

(C) the seller knows the identity of the person asserting the claim and the basis upon which the person has asserted it; and

(States to Select One Alternative)

Alternative A

[(iii) a claim for taxes owing to a governmental unit.]

Alternative B

[(iii) a claim for taxes owing to a governmental unit, if:

(A) a statute governing the enforcement of the claim permits or requires notice of the bulk sale to be given to the governmental unit in a manner other than by compliance with the requirements of this Article; and

(B) notice is given in accordance with the statute.]

(f) "Creditor" means a claimant or other person holding a claim.

(g)(i) "Date of the bulk sale" means:

(A) if the sale is by auction or is conducted by a liquidator on the seller's behalf, the date on which more than ten percent of the net proceeds is paid to or for the benefit of the seller; and

(B) in all other cases, the later of the date on which:

(I) more than ten percent of the net contract price is paid to or for the benefit of the seller; or

(II) more than ten percent of the assets, as measured by value, are transferred to the buyer.

(ii) For purposes of this subsection:

(A) delivery of a negotiable instrument (Section 3–104(1)) to or for the benefit of the seller in exchange for assets constitutes payment of the contract price pro tanto;

(B) to the extent that the contract price is deposited in an escrow, the contract price is paid to or for the benefit of the seller when the seller acquires the unconditional right to receive the deposit or when the deposit is delivered to the seller or for the benefit of the seller, whichever is earlier; and

(C) an asset is transferred when a person holding an unsecured claim can no longer obtain through judicial proceedings rights to the asset that are superior to those of the buyer arising as a result of the bulk sale. A person holding an unsecured claim can obtain those superior rights to a tangible asset at least until the buyer has an unconditional right, under the bulk-sale agreement, to possess the asset, and a person holding an unsecured claim can obtain those superior rights to an intangible asset at least until the buyer has an unconditional right, under the bulk-sale agreement, to use the asset.

(h) "Date of the bulk-sale agreement" means:

(i) in the case of a sale by auction or conducted by a liquidator (subsection (c)(i)), the date on which the seller engages the auctioneer or liquidator; and

(ii) in all other cases, the date on which a bulk-sale agreement becomes enforceable between the buyer and the seller.

(i) "Debt" means liability on a claim.

(j) "Liquidator" means a person who is regularly engaged in the business of disposing of assets for businesses contemplating liquidation or dissolution.

(k) "Net contract price" means the new consideration the buyer is obligated to pay for the assets less:

(i) the amount of any proceeds of the sale of an asset, to the extent the proceeds are applied in partial or total satisfaction of a debt secured by the asset; and

(ii) the amount of any debt to the extent it is secured by a security interest or lien that is enforceable against the asset before and after it has been sold to a buyer. If a debt is secured by an asset and other property of the seller, the amount of the debt secured by a security interest or lien that is enforceable against the asset is determined by multiplying the debt by a fraction, the numerator of which is the value of the new consideration for the asset on the date of the bulk sale and the denominator of which is the value of all property securing the debt on the date of the bulk sale.

(l) "Net proceeds" means the new consideration received for assets sold at a sale by auction or a sale conducted by a liquidator on the seller's behalf less:

(i) commissions and reasonable expenses of the sale;

(ii) the amount of any proceeds of the sale of an asset, to the extent the proceeds are applied in partial or total satisfaction of a debt secured by the asset; and

(iii) the amount of any debt to the extent it is secured by a security interest or lien that is enforceable against the asset before and after it has been sold to a buyer. If a debt is secured by an asset and other property of the seller, the amount of the debt secured by a security interest or lien that is enforceable against the asset is determined by multiplying the debt by a fraction, the numerator of which is the value of the new consideration for the asset on the date of the bulk sale and the denominator of which is the value of all property securing the debt on the date of the bulk sale.

(m) A sale is "in the ordinary course of the seller's business" if the sale comports with usual or customary practices in the kind of business in which the seller is engaged or with the seller's own usual or customary practices.

(n) "United States" includes its territories and possessions and the Commonwealth of Puerto Rico.

(o) "Value" means fair market value.

(p) "Verified" means signed and sworn to or affirmed.

(2) The following definitions in other Articles apply to this Article:

(a) "Buyer."	Section 2–103(1)(a).
(b) "Equipment."	Section 9–102(a)(33).
(c) "Inventory."	Section 9–102(a)(48).
(d) "Sale."	Section 2–106(1).
(e) "Seller."	Section 2–103(1)(d).

(3) In addition, Article 1 contains general definitions and principles of construction and interpretation applicable throughout this Article.

As amended in 1999.

§ 6–103. Applicability of Article.

(1) Except as otherwise provided in subsection (3), this Article applies to a bulk sale if:

(a) the seller's principal business is the sale of inventory from stock; and

(b) on the date of the bulk-sale agreement the seller is located in this state or, if the seller is located in a jurisdiction that is not a part of the United States, the seller's major executive office in the United States is in this state.

(2) A seller is deemed to be located at his [or her] place of business. If a seller has more than one place of business, the seller is deemed located at his [or her] chief executive office.

(3) This Article does not apply to:

(a) a transfer made to secure payment or performance of an obligation;

(b) a transfer of collateral to a secured party pursuant to Section 9–503;

(c) a disposition of collateral pursuant to Section 9–610;

(d) retention of collateral pursuant to Section 9–620;

(e) a sale of an asset encumbered by a security interest or lien if (i) all the proceeds of the sale are applied in partial or total satisfaction of the debt secured by the security interest or lien or (ii) the security interest or lien is enforceable against the asset after it has been sold to the buyer and the net contract price is zero;

(f) a general assignment for the benefit of creditors or to a subsequent transfer by the assignee;

(g) a sale by an executor, administrator, receiver, trustee in bankruptcy, or any public officer under judicial process;

(h) a sale made in the course of judicial or administrative proceedings for the dissolution or reorganization of an organization;

(i) a sale to a buyer whose principal place of business is in the United States and who:

(i) not earlier than 21 days before the date of the bulk sale, (A) obtains from the seller a verified and dated list of claimants of whom the seller has notice three days before the seller sends or delivers the list to the buyer or (B) conducts a reasonable inquiry to discover the claimants;

(ii) assumes in full the debts owed to claimants of whom the buyer has knowledge on the date the buyer receives the list of claimants from the seller or on the date the buyer completes the reasonable inquiry, as the case may be;

(iii) is not insolvent after the assumption; and

(iv) gives written notice of the assumption not later than 30 days after the date of the bulk sale by sending or delivering a notice to the claimants identified in subparagraph (ii) or by filing a notice in the office of the [Secretary of State];

(j) a sale to a buyer whose principal place of business is in the United States and who:

(i) assumes in full the debts that were incurred in the seller's business before the date of the bulk sale;

(ii) is not insolvent after the assumption; and

(iii) gives written notice of the assumption not later than 30 days after the date of the bulk sale by sending or delivering a notice to each creditor whose debt is assumed or by filing a notice in the office of the [Secretary of State];

(k) a sale to a new organization that is organized to take over and continue the business of the seller and that has its principal place of business in the United States if:

(i) the buyer assumes in full the debts that were incurred in the seller's business before the date of the bulk sale;

(ii) the seller receives nothing from the sale except an interest in the new organization that is subordinate to the claims against the organization arising from the assumption; and

(iii) the buyer gives written notice of the assumption not later than 30 days after the date of the bulk sale by sending or delivering a notice to each creditor whose debt is assumed or by filing a notice in the office of the [Secretary of State];

(l) a sale of assets having:

(i) a value, net of liens and security interests, of less than $10,000. If a debt is secured by assets and other property of the seller, the net value of the assets is determined by subtracting from their value an amount equal to the product of the debt multiplied by a fraction, the numerator of which is the value of the assets on the date of the bulk sale and the denominator of which is the value of all property securing the debt on the date of the bulk sale; or

(ii) a value of more than $25,000,000 on the date of the bulk-sale agreement; or

(m) a sale required by, and made pursuant to, statute.

(4) The notice under subsection (3)(i)(iv) must state: (i) that a sale that may constitute a bulk sale has been or will be made; (ii) the date or prospective date of the bulk sale; (iii) the individual, partnership, or corporate names and the addresses of the seller and buyer; (iv) the address to which inquiries about the sale may be made, if different from the seller's address; and (v) that the buyer has assumed or will assume in full the debts owed to claimants of whom the buyer has knowledge on the date the buyer receives the

list of claimants from the seller or completes a reasonable inquiry to discover the claimants.

(5) The notice under subsections (3)(j)(iii) and (3)(k)(iii) must state: (i) that a sale that may constitute a bulk sale has been or will be made; (ii) the date or prospective date of the bulk sale; (iii) the individual, partnership, or corporate names and the addresses of the seller and buyer; (iv) the address to which inquiries about the sale may be made, if different from the seller's address; and (v) that the buyer has assumed or will assume the debts that were incurred in the seller's business before the date of the bulk sale.

(6) For purposes of subsection (3)(l), the value of assets is presumed to be equal to the price the buyer agrees to pay for the assets. However, in a sale by auction or a sale conducted by a liquidator on the seller's behalf, the value of assets is presumed to be the amount the auctioneer or liquidator reasonably estimates the assets will bring at auction or upon liquidation.

As amended in 1999.

§ 6–104. Obligations of Buyer.

(1) In a bulk sale as defined in Section 6–102(1)(c)(ii) the buyer shall:

(a) obtain from the seller a list of all business names and addresses used by the seller within three years before the date the list is sent or delivered to the buyer;

(b) unless excused under subsection (2), obtain from the seller a verified and dated list of claimants of whom the seller has notice three days before the seller sends or delivers the list to the buyer and including, to the extent known by the seller, the address of and the amount claimed by each claimant;

(c) obtain from the seller or prepare a schedule of distribution (Section 6–106(1));

(d) give notice of the bulk sale in accordance with Section 6–105;

(e) unless excused under Section 6–106(4), distribute the net contract price in accordance with the undertakings of the buyer in the schedule of distribution; and

(f) unless excused under subsection (2), make available the list of claimants (subsection (1)(b)) by:

(i) promptly sending or delivering a copy of the list without charge to any claimant whose written request is received by the buyer no later than six months after the date of the bulk sale;

(ii) permitting any claimant to inspect and copy the list at any reasonable hour upon request received by the buyer no later than six months after the date of the bulk sale; or

(iii) filing a copy of the list in the office of the [Secretary of State] no later than the time for giving a notice of the bulk sale (Section 6–105(5)). A list filed in accordance with this subparagraph must state the individual, partnership, or corporate name and a mailing address of the seller.

(2) A buyer who gives notice in accordance with Section 6–105(2) is excused from complying with the requirements of subsections (1)(b) and (1)(f).

§ 6–105. Notice to Claimants.

(1) Except as otherwise provided in subsection (2), to comply with Section 6–104(1)(d) the buyer shall send or deliver a written notice of the bulk sale to each claimant on the list of claimants (Section 6–104(1)(b)) and to any other claimant of which the buyer has knowledge at the time the notice of the bulk sale is sent or delivered.

(2) A buyer may comply with Section 6–104(1)(d) by filing a written notice of the bulk sale in the office of the [Secretary of State] if:

(a) on the date of the bulk-sale agreement the seller has 200 or more claimants, exclusive of claimants holding secured or matured claims for employment compensation and benefits, including commissions and vacation, severance, and sick-leave pay; or

(b) the buyer has received a verified statement from the seller stating that, as of the date of the bulk-sale agreement, the number of claimants, exclusive of claimants holding secured or matured claims for employment compensation and benefits, including commissions and vacation, severance, and sick-leave pay, is 200 or more.

(3) The written notice of the bulk sale must be accompanied by a copy of the schedule of distribution (Section 6–106(1)) and state at least:

(a) that the seller and buyer have entered into an agreement for a sale that may constitute a bulk sale under the laws of the State of _____ ;

(b) the date of the agreement;

(c) the date on or after which more than ten percent of the assets were or will be transferred;

(d) the date on or after which more than ten percent of the net contract price was or will be paid, if the date is not stated in the schedule of distribution;

(e) the name and a mailing address of the seller;

(f) any other business name and address listed by the seller pursuant to Section 6–104(1)(a);

(g) the name of the buyer and an address of the buyer from which information concerning the sale can be obtained;

(h) a statement indicating the type of assets or describing the assets item by item;

(i) the manner in which the buyer will make available the list of claimants (Section 6–104(1)(f)), if applicable; and

(j) if the sale is in total or partial satisfaction of an antecedent debt owed by the seller, the amount of the debt to be satisfied and the name of the person to whom it is owed.

(4) For purposes of subsections (3)(e) and (3)(g), the name of a person is the person's individual, partnership, or corporate name.

(5) The buyer shall give notice of the bulk sale not less than 45 days before the date of the bulk sale and, if the buyer gives notice in accordance with subsection (1), not more than 30 days after obtaining the list of claimants.

(6) A written notice substantially complying with the requirements of subsection (3) is effective even though it contains minor errors that are not seriously misleading.

(7) A form substantially as follows is sufficient to comply with subsection (3):

Notice of Sale

(1) _____ , whose address is _____ , is described in this notice as the "seller."

(2) _____ , whose address is _____ , is described in this notice as the "buyer."

(3) The seller has disclosed to the buyer that within the past three years the seller has used other business names, operated at other addresses, or both, as follows: _____ .

(4) The seller and the buyer have entered into an agreement dated _____ , for a sale that may constitute a bulk sale under the laws of the state of _____ .

(5) The date on or after which more than ten percent of the assets that are the subject of the sale were or will be transferred is _____ , and [if not stated in the schedule of distribution] the date on or after which more than ten percent of the net contract price was or will be paid is _____ .

(6) The following assets are the subject of the sale: _____ .

(7) [If applicable] The buyer will make available to claimants of the seller a list of the seller's claimants in the following manner: _____ .

(8) [If applicable] The sale is to satisfy $ _____ of an antecedent debt owed by the seller to _____ .

(9) A copy of the schedule of distribution of the net contract price accompanies this notice.

[End of Notice]

§ 6–106. Schedule of Distribution.

(1) The seller and buyer shall agree on how the net contract price is to be distributed and set forth their agreement in a written schedule of distribution.

(2) The schedule of distribution may provide for distribution to any person at any time, including distribution of the entire net contract price to the seller.

(3) The buyer's undertakings in the schedule of distribution run only to the seller. However, a buyer who fails to distribute the net contract price in accordance with the buyer's undertakings in the schedule of distribution is liable to a creditor only as provided in Section 6–107(1).

(4) If the buyer undertakes in the schedule of distribution to distribute any part of the net contract price to a person other than the seller, and, after the buyer has given notice in accordance with Section 6–105, some or all of the anticipated net contract price is or becomes unavailable for distribution as a consequence of the buyer's or seller's having complied with an order of court, legal process, statute, or rule of law, the buyer is excused from any obligation arising under this Article or under any contract with the seller to distribute the net contract price in accordance with the buyer's undertakings in the schedule if the buyer:

(a) distributes the net contract price remaining available in accordance with any priorities for payment stated in the schedule of distribution and, to the extent that the price is insufficient to pay all the debts having a given priority, distributes the price pro rata among those debts shown in the schedule as having the same priority;

(b) distributes the net contract price remaining available in accordance with an order of court;

(c) commences a proceeding for interpleader in a court of competent jurisdiction and is discharged from the proceeding; or

(d) reaches a new agreement with the seller for the distribution of the net contract price remaining available, sets forth the new agreement in an amended schedule of distribution, gives notice of the amended schedule, and distributes the net contract price remaining available in accordance with the buyer's undertakings in the amended schedule.

(5) The notice under subsection (4)(d) must identify the buyer and the seller, state the filing number, if any, of the original notice, set forth the amended schedule, and be given in accordance with subsection (1) or (2) of Section 6–105, whichever is applicable, at least 14 days before the buyer distributes any part of the net contract price remaining available.

(6) If the seller undertakes in the schedule of distribution to distribute any part of the net contract price, and, after the buyer has given notice in accordance with Section 6–105, some or all of the anticipated net contract price is or becomes unavailable for distribution as a consequence of the buyer's or seller's having complied with an order of court, legal process, statute, or rule of law, the seller and any person in control of the seller are excused from any obligation arising under this Article or under any agreement with the buyer to distribute the net contract price in accordance with the seller's undertakings in the schedule if the seller:

(a) distributes the net contract price remaining available in accordance with any priorities for payment stated in the schedule of distribution and, to the extent that the price is insufficient to pay all the debts having a given priority, distributes the price pro rata among those debts shown in the schedule as having the same priority;

(b) distributes the net contract price remaining available in accordance with an order of court;

(c) commences a proceeding for interpleader in a court of competent jurisdiction and is discharged from the proceeding; or

(d) prepares a written amended schedule of distribution of the net contract price remaining available for distribution, gives notice of the amended schedule, and distributes the net contract price remaining available in accordance with the amended schedule.

(7) The notice under subsection (6)(d) must identify the buyer and the seller, state the filing number, if any, of the original notice, set forth the amended schedule, and be given in accordance with subsection (1) or (2) of Section 6–105, whichever is applicable, at least 14 days before the seller distributes any part of the net contract price remaining available.

§ 6–107. Liability for Noncompliance.

(1) Except as provided in subsection (3), and subject to the limitation in subsection (4):

(a) a buyer who fails to comply with the requirements of Section 6–104(1)(e) with respect to a creditor is liable to the creditor for damages in the amount of the claim, reduced by any amount that the creditor would not have realized if the buyer had complied; and

(b) a buyer who fails to comply with the requirements of any other subsection of Section 6–104 with respect to a claimant is liable to the claimant for damages in the amount of the claim, reduced by any amount that the claimant would not have realized if the buyer had complied.

(2) In an action under subsection (1), the creditor has the burden of establishing the validity and amount of the claim, and the buyer has the burden of establishing the amount that the creditor would not have realized if the buyer had complied.

(3) A buyer who:

(a) made a good faith and commercially reasonable effort to comply with the requirements of Section 6–104(1) or to exclude the sale from the application of this Article under Section 6–103(3); or

(b) on or after the date of the bulk-sale agreement, but before the date of the bulk sale, held a good faith and commercially reasonable belief that this Article does not apply to the particular sale is not liable to creditors for failure to comply with the requirements of Section 6–104. The buyer has the burden of establishing the good faith and commercial reasonableness of the effort or belief.

(4) In a single bulk sale the cumulative liability of the buyer for failure to comply with the requirements of Section 6–104(1) may not exceed an amount equal to:

(a) if the assets consist only of inventory and equipment, twice the net contract price, less the amount of any part of the net contract price paid to or applied for the benefit of the seller or a creditor; or

(b) if the assets include property other than inventory and equipment, twice the net value of the inventory and equipment less the amount of the portion of any part of the net contract price paid to or applied for the benefit of the seller or a creditor which is allocable to the inventory and equipment.

(5) For the purposes of subsection (4)(b), the "net value" of an asset is the value of the asset less (i) the amount of any proceeds of the sale of an asset, to the extent the proceeds are applied in partial or total satisfaction of a debt secured by the asset and (ii) the amount of any debt to the extent it is secured by a security interest or lien that is enforceable against the asset before and after it has been sold to a buyer. If a debt is secured by an asset and other property of the seller, the amount of the debt secured by a security interest or lien that is enforceable against the asset is determined by multiplying the debt by a fraction, the numerator of which is the value of the asset on the date of the bulk sale and the denominator of which is the value of all property securing the debt on the date of the bulk sale. The portion of a part of the net contract price paid to or applied for the benefit of the seller or a creditor that is "allocable to the inventory and equipment" is the portion that bears the same ratio to that part of the net contract price as the net value of the inventory and equipment bears to the net value of all of the assets.

(6) A payment made by the buyer to a person to whom the buyer is, or believes he [or she] is, liable under subsection (1) reduces pro tanto the buyer's cumulative liability under subsection (4).

(7) No action may be brought under subsection (1)(b) by or on behalf of a claimant whose claim is unliquidated or contingent.

(8) A buyer's failure to comply with the requirements of Section 6–104(1) does not (i) impair the buyer's rights in or title to the assets, (ii) render the sale ineffective, void, or voidable, (iii) entitle a creditor to more than a single satisfaction of his [or her] claim, or (iv) create liability other than as provided in this Article.

(9) Payment of the buyer's liability under subsection (1) discharges pro tanto the seller's debt to the creditor.

(10) Unless otherwise agreed, a buyer has an immediate right of reimbursement from the seller for any amount paid to a creditor in partial or total satisfaction of the buyer's liability under subsection (1).

(11) If the seller is an organization, a person who is in direct or indirect control of the seller, and who knowingly,

intentionally, and without legal justification fails, or causes the seller to fail, to distribute the net contract price in accordance with the schedule of distribution is liable to any creditor to whom the seller undertook to make payment under the schedule for damages caused by the failure.

§ 6–108. Bulk Sales by Auction; Bulk Sales Conducted by Liquidator.

(1) Sections 6–104, 6–105, 6–106, and 6–107 apply to a bulk sale by auction and a bulk sale conducted by a liquidator on the seller's behalf with the following modifications:

(a) "buyer" refers to auctioneer or liquidator, as the case may be;

(b) "net contract price" refers to net proceeds of the auction or net proceeds of the sale, as the case may be;

(c) the written notice required under Section 6–105(3) must be accompanied by a copy of the schedule of distribution (Section 6–106(1)) and state at least:

(i) that the seller and the auctioneer or liquidator have entered into an agreement for auction or liquidation services that may constitute an agreement to make a bulk sale under the laws of the State of _____ ;

(ii) the date of the agreement;

(iii) the date on or after which the auction began or will begin or the date on or after which the liquidator began or will begin to sell assets on the seller's behalf;

(iv) the date on or after which more than ten percent of the net proceeds of the sale were or will be paid, if the date is not stated in the schedule of distribution;

(v) the name and a mailing address of the seller;

(vi) any other business name and address listed by the seller pursuant to Section 6–104(1)(a);

(vii) the name of the auctioneer or liquidator and an address of the auctioneer or liquidator from which information concerning the sale can be obtained;

(viii) a statement indicating the type of assets or describing the assets item by item;

(ix) the manner in which the auctioneer or liquidator will make available the list of claimants (Section 6–104(1)(f)), if applicable; and

(x) if the sale is in total or partial satisfaction of an antecedent debt owed by the seller, the amount of the debt to be satisfied and the name of the person to whom it is owed; and

(d) in a single bulk sale the cumulative liability of the auctioneer or liquidator for failure to comply with the requirements of this section may not exceed the amount of the net proceeds of the sale allocable to inventory and equipment sold less the amount of the portion of any part of the net proceeds paid to or applied for the benefit of a creditor which is allocable to the inventory and equipment.

(2) A payment made by the auctioneer or liquidator to a person to whom the auctioneer or liquidator is, or believes he [or she] is, liable under this section reduces pro tanto the auctioneer's or liquidator's cumulative liability under subsection (1)(d).

(3) A form substantially as follows is sufficient to comply with subsection (1)(c):

Notice of Sale

(1) _____ , whose address is _____ , is described in this notice as the "seller."

(2) _____ , whose address is _____ , is described in this notice as the "auctioneer" or "liquidator."

(3) The seller has disclosed to the auctioneer or liquidator that within the past three years the seller has used other business names, operated at other addresses, or both, as follows: _____ .

(4) The seller and the auctioneer or liquidator have entered into an agreement dated _____ for auction or liquidation services that may constitute an agreement to make a bulk sale under the laws of the State of _____ .

(5) The date on or after which the auction began or will begin or the date on or after which the liquidator began or will begin to sell assets on the seller's behalf is _____, and [if not stated in the schedule of distribution] the date on or after which more than ten percent of the net proceeds of the sale were or will be paid is _____ .

(6) The following assets are the subject of the sale: _____ .

(7) [If applicable] The auctioneer or liquidator will make available to claimants of the seller a list of the seller's claimants in the following manner: _____ .

(8) [If applicable] The sale is to satisfy $ _____ of an antecedent debt owed by the seller to _____ .

(9) A copy of the schedule of distribution of the net proceeds accompanies this notice.

[End of Notice]

(4) A person who buys at a bulk sale by auction or conducted by a liquidator need not comply with the requirements of Section 6–104(1) and is not liable for the failure of an auctioneer or liquidator to comply with the requirements of this section.

§ 6–109. What Constitutes Filing; Duties of Filing Officer; Information from Filing Officer.

(1) Presentation of a notice or list of claimants for filing and tender of the filing fee or acceptance of the notice or list by the filing officer constitutes filing under this Article.

(2) The filing officer shall:

(a) mark each notice or list with a file number and with the date and hour of filing;

(b) hold the notice or list or a copy for public inspection;

(c) index the notice or list according to each name given for the seller and for the buyer; and

(d) note in the index the file number and the addresses of the seller and buyer given in the notice or list.

(3) If the person filing a notice or list furnishes the filing officer with a copy, the filing officer upon request shall note upon the copy the file number and date and hour of the filing of the original and send or deliver the copy to the person.

(4) The fee for filing and indexing and for stamping a copy furnished by the person filing to show the date and place of filing is $ _____ for the first page and $ _____ for each additional page. The fee for indexing each name beyond the first two is $ _____ .

(5) Upon request of any person, the filing officer shall issue a certificate showing whether any notice or list with respect to a particular seller or buyer is on file on the date and hour stated in the certificate. If a notice or list is on file, the certificate must give the date and hour of filing of each notice or list and the name and address of each seller, buyer, auctioneer, or liquidator. The fee for the certificate is $ _____ if the request for the certificate is in the standard form prescribed by the [Secretary of State] and otherwise is $ _____ . Upon request of any person, the filing officer shall furnish a copy of any filed notice or list for a fee of $ _____ .

(6) The filing officer shall keep each notice or list for two years after it is filed.

§ 6–110. Limitation of Actions.

(1) Except as provided in subsection (2), an action under this Article against a buyer, auctioneer, or liquidator must be commenced within one year after the date of the bulk sale.

(2) If the buyer, auctioneer, or liquidator conceals the fact that the sale has occurred, the limitation is tolled and an action under this Article may be commenced within the earlier of (i) one year after the person bringing the action discovers that the sale has occurred or (ii) one year after the person bringing the action should have discovered that the sale has occurred, but no later than two years after the date of the bulk sale. Complete noncompliance with the requirements of this Article does not of itself constitute concealment.

(3) An action under Section 6–107(11) must be commenced within one year after the alleged violation occurs.

Conforming Amendment to Section 2–403

States adopting Alternative B should amend Section 2–403(4) of the Uniform Commercial Code to read as follows:

(4) The rights of other purchasers of goods and of lien creditors are governed by the Articles on Secured Transactions (Article 9), Bulk Sales (Article 6) and Documents of Title (Article 7).

Article 7
Warehouse Receipts, Bills of Lading and Other Documents of Title

Part 1   General

§ 7–101. Short Title.

This Article shall be known and may be cited as Uniform Commercial Code–Documents of Title.

§ 7–102. Definitions and Index of Definitions.

(1) In this Article, unless the context otherwise requires:

(a) "Bailee" means the person who by a warehouse receipt, bill of lading or other document of title acknowledges possession of goods and contracts to deliver them.

(b) "Consignee" means the person named in a bill to whom or to whose order the bill promises delivery.

(c) "Consignor" means the person named in a bill as the person from whom the goods have been received for shipment.

(d) "Delivery order" means a written order to deliver goods directed to a warehouseman, carrier or other person who in the ordinary course of business issues warehouse receipts or bills of lading.

(e) "Document" means document of title as defined in the general definitions in Article 1 (Section 1–201).

(f) "Goods" means all things which are treated as movable for the purposes of a contract of storage or transportation.

(g) "Issuer" means a bailee who issues a document except that in relation to an unaccepted delivery order it means the person who orders the possessor of goods to deliver. Issuer includes any person for whom an agent or employee purports to act in issuing a document if the agent or employee has real or apparent authority to issue documents, notwithstanding that the issuer received no goods or that the goods were misdescribed or that in any other respect the agent or employee violated his instructions.

(h) "Warehouseman" is a person engaged in the business of storing goods for hire.

(2) Other definitions applying to this Article or to specified Parts thereof, and the sections in which they appear are:

"Duly negotiate". Section 7–501.

"Person entitled under the document". Section 7–403(4).

(3) Definitions in other Articles applying to this Article and the sections in which they appear are:

"Contract for sale". Section 2–106.

"Overseas". Section 2–323.

"Receipt" of goods. Section 2–103.

(4) In addition Article 1 contains general definitions and principles of construction and interpretation applicable throughout this Article.

§ 7–103. Relation of Article to Treaty, Statute, Tariff, Classification or Regulation.

To the extent that any treaty or statute of the United States, regulatory statute of this State or tariff, classification or regulation filed or issued pursuant thereto is applicable, the provisions of this Article are subject thereto.

§ 7–104. Negotiable and Non-Negotiable Warehouse Receipt, Bill of Lading or Other Document of Title.

(1) A warehouse receipt, bill of lading or other document of title is negotiable

(a) if by its terms the goods are to be delivered to bearer or to the order of a named person; or

(b) where recognized in overseas trade, if it runs to a named person or assigns.

(2) Any other document is nonnegotiable. A bill of lading in which it is stated that the goods are consigned to a named person is not made negotiable by a provision that the goods are to be delivered only against a written order signed by the same or another named person.

§ 7–105. Construction Against Negative Implication.

The omission from either Part 2 or Part 3 of this Article of a provision corresponding to a provision made in the other Part does not imply that a corresponding rule of law is not applicable.

Part 2   Warehouse Receipts: Special Provisions

§ 7–201. Who May Issue a Warehouse Receipt; Storage Under Government Bond.

(1) A warehouse receipt may be issued by any warehouseman.

(2) Where goods including distilled spirits and agricultural commodities are stored under a statute requiring a bond against withdrawal or a license for the issuance of receipts in the nature of warehouse receipts, a receipt issued for the goods has like effect as a warehouse receipt even though issued by a person who is the owner of the goods and is not a warehouseman.

§ 7–202. Form of Warehouse Receipt; Essential Terms; Optional Terms.

(1) A warehouse receipt need not be in any particular form.

(2) Unless a warehouse receipt embodies within its written or printed terms each of the following, the warehouseman is liable for damages caused by the omission to a person injured thereby:

(a) the location of the warehouse where the goods are stored;

(b) the date of issue of the receipt;

(c) the consecutive number of the receipt;

(d) a statement whether the goods received will be delivered to the bearer, to a specified person, or to a specified person or his order;

(e) the rate of storage and handling charges, except that where goods are stored under a field warehousing arrangement a statement of that fact is sufficient on a non-negotiable receipt;

(f) a description of the goods or of the packages containing them;

(g) the signature of the warehouseman, which may be made by his authorized agent;

(h) if the receipt is issued for goods of which the warehouseman is owner, either solely or jointly or in common with others, the fact of such ownership; and

(i) a statement of the amount of advances made and of liabilities incurred for which the warehouseman claims a lien or security interest (Section 7–209). If the precise amount of such advances made or of such liabilities incurred is, at the time of the issue of the receipt, unknown to the warehouseman or to his agent who issues it, a statement of the fact that advances have been made or liabilities incurred and the purpose thereof is sufficient.

(3) A warehouseman may insert in his receipt any other terms which are not contrary to the provisions of this Act and do not impair his obligation of delivery (Section 7–403) or his duty of care (Section 7–204). Any contrary provisions shall be ineffective.

§ 7–203. Liability for Non-Receipt or Misdescription.

A party to or purchaser for value in good faith of a document of title other than a bill of lading relying in either case upon the description therein of the goods may recover from the issuer damages caused by the nonreceipt or misdescription of the goods, except to the extent that the document conspicuously indicates that the issuer does not know whether any part or all of the goods in fact were received or conform to the description, as where the description is in terms of marks or labels or kind, quantity or condition, or the receipt or description is qualified by "contents, condition and quality unknown", "said to contain" or the like, if such indication be true, or the party or purchaser otherwise has notice.

§ 7–204. Duty of Care; Contractual Limitation of Warehouseman's Liability.

(1) A warehouseman is liable for damages for loss of or injury to the goods caused by his failure to exercise such care in regard to them as a reasonably careful man would exercise under like circumstances but unless otherwise agreed he is not liable for damages which could not have been avoided by the exercise of such care.

(2) Damages may be limited by a term in the warehouse receipt or storage agreement limiting the amount of liability in case of loss or damage, and setting forth a specific liability per article or item, or value per unit of weight, beyond which the warehouseman shall not be liable; provided, however, that such liability may on written request of the bailor at the time of signing such storage agreement or within a reasonable

time after receipt of the warehouse receipt be increased on part or all of the goods thereunder, in which event increased rates may be charged based on such increased valuation, but that no such increase shall be permitted contrary to a lawful limitation of liability contained in the warehouseman's tariff, if any. No such limitation is effective with respect to the warehouseman's liability for conversion to his own use.

(3) Reasonable provisions as to the time and manner of presenting claims and instituting actions based on the bailment may be included in the warehouse receipt or tariff.

(4) This section does not impair or repeal . . .

Note: Insert in subsection (4) a reference to any statute which imposes a higher responsibility upon the warehouseman or invalidates contractual limitations which would be permissible under this Article.

§ 7–205. Title Under Warehouse Receipt Defeated in Certain Cases.

A buyer in the ordinary course of business of fungible goods sold and delivered by a warehouseman who is also in the business of buying and selling such goods takes free of any claim under a warehouse receipt even though it has been duly negotiated.

§ 7–206. Termination of Storage at Warehouseman's Option.

(1) A warehouseman may on notifying the person on whose account the goods are held and any other person known to claim an interest in the goods require payment of any charges and removal of the goods from the warehouse at the termination of the period of storage fixed by the document, or, if no period is fixed, within a stated period not less than thirty days after the notification. If the goods are not removed before the date specified in the notification, the warehouseman may sell them in accordance with the provisions of the section on enforcement of a warehouseman's lien (Section 7–210).

(2) If a warehouseman in good faith believes that the goods are about to deteriorate or decline in value to less than the amount of his lien within the time prescribed in subsection (1) for notification, advertisement and sale, the warehouseman may specify in the notification any reasonable shorter time for removal of the goods and in case the goods are not removed, may sell them at public sale held not less than one week after a single advertisement or posting.

(3) If as a result of a quality or condition of the goods of which the warehouseman had no notice at the time of deposit the goods are a hazard to other property or to the warehouse or to persons, the warehouseman may sell the goods at public or private sale without advertisement on reasonable notification to all persons known to claim an interest in the goods. If the warehouseman after a reasonable effort is unable to sell the goods he may dispose of them in any lawful manner and shall incur no liability by reason of such disposition.

(4) The warehouseman must deliver the goods to any person entitled to them under this Article upon due demand made at any time prior to sale or other disposition under this section.

(5) The warehouseman may satisfy his lien from the proceeds of any sale or disposition under this section but must hold the balance for delivery on the demand of any person to whom he would have been bound to deliver the goods.

§ 7–207. Goods Must Be Kept Separate; Fungible Goods.

(1) Unless the warehouse receipt otherwise provides, a warehouseman must keep separate the goods covered by each receipt so as to permit at all times identification and delivery of those goods except that different lots of fungible goods may be commingled.

(2) Fungible goods so commingled are owned in common by the persons entitled thereto and the warehouseman is severally liable to each owner for that owner's share. Where because of overissue a mass of fungible goods is insufficient to meet all the receipts which the warehouseman has issued against it, the persons entitled include all holders to whom overissued receipts have been duly negotiated.

§ 7–208. Altered Warehouse Receipts.

Where a blank in a negotiable warehouse receipt has been filled in without authority, a purchaser for value and without notice of the want of authority may treat the insertion as authorized. Any other unauthorized alteration leaves any receipt enforceable against the issuer according to its original tenor.

§ 7–209. Lien of Warehouseman.

(1) A warehouseman has a lien against the bailor on the goods covered by a warehouse receipt or on the proceeds thereof in his possession for charges for storage or transportation (including demurrage and terminal charges), insurance, labor, or charges present or future in relation to the goods, and for expenses necessary for preservation of the goods or reasonably incurred in their sale pursuant to law. If the person on whose account the goods are held is liable for like charges or expenses in relation to other goods whenever deposited and it is stated in the receipt that a lien is claimed for charges and expenses in relation to other goods, the warehouseman also has a lien against him for such charges and expenses whether or not the other goods have been delivered by the warehouseman. But against a person to whom a negotiable warehouse receipt is duly negotiated a warehouseman's lien is limited to charges in an amount or at a rate specified on the receipt or if no charges are so specified then to a reasonable charge for storage of the goods covered by the receipt subsequent to the date of the receipt.

(2) The warehouseman may also reserve a security interest against the bailor for a maximum amount specified on the receipt for charges other than those specified in subsection (1), such as for money advanced and interest. Such a security interest is governed by the Article on Secured Transactions (Article 9).

(3)(a) A warehouseman's lien for charges and expenses under subsection (1) or a security interest under subsection (2) is also effective against any person who so entrusted the bailor with possession of the goods that a pledge of them by him to a good faith purchaser for value would have been valid but is not effective against a person as to whom the document confers no right in the goods covered by it under Section 7–503.

(b) A warehouseman's lien on household goods for charges and expenses in relation to the goods under subsection (1) is also effective against all persons if the depositor was the legal possessor of the goods at the time of deposit. "Household goods" means furniture, furnishings and personal effects used by the depositor in a dwelling.

(4) A warehouseman loses his lien on any goods which he voluntarily delivers or which he unjustifiably refuses to deliver.

§ 7–210. Enforcement of Warehouseman's Lien.

(1) Except as provided in subsection (2), a warehouseman's lien may be enforced by public or private sale of the goods in bloc or in parcels, at any time or place and on any terms which are commercially reasonable, after notifying all persons known to claim an interest in the goods. Such notification must include a statement of the amount due, the nature of the proposed sale and the time and place of any public sale. The fact that a better price could have been obtained by a sale at a different time or in a different method from that selected by the warehouseman is not of itself sufficient to establish that the sale was not made in a commercially reasonable manner. If the warehouseman either sells the goods in the usual manner in any recognized market therefor, or if he sells at the price current in such market at the time of his sale, or if he has otherwise sold in conformity with commercially reasonable practices among dealers in the type of goods sold, he has sold in a commercially reasonable manner. A sale of more goods than apparently necessary to be offered to ensure satisfaction of the obligation is not commercially reasonable except in cases covered by the preceding sentence.

(2) A warehouseman's lien on goods other than goods stored by a merchant in the course of his business may be enforced only as follows:

(a) All persons known to claim an interest in the goods must be notified.

(b) The notification must be delivered in person or sent by registered or certified letter to the last known address of any person to be notified.

(c) The notification must include an itemized statement of the claim, a description of the goods subject to the lien, a demand for payment within a specified time not less than ten days after receipt of the notification, and a conspicuous statement that unless the claim is paid within the time the goods will be advertised for sale and sold by auction at a specified time and place.

(d) The sale must conform to the terms of the notification.

(e) The sale must be held at the nearest suitable place to that where the goods are held or stored.

(f) After the expiration of the time given in the notification, an advertisement of the sale must be published once a week for two weeks consecutively in a newspaper of general circulation where the sale is to be held. The advertisement must include a description of the goods, the name of the person on whose account they are being held, and the time and place of the sale. The sale must take place at least fifteen days after the first publication. If there is no newspaper of general circulation where the sale is to be held, the advertisement must be posted at least ten days before the sale in not less than six conspicuous places in the neighborhood of the proposed sale.

(3) Before any sale pursuant to this section any person claiming a right in the goods may pay the amount necessary to satisfy the lien and the reasonable expenses incurred under this section. In that event the goods must not be sold, but must be retained by the warehouseman subject to the terms of the receipt and this Article.

(4) The warehouseman may buy at any public sale pursuant to this section.

(5) A purchaser in good faith of goods sold to enforce a warehouseman's lien takes the goods free of any rights of persons against whom the lien was valid, despite noncompliance by the warehouseman with the requirements of this section.

(6) The warehouseman may satisfy his lien from the proceeds of any sale pursuant to this section but must hold the balance, if any, for delivery on demand to any person to whom he would have been bound to deliver the goods.

(7) The rights provided by this section shall be in addition to all other rights allowed by law to a creditor against his debtor.

(8) Where a lien is on goods stored by a merchant in the course of his business the lien may be enforced in accordance with either subsection (1) or (2).

(9) The warehouseman is liable for damages caused by failure to comply with the requirements for sale under this section and in case of willful violation is liable for conversion. As amended in 1962.

Part 3 Bills of Lading: Special Provisions

§ 7–301. Liability for Non-Receipt or Misdescription; "Said to Contain"; "Shipper's Load and Count"; Improper Handling.

(1) A consignee of a non-negotiable bill who has given value in good faith or a holder to whom a negotiable bill has

been duly negotiated relying in either case upon the description therein of the goods, or upon the date therein shown, may recover from the issuer damages caused by the misdating of the bill or the nonreceipt or misdescription of the goods, except to the extent that the document indicates that the issuer does not know whether any part of all of the goods in fact were received or conform to the description, as where the description is in terms of marks or labels or kind, quantity, or condition or the receipt or description is qualified by "contents or condition of contents of packages unknown", "said to contain", "shipper's weight, load and count" or the like, if such indication be true.

(2) When goods are loaded by an issuer who is a common carrier, the issuer must count the packages of goods if package freight and ascertain the kind and quantity if bulk freight. In such cases "shipper's weight, load and count" or other words indicating that the description was made by the shipper are ineffective except as to freight concealed by packages.

(3) When bulk freight is loaded by a shipper who makes available to the issuer adequate facilities for weighing such freight, an issuer who is a common carrier must ascertain the kind and quantity within a reasonable time after receiving the written request of the shipper to do so. In such cases "shipper's weight" or other words of like purport are ineffective.

(4) The issuer may by inserting in the bill the words "shipper's weight, load and count" or other words of like purport indicate that the goods were loaded by the shipper; and if such statement be true the issuer shall not be liable for damages caused by the improper loading. But their omission does not imply liability for such damages.

(5) The shipper shall be deemed to have guaranteed to the issuer the accuracy at the time of shipment of the description, marks, labels, number, kind, quantity, condition and weight, as furnished by him; and the shipper shall indemnify the issuer against damage caused by inaccuracies in such particulars. The right of the issuer to such indemnity shall in no way limit his responsibility and liability under the contract of carriage to any person other than the shipper.

§ 7–302. Through Bills of Lading and Similar Documents.

(1) The issuer of a through bill of lading or other document embodying an undertaking to be performed in part by persons acting as its agents or by connecting carriers is liable to anyone entitled to recover on the document for any breach by such other persons or by a connecting carrier of its obligation under the document but to the extent that the bill covers an undertaking to be performed overseas or in territory not contiguous to the continental United States or an undertaking including matters other than transportation this liability may be varied by agreement of the parties.

(2) Where goods covered by a through bill of lading or other document embodying an undertaking to be performed in part by persons other than the issuer are received by any

such person, he is subject with respect to his own performance while the goods are in his possession to the obligation of the issuer. His obligation is discharged by delivery of the goods to another such person pursuant to the document, and does not include liability for breach by any other such persons or by the issuer.

(3) The issuer of such through bill of lading or other document shall be entitled to recover from the connecting carrier or such other person in possession of the goods when the breach of the obligation under the document occurred, the amount it may be required to pay to anyone entitled to recover on the document therefor, as may be evidenced by any receipt, judgment, or transcript thereof, and the amount of any expense reasonably incurred by it in defending any action brought by anyone entitled to recover on the document therefor.

§ 7–303. Diversion; Reconsignment; Change of Instructions.

(1) Unless the bill of lading otherwise provides, the carrier may deliver the goods to a person or destination other than that stated in the bill or may otherwise dispose of the goods on instructions from

(a) the holder of a negotiable bill; or

(b) the consignor on a non-negotiable bill notwithstanding contrary instructions from the consignee; or

(c) the consignee on a non-negotiable bill in the absence of contrary instructions from the consignor, if the goods have arrived at the billed destination or if the consignee is in possession of the bill; or

(d) the consignee on a non-negotiable bill if he is entitled as against the consignor to dispose of them.

(2) Unless such instructions are noted on a negotiable bill of lading, a person to whom the bill is duly negotiated can hold the bailee according to the original terms.

§ 7–304. Bills of Lading in a Set.

(1) Except where customary in overseas transportation, a bill of lading must not be issued in a set of parts. The issuer is liable for damages caused by violation of this subsection.

(2) Where a bill of lading is lawfully drawn in a set of parts, each of which is numbered and expressed to be valid only if the goods have not been delivered against any other part, the whole of the parts constitute one bill.

(3) Where a bill of lading is lawfully issued in a set of parts and different parts are negotiated to different persons, the title of the holder to whom the first due negotiation is made prevails as to both the document and the goods even though any later holder may have received the goods from the carrier in good faith and discharged the carrier's obligation by surrender of his part.

(4) Any person who negotiates or transfers a single part of a bill of lading drawn in a set is liable to holders of that part as if it were the whole set.

(5) The bailee is obliged to deliver in accordance with Part 4 of this Article against the first presented part of a bill of lading lawfully drawn in a set. Such delivery discharges the bailee's obligation on the whole bill.

§ 7–305. Destination Bills.

(1) Instead of issuing a bill of lading to the consignor at the place of shipment a carrier may at the request of the consignor procure the bill to be issued at destination or at any other place designated in the request.

(2) Upon request of anyone entitled as against the carrier to control the goods while in transit and on surrender of any outstanding bill of lading or other receipt covering such goods, the issuer may procure a substitute bill to be issued at any place designated in the request.

§ 7–306. Altered Bills of Lading.

An unauthorized alteration or filling in of a blank in a bill of lading leaves the bill enforceable according to its original tenor.

§ 7–307. Lien of Carrier.

(1) A carrier has a lien on the goods covered by a bill of lading for charges subsequent to the date of its receipt of the goods for storage or transportation (including demurrage and terminal charges) and for expenses necessary for preservation of the goods incident to their transportation or reasonably incurred in their sale pursuant to law. But against a purchaser for value of a negotiable bill of lading a carrier's lien is limited to charges stated in the bill or the applicable tariffs, or if no charges are stated then to a reasonable charge.

(2) A lien for charges and expenses under subsection (1) on goods which the carrier was required by law to receive for transportation is effective against the consignor or any person entitled to the goods unless the carrier had notice that the consignor lacked authority to subject the goods to such charges and expenses. Any other lien under subsection (1) is effective against the consignor and any person who permitted the bailor to have control or possession of the goods unless the carrier had notice that the bailor lacked such authority.

(3) A carrier loses his lien on any goods which he voluntarily delivers or which he unjustifiably refuses to deliver.

§ 7–308. Enforcement of Carrier's Lien.

(1) A carrier's lien may be enforced by public or private sale of the goods, in bloc or in parcels, at any time or place and on any terms which are commercially reasonable, after notifying all persons known to claim an interest in the goods. Such notification must include a statement of the amount due, the nature of the proposed sale and the time and place of any public sale. The fact that a better price could have been obtained by a sale at a different time or in a different method from that selected by the carrier is not of itself sufficient to establish that the sale was not made in a commercially rea-

sonable manner. If the carrier either sells the goods in the usual manner in any recognized market therefor or if he sells at the price current in such market at the time of his sale or if he has otherwise sold in conformity with commercially reasonable practices among dealers in the type of goods sold he has sold in a commercially reasonable manner. A sale of more goods than apparently necessary to be offered to ensure satisfaction of the obligation is not commercially reasonable except in cases covered by the preceding sentence.

(2) Before any sale pursuant to this section any person claiming a right in the goods may pay the amount necessary to satisfy the lien and the reasonable expenses incurred under this section. In that event the goods must not be sold, but must be retained by the carrier subject to the terms of the bill and this Article.

(3) The carrier may buy at any public sale pursuant to this section.

(4) A purchaser in good faith of goods sold to enforce a carrier's lien takes the goods free of any rights of persons against whom the lien was valid, despite noncompliance by the carrier with the requirements of this section.

(5) The carrier may satisfy his lien from the proceeds of any sale pursuant to this section but must hold the balance, if any, for delivery on demand to any person to whom he would have been bound to deliver the goods.

(6) The rights provided by this section shall be in addition to all other rights allowed by law to a creditor against his debtor.

(7) A carrier's lien may be enforced in accordance with either subsection (1) or the procedure set forth in subsection (2) of Section 7–210.

(8) The carrier is liable for damages caused by failure to comply with the requirements for sale under this section and in case of willful violation is liable for conversion.

§ 7–309. Duty of Care; Contractual Limitation of Carrier's Liability.

(1) A carrier who issues a bill of lading whether negotiable or nonnegotiable must exercise the degree of care in relation to the goods which a reasonably careful man would exercise under like circumstances. This subsection does not repeal or change any law or rule of law which imposes liability upon a common carrier for damages not caused by its negligence.

(2) Damages may be limited by a provision that the carrier's liability shall not exceed a value stated in the document if the carrier's rates are dependent upon value and the consignor by the carrier's tariff is afforded an opportunity to declare a higher value or a value as lawfully provided in the tariff, or where no tariff is filed he is otherwise advised of such opportunity; but no such limitation is effective with respect to the carrier's liability for conversion to its own use.

(3) Reasonable provisions as to the time and manner of presenting claims and instituting actions based on the shipment may be included in a bill of lading or tariff.

Part 4 Warehouse Receipts and Bills of Lading: General Obligations

§ 7–401. Irregularities in Issue of Receipt or Bill or Conduct of Issuer.

The obligations imposed by this Article on an issuer apply to a document of title regardless of the fact that

(a) the document may not comply with the requirements of this Article or of any other law or regulation regarding its issue, form or content; or

(b) the issuer may have violated laws regulating the conduct of his business; or

(c) the goods covered by the document were owned by the bailee at the time the document was issued; or

(d) the person issuing the document does not come within the definition of warehouseman if it purports to be a warehouse receipt.

§ 7–402. Duplicate Receipt or Bill; Overissue.

Neither a duplicate nor any other document of title purporting to cover goods already represented by an outstanding document of the same issuer confers any right in the goods, except as provided in the case of bills in a set, overissue of documents for fungible goods and substitutes for lost, stolen or destroyed documents. But the issuer is liable for damages caused by his overissue or failure to identify a duplicate document as such by conspicuous notation on its face.

§ 7–403. Obligation of Warehouseman or Carrier to Deliver; Excuse.

(1) The bailee must deliver the goods to a person entitled under the document who complies with subsections (2) and (3), unless and to the extent that the bailee establishes any of the following:

(a) delivery of the goods to a person whose receipt was rightful as against the claimant;

(b) damage to or delay, loss or destruction of the goods for which the bailee is not liable [, but the burden of establishing negligence in such cases is on the person entitled under the document];

Note: *The brackets in (1)(b) indicate that State enactments may differ on this point without serious damage to the principle of uniformity.*

(c) previous sale or other disposition of the goods in lawful enforcement of a lien or on warehouseman's lawful termination of storage;

(d) the exercise by a seller of his right to stop delivery pursuant to the provisions of the Article on Sales (Section 2–705);

(e) a diversion, reconsignment or other disposition pursuant to the provisions of this Article (Section 7–303) or tariff regulating such right;

(f) release, satisfaction or any other fact affording a personal defense against the claimant;

(g) any other lawful excuse.

(2) A person claiming goods covered by a document of title must satisfy the bailee's lien where the bailee so requests or where the bailee is prohibited by law from delivering the goods until the charges are paid.

(3) Unless the person claiming is one against whom the document confers no right under Sec. 7–503(1), he must surrender for cancellation or notation of partial deliveries any outstanding negotiable document covering the goods, and the bailee must cancel the document or conspicuously note the partial delivery thereon or be liable to any person to whom the document is duly negotiated.

(4) "Person entitled under the document" means holder in the case of a negotiable document, or the person to whom delivery is to be made by the terms of or pursuant to written instructions under a non-negotiable document.

§ 7–404. No Liability for Good Faith Delivery Pursuant to Receipt or Bill.

A bailee who in good faith including observance of reasonable commercial standards has received goods and delivered or otherwise disposed of them according to the terms of the document of title or pursuant to this Article is not liable therefor. This rule applies even though the person from whom he received the goods had no authority to procure the document or to dispose of the goods and even though the person to whom he delivered the goods had no authority to receive them.

Part 5 Warehouse Receipts and Bills of Lading: Negotiation and Transfer

§ 7–501. Form of Negotiation and Requirements of "Due Negotiation".

(1) A negotiable document of title running to the order of a named person is negotiated by his indorsement and delivery. After his indorsement in blank or to bearer any person can negotiate it by delivery alone.

(2)(a) A negotiable document of title is also negotiated by delivery alone when by its original terms it runs to bearer.

(b) When a document running to the order of a named person is delivered to him the effect is the same as if the document had been negotiated.

(3) Negotiation of a negotiable document of title after it has been indorsed to a specified person requires indorsement by the special indorsee as well as delivery.

(4) A negotiable document of title is "duly negotiated" when it is negotiated in the manner stated in this section to a holder who purchases it in good faith without notice of any defense against or claim to it on the part of any person and for value, unless it is established that the negotiation is not in the regular course of business or financing or involves receiving the document in settlement or payment of a money obligation.

(5) Indorsement of a nonnegotiable document neither makes it negotiable nor adds to the transferee's rights.

(6) The naming in a negotiable bill of a person to be notified of the arrival of the goods does not limit the negotiability of the bill nor constitute notice to a purchaser thereof of any interest of such person in the goods.

§ 7–502. Rights Acquired by Due Negotiation.

(1) Subject to the following section and to the provisions of Section 7–205 on fungible goods, a holder to whom a negotiable document of title has been duly negotiated acquires thereby:

> (a) title to the document;

> (b) title to the goods;

> (c) all rights accruing under the law of agency or estoppel, including rights to goods delivered to the bailee after the document was issued; and

> (d) the direct obligation of the issuer to hold or deliver the goods according to the terms of the document free of any defense or claim by him except those arising under the terms of the document or under this Article. In the case of a delivery order the bailee's obligation accrues only upon acceptance and the obligation acquired by the holder is that the issuer and any indorser will procure the acceptance of the bailee.

(2) Subject to the following section, title and rights so acquired are not defeated by any stoppage of the goods represented by the document or by surrender of such goods by the bailee, and are not impaired even though the negotiation or any prior negotiation constituted a breach of duty or even though any person has been deprived of possession of the document by misrepresentation, fraud, accident, mistake, duress, loss, theft or conversion, or even though a previous sale or other transfer of the goods or document has been made to a third person.

§ 7–503. Document of Title to Goods Defeated in Certain Cases.

(1) A document of title confers no right in goods against a person who before issuance of the document had a legal interest or a perfected security interest in them and who neither

> (a) delivered or entrusted them or any document of title covering them to the bailor or his nominee with actual or apparent authority to ship, store or sell or with power to obtain delivery under this Article (Section 7–403) or with power of disposition under this Act (Sections 2–403 and 9–307) or other statute or rule of law; nor

> (b) acquiesced in the procurement by the bailor or his nominee of any document of title.

(2) Title to goods based upon an unaccepted delivery order is subject to the rights of anyone to whom a negotiable warehouse receipt or bill of lading covering the goods has been duly negotiated. Such a title may be defeated under the next

section to the same extent as the rights of the issuer or a transferee from the issuer.

(3) Title to goods based upon a bill of lading issued to a freight forwarder is subject to the rights of anyone to whom a bill issued by the freight forwarder is duly negotiated; but delivery by the carrier in accordance with Part 4 of this Article pursuant to its own bill of lading discharges the carrier's obligation to deliver.

As amended in 1999.

§ 7–504. Rights Acquired in the Absence of Due Negotiation; Effect of Diversion; Seller's Stoppage of Delivery.

(1) A transferee of a document, whether negotiable or nonnegotiable, to whom the document has been delivered but not duly negotiated, acquires the title and rights which his transferor had or had actual authority to convey.

(2) In the case of a nonnegotiable document, until but not after the bailee receives notification of the transfer, the rights of the transferee may be defeated

> (a) by those creditors of the transferor who could treat the sale as void under Section 2–402; or

> (b) by a buyer from the transferor in ordinary course of business if the bailee has delivered the goods to the buyer or received notification of his rights; or

> (c) as against the bailee by good faith dealings of the bailee with the transferor.

(3) A diversion or other change of shipping instructions by the consignor in a nonnegotiable bill of lading which causes the bailee not to deliver to the consignee defeats the consignee's title to the goods if they have been delivered to a buyer in ordinary course of business and in any event defeats the consignee's rights against the bailee.

(4) Delivery pursuant to a nonnegotiable document may be stopped by a seller under Section 2–705, and subject to the requirement of due notification there provided. A bailee honoring the seller's instructions is entitled to be indemnified by the seller against any resulting loss or expense.

§ 7–505. Indorser Not a Guarantor for Other Parties.

The indorsement of a document of title issued by a bailee does not make the indorser liable for any default by the bailee or by previous indorsers.

§ 7–506. Delivery Without Indorsement: Right to Compel Indorsement.

The transferee of a negotiable document of title has a specifically enforceable right to have his transferor supply any necessary indorsement but the transfer becomes a negotiation only as of the time the indorsement is supplied.

§ 7–507. Warranties on Negotiation or Transfer of Receipt or Bill.

Where a person negotiates or transfers a document of title for value otherwise than as a mere intermediary under the next following section, then unless otherwise agreed he warrants to his immediate purchaser only in addition to any warranty made in selling the goods

(a) that the document is genuine; and

(b) that he has no knowledge of any fact which would impair its validity or worth; and

(c) that his negotiation or transfer is rightful and fully effective with respect to the title to the document and the goods it represents.

§ 7–508. Warranties of Collecting Bank as to Documents.

A collecting bank or other intermediary known to be entrusted with documents on behalf of another or with collection of a draft or other claim against delivery of documents warrants by such delivery of the documents only its own good faith and authority. This rule applies even though the intermediary has purchased or made advances against the claim or draft to be collected.

§ 7–509. Receipt or Bill: When Adequate Compliance With Commercial Contract.

The question whether a document is adequate to fulfill the obligations of a contract for sale or the conditions of a credit is governed by the Articles on Sales (Article 2) and on Letters of Credit (Article 5).

Part 6 Warehouse Receipts and Bills of Lading: Miscellaneous Provisions

§ 7–601. Lost and Missing Documents.

(1) If a document has been lost, stolen or destroyed, a court may order delivery of the goods or issuance of a substitute document and the bailee may without liability to any person comply with such order. If the document was negotiable the claimant must post security approved by the court to indemnify any person who may suffer loss as a result of non-surrender of the document. If the document was not negotiable, such security may be required at the discretion of the court. The court may also in its discretion order payment of the bailee's reasonable costs and counsel fees.

(2) A bailee who without court order delivers goods to a person claiming under a missing negotiable document is liable to any person injured thereby, and if the delivery is not in good faith becomes liable for conversion. Delivery in good faith is not conversion if made in accordance with a filed classification or tariff or, where no classification or tariff is filed, if the claimant posts security with the bailee in an amount at least double the value of the goods at the time of posting to indemnify any person injured by the delivery who files a notice of claim within one year after the delivery.

§ 7–602. Attachment of Goods Covered by a Negotiable Document.

Except where the document was originally issued upon delivery of the goods by a person who had no power to dispose of them, no lien attaches by virtue of any judicial process to goods in the possession of a bailee for which a negotiable document of title is outstanding unless the document be first surrendered to the bailee or its negotiation enjoined, and the bailee shall not be compelled to deliver the goods pursuant to process until the document is surrendered to him or impounded by the court. One who purchases the document for value without notice of the process or injunction takes free of the lien imposed by judicial process.

§ 7–603. Conflicting Claims; Interpleader.

If more than one person claims title or possession of the goods, the bailee is excused from delivery until he has had a reasonable time to ascertain the validity of the adverse claims or to bring an action to compel all claimants to interplead and may compel such interpleader, either in defending an action for nondelivery of the goods, or by original action, whichever is appropriate.

Revised (1994) Article 8
INVESTMENT SECURITIES

Part 1 Short Title and General Matters

§ 8–101. Short Title.

This Article may be cited as Uniform Commercial Code—Investment Securities.

§ 8–102. Definitions.

(a) In this Article:

(1) "Adverse claim" means a claim that a claimant has a property interest in a financial asset and that it is a violation of the rights of the claimant for another person to hold, transfer, or deal with the financial asset.

(2) "Bearer form," as applied to a certificated security, means a form in which the security is payable to the bearer of the security certificate according to its terms but not by reason of an indorsement.

(3) "Broker" means a person defined as a broker or dealer under the federal securities laws, but without excluding a bank acting in that capacity.

(4) "Certificated security" means a security that is represented by a certificate.

(5) "Clearing corporation" means:

(i) a person that is registered as a "clearing agency" under the federal securities laws;

(ii) a federal reserve bank; or

(iii) any other person that provides clearance or settlement services with respect to financial assets that would require it to register as a clearing agency under the federal securities laws but for an exclusion or exemption from the registration requirement, if its activities as a clearing corporation, including promulgation of rules, are subject to regulation by a federal or state governmental authority.

(6) "Communicate" means to:

(i) send a signed writing; or

(ii) transmit information by any mechanism agreed upon by the persons transmitting and receiving the information.

(7) "Entitlement holder" means a person identified in the records of a securities intermediary as the person having a security entitlement against the securities intermediary. If a person acquires a security entitlement by virtue of Section 8–501(b)(2) or (3), that person is the entitlement holder.

(8) "Entitlement order" means a notification communicated to a securities intermediary directing transfer or redemption of a financial asset to which the entitlement holder has a security entitlement.

(9) "Financial asset," except as otherwise provided in Section 8–103, means:

(i) a security;

(ii) an obligation of a person or a share, participation, or other interest in a person or in property or an enterprise of a person, which is, or is of a type, dealt in or traded on financial markets, or which is recognized in any area in which it is issued or dealt in as a medium for investment; or

(iii) any property that is held by a securities intermediary for another person in a securities account if the securities intermediary has expressly agreed with the other person that the property is to be treated as a financial asset under this Article.

As context requires, the term means either the interest itself or the means by which a person's claim to it is evidenced, including a certificated or uncertificated security, a security certificate, or a security entitlement.

(10) "Good faith," for purposes of the obligation of good faith in the performance or enforcement of contracts or duties within this Article, means honesty in fact and the observance of reasonable commercial standards of fair dealing.

(11) "Indorsement" means a signature that alone or accompanied by other words is made on a security certificate in registered form or on a separate document for the purpose of assigning, transferring, or redeeming the security or granting a power to assign, transfer, or redeem it.

(12) "Instruction" means a notification communicated to the issuer of an uncertificated security which directs that the transfer of the security be registered or that the security be redeemed.

(13) "Registered form," as applied to a certificated security, means a form in which:

(i) the security certificate specifies a person entitled to the security; and

(ii) a transfer of the security may be registered upon books maintained for that purpose by or on behalf of the issuer, or the security certificate so states.

(14) "Securities intermediary" means:

(i) a clearing corporation; or

(ii) a person, including a bank or broker, that in the ordinary course of its business maintains securities accounts for others and is acting in that capacity.

(15) "Security," except as otherwise provided in Section 8–103, means an obligation of an issuer or a share, participation, or other interest in an issuer or in property or an enterprise of an issuer:

(i) which is represented by a security certificate in bearer or registered form, or the transfer of which may be registered upon books maintained for that purpose by or on behalf of the issuer;

(ii) which is one of a class or series or by its terms is divisible into a class or series of shares, participations, interests, or obligations; and

(iii) which:

(A) is, or is of a type, dealt in or traded on securities exchanges or securities markets; or

(B) is a medium for investment and by its terms expressly provides that it is a security governed by this Article.

(16) "Security certificate" means a certificate representing a security.

(17) "Security entitlement" means the rights and property interest of an entitlement holder with respect to a financial asset specified in Part 5.

(18) "Uncertificated security" means a security that is not represented by a certificate.

(b) Other definitions applying to this Article and the sections in which they appear are:

Appropriate person	Section 8–107
Control	Section 8–106
Delivery	Section 8–301
Investment company security	Section 8–103
Issuer	Section 8–201
Overissue	Section 8–210
Protected purchaser	Section 8–303
Securities account	Section 8–501

(c) In addition, Article 1 contains general definitions and principles of construction and interpretation applicable throughout this Article.

(d) The characterization of a person, business, or transaction for purposes of this Article does not determine the characterization of the person, business, or transaction for purposes of any other law, regulation, or rule.

§ 8–103. Rules for Determining Whether Certain Obligations and Interests Are Securities or Financial Assets.

(a) A share or similar equity interest issued by a corporation, business trust, joint stock company, or similar entity is a security.

(b) An "investment company security" is a security. "Investment company security" means a share or similar equity interest issued by an entity that is registered as an investment company under the federal investment company laws, an interest in a unit investment trust that is so registered, or a face-amount certificate issued by a face-amount certificate company that is so registered. Investment company security does not include an insurance policy or endowment policy or annuity contract issued by an insurance company.

(c) An interest in a partnership or limited liability company is not a security unless it is dealt in or traded on securities exchanges or in securities markets, its terms expressly provide that it is a security governed by this Article, or it is an investment company security. However, an interest in a partnership or limited liability company is a financial asset if it is held in a securities account.

(d) A writing that is a security certificate is governed by this Article and not by Article 3, even though it also meets the requirements of that Article. However, a negotiable instrument governed by Article 3 is a financial asset if it is held in a securities account.

(e) An option or similar obligation issued by a clearing corporation to its participants is not a security, but is a financial asset.

(f) A commodity contract, as defined in Section 9–102(a)(15), is not a security or a financial asset.

As amended in 1999.

§ 8–104. Acquisition of Security or Financial Asset or Interest Therein.

(a) A person acquires a security or an interest therein, under this Article, if:

(1) the person is a purchaser to whom a security is delivered pursuant to Section 8–301; or

(2) the person acquires a security entitlement to the security pursuant to Section 8–501.

(b) A person acquires a financial asset, other than a security, or an interest therein, under this Article, if the person acquires a security entitlement to the financial asset.

(c) A person who acquires a security entitlement to a security or other financial asset has the rights specified in Part 5, but is a purchaser of any security, security entitlement, or other financial asset held by the securities intermediary only to the extent provided in Section 8–503.

(d) Unless the context shows that a different meaning is intended, a person who is required by other law, regulation, rule, or agreement to transfer, deliver, present, surrender, exchange, or otherwise put in the possession of another person a security or financial asset satisfies that requirement by causing the other person to acquire an interest in the security or financial asset pursuant to subsection (a) or (b).

§ 8–105. Notice of Adverse Claim.

(a) A person has notice of an adverse claim if:

(1) the person knows of the adverse claim;

(2) the person is aware of facts sufficient to indicate that there is a significant probability that the adverse claim exists and deliberately avoids information that would establish the existence of the adverse claim; or

(3) the person has a duty, imposed by statute or regulation, to investigate whether an adverse claim exists, and the investigation so required would establish the existence of the adverse claim.

(b) Having knowledge that a financial asset or interest therein is or has been transferred by a representative imposes no duty of inquiry into the rightfulness of a transaction and is not notice of an adverse claim. However, a person who knows that a representative has transferred a financial asset or interest therein in a transaction that is, or whose proceeds are being used, for the individual benefit of the representative or otherwise in breach of duty has notice of an adverse claim.

(c) An act or event that creates a right to immediate performance of the principal obligation represented by a security certificate or sets a date on or after which the certificate is to be presented or surrendered for redemption or exchange does not itself constitute notice of an adverse claim except in the case of a transfer more than:

(1) one year after a date set for presentment or surrender for redemption or exchange; or

(2) six months after a date set for payment of money against presentation or surrender of the certificate, if money was available for payment on that date.

(d) A purchaser of a certificated security has notice of an adverse claim if the security certificate:

(1) whether in bearer or registered form, has been indorsed "for collection" or "for surrender" or for some other purpose not involving transfer; or

(2) is in bearer form and has on it an unambiguous statement that it is the property of a person other than the transferor, but the mere writing of a name on the certificate is not such a statement.

(e) Filing of a financing statement under Article 9 is not notice of an adverse claim to a financial asset.

§ 8–106. Control.

(a) A purchaser has "control" of a certificated security in bearer form if the certificated security is delivered to the purchaser.

(b) A purchaser has "control" of a certificated security in registered form if the certificated security is delivered to the purchaser, and:

(1) the certificate is indorsed to the purchaser or in blank by an effective indorsement; or

(2) the certificate is registered in the name of the purchaser, upon original issue or registration of transfer by the issuer.

(c) A purchaser has "control" of an uncertificated security if:

(1) the uncertificated security is delivered to the purchaser; or

(2) the issuer has agreed that it will comply with instructions originated by the purchaser without further consent by the registered owner.

(d) A purchaser has "control" of a security entitlement if:

(1) the purchaser becomes the entitlement holder;

(2) the securities intermediary has agreed that it will comply with entitlement orders originated by the purchaser without further consent by the entitlement holder; or

(3) another person has control of the security entitlement on behalf of the purchaser or, having previously acquired control of the security entitlement, acknowledges that it has control on behalf of the purchaser.

(e) If an interest in a security entitlement is granted by the entitlement holder to the entitlement holder's own securities intermediary, the securities intermediary has control.

(f) A purchaser who has satisfied the requirements of subsection (c) or (d) has control, even if the registered owner in the case of subsection (c) or the entitlement holder in the case of subsection (d) retains the right to make substitutions for the uncertificated security or security entitlement, to originate instructions or entitlement orders to the issuer or securities intermediary, or otherwise to deal with the uncertificated security or security entitlement.

(g) An issuer or a securities intermediary may not enter into an agreement of the kind described in subsection (c)(2) or (d)(2) without the consent of the registered owner or entitlement holder, but an issuer or a securities intermediary is not required to enter into such an agreement even though the registered owner or entitlement holder so directs. An issuer or securities intermediary that has entered into such an agreement is not required to confirm the existence of the agreement to another party unless requested to do so by the registered owner or entitlement holder.

As amended in 1999.

§ 8–107. Whether Indorsement, Instruction, or Entitlement Order Is Effective.

(a) "Appropriate person" means:

(1) with respect to an indorsement, the person specified by a security certificate or by an effective special indorsement to be entitled to the security;

(2) with respect to an instruction, the registered owner of an uncertificated security;

(3) with respect to an entitlement order, the entitlement holder;

(4) if the person designated in paragraph (1), (2), or (3) is deceased, the designated person's successor taking under other law or the designated person's personal representative acting for the estate of the decedent; or

(5) if the person designated in paragraph (1), (2), or (3) lacks capacity, the designated person's guardian, conservator, or other similar representative who has power under other law to transfer the security or financial asset.

(b) An indorsement, instruction, or entitlement order is effective if:

(1) it is made by the appropriate person;

(2) it is made by a person who has power under the law of agency to transfer the security or financial asset on behalf of the appropriate person, including, in the case of an instruction or entitlement order, a person who has control under Section 8–106(c)(2) or (d)(2); or

(3) the appropriate person has ratified it or is otherwise precluded from asserting its ineffectiveness.

(c) An indorsement, instruction, or entitlement order made by a representative is effective even if:

(1) the representative has failed to comply with a controlling instrument or with the law of the State having jurisdiction of the representative relationship, including any law requiring the representative to obtain court approval of the transaction; or

(2) the representative's action in making the indorsement, instruction, or entitlement order or using the proceeds of the transaction is otherwise a breach of duty.

(d) If a security is registered in the name of or specially indorsed to a person described as a representative, or if a securities account is maintained in the name of a person described as a representative, an indorsement, instruction, or entitlement order made by the person is effective even though the person is no longer serving in the described capacity.

(e) Effectiveness of an indorsement, instruction, or entitlement order is determined as of the date the indorsement, instruction, or entitlement order is made, and an indorsement, instruction, or entitlement order does not become ineffective by reason of any later change of circumstances.

§ 8–108. Warranties in Direct Holding.

(a) A person who transfers a certificated security to a purchaser for value warrants to the purchaser, and an indorser, if the transfer is by indorsement, warrants to any subsequent purchaser, that:

(1) the certificate is genuine and has not been materially altered;

(2) the transferor or indorser does not know of any fact that might impair the validity of the security;

(3) there is no adverse claim to the security;

(4) the transfer does not violate any restriction on transfer;

(5) if the transfer is by indorsement, the indorsement is made by an appropriate person, or if the indorsement is by an agent, the agent has actual authority to act on behalf of the appropriate person; and

(6) the transfer is otherwise effective and rightful.

(b) A person who originates an instruction for registration of transfer of an uncertificated security to a purchaser for value warrants to the purchaser that:

(1) the instruction is made by an appropriate person, or if the instruction is by an agent, the agent has actual authority to act on behalf of the appropriate person;

(2) the security is valid;

(3) there is no adverse claim to the security; and

(4) at the time the instruction is presented to the issuer:

(i) the purchaser will be entitled to the registration of transfer;

(ii) the transfer will be registered by the issuer free from all liens, security interests, restrictions, and claims other than those specified in the instruction;

(iii) the transfer will not violate any restriction on transfer; and

(iv) the requested transfer will otherwise be effective and rightful.

(c) A person who transfers an uncertificated security to a purchaser for value and does not originate an instruction in connection with the transfer warrants that:

(1) the uncertificated security is valid;

(2) there is no adverse claim to the security;

(3) the transfer does not violate any restriction on transfer; and

(4) the transfer is otherwise effective and rightful.

(d) A person who indorses a security certificate warrants to the issuer that:

(1) there is no adverse claim to the security; and

(2) the indorsement is effective.

(e) A person who originates an instruction for registration of transfer of an uncertificated security warrants to the issuer that:

(1) the instruction is effective; and

(2) at the time the instruction is presented to the issuer the purchaser will be entitled to the registration of transfer.

(f) A person who presents a certificated security for registration of transfer or for payment or exchange warrants to the issuer that the person is entitled to the registration, payment, or exchange, but a purchaser for value and without notice of adverse claims to whom transfer is registered warrants only that the person has no knowledge of any unauthorized signature in a necessary indorsement.

(g) If a person acts as agent of another in delivering a certificated security to a purchaser, the identity of the principal was known to the person to whom the certificate was delivered, and the certificate delivered by the agent was received by the agent from the principal or received by the agent from another person at the direction of the principal, the person delivering the security certificate warrants only that the delivering person has authority to act for the principal and does not know of any adverse claim to the certificated security.

(h) A secured party who redelivers a security certificate received, or after payment and on order of the debtor delivers the security certificate to another person, makes only the warranties of an agent under subsection (g).

(i) Except as otherwise provided in subsection (g), a broker acting for a customer makes to the issuer and a purchaser the warranties provided in subsections (a) through (f). A broker that delivers a security certificate to its customer, or causes its customer to be registered as the owner of an uncertificated security, makes to the customer the warranties provided in subsection (a) or (b), and has the rights and privileges of a purchaser under this section. The warranties of and in favor of the broker acting as an agent are in addition to applicable warranties given by and in favor of the customer.

§ 8–109. Warranties in Indirect Holding.

(a) A person who originates an entitlement order to a securities intermediary warrants to the securities intermediary that:

(1) the entitlement order is made by an appropriate person, or if the entitlement order is by an agent, the agent has actual authority to act on behalf of the appropriate person; and

(2) there is no adverse claim to the security entitlement.

(b) A person who delivers a security certificate to a securities intermediary for credit to a securities account or originates an instruction with respect to an uncertificated security directing that the uncertificated security be credited to a securities account makes to the securities intermediary the warranties specified in Section 8–108(a) or (b).

(c) If a securities intermediary delivers a security certificate to its entitlement holder or causes its entitlement holder to be registered as the owner of an uncertificated security, the securities intermediary makes to the entitlement holder the warranties specified in Section 8–108(a) or (b).

§ 8–110. Applicability; Choice of Law.

(a) The local law of the issuer's jurisdiction, as specified in subsection (d), governs:

(1) the validity of a security;

(2) the rights and duties of the issuer with respect to registration of transfer;

(3) the effectiveness of registration of transfer by the issuer;

(4) whether the issuer owes any duties to an adverse claimant to a security; and

(5) whether an adverse claim can be asserted against a person to whom transfer of a certificated or uncertificated security is registered or a person who obtains control of an uncertificated security.

(b) The local law of the securities intermediary's jurisdiction, as specified in subsection (e), governs:

(1) acquisition of a security entitlement from the securities intermediary;

(2) the rights and duties of the securities intermediary and entitlement holder arising out of a security entitlement;

(3) whether the securities intermediary owes any duties to an adverse claimant to a security entitlement; and

(4) whether an adverse claim can be asserted against a person who acquires a security entitlement from the securities intermediary or a person who purchases a security entitlement or interest therein from an entitlement holder.

(c) The local law of the jurisdiction in which a security certificate is located at the time of delivery governs whether an adverse claim can be asserted against a person to whom the security certificate is delivered.

(d) "Issuer's jurisdiction" means the jurisdiction under which the issuer of the security is organized or, if permitted by the law of that jurisdiction, the law of another jurisdiction specified by the issuer. An issuer organized under the law of this State may specify the law of another jurisdiction as the law governing the matters specified in subsection (a)(2) through (5).

(e) The following rules determine a "securities intermediary's jurisdiction" for purposes of this section:

(1) If an agreement between the securities intermediary and its entitlement holder specifies that it is governed by the law of a particular jurisdiction, that jurisdiction is the securities intermediary's jurisdiction.

(2) If an agreement between the securities intermediary and its entitlement holder does not specify the governing law as provided in paragraph (1), but expressly specifies that the securities account is maintained at an office in a particular jurisdiction, that jurisdiction is the securities intermediary's jurisdiction.

(3) If neither paragraph (1) nor paragraph (2) applies and an agreement between the securities intermediary and its entitlement holder governing the securities

account expressly provides that the securities account is maintained at an office in a particular jurisdiction, that jurisdiction is the securities intermediary's jurisdiction.

(4) If none of the preceding paragraph applies, the securities intermediary's jurisdiction is the jurisdiction in which the office identified in an account statement as the office serving the entitlement holder's account is located.

(5) If none of the preceding paragraphs applies, the securities intermediary's jurisdiction is the jurisdiction in which the chief executive office of the securities intermediary is located.

(f) A securities intermediary's jurisdiction is not determined by the physical location of certificates representing financial assets, or by the jurisdiction in which is organized the issuer of the financial asset with respect to which an entitlement holder has a security entitlement, or by the location of facilities for data processing or other record keeping concerning the account.

As amended in 1999.

§ 8–111. Clearing Corporation Rules.

A rule adopted by a clearing corporation governing rights and obligations among the clearing corporation and its participants in the clearing corporation is effective even if the rule conflicts with this [Act] and affects another party who does not consent to the rule.

§ 8–112. Creditor's Legal Process.

(a) The interest of a debtor in a certificated security may be reached by a creditor only by actual seizure of the security certificate by the officer making the attachment or levy, except as otherwise provided in subsection (d). However, a certificated security for which the certificate has been surrendered to the issuer may be reached by a creditor by legal process upon the issuer.

(b) The interest of a debtor in an uncertificated security may be reached by a creditor only by legal process upon the issuer at its chief executive office in the United States, except as otherwise provided in subsection (d).

(c) The interest of a debtor in a security entitlement may be reached by a creditor only by legal process upon the securities intermediary with whom the debtor's securities account is maintained, except as otherwise provided in subsection (d).

(d) The interest of a debtor in a certificated security for which the certificate is in the possession of a secured party, or in an uncertificated security registered in the name of a secured party, or a security entitlement maintained in the name of a secured party, may be reached by a creditor by legal process upon the secured party.

(e) A creditor whose debtor is the owner of a certificated security, uncertificated security, or security entitlement is entitled to aid from a court of competent jurisdiction, by injunction or otherwise, in reaching the certificated security, uncertificated security, or security entitlement or in satisfying the claim by means allowed at law or in equity in regard to property that cannot readily be reached by other legal process.

§ 8–113. Statute of Frauds Inapplicable.

A contract or modification of a contract for the sale or purchase of a security is enforceable whether or not there is a writing signed or record authenticated by a party against whom enforcement is sought, even if the contract or modification is not capable of performance within one year of its making.

§ 8–114. Evidentiary Rules Concerning Certificated Securities.

The following rules apply in an action on a certificated security against the issuer:

(1) Unless specifically denied in the pleadings, each signature on a security certificate or in a necessary indorsement is admitted.

(2) If the effectiveness of a signature is put in issue, the burden of establishing effectiveness is on the party claiming under the signature, but the signature is presumed to be genuine or authorized.

(3) If signatures on a security certificate are admitted or established, production of the certificate entitles a holder to recover on it unless the defendant establishes a defense or a defect going to the validity of the security.

(4) If it is shown that a defense or defect exists, the plaintiff has the burden of establishing that the plaintiff or some person under whom the plaintiff claims is a person against whom the defense or defect cannot be asserted.

§ 8–115. Securities Intermediary and Others Not Liable to Adverse Claimant.

A securities intermediary that has transferred a financial asset pursuant to an effective entitlement order, or a broker or other agent or bailee that has dealt with a financial asset at the direction of its customer or principal, is not liable to a person having an adverse claim to the financial asset, unless the securities intermediary, or broker or other agent or bailee:

(1) took the action after it had been served with an injunction, restraining order, or other legal process enjoining it from doing so, issued by a court of competent jurisdiction, and had a reasonable opportunity to act on the injunction, restraining order, or other legal process; or

(2) acted in collusion with the wrongdoer in violating the rights of the adverse claimant; or

(3) in the case of a security certificate that has been stolen, acted with notice of the adverse claim.

§ 8–116. Securities Intermediary as Purchaser for Value.

A securities intermediary that receives a financial asset and establishes a security entitlement to the financial asset in favor of an entitlement holder is a purchaser for value of the financial asset. A securities intermediary that acquires a security entitlement to a financial asset from another securities intermediary acquires the security entitlement for value if the securities intermediary acquiring the security entitlement establishes a security entitlement to the financial asset in favor of an entitlement holder.

Part 2 Issue and Issuer

§ 8–201. Issuer.

(a) With respect to an obligation on or a defense to a security, an "issuer" includes a person that:

(1) places or authorizes the placing of its name on a security certificate, other than as authenticating trustee, registrar, transfer agent, or the like, to evidence a share, participation, or other interest in its property or in an enterprise, or to evidence its duty to perform an obligation represented by the certificate;

(2) creates a share, participation, or other interest in its property or in an enterprise, or undertakes an obligation, that is an uncertificated security;

(3) directly or indirectly creates a fractional interest in its rights or property, if the fractional interest is represented by a security certificate; or

(4) becomes responsible for, or in place of, another person described as an issuer in this section.

(b) With respect to an obligation on or defense to a security, a guarantor is an issuer to the extent of its guaranty, whether or not its obligation is noted on a security certificate.

(c) With respect to a registration of a transfer, issuer means a person on whose behalf transfer books are maintained.

§ 8–202. Issuer's Responsibility and Defenses; Notice of Defect or Defense.

(a) Even against a purchaser for value and without notice, the terms of a certificated security include terms stated on the certificate and terms made part of the security by reference on the certificate to another instrument, indenture, or document or to a constitution, statute, ordinance, rule, regulation, order, or the like, to the extent the terms referred to do not conflict with terms stated on the certificate. A reference under this subsection does not of itself charge a purchaser for value with notice of a defect going to the validity of the security, even if the certificate expressly states that a person accepting it admits notice. The terms of an uncertificated security include those stated in any instrument, indenture, or document or in a constitution, statute, ordinance, rule, regulation, order, or the like, pursuant to which the security is issued.

(b) The following rules apply if an issuer asserts that a security is not valid:

(1) A security other than one issued by a government or governmental subdivision, agency, or instrumentality,

even though issued with a defect going to its validity, is valid in the hands of a purchaser for value and without notice of the particular defect unless the defect involves a violation of a constitutional provision. In that case, the security is valid in the hands of a purchaser for value and without notice of the defect, other than one who takes by original issue.

(2) Paragraph (1) applies to an issuer that is a government or governmental subdivision, agency, or instrumentality only if there has been substantial compliance with the legal requirements governing the issue or the issuer has received a substantial consideration for the issue as a whole or for the particular security and a stated purpose of the issue is one for which the issuer has power to borrow money or issue the security.

(c) Except as otherwise provided in Section 8–205, lack of genuineness of a certificated security is a complete defense, even against a purchaser for value and without notice.

(d) All other defenses of the issuer of a security, including nondelivery and conditional delivery of a certificated security, are ineffective against a purchaser for value who has taken the certificated security without notice of the particular defense.

(e) This section does not affect the right of a party to cancel a contract for a security "when, as and if issued" or "when distributed" in the event of a material change in the character of the security that is the subject of the contract or in the plan or arrangement pursuant to which the security is to be issued or distributed.

(f) If a security is held by a securities intermediary against whom an entitlement holder has a security entitlement with respect to the security, the issuer may not assert any defense that the issuer could not assert if the entitlement holder held the security directly.

§ 8–203. Staleness as Notice of Defect or Defense.

After an act or event, other than a call that has been revoked, creating a right to immediate performance of the principal obligation represented by a certificated security or setting a date on or after which the security is to be presented or surrendered for redemption or exchange, a purchaser is charged with notice of any defect in its issue or defense of the issuer, if the act or event:

(1) requires the payment of money, the delivery of a certificated security, the registration of transfer of an uncertificated security, or any of them on presentation or surrender of the security certificate, the money or security is available on the date set for payment or exchange, and the purchaser takes the security more than one year after that date; or

(2) is not covered by paragraph (1) and the purchaser takes the security more than two years after the date set for surrender or presentation or the date on which performance became due.

§ 8–204. Effect of Issuer's Restriction on Transfer.

A restriction on transfer of a security imposed by the issuer, even if otherwise lawful, is ineffective against a person without knowledge of the restriction unless:

(1) the security is certificated and the restriction is noted conspicuously on the security certificate; or

(2) the security is uncertificated and the registered owner has been notified of the restriction.

§ 8–205. Effect of Unauthorized Signature on Security Certificate.

An unauthorized signature placed on a security certificate before or in the course of issue is ineffective, but the signature is effective in favor of a purchaser for value of the certificated security if the purchaser is without notice of the lack of authority and the signing has been done by:

(1) an authenticating trustee, registrar, transfer agent, or other person entrusted by the issuer with the signing of the security certificate or of similar security certificates, or the immediate preparation for signing of any of them; or

(2) an employee of the issuer, or of any of the persons listed in paragraph (1), entrusted with responsible handling of the security certificate.

§ 8–206. Completion of Alteration of Security Certificate.

(a) If a security certificate contains the signatures necessary to its issue or transfer but is incomplete in any other respect:

(1) any person may complete it by filling in the blanks as authorized; and

(2) even if the blanks are incorrectly filled in, the security certificate as completed is enforceable by a purchaser who took it for value and without notice of the incorrectness.

(b) A complete security certificate that has been improperly altered, even if fraudulently, remains enforceable, but only according to its original terms.

§ 8–207. Rights and Duties of Issuer with Respect to Registered Owners.

(a) Before due presentment for registration of transfer of a certificated security in registered form or of an instruction requesting registration of transfer of an uncertificated security, the issuer or indenture trustee may treat the registered owner as the person exclusively entitled to vote, receive notifications, and otherwise exercise all the rights and powers of an owner.

(b) This Article does not affect the liability of the registered owner of a security for a call, assessment, or the like.

§ 8–208. Effect of Signature of Authenticating Trustee, Registrar, or Transfer Agent.

(a) A person signing a security certificate as authenticating trustee, registrar, transfer agent, or the like, warrants to a purchaser for value of the certificated security, if the purchaser is without notice of a particular defect, that:

(1) the certificate is genuine;

(2) the person's own participation in the issue of the security is within the person's capacity and within the scope of the authority received by the person from the issuer; and

(3) the person has reasonable grounds to believe that the certificated security is in the form and within the amount the issuer is authorized to issue.

(b) Unless otherwise agreed, a person signing under subsection (a) does not assume responsibility for the validity of the security in other respects.

§ 8–209. Issuer's Lien.

A lien in favor of an issuer upon a certificated security is valid against a purchaser only if the right of the issuer to the lien is noted conspicuously on the security certificate.

§ 8–210. Overissue.

(a) In this section, "overissue" means the issue of securities in excess of the amount the issuer has corporate power to issue, but an overissue does not occur if appropriate action has cured the overissue.

(b) Except as otherwise provided in subsections (c) and (d), the provisions of this Article which validate a security or compel its issue or reissue do not apply to the extent that validation, issue, or reissue would result in overissue.

(c) If an identical security not constituting an overissue is reasonably available for purchase, a person entitled to issue or validation may compel the issuer to purchase the security and deliver it if certificated or register its transfer if uncertificated, against surrender of any security certificate the person holds.

(d) If a security is not reasonably available for purchase, a person entitled to issue or validation may recover from the issuer the price the person or the last purchaser for value paid for it with interest from the date of the person's demand.

Part 3 Transfer of Certificated and Uncertificated Securities

§ 8–301. Delivery.

(a) Delivery of a certificated security to a purchaser occurs when:

(1) the purchaser acquires possession of the security certificate;

(2) another person, other than a securities intermediary, either acquires possession of the security certificate on behalf of the purchaser or, having previously acquired possession of the certificate, acknowledges that it holds for the purchaser; or

(3) a securities intermediary acting on behalf of the purchaser acquires possession of the security certificate, only if the certificate is in registered form and is (i) registered in the name of the purchaser, (ii) payable to the order of the purchaser, or (iii) specially indorsed to the purchaser by an effective indorsement and has not been indorsed to the securities intermediary or in blank.

(b) Delivery of an uncertificated security to a purchaser occurs when:

(1) the issuer registers the purchaser as the registered owner, upon original issue or registration of transfer; or

(2) another person, other than a securities intermediary, either becomes the registered owner of the uncertificated security on behalf of the purchaser or, having previously become the registered owner, acknowledges that it holds for the purchaser.

As amended in 1999.

§ 8–302. Rights of Purchaser.

(a) Except as otherwise provided in subsections (b) and (c), upon delivery of a certificated or uncertificated security to a purchaser, the purchaser acquires all rights in the security that the transferor had or had power to transfer.

(b) A purchaser of a limited interest acquires rights only to the extent of the interest purchased.

(c) A purchaser of a certificated security who as a previous holder had notice of an adverse claim does not improve its position by taking from a protected purchaser.

As amended in 1999.

§ 8–303. Protected Purchaser.

(a) "Protected purchaser" means a purchaser of a certificated or uncertificated security, or of an interest therein, who:

(1) gives value;

(2) does not have notice of any adverse claim to the security; and

(3) obtains control of the certificated or uncertificated security.

(b) In addition to acquiring the rights of a purchaser, a protected purchaser also acquires its interest in the security free of any adverse claim.

§ 8–304. Indorsement.

(a) An indorsement may be in blank or special. An indorsement in blank includes an indorsement to bearer. A special indorsement specifies to whom a security is to be transferred or who has power to transfer it. A holder may convert a blank indorsement to a special indorsement.

(b) An indorsement purporting to be only of part of a security certificate representing units intended by the issuer to be separately transferable is effective to the extent of the indorsement.

(c) An indorsement, whether special or in blank, does not constitute a transfer until delivery of the certificate on which it appears or, if the indorsement is on a separate document, until delivery of both the document and the certificate.

(d) If a security certificate in registered form has been delivered to a purchaser without a necessary indorsement, the purchaser may become a protected purchaser only when the indorsement is supplied. However, against a transferor, a transfer is complete upon delivery and the purchaser has a specifically enforceable right to have any necessary indorsement supplied.

(e) An indorsement of a security certificate in bearer form may give notice of an adverse claim to the certificate, but it does not otherwise affect a right to registration that the holder possesses.

(f) Unless otherwise agreed, a person making an indorsement assumes only the obligations provided in Section 8–108 and not an obligation that the security will be honored by the issuer.

§ 8–305. Instruction.

(a) If an instruction has been originated by an appropriate person but is incomplete in any other respect, any person may complete it as authorized and the issuer may rely on it as completed, even though it has been completed incorrectly.

(b) Unless otherwise agreed, a person initiating an instruction assumes only the obligations imposed by Section 8–108 and not an obligation that the security will be honored by the issuer.

§ 8–306. Effect of Guaranteeing Signature, Indorsement, or Instruction.

(a) A person who guarantees a signature of an indorser of a security certificate warrants that at the time of signing:

    (1) the signature was genuine;

    (2) the signer was an appropriate person to indorse, or if the signature is by an agent, the agent had actual authority to act on behalf of the appropriate person; and

    (3) the signer had legal capacity to sign.

(b) A person who guarantees a signature of the originator of an instruction warrants that at the time of signing:

    (1) the signature was genuine;

    (2) the signer was an appropriate person to originate the instruction, or if the signature is by an agent, the agent had actual authority to act on behalf of the appropriate person, if the person specified in the instruction as the registered owner was, in fact, the registered owner, as to which fact the signature guarantor does not make a warranty; and

    (3) the signer had legal capacity to sign.

(c) A person who specially guarantees the signature of an originator of an instruction makes the warranties of a signature guarantor under subsection (b) and also warrants that at the time the instruction is presented to the issuer:

    (1) the person specified in the instruction as the registered owner of the uncertificated security will be the registered owner; and

    (2) the transfer of the uncertificated security requested in the instruction will be registered by the issuer free from all liens, security interests, restrictions, and claims other than those specified in the instruction.

(d) A guarantor under subsections (a) and (b) or a special guarantor under subsection (c) does not otherwise warrant the rightfulness of the transfer.

(e) A person who guarantees an indorsement of a security certificate makes the warranties of a signature guarantor under subsection (a) and also warrants the rightfulness of the transfer in all respects.

(f) A person who guarantees an instruction requesting the transfer of an uncertificated security makes the warranties of a special signature guarantor under subsection (c) and also warrants the rightfulness of the transfer in all respects.

(g) An issuer may not require a special guaranty of signature, a guaranty of indorsement, or a guaranty of instruction as a condition to registration of transfer.

(h) The warranties under this section are made to a person taking or dealing with the security in reliance on the guaranty, and the guarantor is liable to the person for loss resulting from their breach. An indorser or originator of an instruction whose signature, indorsement, or instruction has been guaranteed is liable to a guarantor for any loss suffered by the guarantor as a result of breach of the warranties of the guarantor.

§ 8–307. Purchaser's Right to Requisites for Registration of Transfer.

Unless otherwise agreed, the transferor of a security on due demand shall supply the purchaser with proof of authority to transfer or with any other requisite necessary to obtain registration of the transfer of the security, but if the transfer is not for value, a transferor need not comply unless the purchaser pays the necessary expenses. If the transferor fails within a reasonable time to comply with the demand, the purchaser may reject or rescind the transfer.

Part 4 Registration

§ 8–401. Duty of Issuer to Register Transfer.

(a) If a certificated security in registered form is presented to an issuer with a request to register transfer or an instruction is presented to an issuer with a request to register transfer of an uncertificated security, the issuer shall register the transfer as requested if:

    (1) under the terms of the security the person seeking registration of transfer is eligible to have the security registered in its name;

    (2) the indorsement or instruction is made by the appropriate person or by an agent who has actual authority to act on behalf of the appropriate person;

    (3) reasonable assurance is given that the indorsement or instruction is genuine and authorized (Section 8–402);

(4) any applicable law relating to the collection of taxes has been complied with;

(5) the transfer does not violate any restriction on transfer imposed by the issuer in accordance with Section 8–204;

(6) a demand that the issuer not register transfer has not become effective under Section 8–403, or the issuer has complied with Section 8–403(b) but no legal process or indemnity bond is obtained as provided in Section 8–403(d); and

(7) the transfer is in fact rightful or is to a protected purchaser.

(b) If an issuer is under a duty to register a transfer of a security, the issuer is liable to a person presenting a certificated security or an instruction for registration or to the person's principal for loss resulting from unreasonable delay in registration or failure or refusal to register the transfer.

§ 8–402. Assurance That Indorsement or Instruction Is Effective.

(a) An issuer may require the following assurance that each necessary indorsement or each instruction is genuine and authorized:

(1) in all cases, a guaranty of the signature of the person making an indorsement or originating an instruction including, in the case of an instruction, reasonable assurance of identity;

(2) if the indorsement is made or the instruction is originated by an agent, appropriate assurance of actual authority to sign;

(3) if the indorsement is made or the instruction is originated by a fiduciary pursuant to Section 8–107(a)(4) or (a)(5), appropriate evidence of appointment or incumbency;

(4) if there is more than one fiduciary, reasonable assurance that all who are required to sign have done so; and

(5) if the indorsement is made or the instruction is originated by a person not covered by another provision of this subsection, assurance appropriate to the case corresponding as nearly as may be to the provisions of this subsection.

(b) An issuer may elect to require reasonable assurance beyond that specified in this section.

(c) In this section:

(1) "Guaranty of the signature" means a guaranty signed by or on behalf of a person reasonably believed by the issuer to be responsible. An issuer may adopt standards with respect to responsibility if they are not manifestly unreasonable.

(2) "Appropriate evidence of appointment or incumbency" means:

(i) in the case of a fiduciary appointed or qualified by a court, a certificate issued by or under the direction or supervision of the court or an officer thereof and dated within 60 days before the date of presentation for transfer; or

(ii) in any other case, a copy of a document showing the appointment or a certificate issued by or on behalf of a person reasonably believed by an issuer to be responsible or, in the absence of that document or certificate, other evidence the issuer reasonably considers appropriate.

§ 8–403. Demand That Issuer Not Register Transfer.

(a) A person who is an appropriate person to make an indorsement or originate an instruction may demand that the issuer not register transfer of a security by communicating to the issuer a notification that identifies the registered owner and the issue of which the security is a part and provides an address for communications directed to the person making the demand. The demand is effective only if it is received by the issuer at a time and in a manner affording the issuer reasonable opportunity to act on it.

(b) If a certificated security in registered form is presented to an issuer with a request to register transfer or an instruction is presented to an issuer with a request to register transfer of an uncertificated security after a demand that the issuer not register transfer has become effective, the issuer shall promptly communicate to (i) the person who initiated the demand at the address provided in the demand and (ii) the person who presented the security for registration of transfer or initiated the instruction requesting registration of transfer a notification stating that:

(1) the certificated security has been presented for registration of transfer or the instruction for registration of transfer of the uncertificated security has been received;

(2) a demand that the issuer not register transfer had previously been received; and

(3) the issuer will withhold registration of transfer for a period of time stated in the notification in order to provide the person who initiated the demand an opportunity to obtain legal process or an indemnity bond.

(c) The period described in subsection (b)(3) may not exceed 30 days after the date of communication of the notification. A shorter period may be specified by the issuer if it is not manifestly unreasonable.

(d) An issuer is not liable to a person who initiated a demand that the issuer not register transfer for any loss the person suffers as a result of registration of a transfer pursuant to an effective indorsement or instruction if the person who initiated the demand does not, within the time stated in the issuer's communication, either:

(1) obtain an appropriate restraining order, injunction, or other process from a court of competent jurisdiction enjoining the issuer from registering the transfer; or

(2) file with the issuer an indemnity bond, sufficient in the issuer's judgment to protect the issuer and any transfer agent, registrar, or other agent of the issuer involved from any loss it or they may suffer by refusing to register the transfer.

(e) This section does not relieve an issuer from liability for registering transfer pursuant to an indorsement or instruction that was not effective.

§ 8–404. Wrongful Registration.

(a) Except as otherwise provided in Section 8–406, an issuer is liable for wrongful registration of transfer if the issuer has registered a transfer of a security to a person not entitled to it, and the transfer was registered:

(1) pursuant to an ineffective indorsement or instruction;

(2) after a demand that the issuer not register transfer became effective under Section 8–403(a) and the issuer did not comply with Section 8–403(b);

(3) after the issuer had been served with an injunction, restraining order, or other legal process enjoining it from registering the transfer, issued by a court of competent jurisdiction, and the issuer had a reasonable opportunity to act on the injunction, restraining order, or other legal process; or

(4) by an issuer acting in collusion with the wrongdoer.

(b) An issuer that is liable for wrongful registration of transfer under subsection (a) on demand shall provide the person entitled to the security with a like certificated or uncertificated security, and any payments or distributions that the person did not receive as a result of the wrongful registration. If an overissue would result, the issuer's liability to provide the person with a like security is governed by Section 8–210.

(c) Except as otherwise provided in subsection (a) or in a law relating to the collection of taxes, an issuer is not liable to an owner or other person suffering loss as a result of the registration of a transfer of a security if registration was made pursuant to an effective indorsement or instruction.

§ 8–405. Replacement of Lost, Destroyed, or Wrongfully Taken Security Certificate.

(a) If an owner of a certificated security, whether in registered or bearer form, claims that the certificate has been lost, destroyed, or wrongfully taken, the issuer shall issue a new certificate if the owner:

(1) so requests before the issuer has notice that the certificate has been acquired by a protected purchaser;

(2) files with the issuer a sufficient indemnity bond; and

(3) satisfies other reasonable requirements imposed by the issuer.

(b) If, after the issue of a new security certificate, a protected purchaser of the original certificate presents it for registration of transfer, the issuer shall register the transfer unless an overissue would result. In that case, the issuer's liability is governed by Section 8–210. In addition to any rights on the indemnity bond, an issuer may recover the new certificate from a person to whom it was issued or any person taking under that person, except a protected purchaser.

§ 8–406. Obligation to Notify Issuer of Lost, Destroyed, or Wrongfully Taken Security Certificate.

If a security certificate has been lost, apparently destroyed, or wrongfully taken, and the owner fails to notify the issuer of that fact within a reasonable time after the owner has notice of it and the issuer registers a transfer of the security before receiving notification, the owner may not assert against the issuer a claim for registering the transfer under Section 8–404 or a claim to a new security certificate under Section 8–405.

§ 8–407. Authenticating Trustee, Transfer Agent, and Registrar.

A person acting as authenticating trustee, transfer agent, registrar, or other agent for an issuer in the registration of a transfer of its securities, in the issue of new security certificates or uncertificated securities, or in the cancellation of surrendered security certificates has the same obligation to the holder or owner of a certificated or uncertificated security with regard to the particular functions performed as the issuer has in regard to those functions.

Part 5   Security Entitlements

§ 8–501. Securities Account; Acquisition of Security Entitlement from Securities Intermediary.

(a) "Securities account" means an account to which a financial asset is or may be credited in accordance with an agreement under which the person maintaining the account undertakes to treat the person for whom the account is maintained as entitled to exercise the rights that comprise the financial asset.

(b) Except as otherwise provided in subsections (d) and (e), a person acquires a security entitlement if a securities intermediary:

(1) indicates by book entry that a financial asset has been credited to the person's securities account;

(2) receives a financial asset from the person or acquires a financial asset for the person and, in either case, accepts it for credit to the person's securities account; or

(3) becomes obligated under other law, regulation, or rule to credit a financial asset to the person's securities account.

(c) If a condition of subsection (b) has been met, a person has a security entitlement even though the securities intermediary does not itself hold the financial asset.

(d) If a securities intermediary holds a financial asset for another person, and the financial asset is registered in the name of, payable to the order of, or specially indorsed to the other person, and has not been indorsed to the securities intermediary or in blank, the other person is treated as holding the financial asset directly rather than as having a security entitlement with respect to the financial asset.

(e) Issuance of a security is not establishment of a security entitlement.

§ 8–502. Assertion of Adverse Claim against Entitlement Holder.

An action based on an adverse claim to a financial asset, whether framed in conversion, replevin, constructive trust, equitable lien, or other theory, may not be asserted against a person who acquires a security entitlement under Section 8–501 for value and without notice of the adverse claim.

§ 8–503. Property Interest of Entitlement Holder in Financial Asset Held by Securities Intermediary.

(a) To the extent necessary for a securities intermediary to satisfy all security entitlements with respect to a particular financial asset, all interests in that financial asset held by the securities intermediary are held by the securities intermediary for the entitlement holders, are not property of the securities intermediary, and are not subject to claims of creditors of the securities intermediary, except as otherwise provided in Section 8–511.

(b) An entitlement holder's property interest with respect to a particular financial asset under subsection (a) is a pro rata property interest in all interests in that financial asset held by the securities intermediary, without regard to the time the entitlement holder acquired the security entitlement or the time the securities intermediary acquired the interest in that financial asset.

(c) An entitlement holder's property interest with respect to a particular financial asset under subsection (a) may be enforced against the securities intermediary only by exercise of the entitlement holder's rights under Sections 8–505 through 8–508.

(d) An entitlement holder's property interest with respect to a particular financial asset under subsection (a) may be enforced against a purchaser of the financial asset or interest therein only if:

(1) insolvency proceedings have been initiated by or against the securities intermediary;

(2) the securities intermediary does not have sufficient interests in the financial asset to satisfy the security entitlements of all of its entitlement holders to that financial asset;

(3) the securities intermediary violated its obligations under Section 8–504 by transferring the financial asset or interest therein to the purchaser; and

(4) the purchaser is not protected under subsection (e). The trustee or other liquidator, acting on behalf of all entitlement holders having security entitlements with respect to a particular financial asset, may recover the financial asset, or

interest therein, from the purchaser. If the trustee or other liquidator elects not to pursue that right, an entitlement holder whose security entitlement remains unsatisfied has the right to recover its interest in the financial asset from the purchaser.

(e) An action based on the entitlement holder's property interest with respect to a particular financial asset under subsection (a), whether framed in conversion, replevin, constructive trust, equitable lien, or other theory, may not be asserted against any purchaser of a financial asset or interest therein who gives value, obtains control, and does not act in collusion with the securities intermediary in violating the securities intermediary's obligations under Section 8–504.

§ 8–504. Duty of Securities Intermediary to Maintain Financial Asset.

(a) A securities intermediary shall promptly obtain and thereafter maintain a financial asset in a quantity corresponding to the aggregate of all security entitlements it has established in favor of its entitlement holders with respect to that financial asset. The securities intermediary may maintain those financial assets directly or through one or more other securities intermediaries.

(b) Except to the extent otherwise agreed by its entitlement holder, a securities intermediary may not grant any security interests in a financial asset it is obligated to maintain pursuant to subsection (a).

(c) A securities intermediary satisfies the duty in subsection (a) if:

(1) the securities intermediary acts with respect to the duty as agreed upon by the entitlement holder and the securities intermediary; or

(2) in the absence of agreement, the securities intermediary exercises due care in accordance with reasonable commercial standards to obtain and maintain the financial asset.

(d) This section does not apply to a clearing corporation that is itself the obligor of an option or similar obligation to which its entitlement holders have security entitlements.

§ 8–505. Duty of Securities Intermediary with Respect to Payments and Distributions.

(a) A securities intermediary shall take action to obtain a payment or distribution made by the issuer of a financial asset. A securities intermediary satisfies the duty if:

(1) the securities intermediary acts with respect to the duty as agreed upon by the entitlement holder and the securities intermediary; or

(2) in the absence of agreement, the securities intermediary exercises due care in accordance with reasonable commercial standards to attempt to obtain the payment or distribution.

(b) A securities intermediary is obligated to its entitlement holder for a payment or distribution made by the issuer of a financial asset if the payment or distribution is received by the securities intermediary.

§ 8–506. Duty of Securities Intermediary to Exercise Rights as Directed by Entitlement Holder.

A securities intermediary shall exercise rights with respect to a financial asset if directed to do so by an entitlement holder. A securities intermediary satisfies the duty if:

(1) the securities intermediary acts with respect to the duty as agreed upon by the entitlement holder and the securities intermediary; or

(2) in the absence of agreement, the securities intermediary either places the entitlement holder in a position to exercise the rights directly or exercises due care in accordance with reasonable commercial standards to follow the direction of the entitlement holder.

§ 8–507. Duty of Securities Intermediary to Comply with Entitlement Order.

(a) A securities intermediary shall comply with an entitlement order if the entitlement order is originated by the appropriate person, the securities intermediary has had reasonable opportunity to assure itself that the entitlement order is genuine and authorized, and the securities intermediary has had reasonable opportunity to comply with the entitlement order. A securities intermediary satisfies the duty if:

(1) the securities intermediary acts with respect to the duty as agreed upon by the entitlement holder and the securities intermediary; or

(2) in the absence of agreement, the securities intermediary exercises due care in accordance with reasonable commercial standards to comply with the entitlement order.

(b) If a securities intermediary transfers a financial asset pursuant to an ineffective entitlement order, the securities intermediary shall reestablish a security entitlement in favor of the person entitled to it, and pay or credit any payments or distributions that the person did not receive as a result of the wrongful transfer. If the securities intermediary does not reestablish a security entitlement, the securities intermediary is liable to the entitlement holder for damages.

§ 8–508. Duty of Securities Intermediary to Change Entitlement Holder's Position to Other Form of Security Holding.

A securities intermediary shall act at the direction of an entitlement holder to change a security entitlement into another available form of holding for which the entitlement holder is eligible, or to cause the financial asset to be transferred to a securities account of the entitlement holder with another securities intermediary. A securities intermediary satisfies the duty if:

(1) the securities intermediary acts as agreed upon by the entitlement holder and the securities intermediary; or

(2) in the absence of agreement, the securities intermediary exercises due care in accordance with reasonable commercial standards to follow the direction of the entitlement holder.

§ 8–509. Specification of Duties of Securities Intermediary by Other Statute or Regulation; Manner of Performance of Duties of Securities Intermediary and Exercise of Rights of Entitlement Holder.

(a) If the substance of a duty imposed upon a securities intermediary by Sections 8–504 through 8–508 is the subject of other statute, regulation, or rule, compliance with that statute, regulation, or rule satisfies the duty.

(b) To the extent that specific standards for the performance of the duties of a securities intermediary or the exercise of the rights of an entitlement holder are not specified by other statute, regulation, or rule or by agreement between the securities intermediary and entitlement holder, the securities intermediary shall perform its duties and the entitlement holder shall exercise its rights in a commercially reasonable manner.

(c) The obligation of a securities intermediary to perform the duties imposed by Sections 8–504 through 8–508 is subject to:

(1) rights of the securities intermediary arising out of a security interest under a security agreement with the entitlement holder or otherwise; and

(2) rights of the securities intermediary under other law, regulation, rule, or agreement to withhold performance of its duties as a result of unfulfilled obligations of the entitlement holder to the securities intermediary.

(d) Sections 8–504 through 8–508 do not require a securities intermediary to take any action that is prohibited by other statute, regulation, or rule.

§ 8–510. Rights of Purchaser of Security Entitlement from Entitlement Holder.

(a) An action based on an adverse claim to a financial asset or security entitlement, whether framed in conversion, replevin, constructive trust, equitable lien, or other theory, may not be asserted against a person who purchases a security entitlement, or an interest therein, from an entitlement holder if the purchaser gives value, does not have notice of the adverse claim, and obtains control.

(b) If an adverse claim could not have been asserted against an entitlement holder under Section 8–502, the adverse claim cannot be asserted against a person who purchases a security entitlement, or an interest therein, from the entitlement holder.

(c) In a case not covered by the priority rules in Article 9, a purchaser for value of a security entitlement, or an interest therein, who obtains control has priority over a purchaser of a security entitlement, or an interest therein, who does not obtain control. Except as otherwise provided in subsection (d), purchasers who have control rank according to priority in time of:

(1) the purchaser's becoming the person for whom the securities account, in which the security entitlement is carried, is maintained, if the purchaser obtained control under Section 8–106(d)(1);

(2) the securities intermediary's agreement to comply with the purchaser's entitlement orders with respect to security entitlements carried or to be carried in the securities account in which the security entitlement is carried, if the purchaser obtained control under Section 8–106(d)(2); or

(3) if the purchaser obtained control through another person under Section 8–106(d)(3), the time on which priority would be based under this subsection if the other person were the secured party.

(d) A securities intermediary as purchaser has priority over a conflicting purchaser who has control unless otherwise agreed by the securities intermediary.

As amended in 1999.

§ 8–511. Priority among Security Interests and Entitlement Holders.

(a) Except as otherwise provided in subsections (b) and (c), if a securities intermediary does not have sufficient interests in a particular financial asset to satisfy both its obligations to entitlement holders who have security entitlements to that financial asset and its obligation to a creditor of the securities intermediary who has a security interest in that financial asset, the claims of entitlement holders, other than the creditor, have priority over the claim of the creditor.

(b) A claim of a creditor of a securities intermediary who has a security interest in a financial asset held by a securities intermediary has priority over claims of the securities intermediary's entitlement holders who have security entitlements with respect to that financial asset if the creditor has control over the financial asset.

(c) If a clearing corporation does not have sufficient financial assets to satisfy both its obligations to entitlement holders who have security entitlements with respect to a financial asset and its obligation to a creditor of the clearing corporation who has a security interest in that financial asset, the claim of the creditor has priority over the claims of entitlement holders.

Part 6 Transition Provisions for Revised Article 8

§ 8–601. Effective Date.

This [Act] takes effect . . . .

§ 8–602. Repeals.

This [Act] repeals . . . .

§ 8–603. Savings Clause.

(a) This [Act] does not affect an action or proceeding commenced before this [Act] takes effect.

(b) If a security interest in a security is perfected at the date this [Act] takes effect, and the action by which the security interest was perfected would suffice to perfect a security interest under this [Act], no further action is required to continue perfection. If a security interest in a security is per-

fected at the date this [Act] takes effect but the action by which the security interest was perfected would not suffice to perfect a security interest under this [Act], the security interest remains perfected for a period of four months after the effective date and continues perfected thereafter if appropriate action to perfect under this [Act] is taken within that period. If a security interest is perfected at the date this [Act] takes effect and the security interest can be perfected by filing under this [Act], a financing statement signed by the secured party instead of the debtor may be filed within that period to continue perfection or thereafter to perfect.

Revised Article 9
SECURED TRANSACTIONS

Part 1 General Provisions

[Subpart 1. Short Title, Definitions, and General Concepts]

§ 9–101. Short Title.

This article may be cited as Uniform Commercial Code—Secured Transactions.

§ 9–102. Definitions and Index of Definitions.

(a) In this article:

(1) "Accession" means goods that are physically united with other goods in such a manner that the identity of the original goods is not lost.

(2) "Account", except as used in "account for", means a right to payment of a monetary obligation, whether or not earned by performance, (i) for property that has been or is to be sold, leased, licensed, assigned, or otherwise disposed of, (ii) for services rendered or to be rendered, (iii) for a policy of insurance issued or to be issued, (iv) for a secondary obligation incurred or to be incurred, (v) for energy provided or to be provided, (vi) for the use or hire of a vessel under a charter or other contract, (vii) arising out of the use of a credit or charge card or information contained on or for use with the card, or (viii) as winnings in a lottery or other game of chance operated or sponsored by a State, governmental unit of a State, or person licensed or authorized to operate the game by a State or governmental unit of a State. The term includes health-care insurance receivables. The term does not include (i) rights to payment evidenced by chattel paper or an instrument, (ii) commercial tort claims, (iii) deposit accounts, (iv) investment property, (v) letter-of-credit rights or letters of credit, or (vi) rights to payment for money or funds advanced or sold, other than rights arising out of the use of a credit or charge card or information contained on or for use with the card.

(3) "Account debtor" means a person obligated on an account, chattel paper, or general intangible. The term does not include persons obligated to pay a negotiable instrument, even if the instrument constitutes part of chattel paper.

(4) "Accounting", except as used in "accounting for", means a record:

(A) authenticated by a secured party;

(B) indicating the aggregate unpaid secured obligations as of a date not more than 35 days earlier or 35 days later than the date of the record; and

(C) identifying the components of the obligations in reasonable detail.

(5) "Agricultural lien" means an interest, other than a security interest, in farm products:

(A) which secures payment or performance of an obligation for:

(i) goods or services furnished in connection with a debtor's farming operation; or

(ii) rent on real property leased by a debtor in connection with its farming operation;

(B) which is created by statute in favor of a person that:

(i) in the ordinary course of its business furnished goods or services to a debtor in connection with a debtor's farming operation; or

(ii) leased real property to a debtor in connection with the debtor's farming operation; and

(C) whose effectiveness does not depend on the person's possession of the personal property.

(6) "As-extracted collateral" means:

(A) oil, gas, or other minerals that are subject to a security interest that:

(i) is created by a debtor having an interest in the minerals before extraction; and

(ii) attaches to the minerals as extracted; or

(B) accounts arising out of the sale at the wellhead or minehead of oil, gas, or other minerals in which the debtor had an interest before extraction.

(7) "Authenticate" means:

(A) to sign; or

(B) to execute or otherwise adopt a symbol, or encrypt or similarly process a record in whole or in part, with the present intent of the authenticating person to identify the person and adopt or accept a record.

(8) "Bank" means an organization that is engaged in the business of banking. The term includes savings banks, savings and loan associations, credit unions, and trust companies.

(9) "Cash proceeds" means proceeds that are money, checks, deposit accounts, or the like.

(10) "Certificate of title" means a certificate of title with respect to which a statute provides for the security interest in question to be indicated on the certificate as a condition or result of the security interest's obtaining priority over the rights of a lien creditor with respect to the collateral.

(11) "Chattel paper" means a record or records that evidence both a monetary obligation and a security interest in specific goods, a security interest in specific goods and software used in the goods, a security interest in specific goods and license of software used in the goods, a lease of specific goods, or a lease of specific goods and license of software used in the goods. In this paragraph, "monetary obligation" means a monetary obligation secured by the goods or owed under a lease of the goods and includes a monetary obligation with respect to software used in the goods. The term does not include (i) charters or other contracts involving the use or hire of a vessel or (ii) records that evidence a right to payment arising out of the use of a credit or charge card or information contained on or for use with the card. If a transaction is evidenced by records that include an instrument or series of instruments, the group of records taken together constitutes chattel paper.

(12) "Collateral" means the property subject to a security interest or agricultural lien. The term includes:

(A) proceeds to which a security interest attaches;

(B) accounts, chattel paper, payment intangibles, and promissory notes that have been sold; and

(C) goods that are the subject of a consignment.

(13) "Commercial tort claim" means a claim arising in tort with respect to which:

(A) the claimant is an organization; or

(B) the claimant is an individual and the claim:

(i) arose in the course of the claimant's business or profession; and

(ii) does not include damages arising out of personal injury to or the death of an individual.

(14) "Commodity account" means an account maintained by a commodity intermediary in which a commodity contract is carried for a commodity customer.

(15) "Commodity contract" means a commodity futures contract, an option on a commodity futures contract, a commodity option, or another contract if the contract or option is:

(A) traded on or subject to the rules of a board of trade that has been designated as a contract market for such a contract pursuant to federal commodities laws; or

(B) traded on a foreign commodity board of trade, exchange, or market, and is carried on the books of a commodity intermediary for a commodity customer.

(16) "Commodity customer" means a person for which a commodity intermediary carries a commodity contract on its books.

(17) "Commodity intermediary" means a person that:

(A) is registered as a futures commission merchant under federal commodities law; or

(B) in the ordinary course of its business provides clearance or settlement services for a board of trade that has been designated as a contract market pursuant to federal commodities law.

(18) "Communicate" means:

(A) to send a written or other tangible record;

(B) to transmit a record by any means agreed upon by the persons sending and receiving the record; or

(C) in the case of transmission of a record to or by a filing office, to transmit a record by any means prescribed by filing-office rule.

(19) "Consignee" means a merchant to which goods are delivered in a consignment.

(20) "Consignment" means a transaction, regardless of its form, in which a person delivers goods to a merchant for the purpose of sale and:

(A) the merchant:

(i) deals in goods of that kind under a name other than the name of the person making delivery;

(ii) is not an auctioneer; and

(iii) is not generally known by its creditors to be substantially engaged in selling the goods of others;

(B) with respect to each delivery, the aggregate value of the goods is $1,000 or more at the time of delivery;

(C) the goods are not consumer goods immediately before delivery; and

(D) the transaction does not create a security interest that secures an obligation.

(21) "Consignor" means a person that delivers goods to a consignee in a consignment.

(22) "Consumer debtor" means a debtor in a consumer transaction.

(23) "Consumer goods" means goods that are used or bought for use primarily for personal, family, or household purposes.

(24) "Consumer-goods transaction" means a consumer transaction in which:

(A) an individual incurs an obligation primarily for personal, family, or household purposes; and

(B) a security interest in consumer goods secures the obligation.

(25) "Consumer obligor" means an obligor who is an individual and who incurred the obligation as part of a transaction entered into primarily for personal, family, or household purposes.

(26) "Consumer transaction" means a transaction in which (i) an individual incurs an obligation primarily for personal, family, or household purposes, (ii) a security interest secures the obligation, and (iii) the collateral is held or acquired primarily for personal, family, or household purposes. The term includes consumer-goods transactions.

(27) "Continuation statement" means an amendment of a financing statement which:

(A) identifies, by its file number, the initial financing statement to which it relates; and

(B) indicates that it is a continuation statement for, or that it is filed to continue the effectiveness of, the identified financing statement.

(28) "Debtor" means:

(A) a person having an interest, other than a security interest or other lien, in the collateral, whether or not the person is an obligor;

(B) a seller of accounts, chattel paper, payment intangibles, or promissory notes; or

(C) a consignee.

(29) "Deposit account" means a demand, time, savings, passbook, or similar account maintained with a bank. The term does not include investment property or accounts evidenced by an instrument.

(30) "Document" means a document of title or a receipt of the type described in Section 7–201(2).

(31) "Electronic chattel paper" means chattel paper evidenced by a record or records consisting of information stored in an electronic medium.

(32) "Encumbrance" means a right, other than an ownership interest, in real property. The term includes mortgages and other liens on real property.

(33) "Equipment" means goods other than inventory, farm products, or consumer goods.

(34) "Farm products" means goods, other than standing timber, with respect to which the debtor is engaged in a farming operation and which are:

(A) crops grown, growing, or to be grown, including:

(i) crops produced on trees, vines, and bushes; and

(ii) aquatic goods produced in aquacultural operations;

(B) livestock, born or unborn, including aquatic goods produced in aquacultural operations;

(C) supplies used or produced in a farming operation; or

(D) products of crops or livestock in their unmanufactured states.

(35) "Farming operation" means raising, cultivating, propagating, fattening, grazing, or any other farming, livestock, or aquacultural operation.

(36) "File number" means the number assigned to an initial financing statement pursuant to Section 9–519(a).

(37) "Filing office" means an office designated in Section 9–501 as the place to file a financing statement.

(38) "Filing-office rule" means a rule adopted pursuant to Section 9–526.

(39) "Financing statement" means a record or records composed of an initial financing statement and any filed record relating to the initial financing statement.

(40) "Fixture filing" means the filing of a financing statement covering goods that are or are to become fixtures and satisfying Section 9–502(a) and (b). The term includes the filing of a financing statement covering goods of a transmitting utility which are or are to become fixtures.

(41) "Fixtures" means goods that have become so related to particular real property that an interest in them arises under real property law.

(42) "General intangible" means any personal property, including things in action, other than accounts, chattel paper, commercial tort claims, deposit accounts, documents, goods, instruments, investment property, letter-of-credit rights, letters of credit, money, and oil, gas, or other minerals before extraction. The term includes payment intangibles and software.

(43) "Good faith" means honesty in fact and the observance of reasonable commercial standards of fair dealing.

(44) "Goods" means all things that are movable when a security interest attaches. The term includes (i) fixtures, (ii) standing timber that is to be cut and removed under a conveyance or contract for sale, (iii) the unborn young of animals, (iv) crops grown, growing, or to be grown, even if the crops are produced on trees, vines, or bushes, and (v) manufactured homes. The term also includes a computer program embedded in goods and any supporting information provided in connection with a transaction relating to the program if (i) the program is associated with the goods in such a manner that it customarily is considered part of the goods, or (ii) by becoming the owner of the goods, a person acquires a right to use the program in connection with the goods. The term does not include a computer program embedded in goods that consist solely of the medium in which the program is embedded. The term also does not include accounts, chattel paper, commercial tort claims, deposit accounts, documents, general intangibles, instruments, investment property, letter-of-credit rights, letters of credit, money, or oil, gas, or other minerals before extraction.

(45) "Governmental unit" means a subdivision, agency, department, county, parish, municipality, or other unit of the government of the United States, a State, or a foreign country. The term includes an organization having a separate corporate existence if the organization is eligible to issue debt on which interest is exempt from income taxation under the laws of the United States.

(46) "Health-care-insurance receivable" means an interest in or claim under a policy of insurance which is a right to payment of a monetary obligation for health-care goods or services provided.

(47) "Instrument" means a negotiable instrument or any other writing that evidences a right to the payment of a monetary obligation, is not itself a security agreement or lease, and is of a type that in ordinary course of business is transferred by delivery with any necessary indorsement or assignment. The term does not include (i) investment property, (ii) letters of credit, or (iii) writings that evidence a right to payment arising out of the use of a credit or charge card or information contained on or for use with the card.

(48) "Inventory" means goods, other than farm products, which:

(A) are leased by a person as lessor;

(B) are held by a person for sale or lease or to be furnished under a contract of service;

(C) are furnished by a person under a contract of service; or

(D) consist of raw materials, work in process, or materials used or consumed in a business.

(49) "Investment property" means a security, whether certificated or uncertificated, security entitlement, securities account, commodity contract, or commodity account.

(50) "Jurisdiction of organization", with respect to a registered organization, means the jurisdiction under whose law the organization is organized.

(51) "Letter-of-credit right" means a right to payment or performance under a letter of credit, whether or not the beneficiary has demanded or is at the time entitled to demand payment or performance. The term does not include the right of a beneficiary to demand payment or performance under a letter of credit.

(52) "Lien creditor" means:

(A) a creditor that has acquired a lien on the property involved by attachment, levy, or the like;

(B) an assignee for benefit of creditors from the time of assignment;

(C) a trustee in bankruptcy from the date of the filing of the petition; or

(D) a receiver in equity from the time of appointment.

(53) "Manufactured home" means a structure, transportable in one or more sections, which, in the traveling mode, is eight body feet or more in width or 40 body feet or more in length, or, when erected on site, is 320 or more square feet, and which is built on a permanent chassis and designed to be used as a dwelling with or without a permanent foundation when connected to the required utilities, and includes the plumbing, heating, air-conditioning, and electrical systems contained therein. The term includes any structure that meets all of the requirements of this paragraph except the size requirements and with respect to which the manufacturer voluntarily files a certification required by the United States Secretary of Housing and Urban Development and complies with the standards established under Title 42 of the United States Code.

(54) "Manufactured-home transaction" means a secured transaction:

(A) that creates a purchase-money security interest in a manufactured home, other than a manufactured home held as inventory; or

(B) in which a manufactured home, other than a manufactured home held as inventory, is the primary collateral.

(55) "Mortgage" means a consensual interest in real property, including fixtures, which secures payment or performance of an obligation.

(56) "New debtor" means a person that becomes bound as debtor under Section 9–203(d) by a security agreement previously entered into by another person.

(57) "New value" means (i) money, (ii) money's worth in property, services, or new credit, or (iii) release by a transferee of an interest in property previously transferred to the transferee. The term does not include an obligation substituted for another obligation.

(58) "Noncash proceeds" means proceeds other than cash proceeds.

(59) "Obligor" means a person that, with respect to an obligation secured by a security interest in or an agricultural lien on the collateral, (i) owes payment or other performance of the obligation, (ii) has provided property other than the collateral to secure payment or other performance of the obligation, or (iii) is otherwise accountable in whole or in part for payment or other performance of the obligation. The term does not include issuers or nominated persons under a letter of credit.

(60) "Original debtor", except as used in Section 9–310(c), means a person that, as debtor, entered into a security agreement to which a new debtor has become bound under Section 9–203(d).

(61) "Payment intangible" means a general intangible under which the account debtor's principal obligation is a monetary obligation.

(62) "Person related to", with respect to an individual, means:

(A) the spouse of the individual;

(B) a brother, brother-in-law, sister, or sister-in-law of the individual;

(C) an ancestor or lineal descendant of the individual or the individual's spouse; or

(D) any other relative, by blood or marriage, of the individual or the individual's spouse who shares the same home with the individual.

(63) "Person related to", with respect to an organization, means:

(A) a person directly or indirectly controlling, controlled by, or under common control with the organization;

(B) an officer or director of, or a person performing similar functions with respect to, the organization;

(C) an officer or director of, or a person performing similar functions with respect to, a person described in subparagraph (A);

(D) the spouse of an individual described in subparagraph (A), (B), or (C); or

(E) an individual who is related by blood or marriage to an individual described in subparagraph (A), (B), (C), or (D) and shares the same home with the individual.

(64) "Proceeds", except as used in Section 9–609(b), means the following property:

(A) whatever is acquired upon the sale, lease, license, exchange, or other disposition of collateral;

(B) whatever is collected on, or distributed on account of, collateral;

(C) rights arising out of collateral;

(D) to the extent of the value of collateral, claims arising out of the loss, nonconformity, or interference with the use of, defects or infringement of rights in, or damage to, the collateral; or

(E) to the extent of the value of collateral and to the extent payable to the debtor or the secured party, insurance payable by reason of the loss or nonconformity of, defects or infringement of rights in, or damage to, the collateral.

(65) "Promissory note" means an instrument that evidences a promise to pay a monetary obligation, does not evidence an order to pay, and does not contain an acknowledgment by a bank that the bank has received for deposit a sum of money or funds.

(66) "Proposal" means a record authenticated by a secured party which includes the terms on which the secured party is willing to accept collateral in full or

partial satisfaction of the obligation it secures pursuant to Sections 9–620, 9–621, and 9–622.

(67) "Public-finance transaction" means a secured transaction in connection with which:

(A) debt securities are issued;

(B) all or a portion of the securities issued have an initial stated maturity of at least 20 years; and

(C) the debtor, obligor, secured party, account debtor or other person obligated on collateral, assignor or assignee of a secured obligation, or assignor or assignee of a security interest is a State or a governmental unit of a State.

(68) "Pursuant to commitment", with respect to an advance made or other value given by a secured party, means pursuant to the secured party's obligation, whether or not a subsequent event of default or other event not within the secured party's control has relieved or may relieve the secured party from its obligation.

(69) "Record", except as used in "for record", "of record", "record or legal title", and "record owner", means information that is inscribed on a tangible medium or which is stored in an electronic or other medium and is retrievable in perceivable form.

(70) "Registered organization" means an organization organized solely under the law of a single State or the United States and as to which the State or the United States must maintain a public record showing the organization to have been organized.

(71) "Secondary obligor" means an obligor to the extent that:

(A) the obligor's obligation is secondary; or

(B) the obligor has a right of recourse with respect to an obligation secured by collateral against the debtor, another obligor, or property of either.

(72) "Secured party" means:

(A) a person in whose favor a security interest is created or provided for under a security agreement, whether or not any obligation to be secured is outstanding;

(B) a person that holds an agricultural lien;

(C) a consignor;

(D) a person to which accounts, chattel paper, payment intangibles, or promissory notes have been sold;

(E) a trustee, indenture trustee, agent, collateral agent, or other representative in whose favor a security interest or agricultural lien is created or provided for; or

(F) a person that holds a security interest arising under Section 2–401, 2–505, 2–711(3), 2A–508(5), 4–210, or 5–118.

(73) "Security agreement" means an agreement that creates or provides for a security interest.

(74) "Send", in connection with a record or notification, means:

(A) to deposit in the mail, deliver for transmission, or transmit by any other usual means of communication, with postage or cost of transmission provided for, addressed to any address reasonable under the circumstances; or

(B) to cause the record or notification to be received within the time that it would have been received if properly sent under subparagraph (A).

(75) "Software" means a computer program and any supporting information provided in connection with a transaction relating to the program. The term does not include a computer program that is included in the definition of goods.

(76) "State" means a State of the United States, the District of Columbia, Puerto Rico, the United States Virgin Islands, or any territory or insular possession subject to the jurisdiction of the United States.

(77) "Supporting obligation" means a letter-of-credit right or secondary obligation that supports the payment or performance of an account, chattel paper, a document, a general intangible, an instrument, or investment property.

(78) "Tangible chattel paper" means chattel paper evidenced by a record or records consisting of information that is inscribed on a tangible medium.

(79) "Termination statement" means an amendment of a financing statement which:

(A) identifies, by its file number, the initial financing statement to which it relates; and

(B) indicates either that it is a termination statement or that the identified financing statement is no longer effective.

(80) "Transmitting utility" means a person primarily engaged in the business of:

(A) operating a railroad, subway, street railway, or trolley bus;

(B) transmitting communications electrically, electromagnetically, or by light;

(C) transmitting goods by pipeline or sewer; or

(D) transmitting or producing and transmitting electricity, steam, gas, or water.

(b) The following definitions in other articles apply to this article:

"Applicant."	Section 5–102
"Beneficiary."	Section 5–102
"Broker."	Section 8–102
"Certificated security."	Section 8–102

"Check."	Section 3–104
"Clearing corporation."	Section 8–102
"Contract for sale."	Section 2–106
"Customer."	Section 4–104
"Entitlement holder."	Section 8–102
"Financial asset."	Section 8–102
"Holder in due course."	Section 3–302
"Issuer" (with respect to a letter of credit or letter-of-credit right).	Section 5–102
"Issuer" (with respect to a security).	Section 8–201
"Lease."	Section 2A–103
"Lease agreement."	Section 2A–103
"Lease contract."	Section 2A–103
"Leasehold interest."	Section 2A–103
"Lessee."	Section 2A–103
"Lessee in ordinary course of business."	Section 2A–103
"Lessor."	Section 2A–103
"Lessor's residual interest."	Section 2A–103
"Letter of credit."	Section 5–102
"Merchant."	Section 2–104
"Negotiable instrument."	Section 3–104
"Nominated person."	Section 5–102
"Note."	Section 3–104
"Proceeds of a letter of credit."	Section 5–114
"Prove."	Section 3–103
"Sale."	Section 2–106
"Securities account."	Section 8–501
"Securities intermediary."	Section 8–102
"Security."	Section 8–102
"Security certificate."	Section 8–102
"Security entitlement."	Section 8–102
"Uncertificated security."	Section 8–102

(c) Article 1 contains general definitions and principles of construction and interpretation applicable throughout this article.

Amended in 1999 and 2000.

§ 9–103. Purchase-Money Security Interest; Application of Payments; Burden of Establishing.

(a) In this section:

(1) "purchase-money collateral" means goods or software that secures a purchase-money obligation incurred with respect to that collateral; and

(2) "purchase-money obligation" means an obligation of an obligor incurred as all or part of the price of the collateral or for value given to enable the debtor to acquire rights in or the use of the collateral if the value is in fact so used.

(b) A security interest in goods is a purchase-money security interest:

(1) to the extent that the goods are purchase-money collateral with respect to that security interest;

(2) if the security interest is in inventory that is or was purchase-money collateral, also to the extent that the security interest secures a purchase-money obligation incurred with respect to other inventory in which the secured party holds or held a purchase-money security interest; and

(3) also to the extent that the security interest secures a purchase-money obligation incurred with respect to software in which the secured party holds or held a purchase-money security interest.

(c) A security interest in software is a purchase-money security interest to the extent that the security interest also secures a purchase-money obligation incurred with respect to goods in which the secured party holds or held a purchase-money security interest if:

(1) the debtor acquired its interest in the software in an integrated transaction in which it acquired an interest in the goods; and

(2) the debtor acquired its interest in the software for the principal purpose of using the software in the goods.

(d) The security interest of a consignor in goods that are the subject of a consignment is a purchase-money security interest in inventory.

(e) In a transaction other than a consumer-goods transaction, if the extent to which a security interest is a purchase-money security interest depends on the application of a payment to a particular obligation, the payment must be applied:

(1) in accordance with any reasonable method of application to which the parties agree;

(2) in the absence of the parties' agreement to a reasonable method, in accordance with any intention of the obligor manifested at or before the time of payment; or

(3) in the absence of an agreement to a reasonable method and a timely manifestation of the obligor's intention, in the following order:

(A) to obligations that are not secured; and

(B) if more than one obligation is secured, to obligations secured by purchase-money security interests in the order in which those obligations were incurred.

(f) In a transaction other than a consumer-goods transaction, a purchase-money security interest does not lose its status as such, even if:

(1) the purchase-money collateral also secures an obligation that is not a purchase-money obligation;

(2) collateral that is not purchase-money collateral also secures the purchase-money obligation; or

(3) the purchase-money obligation has been renewed, refinanced, consolidated, or restructured.

(g) In a transaction other than a consumer-goods transaction, a secured party claiming a purchase-money security interest has the burden of establishing the extent to which the security interest is a purchase-money security interest.

(h) The limitation of the rules in subsections (e), (f), and (g) to transactions other than consumer-goods transactions is intended to leave to the court the determination of the proper rules in consumer-goods transactions. The court may not infer from that limitation the nature of the proper rule in consumer-goods transactions and may continue to apply established approaches.

§ 9–104. Control of Deposit Account.

(a) A secured party has control of a deposit account if:

(1) the secured party is the bank with which the deposit account is maintained;

(2) the debtor, secured party, and bank have agreed in an authenticated record that the bank will comply with instructions originated by the secured party directing disposition of the funds in the deposit account without further consent by the debtor; or

(3) the secured party becomes the bank's customer with respect to the deposit account.

(b) A secured party that has satisfied subsection (a) has control, even if the debtor retains the right to direct the disposition of funds from the deposit account.

§ 9–105. Control of Electronic Chattel Paper.

A secured party has control of electronic chattel paper if the record or records comprising the chattel paper are created, stored, and assigned in such a manner that:

(1) a single authoritative copy of the record or records exists which is unique, identifiable and, except as otherwise provided in paragraphs (4), (5), and (6), unalterable;

(2) the authoritative copy identifies the secured party as the assignee of the record or records;

(3) the authoritative copy is communicated to and maintained by the secured party or its designated custodian;

(4) copies or revisions that add or change an identified assignee of the authoritative copy can be made only with the participation of the secured party;

(5) each copy of the authoritative copy and any copy of a copy is readily identifiable as a copy that is not the authoritative copy; and

(6) any revision of the authoritative copy is readily identifiable as an authorized or unauthorized revision.

§ 9–106. Control of Investment Property.

(a) A person has control of a certificated security, uncertificated security, or security entitlement as provided in Section 8–106.

(b) A secured party has control of a commodity contract if:

(1) the secured party is the commodity intermediary with which the commodity contract is carried; or

(2) the commodity customer, secured party, and commodity intermediary have agreed that the commodity intermediary will apply any value distributed on account of the commodity contract as directed by the secured party without further consent by the commodity customer.

(c) A secured party having control of all security entitlements or commodity contracts carried in a securities account or commodity account has control over the securities account or commodity account.

§ 9–107. Control of Letter-of-Credit Right.

A secured party has control of a letter-of-credit right to the extent of any right to payment or performance by the issuer or any nominated person if the issuer or nominated person has consented to an assignment of proceeds of the letter of credit under Section 5–114(c) or otherwise applicable law or practice.

§ 9–108. Sufficiency of Description.

(a) Except as otherwise provided in subsections (c), (d), and (e), a description of personal or real property is sufficient, whether or not it is specific, if it reasonably identifies what is described.

(b) Except as otherwise provided in subsection (d), a description of collateral reasonably identifies the collateral if it identifies the collateral by:

(1) specific listing;

(2) category;

(3) except as otherwise provided in subsection (e), a type of collateral defined in [the Uniform Commercial Code];

(4) quantity;

(5) computational or allocational formula or procedure; or

(6) except as otherwise provided in subsection (c), any other method, if the identity of the collateral is objectively determinable.

(c) A description of collateral as "all the debtor's assets" or "all the debtor's personal property" or using words of similar import does not reasonably identify the collateral.

(d) Except as otherwise provided in subsection (e), a description of a security entitlement, securities account, or commodity account is sufficient if it describes:

(1) the collateral by those terms or as investment property; or

(2) the underlying financial asset or commodity contract.

(e) A description only by type of collateral defined in [the Uniform Commercial Code] is an insufficient description of:

(1) a commercial tort claim; or

(2) in a consumer transaction, consumer goods, a security entitlement, a securities account, or a commodity account.

[Subpart 2. Applicability of Article]

§ 9–109. Scope.

(a) Except as otherwise provided in subsections (c) and (d), this article applies to:

(1) a transaction, regardless of its form, that creates a security interest in personal property or fixtures by contract;

(2) an agricultural lien;

(3) a sale of accounts, chattel paper, payment intangibles, or promissory notes;

(4) a consignment;

(5) a security interest arising under Section 2–401, 2–505, 2–711(3), or 2A–508(5), as provided in Section 9–110; and

(6) a security interest arising under Section 4–210 or 5–118.

(b) The application of this article to a security interest in a secured obligation is not affected by the fact that the obligation is itself secured by a transaction or interest to which this article does not apply.

(c) This article does not apply to the extent that:

(1) a statute, regulation, or treaty of the United States preempts this article;

(2) another statute of this State expressly governs the creation, perfection, priority, or enforcement of a security interest created by this State or a governmental unit of this State;

(3) a statute of another State, a foreign country, or a governmental unit of another State or a foreign country, other than a statute generally applicable to security interests, expressly governs creation, perfection, priority, or enforcement of a security interest created by the State, country, or governmental unit; or

(4) the rights of a transferee beneficiary or nominated person under a letter of credit are independent and superior under Section 5–114.

(d) This article does not apply to:

(1) a landlord's lien, other than an agricultural lien;

(2) a lien, other than an agricultural lien, given by statute or other rule of law for services or materials, but Section 9–333 applies with respect to priority of the lien;

(3) an assignment of a claim for wages, salary, or other compensation of an employee;

(4) a sale of accounts, chattel paper, payment intangibles, or promissory notes as part of a sale of the business out of which they arose;

(5) an assignment of accounts, chattel paper, payment intangibles, or promissory notes which is for the purpose of collection only;

(6) an assignment of a right to payment under a contract to an assignee that is also obligated to perform under the contract;

(7) an assignment of a single account, payment intangible, or promissory note to an assignee in full or partial satisfaction of a preexisting indebtedness;

(8) a transfer of an interest in or an assignment of a claim under a policy of insurance, other than an assignment by or to a health-care provider of a health-care-insurance receivable and any subsequent assignment of the right to payment, but Sections 9–315 and 9–322 apply with respect to proceeds and priorities in proceeds;

(9) an assignment of a right represented by a judgment, other than a judgment taken on a right to payment that was collateral;

(10) a right of recoupment or set-off, but:

(A) Section 9–340 applies with respect to the effectiveness of rights of recoupment or set-off against deposit accounts; and

(B) Section 9–404 applies with respect to defenses or claims of an account debtor;

(11) the creation or transfer of an interest in or lien on real property, including a lease or rents thereunder, except to the extent that provision is made for:

(A) liens on real property in Sections 9–203 and 9–308;

(B) fixtures in Section 9–334;

(C) fixture filings in Sections 9–501, 9–502, 9–512, 9–516, and 9–519; and

(D) security agreements covering personal and real property in Section 9–604;

(12) an assignment of a claim arising in tort, other than a commercial tort claim, but Sections 9–315 and 9–322 apply with respect to proceeds and priorities in proceeds; or

(13) an assignment of a deposit account in a consumer transaction, but Sections 9–315 and 9–322 apply with respect to proceeds and priorities in proceeds.

§ 9–110. Security Interests Arising under Article 2 or 2A.

A security interest arising under Section 2–401, 2–505, 2–711(3), or 2A–508(5) is subject to this article. However, until the debtor obtains possession of the goods:

(1) the security interest is enforceable, even if Section 9–203(b)(3) has not been satisfied;

(2) filing is not required to perfect the security interest;

(3) the rights of the secured party after default by the debtor are governed by Article 2 or 2A; and

(4) the security interest has priority over a conflicting security interest created by the debtor.

Part 2 Effectiveness of Security Agreement; Attachment of Security Interest; Rights of Parties to Security Agreement

[Subpart 1. Effectiveness and Attachment]

§ 9–201. General Effectiveness of Security Agreement.

(a) Except as otherwise provided in [the Uniform Commercial Code], a security agreement is effective according to its terms between the parties, against purchasers of the collateral, and against creditors.

(b) A transaction subject to this article is subject to any applicable rule of law which establishes a different rule for consumers and [insert reference to (i) any other statute or regulation that regulates the rates, charges, agreements, and practices for loans, credit sales, or other extensions of credit and (ii) any consumer-protection statute or regulation].

(c) In case of conflict between this article and a rule of law, statute, or regulation described in subsection (b), the rule of law, statute, or regulation controls. Failure to comply with a statute or regulation described in subsection (b) has only the effect the statute or regulation specifies.

(d) This article does not:

(1) validate any rate, charge, agreement, or practice that violates a rule of law, statute, or regulation described in subsection (b); or

(2) extend the application of the rule of law, statute, or regulation to a transaction not otherwise subject to it.

§ 9–202. Title to Collateral Immaterial.

Except as otherwise provided with respect to consignments or sales of accounts, chattel paper, payment intangibles, or promissory notes, the provisions of this article with regard to rights and obligations apply whether title to collateral is in the secured party or the debtor.

§ 9–203. Attachment and Enforceability of Security Interest; Proceeds; Supporting Obligations; Formal Requisites.

(a) A security interest attaches to collateral when it becomes enforceable against the debtor with respect to the collateral, unless an agreement expressly postpones the time of attachment.

(b) Except as otherwise provided in subsections (c) through (i), a security interest is enforceable against the debtor and third parties with respect to the collateral only if:

(1) value has been given;

(2) the debtor has rights in the collateral or the power to transfer rights in the collateral to a secured party; and

(3) one of the following conditions is met:

(A) the debtor has authenticated a security agreement that provides a description of the collateral and, if the security interest covers timber to be cut, a description of the land concerned;

(B) the collateral is not a certificated security and is in the possession of the secured party under Section 9–313 pursuant to the debtor's security agreement;

(C) the collateral is a certificated security in registered form and the security certificate has been delivered to the secured party under Section 8–301 pursuant to the debtor's security agreement; or

(D) the collateral is deposit accounts, electronic chattel paper, investment property, or letter-of-credit rights, and the secured party has control under Section 9–104, 9–105, 9–106, or 9–107 pursuant to the debtor's security agreement.

(c) Subsection (b) is subject to Section 4–210 on the security interest of a collecting bank, Section 5–118 on the security interest of a letter-of-credit issuer or nominated person, Section 9–110 on a security interest arising under Article 2 or 2A, and Section 9–206 on security interests in investment property.

(d) A person becomes bound as debtor by a security agreement entered into by another person if, by operation of law other than this article or by contract:

(1) the security agreement becomes effective to create a security interest in the person's property; or

(2) the person becomes generally obligated for the obligations of the other person, including the obligation secured under the security agreement, and acquires or succeeds to all or substantially all of the assets of the other person.

(e) If a new debtor becomes bound as debtor by a security agreement entered into by another person:

(1) the agreement satisfies subsection (b)(3) with respect to existing or after-acquired property of the new debtor to the extent the property is described in the agreement; and

(2) another agreement is not necessary to make a security interest in the property enforceable.

(f) The attachment of a security interest in collateral gives the secured party the rights to proceeds provided by Section 9–315 and is also attachment of a security interest in a supporting obligation for the collateral.

(g) The attachment of a security interest in a right to payment or performance secured by a security interest or other lien on personal or real property is also attachment of a security interest in the security interest, mortgage, or other lien.

(h) The attachment of a security interest in a securities account is also attachment of a security interest in the security entitlements carried in the securities account.

(i) The attachment of a security interest in a commodity account is also attachment of a security interest in the commodity contracts carried in the commodity account.

§ 9–204. After-Acquired Property; Future Advances.

(a) Except as otherwise provided in subsection (b), a security agreement may create or provide for a security interest in after-acquired collateral.

(b) A security interest does not attach under a term constituting an after-acquired property clause to:

(1) consumer goods, other than an accession when given as additional security, unless the debtor acquires rights in them within 10 days after the secured party gives value; or

(2) a commercial tort claim.

(c) A security agreement may provide that collateral secures, or that accounts, chattel paper, payment intangibles, or promissory notes are sold in connection with, future advances or other value, whether or not the advances or value are given pursuant to commitment.

§ 9–205. Use or Disposition of Collateral Permissible.

(a) A security interest is not invalid or fraudulent against creditors solely because:

(1) the debtor has the right or ability to:

(A) use, commingle, or dispose of all or part of the collateral, including returned or repossessed goods;

(B) collect, compromise, enforce, or otherwise deal with collateral;

(C) accept the return of collateral or make repossessions; or

(D) use, commingle, or dispose of proceeds; or

(2) the secured party fails to require the debtor to account for proceeds or replace collateral.

(b) This section does not relax the requirements of possession if attachment, perfection, or enforcement of a security interest depends upon possession of the collateral by the secured party.

§ 9–206. Security Interest Arising in Purchase or Delivery of Financial Asset.

(a) A security interest in favor of a securities intermediary attaches to a person's security entitlement if:

(1) the person buys a financial asset through the securities intermediary in a transaction in which the person is obligated to pay the purchase price to the securities intermediary at the time of the purchase; and

(2) the securities intermediary credits the financial asset to the buyer's securities account before the buyer pays the securities intermediary.

(b) The security interest described in subsection (a) secures the person's obligation to pay for the financial asset.

(c) A security interest in favor of a person that delivers a certificated security or other financial asset represented by a writing attaches to the security or other financial asset if:

(1) the security or other financial asset:

(A) in the ordinary course of business is transferred by delivery with any necessary indorsement or assignment; and

(B) is delivered under an agreement between persons in the business of dealing with such securities or financial assets; and

(2) the agreement calls for delivery against payment.

(d) The security interest described in subsection (c) secures the obligation to make payment for the delivery.

[Subpart 2. Rights and Duties]

§ 9–207. Rights and Duties of Secured Party Having Possession or Control of Collateral.

(a) Except as otherwise provided in subsection (d), a secured party shall use reasonable care in the custody and preservation of collateral in the secured party's possession. In the case of chattel paper or an instrument, reasonable care includes taking necessary steps to preserve rights against prior parties unless otherwise agreed.

(b) Except as otherwise provided in subsection (d), if a secured party has possession of collateral:

(1) reasonable expenses, including the cost of insurance and payment of taxes or other charges, incurred in the custody, preservation, use, or operation of the collateral are chargeable to the debtor and are secured by the collateral;

(2) the risk of accidental loss or damage is on the debtor to the extent of a deficiency in any effective insurance coverage;

(3) the secured party shall keep the collateral identifiable, but fungible collateral may be commingled; and

(4) the secured party may use or operate the collateral:

(A) for the purpose of preserving the collateral or its value;

(B) as permitted by an order of a court having competent jurisdiction; or

(C) except in the case of consumer goods, in the manner and to the extent agreed by the debtor.

(c) Except as otherwise provided in subsection (d), a secured party having possession of collateral or control of collateral under Section 9–104, 9–105, 9–106, or 9–107:

(1) may hold as additional security any proceeds, except money or funds, received from the collateral;

(2) shall apply money or funds received from the collateral to reduce the secured obligation, unless remitted to the debtor; and

(3) may create a security interest in the collateral.

(d) If the secured party is a buyer of accounts, chattel paper, payment intangibles, or promissory notes or a consignor:

(1) subsection (a) does not apply unless the secured party is entitled under an agreement:

(A) to charge back uncollected collateral; or

(B) otherwise to full or limited recourse against the debtor or a secondary obligor based on the nonpayment or other default of an account debtor or other obligor on the collateral; and

(2) subsections (b) and (c) do not apply.

§ 9–208. Additional Duties of Secured Party Having Control of Collateral.

(a) This section applies to cases in which there is no outstanding secured obligation and the secured party is not committed to make advances, incur obligations, or otherwise give value.

(b) Within 10 days after receiving an authenticated demand by the debtor:

(1) a secured party having control of a deposit account under Section 9–104(a)(2) shall send to the bank with which the deposit account is maintained an authenticated statement that releases the bank from any further obligation to comply with instructions originated by the secured party;

(2) a secured party having control of a deposit account under Section 9–104(a)(3) shall:

(A) pay the debtor the balance on deposit in the deposit account; or

(B) transfer the balance on deposit into a deposit account in the debtor's name;

(3) a secured party, other than a buyer, having control of electronic chattel paper under Section 9–105 shall:

(A) communicate the authoritative copy of the electronic chattel paper to the debtor or its designated custodian;

(B) if the debtor designates a custodian that is the designated custodian with which the authoritative copy of the electronic chattel paper is maintained for the secured party, communicate to the custodian an authenticated record releasing the designated custodian from any further obligation to comply with instructions originated by the secured party and instructing the custodian to comply with instructions originated by the debtor; and

(C) take appropriate action to enable the debtor or its designated custodian to make copies of or revisions to the authoritative copy which add or change an identified assignee of the authoritative copy without the consent of the secured party;

(4) a secured party having control of investment property under Section 8–106(d)(2) or 9–106(b) shall send

to the securities intermediary or commodity intermediary with which the security entitlement or commodity contract is maintained an authenticated record that releases the securities intermediary or commodity intermediary from any further obligation to comply with entitlement orders or directions originated by the secured party; and

(5) a secured party having control of a letter-of-credit right under Section 9–107 shall send to each person having an unfulfilled obligation to pay or deliver proceeds of the letter of credit to the secured party an authenticated release from any further obligation to pay or deliver proceeds of the letter of credit to the secured party.

§ 9–209. Duties of Secured Party If Account Debtor Has Been Notified of Assignment.

(a) Except as otherwise provided in subsection (c), this section applies if:

(1) there is no outstanding secured obligation; and

(2) the secured party is not committed to make advances, incur obligations, or otherwise give value.

(b) Within 10 days after receiving an authenticated demand by the debtor, a secured party shall send to an account debtor that has received notification of an assignment to the secured party as assignee under Section 9–406(a) an authenticated record that releases the account debtor from any further obligation to the secured party.

(c) This section does not apply to an assignment constituting the sale of an account, chattel paper, or payment intangible.

§ 9–210. Request for Accounting; Request Regarding List of Collateral or Statement of Account.

(a) In this section:

(1) "Request" means a record of a type described in paragraph (2), (3), or (4).

(2) "Request for an accounting" means a record authenticated by a debtor requesting that the recipient provide an accounting of the unpaid obligations secured by collateral and reasonably identifying the transaction or relationship that is the subject of the request.

(3) "Request regarding a list of collateral" means a record authenticated by a debtor requesting that the recipient approve or correct a list of what the debtor believes to be the collateral securing an obligation and reasonably identifying the transaction or relationship that is the subject of the request.

(4) "Request regarding a statement of account" means a record authenticated by a debtor requesting that the recipient approve or correct a statement indicating what the debtor believes to be the aggregate amount of unpaid obligations secured by collateral as of a specified date and reasonably identifying the transaction or relationship that is the subject of the request.

(b) Subject to subsections (c), (d), (e), and (f), a secured party, other than a buyer of accounts, chattel paper, payment intangibles, or promissory notes or a consignor, shall comply with a request within 14 days after receipt:

(1) in the case of a request for an accounting, by authenticating and sending to the debtor an accounting; and

(2) in the case of a request regarding a list of collateral or a request regarding a statement of account, by authenticating and sending to the debtor an approval or correction.

(c) A secured party that claims a security interest in all of a particular type of collateral owned by the debtor may comply with a request regarding a list of collateral by sending to the debtor an authenticated record including a statement to that effect within 14 days after receipt.

(d) A person that receives a request regarding a list of collateral, claims no interest in the collateral when it receives the request, and claimed an interest in the collateral at an earlier time shall comply with the request within 14 days after receipt by sending to the debtor an authenticated record:

(1) disclaiming any interest in the collateral; and

(2) if known to the recipient, providing the name and mailing address of any assignee of or successor to the recipient's interest in the collateral.

(e) A person that receives a request for an accounting or a request regarding a statement of account, claims no interest in the obligations when it receives the request, and claimed an interest in the obligations at an earlier time shall comply with the request within 14 days after receipt by sending to the debtor an authenticated record:

(1) disclaiming any interest in the obligations; and

(2) if known to the recipient, providing the name and mailing address of any assignee of or successor to the recipient's interest in the obligations.

(f) A debtor is entitled without charge to one response to a request under this section during any six-month period. The secured party may require payment of a charge not exceeding $25 for each additional response.

As amended in 1999.

Part 3 Perfection and Priority

[Subpart 1. Law Governing Perfection and Priority]

§ 9–301. Law Governing Perfection and Priority of Security Interests.

Except as otherwise provided in Sections 9–303 through 9–306, the following rules determine the law governing perfection, the effect of perfection or nonperfection, and the priority of a security interest in collateral:

(1) Except as otherwise provided in this section, while a debtor is located in a jurisdiction, the local law of that jurisdiction governs perfection, the effect of perfection or

nonperfection, and the priority of a security interest in collateral.

(2) While collateral is located in a jurisdiction, the local law of that jurisdiction governs perfection, the effect of perfection or nonperfection, and the priority of a possessory security interest in that collateral.

(3) Except as otherwise provided in paragraph (4), while negotiable documents, goods, instruments, money, or tangible chattel paper is located in a jurisdiction, the local law of that jurisdiction governs:

(A) perfection of a security interest in the goods by filing a fixture filing;

(B) perfection of a security interest in timber to be cut; and

(C) the effect of perfection or nonperfection and the priority of a nonpossessory security interest in the collateral.

(4) The local law of the jurisdiction in which the wellhead or minehead is located governs perfection, the effect of perfection or nonperfection, and the priority of a security interest in as-extracted collateral.

§ 9–302. Law Governing Perfection and Priority of Agricultural Liens.

While farm products are located in a jurisdiction, the local law of that jurisdiction governs perfection, the effect of perfection or nonperfection, and the priority of an agricultural lien on the farm products.

§ 9–303. Law Governing Perfection and Priority of Security Interests in Goods Covered by a Certificate of Title.

(a) This section applies to goods covered by a certificate of title, even if there is no other relationship between the jurisdiction under whose certificate of title the goods are covered and the goods or the debtor.

(b) Goods become covered by a certificate of title when a valid application for the certificate of title and the applicable fee are delivered to the appropriate authority. Goods cease to be covered by a certificate of title at the earlier of the time the certificate of title ceases to be effective under the law of the issuing jurisdiction or the time the goods become covered subsequently by a certificate of title issued by another jurisdiction.

(c) The local law of the jurisdiction under whose certificate of title the goods are covered governs perfection, the effect of perfection or nonperfection, and the priority of a security interest in goods covered by a certificate of title from the time the goods become covered by the certificate of title until the goods cease to be covered by the certificate of title.

§ 9–304. Law Governing Perfection and Priority of Security Interests in Deposit Accounts.

(a) The local law of a bank's jurisdiction governs perfection, the effect of perfection or nonperfection, and the priority of a security interest in a deposit account maintained with that bank.

(b) The following rules determine a bank's jurisdiction for purposes of this part:

(1) If an agreement between the bank and the debtor governing the deposit account expressly provides that a particular jurisdiction is the bank's jurisdiction for purposes of this part, this article, or [the Uniform Commercial Code], that jurisdiction is the bank's jurisdiction.

(2) If paragraph (1) does not apply and an agreement between the bank and its customer governing the deposit account expressly provides that the agreement is governed by the law of a particular jurisdiction, that jurisdiction is the bank's jurisdiction.

(3) If neither paragraph (1) nor paragraph (2) applies and an agreement between the bank and its customer governing the deposit account expressly provides that the deposit account is maintained at an office in a particular jurisdiction, that jurisdiction is the bank's jurisdiction.

(4) If none of the preceding paragraphs applies, the bank's jurisdiction is the jurisdiction in which the office identified in an account statement as the office serving the customer's account is located.

(5) If none of the preceding paragraphs applies, the bank's jurisdiction is the jurisdiction in which the chief executive office of the bank is located.

§ 9–305. Law Governing Perfection and Priority of Security Interests in Investment Property.

(a) Except as otherwise provided in subsection (c), the following rules apply:

(1) While a security certificate is located in a jurisdiction, the local law of that jurisdiction governs perfection, the effect of perfection or nonperfection, and the priority of a security interest in the certificated security represented thereby.

(2) The local law of the issuer's jurisdiction as specified in Section 8–110(d) governs perfection, the effect of perfection or nonperfection, and the priority of a security interest in an uncertificated security.

(3) The local law of the securities intermediary's jurisdiction as specified in Section 8–110(e) governs perfection, the effect of perfection or nonperfection, and the priority of a security interest in a security entitlement or securities account.

(4) The local law of the commodity intermediary's jurisdiction governs perfection, the effect of perfection or nonperfection, and the priority of a security interest in a commodity contract or commodity account.

(b) The following rules determine a commodity intermediary's jurisdiction for purposes of this part:

(1) If an agreement between the commodity intermediary and commodity customer governing the commod-

ity account expressly provides that a particular jurisdiction is the commodity intermediary's jurisdiction for purposes of this part, this article, or [the Uniform Commercial Code], that jurisdiction is the commodity intermediary's jurisdiction.

(2) If paragraph (1) does not apply and an agreement between the commodity intermediary and commodity customer governing the commodity account expressly provides that the agreement is governed by the law of a particular jurisdiction, that jurisdiction is the commodity intermediary's jurisdiction.

(3) If neither paragraph (1) nor paragraph (2) applies and an agreement between the commodity intermediary and commodity customer governing the commodity account expressly provides that the commodity account is maintained at an office in a particular jurisdiction, that jurisdiction is the commodity intermediary's jurisdiction.

(4) If none of the preceding paragraphs applies, the commodity intermediary's jurisdiction is the jurisdiction in which the office identified in an account statement as the office serving the commodity customer's account is located.

(5) If none of the preceding paragraphs applies, the commodity intermediary's jurisdiction is the jurisdiction in which the chief executive office of the commodity intermediary is located.

(c) The local law of the jurisdiction in which the debtor is located governs:

(1) perfection of a security interest in investment property by filing;

(2) automatic perfection of a security interest in investment property created by a broker or securities intermediary; and

(3) automatic perfection of a security interest in a commodity contract or commodity account created by a commodity intermediary.

§ 9–306. Law Governing Perfection and Priority of Security Interests in Letter-of-Credit Rights.

(a) Subject to subsection (c), the local law of the issuer's jurisdiction or a nominated person's jurisdiction governs perfection, the effect of perfection or nonperfection, and the priority of a security interest in a letter-of-credit right if the issuer's jurisdiction or nominated person's jurisdiction is a State.

(b) For purposes of this part, an issuer's jurisdiction or nominated person's jurisdiction is the jurisdiction whose law governs the liability of the issuer or nominated person with respect to the letter-of-credit right as provided in Section 5–116.

(c) This section does not apply to a security interest that is perfected only under Section 9–308(d).

§ 9–307. Location of Debtor.

(a) In this section, "place of business" means a place where a debtor conducts its affairs.

(b) Except as otherwise provided in this section, the following rules determine a debtor's location:

(1) A debtor who is an individual is located at the individual's principal residence.

(2) A debtor that is an organization and has only one place of business is located at its place of business.

(3) A debtor that is an organization and has more than one place of business is located at its chief executive office.

(c) Subsection (b) applies only if a debtor's residence, place of business, or chief executive office, as applicable, is located in a jurisdiction whose law generally requires information concerning the existence of a nonpossessory security interest to be made generally available in a filing, recording, or registration system as a condition or result of the security interest's obtaining priority over the rights of a lien creditor with respect to the collateral. If subsection (b) does not apply, the debtor is located in the District of Columbia.

(d) A person that ceases to exist, have a residence, or have a place of business continues to be located in the jurisdiction specified by subsections (b) and (c).

(e) A registered organization that is organized under the law of a State is located in that State.

(f) Except as otherwise provided in subsection (i), a registered organization that is organized under the law of the United States and a branch or agency of a bank that is not organized under the law of the United States or a State are located:

(1) in the State that the law of the United States designates, if the law designates a State of location;

(2) in the State that the registered organization, branch, or agency designates, if the law of the United States authorizes the registered organization, branch, or agency to designate its State of location; or

(3) in the District of Columbia, if neither paragraph (1) nor paragraph (2) applies.

(g) A registered organization continues to be located in the jurisdiction specified by subsection (e) or (f) notwithstanding:

(1) the suspension, revocation, forfeiture, or lapse of the registered organization's status as such in its jurisdiction of organization; or

(2) the dissolution, winding up, or cancellation of the existence of the registered organization.

(h) The United States is located in the District of Columbia.

(i) A branch or agency of a bank that is not organized under the law of the United States or a State is located in the State in which the branch or agency is licensed, if all branches and agencies of the bank are licensed in only one State.

(j) A foreign air carrier under the Federal Aviation Act of 1958, as amended, is located at the designated office of the agent upon which service of process may be made on behalf of the carrier.

(k) This section applies only for purposes of this part.

[Subpart 2. Perfection]

§ 9–308. When Security Interest or Agricultural Lien Is Perfected; Continuity of Perfection.

(a) Except as otherwise provided in this section and Section 9–309, a security interest is perfected if it has attached and all of the applicable requirements for perfection in Sections 9–310 through 9–316 have been satisfied. A security interest is perfected when it attaches if the applicable requirements are satisfied before the security interest attaches.

(b) An agricultural lien is perfected if it has become effective and all of the applicable requirements for perfection in Section 9–310 have been satisfied. An agricultural lien is perfected when it becomes effective if the applicable requirements are satisfied before the agricultural lien becomes effective.

(c) A security interest or agricultural lien is perfected continuously if it is originally perfected by one method under this article and is later perfected by another method under this article, without an intermediate period when it was unperfected.

(d) Perfection of a security interest in collateral also perfects a security interest in a supporting obligation for the collateral.

(e) Perfection of a security interest in a right to payment or performance also perfects a security interest in a security interest, mortgage, or other lien on personal or real property securing the right.

(f) Perfection of a security interest in a securities account also perfects a security interest in the security entitlements carried in the securities account.

(g) Perfection of a security interest in a commodity account also perfects a security interest in the commodity contracts carried in the commodity account.

Legislative Note: Any statute conflicting with subsection (e) must be made expressly subject to that subsection.

§ 9–309. Security Interest Perfected upon Attachment.

The following security interests are perfected when they attach:

(1) a purchase-money security interest in consumer goods, except as otherwise provided in Section 9–311(b) with respect to consumer goods that are subject to a statute or treaty described in Section 9–311(a);

(2) an assignment of accounts or payment intangibles which does not by itself or in conjunction with other assignments to the same assignee transfer a significant part of the assignor's outstanding accounts or payment intangibles;

(3) a sale of a payment intangible;

(4) a sale of a promissory note;

(5) a security interest created by the assignment of a health-care-insurance receivable to the provider of the health-care goods or services;

(6) a security interest arising under Section 2–401, 2–505, 2–711(3), or 2A–508(5), until the debtor obtains possession of the collateral;

(7) a security interest of a collecting bank arising under Section 4–210;

(8) a security interest of an issuer or nominated person arising under Section 5–118;

(9) a security interest arising in the delivery of a financial asset under Section 9–206(c);

(10) a security interest in investment property created by a broker or securities intermediary;

(11) a security interest in a commodity contract or a commodity account created by a commodity intermediary;

(12) an assignment for the benefit of all creditors of the transferor and subsequent transfers by the assignee thereunder; and

(13) a security interest created by an assignment of a beneficial interest in a decedent's estate; and

(14) a sale by an individual of an account that is a right to payment of winnings in a lottery or other game of chance.

§ 9–310. When Filing Required to Perfect Security Interest or Agricultural Lien; Security Interests and Agricultural Liens to Which Filing Provisions Do Not Apply.

(a) Except as otherwise provided in subsection (b) and Section 9–312(b), a financing statement must be filed to perfect all security interests and agricultural liens.

(b) The filing of a financing statement is not necessary to perfect a security interest:

(1) that is perfected under Section 9–308(d), (e), (f), or (g);

(2) that is perfected under Section 9–309 when it attaches;

(3) in property subject to a statute, regulation, or treaty described in Section 9–311(a);

(4) in goods in possession of a bailee which is perfected under Section 9–312(d)(1) or (2);

(5) in certificated securities, documents, goods, or instruments which is perfected without filing or possession under Section 9–312(e), (f), or (g);

(6) in collateral in the secured party's possession under Section 9–313;

(7) in a certificated security which is perfected by delivery of the security certificate to the secured party under Section 9–313;

(8) in deposit accounts, electronic chattel paper, investment property, or letter-of-credit rights which is perfected by control under Section 9–314;

(9) in proceeds which is perfected under Section 9–315; or

(10) that is perfected under Section 9–316.

(c) If a secured party assigns a perfected security interest or agricultural lien, a filing under this article is not required to continue the perfected status of the security interest against creditors of and transferees from the original debtor.

§ 9–311. Perfection of Security Interests in Property Subject to Certain Statutes, Regulations, and Treaties.

(a) Except as otherwise provided in subsection (d), the filing of a financing statement is not necessary or effective to perfect a security interest in property subject to:

(1) a statute, regulation, or treaty of the United States whose requirements for a security interest's obtaining priority over the rights of a lien creditor with respect to the property preempt Section 9–310(a);

(2) [list any certificate-of-title statute covering automobiles, trailers, mobile homes, boats, farm tractors, or the like, which provides for a security interest to be indicated on the certificate as a condition or result of perfection, and any non-Uniform Commercial Code central filing statute]; or

(3) a certificate-of-title statute of another jurisdiction which provides for a security interest to be indicated on the certificate as a condition or result of the security interest's obtaining priority over the rights of a lien creditor with respect to the property.

(b) Compliance with the requirements of a statute, regulation, or treaty described in subsection (a) for obtaining priority over the rights of a lien creditor is equivalent to the filing of a financing statement under this article. Except as otherwise provided in subsection (d) and Sections 9–313 and 9–316(d) and (e) for goods covered by a certificate of title, a security interest in property subject to a statute, regulation, or treaty described in subsection (a) may be perfected only by compliance with those requirements, and a security interest so perfected remains perfected notwithstanding a change in the use or transfer of possession of the collateral.

(c) Except as otherwise provided in subsection (d) and Section 9–316(d) and (e), duration and renewal of perfection of a security interest perfected by compliance with the requirements prescribed by a statute, regulation, or treaty described in subsection (a) are governed by the statute, regulation, or treaty. In other respects, the security interest is subject to this article.

(d) During any period in which collateral subject to a statute specified in subsection (a)(2) is inventory held for sale or lease by a person or leased by that person as lessor and that person is in the business of selling goods of that kind, this section does not apply to a security interest in that collateral created by that person.

Legislative Note: This Article contemplates that perfection of a security interest in goods covered by a certificate of title occurs upon receipt by appropriate State officials of a properly tendered application for a certificate of title on which the security interest is to be indicated, without a relation back to an earlier time. States whose certificate-of-title statutes provide for perfection at a different time or contain a relation-back provision should amend the statutes accordingly.

§ 9–312. Perfection of Security Interests in Chattel Paper, Deposit Accounts, Documents, Goods Covered by Documents, Instruments, Investment Property, Letter-of-Credit Rights, and Money; Perfection by Permissive Filing; Temporary Perfection without Filing or Transfer of Possession.

(a) A security interest in chattel paper, negotiable documents, instruments, or investment property may be perfected by filing.

(b) Except as otherwise provided in Section 9–315(c) and (d) for proceeds:

(1) a security interest in a deposit account may be perfected only by control under Section 9–314;

(2) and except as otherwise provided in Section 9–308(d), a security interest in a letter-of-credit right may be perfected only by control under Section 9–314; and

(3) a security interest in money may be perfected only by the secured party's taking possession under Section 9–313.

(c) While goods are in the possession of a bailee that has issued a negotiable document covering the goods:

(1) a security interest in the goods may be perfected by perfecting a security interest in the document; and

(2) a security interest perfected in the document has priority over any security interest that becomes perfected in the goods by another method during that time.

(d) While goods are in the possession of a bailee that has issued a nonnegotiable document covering the goods, a security interest in the goods may be perfected by:

(1) issuance of a document in the name of the secured party;

(2) the bailee's receipt of notification of the secured party's interest; or

(3) filing as to the goods.

(e) A security interest in certificated securities, negotiable documents, or instruments is perfected without filing or the taking of possession for a period of 20 days from the time it attaches to the extent that it arises for new value given under an authenticated security agreement.

(f) A perfected security interest in a negotiable document or goods in possession of a bailee, other than one that has issued a negotiable document for the goods, remains perfected for 20 days without filing if the secured party makes available to the debtor the goods or documents representing the goods for the purpose of:

(1) ultimate sale or exchange; or

(2) loading, unloading, storing, shipping, transshipping, manufacturing, processing, or otherwise dealing with them in a manner preliminary to their sale or exchange.

(g) A perfected security interest in a certificated security or instrument remains perfected for 20 days without filing if the secured party delivers the security certificate or instrument to the debtor for the purpose of:

(1) ultimate sale or exchange; or

(2) presentation, collection, enforcement, renewal, or registration of transfer.

(h) After the 20-day period specified in subsection (e), (f), or (g) expires, perfection depends upon compliance with this article.

§ 9–313. When Possession by or Delivery to Secured Party Perfects Security Interest without Filing.

(a) Except as otherwise provided in subsection (b), a secured party may perfect a security interest in negotiable documents, goods, instruments, money, or tangible chattel paper by taking possession of the collateral. A secured party may perfect a security interest in certificated securities by taking delivery of the certificated securities under Section 8–301.

(b) With respect to goods covered by a certificate of title issued by this State, a secured party may perfect a security interest in the goods by taking possession of the goods only in the circumstances described in Section 9–316(d).

(c) With respect to collateral other than certificated securities and goods covered by a document, a secured party takes possession of collateral in the possession of a person other than the debtor, the secured party, or a lessee of the collateral from the debtor in the ordinary course of the debtor's business, when:

(1) the person in possession authenticates a record acknowledging that it holds possession of the collateral for the secured party's benefit; or

(2) the person takes possession of the collateral after having authenticated a record acknowledging that it will hold possession of collateral for the secured party's benefit.

(d) If perfection of a security interest depends upon possession of the collateral by a secured party, perfection occurs no earlier than the time the secured party takes possession and continues only while the secured party retains possession.

(e) A security interest in a certificated security in registered form is perfected by delivery when delivery of the certificated security occurs under Section 8–301 and remains perfected by delivery until the debtor obtains possession of the security certificate.

(f) A person in possession of collateral is not required to acknowledge that it holds possession for a secured party's benefit.

(g) If a person acknowledges that it holds possession for the secured party's benefit:

(1) the acknowledgment is effective under subsection (c) or Section 8–301(a), even if the acknowledgment violates the rights of a debtor; and

(2) unless the person otherwise agrees or law other than this article otherwise provides, the person does not owe any duty to the secured party and is not required to confirm the acknowledgment to another person.

(h) A secured party having possession of collateral does not relinquish possession by delivering the collateral to a person other than the debtor or a lessee of the collateral from the debtor in the ordinary course of the debtor's business if the person was instructed before the delivery or is instructed contemporaneously with the delivery:

(1) to hold possession of the collateral for the secured party's benefit; or

(2) to redeliver the collateral to the secured party.

(i) A secured party does not relinquish possession, even if a delivery under subsection (h) violates the rights of a debtor. A person to which collateral is delivered under subsection (h) does not owe any duty to the secured party and is not required to confirm the delivery to another person unless the person otherwise agrees or law other than this article otherwise provides.

§ 9–314. Perfection by Control.

(a) A security interest in investment property, deposit accounts, letter-of-credit rights, or electronic chattel paper may be perfected by control of the collateral under Section 9–104, 9–105, 9–106, or 9–107.

(b) A security interest in deposit accounts, electronic chattel paper, or letter-of-credit rights is perfected by control under Section 9–104, 9–105, or 9–107 when the secured party obtains control and remains perfected by control only while the secured party retains control.

(c) A security interest in investment property is perfected by control under Section 9–106 from the time the secured party obtains control and remains perfected by control until:

(1) the secured party does not have control; and

(2) one of the following occurs:

(A) if the collateral is a certificated security, the debtor has or acquires possession of the security certificate;

(B) if the collateral is an uncertificated security, the issuer has registered or registers the debtor as the registered owner; or

(C) if the collateral is a security entitlement, the debtor is or becomes the entitlement holder.

§ 9–315. Secured Party's Rights on Disposition of Collateral and in Proceeds.

(a) Except as otherwise provided in this article and in Section 2–403(2):

(1) a security interest or agricultural lien continues in collateral notwithstanding sale, lease, license, exchange, or other disposition thereof unless the secured party authorized the disposition free of the security interest or agricultural lien; and

(2) a security interest attaches to any identifiable proceeds of collateral.

(b) Proceeds that are commingled with other property are identifiable proceeds:

(1) if the proceeds are goods, to the extent provided by Section 9–336; and

(2) if the proceeds are not goods, to the extent that the secured party identifies the proceeds by a method of tracing, including application of equitable principles, that is permitted under law other than this article with respect to commingled property of the type involved.

(c) A security interest in proceeds is a perfected security interest if the security interest in the original collateral was perfected.

(d) A perfected security interest in proceeds becomes unperfected on the 21st day after the security interest attaches to the proceeds unless:

(1) the following conditions are satisfied:

(A) a filed financing statement covers the original collateral;

(B) the proceeds are collateral in which a security interest may be perfected by filing in the office in which the financing statement has been filed; and

(C) the proceeds are not acquired with cash proceeds;

(2) the proceeds are identifiable cash proceeds; or

(3) the security interest in the proceeds is perfected other than under subsection (c) when the security interest attaches to the proceeds or within 20 days thereafter.

(e) If a filed financing statement covers the original collateral, a security interest in proceeds which remains perfected under subsection (d)(1) becomes unperfected at the later of:

(1) when the effectiveness of the filed financing statement lapses under Section 9–515 or is terminated under Section 9–513; or

(2) the 21st day after the security interest attaches to the proceeds.

§ 9–316. Continued Perfection of Security Interest Following Change in Governing Law.

(a) A security interest perfected pursuant to the law of the jurisdiction designated in Section 9–301(1) or 9–305(c) remains perfected until the earliest of:

(1) the time perfection would have ceased under the law of that jurisdiction;

(2) the expiration of four months after a change of the debtor's location to another jurisdiction; or

(3) the expiration of one year after a transfer of collateral to a person that thereby becomes a debtor and is located in another jurisdiction.

(b) If a security interest described in subsection (a) becomes perfected under the law of the other jurisdiction before the earliest time or event described in that subsection, it remains perfected thereafter. If the security interest does not become perfected under the law of the other jurisdiction before the earliest time or event, it becomes unperfected and is deemed never to have been perfected as against a purchaser of the collateral for value.

(c) A possessory security interest in collateral, other than goods covered by a certificate of title and as-extracted collateral consisting of goods, remains continuously perfected if:

(1) the collateral is located in one jurisdiction and subject to a security interest perfected under the law of that jurisdiction;

(2) thereafter the collateral is brought into another jurisdiction; and

(3) upon entry into the other jurisdiction, the security interest is perfected under the law of the other jurisdiction.

(d) Except as otherwise provided in subsection (e), a security interest in goods covered by a certificate of title which is perfected by any method under the law of another jurisdiction when the goods become covered by a certificate of title from this State remains perfected until the security interest would have become unperfected under the law of the other jurisdiction had the goods not become so covered.

(e) A security interest described in subsection (d) becomes unperfected as against a purchaser of the goods for value and is deemed never to have been perfected as against a purchaser of the goods for value if the applicable requirements for perfection under Section 9–311(b) or 9–313 are not satisfied before the earlier of:

(1) the time the security interest would have become unperfected under the law of the other jurisdiction had the goods not become covered by a certificate of title from this State; or

(2) the expiration of four months after the goods had become so covered.

(f) A security interest in deposit accounts, letter-of-credit rights, or investment property which is perfected under the law of the bank's jurisdiction, the issuer's jurisdiction, a nominated person's jurisdiction, the securities intermediary's jurisdiction, or the commodity intermediary's jurisdiction, as applicable, remains perfected until the earlier of:

(1) the time the security interest would have become unperfected under the law of that jurisdiction; or

(2) the expiration of four months after a change of the applicable jurisdiction to another jurisdiction.

(g) If a security interest described in subsection (f) becomes perfected under the law of the other jurisdiction before the earlier of the time or the end of the period described in that subsection, it remains perfected thereafter. If the security interest does not become perfected under the law of the other jurisdiction before the earlier of that time or the end of that period, it becomes unperfected and is deemed never to have been perfected as against a purchaser of the collateral for value.

[Subpart 3. Priority]

§ 9–317. Interests That Take Priority over or Take Free of Security Interest or Agricultural Lien.

(a) A security interest or agricultural lien is subordinate to the rights of:

(1) a person entitled to priority under Section 9–322; and

(2) except as otherwise provided in subsection (e), a person that becomes a lien creditor before the earlier of the time:

(A) the security interest or agricultural lien is perfected; or

(B) one of the conditions specified in Section 9–203(b)(3) is met and a financing statement covering the collateral is filed.

(b) Except as otherwise provided in subsection (e), a buyer, other than a secured party, of tangible chattel paper, documents, goods, instruments, or a security certificate takes free of a security interest or agricultural lien if the buyer gives value and receives delivery of the collateral without knowledge of the security interest or agricultural lien and before it is perfected.

(c) Except as otherwise provided in subsection (e), a lessee of goods takes free of a security interest or agricultural lien if the lessee gives value and receives delivery of the collateral without knowledge of the security interest or agricultural lien and before it is perfected.

(d) A licensee of a general intangible or a buyer, other than a secured party, of accounts, electronic chattel paper, general intangibles, or investment property other than a certificated security takes free of a security interest if the licensee or buyer gives value without knowledge of the security interest and before it is perfected.

(e) Except as otherwise provided in Sections 9–320 and 9–321, if a person files a financing statement with respect to a purchase-money security interest before or within 20 days after the debtor receives delivery of the collateral, the security interest takes priority over the rights of a buyer, lessee, or lien creditor which arise between the time the security interest attaches and the time of filing.

As amended in 2000.

§ 9–318. No Interest Retained in Right to Payment That Is Sold; Rights and Title of Seller of Account or Chattel Paper with Respect to Creditors and Purchasers.

(a) A debtor that has sold an account, chattel paper, payment intangible, or promissory note does not retain a legal or equitable interest in the collateral sold.

(b) For purposes of determining the rights of creditors of, and purchasers for value of an account or chattel paper from, a debtor that has sold an account or chattel paper, while the buyer's security interest is unperfected, the debtor is deemed to have rights and title to the account or chattel paper identical to those the debtor sold.

§ 9–319. Rights and Title of Consignee with Respect to Creditors and Purchasers.

(a) Except as otherwise provided in subsection (b), for purposes of determining the rights of creditors of, and purchasers for value of goods from, a consignee, while the goods are in the possession of the consignee, the consignee is deemed to have rights and title to the goods identical to those the consignor had or had power to transfer.

(b) For purposes of determining the rights of a creditor of a consignee, law other than this article determines the rights and title of a consignee while goods are in the consignee's possession if, under this part, a perfected security interest held by the consignor would have priority over the rights of the creditor.

§ 9–320. Buyer of Goods.

(a) Except as otherwise provided in subsection (e), a buyer in ordinary course of business, other than a person buying farm products from a person engaged in farming operations, takes free of a security interest created by the buyer's seller, even if the security interest is perfected and the buyer knows of its existence.

(b) Except as otherwise provided in subsection (e), a buyer of goods from a person who used or bought the goods for use primarily for personal, family, or household purposes takes free of a security interest, even if perfected, if the buyer buys:

(1) without knowledge of the security interest;

(2) for value;

(3) primarily for the buyer's personal, family, or household purposes; and

(4) before the filing of a financing statement covering the goods.

(c) To the extent that it affects the priority of a security interest over a buyer of goods under subsection (b), the period of effectiveness of a filing made in the jurisdiction in which the seller is located is governed by Section 9–316(a) and (b).

(d) A buyer in ordinary course of business buying oil, gas, or other minerals at the wellhead or minehead or after extraction takes free of an interest arising out of an encumbrance.

(e) Subsections (a) and (b) do not affect a security interest in goods in the possession of the secured party under Section 9–313.

§ 9–321. Licensee of General Intangible and Lessee of Goods in Ordinary Course of Business.

(a) In this section, "licensee in ordinary course of business" means a person that becomes a licensee of a general intangible in good faith, without knowledge that the license violates the rights of another person in the general intangible, and in the ordinary course from a person in the business of licensing general intangibles of that kind. A person becomes a licensee in the ordinary course if the license to the person comports with the usual or customary practices in the kind of business in which the licensor is engaged or with the licensor's own usual or customary practices.

(b) A licensee in ordinary course of business takes its rights under a nonexclusive license free of a security interest in the general intangible created by the licensor, even if the security interest is perfected and the licensee knows of its existence.

(c) A lessee in ordinary course of business takes its leasehold interest free of a security interest in the goods created by the lessor, even if the security interest is perfected and the lessee knows of its existence.

§ 9–322. Priorities among Conflicting Security Interests in and Agricultural Liens on Same Collateral.

(a) Except as otherwise provided in this section, priority among conflicting security interests and agricultural liens in the same collateral is determined according to the following rules:

(1) Conflicting perfected security interests and agricultural liens rank according to priority in time of filing or perfection. Priority dates from the earlier of the time a filing covering the collateral is first made or the security interest or agricultural lien is first perfected, if there is no period thereafter when there is neither filing nor perfection.

(2) A perfected security interest or agricultural lien has priority over a conflicting unperfected security interest or agricultural lien.

(3) The first security interest or agricultural lien to attach or become effective has priority if conflicting security interests and agricultural liens are unperfected.

(b) For the purposes of subsection (a)(1):

(1) the time of filing or perfection as to a security interest in collateral is also the time of filing or perfection as to a security interest in proceeds; and

(2) the time of filing or perfection as to a security interest in collateral supported by a supporting obligation is also the time of filing or perfection as to a security interest in the supporting obligation.

(c) Except as otherwise provided in subsection (f), a security interest in collateral which qualifies for priority over a conflicting security interest under Section 9–327, 9–328, 9–329, 9–330, or 9–331 also has priority over a conflicting security interest in:

    (1) any supporting obligation for the collateral; and

    (2) proceeds of the collateral if:

        (A) the security interest in proceeds is perfected;

        (B) the proceeds are cash proceeds or of the same type as the collateral; and

        (C) in the case of proceeds that are proceeds of proceeds, all intervening proceeds are cash proceeds, proceeds of the same type as the collateral, or an account relating to the collateral.

(d) Subject to subsection (e) and except as otherwise provided in subsection (f), if a security interest in chattel paper, deposit accounts, negotiable documents, instruments, investment property, or letter-of-credit rights is perfected by a method other than filing, conflicting perfected security interests in proceeds of the collateral rank according to priority in time of filing.

(e) Subsection (d) applies only if the proceeds of the collateral are not cash proceeds, chattel paper, negotiable documents, instruments, investment property, or letter-of-credit rights.

(f) Subsections (a) through (e) are subject to:

    (1) subsection (g) and the other provisions of this part;

    (2) Section 4–210 with respect to a security interest of a collecting bank;

    (3) Section 5–118 with respect to a security interest of an issuer or nominated person; and

    (4) Section 9–110 with respect to a security interest arising under Article 2 or 2A.

(g) A perfected agricultural lien on collateral has priority over a conflicting security interest in or agricultural lien on the same collateral if the statute creating the agricultural lien so provides.

§ 9–323. Future Advances.

(a) Except as otherwise provided in subsection (c), for purposes of determining the priority of a perfected security interest under Section 9–322(a)(1), perfection of the security interest dates from the time an advance is made to the extent that the security interest secures an advance that:

    (1) is made while the security interest is perfected only:

        (A) under Section 9–309 when it attaches; or

        (B) temporarily under Section 9–312(e), (f), or (g); and

    (2) is not made pursuant to a commitment entered into before or while the security interest is perfected by a method other than under Section 9–309 or 9–312(e), (f), or (g).

(b) Except as otherwise provided in subsection (c), a security interest is subordinate to the rights of a person that becomes a lien creditor to the extent that the security interest secures an advance made more than 45 days after the person becomes a lien creditor unless the advance is made:

    (1) without knowledge of the lien; or

    (2) pursuant to a commitment entered into without knowledge of the lien.

(c) Subsections (a) and (b) do not apply to a security interest held by a secured party that is a buyer of accounts, chattel paper, payment intangibles, or promissory notes or a consignor.

(d) Except as otherwise provided in subsection (e), a buyer of goods other than a buyer in ordinary course of business takes free of a security interest to the extent that it secures advances made after the earlier of:

    (1) the time the secured party acquires knowledge of the buyer's purchase; or

    (2) 45 days after the purchase.

(e) Subsection (d) does not apply if the advance is made pursuant to a commitment entered into without knowledge of the buyer's purchase and before the expiration of the 45-day period.

(f) Except as otherwise provided in subsection (g), a lessee of goods, other than a lessee in ordinary course of business, takes the leasehold interest free of a security interest to the extent that it secures advances made after the earlier of:

    (1) the time the secured party acquires knowledge of the lease; or

    (2) 45 days after the lease contract becomes enforceable.

(g) Subsection (f) does not apply if the advance is made pursuant to a commitment entered into without knowledge of the lease and before the expiration of the 45-day period. As amended in 1999.

§ 9–324. Priority of Purchase-Money Security Interests.

(a) Except as otherwise provided in subsection (g), a perfected purchase-money security interest in goods other than inventory or livestock has priority over a conflicting security interest in the same goods, and, except as otherwise provided in Section 9–327, a perfected security interest in its identifiable proceeds also has priority, if the purchase-money security interest is perfected when the debtor receives possession of the collateral or within 20 days thereafter.

(b) Subject to subsection (c) and except as otherwise provided in subsection (g), a perfected purchase-money security interest in inventory has priority over a conflicting security interest in the same inventory, has priority over a conflicting security interest in chattel paper or an instrument constituting proceeds of the inventory and in proceeds of the chattel paper, if so provided in Section 9–330, and, except as otherwise provided in Section 9–327, also has priority in identifiable cash proceeds of the inventory to the extent the identifiable cash proceeds are received on or before the delivery of the inventory to a buyer, if:

(1) the purchase-money security interest is perfected when the debtor receives possession of the inventory;

(2) the purchase-money secured party sends an authenticated notification to the holder of the conflicting security interest;

(3) the holder of the conflicting security interest receives the notification within five years before the debtor receives possession of the inventory; and

(4) the notification states that the person sending the notification has or expects to acquire a purchase-money security interest in inventory of the debtor and describes the inventory.

(c) Subsections (b)(2) through (4) apply only if the holder of the conflicting security interest had filed a financing statement covering the same types of inventory:

(1) if the purchase-money security interest is perfected by filing, before the date of the filing; or

(2) if the purchase-money security interest is temporarily perfected without filing or possession under Section 9–312(f), before the beginning of the 20-day period thereunder.

(d) Subject to subsection (e) and except as otherwise provided in subsection (g), a perfected purchase-money security interest in livestock that are farm products has priority over a conflicting security interest in the same livestock, and, except as otherwise provided in Section 9–327, a perfected security interest in their identifiable proceeds and identifiable products in their unmanufactured states also has priority, if:

(1) the purchase-money security interest is perfected when the debtor receives possession of the livestock;

(2) the purchase-money secured party sends an authenticated notification to the holder of the conflicting security interest;

(3) the holder of the conflicting security interest receives the notification within six months before the debtor receives possession of the livestock; and

(4) the notification states that the person sending the notification has or expects to acquire a purchase-money security interest in livestock of the debtor and describes the livestock.

(e) Subsections (d)(2) through (4) apply only if the holder of the conflicting security interest had filed a financing statement covering the same types of livestock:

(1) if the purchase-money security interest is perfected by filing, before the date of the filing; or

(2) if the purchase-money security interest is temporarily perfected without filing or possession under Section 9–312(f), before the beginning of the 20-day period thereunder.

(f) Except as otherwise provided in subsection (g), a perfected purchase-money security interest in software has priority over a conflicting security interest in the same collateral, and, except as otherwise provided in Section 9–327, a perfected security interest in its identifiable proceeds also has priority, to the extent that the purchase-money security interest in the goods in which the software was acquired for use has priority in the goods and proceeds of the goods under this section.

(g) If more than one security interest qualifies for priority in the same collateral under subsection (a), (b), (d), or (f):

(1) a security interest securing an obligation incurred as all or part of the price of the collateral has priority over a security interest securing an obligation incurred for value given to enable the debtor to acquire rights in or the use of collateral; and

(2) in all other cases, Section 9–322(a) applies to the qualifying security interests.

§ 9–325. Priority of Security Interests in Transferred Collateral.

(a) Except as otherwise provided in subsection (b), a security interest created by a debtor is subordinate to a security interest in the same collateral created by another person if:

(1) the debtor acquired the collateral subject to the security interest created by the other person;

(2) the security interest created by the other person was perfected when the debtor acquired the collateral; and

(3) there is no period thereafter when the security interest is unperfected.

(b) Subsection (a) subordinates a security interest only if the security interest:

(1) otherwise would have priority solely under Section 9–322(a) or 9–324; or

(2) arose solely under Section 2–711(3) or 2A–508(5).

§ 9–326. Priority of Security Interests Created by New Debtor.

(a) Subject to subsection (b), a security interest created by a new debtor which is perfected by a filed financing statement that is effective solely under Section 9–508 in collateral in which a new debtor has or acquires rights is subordinate to a security interest in the same collateral which is perfected other than by a filed financing statement that is effective solely under Section 9–508.

(b) The other provisions of this part determine the priority among conflicting security interests in the same collateral perfected by filed financing statements that are effective solely under Section 9–508. However, if the security agreements to which a new debtor became bound as debtor were not entered into by the same original debtor, the conflicting security interests rank according to priority in time of the new debtor's having become bound.

§ 9–327. Priority of Security Interests in Deposit Account.

The following rules govern priority among conflicting security interests in the same deposit account:

(1) A security interest held by a secured party having control of the deposit account under Section 9–104 has priority over a conflicting security interest held by a secured party that does not have control.

(2) Except as otherwise provided in paragraphs (3) and (4), security interests perfected by control under Section 9–314 rank according to priority in time of obtaining control.

(3) Except as otherwise provided in paragraph (4), a security interest held by the bank with which the deposit account is maintained has priority over a conflicting security interest held by another secured party.

(4) A security interest perfected by control under Section 9–104(a)(3) has priority over a security interest held by the bank with which the deposit account is maintained.

§ 9–328. Priority of Security Interests in Investment Property.

The following rules govern priority among conflicting security interests in the same investment property:

(1) A security interest held by a secured party having control of investment property under Section 9–106 has priority over a security interest held by a secured party that does not have control of the investment property.

(2) Except as otherwise provided in paragraphs (3) and (4), conflicting security interests held by secured parties each of which has control under Section 9–106 rank according to priority in time of:

   (A) if the collateral is a security, obtaining control;

   (B) if the collateral is a security entitlement carried in a securities account and:

      (i) if the secured party obtained control under Section 8–106(d)(1), the secured party's becoming the person for which the securities account is maintained;

      (ii) if the secured party obtained control under Section 8–106(d)(2), the securities intermediary's agreement to comply with the secured party's entitlement orders with respect to security entitlements carried or to be carried in the securities account; or

      (iii) if the secured party obtained control through another person under Section 8–106(d)(3), the time on which priority would be based under this paragraph if the other person were the secured party; or

   (C) if the collateral is a commodity contract carried with a commodity intermediary, the satisfaction of the requirement for control specified in Section 9–106(b)(2)

with respect to commodity contracts carried or to be carried with the commodity intermediary.

(3) A security interest held by a securities intermediary in a security entitlement or a securities account maintained with the securities intermediary has priority over a conflicting security interest held by another secured party.

(4) A security interest held by a commodity intermediary in a commodity contract or a commodity account maintained with the commodity intermediary has priority over a conflicting security interest held by another secured party.

(5) A security interest in a certificated security in registered form which is perfected by taking delivery under Section 9–313(a) and not by control under Section 9–314 has priority over a conflicting security interest perfected by a method other than control.

(6) Conflicting security interests created by a broker, securities intermediary, or commodity intermediary which are perfected without control under Section 9–106 rank equally.

(7) In all other cases, priority among conflicting security interests in investment property is governed by Sections 9–322 and 9–323.

§ 9–329. Priority of Security Interests in Letter-of-Credit Right.

The following rules govern priority among conflicting security interests in the same letter-of-credit right:

(1) A security interest held by a secured party having control of the letter-of-credit right under Section 9–107 has priority to the extent of its control over a conflicting security interest held by a secured party that does not have control.

(2) Security interests perfected by control under Section 9–314 rank according to priority in time of obtaining control.

§ 9–330. Priority of Purchaser of Chattel Paper or Instrument.

(a) A purchaser of chattel paper has priority over a security interest in the chattel paper which is claimed merely as proceeds of inventory subject to a security interest if:

   (1) in good faith and in the ordinary course of the purchaser's business, the purchaser gives new value and takes possession of the chattel paper or obtains control of the chattel paper under Section 9–105; and

   (2) the chattel paper does not indicate that it has been assigned to an identified assignee other than the purchaser.

(b) A purchaser of chattel paper has priority over a security interest in the chattel paper which is claimed other than merely as proceeds of inventory subject to a security interest if the purchaser gives new value and takes possession of the chattel paper or obtains control of the chattel paper under Section 9–105 in good faith, in the ordinary course of the purchaser's business, and without knowledge that the purchase violates the rights of the secured party.

(c) Except as otherwise provided in Section 9–327, a purchaser having priority in chattel paper under subsection (a) or (b) also has priority in proceeds of the chattel paper to the extent that:

(1) Section 9–322 provides for priority in the proceeds; or

(2) the proceeds consist of the specific goods covered by the chattel paper or cash proceeds of the specific goods, even if the purchaser's security interest in the proceeds is unperfected.

(d) Except as otherwise provided in Section 9–331(a), a purchaser of an instrument has priority over a security interest in the instrument perfected by a method other than possession if the purchaser gives value and takes possession of the instrument in good faith and without knowledge that the purchase violates the rights of the secured party.

(e) For purposes of subsections (a) and (b), the holder of a purchase-money security interest in inventory gives new value for chattel paper constituting proceeds of the inventory.

(f) For purposes of subsections (b) and (d), if chattel paper or an instrument indicates that it has been assigned to an identified secured party other than the purchaser, a purchaser of the chattel paper or instrument has knowledge that the purchase violates the rights of the secured party.

§ 9–331. Priority of Rights of Purchasers of Instruments, Documents, and Securities under Other Articles; Priority of Interests in Financial Assets and Security Entitlements under Article 8.

(a) This article does not limit the rights of a holder in due course of a negotiable instrument, a holder to which a negotiable document of title has been duly negotiated, or a protected purchaser of a security. These holders or purchasers take priority over an earlier security interest, even if perfected, to the extent provided in Articles 3, 7, and 8.

(b) This article does not limit the rights of or impose liability on a person to the extent that the person is protected against the assertion of a claim under Article 8.

(c) Filing under this article does not constitute notice of a claim or defense to the holders, or purchasers, or persons described in subsections (a) and (b).

§ 9–332. Transfer of Money; Transfer of Funds from Deposit Account.

(a) A transferee of money takes the money free of a security interest unless the transferee acts in collusion with the debtor in violating the rights of the secured party.

(b) A transferee of funds from a deposit account takes the funds free of a security interest in the deposit account unless the transferee acts in collusion with the debtor in violating the rights of the secured party.

§ 9–333. Priority of Certain Liens Arising by Operation of Law.

(a) In this section, "possessory lien" means an interest, other than a security interest or an agricultural lien:

(1) which secures payment or performance of an obligation for services or materials furnished with respect to goods by a person in the ordinary course of the person's business;

(2) which is created by statute or rule of law in favor of the person; and

(3) whose effectiveness depends on the person's possession of the goods.

(b) A possessory lien on goods has priority over a security interest in the goods unless the lien is created by a statute that expressly provides otherwise.

§ 9–334. Priority of Security Interests in Fixtures and Crops.

(a) A security interest under this article may be created in goods that are fixtures or may continue in goods that become fixtures. A security interest does not exist under this article in ordinary building materials incorporated into an improvement on land.

(b) This article does not prevent creation of an encumbrance upon fixtures under real property law.

(c) In cases not governed by subsections (d) through (h), a security interest in fixtures is subordinate to a conflicting interest of an encumbrancer or owner of the related real property other than the debtor.

(d) Except as otherwise provided in subsection (h), a perfected security interest in fixtures has priority over a conflicting interest of an encumbrancer or owner of the real property if the debtor has an interest of record in or is in possession of the real property and:

(1) the security interest is a purchase-money security interest;

(2) the interest of the encumbrancer or owner arises before the goods become fixtures; and

(3) the security interest is perfected by a fixture filing before the goods become fixtures or within 20 days thereafter.

(e) A perfected security interest in fixtures has priority over a conflicting interest of an encumbrancer or owner of the real property if:

(1) the debtor has an interest of record in the real property or is in possession of the real property and the security interest:

(A) is perfected by a fixture filing before the interest of the encumbrancer or owner is of record; and

(B) has priority over any conflicting interest of a predecessor in title of the encumbrancer or owner;

(2) before the goods become fixtures, the security interest is perfected by any method permitted by this article and the fixtures are readily removable:

(A) factory or office machines;

(B) equipment that is not primarily used or leased for use in the operation of the real property; or

(C) replacements of domestic appliances that are consumer goods;

(3) the conflicting interest is a lien on the real property obtained by legal or equitable proceedings after the security interest was perfected by any method permitted by this article; or

(4) the security interest is:

(A) created in a manufactured home in a manufactured-home transaction; and

(B) perfected pursuant to a statute described in Section 9–311(a)(2).

(f) A security interest in fixtures, whether or not perfected, has priority over a conflicting interest of an encumbrancer or owner of the real property if:

(1) the encumbrancer or owner has, in an authenticated record, consented to the security interest or disclaimed an interest in the goods as fixtures; or

(2) the debtor has a right to remove the goods as against the encumbrancer or owner.

(g) The priority of the security interest under paragraph (f)(2) continues for a reasonable time if the debtor's right to remove the goods as against the encumbrancer or owner terminates.

(h) A mortgage is a construction mortgage to the extent that it secures an obligation incurred for the construction of an improvement on land, including the acquisition cost of the land, if a recorded record of the mortgage so indicates. Except as otherwise provided in subsections (e) and (f), a security interest in fixtures is subordinate to a construction mortgage if a record of the mortgage is recorded before the goods become fixtures and the goods become fixtures before the completion of the construction. A mortgage has this priority to the same extent as a construction mortgage to the extent that it is given to refinance a construction mortgage.

(i) A perfected security interest in crops growing on real property has priority over a conflicting interest of an encumbrancer or owner of the real property if the debtor has an interest of record in or is in possession of the real property.

(j) Subsection (i) prevails over any inconsistent provisions of the following statutes:

[List here any statutes containing provisions inconsistent with subsection (i).]

Legislative Note: States that amend statutes to remove provisions inconsistent with subsection (i) need not enact subsection (j).

§ 9–335. Accessions.

(a) A security interest may be created in an accession and continues in collateral that becomes an accession.

(b) If a security interest is perfected when the collateral becomes an accession, the security interest remains perfected in the collateral.

(c) Except as otherwise provided in subsection (d), the other provisions of this part determine the priority of a security interest in an accession.

(d) A security interest in an accession is subordinate to a security interest in the whole which is perfected by compliance with the requirements of a certificate-of-title statute under Section 9–311(b).

(e) After default, subject to Part 6, a secured party may remove an accession from other goods if the security interest in the accession has priority over the claims of every person having an interest in the whole.

(f) A secured party that removes an accession from other goods under subsection (e) shall promptly reimburse any holder of a security interest or other lien on, or owner of, the whole or of the other goods, other than the debtor, for the cost of repair of any physical injury to the whole or the other goods. The secured party need not reimburse the holder or owner for any diminution in value of the whole or the other goods caused by the absence of the accession removed or by any necessity for replacing it. A person entitled to reimbursement may refuse permission to remove until the secured party gives adequate assurance for the performance of the obligation to reimburse.

§ 9–336. Commingled Goods.

(a) In this section, "commingled goods" means goods that are physically united with other goods in such a manner that their identity is lost in a product or mass.

(b) A security interest does not exist in commingled goods as such. However, a security interest may attach to a product or mass that results when goods become commingled goods.

(c) If collateral becomes commingled goods, a security interest attaches to the product or mass.

(d) If a security interest in collateral is perfected before the collateral becomes commingled goods, the security interest that attaches to the product or mass under subsection (c) is perfected.

(e) Except as otherwise provided in subsection (f), the other provisions of this part determine the priority of a security interest that attaches to the product or mass under subsection (c).

(f) If more than one security interest attaches to the product or mass under subsection (c), the following rules determine priority:

(1) A security interest that is perfected under subsection (d) has priority over a security interest that is unperfected at the time the collateral becomes commingled goods.

(2) If more than one security interest is perfected under subsection (d), the security interests rank equally in proportion to the value of the collateral at the time it became commingled goods.

§ 9–337. Priority of Security Interests in Goods Covered by Certificate of Title.

If, while a security interest in goods is perfected by any method under the law of another jurisdiction, this State issues a certificate of title that does not show that the goods are subject to the security interest or contain a statement that they may be subject to security interests not shown on the certificate:

(1) a buyer of the goods, other than a person in the business of selling goods of that kind, takes free of

the security interest if the buyer gives value and receives delivery of the goods after issuance of the certificate and without knowledge of the security interest; and

(2) the security interest is subordinate to a conflicting security interest in the goods that attaches, and is perfected under Section 9–311(b), after issuance of the certificate and without the conflicting secured party's knowledge of the security interest.

§ 9–338. Priority of Security Interest or Agricultural Lien Perfected by Filed Financing Statement Providing Certain Incorrect Information.

If a security interest or agricultural lien is perfected by a filed financing statement providing information described in Section 9–516(b)(5) which is incorrect at the time the financing statement is filed:

(1) the security interest or agricultural lien is subordinate to a conflicting perfected security interest in the collateral to the extent that the holder of the conflicting security interest gives value in reasonable reliance upon the incorrect information; and

(2) a purchaser, other than a secured party, of the collateral takes free of the security interest or agricultural lien to the extent that, in reasonable reliance upon the incorrect information, the purchaser gives value and, in the case of chattel paper, documents, goods, instruments, or a security certificate, receives delivery of the collateral.

§ 9–339. Priority Subject to Subordination.

This article does not preclude subordination by agreement by a person entitled to priority.

[Subpart 4. Rights of Bank]

§ 9–340. Effectiveness of Right of Recoupment or Set-Off against Deposit Account.

(a) Except as otherwise provided in subsection (c), a bank with which a deposit account is maintained may exercise any right of recoupment or set-off against a secured party that holds a security interest in the deposit account.

(b) Except as otherwise provided in subsection (c), the application of this article to a security interest in a deposit account does not affect a right of recoupment or set-off of the secured party as to a deposit account maintained with the secured party.

(c) The exercise by a bank of a set-off against a deposit account is ineffective against a secured party that holds a security interest in the deposit account which is perfected by control under Section 9–104(a)(3), if the set-off is based on a claim against the debtor.

§ 9–341. Bank's Rights and Duties with Respect to Deposit Account.

Except as otherwise provided in Section 9–340(c), and unless the bank otherwise agrees in an authenticated record, a bank's rights and duties with respect to a deposit account maintained with the bank are not terminated, suspended, or modified by:

(1) the creation, attachment, or perfection of a security interest in the deposit account;

(2) the bank's knowledge of the security interest; or

(3) the bank's receipt of instructions from the secured party.

§ 9–342. Bank's Right to Refuse to Enter into or Disclose Existence of Control Agreement.

This article does not require a bank to enter into an agreement of the kind described in Section 9–104(a)(2), even if its customer so requests or directs. A bank that has entered into such an agreement is not required to confirm the existence of the agreement to another person unless requested to do so by its customer.

Part 4　Rights of Third Parties

§ 9–401. Alienability of Debtor's Rights.

(a) Except as otherwise provided in subsection (b) and Sections 9–406, 9–407, 9–408, and 9–409, whether a debtor's rights in collateral may be voluntarily or involuntarily transferred is governed by law other than this article.

(b) An agreement between the debtor and secured party which prohibits a transfer of the debtor's rights in collateral or makes the transfer a default does not prevent the transfer from taking effect.

§ 9–402. Secured Party Not Obligated on Contract of Debtor or in Tort.

The existence of a security interest, agricultural lien, or authority given to a debtor to dispose of or use collateral, without more, does not subject a secured party to liability in contract or tort for the debtor's acts or omissions.

§ 9–403. Agreement Not to Assert Defenses against Assignee.

(a) In this section, "value" has the meaning provided in Section 3–303(a).

(b) Except as otherwise provided in this section, an agreement between an account debtor and an assignor not to assert against an assignee any claim or defense that the account debtor may have against the assignor is enforceable by an assignee that takes an assignment:

(1) for value;

(2) in good faith;

(3) without notice of a claim of a property or possessory right to the property assigned; and

(4) without notice of a defense or claim in recoupment of the type that may be asserted against a person entitled to enforce a negotiable instrument under Section 3–305(a).

(c) Subsection (b) does not apply to defenses of a type that may be asserted against a holder in due course of a negotiable instrument under Section 3–305(b).

(d) In a consumer transaction, if a record evidences the account debtor's obligation, law other than this article requires that the record include a statement to the effect that the rights of an assignee are subject to claims or defenses that the account debtor could assert against the original obligee, and the record does not include such a statement:

(1) the record has the same effect as if the record included such a statement; and

(2) the account debtor may assert against an assignee those claims and defenses that would have been available if the record included such a statement.

(e) This section is subject to law other than this article which establishes a different rule for an account debtor who is an individual and who incurred the obligation primarily for personal, family, or household purposes.

(f) Except as otherwise provided in subsection (d), this section does not displace law other than this article which gives effect to an agreement by an account debtor not to assert a claim or defense against an assignee.

§ 9–404. Rights Acquired by Assignee; Claims and Defenses against Assignee.

(a) Unless an account debtor has made an enforceable agreement not to assert defenses or claims, and subject to subsections (b) through (e), the rights of an assignee are subject to:

(1) all terms of the agreement between the account debtor and assignor and any defense or claim in recoupment arising from the transaction that gave rise to the contract; and

(2) any other defense or claim of the account debtor against the assignor which accrues before the account debtor receives a notification of the assignment authenticated by the assignor or the assignee.

(b) Subject to subsection (c) and except as otherwise provided in subsection (d), the claim of an account debtor against an assignor may be asserted against an assignee under subsection (a) only to reduce the amount the account debtor owes.

(c) This section is subject to law other than this article which establishes a different rule for an account debtor who is an individual and who incurred the obligation primarily for personal, family, or household purposes.

(d) In a consumer transaction, if a record evidences the account debtor's obligation, law other than this article requires that the record include a statement to the effect that the account debtor's recovery against an assignee with respect to claims and defenses against the assignor may not exceed amounts paid by the account debtor under the record, and the record does not include such a statement, the extent to which a claim of an account debtor against the assignor may be asserted against an assignee is determined as if the record included such a statement.

(e) This section does not apply to an assignment of a health-care-insurance receivable.

§ 9–405. Modification of Assigned Contract.

(a) A modification of or substitution for an assigned contract is effective against an assignee if made in good faith. The assignee acquires corresponding rights under the modified or substituted contract. The assignment may provide that the modification or substitution is a breach of contract by the assignor. This subsection is subject to subsections (b) through (d).

(b) Subsection (a) applies to the extent that:

(1) the right to payment or a part thereof under an assigned contract has not been fully earned by performance; or

(2) the right to payment or a part thereof has been fully earned by performance and the account debtor has not received notification of the assignment under Section 9–406(a).

(c) This section is subject to law other than this article which establishes a different rule for an account debtor who is an individual and who incurred the obligation primarily for personal, family, or household purposes.

(d) This section does not apply to an assignment of a health-care-insurance receivable.

§ 9–406. Discharge of Account Debtor; Notification of Assignment; Identification and Proof of Assignment; Restrictions on Assignment of Accounts, Chattel Paper, Payment Intangibles, and Promissory Notes Ineffective.

(a) Subject to subsections (b) through (i), an account debtor on an account, chattel paper, or a payment intangible may discharge its obligation by paying the assignor until, but not after, the account debtor receives a notification, authenticated by the assignor or the assignee, that the amount due or to become due has been assigned and that payment is to be made to the assignee. After receipt of the notification, the account debtor may discharge its obligation by paying the assignee and may not discharge the obligation by paying the assignor.

(b) Subject to subsection (h), notification is ineffective under subsection (a):

(1) if it does not reasonably identify the rights assigned;

(2) to the extent that an agreement between an account debtor and a seller of a payment intangible limits the account debtor's duty to pay a person other than the seller and the limitation is effective under law other than this article; or

(3) at the option of an account debtor, if the notification notifies the account debtor to make less than the full

amount of any installment or other periodic payment to the assignee, even if:

(A) only a portion of the account, chattel paper, or payment intangible has been assigned to that assignee;

(B) a portion has been assigned to another assignee; or

(C) the account debtor knows that the assignment to that assignee is limited.

(c) Subject to subsection (h), if requested by the account debtor, an assignee shall seasonably furnish reasonable proof that the assignment has been made. Unless the assignee complies, the account debtor may discharge its obligation by paying the assignor, even if the account debtor has received a notification under subsection (a).

(d) Except as otherwise provided in subsection (e) and Sections 2A–303 and 9–407, and subject to subsection (h), a term in an agreement between an account debtor and an assignor or in a promissory note is ineffective to the extent that it:

(1) prohibits, restricts, or requires the consent of the account debtor or person obligated on the promissory note to the assignment or transfer of, or the creation, attachment, perfection, or enforcement of a security interest in, the account, chattel paper, payment intangible, or promissory note; or

(2) provides that the assignment or transfer or the creation, attachment, perfection, or enforcement of the security interest may give rise to a default, breach, right of recoupment, claim, defense, termination, right of termination, or remedy under the account, chattel paper, payment intangible, or promissory note.

(e) Subsection (d) does not apply to the sale of a payment intangible or promissory note.

(f) Except as otherwise provided in Sections 2A–303 and 9–407 and subject to subsections (h) and (i), a rule of law, statute, or regulation that prohibits, restricts, or requires the consent of a government, governmental body or official, or account debtor to the assignment or transfer of, or creation of a security interest in, an account or chattel paper is ineffective to the extent that the rule of law, statute, or regulation:

(1) prohibits, restricts, or requires the consent of the government, governmental body or official, or account debtor to the assignment or transfer of, or the creation, attachment, perfection, or enforcement of a security interest in the account or chattel paper; or

(2) provides that the assignment or transfer or the creation, attachment, perfection, or enforcement of the security interest may give rise to a default, breach, right of recoupment, claim, defense, termination, right of termination, or remedy under the account or chattel paper.

(g) Subject to subsection (h), an account debtor may not waive or vary its option under subsection (b)(3).

(h) This section is subject to law other than this article which establishes a different rule for an account debtor who is an individual and who incurred the obligation primarily for personal, family, or household purposes.

(i) This section does not apply to an assignment of a health-care-insurance receivable.

(j) This section prevails over any inconsistent provisions of the following statutes, rules, and regulations:

[List here any statutes, rules, and regulations containing provisions inconsistent with this section.]

Legislative Note: States that amend statutes, rules, and regulations to remove provisions inconsistent with this section need not enact subsection (j).

As amended in 1999 and 2000.

§ 9–407. Restrictions on Creation or Enforcement of Security Interest in Leasehold Interest or in Lessor's Residual Interest.

(a) Except as otherwise provided in subsection (b), a term in a lease agreement is ineffective to the extent that it:

(1) prohibits, restricts, or requires the consent of a party to the lease to the assignment or transfer of, or the creation, attachment, perfection, or enforcement of a security interest in an interest of a party under the lease contract or in the lessor's residual interest in the goods; or

(2) provides that the assignment or transfer or the creation, attachment, perfection, or enforcement of the security interest may give rise to a default, breach, right of recoupment, claim, defense, termination, right of termination, or remedy under the lease.

(b) Except as otherwise provided in Section 2A–303(7), a term described in subsection (a)(2) is effective to the extent that there is:

(1) a transfer by the lessee of the lessee's right of possession or use of the goods in violation of the term; or

(2) a delegation of a material performance of either party to the lease contract in violation of the term.

(c) The creation, attachment, perfection, or enforcement of a security interest in the lessor's interest under the lease contract or the lessor's residual interest in the goods is not a transfer that materially impairs the lessee's prospect of obtaining return performance or materially changes the duty of or materially increases the burden or risk imposed on the lessee within the purview of Section 2A–303(4) unless, and then only to the extent that, enforcement actually results in a delegation of material performance of the lessor.

As amended in 1999.

§ 9–408. Restrictions on Assignment of Promissory Notes, Health-Care-Insurance Receivables, and Certain General Intangibles Ineffective.

(a) Except as otherwise provided in subsection (b), a term in a promissory note or in an agreement between an account debtor and a debtor which relates to a health-care-insurance receivable or a general intangible, including a contract, permit, license, or franchise, and which term prohibits, restricts, or requires the consent of the person obligated on the promissory note or the account debtor to, the assignment or transfer of, or creation, attachment, or perfection of a security interest in, the promissory note, health-care-insurance receivable, or general intangible, is ineffective to the extent that the term:

(1) would impair the creation, attachment, or perfection of a security interest; or

(2) provides that the assignment or transfer or the creation, attachment, or perfection of the security interest may give rise to a default, breach, right of recoupment, claim, defense, termination, right of termination, or remedy under the promissory note, health-care-insurance receivable, or general intangible.

(b) Subsection (a) applies to a security interest in a payment intangible or promissory note only if the security interest arises out of a sale of the payment intangible or promissory note.

(c) A rule of law, statute, or regulation that prohibits, restricts, or requires the consent of a government, governmental body or official, person obligated on a promissory note, or account debtor to the assignment or transfer of, or creation of a security interest in, a promissory note, health-care-insurance receivable, or general intangible, including a contract, permit, license, or franchise between an account debtor and a debtor, is ineffective to the extent that the rule of law, statute, or regulation:

(1) would impair the creation, attachment, or perfection of a security interest; or

(2) provides that the assignment or transfer or the creation, attachment, or perfection of the security interest may give rise to a default, breach, right of recoupment, claim, defense, termination, right of termination, or remedy under the promissory note, health-care-insurance receivable, or general intangible.

(d) To the extent that a term in a promissory note or in an agreement between an account debtor and a debtor which relates to a health-care-insurance receivable or general intangible or a rule of law, statute, or regulation described in subsection (c) would be effective under law other than this article but is ineffective under subsection (a) or (c), the creation, attachment, or perfection of a security interest in the promissory note, health-care-insurance receivable, or general intangible:

(1) is not enforceable against the person obligated on the promissory note or the account debtor;

(2) does not impose a duty or obligation on the person obligated on the promissory note or the account debtor;

(3) does not require the person obligated on the promissory note or the account debtor to recognize the security interest, pay or render performance to the secured party, or accept payment or performance from the secured party;

(4) does not entitle the secured party to use or assign the debtor's rights under the promissory note, health-care-insurance receivable, or general intangible, including any related information or materials furnished to the debtor in the transaction giving rise to the promissory note, health-care-insurance receivable, or general intangible;

(5) does not entitle the secured party to use, assign, possess, or have access to any trade secrets or confidential information of the person obligated on the promissory note or the account debtor; and

(6) does not entitle the secured party to enforce the security interest in the promissory note, health-care-insurance receivable, or general intangible.

(e) This section prevails over any inconsistent provisions of the following statutes, rules, and regulations:

[List here any statutes, rules, and regulations containing provisions inconsistent with this section.]

Legislative Note: States that amend statutes, rules, and regulations to remove provisions inconsistent with this section need not enact subsection (e).

As amended in 1999.

§ 9–409. Restrictions on Assignment of Letter-of-Credit Rights Ineffective.

(a) A term in a letter of credit or a rule of law, statute, regulation, custom, or practice applicable to the letter of credit which prohibits, restricts, or requires the consent of an applicant, issuer, or nominated person to a beneficiary's assignment of or creation of a security interest in a letter-of-credit right is ineffective to the extent that the term or rule of law, statute, regulation, custom, or practice:

(1) would impair the creation, attachment, or perfection of a security interest in the letter-of-credit right; or

(2) provides that the assignment or the creation, attachment, or perfection of the security interest may give rise to a default, breach, right of recoupment, claim, defense, termination, right of termination, or remedy under the letter-of-credit right.

(b) To the extent that a term in a letter of credit is ineffective under subsection (a) but would be effective under law other than this article or a custom or practice applicable to the letter of credit, to the transfer of a right to draw or otherwise demand performance under the letter of credit, or to the assignment of a right to proceeds of the letter of credit, the creation, attachment, or perfection of a security interest in the letter-of-credit right:

(1) is not enforceable against the applicant, issuer, nominated person, or transferee beneficiary;

(2) imposes no duties or obligations on the applicant, issuer, nominated person, or transferee beneficiary; and

(3) does not require the applicant, issuer, nominated person, or transferee beneficiary to recognize the security interest, pay or render performance to the secured

party, or accept payment or other performance from the secured party.

As amended in 1999.

Part 5   Filing

[Subpart 1. Filing Office; Contents and Effectiveness of Financing Statement]

§ 9–501. Filing Office.

(a) Except as otherwise provided in subsection (b), if the local law of this State governs perfection of a security interest or agricultural lien, the office in which to file a financing statement to perfect the security interest or agricultural lien is:

    (1) the office designated for the filing or recording of a record of a mortgage on the related real property, if:

        (A) the collateral is as-extracted collateral or timber to be cut; or

        (B) the financing statement is filed as a fixture filing and the collateral is goods that are or are to become fixtures; or

    (2) the office of [ ] [or any office duly authorized by [ ]], in all other cases, including a case in which the collateral is goods that are or are to become fixtures and the financing statement is not filed as a fixture filing.

(b) The office in which to file a financing statement to perfect a security interest in collateral, including fixtures, of a transmitting utility is the office of [ ]. The financing statement also constitutes a fixture filing as to the collateral indicated in the financing statement which is or is to become fixtures.

Legislative Note: The State should designate the filing office where the brackets appear. The filing office may be that of a governmental official (e.g., the Secretary of State) or a private party that maintains the State's filing system.

§ 9–502. Contents of Financing Statement; Record of Mortgage as Financing Statement; Time of Filing Financing Statement.

(a) Subject to subsection (b), a financing statement is sufficient only if it:

    (1) provides the name of the debtor;

    (2) provides the name of the secured party or a representative of the secured party; and

    (3) indicates the collateral covered by the financing statement.

(b) Except as otherwise provided in Section 9–501(b), to be sufficient, a financing statement that covers as-extracted collateral or timber to be cut, or which is filed as a fixture filing and covers goods that are or are to become fixtures, must satisfy subsection (a) and also:

    (1) indicate that it covers this type of collateral;

    (2) indicate that it is to be filed [for record] in the real property records;

    (3) provide a description of the real property to which the collateral is related [sufficient to give constructive notice of a mortgage under the law of this State if the description were contained in a record of the mortgage of the real property]; and

    (4) if the debtor does not have an interest of record in the real property, provide the name of a record owner.

(c) A record of a mortgage is effective, from the date of recording, as a financing statement filed as a fixture filing or as a financing statement covering as-extracted collateral or timber to be cut only if:

    (1) the record indicates the goods or accounts that it covers;

    (2) the goods are or are to become fixtures related to the real property described in the record or the collateral is related to the real property described in the record and is as-extracted collateral or timber to be cut;

    (3) the record satisfies the requirements for a financing statement in this section other than an indication that it is to be filed in the real property records; and

    (4) the record is [duly] recorded.

(d) A financing statement may be filed before a security agreement is made or a security interest otherwise attaches.

Legislative Note: Language in brackets is optional. Where the State has any special recording system for real property other than the usual grantor-grantee index (as, for instance, a tract system or a title registration or Torrens system) local adaptations of subsection (b) and Section 9–519(d) and (e) may be necessary. See, e.g., Mass. Gen. Laws Chapter 106, Section 9–410.

§ 9–503. Name of Debtor and Secured Party.

(a) A financing statement sufficiently provides the name of the debtor:

    (1) if the debtor is a registered organization, only if the financing statement provides the name of the debtor indicated on the public record of the debtor's jurisdiction of organization which shows the debtor to have been organized;

    (2) if the debtor is a decedent's estate, only if the financing statement provides the name of the decedent and indicates that the debtor is an estate;

    (3) if the debtor is a trust or a trustee acting with respect to property held in trust, only if the financing statement:

        (A) provides the name specified for the trust in its organic documents or, if no name is specified, provides the name of the settlor and additional information sufficient to distinguish the debtor from other trusts having one or more of the same settlors; and

        (B) indicates, in the debtor's name or otherwise, that the debtor is a trust or is a trustee acting with respect to property held in trust; and

    (4) in other cases:

(A) if the debtor has a name, only if it provides the individual or organizational name of the debtor; and

(B) if the debtor does not have a name, only if it provides the names of the partners, members, associates, or other persons comprising the debtor.

(b) A financing statement that provides the name of the debtor in accordance with subsection (a) is not rendered ineffective by the absence of:

(1) a trade name or other name of the debtor; or

(2) unless required under subsection (a)(4)(B), names of partners, members, associates, or other persons comprising the debtor.

(c) A financing statement that provides only the debtor's trade name does not sufficiently provide the name of the debtor.

(d) Failure to indicate the representative capacity of a secured party or representative of a secured party does not affect the sufficiency of a financing statement.

(e) A financing statement may provide the name of more than one debtor and the name of more than one secured party.

§ 9–504. Indication of Collateral.

A financing statement sufficiently indicates the collateral that it covers if the financing statement provides:

(1) a description of the collateral pursuant to Section 9–108; or

(2) an indication that the financing statement covers all assets or all personal property.

As amended in 1999.

§ 9–505. Filing and Compliance with Other Statutes and Treaties for Consignments, Leases, Other Bailments, and Other Transactions.

(a) A consignor, lessor, or other bailor of goods, a licensor, or a buyer of a payment intangible or promissory note may file a financing statement, or may comply with a statute or treaty described in Section 9–311(a), using the terms "consignor", "consignee", "lessor", "lessee", "bailor", "bailee", "licensor", "licensee", "owner", "registered owner", "buyer", "seller", or words of similar import, instead of the terms "secured party" and "debtor".

(b) This part applies to the filing of a financing statement under subsection (a) and, as appropriate, to compliance that is equivalent to filing a financing statement under Section 9–311(b), but the filing or compliance is not of itself a factor in determining whether the collateral secures an obligation. If it is determined for another reason that the collateral secures an obligation, a security interest held by the consignor, lessor, bailor, licensor, owner, or buyer which attaches to the collateral is perfected by the filing or compliance.

§ 9–506. Effect of Errors or Omissions.

(a) A financing statement substantially satisfying the requirements of this part is effective, even if it has minor errors or omissions, unless the errors or omissions make the financing statement seriously misleading.

(b) Except as otherwise provided in subsection (c), a financing statement that fails sufficiently to provide the name of the debtor in accordance with Section 9–503(a) is seriously misleading.

(c) If a search of the records of the filing office under the debtor's correct name, using the filing office's standard search logic, if any, would disclose a financing statement that fails sufficiently to provide the name of the debtor in accordance with Section 9–503(a), the name provided does not make the financing statement seriously misleading.

(d) For purposes of Section 9–508(b), the "debtor's correct name" in subsection (c) means the correct name of the new debtor.

§ 9–507. Effect of Certain Events on Effectiveness of Financing Statement.

(a) A filed financing statement remains effective with respect to collateral that is sold, exchanged, leased, licensed, or otherwise disposed of and in which a security interest or agricultural lien continues, even if the secured party knows of or consents to the disposition.

(b) Except as otherwise provided in subsection (c) and Section 9–508, a financing statement is not rendered ineffective if, after the financing statement is filed, the information provided in the financing statement becomes seriously misleading under Section 9–506.

(c) If a debtor so changes its name that a filed financing statement becomes seriously misleading under Section 9–506:

(1) the financing statement is effective to perfect a security interest in collateral acquired by the debtor before, or within four months after, the change; and

(2) the financing statement is not effective to perfect a security interest in collateral acquired by the debtor more than four months after the change, unless an amendment to the financing statement which renders the financing statement not seriously misleading is filed within four months after the change.

§ 9–508. Effectiveness of Financing Statement If New Debtor Becomes Bound by Security Agreement.

(a) Except as otherwise provided in this section, a filed financing statement naming an original debtor is effective to perfect a security interest in collateral in which a new debtor has or acquires rights to the extent that the financing statement would have been effective had the original debtor acquired rights in the collateral.

(b) If the difference between the name of the original debtor and that of the new debtor causes a filed financing statement that is effective under subsection (a) to be seriously misleading under Section 9–506:

(1) the financing statement is effective to perfect a security interest in collateral acquired by the new

debtor before, and within four months after, the new debtor becomes bound under Section 9B–203(d); and

(2) the financing statement is not effective to perfect a security interest in collateral acquired by the new debtor more than four months after the new debtor becomes bound under Section 9–203(d) unless an initial financing statement providing the name of the new debtor is filed before the expiration of that time.

(c) This section does not apply to collateral as to which a filed financing statement remains effective against the new debtor under Section 9–507(a).

§ 9–509. Persons Entitled to File a Record.

(a) A person may file an initial financing statement, amendment that adds collateral covered by a financing statement, or amendment that adds a debtor to a financing statement only if:

    (1) the debtor authorizes the filing in an authenticated record or pursuant to subsection (b) or (c); or

    (2) the person holds an agricultural lien that has become effective at the time of filing and the financing statement covers only collateral in which the person holds an agricultural lien.

(b) By authenticating or becoming bound as debtor by a security agreement, a debtor or new debtor authorizes the filing of an initial financing statement, and an amendment, covering:

    (1) the collateral described in the security agreement; and

    (2) property that becomes collateral under Section 9–315(a)(2), whether or not the security agreement expressly covers proceeds.

(c) By acquiring collateral in which a security interest or agricultural lien continues under Section 9–315(a)(1), a debtor authorizes the filing of an initial financing statement, and an amendment, covering the collateral and property that becomes collateral under Section 9–315(a)(2).

(d) A person may file an amendment other than an amendment that adds collateral covered by a financing statement or an amendment that adds a debtor to a financing statement only if:

    (1) the secured party of record authorizes the filing; or

    (2) the amendment is a termination statement for a financing statement as to which the secured party of record has failed to file or send a termination statement as required by Section 9–513(a) or (c), the debtor authorizes the filing, and the termination statement indicates that the debtor authorized it to be filed.

(e) If there is more than one secured party of record for a financing statement, each secured party of record may authorize the filing of an amendment under subsection (d).
As amended in 2000.

§ 9–510. Effectiveness of Filed Record.

(a) A filed record is effective only to the extent that it was filed by a person that may file it under Section 9–509.

(b) A record authorized by one secured party of record does not affect the financing statement with respect to another secured party of record.

(c) A continuation statement that is not filed within the six-month period prescribed by Section 9–515(d) is ineffective.

§ 9–511. Secured Party of Record.

(a) A secured party of record with respect to a financing statement is a person whose name is provided as the name of the secured party or a representative of the secured party in an initial financing statement that has been filed. If an initial financing statement is filed under Section 9–514(a), the assignee named in the initial financing statement is the secured party of record with respect to the financing statement.

(b) If an amendment of a financing statement which provides the name of a person as a secured party or a representative of a secured party is filed, the person named in the amendment is a secured party of record. If an amendment is filed under Section 9–514(b), the assignee named in the amendment is a secured party of record.

(c) A person remains a secured party of record until the filing of an amendment of the financing statement which deletes the person.

§ 9–512. Amendment of Financing Statement.
[Alternative A]

(a) Subject to Section 9–509, a person may add or delete collateral covered by, continue or terminate the effectiveness of, or, subject to subsection (e), otherwise amend the information provided in, a financing statement by filing an amendment that:

    (1) identifies, by its file number, the initial financing statement to which the amendment relates; and

    (2) if the amendment relates to an initial financing statement filed [or recorded] in a filing office described in Section 9–501(a)(1), provides the information specified in Section 9–502(b).

[Alternative B]

(a) Subject to Section 9–509, a person may add or delete collateral covered by, continue or terminate the effectiveness of, or, subject to subsection (e), otherwise amend the information provided in, a financing statement by filing an amendment that:

    (1) identifies, by its file number, the initial financing statement to which the amendment relates; and

    (2) if the amendment relates to an initial financing statement filed [or recorded] in a filing office described in

Section 9–501(a)(1), provides the date [and time] that the initial financing statement was filed [or recorded] and the information specified in Section 9–502(b).

[End of Alternatives]

(b) Except as otherwise provided in Section 9–515, the filing of an amendment does not extend the period of effectiveness of the financing statement.

(c) A financing statement that is amended by an amendment that adds collateral is effective as to the added collateral only from the date of the filing of the amendment.

(d) A financing statement that is amended by an amendment that adds a debtor is effective as to the added debtor only from the date of the filing of the amendment.

(e) An amendment is ineffective to the extent it:

(1) purports to delete all debtors and fails to provide the name of a debtor to be covered by the financing statement; or

(2) purports to delete all secured parties of record and fails to provide the name of a new secured party of record.

Legislative Note: States whose real-estate filing offices require additional information in amendments and cannot search their records by both the name of the debtor and the file number should enact Alternative B to Sections 9–512(a), 9–518(b), 9–519(f), and 9–522(a).

§ 9–513. Termination Statement.

(a) A secured party shall cause the secured party of record for a financing statement to file a termination statement for the financing statement if the financing statement covers consumer goods and:

(1) there is no obligation secured by the collateral covered by the financing statement and no commitment to make an advance, incur an obligation, or otherwise give value; or

(2) the debtor did not authorize the filing of the initial financing statement.

(b) To comply with subsection (a), a secured party shall cause the secured party of record to file the termination statement:

(1) within one month after there is no obligation secured by the collateral covered by the financing statement and no commitment to make an advance, incur an obligation, or otherwise give value; or

(2) if earlier, within 20 days after the secured party receives an authenticated demand from a debtor.

(c) In cases not governed by subsection (a), within 20 days after a secured party receives an authenticated demand from a debtor, the secured party shall cause the secured party of record for a financing statement to send to the debtor a termination statement for the financing statement or file the termination statement in the filing office if:

(1) except in the case of a financing statement covering accounts or chattel paper that has been sold or

goods that are the subject of a consignment, there is no obligation secured by the collateral covered by the financing statement and no commitment to make an advance, incur an obligation, or otherwise give value;

(2) the financing statement covers accounts or chattel paper that has been sold but as to which the account debtor or other person obligated has discharged its obligation;

(3) the financing statement covers goods that were the subject of a consignment to the debtor but are not in the debtor's possession; or

(4) the debtor did not authorize the filing of the initial financing statement.

(d) Except as otherwise provided in Section 9–510, upon the filing of a termination statement with the filing office, the financing statement to which the termination statement relates ceases to be effective. Except as otherwise provided in Section 9–510, for purposes of Sections 9–519(g), 9–522(a), and 9–523(c), the filing with the filing office of a termination statement relating to a financing statement that indicates that the debtor is a transmitting utility also causes the effectiveness of the financing statement to lapse. As amended in 2000.

§ 9–514. Assignment of Powers of Secured Party of Record.

(a) Except as otherwise provided in subsection (c), an initial financing statement may reflect an assignment of all of the secured party's power to authorize an amendment to the financing statement by providing the name and mailing address of the assignee as the name and address of the secured party.

(b) Except as otherwise provided in subsection (c), a secured party of record may assign of record all or part of its power to authorize an amendment to a financing statement by filing in the filing office an amendment of the financing statement which:

(1) identifies, by its file number, the initial financing statement to which it relates;

(2) provides the name of the assignor; and

(3) provides the name and mailing address of the assignee.

(c) An assignment of record of a security interest in a fixture covered by a record of a mortgage which is effective as a financing statement filed as a fixture filing under Section 9–502(c) may be made only by an assignment of record of the mortgage in the manner provided by law of this State other than [the Uniform Commercial Code].

§ 9–515. Duration and Effectiveness of Financing Statement; Effect of Lapsed Financing Statement.

(a) Except as otherwise provided in subsections (b), (e), (f), and (g), a filed financing statement is effective for a period of five years after the date of filing.

(b) Except as otherwise provided in subsections (e), (f), and (g), an initial financing statement filed in connection with a public-finance transaction or manufactured-home transaction is effective for a period of 30 years after the date of filing if it indicates that it is filed in connection with a public-finance transaction or manufactured-home transaction.

(c) The effectiveness of a filed financing statement lapses on the expiration of the period of its effectiveness unless before the lapse a continuation statement is filed pursuant to subsection (d). Upon lapse, a financing statement ceases to be effective and any security interest or agricultural lien that was perfected by the financing statement becomes unperfected, unless the security interest is perfected otherwise. If the security interest or agricultural lien becomes unperfected upon lapse, it is deemed never to have been perfected as against a purchaser of the collateral for value.

(d) A continuation statement may be filed only within six months before the expiration of the five-year period specified in subsection (a) or the 30-year period specified in subsection (b), whichever is applicable.

(e) Except as otherwise provided in Section 9–510, upon timely filing of a continuation statement, the effectiveness of the initial financing statement continues for a period of five years commencing on the day on which the financing statement would have become ineffective in the absence of the filing. Upon the expiration of the five-year period, the financing statement lapses in the same manner as provided in subsection (c), unless, before the lapse, another continuation statement is filed pursuant to subsection (d). Succeeding continuation statements may be filed in the same manner to continue the effectiveness of the initial financing statement.

(f) If a debtor is a transmitting utility and a filed financing statement so indicates, the financing statement is effective until a termination statement is filed.

(g) A record of a mortgage that is effective as a financing statement filed as a fixture filing under Section 9–502(c) remains effective as a financing statement filed as a fixture filing until the mortgage is released or satisfied of record or its effectiveness otherwise terminates as to the real property.

§ 9–516. What Constitutes Filing; Effectiveness of Filing.

(a) Except as otherwise provided in subsection (b), communication of a record to a filing office and tender of the filing fee or acceptance of the record by the filing office constitutes filing.

(b) Filing does not occur with respect to a record that a filing office refuses to accept because:

(1) the record is not communicated by a method or medium of communication authorized by the filing office;

(2) an amount equal to or greater than the applicable filing fee is not tendered;

(3) the filing office is unable to index the record because:

(A) in the case of an initial financing statement, the record does not provide a name for the debtor;

(B) in the case of an amendment or correction statement, the record:

(i) does not identify the initial financing statement as required by Section 9–512 or 9–518, as applicable; or

(ii) identifies an initial financing statement whose effectiveness has lapsed under Section 9–515;

(C) in the case of an initial financing statement that provides the name of a debtor identified as an individual or an amendment that provides a name of a debtor identified as an individual which was not previously provided in the financing statement to which the record relates, the record does not identify the debtor's last name; or

(D) in the case of a record filed [or recorded] in the filing office described in Section 9–501(a)(1), the record does not provide a sufficient description of the real property to which it relates;

(4) in the case of an initial financing statement or an amendment that adds a secured party of record, the record does not provide a name and mailing address for the secured party of record;

(5) in the case of an initial financing statement or an amendment that provides a name of a debtor which was not previously provided in the financing statement to which the amendment relates, the record does not:

(A) provide a mailing address for the debtor;

(B) indicate whether the debtor is an individual or an organization; or

(C) if the financing statement indicates that the debtor is an organization, provide:

(i) a type of organization for the debtor;

(ii) a jurisdiction of organization for the debtor; or

(iii) an organizational identification number for the debtor or indicate that the debtor has none;

(6) in the case of an assignment reflected in an initial financing statement under Section 9–514(a) or an amendment filed under Section 9–514(b), the record does not provide a name and mailing address for the assignee; or

(7) in the case of a continuation statement, the record is not filed within the six-month period prescribed by Section 9–515(d).

(c) For purposes of subsection (b):

(1) a record does not provide information if the filing office is unable to read or decipher the information; and

(2) a record that does not indicate that it is an amendment or identify an initial financing statement to which it relates, as required by Section 9–512, 9–514, or 9–518, is an initial financing statement.

(d) A record that is communicated to the filing office with tender of the filing fee, but which the filing office refuses to accept for a reason other than one set forth in subsection (b), is effective as a filed record except as against a purchaser of the collateral which gives value in reasonable reliance upon the absence of the record from the files.

§ 9–517. Effect of Indexing Errors.

The failure of the filing office to index a record correctly does not affect the effectiveness of the filed record.

§ 9–518. Claim Concerning Inaccurate or Wrongfully Filed Record.

(a) A person may file in the filing office a correction statement with respect to a record indexed there under the person's name if the person believes that the record is inaccurate or was wrongfully filed.

[Alternative A]

(b) A correction statement must:

(1) identify the record to which it relates by the file number assigned to the initial financing statement to which the record relates;

(2) indicate that it is a correction statement; and

(3) provide the basis for the person's belief that the record is inaccurate and indicate the manner in which the person believes the record should be amended to cure any inaccuracy or provide the basis for the person's belief that the record was wrongfully filed.

[Alternative B]

(b) A correction statement must:

(1) identify the record to which it relates by:

(A) the file number assigned to the initial financing statement to which the record relates; and

(B) if the correction statement relates to a record filed [or recorded] in a filing office described in Section 9–501(a)(1), the date [and time] that the initial financing statement was filed [or recorded] and the information specified in Section 9–502(b);

(2) indicate that it is a correction statement; and

(3) provide the basis for the person's belief that the record is inaccurate and indicate the manner in which the person believes the record should be amended to cure any inaccuracy or provide the basis for the person's belief that the record was wrongfully filed.

[End of Alternatives]

(c) The filing of a correction statement does not affect the effectiveness of an initial financing statement or other filed record.

Legislative Note: States whose real-estate filing offices require additional information in amendments and cannot search their records by both the name of the debtor and the file number should enact Alternative B to Sections 9–512(a), 9–518(b), 9–519(f), and 9–522(a).

[Subpart 2. Duties and Operation of Filing Office]

§ 9–519. Numbering, Maintaining, and Indexing Records; Communicating Information Provided in Records.

(a) For each record filed in a filing office, the filing office shall:

(1) assign a unique number to the filed record;

(2) create a record that bears the number assigned to the filed record and the date and time of filing;

(3) maintain the filed record for public inspection; and

(4) index the filed record in accordance with subsections (c), (d), and (e).

(b) A file number [assigned after January 1, 2002,] must include a digit that:

(1) is mathematically derived from or related to the other digits of the file number; and

(2) aids the filing office in determining whether a number communicated as the file number includes a single-digit or transpositional error.

(c) Except as otherwise provided in subsections (d) and (e), the filing office shall:

(1) index an initial financing statement according to the name of the debtor and index all filed records relating to the initial financing statement in a manner that associates with one another an initial financing statement and all filed records relating to the initial financing statement; and

(2) index a record that provides a name of a debtor which was not previously provided in the financing statement to which the record relates also according to the name that was not previously provided.

(d) If a financing statement is filed as a fixture filing or covers as-extracted collateral or timber to be cut, [it must be filed for record and] the filing office shall index it:

(1) under the names of the debtor and of each owner of record shown on the financing statement as if they were the mortgagors under a mortgage of the real property described; and

(2) to the extent that the law of this State provides for indexing of records of mortgages under the name of the mortgagee, under the name of the secured party as if the secured party were the mortgagee thereunder, or, if indexing is by description, as if the financing statement were a record of a mortgage of the real property described.

(e) If a financing statement is filed as a fixture filing or covers as-extracted collateral or timber to be cut, the filing office shall index an assignment filed under Section 9–514(a) or an amendment filed under Section 9–514(b):

(1) under the name of the assignor as grantor; and

(2) to the extent that the law of this State provides for indexing a record of the assignment of a mortgage under the name of the assignee, under the name of the assignee.

[Alternative A]

(f) The filing office shall maintain a capability:

(1) to retrieve a record by the name of the debtor and by the file number assigned to the initial financing statement to which the record relates; and

(2) to associate and retrieve with one another an initial financing statement and each filed record relating to the initial financing statement.

[Alternative B]

(f) The filing office shall maintain a capability:

(1) to retrieve a record by the name of the debtor and:

(A) if the filing office is described in Section 9–501(a)(1), by the file number assigned to the initial financing statement to which the record relates and the date [and time] that the record was filed [or recorded]; or

(B) if the filing office is described in Section 9–501(a)(2), by the file number assigned to the initial financing statement to which the record relates; and

(2) to associate and retrieve with one another an initial financing statement and each filed record relating to the initial financing statement.

[End of Alternatives]

(g) The filing office may not remove a debtor's name from the index until one year after the effectiveness of a financing statement naming the debtor lapses under Section 9–515 with respect to all secured parties of record.

(h) The filing office shall perform the acts required by subsections (a) through (e) at the time and in the manner prescribed by filing-office rule, but not later than two business days after the filing office receives the record in question.

[(i) Subsection[s] [(b)] [and] [(h)] do[es] not apply to a filing office described in Section 9–501(a)(1).]

Legislative Notes:

1. States whose filing offices currently assign file numbers that include a verification number, commonly known as a "check digit," or can implement this requirement before the effective date of this Article should omit the bracketed language in subsection (b).

2. In States in which writings will not appear in the real property records and indices unless actually recorded the bracketed language in subsection (d) should be used.

3. States whose real-estate filing offices require additional information in amendments and cannot search their records by both the name of the debtor and the file number should enact Alternative B to Sections 9–512(a), 9–518(b), 9–519(f), and 9–522(a).

4. A State that elects not to require real-estate filing offices to comply with either or both of subsections (b) and (h) may adopt an applicable variation of subsection (i) and add "Except as otherwise provided in subsection (i)," to the appropriate subsection or subsections.

§ 9–520. Acceptance and Refusal to Accept Record.

(a) A filing office shall refuse to accept a record for filing for a reason set forth in Section 9–516(b) and may refuse to accept a record for filing only for a reason set forth in Section 9–516(b).

(b) If a filing office refuses to accept a record for filing, it shall communicate to the person that presented the record the fact of and reason for the refusal and the date and time the record would have been filed had the filing office accepted it. The communication must be made at the time and in the manner prescribed by filing-office rule but [, in the case of a filing office described in Section 9–501(a)(2),] in no event more than two business days after the filing office receives the record.

(c) A filed financing statement satisfying Section 9–502(a) and (b) is effective, even if the filing office is required to refuse to accept it for filing under subsection (a). However, Section 9–338 applies to a filed financing statement providing information described in Section 9–516(b)(5) which is incorrect at the time the financing statement is filed.

(d) If a record communicated to a filing office provides information that relates to more than one debtor, this part applies as to each debtor separately.

Legislative Note: A State that elects not to require real-property filing offices to comply with subsection (b) should include the bracketed language.

§ 9–521. Uniform Form of Written Financing Statement and Amendment.

(a) A filing office that accepts written records may not refuse to accept a written initial financing statement in the following form and format except for a reason set forth in Section 9–516(b):

[NATIONAL UCC FINANCING STATEMENT (FORM UCC1)(REV. 7/29/98)]

[NATIONAL UCC FINANCING STATEMENT ADDENDUM (FORM UCC1Ad)(REV. 07/29/98)]

(b) A filing office that accepts written records may not refuse to accept a written record in the following form and format except for a reason set forth in Section 9–516(b):

[NATIONAL UCC FINANCING STATEMENT AMENDMENT (FORM UCC3)(REV. 07/29/98)]

[NATIONAL UCC FINANCING STATEMENT AMEND-
MENT ADDENDUM (FORM UCC3Ad)(REV. 07/29/98)]

§ 9–522. Maintenance and Destruction of Records.

[Alternative A]

(a) The filing office shall maintain a record of the information provided in a filed financing statement for at least
one year after the effectiveness of the financing statement
has lapsed under Section 9–515 with respect to all secured
parties of record. The record must be retrievable by using
the name of the debtor and by using the file number
assigned to the initial financing statement to which the
record relates.

[Alternative B]

(a) The filing office shall maintain a record of the information provided in a filed financing statement for at least
one year after the effectiveness of the financing statement
has lapsed under Section 9–515 with respect to all secured
parties of record. The record must be retrievable by using
the name of the debtor and:

(1) if the record was filed [or recorded] in the filing
office described in Section 9–501(a)(1), by using the
file number assigned to the initial financing statement
to which the record relates and the date [and time] that
the record was filed [or recorded]; or

(2) if the record was filed in the filing office described
in Section 9–501(a)(2), by using the file number
assigned to the initial financing statement to which the
record relates.

[End of Alternatives]

(b) Except to the extent that a statute governing disposition of public records provides otherwise, the filing office
immediately may destroy any written record evidencing a
financing statement. However, if the filing office destroys a
written record, it shall maintain another record of the
financing statement which complies with subsection (a).

*Legislative Note: States whose real-estate filing offices require
additional information in amendments and cannot search their
records by both the name of the debtor and the file number should
enact Alternative B to Sections 9–512(a), 9–518(b),
9–519(f), and 9–522(a).*

§ 9–523. Information from Filing Office; Sale or License of Records.

(a) If a person that files a written record requests an
acknowledgment of the filing, the filing office shall send to
the person an image of the record showing the number
assigned to the record pursuant to Section 9–519(a)(1) and
the date and time of the filing of the record. However, if the
person furnishes a copy of the record to the filing office, the
filing office may instead:

(1) note upon the copy the number assigned to the
record pursuant to Section 9–519(a)(1) and the date
and time of the filing of the record; and

(2) send the copy to the person.

(b) If a person files a record other than a written record,
the filing office shall communicate to the person an
acknowledgment that provides:

(1) the information in the record;

(2) the number assigned to the record pursuant to
Section 9–519(a)(1); and

(3) the date and time of the filing of the record.

(c) The filing office shall communicate or otherwise make
available in a record the following information to any person that requests it:

(1) whether there is on file on a date and time specified by the filing office, but not a date earlier than three
business days before the filing office receives the
request, any financing statement that:

(A) designates a particular debtor [or, if the request
so states, designates a particular debtor at the
address specified in the request];

(B) has not lapsed under Section 9–515 with
respect to all secured parties of record; and

(C) if the request so states, has lapsed under
Section 9–515 and a record of which is maintained
by the filing office under Section 9–522(a);

(2) the date and time of filing of each financing statement; and

(3) the information provided in each financing statement.

(d) In complying with its duty under subsection (c), the filing office may communicate information in any medium.
However, if requested, the filing office shall communicate
information by issuing [its written certificate] [a record that
can be admitted into evidence in the courts of this State
without extrinsic evidence of its authenticity].

(e) The filing office shall perform the acts required by subsections (a) through (d) at the time and in the manner prescribed by filing-office rule, but not later than two business
days after the filing office receives the request.

(f) At least weekly, the [insert appropriate official or governmental agency] [filing office] shall offer to sell or license
to the public on a nonexclusive basis, in bulk, copies of all
records filed in it under this part, in every medium from
time to time available to the filing office.

Legislative Notes:

*1. States whose filing office does not offer the additional service of
responding to search requests limited to a particular address should
omit the bracketed language in subsection (c)(1)(A).*

*2. A State that elects not to require real-estate filing offices to
comply with either or both of subsections (e) and (f) should specify in the appropriate subsection(s) only the filing office described
in Section 9–501(a)(2).*

§ 9–524. Delay by Filing Office.

Delay by the filing office beyond a time limit prescribed by this part is excused if:

(1) the delay is caused by interruption of communication or computer facilities, war, emergency conditions, failure of equipment, or other circumstances beyond control of the filing office; and

(2) the filing office exercises reasonable diligence under the circumstances.

§ 9–525. Fees.

(a) Except as otherwise provided in subsection (e), the fee for filing and indexing a record under this part, other than an initial financing statement of the kind described in subsection (b), is [the amount specified in subsection (c), if applicable, plus]:

(1) $[X] if the record is communicated in writing and consists of one or two pages;

(2) $[2X] if the record is communicated in writing and consists of more than two pages; and

(3) $[½X] if the record is communicated by another medium authorized by filing-office rule.

(b) Except as otherwise provided in subsection (e), the fee for filing and indexing an initial financing statement of the following kind is [the amount specified in subsection (c), if applicable, plus]:

(1) $_____ if the financing statement indicates that it is filed in connection with a public-finance transaction;

(2) $_____ if the financing statement indicates that it is filed in connection with a manufactured-home transaction.

[Alternative A]

(c) The number of names required to be indexed does not affect the amount of the fee in subsections (a) and (b).

[Alternative B]

(c) Except as otherwise provided in subsection (e), if a record is communicated in writing, the fee for each name more than two required to be indexed is $_____.

[End of Alternatives]

(d) The fee for responding to a request for information from the filing office, including for [issuing a certificate showing] [communicating] whether there is on file any financing statement naming a particular debtor, is:

(1) $_____ if the request is communicated in writing; and

(2) $_____ if the request is communicated by another medium authorized by filing-office rule.

(e) This section does not require a fee with respect to a record of a mortgage which is effective as a financing statement filed as a fixture filing or as a financing statement covering as-extracted collateral or timber to be cut under Section 9–502(c). However, the recording and satisfaction fees that otherwise would be applicable to the record of the mortgage apply.

Legislative Notes:

1. To preserve uniformity, a State that places the provisions of this section together with statutes setting fees for other services should do so without modification.

2. A State should enact subsection (c), Alternative A, and omit the bracketed language in subsections (a) and (b) unless its indexing system entails a substantial additional cost when indexing additional names.

As amended in 2000.

§ 9–526. Filing-Office Rules.

(a) The [insert appropriate governmental official or agency] shall adopt and publish rules to implement this article. The filing-office rules must be[:

(1)] consistent with this article[; and

(2) adopted and published in accordance with the [insert any applicable state administrative procedure act]].

(b) To keep the filing-office rules and practices of the filing office in harmony with the rules and practices of filing offices in other jurisdictions that enact substantially this part, and to keep the technology used by the filing office compatible with the technology used by filing offices in other jurisdictions that enact substantially this part, the [insert appropriate governmental official or agency], so far as is consistent with the purposes, policies, and provisions of this article, in adopting, amending, and repealing filing-office rules, shall:

(1) consult with filing offices in other jurisdictions that enact substantially this part; and

(2) consult the most recent version of the Model Rules promulgated by the International Association of Corporate Administrators or any successor organization; and

(3) take into consideration the rules and practices of, and the technology used by, filing offices in other jurisdictions that enact substantially this part.

§ 9–527. Duty to Report.

The [insert appropriate governmental official or agency] shall report [annually on or before _____] to the [Governor and Legislature] on the operation of the filing office. The report must contain a statement of the extent to which:

(1) the filing-office rules are not in harmony with the rules of filing offices in other jurisdictions that enact substantially this part and the reasons for these variations; and

(2) the filing-office rules are not in harmony with the most recent version of the Model Rules promulgated by the International Association of Corporate Administrators, or any successor organization, and the reasons for these variations.

Part 6 Default

[Subpart 1. Default and Enforcement of Security Interest]

§ 9–601. Rights after Default; Judicial Enforcement; Consignor or Buyer of Accounts, Chattel Paper, Payment Intangibles, or Promissory Notes.

(a) After default, a secured party has the rights provided in this part and, except as otherwise provided in Section 9–602, those provided by agreement of the parties. A secured party:

(1) may reduce a claim to judgment, foreclose, or otherwise enforce the claim, security interest, or agricultural lien by any available judicial procedure; and

(2) if the collateral is documents, may proceed either as to the documents or as to the goods they cover.

(b) A secured party in possession of collateral or control of collateral under Section 9–104, 9–105, 9–106, or 9–107 has the rights and duties provided in Section 9–207.

(c) The rights under subsections (a) and (b) are cumulative and may be exercised simultaneously.

(d) Except as otherwise provided in subsection (g) and Section 9–605, after default, a debtor and an obligor have the rights provided in this part and by agreement of the parties.

(e) If a secured party has reduced its claim to judgment, the lien of any levy that may be made upon the collateral by virtue of an execution based upon the judgment relates back to the earliest of:

(1) the date of perfection of the security interest or agricultural lien in the collateral;

(2) the date of filing a financing statement covering the collateral; or

(3) any date specified in a statute under which the agricultural lien was created.

(f) A sale pursuant to an execution is a foreclosure of the security interest or agricultural lien by judicial procedure within the meaning of this section. A secured party may purchase at the sale and thereafter hold the collateral free of any other requirements of this article.

(g) Except as otherwise provided in Section 9–607(c), this part imposes no duties upon a secured party that is a consignor or is a buyer of accounts, chattel paper, payment intangibles, or promissory notes.

§ 9–602. Waiver and Variance of Rights and Duties.

Except as otherwise provided in Section 9–624, to the extent that they give rights to a debtor or obligor and impose duties on a secured party, the debtor or obligor may not waive or vary the rules stated in the following listed sections:

(1) Section 9–207(b)(4)(C), which deals with use and operation of the collateral by the secured party;

(2) Section 9–210, which deals with requests for an accounting and requests concerning a list of collateral and statement of account;

(3) Section 9–607(c), which deals with collection and enforcement of collateral;

(4) Sections 9–608(a) and 9–615(c) to the extent that they deal with application or payment of noncash proceeds of collection, enforcement, or disposition;

(5) Sections 9–608(a) and 9–615(d) to the extent that they require accounting for or payment of surplus proceeds of collateral;

(6) Section 9–609 to the extent that it imposes upon a secured party that takes possession of collateral without judicial process the duty to do so without breach of the peace;

(7) Sections 9–610(b), 9–611, 9–613, and 9–614, which deal with disposition of collateral;

(8) Section 9–615(f), which deals with calculation of a deficiency or surplus when a disposition is made to the secured party, a person related to the secured party, or a secondary obligor;

(9) Section 9–616, which deals with explanation of the calculation of a surplus or deficiency;

(10) Sections 9–620, 9–621, and 9–622, which deal with acceptance of collateral in satisfaction of obligation;

(11) Section 9–623, which deals with redemption of collateral;

(12) Section 9–624, which deals with permissible waivers; and

(13) Sections 9–625 and 9–626, which deal with the secured party's liability for failure to comply with this article.

§ 9–603. Agreement on Standards Concerning Rights and Duties.

(a) The parties may determine by agreement the standards measuring the fulfillment of the rights of a debtor or obligor and the duties of a secured party under a rule stated in Section 9–602 if the standards are not manifestly unreasonable.

(b) Subsection (a) does not apply to the duty under Section 9–609 to refrain from breaching the peace.

§ 9–604. Procedure If Security Agreement Covers Real Property or Fixtures.

(a) If a security agreement covers both personal and real property, a secured party may proceed:

(1) under this part as to the personal property without prejudicing any rights with respect to the real property; or

(2) as to both the personal property and the real property in accordance with the rights with respect to the real property, in which case the other provisions of this part do not apply.

(b) Subject to subsection (c), if a security agreement covers goods that are or become fixtures, a secured party may proceed:

(1) under this part; or

(2) in accordance with the rights with respect to real property, in which case the other provisions of this part do not apply.

(c) Subject to the other provisions of this part, if a secured party holding a security interest in fixtures has priority over all owners and encumbrancers of the real property, the secured party, after default, may remove the collateral from the real property.

(d) A secured party that removes collateral shall promptly reimburse any encumbrancer or owner of the real property, other than the debtor, for the cost of repair of any physical injury caused by the removal. The secured party need not reimburse the encumbrancer or owner for any diminution in value of the real property caused by the absence of the goods removed or by any necessity of replacing them. A person entitled to reimbursement may refuse permission to remove until the secured party gives adequate assurance for the performance of the obligation to reimburse.

§ 9–605. Unknown Debtor or Secondary Obligor.

A secured party does not owe a duty based on its status as secured party:

(1) to a person that is a debtor or obligor, unless the secured party knows:

(A) that the person is a debtor or obligor;

(B) the identity of the person; and

(C) how to communicate with the person; or

(2) to a secured party or lienholder that has filed a financing statement against a person, unless the secured party knows:

(A) that the person is a debtor; and

(B) the identity of the person.

§ 9–606. Time of Default for Agricultural Lien.

For purposes of this part, a default occurs in connection with an agricultural lien at the time the secured party becomes entitled to enforce the lien in accordance with the statute under which it was created.

§ 9–607. Collection and Enforcement by Secured Party.

(a) If so agreed, and in any event after default, a secured party:

(1) may notify an account debtor or other person obligated on collateral to make payment or otherwise render performance to or for the benefit of the secured party;

(2) may take any proceeds to which the secured party is entitled under Section 9–315;

(3) may enforce the obligations of an account debtor or other person obligated on collateral and exercise the rights of the debtor with respect to the obligation of the account debtor or other person obligated on collateral to make payment or otherwise render performance to the debtor, and with respect to any property that secures the obligations of the account debtor or other person obligated on the collateral;

(4) if it holds a security interest in a deposit account perfected by control under Section 9–104(a)(1), may apply the balance of the deposit account to the obligation secured by the deposit account; and

(5) if it holds a security interest in a deposit account perfected by control under Section 9–104(a)(2) or (3), may instruct the bank to pay the balance of the deposit account to or for the benefit of the secured party.

(b) If necessary to enable a secured party to exercise under subsection (a)(3) the right of a debtor to enforce a mortgage nonjudicially, the secured party may record in the office in which a record of the mortgage is recorded:

(1) a copy of the security agreement that creates or provides for a security interest in the obligation secured by the mortgage; and

(2) the secured party's sworn affidavit in recordable form stating that:

(A) a default has occurred; and

(B) the secured party is entitled to enforce the mortgage nonjudicially.

(c) A secured party shall proceed in a commercially reasonable manner if the secured party:

(1) undertakes to collect from or enforce an obligation of an account debtor or other person obligated on collateral; and

(2) is entitled to charge back uncollected collateral or otherwise to full or limited recourse against the debtor or a secondary obligor.

(d) A secured party may deduct from the collections made pursuant to subsection (c) reasonable expenses of collection and enforcement, including reasonable attorney's fees and legal expenses incurred by the secured party.

(e) This section does not determine whether an account debtor, bank, or other person obligated on collateral owes a duty to a secured party.

As amended in 2000.

§ 9–608. Application of Proceeds of Collection or Enforcement; Liability for Deficiency and Right to Surplus.

(a) If a security interest or agricultural lien secures payment or performance of an obligation, the following rules apply:

(1) A secured party shall apply or pay over for application the cash proceeds of collection or enforcement under Section 9–607 in the following order to:

(A) the reasonable expenses of collection and enforcement and, to the extent provided for by agreement and not prohibited by law, reasonable attorney's fees and legal expenses incurred by the secured party;

(B) the satisfaction of obligations secured by the security interest or agricultural lien under which the collection or enforcement is made; and

(C) the satisfaction of obligations secured by any subordinate security interest in or other lien on the collateral subject to the security interest or agricultural lien under which the collection or enforcement is made if the secured party receives an authenticated demand for proceeds before distribution of the proceeds is completed.

(2) If requested by a secured party, a holder of a subordinate security interest or other lien shall furnish reasonable proof of the interest or lien within a reasonable time. Unless the holder complies, the secured party need not comply with the holder's demand under paragraph (1)(C).

(3) A secured party need not apply or pay over for application noncash proceeds of collection and enforcement under Section 9–607 unless the failure to do so would be commercially unreasonable. A secured party that applies or pays over for application noncash proceeds shall do so in a commercially reasonable manner.

(4) A secured party shall account to and pay a debtor for any surplus, and the obligor is liable for any deficiency.

(b) If the underlying transaction is a sale of accounts, chattel paper, payment intangibles, or promissory notes, the debtor is not entitled to any surplus, and the obligor is not liable for any deficiency.

As amended in 2000.

§ 9–609. Secured Party's Right to Take Possession after Default.

(a) After default, a secured party:

(1) may take possession of the collateral; and

(2) without removal, may render equipment unusable and dispose of collateral on a debtor's premises under Section 9–610.

(b) A secured party may proceed under subsection (a):

(1) pursuant to judicial process; or

(2) without judicial process, if it proceeds without breach of the peace.

(c) If so agreed, and in any event after default, a secured party may require the debtor to assemble the collateral and make it available to the secured party at a place to be designated by the secured party which is reasonably convenient to both parties.

§ 9–610. Disposition of Collateral after Default.

(a) After default, a secured party may sell, lease, license, or otherwise dispose of any or all of the collateral in its present condition or following any commercially reasonable preparation or processing.

(b) Every aspect of a disposition of collateral, including the method, manner, time, place, and other terms, must be commercially reasonable. If commercially reasonable, a secured party may dispose of collateral by public or private proceedings, by one or more contracts, as a unit or in parcels, and at any time and place and on any terms.

(c) A secured party may purchase collateral:

(1) at a public disposition; or

(2) at a private disposition only if the collateral is of a kind that is customarily sold on a recognized market or the subject of widely distributed standard price quotations.

(d) A contract for sale, lease, license, or other disposition includes the warranties relating to title, possession, quiet enjoyment, and the like which by operation of law accompany a voluntary disposition of property of the kind subject to the contract.

(e) A secured party may disclaim or modify warranties under subsection (d):

(1) in a manner that would be effective to disclaim or modify the warranties in a voluntary disposition of property of the kind subject to the contract of disposition; or

(2) by communicating to the purchaser a record evidencing the contract for disposition and including an express disclaimer or modification of the warranties.

(f) A record is sufficient to disclaim warranties under subsection (e) if it indicates "There is no warranty relating to title, possession, quiet enjoyment, or the like in this disposition" or uses words of similar import.

§ 9–611. Notification before Disposition of Collateral.

(a) In this section, "notification date" means the earlier of the date on which:

(1) a secured party sends to the debtor and any secondary obligor an authenticated notification of disposition; or

(2) the debtor and any secondary obligor waive the right to notification.

(b) Except as otherwise provided in subsection (d), a secured party that disposes of collateral under Section 9–610 shall send to the persons specified in subsection (c) a reasonable authenticated notification of disposition.

(c) To comply with subsection (b), the secured party shall send an authenticated notification of disposition to:

(1) the debtor;

(2) any secondary obligor; and

(3) if the collateral is other than consumer goods:

(A) any other person from which the secured party has received, before the notification date, an authenticated notification of a claim of an interest in the collateral;

(B) any other secured party or lienholder that, 10 days before the notification date, held a security interest in or other lien on the collateral perfected by the filing of a financing statement that:

    (i) identified the collateral;

    (ii) was indexed under the debtor's name as of that date; and

    (iii) was filed in the office in which to file a financing statement against the debtor covering the collateral as of that date; and

(C) any other secured party that, 10 days before the notification date, held a security interest in the collateral perfected by compliance with a statute, regulation, or treaty described in Section 9–311(a).

(d) Subsection (b) does not apply if the collateral is perishable or threatens to decline speedily in value or is of a type customarily sold on a recognized market.

(e) A secured party complies with the requirement for notification prescribed by subsection (c)(3)(B) if:

(1) not later than 20 days or earlier than 30 days before the notification date, the secured party requests, in a commercially reasonable manner, information concerning financing statements indexed under the debtor's name in the office indicated in subsection (c)(3)(B); and

(2) before the notification date, the secured party:

    (A) did not receive a response to the request for information; or

    (B) received a response to the request for information and sent an authenticated notification of disposition to each secured party or other lienholder named in that response whose financing statement covered the collateral.

§ 9–612. Timeliness of Notification before Disposition of Collateral.

(a) Except as otherwise provided in subsection (b), whether a notification is sent within a reasonable time is a question of fact.

(b) In a transaction other than a consumer transaction, a notification of disposition sent after default and 10 days or more before the earliest time of disposition set forth in the notification is sent within a reasonable time before the disposition.

§ 9–613. Contents and Form of Notification before Disposition of Collateral: General.

Except in a consumer-goods transaction, the following rules apply:

(1) The contents of a notification of disposition are sufficient if the notification:

    (A) describes the debtor and the secured party;

    (B) describes the collateral that is the subject of the intended disposition;

    (C) states the method of intended disposition;

    (D) states that the debtor is entitled to an accounting of the unpaid indebtedness and states the charge, if any, for an accounting; and

    (E) states the time and place of a public disposition or the time after which any other disposition is to be made.

(2) Whether the contents of a notification that lacks any of the information specified in paragraph (1) are nevertheless sufficient is a question of fact.

(3) The contents of a notification providing substantially the information specified in paragraph (1) are sufficient, even if the notification includes:

    (A) information not specified by that paragraph; or

    (B) minor errors that are not seriously misleading.

(4) A particular phrasing of the notification is not required.

(5) The following form of notification and the form appearing in Section 9–614(3), when completed, each provides sufficient information:

NOTIFICATION OF DISPOSITION OF COLLATERAL

To: [*Name of debtor, obligor, or other person to which the notification is sent*]

From: [*Name, address, and telephone number of secured party*]

Name of Debtor(s): [*Include only if debtor(s) are not an addressee*]

    [*For a public disposition:*]

We will sell [or lease or license, *as applicable*] the [*describe collateral*] [to the highest qualified bidder] in public as follows:

    Day and Date: _____

    Time: _____

    Place: _____

    [*For a private disposition:*]

We will sell [or lease or license, *as applicable*] the [*describe collateral*] privately sometime after [*day and date*].

You are entitled to an accounting of the unpaid indebtedness secured by the property that we intend to sell [or lease or license, *as applicable*] [for a charge of $_____]. You may request an accounting by calling us at [*telephone number*].

[End of Form]

As amended in 2000.

§ 9–614. Contents and Form of Notification before Disposition of Collateral: Consumer-Goods Transaction.

In a consumer-goods transaction, the following rules apply:

(1) A notification of disposition must provide the following information:

    (A) the information specified in Section 9–613(1);

    (B) a description of any liability for a deficiency of the person to which the notification is sent;

(C) a telephone number from which the amount that must be paid to the secured party to redeem the collateral under Section 9–623 is available; and

(D) a telephone number or mailing address from which additional information concerning the disposition and the obligation secured is available.

(2) A particular phrasing of the notification is not required.

(3) The following form of notification, when completed, provides sufficient information:

[Name and address of secured party]

[Date]

NOTICE OF OUR PLAN TO SELL PROPERTY

[Name and address of any obligor who is also a debtor]

Subject: [Identification of Transaction]

We have your [describe collateral], because you broke promises in our agreement.

[For a public disposition:]

We will sell [describe collateral] at public sale. A sale could include a lease or license. The sale will be held as follows:

Date: _____

Time: _____

Place: _____

You may attend the sale and bring bidders if you want.

[For a private disposition:]

We will sell [describe collateral] at private sale sometime after [date]. A sale could include a lease or license.

The money that we get from the sale (after paying our costs) will reduce the amount you owe. If we get less money than you owe, you [will or will not, as applicable] still owe us the difference. If we get more money than you owe, you will get the extra money, unless we must pay it to someone else.

You can get the property back at any time before we sell it by paying us the full amount you owe (not just the past due payments), including our expenses. To learn the exact amount you must pay, call us at [telephone number].

If you want us to explain to you in writing how we have figured the amount that you owe us, you may call us at [telephone number] [or write us at [secured party's address]] and request a written explanation. [We will charge you $_____ for the explanation if we sent you another written explanation of the amount you owe us within the last six months.]

If you need more information about the sale call us at [telephone number] [or write us at [secured party's address]].

We are sending this notice to the following other people who have an interest in [describe collateral] or who owe money under your agreement:

[Names of all other debtors and obligors, if any]

[End of Form]

(4) A notification in the form of paragraph (3) is sufficient, even if additional information appears at the end of the form.

(5) A notification in the form of paragraph (3) is sufficient, even if it includes errors in information not required by paragraph (1), unless the error is misleading with respect to rights arising under this article.

(6) If a notification under this section is not in the form of paragraph (3), law other than this article determines the effect of including information not required by paragraph (1).

§ 9–615. Application of Proceeds of Disposition; Liability for Deficiency and Right to Surplus.

(a) A secured party shall apply or pay over for application the cash proceeds of disposition under Section 9–610 in the following order to:

(1) the reasonable expenses of retaking, holding, preparing for disposition, processing, and disposing, and, to the extent provided for by agreement and not prohibited by law, reasonable attorney's fees and legal expenses incurred by the secured party;

(2) the satisfaction of obligations secured by the security interest or agricultural lien under which the disposition is made;

(3) the satisfaction of obligations secured by any subordinate security interest in or other subordinate lien on the collateral if:

(A) the secured party receives from the holder of the subordinate security interest or other lien an authenticated demand for proceeds before distribution of the proceeds is completed; and

(B) in a case in which a consignor has an interest in the collateral, the subordinate security interest or other lien is senior to the interest of the consignor; and

(4) a secured party that is a consignor of the collateral if the secured party receives from the consignor an authenticated demand for proceeds before distribution of the proceeds is completed.

(b) If requested by a secured party, a holder of a subordinate security interest or other lien shall furnish reasonable proof of the interest or lien within a reasonable time. Unless the holder does so, the secured party need not comply with the holder's demand under subsection (a)(3).

(c) A secured party need not apply or pay over for application noncash proceeds of disposition under Section 9–610 unless the failure to do so would be commercially unreasonable. A secured party that applies or pays over for application noncash proceeds shall do so in a commercially reasonable manner.

(d) If the security interest under which a disposition is made secures payment or performance of an obligation, after making the payments and applications required by subsection (a) and permitted by subsection (c):

(1) unless subsection (a)(4) requires the secured party to apply or pay over cash proceeds to a consignor, the secured party shall account to and pay a debtor for any surplus; and

(2) the obligor is liable for any deficiency.

(e) If the underlying transaction is a sale of accounts, chattel paper, payment intangibles, or promissory notes:

(1) the debtor is not entitled to any surplus; and

(2) the obligor is not liable for any deficiency.

(f) The surplus or deficiency following a disposition is calculated based on the amount of proceeds that would have been realized in a disposition complying with this part to a transferee other than the secured party, a person related to the secured party, or a secondary obligor if:

(1) the transferee in the disposition is the secured party, a person related to the secured party, or a secondary obligor; and

(2) the amount of proceeds of the disposition is significantly below the range of proceeds that a complying disposition to a person other than the secured party, a person related to the secured party, or a secondary obligor would have brought.

(g) A secured party that receives cash proceeds of a disposition in good faith and without knowledge that the receipt violates the rights of the holder of a security interest or other lien that is not subordinate to the security interest or agricultural lien under which the disposition is made:

(1) takes the cash proceeds free of the security interest or other lien;

(2) is not obligated to apply the proceeds of the disposition to the satisfaction of obligations secured by the security interest or other lien; and

(3) is not obligated to account to or pay the holder of the security interest or other lien for any surplus.

As amended in 2000.

§ 9–616. Explanation of Calculation of Surplus or Deficiency.

(a) In this section:

(1) "Explanation" means a writing that:

(A) states the amount of the surplus or deficiency;

(B) provides an explanation in accordance with subsection (c) of how the secured party calculated the surplus or deficiency;

(C) states, if applicable, that future debits, credits, charges, including additional credit service charges or interest, rebates, and expenses may affect the amount of the surplus or deficiency; and

(D) provides a telephone number or mailing address from which additional information concerning the transaction is available.

(2) "Request" means a record:

(A) authenticated by a debtor or consumer obligor;

(B) requesting that the recipient provide an explanation; and

(C) sent after disposition of the collateral under Section 9–610.

(b) In a consumer-goods transaction in which the debtor is entitled to a surplus or a consumer obligor is liable for a deficiency under Section 9–615, the secured party shall:

(1) send an explanation to the debtor or consumer obligor, as applicable, after the disposition and:

(A) before or when the secured party accounts to the debtor and pays any surplus or first makes written demand on the consumer obligor after the disposition for payment of the deficiency; and

(B) within 14 days after receipt of a request; or

(2) in the case of a consumer obligor who is liable for a deficiency, within 14 days after receipt of a request, send to the consumer obligor a record waiving the secured party's right to a deficiency.

(c) To comply with subsection (a)(1)(B), a writing must provide the following information in the following order:

(1) the aggregate amount of obligations secured by the security interest under which the disposition was made, and, if the amount reflects a rebate of unearned interest or credit service charge, an indication of that fact, calculated as of a specified date:

(A) if the secured party takes or receives possession of the collateral after default, not more than 35 days before the secured party takes or receives possession; or

(B) if the secured party takes or receives possession of the collateral before default or does not take possession of the collateral, not more than 35 days before the disposition;

(2) the amount of proceeds of the disposition;

(3) the aggregate amount of the obligations after deducting the amount of proceeds;

(4) the amount, in the aggregate or by type, and types of expenses, including expenses of retaking, holding, preparing for disposition, processing, and disposing of the collateral, and attorney's fees secured by the collateral which are known to the secured party and relate to the current disposition;

(5) the amount, in the aggregate or by type, and types of credits, including rebates of interest or credit service charges, to which the obligor is known to be entitled and which are not reflected in the amount in paragraph (1); and

(6) the amount of the surplus or deficiency.

(d) A particular phrasing of the explanation is not required. An explanation complying substantially with the requirements of subsection (a) is sufficient, even if it includes minor errors that are not seriously misleading.

(e) A debtor or consumer obligor is entitled without charge to one response to a request under this section during any six-month period in which the secured party did not send to the debtor or consumer obligor an explanation pursuant to subsection (b)(1). The secured party may require payment of a charge not exceeding $25 for each additional response.

§ 9–617. Rights of Transferee of Collateral.

(a) A secured party's disposition of collateral after default:

(1) transfers to a transferee for value all of the debtor's rights in the collateral;

(2) discharges the security interest under which the disposition is made; and

(3) discharges any subordinate security interest or other subordinate lien [other than liens created under [cite acts or statutes providing for liens, if any, that are not to be discharged]].

(b) A transferee that acts in good faith takes free of the rights and interests described in subsection (a), even if the secured party fails to comply with this article or the requirements of any judicial proceeding.

(c) If a transferee does not take free of the rights and interests described in subsection (a), the transferee takes the collateral subject to:

(1) the debtor's rights in the collateral;

(2) the security interest or agricultural lien under which the disposition is made; and

(3) any other security interest or other lien.

§ 9–618. Rights and Duties of Certain Secondary Obligors.

(a) A secondary obligor acquires the rights and becomes obligated to perform the duties of the secured party after the secondary obligor:

(1) receives an assignment of a secured obligation from the secured party;

(2) receives a transfer of collateral from the secured party and agrees to accept the rights and assume the duties of the secured party; or

(3) is subrogated to the rights of a secured party with respect to collateral.

(b) An assignment, transfer, or subrogation described in subsection (a):

(1) is not a disposition of collateral under Section 9–610; and

(2) relieves the secured party of further duties under this article.

§ 9–619. Transfer of Record or Legal Title.

(a) In this section, "transfer statement" means a record authenticated by a secured party stating:

(1) that the debtor has defaulted in connection with an obligation secured by specified collateral;

(2) that the secured party has exercised its post-default remedies with respect to the collateral;

(3) that, by reason of the exercise, a transferee has acquired the rights of the debtor in the collateral; and

(4) the name and mailing address of the secured party, debtor, and transferee.

(b) A transfer statement entitles the transferee to the transfer of record of all rights of the debtor in the collateral specified in the statement in any official filing, recording, registration, or certificate-of-title system covering the collateral. If a transfer statement is presented with the applicable fee and request form to the official or office responsible for maintaining the system, the official or office shall:

(1) accept the transfer statement;

(2) promptly amend its records to reflect the transfer; and

(3) if applicable, issue a new appropriate certificate of title in the name of the transferee.

(c) A transfer of the record or legal title to collateral to a secured party under subsection (b) or otherwise is not of itself a disposition of collateral under this article and does not of itself relieve the secured party of its duties under this article.

§ 9–620. Acceptance of Collateral in Full or Partial Satisfaction of Obligation; Compulsory Disposition of Collateral.

(a) Except as otherwise provided in subsection (g), a secured party may accept collateral in full or partial satisfaction of the obligation it secures only if:

(1) the debtor consents to the acceptance under subsection (c);

(2) the secured party does not receive, within the time set forth in subsection (d), a notification of objection to the proposal authenticated by:

(A) a person to which the secured party was required to send a proposal under Section 9–621; or

(B) any other person, other than the debtor, holding an interest in the collateral subordinate to the security interest that is the subject of the proposal;

(3) if the collateral is consumer goods, the collateral is not in the possession of the debtor when the debtor consents to the acceptance; and

(4) subsection (e) does not require the secured party to dispose of the collateral or the debtor waives the requirement pursuant to Section 9–624.

(b) A purported or apparent acceptance of collateral under this section is ineffective unless:

(1) the secured party consents to the acceptance in an authenticated record or sends a proposal to the debtor; and

(2) the conditions of subsection (a) are met.

(c) For purposes of this section:

(1) a debtor consents to an acceptance of collateral in partial satisfaction of the obligation it secures only if the debtor agrees to the terms of the acceptance in a record authenticated after default; and

(2) a debtor consents to an acceptance of collateral in full satisfaction of the obligation it secures only if the debtor agrees to the terms of the acceptance in a record authenticated after default or the secured party:

(A) sends to the debtor after default a proposal that is unconditional or subject only to a condition that collateral not in the possession of the secured party be preserved or maintained;

(B) in the proposal, proposes to accept collateral in full satisfaction of the obligation it secures; and

(C) does not receive a notification of objection authenticated by the debtor within 20 days after the proposal is sent.

(d) To be effective under subsection (a)(2), a notification of objection must be received by the secured party:

(1) in the case of a person to which the proposal was sent pursuant to Section 9–621, within 20 days after notification was sent to that person; and

(2) in other cases:

(A) within 20 days after the last notification was sent pursuant to Section 9–621; or

(B) if a notification was not sent, before the debtor consents to the acceptance under subsection (c).

(e) A secured party that has taken possession of collateral shall dispose of the collateral pursuant to Section 9–610 within the time specified in subsection (f) if:

(1) 60 percent of the cash price has been paid in the case of a purchase-money security interest in consumer goods; or

(2) 60 percent of the principal amount of the obligation secured has been paid in the case of a non-purchase-money security interest in consumer goods.

(f) To comply with subsection (e), the secured party shall dispose of the collateral:

(1) within 90 days after taking possession; or

(2) within any longer period to which the debtor and all secondary obligors have agreed in an agreement to that effect entered into and authenticated after default.

(g) In a consumer transaction, a secured party may not accept collateral in partial satisfaction of the obligation it secures.

§ 9–621. Notification of Proposal to Accept Collateral.

(a) A secured party that desires to accept collateral in full or partial satisfaction of the obligation it secures shall send its proposal to:

(1) any person from which the secured party has received, before the debtor consented to the accep-

tance, an authenticated notification of a claim of an interest in the collateral;

(2) any other secured party or lienholder that, 10 days before the debtor consented to the acceptance, held a security interest in or other lien on the collateral perfected by the filing of a financing statement that:

(A) identified the collateral;

(B) was indexed under the debtor's name as of that date; and

(C) was filed in the office or offices in which to file a financing statement against the debtor covering the collateral as of that date; and

(3) any other secured party that, 10 days before the debtor consented to the acceptance, held a security interest in the collateral perfected by compliance with a statute, regulation, or treaty described in Section 9–311(a).

(b) A secured party that desires to accept collateral in partial satisfaction of the obligation it secures shall send its proposal to any secondary obligor in addition to the persons described in subsection (a).

§ 9–622. Effect of Acceptance of Collateral.

(a) A secured party's acceptance of collateral in full or partial satisfaction of the obligation it secures:

(1) discharges the obligation to the extent consented to by the debtor;

(2) transfers to the secured party all of a debtor's rights in the collateral;

(3) discharges the security interest or agricultural lien that is the subject of the debtor's consent and any subordinate security interest or other subordinate lien; and

(4) terminates any other subordinate interest.

(b) A subordinate interest is discharged or terminated under subsection (a), even if the secured party fails to comply with this article.

§ 9–623. Right to Redeem Collateral.

(a) A debtor, any secondary obligor, or any other secured party or lienholder may redeem collateral.

(b) To redeem collateral, a person shall tender:

(1) fulfillment of all obligations secured by the collateral; and

(2) the reasonable expenses and attorney's fees described in Section 9–615(a)(1).

(c) A redemption may occur at any time before a secured party:

(1) has collected collateral under Section 9–607;

(2) has disposed of collateral or entered into a contract for its disposition under Section 9–610; or

(3) has accepted collateral in full or partial satisfaction of the obligation it secures under Section 9–622.

§ 9–624. Waiver.

(a) A debtor or secondary obligor may waive the right to notification of disposition of collateral under Section 9–611 only by an agreement to that effect entered into and authenticated after default.

(b) A debtor may waive the right to require disposition of collateral under Section 9–620(e) only by an agreement to that effect entered into and authenticated after default.

(c) Except in a consumer-goods transaction, a debtor or secondary obligor may waive the right to redeem collateral under Section 9–623 only by an agreement to that effect entered into and authenticated after default.

[Subpart 2. Noncompliance with Article]

§ 9–625. Remedies for Secured Party's Failure to Comply with Article.

(a) If it is established that a secured party is not proceeding in accordance with this article, a court may order or restrain collection, enforcement, or disposition of collateral on appropriate terms and conditions.

(b) Subject to subsections (c), (d), and (f), a person is liable for damages in the amount of any loss caused by a failure to comply with this article. Loss caused by a failure to comply may include loss resulting from the debtor's inability to obtain, or increased costs of, alternative financing.

(c) Except as otherwise provided in Section 9–628:

(1) a person that, at the time of the failure, was a debtor, was an obligor, or held a security interest in or other lien on the collateral may recover damages under subsection (b) for its loss; and

(2) if the collateral is consumer goods, a person that was a debtor or a secondary obligor at the time a secured party failed to comply with this part may recover for that failure in any event an amount not less than the credit service charge plus 10 percent of the principal amount of the obligation or the time-price differential plus 10 percent of the cash price.

(d) A debtor whose deficiency is eliminated under Section 9–626 may recover damages for the loss of any surplus. However, a debtor or secondary obligor whose deficiency is eliminated or reduced under Section 9–626 may not otherwise recover under subsection (b) for noncompliance with the provisions of this part relating to collection, enforcement, disposition, or acceptance.

(e) In addition to any damages recoverable under subsection (b), the debtor, consumer obligor, or person named as a debtor in a filed record, as applicable, may recover $500 in each case from a person that:

(1) fails to comply with Section 9–208;

(2) fails to comply with Section 9–209;

(3) files a record that the person is not entitled to file under Section 9–509(a);

(4) fails to cause the secured party of record to file or send a termination statement as required by Section 9–513(a) or (c);

(5) fails to comply with Section 9–616(b)(1) and whose failure is part of a pattern, or consistent with a practice, of noncompliance; or

(6) fails to comply with Section 9–616(b)(2).

(f) A debtor or consumer obligor may recover damages under subsection (b) and, in addition, $500 in each case from a person that, without reasonable cause, fails to comply with a request under Section 9–210. A recipient of a request under Section 9–210 which never claimed an interest in the collateral or obligations that are the subject of a request under that section has a reasonable excuse for failure to comply with the request within the meaning of this subsection.

(g) If a secured party fails to comply with a request regarding a list of collateral or a statement of account under Section 9–210, the secured party may claim a security interest only as shown in the list or statement included in the request as against a person that is reasonably misled by the failure.

As amended in 2000.

§ 9–626. Action in Which Deficiency or Surplus Is in Issue.

(a) In an action arising from a transaction, other than a consumer transaction, in which the amount of a deficiency or surplus is in issue, the following rules apply:

(1) A secured party need not prove compliance with the provisions of this part relating to collection, enforcement, disposition, or acceptance unless the debtor or a secondary obligor places the secured party's compliance in issue.

(2) If the secured party's compliance is placed in issue, the secured party has the burden of establishing that the collection, enforcement, disposition, or acceptance was conducted in accordance with this part.

(3) Except as otherwise provided in Section 9–628, if a secured party fails to prove that the collection, enforcement, disposition, or acceptance was conducted in accordance with the provisions of this part relating to collection, enforcement, disposition, or acceptance, the liability of a debtor or a secondary obligor for a deficiency is limited to an amount by which the sum of the secured obligation, expenses, and attorney's fees exceeds the greater of:

(A) the proceeds of the collection, enforcement, disposition, or acceptance; or

(B) the amount of proceeds that would have been realized had the noncomplying secured party proceeded in accordance with the provisions of this part relating to collection, enforcement, disposition, or acceptance.

(4) For purposes of paragraph (3)(B), the amount of proceeds that would have been realized is equal to the

sum of the secured obligation, expenses, and attorney's fees unless the secured party proves that the amount is less than that sum.

(5) If a deficiency or surplus is calculated under Section 9–615(f), the debtor or obligor has the burden of establishing that the amount of proceeds of the disposition is significantly below the range of prices that a complying disposition to a person other than the secured party, a person related to the secured party, or a secondary obligor would have brought.

(b) The limitation of the rules in subsection (a) to transactions other than consumer transactions is intended to leave to the court the determination of the proper rules in consumer transactions. The court may not infer from that limitation the nature of the proper rule in consumer transactions and may continue to apply established approaches.

§ 9–627. Determination of Whether Conduct Was Commercially Reasonable.

(a) The fact that a greater amount could have been obtained by a collection, enforcement, disposition, or acceptance at a different time or in a different method from that selected by the secured party is not of itself sufficient to preclude the secured party from establishing that the collection, enforcement, disposition, or acceptance was made in a commercially reasonable manner.

(b) A disposition of collateral is made in a commercially reasonable manner if the disposition is made:

(1) in the usual manner on any recognized market;

(2) at the price current in any recognized market at the time of the disposition; or

(3) otherwise in conformity with reasonable commercial practices among dealers in the type of property that was the subject of the disposition.

(c) A collection, enforcement, disposition, or acceptance is commercially reasonable if it has been approved:

(1) in a judicial proceeding;

(2) by a bona fide creditors' committee;

(3) by a representative of creditors; or

(4) by an assignee for the benefit of creditors.

(d) Approval under subsection (c) need not be obtained, and lack of approval does not mean that the collection, enforcement, disposition, or acceptance is not commercially reasonable.

§ 9–628. Nonliability and Limitation on Liability of Secured Party; Liability of Secondary Obligor.

(a) Unless a secured party knows that a person is a debtor or obligor, knows the identity of the person, and knows how to communicate with the person:

(1) the secured party is not liable to the person, or to a secured party or lienholder that has filed a financing

statement against the person, for failure to comply with this article; and

(2) the secured party's failure to comply with this article does not affect the liability of the person for a deficiency.

(b) A secured party is not liable because of its status as secured party:

(1) to a person that is a debtor or obligor, unless the secured party knows:

(A) that the person is a debtor or obligor;

(B) the identity of the person; and

(C) how to communicate with the person; or

(2) to a secured party or lienholder that has filed a financing statement against a person, unless the secured party knows:

(A) that the person is a debtor; and

(B) the identity of the person.

(c) A secured party is not liable to any person, and a person's liability for a deficiency is not affected, because of any act or omission arising out of the secured party's reasonable belief that a transaction is not a consumer-goods transaction or a consumer transaction or that goods are not consumer goods, if the secured party's belief is based on its reasonable reliance on:

(1) a debtor's representation concerning the purpose for which collateral was to be used, acquired, or held; or

(2) an obligor's representation concerning the purpose for which a secured obligation was incurred.

(d) A secured party is not liable to any person under Section 9–625(c)(2) for its failure to comply with Section 9–616.

(e) A secured party is not liable under Section 9–625(c)(2) more than once with respect to any one secured obligation.

Part 7 Transition

§ 9–701. Effective Date.

This [Act] takes effect on July 1, 2001.

§ 9–702. Savings Clause.

(a) Except as otherwise provided in this part, this [Act] applies to a transaction or lien within its scope, even if the transaction or lien was entered into or created before this [Act] takes effect.

(b) Except as otherwise provided in subsection (c) and Sections 9–703 through 9–709:

(1) transactions and liens that were not governed by [former Article 9], were validly entered into or created before this [Act] takes effect, and would be subject to this [Act] if they had been entered into or created after this [Act] takes effect, and the rights, duties, and interests flowing from those transactions and liens remain valid after this [Act] takes effect; and

(2) the transactions and liens may be terminated, completed, consummated, and enforced as required or per-

mitted by this [Act] or by the law that otherwise would apply if this [Act] had not taken effect.

(c) This [Act] does not affect an action, case, or proceeding commenced before this [Act] takes effect.

As amended in 2000.

§ 9–703. Security Interest Perfected before Effective Date.

(a) A security interest that is enforceable immediately before this [Act] takes effect and would have priority over the rights of a person that becomes a lien creditor at that time is a perfected security interest under this [Act] if, when this [Act] takes effect, the applicable requirements for enforceability and perfection under this [Act] are satisfied without further action.

(b) Except as otherwise provided in Section 9–705, if, immediately before this [Act] takes effect, a security interest is enforceable and would have priority over the rights of a person that becomes a lien creditor at that time, but the applicable requirements for enforceability or perfection under this [Act] are not satisfied when this [Act] takes effect, the security interest:

(1) is a perfected security interest for one year after this [Act] takes effect;

(2) remains enforceable thereafter only if the security interest becomes enforceable under Section 9–203 before the year expires; and

(3) remains perfected thereafter only if the applicable requirements for perfection under this [Act] are satisfied before the year expires.

§ 9–704. Security Interest Unperfected before Effective Date.

A security interest that is enforceable immediately before this [Act] takes effect but which would be subordinate to the rights of a person that becomes a lien creditor at that time:

(1) remains an enforceable security interest for one year after this [Act] takes effect;

(2) remains enforceable thereafter if the security interest becomes enforceable under Section 9–203 when this [Act] takes effect or within one year thereafter; and

(3) becomes perfected:

(A) without further action, when this [Act] takes effect if the applicable requirements for perfection under this [Act] are satisfied before or at that time; or

(B) when the applicable requirements for perfection are satisfied if the requirements are satisfied after that time.

§ 9–705. Effectiveness of Action Taken before Effective Date.

(a) If action, other than the filing of a financing statement, is taken before this [Act] takes effect and the action would have resulted in priority of a security interest over the rights of a person that becomes a lien creditor had the security interest become enforceable before this [Act] takes effect, the action is effective to perfect a security interest that attaches under this [Act] within one year after this [Act] takes effect. An attached security interest becomes unperfected one year after this [Act] takes effect unless the security interest becomes a perfected security interest under this [Act] before the expiration of that period.

(b) The filing of a financing statement before this [Act] takes effect is effective to perfect a security interest to the extent the filing would satisfy the applicable requirements for perfection under this [Act].

(c) This [Act] does not render ineffective an effective financing statement that, before this [Act] takes effect, is filed and satisfies the applicable requirements for perfection under the law of the jurisdiction governing perfection as provided in [former Section 9–103]. However, except as otherwise provided in subsections (d) and (e) and Section 9–706, the financing statement ceases to be effective at the earlier of:

(1) the time the financing statement would have ceased to be effective under the law of the jurisdiction in which it is filed; or

(2) June 30, 2006.

(d) The filing of a continuation statement after this [Act] takes effect does not continue the effectiveness of the financing statement filed before this [Act] takes effect. However, upon the timely filing of a continuation statement after this [Act] takes effect and in accordance with the law of the jurisdiction governing perfection as provided in Part 3, the effectiveness of a financing statement filed in the same office in that jurisdiction before this [Act] takes effect continues for the period provided by the law of that jurisdiction.

(e) Subsection (c)(2) applies to a financing statement that, before this [Act] takes effect, is filed against a transmitting utility and satisfies the applicable requirements for perfection under the law of the jurisdiction governing perfection as provided in [former Section 9–103] only to the extent that Part 3 provides that the law of a jurisdiction other than the jurisdiction in which the financing statement is filed governs perfection of a security interest in collateral covered by the financing statement.

(f) A financing statement that includes a financing statement filed before this [Act] takes effect and a continuation statement filed after this [Act] takes effect is effective only to the extent that it satisfies the requirements of Part 5 for an initial financing statement.

§ 9–706. When Initial Financing Statement Suffices to Continue Effectiveness of Financing Statement.

(a) The filing of an initial financing statement in the office specified in Section 9–501 continues the effectiveness of a financing statement filed before this [Act] takes effect if:

(1) the filing of an initial financing statement in that office would be effective to perfect a security interest under this [Act];

(2) the pre-effective-date financing statement was filed in an office in another State or another office in this State; and

(3) the initial financing statement satisfies subsection (c).

(b) The filing of an initial financing statement under subsection (a) continues the effectiveness of the pre-effective-date financing statement:

(1) if the initial financing statement is filed before this [Act] takes effect, for the period provided in [former Section 9–403] with respect to a financing statement; and

(2) if the initial financing statement is filed after this [Act] takes effect, for the period provided in Section 9–515 with respect to an initial financing statement.

(c) To be effective for purposes of subsection (a), an initial financing statement must:

(1) satisfy the requirements of Part 5 for an initial financing statement;

(2) identify the pre-effective-date financing statement by indicating the office in which the financing statement was filed and providing the dates of filing and file numbers, if any, of the financing statement and of the most recent continuation statement filed with respect to the financing statement; and

(3) indicate that the pre-effective-date financing statement remains effective.

§ 9–707. Amendment of Pre-Effective-Date Financing Statement.

(a) In this section, "Pre-effective-date financing statement" means a financing statement filed before this [Act] takes effect.

(b) After this [Act] takes effect, a person may add or delete collateral covered by, continue or terminate the effectiveness of, or otherwise amend the information provided in, a pre-effective-date financing statement only in accordance with the law of the jurisdiction governing perfection as provided in Part 3. However, the effectiveness of a pre-effective-date financing statement also may be terminated in accordance with the law of the jurisdiction in which the financing statement is filed.

(c) Except as otherwise provided in subsection (d), if the law of this State governs perfection of a security interest, the information in a pre-effective-date financing statement may be amended after this [Act] takes effect only if:

(1) the pre-effective-date financing statement and an amendment are filed in the office specified in Section 9–501;

(2) an amendment is filed in the office specified in Section 9–501 concurrently with, or after the filing in that office of, an initial financing statement that satisfies Section 9–706(c); or

(3) an initial financing statement that provides the information as amended and satisfies Section 9–706(c) is filed in the office specified in Section 9–501.

(d) If the law of this State governs perfection of a security interest, the effectiveness of a pre-effective-date financing statement may be continued only under Section 9–705(d) and (f) or 9–706.

(e) Whether or not the law of this State governs perfection of a security interest, the effectiveness of a pre-effective-date financing statement filed in this State may be terminated after this [Act] takes effect by filing a termination statement in the office in which the pre-effective-date financing statement is filed, unless an initial financing statement that satisfies Section 9–706(c) has been filed in the office specified by the law of the jurisdiction governing perfection as provided in Part 3 as the office in which to file a financing statement.

As amended in 2000.

§ 9–708. Persons Entitled to File Initial Financing Statement or Continuation Statement.

A person may file an initial financing statement or a continuation statement under this part if:

(1) the secured party of record authorizes the filing; and

(2) the filing is necessary under this part:

(A) to continue the effectiveness of a financing statement filed before this [Act] takes effect; or

(B) to perfect or continue the perfection of a security interest.

As amended in 2000.

§ 9–709. Priority.

(a) This [Act] determines the priority of conflicting claims to collateral. However, if the relative priorities of the claims were established before this [Act] takes effect, [former Article 9] determines priority.

(b) For purposes of Section 9–322(a), the priority of a security interest that becomes enforceable under Section 9–203 of this [Act] dates from the time this [Act] takes effect if the security interest is perfected under this [Act] by the filing of a financing statement before this [Act] takes effect which would not have been effective to perfect the security interest under [former Article 9]. This subsection does not apply to conflicting security interests each of which is perfected by the filing of such a financing statement.

As amended in 2000.

The United Nations Convention on Contracts for the International Sale of Goods (Excerpts)

Part I. SPHERE OF APPLICATION AND GENERAL PROVISIONS

* * * *

Chapter II—General Provisions

* * * *

Article 8

(1) For the purposes of this Convention statements made by and other conduct of a party are to be interpreted according to his intent where the other party knew or could not have been unaware what that intent was.

(2) If the preceding paragraph is not applicable, statements made by and other conduct of a party are to be interpreted according to the understanding that a reasonable person of the same kind as the other party would have had in the same circumstances.

(3) In determining the intent of a party or the understanding a reasonable person would have had, due consideration is to be given to all relevant circumstances of the case including the negotiations, any practices which the parties have established between themselves, usages and any subsequent conduct of the parties.

Article 9

(1) The parties are bound by any usage to which they have agreed and by any practices which they have established between themselves.

(2) The parties are considered, unless otherwise agreed, to have impliedly made applicable to their contract or its formation a usage of which the parties knew or ought to have known and which in international trade is widely known to, and regularly observed by, parties to contracts of the type involved in the particular trade concerned.

* * * *

Article 11

A contract of sale need not be concluded in or evidenced by writing and is not subject to any other requirement as to form. It may be proved by any means, including witnesses.

* * * *

Part II. FORMATION OF THE CONTRACT

Article 14

(1) A proposal for concluding a contract addressed to one or more specific persons constitutes an offer if it is sufficiently definite and indicates the intention of the offeror to be bound in case of acceptance. A proposal is sufficiently definite if it indicates the goods and expressly or implicitly fixes or makes provision for determining the quantity and the price.

(2) A proposal other than one addressed to one or more specific persons is to be considered merely as an invitation to make offers, unless the contrary is clearly indicated by the person making the proposal.

Article 15

(1) An offer becomes effective when it reaches the offeree.

(2) An offer, even if it is irrevocable, may be withdrawn if the withdrawal reaches the offeree before or at the same time as the offer.

Article 16

(1) Until a contract is concluded an offer may be revoked if the revocation reaches the offeree before he has dispatched an acceptance.

(2) However, an offer cannot be revoked:

(a) If it indicates, whether by stating a fixed time for acceptance or otherwise, that it is irrevocable; or

(b) If it was reasonable for the offeree to rely on the offer as being irrevocable and the offeree has acted in reliance on the offer.

Article 17

An offer, even if it is irrevocable, is terminated when a rejection reaches the offeror.

Article 18

(1) A statement made by or other conduct of the offeree indicating assent to an offer is an acceptance. Silence or inactivity does not in itself amount to acceptance.

(2) An acceptance of an offer becomes effective at the moment the indication of assent reaches the offeror. An acceptance is not effective if the indication of assent does not reach the offeror within the time he has fixed or, if no time is fixed, within a reasonable time, due account being taken of the circumstances of the transaction, including the rapidity of the means of communication employed by the offeror. An oral offer must be accepted immediately unless the circumstances indicate otherwise.

(3) However, if, by virtue of the offer or as a result of practices which the parties have established between themselves or of usage, the offeree may indicate assent by performing an act, such as one relating to the dispatch of the goods or payment of the price, without notice to the offeror, the acceptance is effective at the moment the act is performed, provided that the act is performed within the period of time laid down in the preceding paragraph.

Article 19

(1) A reply to an offer which purports to be an acceptance but contains additions, limitations or other modifications is a rejection of the offer and constitutes a counter-offer.

(2) However, a reply to an offer which purports to be an acceptance but contains additional or different terms which do not materially alter the terms of the offer constitutes an acceptance, unless the offeror, without undue delay, objects orally to the discrepancy or dispatches a notice to that effect. If he does not so object, the terms of the contract are the terms of the offer with the modifications contained in the acceptance.

(3) Additional or different terms relating, among other things, to the price, payment, quality and quantity of the goods, place and time of delivery, extent of one party's liability to the other or the settlement of disputes are considered to alter the terms of the offer materially.

*　*　*　*

Article 22

An acceptance may be withdrawn if the withdrawal reaches the offeror before or at the same time as the acceptance would have become effective.

*　*　*　*

Part III.   SALE OF GOODS
Chapter I—General Provisions

Article 25

A breach of contract committed by one of the parties is fundamental if it results in such detriment to the other party as substantially to deprive him of what he is entitled to expect under the contract, unless the party in breach did not foresee and a reasonable person of the same kind in the same circumstances would not have foreseen such a result.

*　*　*　*

Article 28

If, in accordance with the provisions of this Convention, one party is entitled to require performance of any obligation by the other party, a court is not bound to enter a judgment for specific performance unless the court would do so under its own law in respect of similar contracts of sale not governed by this Convention.

Article 29

(1) A contract may be modified or terminated by the mere agreement of the parties.

(2) A contract in writing which contains a provision requiring any modification or termination by agreement to be in writing may not be otherwise modified or terminated by agreement. However, a party may be precluded by his conduct from asserting such a provision to the extent that the other party has relied on that conduct.

*　*　*　*

Chapter II—Obligations of the Seller
*　*　*　*

Section II. Conformity of the Goods and Third Party Claims

Article 35

(1) The seller must deliver goods which are of the quantity, quality and description required by the contract and which are contained or packaged in the manner required by the contract.

(2) Except where the parties have agreed otherwise, the goods do not conform with the contract unless they:

(a) Are fit for the purposes for which goods of the same description would ordinarily be used;

(b) Are fit for any particular purpose expressly or impliedly made known to the seller at the time of the conclusion of the contract, except where the circumstances show that the buyer did not rely, or that it was unreasonable for him to rely, on the seller's skill and judgment;

(c) Possess the qualities of goods which the seller has held out to the buyer as a sample or model;

(d) Are contained or packaged in the manner usual for such goods or, where there is no such manner, in a manner adequate to preserve and protect the goods.

(3) The seller is not liable under subparagraphs (a) to (d) of the preceding paragraph for any lack of conformity of the goods if at the time of the conclusion of the contract the buyer knew or could not have been unaware of such lack of conformity.

* * * *

Article 64

(1) The seller may declare the contract avoided:

(a) If the failure by the buyer to perform any of his obligations under the contract or this Convention amounts to a fundamental breach of contract; or

(b) If the buyer does not, within the additional period of time fixed by the seller in accordance with paragraph (1) of article 63, perform his obligation to pay the price or take delivery of the goods, or if he declares that he will not do so within the period so fixed.

(2) However, in cases where the buyer has paid the price, the seller loses the right to declare the contract avoided unless he does so:

(a) In respect of late performance by the buyer, before the seller has become aware that performance has been rendered; or

(b) In respect of any breach other than late performance by the buyer, within a reasonable time:

(i) After the seller knew or ought to have known of the breach; or

(ii) After the expiration of any additional period of time fixed by the seller in accordance with paragraph (1) of article 63, or after the buyer has declared that he will not perform his obligations within such an additional period.

* * * *

Chapter IV—Passing of Risk
* * * *

Article 67

(1) If the contract of sale involves carriage of the goods and the seller is not bound to hand them over at a particular place, the risk passes to the buyer when the goods are handed over to the first carrier for transmission to the buyer in accordance with the contract of sale. If the seller is bound to hand the goods over to a carrier at a particular place, the risk does not pass to the buyer until the goods are handed over to the carrier at that place. The fact that the seller is authorized to retain documents controlling the disposition of the goods does not affect the passage of the risk.

(2) Nevertheless, the risk does not pass to the buyer until the goods are clearly identified to the contract, whether by markings on the goods, by shipping documents, by notice given to the buyer or otherwise.

* * * *

Chapter V—Provisions Common to the Obligations of the Seller and of the Buyer

Section I. Anticipatory Breach and Instalment Contracts

Article 71

(1) A party may suspend the performance of his obligations if, after the conclusion of the contract, it becomes apparent that the other party will not perform a substantial part of his obligations as a result of:

(a) A serious deficiency in his ability to perform or in his creditworthiness; or

(b) His conduct in preparing to perform or in performing the contract.

(2) If the seller has already dispatched the goods before the grounds described in the preceding paragraph become evident, he may prevent the handing over of the goods to the buyer even though the buyer holds a document which entitles him to obtain them. The present paragraph relates only to the rights in the goods as between the buyer and the seller.

(3) A party suspending performance, whether before or after dispatch of the goods, must immediately give notice of the suspension to the other party and must continue with performance if the other party provides adequate assurance of his performance.

Article 72

(1) If prior to the date for performance of the contract it is clear that one of the parties will commit a fundamental breach of contract, the other party may declare the contract avoided.

(2) If time allows, the party intending to declare the contract avoided must give reasonable notice to the other party in order to permit him to provide adequate assurance of his performance.

(3) The requirements of the preceding paragraph do not apply if the other party has declared that he will not perform his obligations.

Article 73

(1) In the case of a contract for delivery of goods by instalments, if the failure of one party to perform any of his obligations in respect of any instalment constitutes a fundamental breach of contract with respect to that instalment, the other party may declare the contract avoided with respect to that instalment.

(2) If one party's failure to perform any of his obligations in respect of any instalment gives the other party good grounds to conclude that a fundamental breach of contract

will occur with respect to future instalments, he may declare the contract avoided for the future, provided that he does so within a reasonable time.

(3) A buyer who declares the contract avoided in respect of any delivery may, at the same time, declare it avoided in respect of deliveries already made or of future deliveries if, by reason of their interdependence, those deliveries could not be used for the purpose contemplated by the parties at the time of the conclusion of the contract.

Section II. Damages

Article 74

Damages for breach of contract by one party consist of a sum equal to the loss, including loss of profit, suffered by the other party as a consequence of the breach. Such damages may not exceed the loss which the party in breach foresaw or ought to have foreseen at the time of the conclusion of the contract, in the light of the facts and matters of which he then knew or ought to have known, as a possible consequence of the breach of contract.

Article 75

If the contract is avoided and if, in a reasonable manner and within a reasonable time after avoidance, the buyer has bought goods in replacement or the seller has resold the goods, the party claiming damages may recover the difference between the contract price and the price in the sub-stitute transaction as well as any further damages recoverable under article 74.

Article 76

(1) If the contract is avoided and there is a current price for the goods, the party claiming damages may, if he has not made a purchase or resale under article 75, recover the difference between the price fixed by the contract and the current price at the time of avoidance as well as any further damages recoverable under article 74. If, however, the party claiming damages has avoided the contract after taking over the goods, the current price at the time of such taking over shall be applied instead of the current price at the time of avoidance.

(2) For the purposes of the preceding paragraph, the current price is the price prevailing at the place where delivery of the goods should have been made or, if there is no current price at that place, the price at such other place as serves as a reasonable substitute, making due allowance for differences in the cost of transporting the goods.

Article 77

A party who relies on a breach of contract must take such measures as are reasonable in the circumstances to mitigate the loss, including loss of profit, resulting from the breach. If he fails to take such measures, the party in breach may claim a reduction in the damages in the amount by which the loss should have been mitigated.

APPENDIX E
The Uniform Partnership Act (Excerpts)

(The Uniform Partnership Act was amended in 1997 to provide limited liability for partners in a limited liability partnership. Over half the states, including District of Columbia, Puerto Rico, and the U.S. Virgin Islands, have adopted this latest version of the UPA.)

Article 1
GENERAL PROVISIONS

SECTION 101. Definitions In this [Act]:

* * * *

(6) "Partnership" means an association of two or more persons to carry on as co-owners a business for profit formed under Section 202, predecessor law, or comparable law of another jurisdiction.

(7) "Partnership agreement" means the agreement, whether written, oral, or implied, among the partners concerning the partnership, including amendments to the partnership agreement.

(8) "Partnership at will" means a partnership in which the partners have not agreed to remain partners until the expiration of a definite term or the completion of a particular undertaking.

(9) "Partnership interest" or "partner's interest in the partnership" means all of a partner's interests in the partnership, including the partner's transferable interest and all management and other rights.

(10) "Person" means an individual, corporation, business trust, estate, trust, partnership, association, joint venture, government, governmental subdivision, agency, or instrumentality, or any other legal or commercial entity.

* * * *

SECTION 103. Effect of Partnership Agreement; Nonwaivable Provisions.

(a) Except as otherwise provided in subsection (b), relations among the partners and between the partners and the partnership are governed by the partnership agreement. To the extent the partnership agreement does not otherwise provide, this [Act] governs relations among the partners and between the partners and the partnership.

(b) The partnership agreement may not:

(1) vary the rights and duties under Section 105 except to eliminate the duty to provide copies of statements to all of the partners;

(2) unreasonably restrict the right of access to books and records under Section 403(b);

(3) eliminate the duty of loyalty under Section 404(b) or 603(b)(3), but:

(i) the partnership agreement may identify specific types or categories of activities that do not violate the duty of loyalty, if not manifestly unreasonable; or

(ii) all of the partners or a number or percentage specified in the partnership agreement may authorize or ratify, after full disclosure of all material facts, a specific act or transaction that otherwise would violate the duty of loyalty;

(4) unreasonably reduce the duty of care under Section 404(c) or 603(b)(3);

(5) eliminate the obligation of good faith and fair dealing under Section 404(d), but the partnership agreement may prescribe the standards by which the performance of the obligation is to be measured, if the standards are not manifestly unreasonable;

(6) vary the power to dissociate as a partner under Section 602(a), except to require the notice under Section 601(1) to be in writing;

(7) vary the right of a court to expel a partner in the events specified in Section 601(5);

* * * *

SECTION 105. Execution, Filing, and Recording of Statements.

(a) A statement may be filed in the office of [the Secretary of State]. A certified copy of a statement that is filed in an office in another State may be filed in the office of [the Secretary of State]. Either filing has the effect provided in this [Act] with respect to partnership property located in or transactions that occur in this State.

(b) A certified copy of a statement that has been filed in the office of the [Secretary of State] and recorded in the office for recording transfers of real property has the effect provided for recorded statements in this [Act]. A recorded statement that is not a certified copy of a statement filed in the office of the [Secretary of State] does not have the effect provided for recorded statements in this [Act].

* * * *

SECTION 106. Governing Law.

(a) Except as otherwise provided in subsection (b), the law of the jurisdiction in which a partnership has its chief executive office governs relations among the partners and between the partners and the partnership.

(b) The law of this State governs relations among the partners and between the partners and the partnership and the liability of partners for an obligation of a limited liability partnership.

* * * *

Article 2
NATURE OF PARTNERSHIP

SECTION 201. Partnership as Entity.

(a) A partnership is an entity distinct from its partners.

(b) A limited liability partnership continues to be the same entity that existed before the filing of a statement of qualification under Section 1001.

SECTION 202. Formation of Partnership.

* * * *

(c) In determining whether a partnership is formed, the following rules apply:

(1) Joint tenancy, tenancy in common, tenancy by the entireties, joint property, common property, or part ownership does not by itself establish a partnership, even if the co-owners share profits made by the use of the property.

(2) The sharing of gross returns does not by itself establish a partnership, even if the persons sharing them have a joint or common right or interest in property from which the returns are derived.

(3) A person who receives a share of the profits of a business is presumed to be a partner in the business, unless the profits were received in payment:

(i) of a debt by installments or otherwise;

(ii) for services as an independent contractor or of wages or other compensation to an employee;

(iii) of rent;

(iv) of an annuity or other retirement or health benefit to a beneficiary, representative, or designee of a deceased or retired partner;

(v) of interest or other charge on a loan, even if the amount of payment varies with the profits of the business, including a direct or indirect present or future ownership of the collateral, or rights to income, proceeds, or increase in value derived from the collateral; or

(vi) for the sale of the goodwill of a business or other property by installments or otherwise.

SECTION 203. Partnership Property.

Property acquired by a partnership is property of the partnership and not of the partners individually.

SECTION 204. When Property is Partnership Property.

* * * *

(d) Property acquired in the name of one or more of the partners, without an indication in the instrument transferring title to the property of the person's capacity as a partner or of the existence of a partnership and without use of partnership assets, is presumed to be separate property, even if used for partnership purposes.

Article 3
RELATIONS OF PARTNERS TO PERSONS DEALING WITH PARTNERSHIP

SECTION 301. Partner Agent of Partnership.

Subject to the effect of a statement of partnership authority under Section 303:

(1) Each partner is an agent of the partnership for the purpose of its business. An act of a partner, including the execution of an instrument in the partnership name, for apparently carrying on in the ordinary course the partnership business or business of the kind carried on by the partnership binds the partnership, unless the partner had no authority to act for the

partnership in the particular matter and the person with whom the partner was dealing knew or had received a notification that the partner lacked authority.

(2) An act of a partner which is not apparently for carrying on in the ordinary course the partnership business or business of the kind carried on by the partnership binds the partnership only if the act was authorized by the other partners.

* * * *

SECTION 303. Statement of Partnership Authority.

(a) A partnership may file a statement of partnership authority, which:

(1) must include:

(i) the name of the partnership;

(ii) the street address of its chief executive office and of one office in this State, if there is one;

(iii) the names and mailing addresses of all of the partners or of an agent appointed and maintained by the partnership for the purpose of subsection (b); and

(iv) the names of the partners authorized to execute an instrument transferring real property held in the name of the partnership; and

(2) may state the authority, or limitations on the authority, of some or all of the partners to enter into other transactions on behalf of the partnership and any other matter.

* * * *

(d) Except as otherwise provided in subsection (g), a filed statement of partnership authority supplements the authority of a partner to enter into transactions on behalf of the partnership as follows:

(1) Except for transfers of real property, a grant of authority contained in a filed statement of partnership authority is conclusive in favor of a person who gives value without knowledge to the contrary, so long as and to the extent that a limitation on that authority is not then contained in another filed statement. A filed cancellation of a limitation on authority revives the previous grant of authority.

(2) A grant of authority to transfer real property held in the name of the partnership contained in a certified copy of a filed statement of partnership authority recorded in the office for recording transfers of that real property is conclusive in favor of a person who gives value without knowledge to the contrary, so long as and to the extent that a certified copy of a filed statement containing a limitation on that authority is not then of record in the office for recording transfers of that real property. The recording in the office for recording transfers of that real property of a certified copy of a

filed cancellation of a limitation on authority revives the previous grant of authority.

(e) A person not a partner is deemed to know of a limitation on the authority of a partner to transfer real property held in the name of the partnership if a certified copy of the filed statement containing the limitation on authority is of record in the office for recording transfers of that real property.

(f) Except as otherwise provided in subsections (d) and (e) and Sections 704 and 805, a person not a partner is not deemed to know of a limitation on the authority of a partner merely because the limitation is contained in a filed statement.

* * * *

SECTION 305. Partnership Liable for Partner's Actionable Conduct.

(a) A partnership is liable for loss or injury caused to a person, or for a penalty incurred, as a result of a wrongful act or omission, or other actionable conduct, of a partner acting in the ordinary course of business of the partnership or with authority of the partnership.

(b) If, in the course of the partnership's business or while acting with authority of the partnership, a partner receives or causes the partnership to receive money or property of a person not a partner, and the money or property is misapplied by a partner, the partnership is liable for the loss.

SECTION 306. Partner's Liability.

(a) Except as otherwise provided in subsections (b) and (c), all partners are liable jointly and severally for all obligations of the partnership unless otherwise agreed by the claimant or provided by law.

(b) A person admitted as a partner into an existing partnership is not personally liable for any partnership obligation incurred before the person's admission as a partner.

(c) An obligation of a partnership incurred while the partnership is a limited liability partnership, whether arising in contract, tort, or otherwise, is solely the obligation of the partnership. A partner is not personally liable, directly or indirectly, by way of contribution or otherwise, for such an obligation solely by reason of being or so acting as a partner. This subsection applies notwithstanding anything inconsistent in the partnership agreement that existed immediately before the vote required to become a limited liability partnership under Section 1001(b).

SECTION 307. Actions by and Against Partnership and Partners.

(a) A partnership may sue and be sued in the name of the partnership.

* * * *

(d) A judgment creditor of a partner may not levy execution against the assets of the partner to satisfy a judgment based on a claim against the partnership unless the partner is personally liable for the claim under Section 306 and:

(1) a judgment based on the same claim has been obtained against the partnership and a writ of execution on the judgment has been returned unsatisfied in whole or in part;

(2) the partnership is a debtor in bankruptcy;

(3) the partner has agreed that the creditor need not exhaust partnership assets;

(4) a court grants permission to the judgment creditor to levy execution against the assets of a partner based on a finding that partnership assets subject to execution are clearly insufficient to satisfy the judgment, that exhaustion of partnership assets is excessively burdensome, or that the grant of permission is an appropriate exercise of the court's equitable powers; or

(5) liability is imposed on the partner by law or contract independent of the existence of the partnership.

(e) This section applies to any partnership liability or obligation resulting from a representation by a partner or purported partner under Section 308.

SECTION 308. Liability of Purported Partner.

(a) If a person, by words or conduct, purports to be a partner, or consents to being represented by another as a partner, in a partnership or with one or more persons not partners, the purported partner is liable to a person to whom the representation is made, if that person, relying on the representation, enters into a transaction with the actual or purported partnership. If the representation, either by the purported partner or by a person with the purported partner's consent, is made in a public manner, the purported partner is liable to a person who relies upon the purported partnership even if the purported partner is not aware of being held out as a partner to the claimant. If partnership liability results, the purported partner is liable with respect to that liability as if the purported partner were a partner. If no partnership liability results, the purported partner is liable with respect to that liability jointly and severally with any other person consenting to the representation.

(b) If a person is thus represented to be a partner in an existing partnership, or with one or more persons not partners, the purported partner is an agent of persons consenting to the representation to bind them to the same extent and in the same manner as if the purported partner were a partner, with respect to persons who enter into transactions in reliance upon the representation. If all of the partners of the existing partnership consent to the representation, a partnership act or obligation results. If fewer than all of the partners of the existing partnership consent to the representation, the person acting and the partners consenting to the representation are jointly and severally liable.

* * * *

Article 4
RELATIONS OF PARTNERS TO EACH OTHER AND TO PARTNERSHIP

SECTION 401. Partner's Rights and Duties.

* * * *

(b) Each partner is entitled to an equal share of the partnership profits and is chargeable with a share of the partnership losses in proportion to the partner's share of the profits.

* * * *

(f) Each partner has equal rights in the management and conduct of the partnership business.

(g) A partner may use or possess partnership property only on behalf of the partnership.

(h) A partner is not entitled to remuneration for services performed for the partnership, except for reasonable compensation for services rendered in winding up the business of the partnership.

(i) A person may become a partner only with the consent of all of the partners.

(j) A difference arising as to a matter in the ordinary course of business of a partnership may be decided by a majority of the partners. An act outside the ordinary course of business of a partnership and an amendment to the partnership agreement may be undertaken only with the consent of all of the partners.

* * * *

SECTION 403. Partner's Rights and Duties with Respect to Information.

(a) A partnership shall keep its books and records, if any, at its chief executive office.

(b) A partnership shall provide partners and their agents and attorneys access to its books and records. It shall provide former partners and their agents and attorneys access to books and records pertaining to the period during which they were partners. The right of access provides the opportunity to inspect and copy books and records during ordinary business hours. A partnership may impose a reasonable charge, covering the costs of labor and material, for copies of documents furnished.

* * * *

SECTION 404. General Standards of Partner's Conduct.

(a) The only fiduciary duties a partner owes to the partnership and the other partners are the duty of loyalty and the duty of care set forth in subsections (b) and (c).

(b) A partner's duty of loyalty to the partnership and the other partners is limited to the following:

(1) to account to the partnership and hold as trustee for it any property, profit, or benefit derived by the partner in the conduct and winding up of the partnership business or derived from a use by the partner of partnership property, including the appropriation of a partnership opportunity;

(2) to refrain from dealing with the partnership in the conduct or winding up of the partnership business as or on behalf of a party having an interest adverse to the partnership; and

(3) to refrain from competing with the partnership in the conduct of the partnership business before the dissolution of the partnership.

(c) A partner's duty of care to the partnership and the other partners in the conduct and winding up of the partnership business is limited to refraining from engaging in grossly negligent or reckless conduct, intentional misconduct, or a knowing violation of law.

(d) A partner shall discharge the duties to the partnership and the other partners under this [Act] or under the partnership agreement and exercise any rights consistently with the obligation of good faith and fair dealing.

(e) A partner does not violate a duty or obligation under this [Act] or under the partnership agreement merely because the partner's conduct furthers the partner's own interest.

*   *   *   *

SECTION 405. Actions by Partnership and Partners.

(a) A partnership may maintain an action against a partner for a breach of the partnership agreement, or for the violation of a duty to the partnership, causing harm to the partnership.

(b) A partner may maintain an action against the partnership or another partner for legal or equitable relief, with or without an accounting as to partnership business, to:

(1) enforce the partner's rights under the partnership agreement;

(2) enforce the partner's rights under this [Act], including:

(i) the partner's rights under Sections 401, 403, or 404;

(ii) the partner's right on dissociation to have the partner's interest in the partnership purchased pursuant to Section 701 or enforce any other right under [Article] 6 or 7; or

(iii) the partner's right to compel a dissolution and winding up of the partnership business under or enforce any other right under [Article] 8; or

(3) enforce the rights and otherwise protect the interests of the partner, including rights and interests arising independently of the partnership relationship.

*   *   *   *

Article 5
TRANSFEREES AND CREDITORS OF PARTNER

SECTION 501. Partner Not Co-Owner of Partnership Property.

A partner is not a co-owner of partnership property and has no interest in partnership property which can be transferred, either voluntarily or involuntarily.

SECTION 502. Partner's Transferable Interest in Partnership.

The only transferable interest of a partner in the partnership is the partner's share of the profits and losses of the partnership and the partner's right to receive distributions. The interest is personal property.

SECTION 503. Transfer of Partner's Transferable Interest.

(a) A transfer, in whole or in part, of a partner's transferable interest in the partnership:

(1) is permissible;

(2) does not by itself cause the partner's dissociation or a dissolution and winding up of the partnership business; and

(3) does not, as against the other partners or the partnership, entitle the transferee, during the continuance of the partnership, to participate in the management or conduct of the partnership business, to require access to information concerning partnership transactions, or to inspect or copy the partnership books or records.

*   *   *   *

SECTION 504. Partner's Transferable Interest Subject to Charging Order.

(a) On application by a judgment creditor of a partner or of a partner's transferee, a court having jurisdiction may charge the transferable interest of the judgment debtor to satisfy the judgment. The court may appoint a receiver of the share of the distributions due or to become due to the judgment debtor in respect of the partnership and make all other orders, directions, accounts, and inquiries the judgment debtor might have made or which the circumstances of the case may require.

*   *   *   *

Article 6
PARTNER'S DISSOCIATION

SECTION 601. Events Causing Partner's Dissociation.

A partner is dissociated from a partnership upon the occurrence of any of the following events:

(1) the partnership's having notice of the partner's express will to withdraw as a partner or on a later date specified by the partner;

(2) an event agreed to in the partnership agreement as causing the partner's dissociation;

(3) the partner's expulsion pursuant to the partnership agreement;

(4) the partner's expulsion by the unanimous vote of the other partners if:

(i) it is unlawful to carry on the partnership business with that partner;

(ii) there has been a transfer of all or substantially all of that partner's transferable interest in the partnership, other than a transfer for security purposes, or a court order charging the partner's interest, which has not been foreclosed;

(iii) within 90 days after the partnership notifies a corporate partner that it will be expelled because it has filed a certificate of dissolution or the equivalent, its charter has been revoked, or its right to conduct business has been suspended by the jurisdiction of its incorporation, there is no revocation of the certificate of dissolution or no reinstatement of its charter or its right to conduct business; or

(iv) a partnership that is a partner has been dissolved and its business is being wound up;

(5) on application by the partnership or another partner, the partner's expulsion by judicial determination because:

(i) the partner engaged in wrongful conduct that adversely and materially affected the partnership business;

(ii) the partner willfully or persistently committed a material breach of the partnership agreement or of a duty owed to the partnership or the other partners under Section 404; or

(iii) the partner engaged in conduct relating to the partnership business which makes it not reasonably practicable to carry on the business in partnership with the partner;

(6) the partner's:

(i) becoming a debtor in bankruptcy;

(ii) executing an assignment for the benefit of creditors;

(iii) seeking, consenting to, or acquiescing in the appointment of a trustee, receiver, or liquidator of that partner or of all or substantially all of that partner's property; or

(iv) failing, within 90 days after the appointment, to have vacated or stayed the appointment of a trustee, receiver, or liquidator of the partner or of all or substantially all of the partner's property obtained without the partner's consent or acquiescence, or failing within

90 days after the expiration of a stay to have the appointment vacated;

(7) in the case of a partner who is an individual:

(i) the partner's death;

(ii) the appointment of a guardian or general conservator for the partner; or

(iii) a judicial determination that the partner has otherwise become incapable of performing the partner's duties under the partnership agreement;

* * * *

SECTION 602. Partner's Power to Dissociate; Wrongful Dissociation.

(a) A partner has the power to dissociate at any time, rightfully or wrongfully, by express will pursuant to Section 601(1).

(b) A partner's dissociation is wrongful only if:

(1) it is in breach of an express provision of the partnership agreement; or

(2) in the case of a partnership for a definite term or particular undertaking, before the expiration of the term or the completion of the undertaking:

(i) the partner withdraws by express will, unless the withdrawal follows within 90 days after another partner's dissociation by death or otherwise under Section 601(6) through (10) or wrongful dissociation under this subsection;

(ii) the partner is expelled by judicial determination under Section 601(5);

(iii) the partner is dissociated by becoming a debtor in bankruptcy; or

(iv) in the case of a partner who is not an individual, trust other than a business trust, or estate, the partner is expelled or otherwise dissociated because it willfully dissolved or terminated.

(c) A partner who wrongfully dissociates is liable to the partnership and to the other partners for damages caused by the dissociation. The liability is in addition to any other obligation of the partner to the partnership or to the other partners.

SECTION 603. Effect of Partner's Dissociation.

(a) If a partner's dissociation results in a dissolution and winding up of the partnership business, [Article] 8 applies; otherwise, [Article] 7 applies.

(b) Upon a partner's dissociation:

(1) the partner's right to participate in the management and conduct of the partnership business terminates, except as otherwise provided in Section 803;

(2) the partner's duty of loyalty under Section 404(b)(3) terminates; and

(3) the partner's duty of loyalty under Section 404(b)(1) and (2) and duty of care under Section 404(c) continue

only with regard to matters arising and events occurring before the partner's dissociation, unless the partner participates in winding up the partnership's business pursuant to Section 803.

Article 7
PARTNER'S DISSOCIATION WHEN BUSINESS NOT WOUND UP

SECTION 701. Purchase of Dissociated Partner's Interest.

(a) If a partner is dissociated from a partnership without resulting in a dissolution and winding up of the partnership business under Section 801, the partnership shall cause the dissociated partner's interest in the partnership to be purchased for a buyout price determined pursuant to subsection (b).

(b) The buyout price of a dissociated partner's interest is the amount that would have been distributable to the dissociating partner under Section 807(b) if, on the date of dissociation, the assets of the partnership were sold at a price equal to the greater of the liquidation value or the value based on a sale of the entire business as a going concern without the dissociated partner and the partnership were wound up as of that date. Interest must be paid from the date of dissociation to the date of payment.

(c) Damages for wrongful dissociation under Section 602(b), and all other amounts owing, whether or not presently due, from the dissociated partner to the partnership, must be offset against the buyout price. Interest must be paid from the date the amount owed becomes due to the date of payment.

* * * *

SECTION 702. Dissociated Partner's Power to Bind and Liability to Partnership.

(a) For two years after a partner dissociates without resulting in a dissolution and winding up of the partnership business, the partnership, including a surviving partnership under [Article] 9, is bound by an act of the dissociated partner which would have bound the partnership under Section 301 before dissociation only if at the time of entering into the transaction the other party:

(1) reasonably believed that the dissociated partner was then a partner;

(2) did not have notice of the partner's dissociation; and

(3) is not deemed to have had knowledge under Section 303(e) or notice under Section 704(c).

(b) A dissociated partner is liable to the partnership for any damage caused to the partnership arising from an obligation incurred by the dissociated partner after dissociation for which the partnership is liable under subsection (a).

SECTION 703. Dissociated Partner's Liability to Other Persons.

(a) A partner's dissociation does not of itself discharge the partner's liability for a partnership obligation incurred before dissociation. A dissociated partner is not liable for a partnership obligation incurred after dissociation, except as otherwise provided in subsection (b).

(b) A partner who dissociates without resulting in a dissolution and winding up of the partnership business is liable as a partner to the other party in a transaction entered into by the partnership, or a surviving partnership under [Article] 9, within two years after the partner's dissociation, only if the partner is liable for the obligation under Section 306 and at the time of entering into the transaction the other party:

(1) reasonably believed that the dissociated partner was then a partner;

(2) did not have notice of the partner's dissociation; and

(3) is not deemed to have had knowledge under Section 303(e) or notice under Section 704(c).

* * * *

SECTION 704. Statement of Dissociation.

(a) A dissociated partner or the partnership may file a statement of dissociation stating the name of the partnership and that the partner is dissociated from the partnership.

(b) A statement of dissociation is a limitation on the authority of a dissociated partner for the purposes of Section 303(d) and (e).

(c) For the purposes of Sections 702(a)(3) and 703(b)(3), a person not a partner is deemed to have notice of the dissociation 90 days after the statement of dissociation is filed.

* * * *

Article 8
WINDING UP PARTNERSHIP BUSINESS

SECTION 801. Events Causing Dissolution and Winding Up of Partnership Business.

A partnership is dissolved, and its business must be wound up, only upon the occurrence of any of the following events:

(1) in a partnership at will, the partnership's having notice from a partner, other than a partner who is dissociated under Section 601(2) through (10), of that partner's express will to withdraw as a partner, or on a later date specified by the partner;

(2) in a partnership for a definite term or particular under-taking:

    (i) within 90 days after a partner's dissociation by death or otherwise under Section 601(6) through (10) or wrongful dissociation under Section 602(b), the express will of at least half of the remaining partners to wind up the partnership business, for which purpose a partner's rightful dissociation pursuant to Section 602(b)(2)(i) constitutes the expression of that partner's will to wind up the partnership business;

    (ii) the express will of all of the partners to wind up the partnership business; or

    (iii) the expiration of the term or the completion of the undertaking;

(3) an event agreed to in the partnership agreement resulting in the winding up of the partnership business;

(4) an event that makes it unlawful for all or substantially all of the business of the partnership to be continued, but a cure of illegality within 90 days after notice to the partnership of the event is effective retroactively to the date of the event for purposes of this section;

(5) on application by a partner, a judicial determination that:

    (i) the economic purpose of the partnership is likely to be unreasonably frustrated;

    (ii) another partner has engaged in conduct relating to the partnership business which makes it not reasonably practicable to carry on the business in partnership with that partner; or

    (iii) it is not otherwise reasonably practicable to carry on the partnership business in conformity with the partnership agreement; or

*   *   *   *

SECTION 802. Partnership Continues after Dissolution.

(a) Subject to subsection (b), a partnership continues after dissolution only for the purpose of winding up its business. The partnership is terminated when the winding up of its business is completed.

(b) At any time after the dissolution of a partnership and before the winding up of its business is completed, all of the partners, including any dissociating partner other than a wrongfully dissociating partner, may waive the right to have the partnership's business wound up and the partnership terminated. In that event:

    (1) the partnership resumes carrying on its business as if dissolution had never occurred, and any liability incurred by the partnership or a partner after the dissolution and before the waiver is determined as if dissolution had never occurred; and

    (2) the rights of a third party accruing under Section 804(1) or arising out of conduct in reliance on the dis-solution before the third party knew or received a notification of the waiver may not be adversely affected.

SECTION 803. Right to Wind Up Partnership.

(a) After dissolution, a partner who has not wrongfully dissociated may participate in winding up the partnership's business, but on application of any partner, partner's legal representative, or transferee, the [designate the appropriate court], for good cause shown, may order judicial supervision of the winding up.

(b) The legal representative of the last surviving partner may wind up a partnership's business.

(c) A person winding up a partnership's business may preserve the partnership business or property as a going concern for a reasonable time, prosecute and defend actions and proceedings, whether civil, criminal, or administrative, settle and close the partnership's business, dispose of and transfer the partnership's property, discharge the partnership's liabilities, distribute the assets of the partnership pursuant to Section 807, settle disputes by mediation or arbitration, and perform other necessary acts.

SECTION 804. Partner's Power to Bind Partnership After Dissolution.

Subject to Section 805, a partnership is bound by a partner's act after dissolution that:

(1) is appropriate for winding up the partnership business; or

(2) would have bound the partnership under Section 301 before dissolution, if the other party to the transaction did not have notice of the dissolution.

SECTION 805. Statement of Dissolution.

(a) After dissolution, a partner who has not wrongfully dissociated may file a statement of dissolution stating the name of the partnership and that the partnership has dissolved and is winding up its business.

(b) A statement of dissolution cancels a filed statement of partnership authority for the purposes of Section 303(d) and is a limitation on authority for the purposes of Section 303(e).

(c) For the purposes of Sections 301 and 804, a person not a partner is deemed to have notice of the dissolution and the limitation on the partners' authority as a result of the statement of dissolution 90 days after it is filed.

*   *   *   *

SECTION 807. Settlement of Accounts and Contributions among Partners.

(a) In winding up a partnership's business, the assets of the partnership, including the contributions of the partners required by this section, must be applied to discharge its obligations to creditors, including, to the extent permitted by law, partners who are creditors. Any surplus must be applied to pay in cash the net amount distributable to partners in accordance with their right to distributions under subsection (b).

(b) Each partner is entitled to a settlement of all partnership accounts upon winding up the partnership business. In settling accounts among the partners, profits and losses that result from the liquidation of the partnership assets must be credited and charged to the partners' accounts. The partnership shall make a distribution to a partner in an amount equal to any excess of the credits over the charges in the partner's account. A partner shall contribute to the partnership an amount equal to any excess of the charges over the credits in the partner's account but excluding from the calculation charges attributable to an obligation for which the partner is not personally liable under Section 306.

*   *   *   *

(d) After the settlement of accounts, each partner shall contribute, in the proportion in which the partner shares partnership losses, the amount necessary to satisfy partnership obligations that were not known at the time of the settlement and for which the partner is personally liable under Section 306.

*   *   *   *

Article 10
LIMITED LIABILITY PARTNERSHIP

SECTION 1001. Statement of Qualification.

(a) A partnership may become a limited liability partnership pursuant to this section.

(b) The terms and conditions on which a partnership becomes a limited liability partnership must be approved by the vote necessary to amend the partnership agreement except, in the case of a partnership agreement that expressly considers obligations to contribute to the partnership, the vote necessary to amend those provisions.

(c) After the approval required by subsection (b), a partnership may become a limited liability partnership by filing a statement of qualification. The statement must contain:

(1) the name of the partnership;

(2) the street address of the partnership's chief executive office and, if different, the street address of an office in this State, if any;

(3) if the partnership does not have an office in this State, the name and street address of the partnership's agent for service of process;

(4) a statement that the partnership elects to be a limited liability partnership; and

(5) a deferred effective date, if any.

*   *   *   *

SECTION 1002. Name.

The name of a limited liability partnership must end with "Registered Limited Liability Partnership", "Limited Liability Partnership", "R.L.L.P.", "L.L.P.", "RLLP," or "LLP".

SECTION 1003. Annual Report.

(a) A limited liability partnership, and a foreign limited liability partnership authorized to transact business in this State, shall file an annual report in the office of the [Secretary of State] which contains:

(1) the name of the limited liability partnership and the State or other jurisdiction under whose laws the foreign limited liability partnership is formed;

(2) the street address of the partnership's chief executive office and, if different, the street address of an office of the partnership in this State, if any; and

(3) if the partnership does not have an office in this State, the name and street address of the partnership's current agent for service of process.

(b) An annual report must be filed between [January 1 and April 1] of each year following the calendar year in which a partnership files a statement of qualification or a foreign partnership becomes authorized to transact business in this State.

*   *   *   *

Article 11
FOREIGN LIMITED LIABILITY PARTNERSHIP

SECTION 1101. Law Governing Foreign Limited Liability Partnership.

(a) The law under which a foreign limited liability partnership is formed governs relations among the partners and between the partners and the partnership and the liability of partners for obligations of the partnership.

*   *   *   *

SECTION 1102. Statement of Foreign Qualification.

(a) Before transacting business in this State, a foreign limited liability partnership must file a statement of foreign qualification. The statement must contain:

(1) the name of the foreign limited liability partnership which satisfies the requirements of the State or other jurisdiction under whose law it is formed and ends with "Registered Limited Liability Partnership", "Limited Liability Partnership", "R.L.L.P.", "L.L.P.", "RLLP," or "LLP";

(2) the street address of the partnership's chief executive office and, if different, the street address of an office of the partnership in this State, if any;

(3) if there is no office of the partnership in this State, the name and street address of the partnership's agent for service of process; and

(4) a deferred effective date, if any.

* * * *

SECTION 1104. Activities Not Constituting Transacting Business.

(a) Activities of a foreign limited liability partnership which do not constitute transacting business for the purpose of this [article] include:

(1) maintaining, defending, or settling an action or proceeding;

(2) holding meetings of its partners or carrying on any other activity concerning its internal affairs;

(3) maintaining bank accounts;

(4) maintaining offices or agencies for the transfer, exchange, and registration of the partnership's own securities or maintaining trustees or depositories with respect to those securities;

(5) selling through independent contractors;

(6) soliciting or obtaining orders, whether by mail or through employees or agents or otherwise, if the orders require acceptance outside this State before they become contracts;

(7) creating or acquiring indebtedness, with or without a mortgage, or other security interest in property;

(8) collecting debts or foreclosing mortgages or other security interests in property securing the debts, and holding, protecting, and maintaining property so acquired;

(9) conducting an isolated transaction that is completed within 30 days and is not one in the course of similar transactions; and

(10) transacting business in interstate commerce.

(b) For purposes of this [article], the ownership in this State of income-producing real property or tangible personal property, other than property excluded under subsection (a), constitutes transacting business in this State.

* * * *

The Revised Uniform Limited Partnership Act (Excerpts)

Article 1
GENERAL PROVISIONS

Section 101. Definitions.

As used in this [Act], unless the context otherwise requires:

(1) "Certificate of limited partnership" means the certificate referred to in Section 201, and the certificate as amended or restated.

(2) "Contribution" means any cash, property, services rendered, or a promissory note or other binding obligation to contribute cash or property or to perform services, which a partner contributes to a limited partnership in his capacity as a partner.

(3) "Event of withdrawal of a general partner" means an event that causes a person to cease to be a general partner as provided in Section 402.

(4) "Foreign limited partnership" means a partnership formed under the laws of any state other than this State and having as partners one or more general partners and one or more limited partners.

(5) "General partner" means a person who has been admitted to a limited partnership as a general partner in accordance with the partnership agreement and named in the certificate of limited partnership as a general partner.

(6) "Limited partner" means a person who has been admitted to a limited partnership as a limited partner in accordance with the partnership agreement.

(7) "Limited partnership" and "domestic limited partnership" mean a partnership formed by two or more persons under the laws of this State and having one or more general partners and one or more limited partners.

(8) "Partner" means a limited or general partner.

(9) "Partnership agreement" means any valid agreement, written or oral, of the partners as to the affairs of a limited partnership and the conduct of its business.

(10) "Partnership interest" means a partner's share of the profits and losses of a limited partnership and the right to receive distributions of partnership assets.

(11) "Person" means a natural person, partnership, limited partnership (domestic or foreign), trust, estate, association, or corporation.

(12) "State" means a state, territory, or possession of the United States, the District of Columbia, or the Commonwealth of Puerto Rico.

Section 102. Name.

The name of each limited partnership as set forth in its certificate of limited partnership:

(1) shall contain without abbreviation the words "limited partnership";

(2) may not contain the name of a limited partner unless (i) it is also the name of a general partner or the corporate name of a corporate general partner, or (ii) the business of the limited partnership had been carried on under that name before the admission of that limited partner;

(3) may not be the same as, or deceptively similar to, the name of any corporation or limited partnership organized under the laws of this State or licensed or registered as a foreign corporation or limited partnership in this State; and

(4) may not contain the following words [here insert prohibited words].

Section 103. Reservation of Name.

(a) The exclusive right to the use of a name may be reserved by:

(1) any person intending to organize a limited partnership under this [Act] and to adopt that name;

(2) any domestic limited partnership or any foreign limited partnership registered in this State which, in either case, intends to adopt that name;

(3) any foreign limited partnership intending to register in this State and adopt that name; and

(4) any person intending to organize a foreign limited partnership and intending to have it register in this State and adopt that name.

(b) The reservation shall be made by filing with the Secretary of State an application, executed by the applicant, to reserve a specified name. If the Secretary of State finds that the name is available for use by a domestic or foreign limited partnership, he [or she] shall reserve the name for the exclusive use of the applicant for a period of 120 days. Once having so reserved a name, the same applicant may not again reserve the same name until more than 60 days after the expiration of the last 120-day period for which that applicant reserved that name. The right to the exclusive use of a reserved name may be transferred to any other person by filing in the office of the Secretary of State a notice of the transfer, executed by the applicant for whom the name was reserved and specifying the name and address of the transferee.

Section 104. Specified Office and Agent.

Each limited partnership shall continuously maintain in this State:

(1) an office, which may but need not be a place of its business in this State, at which shall be kept the records required by Section 105 to be maintained; and

(2) an agent for service of process on the limited partnership, which agent must be an individual resident of this State, a domestic corporation, or a foreign corporation authorized to do business in this State.

Section 105. Records to Be Kept.

(a) Each limited partnership shall keep at the office referred to in Section 104(1) the following:

(1) a current list of the full name and last known business address of each partner, separately identifying the general partners (in alphabetical order) and the limited partners (in alphabetical order);

(2) a copy of the certificate of limited partnership and all certificates of amendment thereto, together with executed copies of any powers of attorney pursuant to which any certificate has been executed;

(3) copies of the limited partnership's federal, state and local income tax returns and reports, if any, for the three most recent years;

(4) copies of any then effective written partnership agreements and of any financial statements of the limited partnership for the three most recent years; and

(5) unless contained in a written partnership agreement, a writing setting out:

(i) the amount of cash and a description and statement of the agreed value of the other property or services contributed by each partner and which each partner has agreed to contribute;

(ii) the times at which or events on the happening of which any additional contributions agreed to be made by each partner are to be made;

(iii) any right of a partner to receive, or of a general partner to make, distributions to a partner which include a return of all or any part of the partner's contribution; and

(iv) any events upon the happening of which the limited partnership is to be dissolved and its affairs wound up.

(b) Records kept under this section are subject to inspection and copying at the reasonable request and at the expense of any partner during ordinary business hours.

Section 106. Nature of Business.

A limited partnership may carry on any business that a partnership without limited partners may carry on except [here designate prohibited activities].

Section 107. Business Transactions of Partners with Partnership.

Except as provided in the partnership agreement, a partner may lend money to and transact other business with the limited partnership and, subject to other applicable law, has the same rights and obligations with respect thereto as a person who is not a partner.

Article 2
FORMATION; CERTIFICATE OF LIMITED PARTNERSHIP

Section 201. Certificate of Limited Partnership.

(a) In order to form a limited partnership, a certificate of limited partnership must be executed and filed in the office of the Secretary of State. The certificate shall set forth:

(1) the name of the limited partnership;

(2) the address of the office and the name and address of the agent for service of process required to be maintained by Section 104;

(3) the name and the business address of each general partner;

(4) the latest date upon which the limited partnership is to dissolve; and

(5) any other matters the general partners determine to include therein.

(b) A limited partnership is formed at the time of the filing of the certificate of limited partnership in the office of the Secretary of State or at any later time specified in the certificate of limited partnership if, in either case, there has been substantial compliance with the requirements of this section.

Section 202. Amendment to Certificate.

(a) A certificate of limited partnership is amended by filing a certificate of amendment thereto in the office of the Secretary of State. The certificate shall set forth:

(1) the name of the limited partnership;

(2) the date of filing the certificate; and

(3) the amendment to the certificate.

(b) Within 30 days after the happening of any of the following events, an amendment to a certificate of limited partnership reflecting the occurrence of the event or events shall be filed:

(1) the admission of a new general partner;

(2) the withdrawal of a general partner; or

(3) the continuation of the business under Section 801 after an event of withdrawal of a general partner.

(c) A general partner who becomes aware that any statement in a certificate of limited partnership was false when made or that any arrangements or other facts described have changed, making the certificate inaccurate in any respect, shall promptly amend the certificate.

(d) A certificate of limited partnership may be amended at any time for any other proper purpose the general partners determine.

(e) No person has any liability because an amendment to a certificate of limited partnership has not been filed to reflect the occurrence of any event referred to in subsection (b) of this section if the amendment is filed within the 30-day period specified in subsection (b).

(f) A restated certificate of limited partnership may be executed and filed in the same manner as a certificate of amendment.

Section 203. Cancellation of Certificate.

A certificate of limited partnership shall be cancelled upon the dissolution and the commencement of winding up of the partnership or at any other time there are no limited partners. A certificate of cancellation shall be filed in the office of the Secretary of State and set forth:

(1) the name of the limited partnership;

(2) the date of filing of its certificate of limited partnership;

(3) the reason for filing the certificate of cancellation;

(4) the effective date (which shall be a date certain) of cancellation if it is not to be effective upon the filing of the certificate; and

(5) any other information the general partners filing the certificate determine.

Section 204. Execution of Certificates.

(a) Each certificate required by this Article to be filed in the office of the Secretary of State shall be executed in the following manner:

(1) an original certificate of limited partnership must be signed by all general partners;

(2) a certificate of amendment must be signed by at least one general partner and by each other general partner designated in the certificate as a new general partner; and

(3) a certificate of cancellation must be signed by all general partners.

(b) Any person may sign a certificate by an attorney-in-fact, but a power of attorney to sign a certificate relating to the admission of a general partner must specifically describe the admission.

(c) The execution of a certificate by a general partner constitutes an affirmation under the penalties of perjury that the facts stated therein are true.

Section 205. Execution by Judicial Act.

If a person required by Section 204 to execute any certificate fails or refuses to do so, any other person who is adversely affected by the failure or refusal may petition the [designate the appropriate court] to direct the execution of the certificate. If the court finds that it is proper for the certificate to be executed and that any person so designated has failed or refused to execute the certificate, it shall order the Secretary of State to record an appropriate certificate.

Section 206. Filing in Office of Secretary of State.

(a) Two signed copies of the certificate of limited partnership and of any certificates of amendment or cancellation (or of any judicial decree of amendment or cancellation) shall be delivered to the Secretary of State. A person who executes a certificate as an agent or fiduciary need not exhibit evidence of his [or her] authority as a prerequisite to filing. Unless the Secretary of State finds that any certificate does not conform to law, upon receipt of all filing fees required by law he [or she] shall:

(1) endorse on each duplicate original the word "Filed" and the day, month, and year of the filing thereof;

(2) file one duplicate original in his [or her] office; and

(3) return the other duplicate original to the person who filed it or his [or her] representative.

(b) Upon the filing of a certificate of amendment (or judicial decree of amendment) in the office of the Secretary of State, the certificate of limited partnership shall be amended as set forth therein, and upon the effective date of a certificate of cancellation (or a judicial decree thereof), the certificate of limited partnership is cancelled.

Section 207. Liability for False Statement in Certificate.

If any certificate of limited partnership or certificate of amendment or cancellation contains a false statement, one who suffers loss by reliance on the statement may recover damages for the loss from:

(1) any person who executes the certificate, or causes another to execute it on his behalf, and knew, and any general partner who knew or should have known, the statement to be false at the time the certificate was executed; and

(2) any general partner who thereafter knows or should have known that any arrangement or other fact described in the certificate has changed, making the statement inaccurate in any respect within a sufficient time before the statement was relied upon reasonably to have enabled that general partner to cancel or amend the certificate, or to file a petition for its cancellation or amendment under Section 205.

Section 208. Scope of Notice.

The fact that a certificate of limited partnership is on file in the office of the Secretary of State is notice that the partnership is a limited partnership and the persons designated therein as general partners are general partners, but it is not notice of any other fact.

Section 209. Delivery of Certificates to Limited Partners.

Upon the return by the Secretary of State pursuant to Section 206 of a certificate marked "Filed," the general partners shall promptly deliver or mail a copy of the certificate of limited partnership and each certificate of amendment or cancellation to each limited partner unless the partnership agreement provides otherwise.

Article 3
LIMITED PARTNERS

Section 301. Admission of Additional Limited Partners.

(a) A person becomes a limited partner on the later of:

(1) the date the original certificate of limited partnership is filed; or

(2) the date stated in the records of the limited partnership as the date that person becomes a limited partner.

(b) After the filing of a limited partnership's original certificate of limited partnership, a person may be admitted as an additional limited partner:

(1) in the case of a person acquiring a partnership interest directly from the limited partnership, upon compliance with the partnership agreement or, if the partnership agreement does not so provide, upon the written consent of all partners; and

(2) in the case of an assignee of a partnership interest of a partner who has the power, as provided in Section 704, to grant the assignee the right to become a limited partner, upon the exercise of that power and compliance with any conditions limiting the grant or exercise of the power.

Section 302. Voting.

Subject to Section 303, the partnership agreement may grant to all or a specified group of the limited partners the right to vote (on a per capita or other basis) upon any matter.

Section 303. Liability to Third Parties.

(a) Except as provided in subsection (d), a limited partner is not liable for the obligations of a limited partnership unless he [or she] is also a general partner or, in addition to the exercise of his [or her] rights and powers as a limited partner, he [or she] participates in the control of the business. However, if the limited partner participates in the control of the business, he [or she] is liable only to persons who transact business with the limited partnership reasonably believing, based upon the limited partner's conduct, that the limited partner is a general partner.

(b) A limited partner does not participate in the control of the business within the meaning of subsection (a) solely by doing one or more of the following:

(1) being a contractor for or an agent or employee of the limited partnership or of a general partner or being an officer, director, or shareholder of a general partner that is a corporation;

(2) consulting with and advising a general partner with respect to the business of the limited partnership;

(3) acting as surety for the limited partnership or guaranteeing or assuming one or more specific obligations of the limited partnership;

(4) taking any action required or permitted by law to bring or pursue a derivative action in the right of the limited partnership;

(5) requesting or attending a meeting of partners;

(6) proposing, approving, or disapproving, by voting or otherwise, one or more of the following matters:

(i) the dissolution and winding up of the limited partnership;

(ii) the sale, exchange, lease, mortgage, pledge, or other transfer of all or substantially all of the assets of the limited partnership;

(iii) the incurrence of indebtedness by the limited partnership other than in the ordinary course of its business;

(iv) a change in the nature of the business;

(v) the admission or removal of a general partner;

(vi) the admission or removal of a limited partner;

(vii) a transaction involving an actual or potential conflict of interest between a general partner and the limited partnership or the limited partners;

(viii) an amendment to the partnership agreement or certificate of limited partnership; or

(ix) matters related to the business of the limited partnership not otherwise enumerated in this subsection (b), which the partnership agreement states in writing may be subject to the approval or disapproval of limited partners;

(7) winding up the limited partnership pursuant to Section 803; or

(8) exercising any right or power permitted to limited partners under this [Act] and not specifically enumerated in this subsection (b).

(c) The enumeration in subsection (b) does not mean that the possession or exercise of any other powers by a limited partner constitutes participation by him [or her] in the business of the limited partnership.

(d) A limited partner who knowingly permits his [or her] name to be used in the name of the limited partnership, except under circumstances permitted by Section 102(2), is liable to creditors who extend credit to the limited partnership without actual knowledge that the limited partner is not a general partner.

Section 304. Person Erroneously Believing Himself [or Herself] Limited Partner.

(a) Except as provided in subsection (b), a person who makes a contribution to a business enterprise and erroneously but in good faith believes that he [or she] has become a limited partner in the enterprise is not a general partner in the enterprise and is not bound by its obligations by reason of making the contribution, receiving distributions from the enterprise, or exercising any rights of a limited partner, if, on ascertaining the mistake, he [or she]:

(1) causes an appropriate certificate of limited partnership or a certificate of amendment to be executed and filed; or

(2) withdraws from future equity participation in the enterprise by executing and filing in the office of the Secretary of State a certificate declaring withdrawal under this section.

(b) A person who makes a contribution of the kind described in subsection (a) is liable as a general partner to any third party who transacts business with the enterprise (i) before the person withdraws and an appropriate certificate is filed to show withdrawal, or (ii) before an appropriate certificate is filed to show that he [or she] is not a general partner, but in either case only if the third party actually believed in good faith that the person was a general partner at the time of the transaction.

Section 305. Information.

Each limited partner has the right to:

(1) inspect and copy any of the partnership records required to be maintained by Section 105; and

(2) obtain from the general partners from time to time upon reasonable demand (i) true and full information regarding the state of the business and financial condition of the limited partnership, (ii) promptly after becoming available, a copy of the limited partnership's federal, state, and local income tax returns for each year, and (iii) other information regarding the affairs of the limited partnership as is just and reasonable.

Article 4
GENERAL PARTNERS

Section 401. Admission of Additional General Partners.

After the filing of a limited partnership's original certificate of limited partnership, additional general partners may be admitted as provided in writing in the partnership agreement or, if the partnership agreement does not provide in writing for the admission of additional general partners, with the written consent of all partners.

Section 402. Events of Withdrawal.

Except as approved by the specific written consent of all partners at the time, a person ceases to be a general partner of a limited partnership upon the happening of any of the following events:

(1) the general partner withdraws from the limited partnership as provided in Section 602;

(2) the general partner ceases to be a member of the limited partnership as provided in Section 702;

(3) the general partner is removed as a general partner in accordance with the partnership agreement;

(4) unless otherwise provided in writing in the partnership agreement, the general partner: (i) makes an assignment for the benefit of creditors; (ii) files a voluntary petition in bankruptcy; (iii) is adjudicated a bankrupt or insolvent; (iv) files a petition or answer seeking for himself [or herself] any reorganization, arrangement, composition, readjustment, liquidation, dissolution, or similar relief under any statute, law, or regulation; (v) files an answer or other pleading admitting or failing to contest the material allegations of a petition filed against him [or her] in any proceeding of this nature; or (vi) seeks, consents to, or acquiesces in the appointment of a trustee, receiver, or liquidator of the general partner or of all or any substantial part of his [or her] properties;

(5) unless otherwise provided in writing in the partnership agreement, [120] days after the commencement of any proceeding against the general partner seeking reorganization,

arrangement, composition, readjustment, liquidation, dissolution, or similar relief under any statute, law, or regulation, the proceeding has not been dismissed, or if within [90] days after the appointment without his [or her] consent or acquiescence of a trustee, receiver, or liquidator of the general partner or of all or any substantial part of his [or her] properties, the appointment is not vacated or stayed or within [90] days after the expiration of any such stay, the appointment is not vacated;

(6) in the case of a general partner who is a natural person,

(i) his [or her] death; or

(ii) the entry of an order by a court of competent jurisdiction adjudicating him [or her] incompetent to manage his [or her] person or his [or her] estate;

(7) in the case of a general partner who is acting as a general partner by virtue of being a trustee of a trust, the termination of the trust (but not merely the substitution of a new trustee);

(8) in the case of a general partner that is a separate partnership, the dissolution and commencement of winding up of the separate partnership;

(9) in the case of a general partner that is a corporation, the filing of a certificate of dissolution, or its equivalent, for the corporation or the revocation of its charter; or

(10) in the case of an estate, the distribution by the fiduciary of the estate's entire interest in the partnership.

Section 403. General Powers and Liabilities.

(a) Except as provided in this [Act] or in the partnership agreement, a general partner of a limited partnership has the rights and powers and is subject to the restrictions of a partner in a partnership without limited partners.

(b) Except as provided in this [Act], a general partner of a limited partnership has the liabilities of a partner in a partnership without limited partners to persons other than the partnership and the other partners. Except as provided in this [Act] or in the partnership agreement, a general partner of a limited partnership has the liabilities of a partner in a partnership without limited partners to the partnership and to the other partners.

Section 404. Contributions by General Partner.

A general partner of a limited partnership may make contributions to the partnership and share in the profits and losses of, and in distributions from, the limited partnership as a general partner. A general partner also may make contributions to and share in profits, losses, and distributions as a limited partner. A person who is both a general partner and a limited partner has the rights and powers, and is subject to the restrictions and liabilities, of a general partner and, except as provided in the partnership agreement, also has the powers, and is subject to the restrictions, of a limited partner to the extent of his [or her] participation in the partnership as a limited partner.

Section 405. Voting.

The partnership agreement may grant to all or certain identified general partners the right to vote (on a per capita or any other basis), separately or with all or any class of the limited partners, on any matter.

Article 5
FINANCE

Section 501. Form of Contribution.

The contribution of a partner may be in cash, property, or services rendered, or a promissory note or other obligation to contribute cash or property or to perform services.

Section 502. Liability for Contribution.

(a) A promise by a limited partner to contribute to the limited partnership is not enforceable unless set out in a writing signed by the limited partner.

(b) Except as provided in the partnership agreement, a partner is obligated to the limited partnership to perform any enforceable promise to contribute cash or property or to perform services, even if he [or she] is unable to perform because of death, disability, or any other reason. If a partner does not make the required contribution of property or services, he [or she] is obligated at the option of the limited partnership to contribute cash equal to that portion of the value, as stated in the partnership records required to be kept pursuant to Section 105, of the stated contribution which has not been made.

(c) Unless otherwise provided in the partnership agreement, the obligation of a partner to make a contribution or return money or other property paid or distributed in violation of this [Act] may be compromised only by consent of all partners. Notwithstanding the compromise, a creditor of a limited partnership who extends credit, or, otherwise acts in reliance on that obligation after the partner signs a writing which reflects the obligation and before the amendment or cancellation thereof to reflect the compromise may enforce the original obligation.

Section 503. Sharing of Profits and Losses.

The profits and losses of a limited partnership shall be allocated among the partners, and among classes of partners, in the manner provided in writing in the partnership agreement. If the partnership agreement does not so provide in writing, profits and losses shall be allocated on the basis of the value, as stated in the partnership records required to be kept pursuant to Section 105, of the contributions made by each partner to the extent they have been received by the partnership and have not been returned.

Section 504. Sharing of Distributions.

Distributions of cash or other assets of a limited partnership shall be allocated among the partners and among classes of partners in the manner provided in writing in the partnership agreement. If the partnership agreement does not so provide in writing, distributions shall be made on the basis of the value, as stated in the partnership records required to be kept pursuant to Section 105, of the contributions made by each partner to the extent they have been received by the partnership and have not been returned.

Article 6
DISTRIBUTIONS AND WITHDRAWAL

Section 601. Interim Distributions.

Except as provided in this Article, a partner is entitled to receive distributions from a limited partnership before his [or her] withdrawal from the limited partnership and before the dissolution and winding up thereof to the extent and at the times or upon the happening of the events specified in the partnership agreement.

Section 602. Withdrawal of General Partner.

A general partner may withdraw from a limited partnership at any time by giving written notice to the other partners, but if the withdrawal violates the partnership agreement, the limited partnership may recover from the withdrawing general partner damages for breach of the partnership agreement and offset the damages against the amount otherwise distributable to him [or her].

Section 603. Withdrawal of Limited Partner.

A limited partner may withdraw from a limited partnership at the time or upon the happening of events specified in writing in the partnership agreement. If the agreement does not specify in writing the time or the events upon the happening of which a limited partner may withdraw or a definite time for the dissolution and winding up of the limited partnership, a limited partner may withdraw upon not less than six months' prior written notice to each general partner at his [or her] address on the books of the limited partnership at its office in this State.

Section 604. Distribution Upon Withdrawal.

Except as provided in this Article, upon withdrawal any withdrawing partner is entitled to receive any distribution to which he [or she] is entitled under the partnership agreement and, if not otherwise provided in the agreement, he [or she] is entitled to receive, within a reasonable time after withdrawal, the fair value of his [or her] interest in the limited partnership as of the date of withdrawal based upon his [or her] right to share in distributions from the limited partnership.

Section 605. Distribution in Kind.

Except as provided in writing in the partnership agreement, a partner, regardless of the nature of his [or her] contribution, has no right to demand and receive any distribution from a limited partnership in any form other than cash. Except as provided in writing in the partnership agreement, a partner may not be compelled to accept a distribution of any asset in kind from a limited partnership to the extent that the percentage of the asset distributed to him [or her] exceeds a percentage of that asset which is equal to the percentage in which he [or she] shares in distributions from the limited partnership.

Section 606. Right to Distribution.

At the time a partner becomes entitled to receive a distribution, he [or she] has the status of, and is entitled to all remedies available to, a creditor of the limited partnership with respect to the distribution.

Section 607. Limitations on Distribution.

A partner may not receive a distribution from a limited partnership to the extent that, after giving effect to the distribution, all liabilities of the limited partnership, other than liabilities to partners on account of their partnership interests, exceed the fair value of the partnership assets.

Section 608. Liability Upon Return of Contribution.

(a) If a partner has received the return of any part of his [or her] contribution without violation of the partnership agreement or this [Act], he [or she] is liable to the limited partnership for a period of one year thereafter for the amount of the returned contribution, but only to the extent necessary to discharge the limited partnership's liabilities to creditors who extended credit to the limited partnership during the period the contribution was held by the partnership.

(b) If a partner has received the return of any part of his [or her] contribution in violation of the partnership agreement or this [Act], he [or she] is liable to the limited partnership for a period of six years thereafter for the amount of the contribution wrongfully returned.

(c) A partner receives a return of his [or her] contribution to the extent that a distribution to him [or her] reduces his [or her] share of the fair value of the net assets of the limited partnership below the value, as set forth in the partnership records required to be kept pursuant to Section 105, of his [or her] contribution which has not been distributed to him [or her].

Article 7
ASSIGNMENT OF PARTNERSHIP INTERESTS

Section 701. Nature of Partnership Interest.

A partnership interest is personal property.

Section 702. Assignment of Partnership Interest.

Except as provided in the partnership agreement, a partnership interest is assignable in whole or in part. An assignment of a partnership interest does not dissolve a limited partnership or entitle the assignee to become or to exercise any rights of a partner. An assignment entitles the assignee to receive, to the extent assigned, only the distribution to which the assignor would be entitled. Except as provided in the partnership agreement, a partner ceases to be a partner upon assignment of all his [or her] partnership interest.

Section 703. Rights of Creditor.

On application to a court of competent jurisdiction by any judgment creditor of a partner, the court may charge the partnership interest of the partner with payment of the unsatisfied amount of the judgment with interest. To the extent so charged, the judgment creditor has only the rights of an assignee of the partnership interest. This [Act] does not deprive any partner of the benefit of any exemption laws applicable to his [or her] partnership interest.

Section 704. Right of Assignee to Become Limited Partner.

(a) An assignee of a partnership interest, including an assignee of a general partner, may become a limited partner if and to the extent that (i) the assignor gives the assignee that right in accordance with authority described in the partnership agreement, or (ii) all other partners consent.

(b) An assignee who has become a limited partner has, to the extent assigned, the rights and powers, and is subject to the restrictions and liabilities, of a limited partner under the partnership agreement and this [Act]. An assignee who becomes a limited partner also is liable for the obligations of his [or her] assignor to make and return contributions as provided in Articles 5 and 6. However, the assignee is not obligated for liabilities unknown to the assignee at the time he [or she] became a limited partner.

(c) If an assignee of a partnership interest becomes a limited partner, the assignor is not released from his [or her] liability to the limited partnership under Sections 207 and 502.

Section 705. Power of Estate of Deceased or Incompetent Partner.

If a partner who is an individual dies or a court of competent jurisdiction adjudges him [or her] to be incompetent to manage his [or her] person or his [or her] property, the partner's executor, administrator, guardian, conservator, or other legal representative may exercise all of the partner's rights for the purpose of settling his [or her] estate or administering his [or her] property, including any power the partner had to give an assignee the right to become a limited partner. If a partner is a corporation, trust, or other entity and is dissolved or terminated, the powers of that partner may be exercised by its legal representative or successor.

Article 8
DISSOLUTION

Section 801. Nonjudicial Dissolution.

A limited partnership is dissolved and its affairs shall be wound up upon the happening of the first to occur of the following:

(1) at the time specified in the certificate of limited partnership;

(2) upon the happening of events specified in writing in the partnership agreement;

(3) written consent of all partners;

(4) an event of withdrawal of a general partner unless at the time there is at least one other general partner and the written provisions of the partnership agreement permit the business of the limited partnership to be carried on by the remaining general partner and that partner does so, but the limited partnership is not dissolved and is not required to be wound up by reason of any event of withdrawal if, within 90 days after the withdrawal, all partners agree in writing to continue the business of the limited partnership and to the appointment of one or more additional general partners if necessary or desired; or

(5) entry of a decree of judicial dissolution under Section 802.

Section 802. Judicial Dissolution.

On application by or for a partner the [designate the appropriate court] court may decree dissolution of a limited partnership whenever it is not reasonably practicable to carry on the business in conformity with the partnership agreement.

Section 803. Winding Up.

Except as provided in the partnership agreement, the general partners who have not wrongfully dissolved a limited partnership or, if none, the limited partners, may wind up the limited partnership's affairs; but the [designate the appropriate court] court may wind up the limited partnership's affairs upon application of any partner, his [or her] legal representative, or assignee.

Section 804. Distribution of Assets.

Upon the winding up of a limited partnership, the assets shall be distributed as follows:

(1) to creditors, including partners who are creditors, to the extent permitted by law, in satisfaction of liabilities of the limited partnership other than liabilities for distributions to partners under Section 601 or 604;

(2) except as provided in the partnership agreement, to partners and former partners in satisfaction of liabilities for distributions under Section 601 or 604; and

(3) except as provided in the partnership agreement, to partners first for the return of their contributions and secondly respecting their partnership interests, in the proportions in which the partners share in distributions.

Article 9
FOREIGN LIMITED PARTNERSHIPS

Section 901. Law Governing.

Subject to the Constitution of this State, (i) the laws of the state under which a foreign limited partnership is organized govern its organization and internal affairs and the liability of its limited partners, and (ii) a foreign limited partnership may not be denied registration by reason of any difference between those laws and the laws of this State.

Section 902. Registration.

Before transacting business in this State, a foreign limited partnership shall register with the Secretary of State. In order to register, a foreign limited partnership shall submit to the Secretary of State, in duplicate, an application for registration as a foreign limited partnership, signed and sworn to by a general partner and setting forth:

(1) the name of the foreign limited partnership and, if different, the name under which it proposes to register and transact business in this State;

(2) the State and date of its formation;

(3) the name and address of any agent for service of process on the foreign limited partnership whom the foreign limited partnership elects to appoint; the agent must be an individual resident of this State, a domestic corporation, or a foreign corporation having a place of business in, and authorized to do business in, this State;

(4) a statement that the Secretary of State is appointed the agent of the foreign limited partnership for service of process if no agent has been appointed under paragraph (3) or, if appointed, the agent's authority has been revoked or if the agent cannot be found or served with the exercise of reasonable diligence;

(5) the address of the office required to be maintained in the state of its organization by the laws of that state or, if not so required, of the principal office of the foreign limited partnership;

(6) the name and business address of each general partner; and

(7) the address of the office at which is kept a list of the names and addresses of the limited partners and their capital contributions, together with an undertaking by the foreign limited partnership to keep those records until the foreign limited partnership's registration in this State is cancelled or withdrawn.

Section 903. Issuance of Registration.

(a) If the Secretary of State finds that an application for registration conforms to law and all requisite fees have been paid, he [or she] shall:

(1) endorse on the application the word "Filed", and the month, day, and year of the filing thereof;

(2) file in his [or her] office a duplicate original of the application; and

(3) issue a certificate of registration to transact business in this State.

(b) The certificate of registration, together with a duplicate original of the application, shall be returned to the person who filed the application or his [or her] representative.

Section 904. Name.

A foreign limited partnership may register with the Secretary of State under any name, whether or not it is the name under which it is registered in its state of organization, that includes without abbreviation the words "limited partnership" and that could be registered by a domestic limited partnership.

Section 905. Changes and Amendments.

If any statement in the application for registration of a foreign limited partnership was false when made or any arrangements or other facts described have changed, making the application inaccurate in any respect, the foreign limited partnership shall promptly file in the office of the Secretary of State a certificate, signed and sworn to by a general partner, correcting such statement.

Section 906. Cancellation of Registration.

A foreign limited partnership may cancel its registration by filing with the Secretary of State a certificate of cancellation signed and sworn to by a general partner. A cancellation does not terminate the authority of the Secretary of State to accept service of process on the foreign limited partnership with respect to [claims for relief] [causes of action] arising out of the transactions of business in this State.

Section 907. Transaction of Business Without Registration.

(a) A foreign limited partnership transacting business in this State may not maintain any action, suit, or proceeding in any court of this State until it has registered in this State.

(b) The failure of a foreign limited partnership to register in this State does not impair the validity of any contract or act of the foreign limited partnership or prevent the foreign limited partnership from defending any action, suit, or proceeding in any court of this State.

(c) A limited partner of a foreign limited partnership is not liable as a general partner of the foreign limited partnership solely by reason of having transacted business in this State without registration.

(d) A foreign limited partnership, by transacting business in this State without registration, appoints the Secretary of State as its agent for service of process with respect to [claims for relief] [causes of action] arising out of the transaction of business in this State.

Section 908. Action by [Appropriate Official].

The [designate the appropriate official] may bring an action to restrain a foreign limited partnership from transacting business in this State in violation of this Article.

Article 10
DERIVATIVE ACTIONS

Section 1001. Right of Action.

A limited partner may bring an action in the right of a limited partnership to recover a judgment in its favor if general partners with authority to do so have refused to bring the action or if an effort to cause those general partners to bring the action is not likely to succeed.

Section 1002. Proper Plaintiff.

In a derivative action, the plaintiff must be a partner at the time of bringing the action and (i) must have been a partner at the time of the transaction of which he [or she] complains or (ii) his [or her] status as a partner must have devolved upon him by operation of law or pursuant to the terms of the partnership agreement from a person who was a partner at the time of the transaction.

Section 1003. Pleading.

In a derivative action, the complaint shall set forth with particularity the effort of the plaintiff to secure initiation of the action by a general partner or the reasons for not making the effort.

Section 1004. Expenses.

If a derivative action is successful, in whole or in part, or if anything is received by the plaintiff as a result of a judgment, compromise, or settlement of an action or claim, the court may award the plaintiff reasonable expenses, including reasonable attorney's fees, and shall direct him [or her] to remit to the limited partnership the remainder of those proceeds received by him [or her].

Article 11
MISCELLANEOUS

Section 1101. Construction and Application.

This [Act] shall be so applied and construed to effectuate its general purpose to make uniform the law with respect to the subject of this [Act] among states enacting it.

Section 1102. Short Title.

This [Act] may be cited as the Uniform Limited Partnership Act.

Section 1103. Severability.

If any provision of this [Act] or its application to any person or circumstance is held invalid, the invalidity does not affect other provisions or applications of the [Act] which can be given effect without the invalid provision or application, and to this end the provisions of this [Act] are severable.

Section 1104. Effective Date, Extended Effective Date, and Repeal.

Except as set forth below, the effective date of this [Act] is _____ and the following acts [list existing limited partnership acts] are hereby repealed:

(1) The existing provisions for execution and filing of certificates of limited partnerships and amendments thereunder and cancellations thereof continue in effect until [specify time required to create central filing system], the extended effective date, and Sections 102, 103, 104, 105, 201, 202, 203, 204 and 206 are not effective until the extended effective date.

(2) Section 402, specifying the conditions under which a general partner ceases to be a member of a limited partnership, is not effective until the extended effective date, and the applicable provisions of existing law continue to govern until the extended effective date.

(3) Sections 501, 502 and 608 apply only to contributions and distributions made after the effective date of this [Act].

(4) Section 704 applies only to assignments made after the effective date of this [Act].

(5) Article 9, dealing with registration of foreign limited partnerships, is not effective until the extended effective date.

(6) Unless otherwise agreed by the partners, the applicable provisions of existing law governing allocation of profits and losses (rather than the provisions of Section 503), distributions to a withdrawing partner (rather than the provisions of Section 604), and distributions of assets upon the winding up of a limited partnership (rather than the provisions of Section 804) govern limited partnerships formed before the effective date of this [Act].

Section 1105. Rules for Cases Not Provided For in This [Act].

In any case not provided for in this [Act] the provisions of the Uniform Partnership Act govern.

Section 1106. Savings Clause.

The repeal of any statutory provision by this [Act] does not impair, or otherwise affect, the organization or the continued existence of a limited partnership existing at the effective date of this [Act], nor does the repeal of any existing statutory provision by this [Act] impair any contract or affect any right accrued before the effective date of this [Act].

The Revised Model Business Corporation Act (Excerpts)

Chapter 2.
INCORPORATION

§ 2.01 Incorporators

One or more persons may act as the incorporator or incorporators of a corporation by delivering articles of incorporation to the secretary of state for filing.

§ 2.02 Articles of Incorporation

(a) The articles of incorporation must set forth:

(1) a corporate name * * * ;

(2) the number of shares the corporation is authorized to issue;

(3) the street address of the corporation's initial registered office and the name of its initial registered agent at that office; and

(4) the name and address of each incorporator.

(b) The articles of incorporation may set forth:

(1) the names and addresses of the individuals who are to serve as the initial directors;

(2) provisions not inconsistent with law regarding:

(i) the purpose or purposes for which the corporation is organized;

(ii) managing the business and regulating the affairs of the corporation;

(iii) defining, limiting, and regulating the powers of the corporation, its board of directors, and shareholders;

(iv) a par value for authorized shares or classes of shares;

(v) the imposition of personal liability on shareholders for the debts of the corporation to a specified extent and upon specified conditions;

(3) any provision that under this Act is required or permitted to be set forth in the bylaws; and

(4) a provision eliminating or limiting the liability of a director to the corporation or its shareholders for money damages for any action taken, or any failure to take any action, as a director, except liability for (A) the amount of a financial benefit received by a director to which he is not entitled; (B) an intentional infliction of harm on the corporation or the shareholders; (C) [unlawful distributions]; or (D) an intentional violation of criminal law.

(c) The articles of incorporation need not set forth any of the corporate powers enumerated in this Act.

§ 2.03 Incorporation

(a) Unless a delayed effective date is specified, the corporate existence begins when the articles of incorporation are filed.

(b) The secretary of state's filing of the articles of incorporation is conclusive proof that the incorporators satisfied all conditions precedent to incorporation except in a proceeding by the state to cancel or revoke the incorporation or involuntarily dissolve the corporation.

§ 2.04 Liability for Preincorporation Transactions

All persons purporting to act as or on behalf of a corporation, knowing there was no incorporation under this Act, are jointly and severally liable for all liabilities created while so acting.

§ 2.05 Organization of Corporation

(a) After incorporation:

(1) if initial directors are named in the articles of incorporation, the initial directors shall hold an organizational meeting, at the call of a majority of the directors,

to complete the organization of the corporation by appointing officers, adopting bylaws, and carrying on any other business brought before the meeting;

(2) if initial directors are not named in the articles, the incorporator or incorporators shall hold an organizational meeting at the call of a majority of the incorporators:

(i) to elect directors and complete the organization of the corporation; or

(ii) to elect a board of directors who shall complete the organization of the corporation.

(b) Action required or permitted by this Act to be taken by incorporators at an organizational meeting may be taken without a meeting if the action taken is evidenced by one or more written consents describing the action taken and signed by each incorporator.

(c) An organizational meeting may be held in or out of this state.

*   *   *   *

Chapter 3.
PURPOSES AND POWERS

§ 3.01 Purposes

(a) Every corporation incorporated under this Act has the purpose of engaging in any lawful business unless a more limited purpose is set forth in the articles of incorporation.

(b) A corporation engaging in a business that is subject to regulation under another statute of this state may incorporate under this Act only if permitted by, and subject to all limitations of, the other statute.

§ 3.02 General Powers

Unless its articles of incorporation provide otherwise, every corporation has perpetual duration and succession in its corporate name and has the same powers as an individual to do all things necessary or convenient to carry out its business and affairs, including without limitation power:

(1) to sue and be sued, complain and defend in its corporate name;

(2) to have a corporate seal, which may be altered at will, and to use it, or a facsimile of it, by impressing or affixing it or in any other manner reproducing it;

(3) to make and amend bylaws, not inconsistent with its articles of incorporation or with the laws of this state, for managing the business and regulating the affairs of the corporation;

(4) to purchase, receive, lease, or otherwise acquire, and own, hold, improve, use, and otherwise deal with, real or personal property, or any legal or equitable interest in property, wherever located;

(5) to sell, convey, mortgage, pledge, lease, exchange, and otherwise dispose of all or any part of its property;

(6) to purchase, receive, subscribe for, or otherwise acquire; own, hold, vote, use, sell, mortgage, lend, pledge, or otherwise dispose of; and deal in and with shares or other interests in, or obligations of, any other entity;

(7) to make contracts and guarantees, incur liabilities, borrow money, issue its notes, bonds, and other obligations (which may be convertible into or include the option to purchase other securities of the corporation), and secure any of its obligations by mortgage or pledge of any of its property, franchises, or income;

(8) to lend money, invest and reinvest its funds, and receive and hold real and personal property as security for repayment;

(9) to be a promoter, partner, member, associate, or manager of any partnership, joint venture, trust, or other entity;

(10) to conduct its business, locate offices, and exercise the powers granted by this Act within or without this state;

(11) to elect directors and appoint officers, employees, and agents of the corporation, define their duties, fix their compensation, and lend them money and credit;

(12) to pay pensions and establish pension plans, pension trusts, profit sharing plans, share bonus plans, share option plans, and benefit or incentive plans for any or all of its current or former directors, officers, employees, and agents;

(13) to make donations for the public welfare or for charitable, scientific, or educational purposes;

(14) to transact any lawful business that will aid governmental policy;

(15) to make payments or donations, or do any other act, not inconsistent with law, that furthers the business and affairs of the corporation.

*   *   *   *

Chapter 5.
OFFICE AND AGENT

§ 5.01 Registered Office and Registered Agent

Each corporation must continuously maintain in this state:

(1) a registered office that may be the same as any of its places of business; and

(2) a registered agent, who may be:

(i) an individual who resides in this state and whose business office is identical with the registered office;

(ii) a domestic corporation or not-for-profit domestic corporation whose business office is identical with the registered office; or

(iii) a foreign corporation or not-for-profit foreign corporation authorized to transact business in this state whose business office is identical with the registered office.

* * * *

§ 5.04 Service on Corporation

(a) A corporation's registered agent is the corporation's agent for service of process, notice, or demand required or permitted by law to be served on the corporation.

(b) If a corporation has no registered agent, or the agent cannot with reasonable diligence be served, the corporation may be served by registered or certified mail, return receipt requested, addressed to the secretary of the corporation at its principal office. Service is perfected under this subsection at the earliest of:

(1) the date the corporation receives the mail;

(2) the date shown on the return receipt, if signed on behalf of the corporation; or

(3) five days after its deposit in the United States Mail, if mailed postpaid and correctly addressed.

(c) This section does not prescribe the only means, or necessarily the required means, of serving a corporation.

Chapter 6.
SHARES AND DISTRIBUTIONS

* * * *

Subchapter B. Issuance of Shares

* * * *

§ 6.21 Issuance of Shares

(a) The powers granted in this section to the board of directors may be reserved to the shareholders by the articles of incorporation.

(b) The board of directors may authorize shares to be issued for consideration consisting of any tangible or intangible property or benefit to the corporation, including cash, promissory notes, services performed, contracts for services to be performed, or other securities of the corporation.

(c) Before the corporation issues shares, the board of directors must determine that the consideration received or to be received for shares to be issued is adequate. That determination by the board of directors is conclusive insofar as the adequacy of consideration for the issuance of shares relates to whether the shares are validly issued, fully paid, and nonassessable.

(d) When the corporation receives the consideration for which the board of directors authorized the issuance of shares, the shares issued therefor are fully paid and nonassessable.

(e) The corporation may place in escrow shares issued for a contract for future services or benefits or a promissory note, or make other arrangements to restrict the transfer of the shares, and may credit distributions in respect of the shares against their purchase price, until the services are performed, the note is paid, or the benefits received. If the services are not performed, the note is not paid, or the benefits are not received, the shares escrowed or restricted and the distributions credited may be cancelled in whole or part.

* * * *

§ 6.27 Restriction on Transfer or Registration of Shares and Other Securities

(a) The articles of incorporation, bylaws, an agreement among shareholders, or an agreement between shareholders and the corporation may impose restrictions on the transfer or registration of transfer of shares of the corporation. A restriction does not affect shares issued before the restriction was adopted unless the holders of the shares are parties to the restriction agreement or voted in favor of the restriction.

(b) A restriction on the transfer or registration of transfer of shares is valid and enforceable against the holder or a transferee of the holder if the restriction is authorized by this section and its existence is noted conspicuously on the front or back of the certificate or is contained in the information statement [sent to the shareholder]. Unless so noted, a restriction is not enforceable against a person without knowledge of the restriction.

(c) A restriction on the transfer or registration of transfer of shares is authorized:

(1) to maintain the corporation's status when it is dependent on the number or identity of its shareholders;

(2) to preserve exemptions under federal or state securities law;

(3) for any other reasonable purpose.

(d) A restriction on the transfer or registration of transfer of shares may:

(1) obligate the shareholder first to offer the corporation or other persons (separately, consecutively, or simultaneously) an opportunity to acquire the restricted shares;

(2) obligate the corporate or other persons (separately, consecutively, or simultaneously) to acquire the restricted shares;

(3) require the corporation, the holders of any class of its shares, or another person to approve the transfer of the restricted shares, if the requirement is not manifestly unreasonable;

(4) prohibit the transfer of the restricted shares to designated persons or classes of persons, if the prohibition is not manifestly unreasonable.

(e) For purposes of this section, "shares" includes a security convertible into or carrying a right to subscribe for or acquire shares.

* * * *

Chapter 7.
SHAREHOLDERS

Subchapter A. Meetings

§ 7.01 Annual Meeting

(a) A corporation shall hold annually at a time stated in or fixed in accordance with the bylaws a meeting of shareholders.

(b) Annual shareholders' meetings may be held in or out of this state at the place stated in or fixed in accordance with the bylaws. If no place is stated in or fixed in accordance with the bylaws, annual meetings shall be held at the corporation's principal office.

(c) The failure to hold an annual meeting at the time stated in or fixed in accordance with a corporation's bylaws does not affect the validity of any corporate action.

     *   *   *   *

§ 7.05 Notice of Meeting

(a) A corporation shall notify shareholders of the date, time, and place of each annual and special shareholders' meeting no fewer than 10 nor more than 60 days before the meeting date. Unless this Act or the articles of incorporation require otherwise, the corporation is required to give notice only to shareholders entitled to vote at the meeting.

(b) Unless this Act or the articles of incorporation require otherwise, notice of an annual meeting need not include a description of the purpose or purposes for which the meeting is called.

(c) Notice of a special meeting must include a description of the purpose or purposes for which the meeting is called.

(d) If not otherwise fixed * * *, the record date for determining shareholders entitled to notice of and to vote at an annual or special shareholders' meeting is the day before the first notice is delivered to shareholders.

(e) Unless the bylaws require otherwise, if an annual or special shareholders' meeting is adjourned to a different date, time, or place, notice need not be given of the new date, time, or place if the new date, time, or place is announced at the meeting before adjournment. * * *

     *   *   *   *

§ 7.07 Record Date

(a) The bylaws may fix or provide the manner of fixing the record date for one or more voting groups in order to determine the shareholders entitled to notice of a shareholders' meeting, to demand a special meeting, to vote, or to take any other action. If the bylaws do not fix or provide for fixing a record date, the board of directors of the corporation may fix a future date as the record date.

(b) A record date fixed under this section may not be more than 70 days before the meeting or action requiring a determination of shareholders.

(c) A determination of shareholders entitled to notice of or to vote at a shareholders' meeting is effective for any adjournment of the meeting unless the board of directors fixes a new record date, which it must do if the meeting is adjourned to a date more than 120 days after the date fixed for the original meeting.

(d) If a court orders a meeting adjourned to a date more than 120 days after the date fixed for the original meeting, it may provide that the original record date continues in effect or it may fix a new record date.

Subchapter B. Voting

§ 7.20 Shareholders' List for Meeting

(a) After fixing a record date for a meeting, a corporation shall prepare an alphabetical list of the names of all its shareholders who are entitled to notice of a shareholders' meeting. The list must be arranged by voting group (and within each voting group by class or series of shares) and show the address of and number of shares held by each shareholder.

(b) The shareholders' list must be available for inspection by any shareholder, beginning two business days after notice of the meeting is given for which the list was prepared and continuing through the meeting, at the corporation's principal office or at a place identified in the meeting notice in the city where the meeting will be held. A shareholder, his agent, or attorney is entitled on written demand to inspect and, subject to the requirements of section 16.02(c), to copy the list, during regular business hours and at his expense, during the period it is available for inspection.

(c) The corporation shall make the shareholders' list available at the meeting, and any shareholder, his agent, or attorney is entitled to inspect the list at any time during the meeting or any adjournment.

(d) If the corporation refuses to allow a shareholder, his agent, or attorney to inspect the shareholders' list before or at the meeting (or copy the list as permitted by subsection (b)), the [name or describe] court of the county where a corporation's principal office (or, if none in this state, its registered office) is located, on application of the shareholder, may summarily order the inspection or copying at the corporation's expense and may postpone the meeting for which the list was prepared until the inspection or copying is complete.

(e) Refusal or failure to prepare or make available the shareholders' list does not affect the validity of action taken at the meeting.

     *   *   *   *

§ 7.22 Proxies

(a) A shareholder may vote his shares in person or by proxy.

(b) A shareholder may appoint a proxy to vote or otherwise act for him by signing an appointment form, either personally or by his attorney-in-fact.

(c) An appointment of a proxy is effective when received by the secretary or other officer or agent authorized to tabulate votes. An appointment is valid for 11 months unless a longer period is expressly provided in the appointment form.

* * * *

§ 7.28 Voting for Directors; Cumulative Voting

(a) Unless otherwise provided in the articles of incorporation, directors are elected by a plurality of the votes cast by the shares entitled to vote in the election at a meeting at which a quorum is present.

(b) Shareholders do not have a right to cumulate their votes for directors unless the articles of incorporation so provide.

(c) A statement included in the articles of incorporation that "[all] [a designated voting group of] shareholders are entitled to cumulate their votes for directors" (or words of similar import) means that the shareholders designated are entitled to multiply the number of votes they are entitled to cast by the number of directors for whom they are entitled to vote and cast the product for a single candidate or distribute the product among two or more candidates.

(d) Shares otherwise entitled to vote cumulatively may not be voted cumulatively at a particular meeting unless:

(1) the meeting notice or proxy statement accompanying the notice states conspicuously that cumulative voting is authorized; or

(2) a shareholder who has the right to cumulate his votes gives notice to the corporation not less than 48 hours before the time set for the meeting of his intent to cumulate his votes during the meeting, and if one shareholder gives this notice all other shareholders in the same voting group participating in the election are entitled to cumulate their votes without giving further notice.

* * * *

Subchapter D. Derivative Proceedings

* * * *

§ 7.41 Standing

A shareholder may not commence or maintain a derivative proceeding unless the shareholder:

(1) was a shareholder of the corporation at the time of the act or omission complained of or became a shareholder through transfer by operation of law from one who was a shareholder at that time; and

(2) fairly and adequately represents the interests of the corporation in enforcing the right of the corporation.

§ 7.42 Demand

No shareholder may commence a derivative proceeding until:

(1) a written demand has been made upon the corporation to take suitable action; and

(2) 90 days have expired from the date the demand was made unless the shareholder has earlier been notified that the demand has been rejected by the corporation or unless irreparable injury to the corporation would result by waiting for the expiration of the 90 day period.

* * * *

Chapter 8.
DIRECTORS AND OFFICERS

Subchapter A. Board of Directors

* * * *

§ 8.02 Qualifications of Directors

The articles of incorporation or bylaws may prescribe qualifications for directors. A director need not be a resident of this state or a shareholder of the corporation unless the articles of incorporation or bylaws so prescribe.

§ 8.03 Number and Election of Directors

(a) A board of directors must consist of one or more individuals, with the number specified in or fixed in accordance with the articles of incorporation or bylaws.

(b) If a board of directors has power to fix or change the number of directors, the board may increase or decrease by 30 percent or less the number of directors last approved by the shareholders, but only the shareholders may increase or decrease by more than 30 percent the number of directors last approved by the shareholders.

(c) The articles of incorporation or bylaws may establish a variable range for the size of the board of directors by fixing a minimum and maximum number of directors. If a variable range is established, the number of directors may be fixed or changed from time to time, within the minimum and maximum, by the shareholders or the board of directors. After shares are issued, only the shareholders may change the range for the size of the board or change from a fixed to a variable-range size board or vice versa.

(d) Directors are elected at the first annual shareholders' meeting and at each annual meeting thereafter unless their terms are staggered under section 8.06.

* * * *

§ 8.08 Removal of Directors by Shareholders

(a) The shareholders may remove one or more directors with or without cause unless the articles of incorporation provide that directors may be removed only for cause.

(b) If a director is elected by a voting group of shareholders, only the shareholders of that voting group may participate in the vote to remove him.

(c) If cumulative voting is authorized, a director may not be removed if the number of votes sufficient to elect him under cumulative voting is voted against his removal. If cumulative voting is not authorized, a director may be removed only if the number of votes cast to remove him exceeds the number of votes cast not to remove him.

(d) A director may be removed by the shareholders only at a meeting called for the purpose of removing him and the meeting notice must state that the purpose, or one of the purposes, of the meeting is removal of the director.

*　*　*　*

Subchapter B. Meetings and Action of the Board

§ 8.20 Meetings

(a) The board of directors may hold regular or special meetings in or out of this state.

(b) Unless the articles of incorporation or bylaws provide otherwise, the board of directors may permit any or all directors to participate in a regular or special meeting by, or conduct the meeting through the use of, any means of communication by which all directors participating may simultaneously hear each other during the meeting. A director participating in a meeting by this means is deemed to be present in person at the meeting.

*　*　*　*

§ 8.22 Notice of Meeting

(a) Unless the articles of incorporation or bylaws provide otherwise, regular meetings of the board of directors may be held without notice of the date, time, place, or purpose of the meeting.

(b) Unless the articles of incorporation or bylaws provide for a longer or shorter period, special meetings of the board of directors must be preceded by at least two days' notice of the date, time, and place of the meeting. The notice need not describe the purpose of the special meeting unless required by the articles of incorporation or bylaws.

*　*　*　*

§ 8.24 Quorum and Voting

(a) Unless the articles of incorporation or bylaws require a greater number, a quorum of a board of directors consists of:

(1) a majority of the fixed number of directors if the corporation has a fixed board size; or

(2) a majority of the number of directors prescribed, or if no number is prescribed the number in office immediately before the meeting begins, if the corporation has a variable-range size board.

(b) The articles of incorporation or bylaws may authorize a quorum of a board of directors to consist of no fewer than one-third of the fixed or prescribed number of directors determined under subsection (a).

(c) If a quorum is present when a vote is taken, the affirmative vote of a majority of directors present is the act

of the board of directors unless the articles of incorporation or bylaws require the vote of a greater number of directors.

(d) A director who is present at a meeting of the board of directors or a committee of the board of directors when corporate action is taken is deemed to have assented to the action taken unless: (1) he objects at the beginning of the meeting (or promptly upon his arrival) to holding it or transacting business at the meeting; (2) his dissent or abstention from the action taken is entered in the minutes of the meeting; or (3) he delivers written notice of his dissent or abstention to the presiding officer of the meeting before its adjournment or to the corporation immediately after adjournment of the meeting. The right of dissent or abstention is not available to a director who votes in favor of the action taken.

*　*　*　*

Subchapter C. Standards of Conduct

§ 8.30 General Standards for Directors

(a) A director shall discharge his duties as a director, including his duties as a member of a committee:

(1) in good faith;

(2) with the care an ordinarily prudent person in a like position would exercise under similar circumstances; and

(3) in a manner he reasonably believes to be in the best interests of the corporation.

(b) In discharging his duties a director is entitled to rely on information, opinions, reports, or statements, including financial statements and other financial data, if prepared or presented by:

(1) one or more officers or employees of the corporation whom the director reasonably believes to be reliable and competent in the matters presented;

(2) legal counsel, public accountants, or other persons as to matters the director reasonably believes are within the person's professional or expert competence; or

(3) a committee of the board of directors of which he is not a member if the director reasonably believes the committee merits confidence.

(c) A director is not acting in good faith if he has knowledge concerning the matter in question that makes reliance otherwise permitted by subsection (b) unwarranted.

(d) A director is not liable for any action taken as a director, or any failure to take any action, if he performed the duties of his office in compliance with this section.

*　*　*　*

Subchapter D. Officers

*　*　*　*

§ 8.41 Duties of Officers

Each officer has the authority and shall perform the duties set forth in the bylaws or, to the extent consistent with the bylaws, the duties prescribed by the board of directors or by direction of an officer authorized by the board of directors to prescribe the duties of other officers.

§ 8.42 Standards of Conduct for Officers

(a) An officer with discretionary authority shall discharge his duties under that authority:

(1) in good faith;

(2) with the care an ordinarily prudent person in a like position would exercise under similar circumstances; and

(3) in a manner he reasonably believes to be in the best interests of the corporation.

(b) In discharging his duties an officer is entitled to rely on information, opinions, reports, or statements, including financial statements and other financial data, if prepared or presented by:

(1) one or more officers or employees of the corporation whom the officer reasonably believes to be reliable and competent in the matters presented; or

(2) legal counsel, public accountants, or other persons as to matters the officer reasonably believes are within the person's professional or expert competence.

(c) An officer is not acting in good faith if he has knowledge concerning the matter in question that makes reliance otherwise permitted by subsection (b) unwarranted.

(d) An officer is not liable for any action taken as an officer, or any failure to take any action, if he performed the duties of his office in compliance with this section.

*　*　*　*

Chapter 11.
MERGER AND SHARE EXCHANGE

§ 11.01 Merger

(a) One or more corporations may merge into another corporation if the board of directors of each corporation adopts and its shareholders (if required *　*　*) approve a plan of merger.

(b) The plan of merger must set forth:

(1) the name of each corporation planning to merge and the name of the surviving corporation into which each other corporation plans to merge;

(2) the terms and conditions of the merger; and

(3) the manner and basis of converting the shares of each corporation into shares, obligations, or other securities of the surviving or any other corporation or into cash or other property in whole or part.

(c) The plan of merger may set forth:

(1) amendments to the articles of incorporation of the surviving corporation; and

(2) other provisions relating to the merger.

*　*　*　*

§ 11.04 Merger of Subsidiary

(a) A parent corporation owning at least 90 percent of the outstanding shares of each class of a subsidiary corporation may merge the subsidiary into itself without approval of the shareholders of the parent or subsidiary.

(b) The board of directors of the parent shall adopt a plan of merger that sets forth:

(1) the names of the parent and subsidiary; and

(2) the manner and basis of converting the shares of the subsidiary into shares, obligations, or other securities of the parent or any other corporation or into cash or other property in whole or part.

(c) The parent shall mail a copy or summary of the plan of merger to each shareholder of the subsidiary who does not waive the mailing requirement in writing.

(d) The parent may not deliver articles of merger to the secretary of state for filing until at least 30 days after the date it mailed a copy of the plan of merger to each shareholder of the subsidiary who did not waive the mailing requirement.

(e) Articles of merger under this section may not contain amendments to the articles of incorporation of the parent corporation (except for amendments enumerated in section 10.02).

*　*　*　*

§ 11.06 Effect of Merger or Share Exchange

(a) When a merger takes effect:

(1) every other corporation party to the merger merges into the surviving corporation and the separate existence of every corporation except the surviving corporation ceases;

(2) the title to all real estate and other property owned by each corporation party to the merger is vested in the surviving corporation without reversion or impairment;

(3) the surviving corporation has all liabilities of each corporation party to the merger;

(4) a proceeding pending against any corporation party to the merger may be continued as if the merger did not occur or the surviving corporation may be substituted in the proceeding for the corporation whose existence ceased;

(5) the articles of incorporation of the surviving corporation are amended to the extent provided in the plan of merger; and

(6) the shares of each corporation party to the merger that are to be converted into shares, obligations, or other securities of the surviving or any other corporation or into cash or other property are converted and the former holders of the shares are entitled only to the rights provided in the articles of merger or to their rights under chapter 13.

(b) When a share exchange takes effect, the shares of each acquired corporation are exchanged as provided in the plan, and the former holders of the shares are entitled only to the exchange rights provided in the articles of share exchange or to their rights under chapter 13.

*   *   *   *

Chapter 13.
DISSENTERS' RIGHTS

Subchapter A. Right to Dissent and Obtain Payment for Shares

*   *   *   *

§ 13.02 Right to Dissent

(a) A shareholder is entitled to dissent from, and obtain payment of the fair value of his shares in the event of, any of the following corporate actions:

(1) consummation of a plan of merger to which the corporation is a party (i) if shareholder approval is required for the merger by [statute] or the articles of incorporation and the shareholder is entitled to vote on the merger or (ii) if the corporation is a subsidiary that is merged with its parent under section 11.04;

(2) consummation of a plan of share exchange to which the corporation is a party as the corporation whose shares will be acquired, if the shareholder is entitled to vote on the plan;

(3) consummation of a sale or exchange of all, or substantially all, of the property of the corporation other than in the usual and regular course of business, if the shareholder is entitled to vote on the sale or exchange, including a sale in dissolution, but not including a sale pursuant to court order or a sale for cash pursuant to a plan by which all or substantially all of the net proceeds of the sale will be distributed to the shareholders within one year after the date of sale;

(4) an amendment of the articles of incorporation that materially and adversely affects rights in respect of a dissenter's shares because it:

(i) alters or abolishes a preferential right of the shares;

(ii) creates, alters, or abolishes a right in respect of redemption, including a provision respecting a sinking fund for the redemption or repurchase, of the shares;

(iii) alters or abolishes a preemptive right of the holder of the shares to acquire shares or other securities;

(iv) excludes or limits the right of the shares to vote on any matter, or to cumulate votes, other than a limitation by dilution through issuance of shares or other securities with similar voting rights; or

(v) reduces the number of shares owned by the shareholder to a fraction of a share if the fractional share so created is to be acquired for cash *   *   * ; or

(5) any corporate action taken pursuant to a shareholder vote to the extent the articles of incorporation, bylaws, or a resolution of the board of directors provides that voting or nonvoting shareholders are entitled to dissent and obtain payment for their shares.

(b) A shareholder entitled to dissent and obtain payment for his shares under this chapter may not challenge the corporate action creating his entitlement unless the action is unlawful or fraudulent with respect to the shareholder or the corporation.

*   *   *   *

Subchapter B. Procedure for Exercise of Dissenters' Rights

*   *   *   *

§ 13.21 Notice of Intent to Demand Payment

(a) If proposed corporate action creating dissenters' rights under section 13.02 is submitted to a vote at a shareholders' meeting, a shareholder who wishes to assert dissenters' rights (1) must deliver to the corporation before the vote is taken written notice of his intent to demand payment for his shares if the proposed action is effectuated and (2) must not vote his shares in favor of the proposed action.

(b) A shareholder who does not satisfy the requirements of subsection (a) is not entitled to payment for his shares under this chapter.

*   *   *   *

§ 13.25 Payment

(a) *   *   * [A]s soon as the proposed corporate action is taken, or upon receipt of a payment demand, the corporation shall pay each dissenter *   *   * the amount the corporation estimates to be the fair value of his shares, plus accrued interest.

*   *   *   *

§ 13.28 Procedure If Shareholder Dissatisfied with Payment or Offer

(a) A dissenter may notify the corporation in writing of his own estimate of the fair value of his shares and amount of interest due, and demand payment of his estimate (less any payment under section 13.25) *   *   * if:

(1) the dissenter believes that the amount paid under section 13.25 *   *   * is less than the fair value of his shares or that the interest due is incorrectly calculated;

(2) the corporation fails to make payment under section 13.25 within 60 days after the date set for demanding payment; or

(3) the corporation, having failed to take the proposed action, does not return the deposited certificates or

release the transfer restrictions imposed on uncertificated shares within 60 days after the date set for demanding payment.

(b) A dissenter waives his right to demand payment under this section unless he notifies the corporation of his demand in writing under subsection (a) within 30 days after the corporation made or offered payment for his shares.

* * * *

Chapter 14.
DISSOLUTION

Subchapter A. Voluntary Dissolution
* * * *

§ 14.02 Dissolution by Board of Directors and Shareholders

(a) A corporation's board of directors may propose dissolution for submission to the shareholders.

(b) For a proposal to dissolve to be adopted:

(1) the board of directors must recommend dissolution to the shareholders unless the board of directors determines that because of conflict of interest or other special circumstances it should make no recommendation and communicates the basis for its determination to the shareholders; and

(2) the shareholders entitled to vote must approve the proposal to dissolve as provided in subsection (e).

(c) The board of directors may condition its submission of the proposal for dissolution on any basis.

(d) The corporation shall notify each shareholder, whether or not entitled to vote, of the proposed shareholders' meeting in accordance with section 7.05. The notice must also state that the purpose, or one of the purposes, of the meeting is to consider dissolving the corporation.

(e) Unless the articles of incorporation or the board of directors (acting pursuant to subsection (c)) require a greater vote or a vote by voting groups, the proposal to dissolve to be adopted must be approved by a majority of all the votes entitled to be cast on that proposal.

* * * *

§ 14.05 Effect of Dissolution

(a) A dissolved corporation continues its corporate existence but may not carry on any business except that appropriate to wind up and liquidate its business and affairs, including:

(1) collecting its assets;

(2) disposing of its properties that will not be distributed in kind to its shareholders;

(3) discharging or making provision for discharging its liabilities;

(4) distributing its remaining property among its shareholders according to their interests; and

(5) doing every other act necessary to wind up and liquidate its business and affairs.

(b) Dissolution of a corporation does not:

(1) transfer title to the corporation's property;

(2) prevent transfer of its shares or securities, although the authorization to dissolve may provide for closing the corporation's share transfer records;

(3) subject its directors or officers to standards of conduct different from those prescribed in chapter 8;

(4) change quorum or voting requirements for its board of directors or shareholders; change provisions for selection, resignation, or removal of its directors or officers or both; or change provisions for amending its bylaws;

(5) prevent commencement of a proceeding by or against the corporation in its corporate name;

(6) abate or suspend a proceeding pending by or against the corporation on the effective date of dissolution; or

(7) terminate the authority of the registered agent of the corporation.

* * * *

Subchapter C. Judicial Dissolution

§ 14.30 Grounds for Judicial Dissolution

The [name or describe court or courts] may dissolve a corporation:

(1) in a proceeding by the attorney general if it is established that:

(i) the corporation obtained its articles of incorporation through fraud; or

(ii) the corporation has continued to exceed or abuse the authority conferred upon it by law;

(2) in a proceeding by a shareholder if it is established that:

(i) the directors are deadlocked in the management of the corporate affairs, the shareholders are unable to break the deadlock, and irreparable injury to the corporation is threatened or being suffered, or the business and affairs of the corporation can no longer be conducted to the advantage of the shareholders generally, because of the deadlock;

(ii) the directors or those in control of the corporation have acted, are acting, or will act in a manner that is illegal, oppressive, or fraudulent;

(iii) the shareholders are deadlocked in voting power and have failed, for a period that includes at least two consecutive annual meeting dates, to elect successors to directors whose terms have expired; or

(iv) the corporate assets are being misapplied or wasted;

(3) in a proceeding by a creditor if it is established that:

(i) the creditor's claim has been reduced to judgment, the execution on the judgment returned unsatisfied, and the corporation is insolvent; or

(ii) the corporation has admitted in writing that the creditor's claim is due and owing and the corporation is insolvent; or

(4) in a proceeding by the corporation to have its voluntary dissolution continued under court supervision.

*   *   *   *

Chapter 16.
RECORDS AND REPORTS

Subchapter A. Records

§ 16.01 Corporate Records

(a) A corporation shall keep as permanent records minutes of all meetings of its shareholders and board of directors, a record of all actions taken by the shareholders or board of directors without a meeting, and a record of all actions taken by a committee of the board of directors in place of the board of directors on behalf of the corporation.

(b) A corporation shall maintain appropriate accounting records.

(c) A corporation or its agent shall maintain a record of its shareholders, in a form that permits preparation of a list of the names and addresses of all shareholders, in alphabetical order by class of shares showing the number and class of shares held by each.

(d) A corporation shall maintain its records in written form or in another form capable of conversion into written form within a reasonable time.

(e) A corporation shall keep a copy of the following records at its principal office:

(1) its articles or restated articles of incorporation and all amendments to them currently in effect;

(2) its bylaws or restated bylaws and all amendments to them currently in effect;

(3) resolutions adopted by its board of directors creating one or more classes or series of shares, and fixing their relative rights, preferences, and limitations, if shares issued pursuant to those resolutions are outstanding;

(4) the minutes of all shareholders' meetings, and records of all action taken by shareholders without a meeting, for the past three years;

(5) all written communications to shareholders generally within the past three years, including the financial statements furnished for the past three years *   *   * ;

(6) a list of the names and business addresses of its current directors and officers; and

(7) its most recent annual report delivered to the secretary of state *   *   *.

§ 16.02 Inspection of Records by Shareholders

(a) Subject to section 16.03(c), a shareholder of a corporation is entitled to inspect and copy, during regular business hours at the corporation's principal office, any of the records of the corporation described in section 16.01(e) if he gives the corporation written notice of his demand at least five business days before the date on which he wishes to inspect and copy.

(b) A shareholder of a corporation is entitled to inspect and copy, during regular business hours at a reasonable location specified by the corporation, any of the following records of the corporation if the shareholder meets the requirements of subsection (c) and gives the corporation written notice of his demand at least five business days before the date on which he wishes to inspect and copy:

(1) excerpts from minutes of any meeting of the board of directors, records of any action of a committee of the board of directors while acting in place of the board of directors on behalf of the corporation, minutes of any meeting of the shareholders, and records of action taken by the shareholders or board of directors without a meeting, to the extent not subject to inspection under section 16.02(a);

(2) accounting records of the corporation; and

(3) the record of shareholders.

(c) A shareholder may inspect and copy the records identified in subsection (b) only if:

(1) his demand is made in good faith and for a proper purpose;

(2) he describes with reasonable particularity his purpose and the records he desires to inspect; and

(3) the records are directly connected with his purpose.

(d) The right of inspection granted by this section may not be abolished or limited by a corporation's articles of incorporation or bylaws.

(e) This section does not affect:

(1) the right of a shareholder to inspect records under section 7.20 or, if the shareholder is in litigation with the corporation, to the same extent as any other litigant;

(2) the power of a court, independently of this Act, to compel the production of corporate records for examination.

(f) For purposes of this section, "shareholder" includes a beneficial owner whose shares are held in a voting trust or by a nominee on his behalf.

The Sarbanes-Oxley Act of 2002 (Excerpts and Explanatory Comments)

Note: The author's explanatory comments appear in italics following the excerpt from each section.

SECTION 302

Corporate responsibility for financial reports[1]

(a) Regulations required

The Commission shall, by rule, require, for each company filing periodic reports under section 13(a) or 15(d) of the Securities Exchange Act of 1934 (15 U.S.C. 78m, 78o(d)), that the principal executive officer or officers and the principal financial officer or officers, or persons performing similar functions, certify in each annual or quarterly report filed or submitted under either such section of such Act that—

(1) the signing officer has reviewed the report;

(2) based on the officer's knowledge, the report does not contain any untrue statement of a material fact or omit to state a material fact necessary in order to make the statements made, in light of the circumstances under which such statements were made, not misleading;

(3) based on such officer's knowledge, the financial statements, and other financial information included in the report, fairly present in all material respects the financial condition and results of operations of the issuer as of, and for, the periods presented in the report;

(4) the signing officers—

(A) are responsible for establishing and maintaining internal controls;

(B) have designed such internal controls to ensure that material information relating to the issuer and its consolidated subsidiaries is made known to such officers by others within those entities, particularly during the period in which the periodic reports are being prepared;

(C) have evaluated the effectiveness of the issuer's internal controls as of a date within 90 days prior to the report; and

(D) have presented in the report their conclusions about the effectiveness of their internal controls based on their evaluation as of that date;

(5) the signing officers have disclosed to the issuer's auditors and the audit committee of the board of directors (or persons fulfilling the equivalent function)—

(A) all significant deficiencies in the design or operation of internal controls which could adversely affect the issuer's ability to record, process, summarize, and report financial data and have identified for the issuer's auditors any material weaknesses in internal controls; and

(B) any fraud, whether or not material, that involves management or other employees who have a significant role in the issuer's internal controls; and

(6) the signing officers have indicated in the report whether or not there were significant changes in internal controls or in other factors that could significantly affect internal controls subsequent to the date of their evaluation, including any corrective actions with regard to significant deficiencies and material weaknesses.

(b) Foreign reincorporations have no effect

Nothing in this section shall be interpreted or applied in any way to allow any issuer to lessen the legal force of the statement required under this section, by an issuer having reincorporated or having engaged in any other transaction that resulted in the transfer of the corporate domicile or offices of the issuer from inside the United States to outside of the United States.

(c) Deadline

The rules required by subsection (a) of this section shall be effective not later than 30 days after July 30, 2002.

---

1. This section of the Sarbanes-Oxley Act is codified at 15 U.S.C. Section 7241.

EXPLANATORY COMMENTS: *Section 302 requires the chief executive officer (CEO) and chief financial officer (CFO) of each public company to certify that they have reviewed the company's quarterly and annual reports to be filed with the Securities and Exchange Commission (SEC). The CEO and CFO must certify that, based on their knowledge, the reports do not contain any untrue statement of a material fact or any half-truth that would make the report misleading, and that the information contained in the reports fairly presents the company's financial condition.*

In addition, this section also requires the CEO and CFO to certify that they have created and designed an internal control system for their company and have recently evaluated that system to ensure that it is effectively providing them with relevant and accurate financial information. If the signing officers have found any significant deficiencies or weaknesses in the company's system or have discovered any evidence of fraud, they must have reported the situation, and any corrective actions they have taken, to the auditors and the audit committee.

SECTION 306

Insider trades during pension fund blackout periods[2]

(a) Prohibition of insider trading during pension fund blackout periods

(1) In general

Except to the extent otherwise provided by rule of the Commission pursuant to paragraph (3), it shall be unlawful for any director or executive officer of an issuer of any equity security (other than an exempted security), directly or indirectly, to purchase, sell, or otherwise acquire or transfer any equity security of the issuer (other than an exempted security) during any blackout period with respect to such equity security if such director or officer acquires such equity security in connection with his or her service or employment as a director or executive officer.

(2) Remedy

(A) In general

Any profit realized by a director or executive officer referred to in paragraph (1) from any purchase, sale, or other acquisition or transfer in violation of this subsection shall inure to and be recoverable by the issuer, irrespective of any intention on the part of such director or executive officer in entering into the transaction.

(B) Actions to recover profits

An action to recover profits in accordance with this subsection may be instituted at law or in equity in any court of competent jurisdiction by the issuer, or by the owner of any security of the issuer in the name and in behalf of the issuer if the issuer fails or refuses to bring such action within 60 days after the date of request, or fails diligently to prosecute the action thereafter, except that no such suit shall be brought more than 2 years after the date on which such profit was realized.

(3) Rulemaking authorized

The Commission shall, in consultation with the Secretary of Labor, issue rules to clarify the application of this subsection and to prevent evasion thereof. Such rules shall provide for the application of the requirements of paragraph (1) with respect to entities treated as a single employer with respect to an issuer under section 414(b), (c), (m), or (o) of Title 26 to the extent necessary to clarify the application of such requirements and to prevent evasion thereof. Such rules may also provide for appropriate exceptions from the requirements of this subsection, including exceptions for purchases pursuant to an automatic dividend reinvestment program or purchases or sales made pursuant to an advance election.

(4) Blackout period

For purposes of this subsection, the term "blackout period", with respect to the equity securities of any issuer—

(A) means any period of more than 3 consecutive business days during which the ability of not fewer than 50 percent of the participants or beneficiaries under all individual account plans maintained by the issuer to purchase, sell, or otherwise acquire or transfer an interest in any equity of such issuer held in such an individual account plan is temporarily suspended by the issuer or by a fiduciary of the plan; and

(B) does not include, under regulations which shall be prescribed by the Commission—

(i) a regularly scheduled period in which the participants and beneficiaries may not purchase, sell, or otherwise acquire or transfer an interest in any equity of such issuer, if such period is—

(I) incorporated into the individual account plan; and

(II) timely disclosed to employees before becoming participants under the individual account plan or as a subsequent amendment to the plan; or

(ii) any suspension described in subparagraph (A) that is imposed solely in connection with persons becoming participants or beneficiaries, or ceasing to be participants or beneficiaries, in an individual account plan by reason of a corporate merger, acquisition, divestiture, or similar transaction involving the plan or plan sponsor.

(5) Individual account plan

For purposes of this subsection, the term "individual account plan" has the meaning provided in section 1002(34) of Title 29, except that such term shall not

---

2. Codified at 15 U.S.C. Section 7244.

include a one-participant retirement plan (within the meaning of section 1021(i)(8)(B) of Title 29).

(6) Notice to directors, executive officers, and the Commission

In any case in which a director or executive officer is subject to the requirements of this subsection in connection with a blackout period (as defined in paragraph (4)) with respect to any equity securities, the issuer of such equity securities shall timely notify such director or officer and the Securities and Exchange Commission of such blackout period.

*   *   *   *

EXPLANATORY COMMENTS: *Corporate pension funds typically prohibit employees from trading shares of the corporation during periods when the pension fund is undergoing significant change. Prior to 2002, however, these blackout periods did not affect the corporation's executives, who frequently received shares of the corporate stock as part of their compensation. During the collapse of Enron, for example, its pension plan was scheduled to change administrators at a time when Enron's stock price was falling. Enron's employees therefore could not sell their shares while the price was dropping, but its executives could and did sell their stock, consequently avoiding some of the losses. Section 306 was Congress's solution to the basic unfairness of this situation. This section of the act required the SEC to issue rules that prohibit any director or executive officer from trading during pension fund blackout periods. (The SEC later issued these rules, entitled Regulation Blackout Trading Restriction, or Reg BTR.) Section 306 also provided shareholders with a right to file a shareholder's derivative suit against officers and directors who have profited from trading during these blackout periods (provided that the corporation has failed to bring a suit). The officer or director can be forced to return to the corporation any profits received, regardless of whether the director or officer acted with bad intent.*

SECTION 402
Periodical and other reports[3]

*   *   *   *

(i) Accuracy of financial reports

Each financial report that contains financial statements, and that is required to be prepared in accordance with (or reconciled to) generally accepted accounting principles under this chapter and filed with the Commission shall reflect all material correcting adjustments that have been identified by a registered public accounting firm in accordance with generally accepted accounting principles and the rules and regulations of the Commission.

(j) Off-balance sheet transactions

Not later than 180 days after July 30, 2002, the Commission shall issue final rules providing that each annual and quar-

---

3. This section of the Sarbanes-Oxley Act amended some of the provisions of the 1934 Securities Exchange Act and added the paragraphs reproduced here at 15 U.S.C. Section 78m.

terly financial report required to be filed with the Commission shall disclose all material off-balance sheet transactions, arrangements, obligations (including contingent obligations), and other relationships of the issuer with unconsolidated entities or other persons, that may have a material current or future effect on financial condition, changes in financial condition, results of operations, liquidity, capital expenditures, capital resources, or significant components of revenues or expenses.

(k) Prohibition on personal loans to executives

(1) In general

It shall be unlawful for any issuer (as defined in section 7201 of this title), directly or indirectly, including through any subsidiary, to extend or maintain credit, to arrange for the extension of credit, or to renew an extension of credit, in the form of a personal loan to or for any director or executive officer (or equivalent thereof) of that issuer. An extension of credit maintained by the issuer on July 30, 2002, shall not be subject to the provisions of this subsection, provided that there is no material modification to any term of any such extension of credit or any renewal of any such extension of credit on or after July 30, 2002.

(2) Limitation

Paragraph (1) does not preclude any home improvement and manufactured home loans (as that term is defined in section 1464 of Title 12), consumer credit (as defined in section 1602 of this title), or any extension of credit under an open end credit plan (as defined in section 1602 of this title), or a charge card (as defined in section 1637(c)(4)(e) of this title), or any extension of credit by a broker or dealer registered under section 78o of this title to an employee of that broker or dealer to buy, trade, or carry securities, that is permitted under rules or regulations of the Board of Governors of the Federal Reserve System pursuant to section 78g of this title (other than an extension of credit that would be used to purchase the stock of that issuer), that is—

(A) made or provided in the ordinary course of the consumer credit business of such issuer;

(B) of a type that is generally made available by such issuer to the public; and

(C) made by such issuer on market terms, or terms that are no more favorable than those offered by the issuer to the general public for such extensions of credit.

(3) Rule of construction for certain loans

Paragraph (1) does not apply to any loan made or maintained by an insured depository institution (as defined in section 1813 of Title 12), if the loan is subject to the insider lending restrictions of section 375b of Title 12.

(l) Real time issuer disclosures

Each issuer reporting under subsection (a) of this section or section 78o(d) of this title shall disclose to the public on a rapid and current basis such additional information concerning material changes in the financial condition or operations of the issuer, in plain English, which may include trend and qualitative information and graphic presentations, as the Commission determines, by rule, is necessary or useful for the protection of investors and in the public interest.

EXPLANATORY COMMENTS: *Corporate executives during the Enron era typically received extremely large salaries, significant bonuses, and abundant stock options, even when the companies for which they worked were suffering. Executives were also routinely given personal loans from corporate funds, many of which were never paid back. The average large company during that period loaned almost $1 million a year to top executives, and some companies, including Tyco International and Adelphia Communications Corporation, loaned hundreds of millions of dollars to their executives every year. Section 402 amended the 1934 Securities Exchange Act to prohibit public companies from making personal loans to executive officers and directors. There are a few exceptions to this prohibition, such as home-improvement loans made in the ordinary course of business. Note also that while loans are forbidden, outright gifts are not. A corporation is free to give gifts to its executives, including cash, provided that these gifts are disclosed on its financial reports. The idea is that corporate directors will be deterred from making substantial gifts to their executives by the disclosure requirement—particularly if the corporation's financial condition is questionable—because making such gifts could be perceived as abusing their authority.*

SECTION 403

Directors, officers, and principal stockholders[4]

(a) Disclosures required

(1) Directors, officers, and principal stockholders required to file

Every person who is directly or indirectly the beneficial owner of more than 10 percent of any class of any equity security (other than an exempted security) which is registered pursuant to section 78l of this title, or who is a director or an officer of the issuer of such security, shall file the statements required by this subsection with the Commission (and, if such security is registered on a national securities exchange, also with the exchange).

(2) Time of filing

The statements required by this subsection shall be filed—

(A) at the time of the registration of such security on a national securities exchange or by the effective date of a registration statement filed pursuant to section 78l(g) of this title;

(B) within 10 days after he or she becomes such beneficial owner, director, or officer;

---

4. This section of the Sarbanes-Oxley Act amended the disclosure provisions of the 1934 Securities Exchange Act, at 15 U.S.C. Section 78p.

(C) if there has been a change in such ownership, or if such person shall have purchased or sold a security-based swap agreement (as defined in section 206(b) of the Gramm-Leach-Bliley Act (15 U.S.C. 78c note)) involving such equity security, before the end of the second business day following the day on which the subject transaction has been executed, or at such other time as the Commission shall establish, by rule, in any case in which the Commission determines that such 2-day period is not feasible.

(3) Contents of statements

A statement filed—

(A) under subparagraph (A) or (B) of paragraph (2) shall contain a statement of the amount of all equity securities of such issuer of which the filing person is the beneficial owner; and

(B) under subparagraph (C) of such paragraph shall indicate ownership by the filing person at the date of filing, any such changes in such ownership, and such purchases and sales of the security-based swap agreements as have occurred since the most recent such filing under such subparagraph.

(4) Electronic filing and availability

Beginning not later than 1 year after July 30, 2002—

(A) a statement filed under subparagraph (C) of paragraph (2) shall be filed electronically;

(B) the Commission shall provide each such statement on a publicly accessible Internet site not later than the end of the business day following that filing; and

(C) the issuer (if the issuer maintains a corporate website) shall provide that statement on that corporate website, not later than the end of the business day following that filing.

*   *   *   *

EXPLANATORY COMMENTS: *This section dramatically shortens the time period provided in the Securities Exchange Act of 1934 for disclosing transactions by insiders. The prior law stated that most transactions had to be reported within ten days of the beginning of the following month, although certain transactions did not have to be reported until the following fiscal year (within the first forty-five days). Because some of the insider trading that occurred during the Enron fiasco did not have to be disclosed (and was therefore not discovered) until long after the transactions, Congress added this section to reduce the time period for making disclosures. Under Section 403, most transactions by insiders must be electronically filed with the SEC within two business days. Also, any company that maintains a Web site must post these SEC filings on its site by the end of the next business day. Congress enacted this section in the belief that if insiders are required to file reports of their transactions promptly with the SEC, companies will do more to police themselves and prevent insider trading.*

SECTION 404

Management assessment of internal controls[5]

(a) Rules required

The Commission shall prescribe rules requiring each annual report required by section 78m(a) or 78o(d) of this title to contain an internal control report, which shall—

(1) state the responsibility of management for establishing and maintaining an adequate internal control structure and procedures for financial reporting; and

(2) contain an assessment, as of the end of the most recent fiscal year of the issuer, of the effectiveness of the internal control structure and procedures of the issuer for financial reporting.

(b) Internal control evaluation and reporting

With respect to the internal control assessment required by subsection (a) of this section, each registered public accounting firm that prepares or issues the audit report for the issuer shall attest to, and report on, the assessment made by the management of the issuer. An attestation made under this subsection shall be made in accordance with standards for attestation engagements issued or adopted by the Board. Any such attestation shall not be the subject of a separate engagement.

EXPLANATORY COMMENTS: *This section was enacted to prevent corporate executives from claiming they were ignorant of significant errors in their companies' financial reports. For instance, several CEOs testified before Congress that they simply had no idea that the corporations' financial statements were off by billions of dollars. Congress therefore passed Section 404, which requires each annual report to contain a description and assessment of the company's internal control structure and financial reporting procedures. The section also requires that an audit be conducted of the internal control assessment, as well as the financial statements contained in the report. This section goes hand in hand with Section 302 (which, as discussed previously, requires various certifications attesting to the accuracy of the information in financial reports).*

Section 404 has been one of the more controversial and expensive provisions in the Sarbanes-Oxley Act because it requires companies to assess their own internal financial controls to make sure that their financial statements are reliable and accurate. A corporation might need to set up a disclosure committee and a coordinator, establish codes of conduct for accounting and financial personnel, create documentation procedures, provide training, and outline the individuals who are responsible for performing each of the procedures. Companies that were already well managed have not experienced substantial difficulty complying with this section. Other companies, however, have spent millions of dollars setting up, documenting, and evaluating their internal financial control systems. Although initially creating the internal financial control system is a onetime-only expense, the costs of maintaining and evaluating it

are ongoing. Some corporations that spent considerable sums complying with Section 404 have been able to offset these costs by discovering and correcting inefficiencies or frauds within their systems. Nevertheless, it is unlikely that any corporation will find compliance with this section to be inexpensive.

SECTION 802 (A)

Destruction, alteration, or falsification of records in Federal investigations and bankruptcy[6]

Whoever knowingly alters, destroys, mutilates, conceals, covers up, falsifies, or makes a false entry in any record, document, or tangible object with the intent to impede, obstruct, or influence the investigation or proper administration of any matter within the jurisdiction of any department or agency of the United States or any case filed under title 11, or in relation to or contemplation of any such matter or case, shall be fined under this title, imprisoned not more than 20 years, or both.

Destruction of corporate audit records[7]

(a) (1) Any accountant who conducts an audit of an issuer of securities to which section 10A(a) of the Securities Exchange Act of 1934 (15 U.S.C. 78j-1(a)) applies, shall maintain all audit or review workpapers for a period of 5 years from the end of the fiscal period in which the audit or review was concluded.

(2) The Securities and Exchange Commission shall promulgate, within 180 days, after adequate notice and an opportunity for comment, such rules and regulations, as are reasonably necessary, relating to the retention of relevant records such as workpapers, documents that form the basis of an audit or review, memoranda, correspondence, communications, other documents, and records (including electronic records) which are created, sent, or received in connection with an audit or review and contain conclusions, opinions, analyses, or financial data relating to such an audit or review, which is conducted by any accountant who conducts an audit of an issuer of securities to which section 10A(a) of the Securities Exchange Act of 1934 (15 U.S.C. 78j-1(a)) applies. The Commission may, from time to time, amend or supplement the rules and regulations that it is required to promulgate under this section, after adequate notice and an opportunity for comment, in order to ensure that such rules and regulations adequately comport with the purposes of this section.

(b) Whoever knowingly and willfully violates subsection (a)(1), or any rule or regulation promulgated by the Securities and Exchange Commission under subsection (a)(2), shall be fined under this title, imprisoned not more than 10 years, or both.

(c) Nothing in this section shall be deemed to diminish or relieve any person of any other duty or obligation imposed

---

5. Codified at 15 U.S.C. Section 7262.

6. Codified at 15 U.S.C. Section 1519.
7. Codified at 15 U.S.C. Section 1520.

by Federal or State law or regulation to maintain, or refrain from destroying, any document.

EXPLANATORY COMMENTS: *Section 802(a) enacted two new statutes that punish those who alter or destroy documents. The first statute is not specifically limited to securities fraud cases. It provides that anyone who alters, destroys, or falsifies records in federal investigations or bankruptcy may be criminally prosecuted and sentenced to a fine or to up to twenty years in prison, or both. The second statute requires auditors of public companies to keep all audit or review working papers for five years but expressly allows the SEC to amend or supplement these requirements as it sees fit. The SEC has, in fact, amended this section by issuing a rule that requires auditors who audit reporting companies to retain working papers for seven years from the conclusion of the review. Section 802(a) further provides that anyone who knowingly and willfully violates this statute is subject to criminal prosecution and can be sentenced to a fine, imprisoned for up to ten years, or both if convicted.*

This portion of the Sarbanes-Oxley Act implicitly recognizes that persons who are under investigation often are tempted to respond by destroying or falsifying documents that might prove their complicity in wrongdoing. The severity of the punishment should provide a strong incentive for these individuals to resist the temptation.

SECTION 804

Time limitations on the commencement of civil actions arising under Acts of Congress[8]

(a) Except as otherwise provided by law, a civil action arising under an Act of Congress enacted after the date of the enactment of this section may not be commenced later than 4 years after the cause of action accrues.

(b) Notwithstanding subsection (a), a private right of action that involves a claim of fraud, deceit, manipulation, or contrivance in contravention of a regulatory requirement concerning the securities laws, as defined in section 3(a)(47) of the Securities Exchange Act of 1934 (15 U.S.C. 78c(a)(47)), may be brought not later than the earlier of—

   (1) 2 years after the discovery of the facts constituting the violation; or

   (2) 5 years after such violation.

EXPLANATORY COMMENTS: *Prior to the enactment of this section, Section 10(b) of the Securities Exchange Act of 1934 had no express statute of limitations. The courts generally required plaintiffs to have filed suit within one year from the date that they should (using due diligence) have discovered that a fraud had been committed but no later than three years after the fraud occurred. Section 804 extends this period by specifying that plaintiffs must file a lawsuit within two years after they discover (or should have discovered) a fraud but no later than five years after*

the fraud's occurrence. This provision has prevented the courts from dismissing numerous securities fraud lawsuits.

SECTION 806

Civil action to protect against retaliation in fraud cases[9]

(a) Whistleblower protection for employees of publicly traded companies.—

No company with a class of securities registered under section 12 of the Securities Exchange Act of 1934 (15 U.S.C. 78l), or that is required to file reports under section 15(d) of the Securities Exchange Act of 1934 (15 U.S.C. 78o(d)), or any officer, employee, contractor, subcontractor, or agent of such company, may discharge, demote, suspend, threaten, harass, or in any other manner discriminate against an employee in the terms and conditions of employment because of any lawful act done by the employee—

   (1) to provide information, cause information to be provided, or otherwise assist in an investigation regarding any conduct which the employee reasonably believes constitutes a violation of section 1341, 1343, 1344, or 1348, any rule or regulation of the Securities and Exchange Commission, or any provision of Federal law relating to fraud against shareholders, when the information or assistance is provided to or the investigation is conducted by—

      (A) a Federal regulatory or law enforcement agency;

      (B) any Member of Congress or any committee of Congress; or

      (C) a person with supervisory authority over the employee (or such other person working for the employer who has the authority to investigate, discover, or terminate misconduct); or

   (2) to file, cause to be filed, testify, participate in, or otherwise assist in a proceeding filed or about to be filed (with any knowledge of the employer) relating to an alleged violation of section 1341, 1343, 1344, or 1348, any rule or regulation of the Securities and Exchange Commission, or any provision of Federal law relating to fraud against shareholders.

(b) Enforcement action.—

   (1) In general.—A person who alleges discharge or other discrimination by any person in violation of subsection (a) may seek relief under subsection (c), by—

      (A) filing a complaint with the Secretary of Labor; or

      (B) if the Secretary has not issued a final decision within 180 days of the filing of the complaint and there is no showing that such delay is due to the bad faith of the claimant, bringing an action at law or equity for de novo review in the appropriate district court of the United States, which shall have jurisdic-

---

8. Codified at 28 U.S.C. Section 1658.

9. Codified at 18 U.S.C. Section 1514A.

tion over such an action without regard to the amount in controversy.

(2) Procedure.—

(A) In general.—An action under paragraph (1)(A) shall be governed under the rules and procedures set forth in section 42121(b) of title 49, United States Code.

(B) Exception.—Notification made under section 42121(b)(1) of title 49, United States Code, shall be made to the person named in the complaint and to the employer.

(C) Burdens of proof.—An action brought under paragraph (1)(B) shall be governed by the legal burdens of proof set forth in section 42121(b) of title 49, United States Code.

(D) Statute of limitations.—An action under paragraph (1) shall be commenced not later than 90 days after the date on which the violation occurs.

(c) Remedies.—

(1) In general.—An employee prevailing in any action under subsection (b)(1) shall be entitled to all relief necessary to make the employee whole.

(2) Compensatory damages.—Relief for any action under paragraph (1) shall include—

(A) reinstatement with the same seniority status that the employee would have had, but for the discrimination;

(B) the amount of back pay, with interest; and

(C) compensation for any special damages sustained as a result of the discrimination, including litigation costs, expert witness fees, and reasonable attorney fees.

(d) Rights retained by employee.—Nothing in this section shall be deemed to diminish the rights, privileges, or remedies of any employee under any Federal or State law, or under any collective bargaining agreement.

EXPLANATORY COMMENTS: *Section 806 is one of several provisions that were included in the Sarbanes-Oxley Act to encourage and protect whistleblowers—that is, employees who report their employer's alleged violations of securities law to the authorities. This section applies to employees, agents, and independent contractors who work for publicly traded companies or testify about such a company during an investigation. It sets up an administrative procedure at the Department of Labor for individuals who claim that their employer retaliated against them (fired or demoted them, for example) for blowing the whistle on the employer's wrongful conduct. It also allows the award of civil damages—including back pay, reinstatement, special damages, attorneys' fees, and court costs—to employees who prove that they suffered retaliation. Since this provision was enacted, whistleblowers have filed numerous complaints with the Department of Labor under this section.*

SECTION 807

Securities fraud[10]

Whoever knowingly executes, or attempts to execute, a scheme or artifice—

(1) to defraud any person in connection with any security of an issuer with a class of securities registered under section 12 of the Securities Exchange Act of 1934 (15 U.S.C. 78l) or that is required to file reports under section 15(d) of the Securities Exchange Act of 1934 (15 U.S.C. 78o(d)); or

(2) to obtain, by means of false or fraudulent pretenses, representations, or promises, any money or property in connection with the purchase or sale of any security of an issuer with a class of securities registered under section 12 of the Securities Exchange Act of 1934 (15 U.S.C. 78l) or that is required to file reports under section 15(d) of the Securities Exchange Act of 1934 (15 U.S.C. 78o(d)); shall be fined under this title, or imprisoned not more than 25 years, or both.

EXPLANATORY COMMENTS: *Section 807 adds a new provision to the federal criminal code that addresses securities fraud. Prior to 2002, federal securities law had already made it a crime—under Section 10(b) of the Securities Exchange Act of 1934 and SEC Rule 10b-5, both of which are discussed in Chapter 41—to intentionally defraud someone in connection with a purchase or sale of securities, but the offense was not listed in the federal criminal code. Also, paragraph 2 of Section 807 goes beyond what is prohibited under securities law by making it a crime to obtain by means of false or fraudulent pretenses any money or property from the purchase or sale of securities. This new provision allows violators to be punished by up to twenty-five years in prison, a fine, or both.*

SECTION 906

Failure of corporate officers to certify financial reports[11]

(a) Certification of periodic financial reports.—Each periodic report containing financial statements filed by an issuer with the Securities Exchange Commission pursuant to section 13(a) or 15(d) of the Securities Exchange Act of 1934 (15 U.S.C. 78m(a) or 78o(d)) shall be accompanied by a written statement by the chief executive officer and chief financial officer (or equivalent thereof) of the issuer.

(b) Content.—The statement required under subsection (a) shall certify that the periodic report containing the financial statements fully complies with the requirements of section 13(a) or 15(d) of the Securities Exchange Act of 1934 (15 U.S.C. 78m or 78o(d)) and that information contained in the periodic report fairly presents, in all material respects, the financial condition and results of operations of the issuer.

---

10. Codified at 18 U.S.C. Section 1348.
11. Codified at 18 U.S.C. Section 1350.

(c) Criminal penalties.—Whoever—

(1) certifies any statement as set forth in subsections (a) and (b) of this section knowing that the periodic report accompanying the statement does not comport with all the requirements set forth in this section shall be fined not more than $1,000,000 or imprisoned not more than 10 years, or both; or

(2) willfully certifies any statement as set forth in subsections (a) and (b) of this section knowing that the periodic report accompanying the statement does not comport with all the requirements set forth in this section shall be fined not more than $5,000,000, or imprisoned not more than 20 years, or both.

EXPLANATORY COMMENTS: *As previously discussed, under Section 302 a corporation's CEO and CFO are required to certify that they believe the quarterly and annual reports their company files with the SEC are accurate and fairly present the company's financial condition. Section 906 adds "teeth" to these requirements by authorizing criminal penalties for those officers who intentionally certify inaccurate SEC filings. Knowing violations of the requirements are punishable by a fine of up to $1 million, ten years in prison, or both. Willful violators may be fined up to $5 million, sentenced to up to twenty years in prison, or both. Although the difference between a knowing and a willful violation is not entirely clear, the section is obviously intended to remind corporate officers of the serious consequences of certifying inaccurate reports to the SEC.*

Sample Answers for End-of-Chapter Questions with Sample Answer

1–2A. QUESTION WITH SAMPLE ANSWER

At the time of the Nuremberg trials, "crimes against humanity" were new international crimes. The laws criminalized such acts as murder, extermination, enslavement, deportation, and other inhumane acts committed against any civilian population. These international laws derived their legitimacy from "natural law." Natural law, which is the oldest and one of the most significant schools of jurisprudence, holds that governments and legal systems should reflect the moral and ethical ideals that are inherent in human nature. Because natural law is universal and discoverable by reason, its adherents believe that all other law is derived from natural law. Natural law therefore supersedes laws created by humans (national, or "positive," law), and in a conflict between the two, national or positive law loses its legitimacy. The Nuremberg defendants asserted that they had been acting in accordance with German law. The judges dismissed these claims, reasoning that the defendants' acts were commonly regarded as crimes and that the accused must have known that the acts would be considered criminal. The judges clearly believed the tenets of natural law and expected that the defendants, too, should have been able to realize that their acts ran afoul of it. The fact that the "positivist law" of Germany at the time required them to commit these acts is irrelevant. Under natural law theory, the international court was justified in finding the defendants guilty of crimes against humanity.

2–2A. QUESTION WITH SAMPLE ANSWER

Trial courts, as explained in the text, are responsible for settling "questions of fact." Often, when parties bring a case to court there is a dispute as to what actually happened. Different witnesses have different versions of what they saw or heard, and there may be only indirect evidence of certain issues in dispute. During the trial, the judge and the jury (if it is a jury trial) listen to the witnesses and view the evidence firsthand. Thus, the trial court is in the best position to assess the credibility (truthfulness) of the witnesses and determine the weight that should be given to various items of evidence. At the end of the trial, the judge and the jury (if it is a jury trial) decide what will be considered facts for the purposes of the case. Trial courts are best suited to this job, as they have the opportunity to observe the witnesses and evidence, and they regularly determine the reliability of certain evidence. Appellate courts, in contrast, see only the written record of the trial court proceedings and cannot evaluate the credibility of witnesses and the persuasiveness of evidence. For these reasons, appellate courts nearly always defer to trial courts' findings of fact. An appellate court can reverse a lower court's findings of fact, however, when so little evidence was presented at trial that no reasonable person could have reached the conclusion that the judge or jury reached.

3–3A. QUESTION WITH SAMPLE ANSWER

(a) After all of the pleadings (the complaint, answer, and any counterclaim and reply) have been filed, either party can file a motion for judgment on the pleadings. This may happen because it is clear from just the pleadings that the plaintiff has failed to state a cause of action. This motion is also appropriate when all the parties agree on the facts, and the only question remaining is how the law applies to those facts. The court may consider only those facts pleaded in the documents and stipulated (agreed to) by the parties. This is the difference between a motion for judgment on the pleadings and a motion for summary judgment (discussed below). In a motion for summary judgment, there may be some facts in dispute and the parties may supplement the pleadings with sworn statements and other materials.

(b) During the trial, at the conclusion of the plaintiff's case, the defendant may move for a directed verdict. If the defendant does this, he or she will argue to the court that the plaintiff presented inadequate evidence that he or she is entitled to the remedy being sought. In considering a motion for a directed verdict (federal courts use the term "motion for a judgment as a matter of law"), the judge looks at the evidence in the light most favorable to the plaintiff and grants the motion only if there is insufficient evidence to raise an issue of fact. These motions are rarely granted at this stage of a trial. At the end of the defendant's case, the parties have another opportunity to move for a directed verdict. This time, either party can seek the motion. The motion will be granted only if there is no reasonable way to find for the party against whom the motion is made. In other words, if, after the defense's case is concluded, the plaintiff asks the court to direct a verdict against the defendant, the court will do so if no reasonable interpretation of the evidence would allow the defendant to win the case.

(c) As noted in part (a) of this answer, a motion for summary judgment is similar to a motion for a judgment on the pleadings in that it asks the court to grant a judgment without a trial. Either party can file a summary judgment motion when the only question is how the law applies to the facts in a case. When a court considers a motion for summary judgment, it can take into account evidence outside the pleadings. The evidence may consist of sworn statements by parties or witnesses as well as documents. The use of this additional evidence distinguishes the motion for summary judgment from the motion for judgment on the pleadings. Summary judgment motions will be granted only when there are no questions of fact that need to be decided and the only question is a question of law, which requires a judge's ruling. These motions can be made before or during a trial.

(d) If a losing party has previously moved for a directed verdict, that party can make a motion for a judgment *n.o.v.* (notwithstanding the verdict) after the jury issues its verdict. The standards for granting a judgment *n.o.v.* are the same as those for granting a motion to dismiss a case or a motion for a directed verdict. Essentially, the losing party argues that even if the evidence is viewed in the light most favorable to the other party, a reasonable jury could not have found in that party's favor. If the judge finds this contention to be correct or decides that the law requires the opposite result, the motion will be granted.

4–2A. Question with Sample Answer

As the text points out, Thomas has a constitutionally protected right to his religion and the free exercise of it. In denying his unemployment benefits, the state violated these rights. Employers are obligated to make reasonable accommodations for their employees' beliefs, right or wrong, that are openly and sincerely held. Thomas's beliefs were openly and sincerely held. By placing him in a department that made military goods, his employer effectively put him in a position of having to choose between his job and his religious principles. This unilateral decision on the part of the employer was the reason Thomas left his job and why the company was required to compensate Thomas for his resulting unemployment.

5–2A. Question with Sample Answer

This question essentially asks whether good behavior can ever be unethical. The answer to this question depends on which approach to ethical reasoning you are using. Under the outcome-based approach of utilitarianism, it is simply not possible for selfish motives to be unethical if they result in good conduct. A good outcome is moral regardless of the nature of the action itself or the reason for the action. Under a duty-based approach, motive would be more relevant in assessing whether a firm's conduct was ethical. You would need to analyze the firm's conduct in terms of religious truths or to determine whether human beings were being treated with the inherent dignity that they deserve. Although a good motive would not justify a bad act to a religious ethicist, in this situation the actions were good and the motive was questionable (because the firm was simply seeking to increase its profit). Nevertheless, unless one's religion prohibited making a profit, the firm's actions would likely not be considered unethical. Applying Kantian ethics would require you to evaluate the firm's actions in light of what would happen if everyone in society acted that way (categorical imperative). Here, because the conduct was good, it would be positive for society if every firm acted that way. Hence, the profit-seeking motive would be irrelevant in a Kantian analysis. In a debate between motive and conduct, then, conduct is almost always given greater weight in evaluating ethics.

6–2A. Question with Sample Answer

To answer this question, you must first decide if there is a legal theory under which Harley may be able to recover. You may recall from your reading the intentional tort of "wrongful interference with a contractual relationship." To recover damages under this theory, Harley would need to show that he and Martha had a valid contract, that Lothar knew of this contractual relationship between Martha and Harley, and that Lothar intentionally convinced Martha to break her contract with Harley. Even though Lothar hoped that his advertisements would persuade Martha to break her contract with Harley, the question states that Martha's decision to change bakers was based solely on the advertising and not on anything else that Lothar did. Lothar's advertisements did not constitute a tort. Note, though, that while Harley cannot collect from Lothar for Martha's actions, he does have a cause of action against Martha for her breach of their contract.

7–2A. Question with Sample Answer

This is a causation question. You will recall from the chapter that four elements must be proved for a plaintiff to recover in a claim for negligence: that the defendant owed a duty of care, the defendant breached this duty, the plaintiff suffered a legally recognizable injury, and the defendant's breach of the duty of care caused the injury. Ruth did breach the duty of care that she owed Jim (and others in society) when she parked carelessly on the hill. Jim also clearly suffered an injury. The only remaining question, then, has to do with causation. Causation is broken down into two parts, causation in fact and proximate cause. In order for Jim to recover, he must prove that both kinds of causation existed in this case. Causation in fact is answered by the "but for" test and readily answered here. Ruth's car set into motion a chain of events without which the barn would not have fallen down. Meeting the proximate cause test will be more difficult for Jim. Recall that proximate cause exists only when the connection between an act and an injury is strong enough to justify imposing liability. Careless parking on a hill creates a risk that a reasonable person can foresee could result in harm. The question here is whether the electric spark, the grass fire, the barn full of dynamite, and the roof falling in are *foreseeable* risks stemming from a poor parking job. In this case, it would be a question of fact for a jury to determine whether there were enough intervening events between Ruth's parking and Jim's injury to defeat Jim's claim.

8–2A. QUESTION WITH SAMPLE ANSWER

(a) Ursula will not be held liable for copyright infringement in this case because her photocopying pages for use in scholarly research falls squarely under the "fair use" exception to the Copyright Act.

(b) While Ursula's actions are improper, they could constitute trademark infringement, not copyright infringement. Copyrights are granted for literary and artistic productions; trademarks are distinctive marks created and used by manufacturers to differentiate their goods from those of their competitors. Trademark infringement occurs when a mark is copied to a substantial degree, intentionally or unintentionally.

(c) As with the answer to (a) above, Ursula's actions fall within the "fair use" doctrine of copyright law. Her use of the taped television shows for teaching is the exact type of use the exception is designed to cover.

9–3A. QUESTION WITH SAMPLE ANSWER

As you read in the text, some torts, including assault and battery, provide a basis for criminal prosecution as well as civil liability. This question aptly demonstrates this principle. Double jeopardy is a criminal law concept and does not constitute a defense against a civil lawsuit. The Fifth Amendment prohibition against double jeopardy means that once Armington has been tried and found guilty or not guilty for this assault, he may not be tried for it again. Nevertheless, Jennings may seek damages for his injuries in a civil lawsuit because Armington's prison sentence will do nothing to reimburse him for his medical bills and disability. Armington's guilty verdict has no bearing on the civil lawsuit. The criminal conviction, however, having been proved beyond a reasonable doubt, will likely improve Jennings's chances of recovering damages from Armington in a civil case. As you will recall, in a civil suit the plaintiff merely has

to prove his or her case by a preponderance of the evidence. For Jennings, this burden of proof will probably be much easier to meet, given Armington's conviction.

10–2A. QUESTION WITH SAMPLE ANSWER

According to the question, Janine was apparently unconscious or otherwise unable to agree to a contract for the nursing services she received while she was in the hospital. As you read in the chapter, however, sometimes the law will create a fictional contract in order to prevent one party from unjustly receiving a benefit at the expense of another. This is known as a *quasi contract* and provides a basis for Nursing Services to recover the value of the services it provided while Janine was in the hospital. As for the at-home services that were provided to Janine, because Janine was aware that those services were being provided for her, Nursing Services can recover for those services under an implied-in-fact contract. Under this type of contract, the conduct of the parties creates and defines the terms. Janine's acceptance of the services constitutes her agreement to form a contract, and she will probably be required to pay Nursing Services in full.

11–2A. QUESTION WITH SAMPLE ANSWER

(a) Death of either the offeror or the offeree prior to acceptance automatically terminates a revocable offer. The basic legal reason is that the offer is personal to the parties and cannot be passed on to others, not even to the estate of the deceased. This rule applies even if the other party is unaware of the death. Thus, Schmidt's offer terminates on Schmidt's death, and Barry's later acceptance does not constitute a contract.

(b) An offer is automatically terminated by the destruction of the specific subject matter of the offer prior to acceptance. Thus, Barry's acceptance after the fire does not constitute a contract.

(c) When the offer is irrevocable, under an option contract, death of the offeror does not terminate the option contract, and the offeree can accept the offer to sell the equipment, binding the offeror's estate to performance. Performance is not personal to Schmidt, as the estate can transfer title to the equipment. Knowledge of the death is immaterial to the offeree's right of acceptance. Thus, Barry can hold Schmidt's estate to a contract for the purchase of the equipment.

(d) When the offer is irrevocable, under an option contract, death of the offeree also does not terminate the offer. Because the option is a separate contract, the contract survives and passes to the offeree's estate, which can exercise the option by acceptance within the option period. Thus, acceptance by Barry's estate binds Schmidt to a contract for the sale of the equipment.

12–2A. QUESTION WITH SAMPLE ANSWER

The legal issue deals with the preexisting duty rule, which basically states that a promise to do what one already has a

legal or contractual duty to do does not constitute consideration, and thus the return promise is unenforceable. In this
case, Shade was required contractually to build a house
according to a specific set of plans for $53,000, and
Bernstein's later agreement to pay an additional $3,000 for
exactly what Shade was required to do for $53,000 is with-
out consideration and unenforceable. One of the purposes of
this general rule is to prevent commercial blackmail. There
are four basic exceptions to this rule:

(a) If the duties of Shade are modified, for example,
by changes made by Bernstein in the specifications, these
changes can constitute consideration and bind Bernstein
to pay the additional $3,000.

(b) Rescission and new contract theory could be
applied, by which the old contract of $53,000 would
mutually be canceled and a new contract for $56,000
would be made. Most courts would not apply this theory
unless there was a clear intent to cancel the original contract. It appears here that the intent to cancel the
$53,000 contract is lacking (there is merely an intent to
modify), so this exception would not apply.

(c) A few states have statutes that allow any modification to be enforceable if it is in writing. The facts stated
give no evidence that Bernstein's agreement to the additional $3,000 is in writing, but, if it is, Bernstein is
bound in those states.

(d) The unforeseen difficulty or hardship rule could
be argued. This rule, however, applies only to unknown
risks not ordinarily assumed in business transactions.
Because inflation and price rises are risks ordinarily
assumed in business, this exception cannot be used by
Shade.

13–2A. QUESTION WITH SAMPLE ANSWER

Contracts in restraint of trade are usually illegal and unenforceable. An exception to this rule applies to a covenant
not to compete that is ancillary to certain types of business
contracts in which some fair protection is deemed appropriate (such as in the sale of a business). The covenant, however, must be reasonable in terms of time and area to be
legally enforceable. If either term is excessive, the court can
declare that the restraint goes beyond what is necessary for
reasonable protection. In this event, the court can either declare the covenant illegal or it can reform the covenant to
make the terms of time and area reasonable and then enforce
it. Suppose the court declares the covenant illegal and unenforceable. Because the covenant is ancillary and severable
from the primary contract, the primary contract is not
affected by such a ruling. In the case of Hotel Lux, the primary contract concerns employment; the covenant is ancillary and desirable for the protection of the hotel. The time
period of one year may be considered reasonable for a chef
with an international reputation. The reasonableness of the
three-state area restriction may be questioned, however. If it
is found to be reasonable, the covenant probably will be
enforced. If it is not found to be reasonable, the court could
declare the entire covenant illegal, allowing Perlee to be
employed by any restaurant or hotel, including one in direct
competition with Hotel Lux. Alternatively, the court could
reform the covenant, making its terms reasonable for protecting Hotel Lux's normal customer market area.

14–2A. QUESTION WITH SAMPLE ANSWER

Four basic elements are necessary to prove fraud, thus rendering a contract voidable: (1) an intent to deceive, usually
with knowledge of the falsity; (2) a misrepresentation of material facts; (3) a reliance by the innocent party on the misrepresentation; and (4) usually damage or injury caused by
the misrepresentation. Statements of events to take place in
the future or statements of opinions are generally not treated
as representations of fact. Therefore, even though the prediction or opinion may turn out to be incorrect, a contract
based on this type of statement would remain enforceable.
Grano's statement that the motel would make at least
$45,000 next year would probably be treated as a prediction
or opinion; thus, one of the elements necessary to prove
fraud—misrepresentation of facts—would be missing. The
statement that the motel netted $30,000 last year is a delib-
erate falsehood (with intent and knowledge). Grano's
defense will be that the books in Tanner's possession clearly
indicated that the figure stated was untrue, and therefore
Tanner cannot be said to have purchased the motel in
reliance on the falsehood. If the innocent party, Tanner,
knew the true facts, or should have known the true facts
because they were available to him, Grano's argument will
prevail.

Finally, the issue centers on Grano's duty to tell Tanner
of the bypass. Ordinarily, neither party in a nonfiduciary
relationship has a duty to disclose facts, even when the information might bear materially on the other's decision to enter
into the contract. Exceptions are made, however, when the
buyer cannot reasonably be expected to discover the information known by the seller, in which case fairness imposes a
duty to speak on the seller. Here, the court can go either way.
If the court decides there was no duty to disclose, deems the
prediction of future profits to be opinion rather than a statement of fact, and also decides there was no justifiable
reliance by Tanner because the books available to Tanner
clearly indicated Grano's profit statement for the last year to
be false, then Tanner cannot get his money back on the basis
of fraud.

15–2A. QUESTION WITH SAMPLE ANSWER

In this situation, Mallory becomes what is known as a
guarantor on the loan; that is, she guarantees to the hardware
store that she will pay for the mower if her brother fails to
do so. This kind of collateral promise, in which the guarantor states that he or she will become responsible *only* if the
primary party does not perform, must be in writing to be
enforceable. There is an exception, however. If the main pur-

pose in accepting secondary liability is to secure a personal benefit—for example, if Mallory's brother bought the mower for her—the contract need not be in writing. The assumption is that a court can infer from the circumstances of the case whether the main purpose was to secure a personal benefit and thus, in effect, to answer for the guarantor's own debt.

16–2A. QUESTION WITH SAMPLE ANSWER

Thrift is a creditor beneficiary. To be a creditor beneficiary one must be the creditor in a previously established debtor-creditor relationship, and then the debtor's subsequent contract terms with a third party must confer a benefit on the creditor. The contract made between the debtor and third party is not made expressly for the benefit of the creditor (as is required for a donee beneficiary). Rather, it is made for the benefit of the contracting parties. In this case, the original mortgage contract created a debtor-creditor relationship between Hensley and Thrift. Hensley's contract of sale in which Sylvia agreed to assume the mortgage payments conferred a benefit on Thrift as to payment of the debt. The primary purpose of the contract was strictly to benefit the contracting parties. Hensley was to receive money for the sale of the house, and Sylvia was to receive the low mortgage interest rate. Thrift still has the house and lot as security for the loan, can hold Hensley personally liable for the mortgage note, and as a creditor beneficiary can hold Sylvia personally liable on the basis of her contract with Hensley to assume the mortgage.

17–2A. QUESTION WITH SAMPLE ANSWER

A novation exists when a new, valid contract expressly or impliedly discharges a prior contract by the substitution of a party. Accord and satisfaction exists when the parties agree that the original obligation can be discharged by a substituted performance. In this case, Fred's agreement with Iba to pay off Junior's debt for $1,100 (as compared to the $1,000 owed) is definitely a valid contract. The terms of the contract substitute Fred as the debtor for Junior, and Junior is definitely discharged from further liability. This agreement is a *novation*.

18–2A. QUESTION WITH SAMPLE ANSWER

Generally, the equitable remedy of specific performance will be granted only if two criteria are met: monetary damages (under the situation) must be inadequate as a remedy, and the subject matter of the contract must be unique.

(a) In the sale of land, the buyer's contract is for a specific piece of real property. The land under contract is unique, because no two pieces of real property have the same legal description. In addition, money damages would not compensate a buyer adequately, as the same land cannot be purchased elsewhere. Specific performance is an appropriate remedy.

(b) The basic criteria for specific performance do not apply well to personal-service contracts. If the identical service contracted for is readily available from others, the service is not unique, and monetary damages for nonperformance are adequate. If, however, the services are so personal that only the contract party can perform them, the contract meets the test of uniqueness; but the courts will refuse to decree specific performance if (1) the enforcement of specific performance requires involuntary servitude (prohibited by the Thirteenth Amendment to the U.S. Constitution), or (2) it is impractical to attempt to force meaningful performance by someone against his or her will. In the case of Amy and Fred, specific performance is not an appropriate remedy.

(c) A rare coin is unique, and monetary damages for breach are inadequate, as Hoffman cannot obtain a substantially identical substitute in the market. This is a typical case in which specific performance is an appropriate remedy.

(d) The key issue here is that this is a closely held corporation. Therefore, the stock is not available in the market, and the shares become unique. The uniqueness of these shares is enhanced by the fact that if Ryan sells her 4 percent of the shares to Chang, Chang will control the corporation. Because of this, monetary damages for Chang are totally inadequate as a remedy. Specific performance is an appropriate remedy.

19–2A. QUESTION WITH SAMPLE ANSWER

Anne has entered into an enforceable contract to subscribe to *E-Commerce Weekly*. In this problem, the offer to deliver, via e-mail, the newsletter was presented by the offeror with a statement of how to accept—by clicking on the "SUBSCRIBE" button. Consideration was in the promise to deliver the newsletter and in the price that the subscriber agreed to pay. The offeree had an opportunity to read the terms of the subscription agreement before making the contract. Whether she actually read those terms does not matter.

20–2A. QUESTION WITH SAMPLE ANSWER

The entire answer falls under UCC 2–206(1)(b), because the situation deals with a buyer's order to buy goods for prompt shipment. The law is that such an order or offer invites acceptance by a prompt promise to ship conforming goods. If the promise (acceptance) is sent by a medium reasonable under the circumstances, the acceptance is effective when sent. Therefore, a contract was formed on October 8, and it required Martin to ship 100 model Color-X television sets. Martin's shipment is nonconforming, and Flint is correct in claiming that Martin is in breach. Martin's claim would be valid if Martin had not sent its promise of shipment. The UCC provides that shipment of nonconforming goods constitutes an acceptance *unless* the seller seasonably notifies the buyer that such shipment is sent only as an accommodation. Thus, had a contract not been formed on October 8, the nonconforming shipment on the 28th would not be treated as an acceptance, and no contract would be in existence to breach.

21–2A. QUESTION WITH SAMPLE ANSWER

There is no question that the suit is in existence and identified to the contract. Nor do the facts indicate that there was an agreement as to when title or risk of loss would pass. Therefore, these situations deal with passage of title and risk of loss to goods that are "to be delivered" without physical movement of the goods by the seller and not represented by a document of title. The rules of law are that title passes to the buyer on the making of the contract, and risk of loss passes from a *merchant* seller to the buyer when the buyer *receives* the goods.

(a) In the case of the major creditor, title is with Sikora, and the major creditor cannot levy on the suit.

(b) The risk of loss on the suit destroyed by fire falls on Carson. Carson is a merchant, and because Sikora has not taken possession, Carson retains the risk of loss. This problem illustrates that title and risk of loss do not always pass from seller to buyer at the same time.

22–2A. QUESTION WITH SAMPLE ANSWER

Topken basically has the following remedies.

(a) Topken can identify the 500 washing machines to the contract and resell the goods [UCC 2–704].

(b) Topken can withhold delivery and proceed with other remedies [UCC 2–703].

(c) Topken can cancel the contract and proceed with other remedies [UCC 2–703 and 2–106(4)].

(d) Topken can resell the goods in a commercially reasonable manner (public or private sale with notice to Lorwin, holding Lorwin liable for any loss and retaining any profits) [UCC 2–706]. If Topken cannot resell after making a reasonable effort, Topken can sue for the purchase price [UCC 2–709 (1)(b)].

(e) Topken can sue Lorwin for breach of contract, recovering as damages the difference between the market price (at the time and place of tender) and the contract price, plus incidental damages [UCC 2–708].

The student should note the combination of remedies that would be most beneficial for Topken under the circumstances.

23–2A. QUESTION WITH SAMPLE ANSWER

If Colt can prove that all due care was exercised in the manufacture of the pistol, Colt cannot be held in an action based on negligence. Under the theory of strict liability in tort, however, Colt can be held liable regardless of the degree of care exercised. The doctrine of strict liability states that a merchant seller who sells a defective product that is unreasonably dangerous is liable for injuries caused by that product (even if all possible care in preparation and sale is exercised), provided that the product has not been substantially changed after the time of sale. Therefore, if Wayne can prove the pistol is defective, unreasonably dangerous, and caused him injury, Colt as a merchant is strictly liable, be-

cause there is no evidence that the pistol has been altered since the date of its manufacture.

24–2A. QUESTION WITH SAMPLE ANSWER

For an instrument to be negotiable, it must meet the following requirements:

(a) Be in writing.

(b) Be signed by the maker or drawer.

(c) Be an unconditional promise or order.

(d) State a fixed amount of money.

(e) Be payable on demand or at a definite time.

(f) Be payable to bearer or order (unless it is a check).

The instrument in this case meets the writing requirement in that it is handwritten and on something with a degree of permanence that is transferable. The instrument meets the requirement of being signed by the maker, as Juan Sanchez's signature (his name in his handwriting) appears in the body of the instrument. The instrument's payment is not conditional and contains Juan Sanchez's definite promise to pay. In addition, the sum of $100 is both a fixed amount and payable in money (U.S. currency). Because the instrument is payable on demand and to bearer (Kathy Martin or any holder), it is negotiable.

25–2A. QUESTION WITH SAMPLE ANSWER

(a) The bank does qualify as a holder in due course (HDC) for the amount of $5,000. To qualify as an HDC under UCC 3–302, one must take the instrument for value, in good faith, and without being put on notice that a defense exists against it, that it has been dishonored, or that it is overdue. In this situation the bank has given full value for the instrument—$4,850 ($5,000 – $150 discount). Therefore, the bank is entitled to be an HDC for the face value of the instrument ($5,000). In addition, the bank took the instrument in good faith and without notice of the original incompleteness of the instrument (completed when purchased by the bank) or the lack of authority of Hayden to complete the instrument in an amount over $2,000. The instrument was also taken before overdue (before the maturity date). Thus, First National Bank is an HDC.

(b) The sale to a stranger in a bar for $500 creates an entirely different situation. One of the requirements for the status of an HDC is that a holder take the instrument in good faith. *Good faith* is defined in the UCC as "honesty in fact in the conduct or transaction concerned" [UCC 1–201(19)]. Although the UCC does not provide clear guidelines to determine what is or is not good faith, both the amount paid (as compared to the face value of the instrument) and the circumstances under which the instrument is taken (as interpreted by a reasonable person) dictate whether the holder honestly believed the instrument was not defective when taken. In this case, taking a $5,000 note for $500 in a bar would raise a serious question of the stranger's good faith. Thus, the stranger would not qualify as a holder in due course.

26–3A. QUESTION WITH SAMPLE ANSWER

Frazier can recover the $1,500 from Kennedy if he is a holder in due course (HDC). He will be an HDC only if he, as a holder, took the check (a) for value, (b) in good faith, and (c) without notice that the check was overdue or dishonored or that a claim or defense against it exists. In this instance, Frazier qualifies for HDC status. First, he is a holder as the check was properly negotiated to him (by indorsement). Second, the facts indicate that he gave value. Third, there is nothing to indicate that he took the instrument in bad faith. Fourth, he was unaware of Niles's fraud (claim or defense), and he took the check before it was overdue (within thirty days of issue). Thus, Frazier is a holder in due course and can hold Kennedy liable.

27–2A. QUESTION WITH SAMPLE ANSWER

Citizens Bank will not have to recredit Gary's account for the $1,000 check and probably will not have to recredit his account for the first forged check for $100. Generally, a drawee bank is responsible for determining whether the signature of its customer is genuine, and when it pays on a forged customer's signature, the bank must recredit the customer's account [UCC 3–401, 4–406]. There are, however, exceptions to this general rule. First, when a customer's negligence substantially contributes to the making of an unauthorized signature (including a forgery), the drawee bank that pays the instrument in good faith will not be obligated to recredit the customer's account for the full amount of the check [UCC 3–406]. In addition, when a drawee bank sends to its customer a statement of account and canceled checks, the customer has a duty to exercise reasonable care and promptness in examining the statement to discover any forgeries and report them to the drawee bank. Failure of the customer to do so relieves the drawee from liability to the customer to the extent that the drawee bank suffers a loss [UCC 4–406(c)]. Therefore, Gary's negligence in allowing his checkbook to be stolen and his failure to report the theft or examine his May statement will preclude his recovery on the $100 check from the Citizens Bank. Under UCC 3–406(b) and 4–406(e), however, the bank could be liable to the extent that its negligence substantially contributes to the loss. Second, when a series of forgeries is committed by the same wrongdoer, the customer must discover and report the initial forgery within fourteen calendar days from the date that the statement of account and canceled checks (containing the initial forged check) are made available to the customer [UCC 4–406(d)(2)]. Failure to discover and report a forged check releases the drawee bank from liability for all additional forged checks in the series written after the thirty-day period. Therefore, Gary's failure to discover the May forged check by June 30 relieves the bank from liability for the June 20 check of $1,000.

28–2A. QUESTION WITH SAMPLE ANSWER

Three basic actions are available to Holiday:

(a) Attachment—a court-ordered seizure of nonexempt property prior to Holiday's reducing the debt to judgment. The grounds for granting the writ of attachment are limited, but in most states (when submitted), the writ is granted on introduction of evidence that a debtor intends to remove the property from the jurisdiction in which a judgment would be rendered. Holiday would have to post a bond and reduce its claim to judgment; then it could sell the attached property to satisfy the debt, returning any surplus to Kanahara.

(b) Writ of execution, on reducing the debt to judgment. The writ is an order issued by the clerk directing the sheriff or other officer of the court to seize (levy) nonexempt property of the debtor located within the court's jurisdiction. The property is then sold, and the proceeds are used to pay for the judgment and cost of sale, with any surplus going to the debtor (in this case, Kanahara).

(c) Garnishment of the wages owed to Kanahara by the Cross-Bar Packing Corp. Whenever a third person, the garnishee, owes a debt, such as wages, to the debtor, the creditor can proceed to have the court order the employer garnishee to turn over a percentage of the take-home pay (usually no more than 25 percent) to pay the debt. Garnishment actions are continuous in some states; in others, the action must be taken for each pay period.

Holiday can proceed with any one or a combination of these three actions. Because the property may be removed from the jurisdiction, and perhaps Kanahara himself may leave the jurisdiction (he may quit his job), prompt action is important.

29–3A. QUESTION WITH SAMPLE ANSWER

Generally, under Article 9, a secured party, on repossession of the collateral, has the right to keep it in full satisfaction of the debt (on proper notice and if no objection is received within twenty-one days) or to sell it or dispose of it, using the proceeds to cancel the debt. If the debtor has paid 60 percent of the cash price of a purchase-money security interest in consumer goods and has not after default signed a waiver of rights, the secured party cannot keep the collateral in full satisfaction of the debt. The secured party is forced to dispose of the collateral within ninety days [UCC 9–620(f)]. *Consumer goods* are defined as those used or bought primarily for personal, family, or household purposes [UCC 9–102(a)(23)]. In this case, Cummings has paid $400 ($100 down plus six $50 payments) of the $600 purchase price. Because the security interest is purchase money in consumer goods and the amount paid exceeds 60 percent of the price, Delgado cannot keep the repossessed set in full satisfaction of the debt. Therefore, Delgado has a duty to sell, lease, or otherwise dispose of the collateral and to apply the proceeds as prescribed in UCC 9–610.

30–3A. Question with Sample Answer

A trustee is given avoidance powers by the Bankruptcy Code. One situation in which the trustee can avoid transfers of property or payments by a debtor to a creditor is when such transfer constitutes a *preference*. A preference is a transfer of property or payment that favors one creditor over another. For a preference to exist, the debtor must be insolvent and must have made payment for a preexisting debt within ninety days of the filing of the petition in bankruptcy. The Code provides that the debtor is *presumed* to be insolvent during this ninety-day period. If the payment is made to an insider (and in this case payment was made to a close relative), the preference period is extended to one year, but the presumption of insolvency still applies only to the ninety-day period. In this case, the trustee has an excellent chance of having both payments declared preferences. The payment to Cool Springs was within ninety days of the filing of the petition, and it is doubtful that Cool Springs could overcome the presumption that Peaslee was insolvent at the time the payment was made. The $5,000 payment was made to an insider, Peaslee's father, and any payment made to an insider within one year of the petition of bankruptcy is a preference—as long as the debtor was insolvent at the time of payment. The facts indicate that Peaslee probably was insolvent at the time he paid his father. If he was not, the payment is not a preference, and the trustee's avoidance of the transfer would be improper.

31–2A. Question with Sample Answer

On creation of an agency, the agent owes certain fiduciary duties to the principal. Two such duties are the duty of loyalty and the duty to inform or notify. The duty of loyalty is a fundamental concept of the fiduciary relationship. The agent must act solely for the benefit of the principal, not in the agent's own interest or in the interest of another person. One of the principles invoked by this duty is that an agent employed to sell cannot become a purchaser without the principal's consent. When the agent is a partner, contracting to sell to another partner is equivalent to selling to oneself and is therefore a breach of the agent's duty. In addition, the agent has a duty to disclose to the principal any facts pertinent to the subject matter of the agency. Failure to disclose to Peter the knowledge of the shopping mall and the increased market value of the property also was a breach of Alice's fiduciary duties. When an agent breaches fiduciary duties owed to the principal by becoming a recipient of a contract, the contract is voidable at the election of the principal. Neither Carl nor Alice can hold Peter to the contract, and Alice's breach of fiduciary duties also allows Peter to terminate the agency relationship.

32–2A. Question with Sample Answer

As a general rule, a principal and third party are bound only to a contract made by the principal's agent within the scope of the agent's authority. An agent's authority to act can come from actual authority given to the agent (express or implied), apparent authority, or authority derived from an emergency. Express authority is directly given by the principal to the agent. Implied authority is deemed customary or inferred from the agent's position. Apparent authority is created when a principal gives a third person reason to believe the agent possesses authority not truly possessed. In this case, no express authority was given, and certainly no implied authority exists for a purchasing agent of goods to acquire realty. Moreover, A & B did nothing to lead Wilson to believe that Adams had authority to purchase land on its behalf. In addition, there was no emergency creating a need for Adams to purchase the land. Therefore, although Adams indicated in the contract that she was an agent, she acted outside the scope of her authority. Because of this, the contract between Adams and Wilson is treated merely as an unaccepted offer. As such, neither Wilson nor A & B is bound unless A & B ratifies (accepts) the contract before Wilson withdraws (revokes) the offer. Ratification can take place only when the principal is aware of all material facts and makes some act of affirmation. If A & B affirms the contract before Wilson withdraws, A & B can enforce Adams's contract. If Wilson withdraws first, Adams's contract cannot be enforced by A & B.

33–2A. Question with Sample Answer

The Occupational Health and Safety Act (OSHA) requires employers to provide safe working conditions for employees. The act prohibits employers from discharging or discriminating against any employee who refuses to work when the employee believes in good faith that he or she will risk death or great bodily harm by undertaking the employment activity. Denton and Carlo had sufficient reason to believe that the maintenance job required of them by their employer involved great risk, and therefore, under OSHA, their discharge was wrongful. Denton and Carlo can turn to the Occupational Safety and Health Administration, which is part of the Department of Labor, for assistance.

34–2A. Question with Sample Answer

The Age Discrimination in Employment Act (ADEA) prohibits discrimination in employment on the basis of age against individuals forty years of age or older. For the ADEA to apply, an employer must have twenty or more employees, and interstate commerce must be affected by the employer's business activities. Because Jones worked at a resort (presumably employing more than twenty persons), the court would probably find that its activities affected interstate commerce because it was frequented by out-of-state travelers. Because Jones was not demoted due to any apparent job-performance problems, the fact that he was replaced by a person half his age coupled with Blair's statement about getting rid of all the "senile" men would be enough to shift the burden to the employer to show that it was not discriminating on the basis of age.

35–2A. QUESTION WITH SAMPLE ANSWER

The court would likely conclude that National Foods was responsible for the acts of harassment by the manager at the franchised restaurant, on the ground that the employees were the agents of National Foods. An agency relationship can be implied from the circumstances and conduct of the parties. The important question is the degree of control that a franchisor has over its franchisees. Whether it exercises that control is beside the point. Here, National Foods retained considerable control over the new hires and the franchisee's policies, as well as the right to terminate the franchise for violations. That its supervisors routinely approved the policies would not undercut National Foods' liability.

36–2A. QUESTION WITH SAMPLE ANSWER

(a) A limited partner's interest is assignable. In fact, assignment allows the assignee to become a substituted limited partner with the consent of the remaining partners. The assignment, however, does not dissolve the limited partnership.

(b) Bankruptcy of the limited partnership itself causes dissolution, but bankruptcy of one of the limited partners does not dissolve the partnership unless it causes the bankruptcy of the firm.

(c) The retirement, death, or insanity of a general partner dissolves the partnership unless the business can be continued by the remaining general partners. Because Dorinda was the only general partner, her death dissolves the limited partnership.

37–2A. QUESTION WITH SAMPLE ANSWER

Although a joint stock company has characteristics of a corporation, it is usually treated as a partnership. Therefore, although the joint stock company issues transferable shares of stock and is managed by directors and officers, the shareholders have personal liability. Unless the shareholders transfer their stock and ownership to a third party, not only are the joint stock company's assets available for damages caused by a breach, but the individual shareholders' estates are also subject to such liability. The business trust resembles and is treated like a corporation in many respects. One similarity is the limited liability of the beneficiaries. Unless by state law beneficiaries are treated as partners, making them liable to business trust creditors, Bateson Corp. can look to only business trust assets in the event of breach.

38–2A. QUESTION WITH SAMPLE ANSWER

(a) As a general rule, a promoter is personally liable for all preincorporation contracts made by the promoter. The basic theory behind such liability is that the promoter cannot be an agent for a nonexistent principal (a corporation not yet formed). It is immaterial whether the contracting party knows of the prospective existence of the corporation, and the general rule of promoter liability continues even after the corporation is formed. Three basic exceptions to promoter liability are:

(1) The promoter's contract with a third party can stipulate that the third party will look only to the new corporation, not to the promoter, for performance and liability.

(2) The third party can release the promoter from liability.

(3) After formation, the corporation can assume the contractual obligations and liability by *novation*. (If it is by *adoption*, most courts hold that the promoter is still personally liable.)

Peterson is therefore personally liable on both contracts, because (1) neither Owens nor Babcock has released him from liability, (2) the corporation has not assumed contractual responsibility by novation, and (3) Peterson's contract with Babcock did not limit Babcock to holding only the corporation liable. (Peterson's liability was conditioned only on the corporation's formation, which did occur.)

(b) Incorporation in and of itself does not make the newly formed corporation liable for preincorporation contracts. Until the newly formed corporation assumes Peterson's contracts by novation (releasing Peterson from personal liability) or by adoption (undertaking to perform Peterson's contracts, which makes both the corporation and Peterson liable), Babcock cannot enforce Peterson's contract against the corporation.

39–2A. QUESTION WITH SAMPLE ANSWER

Directors are personally answerable to the corporation and the shareholders for breach of their duty to exercise reasonable care in conducting the affairs of the corporation. Reasonable care is defined as being the degree of care that a reasonably prudent person would use in the conduct of personal business affairs. When directors delegate the running of the corporate affairs to officers, the directors are expected to use reasonable care in the selection and supervision of such officers. Failure to do so will make the directors liable for negligence or mismanagement. A director who dissents to an action by the board is not personally liable for losses resulting from that action. Unless the dissent is entered into the board meeting minutes, however, the director is presumed to have assented. Therefore, the first issue in the case of AstroStar, Inc., is whether the board members failed to use reasonable care in the selection of the president. If so, and particularly if the board failed to provide a reasonable amount of supervision (and openly embezzled funds indicate that failure), the directors will be personally liable. This liability will include Eckhart unless she can prove that she dissented and that she tried to reasonably supervise the new president. Considering the facts in this case, it is questionable that Eckhart could prove this.

40–2A. QUESTION WITH SAMPLE ANSWER

Ajax apparently has given shareholder Alir notice of the meeting for approval of the merger. In addition, however,

Ajax should have notified Alir of her right to dissent and of her right, should the merger be approved, to be paid a fair value for her shares. The law recognizes that a dissenting shareholder should not be forced to become an unwilling shareholder in a new corporation. If Alir adheres strictly to statutory procedures, she has appraisal rights for the Ajax shares she holds after approval of the merger. Alir's appraisal rights entitle her to be paid by Zeta the "fair value" of her shares. Fair value is the value of the shares on the day prior to the date on which the vote for merger is taken. This value must not reflect appreciation or depreciation of the stock in anticipation of the approval. If $20 is a true value (the market value on the day before the vote), Alir will receive $200,000 for her 10,000 Ajax shares.

41–2A. QUESTION WITH SAMPLE ANSWER

No. Under federal securities law, a stock split is exempt from registration requirements. This is because no *sale* of stock is involved. The existing shares are merely being split, and no consideration is received by the corporation for the additional shares created.

42–2A. QUESTION WITH SAMPLE ANSWER

A court might initially consider whether a member of a limited liability company (LLC) who has a material conflict of interest should be prohibited from dealing with matters of the LLC. Most likely, a court would conclude that a member—even a member with a conflict of interest—can vote to transfer LLC property, but must do so fairly. In this problem, the transfer of BP's sole asset by two of BP's members to themselves, disguised as Excel (a newly created LLC), represented a material conflict of interest. Not only did Amy and Carl engage in self-dealing, but in doing so, they increased their interests in Excel. This conflict did not prohibit Amy and Carl from voting to transfer BP's sole asset to Excel, however, so long as they dealt fairly with Dave. To judge the fairness, a court might consider the members' conduct, the end result, the purpose of the LLC, and the parties' expectations. Here, the transfer was arguably unfair in two respects. First, it was not an "arm's length transaction" because it did not occur on the open market. Second, the sale undercut BP's capacity to carry on its intended business (to own the property as a long-term investment). The court might still rule in favor of Amy and Carl if they could argue successfully that the transaction did not need to be, or could not be, at "arm's length" and that BP's investment capacity was not undercut.

43–2A. QUESTION WITH SAMPLE ANSWER

The court will consider first whether the agency followed the procedures prescribed in the Administrative Procedure Act (APA). Ordinarily, courts will not require agencies to use procedures beyond those of the APA. Courts will, however, compel agencies to follow their own rules. If an agency has adopted a rule granting extra procedures, the agency must provide those extra procedures, at least until the rule is

formally rescinded. Ultimately, in this case, the court will most likely rule for the food producers.

44–3A. QUESTION WITH SAMPLE ANSWER

Yes. A regulation of the Federal Trade Commission (FTC) under Section 5 of the Federal Trade Commission Act makes it a violation for door-to-door sellers to fail to give consumers three days to cancel any sale. In addition, a number of state statutes require this three-day "cooling off" period to protect consumers from unscrupulous door-to-door sellers. Because the Gonchars sought to rescind the contract within the three-day period, Renowned Books was obligated to agree to cancel the contract. Its failure to allow rescission was in violation of the FTC regulation and of most state statutes.

45–2A. QUESTION WITH SAMPLE ANSWER

Fruitade has violated a number of federal environmental laws if such actions are being taken without a permit. First, because the dumping is in a navigable waterway, the River and Harbor Act of 1886, as amended, has been violated. Second, the Clean Water Act of 1972, as amended, has been violated. This act is designed to make the waters safe for swimming, to protect fish and wildlife, and to eliminate discharge of pollutants into the water. Both the crushed glass and the acid violate this act. Third, the Toxic Substances Control Act of 1976 was passed to regulate chemicals that are known to be toxic and could have an effect on human health and the environment. The acid in the cleaning fluid or compound could come under this act.

46–2A. QUESTION WITH SAMPLE ANSWER

Yes. The major antitrust law being violated is Section 7 of the Clayton Act. Section 7 prohibits any person or business organization from acquiring the stock or assets in another business where the effect may be to substantially lessen competition. The removal of a competitor who controls 35 percent of the market, combined with the 40 percent held by the acquiring partnership, definitely could drive out the remaining small competitors and be a barrier to future entrants into this market. Either the U.S. Department of Justice or the Federal Trade Commission could file for divestiture.

47–2A. QUESTION WITH SAMPLE ANSWER

For Curtis to recover against the hotel, he must first prove that a bailment relationship was created between himself and the hotel as to the car or the fur coat, or both. For a bailment to exist, there must be a delivery of the personal property that gives the bailee exclusive possession of the property, and the bailee must knowingly accept the bailed property. If either element is lacking, there is no bailment relationship and no liability on the part of the bailee hotel. The facts clearly indicate that the bailee hotel took exclusive possession and control of Curtis's car, and it knowingly accepted the car when the attendant took the car from

Curtis and parked it in the underground guarded garage, retaining the keys. Thus, a bailment was created as to the car, and, because a mutual benefit bailment was created, the hotel owes Curtis the duty to exercise reasonable care over the property to and to return the bailed car at the end of the bailment. Failure to return the car creates a presumption of negligence (lack of reasonable care), and unless the hotel can rebut this presumption, the hotel is liable to Curtis for the loss of the car. As to the fur coat, the hotel neither knew nor expected that the trunk contained an expensive fur coat. Thus, although the hotel knowingly took exclusive possession of the car, the hotel did not do so with the fur coat. (But for a regular coat and other items likely to be in the car, the hotel would be liable.) Because no bailment of the expensive fur coat was created, the hotel has no liability for its loss.

48–3A. QUESTION WITH SAMPLE ANSWER

Wilfredo understandably wants a general warranty deed, as this type of deed will give him the most extensive protection against any defects of title claimed against the property transferred. The general warranty would have Patricia warranting the following covenants:

(a) Covenant of seisin and right to convey—a warranty that the seller has good title and power to convey.

(b) Covenant against encumbrances—a guaranty by the seller that, unless stated, there are no outstanding encumbrances or liens against the property conveyed.

(c) Covenant of quiet possession—a warranty that the grantee's possession will not be disturbed by others claiming a prior legal right. Patricia, however, is conveying only ten feet along a property line that may not even be accurately surveyed. Patricia therefore does not wish to make these warranties. Consequently, she is offering a quitclaim deed, which does not convey any warranties but conveys only whatever interest, if any, the grantor owns. Although title is passed by the quitclaim deed, the quality of the title is not warranted.

Because Wilfredo really needs the property, it appears that he has three choices: he can accept the quitclaim deed; he can increase his offer price to obtain the general warranty deed he wants; or he can offer to have a title search made, which should satisfy both parties.

49–2A. QUESTION WITH SAMPLE ANSWER

Ajax will probably not be able to void the policy. Most life insurance policies contain what is called an incontestability clause. Such a clause provides that a policy cannot be contested for misstatements by the insured after the policy has been in effect for a given period, usually two years. Even though the application is part of the policy (attached to the policy), Patrick's innocent error in answering the question dealing with heart problems or ailments can no longer be contested by the insurer, as the incontestability clause is now in effect (three years have passed since the issuance of the policy). In addition, a misstatement about age is not grounds

in and of itself for Ajax to avoid the policy. Ajax does, however, have the right to adjust premium payments to reflect the correct age or to reduce the amount of the insurance coverage accordingly. Thus, Ajax cannot escape liability on Patrick's death, but it can reduce the $50,000 coverage to account for the premiums that should have been paid for a person who is thirty-three years old, not thirty-two years old.

50–3A. QUESTION WITH SAMPLE ANSWER

(a) State laws vary on whether a will written and executed before marriage is revoked by the marriage. Some states declare that the will is revoked by a subsequent marriage only if a child is born out of that marriage. Under the Uniform Probate Code, a subsequent marriage does not revoke a will; however, the new spouse is entitled to share the estate as if the deceased has died intestate, and the balance passes under the will. In this case, if the will is revoked by marriage, Lisa will receive the entire estate, and Carol, as James's mother, will receive nothing. If the marriage does not revoke the will, Lisa will probably receive one-half the estate under the laws of intestacy, and the balance will go to Carol.

(b) At common law and under the Uniform Probate Code, divorce does not in and of itself revoke a will made and executed during a previous marriage. If the divorce is accompanied by a property settlement, most states revoke that portion of the will that disposed property to the former spouse. Although this matter is frequently controlled by statute, in the absence of such a statute, if Lisa received a property settlement on divorce, the will of James would be revoked and Mandis would recover the entire estate by the laws of intestacy.

(c) If a child is born after a will has been executed and the child is not provided for in the will, the law will allow the child to inherit as if the testator had died intestate. The philosophy is that unless the child is specifically excluded by the will, the child was intended to inherit and was omitted in error. Therefore, Claire would receive one-half of the estate in most states.

51–2A. QUESTION WITH SAMPLE ANSWER

Assuming that the court has abandoned the *Ultramares* rule, it is likely that the accounting firm of Goldman, Walters, Johnson & Co. will be held liable to Happydays State Bank for negligent preparation of financial statements. There are various policy reasons for holding accountants liable to third parties even in the absence of privity. The potential liability would make accountants more careful in the preparation of financial statements. Moreover, in some situations the accountants may be the only solvent defendants, and hence, unless liability is imposed on accountants, third parties who reasonably rely on financial statements may go unprotected. Accountants, rather than third parties, are in better positions to spread the risks. If third parties such as banks have to absorb the costs of bad loans made as a result of negligently prepared financial statements, then the cost of credit to the public in general will increase. In contrast, accountants are in a better position to spread the risk by purchasing liability insurance.

52–2A. QUESTION WITH SAMPLE ANSWER

Each system has its advantages and its disadvantages. In a common law system, the courts independently develop the rules governing certain areas of law, such as torts and contracts. This judge-made law exists in addition to the laws passed by a legislature. Judges must follow precedential decisions in their jurisdictions, but courts may modify or even overturn precedents when deemed necessary. Also, if there is no case law to guide a court, the court may create a new rule of law. In a civil law system, the only official source of law is a statutory code. Courts are required to interpret the code and apply the rules to individual cases, but courts may not depart from the code and develop their own laws. In theory, the law code will set forth all the principles needed for the legal system. Common law and civil law systems are not wholly distinct. For example, the United States has a common law system, but crimes are defined by statute as in civil law systems. Civil law systems may allow considerable room for judges to develop law: law codes cannot be so precise as to address every contested issue, so the judiciary must interpret the codes. There are also significant differences among common law countries. The judges of different common law nations have produced differing common law principles. The roles of judges and lawyers under the different systems should be taken into account. Among other factors that should be considered in establishing a business law system and in deciding what regulations to impose are the goals that the system and its regulations are intended to achieve and the expectations of those to whom both will apply, including foreign and domestic investors.

GLOSSARY

A

Abandoned property Property with which the owner has voluntarily parted, with no intention of recovering it.

Abandonment In landlord-tenant law, a tenant's departure from leased premises completely, with no intention of returning before the end of the lease term.

Abatement A process by which legatees receive reduced benefits if the assets of an estate are insufficient to pay in full all general bequests provided for in the will.

Abus de droit A doctrine developed in the French courts. The doctrine modified employment at will and protected workers exercising their rights from wrongful discharge and other employer abuses.

Acceleration clause A clause in an installment contract that provides for all future payments to become due immediately on the failure to tender timely payments or on the occurrence of a specified event.

Acceptance (1) In contract law, the offeree's notification to the offeror that the offeree agrees to be bound by the terms of the offeror's proposal. Although historically the terms of acceptance had to be the mirror image of the terms of the offer, the Uniform Commercial Code provides that even modified terms of the offer in a definite expression of acceptance constitute a contract. (2) In negotiable instruments law, the drawee's signed agreement to pay a draft when presented.

Acceptor The person (the drawee) who accepts a draft and who agrees to be primarily responsible for its payment.

Access contract A contract formed for the purpose of obtaining, by electronic means, access to another's database or information processing system.

Accession Occurs when an individual adds value to personal property by either labor or materials. In some situations, a person may acquire ownership rights in another's property through accession.

Accommodation party A person who signs an instrument for the purpose of lending his or her name as credit to another party on the instrument.

Accord and satisfaction An agreement for payment (or other performance) between two parties, one of whom has a right of action against the other. After the payment has been accepted or other performance has been made, the "accord and satisfaction" is complete and the obligation is discharged.

Accredited investors In the context of securities offerings, "sophisticated" investors, such as banks, insurance companies, investment companies, the issuer's executive officers and directors, and persons whose income or net worth exceeds certain limits.

Acquittal A certification or declaration following a trial that the individual accused of a crime is innocent, or free from guilt, and is thus absolved of the charges.

Act of state doctrine A doctrine that provides that the judicial branch of one country will not examine the validity of public acts committed by a recognized foreign government within its own territory.

Actionable Capable of serving as the basis of a lawsuit.

Actual authority Authority of an agent that is express or implied.

Actual malice A condition that exists when a person makes a statement with either knowledge of its falsity or a reckless disregard for the truth. In a defamation suit, a statement made about a public figure normally must be made with actual malice for liability to be incurred.

Actus reus (pronounced *ak*-tus *ray*-uhs) A guilty (prohibited) act. The commission of a prohibited act is one of the two essential elements required for criminal liability, the other element being the intent to commit a crime.

Adequate protection doctrine In bankruptcy law, a doctrine that protects secured creditors from losing their security as a result of an automatic stay on legal proceedings by creditors against the debtor once the debtor petitions for bankruptcy relief. In certain circumstances, the bankruptcy court may provide adequate protection by requiring the debtor or trustee to pay the creditor or provide additional guaranties to protect the creditor against the losses suffered by the creditor as a result of the stay.

Adhesion contract A "standard-form" contract, such as that between a large retailer and a consumer, in which the stronger party dictates the terms.

Adjudicate To render a judicial decision. In the administrative process, the proceeding in which an administrative law judge hears and decides on issues that arise when an administrative agency charges a person or a firm with violating a law or regulation enforced by the agency.

Adjudication The process of adjudicating. *See* Adjudicate

Administrative agency A federal, state, or local government agency established to perform a specific function. Administrative agencies are authorized by legislative acts to make and enforce rules to administer and enforce the acts.

Administrative law The body of law created by administrative agencies (in the form of rules, regulations, orders, and decisions) in order to carry out their duties and responsibilities.

Administrative law judge (ALJ) One who presides over an administrative agency hearing and who has the power to administer oaths, take testimony, rule on questions of evidence, and make determinations of fact.

Administrative process   The procedure used by administrative agencies in the administration of law.

Administrator   One who is appointed by a court to handle the probate (disposition) of a person's estate if that person dies intestate (without a valid will) or if the executor named in the will cannot serve.

Adverse possession   The acquisition of title to real property by occupying it openly, without the consent of the owner, for a period of time specified by a state statute. The occupation must be actual, open, notorious, exclusive, and in opposition to all others, including the owner.

Affidavit   A written or printed voluntary statement of facts, confirmed by the oath or affirmation of the party making it and made before a person having the authority to administer the oath or affirmation.

Affirm   To validate; to give legal force to. *See also* Ratification

Affirmative action   Job-hiring policies that give special consideration to members of protected classes in an effort to overcome present effects of past discrimination.

Affirmative defense   A response to a plaintiff's claim that does not deny the plaintiff's facts but attacks the plaintiff's legal right to bring an action. An example is the running of the statute of limitations.

After-acquired evidence   A type of evidence submitted in support of an affirmative defense in employment discrimination cases. Evidence that, prior to the employer's discriminatory act, the employee engaged in misconduct sufficient to warrant dismissal had the employer known of it earlier.

After-acquired property   Property of the debtor that is acquired after the execution of a security agreement.

Age of majority   The age at which an individual is considered legally capable of conducting himself or herself responsibly. A person of this age is entitled to the full rights of citizenship, including the right to vote in elections. In contract law, one who is no longer an infant and can no longer disaffirm a contract.

Agency   A relationship between two parties in which one party (the agent) agrees to represent or act for the other (the principal).

Agency by estoppel   Arises when a principal negligently allows an agent to exercise powers not granted to the agent, thus justifying others in believing that the agent possesses the requisite agency authority. *See also* Promissory estoppel

Agent   A person who agrees to represent or act for another, called the principal.

Aggressor   The acquiring corporation in a takeover attempt.

Agreement   A meeting of two or more minds in regard to the terms of a contract; usually broken down into two events—an offer by one party to form a contract, and an acceptance of the offer by the person to whom the offer is made.

Alien corporation   A designation in the United States for a corporation formed in another country but doing business in the United States.

Alienation   In real property law, the voluntary transfer of property from one person to another (as opposed to a transfer by operation of law).

Allegation   A statement, claim, or assertion.

Allege   To state, recite, assert, or charge.

Allonge   (pronounced uh-*lohnj*)   A piece of paper firmly attached to a negotiable instrument, on which transferees can make indorsements if there is no room left on the instrument itself.

Alteration   In the context of leaseholds, an improvement or change made that materially affects the condition of the property. Thus, for example, erecting an additional structure probably would (and painting interior walls would not) be considered making an alteration.

Alternative dispute resolution (ADR)   The resolution of disputes in ways other than those involved in the traditional judicial process. Negotiation, mediation, and arbitration are forms of ADR.

Amend   To change and improve through a formal procedure.

American Arbitration Association (AAA)   The major organization offering arbitration services in the United States.

Analogy   In logical reasoning, an assumption that if two things are similar in some respects, they will be similar in other respects also. Often used in legal reasoning to infer the appropriate application of legal principles in a case being decided by referring to previous cases involving different facts but considered to come within the policy underlying the rule.

Annuity   An insurance policy that pays the insured fixed, periodic payments for life or for a term of years, as stipulated in the policy, after the insured reaches a specified age.

Annul   To cancel; to make void.

Answer   Procedurally, a defendant's response to the plaintiff's complaint.

Antecedent claim   A preexisting claim. In negotiable instruments law, taking an instrument in satisfaction of an antecedent claim is taking the instrument for value—that is, for valid consideration.

Anticipatory repudiation   An assertion or action by a party indicating that he or she will not perform an obligation that the party is contractually obligated to perform at a future time.

Antitrust law   The body of federal and state laws and statutes protecting trade and commerce from unlawful restraints, price discrimination, price fixing, and monopolies. The principal federal antitrust statues are the Sherman Act of 1890, the Clayton Act of 1914, and the Federal Trade Commission Act of 1914.

Apparent authority   Authority that is only apparent, not real. In agency law, a person may be deemed to have had the power to act as an agent for another party if the other party's manifestations to a third party led the third party to believe that an agency existed when, in fact, it did not.

Appeal Resort to a superior court, such as an appellate court, to review the decision of an inferior court, such as a trial court or an administrative agency.

Appellant The party who takes an appeal from one court to another.

Appellate court A court having appellate jurisdiction. Each state court system has at least one level of appellate courts. In the federal court system, the appellate courts are the circuit courts of appeals (intermediate appellate courts) and the United States Supreme Court (the highest appellate court in the federal system).

Appellate jurisdiction Courts having appellate jurisdiction act as reviewing courts, or appellate courts. Generally, cases can be brought before appellate courts only on appeal from an order or a judgment of a trial court or other lower court.

Appellee The party against whom an appeal is taken—that is, the party who opposes setting aside or reversing the judgment.

Appraisal right The right of a dissenting shareholder, if he or she objects to an extraordinary transaction of the corporation (such as a merger or consolidation), to have his or her shares appraised and to be paid the fair value of his or her shares by the corporation.

Appropriation In tort law, the use by one person of another person's name, likeness, or other identifying characteristic without permission and for the benefit of the user.

Arbitrary and capricious test The court reviewing an informal administrative agency action applies this test to determine whether or not that action was in clear error. The court gives wide discretion to the expertise of the agency and decides if the agency had sufficient factual information on which to base its action. If no clear error was made, then the agency's action stands.

Arbitration The settling of a dispute by submitting it to a disinterested third party (other than a court), who renders a decision. The decision may or may not be legally binding.

Arbitration clause A clause in a contract that provides that, in the event of a dispute, the parties will submit the dispute to arbitration rather than litigate the dispute in court.

Arraignment A procedure in which an accused person is brought before the court to plead to the criminal charge in the indictment or information. The charge is read to the person, and he or she is asked to enter a plea—such as "guilty" or "not guilty."

Arson The malicious burning of another's dwelling. Some statutes have expanded this to include any real property regardless of ownership and the destruction of property by other means—for example, by explosion.

Articles of incorporation The document filed with the appropriate governmental agency, usually the secretary of state, when a business is incorporated; state statutes usually prescribe what kind of information must be contained in the articles of incorporation.

Articles of organization The document filed with a designated state official by which a limited liability company is formed.

Articles of partnership A written agreement that sets forth each partner's rights and obligations with respect to the partnership.

Artisan's lien A possessory lien given to a person who has made improvements and added value to another person's personal property as security for payment for services performed.

Assault Any word or action intended to make another person fearful of immediate physical harm; a reasonably believable threat.

Assignee The person to whom contract rights are assigned.

Assignment The act of transferring to another all or part of one's rights arising under a contract.

Assignor The person who assigns contract rights.

Assumption of risk A defense against negligence that can be used when the plaintiff is aware of a danger and voluntarily assumes the risk of injury from that danger.

Attachment (1) In the context of secured transactions, the process by which a security interest in the property of another becomes enforceable. (2) In the context of judicial liens, a court-ordered seizure and taking into custody of property prior to the securing of a judgment for a past-due debt.

Attempted monopolization Any actions by a firm to eliminate competition and gain monopoly power.

Attractive nuisance doctrine A common law doctrine under which a landowner or landlord may be held liable for injuries incurred by children who are lured onto the property by something dangerous and enticing thereon.

Authenticate To sign a record, or with the intent to sign a record, to execute or to adopt an electronic sound, symbol, or the like to link with the record. A *record* is retrievable information inscribed on a tangible medium or stored in an electronic or other medium.

Authority In agency law, the agent's permission to act on behalf of the principal. An agent's authority may be actual (express or implied) or apparent. *See also* Actual authority; Apparent authority

Authorized means In contract law, the means of acceptance authorized by the offeror.

Automatic stay In bankruptcy proceedings, the suspension of virtually all litigation and other action by creditors against the debtor or the debtor's property; the stay is effective the moment the debtor files a petition in bankruptcy.

Award In the context of litigation, the amount of money awarded to a plaintiff in a civil lawsuit as damages. In the context of arbitration, the arbitrator's decision.

B

Bail An amount of money set by the court that must be paid by a criminal defendant to the court before the defendant will be released from custody. Bail is set to assure that an individual accused of a crime will appear for further criminal proceedings. If the accused provides bail, whether in cash or in a surety bond, then he or she is released from jail.

Bailee   One to whom goods are entrusted by a bailor. Under the Uniform Commercial Code, a party who, by a bill of lading, warehouse receipt, or other document of title, acknowledges possession of goods and contracts.

Bailee's lien   A possessory lien, or claim, that a bailee entitled to compensation can place on the bailed property to ensure that he or she will be paid for the services provided. The lien is effective as long as the bailee retains possession of the bailed goods and has not agreed to extend credit to the bailor. Sometimes referred to as an artisan's lien.

Bailment   A situation in which the personal property of one person (a bailor) is entrusted to another (a bailee), who is obligated to return the bailed property to the bailor or dispose of it as directed.

Bailor   One who entrusts goods to a bailee.

Bait-and-switch advertising   Advertising a product at a very attractive price (the "bait") and then informing the consumer, once he or she is in the store, that the advertised product is either not available or is of poor quality; the customer is then urged to purchase ("switched" to) a more expensive item.

Banker's acceptance   A negotiable instrument that is commonly used in international trade. A banker's acceptance is drawn by a creditor against the debtor, who pays the draft at maturity. The drawer creates a draft without designating a payee. The draft can pass through many parties' hands before a bank (drawee) accepts it, transforming the draft into a banker's acceptance. Acceptances can be purchased and sold in a way similar to securities.

Bankruptcy court   A federal court of limited jurisdiction that handles only bankruptcy proceedings. Bankruptcy proceedings are governed by federal bankruptcy law.

Bargain   A mutual undertaking, contract, or agreement between two parties; to negotiate over the terms of a purchase or contract.

Basis of the bargain   In contract law, the affirmation of fact or promise on which the sale of goods is predicated, creating an express warranty.

Battery   The unprivileged, intentional touching of another.

Beachhead acquisition   The gradual accumulation of a bloc of a target corporation's shares by an aggressor during an attempt to obtain control of the corporation.

Bearer   A person in the possession of an instrument payable to bearer or indorsed in blank.

Bearer instrument   Any instrument that is not payable to a specific person, including instruments payable to the bearer or to "cash."

Beneficiary   One to whom life insurance proceeds are payable or for whose benefit a trust has been established or property under a will has been transferred.

Bequest   A gift by will of personal property (from the verb—to bequeath).

Beyond a reasonable doubt   The standard used to determine the guilt or innocence of a person criminally charged. To be guilty of a crime, one must be proved guilty "beyond and to the exclusion of every reasonable doubt." A reasonable doubt is one that would cause a prudent person to hesitate before acting in matters important to him or her.

Bilateral contract   A type of contract that arises when a promise is given in exchange for a return promise.

Bill of lading   A document that serves both as evidence of the receipt of goods for shipment and as documentary evidence of title to the goods.

Bill of Rights   The first ten amendments to the U.S. Constitution.

Binder   A written, temporary insurance policy.

Binding authority   Any source of law that a court must follow when deciding a case. Binding authorities include constitutions, statutes, and regulations that govern the issue being decided, as well as court decisions that are controlling precedents within the jurisdiction.

Blank indorsement   An indorsement that specifies no particular indorsee and can consist of a mere signature. An order instrument that is indorsed in blank becomes a bearer instrument.

Blue laws   State or local laws that prohibit the performance of certain types of commercial activities on Sunday.

Blue sky laws   State laws that regulate the offer and sale of securities.

Bona fide   Good faith. A bona fide obligation is one made in good faith—that is, sincerely and honestly.

Bona fide occupational qualification (BFOQ)   Identifiable characteristics reasonably necessary to the normal operation of a particular business. These characteristics can include gender, national origin, and religion, but not race.

Bond   A certificate that evidences a corporate (or government) debt. It is a security that involves no ownership interest in the issuing entity.

Bond indenture   A contract between the issuer of a bond and the bondholder.

Bounty payment   A reward (payment) given to a person or persons who perform a certain service—such as informing legal authorities of illegal actions.

Boycott   A concerted refusal to do business with a particular person or entity in order to obtain concessions or to express displeasure with certain acts or practices of that person or business. *See also* Secondary boycott

Breach   To violate a law, by an act or an omission, or to break a legal obligation that one owes to another person or to society.

Breach of contract   The failure, without legal excuse, of a promisor to perform the obligations of a contract.

Bribery   The offering, giving, receiving, or soliciting of anything of value with the aim of influencing an official action or an official's discharge of a legal or public duty or (with respect to commercial bribery) a business decision.

Brief   A formal legal document submitted by the attorney for the appellant—or the appellee (in answer to the appellant's brief)—to an appellate court when a case is appealed. The appellant's brief outlines the facts and issues of the case, the judge's rulings or jury's findings that should be reversed or modified, the applicable law, and the arguments on the client's behalf.

Browse-wrap terms Terms and conditions of use that are presented to an Internet user at the time certain products, such as software, are being downloaded but that need not be agreed to (by clicking "I agree," for example) before being able to install or use the product.

Bulk transfer A bulk sale or transfer, not made in the ordinary course of business, of a major part of the materials, supplies, merchandise, or other inventory of an enterprise.

Bureaucracy A large organization that is structured hierarchically to carry out specific functions.

Burglary The unlawful entry into a building with the intent to commit a felony. (Some state statutes expand this to include the intent to commit any crime.)

Business ethics Ethics in a business context; a consensus of what constitutes right or wrong behavior in the world of business and the application of moral principles to situations that arise in a business setting.

Business invitees Those people, such as customers or clients, who are invited onto business premises by the owner of those premises for business purposes.

Business judgment rule A rule that immunizes corporate management from liability for actions that result in corporate losses or damages if the actions are undertaken in good faith and are within both the power of the corporation and the authority of management to make.

Business necessity A defense to allegations of employment discrimination in which the employer demonstrates that an employment practice that discriminates against members of a protected class is related to job performance.

Business plan A document describing a company, its products, and its anticipated future performance. Creating a business plan is normally the first step in obtaining loans or venture-capital funds for a new business enterprise.

Business tort The wrongful interference with the business rights of another.

Business trust A voluntary form of business organization in which investors (trust beneficiaries) transfer cash or property to trustees in exchange for trust certificates that represent their investment shares. Management of the business and trust property is handled by the trustees for the use and benefit of the investors. The certificate holders have limited liability (are not responsible for the debts and obligations incurred by the trust) and share in the trust's profits.

Buyer in the ordinary course of business A buyer who, in good faith and without knowledge that the sale to him or her is in violation of the ownership rights or security interest of a third party in the goods, purchases goods in the ordinary course of business from a person in the business of selling goods of that kind.

Buyout price The amount payable to a partner on his or her dissociation from a partnership, based on the amount distributable to that partner if the firm were wound up on that date, and offset by any damages for wrongful dissociation.

Buy-sell agreement In the context of partnerships, an express agreement made at the time of partnership formation for one or more of the partners to buy out the other or others should the situation warrant—and thus provide for the smooth dissolution of the partnership.

Bylaws A set of governing rules adopted by a corporation or other association.

Bystander A spectator, witness, or person standing nearby when an event occurred and who did not engage in the business or act leading to the event.

C

C.I.F. or C.&F. Cost, insurance, and freight—or just cost and freight. A pricing term in a contract for the sale of goods requiring, among other things, that the seller place the goods in the possession of a carrier before risk passes to the buyer.

C.O.D. Cash on delivery. In sales transactions, a term meaning that the buyer will pay for the goods on delivery and before inspecting the goods.

Callable bond A bond that may be called in and the principal repaid at specified times or under conditions specified in the bond when it is issued.

Cancellation The act of nullifying, or making void. *See also* Rescission

Capital Accumulated goods, possessions, and assets used for the production of profits and wealth; the equity of owners in a business.

Carrier An individual or organization engaged in transporting passengers or goods for hire. *See also* Common carrier

Case law The rules of law announced in court decisions. Case law includes the aggregate of reported cases that interpret judicial precedents, statutes, regulations, and constitutional provisions.

Case on point A previous case involving factual circumstances and issues that are similar to the case before the court.

Cash surrender value The amount that the insurer has agreed to pay to the insured if a life insurance policy is canceled before the insured's death.

Cashier's check A check drawn by a bank on itself.

Categorical imperative A concept developed by the philosopher Immanuel Kant as an ethical guideline for behavior. In deciding whether an action is right or wrong, or desirable or undesirable, a person should evaluate the action in terms of what would happen if everybody else in the same situation, or category, acted the same way.

Causation in fact An act or omission without ("but for") which an event would not have occurred.

Cause of action A situation or state of facts that would entitle a party to sustain a legal action and give the party a right to seek a judicial remedy.

Cease-and-desist order An administrative or judicial order prohibiting a person or business firm from conducting activities that an agency or court has deemed illegal.

Certificate of deposit (CD) A note of a bank in which a bank acknowledges a receipt of money from a party and promises to repay the money, with interest, to the party on a certain date.

Certificate of incorporation The primary document that evidences corporate existence (referred to as articles of incorporation in some states).

Certificate of limited partnership The basic document filed with a designated state official by which a limited partnership is formed.

Certification In negotiable instruments law, the act of certifying a check. *See* Certified check

Certification mark A mark used by one or more persons, other than the owner, to certify the region, materials, mode of manufacture, quality, or accuracy of the owner's goods or services. When used by members of a cooperative, association, or other organization, such a mark is referred to as a collective mark. Examples of certification marks include the "Good Housekeeping Seal of Approval" and "UL Tested."

Certified check A check that has been accepted by the bank on which it is drawn. Essentially, the bank, by certifying (accepting) the check, promises to pay the check at the time the check is presented.

Certiorari *See* Writ of *certiorari*

Chain-style business franchise A franchise that operates under a franchisor's trade name and that is identified as a member of a select group of dealers that engage in the franchisor's business. The franchisee is generally required to follow standardized or prescribed methods of operation. Examples of this type of franchise are McDonald's and most other fast-food chains.

Chancellor An adviser to the king at the time of the early king's courts of England. Individuals petitioned the king for relief when they could not obtain an adequate remedy in a court of law, and these petitions were decided by the chancellor.

Charging order In partnership law, an order granted by a court to a judgment creditor that entitles the creditor to attach profits or assets of a partner on dissolution of the partnership.

Charitable trust A trust in which the property held by a trustee must be used for a charitable purpose, such as the advancement of health, education, or religion.

Charter *See* Corporate charter

Chattel All forms of personal property.

Chattel paper Any writing or writings that show both a debt and the fact that the debt is secured by personal property. In many instances, chattel paper consists of a negotiable instrument coupled with a security agreement.

Check A draft drawn by a drawer ordering the drawee bank or financial institution to pay a certain amount of money to the holder on demand.

Checks and balances The national government is composed of three separate branches: the executive, the legislative, and the judicial branches. Each branch of the government exercises a check on the actions of the others.

Choice-of-language clause A clause in a contract designating the official language by which the contract will be interpreted in the event of a future disagreement over the contract's terms.

Choice-of-law clause A clause in a contract designating the law (such as the law of a particular state or nation) that will govern the contract.

Citation A reference to a publication in which a legal authority—such as a statute or a court decision—or other source can be found.

Civil law The branch of law dealing with the definition and enforcement of all private or public rights, as opposed to criminal matters.

Civil law system A system of law derived from that of the Roman Empire and based on a code rather than case law; the predominant system of law in the nations of continental Europe and the nations that were once their colonies. In the United States, Louisiana is the only state that has a civil law system.

Claim As a verb, to assert or demand. As a noun, a right to payment.

Clearinghouse A system or place where banks exchange checks and drafts drawn on each other and settle daily balances.

Click-on agreement An agreement that arises when a buyer, engaging in a transaction on a computer, indicates his or her assent to be bound by the terms of an offer by clicking on a button that says, for example, "I agree"; sometimes referred to as a *click-on license* or a *click-wrap agreement*.

Close corporation A corporation whose shareholders are limited to a small group of persons, often including only family members. The rights of shareholders of a close corporation usually are restricted regarding the transfer of shares to others.

Closed shop A firm that requires union membership by its workers as a condition of employment. The closed shop was made illegal by the Labor-Management Relations Act of 1947.

Closing The final step in the sale of real estate—also called settlement or closing escrow. The escrow agent coordinates the closing with the recording of deeds, the obtaining of title insurance, and other concurrent closing activities. A number of costs must be paid, in cash, at the time of closing, and they can range from several hundred to several thousand dollars, depending on the amount of the mortgage loan and other conditions of the sale.

Closing argument An argument made after the plaintiff and defendant have rested their cases. Closing arguments are made prior to the jury charges.

Codicil A written supplement or modification to a will. A codicil must be executed with the same formalities as a will.

Collateral Under Article 9 of the Uniform Commercial Code, the property subject to a security interest, including accounts and chattel paper that have been sold.

Collateral promise   A secondary promise that is ancillary (subsidiary) to a principal transaction or primary contractual relationship, such as a promise made by one person to pay the debts of another if the latter fails to perform. A collateral promise normally must be in writing to be enforceable.

Collecting bank   Any bank handling an item for collection, except the payor bank.

Collective bargaining   The process by which labor and management negotiate the terms and conditions of employment, including working hours and workplace conditions.

Collective mark   A mark used by members of a cooperative, association, or other organization to certify the region, materials, mode of manufacture, quality, or accuracy of the specific goods or services. Examples of collective marks include the labor union marks found on tags of certain products and the credits of movies, which indicate the various associations and organizations that participated in the making of the movies.

Comity   A deference by which one nation gives effect to the laws and judicial decrees of another nation. This recognition is based primarily on respect.

Comment period   A period of time following an administrative agency's publication or a notice of a proposed rule during which private parties may comment in writing on the agency proposal in an effort to influence agency policy. The agency takes any comments received into consideration when drafting the final version of the regulation.

Commerce clause   The provision in Article I, Section 8, of the U.S. Constitution that gives Congress the power to regulate interstate commerce.

Commercial impracticability   A doctrine under which a seller may be excused from performing a contract when (1) a contingency occurs, (2) the contingency's occurrence makes performance impracticable, and (3) the nonoccurrence of the contingency was a basic assumption on which the contract was made. Despite the fact that UCC 2–615 expressly frees only sellers under this doctrine, courts have not distinguished between buyers and sellers in applying it.

Commercial paper   *See* Negotiable instrument

Commingle   To mix together. To put funds or goods together into one mass so that the funds or goods are so mixed that they no longer have separate identities. In corporate law, if personal and corporate interests are commingled to the extent that the corporation has no separate identity, a court may "pierce the corporate veil" and expose the shareholders to personal liability.

Common area   In landlord-tenant law, a portion of the premises over which the landlord retains control and maintenance responsibilities. Common areas may include stairs, lobbies, garages, hallways, and other areas in common use.

Common carrier   A carrier that holds itself out or undertakes to carry persons or goods of all persons indifferently, or of all who choose to employ it.

Common law   That body of law developed from custom or judicial decisions in English and U.S. courts, not attributable to a legislature.

Common stock   Shares of ownership in a corporation that give the owner of the stock a proportionate interest in the corporation with regard to control, earnings, and net assets; shares of common stock are lowest in priority with respect to payment of dividends and distribution of the corporation's assets on dissolution.

Community property   A form of concurrent ownership of property in which each spouse technically owns an undivided one-half interest in property acquired during the marriage. This form of joint ownership occurs in only nine states and Puerto Rico.

Comparative law   The study and comparison of legal systems and laws across nations.

Comparative negligence   A theory in tort law under which the liability for injuries resulting from negligent acts is shared by all parties who were negligent (including the injured party), on the basis of each person's proportionate negligence.

Compensatory damages   A money award equivalent to the actual value of injuries or damages sustained by the aggrieved party.

Complaint   The pleading made by a plaintiff alleging wrongdoing on the part of the defendant; the document that, when filed with a court, initiates a lawsuit.

Complete performance   Performance of a contract strictly in accordance with the contract's terms.

Composition agreement   *See* Creditors' composition agreement

Computer crime   Any wrongful act that is directed against computers and computer parties, or wrongful use or abuse of computers or software.

Computer information   As defined by the Uniform Computer Information Transactions Act, "information in an electronic form obtained from or through use of a computer, or that is in digital or an equivalent form capable of being processed by a computer."

Concentrated industry   An industry in which a large percentage of market sales is controlled by either a single firm or a small number of firms.

Conciliation   A form of alternative dispute resolution in which the parties reach an agreement themselves with the help of a neutral third party, called a conciliator, who facilitates the negotiations.

Concurrent conditions   Conditions in a contract that must occur or be performed at the same time; they are mutually dependent. No obligations arise until these conditions are simultaneously performed.

Concurrent jurisdiction   Jurisdiction that exists when two different courts have the power to hear a case. For example, some cases can be heard in either a federal or a state court.

Concurrent ownership   Joint ownership.

Concurring opinion   A written opinion outlining the views of a judge or justice to make or emphasize a point that was not made or emphasized in the majority opinion.

Condemnation The process of taking private property for public use through the government's power of eminent domain.

Condition A possible future event, the occurrence or nonoccurrence of which will trigger the performance of a legal obligation or terminate an existing obligation under a contract.

Condition precedent A condition in a contract that must be met before a party's promise becomes absolute.

Condition subsequent A condition in a contract that operates to terminate a party's absolute promise to perform.

Conditional contract A contract subject to a condition that must be met for the contract to be enforceable. *See* Condition precedent

Confession of judgment The act of a debtor in permitting a judgment to be entered against him or her by a creditor, for an agreed sum, without the institution of legal proceedings.

Confiscation A government's taking of privately owned business or personal property without a proper public purpose or an award of just compensation.

Conforming goods Goods that conform to contract specifications.

Confusion The mixing together of goods belonging to two or more owners so that the separately owned goods cannot be identified.

Conglomerate merger A merger between firms that do not compete with each other because they are in different markets (as opposed to horizontal and vertical mergers).

Consent Voluntary agreement to a proposition or an act of another. A concurrence of wills.

Consequential damages Special damages that compensate for a loss that is not direct or immediate (for example, lost profits). The special damages must have been reasonably foreseeable at the time the breach or injury occurred in order for the plaintiff to collect them.

Consideration Generally, the value given in return for a promise or a performance. The consideration, which must be present to make the contract legally binding, must be something of legally sufficient value and bargained for.

Consignee One to whom goods are delivered on consignment. *See also* Consignment

Consignment A transaction in which an owner of goods (the consignor) delivers the goods to another (the consignee) for the consignee to sell. The consignee pays the consignor for the goods when they are sold by the consignee.

Consignor One who consigns goods to another. *See also* Consignment

Consolidation A contractual and statutory process in which two or more corporations join to become a completely new corporation. The original corporations cease to exist, and the new corporation acquires all their assets and liabilities.

Constitutional law Law that is based on the U.S. Constitution and the constitutions of the various states.

Constructive condition A condition in a contract that is neither expressed nor implied by the contract but rather is imposed by law for reasons of justice.

Constructive delivery An act equivalent to the actual, physical delivery of property that cannot be physically delivered because of difficulty or impossibility; for example, the transfer of a key to a safe constructively delivers the contents of the safe.

Constructive discharge A termination of employment brought about by making an employee's working conditions so intolerable that the employee reasonably feels compelled to leave.

Constructive eviction A form of eviction that occurs when a landlord fails to perform adequately any of the undertakings (such as providing heat in the winter) required by the lease, thereby making the tenant's further use and enjoyment of the property exceedingly difficult or impossible.

Constructive trust An equitable trust that is imposed in the interests of fairness and justice when someone wrongfully holds legal title to property. A court may require the owner to hold the property in trust for the person or persons who rightfully should own the property.

Consumer credit Credit extended primarily for personal or household use.

Consumer-debtor An individual whose debts are primarily consumer debts (debts for purchases made primarily for personal or household use).

Consumer goods Goods that are primarily for personal or household use.

Consumer law The body of statutes, agency rules, and judicial decisions protecting consumers of goods and services from dangerous manufacturing techniques, mislabeling, unfair credit practices, deceptive advertising, and so on. Consumer laws provide remedies and protections that are not ordinarily available to merchants or to businesses.

Contingency fee An attorney's fee that is based on a percentage of the final award received by his or her client as a result of litigation.

Continuation statement A statement that, if filed within six months prior to the expiration date of the original financing statement, continues the perfection of the original security interest for another five years. The perfection of a security interest can be continued in the same manner indefinitely.

Contract An agreement that can be enforced in court; formed by two or more parties, each of whom agrees to perform or to refrain from performing some act now or in the future.

Contract implied in law *See* Quasi contract

Contract under seal A formal agreement in which the seal is a substitute for consideration. A court will not invalidate a contract under seal for lack of consideration.

Contractual agreement *See* Contract

Contractual capacity The threshold mental capacity required by the law for a party who enters into a contract to be bound by that contract.

Contribution *See* Right of contribution

Contributory negligence A theory in tort law under which a complaining party's own negligence contributed to or caused his or her injuries. Contributory negligence is an absolute bar to recovery in a minority of jurisdictions.

Conversion The wrongful taking, using, or retaining possession of personal property that belongs to another.

Convertible bond A bond that can be exchanged for a specified number of shares of common stock under certain conditions.

Conveyance The transfer of a title to land from one person to another by deed; a document (such as a deed) by which an interest in land is transferred from one person to another.

Conviction The outcome of a criminal trial in which the defendant has been found guilty of the crime with which he or she was charged and on which sentencing, or punishment, is based.

Cooperative An association that is organized to provide an economic service to its members (or shareholders). An incorporated cooperative is a nonprofit corporation. It will make distributions of dividends, or profits, to its owners on the basis of their transactions with the cooperative rather than on the basis of the amount of capital they contributed. Examples of cooperatives are consumer purchasing cooperatives, credit cooperatives, and farmers' cooperatives.

Co-ownership Joint ownership.

Copyright The exclusive right of authors to publish, print, or sell an intellectual production for a statutory period of time. A copyright has the same monopolistic nature as a patent or trademark, but it differs in that it applies exclusively to works of art, literature, and other works of authorship, including computer programs.

Corporate charter The document issued by a state agency or authority (usually the secretary of state) that grants a corporation legal existence and the right to function.

Corporate governance The system by which corporations are directed and controlled and which governs the relationship of the corporation to its shareholders. The corporate governance structure specifies the distribution of rights and responsibilities among different groups within the corporation and spells out the rules and procedures for making corporate decisions.

Corporate social responsibility The concept that corporations can and should act ethically and be accountable to society for their actions.

Corporation A legal entity formed in compliance with statutory requirements. The entity is distinct from its shareholders-owners.

Cosign The act of signing a document (such as a note promising to pay another in return for a loan or other benefit) jointly with another person and thereby assuming liability for performing what was promised in the document.

Cost-benefit analysis A decision-making technique that involves weighing the costs of a given action against the benefits of the action.

Co-surety A joint surety. One who assumes liability jointly with another surety for the payment of an obligation.

Counteradvertising New advertising that is undertaken pursuant to a Federal Trade Commission order for the purpose of correcting earlier false claims that were made about a product.

Counterclaim A claim made by a defendant in a civil lawsuit that in effect sues the plaintiff.

Counteroffer An offeree's response to an offer in which the offeree rejects the original offer and at the same time makes a new offer.

Course of dealing Prior conduct between parties to a contract that establishes a common basis for their understanding.

Course of performance The conduct that occurs under the terms of a particular agreement; such conduct indicates what the parties to an agreement intended it to mean.

Court of equity A court that decides controversies and administers justice according to the rules, principles, and precedents of equity.

Court of law A court in which the only remedies that could be granted were things of value, such as money damages. In the early English king's courts, courts of law were distinct from courts of equity.

Covenant against encumbrances A grantor's assurance that on land conveyed there are no encumbrances—that is, that no third parties have rights to or interests in the land that would diminish its value to the grantee.

Covenant not to compete A contractual promise to refrain from competing with another party for a certain period of time (not excessive in duration) and within a reasonable geographic area. Although covenants not to compete restrain trade, they are commonly found in partnership agreements, business sale agreements, and employment contracts. If they are ancillary to such agreements, covenants not to compete will normally be enforced by the courts unless the time period or geographic area is deemed unreasonable.

Covenant not to sue An agreement to substitute a contractual obligation for some other type of legal action based on a valid claim.

Covenant of quiet enjoyment A promise by a grantor (or landlord) that the grantee (or tenant) will not be evicted or disturbed by the grantor or a person having a lien or superior title.

Covenant of the right to convey A grantor's assurance that he or she has sufficient capacity and title to convey the estate that he or she undertakes to convey by deed.

Covenant running with the land An executory promise made between a grantor and a grantee to which they and subsequent owners of the land are bound.

Cover A buyer or lessee's purchase on the open market of goods to substitute for those promised but never delivered by the seller. Under the Uniform Commercial Code, if the cost of cover exceeds the cost of the contract goods, the buyer or lessee can recover the difference, plus incidental and consequential damages.

Cram-down provision A provision of the Bankruptcy Code that allows a court to confirm a debtor's Chapter 11 reorganization plan even though only one class of creditors has accepted it. To exercise the court's right under this provision, the court must demonstrate that the plan does not discriminate unfairly against any creditors and is fair and equitable.

Crashworthiness doctrine A doctrine that imposes liability for defects in the design or construction of motor vehicles that increase the extent of injuries to passengers if an accident occurs. The doctrine holds even when the defects do not actually cause the accident.

Creditor A person to whom a debt is owed by another person (the debtor).

Creditor beneficiary A third party beneficiary who has rights in a contract made by the debtor and a third person. The terms of the contract obligate the third person to pay the debt owed to the creditor. The creditor beneficiary can enforce the debt against either party.

Creditors' composition agreement An agreement formed between a debtor and his or her creditors in which the creditors agree to accept a lesser sum than that owed by the debtor in full satisfaction of the debt.

Crime A wrong against society proclaimed in a statute and, if committed, punishable by society through fines and/or imprisonment—and, in some cases, death.

Criminal act *See Actus reus*

Criminal intent *See Mens rea*

Criminal law Law that defines and governs actions that constitute crimes. Generally, criminal law has to do with wrongful actions committed against society for which society demands redress.

Cross-border pollution Pollution across national boundaries; air and water degradation in one nation resulting from pollution-causing activities in a neighboring country.

Cross-collateralization The use of an asset that is not the subject of a loan to collateralize that loan.

Cross-examination The questioning of an opposing witness during the trial.

Cumulative voting A method of shareholder voting designed to allow minority shareholders to be represented on the board of directors. With cumulative voting, the number of members of the board to be elected is multiplied by the total number of voting shares held. The result equals the number of votes a shareholder has, and this total can be cast for one or more nominees for director.

Cure Under the Uniform Commercial Code, the right of a party who tenders nonconforming performance to correct his or her performance within the contract period.

Cyber crime A crime that occurs online, in the virtual community of the Internet, as opposed to the physical world.

Cyber hate speech Extreme hate speech on the Internet. Racist materials and Holocaust denials disseminated on the Web are examples.

Cyber mark A trademark in cyberspace.

Cyber tort A tort committed via the Internet.

Cyberlaw An informal term used to refer to all laws governing electronic communications and transactions, particularly those conducted via the Internet.

Cybernotary A legally recognized authority that can certify the validity of digital signatures.

Cyberstalker A person who commits the crime of stalking in cyberspace. Generally, stalking consists of harassing a person and putting that person in reasonable fear for his or her safety or the safety of the person's immediate family.

Cybersquatting The act of registering a domain name that is the same as, or confusingly similar to, the trademark of another and then offering to sell that domain name back to the trademark owner.

Cyberterrorist A hacker whose purpose is to exploit a target computer for a serious impact, such as the corruption of a program to sabotage a business.

D

Damages Money sought as a remedy for a breach of contract or for a tortious act.

Debenture bond A bond for which no specific assets of the corporation are pledged as backing; rather, the bond is backed by the general credit rating of the corporation, plus any assets that can be seized if the corporation allows the debentures to go into default.

Debit card A plastic card issued by a financial institution that allows the user to access his or her accounts online via automated teller machines.

Debtor Under Article 9 of the Uniform Commercial Code, a debtor is any party who owes payment or performance of a secured obligation, whether or not the party actually owns or has rights in the collateral.

Debtor in possession (DIP) In Chapter 11 bankruptcy proceedings, a debtor who is allowed to continue in possession of the estate in property (the business) and to continue business operations.

Declaratory judgment A court's judgment on a justiciable controversy when the plaintiff is in doubt as to his or her legal rights; a binding adjudication of the rights and status of litigants even though no consequential relief is awarded.

Decree The judgment of a court of equity.

Deed A document by which title to property (usually real property) is passed.

Defalcation The misuse of funds.

Defamation Any published or publicly spoken false statement that causes injury to another's good name, reputation, or character.

Default The failure to observe a promise or discharge an obligation. The term is commonly used to mean the failure to pay a debt when it is due.

Default judgment A judgment entered by a court against a defendant who has failed to appear in court to answer or defend against the plaintiff's claim.

Defendant One against whom a lawsuit is brought; the accused person in a criminal proceeding.

Defense Reasons that a defendant offers in an action or suit as to why the plaintiff should not obtain what he or she is seeking.

Deficiency judgment A judgment against a debtor for the amount of a debt remaining unpaid after collateral has been repossessed and sold.

Delegatee One to whom contract duties are delegated by another, called the delegator.

Delegation   The transfer of a contractual duty to a third party. The party delegating the duty (the delegator) to the third party (the delegatee) is still obliged to perform on the contract should the delegatee fail to perform.

Delegation doctrine   A doctrine based on Article I, Section 8, of the U.S. Constitution, which has been construed to allow Congress to delegate some of its power to make and implement laws to administrative agencies. The delegation is considered to be proper as long as Congress sets standards outlining the scope of the agency's authority.

Delegator   One who delegates his or her duties under a contract to another, called the delegatee.

Delivery   In contract law, the one party's act of placing the subject matter of the contract within the other party's possession or control.

Delivery ex ship   Delivery from the carrying ship. A contract term indicating that risk of loss will not pass to the buyer until the goods leave the ship or are otherwise properly unloaded.

Delivery order   A written order to deliver goods directed to a warehouser, carrier, or other person who, in the ordinary course of business, issues warehouse receipts or bills of lading [UCC 7–102(1)(d)].

Demand deposit   Funds (accepted by a bank) subject to immediate withdrawal, in contrast to a time deposit, which requires that a depositor wait a specific time before withdrawing or pay a penalty for early withdrawal.

Demurrer   *See* Motion to dismiss

De novo   Anew; afresh; a second time. In a hearing *de novo*, an appellate court hears the case as a court of original jurisdiction—that is, as if the case had not previously been tried and a decision rendered.

Depositary bank   The first bank to receive a check for payment.

Deposition   The testimony of a party to a lawsuit or a witness taken under oath before a trial.

Destination contract   A contract in which the seller is required to ship the goods by carrier and deliver them at a particular destination. The seller assumes liability for any losses or damage to the goods until they are tendered at the destination specified in the contract.

Devise   To make a gift of real property by will.

Digital cash   Funds stored on microchips and other computer devices.

Dilution   With respect to trademarks, a doctrine under which distinctive or famous trademarks are protected from certain unauthorized uses of the marks regardless of a showing of competition or a likelihood of confusion. Congress created a federal cause of action for dilution in 1995 with the passage of the Federal Trademark Dilution Act.

Direct examination   The examination of a witness by the attorney who calls the witness to the stand to testify on behalf of the attorney's client.

Directed verdict   *See* Motion for a directed verdict

Disaffirmance   The legal avoidance, or setting aside, of a contractual obligation.

Discharge   The termination of an obligation. (1) In contract law, discharge occurs when the parties have fully performed their contractual obligations or when events, conduct of the parties, or operation of the law releases the parties from performance. (2) In bankruptcy proceedings, the extinction of the debtor's dischargeable debts.

Discharge in bankruptcy   The release of a debtor from all debts that are provable, except those specifically excepted from discharge by statute.

Disclosed principal   A principal whose identity is known to a third party at the time the agent makes a contract with the third party.

Discovery   A phase in the litigation process during which the opposing parties may obtain information from each other and from third parties prior to trial.

Dishonor   To refuse to accept or pay a draft or a promissory note when it is properly presented. An instrument is dishonored when presentment is properly made and acceptance or payment is refused or cannot be obtained within the prescribed time.

Disparagement of property   An economically injurious false statement made about another's product or property. A general term for torts that are more specifically referred to as slander of quality or slander of title.

Disparate-impact discrimination   A form of employment discrimination that results from certain employer practices or procedures that, although not discriminatory on their face, have a discriminatory effect.

Disparate-treatment discrimination   A form of employment discrimination that results when an employer intentionally discriminates against employees who are members of protected classes.

Dissenting opinion   A written opinion by a judge or justice who disagrees with the majority opinion.

Dissociation   Occurs when a partner ceases to be associated in the carrying on of the partnership business. The severance of the relationship between a partner and a partnership.

Dissolution   The formal disbanding of a partnership or a corporation. It can take place by (1) acts of the partners or, in a corporation, of the shareholders and board of directors; (2) the death of a partner; (3) the expiration of a time period stated in a partnership agreement or a certificate of incorporation; or (4) judicial decree.

Distributed network   A network that can be used by persons located (distributed) around the country or the globe to share computer files.

Distribution agreement   A contract between a seller and a distributor of the seller's products setting out the terms and conditions of the distributorship.

Distributorship   A business arrangement that is established when a manufacturer licenses a dealer to sell its product. An example of a distributorship is an automobile dealership.

Diversity of citizenship   Under Article III, Section 2, of the Constitution, a basis for federal court jurisdiction over a lawsuit between (1) citizens of different states, (2) a foreign country and citizens of a state or of different states, or (3) citizens of a state and citizens or subjects of a foreign country. The amount in controversy must be more than

$75,000 before a federal court can take jurisdiction in such cases.

Divestiture   The act of selling one or more of a company's parts, such as a subsidiary or plant; often mandated by the courts in merger or monopolization cases.

Dividend   A distribution to corporate shareholders of corporate profits or income, disbursed in proportion to the number of shares held.

Docket   The list of cases entered on a court's calendar and thus scheduled to be heard by the court.

Document of title   Paper exchanged in the regular course of business that evidences the right to possession of goods (for example, a bill of lading or a warehouse receipt).

Domain name   The series of letters and symbols used to identify site operators on the Internet; Internet "addresses."

Domestic corporation   In a given state, a corporation that does business in, and is organized under the laws of, that state.

Domestic relations court   A court that deals with domestic (household) relationships, such as adoption, divorce, support payments, child custody, and the like.

Donee beneficiary   A third party beneficiary who has rights under a contract as a direct result of the intention of the contract parties to make a gift to the third party.

Double jeopardy   A situation occurring when a person is tried twice for the same criminal offense; prohibited by the Fifth Amendment to the Constitution.

Double taxation   A feature (and disadvantage) of the corporate form of business. Because a corporation is a separate legal entity, corporate profits are taxed by state and federal governments. Dividends are again taxable as ordinary income to the shareholders receiving them.

Draft   Any instrument (such as a check) drawn on a drawee (such as a bank) that orders the drawee to pay a certain sum of money, usually to a third party (the payee), on demand or at a definite future time.

Dram shop act   A state statute that imposes liability on the owners of bars and taverns, as well as those who serve alcoholic drinks to the public, for injuries resulting from accidents caused by intoxicated persons when the sellers or servers of alcoholic drinks contributed to the intoxication.

Drawee   The party that is ordered to pay a draft or check. With a check, a financial institution is always the drawee.

Drawer   The party that initiates a draft (writes a check, for example), thereby ordering the drawee to pay.

Due diligence   A required standard of care that certain professionals, such as accountants, must meet to avoid liability for securities violations. Under securities law, an accountant will be deemed to have exercised due diligence if he or she followed generally accepted accounting principles and generally accepted auditing standards and had, "after reasonable investigation, reasonable grounds to believe and did believe, at the time such part of the registration statement became effective, that the statements therein were true and that there was no omission of a material fact required to be stated therein or necessary to make the statements therein not misleading."

Due negotiation   The transfer of a document of title in such form that the transferee becomes a holder [UCC 7–501].

Due process clause   The provisions of the Fifth and Fourteenth Amendments to the Constitution that guarantee that no person shall be deprived of life, liberty, or property without due process of law. Similar clauses are found in most state constitutions.

Dumping   The selling of goods in a foreign country at a price below the price charged for the same goods in the domestic market.

Durable power of attorney   A document that authorizes a person to act on behalf of an incompetent person—write checks, collect insurance proceeds, and otherwise manage the disabled person's affairs, including health care—when he or she becomes incapacitated. Spouses often give each other durable power of attorney and, if they are advanced in age, may give a second such power of attorney to an older child.

Duress   Unlawful pressure brought to bear on a person, causing the person to perform an act that he or she would not otherwise perform.

Duty of care   The duty of all persons, as established by tort law, to exercise a reasonable amount of care in their dealings with others. Failure to exercise due care, which is normally determined by the "reasonable person standard," constitutes the tort of negligence.

E

E-agent   A computer program, electronic, or other automated means used to perform specific tasks without review by an individual.

E-commerce   Business transacted in cyberspace.

E-contract   A contract that is entered into in cyberspace and is evidenced only by electronic impulses (such as those that make up a computer's memory), rather than, for example, a typewritten form.

E-evidence   A type of evidence that consists of computer-generated or electronically recorded information, including e-mail, voice mail, spreadsheets, word-processing documents, and other data.

E-money   Prepaid funds recorded on a computer or a card (such as a *smart card*).

E-signature   As defined by the Uniform Electronic Transactions Act, "an electronic sound, symbol, or process attached to or logically associated with a record and executed or adopted by a person with the intent to sign the record."

Early neutral case evaluation   A form of alternative dispute resolution in which a neutral third party evaluates the strengths and weakness of the disputing parties' positions; the evaluator's opinion forms the basis for negotiating a settlement.

Easement   A nonpossessory right to use another's property in a manner established by either express or implied agreement.

Ejectment The eviction of a tenant from leased premises. A remedy at common law to which the landlord can resort when a tenant fails to pay rent for leased premises. To obtain possession of the premises, the landlord must appear in court and show that the defaulting tenant is in wrongful possession.

Elder law A relatively new area of legal practice in which attorneys assist older persons in dealing with such problems as disability, long-term health care, age discrimination, grandparents' visitation rights, and other problems relating to age.

Electronic fund transfer (EFT) A transfer of funds with the use of an electronic terminal, a telephone, a computer, or magnetic tape.

Emancipation In regard to minors, the act of being freed from parental control; occurs when a child's parent or legal guardian relinquishes the legal right to exercise control over the child. Normally, a minor who leaves home to support himself or herself is considered emancipated.

Embezzlement The fraudulent appropriation of money or other property by a person to whom the money or property has been entrusted.

Eminent domain The power of a government to take land for public use from private citizens for just compensation.

Employee A person who works for an employer for a salary or for wages.

Employer An individual or business entity that hires employees, pays them salaries or wages, and exercises control over their work.

Employment at will A common law doctrine under which either party may terminate an employment relationship at any time for any reason, unless a contract specifies otherwise.

Employment discrimination Treating employees or job applicants unequally on the basis of race, color, national origin, religion, gender, age, or disability; prohibited by federal statutes.

Enabling legislation A statute enacted by Congress that authorizes the creation of an administrative agency and specifies the name, composition, purpose, and powers of the agency being created.

Encryption The process by which a message (plaintext) is transformed into something (ciphertext) that the sender and receiver intend third parties not to understand.

Endowment insurance A type of insurance that combines life insurance with an investment so that if the insured outlives the policy, the face value is paid to him or her; if the insured does not outlive the policy, the face value is paid to his or her beneficiary.

Entrapment In criminal law, a defense in which the defendant claims that he or she was induced by a public official—usually an undercover agent or police officer—to commit a crime that he or she would otherwise not have committed.

Entrepreneur One who initiates and assumes the financial risks of a new enterprise and who undertakes to provide or control its management.

Entrustment The transfer of goods to a merchant who deals in goods of that kind and who may transfer those goods and all rights to them to a buyer in the ordinary course of business [UCC 2–403(2)].

Environmental impact statement (EIS) A statement required by the National Environmental Policy Act for any major federal action that will significantly affect the quality of the environment. The statement must analyze the action's impact on the environment and explore alternative actions that might be taken.

Environmental law The body of statutory, regulatory, and common law relating to the protection of the environment.

Equal dignity rule In most states, a rule stating that express authority given to an agent must be in writing if the contract to be made on behalf of the principal is required to be in writing.

Equal protection clause The provision in the Fourteenth Amendment to the Constitution that guarantees that no state will "deny to any person within its jurisdiction the equal protection of the laws." This clause mandates that state governments treat similarly situated individuals in a similar manner.

Equitable maxims General propositions or principles of law that have to do with fairness (equity).

Equity of redemption The right of a mortgagor who has breached the mortgage agreement to redeem or purchase the property prior to foreclosure proceedings.

Escheat The transfer of property to the state when the owner of the property dies without heirs.

Escrow account An account that is generally held in the name of the depositor and escrow agent; the funds in the account are paid to a third person only on fulfillment of the escrow condition.

Establishment clause The provision in the First Amendment to the U.S. Constitution that prohibits Congress from creating any law "respecting an establishment of religion."

Estate The interest that a person has in real and personal property.

Estate planning Planning in advance how one's property and obligations should be transferred on one's death. Wills and trusts are two basic devices used in the process of estate planning.

Estop To bar, impede, or preclude.

Estoppel The principle that a party's own acts prevent him or her from claiming a right to the detriment of another who was entitled to and did rely on those acts. *See also* Agency by estoppel; Promissory estoppel

Estray statute A statute defining finders' rights in property when the true owners are unknown.

Ethical reasoning A reasoning process in which an individual links his or her moral convictions or ethical standards to the particular situation at hand.

Ethics Moral principles and values applied to social behavior.

Evidence Proof offered at trial—in the form of testimony, documents, records, exhibits, objects, and so on—

for the purpose of convincing the court or jury of the truth of a contention.

Eviction   A landlord's act of depriving a tenant of possession of the leased premises.

Ex parte contact   Communications with an administrative agency that are not placed in the record.

Ex ship   *See* Delivery ex ship

Exclusionary rule   In criminal procedure, a rule under which any evidence that is obtained in violation of the accused's constitutional rights guaranteed by the Fourth, Fifth, and Sixth Amendments, as well as any evidence derived from illegally obtained evidence, will not be admissible in court.

Exclusive distributorship   A distributorship in which the seller and the distributor of the seller's products agree that the distributor has the exclusive right to distribute the seller's products in a certain geographic area.

Exclusive jurisdiction   Jurisdiction that exists when a case can be heard only in a particular court or type of court, such as a federal court or a state court.

Exclusive-dealing contract   An agreement under which a seller forbids a buyer to purchase products from the seller's competitors.

Exculpatory clause   A clause that releases a contractual party from liability in the event of monetary or physical injury, no matter who is at fault.

Executed contract   A contract that has been completely performed by both parties.

Execution   An action to carry into effect the directions in a court decree or judgment.

Executive agency   An administrative agency within the executive branch of government. At the federal level, executive agencies are those within the cabinet departments.

Executor   A person appointed by a testator to see that his or her will is administered appropriately.

Executory contract   A contract that has not as yet been fully performed.

Export   To sell products to buyers located in other countries.

Express authority   Authority expressly given by one party to another. In agency law, an agent has express authority to act for a principal if both parties agree, orally or in writing, that an agency relationship exists in which the agent had the power (authority) to act in the place of, and on behalf of, the principal.

Express contract   A contract in which the terms of the agreement are fully and explicitly stated in words, oral or written.

Express warranty   A seller's or lessor's oral or written promise, ancillary to an underlying sales or lease agreement, as to the quality, description, or performance of the goods being sold or leased.

Expropriation   The seizure by a government of privately owned business or personal property for a proper public purpose and with just compensation.

Extension clause   A clause in a time instrument that allows the instrument's date of maturity to be extended into the future.

F

F.A.S.   Free alongside. A contract term that requires the seller, at his or her own expense and risk, to deliver the goods alongside the ship before risk passes to the buyer.

F.O.B.   Free on board. A contract term that indicates that the selling price of the goods includes transportation costs (and that the seller carries the risk of loss) to the specific F.O.B. place named in the contract. The place can be either the place of initial shipment (for example, the seller's city or place of business) or the place of destination (for example, the buyer's city or place of business).

Family limited liability partnership (FLLP)   A limited liability partnership (LLP) in which the majority of the partners are persons related to each other, essentially as spouses, parents, grandparents, siblings, cousins, nephews, or nieces. A person acting in a fiduciary capacity for persons so related could also be a partner. All of the partners must be natural persons or persons acting in a fiduciary capacity for the benefit of natural persons.

Federal form of government   A system of government in which the states form a union and the sovereign power is divided between a central government and the member states.

Federal question   A question that pertains to the U.S. Constitution, acts of Congress, or treaties. A federal question provides a basis for federal jurisdiction.

Federal Reserve System   A network of twelve central banks, located around the country and headed by the Federal Reserve Board of Governors. Most banks in the United States have Federal Reserve accounts.

Federal Rules of Civil Procedure (FRCP)   The rules controlling procedural matters in civil trials brought before the federal district courts.

Federal system   A system of government in which power is divided by a written constitution between a central government and regional, or subdivisional, governments. Each level must have some domain in which its policies are dominant and some genuine political or constitutional guarantee of its authority.

Fee simple   An absolute form of property ownership entitling the property owner to use, possess, or dispose of the property as he or she chooses during his or her lifetime. On death, the interest in the property passes to the owner's heirs; a fee simple absolute.

Fee simple absolute   An ownership interest in land in which the owner has the greatest possible aggregation of rights, privileges, and power. Ownership in fee simple absolute is limited absolutely to a person and his or her heirs.

Fellow-servant doctrine   A doctrine that bars an employee from suing his or her employer for injuries caused by a fellow employee.

Felony   A crime—such as arson, murder, rape, or robbery—that carries the most severe sanctions, usually ranging from one year in a state or federal prison to the forfeiture of one's life.

Fictitious payee A payee on a negotiable instrument whom the maker or drawer does not intend to have an interest in the instrument. Indorsements by fictitious payees are not treated as unauthorized under Article 3 of the Uniform Commercial Code.

Fiduciary As a noun, a person having a duty created by his or her undertaking to act primarily for another's benefit in matters connected with the undertaking. As an adjective, a relationship founded on trust and confidence.

Fiduciary duty The duty, imposed on a fiduciary by virtue of his or her position, to act primarily for another's benefit.

Filtering software A computer program that includes a pattern through which data are passed. When designed to block access to certain Web sites, the pattern blocks the retrieval of a site whose URL or key words are on a list within the program.

Final order The final decision of an administrative agency on an issue. If no appeal is taken, or if the case is not reviewed or considered anew by the agency commission, the administrative law judge's initial order becomes the final order of the agency.

Financial institution An organization authorized to do business under state or federal laws relating to financial institutions. For example, under the Electronic Fund Transfer Act, financial institutions include banks, savings and loan associations, credit unions, and other business entities that directly or indirectly hold accounts belonging to consumers.

Financing statement A document prepared by a secured creditor and filed with the appropriate government official to give notice to the public that the creditor claims an interest in collateral belonging to the debtor named in the statement. The financing statement must contain the names and addresses of both the debtor and the creditor, and describe the collateral by type or item.

Firm offer An offer (by a merchant) that is irrevocable without consideration for a period of time (not longer than three months). A firm offer by a merchant must be in writing and must be signed by the offeror.

Fitness for a particular purpose *See* Implied warranty of fitness for a particular purpose

Fixture A thing that was once personal property but that has become attached to real property in such a way that it takes on the characteristics of real property and becomes part of that real property.

Flame An online message in which one party attacks another in harsh, often personal, terms.

Floating lien A security interest in proceeds, after-acquired property, or property purchased under a line of credit (or all three); a security interest in collateral that is retained even when the collateral changes in character, classification, or location.

Forbearance The act of refraining from an action that one has a legal right to undertake.

Force majeure (pronounced mah-*zhure*) **clause** A provision in a contract stipulating that certain unforeseen events—such as war, political upheavals, acts of God, or other events—will excuse a party from liability for non-performance of contractual obligations.

Foreclosure A proceeding in which a mortgagee either takes title to or forces the sale of the mortgagor's property in satisfaction of a debt.

Foreign corporation In a given state, a corporation that does business in the state without being incorporated therein.

Foreseeable risk In negligence law, the risk of harm or injury to another that a person of ordinary intelligence and prudence should have reasonably anticipated or foreseen when undertaking an action or refraining from undertaking an action.

Forfeiture The termination of a lease, according to its terms or the terms of a statute, when one of the parties fails to fulfill a condition under the lease and thereby breaches it.

Forgery The fraudulent making or altering of any writing in a way that changes the legal rights and liabilities of another.

Formal contract A contract that by law requires a specific form, such as being executed under seal, to be valid.

Forum A jurisdiction, court, or place in which disputes are litigated and legal remedies are sought.

Forum-selection clause A provision in a contract designating the court, jurisdiction, or tribunal that will decide any disputes arising under the contract.

Franchise Any arrangement in which the owner of a trademark, trade name, or copyright licenses another to use that trademark, trade name, or copyright, under specified conditions or limitations, in the selling of goods and services.

Franchise tax A state or local government tax on the right and privilege of carrying on a business in the form of a corporation.

Franchisee One receiving a license to use another's (the franchisor's) trademark, trade name, or copyright in the sale of goods and services.

Franchisor One licensing another (the franchisee) to use his or her trademark, trade name, or copyright in the sale of goods or services.

Fraud Any misrepresentation, either by misstatement or omission of a material fact, knowingly made with the intention of deceiving another and on which a reasonable person would and does rely to his or her detriment.

Fraud in the execution In the law of negotiable instruments, a type of fraud that occurs when a person is deceived into signing a negotiable instrument, believing that he or she is signing something else (such as a receipt); also called fraud in the inception. Fraud in the execution is a universal defense to payment on a negotiable instrument.

Fraud in the inducement Ordinary fraud. In the law of negotiable instruments, fraud in the inducement occurs when a person issues a negotiable instrument based on false statements by the other party. The issuing party will be able to avoid payment on that instrument unless the holder is a holder in due course; in other words, fraud in the inducement is a personal defense to payment on a negotiable instrument.

Fraudulent misrepresentation (fraud) Any misrepresentation, either by misstatement or omission of a material fact, knowingly made with the intention of deceiving another and on which a reasonable person would and does rely to his or her detriment.

Free exercise clause The provision in the First Amendment to the U.S. Constitution that prohibits Congress from making any law "prohibiting the free exercise" of religion.

Frustration of purpose A court-created doctrine under which a party to a contract will be relieved of his or her duty to perform when the objective purpose for performance no longer exists (due to reasons beyond that party's control).

Full faith and credit clause A clause in Article IV, Section 1, of the Constitution that provides that "Full Faith and Credit shall be given in each State to the public Acts, Records, and Judicial Proceedings of every other State." The clause ensures that rights established under deeds, wills, contracts, and the like in one state will be honored by the other states and that any judicial decision with respect to such property rights will be honored and enforced in all states.

Full warranty A warranty as to full performance covering generally both labor and materials.

Fungible goods Goods that are alike by physical nature, by agreement, or by trade usage. Examples of fungible goods are wheat, oil, and wine that are identical in type and quality.

G

Garnishment A legal process used by a creditor to collect a debt by seizing property of the debtor (such as wages) that is being held by a third party (such as the debtor's employer).

General jurisdiction Exists when a court's subject-matter jurisdiction is not restricted. A court of general jurisdiction normally can hear any type of case.

General partner In a limited partnership, a partner who assumes responsibility for the management of the partnership and liability for all partnership debts.

General partnership *See* Partnership

Generally accepted accounting principles (GAAP) The conventions, rules, and procedures that define accepted accounting practices at a particular time. The source of the principles is the Financial Accounting Standards Board.

Generally accepted auditing standards (GAAS) Standards concerning an auditor's professional qualities and the judgment exercised by him or her in the performance of an examination and report. The source of the standards is the American Institute of Certified Public Accountants.

Genuineness of assent Knowing and voluntary assent to the terms of a contract. If a contract is formed as a result of a mistake, misrepresentation, undue influence, or duress, genuineness of assent is lacking, and the contract will be voidable.

Gift Any voluntary transfer of property made without consideration, past or present.

Gift *causa mortis* A gift made in contemplation of death. If the donor does not die of that ailment, the gift is revoked.

Gift *inter vivos* A gift made during one's lifetime and not in contemplation of imminent death, in contrast to a gift *causa mortis*.

Good faith Under the Uniform Commercial Code, good faith means honesty in fact; with regard to merchants, good faith means honesty in fact *and* the observance of reasonable commercial standards of fair dealing in the trade.

Good faith purchaser A purchaser who buys without notice of any circumstance that would put a person of ordinary prudence on inquiry as to whether the seller has valid title to the goods being sold.

Good Samaritan statute A state statute that provides that persons who rescue or provide emergency services to others in peril—unless they do so recklessly, thus causing further harm—cannot be sued for negligence.

Grand jury A group of citizens called to decide, after hearing the state's evidence, whether a reasonable basis (probable cause) exists for believing that a crime has been committed and whether a trial ought to be held.

Grant deed A deed that simply recites words of consideration and conveyance. Under statute, a grant deed may impliedly warrant that at least the grantor has not conveyed the property's title to someone else.

Grantee One to whom a grant (of land or property, for example) is made.

Grantor A person who makes a grant, such as a transferor of property or the creator of a trust.

Group boycott The refusal to deal with a particular person or firm by a group of competitors; prohibited by the Sherman Act.

Guarantor A person who agrees to satisfy the debt of another (the debtor) only after the principal debtor defaults; a guarantor's liability is thus secondary.

H

Habitability *See* Implied warranty of habitability

Hacker A person who uses one computer to break into another. Professional computer programmers refer to such persons as "crackers."

Health-care power of attorney A document that designates a person who will have the power to choose what type of and how much medical treatment a person who is unable to make such a choice will receive.

Hearsay An oral or written statement made out of court that is later offered in court by a witness (not the person who made the statement) to prove the truth of the matter asserted in the statement. Hearsay is generally inadmissible as evidence.

Hirfindahl-Hirschman Index (HHI) An index of market power used to calculate whether a merger of two businesses will result in sufficient monopoly power to violate antitrust laws.

Historical school A school of legal thought that emphasizes the evolutionary process of law and that looks to the past to discover what the principles of contemporary law should be.

Holder Any person in the possession of an instrument drawn, issued, or indorsed to him or her, to his or her order, to bearer, or in blank.

Holder in due course (HDC) A holder who acquires a negotiable instrument for value; in good faith; and without notice that the instrument is overdue, that it has been dishonored, that any person has a defense against it or a claim to it, or that the instrument contains unauthorized signatures, alterations, or is so irregular or incomplete as to call into question its authenticity.

Holographic will A will written entirely in the signer's handwriting and usually not witnessed.

Homestead exemption A law permitting a debtor to retain the family home, either in its entirety or up to a specified dollar amount, free from the claims of unsecured creditors or trustees in bankruptcy.

Horizontal merger A merger between two firms that are competing in the same market.

Horizontal restraint Any agreement that in some way restrains competition between rival firms competing in the same market.

Hot-cargo agreement An agreement in which employers voluntarily agree with unions not to handle, use, or deal in nonunion-produced goods of other employers; a type of secondary boycott explicitly prohibited by the Labor-Management Reporting and Disclosure Act of 1959.

Hung jury A jury whose members are so irreconcilably divided in their opinions that they cannot come to a verdict by the requisite number of jurors. The judge in this situation may order a new trial.

I

Identification In a sale of goods, the express designation of the specific goods provided for in the contract.

Identity theft The act of stealing another's identifying information—such as a name, date of birth, or Social Security number—and using that information to access the victim's financial resources.

Illusory promise A promise made without consideration, which renders the promise unenforceable.

Immunity A status of being exempt, or free, from certain duties or requirements. In criminal law, the state may grant an accused person immunity from prosecution—or agree to prosecute for a lesser offense—if the accused person agrees to give the state information that would assist the state in prosecuting other individuals for crimes. In

tort law, freedom from liability for defamatory speech. *See also* Privilege

Implied authority Authority that is created not by an explicit oral or written agreement but by implication. In agency law, implied authority (of the agent) can be conferred by custom, inferred from the position the agent occupies, or implied by virtue of being reasonably necessary to carry out express authority.

Implied warranty A warranty that the law derives by implication or inference from the nature of the transaction or the relative situation or circumstances of the parties.

Implied warranty of fitness for a particular purpose A warranty that goods sold or leased are fit for a particular purpose. The warranty arises when any seller or lessor knows the particular purpose for which a buyer or lessee will use the goods and knows that the buyer or lessee is relying on the skill and judgment of the seller or lessor to select suitable goods.

Implied warranty of habitability An implied promise by a landlord that rented residential premises are fit for human habitation—that is, in a condition that is safe and suitable for people to live in.

Implied warranty of merchantability A warranty that goods being sold or leased are reasonably fit for the ordinary purpose for which they are sold or leased, are properly packaged and labeled, and are of fair quality. The warranty automatically arises in every sale or lease of goods made by a merchant who deals in goods of the kind sold or leased.

Implied-in-fact contract A contract formed in whole or in part from the conduct of the parties (as opposed to an express contract).

Impossibility of performance A doctrine under which a party to a contract is relieved of his or her duty to perform when performance becomes impossible or totally impracticable (through no fault of either party).

Imposter One who, by use of the mail, telephone, or personal appearance, induces a maker or drawer to issue an instrument in the name of an impersonated payee. Indorsements by imposters are not treated as unauthorized under Article 3 of the Uniform Commercial Code.

In pari delicto At equal fault.

In personam jurisdiction Court jurisdiction over the "person" involved in a legal action; personal jurisdiction.

In rem jurisdiction Court jurisdiction over a defendant's property.

Incidental beneficiary A third party who incidentally benefits from a contract but whose benefit was not the reason the contract was formed; an incidental beneficiary has no rights in a contract and cannot sue to have the contract enforced.

Incidental damages Losses reasonably associated with, or related to, actual damages resulting from a breach of contract.

Incontestability clause A provision in an insurance policy that prevents the insurer, after the policy has been in force for a specified length of time (usually two or three years), from disputing the policy's validity based on the policyholder's statements or omissions in the application.

Indemnify   To compensate or reimburse another for losses or expenses incurred.

Independent contractor   One who works for, and receives payment from, an employer but whose working conditions and methods are not controlled by the employer. An independent contractor is not an employee but may be an agent.

Independent regulatory agency   An administrative agency that is not considered part of the government's executive branch and is not subject to the authority of the president. Independent agency officials cannot be removed without cause.

Indictment (pronounced in-*dyte*-ment)   A charge by a grand jury that a reasonable basis (probable cause) exists for believing that a crime has been committed and that a trial should be held.

Indorsee   The person to whom a negotiable instrument is transferred by indorsement.

Indorsement   A signature placed on an instrument for the purpose of transferring one's ownership rights in the instrument.

Indorser   A person who transfers an instrument by signing (indorsing) it and delivering it to another person.

Industry-wide liability   Product liability that is imposed on an entire industry when it is unclear which of several sellers within the industry manufactured a particular product. *See also* Market-share liability

Informal contract   A contract that does not require a specified form or formality in order to be valid.

Information   A formal accusation or complaint (without an indictment) issued in certain types of actions (usually criminal actions involving lesser crimes) by a law officer, such as a magistrate.

Information return   A tax return submitted by a partnership that only reports the income earned by the business. The partnership as an entity does not pay taxes on the income received by the partnership. A partner's profit from the partnership (whether distributed or not) is taxed as individual income to the individual partner.

Infringement   A violation of another's legally recognized right. The term is commonly used with reference to the invasion by one party of another party's rights in a patent, trademark, or copyright.

Initial order   In the context of administrative law, an agency's disposition in a matter other than a rulemaking. An administrative law judge's initial order becomes final unless it is appealed.

Injunction   A court decree ordering a person to do or refrain from doing a certain act or activity.

Innkeeper   An owner of an inn, hotel, motel, or other lodgings.

Innkeeper's lien   A possessory or statutory lien allowing the innkeeper to take the personal property of a guest, brought into the hotel, as security for nonpayment of the guest's bill (debt).

Innocent misrepresentation   A false statement of fact or an act made in good faith that deceives and causes harm or injury to another.

Insider   A corporate director or officer, or other employee or agent, with access to confidential information and a duty not to disclose that information in violation of insider-trading laws.

Insider trading   The purchase or sale of securities on the basis of "inside information" (information that has not been made available to the public) in violation of a duty owed to the company whose stock is being traded.

Insolvent   Under the Uniform Commercial Code, a term describing a person who ceases to pay "his debts in the ordinary course of business or cannot pay his debts as they become due or is insolvent within the meaning of federal bankruptcy law" [UCC 1–201(23)].

Installment contract   Under the Uniform Commercial Code, a contract that requires or authorizes delivery in two or more separate lots to be accepted and paid for separately.

Instrument   *See* Negotiable instrument

Insurable interest   An interest either in a person's life or well-being or in property that is sufficiently substantial that insuring against injury to (or the death of) the person or against damage to the property does not amount to a mere wagering (betting) contract.

Insurance   A contract in which, for a stipulated consideration, one party agrees to compensate the other for loss on a specific subject by a specified peril.

Intangible property   Property that is incapable of being apprehended by the senses (such as by sight or touch); intellectual property is an example of intangible property.

Integrated contract   A written contract that constitutes the final expression of the parties' agreement. If a contract is integrated, evidence extraneous to the contract that contradicts or alters the meaning of the contract in any way is inadmissible.

Intellectual property   Property resulting from intellectual, creative processes. Patents, trademarks, and copyrights are examples of intellectual property.

Intended beneficiary   A third party for whose benefit a contract is formed; an intended beneficiary can sue the promisor if such a contract is breached.

Intentional tort   A wrongful act knowingly committed.

Inter vivos gift   *See* Gift *inter vivos*

Inter vivos trust   A trust created by the grantor (settlor) and effective during the grantor's lifetime (that is, a trust not established by a will).

Intermediary bank   Any bank to which an item is transferred in the course of collection, except the depositary or payor bank.

International law   The law that governs relations among nations. International customs and treaties are generally considered to be two of the most important sources of international law.

International organization   In international law, a term that generally refers to an organization composed mainly of nations and usually established by treaty. The United States is a member of more than one hundred multilateral and bilateral organizations, including at least twenty through the United Nations.

Interpretive rule   An administrative agency rule that is simply a statement or opinion issued by the agency explaining how it interprets and intends to apply the statutes it enforces. Such rules are not automatically binding on private individuals or organizations.

Interrogatories   A series of written questions for which written answers are prepared and then signed under oath by a party to a lawsuit, usually with the assistance of the party's attorney.

Intestacy laws   State statutes that specify how property will be distributed when a person dies intestate (without a valid will); statutes of descent and distribution.

Intestate   As a noun, one who has died without having created a valid will; as an adjective, the state of having died without a will.

Investment company   A company that acts on behalf of many smaller shareholder-owners by buying a large portfolio of securities and professionally managing that portfolio.

Invitee   A person who, either expressly or impliedly, is privileged to enter onto another's land. The inviter owes the invitee (for example, a customer in a store) the duty to exercise reasonable care to protect the invitee from harm.

Irrevocable offer   An offer that cannot be revoked or recalled by the offeror without liability. A merchant's firm offer is an example of an irrevocable offer.

Issue   The first transfer, or delivery, of an instrument to a holder.

J

Joint and several liability   In partnership law, a doctrine under which a plaintiff may sue, and collect a judgment from, one or more of the partners separately (severally, or individually) or all of the partners together (jointly). This is true even if one of the partners sued did not participate in, ratify, or know about whatever it was that gave rise to the cause of action.

Joint liability   Shared liability. In partnership law, partners incur joint liability for partnership obligations and debts. For example, if a third party sues a partner on a partnership debt, the partner has the right to insist that the other partners be sued with him or her.

Joint stock company   A hybrid form of business organization that combines characteristics of a corporation (shareholder-owners, management by directors and officers of the company, and perpetual existence) and a partnership (it is formed by agreement, not statute; property is usually held in the names of the members; and the shareholders have personal liability for business debts). Usually, the joint stock company is regarded as a partnership for tax and other legally related purposes.

Joint tenancy   The joint ownership of property by two or more co-owners in which each co-owner owns an undivided portion of the property. On the death of one of the joint tenants, his or her interest automatically passes to the surviving joint tenants.

Joint venture   A joint undertaking of a specific commercial enterprise by an association of persons. A joint venture is normally not a legal entity and is treated like a partnership for federal income tax purposes.

Judgment   The final order or decision resulting from a legal action.

Judgment n.o.v.   *See* Motion for judgment n.o.v.

Judgment rate of interest   A rate of interest fixed by statute that is applied to a monetary judgment from the moment the judgment is awarded by a court until the judgment is paid or terminated.

Judicial lien   A lien on property created by a court order.

Judicial process   The procedures relating to, or connected with, the administration of justice through the judicial system.

Judicial review   The process by which courts decide on the constitutionality of legislative enactments and actions of the executive branch.

Junior lienholder   A person or business who holds a lien that is subordinate to one or more other liens on the same property.

Jurisdiction   The authority of a court to hear and decide a specific action.

Jurisprudence   The science or philosophy of law.

Justiciable (pronounced jus-*tish*-a-bul) **controversy**   A controversy that is not hypothetical or academic but real and substantial; a requirement that must be satisfied before a court will hear a case.

K

King's court   A medieval English court. The king's courts, or *curiae regis*, were established by the Norman conquerors of England. The body of law that developed in these courts was common to the entire English realm and thus became known as the common law.

L

Laches   The equitable doctrine that bars a party's right to legal action if the party has neglected for an unreasonable length of time to act on his or her rights.

Landlord   An owner of land or rental property who leases it to another person, called the tenant.

Landlord's lien   A landlord's remedy for a tenant's failure to pay rent. When permitted under a statute or the lease agreement, the landlord may take and keep or sell whatever of the defaulting tenant's property is on the leased premises.

Larceny   The wrongful taking and carrying away of another person's personal property with the intent to permanently deprive the owner of the property. Some states classify larceny as either grand or petit, depending on the property's value.

Last clear chance A doctrine under which a plaintiff may recover from a defendant for injuries or damages suffered, notwithstanding the plaintiff's own negligence, when the defendant had the opportunity—a last clear chance—to avoid harming the plaintiff through the exercise of reasonable care but failed to do so.

Law A body of enforceable rules governing relationships among individuals and between individuals and their society.

Lawsuit The litigation process. *See* Litigation

Lease In real property law, a contract by which the owner of real property (the landlord, or lessor) grants to a person (the tenant, or lessee) an exclusive right to use and possess the property, usually for a specified period of time, in return for rent or some other form of payment.

Lease agreement In regard to the lease of goods, an agreement in which one person (the lessor) agrees to transfer the right to the possession and use of property to another person (the lessee) in exchange for rental payments.

Leasehold estate An estate in realty held by a tenant under a lease. In every leasehold estate, the tenant has a qualified right to possess and/or use the land.

Legacy A gift of personal property under a will.

Legal positivists Adherents to the positivist school of legal thought. This school holds that there can be no higher law than a nation's positive law—law created by a particular society at a particular point in time. In contrast to the natural law school, the positivist school maintains that there are no "natural" rights; rights come into existence only when there is a sovereign power (government) to confer and enforce those rights.

Legal rate of interest A rate of interest fixed by statute as either the maximum rate of interest allowed by law or a rate of interest applied when the parties to a contract intend, but do not fix, an interest rate in the contract. In the latter case, the rate is frequently the same as the statutory maximum rate permitted.

Legal realism A school of legal thought that was popular in the 1920s and 1930s and that challenged many existing jurisprudential assumptions, particularly the assumption that subjective elements play no part in judicial reasoning. Legal realists generally advocated a less abstract and more pragmatic approach to the law, an approach that would take into account customary practices and the circumstances in which transactions take place. The school left a lasting imprint on American jurisprudence.

Legal reasoning The process of reasoning by which a judge harmonizes his or her decision with the judicial decisions of previous cases.

Legatee One designated in a will to receive a gift of personal property.

Legislative rule An administrative agency rule that carries the same weight as a congressionally enacted statute.

Lessee A person who acquires the right to the possession and use of another's property in exchange for rental payments.

Lessor A person who sells the right to the possession and use of property to another in exchange for rental payments.

Letter of credit A written instrument, usually issued by a bank on behalf of a customer or other person, in which the issuer promises to honor drafts or other demands for payment by third persons in accordance with the terms of the instrument.

Leveraged buyout (LBO) A corporate takeover financed by loans secured by the acquired corporation's assets or by the issuance of corporate bonds, resulting in a high debt load for the corporation.

Levy The obtaining of money by legal process through the seizure and sale of property, usually done after a writ of execution has been issued.

Liability Any actual or potential legal obligation, duty, debt, or responsibility.

Libel Defamation in writing or other form (such as in a videotape) having the quality of permanence.

License A revocable right or privilege of a person to come on another person's land.

Licensee One who receives a license to use, or enter onto, another's property.

Lien (pronounced *leen*) A claim against specific property to satisfy a debt.

Lien creditor One whose claim is secured by a lien on particular property, as distinguished from a general creditor, who has no such security.

Life estate An interest in land that exists only for the duration of the life of some person, usually the holder of the estate.

Limited jurisdiction Exists when a court's subject-matter jurisdiction is limited. Bankruptcy courts and probate courts are examples of courts with limited jurisdiction.

Limited liability Exists when the liability of the owners of a business is limited to the amount of their investments in the firm.

Limited liability company (LLC) A hybrid form of business enterprise that offers the limited liability of the corporation but the tax advantages of a partnership.

Limited liability limited partnership (LLLP) A type of limited partnership. The difference between a limited partnership and an LLLP is that the liability of the general partner in an LLLP is the same as the liability of the limited partner. That is, the liability of all partners is limited to the amount of their investments in the firm.

Limited liability partnership (LLP) A form of partnership that allows professionals to enjoy the tax benefits of a partnership while limiting their personal liability for the malpractice of other partners.

Limited partner In a limited partnership, a partner who contributes capital to the partnership but has no right to participate in the management and operation of the business. The limited partner assumes no liability for partnership debts beyond the capital contributed.

Limited partnership A partnership consisting of one or more general partners (who manage the business and are liable to the full extent of their personal assets for debts of the partnership) and one or more limited partners (who contribute only assets and are liable only to the extent of their contributions).

Limited-payment life   A type of life insurance for which premiums are payable for a definite period, after which the policy is fully paid.

Limited warranty   A written warranty that fails to meet one or more of the minimum standards for a full warranty.

Liquidated damages   An amount, stipulated in the contract, that the parties to a contract believe to be a reasonable estimation of the damages that will occur in the event of a breach.

Liquidated debt   A debt that is due and certain in amount.

Liquidation   (1) In regard to bankruptcy, the sale of all of the nonexempt assets of a debtor and the distribution of the proceeds to the debtor's creditors. Chapter 7 of the Bankruptcy Code provides for liquidation bankruptcy proceedings. (2) In regard to corporations, the process by which corporate assets are converted into cash and distributed among creditors and shareholders according to specific rules of preference.

Litigant   A party to a lawsuit.

Litigation   The process of resolving a dispute through the court system.

Living will   A document that allows a person to control the methods of medical treatment that may be used after a serious accident or illness.

Loan workout   *See* Workout

Long arm statute   A state statute that permits a state to obtain personal jurisdiction over nonresident defendants. A defendant must have "minimum contacts" with that state for the statute to apply.

Lost property   Property with which the owner has involuntarily parted and then cannot find or recover.

M

Magistrate's court   A court of limited jurisdiction that is presided over by a public official (magistrate) with certain judicial authority, such as the power to set bail.

Mailbox rule   A rule providing that an acceptance of an offer becomes effective on dispatch (on being placed in a mailbox), if mail is, expressly or impliedly, an authorized means of communication of acceptance to the offeror.

Main purpose rule   A rule of contract law under which an exception to the Statute of Frauds is made if the main purpose in accepting secondary liability under a contract is to secure a personal benefit. If this situation exists, the contract need not be in writing to be enforceable.

Majority   *See* Age of majority

Majority opinion   A court's written opinion, outlining the views of the majority of the judges or justices deciding the case.

Maker   One who promises to pay a certain sum to the holder of a promissory note or certificate of deposit (CD).

Malpractice   Professional misconduct or the failure to exercise the requisite degree of skill as a professional.

Negligence—the failure to exercise due care—on the part of a professional, such as a physician or an attorney, is commonly referred to as malpractice.

Manufacturing or processing-plant franchise   A franchise that is created when the franchisor transmits to the franchisee the essential ingredients or formula to make a particular product. The franchisee then markets the product either at wholesale or at retail in accordance with the franchisor's standards. Examples of this type of franchise are Coca-Cola and other soft-drink bottling companies.

Marine insurance   Insurance protecting shippers and vessel owners from losses or damages sustained by a vessel or its cargo during the transport of goods or materials by water.

Mark   *See* Trademark

Market concentration   A situation that exists when a small number of firms share the market for a particular good or service. For example, if the four largest grocery stores in Chicago accounted for 80 percent of all retail food sales, the market clearly would be concentrated in those four firms.

Market power   The power of a firm to control the market price of its product. A monopoly has the greatest degree of market power.

Marketable title   Title to real estate that is reasonably free from encumbrances, defects in the chain of title, and other events that affect title, such as adverse possession.

Market-share liability   A method of sharing liability among several firms that manufactured or marketed a particular product that may have caused a plaintiff's injury. This form of liability sharing is used when the true source of the product is unidentifiable. Each firm's liability is proportionate to its respective share of the relevant market for the product. Market-share liability applies only if the injuring product is fungible, the true manufacturer is unidentifiable, and the unknown character of the manufacturer is not the plaintiff's fault.

Market-share test   The primary measure of monopoly power. A firm's market share is the percentage of a market that the firm controls.

Marshalling assets   The arrangement or ranking of assets in a certain order toward the payment of debts. In equity, when two creditors have recourse to the same property of the debtor, but one has recourse to other property of the debtor, that creditor must resort first to those assets of the debtor that are not available to the other creditor.

Mass-market license   An e-contract that is presented with a package of computer information in the form of a *click-on license* or a *shrink-wrap license*.

Material alteration   *See* Alteration

Material fact   A fact to which a reasonable person would attach importance in determining his or her course of action. In regard to tender offers, for example, a fact is material if there is a substantial likelihood that a reasonable shareholder would consider it important in deciding how to vote.

Mechanic's lien   A statutory lien on the real property of another, created to ensure payment for work performed and materials furnished in the repair or improvement of real property, such as a building.

Mediation   A method of settling disputes outside of court by using the services of a neutral third party, called a mediator. The mediator acts as a communicating agent between the parties and suggests ways in which the parties can resolve their dispute.

Member   The term used to designate a person who has an ownership interest in a limited liability company.

Mens rea (pronounced *mehns ray*-uh)   Mental state, or intent. A wrongful mental state is as necessary as a wrongful act to establish criminal liability. What constitutes a mental state varies according to the wrongful action. Thus, for murder, the *mens rea* is the intent to take a life; for theft, the *mens rea* must involve both the knowledge that the property belongs to another and the intent to deprive the owner of it.

Merchant   A person who is engaged in the purchase and sale of goods. Under the Uniform Commercial Code, a person who deals in goods of the kind involved in the sales contract; for further definitions, see UCC 2–104.

Merger   A contractual and statutory process in which one corporation (the surviving corporation) acquires all of the assets and liabilities of another corporation (the merged corporation). The shareholders of the merged corporation receive either payment for their shares or shares in the surviving corporation.

Meta tags   Words inserted into a Web site's key-words field to increase the site's appearance in search engine results.

Minimum-contacts requirement   The requirement that before a state court can exercise jurisdiction over a foreign corporation, the foreign corporation must have sufficient contacts with the state. A foreign corporation that has its home office in the state or that has manufacturing plants in the state meets this requirement.

Minimum wage   The lowest wage, either by government regulation or union contract, that an employer may pay an hourly worker.

Mini-trial   A private proceeding in which each party to a dispute argues its position before the other side and vice versa. A neutral third party may be present and act as an adviser if the parties fail to reach an agreement.

Mirror image rule   A common law rule that requires, for a valid contractual agreement, that the terms of the offeree's acceptance adhere exactly to the terms of the offeror's offer.

Misdemeanor   A lesser crime than a felony, punishable by a fine or imprisonment for up to one year in other than a state or federal penitentiary.

Mislaid property   Property with which the owner has voluntarily parted and then cannot find or recover.

Misrepresentation   A false statement of fact or an action that deceives and causes harm or injury to another. *See also* Fraudulent misrepresentation (fraud); Innocent misrepresentation

Mitigation of damages   A rule requiring a plaintiff to have done whatever was reasonable to minimize the damages caused by the defendant.

Money laundering   Falsely reporting income that has been obtained through criminal activity as income obtained through a legitimate business enterprise—in effect, "laundering" the "dirty money."

Monopolization   The possession of monopoly power in the relevant market and the willful acquisition or maintenance of that power, as distinguished from growth or development as a consequence of a superior product, business acumen, or historic accident.

Monopoly   A term generally used to describe a market in which there is a single seller or a limited number of sellers.

Monopoly power   The ability of a monopoly to dictate what takes place in a given market.

Moral minimum   The minimum degree of ethical behavior expected of a business firm, which is usually defined as compliance with the law.

Mortgage   A written instrument giving a creditor (the mortgagee) an interest in (a lien on) the debtor's (mortgagor's) property as security for a debt.

Mortgage bond   A bond that pledges specific property. If the corporation defaults on the bond, the bondholder can take the property.

Mortgagee   Under a mortgage agreement, the creditor who takes a security interest in the debtor's property.

Mortgagor   Under a mortgage agreement, the debtor who gives the creditor a security interest in the debtor's property in return for a mortgage loan.

Motion   A procedural request or application presented by an attorney to the court on behalf of a client.

Motion for a directed verdict   In a jury trial, a motion for the judge to take the decision out of the hands of the jury and direct a verdict for the moving party on the ground that the other party has not produced sufficient evidence to support his or her claim; referred to as a motion for judgment as a matter of law in the federal courts.

Motion for a new trial   A motion asserting that the trial was so fundamentally flawed (because of error, newly discovered evidence, prejudice, or other reason) that a new trial is necessary to prevent a miscarriage of justice.

Motion for judgment n.o.v.   A motion requesting the court to grant judgment in favor of the party making the motion on the ground that the jury verdict against him or her was unreasonable and erroneous.

Motion for judgment on the pleadings   A motion by either party to a lawsuit at the close of the pleadings requesting the court to decide the issue solely on the pleadings without proceeding to trial. The motion will be granted only if no facts are in dispute.

Motion for summary judgment   A motion requesting the court to enter a judgment without proceeding to trial. The motion can be based on evidence outside the pleadings and will be granted only if no facts are in dispute.

Motion to dismiss   A pleading in which a defendant asserts that the plaintiff's claim fails to state a cause of action (that is, has no basis in law) or that there are other grounds on which a suit should be dismissed.

Multiple product order   An order issued by the Federal Trade Commission to a firm that has engaged in deceptive advertising by which the firm is required to cease and desist from false advertising not only in regard to the product that was the subject of the action but also in regard to all the firm's other products.

Municipal court   A city or community court with criminal jurisdiction over traffic violations and, less frequently, with civil jurisdiction over other minor matters.

Mutual assent   The element of agreement in the formation of a contract. The manifestation of contract parties' mutual assent to the same bargain is required to establish a contract.

Mutual fund   A specific type of investment company that continually buys or sells to investors shares of ownership in a portfolio.

Mutual rescission   An agreement between the parties to cancel their contract, releasing the parties from further obligations under the contract. The object of the agreement is to restore the parties to the positions they would have occupied had no contract ever been formed. *See also* Rescission

N

National law   Law that pertains to a particular nation (as opposed to international law).

Natural law   The belief that government and the legal system should reflect universal moral and ethical principles that are inherent in human nature. The natural law school is the oldest and one of the most significant schools of legal thought.

Necessaries   Necessities required for life, such as food, shelter, clothing, and medical attention; may include whatever is believed to be necessary to maintain a person's standard of living or financial and social status.

Necessity   In criminal law, a defense against liability; under Section 3.02 of the Model Penal Code, this defense is justifiable if "the harm or evil sought to be avoided" by a given action "is greater than that sought to be prevented by the law defining the offense charged."

Negligence   The failure to exercise the standard of care that a reasonable person would exercise in similar circumstances.

Negligence *per se*   An act (or failure to act) in violation of a statutory requirement.

Negligent   misrepresentation   Any   manifestation through words or conduct that amounts to an untrue statement of fact made in circumstances in which a reasonable and prudent person would not have done (or failed to do) that which led to the misrepresentation. A representation made with an honest belief in its truth may still be negligent due to (1) a lack of reasonable care in ascertaining the facts, (2) the manner of expression, or (3) the absence of the skill or competence required by a particular business or profession.

Negotiable instrument   A signed writing that contains an unconditional promise or order to pay an exact sum of money, on demand or at an exact future time, to a specific person or order, or to bearer.

Negotiation   (1) In regard to dispute settlement, a process in which parties attempt to settle their dispute without going to court, with or without attorneys to represent them. (2) In regard to instruments, the transfer of an instrument in such a way that the transferee (the person to whom the instrument is transferred) becomes a holder.

Nominal damages   A small monetary award (often one dollar) granted to a plaintiff when no actual damage was suffered or when the plaintiff is unable to show such loss with sufficient certainty.

Nonconforming goods   Goods that do not conform to contract specifications.

No-par shares   Corporate shares that have no face value—that is, no specific dollar amount is printed on their face.

Normal trade relations (NTR) status   A status granted through an international treaty by which each member nation must treat other members at least as well as it treats the country that receives its most favorable treatment. This status was formerly known as most-favored-nation status.

Notary public   A public official authorized to attest to the authenticity of signatures.

Note   A written instrument signed by a maker unconditionally promising to pay a fixed amount of money to a payee or a holder on demand or on a specific date.

Notice-and-comment rulemaking   An administrative rulemaking procedure that involves the publication of a notice of a proposed rulemaking in the *Federal Register*, a comment period for interested parties to express their views on the proposed rule, and the publication of the agency's final rule in the *Federal Register*.

Notice of Proposed Rulemaking   A notice published (in the *Federal Register*) by an administrative agency describing a proposed rule. The notice must give the time and place for which agency proceedings on the proposed rule will be held, a description of the nature of the proceedings, the legal authority for the proceedings (which is usually the agency's enabling legislation), and the terms of the proposed rule or the subject matter of the proposed rule.

Novation   The substitution, by agreement, of a new contract for an old one, with the rights under the old one being terminated. Typically, there is a substitution of a new person who is responsible for the contract and the removal of an original party's rights and duties under the contract.

Nuisance   A common law doctrine under which persons may be held liable for using their property in a manner that unreasonably interferes with others' rights to use or enjoy their own property.

Nuncupative will   An oral will (often called a deathbed will) made before witnesses; usually limited to transfers of personal property.

O

Objective theory of contracts A theory under which the intent to form a contract will be judged by outward, objective facts (what the party said when entering into the contract, how the party acted or appeared, and the circumstances surrounding the transaction) as interpreted by a reasonable person, rather than by the party's own secret, subjective intentions.

Obligee One to whom an obligation is owed.

Obligor One that owes an obligation to another.

Offer A promise or commitment to perform or refrain from performing some specified act in the future.

Offeree A person to whom an offer is made.

Offeror A person who makes an offer.

Omnibus clause A provision in an automobile insurance policy that protects the vehicle owner who has taken out the insurance policy and anyone who drives the vehicle with the owner's permission.

Online Dispute Resolution (ODR) The resolution of disputes with the assistance of organizations that offer dispute-resolution services via the Internet.

Opening statement A statement made to the jury at the beginning of a trial by a party's attorney, prior to the presentation of evidence. The attorney briefly outlines the evidence that will be offered and the legal theory that will be pursued.

Operating agreement In a limited liability company, an agreement in which the members set forth the details of how the business will be managed and operated.

Operation of law A term expressing the manner in which certain rights or liabilities may be imposed on a person by the application of established rules of law to the particular transaction, without regard to the actions or cooperation of the party himself or herself.

Opinion A statement by the court expressing the reasons for its decision in a case.

Optimum profits The amount of profits that a business can make and still act ethically, as opposed to maximum profits, defined as the amount of profits a firm can make if it is willing to disregard ethical concerns.

Option contract A contract under which the offeror cannot revoke his or her offer for a stipulated time period and the offeree can accept or reject the offer during this period without fear that the offer will be made to another person. The offeree must give consideration for the option (the irrevocable offer) to be enforceable.

Order for relief A court's grant of assistance to a complainant. In bankruptcy proceedings, the order relieves the debtor of the immediate obligation to pay the debts listed in the bankruptcy petition.

Order instrument A negotiable instrument that is payable "to the order of an identified person" or "to an identified person or order."

Ordinance A law passed by a local governing unit, such as a municipality or a county.

Original jurisdiction Courts having original jurisdiction are courts of the first instance, or trial courts—that is, courts in which lawsuits begin, trials take place, and evidence is presented.

Output contract An agreement in which a seller agrees to sell and a buyer agrees to buy all or up to a stated amount of what the seller produces.

Overdraft A check written on a checking account in which there are insufficient funds to cover the amount of the check.

P

Parent-subsidiary merger A merger of companies in which one company (the parent corporation) owns most of the stock of the other (the subsidiary corporation). A parent-subsidiary merger (short-form merger) can use a simplified procedure when the parent corporation owns at least 90 percent of the outstanding shares of each class of stock of the subsidiary corporation.

Parol evidence A term that originally meant "oral evidence," but which has come to refer to any negotiations or agreements made prior to a contract or any contemporaneous oral agreements made by the parties.

Parol evidence rule A substantive rule of contracts under which a court will not receive into evidence the parties' prior negotiations, prior agreements, or contemporaneous oral agreements if that evidence contradicts or varies the terms of the parties' written contract.

Partially disclosed principal A principal whose identity is unknown by a third person, but the third person knows that the agent is or may be acting for a principal at the time the agent and the third person form a contract.

Partner A co-owner of a partnership.

Partnering agreement An agreement between a seller and a buyer who frequently do business with each other on the terms and conditions that will apply to all subsequently formed electronic contracts.

Partnership An agreement by two or more persons to carry on, as co-owners, a business for profit.

Partnership by estoppel A judicially created partnership that may, at the court's discretion, be imposed for purposes of fairness. The court can prevent those who present themselves as partners (but who are not) from escaping liability if a third person relies on an alleged partnership in good faith and is harmed as a result.

Par-value shares Corporate shares that have a specific face value, or formal cash-in value, written on them, such as one dollar.

Past consideration An act done before the contract is made, which ordinarily, by itself, cannot be consideration for a later promise to pay for the act.

Patent A government grant that gives an inventor the exclusive right or privilege to make, use, or sell his or her invention for a limited time period. The word *patent* usually refers to some invention and designates either the instrument by which patent rights are evidenced or the patent itself.

Payee A person to whom an instrument is made payable.

Payor bank The bank on which a check is drawn (the drawee bank).

Peer-to-peer (P2P) networking The sharing of resources (such as files, hard drives, and processing styles) among multiple computers without necessarily requiring a central network server.

Penalty A sum inserted into a contract, not as a measure of compensation for its breach but rather as punishment for a default. The agreement as to the amount will not be enforced, and recovery will be limited to actual damages.

Per capita A Latin term meaning "per person." In the law governing estate distribution, a method of distributing the property of an intestate's estate in which each heir in a certain class (such as grandchildren) receives an equal share.

Per curiam By the whole court; a court opinion written by the court as a whole instead of being authored by a judge or justice.

Per se A Latin term meaning "in itself" or "by itself."

Per se violation A type of anticompetitive agreement—such as a horizontal price-fixing agreement—that is considered to be so injurious to the public that there is no need to determine whether it actually injures market competition; rather, it is in itself (*per se*) a violation of the Sherman Act.

Per stirpes A Latin term meaning "by the roots." In the law governing estate distribution, a method of distributing an intestate's estate in which each heir in a certain class (such as grandchildren) takes the share to which his or her deceased ancestor (such as a mother or father) would have been entitled.

Perfect tender rule A common law rule under which a seller was required to deliver to the buyer goods that conformed perfectly to the requirements stipulated in the sales contract. A tender of nonconforming goods would automatically constitute a breach of contract. Under the Uniform Commercial Code, the rule has been greatly modified.

Perfection The legal process by which secured parties protect themselves against the claims of third parties who may wish to have their debts satisfied out of the same collateral; usually accomplished by the filing of a financing statement with the appropriate government official.

Performance In contract law, the fulfillment of one's duties arising under a contract with another; the normal way of discharging one's contractual obligations.

Periodic tenancy A lease interest in land for an indefinite period involving payment of rent at fixed intervals, such as week to week, month to month, or year to year.

Personal defense A defense that can be used to avoid payment to an ordinary holder of a negotiable instrument but not a holder in due course (HDC) or a holder with the rights of an HDC.

Personal identification number (PIN) A number given to the holder of an access card (debit card, credit card, ATM card, or the like) that is used to conduct financial transactions electronically. Typically, the card will not provide access to a system without the number, which is meant to be kept secret to inhibit unauthorized use of the card.

Personal jurisdiction *See In personam* jurisdiction

Personal property Property that is movable; any property that is not real property.

Personalty Personal property.

Petition in bankruptcy The document that is filed with a bankruptcy court to initiate bankruptcy proceedings. The official forms required for a petition in bankruptcy must be completed accurately, sworn to under oath, and signed by the debtor.

Petitioner In equity practice, a party that initiates a lawsuit.

Petty offense In criminal law, the least serious kind of criminal offense, such as a traffic or building-code violation.

Pierce the corporate veil To disregard the corporate entity, which limits the liability of shareholders, and hold the shareholders personally liable for a corporate obligation.

Plaintiff One who initiates a lawsuit.

Plea In criminal law, a defendant's allegation, in response to the charges brought against him or her, of guilt or innocence.

Plea bargaining The process by which a criminal defendant and the prosecutor in a criminal case work out a mutually satisfactory disposition of the case, subject to court approval; usually involves the defendant's pleading guilty to a lesser offense in return for a lighter sentence.

Pleadings Statements made by the plaintiff and the defendant in a lawsuit that detail the facts, charges, and defenses involved in the litigation; the complaint and answer are part of the pleadings.

Pledge A common law security device (retained in Article 9 of the Uniform Commercial Code) in which personal property is turned over to the creditor as security for the payment of a debt and retained by the creditor until the debt is paid.

Police powers Powers possessed by states as part of their inherent sovereignty. These powers may be exercised to protect or promote the public order, health, safety, morals, and general welfare.

Policy In insurance law, a contract between the insurer and the insured in which, for a stipulated consideration, the insurer agrees to compensate the insured for loss on a specific subject by a specified peril.

Positive law The body of conventional, or written, law of a particular society at a particular point in time.

Positivist school A school of legal thought whose adherents believe that there can be no higher law than a nation's positive law—the body of conventional, or written, law of a particular society at a particular time.

Possessory lien A lien that allows one person to retain possession of another's property as security for a debt or obligation owed by the owner of the property to the lienholder. An example of a possessory lien is an artisan's lien.

Potential competition doctrine A doctrine under which a conglomerate merger may be prohibited by law because it would be injurious to potential competition.

Potentially responsible party (PRP) A potentially liable party under the Comprehensive Environmental Response, Compensation and Liability Act (CERCLA). Any person who generated the hazardous waste, transported the hazardous waste, owned or operated a waste site at the time of disposal, or currently owns or operates a site may be responsible for some or all of the cleanup costs involved in removing the hazardous chemicals.

Power of attorney A written document, which is usually notarized, authorizing another to act as one's agent; can be special (permitting the agent to do specified acts only) or general (permitting the agent to transact all business for the principal).

Preauthorized transfer A transaction authorized in advance to recur at substantially regular intervals. The terms and procedures for preauthorized electronic fund transfers through certain financial institutions are subject to the Electronic Fund Transfer Act.

Precedent A court decision that furnishes an example or authority for deciding subsequent cases involving identical or similar facts.

Predatory pricing The pricing of a product below cost with the intent to drive competitors out of the market.

Preemption A doctrine under which certain federal laws preempt, or take precedence over, conflicting state or local laws.

Preemptive rights Rights held by shareholders that entitle them to purchase newly issued shares of a corporation's stock, equal in percentage to shares presently held, before the stock is offered to any outside buyers. Preemptive rights enable shareholders to maintain their proportionate ownership and voice in the corporation.

Preference In bankruptcy proceedings, property transfers or payments made by the debtor that favor (give preference to) one creditor over others. The bankruptcy trustee is allowed to recover payments made both voluntarily and involuntarily to one creditor in preference over another.

Preferred creditor In the context of bankruptcy, a creditor who has received a preferential transfer from a debtor.

Preferred stock Classes of stock that have priority over common stock both as to payment of dividends and distribution of assets on the corporation's dissolution.

Prejudgment interest Interest that accrues on the amount of a court judgment from the time of the filing of a lawsuit to the court's issuance of a judgment.

Preliminary hearing An initial hearing used in many felony cases to establish whether or not it is proper to detain the defendant. A magistrate reviews the evidence and decides if there is probable cause to believe that the defendant committed the crime with which he or she has been charged.

Premium In insurance law, the price paid by the insured for insurance protection for a specified period of time.

Prenuptial agreement An agreement made before marriage that defines each partner's ownership rights in the other partner's property. Prenuptial agreements must be in writing to be enforceable.

Preponderance of the evidence A standard in civil law cases under which the plaintiff must convince the court that, based on the evidence presented by both parties, it is more likely than not that the plaintiff's allegation is true.

Presentment The act of presenting an instrument to the party liable on the instrument to collect payment; presentment also occurs when a person presents an instrument to a drawee for acceptance.

Presentment warranties Any person who presents an instrument for payment or acceptance impliedly warrants that (1) he or she is entitled to enforce the instrument or authorized to obtain payment or acceptance on behalf of a person who is entitled, (2) the instrument has not been altered, and (3) he or she has no knowledge that the signature of the drawer is unauthorized.

Pretrial conference A conference, scheduled before the trial begins, between the judge and the attorneys litigating the suit. The parties may settle the dispute, clarify the issues, schedule discovery, and so on during the conference.

Pretrial motion A written or oral application to a court for a ruling or order, made before trial.

Price discrimination Setting prices in such a way that two competing buyers pay two different prices for an identical product or service.

Price-fixing agreement An agreement between competitors in which the competitors agree to fix the prices of products or services at a certain level; prohibited by the Sherman Act.

Prima facie **case** A case in which the plaintiff has produced sufficient evidence of his or her conclusion that the case can go to to a jury; a case in which the evidence compels the plaintiff's conclusion if the defendant produces no evidence to disprove it.

Primary liability In negotiable instruments law, absolute responsibility for paying a negotiable instrument. Makers and acceptors are primarily liable.

Principal In agency law, a person who agrees to have another, called the agent, act on his or her behalf.

Principle of rights The principle that human beings have certain fundamental rights (to life, freedom, and the pursuit of happiness, for example). Those who adhere to this "rights theory" believe that a key factor in determining whether a business decision is ethical is how that decision affects the rights of others. These others include the firm's owners, its employees, the consumers of its products or services, its suppliers, the community in which it does business, and society as a whole.

Privatization The replacement of government-provided products and services by private firms.

Privilege In tort law, the ability to act contrary to another person's right without that person's having legal redress for such acts. Privilege may be raised as a defense to defamation.

Privileges and immunities clause Special rights and exceptions provided by law. Article IV, Section 2, of the Constitution requires states not to discriminate against one another's citizens. A resident of one state cannot be treated as an alien when in another state; he or she may not be denied such privileges and immunities as legal protection, access to courts, travel rights, or property rights.

Privity of contract   The relationship that exists between the promisor and the promisee of a contract.

Pro rata   Proportionately; in proportion.

Probable cause   Reasonable grounds to believe the existence of facts warranting certain actions, such as the search or arrest of a person.

Probate   The process of proving and validating a will and the settling of all matters pertaining to administration, guardianship, and the like.

Probate court   A state court of limited jurisdiction that conducts proceedings relating to the settlement of a deceased person's estate.

Procedural due process   The requirement that any government decision to take life, liberty, or property must be made fairly. For example, fair procedures must be used in determining whether a person will be subjected to punishment or have some burden imposed on him or her.

Procedural law   Rules that define the manner in which the rights and duties of individuals may be enforced.

Procedural unconscionability   Occurs when, due to one contractual party's vastly superior bargaining power, the other party lacks a knowledge or understanding of the contract terms due to inconspicuous print or the lack of an opportunity to read the contract or to ask questions about its meaning. Procedural unconscionability often involves an *adhesion contract,* which is a contract drafted by the dominant party and then presented to the other— the adhering party—on a take-it-or-leave-it basis.

Proceeds   Under Article 9 of the Uniform Commercial Code, whatever is received when the collateral is sold or otherwise disposed of, such as by exchange.

Product liability   The legal liability of manufacturers, sellers, and lessors of goods to consumers, users, and bystanders for injuries or damages that are caused by the goods.

Product misuse   A defense against product liability that may be raised when the plaintiff used a product in a manner not intended by the manufacturer. If the misuse is reasonably foreseeable, the seller will not escape liability unless measures were taken to guard against the harm that could result from the misuse.

Professional corporation   A corporation formed by professional persons, such as physicians, lawyers, dentists, and accountants, to gain tax benefits. Subject to certain exceptions (when a court may treat a professional corporation as a partnership for liability purposes), the shareholders of a professional corporation have the limited liability characteristic of the corporate form of business.

Profit   In real property law, the right to enter onto and remove things from the property of another (for example, the right to enter onto a person's land and remove sand and gravel therefrom).

Promise   A person's assurance that he or she will or will not do something.

Promisee   A person to whom a promise is made.

Promisor   A person who makes a promise.

Promissory estoppel   A doctrine that applies when a promisor makes a clear and definite promise on which the promisee justifiably relies; such a promise is binding if justice will be better served by the enforcement of the promise. *See also* Estoppel

Promissory note   A written promise made by one person (the maker) to pay a fixed sum of money to another person (the payee or a subsequent holder) on demand or on a specified date.

Promoter   A person who takes the preliminary steps in organizing a corporation, including (usually) issuing a prospectus, procuring stock subscriptions, making contract purchases, securing a corporate charter, and the like.

Property   Legally protected rights and interests in anything with an ascertainable value that is subject to ownership.

Prospectus   A document required by federal or state securities laws that describes the financial operations of the corporation, thus allowing investors to make informed decisions.

Protected class   A class of persons with identifiable characteristics who historically have been victimized by discriminatory treatment for certain purposes. Depending on the context, these characteristics include age, color, gender, national origin, race, and religion.

Proximate cause   Legal cause; exists when the connection between an act and an injury is strong enough to justify imposing liability.

Proxy   In corporation law, a written agreement between a stockholder and another under which the stockholder authorizes the other to vote the stockholder's shares in a certain manner.

Proxy fight   A conflict between an individual, group, or firm attempting to take control of a corporation and the corporation's management for the votes of the shareholders.

Public figures   Individuals who are thrust into the public limelight. Public figures include government officials and politicians, movie stars, well-known businesspersons, and generally anybody who becomes known to the public because of his or her position or activities.

Public policy   A government policy based on widely held societal values and (usually) expressed or implied in laws or regulations.

Public prosecutor   An individual, acting as a trial lawyer, who initiates and conducts criminal cases in the government's name and on behalf of the people.

Puffery   A salesperson's exaggerated claims concerning the quality of property offered for sale. Such claims involve opinions rather than facts and are not considered to be legally binding promises or warranties.

Punitive damages   Money damages that may be awarded to a plaintiff to punish the defendant and deter future similar conduct.

Purchase-money security interest (PMSI)   A security interest that arises when a seller or lender extends credit for part or all of the purchase price of goods purchased by a buyer.

Q

Qualified indorsement   An indorsement on a negotiable instrument in which the indorser disclaims any contract liability on the instrument; the notation "without recourse" is commonly used to create a qualified indorsement.

Quantum meruit (pronounced *kwahn*-tuhm *mehr*-oo-wuht)   Literally, "as much as he deserves"—an expression describing the extent of liability on a contract implied in law (quasi contract). An equitable doctrine based on the concept that one who benefits from another's labor and materials should not be unjustly enriched thereby but should be required to pay a reasonable amount for the benefits received, even absent a contract.

Quasi contract   A fictional contract imposed on parties by a court in the interests of fairness and justice; usually, quasi contracts are imposed to avoid the unjust enrichment of one party at the expense of another.

Question of fact   In a lawsuit, an issue involving a factual dispute that can only be decided by a judge (or, in a jury trial, a jury).

Question of law   In a lawsuit, an issue involving the application or interpretation of a law; therefore, the judge, and not the jury, decides the issue.

Quiet enjoyment   *See* Covenant of quiet enjoyment

Quitclaim deed   A deed intended to pass any title, interest, or claim that the grantor may have in the property but not warranting that such title is valid. A quitclaim deed offers the least amount of protection against defects in the title.

Quorum   The number of members of a decision-making body that must be present before business may be transacted.

Quota   An assigned import limit on goods.

R

Ratification   The act of accepting and giving legal force to an obligation that previously was not enforceable.

Reaffirmation agreement   An agreement between a debtor and a creditor in which the debtor reaffirms, or promises to pay, a debt dischargeable in bankruptcy. To be enforceable, the agreement must be made prior to the discharge of the debt by the bankruptcy court.

Real defense   *See* Universal defense

Real property   Land and everything attached to it, such as foliage and buildings.

Reasonable care   The degree of care that a person of ordinary prudence would exercise in the same or similar circumstances.

Reasonable doubt   *See* Beyond a reasonable doubt

Reasonable person standard   The standard of behavior expected of a hypothetical "reasonable person." The standard against which negligence is measured and that must be observed to avoid liability for negligence.

Rebuttal   The refutation of evidence introduced by an adverse party's attorney.

Receiver   In a corporate dissolution, a court-appointed person who winds up corporate affairs and liquidates corporate assets.

Record   According to the Uniform Electronic Transactions Act, information that is either inscribed on a tangible medium or stored in an electronic or other medium and that is retrievable. The Uniform Computer Information Transactions Act uses the term *record* instead of *writing*.

Recording statutes   Statutes that allow deeds, mortgages, and other real property transactions to be recorded so as to provide notice to future purchasers or creditors of an existing claim on the property.

Red herring   A preliminary prospectus that can be distributed to potential investors after the registration statement (for a securities offering) has been filed with the Securities and Exchange Commission. The name derives from the red legend printed across the prospectus stating that the registration has been filed but has not become effective.

Redemption   A repurchase, or buying back. In secured transactions law, a debtor's repurchase of collateral securing a debt after a creditor has taken title to the collateral due to the debtor's default but before the secured party disposes of the collateral.

Reformation   A court-ordered correction of a written contract so that it reflects the true intentions of the parties.

Regulation E   A set of rules issued by the Federal Reserve System's Board of Governors under the authority of the Electronic Fund Transfer Act to protect users of electronic fund transfer systems.

Regulation Z   A set of rules promulgated by the Federal Reserve Board to implement the provisions of the Truth-in-Lending Act.

Reimbursement   *See* Right of reimbursement

Rejection   In contract law, an offeree's express or implied manifestation not to accept an offer. In the law governing contracts for the sale of goods, a buyer's manifest refusal to accept goods on the ground that they do not conform to contract specifications.

Rejoinder   The defendant's answer to the plaintiff's rebuttal.

Release   A contract in which one party forfeits the right to pursue a legal claim against the other party.

Relevant evidence   Evidence tending to make a fact at issue in the case more or less probable than it would be without the evidence. Only relevant evidence is admissible in court.

Remainder   A future interest in property held by a person other than the original owner.

Remanded   Sent back. If an appellate court disagrees with a lower court's judgment, the case may be remanded to the lower court for further proceedings in which the lower court's decision should be consistent with the appellate court's opinion on the matter.

Remedy   The relief given to an innocent party to enforce a right or compensate for the violation of a right.

Remedy at law A remedy available in a court of law. Money damages are awarded as a remedy at law.

Remedy in equity A remedy allowed by courts in situations where remedies at law are not appropriate. Remedies in equity are based on settled rules of fairness, justice, and honesty, and include injunction, specific performance, rescission and restitution, and reformation.

Remitter A person who sends money, or remits payment.

Rent The consideration paid for the use or enjoyment of another's property. In landlord-tenant relationships, the payment made by the tenant to the landlord for the right to possess the premises.

Rent escalation clause A clause providing for an increase in rent during a lease term.

Repair-and-deduct statutes Statutes providing that a tenant may pay for repairs and deduct the cost of the repairs from the rent, as a remedy for a landlord's failure to maintain leased premises.

Replevin (pronounced ruh-*pleh*-vin) An action to recover specific goods in the hands of a party who is wrongfully withholding them from the other party.

Reply Procedurally, a plaintiff's response to a defendant's answer.

Reporter A publication in which court cases are published, or reported.

Repudiation The renunciation of a right or duty; the act of a buyer or seller in rejecting a contract either partially or totally. *See also* Anticipatory repudiation

Requirements contract An agreement in which a buyer agrees to purchase and the seller agrees to sell all or up to a stated amount of what the buyer needs or requires.

Res ipsa loquitur (pronounced *rehs ehp*-suh *low*-quuh-duhr) A doctrine under which negligence may be inferred simply because an event occurred, if it is the type of event that would not occur in the absence of negligence. Literally, the term means "the facts speak for themselves."

Resale price maintenance agreement An agreement between a manufacturer and a retailer in which the manufacturer specifies the minimum retail price of its products. Resale price maintenance agreements are illegal *per se* under the Sherman Act.

Rescind (pronounced reh-*sihnd*) To cancel. *See also* Rescission

Rescission (pronounced reh-*sih*-zhen) A remedy whereby a contract is canceled and the parties are returned to the positions they occupied before the contract was made; may be effected through the mutual consent of the parties, by their conduct, or by court decree.

Residuary The surplus of a testator's estate remaining after all of the debts and particular legacies have been discharged.

Respondeat superior (pronounced ree-*spahn*-dee-uht soo-*peer*-ee-your) In Latin, "Let the master respond." A doctrine under which a principal or an employer is held liable for the wrongful acts committed by agents or employees while acting within the course and scope of their agency or employment.

Respondent In equity practice, the party who answers a bill or other proceeding.

Restitution An equitable remedy under which a person is restored to his or her original position prior to loss or injury, or placed in the position he or she would have been in had the breach not occurred.

Restraint on trade Any contract or combination that tends to eliminate or reduce competition, effect a monopoly, artificially maintain prices, or otherwise hamper the course of trade and commerce as it would be carried on if left to the control of natural economic forces.

Restrictive covenant A private restriction on the use of land that is binding on the party that purchases the property originally as well as on subsequent purchasers. If its benefit or obligation passes with the land's ownership, it is said to "run with the land."

Restrictive indorsement Any indorsement on a negotiable instrument that requires the indorsee to comply with certain instructions regarding the funds involved. A restrictive indorsement does not prohibit the further negotiation of the instrument.

Resulting trust An implied trust arising from the conduct of the parties. A trust in which a party holds the actual legal title to another's property but only for that person's benefit.

Retained earnings The portion of a corporation's profits that has not been paid out as dividends to shareholders.

Retainer An advance payment made by a client to a law firm to cover part of the legal fees and/or costs that will need to be incurred on that client's behalf.

Retaliatory eviction The eviction of a tenant because of the tenant's complaints, participation in a tenant's union, or similar activity with which the landlord does not agree.

Reverse To reject or overrule a court's judgment. An appellate court, for example, might reverse a lower court's judgment on an issue if it feels that the lower court committed an error during the trial or that the jury was improperly instructed.

Reverse discrimination Discrimination against majority groups, such as white males, that results from affirmative action programs, in which preferences are given to minority members and women.

Reversible error An error by a lower court that is sufficiently substantial to justify an appellate court's reversal of the lower court's decision.

Reversionary interest A future interest in property retained by the original owner.

Revocation In contract law, the withdrawal of an offer by an offeror. Unless an offer is irrevocable, it can be revoked at any time prior to acceptance without liability.

Right of contribution The right of a co-surety who pays more than his or her proportionate share on a debtor's default to recover the excess paid from other co-sureties.

Right of entry The right to peaceably take or resume possession of real property.

Right of first refusal The right to purchase personal or real property—such as corporate shares or real estate—before the property is offered for sale to others.

Right of redemption *See* Equity of redemption; Redemption

Right of reimbursement The legal right of a person to be restored, repaid, or indemnified for costs, expenses, or losses incurred or expended on behalf of another.

Right of subrogation The right of a person to stand in the place of (be substituted for) another, giving the substituted party the same legal rights that the original party had.

Right-to-work law A state law providing that employees are not to be required to join a union as a condition of obtaining or retaining employment.

Risk A prediction concerning potential loss based on known and unknown factors.

Risk management Planning that is undertaken to protect one's interest should some event threaten to undermine its security. In the context of insurance, risk management involves transferring certain risks from the insured to the insurance company.

Robbery The act of forcefully and unlawfully taking personal property of any value from another; force or intimidation is usually necessary for an act of theft to be considered a robbery.

Rule of four A rule of the United States Supreme Court under which the Court will not issue a writ of *certiorari* unless at least four justices approve of the decision to issue the writ.

Rule of reason A test by which a court balances the positive effects (such as economic efficiency) of an agreement against its potentially anticompetitive effects. In antitrust litigation, many practices are analyzed under the rule of reason.

Rule 10b-5 *See* SEC Rule 10b-5

Rulemaking The process undertaken by an administrative agency when formally adopting a new regulation or amending an old one. Rulemaking involves notifying the public of a proposed rule or change and receiving and considering the public's comments.

Rules of evidence Rules governing the admissibility of evidence in trial courts.

S

S corporation A close business corporation that has met certain requirements as set out by the Internal Revenue Code and thus qualifies for special income tax treatment. Essentially, an S corporation is taxed the same as a partnership, but its owners enjoy the privilege of limited liability.

Sale The passing of title (evidence of ownership rights) from the seller to the buyer for a price.

Sale on approval A type of conditional sale in which the buyer may take the goods on a trial basis. The sale becomes absolute only when the buyer approves of (or is satisfied with) the goods being sold.

Sale or return A type of conditional sale in which title and possession pass from the seller to the buyer; however, the buyer retains the option to return the goods during a specified period even though the goods conform to the contract.

Sales contract A contract for the sale of goods under which the ownership of goods is transferred from a seller to a buyer for a price.

Satisfaction *See* Accord and satisfaction

Scienter (pronounced *sy-en-*ter) Knowledge by the misrepresenting party that material facts have been falsely represented or omitted with an intent to deceive.

Search warrant An order granted by a public authority, such as a judge, that authorizes law enforcement personnel to search particular premises or property.

Seasonably Within a specified time period, or, if no period is specified, within a reasonable time.

SEC Rule 10b-5 A rule of the Securities and Exchange Commission that makes it unlawful, in connection with the purchase or sale of any security, to make any untrue statement of a material fact or to omit a material fact if such omission causes the statement to be misleading.

Secondary boycott A union's refusal to work for, purchase from, or handle the products of a secondary employer, with whom the union has no dispute, for the purpose of forcing that employer to stop doing business with the primary employer, with whom the union has a labor dispute.

Secondary liability In negotiable instruments law, the contingent liability of drawers and indorsers. A secondarily liable party becomes liable on an instrument only if the party that is primarily liable on the instrument dishonors it or, in regard to drafts and checks, the drawee fails to pay or to accept the instrument, whichever is required.

Secured party A lender, seller, or any other person in whose favor there is a security interest, including a person to whom accounts or chattel paper has been sold.

Secured transaction Any transaction in which the payment of a debt is guaranteed, or secured, by personal property owned by the debtor or in which the debtor has a legal interest.

Securities Generally, corporate stocks and bonds. A security may also be a note, debenture, stock warrant, or any document given as evidence of an ownership interest in a corporation or as a promise of repayment by a corporation.

Security agreement An agreement that creates or provides for a security interest between the debtor and a secured party.

Security interest Any interest "in personal property or fixtures which secures payment or performance of an obligation" [UCC 1–201(37)].

Self-defense The legally recognized privilege to protect one's self or property against injury by another. The privilege of self-defense protects only acts that are reasonably necessary to protect one's self or property.

Seniority system In regard to employment relationships, a system in which those who have worked longest for the company are first in line for promotions, salary increases, and other benefits; they are also the last to be laid off if the workforce must be reduced.

Service mark A mark used in the sale or the advertising of services, such as to distinguish the services of one person from the services of others. Titles, character names, and other distinctive features of radio and television programs may be registered as service marks.

Service of process The delivery of the complaint and summons to a defendant.

Settlor One creating a trust.

Severance pay A payment by an employer to an employee that exceeds the employee's wages due on termination.

Sexual harassment In the employment context, the granting of job promotions or other benefits in return for sexual favors or language or conduct that is so sexually offensive that it creates a hostile working environment.

Sham transaction A false transaction without substance that is undertaken with the intent to defraud a creditor or the government. An example of a sham transaction is the sale of assets to a friend or relative for the purpose of concealing assets from creditors or a bankruptcy court.

Share A unit of stock. *See also* Stock

Shareholder One who purchases shares of a corporation's stock, thus acquiring an equity interest in the corporation.

Shareholder's derivative suit A suit brought by a shareholder to enforce a corporate cause of action against a third person.

Sharia Civil law principles of some Middle Eastern countries that are based on the Islamic directives that follow the teachings of the prophet Muhammad.

Shelter principle The principle that the holder of a negotiable instrument who cannot qualify as a holder in due course (HDC), but who derives his or her title through an HDC, acquires the rights of an HDC.

Sheriff's deed The deed given to the purchaser of property at a sheriff's sale as part of the foreclosure process against the owner of the property.

Shipment contract A contract in which the seller is required to ship the goods by carrier. The buyer assumes liability for any losses or damage to the goods after they are delivered to the carrier. Generally, all contracts are assumed to be shipment contracts if nothing to the contrary is stated in the contract.

Short-form merger A merger between a subsidiary corporation and a parent corporation that owns at least 90 percent of the outstanding shares of each class of stock issued by the subsidiary corporation. Short-form mergers can be accomplished without the approval of the shareholders of either corporation.

Short-swing profits Profits made by officers, directors, and certain large stockholders resulting from the use of nonpublic (inside) information about their companies; prohibited by Section 12 of the 1934 Securities Exchange Act.

Shrink-wrap agreement An agreement whose terms are expressed in a document located inside a box in which goods (usually software) are packaged; sometimes called a *shrink-wrap license*.

Sight draft In negotiable instruments law, a draft payable on sight—that is, when it is presented for payment.

Signature Under the Uniform Commercial Code, "any symbol executed or adopted by a party with a present intention to authenticate a writing."

Slander Defamation in oral form.

Slander of quality (trade libel) The publication of false information about another's product, alleging that it is not what its seller claims.

Slander of title The publication of a statement that denies or casts doubt on another's legal ownership of any property, causing financial loss to that property's owner.

Small claims courts Special courts in which parties may litigate small claims (usually, claims involving $2,500 or less). Attorneys are not required in small claims courts, and in many states attorneys are not allowed to represent the parties.

Smart card Prepaid funds recorded on a microprocessor chip embedded on a card. One type of *e-money*.

Sociological school A school of legal thought that views the law as a tool for promoting justice in society.

Sole proprietorship The simplest form of business, in which the owner is the business; the owner reports business income on his or her personal income tax return and is legally responsible for all debts and obligations incurred by the business.

Sovereign immunity A doctrine that immunizes foreign nations from the jurisdiction of U.S. courts when certain conditions are satisfied.

Spam Bulk, unsolicited ("junk") e-mail.

Special indorsement An indorsement on an instrument that indicates the specific person to whom the indorser intends to make the instrument payable; that is, it names the indorsee.

Special warranty deed A deed in which the grantor only covenants to warrant and defend the title against claims and demands of the grantor and all persons claiming by, through, and under the grantor.

Specific performance An equitable remedy requiring the breaching party to perform as promised under the contract; usually granted only when money damages would be an inadequate remedy and the subject matter of the contract is unique (for example, real property).

Spendthrift trust A trust created to prevent the beneficiary from spending all the money to which he or she is entitled. Only a certain portion of the total amount is given to the beneficiary at any one time, and most states prohibit creditors from attaching assets of the trust.

Spot zoning Granting a zoning classification to a parcel of land that is different from the classification given to other land in the immediate area.

Stale check A check, other than a certified check, that is presented for payment more than six months after its date.

Standing to sue The requirement that an individual must have a sufficient stake in a controversy before he or she can bring a lawsuit. The plaintiff must demonstrate that he or she either has been injured or threatened with injury.

Stare decisis (pronounced *ster*-ay dih-*si*-ses) A common law doctrine under which judges are obligated to follow the precedents established in prior decisions.

Statute of Frauds A state statute under which certain types of contracts must be in writing to be enforceable.

Statute of limitations A federal or state statute setting the maximum time period during which a certain action can be brought or certain rights enforced.

Statute of repose Basically, a statute of limitations that is not dependent on the happening of a cause of action. Statutes of repose generally begin to run at an earlier date and run for a longer period of time than statutes of limitations.

Statutory law The body of law enacted by legislative bodies (as opposed to constitutional law, administrative law, or case law).

Statutory lien A lien created by statute.

Statutory period of redemption A time period (usually set by state statute) during which the property subject to a defaulted mortgage, land contract, or other contract can be redeemed by the debtor after foreclosure or judicial sale.

Stock An equity (ownership) interest in a corporation, measured in units of shares.

Stock certificate A certificate issued by a corporation evidencing the ownership of a specified number of shares in the corporation.

Stock option *See* Stock warrant

Stock warrant A certificate that grants the owner the option to buy a given number of shares of stock, usually within a set time period.

Stockholder *See* Shareholder

Stop-payment order An order by a bank customer to his or her bank not to pay or certify a certain check.

Strict liability Liability regardless of fault. In tort law, strict liability may be imposed on defendants in cases involving abnormally dangerous activities, dangerous animals, or defective products.

Strike An extreme action undertaken by unionized workers when collective bargaining fails; the workers leave their jobs, refuse to work, and (typically) picket the employer's workplace.

Subject-matter jurisdiction Jurisdiction over the subject matter of a lawsuit.

Sublease A lease executed by the lessee of real estate to a third person, conveying the same interest that the lessee enjoys but for a shorter term than that held by the lessee.

Subpoena A document commanding a person to appear at a certain time and place or give testimony concerning a certain matter.

Subrogation *See* Right of subrogation

Subscriber An investor who agrees, in a subscription agreement, to purchase capital stock in a corporation.

Substantial evidence test The test applied by a court reviewing an administrative agency's informal action. The court determines whether the agency acted unreasonably and overturns the agency's findings only if unsupported by a substantial body of evidence.

Substantial performance Performance that does not vary greatly from the performance promised in a contract; the performance must create substantially the same benefits as those promised in the contract.

Substantive due process A requirement that focuses on the content, or substance, of legislation. If a law or other governmental action limits a fundamental right, such as the right to travel or to vote, it will be held to violate substantive due process unless it promotes a compelling or overriding state interest.

Substantive law Law that defines the rights and duties of individuals with respect to each other, as opposed to procedural law, which defines the manner in which these rights and duties may be enforced.

Substantive unconscionability Results from contracts, or portions of contracts, that are oppressive or overly harsh. Courts generally focus on provisions that deprive one party of the benefits of the agreement or leave that party without remedy for nonperformance by the other. An example of substantive unconscionability is the agreement by a welfare recipient with a fourth-grade education to purchase a refrigerator for $2,000 under an installment contract.

Suit *See* Lawsuit; Litigation

Summary judgment *See* Motion for summary judgment

Summary jury trial (SJT) A method of settling disputes in which a trial is held, but the jury's verdict is not binding. The verdict acts only as a guide to both sides in reaching an agreement during the mandatory negotiations that immediately follow the summary jury trial.

Summons A document informing a defendant that a legal action has been commenced against him or her and that the defendant must appear in court on a certain date to answer the plaintiff's complaint. The document is delivered by a sheriff or any other person so authorized.

Superseding cause An intervening force or event that breaks the connection between a wrongful act and an injury to another; in negligence law, a defense to liability.

Supremacy clause The provision in Article VI of the Constitution that provides that the Constitution, laws, and treaties of the United States are "the supreme Law of the Land." Under this clause, state and local laws that directly conflict with federal law will be rendered invalid.

Surety A person, such as a cosigner on a note, who agrees to be primarily responsible for the debt of another.

Suretyship An express contract in which a third party to a debtor-creditor relationship (the surety) promises to be primarily responsible for the debtor's obligation.

Surviving corporation The remaining, or continuing, corporation following a merger. The surviving corporation is vested with the merged corporation's legal rights and obligations.

Syllogism A form of deductive reasoning consisting of a major premise, a minor premise, and a conclusion.

Symbolic speech Nonverbal conduct that expresses opinions or thoughts about a subject. Symbolic speech is protected under the First Amendment's guarantee of freedom of speech.

Syndicate An investment group of persons or firms brought together for the purpose of financing a project that they would not or could not undertake independently.

T

Tag In the context of the World Wide Web, a code in an HTML document. *See* Meta tags.

Takeover The acquisition of control over a corporation through the purchase of a substantial number of the voting shares of the corporation.

Taking The taking of private property by the government for public use. Under the Fifth Amendment to the Constitution, the government may not take private property for public use without "just compensation."

Tangible employment action A significant change in employment status, such as firing or failing to promote an employee, reassigning the employee to a position with significantly different responsibilities, or effecting a significant change in employment benefits.

Tangible property Property that has physical existence and can be distinguished by the senses of touch, sight, and so on. A car is tangible property; a patent right is intangible property.

Target corporation The corporation to be acquired in a corporate takeover; a corporation to whose shareholders a tender offer is submitted.

Tariff A tax on imported goods.

Technology licensing Allowing another to use and profit from intellectual property (patents, copyrights, trademarks, innovative products or processes, and so on) for consideration. In the context of international business transactions, technology licensing is sometimes an attractive alternative to the establishment of foreign production facilities.

Teller's check A negotiable instrument drawn by a bank on another bank or drawn by a bank and payable at or payable through a bank.

Tenancy at sufferance A type of tenancy under which one who, after rightfully being in possession of leased premises, continues (wrongfully) to occupy the property after the lease has been terminated. The tenant has no rights to possess the property and occupies it only because the person entitled to evict the tenant has not done so.

Tenancy at will A type of tenancy under which either party can terminate the tenancy without notice; usually arises when a tenant who has been under a tenancy for years retains possession, with the landlord's consent, after the tenancy for years has terminated.

Tenancy by the entirety The joint ownership of property by a husband and wife. Neither party can transfer his or her interest in the property without the consent of the other.

Tenancy for years A type of tenancy under which property is leased for a specified period of time, such as a month, a year, or a period of years.

Tenancy in common Co-ownership of property in which each party owns an undivided interest that passes to his or her heirs at death.

Tenancy in partnership Co-ownership of partnership property.

Tenant One who has the temporary use and occupation of real property owned by another person, called the landlord; the duration and terms of the tenancy are usually established by a lease.

Tender An unconditional offer to perform an obligation by a person who is ready, willing, and able to do so.

Tender of delivery Under the Uniform Commercial Code, a seller's or lessor's act of placing conforming goods at the disposal of the buyer or lessee and giving the buyer or lessee whatever notification is reasonably necessary to enable the buyer or lessee to take delivery.

Tender offer An offer to purchase made by one company directly to the shareholders of another (target) company; often referred to as a "takeover bid."

Term insurance A type of life insurance policy for which premiums are paid for a specified term. Payment on the policy is due only if death occurs within the term period. Premiums are less expensive than for whole life or limited-payment life, and there is usually no cash surrender value.

Testamentary trust A trust that is created by will and therefore does not take effect until the death of the testator.

Testate The condition of having died with a valid will.

Testator One who makes and executes a will.

Third party beneficiary One for whose benefit a promise is made in a contract but who is not a party to the contract.

Time draft A draft that is payable at a definite future time.

Tippee A person who receives inside information.

Title insurance Insurance commonly purchased by a purchaser of real property to protect against loss in the event that the title to the property is not free from liens or superior ownership claims.

Tombstone ad An advertisement, historically in a format resembling a tombstone, of a securities offering. The ad informs potential investors of where and how they may obtain a prospectus.

Tort A civil wrong not arising from a breach of contract. A breach of a legal duty that proximately causes harm or injury to another.

Tortfeasor One who commits a tort.

Totten trust A trust created by the deposit of a person's own money in his or her name as a trustee for another. It is a tentative trust, revocable at will until the depositor dies or completes the gift in his or her lifetime by some unequivocal act or declaration.

Toxic tort Failure to use or to clean up properly toxic chemicals that cause harm to a person or society.

Trade acceptance A draft that is drawn by a seller of goods ordering the buyer to pay a specified sum of money to the seller, usually at a stated time in the future. The buyer accepts the draft by signing the face of the draft, thus creating an enforceable obligation to pay the draft when it comes due. On a trade acceptance, the seller is both the drawer and the payee.

Trade dress The image and overall appearance of a product—for example, the distinctive decor, menu, layout, and style of service of a particular restaurant. Basically, trade dress is subject to the same protection as trademarks.

Trade fixture The personal property of a commercial tenant that has been installed or affixed to real property for a business purpose. When the lease ends, the tenant can remove the fixture but must repair any damage to the real property caused by the fixture's removal.

Trade libel The publication of false information about another's product, alleging it is not what its seller claims; also referred to as slander of quality.

Trade name A term that is used to indicate part or all of a business's name and that is directly related to the business's reputation and goodwill. Trade names are protected under the common law (and under trademark law, if the name is the same as the firm's trademarked property).

Trade secret Information or a process that gives a business an advantage over competitors who do not know the information or process.

Trademark A distinctive mark, motto, device, or implement that a manufacturer stamps, prints, or otherwise affixes to the goods it produces so that they may be identified on the market and their origins made known. Once a trademark is established (under the common law or through registration), the owner is entitled to its exclusive use.

Transfer warranties Implied warranties, made by any person who transfers an instrument for consideration to subsequent transferees and holders who take the instrument in good faith, that (1) the transferor is entitled to enforce the instrument, (2) all signatures are authentic and authorized, (3) the instrument has not been altered, (4) the instrument is not subject to a defense or claim of any party that can be asserted against the transferor, and (5) the transferor has no knowledge of any insolvency proceedings against the maker, the acceptor, or the drawer of the instrument.

Transferee In negotiable instruments law, one to whom a negotiable instrument is transferred (delivered).

Transferor In negotiable instruments law, one who transfers (delivers) a negotiable instrument to another.

Traveler's check A check that is payable on demand, drawn on or payable through a bank, and designated as a traveler's check.

Treasure trove Money or coin, gold, silver, or bullion found hidden in the earth or other private place, the owner of which is unknown; literally, treasure found.

Treasury shares Corporate shares that are authorized by the corporation but that have not been issued.

Treaty An agreement formed between two or more independent nations.

Treble damages Damages consisting of single damages determined by a jury and tripled in amount in certain cases as required by statute.

Trespass to land The entry onto, above, or below the surface of land owned by another without the owner's permission or legal authorization.

Trespass to personal property The unlawful taking or harming of another's personal property; interference with another's right to the exclusive possession of his or her personal property.

Trespasser One who commits the tort of trespass in one of its forms.

Trial court A court in which trials are held and testimony taken.

Trust An arrangement in which title to property is held by one person (a trustee) for the benefit of another (a beneficiary).

Trust indorsement An indorsement for the benefit of the indorser or a third person; also known as an agency indorsement. The indorsement results in legal title vesting in the original indorsee.

Trustee One who holds title to property for the use or benefit of another (the beneficiary).

Tying arrangement An agreement between a buyer and a seller in which the buyer of a specific product or service becomes obligated to purchase additional products or services from the seller.

U

U.S. trustee A government official who performs certain administrative tasks that a bankruptcy judge would otherwise have to perform.

Ultra vires (pronounced *uhl*-trah *vye*-reez) A Latin term meaning "beyond the powers"; in corporate law, acts of a corporation that are beyond its express and implied powers to undertake.

Unanimous opinion A court opinion in which all of the judges or justices of the court agree to the court's decision.

Unconscionable (pronounced un-*kon*-shun-uh-bul) **contract or clause** A contract or clause that is void on the basis of public policy because one party, as a result of his or her disproportionate bargaining power, is forced to accept terms that are unfairly burdensome and that unfairly benefit the dominating party. *See also* Procedural unconscionability; Substantive unconscionability

Underwriter In insurance law, the insurer, or the one assuming a risk in return for the payment of a premium.

Undisclosed principal A principal whose identity is unknown by a third person, and the third person has no knowledge that the agent is acting for a principal at the time the agent and the third person form a contract.

Unenforceable contract A valid contract rendered unenforceable by some statute or law.

Uniform law A model law created by the National Conference of Commissioners on Uniform State Laws and/or the American Law Institute for the states to consider adopting. If the state adopts the law, it becomes statutory law in that state. Each state has the option of adopting or rejecting all or part of a uniform law.

Unilateral contract A contract that results when an offer can only be accepted by the offeree's performance.

Union shop A place of employment in which all workers, once employed, must become union members within a specified period of time as a condition of their continued employment.

Unitary system A centralized governmental system in which local or subdivisional governments exercise only those powers given to them by the central government.

Universal defense A defense that is valid against all holders of a negotiable instrument, including holders in due course (HDCs) and holders with the rights of HDCs. Universal defenses are also called real defenses.

Universal life A type of insurance that combines some aspects of term insurance with some aspects of whole life insurance.

Unlawful detainer The unjustifiable retention of the possession of real property by one whose right to possession has terminated—as when a tenant holds over after the end of the lease term in spite of the landlord's demand for possession.

Unliquidated debt A debt that is uncertain in amount.

Unreasonably dangerous product In product liability, a product that is defective to the point of threatening a consumer's health and safety. A product will be considered unreasonably dangerous if it is dangerous beyond the expectation of the ordinary consumer or if a less dangerous alternative was economically feasible for the manufacturer, but the manufacturer failed to produce it.

Usage of trade Any practice or method of dealing having such regularity of observance in a place, vocation, or trade as to justify an expectation that it will be observed with respect to the transaction in question.

Usurpation In corporation law, the taking advantage of a corporate opportunity by a corporate officer or director for his or her personal gain and in violation of his or her fiduciary duties.

Usury Charging an illegal rate of interest.

Utilitarianism An approach to ethical reasoning in which ethically correct behavior is not related to any absolute ethical or moral values but to an evaluation of the consequences of a given action on those who will be affected by it. In utilitarian reasoning, a "good" decision is one that results in the greatest good for the greatest number of people affected by the decision.

V

Valid contract A contract that results when elements necessary for contract formation (agreement, consideration, legal purpose, and contractual capacity) are present.

Validation notice An initial notice to a debtor from a collection agency informing the debtor that he or she has thirty days to challenge the debt and request verification.

Vendee One who purchases property from another, called the vendor.

Vendor One who sells property to another, called the vendee.

Venture capital Funds that are invested in, or that are available for investment in, a new corporate enterprise.

Venture capitalist A person or entity that seeks out promising entrepreneurial ventures and funds them in exchange for equity stakes.

Venue (pronounced *ven*-yoo) The geographical district in which an action is tried and from which the jury is selected.

Verdict A formal decision made by a jury.

Vertical merger The acquisition by a company at one stage of production of a company at a higher or lower stage of production (such as its supplier or retailer).

Vertical restraint Any restraint on trade created by agreements between firms at different levels in the manufacturing and distribution process.

Vertically integrated firm A firm that carries out two or more functional phases—such as manufacture, distribution, retailing—of a product.

Vesting Under the Employee Retirement Income Security Act of 1974, a pension plan becomes vested when an employee has a legal right to the benefits purchased with the employer's contributions, even if the employee is no longer working for this employer.

Vicarious liability Legal responsibility placed on one person for the acts of another.

Virtual courtroom A courtroom that is conceptual and not physical. In the context of cyberspace, a virtual courtroom could be a location on the Internet at which judicial proceedings take place.

Virtual property Property that, in the context of cyberspace, is conceptual, as opposed to physical. Intellectual property that exists on the Internet is virtual property.

Void contract A contract having no legal force or binding effect.

Voidable contract A contract that may be legally avoided (canceled, or annulled) at the option of one of the parties.

Voidable preference In bankruptcy law, a preference that may be avoided, or set aside, by the trustee.

Voir dire (pronounced *vwahr deehr*) A French phrase meaning, literally, "to see, to speak." In jury trials, the phrase refers to the process in which the attorneys question prospective jurors to determine whether they are biased or have any connection with a party to the action or with a prospective witness.

Voting trust An agreement (trust contract) under which legal title to shares of corporate stock is transferred to a trustee who is authorized by the shareholders to vote the shares on their behalf.

W

Waiver An intentional, knowing relinquishment of a legal right.

Warehouse receipt A document of title issued by a bailee-warehouser to cover the goods stored in the warehouse.

Warehouser One in the business of operating a warehouse.

Warranty A promise that certain facts are truly as they are represented to be.

Warranty deed A deed in which the grantor guarantees to the grantee that the grantor has title to the property conveyed in the deed, that there are no encumbrances on the property other than what the grantor has represented, and that the grantee will enjoy quiet possession of the property; a deed that provides the greatest amount of protection for the grantee.

Warranty disclaimer A seller's or lessor's negation or qualification of a warranty.

Warranty of fitness *See* Implied warranty of fitness for a particular purpose

Warranty of merchantability *See* Implied warranty of merchantability

Warranty of title An implied warranty made by a seller that the seller has good and valid title to the goods sold and that the transfer of the title is rightful.

Waste The abuse or destructive use of real property by one who is in rightful possession of the property but who does not have title to it. Waste does not include ordinary depreciation due to age and normal use.

Watered stock Shares of stock issued by a corporation for which the corporation receives, as payment, less than the fair market value of the shares.

Wetlands Areas of land designated by government agencies (such as the Army Corps of Engineers or the Environmental Protection Agency) as protected areas that support wildlife and that therefore cannot be filled in or dredged by private contractors or parties.

Whistleblowing An employee's disclosure to government, the press, or upper-management authorities that the employer is engaged in unsafe or illegal activities.

White-collar crime Nonviolent crime committed by individuals or corporations to obtain a personal or business advantage.

Whole life A life insurance policy in which the insured pays a level premium for his or her entire life and in which there is a constantly accumulating cash value that can be withdrawn or borrowed against by the borrower. Sometimes referred to as straight life insurance.

Will An instrument directing what is to be done with the testator's property on his or her death, made by the testator and revocable during his or her lifetime. No interests in the testator's property pass until the testator dies.

Willful Intentional.

Winding up The second of two stages involved in the termination of a partnership or corporation. Once the firm is dissolved, it continues to exist legally until the process of winding up all business affairs (collecting and distributing the firm's assets) is complete.

Workers' compensation laws State statutes establishing an administrative procedure for compensating workers' injuries that arise out of—or in the course of—their employment, regardless of fault.

Working papers The various documents used and developed by an accountant during an audit. Working papers include notes, computations, memoranda, copies, and other papers that make up the work product of an accountant's services to a client.

Workout An out-of-court agreement between a debtor and his or her creditors in which the parties work out a payment plan or schedule under which the debtor's debts can be discharged.

Writ of attachment A court's order, prior to a trial to collect a debt, directing the sheriff or other officer to seize nonexempt property of the debtor; if the creditor prevails at trial, the seized property can be sold to satisfy the judgment.

Writ of *certiorari* (pronounced sur-shee-uh-*rah*-ree) A writ from a higher court asking the lower court for the record of a case.

Writ of execution A court's order, after a judgment has been entered against the debtor, directing the sheriff to seize (levy) and sell any of the debtor's nonexempt real or personal property. The proceeds of the sale are used to pay off the judgment, accrued interest, and costs of the sale; any surplus is paid to the debtor.

Wrongful discharge An employer's termination of an employee's employment in violation of an employment contract or laws that protect employees.

Z

Zoning The division of a city by legislative regulation into districts and the application in each district of regulations having to do with structural and architectural designs of buildings and prescribing the use to which buildings within designated districts may be put.

TABLE OF CASES

INDEX

Helpful Internet Uniform Resource Locators (URLs)

General Legal Resources

http://www.findlaw.com FindLaw, which is a part of West Group, is one of the most comprehensive sources of free legal information. You can access all federal and state cases, codes, and agency regulations, as well as journal articles, newsletters, and links to other useful sites and discussion groups.

http://www.law.cornell.edu The Legal Information Institute (LII) at Cornell Law School also is a great site for legal research and includes federal, state, and international law. You can access materials by topic or by jurisdiction, or you can browse through one of its topical libraries.

http://www.lectlaw.com/bus.html The 'Lectric Law Library has general legal resources.

http://www.lawguru.com/ilawlib The Internet Law Library provides many legal resources relating to American and foreign law.

http://www.law.com/index.shtml This site provides up-to-date legal news articles and information, and has links to other legal news publications, including the *National Law Journal*.

Helpful Government Sites

http://firstgov.gov The U.S. government's official Web site provides links to every branch of the federal government, including federal agencies.

http://www.loc.gov The Library of Congress has links to state and federal government resources, and the THOMAS system allows you to search through several legislative databases.

http://www.sec.gov/edgar.shtml The Web site of the Securities and Exchange Commission offers a searchable electronic database (called EDGAR) of information about public companies.

http://www.gpoaccess.gov/index.html The U.S. Government Printing Office posts official information from each of the three branches of the federal government, including publications such as the *Code of Federal Regulations* and the *Federal Register*.

http://www.uspto.gov The U.S. Patent and Trademark Office has a searchable database of patents and trademarks. This site also provides general information and a way to check the status of pending applications.

http://www.loc.gov/copyright The U.S. Copyright Office provides information on copyrights and a searchable database of copyright records.

http://www.eeoc.gov/index.html The Equal Employment Opportunity Commission (EEOC) posts information on employment discrimination, EEOC regulations, compliance, and enforcement.

http://www.epa.gov The Environmental Protection Agency offers information on environmental laws, regulations, and compliance assistance.

http://www.sbaonline.sba.gov The U.S. Small Business Administration assists in forming, financing, and operating small businesses.

http://www.usdoj.gov The U.S. Department of Justice provides information on many areas of law, including civil rights, employment, crime, and immigration.

http://www.csg.org The Council of State Governments offers state news, information, legislation, and links to state home pages.

http://www.nccusl.org The National Conference of Commissioners on Uniform State Laws posts the text of uniform laws (such as the Uniform Commercial Code) and information on state adoptions and pending state legislation.

Federal and State Courts

http://www.supremecourtus.gov This official site of the United States Supreme Court provides case opinions, orders, and other information about the Court, including its history, procedures, schedule, and transcripts of oral arguments.

http://www.oyez.org/oyez/frontpage This site offers in addition to United States Supreme Court opinions, a multimedia guide to the Court, including a virtual tour of the building and digital audio of selected oral arguments and Court decisions.

http://www.uscourts.gov/index.html The federal judiciary provides access to every federal court (including district courts, appellate courts, and bankruptcy courts).

http://www.ncsconline.org The National Center for State Courts offers links to the Web pages of all state courts.

http://www.abiworld.org The American Bankruptcy Institute is a good resource for bankruptcy court opinions, news, and other information.